et septem angeli qui h̄ent septē tubas pa
rauerunt se ut tuba canerent. Et pimuf
angelus tuba cecinit· et fcā est grando ᵹ igmf

et les·vij·anges qui auoient les·vij·buzmes
saparelleterent a chanter o loz buzmes· Et le
premier ange chanta o sa troumpe· ardē fur fete

mixta in sanguine et missum est in terra
et tertia pars terre combusta est et tertia pf
arborū et omne fenū uiride combustum est·

grisle ᵹ feu mellez o sang· ᵹ fur enuoie ēterre·
ᵹ la tierce partie de la terre est bruillee· ᵹ la tier
ce partie des arbres ᵹ tot fei uert· est ars ᵹ brulle

The Apocalypse, fourteenth-century manuscript illumination.

(© Historical Picture Archive/CORBIS)

NEW
CATHOLIC
ENCYCLOPEDIA

NEW CATHOLIC ENCYCLOPEDIA

SECOND EDITION

1
A–Azt

GALE®

THOMSON
™
GALE

Detroit • New York • San Diego • San Francisco • Cleveland • New Haven, Conn. • Waterville, Maine • London • Munich

in association with
THE CATHOLIC UNIVERSITY OF AMERICA • WASHINGTON, D.C.

THOMSON

GALE

™

The New Catholic Encyclopedia, Second Edition

Project Editors
Thomas Carson, Joann Cerrito

Editorial
Erin Bealmear, Jim Craddock, Stephen Cusack, Miranda Ferrara, Kristin Hart, Melissa Hill, Margaret Mazurkiewicz, Carol Schwartz, Christine Tomassini, Michael J. Tyrkus

Permissions
Edna Hedblad, Shalice Shah-Caldwell

Imaging and Multimedia
Randy Bassett, Dean Dauphinais, Robert Duncan, Leitha Etheridge-Sims, Mary K. Grimes, Lezlie Light, Dan Newell, David G. Oblender, Christine O'Bryan, Luke Rademacher, Pamela Reed

Product Design
Michelle DiMercurio

Data Capture
Civie Green

Manufacturing
Rhonda Williams

Indexing
Victoria Agee, Victoria Baker, Lynne Maday, Do Mi Stauber, Amy Suchowski

While every effort has been made to ensure the reliability of the information presented in this publication, The Gale Group, Inc. does not guarantee the accuracy of the data contained herein. The Gale Group, Inc. accepts no payment for listing; and inclusion in the publication of any organization, agency, institution, publication, service, or individual does not imply endorsement of the editors or publisher. Errors brought to the attention of the publisher and verified to the satisfaction of the publisher will be corrected in future editions.

LIBRARY OF CONGRESS CATALOGING-IN-PUBLICATION DATA

New Catholic encyclopedia.—2nd ed.
        p. cm.
              Includes bibliographical references and indexes.
              ISBN 0-7876-4004-2
              1. Catholic Church—Encyclopedias. I. Catholic University of America.
    BX841 .N44 2002
    282′ .03—dc21
    2002000924

ISBN: 0-7876-4004-2 (set)
0-7876-4005-0 (v. 1)
0-7876-4006-9 (v. 2)
0-7876-4007-7 (v. 3)
0-7876-4008-5 (v. 4)

0-7876-4009-3 (v. 5)
0-7876-4010-7 (v. 6)
0-7876-4011-5 (v. 7)
0-7876-4012-3 (v. 8)
0-7876-4013-1 (v. 9)

0-7876-4014-x (v. 10)
0-7876-4015-8 (v. 11)
0-7876-4016-6 (v. 12)
0-7876-4017-4 (v. 13)
0-7876-4018-2 (v. 14)
0-7876-4019-0 (v. 15)

Printed in the United States of America
10 9 8 7 6 5 4 3 2 1

For The Catholic University of America Press

EDITORIAL STAFF

Foreword

This revised edition of the *New Catholic Encyclopedia* represents a third generation in the evolution of the text that traces its lineage back to the *Catholic Encyclopedia* published from 1907 to 1912. In 1967, sixty years after the first volume of the original set appeared, The Catholic University of America and the McGraw-Hill Book Company joined together in organizing a small army of editors and scholars to produce the *New Catholic Encyclopedia*. Although planning for the *NCE* had begun before the Second Vatican Council and most of the 17,000 entries were written before Council ended, Vatican II enhanced the encyclopedia's value and importance. The research and the scholarship that went into the articles witnessed to the continuity and richness of the Catholic Tradition given fresh expression by Council. In order to keep the *NCE* current, supplementary volumes were published in 1972, 1978, 1988, and 1995. Now, at the beginning of the third millennium, The Catholic University of America is proud to join with The Gale Group in presenting a new edition of the *New Catholic Encyclopedia*. It updates and incorporates the many articles from the 1967 edition and its supplements that have stood the test of time and adds hundreds of new entries.

As the president of The Catholic University of America, I cannot but be pleased at the reception the *NCE* has received. It has come to be recognized as an authoritative reference work in the field of religious studies and is praised for its comprehensive coverage of the Church's history and institutions. Although Canon Law no longer requires encyclopedias and reference

works of this kind to receive an *imprimatur* before publication, I am confident that this new edition, like the original, reports accurate information about Catholic beliefs and practices. The editorial staff and their consultants were careful to present official Church teachings in a straightforward manner, and in areas where there are legitimate disputes over fact and differences in interpretation of events, they made every effort to insure a fair and balanced presentation of the issues.

The way for this revised edition was prepared by the publication, in 2000, of a Jubilee volume of the *NCE*, heralding the beginning of the new millennium. In my foreword to that volume I quoted Pope John Paul II's encyclical on Faith and Human Reason in which he wrote that history is "the arena where we see what God does for humanity." The *New Catholic Encyclopedia* describes that arena. It reports events, people, and ideas—"the things we know best and can verify most easily, the things of our everyday life, apart from which we cannot understand ourselves" (*Fides et ratio,* 12).

Finally, I want to express appreciation on my own behalf and on the behalf of the readers of these volumes to everyone who helped make this revision a reality. We are all indebted to The Gale Group and the staff of The Catholic University of America Press for their dedication and the alacrity with which they produced it.

Very Reverend David M. O'Connell, C.M., J.C.D.
President
The Catholic University of America

Preface to the Revised Edition

When first published in 1967 the *New Catholic Encyclopedia* was greeted with enthusiasm by librarians, researchers, and general readers interested in Catholicism. In the United States the *NCE* has been recognized as the standard reference work on matters of special interest to Catholics. In an effort to keep the encyclopedia current, supplementary volumes were published in 1972, 1978, 1988, and 1995. However, it became increasingly apparent that further supplements would not be adequate to this task. The publishers subsequently decided to undertake a thorough revision of the *NCE*, beginning with the publication of a Jubilee volume at the start of the new millennium.

Like the biblical scribe who brings from his storeroom of knowledge both the new and the old, this revised edition of the *New Catholic Encyclopedia* incorporates material from the 15-volume original edition and the supplement volumes. Entries that have withstood the test of time have been edited, and some have been amended to include the latest information and research. Hundreds of new entries have been added. For all practical purposes, it is an entirely new edition intended to serve as a comprehensive and authoritative work of reference reporting on the movements and interests that have shaped Christianity in general and Catholicism in particular over two millennia.

SCOPE

The title reflects its outlook and breadth. It is the *New Catholic Encyclopedia,* not merely a new encyclopedia of Catholicism. In addition to providing information on the doctrine, organization, and history of Christianity over the centuries, it includes information about persons, institutions, cultural phenomena, religions, philosophies, and social movements that have affected the Catholic Church from within and without. Accordingly, the *NCE* attends to the history and particular traditions of the Eastern Churches and the Churches of the Protestant Reformation, and other ecclesial communities. Christianity cannot be understood without exploring its roots in ancient Israel and Judaism, nor can the history of the medieval and modern Church be understood apart from its relationship with Islam. Interfaith dialogue requires an appreciation of Buddhism and other world religions, as well as some knowledge of the history of religion in general.

On the assumption that most readers and researchers who use the *NCE* are individuals interested in Catholicism in general and the Church in North America in particular, its editorial content gives priority to the Western Church, while not neglecting the churches in the East; to Roman Catholicism, acknowledging much common history with Protestantism; and to Catholicism in the United States, recognizing that it represents only a small part of the universal Church.

Scripture, Theology, Patrology, Liturgy. The many and varied articles dealing with Sacred Scripture and specific books of the Bible reflect contemporary biblical scholarship and its concerns. The *NCE* highlights official church teachings as expressed by the Church's magisterium. It reports developments in theology, explains issues and introduces ecclesiastical writers from the early Church Fathers to present-day theologians whose works exercise major influence on the development of Christian thought. The *NCE* traces the evolution of the Church's worship with special emphasis on rites and rituals consequent to the liturgical reforms and renewal initiated by the Second Vatican Council.

Church History. From its inception Christianity has been shaped by historical circumstances and itself has become a historical force. The *NCE* presents the Church's history from a number of points of view against the background of general political and cultural history. The revised edition reports in some detail the Church's missionary activity as it grew from a small community in Jerusalem to the worldwide phenomenon it is today. Some entries, such as those dealing with the Middle Ages, the Reformation, and the Enlightenment, focus on major time-periods and movements that cut across geographical boundaries. Other articles describe the history and structure of the Church in specific areas, countries, and regions. There are separate entries for many dioceses and monasteries which by reason of antiquity, size, or influence are of special importance in ecclesiastical history, as there are for religious orders and congregations. The *NCE* rounds out its comprehensive history of the Church with articles on religious movements and biographies of individuals.

Canon and Civil Law. The Church inherited and has safeguarded the precious legacy of ancient Rome, described by Virgil, "to rule people under law, [and] to establish the way of peace." The *NCE* deals with issues of ecclesiastical jurisprudence and outlines the development of legislation governing communal practices and individual obligations, taking care to incorporate and reference the 1983 *Code of Canon Law* throughout and, where appropriate, the *Code of Canons for the Eastern Churches*. It deals with issues of Church-State relations and with civil law as it impacts on the Church and Church's teaching regarding human rights and freedoms.

Philosophy. The Catholic tradition from its earliest years has investigated the relationship between faith and reason. The *NCE* considers at some length the many and varied schools of ancient, medieval, and modern philosophy with emphasis, when appropriate, on their relationship to theological positions. It pays particular attention to the scholastic tradition, particularly Thomism, which is prominent in Catholic intellectual history. Articles on many major and lesser philosophers contribute to a comprehensive survey of philosophy from pre-Christian times to the present.

Biography and Hagiography. The *NCE*, making an exception for the reigning pope, leaves to other reference works biographical information about living persons. This revised edition presents biographical sketches of hundreds of men and women, Christian and non-Christian, saints and sinners, because of their significance for the Church. They include: Old and New Testament figures; the Fathers of the Church and ecclesiastical writers; pagan and Christian emperors; medieval and modern kings; heads of state and other political figures; heretics and champions of orthodoxy; major and minor figures in the Reformation and Counter Reformation; popes, bishops, and priests; founders and members of religious orders and congregations; lay men and lay women; scholars, authors, composers, and artists. The *NCE* includes biographies of most saints whose feasts were once celebrated or are currently celebrated by the universal church. The revised edition relies on Butler's *Lives of the Saints* and similar reference works to give accounts of many saints, but the *NCE* also

provides biographical information about recently canonized and beatified individuals who are, for one reason or another, of special interest to the English-speaking world.

Social Sciences. Social sciences came into their own in the twentieth century. Many articles in the *NCE* rely on data drawn from anthropology, economics, psychology and sociology for a better understanding of religious structures and behaviors. Papal encyclicals and pastoral letters of episcopal conferences are the source of principles and norms for Christian attitudes and practice in the field of social action and legislation. The *NCE* draws attention to the Church's organized activities in pursuit of peace and justice, social welfare and human rights. The growth of the role of the laity in the work of the Church also receives thorough coverage.

ARRANGEMENT OF ENTRIES

The articles in the *NCE* are arranged alphabetically by the first substantive word using the word-by-word method of alphabetization; thus "New Zealand" precedes "Newman, John Henry," and "Old Testament Literature" precedes "Oldcastle, Sir John." Monarchs, patriarchs, popes, and others who share a Christian name and are differentiated by a title and numerical designation are alphabetized by their title and then arranged numerically. Thus, entries for Byzantine emperors Leo I through IV precede those for popes of the same name, while "Henry VIII, King of England" precedes "Henry IV, King of France."

Maps, Charts, and Illustrations. The *New Catholic Encyclopedia* contains nearly 3,000 illustrations, including photographs, maps, and tables. Entries focusing on the Church in specific countries contain a map of the country as well as easy-to-read tables giving statistical data and, where helpful, lists of archdioceses and dioceses. Entries on the Church in U.S. states also contain tables listing archdioceses and dioceses where appropriate. The numerous photographs appearing in the *New Catholic Encyclopedia* help to illustrate the history of the Church, its role in modern societies, and the many magnificent works of art it has inspired.

SPECIAL FEATURES

Subject Overview Articles. For the convenience and guidance of the reader, the *New Catholic Encyclopedia* contains several brief articles outlining of scope of major fields: "Theology, Articles on," "Liturgy, Articles on," "Jesus Christ, Articles on," etc.

Cross-References. The cross-reference system in the *NCE* serves to direct the reader to related material in other articles. The appearance of a name or term in small capital letters in text indicates that there is an article of that title elsewhere in the encyclopedia. In some cases, the name of the related article has been inserted at the appropriate point as a *see* reference: (*see* THOMAS AQUINAS, ST.). When a further aspect of the subject is treated under another title, a *see also* reference is placed at the end of the article. In addition to this extensive cross-reference system, the comprehensive index in volume 15 will greatly increase the reader's ability to access the wealth of information contained in the encyclopedia.

Abbreviations List. Following common practice, books and versions of the Bible as well as other standard works by selected authors have been abbreviated throughout the text. A guide to these abbreviations follows this preface.

The Editors

Abbreviations

The system of abbreviations used for the works of Plato, Aristotle, St. Augustine, and St. Thomas Aquinas is as follows: Plato is cited by book and Stephanus number only, e.g., Phaedo 79B; Rep. 480A. Aristotle is cited by book and Bekker number only, e.g., Anal. post. 72b 8–12; Anim. 430a 18. St. Augustine is cited as in the Thesaurus Linguae Latinae, e.g., C. acad. 3.20.45; Conf. 13.38.53, with capitalization of the first word of the title. St. Thomas is cited as in scholarly journals, but using Arabic numerals. In addition, the following abbreviations have been used throughout the encyclopedia for biblical books and versions of the Bible.

Books

Acts	Acts of the Apostles
Am	Amos
Bar	Baruch
1–2 Chr	1 and 2 Chronicles (1 and 2 Paralipomenon in Septuagint and Vulgate)
Col	Colossians
1–2 Cor	1 and 2 Corinthians
Dn	Daniel
Dt	Deuteronomy
Eccl	Ecclesiastes
Eph	Ephesians
Est	Esther
Ex	Exodus
Ez	Ezekiel
Ezr	Ezra (Esdras B in Septuagint; 1 Esdras in Vulgate)
Gal	Galatians
Gn	Genesis
Hb	Habakkuk
Heb	Hebrews
Hg	Haggai
Hos	Hosea
Is	Isaiah
Jas	James
Jb	Job
Jdt	Judith
Jer	Jeremiah
Jgs	Judges
Jl	Joel
Jn	John
1–3 Jn	1, 2, and 3 John
Jon	Jonah
Jos	Joshua
Jude	Jude
1–2 Kgs	1 and 2 Kings (3 and 4 Kings in Septuagint and Vulgate)
Lam	Lamentations
Lk	Luke
Lv	Leviticus
Mal	Malachi (Malachias in Vulgate)
1–2 Mc	1 and 2 Maccabees
Mi	Micah
Mk	Mark
Mt	Matthew
Na	Nahum
Neh	Nehemiah (2 Esdras in Septuagint and Vulgate)
Nm	Numbers
Ob	Obadiah
Phil	Philippians
Phlm	Philemon
Prv	Proverbs
Ps	Psalms
1–2 Pt	1 and 2 Peter
Rom	Romans
Ru	Ruth
Rv	Revelation (Apocalypse in Vulgate)
Sg	Song of Songs
Sir	Sirach (Wisdom of Ben Sira; Ecclesiasticus in Septuagint and Vulgate)
1–2 Sm	1 and 2 Samuel (1 and 2 Kings in Septuagint and Vulgate)
Tb	Tobit
1–2 Thes	1 and 2 Thessalonians
Ti	Titus
1–2 Tm	1 and 2 Timothy
Wis	Wisdom
Zec	Zechariah
Zep	Zephaniah

Versions

Apoc	Apocrypha
ARV	American Standard Revised Version
ARVm	American Standard Revised Version, margin
AT	American Translation
AV	Authorized Version (King James)
CCD	Confraternity of Christian Doctrine
DV	Douay-Challoner Version

ERV	English Revised Version	NJB	New Jerusalem Bible
ERVm	English Revised Version, margin	NRSV	New Revised Standard Version
EV	English Version(s) of the Bible	NT	New Testament
JB	Jerusalem Bible	OT	Old Testament
LXX	Septuagint	RSV	Revised Standard Version
MT	Masoretic Text	RV	Revised Version
NAB	New American Bible	RVm	Revised Version, margin
NEB	New English Bible	Syr	Syriac
NIV	New International Version	Vulg	Vulgate

A

A CAPPELLA

A term referring to choral music without instrumental accompaniment. During the Renaissance the performances of the SISTINE CHOIR in Rome were considered exemplary; and since the use of instruments was forbidden by its statutes, the term came to be used for any performance in a manner similar to those in the Sistine Chapel. The Sistine tradition of unaccompanied voices stems from the monophonic, purely vocal style of plainchant. Although musical historians of the 19th century believed that all music before 1600 was *a cappella,* they ignored the vast amount of evidence, especially that of paintings, to the contrary. Even in liturgical performance the older procedure was to double vocal lines with instruments of disparate tone colors, thus enhancing the individuality of the parts and accenting the music's polyphonic character. The *a cappella* practice is related to polyphony in what is called the ''Palestrina style,'' a term referring not only to works of G. PALESTRINA but also to imitations of his style, e.g., the *stile antico* of the baroque era. Though the *concertato* style with instruments became widespread during the 17th and 18th centuries, the Sistine Choir continued its *a cappella* tradition, thus furnishing a performance model for the revival of liturgical polyphony in the 19th century (*see* CAECILIAN MOVEMENT).

Bibliography: K. G. FELLERER, *The History of Catholic Church Music,* tr. F. A. BRUNNER (Baltimore 1961). J. HANDSCHIN, ''Die Grundlagen des A-capella-Stils,'' *Hans Häusermann und der Häusermannsche Privatchor* (Zurich 1929). P. H. LÁNG, *Music in Western Civilization* (New York 1941). G. REESE, *Music in the Renaissance* (rev. ed. New York 1959). W. APEL, *Harvard Dictionary of Music* (Cambridge, Mass. 1958).

[L. J. WAGNER]

AACHEN

City in north Rhine-Westphalia, west central Germany. The scene of treaties ending the Wars of Devolution (1668) and of the Austrian Succession (1748), it was in great part destroyed in World War II (1944). The Diocese of Aachen (*Aquisgranensis*) has been suffragan to Cologne since 1930. In 2001 it had 590 secular and 176 religious priests, 238 members of men's religious institutes, 1,305 members of women's religious institutes, 539 parishes, and 22 churches or mission stations. There are 1,232,300 Catholics out of a population of 2,012,000. It is 3,937 square kilometers in area. The name *Aquae Grani,* first mentioned at the time of Charlemagne, means water.

The earliest traces of Christianity appear in graves and in a chapel (5th century) at an ancient bath shrine, which King Pepin replaced with a small palace chapel. Charlemagne (786–814) had the palace and chapel rebuilt (*c.* 786), and in the last part of his reign resided in Aachen, the center of the Carolingian Empire. Aachen's importance appears also in the many Carolingian synods held there, the Aachen rule for canons, and the influence of its court academy and palace school during the Carolingian Renaissance. As a result of the tradition of Charlemagne, 30 German kings were crowned in the cathedral (936–1531), which rulers favored with gifts. Until 1802 Aachen belonged to the Diocese of Liège. Under the French it became a diocese (1802–21), suffragan to Mechelen; then it was suppressed and became part of the restored See of COLOGNE (1821). Resurrected as a see by the Prussian Concordat (1929), Aachen was canonically erected in 1930.

The cathedral, a major monument, began with the octagonal building of Charlemagne, modeled after S. Vitale in RAVENNA and the Theodosian tomb chapel at Old St. Peter's in Rome; it was probably dedicated July 17, 800. Gothic side chapels were added in the 15th century; the hall choir was completed in 1414. Cathedral treasures include the throne of Charlemagne (with six steps modeled after Solomon's), Carolingian and Ottonian Gospels, the cross of Lothair, the golden table, the pulpit of Henry II, and the bronze corona chandelier of Frederick I Barbarossa.

Shrine of Charlemagne, detail, 1200–1215, Aachen Cathedral, Aachen, Germany. (©Archivo Iconografico, S.A./CORBIS)

From Pepin's time the palace chapel housed important relics, and the number increased under Charlemagne. Its Great Relics, apparently exhibited in Charlemagne's time, are the swaddling clothes of Christ, the loin cloth of the Lord, the cloth for John the Baptist's head, and the cloak of Mary. Veneration of these increased through the Middle Ages, with pilgrims coming from all central Europe. The seven-year cycle of the pilgrimage is known from the 14th century. At first kept in a Carolingian shrine, the Great Relics have been in a Gothic Marian shrine since 1239. The Shrine of Charlemagne (1215) houses his remains, exhumed in 1165 when a local cult of St. Charlemagne developed. The cathedral also has a 14th-century statue of Our Lady that is venerated as miraculous.

Many spiritual institutions have arisen in Aachen: St. Adalbert chapter, the Benedictine Burtscheid, smaller cloisters, hospitals, and a leprosarium outside the city. Charitable foundations include the 13th-century Alexian Brothers (Beghards) and the 17th-century Sisters of St. Elizabeth. Three pupils of the poetess Luise Hensel, a teacher at St. Leonhard (1827–32), founded orders: Clara FEY (1815–94), Franziska SCHERVIER (1819–76), and Pauline von Mallinckrodt (1818–81). Around Leonhard Nellessen (1783–1859), pastor of St. Nikolaus, arose the

Aachen circle of priests, devoted to pastoral care and works of charity. Aachen was the origin of the May devotion in the 19th century. The Francis Xavier Mission Society (now part of the Society for the PROPAGATION OF THE FAITH) and the Child Jesus Society (now part of the Pontifical Association of the Holy Childhood) were founded there. Philipp Höver founded the Society of the Poor Brothers of St. Francis to care for school dropouts (1857). Recently the administration of Misereor, a work originated by the German episcopacy for spiritual and bodily needs in underdeveloped lands, has been in Aachen.

Bibliography: J. RAMACKERS, "Werkstattheimat der Grabplatte Papst Hadrians I," *Römische Quartalschrift für christliche Altertumskunde und für Kirchenge-schichte* 59 (Freiburg 1964) 36–78; "Das Grab Karls des Grossen und die Frage nach dem Ursprung des Aachener Oktogons," *Historisches Jahrbuch der Görres-Gesellschaft* 75 (Munich 1956) 123–153; *Lexikon für Theologie und Kirche,* eds. J. HOFER and K. RAHNER (Freiburg 1957–65); suppl., *Das Zweite Vatikanishe Konsil: Dokumente und Kommentare,* ed. H. S. BRECHTER et al. (1966) 1: 1–3. *Zeitschrift des Aachener Geschichtsvereins,* v.1–76 (Aachen 1879–1964). *Aachener Heimatgeschichte,* ed. A. HUYSKENS (Aachen 1924). *Handbuch des Bistums A.* (2d ed. Aachen 1962). J. TORSY, *Geschichte des Bistums A. während der französischen Zeit (1802–1814)* (Bonn 1940). C. FAYMONVILLE et al., eds., *Die Kunstdenkmäler der Stadt A.,* 3 v. (Die Kunstdenkmäler der Rheinprovinz, ed. P. CLEMEN, v.10; Düsseldorf 1916–24). *Aachener Kunstblätter,* v.16–29 (1957–64). W. BOECKELMANN, "Von den Ursprüngen der Aachener Pfalzkapelle," *Wallraf-Richartz-Jahrbuch* 19 (1957) 9–38. W. SCHÖNE, "Die künstlerische und liturgische Gestalt der Pfalzkapelle Karls des Grossen in A.," *Zeitschrift für Kunstwissenschaft* 15 (1961) 97–148. H. P. HILGER, *Der Skulpturenzyklus im Chor des Aachener Domes* (Die Kunstdenkmäler des Rheinlands, *op. cit.* Beiheft 8; Essen 1961). J. FLECKENSTEIN, *Die Hofkapelle der deutschen Könige,* v. 1 (Stuttgart 1959). A. SCHULTE, *Die Kaiser- und Königskrönungen zu Aachen, 813–1531* (Darmstadt 1965). E. MEUTHEN, *Aachener Urkunden 1101-1250* (Bonn 1972). V. GIELEN, *Aachen unter Napoleon* (Aachen 1977). W. KAEMMERER, *Aachener Quellentexte* (Aachen 1980). R. SCHLÖGL, *Glaube und Religion in der Säkularisierung: die katholische Stadt—Könl, Aachen, Münster—1700–1840* (Munich 1995). A. HAUSMANN, *Aachen im Mittelalter: königlicher Stuhl und kaiserliche Stadt* (Aachen 1997). D.P.J. WYNANDS, ed., *Der Aachener Marienschrein: eine Festschrift* (Aachen 2000). M. KRAMP, ed., *Krönungen: Könige in Aachen, Geschichte und Mythos* (Mainz 2000).

[J. RAMACKERS]

AARON

Son of Amram and Jochabed; brother of MOSES and Mariam (Ex 6.20); and husband of Elisabe, who bore him Nadab, Abiu, Eleazar, and Ithamar (6.23). The actual role of Aaron has been obscured in the development of the PENTATEUCH. Most scholars question whether Aaron appeared in the original YAHWIST tradition and suggest that a later editor was responsible for linking him with Moses.

An illustration of scenes from Exodus, chapters 5 and 7 in which Aaron and Moses ask Pharaoh to let the Hebrews go to the desert to worship God, and Aaron's staff turns into a snake which eats the staffs of the Egyptian magicians. (©Historical Picture Archive/ CORBIS)

In the ELOHIST tradition Aaron acts as Moses' deputy, holds up his hands at Raphidim (Ex 17.10–12), goes up the mountain with him and sees the Lord (19. 24), and acts as leader with Hur in Moses' absence. He accedes to the wishes of the insecure Hebrews, casts the golden calf, and constructs an altar in its honor (32.1–24). He joins Mariam in a complaint against Moses' marriage to a Chusite woman, although the text indicates their envy of Moses as the instrument of God's revelation (Nm 12.1–15). Later, the Pentateuchal PRIESTLY WRITERS cast Aaron in the role of religious leader who figured prominently in the liberation of Israel. When he and Moses appear before the pharaoh, Aaron brings on the plagues (Ex 7.19–20; 8.1–2, 12–13). As coadjutor of Moses, he too suffers from the complaints of the people (16.2), is likewise consulted by them (Nm 9.6), is addressed by God (Ex 9.8–10), and is forbidden to enter the Promised Land because of the incident at Meriba, where he sinned against the Lord (Nm 20.1–13). The tragic fate of the followers of Core, the checking of the plague (Nm ch. 16), as well as the event of the flowering rod, are presented as the divine witness to the priesthood of Aaron with its exclusive rights and privileges (Nm 17.16–26). Tradition assigns Mt. Hor (Nm 20.22–29) and Moser (Dt 10.6) as the location of his death.

Bibliography: *Encyclopedic Dictionary of the Bible*, tr. and adap. by L. HARTMAN (New York 1963) 1–2. H. JUNKER, *Lexikon für Theologie und Kirche*, ed. J. HOFER and K. RAHNER (Freiberg 1957–65) 1:3–4. F. MAASS, *Die Religion in Geschichte und Gegenwart* (Tübingen 1957–65) 1:2–3. F. S. NORTH, ''Aaron's Rise in Prestige,'' *Zeitschrift für die alttestamentliche Wissenschaft* 6 (1954) 191–199.

[E. ROESSLER]

ABAD CASASEMPERE, AMALIA, AND COMPANIONS, BB.

Lay martyrs; d. Aug. 20, 1936 and Jan. 31, 1937, Valencia, Spain. Although the venom of the Republican Guards was vented primarily against priests and religious during the Spanish Civil War, many devout lay people also fell victim to the rebels' hatred of the Church. These women, members of Catholic Action, are representative of the numerous lay martyrs of the period. Many became suspect because they owned a Rosary or were seen attending Mass. Included below, in chronological order of their martyrdom, are single women, wives, mothers, and widows aging in age from 31 to 83.

María Climet Mateu (b. May 13, 1887, Xátiva; d. there, Aug. 20, 1936) was a self-supporting, single woman, who was actively involved in all aspects of parochial life. She was martyred together with her mother, who has not been beatified.

Francisca Cualladó Baixauli (b. Dec. 3, 1890, Valencia; d. Sept. 19, 1936, Benifaiós) was a seamstress, who openly lived and proclaimed her Catholic faith through her frequent participation in the Eucharist and service to others.

Crescencia VALLS ESPÍ (b. June 9, 1863, Ontinyent; d. there, Sept. 20, 1936) contributed to the support of her family through her embroidery, while participating actively in various parish associations. She was martyred with three of her sisters.

Amalia Abad Casasempere (b. Dec. 11, 1897, Alcoi, Alicante; d. Sept. 21, 1936, Benillup, Alicante) was the widowed mother of two daughters. While fulfilling her familial duties, she was involved with various religious groups and in caring for the poor.

María de la Purificación Vidal Pastor (b. Sept. 14, 1892, Alzira; d. Sept. 21, 1936, Corbera), a committed single woman, lived a life of intense Eucharistic and Marian piety.

Josefina Moscardó Montalvá (b. April 10, 1880, Alzira; d. there, Sept. 22, 1936), like many other unmarried lay women of this group, was known for her generosity to all in need. She openly practiced her faith and participated in many parish activities.

Sofía Ximénez Ximénez (b. Oct. 15, 1876, Valencia; d. Sept. 23, 1936, Paterna), widowed mother of two children, whom she supported by her own labor while still finding time to participate in the apostolic works of the parish. She was killed with her sister, Bl. María de la Purificación Ximénez, and Bl. María Josefa del Rio Messa (*see* TORRENTALLÉ PARAIRE, ELVIRA).

Encarnación GIL VALLS (b. Jan. 27, 1888, Ontinyent; d. Sept. 24, 1936, L'Ollería) was considered especially dangerous by the anti-religious authorities because she taught children and shared with them her profound faith.

Herminia Martínez Amigó (b. July 31, 1887, Puzol; d. Sept. 26, 1936, Gilet), known for her generosity and numerous charitable works, was shot to death with her husband, who has not been beatified.

María Jordá Botella (b. Jan. 26, 1905, Alcoi, Alicante; d. Sept. 27, 1936, Benifallím, Alicante), the youngest of the group, was known for her undaunted optimism and the joy with which she carried out her lay apostolate.

Florencia Caerols Martínez (b. Feb. 20, 1890, Caudete, Albacete; d. Oct. 2, 1936, Rotglá Corbera), an unmarried textile worker, served her parish as a catechist and by visiting the sick.

Ana María Aranda Riera (b. Jan. 24, 1888, Denia, Alicante; d. Oct. 14, 1936, Paterna), a single woman, attended Mass daily, participated in various parish groups, and assisted with the many works of the Church.

Társila Córdoba Belda (b. May 8, 1861, Sollana; d. Oct. 17, 1936, Algemesí) suffered much tragedy in her life. After the deaths of her husband and three children, she found the strength through daily Communion to care for the sick, poor, and needy.

María Teresa Ferragut Roig (b. Jan. 14, 1853, Algemesí; d. Oct. 25, 1936, Alzira), the eldest of this group (83), is called the "Mother of the Maccabbees" because she died with four of her daughters, three of whom were beatified with her (*see* MASIÁ FERRAGUD, JESÚS).

María del Carmen Viel Ferrando (b. Nov. 27, 1893, Sueca; d. Nov. 4, 1936, El Saler de Valencia), an unmarried woman, worked with working-class children and collaborated in parish activities.

María del Olvido Noguera Albelda (b. Dec. 30, 1903, Carcaixent; d. Nov. 30, 1936, Benifairó de Valldigna), an unmarried woman, manifested her faith through diverse apostolates in the parish and secular world.

Luisa María Frías Cañizares (b. June 20, 1896, Valencia; d. Dec. 6, 1936, Paterna), an unmarried professor at the University of Valencia, established her lay apostolate in the college setting and the parish. She is remembered for her loving spirit and desire for social justice.

Pilar Villalonga Villalba (b. Jan. 22, 1891, Valencia; d. Dec. 11, 1936, Burjassot), a committed single woman, lived an intensely spiritual life that manifested itself in her public actions and service to the Church.

María Luisa Montesinos Orduña (b. March 3, 1901, Valencia; d. Jan. 31, 1937, Picassent), an unmarried member of various religious groups, was martyred with her father, three siblings, and uncle, none of whom have been beatified.

These 19 women were beatified by Pope John Paul II with José Aparicio Sanz and 232 companions on March 11, 2001.

Feast: Sept. 22.

Bibliography: V. CÁRCEL ORTÍ, *Martires españoles del siglo XX* (Madrid 1995). W. H. CARROLL, *The Last Crusade* (Front Royal, Va. 1996). J. PÉREZ DE URBEL, *Catholic Martyrs of the Spanish Civil War*, tr. M. F. INGRAMS (Kansas City, Mo. 1993). R. ROYAL, *The Catholic Martyrs of the Twentieth Century* (New York 2000). L'Osservatore Romano, Eng. no. 11 (March 14, 2001), 1–4, 12.

[K. I. RABENSTEIN]

ABANDONMENT, SPIRITUAL

The term can be taken in either an active or a passive sense. In its active sense it refers to a person's self-abandonment to divine providence through the theological virtues. In its passive sense it refers to a condition in which the soul is really, because of sin, or only apparently, forsaken by God. This article refers to abandonment understood as that experience in which it seems to a spiritual person that God has forsaken him. This spiritual abandonment, then, is an interior trial in which the spiritually advanced soul, feeling the painful need of a clearer and stronger possession of God, has the keen impression that God has deserted it and no longer holds it in His favor.

In its less intense form this abandonment makes one feel that God is far away; in its more intense form it makes one feel rejected by God and destined to be lost. Such suffering is experienced only by persons who have reached a high degree of perfection. Although certain forms of abandonment may be experienced as a result of sin or of a lukewarm faith, the real suffering caused by the feeling of being forsaken by God is only conceivable in holy souls for whom God has become the sole object of an intense desire and love.

Christian hagiography from all ages offers examples of spiritual abandonment. Ancient writers such as St. John Climacus and Cassian describe the trial, but references to this suffering are much more abundant among the saints of modern times. This more recent testimony is undoubtedly attributable to the greater number of spiritual biographies and letters of spiritual direction; these manifest more clearly the interior secrets of souls and, notably, the painful aspects of their spiritual lives.

The experience of spiritual abandonment may arise from the purgative contemplation by which God effects

the purification of the soul, especially in the passive night of the spirit; or it may be a means whereby already purified souls suffer as victims in union with Christ. In either case this trial enables the soul to share most intimately in the suffering of Christ's abandonment on the cross. This union with the crucified Christ in turn gives rise in the soul to the most sublime acts of self-abandonment.

See Also: SELF-ABANDONMENT, SPIRITUAL; PURIFICATION, SPIRITUAL.

Bibliography: JOHN OF THE CROSS, "The Dark Night," *Collected Works*, tr. K. KAVANAUGH and O. RODRIGUEZ (Garden City, NY 1964) 295–389. A. POULAIN, *The Graces of Interior Prayer*, tr. L. L. YORKE SMITH, ed. J. V. BAINVEL (St. Louis 1950). L. CHARDON, *The Cross of Jesus*, tr. R. T. MURPHY and J. THORNTON, 2 v. (St. Louis 1957–59). H. MARTIN, *Dictionnaire de spiritualité ascétique et mystique. Doctrine et histoire* 3:504–517, 631–645.

[K. KAVANAUGH]

ABBA

A Greek transliteration of the Aramaic *'abbā'*, a vocative or declarative form of *ab*, "father." The significance of *abba* in the NT continues to be debated in biblical studies and Christology. Its earliest uses in Christian sources, Gal 4.6 and Rom 8.15, depict Christians crying out *Abba* during Spirit-inspired prayer to express *their* adoptive relationship with God. The only other NT occurrence of the term is Mk 14.36, a later witness, where Jesus addresses God as *Abba* during his agony in the garden. Many interpreters have regarded this Aramaic word as used by Jesus as an instance of the *ipsissima vox Iesu*. His prayer in Mk 14.36, however, is witnessed by none (see Mk 14.37), raising uncertainty as to the evangelist's source of the wording.

Each of the NT examples of *abba* is followed in Greek by *ho pater*, "the father." The seeming redundancy of *abba ho pater* has been variously explained: *ho pater* may be understood as a translation into Greek of the Aramaic *'abbā'*. *Abba* could also be taken to mean "God," with the whole expression then meaning "O God, the (or my, or our) Father."

Over the centuries a so-called "*abba*-problem" has centered at various times on philological, historical, and theological issues (see Fitzmyer, "*Abba*," 47–50). Scholars have asked whether the historical Jesus would indeed have used this mode of address (i.e. applied such a familial term to God), from what source(s) the early Christians derived their use of the word, what its relation is to other gospel instances where Jesus simply used the word "Father," and what the theological implications of the term are for Jesus himself and for the NT writers, Paul and Mark.

The research of German biblical scholar Joachim Jeremias gave new life to the debate beginning in the 1950s. Jeremias put forth the thesis that in all of pre-Christian Palestinian literature there is no other use of God being addressed as *abba* by an individual Jew in prayer. He interpreted this as indicating a uniqueness in the relationship between Jesus and God, an idea he linked also with a theory that this particular form of the Aramaic word for "father" had its origin in the chatter of small children, e.g. as in English "Daddy," "Papa" (see biblio. of Jeremias' main works on this subject in Fitzmyer, "*Abba*," 132, n.1). While Jeremias continued to hold in his later writings that Jesus "spoke to God like a child to its father, simply, inwardly, confidently" (*Prayers*, 62), he also called it "a piece of inadmissible naivety" (*ibid.*) to assume, as he had earlier, that Jesus really spoke to his Father like a small child. Nonetheless, popular works and some exegetes have continued to expound Jeremias' original position.

Integral to the important criticisms leading to various degrees of nuancing, or rejecting, Jeremias' approach (see the summary in Ashton, *ABD* 1:7–8) is evidence from Qumran. There are now two known instances, albeit in Hebrew not Aramaic (4Q372 1:16; 4Q460 5:6), where for the first time an individual Jew is seen in pre-Christian Palestinian texts calling upon God as "my father." This still seems to leave open the question, however, of whether Jesus's use of the Aramaic term to call upon God was an expression of unique filiation as early in the first century A.D., as he is portrayed doing so.

While some theologians use Jesus' use of *Abba* as a starting point in their Christology, others question whether he even voiced the word at all. Feminist theologians, concerned with the problem of language and imagery applied to God, often focus on what *abba* meant with respect to issues of patriarchy in early Christian communities where it was used.

Bibliography: J. ASHTON, "ABBA," *ABD* 1:7–8. J. BARR, "'Abba' Isn't 'Daddy,'" *Journal of Theological Studies* 39 (1988) 28–47. M. R. D'ANGELO, "*Abba* and Father: Imperial Theology and the Jesus Traditions," *Journal of Biblical Literature* 111 (1992) 611–30; *idem*, "Theology in Mark and Q: *Abba* and 'Father' in Context," *Harvard Theological Review* 85 (1992) 149–74. J. A. FITZMYER, "*Abba* and Jesus' Relation to God" in *idem, According to Paul* (New York/Mahwah 1993) 47–63 (slightly rev. ed. of "*Abba* and Jesus' Relation to God," in R. GANTOY (ed.), *A cause de l'évangile: Etudes sur les Synoptiques et les Actes offertes au P. Jacques Dupont, O.S.B. à l'occasion de son 70e anniversaire* (*Lectio divina* 123; Paris 1985) 15–38. J. JEREMIAS, *The Prayers of Jesus* (London 1967). A. SAND, "'Abba-Vater' - Gotteserfahrung und Gottesglaube Jesu," *Renovatio* 48 (1992) 204–218; E. SCHULLER, "4Q372 1: A Text about Joseph," *Revue de Qumran* 14 (1989–90) 349–76; *idem*, "The Psalm of 4Q372 1 within the Context of Second Temple Prayer," *Catholic Biblical Quarterly* 54 (1992) 67–79; C. TERNYÁK, "'Abba' nel pensiero di Joachim Jeremias," *Folia Theologica* 2 (Budapest 1991) 29–60.

[F. M. GILLMAN]

'ABBĀSIDS

Descendants of 'Abbās (d. A.D. 653), uncle of Muḥammad the prophet of ISLAM; in A.D. 750 they seized the office of CALIPH earlier held by the UMAYYADS, and reigned at Baghdad until 1258.

As Muḥammad's surviving uncle and head of his clan, 'Abbās would have had a claim to succeed the Prophet after his death in 632, had not 'Abbās's delayed conversion to Islam counted against him. His son 'Abdallāh (d. 687), a prominent religious authority, was governor of Basra under ALI ('ALĪ IBN ABĪ ṬĀLIB), but later was won to the cause of Mu'āwiya.

The family played no public role under Mu'āwiya's family, the Umayyads, but they were able by clandestine religious-political propaganda to turn to their advantage the social unrest of the early Arab Muslim Empire. Their message was egalitarian and messianic and seems to have incorporated certain Iranian religious ideas palatable to the newly converted. It was discreetly directed by agents in Kufa, the stronghold of Shī'ī sympathies in Iraq. Under the able Iranian propagandist Abū Muslim, 'Abbāsid propaganda found greatest response among the half-Islamized Iranian inhabitants of the old eastern marches of the Persian Empire, Khurasan, a frontier area where Zoroastrianism, Buddhism, Mazdakism, Manichaeism, and Nestorian Christianity had met and mixed. Here in 747 local revolts were raised that, by calling for "an Imām [religious leader] of the Prophet's family," grew by 749 into a general rebellion of all disaffected elements in the Umayyad Empire. Shī'īs participated enthusiastically in the belief that a descendant of 'Alī would come to power, but it was the head of the 'Abbāsid House, Abū al-'Abbās al-Saffāḥ (d. 754) who was acclaimed caliph in 749, and who rooted out the Umayyads in every province but Spain.

Like other revolutionary regimes, the 'Abbāsids had, when once in power, to reckon on conflicts with the differing groups and interests that had cooperated to give them the victory. Under al-Manṣūr, brother and successor of al-Saffāḥ, the new regime's power was consolidated. Abū Muslim was put to death and his closest followers crushed. The hostility of the Shī'īs pursued the dynasty through all its history, and succeeding 'Abbāsids were alternately led to employ repression or placation in dealing with them.

Al-Manṣūr's new capital on the Tigris, Madīnat al-Salam (popularly known as Baghdad, after an earlier village on that site), was built at the junction of several trade routes, and within 50 years had become one of the great centers of civilization.

With the 'Abbāsid accession, the transformation of the Islamic polity from an Arab kingdom to the Muslim Empire was completed. The economic base of the dynasty was Mesopotamia, seat of earlier multiracial Middle Eastern empires; it drew heavily on the skills and traditions of the conquered peoples, particularly of converted members of the Sassanian bureaucratic class, and it depended on the military support of the peoples of the eastern frontier. Islamic religion and the Arabic language gave their distinctive stamp to this richly syncretic civilization, but the Arabs had lost their exclusive right to the responsibilities and rewards of empire. Islam, not Arab origin, sufficed for full membership in the Empire, and advancement depended almost solely on the favor of the caliphs, who had now transformed the simplicity of the first caliphs into the elaborate and splendid court of Persian autocrats.

The rapidity with which the cultural brilliance of the 'Abbāsid prime was reached (under Harūn al-Rashīd, 786–809, and his son al-Ma'mūn, d. 833) led Prof. Arnold Toynbee to argue convincingly that in fact under the aegis of Islam the earlier civilization of Achaemenid times had come again into its own.

However, during the subsequent period (836–92) when the court resided at Samarra, a new royal city north of Baghdad, the caliphs became the virtual prisoners of the elite corps they had formed from Central Asian Turkish slaves. Local rulers asserted themselves in the provinces, the clash of new cultural ideas prepared the way for new heretical movements, and a slave uprising of Africans devastated lower Iraq. Caliphal authority was slowly reasserted after 870, but during the long reign of al-Muqtadir (908–32) the central administration of the empire began a period of self-strangulation through corruption and internal rivalries. In 909 the Isma'īlī Shī'īs established an anticaliphate "of the Children of Fāṭima" in Tunisia (capital at Cairo from 969–1171). From 945 to 1055 the 'Abbāsids at Baghdad were puppets of the Buwayhid dictators, Persian Shī'īs of the "Twelver" sect. From 1055 to c. 1194 they were under the patronage of sultans of the house of Seljuk, Turkish chiefs whom they invited to rid them of the Buwayhids. The SELJUKS were at least orthodox in practice and led a Sunnī restoration.

In religious as well as imperial theory the caliph was still the sole fount of all validly exercised power, and most Sunnī Muslim monarchs found it advisable to secure a diploma of investiture from Baghdad. This has led to the caliphate's being rather inaccurately likened to the papacy.

A brief restoration of 'Abbāsid power, in Iraq at least, occurred with the passing of the Seljuks, under the Caliph al-Nāṣir (1180–225). But in 1258 Hulagu, grandson of Genghis Khan, destroyed Baghdad and put the Caliph al-Musta'ṣim to death.

Under the Mamelukes of Cairo, a member of the 'Abbāsid family was established as caliph there in 1261. This shadow caliphate was continued by his descendants until the end of the sultanate in 1517, but it was only a legal device for the legitimization of Muslim rulers, and the Cairo 'Abbāsids were little more than court officials.

Bibliography: P. K. HITTI, *History of the Arabs* (6th ed. New York 1958). W. MUIR, *The Caliphate, Its Rise, Decline and Fall*, rev. T. H. WEIR (Edinburgh 1924). A. J. TOYNBEE, *A Study of History*, 12 v. (New York 1948–61). B. LEWIS, *The Arabs in History* (New York 1950); *Encyclopedia of Islam*, ed. B. LEWIS et al. (2d ed. Leiden 1954–) 1:15–23.

[J. A. WILLIAMS]

ABBELEN, PETER

Controversialist; b. Germany, Aug. 8, 1843; d. Milwaukee, Wisconsin, Aug. 24, 1917. He attended schools at Gaesdonk and Münster in Germany, and St. Francis Seminary, Milwaukee, where he was ordained Jan. 29, 1868. After teaching for a semester, he joined the La Crosse diocese, where he spent eight years in pastorates at Chippewa Falls, La Crosse, and Prairie du Chien. In 1876 he became spiritual director of the School Sisters of Notre Dame, Milwaukee, whose subsequent progress was credited to his zeal. He wrote a life of Mother Caroline Friess, first superior of the Milwaukee mother-house. He was one of the theologians selected to do preliminary work for the Third Plenary Council of Baltimore. He was named vicar-general of the Milwaukee archdiocese in 1906, and a domestic prelate in 1907.

Acting for Abp. Michael HEISS and others, he became absorbed in the controversy between German- and English-speaking Catholics. The conflict involved questions concerning the selection of a coadjutor for Archbishop HENNI, the juridical status of nationalistic parishes, the Bennett Law requiring the use of English in schools, Cahenslyism, and Americanism. Among the items contained in his petition to Rome in 1886 were the recognition of parochial status for national churches and legislation assigning immigrants to national churches and their children to the schools thereof. The Congregation of the Propagation of the Faith delayed a decision; when rendered through Bps. John Ireland and John Keane, it was generally regarded as unfavorable to Abbelen. He constantly maintained that he had always been guided by moral objectives, and remarked that he thought Peter Cahensly's program would serve the good of immigrants. The controversy was not fully resolved until the promulgation of the new Code of Canon Law and the end of World War I.

Bibliography: P. M. ABBELEN, ''Memorial on the German Question. . .,'' in C. J. BARRY, *The Catholic Church and German Americans* (Milwaukee 1953) 289–296, with answers to the same, 296–312.

[P. L. JOHNSON]

ABBESS

Term derived from abbot (Aramaic *abba*, father), ''abbess'' is the title of a female superior of a monastic community of nuns. Superiors were referred to as *mater monasterii, mater monacharum, praeposita*; the term ''abbess'' appeared for the first time in the West on the tomb of a certain ''Serena, abbatissa'' (d. *c.* 514) in the Roman church of St. Agnes-Outside-the-Walls. Growing Benedictine influence endowed the office of abbess with a liturgical character, making it elective by vote of the community, prescribing episcopal benediction, and granting the right to the ring, pectoral cross, and crosier. During the Middle Ages, abbesses of great monastic houses exercised practically all the temporal power of abbots and feudal lords, ranking among the nobles of the realm, sitting in parliament and in councils, and recognizing no ecclesiastical authority other than the pope. Many abbesses assumed spiritual power over their nuns also, to the point of incurring stern papal prohibitions against interference in the administration of penance, conferring the veil, and giving benedictions and even sacramental absolution. For such abuses INNOCENT III rebuked abbesses of the royal monasteries in Burgos (*see* HUELGAS DE BURGOS, ABBEY OF) and Palencia, Spain. The abbess of Conversano in Apulia, Italy, had the right to a quasi-episcopal authority over her clergy until 1810, when PIUS VII abolished her privileges. The abbess of FONTEVRAULT had jurisdiction over both monks and nuns of this monastic establishment, typical of other double MONASTERIES. With the breakdown of the feudal system, the temporal power of abbesses declined.

The title abbess continues to be used in older monastic orders such as Benedictines, Poor Clares, Bridgettines and canonesses, but not in all. In some orders the name is used only in formal communication, and there is no universal legislation concerning the use or non-use of the term. Instead, it is left to each order to state in their Rule or constitutions the title to be used. The 1983 Code of Canon Law of the Latin church uses the generic term ''Supreme Moderator'' for the person who has authority over all provinces, houses and members of the institute.

The term Superior is used for others who have authority according to the constitutions and within the limits of their office. The Code leaves to each institute the right to decide what title to use for those who exercise authority in it, and stipulates only that those in authority are to be in office for a given period of time according to the nature and needs of the institute, unless the constitutions establish otherwise for the Supreme Moderator and for the Superiors of an autonomous house.

Bibliography: T. J. BOWE, *Religious Superioresses: A Historical Synopsis and a Plain Commentary* (Washington 1946). J. BEAL, J. CORIDEN and T. GREEN, *New Commentary on the Code of Canon Law* (New York, NY/Mahwah, NJ 2000).

[M. F. LAUGHLIN/C. BARTONE]

ABBEVILLE, CLAUDE D'

French Capuchin missionary and historian; b. place and date unknown; d. 1616 (not in 1622 or 1623, as some have stated). He entered the order in 1593. In 1611 he volunteered as a missionary in the French expedition to Brazil. He arrived in Maranhão in June 1612 and with six Amerindians returned to France to get aid in December of the same year. With 12 missionaries he returned to Maranhão in June of 1614, but they were expelled in December because of the war between the French and Portuguese. Abbeville's reputation is based on his literary work; he was a keen observer and an impartial historian, the first to write about the Brazilian lands conquered by the French. In August 1612 he was already writing interesting letters about the expedition and the native tribes; these letters were edited six times in French and translated into German (Augsburg 1613) and Italian (Bérgamo-Treviso 1613). His principal work is the history of Maranhão Island and its first evangelization, *Histoire de la mission des Pères Capucins en l'isle de Maragnan et terres circonvoisines* (Paris 1614). It is valuable for its information on evangelization, colonization, ethnology, and linguistics.

Bibliography: *Histoire de la mission des Pères Capucins en l'isle de Maragnan et terres circonvoisines* (Paris 1614), Port. tr. S. MILLIET (São Paulo 1945). F. LEITE DE FARIA, *Os primeiros missionários do Maranhão* (Lisbon 1961).

[M. DE POBLADURA]

ABBO OF FLEURY, ST.

Abbot, writer; b. Orléans, France, *c.* 945–950; d. La Réole Abbey, Nov. 13, 1004. Offered as an oblate in Fleury, he studied at Paris, Reims, and Orléans. He was ordained in England, where he had been called to preside over the school of Ramsey (985–988). From 988 to 1004 he was abbot of Saint-Benoît-sur-Loire (Fleury). One of the most remarkable teachers of his century, he was also a prolific writer and a staunch defender of papal authority against royal and episcopal power. When commissioned by King ROBERT II to treat with the papacy in the royal interest, Abbo achieved harmony between the Church and the Capetian dynasty. A zealous promoter of ecclesiastical reform and a champion of monastic independence, he obtained papal immunity for his own monastery and carried the principles of Cluny into the monasteries of France and England. Abbo was fatally wounded during a quarrel that arose between his followers and the Gascons outside the Abbey of La Réole, where he was undertaking a reform. He is revered as a martyr and has received public veneration since 1031. The most notable of his writings (PL 139:463–582) are: *Apologeticus* to Hugh Capet and his son on the rights and duties of clergy, religious, and laity; *Liber de computo; Collectio canonum; Passio S. Eadmundi*, (ed. Arnold, *Memorials of St. Edmund's Abbey*, London, 1890–96).

Feast: Nov. 13.

Bibliography: *Epistola encyclica de caede A. abbatis, Patrologia Latina* 139:417–418; ABBO OF FLEURY, *Epistolae, Recueil des historiens de Gaule et de la France* 10:434–442. AIMOIN, *Vita s. Abbonis, Patrologia Latina* 139:375–414. A. VAN DE VYVER, ''Les Oeuvres inédites d'A.,'' *Revue Bénédictine* 47 (1935) 125–169. P. COUSIN, *A. de Fleury-sur-Loire* (Paris 1954). M. MOSTERT, *The political theology of Abbo of Fleury: A study of the ideas about society and law of the tenth-century monastic reform movement* (Hilversum 1987). A. FLICHE, *La Réforme grégorienne*, 3 v. (Louvain 1924–37) 1:49–59. E. SACKUR, *Die Cluniacenser*, 2 v. (Halle 1892–94) 1:270–299.

[P. J. MULLINS]

ABBO OF METZ, ST.

Bishop; b. Aquitaine; d. 647. Abbo, or Goericus, was a member of the prominent family of Ansbertina. When St. Arnulf of Metz, a kinsman, resigned from the See of Metz in 629, Abbo succeeded him. The medieval *Vita Goerici* that gives other details of his life is wholly unreliable. Among the letters of St. Desiderius of Cahors, there is a letter to Abbo and one from him (PL 87:253, 262). It is in the will of King Dagobert (d. 639) that he is called Abbo. He built St. Peter's in Metz.

Feast: Sept. 19.

Bibliography: *Acta Sanctorum* Sept. 6:48–55. *Monumenta Germaniae Historica: Scriptores* 2:267–270. *Monumenta Germaniae Historica: Scriptores rerum Merovingicarum* 2:417–425, 442. A. BUTLER, *The Lives of the Saints*, ed. H. THURSTON and D. ATTWATER (New York 1956) 3:597.

[B. L. MARTHALER]

Alcuin, Abbot of Tours (c. 702-804). (©Bettmann/CORBIS)

ABBOT

Name and title of the superior of an autonomous MONASTERY of one of the old monastic orders such as the BENEDICTINES, CAMALDOLESE, VALLOMBROSANS, and CISTERCIANS. BASILIAN monks sometimes employ the term ''hegumen'' (Greek ἡγούμενος), while Russian and other Oriental monasteries style their superior an archimandrite.

The term is derived from the Hebrew ABBA, meaning father, a word found in the Bible often with reference to God. It was employed in the early 4th century as descriptive of the role of some of the Egyptian hermits as guides and teachers of religious life for younger monks who came to live under their direction. The original idea of the abbot's spiritual fatherhood of his monks developed ultimately into the juridical office of abbot, vested with authority as set forth in the BENEDICTINE RULE. In Chapter 2 of the rule St. BENEDICT portrays the ideal abbot, and the traits of both father and officer are recognized in the double form of address the author dictates for him, *dominus et abbas*. As the representative of Christ the abbot is the father of the monastic community and exercises a father's jurisdiction over those under his care. He will be held accountable to God, Benedict points out, for the spiritual welfare of his charges. Chapter 64 of the rule goes on to describe the authority of the abbot over his monks and emphasizes encouragement and understanding, as much as firmness and discipline, in the administration of his office. The monks, for their part, owe the abbot reverence and obedience because they should see in him Christ's deputy in their midst.

The abbot is usually elected by the monks of the monastery, the constitutions of the various congregations setting forth the qualifications of electors, the time and manner of voting and the qualifications for the office itself. It was originally intended that the abbot would hold office for life, although in modern times it is not unusual for his term to be limited to 6, 8, or 12 years (as with the English Benedictines). The election must be confirmed by proper authority, either the Holy See, frequently acting through the superior of the monastic congregation, or the local ordinary. The abbot must then seek episcopal benediction according to the rite prescribed in the Roman PONTIFICAL. Monastic founders who were religious often assumed the position of superior in their foundations and in the Middle Ages, as monasteries came to assume an increasingly important role in the economic and political life of their day, feudal lords often dictated the choice of abbots for houses within their territory. The Benedictine Rule envisioned an abbot ruling a single, independent community, but during certain periods, especially those of great monastic reform, one man came to rule a number of widely scattered houses (BENEDICT OF ANIANE, JOHN OF GORZE, ODO OF CLUNY) and later great monastic congregations came to develop (CLUNY in the 10th and 11th centuries, the MAURISTS in the 17th century). The privilege of EXEMPTION, granted since Merovingian times, gave the abbots more freedom from the control of local bishops and feudal lords and a number of houses established themselves as subject only to the Holy See. Among the Cistercians the father abbot and the abbots of the daughter houses have always had a strong influence on each other's abbatial elections while the modern Benedictines have formed themselves into national congregations. Certain privileges are attached to the office of abbot and he may be granted the right to the use of pontificals such as the ring, pectoral cross, miter, and crozier.

Canon law distinguishes between the following types of abbots. The *abbas regularis de regimine* has *de jure* and *de facto* government of an abbey. Enjoying episcopal exemption, he has ordinary jurisdiction in the external and internal forum over all persons belonging to the abbey. An *abbas nullius* has actual episcopal jurisdiction over all clergy and laity in a specified territory subject directly to the abbey. *Archiabbas* (archabbot), *abbas praeses*, or *abbas generalis* is a designation for an abbot who is head of a monastic congregation. The *abbas primas* or abbot primate is the head of the modern Benedic-

tine confederation. A titular abbot is one who has the rank, title, and insignia of an abbot but does not himself govern the abbey whose name he bears.

A commendatory abbot, or abbot *in commendam*, refers to a personage who was allotted the usufruct of a monastic benefice and its revenues. Such an arrangement was much employed in the late Middle Ages but was forbidden by the Council of TRENT (*see* COMMENDATION).

See Also: ABBESS; ABBOT (CANON LAW).

Bibliography: F. CHAMARD, ''Les Abbés au moyen-âge,'' *Revue des questions historiques* 33 (1885) 71–108. J. M. BESSE, *Dictionnaire d'archéologie chrétienne et de liturgie,* ed. F. CABROL, H. LECLERCQ, and H. I. MARROU, 15 v. (Paris 1907–53) 1.1:39–42. J. DE PUNIET, *Dictionnaire de spiritualité ascétique et mystique. Doctrine et histoire,* ed. M. VILLER et al. (Paris 1932–) 1:49–57. F. CIMETIER, *Catholicisme. Hier, aujourd'hui et demain,* ed. G. JACQUEMET 1:19–22. C. BUTLER, *Benedictine Monachism* (2d ed. 1924; repr. New York 1961). J. BAUCHER, *Dictionnaire de droit canonique,* ed. R. NAZ, 7 v. (Paris 1935–65) 1:29–62. P. SCHMITZ, *Histoire de l'Ordre de Saint-Benoît,* 7 v. (Maredsous, Bel. 1942–56) 1:181–191, 259–262. H. EMONDS, *Lexikon für Theologie und Kirche,* ed. J. HOFER and K. RAHNER, 10 v. (2d, new ed. Freiburg 1957–65) 1:90–93. B. HEGGLIN, *Der benediktinische Abt in rechtsgeschichtlicher Entwicklung und geltendem Kirchenrecht* (Kirchengeschichtliche Quellen und Studien 5; St. Ottilien 1961). P. SALMON, *L'Abbé dans la tradition monastique* (Paris 1962). *Handwörterbuch zur deutschen Rechtsgeschichte,* ed. W. STAMMLER et al. (Berlin 1964–) 1:18–20, with bibliog.

[P. VOLK]

ABBOT (CANON LAW)

The title applied to the religious superior of an abbey; derives from the earliest years of Oriental monasticism when the aspirant to holiness chose a suitable monk, whom he called his *abba* (father), to teach and guide him. Later, monastic rules, especially that of St. Benedict, introduced the term into Western Canon Law and liturgy. Since the mendicant orders and the more modern religious institutes adopted another nomenclature for their superiors, the title of abbot is also found among the Canons Regular and in the monastic orders, particularly those that follow the Benedictine Rule.

Election and Privileges. An abbot is usually selected by the secret vote of the community he will govern. The constitutions of each institute establish the specific requisites in the electorate, candidate, and electoral procedure. Generally the requirement is for a majority vote of the solemnly professed religious, taken by secret ballot, for a priest who has been a professed member of the order for at least ten years, is of legitimate birth, and is at least 30 years of age. Upon acceptance of his election and its confirmation by the competent ecclesiastical authority, the new abbot receives the abbatial blessing from the diocesan bishop. While this rite closely resembles an episcopal consecration, it confers no power of orders, but is a requisite for the use of some prelatial powers.

Although in some communities the term of office is limited, an abbot is elected for life. In the event of old age or other incapacity, he may request a coadjutor, or he may even resign. Some resigned abbots are made titular abbots and hold in empty title an abbey no longer active. In very rare cases the title of abbot is directly granted by the Holy See as an honor.

Since the Middle Ages, abbots have received, by papal privilege, the use of insignia and ceremonial proper to bishops. These prelatial prerogatives are recognized in law and liturgy. An abbot is allowed the use of a ring, pectoral cross, and zucchetto. Vested for pontifical functions or assisting in formal choir, he wears the garb of a bishop, except that its color is proper to his religious order. Thus a Norbertine abbot wears white, a Benedictine abbot wears black. An abbot celebrates Holy Mass and performs other liturgical functions according to the ceremonial of a prelate. He uses a throne with a canopy, wears complete prelatial vesture, and observes the rubrics for a pontiff. While there remain no restrictions on the frequency of his use of these prerogatives, an abbot is normally allowed their use only in churches of his own order, although privilege and custom have modified this limitation. Unless the abbot is a bishop, however, he is not authorized to perform those consecrations that require episcopal power. Thus he does not ordinarily prepare the holy oils or ordain to major orders. He is allowed, after having received the abbatial blessing, to confer tonsure and minor orders on his own religious.

An abbot may be honored by being allowed to wear the cappa magna, a cloak and train, in processions. Less frequently the use of a violet zucchetto is permitted as a special distinction.

In formal address, an abbot is titled "right reverend abbot," but his religious would speak to him as "father abbot." In an assembly of their own institute, ruling abbots take precedence according to the time of their election after officers of the assembly, abbots *nullius,* and archabbots. The name of the abbot is not mentioned in the Canon of the Mass unless he is an abbot *nullius.* For his funeral, an abbot is vested in full pontifical garb, but the Mass is celebrated as for a priest.

Right to Govern. The abbot is, first of all, the religious superior of his community. His authority to instruct and command the religious is ideally a father's care for his sons. Monastic communities cherish their abbot not only as the superior or administrator, but also as the wise and solicitous parent who recognizes in each member of the family his particular talent and endowment, and by means best suited to the individual, develops that potential. Although the work of the apostolate and the care of temporalities demand consideration, the abbot is ever to be aware of spiritual goals as his first concern. The dominative power of the abbot arises from the religious profession of vows.

The authority of the abbot as a major superior in a clerical exempt institute is also jurisdictional. As the ordinary for his religious, he grants faculties for the hearing of their confessions and he can dispense them from certain obligations of the common law, such as fasting. An abbot possesses exclusive authority and responsibility for his community and for each member of it. He chooses the several officials of the monastery, who are responsible to and remain dependent upon him. He has direct and immediate control of each member of the house, while these have the right to approach him directly. This relationship, while sometimes difficult in very large abbeys, is the significant characteristic of abbatial rule.

While each abbey is a separate and independent juridic entity, most are associated into monastic congregations. The authority of its abbot president is specified in the constitutions. Pope Leo XIII provided for the confederation of Benedictine monastic congregations with an abbot primate, whose authority is described in the *Lex propria* of 1952.

If an abbey is to be specially distinguished, particularly as the motherhouse of many abbeys, it may be honored as an archabbey and its abbot called the archabbot. Unless the title is used for the head of a monastic congregation, an archabbot possesses almost no authority over other abbeys and their religious, but does enjoy some precedence. In the United States there are the Archabbeys of ST. VINCENT (Latrobe, Pa.) and of ST. MEINRAD (St. Meinrad, Ind.).

Bibliography: M. DLOUHY, *The Ordination of Exempt Religious* (Catholic University of American Canon Law Studies 271; Washington 1955) 68–87.

[M. J. DLOUHY]

ABBOT, BLESSING OF

In his own monastery and churches belonging to his monastery an abbot may celebrate the liturgy pontifically. To enjoy this privilege he must be blessed by the bishop of the place where the monastery is located or, in his absence, by a bishop of the abbot's own choice.

Mention of a special blessing for abbots is made in the 6th-century Rule of St. Benedict and also in the writings of St. Gregory the Great (d. 604 A.D.). The nucleus of the present rite was already developed by the 8th century, but throughout the Middle Ages the ceremonial was embellished along the lines of an episcopal consecration.

The blessing takes place at Mass, usually a Pontifical Mass concelebrated by the bishop and the new abbot. Two other abbots assist in the ceremony. The rite begins with the presentation of the abbot, who is examined briefly by the bishop. Then the Mass begins and continues up to the Alleluia Verse or Tract following the Epistle. The abbot prostrates himself before the altar for the chanting of the Litany of the Saints. The bishop then recites two orations and sings the Consecratory Preface, in the course of which he imposes hands on the head of the abbot in blessing. The abbot is given a copy of the Holy Rule of St. Benedict, the crozier, and the ring.

The celebration of Mass is resumed and continues as usual until the Offertory, when the abbot presents the bishop with candles, bread, and wine. Following the last blessing, the abbot is given the miter and gloves and is enthroned by the bishop. During the singing of the *Te Deum,* the abbot goes through the church blessing the people. At his throne he receives the homage of his monks and then finally imparts his solemn blessing on all.

Bibliography: J. BAUDOT, *Dictionnaire d'archéologie chrétienne et de liturgie* 2.1:723–727. P. RADÓ, *Enchiridion liturgicum,* 2 v. (Rome 1961) 2:1030–32.

[R. K. SEASOLTZ]

ABBOT, HENRY, BL.

Lay martyr; b. Howden, East Riding, Yorkshire, England; hanged, drawn, and quartered at York, July 4, 1597. Challoner relates his *acta* as follows: ''A certain Protestant minister, for some misdemeanour put into York Castle, to reinstate himself in the favor of his superiors, insinuated himself into the good opinion of the Catholic prisoners, by pretending a deep sense of repentance, and a great desire of embracing the Catholic truth . . . . So they directed him, after he was enlarged, to Mr. Henry Abbot, a zealous convert who lived in Holden in the same country, to procure a priest to reconcile him . . . . Mr. Abbot carried him to Carlton to the house of Esquire Stapleton, but did not succeed in finding a priest. Soon after, the traitor having got enough to put them all in danger of the law, accused them to the magistrates . . . . They confessed that they had explained to him the Catholic Faith, and upon this they were all found guilty and sentenced to die.'' Sentenced with Abbot were BB. George ERRINGTON, William KNIGHT, and William GIBSON. Abbot was declared venerable in 1886 and beatified by Pius XI on Dec. 15, 1929.

Feast of the English Martyrs: May 4 (England).

See Also: ENGLAND, SCOTLAND, AND WALES, MARTYRS OF.

Bibliography: R. CHALLONER, *Memoirs of Missionary Priests,* ed. J. H. POLLEN (rev. ed. London 1924; repr. Farnborough 1969). J. H. POLLEN, *Acts of English Martyrs* (London 1891).

[K. I. RABENSTEIN]

ABBOTT, LYMAN

Congregational clergyman and editor, whose writings offered a popular synthesis of Christianity and Darwinism; b. Roxbury, Mass., Dec. 13, 1835; d. Cornwall-on-Hudson, N.Y., Oct. 22, 1922. He was the son of Rev. Jacob Abbott, a popular writer, who moved to New York City in 1843. After graduating from New York University in 1853, Abbott was admitted to the bar, studied theology under his uncle Rev. John S. C. Abbott, and was ordained in 1860. An active abolitionist, he served as secretary of the American Freedmen's Union, which supported schools for freed slaves. In 1868 he became editor of the *Illustrated Christian Weekly* and literary editor of *Harper's,* resigning both posts in 1879. From 1876 to 1893 he edited the *Christian Union,* known later as the *Outlook* under his son's editorship. After the death of Henry Ward Beecher, Abbott succeeded to the pastorate of Plymouth Church, Brooklyn, N.Y., from which he resigned in 1898. He edited Beecher's collected works and wrote his official biography (1903). Abbott's other writings include the *Dictionary of Religious Knowledge* (1874), *The Spirit of Democracy* (1910), and autobiographical *Reminiscences* (1915). His Lowell Lectures, published as *The Evolution of Christianity* (1892), dealt with the development of theology and the church in Darwinian terms. *Christianity and Social Problems* (1896) called for reforms in the social organism. The *Theology of an Evolutionist* (1897) offered a synthesis of science and religion in Modernist terms.

Bibliography: I. V. BROWN, *Lyman Abbott: Christian Evolutionist* (Cambridge, Mass. 1953).

[R. K. MACMASTER]

ABBREVIATORS

This term was generically applied to one who drew up the first draft of a document, from which a good copy would be made to serve as the original. The ecclesiastical abbreviators were officials of the Apostolic Chancery, one of the oldest and most important offices in the Roman Curia. Their function was twofold: to compose the first, rather abbreviated, draft of papal letters, which were transcribed in proper form by copyists, and then to inspect the finished letter before it received the papal seal.

The origins of this office are uncertain. Mention is made of the existence of abbreviators in the Curia of Innocent III (1198–1216), but the first explicit use of the title abbreviator of apostolic letters occurs in the acts of John XXII (1316–34).

Whatever may be the date of the institution of the office of abbreviator, it is certain that it assumed greater importance upon its erection under Pius II (1458–64) into a college of prelates divided into a higher and a lower rank.

By decree of Leo X (1513–21) abbreviators were created nobles, counts palatine, and members of the papal household. They and their clerics and properties were exempt from all jurisdiction except the immediate jurisdiction of the pope. He also empowered them to confer the degree of doctor, to create notaries, to legitimize children, to ennoble three persons, and to make knights of the Order of St. Sylvester.

In the reforms of Pius VII (1800–23), the abbreviators of the lower rank were suppressed. The abolition of those of the higher rank in the reorganization of the papal chancery under Pius X (1903–14) brought to a close the long history of this institution.

Bibliography: E. FOURNIER, *Dictionnaire de droit canonique* 1:98–106. L. PASTOR, *The History of the Popes from the Close of the Middle Ages* 4:38–39. M. LEGA, *Praelectiones in textum iuris canonici,* 4 v. (Rome 1896–1901) 2.1:289–290. G. CIAMPINI, *De abbreviatorum . . . statu . . .* (Rome 1691).

[L. A. VOEGTLE]

'ABDALLĀH ZĀḤIR

Goldsmith, printer, lecturer, polemicist, deacon; b. Aleppo, Syria, 1680; d. monastery of Mar Hannā, Shuwair, Lebanon, Aug. 20, 1748. He was well educated in classical Arabic, philosophy, theology, and church history. Persecuted in Aleppo, he finally settled in the monastery of Mar Hannā (St. John) where he spent the rest of his life as a lay deacon, refusing priesthood out of humility. His greatest achievement was the construction of one of the very first printing presses for the Arabic language in the Orient, between 1723 and 1726. The first publication, however, dates from 1734. The purpose was to provide apologetic, instructional, and liturgical literature for Eastern Christians. He took an active part in the composition of the religious constitutions of the Basilian Shuwairite Order, vigorously opposed attempts by Patriarch Cyril Tānās to merge the Shuwairite monks and the

Lyman Abbott.

Salvatorian missionaries into one order, and courageously denounced the efforts of Jesuit missionaries to Latinize the Melchite Church. The literary works of 'Abdallāh contain dissertations in reply to attacks of non-Catholic writers, an incomplete introduction to philosophy, a short manual of theology, several sermons, and a number of interesting letters. Also, many books on spiritual matters, edited and printed by him, bear the stamp of his character and zeal. He was buried in the church at St. John's Monastery, Shuwair.

Bibliography: G. GRAF, *Geschichte der christlichen arabischen Literatur* 3:191–201, contains good bibliog.

[L. MALOUF]

ABDIAS OF BABYLON, ST.

According to legend, Abdias was the first bishop of Babylon, appointed by the Apostles Simon and Jude. W. Lazius, in 1552, regarded Abdias as the author of a collection of legends about the Apostles, assuming that he had written them in Hebrew and that they had been translated into Greek by Eutropius, his disciple, and into Latin by Julius Africanus. Actually the collection was drawn up by two anonymous authors in Gaul in the sixth century from earlier sources—one describing the martyrdoms of the Apostles and the other adding their virtues and miracles. It was used at the end of the sixth century in a revision at Auxerre of Jerome's martyrology and in a poem by Venantius Fortunatus. The Abdias of a mutilated epitaph of the fifth century found at Henchir Djezza in Tunisia was probably a martyr under the Vandals.

Bibliography: A. AUDOLLENT, *Dictionnaire d'histoire et de géographie ecclésiastiques*, ed. A. BAUDRILLART et al. (Paris 1912) 1:62–63.

[M. J. COSTELLOE]

ABDINGHOF, ABBEY OF

Paderborn, Westphalia, founded 1015 by Meinwerk, Bishop of Paderborn, with the help of Benedictine monks from CLUNY. The abbatial church, dedicated to SS. Peter and Paul, was consecrated in 1031. The abbey was an important cultural center during the 11th and 12th centuries. The *Carmina Abdinhofensia* probably originated there toward the end of the 11th century, and during the 12th century the monks wrote the *Vita Meinwerci* (*Monumenta Germaniae Historica: Scriptores* 11:104–161), and the *Annales Patherbrunnenses*. In the 13th century, however, a decline began to be apparent, and although various attempts at restoration were made, none produced any lasting improvement. After the plague of 1476, Abbot Henry of Peine (1477–91) united the abbey to the flourishing Bursfeld Union, and it again became a center of discipline and religious life. But by the end of the 16th century signs of decline were again occurring, and once more restoration took place under Abbot Leonard Ruben (1598–1609); after that the abbey remained vigorous until its suppression in 1803.

Bibliography: U. BERLIÈRE, *Dictionnaire d'histoire et de géographie ecclésiastiques*, ed. A. BAUDRILLART et al. (Paris 1912–) 1:64–65. *Westfälische Zeitschrift*, 107 (1957). K. HONSELMANN, *Lexikon für Theologie und Kirche*, ed. J. HOFER and K. RAHNER, 10 v. (2d, new ed. Freiburg 1957–65) 1:12.

[C. FALK]

'ABDISHO IV (EBEDJESU), CHALDEAN PATRIARCH

Abdisho IV (1555–1567) was a monk and bishop of Gezirah, Mesopotamia (upper Tigris), when he suc-

ceeded the Patriarch John Sulaqa. He journeyed to Rome (1561), where he was recognized and given the pallium by Pope Pius IV (April 17, 1562). His profession of faith was read at the Council of TRENT (Sept. 14, 1562). He consecrated many bishops. The Portuguese opposed his attempt to bring the Thomas Christians of India under his jurisdiction. He composed hymns in the honor of his predecessors who were martyred.

Bibliography: J. M. VOSTÉ, "Trois poésies inédites," *Angelicum* 8 (1931) 187–234. G. BELTRAMI, *La chiesa Caldea nel secolo dell'Unione* (Orientalia Christiana 83; 1933). É. AMANN, *Dictionnaire de théologie catholique* 11.1:229–230. E. TISSERANT, *ibid.* 14.2:3101–03. W. DE VRIES, *Lexikon für Theologie und Kirche* 3:626.

[F. X. MURPHY]

'ABDISHO BAR BERĪKĀ

Or Ebedjesu, Nestorian writer and metropolitan of Nisibis (Soba) and Armenia; d. November 1318. A monk (c. 1284) and bishop of Sīghar and Bet 'Arabājē, he became metropolitan of Nisibis in 1291. His voluminous writings in Syriac are listed at the end of his *Catalogue of Writers* (Badger, 361–379). *Commentaries* on the OT and NT, *Book of the Secrets of the Philosophy of the Greeks, Book on the Wonderful Economy of Salvation*, and many letters are lost. His *Book of the Pearl* and an *Introduction to the Trinity and Incarnation* are Nestorian dogmatic treatises; his *Symbolum, Canonical Collection, Table of Church Orders and Laws*, 50 spiritual poems called *Eden-Paradise, Book of Jewels*, and his *Book of the Foundations of Religion* are also preserved, some in Syriac and some in Arabic.

Bibliography: A. BAUMSTARK, *Geschichte der syrischen Literatur* (Bonn 1922) 323–325. J. PARISOT, *Dictionnaire de théologie catholique* 1.1:24–27. B. KOTTER, *Lexikon für Theologie und Kirche* 3:625–626. G. P. BADGER, *The Nestorians and Their Rituals*, 2 v. (London 1852) 2:422. J. M. VOSTÉ, *Orientalia Christiana periodica* 7 (1941) 233–250, Ascension. G. GRAF, *Geschichte der christlichen arabischen Literatur* 1:165; 2:214–216. J. DAUVILLER, *Dictionnaire de droit canonique* (Paris 1935–65) 5:91–134.

[F. X. MURPHY]

ABDISHO OF KASKAR, ST.

Fourth-century Babylonian martyr. According to the Syrian *Passio*, Abdisho (Abdiesus, Ebedjesu, or Hebedjesus) was chorbishop of Kaskar, Babylonia. Accused of conspiracy with the Romans, he suffered martyrdom with Abdas and 38 Christians under the Sassanid King Shapur II in 374 or 375.

Feast: May 16.

Bibliography: J. LABOURT, *Le Christianisme dans l'empire perse* (Paris 1904). A. CHRISTENSEN, *L'Iran sous les Sassanides* (Paris 1937). A. SCHALL, *Lexikon für Theologie und Kirche* 3:626. P. BEDJAN, ed., *Acta martyrum et sanctorum,* 7 v. (Paris 1890–97) 2:325–347.

[F. X. MURPHY]

ABDUCTION (IMPEDIMENT TO MARRIAGE)

Abduction as an impediment to marriage comes into being when a person is forcibly carried off or at least detained, and is retained in the abductor's power for the purpose of contracting marriage. The Latin code speaks of a woman who has been abducted or detained, while the Eastern code speaks more generally of a person who has been abducted or detained (*Codex Iuris Canonicis,* c.1089, *Codex Canonum Ecclesiarium Orientalium,* c. 806). Abduction is a diriment impediment since the law prescribes that there can be no valid marriage between the abductor and the one abducted as long as the abductor retains power over the one abducted.

The impediment of abduction considered in itself, and excluding the defect of consent that is frequently involved in it, is of ecclesiastical law and binds only Catholics. As an ecclesiastical law impediment, the impediment of abduction can be dispensed, however unlikely it might be that such a dispensation would be granted.

The impediment comes into being when a Catholic is either the abductor or the abducted person, because the impediment is intended not only as a protection for the abducted person, but also as a deterrent to the crime of abduction.

The impediment arises whether the abductor acts personally or through agents, either men or women. If a woman is abducted by agents and detained by them up to the actual moment of the marriage, the impediment renders the marriage invalid between the man who ordered the abduction and the woman whom he ordered abducted.

Violent or forceful abduction must be for the sole purpose of contracting marriage. If a woman is taken away and retained for any other purpose, e.g., for extortion or turpitude, the impediment does not arise.

The impediment arises as soon as the abductor perpetrates the abduction, and it continues to exist as long as the abducted person remains in his power. The impediment ceases to exist when the abducted person is separated from the abductor and has been restored to a safe and free place. Separation from the abductor entails a physical separation from him and from his agents. This has a special reference to the dwelling place. The abducted person must no longer be living in the same dwelling with the abductor, but the length of time for which this separation must endure is not established in the law. No change of place is absolutely required. If the abducted person has been detained by the abductor, the place can be said to become free and safe if the abductor departs and absolutely removes his influence and that of his agents over the abducted person. Hence, a safe and free place is one in which the abducted person is able freely to dispose of affairs at will, and in which the abducted person can declare his or her own wishes without external constraint.

Bibliography: B. F. FAIR, *Catholic University of America Canon Law Studies: The Impediment of Abduction* 194 (Washington 1944) 28–83. H. A. AYRINHAC, *Penal Legislation in the New Code of Canon Law* (New York 1920) 293–296. H. A. AYRINHAC and P. J. LYDON, *Marriage Legislation in the New Code of Canon Law* (New York 1957) 145–150.

[W. A. O'MARA]

ABELARD, PETER

Philosopher and theologian (Lat. *Abaelardus, Abeilardus*); b. Pallet, Brittany, 1079; d. Châlons-sur-Saône, April 21, 1142. One of the greatest philosophers of the 12th century, this peripatetic from Pallet, known as *Peripateticus palatinus* and *Doctor scholasticus,* is renowned for his solution of the problem of UNIVERSALS. As a theologian, he outraged his contemporaries by his original use of DIALECTICS. As a man, he is known for his celebrated love affair with HÉLOÏSE.

Life. Peter's father, Berengar, Lord of Pallet, planned a military career for him, but he chose learning instead. When he was about 15, he began the study of logic, probably under ROSCELIN OF COMPIÈGNE. In his autobiographical *Historia calamitatum,* he says that he traveled to any town where a teacher of logic could be found. Finally arriving in Paris, he studied under WILLIAM OF CHAMPEAUX, head of the cathedral school of Notre Dame. Prior to William's arrival, Paris had been considered intellectually inferior to the Benedictine Abbey of Bec and the cathedral schools of Laon and Chartres. Through William, Paris acquired great renown. While enrolled as a student, Abelard defeated William in public debate. On the strength of this victory, Abelard set up his own school in nearby Melun, and later in Corbeil. He was then only 25 years old. His youth and rashness in attacking men of established reputation in such a way that they were publicly disgraced earned him celebrity, devoted followers, and persistent enemies. After about two years

Heloise and Abelard.

5

defiat expectatio dum speratur in quo ñ est finis. sed augis̄ u
amoris. Quicqd desiderabile est si ñ contingat. desideras̄
defiat in illud. & quasi animā deponit qui desiderat.
Io est q̄ desicere in io unūquecq̄ toto studio migrate q̄d diligit
illud cogitat. illi heret. illud p̄sonat. in io quadā anime
defectione transfundit. Lassat affectus. seo amor augec̄.
Et q̄ diutī abest q̄d desiderat. eo expectantis desiderium
magis ignescit. Caro defiat. amor p̄fiat. Sponsa nescit
desiderare aliud quā sponsum. Illum desiderat. illū con
cupisat. in quē totis nirib; intendit. illū gremio mentis
fouet. illi se aperit & effundit. & dum maiori desiderio
exerotat amplī defiat. Ista desertio immunio est fragili
tatis. sed assumptio virtutis. **Amore lang. Cum scīs**
uiuentib; siue iam mortuis. desideriū nr̄m expandimī
orando. ut desideriu nr̄i effectū p̄sentent. xpo. tunc filiat
adiurans ut dilecto an primiores nobis sint nuntient ia
amore languenti.

Rufinus Ad hec uulnera. que infligunt̄ ex hu
gua. int homines medic̄ pene nullus est.

Jnuenit religio. inmusqc sepe laudat. Petr̄ Abailard?
Roncet in principio. si in sine sicatur u.
Sū est erā nec enī qsts̄ī 7 dicox utr̄ucq̄. de a homo
nec ds est nec hō p̄sens quā consus penagat
6; sp est et ho quē scam fugurat y nagu.

as a teacher in the region of Paris, he became ill and returned to his native Brittany. Returning to Paris in 1108, he studied rhetoric under the same man against whom he had previously jousted, William of Champeaux. Public disputations had become a prominent feature of school life; during one of them Abelard forced the master to modify his extreme realist position, according to which there is a separately existent reality corresponding to each of the universal terms in one's vocabulary.

When he was 34, Abelard began to study theology under ANSELM OF LAON. He found fault with Anselm's teaching methods, and to show that he could do better he gave a public lecture on the Book of Ezechiel after only one day's preparation. The novelty of his teaching consisted in the forthright raising of questions suggested by his dialectical studies; this was not the traditional method of communicating the patristic tradition with its heavy emphasis on questions that had affective implications. Once more Abelard earned the resentment of his teacher by arousing the interest of Anselm's students, thus showing that they preferred the work of a gifted amateur to Anselm's traditional mode of teaching.

Paris and Héloïse. When Abelard returned to Paris, he was allowed to teach both theology and dialectics, first at the school of Mont Sainte-Geneviève and then, in 1113, at the cathedral school of Notre Dame. Students flocked to him in such numbers that he acquired both wealth and honors. At this time he fell in love with Héloïse, the niece of Fulbert, a canon of Notre Dame. This unwitting man invited Abelard to live in his house and, ironically, to take charge of the further education of his niece. When Héloïse became pregnant, Abelard had her secretly conveyed to his home in Brittany. The whimsical name Astrolabe was given to their son. Later, to mollify Fulbert, Abelard secretly married Héloïse. This was possible since he had not received major orders at the time. When the marriage became known publicly and when students began to sing love songs and lyrics reputed to have been written by Abelard for Héloïse, Abelard tried to safeguard his position by having Héloïse enter the convent of Saint-Argenteuil, where she had been brought up. Fulbert regarded this as an evasion of responsibility and in anger hired men who, with the connivance of Abelard's servant, entered his room at night and emasculated him.

Abelard's personal fame as a man centers not so much on his philosophical and theological work as it does upon this love affair with Héloïse, told in such detail and with such frankness in letters that are still extant. He is the only philosopher in the Middle Ages who left an autobiography and personal letters, in which historians find details that are very illuminating for the study of social and intellectual life in the 12th century. The information supplied in these is invaluable for destroying false stereotypes set up by 19th-century historians, such as Jules Michelet, about intellectual freedom in the Middle Ages.

St. Bernard's Denunciation. After his downfall, Abelard entered the monastery at Saint-Denis to become a Benedictine monk. Characteristically, he aroused opposition by offering proof that the monastery's patron was not identical with Dionysius the Areopagite. He resumed teaching in Paris until 1121, when the Council of Soissons condemned his teaching on the Blessed Trinity. After spending some time in forced residence in a monastic house, he set up a school in what became the town of Nogent-sûr-Seine. In 1125 he was elected abbot of the Abbey of Saint-Gildas in his native Brittany. Finding his life as abbot difficult and complicated because of the monks of Saint-Gildas, he was back teaching in Paris in 1136. His teaching was denounced to St. BERNARD OF CLAIRVAUX by WILLIAM OF SAINT-THIERRY, who accused him of a rationalist approach that attempted to empty even doctrines such as the Trinity of all mystery. Bernard wrote to Pope Innocent II and to numerous bishops against Abelard and his teaching. Under the illusion that he would have the opportunity of publicly disputing with Bernard, Abelard appeared before the Council of Sens in 1141 only to find that his role was to listen silently while a sentence of condemnation was read to him. He appealed to Pope Innocent, oblivious of the fact that Bernard's letters had closed all doors to him. On his way to Rome, he was received at the monastery of Cluny by PETER THE VENERABLE, who persuaded him to abandon the struggle, attempt reconciliation with Bernard, and accept a papal authorization to pass his remaining years under the protection of Cluny. He died at a Cluniac priory in 1142.

Writings. Abelard's more important extant works are those that treat of logic and theology. In addition, there are extant sermons, poems, and letters, one of which is an autobiography covering his life until about 1129.

Logic. His *Introductiones parvulorum* are short glosses on the logical treatises of Porphyry, Aristotle, and Boethius, probably representing the lessons he gave to beginners. *Logica ingredientibus* contained more elaborate glosses on Porphyry and on the *Categories* and *De interpretatione* of Aristotle. *Dialectica* is his most developed and complete work on logic; the beginning of this work, probably attacking the realist position, has not survived.

Theology. His *Tractatus de fide Trinitatis* is the surviving record of his theological lectures prior to the Council of Soissons (1121). This work is notable for its lack of reference to the Church Fathers and the substitution of personal and seemingly rationalistic attempts to explain the Blessed Trinity. The compilation *Sic et non* lists the opinions of the Fathers, often contradictory, on various theological topics raised in scholastic disputations. This is at the same time an answer to those who said that he was not concerned with the Fathers and a proof that some rational approach was needed to reconcile their differences. One version of this work seems to have been written about 1123, and another toward the end of his life in 1136. *Theologia Christiana* is a reworking of the *Tractatus de fide Trinitatis* with many citations from the Church Fathers and the Scripture. It seems to have been written in 1124. Books 1 and 2 of *Introductio ad theologiam* are a reworking of his earlier books on theology. Book 3 represents an advanced form of his thought and was probably written in 1136. His *Ethics,* or *Scito teipsum,* probably written in 1137, deals with moral theology. *Dialogus inter philosophum, Judaeum et Christianum* was written during the last year of his life and gives his final thought on the problem of reason and faith.

Influence. The importance of Abelard in the history of philosophy rests mainly on his proposed solution to the problem of universals. He stood midway between the ultrarealist position of the Platonic tradition and the nominalist views of Roscelin, saying that universals as such exist only in the mind but that they signify the nature that individual things share in common. His place in theology depends mainly on his contribution toward the SCHOLASTIC METHOD. Historically, he stands close to the origin of the tradition, exemplified by Peter Lombard, that used varying opinions of the Fathers as the starting point for theological synthesis. His speculative pursuit of questions in theology without reference to their affective connotations seems to have outraged William of Saint-Thierry. In a letter to Bernard, the latter accuses Abelard of doing in theology what he had learned to do in dialectics, of being ''a censor of the faith, not a disciple; an improver of it, not an imitator.'' Viewed from the vantage point of the great syntheses of faith and reason established by 13th-century SCHOLASTICISM, in which Abelardian methods had an important place, his work seems more defensible than it did to his contemporaries. As to the orthodoxy of Abelard's theological opinions there are, on the one hand, the condemnations of Soissons and Sens (the latter formally approved by Innocent II) and the firm, lasting hostility of Bernard. On the other hand, modern scholars such as Jean Cottiaux and J. Rozycki, after a careful study of the development of his doctrine on faith and reason and on the Trinity, have found it possible to give a much more benign interpretation. Two things are certain: (1) Abelard wished to reason in such a way as not to be separated from Christ, and (2) much that was condemned at Sens cannot be found, as such, in his writings. This does not mean that Bernard and the bishops were wrong in condemning what they thought his contemporaries would have drawn from his words. Extant MSS of some of Abelard's immediate disciples indicate that the sense of the errors condemned was the very sense defended by the school of Abelard.

Modern scholarship has shown the existence of a school of Abelard both in theology and in logic. Not all of his disciples, however, were like Adam, a canon of the Lateran, who taught the errors of his master concerning the Incarnation before 1135 and who, being attacked by GERHOH OF REICHERSBERG, preferred apostasy to retraction. Direct disciples, such as JOHN OF SALISBURY and PETER OF POITIERS, were orthodox, while others, such as WILLIAM OF CONCHES and GILBERT DE LA PORRÉE, were accused of heresy. Bernard, William of Saint-Thierry, and John of Salisbury attest to the vast divulgation of Abelard's writings and influence, even after the condemnation of 1141. This is confirmed by the discovery of numerous MSS of *summae* of various *Sentences,* theological treatises, and logical works, many of them anonymous, belonging to the school of Abelard. Even after he was long dead, Peter Abelard was attacked by Walter of Saint-Victor as one of France's evils in *Contra quatuor labyrinthos Franciae.* By that time, Abelard's dialectics had taken firm hold in early scholasticism.

See Also: DIALECTICS IN THE MIDDLE AGES, SENTENCES AND SUMMAE.

Bibliography: Works. *Opera omnia, Patrologia Latina,* ed. J. P. MIGNE, v.178; *Ouvrages inédits d'Abélard,* ed. V. COUSIN (Paris 1836); *Opera,* ed. V. COUSIN et al., 2 v. (Paris 1849–59); ''Peter Abelards Philosophische Schriften,'' ed. B. GEYER, *Beiträge zur Geschichte der Philosophie und Theologie des Mittelalters* 21.1–4 (Münster 1919–33) 1–633; *Dialectica,* ed. L. M. DE RIJK (Assen 1956). Studies. Gilson *History of Christian Philosophy* 153–163. J. G. SIKES, *Peter Abailard* (Cambridge, Eng. 1932). É. H. GILSON, *Héloïse and Abelard,* tr. L. K. SHOOK (Chicago 1951). E. PORTALIÉ, A. VACANT et al, ed. *Dictionnaire de théologie catholique,* 15 v. (Paris 1903–50) 1.1:36–55. P. GLORIEUX, A. VACANT et al, ed. *Dictionnaire de théologie catholique,* 15 v. (Paris 1903–50) Tables généraees 1:5–7. E. VACANDARD, *Dictionnaire d'histoire et de géographie ecclésiastiques* 1:71–91. G. PARÉ et al., *La Renaissance du XIIᵉ siècle: Les Écoles et l'enseignement* (Paris 1933). R. E. WEINGART, *The Logic of Divine Love: A Critical Analysis of the Soteriology of Peter Abailard* (London 1970). J. MARENBON, *The Philosophy of Peter Abelard* (Cambridge 1997).

[S. R. SMITH]

ABELL, THOMAS, BL.

Martyr; b. place unknown, toward the end of the fifteenth century; d. July 30, 1540. He was educated at Oxford (M.A., 1516), became a chaplain to Catherine of Aragon, and preached and wrote in her favor. When sent to Spain in 1529 at the time of the divorce question, he performed invaluable work on Queen Catherine's behalf. He was one of her counselors at the divorce trial and probably helped her in making her appeals against the jurisdiction of the Legatine Court. In 1531 he published his vigorous defense of Catherine's marriage, the *Invicta Veritas*. For this he was imprisoned, but was later released. In 1533 he was sent to the Tower because of his counsel to Catherine to persist in refusing the title of "Princess Dowager." His name was included in the attainder of 1534 against the Nun of Kent and others, but he had had no real association with the Nun. He remained in the Tower for more than six years, receiving appalling ill-treatment. He refused to acknowledge the royal supremacy and for this reason was attainted of treason in 1540. He was hanged, drawn, and quartered at Smithfield. He was beatified on Dec. 29, 1886.

Feast: July 30.

Bibliography: B. CAMM, ed., *Lives of the English Martyrs Declared Blessed by Pope Leo XIII in 1886 and 1895*, 2 v. (London 1904–05).

[J. E. PAUL]

ABERCIUS, EPITAPH OF

The oldest monument that mentions the Eucharist, the Epitaph of Abercius is of great theological importance for the history of ecclesiastical doctrine. Two fragments of this inscription were discovered in 1883 by the British archeologist W. Ramsay in Hieropolis, near Synnada, in Phrygia Minor; they are now in the Lateran Museum. The epitaph appears to have been composed at the end of the 2nd century. It existed at the latest before the year 216, because the epitaph of Alexander, found by Ramsay a year before near the same place, quotes a part of the epitaph of Abercius and is dated 216. This epitaph of Alexander and a Greek legendary life of Abercius (4th century) enabled scholars to restore the entire text of the inscription. It contains 22 verses, a distichon, and 20 hexameters that describe the life and deeds of Abercius, Bishop of Hieropolis, who says that he composed and dictated it at the age of 72. The great event of his life was his journey to Rome, of which he gives an account.

The mystical and symbolic style of the inscription reflects the influence of the discipline of the SECRET, and its metaphorical phraseology is responsible for the sharp controversy that followed the discovery. A number of scholars, including G. Ficker, A. Dieterich, and R. Reitzenstein, tried to demonstrate that Abercius was not a Christian, but a venerator of Phrygian divinities Cybele and Attis; A. von Harnack called him a syncretist. The majority of scholars, including W. Ramsay, G. de ROSSI,

L. DUCHESNE, and F. CUMONT, are convinced that the epitaph is of Christian origin. A thorough investigation of its language and style, its content and form by F. DÖLGER has removed all doubt as to its Christian character. Abercius does not call himself a bishop, but "a disciple of the chaste shepherd," i.e., Christ, who "has great eyes that look on all sides." He taught him "faithful writings," i.e., the Holy Scriptures of the Christians and their doctrines. He sent him to Rome to see "the queen with golden robe and golden shoes," i.e., the Church of Christ, His Bride. Abercius saw there "a people bearing a splendid seal," i.e., the seal of Baptism. Faith was "his guide," and for this reason he met friends and fellow Christians everywhere who offered him as a meal the Lord's Supper of bread and wine. He calls Christ "the fish from the spring, mighty and pure," that "the spotless Virgin caught," i.e., whom the Virgin Mary conceived. The Christian teaching appears in the language of a mystery cult and explains why Abercius at the end says: "Let him who understands and believes this pray for Abercius," since only the initiated could comprehend the meaning of these words.

Bibliography: J. QUASTEN, ed., *Monumenta eucharista et liturgica vetustissima* (Bonn 1935–37); *Florilegium Patristicum* 7, ed. J. ZELLINGER et al. (Bonn 1904–) 2–25, text and Lat. tr. F. J. DÖLGER, ΙΧΘΥΣ, v.1 (Rome 1910) 8–138; *ibid.* v.2 (Münster 1922) 454–507. A. ABEL, *Byzantion* 3 (1926) 321–411, complete bibliog. J. QUASTEN, *Patrology*, 3 v. (Westminster, Md. 1950–53) 1:171–173, Eng. tr. A. FERRUA, *Revista di archeologia cristiana* 20 (1943) 279–305; *La civiltà cattolica* (1943) 39–45. H. GRÉGOIRE, *Byzantion* 25–27 (1955–57) 363–368, and Bardesanes.

[J. QUASTEN]

ABERCROMBY, ROBERT

Scottish Jesuit, 19 years on the Scottish mission; b. Scotland, 1532; d. Braunsberg College, East Prussia, April 27, 1613. Robert, of a good Catholic family, was educated at St. Mary's College, Scotland. He was one of five young men who in 1562 went to the Continent to study for the priesthood in the company of the Papal Nuncio Nicholas de Gouda, SJ, who was then returning from an unsuccessful visit to the court of Queen Mary in order to bring Scottish bishops to the Council of Trent. All five became Jesuits and played a distinguished role in the Counter Reformation in Scotland: James Tyrie, William Crichton, John Hay, William Murdoch, and Abercromby. Father Tyrie, who died in Rome in 1597, was especially influential in gaining Abercromby for the mission to Scotland. Meanwhile Abercromby spent 23 years abroad assisting Catholics from England and Scotland and training Jesuit novices. He was a pupil of the celebrated Jesuit Diego LAÍNEZ in the latter's last years and a friend of Cardinal Stanislaus HOSIUS, who built a seminary for priests at Braunsberg, where many Scotsmen came to study and receive their training for the missions from the Jesuits.

In 1586 Elizabeth of England had concluded an alliance with James VI of Scotland that had as a condition the expulsion of the Jesuits from Scotland. But the execution of his mother, Mary Stuart, shortly after, disposed the king to show indulgence to his Catholic subjects. The Jesuit missionaries were not slow to take advantage; Abercromby and William Ogilvie arrived from Poland and went into hiding while administering to the Catholics. Abercromby converted a number of high-born Scots, among them James Lindsay, brother of the Earl of Crawford. His most notable convert was James VI's wife, Anne of Denmark, at Holyroodhouse in 1600. Abercromby's own account, in a letter from Braunsberg, September 1608, gives evidence of James's knowledge of this and tacit consent. ''She [Anne] admitted [to the King] she had dealings with a Catholic priest and named me, an old cripple.'' James made no effort to reclaim Anne, but rather made it possible for her to have secret access to her Jesuit confessor by appointing Abercromby ''Keeper of his Majesty's Hawks.'' In a report on the state of Scotland (1602), Abercromby, then superior of the Scottish mission, remarked that the Queen had received Holy Communion nine or ten times.

The Gunpowder Plot of 1605 caused James, now king of England, to order a special search for Abercromby, offering a reward of 10,000 crowns for his capture, no mean proof of his worth to his enemies and his courage and skill in evading his pursuers. Forced finally to flee, Abercromby was one of the last priests to leave Scotland. He spent the remainder of his life at the Jesuit College at Braunsberg.

Bibliography: A. BELLESHEIM, *History of the Catholic Church of Scotland*, tr. D. O. HUNTER-BLAIR, 4 v. (Edinburgh 1887–90). W. FORBES-LEITH, ed., *Narratives of Scottish Catholics under Mary Stuart and James VI* (Edinburgh 1885). *Recusant History* 5 (1959–60) 205–206, for list of documents and bibliog. H. FOLEY, ed., *Records of the English Province of the Society of Jesus*, 7 v. in 15 (London 1877–82) v.7, pt. 2. G. OLIVER, *Collections towards Illustrating the Biography of the Scotch, English and Irish Members of the Society of Jesus* (London 1845). D. MCROBERTS, ed., *Essays on the Scottish Reformation, 1513–1625* (Glasgow 1962). T. COLLINS, *Martyr in Scotland* (New York 1956).

[J. D. HANLON]

ABGAR, LEGENDS OF

Two letters published by Eusebius of Caesarea as part of the *Acta Edessena* (*Histoire ecclesiastique* 1.13), supposedly discovered in the archives of Edessa. They purport to be an exchange of correspondence between Jesus Christ and King Abgar V called Uchama (the ''black'' according to Tacitus), who reigned in Osrhoene from 4 B.C. to A.D. 7 and from A.D. 13 to 50. The first letter carried by an artist, Ananias, requests Christ to come to Osrhoene and cure the king. In His response Christ excuses Himself, but promises to send the Apostle Thaddeus (the Disciple Thomas the Younger, or Addai) after His Ascension. A version (c. 400) of the legend in the *Acts of Thaddeus* and the Syriac *Doctrina Addaei* or Thaddeus legend has Christ cure Abgar before sending Thaddeus who converts the king.

The legend is further elaborated with the story of the conversion of King Abgar IX (179–216) who became a Roman tributary in 195, and whose court was visited by JULIUS AFRICANUS and the gnostic Bardesanes [*Kestoi* 7, ed. J. Viellefond (Paris 1932) 49]. The so-called portrait of Christ at Edessa was supposedly painted by the messenger Ananias; and the words of Christ quoted in the second letter were used by Syrians and Eastern Egyptians as protective devices (Procopius, *Bell. Pers.* 2.12).

Recent investigation indicates that the Eusebian version that spread in the West through RUFINUS OF AQUILEIA's translation of his Church History antedates the Thaddeus legend. Traces of Tatian's *Diatessaron* in the letters point to an early third-century composition. St. Augustine denied the existence of any letter written by Christ (*C. Faust.* 28.4) and the *Decretum Gelasianum* called this correspondence apocryphal. Considerable doubt now surrounds the conversion of King Abgar IX, which until recently was accepted as historical fact.

Bibliography: H. RAHNER, *Lexikon für Theologie und Kirche* 2 1:43. J. QUASTEN, *Patrology* 1:140–143. LABUBNÅ BAR SENNÅK, *The Doctrine of Addai*, ed. in Syriac and tr. G. PHILLIPS (London 1876). E. VON DOBSCHÜTZ, ''Der Briefwechsel zwischen Abgar und Jesus,'' *Zeitschrift für wissenschaftliche Theologie* 43 (1900) 422–486; *Das Christusbild von Edessa* (*Texte und Untersuchungen zur Geschichte der altchristlichen Literatur* 18, NS 3; 1899). A. VON HARNACK and E. VON DOBSCHÜTZ, eds., *Decretum Gelasianum* (*Texte und Untersuchungen zur Geschichte der altchristlichen Literatur* 38; 1912). S. RUNCIMAN, *Cambridge Historical Journal* 3 (1929–31) 238–252, portraits: H. C. YOUTIE, ''. . . the Letter to Abgar,'' *Harvard Theological Review* 23 (1930) 299–302; 24 (1931) 61–66. I. ORTIZ DE URBINA, ''Le origini del cristianesimo in Edessa,'' *Gregorianum* 15 (1934) 82–91.

[F. X. MURPHY]

ABIDING IN CHRIST

The verb μένειν, which in general means to remain or to abide, occurs about 117 times in the New Testament, and 67 of these are found in the Johannine writings. The phrase ''abiding in Christ'' reflects both the King James and the Douay translations. Contemporary English translations differ, some using ''abide,'' but others favoring ''remain'' and ''dwell.'' St. John employs the Greek word to express hisconviction that the new life of the last age, which the Christian believer possesses here and now, is in itself and in its fundamental orientation permanent and imperishable. This new life is everlasting,precisely because it joins the Christian in an abiding community of life with Christ and, through Christ, with the Father. Christ abides in His disciples, giving them a share in His own divine and everlasting life, which He holds from the Father (Jn 5.26; 6.56–57; 1 Jn 5.11–12). St. John uses with predilection the so-called reciprocal immanence formulas (e.g., ''Abide in me, and I in you,'' John 15.4) to express this deep unchangeable community of life with Christ and, through Him, with the Father (Jn 6.56–57; 15.4–10; 1 Jn 3.24; 4.12–16). In St. John's view the Christian's union with the Father is an extension of his abiding union with the Son (Jn 14.20; 15.9–10; 17.21, 23, 26); and the communion among Christians grounded on their communion with the Son and Father, has as its exemplar the union between Father and Son (Jn 17.11, 21, 22). The abiding new life in Christ is conferred by the Sacraments in FAITH (Jn 3.5; 6.56–57), with the uncreated gift of the Spirit vouching for the fact that ''we abide in God and He in us'' (1 Jn 4.13; see 3.24b). Nevertheless the hostility of the world requires that Christians strive perseveringly to abide in faith, in love, and in the practice of the Commandments; see St. John's urgent imperatives: Jn 8.31; 15.4–27; 1 Jn 2.6, 24, 27, 28; 3.15, 17; 4.12, 16.

See Also: MYSTICAL BODY OF CHRIST; BROTHER IN CHRIST;INCORPORATION IN CHRIST; REBIRTH (IN THE BIBLE); GRACE, ARTICLES ON.

[F. X. LAWLOR/D. M. DOYLE]

ABINGDON, ABBEY OF

Benedictine house, Berkshire, England, founded *c.* 675, refounded *c.* 954, dissolved 1538. Its early history is doubtful, but according to its chronicler it was founded by a certain Cissa, king of Wessex. It was ruined by the Danes in the 9th century and left derelict until King Eadred gave it to St. ETHELWOLD OF WINCHESTER to restore *c.* 954. Regular Benedictine life was restored, and Abingdon became a powerhouse of the English monastic revival, sending colonies of monks to the new minster of WINCHESTER and to the Fenland abbeys of ELY, PETERBOROUGH, THORNEY, and CROWLAND. After the Conquest, a Norman abbot from Jumièges was installed and the Crown imposed a service of 30 knights on the abbey. It possessed extensive estates and church patronage in Berkshire, Oxford, Gloucester, and Warwick. The church and monastic buildings were rebuilt in the 12th century,

but little of these remain. Its income in 1535 was £1,876. The last abbot, Thomas Rowland, formally surrendered the abbey to the Crown on Feb. 9, 1538.

Bibliography: *Chronicon Monasterii de Abingdon,* ed. J. STEVENSON, 2 v. (*Rerum Britannicarum medii aevi scriptores* 2; 1858). *The Victoria History of Berkshire,* ed. P. H. DITCHFIELD and W. PAGE, 4 v. (London 1906–24) v. 2. F. M. STENTON, *The Early History of the Abbey of Abingdon* (Reading, Eng. 1913). D. KNOWLES, *The Monastic Order in England, 943–1216* (2d ed. Cambridge, Eng. 1962) 31–56, *passim.* J. A. ROBINSON, *The Times of Saint Dunstan* (Oxford 1923).

[C. H. LAWRENCE]

ABINGTON, THOMAS (HABINGTON)

Recusant and antiquarian; b. Thorpe, near Chertsey, Surrey, England, Aug. 23, 1560; d. Hindlip, near Worcester, Oct. 8, 1647. He was the son of John Abington, cofferer to Elizabeth I, and he attended Lincoln College, Oxford, and in 1579 went to the Continent to pursue his studies. At Rheims he was converted to the Catholic faith, and some time later he returned to England. The cause of the imprisoned Mary Queen of Scots elicited his devotion, and he became involved, along with his brother Edward, in the Babington Plot. Edward was executed (Sept. 30, 1586), but Thomas was committed to the Tower of London where he remained for six years. Released by order of Elizabeth (he was her godson), he retired to Hindlip Castle, the country seat his father had built in Worcestershire. For harboring priests (the house had 11 priest holes), Abington was arrested in January 1606, when four Jesuits—Fathers Garnet and Oldcorne, and Brothers Owen and Ashley—were found there. On the charge of complicity in the Gunpowder Plot, all four were executed; but Abington, who was tried with them, was released on the intercession of Lord Monteagle, his brother-in-law. Forbidden to leave Worcestershire, he devoted his remaining years to local antiquarian researches.

Bibliography: J. GILLOW, *A Literary and Biographical History or Bibliographical Dictionary of the English Catholics from 1534 to the Present Time,* 5v. (New York, 1885–1902) 3:74–76. H. FOLEY, ed., *Records of the English Province of the Society of Jesus,* 7 v. (London 1877–82) 4.1:33–34. *Dictionary of National Biography, from the Earliest Times to 1900,* 63 v. (London 1885–1900) 8:857–858.

[R. I. BRADLEY]

ABOMINATION OF DESOLATION

This cryptic apocalyptic expression is employed contemptuously in Daniel to describe the profanation of the Temple by the King of Syria, ANTIOCHUS IV EPI-

PHANES, who had the statue of Zeus Olympios placed there; in the New Testament the expression is used in the "little apocalypse" of Christ's eschatological discourse to call attention to the blasphemous activity of the Antichrist (prefigured by Antiochus) that is to be expected prior to the Parousia.

In Daniel. The only Old Testament usage of the now traditional expression "abomination of desolation" or "the horrible abomination" is found in the Book of Daniel (9.27; 11.31; 12.11). Scholars now see in this mysterious expression [Heb. *šiqqûṣ (me)šōmēm*] a veiled description of the blasphemous actions of Antiochus IV, described with clearer detail in Maccabees (1 Mc 1.57; 2 Mc 6.2). Thus, chapter 11 of Daniel describes Antiochus's ruthless persecution climaxed by the erection of the abomination of desolation in the Temple; the texts of Maccabees tell of the desecration of the Temple by the soldiers of Antiochus and the setting up of the idol Zeus Olympios on the altar. Since Baal Shamem (Aramaic, *ba'al šamēm*, lord of the heavens) is the Aramaic title of Zeus Olympios, scholars look on the abomination of desolation as a veiled and contemptuous reference to this idol. By replacing the name of Baal with *šiqqûṣ* (abomination, detested thing) and by eliminating the vowels of *šamēm* (heavens) and substituting those of *bōšet* (shame), the author obtained the Hebrew expression *šiqqûṣ šōmēm* (abomination of desolation). The entire expression would then refer to the statue of Baal Shamem (alias Zeus Olympios) that Antiochus IV erected in the Temple in 167 B.C.

In Christ's Eschatological Discourse. In Mt 24.15 and Mk 13.14 the abomination of desolation is linked with the fall of Jerusalem and the end of the world. Since the abomination of desolation is presented as "standing," with a grammatical switch from the neuter τὸ βδέλυγμα to the masculine participle ἑστηκότα (Mk 13.14; see Taylor, 511–512), the text itself suggests that the abomination is really symbolic of a man. Noting the similarities between the eschatological discourse of Christ in the Synoptics (Mt 24.4–39; Mk 13.5–31) and St. Paul's description of the Antichrist (2 Thes 2.3–12), it is probable that the abomination of desolation is to be identified with the "man of sin," "the son of perdition," "the wicked one," who in the last days "sits in the temple of God and gives himself out as if he were God" (2 Thes 2.4). When Matthew cautions "let him who reads understand," his purpose is to recall the hideous desecration wrought by Antiochus (cf. 1 Mc 1.57) as a warning to his readers concerning the blasphemous activity of the Antichrist. According to earlier commentators, the prophecy was fulfilled when the Emperor Caligula attempted to have his statue erected in the Temple in A.D. 40, or when the fiery zealots turned the Temple into a fortress in A.D.

68, or at the actual destruction of the Holy City and the Temple by Titus in A.D. 70. Although the last opinion merits consideration, recent commentators hold that it is more likely that Matthew and Mark were not so much concerned with indicating a purely historical event, but actualized a traditional expression by applying it to the godless and blasphemous activity of the Antichrist at the end of time.

Bibliography: W. FOERSTER, "Βδέλυγμα," G. KITTEL, *Theologisches Wörterbuch zum Neuen Testament* (Stuttgart 1935–) 1:598–600. R. H. CHARLES, *Commentary on Daniel* (Oxford 1929). J. A. MONTGOMERY, *Daniel* (International Critical Commentary; New York 1927) 388–390. V. TAYLOR, ed., *The Gospel according to St. Mark* (London 1952) 511–515.

[F. J. MONTALBANO/EDS.]

ABONDANCE, MONASTERY OF

Former house of CANONS REGULAR OF ST. AUGUSTINE, and then of Cistercian Feuillants, more properly called the Abbey of Sainte-Marie d'Abondance (Latin, *Abundantia*), in the valley of the Drance, in Haute-Savoie, France, former Diocese of Geneva. Its origin is often attributed to St. COLUMBAN, but none of his biographies mentions it. The ascription probably stems from a confusion of names between it and REMIREMONT (original Latin, *Monasterium Habundense*). It is certain that in 1080 Louis of Féterne established canons regular at Abondance, and that the foundation was richly endowed by his family. Then in 1108, the canons of SAINT-MAURICE gave the lands of Abondance to a group of canons under Prior Herluin. In 1155 these canons were congratulated on their observance in a bull of Pope Adrian IV. Between 1128 and 1144 the monastery had achieved the status of an ABBEY; Rudolph of Vauserier was made first abbot (1144). In 1156 and 1158 the abbots of Abondance and Saint-Maurice signed agreements of association. But between mid-12th and early 13th century, Abondance founded or subordinated to itself five abbeys: Sixt, Entremont, Grandval, Goailles, and Filly, as well as 22 priories. Up to the 14th century, the monastery enjoyed great material prosperity; it held first place in the Diocese of Geneva. But excessive wealth and COMMENDATION (1436) led to a relaxation of discipline. Decadence proceeded at a rapid pace in the 16th century, and the number of religious diminished to half. Though the commendatory Abbot Gaspard Provana opposed the reform attempted there by FRANCIS DE SALES, the future bishop of Geneva, the latter finally won out in 1598. The new reform abbot, Vespasian Aiazza, came to an understanding with the Cistercian FEUILLANTS, and by a brief of Sept. 28, 1606, Pope Paul V sanctioned Abondance's concordat with the Feuillants, who, on May 7, 1607, installed Favre, vicar-general of Francis de Sales, as abbot. But these religious, isolated high up in the valley of the Drance, abandoned themselves in time to unhealthy distractions. Finally, Pope CLEMENT XIII's bull of May 9, 1761, granted King Charles-Emmanuel the right to suppress the Feuillants; another bull of May 4, 1762, allotted the goods of Abondance, with the exception of the benefices, to the Abbey of Sainte-Marie of Thonon. During the French Revolution the abbey was sold. Today, the abbey church (14th and 17th centuries), the cloister (14th century with frescoes), and the rich treasury are all classified as historical monuments. The church serves the needs of the local parish.

Bibliography: L. CIBRARIO, ed., *Scriptorum*, 3 v. (Monumenta historiae patriae 3, 5, 11; Turin 1840–1863) 2:301–318, constitutions, 321–434, necrology. J. GARIN, *Dictionnaire d'histoire et de géographie ecclésiastiques* 1:144–153. L. H. COTTINEAU, *Répertoire topo-bibliographique des abbayes et prieurés* 1:9–10.

[J. DAOUST]

ABORTION

PRACTICE

Medically, abortion is defined as the termination of pregnancy by any means before the fetus is sufficiently developed to survive; it is divided into spontaneous ("miscarriage") and induced. Dictionaries, encyclopedias, and textbooks sometimes follow this definition. However, the practice of induced abortion requires a definition that is properly descriptive of the moral reality. In his landmark encyclical *The Gospel of Life (Evangelium Vitae)* (1995), John Paul II, citing the need to "*call things by their proper name,*" defines abortion—he uses the term "procured abortion"—as "*the deliberate and direct killing, by whatever means it is carried out, of a human being in the initial phase of his or her existence, extending from conception to birth*" (58) (emphasis in original). Approximately 15% of recognized pregnancies end in spontaneous abortions. However, the topic of procured abortion is part of an intense debate that John Paul II calls "an enormous and dramatic clash between good and evil, death and life, the 'culture of death' and the 'culture of life'" (EV 28). At the conclusion of his classical study on abortion, Connery notes that the trend in the 19th century of eradicating abortion has now been reversed and that "in our present society the frequency of abortion is far greater than anything the Roman or ancient world ever knew or dreamed of" (Connery, 313). Indeed, the practice of abortion is unprecedented not only in terms of numbers but in term of methods and motivations.

Procedures. The purpose of abortion is to produce a dead child. Techniques for performing abortion are divided into surgical and what are called medical (involving the use of chemicals).

In surgical abortions the unborn child is killed and removed either through the woman's cervix or, for some late-term abortions, through the abdomen (hysterotomy or hysterectomy). The most common abortion technique reported in the United States for 1997 was the surgical technique of dilation of the woman's cervix and curettage (D&C) (97.4% as reported to the Center for Disease Control for 1997), including sharp curettage but mainly suction curettage (vacuum aspiration). In suction curettage, the cervix is dilated, and a hollow curette tube is inserted through the cervix and into the uterus. Suction causes the baby's body to implode; the body parts are then suctioned through the tube. After 16 weeks, dilation and evacuation (D&E) is used. A variation on D&E is intact dilation and extraction (D&X or partial-birth abortion), used primarily at 20 to 24 weeks, but sometimes later, a technique in which the child is delivered feet-first all except for the head, an instrument is forced into the base of the living child's head, the brain is sucked out, and the delivery of the now-dead child is completed.

In medical abortions, various chemicals—such as oxytocin, saline or urea solutions, prostaglandins, mifepristone (RU-486), misoprostal, or methotrexate—are used in various combinations to kill the unborn child and/or to induce premature labor. Certain contraceptive drugs and devices can also act as abortifacients by preventing implantation of the newly conceived life. This also is one of the principle effects of "morning-after pills," high doses of ordinary birth control pills taken a couple of days after intercourse.

Statistics. The number of illegal or clandestine abortions performed is by definition difficult to determine. Estimates vary widely. Once abortion is made legal, the overall incidence of abortion increases. In the United States, the incidence of legal abortion is tracked by the Center for Disease Control (CDC) and by the Alan Guttmacher Institute (AGI), founded by Planned Parenthood. CDC data are derived primarily from central health agencies and are considered incomplete. To overcome this deficiency, AGI sends questionnaires to all known abortion providers. CDC reported 193,491 legal abortions in 1970. The number increased to a peak of 1,429,577 in 1990, then generally dropped throughout the 1990s to 1,186,039 in 1997 (with a slight increase from 1995 to 1996). AGI's peak number, also in 1990, was 1,608,600, that number dropping in 1996 to 1,365,700 (also with a slight increase from 1995 to 1996). Especially since the 1950s, laws regulating and restricting the practice of

Cardinals standing in front of boxes of petitions during a pro-life rally on Capitol Hill. Left to right: Adam Maida, Detroit; Roger Mahony, Los Angeles; Joseph Bernardin, Chicago; Anthony Bevelaqua, Philadelphia; Bernard Law, Boston; James Hickey, Washington; and William Keeler, Baltimore. (AP/Wide World Photos)

abortion have been overturned in many countries. AGI estimates that the number of legal abortions worldwide in 1995 could have been as high as 25.6 million.

Reasons for Abortion. CDC's report on U.S. abortions for 1997 showed that women obtaining abortions were more likely to be under 25 years of age (51.8%), white (58.4%), and unmarried (81%). Forty-eight percent had repeat abortions. CDC or the AGI surveys do not track reasons for abortions. Specialized surveys indicate that most abortions are elective. In one U.S. study, women on average gave 3.7 reasons for obtaining an abortion, with 76% choosing concern about how having a baby could change their lives. Similar results are found worldwide.

However, reasons for promoting the legalization of abortion extend far beyond making life choices available. Major social forces consider abortion an essential part of an effort to control population growth and size. Others see abortion as a tool to solve a wide variety of social problems, for example, poverty and crime. In these and other cases, the inherent dignity of the unborn child is negated, reduced, or superceded for the sake of other values.

CHURCH TEACHING

Each person is created in the image and likeness of God and is called to a personal relationship with God that will last forever. The life of each person is sacred and must be respected absolutely from the moment of conception to natural death. No one can ever claim the right to directly destroy an innocent human being for any reason. Direct abortion is gravely contrary to the moral law. With respect to care for the mother and her child, the Church's social teaching embraces a deep commitment

Pro-life demonstrators marching in front of the White House, 1979.

to support for families, help for pregnant women in need, and healing after abortion.

Scripture. Neither the Old nor the New Testament explicitly addresses the question of procured abortion. This silence is not a sign of acceptance but of abhorrence. Life is a gift from God, who is the Lord of life and death. Shedding the blood of the innocent was forbidden (Gn 9:4–6; Ex 20:13; Dt 5:17). In some texts it is suggested that God works within the womb (Jb 10:8–12, 31:15; Is 44:24; Ps 139:13–15; 2 Mc 7:22–23) and that God has a personal relationship with the unborn child (Is 49:1, 5; Jer 1:5). In the New Testament, the infancy narratives in particular manifest great respect for fetal and infant life.

Early Church. Abortion was an accepted practice in the Greco-Roman culture. As the early Church moved into this world, an explicit teaching in opposition to abortion developed. The *Didache or Teaching of the Twelve Apostles*, an early book of Christian instruction with roots in the Jewish community (dating perhaps from the 1st century AD), begins with a teaching on the two Ways of Life and Death, and includes the admonition: ''Thou shalt not procure abortion, nor commit infanticide'' (II.2). In the early centuries, the condemnation of abortion was unequivocal.

The first Church legislation prescribing penitential discipline for abortion appears in the early 4th century, beginning a legal tradition that continues to this day. The distinction between the formed and unformed fetus, especially with regard to the time of animation, entered into patristic theological reflections. A primary influence in this regard was the Septuagint (Greek) translation of a text in the Old Testament. One man in the course of fighting with another strikes a woman and causes a miscarriage (Ex 21:22–25). In the Hebrew version, a fine is levied for the miscarriage, but the principle of ''life for life, eye for an eye'' applies to any other injuries. The Greek text introduces a distinction between the unformed and formed child, the penalty for destroying the former being a fine, for the latter ''life for life.'' Here abortion of the formed fetus was homicide. Not all Church Fathers thought the distinction between the formed and unformed fetus was significant. Even for those who did, the time of animation was not seen as a dividing line determining when abortion was permissible. Whether formed or unformed, a new human life was under way and abortion was rejected either as homicide or as anticipated homicide.

Transmission of the Tradition. In the Middle Ages, Aristotle's biology, in which the male was formed at 40

Abortion rights supporters march through Washington. (UPI/Corbis-Bettmann)

days, the female at 90 days, was reintroduced into the West. The distinction between the formed and unformed fetus became a part of Church discipline, law, and theology, but the condemnation of abortion at any stage continued. As Connery notes, "Even during the many centuries when Church penal and penitential practice was based on the theory of delayed animation, the condemnation of abortion was never affected by it" (Connery, 304). The distinction was used mainly for purposes of legal classification and the grading of penances.

Building on an unpublished work of John of Naples, Antoninus (1389–1459) for the first time introduced into theology a discussion of abortion of the unanimated fetus to save the life of the mother. Theologians debated this matter for the next three or four centuries. The issue became obsolete when the distinction between formed and unformed fetus was undercut by the findings of modern science and the theory of delayed animation was displaced by that of immediate animation. Connery argues that a consensus of theologians regarding immediate animation was reached in the second half of the 19th century. "This tended to make the whole question [lregarding abortion of the unanimated fetus] somewhat speculative" (Connery, 223). In 1869, Pius IX removed the distinction

between animated and unanimated fetus as a basis for penalties in Church law.

In the course of the modern debate, Antonius de Corduba (1485–1578) introduced a distinction between acceptable medical therapies that are immediately, directly, and principally conducive to the health of the mother (*de se salutifera*) and unacceptable therapies that are immediately, directly, and principally conducive to the death of fetus (*de se mortifera*). Corduba's distinction met with general acceptance and eventually became known as the distinction between direct and indirect abortion.

Modern Developments. In the second half of the 19th century, an extended debate arose among theologians over craniotomy (collapsing the skull of the child to complete delivery) and medical abortion to save the mother's life. Those in favor argued that the fetus in these circumstances was an unjust aggressor, even if only in a material sense. The intention was to save the mother's life, while the death of the fetus was accidental and unintentional. Through decrees in 1884, 1889, and finally 1895 (DS 3258, 3298), the Holy Office rejected craniotomy and medical abortion. It stated that it cannot be taught that craniotomy is licit, and that the same applies to any

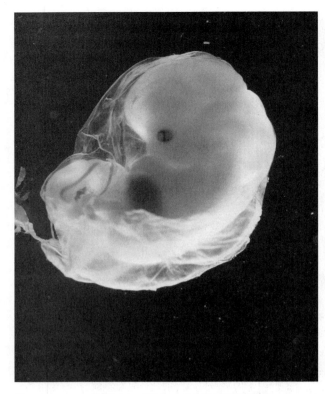

Human embryo. (© Science Pictures Limited/CORBIS)

medical procedure directly lethal either to the fetus or to the mother. After devoting four chapters of his book to these controversies, Connery concluded: ''It may be difficult in many cases to know where to draw the line between accidental and deliberate killing, but church authorities apparently felt that these theologians [arguing for the procedures] had gone over the line'' (Connery, 312).

After the issuance of the encyclical *Casti connubii* by Pius XI (1930), in which abortions for the mother's life or health were addressed at some length, a discussion developed among theologians on the application of the distinction between direct and indirect abortion to the case of the removal of the cancerous uterus of a pregnant woman. Theologians generally came to accept the position that it was legitimate directly to remove the cancerous uterus to save the mother's life, with the indirect effect that the child may die.

In 1898 and 1902, the Holy Office responded to questions about ectopic pregnancies (DS 3338, 3358). It recognized the general permissibility of a laparotomy, as long as serious provision was made for the life of both the fetus and the mother, but it objected to the direct removal of the nonviable fetus. In a work published in 1933, T. Lincoln Bouscaren applied the distinction be-

tween direct and indirect abortion to ectopic pregnancies. He argued that a pathological tube could be directly removed to save the mother's life, with the indirect effect that the child may die. His position was generally accepted by theologians.

In his Oct. 25, 1951 ''Allocution to Midwives,'' Pius XII affirmed that every human being, even the child in the womb, has the right to life directly from God. There is no justification for the direct, deliberate disposal of an innocent human life, whether as an end in itself or as a means. In a Nov. 26, 1951 ''Address to the Family Front Congress,'' Pius XII again affirmed that innocent human life from the first moment of its existence is to be preserved from any direct voluntary attack. He further stated that this principle applies to mother and child; every means must be used to save the life of both. The Holy Father explicitly adopts the distinction between direct and indirect abortion. He notes that he is careful in the use of the expression ''direct killing.''

> The reason is that if, for example, the safety of the life of the future mother, independently of her state of pregnancy, might call for an urgent surgical operation, or any other therapeutic application, which would have as an accessory consequence, in no way desired nor intended, but *inevitable*, the death of the fetus, such an act could not be called a *direct* attempt on the innocent life. In these conditions, the operation can be lawful, as can other similar medical interventions, provided that it be a matter of great importance, such as life, and that it is not possible to postpone it until the birth of the child, or to have recourse to any other efficacious remedy.

Vatican II to the Present. In its ''Pastoral Constitution on the Church in the Modern World,'' the Second Vatican Council summed up the Church's teaching tradition on abortion: ''God, the Lord of life, has entrusted to men the noble mission of safeguarding life, and men must carry it out in a manner worthy of themselves. Life must be protected with the utmost care from the moment of conception: abortion and infanticide are abominable crimes'' (51). Thirty years later, John Paul II authoritatively set forth the teaching that the direct and voluntary killing of an innocent human being is always gravely immoral (EV 57) and then with an equal invocation of authority he applied this teaching to abortion:

> Therefore, by the authority which Christ conferred upon Peter and his Successors, in communion with the Bishops . . . *I declare that direct abortion, that is, abortion willed as an end or as a means, always constitutes a grave moral disorder,* since it is the deliberate killing of an innocent human being. This doctrine is based upon the natural law and upon the written Word of God, is

transmitted by the Church's Tradition and taught by the ordinary and universal Magisterium (EV 62) (emphasis in original).

The worldwide practice and promotion of abortion on a scale unheard of in the history of human society prompted this unprecedented formulation of the Church's teaching. Just as the Church at the end of the 19th century could not be silent about the working classes who were oppressed in their fundamental rights, so today, ''when another category of persons is being oppressed in the fundamental right to life, the Church feels in duty bound to speak out with the same courage on behalf of those who have no voice'' (EV 5).

SPECIAL QUESTIONS

In the process of human generation, God creates and directly infuses the immaterial and eternal soul. The Magisterium has not definitively resolved the issue of when the soul is infused. However, today, as in the past, all direct abortion from fertilization forward is rejected. In *The Gospel of Life*, John Paul II sets forth two basic arguments. First, a new human individual begins at fertilization: ''a life is begun which is neither that of the father nor the mother; it is rather the life of a new human being with his own growth. It would never be made human if it were not human already. . . . Right from fertilization the adventure of a human life begins, and each of its capacities requires time, a rather lengthy time to find its place and to be in a position to act'' (EV 60, quoting the Congregation for the Doctrine of the Faith, ''Declaration on Procured Abortion'' [1974]). John Paul II takes as his own the rhetorical question asked in the CDF's instruction *Donum vitae*, ''How could a human individual not be a human person?'' Second, when human life is at issue, the safer course is required: ''The mere probability that a human person is involved would suffice to justify an absolutely clear prohibition of any intervention aimed at killing a human embryo.'' The Holy Father continues: ''Precisely for this reason, over and above all scientific debates and those philosophical affirmations to which the Magisterium has not expressly committed itself, the Church has always taught and continues to teach that the result of human procreation, from the first moment of its existence, must be guaranteed that unconditional respect which is morally due to the human being in his or her totality and unity as body and spirit'' (EV 60).

In the Middle Ages, Thomas Aquinas was a proponent of delayed animation. According to his biological theory, out of excess nourishment, the male produces semen, which serves as an active instrumental cause of the generative power of the father's soul, the elements, and the heavens (responsible for the species of the one generated). Also out of excess nourishment, the female produces menstrual blood, a passive material. At conception, the semen begins acting on the menstrual blood; through a series of many generations and corruptions, a new life is generated, at first vegetative, then animal, and finally, when the body is sufficiently organized, intellectual. With respect to the completion of the generative process, the parents only dispose the matter, while God directly creates the form. In the *Summa Theologiae*, Thomas espouses the classic Aristotelian view that once generation is complete, the semen dissolves. ''The movement of an instrument ceases when the effect has been produced in being'' (*Summa Theologiae* I, q. 118, a. 1, ad 4).

As noted earlier, with the establishment of the cell theory, the discovery of the female ovum, and a proper understanding of the male sperm and fertilization, the theory of immediate animation became generally accepted. The essential generative act takes place at fertilization. What happens thereafter is self-directed development and growth. From the single-celled zygote stage, the new life is an organized, complex, unique, human, individual person. The new life is not a potential human being but a human being with active potential to grow and develop in accord with the life cycle proper to the human person.

Those who seek to maintain the general theory of delayed hominization—the commonly used term today for delayed animation—in the context of the new biology have difficulties in explaining how a lower form of life is transformed into a higher. If the male semen is not the cause of the ever-evolving generative process, then a new efficient cause must be found. The most economical argument places the nucleus of the zygote as the efficient cause of the developmental process. Ashley and O'Rourke point out that for Aristotle the presence of a highly organized body is dependent on the appearance of a ''primary organ'' (which for him was the heart) through which the soul activated the organism. But today we know that ''a sequence of primordial centers of organization in the embryo goes back continuously to the nucleus of the zygote, long before the brain appears as the final center'' (Ashley and O'Rourke, 236). Only the minimal structure necessary for the active potentiality of self-development is required for an organism to be an actual human person.

Not all who favor some form of delayed hominization adopt the traditional general theory. Some argue that the new human life in its earliest days and even weeks is genetically human but is not a single unified individual. However, a careful look at what is known biologically sheds new light on early human development and casts aside the suggestion that in the early stages the cells of the new life are just an aggregate.

Serra and Columbo argue that the new genome, established at fertilization, is the basis of the structural and functional unity of the embryo developing in a constant direction. In fact, the regulation of the process of development is the result of the hierarchically ordered activity of three main classes of genes: the "coordinate," the "selector," and the "realizator" genes. After reviewing the biological data, Serra and Columbo conclude: "[A]part from fortuitous disturbances, *at the fusion of two gametes, a new real human individual initiates its own existence, or life cycle*, during which—given all the necessary and sufficient conditions—it will autonomously realize all the potentialities with which he is intrinsically endowed" (165).

Johnson examined the arguments that claim irreversible individuality does not occur at fertilization but perhaps 14 or so days later. He reduces the cases giving rise to this view to three: that of the hydatidiform mole, the role of the maternal contribution to human development, and the question of totipotentiality (including the issue of twinning). In the case of hydatidiform moles, no organism is actually present or the organism is profoundly defective and doomed to die. With respect to the maternal role in the developing new life, Johnson argues that any genetic information received from the mother would be subordinate to the dominant role played by the zygote's own directive structures. The most important of these three cases is that of totipotentiality. The cells of the early embryo, perhaps up to when the primitive streak appears, possess an ability to become separate organisms, as occurs in the case of monozygotic twinning (with the subcase the possibility that the twins subsequently recombine). Thus, some argue, until twinning is no longer possible, the new life is a genetic but not a developmental individual. Johnson observes that separated early cells can develop as new individuals (a form of asexual reproduction) but that excessive focus on this "plastic" character can give rise to the idea that the early cells when part of the developing new life have no more than an incidental unity. An examination of the cells as part of the early embryo shows complex ordering, communication, and regulation one in relation to the other. He suggests that "potentially totipotent" would be a better term for the cells that are a part of the developing new life. Serra and Colombo make a similar point when they state that the totipotency present in the zygote does not mean indeterminancy, but an actual capacity for executing a plan according to a given program. Twinning occurs when cells accidentally break off (due, for example, to an error in cell division) and is the exception to the rule. Johnson argues that the claims for delayed hominization that he has examined cannot be used as grounds to justify any proposed action.

CONCLUSION

On many occasions, John Paul II has addressed the question of abortion. In his Oct. 7, 1979 homily on the Mall in Washington, D.C., he poignantly summed up the Church's teaching: "I do not hesitate to proclaim before you and before the world that all human life—from the moment of conception and through all subsequent stages—is sacred, because human life is created in the image and likeness of God. . . . Human life is precious because it is the gift of a God whose love is infinite; and when God gives life, it is forever."

Bibliography: "Law and the Incidence of Abortion," *Documentation on Abortion and the Right to Life II* (Washington, DC 1976), 5–11. A. TORRES and J. D. FORREST, "Why Do Women Have Abortions?" *Family Planning Perspectives* 20 (1988) 69–76. F. G. CUNNINGHAM, et al., eds., *Williams Obstetrics: 20th Edition* (Stamford, Conn. 1997). K. L. MOORE and T. V. N. PERSAUD, *Before We Are Born: Essentials of Embryology and Birth Defects*, 5th ed. (Philadelphia 1998). S. K. HENSHAW, "Abortion Incidence and Services in the United States, 1995–1996," *Family Planning Perspectives* 30 (1998) 263–70, 287; *Sharing Responsibility: Women, Society, and Abortion Worldwide* (New York 1999); "Abortion Surveillance United States, 1997," *Morbidity and Mortality Weekly Report: CDC Surveillance Summaries* 40 (Dec. 8, 2000). Congregation for the Doctrine of the Faith, "Declaration on Procured Abortion," (1974); "Instructions on Respect for Human Life in Its Origins and on the Dignity of Procreation," (1987). *Catechism of the Catholic Church* 2258, 2270–75, 2319, 2322–23. JOHN PAUL II, *The Gospel of Life (Evangelium Vitae)* (1995). "The Didache, or Teaching of the Twelve Apostles," *The Apostolic Fathers*, v. 1, tr. K. LAKE (Cambridge, Mass. 1965). U.S. Catholic Bishops, *Pastoral Plan for Pro-Life Activities: A Reaffirmation (1985); Faithful for Life: A Moral Reflection (1995); Living the Gospel of Life (1998).* J. T. NOONAN, JR., "An Almost Absolute Value in History," in *The Morality of Abortion: Legal and Historical Perspectives* (Cambridge, Mass. 1970), 1–59. G. GRISEZ, *Abortion: The Myths, the Realities, and the Arguments* (New York 1970); *The Way of the Lord Jesus*, v. 2: *Living a Christian Life* (Quincy, Ill. 1993). B. ASHLEY, "A Critique of the Theory of Delayed Hominization," in *An Ethical Evaluation of Fetal Experimentation: An Interdisciplinary Study*, ed. D. G. MCCARTHY and A. S. MORACZEWSKI (St. Louis, Mo. 1976), 113–33. B. ASHLEY and K. D. O'ROURKE, *Health Care Ethics: A Theological Analysis*, 4th ed. (Washington, DC 1997). J. CONNERY, *Abortion: The Development of the Roman Catholic Perspective* (Chicago, Ill. 1977). S. J. HEANEY, ed., *Abortion: A New Generation of Catholic Responses* (Braintree, Mass. 1992). M. JOHNSON, "Delayed Hominization," *Theological Studies* 56 (1995) 743–63. P. LEE, *Abortion and Unborn Human Life* (Washington, DC 1996). T. J. O'DONNELL, *Medicine and Christian Morality*, 3d ed. (Staten Island, N.Y. 1996). I. C. DE PAULA, "The Respect Due to the Human Embryo: A Historical and Doctrinal Perspective," in *Identity and Statute of Human Embryo: Proceedings of Third Assembly of the Pontifical Academy for Life*, ed. J. DE DIOS VIAL CORREA and E. SGRECCIA (Vatican City 1998), 48–73. A. SERRA and R. COLOMBO, "Identity and Status of the Human Embryo: The Contribution of Biology," in *ibid.*, 128–77. W. E. MAY, *Catholic Bioethics and the Gift of Human Life* (Huntington, Ind. 2000). J. DONCEEL, "Immediate Animation and Delayed Hominization," *Theological Studies* 31 (1970) 76–105. N. FORD, *When Did I Begin? Conception of the Human Individual in History, Philosophy, and Science* (Cambridge, Eng. 1988). T. A. SHANNON and A. B.

Pope John Paul II visits grave of Jerome Lejeune, an ardent abortion opponent and leader of Pontifical Academy for Life, an organization with close ties to the Vatican, Chalo-Saint-Mars cemetery outside Paris, August 1997. (AP/Wide World Photos)

WOLTER, "Reflections on the Moral Status of the Pre-Embryo," *Theological Studies* 51 (1990) 603–26.

[M. A. TAYLOR]

ABORTION (CANON LAW)

The Catholic Church has long considered abortion to be not only a grave moral evil but also a crime punishable by canonical sanctions. Any Latin Catholic who successfully procures an abortion incurs an "automatic" (*latae sententiae*) excommunication (*Codex iuris canonici* c. 1398). A major excommunication can be imposed on an Eastern Catholic who procures an abortion. An Eastern cleric can be subjected to additional penalties, including deposition from the clerical state (*Corpus canonum ecclesiarum orientalium* c. 1450.2). One who procures or positively cooperates in the procuration of an abortion is irregular or permanently impeded from the reception of orders and the exercise of orders already received (CIC cc. 1041.4, 1044.3; CCEO cc. 762–763).

The traditional canonical understanding of "abortion" was that it consisted in the intentional and culpable expulsion from the uterus of a living, non-viable fetus. Interpreting the text narrowly, most (but not all) canonists held that the canonical penalty for abortion was not incurred by those who killed a viable fetus in utero or allowed such a fetus to die after causing its expulsion from the uterus. In 1988, the Pontifical Council for the Interpretation of Legal Texts authoritatively construed the term "abortion" to mean the intentional and culpable killing of a fetus "in whatever way or whatever time from the moment of conception it may be procured." Thus, penalties for abortion can now be incurred or imposed even for the destruction of a viable fetus.

The current Codes omit the 1917 Code's explicit reference to the mother as one who incurs the censure for abortion. The explicit mention of the mother in the 1917 Code was intended to resolve a controversy among pre-Code authors. Since the 1917 Code definitively resolved this dispute, mention of the mother in the revised Code was seen as superfluous.

The *latae sententiae* excommunication threatened by the Latin Code for procuration of abortion is often referred to as an "automatic" penalty. It should be noted, however, that only Latin-rite Catholics who have completed their eighteenth year can incur *latae sententiae* penalties. Any legally recognized factor that eliminates or diminishes culpability for an offense also relieves one of the burden of an "automatic" penalty for that offense (CIC c. 1324.3).

The revised Latin Code subjects to the *latae sententiae* penalty of excommunication only those cooperators in an abortion whose cooperation was necessary for the commission of the offense. In other words, only those without whose efforts a particular abortion would not have occurred incur the "automatic" penalty of excommunication (CIC c. 1329.2). Penalties can be imposed on other cooperators in accord with the gravity of their complicity in a "common conspiracy" (CIC c. 1329.1; CCEO c. 1417). One need not be a necessary cooperator to become irregular for the reception or exercise of orders. Culpable positive cooperation suffices.

Remission of censures incurred or imposed for abortion is reserved in the Latin Church (CIC c. 1355) to ordinaries in normal circumstances and in the Eastern Churches (CCEO c. 1420.1) to hierarchs. When a penitent of the Latin Church is in danger of death, any priest, even one lacking the faculty to hear confessions, validly absolves from the censure in the act of sacramental confession (CIC c. 976). For the faithful of Eastern Churches, penalties forbidding the reception of the sacraments are suspended when the guilty party is in danger of death (CCEO c. 1435.1) and any priest can then absolve from the sin of abortion that prompted the penalty (CCEO c. 725).

In the Latin Church, as long as the *latae sententiae* censure for abortion has not been declared, all bishops (CIC c. 1355.2), canons penitentiary, those appointed to fulfill that role in dioceses that do not have cathedral chapters (CIC c. 508), and chaplains in prisons, hospitals, and ocean liners (CIC c. 566.2) may remit the censure in the sacramental forum. In hardship situations, ordinary confessors can temporarily remit the censure, but the penitent reincurs the censure unless he or she makes recourse to one with authority to remit the censure within thirty days (CIC c. 1357). Confessors can be given habitual faculties to absolve unconditionally from this censure in sacramental confession.

Bibliography: T. GREEN, "Sanction in the Church (c. 1311–1399)," in J. CORIDEN et al., eds., *The Code of Canon Law: A Text and Commentary* (New York 1985) 891–942. M. GLENDON, *Abortion and Divorce in Western Law* (Cambridge 1987). R. SAGMEISTER, "Das neue kirchliche Strafrecht und der Schutz des Lebens," in K. LUDICKE et al., eds., *Recht im Dienste des Menschen* (Graz 1986) 493–516. L. WRENN, *Authentic Interpretation on the 1983 Code* (Washington 1993) 48–49.

[J. P. BEAL]

ABORTION (U.S. LAW)

The United States has been making laws about abortion since the 19th century. From the middle to latter decades of that century, distinctions between abortions preformed before and after "quickening" passed away, and the vast majority of states penalized most abortions, as well as the advertising of abortion services and information. While doctors were generally subject to criminal penalties for performing abortions, few states imposed such penalties on the women who sought them.

Beginning in the 1960s, several states enacted laws that permitted abortion in particular circumstances such as rape and incest, and in cases in which a doctor concluded that a pregnancy posed a danger to the mother's life or health. Some states also allowed abortions during approximately the first trimester of pregnancy. In response, a rapidly developing pro-life movement supported referenda and legislation to reverse permissive abortion laws. These pro-life campaigns were largely successful during the late 1960s and the early years of the 1970s.

The Legalization of Abortion. This democratic process at the state level was largely halted in 1973 with the United States Supreme Court's decision in *Roe v. Wade* and its companion case *Doe v. Bolton*. In these cases, the Supreme Court announced that there could be found in the U.S. Constitution a right of "privacy" broad enough to encompass a woman's decision to terminate her pregnancy by abortion; unborn human lives were not "persons" entitled to protection under the Fourteenth Amendment. Furthermore, states could not pass abortion laws shielding unborn life from abortion to a degree greater than the federal constitution without running afoul of women's federal constitutional right to choose abortion.

The *Roe* Court established standards for state regulation of abortion with reference to the three trimesters of pregnancy. On the surface, it appeared that these standards allowed states to restrict abortion to a greater degree as a pregnancy progressed. In effect, however, the Court's standards prohibited states from banning any abortion throughout pregnancy. Even in the last trimester, states could not forbid any abortion if an abortion provider would state that it was necessary for a woman's "health." The *Doe* decision defined "health" in the abortion context very expansively to include "all factors—physical, emotional, psychological, familial, and the woman's age—relevant to the well-being of the patient."

After *Roe v. Wade*. In response to *Roe*, a movement arose in the 1970s to add a "human life amendment" to

"March for Life" Demonstration, Washington D.C., 1975. (AP/Wide World Photos)

the federal constitution. Two leading versions of this amendment were proposed. The first would declare the unborn human life a constitutional "person" entitled to the Fourteenth Amendment's protection of life. A second would allow all states, if they wished, to pass laws protecting the lives of the unborn as they had before *Roe*. While there arose significant momentum for such an amendment over the course of the 1970s and early 1980s, no such amendment has yet passed. The passage of a human life amendment remains an ultimate goal of the pro-life movement.

Also in response to *Roe*, state legislatures passed a great number and variety of laws intended either to restrict legal abortion based on the mother's reasons for seeking abortion or on the length of her pregnancy, or to regulate (usually limit) the conditions under which abortion could take place. Abortion advocates regularly challenged these laws in federal court; as a result, many abortion law cases were appealed to and ultimately decid-

ed by the United States Supreme Court. During the 1970s and 1980s, the Supreme Court most often interpreted the privacy right announced in *Roe* quite expansively, and invalidated state laws regulating or restricting abortion. From 1976 to 1986, for example, the court held: that a husband's interests in his unborn child are not greater than a wife's right to seek an abortion (*Planned Parenthood v. Danforth*); that parents have only a limited right to direct their minor daughters' abortion decisions, which right can be assumed by a judge (*Bellotti v. Baird*); that safety regulations may not be imposed upon abortion clinics if compliance would create significant financial obstacles to women seeking abortions (*Akron v. Akron Center for Reproductive Health*); and that abortionists may not be directed to use the post-viability abortion method most likely to result in a live child (*Colautti v. Franklin*).

The judicial trend to render the abortion right virtually absolute peaked in the decision of *Thornburgh v.*

Pro-life demonstrators from Operation Rescue, Buffalo, New York, 1992. (AP/Wide World Photos)

American College of Obstetricians and Gynecologists. In this case, the Supreme Court struck down a Pennsylvania law requiring abortionists to obtain a woman's informed consent prior to performing an abortion. Dissenting from the majority opinion, *Roe* supporter Justice Warren Burger wrote: "We have apparently already passed the point at which abortion is available merely on demand. If the statute at issue here is to be invalidated, the 'demand' will not even have to be the result of an informed choice."

Roe v. Wade Questioned. In 1989, the tone of Supreme Court abortion jurisprudence changed somewhat in *Webster v. Reproductive Health Services.* In this case, while the Court explicitly refused to reconsider *Roe*, a majority of justices held that the right to choose an abortion should be demoted from the status of a "fundamental" constitutional right to that of a "liberty interest." The Court upheld Missouri laws that: (a) permitted the use of state resources for childbirth, but not for abortion; (b) mandated viability testing at 20 weeks' gestation and later prior to the performance of an abortion; (c) directed that all state laws should be interpreted to protect unborn children, subject to existing constitutional and case law precedents.

After *Webster*, two cases clarified the law concerning parental involvement in minors' abortions. In *Hodg-*

son v. Minnesota and *Ohio v. Akron Center for Reproductive Health*, the Supreme Court held that one or both parents could legally be required to receive notification of an unmarried minor's abortion decision if the daughter was provided the opportunity of a "judicial bypass," i.e. appealing to a judge to go forward with the abortion without parental notification.

It was widely expected that the Supreme Court would continue to weaken *Roe* with its decision in *Planned Parenthood v. Casey* in 1992. The opposite occurred. In a plurality opinion authored by the appointees of two anti-abortion presidents, George Bush, Sr., and Ronald Reagan, *Roe* was reaffirmed, albeit with a bimester (versus a trimester) scheme for reviewing state abortion laws. After viability, the old standard would apply: abortions declared to be for a woman's "life or health" could not be restricted. Pre-viability, abortion laws would be judged according to a new standard: whether or not they imposed an "undue burden" or "substantial obstacle" to any woman's obtaining any abortion. This standard was attacked by the dissenters in *Casey* as one subject to wildly varying and subjective interpretations.

The plurality opinion in *Casey* was silent regarding whether *Roe* had been rightly decided. It opined, instead, that abortion had become necessary for women to plan their lives in the event their birth control should fail. The Court also indicated that it believed that its authority would be undermined by a reversal of *Roe*.

Partial Birth Abortion. The movement to ban a practice known as "partial-birth abortion" began a new chapter in the legal and political struggle over abortion in the United States. In the early 1990s, pro-life advocates learned of the development of a new method for terminating the lives of partially-born children. In a paper delivered at an annual meeting of the National Abortion Federation (a trade association for abortionists and abortion clinics), abortionist Dr. Martin Haskell of Ohio described a procedure he had helped develop called "Dilation and Extraction." Used on unborn human lives from approximately 16 to 32 weeks gestation, the procedure involved: (1) dilating a pregnant mother's cervix over several days; (2) forcibly converting the body of the living unborn child to a breech position in the womb; (3) with forceps, grabbing a leg of the child and dragging its entire body up to the base of the neck outside the mother's body; (4) stabbing the child with a pair of scissors at the base of the brain; (5) with a suction device, evacuating the contents of the skull; (6) crushing the skull and removing the entire body from the mother.

Pro-life groups disseminated information about this procedure widely to the public, the media, and to Congress. In 1995, legislation was introduced in Congress to ban this procedure; it was entitled the ''Partial-Birth Abortion Ban Act.'' The bill commanded support from many self-described ''pro-choice'' members of Congress. It also had bi-partisan support. Public opinion polls showed up to 70 percent of American citizens favoring passage of the bill, including a majority of self-described ''pro-choice'' men and women. Still, after several attempts, the bill did not become law; it was twice vetoed by President William Clinton. While the House of Representatives easily overrode such vetoes, the Senate remained a few votes short of the number needed for an override.

While the federal Congress deliberated, however, 30 states passed legislation banning partial-birth abortion. These laws were immediately challenged by abortion advocates, and in 1999 the U.S. Supreme Court granted certiorari to hear the dispute over the partial-birth ban passed by the legislature of Nebraska. The Court's opinion in that case, *Stenberg v. Carhart*, in the eyes of many veteran legal analysts, marks a return to the days when the constitutional abortion right was interpreted so broadly that it swallowed all attempts at regulation. In *Stenberg*, writing for the 5–4 majority, Justice Breyer stated that Nebraska's law failed the *Casey* test; the law placed an undue burden on women's right to abortion because it could be interpreted to ban the most common form of second trimester abortions, the dismemberment or ''Dilation and Evacuation'' method. He also wrote that—despite the lack of empirical scientific evidence on the medical necessity for partial-birth abortion—the state was required to make a ''health exception'' to the ban in the event that any abortionist might decide that this procedure would be marginally better for any woman seeking an abortion.

The majority's opinion provoked blistering dissents from Chief Justice Rehnquist and Justices Thomas, Scalia, and Kennedy. Justice Scalia compared *Stenberg* with the Supreme Court decisions allowing slavery (*Dred Scott*) and the internment of Japanese American citizens during World War II (*Korematsu*). Justice Kennedy, a member of the *Casey* plurality, argued that the Court had turned its back on *Casey*'s invitation to accord greater weight to states' interests in unborn life. In emotional language, he described partial-birth abortion and argued for Nebraska's right to declare such a procedure a threat to respect for all human life and to the future of the medical profession.

Despite the *Stenberg* decision, the struggle over partial-birth abortion altered the legal and political landscape in ways fundamentally harmful to abortion advocates in the United States. Public opinion polls taken in the late 1990s showed pro-life support even with support for legal abortion for the first time since the early 1970s. During the federal congressional debate over partial-birth abortion, abortion advocacy groups, for the first time in decades, were forced to answer hard questions in the media. False statements made repeatedly by abortion advocates were exposed by reporters and in congressional hearings broadcast live on C-SPAN. While the fate of state and federal bans on partial-birth abortions is not yet decided and the *Stenberg* opinion was a major legal blow to the pro-life movement, the campaign to ban partial-birth abortion advanced the credibility of the pro-life movement in ways that will be felt for years.

Bibliography: The texts of all United States Supreme Court decisions can be found in the official U.S. Supreme Court reports. The legal, political, and social history of abortion in the United States during the nineteenth century can be found in M. GROSSBERG, *Governing the Hearth: Law and the Family in Nineteenth–Century America* (Chapel Hill, N.C. 1985). Abortion law and practice from the nineteenth century to today is found in M. OLASKY, *Abortion Rites: A Social History of Abortion in America* (Wheaton, Ill. 1992).

[H. M. ALVARE]

ABRABANEL, ISAAC (ABRAVANEL)

Portuguese rabbi, biblical scholar, and philosopher; b. Lisbon, 1437; d. Venice, 1508. Born in a rich Jewish family, Isaac ben-Judah Abrabanel received an excellent education and entered politics. He was the minister of finance, first of King Alfonso V of Portugal (1438–81), and then of King Ferdinand V of Castile. The edict of 1492, which expelled all the Jews from Spain, drove him into exile. At first he was welcomed in Naples, where he held an important post at the court of Ferdinand I (1458–94) and Alfonso II (1494–95), but the French invasion forced him to take refuge in Sicily and later in Corfu. After a short stay in Apulia, he finally settled in Venice.

Despite these numerous changes of abode, Abrabanel wrote many works that are as varied as they are original. With his brilliant mind, encyclopedic knowledge, and noble and generous heart, he was an outstanding exception to the general decadence that marked the disastrous end of the Judeo-Spanish epoch. He once said of himself that he was ''a descendant of Jesse of Bethlehem, a scion of the royal house of David''; and there was in fact something princely about him.

His numerous writings show him to have been well versed in Christian and Muslim, Greek and Hebrew literatures, a creative thinker, a careful and exact student of the Bible. While in Portugal, he wrote a commentary entitled *Merkebet Ha-Mishneh* (The Chariot of Deuteronomy); in Castile, he wrote commentaries on Joshua, Judges, and Kings. In Naples, he composed a commentary on Daniel and a sort of ritual on the Passover sacrifice. In Corfu, he wrote a work on Isaiah; in Venice, commentaries on the other Prophets and on the first four books of the Pentateuch. His dissertations on the Messiah influenced the messianic movements among the Jews of the 16th and 17th centuries (*see* SHABBATAIÏSM).

Among his works are also the *Migdol Yeshu'ot* (Tower of Saving Deeds) on the evidence of God's grandeur as shown in His miraculous interventions, the *Lahaqat Nebi'im* (The Company of the Prophets), and the *'Ateret Zeqenim* (The Crown of the Ancients). As a philosopher, Abrabanel brought to a close the line of Jewish Aristotelian thinkers. He knew and respected Christian scholasticism, especially the works of St. Thomas Aquinas, whose treatise *De spiritualibus creaturis* he translated from Latin into Hebrew.

In his biblical exegesis he followed in the footsteps of RASHI and Kimchi, avoiding both a mystical and a rationalistic interpretation of the text, in favor of a natural and simple explanation. He was regarded as an authority in learned matters among the Jews, who called him *Hakam* (the Sage) and *Nasi* (the Prince). His erudite introductions to the Scriptures rendered considerable service to biblical criticism also among Christian scholars. Richard Simon did not hesitate to write emphatically: "We can gain more from him than from any other of the rabbinical scholars for a better understanding of the Scriptures. . . . His clarity and eloquence in Hebrew are not less than Cicero's in Latin." Yet this is tantamount to admitting that he was more of a rhetorician than an exegete. Besides, it must be conceded that his ideas were often oversubtle and his language too prolix, and that he indulged too much in violent diatribes against Christianity.

See Also: JEWISH PHILOSOPHY.

Bibliography: B. NETANYAHU, *Don Isaac Abravanel, Statesman and Philosopher* (Philadelphia 1953). J. SARACHEK, *Don Isaac Abravanel* (New York 1938). A. MELINEK, *Don Isaac Abrabanel: His Life and Times* (London 1952). J. B. TREND and H. M. J. LOEWE, eds., *Isaac Abravanel* (New York 1938). E. I. J. ROSENTHAL, "Don Isaac Abravanel: Financier, Statesman and Scholar, 1437–1937," *Bulletin of the John Rylands Library* 21 (1937) 445–478. J. BAER, "Don Isaac Abravanel and His Relation to Problems of History and Politics," *Tarbiz* 8 (1937) 241–259, in Heb. M. H. SEGAL, "R. Isaac Abravanel as Interpreter of the Bible," *ibid.* 260–299, in Heb. E. E. URBACH, "Die Staatsauffassung des Don Isaak Abrabanel," *Monatsschrift für Geschichte und Wissenschaft des Judentums* 81 (1937) 257–270. J. BERGMANN, "Abrabanels Stellung zur Agada," *ibid.* 270–280. H. FINKELSCHERER, "Quellen und Motive der Staats- und Gesellschaftsauffassung des Don Isaak Abravanel," *ibid.* 496–508. L. GINZBERG, *The Jewish Encyclopedia* (New York 1901–06) 1: 126–128. I. LANDMAN, *Universal Jewish Encyclopedia* (New York 1939–44) 1:53–54. S. A. HORODEZKY, *Encyclopedia Judaica: Das Judentum in Geschichte und Gegenwart* (Berlin 1928–34) 1:588–596.

[A. BRUNOT]

ABRAHAM, PATRIARCH

Ancestor of the Israelites and neighboring peoples. One form of his name, Abram, regarded in Genesis as his earlier name is but a dialectic variant of the other form, Abraham, both meaning "Father [God] is exalted." However, by folk etymology, the form Abraham (Hebrew *'abrāhām*) is made to mean *'ab hǎmôn gôyīm*, "Father of a multitude of nations" (Gn 17.5).

Life. Although the formerly common identification of Amraphel (Gn 14.1) with HAMMURABI is now regarded as very improbable, Abraham can nevertheless be considered roughly contemporaneous with this Babylonian king (18th century B.C.); the background of the Genesis stories of the Biblical PATRIARCHS agrees very well with the known conditions of northern Mesopotamia in the first half of the 2d millennium B.C. Abraham was apparently one of the seminomads of AMORRITE stock who migrated from upper Mesopotamia into Syria and Canaan between 1900 and 1700 B.C. According to the traditions recorded by the YAHWIST and the ELOHIST, his home was in Haran of Aram Naharaim (northern Mesopotamia). The later Pentateuchal PRIESTLY writers locate his original home in "Ur of the Chaldees" in southern Mesopotamia (Gn 11.28, 31; 12.4–5; 15.7; 24.10; Jos 24.2; Neh 9.7). The motive for Abraham's migration was primarily religious, leaving Mesopotamia at Yahweh's command (Gn 12.1–4), to be free from its crass polytheism (Jdt 5.6–9), but political and economic reasons may also have influenced his decision to migrate. In Gn 14.13 Abraham is called "the Hebrew" (*hā'ibrî*), which later generations may have taken to mean "the descendant of Eber" (*'ēber*), (cf. Gn 11.14–26), but which more likely originally meant "the immigrant" (*see* HABIRU).

Biblical genealogies relate Abraham to many Near Eastern peoples: through his brother Nahor to the ARAMAEANS; through his son Ishmael to the Ishmaelites (Gn 16; 21.9–21; 25.12–18); through his son Isaac and his grandson JACOB (Israel) to the Israelites; through his other grandson Esau to the EDOMITES (Gn 36); through his second wife Cetura to several Arabic tribes (Gn 25.1–4); and through his nephew Lot to the MOABITES and Ammonites (Gn 19.30–38). Tradition associated Abraham with several places and sacred trees in Canaan: SHECHEM and its sacred terebinth of More (Gn 12.6), BETHEL and its altar (12.8), Hebron and its terebinths of Mamre (13.18), and Beersheba and its tamarisk (21.33). Besides his wanderings in Canaan, he also went to Gerar in the western Negeb, according to the Elohist (Gn 20), and to Egypt, according to the Yahwist (Gn 12.10–20). According to Gn 25.7–11, Abraham died in his 175th year and was buried in the cave of Machpela, near Hebron.

Abraham in Salvation History. This patriarch marks a significant point in the history of salvation. He is the first to worship the true God. Because of Yahweh's covenant with him, which included the promise that in him all the nations of the earth should be blessed and of which the sign was circumcision, descent from Abraham was considered a necessary condition for belonging to the people of God. Abraham's faith in God's promise of innumerable descendants survived a severe test when God commanded him to sacrifice his only son Isaac (Gn 22). ''Abram believed the Lord, who credited the act to him as justice'' (Gn 15.6). St. Paul cites these words (Rom 4.3, 9, 22; Gal 3.6) to show that it is not carnal descent or circumcision, but faith like that of Abraham that makes men the true descendants of Abraham (Rom 4; Heb 11.17–19). Because they are his offspring, the blessed after death recline at the messianic banquet ''in Abraham's bosom'' (Lk 16.22–23).

Iconography. Perhaps the most frequently reproduced theme from the life of Abraham is that of his impending sacrifice of Isaac. This is found as early as the Synagogue of DURA-EUROPOS (*c.* A.D. 245) and in the Christian catacombs. As a type of the sacrifice of Christ, this scene became increasingly popular in the Middle Ages. It was also interpreted as a type of the Eucharist, as was likewise the frequently depicted encounter of Abraham with Melchizedek (Gn 14.18), e.g., in St. Mary Major in Rome. Another commonly portrayed scene was that of the visit to Abraham of three angels, sometimes represented as the Three Persons of the Blessed Trinity (Gn 18). Various motifs from Abraham's life were utilized by Titian, Tintoretto, Rembrandt, and Rubens.

Bibliography: M. NOTH, *A History of Pentateuchal Traditions* (Englewood Cliffs, NJ 1972). J. VAN SETERS, *Abraham in History and Tradition* (New Haven 1975). B.VAWTER, *On Genesis* (Garden City NY 1977). C. WESTERMANN, *Genesis, 1–11, Genesis 12–36, Genesis 37–50* (Minneapolis 1984–86).

[E. MARTIN]

ABRAHAM ECCHELLENSIS

Maronite scholar; b. Ḥāqil (Mt. Lebanon), Feb. 18, 1605; d. Rome, July 15, 1664. Ibrāhīm al-Ḥāqilānī studied at the Maronite Roman College, was ordained and remained a deacon, taught Syriac and Arabic at Pisa and in Rome, published a Syriac grammar (1628), and became the interpreter for the Propagation of Faith (1635),

Abraham and Isaac. (©Archive Photos)

succeeding the Maronite bishop, Sergius Rezzee, on the project to revise the Arabic translation of the Bible. From 1640 he collaborated with C. LE JAY on the Polyglot edition of the Bible, revised the work of GABRIEL SIONITA, and published the Book of Ruth in Arabic and Syriac with a Latin translation, and Maccabees three in Arabic and Latin. In 1645 he became professor of Syriac and Arabic at the Collège de France and in 1647 published three letters in defense of his book on Ruth. He was appointed by Pope ALEXANDER VII a scriptor for Arabic and Syriac at the Vatican Library (1660), and spent the rest of his life studying and publishing. His private library is conserved in the Vatican under *Fonds Ecchellensis*.

Bibliography: A. SCHALL, *Lexikon für Theologie und Kirche* 2 1:61–62. J. LAMY, *Dictionnaire de théologie catholique* 1.1:116–118. L. PETIT, *Dictionnaire d'histoire et géographie ecclésiastiques* (Paris 1912–) 1:169–171. G. GRAF, *Geschichte der christlichen arabischen Literatur* 3:354–359. Y. I. AD-DIBS, *Al-Ǧāmiʿ al-mufaṣṣal fī taʾrīḥ al-Mawārina al-muʾaṣṣal* (Beirut 1905) 383–386, history of the Maronites. P. RAPHAEL, *Le Rôle du collège maronite romain dans l'orientalisme* (Beirut 1950) 88–92.

[E. EL-HAYEK]

ABRAHAM OF CLERMONT, ST.

Hermit, abbot; d. *c.* 474–481. Abraham was of Persian origins. During the Sassanian persecution of Christians he was imprisoned, regained his freedom, and fled to the West. According to the *Vita patrum,* ch. three, of GREGORY OF TOURS (MGSrerMer 1:672), who seems to have confused him with the Biblical patriarch, Abraham sojourned among the Anchorites in Egypt before arriving in Auvergne. There he lived a hermit's life near Clermont. His reputation for sanctity attracted a number of disciples, and his hermitage became the nucleus of a monastery dedicated to St. Cyriacus with Abraham as abbot. SIDONIUS APOLLINARIS composed his epitaph (*Epist.* 7.17; MGAucAnt 8:123). Abraham was invoked for the cure of fever.

Feast: June 15 (Diocese of Clermont).

Bibliography: *Acta Sanctorum* June 3:534–536. R. AIGRAIN, *Catholicisme* 1:57. J. L. BAUDOT and L. CHAUSSIN, *Vies des saints et des bienhereux selon l'ordre du calendrier avec l'historique des fêtes* (Paris 1935–56) 6:251–252.

[B. L. MARTHALER]

ABRAHAM OF EPHESUS, ST.

Bishop; d. either after 542 or 553. He built a religious house in Constantinople and another in Jerusalem; the former was known as the monastery of the Abrahamites, the latter as that of the Byzantines. He succeeded to the See of Ephesus as metropolitan of Asia, either in 542 after Hypatios, or in 553, after Andrew. Of his works, two homilies, important for the history of the liturgy are extant: one on the feast of the Annunciation (*Euangelismos*) delivered on March 25 instead of the Sunday before Christmas according to earlier custom; the other, on the Presentation (*Hypapante*).

Feast: Oct. 28.

Bibliography: *Acta Sanctorum* Oct. 12:757–769. M. JUGIE, "Abraham d'Éphèse et ses écrits," *Byzantinische Zeitschrift* 22 (1913) 37–59. J. L. BAUDOT and L. CHAUSSIN, *Vies des saints et des bienhereux selon l'ordre du calendrier avec l'historique des fêtes* (Paris 1935–56) 10:929.

[B. L. MARTHALER]

ABRAHAM OF SANCTA CLARA

Discalced Augustinian friar, preacher, and author of popular devotional works; b. Kreenheinstetten near Baden, July 2, 1644; d. Vienna, Dec. 1, 1709. He was the son of Matthew Mergerle or Mergerlin, a tavern keeper in Kreenheinstetten, and received the name John Ulrich at baptism. He received his elementary education at the village school and at Messkirch, and he entered the gymnasium of the Jesuits at Ingolstadt in 1656. Upon the

death of his father he was adopted by an uncle, Abraham von Mergerlin, a canon of Altötting, who transferred him to the Benedictine school at Salzburg in 1659. After three years there John Ulrich entered the Discalced Augustinians and at profession took the name of Abraham, doubtless out of courtesy to his uncle. He made his novitiate and completed his studies at Mariabrunn and was ordained in Vienna on June 8, 1668. After a brief assignment as preacher at the shrine in Taxa, near Augsburg, where he gained some fame for his dramatic sermons, Abraham went to Vienna, which was to be the chief center of his work. Leopold I named him preacher of the imperial court in 1677, and within the order he served as superior and prior of the convent in Vienna, as master of novices at Mariabrunn, and minister provincial of the Vienna province.

Abraham gained a reputation as a forceful orator with an unusual talent for presenting his themes in a graphic manner. Although accused by some of his contemporaries of being a buffoon in the pulpit, he seems in fact to have been a witty, cultivated, and learned man. He utilized his varied store of knowledge and exceptional ability in such a manner as to be an effective preacher.

Abraham was a prolific author and his works include a vast mélange of both sacred and secular writings. He was a literary master of both prose and poetry. Schiller characterized him as a man of marvelous originality, worthy of respect, and not easy to surpass in wit or cleverness. Abraham regarded his writings as an apostolate and even in his most humorous works aimed at the moral elevation of his readers. Abraham began his literary career in response to the plague that devastated Vienna in 1679. He wrote *Merk's Wien!* (Vienna 1680) as a dramatic description of the plague to show how death spares no one. He followed this with two lesser works, *Lösch Wien* (Vienna 1680) and *Die grosse Totenbruderschaft* (Vienna 1681), which exhorted the people to pray for the souls of those killed in the plague and listed personages of prominence who had succumbed. His next work, *Auff, auff, ihr Christen* (Vienna 1683) was an appeal to the Christian world to do battle against the Turks. This is chiefly remembered because Schiller used it as a model for the sermon of the Capuchin Friar in *Wallenstein's Lager.* A four-volume work, *Judas der Erzschelm* (Judas the archknave; Salzburg, 1686–95), is usually considered Abraham's masterpiece. The fruit of a decade of labor, this work sets forth the apocryphal life of Judas with moral applications for the daily spiritual life of the reader. The remaining works, constituting a mixture of the most varied sort, can be found in a collective edition published at Passau in 1846. They range from the serious *Grammatica Religiosa* (Salzburg 1691), a compendium of moral teaching, to *Huy! und Pfuy der Welt* (Ho! and phooey on the world; Würzburg, 1707), which shows the influence of Sebastian Brant's *Narrenschiff* (Ship of fools). Several volumes of literary works were published after his death, and various editions and collections have appeared down to the present century. These must be used with care since there are some doubtful and spurious entries.

Bibliography: G. DUNNHAUPT, ed., *Stern so aus Jacob aufgegangen Maria (Rarissima litterarum)* (Stuttgart 1994). K. BERTS-CHE, *Die Werke Abrahams a Sancta Clara in ihren Frühdrucken* (Schwetzingen 1922). W. BRANDT, *Schwank und Fabel bei Abraham a Sancta Clara* (Münster 1923). L. BIANCHI, *Studien zur Beurteilung des Abraham a Santa Clara* (Heidelberg 1924).

[A. J. CLARK]

ABRAHAM THE SIMPLE, ST.

Called also Abraham the Child; fourth-century desert father. He is identified by John Cassian as one of the great desert fathers known for his simplicity of manner and innocence and for miracles of healing. He was dead by the end of the fourth century. He may be the Abraham who relates Cassian's last *Conference,* a man of strictest austerity. He is not to be confused with the disciple of Pachomius and Theodore, but he may be the Abraham whose three maxims are given in the *Apophthegmata Patrum* PG 65: 129–132.

Feast: Oct. 27.

Bibliography: J. CASSIAN, *Conlationes,* ed. M. PETSCHENIG (*Corpus scriptorum ecclesiasticorum latinorum* 13; 1886) 430–431, 672–711. S. SALAVILLE, *Dictionnaire d'histoire et de géographie ecclésiastiques* 1: 171–172. B. KÖTTING, *Lexicon für Theologie und Kirche* 1:63. S. LE NAIN DE TILLEMONT, *Mémoires pour servir à l'histoire ecclésiastique des six premiers siècles* (Paris 1693-1712) 10:30–32.

[M. C. MCCARTHY]

ABRAHAM'S BOSOM

The place, according to Jewish ideas at the time of Christ, where the just go after death. In the parable of the Rich Man and Lazarus (Lk 16.19–31), the reward of Lazarus after his death is described in terms of his being "borne away by angels into Abraham's bosom." The Greek κόλπος, like its Hebrew equivalent *ḥêq,* can mean either bosom or lap. Some exegetes understand the text in the sense that Abraham received Lazarus as a loving father would take his small son upon his lap or hold him close to his bosom (cf. Jn 1.18); others, that Lazarus was given a place of honor at the Messianic banquet, reclining at the right hand of Abraham (cf. Jn 13.23). The latter interpretation appears more probable, since the banquet

"Paradise with Christ in the Lap of Abraham," miniature painting from a manuscript c. 1239.

image was used in Rabbinic literature (*see* G. Kittel, *Theologisches Wörterbuch zum Neuen Testament* 3:824–826), and Jesus Himself describes the Kingdom of God in terms of the eschatological banquet prepared on top of the Mountain of God (Lk 13.22–29; Is 2.2; 49.12), where the elect will recline with Abraham, Isaac, and Jacob (Lk 13.28–29). At times, however, the repose in Abraham is unrelated to a banquet and signifies blissful happiness enjoyed with the Patriarch (2 Mc 13.17). The common notion of the Fathers of the Church that Abraham's bosom designates a place of happiness not only for Christians in heaven, but also for the just of the OT who there (in the LIMBO of the fathers) await the coming of the Messiah, is foreign to Jewish thought.

Bibliography: *Encyclopedic Dictionary of the Bible,* tr. and adap. by L. HARTMAN (New York 1963), from A. VAN DEN BORN, *Bijbels Woordenboek,* 15. E. W. SAUNDERS, G. A. BUTTRICK, ed., *The Interpreters' Dictionary of the Bible,* 4 v. (Nashville 1962) 1:21–22. J. SCHMID, *Lexikon für Theologie und Kirche,* ed. J. HOFER and K. RAHNER, 10 v. (2d, new ed. Freiburg 1957–65) 1:58–59. W.

STAERK, *Reallexikon für Antike und Christentum,* ed. T. KLAUSER (Stuttgart 1950) 1:27–28.

[J. PLASTARAS]

ABRAXAS

A magico-mystical word occurring in Hellenistic papyri and found also, along with other symbols, on ancient and medieval amulets. The numerical values of the Greek letters making up the word Ἀβράξας or its variant Ἀβράσαξ (Ἀ = 1, β = 2, ρ = 100, α = 1, ξ = 60, α = 1, ς = 200) give a sum of 365. This figure corresponds to the total number of days in the solar year. In the Gnostic system of Basilides the term is employed also to designate the First Principle or Supreme Being, the ultimate source of the 365 heavens. Some scholars consider that there is a connection between *Abraxas* and the magic word *abracadabra,* but the relationship is disputed.

Bibliography: H. LECLERCQ, *Dictionnaire d'archéologie chrétienne et de liturgie,* ed. F. CABROL, H. LECLERCQ, and H. I. MARROU, 15 v. (Paris 1907–53) 1.1:127–155, with illustrations. M. HAIN, *Lexikon für Theologie und Kirche,* ed. J. HOFER and K. RAHNER, 10 v. (2d, new ed. Freiburg 1957–65) 1:66.

[M. R. P. MCGUIRE]

ABRUNCULUS OF TRIER, ST.

Bishop; d. *c.* 527. The only definite information about Abrunculus, or Aprunculus, comes from GREGORY OF TOURS, who says that upon his death Nicetius was elected bishop of Trier (*Vitae patrum,* 6.3, MGSrer Mer 1:682). In the eleventh century his remains were translated from St. Symphorian to the church of St. Paulinus in Trier, and a century later, to the abbey church of Springiersbach.

Feast: April 22.

Bibliography: *Acta Sanctorum* April 3:30–31. *Bibliotheca hagiographica latina antiquae et mediae aetatis* (Brussels 1898–1901) 5985. J. L. BAUDOT and L. CHAUSSIN, *Vies des saints et des bienheureux selon l'ordre du calendrier avec l'historique des fêtes* (Paris 1935–56) 4:556.

[B. L. MARTHALER]

ABSALON OF LUND

Archbishop, founder of Copenhagen; b. Fjenneslev, Denmark, Oct. 1128; d. Sorø, March 21, 1201. A member of one of the most powerful families on the island of Sjaelland, that of Skjalm the White, Absalon studied at Sainte-Geneviève-de-Paris. He was ordained there and

enthusiastically adopted the Latin culture as well as the current ideology of Church reform. Upon his return to Denmark, he became counselor to King Valdemar the Great, founded the monastery at Sorø, was elected bishop of Roskilde (1158), and in 1178 was appointed archbishop of Lund, simultaneously retaining Roskilde up to 1191. He distinguished himself by the zeal with which he introduced into Denmark Western Church customs (e.g., tithing, clerical celibacy) and Western monasticism (Cistercians and Carthusians). He proved to be an administrator and a statesman—even a warrior—as well as a builder and a patron of the arts. In fortifying his diocese against the invasion of the Slavs (Wends), he built at Havn a castle-keep that became the nucleus of the city of Copenhagen. Multiplying the expeditions against these pagan Slavs on the southern coast of the Baltic, he took by storm the temple of Arkona (1169) on the island of Rügen, which was then annexed to Denmark. On the intellectual plane, Absalon dominated the Danish clergy of his time: a runic inscription at Nørre Aasum, Skåne, testifies to his interest in the traditional Scandinavian culture, but it is significant that he was the protector of the best Latin chronicler of his time, Saxo Grammaticus, who dedicated his *Gesta Danorum* to Absalon. While remaining outside the investiture struggle, Absalon was the faithful protector of royal power; this earned him the regency under the young King Canute IV (*c.* 1187–90).

He energetically upheld the interests of his family, promoted the career of his nephews Anders Sunesøn and Peder Sunesøn, like himself former students at Paris, who succeeded him at Lund and Roskilde respectively; Absalon also proclaimed the sanctity of his relative MARGARET OF ROSKILDE.

The city of Copenhagen venerates him as its founder; he can be considered the most brilliant Scandinavian prelate of the Middle Ages.

Bibliography: SAXO GRAMMATICUS, *Gesta Danorum,* ed. J. OLRIK and H. RAEDER, 2 v. (Copenhagen 1931–57). H. OLRIK, *Absalon,* 2 v. (Copenhagen 1908–09). H. KOCH and B. KORNERUP, eds. *Den danske kirkes historie* (Copenhagen 1950–) v.1. L. WEIBULL, *Nordisk Historia* 2 (1948) 526–538.

[L. MUSSET]

ABSOLUTE, THE

From the Latin *ab-solutus,* meaning separated, free from, or complete, that which is independent of conditions, relations, or impediments. In philosophical language the absolute may be said to function adverbially, adjectivally, and substantively. In an adverbial sense, a consideration is said to be absolute when something is discussed without reference to conditions that may *de facto* attach to it but are not essential to it. For example, in comparing intelligence and will, one may maintain that, absolutely speaking, the activity of intelligence is more perfect than that of will, although in man's present condition some objects are attained more perfectly by love than by knowledge. In an adjectival sense, the most important philosophical instance of the absolute is absolute truth. TRUTH is the relation of a mental judgment to reality, and yet some truths are said to be eternal. Finally, in a substantive sense, the Absolute is that which is perfect and complete and preeminently the supreme principle of all things. Absolute truth and absolute being are the most important senses of the term for philosophy. This article summarizes the historical development of the concept from Augustine to Hegel and concludes with a brief evaluation of absolutism as compared to relativism.

Augustine. Although there are many historical precedents to his teaching in this matter, St. AUGUSTINE is among the most notable examples of a thinker who moves from the necessity of eternal truth to a subsistent truth, an absolute being. PLATONISM, through the intermediary of PLOTINUS, is a major source of Augustinian doctrine, and yet the great African bishop had first to formulate a defense against the SKEPTICISM of the Academy, Plato's old school. PLATO had held that the sensible world is incapable of grounding true knowledge but that there are other entities, the Forms or Ideas, that are objects commensurate with the demands of knowledge. The New Academy accepted Plato's teaching with respect to the inadequacy of the sensible world as a cause of knowledge, but it did not share his certitude in the existence of Ideas. In this way, the possibility of knowledge was called into question.

Augustine, in his attack on the new Academicians, appealed to the existence of the doubter as something that escapes doubt. Although this may seem an anticipation of the Cartesian *cogito,* it did not play the role of a truth from which all others are in some way derived. More positively, Augustine appealed to the truths of mathematics, which, being certain and independent of the sensible world, give strength to the belief that there is an intelligible world to respond to knowledge in the full sense—an intelligible world that is independent of the sensible world. Augustine employed the Platonic vocabulary to speak of the intelligible world, the realm of the Ideas. For him, the existence of Ideas is plain from the facts that this is a created world and that God must know what it is He creates. The Ideas are the patterns according to which God fashions creatures. The locus, as it were, of the Ideas is the Second Person of the Trinity; He is the wisdom philosophers are ever seeking. The supreme attribute of God, for Augustine, is truth; God is the truth who grounds all other truths. Thus the recognition of absolute truths, as

in mathematics, led Augustine to the conclusion that there must be an absolute being who is subsistent truth.

Thomas Aquinas. In the teaching of St. THOMAS AQUINAS there is an intimate connection between the notion of eternal or absolute truth and absolute being. This emerges quite clearly from his discussion of the question as to whether created truth is eternal. "Notice that the truth of statements is nothing other than the truth of intellect, for what is stated exists in the mind as well as in speech, and it is insofar as it is in the mind that it has truth properly speaking. As spoken it is said to be a true statement insofar as it expresses some truth in the mind, not because of any truth existing in the enunciation as in a subject. So, too, urine is said to be healthy, not from any health in it but from the health of the animal of which it is a sign. Similarly we have pointed out that things are called true with reference to the truth of understanding. Hence if no mind were eternal, no truth would be eternal. And, because only the divine mind is eternal, in it alone does truth have eternity. Nor does it follow from this that something besides God is eternal, because the truth of the divine mind is God Himself, as we argued earlier" (*Summa Theologiae* 1a, 16.7). The ontology of Aquinas leads to a description of God as that being whose existence is His very nature. Any being other than God is such that it is possible for it not to exist; the cause of its existence must therefore be sought outside itself. God is His existence and His being is therefore absolute, utterly independent of every other being. It should not be thought that this involves something like the Anselmian ONTOLOGICAL ARGUMENT; Aquinas dismisses somewhat curtly the suggestion that, since the term God signifies a being than which nothing greater can be thought, such a being must necessarily exist (*Summa Theologiae* 1a, 2.1 ad 2). St. Thomas holds that man's warrant for asserting that God exists and, indeed, *is* existence, must always be found in creatures. If man knew God directly, this would not be necessary; but the human mode of knowing, which has as its commensurate object the nature of sensible reality, precludes such a direct intuition. In short, man's knowledge of absolute being is relative to his knowledge of dependent or created being.

This analysis may seem to call into question the absoluteness of divine being since, if God is not somehow relative to creatures, it would seem to follow that knowledge of creatures could not lead to knowledge of God. Indeed, many of the names man applies to God seem to imply such a relation to creatures—names such as "Creator," "Savior," and even the word "God" itself insofar as its etymology refers to divine providence. And, of course, if God is related to the world, He cannot be absolute in the desired sense.

St. Thomas's solution to this difficulty involves a distinction between real relations and relations of reason. A real RELATION is had when one thing is dependent on another for its being. Such a relation is often reciprocal. For example, a son is dependent on his father; but the father is dependent on his son as well since, if he had no child, he could not be a father. In the case of God and creatures, St. Thomas argues that while creatures are really related to God, the relation of God to creatures is one of reason alone (*De pot.* 7.11). Thus, in knowing that God's existence is absolute, man does not know Him absolutely, that is, independently of his knowledge of things that are quite distinct from, and inessential to, God. That man comes to know God through His created effects is an indication of the imperfection of man's knowledge of God, since there is an infinite distance between created and divine perfection. "Perfect knowledge of a cause cannot be gained through effects that are not proportioned to the cause, but from any effect it can be clearly demonstrated to us that the cause exists, as we have argued. So it is that from the effects of God we demonstrate that God exists, although they do not permit us to know Him perfectly in His very essence" (*Summa Theologiae* 1a, 2.2 ad 3).

The position of St. Thomas, here as elsewhere, depends on the possibility of distinguishing what man knows from the way in which he knows it. If the human manner of knowing were a complete determinant of what man knows, he could not have knowledge even that an absolute exists. But, given the distinction, it can be maintained that, while the human manner of knowing absolute being necessarily entails relating absolute being to being other than itself—hence preventing man's knowing it absolutely—nevertheless what man knows is absolute being. In the case of God, however, one must quickly add that, since on the level of what is known creatures are the necessary bridge to knowledge of His existence, human knowledge of God is unavoidably imperfect and derived.

Spinoza. The absolute implies an opposite: the non-absolute, or relative; given at least the definition of the absolute, the nonabsolute appears to have but a precarious hold on its claim to reality. For Aquinas, the distinction between the relative and the absolute could be expressed by the dualism of created and uncreated substance. This same dualism, though admittedly on quite another basis, was retained by R. DESCARTES; but, in his wake, B. SPINOZA argued that the very concept of SUBSTANCE leads to the conclusion that there can be but one substance and that substance is absolute. For him, thought and extension—one might simply say, the created—cannot be thought of as substances when compared to God. If they exist, they can exist only as attributes of the one substance. Thus Spinoza's insistence on absolute

substance leads to a monism of substance; the only dualism remaining consists of parallel systems of attributes, mental and physical. Everything is reduced in pantheistic fashion to God (*see* PANTHEISM).

Fichte. The significance of the absolute ego in the thought of J. G. FICHTE has to be understood against the general background of his insistence on the WILL, or ego, as a corrective of Kantian critical idealism. The upshot of the Kantian *Critiques* was that these provided man with a basis for a rational faith in the realm of freedom. The thing-in-itself, originally a postulated and surd element in the Kantian system, became the realm of morality and of God, which is inaccessible to critical reason. For Kant, the moral law within provides a ground for belief in, but not knowledge of, the existence of God, the spiritual order, and the immortality of the soul. In his view, while man cannot know any of these things by way of proof, he does have a warrant that will allow him to accept them on practical grounds.

Fichte refused to accept this relegation of freedom and self to the fringes of true knowledge; his own philosophy began with the assertion of the conception of FREEDOM, of the ego or SELF, as the absolutely basic principle. From this principle must be derived the categories of experience. This was, in its own way, a Copernican revolution. The willing, free self became the source of all knowledge and experience. Freedom, the world order, and God were the basic realities; if anything else was to be admitted as real, it had to be deduced from these. The practical order was not merely saved as a realm unto itself, then; it became the fundamental and regulative order of reality. Fichte, in order to avoid the charge that he was deducing all reality from his own self, introduced a distinction between particular selves and the absolute self of which individual selves are manifestations. For this reason he would have denied that he had developed a system of subjective IDEALISM. He was able to account, to his own satisfaction, for the existence of the external world, since it did not depend in its entirety on his ego. The absolute ego that thus became the center of Fichte's philosophy is God, but God understood as a process, a self-determining spiritual evolution. This absolute self expresses and manifests itself in individual selves; it lives and acts in them as the law of their nature, the ultimate ground of both the phenomenal world and the necessary laws of thought.

Schelling. In Fichte nature is a product of the absolute ego; with reference to the individual ego, however, it is merely an obstacle. F. W. J. SCHELLING attempted to go beneath this remaining dualism to find, in the concept of the absolute as nature or process, a completely monistic ground for reality. Nature, for him, is no longer a dead, mechanical process; it is unconscious intelligence just as man is conscious intelligence. There is therefore an affinity that permits knowledge. The common note of reality, for Schelling, is pure activity, self-determining energy; nature and mind are not parallel aspects but stages in the development of the absolute ego. The absolute is not something that exists, but something that evolves, unfolds, has a history; and nature and mind are moments in that history. Thus, Schelling maintains that individual selves, since they are the loci where blind intelligence becomes self-conscious, cannot be real except as rooted in the absolute. Schelling's nature is thus very much like the pre-Socratic *physis;* the ideal he sets for science is the ultimate identification of the laws of thought and the laws of nature. By such an identity, the whole of reality is reduced to intelligence.

Hegel. The identification of the laws of thought and the laws of reality, taught by Schelling, was accepted by G. W. F. HEGEL. Whether in knowledge or in the world, for Hegel one and the same process or development is taking place and the laws according to which it happens are the same. The real is the rational, the rational is the real. The absolute for Hegel is not something vague and amorphous, as he took Schelling's absolute to be, nor is it substance, as it was for Spinoza. The absolute is process that passes through unconscious moments but whose *telos* is total self-consciousness. The meaning of the process is had in that ultimate goal where the absolute has become completely conscious of itself and recognizes its identity with the ultimate purpose of the universe.

The Hegelian absolute is at once present in, and emerging from, every process. The business of philosophy is therefore to seek and find reason in every process, however apparently irrational and absurd. Hegel's interest in history is predictable: he urges man to seek the absolute in history. He provides religious motives for this search, saying that man is told not only to love God but to know Him as well. God reveals Himself to man in history, which is the theater of providence. One may think that things happen haphazardly and adventitiously in history, but this cannot be. Man must not think that there is any distinction between the way things are and the way they ought to be. In history everything happens necessarily and for the best, and it is the task of the philosopher to show this (*see* HISTORY, PHILOSOPHY OF).

The dialectical process and the claim that the principle of CONTRADICTION rules all are both revealing of Hegel's identification of thought and reality. Just as one might think of thought as a process that moves from global confusion to determination and distinction, so Hegel views reality as progressing from the homogenous and undifferentiated abstract to concrete distinction. Each step of the process looks backward and forward. What is is not what it was or what it will be: a present state is the contradictory of a previous state and drives toward the contradictory of what it now is. Contradiction is the law of life and movement. In the whole, opposites and contradictories are swallowed up and reconciled. World development on the natural plane is unconscious, but the thinker must, so to speak, relive the process by thinking it. The dialectical method of thought begins with an abstract notion that gives rise to its contradiction, and these two are reconciled in a third concept: thesis, antithesis, and synthesis. The movement is from the abstract to the concrete universal. Thus Hegel's description of the progress of thought and the evolution of reality are the same.

Hegel's absolute is the evolutionary process of reality and the goal of that process. God does not exist prior to the world, which Hegel holds is eternally created; God is the logos, the reason, the law of the universe; the evolutionary process is the absolute's progressive consciousness of self. Hegel's absolute, accordingly, is unintelligible without the world.

Absolutism. The opposition between absolutism and RELATIVISM is best understood as indicating epistemological options, even though these are based on ontological judgments. In the discussion of Aquinas, a distinction he would wish to make between absolute being and man's manner of knowing it was indicated. An absolute being is by definition one that exists in utter independence of all else. However, as known by someone other than itself, absolute being is relative to that knower, and it would seem to be doubly relative in a doctrine according to which it can be known only relative to another object of knowledge. Unless one can distinguish a thing's manner of being known from its manner of being, such considerations would effectively do away with the absolute. The relatedness to a knower implicit in all knowledge has been a source both of absolutism and relativism. Thus the observation that sense qualities are relative to sense organs leads to a questioning of their OBJECTIVITY. Some thinkers go on to insist on the existence of other absolute aspects of reality, while others conclude that whatever one knows is relative to his mode of knowing. These latter may then seek to ground the laws of knowing in an absolute subject. A thinker who maintains both that what one knows is essentially colored by his way of knowing and that his way of knowing is simply contingent may be called a relativist. Whether the relativist can ever successfully explain the relativity of knowledge without appeal to at least an ideal of absoluteness must, of course, be asked.

Summary. The Absolute is preeminently a changeless, eternal being, independent of all else. As applied to knowledge, absolute knowledge bears on objects whose being is independent of the knower, even though as known they are related to a knower. Whether in reality or in thought, an absolute is required; but it is not necessary to identify, as Hegel did, what is absolute in knowledge and what is absolute in reality.

See Also: PANENTHEISM; IMMANENCE; HEGELIANISM AND NEO-HEGELIANISM.

Bibliography: F. C. COPLESTON, *History of Philosophy,* v. 7. (Westminster, Md. 1946—). M. C. CAHILL, *The Absolute and the Relative in St. Thomas and in Modern Philosophy* (Washington 1939). R. EISLER, *Wörterbuch der philosophischen Begriffe,* 3 v. (4th ed. Berlin 1927–30) 1:3–6. J. MÖLLER, *Lexikon für Theologie und Kirche,* 10 v. (Freiburg 1957–65) 1:70–71. J. KLEIN, *Die Religion in Geschichte und Gegenwart,* 7 v. (3d ed Tübingen 1957–65) 1:74–76. A. CHOLLET, *Dictionnaire de théologie catholique,* 1.1:134–135. A. CARLINI, *Enciclopedia filosofica* 4 v. (Venice-Rome 1957) 1:406–415.

[R. M. MCINERNY]

ABSOLUTISM

Both a theory of the nature of political authority and a practice that prevailed throughout the 17th and 18th centuries. According to its principles, the ruler possessed an authority that was unconditional and unlimited. He was subject only to his own will and was not restrained in his actions by the laws of God or those of nature or by any other legal limitations.

Essential to the theory of absolutism was the ruler's and the state's relation to law. In the medieval period, the ruler was considered subject to the laws of God and nature. The laws of the state were laws only so far as they were in harmony with the natural law. In the early modern period, law became a thing not of reason but of the will of the ruler. Instead of the state being based upon law, law became solely a command of the state, depending for its efficacy upon the authority of the one who commanded. This concept served the cause of the rising nation-states. It entailed the death of the idea of empire, the rise of the independent sovereign state, the secular state's independence of the church, and the centralization of authority against existing customs and privileges of cities and of the nobility.

The theory of absolutism can be traced from MACHIAVELLI's justification of the separation of morality and politics, through the development of sovereignty in Jean Bodin, to a full-blown absolutism in the legal theory of Thomas HOBBES. The result was the justification of the monarchical absolutism of the dynastic nation-state. During the 18th-century Enlightenment, in writers like Jean Jacques ROUSSEAU, the source of absolute authority was transferred from the monarch to the people, or the "general will," to form a "democratic" absolutism.

Catholic theologians such as BELLARMINE and SUÁREZ upheld the concept of a limited authority. The moral theologians of the 17th century held that the ruler was subject to divine and natural law, but that he was the sole judge of that limitation. Further, a great number of them taught that will was the source of law, that the ruler was above his own law, that the people could not resist a law of the sovereign, and that law was valid without the consent of the people. To that extent they taught a legal theory identical with absolutism and necessary to the rise of the absolute state.

See Also: MONARCHY; DIVINE RIGHT OF KINGS.

Bibliography: M. BELOFF, *Age of Absolutism, 1660–1815* (New York 1954), bibliography 181–182. J. W. ALLEN, *A History of Political Thought in the Sixteenth Century* (3d rev. ed. New York 1957). A. D. LINDSAY, *Encyclopedia of the Social Sciences* 1:380–382. J. N. FIGGIS, *Cambridge Modern History* 3:736–769. S. SKALWEIT, *Cambridge Modern History* 2 5:96–121.

[D. WOLF]

ABSTRACTION

Generally, a mental separation of things, not or at least not necessarily, separated in the real. Looked at from this point of view, abstraction is understood as the psychological act of discarding all but one facet of a thing (or things) to cognize that facet without the others. To be legitimate, this psychological act presupposes an appropriate object: the facet cognized through abstraction must in itself be knowable, apart from that which it is mentally separated. Just as the term abstraction is used to name the psychological act of mentally separating one thing from another, it can also be used to name the abstractability of that which is mentally separated. Thus one may speak of a man abstracting a given object from certain nonessential data, and one may speak of that object itself abstracting from these data. This article first considers the abstraction of the intelligible from the sensible, as well as alternative theories in the history of thought that propose to account for the discovery of the intelligible. It then explains how the intelligible as abstracted is universal, and concludes with a consideration of the various kinds of abstraction.

Abstraction Of The Intelligible. Of the different, though not necessarily unrelated, instances of abstraction the most radical is the abstraction of the intelligible object from the data of sense experience. This abstraction is meaningful, of course, only within a philosophical frame that sees such a thorough difference between the sensible and the intelligible, that they are recognized as objects pertaining to irreconcilably different orders. And even among those who admit this difference there is an abstraction only so long as the sensible and intelligible are somehow given together, with the intelligible somehow cognized by way of an insight in and through the sensible. The sensible is the fluctuating, kaleidoscopic data of man's original cognitive contact with the things of the physical world: their colors and shapes, their sounds, odors and flavors, their temperatures and weights, their motions and rest, and the like. The intelligible, on the other hand, is the stable, definable, potentially scientific object of a cognitive vision radically different from an experience of the sensible. If the sensible is the phenomenal in things, the intelligible is the meaningful in them. The sensible as a datum of experience is exclusively singular, tied to an individual thing in this place at this time. The intelligible is, at least as the object of the direct act of intellection, universal; i.e., it can be said of many, indifferent to individual differences, indifferent to shifts in place and time.

Empiricist View. For those who fail to admit the distinction between the sensible and the intelligible there is no question of the abstraction of an intelligible object from sense data. This is the case, for example, with those empiricists (such as J. LOCKE and D. HUME) who limit knowledge effectively to the realm of sense experience. They may speak of an abstraction, but at best they mean some more or less subtle reworking of sense impressions that yield an image involving an outline simple enough to stand for many things. This notion also underlies the use of the term abstraction by those working in CYBERNETICS. The refined impressions spoken of here, remain on the same plane as the impressions from which they came, the plane of the sensible. There is no question of penetrating to the radically different plane of the meaningful. Therefore, in this there can be no abstraction from the sensible to the intelligible.

Nonabstractive Theories. There are some in the history of thought, however, who do admit the radical difference between the sensible and the intelligible, but they nevertheless explain man's knowledge of each without recourse to a theory of abstraction. Plato and St. Augustine are two such people.

For PLATO, envisioning the intelligible is not the result of seeing into and through the data of sense experience to an underlying intelligibility, but rather, of turning from what is sensible, to the intelligible that is defined apart from and exists independently of the sensible. Plato distinguishes between preexistence in a realm of pure intelligibles, wherein a vision of these intelligibles has once been achieved, and this life, in which there takes place, by way of reminiscence, a conversion from the data of sense experience to these intelligibles. If Plato can be taken literally, for him learning is but a process of remembering ideas from another existence, temporarily forgotten in this existence, but innately present nonetheless.

For St. AUGUSTINE, the intelligible is not innate; it is not apprehended by way of reminiscence, but neither is it seen by way of abstraction from sensible data. In his view, there is a realm of intelligibles to which the human intellect is naturally subject and which a man can know so long as his intellectual vision functions in virtue of an incorporeal light supplied by God. The intellect is thought to be related through this divine ILLUMINATION to the intelligible as the sense of sight is related through corporeal light to the visible. For St. Augustine, as well as for Plato, there is an infinite metaphysical distance between the sensible and the intelligible, but there is no abstraction because the intelligible is not known in and through the sensible. For ARISTOTLE and for St. THOMAS AQUINAS, there is an infinite metaphysical distance between the sensible and the intelligible, and yet the latter can only be cognized through the former; for them a theory of abstraction is a noetic necessity.

Thomistic Account. According to the Thomistic EPISTEMOLOGY, some things are endowed sensibly as well as intelligibly, for example, men, trees and rocks; others, such as angels, are endowed only intelligibly. Men can know both, but the human condition is such that the latter are known only as a function of the former, and the intelligible in the former is known only as a function of the sensible. In other words, the sensible characteristics of the sensibly endowed things are immediately knowable, but the intelligible characteristics are knowable only mediately by way of the sensible.

In Thomistic terms, a thing is said to be actually sensible and only potentially intelligible. As actually sensible it can be actually sensed as it stands; but the potentially intelligible part must be rendered actually intelligible before it can be actually understood. The SENSES are capacities for actually sensing the actually sensible; the INTELLECT (that is, the possible intellect) is the capacity for actually understanding the actually intelligible. The senses need no help since the thing as it stands is actually sensible. The possible intellect stands in need of another capacity on the intellectual level that is able to make the potentially intelligible actually intelligible. This capacity is called the agent intellect. The thing—which is potentially intelligible—is originally present in knowledge through its sensory representation, which is called the PHANTASM. Through this phantasm in sensory experience, only the sensible characteristics of the thing are actually presented to the knower; but just as the thing, while being actually sensible, is potentially intelligible, so through the phantasm the intelligible aspect of the thing is potentially present to the knower. The agent intellect is a spiritual light that, by illuminating the phantasm, actualizes the intelligible so that it can be actually cognized by the possible intellect.

The possible intellect, like the senses, is a passive power, able to operate only after being reduced from potency to act. The thing as it stands, as physical, is able to reduce the senses, themselves in a way physical, from potency to act: no agent sense is needed. But the thing itself, as physical, cannot reduce the wholly spiritual possible intellect to act: only something spiritual can do this, and this is the agent intellect. But the agent intellect is an unspecified light; and since there is no knowing except of something determinate, that which actualizes the possible intellect must simultaneously specify it for the act of knowing something determinate. Thus the agent intellect, as principal cause, uses the phantasm of the thing as instrumental cause (*see* INSTRUMENTAL CAUSALITY). Together they actualize the possible intellect, which—once reduced from potency to act in reference to a given intelligible aspect of some thing—can posit the act of knowing that intelligible object. The intelligible remains an object irreducibly other than the sensible. Intellection is never reduced to sensation. But the intelligible is known only in and through sense experience by way of an intuitive penetration that is most strictly an abstractive act.

The Intelligible As Universal. The object cognized in the abstractive intuition just described can be distinguished from the data of sense experience in several ways, as has already been noted. Perhaps the most obvious difference is that the characteristics present in sense knowledge are incorrigibly singular, while the object intellectually cognized is characteristically universal. This difference demands further comment. For one thing, though this is an obvious difference between the sensible and the intelligible in man's experience, it is not the essential difference. If it were, the intellect would be defined as an appetite for the universal; it is, rather, an appetite for the meaningful. In fact, there is an inverse ratio between the meaningful content of an object and its universality (man being an object much richer in content than substance, but considerably less general). If one were to define the intellect as transcendentally related to universality rather than to intelligible content or meaning, this would strongly suggest that the crowning achievement of the intellectual life would come in the possession of an object involving next to nothing in the way of intelligible content.

It remains true, however, that the object cognized intellectually is, as cognized, universal. The reason is that that which in the thing shrouds its intelligibility (so that it is only potentially intelligible) is MATTER, and this co-incidentally is the principle of the INDIVIDUATION of the physical thing. To get to the intelligible, man must (and does, through the light that is the agent intellect) slough off matter as a principle of nonintelligibility. In doing so, of course, he also sloughs off the principle of individuation and cognizes an object that is universal. The intellect is essentially ordered to the intelligible, but the price of knowing the intelligible is knowing it as a universal.

Further comment is required in reference to the universal character of the object of intellection. It might seem, perhaps, that since in the realm of real subjects only singulars exist, the abstraction that renders an object universal somehow precludes the possibility of knowing things as they are. The question is: Is there something inherently falsifying in the process of abstraction? Not at all. A QUIDDITY that is universal in the mind as object, need not be in itself intelligibly different from this same quiddity individualized in things. Natures or quiddities in themselves are neither singular nor universal, but as such are open to either state. In things, in a first existence outside the mind natures are in the state of singularity; in the mind in a second existence, as objects, they are invested with the relation of reason that is the form of universality. Universality is not real; it is a being of reason. But the nature as known, to which universality accrues in the process of being known, need in no sense be itself intelligibly de-realized simply because it takes on a nonreal relation in the mind. The nature of the thing remains unchanged. However, even though abstraction does not falsify things, man does pay a price because he knows by way of abstraction. Things as they exist as subjects, independently of the mind's knowing them, are highly sophisticated complexes of many intelligible aspects as well as all that is sensible in them and the existential act that makes them be more than a mere possibility. In any given act of abstractive intuition some one (more or less meaningful) intelligible aspect, abstracted from all else, is cognized. Thus knowledge by way of abstraction, in any given instance of abstractive intuition, may be seriously incomplete. However, there is an infinite difference between knowledge that is incorrigibly false and knowledge that is less than complete. (*See* UNIVERSALS.)

Kinds of Abstraction. The discussion thus far has been limited to the abstraction of the intelligible from the sensible. There are other abstractions to consider and certain distinctions to be made, namely, between abstraction by way of simple consideration and abstraction by way of negative judgment, between precisive and nonprecisive abstraction, between total abstraction and formal abstraction, and between the abstraction of the whole, the abstraction of the form and separation.

Simple Consideration vs. Negative Judgment. One important distinction between different types of abstraction is between abstraction by way of simple consideration and abstraction by way of negative judgment. To abstract one thing from another by way of simple consideration is to cognize it without simultaneously cognizing the other. This is legitimate only if the first is definable or able to be understood without the other entering into its definition or meaning. There is no need here for the first to be existentially independent of the other. Some things (for example, the nature of man) are definable apart from other things (such as individuating characteristics) without being able to exist apart from them. They can, of course, be abstracted from these by way of abstraction through simple consideration.

To abstract one thing from another by way of negative judgment is not simply to cognize it independently of the other but to think that it exists without the other. An abstraction of this sort is legitimate only if what is abstracted from another is not only independent in meaning from the other but even existentially independent. The nature of man cannot be abstracted by way of negative judgment from individuating characteristics because, though man is definable apart from them, man cannot exist apart from them. However, man can be abstracted from a tree by way of negative judgment because man is independent of the tree both in meaning and in existence; for a tree does not enter into the definition of man, and men can exist without trees. This distinction is important, as the examples should make clear, for any solution to the problem of the universal. As Aquinas frequently points out, it was a failure to distinguish between abstraction by way of simple consideration and abstraction by way of negative judgment that forced Plato to posit *existing* Forms and Mathematicals.

Precisive vs. Nonprecisive Abstraction. Another distinction between types of intellectual abstraction is that between precisive abstraction that renders an object abstractly expressed and nonprecisive abstraction that renders an object concretely expressed. The difference between ''man'' and ''humanity'' (for an example from the category of SUBSTANCE) and between ''pious'' and ''piety'' (for an example of an ACCIDENT) is at stake. ''Pious'' and ''piety'' do not differ in intelligible content; their difference is one of mode of conception. The formality that is precisely ''piety'' is conceived as belonging to a bearer (in general) in the conception of ''pious.'' ''Pious'' is equivalently ''subject-having-piety.'' Identically this same formality, but abstracted from any reference to a bearer—that is, positively cut off from any subject—is conceived in the notion of ''piety.'' ''Pious'' names a whole, that is, the whole subject that is the bearer of piety, but only from the point of view of its piety. ''Piety'' names the formality as a part, which, with other parts, makes up the whole. ''Pious'' can be said of a con-

crete subject, such as Tom, so long as Tom has piety. ''Piety'' cannot be said of Tom; though it is no less real than ''pious,'' it is conceived in such fashion as to be, as conceived, cut off from concrete subjects.

Formal vs. Total Abstraction. Important among the traditional distinctions between types of intellectual abstraction is that between formal abstraction and total abstraction. In this matter it is necessary to clarify the usage of terms, for ''total abstraction'' and ''formal abstraction'' are used by different philosophers to stand for a variety of different abstractions. Reference here is exclusively to the use to which T. de Vio CAJETAN and JOHN OF ST. THOMAS put them when they discuss abstraction in reference to the specification of the sciences (*see* SCIENCES, CLASSIFICATION OF). Although these commentators on St. Thomas claim to be repeating a distinction already made by St. Thomas, a careful investigation of the relevant texts in St. Thomas suggests this is not the case. Be that as it may, the point they make is consonant with the Thomistic theory of science and helpful in understanding it.

Formal abstraction (*abstractio formalis*) is the abstraction of an intelligible content of thought from the matter that shrouds its intelligibility. Total abstraction (*abstractio totalis*) is the abstraction of a logical whole from its subjective parts. Formal abstraction yields an object qua intelligible; total abstraction, qua universal. Given the inverse ratio between meaningful content and universality the two abstractions work in opposite directions. And yet they are both necessary for human SCIENCE (*scientia*). Human science, as science, needs an object able to be intellectually analyzed. For science, the real must be present to the mind in abstraction from whatever matter stands in the way of its being understood. Formal abstraction abstracts from matter as a principle of nonintelligibility to yield an object rich enough in intelligible content to satisfy the scientific mind. Human science, as human, is achieved in discourse. The objects of scientific analysis must be present to the mind as being able to fit into a discursive pattern: they must be present in the state of universality or of communicability. Total abstraction abstracts from matter as the principle of incommunicability to yield an object that is universal and as such able to fit into a discursive pattern.

To the extent that objects are differently freed from the restrictions of matter as a principle of nonintelligibility they are differently scientific. Freedom from individual sensible matter yields an object that is scientifically relevant on the level of natural science. Freedom from all sensible matter yields an object that is scientifically relevant on the level of mathematics. And freedom from all matter yields the object of metaphysical inquiry. Thus one may speak of the first order of formal abstraction, that is, physical abstraction; the second order of formal abstraction, that is, mathematical abstraction; and the third order of formal abstraction, that is, metaphysical abstraction. These three orders or degrees of formal abstraction respectively constitute the different levels of theoretical science.

Total abstraction admits of different degrees also: some objects are more general and some less general than others. These differences do not constitute differences *among* sciences; they function exclusively *within* a given science. Two objects on the same level of formal abstraction are studied in the same science, but the more general is studied before the more specific. Total abstraction does not help to specify the sciences, but it is a common condition for all the sciences; and, within a given science, it determines the order of proceeding in its particular subject matter.

Abstraction vs. Separation. In distinguishing between the types of speculative science, St. Thomas speaks of an abstraction of the whole (*abstractio totius*) that yields the object of natural science, of an abstraction of the form (*abstractio formae*) that yields the object of mathematics, and a separation (*separatio*) that yields the object of metaphysics. The first two of these are called abstractions in a strict sense because they are abstractions by way of simple consideration. The third is more sharply referred to as a separation because it is an instance of the more radical abstraction by way of negative judgment.

The first of these three abstractions is the abstraction of the whole essence of the natural thing from the matter that individuates it. It yields an object sufficiently free from matter to be intelligible, but an object defined nevertheless in terms of common sensible matter. The second yields the form of QUANTITY that is abstracted from all matter save common intelligible matter. The third yields an object abstracted from all matter and an object seen to be independent of matter both in meaning and existence. The significantly different stances in reference to matter for these objects—resulting in significantly different modes of defining—put each on a different level of theoretical science. St. Thomas, with his distinctions between the abstraction of the whole, the abstraction of the form, and separation, covers the same ground as do Cajetan and John of St. Thomas with their distinctions between physical abstraction (the first degree of formal abstraction), mathematical abstraction (the second degree of formal abstraction), and metaphysical abstraction (the third degree of formal abstraction).

See Also: KNOWLEDGE, PROCESS OF; KNOWLEDGE, THEORIES OF; KNOWLEDGE; EPISTEMOLOGY; UNIVERSALS

Bibliography: THOMAS AQUINAS, *The Division and Methods of the Sciences: Questions 5 and 6 of Commentary on the De Trinitate of Boethius,* tr. with introd. and notes, A. MAURER (Toronto 1953), bibliography 86–93. J. F. PEIFER, *The Concept in Thomism* (New York 1952). E. D. SIMMONS, "In Defense of Total and Formal Abstraction," *The New Scholasticism,* 29 (1955) 427–440; "The Thomistic Doctrine of the Three Degrees of Formal Abstraction," *Thomist,* 22 (1959) 37–67. C. DE KONINCK, "Abstraction from Matter," *Laval Théologique et Philosophique,* 13 (1957) 133–196; 16 (1960) 53–69, 169–188. F. A. CUNNINGHAM, "A Theory on Abstraction in St. Thomas," *The Modern Schoolman,* 35 (1958) 249–270. L. FERRARI, *"Abstractio totius* and *abstractio totalis,"* *Thomist,* 24 (1961) 72–89. M.D. PHILLIPE, "'Α φαίρεσις, πρόσθεσις, χωρίζειν dans la philosophie d'Aristote," *Revue thomiste,* 48 (1948) 461–479. G. VAN RIET, "La Théorie thomiste de l'abstraction," *Revue philosophique de Louvain,* 50 (1952) 353–393. L. B. GEIGER, "Abstraction et séparation d'après S. Thomas: *In De Trinitate,* q.5, a.3," *Revue des sciences philosophiques et théologiques,* 31 (1947) 3–40.

[E. D. SIMMONS]

ABSURDITY

Absurdity is a basic notion for a number of modern thinkers such as A. Malraux (1901–), J. P. Sartre (1905–80), A. Camus (1913–60), F. Kafka (1883–1924), E. Albee (1928–), F. Arrabal (1932–), S. Beckett (1906–89), J. Genet (1910–86), E. Ionesco (1912–94), and H. Pinter (1930–). Whereas dictionaries define the absurd as that which is contrary to reason, as used by these writers it designates that which is without a reason. The absurd is a situation, a thing, or an event that really is, but for which no explanation is possible. Because the affair is inexplicable, it offends reason; it is senseless; it is absurd.

Søren Kierkegaard (1813–55) is the source for this type of thought. Kierkegaard's writings are a constant protest against the excessive RATIONALISM of G. W. HEGEL, who taught that all the mysteries of the Christian faith could be comprehended by reason. To indicate that the Incarnation was beyond the understanding of human reason, Kierkegaard called it the absurd, meaning by that something unintelligible and incomprehensible to reason. He insisted that Christian absurdity was neither nonsense, nor irrationality, nor something meaningless; for notions such as these follow on the judgment of reason examining its legitimate data, whereas the Christian accepts the Incarnation by faith. In the light of faith he sees that the Incarnation is in no way absurd.

The notion was then taken up by modern thinkers, especially by existentialists, but in an atheistic context. Thus, absurdity for Sartre arises from the absolute contingency and complete gratuity of the world. Because there is no God, Sartre argues, there are no reasons for things.

Things just are; and because they are without any reason for being, they are absurd. Ultimately all things come from nowhere and are going nowhere. Camus gives a different meaning. Admitting that there are scientific explanations for the various parts of the universe, Camus denies that there is any ultimate reason for the whole. Absurdity is a feeling that arises from the confrontation between man, who is looking for a unified explanation of all things, and a world that has no basic meaning.

Because of their preoccupation with the absurd, playwrights like Genet, Ionesco, Beckett and the like have been called collectively the Theater of the Absurd. To indicate the role of absurdity in the human situation these dramatists create sections of dialogue that are incoherent; they depict scenes in which the actions of the actors directly contradict the words they are speaking; they construct plays around the weird fantasies of deranged minds. In this they resemble Kafka, whose exuberant and enigmatic symbolism describes man as caught in a nightmare of existence; truth and illusion are so intertwined in his works that life is there seen as wearisome, uncertain, and senseless.

The Christian can well appreciate the loneliness, frustration, and the emptiness engendered by ATHEISM in these men. He can also be grateful for his faith, which enables him to see atheism as the most absurd of all absurdities; for the visible things of this world do declare the hidden attributes of God (Rom 1.20).

See Also: EXISTENTIALISM.

Bibliography: P. PRINI, *Enciclopedia filosofica* (Venice-Rome 1957) 1:416–417.

[V. M. MARTIN]

ABŪ 'L-BARAKĀT

Coptic author; d. May 10, 1324. His full name was Shams al-Ri'āsa abū 'l-Barakāt ibn Kabar. He seems to have taken the added name of Barsauma on the occasion of his priestly ordination. He was a Coptic priest attached to the church called al-Mu'allaqa in Old Cairo. He held, besides, the post of secretary to the prince and Mameluke officer Ruqn al-Dīn Baibars al-Mansūri and collaborated with him on his history of Islam, which comes up to 1325, the year of Ruqn's death. Other works that he left include: a Coptic-Arabic dictionary; a large number of elegant sermons for feasts and occasions; and his principal work, a theological encyclopedia titled *The Lamp of Darkness and the Exposition of the Service.*

The Lamp of Darkness presents all that clergy and laity need to know about the doctrines of the faith, the Scriptures, Canon Law, liturgy. The work has a practical teaching purpose and seeks to hand on the genuine religious tradition. Of 24 chapters the first seven deal with doctrine (1–3), items of church history (4), a list of collections of Church law (5), introduction to the Scripture and an account of the liturgical books (6), and an account of Christian literature in Arabic (7). The remaining chapters treat of cult and Church customs and practices.

Bibliography: G. GRAF, *Geschichte der christlichen arabischen Literatur* 2:438–445. E. TISSERANT, *Dictionnaire de théologie catholique* 8.2:2293–96; *Revue de l'Orient chrétien* 22 (1920–21) 373–394. J. ASSFALG, *Lexikon für Theologie und Kirche* 2 1:101.

[J. A. DEVENNY]

ABUNDIUS OF COMO, ST.

Bishop and patron of Como, Italy; d. April 2 *c.* 462–489, probably 468. Abundius (also called Abundantius), assistant and successor of Bishop Amantius, was consecrated Nov. 17, 449, and sent by Pope Leo I in 450, along with Bishop Eutherius of Capua and the priests Basilius and Senator, to Constantinople to discuss the orthodoxy of its patriarch ANATOLIUS. Theodosius II died before their arrival, but Marcian and Pulcheria received them kindly. On Oct. 21, 450, a synod was held in the baptistery of Hagia Sophia in which all the bishops of the patriarchate, beginning with Anatolius, signed the Tome of Leo to Flavian anathematizing the doctrines of NESTORIUS and EUTYCHES. Abundius performed a similar papal mission to Bishop Eusebius of Milan and his suffragans, and then devoted himself to the conversion of pagans in his own diocese.

Feast: April 2.

Bibliography: R. MAIOCCHI, *Storia dei vescovi di Como* (Milan 1929). P. GINI, *Bibliotheca Sanctorum* 1:23–30.

[M. J. COSTELLOE]

ACACIAN SCHISM

The Acacian Schism (484–519) was caused by a change of policy on the part of the Patriarch of Constantinople, Acacius (472–489), who despite his intimacy with the Monophysites had opposed the anti-Chalcedonian encyclical of the Emperor BASILISCUS in 475. Upon the restoration of the Emperor Zeno (August 476), he collaborated in the deposition of the Monophysite bishops, including Peter the Fuller of Antioch and John Codonatus of Apamea. In 479 he consecrated the Chalcedonian Calandion as bishop of Antioch at the emperor's behest and drew a protest from Pope SIMPLICIUS (468–483) for interfering in another patriarchal jurisdiction (*Epist.* June 22, 479).

In 482, in concert with Peter Mongus, he composed a doctrinal statement called the HENOTICON, or Decree of Union, which Zeno promulgated for the province of Egypt. It was intended to conclude the Christological disputes by citing the authority of the first three ecumenical councils, condemning Nestorius and Eutyches, but it did not mention the natures in Christ. Contrary teaching, ''be it of the Council of Chalcedon or any other council,'' was condemned. Though the symbol of Chalcedon and Leo's *Tome* were not rejected, anti-Chalcedonians were admitted to communion, and Peter Mongus was reinstated as patriarch in Alexandria.

Pope FELIX III wrote a letter of protest to Acacius, then excommunicated him in a Roman synod (July 28, 484) when Acacius recognized Peter Mongus at Alexandria. When the excommunication was reiterated in 485, Acacius erased the name of Felix from the diptychs. The two successors of Acacius, Fravita (490) and Euphemius (490–495), were not hostile to the decrees of Chalcedon. They announced their election to the pope for recognition; but Felix demanded that Acacius's name be struck from the diptychs, and relations were again suspended between Rome and Constantinople. The Patriarch Euphemius, having forced the new Emperor ANASTASIUS I (491–518) to accept the decisions of Chalcedon before his accession to the throne, attempted to heal the rupture with Pope GELASIUS (492–496), but without success since the new pope renewed the demand made by Felix. Meanwhile acceptance of the *Henoticon,* though not universal among the Monophysites, was considered an anti-Chalcedonian gesture. Gelasius, however, entered relations with Constantinople through an embassy sent by the Roman senate (492 and 494); but his successor, ANASTASIUS II (496–498), proved adamant in the request for the removal of Acacius's name from the diptychs.

Emperor Anastasius was encouraged in his anti-Chalcedonian policy during the three-year sojourn in Constantinople (508–511) of the Monophysite propagandist SEVERUS, the future patriarch of Antioch (512–518) and a fervent supporter of the *Henoticon.* The emperor published his *Type,* or formula for union, which he attempted to impose upon the Chalcedonian Patriarch, Flavian of Antioch (510). In 512 Pope SYMMACHUS responded to an imperial letter that attempted, among other accusations, to charge him with favoring Manichaeism.

When the rebel general Vitalian forced the emperor to agree to call a council at Heraclea with the pope presiding, Anastasius was compelled to enter into relations with Rome. But after the defeat of Vitalian, legations sent to Constantinople in 515 and 517 by Pope HORMISDAS were unsuccessful. However the advent of JUSTIN I occasioned immediate negotiations between Hormisdas and the pro-Chalcedonian emperor. The schism was brought to an end on March 28, 519, when Patriarch John in a letter to the pope indicated his acceptance of the formula of Hormisdas and the removal of the names of Zeno and Acacius as well as the latter's five successors from the diptychs. Opposition throughout the East endured only briefly.

Bibliography: E. SCHWARTZ, *Publizistische Sammlungen zum Acacianischen Schisma* (*Abhandlungen der Akademie der Wissenschaften* NS 10; 1934). F. HOFMANN, *Das Konzil von Chalkedon,* ed. A. GRILLMEIER and H. BACHT (Würzburg 1951–54). 2:43–94. R. HAACKE, *ibid.* 117–146. H. BACHT, *ibid.* 266–291. P. CHARANIS, *Church and State in the Later Roman Empire* (Madison, Wis. 1939). S. SALAVILLE, ''L'Affaire de l'Hénotique,'' *Échos d'Orient* 18 (1916–19) 255–266, 389–397; 19 (1920) 49–68, 415–433. L. SALAVILLE, *Dictionnaire de théologie catholique,* 6.2: 2153–78. E. STEIN, *Histoire du Bas-Empire,* tr. J. R. PALANQUE 2:24–39, 224–228.

[H. CHIRAT]

ACACIUS OF BEROEA

Bishop in the province of ANTIOCH who took part in all major ecclesiastical controversies between 360 and 433; b. Syria?, *c.* 322; d. Beroea, after 433. He had been a monk under ASTERIUS OF AMASEA at Gindarus near Antioch, and was renowned as a bishop for his austere life and discipline. He fought Arianism and Apollinarianism at Antioch in the persecution of Valens from 369 to 377. He was consecrated bishop of Beroea in 378, and attended most later councils, including CONSTANTINOPLE I in 381. He took part in two legations from the East to Rome to settle the Antiochian schism, and he was prominent in the intrigues (401–404) that led to the exile of St. JOHN CHRYSOSTOM. He did not attend the Council of Ephesus in 431, but played an important part in the NESTORIAN controversy and helped restore peace between Alexandria and Antioch through the Union formula of 433. When he died shortly after, he was more than 110 years old. Of his writings only six letters remain.

Bibliography: J. QUASTEN, *Patrology* 3:482–83. G. BARDY, ''Acace de Bérée et son rôle dans la controverse nestorienne,'' *Revue des sciences religieuses* 18 (1938) 20–44.

[V. C. DE CLERCQ]

ACACIUS OF CAESAREA

Disciple and successor of EUSEBIUS OF CAESAREA and leader of the Homoean faction in the Arian controversy; d. after 365. Nothing is known of him before he succeeded Eusebius *c.* 340. He was present at the Council of Antioch in 341 and became one of the foremost bishops of the anti-Nicene party. As such he was condemned by name by the orthodox assembly of SARDICA in 343. Later he was involved in a bitter feud with St. CYRIL OF JERUSALEM on jurisdictional and doctrinal grounds. His career reached a climax when the Homoean confession (the Son is "like to" the Father) became the official creed of the empire at the Synod of Constantinople in 360. When orthodoxy prevailed under the Emperor Jovian, Acacius had no scruples in signing the Nicene creed; but he returned to Homoean doctrine when VALENS became Emperor of the East in 364. However, he was condemned by the Homoiousian synod of Lampsacus in the summer of 365 but retained his see until his death (c. 366). He was noted for his eloquence and Biblical scholarship. He renovated the famous library of Caesarea, and he composed several works that are lost, except for a few exegetical fragments on Romans and the Octateuch.

Bibliography: J. QUASTEN, *Patrology* 3:345–46. J. LEBON, "La Position de saint Cyrille de Jérusalem dans les luttes provoquées par l'arianisme," *Revue d'histoire ecclésiastique* 20 (1924) 181–210, 357–86.

[V. C. DE CLERCQ]

ACADEMIC FREEDOM

The nature and purposes of academic freedom have assumed different forms at different points in history and in the contexts of secular and Catholic education, and when applied to professors or to students. This article will examine this complex idea in five steps: (1) some historical precedents to the modern concept of academic freedom before the 20th century; (2) the development of the idea in the United States; (3) the idea in Catholic colleges and universities in the United States; (4) *Ex corde ecclesiae* (1990) and its application in the U.S.; and (5) the continuing tensions regarding academic freedom today, especially with regard to Catholic universities.

Historical Precedents. With the development in the West of cathedral schools in 11th and 12th-century Europe, and then the great medieval universities beginning in the 12th century, questions arose about the relationship between these educational institutions and the surrounding society, including civil rulers and bishops. Theological faculties within universities gained a certain magisterial authority recognized by bishops and the pope. In some instances, for example, at the University of Paris in 1215 and then again in 1231, the popes protected theological faculties from the precipitous intervention of local bishops into their disputes. On the one hand, the theologians generally accepted authoritative Church teaching; on the other hand, they enjoyed considerable freedom in debating "disputed questions." Their influence in the

Church was considerable. In one admittedly unusual situation, John XXII (1316–1334), asked the theologians of Paris not to come too quickly to a judgement about the orthodoxy of several sermons he had preached on the Beatific Vision, explaining that he was only testing his ideas in public, ideas which he thought merited further debate. Often, however, bishops did make determinations about proposed theological propositions, as was the case with Bishop Steven TEMPIER's condemnation (1277) of 100 propositions, including several extracted from the writings of St. THOMAS ACQUINAS. The role of theologians in explaining the faith and putting forth new ways of thinking of it on the one hand, and on the other hand the role of bishops in making judgments as to which explanations and interpretations are orthodox, has continued to be a locus for a distinctively Catholic understanding of academic freedom.

At the time of the REFORMATION, the corporate character of medieval universities largely disappeared. The type of theology taught in a particular university in a confessional state was determined in large part by the ruler of that state. Universities in Europe had become, for all practical purposes, confessional institutions. In the early 18th and 19th centuries, a number of German universities "secularized" themselves, and in that process their faculties developed the concepts of *Lehrfreiheit* (the freedom of professors to do unfettered research and teach their findings) and *Lernfreiheit* (the freedom of students, mostly what we would consider graduate students, to learn from whomever they wished and to live their lives in private quarters without supervision). In the view of these faculty, such freedoms constituted a university in the true sense.

On the eve of the 20th century, academic freedom (though the name was not used until the early 20th century) indicated a thinker's personal commitment to speak what he or she believes to be true, regardless of consequence; the appropriateness of the use of reason for believers trying to think through their faith; the freedom of theologians to debate disputed questions; and the protection of academics from persons of power from outside the university.

Academic Freedom in the United States. An institutional confessional stance marked most of the early American colleges: Harvard and Yale, for example, being Congregationalist, William and Mary Anglican, and Princeton Presbyterian. The medieval universities had been self-governed by guild systems and thus largely protected themselves from various external threats. In the New World, boards composed of clergy and laity rather than faculty retained the power to hire and fire and to set policy. With greater reliance on the empirical research

Students at Columbia University, New York, protest the university's failure to reappoint Donald Henderson, economics instructor, striking in defense of "academic freedom." Violence erupted between strikers and nonstrikers, and police were called to break up the rioting, May 15, 1933. (©Bettmann/CORBIS)

model after the Civil War, the dominance of the clergy as presidents and board members of these colleges declined dramatically. By the end of the 19th century, the development of many of the social sciences as distinct disciplines further strengthened the autonomy of faculty, who now based their research on empirical methods of investigation over which the churches had decreasing authority.

Between 1890 and 1915, presidents of these colleges dismissed a number of faculty, many of whom had done doctoral work in German universities. These cases became widely known, and in 1915 thirteen professors signed a statement on academic freedom, titled "Declaration of Principles." Johns Hopkins philosopher Arthur Lovejoy and Columbia economist Edwin R. Seligman drafted the statement; eight of the 13 signers had studied in Germany and seven were social scientists. They

founded the American Association of University Professors (AAUP), with John Dewey as its first president. Initially, membership was open to "any university or college teacher of recognized scholarship or scientific productivity who holds, and for ten years has held, a position of teaching or research." Administrators were then typically excluded. Academic freedom in the United States became at this time a protection for individual university professors against the arbitrary actions of administrators and those outside the academy who would seek to influence them. Stated more positively, academic freedom defended professors' ability to do research and go wherever their investigations led them, to teach their students what they know and believe, and to address issues in the public forum ("extramural freedom"), but to do so not as spokespersons for the university.

The AAUP insisted on the responsibilities as well as on the rights of individual professors. For example, when dealing with controversial matters, professors were expected to set forth divergent opinions without suppression or innuendo and were to help students learn for themselves rather than indoctrinate them. According to the 1915 Declaration, "the liberty of a scholar to set forth his conclusions, be they what they may, is conditioned by their being conclusions gained in a scholar's method and held in a scholar's spirit; that is to say, they must be fruits of competent and patient and sincere inquiry; and they must be set forth with dignity, courtesy, and temperateness." Moreover, the AAUP stressed that research required evaluation, which could be done competently only by peers who were to follow certain procedures designed to ensure fairness in matters of promotion and tenure. Again, in the 1915 Declaration, the AAUP stated that in all disciplines, "the first condition of progress is complete and unlimited freedom to pursue inquiry and publish its results," and added that "such freedom is the breath in the nostrils of all scientific activity." In the AAUP's vision of the academy, administrators gave permission to hire; professors, who constituted "the community of the competent," decided whom they would hire.

The signers of the 1915 "Report" acknowledged the right of a board of trustees of a denominational college to govern according to its religious tradition, but made it clear that the AAUP had serious reservations about the academic integrity of at least a number of such institutions. They stated that such institutions "do not, at least as regards one particular subject, accept the principles of freedom of inquiry, of opinions and of teaching; and their purpose is not to advance knowledge by the unrestricted research and unfettered discussion of impartial investigations, but rather to subsidize the promotion of the opinions held by persons usually not of a scholar's calling, who provide funds for their maintenance. Concerning the desirability of the existence of such institutions, the committee does not desire to express any opinion. But it is manifestly important that they should not be permitted to sail under false colors. Genuine boldness and thoroughness of inquiry and freedom of speech are scarcely reconcilable with the prescribed inculcating of a particular opinion upon a controverted question." As a result, the AAUP judged that nearly all church-related colleges could not fully embrace academic freedom. In 1940, it stated what came to be known as the "limitations clause," which read: "limitations in academic freedom because of religious and other aims of the institutions should be clearly stated in writing at the time of appointment."

At the time, few church-related institutions had any discussions about academic freedom. A report given at the 1942 meeting of the National Catholic Education Association convention stated that 65% of those Catholic colleges that responded to the questionnaire made no provision for tenure. Since a great majority of Catholic colleges were run and staffed by religious, they never saw the need for tenure. People under the vow of obedience were simply assigned and reassigned, sometimes quite arbitrarily.

The 1960s saw a number of changes in Catholic higher education: the establishment of largely lay boards of trustees, more widespread adoption of the dominant scientific research model, and a decline in Catholic professional associations. By 1970, the AAUP stated that "most such colleges no longer need to state such a limitations clause." It remained, nonetheless, opposed to any forms of indoctrination. In 1983, for example, it stated that a "college or university is a marketplace of ideas, and it cannot fulfill its purpose of transmitting, evaluating and extending knowledge if it requires conformity with any orthodoxy of content or method." In 1988, shortly after moral theologian Fr. Charles Curran had been told by the Catholic University of America trustees, that he could no longer teach Catholic moral theology, a subcommittee of the AAUP clarified further the 1940 statement by affirming clearly two of its main points: "(1) the prerogative of institutions to require doctrinal fidelity; and (2) the necessary consequences of denying to institutions invoking this prerogative the moral right to proclaim themselves as seats of higher learning." Though never formally approved by the AAUP, the subcommittee's conclusions are consistent with the organization's long-standing doubt that some church-related institutions provide their faculty with academic freedom, and, in fact, are universities in the "full sense of the term."

Academic Freedom and Catholic Colleges and Universities in the U.S. Most Catholic educational institutions, beginning with those established by the Ursuline sisters in New Orleans in the 1720s, and John Carroll in Washington in 1789, were little more than primary schools whose mission was to prepare their students for service in the world and equip them with the capacity to defend their Catholic faith. Nearly all of the institutions that eventually grew into colleges were founded by religious communities of men and women. At the turn of the 19th century, nearly all Catholic colleges were small, and even by 1940 typically had no endowments, the religious who ran the majority of them constituting their institutions' "living endowments." Few offered tenure and none endorsed the AAUP's understanding of academic freedom. In 1889, the U.S. bishops founded in Washington, D.C., the Catholic University of America, intended initially to be only a graduate school. Bishops on the board retain full legal control at a pontifically chartered institution. Over the years, the board of the Catholic University dismissed several faculty for opinions judged to be unorthodox (most recently, the 1986 Curran case).

Catholic colleges and universities grew steadily in number and size in the 20th century. In 1916, 32,000 students had enrolled in 84 colleges for men (though more than half these men were actually high school students), and by 1940, 160,000 men and women were enrolled. Shortly after the end of World War II, enrollments at Catholic colleges and universities grew considerably (thanks to the GI Bill and the baby boom). By 1966, nearly 400,000 students had enrolled. In the 1960s, leaders of these institutions began to shift full authority over their institutions to predominantly lay boards of trustees and to adopt the ecumenical emphasis of Vatican II. They promoted the professionalization of their faculties, and, in the process, frequently looked to the AAUP for their understanding of academic freedom and tenure. The year 1966 also marked the beginning of an unexpected and rapid decline in the number of religious men and women who had founded these very institutions.

In July 1967, twenty-six Catholic university and college presidents, faculty, and bishops gathered in Land O'Lakes, Wisconsin, to prepare a statement on the nature and role of a Catholic university. "The Catholic university today must be a university in the full modern sense of the word, with a strong commitment to and concern for academic excellence. To perform its teaching and research functions effectively the Catholic university must have a true autonomy and academic freedom in the face of authority of whatever kind, lay or clerical, external to the academic community itself. To say this is simply to assert that institutional autonomy and academic freedom are essential conditions of life and growth and indeed of survival for Catholic universities as for all universities." This excerpt from the statement has been frequently cited by many leaders of Catholic higher education. Just as frequently overlooked, however, is another affirmation found in the same paragraph: "Distinctively, then, the Catholic university must be an institution, a community of learners or a community of scholars, in which Catholicism is perceptibly present and effectively operative." How to be distinctively Catholic and, at the same time, an autonomous institution which affirms an "academic freedom in the face of authority of whatever kind," has remained a key question ever since.

A series of state and Supreme Court judgments in the 1960s and 1970s made it difficult for Catholic colleges and universities to be explicit about their religious mission and remain eligible for state and federal funding. In the early 1980s, a series of court decisions seemed, at least in the view of some academic leaders, to force Catholic colleges and universities to choose between being sectarian or secular. Some of these leaders thought that if they were to remain eligible for federal funding, they needed to avoid any mention of the religious mission of their institution when hiring new faculty or admitting students, to teach theology only as an academic discipline, and to avoid all proselytizing. Most institutions had already made all religious practices optional and had begun to affirm academic freedom along the lines outlined by the AAUP, if not simply adopting it as their own. Given such understandings, along with the rapid expansion and professionalization of lay faculties, the decrease in the number of priests and religious, the power of accrediting agencies, the restrictions that accompanied an ever-increasing amount of government money for sponsored research, and the market pressures to compete with state subsidized public institutions, many Catholic colleges and universities, by the mid 1980s, struggled to find legal ways to make their identity and mission "perceptibly present and effectively operative."

Ex corde ecclesiae (1990). In 1979, the Vatican Congregation for Education published the apostolic constitution *Sapientia Christiana*, written for all pontifically chartered universities (such as the Catholic University of America). Shortly thereafter, the Congregation initiated a world-wide consultation for a second document that would deal with all non-pontifically chartered institutions—the vast majority of institutions in the U.S. In 1990, Pope John Paul II published the apostolic constitution *Ex corde ecclesiae*, indicating by its title that universities find their origin from the heart of the Church. The document's vision of higher education calls for Catholic institutions to show how various types of knowledge relate to one another, and to develop a coherent undergraduate curriculum in which philosophy and theology provide a framework for integration. It calls for faculty members to learn about each other's work, to search for the ethical and moral implications of both the methods and discoveries of their research, and to promote social justice.

Two essential components of the Land O'Lakes statement appear in the 1990 document: "Every Catholic university possesses that institutional autonomy necessary to perform its functions effectively and guarantees its members academic freedom, so long as the rights of the individual person and of the community are preserved within the confines of the truth and the common good." By institutional autonomy, the document explains in a footnote that "the governance of an academic institution is and remains internal to the institution." Concerning academic freedom, it explains further that it "is the guarantee given to those involved in teaching and research that, within their specific specialized branch of knowledge and according to the methods proper to that specific area, they may search and publish the results of this search, keeping in mind the cited criteria, that is, safeguarding the rights of the individual and of society within the confines of the truth and the common good.''

The Vatican directed national episcopal conferences to take the general norms outlined in the second part of *Ex corde* (the first part dealt with the mission and identity of Catholic higher education), and make whatever adaptations were needed for their local application. A ''pastoral'' application was produced by the U.S. bishops in 1996, but was rejected by the Vatican, which directed that essential juridical elements, outlined in the revised 1983 Code of Canon Law, be included in a new application. Among those juridical elements were the requirement of the *mandatum* for Catholic theologians, the taking of the Oath of fidelity by presidents of Catholic universities, the desirability of at least 50 percent of the faculty and the board of trustees be Catholics, and the clear inclusion of *Ex corde*'s description of the mission and nature of a Catholic university in the by-laws of the local institution. The bishops produced such an application in 1999, which was subsequently approved by the Vatican.

Continuing Tensions Regarding Academic Freedom. Five persistent tensions accompany the idea of academic freedom at Catholic colleges and universities: (1) the differences between the corporate and individual aspects of academic freedom, (2) the AAUP's understanding of academic freedom, (3) institutional autonomy and episcopal authority, (4) the academic freedom of the Catholic theologian, and (5) the practice of hiring for mission.

First, Catholic universities have stressed in practice, though rarely explicitly, a corporate idea of academic freedom. The AAUP understanding of academic freedom emphasizes the rights and responsibilities of the individual professor and the corresponding power of professional peers to determine what counts as knowledge. That understanding arose largely out of a liberal democratic focus on individual rights. Catholic tradition draws on a different understanding of the individual and society. It starts with the understanding that a person is radically social and always a member of a community. It describes society more in organic than contractual terms, though rights continue to belong both to the community and the individual. Given these differences between the AAUP and the Catholic approaches to the individual's relationship to community, it is understandable why the Church has had such difficulty with many of the affirmations of the Enlightenment, particularly the way it formulated the ideas of freedom of conscience and religious liberty. It seemed to Church authorities that both freedoms led inevitably to a kind of philosophical relativism and a rejection of Church tradition and authority. It was only midway through the 20th century that the work of thinkers like John Courtney Murray helped the Church embrace religious freedom, albeit with careful qualifications. Medieval universities retained a strong corporate freedom; they set their own standards and debated controversial issues. Were the university not to have the right to set appropriate standards that strengthen the Catholic character of the institutions, then the emphasis only on the individual professor's rights would weaken the corporate identity of the institution.

Second, the AAUP's concept of academic freedom emphasizes, as has been mentioned, a type of knowledge that relies primarily on scientific methodology. Therefore, it emphasizes new knowledge, acquired by inquiry and experimentation rather than the faithful retrieval and handing on of religious and humanistic traditions. In other words, the authority of a certain type of tradition, a religious tradition, was displaced by another tradition, a certain academic tradition that recognized as valid only that knowledge which is arrived at through scientific methodology. While it is true that very few thinkers now would describe themselves only as empiricists, for a number of secular academics the acceptance of Christian revelation as true still appears to be an indefensible sacrifice of intellectual freedom.

Having underscored these two limitations, it should be added that Catholic institutions can benefit from other characteristics of the AAUP understanding of academic freedom. In particular, its emphases on due process and institutional autonomy are of critical importance for Catholic institutions, which only in recent decades are putting in place procedures to insure both.

Third, *Ex corde* strikes a delicate balance between institutional autonomy on the one hand and episcopal authority on the other when, citing Pope John Paul II's 1987 New Orleans address to the leaders of Catholic higher education, it says that bishops ''should be seen not as external agents but as participants in the life of the Catholic university.'' Except for pontifically chartered universities, nearly all Catholic colleges and universities in the United States (diocesan colleges have a slightly different relationship to their bishop) have predominantly lay boards of trustees. In essence, the local bishop has, as a consequence, no direct authority within the university to hire or fire faculty or employees. The bishop's influence takes the form of persuasion and encouragement, and will be as effective as is his relationship with the leadership and members of a particular Catholic college. On the other hand, if a board of trustees changed its by-laws to permit the bishop some direct authority, the bishop's "influence" would become administrative authority, no longer external but internal. Unfortunately, the mutually exclusive meaning conveyed by the words "external" and "internal" obscure the many ways in which the life of the Church, including the leadership of bishops, and the mission of a Catholic university do and should mutually influence each other. While the Church and the university have distinctive missions, in some ways, not juridical, these missions overlap.

Fourth, some secular academics question seriously whether Catholic theologians have genuine academic freedom. Theologians do not employ the same methods of verification as do scientists; their work, like that done by many in the humanities, is seen as mainly interpretation and opinion, not the result of rigorous and objective methodologies. Their teaching is perceived as "advocacy" or even "proselytization," rather than the dispassionate presentation of knowledge. Their competency is determined not by their peers, but by bishops who are perceived as "external non-academic" agents. The requirement that Catholic theologians teaching Catholic theology have from the local bishop a *mandatum* seems to verify all these perceptions. In response to these concerns, some have criticized the narrow epistemology that privileges the scientific method. Others maintain that many academics have shown that it is possible to teach a discipline enthusiastically and yet critically. It is also pointed out that "realities" outside the academy daily determine what ought to be the subject matter of a discipline—Supreme Court decisions for legal education, business trends for finance curricula, the state of the environment for ecologists, and developments in information technology for those designing communications curricula. More precisely, the lives and experiences of Christian believers in different cultures during different periods of history constitute as important a source for theological work as do the formal doctrinal decisions of Church councils and bishops. Finally, defenders of the *mandatum* point out that it only requires a Catholic theologian to present as Catholic theology what is officially the teaching of the Church—a legitimate professional expectation. Theologians, they continue, may also present other points of view, provide comparisons with other traditions, and raise critical questions, even about official teachings of the Church. If however a Catholic theologian opposes dogmatic teachings of the Church, then he or she ceases to be a Catholic theologian in good standing. Continuing tensions remain and, if Church history is any indication, will continue to remain as to how to insure due process should a difference on doctrine arise between a theologian and a bishop, and as to whether that difference is le-

gitimate or heterodox. Or, tensions will remain over differing interpretations of just what constitutes, in the words of *Ex corde*, the "confines of truth" and "the common good," the two qualities it attaches to academic freedom.

Fifth and finally, in recent years Catholic colleges and universities have increasingly attempted to "hire for mission," that is, to seek out academically qualified candidates for faculty positions who are Catholic or, if not, who nonetheless understand and support the institution's Catholic mission. Such efforts are fraught with difficulties, not the least of which are hiring candidates with religious but not academic qualifications and making all who are not Catholics feel only tolerated. Defenders of the practice of hiring for mission claim that if Catholicism is to be "perceptively present and effectively operative," especially as an intellectual force, then at least some Catholic intellectuals must be hired. As important as Catholic theology is for a Catholic university, other disciplines also must find ways to explore, critique, and embody key insights of Catholic intellectual traditions. Finally, they argue that unless there is a strong and vital non-juridical relationship to the faith and intellectual life of the Church that founded the college or university, it is only a matter of time before that institution begins to move away from its theological tradition to a moral one, and from there to a humanistic tradition, and before long, given the strong secular currents in the academy in the West, to a tradition that has no discernible relationship—intellectual or cultural—to the founding Church at all.

How to understand academic freedom for Catholic colleges and universities, how to benefit from the AAUP understanding of academic freedom aware of its limitations, how to balance institutional autonomy with a vital relationship to the larger Church, how to hire for mission without narrowing the base of faculty talent and the range of views any university should examine, and how to sustain a context in which theologians as well as faculty in other disciplines can creatively work—these challenges, if handled thoughtfully, will continue to ensure that Catholic higher education will provide a truly distinctive alternative to the over 3,000 other institutions of higher learning in the United States.

Bibliography: "Academic Freedom: American and Catholic," in *Origins* 28, no. 35 (18 Feb. 1999). A. GALLIN, ed., *American Catholic Higher Education: Essential Documents, 1967–1990* (Notre Dame 1992). P. GLEASON, *Contending with Modernity* (Oxford 1994). J. HEFT, ed., *A Catholic Modernity? A Discussion with Charles Taylor* (Oxford 1999). R. HOFSTADTER and W. METZGER, *The Development of Academic Freedom in the United States* (New York 1955). W. P. LEAHY, *Adapting to America: Catholics, Jesuits, and Higher Education in the Twentieth Century* (Washington, D.C. 1991). J. T. MCGREEVY, "Thinking on One's Own: Catholicism in the American Intellectual Imagination, 1928–1960," *Journal of American History* 84.1 (June 1997): 97–131.

[J. L. HEFT]

ACCA OF HEXHAM, ST.

Bishop of Hexham; d. Hexham, England, Oct. 20, 740. A Northumbrian, he was fostered by Bosa (d. 705), who was afterward appointed bishop of York (678), and he became the devoted disciple and companion of WILFRID. When the latter was reinstated at Hexham in 705, he made Acca abbot of St. Andrew's monastery there. Acca succeeded Wilfrid as bishop of Hexham in 709. In addition to ruling the diocese with zeal, he concerned himself with the promotion of the liturgy in all its splendor by procuring the service of the cantor Maban (fl. 720), who had inherited the Roman tradition of psalmody of GREGORY THE GREAT, brought to England by the monks of Augustine of Canterbury. He completed, decorated, and richly furnished the churches begun by Wilfrid. He promoted learning, built and equipped a famous library, and, above all, encouraged BEDE, who wrote about him and dedicated several books to him. He was expelled from Hexham in 732 for some unknown reason; he sought refuge in Galloway but returned to die and be buried in his diocese.

Feast: Oct. 20.

Bibliography: BEDE, *Ecclesiastical History* 5:19–20; ed. C. PLUMMER 1:330–332. J. GODFREY, *The Church in Anglo-Saxon England* (Cambridge, England 1962), *passim*. A. S. COOK, "The Old-English Andreas and Bishop Acca of Hexham," *Transactions of the Connecticut Academy of Arts and Sciences* 26 (1924) 245–332. A. M. ZIMMERMANN, *Lexicon für Theologie und Kirche,* ed. J. HOFER and K. RAHNER (Freiburg 1957–65)1:103; *Kalendarium Benedictinum* (Metten 1933–38) 3:200–203.

[C. MCGRATH]

ACCEPTANTS

Members of the clergy, especially in France and in the Netherlands, who accepted the bull *Unigenitus*, dated Sept. 8, 1713, and known in France as early as September 25. At this time, in France, a pontifical declaration had no effect until after it had been accepted by parliament and the Assembly of the Clergy. Parliament discussed the bull *UNIGENITUS* on September 27 and 28. The opposition was led by Attorney General H. F. Daguesseau, who maintained that he saw in it proof of the fallibility of the popes, and parliament refused to endorse the bull, at least for the time being. The King then brought together the bishops present in Paris in an Assembly of the Clergy.

The debates began on October 16. The Acceptants were immediately in the majority; supported by those in power and influenced especially by Cardinals A. G. de Rohan and H. de Bissy, they were nevertheless unable to attain unanimity and subdue their opponents, grouped around Cardinal L. A. de Noailles, Archbishop of Paris. Louis XIV, annoyed, sent the opponents to their dioceses and on Feb. 15, 1714, by a *lettre de cachet,* imposed on parliament the acceptance of the bull. In Aug. 1714, 112 bishops had accepted it, while only 16 refused it. Some Acceptants retracted their submission in 1716, during the brief period in which the Regent was favorably disposed toward Jansenism; but shortly afterward the Acceptants again had the support of those in power, and the Archbishop of Sens, Languet de Gergy, assumed a leading position in the group. The victory was practically assured them after the royal declaration of March 24, 1730, which made *Unigenitus* a law of the land.

[L. J. COGNET]

ACCESSUS

In order to expedite the papal election, each cardinal, immediately after an inconclusive ballot, was allowed an additional vote in favor of a candidate other than the one for whom he had voted in the ballot; such additional votes were added to those cast in the ballot in the hope of effecting a two-thirds majority. This procedure was known as *accessus,* i.e., acceding to the latter candidate. A cardinal could use this right of accessus only once after each ballot; after 1621 he could not use it in his own favor. The complications involved in ensuring that a cardinal did not use it in his own favor or in favor of the candidate for whom he had already voted in the ballot prompted St. Pius X in 1904 to abolish it, replacing it with a second ballot that should take place immediately after each morning and evening ballot.

Bibliography: PIUS X, "Vacante Sede Apostolica" (apostolic constitution, Dec. 25, 1904), *Codex iuris canonici*, Document 1, par. 76. L. PASTOR, *The History of the Popes from the Close of the Middle Ages* (London-St Louis 1938–61) 27:117.

[B. FORSHAW]

ACCIAIOLI

A celebrated Florentine family whose name (spelled also Acciaiuli or Acciajuoli) derives from *acciaio* (steel), in which the family dealt in the Brescia-Bergamo area until Frederick Barbarossa's depredations against the Guelfs of Lombardy forced them to move into Tuscany. From the year 1161, when Guigliarallo Acciaioli settled

"Niccolo Acciaiuoli," painting by Andrea del Castagno. (©Arte & Immagini srl/CORBIS)

in Florence, until his last male descendant died in 1834, the family was renowned for its merchants, bankers, scholars, statesmen, and patrons of the arts. Wealth amassed in their mercantile enterprises, which extended into North Africa and the eastern Mediterranean, became the capital for a lucrative banking business that counted kings and popes among its clients. The most important churchmen in the family were Angelo, Niccolò, and Filippo.

Angelo, cardinal, supporter of the Roman popes during the Great WESTERN SCHISM (1378–1417); b. Florence, April 15, 1340; d. Pisa, May 31, 1408. In 1375 he was named to the bishopric of Rapolla in the Kingdom of Naples by Gregory XI (1371–78), and in 1383 he was appointed archbishop of Florence by Urban VI (1378–89). During this period his eloquent defense of the Roman pontiff against the pretensions of the Avignon claimant, Clement VII (1378–94), was rewarded by his elevation to the cardinalate with the titular see of South Lorenzo in Damaso. In the papal election of 1389 Angelo

was the choice of half of the cardinals, but he directed this support to Cardinal Pietro Tomacelli, who assumed the tiara as Boniface IX (1389–1404). The pope entrusted Angelo with several difficult missions, especially that of assuring the accession of Prince Ladislaus to the throne of Naples and of Hungary, as well as conducting the young king's coronations at Gaeta and at Zara. Angelo restored peace between the pope and the powerful Orsini family and settled ecclesiastical difficulties in Germany and in the Balkans. In common with other cardinals, hitherto unquestioningly loyal to the Roman pontiff, he concluded that a council was the only solution to the Western Schism and was attending a preliminary session of the Council of Pisa at the time of his death. His body was transferred to the Certosa in Florence in the 16th century.

Niccolò, cardinal, papal diplomat; b. Florence, 1630; d. Rome, 1719. Niccolò attended the Roman Seminary and completed his clerical studies at the Roman College, where he received a doctorate in law. Under Alexander VII (1655–67), Niccolò had charge of paying and equipping the militia of the Papal States. In 1667 he administered the papal treasury and two years later was made cardinal deacon of Saints Cosmas and Damian by Clement IX (1667–69). During the reign of Alexander VIII (1689–91), Niccolò, with the clumsy assistance of Cosimo III, grand duke of Tuscany, attempted to prevent the marriage of his nephew Roberto Acciaioli to Elizabeth Mormorai, a widow. When Elizabeth was forcibly placed in a convent, her fiancé delivered an uncomplimentary account of his uncle's part in the episode to each of the cardinals who had assembled to elect a successor to Alexander VIII. The embarrassing narrative did much to defeat Niccolò's otherwise excellent chances of election. In the conclave of 1700 Niccolò, who was identified with the "Zelanti," was again among the favored candidates but was ruled out of contention by the powerful "Imperialist" faction. For 12 years Niccolò served as papal legate to Ferrara, and in 1715, four years before his death, he was made bishop of Ostia and dean of the Sacred College.

Filippo, cardinal, papal nuncio to Portugal at the time of the expulsion of the Jesuits; b. Rome, March 12, 1700; d. Ancona, July 4, 1776. Filippo's first ecclesiastical appointment was as vice legate to Ravenna (1724), where he remained for four years. This was followed by other minor assignments until 1743, when he was made titular archbishop of Petra in Transjordan and sent to Lucerne as papal nuncio to Switzerland. In 1753 he was appointed nuncio to Portugal, where Sebastião POMBAL was beginning his campaign of vilification against the Jesuits. Filippo endeavored to refute or mitigate each charge against the society and kept Pope Benedict XIV (1740–58) informed of developments. Filippo was advised by Benedict to remain near the Spanish border so that he could escape if necessary and send or receive messages with less danger of their interception. Despite Filippo's efforts, all Portuguese Jesuits were either jailed or expelled in January of 1759, eight months before Filippo was elevated to the cardinalate by Clement XIII (1758–69), with the titular see of South Maria degli Angeli. The following year he was ordered to leave Portugal. After his return to Rome, Filippo was made bishop of Ancona.

Bibliography: C. UGURGIERI DELLA BERARDENGA, *Gli Acciaioli di Firenze,* 2 v. (Florence 1962). E. SAPORI et al., *Enciclopedia Italiana di scienzi, littere ed arti,* 36 v. (Rome 1929–39) 1:259–261. *Enciclopedia universal ilustrada Europeo-Americana,* 70 v. (Barcelona 1908–30) 1:967–971. F. BOCK, *Lexikon für Theologie und Kirche,* ed. J. HOFER and K. RAHNER, 10 v. (2d, new ed. Freiburg 1957–65) 1:103–104. L. PASTOR, *The History of the Popes from the Close of the Middle Ages,* 40 v. (London–St. Louis 1938–61) v. 36, 37. G. MOLLAT and P. RICHARD, *Dictionnaire d'histoire et de géographie ecclésiastiques,* ed. A. BAUDRILLART et al. (Paris 1912–) 1:263–265. A. D'ADDARIO and G. PAMPALONI, *Dizionario biographico degli Italiani,* ed. A. M. GHISALBERTI (Rome 1960–) 1:76, 82–83. P. LITTA et al., *Famiglie celebri italiane,* 14 v. (Milan 1819–1923).

[R. F. COPELAND]

ACCIDENT

A word with various meanings in ordinary usage and with precise technical significations in law, philosophy, and theology. The term may generally mean a chance occurrence, or it may be used to describe a fall or collision, as in vehicular traffic, with or without personal injury. The adjectival form, moreover, is frequently used to refer to the less important or more superficial aspect of a thing or event. Though these meanings may be different, there is a common element among them. If used as CHANCE, accident contrasts with the stability of ORDER; if used as less important, accident contrasts with the essential or the necessary. The note of contrast, then, is implicit in most usages of the term. Its varied meanings are set over against a more basic, more important, usually more enduring reality that is implied in the very usage itself.

Ancient and medieval philosophers thus employed the term in enumerating accident among the PREDICABLES and in contrasting accident with SUBSTANCE. In their analysis, man is essentially what his substance is. While this substance remains unchanged, man remains. But man does change accidentally. He may gain weight, increase in size, become tanned in the summer, develop his knowledge, exercise his muscles, and move about from place to place in time. All of these changes are real. The essential sameness of man throughout this type of change indicates a difference of levels, that of independent and dependent, basic and proximate, fundamental and phenomenal, substantial and accidental.

When modern philosophers rejected substance and substituted phenomenon for accident, they eliminated any contrasting note from phenomenon. The phenomenon began to play the dual role of substance or SUBJECT as well as the manifestation or appearance of that subject. Hence, the terms accident and phenomenon cannot always be read simply as translations of each other or as necessarily contrasted with their correlatives, substance and noumenon respectively (*see* NOUMENA; PHENOMENA). The context must be consulted before deciding how the term accident is being used by a particular author.

This article first discusses the historical development of the concept and then presents a systematic analysis that justifies its understanding in the Aristotelian-Thomistic tradition and explains its uses in Catholic theology.

Historical Development

The main stages in the evolution of the concept of accident include its origins in Greek philosophy; its development in the medieval period, particularly by St. Thomas Aquinas; and later formulations that led to the gradual rejection of the concept in modern and contemporary philosophy.

GREEK NOTIONS

The key to the historical development of the meaning of accident is the kind of relation an accident bears to a more fundamental subject. The relative and dependent character of accident was clearly taught by ARISTOTLE in his classic resolution of the Greek philosophical controversy over the fact and nature of change. Accident was to substance as the superficial to the fundamental. But PLATO had prepared for the Aristotelian answer by asking in what sense being (εἶναι, οὐσία) could be predicated of things that were different, such as rest and motion. For Plato, the problem also centered on a plurality of predicates for one subject. In the *Sophist* (*c.* 255) he states that "of those which are, some are per se, and some are related to others."

Aristotle developed these insights. He says in his *Metaphysics* (1030a 20–23), "For as 'is' belongs to all things, not however in the same sense, but to one sort of thing primarily and to others in a secondary way, so too 'what a thing is' belongs in the simple sense to substance, but in a limited sense to the other categories." In contrast with οὐσία for substance as primary being, Aristotle used συμβεβηκός for accident. This Greek term connoted "going along with" or "occurring with" something else. For Aristotle, there were nine different ways, classes or categories in which there was an "occurring with" the primary being, substance. These nine classes of accident together with substance constitute the ten CATEGORIES OF

BEING. When the Greek συμβεβήκος came to be translated into the Latin *accidens,* the latter's etymology of "happening" or "falling upon" accented the notion of relative and dependent; it also provided the form for the later English term.

THOMISTIC CONCEPT

St. THOMAS AQUINAS further emphasized the relative and dependent aspect of accidents. "In the definition of an accident something is placed which is outside the essence of the thing defined; for it is necessary to place the subject in the definition of an accident" (*In 2 de anim.* 1.1). The reason for this necessity is that accidents "do not have a perfect essence; whence it follows that they must admit into their definition the subject, which is outside of their genus" (*De ente* 2).

Essence of accidents. Accident is said not to have a perfect ESSENCE; yet it does have some kind of essence. Its very state of imperfection or of being a lesser essence emphasizes a dual character: its reality as distinct from substance and its dependence on substance. In the Aristotelian and Thomistic view, an accident always has a dependent mode of existence. An accident expresses more than itself in its very aspect of lacking independence: its referent is not size alone, but the size of something; not shape alone, but the shape of something.

Though having an imperfect essence, accident nonetheless has an essence and may thus be compared to substance. As essences, both substance and accident are alike in that they have a capacity for EXISTENCE. "In its own nature being is substance or accident" (*De nat. gen.* 2). Substance and accident are distinguished from each other by the precise, opposite modes of existence proper to each. The mode of existence proper to substance is *per se,* or independent, whereas that proper to accident is *in alio,* or dependent. "Similarly, 'to exist in a subject' is not the definition of accident, but on the contrary 'a thing which is due to exist in another'" (*In 4 sent.* 12.1.1.1 ad 2). What is properly characteristic of accident is its need or aptitude for existence in another. Even in the Eucharist, after the change of the substance of the bread and the wine into the Body and Blood of Christ, the accidents of bread and wine do not cease to have aptitude for inherence in a subject; thus, although sustained by divine power, they never cease to be accidents (*Summa theologiae* 3a, 77.1 ad 2).

In both the natural and supernatural orders, accident is within the order of BEING, and it is most properly called a being of a being (*ens entis*) to emphasize its everpresent dependent mode. It is also characterized as a being *secundum quid* (that is, relatively) in contrast with substance, which is a being *simpliciter* (that is, absolute-ly). This latter contrast also emphasizes a development in the terminology of St. Thomas for substance and accident. In his commentary on the *Sentences,* he uses *res* (THING) when speaking of substance or accident; in his later writings, however, his terminology indicates that substance and accident are principles within the order of being. Each is an essence, but only substance is perfect; accident is imperfect. By reason of the different status of their essence, they have differing capacities for existence. Substance is essence in its capacity for an independent, or *per se,* mode of existence. Accident is essence in its capacity for a dependent, or *in alio,* mode of existence. They are distinguished by their differing capacities for distinct modes of existence, while remaining interrelated as the dependent on the independent.

Distinct existence of accidents. This principle of distinction between substance and accident also serves to answer the controverted question of the distinct existence of the accident. The majority of St. Thomas's commentators, including JOHN OF ST. THOMAS and T. de Vio CAJETAN, hold that in a thing there is one substantial existence with many distinct accidental existences. Some distinguished contemporary commentators, however, point to various passages in St. Thomas and advance their reasons for holding that the one substantial existence is also that whereby accidents exist [R. G. FONTAINE, *Subsistent Accident in the Philosophy of St. Thomas and in His Predecessors* (Washington 1950) 74–76]. The author of this article takes the position that substance and accident have distinct existences within the one concrete thing. The argument for this view may be put as follows: "An accident really exists as a modification of a really existent substance. Only in real dependence upon substantial existence can the accidental existence be had. An identical existence could not be really dependent and really independent in the same respect. The one has to be really distinct from the other" [J. OWENS, *An Elementary Christian Metaphysics* (Milwaukee 1963) 159–160].

THOMISTIC CLASSIFICATION

In treating the real distinction between substance and accident, one may easily create the false impression that there is but a single kind of substance and a single kind of accident. Actually, there are many specifically different substances, and it is the substance itself that specifies the difference. "For when we say that some substance is corporeal or spiritual, we do not compare spirituality or corporeity to substance as forms to matter, or accidents to a subject; but as differences to a genus. Thus it is that a spiritual substance is not spiritual through something added to its own substance, but is such through its own substance. In the same way, corporeal substance is not corporeal through something added to substance, but according to its own substance" (*De subs. sep.* 6).

In a somewhat similar fashion, accident in general is distinguished into ultimate classes or genera. Aristotle, Augustine, and Aquinas treat the nine genera of accidents as classifications of real being. Of these nine genera, Aquinas observes that two points must be noted. "One is the nature belonging to each of them considered as an accident, which commonly applies to each of them as inherent in a subject, for the existence (*esse*) of an accident is existence in another (*inesse*). The other point to note is the proper nature of each one of these genera" (ST 1a, 28.2).

St. AUGUSTINE has given examples of the nine genera. "When the question is asked, how large is he? and I say he is . . . four feet in measure, I affirm according to quantity . . . . I say he is white, I affirm according to quality . . . . I say he is near, I affirm something according to relation . . . . I affirm something according to position when I say he lies down . . . . I speak according to condition (*habitus*) when I say he is armed . . . . I affirm according to time when I say he is of yesterday . . . . And when I say he is at Rome, I affirm according to place . . . . I affirm according to the predicament of action when I say he strikes . . . and when I say he is struck, I affirm according to the predicament of passion" (*Trin.* 5.7).

A list of the predicamental accidents in more precise terminology would include QUANTITY, QUALITY, RELATION, ACTION AND PASSION, position in time (*quando*), LOCATION (*ubi*), SITUATION (*situs*), and condition, or habit (*habitus*). It is well, however, to remember that "the original terms that Aristotle used to name the accidental categories were not substantive in form. . . . The proper designation of the category of quantity, for instance, was *to poson,* the quantitative. That of quality was *to poion,* the qualitative. Corresponding to these adjectival forms, adverbial and verbal forms were used to name the other categories. . . . 'The quantitative' helps keep in mind that it designates not something self-contained and as it were standing in its own right, but rather a way in which a substance happens to be" [J. Owens, *An Elementary Christian Metaphysics* (Milwaukee 1963) 166].

Absolute and intrinsic accidents. Of these predicaments, quantity and quality are absolute accidents and the rest are relative. While each of the predicamental accidents is, as an accident, related to the subject or substance on which it depends, only the accidents other than quantity and quality put the substance in which they inhere into relation with other things. Quantity and quality alone modify the substance in itself, that is, without further reference to other substances. Quantity confers EXTENSION on corporeal substance. Quality modifies a substance, whether spiritual or corporeal, either in itself or in its op-

eration. Both quantity and quality thus serve in an absolute or intrinsic way for the immediate grounding of relative or extrinsic accidents; these enable substance further to relate to other things and to manifest itself in a variety of ways.

Relative and extrinsic accidents. Accidents other than quantity and quality are sometimes designated as extrinsic, a term that serves to contrast them with the two intrinsic accidents. Just as all accidents are in a sense relative, because their very essence is to have aptitude for inherence in a subject, so too are all accidents in a sense intrinsic. A real accident of its very nature belongs to a substance, and in this way is intrinsic. Those accidents, however, that put their substance into relation with other substances are properly called extrinsic. Their role and function are directed outward toward other substances, even though the accident itself is rooted in the relating substance.

The most obvious of the extrinsic or relative accidents is relation. As real, predicamental relation is distinguished from the logical relation, or the relation of reason, which exists only within the mind. As predicamental, it is distinguished from the transcendental relation, which is the very nature of some essence or principle as this relates to a complementary principle. Predicamental relation is a distinct reality by means of which the substance to which it belongs is related to another subject; its very essence is reference or order to another. Such a relation must be distinguished from the foundation that serves as the cause of relation. For example, the quality of tallness is the foundation for the real relation of SIMILARITY between tall people.

The correlative accidents of action and passion are related to the operation of an AGENT, although each stands in different relation to that agent. Action is the second actuality of the creature at the operational level. Since it involves the exercise of CAUSALITY, it cannot be understood without an appreciation of the notion and reality of cause. Action is a further perfection of the agent, but it is extrinsically denominated by reference to the patient upon which the agent operates. Passion, on the other hand, is the accidental modification that the patient undergoes by receiving in itself the efficiency of the agent. Action and passion are really distinct categories, although both are intimately related to the EFFICIENT CAUSALITY of the agent.

Finally, there are four extrinsic accidents based on quantity. The accident "when" (*quando*) is sometimes, although incorrectly, identified with TIME. Time is based on the reality of MOTION, whose inner relationships provide the basis for the measuring or numbering in which time consists. Corporeal objects, existing in the changing world of time, have a type of accidental existence by reason of their temporal situation. "When" is thus a category of real being; it has extrinsic denomination from time as a measure.

Location in PLACE provides the basis for another category, the accident "where" (*ubi*). This inheres in a subject through its quantity, because of the circumscriptive containment of the subject arising from the surrounding quantities of other bodies. The ninth category, situation or posture, is an accident presupposing the category "where," which it further determined by specifying the order of the parts of the body in place. Being a passenger on the subway or bus would answer to the category "where," whereas the various stances one chooses or is forced to take on the vehicle as it becomes crowded are examples of the further determination that is situation or posture.

The tenth category, condition or habit (*habitus*), is the accident proper to a body by reason of something extrinsic and adjacent to it that does not measure it, as does place. An example would be "clothed," in which case the body that is the subject of the accident is denominated by something extrinsic to it, namely, clothing.

LATER CONCEPTIONS

St. Thomas reconciled the unity of a thing with its many divergent characteristics, activities, and changes by acknowledging the complexity within the structure of a finite thing. Unity is preserved through the uniqueness of a specific substantial nature with its proportioned substantial existence, which in turn allows for a variety of lesser perfections or accidents that have a basic exigency for inherence in the substance. Though having real status in the order of being, the accident is nonetheless a lesser being; as has been said, it is but a being of a being.

This delicate balancing of unity and plurality within the one concrete thing was not preserved by much of 14th century scholasticism. The most prominent spokesman was WILLIAM OF OCKHAM, who rejected any real distinction other than between thing and thing. "In creatures there cannot be any distinction whatsoever outside the soul, except where there are distinct things" (*Summulae in lib. phys.* 1.14). Renaissance scholasticism, in the person of F. Suárez, lost still more the Thomistic appreciation for unity within complexity. Suárez's distinctive teaching was that "being can be predicated absolutely and without qualification of the accident" (*Disp. meta.* 32.2.18).

The extreme view of the distinction of accident from substance that thus developed evoked opposing reactions in modern philosophy. Authors tended to suppress either the reality of accident or the reality of substance. Although it would be simplistic to ascribe these two tendencies solely to the teaching of Suárez, it may be noted that R. DESCARTES and G. W. LEIBNIZ read him and that I. KANT knew his teaching through the *Ontologia* of C. WOLFF. The more basic reason for these opposing tendencies in modern philosophy, however, lies in the differing epistemologies of RATIONALISM and EMPIRICISM. Rationalism, by exalting the intellectual power of man, freed man's reason from dependence on the data of sense and ascribed to reason the power of attaining easily the essences of things. Empiricism, reacting against this abandonment of the sense origins of knowledge, so deeply immersed itself in the conditions of the empirical that it precluded any intellectual discovery of the substantial essence.

Thus Descartes opted for two kinds of substance, the bodily and the spiritual, each of which he really identified with its primary property, extension and thought respectively. All other properties he regarded as but varieties of the primary property. B. SPINOZA sought to resolve the basic problem of unity and plurality in things by considering the Cartesian extension and thought as two modes of a unique, infinite substance. Yet Spinoza carefully refrained from calling the modes accidents. All multiplicity and apparent finiteness, for him, are mere modifications of the two attributes of extension and thought that are characteristic of the one, infinite, divine substance.

J. LOCKE opposed the innate ideas of Descartes but accepted the Cartesian criterion of truth as the clear and distinct idea. He applied the criterion of distinctness to the point of isolating empirical qualities from any known bond with the thing of which they were supposed to be qualities. Instead of stressing the interdependence and interrelation between quality and substance, he gave to each a separate and independent status. One may speculate what influence Locke's training in Ockhamist philosophy at Oxford, had on this extreme separation of substance and accident.

Whereas Locke would allow that substance is at least an unknown support of qualities, D. HUME, going further than G. BERKELEY in the rejection of material substance, could find no philosophical need for substance in any sense whatever. Restricting his knowledge to distinct perceptions, each of which he considered as existing independently, Hume in effect identified the accidental with the substantial. Since "every perception may exist separately, and have no need of anything else to support their existence, they are therefore substances, as far as this definition explains a substance" (*Treatise* 1.1.5).

Modern and contemporary philosophers have tended to repeat the position of Hume. A common view is that there is no need of substance to explain reality because everything that substance is supposed to contribute can be ascribed to phenomena. Hence, although Kant provided for the unknowable thing-in-itself, the noumenon, in contradistinction to the empirically known phenomenon, the more dominant theme in contemporary thought has been a rejection of substance.

Systematic Analysis

While many contemporary philosophers thus tend to disregard the distinction between substance and accident, and therefore to reject the concept of accident itself, this concept continues to be important in scholastic philosophy and theology. The following more systematic explanation may serve to justify the retention of the concept in philosophy and to outline its many important uses in Catholic theology.

JUSTIFICATION IN PHILOSOPHY

The various philosophical positions with respect to accident in modern thought may be grouped under four headings, namely, (1) rationalist, (2) empiricist, (3) Kantian and (4) contemporary scientific. Though differing superficially, these positions have much in common; moreover, they must all confront the perennial problem of reconciling unity and plurality as these are found in the concrete existing thing.

Rationalism, as exemplified in the thought of Descartes and Spinoza, really identifies substance and accident or substance and mode while accenting the reality of substance. Empiricism, as exemplified in Hume's formulation, rejects substance while ascribing to perceptions or phenomena the substantial mode of independent existence. Kantian criticism explicitly retains the unknown noumenon, or thing-in-itself, and the known phenomena that, together with the space-time forms within the knower, are materially constitutive of sensible intuition; with the noumenon unknown and unknowable, however, for all practical purposes only the phenomena are retained. Hence rationalism, empiricism, and Kantian criticism effectively retain only one ultimate level of reality. The same may be said of the contemporary scientific view; so far as it accords any objectivity to accident, it regards phenomena such as light, color, heat and sound as various types of motion. Physical scientists and contemporary naturalistic philosophers speak of systems rather than of substance, although they continue to designate the entities and particles within their systems in terms once used to describe substance. Since this manner of thinking equivalently rejects a substance-accident dualism, it amounts to maintaining that matter and motion (or matter in motion) exist either independently or dependently—in other words, are either substances or accidents. Hence, the contemporary scientific position, like its three predecessors, reductively retains but one ultimate level of reality.

The basic issue is whether reality is sufficiently explained when only one level of reality is retained or whether the facts expostulate a radical dualism that accentuates the relatedness and dependence of realities at different levels. In effect, the philosophical problem may be stated either as the problem of substance or as the problem of accident. If substance is rejected, either theoretically or practically, its intelligible characteristics, both generic and specific, are transferred to the phenomena. But then what is to be said of the phenomena? A duality of levels of reality is denied while a term is retained, namely, phenomenon, whose etymological meaning is ''that which appears or is manifest,'' and which itself connotes the presence of something else that does not appear or is not manifest. The same is true of the term accident, which means ''occurring with'' or ''happening to'' something else.

The resulting inference is more than a carry-over of Aristotelian prejudices that have been inherited along with a Greek-derived language. What it indicates is, rather, that the mind dealing with the data of experience recognizes two complementary, mutually related roles within a thing, one of which is dependent, the other independent. Plato sought answers to the problem that arises when one subject is considered to be the recipient of many different predicates. The full answer is more than the substance-accident dualism as elaborated by Aristotle, but this dualism is integral to the solution of the problem. As Aquinas has demonstrated, beneath such diversity there must be something basic, primary, and independent, for this alone can account for the unity that is known. The alternative is a meaningless regression to infinity. The basic and independent source of a thing's unity and the ultimate subject of all predication is substance (ST 1a, 11.1 ad 1).

Substance-accident dualism cannot be appreciated in any epistemology that severs the bond of relatedness between substance and accident and presumes to treat of either as though it were independent of the other. Original knowledge of substance and accident in any explicit way is a simultaneous recognition of the independent-dependent duality found in the things of experience. By a gradual process of increasingly perfected knowledge, the mind comes to know the precise characteristics of substance and of accident in general. Proper knowledge of the specific kind of substance, while varying in its degree of difficulty, corresponds to the perfection of knowledge of its accidents, for these both manifest the substance and are dependent on it.

USES IN CATHOLIC THEOLOGY

A proper understanding of the nature of accident is of special importance for Catholic theology and doctrine. For example, a sound theological statement of the mystery of human and angelic supernatural participation in the divine life requires the utmost precision regarding the substantial and accidental orders, for only if this distinction is maintained can both the reality of the divine indwelling be preserved and the error of PANTHEISM be avoided. The meaning of created grace as a prerequisite for man's living union with God involves a new mode of accidental existence within man, while preserving intact man's essential humanity and God's transcendent deity.

EUCHARISTIC DOCTRINE

The doctrine most commonly associated with philosophical teaching on substance and accident is that of the EUCHARIST. Of this mystery, the Council of Trent declares: ''This Council teaches the true and genuine doctrine about this venerable and divine sacrament of the Eucharist—the doctrine which the Catholic Church has always held and which she will hold until the end of the world, as she has learned it from Christ our Lord himself, from his Apostles, and from the Holy Spirit, who continually brings all truth to her mind. . . . The Council forbids all the faithful of Christ henceforth to believe, teach, or preach anything about the Most Holy Eucharist that is different from what is explained and defined in this present decree'' (H. Denzinger, *Enchiridion symbolorum* 1635). ''If anyone says that the substance of bread and wine remain in the holy sacrament of the Eucharist together with the body and blood of our Lord Jesus Christ and denies that wonderful and singular change of the whole substance of the bread into the body and the whole substance of the wine into the blood, while only the species of bread and wine remain, a change which the Catholic Church has most fittingly called transubstantiation: let him be anathema'' (Denzinger 1652).

Four hundred years after Trent, Pope Pius XII stated in *Humani generis* (1950): ''Some even say that the doctrine of transubstantiation, based on an antiquated philosophical notion of substance, should be so modified that the real presence of Christ in the Holy Eucharist be reduced to a kind of symbolism, whereby the consecrated species would be merely efficacious signs of the spiritual presence of Christ . . .'' (Denzinger 3891). In 1965 some Catholic theologians continued to question the relevance of the substance-accident dualism for Eucharistic theology. They denied that the Council of Trent used substance as a technical philosophical term and maintained, on the basis of contemporary science, that fundamental changes within a thing, such as bread, are not substantial changes. Further, their argument calls attention to the fact that Trent did not use the term accident but the term species.

In reply, one must distinguish the scientific, the philosophical, and the theological levels involved in this questioning. The critique given for the rejection of substance-accident dualism by contemporary science and by modern philosophy may be taken on face value for purposes of argument. But one may add a further question: What evidence is there that contemporary scientists use the expression SUBSTANTIAL change in the same way as philosophers use it, especially scholastic philosophers whose terminology is a requisite for understanding the statements of the Council of Trent? As Pope Pius XII insisted in *Humani generis,* ''the things that have been composed through common effort by Catholic teachers over the course of the centuries to bring about some understanding of dogma are certainly not based on any such weak foundation. These things are based on principles and notions deduced from a true knowledge of created things. . . . Hence, it is not astonishing that some of these have not only been used by the Ecumenical Councils, but even sanctioned by them, so that it is wrong to depart from them'' (Denzinger 3883).

Historical development. The fact is that the Eucharistic teaching of the Council of Trent represents a definitive formulation culminating the gradual growth of the Church's understanding of its traditional belief in the real presence of Christ in the Eucharist. The Fathers of the Church all taught that after the consecration, Christ is truly present and that bread and wine are no longer present. Further statements seeking greater understanding of the mystery were a later development beginning with PASCHASIUS RADBERTUS, who in 844 published the first monograph on the Eucharist, *De corpore et sanguine Domini.* Paschasius raised the problem of the objectivity of the appearances of bread and wine while affirming the real presence of the Body and Blood of Christ. Two centuries later BERENGARIUS OF TOURS, maintaining that his position had the support of the New Testament and the Fathers, taught that the doctrine of the real presence and of substantial conversion is against reason. LANFRANC, in his *De corpore et sanguine Domini,* replied: ''We believe that the earthly substances . . . are converted . . . into the essence of the Lord's body, the species of the things themselves being preserved and certain other qualities.'' The teaching of Berengarius was condemned by several synods, including those at Paris, Tours, and Rome, and also by the Sixth Council of Rome (1079) at which Pope Gregory VII required that Berengarius profess his belief that ''the bread and wine . . . are substantially changed into the true, proper, and life-giving flesh and blood of our Lord Jesus Christ'' (Denzinger 700; cf. 690).

From the middle of the 11th century onward, theologians used accident interchangeably for appearances, species, and qualities when dealing with the Eucharistic transformation of bread and wine into the Body and Blood of Christ. The term TRANSUBSTANTIATION was used by ALAN OF LILLE in his *Theologicae regulae* (c. 1200) to indicate the type of change that is there taking place.

It remained for St. Thomas Aquinas to treat extensively of substance and accident as these relate to the intelligibility of statements concerning the Eucharist. By developing Aristotelian insights on the interdependent, but really distinct, character of substance and accident, and their simultaneous knowability through the natural functioning of the intellect in its dependence on the senses, Aquinas was able to formulate an acceptable accounting of the mystery of transubstantiation. The divine power in and after the consecration, in a manner transcending man's comprehension, sustains the real accidents of bread and wine without their connatural substances. Since the species of bread and wine are the natural objects of the senses and declare to reason the presence of bread and wine, the species serve as a sacramental sign; these require an act of faith in the presence of the Real Food, who is the living Christ physically present beneath the appearances. St. Thomas in his explanation uses the terms accidents and species interchangeably (ST 3a, 75.5).

The formulations of the dogma of the Eucharist as proposed by Trent should thus be understood against the background of their development within the living theology of the Church, which includes not only the work of the great scholastic theologians, but especially other conciliar teachings, such as those of the Councils of Rome, Constance and Florence.

See Also: EUCHARIST (AS SACRAMENT); SUBSTANCE; ACT; FORM; QUALITY

Bibliography: C. FERRO, *Enciclopedia filosofica,* 4 v. (Venice-Rome 1957) 1:29–38. R. J. DEFERRARI et al., *A Lexicon of St. Thomas Aquinas* (Washington 1948–53) 1:9–10. R. E. MCCALL, *The Reality of Substance* (Washington 1956). L. DE RAEYMAEKER, *The Philosophy of Being,* tr. E. H. ZIEGELMEYER (St. Louis 1954) 195–204. C. A. HART, *Thomistic Metaphysics* (Englewood Cliffs, N.J. 1959) 215–239. M. M. SCHEU, *The Categories of Being in Aristotle and St. Thomas* (Washington 1944). A. J. OSGNIACH, *The Analysis of Objects* (New York 1938). C. DAVIS, ''The Theology of Transubstantiation,'' *Sophia* (Melbourne, Australia, April 1964). H. B. GREEN, ''The Eucharistic Presence: Change and/or Signification,'' *Downside Review,* 83 (1965) 32–48. PAUL VI, ''Mysterium fidei'' (encyclical, Sept. 3, 1965), *The Pope Speaks,* 10 (1965) 309–328.

[R. E. MC CALL]

ACCOLTI, MICHAEL

Jesuit missionary; b. Conversano, Italy, Jan. 29, 1807; d. San Francisco, Calif., Nov. 7, 1878. Both of his parents were of ancient and noble families. In 1830 he was appointed to the Pontifical Academy of Noble Ecclesiastics in Rome and enrolled for two years. He then entered the Jesuit novitiate of Sant' Andrea in Rome, and was ordained on Sept. 24, 1842, in the Basilica of St. John Lateran. A year later he was assigned to accompany a group of Jesuits led by Pierre DE SMET to work among the Flathead Indians in the Northwest of North America.

Accolti spent several years working in Jesuit missionary stations in Oregon. With the discovery of gold in California by James Marshall on Jan. 24, 1848, the rapid increase in population there made the need for priests imperative. Accordingly, Accolti and a companion, John NOBILI, arrived in San Francisco on Dec. 8, 1849, marking the first return of the Society of Jesus (SJ) to California since its expulsion in 1768 from the lower, or Mexican, part of the area.

Within a few months Accolti was recalled to Oregon as superior of the Jesuits of the Northwest. Because he was convinced of the need to establish the Jesuits permanently in California, he went to Rome in 1853 and secured from the father general, Peter Beckx, a decree (1854) assigning the Jesuit effort in the Oregon country and California to the care of the Italian Jesuit province of Turin. This arrangement ensured a flow of manpower to the missions confided to Accolti. In 1855 he was relieved of his office of superior in Oregon and returned to San Francisco, where he assisted Anthony Maraschi, SJ, to found St. Ignatius College (later University of San Francisco). From 1860 until his death he served alternately in San Francisco and at Santa Clara College (later University).

Bibliography: G. J. GARRAGHAN, *Jesuits in the Middle United States,* 3 v. (New York 1938). J. W. RIORDAN, *The First Half Century of St. Ignatius Church and College* (San Francisco 1905).

[J. B. MCGLOIN]

ACCOLTI, PIETRO AND BENEDETTO

Members of a Tuscan family notable for its ecclesiastics and poets.

Pietro, cardinal of Ancona; b. Florence, March 15, 1455; d. Rome, Dec. 12, 1532. In 1505 he was consecrated bishop and received the See of Ancona. Pope Julius II made him a member of the college of cardinals on March 17, 1511. Leo X placed Cardinal Accolti in charge of the papal letters during his pontificate, and in this capacity he drew up *Exsurge Domine,* which condemned Martin Luther on 41 accounts of heresy. In keeping with the pluralism of the times, Cardinal Accolti held the bishoprics of suburban Albano and Sabina, and the Sees of Maillezais, Arras, Cadiz, and Cremona. In 1524 Clement VII bestowed upon him the archbishopric of Ravenna. The Cardinal resided in Rome during the last years of his life. He was survived by his brother Bernardo (1465–1536), who gained considerable fame as a poet. Because of confusion with respect to the Accolti family in the 15th and early 16th centuries, Pietro has been mistaken for his nephew Benedetto.

Benedetto, cardinal–archbishop of Ravenna, papal secretary; b. Florence, 1497; d. there, Sept. 21, 1549. Benedetto, the son of Michele Accolti, was named cardinal in 1527 by Clement VII. Much of the confusion resulted from the granting of several of the bishoprics held by Pietro to Benedetto upon his uncle's death. Furthermore, Benedetto has also been identified with the 15th century jurist and historian who bears the same name (Benedetto Accolti, 1415–66). Cardinal Benedetto Accolti made his reputation as a poet and defender of papal rights in the early years of the Protestant revolt.

Bibliography: A. POSCH, *Lexikon für Theologie und Kirche*[2], ed. J. HOFER and K. RAHNER, 10 v. (2d, new ed. Freiburg 1957–65)[2] 1:104–105. P. RICHARD, *Dictionnaire d'histoire et de géographie ecclésiastiques,* ed. A. BAUDRILLART et al. (Paris 1912—) 1:270–271. L. PASTOR, *The History of the Popes From the Close of the Middle Ages,* 40 v. (London–St. Louis 1938–61) v.7, 9–12, *passim.* G. B. PICOTTI, *La Giovinezza di Leone X* (Milan 1928). G. K. BROWN, *Italy and the Reformation to 1550* (Oxford, Eng. 1933). E. P. RODOCANACHI, *Histoire de Rome: Le Pontificat de Léon X* (Paris 1931).

[J. G. GALLAHER]

ACCUSATION

Accusation, commonly, is the act of charging one with a fault or offense (from the Latin *accusare,* to call to account).

In moral theology accusation can be either evangelical (CORRECTION, FRATERNAL) or judicial; the latter is the type of accusation considered here. Public officials, who have been appointed for the preservation of the common good, are obliged, more or less gravely, depending on the possibility of injury to the community resulting from silence, to make accusations against those who violate the law. Such officials, if bound by their oath to the fulfillment of their office, are the more gravely obliged. However, such oaths of office are generally understood to impose no graver obligation than is proportionate to the importance of a case and to its bearing on the common good.

Private individuals also may be bound to accuse violators of the law. Every member of society is obliged to come to the aid of the society when peace and order are endangered. There are times when this duty makes it seriously obligatory to accuse criminals. For example, to keep silent when one has information about persons who are a threat to the community's peace can be a grave sin. Duty to oneself or one's family may also indicate an obligation to lodge an accusation against a wrongdoer. Apart from obligations in justice, anyone may be gravely obliged in charity to save another from a grave evil, especially if this can be done without serious inconvenience to self.

Bibliography: D. M. PRÜMMER, *Manuale theologiae moralis,* ed. E. M. MÜNCH, 3 v. (12th ed. Freiburg-Barcelona 1955) 2:159.

[J. D. FEARON]

ACEDIA

Acedia, more commonly called sloth through confusion with its most notable effect, is a disgust with the spiritual because of the physical effort involved. If the spiritual good from which acedia recoils has a necessary connection with the divine good, which should be the subject of Christian joy, it can be a sin, and even serious. Moreover, acedia is one of the capital sins, a common distraction from virtue, producing other, even quite distinct, sins.

The word describing this constant human phenomenon is found not only in the Septuagint Bible (e.g., Sir 6.26) but in Greek and Latin pagan authors; etymologists show that the word should not be derived from Latin *acidus* but from the Greek α-κήδος (not caring). Whatever its possibly Stoic origins may be, the psychology of the temptation received most careful attention from the desert fathers of the fourth century, who discussed it in the context of other evil thoughts as the *daemon meridianus* (Ps 90.6). Evagrius Ponticus in 383 seems to be the first to have written a description of acedia in his *De octo vitiosis cogitationibus* (*Patrologia Graeca*, ed. J. P. Migne, 40:1274), obviously drawing more from actual experience than literary antecedents. The loneliness of the hermitage in the barren desert, a body worn out by fasting, and a mind fatigued by long prayers were conditions calculated to bring on the ennui and restlessness that was called acedia. John Cassian faithfully reported this fairly common trouble to the West in his *On the Spirit of Acedia* (Conferences 10; *Patrologia Latina*, ed. J. P. Migne, 49:359–369). The description of Cassian luxuriates in psychological detail, showing that acedia can express itself not simply in laziness but even in nervous activity. Evagrius, Cassian, and in fact the entire Oriental tradition had spoken of melancholy (λυπή) as a distinct sin though closely connected with acedia. St. Gregory the Great in his commentary of Job (*Moralia* 31.45; *Patrologia Latina* 76:620) omitted acedia from his list of principal sins and included only sadness (*tristitia*). Nevertheless, as later commentators have pointed out, in one respect the more ancient tradition—the use of the word acedia, or its corruption *accidia*—prevailed. Moreover six "daughter" sins are for the first time explicitly named in connection with this melancholy: malice, rancor, pusillanimity, despair, torpor concerning commandments, and a wandering of the mind around forbidden things. Finally, St. Gregory, or at least the Gregorian pastoral tradition, is responsible for the removal of acedia from its original context in which it was a special temptation for monks, and for viewing it as an interior malaise that expressed itself most frequently in a tardy and slothful performance of religious and other duties (cf., e.g., Rabanus Maurus, *De ecclesiastica disciplina, Patrologia Latina*, 112:1251–53; Jonas of Orleans, *De institutione laicali, Patrologia Latina*, 102:245–246; Alcuin, *Liber de virtutibus* c.32, *Patrologia Latina*, 101:635; St. Antoninus, *Summa theologiae moralis* 2.10:933–938).

St. Thomas Aquinas opposed acedia to the joy of charity, and in a precise study demonstrated its sinfulness by showing the evil of sadness over a genuinely good object and likewise the excessiveness of even legitimate sorrow when it impedes the performance of duty. The specificity of acedia St. Thomas sees in its opposition to the divine good as man may participate in it, but the intimate connection of the other virtues with charity permits a wide scope for acedia. Nevertheless, acedia's direct attack on charity's act of rejoicing in the divine good makes it serious matter, although imperfect acts of acedia are found even in the holy. Finally, St. Thomas justified acedia's right to be called capital from its ability to produce other sins. The "daughter" sins associated with acedia in the Gregorian tradition, as well as their proliferation in the encyclopedic effort of St. Isidore (*In Deut., Patrologia Latina*, 83:366), are ingeniously explained (ST 2a2ae, 35; *De malo* 11). While the commentators have remained faithful to the Thomistic synthesis, a popular tendency to confuse acedia with its principal external effect, sloth (*pigritia*), developed. Those aware of more profound interior implications attempted the spiritualization of acedia by "baptizing" it spiritual sloth. This terminology, adapted from St. John of the Cross (*Dark Night . . .* 1.7), has the disadvantage of making acedia appear to be an exotic sin reserved for the spiritual elite, whereas the tradition and experience show it to be a very common difficulty.

Bibliography: E. VANSTEENBERGHE, *Dictionnaire de théologie catholique*, ed. A. VACANT et al., (Paris 1903–50) 11.2:2026–30.

G. BARDY, *Dictionnaire de spiritualité ascétique et mystique. Doctrine et histoire*, ed. M. VILLER et al. (Paris 1932–) 1:166–169. For an interesting survey of the development of the idea, A. L. HUXLEY, "Accidie," in *On the Margin* (London 1923). E. WAUGH, "Sloth," in A. WILSON et al., *The Seven Deadly Sins,* ed. I. FLEMING (New York 1962). A series of five articles by I. COLOSIO in *Rivista di ascetica e mystica* 2 (1958) 266–287, 495–511; 3 (1959) 185–201, 528–546; 4 (1960) 22–33, 159–169.

[U. VOLL]

ACHARD (AICHARDUS), BL.

Architect; d. *c.* 1170. From CLAIRVAUX, St. Bernard sent him as architect to several new monasteries. The Romanesque church of HIMMEROD was one of Achard's buildings. Two of his writings as novice master, "On the Seven Deserts" and "On All the Saints," are extant in manuscript (Montfaucon 1299).

Feast: Sept. 15 (Cistercians).

Bibliography: A. M. ZIMMERMANN, *Kalendarium Benedictinum: Die Heiligen und Seligen des Benediktinerordens und seiner Zweige* 4:88. P. FOURNIER, *Dictionnaire d'histoire et de géographie ecclésiastiques* 1:306. A. SCHNEIDER, *Die Cistercienserabtei Himmerod im Spätmittelalter* (Himmerod 1954) 131–132. KONRAD VON EBERBACH, *Exordium magnum Cisterciense*, ed. B. GRIESSER (Rome 1961).

[A. SCHNEIDER]

ACHARD OF SAINT-VICTOR

Theologian, bishop; b. England, early 12th century; d. Avranches, France, 1171 or 1172. A canon regular of Saint-Victor, Paris, he was its abbot in 1155, succeeding the abbey's first abbot, Gilduin. In 1162 he was consecrated bishop of Avranches. His major treatise, *De Trinitate*, was known for a long time only through two citations in the *Eulogium ad Alexandrum III* [N. Häring, ed. *Mediaeval Studies* 13 (1951) 267 by John of Cornwall (*c.* 1125 to *c.* 1199)]. It is preserved in a Padua manuscript [cf. M. T. D'Alverny, *Recherches de théologie ancienne et médiévale* 21 (1954) 299–306]. Jean Chatilloln has maintained Achard's authorship of the treatise on spiritual psychology entitled *De discretione animae, spiritus et mentis*, even though Häring, who edited the work, attributes it to Gilbert de la Porrée [*Mediaeval Studies* 22 (1960) 148–191]. Also extant are 15 of Achard's sermons, now edited by Jean Chatilloon, some of which are really treatises, remarkable for their rich philosophical and theological content, especially Achard's christology and theological anthropology. Two of his letters are published in *Patrologia Latina* 196, 1381–82.

Bibliography: J. CHÂTILLON, "Achard de Saint-Victor et les controverses Christologiques du 12e siècle," *Mélanges F. Cavall-*

era (Toulouse 1948) 317–337; ''Les Régions de la dissemblance selon A. de S-V.,'' *Recherches Augustiniennes* 2 (1962) 237–250; ''A. de S-V. et le *De discretione animae, spiritus et mentis, Archives d'histoire doctrinale et littéraire du moyen-âge* 31 (1965). F. BONNARD, *Histoire de l'Abbaye royale et de l'ordre des chanoines réguliers de Saint-Victor*, 2 v. (Paris 1904–08) 1:120, 144, 203–209. P. DELHAYE, *Lexikon für Theologie und Kirche*, ed. J. HOFER and K. RAHNER (Freiburg 1957–65) 1:107. ACHARD OF SAINT-VICTOR, *Sermons inédits*, ed. J. CHÂTILLON (Paris 1970). *L'unité de Dieu et la pluralité des créatures (De unitate Dei et pluralitate creaturarum)*, ed. and tr. E. MARTINEAU, Saint-Lambert des Bois: Franc-Dire, 1987. J. CHÂTILLON, *Théologie, spiritualité et métaphysique dans l'œuvre oratoire d'Achard de Saint-Victor: études d'historie doctrinale précédées d'un essai sur la vie et l'œuvre d'Achard* (Paris 1969). ''Les régions de la dissemblance et de la ressemblance selon Achard de Saint-Victor,'' *Recherches augustiniennes*, 2 (1962) 237–250.

[J. CHÂTILLON/G. ZINN]

ACHARIUS OF NOYON, ST.

Bishop; d. Nov. 27, *c.* 640. Though no medieval hagiographer has left a life of St. Acharius (Aigahardus), he is mentioned in several Merovingian sources. He was a monk at LUXEUIL under St. EUSTACE OF LUXEUIL, the successor of St. COLUMBAN. In 626–627 he signed the acts of the synod of Clichy as Aigahardus, Bishop of Tournai-Noyon. Most probably he was responsible for the appointment of St. OMER to the See of Thérouanne by King Dagobert I. He encouraged the missionary activities of St. AMANDUS, who in turn asked Acharius to have Dagobert force the rebellious pagans to receive Baptism. St. Acharius's successor at Noyon was St. ELIGIUS OF NOYON.

Feast: Nov. 27.

Bibliography: *Monumenta Germaniae Historica: Scriptores rerum Merovingicarum* 4:123 (Colomban); 4:695 (Eligius); 5:437 (Amand); 5:755 (Omer). J. L. BAUDOT and L. CHAUSSIN, *Vies des saints et des bienheureux selon l'ordre du calendrier avec l'historique des fêtes* 11:923–924.

[B. L. MARTHALER]

ACOLYTE

Historically, an acolyte (i.e., one who follows, a companion) referred to the fourth and highest of the minor orders. The ministry of the acolyte, as well as that of the subdeacon, arose from a division of the ministry of the deacon. The chief duties of the acolyte were to assist the deacon and the priest in liturgical celebrations. As an order instituted by the Church, it was not considered a Sacrament, but a sacramental participating in the order of the deacon. By the *motu proprio Ministeria quaedam*, dated Aug. 15, 1972, Pope Paul VI suppressed the four minor orders and, as replacement, instituted the ministries of acolyte and lector, both of which are open to qualified laity. Pope Paul VI laid out the responsibilities of an acolyte as follows: ''The acolyte is appointed in order to aid the deacon and to minister to the priest'' (see *Ministeria quaedam*, VI). *Ministeria quaedam* lists the responsibilities of acolytes as follows: (1) to assist at the altar, by aiding the priest or deacon, at the Preparation of the Gifts in Mass, (2) to assist deacons and priests in other liturgical celebrations, (3) to aid in the distribution of communion, where necessary, (4) in extraordinary circumstances, to be entrusted with publicly exposing the Blessed Sacrament for adoration and afterward replacing it, ''but not with blessing the people,'' and (5) ''to the extent needed, take care of instructing other faithful who by temporary appointment assist the priest or deacon in liturgical celebrations by carrying the missal, cross, candles, etc., or by performing other such duties'' (ibid.).

Although the minor order of acolyte as a stepping stone to the major orders has been abolished, the 1983 Code of Canon Law requires candidates to the permanent or transitional diaconate to have received the ministries of lector and acolyte (*c.* 1035 §1). Canon 1035 §2 stipulates that there is to be ''an interval of at least six months between the conferral of the ministry of acolyte and the diaconate.''

Altar Servers. The substitution of altar servers for minor clerics dates back more than 1,000 years. In the 9th century at the Synod of Mainz it was decreed that ''Every priest should have a cleric or boy (*scholarem*) to read the epistle or lesson, to answer him at Mass, and with whom he can chant the psalms'' (*Admonitio Synodalis, Patrologia Latina,* ed. J. P. Migne, 217 v., indexes 4 v. (Paris 1878–90) 132:456). For more than 1,000 years, only boys were permitted to be altar servers. The 1983 Code of Canon Law confirms the traditional practice of male altar servers when it permitted qualified lay men to be admitted, among other things, to the ministry of acolyte (*Codex iuris canonici* [Rome 1918; repr. Graz 1955] c. 230 §1). At the same time, c. 230 §2 states, among other things: ''All lay persons can also perform the functions of commentator or cantor, or other functions, according to the norm of law.'' By an instruction dated June 30, 1992, the Congregation for Divine Worship and the Discipline of the Sacraments held that the use of female altar servers was permissible under c. 230 §2. Pope John Paul II confirmed this interpretation on July 11, 1992 [see *AAS* 86 (1994) 541, *Origins* 23 (April 28, 1994) 777–779]. The Congregation reminded bishops that boys should remain servers at the altar, since this is a source of vocations to the priesthood.

Bibliography: Bishops' Committee on the Liturgy, *Study Text III, Ministries in the Church: Commentary on the Apostolic Letters of Pope Paul VI, "Ministeria quaedam" and "Ad pascendum"* (Washington, D.C. 1974). *International Commission on English in the Liturgy, Institution of Readers and Acolytes* (Washington, D.C. 1976). Congregation for Divine Worship and the Discipline of the Sacraments, "Instruction on Female Altar Servers," *Origins* 23 (April 28, 1994) 777–779.

[T. J. RILEY/J. A. GURRIERI/EDS.]

ACOSTA, GABRIEL (URIEL)

Jewish rationalist and religious dissenter; b. Oporto, Portugal, *c.* 1590; d. Amsterdam, Holland, April 1640. He was called originally Gabriel da Costa, and he himself always used the family name of da Costa, but he is more generally known by its Latinized form of Acosta. He was born into a family of MARRANOS, his father having escaped the stake by accepting Catholicism. However, according to Gabriel's autobiography, his family observed the tenets of the Catholic faith punctiliously. Young Gabriel was reared as a noble; he studied law and prepared himself for an ecclesiastical career. Despite this background he began to doubt the truth of Christian dogma, became increasingly disenchanted, and found no solace in the resolute doctrines of the Catholic Church. Circumstances, however, had compelled Acosta to conceal his theological views, for in 1615, after the death of his father, in order to support his family, he accepted a semiecclesiastical office as chief treasurer of an abbey, the collegiate church of Oporto. But his spirit became more restless and his conscience more disquieted. Secretly he began to delve into the faith of his ancestors, and the doctrines of Judaism brought repose to his mind. Gabriel then determined to forsake Catholicism and return to Judaism. Cautiously, he conveyed his intention to his mother and brothers, and they too resolved to expose themselves to the great danger of secret emigration and to the perils of an uncertain future. About 1617 the Acosta family arrived in Amsterdam, where they were admitted into the covenant of Abraham and where the baptismal name Gabriel was exchanged for the name Uriel.

Soon, however, it became apparent that in Judaism as well, Uriel's wayward disposition could find no satisfaction. From his readings of the Old Testament he had constructed an ideal of Judaism that clashed sharply with the realities of Jewish life. Liberal Mosaic and prophetic doctrines, he believed, were being discarded for rigid and prosaic ritual and observance, and the religious life of Judaism seemed to be as clogged with petty detail as the Catholic faith that he had abandoned. He had expected that Judaism would resolve for him the puzzles that the Church could not solve and that the rabbis could offer what he could not obtain from his Catholic confessors. Acosta had sacrificed much for his convictions, and he believed he had earned thereby his right to protest and to propagate his views. In a lengthy pamphlet (*Proposals against Tradition*), which he had written from Hamburg and directed to the Sephardic community of Venice, he challenged and denounced the "offensive" traditional laws and customs, and with arrogant expressions he decried their rabbinic guardians and cavilled at their authority. His revolutionary ideas had aroused a vigorous opposition, and upon his refusal to recant he was promptly placed under the ban at Hamburg and publicly excommunicated at Venice (Aug. 14, 1618).

In the interim he had returned to Amsterdam, where he was held in great contempt and isolated from all human intercourse. This forced severance only served to increase his passion for speculation, and he resolved to publish a work in which he would deny the doctrine of immortality and indicate the "glaring contrasts" between the Bible and rabbinical Judaism. But Acosta's intention was anticipated by his former friend, the physician Samuel da Silva, who in 1623 had published a book in Portuguese entitled *A Treatise on the Immortality of the Soul in order to Confute the Ignorance of a Certain Opponent, Who in Delusion Affirms Many Errors.* Believing that the opposition had commissioned Da Silva, he hastened to publish his retort (1624), also in Portuguese, *An Examination of the Pharisaic Traditions Compared with the Written Laws, and a Reply to the Slanderer Samuel da Silva.* He now denied not only the belief in immortality but also the doctrines of the resurrection and of reward and punishment. By denying such concepts he had challenged Christian dogma as well. He was again denounced, arrested, imprisoned for several days, and fined 300 florins, and his work was condemned to the flames. For 15 years (1618–33) Acosta lived as an outcast; unable to bear it any longer, he agreed to recant and to be, as he phrased it, "an ape among apes."

He had submitted not from conviction but from despair, and consequently he became embittered to the point of disbelief in the divine origin of the Bible itself. Word had now gotten out that he dissuaded three Christians from their intention of embracing Judaism, and he was once more placed under the ban. After seven years of total ostracism he succumbed. His tortured spirit now longed for tranquility, and the price required of him this time was severe and cruel. Before huge audiences he was ordered to recite his public penance, was given 39 lashes, and then trampled upon as he lay prostrate upon the threshold of the synagogue. His proud and indomitable spirit had now been broken; with shame and humiliation he arrived home, poured out his feelings in a short autobiographical sketch entitled *Exemplar Humanae Vitae (A Specimen of Human Life)*, and then shot himself. A refutation of the *Exemplar* was made by Philip Limborch, a Dutch theologian, as an appendix to his *Amica collatio cum erudito Judaeo* (Gouda 1687; repr. 1847).

Bibliography: S. BERNSTEIN, *Universal Jewish Encyclopedia* 1:72–74. F. DE SOLA MONDES, *The Jewish Encyclopedia* 1:167–68. C. GEBHARDT, *Encyclopaedia Judaica: Das Judentum in Geschichte und Gegenwart* 5:678–80. J. CANTERA, *Lexikon für Theologie und Kirche* 1:113. I. SONNE, ''Da Costa Studies,'' *Jewish Quarterly Review* 22 (1932) 247–93. H. H. GRAETZ, *History of the Jews*, ed. and tr. B. LÖWY, 6 v. (Philadelphia 1945) 5:56–65. J. WHISTON, *The Remarkable Life of Uriel Acosta* (London 1740).

[N. J. COHEN]

ACOSTA, JOSÉ DE

Philosopher and theologian; b. Medina del Campo, Spain, September or October 1540; d. Salamanca, Feb. 15, 1600. He took vows in the Society of Jesus Sept. 24, 1570. In 1572 he went to Peru, where he was provincial and rector of the Colegio of Lima. He served as theologian of the Third Provincial Council of Lima (1582–83), and participated in the composition and publishing of the books ordered by the council. In 1586 he went to Mexico, where he remained until his return to Spain in May 1587. He was visitor of the provinces of Aragon and Andalusia, and, in 1592, provost of the Casa Profesa of Valladolid. In connection with the convocation of the Fifth Congregation of the Society of Jesus he was in Rome until 1594, engaged in negotiations that caused him difficulties with Father General Claudio Aquaviva. He spent the rest of his life in Spain. In 1597 he was named rector of the Colegio of Salamanca.

Acosta's writings are many and varied, but the following works brought him fame: *De natura novi orbis, De procuranda indorum salute* (both published Salamanca 1588), and the *Historia natural y moral de las Indias* (1590; new ed. Mexico City 1962). He translated *De natura* into Spanish and included it with the *Historia* as books 1 and 2, so that those two works came to form a single whole.

In the *De procuranda* Acosta examined the problems of evangelization in America in his day. He discussed the doubts as to the capacity of the Native Americans (book 1), the legality of the employment of force (book 2), the rights and obligations of the civil authority and of the colonists (book 3), the special requisites for being a missionary in America (book 4), the parochial functions of the missions (book 5), and the casuistic difficulty in the administration of the Sacraments to the Native Americans (book 6). This work was the first systematic and complete presentation of the missionary problems provoked by the appearance of a new and unforseeable pagan world in the midst of the inhabited world. It is noteworthy, also, for the practical and balanced solutions proposed by its author, in contrast to the unfair exaggerations of impassioned men such as Fray Bartolomé de LAS CASAS and Ginés de Sepulveda. The *Historia* (including the *De natura*) reflects Acosta's scientific concerns, which were never divorced from his missionary interests. A new entity, America, had appeared within the heart of Christendom, and it was necessary to show that, despite its novelty, it did not mean any derogation of the order God had assigned to nature and the course of history. This was the great task Acosta performed in his *Historia*. The highly varied subjects are grouped in accordance with the scientific view of reality then current, and thus the author placed the American world within the system of the universe (book 1), the sphere of the world (book 2), the concept of matter (book 3), the hierarchy of living beings (book 4), the idea of man as a spiritual being (book 5) and man as a rational being (book 6), and, finally, within the providential system of history (book 7).

Acosta's two great works represent the ideological culmination of the initial period (16th century) of the religious conquest and the philosophical and scientific conquest of the New World, of the great historical and ontological process of its incorporation into Western culture. For this reason, both works occupy unique positions in early American bibliography and have a historical value that is both irreplaceable and permanent.

[E. O'GORMAN]

ACQUAVIVA

Prominent Neapolitan family, which gave several leading members to the Church.

Giulio, cardinal, of the family of the Duke of Atri; b. Naples, 1546; d. Rome, July 21, 1574. In 1568 he was sent to Spain to settle a controversy between (St.) Charles Borromeo and the governor of Milan, and to offer the pope's condolences to Philip II, recently bereft of his third wife and his son Don Carlos. On May 9, 1570, he was created cardinal deacon of St. Callistus, and later of St. Theodorus, by Pius V, who held him in great esteem and asked for his spiritual assistance at his deathbed.

Ottavio (the elder), cardinal; b. Naples, 1560; d. there, 1612. He was summoned to Rome by Sixtus V, and held various offices under him and his successors. On March 16, 1591, Gregory XIII created him a cardinal and sent him as vice-legate to Campania. Two years later, Clement VIII sent him to Avignon as his representative, a difficult mission because at that time relations were tense between the Church and the neighboring Protestant subjects of Henry IV. The conversion and coronation of this monarch took place while Ottavio was in Avignon. As a tactful and efficient administrator, he reorganized the administration of justice, implementing reforms that lasted until the end of the papal administration. On his return to Rome in March 1597, he was given impressive popular acclaim. Leo XI appointed Ottavio archbishop of Naples in 1605, in which office he distinguished himself by his ability and charity. He sought to alleviate the consequences of the famine of 1607, built two monasteries for the Minorites, and left a few manuscripts, one a commentary on the *Summa.*

Ottavio (the younger), cardinal; b. Naples, 1608; d. Rome, 1674. As governor of Jesi (1638), Orvieto (1642), and Ancona (1643), he organized the defense of these cities against Parma and the French. Innocent VI summoned him to Rome, where he held various posts. In March 1664 he became cardinal with the title of St. Bartholomew-of-the-Island, and later of St. Cecilia (1668). As a papal legate in Bologna, he led a campaign against outlaws; in 1655 he was host to Christine of Sweden.

Trojano, cardinal; b. Naples, Jan. 24, 1695; d. Rome, March 24, 1747. A vice-legate to Bologna under Clement XI, Trojano was appointed governor of Ancona by Innocent XIII, and master of the Sacred Palace by Benedict XIII. Titular archbishop of Larissa, he was created cardinal of St. Cecilia by Clement XII in 1732. At the request of Philip V he became archbishop of Toledo; in 1739, of Monreale. He was on friendly terms with Charles III, and represented Spain and Naples in the Roman Curia. He favored the reforms of B. Tanucci and negotiated the concordat of 1741, which abolished certain privileges of the clergy, among them, exemption from taxation. He played a major role in the conclave of 1740, which elected Benedict XV. The 1744 edition of Giambattista Vico's *Scienze Nuova* was dedicated to him.

Bibliography: P. RICHARD, *Dictionnaire d'histoire et de géographie ecclésiastiques,* ed. A. BAUDRILLART et al. (Paris 1912–) 1:359–363. L. CARDELLA, *Memorie storiche dei cardinali,* 9 v. (Rome 1792–97). L. PASTOR, *The History of the Popes From the Close of the Middle Ages* (London-St. Louis 1938–61): from 1st German ed. *Geschichte der Päpste seit dem Ausgang des Mittelalters* (Freiburg 1885–1933; repr. 1955–) v.17, 18.

[E. J. THOMSON]

ACQUAVIVA, CLAUDIUS

Fifth general of the Jesuits; b. Atri, Sept. 14, 1543; d. Rome, Jan. 31, 1615. He was the youngest son of the Duke of Atri, Giovanni Antonio Donato A. d'Aragona.

Octavo Cardinal Acquaviva, ca. 1612.

He studied jurisprudence in Perugia, entered papal service and was appointed a chamberlain by Pius IV.

On July 22, 1567, he entered the Society of Jesus after learning about it from Francis Borgia and Juan de Polanco. In 1574 he was ordained, and became a professor of philosophy at the Roman College. The next year he was named rector of the Collegium Maximum in Naples. In 1576 he was provincial of the Neapolitan province and three years later, of the Roman province. On Feb. 19, 1581, with 32 of the 57 votes, Acquaviva was elected general of the society; he had the longest term of office to 1964.

His administration was marked by a very sharp increase of the society in Europe and in the missions. The number of members grew from approximately 5,000 to more than 13,000, and colleges, from 144 to 372. To the tasks posed by this expansion, Acquaviva brought a disciplined handling of his office, judged by many to have been too authoritative. He molded the society as no other general had since its founder, Ignatius of Loyola. His chief concern was the maintenance and promotion of religious spirit during this period of rapid growth. In the resultant regimentation that seemed necessary, the individual initiative envisioned by Ignatius was perforce retarded. During Acquaviva's long term, the standardization that had actually begun earlier was conclusively established, e.g., a binding regulation for the daily hour of mental prayer, annual repetition of the Exercises, and a one-year tertianship. Significant is his letter *Quis sit orationis et paenitentiae usus* of 1590, in which Acquaviva, as did his predecessor Everard Mercurian, takes an open-minded attitude on the question of extent and type of mental prayer and external penitential exercises. Differences of opinion on this point led to a clash with the German assistant and admonitor, Peter Hoffaeus, who subsequently was relieved of his office.

In 1599 the final *Directorium* for making and conducting the Spiritual Exercises appeared, which, although in use for centuries, is today not considered to correspond completely with the intentions of St. Ignatius. Acquaviva also provided the definitive text of the Ratio Studiorum, which regulated Jesuit learning and higher studies until the society's suppression on Aug. 16, 1773. He issued as well the *Industriae . . . ad curandos animae morbos*, directed to superiors and reflecting wide experience and genuine piety. Among the many difficulties that tested his brilliant talent for diplomacy and administration were: the movement among Spanish Jesuits toward a national independence which was supported by Phillip II and had an influential advocate in Francesco Toletus, who was elevated to the cardinalate in 1593; the intention of Sixtus V to amend the constitution of the society on very significant points; and the plan of Clement VIII to name Acquaviva archbishop of Naples in order to remove him from control of the society. There were also the controversies on theological questions, such as the doctrine stated by St. Robert Bellarmine on the *potestas indirecta* of the pope; the debates on grace caused by Luis MOLINA's *Concordia liberi arbitrii cum gratiae donis* that led to the *CONGREGATIO DE AUXILIIS*; and the doctrine of Juan de Mariana on the murder of tyrannical leaders. Through these difficulties Acquaviva was able to consolidate the society into its ultimate stability with circumspection and tenacity.

Bibliography: C. SOMMERVOGEL et al., *Bibliothèque de la Compagnie de Jésus* (Brussels-Paris 1890–1931) 1:480–491; 8:1669–70; 12:46–48, 318–319, 910–911. B. SCHNEIDER, *Archivum historicum Societatis Jesu* 26 (1957) 3–56; 27 (1958) 279–306. J. DE GUIBERT, *La Spiritualité de la Compagnie de Jésus*, ed. E. LAMALLE (Rome 1953).

[B. SCHNEIDER]

ACROSTIC

Acrostic is an anglicized Greek word signifying a composition, usually in verse, in which initial (or occasionally middle and final) letters are arranged in such an order as to form words. When middle and final letters are so employed, there is question rather of mesostichs and telestichs respectively. The word type, as well as the alphabetical form of acrostic, is Oriental in origin. The earliest Greek example dates from the beginning of the 2nd century B.C. The word form of acrostic was a characteristic feature of the pagan Sibylline Oracles (*see* Cicero, *Div.* 2.54.171–) and other oracular or magicoreligious texts. Hence, it was only natural that the Christian Sibylline books should make use of the same device. In book 8, 217–250 (written near the end of the 2nd century A.D.), one finds the well-known acrostic: Ἰησοῦς Χριστὸς Θεοῦ Ὑιὸς Σωτὴρ σταυρός (Jesus Christ, Son of God, Savior, Cross), which—with the omission of σταυρός—furnishes also the widespread acrostic ΙΧΘΥΣ (in Greek, fish, a basic early Christian symbol). The passage from the Sibyllines is presented in Latin translation by St. Augustine (*Civ.* 18.23) in such a way that the initial letters of each Latin verse reproduce the Greek verse cited—but without the word σταυρός—in Latin transliteration. In the Pectorius inscription found near Autun, the initial Greek letters of the first five verses furnish the acrostic ΙΧΘΥΣ also. In keeping with the Oriental background, frequent use of acrostics is noted likewise in Christian Syriac poetry, especially in the hymns of St. Ephrem. Optatianus Porphyrius (first half of 4th century A.D.), Ausonius, and Commodian employed elaborate acrostics, and acrostics became common as a device for indicating the name of the deceased in Christian funeral epigrams, especially the name of a martyr.

The alphabetic acrostic, familiar from the Lamentations of Jeremia and from a number of Psalms, is the obvious source for Christian Greek and Latin acrostics of this kind. St. Hilary of Poitiers has two abecedarian hymns, and St. Augustine made use of this form as a memory aid in his famous *Psalmus abecedarius contra partem Donati.* The abecedarian hymn (*A solis ortus cardine*) of Sedulius has become a part of the Christmas liturgy. In the tradition of Optatianus Porphyrius, acrostics were developed to a fantastic degree in the *carmina figurata* of Rabanus Maurus in the Carolingian age. Acrostics of the earlier and simple form continued to flourish throughout the Middle Ages and have had a sporadic life down to the present time (*see* PECTORIUS, EPITAPH OF).

Bibliography: A. KURFESS and T. KLAUSER, *Reallexikon für Antike und Christentum,* ed. T. KLAUSER [Stuttgart 1941 (1950)–] 1:235–238, an excellent treatment with bibliog. H. LECLERCQ, *Dictionnaire d'archéologie chrétienne et de liturgie,* ed. F. CABROL, H. LECLERCQ, and H. I. MARROU, 15 v. (Paris 1907–53) 1.1:356–372, with full texts and plates. F. DORNSEIFF, *Das Alphabet in Mystik und Magie* (2d ed. Leipzig 1925) 146–151. M. MANITIUS, *Geschichte* *der lateinischen Literatur des Mittelalters,* 3 v. (Munich 1911–31), Indexes s.v. ''Akrosticha.''

[M. R. P. MCGUIRE]

ACT

Considered analogically and in its own right, act denotes perfection just as POTENCY denotes imperfection. Hence, potency plays a determining, limiting role in relation to act. Thus we say that God is PURE ACT, because He is not limited by any potency, while the created being is a mixture of potency and act. Since act in itself is said to denote perfection, it is not limited except by a principle distinct from itself, namely, potency; wherefore the axiom: *actus non limitatur a seipso.* Both potency and act should be considered as principles of being, not as beings themselves. It is also important not to confuse potency and act as principles in the structure of being with two successive stages in the development of a being, as when one speaks of being first in potency (*in potentia*) and then in act (*in actu*).

Kinds of Act. To make use of the following classification one must be aware of the ontological scope of its application. The notions of potency and act are basically analogical. Hence, what might perfectly fulfill the notion of act from one point of view might be considered as potency from another point of view, at the same time. Thus the form of a being is act in relation to the matter that it actuates, while the essence of that which is composed of matter and form, in its turn, is potency in regard to the *esse* that actuates it.

Act That Is Neither Received nor Receptive. This is pure act, subsistence act, which is neither received into a limiting potency nor susceptible of receiving an act superior to it.

Act That Is Received but Is Not Receptive. This is substantial existence or *esse,* limited by essence, that in turn, plays the role of limiting potency in its regard. *Esse,* as such, is not in its own turn susceptible of receiving an act in the substantial order that would be superior to it. What is composed of essence and *esse,* however, is said to be ordered to activity as to an accidental act that perfects an individual substance. Operation is also an act in this category, for it perfects the faculty and through it the individual in which it is received and from which it emanates. But it too, in itself and in its own right, is not ordered to a superior act.

Act That Is Receptive but Not Received. The separated form belongs to this classification. It is not received into quantitatively signed matter (*signata quantitate*), which would otherwise make it some type of individual

being, but it does receive an act to which it is ordained and which is its proper substantial *esse.* An act that is not received, inasmuch as it is pure form, is called ''infinite'' because it is not limited by matter. Yet it is ''finite'' in the order of existence since it is not *esse subsistens,* but has a finite mode of existing. This category of act has the role of being a limited potency to *esse.*

Act That Is Received and Receptive. This is the category of all forms received into a limiting principle, that in their turn, are ordained to a further act that perfects them. Such, for example, is the form of a composite being received in the limiting matter that it actuates, but that, together with this matter, is ordained to the act of the composite, namely, the substantial *esse.* The same applies to any accidental form that is act in relation to its subject but is also potency in relation to a superior act that perfects it. An example would be a faculty that perfects an individual but is ordained to operation as to a superior act that in turn perfects the individual.

Pure and Mixed Act. What has been said thus far leads to the distinction between pure act and mixed act (*purus* and *non purus*). In itself the first is not received and limited, whereas the second is. Again one must specify the given context in stating whether an act is pure or not. In relation to *esse,* God alone is Pure Act. In the order of essence, separated forms, that is, beings that are not composed, can be called pure and infinite inasmuch as they are not limited by potency.

First and Second Act. First act is often opposed to second act (*actus primus* and *actus secundus*). This usage designates either form or essence in relation to the *esse* that perfects them, or the individual in relation to the operation that perfects it. That which perfects as an ultimate actualization is called second act.

One can sum up the different kinds of act as follows: (1) MOTION, act of the changeable, (2) substantial or accidental FORM (faculty, HABIT), (3) *esse* (EXISTENCE) and (4) operation. Each in its own way is act and as such conveys the notion of perfection. Substantial *esse* and operation are alone, strictly speaking, terminal acts and are not further receptive in their own proper order.

Historical Development. The notion of potency as opposed to act, and as uniquely definable by it, was introduced into philosophy by ARISTOTLE. He first used these notions in the *Physics* to explain change, which he defined as ''the act of that which is in potency, precisely as such'' (201a, 10). In the *Metaphysics* he introduced act and potency as general divisions of being (1045b 34). Here also he arrived at the notion of pure act (1071b, 20).

Scholastic Thought. St. THOMAS AQUINAS applied the notions of potency and act in a context to which Aristotle could not have given thought, that of the real distinction between essence and existence. Here the notions attain a level of ontological profundity never before known (*see* ESSENCE AND EXISTENCE). Potency and act are also basic to the Thomistic thesis on PARTICIPATION and to the notion of BEING proper to St. Thomas (see below).

With John DUNS SCOTUS one finds an early attempt to introduce an entity, unknown to Aristotle and St. Thomas, intermediate between potency and act, that is, virtual act (*actus virtualis*). Virtual act is that which without the agency of any extrinsic causality, reduces a being from potency to act. Thus it is the complete power to pass into act by itself; all being that possess it are self-moved. Wherefore, Scotus reasons, the inefficacy of Aristotle's attempt to prove that whatever is moved is moved by another; for Scotus, the fact that motion involves passage from potency to act is no proof of that. For arguments against the virtual act of Scotus, see Sylvester of Ferrara, *Comm. in 1 C. gent.,* Leon. ed., c. 13, p. 35, nn. 6–7. Francisco SUÁREZ rejects the distinction between essence and existence as part of his refusal to use the principle of the limitation of act by potency to prove the real distinction. Suárez admits neither this distinction nor the Thomistic concept of being upon which it is based. Instead he attempts to base the fundamental distinction between God as infinite and creature as finite on the notions of *ens a se* and *ens ab alio*. But he does not perceive the ties that unite the thesis of the distinction between *ens a se* and *ens ab alio* with the distinction in the Thomistic tradition between pure act and created being that is necessarily composed of potency (essence) and act (existence). Finally, Suárez subscribes to the notion of *virtual act,* with the consequences inherent in it (confer *Disp. Meta.,* disp. 29, sect. 1, n. 7, ed. Vives, 26:23).

Leibniz and Descartes. Gottfried LEIBNIZ is situated, consciously or not, in the line of Scotus and Suárez inasmuch as he employs the notion of "active force" and replaces the notion of potency with that of "impeded act." For Leibniz, forces are always active. If they appear to be at rest, it is because their activity is impeded.

René DESCARTES' elimination of the notions of potency and act is part of his deliberate rejection of all ontology. He combines both scientific reasons (for example, the principle of inertia) and philosophical arguments to condemn the principle that whatever is moved is moved by another. His reasoning rests generally on his opposition to the notions of potency and act. In all this there is a conscious rejection, a reflective break with the world of the ancients and the Middle Ages, in which the notions of being, act and potency occupy a central place. The consequences of this break were destined to become immeasurable.

Modern and Contemporary Period. Little by little, the notion of act came to be employed in one of its many senses. The moderns designate activity by it, and more particularly, the free intellectual activity of self-proper to man. The metaphysics of act now becomes subjectivistic, and this phenomenon is realized most characteristically in such philosophies as those of HEGEL or GENTILE. The latter attacks Aristotle, gratuitously at that, for regarding act as static, as an object, whereas it is grasped interiorly by consciousness. Louis LAVELLE shows a different emphasis; while maintaining the interiorization of act, he views act in relation to being, potency and choice, and thus avoids the strictly idealistic viewpoint of Gentile.

Recent Thomism. Since the appearance of *Aeterni Patris,* there has been a revival of the classic doctrine of potency and act. At the same time, discussions relative to its interpretation, its role in the Thomistic synthesis, its value in itself and its applications have been encouraged. The same can be said for the principle *actus non limitatur a seipso* and the conclusions that can be drawn from it.

Outside of SCHOLASTICISM, the analogical notions of potency and act have on the whole lost their significance. One cannot, without great equivocation, connect scholastic usage with what contemporary thinkers make of these notions. Regrettable though this may be, it is a fact that must be faced.

Act and Being. The first of all notions is that of being, not of act. Potency and act divide being as such. Also, being is defined as that which is either in potency or in act, and not as that which exists; whence, the definition: *ens est id quod habet relationem ad esse sive actualitatis sive possibilitatis.* With St. Thomas the notion of being is profoundly "existentialized" by the fact that for him *esse* is the act of acts, the most profound, intimate and formal element in being. Unless one reverts to "essentialism," being is inconceivable without this reference to *esse.* Thus the whole metaphysics of St. Thomas is founded upon the notion of being understood with explicit relation to *esse* as act. This notion is what enables him to argue to the real distinction of essence and existence in FINITE being.

Act and Participation. The problem of the one and the many is at the heart of metaphysics. As St. Thomas saw it, PARTICIPATION is in turn basic to the solution of the problem of the one and the many. Numerically multiplied and limited beings are possible because they are beings by participation. They are not instances of *esse per se subsistens,* which is necessarily unique (God), but of *esse* received into limiting potencies, that is, into essences. The notions of potency and act, Aristotelian in origin, enabled St. Thomas to systematize the doctrine of participation, of Platonic origin, into a conceptualization that is precise and free from equivocation. St. Thomas's stroke of genius consists in having united these two perspectives into a new and irreducible synthesis that profoundly transformed the elements it assimilated, thanks in no small part to his distinctive notion of *esse* as act.

This notion also gives an essential profundity to his metaphysics of CAUSALITY. For St. Thomas, the efficient cause touches the *esse rerum,* allowing him to conceive of God as cause of this *esse,* and even its proper cause. Creatures merely confer *esse* as secondary causes under God's premotion (*see* PREMOTION, PHYSICAL). Thus God is not merely a final cause, moving by desire (as was taught by Aristotle), nor merely the first formal and exemplary cause (as for the Platonists). It is in these perspectives that one must locate the *secunda via* of St. Thomas.

Act and Change. Historically in Aristotle and psychologically in human consciousness, act and potency are linked with the perception of movement and with one's own activity. This includes continuous movement, substantial change and the personal operation that precedes any discovery. To be grasped intelligibly and without contradiction, change presupposes: (1) a point of departure—potency, (2) a point of arrival—act, and (3) the imperfect act (*actus imperfectus*) between these—essentially act in relation to the prior potency, that of the point of departure and at the same time potency in relation to the perfect act (*actus perfectus*) at the terminal point of the movement. Wherefore, the classical definition of MOTION as "the act of a being in potency precisely as such."

See Also: POTENCY AND ACT; POTENCY; ACTION AND PASSION; ENTELECHY; EXISTENCE; FORM; PURE ACT; HUMAN ACT; MOTION; PARTICIPATION.

Bibliography: C. A. HART, *Thomistic Metaphysics: An Inquiry into the Act of Existing* (Englewood Cliffs, N.J. 1959). H. REITH, *The Metaphysics of St. Thomas Aquinas* (Milwaukee 1958). F. VAN STEENBERGHEN, *Ontology,* tr. M. FLYNN (New York 1952). A. FOSSATI, *Enciclopedia filosofica,* 4 v. (Venice-Rome 1957) 1:464–475. A. SMEETS, *Actus en potentie in de Metaphysica van Aristoteles* (Conférences d'Histoire et de Philologie ser. 3.49, Louvain 1952). G. MANSER, *Das Wesen des Thomismus* (Thomistische Studien 5; 3d ed. Fribourg 1949). C. GIACON, *Atto e potenza* (Brescia 1947). W. N. CLARKE, "The Limitation of Act by Potency," *The New Scholasticism,* 26 (1952) 167–194. J. D. ROBERT, "Le Principe: Actus non limitatur nisi per potentiam subjectivam realiter distinctam," *Revue philosophique de Louvain,* 47 (1949) 44–70. G. GENTILE, *Genesis and Structure of Society,* tr. H. S. HARRIS (Urbana 1960). L. LAVELLE, *La Dialectique de l'éternel présent: de l'acte* (Paris 1946).

[J. D. ROBERT]

ACT, FIRST

As used in theology indicates the universal principle of all actuality, namely, God. Whatever is finite actuality is so because it participates in the infinite actuality of the first act (St. Thomas, *Summa theologiae 1a,* 75.5 ad 1). Creatures can no more act without a positive divine influence than they can begin or continue in existence independently of it. God as the first act is the cause of created action, not only by giving the created agent its form, which is the principle of action, but by conserving that form and its powers, and by concurring in the operations that flow from those powers. Since every reduction of power to operation, whether in the material or spiritual order, is a transition from POTENCY to ACT, effected by something in act, God must be the first act (ST 1a, 2.3).

While God is first act, the acts of creatures as secondary agents, nevertheless, are real, efficacious, and according to their proper forms and powers (ST 1a, 105.5). Since the cause of an action, however, is more the one whose power effects it than the one who acts, God as first act is more the cause of created action than its secondary agents. How God moves the created free will freely, yet efficaciously, so that it acts freely under divine influence, is a problem about which theologians have speculated through the centuries.

See Also: CAUSALITY; CAUSE, FIRST; FREE WILL AND GRACE; PURE ACT

Bibliography: A. GARDEIL, *Dictionnaire de théologie catholique,* ed. A. VACANT et al., 15 v. (Paris 1903–50; Tables générales 1951–) 1.1:337–339, Tables générales 1:557–560. J. MÖLLER, *Lexikon für Theologie und Kirche,* ed. J. HOFER and K. RAHNER, 10 v. (2d, new ed. Freiburg 1957–65). T. T. PAINE, H. F. DAVIS et al., *A Catholic Dictionary of Theology* (London 1962–) 1:23–25.

[M. R. E. MASTERMAN]

ACT OF SETTLEMENT, IRISH

Decisive legislative measure of 1662; it began the reduction of land owned by Irish Catholics from 61 percent in 1641 to 22 percent in 1688 and 15 percent in 1703. Consequently, the Protestant ascendancy dominated Ireland until, after Catholic Emancipation (1829), Daniel O'CONNELL compelled the English government to give equality to Catholics. Socially and economically, the landed system of Ireland remained stereotyped except for the brief Catholic ascendancy under James II, for 200 years, from Oliver CROMWELL until after the famine of the 1840s.

Provisions of the Act. The act, which was passed on July 31, 1662, virtually confirmed the Cromwellian settlement in favor of the adventurers who invested money in the parliamentarian war in Ireland and the soldiers who fought against the Catholics and Royalists. Charles II was restored on terms that maintained political power in the hands of the English conquerors in the Irish Civil War (1641–53), except for the regicides. Some initial endeavor was made to be favorable to those Catholics who had supported the king in arms, notably in the king's declaration of Nov. 30, 1660, but in Ireland pressure from the ex-Cromwellians was so great that is diminished the chances of Catholic Restoration in succeeding months. Finally, even those who were made secure by the Act of Settlement were denied justice. The government became alarmed at the Puritan Castle Plot of May 1663 that nearly succeeded in capturing James, Duke of Ormond, the Lord Lieutenant; as a result, before the end of 1665 the Act of Explanation was passed, restricting to some 50 the restoration of Catholics under the preceding act, but also compelling the new Protestant interest to surrender one-third. The Declaration of November 1660 had promised to restore royalist Irish who were "innocent" of rebellion against Charles I, but it also had confirmed to the adventurers all lands possessed by them on May 7, 1659, with provision for deficiencies claimed before the following May. In regard to the soldiers, the lands already assigned to them to compound for wages due, even if only in valuation at 13 in every pound sterling (20), were confirmed, except where it could be established before the following December twelvemonth, that there had been bribery or false admeasurements in allotting their land.

Exceptions involved those regicides and others exempted from pardon by the English Act of Oblivion (1660), the Protestant Church of IRELAND lands, the estates of those opposing the Restoration, and the estates restored to "innocent" owners by decree of the king's courts, although previously set out to adventurers and soldiers. Satisfaction would be given to adventurers and soldiers holding lands when it could be proved that these properly belonged to legal encumbrancers from before Oct. 22, 1641 (the day before the outbreak of the Irish Catholic Rebellion). Provision was to be made, where this had not already been done, for those officers who had served Charles II or his father before June 5, 1649, at a rate comparable to the provision for parliamentarian soldiers, but they were to be satisfied with sixpence less on the pound. Protestants were to be restored to their estates where these had been taken from them under the Cromwellian Settlement, and a reprisal of equal value was to be assigned to the adventurers and soldiers who would have to be removed for this purpose. There was to be no benefit for those persons who entered the rebellion before Sept. 15, 1643 (the date of the cessation of hostilities between the Catholic Confederates of Kilkenny and King

Charles I, leading to their payment of subsidies and lending of troops to him). Nor was there to be any benefit for those who had taken out decrees in land in Connaught or Clare (under the Cromwellian provision transporting innocent Catholics from their lands east of the Shannon so as to leave the three other provinces for the adventurers and soldiers).

Special provisions in favor of the Earl of Ormond and his wife and the Earl of Inchiquin safeguarded such actions as they had taken in mortgaging their lands. "Innocent papists" who had never acted against the king since Oct. 22, 1641, were to be restored by May 2, 1661 (subsequently extended by a further Act for one year), provided they restored to the king those transplantees' lands to which they had been removed compulsorily in Connaught and Clare. This provision marked them off from those who had voluntarily taken out decrees for Connaught and Clare land, as these were held bound by their own decision. Again "innocent popish inhabitants" of towns, especially of Cork, Youghal, and Kinsale, were not to be restored specifically to their own property, but instead were to be allotted undisposed lands near these towns. Lands set out to persons for money lent for the army in the beginning of the rebellion were to remain disposable for the most deserving.

Lands allotted by the Cromwellians to certain persons, notably George Monck, Duke of Albemarle; Roger Boyle, Earl of Orrery; and the orphans of Owen O'Connolly, who had revealed the 1641 rising plans, were confirmed. The Declaration provided for a sequence of priorities in accommodating these various interests. Those who had adhered to the articles of peace deserved consideration, but not those who rejected or abandoned them or those who took Connaught certificates, unlike those who served the king's ensigns abroad, some of whom were specifically named for restoration. Many others were also named ("nominees"), but not for immediate restoration.

Enactment. The Declaration of 1660 had provided for action in this order. First, the English who were to be dispossessed were to be settled; then precedence was to be observed in restitution as follows: (1) innocent Protestants and papists without decrees in Connaught and Clare; (2) those with such decrees being innocents; (3) transplanted persons dispossessed hereby of lands decreed in Connaught and Clare; and (4) Irish papists who served the king's ensigns abroad. After these reprisals, the debts for the army before 1649 were to be satisfied. Rents were reserved on lands of every adventurer, soldier, and person settled, restored, or reprised. The Declaration was followed by a commission for its execution on April 30, 1661. Meanwhile, the Catholic position had been worsened by the production at court of the Catholic Confederates' negotiations with Urban VIII in the 1640s, making him their final court of appeal in their disputes with the king. In consequence, the instruction for the execution of the commission discriminated specifically against those who had supported the papal nuncio Giovanni Battista RINUCCINI or who, having opposed him, subsequently sought absolution from excommunication. The act itself, incorporating the Declaration and the commission, was passed only under threat that the government would not pardon activities during the interregnum. Subsequently, the court of claims to determine those who were innocent operated for nine months before the termination of such restorations by the Act of Explanation. An abortive attempt to reopen the question in 1672 by individual royal grants led to parliamentary pressure in England to banish the Catholic clergy. In 1864 a Commission of Grace restored a few others, and the abortive Irish Parliament of James II attempted to repeal the Restoration acts. The Act of Settlement remained a standing grievance with the Catholic aristocracy.

Bibliography: *Statutes at Large, Passed in the Parliaments Held in Ireland,* 20 v. (2d. ed., Dublin 1786–1801). W. S. MASON, *Collation of the Irish Statutes* (Trinity College, Dublin, MSS Add. w.8). *Calendar of the State Papers Relating to Ireland . . . 625–1670,* 8 v. (London 1900–10). Irish Manuscripts Commission, *The Civil Survey . . . 1654–1656,* 10 v. (Dublin 1931–61). J. G. SIMMS, *Williamite Confiscation in Ireland, 1690–1703* (London 1956). W. F. T. BUTLER, *Confiscation in Irish History* (Dublin-London 1917).

[R. D. EDWARDS]

ACTA APOSTOLICAE SEDIS

The official journal of the Holy See, established in accord with the constitution *Promulgandi* of St. Pius X, Sept. 29, 1908. Its first issue appeared Jan. 1, 1909, replacing the *Acta sanctae sedis* which since 1865 had been presenting, on an unofficial basis (until 1904 when it became "official"), the various documents of the Holy See; subsequent issues have generally been issued monthly. The *Acta* is the exclusive and prescribed means for promulgating the laws of the Holy See, unless otherwise provided. Prior to its establishment in 1908, promulgation was often effected by posting documents at the entrance of the papal residence. According to canon 8, §1 of the 1983 *Code of Canon Law*, laws come into force only on the expiry of three months from the date appearing on the particular issue of the *Acta*, unless because of the nature of the case they bind at once (for instance, if the law involves a substantial matter of faith or declares the divine law), or if a shorter or a longer interval has been specifically and expressly prescribed in the law itself (as was the case with the *Code of Canon Law*, which went into effect on Nov. 27, 1983, some ten months after promulgation). Not all laws of the Church are published in the *Acta* (for instance, many liturgical documents are issued elsewhere), nor is every published document a law requiring promulgation (for instance, various allocutions of the pope). Although the official language is Latin, more and more of the documents are published in the language in which they were first given. In general, its contents consist of documents and addresses of the Holy Father; decrees and decisions of the various departments of the Roman Curia, a diary of the Curia, a list of officials appointed or honored by the Holy See, and a necrology of bishops.

Bibliography: R. P. MCBRIEN, ed., *Encyclopedia of Catholicism* (San Francisco 1995). E. MAGNIN, "Acta Sanctae Sedis, Acta Apostolicae Sedis," R. NAZ, ed., *Dictionnaire de Droit canonique* (Paris 1935), I, col. 158. *Annuario Pontificio 2000* (Città del Vaticano 2000) 1934–35.

[F. G. MORRISEY]

ACTION AND PASSION

Two of the ten Aristotelian CATEGORIES OF BEING; ποιεῖν and πάσχει in Greek, *actio* and *passio* in scholastic Latin. The history of these concepts reveals a shift of emphasis between ARISTOTLE himself and modern Aristotelians. In Aristotle, action and passion are uniformly taken for granted. The *Categories*—presumably because action and passion are assumed to be obvious—merely give examples, "to lance," "to cauterize," "to be lanced," "to be cauterized" (2a, 3). The *Physics* is concerned directly with questions about motion, and detailed consideration of action is given only because of a difficulty based on the reality of action (202a, 16; 202b 22). The same is true in the Metaphysics, where the difficulty is based on the actuality of action (1050a, 30). Among the Greek and Latin commentators as well as in St. THOMAS AQUINAS there is no dissent with respect to Aristotle's answer to these difficulties, that action is in the "patient" or recipient of the action. However, St. Thomas does give an occasion for later controversies by devoting a separate, formal consideration to action as being in the patient (*In 3 phys.* 5), and by making incidental statements that seem to contradict Aristotle's opinion (for example, *C. gent.* 2.9; *De pot.* 7.9 ad 7, 7.10 ad 1, 8.2). These apparent contradictions escaped early Thomistic commentators and it was left to T. de Vio CAJETAN to uncover the latent difficulty—though, curiously enough, even this discovery was not based on the difficult texts (*In Summa Theologiae* 1a, 25.1). After Cajetan, the shift in emphasis of the discussion was complete and the focus then shifted to various theories with respect to the subject of inherence of action considered as an ACCIDENT.

This brief history omits the opinion of John DUNS SCOTUS (*Oxon.* 4.13.1) and the Scotists, who, considering action as an extrinsic relation to the patient, maintained against Aristotle that action is in the agent.

Definitions. Action and passion, in this context, are limited to the sphere of physical or predicamental action. Predicamental action, which constitutes the category of action, is regularly distinguished from ''immanent action,'' which belongs to one of the species of QUALITY. The former is often called ''transient'' (or ''transitive'') action, since it affects something outside the AGENT because of its nature, whereas immanent action perfects the agent itself. In general, predicamental or transient action has the meaning of physical activity—any activity that because of its nature brings about some change or MOTION in another body. Thus, pushing, striking, painting, and even feeding are transient actions; knowing, willing and feeling, on the other hand, are not (St. Thomas, *C. gent.* 1.100; *In 9 meta.* 8.1862–65; etc.).

In the older Aristotelian tradition (with the exception of the Scotists), it was generally accepted that Aristotle meant this predicamental action, when he said that the action is in the patient. His argument is straightforward: ''A thing is capable of causing motion because it can *do* this, it is a mover because it actually *does* it. But it is only on the movable that it is capable of acting. Hence there is a single actuality of both'' (*Phys.* 202a, 16–19). The conclusion is stated clearly in the *Metaphysics* in terms of a concrete example: ''The act of building is in the thing being built'' (1050a, 30).

Passion, in this understanding, is simply the reception of the single actuality, motion-action. The sole reality in all three—motion, action and passion—is the motion itself, though each is distinct from the others in definition (*In 3 phys.* 5.7, 5.10). Accordingly, in this straightforward view, action is defined simply as ''motion from an agent''; passion, as ''motion [received from an agent] in a patient.''

It is clear that this doctrine has a direct bearing on the Aristotelian notion of EFFICIENT CAUSALITY. An agent, according to St. Thomas, is denominated such, precisely because of its effect on the patient (*In 3 phys.* 5.15). It would also seem clear that such a notion, of the agents' being determined from the effects they produce, could be of service in responding to difficulties raised by D. HUME against the perception of CAUSALITY in the physical order.

Subject of Predicamental Action. The straightforwardness of Aristotle's view about the subject of inherence of predicamental action, is lost in controversies after the time of Cajetan. Cajetan did not deny Aristotle's sin-

gle actuality of action and motion, nor did he deny that this actuality is in the patient; but he added a second actuality—the perfecting of the agent whereby it actually comes to affect something else—to it and it is this, he claims, that is essential to action as a category and is subjected in the agent (*In ST,* 1a, 25.1). This subtlety, distinguishing two actualities with respect to action, one in the patient and one in the agent, led to a new definition of action as ''the second act by which an agent is rendered actually causing'' [as opposed to first act, in which it is only a potential agent; see F. SUÁREZ, *Disp. meta.* 48.1.15–20 (Vivès, 26:872–873); JOHN OF ST. THOMAS, *Nat. phil* 1.14.3–4 (*Curs. phil.* 2:304–305, 310)].

In the aftermath of Cajetan's formulation, three well-defined schools of thought have developed relative to the subject of inherence of transient action: (1) many Thomists (for example, FERRARIENSIS, F. Suárez and P. FONSECA) continued to maintain the older view, that action is in the patient and the view still has its proponents (T. S. McDermott); (2) at the opposite pole, some Thomists [for example, J. P. Nazarius (1555–1646) and S. MAURUS], followed the lead of Cajetan, holding that action in the true sense is not in the patient but in the agent and again the view has contemporary proponents (J. Gredt, *Elementa philosophiae* 1.281); (3) finally, John of St. Thomas developed an intermediate position, maintaining that action is both in the agent and the patient, though in different senses, a view that also has present-day proponents (W. D. Kane).

Arguments can be proposed both for and against each of these positions, as follows.

Action Is in the Patient. Two arguments are presented in favor of this position. The first is based on the authority of Aristotle and maintains that the doctrine that action is in the patient, was universally held (with the exception of the Scotists) up to the time of Cajetan. Aside from the slighting of the Scotist position, this argument has little force apart from its further doctrinal justification; it can easily be countered, as is implicitly done by Cajetan: the traditional doctrine is not denied, but only complemented by a further consideration that is not touched on explicitly by the older tradition (*In ST* 1a, 25.1.6).

The formal argument in favor of action as in the patient is more cogent. In one form or another, it usually recapitulates the argument of Aristotle: since the whole reality of action is motion as from an agent (it is defined as *motus ab agente*), it follows that action will be found where motion is found. Therefore, since it is solid Aristotelian doctrine that motion is in its subject and not in the agent, action also must be in the subject (now denominated ''patient,'' as receiving motion from the agent). The counterargument proposed against this is that this action is not denied, but it is not the essential constituent of predicamental action. Such a counterargument is not convincing in every way, if only because it is precisely this notion of action in the patient that St. Thomas uses to establish action in his derivation of the categories (*In 3 phys.* 5.15).

Action Is in the Agent. The first argument in favor of this view, proposed by Cajetan, is based on a difficulty in theology. All the divine perfections are in reality identified with the divine essence. If, therefore, the perfection of an agent is in the patient, it is difficult to see how the action of God producing effects in creatures without the intermediate cause can be identified with the divine essence. If, on the contrary, action is taken to be the perfection of the agent as actually causing it, the difficulty vanishes. It is hard to see this as a serious difficulty; the question here is clearly one of an action properly immanent and only virtually transient.

What then of the argument occasioned by this difficulty? It states that, because action is the perfection of the agent as actually (and no longer only potentially) causing it, it must be in the agent. Confirmation is sought from St. Thomas's statement that action is the actualization of a power (*actualitas virtutis*—*ST* 1a, 54.1).

As opposed to this it can be argued that: (1) the distinction between immanent and transient action cannot be adequately sustained in such a formulation; (2) St. Thomas finds no difficulty in placing the perfection of a power in its affecting something outside itself—he does precisely this, in fact, in order to distinguish transient from immanent action (*In 9 meta.* 8.1864); and (3) in Aristotelian doctrine the primary type of motion is local motion. In such motion it is difficult to see what added perfection a moving body would acquire by moving another body in a collision—obviously a most important case of the action of a physical agent.

Action Is in Both the Agent and the Patient. To this formulation is usually added: in the agent "inchoatively," in the patient "formally and terminatively [*consummative*]." Before arguments can be proposed in favor of this position, the very terms in which it is stated must be clarified.

John of St. Thomas, the chief proponent of this view, explains the term "inchoatively" in two ways. First he says that it means "after the manner of an emanation" (though obviously he does not mean this to exclude a secondary aspect of inherence in a subject). Then he shows how it is possible for something to be in two subjects at once, provided that it is formally or *simpliciter* in only one, by appeal to the way in which a virtue can be in the

will as imperating and yet at the same time be formally in the sense appetites (*ST* 1a, 2ae, 50.3; 56.2).

The terms "formally and terminatively" are then clear from the preceding account: action receives its ultimate formality in producing its effect in the patient, and this formality lies in the completing of the emanation from the agent in the patient.

In defending this position, John of St. Thomas feels that the principal burden falls on the defenders of action as only in the patient, to explain away the apparently contrary texts in St. Thomas and to show that an aspect in the agent is unnecessary. (He feels that the position of those holding for action in the agent need not lead them to deny that it is also in the patient, but only to affirm that it is in some way in the agent.) His refutations of arguments in favor of action as only in the patient can be reduced to a distinction between "action-as-effected" and "action-as-effecting," and he is forced to say that both Aristotle and St. Thomas, in the majority of texts, wished to lay such stress on the terminative and formal aspect that they passed over the inchoative or emanational aspect [*Nat. phil.* 1.14.3–4 (*Curs. phil.* 2:304–314)]. Such an argument seems odd for a professed Aristotelian and Thomist, and this aspect of the whole position can be countered by the same arguments proposed earlier against action as in the agent.

A Simpler Position. Finally, against all three positions adopted after the time of Cajetan, it can be objected that they are needlessly subtle and are based on a false notion of what is required to constitute a category (P. Hoenen, 237–247). This view has much to recommend it, both in its simplicity and its return to the traditional view. However, it must explain away the difficulties in St. Thomas's texts if it is to be completely successful as a Thomistic interpretation. In summary, this explanation runs as follows: For St. Thomas and the earlier scholastics in general, a purely extrinsic denomination—without any instrinsic form as foundation—was sufficient to establish the last six categories, and St. Thomas is explicit in affirming that action and passion are based on extrinsic denomination and not on any intrinsic form. Nevertheless, it is still the agent that is denominated by this extrinsic reality, and it is this aspect—the agent as denominated from its effect and as subject of predication—that is referred to whenever St. Thomas refers to action as in the agent (Hoenen, 245–246).

Importance. Whether in its simple or in its subtle form, this question has an important bearing on several areas of scholastic philosophy. One aspect, in the defense of a realistic view of causality against Hume, has already been touched upon. In addition, the theory has an important bearing on the proofs for the existence of God as an unmoved mover and on the way in which free agents move and are moved by God (*see* MOTION, FIRST CAUSE OF). Further, the doctrine is of supreme importance both in explaining the difference between physical action, the acts of knowledge and affectivity, and in explaining the interaction of soul and body, knower and known, in psychology.

See Also: ACTION AT A DISTANCE.

Bibliography: P. H. J. HOENEN, *Cosmologia* (5th ed. Rome 1956). T. S. MCDERMOTT, ''The Subject of Predicamental Action,'' *Thomist,* 23 (1960) 189–210. W. D. KANE, ''The Subject of Predicamental Action according to John of St. Thomas,'' *ibid.* 22 (1959) 366–388. J. A. MCWILLIAMS, ''Action Does Not Change the Agent,'' *Philosophical Studies in Honor of the Very Rev. Ignatius Smith,* ed. J. K. RYAN (Westminster, Md. 1952) 208–221.

[P. R. DURBIN]

ACTION AT A DISTANCE

The action of one material body on another across empty space, i.e., without mutual contact or without the presence of a third body or medium that is in contact with both. Whether such action is possible or not is discussed by both philosophers and scientists. The more common answer is that such action is impossible on both philosophical and empirical grounds; agreement is not unanimous largely because of differences over what is meant by ''action,'' ''matter'' or ''material,'' and ''empty space'' (*see* ACTION AND PASSION; MATTER). The possibility of a spirit's exercising influence upon a material body is not in question because the notions of action, distance, and contact—derived as they are from material and extended being—do not apply to a spirit except in an analogical sense. Two reasons are usually adduced for the necessity of mutual contact or for the presence of an intermediate body: first, to make it possible to speak of localization and distance; and second, to make possible the action of the AGENT upon the receiving subject. The present article discusses only the second reason, the first being treated elsewhere. [*see* PLACE; LOCATION (UBI)].

Various Positions. Among the philosophical proponents of the possibility of action at a distance are usually enumerated dynamists such as I. Kant (1724–1804), with his concept of attractive forces (*Anziehungskräfte*), R. Boscovich (1711–87), and I. J. J. Carbonnelle (1829–89); and various philosophers of science or of nature, including B. Bolzano (1781–1848), R. H. LOTZE (1817–81), K. Gutberlet (1837–1928), and J. Schwertschlager (1853–1924). Chief among those who oppose the possibility are the early Greek philosophers—particularly the atomists, the pre-Socratic cosmologists, and the Hippocratic medical writers—and 17th-century Cartesians and mechanists. Similar opposition stems from Aristotle, St. THOMAS AQUINAS, and most medieval and scholastic thinkers, all of whom reject the possibility on metaphysical grounds.

The founders of modern science were against action at a distance, generally because of the atomist and mechanist suppositions that underlay their thought. Supporters for the concept of such action first arose from the Newtonian theory of gravitation, although Newton himself opposed it. The express formulation of the concept came in the 19th century with various interpretations of the experimental work of A. M. Ampère (1775–1836) and Michael Faraday (1791–1867), and the mathematical theories of J. C. Maxwell (1831–79) and H. R. Hertz (1857–94). At the end of the century, the failure of the Michelson-Morley experiment to detect an ether gave further support to the concept. More recent thinkers variously accept the possibility because of the purely mathematical way in which they interpret field concepts, or reject it because of a realist commitment to fields as existent entities, or regard it as a pseudo-problem because of a positivist view of modern science in its entirety.

Metaphysical Impossibility. The various arguments for the metaphysical impossibility of action at a distance may be summarized as follows: (1) action requires the presence of an agent; (2) contact is necessary for the exercise of influence; (3) action, as an ACCIDENT of both agent and recipient, requires that both be present in the same place; (4) cause and effect must be together; and (5) the actual dependence of the recipient upon the agent requires local contact. Since a number of these arguments are considered elsewhere (*see* ACTION AND PASSION; CAUSALITY; MOTION, FIRST CAUSE OF), only the last is explained here. The argument may be formulated in the following terms.

The action of one subject upon another requires that the recipient be dependent upon the agent in such a way that it be able to receive the agent's action. Where material bodies are involved, however, such dependence is possible only when there is local contact between agent and recipient. Therefore, action at a distance is impossible.

The major premise is universally true of action in general, even that of a spirit upon matter. The mere existence of two subjects is not sufficient for one to act upon the other, but a certain conditioning of the one for the other is required and this conditioning is prior in nature to the action itself.

In order for such mutual conditioning to occur, as stated in the minor premise, the agent and recipient must form one system in a material sense, i.e., one corporeal system with internal local relations. But such a system can be obtained only through local contact, and this either immediately or mediately, i.e., through a material medium that is again in immediate contact with both agent and recipient. If such contact does not exist, the bodies cannot influence one another. Moreover, while an inactive medium can register place and relative direction, it cannot determine an event that originates from one body and influences another at a particular time and with a particular intensity. Thus, when a medium is involved, it must play both an active and a passive role in the bodily interaction.

This argument is metaphysical in the sense that it presupposes the validity of such concepts as action, being, and causality, all of which are verifiable in ordinary experience without recourse to the experimental and conceptual developments of modern science. Those who reject metaphysics, of course, do not subscribe to an argumentation of this type (*see* METAPHYSICS, VALIDITY OF).

Physical Arguments. Physical proofs of the impossibility of action at a distance attempt to show that, as a matter of fact, such action does not take place in the physical universe. For this purpose, one may classify actions as either chemical, or mechanical, or those involving some type of field interaction. Regarding chemical activity, it seems generally agreed that chemical interaction occurs only if reagents are brought into contact, and thus there is no action at a distance. Again, if physical action is transmitted mechanically, either by streams of particles or by collision of macroscopic bodies, there is no action at a distance. This leaves only actions associated with field concepts—among which may be enumerated electricity, magnetism, electromagnetism, gravity, and nuclear and other forces —for detailed discussion.

One characteristic of such actions is their dependence upon the distance between agent and recipient, as, for example, the magnitude of the gravitational force between bodies being inversely proportional to the square of their distance. Again, in the case of the electric and magnetic phenomena, intermediary bodies can exercise influence, as in shielding effects. Moreover, such actions are propagated with a finite velocity, and the implied dependence on space and time is incompatible with action at a distance. Yet again, the existence of standing waves and of radiation quanta cannot be explained solely in terms of empty space. Finally, a field theory itself is opposed to the concept of action at a distance. Fields have properties that differ from point to point and that are describable in terms of potentials; they also contain a definite amount of energy. Thus they function as operational media and have a degree of reality corresponding to the action they transmit. Whatever phenomena urge scientists to admit the action of a field also urge the acceptance of a medium that supports such activity.

Such arguments, while not absolutely conclusive, argue strongly against the hypothesis of action at a distance.

Bibliography: P. H. VAN LAER, *Actio in distans en aether* (Utrecht 1947); *Philosophico-scientific Problems*, tr. H. J. KOREN (Pittsburgh 1953). M. B. HESSE, ''Action at a Distance,'' *The Concept of Matter*, ed. E. MCMULLIN (Notre Dame, Ind. 1963) 372–90; *Forces and Fields: The Concepts of Action at a Distance in the History of Physics* (New York 1962).

[W. A. WALLACE]

ACTION FRANÇAISE

Action Française (A.F.) is the name of a political league and its journal that attempted, during the first four decades of the 20th century, to reestablish the monarchy in France.

Program and Influence. A first committee of A.F. was born in 1898 during the Dreyfus affair. It was transformed in 1905 into a league of A.F., which proposed to combat every republican regime and to re-establish the monarchy. It edited a biweekly periodical, called *L'Action française.* (1899–), and in 1908 launched a daily newspaper, with the same name. An institute of A.F. took charge of doctrinal propaganda. Charles MAURRAS was the unquestioned head and the theorist of the movement, which counted several other very talented leaders, such as Léon DAUDET, Henri Vaugeois, and Jacques Bainville.

A.F. was never a mass movement, and played only a minor legislative role, although Daudet was for a time elected a deputy, but its intellectual influence was considerable, especially among Catholics. Although its principal directors were atheists, they believed that if French society was to prosper as it had in the past, it must return to both the political form and the religious practice of earlier times. The Church quickly became disturbed by the organization's influence over a section of the French clergy and faithful. Its journal taught that political laws proceed from experience, and that the national interest has an absolute primacy in moral matters. Its young partisans grouped under the name ''camelots,'' and swore to promote royalist restoration by any means whatsoever. In brief, it was a political school whose concepts derived from a naturalist view of man, society, and religion; and this intellectual outlook obliterated the moral sense of its members in their concepts of foreign and domestic politics.

Attitude of the Church. Because of the complaints of French bishops, the Holy Office prepared a prohibition of seven books by Maurras, and the periodical, but not the newspaper, of the movement (Jan. 26, 1914). However, A.F.'s combat against anticlerical republicans and its struggle for a conservative type of Catholicism then in favor at the Vatican produced interventions in its favor at Rome. As a result, Pius X (1903–14) suspended publication of the decree. Benedict XV (1914–22) adopted the same attitude because of World War I. Pius XI (1922–39) received new complaints as a result of an investigation that revealed the extraordinary ascendancy of the movement over Belgian youth, and asked Cardinal Andrieu, Archbishop of Bordeaux, to publish a letter of disapproval, which appeared on Aug. 25, 1926, and received papal approbation. The *Osservatore Romano* printed articles on this subject to which A.F. replied violently, branding the editors a "small band of demoniacal agents," and pretending in an article entitled *"Non possumus"* that treason and parricide were being asked of it. A decree of the Holy Office (Dec. 29, 1926) published the text of the 1914 condemnation, and added to it, with the ratification of Pius XI, the newspaper *L'Action française* "as it is published today" because of articles written "these recent days especially . . . namely by Charles Maurras and Léon Daudet, articles which every sensible man is obliged to recognize as written against the Holy Apostolic See and the Roman Pontiff himself."

Reacting with fury, A.F. vilified the *Osservatore Romano* as *"Diffamatore Romano,"* and "an infamous rag"; resurrected all the familiar specters of anticlericalism, such as Galileo, St. Bartholomew's Massacre, Alexander VI, and the Borgias; and accused the pope of being the victim of a plot to restore the Holy Roman Germanic Empire. This led Bishop Ruch of Strasbourg to classify *L'Action française* the most anti-clerical newspaper in France.

Subsequent to the condemnation of Dec. 29, 1926, the Holy See published other documents that fixed the manner of treating the unsubmissive. Priests were forbidden to administer the Sacraments to them and were threatened with canonical sanctions if disobedient. Marriages of the rebellious were merely to be blessed in the sacristy, like mixed marriages. Dying rebels must make honorable amends or be deprived of the last rites, and go to their graves without the Church's prayers.

Several French bishops remained sympathetic to A.F., and at first refrained from commenting on the Roman condemnation or made very fine distinctions in their observations. Undoubtedly at the Holy See's demand, a long declaration appeared with 116 episcopal signatures (Mar. 8, 1927), but without the names of three bishops. One of these was later regarded by the Holy See as having resigned. Sanctions were taken against important ecclesiastics, such as Cardinal BILLOT, who was removed from the Sacred College and went to finish his days at the Jesuit novitiate in Gallora. Priests suspected of favoring the movement were gradually removed from influential posts, especially those dealing with young people. Jacques Maritain, in collaboration with P. Doncoeur and four other ecclesiastics, published a book defending the Holy See, *Pourquoi Rome a parlé* (1927). Maurice Pujo replied to it in a series of articles later gathered in book form as *Comment Rome est trompé* (1929), which drew from V. Bernadot and five authors the reply *Clairvoyance de Rome* (1929). Some bishops closed their eyes, but others applied the sanctions rigorously. Many cases gained notoriety and with the passage of time contributed to building hopes for a gradual appeasement of the affair. Some interventions occurred in Rome. Maurras wrote to Pius XI (January 1937), and received a reply. He then wrote two more letters to the Pope. Their correspondence made it clear, however, that their viewpoints remained irreconcilable.

The pontificate of Pius XII (1939–58) opened new perspectives. After long negotiations, the directive committee of A.F. sent a letter to the pope expressing their sincerest sorrow for anything in their polemies and controversies that had been injurious and even unjust. The Catholics on the committee rejected all their erroneous writings and every precept and theory contrary to Catholic teachings. Pius XII had not demanded the type of retraction required by his predecessor, but the text signed by the committee constituted an implicit retraction since it admitted that the prohibition's motives were just.

The Holy See triumphed in the end, for Catholic youths ceased joining the movement. Its defeat became more evident when the Duke of Guise, pretender to the throne, disassociated himself from A.F. (Nov. 1937). In 1944 the liberation government forbade the publication of *L'Action française* because of its attitude during World War II.

Bibliography: N. FONTAINE, *Saint-Siège: Action française et catholiques intégraux* (Paris 1928). D. GWYNN, *The "Action Française" Condemnation* (London 1928). L. WARD, *The Condemnation of the Action Française* (London 1928) J. BRUGERETTE, *Le Prêtre français et la société contemporaine,* 3 v. (Paris 1933–38) v.3. Dansette 2. S. M. OSGOOD, *French Royalism under the Third and Fourth Republics* (The Hague 1960). E. J. WEBER, *Action Française* (Stanford 1962). E. R. TANNENBAUM, *The Action Française* (New York 1962). H. DANIEL-ROPS, *L'Église des révolutions: Un Combat pour Dieu, 1870–1939* (*Histoire de l'Église du Christ* 6.2; Paris 1963). J. GRISAR, *Lexikon für Theologie und Kirche,* ed. M. BUCHBERGER (Freiburg 1930–38) 1:71–74. H. DU PASSAGE, *Lexikon für Theologie und Kirche,* ed. J. HOFER and K. RAHNER (Freiberg 1957–65) 1:116–117.

[A. DANSETTE]

ACTIVE LIFE, SPIRITUAL

A life of external activity as opposed to contemplation. In the third century, Origen identified the active life with Martha and the contemplative life with her sister Mary. Before the Christian era the Greeks had differentiated the theoretical life from the practical life. The practical life was that which busied itself with the affairs of the family or the city. St. Paul used the Greek word "askein" to express the practical matter of working out one's salvation, of striving for perfection or making a spiritual effort to purify one's conscience in the sight of God. Gradually this word acquired the meaning of an exercise of the spiritual faculties in the acquisition of the virtues of learning, or exercise, in a physical sense. St. Paul often made reference to the efforts of athletes in the games when urging his Christians to the practice of perfection.

Origen was again the first to apply the word "ascetic" to Christians who practiced virginity and devoted themselves to works of mortification. With St. Augustine, the term active life became almost synonymous with ascetical striving, by making it consist of the practice of virtues, as apart from contemplation of truth. St. Gregory the Great, seconded this doctrine by identifying the active life with the practice of the corporal works of mercy, and to some extent the spiritual works and this tradition persisted through St. Thomas and Suárez.

The active life reaches a new plane when it concerns itself with the care of souls. From the time of Augustine authors point out that bishops, to whom the care of souls properly belongs, lead the active life in its fullest sense, as well as the contemplative life, since all their activity must be richly impregnated with contemplation. It follows that those who are not bishops lead the active life more fully, the more they participate in the care of souls, a work that is proper to bishops. That is why St. Thomas can rank those religious orders whose concern is to give to others the fruit of their contemplation in the first place. Historically, religious orders, at the beginning, were concerned only with the perfection of their own members. Gradually, the needs of souls forced them into the apostolate proper to bishops. Religious orders, such as the Franciscans and Dominicans in the 13th century, were founded with a view of doing the work that bishops could no longer handle alone. The revolutionary Society of Jesus (1540), which set the pattern for many of the more modern religious institutes, moved into whatever area was necessary for the good of souls, whether it was the corporal and spiritual works of mercy, or preaching and the administration of the Sacraments. In modern times, the next logical step was taken by the participation of the laity in the apostolate of the hierarchy, or what is known as Catholic Action, a way of living the active life of the spirit while remaining in the world.

The secret of the successful practice of the active life is charity in action. As St. Thomas teaches, charity is the root of merit. Affective charity, consisting in internal acts of the love of God is common to both the active and the contemplative lives, and must be made effective in the external worship of God in the contemplative life. St. Augustine says that it is "only the compulsion of charity that shoulders necessary activity" (Civ. 19.19). Affective charity is the real measure of perfection, but is itself best gauged by this effective charity of good works. Effective charity means carrying out God's commands. The whole purpose of the active life is to attain union with God by service to the neighbor, whom God has commanded us to love. One leading the active life does not so much leave God for God, as the popular phrase puts it, but finds God always and everywhere in activity done for the love of God.

Obviously the term "active life" is an analogous term. In a non-spiritual sense it would be the opposite of quiet. In a spiritual sense it is ambiguous, for it can either mean the opposite of the contemplative life or the life that flows from contemplation. When used in the context of the spiritual as a univocal term, it usually refers to the life of virtue, the pursuit of virtue, the life of the corporal and spiritual works of mercy, and all those things that are indirectly connected with charity.

Bibliography: E. C. BUTLER, *Western Mysticism* (2d ed. London 1927). P. T. CAMELOT and I. MENNESSIER, "The Active Life and the Contemplative Life," *The Virtues and States of Life,* ed. A. M. HENRY, tr. R. J. OLSON and G. T. LENNON (Theology Library 4; Chicago 1957) 645–683. J. DE GUIBERT, *The Theology of the Spiritual Life,* tr. P. BARRETT (New York 1953). E. CORETH, "Contemplative in Action," *Theology Digest,* 3 (1955) 37–45.

[J. F. CONWELL]

ACTIVISM

A teaching or orientation that emphasizes action in contradistinction to passivity. Thus, in a learning situation, the functionalism advocated by John Dewey or the method of teaching children promoted by Maria MONTESSORI is sometimes called activism. As a philosophic notion, it is opposed to intellectualism and gives precedence to practice and activity over theory. In this sense contemporary EXISTENTIALISM can be called activism in that it repudiates speculation in favor of action.

However, in Catholic circles, particularly in the U.S., it has come to denote an excessive activity of the apostolate that is detrimental to the spiritual life, especially in religious orders and congregations: exterior work of the apostolate absorbs the interest of the one engaged in it to the extent that his interior life suffers as a consequence.

It is also referred to as naturalism. Although such activism is not a formal doctrine, but rather a tendency of human nature, it is sometimes called the "heresy of action" and may be said in a general way to have a spirit opposed to the QUIETISM promoted by Miguel de MOLINOS and condemned by Innocent XI in 1687 (H. Denzinger, *Enchiridion symbolorum*, ed. A. Schönmetzer, 2201–69).

Activism should not be confused with the salutary work of the apostolate performed with the proper spiritual motives. Far from being an obstacle to spiritual growth, the giving of oneself in the service of others out of charity fosters the interior life of the soul. Activism, therefore, should not be equated with activity or a multiplicity of works. In its modern connotation, it has reference only to spiritual activity prompted by an indiscreet zeal and lacking a spiritual foundation. In the encyclical *Menti nostrae* Pius XII refers to it as "that kind of activity which is not based on divine grace and does not make constant use of the aids provided by Jesus Christ for the attainment of holiness" [*Acta Apostolicae Sedis* 42 (1950) 677].

Safeguards against activism include proper spiritual formation, the constant exercise of humility and prayer, and a wholesome spiritual outlook concerning the work of the apostolate. Those engaged in the apostolate should keep the words of St. Paul foremost in mind: "So then neither he who plants is anything, nor he who waters, but God who gives the growth" (1 Cor 3.7). The avoidance of activism should not, on the other hand, give way to a negativism characterized by a turning away from the performance of good works. In fact, there is great necessity for an increase in apostolic work to counteract growing materialistic tendencies.

Activism is also called AMERICANISM. Such a spiritual pragmatism was condemned by Leo XIII in the apostolic letter *TESTEM BENEVOLENTIAE*, addressed to Cardinal James Gibbons in 1899. While the pope praised the Church and the people of the U.S. for their spirit of progress and accomplishment, he nevertheless cautioned them, among other things, not to place too great an emphasis on externals and outward activity to the detriment of the spiritual life. Thus the term Americanism is often used, especially by European writers, to denote an excessive apostolic activity lacking the proper spiritual motivation.

See Also: APOSTOLATE AND SPIRITUAL LIFE; GRACE

Bibliography: M. BLONDEL, "Theory and Practice of Action," tr. J. M. SOMERVILLE, *Cross Currents* 4 (1954) 251–61. J. B. CHAUTARD, *The Soul of the Apostolate,* tr. J. A. MORAN (Trappist, Ky. 1941). J. AUMANN, "The Heresy of Action," *Cross and Crown* 3 (1951) 25–45. L. J. PUTZ, "Toward a Spirituality of Action," *Proceedings of the 1958 Sisters' Institute of Spirituality* 6 (1959) 96–105. R. BRADLEY, "Activity or Activism," *Sister Formation Bulletin* 4.2 (1957) 1–6. F. KLEIN, *Americanism: A Phantom Heresy* (Cranford, N.J. 1951) reproduced from W. ELLIOTT's *Life of Father Hecker* (4th ed. New York 1898).

[L. F. BACIGALUPO]

ACTON, CHARLES JANUARIUS

Cardinal; b. Naples, Italy, March 6, 1803; d. there, June 23, 1847. He was the son of Sir John Acton, sometime prime minister of the Kingdom of Naples. After his father's death (1811), Charles went to England, where he studied at Westminster School and then at Magdalene College, Cambridge (1819–23). He then returned to Rome to attend the Academy of Noble Ecclesiastics previous to ordination. In 1828 he was made a papal chamberlain and was appointed secretary to the nuncio in Paris. His next appointment was that of vice legate at Bologna. Before the uprising in Bologna (1831), Gregory XVI named him secretary to the Congregation of Regulars. Later he became auditor of the Apostolic Chamber. He was proclaimed cardinal (June 24, 1842) after being created *in petto* nearly three years previously. At the meeting between Gregory XVI and Czar Nicholas I (1845), Acton was the interpreter and sole witness. Later he wrote an account of the conversation at the pope's request. As adviser to the Holy See on matters concerning England, he recommended in 1840 an increase in the number of English vicars apostolic from four to eight but opposed the restoration of the hierarchy (1850). Although urged by the king of Naples to do so, he refused to accept the archiepiscopal See of Naples.

Bibliography: C. S. ISAACSON, *The Story of the English Cardinals* (London 1907). B. N. WARD, *The Sequel to Catholic Emancipation,* 2 v. (New York 1915) 1:154–66. J. GILLOW, *A Literary and Biographical History or Bibliographical Dictionary of the English Catholics from 1534 to the Present Time* 1:3–6.

[B. FOTHERGILL]

ACTON, JOHN EMERICH EDWARD DALBERG

Historian; b. Naples, Italy, Jan. 10, 1834; d. Tegernsee, Bavaria, June 19, 1902. The later eighth baronet and first baron, Acton was the only child of Sir Richard Acton and Marie Louise Pellini de Dalberg. At the age of three, upon the death of his father, he succeeded to a baronetcy in England. With his mother as his guardian, he was brought to his estate at Aldenham. After spending a year at St. Nicholas, a preparatory school near Paris (1842), he enrolled for four years at St. Mary's College, Oscott, whose president was Nicholas (later Cardinal) WISEMAN. Acton continued his studies at Edinburgh under a private tutor, Dr. Logan, a former vice president of Oscott. Unable to gain admission to Cambridge University, Acton went to Munich in 1850 to become the pupil and traveling companion of Johannes Ignaz von DÖLLINGER. He traveled widely throughout Europe and visited the U.S. in 1855. His German training developed in him a profound love for historical learning and critical scholarship. His cosmopolitan background and knowledge of languages assisted him greatly in his historical pursuits.

Acton returned to England in 1859 with the intention of introducing the isolated English Catholic community to progressive Catholic thought. He believed that England, better than any other Western country, had preserved a true Catholic spirit in its political institutions and that Catholics had a special duty to maintain the Christian character of the English constitution. He sat as a Whig member of Parliament for Carlow, an Irish constituency (1859–65). During this period he formed a close friendship with William GLADSTONE and became his lifelong political supporter and confidant. With his interests and talents, Acton found the world of practical politics thoroughly uncongenial, and he took little part in parliamentary affairs. In 1858 he purchased part ownership of a liberal Catholic journal, the *Rambler* (called in 1862 *The Home and Foreign Review*). Until 1864 he devoted most of his energies to writing articles and reviews for this enterprise. This was his most prolific period as a writer and saw the production of some of his best works.

Encouraged by NEWMAN and ably assisted by Richard SIMPSON, Acton followed a progressive line that gave offense to the ultraconservatives who represented the dominant group in the Church. Because of his insistence, often in provocative, arrogant fashion, that the Catholic scholar should be free to discuss without restriction all religious questions that were not defined doctrines, and his coolness toward the papal temporal power, the English hierarchy and Rome viewed him with suspicion. By 1864, when Pius IX issued the SYLLABUS OF ERRORS, Acton was convinced that the Holy See favored a restrictive policy that ran counter to his own deepest convictions. In a spirit of frustration he withdrew from Catholic journalism. He continued to contribute to the *Chronicle* (1867–68) and the *North British Review* (1867–71), but his most productive period was at an end. On Gladstone's recommendation he was raised to the peerage in 1869.

During VATICAN COUNCIL I, Acton was one of the most vociferous opponents of a solemn definition of papal primacy and infallibility. Despite his close association with Döllinger, he refused to identify himself with the German scholars who repudiated the conciliar defini-

John Emerich Edward Dalberg Acton, ca. 1879, painting by Franz Seraph von Lenbach.

tions of the papal prerogatives and who were, as a result, excommunicated (*see* OLD CATHOLICS). Although fanatically opposed to the growing ULTRAMONTANISM, he taught his son in 1890: "A Church without a pope is not the Church of Christ." He remained a devout Catholic in his private life, but after 1875 he grew more isolated from his coreligionists.

Contemporary ideas of progress and human perfectibility exercised a powerful influence on his thoughts. Acton came to view the course of history as one of progress toward freedom. With a fervor that at times approached hysteria he denounced all forces, past or present, that restricted liberty. He subjected the popes to special condemnation, and he was no less severe on saints who had countenanced the INQUISITION. He collected voluminous notes for a major work on the history of liberty that was never completed. He was one of the founders of the *English Historical Review* (1886). On the nomination of Lord Rosebery, Acton was appointed (1895) regius professor of modern history at Cambridge. As his final project Acton drew up the plans and acted as editor for the *Cambridge Modern History,* but this 14-volume monument of cooperative scholarship appeared (1902–12) only after his death.

Apart from periodical articles, Acton published little during his lifetime. Since his death, however, most of his major essays and lectures have appeared in book form. His writings reflect immense learning and moral earnestness, but they are marred occasionally by a Whig bias that led him to be unfair in his historical judgments. His influence on Catholic thought during his lifetime was minimal, but he has since been recognized as the most farsighted Catholic historical thinker of his generation.

Bibliography: Works. *Lectures on Modern History,* ed. J. N. FIGGIS and R. V. LAURENCE (London 1906; repr. 1930); *Historical Essays and Studies,* ed. J. N. FIGGIS and R. V. LAURENCE (London 1907); *Essays on Freedom and Power,* ed. G. HIMMELFARB (Boston 1948); *Essays on Church and State,* ed. D. WOODRUFF (New York 1953); *Letters to Mary Gladstone,* ed. H. PAUL (New York 1904); *Selections from the Correspondence of the First Lord Acton,* ed. J. N. FIGGIS and R. V. LAURENCE (London 1917); *Lord Acton and His Circle,* ed. F. A. GASQUET (New York 1906). A. WATKIN and H. BUTTERFIELD, "Gasquet and the Acton-Simpson Correspondence," *Cambridge Historical Journal* 10 (1950–) 77–105, points out defects in Gasquet's editing. V. CONZEMIUS, ed., *Ignaz von Döllinger: Briefwechsel 1820–90* (Munich 1963–), to be completed in 5 v., contains D's correspondence with Acton. Literature. U. NOACK, *Katholizität und Geistesfreiheit nach den Schriften von J. Dalberg-Acton, 1834–1902* (Frankfurt 1936). F. ENGEL-JANOSI, "Reflections of Lord Acton on Historical Principles," *American Catholic Historical Review* 27 (1941) 166–85. F. E. LALLY, *As Lord Acton Says* (Newport, R.I. 1942). D. MATHEW, *Acton: The Formative Years* (London 1946). H. BUTTERFIELD, *Lord Acton* (London 1948), pamphlet; "Acton: His Training, Methods, and Intellectual System," in *Studies in Diplomatic History and Historiography in Honour of G. P. Gooch,* ed. A. O. SARKISSIAN (London 1961) 169–98. G. HIMMELFARB, *Lord Acton* (Chicago 1952). H. A. MACDOUGALL, *The Acton-Newman Relations* (New York 1962). G. E. FASNACHT, *Acton's Political Philosophy* (London 1952). L. KOCHAN, *Acton on History* (London 1954). J. L. ALTHOLZ, *The Liberal Catholic Movement in England* (London 1962).

[H. A. MACDOUGALL]

ACTS, NOTIONAL

In Trinitarian theology notions are characteristics proper to each Divine PERSON, by which man is able to know the Persons as distinct. These are innascibility, paternity, filiation, active and passive spiration (ST 1a, 32; Scotus adds the inspirability of the Second Person: *In 1 sent.* 28.1–3). The adjective notional is applied to whatever is proper to one Person and not common to all. In God "all is one, save where there is relative opposition" (Council of Florence; H. Denzinger, *Enchiridion symbolorum,* ed. A. Schönmetzer, 1330); therefore all that is notional is really identical with the divine relations of rigin, but man's abstractive mode of thought makes it necessary to introduce further mental distinctions if he is to think or speak of this mystery.

By the term notional acts theologians designate those divine acts that enable one to come to the knowledge of the distinct Persons; these are the GENERATION OF THE WORD and the SPIRATION of the Spirit. The magisterium unhesitatingly applies the corresponding verbs (*generare, gigni, procedere*) to each Person (Fourth Lateran Council; *Enchiridion symbolorum,* 800, 804). Considered as the way by which the Persons and their opposed relations originate, these enable one to discern each Person. Some theologians speak simply of two acts (generation, spiration); the majority speak of four, considering each act both as emanating from a principle (active generation, spiration) and as received in a term (passive generation, spiration).

Certain conceptual problems arise (ST 1a, 40.4; 41.1–6). (1) One cannot think of origin save in terms of action, but, applied to God, man's concept of action must be purified of all created imperfection. God's immanent activity of knowing and loving is identical with His essence, pure act; one must exclude all idea of motion, passive potency, and determinability and speak simply of God's active power, exercise of activity, the active and actual influence of principle on term. Thus, by a mental distinction, one expresses the dynamic aspect of the relation of producing principle to term produced. (2) Notional acts are necessary, for God's activity is identical with His essence. This is not to suggest coercion; indeed notional acts are voluntary, not that the Father could have refrained from begetting the Son, but because God wills and loves all the perfection that He necessarily is. (3) Does the notional act presuppose (logically) the corresponding property, or vice versa? When one considers generation and spiration as received in the Son and the Spirit, the act is clearly prior to the property (filiation, passive spiration). Active spiration, common to two Persons, obviously presupposes those Persons. But what of active generation? This presupposes the First Person, constituted by the property of paternity. How can that property be logically prior to the act of generation? St. Thomas answers (ST 1a, 40.4 ad 1) by distinguishing between paternity as a property of the First Person (prior to generation) and as a relation to the Second Person (subsequent to generation).

See Also: PROPERTIES, DIVINE PERSONAL; RELATIONS, TRINITARIAN; PROCESSIONS, TRINITARIAN; TRINITY, HOLY, ARTICLES ON

Bibliography: A. MICHEL, *Dictionnaire de théologie catholique,* ed. A. VACANT et al. (Paris 1903–50) 11.1:802–805. Commentaries on ST 1a, 41. *Somme théologique: La Trinité,* ed. and tr. H. F. DONDAINE, 2 v. (Paris 1942–46) 2:354–366. P. VANIER, *Théologie trinitaire chez saint Thomas d'Aquin: Évolution du concept d'action notionelle* (Montreal 1953).

[R.L. STEWART]

ACTS OF THE APOSTLES

A book of the New Testament that presents the life of the early Christian community in Jerusalem after the Ascension of Jesus and narrates the progress of the Christian movement from Jerusalem to Rome.

A Sequel to the Gospel of Luke. The canonical place of the Acts of the Apostles between the gospels and the letters of Paul is appropriate since its narrative of the development of Christianity not only continues the gospel story of Jesus but also provides a framework for understanding the letters of Paul. Although it appears in the canon after the Gospel of John, the Acts of the Apostles is really to be regarded as a sequel to the Gospel of Luke. Both contain a dedicatory preface addressed to a certain Theophilus. The reference to a ''first book'' in prologue of Acts (1:1–5) suggests that Acts was meant as a continuation of an earlier work. The identification of this ''first book'' with the Gospel of Luke is based on the relation of the two prologues as well as the connection between the first chapter of Acts and the last chapter of Luke. Verbal and thematic correspondence exist between Acts 1:4 and Lk 24:49, the instruction of Jesus to the disciples ''not to depart from Jerusalem'' and ''to wait for the promise of the Father''; Acts 1:8 and Lk 24:47–48, they will be witnesses in Jerusalem; Acts 1:2.9 and Lk 24:51, the ascension of Jesus as the conclusion of his earthly career. Apart from these, thematic continuity, parallelisms and geographical pattern substantiate the view that the Gospel of Luke and the Acts of the Apostles were written by the same author who meant them to be two volumes of a single work. The literary unity of Luke-Acts is now generally acknowledged though each represents a different genre. Some would, however, see both works as historical monograph, with the gospel having a biographical interest while Acts is focused on historical events.

Authorship. The name of the author is not mentioned in the text of Acts or in the Third Gospel. The earliest attributions of authorship can be found in the Anti-Marcionite Prologue to Luke; Irenaeus' Adversus Haereses, 3.1.1; 3.14.1; and the Muratorian Canon. These writings of the late second century identify the author with Luke, the physician, an attendant and inseparable companion of Paul. It is said that he was an eyewitness of some of the events narrated in Acts, particularly those in the ''we-passages'' (Acts 16:10–17; 20:5–15; 21:1–18; 27:1–28:16). It was also believed that Luke came from Antioch (cf. Irenaeus and Eusebius), that he wrote for the Gentiles (cf. Origen) and that he composed the Acts of the Apostles in Rome (Jerome, *De Viris Illustribus* 7). The Church Fathers did not mention the source of their information about Luke, but some could be inferred from 2 Tim 4:11 (companion of Paul); Col 4:14 (beloved physician); Phlm 24 (Paul's co-worker).

St. Peter and St. Paul. (©Archive Photos)

It is possible that the Luke mentioned in these letters was the same Luke whom tradition acknowledges as the author of Luke-Acts. It cannot be ascertained, however, that he actually wrote them. Whoever the real author may be, he has come to be known as Luke.

From the text of Luke-Acts, something can be said about the implied author. In the gospel prologue (Lk 1:1–4), he sees himself as a link in the chain of tradition but distinguishes himself from ''the eyewitnesses and ministers of the word.'' His claim to write ''an orderly account'' subtly expresses a critical appraisal of his predecessors and offers a reason for his own literary endeavor. He presents his credential as a historian by assuring his addressees that his composition is based on reliable tradition and his own thorough investigation. His involvement in some of the events he narrates is supported by the impression of an eyewitness report in the ''we-passages'' in Acts.

The prologues and the language of the two-volume work suggest that the (implied) author's native tongue is

Greek, that he is well educated and knows the conventions of Greco-Roman rhetoric. He is aware of the philosophical currents of his time and has a clear knowledge of the Septuagint, of Jewish culture and of Christian traditions. He is a well-traveled, cosmopolitan person with a broad vision of the Christian movement.

Date and Place of Composition. The connection to the Gospel of Luke makes the dating of Acts dependent on the dating of this gospel and the gospel of Mark. Since internal evidence makes it most plausible that Luke made use of the gospel of Mark, written ca. 68–73 CE, his gospel must have been written some time after Mark's gospel had been circulated and attained recognition. Luke's gospel was written after the destruction of Jerusalem but before the persecution of Christians in the latter part of the reign of Domitian (ca. 81–96) and even before the bitter controversy of Christianity and Pharisaic Judaism (ca. 85–90). Thus, the gospel of Luke is dated in the 80s and the Acts of the Apostles must have been written shortly after the gospel. A group of scholars date Acts before 64 CE on the basis of the traditional view of Lukan authorship and the ending of Acts which mentions Paul's house arrest in Rome but not his martyrdom. The lack of any mention of Paul's death cannot be a determining factor in dating Acts since it can be explained by the author's literary purpose and theological intention. A late dating of Acts, ca. 95–100, has also been proposed based on the view that Luke was dependent on Josephus' Antiquties which was published ca. 93. This is a minority opinion. The place of composition is uncertain. It could be Antioch or Rome. Tradition connects Luke with Antioch in Syria. Jerome says the Acts was written in Rome but also suggests other places such as Achaia and Boetia.

Audience. Luke dedicates his two-volume work to Theophilus. There is no reason to doubt that a particular person is meant. The address Luke uses for him, kratiste, indicates a person of high social status. For Luke to write his books with skill and grace, he must have relied on his own financial resources or on the support of a well-to-do person. The dedicatory preface suggests that Theophilus could have been his patron. Luke assumes a shared knowledge between him and his reader. He assumes that the reader has some knowledge of the Christian tradition and can understand his allusions to the Hebrew Scriptures. To appreciate his language and literary style, the reader must have had some Hellenistic education. Theophilus could not have been a total outsider to the Christian movement. He could be a recent convert to Christianity, of Jewish or Gentile origin, with a Hellenistic education. Luke certainly did not intend his works only for Theophilus. Following the literary convention of prologue means that he intended his works for a wider au-

dience. Theophilus, thus, also represents the implied readers of Luke-Acts.

Texts and Sources. The early witnesses for the text of Acts fall into two distinct text types: (1) the Alexandrian text represented by p45 p74 Sinaiticus A B C 81, Clement of Alexandria (2) the so-called Western text represented chiefly by D and the fragmentary papyri p29, p38 and p48, Old Latin, the Harclean apparatus, Irenaeus, Cyprian and Augustine. The Western text is about ten percent longer than the Alexandrian text. Notwithstanding its early date, the Western text appears to be secondary and paraphrastic. Generally the more reliable text is the Alexandrian text. In some instances the Western text may preserve an original reading. Each reading must be judged according to its own merits.

The search for the sources of Acts has not been successful primarily because of Luke's tendency to rewrite his sources thoroughly. In the case of the gospel, if we did have the gospel of Mark with which to compare Luke's gospel, it would be very difficult to ascertain that Luke was using Mark as a source. The detection of sources in the case of Acts is even more difficult since there is no standard of comparison. This is not to deny Luke's use of sources for Acts. It is not improbable that he had access to written sources and oral traditions of Christian communities, stories about Peter and Paul, other personalities in Acts such as Philip, Stephen, Cornelius and other converts to the Christian faith. The "we-passages" could have been based on his own experiences or could have come from a missionary travel diary. Although the narrative of Acts 16–20 agrees with some facts from 1–2 Corinthians, 1 Thessalonians, Galatians and Romans, it is not likely that Luke made use of Paul's letters in constructing his story. The many points of discrepancy in the places of overlap preclude literary dependence. Not only does Luke not mention Paul's letters, his picture of Paul and his theology does not quite agree either with the portrait and theology of Paul in the letters.

Structure and Content. The story of Acts may be divided according to the stages of the progress of the Christian movement. Some scholars have seen in the summaries of growth (6:7; 9:31; 12:24; 16:5; 19:20) an indication of the division of Acts into six panels. There are, however, other summaries which make this division questionable. Recognizing the significance of the Jerusalem council some scholars divide Acts into two parts (1:1–15:35; 15:36–28:31).

Jesus' commission to the disciples in Acts 1:8 is considered a key to the development of the narrative in Acts. Its geographical outline shows how this commission is fulfilled in Jerusalem (1:1–5:42), in Judea and Samaria (6:1–12:25), and to the end of the earth (13:1–28:31).

Following the dedication to Theophilus and a summary of the first book (1:1–2), the prologue provides a background to the narrative of Acts by recalling the final events recounted in the gospel, the appearances, instruction and promise of the Risen Jesus to the disciples. Jesus' response to the disciples' question about the restoration of Israel focuses on what their concern should be. The promise of receiving power when the Holy Spirit comes upon them is coupled with a commission to be witnesses (1:8). After the brief and vivid portrayal of Jesus' ascension, the heavenly messengers challenge the disciples to shift their attention from future concern to present responsibility (1:9–11).

The Community of Believers in Jerusalem. The story of the believers properly begins after the ascension with the return of the disciples to Jerusalem. The community of the eleven, introduced by name, with Mary, the mother of Jesus, the women and the brothers of Jesus, stay in the upper room and devote themselves to prayer (1:12–14). Peter takes the initiative as the leader of the group in the choice of a replacement for Judas Iscariot. The Twelve is reconstituted upon the election of Matthias (1:15–26). In fulfillment of Jesus' promise, the disciples receive the gift of the Holy Spirit on the day of Pentecost. Speaking in tongues, the visible manifestation of this gift, draws reactions of wonder, amazement, doubt and mockery from the crowd. Peter addresses the people and interprets the event in the light of Jesus' resurrection. His proclamation and call to repentance brings about the conversion of three thousand people (2:1–41). The remarkable increase in the number of believers is followed by a summary description of the life of the community (2:42–47). The communal life of the believers is characterized not only by prayer but also by the teaching of the apostles, the fellowship and the breaking of bread. Community solidarity is expressed in the sharing of meals and of possessions. The dynamic impact of the reception of the Holy Spirit is vividly illustrated. From an inconspicuous group gathered in the upper room, the believers now gather in the temple. They begin to witness to Jesus through their communal life and through the signs and wonders of the apostles. The witness of Peter and John is dramatically portrayed in the events that follow (3:1–4:22). The healing of the lame in the name of Jesus (3:1–10) provides the occasion for Peter's proclamation. His teaching in the temple draws the attention of the temple authorities. Peter and John are arrested, imprisoned and brought to trial. The trial becomes another opportunity for Peter to bear witness to Jesus (4:8–12.19–20). They are released without punishment after being warned no longer to speak or teach in the name of Jesus (4:17). Peter and John return to the community and their prayer for boldness is granted with a new outpouring of the Spirit (4:23–30).

A second portrait of the community of Jerusalem (4:32–35) signals a stage in the development of the community. The focus is on the unity of heart and soul of the community manifested in the sharing of possessions. The apostles continue their witness to the resurrection of the Lord (4:33) and take on the role of administrator and distributor of community property. Barnabas' sale of his property is a positive example of the practice of communion of goods. It is done according to the spirit of the community (4:36–37) whereas the act of Ananias and Sapphira is tainted with dishonesty (5:1–11). Their deceit threatens the unity of the community and the credibility of the apostles. Both incur death as punishment when they persist in their deceit even after Peter confronts them. The story of Ananias and Sapphira provides a transition from the theme of communion of goods to the wonders and signs of the apostles, the focus of the third description of the community of Jerusalem (5:12–16). This is followed by another dramatic presentation that parallels the plot of Acts 4. This time, not only Peter and John, but all the apostles arouse the jealousy and opposition of the high priest and the Sadducean party. They are arrested but are miraculously released by an angel. They are found by their captors in the morning teaching in the temple, are again arrested and then brought to trial (5:17–25). The scene before the council becomes another opportunity to bear witness (5:29–32). Heeding Gamaliel's advice, the council releases the apostles after being beaten and charged not to speak in the name of Jesus (5:33–40). The episode ends with the picture of the apostles joyfully and boldly proclaiming Jesus as the Christ (5:42).

Judea and Samaria. The transition from Jerusalem to Judea and Samaria is provided in the story of the Hebrew and Hellenist widows, the institution of the seven deacons and the ministry of Stephen (6:1–8:1). The increase of the disciples also leads to a problem. A conflict ensues because of the neglect of the Hellenist widows in the daily distribution. This is solved by the community through the institution of the seven deacons among whom are Stephen and Philip (6:1–7). Stephen and Philip will be instrumental in the spread of the mission to Judea and Samaria. Stephen's preaching before the council leads to his martyrdom and the disciples are scattered because of the persecution that follows (6:8–8:3; 11:19–21). The scattered disciples continue to preach the word. Philip converts many in Samaria through his preaching and miracles (8:4–13) and baptizes an Ethiopian eunuch (8:26–40). The Samaritan converts receive the Holy Spirit when Peter and John, who are sent by the Jerusalem community, lay their hands on them.

Another significant development is the conversion of a persecutor, Saul, who becomes an active preacher after his conversion (9:1–22). When his life is threatened, he escapes and comes to Jerusalem. Barnabas brings him to the apostles. Saul continues to preach in the name of the Lord and is sent off to Tarsus when his life is again threatened. Peter, on the other hand, is also drawing converts in Lydda, Sharon and Joppa (9:32–43).

To the end of the Earth. The conversion of Cornelius (10:1–49) is an interesting development because it opens the way for the mission to the Gentiles. The story is narrated three times (11:1–18; 15:7–11.14) for emphasis like the threefold repetition of the summary description of the Jerusalem community (2:42–47; 4:32–35; 5:12–16) and the conversion of Saul (9:1–22; 22:1–21; 26:1–23). The story shows how God directs the progress of the Christian movement and how Peter becomes instrumental in the conversion of the first Gentile. The event leads to a conflict as Peter is questioned by the circumcision party. Peter's report to the Jerusalem community silences the objection (11:1–18). The episode is followed by a reference to the martyrdom of Stephen that results in the geographical spread of the Christian message and the formation and growth of the community in Antioch where the believers are first called Christians (11:19–26). The role of Barnabas and Saul in this community and the relation of this community to Jerusalem are also noted (11:27–30). The Jerusalem community experiences famine and persecution. James is killed and Peter is arrested. Peter is then miraculously delivered from prison and justice is served when Herod dies (12:1–23).

Missionary expansion begins with the sending (13:1–3) of Barnabas and Saul, who becomes known as Paul (13:9). They carry the word of the Lord to Asia Minor (13:4–14:26) and returning to Antioch, they report missionary success among the Gentiles. The issue of circumcision and the observance of the Mosaic law raised by some men from Jerusalem is resolved in a meeting in Jerusalem. After Peter, Barnabas and Paul narrate what God has done through them among the Gentiles (15:6–12), James gives his judgment. The decision not to require the Gentile converts to be circumcised is accepted. Judas and Silas are chosen to go to Antioch with Barnabas and Paul and deliver the letter giving the minimum dietary and moral requirements for Gentile converts (15:22–29). This decision gives a greater impetus to the Gentile mission. Barnabas and Paul spend some time in Antioch before embarking in another missionary journey. But a conflict between the two over John Mark results in their separation (15:36–40). Paul takes Silas with him and from this point onward, he emerges as an independent missionary and the main character in the narrative of Acts. Directed by the Spirit (16:6–10), he brings the Christian message beyond Asia Minor to Greece (15:40–18:22). In his third mission journey (18:23–21:16), Paul pays a visit to some of the communities he founded. After winning converts in Ephesus, he heads towards Jerusalem (20:16.22; 21:17). When he reaches Jerusalem and goes to the temple, he is arrested and imprisoned. When he invokes his Roman citizenship and appeals to Roman justice, he is brought to Caesarea before governor Feliz (21:17–26:32). Paul stays two years in prison until Felix is succeeded by Porcius Festus. During the trial, Paul makes an appeal to Caesar (25:11) which is granted by Festus. When King Agrippa arrives in Caesarea to welcome Festus, the latter lays Paul's case before the king. King Agrippa declares to Festus Paul's innocence (26:10–32) but his appeal to Caesar ironically becomes the obstacle to setting him free. Paul, thus, sails to Rome as a prisoner (27:1–28:16). The story of Acts ends with Paul in house custody in Rome still proclaiming his witness to Jesus Christ and the kingdom of God.

Bibliography: C. K. BARRETT, *A Critical and Exegetical Commentary on the Acts of the Apostles.* Vol. 1, *Preliminary Introduction and Commentary on Acts I–XIV* (Edinburgh 1994). Vol 2, *Introduction and Commentary on Acts XV–XXVIII* (Edinburgh 1998). F. F. BRUCE, *The Acts of the Apostles. The Greek Text with Introduction and Commentary,* 3d ed. (Grand Rapids, MI 1990). J. D. G. DUNN, *The Acts of the Apostles* (Peterborough 1996). J. DUPONT, *Nouvelles etudes sur les Actes des Apotres* (Paris 1984). J. A. FITZMYER, *The Acts of the Apostles: A New Translation with Introduction and Commentary* (New York 1998). E. HAENCHEN, *The Acts of the Apostles: A Commentary* (Oxford 1971). L. T. JOHNSON, *The Acts of the Apostles* (Collegeville 1992). G. LUDEMANN, *Early Christianity according to the Traditions in Acts: A Commentary* (Minneapolis 1987). J. B. POLHILL, *Acts* (The New American Commentary, vol. 26. Nashville, Tennessee 1992). C. H. TALBERT, *Reading Acts. A Literary and Theological Commentary on the Acts of the Apostles* (New York 1997). R. C. TANNEHILL, *The Narrative Unity of Luke-Acts. A Literary Interpretation,* Vol. 2, *The Acts of the Apostles* (Minneapolis 1990). J. VERHEYDEN, *The Unity of Luke-Acts* (Bibliotheca ephemeridum theologicarum lovaniensium, 142. Leuven 1999). B. WITHERINGTON, *The Acts of the Apostles. A Socio-rhetorical Commentary* (Grand Rapids, MI 1998).

[S. MARIA ANICIA BATION CO]

ACTS OF THE MARTYRS

The official court records of the trials of early Christians for their faith. Taken in a broader sense, the Acts of the Martyrs, or *Acta Martyrum,* include all the varied accounts (*acta, gesta, passiones, martyria,* and *legenda*) of the arrest, interrogation, condemnation, execution, and burial of the martyrs of the first centuries. These narratives make up an extensive and important body of Christian literature, but are of unequal value, ranging from authentic accounts of trustworthy eyewitnesses to complete fictions, and even forgeries. The Bollandist H. DELEHAYE has divided the Acts into six categories accepted by other hagiographers, even though differences of opinion exist about the value of any particular Acts.

"The Martyrdom of Saint Sebastian," painting by Antonio and Piero del Pollaiuolo, c. 1475, National Gallery, London. (© National Gallery Collection; By kind permission of the Trustees of the National Gallery, London/CORBIS)

Christian martyrs in the Circus Maximus, after a painting by Jean Leon. Gerome. (The Bettmann Archive)

Acta, or Court Proceedings. In a Roman criminal court, the questions asked by the judge and the responses of the defendants, along with the official verdict, were taken down in shorthand by professional notaries (*notarii, exceptores, or censuales*). These notes were then transcribed in regular characters and deposited in the archives (*instrumentum provinciae*) where they could be consulted years, and even decades, later as is attested by Eusebius (*Ecclesiastical History* 5.18.9; 7.11.6), St. Augustine (*Contra Cresconium* 3.70), St. Jerome (*Adv. Rufinum* 2.3), and Lydus (*De magistratibus populi Romani* 3.29). Copies of the proceedings could be obtained for private circulation and were used for public reading in the liturgy. Within less than a year after Cyprian's first interrogation at Carthage the *acta proconsulis* were in the hands of confessors in the mines of Numidia (Cyprian, *Epistles* 77.2). The earliest of the authentic Acts are those of JUSTIN MARTYR and his six companions, executed at Rome *c.* 164 by order of Junius Rusticus, prefect of the city. The *Acta Martyrum Scillitanorum* report the trial and condemnation of 12 Christians from Scilli on July 17, 180, by the proconsul Saturninus at Carthage.

The *Proconsular Acts of Cyprian,* one of the most important and moving documents of the early Church, contains a transcript of his first trial in 257; another of his second the following year; and a description by an eye-witness of his execution on Sept. 14, 258. The *Acts of Fructuosus* preserve the protocol of the trial of the bishop and his two deacons, Augurius and Eulogius, along with a description of their deaths by fire (Jan. 21, 259). Other authentic Acts from the time of Diocletian are those of Maximilianus, who was executed at Theveste in Numidia in 295 for refusing to enter military service, and of the centurion Marcellus, beheaded at Tangier in Mauretania in 298 for throwing away his military belt. A number of other Acts are occasionally placed in this first category, but in general they seem to be interpolated or to be of somewhat doubtful authenticity.

Passiones and Martyria. Accounts of eyewitnesses or well-informed contemporaries are frequently called *passiones* in Latin and in Greek *martyria.* They were written by Christians and are of a more personal and literary character than the *acta.* The earliest of these writings is the *Martyrdom of POLYCARP* of Smyrna, composed by a certain Marcion and sent in the name of the Church of Smyrna to the Christian community at Philomelium in Greater Phrygia. These Acts describe the arrest, trial, and heroic death of the aged bishop in the arena at Smyrna, most likely on Feb. 22, 156. Another report of this same type is the encyclical letter preserved by Eusebius (*Ecclesiastical History* 5.1.1–2.7), sent by the Churches of Lyons and Vienne to the Churches in Asia and Phrygia, describing the persecution of the Christians at Lyons in 177. Among the numerous victims was Bishop Pothinus ''over ninety years of age''; Blandina, a slave girl; Sanctus, a deacon of Vienne; and Ponticus, a boy of 15. This famous letter, the first important document of Gallic Christianity, may have been composed by St. IRENAEUS OF LYONS, disciple of Polycarp and successor of Pothinus. The *Passio SS. Perpetuae et Felicitatis* gives an engaging account of the imprisonment and death in the amphitheater at Carthage on March 7, 202, of Saturus Saturninus, Revocatus, and two young women, a slave Felicitas and her mistress, Vibia Perpetua, 22 years of age, ''well born, liberally educated, honorably married, having father and mother and two brothers, one like herself a catechumen, and an infant son at her breast.'' The longest portion of the *passio* (ch. 3–10) was written by Perpetua herself, and another section, by Saturus, (ch. 11–13) while they were waiting execution. The two documents were given an introduction and conclusion describing the deaths of the saints by a contemporary of considerable literary talent, possibly TERTULLIAN.

The *Acts of SS. Carpus, Papylus, and Agathonice* is a description of the trial and deaths of three saints at Pergamum under Marcus Aurelius and Lucius Verus (A.D. 161–169) or, more likely, during the persecution of Decius (250–251). A similar chronological problem is connected with the death of Pionius at Smyrna. His *passio* was taken by an unskilled editor from three sources: a memorial left by Pionius himself or one of his companions, and two official interrogations. The structural and ideological resemblances between the *passio* of Marion and James, that of Montanus and Lucius, who suffered in Africa (*c.* 259), and that of Perpetua and Felicitas have raised questions regarding their authenticity, but they are probably genuine. The *Acts of Phileas,* Bishop of Thmuis, condemned by Culcianus, Prefect of Egypt, at Alexandria early in the fourth century also belong to this category.

Interpolated Accounts. The third class of martyrs' Acts is much more extensive. It consists of accounts drawn from written documents that have been more or less extensively edited at a later date to suit the purpose of the author. An example of this type of development may be seen in seven different redactions of the *Acts of the Scillitan Martyrs.* Among the pieces in this class are the *passiones* of Maximus, CRISPINA, Irenaeus, Pollio, Euplus, Philip, Quirinus, Julius; of AGAPE and Chionia; of Saturninus, Dativus and their companions, Claudius, Asterius and their companions; and of the Persian martyrs Simeon, Pherbuta, Sadoth, and Bademus. Many of the narratives in the Menology of Symeon Metaphrastes also belong here. Since the mid–19th century, numerous attempts have been made, using both internal and external criteria, to sift the facts from the fiction in these Acts, but the conclusions reached are often uncertain.

Historical and Imaginative Romances. These are late works based on neither written documents nor definite oral traditions. A few facts are set down in an elaborate, imaginary framework. Usually what is historical in these compositions is the saint's name, the date of his feast, and the existence of his shrine. Acts of this type are very numerous. They include those of Vincent, Peter Balsam, George, Cyricus and Julitta, Lucianus and Marcianus, Firmus and Rusticus, and the series of cycles of the Roman *legendarium* that include the martyrdoms of SS. AGNES, CECILIA, HIPPOLYTUS, LAWRENCE, Sixtus, SEBASTIAN, JOHN AND PAUL, and COSMAS AND DAMIAN. Here also belong the Acts of St. Felicitas and her seven sons. The execution of seven martyrs at Rome on July 10 (their feast) is guaranteed by the Philocalian calendar (354); the account of their kinship is probably due to the influence of the Biblical story of the heroic Jewish mother and her seven sons tortured to death by Antiochus the Great (2 Mc 7.1–42).

Imaginative romances were likewise written using the martyr story as a theme. In legends of this type not only are the narrated events fictitious, but the saint's existence has no foundation in fact. The Acts of Didymus and Theodora, of GENESIUS The Comedian who was converted while ridiculing Baptism, and of SS. Barbara and CATHERINE OF ALEXANDRIA are apparently of this category. The Acts of Theodotus of Ancyra were woven about an ancient tale already known to Herodotus (*Hist.* 2.121); and the story of BARLAAM AND JOASAPH, which contains the greater portion of the *Apology* of the second-century ARISTIDES, is essentially a Christian retelling of the ancient Buddha legend from the East. Stories of this type that followed the tradition of the Hellenistic novel were extremely popular in the sixth and seventh centuries. Unfortunately, Christians of later times took these tales for history.

Hagiographical Forgeries. These accounts about the death of martyrs were written for neither the edification nor the amusement of readers, but to deceive them. The *Acts of Paul and Thecla* are the earliest examples of this type. They were composed out of excessive devotion to St. Paul by a priest of Asia who was later deposed for his pains (Tertullian, *De baptismo* 17). Such stories were also fabricated to substantiate the Apostolic founding of Gallic sees; and in most instances it is impossible to determine the real authors of the frauds since the writer may simply be elaborating an already current tale.

Growth of Martyr Literature. Several factors contributed to the growth of martyr literature. There was, first of all, the natural desire to preserve the memory of those who had died for a cause. Jewish counterparts of the Christian Acts are found not only in the Book of Machabees, but also in the martyrdoms of Akiba and Jehuda ben Baba. Pagan parallels existed in the political martyrs of the *Acta Alexandrinorum* and in the trial of Secundus, the Silent Philosopher, at Athens by the Emperor Hadrian. There was an appreciation of the apologetic value of martyrdom as a proof of the divine origin of Christianity (Tertullian, *Apologeticum* 50; Justin, 2 *Apology* 13) and of the theological notion that the martyr was the perfect imitator of Christ in his passion, and there was the edification that could be derived from a reading of the sufferings of the saints.

In Africa, Gaul, and Spain the custom quickly rose of reading in the liturgy the Acts of the martyrs on their feasts. The practice was not introduced at Rome until a much later date. This seems to explain why, with the exception of the account given by Justin Martyr of the condemnation of three Christians by Lollius Urbicus (*c.* 160; 2 *Apology* 2) and the Acts of Justin and his companions, there are no authentic records of the trials and executions of the numerous Roman martyrs. During the centuries following the persecutions, anonymous writers tried to make up for this deficiency. According to a late fifth–century document, the so-called *Decretum Gelasianum* 1 (*Patrologia Latina*, ed. J. P. Migne [Paris 1878–90] 59:171–172), the *gesta sanctorum martyrum* were not read in church at Rome since their authors were unknown and they could be a source of ridicule. Later centuries were less critical; and by the end of the eighth, a martyr's Acts were liturgically read at Rome on his feast (Hadrian I, *Epistolae ad Carolum Regem; Patrologia Latina* 98:1284).

The legendary Acts of the martyrs are historically useful for the knowledge they supply regarding popular beliefs and social, political, and legal institutions during the centuries in which they were composed. The authentic Acts are important for the direct and indirect evidence they afford of practices and beliefs traditional in the early Church: a reverence for Scripture (*Passio SS. Scillitanorum* 12); the preservation of relics (*Acta Procons. Cypriani* 5); infant Baptism (*Martyrdom of Polycarp* 9); martyrdom as a second Baptism (*Passio SS. Perpetuae et Felicitatis* 21; *Passio SS. Jacobi et Mariani* 11); prayers for the souls of the departed (*Passio SS. Perpetuae et Felicitatis* 7–8); devotion to "Mother" Church (*Letter of the Churches of Lyons and Vienne;* in Eusebius,

Ecclesiastical History, 5.2.6–7); the observance of fasts (*Acta SS. Fructuosi, Eulogii et Augurii martyrum* 3), particularly before the reception of the Eucharist (*Passio SS. Jacobi et Mariani* 8); and the essential difference in the veneration shown to Christ and to the saints: "For Him, who is the Son of God, we adore; but the martyrs, we love as disciples and imitators of the Lord" (*Martyrdom of Polycarp* 17). Even more intimately than the arguments of the apologists and the speculations of the Alexandrian theologians, the authentic Acts make contact with our spiritual ancestors, the common Christians called to make a heroic confession. They present the moving spectacle of men and women of every age and every walk of life dying for their faith in the firm hope of attaining everlasting life.

Bibliography: E. C. E. OWEN, ed. and tr., *Some Authentic Acts of the Early Martyrs* (Oxford 1927). H. DELEHAYE, *The Legends of the Saints* tr. D. ATTWATER (New York 1962). H. LECLERCQ, *Dictionnaire d'archéologie chrétienne et de liturgie.* ed. F. CABROL, H. LECLERCQ and H. I. MARROU (Paris 1907–53) 1.1:373–446. A. HAMMAN, *Lexikon für Theologie und Kirche,* ed. J. HOFER and K. RAHNER (Freiberg 1957–65) 7:133–134. W. H. C. FREND, *Martyrdom and Persecution in the Early Church* (Oxford 1965). G. A. BISBEE, *Pre-Decian Acts of Martyrs and Commentarii* (Philadelphia 1988).

[M. J. COSTELLOE]

ACUÑA, CRISTÓBAL DE

Spanish Jesuit missionary, explorer of the Amazon; b. Burgos, 1597; d. Lima, Peru, Jan. 14, 1670. He entered the Jesuit Society in 1612 and made his profession in 1634. In 1630 he was the first rector of the College of Cuenca (Ecuador), the base for the Jesuit mission of Maynas in the upper Amazon. Acuña was appointed by the royal court to take part in a scientific expedition to the Amazon River because he had "journeyed through almost all Provinces of Peru, Quito, Chile, Tucumán, and Paraguay, including the coast of Brazil, La Plata, and Pará," according to reports from his superior, Francisco Fuentes. Acuña and a companion, Father Andrés de Artieda, left Quito on Feb. 16, 1639, investigating the characteristics of the Amazon River, native population, products, and various other items of interest. They arrived in Pará Dec. 12, 1639, and in March 1640 both returned to Spain. In Madrid Acuña gave an account of his observations to Philip IV and the Council of the Indies, and requested permission and assistance to carry out further evangelization along the great river. A result of his exploration was the *Nuevo descubrimiento del Gran Río de las Amazonas* (Madrid 1641), immediately translated into several languages. With the political separation of Portugal from Spain in 1640, projects of colonization and missionary work came to a standstill, and Acuña returned to South America in 1644. He stayed in the New Kingdom of Granada and Quito, until he was persuaded to return to Lima in 1659.

Bibliography: J. JOUANEN, *Historia de la Compañía de Jesús en la antigua provincia de Quito, 1570–1774,* 2 v. (Quito 1941–43). E. TORRES SALDAMANDO, *Los antiguos Jesuítas del Perú* (Lima 1882).

[F. MATEOS]

AD BESTIAS

Beast hunts and fights were a favorite entertainment at Rome from the middle of the 2d century B.C. and subsequently throughout the cities of the Roman world. Gladiators—who were slaves—and criminals were required to fight various kinds of ferocious wild animals in the amphitheater. The gladiators often survived, but criminals, who were under the formal sentence, *datio* or *damnatio ad bestias,* were doomed to die in the arena. This criminal sentence was imposed on men guilty of tampering with coinage, of parricide, murder, or treason, and to some extent also on prisoners of war. In the age of the persecutions, Christians, who were accused of treason for not worshiping the emperor, were often condemned *ad bestias,* as is evident from numerous references to this form of punishment in the passions of the martyrs and in the works of early Christian writers. As the Christians were unpopular, the cry, *Christiani ad leones,* was often raised by spectators. Contrary, however, to the modern widespread view, the majority of the early Christian martyrs did not perish in the arena, but were executed by the sword.

Bibliography: H. LECLERCQ, *Dictionnaire d'archéologie chrétienne et de liturgie,* ed. F. CABROL H. LECLERQ and H. I. MARROU (Paris 1907–53) 1:449–462, with full presentation of the literary, epigraphical, and archeological evidence. A. PILLET, *Étude sur la ''damnatio ad bestias''* (Lille 1902).

[M. R. P. MCGUIRE]

AD LIMINA VISIT

(*Visitatio ad limina apostolorum*) Refers to the periodic visit to Rome required of each residential bishop (CIC c. 400; *Pastor bonus,* no. 28) and military vicar approved by apostolic authority (S.C. Consist., Feb. 28, 1959, AAS 51:272). This visit is directly tied to the quinquennial report that is required of each residential bishop every five years in c. 399, as the visit is to be made the same year as that in which the report is submitted (c. 400 & sect.1). The 1983 Code of Canon Law has made the bishop's obligation to make the *ad limina* visit personal-

ly, and only if he is impeded may he satisfy the obligation through another, i.e. his coadjutor, the auxiliary, or a suitable priest who resides in the diocese (c. 400 & sect. 2). Since auxiliary and other titular bishops are not the primary pastors of a particular church and have no quinquennial report to make, they are not held to the *ad limina* visit. This visit has a sacred meaning, since ''the bishops with religious veneration pay a visit to the tombs of Peter and Paul.'' It has a personal meaning, ''because each individual bishop meets the successor of Peter and talks to him face to face,'' and it has a curial meaning, that is a ''hallmark of community, because the bishops enter into conversation with the moderators of the dicasteries, councils, and offices of the Roman Curia'' (Appendix 1, no. 6, of *Pastor bonus*). The purpose of the visit, for the bishops, is ''the strengthening of their own responsibility as successors of the Apostles and of their hierarchical communion with the Successor of Peter'' (Congregation for Bishops, ''Directory for the 'ad limina' visit,'' in *L'Osservatore Romano,* July 11, 1988). The *ad limina* visit has changed considerably under the pontificate of John Paul II from a canonical formality into a genuine exercise of the pope's care for all the Churches. As stated in the ''Directory for the 'ad limina' visit,'' it is ''an important moment in the exercise of the Holy Father's pastoral ministry,'' because he receives the bishops and discusses personally with them their questions concerning ''their ecclesial mission.'' Though there is no concrete date in which the visits started, ''There are, however, numerous testimonies which speak of its existence from the 4th century'' (Orti, Accompanying Historico-Juridical Notes to the ''Directory for the 'ad limina' visit'').

[T. C. KELLY]

AD MAJOREM DEI GLORIAM (A.M.D.G.)

Often taken to be the sign manual of the Society of Jesus from its frequent use in the writings of St. IGNATIUS OF LOYOLA, the founder. Father Brou says: ''The haunting idea which summons a formula to the tip of a writer's pen reveals the dominant thought of his soul: in the *Constitutions* alone, St. Ignatius makes mention of the greater glory of God 259 times, almost once for every page.'' Another writer, Father Lawlor, says: ''I have made the count twice over, and the truth is that Ignatius uses the formula about 135 times . . . locutions such as 'ad majus servitium Dei,' 'ad majus Dei obsequium,' etc., are repeated about 157 times in the *Constitutions.*'' Probably the most dramatic presentation of the formula is seen in the silver statue, modeled in Rome by Francisco de Ver-

Francis Cardinal Spellman meets with Pope Pius XII in Rome, 1954. (© Bettmann/CORBIS)

gara and erected in 1741 as an *ex voto* over the high altar in the Basilica of St. Ignatius at Loyola. The saint is represented bearing a large open book on his left forearm, and pointing with his right hand to the formula inscribed across both pages. It can be safely assumed that in St. Ignatius's vocabulary, the words *obsequium, servitium,* and *gloria Dei* are practically synonymous, and that consequently the idea occurs 1,000 times or more, if to the *Constitutions* we add the occurrences in the 12 volumes of his letters. Most interpreters agree that the dynamic word is the qualifier *Majorem.*

Bibliography: A. BROU, *The Ignatian Way to God,* tr. W. J. YOUNG (Milwaukee 1952). F. X. LAWLOR, ''The Doctrine of Grace in the *Spiritual Exercises,*'' *Theological Studies* 3 (1942) 513–532. H. RAHNER, *Lexikon für Theologie und Kirche,* ed. J. HOFER and K. RAHNER (Freiburg 1957–65) 1:149.

[W. J. YOUNG]

AD PERENNIS VITAE FONTEM

The first line of the *De gaudio paradisi,* the first part of a rhythmical eschatological tetralogy traditionally ascribed to PETER DAMIAN. Its meter is accentual trochaic tetrameter, maintained flawlessly throughout the 20 three-lined strophes of this rhythm on the joys of paradise, and continued in the 35 additional strophes on death, judgment, and hell. The *Ad perennis* has received several excellent translations into English. Abounding in Biblical imagery, the poem captures the longing of the soul to be released from the bonds of earth to abide in the heavenly Jerusalem, especially in the unending possession of the Source of life itself. Damian's authorship is questioned, not only because of a doubt in the MS ascription in Vat. lat. 3797, fol. 362–363, and of the admittedly dubious claim of Peter the Deacon of Monte Cassino that it was written by Alberic of Monte Cassino, but for the further reason that its meter seems to be foreign to that appearing in the poetic works of Damian that have been definitely authenticated.

Bibliography: *Analecta Hymnica* 48:66–67. O. J. BLUM, "Alberic of Monte Cassino . . . ," *Traditio* 12 (1956) 87–148, esp. 128–130. S. A. HURLBUT, *The Song of St. Peter Damiani* (Washington 1928). F. J. E. RABY, *A History of Christian-Latin Poetry* (Oxford 1953) 250–256; *A History of Secular Latin Poetry in the Middle Ages* (Oxford 1957)1:369–374. J. JULIAN, ed., *A Dictionary of Hymnology* (London 1907) 1:13. J. LECLERCQ, *Revue Bénédectine* 67 (1957) 151–174. P. MEYVAERT, *ibid.*, 175–181. K. REINDEL, *ibid.*, 182–189. J. SZÖVÉRFFY, *Die Annalen der lateinischen Hymnendichtung* (Berlin 1964–65) 1:391–397.

[O. J. BLUM]

AD REGIAS AGNI DAPES

An Ambrosian hymn by an unknown author; it was used for Vespers on the Saturday after Easter and subsequent Sundays and ferials until the feast of the Ascension. The Roman Breviary had an earlier version, *Ad coenam agni providi,* which seemed to reflect the Ambrosian Milanese thought of the sixth century or earlier. It may very well be the work of NICETAS OF REMESIANA, a near contemporary of St. Ambrose. When this hymn was included in the 1632 reform of the Roman Breviary, it lost in its revision much of the rhythm of the primitive text, only three original lines being retained unchanged. The hymn is the song of a people newly redeemed, glorying in the triumph of their Leader, who invites them to a banquet celebration. As the Israelites were spared by the avenging angel (Ex 12.23) and as they passed miraculously through the Red Sea (Ex 14.22–23), so Christ has become Pasch and Victim (1 Cor 5.7–8) to break the bonds of Satan and offer the faithful the trophies of the spirit, especially joy.

Bibliography: H. A. DANIEL, *Thesaurus hymnologicus,* 5 v. (Halle-Leipzig 1841–56) 1:88, text. *Analecta hymnica* 51:87. F. J. E. RABY, *A History of Christian-Latin Poetry* (Oxford 1953) 41. J. CONNELLY, *Hymns of the Roman Liturgy* (Westminster MD 1957) 140–143.

[M. M. BEYENKA]

AD SANCTAM BEATI PETRI SEDEM

A bull of Alexander VII dated Oct. 16, 1656, that states precisely that the five propositions condemned in 1653 by the bull CUM OCCASIONE of Innocent X came from C. JANSEN and that they had been condemned in the sense in which Jansen understood them. The pope recalled that he had, while cardinal, taken part in the commissions held in 1653 and that he had thus formed a personal opinion on the subject. Nevertheless, in Jansenist circles there was a persistent rumor that, in order to obtain this bull, their adversaries had showed the pope a falsified copy of AUGUSTINUS into which had been introduced the last four propositions, which were not there expressed in proper terms. For somewhat obscure reasons, the bull *Ad sanctam* was held in reserve for quite a long time, and it was not until March 2, 1657, that the nuncio Piccolomini sent it to Louis XIV. Cardinal Mazarin had it immediately accepted by the Assembly of the Clergy, and in the following November, not without some difficulty, by parliament.

Bibliography: H. DENZINGER, *Enchiridion symbolorum*, ed. A SCHÖNMETZER (Freiburg 1963) 2010–12.

[L. J. COGNET]

AD TUENDAM FIDEM

Apostolic letter, "To Protect the Faith," issued *motu proprio* by Pope John Paul II, May 28, 1998, adding to the codes of canon law for the Latin and the Eastern churches. The additions add a third distinction in the levels of teaching of the Magisterium, stipulate the adherence this teaching requires and the penalties to be imposed for violation, thereby making the adjusted canons reflective of the levels of teaching set out in the Profession of Faith and Oath of Fidelity issued by the Congregation for the Doctrine of the Faith in 1989.

The first paragraph of the *motu proprio* explicitly states that it is written in response to concern for errors, especially "from among those dedicated to the various disciplines of sacred theology" (Introduction). Following some comments on the history of the Nicene-Constantinopolitan Creed as a summation of the faith, the document turns to an explanation of the 1989 Profession of Faith and Oath of Fidelity, which is composed of not only the Creed but also three paragraphs "intended to describe the truths of the Catholic faith" (no. 2). The text continues with an explanation of these three paragraphs, pointing out that while the levels of teaching described in the first and third paragraphs are provided for in the codes of canon law, the level of teaching mentioned in the second paragraph is not. *Ad tuendam fidem* then supplies for this omission since the level of teaching omitted illustrates "the Divine Spirit's particular inspiration for the Church's deeper understanding of a truth concerning faith and morals, with which they are connected either for historical reasons or by a logical relationship" (no. 3).

The levels of teaching mentioned in the Profession of Faith and Oath of Fidelity and already provided for in the law are found in canons 750, §1, and 752 of the Latin code, and canons 598 and 599 of the Eastern code. Patterned closely on the wording of the Profession of Faith, the *motu proprio* adds the following paragraph to the law:

Each and every thing which is proposed definitively by the magisterium of the Church concerning the doctrine of faith and morals, that is, each and every thing which is required to safeguard reverently and to expound faithfully the same deposit of faith, is also to be firmly embraced and retained; therefore, one who rejects those propositions which are to be held definitively is opposed to the doctrine of the Catholic Church. (Translation from Code of Canon Law: Latin English Edition, rev. ed. [Washington: Canon Law Society of America, 1998] 247.)

The same text is added to the Code of Canon Law for the Eastern Churches. A cross reference to canon 1371 of the Latin code stipulates that violations of this canon are met with a ''just penalty.''

Questions surrounding this document focus on the meaning of the word ''definitive'' as that is applied to official teaching, and also on which teachings fall into this second category of teaching rather than the third. When issued, the *motu proprio* was accompanied by a doctrinal commentary issued by the Congregation for the Doctrine of the Faith. The commentary states that ''the correct explanation'' of the three final paragraphs of the Profession of Faith and Oath of Fidelity deserve ''a clear presentation, so that their authentic meaning, as given by the Church's Magisterium, will be well understood, received and integrally preserved.''

Bibliography: For the text of *Ad tuendum fidem,* see: *Acta Apostolicae Sedis* 90 (1998) 457–461 (Latin); *Origins* 28, no. 8 (16 July 1998) 113–116 (English); *The Pope Speaks* 43 (1998) 327–330 (English).

[E. RINERE]

ADALAR, ST.

Priest and martyr, also known as Adalher; d. Dokkum, Netherlands, June 5, 754. He was a companion of St. BONIFACE and shared the martyrdom of that great missionary in Frisia. Little more is known of him, but there is an unsubstantiated tradition that he was the first bishop of Erfurt, consecrated by Boniface himself in 741. The *Acta sanctorum,* however, lists him as only a priest in its account of Boniface's last days. Adalar's relics were taken to Erfurt *c.* 756, and he was honored by special veneration in that city during the Middle Ages. His relics, along with those of St. EOBAN, rediscovered during the construction of a new church in 1154, were translated, and are now in the Erfurt cathedral.

Feast (of translation): April 20.

Bibliography: *Acta Sanctorum* June 1:450. M. OPPERMANN, *Der hl. Adelarius, Erfurts erster und einziger Bischof* (Paderborn 1897). A. M.. ZIMMERMANN, *Kalendarium Benedictinum: Die Heiligen und Seligen des Benediktinerorderns und seiner Zweige,* 4 v. (Metten 1933–38) 2:78–80. A. BIGELMAIR, ''Die Gründung der mitteldeutschen Bistümer,'' in *Sankt Bonifatius: Gedenkgabe z. 1200. Todestag* (Fulda 1954) 247–287, esp. 279. U. TURCK, *Lexikon für Theologie und Kirche,* ed. J. HOFER and K. RAHNER, 10 v. (2d, new ed. Freiburg 1957–65) 1:119.

[B. J. COMASKEY]

ADALARD, ST.

Carolingian abbot of Corbie, author (known also as Adalhard of Corbie); b. *c.* 750; d. January 2, 826. The grandson of CHARLES MARTEL and the nephew of King PEPIN III, Adalard was educated at the Frankish court. At the age of 20, in protest over CHARLEMAGNE's repudiation of his wife, the daughter of the Lombard king DESIDERIUS, Adalard left the court and entered the Benedictine monastery of Corbie. But for ascetic-monastic, and perhaps, dynastic reasons he soon transferred to Monte Cassino. Later, probably *c.* 780, the monks of Corbie in conjunction with Charlemagne himself brought Adalard back to the Frankish kingdom and made him abbot at Corbie. Thenceforth Adalard, himself an important representative of the CAROLINGIAN RENAISSANCE, was in active intellectual contact with PAUL THE DEACON, ALCUIN, ANGILBERT OF SAINT-RIQUIER and others, and was reputed to be one of the more influential advisers of Charlemagne. In 809 and 810 Adalard was in Rome on the emperor's business and met with Pope LEO III to consider the differences between Rome and the Franks on the filioque question. Possibly chief minister of the young King Pepin of Italy even at this time, Adalard was the tutor of Pepin's son Bernard, and was Charlemagne's *missus* to the Lombard Kingdom from 811 to 814, the year he was banished by Emperor LOUIS THE PIOUS for unknown reasons (perhaps at the instigation of BENEDICT OF ANIANE). He was not recalled from the island monastery of Noirmoutier until 821. Thenceforth he was active in the reorganization of his Abbey of Corbie, in founding (with WALA) the new Abbey of Corvey in Saxony, and as adviser to Louis the Pious on questions of ecclesiastical policy (e.g., his penance at Attigny, 822). As monk and abbot, Adalard enjoyed great prestige (whence his sobriquet ''Antonius''), but he preserved some practices of the monastic *regula mixta* and came out, sometimes rather sharply, against Benedict of Aniane. His remains were elevated Oct. 10, 1040; since then he has been locally venerated as a saint. Adalard's writings include *De ordine palatii,* now lost [but see M. Prou in *Bibl. de l'École des Hautes Etudes* 85 (Paris 1885) and *Monumenta Germaniae Historica: Capitularia* 2:517–530]. His *De ratione lunae paschalis* is also lost (cf.

Monumenta Germaniae Historica: Epistolae 4:566.9 and Flodoard of Reims in *Monumenta Germaniae Historica: Scriptores* 13:531). Extant are Adalard's *Statuta seu brevis Corbeiensis monasterii* [ed. J. Semmler, Corpus Consuetudinum Monasticarum 1 (Siegburg 1963) 355–408] and his *Capitula . . . de admonitionibus in congregatione* (ed. J. Semmler, *ibid.* 408–418).

Feast: Jan. 2

Bibliography: *Vita* by PASCHASIUS RADBERTUS, *Patrologia Latina* 120:1507–56; *Charlemagne's cousins: contemporary lives of Adalard and Wala,* tr. A. CABANISS (Syracuse, N.Y. 1967). *Vita II* and Miracles, J. MABILLON, *Acta sanctorum ordinis S. Benedicti* 5:289–355. B. KASTEN, *Adalhard von Corbie* (Düsseldorf 1986). H. PELTIER, *Adalhard, abbé de Corbie* (Amiens 1969). S. ABEL and B. VON SIMSON, *Jahrbücher des fränkischen Reiches unter Karl dem Grossen,* 2 v. (v.1 2d ed. Leipzig 1883–88), *passim.* B. VON SIMSON, *Jahrbücher des fränkischen Reiches unter Ludwig dem Frommen,* 2 v. (Leipzig 1874–76), *passim.* J.L. BAUDOT and L. CHAUSSIN, *Vies des saints et des bien-heureux selon l'ordre du calendrier avec l'historique des fêtes* 1:35–38. D. A. BULLOUGH, "*Baiuli* in the Carolingian Regnum Langobardorum and the Career of Abbot Waldo," *EngHistRev* 77 (1962) 625–637. J. SCHMIDT, *Hinkmars De ordine palatii und seine Quellen* (Diss. Frankfurt 1962). A. E. VERHULST and J. SEMMLER, "Les Status d'Adalhard de Corbie de l'an 822," *Moyen-âge* 68 (1962) 91–123, 233–269. L. WEINRICH, *Wala: Graf, Mönch und Rebell* (Lübeck 1963). H. PELTIER and H. WIESEMEYER, in *Corbie, abbaye royale* (Lille 1963) 61–94, 105–133. J. SEMMLER, "Die Beschlüsse des Aachener Konzils im Jahre 816," *ZKirchgesch* 74 (1963) 15–82, esp. 76–82. C. BRÜHL, "Hinkmariana," Deutsch v.1 (Düsseldorf 1965) 81.

[J. SEMMLER]

ADALBALD OF OSTREVAND, ST.

Nobleman; d. near Perigueux in Aquitaine, *c.* 650. Information about Adalbald of Ostrevand is mainly derived from the ninth-century *Life of St. Rictrude* by Hucbald of Saint-Amand (*Acta Sanctorum* May 3:81–89). It relates that Adalbald was the grandson of St. Gertrude of Hamage, and the husband of St. Rictrude, by whom he had four children. He was the brother-in-law of St. Bertha, and friend of St. Amandus, the Apostle of Belgium, with whom he founded the abbey of Marchiennes in Flanders. He had been very active in the court of Dagobert I. Vindictive in-laws assassinated him.

Feast: Feb. 2.

Bibliography: L. VAN DER ESSEN, *Étude . . . saints merovingiens* (Louvain 1907). J. L. BAUDOT and L. CHAUSSIN, *Vies des saints et des bienhereux selon l'ordre du calendrier avec l'historique des fêtes* (Paris 1935–56) 2:44–46. A. BUTLER, *The Lives of the Saints* (New York 1956) 1:236.

[B. L. MARTHALER]

ADALBERO OF AUGSBURG, BL.

Bishop; d. April 28, 909. He was highly regarded for his great erudition and his proficiency in liturgical chant, and through his zeal for regular observance the Abbey of LORSCH became a model of monastic discipline under his guidance. He was instrumental in obtaining royal favors for the monastery of SANKT GALLEN, with which he maintained close spiritual ties. Little is known of his activity while bishop of Augsburg from 887 to 909. REGINO OF PRÜM sent his *Chronicon* (*Monumenta Germaniae Scriptores* 1:543–612) to Adalbero for approval and correction where such might seem necessary to the bishop. This prominent churchman supervised the education of Louis the Child (d. 911), the last of the CAROLINGIAN dynasty to rule in Germany, and was his trusted adviser and loyal supporter. The tomb of Adalbero is in the church of St. Afra in Augsburg.

Feast: Oct. 9.

Bibliography: L. BOITEUX, *Dictionnaire d'histoire et de géographie ecclésiastiques,* ed. A. BAUDRILLART (Paris 1912–) 2:429–430. J. L. BAUDOT and L. CHAUSSIN, *Vies des saints et des bienheueux selon l'ordre du calendrier avec l'historique des fêtes,* ed. by The Benedictines of Paris, 12 v. (Paris 1935–56) 10:252–253. F. ZOEPFL, *Neue deutsche Biographie* (Berlin 1953–) 1:39–40; *Lexikon für Theologie und Kirche,* ed. J. HOFER and K. RAHNER, 10 v. (2d, new ed. Freiburg 1957–65) 1:119. J. SZÖVÉRFFY, *Die Annalen der lateinischen Hymnendichtung,* (Berlin 1964–65) 1:268. A. M. ZIMMERMANN, *Kalendarium Benedictinum: Die Heiligen und Seligen des Benediktinerordens und seiner Zweige,* 4 v. (Metten 1933–38) 3:155, 158. F. ZOEPFL, *Das Bistum Augsburg und seine Bischöfe im Mittelalter* (Augsburg 1955) 55–59.

[H. DRESSLER]

ADALBERO OF METZ

Two bishops of the See of Metz.

Adalbero I, bishop, statesman, monastic reformer; d. Saint-Trond, Belgium, April 26, 962. Son of Count Wigerich and brother of Duke Frederick of Upper Lorraine, Adalbero succeeded BENNO as bishop of Metz, the chief see of Lorraine, in 929. Always politically active, he joined the rebellion against OTTO I (938–940), with the intention of transferring Lorraine to French suzerainty. Failing in this enterprise, he thereafter remained on close, friendly terms with the German court. In 950 Adalbero intervened in France as mediator between Hugh the Great and Louis IV. He gave vital support to the monastic reform movement by reforming GORZE ABBEY in 933 and appointing Abbot Ainald. Subsequently he introduced Gorze monks into his own cathedral chapter at St. Arnulf's, and reformed other houses including Moyenmoutier and Saint-Trond, of which Adalbero himself was abbot.

Adalbero II, bishop, monastic reformer; b. *c.* 955–962; d. Dec. 14, 1005. Nephew of Adalbero I, and son of Duke Frederick, he was reared at Gorze and elected bishop of Verdun in 984. He was then transferred immediately to Metz through his mother's influence. More ascetic and less interested in politics than his uncle, he devoted his attention chiefly to his spiritual tasks. He introduced the Cluniac reform into Lorraine, rebuilt the dilapidated Abbey of St. Symphorian, founded three abbeys for women, and seconded, but not always wisely, Emperor HENRY II's ecclesiastical policy. He promoted education and made Metz the intellectual center of Upper Lorraine. He enjoyed a local, unofficial cult as a *beatus.*

Feast: Dec. 15.

[R. H. SCHMANDT]

ADALBERO OF WÜRZBURG, ST.

Bishop; b. *c.* 1010; d. Lambach Abbey, Oct. 6, 1090. Last of the Carinthian counts of Lambach Wels, he studied at Paris, became a canon of the cathedral of Würzburg, and, named by Emperor Henry III, was consecrated bishop of Würzburg (June 30, 1045). He was a zealous if litigious bishop, maintaining his episcopal rights against both the monastery of Fulda (1049) and the Diocese of Bamberg (1052). During the struggle between King (later Emperor) Henry IV and Pope Gregory VII, he remained loyal to the imperial cause until Henry "excommunicated" the pope (1076). He then broke with Henry and participated actively in his deposition (1077). In 1085, forced from his see by an antibishop, Meginhard, he found final refuge at Lambach, his ancestral monastery, which he himself had reestablished as a Benedictine abbey. His cultus was approved in 1883.

Feast: Oct. 6.

Bibliography: *Kirche in der Gesellschaft: Dimensionen der Seelsorge,* eds. R. SCHNEIDER and L. BRANDL (Passau 1992). P.-W. SCHEELE, *Die Herrlichkeit des Herrn: die Lambacher Fresken aus der Zeit des heiligen Adalbero* (Würzburg 1990). P. J. JORG, *Lexicon für Theologie und Kirche,* ed. J. HOFER and K. RAHNER (Freiburg 1957–65) 1:120.

[S. WILLIAMS]

ADALBERT OF BREMEN

Archbishop of Bremen-Hamburg, royal adviser; b. Thuringia, *c.* 1000; d. Goslar, March 16, 1072. Born of noble parents, he was educated at Halberstadt, where he became canon and, by 1032, provost. Then through royal favor he was made archbishop of Bremen-Hamburg (1045–72). Under him the see's efforts to convert the northern Slavs and Scandinavians were intensified. Denmark was deeply influenced by Bremen, Sweden only temporarily, and Norway hardly at all; missionaries sailed to Iceland, Greenland, the Orkneys, and Finland; in 1060 Slavic sees were erected at Mecklenburg and Ratzeburg. After the Council of SUTRI (1046) Adalbert refused Emperor Henry III's offer of the papacy. He hoped instead to establish his see as a patriarchate (probably over a Danish archbishop), but was only appointed papal agent for the evangelization of northern Europe, i.e., he was made legate, and then vicar in 1053. In German politics he played a leading role as adviser to Henry III and guardian to young HENRY IV, and virtually ruled (1064–66) until rival nobles exiled him from court (1066–69). This reversal prevented the realization of his greatest ambition, to make his see into a compact duchy in which the archbishop would be the leading economic, religious, and political power; nonetheless, he enlarged its power and prestige substantially. He is typical of the great German prelates who served the Salians on the eve of the INVESTITURE STRUGGLE. Adam of Bremen's history is the best source for Adalbert's life.

Bibliography: E. N. JOHNSON, "A. of Hamburg-Bremen: A Politician of the Eleventh Century," *Speculum* 9 (1934) 147–79. O. H. MAY, *Regesten der Erzbischöfe von Bremen,* v.1 (Hanover 1928–37) 53–79, with full bibliog.; *Neue deutsche Biographie* 1:42–43. H. FUHRMANN, "Studien zur Geschichte mittelalterlicher Patriarchate," *Zeitschrift der Savigny-Stiftung für Rechtsgeschichte, Kanonistische Abteilung* 41 (1955) 120–70.

[R. KAY]

ADALBERT OF PRAGUE, ST.

Bishop, martyr; b. probably at Libice, the ancestral stronghold of his family, 956; d. near Danzig, April 23, 997. He was baptized Vojtech and was a member of the East Bohemian princely dynasty of Slavnik. At confirmation he took the name Adalbert, the name of the first archbishop of Magdeburg, who had supervised his education. Because of his great piety and demonstrated ability, the young Adalbert was chosen bishop of Prague in 982, after the death of Thietmar, the first bishop of Prague, a German by birth. Thus Adalbert was the first Czech to occupy the See of Prague. His position was particularly important owing to the great influence of the Slavnik family to which he belonged. A man of austerity, energy, and zeal, Adalbert strove to improve and reform his clergy, to suppress abuses and pagan survivals, and to spread Christianity throughout Bohemia and neighboring Hungary. His activity, however, aroused the enmity of the extreme nationalists, who sympathized with the old pagan traditions, and led to a conflict with the Duke of Bohemia,

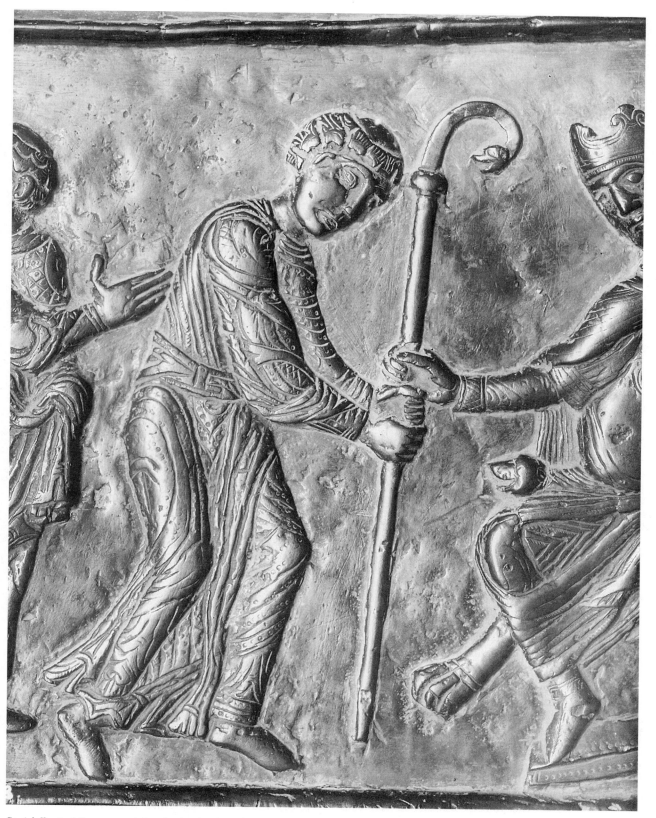

St. Adalbert of Prague receiving the crosier from Otto II, detail of bronze doors, Cathedral at Gniezno, c. 1175.

Boleslas II. Adalbert, when forced to leave Prague, went to Rome, where he became a monk at the Benedictine Abbey of SS. Alexius and Boniface. In 992 he was persuaded to return to Prague, but found it necessary to leave again in 995. In that same year Boleslas II treacherously attacked Libice and massacred all the members of the Slavnik family and their principal supporters. Refused permission to return to his see, Adalbert obtained a release from his episcopal obligations from John XV and dedicated himself entirely to missionary activity. A close friend of Emperor OTTO III, Adalbert was his trusted adviser on problems concerned with the progressive Christianization of the Slavs. Adalbert was also a close friend and collaborator of SS. ROMUALD and BRUNO OF QUERFURT. In 995 he accepted the invitation of King Boleslas I the Great of Poland to organize missionary work among the heathen Prussians on the Baltic coast, where he met a martyr's death. His body was ransomed by King Boleslas and buried at Gniezno, Poland, and in 1039 was translated to Prague.

Feast: April 23.

Bibliography: *Adalbert von Prag: Brückenbauer zwischen dem Osten und Westen Europas*, ed. H. H. HENRIX (Baden-Baden 1997). *Svatý Vojtech: sborník k mileniu*, ed. J. V. POLC (Prague 1997). J. CANAPARIUS, *Vita s. Adalberti* in v.1 of *Fontes rerum Bohemicarum*, 7 v. (Prague 1873–1932). E. JOHANSSON, *Studien zu Nicolaus von Jeroschins Adalbertübersetzung* (Lund 1967). BRUNO OF QUERFURT, *Vita s. Adalberti, ibid.* H. G. VOIGT, *Adalbert v. Prag* (Berlin 1898). F. DVORNIK, *The Making of Central and Eastern Europe* (London 1949); *The Slavs: Their Early History and Civilization* (Boston 1956); *Svatý Vojtech: druhý prazský biskup* (Olomouc 1997). J. KRASÍNSKI, *Milenium sw. Wojciecha, 997–1997* (Sandomierz 1997). J. WYROZUMSKI, *Legenda pruska o swietym Wojciechu* (Krakow 1997). *Ezer év Szent Adalbert oltalma alatt*, ed. A. HEGEDÜS and I. BÁRDOS (Esztergom 2000).

[O. P. SHERBOWITZ-WETZOR]

ADALBERT THE DEACON, ST.

Missionary; b. England, late seventh century; d. Egmond, Holland, June 25, 705. Possibly a member of the English royalty, he devoted himself to missionary work. Under the leadership of St. WILLIBRORD, Adalbert left his monastery in 690 to evangelize Friesland. Though he never advanced beyond the rank of deacon, Adalbert's patience and kindness made him an effective witness to the faith. He became archdeacon of Utrecht, a position entailing considerable responsibility. In about 702 he went to preach in northern Holland and built a church in Egmond, where he is buried. After his death his tomb became a place of pilgrimage, and his cult had the support of the counts of Holland, who in 923 founded the Abbey of Egmond in his honor. Adalbert's first biographer, Rupert, wrote almost 200 years later, and hence the details

of his vita are largely conjectural. He should not be confused with the Abbot Adalbert of Echternach.

Feast: June 25.

Bibliography: J. MABILLON, *Acta sanctorum ordinis S. Benedicti* (Venice 1733-40) 3:586–600. *Acta Sanctorum* June 7:82–95. A. BUTLER, *Lives of the Saints* (New York 1956) 2:641–642.

[J. F. FAHEY]

ADALDAG, ST.

Seventh archbishop of Bremen-Hamburg; b. *c.* 900; d. Bremen, Germany, April 28 or 29, 988 (commemorated, April 28). A Saxon and canon of Hildesheim, Adaldag was the chancellor of Emperor OTTO I when he succeeded UNNI as archbishop of the great northern See of Bremen-Hamburg in 937. Adaldag remained one of Otto's principal advisers, and when Otto deposed and abducted Pope BENEDICT V (964), it was Adaldag who served as the pope's custodian. As archbishop, Adaldag proved energetic and effective and carried on extensive missionary activities. Under him the Danish suffragan Sees of Schleswig, Ribe, Aarhus, and Odense were founded. The Diocese of Oldenburg in Holstein was set up as a base for a reinvigorated mission to the Wends. He successfully warded off the claim of the archbishop of Cologne to metropolitan jurisdiction over Bremen.

Bibliography: ADAM OF BREMEN, *History of the Archbishops of Hamburg-Bremen*, tr. F. J. TSCHAN (New York 1959). O. H. MAY, *Regesten der Erzbishöfe von Bremen*, v.1 (Hanover 1928). G. DEHIO, *Geschichte des Erzbistums Hamburg-Bremen* (Berlin 1877). G. GLAESKE, *Die Erzbischöfe von Hamburg-Bremen als Reichsfürsten* (937–1258) (Hildesheim 1962).

[J. F. FAHEY]

ADALGAR OF BREMEN, ST.

Third archbishop of Bremen-Hamburg; d. Bremen, May 9, 909. Having proved a pious, wise, and zealous monk and deacon at Corvey, he was assigned (865) by his abbot—also named Adalgar—to assist Abp. REMBERT OF BREMEN-HAMBURG. Adalgar became Rembert's coadjutor and then his successor (889) after confirmation by King Louis II and his sons Louis III and Carloman, by Emperor Arnulf, by the abbot and monastery of Corvey, and by a local synod. He received the pallium from Pope STEPHEN V, was consecrated by Abp. Sundrold of Mainz, and received his crozier from Arnulf. Adalgar traveled throughout his see and attended the royal court; his missionary activity was somewhat limited by the Norman wars. He was involved in a dispute with Abp. Herman of Cologne, who forced Bremen into the status of suffragan bishopric by means of the Synod of Tribur (895) presided over by Abp. Hatto of Mainz. However, Pope SERGIUS III abrogated this decision at the end of Adalgar's life. Adalgar appointed a coadjutor, Hoger of Bremen-Hamburg, and five bishops. He is buried in the basilica of St. Michael in Bremen. TRITHEMIUS was the first to call him a saint (*De Viris illustribus* 3.214); northern writers say nothing of canonization. There is a baroque statue of him in the choir at Corvey.

Feast: May 15.

Bibliography: ADAM OF BREMEN, *History of the Archbishops of Hamburg-Bremen*, ed. and tr. F. J. TSCHAN (New York 1959). *Leben der Erzbischöfe Anskar und Rimbert*, ed. W. WATTENBACH (Die Geschichtsschreiber der deutschen Vorzeit 22; 3d ed. Leipzig 1939). A. M. ZIMMERMANN, *Kalendarium Benedictinum* (Metten 1933–38) 2:174.

[G. SPAHR]

ADALGIS OF NOVARA, ST.

Bishop; d. *c.* 850. According to a constant tradition, Adalgis (or Adelgis) was of Lombard origin and possibly belonged to the same family as DESIDERIUS, the last Lombard king. Though nothing is known of his early life, it is likely that Adalgis was a canon of the church of San Gaudenzio in Novara. It is not clear whether his nomination to the episcopacy (*c.* 830) was because of his merits or his family connections. He seems to have been a man of considerable importance, for his name is found on many documents during the years 835 to 848. He was buried in the church of San Gaudenzio, which he had endowed a short while before; his remains were transferred to the cathedral *c.* 1590.

Feast: Oct 7.

Bibliography: *Acta Sanctorum* Oct. 3:945–947. V. G. GREMIGNI and A. CARDINALI, *Bibliotheca sanctorum* (Rome 1961–) 1:194–196.

[J. E. LYNCH]

ADALGOTT, SS.

Two abbots of Disentis with this name.

Adalgott I, abbot; d. Nov. 1, 1031. A Benedictine monk from the abbey of Einsiedeln, he became abbot of Disentis in 1016. He was interested in monastic reform and the elaboration of the liturgy. According to the Einsiedeln chronicler, who preserves a verse epitaph of him, he was popularly honored as a saint immediately after his death. In 1672 his relics were enshrined in a new church at the abbey.

Feast: Oct 26.

Adalgott II, abbot, and bishop of Chur; d. abbey of Disentis, Switzerland, Oct. 3, 1160. A disciple of BERNARD OF CLAIRVAUX, he became abbot of Disentis and bishop of Chur, Switzerland, in 1150 and served in both offices with outstanding devotion until his death. He appears to have been a great benefactor of other religious houses, such as Münster and Schännis, where commemoration of him was later made. He was a figure of some importance in the affairs of the time, being connected with Emperor FREDERICK I BARBAROSSA and the prince bishop of Constance and also with Pope Stephen III, whose fellow student he had been. His feast is still kept in the Diocese of Chur, and his relics were enshrined along with those of Adalgott I in the abbey church in 1672.

Feast: Oct. 3.

Bibliography: Adalgott. *Acta Sanctorum* Nov. 1:385. I. MÜLLER, *Disentiser Klostergeschichte* (Einsiedeln 1942) 75, 81, 236, 268; *Lexicon für Theologie und Kirche*, ed. J. HOFER and K. RAHNER (Freiburg 1957–65) 1:124. A. M. ZIMMERMANN, *Kalendarium Benedictinum* (Metten 1933–38) 3:222, 224. Adalgott II. I. MÜLLER, *Lexicon für Theologie und Kirche*, ed. J. HOFER and K. RAHNER (Freiburg 1957–65) 1:124. J. G. MAYER, *Geschichte des Bist ums Chur* (Stans 1907) 206–212. L. BURGENER, *Helvetia sancta*, 2 v. (New York 1860) 1:7–9. A. M. ZIMMERMANN *Kalendarium Benedictinum* (Metten 1933–38) 3:133, 135.

[J. L. GRASSI]

ADAM

The name given in the genealogical lists of Gn 4.25–5.5 to the first human being, identical in form with the Hebrew word for man, *'ādām*. He is named simply Man, not merely because he was the first man, but rather because he was regarded as the type of all mankind (Gn 5.2). However, in the story of PARADISE and the Fall of Man in Gn 2.4b–3.24 the term is always preceded by the definite article in Hebrew, *hā-'ādām*, ''the man,'' and therefore in this section it should not be translated as if it were a proper noun. The Hebrew word *'ādām* means man in the sense of ''mankind''; to designate an individual man, Hebrew must use the term *ben 'ādām*, son, i.e., member, of the human race. This fact is of some importance in the interpretation of the story of the fall of man, in which the inspired author is speaking not so much about an individual man as about the whole human race typified by this individual.

The derivation of the Hebrew word *'ādām* is uncertain. Probably there is nothing more than a folk etymology in Gn 2.7 where it is implied that man is called *'ādām* because God formed him out of the dirt of the *'ădāmâ* (ground). But in any case, the author of Gn 2.4b–3.24

"Creation of Adam," detail of a fresco cycle by Michelangelo, 1508–1512, Sistine Chapel. (©Bettmann/CORBIS)

makes skillful use of this derivation: because man ('*ādām*) was formed from the ground ('*ădāmâ*), he is destined to till the ground (Gn 2.5) in hard labor (3.17, 23) and ultimately go back to it in death (3.17).

According to the genealogies of the PATRIARCHS, Adam lived for 930 years (Gn 5.5). The children that EVE bore him were Cain, Abel and Seth (4.1–2, 25).

After these first few chapters of Genesis, Adam is not mentioned again in the Old Testament until the books written in the last few centuries before Christ (1 Chr 1.1; Tb 8.6; Sir 17.1–4; 49.16; Wis 2.23–24; 9.2–3; 10.1–2), when people began to speculate about the first man. Several curious tales are told about Adam in the apocryphal and rabbinical writings.

In the New Testament, besides the passing references in Lk 3.38, Acts 17.26, and Jude 14, Adam is mentioned in connection with the Christian doctrine on marriage (Mt 19.4–6; Eph 5.31), the position of women

(1 Cor 11.7–12; 1 Tm 2.13–14), and especially the teachings of St. Paul on the universality of grace (Rom 5.12–21), the resurrection of the dead (1 Cor 15.21–22), and the state of the glorified body (1 Cor 15.45–49). Paul draws an important contrast between "the first, the old, the earthly Adam" of Genesis and "the second, the new, the heavenly Adam" who is Christ; the former is the "figure" (τύπος) of the latter (Rom 5.14). The Christian must "strip off the old Adam and his deeds and put on the new Adam, so that he may be renewed unto perfect knowledge according to the image of his Creator" (Col 3.9–10).

In theology both Greek and Latin fathers affirmed a privileged state for Adam, head of the human race, before his sin, but the enumeration and analysis of his gifts were arrived at slowly. Some, such as Gregory of Nyssa, tended to elaborate; others, such as Irenaeus, tended to attenuate the Genesis paradisal passages. Augustine formulated the traditional gifts: immortality, IMPASSIBILITY, INTEG-

Adam and Eve after the expulsion from paradise, painting by Veronese. (©Francis G. Mayer/CORBIS)

RITY, a marvelous knowledge. He made the gift of origi-nal justice seem the same as sanctifying GRACE. Anselm followed Augustine but saw ORIGINAL JUSTICE as per-taining to the nature of man. Aquinas taught that Adam was created in grace but left room for a distinction be-tween sanctifying grace and original justice, the former regarded not as a formal constituent of original justice but as efficient cause. He followed Augustine's enumeration of the gifts, as did most scholastics up until the present century. A triple subordination existed in Adam. His rea-son was subject to God, the lower powers to reason, the body to the soul; and the first subjection was the cause of both the second and third (St. Thomas, *Summa theologiae,* 1a, 95.1). The Church is more cautious than its theologians. Nowhere are the gifts singly defined. Trent uses the phrase ''holiness and justice'' to indicate them (H. Denzinger, *Enchiridion symbolorum,* 1511).

The theory of evolution and the findings of paleon-tology have proposed many questions about the first man (*see* EVOLUTION). Were there many Adams or just one? Was Adam the paragon of creation or a cave man? Did he know the natures of all created things or was his knowledge very primitive? Contemporary sciences deal-ing with the origin of man seem to contradict the tradi-tional concept of Adam. ''If the details of the evolutionary theory regarding man are still hypothetical, its general direction is uncontestably shown [and] the conception of a primitive paradisal state would seem to be absolutely outside the facts'' (Gardeil).

Contemporary theology on Adam has accepted, in general, this trend in scientific thought. Pius XII in 1950 reminded Catholics that ''the Catholic faith obliges us to believe that souls are immediately created by God'' and that Adam cannot be regarded as representing a certain number of first parents since ''it is in no way apparent how such an opinion can be reconciled with what the fonts of revelation and the pronouncements of the mag-

"Creation of Adam," detail of Freso cycle by Michelangelo. (Scala/Art Resource, NY)

isterium of the Church set forth concerning original sin'' (*Enchiridion symbolorum,* 3896–97).

Toward a harmony of science and revealed truth, theologians make many points. Three may be mentioned here. There is a parallel between the production of the first man and that of any man. As in the latter case biology cannot ascertain the fact of the infusion of the soul by God, so in the former paleontology cannot ascertain the fact of the divine intervention. Again, sanctifying grace is not to be judged or measured by technology. The first man may indeed have been a primitive; this does not rule out his FRIENDSHIP WITH GOD. Finally, the special endowments of Adam may be interpreted now as ''germs or possibilities rather than perfections actually realized'' (Gardeil).

See Also: EVE; CREATION, ARTICLES ON; ORIGINAL SIN.

Bibliography: *Dictionnaire de théologie catholique,* ed. A. VACANT et al., 15 v. (Paris 1903–50; Tables générales 1951-), Tables générales 1:30–33. J. SCHILDENBERGER, *Lexikon für Theologie und Kirche,* ed. J. HOFER and K. RAHNER, 10 v. (Freiburg 1957–65) 1:127–130. A. ROBERT and A. TRICOT, *Guide to the Bible,* tr. E. P. ARBEZ and M. P. MC GUIRE, 2 v. (Tournai-New York 1951–55; v. 1 rev. and enl. 1960) 1:174, excellent bibliog. on European and American lit. to 1960. L. PIROT and J. B. FREY, *Dictionnaire de la Bible,* suppl. ed. L. PIROT et al. (Paris 1928–) 1:86–134. J. JEREMIAS, in G. KITTEL, *Theologisches Wörterbuch zum Neuen Testament* (Stuttgart 1935–) 1:141–143. J. DANIÉLOU, *From Shadows to Reality,* tr. W. HIBBERD (Westminster, Md. 1960). A. VITTI, ''Christus-Adam,'' *Biblica* 7 (1926) 121–145, 270–285, 384–401. C. WESTERMANN, *Genesis 1–11* (Minneapolis, 1984–86). THOMAS AQUINAS, *Summa theologiae,* 1a, 90–102, and commentary by H. D. GARDEIL in *Somme théologique I.90–102: Les Origines de l'homme,* tr. A. PATFOORT (Paris 1963) 423–451. J. COPPENS, *La Connaissance du bien et du mal et le péché du Paradis* (Louvain 1948), also in *Revue biblique* 56 (1949) 300–308. J. DE FRAINE, *The Bible and the Origins of Man* (New York 1962). A. M. DUBARLE, *Le Péché originel dans l'Écriture* (Paris 1958). C. HAURET, *Beginnings: Genesis and Modern Science,* tr. and ed. E. P. EMMANS (Dubuque 1964). M. M. LABOURDETTE, *Le Péché originel et les origines de l'homme* (Paris 1953). J. L. MCKENZIE, *Myths and Realities* (Milwaukee 1963) 146–181. R. J. NOGAR, *The Wisdom of Evolution*

(Garden City, N.Y. 1963). H. RENCKENS, *Israel's Concept of the Beginning*, tr. C. NAPIER (New York 1964). L. F. HARTMAN, "Sin in Paradise," *The Catholic Biblical Quarterly,* 20 (1958) 26–40, with fine bibliog. C. REILLY, "Adam and Primitive Man," *The Irish Theological Quarterly* 26 (1959) 331–345. C. VOLLERT, "Evolution and the Bible," *Symposium on Evolution* (Pittsburgh 1959) 81–119.

[E. H. PETERS/T. R. HEATH/EDS.]

ADAM, KARL

Historian of dogma and dogmatic theologian; b. Pursruck, Bavaria, Oct. 22, 1876; d. Tübingen, April 1, 1966. After ordination in 1900, Adam continued his studies at Munich, later devoting himself to teaching and pastoral duties there and in Strasbourg. In 1919 he became professor for dogmatic theology at the University of Tübingen, a post which he held until his retirement just after World War II.

At Tübingen his lectures and books enjoyed a favorable reception, especially *The Spirit of Catholicism* (1924). This book, his masterpiece, was translated into 11 languages; it communicated to Catholics all over the world a truly theological view of the Church with emphasis on the doctrine of the Mystical Body. Another much-translated work, *The Son of God* (1933), presented Christology in a language suitable to the needs of his contemporaries. His historical sense and sincere piety gave an added dimension not often found in theological popularizations. In his retirement he gave vigorous support to ecumenicism (*One and Holy,* 1948). His last major work was *The Christ of Faith* (1954).

Bibliography: AUBERT in *Tendenzen der Theologie im 20. Jahrhundert,* ed. H. J. SCHULTZ, (Stuttgart, Olten 1966) 156–162. A. AUER, "Karl Adam 1876–1966," *Theologische Qartalschrift* 150 (1970) 130–143. J. STELZENBERGER, "Bibliographie Karl Adam," *Theologie Quartalschrift* 138 (1958) 330–347. R. A. KRIEG, *Karl Adam: Catholicism in German Culture* (Notre Dame 1992).

[P. MISNER]

ADAM EASTON

English cardinal, theologian responsible for the papal condemnation of John Wyclif in 1377, author of several important spiritual and liturgical works; b. Easton, England, *c.* 1330; d. Rome, Sept. 20, 1397. Easton, a monk of Norwich cathedral priory, studied at Oxford and graduated there as master of theology in 1366. Two years later he accompanied the Benedictine cardinal, SIMON LANGHAM of Canterbury, to the papal Curia at AVIGNON and completed there by 1377 his *Defensorium ecclesiastice potestatis,* a systematic refutation of the an-

tipapal writings of MARSILIUS OF PADUA and John WYCLIF. He was an eyewitness of the disputed election of Pope URBAN VI, the validity of which he consistently maintained. In 1381 he was promoted to cardinal and wrote the *Office of the Visitation of the BVM,* promulgated in 1389 in the cause of Church unity. Another major work, *Defensorium s. Birgittae* led to the canonization of BRIDGET OF SWEDEN in 1391. Easton's extant writings reveal him to have been one of the greatest biblical scholars and Hebraists of the 14th century.

Bibliography: L. MACFARLANE, *Dictionnaire de spiritualité ascétique et mystique, Doctrine et histoire* 4.1:5–8; *The Life and Writings of Adam Easton,* 2 v. (U. of London thesis, 1955). A. B. EMDEN, *A Biographical Review of the University of Oxford to* A.D. *1500* 1:620–21.

[L. MACFARLANE]

ADAM MARSH

English theologian (also known as de Marisco); b. in Diocese of Bath and Wells, late 12th century; d. Nov. 18, 1258. He studied arts under ROBERT GROSSETESTE at Oxford, where he had become master by 1226. He became a Franciscan at Worcester in 1232 or 1233. He returned to Oxford to study theology under Grosseteste until the latter became bishop of Lincoln in 1235. As intimate friend and adviser of Grosseteste, he accompanied the bishop to the Council of Lyons (1244–46). Around 1247, he became the first Franciscan master in theology at Oxford, where he taught until 1250. He was constantly summoned by King Henry III for official business; by BONIFACE OF SAVOY, Archbishop of Canterbury, for counsel; and by the pope for settling local disputes. In 1256, the king and the archbishop tried unsuccessfully to secure his appointment to the See of Ely. He explored the possibilities of making peace with France in 1257. In his lifetime he had the title of "Doctor illustris." ROGER BACON spoke of Adam and Grosseteste as "the greatest clerics in the world," (*Opus Tertium,* 22, 23, 25). His 247 letters, published by J. S. Brewer [*Monumenta Franciscana (Rerum Britannicarum medii aevi scriptores* 1858) 1:77–489], are of unusual historical interest, but the theological and exegetical works ascribed to him have not yet been studied or edited.

Bibliography: A. G. LITTLE, *The Gray Friars in Oxford* (Oxford 1892) 134–39; "The Franciscan School at Oxford in the 13th Century," *Archivum Franciscanum historicum* 19 (1926) 831–38. D. DOUIE, "A. de Marisco," *Durham University Journal* 32 (1940) 81–97. G. CANTINI, "Adam de Marisco," *Antonianum* 23 (1948) 441–74. M. CREIGHTON, *The Dictionary of National Biography from the Earliest Times to 1900* 1:79. A. DE SERÉNT, *Dictionnaire d'histoire et de géographie ecclésiastiques* 1:482–84. A. B. EMDEN *A Biographical Register of the University of Oxford to* A.D. *1500* 2:1225–26.

[J. A. WEISHEIPL]

ADAM OF BUCKFIELD

Aristotelian philosopher of Oxford; b. Bockenfield, Northumberland, c. 1220; d. between 1279 and 1294. He was a student at Oxford in 1238, and by 1243 he became a master in arts. In 1249, then a subdeacon, he was recommended by ADAM MARSH to ROBERT GROSSETESTE for the rectory of Iver, Buckinghamshire, and was praised highly for his piety and learning. In 1264 he held a canonry and prebend at Lincoln, probably having abandoned the schools of Oxford. There is no contemporary evidence that he was a master in theology.

All his extant writings relate to his teaching career in the faculty of arts at Oxford. The precise determination of his writings is a delicate matter. Some are ascribed to Adam Buckfield, some to Adam Bouchermefort, others vaguely to *Magister Adam Anglicus;* and six works survive in two versions. M. GRABMANN, the first to consider the problem seriously, assumed that Buckfield and Bouchermefort were distinct individuals and assigned one set of writings to each on the basis of the manuscript tradition. Later, Grabmann himself acknowledged that Buckfield and Bouchermefort are the same person. A diversity of names for a single individual is not unusual, since medieval scribes were frequently unfamiliar with the place name being copied; Emden has noted 22 different forms for Adam of Buckfield.

His works, commonly called *notulae, glosae,* or *sententiae,* cover all the *libri naturales* of Aristotle and the *Metaphysica nova,* the version from the Arabic. His method of exposition was one used early in the schools and later popularized by Averroës. It consists in a literal exposition and analysis of each section of the text that had been divided and subdivided. Buckfield's exposition is remarkable for its clarity, conciseness, and accuracy. He used the Latin version of Aristotle known as the *corpus vetustius,* although he sometimes referred to other versions. Occasionally he inserted short questions to clarify difficult points. A notable one, the only fully developed *quaestio,* occurs at the end of *De anima,* Bk. 1. Although he utilized Avicenna, ALGAZEL, and others, his principal source was Averroës, often to the point of simply paraphrasing him. However, unlike Averroës, Buckfield maintained a plurality of forms in material substance (*see* FORMS, UNICITY AND PLURALITY OF).

Besides commenting on Aristotle he also wrote glosses on the pseudo-Aristotelian *De plantis* and *De differentia spiritus et animae,* and a *Quaestio de augmento.* The authenticity of *In metaph. vetus* and *De causis,* sometimes ascribed to him, is doubtful. The *De anima* in the Berlin manuscript is a compilation drawn from Buckfield and ALBERT THE GREAT.

The 45 surviving manuscripts, widely scattered, indicate that his works were considerably popular in the Middle Ages. The importance of Buckfield lies in the range of his commentaries, the perfection of his technique, and the indication of the curriculum of arts at Oxford in the middle of the 13th century.

Bibliography: ADAM OF BUCKFIELD, ''Super secundum Metaphysicae,'' ed. A. A. MAURER in *Nine Medieval Thinkers,* ed. J. R. O'DONNELL (Toronto 1955) 99–144. D. A. CALLUS, *Revue néoscolastique de philosophie* 42 (1939) 413–24, 433–38; ''Introduction of Aristotelian Learning to Oxford,'' *Proceedings of the British Academy* 29 (1943) 255–56. M. GRABMANN, *Mittelalterliches Geistesleben,* 3 v. (Munich 1925–56) 138–82, 614–16. F. PELSTER, *Scholastik* 11 (1936) 196–224. S. H. THOMSON, *Medievalia et humanistica* 2 (1944) 55–87; 3 (1945) 132–33; 12 (1948) 23–32. L. BATAILLON, ibid. 13 (1960) 35–39. A. B. EMDEN, *A Biographical Register of the University of Oxford to* A.D. *1500* 1:297.

[D. A. CALLUS]

ADAM OF EBRACH, BL.

Abbot; b. near Cologne, c. 1100; d. Nov. 20, 1161. He is probably to be identified with Adam, monk of MORIMOND, to whom BERNARD OF CLAIRVAUX wrote two surviving letters (*Patrologia Latina,* ed. J. P. Migne 182:91–105). Adam was originally a monk of MARMOUTIER who by 1121 had become a CISTERCIAN at Foligny, whence he went to Morimond and became abbot. In 1125 he and many of the monks abandoned Morimond, and only considerable pressure from Bernard induced them to return. Adam founded the Abbey of EBRACH, near Mannheim, in 1127 and became its first abbot. His high and saintly reputation so assured the house of success that he was able to make new foundations: at Reun (1129), HEILSBRONN and Langheim (1133), Nepomuk (1145), Alderspach (1146), and Bildhausen (1158). In his final years he was a correspondent of the mystic St. HILDEGARDE OF BINGEN and an ardent supporter of the CRUSADES. His cult has never been officially recognized, but his feast is kept by the Cistercians.

Feast: Feb. 25.

Bibliography: F. X. VON WEGELE, ''Relacio . . . et . . . Narratio fundationis monasterii Eberacensis,'' *Monumenta Eberacensia* (Nördlingen 1863) 3–7. R. TRILHE, *Dictionnaire d'histoire et de géographie ecclésiastiques,* ed. A. BAUDRILLART (Paris 1912–) 1:461–463. F. J. SCHMALE, *Lexikon für Theologie und Kirche,* ed. J. HOFER and K. RAHNER, 10 v. (2d, new ed. Freiburg 1957–65) 1:131–132. SELNER, *Brevis notitia monasterii B.M.V. Ebracensis* (Rome 1749) 99–102.

[J. L. GRASSI]

ADAM OF ORLETON

Master of arts; doctor of canon law, Oxford (1310); bishop of Hereford (1317), Worcester (1327), Winchester (1333); d. Farnham Castle, Hampshire, July 18, 1345. He sided with the Mortimers against Edward II and engineered the escape of Roger Mortimer of Wigmore from the Tower (1323). When charged with treason, Orleton refused to plead before a civil court and was condemned in absence (1324). Protected meanwhile by the other bishops, he joined Queen Isabella's forces (1326) and played a leading part in securing Edward's abdication (1327). He served on Edward III's regency council as treasurer, and he represented Edward in dealings with JOHN XXII and with France, retaining the king's favor even after Mortimer's fall (1330). His conviction was annulled (1329). He quarreled with Archbishop JOHN STRATFORD (1341) and may have written the king's answer to Stratford's criticisms of the government. Modern writers tend to accept the view of the chronicles of Geoffrey le Baker (ed. E. M. Thompson, Oxford 1889) that Orleton was able, but opportunist and unscrupulous.

Bibliography: *Registrum Ade de Orleton, Episcopi Herefordensis, A.D. MCCCXVII–MCCCXXVII,* ed. A. T. BANNISTER (Canterbury and York Society; London 1908). H. R. LUARD, *The Dictionary of National Biography from the Earliest Times to 1900* 1:79–81. J. C. DAVIES, *Baronial Opposition to Edward II* (Cambridge, Eng. 1918). E. L. G. STONES, "The Date of Roger Mortimer's Escape from the Tower of London," *English Historical Review* 66 (1951) 97–98. A. B. EMDEN, *A Biographical Register of the University of Oxford to A.D. 1500* 2:1402–04. M. MCKISACK, *The Fourteenth Century, 1307–99* (Oxford 1959).

[R. W. HAYS]

ADAM OF PERSEIGNE

Cistercian abbot, spiritual writer; b. Champagne; d. Perseigne, 1221. After entering the clerical state, Adam received an excellent education in philosophy and theology. He was first attached to the court of the Count of Champagne as chaplain and confessor of Countess Marie. The chronology of Adam's life is uncertain but it is generally assumed that he successively joined the Canons Regular, the Benedictines of MARMOUTIER, and finally the Cistercians at PONTIGNY, where he served as master of novices. In 1188 he was elected abbot of Perseigne near Alençon. Adam's public career reached its climax in the service of Innocent III. In 1199 he mediated the feud over royal succession following the death of King Richard I, the Lionhearted. In 1200 he participated in the organization of the Fourth Crusade (*see* CRUSADES); in 1203 he arbitrated the disputed episcopal election at Reims; and in 1208 he acted as peacemaker between PHILIP II AUGUSTUS of France and King JOHN of England. He was venerated in his abbey as blessed. Much of Adam's literary work has been lost. The surviving portion consists of letters of spiritual guidance and of sermons on the

Blessed Virgin or on various scriptural passages. He was a master of medieval Latin style, was well acquainted with the Bible and with patristic and Cistercian sources such as the works of St. Bernard and St. Aelred. He was warm, sympathetic, and sincere, a man of piety and practical wisdom.

Bibliography: Sources. *Lettres (Sources Chrétiennes* 66; Paris 1960-) v.1, *Texte latin, introduction, traduction et notes,* ed. J. BOUVET; *Patrologia Latina* 211:579–779. J. BOUVET, "Correspondance d'Adam, Abbé de Perseigne, 1188–1221," *Archives Historiques du Maine* 13 (1953) 101–60. Literature. L. T. MERTON, "La Formation monastique selon Adam de Perseigne," *Collectanea ordinis Cisterciensium Reformatorum* 19 (1957) 1–17. J. BOUVET, "Biographie d'Adam de Perseigne," *Collectanea ordinis Cisterciensium Reformatorum* 20 (1958) 16–26. B. LOHR, "The Philosophical Life According to Adam of Perseigne," *Collectanea ordinis Cisterciensium Reformatorum* 24 (1962) 225–42; 25 (1963) 31–43. A. MIGNON, *Dictionnaire de théologie catholique* 1:387–88. L. CALENDINI, *Dictionnaire d'histoire et de géographie ecclésiastiques* 1:488–90. A. LE BAIL, *Dictionnaire de spiritualité ascétique et mystique. Doctrine et histoire* 1:198–201.

[L. J. LEKAI]

ADAM OF SAINT-VICTOR

Victorine canon and liturgical poet; b. probably in Britain or Brittany, *c.* 1110; d. apparently *c.* 1180. Little exact biographical information is known about Adam since no account of his life was written before that by William of Saint-Lô (d. 1349). Educated in Paris, Adam entered the monastery of SAINT-VICTOR *c.* 1130; there he followed the lectures of HUGH OF SAINT-VICTOR. His theological ideas are Augustinian, as is evidenced in his poem on mankind, *Haeres peccati (Patrologia Latina,* ed. J. P. Migne [Paris 1878–90] 196:1422), which served as his epitaph. At one time he was thought to be the author of scholastic and Biblical works, but this is now challenged (F. Stegmüller, *Repertorium biblicum medii aevi* [Madrid 1949–61] 1:14). However, he is known and praised for the composition of approximately 45 SEQUENCES, rhythmic pieces to be used in the liturgy of the Mass preceding the Gospel. At the Fourth LATERAN COUNCIL (1215) INNOCENT III gave Adam's Sequences a general approbation. He is credited with having brought to perfection the Sequence poetry that had been initiated by NOTKER BALBULUS and nurtured at Saint-Victor even before Adam's time. His poetry is based on accent, rhyme, and a fixed number of syllables, 4, 6, 8, 10, or 12 (J. De Ghellinck, *L'Essor de la littérature latine au XIIe siècle* [Brussels-Paris 1946] 2:295–298). After the invocation of the first strophe, his Sequences describe the virtues and the miracles of the saint whose feast is being celebrated (e.g., St. Geneviève, the patron of Paris, Sequence 10). In his Sequences on Christ and the Blessed

Virgin, Adam made use of the allegory typical of his day (F. J. E. Raby, *A History of Christian-Latin Poetry from the Beginnings to the Close of the Middle Ages* [Oxford 1953] 345–375).

See Also: HYMNOLOGY.

Bibliography: *Oeuvres poétiques,* ed. L. GAUTIER, 2 v. (Paris 1858–59); *Les Proses: Texte et musique,* ed. E. MISSET and P. AUBRY (Paris 1900); *Sämtliche Sequenzen, lateinisch und deutsch,* ed. and tr. F. WELLNER (2d ed. Munich 1955). *Analecta hymnica* (Leipzig 1886–1922) 8:53–55. *Histoire littéraire de la France* (Paris 1865–) 15:40–45; 29:589–98. M. MANITIUS, *Geschichte der lateinischen Literatur des Mittelalters* (Munich 1911–31) 3:1002–08. F. J. E. RABY, *A History of Christian-Latin Poetry from the Beginnings to the Close of the Middle Ages* (Oxford 1953) 345–375. H. SPANKE, ''Die Kompositionskunst der Sequenzen Adams von St. Victor,'' *Studi medievali* 14 (1941) 1–29.

[P. DELHAYE]

ADAM PULCHRAE MULIERIS

Secular master of theology at Paris; fl. 1210–1250. The personage designated by this perennially enigmatic name is gradually becoming better identified. He was Master Adam who read the *Sentences* at Paris (1243–1245) under Peter of Lamballe (d. 1256), the text of which is preserved in Paris MS, Bibl. Nat. Lat. 15652. He was a contemporary of Eudes Rigauld (fl. 1236–75), Peter the Archbishop (fl. 1245–48), Stephen of Poligny (fl.1242–48), and John Pagus (fl. 1231–46), but older than Bertrand of Bayonne (fl. 1240–59), ALBERT THE GREAT, Eudes of Rosny, and John Pointlasne (*Pungens asinum*; fl. 1245–48). Having been a master of arts, he was probably fairly well known in his day, for he composed *De intelligentiis* (or *Memoriale rerum difficilium*) between 1210 and 1240. In it he manifests knowledge of various writings of ARISTOTLE, notably the *Metaphysics,* and at least one treatise by AVICENNA. He seems to have been inspired by the hierarchical illumination theme of PSEUDO-DIONYSIUS and to have had a profoundly voluntaristic conception of man and life. His activities and influence cannot be fully appreciated until publication of numerous treatises attributed to ''Master Adam,'' including those of ADAM OF BUCKFIELD or Bouchermefort.

Bibliography: P. GLORIEUX, *Répertoire des maîtres en théologie de Paris au XIIIᵉ siècle* (Paris 1933–34) v. 17–18 of Bibliothèque Thomiste, 1:288; ''Les Années 1242–1247 à la Faculté de Théologie de Paris,'' *Recherches de théologie ancienne et médiévale* 29 (Louvain 1962) 234–249. C. BAEUMKER, *Witelo, ein Philosoph und Naturforscher des XIII. Jahrhunderts* (Beiträge zur Geschichte der Philosophie und Theologie des Mittelalters 3.2; Münster 1908); *Miscellanea Francesco Ehrle,* v.1 (Studi e Testi 37; Rome 1924) 87–102.

[P. GLORIEUX]

ADAM WODHAM

English Franciscan theologian; b. *c.* 1295; d. Babwell, England, 1358. Also known as Adam Wodeham. He seems to have studied at Oxford (*c.* 1317–19), for he attended disputations given by WILLIAM OF OCKHAM and WALTER OF CHATTON. He lectured on the *Sentences* in the Franciscan friary in London (1328–30) before presenting a revised version at Oxford (1330–32). A marginal note in manuscript Vat. Latin 955, folio 1v, refers to a collection of the lectures made at Oxford in 1331. Later Adam prepared a definitive text (*Ordinatio*) and a shorter version (*Editio media*). He also lectured on the *Sentences* at Norwich (1332–34). The *Editio media* was abbreviated by Henry (Totting) of Oyta *c.* 1373 (ed. Paris 1512). Adam is also credited with a revised text of disputed questions (*Determinationes*); however, there is no manuscript evidence for the writings on Scripture attributed to him by L. Wadding and others. Adam is frequently called an Ockhamist. Not only did he accept the dedication of Ockham's *Summa logicae,* but he seems to have written the prologue to the work, stating that he was not ashamed to have been under the rod of such a master. Because of this intimacy, he is often called the ''imitator of Ockham.'' However, Adam belonged to no one school, for he criticized Ockham as well as DUNS SCOTUS. He was an independent thinker, quoted by Peter of Candia as on par with THOMAS AQUINAS, Duns Scotus, Ockham, and JOHN OF RIPA.

Bibliography: W. J. COURTENAY, ''Ockhamism Among the Augustinians: The Case of Adam Wodeham'' in *Scientia Augustiniana* (Wurzburg 1975), 267–275; *Adam Wodeham: An Introduction to His Life and Writings* (Leiden 1978). R. WOOD, ed. *Lectura Secunda in Librum Primum Sententiarum* (St. Bonaventure, New York 1990).

[I. C. BRADY]

ADAMNAN OF IONA, ST.

Also known as Adamnan McRonan, Adam, Aunan, and Eunan; abbot; b. Drumhome, County Donegal, Ireland, *c.* 625; d. Iona, 704. Adamnan embraced the monastic life and later went to Scotland to the abbey of Iona, becoming its ninth abbot in 679. When required to go to England in 685 on behalf of some Irish held captive there, he was converted to the Roman system in the Easter controversy and to the Roman tonsure. He went back to Iona and later to Ireland pleading for this latter change, and it was adopted in many places, though not in Iona. At the Synod of Tara (697) he insisted that women should not take part in warfare, and the Old Irish *Cáin Adamnáin* (Canon of Adamnan) is attributed to him. He wrote also the life of his predecessor, COLUMBA OF IONA, as well as the treatise *De locis sanctis,* an account of Arculfus's trip to the Holy Land. The ascription of a Vergil commentary to him is uncertain, and the Old Irish *Fís Adamnáin* is certainly not his. An Old Irish life, the *Betha Adamnáin,* is still extant.

Feast: Sept. 23.

Bibliography: ADAMNAN, *The Life of Columba,* ed. W. REEVES (Dublin 1857), ed. and tr. A. O. and M. O. ANDERSON (New York 1961); *De locis sanctis,* ed. D. MEEHAN (Scriptores latini hiberniae 3; Dublin 1958); *Cáin Adamnáin,* ed. and tr. K. MEYER (Oxford 1905); ''Betha Adamnáin,'' ed. R. I. BEST, in *Anecdota from Irish Manuscripts,* ed. O. J. BERGIN et al., 5 v. (Halle 1907–13) 2:10–20, tr. M. JOYNT *Celtic Review* 5 (1908–9) 97–107. *Betha Adamnáin=The Irish life of Adamnán,* ed. M. HERBERT and P. Ó RIAIN (London 1988). J. HIRSCHMAN, *Adamnan* (Santa Barbara, Ca. 1972). *Acta Sanctorum* Sept. 6:642–649. M. MANITIUS, *Geschichte der lateinischen Literatur des Mittelalters* (Munich 1911–31)1:236–239. J. F. KENNEY, *The Sources for the Early History of Ireland: v. 1, Ecclesiastical* (New York 1929) 283–287.

[R. T. MEYER]

ADAMS, HENRY BROOKS

Writer, novelist, and historian; b. Boston, Mass., Feb. 16, 1838; d. Washington, D.C., March 27, 1918. He was descended on both sides from wealthy and distinguished New England ancestors, two of whom were presidents of the United States. He was raised as a Unitarian, but rejected his Protestant orientation because he felt it was complacent (''Boston had solved the universe . . .'') and unrealistic (''all the problems which had convulsed human thought from earliest recorded time . . . were not worth discussing''). His most significant effort in a lifetime of inquiry was to understand and recover the religious instinct.

At Harvard College (1854–58) he was influenced by Louis Agassiz to devote himself to the intellectual life. He sailed for Germany to study law, but decided to become a writer instead. He returned to America in 1860, and served as private secretary to his father, Charles F. Adams, who had been reelected to Congress. When the elder Adams was appointed minister to Great Britain, Henry accompanied him to London (1861–68). To strike the strongest blows for reform, he became a freelance journalist and covered the Washington political scene (1868–70). He was appointed assistant professor of medieval history at Harvard (1870) and was named editor of the *North American Review* (1870–76). In 1872 he married Marian Hooper.

In 1877, Adams moved back to Washington, where he devoted himself full time to writing and to his self-appointed function as ''stable-companion to statesmen.''

Henry Brooks Adams with his dog. (© Bettman/CORBIS)

The next eight years were highly productive. He started the monumental *History of the United States during the Administrations of Jefferson and Madison* (9 v. 1889–91), which has been hailed by some as the greatest work of its kind since GIBBON's. He was also an able biographer, author of *Albert Gallatin* (1879), a study of Jefferson's secretary of the treasury, and *John Randolph,* a partisan view of the brilliant Southern spokesman. In later life Adams returned to biography, publishing *The Life of George Cabot Lodge* (1911). Both of his novels were published anonymously. *Democracy, An American Novel* (1880), a best-selling *succès de scandale,* was a satire on the Washington of his time, centering on the career of Mrs. Lightfoot Lee. *Esther* (1884) also features a cultivated and charming heroine, probably modeled on his wife, who makes an earnest but futile effort to accept a religious view of life.

His wife's suicide in 1885 was a severe blow to his psychic equilibrium. Although Adams was by nature an inveterate traveler, his journey to Japan (1886) with his close friend, artist John LA FARGE, was meant, in part, to be recuperative. With La Farge he visited Hawaii, the Pacific Islands, Australia, and Europe (1890–92). This journey occasioned one of his most interesting and curious volumes, *Memoirs of Marau Taaroa* (1893), a history of Tahiti from a non-Western perspective, revised and reprinted (1901) as *Memoirs of Arii Taimai E.* During the 1890s he spent much of his time abroad, traveling from the Near East to Russia and Scandinavia. In his mid 60s he undertook the completion of his two most important books— *Mont-Saint-Michel and Chartres* (1902), a study of medievalism rather than medieval history, and *The Education of Henry Adams* (1906), at once an intellectual autobiography in the third person and a study of 20th-century multiplicity. Both books were privately printed. "The Rule of Phase Applied to History" (1908) and "A Letter to American Teachers of History" (1910) were collected along with an earlier essay, "The Tendency of History" (1894), in *The Degradation of the Democratic Dogma* (1919). In 1912 he suffered a heart attack, but recovered sufficiently to go to France, where he remained until the outbreak of World War I. In 1918 he returned to Washington and died there.

Adams was not generally regarded as a literary figure until *Mont-Saint-Michel and Chartres* and *The Education* won an audience after his death. He prophesied the "darkening chaos of the modern world" in *The Education,* predicting the moral bankruptcy of a materialistic society. Using the 12th century, presented poetically and passionately in *Chartres,* as a touchstone by which to judge the 20th century, he looked with nostalgia at the unity of that far time, the Middle Ages, and with fear at the "multiplicity" of the time to come. The Virgin was the chief symbol in his studies of 13th-century unity, "the point of history when man held the highest idea of himself as a unit in the unified universe"; the Dynamo symbolized 20th-century multiplicity, marked by a "great influx of new forces . . . violently coercive" and "rapid in acceleration."

Bibliography: J. BLANCK, *Bibliography of American Literature,* 4 v. (New Haven 1955–63) v.1 contains a descriptive listing of separate editions. *Literary History of the United States,* ed. R. E. SPILLER et al., 3 v. (New York 1948) v.3 and its *Bibliography Supplement,* ed. R. M. LUDWIG (New York 1959), the best general bibliography. H. ADAMS, *Letters of Henry Adams, 1858–1918,* ed. W. C. FORD, 2 v. (Boston 1930–38); *Henry Adams and His Friends,* ed. H. D. CATER (Boston 1947). W. C. FORD, ed., *A Cycle of Adams Letters, 1861–65,* 2 v. (Boston 1920). E. SAMUELS, *The Young Henry Adams* (Cambridge, Mass. 1948); *Henry Adams: The Middle Years* (Cambridge, Mass. 1958); *Henry Adams: The Major Phase* (Cambridge, Mass. 1964). E. STEVENSON, *Henry Adams, a Biography* (New York 1955). W. H. JORDY, *Henry Adams: Scientific Historian* (New Haven 1952). J. C. LEVENSON, *The Mind and Heart of Henry Adams* (Boston 1957). Y. WINTERS, *In Defense of Reason* (New York 1947).

[J. SCHWARTZ]

ADAMS, JOHN, BL.

Priest, martyr; b. ca. 1543 at Winterbourne or Martin's Town, Dorsetshire, England; d. Oct. 8, 1586,

hanged, drawn and quartered at Tyburn (outside London), England. He had been a Protestant minister. Upon his conversion to Catholicism, he went to Rheims, where he was ordained a priest (1580). He returned to England in March 1581, where he labored at Winchester and in Hampshire, especially among the poor. He was also a noted exorcist. Adams was imprisoned in 1584 and banished the following year with 72 other priests. He returned, was again arrested for high treason, and executed, with two others, BB. John LOWE and Robert DIBDALE. According to Anthony Tyrrell's *Confessions,* Adams and Lowe were specifically selected for execution by Justice Young on the advice of Tyrrell, who was chagrined by his failure to implicate the Jesuit William WESTON in the Babington Plot and knew they exercised the greatest influence over imprisoned Catholics. William Warford, who knew Adams, described him as a man of "average height, with a dark beard, a sprightly look and black eyes. He was a very good apologist, straightforward, very pious, and pre-eminently a man of hard work." Adams was beatified by Pope John Paul II on Nov. 22, 1987 with George Haydock and Companions.

Feast: May 4 (England).

See Also: ENGLAND, SCOTLAND, AND WALES, MARTYRS OF.

Bibliography: R. CHALLONER, *Memoirs of Missionary Priests,* ed. J. H. POLLEN (rev. ed. London 1924). J. H. POLLEN, *Acts of English Martyrs* (London 1891).

[K. I. RABENSTEIN]

ADDAI AND MARI, SS.

According to Syrian Christian legend, Addai (Thaddeus) and Mari were two of the Lord's 72 Disciples, and were sent by Christ to establish the Church in Syria and Persia. Addai is named in the *Acta Edessena,* partly preserved by Eusebius (*Hist. eccl.* 1.13), which recounts the legends of ABGAR and part of the "Doctrine of Addai." The Doctrine is a fourth-century apocryphal account of the founding of Christianity in Edessa; it gives the story of the finding of the holy cross by Protonica, describes the Emperor Tiberius as punishing Jews for the crucifixion of Christ, and mentions Palut as one of the earliest bishops of Edessa. The Edessan portrait of Christ attributed in the account to Ananias, the messenger of King Abgar V, must be later than 394 for it is not mentioned by Aetheria in her *Peregrinatio ad loca sancta.*

Mari is considered the disciple of Addai and one of the 72. He is said to have founded the Persian Church in Kōē near Seleucia-Ctesiphon, and the monastery at Dair Qunnā. The *Acta S. Maris* was written probably in the ninth century. The Nestorians trace the foundation of their liturgy to SS. Addai and Mari.

Feast: Aug 5.

Bibliography: LABUBNĀ BAR SENNĀK, *The Doctrine of Addai,* ed. and tr. G. PHILLIPS (London 1876). H. RAHNER, *Lexikon für Theologie und Kirche* 1:136. J. ASSFALG, *ibid.* 7:24. A. BAUMSTARK, *Geschichte der syrischen Literatur* (Bonn 1922). B. BOTTE, ''L'Anaphore Chaldéene des Apôtres,'' *Orientalia Christiana periodica* 15 (1949) 259–276.

[F. X. MURPHY]

ADELA, ST.

Benedictine abbess; b. *c.* 675; d. near Trier, *c.* 734. Probably the daughter of Dagobert II, she is quite surely identical with the abbess Adola, to whom a letter of Abbess Alffled (*Monumenta Germaniae Epistolae selectae* 1.3: letter 8) is addressed. She is said to have founded the Abbey of Pfalzel at Trier. In 722 BONIFACE visited her and took her grandson (later Gregory of Utrecht) away as a student. She died about 734, but her remains were not discovered until 1072. Other information about Adela is based on a will, regarded as unauthentic by Pertz, but accepted by some scholars today. Her cult has not been confirmed, and she is not generally venerated in the liturgy of the Church.

Feast: Dec. 24.

Bibliography: M. WERNER, *Adelsfamilien im Umkreis der frühen Karolinger* (Sigmaringen 1982). R. AIGRAIN, *Catholicisme* 1:136–137. A. HEINTZ, *Lexicon für Theologie und Kirche,* ed. J. HOFER and K. RAHNER (Freiburg 1957–65) 1:140.

[L. MEAGHER]

ADELAIDE OF VILICH, ST.

Abbess. b. Cologne, last half of the tenth century; d. Cologne, Feb. 5, probably 1015. She was the daughter of Count Megingoz of Gelder. At an early age, Adelaide (Adelheid) entered the convent of St. Ursula in Cologne, where the Rule of St. Jerome was observed. As first abbess of the convent founded by her parents in Vilich (Bellich or Willich, today Beuel, near Bonn), on the Rhine River, she introduced the Benedictine Rule, which she considered stricter than that of St. Jerome. It was said that she had her nuns learn Latin so that they might better understand the Divine Office. While remaining abbess of Vilich, Adelaide succeeded her sister Bertrada, after the latter's death, as abbess of St. Maria im Kapitol in Cologne. She was buried in Vilich, where her relics are preserved. Adelaide was the friend and adviser of Heribert, Archbishop of Cologne; and according to legend, she showed great prudence in providing for the poor during a severe famine.

Feast: Feb. 5.

Bibliography: *Acta Sanctorum* Feb. 1:719–727. M. ZIMMERMANN, *Kalendarium Benedictinum* (Metten 1933–83)1:170–173. A. SCHÜTTE, *Handbuch der deutschen Heiligen* (Cologne 1941) 27–28. A. GROETEKEN, *Die l. Aebtissin Adelheid von Vilich* (2d ed. Kevelaer, Ger. 1956). J. TORSY, *Lexicon für Theologie und Kirche,* ed. J. HOFER and K. RAHNER (Freiburg 1957–65) 1:142.

[M. F. MCCARTHY]

ADELARD OF BATH

English translator, writer of scientific treatises, philosopher; b. *c.* 1070; d. after 1142–46. A Benedictine, he was educated at Tours, taught at Laon, and then spent seven years traveling in Italy, Sicily, possibly Spain, and Jerusalem, learning as opportunity offered. He is thought to have taught again in France, and an entry in the Pipe Roll for 1130 indicates that he had already returned to England.

A letter to his nephew, *De eodem et diverso* (*On the Identical and the Diverse*), written between 1105 and 1110, and dedicated to William, Bishop of Syracuse, records a conversation of the author with Philosophia and Philocosmia—the former representing the realm of reason, possibly the liberal arts and unchanging values, the latter the shifting world encountered through the senses. Its main interest lies in its remarks on UNIVERSALS.

His *Quaestiones naturales* or *76 Questions on Nature* composed 1111–16, deal with a variety of the natural sciences based on Arabic learning. [An English translation by H. Gollancz is included in Berechiah Ben Natronai, *Dodi ve-nichdi—Uncle and Nephew* (Oxford 1920)]. He acquired an Arabic copy of Euclid's *Elements* *c.* 1120, and being competent in both Greek and Arabic, he was the first to translate this work into Latin. He also rendered into Latin an Arabic *Introduction to Astronomy,* the astronomical tables, and an *Introduction* by Mohammed ben Moses al Khwarizmi (fl. *c.* 830) either to astronomy or to the quadrivium as a whole, as well as other works of Greco-Arabic science. He is the author of *Rules for the Abacus, Function of the Astrolabe* (*c.* 1141–46), and a treatise *On Falconry.*

Adelard was the first of the twelfth-century scholars to give learning in England its bias toward the investigation of nature and mathematics, a bias later conspicuous in the works of ROBERT GROSSETESTE and ROGER BACON.

Bibliography: H. E. WILLNER, ed. ''Des Adelard von Bath Traktat De eodem et diverso,'' *Beiträge zur Geschichte der Philosophie und Theologie des Mittelalters* 4.1 (1903). L. THORNDIKE, *A History of Magic and Experimental Science* (New York 1923–53) 2:19–49. C. H. HASKINS, *Studies in the History of Medieval Science* (2d ed. Cambridge, Mass. 1927). M. MÜLLER, ''Die Quaestiones naturales des Adelardus. . .,'' *Beiträge zur Geschichte der Philosophie und Theologie des Mittelalters* 31.2 (1934). F. P. BLIEMETZRIEDER, *Adelhard von Bath* (Munich 1935). D. A. CALLUS, ''Introduction of Aristotelian Learning to Oxford,'' *Proceedings of the British Academy* 29 (1943) 229–281. A. C. CROMBIE, *Augustine to Galileo* (London 1952). E. J. DIJKSTERHUIS, *The Mechanization of the World Picture,* tr. C. DIKSHOORN (Oxford 1961).

[E. A. SYNAN]

ADELELM OF BURGOS, ST.

Known also as Lesmes and, in French, Aleaume, patron of Burgos and one of four famous Benedictine abbots in Castile in the eleventh century; b. Loudon, near Poitiers, date unknown; d. Burgos, Jan. 30, 1097. His vita was written soon after his death by Rudolph, a monk of Chaise-Dieu in Auvergne. Adelelm gave up wealth and a military life and at Chaise-Dieu became famous for asceticism and miracles. He sent the Queen of England (Matilda of Flanders) blessed bread that reportedly cured her lethargy. At the request of Alfonso VI and his wife, Constance, he came to Burgos about 1081 and ministered to pilgrims and the sick. He crossed the swollen Tagus River Moses-like (reputedly without getting wet) in front of Alfonso's army when it took Toledo in 1085. The miracles attributed to him in France and in Spain were chiefly cures of sickness effected by means of blessed bread or water.

Feast: Jan. 30.

Bibliography: A. DE VENERO, *Vida del confessor San Lesmes* (Burgos 1563). L. SERRANO, *El obispado de Burgos,* 3 v. (Madrid 1935) v.2. K. LECHNER, *Lexicon für Theologie und Kirche,* ed. J. HOFER and K. RAHNER (Freiburg 1957–65) 1:141.

[E. P. COLBERT]

ADELHELM I, BL.

Abbot; d. Feb. 25, 1131. A BENEDICTINE monk at the Abbey of SANKT BLASIEN, he was chosen *c.* 1122 to be the first abbot of Engelberg, near Stans in Switzerland, soon after its foundation by Conrad of Seldenbüren (d. 1125). He worked to secure the exemption of his abbey from outside controls and won royal and papal confirmation of its status in 1124. Although his life was reputed to have been a saintly one, and miracles and wonders were reported at his tomb, almost no details beyond his activity as abbot are known. Having been venerated from the middle of the 12th century, his relics were enshrined in a chapel at the abbey at Engelberg in 1744.

Feast: Feb. 25.

Bibliography: M. BESSON, *Dictionnaire d'histoire et de géographie ecclésiastiques* 1:528. A. M. ZIMMERMANN, *Lexikon für Theologie und Kirche*² 1:142. *Acta Sanctorum* Feb. 3 (1863) 490. L. BURGENER, *Helvetia Sancta,* 2 v. (New York 1860). H. MAYER, *Geschichte des Klosters Engelburg* (Ei 1891). A. M. ZIMMERMANN, *Kalendarium Benedictinum: Die Heiligen und Seligen des Benediktinerordens und seiner Zweige* (Metten 1933–38) 1:252–254.

[J. L. GRASSI]

ADELPHUS OF METZ, ST.

Bishop; d. fifth century. Apart from the undoubted existence of his cult in Metz from an early date, everything about Adelphus is conjectural. He is believed to have succeeded St. Rufus as bishop of Metz in the fifth century, and to have ruled the diocese for 17 years, converting many pagans. The solemn translation of his relics to Neuweiler in 836 was an occasion of great popular rejoicing. Neuweiler became a center of pilgrimage. A great church was built in the eleventh century to enshrine the relics, but during the Reformation they were restored to their former repository in the abbey church.

Feast: Aug. 29; Sept. 1 in Neuweiler.

Bibliography: *Acta Sanctorum* Aug. 6:504–512. *Bibliotecha hagiographia latina antiquae et mediae aetatis* (Brussels 1898–1901) 1:76. *Pauli Warnefridi Liber de episcopis Mettensibus, Monumenta Germaniae Historica: Scriptores* (Berlin 1826–) 2:260–270. *Gesta episcoporum Mettensium,* ed. G. WAITZ, *Monumenta Germaniae Historica: Scriptores* (Berlin 1826–) 10:531–551, esp. 536. *Translatio et miracula S. Adelphi episcopi Mettensis,* ed. L. DE HEINEMANN, *Monumenta Germaniae Historica: Scriptores* (Berlin 1826–) 15.1:293–296. L. DUCHESNE, *Fastes épiscopaux de l'ancienne Gaul* (Paris 1907–15) 3:45–54. L. PFLEGER, ''Zur Gesch. des Adelphikultus in Elsass,'' *Archiv für elsässische Kirchengeschichte* 2 (1927) 443–444. J. M. B. CLAUSS, *Die Heiligen des Elsass* (Düsseldorf 1935). A. M. BURG, *Lexicon für Theologie und Kirche,* ed. J. HOFER and K. RAHNER (Freiburg 1957–65) 1:144.

[M. B. RYAN]

ADENULF OF ANAGNI

Secular Parisian scholastic; b. Anagni, *c.* 1225; d. Paris, Aug. 26, 1289. A nephew of GREGORY IX, he studied arts and theology at Paris, being regent master in theology *c.* 1272 to 1288. Of his works there are extant two commentaries on Aristotle, a quodlibet, about ten sermons, and a canonical treatise. He may have written the commentaries on the Psalms and Apocalypse published under the name of ALBERT THE GREAT. A canon of Paris, provost of Saint-Omer, a rich and liberal man, he fostered studies, students, and the transcription of manuscripts, among them the commentary of St. THOMAS AQUINAS on St. John. He was twice proposed for a bishopric (Narbonne and Paris), but found refuge among the canons of Saint-Victor. He bequeathed almost 40 magnificent manuscripts to Saint-Victor and the Sorbonne.

Bibliography: P. GLORIEUX, *Répertoire des maîtres en théologie de Paris au XIIIᵉ siècle* (Paris 1933–34) v. 17–18 of Bibliothèque Thomiste, 1:376–377; *La Littérature quodilbétique* v.1 (Kain 1925) 1:99–100. M. GRABMANN, *Traditio* 5 (1947) 269–283. G. MOLLAT, *Dictionnaire d'histoire et de géographie ecclésiastiques*, ed. A. BAUDRILLART et al. (Paris 1912–) 1:541.

[P. GLORIEUX]

ADEODATUS (DEUSDEDIT) II, POPE

Pontificate: April 11, 672 to June 16, 676; b. Rome, the son of Jovinian. Adeodatus succeeded VITALIAN and, like him, defendedorthodoxy against MONOTHELITISM. He was remarkable forhis generosity and for inaugurating the practice of datingevents in terms of his reign. He enlarged and enrichedthe Benedictine monastery of St. Erasmus on the CoelianHill, where he had been a monk. Two letters defending monastic exemptions are attributed to him (*Patrologia Latina*, ed. J. P. Migne 87: 1141–46). Some martyrologies celebrate his feast onJune 26, but the BOLLANDISTS say he had no cult.

Bibliography: *Liber pontificalis*, ed. L. DUCHESNE (Paris 1886–92, 1958) 1:346–347. P. JAFFÉ, *Regesta pontificum romanorum ab condita ecclesia ad annum post Christum natum 1198*, ed. S. LÖWENFELD et al. (Graz 1956) 166. J. F. KEHR, *Regesta Pontificum Romanorum. Italia Pontificia* (Berlin 1906–35) 1:43,176. H. K. MANN, *The Lives of the Popes in the Early Middle Ages from 590 to 1304* (London 1902–32) 1.2:17–19. C. CASPAR, *Geschichte de Paapsttums von den Anfängen bis zur Höhe der Weltherrscchaft* (Tübingen 1930–33) 2:587. G. SCHWAIGER, *Lexikon für Theologie und Kirche*, ed. J. HOFER and K. RAHNER (Freiberg 1957–65) 1:144. J. N. D. KELLY, *Oxford Dictionary of Popes* (New York 1986), 76–77

[C. M. AHERNE]

ADESTE FIDELES

Hymn used during the Christmas season, found neither in the Breviary nor in the Missal. Its origin is variously accounted for, although it is generally thought that both hymn and music were composed together in the early 18th century. Many scholars today think that it was written by John Francis Wade (1711–86), who was a teacher of Latin and church song at Douai, France, between 1740 and 1743. J. Stéphan in 1947 bolstered a plausible theory of Wade's authorship of an earlier version of the hymn and chorus, *Venite, adorate,* and the later more liturgical *Venite, adoremus.* He maintained that the hymn antedated 1744, when in a disguised form it was used as an "Air anglais" in a Paris vaudeville *Acajou.* It exists today in three versions, the first, with four strophes beginning with the words (stanza 1) *Adeste,* (2) *Deum de Deo,* (7) *Cantet,* and (8) *Ergo qui natus;* the second, with additional strophes inserted beginning (3) *En grege relicto,* (4) *Stella duce,* (5) *Magi aeterni patris,* and (6) *Pro nobis egenum;* a third version used in France has strophes 1, 3, 5 and 6. The hymn urges the faithful to approach the crib of the Word made Flesh, in the company of shepherds, magi, and angels. There are numerous English translations of the hymn.

Bibliography: J. STÉPHAN, *The Adeste Fideles* (Buckfastleigh, Eng. 1947). A. MOLIEN, *Catholicisme* 1:140–141. P. DEARMER, *Songs of Praise Discussed* (New York 1952). M. BRITT, ed., *The Hymns of the Breviary and Missal* (new ed. New York 1948).

[M. M. BEYENKA]

ADJUTOR, ST.

Crusader, hermit, and Benedictine monk; b. late eleventh century; d. Tiron, France, April 30, 1131. His parents were Jean, Seigneur de Vernon, and Rosemonde de Blaru. A devoutly religious youth, Adjutor attempted to live as austerely as possible, and HUGH OF AMIENS, Archbishop of Rouen, his friend and biographer, recounts his compassion and charity in great detail. He was one of a group of Norman knights who in 1095 set out on the First Crusade. The expedition was reputedly attended by many miraculous occurrences including Adjutor's escape from a Moslem prison. On his return to France, he became a monk at the Abbey of Tiron, where he earned a reputation for sanctity. He spent his last years as a hermit in a small cell he had built near the monastery.

Feast: April 30 (Rouen, Évreux, Chartres).

Bibliography: A. DELLA PORTA, *S. Adiutore, patrono della diocesi di Cava dei Tirreni* (Cava dei Tirreni 1968). *Acta Sanctorum* April 3:832–836. M. ZIMMERMANN, *Kalendarium Benedictinum* (Metten 1933–83) 2:78–81. H. LAHRKAMP, *Lexikon für Theologie und Kirche*, ed. J. HOFER and K. RAHNER (Freiburg 1957–65) 1:147. J. THÉROUDE, *La Vie et l'office de s. Adjuteur* (Rouen 1864), hist. and bibliog. introd. by R. BORDEAUX; repr. of *Vie de S. Adjuteur,* pub. by D. LANGLOIS in 1638 and of *Officium s. Adjutoris* (Paris 1639).

[V. L. BULLOUGH]

ADMINISTRATOR, APOSTOLIC

In the Latin Church, an apostolic administrator is a priest, and usually a bishop, who is assigned by the pope to govern an apostolic administration (*Codex Iuris Canonicis* [CIC] [Rome 1918; repr. Graz 1955] c. 371 §2). Alternately, by an extraordinary measure, the apostolic administrator may be assigned to govern a diocese in serious spiritual or temporal difficulty. As is evident from the nature of his mission, the history of the office, and canonical discipline, the latter kind of administrator is a papal "troubleshooter" sent to a distressed diocese.

Mission. Ordinarily, an apostolic administrator would be sent to represent the pope to a portion of God's people who are in an area where, due to special and particularly grave reasons, a diocese has not been erected (CIC c. 371 §2). An administrator could also be sent to a diocese whose diocesan bishop might be, for example, under a canonical penalty suspending his jurisdiction, guilty of gross mismanagement in financial affairs, incapacitated by bodily or mental illness, or physically prevented from exercising jurisdiction because of banishment or detention. An administrator's appointment to a vacant diocese might be prompted, for example, by the need for special investigation into past administration or for delicate diplomacy during a period of political discord.

Unlike a diocesan bishop, the administrator has only vicarious power, governing not in his own name, but in the name of the pope whose jurisdiction he exercises (CIC c. 371 §2). When the situation in the diocese has been normalized, administration is resumed by a diocesan bishop who rules by proper power in his own name, not as a delegate of the pope (CIC c. 381 §1).

Historical Evolution. Although the title "apostolic administrator" was stabilized only in 1908 by Pius X's constitution *Sapienti Consilio,* the existence of the office that it represents is discernible as far back as the 5th century. The Fifth Council of Carthage (401) and the Council of Macriana (419) in Africa speak of the interventor or intercessor, appointed by the metropolitan or a provincial council to oversee the smooth succession of government in a vacant diocese. He was usually the bishop of a neighboring diocese whose task as interventor was to conduct the funeral of the deceased bishop, to administer provisionally the affairs of the diocese, and to supervise the election of the new bishop.

In Italy and France a similar office was called that of visitator, the earliest record of which appears in the Council of Riez (439). From this time it became the common practice in France for the metropolitan to send a visitator to a diocese immediately upon its vacancy in order to prevent, among other things, the plundering of the bishop's property by clergy and laity alike. The prerogative of appointing visitators soon devolved to the papacy. From the time of Pope St. Gregory the Great (*c.* 540–604) well into the 9th century there were numerous examples of papal visitators sent throughout Italy and France, as well as Spain where the similar office of commendator had been common since the Council of Valencia (524).

From the 8th century the office began to suffer limitations as the institute of the cathedral chapter developed. When the Second General Lateran Council in 1139 granted the cathedral chapter the right to hold episcopal elec-

tions, the office of visitator became one of extraordinary and less frequent application, and in 1298 Boniface VIII reserved the appointment of administrators to the Holy See (*Corpus iuris canonici,* VI⁰, ed. E. Friedberg, 1.8.4). Sixtus V in 1588 assigned competence over such appointments to the Congregation of Bishops and Regulars, and in 1908 Pius X, in reorganizing the Roman CURIA, reassigned competence to the Congregation of the Consistory and consecrated the title apostolic administrator, which, since the time of decretal law, had been used interchangeably with the title Vicar Apostolic. The two are now distinct offices, the latter generally denoting a papal deputy sent to a missionary territory (CIC c. 371 §1).

Law Governing the office in the Latin Church. In default of special contrary provisions of the Holy See in a particular case, the Code of Canon Law determines various details in the office of apostolic administrator. After taking possession of the government of his territory, the apostolic administrator is a local ordinary (CIC c. 134). The administrator's jurisdiction does not cease on account of the death of the pope; normally it expires according to the wishes of the Holy See and, generally, when a new bishop takes possession of the see.

Unless there are contrary conditions in his mandate, the apostolic administrator generally enjoys the same rights, honors, and duties as a diocesan bishop (CIC c. 381 §2).

Office in the Eastern Churches. In the Eastern Catholic Churches, an apostolic administrator is appointed by the pope to govern an eparchy, whether vacant or not, for serious and special reasons (*Codex Canonum Ecclesiarium Orientalium* [CCEO] c. 234 §1). The apostolic administrator has the rights, honors, and duties that are given to him in his letter of appointment (CCEO c. 234 §2). He is a local hierarch (CCEO c. 984 §2).

Bibliography: T. J. MCDONOUGH, *Apostolic Administrators* (Catholic University of America Canon Law Studies 139; Washington, D.C. 1941). P. HOFMEISTER, "Von den Apostolischen Administratoren der Diözesen und Abteien," *Archiv für katholisches Kirchenrecht* 110 (1930) 337–392. J. A. RENKEN, in *New Commentary on the Code of Canon Law,* ed. J. P. BEAL et al. (New York 2000) 508–509, 518–520.

[J. R. KEATING/J. STAAB]

ADMONT, ABBEY OF

Benedictine abbey on the Enns River, Diocese of Graz-Seckau, central Austria; dedicated to the Blessed Virgin and St. BLAISE. The place (*in valle Ademundi*) is first mentioned in a document of Louis the German (859). In 1074 Abp. Gebhard of Salzburg built the abbey on an earlier cloister of St. Emma of Gurk (d. 1045), who also endowed the monastery of Gurk (1043). A reform cloister in the spirit of CLUNY, Admont reached its first peak under Abbots Gottfried (1138–65) and Irimbert (1172–77) with a scriptorium famous for illuminations and script. The abbey cleared land, founded parishes, opened mines, fostered viticulture, and kept a hospital for the poor, the sick, and lepers; 13 monks became abbots elsewhere. From the 12th century, the abbot was archdeacon of the Enns, Palten, and Liesing valleys. A brief decline was followed by economic and spiritual revival under Henry II (1275–97) and ENGELBERT (1297–1327). Protestantism and the Turks caused great harm; and the cloister of Benedictine nuns, founded in 1120, came to an end. Johann IV Hoffmann (1581–1614), Mathias von Preininger (1615–28), and Urban Weber (1628–59) restored and rebuilt Admont. The Latin school was succeeded by a gymnasium (1644) and a school of theology (1711); monks from Admont taught in the state Gymnasiums of Graz, Leoben, and Judenburg (1750–1900). During the Napoleonic Wars, the abbey was plundered four times (1798–1809). Benno Kreil (1823–63) restored its finances, but a fire destroyed part of the cloister, the abbey church, and the nearby market (1865). Admont was rebuilt, only to be expropriated by Nazis (1938).

Since 1945 Admont has been slowly rebuilding and regaining its lost possessions and art treasures. It now has extensive farms and forests with modern equipment, workshops, and two power plants. The ornate library (236 by 46 feet and 36 feet high) has seven ceiling frescoes by B. Altomonte (1776) and baroque carvings by J. T. Stammel (d. 1765); it holds 130,000 volumes, 1,100 MSS, and 900 early printed works. The archives, a natural history museum with a collection of insects, and an art museum with a 1,000-year-old collection are noteworthy. The neo-Gothic abbey church (1869) has sacred art objects, a Christmas crib by Stammel (1745), and precious vestments from the abbey's embroidery school (17th and 18th centuries).

Bibliography: P. J. WICHNER, *Geschichte des Stiftes Admont,* 4 v. (Graz 1874–80). P. A. KRAUSE, *Die Stiftsbibliothek in Admont* (Linz 1962). U. BERLIÈRE, *Dictionnaire d'histoire et de géographie ecclésiastiques* 1:574–576. A. KRAUSE, *Lexikon für Theologie und Kirche,* ed. J. HOFER and K. RAHNER (Freiburg 1957–65) 1:150. L. H. COTTINEAU, *Répertoire topobibliographique des abbayes et prieurés* (Mâcon 1935–39) 1:19–20. O. L. KAPSNER, *A Benedictine Bibliography: An Author-Subject Union List* (Collegeville, Minn.) 2:184. P. A. KRAUSE, *Das Blasiusmünster in Admont* (Linz 1965).

[A. KRAUSE]

ADO OF VIENNE, ST.

Historian, archbishop of Vienne; b. Archdiocese of Sens, France, *c.* 800; d. Vienne, France, Dec. 16, 875. He

Library of Admont Abbey, designed by Josef Huber with frescoes by Bartolomeo Altomonte. (© Josi F. Poblete/CORBIS)

was born of a Gâtinais family, who offered him as a child to the Benedictine Abbey of Ferrières-en-Gâtinais, where he was trained under Abbot Lupus of Ferrières. He later spent some time studying at Prüm under Abbot Markward, and went also to Rome or Ravenna for some years—perhaps five—to gather hagiographical materials. Given charge of the parish of Saint-Romain in Lyons, Ado was later promoted to the See of Vienne some time between July 6, 859 (when Aglimar, his predecessor, died), and Oct. 22, 860 (when Ado signed the acts of the Council of Thusey).

As archbishop of Vienne he won the esteem of popes NICHOLAS I and ADRIAN II, and kings Charles II the Bald and Louis the German alike, especially for his firm stand against the divorce of King LOTHAIR II. He was active in his archdiocese as well, holding councils to reform clerical morality and to regulate the celebration of the Divine Office. The acts of these reforming councils have disappeared except for a fragment from one held in 870.

Ado is also important as an author. In his *Chronicum sive Breviarium de sex mundi aetatibus ab Adamo usque ad annum 869* (*Patrologia Latina* 123:23–138; *Monumenta Germanica Historica: Scriptores* 2:315–323), a chronicle of world history that depends on similar works by Bede, Orosius, and Isidore and on contemporary Frankish sources, he treated in interesting detail the Diocese of Vienne, listing 47 bishops accurately (Duchesne, *Fastes épiscopaux de l'ancienne Gaule* 150–162). But he identified the first bishop, Crescens, with the person of that name mentioned by St. Paul (2 Tm 4.10). Bishop

Crescens actually lived in the third century. Ado himself may have wrenched the chronology or may simply have repeated an earlier legend. He reedited a life of St. DE-SIDERIUS of Vienne, one of his predecessors in the See of Vienne, who died as a result of courageously rebuking the redoubtable Brunhilde, and composed a life of St. Theuderius, a sixth-century abbot in Vienne. Ado published a martyrology called *Passionum codices undecumque collecti* (*Patrilogia Latina* 123:143–436), nine-tenths of which was taken from a similar work by FLORUS OF LYONS. The remaining text Ado claimed to have derived from an ancient collection copied by him when he was in Italy at Ravenna. This portion of the text has been condemned as sheer forgery on Ado's part; it only added to the already complicated problems concerning martyrologies. USUARD was much influenced by Ado's work.

Feast: Dec. 16.

Bibliography: J. MABILLON, *Acta sanctorum ordinis S. Benedicti* (Venice 1733–40) 6:278–290. W. L. KREMERS, *Ado von Vienne* (Steyl 1911). A. BUTLER, *The Lives of the Saints,* ed. H. THURSTON and D. ATTWATER (New York 1956) 4:571–572. J. L. BAUDOT and L. CHAUSSIN, *Vies des saints et des bienhereux selon l'ordre du calendrier avec l'historique des fêtes* (Paris 1935–56) 12:482–494. A. M. ZIMMERMANN, *Lexicon für Theologie und Kirche,* ed. J. HOFER and K. RAHNER (Freiburg 1957–65) 1:150–51.

[C. M. AHERNE]

ADONAI

This term comes from the Canaanite and Hebrew word *'ādôn,* which means lord. The word is a plural form to which the personal suffix "my" has been added. In order to distinguish this form, which means "my lords," from the same word used in speaking of the one Lord, a special plural form featuring a long "a" before the "i" was evolved. (For an example of these different forms cf. Gn 18.3 with 19.2, Hebrew text.) The suffix "my" gradually lost its significance, as happened also in the case of the word "Rabbi" (my Master). (For Adonai as a substitute for Yahweh, *see* ELOHIM; JEHOVAH; YAHWEH.)

Bibliography: B. W. ANDERSON, *The Interpreter's Dictionary of the Bible,* ed. G. A. BUTTRICK, 4 v. (Nashville 1962) 2:414. H. JUNKER, *Lexikon für Theologie und Kirche,* ed. J. HOFER and K. RAHNER, 10 v. (2d, new ed. Freiburg 1957–65) 1:152. P. VAN IMSCHOOT, *Théologie de l'Ancien Testament,* 2 v. (Tournai 1954–56).

[R. T. A. MURPHY]

ADOPTION (IN THE BIBLE)

The legal action by which a minor is made the equivalent of a child born in a family and given corresponding inheritance rights. Adoption was practiced in the ancient Near Eastern civilizations of the second millennium, and traces of the custom can be found in the Bible, especially in the stories of the PATRIARCHS. For example, Abraham's expectation that Eliezer would be his heir (Gn 15.2–3) seems to reflect the practice of the Hurrians preserved in the Nuzu (Nuzi) documents. From these texts it appears that even a slave could be made an heir when there was no son. Such a person would be considered an adopted child. The action of Sara in giving her servant girl HAGAR to Abraham as a concubine in order that Sarah might accept the child born of this union as her own (Gn 16.2–5) is a case of adoption paralleled in the Nuzu texts. The same is true of the story of the birth of Jacob's sons, Dan and Nephthali, whom Bala, Rachel's maid, bore on her mistress's "knees" (Gn 30.3–8), and of the account of Israel's action in regard to Joseph's sons (Gn 48.5–20); the sons of Machir (the son of Manasseh) also "were born on Joseph's knees" (Gn 50.23). These parallels to the Hurrian practice reflect the ancient Near Eastern background of the patriarchal narratives and are not surprising since HARAN, a patriarchal center, was part of the Hurrian territory. However, it would seem that these practices of adoption were not made part of the Israelite legal traditions, since there is no trace of them in the biblical law codes. Other examples of adoption in the Old Testament are the cases of Moses (Ex 2.10), Genubath (1 Kgs 11.20), and Esther (Est 2.7, 15); these, however, took place in foreign lands and do not necessarily reflect Israelite practice.

Another instance of adoption customs that appears in the Bible is the relationship of the king to Yahweh, expressed by the formula of Ps 2.7, "You are my son; this day I have begotten you," which, in turn, is based on Nathan's oracle to David (2 Sm 7.8–16). Since the king represented the people, the people as a whole share in the adoption. This is not a new idea in Israel, for in the Exodus from Egypt God had already entered into a father-son relationship with the people (Ex 4.22; Dt 32.6). The use of the metaphor of Yahweh as father to Israel is expressed in many other texts (Is 63.16; Jer 3.19; 31.9; Os 11.1; etc.).

This concept reached its full flowering only in the New Testament. There Our Lord taught His disciples to address God as their Father (Mt 6.9; Lk 11.2). Similar references are found in the Gospel of St. John (Jn 20.17), and St. Paul refers to the Christian adoption as sons of God as the result of the indwelling of the Holy Spirit (Rom 8.15, 23; Gal 4.5; Eph 1.5).

Bibliography: *Encyclopedic Dictionary of the Bible,* tr. and adap. by L. HARTMAN, (New York 1963) 36–37. R. DE VAUX, *Ancient Israel, Its Life and Institutions,* tr. J. HCHUGH (New York 1961) 51–52. E. A. SPEISER, *Genesis* (Anchor Bible 1; Garden City,

N.Y. 1964) 112, 120–121, 230. R. T. O'CALLAGHAN, *Aram Naharaim* (Analecta orientalia 26; Rome 1948) 73–74. R. J. TOURNAY, "Nouzi," *Dictionnaire de la Bible* (Paris 1928) 6:646–674. S. O. MOWINCKEL, *The Psalms in Israel's Worship*, tr. D. R. AP-THOMAS (Nashville 1962) 54–58.

[S. M. POLAN]

ADOPTIONISM

A heresy that proclaimed a double sonship of Christ and maintained that as divine He was the natural Son of God, but as man He was only the adopted Son. In origin, the heresy goes back to PAUL OF SAMOSATA, although it has been ascribed to THEODORE OF MOPSUESTIA, and NESTORIUS. Adoptionism was first officially taught by ELIPANDUS, Archbishop of Toledo, Spain, *c.* 785, in his attempt to correct the errors of Migetius concerning the Incarnation. Elipandus believed that he could best safeguard the distinction between the divine and human natures in Christ by designating the eternally begotten Logos as God's natural son; and the Son of Mary, which the Logos assumed, as God's adopted son. Two monks, Beatus and Etherius, challenged the orthodoxy of this explanation and referred the matter to Pope ADRIAN I. In a letter to the Spanish hierarchy the Pontiff condemned the term "adopted son" as applied to Christ because it was contrary to Sacred Scripture and to the teaching of the most reliable Greek and Latin theologians, and because it constituted a revival of Nestorianism.

Elipandus refused to submit and found a staunch supporter in Felix, bishop of Urgel. Since the latter's diocese was in Charlemagne's kingdom, Felix was obliged to appear before a council at Ratisbon in 792 and swear never to employ the words "adopted son" in speaking of Christ. At this point the Spanish hierarchy intervened and wrote a defense of Elipandus to Charlemagne and the bishops of Gaul. The king, with the approval of the Sovereign Pontiff, summoned a council at Frankfort in 794 to settle the controversy.

The council was one of the largest assemblies in the history of the Church, with two papal legates present and representatives of every country of western Europe except Mozarabic Spain. It opened with the reading of a letter from Pope Adrian in which he unconditionally condemned Adoptionism as heretical. In accordance with the papal teaching a definition was drawn up that can be summarized as follows: "The Son of God became the Son of man, but He still kept the title of a real son; there is only one Son and He is not an adopted son." It indicated the basic fallacy of Adoptionism, which applied the word son to a nature and not to a person. Finally, texts from Scripture and quotations from the Fathers of the

Detail of the "Pope Giving Privileges to the Hospital Director," by Domenico di Bartolo. (©Archivo Iconografico, S.A./CORBIS)

Church were cited to prove the correctness of this definition. This patristic section seems to have been the work of the scholarly monk ALCUIN. The condemnation of Adoptionism at Frankfort was repeated at councils in Friuli, Italy (796), Rome (799), and Aix-la-Chapelle (800). As far as is known, Elipandus and the Spanish bishops adhered to their opinion, but did not break formally with the Holy See.

In the 12th century, Abelard, Folmar of Trier, and Gilbert de la Porée maintained that the union between the Logos and His human nature could be only external and accidental; for, if it were substantial, it would constitute a finite quality in the Blessed Trinity. Hence they concluded that Jesus Christ as man was not the natural, but only the adopted, son of God. On Feb. 18, 1177, Pope Alexander III condemned the teaching that Jesus Christ as man is not a substantial reality, and added, "as He is truly God, so He is also truly man, composed of a rational soul and a human body." Two centuries later Durandus and some Scotists taught that Jesus Christ is, at the same time, the natural and the adopted Son of God, because He has received the fullness of sanctifying grace. However this opinion is also to be rejected, for adoption implies that the one adopted was previously a stranger to the person who adopted him, and Christ, as at once God and man, could never be a stranger to His heavenly Father. Besides, one and the same person cannot be both the natural and the adopted son of the same father.

Bibliography: H. QUILLIET and E. PORTALIÉ, *Dictionnaire de théologie catholique*, ed. A. VACANT et al., (Paris 1903–50) 1.1:403–421. J. POHLE, *Christology*, v.4 of *Dogmatic Theology*, tr. and ed. A. PREUSS, 12 v. (St. Louis 1950–53). É. AMANN, A. FLICHE and V. MARTIN, eds., *Histoire de l'église depuis les origines jusqu'à nos jours* (Paris 1935–) 6:129–152. H. DENZINGER, *Enchiridion symbolorum*, ed. A. SCHÖNMETZER (Freiburg 1963) 595, 610–611.

[S. J. MCKENNA]

ADORO TE DEVOTE

A rhymed prayer marked by deep personal faith and theological insight, and addressed to Christ in the Blessed Sacrament. Although never a part of the Breviary, it appeared in various collections of popular devotions until Pope PIUS V inserted it in the Roman Missal among the prayers of thanksgiving after Mass. All extant MSS attribute the poem to St. THOMAS AQUINAS; however, his authorship has been contested. No MS is known from the first 50 years after Aquinas's death, nor does anyone during that time refer to Thomas as its author. Two of the 14th century codices state that Thomas composed or recited the prayer on receiving Viaticum. On this point the silence of the saint's biographer, William de Tocca, is significant. Dom André WILMART, who made the most thorough study of the manuscript and literary tradition of the *Adoro Te,* concluded that documentary evidence is insufficient to affirm Aquinas's authorship. Furthermore, some theologians doubt Thomistic origin because of divergences of thought and expression between the *Summa* and this poem. However, M. GRABMANN has maintained the genuineness of authorship because all MSS indicate it, and in his judgment the poem breathes the Eucharistic theology of Aquinas. F. Raby pointed out that a certain poem of JACOPONE DA TODI (written *c.* 1280–94) would be unexplainable had the *Adoro Te* not existed. Although this fact does not prove Thomistic origin, it makes possible the assigning of a date that falls within the lifetime of Thomas (d. 1274). In Raby's opinion the earliest MSS may be correct in stating that Aquinas wrote the *Adoro Te,* even if they report incorrectly the circumstances of its composition. There are many English translations. One of the most effective is that of Gerard Manley Hopkins beginning ''Godhead here in hiding, Whom I do adore.''

Bibliography: A. WILMART, ''La Tradition littéraire et textuelle de l'*Adoro te devote*,'' *Recherches de Théologie ancienne et médiévale* 1 (1929) 21–40, 149–176; repr. with appendices in *Auteurs spirituels et textes dévots du Moyen Âge latin* (Paris 1932) 361–414. F. J. E. RABY, ''The Date and Authorship of the Poem *Adoro Te Devote*,'' *Speculum* 20 (1945) 236–238. M. GRABMANN, *Die Werke des heiligen Thomas von Aquin* (3d ed. Münster 1949) 367–370, with refs. cited in nn. 184–186. J. P. CAVARNOS, ''Greek Translations of the *Adoro Te Devote* and the *Ave Verum*,'' *Traditio* 8 (1952) 418–423.

[M. I. J. ROUSSEAU]

ADRAGNA, ANTONIO MARIA

Theologian; b. Trapani, Sicily, Oct. 1, 1818; d. Rome, Oct. 14, 1890. He entered the Conventual Franciscans in 1834 and was ordained in 1841. He taught in Würzburg and Assisi, was named consultor of the Holy Office in 1861, and member of the dogmatic commission for Vatican Council I in 1866. Adragna was given the task of preparing a schema on the temporalities of the Church for the council. From 1872 to 1879 he was minister general of his order. As a result of the religious suppressions in Rome he was forced to live in Holland (1876–78). None of his works have been published and many have been lost. He was generally considered a conservative in his theology.

Bibliography: A. M. GHISALBERTI, ed., *Dizionario biographico degli Italiani* 1:306. D. SPARACIO, *Frammenti bio-bibliografici di scrittori ed autori minori Conventuali dagli ultimi anni del '600 al 1930* (Assisi 1931).

[P. FEHLNER]

ADRIAN, ST.

Ninth-century bishop and martyr; b., according to legend, in Hungary, of royal stock. Adrian (Hadrian, Odhran) is supposed to have been consecrated bishop there. No reliable information on him is extant. Apparently he went to the British Isles and as a missionary bishop had no settled see, but preached especially to the Picts of Fifeshire. Legend has it that he was archbishop of St. Andrews in Scotland. However, it may well be that this is the Irish St. Odhran who reputedly arrived in Scotland with 6,606 companions of various nationalities, possibly driven out of Ireland by the invading Danes. Adrian established a monastery on the Isle of May (Firth of Forth). In 875 the Danes and the Scots fought at the Firth of Forth, and most of the Scots were killed. The Aberdeen Breviary (1509) commemorated the martyrs who had died in the monastery on the Isle of May on Holy Thursday.

Feast: March 4.

Bibliography: *Acta Sanctorum* March 1:324–326. L. MACFARLANE, *Lexicon für Theologie und Kirche*, ed. J. HOFER and K. RAHNER (Freiburg 1957–65) 4:1310–11. W. F. SKENE, *Celtic Scotland,* 3 v. (2d ed. Edinburgh 1886–90) 2:311–316.

[R. T. MEYER]

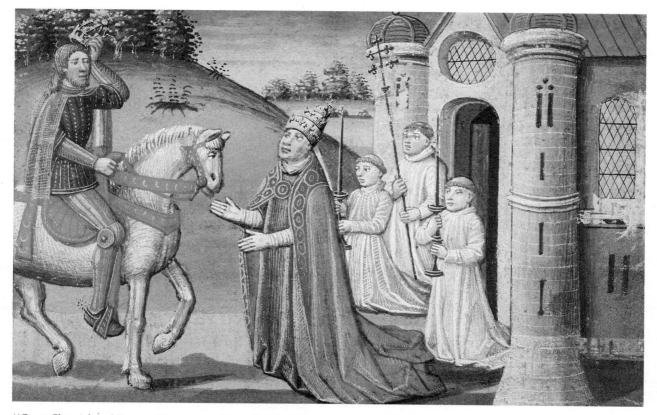

"Great Chronicles of France: Charlemagne Meets Pope Adrian I near Rome," illuminated manuscript. (© Archivo Iconografico, S.A./ CORBIS)

ADRIAN I, POPE

Pontificate: Feb. 1, 772 to Dec. 25, 795. A member of a prominent Roman family representing the military aristocracy, Adrian began his career in the service of the papal bureaucracy, eventually becoming a deacon with a reputation for learning. His election as pope represented a reconciliation of the clerical bureaucracy and the military aristocracy, two elements in the PAPAL STATE whose rivalry for control of the papal office during the pontificate of Pope STEPHEN III (768–772) posed major challenges for Adrian. The Lombard king, DESIDERIUS, had exploited the turmoil in Rome to establish his agent, Paul Afiarta, as the dominant figure in the papal administration. More importantly, Desiderius had taken advantage of developments in the Frankish kingdom to create uncertainty about the Frankish protectorate over the Papal State.

Adrian responded decisively to those challenges. He extended amnesty to those who had suffered as enemies of Paul Afiarta and moved skillfully to eliminate Afiarta from his position of power. The new pope indicated a willingness to establish peace with the LOMBARDS, but only on condition that Desiderius restore territories prom-

ised to the papacy in earlier agreements. The Lombard king responded with renewed assaults on territories claimed by the papacy. One of his goals was to pressure Adrian into anointing the heirs of the recently deceased Frankish king, CARLOMAN, as kings, thereby recognizing their rights to their father's kingdom. Desiderius hoped that success in this venture would disrupt the Frankish-papal alliance by alienating CHARLEMAGNE, who had taken over Carloman's kingdom and whose claim to it would be threatened by papal recognition of the rights of his nephews. Adrian firmly resisted this pressure, all the while continuing his demands for territorial restoration and imploring Charlemagne to fulfill his responsibility as protector of the Papal State. Finally in 773, after Charlemagne's efforts to mediate a peace settlement between the papacy and the Lombards were rebuffed by Desiderius, the Frankish king decided on military action against the Lombards to remove the threat to the realm of St. Peter. While his campaign was in progress Charlemagne traveled to Rome in 774 to celebrate Easter. On that occasion he renewed the promise made in 754 to Pope STEPHEN II by his father, PEPIN III, at Quierzy; the specific terms of that promise, now put into writing, served as the basis for papal claims to territory embracing more than two thirds of the peninsula, including, besides the duchy of Rome, the former Byzantine Exarchate of Ravenna, the Pentapolis, Spoleto, Benevento, Venetia, Istria, Lombard Tuscany, and Corsica. After demonstrating his loyalty to the alliance formed by his father, Charlemagne returned to Pavia, where Desiderius soon surrendered. Charlemagne thereupon deposed the Lombard king and took control of the kingdom, becoming king of the Lombards as well as king of the Franks and *patricius Romanorum*.

During the next few years after 774 Adrian was chiefly concerned with efforts to extend the boundaries of the Papal State and to safeguard papal autonomy in the face of the yet unknown Italian policy of his Frankish protector, now also the neighbor of the Papal State. At first Adrian was persistent in seeking from Charlemagne restoration of all the territories granted to the papacy in the document drawn up in 774. Charlemagne paid little heed to these claims, partly because he was too occupied with his wars against the Saxons and the Muslims to deal with problems in Italy. In time he began to come to grips with his role as king of the Lombards; in doing so he realized that conceding all the territory which Adrian claimed would irreparably damage his Lombard kingdom. As a consequence, Adrian was forced to scale back his claims substantially. On the occasion of trips to Rome in 781 and 787–788 Charlemagne favored Adrian with territorial concessions that enlarged the Papal State, but these concessions fell far short of the claims of the papacy based on its understanding of earlier Frankish promises made in 754 and 774.

In his relationship as ruler of the Papal States with Charlemagne as *patricius Romanorum* Adrian insisted on the autonomy of the Papal State and as a rule acted like an independent ruler in full control of the administration and the resources of his realm. However, there was resistance to papal authority in some parts of the Papal State, especially in Ravenna, where the archbishop sought to establish his own autonomy. Occasionally Adrian clashed with Charlemagne over issues affecting the internal governance of the Papal State, but usually these conflicts were worked out amicably. The Frankish king did put limits on the freedom of Adrian in conducting the external relations of the Papal State, but even in those cases Charlemagne never acted in ways that suggested that he was the pope's overlord. His actions usually worked to the pope's advantage by securing the boundaries of the Papal State.

Freed from the threat of outside intervention and recognized as the unquestioned master of the government of the Papal State, Adrian proved himself an effective ruler. Through skillful management of revenues derived from the patrimonies of St. Peter located within the Papal State

and beyond its borders, he was able to repair the city walls, improve the aqueduct system, and expand the charitable activities of the Church. Especially impressive were his initiatives in restoring old churches and in building new ones. In this respect Adrian gave fresh impetus to efforts begun by his predecessors that resulted in the physical transformation of Rome from a classical to a medieval Christian city, a transformation that had no small effect on the mentality of Rome's citizenry.

All of these activities did not prevent Adrian from discharging the responsibilities implicit in the alliance of friendship, love, and charity made between Stephen II and Pepin III in 754 and renewed between Adrian and Charlemagne. Adrian made special provisions for public prayers for the success of Charlemagne's military undertakings leading to the expansion of Christendom, especially against the Saxons. He repeatedly praised the Frankish ruler for his service in the cause of the Christian community, thereby enhancing Charlemagne's image as guardian of God's people. In 781 Adrian stood as godfather for Charlemagne's son Pepin, and then anointed Pepin and his brother, Louis, as kings of Italy and Aquitaine, thereby helping Charlemagne to put the rulership of his sprawling empire on a sounder footing. He agreed to help Charlemagne maintain control over Bavaria by threatening to excommunicate its rebellious duke unless he abided by his oath of obedience to the Frankish king. He lent his full support to Charlemagne's efforts to reform the Frankish religious establishment, giving advice on proper ecclesiastical organization and providing liturgical texts and a canon law collection known as the *Dionysio-Hadriana* to serve as guides in revitalizing Christian life in Francia.

Despite the mutually friendly and beneficial relationships between Adrian and Charlemagne, tension did emerge in an unexpected area involving the locus of authority in spiritual affairs. At least since the days of Pope GELASIUS I (492–496) it had been widely accepted that there was a unique sphere of human activity involving spiritual affairs over which the Church and its leaders exercised authority. A long succession of popes held that position and resisted the intrusion of secular authorities, including emperors in Constantinople, into spiritual matters, especially those pertaining to the definition of doctrine. Although the liberation of the papacy from imperial control during the eighth century seemed to resolve that issue in favor of papal precedence in spiritual affairs at least in the Latin West, the issue began to emerge in new form during Adrian's pontificate. Increasingly Charlemagne expanded his claim to a directive role in religious affairs, a claim nourished by his actions to renew religious life in his kingdom. Justification for his involvement in religious affairs was provided by religious leaders formed by the intellectual renaissance accompanying Charlemagne's religious reform. They interpreted Old Testament history and St. Augustine's writings in a way that led to a concept of kingship which vested both spiritual and temporal authority in the hands of a single figure, a priest-king responsible to God for the spiritual and temporal well-being of his subjects. Charlemagne increasingly shaped his actions according to this model of ministerial kingship which strongly resembled the CAESAROPAPISM of the imperial government in Constantinople; as a result he assumed undisputed direction of religious life in his realm.

Adrian made no effort to curb Charlemagne's control of ecclesiastical affairs within the Frankish kingdom, partly because he welcomed the success of the king's religious reforms but chiefly because it was beyond his power to restrain Charlemagne. But when matters of doctrine came up, the pope's position was different. One such case involved the Adoptionist heresy which developed in Spain in the 780s. Although Adrian collaborated with the Frankish king in the effort to end this heresy, Charlemagne and his religious advisers took the decisive action by officially condemning ADOPTIONISM at the Council of Frankfurt in 794 and by preparing the theological case upon which the condemnation was based. The issue was posed even more sharply by a significant development surrounding the iconoclastic heresy which took shape during Adrian's pontificate. Like all his predecessors since Pope Gregory II (715–731), Adrian opposed the policy instituted by Emperor LEO III to outlaw the veneration of icons. He thus welcomed the initiative taken by Empress IRENE after she became regent for her infant son in 780 to reverse the iconoclastic policy of the imperial government. He gave his approval to the summoning of the second Council of NICAEA in 787 and sent a letter to Constantinople that provided the theological grounds for the council's condemnation of ICONOCLASM and its sanction of the veneration of images in religious worship. But when a badly translated Latin version of the acts of the council reached Charlemagne's court, the Frankish reaction was anything but approving. Miffed at being denied any part in Nicaea II and confident of the theological prowess of his advisers, Charlemagne took steps to produce a refutation of the acts of the council. The result was a compilation called the *LIBRI CAROLINI,* which among other things condemned the Nicaea II for theological innovations concerning icons, mounted a savage attack on the Greek church and its leaders, and argued for the key role of the Frankish church in guarding orthodoxy and judging departures for it. As work on the *Libri Carolini* proceeded, Adrian was informed of the Frankish position and asked to disavow the acts of the Council of Nicaea despite the fact that he had played an decisive role in

shaping its decisions. Adrian responded in a long document defending the position on images taken at Nicaea, but he did agree to withhold his official approval of the council's position on images until the emperor met certain other conditions. Disregarding Adrian's teaching on images, the Franks officially condemned the position taken at Nicaea II at the Council of Frankfurt in 794. On still another theological issue, the Franks challenged Adrian by insisting that he condemn the Greeks for excluding the *FILIOQUE* phrase from the NICENE CREED used in the liturgy of the Mass. Adrian, whose Roman Church followed the Greek custom, responded by providing evidence from ancient authorities refuting the Frankish position and upholding the Greek-Roman position. In each of these cases the Frankish church and its leader, the king, were claiming a role in the definition of dogma even to the point of challenging positions taken by the pope. Although Adrian stood his ground in this matter, he was by no means able to put limits to the intrusion of an ambitious king and his aggressive, educated clerical supporters into a realm where the Church's spiritual leaders claimed precedence.

Although his pontificate was marked by challenges, Adrian I proved remarkably creative in advancing the interests of the papacy and in shaping a mutually beneficial working arrangement with the increasingly powerful Frankish state and its most famous ruler, Charlemagne. Through Adrian's efforts the Papal State was enlarged, its boundaries secured, its administration given firm direction, and its role in Italian affairs expanded. During his pontificate papal influence spread beyond Rome to contribute to the quickening of religious and cultural life over large areas of the West, especially where the Franks dominated. Perhaps it was his understanding of the magnitude of Adrian's accomplishments that, according to Charlemagne's biographer, Einhard, caused the king to weep like one who had lost a brother or a child when he received news of the death of the pope in 795.

Bibliography: Sources: *Le Liber Pontificalis,* ed. L. DUCHESNE, 3 v., 2d ed. (Paris 1955–1957), 1: 486–523; Eng. tr. in *The Lives of the Eighth-Century Popes (Liber Pontificalis). The Ancient Biographies of Nine Popes from AD 715 to AD 817,* tr. with intro. R. DAVIS (Liverpool 1992) 107–172. *Regesta Pontificum Romanorum ab condita ecclesia ad annum post Christum MCXCVIII,* ed. P. JAFFÉ, 2 v., 2d ed. (Leipzig 1885–1888) 1: 289–306. *Codex Carolinus,* Epp. 49–97, ed. W. GUNDLACH, *Monumenta Germaniae Historica: Epistolae Merowingici et Karolini,* v. 1 (Berlin 1892) 567–648, 654–655. *Epistolae selectae pontificum Romanorum Carlo Magno et Ludowico Pio regnantibus,* ed. K. HAMPE, *Monumenta Germaniae Historica: Epistolae Karolini Aevi,* v. 3 (Berlin 1899) 3–57. J. D. MANSI, *Sacrorum conciliorum, nova et amplissima collectio,* 54 v. (Paris 1901–20; repr. Graz 1960–61), 12: 951–1154; 13: 1–820. **Literature:** L. DUCHESNE, *The Beginnings of the Temporal Sovereignty of the Popes, A.D. 754–1073,* tr. A. H. MATTHEW (London 1908) 87–111. C. J. HEFELE, *Histoire des conciles d'après les documents originaux,* tr. H. LECLERCQ, v. 3, part 2 (Paris 1910),

741–804, 1001–1091. F. X. SEPPELT, *Geschichte des Papsttums. Eine Geschichte der Päpste von den Anfängen bis zum Tod Pius X*, v. 2: *Das Papsttums im Frühmittelalter. Geschichte des Päpste von Regierungsantritt Gregors des Grossen bis zum Mitte des ll. Jahrhundert* (Leipzig 1934) 158–184. O. BERTOLINI, *Roma di Fronte a Bisanzio e ai Langobardi*, (*Storia di Roma* 9, Bologna 1941) 665–698. É. AMANN, *L'Époque carolingienne, Histoire de l' Église depuis les origines jusqu'a nos jours*, ed. A. FLICHE and V. MARTIN 6 (Paris 1947) 49–70, 107–127, 129–148, 173–177. J. HALLER, *Das Papsttums: Idee und Wirklichkeit*, v. 1: *Die Grundlagen* (Basel 1951) 448–462; v. 2: *Der Aufbau* (Basel 1951) 1–16. J. DEÉR, "Die Vorrechte des Kaisers im Rom (772–800)," *Schweitzer Beiträge zur allgemeinen Geschichte* 15 (1957) 5–63. É. GRIFFE, "Aux origines de l'État pontifical: Charlemagne et Hadrian Ier (772–775)," *Bulletin de littérature ecclésiastique* 55, 65–89. W. OHNSORGE, "Der Patricius-Titel Karls des Grossen," *Byzantinische Zeitschrift* 53, 300–321. F. KEMPF, H.-G. BECK, E. EWIG, and J. A. JUNGMANN, *The Church in the Age of Feudalism*, tr. A. BIGGS (New York and London, 1968) 32–41, 54–88. J. T. HALLENBECK, "The Election of Pope Hadrian I," *Church History* 37 (1968) 261–270. W. H. FRITZE, *Papst und Frankenkönig. Studien zu den päpstlich-fränkischen Rechtsbeziehungen von 754 bis 824* (*Vorträge und Forschungen*, Sonderband 10; Sigmaringen 1973) *passim*, especially 44–62. J. JARNUT, "Quierzy und Rom. Bemerkungen zu den *Promissiones Donationis* Pippins und Karls," *Historische Zeitschrift* 220 (1975) 265–297. A. DRABEK, *Die Verträge der fränkischen und deutschen Herrscher mit dem Papsttum von 754 bis 1020* (Vienna, Cologne, Graz 1978) 13–35. G. DUMEIGE, *NICÉE II* (Paris 1978). D. S. SEFTON, "Pope Hadrian I and the Fall of the Kingdom of the Lombards," *Catholic Historical Review* 65: 206–220. R. KRAUTHEIMER, *Rome: Profile of a City 312–1308* (Princeton, N.J. 1980) 109–142. A. ANGENEDT, "Der geistliche Bündnis der Päpste mit dem Karolingern (754–76)," *Historisches Jahrbuch* 100 (1980) 1–94. H. FUHRMANN, "Das Papsttum und der kirchliche Leben im Frankenreich," in *Nascita dell'Europe ed Europa carolingia: Un'equazione de verificare*, 2 v. (Spoleto 1981) 1: 419–456. J. T. HALLENBECK, *Pavia and Rome: The Lombard Monarchy and the Papacy in the Eighth Century* (Philadelphia 1982)132–155. T. F. X. NOBLE, *The Republic of St. Peter. The Birth of the Papal State, 680–825* (Philadelphia 1989) 127–183, 277–290. V. PERI, "Il *Filioque* nei magisterio di Adriano I e de Leone III. Une plausible formulazione del dogma," *Rivista di storia della chiesa in Italia* 41, 5–25. P. DELOGU, "The Rebirth of Rome in the 8th and 9th Centuries," in *The Rebirth of Towns in the West, A.D. 700–1050*, ed. R. HODGES and B. HIBLEY (London 1988) 33–42. M. MACCARRONE, "Il papa Adriano I e il concilio di Nicea del 787," *Annuarium Historiae Conciliorum* 20, (1988) 53–134. G. THOMA, "Papst Hadrian I. und Karl der Grosse. Beobachtungen zur Kommunikation zwischen Papst und König nach den Briefen des Codex Carolinus," in *Festschrift für Eduard Hlawitzschke zum 65. Geburtstag*, ed. K. R. SCHNITH and R. PAULER (Munich 1993) 37–58. P. LLEWELLYN, *Rome in the Dark Ages* (London 1993) 150–156; 227–255. E. LAMBERZ, "Studien zur Überlieferung der Akten des VII. Ökumenischen Konzils: Der Brief Hadrians I. am Konstantin IV. und Irene (JE2448)," *Deutsches Archiv für Erforschung des Mittelalters* 53 (1997) 1–43.

[R. E. SULLIVAN]

ADRIAN II, POPE

Pontificate: Dec. 14, 867 to November or December 872; b. Rome, 792. He was of a distinguished Roman family, from which two previous popes had come— STEPHEN IV (816–817) and SERGIUS II (844–847). In 842 Adrian was named cardinal priest of San Marco. He was elected pope as a compromise candidate in the struggle between those who favored and those who opposed the strong policies of his immediate predecessor, NICHOLAS I (858–867). After approval by German emperor Louis II, Adrian was consecrated on Dec. 14, 867. Though he attempted to maintain the policies of Nicholas, the papal power declined during his reign, for conciliatory by nature and already advanced in age, he was confronted with serious conflicts. Great influence was exercised in papal affairs by the pontifical secretary and archivist, ANASTASIUS THE LIBRARIAN, a member of a powerful family with which Adrian had personal differences. The reason for this difficulty was his daughter, born to him in a marriage contracted before he was ordained a priest. Believing Anastasius to be in part responsible for the subsequent murder of both the daughter and her mother in 868, Adrian dismissed him under the severest ecclesiastical penalties. Not long afterward, however, the secretary was reinstated, and he continued to dominate.

Among Adrian's conflicts with the German princes was that over the attempted divorce of LOTHAIR II, king of Lorraine, who sought to put away his wife, Theutberga, in order to marry his concubine, Waldrada. Adrian's efforts at reconciliation were unsuccessful, and the problem was resolved only upon the death of Lothair in 869. In the subsequent contention over the kingdom of Lorraine, Adrian supported the claims of Louis II against those of Charles II the Bald, who was supported by the redoubtable Bishop HINCMAR OF REIMS. Louis II was excluded when the German princes, Charles the Bald and Louis the German, came to an agreement among themselves at the Treaty of Mersen in 870. Later efforts by Adrian to intervene in the civil and ecclesiastical disputes in the Carolingian domains met with strong rebuffs from Hincmar. Anastasius, then in control of the papal chancellery, was found to be the true author of these attempts at intervention although papal prestige was somewhat restored when Adrian reaffirmed Louis II's imperial title in 872, following a revolt in Benevento.

In his relations with the BYZANTINE EMPIRE, Adrian was only partially successful. A synod held at Rome in June of 869 severely condemned PHOTIUS and his partisans. Three papal legates were dispatched to the Council of Constantinople (*see* CONSTANTINOPLE IV) in 869 and 870, where the position taken by Adrian and his predecessor, in regard to Photius, was upheld. Rome's claims to jurisdiction in the Balkan area were defeated, however, when IGNATIUS, patriarch of Constantinople, accepted the invitation of BORIS I OF BULGARIA to evangelize his people. This defeat was to a degree offset by

Adrian's sponsoring of the mission of CYRIL (Constantine) and Methodius among the Slovak people of Central Europe and his allowing the use of old Slavonic in the liturgy.

Bibliography: *Patrologia Latina*, ed. J. P. MIGNE (Paris 1878–90) 122:1245–1320. P. JAFFÉ, *Regesta pontificum romanorum ab condita ecclesia ad annum post Christum natum 1198*, ed. S. LÖWENFELD (Graz 1956) 368–375. A. NOYON, *Dictionnaire d'histoire et de géographie ecclésiastiques*, ed. A. BAUDRILLART et al. (Paris 1912—) 1:619–624. A. FLICHE and V. MARTIN, eds. *Histoire de l'église depuis les origines jusqu'à nos jours* (Paris 1935—) 6:395–412. F. DVORNIK, *The Photian Schism* (Cambridge 1948); *The Patriarch Photius in the Light of Recent Research* (Munich 1958). F. X. SEPPELT, *Geschichte der Päpste von den Anfängen bis zur Mitte des 20. Jh.* (Munich 1955) 2:289–306, 433–434. *Archivium historiae pontificiae* 1 (1963). L. BELLINGERI, *Diziornario biografico delgi italiani* 41 (Roma 1986), s.v. "Donato, tit. [vesc.]. di Ostia." A. GUILLOU, "Invocation à la Vièrge pour le pape Hadrien II," *Recueil des inscriptions grecques médiévales d'italia* (Rome 1996). W. HARTMAN, "Gespräche in der 'Kaffeepause'—am Rande des Konzils von Attingy 870," *Annuarium Historiae Consiliorum* (Paderborn 1995/1996) 137–145. P. RATKOŠ, "Les lettres disparues d'Adrien II aux princes slaves des années 867–870" *Slovenskà Archivistica* 19 (1984) 75–95. S. SCHOLTZ, *Lexikon für Theologie und Kirche*, (Freiburg 1995) ed. J. HOFER and K. RAHNER 4:524. J.N.D. KELLY, *Oxford Dictionary of Popes* (New York 1986) 109–110.

[A. J. ENNIS]

ADRIAN III, POPE, ST.

Pontificate: May 17, 884 to August or September 885; b. Rome; d. near Modena, Italy. Little is known of him; he was the son of Benedict, member of a Roman family. His brief reign was disturbed by the continuing conflict of contending factions in Rome. It appears that he represented the policies of Pope JOHN VIII (who was assassinated in 882) rather than those of Pope MARINUS I, Adrian's immediate predecessor. In the spirit of the age, Adrian dealt severely with the opposition: by his order a certain George, an official of the Lateran palace, was blinded and a woman named Mary, a member of the aristocracy, was subjected to disgraceful punishment. Adrian's policy regarding the problems with the Byzantine emperor, and especially with PHOTIUS, was probably a conciliatory one, but he did not live long enough to accomplish anything of note. Emperor Charles III the Fat, who at that time was in control of nearly all of the former empire of Charlemagne, invited Adrian to come to an imperial diet, chiefly for the purpose of settling the question of the imperial succession, since Charles had no legitimate male heir. Leaving an imperial *missus* in charge of the government of Rome, Adrian set out for Germany. En route, he fell ill and died. He was buried in the nearby Abbey of Nonantola. His cultus, which developed in the locality, was approved by the Holy See on June 2, 1891.

Pope Adrian II in the procession for the translation of the relics of St. Clement, detail of an 11th-century fresco in the Basilica of S. Clemente at Rome.

Feast: July 8.

Bibliography: P. JAFFÉ, *Regesta pontificum romanorum ab condita ecclesia ad annum post Christum natum 1198* (Graz 1956) 1:426–427; 2:705. *Liber pontificalis*, ed. L. DUCHESNE (Paris 1886–1958) 2:225; 3:127. H. K. MANN, *The Lives of the Popes in the Early Middle Ages from 590 to 1304* v.3 (London 1902–32). P. VIARD, *Catholicisme* 5:474. K. HERBERS, *Lexikon für Theologie und Kirche*, 3d. ed. (1995). J. N. D. KELLY, *Oxford Dictionary of Popes* (New York 1986) 112–113.

[A. J. ENNIS]

ADRIAN IV, POPE

Reigned Dec. 4, 1154, to Sept. 1, 1159; born Nicholas Breakspear, Abbot's Langley, on land belonging to St. Albans' abbey, c. 1100; d. Anagni; buried in St. Peter's, Rome, beside Pope Eugenius III; son of Robert of the Chamber, a clerk in royal service and later monk at St. Albans; created cardinal bishop of Albano (c. 1149–50). The young Breakspear left England to study in France, eventually joining the reformed canonical congregation of St. Ruf near Avignon in the Arelate. Elected prior and then abbot (c. 1135) of this prestigious house, he more than once pursued the community's business at Rome before apparently so alienating his fellow canons that they petitioned the pope for his removal. Eugenius, however, acknowledging his potential by a direct promotion to the cardinalate, later entrusted him with the legation to Scandinavia (1152), his high-profile mission being to reorganize and reform the Church there.

In Norway, he established a metropolitan see at Nidaros (Trondheim), thus breaking the control of the Danish archbishopric of Lund over that country. He introduced the payment of an annual census to Rome and limited royal influence over clerical appointments by insisting on canonical elections. In Sweden, he held a council at Linköping (1152) which facilitated the elevation of Uppsala to metropolitan see (1163) and confirmed the payment of census: however, he failed to impose clerical celibacy in the face of local rivalries between Goths and Swedes. He returned to Rome before November 1153, having earned from the Scandinavians the epithet ''the Good Cardinal,'' and received full support for his work from the recently elected Anastasius IV. On Anastasius's death, he was unanimously chosen as pope, the first Englishman to attain this position.

The pontificate was dominated by interrelated problems, including tensions over the Roman Commune; the imminent coronation of Frederick Barbarossa and the resumption of imperial rights over Lombardy; William I of Sicily's request for papal recognition; the Italian aspirations of Byzantine emperor Manuel I Comnenus; and the security of the Patrimony of St. Peter. Following disturbances among the Romans after his election, Adrian was immediately forced to take refuge inside the Leonine City, placing Rome under interdict until the Wednesday of Holy Week, March 23, 1155. On the following day, the Senate expelled Arnold of Brescia, heretic and chief perpetrator of violence, leaving Adrian free at last to move to the Lateran, where he celebrated Holy Friday with his cardinals. In spite of slightly improved relations with the Commune, nearly half his pontificate of 56 months was spent outside Rome.

Early in 1155, Adrian renewed the Treaty of Constance (March 23, 1153), which was negotiated by his predecessor, Eugenius III, and the German king, Frederick Barbarossa. Adrian's promise of imperial consecration aimed to bind Barbarossa into an agreement to defend the status of the papacy and the integrity of the Patrimony, and he insisted on a sworn undertaking to respect the person of the pope and cardinals. After a destructive progress across Lombardy, the king marched on Rome (April 1155), seeking the promised imperial coronation ''in such haste that he seemed to be an enemy rather than a friend.'' Following complicated diplomatic manoeuvres, Adrian and Barbarossa finally met (June 9,

1155) at Campo Grasso outside Sutri where the king performed the office of *strator*, leading the pope's horse, holding his stirrup, and receiving the kiss of peace. The long-awaited coronation (June 18, 1155), marred by violence between Romans and Germans, was followed by a processional crown-wearing ceremony at Ponte Lucano (June 29, 1155), cordiality between pope and emperor being reinforced by Barbarossa's instruction to the people of Tivoli to maintain their allegiance to the pope. Frederick then returned to Germany to avoid the heat of summer, looting Spoleto on the way.

At precisely the same time a crisis broke out in the south, following William I's failure to obtain prior papal consent for his coronation as king of Sicily (April 5, 1154) and his illegal retention of papal lands. In winter 1154–55, William offered his submission to the new pope, but refused to confirm papal overlordship of his kingdom. In May 1155 William was excommunicated for besieging Benevento and burning several unfortified places in the southern Patrimony. The pope hoped to win Barbarossa's assistance against Sicily through the good offices of Wilbald, abbot of Corvey and Stavelot, who was engaged at the time in sensitive negotiations with Manuel I Comnenus. The increasing significance of Byzantine power in southern Italy was to prove a difficult problem for the pope. The Greeks had never accepted the Norman conquest there, while the Normans had, from time to time, shown themselves willing to attack the Byzantine Empire. Manuel I had agreed to the Treaty of Thessalonica (1148) with Conrad III of Germany whereby the two rulers would together attack Sicily.

However, the ''accord and agreement'' made by Eugenius and Barbarossa in March 1153 at Constance had been intended to keep the Greeks out of the peninsula. Manuel, nonetheless, remained sufficiently confident to send a mission to Ancona late in 1154. In spring 1155, the nobles of Apulia, encouraged by Barbarossa's entry into Italy, launched a rebellion against their new ruler. William I of Sicily appealed for assistance, but the emperor refused and returned to Germany. In September 1155, Adrian gathered an army to march on Benevento and remained there until mid-July 1156, the Greeks offering him unlimited supplies of men and money in return for their acquisition of three cities in Apulia, but ultimately failing in their invasion.

The Treaty of Benevento (June 1156) forced Adrian into recognizing William and his heirs as kings of Sicily in return for liege homage, an annual tribute in gold, and far-reaching concessions over the churches of southern Italy and Sicily. Papal recognition of the Sicilian monarchy ultimately worked to the advantage of Adrian's successors by bringing stability in the south for more than

20 years, but it caused Barbarossa grave displeasure. In 1157 when the Greeks again tried to intervene, Adrian held firm to his agreement with William but, in a famous letter to Patriarch Basil of Ochrida, the pope pursued his idea of a possible future union between the Greek and Latin churches.

In September 1157, Adrian sent a letter to Barbarossa, then at Besançon, complaining that Eskil, archbishop of Lund, being held for ransom in Burgundy, had not yet been released. The pope's use of the word *beneficium* in relation to the imperial crown and its translation into German by Rainald of Dassel, the emperor's chancellor, in such a way as to imply that the empire was a fief of the papacy, helped both to manufacture and inflame this dispute. Relations with the emperor rapidly deteriorated, Fredrick unfairly impugning Adrian's legitimacy by calling him the son of a monk. The pope refused to confirm Barbarossa's nominee to the archbishopric of Ravenna; in April 1159 at Bologna, Adrian protested against the imposition of imperial rights announced at the Diet of Roncaglia (Nov. 12–13, 1158) which involved not only Lombardy, but also parts of the Patrimony. In mid-June 1159, the pope, already known to be unwell, withdrew to Anagni with the so-called Sicilian group of cardinals and made common cause with four anti-imperial cities in Lombardy.

Among Adrian's significant promotions to the cardinalate were figures chosen for their ability to serve the Church: Albert de Morra, later pope Gregory VIII; Walter, successor to the cardinal bishopric of Albano; Boso, papal *scriptor*, friend and biographer, appointed papal chamberlain (1154–55) and cardinal deacon of SS Cosma e Damiano (1156); and Roland Bandinelli, the future Alexander III, retained as chancellor. Adrian made no canonizations, nor have any sermons, treatises or commentaries survived from his pontificate. However, nearly 700 letters and privileges indicate some of the many difficult problems he addressed, attempting to mediate between conflicting claims.

Two particular decisions passed into Canon Law: *Commissum nobis (X, 3.30.4)* restricted monastic exemptions on tithe payments, while *Dignum est (X.4.9.1)* proclaimed the absolute right of the unfree to contract valid marriages. The authenticity of Adrian's letter *Laudabiliter*, once alleged to have permitted the invasion of Ireland by Henry II, is now regarded with much more caution than previously. In collaboration with Boso, Adrian put in place throughout the Patrimony a whole network of *castra specialia*, military and administrative strongholds under the special protection of the Holy See, that bound the local nobles in a system of feudal dependency, and it was this model which Innocent III used to recover the position of the papacy in the early thirteenth century.

Bibliography: *Patrologia Latina*, ed. J. P. MIGNE (Paris 1878–90) 188, 1349–1644; *Regesta Pontificum Romanorum*, ed. P. JAFFÉ, G. WATTENBACH, et al. (Leipzig 1888) 102–145, 760–61. L. DUCHESNE, *Liber Pontificalis* (Paris 1958) 2:388–397. P. FABRE and L. DUCHESNE, *Le Liber Censuum de l'Église romaine* (Paris 1910) 385–400, 425–427. J. M. BRIXIUS, *Die Mitglieder des Kardinalskollegiums 1130–1181* (Berlin 1912) 56, 111. B. ZENKER, *Die Mitglieder des Kardinalskollegiums 1130–1159* (Würzburg 1964) 36–38. D. MACKIE, *Pope Adrian IV* (Oxford 1907). P. RICHARD, *Dictionnaire d'histoire et de géographie ecclésiastiques*, ed. A. BAUDRILLART et al. (Paris 1912–) 1:625–27. A. O. JOHNSEN, *Studier verdrörende Kardinal Nicolaus Breakspears legasjon til Norden* (Oslo 1945). W. ULLMANN, ''Cardinal Roland and Besançon,'' *Miscellanea Historiae Pontificiae* 18 (1954) 107–125; ''The Pontificate of Adrian IV,'' *Cambridge Historical Journal* 11 (1953–55) 233–252. R. MONTINI, *Le tombe dei papi* (Rome 1957) 199–200. M. MACCARRONE, *Papato e Impero dalla elezione di Federico I alla morte di Adriano IV, 1152–1159* (Rome 1959). M. P. SHEEHY, ''Laudabiliter,'' *Pontificia Hibernia, Medieval Papal Chancery Documents concerning Ireland, 640–1261* (Dublin 1962) 15–16. J. G. ROWE, ''Hadrian IV, the Byzantine Empire and the Latin Orient,'' *Essays in Medieval History presented to Bertie Wilkinson*, ed. T. A. SANDQUIST and M. R. POWICKE (Toronto 1969) 3–16. R. W. SOUTHERN, *Medieval Humanism and Other Studies* (Oxford 1970) 234–52. P. TOUBERT, *Les structures du Latium médiéval. Le Latium méridional et la Sabine du IXe siècle à la fin du XIIe siècle*, 2 v. (Rome 1973). M. T. FLANAGAN, *Irish Society, Anglo-Norman Settlers, Angevin Kingship. Interactions in Ireland in the Late Twelfth Century* (Oxford 1989) 7–55, 277–78. R. L. BENSON, ''Political *Renovatio*: Two Models from Roman Antiquity,'' *Renaissance and Renewal in the Twelfth Century*, ed. R. L. BENSON and G. CONSTABLE (Oxford 1982) 339–386. P. LAMMA, *Enciclopedia dei Papi* (Rome 2000) 2:286–26; *Adrian IV (1154–59): The English Pope*, ed B. M. BOLTON and A. J. DUGGAN (Aldershot 2002).

[B. M. BOLTON]

ADRIAN V, POPE

Pontificate: July 11, 1276, to Aug. 18, 1276; b. Ottobono Fieschi, Genoa, Italy, early 13th century; d. Viterbo, Italy. He came from an influential Italian family and was created cardinal deacon of S. Hadrian by his uncle, Pope INNOCENT IV, in September 1244. In May 1265 he was sent to England as the envoy of Pope CLEMENT IV to defend the rights of the Holy See there and to resolve the conflict between King HENRY III and his barons. He successfully completed this task and returned in June 1268 to the Roman CURIA, where he worked in support of the Angevin policy in Italy. Elected to the papacy on the death of INNOCENT V, he died before he could receive either ordination to the priesthood or episcopal consecration. His attempt to repeal the second canon of the Second Council of LYONS concerning papal elections was ignored by his successors. Adrian was buried in the basilica of S. Francesco at Viterbo, where his epitaph may still be seen.

Monument of Pope Adrian V by the 13th-century sculptor Arnolfo di Cambio, in the basilica of S. Francesco, Viterbo, Italy. (Alinari-Art Reference/Art Resource, NY.)

Bibliography: R. GRAHAM, "Letters of Cardinal Ottoboni," *English Historical Review* 15 (1900) 87–120. *Liber pontificalis,* ed. L. DUCHESNE, 2:457. N. SCHÖPP, *Papst Hadrian V* (Heidelberg 1916). A. VACANT, *Dictionnaire de théologie catholique* 1.1:458–459. É. GRIFFE, *Catholicisme* 5:476–477. A. POTTHAST, *Regesta pontificum romanorum inde ab a. 1198 ad a. 1304* 2: 1709–10. F. X. SEPPELT, *Geschichte der Päpste von den Anfängen bis zur Mitte des 20. Jh.* 3:536–540. P. HERDE, *Lexikon für Theologie und Kirche,* 3d. ed., 4 (1995), s.v. "Hadrian V., Papst." J. N. D. KELLY, *Oxford Dictionary of Popes* (New York 1986), 199.

[B. J. COMASKEY]

"Pope Adrian VI," 16th-century portrait by an unknown artist.

ADRIAN VI, POPE

Pontificate: Jan. 9, 1522, to Sept. 14, 1523; b. Adrian Florensz Dedal, Utrecht, March 2, 1459. He was the last non-Italian pope until the election of John Paul II in 1978. His widowed mother secured a good education for him with the Brothers of the Common Life at Zwelle and Deventer, and this enabled him to enter the University of Louvain when he was 17. There he studied and taught theology; in 1497 he became dean of St. Peter's Church, Louvain, and chancellor of the university, of which he was twice rector magnificus. One of his students published his notes on the *Sententiarum Petri Lombardi* (1512), and some of his disputations (*Quaestiones quodlibeticae,* 1515.)

In 1515 Margaret of Burgundy chose him as a member of her household, and Emperor Maximilian appointed him tutor to his grandson, the future Emperor Charles V, who remained grateful throughout his life for Adrian's religious instruction. In the same year Adrian was sent on a difficult diplomatic mission to Spain, where he became the friend of Cardinal XIMÉNEZ OF CISNEROS. Upon the death of Ferdinand V of Castile in 1516, he was appointed sole administrator of the kingdom until the arrival of Charles I. He was named bishop of Tortosa (1516), viceroy of Spain (1517), and inquisitor of Aragon and Navarre (1517) and Castile and Leon (1518). At the request of Emperor Charles he was created cardinal of Utrecht on June 1, 1517.

In Rome, at the death of Leo X and after turbulent deliberations, he was unanimously elected pope. He was shocked by the news, conveyed to him in Spain, but accepted the will of God and took his own name as Pope Adrian VI. As he had labored in Spain in complete ignorance of the language and customs of the country, where he was resented as a foreigner, so in Italy he was a stranger to his environment. He had little sympathy with Renaissance art and culture, though he valued the learning of the humanists, Johann ECK and Juan Luis Vives, and tried to secure the support and advice of Erasmus. The difficulties he encountered in Rome were overwhelming.

The principal Catholic princes, Francis I of France and Emperor Charles V, whose help he needed, were at war with one another. In the Turkish advance, Belgrade had fallen, and the Island of Rhodes was threatened. He was the first pope to face the full impact of the Lutheran revolt, which was making rapid advances, and to deal with the pressing necessity of reform of the Church.

With confusion in the Papal States, lack of financial resources, and reluctant allies, he failed to save Christianity from disunity and from the Turks. The Island of Rhodes fell in December 1522, and the way to Hungary was open. His call for reform alienated the cardinals as well as the members of the Diet of Nuremberg (1522–23), where his "Instructio" to the German nation was ill received and unheeded. Practically alone and exhausted by the opposition on all sides, he died, only 20 months after his accession to the papacy.

Bibliography: L. PASTOR, *The History of the Popes from the Close of the Middle Ages* (London-St. Louis 1938–61). L. P. GACHARD, ed., *Correspondance de Charles-Quint et d'Adrien VI* (Brussels 1859). C. BURMAN, *Hadrianus VI* (Utrecht 1727). E. H. J. REUSENS, *Syntagma Doctrinae Theologicae Adriani sexti* (Louvain 1862). L. E. HALKIN, *La Réforme en Belgique sous Charles-Quint* (Brussels 1957). A. MERCATI, ed., *Dall'Archivio vaticano: . . . Diarii di concistori del pontificato di Adriano VI* (Rome 1951). *Ephemerides theological Lovanienses* (Bruges 1959) 520–629 (commemorative issue on the 500th anniversary of his birth). C. A.

C. VON HÖFLER, *Papst Adrian VI* (Vienna 1880). P. RICHARD, *Dictionnaire d'histoire et de géographie ecclésiastiques,* ed. A. BAUDRILLAT et al. (Paris 1912–) 1:628–630. W. O. O'MALLEY, *Praise and Blame in Renaissance Rome* (Durham, N.C. 1979). P. PARTNER, *Renaissance Rome, 1500–1559* (Berkeley 1976). *Epistolae ad Principes. Leo X–Pius IV (1513–1565)* ed, L. NANNI (Vatican City 1993). C. L. STINGER, *The Renaissance in Rome* (Bloomington, Ind. 1985).

[K. M. SAUM]

ADRIAN OF CASTELLO (DE CORNETO)

Cardinal and humanist; b. Corneto, 1458 or 1459; d. 1521. In 1488 Innocent VIII sent him to Scotland as papal nuncio to reconcile James III and his dissident nobles. James was killed before Adrian's arrival, but Adrian reached England, where he gained favor with King Henry VII and became his agent in Rome. He returned to England in 1489 for the collection of Peter's Pence. He was made bishop of Hereford in England, Feb. 14, 1502, and was raised to the cardinalate, May 31, 1503, by Alexander VI. He also acted as secretary of the Papal Treasury and ambassador of Henry VII. After the death of Alexander VI, his involvement in politics incurred the displeasure of Julius II. In 1509 he left for Venice and later for Trent, where he remained until the death of the pope. In 1511 he returned to Rome for the election of Leo X; became implicated with Cardinal Alfonso Petrucci in a plot to poison Leo X; confessed to being privy to it, and although forgiven by Leo, found it safer to reside in Venice. At the insistence of Henry VIII, he had been deprived of his office as collector of Peter's pence, and on July 5, 1518, he was degraded from the cardinalate and the bishopric of Bath, England, and the honors were given to Thomas Wolsey. A probable rumor mentions that Adrian was murdered in 1521 on his way to Rome after the death of Leo X. Among his writings are *De vera philosophia ex quatuor doctoribus ecclesiae* (Bologna 1507) and *De sermone latino et modo latine loquendi* (Basel 1513).

Bibliography: B. GEBHARDT, *Adrian von Corneto* (Breslau 1886). J. WODKA, *Lexikon für Theologie und Kirche* 1:158.

[M. I. C. DUFFEY]

ADRIANUS

Exegete of the Antiochene School; flourished first half of the fifth century A.D. He was a Greek-speaking Syrian and author of a little work remarkable both in method and content, Ἐισαγωγὴ εἰς τὰς θείας γραφάς (Introduction to Holy Scripture), the first extant work to bear this title. No details whatever are available about his life. He was monk and priest, if he is to be identified with the Adrianus (or Hadrianus) to whom St. Nilus (d. *c.* A.D. 430) addressed three letters. He was certainly mentioned by Cassiodorus in his list of exegetes as coming after St. Augustine, but before Eucherius and Junilius (*Inst.* 1.10.1). Photius (*c.* A.D. 820–91) also speaks of Adrianus in his *Bibliotheca* and characterizes his work as a "book useful to beginners" (*Patrologia Graeca* 103:45 C). The Ἐισαγωγή deals with figures of thought (chiefly anthropomorphisms), word figures, and figures of composition (τῆς συνθέσεως) and their subdivisions. By way of illustration he quotes the Septuagint about 360 times, and the New Testament about 60 times. He was influenced clearly in his work by Theodore of Mopsuestia and Theodoret of Cyr, and possibly by St. John Chrysostom.

Bibliography: J. P. MIGNE, ed., *Patrologia Graeca* 98:1273–1312. ADRIANUS, Ἐισαγωγὴ εἰς τὰς θείας γραφάς, ed. F. GOESSLING (Berlin 1887), this is the modern critical edition that should be used. O. BARDENHEWER, *Geschichte der altkirchlichen Literatur* 4:254–55. G. MERCATI, "Pro Adriano," *Revue biblique* NS 11 (1914) 246–55.

[M. R. P. MCGUIRE]

ADSO OF MONTIER-EN-DER

Benedictine author and teacher (called also Azo, Asso, Hermericus); b. Jura, France, first half of the tenth century; d. at sea, 992. He was a monk at Luxeuil, then schoolmaster at Saint-Evre (Aper) at Toul, and later abbot at Montier-en-Der (Haute-Marne) *c.* 960, before finally becoming abbot of Saint-Bénigne at Dijon. While on pilgrimage to the Holy Land, he died at sea and was buried in the Cyclades. The friend of such important figures as ABBO OF FLEURY, Gerbert (later Pope SYLVESTER II), and Adalbero of Reims, Adso is remembered especially for his writings. The most important is *De Antichristo* (*Patrologia Latina* 101: 1291–98), among the writings attributed to ALCUIN; it is addressed to Gerberga, wife of Louis IV of France. He wrote about the lives of many saints, namely, St. Frodobert (*Acta Sanctorum,* Jan. 1:505–13), St. Mansuetus (*Acta Sanctorum,* Sept. 1:637–51), St. Basolus (*Patrologia Latina* 137:647–68), St. Bercharius (*Acta Sanctorum,* Oct. 7.2:1010–31), and St. Waldebert (*Acta Sanctorum,* May 1:282–87).

Bibliography: J. P. MIGNE, ed., *Patrologia Latina* 137:599–700. *Monumenta Germainae Historica (Scriptores)* 4:487–90, 509–20. A. POTTHAST, *Bibliotheca historica medii aevi* 1:16. E. MARTIN, *Dictionnaire d'histoire et de géographie ecclésiastiques* 1:636. G. HOCQUARD, *Catholicisme* 1:164–65. S. HILPISCH, *Lexikon für Theologie und Kirche* 1:159.

[C. DAVIS]

ADUARTE, DIEGO FRANCISCO

Dominican chronicler and bishop in the Philippines; b. Zaragoza, Spain, 1569; d. Nueva Segovia, 1636. He took the Dominican habit in 1586 and made his profession in the order the next year in Alcalá de Henares. He was already a priest when he went to the Philippines in 1594. In Manila he taught Christianity to the Chinese residents. From there his missionary zeal took him to Cambodia, Canton, Malacca, and Cochin China, where he underwent many hardships and met only failures for his efforts. He was convinced of the need for more missionaries in the Far East and made trips to Spain in 1603 and in 1607 to get them. On the second trip he went to France and got two missionary expeditions sent out. He himself prepared a third group and accompanied it as far as Mexico; he then returned to Spain for a fourth expedition, which he led to Manila. He was named bishop of Nueva Segovia in 1632 and governed wisely and charitably. He died a holy death. His body was found incorrupt, even though it had been buried in such damp soil that the casket was full of water. His chief work was *Historia de la Provincia del Santo Rosario de la Orden de Predicadores en Filipinas, Japón y China,* 2 v. (Manila 1640; Zaragoza, Spain 1693). It was reprinted with many additions in 1742, 1783, and 1870–72. In 1962 an edition containing a biography and bibliography of the author was published in Madrid.

[E. GÓMEZ TAGLE]

ADULTERY

Defined by moral theologians as the act of sexual intercourse between a married man and a woman not his wife, or between a married woman and a man not her husband. The special note here is that at least one of the two parties concerned is married. If both are married, the guilt, of course, is compounded. As to the specific guilt of adultery, it adds a sin against justice to the intrinsically grave malice of fornication, which in itself is a deordination of sex from its true and appointed end. The victim of the injustice is, of course, the innocent spouse, whose marital rights are violated by the sinning parties.

Authors are agreed that the special malice of adultery remains even if the injured spouse should consent to the evil action. The reason is that marriage is an indissoluble contract, and hence no one can waive his rights in this matter, and they are in fact inalienable.

As to the consequences of adultery, Canon Law makes it clear that if one party is guilty of adultery, the other has the right to effect a permanent separation, and this indeed without any intervention of ecclesiastical authority. The marriage bond itself remains, however, and precludes remarriage. Canon 1152 of the code notes also that this right is forfeited if the other party consented to the crime, was the cause of it, expressly or tacitly condoned (i.e., pardoned) it, or was guilty of the same crime. The innocent party is considered to have condoned the crime if, having learned of it, he or she continued to live with the guilty one in marital relations. The law presumes this to be the case unless the innocent party within six months has turned the adulterer out of doors, or has left, or brought legal action against, him or her.

When separation has taken place because of adultery, the innocent party is never again under obligation to readmit the adulterer to a community of married life. If the innocent party freely desires this readmission, however, it is his privilege to grant it, unless the adulterer in the meantime, with the consent of the innocent party, has assumed new obligations, such as the vows of the religious state. In general, it may be said that the Church favors the condoning of the adultery by the innocent party, out of a spirit of Christian charity, for the sake of keeping the family together, unless circumstances clearly make this inadvisable.

If the party accused of adultery denies the crime, objects to the departure of the spouse, and takes his case to an ecclesiastical court, the other party must furnish proof of the adultery.

The right to separate belongs to the innocent party, not to the guilty one, and the adulterer must stay with his spouse if the latter desires this. Once the innocent party has decided on this course of action, the adultery ceases to be a cause of separation, and the innocent party may not at some future disagreement or quarrel threaten to separate because of the adultery.

Bibliography: J. AERTNYS and C. A. DAMEN, *Theologia moralis,* 2 v. (16th ed. Turin 1950). S. WOYWOD, *A Practical Commentary on the Code of Canon Law,* rev. and enl. C. SMITH (New York 1963).

[L. G. MILLER/EDS.]

ADULTERY (IN THE BIBLE)

In the ancient Near East adultery was sexual intercourse between a married or betrothed woman and a man who was not her husband. Adultery was prohibited in the Decalogue (Ex 20:14; Dt 5:8), the Holiness Code of Leviticus (Lv 20:20), and Deuteronomy's collection of miscellaneous laws (Dt 22:22), but is not mentioned in the Covenant Code of Ex 20:22–23:33. The presence of a prohibition of adultery in the Decalogue shows that adultery was not only a matter of concern for the aggrieved

"Christ and the Adultress," oil painting by Lorenzo Lotto, 1530–1535, the Musée du Louvre, Paris. (© Archivo Iconografico, S.A./ CORBIS)

husband, as it was generally considered throughout the ancient Near East, but that it was also and primarily a source of concern for the community. Israel's identity as a covenantal people was at stake when adultery had been committed. A husband's exclusive sexual rights over his wife were violated when his wife committed adultery. What was really at stake, however, was the purity of the family line and the inheritance of a family's possessions by legitimate offspring.

Lv 20:10 and Dt 22:22 portray adultery as a capital crime. The death penalty was to be meted out to both the woman and the man involved in the act. Contemporary scholarship shows that there is considerable debate about this punishment. Some scholars consider that the death penalty was ''on the books'' but that actual practice was somewhat different. Hos 2:4 and later rabbinic texts suggest that divorce was a penalty actually incurred by an adulterous woman. Being stripped of her clothes seems

to be the penalty suggested by Hos 2:5, 12; Jer 13:22–26; Ez 16:37, 39; 23:26, 29. It may be that stripping was either part of the divorce procedure or a preparation for execution. If the penalty of death were actually inflicted, it probably took place by stoning (Sus 62; see Dt 19:16–19; Jn 8:5) but burning may have been the instrument of death (Gn 38:24).

Some of the ambiguity related to the interpretation of the penalty for adultery arises because the Bible's prophetic literature used adultery as an image for Israel's departure from its convenantal relationship with Yahweh (Hos 1–3; Jer 2:23–25; 3:1–13; Ez 16:23; see Rv 17–18). Biblical wisdom literature says that ''the commandment'' preserves a man from the wife of another. The one who commits adultery has no sense and arouses the wrath of the aggrieved husband (Prv 6:20–35; see also Prv 2:16–19, 5:1–23; 7:4–5).

"Christ and the Woman Taken in Adultery," painting by Nicholas Colombel, 1702. (© Archivo Iconografico, S.A./CORBIS)

The New Testament reprises the Decalogue's prohibition of adultery (Mt 5:27; 19:18; Mk 10:19; Lk 18:20; Rom 2:22; 13:9; Jas 2:11). The Sermon on the Mount interprets the commandment "you shall not commit adultery" as also prohibiting lust, probably masturbation, and divorce (Mt 7:27–32). Matthew's explanation of the commandment is similar to the midrashic interpretation of the early rabbinic tradition. Matthew, along with the Book of Revelation, followed the Bible in using adultery as a metaphor for apostasy and religious infidelity (Mt 12:39; 16:4; Rv 2:22; 17:1–18:24; see Mk 8:38).

Hellenistic catalogs of vices listing adultery as a kind of behavior that is inconsistent with discipleship appear in Mt 15:19; Mk 7:22; Lk 18:11; 1 Cor 6:9. Exhortations urging the avoidance of adultery are occasionally found in the New Testament (1 Thes 4:6; Heb 13:4; Jas 4:4). A story of a woman caught in the act of adultery has been incorporated into the Fourth Gospel (Jn 7:53–8:11). While Jesus urges the woman to sin no more (Jn 8:11), the purpose of the story is not to teach about the evil of adultery. Rather, the story is one that contrasts the opponents of Jesus' readiness to condemn others with Jesus' readiness to forgive sinners.

Bibliography: R. F. COLLINS, *Sexual Ethics and the New Testament: Behavior and Belief,* (Companions to the New Testament; New York 2000). E. A. GOODFRIEND, "Adultery," *Anchor Bible Dictionary* (New York 1992) 1:82–86.

[R. F. COLLINS]

ADVENT

From the Latin *adventus*, meaning coming; the season immediately before Christmas, beginning on the Sunday nearest the feast of St. Andrew (November 30) and lasting for four weeks. In about the 9th century the First Sunday of Advent became the beginning of the Church year.

Meaning. Because Advent is so closely related to Christmas it can scarcely be understood apart from that feast. It was not until the birth of Christ was celebrated throughout the Church that Advent came into existence at all. Its name is derived from the ancient name for the feast, for *Adventus, Epiphania* and *Natale* are all synonymous first for the Incarnation itself, then for the feast that commemorates and celebrates the Incarnation. Christmas, as well as Epiphany, is not only the commemoration of the birth of Christ as a historical event, it is also and much more the celebration of the coming of God in the flesh as a saving event. The very celebration itself is a saving event that brings about the coming of Christ among humanity and anticipates his return in glory.

The term Advent gradually came to designate the time before Christmas. The ancient Introit for the Epiphany begins with the words "Ecce *advenit* Dominator Dominus" (Behold the Lord the Ruler is come.) Advent is a comprehensive name for the Incarnation and all that the Incarnation accomplishes.

History. The remote origin of Advent is to be found in the Gallican custom of having a time of preparation for the Feast of the Epiphany, which was a baptismal feast in that part of the West and consequently had its season of preparation for Baptism similar to Lent. This took the form of a period of fasting and prayer that at first lasted three weeks but in time was lengthened to 40 days similar to Lent. It came to be known as St. Martin's Lent because it began on that saint's feast, November 11. This early Advent was an ascetical rather than a liturgical season.

In 380 the Council of Saragossa ordered that there be a three-week fast before the Epiphany, beginning on December 17. About 100 years later the diocese of Tours kept a fast three times a week beginning with St. Martin's Day, a custom that the Council of Mâcon (581) extended to all the dioceses of France. During the next two centuries the practice found its way to England.

At Rome Epiphany had never been a baptismal feast, so the same reason for having a "Lent" preceding it did not exist. When Advent first appeared at Rome it was a preparation for Christmas and not the Epiphany, and it was a liturgical season rather than an ascetical period. There was no Advent at Rome until the second half of the 6th century. The Gelasian Sacramentary (6th century) was the first to provide an Advent liturgy, possibly originating not at Rome but in Ravenna in the 5th century.

Gregory I the Great (d. 604) shortened the season from six weeks to four, composed liturgical texts, and arranged the Lectionary for the Mass and the Office. When the Roman rite was introduced into Gaul in the 9th century, it was enriched there with Gallican prayers and rites. Rome adopted the fast and penitential spirit of the Gallican Advent, along with its emphasis on the second coming of Christ. This fusion of the Roman and Gallican Advents found its way back to Rome in the 10th century.

Liturgy. Advent has a twofold character: as a season to prepare for Christmas when Christ's first coming to us is remembered; as a season when that remembrance directs the mind and heart to await Christ's Second Coming at the end of time. Advent is thus a period for devout and joyful expectation. (*General Norms of the Liturgical Year and Calendar* [GNLYC], no. 39) While the period

up to December 16 more strongly focuses on Christ's return in glory, December 17 to 24 serve more immediately as a preparation for the feast of the incarnation. Throughout, the liturgy celebrates Christ's continual presence in the World (cf. Wednesday of the First Week of Advent, Office of Readings). The first reading for the Sundays of Advent in all three years presents the main messianic prophecies. The gospel reading for the first Sunday exhorts Christians to watch and be ready; the second and third Sundays highlight the figure and message of John the Baptist; and the fourth Sunday of Advent tells of the annunciation to Mary (year A), the annunciation to Joseph (year B), and the Visitation (year C.)

A characteristic feature of the Advent liturgy for December 17 to 23 are the traditional "O" antiphons. Originally found as the antiphon preceding the Canticle of Mary in Evening Prayer, these are popularly known through the hymn, "O Come O Come Emmanuel."

The domestic custom of the wreath has been taken into the liturgy of Advent in many places in North America. The *Book of Blessings*, nos. 1510 to 1513, provides an order for blessing the Advent wreath the first Sunday of Advent, and provides for the silent lighting of the candles on successive Sundays. It indicates that four white candles or three purple and one rose candle may be used. The first purple candle is lit on the first Sunday of Advent, the second purple candle on the second, the rose candle on the third Sunday traditionally known as "Gaudete" ("Rejoice") Sunday, and the fourth purple candle on the fourth Sunday of Advent. A white candle may be lit on Christmas Eve.

The use of rose is a remnant of Medieval practice when Advent was strongly penitential in character. The change of color on *Gaudete* Sunday marked a lessening of the penitential practices in expectation of Christmas joy. The use of all white candles is suggested by the renewal of the whole period of Advent as "one of devout and joyful expectation" (GNLYC, no. 39).

Theology. Advent is a liturgical season, a mystery in the ancient sense of the word, a present reality that contains and mediates salvation. It deepens and strengthens the awareness of Christ's presence in his Church and in its members. Advent is at once a celebration of his first coming and his presence in the midst of his Church, and an anticipation of his full and final coming when he will complete the work of the redemption. The word Advent must therefore be taken in the fullest sense: past, present and future. The Church not only prepares to welcome him at Christmas time or to greet him in the hour of his final triumph; it rejoices even now in the presence of its Lord in its midst. All through the year Christians are summoned to prepare the way of the Lord who will come again by living the mystery of Christ in the present.

Bibliography: A. G. MARTIMORT, *The Church at Prayer IV: The Liturgy and Time* (Collegeville 1986). J. N. ALEXANDER, *Waiting for the Coming* (Washington 1993). F. X. WEISER, *Handbook of Christian Feasts and Customs* (New York 1958).

[W. J. O'SHEA/S. K. ROLL]

ADVENTISTS

Adventists are various groups of Christians who since apostolic times have believed that the Second Coming of the Lord was imminent (*see* PAROUSIA). Adherents of MONTANISM in the 2d century looked for an early end of the world, as did the ANABAPTISTS during the Reformation. Modern adventism began in the early 19th century in America with the biblical prophecies of William MILLER (1782–1849). Seeing signs of widespread moral deterioration, Adventists believe that the world is evil and must soon be destroyed. They foresee a final battle between the forces of good and evil, usually identified as the battle of Armageddon, and the victory of Jesus Christ, who will then establish a kingdom of righteousness that will last for 1,000 years. Miller set definite dates for the Second Coming in 1843 and 1844 but when these dates passed, his followers became disillusioned. Only a remnant continued to proclaim the imminent Second Coming and these adventists usually refused to specify a date.

Largest of the adventist bodies that stem from Miller's preaching is the SEVENTH DAY ADVENTIST Church. Along with adventism it teaches the observance of the Jewish Sabbath, conditional immortality, and the prophethood of Mrs. Ellen G. White (1827–1915). The general conference of the church was organized in 1863 and since then Seventh Day Adventism has spread throughout the world. A much smaller adventist body, the Advent Christian Church, was organized in 1855 by Jonathan Cummings, who taught doctrines similar to those of the Seventh Day Adventists, but his followers observed Sunday instead of Saturday. JEHOVAH'S WITNESSES is an adventist body that denies the Trinity and the deity of Jesus Christ. The founder of this sect, Charles Taze RUSSELL, was influenced by adventist preachers early in his career. The Church of Jesus Christ of LATTERDAY SAINTS originally stressed adventism, but this emphasis in Mormonism gradually diminished. Many of the PENTECOSTAL churches include a strong adventist position among their beliefs, as do the CATHOLIC APOSTOLIC CHURCH and the NEW APOSTOLIC CHURCH. Other small adventist bodies include the Life and Advent Union, the Church of God (Abrahamic Faith), the Primitive Advent Christian Church, and the United Seventh Day Brethren.

[W. J. WHALEN/EDS.]

A close-up of the top of the Church of Seventh Day Adventists in downtown Chicago. (© Sandy Felsenthal/CORBIS)

ADVERTENCE

The act of the mind heeding, attending to, or taking note of something. The term is used by moralists to signify actual attention given by an agent to what he is doing or to some morally significant circumstance. Thus a man who is habitually aware of his obligation to abstain from meat on Friday may eat meat without adverting to the fact that it is Friday. Advertence admits of varying degrees of clarity and of distinctness. Inadvertence is a kind of actual ignorance, and the general principles governing its effect upon the morality of human action are the same as those that determine the influence of ignorance.

See Also: IGNORANCE.

Bibliography: THOMAS AQUINAS, *Summa Theologiae* 1a2ae, 6.8. H. DAVIS, *Moral and Pastoral Theology*, 4 v. (rev. ed. New York 1958) v.1. B. H. MERKELBACH, *Summa theologiae moralis*, 3 v. (8th ed. Paris 1949) 1:351–352, 355–356, 435–438.

[F. D. NEALY]

ADVERTISEMENTS, BOOK OF

A set of instructions regulating the conduct of religious services, issued in 1566 by Matthew PARKER,

Archbishop of Canterbury, as a means of securing uniformity in public worship. The legislation of 1559 had brought about a church compounded of Protestant doctrine and Catholic ceremonial. This compromise was abhorrent to the extreme Protestant reformers who wished to see a form of worship that was purified from all taint of popery (the so-called PURITANS). The Puritan dispute with the established church developed slowly. In its early stages it was concerned with the vestments prescribed for use by the Royal Injunctions of 1559, which the Puritans regarded as the ''livery of Antichrist.'' Neither side was prepared to yield; the Puritan objections were grounded in conscience, and Elizabeth I refused to waive the exercise of her prerogative to regulate worship. Other items were, in time, added to the list of Puritan objections, such as the use of organs, the ring in the marriage service, the sign of the cross in Baptism, and other ''dregs of popery.'' Sympathy with the Puritans was considerable; in 1563 articles embodying their objections were introduced into the lower house of convocation, where they were rejected by only one (proxy) vote.

The disorder prevailing in the church alarmed the Queen, and on Jan. 25, 1565, she instructed Parker to secure ''one manner of uniformity through our whole realm'' and to eradicate variety ''by order, injunction, or censure according to the order and appointment of such laws as are provided by act of parliament.'' Accordingly, in March 1566, he issued a set of instructions, known as the *Book of Advertisements,* which laid down fixed rules for the conduct of public services. The delay in issuing the *Advertisements* was due to the fact that Parker had been anxious, in order to lessen his own difficulties, to obtain royal authority for them; this was, however, withheld by the Queen. From the outset they met with opposition. At a meeting held at Lambeth on March 26, 1566, to which more than 100 of the London clergy were summoned, 37 refused to comply with the *Advertisements*; these men were suspended from office and then deprived. Nevertheless, they continued to preach and conduct services, and they may be regarded as the first English Nonconformists.

Bibliography: R. W. DIXON, *History of the Church of England,* 6 v. (Oxford 1878–1902) v.5, 6. J. STRYPE, *The Life and Acts of Matthew Parker,* 3 v. (Oxford 1821) v.1. V. J. K. BROOK, *A Life of Archbishop Parker* (Oxford 1962). H. GEE and W. J. HARDY, comps., *Documents Illustrative of English Church History* (London 1896) 467–475 (text). J. I. DAELEY, ''Pluralism in the Diocese of Canterbury during the Administration of Matthew Parker, 1559–1575'' *Journal of Ecclesiastical History* 18 (1967) 33–49. M. E. VANDER SCHAAF, ''Archbishop Parker's Efforts Toward a Bucerian Discipline in the Church of England,'' *Sixteenth Century Journal* 8:1 (1977) 85–103. B.S. ROBINSON, '''Darke Speech:' Matthew Parker and the Reforming of History,'' *Sixteenth Century Journal* 29:4 (1998) 1061–1083.

[G. DE C. PARMITER/EDS.]

AELFRIC GRAMMATICUS

Benedictine abbot of Eynsham, greatest Anglo-Saxon author of the 10th and 11th centuries; b. *c.* 950 to 955; d. Eynsham, *c.* 1020. He was trained in the ideals of the 10th-century English Benedictine revival by ETHELWOLD at WINCHESTER and as a monk and priest was sent (*c.* 987) by ALPHEGE OF CANTERBURY, Ethelwold's successor, to Cerne (Dorset), founded by ealdorman Aethelmaer. There Aelfric conducted the monastic school. In 1005 he became first abbot of Eynsham, another foundation of Aethelmaer. His Anglo-Saxon writings, composed in lucid, precise, often alliterative style, included, among other works, the *Catholic Homilies* (991–992), two series of 40 sermons each, dedicated to Abp. Sigeric of Canterbury, derived mainly from Church Fathers and intended for use throughout the liturgical year; *Lives of the Saints* (before 998), a third homiletic collection, concerning saints ''whom monks honor''; paraphrases of parts of the Heptateuch; and a treatise on the Old and New Testaments. His Latin *Grammar,* the source of his appellation ''the Grammarian,'' was the first in a medieval vernacular. This work, his Latin *Glossary* and the famous *Colloquy,* with its informative and amusing conversations, were all educational works for monastic schools. Aelfric also condensed the *Regularis concordia* for Eynsham; he authored a vita of Ethelwold and pastoral letters for Bp. Wulfsige of Sherborne and Abp. Wulfstan of York. Sixteenth-century English reformers believed his Easter homily on the Real Presence supported their views against transubstantiation; but his position, influenced by RATRAMNUS OF CORBIE and affirming the ''spiritual'' (*gastlice*) presence in the Eucharist, antedated the precise distinctions of medieval scholasticism.

Bibliography: W. HUNT, *The Dictionary of National Biography from the Earliest Times to 1900* 1:164–166. C. L. WHITE, *A.: A New Study of His Life and Writings* (Boston 1898). S. H. GEM, *An Anglo-Saxon Abbot: A. of Eynsham* (Edinburgh 1912). M. M. DUBOIS, *A.: Sermonnaire, docteur et grammairien* (Paris 1943). P. CLEMOES, ''The Chronology of A.'s Works,'' *The Anglo-Saxons,* ed. P. CLEMOES (London 1959) 212–247.

[W. A. CHANEY]

AELFRIC OF CANTERBURY, ST.

Archbishop; d. Nov. 16, 1005. A monk of Abingdon and possibly of Glastonbury, he was abbot of St. Alban's and bishop of Ramsbury and Wilton (*c.* 990) before his election to Canterbury on Easter Day 995. Installed in 996, he received GREGORY V's own pallium in Rome (997). The expulsion of secular clergy and the substitution of monks at Canterbury Cathedral are now generally attributed to either Aelfric (Alfrick) or his predecessor,

Sigeric. Buried at Abingdon, his body was translated to St. John's, Canterbury, and (after 1067) to his Cathedral. His will is extant. Reference to Aelfric is found in the *Anglo-Saxon Chronicle*, the *Vita Dunstani auctore B* (dedicated to Aelfric), in Florence of Worcester, the *Chronicon monasterii de Abingdon,* and the *Chronicon monasterii sancti Albani.* Matthew of Paris, however, is unreliable.

Feast: Nov. 16.

Bibliography: J. M. KEMBLE, ed., *Codex diplomaticus aevi saxonici,* 6 v. (London 1839–48). C. COTTON, *The Saxon Cathedral at Canterbury and the Saxon Saints Buried Therein* (Manchester 1929). D. KNOWLES, *The Monastic Order in England, 943–1216* (Cambridge 1962) 696–697.

[W. A. CHANEY]

AELFRYTH OF CROWLAND, ST.

Anglo-Saxon virgin, recluse; d. after 833. She was the daughter of King Offa of Mercia, but unfortunately neither he nor his family found a biographer. Aelfryth (Alfreda, Elfriede, Ethelfreda, Etheldritha, etc.) is said to have been betrothed to St. Ethelbert, King of East Anglia, who was executed on her father's orders *c.* 790. Surviving her father (d. 796) by many years, she seems to have lived a solitary life at Crowland (Croyland), one of the great Midland monasteries. She is often confused with her sister Aelfleda, whose husband was murdered through treachery.

Feast: Aug. 2 (Crowland).

Bibliography: *Acta Sanctorum* August 1:173–175. W. DUGDALE, *Monasticon Anglicanum,* ed. J. CALEY et al. (London 1817–30) 2:109–111. R. STANTON, *A Menology of England and Wales* (London 1887) 22. A. M. ZIMMERMANN, *Kalendarium Benedictinum* (Metten 1933–38) 2:527.

[E. JOHN]

AELRED (AILRED), ST.

Abbot and writer; b. Hexham, Northumberland, 1110; d. Rievaulx, Jan. 12, 1167.

Life. He was of a noble family, the son of Eilaf, the last of the hereditary priests of Hexham in Northumberland on the English-Scottish border. He attended schools at Hexham and Durham, and possibly at the old Scottish capital, Roxburgh. Much of his youth he spent at the court of the half-English King David I of Scotland. Aelred entered the Cistercian Abbey of Rievaulx in Yorkshire probably in 1134. His monastic life falls into three periods: for nine years he was at Rievaulx as novice,

monk, and confidential adviser to Abbot William; for about four years he was abbot of Revesby, a newly established daughterhouse of Rievaulx; and from the end of 1147 until his death he was abbot of Rievaulx.

Aelred was known to his contemporaries as the "Bernard of the North" because of the warmth of his sentiment, the attractive power of his mind, and his wondrous gift of writing and preaching for monks and clergy. He was one of the most influential persons of his time. His life was marked by tireless activity, even during the chronic illness that plagued his later life. The duties of administering a large and prosperous community and the many visitations to the daughterhouses of Rievaulx were a constant responsibility. Moreover, he kept up an extensive correspondence and was much in demand as friend and counselor to abbots, bishops, and kings. His writings reveal Aelred as a person of warmth and simplicity, deeply imbued with the Christian humanism of his day.

His life, the *Vita Aelredi,* was written by a contemporary monk, Walter Daniel, who lived for 17 years under Aelred's rule and who sought to illustrate Aelred's sanctity. The supposed canonization of Aelred by Celestine III in 1191 is false. In 1476 the general chapter at Cîteaux allowed a more solemn celebration of Aelred's feast in England and gave a formal authorization of the local cultus.

Writings. Only part of the literary heritage of Aelred is extant. His extensive correspondence with popes and kings, his rhythmic prose in honor of St. Cuthbert, his homily for the feast of St. Edward the Confessor have been lost. The *Vita Aelredi* is the starting point for the authentic list of Aelred's works. This list does not include the *Oratio pastoralis* and four historical works, although these are well attested by twelfth-century Rievaulx manuscripts. The manuscript tradition of the *corpus aelredianum* tells an interesting story. Some 180 manuscripts have been listed. The great number of thirteenth-century manuscripts (71) is due partly to the fact that several works of Aelred were ascribed to St. Bernard and St. Augustine. The greatest number of manuscripts were copied at the Benedictine Abbey of Reading, and most are preserved today in England.

The first attempt to edit a series of Aelredian works was made by Richard Gibbons in the 17th century. A complete and critical edition of the *Opera Omnia* was published in 1971 for the 800th anniversary of Aelred's death.

The writings of Aelred are usually divided into ascetical or devotional works and historical works.

Ascetical Works. Aelred's first work, *Speculum caritatis,* was written at the instigation of St. Bernard of

Clairvaux while Aelred was novice master. In a fluent and fine style, he treated of the excellence and practice of charity. The *De Iesu puero duodenni* was written at the request of a friend, Ivo of Wardon. Quoting the text of Luke (2.41–52), Aelred gave a literal, an allegorical, and a spiritual or moral exposition. His most famous work, *De spiritali amicitia,* was based on Cicero's *De amicitia* but was influenced also by Augustine and Bernard. Written in dialogue form, it has as its theme that truly spiritual friendship never concerns two persons only. It always involves Christ, who is the source from which the friendship springs, the framework in which it grows, and the final end at which it aims.

The *De institutione inclusarum* is a rule for recluses, written at the request of Aelred's sister. According to the author's own words, it contains "a way of life to govern the body, a way of purifying the inward man of vices, and an example of three-fold meditation." The *De anima* consists solely in a synthesis of Augustinian doctrine and deals with fundamental questions concerning the nature of the soul—a common preoccupation for contemporary Cistercian psychologists. Aelred's ascetical works include also *Sermones de tempore et de sanctis,* 31 *Sermones de oneribus,* and a fine pastoral prayer of the abbot for his monks.

Historical Works. The historical writings of Aelred have long been neglected on the assumption that they are not of spiritual interest. However, they reveal much of Aelred's personality and of the spiritual environment of the country in which he lived. In chronological order, they are: *Genealogia regum anglorum, Vita s. Niniani, De bello standardii, De sanctimoniali de Watton, Vita s. Eduardi Confessoris, De sanctis Ecclesiae Hagulstadensis.*

Doctrine. Aelred's love for Ciceronian literature could no longer predominate after he entered the cloister. The *lectio divina* led him to a love of the Scriptures. As a monk he was oriented toward the writings of the fathers of the desert, the Rule of St. Benedict, and the whole patristic learning, especially the *Confessions* of St. Augustine. Faithful to the Cistercian formation, he showed great devotion to the humanity of Christ, wrote with Bernardine accents about charity and spiritual friendship, composed a treatise on the nature of the soul, and wove beautiful prayers into his sermons for the monks. His meditation on the incidents of Our Lord's life and Passion had a remarkable influence on the later development of Christian spirituality. Aelred's insistence on monastic experience as a way that leads to God, his affective spirituality, his Christocentric devotion, especially to the Child Jesus, make him one of the greatest monastic writers of medieval England.

Feast: March 3 (Dioceses of Liverpool, Hexham, and Middlesbrough and in Cistercian houses).

Bibliography: W. DANIEL, *The Life of Ailred of Rievaulx,* ed. and tr. F. M. POWICKE (New York 1950; reprinted Oxford 1978). M. A. CALABRESE, *Biblioteca sanctorum* 1:276–279. B. P. MCGUIRE, *Brother and Lover: Aelred of Rievaulx* (New York 1994) A. SQUIRE, *Aelred of Rievaulx: A study.* (London 1969; reprinted Kalamazoo, Mich. 1981). C. M. SAGE, "The MSS of St. Aelred," *American Catholic Historical Review* 34 (1949) 437–445. A. HOSTE, *Bibliotheca Aelrediana* (The Hague 1962), a survey of the MSS, old catalog, eds., and studies of Aelred. *Aelredi Rievallensis Opera omnia,* A. HOSTE and C. H. TALBOT (Turnholti, Belgium 1971) in the series *Corpus Christianorum. Continuatio Medievalis. Aelred of Rievaulx, historical works,* ed. J. P. FREELAND and M. DUTTON (Kalamazoo, MI 1994). R. GIBBONS, ed., *Opera divi Aelredi Rievallensis* (Douai 1618; repr. 1655), includes most of the ascetical works. Critical eds. of individual works: *De Iesu puero duodenni,* ed. A. HOSTE, tr. J. DUBOIS, as *Quand Jésus eut douze ans* (Sources Chrétienne 60; 1959); Eng. tr. G. WEBB and A. WALKER, *On Jesus at Twelve Years Old* (London 1956). *De institutione inclusarum,* ed. C. H. TALBOT, in AnalOCist 7 (1951) 167–217; Eng. tr. G. WEBB and A. WALKER, *A Letter to His Sister by Saint Aelred of Rievaulx* (London 1957). *De anima,* ed. C. H. TALBOT, in *Medieval and Renaissance Studies* Suppl 1 (1952). *De spiritali amicitia,* see A. HOSTE, "The First Draft of Aelred of Rievaulx' *De spiritali amicitia,*" *Sacris erudiri* 10 (1958)186–211. For thirteenth- and fourteenth-century summaries of *De spiritali amicitia,* see A. HOSTE, "Le *Speculum spiritalis amicitiae,* compilation du XIII e siècle de deux traités d'Aelred de Rievaulx par Thomas de Frakaham," *Studia monastica* 3 (1961) 291–323, Eng. tr. H. TALBOT, *Christian Friendship by S. Aelred of Rievaulx* (London 1942). C. DUMONT, ed. and tr., *Saint Aelred de Rievaulx* (Les Écrits des saints; Namur 1961), extracts of the ascetical writings. R. TWYSDEN, ed., *Historiae anglicanae scriptores X* (London 1652), includes most of the historical writings. See also A. SQUIRE, "Historical Factors in the Formation of A. of R.," *Collectanea ordinis Cistercienism Reformatorium* 22 (1960) 262–282. CETEDOC, Universitas Catholica Lovaniensis Lovanii Novi, ed., *Aelredus Rievallensis, opera ascetica,* ed. (Turnhout, Belgium 1989); *Aelredus Rievallensis, Sermones I-XLVI* (Turnhout 1989). R. L. G. RITCHIE, *The Normans in Scotland* (Edinburgh 1954) 246–257. A. HALLIER, *Un Éducateur monastique: Aelred de Rievaulx* (Paris 1959), Eng. tr. C. HEANEY as *The Monastic Theology of Aelred of Rievaulx: An experiential theology* (Shannon, Ireland 1969). C. DUMONT, "L'Équilibre humain de la vie cistercienne d'après le Bs. A. de R.," *Collectanea ordinis Cistercienism Reformatorium* 18 (1956) 177–189; "A. de R.," *Théologie de la vie monastique* (Paris 1961) 527–538. A. HOSTE and S. ROSE DE LIMA, *For Crist Luve: Prayers of Saint Aelred, Abbot of Rievaulx* (The Hague 1965). Literature. G. FÖSGES, *Das Menschenbild bei Aelred von Rievaulx* (Altenberge 1994). J. J. JUSSERAND, *English essays from a French Pen* (New York 1970). A. MAIORINO TUOZZI, *La conoscenza di sé nella scuola cisterciense* (Naples 1976). W. M. WRIGHT, *A retreat with Francis de Sales, Jane de Chantal, and Aelred of Rievaulx: Befriending Each Other in God* (Cincinnati, Ohio 1996).

[A. HOSTE]

AEMILIAN, SS.

The Roman martyrology lists eight saints by this name; other martyrologies list more. The most noteworthy are the following:

Aemilian, martyred at Dristra (Romania) under the Emperor Julian the Apostate.

Feast: July 18.

Aemilian of Cogolla (also called Emilian Cucullatus and Emilian-with-the-Hood), hermit, parish priest; d. Tarazon, Aragon, 574; the abbey of S. Millán de la Cogolla was built at his hermitage and has his relics. His life was written by BRAULIO; he is regarded as a patron of Spain.

Feast: Nov. 12.

Aemilian, Bishop of Cyzicus, ninth century; he opposed Emperor Leo V the Armenian in the controversy over iconoclasm and died in exile as a result.

Feast: Aug. 8.

Aemilian, Bishop of Nantes, perhaps in the eighth century; though he is not named in the early lists of bishops of Nantes, legend claims he fought against the Saracens near Autun.

Feast: Sept. 3.

Aemilian (also Eminian) of Lagny, abbot, d. *c.* 648; an Irish disciple of St. FURSEY (FURSEUS), he succeeded him as abbot of Lagny-sur-Marne.

Feast: March 10.

Bibliography: B. DUTTON, *La "Vida de San Millán de la Cogolla" de Gonzalo de Berceo* (London 1967). *Acta Sanctorum* July 4:370–376. J. DUBOIS, *Catholicisme* 4:52. I. M. GOMEZ, *Dictionnaire d'histoire et de géographie ecclésiastiques* 15:406–412. A. BUTLER, *The Lives of the Saints*, ed. H. THURSTON and D. ATTWATER (New York 1956) 4:321–322. A. M. ZIMMERMANN, *Lexicon für Theologie und Kirche*, ed. J. HOFER and K. RAHNER (Freiburg 1957–65) 1:438. *Acta Sanctorum* Aug. 2:353; Oct. 11:196. V. GRUMEL, *Catholicisme* 4:51–52. *Bibliotheca hagiographica latina antiquae et mediae aetatis* 1:105. J. L. BAUDOT and L. CHAUSSIN, *Vies des saints et des bienhereux selon l'ordre du calendrier avec l'historique des fêtes* (Paris 1935–56) 9:75–76. G. BARDY, *Catholicisme* 4:52–53. *Acta Sanctorum* March 2:45.

[B. L. MARTHALER]

AEON (IN THE BIBLE)

An indefinitely long period of time. The Biblical use of the term can be seen best by examining how it is employed in the OT, in intertestamental Judaism, and in the NT.

In the Old Testament. The Greek word αἰών, from which the English word is derived, first occurs in the Greek versions of the Bible as a translation of the Hebrew word *'ôlām,* meaning an indefinitely long period of time of greater or lesser extent. The terms express especially the notion of the duration of time in which one generation succeeds another (Eccl 1.4) or indefinite periods of time long since past (Jos 24.2) and thus come to mean age (Ez 26.20). Moreover, *'ôlām* and αἰών come to take on the more precise meaning of eternity or unlimited, endless time in some passages in which Yahweh is said to live "from of old" (*mê-'ôlām*), as one generation succeeds another. He is "the everlasting God" (*'ēl 'ôlām:* Gn 21.33). He swears "As I live forever. . ." (*le 'ôlām:* Dt 32.40). The eternal King (*melek 'ôlām:* Jer 10.10) is, in the later, deuterocanonical books, He who lives forever (*hê-' 'ôlām:* Dn 12.7; Sir 18.1).

In Intertestamental Judaism. In addition to the two meanings of αἰών, "long duration of time" and "eternity," that later Judaism received from the OT, two new and often related meanings emerged: (1) The apocalyptic literature in particular distinguishes between the present "age," which is "the aeon of injustice" (Ethiopic Enoch 48.7) and the future "age" of holiness (Syriac Baruch 15.7–8). In the eschatology of this period [*see* ESCHATOLOGY (IN THE BIBLE)] there is postulated a moral difference between the present evil aeon and the future aeon with its promise of happiness for the just (cf. even the deuterocanonical Tb 14.5). (2) The present "age" was easily identified with the world that has existed from creation up to the present [*see* WORLD (IN THE BIBLE)] or to the future golden "age," and thus the temporal meaning of αἰών tends sometimes to merge with a purely spatial sense of this material world (4 Esdras 7.50).

In the New Testament. The NT authors use αἰών to mean (1) age in the sense of a certain period of time of greater or lesser duration, (2) age meaning an indefinite period of years or of generations, (3) eternity properly speaking, and (4) world either as the present material world, especially the world of sin and darkness that is opposed to the kingdom of God, or the "world to come" that has already begun.

(1) The word αἰών sometimes means simply age or era as a more or less defined number of years or generations. Thus in 1 Cor 10.11, St. Paul refers to the limited "ages" of the past when he says that "the end of the ages" has come.

(2) As an indefinite duration of time, αἰών may have been used several times (e.g., in 1 Cor 2.7, where "before the ages" may refer to the limited but indefinite period of time between creation and the end of the world), but such usage readily passes over into the following meaning.

(3) The term αἰών can signify eternity in the sense of an unlimited, endless period of time, either backward and forward or simply the future duration of time without

end. Thus in Col 1.26 ἀπὸ τῶν αἰώνων apparently means "from all eternity," but perhaps equivalently, "before the foundation of the world," as in Eph 1.4; Jn 17.24; 1 Pt 1.20; see also εἰς τὸν αἰῶνα (forever) in Jn 6.51; εἰς τὸν αἰῶνα τοῦ αἰῶνος and εἰς τοὺς αἰῶνας τῶν αἰώνων in Heb 1.8; Gal 1.5; 1 Tm 1.17 meaning "forever and ever," and αἰώνιος (everlasting) in Rom 16.26; Heb 9.14.

(4) Finally, αἰών very frequently has the sense of world (Heb 1.2; 11.3), especially in those passages where "this present aeon" is contrasted with "the aeon to come" (Mt 12.32; Mk 10.30; Rom 12.2). As in Jewish usage there is often a moral difference between "this aeon" and "the aeon to come"; so in Lk 16.8, "the children of this aeon" are distinguished from "the children of light." St. Paul expressly speaks of "the present evil aeon" (Gal 1.4), and Jesus refers to its end (Mt 13.39). The future aeon has, indeed, already begun in the present aeon by means of Christ's Redemption (Gal 1.4; Heb 6.5), but there remains the tension between the present world and the growing realization of the kingdom of God.

Bibliography: H. SASSE, G. KITTEL, *Theologisches Wörterbuch zum Neuen Testament* (Stuttgart 1935–) 1:197–209. O. CULLMANN, *Christ and Time*, tr. F. V. FILSON (rev. ed. Philadelphia 1964). J. BARR, *Biblical Words for Time* (Naperville, Ill. 1962). A. LUNEAU, *L'Histoire du salut chez les pères de l'église* (Paris 1964). *Encyclopedic Dictionary of the Bible*, trans. and ed. by L. HARTMAN (New York 1963) 662–664. F. J. SCHIERSE, *Lexikon für Theologie und Kirche*, ed. J. HOFER and K. RAHNER (Freiberg 1957–65) 1:680–683.

[J. L. RONAN]

AEONIUS OF ARLES, ST.

Bishop; fl. 494–500. Little is known of his life before he became bishop and metropolitan of Arles on Aug. 23, 494. On Sept. 29, 500, he was succeeded at his own request by his friend CAESARIUS OF ARLES, with whom he had founded Châlon-sur-Saône. Two important items were settled during his episcopacy, the diocesan boundary with Vienne and the primacy of the See of Arles (Jaffé K 753, 754). Popes ANASTASIUS III and Symmachus corresponded with him on TRADUCIANISM and the date of Easter in certain doubtful cases (Jaffé 751, 754). There are also letters to him from Ruricius I of Limoges (d. 507; PL 58:87, 97). Aeonius contributed much to the development of monasticism in France and was instrumental in bringing Caesarius to Arles. His name does not appear in the Roman Martyrology.

Feast: Aug. 18.

Bibliography: *Monumenta Germaniae Scriptores rerum Merovingicarum* (Berlin) 3:460–462, 469. *Patrologia Latina*

67:1005–06. *Sancti Caesarii opera omnia*, ed. G. MORIN, 2 v. in 3 (Maredsous 1937–42) 2:300. E. EWIG, *Lexicon für Theologie und Kirche*, ed. J. HOFER and K. RAHNER (Freiburg 1957–65) 1:683. G. BARDY, *Catholicisme* 4:279–280. P. JAFFÉ, *Regesta pontificum romanorum ab condita eclesia ad annum post Christum natum 1198*, ed. F. KALTENBRUNNER (Graz 1956).

[T. P. HALTON]

AERTNYS, JOZEF

Redemptorist moral theologian (known also as Josef Aertnijs); b. Eindhoven, in the Diocese of s'Hertogenbosch, Holland, Jan. 15, 1828: d. Wittem, Holland, June 30, 1915. After being educated by the Redemptorists, Aertnys made his profession Oct. 15, 1846, and was ordained Sept. 14, 1854. He served as professor of moral theology at Wittem from 1860 to 1898 and was a consultant in theological and canonical problems for the bishops and priests of his native land. Among his writings, the more important were: *Caeremoniale solemnium functionum juxta liturgiam Romanam* (s'Hertogenbosch 1880; 3d ed. 1921); *Compendium liturgiae sacrae* (Tournai 1895; 11th ed. 1943); and *Theologia moralis juxta doctrinam S. Alphonsi* (Tournai 1886–87), a work that went through 17 editions, of which the ninth to 16th were made by A. Damen and the 17th was provided by J. Visser (1956–58), professor at the Urbaniana University in Rome. The 18th edition is being prepared. Aertnys also wrote *Theologia pastoralis* (Tournai 1892; 6th ed. 1916). He published many articles in scholarly publications and served as one of the original founders of the *Nederlandse Katholieke Stemmen*, for which he wrote frequently on moral questions of the day.

Bibliography: "In Memoriam," *Nederlandse Katholieke Stemmen* 15 (1915) 210–11. M. DE MEULEMEESTER et al., *Bibliographie générale des écrivains Rédemptoristes*, 3 v. (Louvain 1933–39) 2:9–11; 3:246.

[A. SAMPERS]

AESCULAPIUS, CULT OF

Greek hero and god of healing, known also by the Greek form of his name, Asklepios. He is mentioned in the *Iliad* and by Pindar (*Pyth.* 3) and is treated extensively by Pausanias (*Description of Greece*, bk 2). The town of Epidaurus claimed to be his birthplace and here was built the greatest of the temples and healing establishments dedicated to him. Other outstanding centers were on the island of Cos and at Pergamum and Smyrna in Asia Minor. The cult was brought to Rome in 293 B.C.

The practice of healing at temples of Aesculapius usually required that the patient stay within the sacred enclosure of the temple, where the god would send dreams prescribing treatments to effect cures. The treatments prescribed were frequently of an unexpected character and involved physical exertion, regardless of the patient's condition. In addition to balms, poultices, warm baths, purges, bloodletting, diet and fasting, the god frequently prescribed horseback riding, cold baths, going barefoot, smearing the body with mud from the sacred spring, and outdoor exercises, even in the coldest weather.

Many votive inscriptions from the temple at Epidaurus are known (published in *Inscriptiones Graecae* v. 4 and in other collections). These, along with the data supplied by Aristophanes (*Plut.* 653–747) and the great 2d-century Sophist Aelius Aristides (*Sacred Discourses*) and others, furnish a fairly full literature on the kind of ailments treated and miraculous cures attested to. These include cures of barrenness, paralysis of the fingers, blindness, dumbness, removal of branding marks, kidney stones, tumors, skin diseases, fevers, and bronchial ailments—in fact, almost all the diseases known to man.

Some modern scholars have maintained that priests at the temples of Aesculapius often administered medicines and sometimes even performed operations, inducing the patient to believe that such events had occurred while they were asleep and were due to the intervention of the god himself. It is indeed probable that much of the medical lore contained in the so-called Hippocratic Corpus was collected, and perhaps used, at temples of this deity. The cult of Aesculapius was very popular and flourished until it was suppressed by Christian emperors.

Bibliography: F. R. WALTON, *The Oxford Classical Dictionary* (Oxford 1949) 16:106–107. K. PRÜMM, *Religionsgeschichtliches Handbuch für den Raum der altchristlichen Umwelt* (Rome 1954) 447–453. E. J. and L. EDELSTEIN, *Asclepius,* 2 v. (Baltimore 1945). A. M. J. FESTUGIÈRE, *Personal Religion Among the Greeks* (Berkeley 1954) 85–104.

[T. A. BRADY]

AESTHETICS

The term has been used in several significantly different ways since it was first introduced by A. G. Baumgarten (*Meditationes philosophicae de nonnullis ad poema pertinentibus,* 1735), who defined it as "the science of sensory cognition." In one more recent but well-established use (as in the *Journal of Aesthetics and Art Criticism,* Cleveland), it embraces all comparatively broad and searching questions about art, its nature, conditions, and consequences, and is roughly equivalent to the philosophy and psychology of art. Many modern thinkers maintain a sharp distinction between psychological aesthetics, considered as a branch of empirical psychology,

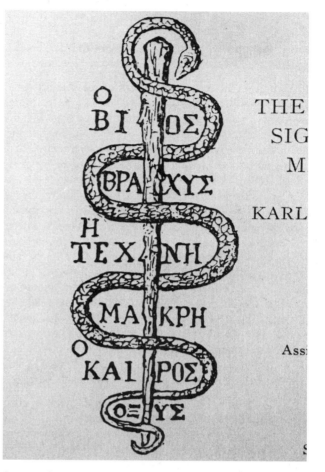

Serpent of Aesculapius. (Bettmann/CORBIS)

and philosophical aesthetics. Of these thinkers, some regard the latter as a special application of philosophical analysis to those problems that arise from reflection on the presuppositions and methodological principles of criticism, i.e., the description, interpretation, and evaluation of works of art. Others would define philosophical aesthetics as the investigation of the nature of art, of beauty, and of aesthetic value.

Each of the arts (and, it might be added, certain aspects of nature and of man) presents its own special problems to the aesthetician, for example, the alleged "meaning" of music, the relation between representation and design in visual art, and the relevance of truth and credibility to the greatness of literature. But there are also general problems that cut across these special ones. The aesthetic study of literature may begin with an examination of the foundations of literary criticism and with such questions as: Are explications of poems objective and interpersonally valid? What reasons can be given for judging a poem to be good, or better than another poem? Such questions, persistently pursued, lead to fundamental problems about the essential nature of poetry and of literature, about the relation of literature to the other arts, and about the values that may be ascribed to art in general. This article reviews three of these broad problems.

Theories of Art. The concept of the fine arts as a special class (comprising such major arts as painting, sculpture, architecture, music and literature as well as hundreds of minor arts, such as flower arranging and the fashioning of jewelry) is a modern achievement. It first clearly appears in *Les beaux arts réduits à un même principe* (1746), by the Abbé C. Batteux, and in D'Alembert's *Discours préliminaire* to the *Encyclopédie* (1751). The formation of this concept made it possible to state one of the fundamental aesthetic problems in the modern way: What is the common and central character of works of fine art (or art, for the purposes of the present discussion)? Much of the thinking about aesthetics in the past 200 years has been a search for a general theory of art. But the earliest sustained reflections on aesthetic problems, by Plato and Aristotle, as well as later medieval and Renaissance discussions of the similarities and differences among the arts, had led to important ideas (such as the idea of "imitation," Batteux's "single principle") that could be put to use by later aestheticians.

The various answers to the question, What is art?, may be placed in three main categories, though it will be evident that within each category there are many divergent views; and it must be borne in mind that individual philosophers may straddle two theories.

Referentialism. It was plain to those who first philosophized about art that at least some works of art are partly derivative from what is to be found in the world: the sculptor gives his figure a recognizable human visage; the dramatic poet presents the words and deeds of actual or possible people. The theory that art is essentially *mimesis* (still, for want of a better term, translated as imitation) was a reasonable generalization from these observations, since ancient visual art was representational and ancient music was wedded to dance and song. Under Plato's dialectical manipulations, *mimesis* took on several senses—most prominently and pejoratively, the sense that the artist makes an image (*phantasma*) or deceptive semblance (see *Soph.* 236B; *Tim.* 19D; *Gorg.* 463–65; *Rep.* 600C). In Aristotle's use of the term (*Poet.* 1447a, 1460b), as applied to poetry and painting, no such denigration is implied.

Whatever else it has come to mean—and it has meant many things in the course of its long history— imitation involves some kind of reference of the work of art to the outside world by means of an important similarity between them, though with something left out or added (abstraction or distortion). Thus HEGEL's view that art embodies the Ideal in sensuous form (see *Philosophy of Fine Art*, tr. F. P. B. Osmaston, London, 1920, 1:53, 77, 154) and SCHOPENHAUER's that art embodies the Platonic Ideas (see *The World as Will and Idea,* book 3, tr. R. B. Haldane and J. Kemp, 4th ed. London, 1896, esp. 1:231, 252, 272) may be regarded as variants of the same theory (*see* PLATO; PLATONISM). Sophisticated 20th-century versions of the theory of "imitation" hold that a work of art is an "iconic sign" [see C. W. Morris, "Esthetics and the Theory of Signs," *Journal of Unified Science (Erkenntnis)*, Leipzig, 8:131–50] or "presentational symbol" (see S. Langer, *Philosophy* in a *New Key*, Cambridge 1942). A musical composition, for example, is said to designate a type of mental state or process in virtue of its kinetic similarity to its referent; in this view, every work of art is or contains a reference to the world outside it.

Expressionism. The source of the artist's creative impulse was the subject of speculation in the earliest times, as for example by Homer and Hesiod, who ascribed it to divine inspiration. Plato's observations on the "madness" or "frenzy" of the poet (see *Phaedrus* 245A; *Ion* 533E, 536B; *Meno* 99C) emphasized the artist's irrationality and lack of genuine wisdom. In this light a work of art has been understood by many as a manifestation, or objectification, of its creator's feelings.

The view of art as essentially expression of emotion was widely accepted during the Romantic period (cf. Wordsworth's description of poetry as "the spontaneous overflow of powerful feelings," 1800 Preface to the *Lyrical Ballads*). In a more complicated form, as developed by Benedetto CROCE (*Estetica*, Milan 1902) and clarified by others (e.g., R. G. Collingwood, *The Principles of Art,* Oxford 1938), the expression theory has become a pervasive influence in 20th-century aesthetics. Croce's identification of expression and intuition is variously interpreted; but his primary thesis, that through the act of expression the artist becomes able to articulate his own feelings and impressions, has been widely accepted.

Formalism. The self-containedness and self-sufficiency (that is, the high degree of unity and order) of works of art were somewhat emphasized by St. Augustine (see *Vera Relig.* 23.59; 41.77; *Musica* 1.13.28; *Ordine* 2.15.42; *Lib. Arb.* 2.16.42). Drawing on suggestions from Plato (*Philebus* 64E, 66AB) and Plotinus (*Enneads* 1.6.2), he developed the connection between beauty, order, and numerical proportion and related art to the divine order. The same interest in the internal nature of the aesthetic object is seen in St. Thomas's three conditions of beauty, *integritas sive perfectio, debita proportio sive consonantia,* and *claritas* (*Summa theologiae* 1a, 39.8; cf. 2a2ae, 145.2, 180.2).

These formal concepts—but detached from metaphysical and theological contexts—commended themselves to some 19th-century aestheticians who were eager to defend the autonomy of art against various encroachments: the neo-Hegelian reduction (or elevation) of art to a sensuous form of religion and philosophy; the realist theory that art is a mirror of social and cultural conditions; the socialist theory that art exists mainly to promote justice and human understanding. Eduard Hanslick, in his highly significant work, *Vom Musikalisch-Schöne* (Leipzig 1854), argued that the beauty of music is peculiar and internal to it, not depending on its relation to anything else.

This so-called formalist theory was generalized to the fine arts by Clive Bell (*Art,* London 1914) and Roger Fry (*Vision and Design*, London 1920) and has been defended in various qualified versions. Its insistence that literary works, for example, should be respected as objects in their own right has inspired such movements as Russian formalism of the prerevolutionary and early postrevolutionary period, and the New Criticism of England and the United States, and it is reflected in such works of the phenomenological school as Roman Ingarden's *Das Literarische Kunstwerk* (Halle 1930).

Highly generalized theories like the foregoing are not always incompatible with each other. Indeed, they may be construed as attempts to answer different questions: the first group, questions about the semantics of art; the second group, questions about the pragmatics of art; and the third group, questions about the syntax of art (to borrow the terminology of C. Morris, "Foundations of the Theory of Signs," *Encyclopedia of Unified Science*, Chicago 1938). Nevertheless, these positions reflect significant differences of opinion about the factors that are basic and decisive in art; and the critic's assumptions about the precise nature and degree of autonomy that can be ascribed to art will have consequences for his practical criticism.

Aesthetic Value. The existence of criticism as a distinctive intellectual activity appears to presuppose that there is a certain "point of view" from which aesthetic objects are most appropriately regarded (the aesthetic point of view) and a special kind of "value" (aesthetic value) to be found, or at least looked for, in them. Criticism has almost always been taken to include the evaluation, or appraisal, of aesthetic objects, issuing in such judgments as "The *Windhover* is a good poem," or "This is a poor painting," which are normally supported by reasons ("The poem is subtle and profound," "The painting is disorganized"). Many of the fundamental issues in the philosophy of criticism concern the logic of critical reasoning—whether, for example, originality or success in fulfilling the author's intention ought to count as a relevant and convincing ground for judging a work to be good.

To justify the critic's appeal to certain reasons—or, in other words, his use of certain criteria of judgment—seems to require the discrimination, or isolation, of aesthetic value. Once we are clear concerning what sort of goodness is to be sought in art, we can ask what features of the work are likely to enhance or to diminish that goodness. This is essentially the procedure followed by Aristotle when he asked what is the proper pleasure (*oikeia hedone*) of tragedy, and proceeded to analyze those elements of tragedy that bear upon its tendency to provide this pleasure (see *Poet.* 1453b, 1459a, 1462b).

The attempt to work out a satisfactory account of aesthetic value encounters a number of very difficult problems, some of them pervasive in general value theory, some of them peculiar to aesthetics. They can be only very briefly indicated here.

Value and Beauty. Is aesthetic value the same as beauty? Until the concept of the sublime came to be considered seriously and carefully in the 18th century, judgments of aesthetic value were characteristically stated as judgments of beauty. In this usage, "This is a beautiful poem" means the same as "This is a good poem." Beauty is today more often considered as a ground of aesthetic value (the painting is good *because* it is beautiful), but not necessarily the sole ground, since expressive distortion may approach ugliness (or, some would say, achieve it); yet its power and vitality may make the painting great. (On this issue, contrast J. Maritain, *Art and Scholasticism,* tr. J. F. Scanlan, New York 1930, with S. C. Pepper, *Aesthetic Quality*, New York 1937.)

Value and Naturalness. Is aesthetic value natural or nonnatural? For some, to give a naturalistic definition of aesthetic value is to equate it with a psychological fact, such as giving pleasure or being desired. Whether it is inherently fallacious to propose such a definition has been much discussed. Many philosophers contend that a normative term (such as value or good) can never be reduced to nonnormative terms (such as pleasure or satisfaction), for any of several reasons: (1) that normative terms refer to a special nonempirical property, (2) that normative terms have a commending function that is absent from nonnormative terms, (3) that normative terms express attitudes and nonnormative terms do not. Others hold that a naturalistic definition framed with sufficient care—that is, by qualifying the conditions of the pleasure, or the nature of the satisfaction, involved—can correctly indicate what a normative term actually means in ordinary usage.

Value—Objective or Subjective? The objectivist regards the aesthetic value of an object as an internal property of it, which it possesses independently of any relation to a human perceiver who enjoys, approves, or admires it. The subjectivist takes aesthetic value to consist in some relation between the object and the perceiver (including the reader). The principal defense of subjectivism is that it is difficult to conceive of an object as having any value apart from some interest that is taken in it or apart from some desire that is satisfied by it. Objectivism, on the other hand, is often supported by the claim that it provides the only escape from relativism.

Value—Relative or Nonrelative? To say that aesthetic value is relative is to say that there can be two persons, one of whom says that a work of art is good and the other that it is not good, yet without really contradicting each other. If aesthetic value is objective, then it is not relative; but the subjectivist can choose between relativistic and nonrelativistic definitions. For example, if the subjectivist can first formulate the concept of the ''perfect critic,'' as one who has all the desirable qualifications we could ask for in a critic—sensitivity, learning, sympathy, impartiality, etc.—then he might define the term ''has aesthetic value'' as ''would be approved and admired by a majority of all perfect critics.'' This definition is subjective, but it is not relative, since whenever A says that a poem is good in this sense and B denies it, A and B are contradicting each other, no matter who A and B may be. On the other hand, the subjectivist might define aesthetic value in relation to a particular culture or historical epoch; by this definition, when a critic praises a poem, he is saying that it is, or will be, or under certain conditions would be, enjoyed and approved by sensitive people in his own culture. According to such a definition, if A and B belong to different cultures, they cannnot contradict each other by respectively affirming and denying that the poem is good.

The relativist usually argues that tastes vary and that what can be enjoyed by some people cannot be enjoyed by others; he urges that our definition of aesthetic value reflect this fact. In rebuttal it may be pointed out that there are all sorts of factors that affect this variability and no particular definition can accommodate them all. The only safe recourse for the relativist, then, is complete personal relativism, which transforms the critical judgment ''This is a good poem'' into something like ''I now like this poem.'' This personal definition does bring out the alleged ''noncognitive'' features of critical evaluations: that their utterance reveals the speaker's attitude, his desire to commend something, or his hope of influencing others. But it seems to leave out the logical features of critical evaluations that allow disputes to arise over them; and it is implausible to claim that the personal definition correctly describes what most people mean when they praise poems.

Value a Capacity? It is also argued that we must distinguish between aesthetic value as something available to those properly prepared for it and the actual realizations of this value in experience. This distinction can be preserved by defining aesthetic value as the capacity to provide a certain kind of (presumably desirable) experience or a certain kind of (desirable) pleasure. This instrumentalist definition of aesthetic value would be subjective, but nonrelative; it would not be a naturalistic definition, since a normative term (desirable) would be retained in the definiendum. Then critical disputes over, say, the merits of a poem, would concern the question how great an aesthetic experience (or how intense an aesthetic pleasure) can be obtained from it under optimum conditions. If someone actually does derive a genuine aesthetic experience of some magnitude from the work, that will be sufficient evidence of its aesthetic value. If no such experience occurs, the critic may be able to show, by an analysis of the work, either that it is unlikely to occur or that it may occur in more adequately prepared perceivers. In any case, it will be possible to support the critical evaluation by reasons. But the appeal to such reasons will presuppose, what the aesthetician must also at some point justify, that the aesthetic experience is itself desirable.

Aesthetic Experience. The experience of listening to music or contemplating a painting is more different from the experience of reading a poem or novel than these are from each other. This is evident to the careful observer, even though there is much that we do not yet understand (but hope in time to learn by psychological investigation) about the exact nature of these experiences. The aesthetician asks whether there is such a thing as an aesthetic experience common to all the arts. It is important to know this if we wish to group all the arts together in one genus, and especially if aesthetic value is to be defined in terms of aesthetic experience.

There is general agreement that aesthetic experience is characterized at least by unusually intense absorption in a phenomenal object—in visual or auditory patterns or, in the case of prose fiction, the ostensible world of the work. Beyond this, the chief point at issue is the remoteness of aesthetic experience from the experiences of everyday life. A number of questions and positions are on hand, difficult to sort out satisfactorily. They range from Clive Bell's claim (in *Art,* 3–7) that there is a unique ''aesthetic emotion''—the response to ''significant form''—utterly different from any other emotion and owing nothing to life experiences, to I. A. Richards's contrary insistence (*Principles of Literary Criticism*, London and New York 1924, chapters 2, 32) that art differs only in degree from other things in its effects upon us.

"Moving" Quality of Art. Ancient and medieval philosophers were aware of something puzzling about the state of mind induced by works of art. That this response involves the emotions in a central way was suggested (and deplored) by Plato, who noted the excited state of the rhapsode (in the dialogue *Ion*) and of the theater audience (*Rep.* 603–10). When psychological aesthetics came into its full development during the 18th century, a major aim of British aesthetic investigation was to explain the characteristic effects of art—its capacity to move us and the special sort of enjoyment it provides. Various contributions to a solution of this problem were made by J. Addison, in his account of the "pleasures of the imagination" (*Spectator*, Nos. 409, 411–21; 1712), by F. Hutcheson (*An Inquiry into the Original of Our Ideas of Beauty and Virtue*, London 1725) and by E. BURKE (*A Philosophical Inquiry into the Sublime and the Beautiful*, London 1756), and by A. Alison (*Essays on the Nature and Principles of Taste*, Edinburgh 1790), among many others. These writers aimed to discover (some of them with the aid of associationist psychology) the nature of our feelings about the beautiful and the sublime and the basis of our pleasure in these qualities.

Detachment of Aesthetic Experience. It was Kant (*Critique of Judgment*, Berlin 1790) who attempted a radical separation of aesthetic enjoyment from ordinary enjoyments and identified the experience of beauty as one in which we take "pleasure without interest" in an object exhibiting "purposefulness without purpose," an object capable, by its form, of arousing the "free play" of the reproductive imagination in harmony with the general cognitive conditions of the understanding. By emphasizing this disinterestedness of aesthetic experience, Schopenhauer made of art an escape from the horror of life under the dominion of the Will to Live, with its ceaseless alternation between boredom and unsatisfied desire. He described aesthetic experience as a state of "will-less contemplation" of timeless Ideas, when the drives are laid temporarily to rest, as the self loses consciousness of itself and is no longer constrained to view the world under the "principle of sufficient reason."

This opposition between the aesthetic point of view and the practical point of view—between, for example, the painter's and the real-estate developer's way of looking at a landscape—has been widely emphasized in modem aesthetics. Several writers have stressed the "isolation" and "detachment" of aesthetic experience, its wholeness and self-sufficiency—notably E. Bullough in his famous paper "'Psychical Distance' as a Factor in Art and an Aesthetic Principle" (*British Journal of Psychology*, 5, Cambridge 1912–13, 87–118). An object, according to Bullough, is psychically "distanced" when disconnected from ordinary practical needs and ends and

regarded for its surface qualities and internal form. Nearly any object can be so regarded, but aesthetic objects are designed to facilitate this response, though they differ considerably in their degree of distance, ranging from geometrical abstraction to pictorial realism.

Intensity of the Aesthetic Experience. Schopenhauer's emphasis on denial of the Will was violently rejected by Nietzsche (see the posthumously collected notes, *The Will to Power*, tr. A. M. Ludovici, 2d ed., New York 1910–11). Art, he insisted, does not induce resignation but "affirmation" of life in all its aspects; it is an expression of the Will to Power. Later writers have tried to make room for something of this view in stressing the intensity of aesthetic experience, its "heightened consciousness" and the sense of increased vitality—not the absence of emotion, or its release, but its ordering into a harmonious tension. This has been called "synaesthesis," the balance or poise of impulses, opposed without frustration (see I. A. Richards et al., *The Foundations of Aesthetics*, London 1922, 72–91).

Attempted Synthesis. A significant attempt to do justice to these divergent (though not necessarily incompatible) points, as well as others, is that by John Dewey in *Art as Experience*, New York 1934, especially chapter 3. Dewey's aim was to show how the special traits of aesthetic experience, those we cherish most, grow out of a natural setting, as intensifications of traits found valuable in all experience. The organism interacts with its environment, doing and undergoing. Sometimes stretches of continuing experience take on an unusual degree of completeness: the impulses that are aroused at the start run their course; there is consummation and fulfillment. Then we have, not just experience, but "an experience." And when an experience is controlled by attention to sensuous quality, and takes on a pervasive and distinct character, it is aesthetic experience, continuous but articulated, coherent but rhythmic, dynamic, cumulative, and inherently satisfying.

The Thomistic Tradition. This tradition also, as carried on by a number of contemporary thinkers (see e.g., J. Maritain, *Art and Scholasticism*; É. Gilson, *Painting and Reality*, New York 1957), has aimed to do justice to the dominant traits, as well as the wide range, of aesthetic experiences and to correct other accounts by keeping more firmly in view the intellectual aspect of aesthetic enjoyment. St. Thomas's pregnant definition of beauty as *id quod visum placet* (*Summa theologiae* 1.5.4 ad 1; cf. 1a2ae, 27.1) implies that in the perception of beauty, the exquisite intelligibility of the object, its possession of a form proportionate to the intellect itself (*proportio sive consonantia*), affords that delight mixed with exaltation that characterizes aesthetic experience. This relation to the cognitive faculty, which is essential to beauty, explains its restriction to sight and sound—we derive sensuous pleasure from perfumes, for example, but odors are not (strictly speaking) beautiful.

General Conclusion. These theorists and others have guided us to an understanding of many important features of aesthetic experience, though some questions remain unsettled. Roughly speaking, we can locate the peculiar character of that experience in the combination of two distinguishable objects of delight. First, we respond to pattern or gestalt as such; we desire the perception of order: symmetry, geometrical regularity, rational arrangement. Second, we respond to human qualities that emerge in the phenomenal field: to embodied energy, calmness, joy, force, tenderness, etc. With the first is connected the unity and repose of aesthetic experience; with the latter, our capacity to be moved and shaken. Works of art differ enormously according to which aspects are dominant. But speaking generally, in art we confront and cognize a complex of elements and relations making up, through formal cooperation, a satisfactory whole. Out of this whole emerge certain qualities, of various degrees of intensity, that engage our attention and our feelings. In a way subtly different from the feeling of ordinary life, we are lifted to a fresher and more vital plane of awareness, the joy of the spirit answering to the radiance of the object.

See Also: ART (PHILOSOPHY); BEAUTY.

Bibliography: Among the useful anthologies in English are E. VIVAS and M. KRIEGER, eds., *The Problems of Aesthetics* (New York 1953). M. M. RADER, ed., *A Modern Book of Esthetics* (3d ed. New York 1960). M. WEITZ, ed., *Problems in Aesthetics* (New York 1959). W. ELTON, ed., *Aesthetics and Language* (New York 1954). W. E. KENNICK, ed., *Art and Philosophy* (New York 1964). A. HOFSTADTER and R. KUHNS, eds., *Philosophies of Art and Beauty* (New York 1964). K. ASCHENBRENNER and A. ISENBERG, eds., *Aesthetic Theories* (New York 1965). A. SESONSKE, ed., *What Is Art?* (London 1965). On the history of aesthetics, see K. E. GILBERT and H. KUHN, *A History of Esthetics* (rev. ed. Bloomington 1953). M. C. BEARDSLEY, *A Short History of Western Aesthetics* (New York 1965). E. DE BRUYNE, *Études d'esthétique médiévale*, 3 v. (Bruges 1946). A. FONTAINE, *Les Doctrines d'art en France* (Paris 1909). S. H. MONK, *The Sublime: A Study of Critical Theories in 18th Century England* (New York 1935; Ann Arbor pa. 1960). E. CASSIRER, *The Philosophy of the Enlightenment*, tr. C. A. KOELLN and J. P. PETTEGROVE (Princeton 1951). W. J. HIPPLE, *The Beautiful, the Sublime, and the Picturesque in Eighteenth-Century British Aesthetic Theory* (Carbondale, Illinois 1957). G. MORPURGO-TAGLIABUE, *L'Esthétique contemporaine* (Milan 1960). On classical and contemporary problems of aesthetics, see M. C. BEARDSLEY, *Aesthetics* (New York 1958). F. E. SPARSHOTT, *The Structure of Aesthetics* (Toronto 1963). J. STOLNITZ, *Aesthetics and Philosophy of Art Criticism* (Boston 1960).

[M. C. BEARDSLEY]

AETERNA CAELI GLORIA

The office hymn that was historically assigned for Lauds in the ferial office on Fridays throughout the year. Originally the initial letter of each line was in alphabetic sequence through the letter "T," except that the fourth line repeated initial "C." To maintain the correct alphabetic sequence the orthography of the manuscript tradition must be retained in lines 9 and 11 (see Anal Hymn 51:33). The meter of the hymn is the iambic dimeter. The author, once thought to be Pope Gregory I (the Great), is unknown. In content this hymn is a prayer to Christ for light to see one's duties and for the increase of the three theological virtues of faith, hope, and charity.

Bibliography: J. JULIAN, *A Dictionary of Hymnology* (New York 1957) 24–25. *Analectica Hymnica* (Leipzig 1886–1922) 51:32–34. A. S. WALPOLE, ed., *Early Latin Hymns* (Cambridge, Eng. 1922) 276–279. M. BRITT, ed., *The Hymns of the Breviary and Missal* (new ed. New York 1948) 68–69. J. SZÖVÉRFFY, *Die Annalen der latenische Hymnendichtung* (Berlin 1964–65) 1:142, 214.

[H. DRESSLER]

AETERNA CHRISTI MUNERA

An Ambrosian hymn written in iambic dimeter. The authorship of this hymn is generally attributed to St. AMBROSE. The author intended this composition of eight strophes to be used on the feast days of martyrs. In the course of time, however, the hymn was selected for use on the feast days of Apostles also, and this entailed certain changes in the sequence of lines and adaptations especially notable in the first strophe. The first (with adaptations), second, sixth, and seventh strophes, with an added doxology, was traditionally used as the breviary hymn for Matins in the Common of Apostles outside of Easter-tide. In the Common of Martyrs both in and out of Easter time the first (with adaptations), third, fourth, fifth, and eighth strophes was traditionally used for the hymn at Matins. In each case the hymn praises the victory of the Apostles or martyrs and expresses admiration for their constancy in specifically described trials and sufferings.

Bibliography: J. JULIAN, *A Dictionary of Hymnology* (New York 1957) 24–25. A. S. WALPOLE, ed., *Early Latin Hymns* (Cambridge, Eng. 1922) 104–108. M. BRITT, ed., *The Hymns of the Breviary and Missal* (new ed. New York 1948) 325–326. W. BULST, ed., *Hymni Latini antiquissimi LXXV* (Heidelberg 1956) 52, 185. J. SZÖVÉRFFY, *Die Annalen der latenische Hymnendichtung* (Berlin 1964–65) 50–52, 62, 66, 116, 174.

[H. DRESSLER]

AETERNE RERUM CONDITOR

The words of the opening line of the first strophe of the office hymn which was historically assigned for Lauds for the Sundays from Jan. 14 to the first Sunday in Lent and from Oct. 1 to the first Sunday in Advent. The use of this hymn at the early canonical hours goes back to CAESARIUS OF ARLES (d. 542), who prescribed its use in his Rule (*Sanctarum virginum regulae* 69; *S. Caesarii opera omnia* 2:121). The text in the Roman Breviary of 1632 altered the older reading in the second, third, and seventh strophes. This hymn is generally acknowledged as an authentic work of St. AMBROSE. Augustine (*Retract.* 20.2; *Corpus scriptorum ecclesiasticorum latinorum* 36:97–98) quotes two lines of the fourth strophe and names Ambrose as the author. The thought and at times the very wording of several lines bear a striking similarity with passages in Ambrose's *Hexaemeron* (CSEL 32.1:201). The meter of the hymn is the iambic dimeter. In five successive strophes, Ambrose gives a mystical interpretation of the significance of the crowing of the cock (*gallicinium*). Barring the purely scriptural animal metaphors, such as the lamb, the wolf, and the lion of Juda, the usage of this hymn is one of the few animal motifs in early Latin hymnology.

Bibliography: U. CHEVALIER, *Repertorium hymnologicum* (Louvain-Brussels 1892–1921) 1:647. J. JULIAN, *A Dictionary of Hymnology* (New York 1957) 1:26. A. S. WALPOLE, ed., *Early Latin Hymns* (Cambridge, Eng. 192) 27–34. A. M. BRITT, ed., *The Hymns of the Breviary and Missal* (new ed. New York 1948). F. J. E. RABY, *A History of Christian-Latin Poetry from the Beginnings to the Close of the Middle Ages* (Oxford 1953) 33–41. W. BULST, ed., *Hymni Latini antiquissimi LXXV* (Heidelberg 1956) 39, 162. J. SZÖVÉRFFY, *Die Annalen der latenische Hymnendichtung* (Berlin 1964–65) 1:56–58.

[H. DRESSLER]

AETERNE REX ALTISSIME

Opening words of three hymns written in iambic dimeters. The best known of the three is that which was historically prescribed for the Feast of the Ascension. This hymn celebrates Christ's victory over death, recalls the homage due to Him from those in heaven, on earth, and beneath the earth, and begs Him for forgiveness and the crown of eternal glory when He shall come again as Judge. Two forms of this hymn are extant. There is a shorter eight-strope form that was assigned in the Breviary for Matins in the ferial and Sunday Offices during Ascension time. The text in the 1632 revision of the Roman Breviary was heavily edited; only the third and sixth strophes follow the manuscript reading. The author of this hymn is unknown. F. J. Mone conjectured that originally it consisted of the present first four strophes written by

St. AMBROSE and that an inferior fifth-century poet added four more strophes. The longer text of 14 strophes is the form of the hymn as found in the MOZARABIC RITE.

The second hymn dates from the 13th century and was written for use at Vespers on the feast of Christ's crown of thorns, which was reputedly brought to France by King Louis IX and venerated in the Ste. Chapelle in Paris. The author is unknown. The hymn has five strophes, of which the first four have alternating rhyme. The composition expresses the great joy of Paris at being the repository of Christ's crown, which mystically signifies Christ Himself, the crown of men and women living in chastity and the reward of those living in the married state.

The third hymn also honors the crown of thorns. Similar in structure and content to the previous composition, it incorporates two complete strophes from yet another hymn in honor of the crown of thorns, *Corona Christi capitis*.

Bibliography: F. J. MONE, ed., *Lateinische Hymnen des Mittelalters*, 3 v. (Freiburg 1853–55) 1:228–229. *Analecta Hymnica* (Leipzig 1886–1922) 12: 20–21; 27:96–97; 51:94–95; 52:15. G. M. DREVES and C. BLUME, eds., *Ein Jahrtausend lateinischer Hymnendichtung*, 2 v. (Leipzig 1909) 2:136. J. JULIAN, *A Dictionary of Hymnology* (New York 1957) 1:26–27. A. S. WALPOLE, ed., *Early Latin Hymns* (Cambridge, Eng. 1922) 361–364. M. BRITT, ed., *The Hymns of the Breviary and Missal* (new ed. New York 1948). Connelly Hymns 102–103. J. SZÖVÉRFFY, *Die Annalen der lateinische Hymnendichtung* (Berlin 1964–65) 202–203; 254–255; 258; 449.

[H. DRESSLER]

AETERNI PATRIS

The name of two papal documents of Pius IX and Leo XIII. The first is the apostolic letter of June 29, 1868, convoking the Vatican Council I; it indicates the office of the pope as guardian of faith and morals, the role of ecumenical councils, and summarizes the then prevailing dangers to faith and morals. The second document is the encyclical of Leo XIII, dated Aug. 4, 1879, and written to restore scholastic philosophy in general and that of St. Thomas Aquinas in particular. Beginning with a consideration of the Church's concern for teaching true philosophy because of its relation to theology, the pope declares that many modern evils stem from false philosophy. The encyclical mentions the esteem in which St. Thomas has been held and urges the revival of St. Thomas's philosophy and of his spirit of investigation.

Bibliography: PIUS IX, *Acta Pii IX* 4:412–423. R. AUBERT, *Le Pontificat de Pie IX, 1846–1878* (Paris 1952). LEO XIII, *Acta Leonis XIII* 1 (1878–79) 255–285. *Denz* 3135–40. J. COLLINS, "Leo XIII and the Philosophic Approach to Modernity," *Leo XIII and the Modern World*, ed. E. GARGAN (New York 1961) 181–209. C. A.

HART, ''America's Response to the Encyclical *Aeterni Patris*,'' *American Catholic Philosophical Association Bulletin* (1929) 98–117. G. F. RITZEL, ''Some Historical Background of the Encyclical *Aeterni Patris*,'' *Nuntius Aulae* 38 (1956) 135–155. A. ALEXANDER, ''Thomas Aquinas and the Encyclical Letter,'' *Princeton Review* N.S. 5 (Jan. 1880) 245–326. PEDRO RODRIGUEZ, *Fe, razon y teologia en el I Centenario de la Enciclica ''Aeterni Patris''* (Pamplona, Spain 1979); *Atti del'VIII Congresso Tomistico Internaziole: L'Enciclica Aeterni Patris* (Studi Tomistici, 10–12, Vatican City 1981). V.B. BREZIK, CSB (ed.), *One Hundred Years of Thomism: Aeterni Patris and Afterwards, A Symposium* (Houston 1981).

[W. F. HOGAN]

ÆTHELFLÆD, LADY OF THE MERCIANS

Æthelflæd, Lady of the Mercians, was the first-born child of King Alfred the Great (r. 871–99) and his wife Ealswith, a princess of Mercia. Throughout her life, Æthelflæd worked with her father, brother, and husband to reclaim English Mercia from the Danes. Her birth date is unknown, but she married Ethelred, Ealdorman of Mercia, in 886, and had one daughter, Ælfwyn. Both she and Ethelred were fiercely loyal to Alfred, who placed the governance of London in their hands.

Æthelflæd supported her father, and later her brother Edward the Elder (r. 899–925) through a vigorous program of building fortresses and fortifying towns, and by actually leading campaigns against the Danes. A charter (S223) issued by Ethelred at some time during the decade before Alfred's death states that he and his Lady ''ordered the borough at Worcester to be built for the protection of all the people and also to exalt the praise of God therein.'' They also fortified the walls of Chester and refurbished London's defenses. The boroughs were designed to act as points of defense, and also to work in conjunction with Alfred's reformed *fyrd,* or standing army. These boroughs were part of England's national defense, marking an offensive line against the Danes while protecting the English frontier.

Æthelflæd and her husband were supported the Church in many ways. Several of their charters consist of grants to religious communities; one in particular (S223), in response to a request from Wærferth, Bishop of Worcester, states that ''they will grant to God and St. Peter'' and to the Lord of that Church half of their rights within the newly fortified borough of Worcester. Another charter (S221) refers to a grant of a gold chalice in honor of an Abbess Mildburg. Æthelflæd also used relics to provide spiritual blessings and protection. When she encountered various saints' relics during her campaigns against the Danes, she moved them to the West Saxon boroughs.

St. Oswald was translated from Bardney to Gloucester, St. Werburg from Hanbury to Chester, and St. Ealhmund from Derby to Shrewsbury, all from Danish lands into those held by the West Saxons.

A contemporary source, *The Three Fragments,* implies that Ethelred was ill from 902 onwards and incapable of governing Mercia on his own. Æthelflæd, being half Mercian by birth, was accepted by the people of Mercia and began to act in Ethelred's stead. In 907 she granted land to Ingemund, a leader of the Norse-Irish, in Wirral and rebuilt Chester to ensure their loyalty. The *Mercian Register* records that in 910 the English successfully fought the Danes, and Æthelflæd built a fortress at Bremesburh. Ethelred died in 911, and Æthelflæd was immediately acclaimed *Myrcna Hlæfdige,* Lady of the Mercians, which was the exact feminine equivalent of Ethelred's title.

Æthelflæd continued her building program, working closely with her brother Edward to destroy the independent Danish armies in England. Between 912 and 915 she built fortresses at Scergate, Bridgnorth, Tamworth, Stafford, Chirbury, Weardburh, and Runcorn, and refortified existing strongholds at Eddisbury and Warwick.

Toward the end of her life, Æthelflæd began to take an active part in battle. On June 16, 916, an English abbot, Ecgberht, was murdered along with his companions on a trip to Wales. Three days later, Æthelflæd sent an army into Wales to punish the king of Brycheiniog, who was responsible, and took the king's wife and 33 other people hostage. In July 917, when the main army was away fighting Edward, Æthelflæd captured the Danish military center at Derby. In the early part of 918, Æthelflæd peacefully took possession of the borough of Leicester, and accepted the submission of many of the Danish forces that were stationed there. The people of York had also promised to accept her rule, but she died before receiving their submission.

Æthelflæd died on June 12, 918, and was buried in the east chapel of the monastery of St. Peter at Gloucester, which she and Ethelred had built.

Bibliography: R. ABELS, *Lordship and Military Obligation in Anglo-Saxon England* (Los Angeles 1988). P. BLAIR, *An Introduction to Anglo-Saxon England* (2d ed. Cambridge 1977). C. BROOKE, *From Alfred to Henry III 871–1272* (London 1969). G. GARMONSWAY, ed. *The Anglo-Saxon Chronicle* (London 1992). D. ROLLASON ''Relic Cults as an Instrument of Royal Policy, *c.* 900–*c.*1050'' *Anglo-Saxon England* 15 (1986). F. STENTON, *Anglo-Saxon England* (Oxford 1971). R. THOMSON and M. WINTERBOTTOM, eds., *William of Malmesbury: Gesta Regum Anglorum* (Oxford 1999). F. WAINWRIGHT, *Scandinavian England. Collected Papers* (Chichester 1975).

[L. A. LEHTOLA]

AETHELRED II, KING OF ENGLAND

Reigned from March 978 to December 1013 and March/April 1014 to April 23, 1016. Born to Edgar the Peaceable and to Edgar's second wife, Aelfthryth, in or near 968, Aethelred became the center of factional strife along with his older half brother, Edward, when their father died in 975. Edward and his supporters were successful in securing the crown, but his reign was brief, less than three years. At Corfe Passage in March of 1078, Edward was murdered. *The Anglo-Saxon Chronicles* do not identify his murderers, but instead state that Aethelred came to the throne very soon thereafter and was consecrated king. Although the chroniclers condemned the murder of Edward and reported disapprovingly that it was not avenged, they attached no blame to the young Aethelred.

The monastic reform, begun in earnest under his father, Edgar, continued under Aethelred. The idea that the disputed succession between Edward and Aethelred grew out of a party that opposed reform seems unlikely since the movement went forward under both men with the exception of some disputed lands that specific magnates attempted to recover during the confusion following Edward's murder. Aelfthryth had supported the reform under Edgar, and she founded two nunneries, Amesbury in Wilshire and Wherwell in Hampshire, during Aethelred's reign. Aelfhere, a magnate often suspected of complicity in the murder, was a notable benefactor of Glastonbury. There was a brief period that Aethelred was visibly at odds with particular members of the clergy, demonstrated particularly in his abuse of the diocese of Rochester in 986, which was ostensibly caused by a dispute with the bishop. However, he attempted to correct any indiscretions or illegal appropriations of church lands as he reached maturity and recognized that some of the lay leaders at court had misled him. By 995 Aethelred was supporting the replacement of all secular clergy with regular clergy. The church leaders, though critical of Aethelred's ineptness at prosecuting the war against the Danes, supported him tirelessly as their true Christian king, since his defeat spelled an unknown but dreaded fate at the hands of a heathen Viking king.

Had the pacific times of his father, Edgar, continued, Aethelred may have had a very unremarkable career. However, the opportunistic Vikings, recognizing the potential for weakness in a young king, returned to England within two years of Aethelred's coronation after a hiatus of nearly 50 years. The renewed attacks, which developed into a serious design to conquer the whole island under the leadership of the Danish king, Swegn Forkbeard, eventually brought an element of treachery to Athelred's court that went beyond the normal intriguing for power and place. Many at court died of natural causes throughout the long and conflicted reign, but others fell violently if not in the many battles that decimated the nobles regularly, then in political murders that were often sanctioned by the king. These murders occurred within the context of relationships between the south of England and the House of Wessex, out of which Aethelred came, and the north of England, which was still a very recent and vulnerable part of the realm. Not only was Aethelred's father the first to establish a peaceful hegemony over the north, the north had a very large population of Norwegian and Danish descent. He and Aethelred both promoted accord among the disparate parts of the realm by integrating northern leadership into the king's court.

The harmony between north and south was often accomplished through marriage, a practice Aethelred was following when he married Aelfgifu, traditionally identified as the daughter of Thored, earl of Northumbria, whom Aethelred then made an important member of the court. The date of this marriage is not recorded, but it occurred early in the reign since Aethelred had sons and daughters approaching marriageable ages by the time he made a second political marriage in 1002 to Emma, sister of the Duke of Normandy. Three of the daughters married earls appointed to northern areas, and a fourth married a nobleman presumably of the north, since he died at the Battle of Ringmere in 1010. Such marriages were intended to signal a sharing of power between the king from the south and his northern magnates. However, the Vikings easily exploited any weaknesses that appeared between the king and local leaders; local leaders, on the other hand, had difficulty putting their resources together in the interests of a realm that still consisted of diverse and differing parts.

Aethelred departed England after Christmas in 1013, following his wife, Emma, and their two sons into exile at the Norman court of her brother. Defections to Swegn had begun in the north in 1012 and by December 1013, even Wessex and finally London had submitted to him. Aethelred returned to England after Swegn died in February 1014, at the behest of the English magnates. The struggle for the crown continued when Swegn's son, Cnut, chose to press his own claim as Swegn's heir. The realm suffered as previously from the same lack of cohesive determination to fight the Danes and ineffective leadership from the king. Aethelred died at Cosham April 23, 1016, leaving an unresolved conflict and a kingdom divided in its loyalty between his son by Aelfgifu, Edmund Ironside, and Swegn's son, Cnut.

Bibliography: G. N. GARMONSWAY, *The Anglo-Saxon Chronicle* (Rutland, Vermont 1992) 118–149. E. JOHN, *Reassessing Anglo-Saxon England* (Manchester 1996) 139–150. S. KEYNES, *The Diplomas of King Aethelred 'the Unready' 978–1016* (Cambridge

1980) 176–186. P. STAFFORD, *Unification and Conquest: A Political and Social History of England in the Tenth and Eleventh centuries* (London 1989) 45–68.

[P. TORPIS]

AFFINITY

Affinity is a relationship of persons deriving from marriage. It arises from a valid marriage, whether consummated or not, and constitutes an impediment to subsequent marriages between a man and blood relations of his wife, and vice versa (Codex Iuris Canonicis cc. 109, 1092; Codex Canonum Ecclesiarium Orientalium cc. 919, 809). Affinity does not beget affinity; therefore, the blood relations of a man are not impeded by affinity from contracting marriage with the blood relations of his wife, nor are those of the woman with the blood relations of her husband.

In the direct line, the impediment of affinity extends indefinitely either ascending or descending. The impediment of affinity in the collateral line was abrogated in the Latin Church by the 1983 *Code of Canon Law*, but this impediment is retained in *The Code of Canons of the Eastern Churches*. Affinity in the second degree of the collateral line invalidates marriage in the Eastern Catholic churches (Codex Canonum Ecclesiarium Orientalium c. 809 §1).

History. Affinity was an impediment to marriage already in the Mosaic Law. A man was prohibited in the direct line from marrying his stepmother (Lv 18.8, 20.11; Dt 22.30, 27.20); his daughter-in-law (Lv 18.15, 20.12), his stepdaughter, stepson's daughter and stepdaughter's daughter (Lv 18.17), his mother-in-law (Lv 18.17, 20.14, Dt 27.23), and his stepsister (Lv 18.11); in the collateral line, his paternal uncle's wife (Lv 18.14, 20.20), his brother's wife (Lv 18.16, 20.21) except where the levirate law would apply, and the sister of his wife, the latter still living (Lv 18.18). Contrary to the last example, a man could marry two sisters simultaneously before the time of Moses; e.g., Jacob married Leah and Rachel simultaneously (Gn 29).

Although the above texts are addressed to the male, they are applicable reciprocally to the female also. Affinity in each case did not cease through death or divorce of the spouses who created it. The penalty for disregarding the impediment in the direct line was most frequently death (Lv 20.11, 12, 14). In the collateral line the penalty probably did not exceed the legal illegitimizing of offspring.

Carnal relations, licit or illicit, did not produce affinity. Nor was it marriage alone that created affinity but rather the contract of solemn engagement or sponsalia, which would be the equivalent of a ratified marriage. Reasons for declaring affinity an impediment might be cited as: (1) the respect and reserve that a person should naturally possess toward near relatives through blood or marriage, for marriage identified husband and wife in their unity of flesh (Gn 2.24); (2) the scandals that could arise from marriages between persons of close familial ties, in view of Oriental residence customs.

In the New Testament two instances reflect the application of affinity to marriage. The first was Herod Antipas's marriage with his brother's wife, Herodias (Mt 14.3, 4). The union was both adulterous, since Herod's brother was probably still living, and incestuous, as violating the Mosaic Law of affinity, which also obligated strangers living among the Jews (Lv 18.26). The second was the case of incest at Corinth mentioned in 1 Corinthians 5.1, in which a man was rebuked for marrying his stepmother, a crime punished by excommunication. Outside of these two cases, nothing more about affinity appears in the New Testament.

Roman Law. The Roman law concerning affinity (*adfinitas*) was founded upon valid marriage (*justae nuptiae*) and related one consort to the kin of the other (*Corpus iuris civilis, Digesta,* ed. T. Mommsen and P. Krueger, 38.10.4.3, 8; Inst 1.10.6–10). Apparently affinity was considered an impediment only in the direct line reaching to infinity, but not in the collateral line (Dig 23.2.14.4). Prohibition of marriage was limited to affinity involving one's stepfather or stepmother and stepdaughter or stepson; and between father-in-law or mother-in-law and daughter-in-law or son-in-law (Dig 38.10.4.3–5), not descending one from another or from a common stock.

Conciliar Decrees. The Mosaic Law and Roman law were the sources used by the Church to formulate its own rules of affinity. For the first three centuries, the Mosaic Law was probably the only source. With decrees of Church councils such as those of Elvira (300–06) and Neo-Caesarea (314–25), and the Council of Rome (402), there were departures made from the Mosaic law, extending the impediment beyond the limits set by the Old Testament. Elvira forbade marriage with a stepdaughter and stepsister (c. 61, 66; J. D. Mansi, *Sacorum Conciliorum nova et amplissima collectio* 2.15, 16; C. J. von Hefele, *Histoire des conciles d'après les documents originaux* 1.256–57); Neo-Caesarea forbade marriage of a woman with her brother-in-law (c. 2; *Sacorum Conciliorum nova et amplissima collectio* 2.540; *Histoire des conciles d'après les documents originaux* 1.328). The Council of Rome forbade marriage with the deceased wife's sister and a deceased uncle's wife (c. 9, 11; *Sacorum Concili-*

orum nova et amplissima collectio 3.1137; *Histoire des conciles d'après les documents originaux* 2.136–37). These decrees easily passed into the civil codes in the middle of the 4th century (*Corpus iuris civilis, Codex Iustinianus,* ed. P. Krueger, 1.5.5.9). Later councils extended the impediment still further to the widow of the paternal or maternal uncle, reaching as far as the seventh degree, and civil codes followed suit (e.g., Law of Visigoths 1.3.5.1 in *Monumenta Germaniae Historica: Leges* 1).

The ambit of affinity gradually evolved, particularly in the collateral line. From the 8th century the basis of affinity was changed from the marital contract (*justae nuptiae*) to carnal intercourse (*unitas carnis*). With corroboration from Scripture (Gn 2.24; 1 Cor 6.16), Saint Basil (379) had condemned marriage between a brother-in-law and sister-in-law (Letter 160, *Patrologia Graeca,* ed. J. P. Migne, 32:623). Saint Augustine mentioned the case later (*Contra Faustum* 1.22.61; *Patrologia Latina,* ed. J. P. Migne, 42:438; *Corpus scriptorum ecclesiasticorum latinorum* 25.1.656–57; *Civ Corpus scriptorum ecclesiasticorum latinorum* 40.2), and so did the author of a letter attributed by Saint Bede to Saint Gregory (*Sacorum Conciliorum nova et amplissima collectio* 10.407; Bede, *Ecclesiastical History* 1.27 in *Patrologia Latina* 95.60). The practical rule that resulted from this was that *unitas carnis*—carnal intercourse—made two persons one and established identity of relationship between oneself and relatives of a spouse, hence putting affinity on a plane with consanguinity. The Synod of Rome (721) then made this a juridic rule (*Sacorum Conciliorum nova et amplissima collectio* 12.263), and Gratian made it an adage of law (*Corpus iuris canonici,* ed. E. Friedberg, C.35 q.2, 3 c.15; C.35 q.5 c.3). The classical definition of affinity through Gratian became relationship of persons emanating from carnal intercourse.

By the 10th century the similarity between the impediments of affinity and those of consanguinity became complete. Roland Bandinellus (Pope Alexander III, 1159–81), a disciple of Gratian, concerning their mutual computation of degree stated: "The first type of affinity walks abreast [*aequis passibus ambulat*] with consanguinity" (*Corpus iuris canonici* C.35 q.1). In the many vicissitudes during this period the two impediments reached as far as the seventh degree, although the actual force of the last two degrees fluctuated from one area to the next between diriment and impedient.

Since carnal relations (*unitas carnis*) alone formed the basis of affinity, it was calculated identically with consanguinity. Most commentators became adherents of this principle with, however, some notable exceptions such as Saint Thomas, who maintained against the majority that it was marriage and not copula that formed the

true basis of affinity (*Summa theologiae* Supplement 55.4.2). From the basis of *unitas carnis,* logic pushed the experts to develop their speculations about affinity unhindered. They distinguished four kinds of affinity. The first was that arising from marital (licit) or extramarital (illicit) sexual relations. Just when or where the concept of illicit affinity arose is unknown; however, some authors find the first trace in the Pseudo-Isidorian decretals of the 9th century. Once affinity was based upon sexual intercourse, the lack of ecclesiastical precepts respecting a public form of marriage created the difficulty of distinguishing between licit and illicit affinity.

The second kind of affinity arose between the man and the affines of the woman by the first type of affinity and vice versa. In this type a man could become related to the affines of a widow whom he married, and viceversa. Extending this still further, the third kind of affinity would appear in a marriage between a man and the affines related to the woman by the second kind of affinity. These three main classes of affinity are illustrated by this example: Roger and Sylvia are married. The latter's first cousin, Catherine, is married to Julius. Catherine is associated with Roger by the first kind of affinity, Julius with Roger by the second kind of affinity, and following the death of Julius's wife and his remarriage, his new wife will be associated to Roger by the third type of affinity. The fourth type arose not from the sexual act but from generation and touched the offspring born of a second marriage, making them affines to the relatives of the first parent within the fourth degree (*soboles ex secundis nuptiis*).

The principle of exogamy was not without benefit in the fusing of diverse peoples, but it caused inconveniences also in its subtle and complicated computations. The fourth Council of the Lateran (*Sacorum Conciliorum nova et amplissima collectio* 22.1028) in its 50th canon abolished all but the first kind of affinity and restricted its prohibitive power to the fourth degree in the collateral line arising from conjugal or extramarital carnal intercourse. The ancient rule had stated: affinity begets affinity. The new position stated the contrary: affinity does not beget affinity. The simple ancient definition of affinity, "relationship of persons proceeding from sexual intercourse" had to be augmented to read, "between a man and the blood relations of the woman, and vice versa." However valuable were these changes, illicit affinity remained to vex legalists. Also, legitimate affinity upheld to the fourth degree in the collateral line and to infinity in the direct line was still somewhat awkward to deal with.

The Council of Trent (1563) was unsatisfied with the work of the Lateran Council. In the collateral line it limited illicit affinity to the second degree. It upheld licit affinity to the fourth degree, as had the Lateran Council. It did not completely solve the difficulties of which it so vehemently complained in reforming the former law, and subsequent appeals from many bishops appeared in the Curia for relaxation of the impediment. Vatican Council I (1869–70) made no further changes.

It was left to the 1917 *Code of Canon Law* to make radical and far-reaching changes. Its most extreme modification was the change of the very basis of affinity from sexual intercourse to valid marriage entered into according to proper form. This represented a regression to the Roman civil law. As an impediment, it bound each spouse to the blood relations of the other. In the direct line the impediment extended to infinity but was limited in the collateral line to the second degree of affinity (1917 Codex Iuris Canonicis c.1077). The 1983 *Code of Canon Law* further refined church discipline regarding affinity.

Extent of Impediment. Because the marital impediment of affinity is a merely ecclesiastical law, it applies only to Catholics. Non-Catholic Christians and non-Christians are not considered bound by this impediment. However, the impediment would invalidate the marriage of a Catholic who has left the Church by a formal act.

Dispensation. Affinity is perpetual as an impediment and is not extinguished by passage of time or death of one of the parties. It is certain that it is an impediment of merely ecclesiastical law, therefore, the Church can and has dispensed from it. Dispensation from the impediment may be granted by a local ordinary or according to other provisions in Codex Iuris Canonicis cc. 1079–80 or Codex Coannonm Ecclesiarium Orientalium cc. 796–97.

Bibliography: P. DIB, *Dictionnaire de droit canonique,* ed. R. NAZ, 7 v. (Paris 1935–65) 1:264–85.

[C. HENRY]

AFFLIGEM, ABBEY OF

Benedictine abbey in Hekelgem, Brabant, Archdiocese of Mechelen-Brussels, Belgium; dedicated to SS. Peter and Paul. It owes its origin to the conversion (*c.* 1083) of six thieving knights who were moved by the preaching of Wéry, a monk of Saint-Pierre (Ghent). They were soon joined by two monks from Saint-Airly (Verdun), one of whom, Fulgentius, became the first abbot (1088). In 1519 monks from EGMOND introduced at Affligem the reform of BURSFELD. Affligem was incorporated into the episcopal *mensa* (mensal income) of Mechelen (1560) and governed thereafter by provosts, among whom was Benedict of Haeften. In 1628 Affligem adopted the reform of Lorraine and affiliated with the Congregation of the Presentation of Notre Dame, which was dissolved in 1654. The abbey was suppressed by French revolutionaries (1796), but the community regrouped at Termonde (1838) and affiliated with the Congregation of Subiaco (1857). A colony from Termonde regained possession of the ruins of Affligem (1870). Many priories depended on this abbey; three of them became abbeys—Vlierbeek (near Louvain), MARIA LAACH, and SAINT-ANDRÉ-LEZ-BRUGES. Currently the monks of Affligem participate actively in the LITURGICAL MOVEMENT in the Dutch-speaking provinces of Belgium. Affligem missionaries have gone to South Africa.

Bibliography: U. BERLIÈRE, *Dictionnaire d'histoire et de géographie ecclésiastiques,* ed. A. BAUDRILLART et al. (Paris 1912–) 1:672–674. A. M. ZIMMERMANN, *Lexikon für Theologie und Kirche,* ed. J. HOFER and K. RAHNER, 10 v. (2d, new ed. Freiburg 1957–65) 1:168–169. L. H. COTTINEAU, *Répertoire topobibliographique des abbayes et prieurés,* 2 v. (Mâcon 1935–39) 1:23–24.

[N. N. HUYGHEBAERT]

AFGHANISTAN, THE CATHOLIC CHURCH IN

A landlocked, mountainous country in south-central Asia, the Islamic State of Afghanistan is bounded on the north by Turkmenistan, Uzbekistan and Tajikistan, on the northeast by China, on the east and south by Pakistan, and on the west by Iran. Although the region is crossed by several fertile river valleys, rugged terrain to the north, frequent earthquakes, expanding desert areas to the south, and an arid climate punctuated with violent rains have done little to aid Afghan natives in advancing beyond subsistence farming or the raising of sheep and goats. Crops include wheat, barley, and fruit and nuts; deposits of iron ore, coal, copper, natural gas, and oil provide the region with some natural resources. While the economy was devastated by years of civil war at the end of the 20th century, the production of opium poppies and narcotics trafficking did provide the economy with a stabilizing source of revenue.

The country, known in ancient times as Aryana or Khorasan, was first conquered by Alexander the Great, then formed part of the Kingdom of Bactria *c.* 150 B.C. Persia and India later influenced Afghanistan, which was overrun by ISLAM in the 7th century A.D. Political unity was achieved in 1747 under the Arab leader Ahmad Shah. Great Britain gained control over Afghan foreign affairs in 1879 as a way of controlling the Khyber Pass, a strategic trade route between India and Asia. At the end of World War I, on Aug. 19, 1919, the country achieved complete independence from Britain, and was governed by a constitutional monarchy until 1973. After 1973 a series of military governments formed a dependency on Soviet military assistance which culminated in the December 1979 invasion of Afghanistan by the USSR. However, Soviet forces were forced to withdraw on Feb. 15, 1989, a result of U.S. and Arab backing of the armed resistance of Islamic Mujahidin rebels. The fragmented region gradually fell under the control of various political factions, the most powerful of which were the Islamic Taliban fundamentalists, who declared victory over both the communists and the Mujahidin in 1996. In 1999 the Taliban drafted a new constitution based on Islamic law.

The Christian Church in Afghanistan. There is a tradition that the Apostles Thomas and Bartholomew first brought Christianity to this region. Mention is made of the Diocese of Herat, which existed in the 5th century and which was a metropolitan see in the 6th, 10th, and 11th centuries. Christian communities, largely Nestorian, flourished in Afghan cities located along caravan routes, but they eventually disappeared. Balkh, in the northern section, served as an important mission center from whence Christians of the Syrian rite spread the faith to China. Jesuit missionaries came to Kabul in the 17th century, but the number of conversions within this predominately Muslim country was small.

After 1932 a Barnabite priest was attached to the Italian embassy and resident in Kabul, the capital. After the government fell into the hands of Islamic fundamentalists in the late 20th century, Christian missionaries were forbidden to proselytize, their presence in Afghanistan only tolerated because of their willingness to provide humanitarian aid. While Catholic chaplains from Pakistan regularly visited Afghanistan, their purpose was only to minister to the few Catholic non-residents living in the country while engaged in technical work. In 1999 non-Muslims were ordered to mark their homes with a yellow cloth placed on the rooftop, and to identify themselves with yellow clothing so that they might be avoided by Muslims. In January 2001 Taliban government leader Mullah Mohammad Omar announced that conversion to Christianity was punishable by death, the government's reaction to reports that aid workers had engaged in missionary activity proscribed by Afghan law. Church officials around the world were alarmed not only by the lack of religious freedom in Afghanistan, but also by the increasing repression of all Afghan citizens, and in particular women, who were being gradually excluded from public life. In response, in February of 2001, Pope John Paul II cited the ''grave humanitarian crisis'' taking place in Afghanistan, and encouraged human rights organizations to continue their attempts to aid the Afghan people. But in August 2001, eight Christian aid workers were charged by the Taliban with spreading Christianity in the fundamentalist Muslim country and imprisoned.

Capital: Kabul.
Size: 251,825 sq. miles.
Population: 25,838,797 in 2000.
Languages: Afghan Persian (Dari) and Pashtun; Turkic and other languages are spoken in various regions.
Religions: 21,904,589 Sunni Muslims (84%), 3,875,820 Shi'a Muslims (15%), 58,388 other (1%)

Following the September 11, 2001, terrorist attacks on New York City and the Pentagon in Washington, DC, the international community gave the United States government its full backing to pursue military action against the Taliban government and the Al Qaeda terrorist network that operated out of Afghanistan, Al Qaeda being held responsible for the September 11 attacks.

On November 14, 2001, as coalition and anti-Taliban forces swept across the country, US forces freed the eight Christian aid workers from a location outside Kabul and moved them to safety into Pakistan, and then on to their individual countries.

With the collapse of the Taliban and the installation of Hamid Karzai as the interim leader of a new Afghan coalition government in 2002, it was hoped that Afghan people might return to a life of greater intellectual freedom, religious freedom and tolerance as they moved forward in the 21st century.

Bibliography: K. S. LATOURETTE, *A History of the Expansion of Christianity* (New York 1937–45). *Bilan du monde* 2:23–24.

[L. MASCARENHAS]

AFRA, ST.

Martyr at Augsburg during the persecution of DIOCLETIAN, patron of the Diocese of Augsburg. The *Martyrology of St. Jerome* witnesses to her life and martyrdom, and this information is confirmed by Venantius Fortunatus, who visited her grave in 565. A *passio* represented by a long and short recension and a *conversio* depict her as a repentant prostitute. This legend began apparently in the eighth century and spread rapidly (there is even an Armenian version) but has no historical foundation. It arose through confusion with the martyr of Antioch, Venerea, whose name was interpreted in relation to Venus, and was inscribed in the Martyrology of St. Jerome on the same day as Afra's. Several ancient calendars of Augsburg assert that Afra was a virgin. The body of a woman discovered in a sarcophagus in the Roman Church of St. Afra in the eleventh century is honored today under the altar dedicated to the saint. In a later *pas-*

AFGHANISTAN

0   50   100   150 Miles

0   50   100   150 Kilometers

KYRGYZSTAN

CHINA

UZBEKISTAN

TAJIKISTAN

Dushanbe

TURKMENISTAN

PAMIRS

Khorugh

Amu Dar'ya

Termez

Panj

Kcwkcheh

Feyzābād

Qal'eh-ye Panjeh

Vākhān

Balkh

Kondūz

Sheberghān

Mazār-e Sharif

Tāloqān

HINDU KUSH

Sar-e
Pol

Dowlatābād

Baghlān

*Nowshāk
24,557 ft.
7485 m.*

Meymaneh

Qonduz

Morghāb

Chārıkar

Asmār

N

IRAN

PAROPAMISUS MTS.

*Kūh-e Fūlādī
16,847 ft.
5135 m.*

Kabul

Kabul

W   E

Towraghondi

Kabul

S

Tayyebāt

Harīrūd

Chaghcharān

Kowt-e
'Ashrow

Jalālābād

Konar

Peshawar

Herāt

Baraki

*Khyber
Pass*

Islāmābād

Shindand

Farāh

Gardēyz

Ghaznī

Khowst

Zareh
Sharan

Farāh

Helmand

Arghandāb

Qalāt

*Hāmūn-e
Şabērī*

Zaranj

Lashkar
Gāh

Qandahār

PAKISTAN

Afghanistan

Zābol

*Rīgestān
Desert*

*Khojak
Pass*

Helmand

Quetta

Gowd-e Zereh

Chagai   Hills

sio the martyrdom of an Afra at Brescia is fused with that of SS. Faustinus and Jovita. It is obviously a version developed from the original legend of the eighth century.

Feast: Aug. 5.

Bibliography: A. BIGELMAIR and A. P. FRUTAZ, *Lexicon für Theologie und Kirche,* ed. J. HOFER and K. RAHNER (Freiburg 1957–65) 1:169–170. A. BIGELMAIR, "Die heilige Afra," *Lebensbilder aus dem bayerischen Schwaben,* ed. G. VON PÖLNITZ, 4 v. (Munich 1952–55) 1:1–29. W. BRAMBACH, *Die verloren geglaubte Historia de Sancta Afra martyre und das Salve regina des Hermannus Contractus* (Karlsruhe 1892). H. GOUSSEN, *Theologie und Glaube* 1 (1909) 791–794. H. ROSENFELD, Archiv für Kulturgeschichte 37 (1955) 306–335. F. SAVIO, *Analecta Bollandiana* 15 (1896) 5–72, 113–159, Afra of Brescia.

[P. ROCHE]

AFRICAN AMERICAN CATHOLICS IN THE UNITED STATES (HISTORY OF)

Catholics first arrived in what is now the United States in the middle of the sixteenth century. The settlement, named in honor of St. Augustine, was made in what is now the northern part of Florida by Pedro Menéndez de Avilés in 1565. These first settlers were Spanish speaking, all were Catholics, and some were white and others black. In fact, on the first page of the baptismal register appear the names of infants who are described as black or mulattoes. The history of African American Catholics has its beginning with the history of the Catholic Church in America.

Colonial period in Florida. The Spanish government considered the Florida settlement as an outpost against attacks by the British and the French to guard its Caribbean possessions in Cuba and the Gulf of Mexico. The black settlers who settled in Florida in the second half of the sixteenth century were mainly from Spain. Many were free; others were slaves. From the beginning the slaves in the Florida territory enjoyed certain rights and privileges coming from the slave codes based on Roman Law drawn up by Alfonso the Wise (1221–1284) known as the *Siete Partidas*. By 1683 free blacks had formed a militia in St. Augustine. A decade later, the crown promised freedom to runaway slaves from the English colonies who reached the Spanish settlement and converted to the Catholic faith. In 1738 the Spanish governor built the first all-black town in the future United States. Known as the *Gracia Real de Santa Teresa de Mose*, this *palenque*, that is a settlement of freed persons, had Francisco Menéndez as its designated black leader. A courageous soldier and a daring leader, he led both blacks and the Yamassee Indians against the English settlements in Georgia. In 1763 the Spanish in Florida, both whites and blacks, free and slave, were forced to withdraw to Cuba, leaving Florida to the British. This was the result of the Spanish defeat in the Seven Years War. In 1784 the Spanish returned, but the town of Fort Mose was not restored. The baptismal, marriage, and death registers of blacks reveal a society that was bi-racial, Catholic, and Latin. The registers reveal that the soldiers garrisoned in St. Augustine were blacks and mulattoes from Cuba with one or the other coming from West Africa. The Spanish laws governing slavery were more tolerant and emancipation much easier to win than in the British and American societies. In 1793 there were 2,000 whites and 1,600 blacks of whom 1,500 were slaves. In 1814 there were 1,300 whites and 1,770 blacks of whom 1,600 were slaves. Over half of the population was black.

Colonial period in the Southwest and the Louisiana Territory. In 1781 the city of Los Angeles was settled with families from two villages in northern Mexico. Of the eleven families that settled in Los Angeles, only two persons were white and two were blacks, seven were Native Americans, four were *mestizos*, and seven were mulattoes. Not only in Los Angeles but in much of the Southwest a large proportion, especially soldiers, were of mixed race.

The French began the settlement of the Gulf Coast at the end of the seventeenth century. African slaves were introduced into the colony in the first quarter of the eighteenth century. On the eve of the Civil War there were 330,000 slaves; 18,000 free blacks, and 360,000 whites. The *Code Noir* was the slave code drawn up by the authority of Colbert in the France of Louis XIV to control the slave population in the French colonies. The code made slaveholders responsible for the baptism and the religious instruction of their slaves, slaves were to have opportunity to attend church and were to be free from labor on Sundays and feasts, neither marriage nor concubinage was permitted between whites and blacks, and children under fourteen could not be sold away from their parents. Other provisions in the code were extremely harsh and even inhuman. Despite the *Code Noir*, concubinage between white men and black women was a salient feature of Louisiana society. French slaveholders very often freed their slave children, thereby creating a distinct social class known as the "free people of color."

The free people of color or Afro-Creoles were to be found in the cities of the Gulf Coast and in Florida. This social and ethnic class created a distinct Afro-French culture that was Catholic, African, and Latin in religion, language, and art. From this social class came entrepreneurs, skilled craftsmen, business women and men, landowners, and philanthropists. Specific Afro-Creole settlements like Mon Luis Island south of Mobile, Chastang in southern Alabama, and Isle Brevelle outside of Natchitoches in northern Louisiana presented a distinctive Afro-Creole Catholic folk culture.

Many free people of color, like many blacks in other parts of the country, owned slaves. This would include people who were themselves former slaves. The reasons were not always simple. Many free blacks had funds sufficient to purchase a slave, often one's own children, or relatives, or one's spouse. Having funds to purchase a slave did not mean having sufficient funds to post a bond often demanded by local governments to insure that the former slave would not become a public charge. In some places, the freed slave was forced to leave the state or risk being enslaved again. In the years leading up to the Civil War, it became increasingly difficult to free a slave. Finally, there were free blacks who bought and sold slaves for the same reasons that many whites owned slaves. They bought and sold slaves for profit and one's own service.

French settlements in the Midwest, like St Louis, Vincennes, Cahokia, Kaskasia, and Ste.-Genevieve, were also settlements of black Catholics, slave and free. One of the best-known black Catholic leaders of the antebellum period was Jean-Baptiste Pointe du Sable. A trapper, a trader, a wealthy merchant, married to a member of the Potawatomi tribe, he was a French-speaking black man possibly of Haitian origin. Considered to be one of the first settlers of Chicago, he was buried in 1818 in a Catholic cemetery in St. Charles, Missouri.

Slavery and the Catholic Church. Four years before he became the bishop of Baltimore in 1889, John

CARROLL in a letter to the Holy See described the situation of Catholics in the newly established United States. He noted that there were 3,000 African slaves in Maryland in a population of 15,000 Catholics. They were a concern for him. The Jesuits had arrived in Maryland in the seventeenth century. With land grants received from Lord Baltimore, they relied upon slave labor to exploit the land and bring in the income needed for their pastoral work. By the early nineteenth century, the ownership of many slaves who were elderly or children was no longer profitable. In 1837, the Jesuits had sold almost 300 slaves to slave brokers in the South. Assurances were given that families would be kept together and the slaves would be sold to Catholic slaveowners. Nevertheless, some families were divided and more seriously, many were sold to non-Catholics, which meant that they would not be able to practice the Catholic faith. In Maryland, this action scandalized even the slaveholding Catholic laity.

The Catholic Church in the United States was implicated in slavery on many levels. The slaveholding class included members of the clergy and religious orders as well as laypersons. Bishops like John Carroll (1735–1815), Louis William DUBOURG (1766–1833) of Louisiana, Benedict FLAGET (1763–1850) of Louisville, Michael PORTIER (1795–1859) of Mobile owned slaves. The VINCENTIANS in Missouri and the Sulpicians in Maryland and Kentucky were served by slaves in their seminaries. The Carmelite nuns in Maryland; the Ursulines in New Orleans; the Dominican sisters, the Sisters of Charity of Nazareth, and the Sisters of Loretto in Kentucky were all slave owners. Most of the religious communities in the South were slaveowners. It can be said that in the period before the Civil War, the Catholic Church in the South was built and maintained by the labor of black Catholic slaves.

Abolitionism. In the United States, the opposition to slavery and the call for its abolition was the work of Protestant religious leaders, most of whom were Quakers, Presbyterians, and Methodists. Many Protestant churches were split in half over the slavery issue. The opponents to slavery were, for the most part, motivated by deep religious convictions regarding the morality of slavery. These same religious leaders were often harsh critics of the Catholic Church, which they saw as a narrow-minded religious faith, foreign to an American mentality. Catholics in the United States reciprocated with suspicion of the abolitionists, whom they saw as fanatics. Many Catholics, especially members of the hierarchy, considered slavery to be a political issue.

In 1839, Pope Gregory XVI wrote an apostolic letter condemning the slave trade and by implication the institution of slavery itself. John ENGLAND (1786–1842),

bishop of Charleston, wrote a series of letters in his diocesan newspaper (the first of its kind in the United States) in which he sought to prove that the pope was not an abolitionist as some had charged and had no intention of condemning the domestic slavery that existed in the United States. He sought to prove that the Church had never condemned slavery. Finally, acknowledging that he personally did not approve of slavery, he added that he saw no way of bringing it to an end.

On the eve of the Civil War, the first bishop of Natchitoches in Louisiana, Auguste Martin (1803–1875) wrote a pastoral letter in French, defending slavery as a blessing in disguise whereby God in his providence had brought the "children of the race of Canaan" to these shores to receive the blessings of faith and grace. The authorities in Rome were ready to condemn the bishop's theological conclusions when the war ended and the issue was no longer relevant. Only two American bishops publicly called for an end to slavery, John Baptist PURCELL (1800–1883), archbishop of Cincinnati, who called for an end to slavery in 1862, and Josue Moody Young (1808–1866), bishop of Erie. It would take leaders in Europe, like the champion of Irish freedom, Daniel O'Connell (1775–1847), and Félix-Antoine-Philibert DUPANLOUP (1802–1878), bishop of Orléans in France, to speak out against the inhumanity of slavery in the context of Catholic teaching.

Although the 54th Massachusetts Regiment is seen as the first regular all black Union regiment in the Civil War, the first black troops to fight and die in the Civil War were the Louisiana Native Guards. Organized by free men of color as a regiment in the Confederate forces in Louisiana, many of the same Native Guards offered themselves to the Union General Benjamin Butler after New Orleans was captured by the Union Army in April of 1862. They were mustered into the Union Army as the Louisiana Native Guards, forming three regiments. Most of them were French-speaking blacks, and most were Catholics.

The great hero of the African American community in New Orleans was André Cailloux., captain in the First Regiment of the Louisiana Native Guards. A former slave, he was a daring, fearless, natural-born leader, whose finest hour was the moment when he led his men up the bluff at Port Hudson. His regiment was to lead the attack. There André Cailloux was the first of the black soldiers to die on May 27, 1863. The bodies of the black soldiers were left unburied on the battle ground for almost a month. The black soldiers were scorned and they and their families were openly insulted by the general New Orleans populace. The white clergy of New Orleans, like the white population, were in opposition to the

Union forces occupying the city. Consequently, the only priest who would minister to the black soldiers and their families was Claude Pascal Maistre (1820–1875). Maistre, who had been born in the *département* of Aube in the northwest of France, regularly condemned slavery in his sermons, despite the summons of his archbishop to desist. He gave aid and comfort to the black soldiers and full support to the black community as the free people of color rallied to the Union cause. Despite his suspension by the archbishop of New Orleans, Jean-Marie Odin (1800–1870), Maistre continued his ministry to the black community and in that capacity he preached at the public military funeral of André Cailloux.

Second Plenary Council of Baltimore. The American bishops came together for the second Plenary Council in Baltimore in October of 1866. Martin J. Spalding (1810–1872), archbishop of Baltimore, had expressed his concern for ministry to the freed slaves. He spoke of the "golden opportunity for a harvest of souls." In planning for this council with the approval of Rome, he suggested to the members of the Curia that there should be a discussion on the possibility of a prefect apostolic or some other ecclesiastical official, preferably with the status of a bishop, who might coordinate on a national basis the pastoral work for African Americans. The Curia considered this a capital idea. It was included in the agenda. The bishops did not take up the subject until the very end of the allotted time for discussion. In fact, the meeting was held in an extraordinary session on October 22. The minutes of the extraordinary session were never translated into English or published in Latin. The bishops were most unhappy with such a proposal because they felt that it would diminish their authority. The proposal was met with sarcasm, anger, ridicule, and also some bitterness was expressed toward the ex-slaves themselves. The tenor of the discussion was such that Spalding never revealed during the meeting that the idea was originally his own. Ultimately, the assembled bishops made no move to adopt the proposal. It was decided to leave the evangelization of the African American community in the hands of the individual bishops who had African Americans in their respective dioceses. The bishops expressed the hope that missionaries might come from Europe to evangelize the black population.

In 1871, Spalding welcomed the MILL HILL FATHERS, a missionary society from England, into his archdiocese. In 1892, the American branch of Mill Hill separated from the English headquarters and became the Society of St. Joseph of the Sacred Heart. Dedicated exclusively to the apostolate among blacks, they had their headquarters in Baltimore but with parishes and missions throughout the South. Later in 1906 the Society of the Divine Word, a German missionary congregation, came to the United States and also began work in the African American Apostolate. A community of sisters was founded by St. Katherine DREXEL (1858–1955), a Philadelphia-born heiress, who used her immense fortune to establish a religious community known as the Sisters of the Blessed Sacrament in 1891. St. Katherine Drexel opened schools and began missions for both Native Americans and African Americans.

Religious congregations of black women. The African American Catholic community also played an active role in its own evangelization. Two religious orders of women were successfully established in the darkest days of slavery. As early as 1824 a community of black religious women was established in Kentucky. Unfortunately, the effort was unsuccessful.

The second attempt was made possible by the arrival of black refugees from the revolutionary turmoil of Haiti (then referred to as St.-Domingue) into Baltimore. They worshipped together in the lower chapel of St. Mary's Seminary on Paca Street in Baltimore. A Sulpician priest, Jacques Joubert de la Muraille, was assigned to minister among them. After he noted that a group of young black women, three of whom were originally from Haiti, had begun teaching the young children in the community, Joubert inquired about the possibility of their forming a sisterhood and discovered that this was their fondest desire. With Elizabeth Lange (d.1882) as their leader, the women became a religious community in 1829. Two years later in 1831, they received papal approval. Joubert gave them the name of OBLATE SISTERS OF PROVIDENCE. From the beginning, the education of black children was their ministry. At the same time an orphanage was created. The community attracted vocations. Some who were ex-slaves came to the community with their manumission papers in their hands. Nevertheless, the sisters often faced insults and contempt from the wider community. As time went on, the convent played a central role in the religious life of black Catholic community of Baltimore.

One of the original group who founded the Oblates was Therese Duchemin Maxis, who left the Oblates with another sister and went to Monroe, Michigan, where with the assistance of a Belgian Redemptorist priest, she founded the Sisters, Servants of the IMMACULATE HEART OF MARY. Because of a misunderstanding about roles, Therese Maxis was forced to leave the community by the bishop of Detroit, Peter Paul Lefevere (1804–1869); she eventually found refuge with the Grey Nuns in Canada. Toward the end of her life, in 1885, she was allowed to return to a convent of the I.H.M. Sisters in West Chester, Pennsylvania, where she died in 1892.

In New Orleans, a young woman of color, Henriette Delille (1812–1862), a descendant of one of the first settlers in New Orleans and his slave, began to live a life of devotion and service with two other women of color, Juliette Gaudin (1808–1887), originally from Haiti, and Josephine Charles (1812–1885). Under the leadership of Henriette, the three women organized catechism classes for young girls of color and for slaves. Classes were also given to the young girls. The three women acted as sponsors for the baptism of slaves and as witnesses for their marriages. They nursed the sick, especially the poor and the derelict among the abandoned slaves. The community grew and during the 1840s the community evolved from the status of pious women to sisters living a consecrated life. They would become known as the Sisters of the HOLY FAMILY. Racial feelings prevented them from wearing the religious habit on the streets of New Orleans until 1872, ten years after the death of Henriette Delille.

Both the Oblate Sisters of Providence and the Sisters of the Holy Family had to fight for recognition. For many the concept of black nuns was difficult to accept. But their very existence is a testimony to the deep religious faith within the African American community. Today they continue their works of service and education primarily on behalf of the African American community. In 1916 another community of black sisters was founded by Ignatius Lissner, SMA and Mother Theodore Williams (1868–1931) in Savannah, Georgia. Originally founded to teach in the black Catholic schools of the Savannah diocese, the Handmaids of Mary found little opportunity for this task. Mother Theodore Williams relocated the community to New York at the invitation of Cardinal Hayes (1867–1938). There in Harlem, the third religious congregation of black sisters, now known as the Franciscan Handmaids of Mary (see FRANCISCAN SISTERS), continue their work of service to the poor and education for black children in the heart of the city.

African American priests. The first African American priests were three sons of an Irish slaveholder and his female slave. Michael Morris Healy, a former soldier from Ireland who fought with Great Britain during the War of 1812, built for himself a plantation in central Georgia. His slave, Mary Eliza, bore him ten children. Through his friendship with the future bishop of Boston, John Fitzpatrick (1812–1866), he was able to send his children for education in the North. Although his children were legally still slaves, his first four sons were among the first graduates of Holy Cross College in Massachusetts. Three of them studied abroad and became priests. James Augustine Healy (1830–1900) studied for the priesthood in Paris and was ordained in 1854 for the diocese of Boston. He would be named the second bishop of Portland, Maine in 1875 and the first black bishop in the United States. His younger brother, Alexander Sherwood Healy (1836–1874), was also ordained a priest for

the diocese of Boston in Rome in 1858. Sherwood was a brilliant canonist, who was secretary of Bishop John Williams (1822–1907), and who served as his theologian at the First Vatican Council in 1870. He had a brilliant future before him, when he died in 1875. The second oldest brother, Patrick Francis Healy (1834–1910), became a Jesuit and was ordained a priest in Liège in 1864. Patrick Healy became the rector of Georgetown University in Washington, D.C., and was later named its first president. He was responsible for making the university a modern, updated seat of higher learning. Patrick Healy passed for white; Georgetown University would accept no black students until the Civil Rights Movement in the mid-twentieth century. Two of the Healy sisters became nuns in Canada. One of them, Eliza Healy (1846–1919), known as Sister St. Mary Magdalen, became a nun in the Congregation of Notre Dame in Montreal. She served as superior in several of the congregation's foundations. Another sister, Amanda Josephine (1845–1879), became a religious in a nursing community, the Religious Hospitallers at the Hospital of the Hôtel-Dieu in Montreal. Although born in slavery, the Healy children had little contact with the African American population. Although both Bishop Healy and his brother, Alexander Sherwood Healy, were recognized as black, neither the bishop nor any of the other children truly identified with the black Catholic community.

On the other hand, Augustus Tolton (1854–1897), born a slave in Ralls County, Missouri, was clearly recognizable as an African American. Despite many setbacks, Tolton was finally admitted into the Urban College in Rome, where he studied for the priesthood and was ordained in 1886. Stationed first in Quincy, Illinois, he soon moved to Chicago as a result of the hostility of a neighboring priest. In Chicago he organized the parish of St. Monica, the first black parish in the city. Tolton's career was short but impressive. During the eleven years of his priesthood, he became for so many black Catholics a sign of hope and pride. He did not spare himself in responding to the needs of black Catholics both in Chicago and throughout the nation. He died suddenly from heat stroke in July of 1897.

The condition of the first black priests in the United States was an unenviable one. Unlike the tradition of the Church elsewhere, the American Catholic Church would not encourage a native clergy from the African American Catholic community. Between 1891 and 1910 only five black priests were ordained. From 1910 to 1930 only three priests were ordained. Thanks to the insistence of the Holy See, the number of black priests gradually increased. In 1934 four black priests of the Society of the Divine Word were ordained in St. Augustine Seminary in Bay St. Louis, Mississippi. A first all-black seminary had been established by the Divine Word Fathers first in 1920 in Greenwood, Mississippi, and was later moved to Bay St. Louis in 1923. Between the years 1934 and 1944, twenty-three black men were ordained to the priesthood.

Piety of black Catholics. In the Sulpician archives in Baltimore are found two notebook-size documents that reveal the piety of the black Catholic community. At the end of the eighteenth century and in the first part of the following, African American Catholics along with their fellow Catholics joined the different confraternities, the oldest of which was the Confraternity of Our Lady of Mount Carmel, begun by Bishop Carroll in 1796. Fifty-five pages of the notebook list the names of over 1,000 members from 1796 to 1858. Roughly a third of the names were blacks or mulattoes, men and women, slave and free. In two other confraternities, Our Lady of Help and of the Holy Rosary, both of which began in the early nineteenth century, the lists contained a representative number of members, who were designated as black or mulatto. The appearance of these names might serve as a barometer suggesting that the level of piety and devotion was as elevated among black Catholics as it was among whites.

In the same archives is found the *Journal of the Commencement and of the Proceedings of the Society of Coloured people*, a handwritten account of the weekly meetings of some 200 or more black men and women who met from 1843 to 1845 in the basement of Calvert Hall, attached to the Baltimore cathedral. The journal, kept by the white priest who acted as chaplain, gave detailed information regarding the prayers, the hymns, the spiritual conferences, and such practical affairs as the disbursement of funds to those in need and the maintenance of a lending library. The notebook affords one a bird's-eye view of a gathering of very pious black Catholics who were doing more than the minimum in their religious practice.

The Society of the Holy Family was in the form of a mutual benefit society for black Catholics. Prior to the Civil War, there were many such societies among black Catholics. These self-help organizations, although prevalent among African American Protestants, have been little studied among black Catholics. In the *Catholic Directory* for Baltimore at least three other mutual benefit societies were mentioned, one of which was named the Tobias Society. Other examples of black Catholic mutual benefit societies were found in New Orleans.

From the pain and humiliation that was the experience of all American blacks, there emerged individual examples of holiness and piety. The Venerable Pierre TOUSSAINT (*c.* 1756–1853) was born a slave in Haiti. His owner, Jean Bérard, his owner's wife, his sister, and his aunt were brought to New York in 1787. Toussaint, like most urban slaves, learned a trade which would bring remuneration to his owner. He learned the trade of coiffeur or hairdresser, a lucrative trade for those who worked for the distinguished women of New York society. Jean Bérard returned to Haiti to wind up his affairs and unexpectedly died, leaving his wife practically penniless. Madame Bérard, without knowing it, was totally indebted to Toussaint, who supported her by his earnings. Eventually freed in 1807 by Madame Bérard on her deathbed, Toussaint bought the freedom of the woman he married and that of his sister. He was not poor, for he owned his own home and had adequate funds to support his family. He was childless but he reared his niece, who died young. Toussaint exercised a very practical charity. He disbursed funds to those in need, lent money to those who sought help, nursed the sick even in his own home, and offered violin lessons and shelter to young homeless black youths. His charity, his piety and cheerfulness, his deep attachment to his wife, his friendship to many of all stations and background revealed a man who was considered a saint by both blacks and whites, and even by Protestants at the time of his death in 1853. From that time his reputation for sanctity has not not ceased to grow and his cause has been introduced in Rome.

Black Catholic lay leadership. Unlike other ethnic groups within the American Catholic Church in the nineteenth century, black Catholics did not have the clerical leaders as had other ethnic groups in which clerical leaders wielded influence over many aspects of religious and civic life. Black Catholics are almost unique in that from the end of the nineteenth century to the middle of the twentieth century, the leadership role was carried out by lay persons. At the end of the nineteenth century, it was a man named Daniel Rudd, a journalist, a lecturer, a polemicist, and a devout Catholic who spoke out on behalf of the black Catholic community. He was born a slave in 1854 in Bardstown, Kentucky. One of twelve children, he was baptized and reared as a Catholic from infancy. After the Civil War, he joined his brother in Springfield, Ohio and finished there his secondary schooling. He began publishing a black newspaper in Springfield that in 1886 was transformed into *The American Catholic Tribune*, a black Catholic weekly newspaper, the first of its kind. Rudd moved to Cincinnati and then to Detroit, and finally the newspaper ceased publication after 1895. Rudd was convinced that the Catholic Church would become the champion for the rights and the improvement of the black race. He had a vision of a massive conversion of blacks to Catholicism and that this would raise up the entire race just as the Church had done so for other racial groups in the past.

In 1889 there was held in Washington, D.C., the first black Catholic lay congress. There would be four more such congresses, the second one in Cincinnati in 1890, Philadelphia in 1892, Chicago in 1893, and Baltimore in 1894. Inspired by the Catholic lay congresses in Germany and Belgium, the congresses were Rudd's idea. He wished to bring together black Catholic lay leaders from all over the country. Rudd succeeded better than he knew. He was able to imbue the congress members with his own vision of the Catholic Church's role in lifting up the African American race. The Congress members went even further. They began to initiate several actions. They called for better urban living conditions, for education, especially vocational schools that would train black youth to be skilled laborers, and for an end to unions' blocking the entry of blacks to membership. They sent questionnaires to all of the United States bishops, inquiring about the presence of racial discrimination among the institutions of their respective dioceses. More than two-thirds of the bishops responded. It was the intention of the committee of grievances set up by the fourth black lay Catholic congress to report the results to the Holy See.

The present state of research does not allow any clear-cut conclusions as to which communications regarding the status of black Catholics influenced the Roman authorities. Documentation in the apostolic delegation files clearly indicates that the curial officials did know of the complaints regarding the situation of black American Catholics. In 1904, Archbishop Falconio, OFM (1842–1917), apostolic delegate, received a letter from the Prefect of the Congregation of the Propaganda, concerning the "humiliating" way that black Catholics were treated by the clergy and the bishops. The letter went on to say that this treatment was to be "lessened and thus little by little entirely removed." The apostolic delegation files now in the Vatican Archives reveal that between 1912 and 1921, the Roman Curia in its missives to the apostolic delegate were not impressed by the efforts made on behalf of black Catholics by the bishops in the United States. The curial officials could not understand why there were not more black priests and how a pontifical university like the Catholic University of America could refuse to admit black Catholics.

Thomas Wyatt Turner and the Federated Colored Catholics. After 1894, the black Catholic lay congresses ceased to exist and would not be revived until the end of the twentieth century. Daniel Rudd died relatively unknown in the town of his birth in 1933. Many of the congress members, like Fredrick McGhee (1861–1912), of St. Paul, Minnesota, friend of both Booker T. Washington and W. E. B. DuBois, one of the founders of the NAACP Legal Fund and William Henry Smith (1833–1903) of Washington, D.C., assistant librarian of the House of Representatives, highest ranking black in the federal government, were both significant leaders in their respective communities. In their talks and speeches at the congresses and in the mutual addresses to their fellow Catholics delivered at the end of most of the congresses, these leaders expressed a deep sense of loyalty to their Church. They articulated the meaning of this faith to their situation as blacks. In fact, it could be said that a design for black Catholic theology emerged from these congresses at this time.

Thomas Wyatt Turner (1877–1978), college professor, activist, founder of the Federated Colored Catholics in 1924, was a man ahead of his time. Firmly attached to his Catholic faith, he did not hesitate to denounce racism and discrimination within the Catholic Church in the United States. He believed in direct action. He believed that blacks must be in charge of their own battles and that whites should cooperate under black leadership. Turner and his followers had three important goals: making Catholic education available to all black Catholics, opening the Catholic University of America to black students, and opening the seminaries for the education of more black priests. Turner's direct action methods brought him into conflict with two leading Jesuit priests who were also working on behalf of blacks and interracial justice. William Markoe, SJ (1892–1969) of St. Louis, pastor of St. Elizabeth Parish, led the charge against racial discrimination and injustice in St. Louis. In the beginning he sought to collaborate with Turner, but later he denounced Turner's program as establishing a "Jim Crow" organization. He saw "integration" and "interracial" as the watchwords for the movement. John LaFarge, SJ (1880–1963), intellectual leader and spokesman for interracial justice within the Catholic Church, gave support to Markoe's strategy to take over the Federated Colored Catholics. LaFarge saw the importance of providing a space for black Catholics and white Catholics to meet and discuss the issues of justice and Catholic social teaching so that through dialogue racial discrimination and injustice could be eliminated. From this sprang the Catholic Interracial Councils. Unwittingly, the work of the two priests helped destroy the organization built by Turner. Turner realized that in the issue of race relations, black empowerment, black leadership, and black direction would be the only way racist practices would be stopped.

Civil Rights Movement. Turner's methods and goals were taken up again by black Catholic leaders in the post–World War II movement for civil rights. Black Catholics were not on the forefront of the Civil Rights Movement. By and large it was Protestant clergymen who worked with Martin Luther King, Jr. On the local level many Catholics did play an important part, but further research is still necessary to reveal more specific examples. One of the most important civil rights attorneys was Alexander Pierre Tureaud (1899–1972), who successfully fought in the courts to bring about the desegregation of the schools in Louisiana. He was a close collaborator with Thurgood Marshall and his partners.

Following the assassination of Martin Luther King, Jr. in April of 1968, black Catholic priests were called to meet as a caucus to respond to the deteriorating situation where some had called for the shooting of looters. This meant the killing of young people, many of whom would have been minorities. A scheduled meeting of the Catholic Clergy Conference on the Interracial Apostolate, an organization for white and black priests working in black parishes, was to begin its meeting in Detroit on April 16. A message was sent to all of the African American priests to come a day earlier in order to discuss the civil disturbances in the inner cities across the nation. The one day was lengthened to a night and another day. Some 60 or more black priests who had never met with each before began to look at the issues of what it meant to be a black priest in the time of black consciousness. It was a time for many to share their experiences of racial injustice and racial animosity in the seminary, religious congregations, or with their fellow white priests. For many it was a time to reveal hidden wounds and and talk about deeply felt pain. The newly found unity encouraged many of the black clergy to look at plans of action. It was agreed that a letter from the black clergy should be directed to the hierarchy of the Catholic Church in the United States. In it were a series of demands. Many of the demands were the same as blacks across the nation were addressing to white American authority figures. The letter began with the jolting words that the Catholic Church in the United States was a white racist institution.

April of 1968 was a turning point in the history of black Catholics in the United States. For the first time black priests as a body had addressed the issue of race and racism in the Catholic Church. Although agreement was not unanimous, it was clear that the issue of race was a hidden wound in the hearts of nearly all of the black Catholic clergy. It is for this reason that the caucus was transformed into a permanent organization of black priests, now known as the National Black Catholic Clergy Caucus. It continues under this title as a fraternal organization of priests. It seeks to offer support and on-going education to its members. The National Black Clergy Caucus still seeks to be an advocate for issues dealing with race and to serve as a reminder of the Catholic Church's teaching on racial justice and related social issues. The action of the black priests resulted in the formation of the National Black Sisters' Conference later that same year. Later black seminarians organized the National Black Catholic Seminarians' Association. In 1970 the National Office of Black Catholics was established as a coordinating committee for dialogue with the American bishops. In 1988 this task would be taken over by the creation of the Secretariat of African American Catholics for the National Council of Catholic Bishops.

African American Catholics come of age. American Catholics have experienced the same forces of resistance and change that have characterized the modern world. With the creation of more black bishops beginning with the ordination of Harold Perry, SVD, as auxiliary bishop of New Orleans in 1966, the number of bishops has reached the total of thirteen bishops with one retired bishop and three deceased at the beginning of the twenty-first century. The number of African American Catholics is close to 2.5 million. The current influx of Africans into the black community has slowly increased this number. While the number of African American priests has dwindled to fewer than 300, the number of permanent deacons is more than twice that number. The number of African priests working in the African American community, along with an increase in African religious women, has almost doubled the number of black priests and sisters.

The new millenium and the black community. W. E. B. DuBois wrote at the beginning of the twentieth century that the problem of the twentieth century is the problem of the color line. The same problem exists at the beginning of the twenty-first century. The American bishops addressed the issue of racism in a pastoral letter entitled *Brothers and Sisters to Us* in 1979. This letter charged that racism was a sin. The changing face of racism in the United States in the last quarter of the twentieth century has lessened the impact of the document, although the problem has not ended. In 1984 the black bishops issued a pastoral letter *What We Have Seen and Heard*. The bishops spoke of the black Catholic community as having "come of age," and these same black Catholics were now called upon to evangelize themselves, their community, and the Church.

Race was not absent from the schismatic movement when George Stallings, a priest of the archdiocese of Washington, D.C., and Bruce Greening, a Salvatorian, severed ties with the Catholic Church in 1989. Because the cardinal archbishop of Washington would not authorize an independent congregation for the African American Rite, George Stallings broke with the Catholic Church and established the African American Catholic Congregation. Stallings was ordained a bishop by an Old Catholic archbishop.

Bruce Greening, who followed Stallings in his criticism of the Catholic Church, broke ranks with Archbishop Stallings when the initial break with Rome was made. Bruce Greening formed the Independent African American Catholic Rite. His initial desire to remain within the bounds of the Catholic Church had not been possible. Much smaller in number than the Imani Temple of Archbishop Stallings, Greening was ordained a bishop by the patriarch of the African Orthodox Church.

The theological movement begun by black Protestant thinkers (e.g. James Cone) created a like movement among black Catholic theologians who met as a group called the Black Catholic Theological Symposium in 1978. This was the beginning of a permanent summer school institute at Xavier University in New Orleans, the first and only black Catholic university founded by St. Katherine Drexel in 1925. The Institute for Black Catholic Studies began in 1980 with courses in Black Approaches to Theology, Sacraments, and Scripture, Catechetics, History of Black Catholicism, and related subjects. Among the first faculty members was Sister Thea Bowman, FSPA (1937–1990), a gifted teacher and a charismatic speaker who enthralled her listeners.

At the same time, a new organization began to reinstate the meetings of the Black Catholic Congress. The sixth Black Catholic Congress was held in Washington, D.C., in 1987, the seventh was held in New Orleans in 1992, and the eighth was held in Baltimore in 1997. These congresses have revealed the extraordinary liturgical and aesthetic gifts of African American Catholics. The black Catholic Hymnal, *Lead Me Guide Me* (published in 1987), is a reminder of the impact made by black Catholic musicians like Clarence Rivers, Rawn Harbor, Edward Bonnemere, Grayson Brown, and others on the Catholic Church in the United States and abroad.

Black Catholics were among the first who figuratively and literally helped lay the foundations of Catholicism in the territory that would become the United States. Their contribution to American Catholicism, so often overlooked and unsung, has been ongoing and substantial, both spiritually and tangibly. Without their presence, much of the movement, tempo, and vibrant colors of American Catholicism would have been muted and less dynamic. Without their presence, the note of catholicity would have been less evident, the story of faith would have been less apparent, and the mystery of the cross less powerful.

Bibliography: C. DAVIS, *The History of Black Catholics in the United States* (New York 1990). J. LANDERS, ''Free and Slave,'' in *The New History of Florida*, ed. M. GANNON (Gainesville, Fla. 1996) 167–82. M. J. MACGREGOR, *The Emergence of a Black Catholic Community: St. Augustine's in Washington* (Washington, D.C. 1999). M. NICKELS, *Black Catholic Protest and the Federated Colored Catholics, 1917–1933: Three Perspectives on Racial Justice* (New York 1988). S. J. OCHS, *A Black Patriot and a White Priest: André Cailloux and Claude Paschal Maistre in Civil War New Orleans* (Baton Rouge, La. 2000); *Desegregating the Altar: The Jose-phites and the Struggle for Black Priests, 1871–1960* (Baton Rouge, La. 1990). D. W. SOUTHERN, *John LaFarge and the Limits of Catholic Interracialism, 1911–1963* (Baton Rouge, La. 1996).

[C. DAVIS]

AFRICAN MISSIONS, SOCIETY OF

The Society of African Missions (SMA, Official Catholic Directory #0110), of pontifical right, was founded in Lyons, France, on Dec. 8, 1856, by Bp. Melchior de MARION-BRÉSILLAC for missionary work in Africa. It is a clerical society of apostolic life.

In 1858, as its first mission, the society was given the vicariate apostolic of SIERRA LEONE, where, the following year, Brésillac and most of his missionaries perished during a fever epidemic. Leadership then passed to Father Augustin Planque, whom Pius IX confirmed as the first superior general of the society. In 1861 a group of missionaries left for the newly erected vicariate of Dahomey, where successful foundations were made at Ouidah, Porto-Novo, and Lagos. The missionaries established stations along the West Coast of Africa, from Liberia to the Niger River. In 1875 Planque founded the Congregation of Our Lady of the Apostles to provide sisters to assist in establishing schools, orphanages, dispensaries, model farms, and workshops.

The society spread throughout Europe and the U.S.; in 1912 the Irish province was established; in 1923 the Dutch province; in 1927 Eastern France (Alsace); in 1941 the American province. The motherhouse was transferred to Rome in 1937. The U.S. provincialate is in Tenafly, NJ.

The society arrived in the U.S. in 1904, answering a call from Bp. Benjamin J. Keiley of Savannah, Ga., who had appealed to the society for priests to work among the African-Americans of his diocese. From the Savannah mission, begun in 1904 and directed by Rev. Ignatius Lissner, priests spread to various parishes throughout the U.S. In 1917, Lissner founded the FRANCISCAN HANDMAIDS OF THE MOST PURE HEART OF MARY, a congregation for black American sisters. In 1941, when the American province was canonically erected in Tenafly, N.J., he was named its first provincial.

Bibliography: R. F. GUILCHER, *La Société des missions africaines: Ses origines, sa nature, sa vie, ses oeuvres* (Lyon 1956). J. BONFILS, *L'Oeuvre de Msgr. De Marion Brésillac en faveur du clergé local dans les missions de l'Inde au XIXᵉ siècle* (Lyon 1959). M. J. BANE, *Catholic Pioneers in West Africa* (Dublin 1956); *Heroes of the Hinterland* (New York 1959). J. M. TODD, *African Mission* (London 1962).

[E. J. BIGGANE/EDS.]

AFTERLIFE

Although belief in a continuing or new life after death is widespread among the peoples of the world, there are profound differences among cultural traditions in conceptions of this afterlife; and even in those civilized societies in which a sharp division between the here and the hereafter is theologically postulated and conventionally accepted, there are personal variations in specific images of the afterlife. Despite the latter, two elements—belief in a final moral judgment of personal conduct in the world and belief in the specific existence of an afterworld distinct from this world—define Christian, Christian-influenced, and to a lesser degree Jewish and Islamic conceptions of the afterlife. For the developed doctrinal and theological concepts, *see* HEAVEN (THEOLOGY OF); HELL (THEOLOGY OF); JUDGMENT, DIVINE (IN THEOLOGY); PURGATORY. This article treats within the perspective of the comparative study of religion the differing conceptions found (1) in primitive societies, (2) in the Bible, and (3) in Greco-Roman religion.

1. In Primitive Societies

Generally speaking, primitive peoples do not share the twin assumptions of a final moral judgment of behavior in the world and the specific existence of an afterworld. Accordingly, most anthropologists would not agree with Wilhelm SCHMIDT's assumption of moral judgment and an associated belief in an afterworld as coextensive with primitive MONOTHEISM. It seems more acceptable historically to reason that as society becomes increasingly secularized, and in the literal sense civilized, the sphere of moral action contracts and grows more complex; correlatively, the idea that the ultimate *loci* of the consequences of morality and immorality are in the afterworld emerges with great clarity.

Continuity of the Self. Primitive societies are, as Robert Redfield and Paul Radin have indicated, moral at their core; persons relate to each other in a moral nexus, not as contracting partners in a legal, technical, commercial, that is, civilized order. This *sacred* quality of primitive life is evident in the ritually celebrated cycles of birth, death, and rebirth of the person, of society, and of nature at large. In these primitive rites of passage and ritual dramas, persons may be, for example, conceived as dying to a given status in the world and being reborn into another status, but without destroying the continuity of self. The self is never merely reduced to the status; rather, it is enriched by experiencing the pain of internal growth and diversification. In a sense, the passage of the person through primitive societies can be understood as a progressive spiritualization. In the Winnebago medicine rite described by Radin, the goal is what Mircea Eliade has

called the "perpetual regeneration of the initiate," the "eternal return" to mythical origins, implying an abolition of time and a "reinstatement of the miraculous moment of creation" (*Shamanism* 319–20). Historical, progressive, lineal time, central to the modern scientific world view and expressed in the Hebraic and Christian cosmogonies (in the Christian context based on the historicity of Jesus), is not a primitive conception.

The cyclic and sacred character of primitive life is similarly evident in the common belief, as among the Anaguta of Northern Nigeria, that an infant is the reincarnation of an ancestral spirit in the grandparental generation; hence the person, who has literally died to the world, begins a new spiritual existence, is reborn. The critical point is that primitive society itself emerges as the arena of the original drama of creation and transcendence, of Eliade's "irruption of the sacred into the world" occurring in "primordial" time (*The Sacred and the Profane* 72). The passage through life takes on the aspect of a moral drama, culminating, as among the Winnebago people of Wisconsin, in the initiate's ultimate effort to grasp the meaning of creation and so win eternal life or rebirth. In these primitive rites, the forerunners of the more explicit and historically specific Christian Sacraments, that which Eliade terms a "nostalgia for Paradise" (*Shamanism* 508), for the instant of pure being, is evident.

Identity of World and Afterworld. It is clear that the antinomies life-death, natural-supernatural, sacred-profane, and spirit-flesh that weigh so heavily in civilized Christian thought are, in primitive societies, largely irrelevant. Life moves on all levels simultaneously. Ordinary events are suffused with sacred meaning, everything has personality; God, spirits, ancestors—dreamt of, seen, or felt—*exist*. The mode of primitive thinking is existentialist in the most comprehensive sense. Therefore, the split between this world and the afterworld is of little moment. Where conceptions of the afterlife are present, they typically assimilate, as Franz Boas put it, the "social life of the dead [to] . . . the living" (606–07). The deceased may maintain an active position in the kinship structure. The afterworld is, with minor exceptions, quite the same as this world; throughout North Asia, as elsewhere, the former is simply a mirror image of the latter. Frequently, the souls of the dead, on their passage to this inverted world, must pass over some obstacle or across a narrow bridge. But this seems to be related to the psychology of mourning and the consequent need for ritualizing the trauma of separation, rather than to a permanent journey to a distinctly conceived afterworld.

Despite the contradictions inherent in certain technical aspects of the primitive view of the afterlife (e.g., the social immediacy of souls versus their indeterminate ex-

.istence in a ''double'' of this world), neither the idea of hell nor of other-worldly reward for moral behavior are important themes in primitive religions. This is true even where, as among the Anaguta, there is a clear-cut belief in an accessible supreme creator.

See Also: RELIGION (IN PRIMITIVE CULTURE).

Bibliography: F. BOAS, *Race, Language and Culture* (New York 1940). S. DIAMOND, ''Plato and the Definition of the Primitive'' in *Culture in History: Essays in Honor of Paul Radin,* ed. S. DIAMOND (New York 1960) 118–141; ''The Search for the Primitive'' in *Man's Image in Medicine and Anthropology,* ed. I. GALDSTON (New York 1963) 62–115. M. ELIADE, *The Sacred and the Profane,* tr. W. R. TRASK (New York 1959; Torchbook 1961); *Shamanism: Archaic Techniques of Ecstasy,* tr. W. R. TRASK (Bollingen Series 76; rev. ed. New York 1964). R. FIRTH, ''Fate of the Soul'' in *Anthropology of Folk Religion,* ed. C. M. CHARLES (pa. New York 1960). P. RADLIN, *The World of Primitive Man* (New York 1953; repr. 1960). R. REDFIELD, *The Primitive World and Its Transformations* (Ithaca, New York 1953). W. SCHMIDT, *The Origin and Growth of Religion,* tr. H. J. ROSE (2d ed. London 1935).

[S. DIAMOND]

2. In The Bible

The Israelites believed in some kind of ghostlike afterlife. According to their ideas, all the dead go to SHEOL, the nether world. Kings and slaves, old and young, ''all go to one place'' [Eccl 6.6; Ps 88(89).49; Jb 3.13–19; 30.23].

Location and Nature of the Abode of the Dead. The Babylonians refer in their myths, e.g., the GILGAMESH EPIC, to the abode of the dead as a place under the earth or on the other side of the world sea. The dead reach it by descending into the earth or by traveling to the farthest point west. Before entering, they must cross the underground river or the ''waters of death.'' The Scriptures, too, refer to its locality by the direction in which the dead go, ''down to Sheol'' (Is 38.18; Ez 31.14; 1 Kgs 2.9). Even the New Testament localizes the abode of the dead in the depths of the earth (Mt 16.18; Lk 16.26; Acts 2.24, 27, 31; Rom 10.7; Rv 1.18; 20.13). According to mythico-dynamic thinking, this realm of death is constantly overflowing its banks. It is present wherever death exercises its sovereignty. Consequently, not only the grave [Ps 39(40).3; 54(55).24; 142(143).7; etc.] and the depth of the earth are linked with it [Ps 62(63).10; 138(139).8; Is 7.11], but also the sea [Ps 68(69).2, 16; Jon 2.4] and the desert (Jer 2.6, 31; Hos 2.5). These ''three nonworlds'' (J. Pedersen) are considered manifestations of death and belong to the realm of death. In each diminishing of life, the realm of death disrupts the world of the living. Thus illness [Ps 12(13); 21(22); 29(30); 87(88); etc.], captivity [Ps 141(142); 142(143)], persecution and hostility [Ps 17(18); 143(144)], misfortune, poverty, and hunger are all a foretaste of the descent into Sheol and abandonment by Yahweh. The sinner is already living in Sheol (Ps 9A.16–18).

The texts of the preexilic as well as most of the postexilic books draw a most uninviting picture of Sheol. This realm of death is described as an eternal house (Eccl 12.5) with chambers and rooms (Prv 7.27) and gates [Ps 9A.14; 106(107).18; Jb 38.17; Sir 51.9; Wis 16.13; Is 38.10; Mt 16.18; Rv 1.18], a prison (Eccl 9.10) with bars (Jon 2.7) and bolts and bonds [Ps 115(116).3], the land of oblivion [Ps 87(88).13; 114(115).17], a land whence no one can return (Jb 7.9–10; 10.21; Prv 2.19; Sir 38.21). Sheol is called the ''no more'' (Is 38.11), destruction [Ps 87(88).12], dust [Ps 21(22).30; 29(30).10; 145(146).4; Is 26.19; Jb 17.16; Dt 12.2]. It is a place of horror [Ps 115(116).3], complete darkness [Jb 10.21–22; 17.13; 18.18; 38.17; Ps 87(88).7; 142(143).3], and remoteness from Yahweh. Even so, Satan does not have any influence in the abode of the dead, but Yahweh controls Sheol through His power [Ps 138(139).8; Jb 26.6; Prv 15.11; Is 7.11; Am 9.2].

State of the Dead in the Afterlife. In the Old Testament, death is conceived as the end of the entire living man. Yet this basic conception does not exclude a further existence of the deceased in the realm of the dead, as can be shown by the frequent mention of the dead, of graves, and of funeral customs. For the Israelite, life is life only as it is filled with joy, fortune, wealth, and Yahweh's presence. [*See* LIFE, CONCEPT OF (IN THE BIBLE).] These marks of life are not present in the deceased, who are referred to as $r^e p\bar{a}\hat{i}m$, the ''weak'' [Jb 26.5; Ps 87(88).11; Is 14.9] or as those who have descended into the pit [Ps 27(28).1; 29(30).4; Is 38.18; Ez 26.20; 31.14, 16]. In Sheol, the dead were thought to remain in a state of suspended animation, phantoms of the entire former living man, devoid of all power and vitality (Is 14.10). There is no activity (Eccl 9.10), no pleasure (Sir 14.11–17), no participation in or knowledge of what is happening on earth (Eccl 9.5; Jb 14.12–17; 21.21). In the older books of the Old Testament there is no doubt that the deceased are taken away from the vital union with Yahweh. In the nether world, no one praises God any more [Ps 6.6; 29(30).10; 113B(115).17; Sir 17.22–23; Is 38.18b].

However, the older, pessimistic concept of Sheol as the one place for all the dead, irrespective of the moral value of their lives, begins to change in the later books of the Old Testament. The doctrine of RETRIBUTION gradually leads to a distinction between the lot of the good and that of the wicked [Ez 32.17–32; Is 26.8, 14–21; 66.24; Ps 33(34).22–23; Wis 3.2–10, 19; Prv 14.32]. The just man has hope because there will be a reward for his work (2 Chr 15.7; Wis 4.7–17, 20). In the writings of the postexilic period, a real change in the attitude toward afterlife is observable in the expectancy of resurrection (*see* RESURRECTION OF THE DEAD, 1). Israel's faith in its election by Yahweh and in His mercy and omnipotence, a faith that was justified by His constant intervention in the nation's history and by its experience of the loving union between God and the pious man, had to develop into a trust in Yahweh that amounted to an undocumented guarantee of resurrection and immortality (*see* IMMORTALITY, 3). This doctrine developed gradually [Jb 14.14–17; Hos 13.14; Is 25.9; 57.1–2; Wis 1.13–16; Ps 36(37).3–7; 64(65).5a], and some of its theological reasonings were worked out by Isaiah. One finds it in plain words in Dn 12.1–3; Jb 19.25–27; Is 26.19–21; 2 Mc 7.9–11, 14, 22–23, 34–36. However, even at the time of Christ, the doctrine of individual resurrection, which was explicitly rejected by the SADDUCEES, was not commonly accepted in Israel (Mt 22.23–34 and parallels; Acts 23.6–10). The New Testament hardly speaks about the state of the dead. The afterlife was of little concern for the primitive Christian community because the parousia of the Lord (*see* PAROUSIA, 1) and the fulfillment of the eschatological promises were really the heart of the Christian expectation for the future: union with Christ, experienced in faith and in the sacramental life, is but an anticipation of eschatological salvation; this union will be continued, intensified, and fulfilled in the life to come (Phil 1.21–26; etc.).

See Also: HEAVEN (IN THE BIBLE); HELL (IN THE BIBLE); PURGATORY; ABRAHAM'S BOSOM; HADES; GEHENNA; PARADISE; JUDGMENT, DIVINE (IN THE BIBLE).

Bibliography: *Encyclopedic Dictionary of the Bible,* tr. and adap. by L. HARTMAN (New York 1963) 508–10. P. ANTOINE, *Dictionnaire de la Bible,* suppl. ed. L. PIROT, et al. (Paris 1928–) 2:1063–76. J. SCHMID, *Lexikon für Theologie und Kirche,* ed. J. HOFER and K. RAHNER, 10 v. (2d, new ed. Freiburg 1957–65) 5:890–92. H. EISING, *ibid.* 9:391–93. H. J. KRAUS and B. REICKE, *Die Religion in Geschichte und Gegenwart,* 7 v. (3d ed. Tübingen 1957–65) 3:403–06. A. JEREMIAS, *Die babylonisch-assyrischen Vorstellungen vom Leben nach dem Tode* (Leipzig 1887). P. DHORME, ''Le Séjour des morts chez les Babyloniens et les Hébreux,'' *Revue biblique* 16 (1907) 59–78; ''L'Idée de l'au-delà dans la religion hébraïque,'' *Revue de l'histoire des religions* 123 (1941) 113–42. J. P. E. PEDERSEN, *Israel: Its Life and Culture,* 4 v. in 2 (New York 1926–40; repr. 1959). E. F. SUTCLIFFE, *The Old Testament and the Future Life* (2d ed. Westminster, Maryland 1947). O. KUSS, *Der Römerbrief* (Regensburg 1957) 1:241–75, with bibliography. A. FEUILLET, ''Mort du Christ et mort du chrétien d'après les épîtres pauliniennes,'' *Revue biblique* 66 (1959) 481–513. R. H. CHARLES, *Eschatology* (New York 1963).

[H. KÖSTER]

3. In Greco-Roman Religion

At the outset, from an extrinsic point of view, it should be observed that Greco-Roman beliefs on the life after death did not come from a revealed religion; they were not fixed once and for all in sacred books; nor were they dictated, maintained, and controlled as dogmas by a religious authority. They were the product of a slow and steady evolution that corresponded closely, although often with marked lags and uncertainties, to the trends or stages in the development of classical culture in general. Belonging as they did to the domain of tenacious traditions no less than to that of innate anxieties and forebodings, they were in no wise monolithic. New beliefs were superimposed on old conceptions without adjustment or elimination. Rites that belonged to an outmoded faith continued to be performed, even when no one any longer understood their precise bearing or original signification. Conceptions that were basically divergent were found not only side by side in a given cultural period but also together, apparently without conflict, in the soul of one and the same individual.

In General. The mingling of markedly diversified ethnic elements, especially in the great Hellenistic and Roman centers, created a mixture of opinions and beliefs that would be difficult to reduce to its primary components. In view of the shortcomings of official religion in the sphere of death and the hereafter, religious conceptions were so exposed to the strong influences of old wives' tales, superstitions, and black magic, that, in the Hellenistic Age and under the early empire, the educated classes abandoned themselves to unbelief, skepticism, or indifference. The masses, who were long isolated from the progress of philosophy and literature, were too deeply engulfed in the precarious conditions of material subsistence to attempt—at least on their own initiative—a separation of religious rites from superstitious practices or of sound religious sentiments from chimerical fictions.

Intrinsically, Greco-Roman views on the life beyond the grave were conditioned by the evolving ideas of ancient man respecting anthropology, the image of the universe, ethics, and human destiny. From the viewpoint of the earliest beliefs on death, the earliest notions on man were neither spiritual nor materialistic in the modern sense of the terms, but simply ''human,'' in the sense that man did not originally think of himself as a being composed of two ''principles.'' The human being was one, possessing a unity that death did not split into a ''lifeless body'' and a ''surviving soul.'' The shade in the lower world or the soul in heaven was most commonly only man in his entirety, viewed from the angle of his corporeal dematerialization. The development of the concept of man gradually arrived at an increasingly sharp dichotomy between body and soul. The explanation for the distinction is not to be sought in the different opinions that were held on the nature of the vital principle (breath, blood, heat, eidolon, spark), but rather, on the one hand, in the practice of incineration, which by the very fact that it destroyed the body emphasized the soul, and, on the other, in the influence exercised by dualistic currents in philosophy.

The ancient image of the world passed from the stage in which the earth was looked upon as a flat disk floating on the waters of Ocean to the lofty concept of a universe consisting of concentric spheres in harmonious movement, circumscribed by the sphere of the fixed stars. Yet it did not detach itself from the proud and touching idea that the earth, where man reigned as master, formed the center of the universe in question. Since what survived of man did not attain a degree of dematerialization that would have permitted it to escape the category of "place," the soul found a localization beyond the grave in the precise region to which the scientific image of the world and the ideas on the survival and nature of the soul suggested that it be assigned.

Ethical concepts acquired real influence only from the time when death ceased to be considered a mere passage to another world, where the lot of the dead man was simply a repetition of his social condition on earth. Notions of moral responsibility, of personal conscience, of virtuous conduct, and of sinful life could not make their appearance, however, before the individual as such became conscious of himself. From that time he had to abandon the idea that life was lived on earth only, and he had to submit to moral demands with their inevitable sanctions whereby he could hope, in an existence beyond the grave, for the stern justice and the strict recompense that he had vainly expected on earth.

Human destiny was at first confined within the narrow limits of a terrestrial life, from which man escaped only to the extent to which he, on his part, assured the continuity of his family, tribe, and community. When this restricted cadre was broken to the benefit of the emerging individual human person, the way was open for a concept of survival that, in combining the idea of a reward beyond the grave with the notion of an immortal soul, eventually far surpassed in both duration and intensity the possibilities of life on earth. Thus, the true life could begin or rebegin only after death, which, far from diminishing the significance of the human soul, sent it back to its heavenly and divine home.

Early and Classical Greek Beliefs. According to a notion that was held for many centuries, the dead man survived in his tomb. This notion was the source of the meticulous care devoted to funerals, funeral furniture and offerings, and the cult connected, on certain days of the year (e.g., at the *Anthesteria* at Athens), with the tomb of the dead individual or with the tombs of the dead in general. This was the source too, from Mycenaean times, of the family cult, and then of the community cult of dead men who were especially significant, namely, the "heroes." Subsequently, society, cut off from its ancestral tombs by emigration, apparently was not acquainted with either the cult of the dead or that of heroes. Hence arose the general Greek belief—reinforced by the authority of Homer—that the dead were all found together in the subterranean realm of Hades. In the absence of any moral perspective, Hades was not yet a place of retribution. Given the absolute value of life on earth, it was the exact negative replica of that life. It was marked by the absence of the positive features of earthly existence both on the physical plane—countryside, light, warmth, color, and sound—and on the psychological plane—security, freedom, and joy of existence. It was a life in which, by the law of repetition, shades continued the shadow of their earthly sojourn. However, Minoan religion had postulated the existence of Isles of the Blest, located at the end of the world beyond Ocean, to which the gods transported men of divine lineage while they were still alive. This transatlantic eden of living heroes was subsequently changed into the underworld Elysium of the blessed dead—most probably under the influence of the Mysteries of Eleusis. The initiates, in keeping with the law of repetition, continued to celebrate their joyous feasts in their new abode, while the noninitiates had to be satisfied with a shadowy existence in mire (ἐν βορβόρῳ). This, however, was not yet a form of punishment in the strict sense but a deprivation of true life.

Orphic Conceptions. From the 7th to the 6th century B.C., the Orphics, taking over certain popular beliefs regarding the hereafter, went beyond the ritual demands of the Eleusinian Mysteries and substituted for them prescriptions of moral purity. They spread the idea that the noninitiates would be punished in hell for their unworthy lives. Developing also a vague popular notion respecting the transmigration of the soul, the Orphics, from the 6th century, adopted the doctrine of metempsychosis. They maintained that the soul, divinely immortal and essentially independent of the body in which it was entombed (σῶμα, σῆμα), was able, by virtue of upright conduct in the course of successive incarnations, to free itself finally from all dependence on a carnal body. It could then live its own proper and true life in an Elysium, which Orphic "teaching" (except in Pindar) has not described in detail.

Pythagorean Conceptions. From the end of the 6th century, Pythagoreanism borrowed from the Orphic Mysteries its views on metempsychosis and the popular notion of a recompense after death. It thus contributed in its turn to the establishment of the belief according to which, in the lower world, Elysium was reserved for the pious, while Tartarus in Hades was a place of punishment for sinners.

Judgment, and Reward or Punishment in the Hereafter. In the classical period (5th and 4th centuries B.C.) the Orphico-Pythagorean belief in the punishment of **Hades** spread widely, as is evidenced by literature (Aristophanes, Plato) and art (vase paintings). The majority of people were hardly reached by the philosophical arguments of Plato, who sought to prove scientifically the immortality of the soul, but they were deeply influenced by the mythico-religious representations of a rewarding hereafter, of which they learned from mythology and the mysteries. Thus most probably *c.* 400 B.C., the idea of a *iudicium post mortem* took definite shape, as is known through the writings of Plato and the south Italian funerary vases of the 4th century. After death every soul appeared before a tribunal in Hades, where a college of three heroes (Minos, Rhadamanthus, and Aeacus) judged it according to its merits. Pious souls were rewarded with the Elysian dwellings as their abode; those of less perfect conduct had to undergo a kind of purgatory; and hardened sinners were condemned for all eternity to the punitive and exemplary tortures of Tartarus.

Hellenistic Beliefs. Plato's affirmation of the divine affinity and immortal nature of the soul ended in the skepticism of the New Academy, while EPICURUS, following the atomic theory of Democritus, taught that after death the soul, like the body, dissolved into atoms. The early Stoics recognized in their vital principle, which was related to the fiery ether, a vague form of survival, but it was quite impersonal and limited in time. However, with Posidonius and his Platonic leanings, the soul regained a true immortality. The mystery religions and the strong Orphico-Pythagorean beliefs in Magna Graecia promised a hereafter to their adherents. The aspects of this paradise were not so much an indication of a relatively low level of morality as they were a reflection of and transfer of deep longings for a felicity that was no longer threatened by trials or death. According to popular belief, the firmness of which was not influenced by skepticism or by the denials of the educated class, the hereafter was usually located under the earth. This fact is indicated by metrical epitaphs, curse tablets consigning their victims to the infernal deities, Orphic gold plates found in south Italy, and paintings on funerary vases from the same region, etc. Similarly, the allegorical interpretation of the punishments of Tartarus as worked out by the Pythagoreans had no effect whatever on the popular notions respecting reward or punishment in the next world.

Nevertheless, the progress of Hellenistic civilization brought about marked changes regarding the location of the hereafter. On the one hand, in accordance with the new scientific theories on the structure of the earth and the universe, Hades had to be moved either to the dark antipodes of the inhabited earth or to the non-illuminated hemisphere of the world. On the other hand, philosophico-religious teaching on the divine, and therefore heavenly, origin of the soul; astrological cosmology, which turned man's eyes heavenward; the increasing importance of the symbolism of fire and light; and the astral myths telling of great mortals being changed into stars, all combined to exert an influence on beliefs. Men gradually adopted the revolutionary idea that after death souls were changed into stars, or rather flew off to the starry sky. Under the Roman Empire, this lunisolar or astral immortality received support from solar pantheism. It would be wrong, however, to exaggerate the expansion of the new belief. Only limited circles were affected. In the leisured class as a whole, skepticism was the rule, whereas the lower strata of the population continued to stick to their old idea of an underworld Hades.

In Early Rome. Primitive Roman beliefs regarding the hereafter were very restricted in scope and character. The dead man was placed in a tomb that was built in the form of a house. He led there a kind of weak existence, and the living had to sustain him by funeral offerings. At the same time he was to be feared, as is evidenced by references to apparitions in dreams, to ghosts, to the role of the *ahori* or premature dead, and to necromancy. On certain days of the year, too, the dead had official access to the world of the living by the removal of the *lapis manalis* covering the entrance to the lower world (*mundus*). In so far as the dead man was a link in the long chain of his *gens* or clan, he belonged to the divine ancestral spirits, the *Di Parentes*. Mixed in the mass of the dead, he formed a part of the *Lemures,* spirits of the dead who were divided into *Lares* and *Larvae* according as they were benevolent or malevolent, respectively. Furthermore, these various connections were all brought under the head of *Di Manes,* to whom specific rites were assigned: the *Parentalia, Lemuria, Larentalia,* and later the *Rosalia* and *Dies Violares.*

Before the 4th century B.C., the Romans do not seem to have been familiar with an infernal lower world common to all the dead nor with any form of punishment beyond the grave. From this time the Etruscans acquainted them with the Greek representation of Hades, but in the form that the terrifying Etruscan demonology had given it. In the course of the 3d century B.C., Magna Graecia invested this Etrusco-Roman world of the dead, *Orcus,* with all its rich infernal mythology and with all the Orphico-Pythagorean acquisitions to which the Greek genius had given birth. Through the direct contact between the Greco-Oriental and Roman civilizations, all these ideas and beliefs became more and more thoroughly acclimated at Rome. They received a quasi-sacred and definitive expression in the 6th book of Vergil's *Aeneid.*

Greco-Roman Beliefs. From the end of the republic, the Greco-Oriental and Roman worlds were fused into a great cultural commonwealth in which the active, general circulation of religious ideas occasioned the flourishing of various forms of syncretistic religion. Still, old conceptions persisted, whether they took on a new life under their old patrons (the various philosophies), whether they adjusted themselves to the form and organization of religious practices coming from the East (the mystery cults), or whether they simply maintained themselves against the winds and waves of innovation, firmly anchored as they were in the hearts of the masses (popular beliefs).

With regard to the concern of philosophy with the problem of the hereafter, Neo-Pythagoreanism (1st century B.C.–2d century A.D.) and Neoplatonism (c. A.D. 250–c. 500)—despite some Oriental elements—represented basically currents and ideas of Greek origin. According to the Neo-Pythagoreans, souls, on being freed from the body, escaped into the atmosphere, where they were purified by the winds before they re-entered their original home, the starry spheres. The Neoplatonists taught that the soul, buffeted in some way between the material many and the spiritual One, had the duty to apply itself to the noble task of regaining suprasensible divine life. The syncretistic teachings of the Hermetic literature and of Gnosticism (2d and 3d centuries A.D.) held in common that the soul, having once been cast into matter, could return to its heavenly source only through ''true knowledge.'' Besides the old mysteries, whose promise of immortality was reinforced through contact with Orphico-Pythagorean and Neoplatonic elements, various cults, under a flexible form of mystery religion probably borrowed from the Greek mysteries, honored divinities imported from the East (Cybele-Attis, Isis-Osiris, Sabazios, Mithras), and they attracted the intensely emotional devotion of the masses, among whom the earlier native stock was being submerged by cosmopolitan elements.

It is desirable, however, to give a just evaluation of the expansion of the philosophico-religious doctrines, which appealed strictly to the intellectual aristocracy insofar as it had not limited its hopes to the immortality of fame, and also to appraise the content of the message of salvation afforded by the mystery religions. Several lofty ideas that belonged to philosophy and the mysteries—freedom from death of the body by resurrection, deliverance from the death of the soul by spiritual rebirth and divine illumination, deification, divine filiation—had little or no influence on the rank and file of people before Christianity spread among them. Such ideas acquired their real efficacy, expansion, depth, and, in a certain measure, their existence only through the victorious progress of Christianity.

The popular conceptions, which are so vividly revealed by the metrical funeral inscriptions, indicate that common people were practically impervious to the Pythagorean idea that placed Hades in the sublunary region or in the moon itself, and that they had no interest in the system of solar pantheism or in the Gnostic teachings on the fall and ascent of souls through the planetary spheres. The old believers clung obstinately to the cult of the dead at the tomb and to the idea of a lower world in which the shades lived the barest kind of existence in darkness, although they granted that in rare cases the dead, as a reward for a pious life, enjoyed in the Elysian Fields a happy existence of eternal feasting. However, as the gods—and light—had their abode in the heavens, the blessed Hereafter tended to be moved to the celestial heights. There the elect received as their portion the immortal happiness that the philosophicoreligious teachings, the mysteries of Gnostic coloring, and imperial apotheosis had offered to a select few. Hell, in the modern sense, remained fixed in the traditional lower world; its punishments, to which Christianity made its contribution (e.g., in the *Apocalypse of Peter*), attained a diversity and refinement that emanated less from a conscience motivated by the unfulfilled desire for perfect justice than from the lower level of human thinking, over which neither the noblest pagan ideas nor the Christian gospel of salvation had effective control.

See Also: CRETAN-MYCENAEAN RELIGION; ETRUSCAN RELIGION; GREEK PHILOSOPHY (RELIGIOUS ASPECTS); GREEK RELIGION; MYSTERY RELIGIONS, GRECO-ORIENTAL; NEOPLATONISM; NEO-PYTHAGOREANISM; ORPHISM; ROMAN RELIGION; STOICISM.

Bibliography: J. T. ADDISON, *Life Beyond Death in the Beliefs of Mankind* (Boston and New York 1932). F. CUMONT, *Lux perpetua* (Paris 1949). A. DIETERICH, *Nekyia* (2d ed. Leipzig 1913). L. R. FARNELL, *Greek Hero Cults and Ideas of Immortality* (Oxford 1921). F. HEILER, *Unsterblichkeitsglaube und Jenseitshoffnung in der Geschichte der Religionen* (Munich 1950). O. KERN, *Die Religion der Griechen,* 3 v. (2d ed. Berlin 1963). K. LATTE, *Römische Religionsgeschichte* (Munich 1960). R. A. LATTIMORE, *Themes in Greek and Latin Epitaphs* (2d ed. pa. Urbana, Illinois 1962). M. P. NILSSON, *Geschichte der griechischen Religion,* 2 v. (2d ed. Munich 1955–61). W. F. OTTO, *Die Manen oder von den Urformen des Totenglaubens* (3d ed. Darmstadt 1962). C. PASCAL, *Le credenze d'oltretomba nelle opere letterarie dell' antichità classica,* 2 v. (Catania 1912). G. PFANNMUELLER, *Tod, Jenseits und Unsterblichkeit* (Basel 1953). E. ROHDE, *Psyche: The Cult of Souls and Belief in Immortality among the Greeks,* tr. W. B. HILLIS from 8th German ed. (New York 1925).

[G. SANDERS]

AGABUS, ST.

An early Judaeo-Christian endowed with the charism of prophecy. Agabus is first mentioned in Acts 11.27–28, where he is spoken of as accompanying a group of prophets who journeyed from Jerusalem to Antioch. There he predicted that a famine would soon overtake the world. Luke notes the fulfillment of his prophecy in the reign of the Emperor Claudius (A.D. 41–54). This is most probably the famine of Judea that Josephus describes in *Ant.* 3.15.3; 20.2.5; 5.2. As a result of Agabus's prediction, the Antiochian community collected alms for the Jerusalem Church, which had become impoverished through its charity to the poor. Agabus is almost certainly the same prophet who met Paul at Caesarea *c.* A.D. 58 and, through a symbolic action, predicted that Paul would be imprisoned in Jerusalem and given over to the Gentiles (Acts 21.10–11). In the Eastern Church Agabus is venerated as a martyr whose feast day is celebrated on March 8; in the West, he is included as a confessor in the Roman Martyrology on February 13.

Bibliography: A. WIKENHAUSER, *Lexikon für Theologie und Kirche*, ed. J. HOFER and K. RAHNER (Freiburg 1957–65) 4:1314; *Die Apostelgeschichte und ihr Geschichtswert* (Münster 1921) 407–409. B. H. THROCKMORTON, *The Interpreters Dictionary of the Bible*, G. A. BUTTRICK, ed. (Nashville 1962) 1:52. K. S. GAPP, ''The Universal Famine under Claudius,'' *Harvard Theological Review* 28 (1935) 258–265.

[J. A. GRASSI]

AGAGIANIAN XV, GREGORY PETER

Cardinal and Catholic Armenian patriarch; b. Akhaltsikhe, Russian Georgia, Sept. 18, 1895; d. Rome, May 16, 1971. Agagianian's intellectual gifts were recognized early, and at 11 he was sent to Rome for education at the Urbanian Athenaeum. He received doctorates in philosophy, theology, and Canon Law.

After ordination in 1917, Agagianian taught for two years in Rome and then from 1919 to 1921 did pastoral work among Armenian Catholics in Tiflis, Georgia. He was recalled to Rome and appointed vice rector of the Pontifical Armenian College, becoming rector in 1932. He also taught at the Urbanian. In 1935 he was consecrated titular bishop of Comana and appointed papal emissary to Lebanon. In 1937 the Synod of Catholic Armenian Bishops elected him patriarch of the Catholic Armenians and catholicos of Cilicia, near Beirut. Baptized Lazarus A., he assumed the name Gregory, along with Peter, which Catholic Armenian patriarchs take as a symbol of loyalty to Rome.

In 1946 Pope Pius XII made Agagianian a cardinal. In 1958 he became proprefect of the Congregation for the

Cardinal Agagianian, 1961, Rome. (© David Lees/CORBIS)

Propagation of the Faith, and in 1960, prefect, holding the post until his retirement in 1970. As head of the Vatican congregation concerned with mission work he traveled widely, and because of this and his duties on other Vatican congregations and commissions he resigned his office as patriarch. He was a key figure at the Second Vatican Council, serving as a presiding officer and helping to draw up the missionary decree *Ad Gentes.*

[T. EARLY]

AGAPE

Technical name for a love feast in the early Christian Church.

Origin of the Term. The verb ἀγαπάω (to love) was common in classical Greek, but the derivative noun ἀγάπη was unknown. Borrowed from the popular Egyptian dialect, the noun occurred in the Septuagint (LXX) version of the Scriptures (e.g., Jer 2.2; Ct 3.5, 10). In the NT it was used to designate a beneficent love, a predilection of God for men, or a love of men for God or of men among themselves, i.e., a fraternal charity. In all three meanings it was suitable for appropriation by the early Christians as a technical term or proper name for various forms of fraternal meals of a semi-liturgical nature. Although not without certain analogies in the Jewish and pagan world of antiquity (e.g., *The Letter of Aristeas* 187–300; the sacred meals of the QUMRAN COMMUNITY, *Manual of Discipline* 1QS 6.2–5; Plato's *Symposium*; and the meals of Greek religious fraternities), the Christian love feasts had as their specific and basic purpose a practical imitation of Christ's love for men (Lk 14.12–14; 22.26–27) by expressing and fostering fraternal love. The poor and widows were invited to share in both the charitable agapae and those celebrated to honor the dead and the martyrs. Since they were inspired by Christ's love for men, the agapae were related also to the Eucharist, even when they did not include a Eucharistic banquet. Jesus had instituted the Eucharist at the LAST SUPPER in the form of a banquet at which His love attained its full perfection (Jn 13.1), and it was at Eucharistic feasts that the union of Christians in Christ's love was most concretely manifested (1 Cor 10.16–17).

Agape in the New Testament. If agape is understood in a wide sense, many of the communal meals in the NT may be classified as love feasts. The only certain instance of the use of agape as a technical term for love feast in the NT is found in the Epistle of St. Jude, v. 12, "These men are stains [or hidden reefs] at your love feasts, carousing impudently and feeding themselves alone." (The plural form ἀγάπαις occurs here for the first time in extant Greek literature and for the only time in the NT.) However, in a passage suggesting literary dependence, 2 Pt 2.13 reads, "These men are stains and blemishes, reveling in their deceits [or lusts, ἀπάταις, instead of ἀγάπαις, which occurs in some MSS as a variant reading], while they carouse with you" (author's translations).

According to Acts 2.42–47 the primitive Jerusalem community habitually practiced the breaking of bread, an early name for the Eucharist. This Eucharistic rite was probably the essential part of a fraternal meal that recalled and continued the meals of Jesus' public ministry (Mk 6.34–44; Jn 12.1–2), the Last Supper (at which Jesus had gathered with His disciples according to Jewish custom in a *ḥăbûrâ*, a religious fellowship, for the PASSOVER Meal), and the joyful, post-Resurrection feasts with the risen Lord (Lk 24.30–35, 41–43; Jn 21.9–13; Acts 1.4). It was quite fitting and convenient that such feasts, since they reenacted Christ's loving and victorious presence among His disciples, should have included the Eucharist, as a general rule. In Acts 6.1–6, however, the "daily ministration" to widows was simply a work of mercy rather than a liturgical service that included prayer, preaching (the service of the word), and, very likely, the Eucharist.

That abuses occurred when such fraternal feasts were being adapted for recently converted Greeks is clear from 1 Cor 11.17–34. Drunkenness, factions, and dishonoring of the poor at these meals led St. Paul to complain that the sacred meaning of the Lord's Supper was being ignored and corrupted; he insisted on the reform of such gatherings (on their complete elimination according to W. Goossens and L. Thomas) and reemphasized the traditional doctrine about the Eucharist: it was a proclamation of the value of the Lord's death in view of His final PAROUSIA (v. 26). Their meals were to be sober and sacred feasts, convoked not to satisfy hunger (v. 34), but to express fraternal love: "Wherefore, my brethren, when you come together to eat [the meal that signifies your unity], wait for one another" (v. 33). In this way they would not ". . . despise the church of God and put to shame the needy" and would merit Paul's commendation (v. 22). A communal breaking of bread at Troas is also described in Acts 20.7–11.

Agape in the Post-Apostolic Church. The letter of Pliny the Younger to Trajan (10.96, *c*. A.D. 112) describes a Christian fraternal meal, at which food of a "common and innocent" kind was eaten. The quoted words do not necessarily exclude an accompanying Eucharist. In the DIDACHE (ch. 9–10) certain prayers have been interpreted as referring either to the Eucharist, or an agape, or both together, a fact that indicates the rites were similar and not mutually exclusive. The phrase, "to celebrate an agape," of St. IGNATIUS OF ANTIOCH's Epistle to the Smyrnaeans (8.2) refers apparently to a love feast that was related to, but distinct from, the Eucharist. Other Ignatian references to agape as a meal (e.g., *Smyrn.* 6.2; 7.1) are uncertain. TERTULLIAN (*Apology* ch. 39, late 2d century), after speaking of monetary contributions for the relief of the poor, gives the name agape to a meal of which the main purpose, probably on private initiative, was such relief. In this most celebrated description of an agape, prayers were said, food was eaten in moderation, the Scriptures were read, and hymns were sung, although there is no mention of an officiating cleric. In the *First Apology* of St. JUSTIN MARTYR (ch. 65–67) it is the Eucharist itself, not an agape, that served as the occasion for social relief of the needy. An agape for widows is mentioned in the *Apostolic Tradition* of HIPPOLYTUS OF ROME (early 3d century), as well as in the dependent *Canons of Hippolytus* (183). Other forms of agapae in which the poor could share were adapted from pagan funeral feasts, such as those on the Roman feast of the *Parentalia* held in honor of the dead, or on the feasts of martyrs (*Canons of Hippolytus* 169). The so-called *fractio panis* (breaking of bread) scene of the Cappella Greca of the catacomb of Priscilla illustrates a Christian funeral banquet. Such a banquet symbolized the heavenly meal desired for the dead in the place of peace and refreshment (*REFRIGERIUM*) and recalled Jesus' words, ". . . that you may eat and drink at my table in my kingdom'' (Lk 22.29–30). The Church defended the legitimacy of such practices (St. Augustine, *Contra Faustum Manichaeum* 20.21; *De civitate Dei* 8.27), but abuses often caused their regulation or suppression (St. Augustine, *Conf.* 6.2; Council of Laodicea cc.27–28). After the 4th century, social changes and the growth of ecclesiastical organization brought about the gradual disappearance of the agape.

The fragmentary nature of the early texts and their difficulty of interpretation make it impossible to trace a really systematic view of the history of the agape. As seen from the foregoing considerations, the practice seems to have followed few general rules and differed widely according to the various local churches. Never a universal custom, it was replaced by more efficient, if less personal, manifestations of Christian charity.

Bibliography: B. REICKE, *Diakonie, Festfreude und Zelos in Verbindung mit der altchristlichen Agapenfeier, Uppsala Universitets Årsskrift* No. 5 (1951), a fundamental work with many penetrating insights. C. SPICQ, *Agapè: Prolégomènes à une étude de théologie néo-testamentaire* (Studia hellenistica 10; Louvain 1955), presenting the pre-Christian background of the term. W. GOOSSENS, *Les Origines de l'Eucharistie: Sacrement et sacrifice* (Paris 1931) 127–146. DENIS-BOULET, *Catholicisme. Hier, aujourd'hui, et demain,* ed. G. JACQUEMET (Paris 1947) 1:192–193. J. A. JUNGMANN, *Lexikon für Theologie und Kirche,* ed. J. HOFER and K. RAHNER (Freiburg 1957–65) 1:180–181. J. LEIPOLDT, *Die Religion in Geschichte und Gegenwart* (3d ed. Tübingen 1957–65) 1:169–170. L. THOMAS, *Dictionnaire de la Bible* supplement, ed. L. PIROT et al. (Paris 1928) 1:134–153. H. LECLERCQ, *Dictionnaire d'archéologie chrétienne et de liturgie,* ed. F. CABROL, H. LECLERCQ, and H. I. MARROU (Paris 1907–53) 1.1:775–848.

[C. BERNAS]

AGAPE, SS.

The name of several saints honored as martyrs in the early Church. The name Agape (Charity) is sometimes confused with Agatha.

Agape (Charity), daughter of St. Sophia (Wisdom), is associated with SS. Pistis (Faith) and Elpis (Hope) and, according to a seventh- or eighth-century *passio* written by John the Priest, she was allegedly put to death at Rome during the persecution of Hadrian. The ITINERARIA located her grave on the Via Aurelia, while the *Notula* of Olea of Monza placed it on the Via Appia. Ansa, wife of King Desiderius of the Lombards (756–774), gave her relics to the monastery of St. Giulia in Brescia.

Feast: Aug. 1 in the Roman Church; Sept. 17 in the Greek Church.

Agape of Thessalonika, honored with her sisters SS. Chionia and Irene in the Syrian Breviary on April 2, in the Roman Martyrology on April 3, and among the Greeks on April 16. The sisters, after a legal process under the Roman prefect Dulcitius on April 1, 304, were allegedly burned to death for refusing to eat food sacrificed to the Roman gods and for hiding Christian books. Irene survived her sisters and companions for two days. The Basilica of Thessalonica was erected in their honor. The acts of the three judicial processes have been preserved.

Agape, associated with St. Marina, is mentioned in the Syrian martyrology as having been martyred at Antioch on March 11, 411. According to later Spanish legends she is said to have been put to death with the Bithynian martyrs in Spain during the Decian persecution, but this story resulted from a misreading of the Roman martyrology by the Spanish hagiographer Galesinius.

Agape of Terni, mentioned in the Roman martyrology as a virgin and martyr for Feb. 15. A protégé of Bishop Saint Valentine of Terni, she was reputedly beheaded in the Aurelian persecution on Feb. 15, 273, and her body buried on a spot known as *Inter Turres.* In 550 Bishop Anastasius erected a church there in her honor, confiding the body to a Benedictine monastery. In 1174 the church was in ruins; St. Agape's head was then sent to Rome and kept in the Basilica of the Apostles.

St. Jerome's martyrology mentions another St. Agape for Aug. 8, supposedly honored at Trier, but there is no mention of her in the liturgical books of the diocese.

Bibliography: A. FRUTAZ, *Lexikon für Theologie und Kirche,* ed. J. HOFER and K. RAHNER (Freiburg 1957–65) 1:182; G. DE TERVARENT, *Analecta Bollandiana* 68:419–423; ''Passio'' in *Bibliotheca hagiographica latina antiquae et mediae aetatis* (Brussels 1898–1901) 2966–73. A. PALMIERI, *Dictionaire d'histoire et du géographie ecclésiastiques,* ed. A. BAUDRILLART et al. (Paris 1912) 1:876–877. S. SALAVILLE, *Dictionaire d'histoire et du géographie ecclésiastiques,* ed. A. BAUDRILLART et al. (Paris 1912)1:875–876. H. DELEHAYE, ''Les Martyrs d'Interamna,'' *Bulletin d'ancienne littérature et d'archéologie chrétiennes* 1 (1911) 161–168; *Synaxarium ecclesiae Constantinopolitanae* (Brussels 1902) 605–606. F. DE' CAVALIERI, ed., ''Nuove note agiografiche: Martyrium SS. Agapes, Irenes et Chiones,'' *Studi e Testi* 9 (1902) 1–20.

[E. G. RYAN]

AGAPETUS I, POPE, ST.

Pontificate: May 13, 535 to April 22, 536. The successor of Pope JOHN II was the archdeacon Agapetus, member of an old Roman family and the son of Gordianus, priest of the titular church of SS. Giovanni e Paolo. He appears to have been the candidate of the party that had supported DIOSCORUS some years before. Immediately after the election, a council was held, and the document that Pope BONIFACE II had forced the supporters of Dioscorus to sign was solemnly burned. This was a conciliatory gesture that was much appreciated by the clergy. So too was his repudiation of the uncanonical attempts of recent popes to appoint their own successors. He took a hard line against Arianism, even forbidding converts from Arianism to serve as clergy.

Since Queen Amalasuntha had placed herself under imperial protection, Justinian I decided to use her assassination by King Theodatus (535) as an excuse for liquidating Ostrogothic rule in Italy. He ordered his commanders to occupy Sicily and Dalmatia. King Theodatus threatened to put to death all the Roman senators, with their wives and children, unless the emperor desisted from his purpose. Under this pressure Agapetus agreed to the king's request to go to Constantinople and persuade the emperor to give up his plans. The Byzantines gave him a triumphant reception, but the emperor ignored his request to cancel the invasion. Nothing could deflect the emperor from his designs, and BELISARIUS began the reconquest of Italy in July 536. During his brief stay in Constantinople, however, Agapetus was able to accomplish a few successes. Either shortly before or soon after his arrival, he was informed by some of the clergy that Patriarch ANTHIMUS, installed on the throne of Constantinople through the influence of Empress THEODORA (1), was tainted by the Monophysite heresy. When the fact came to light, Agapetus ordered the patriarch's deposition on the grounds that he had been uncanonically translated from the See of Trebizond to Constantinople. The emperor supported this order. Agapetus then secured the election of an orthodox patriarch, MENNAS, whom he personally consecrated (March 13, 536). His firm stand strengthened the Chalcedonian cause in Constantinople.

Agapetus praised the profession of faith that the emperor submitted to him, but refused to acknowledge the right of laymen to teach in the Church. Shortly afterward he became ill and died. Before expiring, he begged the emperor to summon a general council to condemn Anthimus and submitted to him a petition from the monasteries of Constantinople, Syria, and Palestine, urging that the Monophysites, protected by Empress Theodora, should be expelled from Constantinople. But Theodora's influence upon her husband was immense, and nothing came of this request. The pope's body was sealed in a leaden coffin and taken back to Rome, where he was buried in the portico of St. Peter's. Agapetus converted his own family house on the Clivus Scauri into a library, which was intended to form part of a Roman university he hoped to found with the help of CASSIODORUS. The library was later incorporated by Pope GREGORY I in his own monastery nearby on the Caelian. Six genuine letters of Agapetus are extant.

Feast: April 22 and Sept. 20.

Bibliography: *Clavis Patrum latinorum*, ed. E. DEKKERS (Streenbrugge 1961)1693. *Patrologia Latina*, ed. J. P. MIGNE (Paris 1878–90) 66:35–76. *Liber Pontificalis*, ed. L. DUCHESNE (Paris 1886–1958) 1:287–289; 3:91. H. LECLERCQ, *Dictionnaire d'archéologie chrétienne et de liturgie*, ed. F. CABROL, H. LECLERCQ, H. I. MARROU (Paris 1907–53)13.1:1217–18. F. DVORNIK, *Byzance et la primauté romaine* (Paris 1964). E. FERGUSON, ed., *Encyclopedia of Early Christianity* (New York 1997) 1:25–26. H. JEDIN, *History of the Church* (New York 1980) 2:444–445; 627. J. N. D. KELLY, *Oxford Dictionary of Popes* (New York 1986) 58–59. J. RICHARDS, *Popes and Papacy the Early Middle Ages* (London 1979) 126–127.

[J. CHAPIN]

AGAPETUS II, POPE

Pontificate: May 10, 946 to December 955; b. Rome. He was lauded in contemporary sources as "sanctissimus" and as a man "of wondrous sanctity." Interested in monastic reform, Agapetus, with the help of the despot of Rome, Alberic II of Spoleto, established a Cluniac foundation at ST. PAUL-OUTSIDE-THE-WALLS with monks from the Abbey at GORZE. Despite the political preponderance of Alberic in Rome, Agapetus—at least at the beginning of his pontificate—made some notable decisions demonstrating independent papal action and real authority. A struggle over the archbishop of REIMS had developed when Count Herbert of Vermandois appointed his five-year-old son Hugh as archbishop. Raoul, one of the later Carolingians, conquered Reims and appointed the monk Artaud archbishop. At first the pope supported Artaud; then deceived by forged documents, he turned to Hugh. But when several synods (Verdun, 947; Mousson, 948) and especially the council of Ingelheim (948) called by OTTO I and presided over by Marinus, papal legate, decided in favor of Artaud, Agapetus confirmed their decisions at a council in Rome (949). The pope in effect ratified Otto's wide powers of administration over Danish bishops in a bull of 948 extending the jurisdiction of the metropolitan of Hamburg over Denmark. Within Germany he likewise gave Otto broad jurisdiction over monasteries and sent Otto's brother, Abp. BRUNO OF COLOGNE, the PALLIUM, which he permitted Bruno to wear at will. But in spite of the pope's desires to crown Otto I emperor during Otto's Italian expedition (951–952) to rescue Adelaide, dispossessed widow of Lothair II of Italy, Alberic would have none of it. Alberic effectively controlled Rome until his death in 954, and Agapetus played a continually diminishing role in Roman affairs. In the pope's presence Alberic had the nobles and clergy swear they would elect his son Octavian (later JOHN XII) as Agapetus's successor. Octavian succeeded to the temporal government of Rome in 954 and awaited only the pope's death to gain the papacy itself. Agapetus was buried in the Lateran basilica.

Bibliography: *Liber pontificalis*, ed. L. DUCHESNE (Paris 1886–1958) 2:245. P. JAFFÉ, *Regesta pontificum romanorum ab condita ecclesia ad annum post Christum natum 1198* (Graz 1956)1:459–463. C. J. VON HEFELE, *Histoire des conciles d'après les documents originaux* (Paris 1907–38) 4.2:757–788. H. K. MANN, *The Lives of the Popes in the Early Middle Ages from 590 to 1304* (London 1902–32) 4:224–240. J. P. KIRSCH, *Dictionnaire d'historie et de géographie eccléastiques*, ed. A. BAUDRILLART et al. (Paris 1912–) 1:890–892. F. X. SEPPELT, *Geschichte der Päpste von den Anfängen bis zur Mitte des 20. Jh.* (Munich 1954–59) 2:357–362, 366. P. BREZZI, *Roma e l'Impero medioevale* (Bologna 1947). A. ERLER, "Die Synode von Ingelheim [948] und die Kirchengeschichte" in *In memoriam Adalbert Erler* (1994) 145–150. E. D. HEHL, "Erzbischof Ruttbert von Trier und der Reimser Streit," in *Deus qui mutat tempora. Menschen und Institutionen im Wandel des Mittelalters. Festschrift für Alfons Becker zu seinem 65. Geburstag* (1987) 55–68. F. LOTTER, *Lexikon für Theologie und Kirche*, 3d. ed. (1995). J. N. D. KELLY, *Oxford Dictionary of Popes* (New York 1986) 125–126.

[C. M. AHERNE]

AGAPIOS OF HIERAPOLIS

Bishop of Hierapolis in Syria (Manbij, northeast of Aleppo), whose Arabic name was Mahbūb ibn Qustantin, a contemporary of EUTYCHIOS OF ALEXANDRIA (877–940), whom he outlived by some years. His general history, *Kitāb al-'Unwān* (Book of the Title), for which he is known, is quite independent of the *Annals* of Eutychios. It covered the period from the beginning of the world to A.D. 941 or 942. The original text is no longer extant, however, beyond the year 776 or 777, the second year of the caliphate of al-Mahdī. For the ancient history of Christianity Agapios uses, without criticism, a great deal of the apocryphal and popular legendary literature. For later ecclesiastical and profane history, he uses the Syrian sources, including the Maronite chronographer Theophilos of Edessa (785), whose *World Chronicle* was amply exploited by Agapios in explaining the downfall of the dynasty of the UMAYYADS and the rise of the 'ABBĀSIDS. He knew also the *Church History* of Eusebius of Caesarea, which he uses indirectly by short citations. His special merit lies, however, in his sometimes unidentifiable source materials, offering at times historical details no longer preserved in other extant sources. Most important are his list of the Eastern metropolitans, and his references to the famous text of Papias of Hierapolis in Phrygia (whom he does not cite by name) concerning the four Gospels. Agapios is MICHAEL I THE SYRIAN's source on Bardesanes.

Bibliography: AGAPIOS OF HIERAPOLIS, *Kitāb al-'Unwān*, ed. and French tr. A. VASILIEV, *Patrologia orientalis* 5:565–691; 7:459–591; 8:399–547. C. KARALEVSKY, *Dictionnaire d'histoire et de géographie ecclésiastiques* 1:899–900. G. GRAF, *Geschichte der christlichen arabischen Literatur* 2:39–41.

[L. MALOUF]

AGATHA, ST.

Martyr and patroness of Catania, Sicily; d. possibly in the Decian persecution, 249 to 251. The martyrology of Carthage and that of St. Jerome mention her death on February 5. Legend alleges that she was sent to a brothel to induce her to repudiate her faith. After the removal of her breasts, the Apostle Peter is supposed to have appeared and cured her; but the next day she died in prison of new cruelties. From the sixth century, claims were made for Palermo as the place of her birth; but the older versions of the legend testify for Catania. Her *passio* is recorded in many Greek and Latin versions, but the Greek seems to be the oldest.

The cult of St. Agatha quickly spread beyond Sicily, and her name was inscribed in the Canon of the Roman Mass. It is probable that her remains were translated to Constantinople. Pope Symmachus had a church erected in her honor on the Via Aurelia; and Gregory I (d. 604) reconsecrated an Arian church as S. Agata dei Goti in her name. Her intervention was credited with stilling an eruption of Mt. Etna the year after her burial; and in the Middle Ages, particularly in south Germany, bread, candles, fruits, and letters were blessed in her name to ward off destruction by fire. The popular merrymaking that accompanied her cult in Sicily was probably related to ancient pagan festivals, but the claim that her cult prolonged that of Isis is untenable. She is considered the patron of foundrymen, miners, Alpine guides, and nurses. Since the fourteenth century she has been depicted with her severed breasts on a plate, with a candle, or with a house in flames.

Feast: Feb. 5.

Bibliography: S. D'ARRIGO, *Il martirio di sant'Agata nel quadro storico del suo tempo*, 2 v. (Catania 1988). V. J. CAMILLERI, *Saint Agatha: an archaeological study of the ancient monuments at St Agatha's building complex, crypt, catacombs, church, and museum* (Rabat, Malta 1984). B. KÖTTING, *Lexikon für Theologie und Kirche*, ed. J. HOFER and K. RAHNER (Freiburg 1957–65) 1:183–184. H. DÖRRIE, *Reallexikon für Antike und Christentum*, ed. T. KLAUSER (Stuttgart 1970) 1:179–184.

[P. ROCHE]

AGATHO, POPE, ST.

Pontificate: June 27, 678 to Jan. 10, 681. He helped conclude the struggle against MONOTHELITISM, support-

ing the council convened by CONSTANTINE IV POGONA-
TUS, 680–681 (*see* CONSTANTINOPLE III, COUNCIL OF).
Agatho achieved fullest Western participation through
local synods in Milan, England, Gaul, and in Rome (Easter, 680), where 125 bishops, mostly from Italy, met and
appointed three legates to Constantinople. Presiding over
the council, which also condemned HONORIUS I, they
signed its acts and delivered a letter from the Roman
synod describing the lack of clerical education resulting
from poverty in the western Church and the consequent
obligations upon clerics to support themselves. A second
letter from Agatho to Constantine IV, inspired by the
Tome of LEO I, combined clear teaching with a firm proclamation of Roman infallibility. He likewise praised Constantine's toleration of Monothelites. Agatho upheld
Bishop WILFRID OF YORK's appeal to Rome against his
metropolitan's unexpected division of Wilfrid's diocese,
sent the archcantor John to introduce the Roman liturgy
into England, secured the remission of an imperial tax on
newly elected popes, and regularized the See of RAVEN-
NA.

Feast: Jan. 10.

Bibliography: *Liber pontificalis*, ed. L. DUCHESNE (Paris
1886–1958) 1:350–358. P. JAFFÉ, *Regesta pontificum romanorum
ab condita ecclesia ad annum post Christum natum 1198* (Graz
1956) 1:238–240; 2: 699, 741. C. J. VON HEFELE, *Histoire des conciles d'près les documents originaux* (Paris 1907–38) 3.1:475–484.
J. P. KIRSCH, *Dictionnaire d'histoire det de géographie eccléastiques* (Paris 1912–) 1:916–918. H. K. MANN, *The Lives of the Popes
in the Early Middle Ages from 590 to 1304* (London 1902–32)
1.2:23–48. J. HALLER, *Das Papsttum* (Stuttgart 1950–53)
1:332–339; 545. S. BROCK, *Syriac Perspectives on Late Antiquity*
(London 1984). H. CHADWICK, "Theodore of Tarsus and Monotheism" in *Logos. Festschrift für Luise Abtramowski zum 8. Juli 1993*
(Berlin/New York 1993) 534–44. A. CHAVASSE, "Le sanctoral et
le temporal grégoriens, vers 680. Distribution et origine des pièces
utilisées," *Ecclesia: orans* 3 (Rome 1986) 263–88. M. GIBBS, "The
Decrees of Agatho and the Gregorian Plan for York" *Speculum* 48
(Cambrige, MA 1973) 213–46. C. O'DONNELL, *Ecclesia: A Theo-
logical Encyclopedia of the Church* (Collegeville MN 1996). I. G.
ROSESCU, "Principes et dispositions d'organisation et de discipline
dans les canons du VIᵉ Concile oecuménique [roumain]," *Studii
Theologica Varsaviensia* (Warsaw 1983) 64–78. G. SCHWAIGER,
Lexikon fü Theologie und Kirche, 3d. ed. (1993). J. N. D. KELLY, *Ox-
ford Dictionary of Popes* (New York 1986) 77–78.

[C. M. AHERNE]

AGE (CANON LAW)

Age is one of the elements, along with mental condition, residence, legal relationship, and rite, which qualify
the status of a "person." It is the intent of the Roman
Catholic Church in its 1983 Code of Canon Law to harmonize the provisions of ecclesiastical law with those of
civil law regarding age.

The 1983 code considers an "adult" to be anyone
who has completed 18 years of age (c. 97.§1). Those who
*have completed seven years of age until their eighteenth
year of age are considered to be "minors."* An "infant"
is one who has not yet completed seven years of age (c.
97.§2). This same canon of the code decrees that a
"minor" is presumed to have the use of reason, while an
"infant" is not responsible for his or her actions.

Provisions concerning age appear frequently in the
code. These provisions are governed by the principle that
the more difficult the office or state of a person, the greater the maturity that is required. For example, a bishop
must be 35 years of age (c. 378.§1,3) as must the diocesan
administrator (c. 425.§1). However, the vicar general of
a diocese (c. 478.§1) and the judicial vicar (c. 1420.§4)
need be only 30 years of age. A priest may be ordained
at age 25 (c. 1031.§1), and a religious may make final
profession of vows at 21 (c. 658.§1).

The new code states the minimum age for reception
of the Sacrament of Confirmation, but grants to the conference of bishops the jurisdiction to determine the actual
age for reception of this sacrament (c. 891.§1). The 1983
code also gives the minimum age for *valid* marriage as
14 years for a woman and 16 years for a man (c.
1083.§1), but, again, permits the conference of bishops
to establish a higher age for the licit celebration of marriage (c. 1083.§2).

The law of abstinence binds those who have completed their fourteenth year until completion of their fifty-
ninth year, while the law of fasting now binds those who
are "adults" through their fifty-ninth year of age (c.
1252).

[G. CARIE]

AGE (IMPEDIMENT TO MARRIAGE)

In legislating for the minimum age at which her subjects are capable of a valid marriage, the Church declares
that males must have completed their 16th year and fe-
males their 14th year of age (*Codex iuris canonici* c. 1083
§1; CCEO c. 800). Nonage is, therefore, one of the diriment impediments to marriage in the Latin Church as
well as in the Eastern Churches; it has its origin in Roman
law that required puberty for *iustae nuptiae*. Natural law
imposes no such impediment of nonage; it requires only
that the parties be capable of marriage and have sufficient
psychological maturity to give matrimonial consent (cf.
Codex iuris canonici c. 1095; CCEO c. 818). Since the
impediment of nonage established in canon law is a merely ecclesiastical law, it binds only in marriages involving
those baptized into the Catholic Church or received into

it (*Codex iuris canonici* c. 11; CCEO c. 1490). The unbaptized are, however, bound by a reasonable and just impediment of nonage established by the competent civil authority. In addition, non-Catholic Eastern Christians are bound by an impediment of nonage in their own law (CCEO c. 780 §1, 2°). As a matter of ecclesiastical law, this impediment can be dispensed by a local ordinary if the occasion and sufficiently grave causes warrant it. In the Latin Church, conferences of bishops may establish a higher age for the licit celebration of marriage in their territories (*Codes iuris canonici* c. 1083 §2). While regulating the minimum age for a valid marriage, the Catholic Church establishes no age after which a marriage would be invalid.

Bibliography: J. C. O'DEA, "The Matrimonial Impediment of Nonage" *Catholic University of America Canon Law Studies* 205 (Washington 1944). J. ABBO and J. HANNAN, *The Sacred Canons* 2:1067. J. P. BEAL et al., *New Commentary on the Code of Canon Law* (New York 2000) 1283–1284.

[J. D. MCGUIRE]

AGENNĒTOS

In the early formative period of Christian doctrine prior to NICAEA I (325) ἀγέννητος was a Greek adjective employed to signify the self-existence or uncreatureliness of the Godhead. And ἀγέννητος (spelled with two ν's) was indeed a term used in the philosophy of the day to designate God's self-existence. Etymologically, however, the adjective with the two ν's would not have meant self-existence or uncreatureliness—as ἀγένητος (spelled with one ν)—but ungenerateness.

Now if, regardless of etymology, the sense is to be uncreated, ἀγέννητος must be said of both Father and Son. But if, on the other hand, etymology is restored and the sense is ungenerated, then ἀγέννητος can be said only of the Father. For obviously, the Son, precisely as Son, is generated from the Father. ARIANISM, however, almost systematically blurred this difference: first, by using the term in the etymological sense of ungenerated; but then, by taking ungenerated to mean the same thing as uncreated. But the Son was generated, not ungenerated; hence, the Son was a creature.

In its rejection of Arianism, the NICENE CREED clarified the problem (H. Denzinger, *Enchiridion symbolorum* 125–126). The Son is generated (γεννηθέντα); by implication, ἀγέννητος in this context can be said only of the Father. Yet, if the Son is "begotten," the Son is nevertheless "not made" (οὐποιηθέντα); again by implication, ἀγέννητος in this further context, that of creation, characterizes not only the Father but the entire Godhead as such.

See Also: ASEITY; GOD THE FATHER; PATERNITY, DIVINE; PROPERTIES, DIVINE PERSONAL; GENERATION; GENERATION OF THE WORD; LOGOS; GOD (SON); TRINITY, HOLY; TRINITY, HOLY, ARTICLES ON; WORD, THE.

Bibliography: M. SCHMAUS, *Lexikon für Theologie und Kirche*, 10 v. (2d, new ed. Freiburg 1957–65) 1:187–188. J. N. D. KELLY, *Early Christian Doctrines* (2d ed. New York 1960) 226–237. G. W. H. LAMPE, ed., *A Patristic Greek Lexicon* (New York 1961–).

[R. L. RICHARD]

AGENT

A transliteration of the scholastic Latin *agens*, in general having the same meaning as mover (*movens*), efficient cause, or simply cause. St. THOMAS AQUINAS regularly uses agent and efficient cause indiscriminately, often combining them as *causa agens* or *causa movens*. In dependence on Aristotle, he defines an agent as "that whereby a change or state of rest is first produced" (*a quo est principium motus vel quietis—In 2 phys.* 5.5). In this St. Thomas differs in no significant respect from the general scholastic tradition. At least the older scholastic tradition is also in agreement that agents in the physical order are denominated such from the effect produced by their action in the "patient," or recipient (*see* ACTION AND PASSION).

Other aspects of the scholastic notion of agent can be seen in the various assertions commonly accepted with respect to agents: "Every agent acts for an end." "Every agent acts insofar as it is in act, and according to its form." "An agent, precisely as such, is more noble than its patient or effect." "Every agent produces an effect similar to itself." "Agent and patient must exist together," and "every physical agent acts by contact" (*see* SCHOLASTIC TERMS AND AXIOMS).

The principal kinds of agent recognized by the scholastics include: (1) The perfecting (*perficiens*), counseling (*consilians*), and disposing agents—the last being subdivided into primary (*praeparans*) and secondary (*adjuvans*). (2) Equivocal (or analogical) and univocal agents, depending on whether or not the agent is on the same metaphysical level as the patient; this distinction is closely related to that between universal and particular agents and that between incorporeal and corporeal agents. (3) Principal or instrumental and primary or secondary (sometimes "first" and "second") agents. (4) Natural and nonnatural agents, the latter including many other types, such as violent, chance, artificial, and voluntary; a related distinction contains necessary, chance, and free agents. (5) Finally, agents that are causes of BEING or causes merely of BECOMING, according as the effect continues to depend on the cause after it is produced or not.

Intellectual agents are included in this list, especially under artificial and voluntary nonnatural agents, but the "agent intellect" (*intellectus agens*) is not. The latter is the intellectual faculty rendering abstract knowledge possible, and it is treated under INTELLECT.

See Also: CAUSALITY; EFFICIENT CAUSALITY.

Bibliography: R. J. DEFERRARI et al., *A Lexicon of St. Thomas Aquinas* (Washington 1948–53). L. SCHÜTZ, *Thomas-Lexikon* (New York 1957).

[P. R. DURBIN]

AGGRESSION

An act of hostility in which the individual clashes with some facet of reality (persons, things, himself) to reduce tension arising from frustration. This distinguishes aggression from aggressiveness, which aims at the completion of a task with energy, initiative, and determination. Aggressive behavior ordinarily fits the pattern of normal adjustment, while aggression veers toward maladjustment and abnormality. Aggression is direct if the attack is against the frustrating object; displaced, if against a neutral object. Sometimes it is directed inward, and the aggressor punishes himself or herself. When fear inhibits a frontal attack, displaced aggression occurs. The object of the displaced aggression must resemble the original and yet be dissimilar enough that the inhibitions against the act of aggression are overcome.

Some signs of aggression are fighting, bullying, teasing, swearing, carrying of grudges, and ridiculing. They range from self-assertiveness and dominance to revenge and brutality. Some internal determinants of aggression are feelings of guilt, inadequacy, and inferiority; some external are lack of discipline and self-control, rejection, overprotection, and frustrating home or school situations. To the extent that aggression is disruptive of social, psychological, or moral life, it is maladjustive and abnormal.

Bibliography: A. A. SCHNEIDERS, *The Anarchy of Feeling* (New York 1963) 65–79; *Personal Adjustment and Mental Health* (New York 1955) 329–363. N. R. F. MAIER, *Frustration: A Study of Behavior without a Goal* (New York 1949). J. DOLLARD et al., *Frustration and Aggression* (New Haven 1939). L. J. SAUL, *The Hostile Mind: The Sources and Consequences of Rage and Hate* (New York 1956).

[E. J. RYAN]

AGIL, ST.

Missionary and abbot; b. Franche-Comté, *c.* 580; d. Abbey of Rebais near Meaux, France, *c.* 650. At the age of about seven, Agil (also called Aile, Ail, Aisle, Ayeul, Ely) was received at the abbey of Luxeuil by COLUMBAN and trained there in the religious life by EUSTACE OF LUXEUIL. He probably followed Columban into exile in 610, returning to Luxeuil with Eustace, and after his ordination as a priest accompanying Eustace on a missionary journey to Bavaria *c.* 617. When elected bishop of Langres in 628, Agil refused the dignity. OUEN OF ROUEN chose him to be the first abbot of his new foundation at Rebais, and Agil was consecrated in the presence of Dagobert I at Clichy in 636, when the king also granted the abbey a charter of immunity (*Monumenta Germaniae Historica: Diplomata* 1:16). Agil died at the age of 66 and was buried in St. Peter's church at Rebais. There are two biographies of the saint, one from the late seventh century and the other a composite of the eleventh and twelfth centuries.

Feast: Aug. 30.

Bibliography: J. MABILLON, *Acta sanctorum ordinis S. Benedictii* (Venice 1733–40) 2:301–320. *Acta Sanctorum* Aug. 6:574–597. *Bibliotheca hagiographia latina antiquae et mediae aetatis* (Brussels 1898–1901) 148–149. E. VACANDARD, *Vie de saint Ouen, évêque de Rouen* (Paris 1902) 61–69, 169. P. FOURNIER, *Dictionnaire d'histoire et de géographie ecclésiastiques*, ed. A. BAUDRILLART et al. (Paris 1912) 1:957–958. A. M. ZIMMERMANN, *Kalendarium Benedictinum* (Metten 1933–38) 2:634. R. AIGRAIN, *Catholicisme* 1:245–246.

[B. J. COMASKEY]

AGILITY

That quality or endowment in virtue of which the risen body of the just "will be freed from the heaviness that now presses it down and will take on a capability of moving with the utmost ease and swiftness wherever the soul pleases" (*Catechism of the Council of Trent* 1.12.13). According to St. Paul, in the resurrection of the just "what is sown in weakness rises in power" (1 Cor 15.43). In these words Catholic theologians have seen a reference to the agility of the risen GLORIFIED BODY.

St. Thomas explains why this quality is postulated and what its nature is: "The soul which will enjoy the divine vision, united to its ultimate end, will in all matters experience the fulfillment of desire. And since it is out of the soul's desire that the body is moved, the consequence will be the body's utter obedience to the soul's slightest wish. Hence, the bodies of the blessed when they rise are going to have agility. . . . For weakness is what we experience in a body found wanting in the strength to satisfy the desire of the soul in the movements and actions which the soul commands, and this weakness will be entirely taken away then, when power overflows into the body from a soul united to God'' (*C. gent.* 4.86).

Traditional scholastic authorities are in substantial agreement with St. Thomas concerning the nature of this mysterious quality; its future existence, they maintain, is implicitly contained in the revealed fact of the glorious resurrection at the world's end. Agility therefore will be present in the complete and definitive transformation of the body of man's lowliness, which ''our Lord Jesus Christ . . . will refashion . . . conforming it to the body of his glory by exercising the power by which he is able to subject all things to himself'' (Phil 3.21).

See Also: RESURRECTION OF THE DEAD.

Bibliography: A. CHOLLET, *Dictionnaire de théologie catholique* 3.2:1879–1906. J. F. SAGÜES, *Sacre Theologiae summa: Biblioteca de autores cristianos* 4.6:295–309. M. A. GENEVOIS, *Entre dans la joie* (Paris 1960).

[C. J. CORCORAN]

AGILULF OF COLOGNE, ST.

Bishop; d. 750 or 751. He became bishop of Cologne after 745–746, supported the reforms of St. Boniface, and attended the Frankish Synod in 747. The cult of St. Agilulf (Agilulph) did not flourish until after July 9, 1062, when Archbishop ANNO II of Cologne translated the relics of St. Agilulf from the Abbey of Malmédy to St. Maria ad Gradus in Cologne, where they remained until their removal to the cathedral in 1846. According to the *Passio sancti Agilolfi,* composed probably before 1062, this Agilulf was a simple monk, martyred by the Neustrians at Amblève (Amel) on March 31, 716. Later sources wrongly identified him with Bishop Agilulf. Thus, *c.* 1160, Dietrich of Deutz added the title ''martyr'' to the entry *Agilolfus episcopus* in the list of bishops of Cologne. According to another account, the *Miracula sancti Quirini,* written at Malmédy late in the eleventh century, Agilulf was a Benedictine monk at the Abbey of Stavelot under Abbot Anglinus, whom he succeeded, apparently in 745, remaining abbot even after he became bishop of Cologne. This, too, is plainly inaccurate, since Anglinus was certainly abbot as late as 751.

Feast: July 9.

Bibliography: W. NEUSS, ed., *Geschichte des Erzbistums Köln,* v.1. *Das Bistum Köln von den Anfängen bis zum Ende des 12. Jahrhunderts* (Cologne 1964) 134–135. W. LEVISON, ''Bischof Agilolf von Köln und seine *Passio,*'' *Annalen des hist. Vereins für den Niederrhein* 115 (1929) 76–97; repr. in W. LEVISON, *Aus rheinischer und fränkischer Frühzeit. Ausgewählte Aufsätze* (Düs-

seldorf 1948) 76–95. A. STEFFENS, *Der heilige Agilolfus* (Cologne 1893). *Monumenta Germaniae Historica: Scriptores* (Berlin 1826–) 11:438–439, 482; 13:293. *Acta Sanctorum* July 2:714–726.

[M. F. MCCARTHY]

AGNELLI, GIUSEPPE

Jesuit writer of catechetical and devotional works; b. Naples, April 1, 1621; d. Rome, Sept. 8, 1706. Agnelli entered the Society of Jesus in 1637. For a time he was professor of moral theology, and was later rector of the colleges of Montepulciano, Macerata, and Ancona, where he was also consultor of the Inquisition of the March of Ancona. He spent the last 33 years of his life in the professed house in Rome. His chief writing was *Il Catechismo annuale* (Macerata 1657), or *Il Parrocchiano istruttore* (Rome 1677, Venice 1731), which was an adaptation for parish priests and contained an explanation of the Gospel for every Sunday in the year. In addition he wrote a week's devotion to St. Joseph for the Bona Mors Sodality, four commentaries on the *Exercises* of St. Ignatius, a collection of meditations for a triduum, a tenday retreat for Jesuits about to make profession, and a series of sermons for Advent and Lent.

Bibliography: T. J. CAMPBELL, *The Catholic Encyclopedia* 1:212. C. SOMMERVOGEL, et al., *Bibliothèque de la Compagnie de Jésus* 1:65–68.

[B. CAVANAUGH]

AGNELLUS OF PISA, BL.

First Franciscan superior in England; b. Pisa, *c.* 1194; d. Oxford, March 3, 1232. He was sent (*c.* 1217) by St. FRANCIS to France, where he became *custos* of Paris. As a deacon in 1224 he was appointed to introduce the FRANCISCANS into England, where he became the first minister provincial. At the urging of his superior, he became a priest (before 1229). He successfully defended the rights of his order against the claims of the bishops (1231). He propagated the order throughout much of England and is chiefly responsible for the reputation for science of the English Franciscans, since he obtained ROBERT GROSSETESTE as a teacher for the Franciscan house of studies in Oxford. Agnellus was declared blessed in 1892.

Feast: March 13 (Archdiocese of Birmingham, Eng.).

Bibliography: FR. GILBERT, *B. Agnellus and the English Grey friars* (London 1937). J. HARDING, *Agnellus of Pisa* (Canterbury 1979). THOMAS OF ECCLESTON, *De adventu Fratrum Minorum in Angliam,* ed. A. G. LITTLE (2d ed. Manchester, Eng. 1951). C. MARI-

Statue of St. Agnes, 14th century, Church of Notre Dame, Ecouis, France. (© Geoffrey Taunton; Cordaiy Photo Library Ltd./CORBIS)

OTTI, *Il b. Agnello da Pisa ed i Frati Minori in Inghilterra* (Rome 1895). L. HARDICK, ed., *Nach Deutschland und England* (Werl 1957) 115–214.

[L. HARDICK]

AGNES, ST.

Virgin and martyr of Rome. Little is known about this popular Roman saint who was martyred in the middle of the third or in the early fourth century. Her feast is recorded in the *Depositio martyrum* contained in the Chronograph of 354. She is mentioned by Ambrose (*De virginibus* 1.2; *De officiis* 1.41), in the Ambrosian hymn "Agnes beatae virginis," by Pope DAMASUS in a still extant epitaph, and by Prudentius (*Peristephanon* 14). According to Ambrose and Prudentius she was beheaded, according to Damasus, burned to death, and according to the *Agnes beatae virginis,* she was strangled. Despite this contradictory evidence, the sources agree in that she was young, only 12 or 13, when martyred. A fully developed legend of the sixth century describes her as a beautiful young girl with many rivals for her hand. When she rejected them, she was delated to the governor as a Christian and sent to a house of prostitution. Those who came to see her were struck with awe. One who looked lustfully at her lost his sight but regained it through her prayers. Brought before the judge, she was condemned and executed and buried on the Via Salaria, in a catacomb eventually named after her. Before 349 a basilica was built over her tomb by Constantina, daughter of Constantine. This was restored by Pope SYMMACHUS (498–514) and completely rebuilt by HONORIUS I (625–638). In the fourth century, Agnes was represented as an orant with arms outstretched in prayer. From the sixth century on she was portrayed as a young girl with a lamb in her arms or at her feet. Before the ninth century her head was removed from her tomb to the *Sancta Sanctorum* of the Lateran palace. When this was examined on April 19, 1903, it was seen to be that of a girl about 12 years old. Pius X gave the relic to the church of St. Agnes *in Agone* on the Piazza Navona in Rome.

Feast: Jan. 21.

Bibliography: L. ANDRÉ-DELASTRE, *Saint Agnes*, tr. R. SHEED (New York 1962). F. P. KEYES, *Three Ways of Love* (New York 1963). E. JOSI, *Bibliotheca Sanctorum* (Rome 1961) 1:382–407. A. BUTLER, *The Lives of the Saints*, ed. H. THURSTON and D. ATTWATER (New York 1956) 1:133–137.

[M. J. COSTELLOE]

AGNES OF ASSISI, ST.

Poor Clare abbess; b. Assisi, 1197; d. Assisi, Aug. 27, 1253. Sixteen days after her older sister, CLARE OF ASSISI, fled from home to follow (St.) FRANCIS OF ASSISI, Agnes joined her, first at San Angelo di Panzo, where she heroically withstood family opposition, and then at San Damiano. When the Benedictines of Monticelli asked to become POOR CLARES, Francis sent Agnes to them as abbess (1219 or 1221). After returning to San Damiano in 1253, she witnessed the death of Clare and died soon after. She is said to have had a vision of the Christ Child, which her iconography sometimes depicts. Benedict XIV approved her cult in 1753. She is buried in S. Chiara, Assisi.

Feast: Nov. 16.

Bibliography: "Vita . . . ," *Analecta Franciscana* 3 (1897) 173–182. THOMAS OF CELANO, *Legenda Sanctae Clarae virginis,* ed. F. PENNACCHI (Assisi 1910). L. WADDING, *Scriptores Ordinis Minorum* 1:141–142; 2:18–19; 3:350–351. *Vita di. s. Agnese di Assisi, compilata da una suora Clarissa* (Lecce 1913). A. BUTLER, *The*

Lives of the Saints, rev. ed. H. THURSTON and D. ATTWATER (New York 1956) 4:358–359. *Leben und Schriften der heiligen Klara von Assisi*, ed. E. GRAU (2d ed. Werl 1953), legend ascribed to Thomas of Celano; Eng. tr. I. BRADY and M. F. LAUGHLIN (St. Bonaventure, N.Y. 1953) 35–37. C. GENNARO, "Clare, Agnes, and Their Earliest Followers: From the Poor Ladies of San Damiano to the Poor Clares," in D. BORNSTEIN and R. RUSCONI, eds., *Women and Religion in Medieval and Renaissance Italy* (Chicago, 1996) 39–55. M. CARNEY, *The First Franciscan Woman: Clare of Assisi & Her Form of Life.* (Quincy, IL 1993). E. PETROFF, "A Medieval Woman's Utopian Vision: The Rule of St. Clare of Assisi," in *Body and Soul: Essays on Medieval Women and Mysticism* (New York 1994) 66–82. P. RANFT, "An Overturned Victory: Clare of Assisi and the Thirteenth-century Church," in *Journal of Medieval History* 17 (1991), 123–134. R. ARMSTRONG, *Clare of Assisi: Early Documents* (St. Bonaventure, N.Y. 1993).

[M. F. LAUGHLIN]

AGNES OF BOHEMIA, ST.

Also known as Agnes of Prague; princess; Poor Clare abbess; b. Prague, Bohemia, *c.* 1200–1205?; d. Prague, Bohemia, March 2, 1281 or 1282; canonized by Pope John Paul II, Nov. 12, 1989.

Agnes, daughter of Ottokar I, King of Bohemia, and Constance of Hungary, the sister of King Andreas II of Hungary, received her early education from the Cistercian nuns of Trebnitz. This cousin of St. Elizabeth of Hungary (1207–1231) was betrothed at the age of three to Boleslaus, son of Duke Henry of Silesia. Later she appealed to Pope Gregory IX, and he intervened on her behalf to allow her to consecrate herself to virginity.

Agnes established two hospitals for the poor, and she persuaded members of the Military Order of Crusaders of the Red Star (Bethlehemites) to staff them. In 1232, Agnes accomplished the building of a Franciscan friary and the Poor Clare convent of Saint Savior in Prague. Saint Clare sent her five nuns from Assisi to help establish the convent, where Agnes received the veil in 1234 or 1236 and was later elected abbess. Four letters from St. Clare addressed to Agnes are extant.

Agnes is known for her humility and loving service to others. She enjoyed cooking for the sisters and mending the clothes of lepers. She is said to have been gifted with the working of miracles and prescience. She predicted the victory of her brother Wenceslaus over the Duke of Austria. Before her peaceful death, Agnes obtained permission to give up all revenues and property held in common.

Agnes was buried near her convent. About 1322, her body was exhumed and transferred to a special coffin that was lost during the Hussite uprising.

Feast: March 2 (Franciscans).

Bibliography: I. BRADY, ed., *The Legend and Writings of St Clare of Assisi* (New York 1953), 9–10, 88–98, 157–159. M. FASSBINDER, *Die selige Agnes von Prag, eine königliche Klarissin* (Werl 1957). T. JOHNSON, "To Her Who Is Half of Her Soul: Clare of Assisi and the Medieval Epistolary Tradition [Analysis of Clare's Letters to Agnes of Prague]," *Magistra: A Journal of Women's Spirituality in History* 2, no. 1 (Summer 1996): 24–50. J. NEMEC, *Agnese Di Boemia: La Vita, Il Culto, La Legenda* (Milan 1987). W. W. SETON, *Some New Sources for the Life of Bl. Agnes of Bohemia* (Aberdeen, Scotland 1915; New York 1966).

[K. I. RABENSTEIN]

AGNES OF MONTEPULCIANO, ST.

Dominican nun, patroness of Montepulciano; b. Agnes Segni, Gracciano-Vecchio, Tuscany, *c.* 1268; d. Montepulciano, Italy, April 4, 1317. At the age of nine she induced her parents to let her join a community at Montepulciano called "Sisters of the Sack" because of their coarse garments. Her holiness and intelligence impressed the nuns, and she was made bursar when only 14. A year later she accompanied an older nun to Proceno to found a new convent. She was soon elected abbess. In her new position she increased her austerities, fasting on bread and water, and sleeping on the ground. The citizens of Montepulciano, desiring her return, offered to build a convent in a place formerly occupied by a house of ill fame. Agnes became prioress there (1306) and placed the convent under Dominican patronage. She was a competent administrator, often providing miraculously for the needs of her sisters.

Simplicity and ardor were the keynotes of her spirituality. Her vita reports that she was favored by apparitions of the Blessed Virgin, the Christ Child, and the angels, and that showers of white, cross-shaped particles "like manna" fell upon her and the places where she prayed. She died after a painful illness. As patroness of Montepulciano, she is represented with a model of the city in her hands; in Italian art she is associated with CATHERINE OF SIENA and ROSE OF LIMA. She was canonized by Benedict XIII in 1726.

Feast: April 20.

Bibliography: RAYMOND OF CAPUA, *Vita, Acta Sanctorum* April 2:790–810. *Année Dominicaine*, 23 v. (Lyons 1883–1909) April 2: 519–546. A. WALZ, *Die hl. Agnes v. Montepulciano* (Dülmen 1922). A. BUTLER, *The Lives of the Saints*, ed. H. THURSTON and D. ATTWATER (New York 1956) 2:135–137. G. DI AGRESTI and D. VALORI, *Bibliotheca sanctorum* (Rome 1961) 1:375–381.

[M. J. FINNEGAN]

AGNES OF POITIERS, ST.

Abbess; d. *c.* 589. She was the adopted daughter of St. RADEGUNDA, the wife of Chlotar I, King of the Franks

(d. 561). In 550 Radegunda fled from her husband after he killed her brother. She found temporary refuge in several communities and finally founded the convent of the Holy Cross in Poitiers, which was consecrated by St. GERMAIN in 561. About 570 Radegunda and Agnes visited Arles to study the rule of St. CAESARIUS. Subsequently the rule was adopted at Poitiers, and Agnes became the first abbess, but she was replaced in 589 after a revolt by dissatisfied elements in the convent. Agnes is remembered for her connection with the poet Venantius Fortunatus, who was also a correspondent of her mother. Her relics are preserved in the church of St. Radegunda, and her tomb is a popular place of pilgrimage in the area.

Feast: May 13 (Diocese of Poitiers).

Bibliography: GREGORY OF TOURS, *Historia Francorum* 9.39–42 in *Monumenta Germaniae Historica: Scriptores rerum Merovingicarum* 1:393–404. F. G. HOLWECK, *A Biographical Dictionary of the Saints* (St. Louis 1924) 33. R. AIGRAIN, *Catholicisme* 1:216. A. MERCATI and A. PELZER, *Dizionario ecclesiastico* (Turin 1954–58) 1:56. P. DE MONSABERT, *Dictionnaire d'histoire et de géographie ecclésiastiques*, ed. A. BAUDRILLART et al. (Paris 1912) 1:973–974. G. ALLEMANG, *Lexicon für Theologie und Kirche*, ed. J. HOFER and K. RAHNER (Freiburg 1957–65) 1:199.

[J. F. FAHEY]

AGNOSTICISM

An attitude of mind toward man's knowledge of God; namely, that God is humanly unknowable. Etymologically, agnosticism (Gr. *agnostos*) means an unknowing, a profession of ignorance. Historically, the word ''agnostic'' was first used by T. H. Huxley in 1869. Having joined the Metaphysical Society, a society whose members professed knowledge on all kinds of mysteries, and wishing to show his opposition to such extravagant claims, Huxley adopted the name ''agnostic.'' Since his time, the term has been used to designate anyone who denies a knowledge of immaterial reality, and especially of the existence and nature of God.

Kinds of Agnosticism

An agnostic is not an atheist. An atheist denies the existence of God; an agnostic professes ignorance about His existence. For the latter, God may exist, but reason can neither prove nor disprove it. Agnostics have been divided into two groups: those who deny that reason can know God and make no judgment concerning that existence and those who deny that reason can prove it but nonetheless profess a belief in God's existence. A well-known contemporary instance of the first group is Bertrand RUSSELL; a famous example of the second is Immanuel KANT. With few exceptions, modern and contemporary agnostics belong to the second group.

Another division of agnosticism may be made in terms of the philosophical commitments that cause their adherents to deny the possibility of knowing God. These commitments are many and varied, but the principal ones in the history of thought may be enumerated as nominalism, empiricism, Kantianism, the theory of the unconditioned, logical positivism, and existentialism. The remainder of this article explains the philosophical grounds for agnostic attitudes within these schools and gives a critical evaluation of each.

NOMINALISM

WILLIAM OF OCKHAM, the father of philosophical NOMINALISM, denied that the human intellect could with certitude demonstrate the existence of One, Infinite God. For Ockham, universality or community is only a condition of thought and in no sense a truth about being. There is nothing in things that allows the mind to transcend from them to God.

Argument. The line of reasoning for Ockham and his followers is clear. Unless there resides in the beings of man's experience a RELATION that orders them to God, the mind cannot demonstrate the existence of God from the existence of these beings. For the nominalist no such relation exists. Relation bespeaks an order between two things. And since order must include the things ordered, it implies a pattern of inclusiveness, or universality. Universality, however, cannot be part of the structure of being, but only of the signification of words. Nominalism thus erases universality from being. Each individual is simply itself—a singular instance of existence. To put universality in things, argue the nominalists, is to confuse the order of being with the order of signification. Things may be really dependent on God, but the mind could know this only if it could intuit some relation between things and God. But because of the atomistic (nonuniversal) nature of the singular, this is impossible. The singular can reveal to the intellect no illative force, no moment of trancendence. Analysis of the singular never uncovers objective universality. Thus does nominalism block off any philosophical ascent to God by way of intellectual inference. The fruit of nominalism in natural theology is agnosticism (*see* OCKHAMISM; UNIVERSALS).

Evaluation. What the nominalists fail to recognize is that, while each being is indivisibly singular, the INTELLECT has the power to consider one aspect of the singular while leaving others out of consideration. Thus the intellect can attain universal notions, such as man, animal, substance and so forth. Universality is in the thing, in the sense that the perfection that is considered is in the thing; but *as* in the thing, the perfection is inseparable from the very singularity of the thing. Moreover, the order that results from received existence is an intelligible datum that can be grasped by the intellect, though not by the SENSES. Change, imperfection, limitation, composition—these are all intelligible facts about the things of man's experience that spell out for his intellect the contingent condition of their being. Contingency, and hence order and dependence, may be impervious to his senses, for they are not sensible facts; but they are open to his intellect, because they are facts of existence. Thus the intellect is not only justified but necessitated to make an inference from caused to Uncaused Being.

EMPIRICISM

The central teaching of EMPIRICISM is that all knowledge comes through experience. While such a truism need not lead to agnosticism, historically it did so, because of the empiricists' quarrel with rationalism.

Argument. RATIONALISM maintained that such terms as ''contingent'' and ''necessary'' were both true in what they defined and actually descriptive of the real world. For the empiricist this is impossible. Man experiences what happens in the world, not that it must so happen, that is, happen contingently or necessarily. ''Necessity,'' writes D. HUME, ''is something that exists in the mind, not in objects.'' And since man does not experience necessity, he cannot say that the causal proposition, ''every event has a cause,'' has been gained from experience. The necessity and universality found in the causal proposition is not grounded in objects, but in some condition of man's thinking about objects. Empiricism explains the origins of the causal proposition in terms of human habits of thought. Repeatedly experiencing B following A, one comes to anticipate B whenever he experiences A. But since he does not experience a connection between them, he cannot say that B *must* follow A.

This obviously means that the human mind can never reason with certitude to the existence of God. For this would be asserting a necessary connection between mundane events and a supramundane Being, a connection that falls outside human experience. To assert this connection is to commit the fallacy of rationalism; one inserts a necessity derived from his concepts into the world of events. As with nominalism, empiricism precludes a transcendence from effect to cause by rejecting for knowledge the objective value of the causal principle or of CAUSALITY.

Evaluation. The empiricists are guilty of a one-dimensional interpretation of human experience. As has been seen, imperfection, limitation, composition, relations, differences and so forth, are just as clearly facts about a thing as are its color, size, shape, motion, etc. While the former are not sense data, it would be arbitrary to argue that they are not facts of human experience. To

Robert Green Ingersoll (1833–1899), Illinois attorney general and agnostic lecturer. (©CORBIS)

limit experience to what is directly perceptible by the five senses is to eliminate a large part of experience and to go against experience itself. It is true that man does not sense causality, that he does not sense relations; but he does experience them, not with his senses but with his intellect. Sense experience is only one kind of experience. The activities one experiences among beings is attended by the intellectual INSIGHT that these beings are really related and hence are true causes and effects. The demonstration for the existence of God is grounded, above all, in an intellectual, rather than sensible, experience of reality (*see* EXPERIENCE).

KANTIANISM

Kant subscribed to the Humean critique of causality. Yet he viewed the construction of his critical philosophy as the proper synthesis of rationalism and empiricism. The importance of Kant in the history of agnosticism cannot be overstressed. In the minds of most non-Catholic thinkers, Kant's *Critique of Pure Reason* has given the *coup de grâce* to any possible proof for the existence of God.

Kant's criticism. In removing necessity from things themselves, Hume seemed to be destroying the objective value of the necessary truths of the physical sciences, mathematics, and metaphysics. To justify the necessity and universality of such truths (at least for science and mathematics), Kant proposed his theory of the synthetic a priori judgment. A judgment is synthetic, rather than analytic, when its content refers to empirical reality; and it is a priori when it involves elements not drawn from that reality. ''Every event has a cause,'' is an example of a synthetic a priori judgment. It is a judgment that deals with events and hence refers to empirical reality; but it has elements not drawn from empirical reality, namely, universality (*every* event) and necessity (has a *cause*), and so is a priori. For as Hume had correctly pointed out, universality and necessity are not concepts drawn from the object (*see* CRITICISM, PHILOSOPHICAL; KANTIANISM).

The important fact about such a judgment is that, though not drawn completely from empirical reality, it is always applicable to it. This is so because the judgment ''every event has a cause'' expresses a condition for the very experiencing of events, at least in a unified way. In a word, a synthetic a priori judgment contains two elements: one formal, the work of the understanding; the other material, the product of experience. Since such judgments express the very conditions that make knowledge of the world possible, they have objective validity whenever applied to this world. The way man knows empirical reality, and must know it, is as objective as the thing known. It now remains to be seen how this view of knowledge leads of necessity to agnosticism.

Argument. In order to be perceived, a thing must be experienced here and now. The here and now, or space and time, are not intrinsic properties of the thing, but necessary conditions for perceiving the thing. In like manner, cause, substance, and relation are not intrinsic properties of the thing, but necessary conditions for understanding it. And only those things that can be perceived in space and time can be understood. But God is a reality that is entirely outside space and time and so there are no conditions that could make any knowledge of Him possible. There is no way for the intellect of man to have an objective knowledge of God.

But obviously, says Kant, man can form an idea of God. The mind forms such an idea whenever it seeks for the cause of causes, for the ultimate unifying principle of all beings and of all thought. But God as a unifying principle is merely an idea, that is to say, a concept formed by the transcendental activity of human reason with no guarantee of an objective correlate outside the reason. To form an idea of God, then, is in no way to prove that there is a God. For as not subject to the conditions of space and time, God is not perceivable; and as unperceivable through sensibility, He must remain forever unknowable to understanding.

If all Kant were saying is that God in His own Being is in no way subject to the senses or intellect of man, so that one can never have any direct natural knowledge of Him, he would be no more agnostic than the most orthodox Catholic philosopher. His agnosticism consists in his absolute refusal to give to the understanding of man even an indirect knowledge of God. God cannot be known either in Himself (which all admit) or through creatures. The objective reality of God can never in any sense become a term for human understanding. Since God is outside all the conditions for human understanding, no category of the mind can be applied to Him. Thus the category of cause cannot be applied to Him. The application of causality is valid among the beings of empirical reality (PHENOMENA), but not among those of transempirical reality (NOUMENA). God's existence cannot be inferred or concluded to; for the reason in passing from phenomenal reality to noumenal steps outside the conditions of human understanding. Hence this transition results in no objective knowledge of reality, but only in empty concepts.

It is true that Kant, on moral grounds, saw the necessity for postulating a belief in God (or in the idea of God), but since such a postulate has no cognitive content and does not guarantee the actual existence of God, this aspect of Kant's critical philosophy in no way mitigates his agnosticism.

Evaluation. An analysis of Kant's epistemology makes it clear that he equated BEING with ''being-sensible.'' If an absolute condition for knowing anything is that it be *first* perceived in human sensibility, then, of course, only sensibles are knowable. This would mean that all other facts in man's knowledge of being, for example, its distinction from other beings, its limitations, its composition, and so forth, belong not to the thing but only to the way man knows the thing. He could not predicate them about the thing itself, but only about the thing as in his knowledge. He could not say ''man *is* limited,'' but only ''man must be *known* as limited.'' In the view of Kant, one cannot say that limitation, imperfection, and composition (all the facts of being that lead one to God) are facts about being independent of the knowing process. And this is to equate being with ''being-sensible.'' Admittedly, to grasp these facts (including the fact of existence itself) an intellect is needed; the senses are not enough. But to say that therefore they are the product of the intellect, they are due *merely* to the way the intellect knows, is a false conclusion. The way the eye sees color or the ear hears sound is certainly not the way color or sound is present in objects; but no one denies that there is in the object, the proper and sensible correlate of color and sound. So, too, with the intelligible elements of being. They will yield their presence only to an intellect, and in an intellectual way. But they are as much facts about a being as are its sensible facts. To deny this is to deny the very existence of things, for existence is not a sensible fact.

THEORY OF THE UNCONDITIONED

Under the influence of Kant, agnosticism began to assume the form of a philosophical theory, the theory of the unconditioned. The two names most commonly associated with this theory are Sir WILLIAM HAMILTON and Herbert SPENCER. The former develops it in his main work, *Philosophy of the Unconditioned* (Edinburgh 1829), and Spencer devotes the first 100 pages of his *First Principles* (London 1862) to "The Unknowable." While neither man is read much in the mid-20th century, their influence during their lifetime was considerable, and their views on man's knowledge of God have become accepted teaching.

Argument. The theory of the unconditioned is in its essentials, Kantian, and briefly it comes to this. To think of an object is to condition it, either by putting it into some class, as when one says "God is a substance," or by relating it to some other object, as when one says "God is a cause." Since all knowledge goes from the known to the unknown, every object must be known in terms of something else. An object that cannot be conditioned by either classification or relation is unknowable. For, to know, is to condition. But God, as Infinite and Absolute Being, transcends every condition. Thus God is unknowable and is the very negation of thought. To classify the infinite is to make it finite; and to relate the absolute is to make it relative. To say, therefore, that God is a substance, or a cause, or a being, are so many meaningless statements. There is only one meaningful statement that can be made about the unknowable—it cannot be known.

If this teaching simply meant that man can have no direct knowledge of God, in the sense that God in Himself can never be grasped as a term within man's knowledge, it would be acceptable. But it means more than this. For in an indirect knowledge of God through creatures, either God becomes a term of knowledge or not. If He does not, man does not know God, but only creatures; if He does, then He has been conditioned by a relation (cause), and so once more it is not God man is thinking about but only some subjective notion he calls God.

Evaluation. How does one break through the dilemma presented by this theory? By a close look at the act of existing of a finite being and a closer look at what it means to know. The very CONTINGENCY of an imperfect act of existing demands that it has grounds for existing that are outside itself. Its EXISTENCE is received existence. Contingent existence is a contradiction in terms

unless it has its source in Necessary Existence. But can man know this Necessary Being? He cannot know it in itself, but he can know that there must be such a Being. In affirming the necessity of such a Being, what terminates his knowledge is not the being of God but the truth of the proposition "There must be a God." Thus the being of God is left unconditioned, but man's knowledge has been conditioned and determined to a *truth* about God, namely, that He exists. Moreover, this is a truth about an actually existing being (and not an empty concept), for man's knowledge has been determined by actually existing beings precisely as caused by God. And in this sense one can say that God is the indirect object, and the object that logically terminates one's thinking, for it is through His being that the things that determine one to know Him exist. The error of the theory of the unconditioned is that it equates conditioning in knowledge with conditioning in being. Man can know God through creatures without affecting God's being. In fact, though this is not the present concern, even a direct vision of God such as the angels and saints have in heaven, leaves the divine being completely unconditioned, unaffected; for the whole act of knowledge as such is in, and hence affects, the knower. Conditions concern the way one knows, not what one knows. The agnostics fail to make this important distinction.

LOGICAL POSITIVISM

A fashionable form of contemporary agnosticism, especially in the United States and Britain, is LOGICAL POSITIVISM. This school, whose methodology is linguistic analysis and whose theory of knowledge is empiricism, teaches that a proposition is true if its language elements are reducible to, or verifiable in terms of, some direct or indirect sense experience. Propositions that make no claim to describe reality, such as those of logic and mathematics, are true if consistent with themselves. Factual propositions belong to the empirical sciences and formal propositions to the logical and mathematical sciences. Both sets of propositions can be either true or false and both have their proper meaning; for they can be seen as either reducible to sense experience, as in the case of factual propositions, or as self-consistent, as with formal propositions.

Argument. Statements about God are neither factual nor formal. Since the subject of such propositions falls outside both direct and indirect sense experience, the elements of such propositions are not verifiable in terms of any knowable experience. They can be shown to be neither true nor false. Thus they are empty of all meaning; they are meaningless, "nonsensical" bits of language. Nor are they formally true, since they claim to bear upon a real object. If no such claim were made, the logical positivists would grant that statements about God would have formal (not factual) truth. For they could be viewed as instances of a consistent use of language or a possible way that ideas could be related.

Evaluation. As is clear, the agnosticism espoused by the logical positivists is simply a restatement, in terms of the analysis of language, of the basic positions of Hume on the origin of knowledge and of Kant on the noncognitive value of "transcendental ideas" (*see* VERIFICATION).

EXISTENTIALISM

The most important philosophical movement of the mid-20th century is undoubtedly EXISTENTIALISM. Briefly, this doctrine teaches that the only essence the individual man has is that which he freely creates for himself through the decisive realization of his human possibilities. Man in his existence is free tendency. He makes himself what he is. To say that he possesses a stable and determined essence is to rob him of his freedom and to make his being a fixed and formalized unfolding of a predetermined pattern. Moreover, as a continual flux of existential tendencies, man cannot grasp himself through any conceptual knowledge; for a concept immobilizes and so falsifies, reality. Man's being, rather, is grasped by an encounter of experience with himself and others, and not by an insight into intelligible patterns, for there are none.

Argument. Existentialism is agnostic for several reasons. First, it refuses to man any rational or conceptual understanding of God. Second, even when some awareness of a ground of Being is suggested, one can never identify this ground with God. For these objects of "transcendence" (the All-Embracing in K. Jaspers, Being Itself in M. Heidegger, Nothingness in J. P. Sartre) are described in terms philosophically incompatible with a personal and genuinely transcendent God. Furthermore, one can never be sure, because of the type of awareness involved in PHENOMENOLOGY, that these objects are not the product of one's own CONSCIOUSNESS. Third, existentialism is agnostic because in the horizontal movement of phenomenological awareness one never attains a moment of seen inference to a source of being. The roots of intelligibility having been removed from being, nothing remains in the flux of existential moments by which man can grasp a relationship to a Being that transcends the flux. In spite of their great concern for the freedom and openness of the human spirit, existentialists are still the victims of Humean empiricism; but now it is an inverted empiricism, the empiricism of consciousness.

Evaluation. The error of the existentialists is twofold. First, they fail to recognize that a FINITE BEING without an ESSENCE is a contradiction. For finite existence is always the existence of something, and this from its very beginning. Man without an intrinsic limit or essence would be an act of infinite existence. The second error is their failure to recognize that unless human FREEDOM is grounded in intelligence and dependent upon it, man cannot know the possibilities among which he *can* choose. Finally, these possibilities of man are really surreptitiously reintroduced essences; for an essence is a POTENCY that can be realized (made actual) through existence. There are many excellent and profound things in existentialism. But the suppression of the human essence and the apotheosis of freedom are not among them.

CONCLUSION

An interesting phenomenon attends the writings of an agnostic. He describes the Unknown God in the same terms as the theist: infinite, absolute, necessary, transcendent, and so forth. The impression is given that the agnostic knows no less about God than the theist and the theist no more than the agnostic. If God is unknowable, why does the agnostic know so much about Him? The touchstone of an agnostic is not what he says about God, but what he intends these statements to mean. The all-important difference is this: the theist claims his statements about God legitimately bear upon an existing object and give him true and valid knowledge of this object. The agnostic denies that his statements about God have any of these characteristics. They are not statements about an existing object at all, but only about an idea wholly constructed by his mind.

See Also: GOD 2; GOD, PROOFS FOR THE EXISTENCE OF; GOD IN PHILOSOPHY; ATHEISM; DEISM; HUMANISM, SECULAR; NATURALISM; THEISM; THEOLOGY, NATURAL.

Bibliography: *Encyclopedia of Religion and Ethics,* ed. J. HASTINGS, 13 v. (Edinburgh 1908–27) 1:214–220. R. FLINT, *Agnosticism* (London 1903). J. WARD, *Naturalism and Agnosticism,* 2 v. (New York 1899). J. D. COLLINS, *God in Modern Philosophy* (Chicago 1959). H. DE LUBAC, *The Drama of Atheist Humanism,* tr. E. M. RILEY (New York 1949). R. JOLIVET, *The God of Reason,* tr. M. PONTIFEX (New York 1958). *New Essays in Philosophical Theology,* eds. A. G. N. FLEW and A. MACINTYRE, (New York 1955). A. E. TAYLOR, *Does God Exist?* (New York 1947). E. S. BRIGHTMAN, *The Problem of God* (New York 1930). A. C. COCHRANE, *The Existentialists and God* (Philadelphia 1956). F. E. ENGLAND, *Kant's Conception of God* (New York 1930). T. H. L. PARKER, *The Doctrine of the Knowledge of God* (London 1952). F. R. TENNANT, *Philosophical Theology,* 2 v. (New York 1928–30). C. C. J. WEBB, *Studies in the History of Natural Theology* (Oxford 1915).

[M. R. HOLLOWAY]

AGNUS DEI

In the Roman Catholic Eucharist, the Agnus Dei ("Lamb of God") is sung during the fraction rite when the consecrated bread is broken and the wine poured. According to the *Liber pontificalis* (ed. L. Duchesne, 1:376) it was Pope Sergius I (687–701) who first ordered that during the fraction rite, the clergy and people should sing ''Lamb of God [Agnus Dei], who take away the sins of the world, have mercy on us.'' (In the Ambrosian Rite a variable *confractorium* is chanted at this point in the liturgy). According to J. Froger, it is possible that Pope Sergius did nothing more than replace a variable chant in the earlier Roman liturgy with this fixed formula. M. Righetti (*Manuale di storia liturgica*, 3:444 and n.81), on the other hand, insists that the variable texts for the Fraction contained in many early Roman documents are of a later Gallican origin (*see* GALLICAN RITES). Thus, up to the time of Pope Sergius the Roman rite Fraction would have been carried out in silence. The *Capitulare* (ed. Silva-Tarouca, 200), which dates from a few years after the prescriptions of Pope Sergius, states that the Agnus Dei was to be sung by the entire assembly. Soon afterward, however, the *Ordo Romanus* I (ed. M. Andrieu, *Les Ordines Romani* 2:101) and the *Ordo of St. Armand* (ed. M. Andrieu, 2:165) directed that the clergy or the SCHOLA CANTORUM (also composed of clerics) were to sing the Agnus Dei. It seems, therefore, that by the second half of the eighth century it was a chant reserved to the clerics.

The phrase ''qui tollis peccata mundi, miserere nobis'' is found also in the Gloria; both texts, however, are based on the testimonial of John the Baptist (Jn 1.29) with two grammatical changes. The vocative form ''agnus'' is treated as indeclinable because of a sense of reverence for religious terms. The plural ''peccata'' is substituted for the Biblical ''peccatum.'' The phrase ''dona nobis pacem'' does not occur in any of the ancient texts. The petition ''miserere nobis'' was always the same, and the entire invocation was repeated as often as needed until the fraction was finished.

When multiple fractions disappeared in the ninth century, the petitions were gradually reduced to the hallowed number three. According to classic Roman usage, only one all-inclusive petition, ''miserere nobis,'' was added to the invocation. Around the tenth and eleventh centuries the petition ''dona nobis pacem'' was substituted as the third and final response. The first occasion for this substitution was most probably the transfer of the Agnus Dei to accompany the Kiss of Peace (see Rabanus Maurus, *De inst. cler.* 1:33; *Patrologia Latina*, ed. J. P. Migne, 107:324). As early as the eleventh century the words ''dona eis requiem'' were found in REQUIEM MASSES, while the third petition closed with ''requiem sempiternam.''

The oldest melody for the Agnus Dei (Mass 18 in the *Graduale romanum*) is identical to that given for the

Page from the 14th-century Graduale of the monastery of Saint-Corneille at Compiègne, France (MS lat. 16823, fol. 222v). Two tropes for the ''Agnus Dei'' can be seen in the right-hand column.

same text in the Litany of the Saints. The only change is the addition of a note on the accent of ''nobis'' in the Mass melody. The ''Agnus Dei'' at the end of the litany is a self-sufficient song, giving a festive climax to the litany. The dating (twelfth century) given in the *Graduale romanum* for the Agnus Dei of Mass 18 is very misleading, since it refers to the earliest MS in which this melody is found; whereas the melody is actually of a much earlier origin. According to A. Gastoué (*Le Graduel et l'antiphonaire* 278), it is related to ancient Byzantine psalmody. The Agnus Dei in the Mass of the Dead is an adaptation of that of Mass 18. This melody is known as the *minor* in a twelfth-century Rheinau MS, to distinguish it from a more complex one (the *major*) in the same MS, destined to be sung by the *schola* on great feast days [M. Gerbert, *De cantu et musica sacra* (St. Blasien 1774) 1.1:457].

The simple Agnus melodies (Mass 18, Mass of the Dead, Mass 16) show a structural relation to the simple Sanctus melodies (Masses 15, 16, 18) by their use of recitative patterns. Just as these simple Sanctus melodies are an extension of the dialogue recitation of the Preface, so also the Agnus melodies are an extension of the dialogue recitation of the Pax Domini. Among the chant settings (*c.* 300) of the Ordinary, as B. Stäblein notes, the Agnus melodies are most often related to the Sanctus but very seldom to the Kyrie melodies (*Die Musik in Geschichte und Gegenwart*, ed. F. Blume, 1:150).

TROPES for the Agnus Dei began to appear as early as the tenth century. Eighty-six of these have been found, consisting mostly of three verses and, in great part, hexameters. One verse was inserted each time between the invocation and the petition. The following is an example (from MS BN lat. 16823, fol. 1.222v):

> Agnus Dei . . . Fons indeficiens pietatis—Miserere nobis. Agnus Dei . . . Actor summe bonus bonitatis—Miserere nobis. Agnus Dei . . . Pax eterna dator claritatis—Dona nobis pacem.

In the wake of the Vatican II liturgical reform, the *Agnus Dei* was restored to its original usage as an expandable litany to cover the entire fraction rite. Many vernacular musical settings in expandable litany form with variable invocations of the Lord's name have been introduced in different parts of the world.

Bibliography: J. FROGER, *Les Chants de la Messe aux VIIIe et Ixe siècles* (Tournai 1950). J. A. JUNGMANN, *The Mass of the Roman Rite,* tr. F. A. BRUNNER, 2 v. (New York 1951–55) 2:332–340. *General Instruction to the Roman Missal. Music in Catholic Worship. Liturgical Music Today.*

[C. KELLY/EDS.]

AGOBARD OF LYONS, ST.

Archbishop; b. Spain, 769; d. Lyons, France, 840. In 782 he moved to Narbonnaise, Gaul, and in 792 he went to Lyons as a companion to LEIDRADUS, Charlemagne's *missus* (delegate), on one of his tours of duty in the region of Narbonne and Seo de Urgel. Ordained a priest in 804 and named chorbishop for Leidradus in 813, Agobard ruled the See of Lyons at the retirement of Leidradus to Soissons (814), and in 816 was named his successor. Agobard was one of the greatest prelates of his day. Because of his opposition to Emperor Louis the Pious in the Council of Compiègne (833), he was compelled to leave Lyons after the Emperor's coronation in 835, taking refuge with Lothair I in Italy. In the meantime his position in Lyons was given to his opponent, AMALARIUS OF METZ. In 838, after his reconciliation with the Emperor, Agobard returned to Lyons. He composed many theological writings, e.g., against Felix de Urgel *De insolentia Judaeorum* against the Jews, and numerous political, juridical, and liturgical works. He wrote also against superstition. The *Liber de imaginibus,* often attributed to him, was composed by CLAUDIUS OF TURIN. His other authentic works—official documents from his see—are the product of collaboration with his deacon FLORUS OF LYONS. The *De divina psalmodia, Contra libros IV Amalarii,* and the hymn *Rector magnificus* are exclusively the work of Florus. His presence at the Council of Paris in 825 is uncertain, but it is clear that he did not participate in drawing up the synodal *Libellus* against images addressed to Pope EUGENE II.

Feast: June 6.

Bibliography: *Annales Lugdunenses,* in *Monumenta Germaniae Historica: Scriptores* 1:110, autobiographical notes from the margin of Codex Vallicellianus E 26. *Patrologia Latina,* ed. J. P. MIGNE (Paris 1878–90) 104:29–352. *Monumenta Germaniae Historica: Scriptores* 15.1:274–279. *Monumenta Germaniae Historica: Epistolae* 5:150–239. E. BOSHOF, *Erzbischof Agobard von Lyon. Leben und Werk* (Cologne 1969). A. BRESSOLLES, *Saint Agobard, évêque de Lyon, 769–840,* v.1 of *Doctrine et action politique d'Agobard* (Paris 1949). J. A. CABANISS, *Agobard of Lyons* (Syracuse 1953). P. BELLET, "El *Liber de imaginibus sanctorum* bajo el nombre de Agobardo de Lyon obra de Claudio de Turín," *Analecta Sacra Tarraconensia* 26 (1953) 151–194. L. SCHEFFCZYK, *Lexicon für Theologie und Kirche,* ed. J. HOFER and K. RAHNER (Freiburg 1957–65) 1:204.

[P. BELLET]

AGOSTINI, ZEFERINO, BL.

Founder of the Ursuline Daughters of Mary Immaculate; b. Verona, Venetia, Italy. Sept. 24, 1813; d. Verona, April 6, 1896. Agostini was the elder child of Antonio Agostini, a doctor, and Angela Frattini. His father died while Zeferino was still young, but his mother ensured that her two sons received a Christian education at local schools. Agostini entered the seminary as a day student and was distinguished by his piety, concern for contemporary problems, discipline, and success in his studies. He was ordained on March 11, 1837. Assigned to parish work, he took charge of catechesis and the recreational program for boys. In 1845, he was named pastor of a large, poor parish, a position he maintained until his death 50 years later. He started many social and pastoral initiatives in this highly populated district of the city, but his special concern was for the education of women and girls. He founded the Pious Union of Sisters, dedicated to St. Angela MERICI, in response to three young women who were volunteering themselves as religious to serve the poor; the rule received episcopal approbation in 1856. That same year, he founded a school for destitute girls and the congregation of the Ursuline Daughters of Mary Immaculate, primarily for those assistants in the school who wished to live in community. The first 12 Ursulines professed their vows in 1869. Agostini was beatified in Rome by John Paul II, Oct. 25, 1998.

Feast: April 6.

Bibliography: *Acta Apostolicae Sedis,* 21 (1998): 1049. *L'Osservatore Romano,* English edition, no. 43 (1998): 3.

[K. I. RABENSTEIN]

AGRAMUNT RIERA, JUAN, BL.

Martyr, priest of the Order of Poor Clerics Regular of the Mother of God of the Pious Schools (Piarists); b. Feb. 13, 1907 in Alzamora, Castile, Spain; d. Aug. 14, 1936. Fr. Juan was assigned to the Castellon school four kilometers from his home in Almazora. He fled to his parents' home at the end of July where he was arrested. The night of August 13–14, he was taken to prison along with a diocesan priest. They were shot en route, six kilometers from Almazora at the intersection of two roads. He was beatified on Oct. 1, 1995 by Pope John Paul II together with 12 other Piarists (*see* PAMPLONA, DIONISIO AND COMPANIONS, BB.).

Feast: Sept. 22.

Bibliography: "Decreto Super Martyrio," *Acta Apostolicae Sedis* (1995): 651–656. *La Documentation Catholique* 2125 (Nov. 5, 1995): 924.

[L. GENDERNALIK/EDS.]

ÁGREDA, MARY OF

Also known as Mary of Jesus, Poor Clare mystical writer; b. Ágreda, province of Burgos (Spain), April 2, 1602; d. Ágreda, May 24, 1665.

Mary was one of the 11 children of Francisco Coronel and Catalina de Arana. She is said to have made a vow of chastity at the age of eight and to have had a desire for religious life from early youth. In 1619 she became a Poor Clare at Ágreda. Her mother and one of her sisters entered with her; her father, although 63 years of age, took the Franciscan habit and thus made her mother's admission possible. Mary was made abbess at the age of 25 by papal dispensation. Except for a period of three years, she remained in office for life. In 1633 she founded a new monastery outside Ágreda, to which she transferred her nuns. In 1672, seven years after her death, Mary's cause was introduced at the request of the Spanish court, and she was declared venerable.

Mary of Ágreda's principal work was *The Mystical City of God and the Divine History of the Virgin Mother of God* (3 v. Madrid 1670). A concise narrative, written in a polished style (though critics differ on this), it is a life of Our Lady as seen by Mary in vision. It aroused considerable opposition in the Sorbonne, particularly the chapter on the Immaculate Conception, which, though perhaps crude, was not, as was alleged, immoral. Mary supported the doctrine. The book was condemned by the Inquisition and put on the Index of Prohibited Books on June 26, 1681. Almost immediately there were earnest appeals from Spain, and at the request of the king, Innocent XI suspended the decree of condemnation and had it removed on Aug. 4, 1681. Some held that this suspensory decree was intended only for Spain, but a decree of the Holy Office (Sept. 19, 1713) in reply to a query put by the bishop of Ceneda appears to have declared the decree to have the force of law throughout the whole Church.

Prominent among the opponents of the book were Bossuet and particularly Eusebius Amort. It was alleged that more importance was given to private revelations than to the Incarnation, that the term "adoration" was used for devotion to Our Lady, that the government of the Church was attributed to her, etc. On the other hand, it is said that the Sorbonne condemnation was based on a faulty translation and that evidence exists that Amort misunderstood the Spanish in 80 places.

Though the *Mystical City of God* was attacked, even Mary of Ágreda's enemies respected her holy life, and no accusation was ever made against her sincerity. In 1729, after a new examination, the work was approved by the universities of Salamanca, Alcalá de Henares, Toulouse, and Louvain.

Mary's letters to Philip IV cover a period of 22 years and deal with morals, asceticism, and politics. She is said to have been instrumental in the dismissal of the Conde-Duque de Olivares.

Bibliography: T. D. KENDRICK, *Mary of Ágreda: The Life and Legend of a Spanish Nun* (London 1967).

[K. E. POND]

AGRICIUS OF TRIER, ST.

Fourth-century bishop of Trier; d. *c.* 335. Agricius (Agrecius, Agritius) took part in the Council of Arles (314) and was possibly the master and predecessor of Bishop Maximinus, who welcomed the exiled St. ATHANASIUS to Trier. The name of Agricius is connected with the legend of the "Holy Tunic of Trier," which he allegedly received from the Empress (St.) Helena and brought to Trier along with the bones of St. MATTHIAS and other relics. An eleventh-century legend speaks of him as originally bishop of Antioch and says he changed Helena's palace into a cathedral.

Feast: Jan. 13.

Bibliography: *Acta Sanctorum* Jan. 2:55–63. H. V. SAUERLAND, *Trierer Geschichtsquellen des XI. Jahrhunderts* (Trier 1889)

55–212. E. EWIG, *Trierer Zeitschrift* 21 (1952) 30–33. A. HEINTZ, *Lexicon für Theologie und Kirche*, ed. J. HOFER and K. RAHNER (Freiburg 1957–65) 1:207.

[P. ROCHE]

AGRIPPA I AND II

The last two Jewish kings of Palestine. Agrippa I, b. *c.* 10 B.C.; d. A.D. 44. His father was Aristobulus, son of HEROD THE GREAT and Mariamme I, and his mother was Berenice, daughter of Herod's sister Salome and her second husband, Costobar. Agrippa came to the throne of his grandfather Herod by a series of fortunate chances and useful friendships. His mother Berenice was intimate with Antonia, Tiberius's sister–in–law, and during his education in Rome, Agrippa cultivated his contemporaries in the emperor's family, Germanicus, Drusus, and Claudius. When the premature deaths of Germanicus and Drusus disappointed his prospects, Agrippa, along with his wife Cyprus, went to IDUMEA and later accepted a post in TIBERIAS under his uncle HEROD ANTIPAS, who had married Agrippa's sister HERODIAS. A quarrel with Antipas caused Agrippa to go to Flaccus, the Roman legate in Syria; expelled for bribery, he made his way with difficulty back to Italy in A.D. 36, borrowing money at every turn on his expectations and his connections with Antonia. During Tiberius's last year, Agrippa cultivated a friendship with the emperor's grandnephew Gaius Caligula. An indiscreet remark, expressing the hope that Gaius would soon succeed Tiberius, put Agrippa in prison for six months, but he was saved by Tiberius's death (A.D. 37) and Gaius's accession. Agrippa was awarded a kingship over the tetrarchy of his late uncle PHILIP and the tetrarchy of Abilene, with the titular rank of praetor; to this was added, in A.D. 39, the tetrarchy of Antipas, whom he had accused of treason. As king, Agrippa resisted Gaius's insistence that his imperial image be set up in Jewish places of worship, especially in the Jerusalem temple, and strove to protect the traditional privileges granted Jews throughout the empire. To win approval of the Pharisaic party, Agrippa persecuted the Christians in Palestine (Acts 12.1–6). Gaius's assassination (A.D. 41) found Agrippa in Rome, and by his immediate support of the reluctant Claudius he ensured his favor as emperor. Claudius added Judea, Samaria, and Idumea to Agrippa's kingdom and raised him to the titular rank of consul. Agrippa thus ruled over a territory equal to that of Herod the Great. His reign was, however, inefficient and extravagant. Moreover, by taking initiatives forbidden to a vassal king, Agrippa foolishly strained relations with Rome. He died prematurely, after being seized by a sudden illness at a public event in Caesarea (Acts 12.20–23).

Agrippa II, b. A.D. 27; d. probably *c.* 93. Since he was only 17 at the death of his father Agrippa I, he was too young to succeed to the throne. Claudius placed the whole of the kingdom again under a Roman procurator; supervision of Jewish religious affairs was given over to Herod, King of Chalcis, Agrippa I's brother. In A.D. 50, two years after the latter's death, Claudius appointed Agrippa to take his uncle's place, and three years later he enlarged his holdings by substituting for Chalcis the former tetrarchy of Philip and the tetrarchies of Abilene and Noarus; Nero in the following year added four toparchies in Galilee and the Perea. Agrippa, though using the Roman name M. Julius Agrippa, conformed externally to the Jewish Law. He required that his sisters' non–Jewish husbands be circumcised; yet his sister Berenice lived with him, giving scandal to his Jewish subjects. In A.D. 60 the newly appointed Roman procurator Porcius Festus asked Agrippa to help him assess the case of Paul (Acts chapters 25–26). The high–handed behavior of Festus' successor Gessius Florus stirred the people to rebellion, and Agrippa was unable to persuade them to submit to Roman authority. In the revolt Agrippa consistently took the side of Rome; he accompanied both Cestius Gallus and Vespasian in their campaigns. Agrippa's close ties to both Vespasian and Titus served him well after the end of the revolt. Visiting Rome in A.D. 75 with Berenice, he was given the titular rank of praetor. He remained king until his death; his territory was afterward put under direct Roman administration.

Bibliography: J. BLINZLER, *Lexikon für Theologie und Kirche,* ed. J. HOFER and K. RAHNER, 10 v. (2d, new ed. Freiburg 1957–65) 5:265–266. *Encyclopedic Dictionary of the Bible,* tr. and adap. by L. HARTMAN (New York 1963) 43–45. A. ROSENBERG, *Paulys Realenzyklopädie der klassischen Altertumswissenschaft,* ed. G. WISSOWA et al., 10.1 (1917) 143–150. A. H. M. JONES, *The Herods of Judaea* (Oxford 1938) 184–261. S. H. PEROWNE, *The Later Herods* (New York 1959).

[J. P. M. WALSH]

AGUADO, PEDRO DE

Chronicler of the conquest of Venezuela and Colombia; b. Valdemoro (Madrid), 1538; d. probably Bogotá, 1609? He became a Franciscan and in 1560 was included in an expedition of 50 missionaries who were being sent to Peru. He left Spain in 1561 and disembarked in Cartagena. After doing missionary work among the native tribes, he became guardian of the Franciscan convent in Bogotá and enlarged the establishment. As provincial, he went to Spain in 1573 on important business. He must have just written the *Recopilación historial,* based on Medrano's account, for he referred to it as having been completed in the petition he presented at court in 1575.

After reworking the chronicle, he presented it in 1579 to obtain permission for publication. Although permission was granted, the work was not published then. In 1583 he was back in Bogotá and in 1589 he was commissary in Cartagena.

Aguado wrote with the ideas of the COUNTER REFORMATION, presenting events as being the work of men in the exercise of their free will and asserting that therefore men were subject to disciplinary punishment if they acted against the right conscience. The work was divided into two parts, and it was not until 1906 that a partial version of the first part was published in Bogotá. In 1913 and 1915 the second part was published in Caracas. The entire work was published by the Academy of Madrid as *Historia de Santa Marta* (1916–17) and *Historia de Venezuela* (1918–19). It was published under the title *Recopilación historial* in Bogotá in 1956. The manuscripts have been preserved in the Academy of Madrid, and copies are in the library of the Royal Palace.

Bibliography: P. DE AGUADO, *Recopilación historial*, 4 v. (Bogotá 1956–57) 1:14–23. A. LÓPEZ, "Historiadores franciscanos de Venezuela y Colombia: Fray Pedro de Aguado y Fray Pedro Simón," *Archivo Ibero-Americano* 14 (1920) 207–235. G. MORÓN, *Los cronistas y la historia* (Caracas 1957). O. FALS BORDA, "Odyssey of a Sixteenth-Century Document: Fray Pedro Aguado's *Recopilación historial*," *Hispanic American Historical Review* 35 (1955) 203–220. D. RAMOS, "El cronista Pedro Simon," in *Noticias historiales* (Caracas 1963).

[D. RAMOS]

AGUILAR, NICOLÁS

Priest and revolutionist; b. Tonacatepeque, El Salvador, Dec. 15, 1741; d. San Salvador, Sept. 12, 1818. In 1755 he was sent to Guatemala, where he studied under the Jesuits. On April 18, 1767, he was ordained in Olocuilta, El Salvador. Shortly afterward, in a competition, he won the post of pastor of San Salvador and performed his duties faithfully there until his death. In 1811 when San Salvador was governed by the unpopular intendant Don Antonio Gutiérrez Ulloa, Aguilar and José Matías DELGADO led a group that rose, on November 5, in armed rebellion in favor of independence. Their plan was to depose the intendant and take possession of 1,000 new muskets in the court of arms and some 200,000 pesos in the royal treasury. The insurrection failed because it was not well planned. Later, from the pulpit, Aguilar urged the populace to be tranquil and urged obedience to the captive king, Ferdinand VII. Although he continued to be active, he vacillated: sometimes he harangued the crowds to rise up in arms; other times he tried to subdue them, preaching love of neighbor and pardon of one's enemy. In 1814 he directed a new uprising, which failed also. In

his last years, although he was respected because of his advanced age, he suffered bitterly because of what happened to his two brothers, Manuel and Vicente, exemplary priests and patriots. Manuel was deported to Guatemala, and Vicente, who was blind, was imprisoned.

[S. MALAINA]

AGUILAR ALEMÁN, RODRIGO, ST.

Martyr, pastor; b. Mar. 13, 1875, Sayula, Jalisco, Diocese of Ciudad Guzmán, Mexico; d. Oct. 28, 1927, Unión de Tula, Jalisco, Diocese of Autlán. He studied at the auxiliary seminary of Ciudad Guzmán, where he showed exceptional literary talent. Following his ordination to the priesthood (1905), Fr. Aguilar served in various parishes. He was serving as interim pastor of the Unión de Tula when he was persecuted for his priesthood. He took refuge on a farm from where he continued to minister to the faithful and direct spiritual exercises. He was betrayed by one of his flock and arrested by troops under the command of Brigadier General Juan Izaguirre. He was hanged from a mango tree in the town square the following day. Thereafter his body was translated to the parish church at Tula. Aguilar was both beatified (Nov. 22, 1992) and canonized (May 21, 2000) with Cristobal MAGALLANES [*see* GUADALAJARA (MEXICO), MARTYRS OF, SS.] by Pope John Paul II.

Feast: May 25 (Mexico).

See Also: MEXICO, MODERN.

Bibliography: J. CARDOSO, *Los mártires mexicanos* (Mexico City 1953). J. DÍAZ ESTRELLA, *El movimiento cristero: sociedad y conflicto en los Altos de Jalisco* (México, D.F. 1979).

[K. I. RABENSTEIN]

AGUSTÍN, ANTONIO

Humanist, scholar, reform bishop; b. Saragossa, Feb. 26, 1517; d. Tarragona, May 31, 1586. He studied at Alcalá, Salamanca, Bologna (1536) and Padua (1537). In 1541 he became a doctor of laws at Bologna and three years later, at the request of Emperor Charles V, was appointed auditor of the Roman Rota. In 1555 Paul IV dispatched him to England as nuncio to Queen MARY TUDOR and councilor to Cardinal Reginald POLE. The following year he was appointed bishop of Alife, Kingdom of Naples, and in 1561 was made bishop of Lérida in his native Spain. His participation in and support of the Council of TRENT and its ecclesiastical reforms prompted Gregory XIII to create him archbishop of Tarragona (1576). Throughout his life Agustín was concerned with the history and study of Roman and canon law; his best-known work in Roman law is *Emendationum et opinionum libri IV ad Modestinum.* His critical work, *De emendatione Gratiani,* is noteworthy in canon law. Agustín was also a scholar of liturgical and catechetical theology, classical philology, and heraldry. His collected works were published in eight volumes at Lucca (1768–74).

Bibliography: J. F. VON SCHULTE, *Die Geschichte der Quellen und der Literatur des kanonischen Rechts* 3.1:723–28. L. SERRANO, *Dictionnaire d'histoire et de géographie ecclésiastiques* 1: 1077–80. E. MAGNIN, *Dictionnaire de droit canonique* 1:628–30.

[C. L. HOHL, JR.]

AHERN, BARNABAS MARY

Passionist priest, Old Testament scholar and writer; b. Chicago, IL, Feb. 18, 1915; d. Chicago, IL, Jan. 9, 1995. Barnabas Mary Ahern entered the Passionist Preparatory Seminary at Normandy, Missouri, in 1928, was clothed as a novice in Louisville in 1932, and simply professed in 1933. Following his ordination to the priesthood on June 7, 1941, he pursued further theological, biblical, and Semitic studies at the Catholic University of America, where he received the S.T.L. (1942); at the École Biblique in Jerusalem (1947–48); and at the Pontifical Biblical Institute in Rome (1956–58). He received his S.S.D. from the Pontifical Biblical Commission.

Ahern taught scripture in Chicago 1943–1947, again from 1948 to 1956, and in Louisville 1959–1962. From 1962 to1966, he was called to Rome to serve as peritus at Vatican II. He taught again in the United States from 1965 to 1970 (St. Meinrad's and the Catholic Theological Union). Ahern then returned to Rome, where he was involved with various congregations and commissions, and taught at both the Gregorian University and the Regina Mundi Institute. Poor health resulted in his returning to the U.S. in 1978, until he was able to travel to Africa to teach in Kenya from 1984 to 1989.

Among other scholarly activities, Ahern was involved in work on the Confraternity of Christian Doctrine's translation of the scriptures (later known as the New American Bible). He was president of the Catholic Biblical Association of America (1964–65), a member of both the Pontifical Biblical Commission (1969–75) and the International Theological Commission (1970–85). In addition to his scholarly contributions, Ahern is equally known for his work in publications such as the commentary series *The New Testament Reading Guide,* of which he became editor in 1960, and the periodical *The Bible Today,* which he edited from 1962 to 1975.

Bibliography: A bibliography of Ahern's publications, listing 12 books and 69 articles, can be found in *A Voice Crying out in the Desert: Preparing for Vatican II with Barnabas M. Ahern, C.P.,* ed. C. STUHLMUELLER and S. MACDONALD (Collegeville 1996).

[J. JENSEN]

AHIKAR (ACHIOR)

Hero of a story found in several forms and in many places of the ancient Near East. The story itself is accompanied by a long series of maxims typical of the wisdom literature of that part of the world [*see* WISDOM (IN THE BIBLE)]. This article treats first of the story, then considers the relationship between the Ahikar of the story and the Achior of the Books of Tobit and Judith.

Ahikar of the Aramaic Story. The narrative portion of the text relates the experiences of Ahikar who was purportedly chancellor and adviser of the Assyrian Kings Sennacherib (705–682 B.C.) and Esarhaddon (681–670). Being childless, he adopted a nephew, Nadan (Nadab), to whose education he devoted much time and effort. Thanks to this careful grooming, Nadan was chosen his uncle's successor. Once established in power, Nadan forgot his benefactor and eventually became so antagonistic toward him that he had him condemned to death. By a clever ruse, however, Ahikar escaped execution and found safe refuge in a cave.

Sometime later, the pharaoh of Egypt sought the aid of Esarhaddon in his quest of a man wise enough to solve several profound riddles (such as how to construct a castle in the air). Esarhaddon turned to Nadan, but he declined the challenge, whereupon the king sorely regretted having consented to Ahikar's execution. At this propitious moment, the executioner presented himself and told how the doomed man had been spared. Ahikar was found; he readily solved all the riddles and was promptly restored to power. Nadan was flogged and cast into prison where he died miserably.

As might be expected, the 142 maxims that accompany the story are sage observations on such matters as education, obedience, filial respect, gratitude, and retribution. Both the story and the maxims enjoyed extraordinary popularity, as is evidenced by the traces of those that have been found in such varied sources as the Arabic *Thousand and One Nights,* the Greek edition of *Aesop's Fables,* the QUR'AN, and the Bible.

The oldest known text of the story is a fragmentary Aramaic version found among the Elephantine Papyri and dated in the late fifth century B.C. (tr. by H. L. Ginsberg, J. B. Pritchard, *Ancient and Near Eastern Texts Relating to the Old Testament* [Princeton 1955] 427–430). Other texts are available in Syriac, Arabic, and other languages (see F. C. Conybeare, J. R. Harris, and Agnes S.

Lewis, *The Story of Ahikar from the Syriac, Arabic, Armenian, Ethiopic, Greek and Slavonic Versions*, 2d ed., Cambridge 1913).

Scholars generally agree that the original story was written in Aramaic, in an Akkadian (Mesopotamian) milieu, perhaps as early as the seventh century B.C. and certainly no later than the sixth century B.C. They vary considerably, however, on their estimate of its historical reliability. All admit a degree of literary embellishment; some maintain that the essential elements of the narrative should be accepted as factual. This position has been strengthened by a text recently discovered at Uruk in which there is reference to a certain "Ahuqar" who was royal adviser under Esarhaddon. [Text first published by J. J. van Dijk. See report by J. C. Greenfield in *The Journal of the American Oriental Society* 82 (1962) 293].

Ahikar and the Achior of Tobit and Judith. A certain Achior is mentioned in four passages of the Book of TOBIT. He is presented as chief administrator and royal adviser ("keeper of the seal") under Esarhaddon and is claimed as Tobit's nephew (1.21–22) and friend (2.10). Both Achior and his nephew, Nadab, were among the guests at Tobias's wedding (11.18), and explicit mention is made of Nadab's ingratitude and disgrace (14.10). In view of these striking similarities there can be little doubt that this Achior is to be identified with Ahikar of the Aramaic Story. Moreover, the spelling of the name in the Greek text ['Αχι(α)χαρος] eliminates any difficulty on that score.

Some scholars have suggested that the story of Tobit was in fact a mere adaptation of the Ahikar story. However, a careful reading of Tobit reveals almost no similarity between the themes of these two works. In Tobit, there are no riddles to be solved and, more important, there is no ungrateful nephew; rather, there is a most obedient son. There is some slight evidence of literary influence (e.g., 4.17); beyond that, one can say only that the author of Tobit wished to associate his hero with a famous sage who had also known adversity and was rewarded at the end.

In the Book of JUDITH, one of the main characters is an Ammonite leader called Achior (Αχιωρ). He expounds at length on the theological implications of Israel's history for the benefit of a skeptical Holofernes (5.5–21), is scorned and reproached for his efforts (6.2–13), and is forced to share Israel's lot (6.14–21). Thus he shares eventually in her victory also (14.6–10). There does not appear to be any demonstrable connection between this Achior and the Ahikar of the Aramaic Story.

Bibliography: *Dictionnaire de la Bible*, suppl. ed. L. PIROT, et al. (Paris 1928–) 1:198–207. A. E. GOODMAN, in *Documents from Old Testament Times*, ed. D. W. THOMAS (London 1958) 270–275. T. NÖLDEKE, *Untersuchungen zum Achiqar-Roman* (Berlin 1913).

[D. R. DUMM]

AḤMADIYYA

A sect claiming to be part of Orthodox Islam, although repudiated by both the Sunni and Shī'a branches of ISLAM. The Aḥmadiyya movement was founded by Mīrzā Ghulām Aḥmad (1839–1908) at Qādiyān in the Punjab (India). In 1891 he formally claimed the titles "al- MAHDĪ" (the leader who is to return to humanity according to Islamic and, more emphatically, Shī'a doctrine) and "al-Masīḥ" (the Messiah). The main lines of his doctrine, embodied in the *Bay'ah,* followed Islam more or less closely. However, his personal claims to messiahship were so offensive and so far exceeded the bounds of Islamic orthodoxy that the Aḥmadiyya came to be regarded by Orthodox Muslims generally as simply another syncretistic sect of a type frequently bred in western India. After the death of Mīrzā Ghulām Ahmad's first caliph (Arabic *khalīfah,* "successor") in 1914, the Aḥmadiyya was split by a schism that separated from the so-called Qādiyāni Aḥmadiyya repudiating some of the founder's claims and the political activity of the movement. Since then, further schisms have occurred.

Bibliography: H. A. WALTER, *The Ahmadiya Movement* (London 1918). M. BASHIR-AL-DIN, *The Ahmadiyya Movement in Islam* (Chicago n.d.). J. S. TRIMINGHAM, *Islam in West Africa* (Oxford 1959) 230–232.

[J. KRITZECK/EDS.]

AHURA MAZDA (OHRMAZD) AND AHRIMAN

The good God and the Evil Spirit in Zoroastrianism. In ZOROASTER's *Gāthās,* Ahura Mazda, "The Wise Lord" (the ancient name of Ohrmazd, and used by Darius and his successors), was the father of the twin spirits—the Holy One (Spenta Mainyu) and the Destructive One (Anra Mainyu, hence Ahriman), who at the origin of the world made a choice, respectively, in favor of good and evil. Later, in more recent parts of the *Avesta,* Ahura Mazda became identified with the Holy One, thus becoming the direct opposite of Anra Mainyu, and on a level with him. The origin of evil is no longer explained as the consequence of a choice, but is either left unaccounted for, Ohrmazd and Ahriman being coeval, or reinterpreted in the light of ZERVANISM, a Persian speculative doctrine on time. Zervan, "Time," is said to have offered sacrifice for 1,000 years before the world existed, in order to have an offspring. At the end of this period, Ohrmazd was born to him, but also Ahriman—the latter as the result of a doubt that came to Zervan about the efficacy of his sacrifice.

Bibliography: R. C. ZAEHNER, *The Dawn and Twilight of Zoroastrianism* (New York 1961). J. DUCHESNE-GUILLEMIN, *La Religion de l'Iran ancien* (Paris 1962).

[J. DUCHESNE-GUILLEMIN]

AIDAN OF LINDISFARNE, ST.

Monastic bishop; d. Bamborough, Aug. 31, 651. Aidan (Aedan) was of Irish descent and while a monk at Iona, was invited by King OSWALD to reconvert the lapsed Northumbrian race. Consecrated bishop in 635, he established his see in Lindisfarne. BEDE, almost the sole source of knowledge of the saint, praised his ascetic life and evangelical fervor, and told of his many miracles, but regretted his adherence to the schismatic practices of the Celtic Church, especially over the dating of Easter. Aidan had several famous pupils including SS. CHAD, Eata, and Hilda. Cuthbert, while keeping sheep, saw his soul being carried to heaven by angels. Some of Aidan's relics were taken to Ireland in 664. Others were removed from Lindisfarne in 875; in 995 they were translated to Durham with the body of St. Cuthbert of Lindisfarne.

Feast: August 31.

Bibliography: D. ADAM, *Flame in my heart: St Aidan for today* (Harrisburg, Pa. 1998). BEDE, *Ecclesiastical History* 3.5, 14–17. *Acta Sanctorum* Aug. 6: 688–694. L. GOUGAUD, *Christianity in Celtic Lands*, tr. M. JOYNT (London 1932). A. THOMAS, *Brands from the burning* (London 1937). M. CREIGHTON, *Dictionary of National Biography* 1:182–183. A. M. ZIMMERMANN, *Kalendarium Benedictinum* (Metten 1933–38) 2:644. A. BUTLER, *The Lives of the Saints*, ed. H. THURSTON and D. ATTWATER (New York 1956) 3:451–452.

[B. COLGRAVE]

AIDS

An acronym for Acquired Immune Deficiency Syndrome, AIDS refers to a terminal condition of opportunistic infections resulting from the suppression of the immune system. In 1983, researchers working independently at the American Cancer Institute in the U.S. and at the Pasteur Institute in France simultaneously identified the cause of this immune suppression. Commonly known as the Human Immunodeficiency Virus (HIV), this human retrovirus infects the T-4 Helper cells of the immune system, gradually destroying the person's ability to fight off what would normally be common infections.

It is estimated that between 20% and 30% of those who become infected with HIV will develop AIDS within five years. Others who become infected may develop AIDS Related Complex (ARC), a condition similar to AIDS, though generally less severe. A third group who become infected, while able to infect others, will remain healthy indefinitely.

Transmission. HIV is transmitted only through direct contact of one's own blood with infected blood, blood products, and bodily fluids which contain a large volume of white blood cells, such as seminal and vaginal fluids. The virus has been isolated in other bodily fluids such as tears and saliva, but this is rare, and only in situations where the person had AIDS rather than ARC or test HIV-positive. Infection through blood contact with these bodily fluids has never been proven, and has been deemed by the Center for Disease Control as extremely unlikely.

A primary means of infection is through the shared use of non-sterile needles and syringes by intravenous drug users. The other most common means of transmission is through sexual intercourse with an infected person. Lesions, often imperceptible, caused by penile penetration of the vagina or the anus may allow HIV infected seminal fluid to enter a person's blood. Studies have shown that transmission is most likely during anal intercourse with an infected male due to the more sensitive anal lining, and during vaginal intercourse when the woman has a history of previous sexually transmitted diseases which leave lesions likely to increase bleeding during intercourse. Infection of the male by the female during vaginal intercourse is less likely, but may result if infected vaginal fluid enters any sores along the penis or within the urethra which may result from intercourse or another sexually transmitted disease. Infection may also result when seminal or vaginal fluid is taken into the mouth, and if there are sores or cancers present which may bleed.

In the early stages of the AIDS epidemic some cases of infection were reported to have resulted from blood transfusions and clinical contact with infected specimens. Improved screening and blood testing procedures have effectively protected the national blood supply, and medical literature reports that, if normal procedures are followed for the handling of infectious patients and specimens, the risk of contracting HIV is actually less than that of contracting other infectious diseases.

Finally, children born to mothers who are HIV infected are at a high risk for themselves becoming infected. The child may become infected during pregnancy, during child birth, or during breast feeding.

Health Care. Although studies show a great concern among health care workers and their families about infection, the risks involved in caring for AIDS or HIV infected patients are well within the range deemed acceptable for other infectious diseases. Researchers have focused attention on the development of a vaccine to prevent infection, as well as treatment to prevent the development of AIDS among those who become infected.

Of great concern to health care workers is the successful treatment of opportunistic infections among those with AIDS. Care has been complicated by the fact that, among those with AIDS, conventional treatments for infections are often unsuccessful, and there is a high incidence of recurrence when infections are successfully treated. In addition, similar treatments for similar infections among different people, or even the same person in the case of recurrence, do not always result in similar responses. Decisions concerning appropriate treatment or prognosis are, therefore, difficult to make.

Moral and Pastoral Issues. The incidence of AIDS raises many moral and pastoral issues concerning an appropriate Christian response. A number of American dioceses, especially in metropolitan areas where the incidence of AIDS is high, have sought to address this issue. For example, they have sponsored Hospice care for AIDS patients, and have taken a leadership role in protecting such civil rights as housing, employment, insurance and education for those who become infected. The 1988 letter of the California Conference of Catholic Bishops, ''A Call to Compassion: Pastoral Letter on AIDS to the Catholic Community of California,'' is just one example of the local church's involvement in the formation of educational, health care and public policy to address this issue.

Nationally, the administrative board of the United States Catholic Conference published ''The Many Faces of AIDS: A Gospel Response'' in November 1987. Although this letter precipitated a great deal of controversy over its statement that a discussion of condoms could be included as part of the broad factual picture concerning the spread of HIV, the principal focus of the letter concerned the protection of the dignity and rights of those who become infected. For example, they affirmed that AIDS is not the result of sin, expressed alarm concerning the increased violence against the gay and lesbian community as a result of AIDS, opposed quarantining persons infected with HIV, decried the exclusion of people infected from health insurance coverage, opposed mandatory antibody testing, and expressed concern that some in the healthcare industry refuse to provide medical or dental care to those with AIDS or presumed to be at risk.

The AIDS Quilt on Central Park's Great Lawn, New York City, June 1988. The quilt consists of panels bearing the names and images of people who have died of AIDS. (©Bettmann/CORBIS)

They conclude by stating that ''persons with AIDS, their families, and their friends need solidarity, comfort, and support,'' and encourage each local diocese to appoint a person responsible for coordinating its ministry to persons with AIDS and their loved ones. Quoting Pope John Paul II, they remind the reader to love others as God loves us, and that ''God loves those of you who are sick, those who are suffering from AIDS and from AIDS-related complex.''

Bibliography: D. BADER, OP, and E. MCMILLAN, *AIDS: Ethical Guidelines for Healthcare Providers* (St. Louis 1987). M. L. BROWN, ''AIDS and Ethics: Concerns and Considerations,'' *Oncology Nurses Forum* 14 (January/February 1987) 69–73. R. C. GALLO, ''The AIDS Virus,'' *Science* 256 (January 1987) 46–56. G. W. MATTHERS and V. S. NESLUND, ''The Initial Impact of AIDS on Public Health Law in the United States-1986.'' *Journal of the American Medical Association* 257 (January 1987) 344–351. R. H. SUNDERLAND and E. E. SHELP, *AIDS: A Manual for Pastoral Care* (Philadelphia 1987). ''Surgeon General's Report on Acquired Immune Deficiency Syndrome,'' *Journal of the American Medical Associa-*

tion 256 (November 1986) 2764–2789. USCC, *The Many Faces of AIDS: A Gospel Response* (Washington, D.C. 1987).

[J. F. TUOHEY]

AIGUANI, MICHELE (ANGUANI, ANGRIANI)

Theologian; b. Bologna, *c.* 1320; d. Bologna, Nov. 16, 1400. He is commonly known as Michael of Bologna. After joining the Carmelite Order, he studied Scripture (1360) and theology (1362–63) at Paris, where in 1364–65 he obtained his master's degree. For years he taught theology at Bologna. He was elected definitor (1372) and provincial (1375 and 1379) of his own province of Bologna. In 1380, when the WESTERN SCHISM had divided also the Carmelite Order, Aiguani was nominated vicar-general of the whole order by Urban VI (d. 1389). In 1381 Aiguani was elected prior general, an office he retained until 1386 when Urban deposed him, probably because he was unjustly accused of opposition to the pope. However, he was vindicated by Boniface IX (d. 1404), who in 1395 nominated him again as vicar-general for the province of Bologna. Aiguani held a philosophical position between voluntarism and seminominalism. He long remained one of the main theologians of his order; this explains why so many manuscripts of his works are extant and why his principal works have been reprinted so often. His chief works were: *Lectura Sententiarum* (Milan 1510), *Lectura super Psalterio* (Compluti 1524).

Bibliography: B. M. XIBERTA Y ROQUETA, *De Scriptoribus scholasticis saec. XIV ex Ordine Carmelitarum* (Louvain 1931) 324–93.

[H. SPIKKER]

AIGULF OF LÉRINS, ST.

Abbot; b. Blois *c.* 630; d. *c.* 674. At 20, Aigulf (Aigulphus, Ayou, Ayoul) entered the monastery of Fleury. Abbot Mummolus commissioned Aigulf to go to Monte Cassino, which had been ravaged by the Lombards, and to bring back the remains of SS. Benedict and Scholastica. The success of his mission is questionable (Leccisotti, *Il Sepolcro di s. Benedetto,* Monte Cassino, 1951). In 671 Aigulf was made abbot of Lérins. His severe rule led to his abduction and martyrdom on Capri.

Feast: Sept. 3.

Bibliography: *Vita,* J. MABILLON, *Acta sanctorum ordinis S. Benedictii* (Venice 1733–40) 2:627–643, see also 338–344 for account of the *translatio. Passio, Acta Sanctorum* Sept. 1:728–763. H. LECLERCQ, *Dictionnaire d'archéologie chrétienne et de liturgie,*

ed. F. CABROL, H. LECLERCQ, and H. I. MARROU (Paris 1907–53) 5.2:1709–60. J. L. BAUDOT and L. CHAUSSIN, *Vies des saints et des bienhereux selon l'ordre du calendrier avec l'historique des fêtes* (Paris 1935–56) 9:77–79. R. AIGRAIN, *Catholicisme* 1:244–245. E. EWIG, *Lexicon für Theologie und Kirche,* ed. J. HOFER and K. RAHNER (Freiburg 1957–65) 1:226. C. LEFEBVRE, *Bibliotheca Sanctorum* 1:633–634.

[B. F. SCHERER]

AIKENHEAD, MARY

Foundress of the Irish Sisters of Charity; b. Cork, Ireland, Jan. 19, 1787; d. Dublin, July 22, 1858. Because of her early attraction toward the service of the poor, Daniel MURRAY, then coadjutor bishop of Dublin and later archbishop there, persuaded her to form a religious congregation and received authorization from the Holy See to establish it. Mary and one associate then spent a three-year noviceship at the Bar Convent of the Institute of the Blessed Virgin Mary, York, England. The Irish SISTERS OF CHARITY began their institutional existence when the two women returned to the North William Street Orphanage, their new home in Dublin, and took the usual three vows of religion, plus a fourth vow of dedication to the poor. The sisters cared for the orphans, set up a day school, and visited neighboring poor families. Steady growth in numbers of recruits and of houses enabled the congregation to teach religion in parochial schools and to staff additional free schools and a Magdalen refuge. In 1834 the sisters opened St. Vincent's Hospital in Dublin, the first Catholic hospital in Ireland. In 1838 they became the first religious women to labor in Australia. For the last 27 years of her life, Mother Aikenhead directed her institute while prostrate on her bed with chronic spinal trouble. The decree introducing her cause of beatification in Rome was issued in 1921. Since her death the congregation has spread to England, Scotland, the United States, and Africa.

Bibliography: M. B. BUTLER, *A Candle Was Lit: The Life of Mother Mary Aikenhead* (Dublin 1953). *Acta Apostolicae Sedis* 13 (1921) 234–38.

[E. MCDERMOTT]

AIMERIC OF PIACENZA

Dominican master general; b. Lombardy; d. Bologna, Aug. 19, 1327. He entered the DOMINICANS at Bologna (1267), studied at Milan, and taught for 24 years at Bologna. He also served as provincial of the province of Greece. He was active in organizing studies in the order, but is best known for his role in the trial of the TEMPLARS. Ordered by Clement V (1309) to proceed against the

Templars in Castile and Leon, Aimeric exonerated them after an investigation conducted without torture. He believed that his order's exemption allowed him to dispense with torture, evidently unaware that Clement had explicitly ordered it in a bull dated March 17, 1310. He was summoned to the Council of Vienne but did not attend. It is probable that he resigned as master general (May 30, 1311) rather than take part in the process against the Templars.

Bibliography: J. QUÉTIF and J. ÉCHARD, *Scriptores Ordinis Praedicatorum* (New York 1959) 1.2:494–496. D. A. MORTIER, *Histoire des maîtres généraux de l'ordre des Frères Prêcheurs,* 8 v. (Paris 1903–20) 2:421–473.

[P. M. STARRS]

AIN-TRAZ, SYNODS OF

Ain-Traz is the summer residence of the Melchite patriarch of Antioch when he is in Lebanon. This residence was purchased in 1811 by Patriarch Agapios Matar to be used as a seminary for married priests. It is here that the Melchite patriarch convenes with his bishops to study, discuss, and decide on the major issues concerning their community. In the course of modern Melchite history, two of the synods held at Ain-Traz deserve particular attention.

Ain-Traz Synod I was convoked and presided over by the then newly elected patriarch Maximos Mazloum on Dec. 13, 1835. The canons outlined by this synod relate to the Melchite discipline. They regulate Baptism, Confirmation, the Liturgy of the Presanctified, Confession, Extreme Unction, Holy Orders, Matrimony, communication in sacris, the holy days of obligation, the clergy (garb, commerce, residence, catechism, exercise of medicine, inheritance), the religious (garb, exclaustration), pastoral visits of the bishops, alms to the seminary of Ain-Traz, charitable foundations, fast and abstinence, pilgrimages to different churches, usury, etc. The Congregation for the Propagation of the Faith confirmed *in forma generali* the 25 canons listed above with few modifications of the text submitted. In this manner the Melchite discipline, outlined at the Synod of Saint-Sauveur in 1790 and reaffirmed at the Synod of Qarqafee in 1806, received the official stamp of the Church on Jan. 13, 1838.

While the Congregation for the Propagation of the Faith was studying the acts of this synod, Patriarch Maximos Mazloum received a diploma from the sultan in Constantinople recognizing him as the sole civil leader of all the Melchites in the Turkish Empire, and from the Holy See in Rome, the right to add to his title the words "Alex-

Mary Aikenhead on commemorative postage stamp.

andria and Jerusalem." As a result, his jurisdiction was extended to encompass the territories of the old patriarchates of the East.

Ain-Traz Synod II was called by Patriarch Cyril Jehunla and was held from May 30 to July 8, 1909. The acts are not printed. It is certain, however, that they have served as *fontes* to the modern codification of the Eastern Churches as it concerns the Melchite congregation.

Besides these two official synods, each successive patriarch meets regularly with his bishops at Ain-Traz to discuss current events. Their directives are printed in the major publications of the community, mainly *Al Masarrat,* published by the Paulist Fathers at Harrissa; *Ar Risalat Al Muḥalisiat,* published by the Salvatorian Fathers at Saida; and *Le Lien,* published by the Patriarchal clergy in Cairo.

Bibliography: C. J. VON HEFELE, *Histoire des conciles d'après les documents originaux,* tr. and continued by H. LECLERCQ, 10 v. in 19 (Paris 1907–38) 11:339–379. J. CHAMMAS, *Ḥulasat Ṭarîḫ al-Kanîsat al-Malakîyat,* 3 v. (Sidon, Leb. 1952) 3:185.

[L. MALOUF]

AINAY, ABBEY OF

Former BENEDICTINE monastery of Saint-Martin and former collegiate church, located in the marshy peninsula between the Rhone and the Saône, slightly upstream from the junction of the two rivers, in present-day Lyons, France, Diocese of Lyons (Latin, *Athanacum monasterium* or *Interamnense mon.*). Founded in the 6th century, it suffered a serious crisis in the mid-9th century, and was resettled by Benedictine monks who came apparently from the Paris area. The abbey church, wholly preserved today, was consecrated by Pope Paschal II on Jan. 27, 1107. The abbey prospered in subsequent centuries, and at the end of the 13th century it controlled 200 parishes in the southeastern part of present-day France. Yet this powerful abbey produced no great ecclesiastical writer and gave the Church no saint. Its temporal power, as well as its spiritual influence, was severely curtailed by the WARS OF RELIGION. It was secularized by a papal bull of Dec. 4, 1685, becoming a collegiate church; the former religious became a chapter of CANONS. During the French Revolution three of its canons were guillotined. The church is still used as a parish church and is the seat of an archpriest of the city of Lyons. It has been elevated to the rank of a minor basilica.

Bibliography: *Gallia Christiana,* v. 1–13 (Paris 1715–85), v. 14–16 (Paris 1856–65) 4:233–241. H. A. CHARPIN-FEUGEROLLES and M. C. GUIGUE, eds., *Grand cartulaire de l'abbaye d'Ainay,* 2 v. (Lyons 1885). J. B. VANEL, *Dictionnaire d'histoire et de géographie ecclésiastiques,* ed. A. BAUDRILLART et al. (Paris 1912–) 1:1195–1201. R. GAZEAU, *Catholicisme,* 1:248–249.

[L. GAILLARD]

AIRVAULT, MONASTERY OF

Former monastery of Canons Regular of St. Augustine in the Diocese of POITIERS, west central France. It was founded as a collegiate chapter *c.* 991 by Audéarde (d. *c.* 1013) and reformed with Augustinian canons from Lesterp by Bp. Peter II of Poitiers (1087–1115). It declined and was impoverished by the Hundred Years' War; the conventual buildings were destroyed in the Wars of Religion (1568). In 1477 the first commendatory abbot appeared, and by 1546 Airvault was definitely in COMMENDATION. The community of 12 canons, appointed by the abbot, joined none of the reform congregations of canons in the 17th century. The suppression ordered in 1768 by the COMMISSION OF REGULARS was not enforced, and the canons continued their services in the church of St-Pierre until 1791. The 11th-century church, redone in the 13th century, now serves a parish.

Bibliography: L. H. COTTINEAU, *Répertoire topobibliographique des abbayes et prieurés,* 2 v. (Mâcon 1935–39) 1:39. P. DE MONSABERT, *Dictionnaire d'histoire et de géographie ecclésiastiques,* ed. A. BAUDRILLART et al. (Paris 1912–) 1:1219–23. H. BEAUCHET-FILLEAU, ''Recherches sur Airvault: Son château et son abbaye,'' *Memoires de la Société des antiquaries de l'Ouest,* 24 (1857) 177–369. J. BERTHELÉ, ''Les Voûtes Plantagenet des églises d'Airvault et de St. Jouin,'' *Revue poitevine et Saintongeaise,* 4 (Melle 1887) 1–15.

[N. BACKMUND]

AIX, ARCHDIOCESE OF

Also known as *Aquensis In Gallia*; located in southeastern France, 20 miles north of Marseilles; it corresponds to the arrondissements of Aix and Arles in Bouches-du-Rhône department and is 1,768 square miles in area; metropolitan see since 445. Since 1822 the archbishop has also held the titles of ARLES (once a metropolitan and for a while a primatial see) and Embrun (once a metropolitan see). The area of the diocese has varied greatly. Until 1789 it corresponded to the old Roman *civitas* (96 parishes). In 1802 it included the departments of Var and Bouches-du-Rhône. In 1822 it lost Marseilles arrondissement and Var department. Its suffragans *c.* 800 (Apt, Fréjus, Gap, Riez, and Sisteron) comprised the old Roman province *Narbonensis II*, less Antibes. ALGIERS (1838–67) and Nice (1860) were added later.

The 11th-century legend that the sees of the lower Rhône were founded by disciples of Christ (Lazarus, Mary Magdalen, and Martha) is without value. The first known bishop dates from *c.* 379. Until *c.* 1000 the history of Aix is very obscure. Many lacunae in its list of bishops correspond with the domination of the Arian Goths and to the years when Saracens raided from their base at Garde-Freinet (until 972). After the Muslims were expelled, Aix revived and became the capital of the County of Provence, with which its history then merged. Despite Abp. Jean de Saint-Chamond, who in 1566 announced from the episcopal throne his apostasy to Protestantism and married, the diocese remained strongly Catholic. The Catholic reform followed the rulings of the Council of Aix (1585); but Jansenism, supported by members of the Parlement of Provence (1501–1789), troubled the diocese, especially in the 17th century.

Of 34 synodal statutes known (1362–1760), 22 date from the 18th century. Provincial councils were held in 1103, 1112, 1409, 1585, 1838, and 1850. The most important was that of 1585, under Abp. Alexandre Canigiani (1576–91), an Italian who attended the Councils of Milan held by St. Charles BORROMEO, whose disciple he was. The decisions at Aix in 1585 contained the essence of Borromeo's rules and spirit: definition of an ideal bishop, rules of the episcopal life, and relations with clergy and faithful; pastoral duties, which were also insisted upon, included preaching, administration of the Sacraments, pastoral visitations, validation of Baptism, strict rules on the Sacrament of Reconciliation, the spirit of

Rome in the liturgy, rules for seminaries (Canigiani founded one in 1580), and division of the diocese into itinerant vicariates with regular inspection. Borromeo's spirit and methods thus were introduced before the spirit of French reform developed. Other archbishops of Aix were PETER AUREOLI (1321–22), Guillaume FILLASTRE (1420–22), Gilbert GÉNÉBRARD (1593–97), Alphonse du Plessis de Richelieu (1626–29, Carthusian brother of Cardinal Richelieu and later archbishop of Lyons), Jérôme de Grimaldi (1648–85, who left his goods to the seminary he started), Charles de Vintimille (1708–29, transferred to Paris), Jérôme Champion de Cicé (1771–1801, ecclesiastical minister of Louis XVI who played a role in the Estates General of 1789), and François Xavier Gouthe-Soulard (1886–1900).

Famous people in Aix's history include St. EUCHERI- US OF LYONS (d. *c.* 450); St. ELZÉAR OF SABRAN (1285–1323), canonized with his wife Delphine in 1369; Abp. Honoré de Laurens of Embrun (1600–12); Ignace Cottolendi, vicar apostolic of Nanjing (1630–62); and Cardinal Abp. J. H. Guibert of Paris (1871–86). The for- mer Cistercian Abbey of Silvacane (1147–1440) and the 12th-century Benedictine MONTMAJOUR in Arles were distinguished. The archbishop was chancellor of the uni- versity founded in Aix (1403) by the Pisan Pope Alexan- der V, with faculties of theology, law, and medicine. Aix, once known for baths (*Aquae Sextiae,* after the consul Sextius who founded it in 123 B.C.), has beautiful monu- ments: the 12th-century Cloister of Saint-Sauveur; the composite (5th–16th century) Cathedral of Saint-Sauveur with a 5th-century tomb of St. Mitrias (d. *c.* 300) and a 5th-century baptistery; Sainte-Madeleine and the Jesuit chapel (17th century); and Saint-Jean-de-Malté (13th–15th century). Arles has the church and cloister of Saint-Trophime (11th–15th century), Notre-Dame de la Major (12th century), and the Romanesque Saint- Honorat. Sainte-Marthe is a shrine in Tarascon. Among other shrines in the diocese, many to the Blessed Virgin, is that of Saintes-Maries of the Sea (for gypsies) in honor of St. Sarah, the gypsy (servant) of Mary Magdalen and Martha.

Bibliography: É. GRIFFE, *La Gaule chrétienne à l'époque ro- maine,* 2 v. (Paris 1947–58; rev. ed. 1965–).

[E. JARRY/EDS.]

AKATHISTOS

From the Greek ἀ-κάθιστος, meaning not seated, standing. It is perhaps the most celebrated hymn of the Byzantine Church, and belongs to the poetical genre known as kontakion (*see* BYZANTINE RITE, CHANTS OF). It is performed at the vigil service of the fifth Saturday in

Church in Aix-en-Provence, France. (©Ric Ergenbright/ CORBIS)

Lent, a calendar position that it occupied from an early date; its original association, however, was more proba- bly with the Feast of the Annunciation, March 25.

The body of the poem comprises 24 stanzas (*oikoi*) linked by an alphabet acrostic—the first 12 treating of the Incarnation and the infancy of Christ, the last 12 alternat- ing the praises of God and His Mother in the even- and odd-numbered stanzas respectively; the concluding stan- za, by exception, is addressed to the Virgin. Each of the stanzas presents the same seven-line metric pattern, but the odd ones add to this a series of salutations to the Vir- gin: 12 lines in metrically matching pairs, each line be- ginning with Χαῖρε (Hail), and the entire stanza concluding with the unvarying refrain Χαῖρε, νύμφη ἀνύμφευτε (Hail, unwedded Bride). The even stanzas have simply "Alleluia" as refrain. As an intro- duction (*prooimion*) to the 24 stanzas, early MSS give an- other stanza, of independent metrical design and standing outside the alphabet acrostic: τῇ ὑπερμάχῳ στρατηγῷ . . . (To the invincible Leader. . .), a hymn of thanks- giving to the Virgin for the delivery of Constantinople from siege; in fact, the chronicles mention several such occasions at which the *Akathistos* was presumably sung. It has been conjectured that the original *prooimion* was not this but another stanza, now found as an independent hymn for the same office: Τὸ προσταχθὲν μυσ- τικῶδ λαβών . . . (Receiving secretly the com- mand. . .), which corresponds more closely to the 24 stanzas in wording and theme. But quite possibly neither stanza was part of the original composition of the hymn.

The authorship and date of the *Akathistos* have been the subject of much discussion; the medieval sources offer different attributions, and modern scholars in turn have advanced the claims of various candidates for the honor: Romanos in the sixth century, Patriarch Sergios and George Pisides in the seventh, Patriarchs Germanos and Photios in the eighth and ninth centuries respectively. The latest of these claimants has been eliminated by the discovery of a Latin translation of the *Akathistos* that can hardly be later than the early ninth century. As for the others, the prevailing tendency in more recent scholarship has been to assign the hymn to the sixth century, or even somewhat earlier; and the case for the authorship of Romanos himself has been forcefully argued, notably by Wellesz, despite its weakness in the MS tradition. For other scholars the hymn remains anonymous, perhaps the work of some imitator of Romanos; thus the question of attribution seems unlikely to receive any definitive solution.

The earliest extant musical sources for the *Akathistos,* completely notated, date from the thirteenth century; there is little reason to suppose that the music they contain was that originally accompanying the text. The melody conforms to the highly ornate and formulaic style characteristic of the kontakion in that period; the service book in which it occurs was, in all likelihood, of a type designed for the use of soloists. The music is written out in full over the individual stanzas, suggesting that, at a time when virtually all kontakia had been reduced to *prooimion* and a single *oikos,* the *Akathistos,* at least on occasion, was performed in its musical entirety. In the present-day service the medieval melody has been replaced by one of more recent origin, and the stanzas succeeding the first are generally read, not sung.

As mentioned previously, the *Akathistos* existed in a Latin version by the late eigth or early ninth century; thereafter, its rhetoric and imagery appear as the inspiration of a considerable repertory of Latin hymns. The subject is given detailed exposition in the study of G. G. Meersseman cited below.

Bibliography: E. WELLESZ, *A History of Byzantine Music and Hymnography* (2d ed. Oxford 1961). *The Akathistos Hymn,* introd. and transcribed by E. WELLESZ (*Monumenta musicae byzantinae, Transcripta* 9; Copenhagen 1957). E. WELLESZ, ''The 'Akathistos': A Study in Byzantine Hymnography,'' *Dumbarton Oaks Papers* 9 and 10 (1956) 141–174. C. DE GRANDE, *L'Inno acatisto* (Florence 1948). G. G. MEERSSEMAN, ''Der Hymnos Akathistos im Abendland,'' in *Spicilegium Friburgense,* v. 2–3 (Fribourg 1956–60). P. MAAS, ''Das Kontakion,'' *Byzantinische Zeitschrift* 19 (1910) 285–306. P. F. KRYPIAKIEWICZ, ''De Hymni Acathisti auctore,'' *Byzantinische Zeitschrift* 18 (1901) 357–382. M. HUGLO, ''L'Ancienne version latine de l'hymne acathiste,'' *Muséon* 64 (1951) 27–61. For a more recent English translation, see MOTHER MARY and K. WARE in *The Lenten Triodion* (London-Boston, 1978) 422–37.

[I. THOMAS/EDS.]

AKHNATON (AMENHOTEP IV)

Akhnaton is the name that Amenhotep IV gave to himself, although Egyptologists, following the practice of Manetho, usually call him Amenophis IV. He was the son and successor of Amenhotep III and ruled for some 17 years, about the middle of the 14th century B.C. (1372–1354, according to E. Drioton and J. Vandier, *L'Égypte,* 3d ed., 631; 1353–1336, according to W. Helck-E. Otto, *Kleines Wörterbuch der Ägyptologie* 37). His mother was Tiye. His wife, Nefertiti, cannot be identified, as some have claimed, with Princess Tadukhepa, the daughter of the Mitannian King Tushratta; her nurse was Teye, the wife of Ay, and she had a sister in Egypt named Benremut. The history of the reign of Amenhotep IV is dominated by the religious revolution that he unleashed against Amon and the other Egyptian gods. This revolt so engaged his energies that it caused the collapse of the empire that Thutmosis III had built up in Syria and Phoenicia.

The Aton Reform. From the beginning of his reign, Amenhotep IV showed his devotion to a particular form of the sun-god, the solar disk, which was called Aton. Aton appears more and more frequently on the monuments and in the texts that date from the beginning of the New Empire, especially under Amenhotep III; but from this it does not follow that the solar disk had already been the object of a special cult. East of the temple of Amon at Karnak, Amenhotep IV built for Aton a solar temple like the one in Heliopolis. Its god was represented under the form of a solar disk, the rays of which ended in human hands. It is important to note that the colossal statues of the king that adorned this temple were made in a new style that was to become characteristic of the Amarna Art, as it is called. In the tombs of his officials, e.g., that of the vizier, Ramose, the traditional art is also suddenly replaced by this realistic style. This shows that the sovereign was able to impose his novel ideas on his contemporaries, and we can suppose that these art forms served merely as means to express his equally revolutionary notions in religious matters. Thereupon the conflict that this involved with the traditionalists reached a critical point, and things began to happen quickly. In the sixth year of his reign Amenhotep IV left Thebes and founded a city, halfway between Luxor and Cairo, on a site that is currently known as el-Amarna, but that he called Akhetaton (the Horizon of Aton). Here he surrounded himself with officials who were *homines novi* and were totally devoted to him. Soon he proscribed the cult of most of the other gods, particularly that of Amon. Their temples were closed, their statues smashed, and their names chiseled out of every monument, whether big or little. His own name, Amenhotep, "Amon is merciful," he changed to Akhnaton, "Useful to Aton."

Akhnaton's new doctrine finds its best expression in the famous hymn to Aton that appears in certain tombs of his officials at el-Amarna, most notably the tomb of Ay, who later succeeded Tut-ankh-Amon on the throne of Egypt (see J. B. Pritchard's *Ancient Near Eastern Texts Relating to the Old Testament* 369–71). Akhnaton himself is credited with its composition. The tenor of this hymn is thoroughly monotheistic; yet a careful study of it shows that it does not really contain much that had not been said before in the hymns to Amon and various other gods. Actually, the traditional cults also showed a strong monotheistic tendency (*see* EGYPT, ANCIENT), but the syncretism that is the basis of the old religion is entirely absent here, and it is precisely this that constitutes, above all else, the novelty of the hymn. The new faith ignored all the old gods that were venerated under animal or human forms and worshiped only the sun-god, under the form of the solar disk. An exception, however, must be made for the cult of the bull, Mnevis, which was also introduced at Akhetaton. This detail shows how much the religion of Akhnaton was indebted to the Heliopolitan cult. The conclusion can be drawn that what the king really did was to carry to its extreme the ideology of the ancient solar religion by abolishing, as E. Drioton expresses it, "the contradiction, that had always been felt by the more enlightened thinkers, between the monotheism professed by the educated classes and their official polytheism" ["Le monothéisme de L'Ancienne Égypte" *Cahiers d'histoire égyptienne* (Cairo 1949) 167]. There is no need, therefore, to look outside of Egypt, as some have done, for the motives that inspired this reform.

The relations with Heliopolis are evident also in the plan of the sanctuary at Akhetaton, which, though more complicated, belongs to the general type of solar temples. The first part consisted of the *per-hat,* "house of jubilation," a courtyard with two altars, and of the *gem-Aton,* "Aton was found," a series of courtyards with altars. The second part, the house of *benben,* likewise comprised two courtyards, one of which was enclosed with a peristyle within which was probably an obelisk.

End of the Reign. Such simple and rational doctrine, however, proved insufficient, even though it was propagated by a fanatical prophet, who was at the same time both a poet and an originator of a new aesthetic ideal. Immemorial tradition showed itself still stronger. The Aton doctrine won few adepts apart from Akhnaton himself,

and scarcely was he dead when even his former friends returned to the old religion. The last years of his life were not happy. His second daughter, Meketaton, died. His wife, Nefertiti, fell into disgrace, and in her palace to the south of Akhetaton her name and image were everywhere replaced by those of her oldest daughter, Meritaton, the wife of Akhnaton's younger brother, Smenkhkarē, who began to make conciliatory gestures to the Amon priesthood. Tut-ankh-Aton, the husband of Akhnaton's third daughter and later his successor, changed his name to Tut-ankh-Amon for his short reign at Thebes, during which he officially restored the Amon cult. Horemheb, when ascending the throne, wiped out the last traces of the Aton heresy. It was probably at this time that Akhnaton suffered his *damnatio memoriae* and that his body was doomed to destruction, though perhaps secretly saved by some of the small group of his loyal followers. Succeeding generations regarded him merely as "the enemy at Akhetaton."

Bibliography: J. A. WILSON, *The Burden of Egypt: An Interpretation of Ancient Egyptian Culture* (Chicago 1951) ch. 9; also available as *The Culture of Ancient Egypt* (Chicago 1956). A. H. GARDINER, *Egypt of the Pharaohs* (Oxford 1961) ch. 9. L. G. LEEUWENBERG, *Echnaton* (The Hague 1946).

[J. VERGOTE]

AKIBA BEN JOSEPH

The leading rabbi of his time and one of the founders of Talmudic JUDAISM; b. Palestine *c.* A.D. 50; d. there, *c.* 135. He took no interest in learning until he was well on in years, when he studied under Rabbi JOHANAN BEN ZAKKAI at Jabneh (Jamnia). Later he founded his own academy, first at Lydda (Lod) and then at Bene Barak. He was the main spiritual force behind BAR KOKHBA in the latter's revolt against the Romans (132–35). After being arrested and tortured by the Romans, he died reciting the Shema Yisrael ("Hear, O Israel . . . ," Judaism's profession of faith, citing Deuteronomy 6.4).

Rabbi Akiba (Akiva, Aqiba) was the first to make a systematic collection of the halakic traditions (*see* HALAKAH) of the Tannaim ("repeaters," the rabbis of the first two Christian centuries) who handed down the Oral Law (as distinct from the Written Law of Moses); this work of his, as continued by his disciple Rabbi Meïr and still in oral form, was further systematized and recorded in writing in Rabbi JUDAH HA-NASI's MISHNAH. Another original contribution made by Akiba was his doctrine that the Oral Law was not immutable, but could be adjusted to changing conditions; since this is the basic principle guiding all Talmudic development, he is regarded as father of the TALMUD.

Exterior of Spring Hill College, Mobile, Alabama, 1830.

Bibliography: L. GINZBERG, *The Jewish Encyclopedia* 1:304–10. D. J. BORNSTEIN, *Encyclopaedia Judaica: Das Judentum in Geschichte und Gegenwart* 2:7–22. S. COHEN, *Universal Jewish Encyclopedia* 1: 144–50. J. SCHMID, *Lexikon für Theologie und Kirche* 1:778–79. L. FINKELSTEIN, *Akiba: Scholar, Saint and Martyr* (New York 1936). A. GUTTMANN, ''Akiba, 'Rescuer of the Torah,''' *Hebrew Union College Annual* 17 (1942–43) 395–421. S. A. BIRNBAUM, ''Bar Kokhba and Akiba,'' *Palestine Exploration Fund Quarterly Statement* 86 (1954) 23–32. P. BENOIT, ''Rabbi Aqiba ben Joseph, sage et héros du Judaïsme,'' *Revue biblique* 54 (1947) 54–89.

[J. J. DOUGHERTY]

ALABAMA, CATHOLIC CHURCH IN

Initially designated a part of the Diocese of Quebec, the region that now constitutes the State of Alabama was organized as the Vicariate-Apostolic of Alabama and the Floridas in 1825. The Diocese of Mobile was erected on May 15, 1829, and its name was changed to the Diocese of Mobile-Birmingham on July 9, 1954. The Diocese of Birmingham was created as a separate entity in 1969. Finally, the Archdiocese of Mobile was established on November 16, 1980, comprising the lower 28 counties of the State of Alabama (22,969 square miles), with the suffragan dioceses of Birmingham, and Biloxi and Jackson, Mississippi. Though Catholicism in the region remained below five percent of the total population at the beginning of the new millennium, it has enjoyed steady growth amid varied challenges, which have included economic, political and anti-Catholic sentiment.

Catholic Origins. Catholicism first came to the region with early Spanish and French exploration and a permanent settlement at Mobile in 1702, with Father Henry Rolleaux de las Vente as its first pastor. The parish register, intact from 1704, documents the unsettled conditions of those early years in which the faith expanded. One such condition was the dilemma of maintaining an adequate number of clergy to minister to the growing Catholic population. Yet, amid the transition of the varied political entities (French, Spanish and British) governing the region, secular and religious priests, in turn, functioned as pastors, without too much interference from civil authorities.

With the territory passing from French, British and Spanish rule, the ecclesiastical responsibility shifted from Quebec, Canada, to Santiago de Cuba, and finally in 1793, to the mainland diocese of New Orleans. With the Gulf Coast area becoming part of the United States, the State of Alabama and the Territory of Florida were erected into a vicariate apostolic in August 1825, and Bishop Michael PORTIER (1795–1859) was appointed to head the new jurisdiction.

Diocese. Portier, a native cleric of Lyon, France, developed and structured religious life in the Gulf Coast area. The vicariate was raised to a diocese in May 1829, and in 1850 was reduced in geographical size, when part of the panhandle of Florida was transferred to the ecclesiastical jurisdiction of the Diocese of Stt. Augustine, Florida. Portier was most successful in founding institutions of education and welfare, which allowed the Catholic presence further influence and visibility in the greater community. Such institutions included Spring Hill College, founded in 1830, and entrusted to the Jesuits in 1847. At the time of Portier's death in 1859 there were 10 priests serving nine parishes and nine missions, and the Catholic population had grown from 6,000 to an estimated 10,000, most of it centered along the Alabama-Florida Gulf coast.

Bishop John Quinlan (1826–83) was consecrated as the second bishop of Mobile in New Orleans on December 4, 1859. A native of County Cork, Ireland, Quinlan immigrated to the United States in 1844, and was ordained for the Diocese of Cincinnati, Ohio, in 1852. He spent his early years in the diocese shepherding a region in turmoil due to the national debate over slavery and "states' rights." With the coming of the Civil War, and the consequent economic plights during and after the conflict, there was a greater commitment of Church resources to the poor. Yet, this commitment also hampered efforts to expand a parochial Catholic presence in the region.

Amid such challenges Quinlan secured clergy from Ireland, attained financial resources, and furthered construction on the cathedral. The northern half of the diocese received resident pastors for the first time, thanks to the arrival of monks from the Benedictine abbey of St. Vincent Abbey (later arch-abbey), Latrobe, Pennsylvania. The eventual establishment of the independent Benedictine Abbey of St. Bernard's in Cullman (1891) also provided the diocese with a second Catholic college, St. Bernard's. By the time of Quinlan's death, the clergy population had increased to 45, evenly divided between secular and religious priests. The Catholic population had also increased to about 18,000. Unfortunately, the diocese continued to be burdened with significant financial obligations.

Although growth of the Catholic population continued in the Diocese of Mobile, throughout the 1800s the local church could be characterized more by retrenchment and consolidation than by new gains. The vast majority of the relatively small Catholic population remained along the Gulf coast of Alabama, primarily in the city of Mobile, but small and steadfast Catholic populations were found in Montgomery, Tuscaloosa, and the expanding "new city" of Birmingham.

The third bishop, Dominic Manucy (1823–85), was born in St. Augustine, Florida, and had been ordained by Portier in 1850. He was transferred to Mobile in March 1884, while retaining the administration of his former jurisdiction, the Vicariate Apostolic of Brownsville in Texas. But ill health and difficulties in Mobile led Manu-

cy to resign before the end of 1884. Jeremiah O'Sullivan (1844–96), a native of Ireland and priest of the Archdiocese of Baltimore, was consecrated the fourth bishop of Mobile, Sept. 20, 1885. He was instrumental in resolving the financial difficulties of the diocese, yet no substantial growth of institutions or Catholic population took place. Hard economic times in the South, particularly in Mobile, made immigration to the region unlikely. By the close of the 19th century, the State of Alabama had suffered a slight decline in Catholic population.

The cultural and political situation in the United States at the beginning of the following century, as well as the leadership of the next two bishops, were instrumental in the expansion of Catholic institutions and the spiritual good of the slowly growing Catholic population. Edward Patrick Allen, who had been president of St. Mary's College in Emmitsburg, Maryland, was consecrated bishop in Baltimore on May 16, 1897. During his 30 years as bishop in Mobile the Catholic population grew to 48,000, new churches were built, and there was an increase in the number of clergy. Particular emphasis was placed upon the spiritual well being of Catholics in the rural areas outside of Mobile, and the Josephite Fathers began their ministry to the African American population in the area.

Efforts by the Josephite, the Trinitarian, and the Edmundite Fathers fostered an environment of evangelization in the African American community, as well as in the general Alabama population, particularly in the rural areas and among the poor. These religious communities of men also promoted the development of Catholic education throughout the diocese, especially in the Black communities, which at this time were denied quality education, due to segregation and the infamous "Jim Crow" laws. The diocese also benefited from the endowments established by the McGill family of Mobile.

The 20th century brought monumental change for the State of Alabama and her Catholic population. The city of Mobile experienced steady growth throughout the century, due in part to the expanding paper and chemical industry, as well as the construction of a military air base. The city of Birmingham had the greatest increase in population thanks to the expansion of the steel and coal industries found there. This increase included Catholic immigrants, particularly Italians, attracted to the region by the new employment opportunities.

The city of Montgomery, also witnessed an increased Catholic population due to the expansion of Maxwell Field (now Maxwell Air Force Base) at the onset of World War II. This military base eventually became the home of the United States Air Force War College, which has continued to draw Catholics to the region. The Cold

War period created the conditions for the rapid expansion of the Catholic population, through the continued building of the chemical and steel industries, as well as the increasing military presence in the region. Yet in rural Alabama, the Catholic community struggled to maintain a visible presence in the midst of an anti-Catholic environment. At the same time that the State of Alabama witnessed new economic opportunities, it was also faced with the challenge to address the tragic historical issue of racial inequality.

For the first half of the 20th century the man who personified "Catholic" in Alabama was Bishop Thomas Joseph TOOLEN (1886–1976). From the time of his appointment as the sixth bishop of Mobile on February 28, 1927 until his retirement in 1969, Toolen instilled and fostered a greater unity and self-respect among the Catholic faithful. Toolen mandated religious education in every parish and established parochial schools, as well as Catholic healthcare facilities in the three metropolitan areas of the State of Alabama. He also addressed the plight of the poor through the establishment of the Catholic Charities Office during the Great Depression. Toolen also expanded the participation of the laity through the efforts of the Diocesan Council of Catholic Women, the Holy Name of Jesus Fraternity, and grand Catholic gatherings such as Christ the King celebrations, held throughout the diocese. In 1954 Pope Pius XII designated Toolen an "archbishop ad Personam."

Catholic Life Today. Archbishop Toolen continued the expansion of Catholic institutions and presence throughout Alabama. He gave particular attention to Catholic education in the African American parishes, and invited religious communities to serve in ministry to the rural areas of the diocese. He sought to maintain Catholic social agencies concerned with the poor and healthcare facilities. By 1969, an extensive "Catholic structure" has been developed to address the pastoral and fiscal needs of the Catholic population, as well as those of the greater community. These developments and the rapid growth in the Catholic population following World War II caused the Holy See to establish two new dioceses from out of the territorial jurisdiction of Diocese of Mobile: the Diocese of Pensacola-Tallahassee was established in 1968, and in 1969, the Diocese of Birmingham.

The newly created Diocese of Birmingham experienced an amazing growth in Catholic population through the migration of Catholics into the northern half of the state, mainly due to the relocation of the steel industry to the South, the growth of technological and medical research in the Birmingham metropolitan area, and the establishment of NASA's jet propulsion headquarters in Huntsville. Prior to the mid-20th century, Catholicism in Alabama had been shaped and identified along the Gulf Coast region of the state, primarily in the city of Mobile. But the once "Protestant interior" of the state saw a dramatic increase in the Catholic population in Birmingham, Anniston, and in other once-small communities throughout the northern tier of the state. By the late 1950s the Catholic population in northern Alabama was growing at a faster rate than that of the Gulf Coast region. Thus there came to be a pattern of two experiences of Catholic life in the State of Alabama: a predominance of native, Southern Catholics along the Gulf Coast, with long roots in the coastal region, and the more recent immigrant Catholics in the northern part of the state, with family roots in other areas of the country as well as other nations. The only "ethnic parishes" in the state are found in Birmingham.

When Pope Paul IV established the Diocese of Birmingham on June 28, 1969, the newly created diocese included the upper 39 counties of the state and had an initial Catholic population of 39,828 among the general population of 2,134,396. By 2000, the Catholic population of the diocese had nearly doubled, to 76,941. Thus, the once "mission" area of the state that a few years previously had only a few established Catholic communities in Tuscaloosa, Birmingham, and Cullman came to have a greater Catholic population than the "mother diocese" of Mobile. Catholics in the region, with strong Eucharistic and Marian devotions, often still face misconceptions about Catholics beliefs as well as direct and indirect anti-Catholicism.

In 1969 John L. May was appointed the seventh bishop in Mobile. He was a native of Chicago and head of the Catholic Extension Society, which has continued to forward grant monies to many of the mission parishes in the state. Bishop May was noted for implementing the "vision" of the Second Vatican Council, being an advocate of adult faith formation, and for the establishment of mission parishes in counties with growing, yet small Catholic populations. He also helped in the formation of the longest ongoing Christian-Jewish dialogue in the United States: Mobile Christian-Jewish Dialogue.

In January 1980 May was appointed Archbishop of St. Louis, Missouri. In that same year the Holy See raised the Diocese of Mobile to an archdiocese. And on July 29, 1980, Monsignor Oscar H. Lipscomb, a native Mobilian and chancellor of the diocese, was appointed the first archbishop of Mobile. Lipscomb provided a continued vision for the newly established Archdiocese of Mobile, bringing qualities nurtured in his own experience of Catholic culture in the Deep South and his understanding of the documents of the Second Vatican Council.

At the beginning of the new millennium the Catholic population continued to grow, though not at the accelerated rate of that found immediately after World War II. Also, the efforts to establish a Catholic ethos in rural Alabama began to see fruit in the southeastern and northern regions of the state, where once-mission parishes were becoming large and dynamic centers of Catholic worship, contributing to the greater community. The Archdiocese of Mobile and the Diocese of Birmingham in Alabama continue to provide ministry to the poor of the region, most of whom are non-Catholics. Thus, the Catholic faithful continue to create ecumenical bridges, while still offering ongoing formation in and the celebration of Catholic culture in a rapidly changing ''Deep South'' state.

Bibliography: M. T. A. CARROLL, *A Catholic History of Alabama and the Floridas* (New York 1908). *Catholic Culture in Alabama: Centenary Story of Spring Hill College* (New York 1931). REVEREND O. H. LIPSCOMB, *The Administration of Michael Portier, Vicar Apostolic of Alabama and the Floridas, 1825–1829, and First Bishop of Mobile, 1829–1859* (unpublished thesis, Catholic University of America, 1965). R. G. LOVETT, *Catholic Church in the Deep South* (Birmingham, Ala. 1981).

[M. FARMER]

ALACOQUE, MARGARET MARY, ST.

Contemplative nun of the VISITATION order; b. Lauthecourt, France, July 22, 1647; d. Paray-le-Monial, Oct. 17, 1690. Margaret was the fifth of seven children of Claude Alacoque, a royal notary, and Philiberte Lamyn. The family was esteemed by members of the nobility, whose names appear frequently as sponsors on the Baptism register. Margaret's education was limited to the training received in the home of her godmother and, after the death of her father, to the two years spent at the boarding school of the Urbanists, where she made her first Communion. Illness required her withdrawal, and the next 15 years were spent with her mother in painful dependence on nearby relatives. During this period, her attraction to suffering and her grace of contemplative prayer were intensified. On July 20, 1671, Margaret Mary entered Paray-le-Monial, and was professed Nov. 6 of the next year. Between 1673 and 1675 she received the revelations. The first commissioned her to spread devotion to the SACRED HEART; the second requested Communion and the HOLY HOUR of reparation; the last expressed a wish for a special feast day in honor of the Sacred Heart. Margaret Mary lived the devotion, and amid contradiction and opposition worked for its recognition within her order. The exterior apostolate was confided to the Jesuits, among whom Saint Claude de la COLOMBIÈRE had been chosen to sanction the revelations. She was beatified by Pius IX, Sept. 18, 1864, and canonized by Benedict XV, May 13, 1920.

Feast: Oct. 16.

Bibliography: M. M. ALACOQUE, *Letters*, tr. C. A. HERBST (Chicago 1954); *The Autobiography*, tr. V. KERNS (Westminster, Md. 1961); *Vie et oeuvres de sainte Marguerite-Marie Alacoque*, ed. R. DARRICAU, 2 vols. (Paris 1990–1993). P. BLANCHARD, *Sainte Marguerite-Marie: Expérience et doctrine* (Paris 1961). L. CRISTIANI, *Saint Margaret Mary Alacoque and the Promises of the Sacred Heart*, tr. M. A. BOUCHARD (Boston 1975). J. CROISET, *The devotion to the Sacred Heart of Our Lord Jesus Christ*, tr. P. O'CONNELL from the French of the final edition published at Lyons, 1694 (Milwaukee 1976). H. GHÉON, *Secrets of the saints*, tr. F. J. SHEED and D. ATTWATER (London 1973). A. HAMON, *Vie de Ste. Marguerite Marie* (Paris 1924), with full bibliography. J. LADAME, *Doctrine et spiritualité de sainte Marguerite-Marie* (Montsûrs 1979); *Les faits de Paray-le-Monial* (Paris 1970). H. MONTAIGU, *Paray-le-Monial, ou, Le Ciel intérieur* (Paris 1979). A. BUTLER, *The Lives of the Saints*, ed. H. THURSTON and D. ATTWATER (New York 1956) 4:134–138. J. BAINVEL, *Dictionnaire de théologie catholique* (Paris 1903–50) 3.1: 320–351.

[M. L. LYNN]

ALAIN (ÉMILE AUGUSTE CHARTIER)

French philosopher, essayist, and schoolmaster, one of the great intellectual forces in France during the first half of the 20th century; b. Mortagne, France, March 3, 1868; d. Le Vésinet, June 3, 1951. Of Norman ancestry, he inherited the rugged common sense and obstinacy of the Norman peasant. Of Catholic parentage, he gave up his religious beliefs in youth and never became fully reconciled with Catholic dogma. After graduation from École Normale Supérieure, he taught in various lycées, finally becoming a professor of philosophy at Lycée Henry IV in Paris. His renown as philosopher and teacher extended to all parts of France, and many of his pupils attained eminence, among them the later biographer and historian André Maurois. Although after his retirement his home became a rendezvous for distinguished Frenchmen, he is not well-known outside his own country.

He wrote daily *propos* for the *Dépêche de Rouen*. These short essays, embodying his views on a variety of subjects, were collected from time to time and reissued. They form about half of his complete works and include *Les propos d'Alain* (1920), *Propos de littérature* (1933), and *Propos de politique* (1934). Among Chartier's other published works are *Le Citoyen contre les pouvoirs* (1925) and *Histoire de mes pensées* (1936).

Although his life was devoted to teaching and many of his works contain references to education, he wrote only one book on the subject, his *Propos sur l'éducation*. The style, though informal, is forceful, displaying an original mind. His educational philosophy shows the influence of G. F. Hegel rather than of J. J. Rousseau. His educational views followed few of the accepted patterns of his day. The task of the school was twofold: (1) making of citizens; and (2) integration, by which he meant the maintenance of the moral and intellectual man, who in turn makes the nation. To achieve this end, he favored the Napoleonic system of centralized control in education and austere educational surroundings. He advocated the early intense and detailed study of the best literature, and stressed mathematics, history, and geography with particular emphasis on geometry and Latin. He aimed to induce pupils to think long and deeply on worthwhile things and insisted that progress be slow and thorough with excellence as the main goal.

Chartier was mainly a conservative and looked askance at the "new education." He objected to observation lessons, so much insisted upon in the Decroly system. He considered wasteful many of the motivational devices used in the modern school, holding that the child responds best to something challenging, and lightly dismissed the findings of psychology on individual differences. His own ideas on pupils' capacities were formed from his experiences with the select group that attended the French lycée. The concept of equality of opportunity did not interest him. The aim, he insisted, should be to discover and concentrate on excellence. He disregarded parental rights in education, holding that centralized state authority was best fitted to use the school as an instrument for achieving the "glory of France."

In France, between World Wars I and II, his teaching and extensive publications exercised a wide influence. This lay largely in strengthening and conserving the prevailing classical and French tradition of an elite excelling in scholarship and indirectly, therefore, obstructed the liberalizing and democratizing efforts of other educational leaders. He contributed nothing to furthering distinctly Christian ideals in French education.

Bibliography: J. CHATEAU, ed., *Les Grands pédagogues* (Paris 1956). A. MAUROIS, *Alain* (Paris 1949). G. PASCAL, *La Pensée d'Alain* (Paris 1946). "Hommage à Alain," *Mercure de France* 313 (1951) 581–661, made up of seven articles on various phases of Chartier's life and thought. C. L. HALL, "Alain, 1868–1951," *School and Society* 76 (1952) 289–92.

[M. R. MCLAUGHLIN]

ALAMANNI, COSMO

Italian philosopher, theologian, and commentator on the works of St. THOMAS AQUINAS; b. Milan, Aug. 30, 1559; d. Milan, May 24, 1634 (according to Sotwell) or July 24, 1634 (according to Ehrle). Alamanni entered the Jesuit novitiate at Novellara on Sept. 11, 1575, one of five brothers to do so; he studied theology at the Roman College under F. SUÁREZ and G. VÁZQUEZ, and taught at

Brera College in Milan. In 1590 he prepared for publication a theological opusculum entitled *Correctiones in Fonescam,* but it remained in manuscript only. Delicate health forced him to interrupt his teaching career in Milan after 17 years. In 1606 he was called to be the bishop's theologian at the Pavia curia, where he remained for 17 years also. During his sojourn in Pavia, Alamanni completed his *Summa totius philosophiae e divi Thomae Aquinatis doctrina* (Pavia 1618–23). This was edited a second time with augmentations by J. Frontenau (Paris 1640) and again by F. Ehrle (Paris 1885–94). The *Summa* presented a clear and accurate exposition of the teaching of St. Thomas, and was considerably influential in the revival of THOMISM in the twentieth century.

Bibliography: *Summa philosophiae,* ed. F. EHRLE, 3 v. (Paris 1885–1894), pref. vi–viii. N. SOTWEL, *Bibliotheca scriptorum Societatis Jesu* (Rome 1676) 161–162, 519.

[F. J. ROENSCH]

ALAN DE LA ROCHE

A.k.a. Alanus de Rupe, founder of the modern rosary devotion and of the Confraternities of the Rosary; b. somewhere in Brittany, date unknown; d. Zwolle (Holland), Sept. 8, 1475. Although called blessed, he was never officially beatified. Little information about his life is historically certain. He entered the Dominicans probably at an early age at Dinan in Brittany. After his profession he was sent to the convent of St. Jacques in Paris for his philosophical and theological studies, and subsequently he lectured there. The date of his ordination is not known. He filled professorships in different convents of his order: from 1462 he was at Lille, where, from 1464, the Dominican convent belonged to the *Congregatio Hollandica*; in 1464 he was at Douai, and in 1468, at Ghent. It is questionable whether he went to the University of Rostock (Germany) in 1470. In 1474 he went to Zwolle. Along with his teaching he may have preached often, though there is no solid historical information on this point.

Alan's works on the rosary were printed after his death by J. A. Coppenstein, OP (*B. Alanus de Rupe Redivivus,* Freiburg 1619), but this edition exhibits a worked-over text and is uncritical and incomplete. Alan gave the Hail Mary, which existed in various forms, the precise form in which it became popular. He divided 150 Ave's into three series of 50, introduced the Our Father before each 10, and treated in accompanying articles or statements the mysteries of the birth, Passion, and glory of Christ. In 1470 he founded at Douai the first Confraternity of the Rosary. His fantastic visions, in which, for example, it was said that the Blessed Virgin commissioned

St. Dominic to institute the rosary, should be regarded as a quite normal means of religious propaganda in Alan's period.

Bibliography: *Beatus Alanus de Rupe Redivivus,* ed. J. A. COPPENSTEIN (Naples 1630), the most accessible ed. and later reprints. R. COULON, *Dictionnaire d'histoire et de géographie ecclésiastiques,* 1:1306–12. J. QUÉTIF and J. ÉCHARD, *Scriptores Ordinis Praedicatorum,* 1.2:849–852. B. DE BOER, ''De Souter van Alanus de Rupe,'' *Ons Geestelijk Erf* 29 (1955) 358–388; 30 (1956) 156–190; 31 (1957) 187–204; 33 (1959) 145–193, best study to date, with detailed bibliog.

[C. BRAKKEE]

ALAN OF LILLE

Alan of Lille (Alanus Insulis), Doctor Universalis, theologian, philosopher, poet, preacher, and polemist; b. Lille, *c.* 1116–1120; d. Cîteaux, 1202. During his life, Alan was renown for being the most widely learned person of his day. Although his fame during his life lay in teaching the liberal arts at Paris, he had great influence as a poet and theologian on later thinkers like Dante and Chaucer.

Life. It is difficult to create a sharp chronology of Allan's life; his early years are especially obscure. Yet, it is clear that Alan had exceptional training in the liberal arts and theology. Most likely he studied under Gilbert of Poitiers, at Paris or perhaps at Chartres, sometime between 1140 and 1142, before Gilbert became Bishop of Poitiers. Allan was a prominent teacher at Paris from around 1157 to 1170, which marked the apex of his career. Present scholarship points to his being at Montepellier perhaps first as student and later as teacher from *c.* 1171–85. At some point in the next decade he retired and lived with the Cistercians at Cîteaux, where he remained until his death in 1202. His remains were exhumed in 1960, when it was determined that he had been around 86 years old at the time of his death. Based on the pastoral tone of his writings as well as interest in the art of preaching, Alan appears to have been a secular cleric.

Works. Alan's literary production was large and diverse. His theological writings include his *Summa, Quoniam homines*, numerous *Questiones disputatae*, and his *Theologicae regulae*. In the last of these Alan sets out to prove theological truths by using the methods of geometry, a proto-scholastic method similar to Peter Lombard. Some of his conclusions are original, although others are borrowed. It is one of the first attempts to make a clear and systematic presentation of orthodox theological principles. We also have over seventy of his sermons, a Biblical dictionary entitled *Distinctiones dictionum theologicarum*, a small treatise on the *De sex alis Cherubim*, a confessional manual, and a commentary on the Song of Songs called *Elucidatio in Cantica Canticorum.* Other works include a list of moral principles, the *Liber parabolarum,* and his *Ars praedicandi,* one of the first works on the art of preaching. Alan also wrote an apologetic refutation of Christian heresies and against the Jewish and Islamic faiths entitled *Contra haereticos.*

The two of Alan's works that had the most lasting influence were his cosmological mythic poems, *De Planctu naturae* (*c.* 1160–70) and *Anticlaudianus* (*c.* 1183). In the former the goddess Nature, modeled on Boethius' Philosophia and Bernard Silvester's Natura, is the major protagonist. All of creation celebrates her arrival, but she complains to the narrator/poet that the actions of humanity violate reason and the natural order of the universe. This behavior is described in the language of sexual perversion and is symbolized by Nature's torn tunic, which is covered with the content of the cosmos. The poet, who plays both the foil and the representative of humanity, has a dialogue with her. Then the cosmos is once again brought into harmony with divine plan with the help of Genius, Nature's scribe and priest, who excommunicates the vices from the created order, and Hymen, who reconciles opposite forces of nature.

In the *Anticlaudianus*, Nature again is the main character who seeks to make a person who will renew the created order and fulfill the promise of humanity's destiny. This renewal is accomplished with the help of the heavenly virtues of Prudence and Ratio, who ascend into the heavenly spheres on a chariot made of the seven liberal arts, having been guided there by the five senses. Theologia and Fides lead them to God, who creates a perfect soul in His own image through the divine Noys. Nature then uses the elements to create the perfect body, which is bound together with the soul by Concordia, Music, and Arithmetic. After conquering an onslaught of Vices, this person becomes the archetypal human being and the new ruler of the new earth.

In both poems, pagan authors like Plato are vehicles for understanding Christian ideas. In doing this Alan follows Boethius, as well as his predecessor and inspiration Bernard Silvester. Allan's mythic poetry expresses his vision of the cosmos as a way by which the human race can approach divine truth. But our actions require more than reason, and ultimately it is theology and faith that will lead us to wisdom.

Bibliography: Most of Alan's works are compiled in *Patrologia Latina,* ed. J. P. MIGNE [Paris 1878–90] 210. These include *Distinctiones dictionum theologicarum* (*Patrologia Latina* 210 685–1012), *De sex alis Cherubim* (*Patrologia Latina* 210 269–280), *Elucidatio in Canticum Canticorum,* (*Patrologia Latina* 210 51–110), *Ars praedicandi* (*Patrologia Latina* 210 111–195), *Contra haereticos* (*Patrologia Latina* 210 305–430). Several of

Alan's sermons and other smaller works are edited by M. T. D'ALVERNY, *Alain de Lille: Textes inédits* (Paris 1965). *Summa Quoniam homines*, ed. P. GLORIEUX, *AHDLMA* xx: (1954) 113–364. *Numerous Questiones disputatae*, unedited but see L. THORNDIKE, *Isis* 51 (1950) 181–185. *Theologicae regulae*, ed. N. HARING, "Magister Alanus de Insulis, Regulae caelestis iuris," *AHDLMA* XLVIII (1981) 97–226. *De Planctu Naturae*, ed. N. HARING, *Studi Medievali* ser 3, xix: (1978) 797–879. *Anticlaudianus* ed. R. BOSSUAT (Paris 1955), trans. J. J. SHERIDAN (Toronto 1973). *De virtutibus et vitiis* ed. O. LOTTIN in *Psychologie et morale aux XIIe et XIIIe siècles* VI (Gembloux 1960). Literature. G. RAYNAUD DE LAGE, *Alain de Lille, poète du xii siècle* (Paris 1951). R. GREEN, "Alan of Lille's Anticlaudianus: Ascenus mentis ad Deum" *Annuale medievale* 8 (1976) 3–16. A. CIOTTI, "Alano e Dante." *Convivium* 28 (1960) 257–88. M. T. D'ALVERNY, "Alain de Lille et la Theologia" in *L'homme devant Dieu: Mélanges offerts au Père Henri de Lubac* (Paris 1964) 111–28. Also see the extensive introduction in d'Alverny's critical edition of Alan's sermons listed above. P. G. WALSH, "Alan of Lille as a Renaissance Figure" in *Renaissance and Renewal in Christian History* (Oxford 1989). W. WETHERBEE, *Platonism and Poetry in the Twelfth Century* (Princeton 1972). G. EVANS, *Alan of Lille: The Frontiers of Theology in the Late Twelfth Century* (Cambridge 1983).

[P. ELLARD]

ALAN OF TEWKESBURY

Benedictine abbot, writer; d. 1202. Alan entered the monastery at Canterbury in 1174 on his return from Benevento where he had been a canon. When Herlewin resigned in 1179, Alan became prior. He incurred the enmity of HENRY II because he supported Thomas Becket, obtained the privilege of collecting PETER'S PENCE, and objected to the choice of Baldwin as archbishop of Canterbury. Though Alan later recognized BALDWIN OF CANTERBURY, the latter transferred him to the abbey of TEWKESBURY, where he was abbot in 1186. Alan wrote a life of Becket and an account of the Clarendon Council (*see* CLARENDON, CONSTITUTIONS OF). Also extant are his letters to Henry concerning the translation of Becket's remains, and to Baldwin claiming for Canterbury certain rights over the see of ROCHESTER.

Bibliography: *Materials for History of Archbishop Thomas Becket*, ed. J. C. ROBERTSON, *Rerum Britannicarum medii aevi scriptores* 67.2:299–352. GERVAISE OF CANTERBURY, *Historical Works*, ed. W. STUBBS, *Rerum Britannicarum medii aevi scriptores* 73.1:293. J. B. MULLINGER, *The Dictionary of National Biography from the Earliest Times to 1900* 1:214–15. R. BIRON, *Dictionnaire d'histoire et de géographie ecclésiastiques* 1:1318. J. DE GHELLINCK, *L'Essor de la littérature latine au XIIe siècle* 1:132; 2:174–75.

[M. L. MISTRETTA]

ALANS

A nomadic Iranian people occupying the steppe region between the Caucasus Mts. and the Don and Ural Rivers early in the Christian era. They figured occasionally in Roman affairs before falling under the domination of the Huns *c.* A.D. 350, with whom they moved westward into Ostrogothic territory. One group advanced into central Germany, joined the Vandals in Gaul 406–409, and crossed into Spain under their chieftain, Respendial. Decimated there by Visigothic *foederati* in 418, the survivors merged with the Vandals and accompanied Gaiseric into Africa. Another Alan contingent near Orleans fought with the Roman general Aetius against Attila in 451. Liberated from the Huns after 455, the main body of Alans drifted back to the steppes. Muslims and Mongols dominated them during the Middle Ages. They finally withdrew into the central Caucasus where their descendants survive as the Osset nation. The only ancient report of the Alans' religion says that they worshiped a sword fixed in the ground. Those who associated with the East Germans probably absorbed some Arianism, but their conversion as a tribe came only after Patriarch NICHOLAS I OF CONSTANTINOPLE (901–925) sent the monk Euthymius to evangelize them. Nicholas then established the metropolitan see of Alania whose Orthodox history can be traced to 1590.

Bibliography: S. VAILHÉ, *Dictionnaire d'histoire et de géographie ecclésiastiques* 1:1334–38. E. A. THOMPSON, *A History of Attila and the Huns* (Oxford 1948). F. DVORNIK, *The Making of Central and Eastern Europe* (London 1949). G. DEETERS, *Lexikon für Theologie und Kirche*, 10 v. (2d, new ed. Freiburg 1957–65) 1:265.

[R. H. SCHMANDT]

ALANUS ANGLICUS

A medieval canonist of Welsh origin, date and place of birth and death unknown. He was one of the leading professors at Bologna in the decade preceding the Fourth Lateran Council (1215); possibly he and his fellow countryman GILBERTUS ANGLICUS ended their days as Dominicans. Both DECRETIST and decretalist, his collection of decretals suggests English affiliations: he may have studied or taught law in England before the Bologna period or at least may have had some connection with John of Tynmouth and his associates in the English schools (*see* CANON LAW, HISTORY OF). Tancred, in the preface of his *Apparatus* to the *Compilatio tertia antiqua*, speaks of him simply as an English professor in the schools of Bologna. The extant works of Alanus are: *Collectio decretalium* (*c.* 1206), a critical register of which has been published by R. von Heckel (see bibliography); *Apparatus* to *Compilatio prima antiqua* (after 1207); glosses on *Compilatio secunda antiqua* (shortly after 1210 or 1212); and *Apparatus Decretorum* (*Ius naturale*). Some have held that he was the author of *Compilatio quarta antiqua*, but this was definitely JOANNES TEUTONICUS.

The apparatus *Ius naturale* is one of four great apparatuses on Gratian's *Decretum* that appeared at Bologna between 1190 and 1210. A first recension dates from about 1192, a second from some ten years later. As Stickler has shown (1959), the two recensions differ doctrinally: whereas, for example, Alanus originally was in the Gelasian-Gratian tradition of the juridical independence of the spiritual and secular powers, he had shifted by 1202 to a theocratic position. However, although some consider Alanus to be the architect of those curialist doctrines of papal sovereignty that eventually crystallized in the UNAM SANCTAM of Boniface VIII, he was simply responding to a wind that was blowing from the *Summa* of HUGUCCIO (*see* CHURCH AND STATE). The *Collectio Decretalium* of Alanus is one of the many systematic collections of decretals that appeared about this time. A first version had an appendix of 111 chapters; in a second version, which was that "received" at Bologna, Alanus inserted these chapters into the body of his collection, distributing 412 decretals in 484 chapters. Except for a division into six books instead of the classic five and some additional decretals, it follows the layout of the collection (1202–03) of Gilbertus Anglicus and appears to owe something to Anglo-Norman collections. With that of Gilbertus, the *Collectio Alani* is the principal source from which JOHN OF WALES formed his *Compilatio secunda antiqua* (1210–12) after the publication of Innocent III's official *Compilatio tertia antiqua* in 1210 (*see* QUINQUE COMPILATIONES ANTIQUAE).

Bibliography: J. F. VON SCHULTE, *Die Geschichte der Quellen und der Literatur des kanonischen Rechts* 1:84, 188–89. S. KUTTNER, *Repertorium der Kanonistik* 67–75, 316, 325, 346. R. VON HECKEL, "Die Dekretalensammlungen des Gilbertus und Alanus nach den Weingartener Handschriften," *Zeitschrift der Savigny-Stiftung für Rechtsgeschichte, Kanonistische Abteilung* 29 (1940) 116–357. A. M. STICKLER, *Historia iuris canonici latini*: v.1, *Historia fontium* 231. S. KUTTNER, "The Collection of Alanus: A Concordance of Its Two Recensions," *Rivista di storia del diritto italiano* 26–27 (1953–54) 39–55. A. M. STICKLER, "Alanus Anglicus als Verteidiger des monarchischen Papsttums," *Salesianum* 21 (1959) 346–406; *Lexikon für Theologie und Kirche* 1:265–66. "Bulletin of the Institute for Research and Study in Medieval Canon Law," *Traditio* 16 (1960) 557–58; 17 (1961) 534–36.

[L. E. BOYLE]

ALASKA, CATHOLIC CHURCH IN

Evolution of Ecclesiastical Jurisdiction. *Alaska* (spelled variously during earlier times) is the name the native inhabitants of the Aleutian Islands, the Aleuts, gave to the landmass lying to the east of their ancestral homeland. It translates basically as "the Great Land." Comprising 591,004 square miles, this massive peninsula at the northwestern extremity of the North American con-

Archdiocese/Diocese	Year Created
Archdiocese of Anchorage	1966
Diocese of Fairbanks	1962
Diocese of Juneau	1951

tinent is nearly one-fifth the size of the rest of the continental states. "Discovered" in July 1741 by Vitus Bering sailing under the Russian flag, Alaska was known as "Russian America" up to the time of its purchase from Russia by the United States in 1867 for $7,200,000. Organized as a Territory in 1912, Alaska was admitted into the Union in 1959 as the 49th state.

According to reliable records, the first formal act of Christian worship in what is today the State of Alaska took place on Ascension Thursday, May 13, 1779, when the Franciscan priest Juan Riobó—a member of a Spanish exploratory expedition sailing out of San Blas, Mexico—celebrated Mass near present-day Craig in southeastern Alaska. Alaska remained, in terms of ecclesiastical jurisdiction, a "no-man's land" until 1847, when Modest Demers was consecrated the first bishop of Vancouver Island, Canada, and given jurisdiction "over the island of that name and all British and Russian possessions as far north as 'the glacial sea.'"

The first Catholic missionary priest to enter Alaska was an OBLATE OF MARY IMMACULATE, Jean Séguin, who, coming from Canada, spent a fruitless winter, 1862–63, at Fort Yukon. In 1870 Oblate Father Émile Petitot visited Fort Yukon briefly. Two years later Oblate Bishop Isidore Clut and Auguste Lecorre (still a diocesan priest) traveled to Fort Yukon in hopes of establishing a permanent mission there. Owing to an Anglican presence there, they met with little success. In the summer of 1873, the two went down the Yukon River to St. Michael, where they were favorably received and enjoyed a modest degree of evangelizing success. Lecorre spent the winter 1873–74 at St. Michael. In the summer of 1874, when he learned that Alaska was under the jurisdiction of the bishop of Vancouver Island, he returned to Canada. It was at the invitation of and thanks to the support of Francois X. Mercier, a French-Canadian Catholic from Montréal and agent of the Alaska Commercial Company, that the Oblates entered Alaska from Canada and were able to achieve some positive, if limited, evangelizing results there.

While Oblate missionaries were active in northern Alaska, diocesan priests from Vancouver Island were visiting Alaska's southeastern part and establishing missions there. In 1867 Father Joseph Mandart made a brief

First Roman Catholic Church in Fairbanks, Alaska. (©Vince Streano/CORBIS)

trip to the panhandle, and in 1873 Charles J. SEGHERS—born Ghent, Belgium, Dec. 26, 1839, and newly consecrated bishop of Vancouver Island as of June 29, 1873—made his first of five trips to Alaska, visiting Sitka, Kodiak, and Unalaska. In 1877, accompanied by Mandart, he traveled to the northern interior, arriving at Nulato in August. The two spent the next 12 months there, engaged in missionary activity in Nulato and in the surrounding area. In May 1879 Seghers founded a mission at Wrangell and put Father John Althoff in charge. In 1885 Seghers—now an archbishop—established a mission at Sitka with Father William Heynen in charge.

In 1886 Seghers—rightly honored as "the Apostle of Alaska"—set out for Alaska on what was to be the last journey of his life. He had with him two Jesuits, Paschal Tosi and Aloysius Robaut. The party had as its goal the establishment of missions in Alaska's northern interior, especially at Nulato, which Seghers fondly remembered from his earlier stay there. The archbishop, the two Jesuits, and a Catholic layman, Francis Fuller, left Victoria on July 13, 1886. On September 7, via the Chilkoot Trail, they arrived at the confluence of the Stewart and Yukon Rivers, still in Canada. It was decided that the two Jesuits would spend the winter there, while Seghers and Fuller pushed on downriver toward Nulato. It was getting late

in the season for river travel, but Seghers was most eager to get to Nulato, driven, as he was, by the fear that Protestant ministers might get there before him and take over the area.

As Seghers and Fuller—who had already given clear signs of mental instability soon after the party left tidewater—made their way down the Yukon, their boat, traveling conditions, and Fuller's mind deteriorated rapidly. On October 4 they arrived at the confluence of the Yukon and Tanana Rivers, where they abandoned their boat and waited for the river to freeze solid enough for sled travel. On November 19 they again set out for Nulato. On November 27, with Nulato still a good distance away and travel difficult because of deep snow, the party camped. Early the next morning, the demented Fuller fired a shot into Seghers as he bent over to pick up his mittens. He died instantly.

The following spring, 1887, Tosi and Robaut came down the Yukon into Alaska, where they learned of Seghers's death. Immediately Tosi sailed for the Pacific Northwest to confer with Rocky Mountain Mission Superior Joseph M. Cataldo, S.J. When Seghers was given Tosi and Robaut for the trip north in 1886, they were intended simply as traveling companions. There was no intention to commit Jesuits to the Alaska Mission. Divine Providence ordained otherwise. Upon Tosi's urging, Cataldo decided then and there that the Jesuits would, for the time being, take charge at least of parts of Alaska. A long-term commitment would need Rome's approval. Armed with all the faculties the Vicar General of Vancouver Island could give him, Tosi returned to Alaska in the summer of 1887 to organize the systematic development of missions in northern Alaska. In 1892, during a private visit with Pope Leo XIII in Rome, Tosi so moved him with his account of Alaska that Leo told him: "Go, and make yourself the pope in those regions!"

Formal ecclesiastical jurisdiction within the whole of Alaska first came about in 1894, when the Holy See separated Alaska from the Diocese of Vancouver Island and made it a prefecture apostolic with Tosi as prefect apostolic. At the same time, Alaska became an independent mission, entrusted to the Jesuits, with Tosi as general superior. Failing health led to his being replaced as prefect apostolic in 1897 by John B. René, S.J. He, in turn, was replaced in 1904 by Joseph R. Crimont, S.J. In 1916 Alaska was raised to the next ecclesiastical level, that of a vicariate apostolic, and the following year Crimont was consecrated a bishop to serve as Alaska's first vicar apostolic. (It was Crimont, who, in 1920, five years before she was declared a saint, placed the whole Alaska Mission under the protection of St. Thérèse.) Upon his death in 1945, he was succeeded by his coadjutor since 1939,

Bishop Walter J. Fitzgerald, S.J., who died two years later. He was followed in 1948 by Bishop Francis D. Gleeson, S.J., Alaska's last vicar apostolic.

From time to time—beginning already during the Crimont years—Alaska's vastness and its varied geographic and ethnic makeup prompted those in authority, both in Rome and in Alaska, to consider the desirability of dividing it into several ecclesiastical districts. In 1951 Rome decreed the erection of Alaska's first diocese, the Diocese of Juneau, comprising at the time Alaska's panhandle—a coastal region, consisting in large part of many heavily forested, mist-shrouded islands sculpted by glaciers, and inhabited by a mix of many peoples, including some of Alaska's first people, the Haida and Tlingit—and much of south-central Alaska. Dermot O'Flanagan, a long-time diocesan priest in Alaska, was consecrated its first ordinary. He was the first bishop to be consecrated in Alaska, in Anchorage, by Bishop Gleeson on Oct. 3, 1951.

Up to 1951 all of Alaska's ecclesiastical leaders after Tosi had made Juneau their headquarters. When the Juneau diocese was established, Gleeson moved to Fairbanks, where he continued on as vicar apostolic of the rest of Alaska. In 1962, however, the vicariate became the missionary Diocese of Fairbanks (directly under the *Propaganda Fidei* in Rome) with Gleeson as its ordinary. In 1966 the 138,985-square-mile Archdiocese of Anchorage was established with Joseph T. Ryan as its first archbishop. This left the Juneau diocese with 37,566 square miles and the Fairbanks diocese with 409,849.

O'Flanagan resigned the Juneau See in June 1968, and for two years it was administered by Ryan. Gleeson retired in November 1968, and was succeeded as Bishop of Fairbanks by Robert L. Whelan, S.J. (George T. Boileau, S.J., was consecrated a coadjutor bishop with right of succession on July 31, 1964. However, he died soon thereafter, on Feb. 25, 1965.) In 1970 Francis T. Hurley was named auxiliary bishop for Anchorage and administrator of Juneau (as Ryan's vicar). In 1971 he was appointed ordinary of the Juneau diocese. In December 1975 Ryan became coadjutor military vicar of the U.S. Armed Forces, and the following year Hurley became Archbishop of Anchorage and administrator of Juneau. From 1979 to 1995—the year of his sudden death in Jordan—Michael H. Kenny was Juneau's Ordinary. Michael W. Warfel succeeded him in 1996. When, in 1985, Whelan retired as Bishop of Fairbanks, Michael J. Kaniecki, S.J., began his 15-year term as Bishop of Fairbanks. In the Eskimo village of Emmonak near the mouth of the Yukon River, on August 6, 2000, Kaniecki died suddenly of a massive heart attack. On Jan. 18, 2000, Roger L. Schwietz, O.M.I., was appointed Coadjutor Archbishop of Anchorage, taking possession of the archdiocese on March 4, 2001.

Apostolic Works. The first Religious women to undertake apostolic works in Alaska were the Sisters of St. Ann. In 1886 they opened a school and a hospital in Juneau. By the time they left Alaska over a century later, they had staffed schools and hospitals in various other places, but it was especially at Holy Cross on the Yukon that they had their greatest impact in Alaska, serving there for decades as teachers—along with Jesuits and, for a few years, with Brothers of Christian Instruction—and nurses. The Holy Cross Mission was founded in 1888 by Father Robaut, who died there in 1930 and lies buried there. In northern Alaska, however, it is Nulato, founded in 1887 by Father Tosi, that rightly claims primacy. Inseparably connected with the name of Nulato is the name of Fr. Julius Jetté, S.J. It was at Nulato that Jetté—who spent over 25 years in northern Alaska and was hailed as "the most distinguished scholar in Alaska"—began, in 1898, work on his monumental dictionary of the Koyukon Athabaskan language. He never lived to see it in print. A century later the Alaska Native Language Center at the University of Alaska, Fairbanks, published it—all 1212 pages of it—under the title of *Koyukon Athabascan Dictionary*.

Evangelization among the Central Yup'ik people of western Alaska began in 1889 with the founding of the mission on Nelson Island by Joseph M. Tréca, S.J., "the Apostle of the Tundra." The mission and boarding school at Akulurak near the mouth of the Yukon, St. Joseph's, staffed by Sisters of St. Ann and Jesuits, was opened in 1894. It was closed four years later. The mission at St. Michael dates from 1898. (At St. Michael lies buried Jesuit Brother Ulric Paquin, who froze to death on the trail, while bringing building supplies from St. Michael to Stebbins by sled and dogteam.)

The Nome parish was founded in 1901 for the whites and natives of the area. The Sisters of Providence operated a hospital there from 1902 to 1918, and a day school from 1904 to 1918. The Little Sisters of Jesus have been in Nome since 1952. In 1971 Nome's Catholic radio station, KNOM, went on the air. Now the oldest Catholic station in the United States, it has been winning top awards ever since.

The Fairbanks parish was founded in 1904 by Francis M. Monroe, S.J., "the Alaskan Hercules." A hospital followed two years later. This was staffed briefly by Sisters of St. Ann, then by Benedictine Sisters, then, from 1910 to 1968 by the Sisters of Providence. When Immaculate Conception grade school opened in Fairbanks in 1946, it was Sisters of Providence that staffed it; and when Monroe Catholic High opened in 1951, Sisters of

Providence—along with Jesuits and lay volunteers—served on the faculty for many years.

In 1905 the boarding school at Akulurak—staffed by Ursuline Sisters and Jesuits—was reopened, and renamed St. Mary's. The school flourished until 1951, when it was moved into new facilities built by James C. Spils, S.J., (known as "God's Builder," who also built Copper Valley School and Fairbanks' Sacred Heart Cathedral) and crew at the site of new St. Mary's on the Andreafsky River. There, still staffed by Ursulines and Jesuits, and assisted by many dedicated members of the Jesuit Volunteer Corps—who at the time were serving also in many other places throughout Alaska—it continued to flourish until the 1980s. It graduated its last class of high school seniors and was closed in the spring of 1987.

In Alaska's north, other missions, schools, and programs continued to spring into being. In 1918 the Pilgrim Springs mission and boarding school north of Nome began to care for many children left orphaned by the influenza epidemic of that year. The mission, staffed by Ursuline Sisters and Jesuits, closed in 1941. Frederick A. Ruppert, S.J., lies buried there. He froze to death, in December 1923, while on the trail with sled and dogteam, headed for the mission with oranges for the orphans for Christmas.

The mission on King Island was founded in 1929 by Fr. Bellarmine Lafortune, S.J. It was he who—during the course of his 44 years in the Seward Peninsula area—had founded, among others, the Pilgrim Springs mission. By the time he built the church on the island and spent his first winter there, most of the King Islanders were Catholic, having been received by him into the Church during their summer sojourns in Nome. The Kotzebue Mission—the first Alaskan mission beyond the Arctic Circle—was also founded in 1929, by the diocesan priest William F. Walsh. Walsh, along with Philip I. Delon, S.J., and pilot Ralph Wien, died the following year in an airplane crash at Kotzebue.

The last mission of major importance to be established in northern Alaska is that of St. Patrick's at Barrow, established in 1954 by the legendary Thomas P. Cunningham, S.J. Cunningham, widely known as "Father Tom," also pioneered the mission on Little Diomede Island, and served on King Island. He became a recognized expert on polar pack ice, and the United States Air Force turned to him as its principal adviser, when it set up scientific stations on the polar ice cap.

In 1956 Copper Valley School, near Glennallen, opened. It was staffed by Sisters of St. Ann, Jesuits, and numerous lay volunteers. Its founder, John R. Buchanan, S.J., intended the primary purpose of the school to be that

of preparing Alaska Natives for college and for positions of leadership in Alaska. It—as did the other Catholic schools in northern Alaska—had the strong support of Gleeson, a promoter of education on all levels. (For a time he had four different priests on the faculty at the University of Alaska-Fairbanks.) Copper Valley School closed in 1971.

Gleeson is given credit not only for supporting a tradition of solid Catholic education in northern Alaska, but also for the restoration of the permanent diaconate in the United States. Upon his urging, the U.S. bishops petitioned Rome in 1968 for approval of the restoration of the permanent diaconate. Approval was given. Under Whelan, Gleeson's successor, the Diocese of Fairbanks's diaconate program came to full flower. In the year 2000 there were 18 native deacons, all Inuit, and seven urban deacons serving in the Fairbanks Diocese. The deacons, a nucleus of diocesan priests, Franciscan Friars (serving in Alaska's northern interior since 1986), and religious men and women of various communities have all served to lessen the long dominance in northern Alaska by Jesuits as apostolic workers and helped the diocese along its road to becoming a diocese of age.

Meanwhile, pioneer parishes and apostolic works were being founded also in Alaska's panhandle. The Wrangell parish dates from 1879, those of Sitka and Juneau from 1885. The Skagway parish was founded in 1898. Skagway's Pius X Mission, a boarding school founded by Father G. Edgar Gallant—the first Catholic priest ordained in Alaska, by Crimont, in Juneau, on March 30, 1918—opened in 1931. The Ketchikan parish was founded in 1903. In 1923 the Sisters of St. Joseph of Peace began operating a hospital there.

In Alaska's South-Central area the parishes of Seward and Valdez were established in 1905, that of Cordova in 1908, that of Anchorage in 1915. Anchorage's Providence Hospital under the care of the Sisters of Providence opened in 1939. Parochial schools, a retreat house, and social outreach programs have been part of the Anchorage scene for decades. The parish of Kodiak came into being in 1944. That same year the Grey Nuns of the Sacred Heart took over the management of the hospital there. A Catholic grade school flourished there for decades. The Dillingham parish dates from 1948. For some years there was also a Catholic day-boarding school in Dillingham.

Needless to say, during the latter half of the 20th century many additional parishes and apostolic works, too numerous to mention, came into being in all three of Alaska's dioceses. While Catholic Alaska is not overly impressive in terms of numbers (according to the 2000 *Official Catholic Directory,* the Archdiocese of Anchorage had 20 parishes and eight missions serving 31,071 out of a total population of 396,801; Fairbanks had 46 parishes and seven missions serving 17,068 out of total population of 155,224; and Juneau had 10 parishes and 10 missions serving 6,049 out of a total population of 73,302), it has achieved a certain degree of maturity, and its three dioceses resemble for the most part other U.S. dioceses. However, the geographic and ethnic makeup of Alaska gives rise to some major differences. Many communities are ''bush'' communities—communities widely separated from one another and unconnected by roads. They can be reached only by airplane, boat, or snow machine. At certain times of the year, Little Diomede Island can be reached only by helicopter. To save time and to cut costs several of Alaska's bishops and many of its priests have flown and fly their own airplanes. The Anchorage and Juneau dioceses have relatively few Alaska Native Catholics, while Fairbanks has many—most of them Athabaskan and Central Yup'ik.

From the day they first set foot in Alaska to the present, Catholics have, in all areas of life—whether in academia, in the business world, in the arts—been part of mainstream Alaskan life. This is strikingly evident, above all, in the area of politics. Among the more prominent Catholics in Alaska's political life have been: Mike Stepovich, Alaska's last territorial governor; William A. Egan, the state of Alaska's first governor; Walter J. Hickel, twice Alaska's governor and Secretary of the Interior under President Nixon; Frank Murkowski, U.S. Senator; George Sullivan and Tom Fink, mayors of Anchorage; Edward Merdes, President of the International Junior Chamber of Commerce and Alaska State Senator.

As with the state of Alaska, the Catholic Church in Alaska is still young and still on the road to full maturity.

Bibliography: M. CANTWELL, *North to Share* (Victoria, Canada 1992). J.-É. CHAMPAGNE, ''First Attempts at the Evangelization of Alaska,'' *Études Oblates* 2 (1943) 13–22. P. HIGGINS, *Providence in Alaska: Sisters of Providence Education Ministry in Alaska, 1902–1978* (Seattle 1999). S. LLORENTE, *Jesuits in Alaska* (Portland, Ore. 1969). G. MOUSSEAU, ''L'Affaire d'Alaska. À propos du Voyage de Msgr. Clut dans l' Amérique Russe en 1872,'' *Études Oblates* 5 (1946) 161–88. L. L. RENNER, *Pioneer Missionary to the Bering Strait Eskimos: Bellarmine Lafortune, S.J.* (Portland, Ore. 1979); ''Fr. Aloysius Robaut, S.J.: Pioneer Missionary in Alaska.'' *Eskimo* 37 no. 20, (New Series, 1980–81) 5–16; ''Diocese of Fairbanks, Alaska: The Eskimo Diaconate Program.'' *Eskimo* 37 no. 20 (New Series, 1980–81) 5–16. A. H. SAVAGE, *Dogsled Apostles* (New York 1942). W. P. SCHOENBERG, *Paths to the Northwest: A Jesuit History of the Oregon Province* (Chicago 1982). J. C. SHIDELER and H. K. ROTHMAN, *Pioneering Spirit: The Sisters of Providence in Alaska* (Anchorage 1987). G. G. STECKLER, ''The Diocese of Juneau, Alaska,'' *Historical Records and Studies* 47 (1959) 234–54; ''The Foundation of the Alaskan Catholic Missions,'' *Studies in Mediaevalia and Americana: Essays in Honor of William Lyle Davis, S.J.* (Spokane, Wash. 1973) 129–50; *Charles John Seghers, Priest and Bishop in the Pacific Northwest,*

Sketch of priest tying alb with cincture. (The Catholic University of America)

1839–1886: A Biography (Fairfield, Wash. 1986). V. A. YZERMANS, *St. Rose of Wrangell: The Church's Beginning in Southeast Alaska* (St. Paul, Minn. 1979).

[L. RENNER]

ALB

A long white linen tunic worn as an undergarment for most liturgical functions. It is gathered in about the waist by means of a cincture. It has its origin in the Greco-Roman *tunica talaris,* a garment of daily use reaching to the ankles and decorated at the bottom and extremities of the sleeves with colored bands. Even though the influence of the short garments of the Germanic peoples brought about a change in fashion, the clergy did not follow it, continuing instead to dress in the traditional Roman style. By the 6th century, the wearing of albs was an established custom for the celebration of the liturgy. Although the interest in color during the Gothic

NEW CATHOLIC ENCYCLOPEDIA

211

period brought about the appearance of colored albs, white has always been traditional. The 16th century saw the rise of the lace industry; only then did lace appear on albs—an innovation that was a regression from the masculine and dignified robe of the past. Eventually lace, at first a mere ornament, covered most of the garment. The liturgical renewal of the 20th century brought about the return of the all-linen alb.

Bibliography: H. NORRIS, *Church Vestments* (New York 1950). E. A. ROULIN, *Vestments and Vesture,* tr. J. MCCANN (Westminster, Md. 1950). J. BRAUN, *Die liturgische Gewandung im Occident und Orient* (Freiburg 1907).

[M. MCCANCE]

ALBAN, ST.

Protomartyr of the English Church. He was a pagan soldier serving in the Roman army at Verulamium (now the city of Saint Albans, Hertfordshire, England). GILDAS and BEDE, both of whom wrote their histories long after the episode, relate Alban's martyrdom to the persecution of DIOCLETIAN (302–305). Some historians doubt that this movement reached England and have attempted to connect the death with the earlier persecution of Decius (249–251). Still others have suggested that the execution was carried out under martial law in 283 or 286 and not as a result of a general edict against Christians. According to tradition Alban protected a Christian priest from his persecutors and was converted by him. Alban was then summoned before a military tribunal, where he admitted to being a Christian and was scourged and later beheaded. A church and, later, the Abbey of Saint Albans were erected on the site of his martyrdom.

Feast: June 21.

Bibliography: R. G. COLLINGWOOD and J. N. L. MYRES, *Roman Britain and the English Settlements* (2d ed. Oxford 1937). J. A. DUKE, *The Columban Church* (London 1932; repr. 1957). L. F. RUSH-BROOK WILLIAMS, *St. Alban in history and legend: A critical examination* (Kingston 1914). K. MORVAY, *Die Albanuslegende: dt. Fassungen u. ihre Beziehungen zur lat. überlieferung* (Munich 1977). C. E. STEVENS, ''Gildas Sapiens,'' *English Historical Review* 56 (1941) 353–373, esp. app. W. LEVISON, ''St. Alban and Saint Albans,'' *Antiquity* 15 (1941) 337–359. A. BUTLER, *The Lives of the Saints,* ed. H. THURSTON and D. ATTWATER (New York 1956) 2:612–614.

[B. F. BYERLY]

ALBANI

Distinguished Umbrian family of Urbino who were prominent in the Church in the 18th and 19th centuries. The most influential member of the family was Pope

CLEMENT XI (1700–21); three of his nephews and a grandnephew were cardinals, all of them closely associated with the papal curia.

Annibale, papal diplomat; b. Urbino, Aug. 15, 1682; d. Rome, Sept. 21, 1751. He was created cardinal in 1711 by his uncle and was appointed bishop of Sabina in 1730. During most of Clement's reign, Annibale was one of the most active diplomats in the Vatican service, occupying in succession the post of nuncio in Vienna, Dresden, and Frankfurt. He exerted considerable influence in the elections of both Innocent XIII and Benedict XIV. He left a valuable library, gallery of paintings, and a collection of coins and antiques to the Vatican collection. Among his literary works was the edition of the writings of Clement XI.

Alessandro, brother of Annibale; b. Urbino, Oct. 19, 1692; d. Rome, Dec. 11, 1779. He was created cardinal by Innocent XII (1721), after he had distinguished himself in the papal diplomatic service. While he was always involved in the political life of the curia, he was primarily a scholar, and after 1761 he was director of the Vatican Library. He was a patron of the arts and a friend of the foremost collectors of antiques; he gained renown for his building of the Villa Albani in Rome, in which he housed a valuable collection of Greek and Roman sculpture.

Giovanni Francesco, a third nephew of Clement; b. Rome, Feb. 26, 1727; d. Rome, September 1803. He was cardinal bishop of Ostia. He was spokesman for the Austrians in the papal curia, and toward the end of his career, was dean of the Sacred College of Cardinals and particularly influential in the election of PIUS VII.

Giuseppe, Giovanni Francesco's nephew; b. Rome, Feb. 26, 1750; d. 1834. He, too, was created cardinal (1801) after some years of service in Vienna. He was secretary of state to PIUS VIII.

Bibliography: E. RE, *Enciclopedia Italiana di scienzi littere ed arti* (Rome 1929–39) 2:95. L. PASTOR, *The History of Popes from the Close of the Middle Ages* (London-St. Louis 1938–61): from the 1st German ed. *Geschichte der Päpste seit dem Ausgang des Mittelalters* (Freiburg 1885–1933; repr. 1955–) v.33, 34, 35. P. RICHARD, *Dictionnaire d'histoire et de géographie ecclésiastiques,* ed. A. BAUDRILLART et al. (Paris 1912–) 1:1369–73.

[C. B. O'KEEFE]

ALBANIA, THE CATHOLIC CHURCH IN

Bordered by Yugoslavia to the north, Macedonia to the east, and Greece to the south, Albania lies across the Adriatic Sea from Italy. A mountainous country, Albania's northern regions contain the Dinaric Alps, while small plains dot the coastal regions. Although Albania is among the poorest of European countries, it contains petroleum, natural gas, coal, and mineral resources; industries include lumber, textiles, and mining. Ethnic Albanians were originally a tribal people descended of the ancient Illyrians; they refer to themselves as *Shquipëtars* and to their country as *Shqipëria*. The Albanian language belongs to the Indo-European family, and is written in Latin characters with numerous diacritical marks.

Most Catholics living within Albania are members of the Orthodox Church. The Orthodox Church has a metropolitan see in Tirana that oversees suffragans Berat, Korrçë (Korçë), and Gjinokastër. The Latin rite Church has as its metropolitan archdiocese Shkodër, which oversees suffragan sees Lesh (Lezhë), Pult, Rreshen, and Sapë. The Archdiocese of Durrës-Tirana is immediately subject to the Holy See. The Byzantine rite Church, with a membership of only 2,500, has an apostolic administration located in southern Albania.

A History of Conquest. As a combined result of the Roman occupation from the north in the 2d century B.C. and the adoption of a Hellenistic tradition to the south as a result of its proximity to Greece, Albania developed divergent cultures north and south, with the line of demarcation the Skhumbi River. In Gratian's administrative division of the Roman Empire in 379, under the Roman emperor Theodosius I, Albania was placed in the eastern section, then later pertained to the Byzantine Empire. As part of the Prefecture of Illyricum Orientale, it formed the provinces of Epirus Vetus (with its capital in Nicopolis, modern Preveza), Epirus Nova (with its capital in Dyrrhacium, modern Dürres), and Praevalitana (with its capital in Scodra, modern Shkodër). During the Middle Ages this area changed masters several times, being subject to Goths, Slavs, Avars, Serbs, Bulgaro-Macedonians, Normans, and Venetians. From the 15th century to 1912 Albania was under Turkish rule; it became a principality in 1912, a republic in 1925, and a kingdom in 1928. From 1946 to 1991 the country was under communist domination and was known as the People's Republic of Albania. A new democratic government came to power during elections held in 1992.

Development of Christianity in Albania. Christianity came to northern Albania from Rome in the form of the LATIN RITE and to southern Albania from Greece in the form of the BYZANTINE LITURGY. There is, however, no evidence about the time and manner of its arrival. It antedated the Council of Sardica (343–344), since five bishops attended this synod from Epirus Nova and Dardania. The Slav invasion (c. 600) destroyed the ecclesiastical organization and caused the inhabitants to retire to

---

Capital: Tirana.
Size: 11,100 sq. miles.
Population: 3,490,435.
Languages: Albanian.
Religions: 2,443,305 Muslims (70%); 698,087 Orthodox (20%); 346,543 Latin rite Catholic (9.5%); 2,500 Byzantine rite Catholics (.5%).

---

the mountainous districts, where they lived as shepherds, gradually reverting to primitivism. Mention of Albanians in the Church's historical record is nonexistent from the 7th to the 11th centuries, when it is known that groups moved southward and settled extensively in Greece as far south as Attica, where they adopted the Byzantine rite and adhered to the EASTERN SCHISM of 1054. Northern Albania remained Catholic and retained the Latin rite. After the formation of the Slav principality of Dioclia (modern Montenegro), the metropolitan See of BAR was created (1089), and dioceses in northern Albania became its suffragans. From 1019 Albanian dioceses of the Byzantine rite were suffragans of the autocephalous (independent) Archdiocese of Ohrid (or Okhrida) until Dyrrhacium and Nicopolis were reestablished as metropolitan sees. Thereafter only the dioceses in inner Albania remained attached to Ohrid. In the 13th century during the Venetian occupation, the Latin Archdiocese of Dyrrhacium was founded.

Turkish invaders in the 15th century met heroic resistance in northern Albania from the Catholic tribes under the leadership of George Castriota (1403–68), known as Scanderbeg. After Scanderbeg's death the Turks occupied Albania, except for some sections held by Venice, until 1912. During over four centuries of Turkish rule most Albanians converted to Islam, especially in central Albania during the 17th and 18th centuries. Frequently this change of religion was merely external; many families remained crypto-Catholics and preserved Christian traditions and usages, such as Baptism, veneration of saints, pilgrimages, and dietary regulations. As a result there evolved a kind of Islamo-Christian syncretism. The expansion of Islam diminished during the 19th century under Austrian protection, but it did not cease until 1912, after Albania proclaimed its independence.

Latin-rite Catholics. For several centuries the care of Catholics in northern Albania was confined almost exclusively to the Franciscans. Pope Clement XI (1700–21) was particularly eager to help these Catholics, because his family, the Albani, had migrated from Albania to Italy in the 15th century. At his insistence the first Albanian national synod convened in Shkodër in 1703. Attempts

ALBANIA

to establish a seminary were made in the 18th century, but they did not succeed until 1856, when Italian Jesuits opened in Shkodër a pontifical college, to which a seminary was later attached. The Jesuits set up a printing press. In their popular missions they strove to abolish the custom of blood vendetta. The Archdiocese of Bar became part of the newly established principality of Montenegro in 1878, and by the terms of the concordat with Montenegro (1886) it ceased to be the metropolitan see for Albania. Shkodër replaced it the same year, with all Albanian dioceses except Durrës as its suffragans.

Orthodox Christians. The Byzantine tradition established in the Orthodox Patriarchate of CONSTANTINO-PLE prevailed in southern Albania and among the Albanians in Greece and Italy. The Eastern Schism entered Albania gradually. Union with Rome persisted in some mountainous districts until the 17th century; it was supported by national opposition to the Greek and Slav hierarchy, by some archbishops of Ohrid, and especially by the populace in the Chimarra district that repeatedly petitioned during the 16th and 17th centuries to have clergy sent there from Rome. In 1628 the Italian Congregation for the Propagation of the Faith dispatched both graduates of the Greek College in Rome and a group of Basilian monks to Chimarra. Athanasius II, Archbishop of Ohrid and a refugee in Chimarra, united with Rome in 1660 and consecrated one of the missionaries as bishop of the Byzantine rite. This mission was abandoned in 1765 when entry was barred to Catholic missionaries; it was not restored until Basilian monks came from Italy (1938–45).

By the early 1900s, following the country's independence, the religious composition of Albania was estimated as 70 percent Muslim, 20 percent Orthodox, and 10 percent Roman Catholic. Muslims were present throughout the country, but especially in central and southern Albania (a mufti was located at Tiranë; other strongholds were Elbasan and Vlora). Orthodox Christians were concentrated mainly in the south around the city of Korçë, while a small but unified Catholic community was centered in the northern city of Shkodër and the surrounding area, including Montenegro, Kosova, and Macedonia. Albania's status as an independent state prompted Fan Noli, a priest, to claim for the Albanian Orthodox the status of an autocephalous church. Noli also replaced the traditional Greek of the Byzantine liturgy with the vernacular, although this change was not recognized by the Patriarchate of Constantinople until 1937.

The Arrival of Communism. During World War II Albania was invaded, first by Italy, then by Greece, and then finally by the German Army. In November 1944 the country found itself independent but in financial ruin, and by January 1946 had declared itself a communist republic. Immediately, communists began a severe persecution of the Catholic Church on the pretext that Catholics sided with the former occupying government of Italy. All Italian missionaries were imprisoned, several were eventually put to death, and others were banished, including the apostolic delegate. The persecution extended equally to the native hierarchy and clergy and to Catholic schools and the seminary. Two Albanian bishops were sentenced to death; others were imprisoned. The Apostolic Administration of South Albania, which had been established in 1939 for Catholics of the Byzantine rite, was destroyed

A small chapel on the hills above the Muslim town of Berat, Albania. (©Arne Hodalic/CORBIS)

and its administrator expelled. The Albanian Catholic Church was cut off from all contact with Rome or with other countries. While in 1951 a law enforcing intervention in church matters still permitted Catholic clergy to continue relations with the Holy See, such permission would be rescinded several years later. The Orthodox Church imitated the Russian Church's method of adapting to the onset of communism by recognizing the Communist government and its proceedings. As a result it received better treatment than the Catholic Church.

Bibliography: D. FARLATI and G. COLETI, *Illyricum sacrum,* 8 v. (Venice 1751–1819), v.7. L. VON THALLÓCZY et al., *Acta et diplomata res Albaniae mediae aetatis illustrantia,* 2 v. (Vienna 1913–18), contains documents for period 344–1406. M. ŠUFFLAY, "Die Kirchenzustände in vortürkischen Albanien," *Illyrisch-albanische Forschungen,* ed. K. JIREČEK, 2 v. (Munich 1916) 1:188–281. M. E. DURHAM, *Some Tribal Origins, Laws, and Customs of the Balkans* (London 1928). G. PETROTTA, "Il cattolicesimo nei Balkani. L'Albania," *La Tradizione* 1 (1928) 165–203; *Popolo, lingua, e letteratura albanese* (2d ed. Palermo 1932). F. W. HASLUCK, *Islam and Christianity under the Sultans,* ed. M. HASLUCK (Oxford 1929). M. SPINKA, *A History of Christianity in the Balkans* (Chicago 1933). N. BORGIA, *I monaci basiliani d'Italia in Albania,* 2 v. (Rome 1935–42). G. STADTMÜLLER, "Altheidnischer Volksglaube und Christianisierung in Albanien," *Orientalia Christiana periodica* 20 (1954) 211–246; "Die Islamisierung bei den Albanern," *Jahrbücher für Geschichte Osteuropas,* NS 3 (1955) 404–429; "Das albanische Nationalkonzil vom Jahre 1703," *Orientalia Christiana periodica* 22 (1956) 68–91.

[M. LACKO]

Religious Persecution. The persecution and isolation of the Catholic Church that began in 1944 under the Communist regime grew more intense with the passage of time. In 1966 the Albanian government promulgated Decree Number 4337, which extended the 1951 law empowering the state to control religious activity and annulled the Church's ability to maintain spiritual ties with the Holy See. The new decree prohibited all public and private religious rites and imposed great penalties on violators. Within a short time, the government seized and closed all churches and mosques in the country. In 1967 officials proclaimed Albania "the first atheistic state in the world." Of the 2,000 churches and mosques seized, 327 were Catholic churches. Most churches were destroyed while some were converted to secular uses or retained as historical monuments. The Shkodër Cathedral was converted to a sports arena; the Jesuit National Shrine of the Sacred Heart in Tiranë became a concert hall, while the National Shrine of Our Lady of Shkodër was razed.

Catholic bishops and priests courageously resisted the closing and destruction of churches and other religious buildings. In retaliation many of the clergy were publicly humiliated. Priests who spoke out were arrested and, after show trials, condemned to hard labor or executed. In 1968 Bishop Antonin Fishta was arrested for conducting religious services, and soon after he died in a labor camp. Bishop Ernest Çoba was arrested in 1976 and died under torture in prison in 1980. At this point Bishop Nikollë Troshani, who was serving a 25-year prison sentence, remained the sole surviving member of the Albanian hierarchy.

In 1975, emboldened by the failure of the world community to act on behalf of Albanian believers, Albanian dictator Enver Hoxha led the communist government in taking yet another step to eradicate all religious influence from society. Decree Number 5339 prohibited religious names for newly born children. By 1976 the government judged that it had achieved its goal of eliminating religion. Antireligious policies were written into the new Albanian constitution: article 37 declared, "The State recognizes no religion whatever and supports atheist propaganda"; article 55 forbade the formation of any religious organization. Meanwhile, Albanian exiles in the diaspora attempted to counteract this persecution by enlisting the support of Amnesty International, the International Association for the Defense of Religious Freedom, Pax Christi, and the U.N. Human Rights Commission.

The Underground Church. Despite the constitutional ban on religion, the Church continued to operate underground. Priests and bishops who had not been imprisoned or exiled secretly ministered to the faithful. The famous 15th-century baptismal formula of Pál Engjulli, archbishop of Durrës, was used by parents and elderly Catholics to baptize infants when a priest could not be found. The formula, the oldest extant written document in the Albanian language, had been used by the faithful during the many centuries of Turkish rule. The blessings of marriages and prayers for the dead were conducted by elderly Catholics. Devout holy women and men became active in towns and villages, serving as indispensable helpers to the few priests who were still free and who would dare to officiate in the underground Church.

Because of the Church's isolation from Rome during the country's period of communist persecution, no Albanian bishops were allowed to participate in the deliberations of the Second Vatican Council. In fact, Catholics were prevented from learning about, let alone implementing the decrees of the council. Catholic prayer books and catechisms were also forbidden to be published or circulated in Albania. However, the Albanian Catholic Archdiocese of Bar and the Diocese of Shkup-Prizren, both in what was then the bordering nation of Yugoslavia, published several pocket catechisms and manuals in Albanian. These books were intended for Albanian Catholic refugees living in these diocese, but copies were also smuggled into communist-dominated Albania.

New Freedom. In April 1985 Albanian dictator Hoxha, the man behind the antireligious movement, died. Gradually the faithful began to identify themselves as Christians and practice their faith openly. Under international pressure from human rights organizations, the government's total ban on religion weakened. In May 1990 the government announced reforms, one of which was the lifting of the ban on religious practice. Religion could be practiced in private. In defiance of the still-existing ban on public practice of religion, Simon Jubani, who had spent 26 years in prison, illegally celebrated mass in the old cemetery of Shkodër in November 1990. Some 50,000 faithful, including Orthodox and Muslims, joined in the liturgy, ignoring the security police who surrounded the cemetery grounds.

In March 1991 the first free elections in over 40 years were held, and newly elected socialist prime minister Ylli Bufi visited Pope John Paul II in Rome. There Bufi apologized to the pontiff for the harmful and unjust policies of the previous government toward the Catholic community, paving the way for diplomatic relations to be reestablished between Albania and the Vatican. In 1992 elections brought to power the democratic party—which included several Catholics—and initiated a social order based on freedom and democracy, with full religious rights.

With the new freedom, the Catholic Church stirred to life. The Jesuits and Franciscans reopened their seminaries in Shkodër. The Albanian clergy began the re-evangelization of the faithful aided by Albanian priests and sisters from Kosovo in the Yugoslavian Federation. Clergy, religious, and laity from Italy, Malta, other European countries, and the United States arrived to assist. Albanian parishes in New York City and Detroit sent help, which was badly needed given that only Bishop Troshani, 31 priests, and 44 sisters had survived the five decades of communist persecution. Many churches that had escaped destruction in 1967 were reopened and those damaged restored.

Albanian-born Nobel Peace Prize winner MOTHER TERESA opened the first house of her Missionaries of Charity in Albania in 1991; by 1994 the number had grown to 11. Although she was not directly involved in the movement for religious freedom, Mother Teresa served as an ambassador for the Albanian Church throughout the period of persecution and in 1997, shortly before her death, addressed the nation in an effort to help end outbreaks of street violence.

The resurrected Catholic Church in Albania, eager to reunite itself with the universal Church, quickly introduced the reforms of Vatican II throughout the country. New missals were translated into Albanian and published by the Congregation for the Evangelization of the People, under whose jurisdiction Albania belongs. Copies of sacramentaries and lectionaries printed in Albanian were a personal gift of Pope John Paul II to the Church, and were distributed to Albanian Catholics through their dioceses and parishes. An Albanian translation of all the major documents of Vatican II became available in 1993. The Catholic press in Albania, which enjoyed considerable prestige in the precommunist era, returned to publishing. A translation of the *Catechism of the Catholic Church* into Albanian was published in 1996.

The Bill of Rights adopted by the Albanian parliament in March 1993 guaranteed among its articles the freedom of thought, conscience, and religion; the freedom to change one's religion; and the freedom to manifest one's religion privately and publicly. A month later, Pope John Paul II visited Albania, where he was greeted by President Sali Berisha who pledged that the past wrongs inflicted on the Church by the previous government would never be repeated. During his visit, the pope ordained four bishops to fill sees vacant since the communist insurgence. The creation of the first Albanian cardinal, Msgr. Mikel Koliqi, by the pope in November of the following year gave new impetus to evangelization among the Albanian people. Koliqi, a living witness among the Catholics in communist prisons and labor camps for 41 years, represented for all Albanians not only a symbol of courage and hope in the face of persecution, but also a shining example of the traditional Albanian values of faith and homeland. By early 2000 there were two archbishops, four bishops, 97 priests, 13 brothers, and 277 sisters in Albania, and in June of that year the ordination of more five priests trained in Albania was deemed by the Archbishop of Scutari ''a sign of hope that shows how the Albanian Church is growing rapidly after so many years of state atheism and martyrdom.''

As the Church made great progress in reclaiming its place in the national life of Albania, it also renewed its traditionally cordial ecumenical ties with the Albanian Orthodox Church and reopened a friendly dialogue with Muslim leaders. Catholics and Orthodox cooperated with a small Evangelical Christian Brotherhood to make available for the first time an Albanian translation of the entire Bible, the work of a Catholic priest in Montenegro. However, competition in the form of new Protestant groups and other religious sects entering the country and threats from anti-Christian Muslim groups showed religious freedom to be somewhat of a double-edged sword to a Church attempting to reestablish its footing after so many years of suppression.

Continuing Political Turmoil. Unfortunately, the new freedoms failed to bring peace and prosperity to the Albanian people. During the 1990s, a failed nationwide pyramid scheme left many citizens bereft of life savings and others desperate enough to vandalize private, public, and even Church property. On June 29, 1997, with help from the European Union, free elections were held that brought to power a socialist president and the hope that the new government could restore public order. In October 1997 a high-ranking representative of the Albanian government traveled to the Vatican, receiving the support of the Church in all efforts at ''material and spiritual reconstruction'' during a private audience with John Paul II.

As acts of religious intolerance and other social protests continued to surface within Albania, they were dramatically overshadowed by events a few miles away, in the Serbian province of Kosovo, where ethnic Albanians—most of them practicing Muslims— were subjected to Serbian violence following a regional request for political autonomy from the Yugoslavian Federation. Many thousands fled to their historic home in Albania, where they were welcomed by the Church. Catholics responded to the crisis by sending humanitarian aid to ethnic Albanians within Kosovo, resulting in the bombing of an Orthodox Church in northern Albania in 1998 and the vandalization of three other churches in 1999. Communications between the pontiff and the Albanian government continued throughout the crisis, as both representatives of the Albanian people sought a way to end what quickly turned into an effort at ''ethnic cleansing'' The Church was also involved in ecumenical councils formed to address the needs of the over 270,000 Kosovar refugees that remained sheltered in Albania until the end of the Serbian violence in 1999.

Bibliography: The *Albanian Catholic Bulletin* 1–15 (1980–94), published by the Albanian Catholic Institute, University of San Francisco, contains Albanian documents from 1966–94. AMNESTY INTERNATIONAL, *Albania, Political Imprisonment, and the Law* (London 1984). R. BEQAJ, *Veprimtarija Antikombetare e Klerit Katolik Shqiptar* (Tiranë 1969); *Veprimtarija Armiqësore e Klerit Katolik Shqiptar 1945–1971* (Tiranë 1973). S. BOWERS, ''Church and State in Albania,'' *Religion in Communist Lands* 6:3 (1978) 148–152. J. BROUN, ''The Status of Christianity in Albania,'' *Journal of Church and State* 28 (1986) 43–60; *Conscience and Captivity: Religion in Eastern Europe* (Washington DC 1988). G. CARRARO, *Albania Cristiana* (Padova 1985). G. GARDIN, *Banishing God in Albania* (San Francisco 1988). C. GIRAUDO, *Già dato per martire: i fioretti di un gesuita albanese* (Rome 1993). I. GOGAJ, *Mbi Qendrimin Reaksionar të Klerit në Fushen e Arësimit* (Tiranë 1972). A. GUIDETTI, *Padre Fausti-Martire in Albania* (Rome 1974). L. GUSSONI and A. BRUNELLO, *The Silent Church* (New York 1954). P. HODGES, ''Albania after Hoxha's Death,'' *Religion in Communist Lands* 14:3 (1986) 268–272. *Human Rights in the People's Socialist Republic of Albania,* Minnesota Lawyers International Human Rights Committee Report (Minneapolis 1990). J. J. OROSHI, ''The Twentieth Anniversary of the Elimination of the Catholic Hierarchy and the Final Blow to All Religions in Albania,'' *Catholic Albanian Life* 11 (1968) 1–14. PUEBLA INSTITUTE, *Albania: Religion in a Fortress State* (Washington DC 1988). G. RULLI, ''Dove va l'Albania?'' *Civiltà Cattolica* 136 (1985) 496–506. Z. SIMONI, ET AL., *Martirizimi në Shqipni 1944–1990* (Shkodër 1993). G. SINISHTA, *The Fulfilled Promise: A Documentary Account of Religious Persecution in Albania* (Santa Clara, CA 1976). G. SINISHTA and B. GRAHAM, *Sacrifice for Albania 1946–1966* (Detroit 1967). B. TÖNNES, ''Religious Persecution in Albania,'' *Religion in Communist Lands* 10:3 (1982) 242–255. J. TORRENS, ''Albania: Never or Next?'' *America* 164:8 (1991) 232–235; ''Albania, Here Come the Missionaries,'' *America* 171:1 (1994) 6–9.

[G. SINISHTA/EDS.]

ALBELDA, ABBEY OF

Former Benedictine monastery of St. Martín in the Diocese of Calahorra, Spain, six miles south of Logroño. The fortress *Albailda* (Arabic: ''white'') built by Muza II of Saragossa in 850 was destroyed by Ordoño I of Oviedo in 851. Hermits, however, there as monks probably before 850, formed a monastery soon afterward and in 924 grouped themselves under the Benedictine rule with a large number of monks sent there from León by Ordoño II. In 951 the abbey had 200 monks and was a famous center of learning. In 976 the monks (Vigila) completed the beautifully illuminated codex *Albeldensis* (Escorial d-I-2) that contains a collection of 61 councils, the valuable *Chronicle of Albelda* of 883, and other items in Visigothic script. A copy of the *Albeldensis* (Escorial d-I-1) completed in 994, a *Liber ordinum* of 1052 (now in SILOS) sent to Rome in 1064 for the approval of the Mozarabic liturgy, several other extant codices of the 10th century, and several lost codices (including works by Salvus, d. 962) gave the scriptorium of Albelda a fame that Alfonso X recognized in 1270. From 1033 to 1092 the bishops of Calahorra-Nájera resided in Albelda, and the monks became secularized canons. In 1435 the canons, the treasure, and many documents of Albelda were moved to Santa María la Redonda in Logroño. The cartulary of the abbey (891–1092) went to Simancas. Archeological remains of the monastery, recently discovered, seem to be Visigothic in style.

Bibliography: C. J. BISHKO, ''Salvus of Albelda . . . ,'' *Speculum. A Journal of Mediaeval Studies* 23 (1948) 559–590. M. ALAMO, *Dictionnaire d'histoire et de géographie ecclésiastiques,* ed. A. BAUDRILLART et al. (Paris 1912–) 11:327–333.

[J. PÉREZ DE URBEL]

ALBERDINGK THIJM, JOSEPHUS ALBERTUS

Dutch poet and pioneer of Catholic emancipation; b. Amsterdam, Aug. 13, 1820; d. Amsterdam, March 17, 1889. He grew up in a middle-class family and embarked on a business career, but he soon started to write romantic poems with a mystical tinge. He later developed a theory that the connection of art and beauty with religion should be an intrinsic part of human life and of society. A militant Catholic, he combatted the mediocrity and narrowmindedness of many fellow Catholics. Against them he defended the necessity of good theater and a friendship with non-Catholic authors, in whose periodicals he wrote essays and poetry. He equally contested growing agnostic materialism, for example, in *Het Voorgeborchte* (1851) and *Magdalena van Vaernewijck* (1851). In this respect he followed his admired master, Willem Bilderdijk (1756–1831), Holland's first romantic poet and the protagonist of a Protestantism based on sentiment. The poet E. J. Potgieter (1808–75) gave his friend Thijm the title of Catholic romantic and encouraged him to elevate Catholic culture.

Under this impulse, Thijm began to understand the greatness of Holland's 17th-century ''golden age,'' a period he had considered pagan and heretical. He became the enthusiastic admirer of Vondel, Holland's greatest poet. Thijm's *Portretten van Joost van den Vondel* (1876) inaugurated a long series of studies of Vondel by Catholic scholars. Prior to his interest in the 17th century, Thijm had seen in the Middle Ages, then generally thought of as ''dark,'' support for his ideals of Catholic unity and harmony. Several of his short stories recapture medieval life and thought, e.g., *De klok van Delft* (1846), *Legenden en Fantasien* (1847), *De organist van de Dom* (1849), *Karolingische verhalen* (1851, Carolingian Tales), and *Geertrude van Oosten* (1853). He was also active in the field of art, especially in architecture. One of his best essays, *De heilige Linie* (1875, The Holy Line), discusses the symbolism of church architecture. In 1876 he was appointed professor in art history at the Academy of Arts in Amsterdam. He was unable to understand younger authors, however, including his own son, Karel (pseudonym, Lodewijk van Deyssel), and lost contact with the young painters, who, like the authors, tended toward naturalism. They in their turn respected him, but considered him the representative of an era that had lost its reason for existence.

Bibliography: *Werken,* ed. J. F. M. STERCK, 7 v. (The Hague 1908–20). A. J. (pseud.), *J. A. Alberdingk Thijm* (Amsterdam 1893), biog. by his son. W. BENNINK, *Alberdingk Thijm: Kunst en Karakter* (Nijmegen 1952). G. BROM, *Alberdingk Thym* (Utrecht 1956).

[J. I. MENDELS]

ALBERGATI, NICCOLÒ, BL.

Carthusian bishop and cardinal; b. Bologna, 1375; d. Siena, May 9, 1443. Nobly born, Albergati abandoned the law for the Carthusian house of San Girolamo di Casara, where he became prior (1407) and visitor (1412). Appointed bishop of Bologna (1417), cardinal (1426), and eventually grand penitentiary and camerlengo, he served both MARTIN V and EUGENE IV as legate to England, France, Germany, and Italy and at the councils of Basel, Ferrara, and Florence. For example, in 1422 Martin V sent him—albeit unsuccessfully—to reconcile the rulers of England, France, and Burgundy. Later (1435), Albergati won Philip the Good of Burgundy over to Charles VII, thus contributing materially to the Peace of Arras. He was buried in the Charter House at Florence. Benedict XIV authorized his cultus on Oct. 6, 1744.

Feast: May 9.

Bibliography: M. ZANOTTI, *Vita del b. Niccolò Albergati* (Bologna 1757). S. AUTORE, *Dictionnaire d'histoire et de géographie ecclésiastiques,* ed. A. BAUDRILLART et al. (Paris 1912) 1:1396–97. P. DE TÖTH, *Il beato cardinale Niccolò Albergati e i suoi tempi, 1375–1444,* 2 v. (Acquapendente 1934). J. G. DICKINSON, *The Congress of Arras, 1435* (Oxford 1955) *passim.*

[J. G. ROWE]

ALBERIC OF OSTIA

Cardinal bishop, papal legate; b. Beauvais, France, c. 1080; d. Verdun, 1148. Alberic became a monk in Cluny, where he rose to the rank of subprior; he held the same office at the Abbey of Saint-Martin-des-Champs. At the instance of PETER THE VENERABLE, he was appointed abbot of Vézelay (1131) despite the opposition of the monks of that abbey. In the schism of Anacletus II (*see* PIERLEONI) he supported Pope INNOCENT II, who created him cardinal bishop of Ostia and papal legate (1138) to England. A strong representative of the Gregorian Reform, Alberic was the first papal legate in more than 70 years to enter England with unrestricted powers. In Scotland he won the clergy to recognition of Innocent (Synod of Carlisle, Sept. 26, 1138); but his primary business was to visit the chief monastic and episcopal centers of England and Scotland, to hold a council in which recent reform decrees might be applied, and to supervise the election of the archbishop of Canterbury. Assisted by two assessors, the Austin Canon Robert of Hereford and Abbot Richard of Fountains, he brought the mission to a successful conclusion with the synod of Westminster (Dec. 11, 1138) and the election of THEOBALD OF CANTERBURY, the former abbot of Bec. After affording his good offices to the establishment of peace between England and Scotland, he returned to Rome (January 1139), where he participated in the Second Lateran Council.

Appointed legate to Antioch, he deposed Radulph, the second Latin patriarch (Nov. 30, 1139), and in 1140 presided at a synod in Jerusalem. His last years were spent as legate in southern France, where he opposed the Albigenses, Éon of Stella, and the followers of Henry of Lausanne.

Bibliography: JOHN OF HEXHAM, *Chronicle* in *The Priory of Hexham,* ed. J. RAINE, 2 v. (Surtees Society 44, 46; London 1864–65) 1:107–172. RICHARD OF HEXHAM, *ibid.* 1:63–106. C. J. VON HEFELE, *Histoire des conciles d'après les documents originaux* (Paris 1907–38) 5:721, 745–746, 817. H. TILLMANN, *Die päpstlichen Legaten in England* (Bonn 1926). D. KNOWLES, *The Monastic Orders in England, 943–1216* (Cambridge, Eng. 1962) 237, 253.

[O. J. BLUM]

ALBERIC OF ROSATE

Italian jurist; b. Rosciate, near Bergamo, Italy, 1290; d. Bergamo, Sept. 14, 1360. He was descended from a family of judges and notaries, and he studied law in Padua under Oldradus de Ponte and Richard Malombra. After returning to Bergamo in the second decade of 1300, he practiced law and continued to cultivate juridical and literary studies, though it appears he never taught. He was one of the principal exponents of the Italian juridical school of commentators at the time of its most glorious flourishing and was the promoter of the first real lexicographic attempt in the juridical field. In his *Quaestiones statutorum,* which had several reprints, he left a fundamental work in statutory legislation, and perhaps the first doctrinal treatise on private international law. His contemporaries and posterity described him as *summus practicus;* he wrote commentaries on various parts of Justinian's Digest and Code. The influence of the *De regulis iuris,* included in the *Liber Sextus* of Boniface VIII, is clearly evident in Alberic's commentary on title *De regulis iuris* of the *Digesta* (*Corpus iuris civilis, Digesta,* ed. T. Mommsen and P. Krueger [Berlin 1928] 50.17). His *Dictionarium iuris,* which was reprinted several times, is the first ample lexicon of civil and canon law. Finally, he revised in Latin the commentary of Jacopus della Lana to Dante's *Comedy* (the work is not edited).

Bibliography: G. CREMASCHI, ''Contributo alla biografia di Alberico da Rosciate,'' *Bergomum* 30 (1956) 3–102. G. BILLANOVICH, ''Epitafio, libri e amici di Alberico da Rosciate,'' *Italia Medioevale e Umanistica* 3 (1960) 251–261.

[R. ABBONDANZA]

ALBERIC OF UTRECHT, ST.

Benedictine monk, bishop of Utrecht; d. Aug. 21 or Nov. 14, 784. He was a nephew of an earlier bishop of Utrecht, St. GREGORY, the successor of BONIFACE. Alberic participated in the mission to the Frisians, directing LUDGER OF MÜNSTER's activity there. He was a friend of such intellectual leaders of the Carolingian Renaissance as ALCUIN and Ludger. He received episcopal consecration in 780 at Cologne. As bishop of Utrecht he reorganized the cathedral school, dividing the teaching among four masters. Alberic's relics are preserved at Susteren.

Feasts: Nov. 14, Aug. 21, March 4 (translation).

Bibliography: *Monumenta Germaniae Historica: Scriptores* 16:497. J. TORSY, *Lexikon für Theologie und Kirche*, ed. J. HOFER and K. RAHNER (Freiburg 1957–65) 1:277.

[R. BALCH]

ALBERONI, GIULIO

Cardinal and statesman; b. Firenzuola d'Arda, Piacenza, Italy, May 31(?)1664; d. Piacenza, June 27, 1752. Although of humble origins, Alberoni was educated by Barnabites and Jesuits and enjoyed the protection of Bishop Barni, who sponsored his ecclesiastical career. Alberoni, ordained and appointed a canon (1698), began his diplomatic apprenticeship as a secretary to the Duke of Vendôme, supreme commander of the French army in Italy, whom he followed to France (1706), Holland, and Spain (1711). After the general's death (1712), Alberoni remained in Madrid as an agent of the duchy of Parma. In 1714 he successfully negotiated the marriage of Philip V, a widower, to Elizabeth Farnese of Parma.

As prime minister (1716) and cardinal (July 12, 1717), Alberoni implemented domestic reforms in agriculture, trade, manufacturing, and welfare that were decidedly in advance of his times. In foreign policy, fully cognizant of the ambitions of Philip V, he boldly sought to restore Spanish prestige in Italy and to vindicate his sovereign's rights to the French throne. To this end, he reorganized the army and navy and engaged in intrigues against the empire and its allies. Compelled to declare war prematurely by the irresponsible actions of Parma and the urging of Philip, Alberoni ordered the invasion of Sardinia (1717) and Sicily (1718), in spite of formal assurances to the contrary given to Clement XI. Diplomatic and military disasters followed. Alberoni failed to secure the support of Russia and Sweden in restoring James Stuart, ''the Old Pretender,'' and in overthrowing Philip, Duke of Orléans. The Quadruple Alliance (Empire, France, England, and Holland) reconquered the islands of Sardinia and Sicily and invaded Navarre. Alberoni, held responsible by the king, the pope, and the Quadruple Alliance for this ill-starred venture, was expelled from Spain (Dec. 5, 1719). Hiding in Italy, he evaded arrest and assassination, while a commission of 15 cardinals investigated charges of treason brought against him.

Alberoni attended the conclave that elected Innocent XIII (1721); he was given a relatively mild sentence of four years' imprisonment but was completely exonerated by the pope (Sept. 18, 1723). When created bishop of Malaga and reconciled with Philip V (1725), the aging cardinal hoped to spend his remaining years in peaceful retirement in his estate of Castelromano. Instead, he was appointed by Clement XII to the legation of Ravenna (1735), where he promoted public works. In 1739 he occupied San Marino, a controversial move that was later disavowed by the pope for political reasons. His last post was the legation of Bologna (1740–43). He spent the last years of his life in Piacenza in charitable and scholarly pursuits. Alberoni is buried in the church of the college San Lazzaro-Alberoni, which he founded in 1732 for the education of clerics.

Bibliography: S. BERSANI, *Storia del Cardinale G. Alberoni* (Piacenza 1861). A. ARATA, *Il processo del Cardinale Alberoni* (Piacenza 1923). P. CASTAGNOLI, *Il Cardinale G. Alberoni*, 3 v. (Piacenza 1929–32). S. HARCOURT-SMITH, *Cardinal of Spain: The Life and Strange Career of Alberoni* (New York 1944). G. F. ROSSI, *Cento studi sul cardinale Alberoni*, 4 v. (Piacenza 1978). E. BOURGEOIS, *Le Secret des Farnèse: Philippe V et la politique d'Alberoni* (Paris 1909). P. RICHARD, *Dictionnaire d'histoire et de géographie ecclésiastiques*, ed. A. BAUDRILLART et al. (Paris 1912) 1:1425–28.

[E. J. THOMSON]

ALBERT (ADALBERT), ANTIPOPE

Pontificate: 1101. Albert was probably made bishop and then cardinal bishop of Silva Candida by the antipope Clement III (1080–1100). After Clement died and his first successor, Theodoric (1100–01), had been imprisoned by Pope Paschal II (1099–1118), Clement's Roman followers elected Albert as the third in what was now a line of antipopes. For his part, Emperor Henry IV (1056–1106) was uninterested in supporting a Roman antipope, and riots broke out when news of Albert's election became public. Albert hid in the home of a

Clementine sympathizer, who quickly turned him over to Paschal in exchange for a bribe. He was imprisoned for a time at the Lateran. Finally, like his predecessor Theodoric, Albert was sentenced to confinement in a monastery in Norman territory, in this case the monastery of St. Lorenzo at Aversa (a few miles north of Naples). Nothing more is known of his life or death.

Bibliography: L. DUCHESNE, ed. *Liber Pontificalis* (Paris 1886–92; repr. 1955–57) 2.298, 345. P. JAFFÉ, *Regesta pontificum Romanorum* (Leipzig 1885–88; repr. Graz 1956) 1.773. *Monumenta Germaniae historica, Libelli de lite* 2.405–07. P. KEHR, "Zur Geschichte Wiberts von Ravenna (Clemens III)," *Sitzungsberichte der Preussischen Akademie der Wissenschaften zu Berlin* (1921) 980–88. P. BREZZI, *Roma e l'impero medioevale* (Bologna 1947). C. SERVATIUS, *Paschalis II* (Stuttgart 1979) 42ff, 70ff, 339. J.N.D. KELLY, *The Oxford Dictionary of Popes* (New York 1986) 162.

[P. M. SAVAGE]

ALBERT, FEDERICO, BL.

Priest and founder of the Congregation of Vincentian Sisters of the Immaculate Conception (Albertines); b. Turin, Piedmont, Italy, Oct. 16, 1820; d. Lanzo, Torinese, Italy, Sept. 30, 1876. Although Federico Albert recognized his vocation to the priesthood early in life, he could not afford to attend seminary. As an adult he passed the required examinations for candidates to the priesthood and was ordained. Albert was an able pastor of souls in several Torinese parishes, as well as a spiritual guide for other priests. He was a friend and early collaborator of St. John BOSCO, and himself served the young and old with special zeal. To provide the needy with further assistance, Albert founded and directed the Albertines. He was beatified by John Paul II, Sept. 30, 1984.

Feast: Sept. 30.

Bibliography: *Acta Apostolicae Sedis* 77 (1985): 1020–1023. *L'Osservatore Romano,* English edition, 44 (1984): 6–7.

[K. I. RABENSTEIN]

ALBERT I OF RIGA, ST.

Bishop; b. near Bremen, Germany, *c.* 1165; d. Riga, Latvia, Jan. 17, 1229. He came from a Buxhövden ministerial family, was a canon at Bremen after 1189, and was consecrated bishop of Livonia by Archbishop Hartwig II on March 28, 1199. After negotiations with the pope, the king, and Denmark, he landed at the mouth of the Düna in 1200 with a large force of crusaders. He founded the city of Riga in 1201 and made it a bishopric. By 1207 the area between the Düna and the Aa (Lielupe) Rivers was under his control. Soon Albert became involved in the great controversies in the territory during that time. The Roman Curia wished to establish a protective state (Marienland) itself and distrusted Albert because of his connection with the Hohenstaufen, who had recognized him as an imperial prince in 1207 and 1225; therefore the Holy See strengthened the Order of the KNIGHTS OF THE SWORD, which was supported by the empire (1210) as well. Although Riga remained a bishopric, it was no longer a suffragan of Bremen after 1214, and received metropolitan privileges over mission dioceses. It became an archbishopric only in 1253. Rome supported the Danes in Estonia. Meanwhile Albert, forced against his will by the Knights of the Sword to submit temporarily (1219–22) to Waldemar II, came into conflict with the Russians, who supported an aimless pagan revolt (1217–24). This ultimately led to a compromise among the Germans, so that the conquered territory was divided between Albert and the Knights. This division became a source of future weakness for the region, a part of which the city of Riga later claimed as its territory.

Feast: June 1 (prior to the Reformation).

Bibliography: HEINRICUS LETTUS, *Chronicon Livoniae,* ed. A. BAUER (2d ed. Würzburg 1959). *Baltische Lande* 1 (Riga 1939). F. KOCH, *Livland und das Reich bis zum Jahre 1225* (Posen 1943). M. HELLMANN, *Das Lettenland im Mittelalter* (Münster 1954). G. ALLMANG, *Dictionnaire d'histoire et de géographie ecclésiastiques,* ed. A. BAUDRILLART et al. (Paris 1912) 1:1440–41.

[H. WOLFRAM]

ALBERT II OF RIGA

Archbishop of Riga; b. Cologne, late 12th century; d. 1273. Albert Suerbeer is frequently said to have been a Dominican, though this is probably an error. The assertion that he studied at Paris and took a master's degree there is also doubtful. He taught at the cathedral school in Bremen and in 1229 was nominated bishop of Livonia, but the chapter at Riga refused to accept him, choosing instead a Premonstratensian, Nicholas. In 1240 Albert was appointed archbishop of ARMAGH, where he supported the English king, Henry III, against the rebellious barons in the struggle over church property and promoted the canonization of EDMUND OF ABINGDON. Albert took part in the First Council of Lyons, 1245, and in 1246 was appointed archbishop of Prussia, Livonia, and Esthonia and papal legate for these countries and adjacent lands. Local opposition prevented him from exercising his authority in these posts, and from 1247 to 1253 he acted as apostolic administrator of the See of Lübeck. In 1253, on the death of the incumbent Nicholas, he was elected by the chapter to the See of Riga; two years later he was confirmed by ALEXANDER IV as archbishop and metropolitan.

His efforts to extend the influence of his see met with strong opposition from the powerful local military order, the KNIGHTS OF THE SWORD, which in 1238 had been assimilated to the TEUTONIC KNIGHTS. This opposition caused the archbishop to be imprisoned briefly in 1268, though his cause was supported by the citizens of Riga.

Bibliography: P. VON GOETZE, *Albert Suerbeer, Erzbischof von Preussen, Livland, und Ehstland* (St. Petersburg 1854). M. H. MACINERNY, *A History of the Irish Dominicans* (Dublin 1916). G. ALLMANG, *Dictionnaire d'histoire et de géographie ecclésiastiques* 1:1563. M. HELLMANN, *Lexikon für Theologie und Kirche* 1:281.

[P. M. STARRS]

ALBERT BEHAIM

Papal legate, anti-imperialist; b. Bavaria, *c.* 1180; d. probably in Passau, *c.* 1260. In 1212 Albert received a canonry at Passau, the first of many benefices he accumulated, shortly after entering the papal Curia, where he served under INNOCENT III and HONORIUS III. Later, after returning to Germany, he became a violent agitator against the Hohenstaufen dynasty even before the final papal controversy with FREDERICK II. When GREGORY IX excommunicated the emperor in 1239, he commissioned Albert to promulgate the sentence in Bavaria and compel obedience, which brought Albert into conflict with almost all the Bavarian clergy. Albert employed so many excommunications and interdicts that Duke Otto expelled him in 1241. He finally found refuge at Lyons in 1244 with INNOCENT IV, whom he advised on German affairs, playing a part in the election of the antikings. Not until 1250, after the emperor's death and the forceful deposition of Albert's chief foe, Bishop Rudiger of Passau, could he return home and recover his prebends. Always aggressive and anxious to promote his own interests, Albert continued to make enemies. His own bishop imprisoned him for some obscure reason, but in 1258 Pope ALEXANDER IV intervened to secure his release. Details of his death are not known.

Bibliography: *Alberts von Beham Conceptbuch,* ed. C. HÖFLER (Stuttgart 1847). R. BAUERREISS, *Kirchengeschichte Bayerns,* 5 v. (St. Ottilien, Ger. 1949–55; 2d ed. 1958). A. HAUCK, *Kirchengeschichte Deutschlands* v. 4. J. OSWALD, *Neue deutsche Biographie* 2:1.

[R. H. SCHMANDT]

ALBERT OF JERUSALEM, ST.

Patriarch of Jerusalem; b. Parma, Italy, *c.* 1149; d. Acre, Holy Land, Sept. 14, 1214. He studied theology, civil law and Canon Law before becoming a canon regular in the monastery of the Holy Cross in Mortara. In 1184 he was made bishop of Bobbio whence he was soon transferred to Vercelli in Lombardy. A skilled diplomat, he served as mediator between Pope CLEMENT III and Emperor FREDERICK I Barbarossa, and later as a legate of Pope INNOCENT III in the north of Italy, where he brought about peace between Parma and Piacenza.

His reputation for diplomacy and piety led to his selection as patriarch of Jerusalem in 1205. Since the Muslims held Jerusalem after 1187, he established his residence in St. Jean d'Acre where he worked hard to keep peace between all factions. In his capacity as patriarch he was requested by Burchard (d. 1221), prior of the hermits living on Mt. Carmel, to give them a rule, which he did in 16 short chapters (*see* CARMELITES). He was assassinated on the Feast of the Exaltation of the Cross by a disgruntled former master of the Hospital of the Holy Spirit at Acre whom he had deposed (*see* HOSPITALLERS). His feast was first introduced by the Carmelites in 1411 and was formally approved in 1666.

Feast: Sept. 25.

Bibliography: B. EDWARDS, tr., *The Rule of St. Albert,* Latin text with an English tr. (London 1973). V. MOSCA, *Alberto Patriarca di Gerusalemme: tempo, vita, opera* (Rome 1996). *Acta Santorum* April 1:764–799. P. MARIE-JOSEPH, *Dictionnaire d'histoire et de géographie ecclésiastiques,* ed. A. BAUDRILLART et al. (Paris 1912) 1:1564–67. J. BAUR, *Lexicon für Theologie und Kirche,* ed. J. HOFER and K. RAHNER (Freiburg 1957–65) 1:279.

[V. L. BULLOUGH]

ALBERT OF PONTIDA, ST.

Monastic reformer; d. Pontida, Italy, May 1, 1095. After recovering from a near mortal wound, he gave up the life of a soldier, made a pilgrimage to SANTIAGO DE COMPOSTELA, and entered the BENEDICTINE Order during the height of the reform movement led by HUGH OF CLUNY. He founded the monastery of Saint James at Pontida, located between the towns of Bergamo and Lecco, *c.* 1080 and became its first prior. He continued to direct the fortunes of this foundation as part of the Cluniac organization until his death, and he was buried there. When the monastery was destroyed by fire in 1373, his remains were transferred to the church of St. Mary Major in Bergamo, where they were honored until 1911, when they were returned to Pontida to the restored abbey church.

Feast: Sept. 5, Sept. 2 in Pontida.

Bibliography: J. MABILLON, *Annales Ordinis S. Benedicti,* 6 v. (Lucca 1739–45) 5:322. L. SECOMANDI, *S. Alberto di Pontida ed il suo monasterio* (Bergamo 1895). P. F. KEHR, *Regesta Pontificum Romanorum. Italia Pontifica.* (Berlin 1906–35) 6.1:392–394. R. BIRON, *Dictionnaire d'histoire et de géographie ecclésiastiques,* ed.

A. BAUDRILLART et al. (Paris 1912) 1:1545–46. G. MORIN, in *Revue Bénédictine* 38 (1926) 53–59. J. BAUR, *Lexicon für Theologie und Kirche*, ed. J. HOFER and K. RAHNER (Freiburg 1957–65) 1:280.

[K. NOLAN]

ALBERT OF SARTEANO, BL.

Franciscan missionary; b. Sarteano, near Siena, Italy, 1385; d. Milan, Italy, Aug. 15, 1450. He received his early education from Guarino of Verona and in 1415 joined the FRANCISCAN order. From 1435 to 1437 he worked as a preacher under the direction of BERNARDINE OF SIENA in the Holy Land. As a delegate of Pope EUGENE IV, Albert made a second journey to the Near East (1439–41), during which he helped win the good will of the Coptic Patriarch John of Alexandria, and so prepared the way for the reunion realized at the Council of FLORENCE in 1442. He was vicar general of the Franciscan Order from 1442 to 1443. His cult has not been publicly approved, but he is honored in the Franciscan order as blessed.

Feast: Aug. 15.

Bibliography: B. NERI, *La vita e i tempi beato Albertio da Sarteano* (Florence 1902). A. DE SÉRENT, *Dictionnaire d'histoire et de géographie ecclésiastiques,* ed. A. BAUDRILLART (Paris 1912–) 1:1554–56. L. WADDING, *Scriptores Ordinis Minorum,* 86 v. (Lyons 1625–54) v.9, 10, 11. G. HOFMANN, "Kopten und Aethiopier auf dem Konzil von Florenz," *Orientalia Christiana periodica* 8 (1942) 5–39. G. FUSSENEGGER, *Lexikon für Theologie und Kirche,* ed. J. HOFER and K. RAHNER, 10 v. (2d, new ed. Freiburg 1957–65) 1:282.

[K. NOLAN]

ALBERT OF SAXONY

Nominalist philosopher of Paris and bishop; b. Rickmersdorf, lower Saxony, 1316; d. 1390. He was an outstanding master in arts at the University of Paris from 1351 to 1362 and rector of the University in 1357 and 1362. In his *Quaestiones super libros Physicorum* (Venice 1504), *Quaestiones in libros de caelo et mundo* (Venice 1520), and *Quaestiones in libros de generatione* (Venice 1504) he was much influenced by the teaching of JOHN BURIDAN and NICHOLAS ORESME, notable on the theory of IMPETUS and on the configuration of forms that can be increased and decreased. In his *Logica* (Venice 1522), *Quaestiones super libros Posteriorum* (Venice 1497), and *Sophismata* (Paris 1489) he was greatly influenced by the NOMINALISM of WILLIAM OF OCKHAM. His *Tractatus obligationum* and *Insolubilia* (Paris 1490) clearly show the influence of Oxford logicians. He promulgated and developed the new physics initiated by

THOMAS BRADWARDINE and John Buridan. He wrote a number of short treatises on proportionality and the square of the circle that became popular textbooks in universities. In his unedited commentary on the *Nicomachean Ethics* of Aristotle he followed closely the commentary of WALTER BURLEY. In 1365 he was named the first rector of the new University of Vienna. In 1366 he was nominated and consecrated bishop of Halberstadt; he served in this office until his death. His writings in natural philosophy were widely read until the 17th century.

Bibliography: B. NARDI, *Enciclopedia filosofica* 1:128. A. MAIER, *Die Vorläufer Galileis im 14. Jahrhundert* (Rome 1949); *An der Grenze von Scholastik und Naturwissenschaft* (2d ed. Rome 1952). M. CLAGETT, *The Science of Mechanics in the Middle Ages* (Madison, Wis. 1959). É. H. GILSON, *History of Christian Philosophy in the Middle Ages* 516–20. P. HOSSFELD, *Lexikon für Theologie und Kirche* 1:281.

[J. A. WEISHEIPL]

ALBERT OF TRAPANI, ST.

Carmelite; b. Trapani, Sicily, *c.* 1240; d. Messina, Sicily, Aug. 7, 1307. By 1280 he had entered the CARMELITE monastery in his native town, and despite his own humble opinion of himself he prepared for the priesthood and was ordained by 1289. He effected numerous conversions throughout Sicily and was made religious superior of the Sicilian province in 1296. By the time of his death, he had gained an extraordinary reputation for sanctity. He was buried at Messina, where he is honored as the patron because of his miraculous assistance to the city during a siege in 1301. His head is preserved at Trapani. His cult was approved by CALLISTUS III in 1457 and by SIXTUS IV in 1476. His relics are widely disseminated because of the currently used blessing of the water of St. Albert in the Carmelite ritual; his aid is invoked against fever. The oldest biography dates from 1385, and few details of his life are certain. He is often shown holding a lily, or receiving the Christ Child from Our Lady. There are paintings of him by Francesco Francia and Bernardo Monaldi.

Feast: Aug. 7.

Bibliography: L. M. SAGGI, *Dizionario biographico degli Italiani,* ed. A. M. GHISALBERTI (Rome 1960–) 1:740–741. B. M. XIBERTA Y ROQUETA, "Catalogus sanctorum ordinis carmelitarum," *De visione sancti Simonis Stock* (Rome 1950) 281–307. P. MARIE-JOSEPH, *Dictionnaire d'histoire et de géographie ecclésiastiques,* ed. A. BAUDRILLAT et al. (Paris 1912–) 1:1558–59. G. MESTERS, *Lexikon für Theologie und Kirche,* ed. J. HOFER and K. RAHNER, 10 v. (2d, new ed. Freiburg 1957–65) 1:282–283. L. RÉAU, *Iconographie de l'art chrétien* (Paris 1955–59) 3.1:47. *Acta Santorum,* Aug. 2:215–239.

[E. R. CARROLL]

ALBERT THE GREAT, ST.

Dominican bishop, Doctor of the Church, patron of scientists, and philosopher; b. Lauingen on the Danube, near Ulm, Germany, c. 1200; d. Cologne, Nov. 15, 1280; variously referred to as Albertus Magnus, Albert of Lauingen, Albert of Cologne, and Albert the German; honored under the scholastic titles of *Doctor universalis* and *Doctor expertus.* Although in his own right Albert was an outstanding figure of the Middle Ages, he is best known as the teacher of St. THOMAS AQUINAS and as a proponent of ARISTOTELIANISM at the University of Paris. He combined interest and skill in natural science with proficiency in all branches of philosophy and theology.

LIFE

Early Life. Albert was the eldest son of a powerful and wealthy German lord of military rank. After his elementary training, he studied the liberal arts at Padua while his father fought in the service of Frederick II in Lombardy. Early in the summer of 1223, JORDAN OF SAXONY, the successor to DOMINIC as master general of the Order of Preachers, came to Padua in the hope of bringing young men into the order by his preaching. At first he found "the students of Padua extremely cold," but ten of them soon sought admission, "among them two sons of two great German lords; one was a provost-marshall, loaded with many honors and possessed of great riches; the other has resigned rich benefices and is truly noble in mind and body" (Jordan, *Epistolae* 20). The latter has always been identified as Albert of Lauingen.

After overcoming fierce opposition from his family, he entered the novitiate and later was sent to Germany to study theology. Shortly after 1233 he was appointed lecturer of theology in the new priory at Hildesheim, then, successively, at Freiburg im Breisgau, at Regensburg for two years, and at Strassburg. During these years he wrote his treatise *De natura boni,* influenced largely by HUGH OF SAINT-VICTOR and WILLIAM OF AUXERRE.

Teaching at Paris. Around 1241 he was sent to the University of Paris to prepare for the mastership in theology. The intellectual climate of Paris, "the city of philosophers," was vastly different from his native Germany, for here he encountered the "new Aristotle," recently translated from Greek and Arabic, and the wealth of Arabic learning introduced from Spain. Albert arrived in Paris just as the commentaries of Averroës on Aristotle were becoming available. At the Dominican convent of St. Jacques, he fulfilled the university requirements for bachelors in theology, lecturing cursorily on the Bible for two years, responding in disputations, and then expounding the *Sentences* of PETER LOMBARD for two years (c. 1243–45), but Albert was more interested in acquiring the new learning than in lecturing on the *Sentences.* In 1245 he incepted as a master in theology under Guéric of St. Quentin, and continued to lecture as master in the Dominican chair "for foreigners" until the end of the academic year 1248. Albert was, in fact, the first German Dominican to become a master.

Most probably it was at Paris that he began his monumental presentation of the whole of human knowledge to the Latin West, paraphrasing and explaining all the known works of Aristotle and pseudo-Aristotle, adding contributions from the Arabs, and even entirely "new sciences" (*Phys.* 1.1.1). Apparently asked by his younger confreres to explain Aristotle's *Physics* in writing, he undertook to explain systematically all the branches of natural science, logic, rhetoric, mathematics, astronomy, ethics, economics, politics, and metaphysics. "Our intention," he said, "is to make all the aforesaid parts of knowledge intelligible to the Latins" (*ibid.*). This vast project took about 20 years to complete and is one of the marvels of medieval scholarship. While working on it, he probably had among his disciples the young Aquinas, who arrived in Paris in the autumn of 1245.

Years in Germany and Italy. In the summer of 1248 Albert was sent to Cologne to organize and preside over the first *studium generale* in Germany, which had been authorized by the Dominican general chapter in June. At Cologne he devoted his full energies to teaching, preaching, studying, and writing until 1254. Among his disciples at this time were Thomas Aquinas, who studied under Albert (1245–52), and ULRIC OF STRASSBURG. In 1253 Albert was elected provincial of the German Dominicans, a position he faithfully filled for three years. Despite the administrative burdens, the yearly visitation of each priory and nunnery, and lengthy journeys on foot, he continued his prolific writing and scientific research in libraries, fields, ore mines, and industrial localities.

In 1256 he was in the papal curia at Anagni with Aquinas and BONAVENTURE to defend the cause of mendicant orders against the attacks of WILLIAM OF SAINT-AMOUR and other secular masters. Here also he held a disputation against Averroist doctrine on the intellect (*see* INTELLECT, UNITY OF). He lectured to the curia on the whole of St. John's Gospel and on some of the Epistles; for this reason he is listed among the "Masters of the Sacred Palace." Resigning the office of provincial, he resumed teaching in Cologne (1257–60). In 1259 the general chapter requested him and four other masters in theology to draw up a plan of study to be followed throughout the order.

Late that same year irregularities in the Diocese of Regensburg led to the appointment of Albert to succeed the removed bishop. His own reluctance and the plead-ings of Humbert of Romans, general of the order, were of no avail. On Jan. 5, 1260, Alexander IV ordered his installation as bishop of Regensburg. With the settling of conditions in this diocese and the election of a new pope, he was able to resign in 1262; he then chose the house of studies at Cologne for his residence. Albert voluntarily resumed teaching, but in the following year he was ordered by Urban IV to preach the crusade throughout Germany and Bohemia (1263–64). From 1264 to 1266 he lived in the Dominican house in Würzburg. In 1268 he was in Strassburg, and from 1269 until his death he resided in Cologne, writing new works and revising earlier ones.

Only two more times, as far as is known, did he undertake long journeys from Cologne. He took part in the Council of Lyons in 1274, and in 1277 he traveled to Paris, at the height of the Averroist controversy, to forestall the hasty condemnation of certain Aristotelian doctrines that both he and Thomas (d. 1274) held to be true (*see* AVERROISM, LATIN; FORMS, UNICITY AND PLURALITY OF). This last journey was apparently a failure. Some time after he drew up his last will and testament in January 1279, his health and memory began to fail him. Weakened by manifold labors, austerities, and vigils, he died at the age of ''eighty years or more,'' to quote BARTHOLOMEW OF LUCCA and BERNARD GUI. His body was laid to rest in the Dominican church at Cologne where it remains today.

Cult and Canonization. Not only was Albert the only man of the High Middle Ages to be called ''the Great,'' but this title was used even before his death (*Annal. Basil., Monumenta Germaniae Historica: Scriptores* 17:202). Long before the canonization of Thomas in 1323, Albert's prestige was well established. SIGER OF BRABANT, a contemporary, considered Albert and Thomas ''the principal men in philosophy'' (*De anim. intel.* 3). In the words of Ulric of Strassburg, Albert was ''a man so superior in every science, that he can fittingly be called the wonder and the miracle of our time'' (*Sum. de bono* 4.3.9).

In Germany there has always existed a deep devotion to the venerable bishop. He was beatified by Gregory XV in 1622. By the decree *In Thesauris Sapientiae* (Dec. 16, 1931) Pius XI declared him a saint of the universal Church with the additional title of doctor. In the solemn decree *Ad Deum* (Dec. 16, 1941) Pius XII constituted him the heavenly patron of all who cultivate the natural sciences.

DOCTRINE

Aristotelianism. The Christian centuries preceding Albert were fundamentally Augustinian in philosophy and theology, transmitting the Christian Platonism of the Fathers through the monasteries and the schools (*see* PLATONISM). The 12th-century Latin translations of AVICENNA, Avicebron, COSTA BEN LUCA, ISAAC ISRAELI, and the *LIBER DE CAUSIS*, together with the paraphrases of DOMINIC GUNDISALVI, could easily be accommodated to Christian philosophy, since Platonic thought was a common element. When the new Aristotle reached the schools, the obscure Latin versions of the Stagirite from Arabic and Greek were studied and taught with every aid at hand, including JOHN SCOTUS ERIGENA, Avicenna, Avicebron and AUGUSTINE. The earliest teachers of the Aristotelian books at Paris, AMALRIC OF BÈNE and DAVID OF DINANT, made a pantheist of Aristotle, and incurred a deserved censure until the new Aristotle could be examined more carefully. Later masters in the faculty of arts, such as ROBERT GROSSETESTE, JOHN BLUND, ADAM OF BUCKFIELD, Geoffrey of Aspall, ROBERT KILWARDBY and ROGER BACON, were more orthodox, although they interpreted Aristotle through the teaching of Avicenna and in Platonist fashion.

However, there is a fundamental divergence between Platonic and Aristotelian views, particularly concerning scientific thought and the nature of man. For PLATO, the study of nature is not strictly scientific, but only problematic, a ''likely story''; for certainty one must go to mathematics, and thence to the contemplation of pure forms in metaphysics. Further, Plato conceived man as a soul imprisoned in a body, rather than a unique composite of body and soul. Aristotle, on the other hand, considered the study of nature to be autonomous in its own domain, independent of mathematics and metaphysics, worthy of pursuit in its own right, and truly ''scientific'' in the technical sense employed by the Greeks. Moreover, Aristotle was the first to elaborate fully the doctrine of potency and act, using this to explain how the body and soul of man constitute an absolute unity in nature. The arrival of Averroës's commentaries in the schools after 1230 helped to bring out the difference between the two Greeks, for Averroës was the most Aristotelian of the Arabic commentators.

Among the Latin schoolmen, Albert was the first to make the Aristotelian approach to the physical world his own and to defend its autonomy against ''the error of Plato'' (*Meta.* 1.1.1, *et passim*) maintained by his contemporaries. Strictly speaking, Albert's expositions of Aristotle are neither commentaries nor paraphrases; they are really original works in which ''the true view of Peripatetic philosophers'' is rewritten, erroneous views refuted, new solutions proposed, and personal observations (*experimenta*) incorporated. This, at least, was the opinion of Roger Bacon's contemporaries at Paris, who thought that ''now a complete philosophy has been given to the Latins, and composed in the Latin tongue'' (*Opus tertium* 9). For this reason, as Bacon tells us, Albert's views had as much authority in the schools as those of Aristotle, Avicenna, or Averroës, ''and he is still alive and he has had in his own lifetime authority, which man has never had in doctrine'' (*ibid.*).

Scientific Method. Yet Albert did not blindly follow the authority of Aristotle. In his philosophical as well as theological works, he does not hesitate to reject certain views, such as the eternity of the world and the animation of the spheres, and observational errors. ''Whoever believes that Aristotle was a god, must also believe that he never erred; but if one believes that Aristotle was a man, then doubtless he was liable to error just as we are'' (*Phys.* 8.1.14). In matters of experimental science, he frequently rejects a supposed observation of the Stagirite, saying that it is contrary to his own observations (*Meteor.* 3.4.11, *Animal.* 23.1.1. 104, etc.). In his treatise on plants he insists, ''Experiment is the only safe guide in such investigations'' (*Veg.* 6.2.1). In practice as well as in theory, he realized that ''the aim of natural science is not simply to accept the statements of others, but to investigate the causes that are at work in nature'' (*Mineral.* 2.2.1).

Albert was an indefatigable student of nature, and applied himself so sedulously that he was accused of neglecting the sacred sciences (HENRY OF GHENT, *De script. eccles.* 2.10). Even in his own lifetime incredible legends were circulated, attributing to him the power of a magician or sorcerer. In later generations such legends were multiplied and spurious treatises were circulated under his name. The real influence of Albert, felt throughout the Renaissance, comes from his establishing the study of nature as a legitimate science in the Christian tradition. *See* SCIENCE (IN THE MIDDLE AGES).

Sacred Theology. In theology he was not as successful as his illustrious disciple in presenting a new synthesis. Aquinas's famous *Summa* is a perfect application of Aristotle's *Posterior Analytics* to the deposit of faith, employing from the very beginning the profound implications of Aristotelian metaphysical principles. This cannot be said of Albert's theological works. Nonetheless these are outstanding in medieval literature for their sound scholarship, breadth of inquiry, and clarity of presentation. Considering the milieu in which he wrote, it is most significant that he strongly defended the distinction between the realm of revelation and that of human reason (*see* FAITH AND REASON).

Unlike many of his contemporaries, he defended the autonomy of philosophical investigation, insisting that no truth of reason could contradict revelation. At the same time, he maintained the superiority of revelation and the right of theologians to use all of human knowledge to search the divine mysteries. This view was continued by Aquinas and others so that today it is an integral part of Catholic theology.

Albertists. Among the immediate students of Albert, apart from Aquinas and Ulrich of Strassburg, should also be enumerated Hugh of Strassburg, JOHN OF FREIBURG, JOHN OF LICHTENBERG, and GILES OF LESSINES. Other German Dominicans favorably disposed toward Neoplatonic thought developed mystical elements in Albert's teaching. These were transmitted through THEODORIC OF FREIBERG and Berthold of Mosburg to Meister ECKHART and other 14th-century mystics, namely, Johannes TAULER, HENRY SUSO, and Jan van RUYSBROECK. In the 15th century, small groups of thinkers at Paris and Cologne, identifying themselves as ''Albertists,'' set up a philosophical school in opposition to Thomism. Founded by Heymericus de Campo (Van de Velde), they opposed the traditional Thomistic teaching on the real distinction between essence and existence, as well as that on universals. In so doing they actually returned to the teaching of Avicenna, and made extensive use of Albert's commentaries on the *Liber de Causis* and the works of PSEUDO-DIONYSIUS.

That Albert's teaching is not to be completely identified with that of his famous student is clear from his response to the 43 questions of JOHN OF VERCELLI (*43 Problemata determinata*), one of his last writings. Some have even held that an occasional *quidam* in the works of Albert is a disparaging reference to Thomas, but on the whole there is broad doctrinal agreement between master and student. This has led to a gradual assimilation of the Albertist tradition within the Dominican Order into the mainstream of Thomism, with the result that Albertism and Thomism have become practically indistinguishable.

WRITINGS

The reputation of Albert was so widespread that not only were his authentic works frequently copied in manuscript and abundantly reproduced in print, but an incredible number of spurious works, some even fantastic, have been attributed to him. On the other hand many works known to have been written by him have not yet been discovered. Two editions of ''complete works'' have been published: one at Lyons in 1651, in 21 folio volumes edited by Peter Jammy, OP; the other at Paris (Vivès), 1890–99, in 38 quarto volumes edited by the Abbé Auguste Borgnet, of the Diocese of Reims. The first volume of a new and critical edition that will comprise 40 volumes, under the direction of Bernhard Geyer, President of the Albertus Magnus Institute of Cologne, appeared in 1951. The following list gives the volume of the Borgnet edition (B), and the actual or projected volume of the Cologne edition (C). The dates in brackets are the certain or probable dates of composition.

Logic. *Super Porphyrium de 5 universalibus,* B.1, C.1; *De praedicamentis,* B.1, C.1; *De sex principiis,* B.1, C.1; *De divisione,* C.1; *Peri hermeneias,* B.1, C.1; *Analytica priora,* B.1, C.2; *Analytica posteriora,* B.2, C.2; *Topica,* B.2, C.3; *De sophisticis elenchis,* B.2, C.3 [all between 1248–1264].

Natural Science. *Physica,* B.3, C.4 [between 1245–48]; *De caelo et mundo,* B.4, C.5 [between 1248–60]; *De natura locorum,* B.9, C.5 [before 1259]; *De causis proprietatum elementorum,* B.9, C.5 [between 1248–59]; *De generatione et corruptione,* B.4, C.5 [before 1260]; *Meteora,* B.4, C.6 [before 1259]; *Mineralia,* B.5, C.6 [before 1263]; *De anima,* B.5, C.7 [c. 1256]; *De nutrimento,* B.9, C.7 [before 1263]; *De intellectu et intelligibili,* B.9, C.7 [before 1259]; *De sensu et sensato,* B.9, C.7 [before 1260]; *De memoria,* B.9, C.7 [before 1263]; *De somno et vigilia,* B.9, C.7 [before 1259]; *De spiritu et respiratione,* B.9, C.7 [before 1259]; *De motibus animalium,* B.9, C.7 [before 1259]; *De aetate,* B.9, C.7 [before 1259]; *De morte et vita,* B.9, C.7 [before 1259]; *De vegetabilibus et plantis,* B.10, C.8 [before 1259]; *De animalibus,* B.11–12, C.9–1 [1258–62]; *De natura et origine animae,* B.9, C.12 [c. 1263]; *De principiis motus processivi,* B.10, C.12 [c. 1261]; *QQ. super de animalibus,* C.12 [c. 1258]

Moral Sciences. *Ethica,* B.7, C.13 [before 1261]; *Super Ethica commentum et quaestiones,* C.14 [between 1248–52]; *Politica,* B.8, C.15 [between 1265–75].

Metaphysics. *Metaphysica,* B.6, C.16 [between 1261–66]; *De causis,* B.10, C.17 [between 1266–71]; *De unitate intellectus,* B.9, C.17 [c. 1270]; *De 15 problematibus,* C.17 [c. 1270]; *43 Problemata determinata,* C.17 [April 1271].

Sacred Scripture. *Super Iob,* C.18 [1272 or 1274]; *Super Isaiam,* C.19; *Super Ieremiam* (frag.), C.20; *Super Threnos,* B.18, C.20; *Super Baruch,* B.18, C.20; *Super Ezechielem* (frag.), C.20; *Super Danielem,* B.18, C.20; *Super Prophetas minores,* B.19, C.20; *Super Mattheum,* B.20–21, C.21 [definitive version after 1270]; *Super Marcum,* B.21, C.22 [definitive version between 1272–5]; *Super Lucam,* B.22–23, C.23 [1261–62; rev. 1270–75]; *Super Ioannem,* B.24, C.24 [1256; rev. 1272–75]. Albert's commentaries on St. Paul and on Apocalypse have not yet been found; the printed Apocalypse is spurious.

Systematic Theology. *De natura boni,* C.25 [before 1240]; *Super 4 sententiarum,* B.25–30, C.29–32 [rev. version completed in 1249]; *QQ. theologicae,* C.25 [1245–48]; *De sacramentis, De incarnatione, De resur-* rectione, C.26 [1245–50]; *De 4 coaequaevis,* B.34, C.26 [1245–50]; *De homine,* B.35, C.27 [1244–48]; *De bono,* C.28 [1244–48]; *In corpus Dionysium,* B.14, C.36–37 [1248–60]; *Summa theologiae,* B.31–33, C.34–35 [after 1270]; *De mysterio missae,* B.38, C.38 [after 1270]; *De corpore domini,* B.38, C.38 [after 1270].

Sermons and Letters. C.39 (see J. P. Schneyer).

Spurious and Dubious Works. C.40. It is certain that Albert wrote on mathematics, astronomy, and rhetoric, but these writings have not yet been found. Among the definitely spurious works, the best known are the *Compendium theologiae veritatis,* B.34, which is by Hugh of Strassburg; *De laudibus B. Mariae Virginis,* B.36; *Mariale,* B.37; *Biblia Mariana,* B.37; the *De secretis naturae, De secretis mulierum,* and other occult works. The authenticity of many other works is still disputed among scholars, principally that of the *Speculum astronomiae.*

Feast: Nov. 15.

See Also: THOMISM; SCHOLASTICISM; NEOPLATONISM.

Bibliography: M. ALBERT, *Albert the Great* (Oxford 1948). M. J. DORCY, *Master Albert; the Story of SaintAlbert the Great* (New York 1955). T. M. SCHWERTNER, *Saint Albert the Great* (Milwaukee 1932). F. C. COPLESTON, *History of Philosophy* (Westminster, Md. 1946–) 2:293–301. F. L. CROSS, *The Oxford Dictionary of the Christian Church* (London 1957) 30. F. UEBERWEG, *Grundriss der Geshichte der Philosophie,* ed. K. PRAECHTER et al. (Berlin 1923–28) 2:400–416. *Enciclopedia filosofica* (Venice-Rome 1957) 1:121–127. W. KÜBEL, *Lexikon für Theologie und Kirche,* ed. J. HOFER and K. RAHNER (Freiberg 1957–65) 1:285–287; *see* 284 under "Albertismus." P. MANDONNET, *Dictionnaire de théologie catholique,* ed. A. VACANT et al., (Paris 1903–50) 1.1:666–675. Institutum Alberti Magni Coloniense, B. GEYER, president, *Opera omnia ad fidem codicum manuscriptorum edenda, apparatu critico . . .,* ed. W. KÜBEL, 37 v. (Aschendorff, Germany 1951–1993). P. G. MEERSSEMAN, *Introductio in opera omnia Beati Alberti Magni* (Bruges 1931). "De vita et scriptis B. Alberti Magni," ed. P. DE LOË, *Analecta Bollandiana* 19 (Brussels 1900) 257–284; 20 (1901) 273–316; 21 (1902) 361–371. J. QUÉTIF and J. ÉCHARD, *Scriptores Ordinis Praedicatorum* (Paris 1719–23) 1:162–183. *Albert der Grosse in Köln: gehalten auf der Feierstunde zur 750sten Wiederkehr . . .,* ed. J. A. AERTSEN (Cologne 1999). *Albertus Magnus, Doctor universalis,* ed. G. MEYER and A. ZIMMERMANN (Mainz 1980). T. M. BONIN, *Creation as Emanation: The Origin of Diversity in Albert the Great's On the Causes and the Procession of the Universe* (Notre Dame, Ind. 2000). G. EMERY, *La Trinité créatrice: Trinité et création dans les commentaires aux Sentences de Thomas d'Aquin et de ses précurseurs Albert le Grand et Bonaventure* (Paris 1995). K. ILLING, *Alberts des Grossen "Super Missam" - Traktat in mittelhochdeutschen Übertragungen: Untersuchungen und Texte* (Munich 1975). A. DE LIBERA, *Albert le Grand et la philosophie* (Paris 1990). F.-J. NOCKE, *Sakrament und personaler Vollzug bei Albertus Magnus* (Münster 1967). A. PIOLANTI, *Il corpo mistico: e le sue relazioni con l'eucaristia in S. Alberto Magno* (Rome 1969). H. C. SCHEEBEN, "Albertus der Grosse: Zur Chronologie seines Lebens," *Quellen und Forschungen zur Gesch-*

ichte des Dominikanerordens in Deutschland 27 (Vechta 1931). "Le Bienheureux Albert le Grand," *Revue thomiste* 36 (1931), esp. M. H. LAURENT and Y. CONGAR, "Essai de bibliographie albertinienne," 422–468. M. SCHOOYANS, "Bibliographie philosophique de saint Albert le Grand (1931–60)," *Revista da Universidade Católica de São Paulo* 21 (1961) 36–88. J. P. SCHNEYER, "Predigten Alberts des Grossen in der Hs. Leipzig, Univ. Bibl. 683," *Archivum Fratrum Praedicatorum* 34 (1964) 45–106. J. P. TILMANN, *An Appraisal of the Geographical Works of Albertus Magnus and His Contributions to Geographical Thought* (Ann Arbor 1971). P. ZAMBELLI, *The Speculum Astronomiae and Its Enigma* (Dordrecht 1992). *Albert and Thomas: Selected Writings*, tr. S. TUGWELL, *The Classics of Western Spirituality* (New York 1988).

[J. A. WEISHEIPL]

ALBERTARIO, DAVIDE

Priest, editor; b. Filighera (Pavia), Italy, Feb. 16, 1846; d. Carenno (Bergamo), Italy, Sept. 21, 1902. Albertario became a journalist the year he was ordained (1868), after earning his doctorate in theology at Rome's Pontifical Gregorian University. In 1872, he became part owner and associate editor, then editor, of the daily *Osservatore Cattolico,* of Milan and of the weekly *Il Popolo Cattolico.* He defended zealously, if not always temperately, the principles of the SYLLABUS OF ERRORS and of VATICAN COUNCIL I, and opposed not only liberal intolerance and "irreligious tyranny" but also the "liberal Catholicism" of some priests and bishops. This position set him against men of outstanding reputation such as Bishop BONOMELLI of Cremona and Bishop SCALABRINI of Piacenza, and well-known priests such as the noted geologist, Antonio Stoppani.

In 1894, at a time when relations between Church and State had become less stormy, Albertario invited to the OSSERVATORE CATTOLICO Filippo Meda, who was to succeed him as editor and give a new impetus to public action by Catholics. During this period the paper continually advised its readers to prepare for the time when the Holy See might permit Italian Catholics to reenter political life (*see* MARGOTTI, GIACOMO).

In 1898, during a disproportionate reaction of the government to certain social movements which led to the temporary dissolution of Catholic organizations, Albertario, who had bravely defended the poorer classes, was arrested. Together with certain Syndicalist Socialists, he was tried and condemned to three years in prison, a sentence generally regarded as unjust. After one year he was released following the lively agitation that the sentence had aroused among Italian Catholics. He told the story of his imprisonment in two volumes titled *Un anno di carcere* (1900).

[E. LUCATELLO]

ALBERTI, LEANDRO

Italian Dominican, historian and inquisitor; b. Bologna, 1479; d. Bologna, 1552? As a young religious at Forlì and then at Bologna, he studied under the humanist G. Garzoni and the theologian S. Mazzolini of Priero. In 1514–15 and in 1525 as socius to two masters general, the celebrated Cajetan and the noted theologian Francesco Silvestri of Ferrara, called "Ferrariensis," he traveled through Italy, France, and Germany. After 1532, apart from a brief period as vicar of Santa Sabina in Rome, he was involved almost exclusively with duties of the office of the Inquisition at Bologna. Among Alberti's literary productions, several works have merited distinction: *De viris illustribus Ordinis Praedicatorum* (Bologna 1517), still profitably consulted; *Descrittione di tutta Italia* (Bologna 1550), his principal work, published in 12 editions; and the *Historie di Bologna* (Bologna and Vicenza 1541–91).

Bibliography: J. QUÉTIF and J. ÉCHARD, *Scriptores Ordinis Praedicatorum* (New York 1959) 2.1:137–139. G. M. MAZZUCHELLI, *Gli scrittori d'Italia*, v.1 (Brescia 1753) 306–310.

[A. L. REDIGONDA]

ALBERTINUS OF FONTE AVELLANA, ST.

Abbot; d. April 13, 1294. He became a BENEDICTINE monk *c.* 1250 and was an outstanding prior general of the congregation of Fonte Avellana in the Marches from 1275 until his death. He was buried in the monastery church at Fonte Avellana and was soon honored as a saint. His cult was approved by Pope Pius VI on Aug. 21, 1782. He is regarded as a holy protector against hernia.

Feast: Aug. 31.

Bibliography: G. B. MITTARELLI and A. COSTADONI, *Annales Camaldulenses,* v.5 (Venice 1760) 207–210. A. GIBELLI, *Monografia dell'antico monastero di S. Croce di Fonte Avellana: I suoi priori ed abbati* (Faenza 1895). R. BIRON, *Dictionnaire d'histoire et de géographie ecclésiastiques*, ed. A. BAUDRILLART et al. (Paris 1912) 1:1585–86. A. M. ZIMMERMANN, *Kalendarium Benedictinum* (Metten 1933–38) 2:50–51. A. MERCATI and A. PELZER, *Dizionario ecclesiastico* (Turin 1954–58) 1:80. A. M. ZIMMERMANN, *Lexicon für Theologie und Kirche*, ed. J. HOFER and K. RAHNER (Freiburg 1957–65) 1:283.

[K. NOLAN]

ALBERTO CASTELLANI

Historian and editor; b. *c.* 1459; d. 1552. He entered the Dominican priory of Saints John and Paul in Venice, and although the details of his life are obscure, his name appears often in connection with writings that cover a wide field of interest, most of them concerned with the history of his order. These include the *Catalogus sanctorum a Petro de Natalibus Veneto e regione Castellana episcopo Equilino concinnatus* (Venice 1501), *Catalogus illustrium Ordinis virorum* (Venice 1501), and *Chronica brevis ab initio Ordinis usque ad praesens tempus* (Venice 1504). Besides these historical accounts of the prominent Dominicans from the foundation of the order to his own time, he edited the constitutions of the Order of Preachers; the formularies for the election of priors, visitation of convents, and conduct of chapters; and the valuable *Tabula super privilegia papalia Ordini Praedicatorum concessa* (1507). In 1519 he edited a Biblical concordance of the Old and New Testament, and he is famous for his revision of the *Pontificale Romanum.* Among the many ascetical, patristic, and apologetical works he published were some of the sermons of Caesarius of Arles and Zeno, Bishop of Verona (Venice 1508), and an interesting example of devotional iconography, the *Rosario de la gloriosa Vergine Maria* (Venice 1521), in which the mysteries of the rosary were incised in wood for popular use.

Bibliography: J. QUÉTIF and ÉCHARD, *Scriptores Ordinis Praedicatorum* 2:48–49. U. MANNUCCI, *Enciclopedia Italiana di scienzi, littere ed arti* 2:192–93.

[E. D. MCSHANE]

ALBI, ARCHDIOCESE OF

Also known as Albiensis; Located in southwest France, 2,232 square miles in area, corresponding to Tarn department; Metropolitan see since 1678.

Albi was detached from the *civitas Ruthenorum* (Rodez) in the fourth century as the *civitas Albigensium* and included in *Aquitania I.* The see was created after the *civitas,* at the end of the fourth century; the first known bishop, Diogenianus, appeared in the fifth century. Albi was held by the Visigoths (who detained St. Eugene, bishop of Carthage, there in 475) until CLOVIS took it (507). Feudal lords seized the bishopric in the 10th century, but in the 11th-century Gregorian reform, the churches were freed. Rather unjustly, Albi's name has been given to the Manichaean heretics (ALBIGENSES) of the 12th and 13th centuries, rampant throughout south France. Bishops and mendicant orders (Dominicans and Franciscans) fought the heresy, and Simon de Montfort and LOUIS VIII led crusades against its protectors. In 1264 the bishops became temporal lords of the city under the suzerainty of the Holy See. The 16th-century Wars of Religion brought grave troubles, but a religious renaissance

took place at the end of the 16th and in the 17th century (convents and episcopal activity). Albi's bishops include St. Salvius (574–584), the reformer Louis d'Amboise (1474–1503), the reformer Hyacinthe Serroni (1678–87) who founded the seminary, Cardinal François de BERNIS (1764–94), and Eudoxe MIGNOT (1900–18) who renewed ecclesiastical studies.

The red-brick, fortified Cathedral of Sainte-Cécile (1282–1514) symbolized the temporal power of the bishops. The late 13th-century episcopal palace (*La Berbie*) adjoins it. The sixth-century monastery of Saint-Salvy, with a 10th–13th century church, has a crypt and a cloister of note.

Albi, suffragan to Bourges, was divided in 1317 to form Castres, and in 1678 was made an archbishopric by Innocent XI. Suppressed by the CONCORDAT OF 1801 and united to Montpellier, it was restored as a see and a metropolitan with its present suffragans (1817–22). The diocese now comprises the old See of Albi and the former Sees of Castres and Lavaur (1317). Former monasteries outside the city include Vieux (a double monastery founded by St. Eugene), Troclar (the late seventh-century double monastery of St. Sigolène), Castres (seventh–nineth century, which became a see), Gaillac (tenth century), Sainte-Marie of Vielmur (tenth), Sainte-Marie of Ardorel (12th, Cistercian in 1138), and Sainte-Marie of Candeil (12th century). The council of 1254, attended by bishops of the provinces of Narbonne, Bourges, and Bordeaux,, dealt with heresy ecclesiastical discipline, usury, and the rights and obligations of Jews. Albi has ten diocesan statutes (1230–1762).

Outside the city are the cathedrals of Castres (17th–18th century) and Lavaur (14th–16th, fortified), the former abbey church of Saint-Michel in Gaillac (16th-century Romanesque, fortified), and the fortified church of Rabastens (13th–14th). There are shrines to Our Lady near Albi and in Grazac, as well as Saint-Crucifix at Cordres.

Bibliography: C. DE VIC and J. VAISSETE, *Histoire générale de Languedoc,* ed. E. DULAURIER et al., 16 v. in 17 (new ed. Toulouse 1872–1904). L. DE LACGER, *États administratifs des anciens diocèses d'Albi, de Castres, et de Lavaur* (Paris 1921). E. JARRY, *Catholicisme* 1:273–275.

[E. JARRY]

ALBIGENSIANS

The name is taken from Albi, Department of Tarn, France. It refers to several small groups of heretics in the Languedoc region of France, Catharists and sometimes WALDENSIANS among them, who played an important

"Albigensian Heretics Disputing with Dominicans," detail of a 14th-century fresco by Simone Martini in the church of Santa Maria Novella, Florence, Italy.

role in the religion and politics of the region from the mid-twelfth to the late fourteenth century. The CATHARI were eastern heretics with roots in Gnosticism who had made inroads in Western Europe around the middle of the twelfth century. Another principal group were the BOGOMILS from Bulgaria, but there were probably multiple sources.

What characterized these groups was their dualistic belief, either absolute or limited, which maintained that God was responsible only for the spiritual world while Satan ruled the material world. In its absolute form, God created only the spiritual world, Jesus had no real human form, matter having been created by the devil. There were no positive values to marriage nor were there any material goods. These ideas were not new—they had been present in Manichaeism in the fourth century, when St. Augustine had at first joined them for nine years and later argued against them after his conversion. Westerners, therefore, identified Catharism with Manichaeism, though there was no direct connection. The indirect link was through Gnosticism, which had remained influential in the East, especially in monastic circles. The appeal of Gnosticism lay both in its strict separation of good and evil as well as in its rich myth-making tradition, which

reworked and elaborated the Christian story to fit its view of the world and to broaden its appeal.

Catharism found fertile soil in many places in the West during periods of monastic reform in the eleventh and twelfth centuries. During this time there was increased contact between East and West and a greater receptivity to eastern forms of monasticism. During the twelfth century, the monastic revival began to impact the laity, finding a welcome among those belonging to confraternities. Recent research has also shown how this piety influenced members of the lesser nobility. Catharism did not, however, spread evenly throughout Europe. Its largest following was to be found in Mediterranean Europe.

One of the most difficult, but very important problems in measuring the Catharist influence lies in assessing their numbers. The popularly accepted statements based on contemporary sources regarding the extent of heresy have almost always proved wrong when examined closely. Even where they were numerous, as in parts of Languedoc, it is unlikely that the Catharists formed a majority save in some relatively small places. Where studies have examined this issue in detail, it seems clear that their influence was chiefly due to family members, who gave them shelter, or a measure of power they received from local authorities whom they supported against their enemies. This factor became more important as the intentions of the French monarchy in the Midi became clearer.

It is evident that neither the popes nor the bishops had a definite policy regarding heresy in the twelfth and early thirteenth centuries. Their efforts to establish a policy was complicated by numerous groups of lower clergy and laity who sought to embrace the apostolic life (*vita apostolica*), and whose zeal led them to preach at times without permission from their bishops. The most noted group, though by no means the only, were the followers of Peter Valdes (Waldo), a pious merchant of Lyons, whose zeal brought him into conflict with the episcopacy and the papacy. Although sometimes lumped with the Catharists as noted above, the Waldensians were not dualists. They opposed clerical abuses, and, in some cases, rejected priestly authority, but they were generally orthodox. Many were reconciled to the church in the early thirteenth century. Although St. Francis of Assisi and his followers were strong opponents of the Cathari, they did appeal directly to Christians who might otherwise have followed the Waldensians through their emphasis on apostolic poverty and their profound religious enthusiasm.

The rise of heresy in this period had a profound impact on the church. In 1184, Pope Lucius III, then in Verona, condemned various heretical groups by name in *Ad abolendam*. Among those mentioned were the followers of ARNOLD OF BRESCIA, the HUMILIATI, and the Cathari. But *Ad abolendam* seems to have been directed chiefly to the concerns of Bishop Adelard of Verona. It had no effect on Humiliati outside that area, but it may have tinged their reputation, as evidenced by a letter of Innocent III which recognized them as Catholic religious. This letter did not shape papal policy in the late twelfth century, however. Of much greater importance were Innocent III's efforts to develop a policy that combined strict penalties for heresy with efforts to reconcile as many heretics as possible and to broaden the view of the church in regard to the laity who were pursuing the *vita apostolica*. Canon Law, which developed rapidly in importance in this period, however, reflected only part of this policy. It is represented in the decretal *Vergentis in senium* (1199), which was directed against the problem of persistent heretics in Viterbo, within the papal state, where Innocent exercised both spiritual and temporal authority. This decretal was in response to the murder of the podestà, Parenzo. Its provisions were, however, somewhat mitigated by the decree ''Excommunicamus,'' at the Fourth Lateran Council in 1215. By that time, moreover, Innocent had behind him the experience of the Albigensian Crusade (1208–), triggered by the assassination

of the Cistercian PETER OF CASTELNAU, one of his legates in Languedoc, by an official of Count Raymond of Toulouse's court. This crusade, which was an obstacle to the successful preaching of the Cistercians and of Bishop Diego de Osma and his associate, Dominic de Guzman, also hindered Innocent's plans for a crusade to free the holy places in the East. Moreover, it led indirectly to the French monarchy's dominance over the region. Innocent's effort to resolve the issues of succession in the south of France at the Fourth Lateran Council ran afoul of the opposition of the French bishops. His efforts at compromise failed.

By the 1220s, the papacy had enlisted the support of the Dominicans and Franciscans. The work of popular preaching continued and was probably the most effective instrument in combating heresy. Ironically, as heresy seems to have declined, the church placed more reliance on judicial means to seek out heretics. The INQUISITION, which evolved gradually around the middle of the thirteenth century, resulted from the recognition that it was becoming more difficult to identify heretics. This technique of judicial inquiry enabled the inquisitors, usually members of the mendicant orders, to secure testimony about suspected heretics. Although Catharism had virtually ceased to exist in Languedoc by the end of the fourteenth century, the effects of the crusade had transformed the region politically, and the Inquisition had led many to view repression as almost the only effective means to combat heresy.

Bibliography: Sources. J. VON DÖLLINGER, *Beiträge zur Sektengeschichte des Mittelalters*, 2 v. in 1 (Munich 1890; repr. New York, 1960). C. DOUAIS, *Documents pour servir . . . l'histoire de l'Inquisition dans le Languedoc*, 2 v. (Paris 1900). W. WAKEFIELD and A. P. EVANS, *Heresies of the High Middle Ages* (New York 1969). E. M. PETERS, *Heresy and Authority in Medieval Europe* (London 1980). Literature. F. ANDREWS, *The Early Humiliati* (Cambridge 1999). A. BORST, *Die Katharer* (Stuttgart 1953). *Cahiers de Fanjeaux*, 1966–. J. DUVERNOY, *Le Catharisme*, 2 v. (Toulouse 1976–9). B. HAMILTON, *The Medieval Inquisition* (London 1981). G. ROTTENWÖHRER, *Der Katharismus*, 4 v. (Bad Honnef, 1982–1993); *Unde Malum? Herkunft und Gestalt des Bösen nach heterdoxer Lehre von Markion bis zu den Katharern* (Bad Honnef 1986). M. LAMBERT, *The Cathars* (Oxford 1998). E. M. PETERS, *Inquisition* (Berkeley 1988). K. RUDOLPH, *Gnosis: The Nature and History of Gnosticism* (San Francisco 1987). J. STRAYER, *The Albigensian Crusades*, 2nd ed. (Ann Arbor 1992). W. WAKEFIELD, *Heresy, Crusade and Inquisition in Southern France* (Berkeley 1974).

[J. M. POWELL]

ALBINUS (AUBIN) OF ANGERS, ST.

Abbot and bishop; b. Vannes, France, 469; d. March 1, 550. He entered the monastery of Tincillac at an early age and was elected abbot in 504 at age 35. Under his rule the community prospered, and in 529 he was made bishop of Angers. In that office he proved himself zealous and capable as well as devout. As bishop, Albinus gave particular attention to the poor, spending large sums for the ransoming of captives. He was energetic in putting into effect the decrees of the Synods of Orléans (538 and 541), in which he had participated. His remains are enshrined in the church dedicated to his memory in 556, and his intercession is credited with many miracles, as a result of which he has become the object of popular veneration, not only in France, but throughout Europe. His vita was composed by FORTUNATUS (*Monumenta Germaniae Hisorica: Auctores Antiquissimi* 4:27–33).

Feast: March 1.

Bibliography: *Acta Sanctorum* March 1:54–63. F. UZUREAU, *Dictionnaire d'histoire et de géographie ecclésiastiques,* ed. A. BAUDRILLART et al. (Paris 1912) 5: 254–255. A. M. ZIMMERMANN, *Kalendarium Benedictinum* (Metten 1933–38) 1:273. R. AIGRAIN, *Catholicisme* 1:1012–13. A. MERCATI and A. PELZER, *Dizionario ecclesiastico* (Turin 1954–58) 1:83. A. BUTLER, *The Lives of the Saints,* ed. H. THURSTON and D. ATTWATER (New York 1956) 1:452. G. ALLEMANG, *Lexicon für Theologie und Kirche,* ed. J. HOFER and K. RAHNER (Freiburg 1957–65) 1:289.

[J. F. FAHEY]

ALBO, JOSEPH

Spanish-Jewish philosopher, theologian, and polemicist; b. *c.* 1380; d. *c.* 1440. Not much is known of his life. He lived for a while at Daroca (province of Saragossa) and later at Soria (province of Castile). One of his teachers was Hasdai CRESCAS. At the celebrated theological Disputation of Tortosa (1413–14), which had been convoked by the antipope BENEDICT XIII during his self-imposed exile in Spain, Albo was one of the leading spokesmen in defense of Judaism against the attacks on it by the convert from Judaism, Gerónimo de Santa Fe (called before his conversion Joshua ben Joseph ibn Vives de Lorca and commonly known as Lorki).

As a result of the debate, Albo, recognizing the need for a good theological work for the defense of Judaism, composed his best-known book, the *Sefer ha-Ikkarim* (Book of Principles), completed in 1425. It soon became one of the most popular works on Jewish theology. It was first printed at Soncino in 1485, and later editions with commentaries were published at Fribourg (1584) and at Venice (1618). In this work Albo attempted to determine precisely the essential beliefs of Judaism. Four tractates make up the work. The first, which serves as a general introduction, discusses the bases of all true religion, which are Albo's three ''principles'': the existence of God, divine revelation, and reward and punishment. In

the three following tractates the author studies in detail each of these three basic principles and their consequences. In this way he sets forth a complete system of Jewish theology, sometimes following MAIMONIDES and sometimes Crescas and borrowing much from his contemporary Simeon ben Tzemah Duran. Like Crescas, he detached himself from the pure intellectualism of the earlier Jewish philosophers and placed the goal of human life not only in intellectual but also in religious and moral perfection. Jewish writers, e.g., Isaac ABRABANEL, have noted Albo's seeming indifference toward the Jewish belief in a coming Messiah.

See Also: JEWISH PHILOSOPHY.

Bibliography: J. ALBO, *Sefer ha-Ikkarim,* tr. I. HUSIK, 5 v. in 4 (Philadelphia 1929–30), a critical ed. of the Hebrew text with Eng. tr. I. HUSIK, *A History of Medieval Jewish Philosophy* (2d ed. New York 1930; pa. 1958); ''Joseph Albo: The Last of the Jewish Mediaeval Philosophers,'' *Proceedings of the American Academy for Jewish Research* 1 (1928–30). G. VAJDA, *Introduction à la pensée juive du moyen âge* (Paris 1947) 186–89, 286. A. TÄNZER, *Die Regionsphilosophie des Joseph Albo* (Frankfurt 1896).

[A. BRUNOT]

ALBORNOZ, GIL ÁLVAREZ CARRILLO DE

Archbishop of Toledo, cardinal legate, restorer of the Papal States; b. Cuenca, Spain, *c.* 1295; d. near Viterbo, Italy, Aug. 23, 1367. He studied Canon Law in Toulouse and rose in the service of Alfonso XI to succeed his uncle as archbishop of Toledo in 1338. As royal chancellor and ecclesiastical primate, he pursued reforms in his diocese, crusaded against the Muslims, and played an important part in the unification of Castile. When Peter I (1350–69) reversed the policies of Alfonso, Albornoz in June 1350 left a vicar in his see and went to Avignon, where CLEMENT VI made him a cardinal in December 1350. In June 1353 INNOCENT VI gave him extensive powers as legate in Italy to prepare the Papal States for the return of the popes. By mid-1357 Albornoz had defeated the petty tyrants and modernized the government of the STATES OF THE CHURCH, centralizing authority territorially and favoring parliaments and communal rights against individual privileges. Innocent then yielded to the Visconti of Milan, to whom Albornoz would not cede Bologna, and replaced him. Albornoz, however, returned to Italy in October 1358 to regain the papal position. His second mission was made difficult as foreign powers became involved in the dispute over Bologna and the return of the popes to Rome. In November 1363 URBAN V replaced Albornoz a second time. The cardinal remained in the Papal States as legate to Naples; he died escorting Urban to

Rome. The *Constitutiones Aegidianae,* which Albornoz promulgated for the Marches of Ancona in 1357, were later extended to all the Papal States and lasted until 1816. He bequeathed his enormous wealth in four countries to a multitude of pious causes. In 1365 he founded a college for Spanish students in Bologna where many of his papers remain to be studied.

Bibliography: P. SELLA, *Costituzioni Egidiane dell' anno 1357* (Rome 1912). G. MOLLAT, *Dictionnaire d'histoire et de géograhpie ecclésiastiques* 1:1717–25; 2:1770–73. F. FILIPPINI, *Il cardinale Egidio Albornoz* (Bologna 1933). J. BENEYTO PEREZ, *El cardenal Albornoz* (Madrid 1950). G. MOLLAT, *Popes at Avignon 1305–1378* (Camden, N.J. 1963).

[E. P. COLBERT]

ALBRECHT OF BRANDENBURG

Cardinal archbishop of Mainz, elector of the Holy Roman Empire; b. Berlin, June 28, 1490; d. Mainz, Sept. 24, 1545. He was the younger son of Johann Cicero, Elector of Brandenburg, and Margareta, daughter of Duke Wilhelm III of Saxony; his brother, Joachim I, succeeded to the electorate upon the father's death. Through the influence of his father and brother, Albrecht became archbishop of Magdeburg (1513) and bishop of Halberstadt. When the archbishopric of Mainz, which carried with it the title of Elector, became vacant in 1514, Albrecht put forth his candidacy. In order to raise the necessary 24,000 ducats (14,000 to pay the installation tax for Mainz and 10,000 to receive the needed dispensation for the plural holding of sees), he made an arrangement with the FUGGER banking house. Genial Jacob Fugger advanced the money to Pope LEO X in return for one–half of the sum that would be collected from the preaching of an indulgence in Albrecht's dioceses. As the indulgence (for the building of St. Peter's in Rome) had not been allowed to be preached in these dioceses as yet, it was believed that large sums would be raised. In January of 1517 Albrecht authorized Johann TETZEL to preach the indulgence. Martin LUTHER posted his 95 theses in protest against the indulgence, Tetzel, and the archbishop.

Albrecht had been strongly influenced by the humanistic atmosphere of the University of Frankfurt–on–der–Oder, which his brother, Joachim I, founded with Albrecht's assistance in 1506. As an admirer of Erasmus he did not hesitate to criticize the Church and advocate reform. Thus he was not unsympathetic to the attacks upon the Church by Luther and his followers in their early stages. However, there was more of Erasmus than Luther in the young humanist and, rather than break with Rome, as did the latter, he supported reform within the Church. As the Protestant Revolt gained momentum, Al-

brecht aligned his religious and political policies closer to those of his brother in support of the papacy. He founded the University of Halle (papal permission granted in 1531) and introduced reforms in the University of Mainz. In 1541 he invited (Blessed) Peter Faber, SJ, to Mainz, where the Jesuit quickly became the heart of the Counter Reformation in western Germany. A lover of the arts and music, with good taste in architecture, Albrecht is one of the finest examples of a 16th century German Renaissance prince.

Bibliography: J. JANSSEN, *History of the German People at the Close of the Middle Ages,* tr. M. A. MITCHELL and A. M. CHRISTIE, 17 v. (London 1896–1925). J. HEIDEMANN, *Die Reformation in der Mark Brandenburg* (Berlin 1889). L. PASTOR, *The History of the Popes From the Close of the Middle Ages,* 40 v. (London–St. Louis 1938–61). J. LORTZ, *Die Reformation in Deutschland,* 2 v. (Freiburg 1940). H. HOLBORN, *A History of Modern Germany: The Reformation* (New York 1959). E. W. ZEEDEN, *Lexikon für Theologie und Kirche*[2], ed. J. HOFER and K. RAHNER, 10 v. (2d, new ed. Freiburg 1957–65) 1:291–292. J. PIETSCH, *Dictionnaire d'histoire et de géographie ecclésiastiques,* ed. A. BAUDRILLART et al. (Paris 1912—) 1:1494–96. W. DELIUS, *Die Religion in Geschichte und Gegenwart*[3], 7 v. (3d ed. Tübingen 1957–65) 1:218.

[J. G. GALLAHER]

ALBRECHT OF BRANDENBURG–ANSBACH

First duke of Prussia, margrave of Ansbach, and last grand master of the Teutonic Knights; b. Ansbach, May 17, 1490; d. Tapiau, East Prussia (present–day Gvardiesk, Russia), March 20, 1568. A distinguished member of the Hohenzollern family, he was the nephew of King Sigismund of Poland through his mother. He was already Margrave of Ansbach when he was elected grand master of the TEUTONIC Knights of East Prussia in 1511, a position he held until April 9, 1525, when he announced his conversion to Lutheranism, suppressed the order, and secularized its property along with the adjacent lands of Samland and Ermland as his personal fief under the suzerainty of the king of Poland. His initial contact with Lutheranism came at the Diet of Nuremberg in 1522, when he met Andreas OSIANDER. Later, he married (1526) at LUTHER's suggestion. His first wife was Dorothy of Denmark, and by this union he linked LUTHERANISM with the Scandinavian countries. His second wife, whom he married in 1550, three years after the death of his Danish wife, was Marie of Braunschweig–Calenberg. Under Albrecht's active leadership Lutheranism spread into Kurland, Livonia, and Estonia. His brother William became archbishop of Riga and in 1539 emulated the actions of Albrecht. The University of Königsberg (*Collegium Albertinum*) was founded by Albrecht in 1544 as an academic institution to study and propagate the Lutheran faith. In 1549 he appointed Osiander as professor of theology, and immediately the university was plunged into theological controversy over Osiander's preaching. In the controversy Albrecht supported Osiander and thus helped to widen the split within the ranks of Lutheranism. He died in 1568 lamenting, "We have, alas, very few pastors of souls, but quite a swarm of hirelings and storks." His biographers agree that he saved Prussia from possible absorption by Poland and paved the way for the eventual union of Brandenburg and Prussia in 1618, thus contributing to the rise of Prussia.

Bibliography: ALBRECHT OF BRANDENBURG–ANSBACH, *Vertrau Gott allein,* ed. E. ROTH (Würzburg 1956). P.G. THIELEN, *Die Kultur am Hofe Herzog Albrechts von Preussen* (Göttingen 1953). W. HUBATSCH, *Die Religion in Geschichte und Gegenwart*[3], 7 v. (3d ed. Tübingen 1957–65) 1:218–219. *Kardinal Stanislaus Hosius, Bischof von Ermland, und Herzog Albrecht von Preussen,* ed. E. M. WERMTER, (Reformationsgeschichtliche Studien und Texte 83; Münster 1957). *Lexikon für Theologie und Kirche*[2], ed. J. HOFER and K. RAHNER, 10 v. (2d, new ed. Freiburg 1957–65) 1:292.

[C. L. HOHL, JR.]

ALBRECHTSBERGER, JOHANN GEORG

Influential composer, theorist, and virtuoso of the classical school; b. Klosterneuburg (near Vienna), Austria, Feb. 3, 1736; d. Vienna, March 7, 1809. After receiving music training as a chorister in St. Martin's Church in Klosterneuburg and at the Abbey of MELK, he was a fellow student with M. HAYDN at the Jesuit college in Vienna and later a student of F. J. HAYDN. He was organist successively in Raab (Hungary), Maria-Taferl (Lower Austria), and Melk (to 1766). His musicianship had been noted by Joseph II as crown prince, and he was named court organist in Vienna in 1772 and also choirmaster at St. Stephen's Cathedral from 1793 until his death. Among his students were Joseph von Eybler, J. N. HUMMEL, and notably Ludwig van BEETHOVEN, who profited immensely from his contrapuntal exercises. Although he turned out a considerable body of sacred vocal and organ music as well as concert compositions, he was more important for his theoretical writings, such as *Gründliche Anweisung zur Composition* and *Clavierschule für Anfänger.* As with J. J. FUX, in theory he preferred *stile antico,* yet often applied *stile moderno* in his instrumentally accompanied sacred music. Many of his settings of the Mass Proper and the Office make use of Gregorian *cantus firmi;* all of them exhibit his great contrapuntal skill. Yet in neither his creative nor his theoretic work was he successful in synthesizing the vocal polyphonic style of Palestrina with that of subsequent instrumental polyphony, and in his oratorios he dropped counterpoint in favor of the *galant* style that was then emerging into fashion.

Bibliography: *Organ and instrumental compositions,* ed. O. KAPP, *Denkmäler der Tonkunst in Österreich* (1893–; repr. Graz 1959–) 33. Individual works also pub. in modern eds. *Complete Works,* ed. I. RITTER VON SEYFRIED (Vienna 1826–37), with biog. E. TITTEL, *Österreichische Kirchenmusik* (Vienna 1961). H. GOOS, *Die Musik in Geschichte und Gegenwart,* ed. F. BLUME (Kassel-Basel 1949–) 1:303–307. F. GEHRING, *Grove's Dictionary of Music and Musicians,* ed. E. BLOM, 9 v. (5th ed. London 1954) 1:97. R. N. FREEMAN, "Johann Georg Albrechtsberger's *26 canoni aperti dei varii autori:* The Edition," *Theoria: Historical Aspects of Music Theory,* 8 (1994) 1–52; "Johann Georg Albrechtsberger," in *The New Grove Dictionary of Music and Musicians,* v. 1, ed. S. SADIE (New York 1980) 224–226. P. GRIFFITHS, *The String Quartet: A History* (New York 1983) 50–51. G. KROMBACH, "Modelle der offertoriumskompositonen bei Antonio Caldara, Johann Georg Albrechtsberger, und Joseph Preindl," *Kirchenmusikalisches Jahrbuch,* 71 (1988) 127–136. D. SCHRODER, *Die geistlichen Vokalkompositionen Johann Georg Albrechtsbergers* (Hamburg 1987). YO TOMITA, "Bach Reception in Pre-Classical Vienna: Baron van Swieten's Circle Edits the *Well-Tempered Clavier II,*" *Music and Letters,* 81 (2000) 369–391.

[K. G. FELLERER]

ALBRIGHT, JACOB

Founder of the Evangelical Association; b. Pottstown, Pennsylvania, May 1, 1759; d. Pottstown, May 18, 1808. The son of German immigrants, he received little formal education, was apprenticed to a brick maker, and followed this trade throughout his life. Albright was originally a Lutheran, but was converted to Methodism in 1790 and began to preach in German among his neighbors. In 1796 he was licensed as an exhorter and preached among the German settlers of Pennsylvania, Maryland, and Virginia. He began forming classes on the Methodist pattern in 1800, and three years later he was ordained a minister by his congregation. When the language barrier separated his German congregations from the mainstream of American Methodism, Albright organized his followers as "The Newly Formed Methodist Conference" (1807) and was chosen by them as their first bishop. The Methodists made no effort to unite with them, and in 1813 the independent conference, subsequently known as the Evangelical Association and still later as the EVANGELICAL CHURCH, severed its nominal ties with Methodism.

Bibliography: R. YEAKEL, *Albright and His CoLaborers* (Cleveland 1883); *History of the Evangelical Association* (Cleveland 1909). R. W. ALBRIGHT, *History of the Evangelical Church* (Harrisburg 1942).

[R. K. MACMASTER]

ALBRIGHT, WILLIAM FOXWELL

American archeologist and Orientalist; b. Coquimbo, Chile, May 24, 1891; d. Baltimore, Maryland, Sept. 19,

1971. Son of a self-supporting Methodist minister, his early education took place in American schools in Chile. He became interested in archeology in his childhood and pursued these interests through a major in classics at Upper Iowa University where he received his A.B. in 1912. He was admitted to the Oriental Seminary of the Johns Hopkins University in 1913 as a candidate for the doctorate of philosophy under Professor Paul Haupt. He received his doctorate in 1916 and for several years he continued his studies through grants and fellowships. In 1921 he was appointed director of the American Schools of Oriental Research in Jerusalem. He remained in that capacity until 1929, when he became professor of Semitic languages at Johns Hopkins. From 1933 to 1936 he served both as a professor and as director of the Jerusalem School. During this period he also completed major excavations at Tell Beit Mirsim in southern Palestine. He served as president of the American Oriental Society (1935–36) and the Society of Biblical Literature (1938–39). He was the recipient of an unparalleled series of honorary degrees and other awards from institutions around the world.

His major contribution to Palestinian archeology was *The Excavations of Tell Beit Mirsim,* which was completed by 1943. Other major works include *Archaeology and the Religion of Israel* (1942), *The Archaeology of Palestine and the Bible* (1949), and *Yahweh and the Gods of Canaan* (1968).

At roughly the midpoint of his scholarly career (1940), Albright wrote *From the Stone Age to Christianity,* in which he formulated his basic positions of a philosophical, historical, and philological nature. He believed there were two key developments in human culture in historic times: the religion of Israel and the philosophy of Greece. In Mosaic monotheism he saw a revolution that involved the repudiation of magic and myth and the multiplicity of competing gods in favor of the unity of God, and the description of the divine-human relationship in terms of an open covenant, morally conditioned and legally defined. Biblical religion has proved powerful enough to survive an age of mass superstition on the one hand and of equally pervasive skepticism on the other. Greek thought represented the second significant breakthrough in the history of human culture. The development of formal logic had the most profound effect on human thought and activity: it directly ushered in the scientific age and was a congener of an entirely new discipline, philosophy. Albright saw this powerful rational tool as the key to progress in the analysis and interpretation of data. Ultimately these two key developments would be indispensable ingredients in the reconstitution of a unified human culture. A universal society whose faith and practice were shaped by the biblical imperatives and whose letters, science, and arts were sustained by the standards and methods of Greek thought would be an appropriate goal for mankind and would lie at the end of the evolutionary trail.

Albright's place as a scholar in archeological history is assured. From 1920 to 1970 he produced a monumental amount of work in the field of ancient Near Eastern studies, reviewing current work, classifying and synthesizing available data, opening new areas of inquiry, refining applicable methods of the natural sciences, and shattering established configurations of an older scholarly consensus. During the half century after World War I, he steadily raised the standards of scholarly discussion in the field. He insisted on the highest possible accuracy in recording data and reasoning from them, his objective being to establish the multiple disciplines of Near Eastern studies on a solid scientific foundation, and then to assemble and organize all pertinent material into a large synthetic structure.

Bibliography: *The Bible and the Ancient Near East,* essays in honor of W. F. Albright, ed. G. E. WRIGHT (Garden City, 1961) bibliography of Albright, 1911–1955. *Near Eastern Studies in Honor of William Foxwell Albright,* ed. H. GOEDICKE (Baltimore, 1971). F. M. CROSS in *The Biblical Archaeologist,* 36 (1973) 1–3, with picture of Albright. D. N. FREEDMAN in *Bulletin of The American Schools of Oriental Research,* 205 (1972) 3–13 (picture).

[D. N. FREEDMAN/L. LEDERER]

ALBUIN OF SÄBEN-BRIXEN, ST.

Bishop; d. Feb. 3 or 5 c. 1005. Albuin (or Albwin), one of the aristocratic Aribonen family of Carinthia, received his education in the cathedral school at Brixen. He became bishop of Säben in the Tirol about 977, and transferred the episcopal residence to nearby, more accessible Brixen. In 978 Emperor OTTO II confirmed and enlarged the bishopric's immunity. Albuin was on excellent terms with Otto II and the Emperor HENRY II, and received extensive grants of land from them and other nobles. He played a considerable part in political life, since his see lay on the main route from Germany to Italy. Shortly after his death Albuin was venerated as a saint. In 1141 he was proclaimed one of the diocesan patron saints. His relics are in the cathedral.

Feast: Feb. 5, together with Bishop Saint Genuinus.

Bibliography: A. W. A. LEEPER, *A History of Medieval Austria* (New York 1941). A. SPARBER, *Kirchengeschichte Tirols* (Innsbruck 1957).

[R. H. SCHMANDT]

ALCALÁ, UNIVERSITY OF

An institution of higher learning founded in 1509 in the ancient Spanish city called Complutum by the Romans and renamed Alcalá de Henares (Alkalá Nahar, fortress or castle) by the Moors. In 1836 the University was transferred from Alcalá to the Spanish capital, where it was replaced by the Central University of Madrid, a state institution under the jurisdiction of the Ministry of Education.

The original idea of a university dates back to 1293, when the Archbishop of Toledo, Gonzalo Gudiel, obtained from the king of Castile, Sancho IV, surnamed the Brave, permission to found a *studium generale* in Alcalá. In 1459, during the reign of John II, Abp. Alonso Carrilo y Acuña, with the approval of Pius II, established and endowed three chairs of grammar and the arts. The true founder of the university, however, was the renowned Franciscan archbishop of Toledo, Francisco XIMÉNEZ DE CISNEROS, prime minister of Spain, to whom the Spanish pope, Alexander VI, granted a bull on April 13, 1499, for the erection of the College of San Ildefonso.

At the outset, only clerical studies were planned: liberal arts and philosophy, theology, the elements of canon law, classical and biblical languages required for the direct study of Sacred Scripture and the Fathers of the Church. Civil law, considered less useful for clerics, was expressly forbidden by the founder, who for the same reason also omitted medicine, which was later added (1514) with the approval of Leo X. Civil law, however, was not included by royal commission until 1672.

The University of Alcalá was a Renaissance institution, a characteristic that differentiated it from all other then existing Spanish universities, and particularly from the famous University of Salamanca, which adhered to scholastic ideals (*see* SCHOLASTICISM). Alcalá's involvement in the renaissance movement is seen in its two most important accomplishments: the establishment of chairs of biblical languages that constituted the Trilingual College and the publication of the POLYGLOT BIBLE prepared by masters incorporated with the university.

In keeping with Cisneros' plans, a major college and 18 minor colleges made up the university city. The major college, San Ildefonso, occupied the same building as the university. The minor colleges were built on nearby streets. Since the plan was carried out in haste (the university was to open in 1508), inferior materials were used. However, in 1543 the original building was replaced by an imposing stone structure, the work of Rodrigo Gil de Ontañón. Besides classrooms and a dining hall for the major college, the university complex included a richly ornamented college hall, the Chapel of San Ildefonso, a library so large that "not even the majority of European [libraries] could vie with it," and a prison, neither dark nor often used, a kind of detention room for fatherly correction. In addition, among the minor colleges was St. Luke's, a student infirmary that later became a student hospital. One college was founded in 1590 by a Portuguese nobleman, Jorge Sylveira, a descendant, through his mother, of the MacDonnels of Ulster in Ireland. He bestowed on the college an endowment of £2000 and at the cost of £1000 built a chapel dedicated to his patron, St. George.

There is some question regarding the authentic statutes, and several dates of issue are cited. The statutes, however, generally accepted as those regulating the first ten years of the university, are those dated Oct. 17, 1517. The date of inauguration was certainly July 26, 1508, and the first scholastic year 1508–09. The course of studies, organized the following year, included the Faculties of Philosophy, Theology, Letters, and Medicine, modeled very closely after the University of Paris.

Administration was vested in the rector of the College of San Ildefonso and the vice rectors of the minor colleges, the councilors, and eventually the visitors sent by the king. The curriculum was controlled by the chairmen of the various departments, also called regents or masters. The rector of the major college (San Ildefonso) was elected each year by the students and received his authority from the pope rather than from the king, according to the constitutions. The students were exempt from all other authority. The rector acted as "ordinary and proper judge," a custom that gave rise to the "university forum" or "tribunal."

A rigid system of examinations, which was completely separate from teaching, was entrusted to a board of doctors not connected with instruction. This necessitated choosing the best-prepared students for the severe ordeal of examination. Those who passed were awarded successively the degree of bachelor, licentiate, and doctor, or in philosophy, master.

Among outstanding masters at the University of Alcalá were Antonio de Nebrija in humanities; THOMAS OF VILLANOVA and Gaspar Cardello in philosophy; and Francisco Valles in medicine—all of whom were deans of their faculties and had the satisfaction of teaching students who were also outstanding in sanctity, such as IGNATIUS OF LOYOLA and JOHN OF AVILA; in diplomacy, Próspero Espínola Doria; in the pacification of Peru, Pedro Lagasca; in Sacred Sciences, Diego LAÍNEZ, theologian at Trent, and Luis de MOLINA, founder of Molinism; and in letters, Francisco de Quevedo, and perhaps Felix de Vega Carpio.

The reform, introduced by the centralized state in the 18th century, sapped the autonomous vitality of the university and finally, in the early 19th century, brought to an end this famous center of culture.

Bibliography: H. RASHDALL, *The Universities of Europe in the Middle Ages,* ed. F. M. POWICKE and A. B. EMDEN, 3 v. (new ed. Oxford 1936). J. URRIZA, *La preclara Facultad de Arte y Filosofía de la Universidad de Alcalá de Henares en el siglo de oro, 1509–1621* (Madrid 1941). F. C. SÁINZ DE ROBLES, *Esquema de una historia de las universidades españolas* (Colección Crisol 74; Madrid 1944). C. M. AJO G. Y SÁINZ DE ZÚÑIGA, *Historia de las universidades hispánicas* (Madrid 1957–). S. D'IRSAY, *Histoire des universités françaises et étrangères des origines à nos jours,* 2 v. (Paris 1933–35). L. A. MUNOYERRO, *La Facultad de Medicina de Alcalá de Henares* (Madrid 1945).

[J. URRIZA]

ALCHEMY

Alchemy is a pseudo-science based on the premise that base matter can be transmuted into gold by chemical means. Although scattered individuals may still be found who take the idea seriously, alchemy as an important cultural movement died out in the 18th century. The "Work" (as it came to be called) has always had both a practical and a mystical side. Realistic (or greedy) experimenters conceived their "gold" as identical with mined gold, while their more mystical brethren, adapting their design to the fact that genuine gold was never produced in the laboratory, vaguely envisioned the end product as a marvelous substance, either solid (hence, "philosopher's stone") or liquid (the "elixir" or the "tincture"), which could variously heal, ennoble, sanctify, or multiply wealth. Alchemy enjoyed no historical "development" as a science; one can, for instance, find that a typical treatise written in the 17th century is no more than a vague congeries of notions drawn from ancient and medieval authors, uncorrected by observation and experiment. The ensuing outline, therefore, consists of only a brief chronological sketch, emphasizing important names and places, followed by a summary of the basic principles of alchemy, a discussion of its theological and mystical pretensions, and, finally, a brief register of the attitudes taken toward alchemy by responsible thinkers from the 13th to the 17th centuries, when the science flourished most widely.

Historical Outline. The term "alchemy" comes from medieval Latin *alchimia,* a version of Arabic *al-kimia,* which is in turn connected with *Khem* (black earth), the old Egyptian term for their own land, through Greek χημία, although this was probably confused with Greek χυμεία, which refers to the pouring or casting of metals. This etymology epitomizes the history of the sci-

Woodcut illustrating alchemical concept of the world.

ence, which may be said to have been born in Hellenistic Alexandria from the imposition of Greek philosophy (mainly the Aristotelian doctrines of ENTELECHY and of the four elements with their "quintessence,"—and later, Gnostic theology) on the arts of metalworking and glassmaking as they had developed in Egypt. (*See* GNOSTICISM.) The original alchemists were probably members of a secret cult whose practices derived largely from the mystical lore of the Hebrews, Egyptians, and Chaldeans. To this period (*c.* A.D. 200–400) belong the writings of a pseudo-Democritus and of Zosimos the Panopolitan; these contain recipes for the superficial coloring of metals to resemble gold, but they also express a belief in the possibility of genuine transmutation. After the fall of the Alexandrian schools alchemists continued to work in Syria and Byzantium (e.g., Theophrastos and Stephanos of Alexandria), but their treatises simply transmit Alexandrian teaching. The rise of Islam saw the translation of Greek alchemical works into Arabic, and the further elaboration of the mystical element by Jâbir ibn Hayyân (9th century) and by his Sufite sect (*see* SUFISM). More practical aspects, especially the classification of mineral and animal substances and the development of pharmaceuticals, were extended by the physician RHAZES (865?–925). Arabic treatises, brought into Sicily and Moorish Spain in the 12th century, were turned into Latin by Robert of Chester and other translators of the Toledo school, while a number of original pseudonymous works were composed also, notably the *Summa perfectionis* of Geber, probably the most widely known alchemical treatise of the Middle Ages. Geber's work has a specious sort of scholastic logic to it, and on practical matters such as the preparation of reagents or the design of a sublimatory furnace he shows a commendable accuracy. But the *Summa* is filled with mystical cant and is finally vitiated by the misguided hope of producing the elixir. Except for PARACELSUS, who turned alchemy to the service of medicine (iatrochemistry), practically nothing was added to the ideas found in Geber, and in the Enlightenment of the 18th century, interest in the science almost entirely died out. There was a parallel growth in China, although it was there related to DAOISM and the notion that Dao-infused substances were productive of long life. Chinese and Western alchemy have a number of secondary features in common, namely, the theory that metals grow in the earth, the doctrine that physical discipline is essential to the successful alchemist, the idea of planetary influence, and frequent allegorical and mystical designations for ingredients and processes.

Relationship to Orthodox Science. In a justly famous phrase, ''the story of alchemy is the history of a mistake.'' From the standpoint of the modern chemist its solid achievements are few. Some pieces of equipment—special furnaces, stills, water-baths, the mortar and pestle—owe their invention to alchemists; a few elementary processes, like sublimation, go back to the earliest days of experimentation; and there are scattered instances of unusually precise technique, as in the distillation of alcohol (*aqua ardens*) in 12th-century Salerno. But these were merely by-products of a quest that was destined to fail because it was founded on a faulty idea and bedeviled by the habit of analogical thinking. In theory, a substance had its individualizing properties removed by heating, so that it became a *prima materia,* a black, formless mass, which could then have qualities added to it in successive stages (represented by changing colors) until it took on the characteristics of gold. Experiment by inductive methods was precluded on principle, the pattern of the ''Work'' being altered only as chance or fashion caused one allegorical statement to succeed another. Even the most widely acknowledged principles of the science were clouded by the same sort of allegorical obscurantism. Such was the doctrine of ''contraries,'' which directed that the ''Work'' must be initiated with a union of con-

trary substances (e.g., mercury, principle of liquidity, and sulfur, principle of fire). This may go back ultimately to primitive superstitions concerning the origin of the universe from an original splitting of a primal chaos. The persistent belief that metals grow in the ground, slowly approaching the perfection of gold, led alchemists to think that they could accelerate nature's processes in the laboratory. The great stress on a color sequence (normally: *nigredo, albedo, rudedo*) probably stems from a primitive animistic belief patterned on the yearly cycle of nature. So, too, the idea of a sympathetic relationship between the macrocosm and the microcosm, perhaps best known for its influence on medieval medicine, was an ancient doctrine implicit in alchemical theory from the earliest times, as in the *Emerald Table of Hermes* (probably composed as early as the 2d century), a cryptic ''revelation'' expounding a vague declaration that ''that which is above is like to that which is below . . . to accomplish the miracles of one thing.'' The correspondence between the seven metals and the seven planets with their related deities (e.g., Sun = gold, Venus = copper) also tended to inhibit free experimentation. The few refinements in equipment and processes were small recompense for this expenditure of misdirected energy, and it was not until the appearance of Boyle's *The Sceptical Chymist* (A.D. 1661) that chemistry had a chance to flourish.

Mystical and Theological Aspects. Such analogies as the above, supported by a natural leaning toward mythopoeic expression and by an alleged desire to conceal the secrets of alchemy from the ''unworthy,'' produced an esoteric jargon and a flood of allegorical explanations of the ''Work.'' And there was an astonishing multiplication of alchemical books in the 13th and 14th centuries, as interest in alchemy kept pace with the burgeoning scientific spirit. There was, however, this important difference—the composition of an alchemical treatise was very much a rhetorical exercise in which the author ''amplified'' his matter by stock figures like the following: rules of conduct (e.g., the ''philosopher'' had to carry on the ''Work'' in isolation, or with absolutely trustworthy assistants); extended citations of ancient authorities such as Hermes, Moses, and Mary the Jewess; inordinately lengthy inventories of ingredients; formulas recommending ceaseless study or perseverance, and others stressing the unity of the ''Work'' (in one treatise it is said to consist of ''*one* thing, *one* substance, *one* vessel, *one* essence, and *one* agent, which begins and ends the ''Work''), the commonness of the stone, or the need of assiduous care of the fire. The tone of address varies from intemperate abuse of foolish ''sophists'' who do not understand what they read to opaque flights of mystical fancy. The quasi-theological element fell into a bizarre combination with the allegorical, at least as early as the

13th century, in works such as the *Pretiosa margarita novella* of Petrus Bonus and the *Aurora consurgens* attributed (certainly wrongly) to St. THOMAS AQUINAS, in both of which it is difficult to tell whether the author is speaking of Christian or alchemical mysteries. Two most curious manifestations of this strain can be seen in the alchemical "mass" of Nicholas Melchior (fl. A.D. 1500) and in the triptych, "The Millennium," of Hieronymus BOSCH, whose interest in alchemy was inspired by the teachings of the heretical Adamites of the 15th century.

Attitudes toward Alchemy. In every age most serious thinkers tended to be critical of both the theory and the practice of alchemy, although occasional strong voices defended the basic idea. Both St. ALBERT the Great and St.Thomas Aquinas admitted the possibility of the transmutation of elements, yet they believed that it had not yet been accomplished. Dante placed the alchemists in the lowest circle of the Inferno because they "ape creative Nature by their Art"; and Petrarch, Jean de Meun, Langland, Chaucer, Sebastian Brant, Erasmus, and Ben Jonson are in the mainstream of a tradition of vitriolic satire against alchemy, based mainly on its antisocial effects but frequently stressing its theoretical absurdity. The decretal of Pope JOHN XXII, beginning "Spondent quas non exhibent," is directed against the illegal practice of alchemy, yet the conclusion of Oldrado da Ponte, consistorial advocate in the papal Curia under John, namely, that alchemy is a true art and that alchemists do not sin as long as they attribute their power to God, was quoted with approval by a number of later canon lawyers. The 14th century saw a spate of trials against ecclesiastics for practicing alchemy and other "occult arts"; in 1323 a sentence of excommunication was passed against all Dominicans who did not renounce alchemy and burn their books within eight days; and the Inquisitor Nicholas Eymeric carried on a vigorous prosecution of alchemists for their heretical beliefs. The religious heretic later gave way to the charlatan, who flowered in the 16th and 17th centuries in such famous quacks as Edward Kelly and John Dee, succeeded in our own day by relatively obscure and harmless mystery-mongers who busy themselves in the attempt to prove that great medieval works of literature and art were in reality designed as alchemical hieroglyphs. Stimulating modern approaches to the problems of alchemy are those of Carl Gustav JUNG, who sees in the "Work" a version of the psychological process of individuation, and Mircea Eliade, who has examined alchemy as a "spiritual technique." These investigators, while they make it clear that alchemy is no mere "prelude to chemistry," both raise problems for the theologian.

A proper history of alchemy awaits the cataloguing and identification of alchemical treatises—a massive undertaking, which is far from complete. It now seems unlikely, however, that the greater part of the treatises attributed to St. Albert the Great, St. Thomas Aquinas, Raymond LULL, and Arnold of Villanova have been correctly ascribed, although Michael Scot and ROGER BACON did have unusual interests and may have composed works on alchemy. The difficulty of achieving scholarly objectivity in texts and studies is compounded by the fact that the freakish history of alchemy has a strong attraction for occultists as well as a legitimate interest for students of chemistry, theology, psychology, and literature. Finally, mention should be made of the frequent claim that modern transmutation of matter through nuclear transformation is a justification of the alchemists' dream. This is certainly not transmutation in any sense comparable to that sanguine hope of elevating base substances to golden perfection comprised in the "philosophers'" command to "cook, cook, cook, and weary not of it." Such comparisons merely obscure the essentially antiscientific character of alchemy.

Bibliography: E. O. VON LIPPMANN, *Entstehung und Ausbreitung der Alchemie,* 3 v. (v.1, 2, Berlin 1919; 1931; v.3, Weinheim 1954), a basic scholarly study. L. THORNDIKE, *A History of Magic and Experimental Science,* 8 v. (New York 1923–). H. M. LEICESTER, *The Historical Background of Chemistry* (New York 1956), a lucid account of chemical operations known to early alchemists. E. J. HOLMYARD, *Alchemy* (Baltimore, MD 1954), a readable short history from a chemist's standpoint. C. G. JUNG, *Psychology and Alchemy,* tr. R. F. HULL (New York 1953), v.12 of *Collected Works* (Bollingen Series 20; New York 1953), contains a useful bibliography of collections and individual works in Latin of the medieval period. M. ELIADE, *The Forge and the Crucible,* tr. S. CORRIN (New York 1962). O. S. JOHNSON, *A Study of Chinese Alchemy* (Shanghai 1928). J. READ, *Prelude to Chemistry* (New York 1937), an interesting survey of the vagaries of the alchemical mind, though it relies to some extent on the writings of occultists such as A. E. Waite.

[J. E. GRENNEN]

ALCHER OF CLAIRVAUX

Cistercian monk at the Abbey of Clairvaux *c.* 1150 to 1175. Certain works that have been attributed to him fall within the framework of the monastic literature of the day; one that seems the most authentic is a treatise on the love of God (*De diligendo Deo; Patrologia Latina,* 40:847). He is known chiefly for the opusculum *De spiritu et anima,* written in the tradition of speculative mysticism as a treatise on the nature and functions of the soul and ordered to the practice of the virtues of a Christian and religious life (*Patrologia Latina,* 40:779–832). During the high scholastic era this work was attributed to St. AUGUSTINE, hence its importance in the history of psychology. In their commentaries on the *Sentences, c.* 1250, ALBERT the Great (*In 1 sent.* 8.25) and THOMAS AQUINAS

(*In 4 Sent.* 44.4.3) recognized that it could not be the work of Augustine, but it had already exerted strong influence.

The *De spiritu et anima* is "a compilation of the doctrines of Augustine" (Aquinas) with additions from Boethius, Macrobius, Hugh of Saint–Victor, Cassiodorus, and St. Isidore of Seville. Alcher limited himself to juxtaposing the borrowed elements; as a result the coherence of his work suffered. Yet from this confused mass some great ideas emerged. The soul is a unique substance, and its so–called powers are only the functions by which its activity is manifested without impinging upon its absolute simplicity. The soul governs everything that constitutes human life, even its most humble functions. The higher functions are affectivity and knowledge: the first operates through the concupiscible and irascible appetites, which act as the seat of the four passions of love, hate, hope, and fear and which give birth to vice or to virtue, according to the use that men make of them. Knowledge includes five hierarchical degrees, from sense, whose object is material things, to intelligence (*intelligentia*), which is direct contact with God. Alcher insisted also that the images of the Trinity are realized in the soul.

Bibliography: E. GILSON, *History of Christian Philosophy,* 168–169, 632, 658. P. MICHAUD–QUANTIN, "Une Division 'augustinienne' des puissances de l'âme au moyen–âge," *Revue des études augustiniennes,* 3 (1957) 235–248. G. THÉRY, "L'Authenticité du *De spiritu et anima* dans S. Thomas et Albert le Grand," *Revue des sciences philosophiques et théologiques,* 11 (1921) 373–377. L. LEWICKI, *Collectanea ordinis Cisterciensium Reformatorum,* 18 (1956) 161–164, summary of Polish theses.

[P. MICHAUD–QUANTIN]

ALCOBAÇA, ABBEY OF

Former Cistercian abbey, once the greatest in Portugal, two miles from the Atlantic, near Leiria. It was founded in 1153 by King Alfonso Henriques after the reconquest of Estremadura and settled from CLAIRVAUX, but it had to be rebuilt after a Moorish raid in 1195. The church, consecrated in 1252, was modeled after that of Clairvaux. The abbey, which reached its peak in the 14th century with 300 monks, founded many daughter houses in Portugal; its possessions included 13 towns and three seaports. The abbot belonged to the Cortes, was Grand Chaplain of the court, and had spiritual jurisdiction over the ORDERS OF CHRIST and of AVIZ. Alcobaça was of major importance in the cultural and economic history of Portugal. Besides promoting the foundation of the University of Lisbon, it established the first public college (1269), the first pharmacy, and one of the first printing presses in Portugal; it maintained an agricultural school and model farms, opened mines, and pioneered in metal-

lurgy, ceramics, glasswork, weapons manufacture, and other industries. From 1475 the abbatial title, with some of the revenue, was granted in COMMENDATION to Portuguese nobles, while monastic life was directed by triennial abbots. In 1567 Alcobaça became the head of the Portuguese Congregation of St. Bernard with its own abbot general and triennial chapters. It lost its moral leadership in the 17th and 18th centuries but prospered until the Napoleonic invasion. After a Liberal revolution the abbey was suppressed and sacked (1834). The buildings were unharmed, but the rich library and archives suffered irreparable damage. Most surviving MSS are in Lisbon's National Library. Alcobaça is now a national monument; the medieval cloister is a tourist attraction, the vast baroque complex is a home for the aged, and the church serves a parish.

Bibliography: VIEIRA NATIVIDADE, *O monasterio de Alcobaça* (Porto 1937). A. GUSMÃO, *A Real Abbadia de Alcobaça* (Lisbon 1948). M. COCHERIL, "L'Ordre de Cîteaux au Portugal. Le problème historique," *Studia Monastica* 1 (1959) 51–95. U. CHEVALIER, *Répertoire des sources historiques de moyen–âge. Topobibliographie* (Paris 1894–1903) 44. L. H. COTTINEAU, *Répertoire topobibliographique des abbayes et prieurés* (Mâcon 1935–39) 1:50–51. R. TRILHE, *Dictionnaire d'histoire et de géographie ecclésiastiques,* ed. A. BAUDRILLART et al. (Paris 1912–) 2:25–29. M. HARTIG, *Lexikon für Theologie und Kirche,* ed. J. HOFER and K. RAHNER (2d, new ed. Freiburg 1957–65) 1:297–298.

[L. J. LEKAI]

ALCOBER FIGUERA, JUAN TOMAS, ST.

Dominican priest, martyr; b. Dec. 21, 1694, Girone (Granada), Andalucia, Spain; d. Oct. 28, 1748, Fukien (Fuzhou), Tunkien, China.

Juan Alcober joined the Dominicans in his hometown (1708) and was ordained priest (1718). He and St. Francis Serrano had planned to work together in the Chinese missions, but Fr. Alcober was delayed in Lorca, where he preached until he was able to set sail. Having gained a reputation as a popular preacher there, only a miracle reminded him of his original purpose. In 1726, he left for the Philippines to study Chinese and work in Binondo until beginning his mission in China in 1728.

Following the publication of a libel against the Christians of Fu-ngan, Fu-kien, Emperor K'ien Lung initiated a prosecution in 1746. Like Fr. Serrano, Alcober was adept at evading the pursuing authorities. He hid in the homes of native Christians, spent a night hiding in a tree, and wandered about the city in the disguise of a water seller. His luck ran out on June 26, 1746.

He baptized a woman, to whom the Blessed Virgin had appeared in an apparition, on her deathbed. The situation drew her neighbors, and soon Fr. Alcober was recognized, captured, and imprisoned at Fukien. He was sentenced to death by the viceroy on Nov. 1, 1746.

Alcober was strangled one night in his prison cell together with Joachim Royo Pérez, Francisco Diaz, and Francisco Serrano to prevent them from converting their jailors. Local Christians collected and preserved their relics.

He was beatified by Pope Leo XIII (May 14, 1893) and canonized (Oct. 1, 2000) by Pope John Paul II with Augustine Zhao Rong and companions.

Feast: June 5.

See Also: CHINA, MARTYRS OF, SS.

Bibliography: M. J. SAVIGNOL, *Les Martyrs dominicains de la Chine au XVIIIᵉ siècle* (Paris 1893). H. I. IWEINS, *Le Bl. Pierre Sanz et ses quatre compagnons* (Ostende 1893). J. M. GONZÁLEZ, *Misiones dominicanas en China, 1700–1750* (Madrid 1952). M. J. DORCY, *Saint Dominic's Family* (Dubuque, Iowa 1963), 484–87.

[K. I. RABENSTEIN]

ALCOCK, JOHN

Cambridge scholar, bishop; b. Beverley, Yorkshire, England, 1430; d. Wisbech Castle, Isle of Ely, Oct. 1, 1500. The son of William Alcock of Beverley, he studied at CAMBRIDGE, where he was a doctor of civil law by 1459. In 1461 he became rector of St. Margaret's, Fish Street, London, after which he rapidly accumulated benefices. In 1472 he became bishop of ROCHESTER by papal provision, keeper of the great seal (until June 1473), tutor of Edward, Prince of Wales, and president of his council. He was transferred to the bishopric of WORCESTER in 1476 and to ELY (1486), where he proved an able administrator. At Ely cathedral he began his own chantry chapel in 1488 and built the great hall in the episcopal palace; at Downham he rebuilt the episcopal residence. His greatest fame rests in his founding of Jesus College, Cambridge (1496), upon the site of the dissolved convent of St. Radegund. His original endowment was small, and the college was limited to six priest–fellows in residence; a boys' grammar school was attached to the college. Still in evidence, decorated with his device of a cock on a globe, are the college buildings, principally remodeled conventual structures. His educational interests are further revealed by his residing at Peterhouse, Cambridge, in the early 1490s and by his foundation of a chantry and grammar school at Hull, Yorkshire. His literary remains include: (1) *Mons perfeccionis, the hyll of perfeccion*, (2) *In die innocencium sermo pro episcopo puerorum*, (3) an English sermon on the text of Luke 8.8, (4) *Desponsacio virginis Christo: Spousage of a virgin to Cryste* (all print-

Alcoholics Anonymous key ring with two keys attached. Round medallion has praying hands above motto reading "A Day at a Time." (Field Mark Publications)

ed by Wynkyn de Worde, 1496–97), (5) *Gallicantus ad confratres suos curatos in sinodo apud Barnwell*, Sept. 25, 1499, (6) *The Abbay of the Holy Gost*, an English commentary on the seven penitential Psalms, and (7) *Castle of Labour* translated from the French by P. Gringoire.

Bibliography: J. ALCOCK, Register as Bishop of Worcester in the Worcester Diocesan Record Office, St. Helen's Church, Worcester; Register as Bishop of Ely in the University Library, Cambridge, with a printed calendar by J. H. CROSBY in *Ely Diocesan Remembrancer* (1908–1910). J. B. MULLINGER, *The Dictionary of National Biography From the Earliest Times to 1900*, 63 v. (London 1885–1900) 1:236–237. *The Victoria History of the County of Cambridgeshire and the Isle of Ely*, ed. L. F. SALZMAN et al. (London 1938–59) v.2, 3, 4. A. GRAY and F. BRITTAIN, *A History of Jesus College, Cambridge* (London 1960). A. B. EMDEN, *Biographical Register of the Scholars of the University of Cambridge before 1500* (Cambridge, Eng. 1963) 5–6, 669.

[H. S. REINMUTH, JR.]

ALCOHOLICS ANONYMOUS

A society, commonly referred to as AA, established to help victims of alcoholism. AA describes itself as a ''fellowship of men and women who share their common wisdom, strength and hope.'' It assumes that alcoholism is an addiction having three dimensions—physical, emotion, and spiritual—all of which require attention. It accepts the premise that alcoholism is disease that, though basically incurable, can nevertheless be arrested, but only by total abstinence from alcohol.

AA was established in 1935 in consequence of a fortuitous conversation between two alcoholics in Akron,

Ohio: Bill Wilson, a failed stock broker from New York, and Bob Smith, an Akron physician. The first AA group consisted of these two men, and they were shortly joined by a third, who gave up drinking as a result of meeting with them. A second small group quickly took shape in New York, and a third was begun in 1936 in Cleveland, Ohio. By late 1937, the number of members having a substantial record of sobriety was sufficient to convince the membership that their program offered new hope to the alcoholic.

To bring the message of the group to those who needed it, in 1939 pioneers in the movement published *Alcoholics Anonymous* known popularly as "The Big Book." They borrowed principles from a number of sources. From the Oxford Group, an evangelical sect founded by Frank Buckman, a Lutheran minister, they learned the importance of taking responsibility for past ill behavior and invocation of a Higher Power. They borrowed from William James's *Variety of Religious Experience* to describe the phenomenon of conversion, and they corresponded with Carl Jung to gain an understanding of the spiritual dimension of recovery. The Big Book codified the spiritual ideas in the Twelve Steps, and applied them to the alcoholic's situation. The message of the society came to the attention of many through this book, which was given wide and continuous publicity by magazines and newspapers throughout the world. Clergymen and physicians alike rallied to the movement, giving it strong support and endorsement beyond the United States and North America.

The experience of the members of AA is that the Twelve Steps, if practiced as a way of life, expel the obsession to drink and enable the sufferer to become happily and usefully integrated. The Twelve Suggested Steps of Recovery are the following:

1. We admitted we were powerless over alcohol—that our lives had become unmanageable.
2. We came to believe that a Power greater than ourselves could restore us to sanity.
3. We made a decision to turn our will and our lives over to the care of God, as we understood Him.
4. We made a searching and fearless inventory of ourselves.
5. We admitted to God, to ourselves, and to another human being, the exact nature of our wrongs.
6. We were entirely ready to have God remove all these defects of character.
7. We humbly asked Him to remove our shortcomings.
8. We made a list of all persons we had harmed, and became willing to make amends to them all.
9. We made direct amends to such people whenever possible, except when to do so would injure them or others.

10. We continued to take personal inventory and when we were wrong promptly admitted it.
11. We sought through prayer and meditation to improve our conscious contact with God as we understood Him, praying only for knowledge of His Will for us and the power to carry that out.
12. Having had a spiritual awakening as the result of these steps, we tried to carry this message to alcoholics, and to practice these principles in all our affairs.

AA also has its Twelve Traditions. These succinctly explain the organizational operation of the society and its means of achieving unity and of relating itself to the world about it. Attendance at regular meetings is one of the most cherished traditions of the movement. Each major city has a central AA office that directs callers to appropriate meetings in the area.

When husbands and wives of AA members found themselves dealing with the effects of the behaviors of their addicted spouses, a group organized Al-Anon. Al-Anon is completely separate from AA, but it follows the Twelve Steps and other AA principles. Over time the principles have been adapted to other addictions. The Twelve Steps have been adapted to deal with problematic behaviors such as overeating, out-of-control sexual behaviors, and smoking.

Bibliography: B. WILSON, *Alcoholics Anonymous* (3d ed.; 1976). E. KURTZ, *Not God: A History of Alcoholics Anonymous* (exp. ed.; Center City, Minn. 1991). G. VALIANT, *The Natural History of Alcoholism* (Cambridge, Mass. 1983). F. HARTIGAN, *Bill W.: A Biography of Alcoholics Anonymous Cofounder Bill Wilson* (New York 2000). *The Al-Anon Family Groups: A Guide for the Families of Problem Drinkers* (New York 1955).

[E. M. ROGERS/P. KELLY]

ALCUIN, BL.

Educator and theologian, adviser and friend of CHARLEMAGNE; b. Northumbria, England, *c.* 735; d. Tours, France, May 19, 804. Alcuin (in Saxon Ealh-wine, Latinized as Alcuinus and Albinus) was educated in the tradition of Anglo-Saxon humanism at the cathedral school of York (the old Roman legionary fortress of Eboracum), of which he became librarian and magister in 778 as the successor of his teacher Aelbert. Charlemagne met Alcuin at Parma and secured his services for the Frankish state, where he lived and worked, with the exception of two journeys to his native England, from 782 until his death at his abbey of St. Martin at Tours, to which he had retired in 796. Though he extolled the monastic ideal, he never became a monk, and his career as a secular cleric never went beyond the diaconate.

Alcuin as Educator. Alcuin's activities profoundly influenced the cultural development of a rude, if not bar-

barous age. His active contribution as a scholar in speeding up the intellectual, religious, and political regeneration and growth of a period commonly called the Carolingian Renaissance was not paralleled by any of his learned contemporaries and friends in the Frankish palace schools attended by members of the royal family and their entourage. His writings—except perhaps his voluminous correspondence of more than 250 letters and his occasional poetry—lay no claim to special artistic merit; they are for the most part the practical result of his educational and political endeavors in the service of Charlemagne. His originality as an educator found expression in his mastery of the traditional learning according to CASSIODORUS's formula of the seven liberal arts; emphasizing the trivium he compiled textbooks on grammar, rhetoric, dialectic, and orthography. Alcuin's edition of the pseudo-Augustinian *Categoriae decem* is the first contribution to the study of the Latin Aristotle since Boethius. Commentaries on Genesis, on certain Psalms, the Canticles, and Ecclesiastes, on John, the Apostolic letters, and the Apocalypse, may have been intended as reading texts designed to acquaint clerics with traditional patristic exegesis. Lives of SS. MARTIN OF TOURS, Richarius, VEDAST, and WILLIBRORD are older vitae rewritten by Alcuin in a better Latin.

The real stature of Alcuin as Charlemagne's counselor in political matters is apparent in the activities undertaken by him either at the King's express request or with his obvious approval.

Theological and Liturgical Writings. The ADOPTIONISM of Felix of Urgel and ELIPANDUS of Toledo was refuted by Alcuin in three apologetic treatises. He publicly rebuked heretical doctrines at synodal meetings, and is now recognized as the author of the Frankish episcopate's *Synodica* and of Charlemagne's letter sent from the Council of Frankfurt to Spain in 794. Alcuin, not THEODULF OF ORLÉANS, was the author of the *LIBRI CAROLINI* in which Charlemagne rejected Byzantine veneration of images restored by the seventh ecumenical council (Nicaea II) in 787.

Alcuin's various reforms introduced into liturgical service books used in the Frankish empire culminated in his edition of a lectionary, and especially in his revision of the Gregorian Sacramentary with his appended supplement and the famous preface *Hucusque*. This revision preserved elements of the Gallican rites and inserted them into the Roman Missal. Irish-Northumbrian customs such as the chanting of the Creed at Mass and the celebration of the Feast of All Saints were introduced by him into the Frankish liturgy. Some of the liturgical texts and formulas used in his revision and supplements are drawn from the Mozarabic rite, whose textual traces he

encountered in his fight against the writings and doctrines of the adoptionists. Recent research has shown for the first time Alcuin's share in the writing of some of Charlemagne's capitularies and letters. This constitutes important evidence for the leading role played by the foreigner from Northumbria in the political life of the Frankish empire. Alcuin's recension of Jerome's Vulgate undertaken upon Charlemagne's wish was presented by Alcuin's pupil Fredugise to the Frankish king at Rome on Christmas Day, 800—the same day on which he became emperor. The contributions of Alcuin to the editing of better Latin texts undoubtedly led to increased activities in Frankish scriptoria, and his name is therefore connected with the creation of the Carolingian minuscule, the new calligraphic book hand that became the prototype of the modern Roman script. But such a dependence is far from certain, and cannot be maintained conclusively. The leading position occupied by Alcuin in the events preceding the coronation of Charlemagne as emperor rests upon firmer grounds. There is much information concerning Alcuin's personal influence on the Frankish king, who had visited him at Tours toward the end of May 800 on his way to Italy. On the other hand, recent research has now made it possible to recognize rather clearly the influence exerted on the events of December 25, 800, by a group of Alcuin's friends who were then in attendance at Rome. The contention, first made by A. Kleinclausz in 1902, that Charlemagne's coronation was the work of imperialistic clerics led by Alcuin and his circle has been accepted in the meantime by both French and German historians. To be sure, Alcuin was neither a meek stay-athome nor "a dedicated bookworm" (*ein Stubengelehrter*), but (as E. E. Stengel observes) a scholar who was thoroughly grounded in the management of political affairs.

Although Alcuin's cultus has never been formally recognized, he is named as a *beatus* in many martyrologies.

Feast: May 19.

Bibliography: Alcuin's works in *Patrologia Latina* v.100 and 101; modern critical editions of letters, saints' lives, poems, and treatises by E. DÜMMLER, B. KRUSCH, K. HALM, W. LEVISON, A. MARSILI, A. PONCELET are listed by L. WALLACH, *Alcuin and Charlemagne: Studies in Carolingian History and Literature* (Cornell Studies in Classical Philology 32; Ithaca 1959) 286–287; newly found letters and documents written by Alcuin: *ibid.* 273–274. *Alcuin of York . . . his life and letters*, tr. S. ALLOTT (York 1974). *Two Alcuin letter-books*, ed. C. CHASE from the British Museum ms. Cotton Vespasian A XIV (Toronto 1975). *Son well-beloved: Six poems*, tr. BENEDICTINES OF STANBROOK (Worcester, Eng. 1967). *Libri Carolini*, ed. H. BASTGEN, *Monumenta Germaniae Historica: Concilia 2*, suppl. Pseudo-Augustine, *Categoriae decem*, ed. L. MINIO-PALUELLO, *Aristoteles latinus I 1–5: Categoriae vel praedicamenta* (Bruges-Paris 1961) 129–192. H. LÖWE, *Die karolingische Reichsgründung und der Südosten* (Stuttgart 1938), ch. on Alcuin rejected by F. L. GANSHOF, *Revue belge de philologie et d'histoire* 17 (1938) 977 and by P. GRIERSON, *English Historical Review* 54 (1939) 525–526. A. KLEINCLAUSZ, *Alcuin* (Paris 1948). E. S. DUCKETT, *Alcuin, Friend of Charlemagne: His World and His Work* (New York 1951). W. WATTENBACH, *Deutschlands Geschichtsquellen im Mittelalter* 2:225–236, and the *additio* in the review by L. WALLACH, *Speculum* 29 (1954) 820–825. I. DEUG-SU, *Cultura e ideologia nella prima età carolingia* (Rome 1984); *L'opera agiografica di Alcuino* (Spoleto 1983). M. S. DRISCOLL, *Alcuin et la pénitence à l'époque carolingienne* (Münster 1999). G. ELLARD, *Master Alcuin: Liturgist* (Chicago 1956). C. J. B. GASKOIN, *Alcuin; his life and his work* (New York 1966). F. C. SCHEIBE, ''Alcuin und die *Admonitio generalis,*'' *Deutsches Archiv für Erforschung des Mittelalters* 14 (1958) 221–229; ''Alcuin und die Briefe Karls des Grossen,'' *ibid.* 15 (1959) 181–193. B. FISCHER, *Die Alkuin Bibel* (Freiburg 1957). A. F. WEST, *Alcuin and the Rise of the Christian Schools* (New York 1971, reprint of 1892 ed.). E. BOURQUE, *Études sur les sacramentaires romains,* pt. 2, *Les Textes remaniés,* v.2, *Le Sacramentaire d'Hadrien: Le Supplément d'Alcuin et les Grégoriens mixtes* (Rome 1958). L. WALLACH, *op. cit.;* ''Libri Carolini and Patristics, Latin and Greek: Prolegomena to a Critical Edition,'' in his *The Classical Tradition: Literary and Historical Studies in Honor of Harry Caplan* (Ithaca 1966). P. MUNZ, *The Origin of the Carolingian Empire* (Leicester 1960). E. E. STENGEL, ''Imperator und Imperium bei den Angelsachsen,'' *Deutsches Archiv für Erforschung des Mittelalters* 16 (1960) 45. F. L. GANSHOF, ''Le Programme de gouvernement impérial de Charlemagne,'' *Renovatio Imperii: Atti della Giornata internazionale di studio per il millenario: Ravenna, 4–5 novembre 1961* (Faenza 1963) 63–96. R. FOLZ, *Le Couronnement impérial de Charlemagne: 25 Décembre 800* (Paris 1964).

[L. WALLACH]

ALDEBERT AND CLEMENT

Pseudosaints; fl. first half of the 8th century, in Neustria. Aldebert (or Adalbert) had himself and his Irish disciple Clement ordained by ignorant Gallic bishops in defiance of regular canonical forms. He claimed to have visions, to have special knowledge of the angels, to be able to read consciences, and to perform miracles. As proof he exhibited a letter from Christ, which he said had fallen from heaven at Jerusalem. Ignorant country people, especially women, proclaimed his virtues those of a saint and a prophet. At the urging of BONIFACE he was condemned (March 744) at the Synod of Soissons. The condemnation was repeated at general Frankish councils in 745 and 747 and at a Roman council in October of 745. After 747 Aldebert and Clement disappeared from history.

Bibliography: *Die Briefe des heiligen Bonifatius und Lullus,* ed. M. TANGL, *Monumenta Germaniae Historica Epistolae selactae,* 1:109–118, 160. *Monumenta Germaniae Historica Concilia,* 2.1:33–50. C. J. VON HEFELE, *Histoire des conciles d'après les documents originaux,* tr. and continued by H. LECLERCQ, 3:846, 874. C. DE CLERCQ, *La Législation religieuse franque . . . ,* 2 v. (Paris-Antwerp 1936–58) 1:123–124. T. SCHIEFFER, *Winfrid-Bonifatius und die christliche Grundlegung Europas* (Freiburg 1954). A. M.

LANDRAF, *Lexikon für Theologie und Kirche,* ed. J. HOFER and K. RAHNER, 10 v. (2d ed. Freiburg 1957–65) 1: 298.

[C. P. LOUGHRAN]

ALDEGUNDIS, ST.

Abbess; b. *c.* 630; d. Jan. 30, 695 or 700. She was the daughter of SS. Walbert, Count of Hainaut (d. *c.* 660), and Bertilda, and the sister of WALDETRUD. Aldegundis became the foundress and first abbess of the convent of Maubeuge, where her niece, ALDETRUDE, received spiritual formation and later succeeded her in office. The many biographies of Aldegundis, all rather legendary, report numerous visions with which she is said to have been favored. There is, however, no doubt about the continuous and widespread cult of this saint, whose intercession is sought for the cure of diseases of the eye and the illnesses common to childhood. She is invoked also as the patroness of cancer victims, probably because she is reported to have suffered greatly from this malady in the last years of her life. Her cult was already well established by the tenth century.

Feast: Jan. 30.

Bibliography: *Patrologia Latina,* ed. J. P. MIGNE (Paris 1878–90) 132:858–876. *Acta Sanctorum* Jan. 3:655–662. J. MABILLON, *Acta sanctorum ordinis S. Benedicti* (Venice 1733–40) 2:773–782. *Monumenta Germaniae Historica: Scriptores rerum Merovingicarum* 6:85–90. E. LEROY, *Histoire de sainte Aldegonde* (Valenciennes 1883). L. VAN DER ESSEN, *Étude critique et littéraire sur Les Vitae des Saints Mérovingiens* (Louvain 1907) 219–231. H. DUBRULLE, *Dictionnaire d'histoire et de géographie ecclésiastiques,* ed. A. BAUDRILLART et al. (Paris 1912) 2:46–47. A. M. ZIMMERMANN, *Kalendarium Benedictinum* (Metten 1933–38) 1:144–146. A. M. ZIMMERMANN, *Lexicon für Theologie und Kirche,* ed. J. HOFER and K. RAHNER (Freiburg 1957–65) 1:141. J. L. BAUDOT and L. CHAUSSIN, *Vies des saints et des bienhereux selon l'ordre du calendrier avec l'historique des fêtes* (Paris 1935–56) 1:619–621. J. DUBOIS, *Analecta Bollandiana* 79 (1961) 270, 287. M. COENS, *ibid.* 80 (1962) 149. R. AIGRAIN, *Catholicisme* 1:285.

[H. DRESSLER]

ALDEIAMENTO SYSTEM IN BRAZIL

Aldeiamento was the name given to a plan to domesticate and Christianize nomadic native Brazilians by gathering them into village mission-settlements *(aldeias)*. In the early years of Portuguese settlement there was no concerted effort to congregate native peoples. Christianization of a few was attempted through visitation by missionaries in the wilderness. Soon after the arrival of the Jesuits in 1549 a more determined effort was made. Members of the Society, not knowing the native languages, at first trained young boys, both native and

Portuguese, to act as interpreters. The youths were taught to read and write, to sing plainchant and other music, to read aloud in Portuguese, play musical instruments, and to serve Mass. With these boys, the Jesuits visited the existing native villages and attempted to introduce Christianity. This method was also unsatisfactory.

Finally the system of *aldeias,* or reductions, was tried. Through persuasion and, at times, a show of force by soldiers, native peoples were gathered into new strategically placed villages. There was catechetical instruction morning and evening for all. After 1583 afternoon instruction was kept for those already Christian or those who were preparing for Holy Communion. The morning instruction consisted mainly of learning essential prayers. The articles of faith and preparation for Confession and Communion were taught in the afternoon. The Jesuits believed that only in this way could the Europeans Christianize and civilize these Stone Age Indians. The natives were treated as minors and not as adults. It was particularly important to keep the neophytes from contact with the pagans. As Manuel NÓBREGA expressed it: "We want to congregate all those baptized and keep them separated from the rest." Through force of circumstances the missionaries were compelled to allow their charges to perform manual labor for the Portuguese, but they always strove to limit this concession and to shield their neophytes from whites and mestizos as far as possible. In the 17th and 18th centuries, the Jesuits and other religious established the *aldeias* far in the interior, at greater distances from white settlements, in order to protect their charges from more demoralization.

Aldeiamento was used particularly in Maranhão, Pará, Amazonas, and, farther south, in the São Paulo area. The system, which was relatively successful after 1680 and included as many as 60,000 people in the Amazon area, came to an abrupt end between 1755 and 1759 with the secularization of all missions by Pombal.

See Also: MISSION IN COLONIAL AMERICA, I (SPANISH MISSIONS).

Bibliography: S. LEITE, *História da Companhia de Jesús no Brasil,* 10 v. (Lisbon 1938–50). C. R. BOXER, *Race Relations in the Portuguese Colonial Empire, 1415–1825* (London 1963).

[M. C. KIEMEN]

ALDEMAR, ST.

Benedictine abbot; b. Capua, Italy, *c.* 950; d. in village of San Martino near Bucchianico, Italy. As a youth he became a monk at Monte Cassino and was ordained deacon. Aloara of Capua (d. 992), widow of Pandolf of Benevento (d. 981), put him in charge of the Capuan

monastery of San Lorenzo, which she had founded in 982. Later he moved to Boiano, where he was ordained a priest. Persecutions drove him first to San Liberatore and then to Farafiliorumpetri, where he built the monastery of Santa Eufemia and he founded other monasteries in the region of Chieti and in Piceno. After his death his body was translated to Bucchianico, where it rests today, and he is venerated locally as a patron saint.

Feast: March 24.

Bibliography: *Bibliotecha hagiographica latina antiquae et mediae aetatis* (Brussels 1898–1901) 251–252. *Acta Sanctorum* March 3:487–490. E. GATTOLA, *Historia abbatiae Cassinensis,* 2 v. (Venice 1733). L. TOSTI, *Storia della badia di Montecassino,* 3 v. (Rome 1888–90) 1:98. A. M. ZIMMERMANN, *Kalendarium Benedictinum* (Metten 1933–38) 1:367–369. U. BERLIÈRE, *Dictionaire d'histoire de géographie ecclésiastiques,* ed. A. BAUDRILLART et al. (Paris 1912–) 2:47. J. BAUR, *Lexicon für Theologie und Kirche,* ed. J. HOFER and K. RAHNER (Freiburg 1957–65) 1:298.

[A. LENTINI]

ALDETRUDE, ST.

Also called Adeltrudis; abbess; b. between 628 and 639; d. Feb. 25, *c.* 696. She was the daughter of VINCENT MADELGARIUS and WALDETRUD. At an early age she was placed in the convent of Maubeuge, where ALDEGUNDIS, her aunt, was abbess. The *Vita Aldetrudis* (*Acta Sanctorum* Feb. 3:514–516), written by a tenth-century monk, contains so many legendary elements that it is practically impossible to gain an accurate account of the spiritual formation of the saint. It is generally agreed, however, that she succeeded her aunt in the office of abbess at Maubeuge and creditably fulfilled the duties of this position for more than a decade. If the early hagiographers are worthy of belief, Aldetrude came from an exceptional family in which father, mother, and four children are venerated as saints.

Feast: Feb. 25.

Bibliography: L. VAN DER ESSEN, *Études critique et littéraire sur les Vitae des saints mérovingiens* (Louvain 1907) 237–240. H. DUBRULLE, *Dictionnaire d'histoire et de géographie ecclésiastiques,* ed. A. BAUDRILLART et al. (Paris 1912) 2:52. J. L. BAUDOT and L. CHAUSSIN, *Vies des saints et des bienheureux selon l'ordre du calendrier avec l'historique des fêtes* (Paris 1935–56) 2:526–527. R. AIGRAIN, *Catholicisme* (Paris 1948) 1:286. G. ALLEMANG, *Lexikon für Theologie und Kirche,* ed. J. HOFER and K. RAHNER (Freiburg 1957–65) 1:299. A. D'HAENENS, *Bibliotheca sanctorum* 1:750–751.

[H. DRESSLER]

ALDHELM, ST.

Abbot, bishop, first notable Anglo-Saxon writer; b. *c.* 640; d. Doulting (Somerset), May 25, 709. Kinsman of INE, King of Wessex, he was educated by Maildubh, Irish founder of Malmesbury, and in Kent by the African Abbot HADRIAN, companion of St. THEODORE OF CANTERBURY. As abbot of Malmesbury (from *c.* 675) he rebuilt the church and monastery and made foundations at Frome and Bradford-on-Avon. When the Wessex Diocese was divided in 705, he ruled the western half (roughly Wiltshire, Dorset, and Somerset) while remaining abbot of Malmesbury. He built churches in his cathedral town of Sherborne and on his Dorset estates at Corfe and Wareham, near which a headland still bears his name. He was buried at Malmesbury, whose principal saint he remained for the Middle Ages, in spite of the short suspension of his cult by LANFRANC.

His principal works include: *De virginitate*, a study of saints of the Bible and the early Church in both prose and verse; *De metris et enigmatibus ac pedum regulis*, a treatise on grammar; *Letters*, including one to the Britons on the date of Easter and one to the clerics of St. Wilfrid on loyalty in persecution; and *Carmina ecclesiastica*, a collection of religious poems. All of these were widely read in England and on the Continent until the eleventh century. Their turgid Latin influenced St. BONIFACE and charter writers. King ALFRED highly praised his Anglo-Saxon poems, sung to harp accompaniment to attract hearers to church, but these have not survived. Highly esteemed by St. BEDE, Aldhelm's learning and piety inspired many followers, including William of Malmesbury.

Feast: May 23; May 28 (Dioceses of Clifton and Plymouth, and Southwark).

Bibliography: *Aldhelmi opera*, ed. R. EHWALD, *Monumenta Germaniae Historica: Auctores Antiquissimi* 15. *Aldhelm, the poetic works*, tr. M. LAPIDGE and J. L. ROSIER (Cambridge 1985). *Aldhelm, the prose works*, tr. M. LAPIDGE and M. HERREN (Cambridge 1979). BEDE, *Historia ecclesiastica*, ed. C. PLUMMER (Oxford 1896, reprint 1956) 5:18. WILLIAM OF MALMESBURY, *Gesta Pontificum Anglorum*, ed. N. E. HAMILTON, *Rerum Britannicarum medii aevi scriptores* 52 (1870) 330–443. G. F. BROWNE, *St. Aldhelm* (London 1903). A. S. COOK, *Sources of the Biography of Aldhelm* (Transactions of the Connecticut Academy of Arts and Sciences 28; New Haven 1927). E. S. DUCKETT, *Anglo-Saxon Saints and Scholars* (New York 1947, reprinted Hamden, Conn. 1967). A. ORCHARD, *The Poetic Art of Aldhelm* (Cambridge, England 1994). N. P. STORK, *Through a Gloss Darkly: Aldhelm's Riddles in the British Library MS Royal 12.C.xxiii* (Toronto, Canada 1990). M. GRETSCH, *The intellectual foundations of the English Benedictine reform* (Cambridge 1999).

[H. FARMER]

ALDOBRANDINI

Distinguished Italian family prominent in Vatican affairs in the 16th and 17th centuries.

Silvestro, jurist; b. Florence, 1499; d. 1558. Of old Florentine nobility, he studied law at Pisa under Filippo Decio and received his doctorate in 1521. Active politically against the Medici, he was forced into exile in 1531. His distinguished career as a jurist led him to Venice, to Faenza, and to Rome (1534), where Paul III appointed him to various legal and administrative offices. He then served the dukes of Ferrara and Urbino before being appointed consistorial advocate in 1548. Under Paul IV he rose with the influence of the Pope's nephew Cardinal Carafa and enthusiastically supported anti-Spanish policy. However, in 1557 he was disgraced and lost his position. His writings include *Addizioni ai commentarii di Filippo Decio sulle Decretali* (Lyons 1551) and *Trattato dell'usura* (Venice 1604).

By Silvestro's marriage with Lisa Deto he had one daughter, Julia, and six sons, four of whom held high positions in the Vatican. Tommaso (d. 1572) was secretary of briefs under Paul IV. Giovanni (d. 1573) became bishop of Imola under Pius V and was made cardinal in 1570. Pietro (d. 1587) was a distinguished jurist and succeeded his father as fiscal advocate in 1556. Ippolito became CLEMENT VIII. During Clemment's pontificate, three of his nephews were raised to prominence.

Two of the nephews, Cinzio Passeri (b. Sinigaglia, 1551; d. Rome, Jan. 1, 1610), Julia's son, and Pietro (b. Rome, 1571; d. there, Feb. 21, 1621), son of Clement's brother Pietro, were made cardinals on Sept. 17, 1593, and were appointed to administer jointly the office of secretary of state. Although Cinzio was the elder and the earlier favored by Clement, Pietro soon established himself as the real authority in the office and the most powerful man in the Vatican next to the pope. He had the natural skills of a diplomat combined with prudence, zeal, and strength of mind. He was a man of affable disposition, deftly handling intricate political affairs and always retaining the close confidence of Clement. As legate *a latere* he received the annexation of the Duchy of Ferrara to the Papal States in 1598. He cultivated harmony with Henry IV of France, personally blessing Henry's marriage to Marie de' Medicis; in 1600 Pietro also secured peace between France and Savoy. Clement rewarded him by making him camerlengo and in 1604, archbishop of Ravenna. After the death of Clement, Pietro fell from papal favor and retired to Ravenna, where he effected important Church reforms.

A third nephew, Gian Francesco (1545–1601), also favored by Clement, was made general of the papal armies. He died while commanding troops against the Turks in Hungary. Of his many children, the eldest son, Silvestro (1587–1612), at the age of 16 years was made cardinal by Clement. Ippolito, the younger (1592–1638),

"Funeral Monument of Silvestro Aldobrandini," sculptural group by Giacomo della Porta, located in S. Maria sopra Minerva, Rome. (Alinari-Art Reference/Art Resource, NY)

became cardinal under Gregory XV. The male line died out in 1638, but the granddaughter of Gian Francesco, Olympia, married Paolo Borghese in 1638, and the Aldobrandini fortunes thereby passed to the Borghese family.

Other distant relatives include Giacomo Aldobrandini (d. 1606), bishop of Troia and nuncio to Naples; Cardinal Baccio Aldobrandini (1613–1665), protégé of Ippolito, the younger; and Alessandro Aldobrandini (1667–1734), nephew of Baccio.

Bibliography: P. LITTA et al., *Famiglie celebri italiane*, 14 v. (Milan 1819–1923). P. E. VISCONTI, *Città e famiglie nobili e celebri dello stato pontificio*, 3 v. in 4 (Rome 1847). P. RICHARD, *La Légation Aldobrandini et le traité de Lyon* (Lyons 1903); et al., *Dictionnaire d'histoire et de géographie ecclésiastiques*, ed. A. BAUDRILLART et al. (Paris 1912–) 2:55–60. L. PASSARINI, *Memorie intorno alla vita di Silvestro Aldobrandini* (Rome 1878): L. PASTOR, *The History of the Popes from the Close of the Middle Ages*: from 1st German ed. *Geschichte der Päpste seit dem Ausgang des Mittelalters* (Freiburg 1885–1933; repr. 1955–) v.23 and 24, *passim*. F. BOCK, *Lexikon für Theologie und Kirche*, ed. J. HOFER and K. RAHNER (2d, new ed. Freiburg 1957–65) 1:300–301.

[J. C. WILLKE]

ALDRIC OF LE MANS, ST.

Bishop; b. *c.* 800; d. March 24, 856. The son of half-Saxon, half-Bavarian parents, Aldric spent his youth at the court of CHARLEMAGNE at Aachen, where he became a friend of Louis the Pious. Bishop DROGO of Metz ordained him priest, named him precentor, and placed him in charge of the cathedral school. But when Louis the Pious became emperor, he recalled Aldric (Aldericus, Audry) to Aachen, making him his chaplain and confessor. Named bishop of Le Mans and consecrated Dec. 22, 832, by the metropolitan of Tours, Aldric received the emperor, who came to celebrate Christmas with him. As bishop Aldric distinguished himself by his charity, disciplined his clergy, and built the monastery of Saint-Martin in his city, as well as the Saint-Julian fountain. He fought with the monks of Saint-Calais, compelling them to recognize his authority over their abbey. On the death of Louis the Pious (840) they allied themselves with the enemies of Emperor Charles II the Bald and had Aldric exiled from Le Mans. In 846, however, a royal charter restored him to his see. However, when Rainald became abbot of Saint-Calais he succeeded, a few years before Aldric's death, in winning from Charles the Bald and the synod of Bonneuil recognition of his abbey's episcopal exemption (855). Aldric is buried in the abbey church of Saint-Vincent in Le Mans. In addition to three testaments (the first two confirm legacies to various churches and counsel on how to maintain peace between clerics and monks; the third is an ascetic piece) the bishop composed the *Gesta Aldrici*, in which he reports on his management of the diocese in the first 44 chapters, the rest of the work being a later addition.

Feast: Jan. 7.

Bibliography: A. E. MOLINIER, et al., *Les Sources de L'histoire de France* (Paris 1901–06) No. 8121–22. *Gesta domni Aldrici*, ed. R. CHARLES and L. FROGER (Mamers 1889). J. P. E. HAVET, *Oeuvres*, 2 v. (Paris 1896) 1:271–317, the *Actus pontificum* usually attributed now to the Chorbishop David. L. DUCHESNE, *Fastes épiscopaux de l'ancienne Gaule* v.2. A. BUTLER, *The Lives of the Saints*, ed. H. THURSTON and D. ATTWATER (New York 1956) 1:48. M. BESSON, *Dictionnaire d'histoire et de géographie ecclésiastiques*, ed. A. BAUDRILLART et al. (Paris 1912) 2:68–69.

[J. DAOUST]

ALDRIC OF SENS, ST.

Monk, abbot, then archbishop of Sens; b. Gâtinais, 775; d. Ferrières, Oct. 10, either 836, according to Duchesne and Levillain, or 841, according to Stein and others. Aldric (Aldericus or Audri) was of noble birth, and was educated at Saint-Martin of Tours, became monk at Ferrières (Gâtinais), was appointed to the clergy of Sens by its Archbishop Jeremiah, was called to the court of Aachen by King Louis the Pious, and was named director of the Palace School and member of the Council. In 821 he succeeded Abbot Adalbert at Ferrières; in 828 he was chosen archbishop of Sens, and was consecrated at the Council of Paris in 829. Concerned about clerical discipline, he effected a reform at the abbey of Saint-Amand in Flanders, and with Ebbo of Sens he reformed Saint-Denis. He sent his disciple Servatus LUPUS of Ferrières to complete his studies with Rabanus Maurus at Fulda. Preoccupied with the prosperity of his own abbey, he obtained during a visit of Louis the Pious to Ferrières the monastery of Saint-Josse in Ponthieu. He participated in the Council of Thionville rehabilitating Louis the Pious. He was buried at the abbey of Ferrières. His magnificent reliquary disappeared, and his remains were scattered when the Calvinists pillaged the abbey in 1569.

Feast: June 7.

Bibliography: J. MABILLON, *Acta sanctorum ordinis S. Benedictii* (Venice 1733–40) v.2. *Gallia Christiana* 12:19–21. *Patrologia Latina*, ed. J. P. MIGNE (Paris 1878–90) 105: 809–811. E. JAROSSAY, *Histoire d'une abbaye à travers les siècles: Ferrières en Gatinais* (Orléans 1901). L. LEVILLAIN, ''Étude sur les lettres de Loup de Ferrières,'' *Bibliothèque de l'École des Chartres* 63 (1902) 85–86. G. HOCQUARD, *Catholicisme* 1:288.

[P. COUSIN]

ALEGAMBE, PHILIPPE

Historiographer and bibliographer; b. Brussels, Jan. 22, 1592; d. Rome, Sept. 6, 1652. At the completion of his literary studies, he traveled to Spain where he entered the service of the Duke of Osuna. In 1611 Alegambe accompanied the duke to Sicily. On Sept. 7, 1613, Alegambe was admitted into the Jesuit novitiate at Palermo. He studied theology at the Roman College and was sent to the University of Graz, Austria, to lecture in philosophy and theology. Then, as tutor of the young Prince of Eggenberg, he traveled for five years throughout Europe until he was called to Rome by the Jesuit General Mutius VITELLESCHI to become secretary to the German assistant. After four years he was relieved of this post and worked on the continuation of the *Bibliotheca scriptorum S.J.* (Antwerp 1643), begun by P. Ribadeneira, SJ. He also published the *Mortes illustres et gesta eorum de S.J. qui in odium fidei. . . confecti sunt* (Rome 1657), *Heroes et victimae charitatis S.J.* (Rome 1658), and the *Compendium vitarum Saints Justini, Felicis, Florentii et Justae. . . ex manuscript ecclesiae colleg. S. Justae Aquilae.*

Bibliography: C. SOMMERVOGEL et al., *Bibliothèque de la Compagnie de Jésus,* 11 v. (Brussels–Paris 1890–1932) 1:151–153. E. M. RIVIÈRE, *Dictionnaire d'histoire et de géographie ecclésiastiques,* ed. A. BAUDRILLART et al. (Paris 1912—) 2:80–81. B. SCHNEIDER, *Lexikon für Theologie und Kirche*[2], ed. J. HOFER and K. RAHNER, 10 v. (2d, new ed. Freiburg 1957–65) 1:302.

[E. D. MCSHANE]

ALEGRE, FRANCISCO JAVIER

Historian and Latinist of Mexico; b. Veracruz, Nov. 12, 1729; d. near Bologna, Aug. 16, 1788. He entered the Society of Jesus on March 19, 1747, and was ordained on Sept. 29, 1754. He taught classics and mathematics in Havana (1755–62) and Canon Law in Mérida, Yucatán (1762–64). Then he was summoned to Mexico City by his provincial superior to write a history of the Jesuit Mexican province. By 1766 he had finished the first draft into which he incorporated hundreds of original documents. Because of his great talent for writing, Alegre rarely had to correct any part of the text, some 1,500 folio pages. Titled *Historia de la provincia de la Compañía de Jesús de Nueva España,* it spans two centuries, for it prefixes to the history of the Mexican province proper (1572–1766) and the tragic Florida mission (1566–72). This thoroughly documented history in which he preserved a vast number of documents now lost or unavailable is Alegre's greatest contribution. Even in the unsatisfactory edition of Bustamante (Mexico City 1841–42) it furnished the principal source of information on northern colonial Mexico to historians from H. H. Bancroft to P. M. Dunne. After the expulsion of the Jesuits in 1767, Alegre went into exile in Bologna, Italy. Here he devoted his last two decades to literary and scientific studies and publications.

Bibliography: F. J. ALEGRE, *Historia de la provincia de la Compañía de Jesús de Nueva España,* ed. E. J. BURRUS and F. ZUBILLAGA, 4 v. (Rome 1956–60). E. J. BURRUS, ''Francisco Javier Alegre: Historian of the Jesuits in New Spain,'' *Archivum historicum Societatis Jesu,* 22 (1953) 439–509.

[F. ZUBILLAGA]

ALEMANY, JOSEPH SADOC

Dominican missionary, first archbishop of San Francisco, Calif.; b. Vich, Spain, July 13, 1814; d. Valencia, Spain, April 14, 1888. He joined the Order of Preachers in 1829. Six years later secularization laws closed the Spanish religious houses, and he completed his studies in Italy. Ordained at Viterbo, Italy, in March 1837, he engaged in further study and pastoral work in Rome.

In 1840 Alemany was sent to the United States to serve the Dominican foundations in Ohio, Kentucky, and Tennessee. He soon perfected his English and became an American citizen (1845) while gaining experience as curate and pastor in several frontier parishes and as rector of Nashville's diocesan seminary. In 1849 he was named American provincial and left for Rome the following spring to attend a general chapter of his order. While there he learned of his appointment by Pius IX as bishop of Monterey in Upper California. After remonstrating unsuccessfully with the pope, Alemany was consecrated in the Church of San Carlo al Corso, Rome, on June 30, 1850 (nine weeks before California became a state). En route to California, he stopped in France and Ireland to seek recruits and help for his distant see. He arrived in San Francisco in December 1850, and by the end of January 1851 was established at Monterey, where the chapel of the presidio served as cathedral. As bishop of Monterey, the 36-year-old Dominican had jurisdiction over both Upper and Lower California as well as much of the land now comprising Nevada and Utah. The Mexican government protested his control over Lower California (Mexican territory) and withheld the proceeds of the PIOUS FUND, an important source of income. Although he had few priests and fewer usable churches in the area, he was still able to report some progress at the First Plenary Council of Baltimore (1852).

On July 29, 1853, Alemany was named archbishop of the new provincial See of San Francisco, and Lower California was removed from his jurisdiction. As archbishop, he attended Vatican Council I (1869–70), where he was a member of the 24-man commission to explore the teaching on papal infallibility. At the Third Plenary Council of Baltimore (1884), he was chairman of the commission of bishops reporting on the expediency of a uniform catechism. After directing his rapidly growing archdiocese for three decades Alemany requested a coadjutor, and on Sept. 16, 1883, Patrick William Riordan, of Chicago, was consecrated for this post. In November, Alemany traveled 1,000 miles to Ogden, Utah, to meet Riordan and welcome him to San Francisco, and from that meeting a close friendship developed. On Dec. 28, 1884, Alemany resigned his charge into the hands of his coadjutor and retired to Spain. He was appointed titular archbishop of Pelusium and devoted his efforts to restoring the Dominican Order in his native country. He served in the parish of Nuestra Señora de la Pilar, Valencia, until his death. At his request, his remains were entombed in the ancient church of Santo Domingo in Vich, where he had been received into the Dominican Order 60 years before. In 1965 Alemany's remains were returned to San Francisco for interment in nearby Holy Cross Cemetery.

Bibliography: A complete biographical study is J. B. MC-GLOIN, *California's Pioneer Archbishop: The Life of Joseph Alemany, O.P., 1814–1888* (New York 1965). An earlier monograph is F. J. WEBER, *A Biographical Sketch of Right Reverend Joseph Sadoc Alemany, Bishop of Monterey 1850–1853* (Van Nuys, Calif. 1961).

[J. B. MCGLOIN]

ALEN, JOHN

Archbishop of Dublin, chancellor of Ireland; b. Cottenshall, Norfolk, 1476; d. Hollywood's of Artane, Ireland, July 28, 1534. Alen (Alan, Allen) was the son of Edward Alen and Catherine St. Leger. He took his master of arts degree at Cambridge and was ordained on Aug. 25, 1499. His doctorate of civil and canon law was acquired at Rome, where for 11 years he acted as proctor of the archbishop of Canterbury. He held a variety of benefices, among them the treasurership of St. Paul's and the living of Galby in Leicestershire into which he was inducted by Wolsey. He played his part as minister of the royal supremacy in reducing the clergy to subjection and in the dissolution of the monasteries. After he was consecrated archbishop of Dublin on March 13, 1529, his indefatigable interest in the rights of his see resulted in the *Reportorium Viride,* a full description of the diocese in 1532–33, and his register (*Liber Niger Alani*). His end came violently, as a result of a false rumor that Gerald Fitzgerald, ninth Earl of Kildare, had been put to death. He sought refuge at Hollywood's of Artane but two retainers of the Fitzgeralds murdered him there.

Bibliography: F. E. BALL, *The Judges in Ireland 1221–1921,* 2 v. (London 1926) 1:125–127, 155–156, 198–199, *passim.* C. MAC-

NEILL, ed., *Calendar of Archbishop Alen's Register* (Dublin 1950). *Analecta Hibernica,* 10 (1941) 173–222. J. GAIRDNER, *The Dictionary of National Biography From the Earliest Times to 1900,* 63 v. (London 1885–1900) 1:305–307.

[J. J. MEAGHER]

ALENI, GIULIO

Italian missionary; b. Brescia, 1582; d. Fuchow, China, Aug. 3, 1649. He entered the Jesuits in 1600. In 1610, having been assigned to the Chinese mission, he arrived at Macao, where he spent three years before gaining entrance into the southeastern provinces of China. Meanwhile he taught mathematics and published his observation of a lunar eclipse, *Resultat de l'observation sur l'éclipse de lune du 8 Novembre, 1612, faite à Macao.* He was the first Christian missionary in Kiang–si and Fukien and labored in those provinces for 30 years. To promote good will toward Christianity, he adopted the dress and manners of the Chinese and became, after Matteo Ricci, the most famous Italian missionary to China; he was honored with the title of "Confucius of the West." He wrote a number of books, mainly theological in content, which were published in Chinese. His chief work, *The Life of God, the Savior, from the Four Gospels* (8 v. Peking 1635–37) was often reprinted and used even by Protestant missionaries. Also notable is a cosmography *Tchi fang wai ki* (The True Origin of 10,000 Things, 6 v. Hangchow 1623).

Bibliography: C. SOMMERVOGEL et al., *Bibliothèque de la Compagnie de Jésus,* 11 v. (Brussels–Paris 1890–1932) 1:157–160; 8:1603; 12:915. E. M. RIVIÈRE, *Dictionnaire d'histoire et de géographie ecclésiastiques,* ed. A. BAUDRILLART et al. (Paris 1912—) 2:99–100. G. H. DUNNE, *Generation of Giants* (Notre Dame, Ind. 1962).

[J. V. MENTAG]

ALERDING, HERMAN JOSEPH

Bishop, historian; b. Ibbenbueren, Westphalia, Germany, April 13, 1845; d. Fort Wayne, Indiana, Dec. 6, 1924. He was the son of Bernard Herman and Theresa (Schrameier) Alerding, who settled in Newport, Kentucky, during his infancy. He entered St. Gabriel Seminary, Vincennes, Indiana, in 1858, and continued his studies at St. Thomas Seminary near Bardstown, Kentucky, and St. Meinrad Seminary, St. Meinrad, Indiana. After he was ordained for the Diocese of Vincennes on Sept. 22, 1868, he did pastoral work in Terre Haute, Indiana, and Cambridge City, Indiana, until 1874. That year he was transferred to Indianapolis, Indiana, where he served as procurator of St. Joseph Seminary during the one year of its existence, and as pastor of St. Joseph Church. On Nov. 30, 1900, Alerding was consecrated as bishop of Fort Wayne by archbishop William H. Elder of Cincinnati, Ohio. The new bishop promoted secondary schools and furthered consolidation of the parochial system. During his episcopacy the Catholic population in the diocese almost doubled, largely because of the influx of foreign–born Catholics to work in the steel mills of northern Indiana.

Alerding gained recognition among Church historians with the publication of *The History of the Catholic Church in the Diocese of Vincennes* (1883). It was the first general history of the Church in Indiana, and, although not scientifically written or well organized, it contained a wealth of material. He published a second work, *The Diocese of Fort Wayne*, in 1907.

Bibliography: *History of the Catholic Church in Indiana*, ed. C. BLANCHARD, 2 v. (Logansport, Ind. 1898). J. F. NOLL, *The Diocese of Fort Wayne: Fragments of History* (Fort Wayne 1941).

[M. C. SCHROEDER]

ALÈS, ADHÉMAR D'

Jesuit theologian and patrologist; b. Orléans, France, Dec. 2, 1861; d. Paris, Feb. 24, 1938. He entered the Society of Jesus in 1880 and was ordained in 1896. As a scholastic and young priest he taught philosophy and both Greek and Latin literature. He inaugurated the *Bibliothèque de théologie historique* in collaboration with P. Bainvel and published detailed theological studies on TERTULLIAN (1905), HIPPOLYTUS (1906), the Edict of Callistus (1914), CYPRIAN (1922), and NOVATIAN (1925). He became professor of theology at the Institute Catholique in Paris in 1907 and dean of the faculty in 1925. He served as principal director of the *Dictionnaire Apologétique de la Foi Catholique* (4 v. Paris 1911–28), to which he contributed many articles dealing with the development of theology in the early and medieval Church. He was an exact and careful scholar whose analyses of theological problems in their historical development have proved invaluable. As a result of a controversy over divine providence and free will he published *Providence et libre arbitre* (Paris 1927). He also contributed to the *Bibliothèque des sciences religieuses* with: *Baptême et Confirmation* (Paris 1928), *Eucharistie* (Paris 1930), *Le Dogme de Nicée* (1925), *Le Dogme de Éphèse* (1931), *De Verbo Incarnato* (1930), and *De Deo Trino* (1935) and wrote articles and reviews for scholarly periodicals.

Bibliography: R. METZ, *Lexikon für Theologie und Kirche*[2], ed. J. HOFER and K. RAHNER, 10 v. (2d, new ed. Freiburg 1957–65) 1:304–305. *Dictionnaire de théologie catholique*, ed. A. VACANT et al., 15 v. (Paris 1903–50) Tables générales 1:70–71. J. LEBRETON, *Catholicisme* 1:294–295. "*In Memoriam:* Le. R. P. D'Alès," *Recherches de science religieuse*, 28 (1938) 129–133.

[F. X. MURPHY]

ALEXANDER, ARCHIBALD

Presbyterian theologian; b. Lexington, Virginia, April 17, 1772; d. Princeton, New Jersey, Oct. 22, 1851. He was the son of William and Ann (Reid) Alexander. After studying at Liberty Hall College (later Washington College), Chestertown, Maryland, under Reverend William Graham, he was ordained in 1794. He served as president of Hampden–Sydney College, Virginia, from 1796 to 1807, when he accepted a call to Pine Street Presbyterian Church, Philadelphia, Pennsylvania. As moderator of the general assembly (1807), he advocated the establishment of the Princeton Theological Seminary. Installed as its first professor in 1812, he taught didactic and polemic theology there until his death. With the works of Turretini and other Calvinist scholastics as the basis of his courses, Alexander was the chief theologian of the Old School party, opposing the New School in his *Thoughts on Religious Experience* (1841) and in the columns of the *Biblical Repertory*, which he founded in 1825. His *Brief Outline of the Evidences of the Christian Religion* (1825) was widely adopted as a college text. In *The Canon of the Old and New Testaments* (1826) he taught verbal inspiration and inerrancy. He was also influential in advocating foreign missions and in the American Colonization Society.

Bibliography: J. W. ALEXANDER, *The Life of Archibald Alexander* (New York 1854). *Sons of the Prophets*, ed. H. T. KERR (Princeton 1963).

[R. K. MACMASTER]

ALEXANDER, SAMUEL

English educator and neorealist philosopher; b. Sydney, Australia, Jan. 6, 1859; d. Manchester, England, Sept. 11, 1938. Alexander was educated at the University of Melbourne and at Balliol College, Oxford, and served as a teaching fellow of Lincoln College from 1882 to 1893. He was then professor of philosophy at Victoria University of Manchester until 1924, during which time he was president of the Aristotelian Society (1908–11), fellow of the British Academy (1913), and Gifford lecturer at the University of Glasgow (1916–18). In 1927, he was appointed the Herbert Spencer lecturer at Oxford. He published many philosophical and literary works, among which *Space, Time, and Deity* (2 v., London 1920) is the most important.

In revolt against traditional materialism, Alexander formulated his epistemology and metaphysics in the context of naturalism and realism. His principal synthesis may be summarized as follows: (1) space and time are infinite, continuous, and inseparable—the universal matrix of all reality; (2) all being originates by "emergent evolution," an intrinsic urge (*nisus*) to develop into a more complex form of reality; (3) reality is creative; each emergent level is known by the "perspective" enjoyed by the mind; (4) just as mind emerges from life, and life from a lower physico-chemical level of existence, so the values of truth, beauty, freedom, and goodness emerge from mind; (5) deity is not a transcendent Creator, but the last emergent quality of mind.

While Alexander's pantheistic evolutionism directly opposed the materialistic, agnostic evolutionism of Spencer and T. H. Huxley, it can be identified with other currents of contemporary thought. Alexander associated his space-time matrix with the four-dimensional continuum arrived at mathematically by Einstein. He allied his "emergent evolution," a concept used independently by the British zoologist, C. Lloyd Morgan, with H. Bergson's "creative evolution." His empirical "perspectivism" was closely akin to the direct realism of G. E. Moore, B. RUSSELL, and the pragmatists, while leaving place for the a priori and nonempirical as found in Plato and Kant. His concept of value, human freedom, and deity has much in common with the pantheistic naturalism of B. SPINOZA, the French philosophy of the spirit, and the absolute idealism of F. H. BRADLEY and B. Bosanquet. Again, his psychic evolutionism is not unlike that proposed by A. N. WHITEHEAD.

The defects of Alexander's evolutionism were two: his system remained basically eclectic and he never unified in principle, logically or ontologically, the world of spirit and of matter. In spite of his instinct against materialism and agnosticism, his thought never truly attained to spiritual substance and the transcendence of God.

See Also: EVOLUTIONISM; PANTHEISM.

Bibliography: Works. *Moral Order and Progress* (3d ed. London 1899); *Locke* (London 1908); *The Basis of Realism* (London 1914); *Space, Time, and Deity,* 2 v. (London 1920); *Artistic Creation and Cosmic Creation* (London 1928); *Spinoza and Time* (London 1921); *Spinoza* (Manchester 1933); *Philosophical and Literary Pieces,* ed. J. LAIRD (London 1939), bibliog. Literature. P. DE-VAUX, *Le Système d'Alexander* (Paris 1929). M. R. KONVITZ, *On the Nature of Value: The Philosophy of Samuel Alexander* (New York 1946). A. F. LIDDELL *Alexander's Space, Time, and Deity* (Chapel Hill, N.C. 1925). J. W. MCCARTHY, *The Naturalism of Samuel Alexander* (New York 1948), bibliog.

[R. J. NOGAR]

ALEXANDER I, EMPEROR OF RUSSIA

B. St. Petersburg, Dec. 12, 1777; d. Taganrog, Nov. 19, 1825. Alexander, the son of Czar Paul I (1754–1801) and Sophia Dorothea of Württemberg, was much influenced by his Swiss tutor Frédéric Laharpe, a rationalist. Until 1812 Alexander was inclined toward deism and was also affected by traditional Russian autocracy. After succeeding to the imperial throne upon his father's assassination (1801), he relaxed some of the rigid state controls and initiated important government reforms. During the first half of his reign, Russia was involved in the Napoleonic wars. At the subsequent Congress of Vienna, Alexander I was the most powerful monarch. Influenced by Metternich, he became extremely conservative both in domestic and foreign policy after 1815.

Alexander I was deeply impressed by ROUSSEAU's adulation of humanity and envisioned a syncretistic Christianity united under his political rule. He sought unsuccessfully to have Pope PIUS VII bless the HOLY ALLIANCE. Within his own realm, he maintained a policy of tolerance toward Latin Catholics but seriously interfered with the correspondence between Rome and the bishops. He supported the scheme, originated under CATHERINE II, to make the metropolitan of Mogilev a veritable Latin patriarch for Russia, with power to nominate and to dispose bishops, to inspect and even to suppress religious houses, and to be the ultimate court of appeal in ecclesiastical cases. By the decree of Nov. 9, 1801, the Czar established the Roman Catholic Ecclesiastical College, which lacked the approval of the Holy See but regulated the affairs of the Latin Church, as the HOLY SYNOD did for the Orthodox Church. Alexander I pursued the policy of subjecting the Ruthenians to Latin jurisdiction. He expelled the JESUITS from St. Petersburg (1815) and from the empire (1820). During his reign, however, he never objected to the conversion of his courtiers to Catholicism, and he even maintained a correspondence with Madame Swetchine. At the time of Alexander's death, General Michaud, his aide–de–camp, was in Rome requesting that Pope LEO XII send a trustworthy priest to St. Petersburg. It was thought that Alexander was contemplating reunion. But he died before a papal mission could be organized. The story that Alexander became a Catholic upon his deathbed lacks foundation.

See Also: RUSSIA

Bibliography: L. I. STRAKHOVSKY, *Alexander I of Russia* (New York 1947). P. PIERLING, *La Russie et le Saint–Siège,* 5 v. (Paris 1896–1912) v.5. A. BOUDOU, *Le Saint–Siège et la Russie,* 2 v. (Paris 1922–25). M. J. ROUËT DE JOURNEL, *Nonciature d'Arezzo, 1802–1806,* 5 v. (Rome 1922–57) v.3, 4. L. KOCH, *Jesuiten–Lexikon: Die Gesellschaft Jesu einst und jetzt* (Paderborn

1934) 37–38, 1574–78. I. SMOLITSCH, *Lexikon für Theologie und Kirche*[2], ed. J. HOFER and K. RAHNER, 10 v. (2d, new ed. Freiburg 1957–65) 1:311–312.

[R. F. BYRNES]

ALEXANDER I, POPE, ST.

Pontificate: 108 or 109 to 116 or 119. Another pope with a Greek name, Alexander, was the fifth successor to Peter. Ancient lists make him successor to Evaristus. Eusebius says that he became bishop in the eighth year of Trajan's reign (*Chronicles*) and died in the third year of Hadrian (*Histoire ecclesiastique* 4.1, 5.6). Jerome says that he became bishop in the twelfth year of Trajan. These dates do not agree with Eusebius's statement (*Histoire ecclesiastique* 4.4) that Alexander reigned ten years: the Liberian catalogue says seven; the *Liber pontificalis*, ten. It also says he was a Roman, the son of an Alexander, and ascribes to him the introduction of the *Qui Pridie* into the Canon of the Mass, an arbitrary attempt to assign an early origin to a liturgical practice. The custom of blessing houses with holy water and salt was inherited from pagan practices rather than introduced by Alexander. The Roman tradition that he was decapitated and buried near Rome apparently confuses him with the Roman martyr, Alexander, whose tomb was discovered in 1855. IRENAEUS knows of no martyrdoms among Roman bishops before Telesphorus.

Feast: May 3.

Bibliography: L. DUCHESNE, *Liber pontificalis* 1:lxxxix–xcii, 54–55, 127. *Acta Sanctorum*, May 1:371–380. E. CASPER, *Geschichte des Papsttums von den anfängen bis zur Höhe der Weltherrschaft* 1:8–16. J. HALLER, *Das Papsttum* 1:18–20. A. DUFOURCQ, *Dictionnaire d'histoire et de géographie ecclésiastiques* 2:204–206. G. SCHWAIGER, *Lexicon für Theologie und Kirche*, 10 v. (2d, new ed. Freiburg 1957–65) 1:315. J. N. D. KELLY, *Oxford Dictionary of Popes* 8–9. T. VEGLIANI, ed., "Alesandro I papa (Epistolae)," *Test I patristici sul sange di Cristo* 4 (Rome 1996) 58–62.

[E. G. WELTIN]

ALEXANDER II, POPE

Pontificate: Sept. 30 to April 21, 1073; b. Anselm, son of Arderico of Baggio, in Baggio, near Milan, date unknown. Educated and ordained a priest in Milan (1055), and onetime disciple of LANFRANC at BEC (1045), he cooperated with the reform aims of the PATARINES. He was made bishop of Lucca in 1057, retaining the see as pope, and served NICHOLAS II as legate to Milan, with Cardinals Hildebrand (GREGORY VII) in 1057 and PETER DAMIAN in 1060, in support of the reform and papal au-

thority there. Disorders after the death of Nicholas II (July 27, 1061) delayed election of a successor. Upheld by Hildebrand and protected by Norman arms, Anselm was elected in Rome and enthroned without participation of the German king, whose role had been canonically recognized, if not clearly defined, in the PAPAL ELECTION DECREE OF 1059. Certain Roman civilians and dissident bishops, seconded by the German court, elected Cadalus of Parma (antipope Honorius II), who was proclaimed by the future emperor, HENRY IV, at a Basel synod, October 28, and was abandoned only after condemnation by the Council of Mantua in 1064. Despite this harassment, the reform objectives and vigorous exercise of papal authority were pressed throughout Latin Christendom, under the steadily increasing influence of Hildebrand, through a growing volume of papal correspondence and the unprecedented activity of legates: in Lombardy, France, Spain (HUGH OF REMIREMONT), England (where WILLIAM I's conquest was approved), Germany, Bohemia, Croatia-Dalmatia, and Scandinavia. Relations with the Church of CONSTANTINOPLE in 1061 and 1062 were the first since Patriarch MICHAEL CERULARIUS was excommunicated in 1054 (cf. V. Grumel, *Les Regestes des actes du patriarcat de Constantinople*). PETER OF ANAGNI was sent to Emperor Michael VII Ducas after his accession in 1071, but unhappily, ecclesiastical concord was not achieved. The Latinization of Greek sees proceeded with the Norman conquest of Byzantine territories in south Italy, in some instances in the name of reform (cf. W. Holtzmann, *Papsturkunden in England*). The reconquest of Muslim dominions, begun at this time with full papal sanction, was an important prelude to the CRUSADES (*see* SPAIN). In 1063 the pope intervened in defense of the Jews in southern France and Spain, who suffered grievously in these campaigns, and renewed the prohibition of Pope GREGORY I against their maltreatment (P. Jaffé, *Regesta pontificum romanorum ab condita ecclesia ad annum post Christum natum 1198* 4528, 4532, 4533). The claim that the territories conquered by French knights in Spain and by NORMANS in Sicily respectively were to be held of the pope in feudal tenure (*ex parte s. Petri*) rested in part on the spurious DONATION OF CONSTANTINE, in wider use from that time on. After a confident appeal to Henry IV for military aid in a conflict with the pope's Norman supporters (settled at the synod of Melfi, 1067), relations with the German court deteriorated. A dispute over the See of Milan (*see* ATTO OF MILAN) was among the causes of growing tension inherited by his successor, Gregory VII, that culminated in the INVESTITURE STRUGGLE.

Bibliography: P. JAFFÉ, *Regesta pontificum romanorum ab condita ecclesia ad annum post Christum natum 1198*, ed. S. LÖWENFELD, et al. (Graz 1956) 1:566–592. *Patrologia Latina*, ed. J. P. MIGNE (Paris 1878–90) 146:1271–1430, letters. H. K. MANN, *The Lives of the Popes in the Early Middle Ages from 590 to 1304*

(London 1902–32) 6:261–369. A. FLICHE and V. MARTIN, eds., *Histoire de l'église depuis les origines jusqu'à nos jours* (Paris 1935—) v.8. C. VIOLANTE, *La pataria milanese e la riforma ecclesiastica* (Rome 1955); *Dizionario biographico degli Italiani*, ed. A. M. GHISALBERTI (Rome 1960—) 2:176–183, both essential. V. GRUMEL, "Le Premier contact de Rome avec l'Orient après le schisme de Michel Cérulaire," *Bulletin de littérature ecclésiastique* 43 (1942) 21–29. W. HOLTZMANN, "Il Papato, i Normanni e la Chiesa greca," *Almanacco calabrese* 13 (Rome 1963) 53–66. F. BAIX, *Dictionnaire d'histoire et de géographie ecclésiastiques*, ed. A. BAUDRILLART et al. (Paris 1912—) 11:53–99. H. HOUBEN, "Die Teilnehmer der Synoden Alexanders II (1061–1073). Mit Neuedition von JL 4651," *Quellen und Forschungen aus Italienischen Archiven und Bibliotheken* (Tübingen 1997) 1–17. E. HOUTS, "The Norman Conquest Through European Eyes" *The English Historical Review* (London 1995) 832–53. J. LAUNDAGE, *Lexikon für Theologie und Kirche* 1 (1995). G. MICCOLOI, "Per la storia della pataria Milanese. Appendice: La legazione dei cardinali Mainardo e Giovanni Minuto e l'atteggiamento di Alessandro II nei confronti della pataria," *Chiesa gregoriana. Ricerche sulla Riforma del secolo XI* (Rome 1999). C. MORTON, "Pope Alexander II and the Norman Conquest," *Latomus* 34 (Bruxelles 1975) 362–82. M. POLOCK, "Zum Rechtsstreit zwischen den Bistümern Siena und Arezzo und zum sog. 'Registrum pape Alexandri' vom Monte Soratte. Ein Diskussionsbeitrag." *Archiv für Diplomatik, Schriftgeschichte, Siegelkunde und Wappenkunde* (Köln; Wein 1996). T. SCHMIDT, *Alexander II. 1061–1073 und die römische Reformgruppe seiner Zeit* (Stuttgart 1977). J. N. D. KELLY, *Oxford Dictionary of Popes* (New York 1986) 152–53.

[J. J. RYAN]

ALEXANDER III, POPE

Pontificate: Sept. 7, 1159 (consecrated and crowned at Ninfa, Sept. 20, 1159) to Aug. 30, 1181; born Rolandus, son of Ranutius (Bandinelli is a late attribution), Siena *c.*1100–05; died "of old age" at Civita Castellana; buried in St. John Lateran, in the right aisle before the pulpit. For more than a century, scholars erroneously confused the Sienese Rolandus with another Master Rolandus, probably from Modena and now identified as disciple of ABELARD, critic of St. BERNARD, teacher of canon law in Bologna and author of both the *Stroma Rolandi*, a commentary on the *Decretum* of GRATIAN, and the *Sententiae Rolandi*, a theological treatise. Little is known of the early career of the Rolandus who became pope: he studied theology and possibly canon law at Bologna but it was his subsequent high profile as a canon in Pisa that recommended him to Eugenius III for rapid promotion to curial office (?1148); cardinal deacon of SS. Cosma e Damiano (by Oct. 23, 1150); created cardinal priest of S. Marco (by March 30, 1151); legate and negotiator at the Treaty of Constance (March 23, 1153); Chancellor of the Roman Church (before May 1153). Retaining office as trusted advisor to Adrian IV, he helped to negotiate the Treaty of Benevento (June 1156) with William of Sicily and challenged Frederick Barbarossa at the Diet of Besançon (October 1157). As chancellor, together with Boso, the papal Chamberlain, he witnessed many charters (1155–59), establishing *castra specialia* throughout the patrimony and bringing the local feudal nobility under the special protection of the Holy See.

On Adrian IV's death, the cardinals' three-day deliberation at St. Peter's (Sept. 4–7, 1159) over his successor achieved a large majority for Rolandus, who took the name of Alexander III. Meanwhile, a small but vociferous minority, including cardinals Guy of S. Callisto and John of S. Martino, forcibly claimed the election for Octavian of Sta. Cecilia, named Victor IV. Boso chronicled the dramatic events of the schism in his *Vita* of Alexander, beginning with the papal conclave imprisoned for two weeks by the Roman mob in the Leonine City and Trastevere; the pope's escape, consecration and coronation at Ninfa (Sept. 20, 1159) by the cardinal bishop of Ostia; and Barbarossa's support for Victor, the anti-pope, whose consecration at Farfa (Oct. 4, 1159) was subsequently endorsed by the imperial councils of Pavia (February 1160) and Lodi (June 1161). Alexander risked danger by excommunicating Victor and his followers (March 24, 1160), but he was fortunate in being served by loyal and exceptionally able legates who won wide support for him throughout Christendom. The episcopal councils of London (June 1160) and Neufmarché (July 1160) jointly declared for Alexander at Beauvais (July 22, 1160), while Louis VII of France and Henry II of England pronounced formally in his favor at the Council of Toulouse (October 1160).

Alexander was forced to spend much of his pontificate outside Rome; his weak position requiring the exercise of consummate diplomacy, his penury forcing him to seek money gifts in order to survive. During this period, two further anti-popes were elected: Paschal III on Victor's death (April 20, 1164), and on Paschal's death (Sept. 20, 1168), Callixtus III, who was finally abandoned in 1176 by Barbarossa. Imperial hostility caused Alexander to flee the Italian peninsula to France (by April 12, 1162), where he summoned a council at Montpellier (May 15–17,1162) to remind secular rulers of their duties towards the Church. He conducted the normal business of the Curia from Sens (1163–65) and presided over an important episcopal Council at Tours (May 19, 1163), also attended by legates of the Byzantine emperor. This council recognized Alexander as the legitimate pope, not only in France and England, but also in Iberia, Hungary, Scotland and Ireland; nine new decrees were promulgated, particularly in relation to the treatment of heretical groups in Languedoc, and a long debate was held on Peter Lombard's Christology.

In November 1165, the Romans invited Alexander to return to the city, receiving him with customary honor

Pope Alexander III returns to Rome, 1177, detail of a fresco by the 15th-century artist Aretino Spinello, Palazzo della Signoria, Siena.

in an *adventus* ceremony, but within the year, just as the desperate financial situation of the Curia was beginning to improve through papal exploitation of Patrimonial revenues, Barbarossa mounted his fourth invasion of the Italian peninsula (November 1166). An imperial victory at Monteporzio (May 29, 1167) and the occupation of Monte Mario permitted the capture of St. Peter's, where Barbarossa and Beatrice, his wife, had themselves crowned by the anti-pope, Paschal III (July 30, 1167). Almost immediately, plague decimated the imperial troops and incidentally killed Rainald of Dassell, the emperor's chancellor. Alexander, who had bravely resisted the occupation of Rome, was eventually forced to escape to Benevento. At the same time, Manuel I Comnenus offered aid against Barbarossa in return for coronation as universal emperor. His offer was declined but the respective legates of both sides continued to discuss the possibility of reunion between Greek and Latin churches.

Alexander supported the anti-imperial Lombard League, whose strength lay in certain north Italian cities, and he was rewarded when the new town of Alessandria was named in his honor (1168). The League's victory at Legnano (May 29, 1176) made possible the Peace of Venice (July 24, 1177), by which Alexander's canonical election was at last recognized by Barbarossa after almost 18 years, and the emperor's excommunication withdrawn. On his return to Rome, the pope experienced a second and even more impressive *adventus* ceremony (March 12, 1178), led by clergy with banners and crosses, all chanting the papal *laudes*, and citizens bearing olive branches. Boso's *Vita* of Alexander reaches its triumphant conclusion at this point. The Peace, however, proved distasteful to a group of dissident nobles who elected Lando of Sezze as Innocent III (Sept. 29, 1179). Although this fourth anti-pope of the pontificate was rapidly dispatched to a papal fortress, Alexander left Rome, choosing to spend his last two years in the patrimony, and died in August 1181 at Civita Castellana.

The weakness of his position did not inhibit Alexander from attempting to assert papal authority. At the beginning of the crisis between Becket and Henry II (1164–70), the pope was at Sens in the kingdom of France, unable to respond vigorously either to royal threats or archiepiscopal pleas and constrained to tread a thin line between principle and compromise. Yet he conceded nothing of substance to the English king, for the Constitutions of Clarendon were not confirmed, nor was Becket deposed; instead the pope insisted on reconciliation and, through various legations, an accommodation was finally agreed after Becket's murder (Dec. 29, 1170). In 1178, Alexander had William I of Scotland (1165–1214) excommunicated and his kingdom placed under interdict for interfering in the election to the bishopric of St. Andrews and, in 1179, confirmed Count Alfonso Henriques (1139–79) as Alfonso I of Portugal (1179–85). In return, Alfonso conceded his kingdom as an apostolic fief and promised to pay an annual census.

The image of the pope exercising his legislative authority, however, was most clearly demonstrated at the Third Lateran Council (March 5–17, 1179). In the opening discourse by the famous canonist, Rufinus, bishop of Assisi, the importance of this view was stressed when he revealed that he envisaged the Council as an assembly in which the pope alone made laws for Christendom. Most important of the 27 decrees was the first, henceforth requiring a two-thirds' majority of cardinals at a papal election to avoid any future schism. Other decrees dealt with reform of the Church, action against heretics and the provision of a teacher in each cathedral school. One decree forbade anyone to demand money for the *licentia docendi* or licence to teach.

Alexander's pontificate was crucial in developing coherent rules in a number of important areas and his decisions passed into more than 700 decretals. Sixty of his marriage decretals appear in the *Liber Extra*, involving betrothal, mutual marital consent, consummation, consanguinity and legitimization. These made it possible to define as true marriage a wide variety of unions that might otherwise have remained outside the Christian community. He sought equitable solutions to situations as they arose and provided a framework for decisions that were both practical and theologically acceptable. In regard to canonization, the papacy's exclusive prerogative in this matter was becoming more generally accepted and Alexander considered no fewer than 12 cases brought before him. He made three canonizations: Edward the Confessor (Feb. 7, 1161), Thomas Becket (March 10, 1173) and Bernard of Clairvaux (Jan. 18, 1174), deliberating on the other nine candidates but giving no verdict. His decisions took the process further than ever before by requiring the presentation of detailed written evidence: the saint's *Life*, a catalogue of miracles and official letters attesting to the authenticity of both miracles and virtues.

Although his pontificate occurred at a time of considerable demoralization following the failure of the Second Crusade, Alexander was in agreement with St. Bernard that the requirement to crusade was explicable as God's test for his people and made his own considerable contribution to crusade ideology, particularly in relation to the indulgence. His encyclicals were issued to summon the faithful to crusade in the East in 1165, 1166, 1169, probably 1173 and 1181. The encyclical *Inter omnia* (July 29, 1169) was significant in referring to the crusade as the expression of God's love while *Cor nostrum* (Jan. 16, 1181) gave the crusade indulgence its mature form, its unequivocal definition being the remission of all or part of the punishment imposed by God in this world or the next. In 1171 or 1172, Alexander authorized crusading against the Finns and Estonians but offered only a limited indulgence, while his only authorization to a crusade in Iberia was made in 1175.

While unable to advance his crusade to the Holy Land, Alexander realized one project as being of equal value when he approved the mission of Henry de Marcy, abbot of Clairvaux, to the County of Toulouse in 1178, empowering him to preach there. The pope recognized the problem of rapidly spreading Catharism and the urgent need to establish a credible distinction between heresy and popular religion. Indeed, a decree of the Council of 1179 permitted bishops to levy troops and to issue indulgences as if for a crusade against the infidel. Alexander believed that the punishment of heretics should be carried out in a spirit of charity; various forms of persuasion being used to encourage their return to the Church, whether isolation, excommunication, compulsion or confiscation of goods and possessions. In 1162, in dealing with some Flemings who sought papal approval of their way of life, he warned the examining archbishop of Rheims to inquire into them and report to him, significantly preferring to risk absolving the guilty than to risk punishing the innocent. In 1179, he received Valdes, whose popular preaching and vernacular translations had brought a ban from the archbishop of Lyons. The pope approved his voluntary renunciation of property and lifestyle but refused to grant him the right to preach. Alexander, in his conciliar decrees, accepted that similar rigorous behavior by clerics was essential in order to command a fraction of the respect given to groups such as the Waldensians or the Humiliati of Lombardy, yet even he, in the last resort, was unable to keep Valdes and others within the Church.

Throughout a long and difficult pontificate, Alexander III demonstrated focused and inclusive leadership, whether as an innovator, particularly in marriage law, a determined advocate of persuasion and negotiation against excessive discipline, violence or threats, or in his 34 promotions to the cardinalate, most notably, Paolo Scolari, the future pope Clement III.

Bibliography: *Patrologia Latina*, 200: 1349–1644. J. M. WATTERICH, ed. *Pontificum Romanorum vitae* (Leipzig 1862) 2: 377–649. *Regesta Pontificum Romanorum*, ed. P. JAFFÉ and G. WATTENBACH, et al., 2 (Leipzig 1888), 145–418, 761–66. L. DUCHESNE, *Liber Pontificalis* 2: 281, 397–446. *Boso's Life of Alexander III,* trans. G. M. ELLIS & intro. P. MUNZ (Oxford 1973). *Codex constitutionum quas summi pontificium ediderunt in solemne canonizatione sanctorum a Johanne XV ad Benedictum XIII (993–1729)*, ed. G. FONTANINI, (Rome 1729) 15–23. J. M. BRIXIUS, *Die Mitglieder des Kardinalskollegiums 1130–1181* (Berlin 1912), 56–57, 112. B. ZENKER, *Die Mitglieder des Kardinalskollegiums 1130–1159* (Würzburg 1964), 85–88. V. ERMONI, ''Alexandre III'', *Dictionnaire d'histoire et de géographie ecclésiastiques,* ed. A. BAUDRILLAT et al. (Paris 1912–) 1:208–14. G. MORIN, ''Le discours d'ouverture du Concile general de Latran (1179) et l'oeuvre littéraire de Maître Rufin, évêque d'Assisi'', *Atti della pontificia Accademia romana di Archeologia,* 3 series, *Memorie,* 2 (1928). S. KUTTNER, 'La réserve papale du droit de canonisation', *Revue historique de droit français et étranger,* 4th ser., 18 (1938), 172–228. E. KEMP, *Canonization and Authority in the Western Church* (London 1948). W. ULLMANN, ''Cardinal Roland and Besançon'', *Miscellanea Historiae Pontificiae* 18 (1954) 107–125. M. PACAUT, *Alexandre III* (Paris 1956). R. MONTINI, *Le tombe dei papi* (Rome 1957), 200–203. P. BREZZI, ''Alessandro III, papa'', *Dizionario Biografico degli Italiani,* 2 (Rome 1960) 183–189. M. BALDWIN, *Alexander III and the Twelfth Century* (Baltimore 1966). M. G. CHENEY, ''The Recognition of Pope Alexander III: Some Neglected Evidence'', *English Historical Review,* 84 (1969), 474–497. B. BOLTON, ''Tradition and Temerity: Papal Attitudes to Deviants, 1159–1216,'' *Studies in Church History,* 9; *Schism, Heresy and Religious Protest,* (Cambridge 1972), 79–91. P. TOUBERT, *Les structures du Latium médiéval. Le Latium méridional et la Sabine du ix siècle à la fin du xii siècle,* 2 vols (Rome 1973). C. DONAHUE JR., ''The Policy of Alexander the Third's Consent Theory of Marriage'', *Proceedings of the Fourth International Congress of Medieval Canon Law,* ed. S. KUTTNER (Vatican City 1976), 251-281. J. T. NOONAN JR., ''Who was Rolandus?'' *Law, Church and Society: Essays in Honor of Stephan Kuttner,* eds. K. PENNINGTON and R. SOMERVILLE (Philadephia 1977), 21–48. R. SOMERVILLE, *Pope Alexander III and the Council of Tours (1163)* (Berkeley 1977). W. MADERTONER, *Die zweispältige Papstwahl des Jahres 1159* (Vienna 1978). R. WEIGAND, ''*Magister Rolandus* und Papst Alexander III,'' *Archiv für Katholisches Kirchenrecht,* 149 (1980), 3–44. *Miscellanea Rolando Bandinelli: Papa Alessandro III,* ed. F. LIOTTA (Siena 1986); R. FOREVILLE, ''Alexandre III et la canonization des Saints,'' ibid., 217–235. *Decrees of the Ecumenical Councils. Volume I, Nicea to Lateran V,* ed., N. J. TANNER, original text established by G. ALBERIGO et al. (London & Georgetown 1990), 205–225. J. LAUDAGE, ''Alexander III.'', *Lexikon für Theologie und Kirche,* II (Freiburg 1994), cols. 367–368. P. BREZZI and A. PIAZZA, ''Alessandro III'', *Enciclopedia dei Papi* (Rome 2000) 2: 291–298. A. DUGGAN, *The Correspondence of Thomas Becket, Archbishop of Canterbury, 1162–1170,* 2 v., Oxford Medieval Texts (Oxford 2000). S. TWYMAN, *Papal Ceremonial at Rome in the Twelfth Century,* Henry Bradshaw Society Subsidia (Woodbridge 2002).

[B. M. BOLTON]

ALEXANDER IV, POPE

Pontificate: Dec. 12, 1254 to May 25, 1261; b. Rainaldo dei Conti di Segni. His illustrious family had produced two earlier popes, INNOCENT III and GREGORY IX. He was named cardinal deacon (1227) by his uncle, Gregory IX, and became cardinal bishop of Ostia in 1231. Although by nature devout and peaceful, Alexander IV nevertheless prosecuted the war begun by his predecessor, INNOCENT IV, against the heirs of Emperor FREDERICK II in Germany, Italy, and Sicily. He allocated Sicily to Alfonso of Castile, and Conradin's heritage he assigned to Edmund, son of Henry III of England. Alexander spent much of his pontificate outside Rome, because of the GUELF–GHIBELLINE struggles in central Italy and Manfred's war against the STATES OF THE CHURCH. During the interregnum in Germany, Alexander at first supported the claims of William of Holland to the imperial throne; after 1257 he switched his support to Richard of Cornwall. In negotiations with the Byzantine Emperor Theodore II Lascaris, Alexander attempted to reunite the Greek and Latin Churches. In Cyprus he successfully settled the rival claims of the two churches. In Syria he made the head of the recently reconciled Maronites patriarch of Antioch. A patron of the FRANCISCANS, Alexander restored to them many privileges that his predecessor had suppressed. He died at Viterbo and is buried in the cathedral.

Bibliography: ALEXANDER IV, *Les Registres,* ed. C. BOUREL DE LA RONCIÈRE et al., 3 v. (Paris 1902–53). A. POTTHAST, *Regesta pontificum romanorum inde ab a. 1198 ad a. 1304* (Graz 1957) 2:1286–1473, 2124–29. F. TENCKHOFF, *Papst Alexander IV* (Paderborn 1907). J. HALLER, *Das Papsttum* (Stuttgart 1950–53) 4:272–296. G. SCHWAIGER, *Lexikon für Theologie und Kirche,* ed. J. HOFER and K. RAHNER (Freiburg 1957–65) 1:316–317. M. GROTEN, ''Konrad von Hochstaden und die Wahl Richards von Cornwall,'' in *Kön. Stadt und Bistum in Kirche und Reich des Mittelalters. Festschrift für Odilo Engels zum 65 Gebürstag* (Böhlau 1993) 483–510. H.-E. HILPERT, ''Richard of Cornwall's Candidacy for the German Throne and the Christmas 1256 at Westminister,'' *Journal of Medieval History* 6 (Amsterdam 1980) 185–98. F. A. C. MANTELLO, ''Letter CXXX of Bishop Robert Grosseteste: A Problem of Attribution,'' *Medieval Studies* 56 (Toronto 1974) 14–59. J. N. D. KELLY, *Oxford Dictionary of Popes* (New York 1986) 194.

[J. A. BRUNDAGE]

ALEXANDER V, ANTIPOPE (PETER OF CANDIA)

Pontificate (Pisan obedience): June 26, 1409–May 3, 1410. A Greek, he was born Peter Philarghus (Petros Phalargis) *c.* 1340 in the northern part of Crete (i.e., Candia, thus his more widely known name, Peter of Candia). Orphaned at an early age, Peter was raised by a Capuchin friar who gave him an elementary education; he died in Bologna on May 3, 1410. Peter joined the Franciscans *c.* 1357 and studied in Padua and Norwich. He received his bachelor of theology degree from Oxford, and taught in Franciscan houses in Russia, Bohemia, and Poland. In 1381, he received his doctorate of theology from Paris, and by the middle 1380s he was in Italy at the court of

Gian Galeazzo Visconti. Over the next three decades, with the patronage of Visconti, Peter held a chair of theology at Pavia, and became bishop of Piacenza (1386), Vicenza (1388), and Novara (1389); he was eventually named archbishop of Milan in 1402. In the midst of this ecclesiastical activity, in 1395 he obtained for Visconti the title duke of Milan from the German king Wenceslas (1378–1400).

From his days in Paris, Peter allied himself with the Roman obedience in the Great Schism (1378–1417), and in 1405 Pope Innocent VII (1404–06) named him cardinal priest of SS. Apostoli and papal legate to Lombardy. Innocent died the following year and was succeeded by Pope Gregory XII, who showed little interest in ending the 26-year-old schism. As a result, Peter approved of those cardinals who were slowly distancing themselves from Gregory's curia; he also encouraged England to take a neutral position regarding the schism, in effect a withdrawal of obedience to Gregory. Because of this Gregory removed Peter as archbishop of Milan and rescinded his cardinalate. In May 1408, after the antipope Benedict XIII lost his French support and Gregory had created four new cardinals (considered a sign that he did not intend to end the schism), all but seven of Gregory's cardinals left for Pisa. At this point Peter (along with Baldassare Cossa, later antipope John XXIII) became one of the leading voices for the *via concilis* (i.e., that a council of the entire church should decide the legitimate pope). He was among the primary organizers of the Council of Pisa (1409); delivered its opening address; secured English, Bohemian, and much German support for the council; and presided at the sessions that declared Benedict XIII and Gregory XII heretics. Peter was then unanimously elected pope (June 26, 1409) after a pledge to keep the council in session until church reform was complete. He took the name Alexander V.

Alexander's authority as pope was problematic from the start. Although he had wide support (France, England, Bohemia, the eastern Empire, and northern and central Italy), each of the supposedly deposed popes still had a limited degree of recognition. Furthermore, Alexander was not in Rome; the city was occupied by King Ladislaus of Durazzo-Naples (1386–1414), who recognized Gregory XII. Finally, in the eyes of some, Alexander did not encourage the church reform he had promised at Pisa. In the first weeks of his papacy, several of the bishoprics and benefices he named went to Franciscans who received the offices to the detriment of local parish clergy, canons, and various university faculties. On July 1, 1490 Alexander ratified and published the decrees of the council, and on August 7 he dissolved it, announcing that a new council would meet in three years. While some saw these policies as legitimate attempts to solidify his power base in order to then end the Great Schism, Alexander's moves appeared to many as directly opposed to church reform. Either way he had broken the letter of his oath to keep the council in session.

In an effort to regain Rome (and thus weaken Gregory), Alexander excommunicated Ladislaus and invested Louis II of Anjou as king of Naples. Louis captured Rome in the name of the Pisan obedience in January 1410. For some reason, probably due to pressure from Baldassare Cossa (whom many contemporaries and modern scholars consider an opportunist), Alexander stayed in Bologna, even after a delegation from Rome pleaded with him to come to the city (Feb. 2, 1410). Alexander died suddenly in Bologna three months later (May 3). Rumors that Cossa, who would become Alexander's successor, had poisoned the antipope circulated immediately and the charge (now largely considered false) was even brought before the Council of Constance. Alexander was buried in the church of St. Francis in Bologna. His tomb was restored in 1889 at the direction of Leo XIII.

Peter of Candia/Alexander V remains a controversial figure. He appears to have been a serious Franciscan and was considered a fine theologian and teacher. His works include a *Principia*, treatises on the immaculate conception, and a well-regarded commentary on Peter Lombard's *Sentences* (which he taught in Paris). His theology was nominalist in approach and has received renewed interest for its place in the development of late medieval thought and the schools. Peter's successful career with Visconti indicates real diplomatic and administrative ability, but he clearly had more mixed results within the ecclesiastical world as Alexander V. Contemporaries like Jean Gerson, and near-contemporaries like Platina and Giles of Viterbo viewed him with some respect. Alexander's greatest liability may have been his early death. He was pope long enough to make many enemies (e.g., on Oct. 12, 1409 he promulgated a bull that broadly extended the right to preach and hear confession to the mendicant orders; this turned many secular clergy against him), but not so long as to end the schism or accomplish any church reform he might have envisioned.

Bibliography: L. DUCHESNE, ed. *Liber Pontificalis* (Paris 1886–92; repr. 1955–57) 2.536. B. PLATINA, *De vita Christi ac omnium pontificum* 212 (207) ed. G. GAIDA, in *Rerum italicarum scriptores* 3.1, ed. L. A. MURATORI (Città di Castello and Bologna 1913–32). L. WADDING, *Scripores Ordinis Minorum* (Lyons 1625–54; Rome 1731–1886; Quaracchi-Florence 1931) 9.221–245, 406–412, 623–27. F. EHRLE, *Der Sentenzenkommentar Peters von Candia, des Pisaner Papstes Alexanders V* (Münster 1925). PETER OF CANDIA, *Petri de Candia (Alexandri V Papa) Tractatus de immaculata Deiparae conceptione*, A. EMMEN, ed. (Florence 1955). A. B. EMDEN, *A Biographical Register of the University of Oxford to AD 1500* (Oxford 1957) 1.345–46. M. CREIGHTON, *A History of the Papacy from the Great Schism to the Sack of Rome* (London 1897;

New York 1969) v. 1. E. WILSON, *The Life and Obligationes of Petrus de Candia* (New York, diss. St. Bonaventure Univ. 1956). A. BUSIO, *Ricerche su Pietro Filargo, Alessandro V* (thesis, Universita' Cattolica del Sacro Cuore 1959). A. PETRUCCI, *Dizionario biografico degli Italiani* (Rome 1960) 2.193–6. J. SMITH, *The Great Schism, 1378: The Disintegration of the Papacy* (New York 1970). S. F. BROWN, ''Peter of Candia's Sermons in Praise of Peter Lombard,'' in *Studies Honoring Ignatius Charles Brady* (St. Bonaventure 1976) 141–76. J.N.D. KELLY, *The Oxford Dictionary of Popes* (New York 1986) 236–37. W. J. COURTENAY, *Schools and Scholars in Fourteenth-Century England* (Princeton 1987). S. F. BROWN, ''Peter of Candia's Hundred-Year History of the Theologian's Role,'' *Medieval Philosophy and Theology* 1 (1991) 156–90. T. E. MORRISEY, ''The Humanist and the Franciscan: A Letter of Giovanni Conversino da Ravenna to Peter Philargus,'' *Franciscan Studies* 52 (1992) 183–89. C. SCHABEL, ''Peter of Candia and the Prelude to the Quarrel at Louvain,'' in *Annual Review of the Cyprus Research Centre* (Nicosia 1998) 87–124.

[P. M. SAVAGE]

ALEXANDER VI, POPE

Pontificate: night of Aug. 10–11, 1492, to Aug. 18, 1503; b. Rodrigo de Borja y Doms (Borgia) in Játiva (Xátiva), Valencia, Spain, *c.* 1431; d. Rome. His uncle, Pope CALLISTUS III, showered him with ecclesiastical benefices, sent him to study law in Bologna (1455), and, along with his cousin Lluís-Joan del Milà, made him a cardinal (Feb. 22, 1456). He was bishop of Valencia (June 30, 1458) and vice chancellor of the Church under popes Callistus III, PIUS II, PAUL II, SIXTUS IV, and INNOCENT VIII, even though his private life brought stern rebukes from Pius II. [*See* BORGIA (BORJA).] A man of great political talent, he was elected pope in the conclave of Aug. 6–11, 1492, employing a form of simony. Ruling in an era of turbulence for Italy and the papacy, before 1498, he pursued a papal, Italian, and family policy that differed from his course of action during the last five years of his pontificate.

Italian Policy before 1498. Until 1498 he strove to consolidate the Italian league, dear to Callistus. This league with Venice and Milan, joined eventually by Siena, Ferrara, and Mantua, was made public April 25, 1493. Then, threatened with an invasion of Italy by King Charles VIII of France, Alexander sealed a treaty of friendship with Alfonso II of Naples through marriage of Alfonso's daughter, Sancha of Aragon, with Jofré Borja; the couple received the principality of Squillace from Alfonso. Alexander gained the support of King Ferdinand V (II of Aragon) and Queen ISABELLA I OF CASTILE by the marriage of Joan (Juan) Borja, Duke of Gandia, to María Enríquez, first cousin of Ferdinand, and by granting the famous bulls that regulated Castilian and Portuguese conquests in America and granted the PATRONATO REAL over all new churches in the Americas.

When Charles VIII invaded Italy with the support of Ludovico el Moro of Milan and the approval of Florence, Alexander was forced to give him free passage for the expedition, in which Charles conquered the Kingdom of Naples (February 1495). Charles entered Rome on Dec. 31, 1494. But eventually papal troops and the *condottiere* Virginio ORSINI drove the French and their allies out of Italy. After the battle of Fornovo (July 6, 1495) and the retreat of Charles to France, Alexander continued his policy of alliance with Spain (he granted the sovereigns the title ''Catholic'' in 1496), and with Naples. He sent his son, Cesare Borja, who he had made a cardinal in 1493, as cardinal-legate for the coronation of Frederick III of Naples in 1497 and arranged the marriage of his daughter, Lucrezia (whose first marriage with Giovanni SFORZA, Lord of Pesaro, he had annulled as unconsummated) with Alfonso of Aragon, Duke of Bisceglie and brother of the above-mentioned Sancha. It was during these years (1495–98) that Alexander was engaged in his struggle with Girolamo SAVONAROLA, who, after his excommunication, was tried and condemned by the government of Florence, then in the hands of his enemies, the *arrabbiati*.

French-Papal Alliance. In 1497 Alexander planned serious plans for the reform of the Church, but his irregular life and the ambitions of Cesare, who resigned the cardinalate in 1498 and took up politics in a practical way, frustrated his good intentions. In preferring Cesare's marriage to Charlotte d'Albret rather than Naples' Carlotta of Aragon, Alexander initiated his new policy in which he relied more on Louis XII of France. It was further characterized by the abandonment of the Kingdom of Naples to its fate, and by the plan to unify the Romagna, Emilia, Umbria, and the Marches, the four feudatories (at least nominally) of the Holy See. Cesare, then Duke of Valentinois, accompanied Louis XII in the occupation of Milan (1499), and later undertook the conquest of central Italy, a campaign comparable to that waged by Alexander in Rome against the feudal nobility (Orsini and COLONNA). The Renaissance plan for greater cohesion in the STATES OF THE CHURCH shows Alexander's political ability, but its execution is open to serious criticism, e.g., the excesses of Cesare and his troops, the danger of a greater separation of central Italy from Rome under Cesare, and the open support of a French king who, after conquering Milan, aspired to Naples as well. Although Cesare's rule of the Romagna vanished with the pope's death, and feudal anarchy returned, the later conquests of Pope JULIUS II and his reorganization of the States of the Church were made possible by the internal collapse of those provinces in the wake of Cesare's conquests. Amid such fighting, however, the HOLY YEAR OF 1500 could still be celebrated with splendor.

"Pope Alexander VI," detail of the *"Resurrection"* fresco by Pinturicchio, 1492–1494, in the Borgia rooms of the Vatican Palace.

After fruitless talks in Rome with ambassadors of various European states, Alexander—as had his uncle Callistus III—published a bull proclaiming a crusade against the OTTOMAN TURKS (June 10, 1500). But only Venice and Spain took part, conquering the islands of Cephalonia and Leukas. On the excuse that Frederick III of Naples was intriguing with the Turks, Louis XII and Ferdinand of Aragon and Castile divided his Neapolitan kingdom by the Treaty of Granada (Nov. 11, 1500). When the two kings disputed over the border, Alexander sided with Louis, for whom Cesare campaigned in Naples. During Cesare's domination of central Italy, Lucrezia married (1501) Alfonso d' ESTE, firstborn of Ercole I, Duke of Ferrara, as a guarantee of the independence of the duchies.

Evaluation. In August 1503 Alexander and Cesare both fell ill during an epidemic in Rome. The pope died after confessing and receiving Viaticum and Extreme Unction. Despite his dissipated life, both as cardinal and pope, Alexander can be credited with several achievements during his pontificate. Better educated and more refined than Callistus III, he entrusted the decoration of the main floor of the VATICAN palace to Pinturiccio, restored the Castel Sant' Angelo, and provided a new building for the University of Rome. Michelangelo created his Pietà for Alexander, and drafted plans for rebuilding St. Peter's Basilica. The Monumental Apostolic chancery palace was built during his pontificate.

In the evangelization of the New World, his actions conformed to the best papal traditions: he promoted the re-Christianization of GREENLAND, supported Portuguese missionary work, and with his ALEXANDRINE bulls, ensured peace between Portugal and Castile in both the Far East and the Americas, as well as the spread of the Gospel. (*See* PAPAL LINE OF DEMARCATION.) Criticism of the bulls has, perhaps, not always taken into account the political rights claimed by popes from the Middle Ages or the interplay of ecclesiastical, papal, and family policies involved in their concession. Alexander's piety seems to have been more sincere than his life would indicate. Still, any overall judgment of him and his pontificate from an ecclesiastical and religious point of view remains negative, even though his enemies have often calumniated him through exaggeration. Recent uncritical excesses of those seeking naively to vindicate him have provoked a reaction, frequently as unrestrained as that of the revisionists.

Bibliography: Sources. O. RAYNALDUS, *Annales ecclesiastici,* ed. J. D. MANSI, 15 v. (Lucca 1747–56) 11:208–416. *Bullarium Romanum* (Magnum), ed. H. MAINARDI and C. COCQUELINES (Rome 1733–62), v. 5. A. DE LA TORRE, ed., *Documentos sobre relaciones internacionales de los Reyes Católicos,* 4 v. (Barcelona 1949–62). J. FERNÁNDEZ ALONSO, *Legaciones y nunciaturas en España de 1466 a 1521,* 2 v. (Rome 1963–66). For further source material, *see* BORGIA. Literature. L. PASTOR, *The History of the Popes From the Close of the Middle Ages* (London–St. Louis 1938–61) v. 5, 6. M. GIMÉNEZ FERNÁNDEZ, "Las bulas alejandrinas de 1493 referentes alas Indias," *Anuario de estudios americanos* 1 (1944) 171–387. G. SORANZO, *Studi intorno a papa Alessandro VI (Borgia)* (Milan 1950); *Il tempo di Alessandro VI papa e di Fra Girolamo Savonarola* (Milan 1960). G. B. PICOTTI, in *Rivista di storia della Chiesa in Italia* (Rome 1951) 5:169–262; 8 (1954) 313–355. A. M. ALBAREDA, "Il vescovo di Barcellona Pietro Garsias bibliotecario della Vaticana sotto Alessandro VI," *La bibliofilia* 60 (1958) 1–18. A. GARCÍA GALLO, "Las bulas de Alejandro VI y el ordenamiento jurídico de la expansión portuguesa y castellana en Africa e Indias," *Anuario de historia del derecho español* 27–28 (1957–58) 461–829. C. M. DE WITTE, "Les Bulles pontificales et l'expansion portugaise au XVᵉ siècle," *Revue d'histoire ecclésiastique* (Louvain 1958) 53: 443–471. P. DE LETURIA, *Relaciones entre la Santa Sede e Hispanoamérica,* 3 v. (*Analecta Gregoriana* [Rome 1930–] 101–103; 1959–60), v.1. M. BATLLORI, *Alejandro VI y la casa real de Aragón, 1492–1498* (Madrid 1958); *Estudis d'història i de cultura catalanes,* v.2 *L'humanisme i els Borja* (Rome). *At the Court of the Borgia, Being an Account of the Reign of Pope Alexander VI Written by . . . Johann Burchard,* ed. and tr. G. PARKER (Folio Society; London 1963). M. MALLET, *The Borgias* (London 1981). H. MARC-BONNET, *Le Papes de la Renaissance, 1447–1527* (Paris 1969).

[M. BATLLORI]

ALEXANDER VII, POPE

Pontificate: April 7, 1655, to May 22, 1667; b. Fabio Chigi, Siena, Feb. 13, 1599. The Sienese Chigi family had been prominent since the Middle Ages. Fabio was a brilliant boy, given to writing verses; for nine years he studied philosophy, law, and theology at the University of Siena, receiving his doctorate in theology in 1626. After two years more of private study at Rome, where he became acquainted with a number of intellectual leaders, Chigi entered the papal service. He rose steadily from a referendary in 1629 to vice-legate of Ferrara, bishop of Nardo in 1635, and apostolic visitor to Malta. When appointed a bishop he became a priest. His diplomatic ability was to receive a sterner test when Urban VIII sent him to troubled Germany. He spent thirteen years as nuncio to Cologne (1639–51), and also served as the pope's representative at the Peace Conference of Münster. This was a most difficult task and if Chigi did not bring about the success of the papal policy, he did win the esteem of the pope and Curia. Innocent X made him secretary of state in 1651 and a year later he received the red hat. The Conclave of 1655 that followed the death of Innocent X was a long one—January 17 to April 7. Upon election Chigi took the name Alexander VII in memory of the great twelfth-century pope, ALEXANDER III. Alexander suffered from poor health, but he was a hard worker. He was charitable to the poor and was a great help to his people in the plague of 1656. He encouraged scholarship and aided the work of historians by setting up sensible regulations for the use of archival materials. A splendid patron of the arts, Alexander is remembered for commissioning the construction of the great colonnade of Bernini.

Alexander and Louis XIV maintained poor relations, and the king went to some pains to humiliate the pope over a clash between Alexander's Corsican guards and the French embassy. But this was not all the trouble Louis caused Alexander. The pope tried hard to help beleaguered Christians beat back the Turks, but Louis XIV, more interested in weakening the Hapsburgs, did not cooperate; thus, papal plans foundered on Bourbon ambitions. Alexander's relations with Venice were better, and he persuaded the Republic to have the Jesuits, who were earlier expelled, return.

Like his predecessors, Alexander was forced to take action against the Jansenists. Innocent X had condemned the Five Propositions, but then Antoine ARNAULD, the great Jansenist leader, decided that while the Five Propositions were indeed wrong, and one could accept the pope's condemnation of them, they were not to be found in Cornelius JANSEN'S *AUGUSTINUS*. Alexander countered by a bull in which he said that the Five Propositions were contained in Jansen's *Augustinus* and condemned Jansen's presentation of them.

Alexander welcomed the illustrious convert, Christina, Queen of Sweden, and gently corrected some of her odd ideas. He encouraged foreign missions allowing the Jesuits in China to utilize Chinese rites, and gave increased power to the Congregation for the Propagation of the Faith.

Bibliography: L. PASTOR, *The History of the Popes From the Close of the Middle Ages* (London-St. Louis 1938–61):1–313. A. L. ARTAUD DE MONTOR, *The Lives and Times of the Popes*, 10 v. (New York 1910–11) 6:71–106. N. J. ABERCROMBIE, *The Origins of Jansenism*, (Oxford 1936). *Bullarium Romanum* (Magnum), ed. H. MAINARDI and C. COCQUELINES, 18 folio v. (Rome 1733–62), v.16–17. J. ORCIBAL, *Les Origines du jansénisme*, 5 v. (Louvain 1947–62). K. REPGEN, *Lexikon für Theologie und Kirche*, ed. J. HOFER and K. RAHNER, 10 v. (2d, new ed. Freiburg 1957–65) 1:318. H. HEMMER, *Dictionnaire de théologie catholique*, ed. A. VACANT et al., 15 v. (Paris 1903–50; Tables générales 1951–) 1.1:727–747. R. KRAUTHEIMER, *The Rome of Alexander VII* (Princeton 1985). E. CROPPER, *Florence and Rome from Grand Duke Ferdinand I to Pope Alexander VII* (Bologna 1992).

[J. S. BRUSHER]

ALEXANDER VIII, POPE

Oct. 6, 1689, to Feb. 1, 1691; b. Pietro Vito Ottoboni, Venice, April 22, 1610. Descendant of a noble Venetian family; his father Marco was chancellor of Venice. Pietro showed brilliance in his studies and at 17 won a doctorate in civil and Canon Law at the University of Padua. In 1630 he went to Rome and was made governor of Terni, Rieti, and Spoleto and auditor of the Rota (1643–42). Innocent X named him cardinal in 1652 and bishop of Brescia in 1654. He returned to Rome in 1664 and, under Innocent XI, he became grand inquisitor of Rome and secretary of the Holy Office. When elected pope in 1689, Alexander was an octogenarian. He used the 18 months of his pontificate to diminish the tensions with France, and in a mood of conciliation brought LOUIS XIV to restore Avignon, seized during the reign of INNOCENT XI, and to renounce the privilege of diplomatic residence. He did not give way, however, on the four articles of the ASSEMBLY OF THE FRENCH CLERGY of 1682 (Gallican Articles). In the bull *Inter multiplices,* signed Aug. 4, 1690, but promulgated just two days before his death, he declared them null and invalid. His improved relations with France decreased his friendship with Emperor Leopold I, who recalled his ambassador from the Vatican court and refused to receive the papal chargé d'affaires in Vienna. He was interested also in a possible Stuart restoration in England and established a group to study English affairs. His reign was conspicuous for generous aid to Venice in the Turkish wars, for excessive nepotism, and for his patronage of the Vatican Library. He is also remembered for his condemnation of 31 Jansenist propositions (Denzinger 2301–32), certain errors about the so-called philosophical sin (Denzinger 2290–93), and errors about the love of God (Denzinger 2311–13, 15).

Bibliography: H. DENZINGER, *Enchiridion symbolorum*, A. SCHÖMETZER (32d. ed. Freiburg 1963). L. PASTOR, *The History of the Popes from the Close of the Middle Ages,* (London-St. Louis 1938–61) 32:530–560. P. RICHARD, *Dictionnaire d'histoire et de géographie ecclésiastiques*, ed. A. BAUDRILLAT et al. (Paris 1912–) 2:243–251. X. M. LE BACHELET, *Dictionnaire de théologie catholique*, ed. A. VACANT et al., 15 v. (Paris 1903–50; Tables générales 1951–) 1:747–763. G. A. HANOTAUX, *Recueil des instructions données aux ambassadeurs et ministres de France*, 3 v. (Paris 1888–1913). *Bullarium Romanum* (Magnum), ed. H. MAINARDI and C. COCQUELINES, 18 folio v. (Rome 1733–62) 20:1–167. L. COGNET, *Le Jansenisme* (Paris 1961). J. DULUMEAU, *Catholicism between Luther and Voltaire* (London 1977).

[S. V. RAMGE]

ALEXANDER NECKHAM

Augustinian theologian, scientist, and poet (also spelled Neckam; nicknamed *Nequam*, meaning worthless); b. Sept. 13, 1157, St. Alban's, Herefordshire, England; d. March 31, 1217, Kempsey, Worcestershire. He studied arts at Paris, probably between 1175 and 1182, and taught at Dunstable (*c.* 1182) and St. Alban's (*c.* 1183–90). Having studied theology at Oxford between 1190 and 1197, he entered the Order of the Augustinian

Canons about 1200. He acted as papal judge delegate (1203 and 1205), and became abbot of Cirencester in 1213. His works include *De nominibus utensilium; Novus Aesopus* and *Novus Avianus; Super Marcianum de nuptilis Mercurii et Philosophiae; Repertorium vocabulorum Bibliae; De naturis rerum libri duo (Rerum Britannicarum medii aevi scriptores* 34:1–354); *Commentarius in Ecclesiastem* (cf. Stegmüller 2:1172); *Commentarius in Canticum; Corrogationes novi Promethei*, or *Summa super Bibliam; De laudibus divinae sapientiae (Rerum Britannicarum medii aevi scriptores* 34:357–503); *Glossae in Psalterium; Commentarius in Parabolas Salomonis; Speculum speculationum; Quaestiones de rebus theologicis; Sacerdos ad altare*; as well as some sermons. Alexander, as a typical exponent of encyclopedic learning in medieval England, influenced later English thought, particularly that of the poet, Edmund SPENSER [cf. *Studies in Philology* 22 (1925) 222–225]. His works display considerable erudition, including knowledge of the natural sciences. His prestige may be judged from the fact that his change of opinion in favor of the celebration of the Virgin Mary's conception [*English Historical Review* 47 (1932) 260–268] was influential in spreading that feast in England [cf. *Franziskanische Studien* 39 (1957) 115, 179].

Bibliography: F. M. POWICKE, "Alexander of S. Albans," *Essays in History Presented to Reginald Lane Poole* (London 1927) 246–260. H. KANTOROWICZ, "A Medieval Grammarian on the Sources of Law," *Tijdschrift voor rechtsgeschiedenis* 15 (1937) 25–47. P. W. DAMON, "A Note on the Neckham Canon," *Speculum* 32 (1957) 99–102. F. STEGMÜLLER, *Repertorium biblicum medii aevi* 2:1158–72. *Lexikon für Theologie und Kirche* ² 1:308. A. B. EMDEN, *A Biographical Register of the University of Oxford to A.D. 1500* 2:1342–43.

[A. EMMEN]

ALEXANDER NEVILLE

Archbishop of York, bishop of Saint Andrews; b. *c.* 1332; d. May 16, 1392. Having studied at Oxford by 1348–49, he was a master of arts by 1357 and a scholar of civil law by 1361. He became master of the hospital of St. Thomas the Martyr at Bolter–in–Allendale, Northumbria, that year, and he was made archbishop of YORK in 1374. A clerk of King Edward III by 1361, he was a royal curialist from 1386 when he became a member of Parliament's continual council under King Richard II. As such he was involved in the crisis of 1387–88 that issued in the Merciless Parliament of 1388. Neville supported the king; hence the chronicler Knighton described him as one of the *nephandi seductores regis*. A bitter opponent of the chief Lord Appellant, Thomas, Duke of Gloucester, he was four times appealed of high treason: at a pre-liminary meeting of the Appellants at Waltham Cross on Nov. 14, 1387; before Richard at Westminster on Nov. 17, 1387; before Richard in the Tower of London on Dec. 28 or 29, 1387; in Parliament on Feb. 3, 1388. He was found guilty of treason and his property and temporalities were declared forfeit. Neville's life was spared, but Pope Urban VI translated him from the archbishopric of York to the Diocese of Saint Andrews, Scotland, at the Appellants' request (bull of translation, April 30, 1388). But since Scotland did not recognize Pope Urban (*see* WESTERN SCHISM), Neville sought refuge in Louvain. He is buried in the church of the Carmelites, Louvain, Belgium.

Bibliography: W. HUNT, *The Dictionary of National Biography From the Earliest Times to 1900*, 63 v. (London 1885–1900) 14:243–244. T. F. TOUT, *Chapters in the Administrative History of Mediaeval England*, 6 v. (New York 1920–33). A. B. STEEL, *Richard II* (Cambridge, Eng. 1941; repr. 1963). M. MCKISACK, *The Fourteenth Century* (Oxford 1959).

[V. MUDROCH]

ALEXANDER NEVSKI

Grand Duke of Vladimir and Kiev, 1252 to Nov. 19, 1263; b. May 30, 1220. The son of Grand Duke Yaroslav II, Alexander proved to be the most outstanding of the Russian princes at the beginning of the Mongol domination of Russia. His father made him Prince of Novgorod in 1228, and from there Alexander witnessed the conquest of Russia by the Mongol armies of Batu Khan (1237–42). The mongol invasion completely destroyed the southern part of Russia (Kiev and Chernigov) and a great part of east Russia (Riazan); but northern Russia, centered around Novgorod, was protected by swamps and woodland and fared better, becoming the pivot of consolidation for whatever survived the Mongol disaster. On the western borders of Novgorod Alexander was eminently successful in repulsing the attacks of Swedes, Lithuanians, and the Livonian Knights—it was his victory over the Swedes on the Neva River that gained him the surname Nevski (of the Neva). Recognizing, however, the hopelessness of any open resistance to the overwhelming power of the MONGOLS, Alexander remained a loyal vassal of the Mongol Empire, and discouraged all insubordination and rebellion; he was thus able to reduce further Mongol ravages and to protect his people. He journeyed to the court of the Great Khan in Mongolia and to the Golden Horde, settling disputes and pleading the cause of his country. In 1252 the Great Khan appointed him Grand Duke of Vladimir and Kiev and thus the senior Russian Prince. He is venerated as a saint in the Russian Church.

Feast: Nov. 23 and Aug. 30.

Bibliography: V. O. KLÎUCHEVSKIĬ, *A History of Russia,* tr. C. J. HOGARTH, 5 v. (New York 1911–31) v.1. A. PALMIERI, *Dictionnaire d'histoire et de géographie ecclésiastiques,* ed. A. BAUDRILLART et al. (Paris 1912—) 2:261–262. N. DE BAUMGARTEN, "Généalogies des branches régnantes des Rurikides du XIIIe au XVI e siècle," *Orientalia Christiana* 35 (1934) 5–150.

[O. P. SHERBOWITZ–WETZOR]

ALEXANDER OF ABONOTEICHOS

Founder and prophet of a pagan oracle and mystery cult in Paphlagonia, Asia Minor, *c.* A.D. 105–175. Except for a few coins of Lucius Verus and Marcus Aurelius, and inscriptions attesting the fact of his existence, our knowledge of him comes from a bitterly antagonistic biography by Lucian of Samosata called *Alexander the False Prophet.* The Alexander ambiguously mentioned by Athenagoras in his *Embassy for the Christians* (*Ancient Christian Writers,* ed. J. H. Crehan, 23:65–66, 157) may be the same man, although the identity is disputed. As a youth he consorted with a healer who was a disciple of the philosopher Apollonius of Tyana. Later he conspired with a charlatan named Cocconas to found an oracle and begin a cult.

At Chalcedon Alexander invented several prophecies to the effect that the god Asclepius or Aesculapius, the son of Apollo, would become incarnate at Abonoteichos and that Alexander would be his prophet. He then arranged a spectacular "birth" of the god, whom he called Glycon, in the form of a snake emerging from a goose egg. Using a tame serpent, a network of spies and helpers, and an ingenious method of opening sealed scrolls with heated needles, he began to issue oracles in return for payment (a drachma and two obols).

The renown of Glycon and Alexander spread through Asia Minor and reached Rome, where the influential Rutilianus became an ardent follower and was inveigled into marriage with Alexander's daughter "by the goddess Selene." With the oracle firmly established, Alexander introduced an annual three day celebration of some of the classical mystery themes and some invented by the prophet himself. His chief opponents apparently were the Epicureans, whom he fought through oracles and through the influence of his followers. By his own orders, Epicureans, Christians, and atheists were rigidly banned from attending the mysteries or consulting Glycon. The cult of Glycon was not confined to healing, but was more properly a form of worship and an imitation of the great oracles of the ancient world.

After amassing wealth, Alexander died of an infection when he was nearly 70. The cult outlasted him by at least a century, as 3rd century coins of the region show.

Bibliography: LUCIAN, *Alexander the False Prophet,* ed. and tr. A. M. HARMON [*Loeb Classical Library,* (London–New York–Cambridge, Mass. 1912—) 4] 173–253. S. DILL, *Encyclopedia of Religion and Ethics,* ed. J. HASTINGS, 13 v. (Edinburgh 1908–27) 1:306. K. PRÜMM, *Religionsgeschichtliches Handbuch für den Raum der altchristlichen Umwelt* (2d ed. Rome 1954) 460–62. J. LEIPOLDT, *Reallexikon für Antike und Christentum,* ed. T. KLAUSER [Stuttgart 1941 (1950)—] 1:260–261.

[G. W. MAC RAE]

ALEXANDER OF COMANA, ST.

Also called Alexander Carbonarius ("the charcoal burner"); first bishop of Comana in Pontus; martyred *c.* 275. According to GREGORY OF NYSSA (*Patrologia Graeca* 46:933–940), St. GREGORY THAUMATURGUS, when invited to organize a Christian community and preside over the election of a bishop in Comana, rejected all the proposed candidates, pointing out that the apostles had been poor and ordinary men. Someone proposed Alexander, and Gregory questioned him to discover that beneath the grime of his trade he was an educated man of good birth, who had given up his possessions to follow Christ. Alexander was consecrated. Later, he was burned to death, probably under Aurelian (270–275). As the patron of charcoal burners, he was first inserted into the Roman martyrology by BARONIUS.

Feast: Aug. 11.

Bibliography: G. ELDAROV, *Bibliotheca sanctorum* 1:776–777.

[M. J. COSTELLOE]

ALEXANDER OF FIESOLE, ST.

Bishop and martyr; b. Fiesole?, Tuscany, Italy; d. near Bologna, *c.* 833–841. Having been consecrated in Rome, he succeeded to the episcopacy of his native city. In that office he was remarkable for all the pastoral virtues. He persuaded the Emperor LOTHAIR I to restore certain properties of which the Church had been despoiled. As Alexander was returning from this successful mission, he was attacked by those who had been forced to surrender their ill-gotten possessions. In the encounter he was drowned in the River Reno. His relics were brought to Fiesole where he quickly became one of the principal patrons.

Feast: June 6.

Bibliography: *Acta Sanctorum* June 1:738–740. *Bibliotheca hagiograpica latina antiquae et mediae aetatis* (Brussels 1898–1901) 1:278. J. L. BAUDOT and L. CHAUSSIN, *Vies des saints et des bienhereux selon l'ordre du calendrier avec l'historique des* *fêtes* (Paris 1935–56) 6:105. G. RASPINI, *Bibliotheca sanctorum* 1:781–782.

[J. E. LYNCH]

ALEXANDER OF HALES

English Franciscan theologian known by the scholastic titles of *Doctor irrefragabilis* and *Doctor doctorum*; b. Hales Owen, Shropshire, *c.* 1185; d. Paris, Aug. 21, 1245.

Life. Born of a wealthy agrarian family, he studied arts at the University of Paris, where he became a master before 1210. About 1210 he began to study theology and became regent master *c.* 1220–22. He retained his professorship until 1241, when he relinquished it to JOHN OF LA ROCHELLE. As a theologian he acquired a considerable reputation. Early in his teaching career as regent master in theology he replaced the custom of lecturing on the Bible with lectures on the *Sentences* of PETER LOMBARD. Because of this unprecedented procedure, ROGER BACON, who originally had the highest admiration for him, mentioned Alexander's innovation as one of the causes for the decline of theology. In fact, however, Alexander's emphasis on speculative theology, use of philosophy, and study of the Fathers initiated the golden age of medieval scholasticism (*see* SCHOLASTICISM). Later this custom was reserved for bachelors in theology. Between 1226 and 1229 he became a canon of St. Paul's in London with the prebend of Holborn, even though he remained in Paris. He played an important part in the struggle between university and crown; the reorganization of the university effected by the bull *Parens scientiarum* of GREGORY IX, April 13, 1231, was partly the work of Alexander. Toward the end of 1231 and the beginning of 1232 he was in England, where contemporary documents record him as canon of Lichfield and archdeacon of Coventry. From August 1235 until February 1236 he helped to negotiate peace between France and England. At the beginning of the academic year 1236–37, Alexander, already more than 50 years of age, disposed of his wealth and entered the Franciscan Order, thereby securing a chair in the university for the order. Among his outstanding Franciscan disciples were John of La Rochelle, Odo Rigaldus, and St. BONAVENTURE. As a Franciscan master he participated in the general chapter at Rome, collaborated on the first exposition of the Rule (1241–42), and was probably dean of regent masters. He took an active part in censuring doctrines of the Dominican Étienne de Venizy (1241) and of the secular John Pagus (1244). Attending the Council of Lyons in 1244, he and ROBERT GROSSETESTE were part of a commission charged with examining documents preparatory to canonizing St. ED-MUND OF ABINGDON. His sudden death was mourned throughout Paris. The solemn funeral rites, held on Aug. 25, 1245, were presided over by ODO OF CHÂTEAUROUX, papal legate to France. The poet John of Garland sang his praises (*Histoire littéraire de la France* 21:372).

Works. Five major writings can be ascribed to him with certainty. (1) *Exoticon*, a youthful work about difficult words, is attributed to him in Cambridge, Glanville, and Caius College MS 136. (2) *Glossa in 4 libros sententiarum*, apparently a *reportatio* that was discovered in 1946, is a *lectio cursoria*, midway between a literal commentary and a fully developed series of questions on the text of Peter Lombard. (3) *Quaestiones disputatae 'antequam esset frater,'* including 68 questions of various length, were written between 1220 and 1236. They touch almost the whole domain of theology and demonstrate convincingly the author's propensity for speculative theology. (4) *Quaestiones quodlibetales*, of which four are known to be extant. (5) The *Summa theologica*, sometimes known as the *Summa pseudo-Alexandri*, must be discussed in terms of the *Summa* left incomplete by Alexander in 1245 and the expanded version issued in 1260 and published at Quaracchi. Of the present version only the following seem to have been in the original *Summa fratris Alexandri*: bk. 1, all except perhaps q. 74, *De missione visibili*; bk. 2, all except the tracts *De corpore humano* and *De coniuncto*; bk. 3, fragments. The work is called *Summa fratris Alexandri* in the manuscript tradition and in the bull *De fontibus paradisi* of Alexander IV, Oct. 7, 1255. The bull ordered that the *Summa* be completed by the Franciscans. WILLIAM OF MELITONA (Middleton) and his collaborators worked until 1260 without completing it. They utilized Alexander's *Glossa* and *Quaestiones disputatae* and incorporated many parts of their own writings, as well as those of Prevostino, or Praepostinus (*c.* 1145–1210); WILLIAM OF AUXERRE; and PHILIP THE CHANCELLOR. The final version of the *Summa* was imposed on the Franciscan school by two ministers general, Guiral Ot in 1331 and Leonard of Gaffoni in 1373. Alexander collaborated with John of La Rochelle, Robert of La Bassée and Odo Rigaldus in the *Expositio super regulam* of 1241–42. Although numerous biblical commentaries have been attributed to him (F. STEGMÜLLER, *Repertorium biblicum medii aevi* 1117–57), only a *Postillae super quatuor Evangelia* and a *Commentarius super Psalmos* are generally accepted as his; but this question needs to be further investigated. Three *Sermones* can also be attributed to him with some certainty.

Thought. Although Alexander quoted freely from almost all the works of ARISTOTLE, including the pseudo-Aristotelian *De causis*, and had access to the full text of these works, he had no clear idea of the true meaning of Aristotelian philosophy. In his writings he adapted fragmentary texts of Aristotle to the teaching of St. AUGUSTINE. His work belongs to a period when no collective theological effort had been made to assimilate the newly discovered Aristotelian world. His main theological authorities were Augustine, PSEUDO-DIONYSIUS, BOETHIUS, and many 11th- and 12th-century theologians, notably St. ANSELM OF CANTERBURY, St. BERNARD OF CLAIRVAUX, GILBERT DE LA PORRÉE, and the pseudo-hermetic *Liber 24 philosophorum*.

His psychological notions, introduced when he was discussing the image of God in man, are strictly Augustinian or are inspired by the pseudo-Augustinian *De spiritu et anima*. Against William of Auxerre, Alexander maintains that the powers of the soul are not distinct from the substance, but only from the essence. Since essence is that by which the soul is what it is, its powers are not what makes the soul to be what it is; on the other hand, since substance is what makes a thing subsist in its indivisible unity, the soul cannot be complete without its powers or faculties (*see* FACULTIES OF THE SOUL). This position was characteristic of the Franciscan school until the time of DUNS SCOTUS. Alexander followed Augustine in his discussion of the problem of evil and in his notion of wisdom. The *Summa theologica* of 1260 remarkably illustrates what may be called the spirit of the 13th-century Franciscan school of theology at the University of Paris.

Bibliography: "Alexander of Hales," *The History of Franciscan Theology*, ed. K. OSBORNE (St. Bonaventure, N.Y. 1994), 1–38. V. DOUCET, "A New Source of the *Summa fratris Alexandri*: The Commentary on the Sentences of Alexander of Hales," *Franciscan Studies* 6 (1946) 403–417; ALEXANDER OF HALES, "Prolegomena," *Summa Theologica*, v.4. (Quaracchi-Florence 1948).

[A. EMMEN]

ALEXANDER OF JERUSALEM, ST.

Bishop and martyr; d. Caesarea, Palestine, 250–251. One of the great bishops of the early Church, he was trained in Alexandria, where he was a pupil of Pantaenus (d. *c.* 200) and CLEMENT of Alexandria and where he became the friend of ORIGEN. After becoming bishop of an unknown see in Cappadocia *c.* 200, he was imprisoned *c.* 204 during the persecution of Septimius Severus (d. 211) and not released until 211. In the following year he was made coadjutor and later successor of the aged Narcissus (d. 222), Bishop of Jerusalem, both unusual proceedings at that early date. At Jerusalem he founded the library later used by EUSEBIUS OF CAESAREA in preparing his great history of the early Church. When Origen was condemned by the bishop of Alexandria, Alexander invited him to Jerusalem, ordained him, and put him in charge

of the teaching of Scripture and theology in the diocese. Alexander died in prison at Caesarea during the persecution of Decius (d. 251).

Feast: March 18 and Jan. 30.

Bibliography: EUSEBIUS, *Historia ecclesiastica* 6.8, 11, 14, 19, 39, 46. G. BAREILLE, *Dictionnaire de théologia catholique* 1.1:763–764.

[J. L. GRASSI]

ALEXANDER, PATRIARCH OF ALEXANDRIA, ST.

Patriarchate, 312 to April 328, during which the controversy over ARIANISM erupted; b. *c.* 250; d. Alexandria, April 18, 328. He served prominently under bishops Peter and Achillas and was probably rector of the famous school of Alexandria. In 312 he was elected to succeed Achillas: PHILOSTORGIUS affirmed that ARIUS supported the candidacy of Alexander; Epiphanius of Constantia blamed Arius's frustrated ambition for the subsequent enmity. Alexander gave Arius charge of the important parish of Baucalis. He first encountered opposition from Meletius of Lycopolis, whose rigoristic attitude toward the lapsed had led him into schism against the former bishop, Peter. Alexander had difficulty also with the priest Kolluthus, who had usurped the power to ordain priests and deacons.

In about 318 he received complaints concerning the teachings of Arius, who denied the true divinity of Christ. Alexander first called a conference of the local clergy, and Arius was asked to explain his views. When discussion and persuasion failed to convince him of his errors, Alexander convened a synod of all Egyptian bishops, which condemned and excommunicated Arius. There followed a period of feverish activity on both sides. Arius went to Palestine and Bithynia, where he received support from both Bishop EUSEBIUS OF CAESAREA and Bishop EUSEBIUS OF NICOMEDIA, who wrote to many fellow bishops in Arius's favor. To counteract this propaganda, Alexander circulated numerous letters to expose the erroneous doctrine of Arius and to defend his own course of action. In these he showed himself an adherent of moderate Origenism and insisted especially on the natural, eternal generation of the Son and on His perfect likeness to the Father.

After conquering the East in 324, Constantine I intervened in the conflict and sent HOSIUS OF CÓRDOBA, his ecclesiastical adviser, to Egypt with a letter for Alexander and Arius, exhorting them to make peace. On Hosius's arrival, Alexander informed him of the true issue at stake and gained a powerful ally. Another Egyptian synod was called; when it failed to bring Arius to submission both prelates suggested holding a general council. At Nicaea I (325), Alexander was among the leaders of the orthodox party and may have had a hand in the inclusion of the term homoousios in the NICENE CREED.

After the Council, Alexander met with continued opposition from the Meletians, although they had been treated leniently by the decisions of Nicaea. He designated ATHANASIUS as his successor. Alexander is venerated as a saint in the Coptic Church. Epiphanius mentions a collection of 70 letters of Alexander, but only two, dealing with the Arian crisis, have survived. A sermon on the soul and body, and one on the Passion of Christ, and fragments of others are also preserved in Coptic and Syriac translations.

Feast: Feb. 26.

Bibliography: H. G. OPITZ, ed., *Athanasius' Werke*, v. 3.1 (Berlin 1934) 6–11; 19–29, works. X. LE BACHELET, *Dictionnaire de théologie catholique* 1.1:764–766. R. JANIN, *Dictionnaire d'histoire et de géographie ecclésiastiques*, ed. A. BAUDRILLART et al. (Paris 1912) 2:182–183. J. N. D. KELLY, *Early Christian Doctrines* (2d ed. New York 1960) 224–225. J. QUASTEN, *Patrologie* (Westminster, MD 1950) 3:13–19. V. C. DE CLERCQ, *Ossius of Cordova* (Washington 1954) 189–206. J. R. PALANQUE et al., *The Church in the Christian Roman Empire*, tr. E. C. MESSENGER, 2 v. in 1 (New York 1953) 1:73–109.

[V. C. DE CLERCQ]

ALEXANDRE, NOËL

Theologian, historian, (also known erroneously as Alexander Natalis); b. Rouen, Jan. 19, 1639; d. Paris, Aug. 21, 1724. In 1654 Alexandre entered the Dominican Order at Saint-Jacques in Rouen. He undertook his ecclesiastical studies in 1656 at Paris, received the baccalaureate in 1668 and the licentiate in 1674, (he was also awarded a Dominican master of theology in 1674), and was received doctor of theology of the faculty of Theology of Paris (Feb. 21, 1675).

After taking his academic degrees, he taught philosophy and theology for the Paris province of his Order, was regent of studies for his own and other provinces (1673–?), and was provincial of his province (1706–10). He tutored J. N. Colbert, son of the minister of Louis XIV.

In 1675, when Jean de Launoy, also of the Parisian faculty of theology equated the payment of ANNATES with SIMONY and questioned the Aquinian authorship of the *Summa Theologiae*, Alexander defended the payment of annates and vindicated the authorship of Aquinas in

the work, *Summa S. Thomae vindicata*. He also wrote his *Dissertatio polemica de confessione* (1678) and the *Dissertationum ecclesiasticarum trias*, which included his thoughts on episcopal supremacy over priests, clerical celibacy, and the Vulgate (1678).

Alexandre's success as a lecturer in history prompted him to compose his great historical work *Selecta historiae capita et in loca ejusdem insignia dissertationes historicae, chronologicae, criticae, dogmaticae* (1676–86). Volumes covering the Church's first ten centuries were highly praised, but those dealing with the 11th and 12th centuries aroused indignation in Rome because of their Gallican tinge. In 1684 Innocent XI condemned the entire work as well as the *Summa . . . vindicata*, the *Trias*, and Alexander's polemical dissertation on confession. The penalty of excommunication was threatened for reading, retaining, or printing these works. A second prohibition came in 1685 with the condemnation of the volumes of the *Selecta historiae capita* devoted to the 13th and 14th centuries. The Dominican Master General Monroy deprived Alexander of all his privileges, but the French government interceded for him in Rome. Nevertheless, in 1687 a third prohibition censured the volumes of the history dealing with the 15th and 16th centuries. Benedict XIII withdrew the prohibition of Alexander's works (1724) and Benedict XIV removed the excommunication on the use of all editions (1754); yet the books remained on the Index, except the edition of the *Selecta . . . capita* of July 8, 1754, with notes and animadversions by Roncaglia (Hänggi, 161).

In 1686, Alexander turned to theology, writing his *Theologia dogmatica et moralis secundum ordinem Catechismi Tridentini* (1693), his last major work. It was intended not only for the theologians, but also for parish priests, confessors, and preachers. In its preface, he indicated a desire for reconciliation with Rome. He published many short treatises (mostly in French), engaged in polemics with the Jesuits, especially Gabriel Daniel, on PROBABILISM, LAXISM, and MOLINISM. The controversy was eventually stopped by the king. Alexander also entered the CHINESE RITES CONTROVERSY: his *Apologie des Dominicains missionaires de la Chine* (1699) was followed by *Conformité des cérémonies chinoises avec l'idolatrie grecque et romaine* (1700).

In 1701, he dedicated himself to providing guideposts for preachers, writing a literal and moral commentary on the New Testament (1703–10). In 1701 he became suspected of Jansenism by signing the *Cas de Conscience*, maintaining that absolution could be given to a cleric who declared that he held on certain points the sentiments of "those called Jansenists," especially that of respectful silence on the question of fact (*see* JANSEN-

ISM). He later wrote letters of explanation and made a retraction.

His third conflict with Rome arose over the bull *Unigenitus* (1714), not because he was a Jansenist, but because, with Archbishop Noailles, he thought some of Quesnel's condemned propositions were representative of Thomistic thought; he considered the bull not the work of the pope, but of the Molinists. Alexander's name was included in the list of "Appellants" to the next general council.

In his last years, blind and worn out, he lived at Saint-Jacques, Paris. On the feast day of St. Dominic in 1724, he renounced his appellancy, less than a month before he died at peace with the Church.

Bibliography: A. HÄNGGI, *Der Kirchenhistoriker Natalis Alexander (1639–1724)* (Fribourg 1955). J. M. GRES-GAYER, *Théologie et pouvoir en Sorbonne* (Paris 1991). D. A. MORTIER, *Histoire des Maîtres Généraux de l'Ordre des Frères Prêcheurs,* 8 v. (Paris 1903–20). J. QUÉTIF and J. ÊCHARD, *Scriptores Ordinis Praedicatorm* (Paris 1719–23) 2.2:810–813.

[J. A. DOSHNER/J. M. GRES-GAYER]

ALEXANDRIA

Greek, Ἀλεξάνδρεια; Latin, Alexandria. "The Paris of the ancient Mediterranean world," it was founded by Alexander the Great in 331 B.C. and became an important commercial, industrial, and cultural center and the chief city of Egypt.

Greek Learning. The museum and library founded by Ptolemy I *c.* 280 B.C., providing for 100 research scholars in the humanities and sciences, made the city one of the most influential centers of Greek learning. A flourishing Jewish colony produced the important scholar PHILO JUDAEUS and made Jewish doctrine available to Gentiles and to Jews ignorant of Hebrew through the translation of the Old Testament into Greek, known as the Septuagint, which was completed in the 2d century B.C. Thus Alexandria was to some extent prepared for the arrival of Christian teaching, which, according to tradition, was brought there by Saint Mark, who was buried in the city. Apollos, one of Saint Paul's collaborators, was a Jew of Alexandria (Acts of the Apostles 18.24), and Paul on the voyage to Rome could talk with the sailors on two Alexandrian ships (Acts of the Apostles 27.6; 28.11). The Gnostic teachers BASILIDES, Isidorus, and CARPOCRATES found followers at Alexandria.

A landmark in the local Christian history was the founding of a Christian school of philosophy by PANTAENUS (late 2d century). Under its famous directors CLEMENT OF ALEXANDRIA (d. *c.* 215) and ORIGEN (185–254), the school became an influential center of Christian scholarship. Alexandria was still a center of Greek learning, and Ammonius Saccas (*c.* 175–242), the founder of Neoplatonism, lectured there. In this setting one of Clement's important achievements was to show that Greek learning could be put to the service of Christianity. Origen after a distinguished career was obliged to leave for Palestine over the question of his qualifications to be a teacher and a priest, and an Alexandrian council of 231 supported his bishop's disapproval of his activities.

Alexandrian Christians suffered persecution under Septimius Severus (202 and after), attacks from the pagans of the city under Philip (249), and persecution again under Decius (250), Valerian (257–62), Diocletian (304–05), and Maximinus Daia (310–12). The MELETIAN schism arose when Meletius, Bishop of Lycopolis, performed ordinations in Alexandria although it was not his diocese. He was condemned at a council at Alexandria in 306.

Heresies. Much of the ecclesiastical history of Alexandria was concerned with the conflicts caused by the heresies of ARIANISM, NESTORIANISM, EUTYCHIANISM, and MONOPHYSITISM. Arius, a parish priest of the city, began his heretical teaching about 319, and after disputes with ALEXANDER, PATRIARCH OF ALEXANDRIA, he was excommunicated by a local synod (321) and left the city. The opposition to Arianism was vigorously led by (Saint) ATHANASIUS OF ALEXANDRIA, who, succeeding Alexander, served as bishop from 328 to 373, with several intervals when he was driven into exile or had to flee for safety. A council was called in 362 to deliberate on the divinity of the Holy Spirit, and two councils in 363 and 364 formulated definitions of the faith addressed to the Emperor Jovian. An anti-Arian council met in 370. Bishop THEOPHILUS OF ALEXANDRIA (385–412) led a campaign against paganism that included the destruction (389) of the temple of Serapis, one of the most venerated pagan shrines. In 415 Hypatia, a noted pagan teacher of classical philosophy, was killed by a Christian mob. SYNESIUS OF CYRENE, later bishop of Ptolemais (*c.* 410– *c.* 414), was one of her pupils before his conversion to Christianity.

The next important chapter in Alexandrian Church history was the patriarchate of Saint Cyril (412–444), who led the fight against Nestorianism. Nestorius's teaching was rejected by a council at Alexandria in 430, and Cyril presided at the Council of Ephesus (431), where Nestorianism was condemned. This condemnation caused a breach between Antioch and Alexandria, which was healed on the basis of a council at Antioch (432).

Out of the controversy over Nestorianism grew the heretical doctrine of Eutyches concerning the nature of

Christ (448), which was the real beginning of the Monophysite heresy. At the Council of Chalcedon (451) DIOSCORUS, Patriarch of Alexandria, was deposed for his support of Eutyches, and his condemnation was followed by rioting and bloodshed in Alexandria. The Monophysite teaching found strong support in Alexandria and the rest of Egypt, as it did in Syria. To the ancient ecclesiastical rivalry between the sees of Alexandria and Constantinople was added the theological antagonism of the Egyptians to the orthodox leaders who represented the Byzantine imperial government and were dispatched from Constantinople to impose official orthodoxy on the Alexandrian Church. Further friction arose out of the racial aversion of Upper Egypt to the Greek culture of Alexandria and out of the ancient nationalistic sentiment of the Egyptian people, who had long been subjected to foreign domination. There were protracted disorders in Alexandria, and the anti-Byzantine kept control of the local Church by violent means, especially under the Coptic Patriarchs Timothy ''the Cat'' (457–77) and Peter ''the Stammerer'' (477–90). The Orthodox Emperor Justinian (527–565), intent on restoring peace in the empire, supported the Orthodox patriarch in Alexandria by force, and the orthodox patriarchs had to be protected by imperial troops. The result of this prolonged experience was that Egypt, like Jacobite Syria, developed well-recognized separatist tendencies; and when the Arabs invaded Egypt (648), they were welcomed as prospectively less oppressive than the hated Byzantine emperor.

A celebrated figure in the Church at Alexandria at this time was the Patriarch (Saint) JOHN THE ALMSGIVER, noted for the simplicity of his personal life and for his extensive charities, which he supported from the profits of the patriarchate's properties and commercial activities, notably, the cargo fleet owned by the Church.

The final years of the local Church before the Arab conquest were troubled by the heresy of MONOTHELITISM, which recognized the existence of only one will in Christ. A Monothelite council was held in the city in 633. In 828 some Venetian merchants, visiting Alexandria, secretly carried off the body of St. Mark to Venice.

Theological School. The museum and library had attracted leading classical scholars, and the Christian theologians of Alexandria were naturally influenced by the local pagan scholarly tradition. Philo Judaeus (d. *c.* A.D. 50) conceived an effort to harmonize Greek philosophy and the Old Testament with a philosophical mysticism that strongly influenced Alexandrian theology. His method of allegorical exegesis of the Bible spread to Christian theological schools elsewhere. Christian thought in Alexandria was strongly influenced also by the Platonic tradition. Clement, Origen, and their colleagues adapted the

Library at Alexandria, Egypt. (©The Bettmann Archive)

Platonic tradition and the allegorical method to Christian thought. The contribution of Alexandria to the development of systematic theology was also important; Origen's *De principiis* was the first systematic exposition of Christian doctrine. Alexandrian thought differed from Antiochene theology, which was Aristotelian, pragmatic, and critical. Similarly, Biblical exegesis at Alexandria was allegorical and mystical, while that at Antioch was historical and literal. Platonic dualism was reflected in the emphasis upon the transcendence of God and the divinity of Christ in Alexandrian teaching. This was the basis of Alexandrian controversies with ANTIOCH, where the humanity of Christ was stressed. Thus Athanasius was the Alexandrian champion of orthodoxy against the Arian teaching, favored at Antioch, that the Son of God was a creature. The same perspective was the basis of the opposition of Cyril to the doctrine of Nestorius of Antioch that there were separate divine and human persons in Christ. The extreme form of the Alexandrian tendency resulted in Monophysitism, which maintained that there was only one, divine, nature in Christ. One of the distinguished Alexandrian scholars of the early 5th century was JOHN PHILOPONUS, typical of his time in working simultaneously as theologian, commentator on Aristotle, and grammarian.

Art and Archeology. Hellenistic Alexandria, with its wealthy and cultivated atmosphere, developed a distinctive artistic style of its own that reflected the sophisticated and cosmopolitan character of the city. The artistic tradition of classical Greece served as the basis for the new Alexandrian manner, but the Alexandrian artists, with a realism unknown in classical Greece, sought to emphasize the individuality of their subjects.

When Christian art appeared in Alexandria, the Christian artists naturally worked in the local style. The earliest preserved Christian monuments in the city are the frescoes in the catacomb of Karmuz, painted in a characteristic style that was carried to Rome and used in the catacombs there. In Egypt and Italy in the early centuries Christ was portrayed as a youthful Hermes, with short curly hair; the bearded oriental type emerged later in Syria and Palestine. The illustrated *Christian Topography* of Cosmas Indicopleustes is a typical example of Alexandrian theology and art of the 6th century. The Christian artists of Alexandria, like their pagan predecessors, produced elegant textiles, glass, gold and silver work, and ivory carving, which they exported throughout the ancient world. There was always opposition between the Hellenic artistic tradition of Alexandria itself and the indigenous COPTIC ART of the rest of Egypt, which represented a totally different artistic tradition.

Bibliography: H. A. MUSURILLO, ed., *The Acts of the Pagan Martyrs: Acta Alexandrinorum* (London 1954). C. BIGG, *The Christian Platonists of Alexandria* (2d ed. London 1913). R. B. TOLLINTON, *Alexandrine Teaching on the Universe* (New York 1932). E. MOLLAND, *The Conception of the Gospel in the Alexandrian Theology* (Oslo 1938). R. V. SELLERS, *Two Ancient Christologies* (London 1940). E. R. HARDY, *Christian Egypt: Church and People* (London 1952). J. MASPERO, *Histoire des patriarches d'Alexandrie* (Paris 1923). C. R. MOREY, *Early Christian Art* (2d ed. Princeton 1953). E. A. PARSONS, *The Alexandrian Library* (New York 1952). G. DOWNEY, ''Coptic Culture in the Byzantine World,'' *Greek and Byzantine Studies* 1.2 (1958) 119–35. H. I. BELL, *Cults and Creeds in Graeco-Roman Egypt* (Liverpool 1953).

[G. DOWNEY/EDS.]

ALEXANDRIA, DIOCESE OF

(*Alexandrinensis*) suffragan of the metropolitan See of New Orleans, was originally established as the Diocese of Natchitoches by Pius IX on July 29, 1853, and at the time covered the parishes (counties) in the northern tier of Louisiana. The see city was transferred to Alexandria, Aug. 6, 1910, and in 1977 it was redesignated as the diocese of Alexandria-Shreveport. When Shreveport became a diocese in 1986, it was again designated as the Diocese of Alexandria.

Missionary Activity. Catholic missionary work in the territory dates from 1682, when the Franciscan Zenobius Membre, chaplain to R. LA SALLE's expedition down the Mississippi River, stopped at the village of the Tensas native tribe, near present-day Newellton, La. The next missionaries in Northern Louisiana were priests from the Seminary of Quebec, Canada, who arrived in the Lower Mississippi Valley in 1699. Francis de Montigny, their superior, took up residence among the Tensas, and in the vicinity of Newellton built what was probably the first chapel within the future Diocese of Alexandria. The oldest town in the diocese and in the entire state originated in 1716 when J. B. le Moyne de Bienville sent a military force to establish Fort St. John the Baptist on an island in the Red River. The settlement became known as ''Le Poste de Natchitoches.''

In 1853 when Louisiana's second diocese was created from the Archdiocese of NEW ORLEANS with Natchitoches as its see city, Auguste Marie Martin was named first bishop. At that time the diocese, covering three-fifths of the state, had five priests, six parish churches, about three mission chapels, one school, and 22,000 Catholics. Martin died Sept. 29, 1875, and was succeded by Francis Xavier Leray, who was consecrated April 22, 1877. Two years later he was named coadjutor of New Orleans, but he remained administrator of Natchitoches until 1883 when he became ordinary of New Orleans. His successor was the Bishop Antoine Durier (1885–1904) who in turn was succeeded by Bishop Cornelius Van de Ven (1904–32). In the spring of 1910, Bishop Van de Ven petitioned the Holy See to transfer the see city of the diocese to Alexandria, citing the latter's advantages of better road and railroad communications to all parts of northern Louisiana, and its closer proximity to the large percentage of French Catholics living in the southern part of the diocese.

Bishop Van de Ven's immediate successor was Bishop Daniel F. Desmond (1933–45). Alexandria's next two bishops, Charles P. Greco (1946–73) and Lawrence P. Graves (1973–82) both retired because of age. (Bishop Greco died on Jan. 20, 1987; Bishop Graves, Jan. 15, 1994). It was during Bishop Graves' tenure that the diocese was redesignated in 1977 as Alexandria-Shreveport. His successor, the Most Reverend William B. Friend, was bishop of Alexandria-Shreveport until the diocese was divided and he became the first bishop of the new diocese of Shreveport, while the Most Reverend John C. Favalora became the bishop of Alexandria. After the separation, the diocese of Alexandria encompassed 11,116 sq. miles, comprising the civil parishes of Rapides, Avoyelles, Concordia, Catahoula, LaSalle, Grant, Natchitoches, Vernon, Tensas, Caldwell, Winn, Franklin, and Madison. Approximately 12 percent of the population were Catholics, distributed among 48 parishes and 24 missions. When Bishop Favalora was transferred to the diocese of St. Petersburg, Florida in 1989, he was succeeded by Bishop Sam G. Jacobs.

Bibliography: R. BAUDIER, *The Catholic Church in Louisiana* (New Orleans 1939).

[C. M. CLAYTON/M. G. GUIDRY/EDS.]

ALEXANDRIA, PATRIARCHATE OF

One of the oldest patriarchates to be formed in the early Church. In the Council of CONSTANTINOPLE I (381) the patriarch of Alexandria was granted second place of honor after the pope of Rome, and his jurisdiction spread over Egypt, Libya, and Pentapolis, which at that time possessed more than 100 bishoprics. ALEXANDRIA was a city of capital importance as a civil center and for its extraordinary library and renowned schools of philosophy and theology. Ecclesiastically, it possessed a tightly organized hierarchy that radiated its jurisdiction over thousands of monks in the Egyptian desert who were renowned all over the then Christian world.

Aftermath of the Council of Chalcedon. Its unity split asunder after the Council of Chalcedon (451) condemned the MONOPHYSITISM of Dioscorus. From 457 there existed two parallel churches. The majority of the Christians living in Alexandria followed their patriarch, Dioscorus, thus forming what today is called the indigenous COPTIC ORTHODOX CHURCH (Oriental Orthodox). Those in the minority who remained faithful to the teachings of Chalcedon formed the Byzantine (MELKITE) Church.

The patriarchal see was disputed between the pro-Chalcedonian and anti-Chalcedonian factions, and from 482 to 538 the latter prevailed. After 538 there was a double patriarchal hierarchy, Byzantine Orthodox (Chalcedonian) and the Coptic Oriental Orthodox (Non-Chalcedonian). The Coptic patriarchs were frequently forced into exile under JUSTINIAN I (527–565), who supported the Byzantine Orthodox. HERACLIUS (610–641) strove to establish MONOTHELITISM as a compromise between strict Monophysitism and Byzantine Orthodoxy to create at least the outer appearance of religious unity.

During the Arab conquest of Egypt, the Coptic patriarch was allowed to exercise his jurisdiction, and through financial and social pressure the number of Byzantine Orthodox was greatly reduced, principally because the Arabs distrusted their loyalty to the Byzantine emperors. The Byzantine patriarchate of Alexandria remained vacant from 652 to 737; and candidates for the episcopacy had to be sent to Tyre for consecration.

At one time, the two churches preserved the same liturgy of Alexandria (*see* ALEXANDRIAN LITURGY), but gradually the Byzantine liturgical rite was accepted by the Melkites. From 639 to 1811 the Copts were oppressed as much as the Byzantine Orthodox under the domination of the Mussulman caliphs. The year 1811 marks the beginning of contemporary history of Egypt under the Sultan Muḥammad Ali and his successors, who granted religious liberty to all Christians.

Great schism. The close relationship between the orthodox patriarch of Alexandria and the ecumenical patriarch of Constantinople caused the Alexandrian patriarchate to rally behind the ecumenical patriarch at the time of the Great Schism of 1054. In 1219 the Latin Crusaders established a Latin patriarch for Alexandria in expectation of their capturing the city, but he was never able to reside there. During the Latin occupation, the orthodox patriarch of Alexandria took up residence in Constantinople, thus increasing his dependence on the Byzantine Church. The Alexandrian patriarch, together with those of Antioch and Jerusalem, sent a representative to the Council of FLORENCE (1439) and through him agreed to enter into communion with the See of Rome. It is difficult to know whether the patriarch of Alexandria repudiated this union with Rome along with the antiochene patriarch in the Synod of Constantinople in 1484. But the Alexandrian Melkites finally severed relations with Rome after the Turkish conquest of Alexandria in 1517. It is probable that a faction favoring communion with Rome always existed and that from time to time one of them held the patriarchal see. But by decision of the Turkish caliph, the patriarch of Constantinople became head of all orthodox subjects in the Ottoman Empire. From this point, the Alexandrian orthodox patriarchate was completely Hellenic.

With the reunion of 1724, a Melkite Greek Catholic patriarchate was established in Antioch. In 1833 Patriarch MAXIMOS III Mazlūm obtained from Pope Gregory XVI the personal privilege (which has been handed down uninterruptedly) of adding the title of patriarch of Alexandria and Jerusalem along with jurisdiction over the Melkite Catholic churches in these areas. From 1895, when a Coptic Catholic patriarchate was established for the Alexandrian patriarchate, until the present there have been four separate patriarchal sees of Alexandria: the Coptic Oriental Orthodox, the Coptic Catholic, the Orthodox, and the Melkite Greek Catholic.

Bibliography: D. ATTWATER, *The Christian Churches of the East,* 2 v. (rev. ed. Milwaukee, Wis. 1961–62). C. DE CLERCQ, *Les*

Églises unies d'Orient (Paris 1934). R. JANIN, *Les Églises Orientales et les Rites Orientaux* (Paris 1955). C. KARALEVSKIJ, *Histoire des Patriarcats Melkites*, 3 v. in 2 (Rome 1909–10). A. A. KING, *The Rites of Eastern Christendom*, 2 v. (London 1950). E. R. HARDY, *Christian Egypt* (New York 1952). W. DE VRIES et al., eds., *Rom und die Patriarchate des Ostens* (Freiburg 1963). R. ROBERSON, *The Eastern Christian Churches: A Brief Survey*, 6th ed (Rome 1999).

[G. A. MALONEY/EDS.]

ALEXANDRIA, SCHOOL OF

The name for both the catechetical institution and the theological tradition characteristic of Alexandria during the patristic age. Alexandria was one of the most important cultural centers of the ancient world and the focal point for the mutual influence exercised in the conjunction of CHRISTIANITY and Hellenism. Before the introduction of Christianity, Alexandria possessed great libraries in its museum, the Serapeum, and the Sebasteon. It was also the center of Hellenistic Judaism; the Books of Ecclesiasticus and Wisdom were probably produced there before the Christian Era. PHILO JUDAEUS, the great doctor of Hellenistic Judaism, worked there. Hence, it is not astonishing that Alexandria early became a Christian intellectual center.

Catechetical School. The origin of the Christian School of Alexandria is obscure. It is obvious that from the start the bishops of Alexandria used collaborators in preparing the catechumens for Baptism, although none of these is known. In the late second century PANTAENUS, a convert philosopher, is cited as the head of a Christian school in Alexandria (*c.* 150); and CLEMENT OF ALEXANDRIA has been considered his successor. These scholars conducted philosophical schools in which they taught the Christian faith as a philosophy (*gnosis*) or way of life. They do not appear to have had anything to do with the catechetical school as such. This was conducted by the bishop; and the first certain information is supplied in relation to ORIGEN, whom Bishop Demetrius charged with the instruction of catechumens (*c.* 203). Origen enlisted the aid of Heraclas, who evidently gave basic instruction in the CHRISTIAN WAY OF LIFE while his master concentrated his attention on the formation of a superior school of sacred science (*didascaleion*) that is generally designated as the School of Alexandria. GREGORY THAUMATURGUS, Origen's student in Caesarea, described the courses taught in the *didascaleion*—logic, dialectic, and physics (including mathematics and astronomy)—as a propaedeutic to Christian theology. This included the analysis of current philosophies, but principally the exegesis of the Scriptures.

Philip Sidetes, a fifth-century historian, records the names of the so-called heads of the school. He does not mention Pantaenus or Clement, but cites Athenagoras; Origen; Heraclas, who was bishop of Alexandria in 232; Dionysius, bishop in 248; Theognostus (247–282); Pierius; and Peter, bishop from 300. Although it is known that many fourth-century Fathers of the Church, such as JEROME, GREGORY OF NAZIANZUS, and BASIL OF CAESAREA, studied for a time at Alexandria, the only fourth-century teacher of whom there is positive knowledge is Didymus the Blind.

Theological School. The current of Christian thought represented by a group of scholars and propagandists with similar intellectual interests and a more or less uniform procedure in exegesis of the Scriptures, formed what is generally referred to as the theological School of Alexandria. Its members did not necessarily belong to the catechetical school. The relationship between Athanasius and Cyril of Alexandria and this school, for example, is not known; both Apollinaris and Eutyches represent Alexandrian Christological thought, although Apollinaris originated in Laodicea, near Antioch, and Eutyches was from Constantinople. The School of Alexandria is represented by two distinct phases: Clement and Origen were intent on presenting the Christian religion to the cultivated people of their epoch, Christians and non-Christians alike, and wanted to show them that Christ was the summit of all human knowledge; on the other hand, the authors of the fourth and fifth centuries, such as Athanasius and Cyril, had to defend the Christian truths concerning the Trinity and the divinity of Christ against heretical Christian theologians.

From the start, Alexandrian exegesis distinguished itself from that of Antioch. The latter was generally attached to the literal sense of the Bible. The Alexandrians recognized this sense, but their primary interest was concentrated on the mystery of divine revelation as revealed in the historical and literary details of the Old Testament. It was therefore a question of discovering Christ in the older revelation. With joyful sagacity, the Alexandrian authors sought out in the Old Testament SYMBOLS of the New. Their preference lay in the more profound, mystical, spiritual sense that is still termed typological or allegorical. Philo placed them on the path of this exegesis, which was, however, immediately inspired by a distinctly Christian principle, that of the unity of the two Testaments, such as Christ Himself expressed when He said that it was of Him that Moses and the Prophets had spoken.

In their Trinitarian doctrine, Clement and Origen were influenced by the Platonism of their epoch. They insisted on the divine transcendence. This at times forced them into expressing themselves as if the Son and the Holy Spirit were inferior to the Father. Origen emphasized the distinction of the divine Persons and spoke of three *hypostases*. Denis the Great did the same, and in so doing was accused of destroying the unity of the divine nature; but the Alexandrian tradition as presented by Athanasius went directly the other way: against Arius, who likewise lived in the Egyptian capital, Athanasius defended the consubstantiality of the Father and the Son, and although he recognized the possible orthodoxy of the formula of the three hypostases, he personally held to the Nicene terminology of the single *ousia,* or substance, and of the single hypostasis.

In Christology, the Alexandrians were guided by the Fourth Gospel. For them, as for St. John, Christ was, above all, the Word. Their soteriology controlled this conception. For them, Redemption consists essentially in the divinization that Christians are to obtain in Christ. This insistence on the divinity of Christ left the aspect of His humanity somewhat obscure. The Alexandrians generally did not see, for example, the importance of attributing a human soul to Christ. However, this aspect was appreciated by Didymus the Blind who stressed the perfect human consubstantiality of Christ. Cyril defined Christ as one nature of the Word Incarnate. This formula was repeated literally by Eutyches and the MONOPHYSITES, and tended to be interpreted by their adversaries as the negation of the human nature in Christ.

Bibliography: R. NELZ, *Die theologischen Schulen der morgenländischen Kirchen* (Bonn 1916). G. BARDY, *Recherches de science religieuse* (Paris 1910–) 27 (1937) 65–90; *Catholicisme* 1:310–314; *Vivre et penser* 2 (1942) 80–109. A. KNAUBER, *Trier theologische Zeitschrift* 60 (1951) 243–266. F. PERICOLI RIDOLFINI, *Revista degli studi orientali* 37 (1962) 211–230. O. BARDENHEWER, *Geschichte der altkirchlichen Literatur* (Freiburg 1913–32) 2:5–10. J. QUASTEN, *Patrology.* (Westminster, Maryland 1950–) 2:2–4. H. RAHNER, *Lexikon für Theologie und Kirche,* ed. J. HOFER and K. RAHNER (Freiberg 1957–65) 1:323–325. F. L. CROSS, *The Oxford Dictionary of the Christian Church* (London 1957) 35. J. DANIÉLOU, *Origène* (Paris 1948). H. DE LUBAC, *Origène: Homélies sur l'Exode (Sources Chretiennes* 16; 1947); "'Typologie' et 'allégorisme,'" *Recherches de science religieuse* 34 (1947) 180–226; 47 (1959) 5–43. J. GUILLET, *ibid.* 34 (1947) 257–302. W. J. BURGHARDT, *Theological Studies* 11 (1950) 78–116. W. GRUBER, *Die pneumatische Exegese bei den Alexandrinern* (Graz 1957). E. MOLLAND, *The Conception of the Gospel in the Alexandrian Theology* (Oslo 1938). R. V. SELLERS, *Two Ancient Christologies* (London 1940).

[A. VAN ROEY]

ALEXANDRIAN LITURGY

The Alexandrian liturgical family, parent of all other Egyptian liturgies, is said to have come from St. Mark the Evangelist. Before the Council of Chalcedon (541), the liturgical rite of Alexandria, Greek-speaking capital of the Egyptian church and cultural center of the Eastern Roman Empire, was the liturgy of St. Mark in Greek. In the aftermath of Chalcedon, the Chalcedonian Christians (Melkites) opted gradually for the Byzantine liturgical rite, while the Non-Chalcedonians (Copts and Ethiopians) modified forms of the Alexandrian liturgy in their own languages, Coptic and Ge'ez. Constantinople's subsequent importance among the Orthodox Christians of the East caused the Byzantine liturgy to intrude upon and finally displace the Alexandrian liturgy among the Melkites. Since the 12th century, the original liturgy of St. Mark in Greek, commonly identified with the original Alexandrian rite, has fallen into disuse. By distilling the layers of Coptic and Byzantine accretions, one can reconstruct an approximation of the original Alexandrian liturgical rite. Earliest known documents include the so-called Strasbourg Papyrus (Gr. 254), a 4th century papyrus containing fragments of what many scholars believe to be the earliest recession of the Anaphora of St. Mark, the *Dêr-Balyzeh Papyrus* (6th–7th century), and an 11th-century manuscript of the *Euchologion* of Serapion of Thmuis (d. 362).

Bibliography: A. HÄNGGI and I. PAHL, *Prex Eucharistica* (Freibourg 1968). R. C. D. JASPER and G. J. CUMING, *Prayers of the Eucharist: Early and Reformed*, 3rd edition (New York 1987). G. J. CUMING, "Thmuis Revisited: Another Look at the Prayers of Bishop Sarapion," *Theological Studies,* 41 (1980) 568–575. G. J. CUMING, "The Anaphora of St. Mark: A Study in Development," *Le Muséon,* 95 (1982) 115–129. B. D. SPINKS, "A Complete Anaphora? A Note on Strasbourg Gr. 254," *Heythrop Journal,* 25 (1984) 51–55.

[E. E. FINN/EDS.]

ALEXANDRINE BULLS

The name usually given to the papal bulls of Pope Alexander VI (1492–1503) that divided the Americas between the Spanish and Portuguese Crowns, on the condition that they assume the obligation of converting the indigenous people within their territories to Christianity. Portugal began exploring the west coast of Africa in 1418. Spain recognized Portuguese control of the Cape Verde Islands in the Treaty of Alcaçovas (1479), and Portugal acknowledged Spanish ownership of the Canaries. Pope Sixtus IV extended the blessings given Portugal in five earlier bulls and confirmed the treaty (1481). Forced into Lisbon by bad weather while returning from his first voyage, Columbus explained his discoveries to King John II (March 9, 1493). John asserted exclusive rights south of the Canaries and west of Africa in the Atlantic. Before Columbus reached the court at Barcelona, the Spanish sovereigns reported to the new pope, Alexander VI, and a bull of May 3, 1493 confirmed Spanish title to lands newly discovered or to be discovered, provided

First page of the bull "Dudum siquidem" of Pope Alexander VI, in an early 16th-century manuscript awarding Christopher Columbus charter and privileges by King Ferdinand II and Queen Isabella I.

they had never been in the possession of any Christian prince. Rights previously granted to Portugal were reserved, and the two governments were treated as equals.

But King Ferdinand V demanded more. A second bull, predated May 3, was more emphatic than the first. A third bull, predated May 4, contained the Line of Demarcation between the spheres of influence of Spain and Portugal. Columbus suggested a line 100 leagues west of the Azores, believing he found there "a great change in the sky, the stars, the air temperature, and in the ocean. . . ." A fourth bull (Sept. 26, 1493) unfairly revoked earlier papal grants that seem to have given Portugal title to lands not in her possession on Christmas Day 1492. Serious diplomatic discussions opened (Aug. 18, 1493) after John began obvious preparations for war. Ferdinand and Isabella wrote to Columbus (Sept. 5) concerning modification of the Demarcation Line. Spain and Portugal agreed on a line 370 leagues west of the Cape Verde Islands, longitude 46° 30' west, in the Treaty of Tordesillas (June 7, 1494).

Earlier bulls, as well as that of 1481, recognized Portugal's exploring efforts, gave papal blessings to the declared intention of Christianizing the indigenous people, and attempted to preserve peace by asking observance of Portugal's commercial laws. The first two bulls of Alexander VI followed these precedents. The idea of the Line of Demarcation was a logical definition of spheres of influence, and not an attempt to divide the world between two nations. The great colonial expansion of Portugal and Spain was carried on with remarkably little friction. It is clear, however, that Ferdinand of Aragon applied pressures to obtain the unreasonable fourth bull. He "used the pope" as other statesmen have done before and since.

At the time the Alexandrine Bulls were issued, it was thought that the islands discovered by Columbus were located along the eastern coast of Asia. Therefore, those documents must be regarded as "pseudo-Asiatic," more than American, and could not really have provided any basis for an exclusive right of sovereignty over the Western Hemisphere on the part of Spain and Portugal. The remote antecedent of the bulls is found in the Donation of Constantine, a famous eighth century forgery, in which that Roman emperor is said to have given the popes, among other privileges, dominion over "the various islands." On this basis, the papal chancery elaborated what is now called by medievalists an "omni-insular doctrine," applied for the first time in 1091 when Urban II gave the Archipelago of Lipari to a local abbot and the island of Corsica to the bishop of Pisa. Afterward, Adrian IV and other popes granted dominion over various islands in European seas to several princes, demanding in exchange the payment of feudal tribute. In some of the final stages of its evolution during the Middle Ages, the collection of Peter's pence was linked to papal sovereignty over islands. Among the areas feudatory to the Holy See were England, Sicily, Sardinia, Cyprus, Castelrosso, the archipelagos of the Tyrrhenian and North African seas, Scandinavia (considered an island by the imperfect geography of the time), and finally, in the fourteenth century, the Canary Islands. The "omni-insular doctrine" was still a part of the public law of Europe when America was discovered.

Bibliography: F. G. DAVENPORT, ed., *European Treaties Bearing on the History of the U.S. and Its Dependencies,* 4 v. (Washington 1917–37) 1:33–100, texts and Eng. trs. of the treaties and bulls. H. VANDER LINDEN, "Alexander VI and the Demarcation of the Maritime and Colonial Domains of Spain and Portugal," *American Historical Review* (New York 1896–) 22 (1916–17) 1–20. D. J. HILL, *A History of Diplomacy in the International Development of Europe,* 3 v. (New York 1905–14). G. ZELLER, *Les Temps modernes,* 2 v. (Paris 1953–55) v.1. L. WECKMANN, *Las bulas alejandrinas de 1493 y la teoría política del Papado medieval* (Mexico City 1949).

[L. WECKMANN/J. B. HEFFERNAN/EDS.]

ALEXIAN BROTHERS

The Congregation of Cellites, or Alexian Brothers (CFA), evolved from the needs of the victims of the Black Death of 14th-century Europe. The work of caring for the sick and burying the dead fell to the lot of men and women whose heroic charity overcame a natural fear of infection and death. One such group, founded in Brabant, Belgium, became known as the Poor Brothers, Bread Brothers, or Cellite Brothers. Those living in St. Alexius House at Aix-la-Chapelle (Aachen, Germany) bound themselves by the vows of religion, according to the Rule of St. Augustine. In 1469 the Holy See raised the society to a religious order. They chose St. Alexius, who worked among the poor, as their chief patron and have since been known as the Alexian Brothers.

Despite European wars and political upheavals, the congregation at its peak had several thousand brothers working in Germany, Holland, Belgium, Luxemburg, and northern France in establishments that were closely affiliated, but locally independent. At a low point, following the French Revolution, the Alexians were revitalized chiefly through the efforts of the superior of the Aachen house, Brother Dominic Brock, known as the ''Pater.'' In 1854 he and four others renewed their vows, which had become almost meaningless because of government interference. Vocations increased and new institutions for the physically and mentally ill were established. In 1870 Clement Wallrath (Pater Dominic's successor) obtained full papal approval from Pius IX, becoming the first superior general responsible directly to the Holy See. Leo XIII urged the independent Alexian houses to unite under Pater Clement, but few actually did so.

Meanwhile, Brother Bonaventure Thelen, who in 1865 was sent to establish the congregation in the U. S., opened Alexian Brothers Hospital in Chicago, Ill., the following year. During the next few years, the brothers pioneered many medical advances and erected hospitals in St. Louis, Mo., Oshkosh, Wis., and Elizabeth, N.J. Under Brother Aloysius Schyns, they incorporated their school of nursing in Chicago in 1898, the only Catholic school of nursing for male students in the nation. In 1938 a home for retired men and women was opened in Signal Mountain, near Chattanooga, Tenn.; in 1955 the brothers took over the operation of the clinic for Father Edward Flanagan's Boys Home at Boys Town, Nebr.

At the beginning of the 21st century, the Brothers operate medical and healthcare facilities in Germany, Belgium, England, Ireland, and the United States, with missions in the Philippines and India.

Bibliography: Official Catholic Directory #0120; C. J. KAUFFMAN, *Tamers of Death: The History of the Alexian Brothers from 1300 to 1789* (New York 1976). C. J. KAUFFMAN, *The Ministry of Healing: The History of the Alexian Brothers from 1789 to the Present* (New York 1978). W. B. FAHERTY, *To Rest In Charity: A History of the Alexian Brothers in Saint Louis (1869–1984)* (St. Louis 1984). L. DAVIDSON, *The Alexian Brothers in Chicago: An Evolutionary Look at the Monastery and Modern Health Care* (New York 1990).

[A. SANFORD/EDS.]

ALEXIUS I COMNENUS, BYZANTINE EMPEROR

Reigned: 1081 to 1118; b. 1048, nephew of Emperor Isaac I Comnenus, he inherited the traditions of a military family. Early in his career, he led small Byzantine forces against bands of Turkish marauders who swarmed over Anatolia after Byzantium's defeat at Mantzikert (1071). In April 1081, he usurped the throne, with support from the army, his family (especially his mother, Anna Dalassena), and his wife's relatives, the Doukas family. Subsequently, he alienated state land to his and his wife's relatives, along with titles and incomes; by marriages, he allied other powerful families to the dominant clan. By restoring the currency (1092), he improved the empire's economic situation, but his heavy taxation oppressed the peasantry.

In 1081, he faced Seljuk Turks in Anatolia, Pechenegs from Central Asia on the Danube, and the Norman conqueror of Southern Italy, Robert Guiscard. Since only Robert threatened Constantinople, Alexius made agreements with the Turks and Pechenegs, and enlisted the Venetians against the Norman invasion (1081) of the western Balkans. Only Robert's death (1085) freed the empire from the Norman menace. The Pechenegs were crushed in 1091 with the aid of the Cumans, a rival Asiatic people. The coming of the First Crusade (1096–97) enabled Alexius to regain Nicaea and repel the Turks from the Anatolian coastlands.

The crusaders, who came in part because of Alexius's appeal to the pope, posed severe problems for the empire. The hordes of commoners who followed Peter the Hermit and Walter the Penniless (1096) were transferred to Anatolia, where the Turks soon decimated them. Most of the nobles, including Bohemund (Guiscard's son) and Godfrey of Bouillon, were induced to pledge fealty to Alexius, who in return promised military support to them. Because Alexius's assistance proved insufficient, rumor claimed that the Byzantines had covertly aided the Turks. After Bohemund seized Antioch, Alexius struggled to regain it. In 1107–8, Bohemund secured Pope Paschal II's support for a crusade against the Byzantine Empire; Alexius defeated the Norman forces in the western Balkans.

With regard to the papacy, Alexius endeavored to heal the schism of 1054. Pope Urban II was interested, and dispatched the First Crusade partially to rescue the Eastern Church. But Paschal II repelled the Byzantines when he insisted that they acknowledge papal primacy before discussing other issues. Internally, Alexius strove to repress such heretics as John Italus and Basil the Bogomil. To reinforce Orthodoxy, he instituted a staff of preachers and teachers at Sancta Sophia and other churches in Constantinople.

After 1112, Alexius was repeatedly ill, and his wife, daughter Anna Comnena, and her husband assumed a dominant role. But at his death in 1118, Alexius left his son John II a larger, more secure, and reinvigorated empire. Anna Comnena wrote a laudatory history of the reign, while John Oxites (ca. 1091) and John Zonaras (who wrote ca. 1140–60) criticized Alexius's appropriation of church treasures and his enrichment of his own family at the empire's expense.

Bibliography: A. COMENA, *The Alexiad,* tr. E. R. A. SEWTER (Harmondsworth 1969). M. ANGOLD, *The Byzantine Empire 1025–1204: A Political History,* 2nd ed. (London 1997). M. MULLETT and D. SMYTHE, eds., *Alexios I Komnenos,* vol. I, Papers (Belfast 1996). R.–J. LILIE, *Byzantium and the Crusader States 1096–1204,* tr. J. C. MORRIS and J. E. RIDINGS (Oxford 1993). M. ANGOLD, *Church and Society in Byzantium under the Comneni, 1081–1261* (Cambridge, 1995). T. GOUMA-PETERSON, ed., *Anna Komnene and Her Times* (New York 2000).

[C. M. BRAND]

ALEXIUS THE STUDITE, PATRIARCH OF CONSTANTINOPLE

Abbot at the monastery Studion from 1025 to 1043, (hence "the Studite"); birth and death dates unknown. Alexius was appointed patriarch by Emperor Basil II on the latter's death bed without the sanction or knowledge of the metropolitan; he was immediately enthroned on Dec. 15, 1025. As his appointment was not in accordance with Canon Law, his entire reign was marred by arguments and altercations. In 1037 Alexius withstood the attempts of John, brother of the reigning Emperor Michael IV, to remove him from the patriarchal throne by asserting that his removal would automatically bring about the removal of the bishops he had consecrated and the priests he had ordained. When John, eager to secure the patriarchy for himself, persisted in efforts to unseat him, Alexius threatened to declare his coronation of Michael IV null and void, and thus he successfully maintained his throne.

The importance of his patriarchate lies in his administrative policies, which were marked in numerous edicts, synods, and disciplinary laws. He concerned himself ex-

tensively with the doctrines of the Monophysites and the Messalians and with Byzantine marriage laws; but he showed weakness by not opposing the second and third marriages of Empress Zoë, daughter of Constantine VIII; these marriages were against Canon Law and the tradition of his monastery. In 1034, Alexius founded a monastery patterned after those of the Studite Order and devoted to the Blessed Virgin; it was later named after him.

Bibliography: *Patrologia Graeca,* ed. J. P. MIGNE, 161 v. (Paris 1857–66) 119:744–748, 827–850. T. BALSAMON, *ibidem* 137:1245. S. PÉTRIDÈS, *Dictionnaire d'histoire et de géographie ecclésiastiques,* ed. A. BAUDRILLART et al. (Paris 1912—) 2:398. K. BAUS, *Lexikon für Theologie und Kirche*[2], ed. J. HOFER and K. RAHNER, 10 v. (2d, new ed. Freiburg 1957–65) 1:328. É. AMANN, *Histoire de l'église depuis les origines jusqu'à nos jours,* eds., A. FLICHE and V. MARTIN (Paris 1935—) 7:136–138. G. FICKER, *Erlasse des Patriarchen von Konstantinopel Alexios Studites* (Kiel 1911).

[G. LUZNYCKY]

ALFARABI (FĀRĀBĪ, AL-)

Arab philosopher and theologian, fuller name Abū Naṣr Muḥammad ibn Muḥammad Al–Fārābī; b. Wasig, Transoxania, in the district of Fārāb, *c.* 870; d. Damascus, 950. Of Turkish descent, he spent most of his life in Iraq and Syria. At Baghdad, where he came in contact with Christian scholars, he acquired a knowledge of Greek philosophy. His works on philosophy, particularly his commentaries on Aristotle, gained him wide notice; he was considered the "second Teacher" after Aristotle himself. He wrote on other subjects, however, including mathematics, music, medicine, and astronomy. He passed several years at the court of Saif ad–Dawlah, ruler of Aleppo, engaged mostly in study. Otherwise his life was uneventful.

Emanation. NEOPLATONISM and the Islamic religious tradition offered Alfarabi the notion of a first being, the One, who is absolute unity, perfect transcendence, and pure existence, and thus a necessary being who is present to himself in an act of knowledge where intellect, object of intellect, and act of intellect are absolutely one. From this being, according to the Neoplatonic principle accepted by Alfarabi, only one creature could derive immediately, and this by a process of "emanation" (Faid). Emanation, however, proceeds by degrees. Thus a first intellect, supremely perfect and yet essentially inferior to the One, is the first creature. He is also the first form of multiplicity, for his essence is necessary when viewed in relation to God (the One) and contingent when viewed in itself. This duality of aspect, distant ancestor of the real distinction between essence and existence, leads to a duality in the act of knowledge. The first intellect knows God and itself by two acts, which themselves are creative: the act by which he knows God is the cause of a second intellect, and that by which he knows himself gives rise to a heavenly sphere with its own soul and body. The process continues, according to common Neoplatonic doctrine, until the spheres of the planets and the fixed stars are produced. The lowest of these pure intellects, the active intellect, tenth in rank after the first cause, is the author of the matter and form in the sublunar world. Finally, under the influence of the heavenly bodies, common matter is prepared to bring forth the forms given it by the active intellect (*dator formarum*). A gradual growth in perfection takes place, culminating in the emergence of the human soul, the highest form associated with matter.

Man and Society. At this point, Alfarabi describes the growth of human consciousness. The activity of the senses furnishes the materials for universal ideas, and illumination by the active intellect puts the human intellect in act. Man's grasp of universals grows as he frees himself from matter and comes more under the influence of the active intellect. The final step in the process is reached when man has an "acquired intellect," which for Alfarabi is almost on a level with the active intellect.

In all this Alfarabi depends heavily on his Greek predecessors, above all on Alexander of Aphrodisias. But there is present in most of his writing a mystical element that reminds one of PLOTINUS. The difference, of course, lies in the fact that Alfarabi considers union with the active intellect as the highest form of existence for man, and not union with the One, as Plotinus held. Alfarabi defines man's happiness as a permanent state of being wherein he is freed from matter and enjoys the society of pure spirits. He insists on the collaboration of intellect and will in the tendency toward this goal.

Moreover, for Alfarabi man is a social being who needs the society of other men to grow toward happiness. In his notion of society Alfarabi is greatly indebted to Plato, particularly to the *Republic.* The "virtuous state" he sees as analogous to the human body, with the ruler as the heart. The ideal ruler is both philosopher and prophet—philosopher to have attained the perfection of the theoretical intellect, prophet to be able to receive inspiration that will lead men to happiness. Since this ideal is almost impossible to realize, Alfarabi was satisfied if the ruler were to possess only the essential qualities. Again, like Plato, he contrasted the ideal state with its imperfect imitations, for example, democracy, timocracy, and tyranny.

Appreciation. In general, Alfarabi relied heavily on the Greek tradition as he knew it. Although he made fre-

quent references to Plato and Aristotle, the extent of his knowledge of their works is not easy to assess. He did write a commentary on Aristotle's *De interpretatione,* gave a summary of the *Metaphysics,* and claimed to have read nine books of Plato's *Laws.* But in most cases his knowledge came from the commentators Alexander and Themistius and from the many manuals of philosophy then available.

Alfarabi's influence in Islam was considerable, for he determined the principal lines of its philosophical speculation. He was generally appreciated by his successors, despite the attacks of ALGAZEL. His works were frequently translated into Latin and Hebrew in the Middle Ages. He seems to have influenced the political theories of MAIMONIDES, but for the most part ranks far behind Avicenna and Averroës in importance for medieval philosophy.

Bibliography: Works. *Philosophische Abhandlungen,* ed. and tr. F. H. DIETERICI (Leiden, Arab. text 1890; Ger. tr. 1892). *Abhandlung: Der Musterstaat,* ed. and tr. F. H. DIETERICI (Leiden, Arab. text 1895; Ger. tr. 1900). *De intellectu et intellecto,* critical edition of Arab. text M. BOUYGES (Beirut 1938). *Commentary on Aristotle's "De interpretatione,"* ed. W. KUTSCH and S. MARROW (Beirut 1960). *Católogo de las ciencias,* ed. and tr. A. GONZÁLEZ PALENCIA (2d ed. Madrid 1953), Span., Arab. and 2 Lat. Versions. *De Platonis philosophia,* ed. F. ROSENTHAL and K. WALZER (Plato arabus 2; London 1943), Lat. and Arab. *Compendium legum Platonis,* ed. and tr. F. GABRIELI, (*ibidem* 3; 1952), Lat. and Arab. *Alfarabi's Philosophy of Plato and Aristotle,* tr. with introd. M. MAHDI (New York 1962). English selections in R. LERNER and M. MAHDI, *Medieval Political Philosophy: A Sourcebook* (Glencoe, Ill. 1963). Literature. M. STEINSCHNEIDER, *Al–Farabi des arabischen Philosophen Leben und Schriften* (Memoires de l'Academie Imperial des Sciences de St. Petersburg 13.4; 1859). I. MADKOUR, *La Place d'al–Fârâbi dans l'école philosophique musulmane* (Paris 1935). E. I. J. ROSENTHAL, *Political Thought in Medieval Islam* (Cambridge, Eng. 1958). N. RESCHER, *Al–Fārābī: An Annotated Bibliography* (Pittsburgh 1962). R. WALZER, *Enciclopedia filosofica,* 4 v. (Venice–Rome 1957) 2:269–270.

[J. FINNEGAN]

ALFERIUS, ST.

Cluniac abbot; b. Salerno; d. La Cava, April 12, 1050. Alferius (Adalfericus, Alpherius) was a member of the Pappacarbone family and received an excellent education. Introduced to the court of Prince Waimar III of Salerno, he was sent on diplomatic missions to France and Germany, *c.* 1002–03. While traveling, he fell ill and stopped at the monastery of S. Michele della Chiusa (Piedmont), where he met ODILO OF CLUNY. To fulfill a vow, Alferius became a monk at Cluny in 1003. He was recalled to Salerno by Waimar III and charged with the reform of the monasteries in this area. His hermitage became the Abbey of La Cava (SS. Trinità) when he was joined by a number of disciples. His cult was approved by Leo XIII in 1893, and confirmed again in 1928.

Feast: April 12.

Bibliography: HUGH OF VENOSA, *Vitae quatuor priorum abbatum Cavensium,* ed. L. MATTEI CERASOLI in *Rerum italicarum scriptores, 500–1500* (Città di Castello 1900) 6.5:3–12. *Acta Sanctorum* April 2:96–101. P. F. KEHR, *Regesta Pontificum Romanorum. Italia Pontificum.* (Berlin 1906–35) 8:311. F. M. MEZZA, *L'ambasciatore che fondò un monastero* (Cava, Italy 1952), popularization. A. BUTLER, *The Lives of the Saints,* ed. H. THURSTON and D. ATTWATER (New York 1956) 2:80.

[R. GRÉGOIRE]

ALFIELD, THOMAS, BL.

Priest martyr; name also given as Aufield, Alphilde, Hawfield, Offeldus; *alias* Badger; b. Gloucestershire, England; hanged at Tyburn (London), July 6, 1585. Thomas and his brother Robert, who was St. Edmund CAMPION's servant and betrayer, were born into a Protestant family. Thomas was educated at Eton and Cambridge. Following his conversion to Catholicism, he studied at Douai and Rheims, where he was ordained (1581). While working in the north of England, he was arrested and sent to the Tower of London, May 2, 1582. Although he remained resolute even under torture, he was released. Captured a second time, he apostatized in prison. Repenting of his lapse, he lived for a time in Rheims before returning to the English mission to circulate Dr. Allen's booklet, *True and modest Defence* (August 1584), in response to Burghley's *Execution of Justice.* For this he was arrested with Ven. Thomas Webley, a dyer's apprentice, and a man named Crabbe. They were imprisoned in the Tower of London, then at Newgate. Crabbe was released after renouncing allegiance to the pope; Alfield and Webley were executed together. Both were beatified by Pius XI on Dec. 15, 1929.

Feast of the English Martyrs: May 4 (England).

See Also: ENGLAND, SCOTLAND, AND WALES, MARTYRS OF.

Bibliography: R. CHALLONER, *Memoirs of Missionary Priests,* ed. J. H. POLLEN (rev. ed. London 1924; repr. Farnborough 1969). J. H. POLLEN, *Acts of English Martyrs* (London 1891).

[K. I. RABENSTEIN]

ALFONSO DE CASTRO

Theologian; b. Zamora, Spain, 1495; d. Brussels, Feb. 3, 1558. De Castro entered the Franciscan Order at Salamanca in 1511; he studied theology there and later at the University of Alcalá. He occupied a chair of theology at Salamanca for 30 years, meanwhile doing occasional preaching in Germany, England, and at the court of Charles V. In 1530 he took part in a debate on the validity of the marriage of Henry VIII and wrote a treatise on the subject that was posthumously published at Lyons in 1568. As theologian to Cardinal Pacheco at the first session of the Council of Trent, he was active in the discussions of original sin and the canon of Sacred Scripture. He became so skilled in the knowledge of penal law that he came to be known as "princeps poenalistarum." In 1557 he was named archbishop of Compostela, but died before being consecrated. Among his works are: *Adversus omnes haereses lib. XIV* (Paris 1534), which catalogues and refutes the heresies from the time of the Apostles to the 16th century; *Homiliae 25 in Ps. 50* (Salamanca 1537); *Homiliae 24 in Ps. 31* (Salamanca 1540); *De justa haereticorum punitione* (Salamanca 1547); and *De potestate legis poenalis* (Salamanca 1550).

Bibliography: L. WADDING, *Scriiptores Ordinis Minorum* (Quaracci-Florence 1931–) 18:132–134.

[B. CAVANAUGH]

ALFONSUS, BONIHOMINIS

Also known as de Buenhombre. Spanish Dominican Hebraist and Arabist; b. Cuenca or Toledo; d. before Aug. 12, 1353. He is known chiefly for his Latin translation of two Arabic works of a Jewish Rabbi converted to Christianity: *Tractatus Rabbi Samuelis ad Rabbi Isaac per quem probatur adventus Christi,* translated while he was in Paris in 1339 (many eds.; *Bibl. vet. Patrum* 18:518); and *Disputatio Abutalib Saraceni et Samuelis Judaei quae fides praecellat* (uned. MS Madrid Nac. 4402 f. 103–110), translated while he was bishop of Marrakech in Morocco (1344 to death). Both are Christian apologies in dialogue form. His other translations from Arabic into Latin are *Historia Joseph* (uned.), done probably in Egypt (1336) and the *Legenda S. Antonii abbatis Thebaidis* (ed. *Bibl. vet. Patrum* 18).

Bibliography: J. QUÉTIF and J. ÉCHARD, *Scriptores Ordinis Praedicatorum* 1:594–595. S. RUIZ, *Dictionnaire d'histoire et de géographie ecclésiastiques* 9: 1135–36. M. H. LAURENT, *ibid.* 10:1061. F. STEGMÜLLER, *Lexikon für Theologie und Kirche*2 1:334.

[M. J. FINNEGAN]

ALFORD, MICHAEL

Jesuit historian; b. London, 1587; d. Saint–Omer, Flanders, Aug. 11, 1652. After a novitiate begun at Louvain (1607), and after the usual course of philosophy in the English College, Seville, and theology at Louvain, during which he was ordained, Alford (originally Griffith), spent two years among the English at Naples. For five years (1615–20) he was English penitentiary at St. Peter's, Rome. He was socius to the master of novices at Liège (1620) and later rector of the tertians at Ghent before going to England in the winter of 1628–29. Upon landing, he was mistaken for Richard Smith, Bishop of Chalcedon, and arrested, but he was released at the intervention of Queen Henrietta Maria. Alford worked in Leicestershire and Herefordshire, becoming superior of the residence of St. Anne in 1636. He spent his leisure mainly in historical studies and writing, and retired to Saint–Omer in 1652 to finish his three–volume *Fides Regia Britannica sive Annales Ecclesiae Britannicae* (Liège 1663). He wrote also a life of St. Winefride (1635) and *Britannia Illustra* (1641).

Bibliography: H. MORE, *Historia Provinciae anglicanae Societatis Jesu* (Saint–Omer 1660) 394–395. G. OLIVER, *Collections toward Illustrating the Biography of the Scotch, English, and Irish Members of the Society of Jesus* (London 1845). A. DE BACKER, *Bibliothèque des écrivains de la compagnie de Jésus*, 3 v. (Paris 1869–76) 1:71. T. COOPER, *The Dictionary of National Biography From the Earliest Times to 1900*, 63 v. (London 1885–1900) 1:284. C. SOMMERVOGEL et al., *Bibliothèque de la Compagnie de Jésus*, 11 v. (Brussels–Paris 1890–1932) 1:175–176.

[F. EDWARDS]

Alfred the Great, King.

ALFRED THE GREAT

Reigned 871–899. Alfred the Great, King of Wessex, was the first king in England to identify himself with the ''English''; during his reign, he laid the foundations for the eventual political unification of England. The Viking invasions, which began again shortly before Alfred's reign, provided an opportunity for Alfred to unify the Englishmen against a common enemy; he then organized and implemented England's first plan of national defense. His conception of kingship led to the foundation of the English monarchy. Alfred respected education and worked to recover that which had been lost through the Viking depredations.

Alfred was born in 849 in Berkshire. He was the youngest of six children and spent his early years traveling around the kingdom with his parents, King Æthelwulf and Queen Osburh. They were very pious and passed on their religious devotion to their children. Alfred visited Rome twice; the first time he was only four years old and was received by Pope Leo IV, who designated him as a spiritual son. Alfred's second journey to Rome was even more fruitful. At the time, Pope Leo was fortifying the area around St. Peter's against the Saracens, and it is possible that Alfred learned some valuable military strategies

from the Pope, i.e., the best defense against invaders was to meet them at sea and defeat them there. He also became devoted to the papal see and remained so for the rest of his life. Both on the way to and from Rome, Alfred and his father, who was newly widowed, spent time at the court of Charles the Bald, king of the Franks. On the return journey, Æthelwulf married Charles' daughter, Judith, and brought her back to England. Alfred was very impressed by the scholars he found at the Frankish court, which became a model for his own kingdom many years later.

According to the *Anglo-Saxon Chronicle*, Æthelwulf died in 858, two years after returning from Rome, and was succeeded by his son Æthelberht. Five years later, Æthelberht too, was dead, and England was facing the threat of Norse invasions. Alfred's only surviving brother, Æthelred, became king, and during his reign the Vikings moved further and further into England each year, ''making peace'' with the weaker English kingdoms around Wessex. Alfred, meanwhile, had married Ealswith, a Mercian noblewoman, thus strengthening the alliance between the kingdoms. In 867, the Vikings took up winter quarters in Mercia. The *Chronicle* records that the Mercian king, Burgred ''begged Æthelred, king of Wessex, and his brother Alfred to help them fight against the host''. However, despite receiving their aid, Burgred was eventually forced to make peace with the Vikings.

The Vikings soon conquered East Anglia and by 870 they were attacking Wessex from their base at Reading. Æthelred and Alfred fought against them but to little avail; despite winning several important battles, the brothers were unable to gain a definitive advantage over their enemies. For Alfred, this situation became desperate when another Norse army arrived at Reading, and his brother Æthelred died shortly thereafter from wounds received during battle.

Alfred became king during one of the darkest times in England's history. Of the major English kingdoms, only Wessex survived, and the Danes had established armies in over one-third of England. His biographer, Asser, wrote that Alfred "did not think that he alone could ever withstand such great ferocity of the Vikings, unless strengthened by divine help, since he had already sustained great losses of many men while his brothers were alive" and after much fighting, Alfred made peace with the enemy. Several years later, in 873, the Vikings drove King Burgred out of Mercia; he went to Rome and the Saxon leadership in that kingdom passed to an ealdorman, Ethelred, who later became one of Alfred's strongest allies.

During the next five years the Vikings continued to move into England, creating what was known as the *Danelaw* and forcing the English to make peace with their armies. In 878, the third invasion of Wessex began simultaneously with an attack on Devon, and Alfred was forced into hiding in the Somerset levels. He fortified Athelney and in May of 878, rallied the men of Somerset, Wiltshire and parts of Hampshire. Two days later, there was a great battle at Edington in Wiltshire, from which Alfred emerged victorious. As part of the resulting peace treaty the Viking leader Guthrum and many of his comrades converted to Christianity. Alfred stood as his sponsor and later honored Guthrum and his soldiers with feasting and gifts. The Vikings promised to leave Wessex at once, and they returned to East Anglia.

Alfred had nearly 14 years of relative peace, and he used that time to create a plan of national defense for England. He began a thorough military reorganization consisting of three major innovations. The first was the division of the *fyrd* (standing army) into two halves, each serving six months. This was designed to give some continuity to the English military actions; mounted warriors fought in the field while the *fyrdmen* at home guarded the land from sudden raids. The second, and possibly most important of Alfred's measures, was the building of large fortifications (*burhs*) at strategic locations to defend against the Vikings and later to serve as bases in the re-

conquest of the *Danelaw*. Alfred's defensive measures were very similar to those taken by Charles the Bald, and he adopted the Carolingian tactic of controlling movement along a river by building along both banks and connecting them with bridges. The third innovation was establishing a fleet of large, fast ships to challenge the Vikings on the seas.

After ensuring the survival and protection of the English, Alfred set about restoring the monastic life of the Church in England and actively pursued the revival of literature and learning. For two generations England had seen little but warfare and was a ruined landscape of burnt monasteries and churches, squalid farms, and poor, ignorant people. Alfred began to remedy that through a vigorous program of religious revival and scholarship. Nearly half of his revenue was devoted to educational ends. He brought foreign scholars and craftsmen to his court from every country in Christendom and established a great school for teaching the sons of thanes and free men to read and write. Alfred also made himself a master of Latin. He translated what he considered the most useful works of Christian and classical knowledge into the vernacular, including Pope Gregory I's *Pastoral Care*, Boethius's *Consolation of Philosophy*, and St. Augustine's *Soliloquies*. As part of his religious program Alfred founded two religious houses. One was at Athelney, where he had sheltered during the Viking invasions, and the other at Shaftesbury, where his daughter Æthelgifu was made Abbess. He supported those religious houses that had survived the Viking depredations, and created an environment within the Church as a whole where the visual and literary arts could flourish.

Alfred also enacted a uniform law code for the good of his subjects, with great emphasis on oath keeping and settling of feuds, and horrible punishment for treason. But Alfred's law codes were more than just a means for keeping social order; according to Simon Keynes, "The act of law-making was a public display of the king's royal power, and provided an opportunity for him to express his political and ideological aspirations in legal form."

In 886, Alfred recovered London from the Danes and entrusted it to his ally and soon to be son-in-law, Ethelred of Mercia. The *Chronicle* records that "all the English people submitted to him except those who were under the Danish yoke." Alfred was now not only king of Wessex but of all free Englishmen, and their acceptance of him as such expressed a feeling that he represented interests common to the entire race. This event can be seen as the beginning of English unity; in charters of the late 880s and early 890s, Alfred is referred to as "king of the Anglo-Saxons."

The Vikings returned to England in 892 but made little headway against Alfred's fortified kingdom, and many of them settled instead in the *Danelaw*. Alfred continued to improve the *burghal* defenses of England, working closely with his son Edward, his daughter Æthelflaed, and her husband, Ethelred of Mercia. Together, they laid the foundations for the eventual conquest of the *Danelaw* and unification of the Anglo-Saxon kingdoms.

Alfred died on Oct. 26, 899, and was buried at Winchester. In his 28-year reign, he had preserved Wessex from the Viking invasions and thus saved England. He also took innovative military measures to protect England from further invasions, emerging as perhaps the first ''English'' king. He rescued many religious houses and began the restoration of learning and literature. In the words of Arthur Bryant, Alfred not only saved a Christian state by his exertions, but made it worth saving.

Bibliography: R. ABELS, *Lordship and Military Obligation in Anglo-Saxon England* (Berkeley 1988). R. ABELS, *Alfred the Great: War, Kingship and Culture in Anglo-Saxon England* (New York 1998). C. BROOKE, *From Alfred to Henry III 871–1272* (New York 1969). J. CAMPBELL, ed. *The Anglo-Saxons* (Ithaca 1982). D. DUMVILLE, *Wessex and England from Alfred to Edgar: Six Essays on Political, Cultural, and Ecclesiastical Revival* (Woodbridge 1992). D. DUMVILLE and S. KEYNES, gen. eds. *The Anglo-Saxon Chronicle: A Collaborative Edition* (Cambridge 1996). D. FISHER, *The Anglo-Saxon Age* (London 1973). S. KEYNES and M. LAPIDGE, *Alfred the Great: Asser's 'Life of King Alfred' and Other Contemporary Sources* (Hammondsworth 1983). A. P. SMYTH, *Alfred the Great* (Oxford 1995). F. STENTON, *Anglo-Saxon England* (Oxford 1989). M. SWANTON, ed. *The Anglo-Saxon Chronicle* (Routledge 1996).

[L. A. LEHTOLA]

ALGAZEL (GHAZZĀLĪ, AL-)

Arab philosopher and theologian; b. Ṭūs, province of Khorāsān, Persia, 1058; d. Ṭūs, 1111.

Life. Algazel received his early education in his native city and at Jurjan, where the teaching of the mystics, or Sufis, was emphasized (*see* SUFISM). The decisive period of his formation began, however, when he attended the lectures of a famous theologian, al-Juwaynī, at Nisāpour. There he acquired a deep knowledge of Islamic theology and law and was initiated into the philosophical speculations of ALFARABI and AVICENNA. From the beginning, Algazel shared with his teacher a distrust for authority in matters of religion. This distrust accompanied him all his life, explaining in great part the distinctive features of his intellectual and spiritual evolution.

When al-Juwaynī died in 1085, Algazel joined the scholars whom the vizier, Niẓām al-Mulk, had gathered around him. After six years in this group, he was named professor of Muslim law at the famous Niẓāmiya College in Baghdad. In 1095 he resigned his post, left Baghdad, and on the pretext of making the pilgrimage to Mecca retired to Damascus. In his *Al-Munqidh min aḍ-ḍalāl* (Deliverance from Error), he explains this decision on religious grounds as a need to deepen his spiritual life and to free himself from worldly preoccupations; scholars suggest, however, that political considerations had something to do with his retirement. Following this, he spent two years in Syria, made the pilgrimage to Mecca, visited Jerusalem, and lived the life of an ascetic, studying and practicing mysticism. He then returned to Ṭūs, probably before 1098 or 1099. He abandoned his life of private teaching and ascetical practices in 1106 when, on demand of the vizier, Fakhr al-Mulk, he returned to Nisāpour as professor at the Niẓāmiya College there. This second period of teaching lasted until 1109, when he retired to Ṭūs, to remain until his death.

Thought. Algazel is among the profound religious teachers of Islam. A polemist of first rank, he is mainly responsible for the intellectual orientation taken by orthodox Islam since his day. He assured the triumph of the theology of al- ASH'ARĪ; at the same time, he contributed to the decadence of philosophical speculation by his attacks on certain classical Neoplatonic doctrines held by Alfarabi and Avicenna. He also endorsed mysticism, thitherto the object of suspicion and condemnation by the orthodox followers of Islam.

Algazel's writings, especially *Al-Munqidh min aḍ-ḍalāl*, show that his conversion expressed itself in the form of universal doubt, somewhat similar to that of R. DESCARTES but arising in a different context. Algazel was convinced that there is in man an innate ground of religious experience that is generally oriented by parental authority. Thus children born of Christians become Christians; those born of Jews become Jews. Such influence cannot be justified, particularly since it would put all religions, Islam included, on the same footing. To found his own religious life and to work for the revival of the true religion, for him Islam, it was necessary for Algazel to uncover the fundamental experience that would justify all the rest. In describing his search for this, he follows a logical rather than a chronological pattern. He begins by doubting sense knowledge, which, as the intellect shows, contains contradictory elements. But he holds that even clear intellectual concepts cannot be accepted at face value, for they too might be found wanting if they could be examined by a higher faculty.

Algazel finally escapes from these harassing doubts not by argument and demonstration, but by the light that God has given him. Once received, this light from God allows him to evaluate the four principal positions that have been defended by the theologians, the philosophers, the Batinites, and the mystics. In weighing each position,

Algazel is not purely negative, but seems conscious that the shortcomings of any one explanation do not render it valueless. It is this attitude that caused Algazel to be accused of insincerity, for his adversaries were not slow to point out that, after attacking them, he incorporated much of their doctrine in his own synthesis.

Algazel criticizes the theologians for adopting principles admitted by their adversaries and for using arguments based merely on universal consent. His criticism of the philosophers is that they have some excellent logical principles but fail to live up to them in proving their own positions, being content merely to echo a long tradition taken over from the Greeks. The third group whose doctrine Algazel rejects is the Batinite Sect, which claimed that all religious truth must be received for no other reason except the infallible authority of a teacher (their infallible Imām, at that time the Fatimite Caliph of Cairo); their position is a radical denial of his own, which claims that authority can never replace experience. The fourth group, the mystics, receives Algazel's full adherence. In his view, purity of heart obtained by recollection is the first condition of progress in the mystic way, which leads to complete absorption in God (*fanā*). At this point there is a period of visions and revelations, later reaching its perfection in a nearness to God. The prophets are those who reach the highest degree of experience and are thus constituted physicians of the heart. It is through their influence and the following of their precepts that a man can eventually hope to attain light.

Works. A great number of works have been attributed to Algazel (see Bouyges). During his first teaching period, up to 1095, he wrote some treatises on logic and composed the *Maqāṣid al-Falācifa,* a summary of philosophical doctrines, which he then refuted in the *Tahāfut al-Falācifa* (Incoherence of the Philosophers). He wrote also some works on Moslem canon law and a treatise on theology, the *Iqtisād.* During his retreat (1095–1105) he composed his principal work, *Iḥyā 'Ulūm ad-Dīn* (Revival of the Religious Sciences), together with numerous minor works dealing with the spiritual life. In 1105–06, while teaching at Nisāpour, he wrote his intellectual autobiography and later *Mishkāt al-Anwār* (Niche of Lights), a highly esoteric account of his religious thought. In the years preceding his retirement from teaching in 1095 and immediately following it, he wrote several works against the Batinite Sect, among others, *Al-Qisṭās al-Mostiqīm* (The Just Balance).

See Also: ARABIAN PHILOSOPHY; ISLAM.

Bibliography: Works in translation. *The Faith and Practice of al-Gazālī,* tr. W. MONTGOMERY WATT (London 1953); *Streitschrift des Gazali gegen die Bātinijja-Sekte,* ed. I. GOLDHIZER (Leiden 1916; repr. 1956); *The Alchemy of Happiness,* tr. C. FIELD (London 1910); *Mishkat al-Anwār (The Niche for Lights),* tr. W. H. T. GAIRDNER (London 1924; Lahore 1952); *O Disciple* (Beirut 1951); *Al Qistās al Mostiqīm* (Damascus 1955–57); *Worship in Islam,* tr. and commentary E. E. CALVERLY of *Book of the Ihyā on the Worship* (Madras 1925; 2d ed. London 1957); *Ihyā ouloûm ed-din ou Vivification des sciences de la foi,* analyzed by H. BOUSQUET (Paris 1955). AVERROËS, *Tahāfut al-Tahāfut,* tr. S. VAN DEN BERGH, 2 v. (London 1954), contains text of Algazel's *Tahāfut* quoted by Averroës. Studies. A. BOUYGES, *Essai de chronologie des oeuvres de al-Ghazali* (Algazel) (Beirut 1960). A. J. WENSINCK, *La Pensée de Ghazzâlî* (Paris 1940). D. B. MACDONALD, ''The Life of al-Ghazzālā with Especial Reference to His Religious Experiences and Opinions,'' *The Journal of the American Oriental Society* (New Haven 1843–) 20 (1899) 71–132. S. M. ZWEMER, *A Moslem Seeker after God* (New York 1920). M. ASINPALACIOS, *''Algazel'' dogmatica, moral, ascetica* (Zaragoza 1901); *La Mystique d'al-Gazzali* (Beirut 1914); *La espiritualidad de Algazel y su sentido Cristiano,* 4 v. (Madrid 1934–41). J. OBERMANN, *Der philosophische und religiöse Subjektivismus Ghazalis* (Vienna 1921). M. SMITH, *Al-Ghazālī: The Mystic* (London 1944). F. JABRE, La Notion de la ma'rifa chez Ghazali (Beirut 1958).

[J. FINNEGAN]

ALGER OF LIÈGE (ALGER OF CLUNY, ALGERUS MAGISTER)

Theologian, whose writings influenced the development of Canon Law; b. Liège, Belgium, in the mid–11th century; d. Cluny, France, about 1131 or 1132. According to his biographer, Nicholas of Liège, Alger received his education in his native city and was first appointed deacon and teacher at St. Bartholomew's, Liège. About 1101 he was transferred to St. Lambert's Cathedral, became a canon, and served as secretary to Bishop Otbert (1092–1117) and his successor, Frederick (1119–21). After Frederick's death on May 27, 1121, Alger entered Cluny and, though already advanced in years, was ordained.

Writings. Presumably while he was at St. Lambert's (1101–21), Alger wrote the *Tractate Concerning the Legal Rights of the Cathedral.* Before 1094 he had written a more important work, *On Mercy and Justice (Liber de misericordia et justitia)*, in which he criticized certain sacramental doctrines of St. PETER DAMIAN (d. 1072) as too lax, and advocated a more thorough study of St. Augustine's sacramental teaching. Some 124 quotations from the works of St. Augustine serve to underline his own effort in this regard.

In later life, Alger wrote *On The Sacraments of the Lord's Body and Blood (De Sacramentis corporis et sanguinis dominici),* generally dated 1110 to 1121. Much of its source material is derived from Ivo's *Decretum.* In addition to these works, his short treatise, *On Free Will (Libellus de libero arbitrio),* of unknown date, and a number of Alger's letters are still extant. But it is more than doubtful that the little tract *On the Sacrifice of the Mass,* attributed to him, and the so–called *Sentences of Master A.,* also often assigned to him, are actually his works.

Although Alger's work on the Eucharist was considered by PETER THE VENERABLE to be far superior to the writings of LANFRANC (d. 1089) and GUITMAND OF AVERSA (d. 1095) on the same subject, its influence on later authors was not strong. His work *On Mercy and Justice,* however, lived on through Gratian's *Decretum* (*see* GRATIAN, DECRETUM OF). It has been estimated that Gratian borrowed about 100 texts from it. More important, the *Dicta Gratiani* contain numerous explanations often copied verbatim from Alger. When Peter Lombard used Gratian's *Decretum* in the compilation of his *Sentences,* Alger's influence on theology was further intensified.

Doctrinal Teachings. In his search for a solution to the doctrinal problems conjured up by the contradictory claims of the GREGORIAN REFORM, Alger points to the "invocation of the divine name" in Baptism as a constructive sacramental principle. Accordingly, he formulates the general rule: "All sacraments, no matter who administers them in the name of the Trinity, are in themselves true and holy" (*De Sacramentis* 2.10). He considers it "a crime to believe that the invocation of the divine name in His sacraments may be frustrated" (*De Sacramentis* 3.2). If administered by heretics, sacraments are valid but without divine grace. An exception to this rule is Baptism administered even by a pagan in case of necessity, for "necessity knows no law" (*De Misericordia* 1.55). In Alger's time the word "sacrament" was neither clearly defined nor restricted to only seven liturgical rites; it must also be noted that in formulating his rule Alger had Baptism, Holy Orders, and the celebration of the Mass in mind.

Alger heavily underlines the importance of faith and intention. By faith, he holds, all sacraments of the Church are brought to completion. The perfection and sum total of the Christian faith are found in the use of the Trinitarian name. Although Alger insists that God examines our intention and faith rather than our external actions, he stresses that to be valid the liturgical rite of the Church must be observed. Any ritual changes made outside the Church must be rejected as heretical. However, regional differences in the liturgical customs of the Church do not affect sacramental validity, for the unifying element is the unity of faith and changes should be judged according to the intention of those responsible for them. Similar clarifications account for an unusual amount of casuistry in Alger's work on the Eucharist. Unfortunately Hugh of Saint–Victor, Gratian, and Peter Lombard did not make

---

Capital: Algiers.
Size: 952,444 sq. miles, 838,315 sq. miles of which are Sahara.
Population: 31,193,917 in 2000.
Languages: Arabic; French and Berber dialects are spoken in various regions.
Religions: 20,000 Catholics (.01%), 31,168,817 Sunni Muslims (99.9%), 1,100 other.

---

use of this work, but a number of manuscripts still extant in the libraries of Europe attest to its widespread popularity in the 12th century. The *Sentences of Master A.,* which provided source material for the compilation of Gratian's *Decretum,* dates back to the School of ANSELM OF LAON rather than to Alger of Liège.

Bibliography: Alger's works are collected in *Patrologia Latina,* ed. J. P. MIGNE, 217 V., indexes 4 v. (Paris 1878–90) 180:739–972. His letters are collected in P. JAFFÉ, *Bibliotheca rerum germanicarum,* 6 v. (Berlin 1864–73) 5:262–267, 373–379. The *Eulogy* by Nicholas of Liège is found in *Patrologia Latina,* ed. J. P. MIGNE, 217 V., indexes 4 v. (Paris 1878–90) 180:737–738. G. LE BRAS, "Le liber de misericordia et justitia d'Alger de Liège," *Nouvelle revue historique de droit français et étranger,* 45 (1921) 80–118. "Alger de Liège et Gratien," *Revue des sciences philosophiques et théologiques,* 20 (1931) 5–26. S. KUTTNER, "Zur Frage der theologischen Vorlagen Gratians," *Zeitschrift der Savigny–Stiftung für Rechtsgeschichte, Kanonistische Abteilung,* 23 (1934) 243–268. L. BRIGUE, *Alger de Liège* (Paris 1936). N. M. HARING, "The *Sententiae Magistri A.* and the School of Laon," *Mediaeval Studies,* 17 (1955) 1–45; "A Study in the Sacramentology of Alger of Liège," *Mediaeval Studies* 20 (1958) 41–78.

[N. M. HARING]

ALGERIA, THE CATHOLIC CHURCH IN

A republic in northwest Africa, Algeria is bordered on the east by Tunisia and Libya, on the south by Niger and Mali, on the west by Mauritania, Western Sahara, and Morocco, and on the north by the Mediterranean Sea. A semi-arid climate and predominantly desert conditions limit Algeria's agricultural output to wheat, barley, and olives. Fortunately, large oil and natural gas reserves began to provide the country with a stable economy during the second half of the 20th century. Nevertheless, despite the healthy revenues generated by such exports, Algeria remained burdened by high unemployment and widespread poverty into the 21st century.

Ecclesiastically, a metropolitan archdiocese is located in Algiers, with suffragans at Constantine and Oran. The diocese of Laghouat, which encompasses most of inland Algeria, was created in 1955 and is immediately

subject to the Holy See. Established in 1901 as the Prefecture of Ghardaïa, two decades later it was detached from the Prefecture of the Sahara and the Sudan; it served the region as a vicariate from 1948 to 1955.

A land of Berber tribes, Algeria had early Phoenician settlements on its northern coast and came under the sway of CARTHAGE before it flourished under Roman rule as *Numidia* and *Mauretania Caesarea*. It suffered from DONATISTS and was conquered by invading Vandals, who were besieging Hippo when St. Augustine died there (430). Byzantine rule after 533 restored order to the area,

but the tribes would not accept the Christianity of the eastern Roman Empire. The Arab conquest of 709 brought with it Islam, which the tribes accepted.

The few Christian communities in Algeria having ties with Rome sustained themselves until *c.* 1150; Gregory VII appointed a bishop of Bône in 1076. Missionaries, especially those from Spain, cared for Christian captives, soldiers, and merchants along the Algerian coast, but by 1512 there were so few Christians in the region that a bishop of Constantine appointed by Julius II did not venture to occupy his see. Beginning in the late

A catholic church in Algeria, c. 1870–1890. (©Michael Maslan Historic Photographs/CORBIS)

16th century, French and Spanish Trinitarians and French Vincentians cared for Christian slaves in Algeria and functioned as French consuls. However, the state of things had little changed; the Vincentian Vicariate Apostolic of Algeria (1650–1827) made little effort to convert Muslims or Christian renegades.

Spain attempted to hold the Algerian coast (1505–29), XIMÉNEZ DE CISNEROS restoring the See of Bougie and planning to restore that of Oran until the Mediterranean was abandoned as a field of expansion in favor of the New World. The coastal city of Oran, a refuge of Moors forced out of Spain, remained under Spain's control (1509–1708, 1732–91), but the rest of the Algerian coast became overrun by Barbary pirates under the loose hand of the Ottoman Empire. In 1830 French troops marched on Algiers, the main port from which the pirates had menaced European coasts and shipping, and from there took control of the country.

The bishopric of Algiers (Roman *Icosium*), one of many small early Christian dioceses in North Africa, was restored by the French in 1838 and became a metropolitan archdiocese in 1866. Another early Christian see, Constantine (Roman *Julia Cirta*), which united to its title that of HIPPO, became, together with Oran, the suffragan sees in 1866. Algiers cared mostly for immigrant French settlers and was deterred by the government from extending its activity to the Moslem population until Cardinal LAVIGERIE, founder of the MISSIONARIES OF AFRICA and MISSIONARY SISTERS OF OUR LADY OF AFRICA (1868), became archbishop (1867–92). The first bishop of Algiers and the first bishop of Constantine resigned because of financial difficulties. Jesuits began missionary work in Kabylia (1839), which had been conquered in 1857. Vincentians returned in 1842 to direct seminaries in Algiers, Constantine, and Oran.

Remaining under French control despite several uprisings, Algeria fell into the hands of the Vichy government during World War II. In November 1942 it was occupied by Allied forces; the following two decades found Algerians in bloody revolt against waning French colonial influence. Algeria finally won independence on July 5, 1962, and was renamed the Democratic and Popular Republic of Algeria. A coup d'etat followed in 1965, foreshadowing the political instability that would haunt the new nation.

Independence prompted a mass exodus of the European population; between 1962 and 1964 more than 800,000 Catholics left the country. Under a constitution first made effective in November 1976, Islam was declared the state religion, although discrimination on the basis of religion was prohibited and Catholic practices were tolerated. All students, even those of non-Islamic faiths, attending primary and secondary schools were required to study Islam; private schools were not permitted to operate within Algeria. While public assembly to worship a faith other than Islam was prohibited by law, the government continued to tolerate Catholic services at the cathedral in Algiers and elsewhere.

During the 1990s Algeria underwent drastic political changes that dramatically altered the country's religious landscape. On the eve of a national election in 1991, the electoral successes of the radical fundamentalist Islamic Salvation Front (FIS) prompted the government to postpone the election process in an attempt to halt further FIS inroads. While censored elections were eventually resumed, FIS candidates were forced underground; in response sympathizers turned to violence, directing their wrath at those they considered impediments to their control of the government, primarily moderate Muslims and Christians. Terrorists took the lives of more than 100,000 people between 1992 and 2000, targeting religious, political, and random civilians for death. Many Catholics were among their victims. By 2000 the Catholic population had been reduced to approximately 20,000 (one source put it at 3,000), only a fifth of their number 40 years earlier. Catholics formed communities around larger churches in the cities of Oran, Constantine, and Algiers for reasons of safety, abandoning some of the 37 parishes that remained in the country.

The situation deteriorated further when, in April 1996, seven Trappists monks were kidnaped by Algerian Islamic guerillas. Despite pleas by Pope John Paul II for their safe release, on May 21 they were murdered in retaliation for the French government's failure to release a political terrorist. Shortly after reports of their deaths were made, Bp. Pierre Claverie of Oran was killed, along with his driver, in a terrorist bombing. Dozens more priests, monks, and nuns were killed in the violence, according to Amnesty International. In 1997 the pope made a public plea for people to "avoid provocations and attitudes which wound human dignity, and the legitimate rights and aspirations of all people," ending his statement by calling the acts of the terrorists "ferocious barbarity." Amid proposals for international peace talks to resolve the situation in Algeria, in late 1999 the pope met with Algerian President Abdelaziz Bouteflika to discuss the situation. Fortunately, no more Catholic clergy lost their life through terrorism following Bp. Claverie's murder in 1996.

In January 2000 the FIS's armed contingent disbanded and many surrendered their weapons under an amnesty sponsored by Bouteflika's government. As the Church looked to the new millennium, it saw its membership drastically decreased: more than half the country's 177 nuns had left, while over 40 missionary centers had been abandoned. However, those remaining perceived a new openness to their faith, perhaps in reaction to the violence they had suffered earlier.

Bibliography: A. PONS, *La Nouvelle Église d'Afrique* (Tunis 1930). *Annuaire du diocese d'Alger* (1930—). L. E. DUVAL, *Messages de Paix* 1955–1962 (Algiers 1961). E. JARRY, *Catholicisme* 1:317–319; 3:100–102. *Bilan du Monde* 2:41–49.

[J. CUOQ/EDS.]

ALHAMBRA, INTERNATIONAL ORDER OF

The International Order of Alhambra is a Catholic fraternal and social organization established for the marking and preservation of Catholic historical sites. Founded in Brooklyn, New York, on Feb. 29, 1904, by William Harper Bennett (1861–1931), it derived its name from the Moorish stronghold in Granada, Spain, which surrendered to the Christian forces of Spain on Jan. 22, 1492. This turning point, which ended the Moorish occupation of Christian Europe that had begun in 711, was a significant event which was not lost on Alhambra's founder who saw the advantage of having an organization devoted to marking significant events, places, and sites associated with the history of Christianity in North America.

Originally envisioned as a higher level of the Knights of Columbus, Alhambrans had to be members of that organization, a requirement that was terminated in 1961. Unlike the Knights, the Alhambrans wear white fezzes and, understandably, are mistaken for Masons by those who do not know of them. That much of the terminology (caravans, divan, and viziers) of the order's governing structure is reflective of the time when Spain was under the Moors lends to Alhambra's attraction.

While the Order of Alhambra is an organization that is concerned about historical landmarks, it is unique in that since 1959 it has been primarily interested in helping the developmentally disabled. The Order of Alhambra provides scholarships to individuals interested in teaching the developmentally disabled, small grants to institutions willing to help them, support for medical research into the causes of Down's syndrome, and setting up housing to care for these persons.

At the same time, while concentrating on its goals relative to the developmentally disabled and to historical memorials, the Order of Alhambra promotes social and fraternal activities among its members who include cardinals, bishops, priests, and deacons as well as lay persons. From a peak membership of more than 11,000 members before the Great Depression, at the beginning of the 21st century it continues its charitable and social works with about half that number. The supreme office of the Order is located in Baltimore, Md., and it has more than 100 caravans or subsidiary units in at least 30 states in the United States and in two provinces (Ontario and Quebec) of Canada.

Bibliography: W. H. BENNETT, "The Order of Alhambra," *Historical Records and Studies*, 16 (May 1924), 94–105. J. L. BORDAS, "History of the Order of Alhambra," *The Alhambran* (July/August 1979: 6–11). V. A. LAPOMARDA, *The Order of Alhambra* (Baltimore 1994).

[V. A. LAPOMARDA]

ALI ('ALĪ IBN ABĪ TĀLIB)

Son-in-law of Muḥammad; b. Mecca, *c.* A.D. 600; d. Kūfa, Jan. 24, 661. 'Alī was taken into his cousin Muḥammad's household at 10, and became one of the first converts to Islam from paganism. He joined the HEGIRA to Medina A.D. 622, was married to the Prophet's daughter Fāṭima, and fathered the Prophet's only surviving grandsons, al–Ḥasan and al–Ḥusayn. Muḥammad's unexpected death in 632 was the first great crisis of Islam. Political, judicial, and religious head of the new Islamic state, Muḥammad left no sons and apparently had appointed no successor. While 'Alī and his kin prepared the body for burial, a group of the Prophet's companions elected Abū Bakr, father of Muḥammad's favorite wife, 'Ā'isha, as successor to the Prophet. 'Alī kept aloof, but the choice was ratified by the people of Medina. Abū Bakr (d. 634) appointed 'Umar, once an enemy, later Father-in-law to Muḥammad, as his own successor; and under their leadership Egypt, the Fertile Crescent, and Persia were taken by Arab armies. 'Umar was assassinated in 644 and the electoral conclave of the six most prominent companions of the Prophet passed over 'Alī in favor of 'Uthmān ibn 'Affān, an early convert of the aristocratic Banū Umayya family, who had led the Meccan

opposition to the Prophet. In 656 'Uthmān, in the face of general discontent with his caliphate, was blockaded in Medina and murdered when he refused to abdicate.

'Alī, then acclaimed caliph, defeated his opponents who accused him of illegal election and collusion with the murderers, and made his capital in Kūfa. Mu'āwiya, Governor of Syria, claiming vengeance for his cousin 'Uthmān, maneuvered 'Alī into a position in which he felt constrained to negotiate. At this, some of 'Alī's party withdrew allegiance, accusing him of forsaking Islam by negotiating on what should be religious principle. 'Alī was forced to take up arms against these "Seceders," (Khārijites) and in revenge was assassinated by one of them in 661. A mosque called Meshed 'Alī was afterward erected to his memory near the spot.

From 'Alī's reign came a major sectarian rift in Islamic theology. The "Partisans" (*Shī'a*) of 'Alī formed the chief division of Islam opposed to the "Traditionalist" (*Sunnī*) majority (*see* SHī'ITES; SUNNITES). After his death, his followers did not accept Mu'āwiya's claim to the caliphate. They insisted that 'Alī and his heirs were divinely appointed IMĀMs, leaders of the Muslim community.

While first an Arab political faction, the Shī'a came to differ markedly from the Sunnīs in metaphysics and doctrine; they have seen the imāms as infallible and impeccable, and at times even as emanations of the Godhead. The Shī'a have subdivided repeatedly over the claims of descendants of 'Alī, and have formed new sects and versions of the doctrine, ranging from the Zaydīs of Yemen, who simply hold that some descendant of 'Alī should rule, to the Nuṣayrīs of North Syria, for whom 'Alī is a member of a Gnostic divine trinity. The Sunnīs hold that he was one of the pious first caliphs, who came legally to power in a troubled time and died a tragic death. The polemic has led to much forged documentation.

Bibliography: L. VECCIA VAGLIERI, *Encyclopedia of Islam*, ed. B. LEWIS et al. (2d ed. Leiden 1954—) 1:381–386. *Annali dell'Islam*, comp. L. CAETANI, 10 v. (Milan 1905–26) v.9 and 10.

[J. A. WILLIAMS]

ALINSKY, SAUL DAVID

Community organizer and sociologist; b. Chicago, Ill., Jan. 30 1909; d. Carmel, Calif., June 12, 1972. The son of Benjamin and Sarah (Tannenbaum) Alinsky, immigrant Orthodox Jews from Russia, Saul enrolled in the famous Chicago School of Pragmatic Sociology (1915–1950) at the University of Chicago in 1926. Upon graduation in 1930, Alinsky received a fellowship for graduate studies in criminology that led him to the Capone gang and Clifford Shaw's Institute for Juvenile Research (IJR). In 1931, he became a staff sociologist and parole classification officer for the Illinois State Penitentiary. He returned to IJR in 1936 and was assigned by Shaw to the Chicago neighborhood known as ''Back of the Yards'' in 1938 to organize the community on delinquency issues (the classic description of Chicago's stockyard and immigrant life in the Back of the Yards is Upton Sinclair's *The Jungle*). In 1939, along with Joseph Meegan, Alinsky organized the ''Back of the Yards Council,'' a unique community organization built by the use of democratic power with the support of organized labor and the Catholic Church, the two chief power blocs in the Back of the Yards.

Alinsky authored three books and numerous articles. His most popular work, *Reveille for Radicals* (1946), became a bestseller. (One reviewer called it the filthiest piece of writing since Tom Paine.) His other published writings include, ''A Sociological Technique in Clinical Criminology,'' in *Proceedings of the Sixty-fourth Annual Congress of the American Prison Association 17-21 September 1934*, 176–187, (Chicago); ''Community Analysis and Organization,'' *American Journal of Sociology* 46, 6 (1941):797–800; *John L. Lewis: An Unauthorized Biography* (New York 1949); ''The Urban Immigrant,'' in *Roman Catholicism and the American Way of Life*, ed. Thomas T. McAvoy, C.S.C., 142–155 (Notre Dame 1960); and *Rules for Radicals* (New York 1971).

Alinsky is regarded as the founder of modern community organizing and his work continues through the Industrial Areas Foundation, a national organizing network, he founded in 1940. Alinsky's enduring contribution is the melding of John Lewis' labor organizing principles with those of the Chicago School of Pragmatic Sociology. The result was and is a distinctive experimental organizing model focused on the attainment of institutional power.

It is clear that Alinsky, a self-professed agnostic, had a profound impact upon American Catholicism. His influence has been noted in the development of such organizations as the Catholic Campaign for Human Development and Catholic Charities, U.S.A., and in parish ministry and leadership-development programs. Criticized from both the left and the right, Alinsky has been variously identified as a dupe of the Catholic Church, a mastermind of a Catholic conspiracy, a Machiavelli in modern dress, and an authentic revolutionary. Prominent Catholic friends included Chicago Auxiliary Bishop Bernard Sheil, Neo-Thomist philosopher Jacques Maritain, Urban Affairs Director Monsignor Jack Egan, and Catholic Charities Director Monsignor John O'Grady.

Bibliography: *Alinsky Papers*. Special Collections, University of Illinois at Chicago; *Saul David Alinsky Collection*, Watkinson Library, Trinity College; unarchived papers located at the Chicago office of the Industrial Areas Foundation. C. E. CURRAN, ''Saul D. Alinsky, Catholic Social Practice, and Catholic Theory,'' in *Directions in Catholic Social Ethics* (Notre Dame 1985) 147–176. B. E. DOERING, ''Jacques Maritain and His Two Authentic Revolutionaries,'' in *Thomistic Papers III*, ed. L. A. KENNEDY, C.S.B. (Notre Dame 1987) 91–116. B. E. DOERING, ed., *The Philosopher and the Provocateur: The Correspondence of Jacques Maritain and Saul Alinsky* (New York 1989). L. J. ENGEL, ''The Influence of Saul Alinsky on the Campaign for Human Development'' *Theological Studies* 59 (1998): 631–661.

[L. J. ENGEL]

ALIPIUS, ST.

Bishop, b. Tagaste, North Africa, *c.* 360; d. after 429. Alipius (or Alypius) was a student and close friend of ST. AUGUSTINE and a fellow Manichean, who pursued a law career at his parents' wish. He joined Augustine at Rome in 383 and journeyed with him in 384 to Milan, where they were baptized by AMBROSE of Milan in 387. Returning to Africa (388) Alipius spent three years at Tagaste in prayer and penance before going to Hippo to be ordained a priest. On a pilgrimage to Palestine he met Jerome and was instrumental in fostering a relationship between Jerome and Augustine. Upon his return to Africa, Alipius became bishop of Tagaste (*c.* 394) and struggled against the Pelagians and the Donatists. He visited Italy again in 419 and 428, on business for the Church and the government. During much of his life, he served as Augustine's assistant in his public activities. Augustine, writing in 429, called him old; and Alipius seems not to have survived long after that.

Feast: Aug. 15 or 18.

Bibliography: *Acta Sanctorum* Aug. 3:201–208. AUGUSTINE, *Conf.* 6, 8, 9. S. LE NAIN DE TILLEMONT, *Mémoires pour servir à l'histoire ecclésiastique des six premiers siècles* (Paris 1693–1712) 12:565–580. A. P. FRUTAZ, *Lexikon für Theologie und Kirche*, ed. J. HOFER and K. RAHNER (Freiburg 1957–65) 1:410. F. MOURRET, *A History of the Catholic Church,* tr. N. THOMPSON, v. 2 (St. Louis 1935) 416.

[R. K. POETZEL]

ALL SAINTS, SOLEMNITY OF

A feast in honor of all the saints, celebrated on November 1 in the West. The origins of this feast are uncertain. First mention comes from the East, in a hymn composed by St. Ephraem in c. 359, where a commemoration of all the martyrs at Edessa on May 13 is mentioned (*Carmen* 6; *Corpus scriptorum Christianorum orientalium* [Paris-Louvain 1903] 219:27). By 411, however, the East Syrians kept this commemoration on the Friday after Easter [*Breviarium Syriacum*, ed. Mariani (Rome 1956) 34]). A sermon of St. John Chrysostom marks the observance of a feast of all the martyrs on the first Sunday after Pentecost (*Patrologia Graeca*, ed. J. P. Migne, 50:705). When Chrysostom preached this sermon is not known, and therefore whether the feast occurred in Antioch or Constantinople is uncertain. If he preached it at Constantinople after he became patriarch (398), this would be the earliest reference to the feast there, still observed by the Byzantine Rite on the Sunday after Pentecost.

An observance of all the martyrs on the Sunday after Pentecost also appears in the West. St. Maximus of Turin (5th century) preached in honor of all the martyrs on the same Sunday (*Hom.* 81; *Patrologia Latina*, ed. J. P. Migne (Paris 1878–90) 57:427). The commemoration soon included nonmartyrs as well, for the *Comes of Würzburg*, the earliest epistle list for Rome (an 8th-century manuscript witnessing to readings used in the late 6th or early 7th century), lists this Sunday as *dominica in natale sanctorum* or Sunday of the Nativity of the Saints (*Dictionnaire d'archéologie chrétienne et de liturgie*, ed. F. Cabol, H. Leclercq, and H. I. Marrou (Paris 1907–53) 8.2:2292). It seems to serve as an octave day for Pentecost. The feast is encountered again in the *Comes* of Murbach, which lists readings accompanying the 8th-century family of mixed sacramentaries that preceded the Charlemagne's reform.

Rome also knew of another feast of all the martyrs before adopting November 1. In 609 or 610, Boniface IV received the Roman Pantheon from the Emperor Phocas (d. 610) and dedicated it under the title *S. Maria ad Martyres* [*Liber Pontificalis*, ed. L. Duchesne (Paris 1955) 1:317]. The dedication occurred on May 13, and the anniversary was later observed with great festivity. Many see in this the origin of All Saints' Day. It may be, however, that the feast of May 13 was simply the anniversary of the dedication, or that Boniface chose this date because it was already associated with all the martyrs in the East. Some scholars have suggested that the date was chosen to offset the pagan *Lemuria* (placating of the gods), observed on May 9, 11, and 13 (P. Radó). The liturgical books that witness to this period make no mention of a feast of all the martyrs that would be in continuity with the Syriac feast mentioned by Ephraem.

How a feast of all the saints came to be celebrated on November 1 has not yet been demonstrated. Gregory III (731–41) dedicated an oratory in St. Peter's Basilica to ''all the apostles, martyrs, confessors, and all the just and perfect who are at rest throughout the whole world.''

(*Liber Pontificalis* 1:417). The precise date of the dedication in early 732 is not known. In England, Bede mentioned a feast of all the saints in his two martyrologies (e.g., *Patrologia Latina* 94:1087). Egbert of York had been ordained deacon in Rome in 732 and had received the pallium from Gregory himself. If Egbert is the founder of the English feast, he may have accepted November 1 as the dedication of Gregory's oratory. Arno of Salzburg called for a festival of all saints on November 1 for Southeast Germany in 798. In 799, Alcuin, who was educated at Egbert's cathedral of York, commended Arno, Archbishop of Salzburg, for observing the feast of November 1 (*Epist.* 91; *Patrologia Latina* 100:296). The feast, however, does not appear in Alcuin's supplement to the Gregorian Sacramentary.

According to John Beleth (d. *ca.* 1165), Gregory IV (827–44) transferred the feast of May 13 to November 1 because provisions were inadequate for the numerous pilgrims coming to Rome for the feast in May (*Rationale divinorum officiorum*, 127; *Patrologia Latina* 202:133–134). There is no scholarly consensus on the matter. H. Schmid denied any connection between the two dates, positing that the November feast originated in Gaul and was immediately adopted in Rome.

According to Ado of Vienne (800–75), this same pontiff asked Louis the Pious (778–840) to extend the feast of November 1 throughout the empire (*Martyrologium, Patrologia Latina* 123:387). Sigebert (d. 1112) in his chronicle, for some unknown reason, assigns the year 835 to this event (*Patrologia Latina* 160:159). In fact, in the 9th and 10th centuries, November 1 is listed as *Natale omnium sanctorum*, e.g., in the Sacramentary of Corbie (*Patrologia Latina* 78:146). According to Sicard of Cremona (d. 1215), it was Gregory VII (1073–85) who definitively suppressed the feast of May 13 in favor of November 1 (*Mitrale, Patrologia Latina* 213:414). Indeed, in the 12th century, May 13 disappears from the liturgical books.

Other scholars, however, with good reason oppose such attempts to connect May 13 and November 1. J. Hennig believes May 13 was simply the anniversary of a dedication and not a feast of all the martyrs. He places the origin of November 1 in Ireland, whence the feast passed to Northumberland and then to the Continent. There is an allusion to a feast of all the saints on November 1 in the oldest Irish martyrology, the *Félire of Oengus*. This book also gives a feast of all the saints of Europe on April 20 and of all the saints of Africa on December 23. Ireland and Britain were considered apart from Europe and so would want a feast of their own saints. The Irish often assigned the first of the month to important feasts, and since November 1 was also the beginning of the Celtic winter, it would have been a likely date for a feast of all the saints. The feast may also have been Christian response to the Druid festival of the dead, Samhain.

The feast had a vigil from early times, and an octave was introduced by Sixtus IV (1471–84), who established the feast for the whole Latin Rite. Both vigil and octave were suppressed in 1955. All Saints is ranked as a solemnity and classified as a holy day of obligation (CIC c. 1246). The euchology of the Mass speaks of the holiness of the people of God through the images of joy, forgiveness, beatitude, and mutual love. Not only does the Church praise God for all the dead who have obtained heavenly glory, but commits itself to the journey to the heavenly Jerusalem, the place where all God's people are in communion (Rv 7.9 [Second reading]).

Bibliography: J. H. MILLER, *Fundamentals of the Liturgy* (Notre Dame, Ind. 1960) 418–19. P. RADÓ, *Enchiridion liturgicum,* 2 v. (Rome 1961) 2:1391–95. M. RIGHETTI, *Manuale di storia liturgica,* 4 v. (Milan): v.2 (2d ed. 1955) 2:207–09. H. A. P. SCHMIDT, *Introductio in liturgiam occidentalem* (Rome 1959). J. HENNIG, ''The Meaning of All The Saints,'' *Mediaeval Studies* 10 (1948) 147–61. P. JOUNEL, ''Le Sanctoral romain du 8e au 12e siècles,'' *Maison-Dieu* 52 (1957) 59–88. OENGUS THE CULDEE, *Martyrology* (*Félire*), ed. W. STOKES (Henry Bradshaw Society 29; London 1905). T. J. TALLEY, ''The Evolution of a Feast,'' *Liturgy* 5, no. 2 (1985) 43–48.

[C. SMITH/EDS.]

ALL SOULS' DAY

A liturgical day of the Roman rite commemorating all the faithful departed. It is observed on November 2, and since 1970 takes precedence if it falls on a Sunday. The Byzantine Churches observe a similar feast before Lent and Pentecost, the Armenian Church on Easter Monday.

Christians retained customs and patterns of memorial for the dead from pagan antiquity. They celebrated the memory of the deceased on the third day after death and the yearly anniversary; later, observance was made on the seventh and thirtieth day and in some places the fortieth day after a person's death. Attempts of local churches to observe a feast commemorating all the departed can be traced back to the early Middle Ages, possibly arising in imitation of the commemorations of deceased members customary in monastic communities. In Spain, for example, the Monday after Pentecost was dedicated to the commemoration of the deceased in the time of St. Isidore of Seville (d. 636). Abbot Eigil of Fulda prescribed December 17, the anniversary of the monastery's founder, as commemoration of all the deceased at the beginning of the ninth century.

The choice of November 2 is traditionally attributed to St. ODILO, the fifth abbot of Cluny (d. 1048). Odilo decreed in 998 that all Cluniac monasteries should follow the example of Cluny in offering special prayers and singing the Office for the Dead on the day following the feast of ALL SAINTS. Due to the influence of Cluny, the custom spread quickly through France, Germany, and England and was finally adopted in Italy and Rome in the thirteenth century.

The custom of having each priest celebrate three Masses seems to have originated among the Spanish Dominicans during the fifteenth century. After this privilege was approved by BENEDICT XIV in 1748, it was rapidly adopted throughout Spain, Portugal, and Latin America. During World War I, BENEDICT XV, moved by the number of war casualties, granted to all priests the privilege of celebrating three Masses: Of these one could be said for a particular intention; another celebrated for all the faithful departed, particularly for all the Mass foundations that had been unfulfilled or forgotten over time; and the third for the intentions of the pope.

Throughout the Middle Ages it was popular belief that the souls in purgatory could appear on this day as will-o'-the-wisps, witches, toads, etc., to persons who had wronged them during their life. Genuine Christian concern for the deceased along with folkloric culture were the reasons for the great number of pious foundations for Masses and prayers on their behalf. Many different popular customs and practices, especially various forms of food offerings, were associated with All Souls' Day. Among religious traditions, the parish procession to the cemetery, visiting the graves of relatives and friends, and leaving flowers and lights on the graves have remained almost universal.

The liturgy of All Souls' Day was revised to express more clearly the paschal character of Christian death and proclaim the paschal mystery of Christ as the foundation of hope and consolation (cf. *Sacrosanctum Concilium,* no. 81). The Sacramentary contains three Mass formularies, but the rubrics that each priest may offer three Masses and that the first formulary should be used for the principal Mass are omitted. The readings are taken from the Lectionary for the Masses for the Dead, and the prefaces of Christian Death are prescribed. The prayers speak of the reality and sadness of death, always in the context of the hope given in Christ Jesus, the resurrection and the life, that all who die in faith share the promise of immortality. The *Book of Blessings* (1989) provides an order for visiting the cemetery recommended for All Soul's Day (nos. 1734–1754), and the *Ceremonial of Bishops* recommends a rite of sprinkling and incensation of burial sites (nos. 395–403) using texts from the *Order of Christian Funerals.*

Bibliography: A. ADAM, *The Liturgical Year*, trans. M. O'CONNELL (New York 1981). K. A. H. KELLNER, *Heortology* (St. Louis 1908) 326–328. T. MAERTENS and L. HEUSCHEN, *Doctrine et pastorale de la liturgie de la mort* (Bruges 1957). C. A. KNELLER, "Geschichtliches über die drei Messen am Allerseelentag," *Zeitschrift für katholische Theologie* 42 (1918) 74–113. D. K. TRIPP, "The Spirituality of the Little Office of the BVM and the Office for the Dead," *Worship* 63 (1989) 218–221.

[A. CORNIDES/EDS.]

ALLAMANO, GIUSEPPE, BL.

Priest; founder, Consolata Society for Foreign Missions and the Missionary Sisters of the Consolata; b. Castelnuovo d'Asti, Piedmont, Italy, Feb. 21, 1851; d. Turin, Piedmont, Italy, Feb. 16, 1926; beatified, Oct. 7, 1990.

Giuseppe Allamano was the fourth of five children born to Joseph Allamano and Marianna Cafasso. His mother, Marianna, was the sister of St. Joseph CAFASSO. While a secondary school student at Valdocco, John BOSCO served as his spiritual mentor. Allamano later entered the diocesan seminary and was ordained a priest in Turin in 1873. At the age of 24 he was appointed spiritual director in the diocesan seminary. In 1880 Allamano became rector of the "Santuario della Consolata," a Marian shrine in Turin, which houses what is believed to be one of the earliest known icons of the Blessed Mother (4th century). Under his direction, the Consolata Shrine became an important center of Marian piety. He remodeled the building, and renewed the devotion to Our Lady, providing a group of priests for confessions and spiritual direction. He won wide popularity as a confessor and spiritual director, and he promoted many charitable works such as the Catholic Action, labor unions, and the Catholic press.

From his youth Allamano was inspired by the missionary life and activities of the Capuchin missionary Cardinal Massaia in Ethiopia. His poor health, however, prevented him from following his dream of being a missionary. After a long period of prayer and planning in 1901, with the encouragement of his Archbishop A. Richelmy and the approval of the bishops of Piedmont he founded the Institute of the Consolata Foreign Missions. In 1902 the first CONSOLATA MISSIONARIES, two priests and two religious brothers, left Turin for Kenya, in East Africa.

As the first Consolata Missionaries were making progress in Kenya, there was an urgent need for more personnel. Allamano started a formation program to train his missionaries and, in 1910, he also founded the Consolata Missionary Sisters, an indispensable presence together with the priests and the brothers, in the evangelization of Kenya. Both in his rectorship of the shrine and in his leadership of the Consolata Missionaries, Allamano was supported by his close co-worker James Camisassa, the vice-rector of the shrine and the co-founder of the Consolata Missionaries. Their continuous cooperation of 43 years is a moving example of priestly friendship.

Though superior general of the Consolata Missionaries, Allamano remained a diocesan priest of Turin all his life, involving himself in every aspect of the diocesan life. He viewed his missionary involvement as a direct consequence of his priesthood. Allamano's spirituality is best characterized as one trusting in God's guidance and provision, and is marked by a deep devotion to the Blessed Virgin Mary. Mary, Mother of Consolation, who experienced God's tender love and responded in total commitment, became a model and companion for his life and mission. Allamano died in Turin where his relics are enshrined in a chapel dedicated to him at the motherhouse of the Consolata Missionaries.

Feast: Feb. 16.

Bibliography: *Acta Apostolicae Sedis*, 82 (1990): 1020. *L'Osservatore Romano*, English edition, nos. 41, 42 (1990); L. SALES, *Il servo di Dio Giuseppe Allamano*, 3rd ed. (Turin 1944); *The Spiritual Life From the Spiritual Conferences of Joseph Allamano* (Rome 1982); I. TUBALDO, *Giuseppe Allamano*, 4 v. (Turin 1982–87); D. AGASSO, *Joseph Allamano* (Middlegreen 1991).

[M. BARBERO]

ALLEGORY

Derived from the Greek words *allos* (other) and *agoreuein* (to speak), allegory refers to a literary and rhetorical style that uses fictitious persons, things and events symbolically as indirect references to real people and situations, or to abstract ideas such as "the Christian life" or "virtue." The first level, but less important, is the actual story told by the narrative (e.g., Gulliver's adventures in a kingdom of tiny people); the second, which carries the author's intended message, lies behind and runs parallel to the literal sense of the narrative. Because this second level of meaning is not spelled out, the text of an allegory is open to multiple interpretations. In a religious context, allegory refers to the meaning given to a narrative or work of art when its elements are interpreted as being symbols for moral and theological values.

The idea that the written word can carry several levels of meaning has had great influence on the Western literary tradition, especially during the late Middle Ages and the Renaissance. From antiquity, works have been written expressly as allegories. Dante's *Divine Comedy*, *Roman de la Rose*, by Guillaume de Lorris and Jean de

*"Allegory of Poverty" from "Three Virtues of Saint Francis,"
detail of fresco, attributed to Maestro delle Vele and Stefano
Fiorentino.* (©Elio Ciol/CORBIS)

Meunand, *Piers Plowman*, attributed to William Langland, and John Bunyan's *Pilgrim's Progress* are often cited examples that illustrate allegory's use in both secular and religious contexts. Allegory has not played so large a role in the modern Western literary tradition, although George Orwell's *Animal Farm*, James Joyce's *Ulysses*, and the works of Franz Kafka and C. S. Lewis do continue the tradition.

Allegorical Interpretation. The fact that some literary works carry two levels of meaning gives rise to a method of interpretation that looks for a second, hidden meaning behind a given text even when there is no indication that the author intended such a meaning. As early as the 5th century B.C., Greek philosophers such as Metrodorus of Lampsacus were searching for hidden meaning in the works of Homer and Hesiod. They were convinced that the ancient poets were great sages who had hidden moral and spiritual truths from the ignorant in their stories. The early Stoics (4th to 1st centuries B.C.) were especially instrumental in developing allegorical interpretations for the mythical legends recorded by Homer and Hesiod. At the beginning of our era, the Neoplatonists revived the allegorical method of interpretation, producing interpretations of Greek mythology that included such things as saying that Helen personifies the beauty of the world that lures souls from their true spiritual home into the world of matter.

Philo Judeaus of Alexandria (*c.* 30 B.C. to *c.* 40 A.D.) applied this "allegoresis" to the Old Testament in an ef-

fort to harmonize its anthropomorphic descriptions of God with Greek philosophical ideas about the true nature of divinity. The early Christian fathers also took up this method of interpreting the Old Testament "[a]s a way of eliminating the scandal which particular passages of the Bible might provide for certain Christians, not to mention pagan adversaries of Christianity" (*The Interpretation of the Bible in the Church*, The Pontifical Biblical Commission, 1994; III.B.2). However, the patristic exegetes did not abandon the literal, historical meaning of biblical texts as the Greek philosophers had done with their own mythology. They held that, since it is the word of God, Scripture is an inexhaustible font of revelation for every time and place. The truth it contains cannot be confined to its literal meaning, but must also be sought behind and under the text. Origen (c. 185 to c. 254) is one of the most influential of the early Christian exegetes, famous for his use of allegory when interpreting the Old Testament. Such interpretation, especially the use of typology (e.g. finding in Abraham's sacrifice of Isaac a "type," or prefiguring, of Christ's sacrifice on the cross), allowed the church fathers to counter the Marcionite heresy, which called for abandoning everything Jewish, including the Old Testament, by pointing out how the Old Testament prefigures and points to Christ. St. Augustine (354 to 430) wrote that Scripture contains both a hidden meaning that exercises the intellect and teaches us to value the truth found with effort, and a literal meaning that provides everything necessary for salvation, so that even the unlearned may be saved (*On Christian Doctrine*, Bk 1). This attitude toward the richness of meaning that can be found in Scripture led to the idea that there are four "senses" of Scripture; the historical or literal, the allegorical or spiritual, and the tropological or moral, and the anagogic or mystical.

Even though the emphasis in biblical study in recent years has been on its literal meaning, especially on trying to discover as nearly as possible the original language and context of the texts, allegorical interpretation continues to be an important way of understanding Scripture. The modern reader may find the patristic use of allegory as an interpretive tool somewhat incredible, but "[t]he fathers of the church teach [us] to read the Bible theologically, within the heart of a living tradition, with an authentic Christian spirit" (Pontifical Biblical Commission, III.B.2). Because it is the word of God, the richness of Scripture's message is inexhaustible; both the text of Scripture and the realities and events it describes can be signs of God's plan of salvation. The allegorical sense of Scripture allows us to "acquire a more profound understanding of [those] events by recognizing their significance in Christ" (*Catechism of the Catholic Church* 117).

Bibliography: M. W. BLOOMFIELD, ed., *Allegory, Myth and Symbol* (Cambridge, Mass. 1981). H. DE LUBAC, *Exégèse médiévale,* 2 v. (Paris 1959–64). A. J. S. FLETCHER, *Allegory: The Theory of a Symbolic Mode* (Ithaca, NY 1964). J. C. JOOSEN and J. H. WASZINK, *Reallexikon für Antike und Christentum,* ed. T. KLAUSER (Stuttgart 1950—) 1:283–293, with bibliog. C. S. LEWIS, *The Allegory of Love: A Study in Medieval Tradition* (New York 1936). J. PÉPIN, *Mythe et allégorie* (Paris 1957). The Pontifical Biblical Commission, *The Interpretation of the Bible in the Church* (1994). J. TATE, *The Oxford Classical Dictionary,* ed. M. CARY et al. (Oxford 1934—) 38–39. J. WHITMAN, *Allegory: The Dynamics of an Ancient and Medieval Technique* (Cambridge, Mass. 1987). H. A. WOLFSON, *The Philosophy of the Church Fathers,* v.1 (Cambridge, Mass. 1956) 24–72.

[L. HARRINGTON]

ALLEGRANZA, JOSEPH

Theologian, archeologist; b. Milan, 1713; d. there, 1785. He belonged to the Milanese Dominican monastery of San Eustorgio and took the habit at Brescia in 1731. After teaching theology at Novara and Vercelli, he took his doctorate in theology at Rome in 1746. He then directed his efforts particularly to archeological researches. His extensive travels in Italy, southern France, and on the Island of Malta provided him with many archeological finds as well as useful friendships. After 1755 he lived almost entirely at Milan, where in 1765 he had the responsibility for cataloging the Pertusati library. For this he was awarded a gold medal from the Empress Maria Theresa. Among his numerous writings of a historical–archeological and antiquarian nature are: *Spiegazione, e riflessioni sopra alcuni sacri monumenti antichi di Milano* (Milan 1757); *De sepulcris christianis in aedibus sacris* (Milan 1773); and *Opusculi eruditi latini ed italiani* (Cremona 1781).

Bibliography: R. COULON, *Dictionnaire d'histoire et de géographie ecclésiastiques,* ed. A. BAUDRILLART et al. (Paris 1912—) 2:489–493. G. FERRETTO, *Note storico–bibliografiche di archeologia cristiana* (Vatican City 1942) 280–282, 339.

[A. L. REDIGONDA]

ALLEGRI, GREGORIO

Priest, composer of the Roman baroque; b. Rome, 1582; d. Rome, Feb. 17, 1652. As a boy he sang under G. B. Nanino at S. Luigi dei Francesi church in Rome from 1591 until his voice changed; he also sang and studied under G. M. Nanino. In 1629, after he had established his reputation as a composer, he was appointed to the papal choir by Urban VIII. As a composer of the late Roman school, Allegri favored the *stile antico*, with a view to preserving the PALESTRINA tradition, already re-

garded as the model for liturgical purposes. His most notable work is the nine-voice, two-choir *Miserere*, which was written down from memory by both MOZART and MENDELSSOHN and is still performed in the Sistine Chapel during Holy Week. Many other sacred works exist in manuscript, and concertini for various voice groupings, motets for two to six voices, and a forerunner of the string quartet were published during his lifetime.

Bibliography: G. ALLEGRI, *Miserere,* ed. F. HABERL (Augsburg 1936). A. CAMETTI, *Rivista musicale Italiana* 22 (1915) 596–608. K. G. FELLERER, *Die Musik in Geschichte und Gegenwart* 1:329–330. B. BYRAM-WIGFIELD, ''An Unknown Quantity,'' *The Musical Times* 12 (1997) 12–21. DON MICHAEL RANDEL, ed., *The Harvard Biographical Dictionary of Music,* 14–15. (Cambridge, Massachusetts 1996). J. ROCHE, ''Gregorio Allegri'' in *The New Grove Dictionary of Music and Musicians, v.1,* ed. S. SADIE (New York 1980) 266–67. NICOLAS SLONIMSKY, ed., *Baker's Biographical Dictionary of Musicians, Eighth Edition* 27 (New York 1992).

[F. J. GUENTNER]

ALLELUIA

A Hebrew word derived from *hallelû* (imperative of *hillel,* to praise) and *Jah* (abbreviated form of *Jahvè*: God) and frequently used as a means to praise God in Jewish and Christian liturgies. It is found in the following forms: (i) as a responsory, (ii) as an acclamation added to or inserted in a liturgical text, and (iii) as an antiphon. In the Roman Catholic Eucharist, it is sung before the Gospel at all times, except in the season of Lent, when its joyful character excludes its use. During the Easter season, the Alleluia is often added to the antiphons, acclamations and responses in the Eucharist and other liturgical celebrations.

History before Musical Notation. From the beginning of the Christian liturgy there seemed no need to translate this Hebrew word of joy. The present spelling is taken from the Septuagint form Ἀλλελούια. Many patristic texts show that the primitive Church preserved the melismatic character of the Alleluia as found among the Jews. ''Nam sicut in melodia hoc compositum nomen [Alleluia] diversos tonos recipit, ita et multiplies causas ad vim suae praedicationis assumit'' (Cassiodorus, Pal-Lat 70.811). *Jubilatio, melodiae tropi,* and even *toni* are terms used to express the musical vocalizations characteristic of the execution of the Alleluia. Other texts indicate the early use of the word as an acclamation. (See Rv 19.1–7.) ''Diligentiones in orando subjungere in orationibus Alleluia solent'' (Tertullian, PalLat 1.1304). Later, Cassian and St. Benedict indicate the frequent addition of the word to Psalm verses in the recitation of the Office. Amalarius, writing about 840, is the first to describe the substitution of the word Alleluia for the texts of standard antiphons. "Antiphonae aliquae sunt post responsorios collectae, quarum sonus redactus est in sola Alleluia sibi invicem conjuncta" (*Studi e testi* 140: 108).

Two problems have been much discussed by scholars: the role of St. Gregory in specifying the times when the Alleluia could be used and the origin of the verse of the Mass Alleluia. The theory generally accepted is that the Alleluia became a part of the Mass by order of Pope Damasus (368–84) at the request of St. Jerome and in imitation of the Church of Jerusalem. Later it was restricted to Easter, but in the 5th century extended to the whole Easter season. St. Gregory, in turn, extended its use to the entire year with the exception of the penitential season. (For the controversy, see Froger and Wellesz in the bibliography.) The oldest references to the Alleluia do not mention the verses, but they are always present in the MS tradition. From the evidence available it is impossible to establish the exact date when the Alleluia as a responsory assumed the form it now has.

History of the Alleluia in Gregorian Chant. In the earliest chant MSS only the Alleluias for Masses on principal feasts were written in the body of the MS; the others were placed in a special fascicle at the end. The selection of the Alleluia for the Sundays and most of the feasts was left to the cantor. For this reason, the first attempts to assign a specific Alleluia for each Mass were not uniform and resulted in various medieval traditions, important for determining the scriptorium from which a MS comes.

The responsorial Alleluia of the classical Roman Rite of the Mass was sung as follows: Alleluia (intoned by soloist), alleluia with jubilus (sung by choir), verse (sung by soloist with the choir joining in at the end), alleluia with jubilus (sung by the choir). In the Middle Ages the Alleluia was not repeated after the verse on ferial days, and on special feasts two verses were sometimes sung as in the Byzantine tradition. The musical structure of the Alleluia and its verses showed great variety. The Alleluia melody may be simple or contain several melodic repetitions, especially in the melisma or jubilus, while the melody of the verse may be new or derived from the Alleluia melody. Frequently the end of the verse repeated the jubilus only, sometimes it repeated the entire melody of the Alleluia plus jubilus, while other verses showed no melodic relationship to the Alleluia and jubilus but had a different melody (such as *Venite exultemus, Te decet,* and *Paratum cor*). The frequent statement that the form of the Alleluia was a simple A-B-A is textually correct but musically erroneous. The protus and tetrardus modes were most frequent; the tritus—as in Byzantine chant—was rare. The responsory Alleluia was used only at Mass in the Roman rite, although Amalarius mentioned (*op. cit.* 105) three Alleluia responses he had found but had not copied into his own antiphonary.

The addition of two or three Alleluias to the texts of the Mass and Office was common in Gregorian chant. Musically they were distinct from the responsory Alleluia in that they were more simple; if they had a melisma it was generally found on the syllable "le" and not the last syllable. Some of these are thought to be of Gallican origin. The substitution of the word Alleluia for the texts of antiphons was most common in the Roman rite as the example shows.

In the Old Roman repertory the number of Alleluias in the Mass was indeed much smaller, only 13 melodies being found for the Alleluia that precedes the verse. When the Alleluia was repeated after the verse, a new and longer jubilus was found on larger feasts, but one that was generally related musically to the first jubilus in that it was enlarged by melodic repetitions and ornaments. The jubilus melisma was not found at the end of the verse except for the Alleluia *Beatus vir.* The interesting Alleluias for Vespers of Paschal week had two or three verses and highly developed melismas.

History of the Alleluia in Mozarabic Chant. The Alleluia of the Mozarabic Mass was sung after the Gospel, not before. More than one verse was not found, and frequently the jubilus was also found at the end of the verse. The Alleluia jubilus when repeated after the verse may be new (as in *Vincenti dabo* and *In die resurrectionis*) or a development of the first. The Mozarabic repertory of Mass Alleluias was richer than the Old Roman and Ambrosian. The addition of Alleluias to the *Sono* (verse sung at beginning of Vespers) and *Sacrificium* (Offertory) showed long and varied melismas on the syllable "le." The substitution of the text Alleluia for standard antiphons, however, was not found.

History of the Alleluia in Ambrosian Chant. The Ambrosian Mass Alleluias ignored the tritus modes and, like the Old Roman, were few in number. Each one, however, had three different melismas or jubiluses. The first had no name, but the second was called *melodiae primae* and the third *melodiae secundae,* the latter being quite developed. A special melisma called the *francigena* was sometimes added to make a fourth. The ritual for singing all of this was complicated and cannot be totally unraveled. The same type of responsorial Alleluia was found also in the Ambrosian Office, especially at Vespers. The other phenomena, i.e., additional Alleluias and substitution for standard texts, were also found in the Ambrosian chant.

The "Longissimae Melodiae." As early as the 9th century there developed in the Gregorian chant a body of elaborate Alleluia melodies, not confused with the liturgical Alleluias but written as a separate collection; they were given strange and suggestive names—*Frigdola,*

Graeca, Hypodiaconissa, Organa, Nostra tuba, Romana, etc. They were called "longissimae melodiae" by Notker and certainly were related to the phenomenon of the longer melismas of the Old Roman, Mozarabic, and Ambrosian liturgical Alleluias. These "longissimae melodiae" are important for the history of the SEQUENCE into which they evolved into.

Bibliography: J. GLIBOTIC, "De cantu Alleluia in patribus saeculo VII antiquioribus," *Ephemerides liturgicae* (Rome 1887–) 50 (1936) 101–23. J. FROGER, "L'Alleluia dans l'usage romain et la réforme de St. Grégoire," *ibid.* 62 (1948) 6–48. E. WELLESZ, "Gregory the Great's Letter on the Alleluia," *Annales musicologiques* 2 (1954) 1–26. B. STÄBLEIN, *Die Musik in Geschichte und Gegenwart,* ed. F. BLUME (Kassel-Basel 1949–) 1:331–50. L. BROU, "L'Alleluia dans la liturgie mozarabe," *Annuario musical* 6 (1951) 3–90. F. GENNRICH, *Grundiss einer Formenlehre des mittelalterlichen Liedes* (Halle 1932) 107–18. D. HILEY, *Western Plainchant* (Oxford 1993) 130–39, 500–05.

[R. G. WEAKLAND/EDS.]

ALLEN, EDWARD PATRICK

Bishop; b. Lowell, Massachusetts, March 17, 1853; d. Mobile, Alabama, Oct. 21, 1926. The son of John and Mary (Egan) Allen, he attended the public schools of Lowell and Lowell Commercial College before entering Mt. St. Mary's College, Emmitsburg, Maryland, where he received the Master of Arts (1878). After completing his studies for the priesthood, he was ordained at Emmitsburg on Dec. 17, 1881, by Bishop Thomas A. Becker. Allen first taught at Mt. St. Mary's, then worked for two years in the Archdiocese of Boston, Massachusetts, returning to Emmitsburg in 1884. After serving briefly as vice president and treasurer of the college, he was elected president in June 1885. On Jan. 26, 1897, he was appointed fifth bishop of Mobile (redesignated MOBILE–BIRMINGHAM in 1954); he was consecrated by Cardinal James Gibbons in Baltimore, Maryland, on May 16 and installed in his diocese on May 30. During the next 30 years the Catholic population in the diocese increased from 17,000 to 48,000; Allen's administrative ability and sound fiscal policy enabled the diocese to keep pace with this growth by an adequate expansion of clergy, churches, and social services. Particular effort was made in the Negro apostolate through the introduction of the JOSEPHITE fathers, and significant progress was achieved in the hitherto undeveloped rural areas of the diocese.

Bibliography: Archives, Diocese of Mobile–Birmingham.

[O. H. LIPSCOMB]

ALLEN, FRANCES MARGARET, SISTER

Nurse; b. Sunderland, Vermont, Nov. 13, 1784; d. Montreal, Canada, Dec. 10, 1819. She was the first daughter of Revolutionary War hero Ethan Allen and his second wife, Frances Montresor Buchanan. Three years after her birth, the family moved to Burlington, Vermont, and two years later her father died. She grew up in a period of religious revival prompted in part by reaction against her father's deistic work, *Reason: The Only Oracle of Man* (1784). Although the revival affected her mother and her stepfather, Jabez Penniman, she remained skeptical. In 1807 she entered the school of the Sisters of Notre Dame in Montreal, where she experienced a spiritual crisis that led her to embrace Catholicism. When she announced her desire to become a nun, Dr. and Mrs. Penniman brought her home. Nevertheless, she returned to Montreal, accompanied by her mother, and on Sept. 20, 1809, entered the nursing order of the Sisters of the Hôtel–Dieu of St. Joseph. She pronounced her vows on March 18, 1811, and devoted herself to pharmacy. During the War of 1812, when the Hôtel–Dieu became a military hospital, she was instrumental in bringing converts into the Catholic Church. Long after her death, a hospital was erected (1894) on a plot that once formed a part of her father's farm, and the Sister Hospitallers of the Hôtel–Dieu were requested to operate it.

Bibliography: Archives, Hôtel–Dieu, Montreal. L. GIBSON, *Some Anglo–American Converts to Catholicism Prior to 1829* (Washington 1943) 171–190. H. MORRISSEY, *Ethan Allen's Daughter* (Quebec 1941).

[L. GIBSON]

ALLEN, WILLIAM

Cardinal, founder of the college at Douai; b. Rossall, Lancashire, 1532; d. Rome, Oct. 16, 1594. He was admitted to Oriel College, Oxford (1547) and took his Master of Arts in 1554. He became principal of St. Mary's Hall, Oxford, in 1556 but resigned soon after the accession of Elizabeth I. He remained in Oxford until 1561 and then went to Louvain to join the distinguished group of English scholars in exile. He returned to England for health reasons in 1562 and spent three years in Lancashire, Oxfordshire, and Norfolk attempting to stiffen Catholic resistance to the religious changes, taking what was then an unusual line among English Catholics, that it was not permissible to be present at Anglican services. He went into exile for the second time and was ordained in 1565. In 1568, with the help of John Vendeville, one of the professors in the new University of DOUAI (DOUAY), he established, by his own initiative and in the face of considerable criticism and opposition, a college at Douai for the training of priests for England. Douai became the major educational center for English Catholics, and its long–term significance is summed up by Philip Hughes's comment: "Here, under God, was the principal means of preserving the Catholic Church in England for the next two hundred years."

Leader of the Exiles. William Allen was regarded as the leader of English Catholics and was called to Rome as adviser on English affairs in 1575, 1579, and 1585, after which he remained in Rome until his death. In 1587, at the request of Philip II, King of Spain, and because of the role he was intended to play as archbishop of Canterbury and Lord Chancellor if the Armada succeeded, Sixtus V made him a cardinal.

Probably from about the mid–1570s Allen was deeply involved in various enterprises to overthrow the Elizabethan government and to support a rival claimant to the throne when Elizabeth I was removed from the scene. With Robert PERSONS and others he was a leader of the "Spanish party" among English Catholics abroad. Allen maintained that the seminary priests sent to England came purely for religious reasons and had no political intentions. In his *Defence of the English Catholics* (1584), he argued that the priests were not traitors and were not working for the overthrow of the regime. With few exceptions this is undoubtedly true, but Allen and his associates were certainly using political means to try to secure their end—the preservation of the Catholic religion in England. They believed that unless action were taken by Catholic rulers in Europe, English Catholicism would be destroyed. Allen's own actions from the mid–1570s and his own statements in his *Defence of Sir William Stanley's Surrender of Deventer* (1587) and in his *Admonition to the Nobility and People of England and Ireland* (1588), which was intended for distribution if the Armada secured a bridgehead, show clearly that he considered that Elizabeth had forfeited any claim to the loyalty of Catholics. This attitude is logical and understandable, but it placed the seminary priests and the Jesuits in an awkward position in relation to the government and lent weight to the charge that the priests were softening up English Catholics so that they would become traitors as soon as the invaders landed.

Allen's Achievements. Allen's varied activities included important contributions to contemporary controversial writing. His profound interest in the Scriptures led, among other work, to the production of the Rheims–Douay New Testament. His remarkable personality and his deep charity helped to ensure the success of Douai and the holding together of the English Catholic body. After his death the college ran into many difficulties, partly because of the absence of any formal regulations, which he had considered unnecessary. The divisions among English Catholics at home and abroad, which were already considerable in his lifetime, became even more deep–seated after his death and did lasting harm to the Catholic cause in England.

Bibliography: Works. *Letters and Memorials,* ed. T. F. KNOX (London 1882). *The First and Second Diaries of the English College, Douay,* ed. T. F. KNOX (London 1878). "Some Correspondence of Cardinal Allen, 1579–85," ed. P. RYAN in *Publications of the Catholic Record Society* (Aberdeen 1911) 7:12–105, additional letters. Literature. P. K. GUILDAY, *The English Catholic Refugees on the Continent 1558–1795* (New York 1914). A. C. SOUTHERN, *Elizabethan Recusant Prose,* 1559–1582 (London 1950). B. CAMM, *Cardinal William Allen* (New York 1909). M. HAILE, *An Elizabethan Cardinal* (New York 1914). G. MATTINGLY, *The Armada* (Boston 1959). "William Allen and Catholic Propaganda in England," *Travaux d'Humanisme et Renaissance,* 28 (1957) 325–339. P. HUGHES, *The Reformation in England,* 3 v. in 1 (5th, rev. ed. New York 1963). T. COOPER, *The Dictionary of National Biography from the Earliest Times to 1900,* 63 v. (London 1885–1900) 1:314–322. F. STEGMÜLLER, *Lexikon für Theologie und Kirche*[2], ed. J. HOFER and K. RAHNER, 10 v. (2d, new ed. Freiburg 1957–65) 1:346–347.

[P. MCGRATH]

ALLOUEZ, CLAUDE JEAN

Jesuit missionary; b. Saint Didier-en-Forez, France, June 6, 1622; d. near Niles, Mich., Aug. 27–28, 1689. He joined the Jesuits at Toulouse (1639), studied there and at Billom and Rodez, and was ordained in 1655. He was 36 when he arrived in Canada, where he spent the next seven years ministering to the settlers in the Saint Lawrence area. In 1665 he was named vicar-general to Bishop François de Montmorency Laval of Quebec. Allouez's assignment to the Great Lakes region marked the first step toward the organization of the hierarchy in the central part of what later became the United States. From 1665 to 1689 he traveled the Great Lakes region in all directions—Huron, Superior, Erie, Michigan—covering 3,000 miles, preaching to more than 20 native tribes, and, it is said, baptizing about 10,000 persons. In 1667 he went to Lake Nipigon and celebrated the first Mass to be offered within the boundaries of the present Diocese of Fort-William, Ontario. He worked among the Illinois, prepared a prayer book in Illinois and French, laid the foundations for St. Francis Xavier Mission (1673), and wrote *Récit d'un 3(e) voyage fait aux Illinois* (c. 1679). The *Relations* of 1667 to 1676 have preserved numerous extracts from his journals; the edition of 1671 contains a portion of the address he delivered the preceding year at Sault Sainte Marie, Michigan, when M. S. F. de Saint-Lusson took possession of the territories of the West in the name of the King of France. Allouez is honored in the

U.S., especially in Wisconsin, where in 1899 the Wisconsin Historical Society raised a monument to him at De Pere, the center of his missionary activities.

Bibliography: "Narrative of a 3rd Voyage to the Illinois made by Father Claude Allouez," *Jesuit Relations and Allied Documents,* ed. R. G. THWAITES, 73 v. (Cleveland 1896–1901; New York 1959–) 60:148–167, and general intro. G.J. GARRAGHAN, *Jesuits of the Middle U.S.* (New York 1938) 1:3–4. T. J. CAMPBELL, *Pioneer Priests of North America,* 3 v. (New York 1908–19) 3:147–164. F. J. NELLIGAN, "The Visit of Father Allouez to Lake Nipigon in 1667," *Canadian Catholic Historical Association Report* (1956) 41–52.

[L. POULIOT]

ALMA

The Hebrew word *'almâ* used to describe the mother of EMMANUEL in the divine oracle delivered to King Ahaz of Juda (735–715 B.C.) by the prophet ISAIAH (Is 7.14). The Hebrew substantive is the feminine counterpart of the rare *'elem,* "young lad," and ordinarily designates a young girl of marriageable age until the birth of her first child, prescinding entirely from her actual marital or virginal status. (The Hebrew word for expressing "virgin" as such is *bᵉ tûlâ.*) A Ugaritic cognate, *ġlmt,* is attested in approximately the same meaning as *alma;* but the Ugaritic literary parallel adduced for the prophecy in the poem of Nikkal is based on a highly questionable textual restoration. In the OT itself, this prophecy exhibits the literary characteristics of the genre known as "birth ORACLE" (*Geburtsorakel*), foretelling a child's birth, name, food, and future circumstances of life (cf. Jgs 13.3–5; Lk 1.13–17).

The Septuagint translation in choosing to render *alma* in this passage by παρθένος (rather than νεᾶνις) furnishes a pre-Christian interpretation and greater specification of the somewhat neutral Hebrew expression by making explicit the notion of "virginity" connected with the mother of Emmanuel. In Mt 1.23 the angel appearing to Joseph in a dream is portrayed as citing the Septuagint version of the prophecy of Emmanuel and his virgin mother and applying it to Mary and her expected child. Subsequent Christian translations and interpretations of the passage in antiquity generally followed the lead of the Septuagint.

Because of its use in Matthew, this prophecy has usually been held to refer to Mary and her Son in at least a typical sense (implicitly demanded by Pius VI in his brief *Divina,* Sept. 20, 1779, *Enchiridion biblicum* 74). But the literal sense of the passage has often been disputed, and no single theory has been able to win general acceptance. The following points describe briefly the four opinions most commonly held at present. (1) The prophecy may be taken as literally messianic (*see* MESSIANISM). Isaiah was promising as a sign for the king a future savior of Israel, even though the prophet may not have fully understood the import of his words. (2) The literal sense of the prophecy may involve no specific woman and child, but may simply be a figurative way of expressing passage of time in a broader context. Isaiah 7.14–16 should be interpreted as a whole: "Before the unborn child of any woman now pregnant has had time to reach the age of discretion, the two kings whom [Ahaz] fears will be destroyed." (3) The prophecy may be viewed as referring to Isaiah's own wife (cf. Is 8.3) and his own unborn child. The child's birth and naming are wholly within the prophet's power because Emmanuel is in fact to be his own son. This opinion sees ch. 6–8 of Isaiah as the proper context for interpreting the oracle and tends to regard 7.18–25 (and perhaps also 7.15, 17) as later literary additions. (4) The oracle may refer literally to Ahaz's queen Abi(a) and the unborn prince who will reign as Hezekiah (715–686 B.C.). The birth of the heir to David's throne would be a mighty portent for the king and provide a fitting type for the Messiah to be born of the same Davidic royal line. The prophecies of the "Prince of Peace" and the "Root of Jesse" in ch. 9 and 11 of Isaiah would thus be fulfilled in varying degrees in both the literal, present heir and in his messianic antitype.

See Also: VIRGIN BIRTH.

Bibliography: J. LINDBLOM, *A Study of the Immanuel Section in Isaiah* (Lund 1957). N. K. GOTTWALD, "Immanuel as the Prophet's Son," *Vetus Testamentus* 8 (1958) 36–47. J. J. STAMM, "Neuere Arbeiten zum Immanuel-Problem," *Zeitschrift für die alttestamentliche Wissenschaft* 68 (1956) 46–53. M. MCNAMARA, "The Emmanuel Prophecy and Its Context," *Scripture* 14 (1962) 118–125; 15 (1963) 19–23, 80–88.

[J. A. BRINKMAN]

ALMA REDEMPTORIS MATER

One of the four Marian antiphons, this chant was traditionally sung at the end of Compline from the Vespers of Saturday before the first Sunday of Advent to the second Vespers of the Feast of the Lord's Presentation (Feb. 2). HERMANNUS CONTRACTUS, a monk of Reichenau (1013–54), is believed to have composed both the words and the music. Although now sung as an independent piece, this chant was originally performed in the manner characteristic of antiphons, i.e., it preceded and followed the chanting of a psalm or canticle on a simple formula. The 13th century MS Worcester Cathedral F. 160 (*Paléoographie musicale* 12:303), assigns it to Terce of the Feast of the Assumption and provides it with a *differ-*

entia, an ending formula for the psalm tone to be used with it. The more elaborate of the two chant melodies for this antiphon is apparently the original one; it served as the basis for numerous medieval and Renaissance compositions. It is found as the tenor of 13th century motets in the Montpellier, Bamberg, and Las Huelgas MSS; in these works the upper voices have different texts. The chant is composed in the major scale rather than in one of the medieval modes, and has often been said to be of particular beauty.

Bibliography: G. REESE, *Music in the Middle Ages* (New York 1940); *Music in the Renaissance* (New York 1959). W. APEL, *Gregorian Chant* (Bloomington, Ind. 1958). P. WAGNER, *Einführung in die gregorianischen Melodien* (Leipzig 1911–21). B. STÄBLEIN, ''Antiphon,'' *Die Musik in Geschichte und Gegenwart,* ed. F. BLUME (Kassel-Basel 1949) 1:523–545.

[R. STEINER]

ALMAIN, JACQUES

Theologian whose works influenced Gallican theories; b. Sens, *c.* 1480; d. Paris, 1515. At first he taught dialectics and natural philosophy at the University of Paris, but then entered the College of Navarre in 1508 to pursue theology, and three years later received his doctorate. In 1512 he was commissioned to teach theology at the college, a task he continued until his death, expounding, as was the custom of the day, the *Books of Sentences.* Almain's rise to prominence was occasioned by Cajetan's treatise *De comparatione auctoritatis papae et concilii,* in which the eminent Thomist personally defended the authority of the pope at the Pseudo–Council of Pisa against the advocates of the conciliar theory. (*See* CONCILIARISM.) Almain was assigned the task of censuring Cajetan's position. His work, *De auctoritate ecclesiae et conciliorum generalium adversus Thomam de Vio,* appeared in 1512. Among other doctrinal points, he maintained that the authority of a general council is superior to that of the pope. Invoking Matthew 18.17, he argued that the bishops gathered in a general council have divine power to judge all the faithful including the pope, because the latter is a member of the Church; that they have the right to impose their will upon him and even to depose him if need be; that the pope is superior to bishops taken individually, but inferior to them gathered in a council. Besides several purely philosophical works, seven of Almain's theological treatises, of unequal value and interest, are extant.

Bibliography: V. OBLET, *Dictionnaire de théologie catholique,* ed. A. VACANT et al., 15 v. (Paris 1903–50) 1:895–897.

[G. M. GRABKA]

ALMERÍA, MARTYRS OF, SS.

D. Aug. 29-Sept. 12, 1936, Almería, Andalucia, Spain. At the outbreak of the three-year Spanish Civil War, 19 Lasallian Brothers of the Christian Schools (Christian Brothers) ran a free school and St. Joseph's College in Almería in the southeastern-most corner of the Iberian Peninsula. On July 22, 1936, members of the Popular Front arrested and confined in makeshift prisons the local religious as enemies of the revolution. Although some survived the privation and mistreatment, two bishops and seven Christian Brothers did not. Each of these martyrs was shot to death without a trial for the crime of professing and teaching the faith.

Herrero, Valerio Bernardo, Bl., baptized Marciano Herrero Martínez, brother; b. July 11, 1909, Porquera de los Infantes, Spain; entered the novitiate Feb. 1, 1926; d. Aug. 30, 1936 near Tabernas. Together with Brother Edmigio and Amalio, he was transferred on Aug. 3, 1936 to the crowded Astoy Mendi prison where their names were added to a list of religious. At the end of August the trio was loaded on a truck, presumably bound for Cartagena, but they were executed en route, and their bodies thrown in a well or mine shaft.

Medina Olmos, Emmanuel (Manuel), St., bishop of Guadix (Spain), the diocese just west of Almería; d. Aug. 29, 1936. Bishops Medina and Ventaja were the first of this group to suffer. They were taken to an isolated spot with fifteen other prisoners and executed.

Mendoza, Amalio, St., baptized Justo Zariquiegui Mendoza, brother; b. Aug. 6, 1886, Salinas de Oro, Spain; entered the novitiate Sept. 13, 1902; d. Aug. 30, 1936 near Tabernas.

Rodríguez, Edmigio, St., baptized Isidoro Primo Rodríguez González, brother; b. April 4, 1881, Adalia, Spain; entered the novitiate Oct. 8, 1898; d. Aug. 30, 1936 with Brs. Amalio and Valerio near Tabernas.

Rodríguez, José Cecilio, St., baptized Bonifacio Rodríguez González, brother; b. May 14, 1885, La Molina de Ubierna, Spain; entered the novitiate Nov. 21, 1901; d. Sept. 12, 1936, Almería. Brothers José Cecilio and Aurelio María were the last to die. They were briefly detained in a convent, then transferred to Capitan Segarra prison. They were among 28 prisoners executed by a firing squad. Their bodies were thrown into a mine shaft.

Säiz, Teodomiro Joaquín, St., baptized Adrián Säiz Säiz, brother; b. Sept. 8, 1907, Puentedey, Spain; entered the novitiate Aug. 15, 1923; d. Sept. 8, 1936, Almería. Like three others of this group, Brothers Teodomiro Joaquín and Evencio Ricardo were transferred to Astoy Mendi prison. They were shot on the roadside. Their discarded bodies were never found.

Uyarra, Evencio Ricardo, St., baptized Eusebio Alonso Uyarra, brother; b. March 5, 1907, Viloria de Rioja, Spain; entered the novitiate Feb. 2, 1923; d. Sept. 8, 1936, Almería.

Ventaja Milan, Diego (James) St., bishop of Almería; d. Aug. 29, 1936. Bishop Ventaja was given several opportunities to flee the war zone, but insisted upon remaining with his flock. He died with Bishop Medina and 15 other prisoners. A monument to his courage stands in Almería.

Villalón, Aurelio María, St., baptized Bienvenido Villalón Acebrón, brother; b. March 22, 1890, Zafra de Záncara, Spain; entered the novitiate Aug. 22, 1906; d. Sept. 12, 1936, Almería. Brother Aurelio María was director of St. Joseph's College. When he was shot, his prayer of several years was heard: "What happiness for us if we could shed our blood for the lofty ideal of Christian education. Let us double our fervor and thus become worthy of such an honor." *See* José Cecilio Rodríguez above.

This group was both beatified (Oct. 10, 1993) and canonized (Nov. 21, 1999) by John Paul II.

Feast: Nov. 16.

Bibliography: J. PÉREZ DE URBEL, *Catholic Martyrs of the Spanish Civil War*, tr. M. F. INGRAMS (Kansas City, Mo. 1993).

[K. I. RABENSTEIN]

ALMICI, CAMILLO

Oratorian scholar; b. Brescia, Italy, June 2, 1714; d. there, 1779. Camillo, inclined from boyhood to learning and piety, joined the Brescia Oratory at the age of 19. After his ordination he spent his life in this community, becoming a distinguished theologian, apologist, and critical scholar, expert particularly in Hebrew, Greek, and Scripture. He was also well acquainted with church history and patristic writings, in fact with the whole field of secular history and archeology. As a scholar, he made himself accessible to other scholars and students, and was much consulted. As an Oratorian priest, he was a popular preacher and confessor. His writings include *Riflessioni su di un libro di Giustino Febronio* (Lucca 1766); *Critica contro le opere del pericoloso Voltaire* (Brescia 1771); *Dissertazione sopra i martiri della Chiesa cattolica* (Brescia 1765); *Meditazione sopra la vita e gli scritti di Paolo Sarpi* (Brescia 1765), in which he points out the tendentiousness and unreliability of Sarpi's history of the Council of Trent; and a dissertation on the art of writing biography and autobiography. Almici published some small works under the anagrammatic pseudonyms Callimaco Limi, and Callimaco Mili.

Bibliography: C. TOUSSAINT, *Dictionnaire de théologie catholique*, ed. A. VACANT et al., 15 v. (Paris 1903–50) 1.1:898. P. GUERRINI, *Le Congregazione dei Padri della Pace* (Brescia 1933). *Hurter Nomencl* 5.1:224–225. A. PALMIERI, *Dictionnaire d'histoire et de géographie ecclésiastiques*, ed. A. BAUDRILLART et al. (Paris 1912—) 2:658.

[J. CHALLENOR]

ALMOND, JOHN, ST.

English martyr; b. Allerton, near Liverpool, *c.* 1577; d. Tyburn, Dec. 5, 1612. At the age of eight, having already attended Much Wootton Grammar School, he went to Ireland, where he remained until 1597. He then entered the English College at Rome and in April 1601 he was ordained. To gain his Doctor of Divinity degree he gave a public disputation that won great applause, since he was exceptionally clever and quick at debate. Almond left Rome for England in September of 1602 and became a successful missionary—discreet, forceful, and holy. In 1607 he was tracked down by pursuivants in Holborn, taken to Newgate, and then transferred to the Gatehouse Prison. He either escaped or was released, for he was heard of in Staffordshire in 1609. In 1612 he was again arrested and brought before Dr. John King, Bishop of London. Part of the extant record of the examination reads:

BISHOP: In what place were you born?

JOHN ALMOND: About Allerton.

BISHOP: About Allerton! Mark the equivocation; then not in Allerton?

JOHN ALMOND: No equivocation. I was not born in Allerton but on the edge or side of Allerton.

BISHOP: You were born under a hedge then were you?

JOHN ALMOND: Many a better man, than I or you either, has been born under a hedge.

BISHOP: You cannot remember that you were born in a house?

JOHN ALMOND: Can you?

BISHOP: My mother told me so.

JOHN ALMOND: Then you remember not that you were born in a house but only that your mother told you so. So much I remember too.

He was committed to Newgate, where the prisoners were in danger of suffocation from the stench of the dungeon. Because of his reputation for cleverness and sanctity, Protestant ministers, including the archbishop of Canterbury, carried on disputes with Almond in the hope of winning a recantation; but they always retired, beaten in argument. On Dec. 3, 1612, he was brought for trial under his own name and two aliases, Mollinax and Ladome. Although no proof was brought, he was found guilty of being a priest and on December 5 he was drawn to Tyburn. His last words on the scaffold were, ''In manus tuas Domine . . .''; he was canonized on Oct. 25, 1970. (*See* ENGLAND, SCOTLAND, AND WALES, MARTYRS OF.)

Feast: Dec. 5; Oct. 25; May 4.

Bibliography: A. BUTLER, *The Lives of the Saints,* rev. ed. H. THURSTON and D. ATTWATER, 4 v. (New York 1956) 4:502–503. J. H. POLLEN, *Acts of English Martyrs* (London 1891) 170–193. R. CHALLONER, *Memoirs of Missionary Priests,* ed. J. H. POLLEN (rev. ed. London 1924). J. GILLOW, *A Literary and Biographical History or Bibliographical Dictionary of the English Catholics from 1534 to the Present time,* 5 v. (London–New York 1885–1902) 1:26–27. W. J. STEELE, *Blessed John Almond* (Postulation pamphlet; London 1961).

[G. FITZHERBERT]

ALMS AND ALMSGIVING (IN THE BIBLE)

A religious act, inspired by compassion and a desire for justice, whereby an individual who possesses the economic means helps in a material way his less fortunate neighbor. In the earlier history of Israel when society was predominantly seminomadic and all members were more or less economically equal, there was no need of almsgiving. But with the possession of landed property, the growth of aristocracy, and the centralization of government, a large mass of debt-ridden farmers arose in contrast to a small urban nobility. Such a society offended the ideal of social justice that the covenant of Yahweh demanded. Hence, the Prophets, beginning with Amos, denounced oppression of the poor (Am 5.11–12, 24; 8.4; Is 10.2; Mi 2.2) and vigorously demanded social justice (Am 5.24).

Throughout the Old Testament the notion of alms (concrete aid given the poor) is understood primarily in the context of justice; just as Yahweh acts with justice, so, too, must his worshipers. The Hebrew word for alms, *ṣ^edāqâ,* means justice or righteousness; giving to the poor helps reestablish the right order; it produces justice. To return to the poor man his pledged cloak at nightfall that he may sleep in comfort is justice (*ṣ^edāqâ*) before Yahweh (Dt 24.13). Mindful of the poor, the Law prescribed that the land should lie fallow every 7th year (Ex 23.11) and that the gleanings from the harvest should be left for the poor in the field and vineyard (Lv 19.9–10; 23.22; see also Ru 2.2–8). After the Exile there was a growing emphasis on the religious nature of personal almsgiving.

Job, in his plea of a clean conscience, asserts that his reverence for God prompted him to give food, clothing, and shelter to the needy (Jb 31.16–23). Alms purge away sin, deliver from death (Tb 12.9; see also Dn 4.24), and bring God's favor on the giver (Tb 4.7); on the other hand, refusing alms to the poor brings a just retribution (Prv 21.13) because God, who created the poor man, too, will hear the latter's cry (Sir 4.1–6).

In the New Testament almsgiving is considered primarily as an act of religion springing from love and compassion; its note of social justice also is alluded to, especially in the writings of St. Luke and in the Epistle of James. Jesus enjoins unostentatious almsgiving, together with prayer and fasting, as one of the pillars of the religious life (Mt 6.1–2, 5, 16, 19). It merits a heavenly reward (Mt 6.4, 20; 19.27–29; 25.40; Lk 12.33; 16.1–9) and makes the donor a true son of the Most High (Lk 6.35). Luke's writings, in particular, commend almsgiving; he alone relates the stories of Zachaeus, a chief tax collector, who gave half his possessions to the poor (Lk 19.1–10), of the Baptist's advice to share food and clothing with the needy (Lk 3.11), and of Christ's advice to lend money without thought of return (Lk 6.35). Luke also takes the opportunity of relating that Paul worked with his hands to provide for the needs of others as well as his own (Acts 18.3; 20.34–35). St. Paul organized collections for the poor (Rom 15.25–28; 1 Cor 16.1; 2 Cor 8–9), in order not only to alleviate want, but to break down prejudices between Jew and Gentile and to knit the members of Christ into a community of good will. According to St. James, true religion demands that those in the Christian community who possess the means should help their needy brethren (Jas 1.27; 2.14–17; see also 1 Jn 3.17; 1 Pt 4.8–10).

Bibliography: *Encyclopedic Dictionary of the Bible,* tr. and adap. by L. HARTMAN (New York, 1963), from A. VAN DEN BORN, *Bijbels Woordenboek* 55–56. G. A. BUTTRICK, ed., *The Interpreters' Bible,* 4 v. (Nashville 1962) 1:87–88. O. CONE, *Rich and Poor in the New Testament* (New York 1902). R. BULTMANN, ''ἐλεημοσύνη,'' G. KITTEL, *Theologisches Wörterbuch zum Neuen Testament* (Stuttgart 1935–) 2:482–83. H. J. CADBURY, *The Making of Luke—Acts* (2d ed. London 1958) 260–63.

[M. RODRÍGUEZ]

ALMS AND ALMSGIVING (IN THE CHURCH)

The word alms can be traced back to the Greek word ἐλεημοσύνη (pity). This word is found in the Septuagint, a fact of importance since it is especially in Holy Scripture that the divine perspective on alms can be seen. From this point of view, the Christian is led to reflect on his duties in regard to those less favored than himself, and especially on the responsibilities of his Christian stewardship over material goods. St. Thomas Aquinas considered almsgiving the general and principal work of mercy (*Summa theologiae* 2a2ae, 32).

The Value of Alms. Alms assume so large a place in the design of eternal love that Holy Scripture considers a heart attentive to the poor a genuine blessing. "Happy is he who has regard for the lowly and the poor; in the day of misfortune the Lord will deliver him. The Lord will keep and preserve him, He will make him happy upon the earth, and not give him over to the will of his enemies. The Lord will help him on his sick bed, He will take away all his ailment when he is ill" [Ps 40(41). 1–4]. Such blessings are hardly surprising since an alms given to a fellow man is received by God Himself. As the Old Testament puts it, "He who has compassion on the poor lends to the Lord, and He will repay him for his good deed" (Prv 19.17), but the New Testament incomparably enhances this value of alms since there it is Jesus Christ Himself who is the recipient of alms. This truth is repeatedly illustrated in the legends of the saints. For example, Christ, disguised as a poor man who was clothed by St. Martin of Tours, was to make Martin a great missionary to the pagans and the founder of the Church of Gaul. The first miracle after Pentecost, which had an enormous effect in Jerusalem, was performed by Peter, who, when asked for an alms, gave not silver and gold, but what he had (see Acts 3.6).

Since God sees as His own the needs of the poor, alms have an eternal value, meriting a treasure in heaven. "Sell what you have and give alms. Make for yourselves . . . a treasure in heaven" (Lk 12.33). Alms also have the redemptive value of blotting out sins. "Water quenches a flaming fire and alms atone for sin" (Sir 3.29). In this spirit Daniel gives advice to a king who is in agony over his own weakness: "Atone for your sins by good deeds and for your misdeeds by kindness to the poor, then your posterity will be long" (Dn 4.24). The Archangel Raphael affirms this value of alms to the family of Tobit; in fact, this is one of the most important lessons given by this Biblical work. "Prayer is good with fasting and alms more than to lay up treasures of gold, for alms delivereth from death, and the same is that which purgeth away sin, and maketh to find mercy and life everlasting" (Tb 12.8–9). Another aspect of the value of alms is that of sacrifice, as taught by Sirach. "In works of charity one offers fine flour, and when he gives alms he presents his sacrifice of prayer" (Sir 35.2).

Alms Purify the Heart. The portions of personal possessions so shared are detached from what is kept, and this tends to create an interior detachment. This may be the meaning of the somewhat obscure text of St. Luke: "Nevertheless, give that which remains as an alms; and behold, all things are clean to you" (Lk 11. 41).

Alms have still other values, for they enrich not only the giver, but the Church, since its charity is in this way enlarged. Alms increase brotherly love in the recipient, who in his turn prays for his benefactor. More particularly, in the exchange of mutual aid between the churches, the entire Mystical Body is blessed. This idea was the foundation of St. Paul's totally apostolic concern for Jerusalem's poor. He considered alms to be a means of eliminating the causes of disunity among Christians. "Now, however, I will set out for Jerusalem to minister to the saints. For Macedonia and Achaia have thought it well to make a contribution for the poor among the saints at Jerusalem" (Rom 15.25–26). Such an idea might have splendid applications to the bonds between parishes and dioceses with the help of papal direction. It would be a witnessing before the world to the mutual aid existing among Christ's disciples so that at least among them there would be no distinction based either on race or on country.

The final words of Paul lead to an even higher sphere: human alms become a divine revelation since God both inspires the good action and is glorified by it. "He . . . will increase the growth of the fruits of your justice that, being enriched in all things, you may contribute with simplicity of heart, and thus through us evoke thanksgiving to God; for the administration of this service not only supplies the wants of the saints, but overflows also in much gratitude to the Lord. The evidence furnished by this service makes them glorify God for your obedient profession of Christ's gospel and for the sincere generosity of your contributions to them and to all; while they themselves, in their prayers for you, yearn for you, because of the excellent grace God has given you" (2 Cor 9.11–14).

Qualities of Alms. In order to have such value and to merit these promises, alms should correspond to the divine pattern. First, the primacy of intention must be emphasized, for intention is the soul of human action and gives it its real value. Christ Himself emphatically taught that alms should be given "in secret and thy Father, who sees in secret, will reward thee" (Mt 6.2–4). Christian alms then, should be a communion in merciful love. From this point of view, almsgiving has a delicacy that excludes ostentation and avoids the display of any superiority. St. Jerome once said that alms should be given as if the giver were the real recipient (*Letter to Hedibian.*) More emphatically yet, the Lord taught, "When thou givest alms, do not let thy left hand know what thy right hand is doing" (Mt 6.3).

Almsgiving must also be totally disinterested, "not hoping for anything in return" (Lk 6.35; cf. Lk 14.4). The Old Testament had already mentioned the importance of promptness in the reception of a needy friend: "Refuse no one the good on which he has a claim when it is in your power to do it for him. Say not to your neighbor, 'Go and come again tomorrow, tomorrow I will give,' when you can give at once" (Prv 3.27–28).

Almsgiving was commanded by the Lord, but not simply in the sense of material assistance; it includes rather, the realization of the compassionate intention of love. St. Paul expressly adds joy to the eagerness of generosity: "He who shows mercy [should do so] with cheerfulness" (Rom 12.8). In a word, alms should reflect the realism of a love that is attentive in its search for the opportunity of fraternal service, since the brother with whom we share what we have is a child of the same Father from whom we have all received. The example of Christ Himself speaks volumes. Living on alms, He nonetheless gave alms to those poorer than Himself (Jn 13.29). Even more, Christ is God's gift for the enrichment of the world: "For you know the graciousness of our Lord Jesus Christ—how being rich he became poor for your sakes, that by his poverty you might become rich" (2 Cor 8.9).

Obligation to Give Alms. St. John has formulated the principle: "He who has the goods of this world and sees his brother in need and closes his heart to him, how does the love of God abide in him?" (1 Jn 3.17). True love demands a sharing when there is an abundance on one hand and a need on the other. To refuse to meet this demand is incompatible with charity. In the parable, the priest and the levite saw the unfortunate Samaritan; they could have helped him, but they passed by. It is seldom that a man's life depends so entirely on help from his neighbor, but when it does, the obligation is quite clear. This obligation would be so great that to refuse or deny it would be to destroy charity.

Conditions for the Obligation. "Abundance" exists when one has more than is necessary and strictly useful for his own life, for that of his family, or for the maintenance of his social position. Provision for one's social position is not necessarily a matter of snobbery or ostentation. Social life can impose real obligations. What these may be in any particular case may be determined by reasonable custom and special circumstances as these are evaluated by the Christian conscience of the individual. The logic of his faith and the operation of the gifts of the Holy Spirit will enable him to reach decisions about what is necessary to himself and what should be shared with his neighbor.

Extreme necessity means the absence or insufficiency of goods required for human life. The standard of liv-

ing varies in different situations. Three stages and forms of theological thought upon this subject can be distinguished. The Fathers were preoccupied with preaching the necessity of almsgiving; the scholastics, with the analysis of its theological foundations; the casuists, with the practical application of the theological conclusions.

The Fathers, as in fact Christian preachers of every age have done, sought to inspire love of the poor and horror of greed and selfishness. They insisted upon the responsibility of the rich, who, as stewards of God, owed their superabundance to the poor. St. Thomas and the scholastics in general worked out the connection between mercy and alms and analyzed the essential reasons why almsgiving is obligatory. From the 14th to the end of the 18th century the major concern of moralists was the problem of conscience in the determination to the extent of the obligation in concrete situations. An effort was made to achieve precision. When exactly is there real abundance? When are alms a matter of strict precept, and when are they more a matter of counsel? St. Alphonsus Liguori studied, edited, and criticized the thought of his predecessors; and his conclusions on the subjects of extreme need and abundance have become classic. With a view to the circumstances of his own time and society, St. Alphonsus taught that the rich should give in charity a 50th part, that is, 2 per cent, of what they could save. In defense of this and other similar theological conclusions in this matter—some propositions were in fact condemned by the Church as too lax—it should be noted that although the sum demanded for charity appears small, these authors did not lose sight of the wider horizons of the Gospel; and they were striving to determine what charity required as a matter of course and independently of extreme need. Confronted by a neighbor in extreme need, no Christian is really faithful to the Gospel when he is not prepared to sacrifice his abundance.

Alms are a matter of counsel when fraternal charity can be genuine without them, for instance, when the necessity of one's neighbor is not at the moment so pressing that a refusal to help him would be equivalent to a denial of love. On the other hand, there would be a serious obligation when the withholding of help would keep another from a good absolutely necessary to him. In this case, the lack of love would constitute a mortal sin against fraternal charity.

Generally speaking, then, the obligation of almsgiving is measured both by the extent of one's abundance, and by the kind of necessity the abundance would alleviate. If this necessity is extreme and one's assistance is the only possible way to relieve it, the duty is strict, but if the condition of need is known to others or if it is not really extreme, determination of the extent and force of the obligation calls for the exercise of prudence. The obligation itself is clear because of its connection with fraternal charity; the assessment of the obligation in concrete situations is often not easy to make.

Difficulty in Assessing. This may be due not only to variable circumstances but also, perhaps, to the very nature of things. An adequate Christian judgment in this matter can proceed only from a genuinely spiritual estimate of one's own resources. Certainly God's plan involves the provision of room in human life for creativeness and the generous use of freedom. However, this should not be used as a pretext to evade imperative duty where it clearly exists. Any uncertainty about the extent of a man's obligation should move him to develop the habit of seeing Christ in those poorer than himself. One's final welcome into the kingdom—or his rejection—will depend upon the criterion of his effective love for his brethren (Mt 25.34–46). The complexity of life's circumstances shows only that Christ wants His disciples to be free and to use their real liberty in a life of charity, with their conscience enlightened by the divine mercy.

Application to Contemporary Life. The two roots of the obligation of almsgiving indicated by St. John are having the goods of this world and seeing the need of a brother (1 Jn 3.17). In the contemporary world the "having" and "wanting" are viewed in relation to an expanding economy that is not only national but international in scope. In the scale of needs there is almost infinite variation, and while the duties of love have not lost their ancient urgency, their application must undergo modification.

The State's Assumption of the Burden of Providing for Many Needs. Modern civilization has become conscious of at least some of the human rights consonant with human dignity, and in genuine democracies these rights are clearly seen. The state either directly or indirectly takes over more and more of the responsibility for meeting such needs as arise from unemployment, illness, old age, and so on. In consequence of this, many people do not require the help of private charity. To pay taxes or to take out insurance is to participate in the assistance the state and other institutions offer. When these factors are taken into consideration, it can be seen that there has been reduction in the frequency of instances of clearly assessable obligation to give alms.

Nevertheless, there will always be cases in which a Christian cannot rely on the community to assume his personal duty to give alms any more than he can expect the community to assume his personal obligation to love his brother. Laws cannot cover every situation (unforeseen accidents, immediate urgencies, and the like). In addition to obligations arising in such circumstances, a

sense of charitable responsibility for his brethren should penetrate and illumine the Christian's performance of his civic duties and particularly the exercise of his right to vote.

Personal Knowledge of the Universality of Human Misery. The newspapers, radio, and television present the public with a spectacle of worldwide need, and this the Christian will see as a call upon his charity. No national or political limits exist for Christian charity. In most situations, only well-organized community effort can make an adequate response to the enormous needs. In the multitude of appeals and of possibilities offered, a 20th-century Christian may need to make a choice; bearing in mind the order of charity, he may have to consider which neighbors are closest to him spiritually. One such spiritual consideration might be "his brethren in the faith." "Therefore, while we have time, let us do good to all men, but especially to those who are of the household of the faith" (Gal 6.10). Those of the household will recognize the help more clearly as an expression of faith. But in general, discernment and an interior spirit become increasingly necessary for the Christian as he finds himself assailed with more multiple and varied appeals.

Need for Collective Organizations. In the mid-20th century it was said that almost any aid project involves so many costly measures that only an organization could undertake it. This is true, especially in cases in which aid must be sent to distant places. This kind of situation should broaden the scope of a Christian's compassionate intentions. He should be conscious of the complexities of the problem and take these into account in his thinking about economics, politics, and international relations. He may feel himself (and be) obligated to personal participation in collective effort and in interesting others by information and appeal. Yet in all this the Christian must take constant care that his participation remains an expression of fraternal love, without which no alms are pleasing to God. The qualities stated above that should mark Christian almsgiving should also characterize participation in the different forms of collective effort to bring aid to others. Otherwise these efforts will degenerate into mere philanthropic enterprises.

While he busies himself by having a share in large and collective undertakings, the Christian will try to keep alert in order not to miss the occasional opportunity that may occur to exercise charity in a direct, immediate, and personal way. He will remember that alms can be in forms other than money. His time, influence, friendliness, sympathy, and encouragement can also be a kind of alms and will give him much opportunity to prove his love for Christ and His Gospel.

See Also: MERCY; MERCY, WORKS OF; CHARITY.

Bibliography: THOMAS AQUINAS, *Summa theologiae* 2a2ae, 30–33. ALPHONSUS LIGUORI, *Theologia moralis*, ed. L. GAUDÉ, 4 v. (new ed. Rome 1905–12) 1.2:3.2. A. BEUGNET, *Dictionnaire de théologie catholique*, ed. A. VACANT et al., (Paris 1903—50) 1.2:2561–71. R. BROUILLARD, *Catholicisme* 1:1050–56; "La Doctrine Catholique de l'aumône," Nouvrevth 54 (1927) 5–36. L. BOUVIER, *Le Précepte de l'aumône chez saint Thomas d'Aquin* (Montreal 1935). G. J. BUDDE, "Christian Charity, Now and Always: The Fathers of the Church and Almsgiving," *American Ecclesiastical Review,* 85 (1931) 561–579. J. D. O'NEILL, *The Catholic Encyclopedia*, ed. C. G. HERBERMANN et al. (New York 1904–14; suppl. 1922) 1.1:328–331.

[J. M. PERRIN]

ALOGOI

The name given to heretics who denied the divinity of Christ as the Logos, as in St. John's Gospel, Epistles, and the Apocalypse. They were first named by EPIPHANIUS OF CONSTANTIA (*Panarion* 51; *Ancor.* 13.5). They were mentioned by IRENAEUS (*Adv. haer.* 3.11. 9–17) as Montanists misusing the Johannine teaching on the Paraclete. Eusebius (*Hist. eccl.* 3.28.1) and Hippolytus (*Die griechischen christlichen Schriftsteller der ersten drei Jahrhunderte* 1.2:241–247) described the Roman priest Gaius in the reign of Pope ZEPHYRINUS (199–217) as attributing the Johannine writings to the Gnostic Cerinthus. A type of enthusiastic spirituality, the Alogoi doctrine was current in the West in the 2nd and 3rd centuries; the necessity of defending the Johannine writings then is evident in Hippolytus and the MURATORIAN CANON (lines 16–26). The name Alogoi has a double meaning: men denying the Logos, and lacking reason.

Bibliography: A. GRILLMEIER, *Lexikon für Theologie und Kirche*, 10 v. (2d, new ed. Freiburg 1957–65) 1:363–364. C. SCHMIDT and J. WAYNBERG, eds. and trs., *Gespräche Jesu* (*Texte und Untersuchungen zur Geschichte der altchristlichen Literatur* 3d ser. 13; 1919) 420–452. A. BLUDAU, *Die ersten Gegner der Johannesschriften* (Biblische Studien 22; Fribourg 1925). G. BAREILLE, *Dictionnaire de théologie catholique* 1.1:898–901. A. WIKENHAUSER, *Einleitung in das Neue Testament* (3d ed. Freiburg 1959).

[F. X. MURPHY]

ALONSO DE ESPINA

Franciscan friar and author; b. c. 1412, Palencia, Spain; d. early 1460s. Alonso was most likely a student at the University of Salamanca, where he eventually became regent of studies at the *Studium Generale* of the Franciscan Order. He is associated with the Franciscan (Observant or Villacretian) reform movement in Spain which stressed the vow of poverty and strict asceticism. He is said to have been present at the death of Alvaro de Luna (1453), the condemned Constable of Juan II, and to have been the confessor of King Enrique IV of Castile (1454–74). He is best known as a proponent of the Spanish Inquisition. The plan that he set forth in the *Fortalitium Fidei*, his most important work, for the eradication of heresy, especially heresies associated with Jews and *conversos* (or "New Christians"), became the basic program for the Spanish National Inquisition. *Fortalitium Fidei* was written between 1459 and 1461, and was translated into French, German, and Italian in the first half of the 16th century. It is divided into five books: the first addresses general spiritual-theological principles, while the other four address what Alonso considered to be the four principal "enemies" of the Church: heretics, Jews, Muslims, and demons. Each one of these books is encyclopedic in form. For example, Book Three is entitled "de bello Judeorum," ("concerning the war of the Jews") and is made up of 12 chapters or considerations which, viewed in their entirety, constitute an "encyclopedia" of the different types of polemics against the Jews. The first three considerations cover the spiritual blindness, the demonic heritage and the confused state—reflected in the great diversity of beliefs—of the Jewish people. Considerations four through six address many exegetical, theological and philosophical arguments against the Jews. Considerations seven through 11 treat material that is more historical in nature, such as the laws imposed on the Jews, the expulsions of the Jewish people from various lands, miracles that happened to convince them of the truth of Christianity, etc. The 12th and final consideration discusses the eschatological role of the Jews at the end of time.

Bibliography: A. GINIO, *La forteresse de la foi: La vision du monde d'Alonso de Espina, moine espagnol (?–1466)* (Paris 1998); *De bello iudaeorum: Fray Alonso de Espina y su Fortalitium fidei*, Fontes Iudaeorum Regni Castellae, VIII (Salamanca 1998). A. ECHEVARRIA, *The Fortress of Faith: The Attitude toward Muslims in Fifteenth Century Spain* (Leiden 1999). S. J. MCMICHAEL, *Was Jesus of Nazareth the Messiah? Alphonso de Espina's Argument Against the Jews in the "Fortalitium Fidei"* (c.1464) (Atlanta 1994).

[S. J. MCMICHAEL]

ALOYSIUS GONZAGA, ST.

Patron of youth; b. Castiglione, near Mantua, Italy, March 9, 1568; d. Rome, June 21, 1591. The firstborn of Ferrante Gonzaga, Marquis of Castiglione and Prince of the Empire, and Marta Tana Santena, Aloysius grew up amid the brutality and license of Renaissance society, which witnessed the murder of two of his brothers. Between Aloysius and his devout mother a tender affection developed, while his father began early to prepare him for the military life envisioned for him. In Pierfrancesco del Turco he had a wise and competent tutor. In 1577 Aloysius was sent to attend the court of Francesco de' Medici, Grand Duke of Tuscany. In 1581, he accompanied his parents, who joined Empress Maria of Austria on a visit to Spain. At the court of Philip II he acted as page to the heir apparent, Don Diego, and pursued the study of philosophy. At Alcalá he was invited to participate in a public debate. While in Spain Aloysius decided to enter the Society of Jesus. His father firmly resisted his decision and began a struggle of wills that lasted for several years and still continued after their return to Castiglione in 1584. Aloysius prevailed, renounced the rights to his inheritance, and entered the novitiate in Rome on Nov. 25, 1585. As a novice he studied philosophy at the Roman College and gave a public defense in that subject. He pronounced his first vows on Nov. 25, 1587. For four years he studied theology, having as one of his masters the brilliant Gabriel Vázquez. In 1589 he returned to Castiglione for a brief stay in order to settle some intricate family affairs. While attending the sick during an epidemic in Rome in March 1591, he contracted the plague, and died three months later.

The steps in the spiritual growth of Aloysius are clear. At seven he manifested a strong sense of responsibility and love for vocal prayer. A book by Gaspar Loarte, SJ, and his later reading of Louis of Granada, opened up for him the area of mental prayer to which he gave several hours a day. With intensity, calmness of judgment, and power to face facts he firmly decided on a life of holiness. His calm purpose to conquer himself was expressed in severe penance. At Florence, before the Madonna in the Church of Annunziata, he made a vow of virginity. A distaste for court life at Mantua led him to read the lives of the saints. In 1580 he received First Holy Communion from St. Charles Borromeo, and this inspired him to a lasting devotion to the Holy Eucharist. He showed his basic humility and obedience in the novitiate by surrendering his own ideas about prayer and penance. His charity, which was practical, was revealed in the catechetical lessons he gave and in his care for the sick. While he was at the Roman College his spiritual director was St. Robert Bellarmine. His letters, uneffusive and unpretentious, reveal a direct and calm soul.

He never signed himself Aloisio or Aloysius, but Aluigi or Luigi. Francesco Sacchini, competent historian of the early Society of Jesus, objected to the form Aloysius in 1612, arguing for Ludovicus or Louis. However, Francesco Gonzaga, head of the family at the time, insisted on Aloysius. Benedict XIII canonized Aloysius in 1726, and three years later declared him patron of youth, an honor confirmed by Pius XI in 1926.

Feast: June 21.

Bibliography: A. GONZAGA, *Lettere ed altriscritti,* ed. E. ROSA (Florence 1926). *Aloysius,* ed. C. STEVENS and W. H. MCNICHOLS (Huntington, Ind. 1993). C. C. MARTINDALE, *The Vocation of Aloysius Gonzaga* (New York 1927). P. BLANC, *Saint Louis de Gonzague: un saint de 23 ans* (Paris 1977). V. CEPARI, *Life of Saint Aloysius Gonzaga,* tr. F. SCHROEDER (Einsiedeln 1891). E. DELPIERRE and A. NOCHÉ, *St. Louis de Gonzague et la Renaissance italienne* (Le Puy 1945). E. FERRI, *Luigi Gonzaga* (Milan 1991). A. LAMBRETTE, *St. Louis de Gonzague* (Museum Lessianum, Section Ascétique et Mystique 22; Louvain 1926). M. MESCHLER, *Leben des hl. Aloysius von Gonzaga* (Freiburg 1891). M. PAGANELLA, *San Luigi Gonzaga: un ritratto in piedi* (Milan 1991). M. SCADUTO, *Il mondo di Luigi Gonzaga* (Rome 1968). R. SIMONI, *Luoghi aloisiani: IV centenario della morte di San Luigi Gonzaga* (Castiglione delle Stiviere, Italy 1990). G. VIGNA, *Il santo dei Gonzaga: San Luigi e il suo tempo* (Milan 1991).

[W. V. BANGERT]

ALOYSIUS RABATÁ, BL.

Carmelite prior; b. Monte San Giuliano, Sicily, *c.* 1430; d. Randazzo, Sicily, 1490. He entered the CARMELITE ORDER at Trapani and became prior of the Randazzo monastery. Even as superior he continued to engage in manual labor and begging. He was noted especially for his love of neighbor and for the forgiveness of his enemies, as was exemplified in his refusal to reveal the identity of the assailant from whose wounds he died. The process of beatification was begun in 1533, the cult approved in 1841 by Gregory XVI, and an Office and Mass assigned in 1842. His relics were translated to the collegiate church of St. Mary, Randazzo, in 1912.

Feast: May 11.

Bibliography: *Acta Sanctae Sedis* May 2:707–721. P. SIMONELLI, *Il beato Luigi Rabatà carmelitano* (Rome 1968). L. M. SAGGI, *Lexicon für Theologie und Kirche,* ed. J. HOFER and K. RAHNER (Freiburg 1957–65) 1:365. A. BUTLER, *The Lives of the Saints,* ed. H. THURSTON and D. ATTWATER (New York 1956) 2:275–276.

[E. R. CARROLL]

ALPHABETIC PSALMS

Poems of an acrostic formation in which the first letter of the word that begins a line or a couplet or even a strophe follows the succession of the 22 letters of the Hebrew alphabet: *'ālep, bêt, gīmel, dālet,* etc. This artificial form is found in Ps 9 (9–10); 24 (25); 33 (34); 36 (37); 110 (111); 111 (112); 118 (119); and also in Prv 31.10–31; Lam 1–4, and partially (because of the poorly preserved text) in Na 1.2–8 and Sir 51.13–30. Occasionally the poet adds, at the end of the alphabetic series, another verse beginning with the letter *pē',* as in Ps 24(25); 33(34). With regard to the choice of this letter, P. W. Skehan has pointed out [*Catholic Biblical Quarterly* 23 (1961) 127] the quasi-alphabetic form also of the poems in the Book of Job. The most plausible reason for the device is that it might serve as an aid to memory or some other didactic purpose.

See Also: PSALMS, BOOK OF.

Bibliography: S. HOLM–NIELSEN, "The Importance of Late Jewish Psalmody for the Understanding of Old Testament Psalmodic Tradition," *Studia Theologica* 14 (1960) 1–51.

[R. E. MURPHY]

ALPHANUS OF SALERNO, ST.

Scholar and archbishop; b. Salerno, Italy, *c.* 1015–1020; d. there, Oct. 9, 1085. He was a teacher at the University of Salerno (*c.* 1050), and together with Desiderius, later Pope Victor III, he entered the BENEDICTINE Order at the monastery of Monte Cassino in 1056. This foundation was, under the abbacy of Desiderius (1058–1087), the most advanced center of culture in Italy. In 1057 Alphanus (or Alfanus) was an abbot in Salerno, and in 1058 he became archbishop. Salerno's fame rested essentially in the field of medicine, the study of which Alphanus strongly encouraged; he also established for himself a considerable reputation as a theologian, hagiographer, and hymnist. He showed unusual skill in the meter of his Latin verse, which covers a wide variety of subjects and indicates considerable acquaintance with the Roman poets (*Analecta hymnica* 22.24, 50). An ode addressed to Hildebrand, while the future GREGORY VII was still an archdeacon, calls on the papacy to crush with spiritual weapons the forces of barbarism that opposed the Church, and it compares Hildebrand himself to the Roman heroes of the past. It was in Salerno that the pope found refuge when the army of Emperor Henry IV forced him to flee Rome (1085). Alphanus was an important figure both in politics and in the development of Christian humanism in the eleventh century.

Bibliography: N. ACOCELLA, *Salerno medioevale ed altri saggi,* ed. A. SPARANO (Naples 1971); *La decorazione pittorica di Montecassino dalle didascalie di Alfano I* (Salerno 1966). F. UGHELLI, *Italia sacra,* ed. N. COLETI, 10 v. in 9 (2d ed. Venice 1717–22). F. J. E. RABY, *A History of Christian-Latin Poetry from the Beginnings to the Close of the Middle Ages* (Oxford 1953); *A History of Secular Latin Poetry in the Middle Ages* (Oxford 1957). C. DAWSON, *Religion and the Rise of Western Culture* (New York 1950). J. M. VIDAL, *Dictionnaire d'histoire et de géographie ecclésiastiques,* ed. A. BAUDRILLART et al. (Paris 1912) 2:401–403. A. LENTINI, "Rassegna delle poesie di Alfano da Salerno," *Bulletino dell' Istituto storico italiano* 69 (1957) 213–241. J. SZÖVÉRFFY, *Die Annalen der lateinischen Hymnendichtung* (Berlin 1964–65) 1:398–402.

[B. D. HILL]

ALPHEGE OF CANTERBURY, ST.

Benedictine, archbishop, honored as a martyr; b. 954; d. Greenwich, England, April 19, 1012. Alphege, who is known also as Aelfheah, Elphege, or Godwine, entered the monastery of Deerhurst in Gloucestershire against his parents' wishes. He left to become an anchorite near Bath; later he was abbot until DUNSTAN called him to succeed ETHELWOLD as bishop of WINCHESTER in 984. In 1006 he was translated to the archbishopric of Canterbury and visited Rome for his PALLIUM. Five years later the Danes sacked Canterbury and held Alphege for ransom, which he agreed to pay until he remembered the poor who must raise the sum. Apparently he sometimes preached to his captors, who in 1012 during a drunken orgy pelted him to death with the bone remains of their feast. In 1023 King CANUTE ceremoniously carried the body of Alphege to Canterbury. Years later Alphege was one of the saints LANFRANC wished to remove from the English calendar, but ANSELM OF CANTERBURY felt that to die for justice and charity was tantamount to martyrdom. The best sources include Osbern of Canterbury's *Life* (ed. H. Wharton, *Anglia Sacra,* 2:122–147), the *Anglo-Saxon Chronicle* and FLORENCE OF WORCESTER, for the year 1012, and THIETMAR OF MERSEBURG (*Monumenta Germaniae Scriptores* 3:849).

Feast: April 19 (Dioceses of Westminster, Clifton, Portsmouth, and Southwark).

Bibliography: W. HUNT, *Dictionary of National Biography from the Earliest Times to 1900,* 63 v. (London 1885–1900) 1:150–152. C. COTTON, *The Saxon Cathedral at Canterbury and the Saxon Saints Buried Therein* (Manchester, England 1929). W. A. PANTIN in *For Hilaire Belloc,* ed. D. WOODRUFF (London 1942). A. BUTLER, *The Lives of the Saints,* ed. H. THURSTON and D. ATTWATER, 4 v. (New York 1956) 2:129–131. D. KNOWLES, *The Monastic Order in England, 943–1216* (2d ed. Cambridge, England 1962), *passim.*

[E. J. KEALEY]

ALPHEGE OF WINCHESTER, ST.

Called Aelfheah, "the Bald"; d. March 12, 951. A priest and monk, perhaps at Glastonbury although the date and circumstances of his monastic profession are unknown, he was chaplain and secretary to his kinsman King Athelstan. Alphege, who succeeded Byrnstan as bishop of Winchester (934), is important primarily for his influence on the English monastic revival, encouraging and eventually investing his relative DUNSTAN as monk. He ordained Dunstan and ETHELWOLD, the latter commended to Alphege by Athelstan, on the same day, prophesying their future episcopates (*c.* 939). Dunstan may have been offered Alphege's see on the latter's death, but Aelfsige succeeded to it. The chief sources are: The *Anglo-Saxon Chronicle;* the *Vita Dunstani auctore B;* Aelfric, *Vita sancti Aethelwoldi;* Adelard, *Vita sancti Dunstani;* WILLIAM OF MALMESBURY; and SIMEON OF DURHAM.

Feast: March 12.

Bibliography: W. BIRCH, ed., *Cartularium Saxonicum,* 4 v. (1885–99). E. S. DUCKETT, *Saint Dunstan of Canterbury* (New York 1955). A. BUTLER, *The Lives of the Saints,* ed. H. THURSTON and D. ATTWATER (New York 1956) 1:577.

[W. A. CHANEY]

ALPHONSUS LIGUORI, ST.

Theologian, founder of the Congregation of the Most Holy Redeemer, bishop, Doctor of the Church; b. Marianella, near Naples, Sept. 27, 1696; d. Pagani, near Salerno, Aug. 1, 1787.

Life. He was the eldest son of Giuseppe de Liguori, of a noble and ancient Neapolitan family and an officer of the royal navy, and Anna Cavalieri. After receiving his early education at home under the care of tutors, Alphonsus was enrolled in 1708 at the University of Naples, where he studied until Jan. 21, 1713, when at the age of 16 he received his doctorate *in utroque jure.* He practiced at the bar for some years, leading the while an exemplary Christian life under the direction of the Oratorians. When charged in 1723 with the defense of the interests of the Duke of Gravina against the Grand Duke of Tuscany, he lost confidence in the justice of his client's cause, perhaps in consequence of intrigues. Shocked by this experience he renounced the world and put on clerical dress, Oct. 23, 1723. He began his theological studies at home under the direction of Don Julio Torni and joined a group of secular priests (Congregation of the Apostolic Missions), in whose missionary activities he took part from 1724. Ordained Dec. 21, 1726, he devoted himself in a special way to the work of hearing confessions and preaching. In 1727 he organized the Evening Chapels (*Cappelle Serotine*), an association of workers and artisans formed for the purpose of mutual assistance, religious instruction, and works of apostolic zeal. In 1729 he left his home and took up residence in the College of the Holy Family, known also as the Chinese College, founded in Naples by Matteo RIPA. There he devoted himself to the pastoral ministry by giving missions and working in the church connected with the college. After a sojourn at Scala and providential meetings with Thomas Falcoia of the society of *Pii Operarii,* who was made bishop of Castellamare di Stabia in 1730, and Sister Maria Celeste Crostarosa (1696–1755), he took an effective part in the foundation

St. Alphonsus Liguori, portrait by an unknown Italian artist, painted in 1768.

at Scala of the Institute of the Most Holy Savior, an order of contemplative nuns dedicated to the imitation of Jesus Christ, which was approved by Benedict XIV in 1750. On Nov. 9, 1732, he founded at Scala, under the direction of Bishop Falcoia, a congregation of priests under the title of the Most Holy Savior (known, after 1749, as the Congregation of the Most Holy Redeemer). It was intended as an association of priests and brothers living a common life and sharing in the desire to imitate Jesus Christ, particularly in the work of preaching the divine word. This congregation was formed with a special view to the needs of country people, who so often lacked the opportunities of missions, catechetical instruction, and spiritual exercises. Alphonsus gave himself to the work of the missions, to the organization of his congregation, and to the composition of his rule. His first companions deserted him, but he stood firm and before long vocations increased in number and new foundations multiplied; among the earliest were Villa Liberi (1734), Ciorani (1735), Pagani (1742), Deliceto (1745), and Mater Domini (1746).

On Feb. 25, 1749, Benedict XIV by his brief *Ad pastoralis dignitatis fastigium* approved the Congregation of the Most Holy Redeemer. Alphonsus was elected superior general for life at the general chapter held that same year. In consequence of the hostility of Marquis Tanucci and of the government, which was opposed to religious orders, Alphonsus could not obtain the royal exequatur in Naples to the brief of Benedict XIV. A royal decree of Dec. 9, 1752, gave limited assurance to the future of the institute, which at the time was extending its activity in the Papal States and in Sicily. Alphonsus governed his congregation, preached missions, and busied himself in writing and other apostolic work. He was appointed bishop of Sant' Agata dei Goti and was consecrated in Rome, June 20, 1762. As a bishop he soon distinguished himself for his work of reform. He put a stop to abuses, restored churches, fought for the liturgy, reformed his seminary, visited his diocese, promoted missions and often took a personal part in them, and exercised charity toward all, especially during the great famine of 1763–64. He kept an eye on the government of his congregation, which at the general chapter of 1764 adopted the completed constitutions, and continued with his writing. He was stricken in 1768 with a painful illness that made the pastoral ministry difficult; he offered his resignation from his see, and it was accepted by Pius VI in 1775. He then retired to Pagani, where he devoted himself to the governing of his congregation. Troubles concerning the rule caused by authorities of the Kingdom of Naples saddened his last years. The future of the congregation seemed precarious after the suppression of the Jesuits. He negotiated through an intermediary with the government to obtain its approbation, but the rule approved by the king and imposed on the congregation— the *regolamento*—differed notably from the rule approved by Benedict XIV. The Holy See, in its struggle with the Kingdom of Naples, took their canonical status away from the houses in the kingdom and gave to the houses in the Papal States their own superior. Alphonsus died before the reunion of the two branches of his congregation, which subsequently expanded to the whole world. Beatified Sept. 15, 1816, by Pius VII, canonized May 26, 1839, by Gregory XVI, declared Doctor of the Church by Pius IX in 1871, Alphonsus was finally made patron of confessors and moralists by Pius XII, April 26, 1950.

The Man. Ardent and richly endowed by nature, of delicate sensibility, tenacious of will, and profoundly intelligent, Alphonsus was given more to practical thinking than to pure speculation. He had to a rare degree an awareness of the concrete, a sense of the practical. In his relationship with others he combined nobility of manner with affability and benevolence toward all, especially the poor, and smiling good humor: "a model of moderation and of gentleness" [B. Croce, *Uomini e cose della vecchia Italia,* v.21 (Bari 1927) 123].

The will of God, obeyed even in its most crucifying demands, was the only rule of his life. His prayer attained

the summit of union with God, but it also expressed itself in apostolic action. He could in fact be described as a mystic of action. All his activity is explained by his determination to consecrate himself to the work of the Redemption and to the salvation of men. In this cause he employed all his artistic gifts. He was a talented musician and composed, in the style of the great Neapolitan school of the 18th century, a duetto of merit called *Duetto tra l'anima e Gesù Cristo.* He composed *Tu scende dalle stelle,* the lovely Christmas hymn that is still the most popular of Italian carols. In his *Canzoncine spirituali* he expressed in authentic poetry the sentiments of his mystical soul. An excellent picture of his psychology and intimate life can be gathered from the three volumes of his letters (Rome 1887–90).

Missions. Popular missions were for Alphonsus the means par excellence of procuring the salvation of souls. As a member of the Congregation of Apostolic Missions he took part in missionary work before he was a priest. His apostolate intensified with his ordination, and still more with the foundation of his congregation, which was dedicated in a special way to that work. It is estimated that he gave no fewer than 150 missions, and he himself once acknowledged that he had had 34 years of missionary experience. As a bishop he promoted missions in his diocese, and until his death he remained interested in the work. Alphonsus borrowed many of the elements of existing systems of conducting missions, but two features marked his own: (1) its concern that in the general structure of the mission and in the plan of the sermons there should be a continual adaptation to the concrete situation of the faithful; and (2) its effort to assure the perseverance of the participants by putting a major stress upon the love of God as the principal motive for conversion, and by calling for "renewals of the mission" to be preached some months after a mission, this last point being an original contribution to mission planning that won much acclaim.

Writing. No complete listing of the literary productions of St. Alphonsus is possible. Between 1728 and 1778 there appeared 111 works, and in addition to these there were posthumous publications. As to editions and translations, P. De Meulemeester in 1933 counted 4,110 editions of the original text (402 appeared before the death of Alphonsus) and 12,925 editions of translations into 61 languages. Since that time the number has continued to grow.

Works on Preaching. His principal work in this field was his *Selva di materie predicabili . . .* (1760), a complete treatise on sacerdotal perfection, the pastoral work of the missions, and the substance and form of preaching. In addition to this he published *Lettera ad un religioso amico ove si tratta del modo di predicare* (1761) in which he insisted on the necessity of preaching the gospel in a simple manner, without superfluous ornamentation, so that all, even the simplest of men, could understand the preacher. Mention should also be made of his sermons, and especially the *Sermoni compendiati per tutte le domeniche del anno* (1771), which were much admired by Newman.

Spiritual Works. These were markedly ascetical in character, but were solidly founded upon theology. They were the fruit of his interior life and of his preaching. The point of departure for his spirituality was the revelation of the love of God for man. Contrary to the teaching of the Jansenists, God offers to every man the possibility of salvation and of sanctification. This consists essentially in the loving response that man makes to the gift of God's love. To man turning toward God and detaching himself from creatures and the disordered impulses of concupiscence, Alphonsus presented the themes proposed by St. Ignatius in the First Week of the SPIRITUAL EXERCISES: death, judgment, heaven, and hell. Such was the subject of his *Apparecchio alla morte* (1758) and of the *Via della salute* (1766). But the supreme motive of the Christian's love for God is Christ, the perfect revelation of God's love for man. The spirituality of St. Alphonsus was resolutely Christocentric. In his works devoted to the mysteries of Christ—*Santo Natale* (1758), *Riflessioni ed affetti sopra la passione di Gesù Cristo* (1761), *Riflessioni sulla passione di Gesù Cristo* (1773), and *Novena del Cuore di Gesù* (1758)—it is always the love of Christ that is emphasized, a love that man must requite by loving Christ in return. The most perfect synthesis of this spirituality is to be found in the *Pratica di amar Gesù Cristo* (1768), written in the manner of a commentary on the hymn of charity of St. Paul (1 Corinthians ch. 13). The love of God is not authentic if it does not express itself—here one can recognize the characteristically Alphonsian propensity for concreteness—in doing the will of God in the state and condition to which one is called. Hence the importance of the choice of state. Alphonsus developed this doctrine for all the states of life in his little work *Uniformità alla volontà di Dio* (1755). A fortiori, this principle is applicable to particular vocations: sacerdotal, as in the above mentioned *Selva;* religious, as in *Avvisi spettanti alla vocazione* (1749), and *La vera sposa di Gesù Cristo* (1760–61), a complete treatise on religious perfection.

What means did God give to Christians to attain holiness? The Sacraments, first of all. Alphonsus insisted particularly upon Penance and the Eucharist. In his volume *Del sagrificio di Gesù Cristo* (1775) he studied the essence of the Mass and the means of participating in it fully. Against the Jansenists he recommended frequent Communion. Devotion to the Blessed Sacrament occu-

pied a place of prime importance in his spirituality. His book *Visita al SS. Sacramento* (1745) became a best seller and went through 40 editions during his lifetime. It gave to the practice of the visit a form that thenceforth became classic and definitive, and by means of it generations of Christians have come to find the nourishment of their daily prayer in the Eucharistic presence.

Prayer has a place of central importance in the economy of salvation and sanctification. Alphonsus gave magisterial treatment to the topic in what was, from the theological point of view, his most important work, *Del gran mezzo della preghiera* (1759). The first, and ascetical, part shows the absolute necessity of prayer for salvation. The second, and theological, part is directed against the Jansenist teaching on salvation and predestination. God wills the salvation of all men; Christ died for all; God gives to all the grace necessary for salvation, and one will certainly be saved if he corresponds with it. Faced with Jansenism and the teaching of the different theological schools on the subject of grace, Alphonsus expounded his own understanding of it. On the one hand there is an efficacious grace necessary for salvation; normally this acts by a kind of moral movement, determining infallibly by its own intrinsic power the consent of man's will, but leaving his liberty intact. But there is also a sufficient grace, which is truly active and gives man the power to perform psychologically easy acts in the order of salvation, such as that of imperfect prayer. One who corresponds with this sufficient grace will necessarily obtain efficacious grace. But sufficient grace is fallibly active. Man can fail to correspond with it and so in effect deprive himself of it. How is this grace fallibly active? St. Alphonsus never pretended to resolve this question explicitly; it is a point upon which one is simply referred to the conclusions of the commentators. F. MARIN-SOLA, OP, and J. Maritain have proposed possible metaphysical extensions of the Alphonsian doctrine. As in other matters, St. Alphonsus was inspired by a number of authors and incorporated their teaching into his own view of the problem. But if, in fact, he often cited H. NORIS and Claude-Louis de Montaigne, the continuator of H. TOURNELY, he went back beyond these and other immediate sources to the scholasticism of the 12th and 13th centuries and to St. Augustine. "Never did anyone bring together so compactly and so accurately the thought of St. Augustine on prayer and its necessity. The bishop of Sant' Agata was only an echo of the bishop of Hippo on this subject. . . . He had the genius to read with suprising clarity what the intellectual Jansenists had neglected in the writings of St. Augustine" [F. Cayré, *Patrologie et histoire de la théologie* v.3 (Paris 1944) 294].

The object of Christian prayer was first the love of God—i.e., the fulfillment of His will—then perseverance in that love, and finally the grace to pray always. Among the forms of prayer recommended by the saint was liturgical prayer (for which in 1774 he edited an Italian translation of the psalter *Traduzione de' Salmi e Cantici*) and mental prayer. For him mental prayer was morally necessary to assure the effective practice of prayer and consequently for perseverance in the grace of God, progress in charity, and union with God. The extremely flexible and easy method of mental prayer described in a number of his works led to the little masterpiece *Modo di conversare continuamente ed alla familiare con Dio* (1753). He would not hesitate to lead a disciple who corresponded with the grace of God to the height of mystical union with God by means of infused prayer [see *Pratica del confessore* (1755)].

The Virgin Mary appears in all the spiritual works of Alphonsus. To her he devoted the most elaborate of his books, *Le glorie di Maria* (1750), which is one of the great works of Catholic Mariology. Replying to L. A. MURATORI's criticism of the deviation of Marian devotion, Alphonsus firmly established the role of Mary in the history of salvation and solidly based devotion to her on theology. By the grace of the Redeemer immaculate in her conception (by his argumentation Alphonsus helped prepare the way for the definition of this dogma by Pius IX), Mary directly cooperated in the redemption of the world effected by Jesus on Calvary; she is the Co-Redemptress and consequently the universal, but not exclusive, mediatrix of grace. Through her one obtains especially the grace of prayer, and thus prayer to Mary leads to Jesus. St. Alphonsus considered authentic devotion to Mary an assurance and sign of salvation. *Le glorie di Maria* had an enormous influence on the 19th century and contributed to the great development of Marian devotion at that time.

In the development of his spiritual teaching Alphonsus was inspired by the spiritual writers of the 16th to the 18th centuries and freely incorporated things gathered from them into his own writings. In the *Biblioteche predicabili* and the *Prontuarii* he drew abundantly from these writers, the authors most frequently cited being the Jesuits Alfonso RODRIGUEZ, G. B. SCARAMELLI, and J. B. SAINT-JURÉ, who transmitted to him the spirituality of the *Exercises* of St. Ignatius, and the spiritual doctrine of SS. Teresa of Avila, Francis de Sales, and, in lesser measure, that of John of the Cross.

Dogmatic Works. These, for the most part, were composed during his episcopate, and they are principally works of controversy. With a pastoral end in view, Alphonsus refuted the principal errors of his time and addressed himself to unbelievers for the purpose of showing them the truth of the Catholic religion. He resorted to psychological and moral as well as to intellectual arguments, wishing to reach the whole man. His *Verità della fede* (1767) is divided according to a threefold purpose, a structure not common in apologetical works of the time. For materialists he sought to prove, against the arguments of Hobbes, Locke, and Spinoza, the existence of a personal God and the spirituality of the soul; for theists, he showed both the necessity of a revealed religion and the truth of the Christian religion; for Christians separated from the Church, he argued that the Catholic Church was the only Church of Christ authenticated by the signs of truth. He stressed the necessity of a supreme authority in the Church provided with the privilege of infallibility. This theme was developed in the *Vindiciae pro suprema pontificis potestate contra Febronium,* printed in 1768 under the pseudonym of Honorius de Honoriis. He brought decisive support to the doctrine of the infallibility of the pope, which Vatican Council I was to recognize. His *Opera dommatica contro gli eretici pretesi riformati* (1769) took the canons and decrees of the Council of Trent and expounded their theological import as opposed to Protestant doctrine. These studies show that Alphonsus was an excellent dogmatic theologian. In his *Trionfo della Chiesa ossia istoria delle eresie colle loro confutazioni* (1772) he traced the history of heresies and their refutation through the centuries from antiquity to Jansenius and Molinos. In his *Condotta ammirabile della divina Providenza* (1775) he expounded his views on the history of salvation and on the unity and perpetuity of the Church in the manner of the *Discours sur l'histoire universelle* of Bossuet, but in a manner that made his thought much more accessible to the generality of Christians.

Moral Works. A third of the writing of Alphonsus was devoted to moral theology, and this fitted smoothly into place in the ensemble of his pastoral and spiritual thought. Writing with an eye upon the daily pastoral necessities of the ministry, he elaborated his moral theology for the use of his religious and of priests engaged in pastoral work, especially that of the confessional. It complemented his spiritual doctrine inasmuch as it searched out the will of God in all the circumstances of life. His great work in the moral field was his *Theologia moralis,* which began as simple annotations on the *Medulla theologiae moralis* of H. BUSENBAUM (1st ed., 1748); in the second edition (1753–55) it became more properly the work of Alphonsus himself, although it adhered to the plan of the *Medulla* and the *Institutiones morales.* With the appearance of the third edition (1757) the *Theologia moralis* in three volumes took on its definitive aspect. Alphonsus, however, labored unceasingly to perfect the successive editions (4th ed., 1760; 5th, 1763; 6th, 1767; 7th, 1772; 8th—which Alphonsus considered definitive—1779; 9th, 1785). From 1791 to 1905, the date of the critical edition by P. Gaude, there were 60 complete editions. In 1755 there appeared his *Pratica del confessore per ben esercitare il suo ministero,* which constituted the soul, so to speak, of his great work on moral theology. The *Istruzione e pratica per un confessore* (1757), translated into Latin under the title *Homo apostolicus,* was an original work, the most perfect, perhaps, of all the writings of the saint for its unity of tone and the firmness of its thought; it was intended as an example of what a manual of moral theology ought to be. *Il confessore diretto per le confessioni della gente di compagna* (1764) was written by the bishop of Sant' Agata for the priests of his diocese. A series of notes and "dissertations," 18 in all, devoted to probabilism and the exposition of his own system of MORALITY, was published between 1749 and 1777. The most important of these was entitled *Dell' uso moderato dell' opinione probabile* (1765). Certain of these papers were written against the theories of Giovanni Vincenzo Patuzzi, OP, with whom Alphonsus engaged in vigorous controversy. The work of St. Alphonsus contained numerous citations, as did all the works of moral theology of the time. In the *Theologia moralis* more than 800 authors were cited, and the number of citations amounted to 70,000. All could not have been made at firsthand. No moralist after 1550 escaped Alphonsus' attention. His work, therefore, provides a complete panorama of the literature of moral theology of that time. His most immediate sources were St. Thomas Aquinas, Lessius, Sanchez, Castropalao, Lugo, Laymann, Bonacina, Croix, Roncaglia, Suarez, Soto, Collet, Concina, and most especially the *Cursus moralis* of the Salmanticenses.

Equiprobabilism. Alphonsus gave much time to the elaboration of his system, known as EQUIPROBABILISM, which sought to steer a middle course between PROBABILISM and PROBABILIORISM. Having used F. Genet (1640–1703), a probabiliorist, as his guide at the beginning of his missionary experience, Alphonsus was won over to ordinary probabilism in practice. But he was not satisfied with it. Beginning in 1749 he wrote a series of dissertations on the subject. His thought became definitively fixed between 1759 and 1765, during his controversy with Patuzzi, which proved to be a fruitful experience for Alphonsus and provided him with an occasion for the consolidation of his thought. From 1767 to 1778, when his literary activity came to an end, he was constrained to veil his thought somewhat because of the anti-Jesuit persecutions, but he did not modify it substantially. Equiprobabilism, opposed to either a lax or a rigorous moral position, was not a compromise between the two, but a higher equilibrium. In recognizing the obligation of the more probable opinion in favor of the law, Alphonsus recognized also the law as a moral value. Rejecting probabilism as a universally valid and mechan-

ically applicable solution of cases of conscience, Alphonsus proclaimed the necessity of a personal decision of conscience. In the case in which two equiprobable opinions, one favoring the law and the other liberty, are presented, Alphonsus, in leaving a man free to make his own decision, affirmed at the same time the moral value of human liberty. Man, who is created to the image of God, imitates his Creator in doing good freely. In support of his system, St. Alphonsus appealed to E. AMORT and St. Thomas. A. G. Sertillanges has said of it: "Equiprobabilism, properly understood, can rightly pass for a Thomist solution" [*La Morale de saint Thomas d'Aquin* (Paris 1942) 401].

In Alphonsian moral theory the study of the concrete circumstances of action rules out the mechanical application of a system, however sound it may be. Always disposed to prefer reason to the authority of moralists, he resolved most of his cases in terms of intrinsic evidence and in the light of Christian charity and prudence. As a result of his labor the Christian world was presented with a compilation of truly sound moral opinion, equally removed from the extremities either of laxism or rigorism, scrupulously weighed by the conscience of a saint. This has been a brilliant service to the Church [M. Labourdette, *Revue thomiste* 50 (1950) 230].

Influence. The influence of St. Alphonsus on moral theology has proved durable, and the practical direction traced by him has been substantially adopted by the Church (Lanza-Palazzini). Among the major events in the history of the Church in the 19th century was the progressive rallying of moralists and of the clergy to the moral thinking of St. Alphonsus. In eliminating rigorism, in facilitating access to the Sacraments, he infused a new youth into Christianity. In France the penetration of Alphonsian thought was perhaps more rapid than elsewhere. Among its propagators in that country were Jean Marie de Lamennais; Bruno Lanteri, the apostle of Turin; and Cardinal Gousset, Archbishop of Reims, who evoked in 1831 the response of the Sacred Penitentiary favorable to Alphonsian moral theology. The Curé d'Ars mitigated his rigor after coming to know Liguorian principles. At the same time the Swiss, Belgians, Germans, and Spaniards welcomed this moral doctrine, the proclamation of St. Alphonsus as a Doctor of the Church lending encouragement to the movement. To the criticism of the system by A. Ballerini, SJ, the Redemptorists responded with a voluminous dossier, *Vindiciae alfonsianae* (1873). Among the manuals of moral theology written by Redemptorists were those of J. AERTNYS, C. Marc, and, in the U.S., A. KONINGS. Many of the manuals used in the seminaries of Europe and America either adopt the Alphonsian system or are marked by its influence in their solutions of cases.

It can be said that the influence of St. Alphonsus on Catholicism in the 19th century was very generally and very deeply felt. What he had written contributed to the definition of the dogmas of the Immaculate Conception and of the infallibility of the pope. He did much to shape the form that popular devotion took, especially the devotion toward the Eucharist and the Virgin Mary. His teaching on prayer reached even beyond the Church to thinkers such as Kierkegaard. He defended the Church against rationalism and enlightened despotism. Above all, he gave Jansenism in its practical form a blow from which it could not recover. His spirituality recalled the great message of the love of God for all men; his moral doctrine, inspired by the gospel, made it possible for Christians everywhere to deal with perplexities that had to be faced if they were to adjust successfully to the world in which they found themselves. "St. Alphonsus was more than a great personage of history. He is a symbol, and a very significant one" [H. X. Arquillière, *Histoire illustrée de l'Eglise,* v.2 (Geneva-Paris 1948) 196].

Feast: Aug. 2

Bibliography: *Complete Works,* ed. E. GRIMM, 22 v. (New York 1886–97; 2d ed. of v.1–5, 12, Brooklyn 1926–28); *Opere ascetiche,* ed. F. DELERUE et al. (Rome 1933–); *Opera dogmatica,* Lat. tr. A. WALTER, 2 v. (Rome 1903); *Theologia moralis,* ed. L. GAUDÉ, 4 v. (Rome 1905–12; repr. 1953); *Lettere,* 3 v. (Rome 1887–90); *Canzoniere Alfonsiano,* ed. O. GREGORIO (Angri 1933); *The Way of Saint Alphonsus Liguori,* ed. B. ULANOV (London 1961), selected writings. Bibliographies. M. DE MEULEMEESTER et al., *Bibliographie générale des écrivains Rédemptoristes,* 3 v. (Louvain 1933–39) v.1, 3. A. SAMPERS, "Bibliographia Alphonsiana 1938–53," *Spicilegium historicum C.SS.R.* 1 (1953) 248–271; "Bibliographia scriptorum de systemate morali S. Alphonsi et de probabilismo in genere, ann. 1787–1922 vulgatorum," *ibid.* 8 (1960) 138–172. Biographies. A. TANNOIA, *Della vita ed istituto del ven. servo di Dio, Alfonso M. de Liguori,* 3 v. (Naples 1798–1802; new ed. Turin 1857). R. TELLERÍA, *S. Alfonso Maria de Ligorio,* 2 v. (Madrid 1950–51). N. FEARON, *Never Stop Walking: The Life and Spirit of Saint Alphonsus Liguori* (Liguori, Mo. 1996). O. GREGORIO et al., *S. Alfonso de Liguori: Contributi biobiliografici* (Brescia 1940). F. M. JONES, *Alphonsus de Liguori* (Liguori, Mo. 1999). A. BERTHE, *St. Alphonsus de Liguori,* tr. H. CASTLE, 2 v. (Dublin 1905). D. F. MILLER and L. X. AUBIN, *Saint Alphonsus* (Brooklyn 1940). H. F. G. SWANSTON, *Saint Alphonsus and His Brothers* (Liguori, Mo. 2000); *Celebrating Eternity Now: A Study of the Theology of Saint Alphonsus Liguori* (Liguori, Mo. 1995). G. VELOCCI, *Sant'Alfonso de Liguori* (Cinisello Balsamo 1994). M. DE MEULEMEESTER, *Origines de la Congrégation du Très Saint Rédempteur,* 2 v. (Louvain 1953–57). H. CASTLE, *The Catholic Encyclopedia,* ed. C. G. HERBERMANN et al., 16 v. (New York 1907–14; suppl. 1922) 1:334–341. B. HÜRING and E. ZETTL, *Lexikon für Theologie und Kirche,* ed. J. HOFER and K. RAHNER, 10 v. (2d, new ed. Freiburg 1957–65) 1:330–332. G. LIÉVIN, *Dictionnaire de spiritualité ascétique et mystique. Doctrine et histoire,* ed. M. VILLER et al. (Paris 1932–) 1:357–389. S. O'RIORDAN, H. F. DAVIS et al., *A Catholic Dictionary of Theology* (London 1962–) 1:60–62. Literature. J. AERTNYS, *Theologia moralis secundum doctrinam S. Alfonsi De Ligorio doctoris Ecclesiae,* 4 b. (n.s. 1967–69). K. C. M. VAN WELY, *Gestalte en structuur van de Missie bij S. Alfonsus* (Amsterdam 1964). G. CACCIATORE, *S. Alfonso de' Liguori e il giansenismo* (Florence 1944). J. F. HIDALGO, *Doctrina alfonsiana acerca de la acción de la gracia actual eficaz y suficiente* (Rome 1951). K. KEUSCH, *Die Aszetik des hl. Alfons von Liguori* (2d ed. Paderborn 1926). H. MANDERS, *De liefde in de spiritualiteit van Sint Alfonsus* (Brussels 1947). T. REY-MERMET, *Moral Choices: The Moral Theology of Saint Alphonsus Liguori,* tr. P. LAVERDURE (Liguori, Mo. 1998). D. CAPONE, "Dissertazioni e note di S. Alfonso sulla probabilitè e la coscienza," *Studia moralia* 1 (Rome 1963) 265–343; 2 (Rome 1964) 89–155; 3 (Rome 1965) 82–149; *Suor Celeste Crostarosa e Sant'Alfonso* (s.n. 1992). C. DILLENSCHNEIDER, *La Mariologie de Saint Alphonse de Liguori,* 2 v. (Fribourg 1931–34). R. S. CULHANE, "Alphonsus and the Immaculate Conception," *The Irish Ecclesiastical Record* 82 (1954) 391–401. J. A. CLEARY, "The Return to St. Alphonsus," *The Irish Theological Quarterly* 18 (1951) 161–176.

[L. VEREECKE]

ALPIRSBACH, ABBEY OF

Former BENEDICTINE abbey in Württemberg, Germany, former Diocese of Constance, present-day Diocese of Rottenburg. Its name came either from the demesne of Count Adalbert I of Uffgau (1041–45) or, according to another interpretation, from the phrase "old deer-hunting." Its founders were Ruotmann of Hausen, Adalbert of Zollern, and Alwig of Sulz. The first monks and the first abbot, Kuno, were of the FRUTTUARIA/SANKT BLASIEN tradition; the third abbot came from HIRSAU. Lands were granted the abbey by Bp. GEBHARD III of Constance when the temporary wooden church was dedicated in 1095; the dedication of the extant Romanesque church followed on Aug. 28, 1099. In 1101 Adalbert of Zollern entered the abbey and donated more land. The foundation was confirmed in 1101 by Pope Paschal II as an abbey with free election of abbot and bailiff (*Vogt*); it received confirmation and protection from Emperor Henry V in Strasbourg on Jan. 23, 1123. The abbey bailiffs included the counts of Zollern, the dukes of Teck, and the counts of Württemberg. It was noted for its liturgy and pastoral work; it assarted the forests of the Kinzigtal area. Alpirsbach reached the high point of its development in the 12th century. It had a worthy and able abbot in Bruno (1338–80). In 1482 it was incorporated into the BURSFELD congregation; the dormitory, abbot's quarters, and cloister were remodeled; the south aisle of the church was widened; the bell tower was completed; and the high altar was commissioned. The abbey was much damaged by fires in 1508 and 1513 and by the PEASANTS' WAR. In 1534 the REFORMATION came to Alpirsbach in the person of Ambrose Blarer, a former Alpirsbach monk become Württemberg reformer. From 1556 to 1595 the abbey was a Protestant convent-school. From 1629 to 1648 it was inhabited by Catholic monks from Ochsenhausen, then it again became Protestant. In

1807 all church property was secularized, including Alpirsbach's holdings in 297 localities. The abbey church is now Lutheran; the refectory, a Catholic chapel.

Bibliography: G. ALLMANG, *Dictionnaire d'histoire et de géographie ecclésiastiques*, ed. A. BAUDRILLART et al. (Paris 1912–) 2:765–768. W. HOFFMANN, *Die ehemalige Benediktinerabtei Alpirsbach* (Munich 1955). *Weingarten, 1056–1956*, ed. G. SPAHR (Weingarten 1956). K. HOFMANN, *Lexikon für Theologie und Kirche*, ed. J. HOFER and K. RAHNER (2d, new ed. Freiburg 1957–65) 1:367.

[G. SPAHR]

ALT, ALBRECHT

OT scholar and Biblical historian; b. Stübach, Bavaria, Sept. 20, 1883; d. Leipzig, April 24, 1956. From 1922 until his death he was a member of the OT faculty at the University of Leipzig. But he often sojourned in Palestine. For some time he edited the *Palästinajahrbuch.* He knew Palestine well, and this familiarity pervaded his geographical and topographical studies; in such historical studies as *Die Landnahme der Israeliten in Palästina* (1925) Alt made much of regional or territorial history and its continuity. In his celebrated collection of historical essays, *Kleine Schriften zur Geschichte des Volkes Israel* (1953–59), Alt's competence extended to the histories of the neighboring peoples also, especially to the histories of Egypt and Syria. A master epigraphist and philologist, he interpreted not only Semitic and cuneiform material but also late Greek, Roman, and Byzantine sources. He was a coeditor of the fourth edition of R. Kittel's *Biblia Hebraica*. In 1929 he published *Der Gott der Väter* on the early religion of the Hebrews.

Alt made major contributions to the understanding of Israelite legal and political institutions. In *Die Ursprünge des israelitischen Rechts* (1934) he distinguished clearly between the types of apodictic law and casuistic law in the Pentateuchal legislation. *Die Staatenbildung der Israeliten in Palästina* (1930) and related studies advanced understanding of Israel's political institutions.

Bibliography: K. H. MANN, "Bibliographie Albrecht Alt," *Beiträge zur historischen Theologie* 16 (1953) 211–223. "Festschrift A. Alt zum 70. Geburtstag," *Wissenschaftliche Zeitschrift* 3 (1953–54) 173–178. M. NOTH, *Die Religion in Geschichte und Gegenwart*, 7 v. (3d ed. Tübingen 1957–65) 1:247–248. M. KÖCKERT, *Vätergott und Väterverheissungen: Eine Auseinandersetzung mit Albrecht Alt und seinen Erben* (Göttingen, 1988). J. DUS, *Israelitische Vorfahren: Vasallen palästinischer Stadtstaaten?: Revisionsbedürftigkeit der Landnahmehypothese von Albrecht Alt* (Frankfurt am Main and New York, 1991).

[T. W. BUCKLEY]

ALTAMIRANO, DIEGO FRANCISCO DE

Jesuit missionary; b. Madrid, Oct. 26, 1625 (or possibly Oct. 18 or 26, 1626); d. Lima, Dec. 22, 1715. He entered the Society of Jesus in 1642. For some ten years he lived as a member of the province of the Philippines, and he made his solemn profession on Sept. 11, 1661. He was professor of theology at the University of Córdoba del Tucumán, Argentina, and rector of the major seminary. As a missionary to the Chaco, he founded the reduction of St. Francis Xavier, and he was provincial of Paraguay from 1677 to 1681. He served as procurator for Madrid and Rome in 1683, visitor of the Nuevo Reino (Colombia and Ecuador), visitor and provincial of Peru, and rector of the College of Lima. An outstanding religious superior, he was a staunch advocate of Jesuit rights in their internal government and in their relationship with the crown and the bishops. He was a historian of the society in the regions with which he was personally acquainted. His contribution to missionary activity ranged from writing a catechism in the Mocobí tongue to supervising the strategic location of missions as far south as the Strait of Magellan. He supported military protection for missions and protected the missions against the incursions of the Paulistas and of other tribes. He tried to stop the king from compelling the natives to grow maté and to export it from their own territory.

Bibliography: E. TORRES SALDAMANDO, *Los antiguos Jesuítas del Perú* (Lima 1882). C. SOMMERVOGEL et al., *Bibliothèque de la Compagnie de Jésus,* 11 v. (Brussels–Paris 1890–1932) 1:208–209.

[A. DE EGAÑA]

ALTANER, BERTHOLD

Catholic historian and patristic scholar, educator, author; b. St. Annaberg (Silesia), Sept. 10, 1885; d. Bad Kissingen (Bavaria), Jan. 30, 1964. After being ordained in 1910, he took his doctorate in theology at the University of Breslau, where he began to teach church history in 1919; in 1929 he was appointed ordinary professor of patrology, ancient church history, and Christian archeology. He was the first theologian to be deprived of his university position by the Nazi government for political reasons (1933). Cardinal Bertram thereupon provided him with a position at the cathedral of Breslau in order to enable him to continue his research. But he lost his very valuable library when the Gestapo expelled him from Breslau in 1945. He found refuge in Bavaria and after the war was appointed to the chair of patrology and the history of the liturgy at the University of Würzburg, which he occupied until his retirement in 1950. His early works deal with the history of the Dominican Order: *Venturino von Bergamo O.P.* (Breslau 1911), *Der hl. Dominikus* (Breslau 1922), *Die Dominikanermission des 15. Jahrhunderts* (Habelschwerdt 1924), and *Die Briefe Jordans von Sachsen* (Leipzig 1925). He became best known because of his one–volume textbook *Patrologie*, which he published in 17 editions and six languages (Eng. ed. by H. Graef, New York 1960). The volume *Kleine patristische Schriften* [*Texte und Untersuchungen zur Geschichte der altchristlichen Literatur*, 83 (Berlin 1965)] collects 48 articles dealing with the influence of Eastern theology on Western writers, especially St. Augustine, published previously in various periodicals.

Bibliography: B. ALTANER, *Verzeichnis meiner Veröffentlichungen 1907–53* (Würzburg 1953). ''Bibliographie B. Altaner,'' *Historisches Jahrbuch der Görres–Gesellschaft*, 77 (1958) 76–600. J. QUASTEN, *Theologische Revue*, 51 (1955) 213–214; *American Catholic Historical Review*, 50 (1964) 92–93.

[J. QUASTEN]

ALTAR IN CHRISTIAN LITURGY

1. In The Liturgy

The early Church spoke of the Lord's table (τράπεζα κυρίου; 1 Cor 10.21), which stressed the meal aspect of the Eucharist. A less common term, θυσιαστήριον (Heb 13.10), emphasized the sacrificial aspect of the Eucharist. With the gradual separation of the Eucharist from its meal context the second century, the idea of sacrifice gradually received more emphasis. Latin Christians then spoke of an *altare* (sing.), distinct from the pagan form, *altaria* (pl.). *Ara* remained a pre-dominantly pagan term for altar.

Historical Developments. The altars in the first three centuries were wooden, and only rarely stone, tables. A third-century representation of a wooden altar exists in the cemetery of St. Callistus. Deacons moved the table to and from the place of the liturgy; however, fixed altars did exist.

Transition to Fixed Stone and Metal Altars. Fixed altars became customary in the fourth century when stone and metal altars began to replace the wooden altars. In 517, the Council of Epaon in Bourgogne forbade wooden altars (can. 26), yet some were still used in the 12th century. Various reasons exist for the transition from wood. The danger of persecution no longer necessitated movable altars, basilicas called for more fitting altars, and the rock or stone theme in Scripture, as well as increased reverence for altars, possibly exerted some influence. Down to the Carolingian era the altar remained small with space enough for the chalice, bread, and book. The mensa (top part) was usually square, but sometimes rounded. Frequently, until the 13th century, it was slightly concave.

Association with Relics. The cult of martyrs provoked the next important development in the history of the altar. It was an ancient custom to honor deceased heroes; with all the more reason did Christians honor their martyrs (*Martyrium Polycarpi* 17.1; 18.2). Cyprian tells of the Eucharist being celebrated at grave sites (*Epistles* 39.3; 12.3). The tombs themselves, however, were not used as altars; instead, portable altars were used. Later, churches and altars were built over the tombs (e.g., St. Peter's and St. Paul's at Rome). Among the reasons for associating relics with the altar were reverence and a desire to retain communion with the martyrs, to obtain their intercessory protection, and to highlight the relation of their sacrifice to the altar's (see, Rv 6.9–11).

This association took place when many new churches were being built. Since not all the new churches could be built over martyr tombs, relics were brought to altars. In Rome and parts of Gaul, however, there often was recourse to second-class relics, such as pieces of cloth touched to reliquaries (*brandea, palliola*), because Roman law strictly forbade the disturbance of the dead. Although it is said that the threat of barbarian invasions (fifth to sixth centuries) led to the translation of some relics to safety within cities, we know that popes Hormisdas (514–523) and Gregory I (590–604) forbade any such translation; yet Boniface IV (608–615) brought a large number of relics to Rome for the dedication of St. Mary of the Martyrs. In any event, the spread of relics from Rome was slow. In the East and in northern Italy, relics were divided and translated with little hesitation. Although Theodosius I (375–395) outlawed it (*Cod. Theod.* 9.7.7), his law was ineffective; the practice continued and eventually prevailed in the West. From the ninth century on, even the Eucharist and corporals were sometimes misused as altar relics till this practice was forbidden in the 14th century.

Types of Altars Resulting from the Association with Relics. This association caused some changes in the structure of altars. Three forms of altars became common. (1) The table altar continued in use with the relics placed either in the base of its main support or in a hollowed out part of the mensa. This type of altar became less common in the Carolingian era because it was impractical for the entombment of relics. (2) There appeared a hollowed box-shaped altar with a window opening on its front or back, permitting access to the reliquary within it. (3) A solid box-shaped altar was built over tombs. Access to the tomb below could be had through a confession in front of the altar. If there was no tomb below the altar,

"The Adoration of the Shepherds," central panel of *"The Portinari Altarpiece"* by Hugo van der Goes, c. 1476, oil on wood panel, Uffizi Gallery, Florence, Italy.

the relics might have been housed in a sepulcher carved out of the mensa or in a niche carved into the front. It was not until the late Middle Ages that the present practice prevailed of placing the sepulcher in the mensa. In 1596 Church law required a sepulcher for every altar.

Altars made out of, or in the form of, sarcophagi did not exist before the 16th century, and were in vogue only during the baroque and rococo period. Wooden portable altars used by missionaries are mentioned as early as the sixth century. The earliest example of one comes from the tomb of St. Cuthbert in Durham (d.687). In the 14th century the portable altarstone become common.

From One Altar to Many Altars. One altar to a church was the rule in the early Church (Ignatius *Ad Phil.* 4.1; Eusebius, *Ecclesiastical History* 10.4.68); and this remains the practice in the Christian East. The one altar gave symbolic expression to the unity of the Church— one people assembled around one altar table in common

worship. In the fifth and sixth centuries altars began to multiply in Western churches. Although the orations *super oblata* (Secret prayers) in the LEONINE SACRAMENTARY speak of *altaria* (pl.), this plural reference was to the altar used to receive the offerings. Altars were first multiplied to provide a place for the numerous relics. This change occurred in the time of Pope Symmachus (498–514), and possibly even before. In the seventh century an increase in the number of low Masses for votive intentions and the practice of ordaining monks were factors in the multiplication of altars, especially since it was often the custom to celebrate only one Masss a day at an altar. Gregory had no objection to a church with 13 altars (*Epistle* 6.49). A Carolingian prescription did try to control this multiplication, but at the end of the Middle Ages the Cathedral of Magdeburg and the Marian Church of Danzig each had 48 altars. Nevertheless, the principle of one altar has been preserved to the extent that there still is only one main altar to a church.

Priests and altar boys at Mass, Guangzhou, China. (©Owen Franken/Corbis)

Position of Altar. In the pre-Carolingian period, the altar was situated away from the apse wall: at the edge of the apse, between the apse and the nave, or in the middle of the nave. Moreover, it might have been built on the floor of the elevated apse or on the floor of the nave, in either case with or without a few steps elevating it. At all events, it was most visible. Two developments played a large part in shifting the altar to the rear or apse wall: orientation and the development of retables. Perhaps an exaggerated reverence for the Eucharistic mystery also played a part in moving the altar away from the people.

As regards orientation, the basilicas in Rome were usually portal-oriented, i.e., the church entrance faced the east (vs. apse-oriented churches). When the bishop went to the altar from his throne in the apse, he would be facing the people. However, the Eastern custom of apse-oriented churches spread to the West, especially from the early fifth century on. The apse-oriented churches in Gaul and the emphasis on orientation in prayer there caused

changes in the ceremony books that originally came from Rome. The celebrant then stood facing the apse, leading the people behind him. The use of this position was brought to Rome with the Roman-Germanic ceremony books of the tenth century. It was eventually accepted by Roman churches, unless other conditions prevented celebrating Mass on the people's side of the altar (e.g., the confession at St. Peter's). This change brought the bishop's throne from behind the altar to the front gospel side of the altar. The clergy moved to the front or people's side of the altar. Thus, orientation contributed to moving the altar to the rear.

However, a second factor contributed to this movement of the altar, namely, the placing of martyr's relics on it in reliquaries that often were quite large. Churches without first-class relics began to substitute retables, vertical structures of varying height, built onto the rear of the altar (or later, from the floor up). At first they were of modest dimensions and painted with religious scenes, especially scenes from the life of a saint. They appeared gradually in the 10th and 11th centuries and flourished in the Gothic period (12th–15th centuries). The oldest extant retables are from the 12th century. Retables grew in size as panneling became common (triptychs and polyptychs). Carved figures were also added to them. Some retables allowed for changes in keeping with the liturgical season. By the end of the Middle Ages, hardly an altar was without a retable. Some cathedral churches built in the 12th and 13th centuries continued to place the bishop's throne behind the altar. In these churches the retable was a subsequent development that blocked out the bishop's throne and made its location useless for the liturgy. The retable in these instances was an additional factor in moving the throne from behind the altar, and thus permitting the location of the altar against the apse wall, farther from the congregation.

The distance between the laity and the altar was further accented by the chancel or rood screen. Even in the early churches a division of some sort separated laity and clergy (Eusebius, *Ecclesiastical History* 10.4). In both East and West this dividing piece grew. In the East it developed into the iconostasis that blocked out the view of the altar except when its center door was opened. In the West the altar could still be seen, but the chancel grew large enough to provide an elevated platform for Scripture readings, preaching, cantors, and even the organ. Since in the late Middle Ages the bishop's throne and choir of canons or monks separated the laity from the altar, an altar for the laity (rood altar) was placed in front of the chancel in many churches. The baroque period was largely responsible for clearing the churches of chancels and replacing them with the altar railing.

Tabernacles and Gradines. Until the 16th century the Eucharist was reserved in various parts of the church. In the 16th century the TABERNACLE become a permanent fixture of the altar. Its presence on the main altar was mandated by law during that time, although provision is made for reserving the Sacred Species elsewhere if there is another place more convenient and fitting for veneration and worship. The presence of the tabernacle has distracted attention from the altar and to some extent made of it a support for the tabernacle and a place for exposition of the Blessed Sacrament.

In the 16th century one or more gradines (steps) were added to the rear of the mensa. These gradines have served as pedestals for candles, flowers, relics, statues, etc. Again, they tend to obscure the nature of the altar.

In the Renaissance and baroque periods, large paintings flanked with pillars and statuary served as retables. Another favorite motif, especially in the baroque period, was the exposition throne for the Blessed Sacrament. The

Altar and sanctuary within a brick apse, mid-5th century Chapel of SS. Teuteria e Fosca, Verona, Italy.

retables often became monumental in their proportions so that the altar seemed a mere appendage. This development, with various modifications, persisted until the early 20th century when the altar has again begun to receive the emphasis it deserves.

Altar Accessories. Retables, chancels, and tabernacles have been discussed in treating the historical development of the Altar. But there are many other altar accessories that deserve special mention.

Civory and Baldachino. The civory is a canopy structure over the altar supported by four columns. Various reasons have been given for its use, but most likely it was adopted from profane use to express the sovereign dignity and liturgical importance of the altar. This seems especially true for the small altar in the large fourth-century basilicas. The popularity of the civory, however, lessened in proportion to the growth of retables. In the late 15th century the BALDACHINO developed from the civory as a canopy supported from above or from behind the altar.

Curtains are sometimes related to the civory. St. John Chrysostom (344?–407) speaks of curtains in conjunction with the liturgy (*Homil. in 1 Cor.* 36.5). In the East, they were frequently attached to the chancel rather than to the civory. They served to hide the altar from catechumens and, later, to hide the mysteries themselves from the laity, as the iconostasis does today. In the West, curtains attached to the civory are mentioned in the time of Sergius I (687–701), but they served a decorative, not liturgical, purpose.

Spanish Romanesque altarpiece depicting Saint Bernard, 13th century, Museo de Mallorca, Palma de Mallorca, Spain. (©Archivo Iconografico, S.A./CORBIS)

Altar Cloths. A cloth completely covering the altar dates back to at least the fourth century. Sometimes a separate white linen cloth, the ancestor of the corporal, was placed on this covering cloth. The back-part of the upper cloth was raised and folded back over the chalice to serve as a pall, but soon the pall became a separate piece. By the eighth century, two or four linen cloths were used to cover the altar in case of spillage. At this time the uppermost cloth came to be called "corporal" since it held the Body (*Corpus*) of Christ. Meanwhile, when the altar received a retable and was moved against the back wall, the original cloth that covered the altar completely became the frontal (or ANTEPENDIUM), for only the front could then be covered.

Candles and Cross. CANDLES (see LIGHT, LITURGICAL USE OF) provided light for the altar from earliest times, but did not appear on the altar until the 11th century. The CROSS appeared on the altar around the 11th century; the CRUCIFIX became increasingly common from the 14th century on.

Vatican II Reforms. The *Instruction for the Proper Implementation of the Constitution on the Sacred Liturgy,* Sept. 26, 1964, prescribed that the main altar be freestanding in such a way that Mass might be celebrated with the priest facing the congregation. The actual decision of whether or not Mass would be celebrated facing the people was left as a local option. Mass facing the people became the common practice following the rationale that facing the people better promotes active participation, the primary goal of the liturgical renewal, and better symbolizes that the Eucharistic Sacrifice occurs under the sacramental sign of a meal.

Postconciliar instructions and documents favor the reservation of the Blessed Sacrament in a special Eucharistic chapel, or, if that is not possible, on a separate "altar of reposition", rather than on the principal altar where the Eucharist is celebrated. Restoration of the practice of concelebration has obviated the need for secondary altars.

According to the reformed Roman Rite of the Mass, only the liturgy of the Eucharist takes place at the altar, while the introductory and concluding rites are led from the presidential chair, and the liturgy of the Word from the ambo. Thus the altar, which has always been regarded as a sign of Christ, becomes more clearly a sign of his special presence in the Eucharistic Sacrifice.

The revised order for the dedication of churches and altars according to the Roman rite (May 29, 1977) sums up the postconciliar doctrine concerning the altar. The altar is a symbol of Christ the Lord, who is the living altar of the heavenly temple (Heb 4.14; 13.10). Its function is as "the table of the sacrifice and of the paschal banquet." It is defined as the "center of the thanksgiving which is achieved through the Eucharist, to which all the other rites of the Church are in some way directed." An older tradition is restored: new churches should have only one altar, to signify the one Savior Jesus and the one Eucharist of the Church—although there may be a second altar in a separate chapel for weekday celebrations.

The Roman document, which is part of the Roman PONTIFICAL, repeats the 1969 norm that the altar, rather than the ambo or the tabernacle, should occupy a position in the church building that is truly central and to which the attention of the entire assembly is spontaneously directed. Thus, in newer churches the altar is brought forward, ideally located at the crossing, close to the congregation; it is the place where the bishop or priest (facing the congregation) and other ministers meet the assembled body of the faithful. In the restoration of older churches, if it is not desirable to completely remove the altar near the east wall of the sanctuary area, it has often been possible to retain its reredos or other altar piece while changing its appearance so that the altar near the congregation is the central focus of the church.

Bibliography: E. BISHOP, *Liturgica historica* (Oxford 1918; repr. 1962) 20–38. J. B. O'CONNELL, *Church Building and Furnish-*

ing (Notre Dame, Ind. 1955) 133–218. Congregation of Rites, *Instruction for the Proper Implementation of the Constitution on the Sacred Liturgy* (Sept. 26, 1964). L. BOUYER, *Liturgy and Architecture* (Notre Dame 1967). J. D. CRICHTON, *Changes in the Liturgy* (New York 1965) 87–98. G. DIEKMANN, "The Place of Liturgical Worship." *Concilium* 2 (New York 1965) 67–107. J. JUNGMANN, "The New Altar," *Liturgical Arts* 37 (1969) 36–40. C. NAPIER, "The Altar in the Contemporary Church," *Clergy Review* 57 (1972) 624–632.

[R. X. REDMOND/F. KRAUSE/F. R. MCMANUS/EDS.]

2. In The Bible

The article will be developed in four parts: terminology, pagan altars in the Bible, altars of Israel, and altars in the N T.

Terminology. The most common Hebrew word for altar in the OT is *mizbēaḥ* from the root *zbḥ*, meaning "to slaughter." Though *mizbēaḥ* probably meant at first that upon which the victim was slaughtered (Gn 22.9), later the victim was slaughtered at a distance from the altar and then placed upon it (Lv 9.13). The altar came to be even more dissociated from slaughter when grain offerings were made upon it, and when the term *mizbēaḥ* was applied to the altar of incense and even to the altar of the Transjordanian tribes, a mere memorial not used for sacrifice (Jos 22.26–27). Less common is *šulḥān*, the "table" of the Lord (Mal 1.12). The Greek equivalent of *mizbēaḥ* is θυσιαστήριον likewise linked with the root "to sacrifice," θύω. In the Books of Maccabees θυσιαστήριον is the characteristic word for the altar of the true God, carefully distinguished from βωμός, a pagan altar (1 Mc 1.54, 59, in Septuagint). In the NT altars of sacrifice are called both θυσιαστήριον (Mt 5.23) and τράπεζα "table" (1 Cor 10.21), the first term being applied also to the altar of incense (Lk 1.11).

Pagan Altars in the Bible. Solomon offered sacrifice at the "great high place" in Gibeon (1 Kgs 3.4), most likely an ancient Canaanite sanctuary. Danger of harmful pagan influence, however, led to laws calling for the destruction of pagan altars (Ex 24.13; Dt 7.5), an attack renewed in the postexilic hostility to the small pagan incense altars known as *ḥammānîm* (2 Chr 34.4). In time, the contamination of pagan worship became so abhorrent that the altar of holocausts defiled by Antiochus Epiphanes (1 Mc 1.57) was entirely dismantled and a new altar constructed in its place (1 Mc 4.44–47).

The Altars of Israel. A large stone in its natural condition could serve as an altar (1 Sm 6.14); most often, however, altars were constructed either of mud brick or unhewn stones. The ancient legislation of Ex 20.24–26 permitted either material, but there is no clear indication as to which was more generally used. Just as a heifer not yet yoked to the plow was suitable for sacrifice (Nm 19.2), so unhewn stones not yet removed from the divine sphere by human industry were proper altars. This desire to separate the divine from the human is probably the origin of the law against steps leading up to the altar (Ex 20.26): such steps would have been hewn out by human labor and would also have been trodden by the priest. The danger of indecent exposure as the priest mounted the steps clad in just a loincloth seems to be a secondary explanation. In time the ancient prescriptions lost their force, and the most sacred parts of the altar became the carved horns at its four corners (Ex 29.12), while the priest, now fully clad, used steps to ascend to the altar (Ex 28.42–43).

Despite changing custom, the symbolism of the altar remained constant. Above all, it was a symbol of God's presence. Thus Abraham and Jacob built altars to commemorate a theophany (Gn 13.18; 35.7), as did Gideon, even giving a theophoric name to his altar: "Yahweh-Peace" (Jgs 6.24). At the altar, communion was achieved with God, as the offerings were removed from the human sphere to the divine, and blessings were received from God in return (Ex 20.24). The sprinkling of blood (*see* BLOOD, RELIGIOUS SIGNIFICANCE OF) on the worshipers and the altar brought the people into communion with God Himself (Ex 24.6).

The horns of the altar were a special sign of God's protective presence, and thus afforded sanctuary to the fugitive who grasped them (1 Kgs 2.28). Their origin is not clear. Perhaps they are vestiges of the ancient memorial pillars (Gn 28.18). They may have been used originally for holding the animal in place, or may merely be considered the altar's extremities prolonged to express a religious respect parallel to that shown for the extremities of the priest's body (Ex 29.20). In any case, they were characteristic of the two altars in the Temple of Jerusalem, the altar of holocausts and the altar of incense. [*See* TEMPLES (IN THE BIBLE).]

The Altar of Holocausts. Although traditions about sacrifice date from the desert period (Ex 10.25; 18.12; 32.6, 8), there is no proof that such sacrifices were performed on a fixed altars. The desert altar of holocausts described in Ex 27.1–8 and 38.1–7 is more accurately understood as a movable likeness of the Temple's altar, which the author assumes to have been in use in the desert period. Since it was wooden and hollow, high but without steps, it is not clear how such an altar could have been used for holocausts. It also contained a bronze grating that gave it the name "the bronze altar." It is not clear what the position or function of this grating was.

The Books of 1 and 2 Kings contain several allusions to the altar of holocausts in Solomon's Temple, though it is noticeably absent from the lengthy description of the temple furnishings in 1 Kgs 6–7. It was made of bronze (1 Kgs 8.64) and was movable (2 Kgs 16.14); similar altars are familiar from Phoenician inscriptions. The sacred writer may have omitted his description of the altar because of its Phoenician origin. Data on the altar measurements are supplied by 2 Chr 4.1; however, these may be taken from the altar built later by Ahaz (2 Kgs 16.10–11) or from the postexilic altar of the author's own time. The precise relationship between this altar in 2 Chronicles, ch. 4, Ahaz's altar, the altar in Ezekiel's vision (Ez 43.13–17), and the postexilic altar of holocausts remains obscure. Ahaz moved Solomon's altar somewhat to the north and installed a much larger one, built on different levels and modeled on one he had seen in Damascus, and therefore probably Syrian in origin. Whether it should be related to Ezekiel's altar, also constructed on various levels but Babylonian in its inspiration, is doubtful. The names Ezekiel gives his altar's different levels (''bosom of the earth,'' ''the divine mountain'') came from the various levels of Babylonian temples and were employed by Ezekiel to make the altar a temple in miniature. The altar in 2 Chr 4.1 has almost the same dimensions as Ezekiel's but its description may have been taken from the postexilic altar, about which further information is lacking.

The Altar of Incense. The incense altar of the TENT OF MEETING is described in Ex 30.1–5 and 37.25–28, but is probably a projection of the temple altar into the desert period. The arrangement of the tent's furnishings is found in Ex 25–27, but, here, there is no mention of the incense altar, described later and out of context in Ex 30.1–5. Nor is it mentioned in texts describing the offering of INCENSE in the desert (Nm 16.6–7, 17–18; 17.11–12), where individual CENSERS are used. Like the desert altar of holocausts, it is a portable altar, built of wood and carried with poles. It is, however, also plated with gold, and so is known as ''the golden altar.''

The existence of this altar just outside the Holy of Holies in Solomon's Temple is well documented in 1 Kgs 7.48 and Is 6.6. Excavations in Mageddo and Shechem have also yielded small stone incense altars that can be said to date back as early as the 10th century B.C.

No mention is made of the incense altar among the precious appurtenances restored by Cyrus to the returning exiles (Ezr 1.6–11), but Antiochus Epiphanes later removed the golden altar when he plundered the second Temple (1 Mc 1.23). Under the Maccabees, an incense altar was reinstalled (1 Mc 4.49), undoubtedly the same one at which Zachary offered incense (Lk 1.8–10).

In the New Testament. The ancient symbolism of the altar as the sign of God's presence is reflected in the words of Jesus: the altar sanctifies the gift (Mt 23.18). The symbolism now lessened the altar's importance, for the NT sacrifice was already sanctified without the altar. The new sacrifice is Jesus who sanctifies Himself (Jn 17.19). Thus, in 1 Cor 10.16–17, St. Paul affirms that Christians partake of the Lord's Body and Blood without reference to the altar. In Hebrews also the author shows no concern for an altar for the Eucharistic sacrifice. When he asserts, ''We have an altar, from which they have no right to eat who serve the tabernacle'' (Heb 13.10), he means the cross, or more likely he means the person of Jesus Himself.

The imagery of the Revelation recalls the Temple's altars, although it is not always clear which is meant, the one for holocausts or for incense. In Rv 11.1, the author is told to measure the Temple and the altar. In its context the image refers to the small group of men who remain faithful to Christ. Other references to altars found in the Revelation (Rv 6.9; 8.3, 5; 9.13; 14.18; 16.7) seem to envisage the altar of holocausts from which the prayers of the martyred saints arise. In any case, even in the Revelation, the altar's value is ultimately eclipsed, for in the vision of the new Jerusalem there is no temple or altar, ''for the Lord God almighty and the Lamb are the temple thereof'' (Rv 21.22).

Bibliography: R DE VAUX *Ancient Isreal, Its Life and Institutions* (New York 1961) 406–414. K. GALLING, *The Interpreters' Dictionary of the Bible* ed. G. A. BUTTRICK 4 v. (Nashville 1962) 1:96–100; 2:699–700. ''Le Mystère de l'Autel,'' *Maison-Dieu* 29 (1952) 9–31.

[P. J. KEARNEY]

ALTDORF, ABBEY OF

Former Benedictine abbey in Alsace, Diocese of STRASBOURG, France; it was important for pastoral care and as a pilgrimage center. Founded by Count Hugo III as a cloister and burial place for his family, it was built under Count Eberhard V and rebuilt several times—*c.* 1192; after it had been pillaged by Strasbourgers, 1262; after the Peasants' War; *c.* 1600; and in 1700. The wooden cloister church, consecrated by Bp. Erchenbald of Strasbourg in the presence of Abbot Maiolus of Cluny, was dedicated to St. Bartholomew (974); a member of the family had taken part in Rome at the translation of relics of St. Bartholomew, who became the family patron saint. Before 1049, it seems, Bishop Werner reconsecrated the church in honor of St. Cyriacus (d. 303), a favorite with Benedictines, and the FOURTEEN HOLY HELPERS. Pope Leo IX, a member of the family, consecrated the altar. In the 12th century Altdorf was a double monastery (*see* MONASTERIES, DOUBLE). The Romanesque church was built *c.* 1200; choir and transept were rebuilt by the Vorarlberg Peter Thumb (1720–33). The Cluniac cloister joined the congregations of Mainz-Bamberg (1417), BURSFELD (1607), and Strasbourg (1608). In the 15th century Altdorf was individually united with SANKT GALLEN. Frescoes of the 12th century, whitewashed when the abbey was suppressed (1790), have been uncovered recently.

A second Abbey of Altdorf in south Württemberg, west Germany, originally housed Benedictine nuns or canonesses (*sanctimoniales*); it seems to have been founded after 934. The cloister was the burial place of the founder's family. The present cemetery of the Abbey of WEINGARTEN occupies the site. Altdorf seems to have died out *c.* 1000; but clerics, perhaps canons, continued divine services. It was revived as a convent of women (1036), which moved to Weingarten after a fire (1053) and then to Altomünster (1056).

Bibliography: A. SIEFFERT, *Altdorf: Geschichte von Abtei und Dorf* (Strasbourg 1946). G. SPAHR, "Die Reform im Kloster St. Gallen," in *Schriften des Vereins für Geschichte des Bodensees* 76 (1958) 1–62. C. BUHL, "Weingarten-Altdorf," in *Weingarten, 1056–1956,* ed. G. SPAHR (Weingarten 1956) 22.

[G. SPAHR]

ALTENBURG, ABBEY OF

Benedictine abbey in the Diocese of St. Pölten, Austria; its patron is St. Lambert. It was founded (1144) by Countess Hildburg of Rebgau-Poigen and settled with 12 monks from SANKT LAMBRECHT in Styria, and has always been the pastoral and cultural center of the former "Horn County." Six incorporated parishes include the pilgrimage parish Maria Dreieichen and the city parish of Horn. In 1964 the abbey had a boys' choir school and a boarding school, and 20 monks devoted themselves to pastoral care and scholarship. The cloister, one of the most splendid baroque monuments in Austria, was built (1650–1742) after its total destruction (1645) in the Thirty Years' War. Its present form is the work of the architect Joseph Mungenast (1729–41). There are many frescoes by Paul Trogers (church, library, prelates' hall, and emperors' stairway) and valuable stucco work of the WESSOBRUNN school (Franz Josef Holzinger and Michael Flor). Excavations in 1932 revealed part of the early Romanesque cloister.

Bibliography: *Urkunden der Benedictiner-Abtei zum heiligen Lambert in Altenburg,* ed. H. BURGER (Fontes rerum Austriacarum 21; Vienna 1865). H. BURGER, *Geschichtliche Darstellung der Gründung und Schicksale des Benedictinerstiftes St. Lambert zu Altenburg in Nieder-Österreich* (Vienna 1862). F. ENDL, *Stift Altenburg* (Augsburg 1929). G. SCHWEIGHOFER, *Stift Altenburg* (Vienna 1963). O. L. KAPSNER, *A Benedictine Bibliography: An Author-*

Subject Union List, 2 v. (2d ed. Collegeville, Minn. 1962) 2:184–185. L. H. COTTINEAU, *Répertoire topobibliographique des abbayes et prieurés,* 2 v. (Mâcon 1935–39) 1:68–69.

[G. SCHWEIGHOFER]

ALTERNATIVA

An institution found in Spain, later transplanted to Spanish America. In Spain, it demanded that an office or offices be alternated between members of different regions or nations. In Spanish America, it usually meant the alternation in office between a native of Spain, called *chapetón* (tenderfoot), and a native of America, called Creole. In Spanish America, the *alternativa* is found both in civil and in Church life; however, it was employed most widely in Spanish America in the religious orders. There it meant that the most important offices in a province had to be filled alternately by Spanish and Spanish-American religious respectively: the head of the province, at least half the members of his council, the heads of the more important houses as well as the occupants of the key posts in the province, such as regent of studies and master of novices. In other words, 10 to 12 posts alternated in each chapter by force of law. In the state of present research, it is not known when the *alternativa* was first established in Spanish America. The earliest known date is 1601, when it was imposed on the Dominicans of Quito. Soon thereafter, it was found officially in Mexico, Central America, Colombia, Venezuela, Peru, Bolivia, and in the Philippines. In 1627 the Franciscans in Mexico even received the *alternativa,* the alternation of office between three parties: the friars who had received the habit in Spain, Spanish boys who entered the order in Mexico, and the Mexicans. The *alternativa* was not found among either the Mercedarians or the Jesuits; the first were governed usually by Spanish superiors, and the second by direct appointees of their general. Most frequently, the *alternativa* was requested by the Spanish friars because they were the minority party. In Guatemala, however, both the native Dominicans and Franciscans asked for it because they were the minority. Theoretically, the *alternativa* could have been advantageous since it could have ensured broadening intellectual contacts. Actually, it was a source of endless friction and dissension and is one of the factors which helped to weaken and corrupt the religious orders in Spanish America wherever it was found. Essentially, it predicated that election to office was less dependent on merit than on race.

Bibliography: A. S. TIBESAR, "The *Alternativa:* A Study in Spanish-Creole Relations in Seventeenth Century Peru," *Americas* 11 (1954–55) 229–283. J. GONZÁLES ECHENIQUE, "Notas sobre la *Alternativa* en las provincias religiosas de Chile indiano," *Historia* 2 (1962–63) 178–196.

[A. S. TIBESAR]

ALTMANN OF PASSAU, ST.

Bishop; b. Westphalia, Germany, *c.* 1015; d. Zeiselmauer, near Vienna, Austria, Aug. 8, 1091. He became canon and teacher at Paderborn, provost of the canons of Aachen *c.* 1051, and then chaplain to Empress Agnes (d. 1114). After a pilgrimage to Jerusalem, he was named bishop of Passau in 1065. His concern for the purity and pastoral zeal of his clergy made him a champion of the *vita communis* according to the Rule of St. Augustine, and he introduced this rule when founding Sankt Nikola outside Passau (*c.* 1070) and Göttweig (1083) and when reforming Sankt Florian (1071) and Sankt Pölten (1081). He was also instrumental in the foundation of the Augustinian houses of Rottenbuch (1073) and Reichersberg (1084). Altmann courageously published the papal decrees against married priests in 1074 and was the first to announce Emperor Henry IV's excommunication in Germany in 1076. As papal legate, he attended the princes' meeting at Tribur in October 1076. Driven from his diocese in 1077 or 1078 by the imperial party, Altmann fled to Rome. In 1080 he returned to the eastern part of his diocese, where he continued his political and pastoral efforts under the protection of Margrave Leopold II (d. 1095) until his death. He was buried in the Abbey of Göttweig, and a monk of this monastery wrote his vita (*Monumenta Germaniae Historica: Scriptores* 12:226–243). Since the late nineteenth century, his cult has been permitted in the dioceses of Passau, Linz, and Sankt Pölten.

Feast: Aug. 8.

Bibliography: *Acta Sanctorum* Aug. 2:356–389. ALTMANN OF PASSAU, *Streitschriften,* ed. M. SDRALEK (Paderborn 1890). A. LINSENMAYER, *Zur Erinnerung an den seligen Bischof Altmann v. Passau, 1065–1091* (Munich 1891). E. TOMEK, *Kirchengeschichte Österreichs* (Innsbruck 1935–59) 1:138–143. J. HALLER, "Der Weg nach Canossa," *Historische Zeitschrift* 160 (1939) 229–285, esp. 280–283. W. WATTENBACH, *Deutschlands Geschichtsquellen im Mittelalter,* ed. R. HOLTZMANN (Tübingen 1948) 1:385–389, 541–545. R. BAUERREISS, *Kirchengeschichte Bayerns,* v.2 (St. Ottilien 1951) 98–103, 233–236. J. OSWALD, *Lexicon für Theologie und Kirche,* ed. J. HOFER and K. RAHNER (Freiburg 1957–65) 1:402–403, bibliog. G. ALLMANG, *Dictionnaire d'histoire et de géographie ecclésiastiques,* ed. A. BAUDRILLART et al. (Paris 1912) 2: 826–827.

[A. A. SCHACHER]

ALTO, ST.

Hermit and monastic founder; d. *c.* 770. According to tradition, he came to the region near modern Dachau shortly after the middle of the eighth century and lived for a time as a hermit on some forest land given him by Pepin III. He was not, it would appear, one of the early missionaries who labored with VIRGILIUS OF SALZBURG in southern Bavaria. After a few years he built the monastery of Altomünster, which was destroyed in the tenth century during the Hungarian invasion. St. BONIFACE is said to have consecrated the monastic church erected during the lifetime of Alto. The authenticity of the saint's relics preserved today at Altomünster is not fully established. Sometime in the eleventh century OTHLOH of Sankt-Emmeram wrote his *Vita s. Altonis* (*Monumenta Germaniae Historicum: Scriptores* 15:843–846), which preserved the local traditions concerning the life of the saint.

Feast: Feb. 9.

Bibliography: A. BAYOL, *Dictionnaire d'histoire et de géographie ecclésiastiques,* ed. A. BAUDRILLART et al. (Paris 1912) 2:830–831. M. MANITIUS, *Geschichte der lateinischen Literatur des Mittelalters* (Munich 1911–31) 2:101. A. M. ZIMMERMANN, *Kalendarium Benedictinum* (Metten 1933–38) 1:190, 192. J. L. BAUDOT and L. CHAUSSIN, *Vies des saints et des bienhereux selon l'ordre du calendrier avec l'historique des fêtes* (Paris 1935–56) 2:216. R. BAUERREISS, *Lexikon für Theologie und Kirche,* ed. J. HOFER and K. RAHNER (Freiburg 1957–65) 1:403.

[H. DRESSLER]

ALTÖTTING, MONASTERY OF

Famous place of pilgrimage in honor of Our Lady, located in Upper Bavaria near the Austrian frontier, in the present Diocese of Passau, former Diocese of Salzburg. The name "Oetting" is said to derive etymologically from *Otto,* name of a Bavarian leader baptized by St. RUPERT OF SALZBURG (*c.* 700); the prefix *Alt-* (Old) was added in 1231 to distinguish the original structure from the new church built at that time. It is estimated that more than 600,000 pilgrims a year now visit the Holy Chapel (*Gnadenkapelle*) at Altötting, which contains the 13th-century statue of Our Lady of Grace (about 26 inches high, of linden wood, vested in jewel-studded robes).

The chapel, octagonal in shape and possibly modeled on the cathedral at AACHEN, was enlarged (1499–1511) by a small nave and arcade. Among its art treasures, special mention should be made of the "Golden Horse," a work of French Gothic workmanship dating from *c.* 1400. Attached to the Bavarian ducal palace in the Carolingian period, the Holy Chapel was endowed in 876 by King Carloman of Bavaria (d. 880), who erected a Benedictine monastery and church adjacent to it. In 907 the chapel survived the attack of the Hungarians that destroyed the Benedictine foundation. Nothing further is known of it until 1231, when Duke Louis the "Kelheimer" founded a new collegiate church there; the provost and the chapter of CANONS were in charge of pilgrimages until 1803, when they were suppressed.

Present-day religious houses in Altötting include St. Mary Magdalene, which has been served successively by Jesuits (1591–1773), secular priests (1773–1841), Redemptorists (1841–1873), and now the Capuchins. St. Anne was a Franciscan friary from 1653 to 1803, when it became a provincial house of Capuchins, who were put in charge of the pilgrimages. St. CONRAD OF PARZHAM (d. 1894) was lay-brother and porter at this Capuchin friary. St. Anne's new church, built in 1911, was made a minor basilica in 1913. The Mary Ward Sisters (*Englische Fräulein*) and the Missionary Sisters of the Holy Cross both have their mother houses there; the Sisters of St. Vincent de Paul have been in Altötting since 1862.

Bibliography: L. BOITEUX, *Dictionnaire d'histoire et de géographie ecclésiastiques*, ed. A. BAUDRILLART et al. (Paris 1912–) 2:834–841. H. GEISELBERGER, *Der Gnadenort Altötting* (6th ed. Altötting 1950). H. M. GILLETT, *Famous Shrines of Our Lady,* 2 v. (Westminster, Md. 1952) v.2. M. A. KÖNIG, *Lexikon für Theologie und Kirche*, ed. J. HOFER and K. RAHNER (2d, new ed. Freiburg 1957–65) 1:404–405.

[M. F. MCCARTHY]

ALUMBRADOS (ILLUMINATI)

Name given to the adherents of a Spanish pseudomysticism of the 16th century and deriving from their claim to act always under the immediate illumination of the Holy Spirit. The name was first so used in a letter from a Franciscan friar to Cardinal XIMÉNEZ DE CISNEROS in 1494. The movement itself was but a recurrence of the bizarre parody of true mysticism that is never long absent from the Church in the world. Proximately, its sources would most probably be found in the voluntarism of medieval Teutonic theology and in the Averroistic strains of Arabian mysticism, as well as in a Reformation anticlericalism. The movement was confined mostly to the Dioceses of Cadiz and Seville. Its doctrines, which are known in later times chiefly in the form of opinions condemned by the Inquisition in 1623, seem to have infected all classes of people.

The basic flaw in the teaching of the Alumbrados lay in the exaggerated importance they attached to mental prayer. They held that mental prayer is commanded by divine law and that in it all other precepts are fulfilled. Thus not even attendance at Mass, obligations arising from charity, or obedience to lawful authority must be allowed to impede the existence of mental prayer. This devotion was described simply as the recollection of God's presence, in which there is no discursive movement of the mind, no meditation properly so called, and no reflection on mental images such as the Sacred Passion or humanity. It is by the practice of this quietistic prayer of nothing-

ness that the soul arrives at a state of perfection in which its faculties are so submerged that the soul can no longer act. To one constituted in this highest degree of spirituality, there comes the ravishment of the Spirit, so that in ecstasy the soul sees the divine essence, beholds the Blessed Trinity even as the elect in heaven. When this beatifying vision has been achieved, all the properties of beatitude logically follow. The soul is freed from the weakness of wounded nature; it is rendered impeccable; it is, in short, consciously confirmed in grace. Thus elevated, a man does not act as of himself; willingly or unwillingly he is moved by the illumination of the Spirit.

In the moral order, such principles could lead only to catastrophe. The investigations of the Inquisition provide a sordid account of the grossest carnal sins indulged in by the "perfect" under the guise of "communications of the Holy Spirit and divine love between souls." As a result of these shocking disclosures, it is not surprising that the Inquisition's judgment of the type of mysticism practiced by the Alumbrados was extremely unfavorable. Certainly the hypercritical attitude of some of the theologians of the next century toward even true spirituality was a result in no small degree of the aberrations of the Alumbrados.

Bibliography: P. POURRAT, *Dictionnaire de théologie catholique*, ed. A. VACANT, 15 v. (Paris 1903–50; Tables générales 1951–) 13.2:1552–54. F. CAYRÉ, *Manual of Patrology and History of Theology*, tr. H. HOWITT, 2 v. (Paris 1936–40) 2:790. R. A. KNOX, *Enthusiasm* (New York 1950; repr. 1961) 241–242. V. BELTRÁN DE HEREDIA, "La Beata de Piedrahita no fué alumbrada," *Ciencia tomista* 63 (1942) 294–311.

[T. K. CONNOLLY]

ALVA Y ASTORGA, PEDRO DE

Lecturer on theology, procurator general of the Franciscans in Rome, one of the most outstanding figures of the 17th century in the debates on Immaculate Conception; b. 1602; d. 1667. He was of Spanish origin, and belonged to the Franciscan Province of the Twelve Apostles of Peru. With the aid of his own press in the Low Countries he was able to publish his copious theological writings. All these centered about the tradition of the Immaculate Conception; he was critic, debater, and editor of collected writings on this subject. Some of these compilations are still of basic interest [compare X. Le Bachelet, "Immaculée Conception," *Dictionnaire de théologie catholique,* ed. A. VACANT et al., 15 v. (Paris 1903–50) 7:1094]. With his contribution the controversy entered upon a decisive period. Another phase of his work, less studied, is his contribution to the history of his order, with his great *Bullarium* in ten volumes and 16,000 documents. The *Indiculus* and a draft of it are well known, but the major work remained unedited, and its present whereabouts are unknown.

Bibliography: A. EGUILUZ, ''Fr. Pedro de Alva y Astorga, O.F.M., en las controversias inmaculistas,'' *Verdad y Vida,* 12 (1954) 247–272. ''El P. Alva y Astorga y sus escritos inmaculistas,'' *Archivo Ibero Americano,* 15 (1955) 497–594. L. CEYSSENS, ''Pedro de Alva y Astorga, O.F.M., y su imprenta de la Inmaculada Concepción de Lovaina (1663–66),'' *ibid.,* 11 (1951) 5–35.

[A. EGUILUZ]

ALVARADO CARDOZO, LAURA EVANGELISTA, BL.

Baptized on Oct. 3, 1875, as Laura Evangelista, called in religion María of San José; is also known as María of Venezuela; co-founder of the AUGUSTINIAN RECOLLECTS of the Heart of Jesus; b. April 25, 1875, at Choroní, Girardot District, Aragua (then called Estado Guzmán Blanco), Venezuela; d. April 2, 1967, at Maracay, Venezuela.

Laura Evangelista was the eldest of the four children of Clemente Alvarado and his then common-law wife Margarita Alvarado Cardozo. When Laura was three, the family moved to Maracay, where she received her early Christian education at home. From ages five to 16, she attended a private school, where she earned the esteem of her teachers and classmates. At her first communion she promised to serve God. Four years later on that feast she made a private vow of her virginity to Christ.

Shortly thereafter, she began instructing poor children at home, supporting the project financially with her own labor. Together with her spiritual director Fr. Vicente López Aveledo she worked to found the first hospital in Maracay, Saint Joseph's. She devoted herself to the care of the sick in spite of the difficulty of the work, the opposition of her parents, and the demoralizing poverty that surrounded her. In 1896, she was named director of the hospital.

Together with Fr. López she founded the Congregation of the Sisters of the Poor of Saint Augustine (1901), better known as the Augustinian Recollects of the Heart of Jesus. They assumed the Rule of Saint Augustine and the habit of Santa Rita. Laura was named superior general and confirmed her vow of virginity in 1902. The following year she made her perpetual vows and took the name María of San José. Until 1960 when she was succeeded by Sister Lourdes Sanchez, Mother María guided the congregation's work of caring for the sick, the elderly and orphans in thirteen hospitals and thirty-seven houses throughout Venezuela. After a long illness patiently

borne, Mother María died at age ninety-two. She was buried with her wooden cross in her hands in the chapel of the Immaculate Conception Home in Maracay. At her beatification by John Paul II on May 7, 1995, María de San José became the first Venezuelan blessed.

Feast: April 25.

Bibliography: *Acta Apostolicae Sedis* (1995): 564. *L'Osservatore Romano,* English edition, no. 19 (1995): 1, 2, 4; no. 20 (1995): 2–3.

[K. I. RABENSTEIN]

ÁLVARES, FRANCISCO

Priest and missionary; d. *c.* 1540. As chaplain of the first official Portuguese royal embassy to Ethiopia (1520–26), he wrote a monumental description of the Eastern Christian nation, *Verdadera* [sic] *informaçam das terras do Preste Joam,* published in reduced form in Portuguese in 1540. Translated into several European languages, it provided 16th-century Europe with frank, honest, accurate information that supplemented what Damião de GÓIS had made available at second hand. It is highly esteemed in Ethiopia today.

Ethiopia's ambassador to Portugal reached Lisbon early in 1514. The following year King Manuel I sent his mission in reply, and the Ethiopian ambassador was in the company as the group proceeded to Goa. In 1517 they tried to land in the Massaua area on the west side of the Red Sea, but bad weather and worse leadership nearly wrecked the whole expedition, and the Portuguese ambassador, Duarte Galvão, died. The survivors returned to India, and only in April 1520 did the embassy, now headed by Dom Rodrigo de Lima, finally land at Massaua.

Álvares's narrative, published in Lisbon long after his return, begins at this point. Its lengthy first book, the major part of the entire volume, concerns the six years the embassy spent in Ethiopia. It ends in April 1526, when the Portuguese, returning home, were picked up by a Portuguese fleet from India. The second book describes the subsequent journey to Goa and the passage to Lisbon, where the travelers arrived in July of 1527.

The Ethiopian emperor, Lebna Dengel (David II), had sent Zagazabo on this same journey as his ambassador to King João III, who had succeeded Manuel in 1521. Perhaps more important, he named Álvares his ambassador to the pope and instructed him to render Ethiopian obedience to the Holy See. For reasons of his own João III forced Álvares to wait in Portugal for five years before permitting him to proceed to Rome in the company of João's ambassador to the pope, Dom Martinho de Portugal.

Finally on Jan. 29, 1533, at a consistory in Bologna, in the presence of Emperor Charles V, Álvares rendered David II's obedience to Pope Clement VII. News of this event electrified Europe, where it circulated in a little Latin book published in Bologna within a month and reprinted many times in several languages. The Latin volume, at least partly written by Paolo Giovio, contains information on Ethiopia unquestionably taken from Álvares's larger treatise.

Nothing came of the Ethiopian submission, for the pope (Giulio de' Medici) had other matters on his mind, as did the Portuguese. Álvares remained in Italy, apparently in Rome, where he is said to have died. His great treatise remained unpublished and is lost. The version printed in 1540, probably without his authorization, is only a portion of the larger study. Published at the king's order, it reveals the workings of a great mind, tolerant and critical, Portuguese and ecumenical.

Bibliography: F. ÁLVARES, *The Prester John of the Indies,* tr. H. E. J. STANLEY, ed. C. F. BECKINGHAM and G. W. B. HUNTINGFORD, 2 v. (Cambridge, Eng. 1961). F. M. ROGERS, *The Quest For Eastern Christians: Travels and Rumor in the Age of Discovery* (Minneapolis 1962).

[F. M. ROGERS]

Title page, *"Verdadera informaçam das terras do Preste Joam"* *(True Information about the Lands of the Prester John), 1540, Portuguese edition, by Francisco Álvares.*

ÁLVAREZ, BALTASAR

Jesuit spiritual writer; b. Cervera del Rio Alhama (Logroño), 1533; d. Belmonte, July 25, 1580. Álvarez entered the Society of Jesus at Alcalá, on May 3, 1555. After a period in the apostolic ministry in Avila (1558–66), he was made rector in Salamanca (1573–76) and from 1576 to 1580 held the posts of both rector and novice master at Medina del Campo and Villagarcía. He was also visitor for the province of Aragón, designated provincial of Peru, and finally, for a few months, provincial of Toledo. St. Teresa of Avila called upon him for counsel in certain critical moments of her life, and for six years he was her confessor.

Álvarez's prayer of silence was considered incompatible with the spirit of the society and was condemned by the Superior General E. Mercurian at the instigation of the provincial Juan Suarez and the visitor Diego Avellaneda. The opposition stemmed in part from caution begotten by the then recent condemnation of the illuministic ideas of the Alumbrados, and in part from the disfavor with which superiors in the society at the time viewed the tendency of some Jesuits to encourage involvement in contemplation at the expense of the apostolic ministry, which was the principal end of the society.

The influence of the spiritual doctrine of Álvarez was due not only to his own accomplishment but also to the popularity of his biography, which was written by Luis de LA PUENTE, SJ. His frequent assignments to administrative office in the society prevented him from dedicated and extensive writing. His works include commentaries on the rule for novices; retreat sermons; two "reports" about his prayer, short but valuable treatises on the prayer of silence. He excelled in the expression of true fervor and the intensity of his personal spiritual experience.

Bibliography: B. ÁLVAREZ, *Escritos espirituales: Introducción biográfica,* ed. C. M. ABAD and F. BOADO (Barcelona 1961), complete ed. of his works. L. DE LA PUENTE, *Vida del v. p. B. Álvarez* (new ed. Madrid 1882). I. IPARRAGUIRRE, *Répertoire de spiritualité ignatienne* (Rome 1961) 177–178. E. HERNÁNDEZ, *Dictionnaire de spiritualité ascétique et mystique. Doctrine et histoire,* ed. M. VILLER et al. (Paris 1932—) 1:405–406. H. BREMOND, *Histoire littéaire du sentiment réligieux en France depuis la fin des guerres de religion jusqu'à nos jours,* 12 v. (Paris 1911–36) 8:228–269. J. TARRAGO, "La oración de silencio . . . del Padre Baltasar Álvarez y los ejercicios . . . ," *Manresa,* 4 (1928) 165–174, 258–270.

[I. IPARRAGUIRRE]

ÁLVAREZ, DIEGO

Theologian; b. Medina del Rio Secco (Diocese of Palencia), date unknown; d. Trani, 1631 (and not in

1635). He entered the Dominican Order at Medina, and taught theology at Burgos, Palencia, Toto, and Valladolid. On Nov. 7, 1596, he arrived at Rome where his superiors had sent him to defend the Thomist school in the controversies on grace and free will. While serving as regent of theological studies at the Minerva, he participated in the work of the CONGREGATIO DE AUXILIIS with Tomás de LEMOS. He was named bishop of Trani (Southern Italy) in 1606, where he remained until his death. His main works deal with the controversies on grace: *Commentarii in Isaiam* (Rome 1599), *De auxiliis divinae gratiae et humani arbitrii viribus et libertate* (Rome 1610), *Responsiones ad objectiones adversus concordiam liberi arbitrii cum divina praescientia* (Trani 1622), *De origine pelagianae haeresis et eius progressu* (Trani 1629). All these works were edited several times in the 17th century. Álvarez also published his courses on theology, on the third part of the *Summa theologica* of St. Thomas, *De incarnatione divini verbi* (Lyons 1614), and on the second part, *Disputationes theologicae in primam secundae S. Thomae* (Trani 1617). His *Manuale concionatorum* (Rome 1622) deals more directly with his episcopal activity. There are many texts and documents at the archives of the order in Rome that remain unedited.

Bibliography: J. QUÉTIF and J. ÉCHARD, *Scriptores Ordinis Praedicatorum,* 5 v. (Paris 1719–23) 2.1:481–482. P. MANDONNET, *Dictionnaire de théologie catholique,* ed. A. VACANT et al., 15 v. (Paris 1903–50) 1.1:926–927. R. COULON, *Dictionnaire d'histoire et de géographie ecclésiastiques,* ed. A. BAUDRILLART et al. (Paris 1912—) 2:872–873.

[A. DUVAL]

ÁLVAREZ DE PAZ, DIEGO

Jesuit spiritual writer; b. Toledo, 1560; d. Potosí, Jan. 17, 1620. Álvarez de Paz entered the Society of Jesus in Alcalá, Feb. 24, 1578, and in 1589 went to Peru as a student of theology and remained there for the rest of his life. He began his active career as professor of philosophy, theology, and Sacred Scripture, and then served as rector in different colleges, vice provincial in Tucumán (1605–07), and provincial in Peru from 1616 until his death. His work as a spiritual writer is contained in three extensive volumes that treat, respectively: perfection; the overcoming of sin, vices, passions, and the practice of virtues, especially humility; and the search for peace through prayer. This trilogy is like a vast spiritual encyclopedia, noteworthy for the depth of insight, theological precision, clearness, and richness in dogmatic content, although from a literary viewpoint it is somewhat too profuse. His doctrine on affective prayer was based on the influence of A. Cordeses, SJ. Álvarez de Paz was the first Jesuit to make a detailed study of infused contemplation.

Bibliography: C. SOMMERVOGEL, *Bibliothèque de la Compagnie de Jésus* 1:252–258. J. E. DE URIARTE and M. LECINA, *Biblioteca de escritores de la Compañía de Jesús a la antigua asistencia de España desde sus orígenes hasta el año de 1773,* v.1 (Madrid 1925) 155–162. I. IPARRAGUIRRE, *Répertoire de spiritualité ignatienne de la mort de S. Ignace à celle du P. Aquaviva, 1556–1615* (Rome 1961). J. DE GUIBERT, *The Jesuits: Their Spiritual Doctrine and Practice* tr. W. T. YOUNG (Chicago 1964). A. ASTRÁIN in *Gregoriana* 1 (1920) 394–424. E. UGARTE DE ERCILLA in *Razón y Fe* 58 (1920) 465–473; 59 (1921) 186–187. E. HERNÁNDEZ, *Dictionnaire de spiritualité ascétique et mystique* 1:407–409.

[I. IPARRAGUIRRE]

ALVAREZ MENDOZA, JULIO, ST.

Martyr, pastor; b. Dec. 20, 1866, Guadalajara, Jalisco, Mexico; d. Mar. 30, 1927, San Julián, Jalisco. He studied in the seminary of Guadalajara with the financial help of benefactors and was ordained in 1894. Thereafter he was assigned to Mechoacanejo, Jalisco (Diocese of Aguascalientes), where he served with kindness and simplicity the rest of his life. He had an opportunity to leave his parishioners at the beginning of the clerical persecution but chose to stay with his flock. En route to celebrate Mass at a farm, he was identified as a priest and apprehended (Mar. 26, 1927). The following morning he was taken to San Julián, where he was shot after pardoning his executioners. His cadaver was left on the trash heap near the church, where a monument has been erected in his honor. Fr. Alvarez was both beatified (Nov. 22, 1992) and canonized (May 21, 2000) with Cristobal MAGALLANES [*see* GUADALAJARA (MEXICO), MARTYRS OF, SS.] by Pope John Paul II.

Feast: May 25 (Mexico).

Bibliography: J. CARDOSO, *Los mártires mexicanos* (Mexico City 1953). J. DÍAZ ESTRELLA, *El movimiento cristero: sociedad y conflicto en los Altos de Jalisco* (México, D.F. 1979). Y. PADILLA RANGEL, *El Catolicismo social y el movimiento Cristero en Aguascalientes* (Aguascalientes 1992).

[K. I. RABENSTEIN]

ÁLVAREZ OF CÓRDOBA, BL.

Dominican preacher and reformer; b. Córdoba (Lisbon) 1360; d. Córdoba, Feb. 19, 1430. He preached extensively in Andalusia and in Italy. Once the Spanish kingdoms broke with the antipope BENEDICT XIII, Álvarez preached tirelessly against him. Having been counselor for a brief period to King Henry III of Castile, he was instrumental at Henry's death, 1406, in securing the election of King John II in preference to Ferdinand, the king's brother. Álvarez acted as confessor and counselor to

Queen Catherine and King John until his retirement to Córdoba in 1423, when he founded the observant priory of Scala Coeli. His devotion to the Passion of Christ, which had been engendered during a pilgrimage to Palestine in 1405, moved him to erect in the priory gardens tableaux of the Passion that were forerunners of the STATIONS OF THE CROSS. In 1427, Martin V appointed him vicar of the Spanish Dominican Observants. He was beatified in 1741.

Feast: Feb. 19.

Bibliography: D. A. MORTIER, *Histoire des maîtres généraux de l'ordre des Frères Prêcheurs*, 8 v. (Paris 1903–20) 4:210–214. P. ÁLVAREZ, *Santos, bienaventurados, venerables de la orden de los Predicadores*, 4 v. (Vergara, Spain 1920–23) 1:495–508. G. GIERATHS, *Lexikon für Theologie und Kirche*, ed. J. HOFER and K. RAHNER, 10 v. (2d, new ed. Freiburg 1957–65) 1:408.

[A. H. CAMACHO]

ALVARO PELAYO

Franciscan (1304), doctor of Canon and civil law in Bologna; b. Galicia, *c.* 1275; d. Seville, *c.* 1349. As papal penitentiary in AVIGNON (1330–32) and as bishop of Silves in Portugal (1332), he knew firsthand the evils plaguing Christendom that are described in his writings. He sought to open the eyes of his readers with exhaustive examinations of conscience (potentially political constitutions) so that reason under canonical guidance might achieve a state of universal order in society. His thought, for the most part theocratic, accords certain basic rights to the state. The first part of *De statu et planctu ecclesiae* (Avignon 1330–32; revised, 1335–40) is a defense of JOHN XXII and the papacy against Louis IV of Bavaria and MARSILIUS OF PADUA. The second part deals with the condition of the Church as it was and as it should be. The *Speculum regum* (*c.* 1341), citing classical authors more frequently than Christian, was meant for the Spain of Alfonso XI, and perhaps his chancellor, Archbishop ALBORNOZ. Alvaro urges Alfonso to continue the Reconquista into Morocco, *de iure* Christian. The *Collirium fidei adversus hereses* (1344) is an annotated catalogue of heresies, ancient and medieval. Although widespread in manuscripts and in print, Alvaro's writings lack definitive editions and studies. A *Quinquagesilogium* dealing with the Franciscan rule and a commentary on St. Matthew exist in manuscripts. A sermon on the beatific vision and a commentary on the *Four Books of Sentences* are lost.

Bibliography: *Bibliographia Franciscana* 9–11 (1954–63). G. DELORME, *Dictionnaire d'histoire et de géographie ecclésiastiques*, ed. A. BAUDRILLART et al. (Paris 1912—) 2:857–861. A. MICHEL, *Dictionnaire de sociologie* 1:488–491. A. VACANT, *Dictionnaire de théologie catholique*, ed. A. VACANT et al., 15 v. (Paris 1903–50) 1.1:926. J. LAHACHE, *Dictionnaire de droit cannonique*, ed. R. NAZ, 7 v. (Paris 1935–65) 6:1312. L. AMORÓS, *Lexikon für Theologie und Kirche*[2], ed. J. HOFER and K. RAHNER, 10 v. (2d, new ed. Freiburg 1957–65) 1:409. M. A. SCHMIDT, *Die Religion in Geschichte und Gegenwart*[3], 7 v. (3d ed. Tübingen 1957–65) 1:301.

[E. P. COLBERT]

ALVASTRA, ABBEY OF

A former CISTERCIAN monastery dedicated to Our Lady, situated near Lake Vättern in the Province of Östergötland, Sweden, in the old Diocese of Linköping. The oldest and most important Cistercian monastery of medieval Sweden, it was founded in 1143 on the advice of Archbishop ESKIL OF LUND by King Sverker the Elder (d. 1156), who granted property for its erection on the estate of his late wife Ulfhild. At her request St. BERNARD had already sent monks from CLAIRVAUX. Alvastra was the 40th abbey to be affiliated with Clairvaux. From Alvastra the monasteries of Varnhem, Julita (Saba), and Husby (Gudsberga) were founded. A monk from Alvastra, Stephen (d. 1185), was appointed the first archbishop of Uppsala in 1164. Both the Sverker family and the succeeding Folkung dynasty were favorably disposed toward the monastery, and the royal tomb of the Sverker family was later built in front of the high altar of the abbey church. St. BRIDGET received visions during her stay at Alvastra, and her husband and one of her sons are buried in its chapel. One of her most devoted friends and her confessor was the prior, Peter Olavi (d. 1390), who recorded most of her revelations from her own dictation. The abbey was abandoned in 1527 when Gustavus I Vasa (d. 1560), who was moving toward imposing the Protestant REFORMATION in Sweden, took control of its estates. Only a few volumes remain from the old monastic library, but parts of the buildings and of the church are still preserved. Layers from fires in 1312 and 1415 have been of importance for the dating of the many articles found during excavation projects carried on at the site since the end of the 19th century.

Bibliography: L. H. COTTINEAU, *Répertoire topobibliographique des abbayes et prieurés*, 2 v. (Mâcon 1935–39) 1:75–76. U. BERLIÉRE, *Dictionnaire d'histoire et de géographie ecclésiastiques*, ed. A. BAUDRILLART et al. (Paris 1912–) 2:892. E. ORTVED, *Cistercieordenen og dens klostre i Norden*, 2 v. in 1 (Copenhagen 1927–33) 2:53–141. K. SPAHR, *Lexikon für Theologie und Kirche*, ed. J. HOFER and K. RAHNER (2d, new ed. Freiburg 1957–65) 1:409. I. SWARTLING, *Alvastra kloster* (Stockholm 1962). H. JOHANSSON, *Ritus cisterciensis* (Lund 1964).

[O. ODENIUS]

ALZOG, JOHANN BAPTIST

Historian, and patrologist; b. Ohlau, Silesia, June 29, 1808; d. Freiburg, Germany, March 1, 1878. Alzog studied at Breslau and at Bonn. He was ordained in Cologne on July 4, 1834, and received the doctor's degree at Münster in 1835. He then taught at Posen (1836–44) and Hildesheim until called to the University of Freiburg im Breisgau (1853), where he remained until his death.

Alzog was a voluminous writer of sure theological sense and scientific method in research. In 1841 he published his *Lehrbuch der Kirchengeschichte,* which went through nine editions and was translated into seven languages. In 1866 he published his *Handbuch der Patrologie,* a model of exactness in biographical detail, conciseness of doctrinal exposition and bibliographical citation. He edited the *Oratio apologetica de fuga sua* of St. Gregory of Nazianzus, and also contributed to various periodicals and lexica. He vigorously supported the archbishop, Martin de Dunin, in the controversy over mixed marriages. In 1869 he was called to Rome by Pius IX to take part in the preparation for Vatican Council I. Alzog's work was noted for impartiality and equanimity. After Johann A. MÖHLER, he was a principal influence in the revival of studies concerned with positive theology in Germany. He also helped to found the GÖRRES–GESELLSCHAFT.

Bibliography: H. HEMMER, *Dictionnaire de théologie catholique,* ed. A. VACANT et al., 15 v. (Paris 1903–50) 1:931–932. P. SÄGER, *Lexikon für Theologie und Kirche*2, ed. J. HOFER and K. RAHNER, 10 v. (2d, new ed. Freiburg 1957–65) 1:410–411.

[F. X. MURPHY]

AMABILIS, ST.

Priest of Auvergne; b. probably Riom (Auvergne), France *c.* 397; d. Nov. 1. *c.* 475. In the sixth century, GREGORY OF TOURS (*In gloria confess.* 33) described the popular belief in this saint's power over serpents as well as the veneration at his tomb. Gregory reports that he himself witnessed two miracles there. Amabilis served as precentor at Clermont and later as parish priest at Riom where, in 1120, a church was dedicated to him. In the seventh century his relics were transferred to Riom; in the eighteenth century a dispute occurred over these relics between neighboring Clermont and Riom, where Amabilis is patron. Public processions in his honor have been traditional in Riom, where he is invoked against fire and snakes.

Feast: June 11; Oct. 19 (Clermont).

Bibliography: *Acta Sanctorum* June 2:460–467. L. BERNET-ROLLANDE, *Saint Amable: Sa vie, son église, son culte* (Clermont-

Ferrand 1891). M. PREVOST, *Dictionnaire d'histoire et de géographie ecclésiastiques,* ed. A. BAUDRILLART et al. (Paris 1912) 2:913. R. AIGRAIN, *Catholicisme* 1:387–388.

[L. M. COFFEY]

AMADEUS IX OF SAVOY, BL.

Duke of Savoy; b. Thonon, France, Feb. 1, 1435; d. Vercelli, Italy, March 30, 1472. He was the first of 18 children born to Louis I of Savoy and Anne of Cyprus. In 1451 he married the daughter of Charles VII of France, Yolanda, to whom he had been betrothed as an infant. He succeeded to the throne in 1456, but later (1469) relinquished control to his wife because he was subject to epilepsy. He was a wise and able ruler, a friend of the poor, and a peacemaker. He meditated and attended Mass daily and received the Sacraments more frequently than was the common practice in his time. He showed great forbearance and forgiveness toward his adversaries, the SFORZAS, and some of his own brothers. He was beatified in 1677.

Feast: March 30.

Bibliography: E. FEDELINI, *Les Bienheureux de la Maison de Savoie* (Chambéry 1925). A. BUTLER, *The Lives of the Saints* 1:706–707. J. GRISAR, *Lexikon für Theologie und Kirche*2 1:413.

[N. G. WOLF]

AMADEUS OF LAUSANNE, ST.

Cistercian abbot of Hautecombe (1139–44), bishop of Lausanne (1144 or 1145–59); b. chateau of Chatte in the Dauphiné, Jan. 21, 1110; d. Lausanne, Aug. 27, 1159. Schooled at the imperial court, Amadeus followed the example of his father, Amadeus the Elder of Clermont-Hauterive, in quitting noble rank for cloistered anonymity (1125), but he did not find the obscurity he sought, for his abbot, St. BERNARD OF CLAIRVAUX, urged him into posts of leadership. He was often imperial counselor, papal legate, and local arbiter. As bishop he put into practice the monastic ideals of personal piety, devotion to communal peace, and attention to practical detail. He was the author of eight homilies in honor of the Blessed Virgin, the seventh of which was cited twice in the 1950 papal definition of the Assumption. After his death he was acclaimed blessed by his people and his order, and his cult was confirmed by St. Pius X. In 1911 his tomb was discovered in the old Lausanne cathedral, and his relics were taken to Fribourg.

Feast: Jan. 28.

Bibliography: *Huit homélies mariales,* ed. G. BAVAUD et al. (*Sources Chrétiennes,* ed. H. DE LUBAC et al., 72; Paris 1960). A. DI-

MIER, *Amédée de Lausanne, disciple de saint Bernard* (S. Wandrille 1949). *Collectanea ordinis Cisterciensium Reformatorum* (Rome-Westmalle 1934–) 21:1–65, commemorative issue, 8th centenary of St. Amadeus's death.

[P. EDWARDS]

AMALARIUS

Bishop; b. in the area of Metz, *c.* 775; d. Metz, *c.* 850. He was educated by Alcuin, and later taught at the palace school at Aachen. From 809 to 813 he was the archbishop of Trier; he also served as a Carolingian ambassador to Constantinople (*c.* 813) and Rome (831). After the exile of Agobard, he administered the diocese of Lyon from 835 to 838. In 838 the Synod of Quierzy, following the leadership of Florus of Lyons, removed him for teaching theology that was "contrary to tradition." Amalarius's most significant work is the *Liber officialis* (823), the most influential liturgical book of the early Middle Ages in the West. Amalarius was the first to apply a fully developed vocabulary of symbolic interpretation to Latin *expositiones missae,* or commentaries on the Mass. Such exegetical methods had long been used as a tool for understanding the Scriptures, and were first extended to the understanding of Christian worship in the mystagogical catecheses of the fourth century. Amalarius was not the first Westerner to utilize such an interpretive language in liturgical explanations, but his use of a figurative hermeneutic captured the imagination of nearly all Western thinkers of the Middle Ages.

Bibliography: J. M. HANSSENS, *Amalarii episcopi opera liturgica omnia,* 3 v. in *Studi e Testi* 138–140 (1948–50). J. A. CABANISS, *Amalarius of Metz* (Amsterdam 1954). J. A. CABANISS, "Agobard and Amalarius: A Comparison," 3 (1952) 125–131. A. KOLPING, "Amalar von Metz und Florus von Lyon," *Zeitschrift für katholische Theologie* 73 (1951) 424–464.

[P. JACOBSON]

AMALBERGA, SS.

Two saints with this name are venerated on the same day, July 10. Because the events of both their lives have been embellished with legendary details, it is quite difficult to distinguish between them, much less to separate fact from fiction in their biographies. It seems quite clear, however, that one St. Amalberga (seventh century, variants: Amalburga, Amelberga, Amalia, Amelia) was the wife of Count Witger and mother of Gudula, Reinelde, and Bishop Emebert of Cambrai (d. *c.* 715). When her husband became a BENEDICTINE monk at the Abbey of Lobbes, she entered the convent at Maubeuge. She died at Maubeuge, and her body was later transferred to Lobbes.

The second Amalberga (eighth century) was a nun of the community of Münsterbilzen in Belgium. Because of her beauty she was approached by King PEPIN III who wished her to marry his son Charles (CHARLEMAGNE). Reportedly she once suffered a broken arm in resisting Charles's attentions, and perhaps for that reason her name has been invoked for the cure of bruises. She died at the convent of Tamise in Flanders, but her relics were solemnly translated to the church of St. Pierre in Ghent in 1073.

A third Amalberga lived in the tenth century. She was the abbess of Susteren, where she educated two of the daughters of the king of Lorraine. Her feast is celebrated on November 21.

Bibliography: A. BUTLER, *The Lives of the Saints,* ed. H. THURSTON and D. ATTWATER (New York 1956) 3:64–65. A. PONCELET, "Les Biographes de Ste. Amelberge," *Analecta Bollandiana* 31 (1912) 401–409. *Acta Sanctorum* July 3:61–68, 70–107. A. MERCATI and A. PELZER, *Dizionario ecclesiastico* (Turin 1954–58) 1:108, 109. U. BERLIÈRE, *Dictionnaire d'histoire et de géographie ecclésiastiques,* ed. A. BAUDRILLART et al. (Paris 1912) 2:924–925. L. VAN DER ESSEN, *Études critique et littéraire sur les vitae des saints mérovingiens de l'ancienne Belgique* (Louvain 1907) 177–182, 301–302. A. M. ZIMMERMANN, *Kalendarium Benedictinum* (Metten 1933–38) 2:427–431.

[J. F. FAHEY]

AMALRIC AUGERIUS

Fourteenth century historian and theologian; b. Béziers, France, date unknown; d. after 1362. He was a doctor of theology from the University of MONTPELLIER, prior of Santa Maria de Aspirano in the Diocese of Perpignan, and chaplain to URBAN V. Although he is commonly identified as an AUGUSTINIAN, A. Zumkeller claims that this is uncertain. His only known work, *Actus romanorum pontificum a primo usque ad Johannem papam XXII sive annum 1321,* is an alphabetical chronicle of the popes, written at Avignon in 1362 (*see* AVIGNON PAPACY) and dedicated to Urban V. It has been edited by J. G. Eccard, *Corpus historicum medii aevi* (Leipzig 1723) 2:1641–1824, and by L. A. Muratori, *Rerum italicarum scriptores* (Milan 1734) 3.2.

Bibliography: A. ZUMKELLER, "Manuskripte von Werken der Autoren des Augustiner–Eremitenordens in mitteleuropäischen Bibliotheken," *Augustiniana,* 11 (1961) 90. L. BOEHM, *Lexikon für Theologie und Kirche*[2], ed. J. HOFER and K. RAHNER, 10 v. (2d, new ed. Freiburg 1957–65) 1:415. H. HURTER, *Nomenclator literarius theologie catholicae,* [13] 2:644. A. PALMIERI, *Dictionnaire d'histoire et de géographie ecclésiastiques,* ed. A. BAUDRILLART et al. (Paris 1912—) 5:387.

[A. J. ENNIS]

AMALRIC OF BÈNE

Theologian, with pantheistic and materialistic inclinations; b. Bène, near Chartres, mid–12th century; d. Paris, *c.* 1206. He was also known as Amaury, and was a student and later teacher of theology at Paris. He showed the influence of the school of CHARTRES and derived his idea partially from misinterpreted writings of JOHN SCOTUS ERIGENA, but especially from ARISTOTLE. Amalric was called to Rome by INNOCENT III who censured his theories. Amalric retracted them upon his return to Paris. Although he left no writings, he attracted a number of disciples called AMALRICIANS, whose writings indicate that basically Amalric identified God with the universe. In 1210 his body was exhumed and, by order of a council of Paris, was reburied in unconsecrated ground.

Bibliography: F. G. HAHN, *Über Amalrich von Bena und David von Dinant* (Villach, Austria 1882). G. C. CAPELLE, *Amaury de Bène* (Paris 1932). F. VERNET, *Dictionnaire de spiritualité ascétique et mystique. Doctrine et histoire,* ed. M. VILLER et al. (Paris 1932—) 1:422–425.

[B. CHUDOBA]

AMALRICIANS

An early 13th-century sect centered in Paris, disciples of AMALRIC OF BÈNE. The disciples were more extreme than their master. Their pantheistic concept of a God who is identical with the universe made them reject TRANSUBSTANTIATION, as they held that God was already present in the bread and wine. Their abstract pantheism ultimately led them to a denial of the essential difference between good and evil, and to the substitution of knowledge of the natural processes for faith. According to their Trinitarian concept of history, the Father ruled over ancient times and the Son over the first 12 centuries of Christianity, while the reign of the Holy Ghost began with Amalric. Having been condemned by a council in Paris (1210) as heretical, and five years later by the Fourth LATERAN COUNCIL, the sect quickly disappeared (*See* JOACHIM OF FIORE).

Bibliography: See references under AMALRIC OF BÈNE. C. J. VON HEFELE, *Histoire des conciles d'après les documents originaux* 5.2:1303–05. M. T. D'ALVERNY, ''Un Fragment du procès des Amauriciens,'' *Archives d'histoire doctrinale et litéraire du moyen-age* 25 (1950–51) 325–336. E. HAMMERSCHMIDT, *Lexikon für Theologie und Kirche,* 10 v. (2d, new ed. Freiburg 1957–65) 1:415–416.

[B. CHUDOBA]

AMANA SOCIETY

The Amana Society, also known as the Community of True Inspiration, is one of the oldest communal sects in America. Deeply influenced by German PIETISM of the early 18th century, Johann Rock and Eberhard Grüber protested against what they considered the rigid dogmatism and ritualism of the Lutheran Church. Claiming that divine inspiration had been given to them, they organized a community of True Inspirationists in 1714. Its principal tenets maintained that God deals directly with the human race through inspiration and revelation and that true Christian living is characterized by simplicity. At first Rock and Grëber gained many adherents, but after their deaths the community steadily declined because no one claimed the charism of inspiration. In 1817, however, the sect experienced a revival, when Christian Metz and Barbara Heineman, both claiming inspiration, became its leaders. Metz, an excellent organizer, set about establishing communities, but the Inspirationists soon ran into difficulties with the German government because of their pacifist beliefs. In 1842 they immigrated to America, establishing themselves in Erie County, N.Y., as a cooperative type community, called Ebenezer. In 1850 they adopted a pure communistic form of living that was closer to their ideal of Christian simplicity.

When more land was needed to support its 1,200 members and to maintain its ''isolation from worldliness,'' the sect migrated west (1854), purchasing 25,000 acres near Iowa City, Iowa. Five years later the settlement, Amana, or ''Believe Faithfully,'' was incorporated under Iowa state laws. For the next 70 years the communal economy proved successful, but in 1932 the community voted in favor of conversion to a joint stock corporation. Legally known as the Amana Society, it holds all real property; ecclesiastical matters are handled by the Amana Church Society, which is governed by elected elders. Members of the Amana community are Christians in the Evangelical tradition, but distinguished by the following: ''We believe . . . in the Holy Ghost . . . who has spoken and operated through the prophets of old and who even now operates audibly through the instruments of true inspiration. . . .'' Their worship is simple; the Lord's Supper, with the washing of feet, is celebrated only rarely. They do not baptize with water, since they hold that baptism is a spiritual practice. Celibacy is highly recommended, marriage is permitted, and divorce is prohibited. Older rules against participation in warfare have been modified.

Bibliography: B. M. SHAMBAUGH, ''The Amana that was and the A. that is,'' *Palimpsest* 31 (1950) 215–248. B. S. YAMBURA and E. W. BODINE, *A Change and a Parting* (Ames, Iowa 1960). J. G. ANDELSON, ''The Community of True Inspiration from Germany to the Amana Colonies,'' in *America's Communal Utopias* (Chapel Hill, NC 1997) 181–203.

[T. HORGAN/EDS.]

AMANDUS, ST.

Apostle of Belgium; b. Aquitaine, France, late 6th century; d. Feb. 6, after 676. His life is known principally from the *Vita prima* [*Monumenta Germaniae Scriptores rerum Merovingicarum* (Berlin 1826–), 5:428–449], which Krusch assigns to the latter half of the 8th century, but which Stracke attributes to Amandus' contemporary Baudemund (d. *c.* 700), and de Moreau [*Analecta Bollandiana* 67 (1949) 449] places in the late 7th or early 8th century. Here the saint is depicted as a native of Aquitaine, son of Serenus and Amantia, who became a monk at Yeu, was tonsured at Tours, and lived as an ascetic at Bourges under Bishop Austregisil (d. *c.* 624). A visit to Rome *c.* 620 launched him on a missionary career in the northern Frankish domains where, probably before 630, he was consecrated a bishop without fixed see. There followed a second journey to Rome and an apostolate along the River Schelde and at Ghent, wherein he was sustained by King Dagobert I (d. 638). It is not certain that his censure of this monarch's morals brought about his exile or that he preached in the Danube region, in the Pyrenees, and in the country about Narbonne. During the years from 639 to 642, operating out of his monastery at Elnone (later to be known as SAINT-AMAND-LES-EAUX), he had the aid of JONAS OF BOBBIO in evangelizing along the Scarpe and Schelde Rivers as far as the North Sea [*Monumenta Germaniae Scriptores rerum Merovingicarum* (Berlin 1826–), 4:62]. That Amandus was constrained to accept the bishopric of Tongeres-Maastricht seems to find support in a 649 letter of Pope MARTIN I dissuading him from resigning his see [P. JAFFÉ, *Regesta pontificum romanorum ab condita ecclesia ad annum post Christian natum 1198,* ed. S. LÖWENFELD et al., 2 v. (2d ed. Leipzig 1881–88; repr. Graz 1956): Jaffé E, ed. P. EWALD, 590–882; 2059]. De Moreau sees evidence that Amandus founded monasteries at Elnone, Ghent, Nivelles, and Barisis-au-Bois [*Monumenta Germaniae Diplomata* (Berlin 1826–), 1:25], and probably also at Marchiennes, Leuze, Renaix, and Moustier-sur-Sambre. At Elnone, on April 17, 674 or 675, he drew up his *Testament* [*Monumenta Germaniae Scriptores rerum Merovingicarum* (Berlin 1826–), 5:483–485], but the year of his death is unknown. Medieval calendars [see *Analecta Bollandiana* 79 (1961) 80] keep his feast on Feb. 6, the traditional date of his death, or on Oct. 26, the date of his episcopal consecration.

Feast: Feb. 6 and Oct. 26.

Bibliography: *Monumenta Germaniae Poetae* (Berlin 1826–), 3:561–610. É. DE MOREAU, *S. Amand, le principal évangélisateur de la Belgique* (Brussels 1942); *Histoire de l'église en Belgique* (2d ed. Brussels 1945) 1:78–92; ''La Vita Amandi prima,'' *Analecta Bollandiana* 67 (1949) 447–464. D. A. STRACKE, ''Over de *Vita sancti Amandi,*'' *Handelingen van den Kon. geschieden oudheidkundigen Kring van Kortrijk* NS 26 (1953) 99–179. E. LESNE, *Dictionnaire d'histoire et de géographie ecclésiastiques,* ed. A. BAUDRILLART et al. (Paris 1912) 2:942–945. W. LAMPEN, *Lexikon für Theologie und Kirche,* ed. J. HOFER and K. RAHNER, 10 v. (2d, new ed. Frieburg 1957–65) 1:416–417. R. AIGRAIN, *Catholicisme. Hier, aujourd'hui et demain,* ed. G. JACQUEMET (Paris 1947–) 1:398–400.

[H. G. J. BECK]

AMANDUS OF WORMS, ST.

Bishop; fl. 7th century. A royal charter of doubtful authenticity by Dagobert I (d. 639) in 627 supposedly granted certain lands and revenues to the church of Worms, of which Amandus, an apostolic man, was said to be bishop (*Monumenta Germaniae Diplomata* [Berlin 1826–] 1:139). According to later reports, RUPERT OF SALZBURG brought the relics of the saint to the monastic church of SANKT PETER in Salzburg during the 8th century. Subsequently doubts arose whether these relics were those of the holy bishop of Worms or of another AMANDUS, the apostle of Belgium, and only in a 17th-century notice in the *Catalogus abbatum S. Petri* are the relics clearly identified as those of St. Amandus, the Bishop of Worms. The first reference to a church at Worms in honor of the saint dates from the early 11th century, and the original cult of the bishop kept his feast day October 26.

Feast: Oct. 2.

Bibliography: *Acta Santorum,* Oct. 11:910–922. G. ALLMANG, *Dictionnaire d'histoire et de géographie ecclésiastiques,* ed. A. BAUDRILLAT et al. (Paris 1912–) 2:937–938. H. SCHMITT, *Lexikon für Theologie und Kirche,* ed. J. HOFER and K. RAHNER, 10 v. (2d, new ed. Freiburg 1957–65) 1:417. I. POLC, *Biblioteca sanctorum* (Rome 1961–) 1:924–925. E. ZÖLLNER, *Geschichte Österreichs* (Munich 1961) 49–50.

[H. DRESSLER]

AMANTIUS OF RODEZ, ST.

Bishop of Rodez, France; fl. 5th century. Nothing is known of his life and episcopate beyond the fame of his miracles. His name seems to be first known for the See of Rodez where he was bishop before 471, when Euric (d. 484), king of the VISIGOTHS, took the city. His biography, attributed falsely to FORTUNATUS, is from at least the 7th, probably the 9th century, and is not trustworthy. A near successor in Rodez, QUINCTIAN OF CLERMONT, who attended the synod of Agde in 506, paid great honor to his relics, building a church over his tomb.

Feast: Nov. 1 and 13 (Martyrology of St. Jerome), Nov. 4 (Roman Martyrology).

Bibliography: *Acta Sanctorum* Nov. 2.1:270–287. R. AIGRAIN, *Catholicisme* 1:400–401. *Bibliotheca hagiographica latina antiquae et mediae aetatis* 1:351–352. A. P. FRUTAZ, *Lexikon für Theologie und Kirche* 1:418. GREGORY OF TOURS, *Vitae patrum* 4.1 in *Monumenta Germaniae Historica: Scriptores rerum Merovingicarum* 1:674. U. ROUZIÈS, *Dictionnaire d'histoire et de géographie ecclésiastiques* 2:949–950.

[M. C. MCCARTHY]

AMAT, THADDEUS

Missioner, educator, second bishop of Monterey (California) diocese, now the Archdiocese of LOS ANGELES; b. Barcelona, Dec. 31, 1811; d. Los Angeles, May 12, 1878. Son of Pedro and Maria (Brusi) Amat, he entered the Congregation of the Mission (Vincentians) in Barcelona on Dec. 30, 1831 where he pronounced his vows on Jan. 16, 1834, and after further training in Barcelona and at Saint Lazare in Paris, was ordained on Dec. 23, 1837. Upon arriving in the United States in 1838, he did missionary work in Louisiana for three years. From 1841 to 1847 he was superior at St. Mary's Seminary in Perryville, Missouri, and St. Vincent's College, Cape Girardeau, Missouri, also serving briefly (1842–43) as pastor of Holy Trinity Church and administrator of the diocesan seminary in St. Louis. In 1848 he became superior of St. Charles Seminary, Philadelphia.

When on July 29, 1853, Bishop Joseph Alemany was transferred to the new See of San Francisco, Amat was named bishop of Monterey, where his familiarity with Spanish and American cultures was useful. He was consecrated in Rome on March 12, 1854. After stopping in Spain to enlist clergy and religious and in San Francisco (November 1855) to deliver the pallium to Archbishop Alemany, he hastened to his own diocese with the personnel he had recruited. Amat had headquarters at Santa Barbara, but soon perceived that rapidly growing Los Angeles would become the population nucleus of his area. In 1856 he sent Blasius Raho, CM, there as his vicar–general. While in Rome in 1859, he obtained authorization to entitle his diocese Monterey–Los Angeles and to reside in Los Angeles. He secured legal recognition of diocesan claims to mission properties in 1856, and later, to the PIOUS FUND of the Californias. In 1862, 1869, and 1876 he held synods to cope with the problems of the growing diocese. He attended the Second Plenary Council of Baltimore (1866) and Vatican Council I (1869–70).

There he participated actively in discussions on the constitutions "On Catholic Faith" and "On Primacy." When a spinal injury restricted his activity, he asked for a coadjutor, and his vicar–general, Francis Mora, was appointed and consecrated on Aug. 3, 1873. Amat was buried in St. Vibiana Cathedral, whose cornerstone he had laid and whose dedication he had witnessed on April 30, 1876.

Bibliography: R. BAUDIER, *The Catholic Church in Louisiana* (New Orleans 1939). G. E. O'DONNELL, *Saint Charles Seminary, Overbrook,* 2 v. (Philadelphia 1943–53). R. BAYARD, *Lone–Star Vanguard: The Catholic Reoccupation of Texas, 1838–1848* (St. Louis 1945).

[N. C. EBERHARDT]

AMATOR, SS.

Amator of Auxerre, also known as Amatre and Amadour, bishop; d. May 1, 418. The details of the sixth-century biography written by an African priest named Stephen, are quite fabulous. There is, however, ample evidence of Amator's historical existence as an early bishop at Auxerre. He is said to have been married to a woman locally venerated as St. Martha prior to his ordination.

Feast: May 1.

Amator, priest and martyr; d. April 30, 855. He had gone to study at Córdoba, and with SS. Peter and Louis he was killed there by the Mohammedans, according to the *Memoriale Sanctorum (Patrologia Latina* 115:814) of EULOGIUS OF CÓRDOBA.

Feast: April 30.

Amator of Lucca, hermit. He is considered a saint in San Michele in Borgo San Lorenzo. Another (the same?) St. Amator is honored the same day in Quercy and in the Limousin. Probably the two are identical, but the historical existence of either is most improbable.

Feast: Aug. 20.

Bibliography: Amator of Auxerre. *Acta Sanctorum* May 1:51–61. L. DUCHESNE, *Fastes épiscopaux de l'ancienne Gaule* (Paris 1907–15) 2:430. M. BESSON, *Dictionnaire d'histoire et de géographie ecclésiastiques,* ed. A. BAUDRILLART et al. (Paris 1912) 2:981–982. Amator, Martyr. *Acta Sanctorum* April 3:815. P. SICART, *Dictionnaire d'histoire et de géographie ecclésiastiques,* ed. A. BAUDRILLART et al. (Paris 1912) 2:982. E. P. COLBERT, *The Martyrs of Córdoba, 850–859* (Washington 1962). Amator of Lucca. *Acta Sanctorum* Aug. 4:16–25. E. ALBE, "La Vie et les miracles de s. Amator," *Analecta Bollandiana* 28 (1909) 57–90; *Dictionnaire d'histoire et de géographie ecclésiastiques,* ed. A. BAUDRILLART et al. (Paris 1912) 2:920–922, 990.

[W. A. JURGENS]

AMATUS OF NUSCO, ST.

Bishop and abbot; b. Nusco, Italy, *c.* 1104; d. Aug. 6, 1193. The chronology of his life and many of its details are uncertain because there are two quite different versions, the earliest of which was written after 1460. The later version appears the more reliable and was favored by the BOLLANDISTS. According to this account (*Acta Sanctorum* Aug. 6:901–928) Amatus was born at Nusco in southern Italy of noble parents. He entered the religious life and after a short period as archpriest of Nusco became a BENEDICTINE. In 1142 he founded the Abbey of Fontignano near Orvieto, and in 1154 he was made bishop of Nusco. He was a zealous and popular bishop and a generous benefactor of religious houses. He is said to have worked many miracles both before and after his death. The other version of the saint's life (*Acta Sanctorum* Aug. 6:844–847) states that he was born in the early eleventh century, was consecrated bishop in 1048 or 1071, when the Diocese of Nusco was created, and died in 1093.

Feast: Sept. 30 (Nusco); Aug. 31 (Benedictines).

Bibliography: A. PALMIERI, *Dictionnaire d'histoire et de géographie ecclésiastiques*, ed. A. BAUDRILLART et al. (Paris 1912) 2:993–994. A. M. ZIMMERMANN, *Lexicon für Theologie und Kirche*, ed. J. HOFER and K. RAHNER (Freiburg 1957–65) 2 1:420. A. M. ZIMMERMANN, *Kalendarium Benedictinum*, (Metten 1933–38) 2:642, 644. G. TAGLIALATELA, *Orazione panegirica di s. Amato, primo vescovo e patrono di Nusco* (Naples 1890). G. PASSARO, *Un testamento e una compravendita: analisi paleografica comparata* (Naples 1973). *Enciclopedia ecclesiastica*, ed. A. BERNAREGGI (Milan 1942–) 1:130.

[J. L. GRASSI]

AMATUS OF REMIREMONT, ST.

Abbot; b. Diocese of Grenoble, France, *c.* 565–570; d. Abbey of Remiremont, France, *c.* 628. About 581, while still very young, Amatus (variants: Amat, Aimé, Amé, Amado) entered the monastery at *Agaunum*, now known as the Abbey of Saint-Maurice, and he eventually became a hermit there. In 614 he went to the monastery of Luxeuil with its abbot, EUSTACE OF LUXEUIL, but he left *c.* 620 with his friend and convert Romaric (d. 653) to found a monastery at Castrum Habendi that soon became known as the Abbey of Romarici Mons, or Remiremont. This foundation became one of the most fruitful of the foundations from Luxeuil, and Romaric succeeded Amatus as abbot. In the dispute between the monk Agrestius and the followers of St. COLUMBAN and Abbot Eustace of Luxeuil, the two founders sided with Agrestius, but after a series of misfortunes and the downfall of Agrestius, they made peace with their former superior.

Amatus died shortly afterward in semi-retirement at Remiremont. He is sometimes mistakenly identified with another Amatus, Bishop of Sion, who died near the close of the century.

Feast: Sept. 13.

Bibliography: *Vita Sancti Amati*, J. MABILLON, *Acta sanctorum ordinis S. Benedicti* (Venice 1733–40) 2:120–127. E. EWIG, *Lexicon für Theologie und Kirche*, ed. J. HOFER and K. RAHNER (Freiburg 1957–65) 1:420–421. A. M. BURG, *ibid.* 9:25–26. A. MERCATI and A. PELZER, *Dizionario ecclesiastico* (Turin 1954–58) 1:111. J. MABILLON, *Lettre . . . touchant le premier institut de l'abbaye de Remiremont* (Paris 1687). M. A. GUINOT, *Étude historique sur l'abbaye de Remiremont* (Paris 1859) 377–388. M. BESSON, *Monasterium Acaunense* (Fribourg 1913) 173–184. A. M. ZIMMERMANN, *Kalendarium Benedictinum* (Metten 1933–38) 3:49–50. *Bibliotheca hagiograpica latina antiquae et mediae aetatis* (Brussels 1898–1901) 1:358. A. BUTLER, *The Lives of the Saints*, ed. H. THURSTON and D. ATTWATER (New York 1956) 3:549–550.

[G. E. CONWAY]

AMBARACH, PETER (MUBARACH, BENEDICTUS)

Seventeenth century Maronite Jesuit, Oriental scholar; b. Gusta, Lebanon, June 1663; d. Rome, Aug. 25, 1742. Ambarach, known in Italy as Pietro Benedetti, studied at the Maronite College in Rome (1672–85), and was ordained in Lebanon by the Maronite Patriarch Stephen al–Duwaihi (Aldoensis) who sent him back to Rome in 1691 to defend the validity of Syriac ordinations against the charges of Jean MORIN. Cosimo III, Grand Duke of Tuscany, named him director of the Oriental Press at Florence, and he accepted the chair of Sacred Scripture at Pisa. He entered the Jesuit novitiate in Rome on Oct. 30, 1707, and became a member of Pope Clement XI's commission for the critical edition of the Greek Bible. At the request of Cardinal Querini he started a Latin translation of the work of St. EPHREM, which he left unfinished. Among his publications are a Latin translation of Stephen al–Duwaihi's *Defense of Syriac Ordinations and the Maronite Liturgy;* a *Vita Arabica S. Alexii* [*Acta Sanctorum,* July 4 (1725) 266–270]; a partial edition of the Menologium of the Emperor BASIL II in Greek and Latin (completed by Clement XI and published, Urbino 1727); a history of the persecutions under the Persian King Sapor and his successors, written with the aid of C. Maiella; a revision of the *Works of St. Ephraem* in Greek and Syriac (3 v. 1737–43; *see* ASSEMANI, JOSEPH SIMON); and some verse and letters, including an exchange with Apollonio Bassetti.

Bibliography: C. SOMMERVOGEL et al., *Bibliothèque de la Compagnie de Jésus,* 11 v. (Brussels–Paris 1890–1932) 1:1295–98. E. M. RIVIÈRE, *Dictionnaire d'histoire et de géographie ecclésias-*

tiques, ed. A. BAUDRILLART et al. (Paris 1912—) 2:1014–15. A. FABRONI, *Vitae Italorum doctrina excellentium,* 18 v. (Pisa 1778–99) 11:174–185.

[P. JOANNOU]

AMBIGUITY

An obscurity of meaning that leaves a statement open to contrary interpretations, often as a result of faulty grammar or insufficient context (*see* FALLACY). The phrase "systematic ambiguity" has been used by Bertrand RUSSELL to characterize the function of certain key words in formal logic. According to Russell, the word "true," for example, applies to statements belonging to a number of logically distinct types. If we apply it to a sentence that combines statements of different types, contradiction may result. By avoiding such combinations the logician can guard against this (*see* ANTINOMY). Some scholastic philosophers speak of the systematic ambiguity of terms used in metaphysics. Such everyday words as "being" and "good" can be applied to the divine order, but at the risk of hidden equivocation. To eliminate this risk, the metaphysician takes note of whatever in the term's original signification carries over into its other uses (*see* ANALOGY).

[H. A. NIELSEN]

AMBITION

Ambition has two extreme senses, one good, the other bad, with interesting mixtures of legitimate thrustfulness and self-regarding pride falling between the two. The term comes from Latin *ambitio* (*ambire, ambitus*), a going about seeking votes for an office; and as representing a desire for success according to the order of right reason, it is laudable and indeed obligatory, for such a desire is inseparable from a brave tackling of difficulties. Thus a man should resolutely prosecute the causes that will give him a full and rounded life, promote the standing of his family, enlarge and dignify the work on which he has set his heart, redound to the credit and glory of his country, and show forth the beauty of the Church. Above all, in a Christian sense, he will not be half-hearted in his response to the call to holiness and the apostolate: "Let your light shine before men" (Mt 5.16).

So considered, ambition is characteristic of the great-hearted man of the Nichomachean Ethics, of the MAGNANIMITY that is the first potential part of the cardinal virtue of FORTITUDE as described in the *Summa theologiae* of St. Thomas Aquinas (ST 2a2ae, 129), or the large-mindedness and grandeur praised by Massillon and the court preachers in the high century of Louis Quatorze. Found in people of spirit who seek nothing but the best, its character, according to Aristotle, the Stoics, and the medieval theologians, appears both from its positive notes and the contrary vices it disdains. It is the love of honor as this implies the resplendence of virtue rather than its fame. Indeed on occasion magnanimity will fight with the enterprise and doggedness of fortitude, and the authors note its special connection with *fiducia* in the sense of the keeping of one's word whatever befalls, and with *securitas,* the steady confidence that is never down-hearted. Yet always it keeps a sense of proportion and acts between the vices of excess and defect. On the one hand it avoids the pushfulness (*praesumptio*) of acting for what is out of the question or not deserved, and the vain-gloriousness (*inanis gloria*) that sets too great a store on human approbation. On the other hand it masters the faint-heartedness (*pusillanimitas*) that causes one to fail to attempt to do what he can. "The kingdom of heaven suffers violence" (Mt 11.12). Yet as bound up with men's contending emotions, the passions of the irascible appetite, magnanimity is turned into sin. So the poet sees ambition as the last infirmity of a noble mind, and St. Thomas treats *ambitio* as a disorder and vice.

Charity is not ambitious; it does not seek its own (1 Cor 13.5). This indeed is the keynote of the sin, a self-seeking that takes honor out of its context and isolates it as a good for oneself, wanting praise for an excellence that is not possessed, or hugging the praise to oneself as if one's efforts deserved it without the help of God, or as if it could be hoarded and not turned to the benefit of others. It is this inordinateness that makes it a moral failure or sin, and it is this extravagance in honor-seeking that makes it a sin against magnanimity.

Bibliography: T. AQUINAS, *Summa theologiae* 2a2ae, 131. R. A. GAUTHIER, *Magnanimité: L'Idéal de la grandeur dans la philosophie païenne et la théologie chrétienne* (Paris 1951); "Fortitude," *The Virtues and States of Life,* ed. A. M. HENRY, tr. R. J. OLSEN and G. T. LENNON (Theology Library 4; Chicago 1957) 487–531. A. BEUGNET, *Dictionnaire de théologie catholique,* ed. A. VACANT et al. (Paris 1903–50) 1:940–942. R. BROUILLARD, *Catholicisme. Hier, aujourd'hui et demain,* ed. G. JACQUEMET (Paris 1947–) 1:407–409.

[T. GILBY]

AMBO

The raised platform for reading and preaching, also referred to as a pulpit. The term ambo (ὄμβων) is derived probably from ἀναβαίνειν (to mount). The elevated reading platform was designated by other terms as well: βῆμα, πύργος, *pulpitum, suggestus, auditorium, tribunal, exedra, dicterium* and in late Latin usage, *lectricium,*

Outdoor ambo carved by Donatello, 15th century, on the cathedral at Prato, Italy. (Alinari-Art Reference/Art Resource, NY)

Ambo on the Gospel side, 9th century, basilica of S. Clemente, Rome. (Alinari-Art Reference/Art Resource, NY)

legitorium, analogium. Since the scriptural service had its origin in the synagogue the ambo had possible precedent in synagogue service where a platform was sometimes provided for the reading of Sacred Scriptures. Its early use in the Christian Church in Africa is attested by both Augustine and Cyprian.

Positions and Development. In the Syrian Church the ambo was usually combined with the clergy's bench in the nave of the church. In the Greek Church it often assumed a prominent position in the nave, outside the sanctuary, and had stairways for ascent and descent. In Rome, the ambo appeared rather late. None of the Fathers make reference to ambo at Rome prior to the 7th century. At this time numerous Byzantine foundations in Rome may have brought the ambo into use. Even then there was as a rule but a single ambo, which served for all lessons. It was used for reading, chanting the intervening Psalms, and preaching. The Service of the Word took place at the same ambo. An example of such an ambo (6th century) is the carved marble one at Castel Sant'Elia, near Nepi. There are eight steps for ascent to the upper tier of a two-tiered balustrade. The use of separate ambos for Epistle and Gospel is medieval in origin and based on an allegorical interpretation introduced by Amalarius of Metz (d. c. 850). During the time when the division of the readings

were rendered on the right and on the left, and two ambos were constructed, an ornamental one on the Gospel side, a more modest structure on the Epistle side.

The separation of places for proclaiming the readings from the places for preaching was a consequence of the medieval introduction of chancel screens and the relegation of the liturgical celebration to the clergy alone. When only priests do the reading the place for reading Scripture is reduced to a simple lectern or, in private Masses, to a mere bookstand on the altar, while the place for the preaching becomes more ornate. In the 11th century the ambo was made a part of the rood screen separating the choir from the nave. Figures of the Savior and His Apostles, representing the Last Judgment and the Passion, frequently ornamented the screen on the side toward the nave. Such ambos were built in Italy as early as the 13th century. The ambo at Pisa, completed by Nicola Pisano in 1260 is an unattached structure resting on seven columns. It opened the way to a new development in Italian sculpture. The first examples of Renaissance ambos are those of Donatello in the 15th century. For funeral orations in the churchyard, for preaching to pilgrimage groups, or for the exhibition of relics, ambos were often built outside of the churches, as at the cathedral of Prato. Ambos of the baroque period were well toward the center of the nave; the base, stairway, and sounding board were covered with luxurious and ornate carving.

The Ambo Today. The renewed liturgy welcomes the reunion of the place of preaching and the place of reading since these elements clearly constitute the Service of the Word. The *Constitution on the Sacred Liturgy* of Vatican Council II instructs: "It is fitting that there be an ambo for the proclamation of the sacred readings, so arranged that the ministers can be easily seen and heard by the faithful." The *General Instruction to the Roman Missal* has directed that the Liturgy of the Word is normally proclaimed from the ambo, while at the same time preserving the ancient practice of proclaiming the Gospel and homily from the presider's chair. The ambo must be dignified, functional, and properly related to altar, chair, and assembly.

Bibliography: A. DAMBLON, *Zwischen Kathedra und Ambo: Zum Predigtverständnis des II Vatikanums—aufgezeigt an den liturgischen Predigtorten* (Dusseldorf 1988). T. MANNOORAM-PARAMPIL, "Bema in the East Syrian Church," *Christian Orient* 19 (1998) 84–99. E. RENHART, *Das syrische Bema: Liturgisch-archäologische Untersuchungen* (Graz, 1995). R. TAFT, "On the Use of the *bema* in the East—Syrian Liturgy," *Eastern Churches Review* 3 (Spring 1970) 30–39. T. MATHEWS, "Early Christian Chancel Arrangement in Rome," *Revista de archeologia cristiana* 38 (1962) 73–95. Vatican Council II, *Constitution on the Sacred Liturgy,* and Instruction of Oct. 16, 1964. J. A. JUNGMANN, *The Mass of the Roman Rite,* tr. F. A. BRUNNER, 2 v. (New York 1951–55) 1:391–461.

[W. M. MARSHALL/EDS.]

AMBROSE, ST.

Bishop of Milan, Father, and Doctor of the Church; b. Trèves (Trier, Germany), *c.* A.D. 339; d. Milan, Italy, April 4, 397. His family, perhaps in part ultimately of Greek origin, belonged to the high Roman aristocracy. At the time of his birth his father was praetorian prefect of the Gauls, one of the chief civil offices in the Roman Empire. Following Ambrose's father's death, his brother St. Satyrus, his sister St. Marcellina, and he were brought to Rome, where the brothers received an excellent education in the liberal arts and in law. Their education both in the family household and at school included a thorough training in Greek, which was to stand Ambrose in good stead later. He must have received a solid training in Christian doctrine also in a household in which Christian conduct and piety were emphasized. His sister Marcellina took the veil from Pope Liberius in 353. About 365 Ambrose and Satyrus entered the civil service as advocates, and *c.* 370 both were promoted to provincial governorships, Ambrose being made *consularis,* or governor, of Liguria and Aemilia with his residence at Milan, the imperial capital of the Roman Empire. He soon acquired a reputation for uprightness in administration and for blameless character. On the death of the Arian Bishop Auxentius, he had to quell the violence that arose regarding the choice of a successor among Catholics and Arians, and then, much against his will, he was unanimously chosen as bishop by both sides. Although brought up in a Christian family, he was still a catechumen. Within a few days after his Baptism he was ordained to the priesthood and consecrated as bishop of Milan (Dec. 7, 374).

Episcopate. He immediately distributed his share of the family wealth to the poor and set an example of strict asceticism in the episcopal household, which was organized on a kind of semimonastic basis. In the administration of his charities he received the enthusiastic and self-sacrificing support of his brother Satyrus (d. 378). Under the tutelage of the learned priest St. Simplicianus, who later succeeded him in the See of Milan, he applied himself to the systematic study of theology. In exegesis he was profoundly influenced by the allegorical method of interpretation as developed by Philo and Origen. His chief guides in theology were St. Athanasius, Didymus the Blind, St. Cyril of Jerusalem, St. Basil, and Hippolytus. The investigations of P. Courcelle have shown, too, that he was well acquainted with Plotinus and made fruitful use of Neoplatonic ideas in his development of Christian thought.

However, Ambrose remained typically Roman in thought and language. In his exegesis and in his theological expositions, as well as in the homilies that underlie most of his works, and even in his letters, he exhibits a

St. Ambrose barring Theodosius from the cathedral at Milan, painting on panel by Ambrogio Borgognone (c. 1450 or 1460 to 1523).

marked predilection for moral teaching and exhortation. All his writings were composed at short notice, as the occasion demanded, in the course of an extraordinarily busy and difficult episcopate. From the days of his election, he was repeatedly involved in problems of the gravest import for the Church and for the State, and he soon came to be recognized throughout the Western Empire as the great champion of orthodoxy and of the rights of the Church.

Altar of Victory. On his accession, the young Emperor GRATIAN (375–383) refused to accept the pagan title *pontifex maximus;* and some years later (381), in his second edict against paganism, he ordered the removal of the altar and statue of Victory from the Senate house in Rome. The powerful pagan party sent a delegation headed by SYMMACHUS to Milan to protest; but, under the influence of Ambrose, it was refused an audience at court. In the summer of 384, after the murder of Gratian (383), a new delegation under the leadership of Symmachus, then Praetorian Prefect, presented an eloquently written *Relatio,* or *Memorial,* to the imperial consistory and the boy-emperor VALENTINIAN (383–392), again pleading for the restoration of the altar and statue. Ambrose hastily prepared a strong refutation of the petition, and the request for restoration was denied. Both the *Memorial* of Symmachus and the reply of Ambrose (*Epist.* 18) are extant—at least in the revised form that was eventually given them.

Conflict with the Arian Empress Justina. Despite the aid rendered to the position of Valentinian by Ambrose's mission to the usurper Maximus at Treves in 383, Valentinian's mother, the Empress Justina, fearing the growing ascendancy of the bishop over her son, and as a staunch Arian, organized a coalition against Ambrose. She raised an issue by demanding that one basilica in Milan, namely, the Basilica Portiana outside the walls, be given to the Arians. Ambrose was summoned to the imperial palace near the beginning of Lent in 385, but refused to give up the basilica. The incident created a riot in the city, and Ambrose himself had to be asked to calm his people. A few weeks later, just before Easter, Justina boldly demanded that the new basilica within the walls, Ambrose's own cathedral church, be turned over to the Arians, but he refused with the curt statement that "a bishop cannot give up the temple of God" (*Epist.* 20.1). Beginning on Palm Sunday there was a series of clashes between the imperial troops and Ambrose's congregations at the new and old basilicas, and at the Portiana, accompanied by destruction of property. The bishop, however, stood his ground, and on Holy Thursday news was brought to him at the Portiana that the court had abandoned its attempt to seize any of his churches at that time.

The struggle was not over. With the help of the Arian Bishop Mercurinus Auxentius, Justina had an imperial edict passed against the Catholics in January 386, and Ambrose was summoned to appear before the emperor and his council to dispute the points at issue with Auxentius. He refused, explaining his position at length, and finally, to avoid arrest, remained within the precincts of the new basilica. For several days and nights the church was surrounded by imperial troops, but they did not force an entrance. To relieve tension and to encourage his flock, Ambrose introduced the antiphonal singing of Psalms and of hymns of his own composition. It was on this occasion also that he delivered his *Sermon against Auxentius,* in which, in terse juridical style, he enunciated the epoch-making principle in the relations of Church and State: *imperator enim intra ecclesiam, non supra ecclesiam est* (par. 3). The court was forced to capitulate; the anti-Catholic edict was rescinded, and no further action was taken against Ambrose. After the deaths of Maximus

(388) and Justina, the young Emperor Valentinian again turned to Ambrose for counsel, and Ambrose treated him with fatherly affection until Valentinian's murder in 392.

Ambrose and the Emperor Theodosius (379–395). Only two incidents marred temporarily the cordial relations of Ambrose and Theodosius, the greatest personalities of their age in Church and State, namely, the Callinicum affair and the massacre of Thessalonica. At Callinicum on the Euphrates the Christian congregation with the connivance of their bishop had burned a Jewish synagogue (late in 388), and Theodosius ordered that the bishop restore the synagogue at his own expense. Ambrose opposed this order in vehement terms on the ground that Christians, in rebuilding a synagogue, would be committing an act of apostasy, and the emperor reluctantly withdrew his order. In this case, however, excessive zeal led Ambrose to neglect the demands of strict justice, for he suggested no possible alternatives for redressing the wrong done.

In 390 several imperial officers were killed in a riot at Thessalonica, and Theodosius, influenced primarily by his Master of the Offices, Rufinus, ordered a savage reprisal that led to the massacre of 7,000 defenseless persons in the circus of the Macedonian city. Ambrose left Milan at the news, but in a letter to the emperor he reproached him for his crime and told him that, under threat of excommunication, he must do public penance. Theodosius complied some months later, even if some of the dramatic details furnished by the historian THEODORET are to be discounted. A few years later (in 392 and 395) Ambrose delivered his great funeral orations on Valentinian II and Theodosius, which contain so much precious information on his part in the political affairs of his time.

Ambrose as Pastor. Despite his heavy involvement in political affairs of concern to the Church, Ambrose was a zealous defender of orthodoxy and, above all, a zealous pastor of souls. In his homilies he attacked severely all the social abuses of his age. With the courage and eloquence of a Hebrew Prophet, he denounced especially evil conduct in the upper classes and its deplorable results. But he also expounded theological doctrine very effectively in his homilies. Augustine came to listen to his eloquence, but was led to a new understanding of the Scriptures and of Christian faith by the bishop's explanations (*Confessions* 6.1.1–6.4.6). Augustine was baptized by Ambrose at Easter 386. Ambrose had distributed his own wealth to help the poor and urged others to do the same. Following the battle of Hadrianople in 378, and the subsequent Gothic invasion, he did not scruple to sell the sacred Church vessels to redeem captives. In his advocacy of Christian ideals, he was one of the most zealous and influential promoters of virginity in his age. He gave a new impetus to the cult of the martyrs with the discovery of two skeletons, which were thought to be those of Gervase and Protase, in the course of the excavations for his own great basilica in 386.

Writings. The volume of his extant works is noteworthy when one considers that they were all written in the midst of an extraordinarily demanding episcopate. They often reveal, on the dogmatic and scriptural side, especially, a heavy dependence on Greek works, but the borrowing is freely acknowledged. Ambrose was primarily concerned not with originality but with meeting the practical needs of dogmatic and moral instruction and exhortation. For the most part his treatises were assembled from homilies, and the revision was hastily done. However, he was splendidly trained in Latin literature, and many passages in his works exhibit Christian Latin literary style at its best. Like Leo the Great, he had a happy facility for coining clear and pithy phrases and definitions.

Exegetical Works. All his Old Testament exegesis is based essentially on Philo and Origen. Even the most literal of scriptural texts is given an allegorical or typological meaning. In view of the homiletic origin of his exegetical works, moral application is invariably a primary concern. His major contributions are: *Exameron* (six bks.), based on the corresponding work of St. Basil; *Expositio evangelii secundum Lucam* (ten bks., of which one and two are taken over directly from Origen); and *Expositio in Psalmum 118*. His shorter works include *De Cain et Abel, De Noe, De Abraham* (two bks.), *De Isaac et anima, De bono mortis, De Iacob et vita beata* (two bks.), *De Ioseph, De patriarchis, De fuga saeculi, De Helia et ieiunio, De Nabuthae, De Tobia, De interpellatione Iob et David, Apologia prophetae David,* and *Explanatio super Psalmos 12*.

Moral-Ascetical Works. The *De officiis* (three bks.), written for the clergy of Milan, is the most important. As its title indicates, it is modeled on the corresponding predominantly Stoic treatise of Cicero. However, resemblance is more external than real. The work is thoroughly Christian and, as is usual in Ambrose, relies heavily on Scripture for examples and authority. The other writings in this category are: *De virginibus ad Marcellinam sororem* (three bks.), *De viduis, De virginitate, De institutione virginis,* and *Exhortatio virginitatis*. In these treatises Ambrose reveals greater independence in developing his arguments in favor of the life of virginity. Through his emphasis on the Blessed Virgin as the ideal and patron of virginity, he is one of the chief founders of devotion to Mary in this respect. The *De lapsu virginis consecratae* is definitely recognized as pseudo-Ambrosian.

Dogmatic Works. Three of these are against Arianism: *De fide ad Gratianum* (five bks.), on the divinity of the Son; *De Spiritu Sancto* (three bks.), based essentially on Didymus the Blind, St. Athanasius, and St. Basil; and *De incarnationis dominicae sacramento*. Three others deal primarily with the exposition of the Sacraments and of the faith to catechumens and are of great importance for the history of the liturgy: *De sacramentis* (six bks.), *De mysteriis,* and *Explanatio symboli*. The last two are now definitely assigned to Ambrose. Finally, he composed the *De paenitentia* to refute Novatianism.

Orations and Letters. The two orations *De excessu fratris* (*Satyri*), the *De obitu Valentiniani,* and *De obitu Theodosii* are masterpieces of their genre. The invective *Sermo contra Auxentium de basilicis tradendis* is to be regarded also as a formal oration. Only 91 of Ambrose's *Epistulae* are extant. Apart from a few, private letters, they are official or semiofficial in character, or are little exegetical or moral treatises in epistolary form.

Hymns and Other Works. Of the numerous hymns ascribed to Ambrose, the *Deus Creator omnium, Aeterne rerum conditor, Iam surgit hora tertia,* and *Intende, qui regis Israel* are certainly genuine. By these compositions he has justly earned the title "father of liturgical hymnody" in the West. He seems also to have given definitive form to the Exsultet. Several inscriptions and 21 Tituli in verse also have good claims to Ambrosian authorship. The *Hegesippus sive de bello Iudaico* (five bks.), a free translation and adaptation of the *De bello Iudaico* of Flavius Josephus, may be regarded with some probability as being a work from the early life of Ambrose.

Appreciation. Ambrose exhibited little originality in the field of dogma or exegesis, but he was a courageous and effective defender of orthodoxy, a great moral teacher, and an exemplary pastor of souls. Above all, he was the first of the Fathers and Doctors of the Church to deal formally with the relations of Church and State. He enunciated the principle that the Church is supreme in its own domain and is the guardian of morality. Even the emperors, despite their lofty dignity and absolutism, are subject to the moral laws as defined and put into practice by the Church. The penance of Theodosius and the principle underlying and demanding it were phenomena found in the sacred history of Israel. However, they were entirely new in the Greco-Roman world, and they were to be of the greatest significance for the future.

Feast: Dec. 7.

Bibliography: *Clavis Patrum latinorum,* ed. E. DEKKERS (Streenbrugge 1961) Nos. 122–183. *Hymnes,* tr. and ed. J. FONTAINE and J.-L. CHARLET (Paris 1992). J. HUHN, *Lexicon für Theologie und Kirche,* ed. J. HOFER and K. RAHNER (Freiburg 1957–65) 1:427–430, with bibliog. A. LARGENT, *Dictionnaire de théologie catholique,* ed. A. VACANT et al. (Paris 1903–50) 1.1:943–951, and A. MICHEL, *ibid.* Tables générales 1:111–115, with bibliog. H. VON CAMPENHAUSEN,

Die Religion in Geschichte und Gegenwart (Tübingen 1957–65) 1:307–308. A. GASTOUÉ and P. DE LABRIOLLE, *Dictionnaire d'histoire et de géographie ecclésiastiques*, ed. A. BAUDRILLART et al. (Paris 1912) 1:1091–1108. W. WILBRAND, *Reallexicon für Antike und Christentum* 1:365–373. B. ALTANER, *Patrology* (New York 1960) 443–457, with an excellent summary of Ambrose's teachings and copious bibliog. F. CAYRÉ, *Manual of Patrology and History of Theology*, tr. H. HOWITT, v.1 (Paris 1936) 520–547. O. Bardenhewer, *Geschichte der alt Kirchlichen Literatur*, 5 v. (Freiburg 1913–32) 3:498–547. J. R. PALANQUE, *Saint Ambroise et l'Empire romain* (Paris 1933), with bibliog. F. H. DUDDEN, *The Life and Times of St. Ambrose,* 2 v. (Oxford 1935). Y.-M. DUVAL, *L'extirpation de l'Arianisme en Italie du Nord et en Occident* (Brookfield 1998). G. GOTTLIEB, *Ambrosius von Mailand und Kaiser Gratian* (Göttingen 1973). A. PAREDI, *St. Ambrose*, tr. J. COSTELLO (Notre Dame, Ind. 1963). C. MARINO, *Chiesa e stato nella dottrina di S. Ambrogio* (Rome 1963). D. MATACOTTA, *Simmaco: l'antagonista di Sant'Ambrogio* (Florence 1992). N. B. MCLYNN, *Ambrose of Milan: Church and Court in a Christian Capital* (Berkeley 1994). J. MOORHEAD, *Ambrose: Church and Society in the Late Roman World* (New York 1999). C. PASINI, *Ambrogio di Milano: azione e pensiero di un vescovo* (Milan 1996). B. RAMSEY, *Ambrose* (London 1997). H. M. RILEY, *Christian Initiation: A Comparative Study of the Interpretation of the Baptismal Liturgy* (Washington 1974). J. HUHN, *Das Geheimnis der Jungfrau-Mutter Maria nach Ambrosius* (Würzburg 1954). V. R. VASEY, *The Social Ideas in the Works of St. Ambrose* (Rome 1982). P. COURCELLE, *Recherches sur les "Confessions" de Saint Augustin* (Paris 1950), esp. 91–174 and 211–221. On the language and style of St. Ambrose, see esp. *Patristic Studies* (Catholic University of America) v. 10, 12, 15, 19, 20, 27, 29, 30, 35, 40, 43, 49, 56, and 58, and E. LUCCHESI, *L'usage de Philon dans l'oeuvre exégétique de Saint Ambroise* (Leiden 1977). A. FRANZ, *Tageslauf und Heilsgeschichte: Untersuchungen zum literarischen Text und liturgischen Kontext der Tagzeitenhymnen des Ambrosius von Mailand* (St. Ottilien, Germany 1994). C. MARKSCHIES, *Ambrosius von Mailand und die Trinitätstheologie: kirchen– und theologiegeschichtliche Studien zu Antiarianismus und Neunizänismus bei Ambrosius und im lateinischen Westen* (Tübingen 1995). C. MOHRMANN, "Langue et style de la poésie chrétienne," *Études sur le latin des chrétiens* v.1 (Rome 1961) 151–168, esp. 165–168. For new Eng. tr. see *The Fathers of the Church*, ed. R. J. DEFERRARI et al. (Washington 1961) v.22, 26, 42, and 44. On the *Vita S. Ambrosii*, written at the suggestion of St. Augustine by Ambrose's former secretary, Paulinus of Milan, in 422, see A. STUIBER, *Lexicon für Theologie und Kirche*, ed. J. HOFER and K. RAHNER (Freiburg 1957–65) 8:208, with bibliog. H. AUF DER MAUR, *Die Psalmenverständnis des Ambrosius von Mailand* (Leiden 1977).

[M. R. P. MCGUIRE]

AMBROSE OF CAHORS, ST.

Bishop?; d. near Bourges, France, *c.* 770. In the account of his life that has come down to us it is impossible to sort out any certain historical information. According to a doubtful tradition he held his episcopal office at Cahors under PEPIN III the Short. Slandered and persecuted despite his works of charity, he gave up his see and lived for three years in a cave near the Lot River. While returning from a pilgrimage to Rome, he died at Ernotrum (now Saint-Ambroise-sur-Arnon). His cultus, dating from the tenth century, is perhaps the best evidence for his saintly career.

Feast: Oct. 16.

Bibliography: *Acta Sanctorum* Oct. 7.2:1031–50. *Bibliotheca hagiographica latina antiquae et mediae aetatis* (Brussels 1898–1901) 1:369–374. L. DUCHESNE, *Fastes épiscopaux de l'ancienne Gaule* (Paris 1907–15) 2:13. E. ALBE, *Dictionnaire d'histoire et de géographie ecclésiastiques*, ed. A. BAUDRILLART et al. (Paris 1912) 2:1110–11. C. LEFEBVRE, *Bibliotheca sanctorum* 1:943. J. L. BAUDOT and L. CHAUSSIN, *Vies des saints et des bienheureux selon l'ordre du calendrier avec l'historique des fêtes* (Paris 1935–56) 10:484–485.

[J. E. LYNCH]

AMBROSE TRAVERSARI, BL.

CAMALDOLESE monk and early Christian humanist; b. Portico, southwest of Ravenna, Sept. 16, 1386; d. Fontebuono, Nov. 17, 1439. He entered the Camaldolese cenobitic monastery, St. Mary of the Angels, at Florence, Oct. 8, 1400, and was professed Nov. 6, 1401. Soon Florentine humanists such as Niccoli, Strozzi, and Cosimo de Medici visited his cell to discuss classical and patristic literature, philosophy, and theology. Ambrose gathered and emended ancient texts and translated many works of the Greek Fathers. He became subprior in January 1431, and prior general of his order on Oct. 26, 1431, because of his interest in reform. The *Hodoeporicon* is a diary of the resulting visitations from December 1431 to 1433. He represented Pope EUGENE IV at the Council of BASEL, and before Emperor SIGISMUND. At Ferrara and Florence in 1438 he effectively employed his knowledge of Greek in negotiating with Byzantine representatives leading to reunion of the Roman and Orthodox Churches.

Feast: Nov. 20.

Bibliography: *Hodoeporicon*, ed. V. TAMBURINI (Florence 1985). *Ambrogio Traversari: un monaco e un monastero nell'umanesimo fiorentino*, ed. S. FRIGERIO (Camaldoli 1988). A. DINI-TRAVERSARI, *Ambrogio Traversari e i suoi tempi* (Florence 1912). G. MERCATI, *Ultimi contributi alla storia degli umanisti*, 2 v. (*Studi e Testi* 90, 91; 1939) v.1. C. L. STINGER, *Humanism and the Church Fathers: Ambrogio Traversari (1386–1439) and Christian Antiquity in the Italian Renaissance* (Albany, N.Y. 1977). J. WODKA, *Lexikon für Theologie und Kirche*, ed. J. HOFER and K. RAHNER, 10 v. (2d, new ed. Freiburg 1957–65) 1:431.

[N. G. WOLF]

AMBROSIAN CHANT

In addition to textual and structural differences from the Roman rite, the Milanese Church also developed a special repertory of chants, commonly called Ambrosian chant.

Except for some fragments in chironomic notation, the first written examples of this chant came from the 12th century, the chief witnesses being British Museum Add. 34209, for the winter season (published in facsimile and transcription *Paléographie musicale* v. 5, 6) and Bedero Val Travaglia, S. Vittore, for the summer season. Numerous later MSS exist and attest to a highly stable musical tradition. Some literary testimony and the existence of numerous manuals prior to the notated sources show that much of the 12th-century repertory must go back to the Carolingian period, if not earlier.

Many scholars of the 19th century too easily assumed that Gregorian chant and Ambrosian chant came from a common stem, since lost, while others, such as Dom Germain Morin, postulated the priority of the Ambrosian chant, from which the Gregorian evolved. More recent trends among scholars tend to differentiate between borrowed chants inserted much later into the Ambrosian chant from the Gregorian and a primitive Ambrosian nucleus that must be pre-Carolingian. This latter shows a kind of music-making similar to Gregorian chant but less rigid, less polished, and less systematic. That this nucleus goes back to the time of St. Ambrose cannot possibly be proved. It is clear, however, that by the Carolingian period the Ambrosian musical practice differed from the Gregorian and that further developments of it were made mostly by borrowings from the Gregorian and adaptations of older chants. The 12th-century MSS thus show a complete but heterogeneous repertory. The fact that the Milanese never developed a musical theory to explain their chants also helps to account for its diversified nature.

Among the chants of the Mass the *Ingressa* (i.e., Introit) and *Offertorium* show the most borrowings from Gregorian chant and were thus the last to be stabilized. No verses were found with the *Ingressa,* showing that it did not function as a processional chant. Several borrowings from post-Carolingian Byzantine chants are also found. The *Psalmellus* (i.e., Gradual) is distinctly Ambrosian, highly ornate and soloistic in nature. The same can be said of the Ambrosian ALLELUIA. The chants sung after the Gospel, during the breaking of the bread (*Confractorium*), and after Communion (*Transitorium*) are related to Office chants and are simpler. They too, however, lack any traces of psalmody. Only the Gloria (with the addition of three Kyries), the Creed, and the Sanctus form the Ambrosian ordinary and a simple and solemn version of each of these was sufficient.

Antiphons, responsories, and hymns form the largest categories of musical compositions in the Office. Because of the late date of the Ambrosian MSS with musical notation, it is difficult to establish the age of the melodies of the Ambrosian hymns. That the melodies of the hymns composed by St. Ambrose also came from the 4th century is possible but cannot be proved. The melodies of the hymns for the feasts of saints have similar features that seem more primitive. Later hymns are certainly adaptations of these earlier melodies. The 40 liturgical hymns are thus adapted to about 28 different melodies. Another feature pointing to the antiquity of these melodies is their avoidance of the tritus modes.

The antiphons of the Office are divided into the following categories: Psalter antiphons used for the recitation of the Psalms, processional antiphons (*psallenda* and *psallentium*), *antiphonae ad crucem,* and *antiphonae in choro.* The Psalter antiphons are the most numerous, about 775 in all, and are generally simple. Many of them can be classified according to melodic types or formulas, even more rigorous in their structure than the Gregorian types. The psalmody that accompanies these antiphons is also of an unornate kind and shows little consistency in the MS tradition. Since no modal theory was worked out by the Ambrosian cantors, no set system of psalmody was developed, the only criterion being that a smooth connection between the end of the Psalm and the repetition of the antiphon was desired. No mediant cadence is found in the psalmody.

The processional antiphons are more varied in style but frequently use psalter antiphons to augment their number. Their use is more frequent in the Ambrosian rite than in the Roman. The famous procession with the cross gave birth to the elaborate *antiphonae ad crucem* with their more elaborate psalmody. They seem more closely connected with Eastern than Western practice. The *antiphonae in choro* show some remnants of psalmody but are peculiarly Ambrosian in style and origin.

The responsories are frequent in the Ambrosian rite, not only at Matins but at the other hours as well. On larger feasts they tend to be extremely ornate in character. A series of long melismas with names to identify them is sung with the responsories on the greater feasts. They tend to be soloistic in nature and contrast with the simplicity of the antiphons.

In sum, Ambrosian chant is less rigid in its modal implications and more heterogeneous than Gregorian chant. On the other hand, its primitive core may thus be preserved in a manner that represents an earlier period than the Gregorian. The late date of its musical MSS is unfortunate, but the uniformity of the tradition and the tenacious attempts to maintain it attest to an older practice.

Bibliography: P. BORELLA, ''Influssi carolingi e monastici sul messale ambrosiano,'' *Miscellanea liturgica in honorem L. Cunibert,* 2 v. (Rome 1948–49) 1:73–115. P. CAGIN, ''Antiphonaire ambrosien,'' *Paléographie musicale* 5 (1896). A. GATARD,

"Ambrosien (chant)," *Dictionnaire d'archéologie chrétienne et de liturgie*, ed. F. CABROL, H. LECLERCQ, and H. I. MARROU, 15 v. (Paris 1907–53) 1:1353–73. B. STÄBLEIN, "Ambrosianisch-Gregorianisch," *Compte rendu de l'International Musicological Society, 4th, 1949* (Basel 1951) 185–89. G. SUÑOL, "La restaurazione ambrosiana," *Ambrosius* 14 (1938) 145–50, 174–77, 196–200, 296–304; 15 (1939) 113–16. *Antiphonale missarum juxta ritum sanctae ecclesiae mediolanensis*, ed. G. N. SUÑOL (Rome 1935); *Liber vesperalis juxta ritum sanctae ecclesiae mediolanensis* (Rome 1939). M. HUGLO, *Fonti e paleografia del canto ambrosiano* (Milan 1956). R. JESSON, W. APEL, *Gregorian Chant* (Bloomington, Ind. 1958) 465–83. E. CATTANEO, *Note storiche sul canto ambrosiano* (Milan 1950). T. BAILEY and P. MERKLEY, *The Antiphons of the Ambrosian Office* (Ottawa 1989). A. PAREDI, *Storia del rito ambrosiano* (Milan 1990). T. BAILEY, *Antiphon and Psalm in the Ambrosian Office* (Ottawa 1994). T. BAILEY, "Ambrosian Double Antiphons," *Laborare fratres in unum: Festschrift Láászlóó Dobszay zum 60. Gerburtstag*, ed. J. SZENDREI and D. HILEY (Hildesheim 1995) 11–24. T. BAILEY, "Antiphon Classification and the Development of the Ambrosian Sanctorale," *The Divine Office in the Latin Middle Ages: Methodology and Source Studies, Regional Developments, Hagiography*, ed. M. FASSLER and R. A. BALTZER (New York 2000). V. A. LENTI, "The Revised Ambrosian Divine Office," *Studia Liturgica* 29 (1999) 116–26. V. A. LENTI, "Liturgical Reform and the Ambrosian and Mozarabic Rites," *Worship* 68 (1994) 417–26. N. A. MÁRQUEZ, "Music at the Crossroads of Empire: Ambrose and Milanese Chant," *Pastoral Music* 25:4 (April-May 2001) 34–37.

[R. G. WEAKLAND]

AMBROSIAN RITE

The Ambrosian Rite is one of three surviving distinct liturgical rites in regular use in the Latin Church, the other two being the Mozarabic Rite and the Roman Rite. Today, it is the principal liturgical rite of the Archdiocese of Milan, as well as the neighboring Italian dioceses of Bergamo and Novara, and the Swiss diocese of Lugano.

HISTORY

The beginnings of the Ambrosian Rite have been much discussed. Many questions that have arisen have not always received conclusive answers. What was St. Ambrose's role in the history of the rite? Is the rite of Greek inspiration, or is it fundamentally of Western character?

Witness of St. Ambrose. The Ambrosian Rite has been called Ambrosian not because St. Ambrose originated it, but because he was the most illustrious of the bishops of Milan and thus personifies the traditions of his see. The attribution to him of the rite's beginnings is found for the first time in an eighth-century *Cursus Scottorum* (contained in *Ordo Rom.* 19; M. Andrieu, *Les 'Ordines Romani' du haut moyen-âge*, 5 v. [Louvain 1931–61] 3:225) and even more clearly in WALAFRID Strabo (d. 849) "Ambrose, Bishop of Milan, arranged the order of Mass and other services for his church and for other churches in Liguria; the Milanese church maintains it to this day" (*De rebus eccl.* 22; *Patrologia Latina*, 217 v. [Paris 1878–90] 114:944).

In about 396, Ambrose wrote that Dionysius, his predecessor who was sent into exile in 355, had asked God to let him die far from Milan so that he would not have to see the Christian traditions of his clergy and people overthrown and trampled upon by the infidels (*Epist.* 63.70; *Patrologia Latina*, 16:1260). Ambrose is here referring to the government of the Church of Milan by the Arian Auxentius (d. 374), who had come from the East.

Elsewhere Ambrose affirmed that his Church followed the leadership of Rome in all things: "cuius (id est ecclesiae Romanae) typum in omnibus sequimur et formam" (*De sacramentis* 3.1.5). By means of such conformity to the liturgy of Rome, he attempted to defend the legitimacy of certain special customs in Milan, for example, the washing of the feet of the newly baptized.

From these two passages of St. Ambrose one must conclude that (1) the liturgy of Milan in the fourth century was substantially the same as that of Rome, and therefore that Milan received it from Rome; (2) the Arian Bishop Auxentius introduced many changes into Milan's worship, and that he was perhaps the source of certain affinities of the Ambrosian Rite with that of the Greeks; and (3) in certain instances the practice of Milan differed from that of Rome (e.g., the feet of the newly baptized are washed; there has never been fasting on Saturday in Milan although there was in Rome: Augustine, *Epist.* 36.32; *Corpus scriptorum ecclesiasticorum latinorum* 34:62).

Innovations Ambrose made in the liturgy of Milan were the use of the antiphon, the singing of hymns, and perhaps a new arrangement of the vigils [A. Paredi, *La liturgia di S. Ambrogio* (Milan 1940) 152–155]. The use of both antiphons and hymns spread from Milan to other Churches of the West (Augustine, *Conf.* 9.7) and finally to Rome itself. The few peculiarities in Baptism and the Eucharist referred to in the *De sacramentis* of the fourth century concord substantially with the Milanese service books coming from the ninth to the eleventh centuries [L. L. Mitchell, "Ambrosian Baptismal Rites," *Studia Liturgica* 1 (1962) 241–253]. As for the Canon of the Mass, it must be remembered that the *De sacramentis* offers only a fragment quoted from memory in a discourse, and therefore one should not make too much of differences between it and the text of the canon found in Milanese liturgical books of the Carolingian era.

Origins. The thesis proposed by L. Duchesne in 1889 [*Christian Worship, Its Origin and Evolution* (5th ed. London 1949) 93–94], that the Ambrosian Rite was of Greek origin imported to Milan by Auxentius, is untenable if one admits, as everyone now does, Ambrose's authorship of *De sacramentis*. Nor is there any probability in the recent thesis that Rome adopted the primitive Mass Canon from Milan. Just as all the churches of the West received the faith and Scriptures from Rome, so also from the same sources must they have accepted the first simple and essential liturgical formulas and rites. The fourth and fifth centuries, however, witnessed a phenomenal development in the liturgy everywhere. In the same way as other shepherds, the bishops of Milan— Eustorgius (until *c.* 350), Dionysius (until 355), Ambrose (d. 397), Simplicianus (d. 401), and Eusebius (d. 460)— made adaptations, composed new prayers, introduced new rites to meet the pastoral needs of their flocks. Very probably the first Milanese service book was systematized and edited shortly after the death of Simplicianus, for he is the last bishop of the diocese to be given a proper Mass in the oldest extant Milanese Missals (9th–11th centuries). In that first service book many prayers could have been the traditional, common Latin compositions, not newly composed ones.

So great was the prestige of St. Ambrose that not only his writings but also the prayers and chants of his church were known in other areas. The developments of the fourth and fifth centuries, particularly Ambrose's innovations, made these variations from Roman practice more obvious. Ambrose alluded to Roman criticism of Milanese peculiarities (*De sacramentis* 3.1.5–6), and this criticism mounted. Innocent I (d. 417) wrote to the bishop of Gubbio, censuring those who followed liturgical usages of churches other than Rome (*Epist.* 25 *ad Decentium; Patrologia Latina,* 20: 551–561). The very customs criticized were to be found in the Milanese service books, which shows that at that time Milan's liturgy was already being imitated by other churches, even those near Rome. Furthermore, seventh-century Gallican service books such as the Bobbio Missal and the *Missale Gothicum* contain prayers clearly of Milanese derivation. On the other hand, it has not been proved that Milan borrowed any prayers from the Gallican books.

Hence Duchesne's thesis can be accepted in the sense that Milan was the center from which a Gallican type liturgy took its origin. By Gallican is meant a Latin (not Eastern) liturgy different from that of Rome in certain particulars [see J. A. Jungmann, *The Early Liturgy* (Notre Dame, Ind. 1959) 227–237].

Development. Aside from the addition of the *Communicantes* and *Nobis quoque peccatoribus,* which were probably adopted from Rome about 570 [V. L. Kennedy, *The Saints of the Canon of the Mass* (Vatican City 1938)

197], the rite tended to be stable partly owing to the exile of Milan's bishops and officials at Genoa from 569 to 649. Its stability was also due partly to the isolation Milan brought upon itself during the schism involved in its (and Aquileia's) refusal to accept the decision of Vigilius (d. 555) and Pelagius (d. 561) confirming the Second Council of Constantinople's condemnation of the THREE CHAPTERS.

Toward the end of the eighth century, however, the Ambrosian Rite probably underwent a revision. All the oldest extant codices (of Milan, Bergamo, Vercelli, and Biasca) enjoy an amazing uniformity in both prayer texts and the arrangement of the sanctoral cycle. Such uniformity cannot be explained without admitting a revision of Milan's Sacramentary, a revision that introduced many new formularies for new feasts, taking them chiefly from the eighth-century Gelasian Sacramentary, basically a Roman book.

A few decades after the revision of the Sacramentary, possibly in the last half of the ninth century, the Milanese Office also received a definitive arrangement. While the chant texts of the Mass use the *Vetus Latina* version of the Psalms, the Office follows the Old Roman Psalter, that is, St. Jerome's correction of the *Vetus Latina* [A. Nohe, *Der Mailänder Psalter* (Freiburg 1936)]. Between the fourth and ninth centuries there must have been two successive reforms of the Office, one due to Greek influence, another to the Benedictines [H. Schneider, *Die altlateinischen biblischen Cantica* (Texte und Arbeiten 29–30; Beuron 1938) 99–126].

These revisions coincide with the limitation of the geographical ambit of the rite during the Carolingian reforms. A tradition going back at least to the eleventh century claims that Charlemagne intervened in the fortunes of the Ambrosian Rite. According to Landulf the Elder (*Hist. Mediolanensis* 11.10; *Patrologia Latina,* 147:583), the emperor tried to abolish the rite by imposing the Roman books and chant. On the other hand, a Cassinese poem (manuscript 318 in the archives of Monte Cassino) says that Charlemagne merely restricted the use of the rite and its chant to the Diocese of Milan. It is not true, however, that Nicholas II (d. 1061) or Gregory VII (d. 1085) attempted to suppress the rite. Also legendary is the alleged attempt of Cardinal Branda da Castiglione (d. 1443) to do the same [A. Paredi, *La biblioteca del Pizolpasso* (Milan 1961) 60].

From the tenth to the fourteenth centuries one finds at work in the Ambrosian Rite the same forces that brought about the accumulation of private prayers and special devotions as in the Roman liturgical books. The chief difficulty was that during this period no typical edition of Milanese service books was made obligatory by episcopal authority, especially for Office and calendar. Consequently the traditions followed varied according to locality. It was only with Archbishop Francesco Pizolpasso in 1440 that the first decree regulating the calendar appeared [E. Cattaneo, *Il breviario ambrosiano* (Milan 1943) appendix].

When Pius V in 1568 and 1570 declared the Roman Breviary and Missal obligatory, he made an exception for those rites that had been in existence for 200 years or more. Hence the Ambrosian Rite was allowed to continue, but the archbishop of Milan had to carry out a reform of the liturgical books and eliminate abuses. To this end a commission was appointed by (St.) Charles Borromeo, who had defended the legitimacy of the rite and ensured its juridical existence. Borromeo thus removed the editing of service books from private initiative and had published the first official *Calendarium* (1567) and Breviary (1582); after his death the Ritual (1589) and Missal (1594) appeared. His chief aim in this reform was to restore the rite to its original state. His commission did not execute his wishes, however, but introduced serious changes contrary to ancient tradition, for example, owing to dogmatic scruples, the Ambrosian form for Anointing of the Sick was replaced by the Roman.

Toward the end of the nineteenth century, there was begun a new reform seeking the primitive purity of the rite. By 1964 there had appeared new editions of the *Missale Ambrosianum* by A. Ceriani in 1901, the *Antiphonale Missarum* (1935) and *Liber Vesperalis* (1939) by G. M. Suñol. In 1930 studies were begun by the Benedictines of Maria Laach for a new edition of the Breviary. In 1976, the revised Ambrosian missal (*Messale Ambrosiano*) and the lectionary (*Lezionario Ambrosiano*) were published together in Italian. This was followed by the promulgation of the Latin text (*Missale Ambrosianum iuxta ritum Sanctae Ecclesiae Mediolanensis*) in 1981, and a second Italian edition of the Ambrosian Missal in 1986.

Sources. The oldest extant manuscripts of Milanese service books date to the ninth to eleventh centuries. Besides early references to the rite in the writings and homilies of Ambrose, Gaudentius of Brescia (d. 427), Peter Chrysologus (d. 450), and Maximus II of Turin (d. 465), there is available an eleventh-century commentary on the Milanese Mass, the *Expositio Missae Canonicae* [ed. A. Wilmart, *Jahrbuch für Liturgiewissenschaft* 2 (1922) 47–67]. Also edited are the ninth-century *Sacramentarium Bergomense* (ed. A. Paredi, Bergamo 1962) and the eleventh-century Sacramentary of Aribert [ed. A. Paredi, *Miscellanea Bernareggi* (Bergamo 1958) 329–488]. M. Magistretti edited a ninth-century Ordinal describing the Church year, *Beroldus sive ecclesiae Ambrosianae Me-*

diolanensis kalendarium et ordines (Milan 1894), and a combined Breviary and Ritual, *Manuale Ambrosianum* (2 v. Milan 1905).

DESCRIPTION OF RITUAL

This section gives a description of the chief characteristics of the celebration of the Eucharist, Sacraments, liturgical year, and vestments in the classical Ambrosian Rite. The 1976 reforms of the Ambrosian Rite has retained many of the principal elements of the classical structure, while simplifying and pruning accretions that were added over the centuries.

Mass. Traditionally, the festive celebration of the Mass was preceded by a procession during which antiphons are sung. The procession ended with a short litany. The prayers of the *Confiteor* began to appear from the thirteenth century on. The Psalm *Iudica me Deus,* wanted by Charles Borromeo and introduced into the *Missale Ambrosianum* of 1594 but omitted in the 1618 edition, is no longer said. The 1976 revisions removed these preparatory ceremonies that were incorporated during the medieval period, and the Ambrosian Rite of the Mass begins with the *Ingressa* or Entrance Antiphon, as was the case in the earliest form of the Ambrosian Rite of the Mass.

The chant for the Ingressa corresponds to the Roman Introit, but has neither verse nor Gloria Patri. After the Gloria in excelsis there is threefold Kyrie eleison. Traditionally, on the Sundays of Lent, instead of the Gloria in excelsis, there are special litanies sung by the deacon; all the people answer "precamur te" or "Kyrie eleison" as a response. Since the altar, as a rule, is kept turned toward the people, the celebrant never turns around for the Dominus vobiscum, even when the altar is not actually turned toward the people. The first oration is called "super populum."

The readings follow. In festive and Sunday Masses there are three readings, the first of which is usually taken from the Old Testament and the second from the New Testament Epistles. The Psalmellus follows the singing of the Old Testament, while the Alleluia Verse follows the Epistle. The Sequence has never been accepted in the Ambrosian Rite, as is the case with the Roman Rite. After the Gospel the homily or Tractatus always follows.

The Preparation of Gifts begins with a triple Kyrie eleison and an antiphon "post evangelium," remnants probably of the ancient litany prayer. An invitation by the deacon follows: "Pacem habete," probably a remnant of the ancient practice of giving the kiss of peace before the Offertory. There follows the Oratio super sindonem, sung after the table-cloth (sindon) has been set on the altar. (This corresponds in the Gelasian Sacramentary to the second oration, which was later abolished in the Gregorian Sacramentary.) The ceremony of the laity's offering the bread and wine was always maintained throughout the centuries, although it fell into disuse in the medieval Roman Rite. During this ceremony there takes place the singing of the Offertorium, or offertory chant. The private prayers of the celebrant during the Offertory are found already in the Missals of the eleventh century. While the Credo is not spoken of in the eleventh-century *Expositio missae canonicae,* it is found in all the ancient Missals of the rite. In Milan it is sung after and not before the Offertory prayers, a practice that is still maintained in the 1976 revision. The prayer Super oblata, ends the Offertory; it is recited or sung aloud.

While the Ambrosian Rite still enjoys the ancient variety of Prefaces, each Mass having its proper Preface, the Ambrosian Canon as cited by St. Ambrose (*De sacramentis* 4.5.21–23, 6.26–27) is in substantial agreement with the most ancient Roman Canon found in the Gelasian Sacramentary. Milan, however, never accepted modifications introduced later into the Roman Canon.

Prior to the 1976 revision, the Ambrosian Rite of the Mass had three Eucharistic prayers, the first being a variant of the Roman Canon, and the other two were specific Eucharistic prayers for Holy Thursday and the Easter Vigil. All three ancient Eucharistic prayers have been retained in the 1976 revision, with the addition of Eucharistic Prayers II, III and IV from the Roman Missal (1969).

One unique peculiarity of the Ambrosian Rite is the practice of the celebrant washing his hands (*lavabo*) before the words of consecration without saying anything. It is not known how old this practice is, but in the books of the thirteenth century the Lavabo comes after the celebrant has received the offerings. The 1976 revision maintains the *lavabo* at this unique position, rather than the more ancient practice after the celebrant receives the offering, a practice that has always been part of the Roman Rite and attested to in the *Ordo Romanus Primus.* The Elevations date from the thirteenth century. Immediately after the second Elevation, the celebrant extends his arms straight out while he says the first words of the Unde et memores. The Fraction of the Host has been kept *before* the Lord's Prayer, as it probably was in the Roman Mass before the time of Gregory the Great (d. 604). During it the Confractorium is sung by the choir.

Communion under both species seems to have been preserved for a long time, far longer than the Roman Rite of the Mass. In fact, in eleventh-century manuals the formula for giving Communion to a person baptized in case of sickness is "Corpus Domini nostri Jesu Christi sanguine tinctum. . . ." The Communion chant is called the *Transitorium.* After the Postcommunion Prayer we find another triple Kyrie, probably the remnant of an early Byzantine-style postcommunion litany. Unlike the Roman Rite, the ancient dismissal of the Ambrosian Rite of the Mass is "Procedamus cum pace" (Let us go [proceed] in peace), to which the assembly responds "In nomine Christi" ("In the name of Christ").

Sacraments. The ceremonies of Baptism differ from those of the Roman rite only in their order and the practice of immersion. The ancient Milanese ritual for Anointing of the Sick was replaced at the time of Charles Borromeo by the Roman ritual. The differences in administration of the other Sacraments are very slight.

Liturgical year. The Ambrosian Rite has never observed a fast on Saturdays, not even during Lent. The arrangement of the Gospel pericopes seems to be a pre-Gregorian type and is common to Milan, Benevento, and Spain. Advent has six Sundays beginning with the First Sunday after the feast of St. Martin (November 11); the Sixth Sunday is the great feast of Mary, which antedates the determination of March 25 as the feast of the Annunciation. The Milanese custom of blessing homes at Christmas rather than at Easter was already practiced in the eleventh century.

Traditionally, no saints' feasts are permitted during Lent. Ancient Ambrosian liturgical usage dictated that the Fridays of Lent were always aliturgical: neither Mass nor reception of Communion was allowed. On Holy Saturday a text of the Exsultet is used, which if not actually written by St. Ambrose, is certainly older than the Roman text. At the very beginning of the Holy Saturday Mass the celebrant announces the Resurrection by singing three times: "Christus Dominus resurrexit"; the people respond thrice with "Deo gratias."

Liturgical vestments. The deacon's stole is always worn outside the dalmatic as in Spain and Gaul before the Carolingian reform. Red is the color used for vestments during Holy Week and for Eucharistic functions.

Bibliography: A. PAREDI, "Messali antichi ambrosiani," *Ambrosius* 35 (1959) 1–25. P. BORELLA, *Il rito Ambrosiano* (Brescia 1964). P. BORELLA, "L'evoluzione dei riti sacramentali nell' antica liturgica ambrosiana," *Liturgie* (München 1963) 48–59. O. HEIMING, "Kleinere Beiträge zur Geschichte der ambrosianischen Liturgie," *Archiv für Liturgiewissenschaft* 12 (1970) 130–147 (Pt. I); 13 (1971) 133–140 (Pt II). E. CATTANEO, "Tradizione e il rito ambrosiani nell'ambiente lombardo-medioevale," *Ambrosius Episcopus,* 2 (Milan 1976) 5–47. A. M. TRIACCA, "Liturgie ambrosienne: amalgame hétérogène ou 'specificum' influent," in *Liturgie de l'église particulière et liturgie de l'église universelle* (Rome 1976) 289–327. A. M. TRIACCA, "Mater omnium viventium: contributo metodologico ad una ecclesiologia liturgica dal nuovo Messale Ambrosiano," in *In ecclesia* (Rome 1977) 353–383. A. M. TRIACCA, "La 'méthexis' dans l'ancienne liturgie ambrosienne: contribution des sources eucologiques ambrosiennes," in *L'assemblée liturgique et les différents rôles dans l'assemblée* (Rome 1977) 269–305. A. M. TRIACCA, "L'eucologie ambrosienne dans la structure du nouveau Missel de la 'Sancta Ecclesia Mediolanensis,'" in *Gestes et paroles dans les diverses familles liturgiques* (Rome 1978) 301–328; "'Ecclesia Mater omnium vivetium': liturgie ambrosienne et ecclésiologie universelle," in *L'église dans la liturgie* (Rome 1980) 295–323; "La structure trinitaire des 'Preces Eucharisticae' dans la liturgie ambrosienne (hier et aujourd'hui)," in *Trinité et liturgie* (Rome 1984) 301–384; "Le 'sanctoral' de la liturgie ambrosienne: des données à théologie liturgique," in *Saints et sainteté dans la liturgie* (Rome 1987) 325–356; "Teologia dell'anno liturgico nelle liturgie occidentali antiche non romane," in *L'anno liturgico* (Genoa 1988) 307–363. V. A. LENTI, "Liturgical Reform and the Ambrosian and Mozarabic Rites," *Worship* 68 (1994) 417–426; "The Revised Ambrosian Divine Office," *Studia Liturgica* 29 (1999) 116–126. A. WARD, "Holy Week in the Ambrosian Liturgy," in *Hebdomadae sanctae celebratio* (Rome 1997) 187–235.

[A. PAREDI/EDS.]

AMBROSIANS

A term applied to various religious congregations under the protection of St. AMBROSE, Bishop of Milan (374–397), especially to two groups of women and three groups of men, although neither Augustine nor Ambrose's biographer, Paulinus, says that Ambrose himself founded a religious order. His *Treatises on Virginity* are exhortations to purity of life and personal sanctity, but not a rule for a religious community.

1. The first known "Ambrosians," the *Oblationaries of St. Ambrose,* appeared in the 9th century in Milan as a group of ten poor men and ten poor women at the Scuola dei Vecchioni in Milan who were entrusted, on feast days, with bringing the people's oblation of bread and wine to the altar at the offertory of an AMBROSIAN RITE Eucharist.

2. In the 14th century, three Milanese noblemen, Alexander Crivelli, Anthony Pietrasancta, and Alber Besozzi, sought retreat and solitude in a wooded glen outside the city walls. Clothed in a chestnut-colored habit of tunic, scapular, and cowl, they practiced works of charity and preached to the people. They were joined by others, and in 1375 Gregory XI, before his return from Avignon, gave the growing community of priests and solitaries the Rule of St. AUGUSTINE, the Ambrosian Rite, and a special constitution under the title of *Fratres Sancti Ambrosii ad Nemas.* Similar groups began to dot the countryside but the only bond of unity was community custom. In 1441, Eugene IV merged all members into the *Congregatio Sancti Ambrosii ad nemus Mediolanensis,* designating the original monastery as the motherhouse. Laxity of discipline led to a reform by St. Charles BORROMEO in 1579. Sixtus V in 1589 added to the congregation the monasteries of the Brothers of St. Barnabas, which had been founded by John Scarpa, and included the name of St. Barnabas in the title. The congregation was dissolved by Innocent X in 1646.

3. In 1408, the *Annunciatae of Lombardy,* or Nuns of St. Ambrose, were founded by Dorothea Morosini, Eleanore Contarini, and Veronica Duodi at Pavia. Daughterhouses spread throughout Lombardy and Venetia. Guided by the Rule of St. Augustine, the nuns lived a cloistered life of prayer and poverty under the jurisdiction of the local bishop. Nicholas V and Pius V approved their constitutions. They were suppressed by Napoleon.

4. Another congregation of Ambrosian sisters was founded by Catherine Morigia in 1474 at Mt. Varese in Lombardy, as a branch of the Ambrosian *Fratres.* These sisters, dedicated to a life of prayer and penance, wore a chestnut-colored habit, followed the strict rule of St. Augustine, lived in cloister, and used the Ambrosian liturgy. In 1474 they were given canonical status by Sixtus IV under the title *Nuns of St. Ambrose.* A rapid decline in the 17th century led Innocent X to abolish them, also in 1646.

5. In implementing the decrees of the Council of Trent in his Diocese of Milan, Charles Borromeo, the "second Ambrose," organized a society of priests under the patronage of Our Lady and St. Ambrose, called *Oblates of St. Ambrose,* in 1578. He consulted Philip NERI and FELIX OF CANTALICE on the rule for his community, which was approved by Gregory XIII. Living in community and owing obedience to the bishop, they became the bishop's associates in the work of the ministry. In 1810, Napoleon dispersed the congregation but Archbishop Romilli restored it in 1854. The oblate ideal spread to Poitiers in France, to Paderborn in Germany, and, in 1857, to England, under Cardinal Nicholas WISEMAN, where the community became known as the *Oblates of St. Charles.*

[M. A. MULHOLLAND]

AMBROSIASTER

The name coined by ERASMUS to designate the author of a commentary on the Epistles of St. Paul that had traditionally been ascribed to St. Ambrose, but that Erasmus was convinced could not be by him. Most scholars agreed that the commentaries were quite unlike the work of Ambrose, and in 1905 A. Souter proved to general satisfaction that a collection of 127 *Quaestiones Veteris et Novi Testamenti,* commonly attributed to Augustine, was in fact by the same author as the Pauline commentaries. In 1908 Souter produced a critical text of this work (*Corpus scriptorum ecclesiasticorum latinorum* v. 50). It was planned that a similar edition of the Pauline commentaries should be produced by H. Brewer, but Brewer died before the work was far advanced. The Maurists' edition (reproduced in *Patrologia Latina* v. 17) was made from 13 MSS, all of French provenance. In recent years a survey of H. J. Vogels has shown that some 72 MSS exist and that they show that there were three versions of the commentary on Romans produced by the author himself: two versions of what he had to say on 1 and 2 Corinthians and a single version of the commentary on the other Epistles, except Hebrews, for which the commentary has been supplied by Alcuin. In the *Quaestiones* Souter indicated that the same procedure was followed. There was a first edition of 150 *quaestiones* by the author himself; then a definitive 127 *quaestiones;* and finally, though much later, a version in which only 115 are found. Souter considered that the author worked on Romans and on 1 and 2 Corinthians and finally made the first edition of his *Quaestiones.* He then turned to the rest of Paul and brought out the second edition of the *Quaestiones,* and all this between 370 and 384. The silence of St. JEROME about such an important work on the Epistles is hard to explain and has been put down to jealousy. Augustine did cite the work (*contra duas epp. Pelagii* 4.4.7; *Corpus scriptorum ecclesiasticorum latinorum* 60:528) but ascribed it to HILARY OF POITIERS. The Irish knew it as Hilary's, for the *Codex Ardmachanus* has *Incipit prologus Hilari in Apostolum* as a heading, and the library at Bobbio had a copy of *Hilarii in ep. ad Romanos.* Guesses have been made as to the identity of the author, but without achieving any firm result. He was versed in Roman law, betrayed an interest in things Jewish (but was not of Jewish origin), had lived in Rome, disliked allegorical interpretations of Scripture, wrote astringently in Latin, and had read Irenaeus, Tertullian, Cyprian, Victorinus of Pettau, and Eusebius of Vercelli.

Bibliography: A. SOUTER, *A Study of Ambrosiaster* (Texts and Studies 7.4; Cambridge, Eng. 1905); *The Earliest Latin Commentaries on the Epistles of St. Paul* (Oxford 1927). G. BARDY, *Dictionnaire de la Bible*, suppl. ed., L. PIROT et. al., (Paris 1928) 1:225–241. H. J. VOGELS, "Die Überlieferung des Ambrosiasterkommentars zu den Paulinischen Briefen," *Nachrichten der Akademie der Wissenschaften in Göttingen. Philologischhistorische Klasse* 1.7 (1959) 107–142; "Ambrosiaster und Hieronymus," *Revue Bénédictine* 66 (1956) 13–19; ed., *Das Corpus Paulinum des Ambrosiaster* (Bonn 1957). D. G. HUNTER, "The Paradise of Patriarchy: Ambrosiaster on Woman as (not) God's Image [Response to Egalitarian Asceticism in Rome]," *Journal of Theological Studies* ns 43 (October 1992): 447–469; "On the Sin of Adam and Eve: A Little-Known Defense of Marriage and Childbearing by Ambrosiaster," *Harvard Theological Review* 82 (July 1989): 283–299. L. A. SPELLER, "New Light on the Photinians: The Evidence of Ambrosiaster," *Journal of Theological Studies* ns 34 (April 1983): 99–113.

[J. H. CREHAN]

AMBROSIUS CATHARINUS (LANCELOT POLITI)

Dominican theologian and bishop; b. Siena, *c.* 1484; d. Naples, Nov. 8, 1553. A doctor of civil and canon law and consistorial lawyer under Leo X, he became a Dominican in 1517 because of Savanarola's preaching. Recognizing the dangers of nascent Lutheranism, he was one of the first (1520, 1521) to write against it. While prior of Siena, he waged a controversy with his superiors in favor of the feast of the Immaculate Conception. This resulted in his removal from office.

In 1532 he went to France where, prior to the Council of Trent, he published several works on problems raised by Protestantism—predestination, justification, purgatory, veneration of the saints, and episcopal residency. Pallavincino declared that Catharinus "was second to none among his contemporaries in contest with heretics." He attended the council from 1545 to 1547 as papal theologian, manifesting his intellectual independence, especially in controversies with his confreres Carranza, D. SOTO and B. Spina. At the petition of the conciliar fathers, Catharinus was appointed bishop of Minori in 1546; he was made archbishop of Conza in 1552.

During the Tridentine period he produced many works concerning the problems that arose during the sessions. His original and extensive writings (50 edited and unedited works), often concerned uncharted areas of theology. Concerning the intention of the minister in conferring the sacraments, he defended the thesis of external intention; on the value of the words *Hoc est corpus meum,* he held that the consecration is effected by the preceding epiclesis, "Quam oblationem . . ." of the Roman Mass. His juridico-moral theory concerning the transmission of original sin found adherents among such theologians as BANEZ, BILLUART, SUAREZ, and the SALMANTICENSES. His works are characterized by an emphasis upon the teaching authority of the Church and a thematic return to the Scriptures and the Fathers.

Bibliography: J. SCHWEIZER, *Ambrosius Catharinus Politus* (Münster 1909).

[J. R. COONEY]

AMBRY (ARMARIUM)

A niche, usually in the wall, with or without a door, for storing or showing books, clothes, food, jewelry, money, precious objects, small statues, vessels, etc. This function was known from antiquity. In Christian usage, the ambry served for the reservation of altar bread and wine, sacred vessels, liturgical books, HOLY OILS, RELICS, and the Eucharist. From the 4th century, sacred objects were kept in church (preferably in the sanctuary or high up in a nearby pillar) or SACRISTY. At least from the early 6th century, ambries were made in the stems of ALTARS. After the decree *Sane* of INNOCENT III, the doors of Eucharistic ambries had locks and keys. As devotion to the Holy Eucharist grew, ambries were placed in more prominent places in church and often had barred windows. The TABERNACLE for reservation upon the altar (9th century) superseded the ambry from the 16th century onward. Documentary and archeological evidence of many varieties of ambry abounds all over the West from the 12th century.

Bibliography: C. DU CANGE, *Glossarium ad scriptores mediae et infimae latinitatis,* ed. L. FAVRE, 10 v. (Niort 1883–88) 1:701–702; 3:372. L. KÖSTER, *De custodia sanctissimae Eucharistiae* (Rome 1940). E. MAFFEI, *La Réservation eucharistique jusqu' à la Renaissance* (Brussels 1942). G. DIX, *A Detection of Aumbries* (4th ed. London 1955). S. J. P. VAN DIJK and J. H. WALKER, *The Myth of the Aumbry: Notes on Medieval Reservation Practice and Eucharistic Devotion* (London 1957) 15–66.

[S. J. P. VAN DIJK]

AMELRY, FRANCIS

Carmelite spiritual writer and mystic; b. *c.* 1498; d. *c.* 1552. Not much is known of his life except that he held a bachelor's degree in theology and was prior at the Carmel at Ieper. The Index of 1558 mentions a mystery play of his, and he is known to have written about ten spiritual works in which love and its mystical experience is the dominant theme. Two of his tracts, *Wat de Liefde Gods can bedrgven* (What the Love of God Can Do) and *Een Dialogus of Tsame sprekinghe der ziele* or *De minnende ziel* (The Loving Soul), have been transposed from Old Dutch into modern Dutch and are published in the series "Bloemen von One Geestelijk Erf." The first tract is a handbook of the spiritual life. The second work, his masterpiece, has been translated into Latin by Antonius von Hemert (1552) and into other languages. It is a systematic and logical presentation of the stages of love, in seven steps, which describe love's progressively enveloping nature. Although based on sound theology, his mystical doctrine was much influenced by personal experience and is expressed in a mystical, ardent, forceful, analogous style.

Bibliography: A. AMPE, *Franciscus Amelry, de edele zanger der liefdle* (Antwerp 1951). C. JANSSEN, *Carmelklius en Carmelwereld* (Bussum 1955) 111–112. *De katholieke encyclopaedie,* ed. P. VAN DER MEER et al., 25 v. (Amsterdam 1949–55) 2:187.

[B. CAVANAUGH]

AMEN

A Hebrew word from a root (*'mn*) meaning "to be trustworthy," used to signify "surely," "so it is," "so may it be," "I ratify." (*See* FAITH.) In the Old Testament, the term has several significations. In Nm 5.22 it is used to signify assent to an administered oath, the one using the term thereby agreeing to accept the consequences of a curse or punishment in the event the crime be committed. In Dt 27.15–26 the word is used to indicate ratification of each of 12 curses for 12 specified possible crimes. It is similarly used in Neh 5.13 and Jer 11.5. In 2 Kgs 1.36, Tb 9.12, and Jer 28.6, it is used to signify agreement with a blessing. In synagogue practice, Amen was used by the people to ratify a prayer or doxology pronounced by the rabbi or leader [Neh 8.6; Ps 105(106).48]; often in such usage it was doubled [Ps 40(41).14; 71(72).19; 88(89).53].

In the New Testament, Christ's statements are often introduced with Amen, thereby guaranteeing their absolute certitude and divine authority. Such meaning was unknown in previous usage of the word. In the Gospel of St. John, such statements are introduced by a double Amen (Jn 1.51; 13.16, etc.), the other evangelists retaining single use of the term. The word was pronounced in apostolic liturgical assemblies to ratify the priestly eucharistic prayer (1 Cor 14.16), even by Greek-speaking Christians. Frequent passages in the Epistles indicate the use of the word to conclude private petitions and doxologies, as well as liturgical ones (Rom 1.25; 9.5; 1 Tm 1.17; Heb 13.21; 1 Pt 4.11; 5.11; 5.14; Jdt 1.25; Phil 1.25; 2 Pt 3.18; 1 Thes 5.28; 2 Thes 3.18; etc.). According to St. Paul, through Christ "also rises the 'Amen' to God unto our glory" (2 Cor 1.20), since all the divine promises find their fulfillment and ratification in the Word Incarnate. The Book of the Revelation states that those in glory, when hearing the heavenly doxologies before the throne of God, will respond with Amen (Rv 5.14).

Liturgical usage. The use of "Amen" as an acclamation of assent to prayers and doxologies in liturgical worship dates back to the apostolic period. In 2 Cor 1:20, Paul asserted that "we utter Amen through Christ to the glory of God." It appeared that early Christians adopted the Jewish practice of assenting to prayer by the invocation "Amen." In his description of the eucharistic prayer in First Apology, Justin Martyr noted that the presider prayed the eucharistic prayer to the best of his ability, and the assembly assented to his prayer with a resounding Amen. Over time, this practice developed into the Great Amen which concludes the eucharistic prayer in the East and West.

Bibliography: L. GILLET, *Ephemerides theologicae Lovanienses* 56 (Bruges 1944–45) 134–136. K. BERGER, "Zur Geschichte der

Einleitungsformel 'Amen, ich sage euch''' *Zeitschrift für die Neu-testamentliche Wissenschaft und die Kunde der Älteren Kirche* 63:1–2 (1972) 45–75. J. M. ROSS, "Amen," *Expository Times* 102 (1991) 166–171. K. SEYBOLD, "Zur Vorgeschichte der liturgischen Formel 'Amen'" *Theologische Zeitschrift* 48 (1992) 109–117.

[M. R. E. MASTERMAN/EDS.]

AMERBACH, VEIT

Humanist and Lutheran convert to Catholicism; b. Wembding, 1503; d. Ingolstadt, Sept. 13, 1557. Amerbach (known also as Trolman) studied at Ingolstadt, Freiburg, and Wittenberg, taught in the Latin school at Eisleben, and was made professor on the arts faculty in Wittenberg in 1530. He became disaffected with his colleagues, concluded that the patristic writings did not support Luther's doctrine of justification by faith, and was moved by Johann Eck's arguments for the primacy of the pope. In November of 1543 he left Wittenberg and embraced Catholicism. He taught briefly in the Latin school in Eichstätt, and then became a professor of philosophy and rhetoric at Ingolstadt. He published commentaries on Cicero, Ovid, Chrysostom, and other writers of classical and Christian antiquity.

Bibliography: L. FISCHER, *Veit Trolmann von Wemding, genannt Vitus Amerpachius, als Professor in Wittenberg* (Freiburg 1926). T. FREUDENBERGER, *Lexikon für Theologie und Kirche*[2], ed. J. HOFER and K. RAHNER, 10 v. (2d, new ed. Freiburg 1957–65) 1:433–434. M. SIMON, *Die Religion in Geschichte und Gegenwart*[3], 7 v. (3d ed. Tübingen 1957–65) 1:310.

[L. W. SPITZ]

AMERICAN ACADEMY OF RELIGION

The American Academy of Religion (AAR) is the major learned society and professional association of research scholars and teachers in the field of religious studies. The Academy serves over 7,500 members, the great majority of whom teach in some 1,500 college and university departments and schools in North America. Its mission is to promote excellence in scholarship and teaching in the field by fostering reflection upon and understanding of religious traditions, issues, questions, and values. Within a context of free inquiry and critical examination, the Academy welcomes all disciplined reflection on religion—from both within and outside of communities of belief and practice—and seeks to enhance its broad public understanding. It is inclusive of the whole range of methodologies and theories used to study religion. The Academy does not endorse or reject any religious tradition or set of religious beliefs or practices. Its commitment is, rather, to the highest standards of scholarship.

The AAR's history is one of development from a small group of biblical scholars to its current status as the largest, most comprehensive association dedicated to promoting the academic study of religion. In 1909 four professors of biblical studies formed the Association of Biblical Instructors in American Colleges and Secondary Schools. Intended as a sister organization to the already-established Society of Biblical Literature, its purpose was to promote excellence in teaching. The group continued to meet under the original name until 1922, when members voted to change the name to the National Association of Biblical Instructors (NABI or "prophet" in Hebrew). Dramatic expansion of the study of religion in the post-World War II period led to NABI's transformation into the American Academy of Religion in 1964 and to the AAR's rapid growth during the succeeding decades.

Activities. The AAR fosters knowledge of religion and religious institutions in all their forms and manifestations through a wide variety of programs and membership services. Among these are an annual scholarly conference, a major publishing program, research grants and book awards, professional services, teaching workshops, and annual regional meetings. The annual conference, held jointly with the Society of Biblical Literature (SBL), attracts scholars from all over the world. *The Journal of the American Academy of Religion* publishes current scholarships across the spectrum of the field. Through the *Spotlight on Teaching* periodical and an ongoing series of teaching workshops, the AAR provides its members with opportunities to learn more about recent pedagogical innovations and to improve their teaching craft. To inform members about current issues of interest to religionists, AAR and SBL jointly publish *Religious Studies News* quarterly. The two societies also offer a comprehensive Employment Information Services program that helps coordinate the efforts of position-seekers and employers. The Association of Department Chairs offers a range of services at the departmental and institutional levels.

A member of both the American Council of Learned Societies and the National Humanities Alliance, the Academy works to improve support for all the humanities and to foster the role of religious studies as an integral part of the humanities. The Academy's executive offices are located in Atlanta.

[B. DECONCINI/EDS.]

AMERICAN BOARD OF CATHOLIC MISSIONS

The ABCM traces its origins back to 1919, when 17 directors of Catholic home and foreign missionary societies met at the University of Notre Dame, Ind., to discuss feasible ways of cooperating in the solicitation of contributions. They recommended a plan of organization to the bishops of the U.S., who at their annual meeting the same year appointed a committee to coordinate and stimulate the missionary endeavors of the whole country. This committee, under the chairmanship of Henry Moeller, archbishop of Cincinnati, Ohio, assumed the title of American Board of Catholic Missions.

Although the board, with the assistance of an advisory council of priests representing various missionary bodies, intended to aid and promote Catholic missions in every part of the world, it had to alter its program and to confine its support to the home missions after the Holy See (1922) reorganized the Pontifical Society for the PROPAGATION OF THE FAITH, which was thenceforth in the U.S. and elsewhere to operate independently under its own director for the benefit of the foreign missions.

After negotiations with the Holy See, a new plan of organization, drawn up under the leadership of Francis C. Kelley, Bishop of Oklahoma, was adopted by the American hierarchy at their annual meeting of 1924 and was approved by Pius XI on November 7 of the same year. At their next annual meeting the bishops elected a new board of six members; the first meeting was held in Washington, D.C., on Sept. 15, 1925, and Cardinal George Mundelein, archbishop of Chicago, Ill., was chosen as president, Bishop Kelley as secretary, and John Francis Noll, bishop of Fort Wayne, Ind., as treasurer; headquarters were located permanently in Chicago.

In 1946 it was resolved that the archbishop of Chicago should be *ipso facto* the president of the ABCM; at the same time William D. O'Brien, auxiliary bishop of Chicago and president of the Catholic Church Extension Society, was appointed permanent secretary, and Bishop Noll was appointed permanent treasurer; they both held these offices until their deaths in 1962 and 1956 respectively. In 1965 there were nine nonpermanent members, elected for five-year terms by the bishops of the U.S. at their annual meetings. The board meets regularly once a year, usually in November; it issues a printed financial report to the bishops of the United States.

The ABCM serves principally as a center for the collection and distribution of funds for the "missions in the territory and for the inhabitants of the United States and of its possessions which do not receive aid from the Society for the Propagation of the Faith." As its main source of income it receives 40 percent of the dues paid for membership in the Society for the Propagation of the Faith and of the collection taken up in all the parishes once a year on Mission Sunday. In distributing the money the board correlates its allotments with those of the Extension Society and other Catholic national institutes and agencies.

The board gives two sorts of grants, namely, ordinary grants to bishops who have requested subventions for the missions in their dioceses and extraordinary grants for work among the Spanish-speaking Catholics in the Southwest and among the African American Catholics in the South. Moreover, even after the Philippines became independent, the board continued to send subsidies to the Church in that country until 1964. In that same year it was also decided that bishops who have priests or laymen working in Latin America may be given some financial aid upon application.

In 1972, the ABCM was reconstituted as a standing committee of the National Conference of Catholic Bishops (NCCB). Subsequently, it was renamed the Bishops' Committee on the Home Missions.

[R. TRISCO/EDS.]

AMERICAN CATHOLIC HISTORICAL ASSOCIATION

The American Catholic Historical Association was founded by a small group of historians assembled under the leadership of Peter Guilday in Cleveland, Ohio, in December 1919. At that time there were diocesan historical societies in New York, Philadelphia, St. Louis, and St. Paul and a state society in Illinois, all interested mainly in local history and composed mostly of amateurs, but a national society of professional historians devoted to the history of the universal Church and qualified to interact with their peers in secular and Protestant history had been lacking. The founders were advised and encouraged by J. Franklin Jameson, a former president of the American Historical Association, with which the new organization became affiliated. The association, incorporated under the laws of the District of Columbia and recognized by the United States Conference of Catholic Bishops, has its headquarters at the Catholic University of America in Washington, D.C.

From its inception the association has pursued two main objectives. One is to promote a deeper and more widespread knowledge of the history of the Catholic Church broadly considered, that is, its internal reality and its relations with civil governments, the influence of its members, individually and collectively, on the intellectual, cultural, political, and social progress of the human race. The other aim is the advancement of historical scholarship in all fields among its members. Membership is open to professional church historians, Catholics and non-Catholics in the United States and in other countries, especially Canada, as well as nonprofessional supporters and students.

The association adopted as its official organ the *Catholic Historical Review,* published quarterly since April 1915 by the Catholic University of America Press. The annual presidential address, the reports of the secretary and treasurer and of the several committees, and current information about the association are published in the *Review.* The association launched the editing of the papers of Archbishop John Carroll, which were published in three volumes for the Bicentennial of American Independence in 1976.

The association holds an annual meeting jointly with the American Historical Association and other affiliated societies, notably the American Society of Church History. Since 1972 the association has held a two-day meeting each spring.

The association annually awards two book prizes, namely, (1) the John Gilmary Shea Prize, established in 1944 to commemorate the association's 25th anniversary and first conferred in 1946, which recognizes the author, American or Canadian, whose book, published within the preceding 12-month period, is judged by a committee of scholars to be the most distinguished contribution to the history of the Catholic Church among the books entered in the competition, and (2) the Howard R. Marraro Prize, funded by a bequest of Professor Marraro of Columbia University, who died in 1972; it is given to an author whose book is considered by a separate committee to be the best of the works published during the preceding year in the field of Italian history or Italo-American history or relations. In years when it is merited, the Peter Guilday Prize is awarded to the writer of an article that has been accepted for publication in the *Review* and is deemed by the editors to be the most outstanding of the articles submitted in any given year by writers who have not previously published any scholarly work. In 1995 the association initiated the John Tracy Ellis Memorial Fund, which each year grants to a doctoral student an award for dissertation research.

The association is the recognized Catholic voice in the historical profession in the United States. It is one of the three constitutive societies of the American National Commission of the International Commission of Comparative Church History.

[R. TRISCO]

AMERICAN COUNCIL OF CHRISTIAN CHURCHES

Founded by the Rev. Carl McIntire, Sept. 17, 1941, the American Council of Christian Churches (ACCC) is an organization of Bible fundamentalist Christian churches, associations and individuals, organized on the basis of a commonly accepted statement of inerrant Biblical truths and on the need to unite against what they consider the errors of other churches and groups of churches. Its constituent members include the Bible Presbyterian Churches (BPC), Evangelical Methodist Churches (EMC), Fellowship of Fundamental Bible Churches (FFBC), Fellowship of Independent Methodists, Fundamental Methodists, General Association of Regular Baptist Churches (GARBC), Independent Churches Affiliated, Independent Fundamental Bible Churches, Tioga River Christian Conference, Ukrainian Evangelical Baptist Conference, and the World Baptist Fellowship.

Noted for its strong anti-ecumenical and anti-charismatic stance, a major preoccupation of the ACCC is opposition to the NATIONAL COUNCIL OF CHURCHES OF CHRIST IN THE U.S.A., the WORLD COUNCILS OF CHURCHES, the NATIONAL ASSOCIATION OF EVANGELICALS, the World Evangelical Fellowship, and all charismatic and ecumenical movements. The ACCC accuses these organizations of compromising the ideals of biblical fundamentalism and of propagating theological falsehoods and errors. Although similar to the NAE on theological and doctrinal principles, the ACCC takes a hard line stance against any collaboration or cooperation with organizations which disagree with its views, including the NAE itself.

[R. MATZERATH/EDS.]

AMERICAN FEDERATION OF CATHOLIC SOCIETIES

Catholic societies existed in the U.S. as early as the 1830s, but the notion of a federation of these societies developed only after Pius IX commended the work of the Belgian Catholic Union in 1871. Influenced by the pope's recommendation that unions be formed throughout the world, Richard Clarke, a New York lawyer, drafted a constitution for local unions, hoping to federate them into a national union. Although this hope was not realized, attempts to unite Catholics continued. In 1889 and 1893 Catholics met at LAY CONGRESSES where the delegates were urged to join Catholic societies. Before the first congress, Martin GRIFFIN, editor of the Irish Catholic Benevolent Union *Journal,* suggested a federation of Catholic societies, and a diocesan federation began in Pittsburgh, Pa., in 1890. For the next 11 years agitation continued for a national federation to muster forces against the "violation of Catholic rights" in education, native missions, employment, and other areas. Finally in 1900 and 1901, organizational meetings were held for this purpose in Philadelphia, Pa.; New York, N.Y.; and at Trenton and Long Branch, N.J.

The result of these efforts was the American Federation of Catholic Societies, a loose union of organizations wherein the members retained their autonomy and identity. It existed until 1920, although the last public meeting took place in 1917. Except for 1905, annual conventions were held; between conventions Anthony Matre, national secretary, handled routine matters, aided by the executive and advisory boards composed of officers and members of the hierarchy. In 1911 the federation formed a social service commission with Bp. Peter MULDOON, of Rockford, Ill., and Rev. Peter DIETZ, of Milwaukee, Wis., as chairman and secretary, respectively. During its 18 active years, the federation tried to mold Catholic public opinion; it informed its members on pertinent topics, both Catholic and secular, and worked to block harmful and aid helpful legislation both locally and nationally. Outstanding Catholic laymen such as James Edward Hagerty, sociologist at Ohio State University; Frederick Kenkel of the Catholic Central Union; and David GOLDSTEIN, converted socialist, were featured by the federation in its *Bulletin*, in its *Weekly Newsletter*, and on its lecture platforms. The federation also conducted a campaign of decency in entertainment and inaugurated an early system of evaluating the morality of motion pictures. To some extent it contributed to the Americanization of immigrant Catholics and provided some early precedents for cooperation between the clergy and laity.

When Catholic action was needed at the beginning of World War I, the federation failed to take the initiative because it was busy reorganizing. However, it did pledge its wholehearted support to the Knights of Columbus and the newly formed National Catholic War Council. When the latter was continued after the war as the NATIONAL CATHOLIC WELFARE CONFERENCE (NCWC), the federation was absorbed into it and eventually disappeared with the formation of the National Councils of Catholic Men and Women, NCCMW.

Bibliography: A. F. GORMAN, *Federation of Catholic Societies, 1870–1920* (Doctoral diss. unpub. U. of Notre Dame 1962).

[A. F. GORMAN]

AMERICAN PROTECTIVE ASSOCIATION

A secret anti-Catholic organization, the American Protective Association (A.P.A.) was active especially in the Midwest between 1893 and 1896. Like the earlier Know-Nothing movement, the A.P.A. relied primarily on political activities to combat the alleged menace of Catholicism in America (*see* KNOW-NOTHINGISM).

The A.P.A. was founded in 1887 in Clinton, Iowa, by Henry F. Bowers. About 70,000 members had been recruited in the upper Mississippi Valley by 1892. The following year a number of factors inspired a great surge in A.P.A. activity and strength. These included the appointment of Abp. Francis Satolli as first permanent papal delegate to the U.S.; the replacement of Bowers by William J. Traynor, a more practical and politically astute leader; and, most important, the Panic of 1893, which A.P.A. propagandists ascribed to papal plots.

These developments occurred at a time when Irish political power was increasing in such cities as Boston and New York and when the prolonged school controversy was aggravating anti-Catholic sentiment. The rapid expansion of parochial schools after the Third Plenary Council in 1884 had induced several states to attempt public regulation of private schools. Compromise solutions, such as the POUGHKEEPSIE PLAN and the FARIBAULT PLAN, only provoked further controversy.

Encouraged by these circumstances the A.P.A. launched a membership drive and by 1896 claimed a total of 2.5 million members. To aid its campaign the society established the *A.P.A. Magazine* and about 70 weekly newspapers, including Traynor's *Patriotic American*, which published a bogus encyclical in which the date was set for American Catholics to slay their fellow citizens in a holy massacre. Propaganda efforts were reinforced by economic pressure against Catholic businessmen and workers.

Political action, however, was the principal A.P.A. concern. Usually endorsing Republican candidates, the A.P.A. influenced elections in 1894 in Ohio, Wisconsin, Indiana, Missouri, and Colorado. In Michigan the society elected a congressman, William S. Linton. Yet, in a year of Republican victories, the strength of the A.P.A. was deceptive. Many of the candidates endorsed by its state and municipal advisory boards ignored the organization after the election. Most of its triumphs were confined to purely municipal offices. Nationally the A.P.A. was denounced by numerous responsible leaders, notably Washington Gladden, a Congregational clergyman. Its appeal was further limited by a legislative program that included little more than opposition to federal grants secured by the Bureau of Catholic Indian Missions and by its objection to Congressional acceptance of the Marquette statue presented by Wisconsin.

The A.P.A. was weakened also by internal strife. A growing nativist faction clashed with the Scotch-Irish and Scandinavian membership. The A.P.A. was then hopelessly wrecked by disagreement over the election of 1896. Traynor refused to endorse William McKinley and attempted, unsuccessfully, to create a third party. McKinley's victory virtually ended the career of the A.P.A., although, again under Bowers's leadership, it remained in existence until 1911.

Bibliography: J. HIGHAM, *Strangers in the Land* (New Brunswick 1955) 62–63, 80–87. C. WITTKE, *We Who Built America* (New York 1940) 498–505. H. J. DESMOND, *The A.P.A. Movement* (Washington 1912). D. L. KINZER, *The American Protective Association: A Study of Anti-Catholicism* (University Microfilms 8097; Ann Arbor 1954; Seattle 1964).

[J. L. MORRISON]

AMERICAN SCHOOLS OF ORIENTAL RESEARCH

A consortium of Catholic, Protestant, Jewish and non-sectarian institutions and individuals, founded 1900 to promote the study and to extend the knowledge of Biblical literature, and of the history, geography, archaeology, and ancient and modern languages and literatures of Palestine, Mesopotamia, and other Near Eastern regions. It fulfills its purpose by undertaking original research, explorations, and excavations in the Near East. These projects may be carried out by the ASOR alone, in cooperation with other institutions, or jointly. The organization also provides opportunities for qualified students to pursue research at its three overseas research centers in Jerusalem (Israel), Amman (Jordan) and Nicosia (Cyprus).

Since its inception in 1900, membership in ASOR has grown to number 140 universities, colleges, seminaries and museums in North American, and some 1,500 individuals by the end of 2000. It disseminates important findings in its journals and publications—the *Bulletin of the American Schools of Oriental Research,* the *Journal of Cuneiform Studies, Near Eastern Archaeology,* the *Annual* and several monograph series. Research by the Jerusalem School has yielded much new knowledge concerning the early history of the alphabet and of Jewish, Islamic and early Christian archaeology. Representatives of the Jerusalem School have been outstanding in the research and exploration connected with the DEAD SEA SCROLLS.

Bibliography: P. J. KING, "American Archaeological Heritage in the Near East," *American Schools of Oriental Research Bulletin* 217 (1975) 55–65. P. J. KING, "Diamond Jubilee, American Schools of Oriental Research," *Catholic Biblical Quarterly* 37 (1975) 370–372. K. J. O'CONNELL, "ASOR Prepares for the Third Millennium," *American Schools of Oriental Research Newsletter* 45 (spr. 1995) 2–5.

[R. G. VINCENT/EDS.]

AMERICAN SOCIETY OF MISSIOLOGY

Founded in 1973, the American Society of Missiology (ASM) is dedicated to providing academic and professional support to scholars in the field of mission studies with membership open to professors, leaders of missionary orders and agencies, and missionaries. Founding members included Roman Catholics, conciliar Protestants, and independent Protestants from Canada and the United States. Parity among the traditions is maintained by electing office holders on a rotating basis from each.

In North America, except for Roman Catholics, the term missiology was rarely used before 1960. European Protestants and Roman Catholics understood missiology to be the scientific study of Christian missions while Anglo-American Protestants emphasized the history and practice of missions. The 1960s were a period of crisis for both Protestants and Roman Catholics. Missionary vocations declined among conciliar Protestants and Roman Catholics. Mission training schools were closed and seminaries discontinued chairs of mission studies. Many mission studies programs were consolidated, e.g., the merger of various Catholic mission studies programs at the Catholic Theological Union in Chicago.

A new thrust emerged among evangelical Protestants symbolized by the founding of Fuller Seminary's School of World Mission (1965) and the School of World Mission and Evangelism of Trinity Evangelical Divinity School (1965). These new schools described their programs as applied missiology, but they also recognized the need to develop academically recognized programs.

The ASM was organized to promote the scholarly study of theological, historical, social and practical questions relating to the missionary dimension of the Christian church in terms of: (1) the relationship of missiology to other scholarly disciplines; (2) promoting fellowship and cooperation among individuals and institutions engaged in activities and studies related to missiology; (3) facilitating mutual assistance and exchange of information among those thus engaged; and (4) encouraging research and publication. The work of the society is conducted through an annual meeting held the third week of June. The Association of Professors of Mission (founded 1952) meets annually in conjunction with ASM. Besides conducting the society's official business, the annual meeting provides opportunity for members to meet for study and fellowship. Since 1988 these sessions have been held at the Society of the Divine Word Techny Towers, Techny, Illinois.

ASM has published *Missiology: An International Review* since 1973, a leading scholarly quarterly in the field of mission studies. Through Norman Thomas, book review editor of *Missiology*, 1985 to 1999, ASM has participated in several bibliography projects, including the international Documentation, Archives and Bibliography (DAB) and a comprehensive annotated bibliography of the 12,500 most important books published in the field of missiology between 1960 and 1990. The latter was published in cooperation with the American Theological Library Association (ATLA) Series. In addition, since 1980, 30 titles have been published in the ASM/Orbis Books series. Several of these works have become standard works in the field of mission studies, including David J. Bosch, *Transforming Mission: Paradigm Shifts in the Theology of Mission* (1991) and Louis Luzbetak, SVD, *The Church and Cultures: New Perspectives in Missiological Anthropology* (1988). In 1997 a dissertation series was started.

Bibliography: W. R. SHENK and G. R. HUNSBERGER, *The American Society of Missiology: The First Quarter Century* (Decatur, Georgia 1998).

[W.R. SHENK]

AMERICANISM

The name given to certain doctrines reprobated by Leo XIII in his apostolic letter *Testem benevolentiae* of Jan. 22, 1899. The pope carefully excluded from condemnation the legitimate use of the word to signify ''the characteristic qualities which reflect honor on the people of America.'' As indicated in the papal letter, the censured doctrines had been discussed in France as a result of the French translation and adaptation of *The Life of Isaac Thomas Hecker* by Walter ELLIOTT, CSP. The basic principle of the censurable Americanism was that the Church should modify her doctrines to suit modern civilization, to attract those not of the faith to the Church, passing over some less attractive doctrines and adapting the Church's teachings to popular theories and methods. Leo summarized five specific errors: the rejection of external spiritual direction as no longer necessary; the extolling of natural over supernatural virtues; the preference of active over passive virtues; the rejection of religious vows as not compatible with Christian liberty; and the adoption of a new method of apologetics and approach to non-Catholics.

U.S. Elements. While the immediate controversy that brought about the papal letter existed chiefly in France it also had roots in the U.S. Bishops and priests there were divided between those who advocated greater Catholic participation in American public life, particularly the public movements for social and economic reform, and the more conservative group who thought American life was Protestant and tainted with the liberalism condemned in the SYLLABUS OF ERRORS of Pius IX. In November of 1886 certain German priests led by Father P. M. ABBELEN, of Milwaukee, Wis., presented a petition to the Congregation of the Propagation of the Faith in Rome, protesting the treatment of foreign language groups and members of national parishes in the U.S. Bishops (later Archbishops) John IRELAND, of St. Paul, Minn., and John J. KEANE, then of Richmond, Va., in Rome at the time to prepare for the foundation of The Catholic University of America, Washington, D.C., published a refutation of the Abbelen petition and sent a warning to Cardinal James GIBBONS, of Baltimore, Md. Gibbons called a meeting of the eastern archbishops in Philadelphia, Pa., on December 19, to protest the petition, which was rejected by the Congregation of Propaganda June 8, 1887.

In 1890 and 1891 certain European societies interested in immigrants to the U.S. met in Lucerne, Switzerland, under the chairmanship of Peter Paul CAHENSLY, and petitioned Rome for better representation of foreign nationalities in the American hierarchy. Archbishop Ireland protested publicly. At a meeting of the National Educational Association in St. Paul in 1890, he praised the public schools and expressed regret that there had to be separate Catholic schools. When he inaugurated the FARIBAULT and Stillwater school plans to get state aid, he was accused of being opposed to Catholic parochial schools. After defending himself at the meeting of the archbishops in 1891 at St. Louis, Mo., he went to Rome to clarify his position on the school question.

In these controversies Ireland's chief associates were John J. Keane, since 1889 rector of Catholic University, and Denis O'Connell, rector of the North American College in Rome. The leaders of the conservatives were Abp. Michael A. CORRIGAN, of New York, and Bps. Bernard MCQUAID, of Rochester, Winand WIGGER of Newark, and the German bishops of Wisconsin, especially Abp. Frederick KATZER and Bp. Sebastian MESSMER. Moreover, among the faculty of Catholic University, the chief conservatives were Msgr. Joseph SCHROEDER, Joseph POHLE, and Abbé Georges Périès. Professors supporting Keane were chiefly Thomas BOUQUILLON, Charles P. Grannan, and Edward PACE. Others who supported the conservatives were Thomas PRESTON, vicar-general of New York, and René HOLAIND, SJ. Gibbons, despite his friendship for Ireland, endeavored to keep peace between the two groups. The N.Y. *Freeman's Journal,* the *Northwestern Chronicle* of St. Paul, and the *Western Watchman* of St. Louis supported Ireland. The *Review* of Chicago and later of St. Louis, edited by Arthur PREUSS; *Church Progress,* edited by Condé PALLEN of St. Louis; and most of the German Catholic papers opposed Ireland's policies.

European Influence. In France, Ireland and Gibbons were admired by the more progressive Catholics, especially those who had accepted the urging of Leo XIII for a reconciliation between the Church and the French Republic, called the RALLIEMENT. When they invited him to speak in Paris in the spring of 1892, Ireland praised the democracy and civic activities of the American priests and gave them credit for the remarkable progress of the Church in the U.S. After he left France a young lecturer in the Institut Catholique, Abbé Félix KLEIN, gathered a selection of Ireland's speeches and translated them into a small volume published in 1894.

Back in the U.S., Ireland welcomed Abp. Francesco Satolli as the papal legate to the World's Fair in Chicago, and heard Satolli support his program for Catholic schools at the archbishops' meeting in New York in November of 1892. Suddenly, on Jan. 14, 1893, Satolli announced the erection of the Apostolic Delegation to the U.S. in Washington, with himself as the delegate. In September of 1893 the delegate appeared in Ireland's company at the Catholic Columbian Congress in Chicago, but refused to take part in the World's Congress of Religions in which Ireland, Keane, Gibbons, and other Catholics participated against the wishes of the conservatives. Two years later, the delegate announced that Rome had forbidden Catholic participation in further congresses of religions. The occasion of this prohibition was the effort of certain French clergymen to promote such a congress at the Paris World's Fair in 1900. In 1895 O'Connell was forced to resign as rector of the North American College, followed in September of 1896 by Keane's enforced resignation from the rectorship of Catholic University. Keane's supporters in the university in turn brought about the resignation of Schroeder, whom they accused of being the chief factor in the rector's removal.

The Catholic Press. During the next two years, the Catholic press carried frequent exchanges between the two groups, with the conservatives making vague charges that their opponents were guilty of the condemned liberalism of the Syllabus, and the progressives insisting that the conservatives were *refractaires,* opposing the policies of Leo XIII. In 1890–91, Father Elliott published in the *Catholic World,* and later in book form, a biography of the founder of the Paulists, Father Isaac HECKER, with an introduction by Archbishop Ireland. Elliott also arranged for a French translation. In 1897 the more progressive Catholics in Paris decided to publish the French translation and asked Klein to shorten it and make it more attractive. He complied, adding an enthusiastic preface in which he praised Hecker as the priest of the future and lauded the American Catholic way of life. The book went quickly into six printings and received wide notice in the religious press.

In addressing the International Scientific Congress in Fribourg, Switzerland, in August of 1897 O'Connell, now rector of Cardinal Gibbon's titular church, Santa Maria in Trastevere, Rome, took as his theme the Americanism in the life of Father Hecker, stressing Hecker's acceptance of American democracy and relations between Church and State. Bp. Charles Turinaz of Nancy, France, demanded permission to answer him. The next fall, beginning November 6, a series of sermons were given in Paris churches by Jesuits who attacked certain dangers to the Church from within, especially "Father Hecker's Americanism." In *La Vérité,* the conservative Catholic newspaper of Paris, under the pen name "Martel," an article appeared March 3, 1897, entitled "L'Americanism Mystique" and was followed by other articles on "Americanism." "Martel" was Abbé Charles Maignen, a priest of the Society of the Brothers of St. Vincent De Paul, a writer who opposed the *ralliement.* Abbé Georges Périès, the former professor of Canon Law at The Catholic University of America, under the name "Saint Clement" occasionally contributed an article to the series, but for the most part the articles were composed by Maignen.

The articles ridiculed the claim of Ireland and Klein that Hecker exemplified the priest of the future, and quoted in derision passages from the biography on Hecker's illnesses and his dismissal from the Redemptorists. Maignen also attacked O'Connell's speech at Fribourg, an article by Keane in the *Catholic World,* some of the articles written to sell the Hecker biography, and the writings of clergymen who had left the Church, such as Abbé Victor Charbonnel. In April other articles in *La Vérité* described "Les Champaignes de L'Américanisme," and how the Americanists were undermining the defense of the Church. The campaigns included the Congress of Religions; the efforts of Charbonnel to hold a second Congress of Religions at the Paris Fair; the activities of Keane in Rome; an article of M. Brunetière praising American Catholicism in *Revue des Deux Mondes;* a newspaper story predicting that Cardinal Gibbons would be the next pope; and an article in the *Contemporary Review* by "Romanus," who Maignen implied was an Americanist.

Maignen found other evidence of the Americanists' doctrines in Keane's addresses at the Congress of Religions and his defense of that congress at the Brussels International Catholic Congress of 1894. Maignen collected these articles, to which he added a few other essays, for a book entitled *Études sur l'Américanisme, Le Père Hecker, est-il un Saint?* When Cardinal Richard of Paris refused his imprimatur to the book, Maignen took it to Rome, where he obtained the imprimatur of the Master of the Sacred Palace, Père Albert Lepidi, OP, which some interpreted as a papal approval of the book. The controversy over the biography and the movement vaguely described as Americanism raged through the French Catholic press and was mentioned in the secular press. The discussion reached into Belgium. Some discussions appeared also in Germany, and then the controversy moved into Italy, where it became confused with the local quarrel over the temporal power of the papacy.

Testem Benevolentiae. Leo XIII opposed the move to put the Hecker biography on the Index and appointed a committee of cardinals to study the question. The committee reported adversely on the doctrines called "Americanism." The pope changed the report in its opening and closing passages so that no one was accused of holding the condemned doctrines, and the ordinary political and social Americanism were exempted from the disapproval. Although Gibbons sent a cable to stop the condemnation and Ireland rushed to Rome, both arrived too late to head off the papal letter, *Testem benevolentiae,* which was dated Jan. 22, 1899. Ireland, Keane, and Klein immediately submitted but denied that they held the condemned doctrines. The Hecker biography was withdrawn from sale. The conservative bishops in the U.S. thanked the pope for saving the American Church from the dangerous doctrines. Gibbons, to whom the pope's letter was addressed, denied in his reply that any educated American Catholic held the condemned doctrines.

Bibliography: T. T. MCAVOY, *The Great Crisis in American Catholic History 1895–1900* (Chicago 1957) with annotated bibliography in "Essay on Sources."

[T. T. MCAVOY]

AMERICANS UNITED FOR SEPARATION OF CHURCH AND STATE

Americans United is an advocacy group working through education, research, litigation, and lobbying to encourage the maintenance of a strict, Jeffersonian interpretation of church-state separation. Originally named Protestants and Other Americans United for Separation of Church and State, Americans United was founded in 1947 in the aftermath of the Supreme Court's Everson decision. That decision, permitting the use of public funds to provide transportation for parochial school students, and the presidential nomination of General Mark Clark as ambassador to the Vatican in 1951 served as symbols of the decline of Protestant hegemony in the United States and galvanized opposition to the growing influence of Catholicism among those who assumed that a stronger Catholic Church would threaten church-state separation.

Americans United was launched with the publication of a manifesto signed by many prominent Protestant churchmen setting forth its objectives: enlightenment of public opinion on religious liberty, prevention of further breaches in the wall of separation between Church and State, opposition to diplomatic relations with the Vatican, repeal of laws granting public funds to parochial schools, invoking the aid of the courts in maintaining the separation of Church and State, opposition to federal aid to parochial schools, and protection of the public schools from sectarian domination. Though its original name suggests a close tie to Protestant churches, Americans United is an independent association that draws its support from a variety of individuals and groups sharing its interest in the church-state issue. Its activities are informed by commitment to a strict interpretation of the establishment and free exercise clauses of the First Amendment to the U.S. Constitution, and its support derives from those who fear the encroachment of government in the affairs of the churches as well as those troubled by the involvement of churches in the affairs of state.

Americans United initially focused on what it perceived to be the Catholic threat to church-state separation. It judged the Catholic Church to be hostile to the concept of church-state separation as enunciated in the First Amendment and was particularly troubled by efforts to secure public funding for parochial schools either directly or through funding for transportation, textbooks, special education, etc. As recently as the 1960 presidential election, Americans United posed "Questions for a Catholic Candidate," compelling John Kennedy to explicate his commitment to church-state separation and the common schools and his opposition "to the federal government's extending support to sustain any church or its schools." At least three events of the 1960s combined to alter the national discourse on church-state issues. First was the election of the nation's first Catholic president and his maintenance of a church-state posture that many Protestants regarded as their own. Another was the Second Vatican Council and its decisive "Declaration on Religious Freedom," which served to assure critics that Catholicism could support a liberal society in which

Church and State were separate. Finally, the Great Society programs of the Lyndon Johnson administration greatly enlarged the sphere of church-state interrelationships in broad areas of social services and higher education and compelled Protestant churches to face problems that had hitherto appeared to be uniquely Catholic.

In the 1990s, the picture was complicated by the emergence on the conservative wing of Protestantism of churches and organizations advocating governmental support for religiously based moral values and sometimes for religious schools. As a result of these fundamental changes, Americans United cannot now, if it ever could, be regarded as the voice of Protestantism. Nor is it now likely to be regarded as simply anti-Catholic, in the light of its strident rhetoric against faith-based initiatives by the State. In continuing its traditional advocacy of strict separation, Americans United has turned its focus to perceived threats to church-state separation from Protestant and governmental sources.

The organization's monthly magazine, *Church and State*, includes articles, reviews, editorials, accounts of state and federal governmental activities, and news of interesting activities and statements relative to the church-state issue. Its head office is in Washington, D.C.

Bibliography: G. L. ARCHER and A. J. MENENDEZ, *The Dream Lives On: The Story of Glenn L. Archer and Americans United* (Washington 1982); *Church and State* (Silver Spring, Md. 1948–). L. P. CREEDON and W. D. FALCON, *United for Separation: An Analysis of POAU Assaults on Catholicism* (Milwaukee, Wis. 1959). R. F. DRINAN, *Religion, the Courts, and Public Policy* (New York 1963). C. S. LOWELL, *The Great Church-State Fraud* (Washington 1973). E. A. SMITH, *Religious Liberty in the United States* (Philadelphia, Pa. 1972). M. S. STEDMAN, JR., *Religion and Politics in America* (New York 1964). R. BOSTON, ''Watchdog on the Wall: The Americans United Story,'' *Church and State* 50 (Nov. 1997) 223–226.

[S. C. PEARSON/EDS.]

AMESHA SPENTA

''The Beneficent Immortals,'' as they are called in the Avesta. According to the teaching of Zoroaster they are the ''archangels'' of Ahura Mazda. From the Indo-Iranian period, the classes and functions of society were threefold, and each had divine patrons. The most important function, sovereignty, had as patrons two principal gods, Varuna, guardian of the True Order, and Mitra (the Contract, the Friend). In Zoroaster's system, Ahura Mazda combines the two aspects of sovereignty. However, this function, like the other functions, continues to be under a hierarchy of archangels in which the True Order, Arta, holds the highest place, above Vohu Manah (Good Mind), which holds the position previously held by

Mitra. The second function, physical force and fighting, had Indra as patron. In Zoroaster's system, Khshathra (Dominion) corresponds to it, while Indra himself persists as a *daēva*. The third function, fecundity, had as patron a variable and multivalent goddess, to whom the archangel Ārmaiti (Devotion) corresponds. The counterparts of the twin patrons, Nāsatya (Healers), are the archangels Haurvatāt and Ameretāt (Health and non-Death). One of the twins survived as a *daēva* named Nāonhaithya. Also there is the god Vāyu (Cosmic Wind), a kind of Janus, ruling over ambiguous beginnings, which in Zoroaster became the initial Choice between Good and Evil, represented by the two Mainyus or Spirits, *Spenta Mainyu* (the Beneficent or Holy Spirit) and Anra Mainyu (the Destructive Spirit).

See Also: DAEVAS; PERSIAN RELIGION, ANCIENT; ZOROASTER (ZARATHUSTRA).

Bibliography: G. DUMÉZIL, *Les Dieux des Indo-Européens* (Brussels 1952); *L'Idéologie tripartie des Indo-Européens* (Brussels 1958). J. DUCHESNE-GUILLEMIN, *La Religion de l'Iran ancien* (Paris 1962).

[J. DUCHESNE-GUILLEMIN]

AMETTE, LÉON ADOLPHE

Cardinal, archbishop of Paris; b. Douville (Eure), Sept. 6, 1850; d. Antony (Seine), Aug. 29, 1920. Born in very modest circumstances, he studied at the seminary of Saint-Sulpice in Paris, was ordained (1873), and became a private secretary to Bishop Grolleau of Evreux (1873) and then vicar-general under a succession of bishops (1889–98). He became bishop of Bayeux (1898); coadjutor to Cardinal RICHARD DE LA VERGNE of Paris (Feb. 21, 1906), whom he succeeded (Jan. 28, 1908); and cardinal (Nov. 27, 1911). In both sees he had to confront the results of the law separating Church and State (1905) but he adopted a peaceful attitude toward the civil power in order to prepare a reconciliation. During World War I he was a promoter of the *Union sacrée* and frequently served as intermediary between the French government and the Holy See. In his archdiocese he erected 16 new parish churches and 29 chapels and gave a great impetus to diocesan works. Amette was very pious, a Dominican tertiary, and a talented orator. He published a number of his pastoral letters and sermons as well as several short tracts on varied religious topics and current problems.

Bibliography: C. CORDONNIER, *Le Cardinal Amette, archevêque de Paris*, 2 v. (Paris 1949). J. RUPP, *Histoire de l'Église de Paris* (Paris 1948) 303–311. H. CHOMON, *Dictionnaire de biographie française* (Paris 1929—) 2:637–640.

[R. LIMOUZIN–LAMOTHE]

AMIAS, JOHN, BL.

Priest, martyr; b. Wakefield, England; hanged, drawn, and quartered at York, March 15, 1589. After the death of his wife (sometimes given as Anne), John Amias, a textile merchant, divided his property among his children and left for the Catholic College at Rheims. There he was ordained in 1581. Thereafter he labored in the English Mission until his arrest in the home of a Mr. Murton in Lancashire. Taken to York, he was tried in company with two other martyrs, Bb. Robert Dalby and Robert DIBDALE. Anthony (Dean) Champney, who was present at their execution, has left an account in his history. Other accounts note that he went to death ''as joyfully as if to a feast.'' He was declared venerable in 1886, and beatified by Pius XI on Dec. 15, 1929.

Feast of the English Martyrs: May 4 (England).

See Also: ENGLAND, SCOTLAND, AND WALES, MARTYRS OF.

Bibliography: R. CHALLONER, *Memoirs of Missionary Priests,* ed. J. H. POLLEN (rev. ed. London 1924; repr. Farnborough 1969). J. H. POLLEN, *Acts of English Martyrs* (London 1891) 331.

[K. I. RABENSTEIN]

AMICE

A rectangular piece of linen used to wrap around the neck and shoulders of the wearer to protect the outer liturgical garments from being soiled by the face and neck. In medieval days, the alb was the first vestment to be put on. The amice was added as a scarf, part of which covered the head, keeping the hair in place until the stole and chasuble were put on and arranged properly. There was no common usage as to when the amice thus worn should be brought back off the head. Some removed it after putting on the chasuble; others kept it on the head until the beginning of the Canon of the Mass. When resting on the shoulders the amice was thought to look untidy. This problem was taken care of by the ornamentation of the upper edge with a band of stiff, rich material, or a narrow strip of embroidery that formed a collar called *Aurifrisium* or apparel. In the wake of the liturgical reforms of Vatican II, the use of the amice is no longer required.

Bibliography: E. A. ROULIN, *Vestments and Vesture,* tr. J. MC-CANN (Westminster, Md. 1950). J. BRAUN, *Die liturgischen Paramente in Gegenwart und Vergangenheit* (2d ed. Freiburg 1924); *Die liturgische Gewandung im Occident und Orient* (Freiburg 1907).

[M. MCCANCE]

AMICO, FRANCESCO

Jesuit theologian; b. Naples, April 5, 1578; d. Graz, Austria, Jan. 31, 1651. He entered the Society of Jesus on Oct. 27, 1596, and after teaching the humanities, philosophy, and theology, he became chancellor of the University of Graz. Adapting his theological treatises to a four years' course of seminary teaching, he wrote his famous *Cursus theologici juxta scholasticam hujus temporis methodum.* The fifth volume of this work (*De iure et iustitia*) contained three propositions censured by the Congregation of the Index, June 18, 1651, and later condemned by Alexander VII and Innocent XI [H. DENZINGER, *Enchiridion symbolorum,* ed. A. SCHÖNMETZER (32d ed. Freiburg 1963) 2037, 2132–33]. A decree of July 6, 1655, permitted the reading of a corrected edition of the work, such as the Antwerp edition of 1650.

Bibliography: C. SOMMERVOGEL et al., *Bibliothèque de la Compagnie de Jésus,* 11 v. (Brussels–Paris 1890–1932) 1:280–282. E. M. RIVIÉRE, *Dictionnaire d'histoire et de géographie ecclésiastiques,* ed. A. BAUDRILLART et al. (Paris 1912—) 2:1234. H. HURTER, *Nomenclator literarius theologiae catholicae,* 5 v. in 6 (3d ed. Innsbruck 1903–13) 3:933–934.

[F. C. LEHNER]

AMIDISM

A form of Mahāyāna Buddhism popular among the laity and especially important in Japan. It was founded by the Pure Land (Ch'ing T'u) or Lotus School in China in the 4th century A.D., if not earlier. Its three basic tenets are contained in three Sanskrit *sūtras* that were translated into Chinese, whence they passed into Japanese. Amida is the Japanese adaptation of the Sanskrit epithets of Buddha: *Amitābha,* ''immeasurable light,'' and *Amitāyus,* ''immeasurable life.'' The idea of the Pure Land is central in the Chinese Lotus School and in the *Jôdo* (Pure Land) doctrine developed in Japan in the 12th and 13th centuries. Salvation is offered to all men who have faith in Amida and invoke his name as ''the Lord of immeasurable light and immeasurable life.'' Through this faith and repeated invocation the humblest layman is assured a rebirth in the Pure Land, the Western paradise. Amidism is the largest Buddhist sect in Japan.

See Also: BUDDHISM.

Bibliography: R. MASUNAGA, ''Amida,'' F. KÖNIG, ed., *Religionswissenschaftliches Wörterbuch* 47–48. J. A. HARDON, *Religions of the World* (Westminster, MD 1963) 124–126. A. LLOYD, *The Creed of Half Japan* (New York 1912). H. DE LUBAC, *Amida* (Paris 1955). F. KIICHI, ''Die Jōdo-Lehre,'' *Christus und die Religionen der Erde,* ed. F. KÖNIG (Vienna 1961) 3:428–432. A. HAUCHECORNE, ''Les Religions du Japon'' in *Histoire des religions,* ed. M. BRILLANT and R. AIGRAIN, v.2 (Paris 1954) 212–215.

[M. R. P. MCGUIRE]

AMIENS

City on both banks of the Somme River in north France; capital of Somme department, which comprises the present diocese, and of Picardy, which comprised the medieval diocese.

The Celtic *Samarobriva* was the capital of the Gallic *Ambiani*, in the Roman province of *Belgica II c.* 400. Its commercial, military, and industrial importance meant an early Christian evangelization, but neither dates nor data can be assigned to the two SS. FIRMIN, traditionally the first apostles of Amiens. The first St. Firmin seems to have been a traveling missionary from Navarre who left traces in Pamplona, Agen, Clermont, ANGERS, BEAUVAIS, and Amiens, where he is supposed to have been martyred *c.* 303; his relics may have been translated to Pamplona (1186) after Philip II Augustus added Amiens to the French realm in 1185. Amiens considers him the founder and first bishop of its church. There is also a tradition of the evangelization of Amiens from Rome, marked by the martyrdoms of SS. Fuscian, Victoricus, and Quentin.

St. MARTIN OF TOURS cut his cape to give half of it to a poor man; the site was marked by a chapel that became the Abbey of Saint-Martin-aux-Jumeaux (1073). No bishops are known between Eulogius (346) and Edibius (511). Until the 11th century Amiens, a prize for Normans (859, 881, 883, 891) and a strong-point in the war between Flanders and Normandy, kept within its Roman walls. Bishop Jesse (799–830, 833–834) was one of Charlemagne's *missi*. The bishop *c.* 1000 shared seigneurial rights with the count, who in the 12th century was his vassal. Episcopal holdings, shared with the chapter, were few outside the city, where the Abbeys of CORBIE (622) and SAINT-RICQUIER (625) held most of the land; in 1301 the bishop disposed of far fewer benefices than did the abbeys. St. Simon, count of Amiens (1072–77), became a monk at St. Claude in the Jura mountains and died in Rome (1082). PETER THE HERMIT, preacher of the First Crusade, was from Amiens. Bishop St. Godefroy (1104–15) supported church reform. When the cathedral was built (1220–69), Amiens was a town rich from the cloth trade.

Picardy was a center of Calvinism, combated by Bp. Geoffroy de la Marthonie (1577–1601). A seminary was founded in 1655. After the revocation of the Edict of Nantes (1685), many of the Huguenots fled to London and Edinburgh. Jansenism was opposed by Bps. François Faure (1653–87), Pierre Sabatier (1706–34), and François Gabriel d'Orléans de la Motte (1734–74). Only two clerics were executed during the French Revolution, when Amiens was a Constitutional see under ROUEN. The CONCORDAT OF 1801 made Amiens, united with Beauvais and Noyon, suffragan to PARIS. In 1822 it became suffra-

gan to Reims again. The major seminary was reorganized in 1805, the minor in 1828. Most of the 12 bishops of the 19th century were in transit to other sees. Pastoral problems differ in the many agricultural villages and in industrial centers.

The beautiful Gothic cathedral ranks with Reims and Chartres; built by the architect Robert de Luzarches, it has five monumental portals (three on the west façade and two at ends of the transept) and two towers 215 feet high. Its treasure includes a replica of a relic of the head of St. John the Baptist brought from Constantinople (1206). Former abbeys include the Benedictine Saint-Valery (613), Saint-Sauve in Montreuil (7th century), Saint-Josse-sur-Mer (793), Forestmontier (10th century), Saint-Fuscien (1105), and Saint-Vast in Moreuil (1109) for men; and Sainte-Austreberte in Montreuil (7th century), Bertaucourt (1095), and Saint-Michel in Doullens (12th century) for women; the Cistercian Le Gard, Cercamp, Valloire (all 1137), and Lieu-Dieu (1191) for men; and Villancourt (12th century), Épagne (1178), and the Paraclet (1219) for women; the Augustinian Saint-Acheul (1085) and Clerfay (1136) for men; and the Premonstratensian Saint-Jean (1115), Dommartin (1120), Séry (1127), Selincourt (1131), and Saint-André-au-Bois (12th century).

Bibliography: H. MACQUERON, *Bibliographie du département de la Somme*, 2 v. (Amiens 1904–07). A. DE CALONNE, *Histoire de la ville d'Amiens*, 3 v. (Amiens 1899–1906). H. PELLETIER, *Histoire religieuse de la Picardie* (Abbeville 1961). F. I. DARSY, *Bénéfices de l'église d'Amiens*, 2 v. (Amiens 1869–71). G. DURAND, *Monographie de l'église Notre-Dame, cathédral d'Amiens*, 3 v. (Amiens 1901–03). *Cartulaire du chapitre de la cathédral d'Amiens*, 2 v. (Amiens 1905–12). F. VERCAUTEREN, *Étude sur les civitates de la Belgique seconde* (Brussels 1934). H. P. EYDOUX, *Réalités et énigmes de l'archéologie* (2d ed. Paris 1964). M. GODET, *Dictionnaire d'histoire et de géographie ecclésiastiques*, ed. A. BAUDRILLART et al. (Paris 1912–) 2:1254–72. E. JARRY, *Catholicisme* 1:466–469. G. BARDY, *ibid.* 4:1318–19. *Annuario Pontificio* (1965) 29.

[J. ESTIENNE]

AMIOT, JEAN JOSEPH MARIE

Missionary to China; b. Toulon, Feb. 8, 1718; d. Peking, Oct. 8, 1793. He entered the Jesuits in 1737 and spent 42 years as a priest in China. He was a prolific writer on Chinese and Tartar art and history. As an astronomer and mathematician he served at the court of the Emperor Ch'ien Lung. His Paris correspondent, Bertin, published many of his writings in *Memoires concernant l'histoire des Chinois, par les missionaires de Pekin* (16 v. 1776–1814), of which volume 12 is his study of Confucius, based on the best Chinese accounts of the philosopher. Amiot translated a history of Chinese music and

Amish farmers, 1986, Lancaster County Pennsylvania. (AP/Wide World Photos)

compiled a Manchu–French dictionary. The Manchu grammar attributed to him is a translation and abridgement of a Latin work, probably by F. Verbiest.

Bibliography: H. CORDIER, *La Grande encyclopédie,* 2:758–759. E. M. RIVIÈRE, *Dictionnaire d'histoire et de géographie ecclésiastiques,* ed. A. BAUDRILLART et al. (Paris 1912—) 2:1275–77. H. CHOMON, *Dictionnaire de biographie française* (Paris 1929—) 2:674–677. *Enciclopedia de la Religión Católica,* 7 v. (Barcelona 1951–56) 1:567. J. A. OTTO, *Lexikon für Theologie und Kirche*[2], ed. J. HOFER and K. RAHNER, 10 v. (2d, new ed. Freiburg 1957–65) 1:439.

[B. LAHIFF]

AMISH CHURCHES

Amish churches are a reform group founded under the leadership of a Swiss Mennonite bishop, Jacob Amman, who withdrew from the Mennonite fellowship in 1693, accusing his fellow MENNONITES of laxity in doctrine and practice. In particular he advocated the strict enforcement of "shunning" excommunicated persons. Following this practice, the Amish avoid all social interaction with such persons, even if they are members of their own family.

Amish immigrants began arriving in America in 1720. They settled in Pennsylvania and later in Indiana, Ohio, Illinois, Nebraska, and Canada. They were popularly known as the "hooks and eyes" Mennonites because they oppose the use of buttons. The Old Order Amish refuse to use such inventions as electricity, telephones, radio and television, and automobiles. They wear plain black clothing, drive horse-drawn buggies, insist on marriage within the sect, oppose participation in war, and try to educate their children in their own schools up to the eighth grade. The men cut their hair in a bob and let their beards grow; the women wear capes and bonnets. Amish farmers attempt to preserve their Swiss-German culture and continue to speak their own "Pennsylvania Dutch" dialect.

The Old Order Amish Mennonite Church was organized in 1865. Church government is of the congregational type, and there are three grades of clergy: *Voll Diener* (bishop), *Diener zum Buch* (preacher), and *Armen Diener* (deacon), all of whom are chosen by lot. Biweekly morning services of worship are held, including hymns, sermons, scriptural reading, testimonies, liturgical prayers, and benediction. During the benediction, everyone genuflects when the name of Jesus Christ is mentioned. Afternoon meetings are scheduled only on the days when the Lord's Supper is celebrated; then the service is in two parts—before and after dinner. The Old Order Amish worship in private homes, subscribe to the Confession of Dortrecht (1632), prescribe strict shunning of backsliders, and try to remain free from the secular community.

Over a period of years some Amish separated from the Old Order Amish and formed the Conservative Mennonite Conference. They held their first conference at Pigeon, Mich., in 1910. These Amish introduced meetinghouses, Sunday schools, and the use of English in worship. They use modern conveniences and cooperate with the larger Mennonite Church.

A smaller group of Amish who also left the parent body formed the Beachy Amish Mennonite Churches. This schism originated in Somerset County, Pa., in 1927 and was led by Bp. Moses M. Beachy. The Beachy Amish have abandoned restrictions against modern inventions and offer a mitigated discipline.

Bibliography: J. A. HOSTETLER, *Amish Society* (Baltimore, Md. 1963). C. G. BACHMAN, *The Old Order Amish of Lancaster County* (Lancaster, Pa. 1961). *The Mennonite Encyclopedia,* ed. H. S. BENDER and C. H. SMITH, 4 v. (Scottdale, Pa. 1955–60). D. B. KRAYBILL and M. A. OLSHAN, eds., *The Amish Struggle with Modernity* (Hanover, N.H. 1994).

[W. J. WHALEN]

AMMANATI DE' PICCOLOMINI, JACOPO

Cardinal, patron of the arts, papal official; b. Villa Basilica near Lucca, Italy, March 8, 1422; d. San Lorenzo, Sept. 10, 1479. Jacopo Ammanati, who came from a poor family, owed his advancement to his classical studies in Florence. Cardinal Domenico Capranica made him his private secretary in 1450. Subsequently, he became secretary of briefs under CALLISTUS III and PIUS II. Pius valued him highly, adopting him into the Piccolomini family, and investing him with the rights of a citizen of Siena. In turn he had great admiration for Pius and wrote a continuation of his *Commentarii,* which gives much information about the intrigues in the papal court. He was named bishop of Pavia in 1460 and cardinal in 1461. He soon disagreed with PAUL II and was even imprisoned on a charge of conspiracy. In 1470 he was transferred to Lucca and named papal delegate to Umbria. Pope SIXTUS IV sent him as legate to Perugia in 1471. He was a conscientious ecclesiastic and a Christian humanist.

Bibliography: S. PAULI, *Disquisizione istorica della patria, e compendio della vita di Giacomo Ammanati Piccolomini* (Lucca 1712). G. CALAMARI, *Il confidente di Pio II,* 2 v. (Rome 1932). J. WODKA, *Lexikon für Theologie und Kirche*[2], ed. J. HOFER and K. RAHNER, 10 v. (2d, new ed. Freiburg 1957–65) 1:439–440.

[N. G. WOLF]

AMMIANUS, MARCELLINUS

Roman historian; b. Antioch, between A.D. 325 and 335; d. probably in Rome, *c.* 400. A Greek of a prominent upper–middle–class family, he served as a military officer under Ursicinus in Italy, on the Rhine, and in the East (353–360); took part in the Persian campaign of JULIAN THE APOSTATE (363); spent time in Antioch; and settled in Rome after 378. Intense Roman patriotism led him to write in Latin and fill the void after Tacitus. His *Res gestae* in 31 books runs from Nerva to the death of Valens (96–378); extant are books 14 (353) to 31, published between 392 and 397.

Ammianus's sources were his memory, notes, interrogations of eyewitnesses (often mentioned by name), and a complex variety of written material. His general accuracy is great as checked against the independent history of Faustus of Byzantium. His knowledge of ancient history and literature is impressive. The *History* reveals a general "faithfulness to facts, based on clear proofs." He is usually objective and fair–minded. Closeness to Ursicinus sometimes clouded his judgment, and he did not do complete justice to Gallus, but his eulogistic tone toward Julian did not blind him to that emperor's faults. The oppression of the pagans by THEODOSIUS I (392) made Ammianus cautious in treating him and his family. His many, though frequently uncritical, excursuses reflect in part his wide travel. His tone is critical of the luxury of the times, but he was blind to the real decline of Rome and the seriousness of the barbarian threat. In style, he shows best in his excellent characterizations and the vitality of his dramatic narratives, but he is often excessively rhetorical. His language is diffuse and poetical, anticipating the style of the literature of the century to follow.

A pagan, Ammianus is respectful of martyrs and generally fair to Christianity insofar as it is a "plain and simple religion." Although critical of Julian for an edict against Christian teachers of rhetoric, he is just as critical of ecclesiastical politics, the "deadly hatred" of Christians for one another, the bloody rivalry of specific bishops, and the widespread luxury of the urban hierarchy. De Labriolle classes him with those cultured pagans, so numerous at the time, who from contempt or indifference looked at the contemporary Christian revolution without understanding it or being impressed by it. For all his limitations, Ammianus is one of the greatest of the Roman historians.

Bibliography: *Rerum gestarum libri,* ed. C. U. CLARK, 2 v. (Berlin 1910–15); Latin–English edition, ed. and tr. J. C. ROLFE, 3 v. (*Loeb Classical Library,* rev. ed. 1950–1956). E. A. THOMPSON, *The Historical Work of Ammianus Marcellinus* (Cambridge, Eng. 1947). M. L. W. LAISTNER, *The Greater Roman Historians* (Berkeley 1947) 141–161, 180–183. P. C. DE LABRIOLLE, *La Réaction païenne* (6th ed. Paris 1942) 433–436. G. B. PIGHI, *Reallexikon für Antike und Christentum,* ed. T. KLAUSER [Stuttgart 1941 (1950)—] 1:386–394.

[W. R. F. TONGUE]

AMON

National god of Egypt. His name is spelled also as Amun. Amon was originally one of the local gods of THEBES (Noh), but when that city became prominent in the Twelfth Dynasty (1991–1786 B.C.), he became the chief god of Thebes, which then became known as No-Amon (City of Amon), as it is called in Nehemiah 3.8; see also Jeremiah 46.25. ST. JEROME translated *nō' 'āmôn* in Nehemiah 3.8 erroneously as *Alexandria populorum* (Alexandria of the nations); therefore Amon's name does not appear in the Vulgate. In the Eighteenth Dynasty (1570–*c.* 1304) Amon emerged as the supreme god of the whole nation, having been identified with RA (Re) the sun-god and called Amon-Ra, "the King of the gods." The main sanctuary of Amon was the enormous temple in the section of Thebes now known as Karnak, but he was worshiped throughout Egypt and even in Libya and Nubia (Biblical Ethiopia). His wife Mu (the mother) and his son Chonsu (the wanderer, i.e., the moon) formed a triad of gods. Amon's name (Egyptian *i'mn,* "hidden") stresses his mysterious and inscrutable nature; he was difficult to find and was often associated with the invisible wind that could only be heard and that, as breath, was the mysterious source of life in man and beast. Amon was also worshiped under several names with different attributes. As Khen or Kin he was the god of reproduction, and as Khnum he was "the maker of gods and men." He was sometimes represented by a human body with the head of a ram, the animal sacred to him, or simply by a pair of ram's horns. More often, however, he was featured in wholly human form with two long feathers on his head. The Greeks and Romans identified Amon with Zeus or Jupiter and called the Egyptian city of Thebes Διόσπολις (city of Zeus).

See Also: EGYPT, ANCIENT, 1

Bibliography: *Encylopedic Dictionary of the Bible,* tr. and adap. by L. HARTMAN, (New York 1963), from A. VAN DEN BORN, *Bijbels Woordenboek,* 70–71. H. JACOBSOHN, *Die Religion in Geschichte und Gegenwart,* 7 v. (3d ed. Tübingen 1957–65) 1:327. H. STOCK, *Lexikon für Theologie und Kirche,* ed. J. HOFER and K. RAHNER, 10 v. (2d, new ed. Frieburg 1957–65) 1:464. K. SETHE, *Amun und die acht Urgötter von Hermopolis* [*Abhandlungen der Deutschen (Preussischen, to 1944) Akademie der Wissenschaften zu Berlin* 4; 1929]. J. A. WILSON, *The Burden of Egypt: An Interpretation of Ancient Egyptian Culture* (Chicago 1951) 130–131, 169–172. H. FRANKFORT, *Ancient Egyptian Religion* (New York 1961).

[H. MUELLER]

AMORRITES

This name suggests that the Amorrites (Amorites) of the OT were the same as the Amorrites who invaded Mesopotamia and Syria *c.* 2000 B.C. At the time of the invasion they were a nomadic people; Egyptian paintings represent them with short beards and dressed in sandals and varicolored tunics. They became urbanized in ancient MESOPOTAMIA, and the OT does not represent them as nomadic. The name is connected with Sumerian MAR.TU and Akkadian Amurru, "west"; Amurru appears in Assyrian records only as a geographical designation. Hence the name must have entered the Israelite vocabulary from Mesopotamia, since the Amorrites did not enter Palestine from the west. The term in Syria and Palestine has its own meaning, which is not derived from Mesopotamian usage. In the AMARNA LETTERS, Amurru signifies both a geographical district in Syria (north of modern Beirut) and a state ruled by Abdi-Ashirta that does not clearly lie in the same geographical district. The Hittite King Mursilis made a treaty with Duppi-Tešub, King of Amurru; the name of this ruler is not Amorrite. The district of Amurru was the objective of a campaign of Seti I of Egypt (1318-1301 B.C.).

Data on Amorrites in Syria and Palestine do not indicate such a wide diffusion as is suggested by Biblical occurrences of the name. The Amorrites are classified with certain Canaanite tribes as sons of Canaan and descendants of Ham (Gn 10.16). The classification is geographical, however, not ethnic; the Amorrites lived in the territory of Canaan but were not of the same ethnic origin as the Canaanites. They are mentioned as living near the Dead Sea at Hasason-Thamar (Gn 14.7), and Mamre is called an Amorrite (Gn 14.13). Mamre, however, is not a personal name but a place name. There are signs that Genesis ch. 14 does not preserve historical memories in their purity. SHECHEM is called an Amorrite city, but only once (Gn 48.22). Other data are not entirely consistent. The Amorrites dwelt in the mountains (the central highlands of Palestine) while the Canaanites dwelt in the Jordan Valley and on the coastal plain (Nm 13.29). The Amorrite kings of western Palestine mentioned in the narratives of the conquests of Joshua resided in the highlands (Jos 5.1; 10.5–7). According to Jgs 1.34–35, on the other hand, the Amorrites of the coastal plain prevented the tribe of Dan from expanding westward and retained cities which they held in the foothills of the central highlands. In Nm 21.21–23 there is an Amorrite kingdom of eastern Palestine east of the Dead Sea and north of the Arnon. It is to be noted, however, that the tradition placed the fall of this kingdom before the Israelite settlement in Palestine. A later writer connects Jerusalem with the Amorrites (Ez 16.3, 45). Hence the Amorrites appear to be distributed over much of the territory of Palestine.

The identity of these Amorrites with the Amorrites of Mesopotamia would be more assured if a representative number of their personal names were mentioned in the Bible. The type of small kingdoms that they established in Palestine corresponds to the type of state that the Amorrites established in northwest Mesopotamia and north Syria. Archeology so far has not disclosed any specifically Amorrite traces; however, the nomadic incursions into Transjordan and the Jordan Valley, particularly at Jericho, that are evidenced for the 21st to 19th centuries B.C. conform very well to what is known of Amorrites from elsewhere. But the allusions to the diffusion of the Amorrites in other sources suit their presence and diffusion in Palestine, where they seem to have survived longer as a distinct group than elsewhere. It is probable that the OT use of the name is somewhat loose, particularly in documents considerably removed in time from the living traditions of the settlements, and that the Amorrites were mistakenly said to have been in some places where they never actually were.

Bibliography: W. F. ALBRIGHT, *From the Stone Age to Christianity* (2d ed. New York 1957). J. BRIGHT, *A History of Israel* (Philadelphia 1959). J. FINEGAN, *Light from the Ancient Past* (2d ed. Princeton 1959). K. KENYON, *Archaeology in the Holy Land* (New York 1960) 135–161.

[J. L. MC KENZIE]

AMORT, EUSEBIUS

Philosopher, theologian; b. Bibermühle, Bavaria, Nov. 15, 1692; d. Polling, Feb. 5, 1775. He received his early education from the Jesuits at Munich and entered the canons regular at Polling, where in 1717 he was assigned to teach philosophy and, later, theology and Canon Law. In 1722 he founded an influential scientific and literary review, *Parnassus boicus,* which he continued for some years. Amort spent the years from 1733 to 1735 as theologian to Cardinal Lercari in Rome, where he became acquainted with many distinguished scholars and theologians. Among his correspondents were numbered such men as Benedict XIII and Benedict XIV, cardinals Lercari, Orsi, and Galli, St. Alphonsus Liguori, and Daniel Concina. After his return from Rome, Amort devoted the last 40 years of his life to writing. Seventy

volumes came from his pen, embracing an almost encyclopedic range of subjects: philosophy, apologetics, dogmatic, moral, and mystical theology, history, Canon Law, prayer books, catechisms, and hagiography. Engaging in the controversy on PROBABILISM, he sought to maintain a middle course between rigorism and laxism, and he is credited with being a cofounder of EQUIPROBABILISM, inasmuch as St. Alphonsus appealed to his authority in support of that system. He took a very critical view of the *Mystical City of God* of Mary of AGREDA, against which he devoted the best known of his works, *De revelationibus, visionibus et apparitionibus regulae tutae. . .* (Augsburg 1744), a book that brought him into conflict with the supporters of Mary. Amort also entered into the controversy that was being waged at the time with regard to the authorship of the IMITATION OF CHRIST. He vigorously defended the claims of Thomas à Kempis against the Benedictine champions of Jean Gerson, and filled seven books with his views upon the matter. His more important moral treatises were: *Theologia eclectica, moralis et scholastica* (4 v. Augsburg 1752), an edition of which, revised by Benedict XIV, was published in Bologna in 1753; *Theologia moralis inter regorem et laxitatem media* (Augsburg 1739); and *Ethica christiana* (Augsburg 1758). His *Vetus disciplina canonicorum regularium et saecularium* (Venice 1748) is still considered a valuable contribution to the history of religious orders.

Bibliography: No thorough biographical study of Amort has been written. H. HURTER, *Nomenclator literarius theologiae catholicae,* 5 v. in 6 (3d ed. Innsbruck 1903–13) 5.1:228–232. C. TOUSSAINT, *Dictionnaire de théologie catholique,* ed. A. VACANT et al., 15 v. (Paris 1903–50) 1.1:1115–17. L. HERTLING, *Dictionnaire de spiritualité ascétique et mystique. Doctrine et histoire,* ed. M. VILLER et al. (Paris 1932—) 1:530–531. T. J. SHAHAN, *The Catholic Encyclopedia,* ed. C. G. HERBERMANN et al., 16 v. (New York 1907–14; suppl. 1922) 1:434–435.

[P. K. MEAGHER]

AMOS, BOOK OF

The third in the series of the 12 MINOR PROPHETS, though actually the earliest one. Although the institution of prophecy was already ancient in the days of Amos, the book bearing his name represents the first written collection of a prophet's oracles, thus ushering in a new epoch in the literature of Israel [*see* PROPHECY (IN THE BIBLE)]. The book is composed almost wholly of oracles pronounced by Amos in the middle of the 8th century B.C. primarily predicting doom for the Northern Kingdom because of social injustice and perversion of cult, emphasizing as it does Yahweh's ethical demands. It also holds some promise of hope, although this is not elaborated on by the prophet. This article will treat of the book in Israel's history, its division, composition, content, and doctrine.

Historical Setting. About midway in the reign of Jeroboam II (783–743), when Israel had reached the zenith of its recovered prosperity, the spirit of the Lord summoned the shepherd Amos from Thecua, an obscure village on the margin of the desert of Judah, to pronounce impending doom upon the Northern Kingdom (Am 1.1; 7.14). Like the roaring of a lion, as described in 3.8, the message of the prophet resounded through the sanctuary at Bethel and in the gates of the capital. The response was an angry rejection of Amos by officialdom in the person of Amasia, priest of the sanctuary (7.13), as had happened on previous occasions (2.12). Yet the call of Amos to the office of prophet was the providential work of Yahweh; it was neither by reason of personal choice nor inheritance that Amos prophesied at the sanctuary of Bethel. He emphatically denied that he was a prophet by profession, i.e., a member of the prophetic guilds that ministered at the sanctuaries (7.14; *see* H. H. Rowley, 114–115). Rather, his call was immediately from Yahweh, who had taken him from following the flock and from dressing sycamore trees to prophesy to Israel (7.15). The oracles of Amos were soon written down, probably by a disciple, and, for the first time in Israel, the force of the written word was effectively carrying the prophetic message. The prophetic faith had found a new instrument to convey its message, and succeeding prophets built upon the solid foundation set by Amos.

Division. In an introduction (1.1–2), the editor identifies the prophet and the general period of his ministry, and with a single verse characterizes the tenor of the entire prophecy.

In the first part (1.3–2.16) is presented a series of oracles, all of the same literary construction and directed against the hostile neighbors of Israel. This reaches a dramatic climax in the judgment of the Lord against the Northern Kingdom itself (2.6–16).

The second part (3.1–6.14) contains a collection of oracles that elaborate upon the sinfulness of Israel and the determination of Yahweh to chastise these transgressions. A third group of minatory oracles (8.4–14) logically pertains to this section, but they apparently have been misplaced, since they interrupt the continuity of the passage in which they now stand.

The last part (7–9) is taken up with a succession of visions, each of which depicts a dire punishment about to overtake the people. Inserted after the third vision is a brief biographical account of Amos (7.10–17). A messianic epilogue concludes the book (9.8–15).

Composition. Modern scholarship attributes the bulk of the prophecy to Amos (*see* W. S. McCullough,

247–248). There is evidence of certain later additions, e.g., the references to Judah (1.2; 2.4–5) and several lyrical passages that may be fragments of a hymn glorifying Yahweh as Lord of the physical universe (4.13; 5.8; 8.9; 9.5–6). The messianic promise of restoration of the "fallen hut of David" at the end of the prophecy (9.8c–15) breathes an optimism difficult to harmonize with what precedes it, which seems to presuppose the destruction of both kingdoms. This messianic part was perhaps added during the Exile. Thus the work as we now possess it comes from the hands of a redactor, probably a disciple of the prophet, who collected the oracles and arranged them in an order that is not necessarily chronological. This work was very likely done in the Southern Kingdom after the fall of Samaria. The text of Amos has been preserved in good condition with a few minor exceptions.

Content and Doctrine. Amos exposes with rustic candor the sins of the wealthy of Samaria, particularly their avarice and greed (2.6; 8.5–6), the perversion of judgment (5.7, 12), oppression of the weak (2.7; 3.10; 5.11), and sensuality (2.7; 6.4–6). These excesses outrage Amos's sense of justice because they are enjoyed at the expense of the defenseless poor of the land.

The sanctuaries of BETHEL, Galgal, and the city of Dan are objects of God's displeasure (4.4–5; 5.5, 21–23; 7.9; 8.10, 14). Here cult is offered to foreign deities (5.26; 8.14) in a kind of syncretism with the religion of Moses. The priests are guilty of fostering formalism in worship rather than a true religion of the heart (5.21–24). Indeed, they have become so self-complacent in their privilege as the chosen people that they have forgotten the obligations that election carries with it (3.2).

Jeroboam II shares this guilt (6.13) and his dynasty will fall (7.9); so too, will the lives of his officials be forfeited (6.1, 7). The whole nation must suffer for the sins of its leaders at the hands of an unnamed oppressor (6.14), which is clearly Assyria (7.17).

A sincere repentance and return to Yahweh could save them (4.6–11). "Seek me, that you may live" is the plaintive refrain of God's last desperate plea (5.4, 6, 14–15). But amidst a people enamoured of luxury, these overtures fall upon deaf ears. Amos, abandoning hope of any true conversion, proclaims a punishment approaching with inexorable certainty (4.12; 5.26–27; 8.3; 9.1–4). In this context, the "DAY OF THE LORD," longed for by the Israelites as a glorious event, is given a new and terrifying meaning by Amos (5.18, 20). It is henceforth to be a day of wrath when Yahweh will visit just retribution upon all sinners (8.9–14). Intimately allied with this is the inchoate theme of the Remnant of Israel to be spared (3.12; 5.15; 9.8).

The leitmotif of Amos's prophecy is "righteousness," the necessary condition for worship that is acceptable to God (5.24). Amos in insisting upon justice contrasts with his contemporary, Hosea, who extols God's steadfast love (Heb. *hesed*), a term that never occurs in Amos [*See* N. Snaith, *The Distinctive Ideas of the OT* (Philadelphia 1946) 65–69].

Amos professes strict monotheism. Yahweh is the sole ruler of the universe (4.13; 5.8; 8.9, 11). He requites evil among the pagans (1–2), directs the course of the history of Israel as well as the nations (9.7), and uses the Assyrians as His instrument (6.14). His wonderful deeds in behalf of His people, especially in the Exodus (2.10; 3.1; 4.10; 5.25; 9.7), increase the responsibility of the Israelites to observe the moral precepts of the covenant.

Bibliography: G. A. BUTTRICK, ed. *The Interpreters' Dictionary of the Bible,* 4 v. (Nashville 1962) 1:116–121. W. R. HARPER, *Amos and Hosea* in *International Critical Commentary* (New York 1905). R. S. CRIPPS, *The Book of Amos* in *ibid.* T. H. SUTCLIFFE, *The Book of Amos* (London 1955). J. MORGENSTERN, *Amos Studies,* 3 v. (Cincinnati 1941—). H. H. ROWLEY, "The Nature of Old Testament Prophecy in the Light of Recent Study," *The Servant of the Lord and Other Essays on the O. T.* (London 1952). A. NEHER, *Amos: Contribution à l'étude du prophétisme* (Paris 1950). W. S. MCCULLOUGH, "Some Suggestions about Amos," *Journal of Biblical Literature* 72 (1953) 247–254. J. D. W. WATTS, "The Origin of the Book of Amos," *Expository Times* 66 (1954–55) 109–112. A. S. KAPELRUD, *Central Ideas in Amos* (Oslo 1961). B. VAWTER, *The Conscience of Israel* (New York 1961) 61–97.

[J. K. SOLARI]

AMPHILOCHIUS OF ICONIUM, ST.

Fourth-century bishop of Iconium, Pisidia; b. Caesarea, *c.* 340; d. after 394. Amphilochius studied rhetoric under Libanius at Antioch, practiced as a lawyer in Constantinople for six years, and decided to become a hermit. His decision was frustrated by Basil of Caesarea, who forced on him the Diocese of Iconium. As bishop, Amphilochius campaigned against Arianism and the crypto-Manichean ascetical sects of the Apotactites, Encratites, and Messalians.

Basil dedicated his *De Spiritu Sancto* to Amphilochius, who used it to combat the propaganda of the Macedonians, against whose teachings he summoned a council at Iconium in 376. Amphilochius himself wrote a similar treatise on the Holy Spirit, but it has not been preserved. Basil's letters 190, 218, 188, 199, and 217 were addressed to Amphilochius; but virtually all of Amphilochius's letters and almost his entire literary output have been lost. A notable exception is his synodal letter to the bishops of another province, following the Council of Iconium (376), in which he explicitly defended the divinity of the Holy Spirit (*Patrologia Graeca* 39:93–98). In 381 Amphilochius attended the Council of Constantinople I; he revisited the capital in 383 and 395, the last time probably shortly before his death and just after presiding at the anti-Messalian Council of Sidon in 394.

His 333 iambic verses to Seleucus are a treatise on the combination of the devout life with contemplative study that was preserved among the works of Gregory of Nazianzus. It has special importance for the history of the canon of the Bible. Eight of his sermons also have been preserved, dealing primarily with liturgical feasts. His authority as a theologian grew during the early fifth century, and all the major councils after Ephesus (431) appeal to him as a source of patristic doctrine.

Feast: Nov. 23.

Bibliography: *Patrologia Graeca,* ed. J. P. MIGNE (Paris 1857—66) 39:9–130. K. HOLL, *Amphilochius von Ikonium in seinem Verhältnis zu den grossen Kappadoziern* (Tübingen 1904; reprinted Darmstadt 1969). G. FICKER, ed., *Amphilochiana* (Leipzig 1906). Altaner 357–358. J. QUASTEN, *Lexicon für Theologie und Kirche,* ed. J. HOFER and K. RAHNER (Freiburg 1957–65) 1:448–449. H. M. WERHAHN, *Byzantinische Zeitschrift* 47 (1954) 414–418. G. BARDY, *Dictionnaire de spiritualité ascétique et mystique,* ed. M. VILLER et al. (Paris 1932–) 1:544.

[A. G. GIBSON]

AMPLEFORTH, ABBEY OF

St Laurence's Abbey, Ampleforth, near York, Diocese of Middlesbrough, part of the English Benedictine congregation. The community of St. Laurence traces its descent from the medieval monastic community of Westminster, restored by Queen Mary and finally suppressed in 1559. It was the last monk of the restored Westminster Abbey, Sigebert Buckley, who in 1607 aggregated a group of monks to Westminster, thereby establishing a certain continuity with pre-Reformation English monasticism. Some of these monks helped in the foundation of the monastery of St. Laurence at Dieulouard in Lorraine (1608). This monastery was primarily missionary in character, and most of the monks served as priests to the recusant communities of England. One of them, St. Alban ROE, was canonized among the martyrs of England and Wales. This form of apostolic monasticism has remained at the core of the community's mission, though the seventeenth century also saw the flourishing of a tradition of spirituality inspired by Fr. Augustine Baker. When Dieulouard was forcibly closed in 1793, the monks returned to England, settling at Ampleforth in 1802. The community has continued its missionary work through the care of a number of parishes, and also has developed a school, which in the twentieth century became one of the leading Roman Catholic public schools. It now numbers over 500 pupils, and includes a Junior School at Gilling Castle. The community also has a guest apostolate and offers an annual retreat program. Ampleforth was elevated to an abbey in 1900, and is today a community of over 90 monks. Its foundations include St. Benet's Hall, Oxford (1897), St. Louis Abbey, Missouri (1955), the monastery of Our Lady of Mount Grace, Osmotherley (1994), the monastery of Christ the Word, Zimbabwe (1996), and St Benedict's monastery, Bamber Bridge (1999). From 1963 to 1976 the community was lead by Abbot Basil HUME, who thereafter became cardinal archbishop of Westminster. From 1976 to 1984, the abbot was Ambrose Griffiths, who was appointed bishop of Hexham and Newcastle in 1992.

Bibliography: J. MCCANN and C. CARY-ELWES, eds., *Ampleforth and Its Origins* (London 1952).

[A. MARETT-CROSBY]

AMPULLAE

The diminutive of amphora [properly, amp(h)orula, from *amphi,* or both, and *phero* or *porto,* bear], a small globular flask with two handles for carrying, another name for cruets. The term is used of those clay or glass vessels found at tombs in the catacombs. It is probable that these vessels were used to preserve portions of the oil or perfume used to anoint the bodies of the dead. Another class of this type of vessel was used to preserve oil for the lamps burning at the shrines of martyrs, a custom generally observed in the Middle Ages. Some image or symbol usually identified the saint from whose tomb the ampullae were taken. Several of those containing oil from the tombs of famous Roman martyrs are still preserved at the Cathedral of Monza. These were the gift of Pope Gregory the Great to Queen Theodolinda. A greater number of ampullae of this type were brought to Europe by pilgrims from the tomb of St. Mennas in Egypt. A third class of ampullae made of clay, metal, or glass was used to preserve the oils consecrated by the bishop (Optatus of Milevis, *Contra Parmenianum Donatistam* 2.19, ''Ampulla Chrismatis'').

Of the ampullae found in the catacombs, many contained a dark-red sediment that was thought to be blood, thus marking the tomb of a martyr. Negative results obtained by chemical analysis have rendered this theory untenable. The sediment found in a test group of so-called blood vases revealed the presence of elements vastly disproportionate to those that might be found in blood. While it is not improbable that a few of the ''ampullae sanguinis'' did contain blood, they cannot be considered one of the marks of a martyr's tomb, since a number of

such ampullae were found at the tombs of children under seven, and many date from the latter half of the fourth century, long after the era of persecution. Moreover, ampullae have been found in Jewish catacombs, e.g., on the Via Labicana, fastened to the tombs in the same way as in the Christian cemeteries.

Bibliography: F. OPPENHEIMER, *The Legend of the Ste. Ampoule* (London 1953). C. BAKIRTZIS, ''Byzantine Ampullae from Thessaloniki,'' in *The Blessings of Pilgrimage,* ed. R. OUSTERHOUT (Urbana, IL 1990) 140–149. M. DUCAN-FLOWERS, ''A Pilgrim's Ampulla from the Shrine of St. John the Evangelist at Ephesus,'' in *The Blessings of Pilgrimage,* ed. R. OUSTERHOUT (Urbana, IL 1990) 125–139.

[M. A. BECKMANN/EDS.]

AMSDORF, NIKOLAUS VON

Lutheran theologian and bishop, important for the early organization of Protestantism; b. probably Torgau, Dec. 3, 1483; d. Eisenach, May 14, 1565. Amsdorf received his M.A. at the University of Wittenberg and lectured there on philosophy and theology. When Luther arrived at Wittenberg, the two became close friends and coworkers, Amsdorf assisting in the translation of the Bible. Amsdorf became an evangelical preacher in Magdeburg, Goslar, Einbeck, Meissen, and elsewhere. In 1542 Elector John Frederick appointed him first bishop of the Lutheran diocese of Naumburg-Zeitz (1542–47), a post that he lost at the outset of the SCHMALKALDIC War. After a period in Weimar, he lived in Eisenach from 1552 until his death, the unofficial leader of the Lutherans there. He was unwavering in holding to a conservative Lutheran position in theology and was instrumental in founding the University of Jena, a Lutheran stronghold.

See Also: GNESIOLUTHERANISM; INTERIMS; CONFESSIONS OF FAITH.

Bibliography: *Ausgewählte Schriften,* ed. O. LERCHE (Gütersloh 1938). O. LERCHE, *Amsdorf und Melanchthon: Eine kirchengeschichtliche Studie* (Berlin 1937). P. BRUNNER, *Nikolaus von Amsdorf als Bischof von Naumburg* (Gütersloh 1961). F. LAU, *Die Religion in Geschichte und Gegenwart* (Tübingen 1957–65) 1:333–334.

[L. W. SPITZ]

AMYOT, JACQUES

Bishop of Auxerre, one of the four great French prose stylists of the 16th century; b. Melun, France, Oct. 30, 1513; d. Auxerre, Feb. 6, 1593. His parents, it seems, were of some means, and he studied at the Collège de France, graduating at age 19 more as the result of hard work than brilliance. He was at Bourges from 1534 to 1547, teaching Greek and Latin. Francis I, to whom he dedicated his first works, conferred on him the abbey of Bellozane-en-Bray on March 18, 1547 (N.S.; 1546 O.S.). It is not known when or where he was ordained. He was in Rome (1550–51) and performed a diplomatic mission of a few days to the Council of Trent before he became tutor to the sons of Henry II. Charles IX made him grand chaplain of France on Dec. 6, 1560, an office he held until Henry IV deposed him in 1590. He received other royal favors from Charles, including the See of Auxerre in 1570. In 1578 Henry III made him grand chaplain of the Order of the Holy Spirit. Charges that he held Protestant beliefs have not been established. His literary work consists mostly of translations: *Histoire aethiopique d'Heliodorus* (1547), *Sept livres des histoires de Diodore Sicilien* (1554), *Amours pastorales de Daphnis et Chloé* (1559), and Plutarch's *Lives* and *Morals* (1559, 1565, 1579), the translation of which by Sir Thomas North in 1579 was used by Shakespeare. Amyot's translations are quite free and contain errors, but it seems that he used the Greek rather than Latin or Italian translations available. The works became very popular and exerted an influence on French moral thought and literary style for some time. Amyot wrote several original works, including prayers before and after Holy Communion, published after his death.

Bibliography: R. STUREL, *Jacques Amyot: Traducteur des Vies parallèles de Plutarque* (Paris 1908). C. URBAIN and M. CITOLEUX, *Dictionnaire de biographie française* (PARIS 1929) 2:751–761.

[D. R. PENN]

AMYRAUT, MOÏSE

Calvinist theologian; b. Bourgeuil, Touraine, September 1596; d. Saumur, Jan. 8, 1664. He was intended for a legal career and became at 21 a licentiate of law at Poitiers; but, having been introduced to Calvin's *Institutes*, he studied theology at Saumur under John CAMERON, whose doctrine of divine election he was to develop and defend. After pastorates at Saint-Agnan and Saumur, he was from 1633 a professor in the Saumur academy. For the Synod of Charenton, 1631, he presented King Louis XIII with a memorandum on infractions of the Edict of NANTES. A man of courtly manners, he moved with ease among eminent persons and was on occasion consulted by Richelieu and Mazarin. He was twice acquitted of heresy before national synods of his church. He was a prolific and in his time an influential writer, firm in his principles and courteous to his opponents. His ''hypothetic universalism'' on divine election is set forth in

Jacques Amyot, engraving. (©Bettmann/CORBIS)

his *Echantillon de la doctrine de Calvin sur la prédestination* (c. 1634), and other treatises. His ecumenical proposals appear best in his Ἐἰρηνικόν (1662), but his whole work is irenic in tone.

Bibliography: E. and É. HAAG, *La France protestante*, 10 v. (Paris 1846–59) 1:72–80, lists and describes his works. R. STAUFFER, *Moïse Amyraut: Un Précurseur français de l'oecuménisme* (Paris 1962). O. E. STRASSER, *Die Religion in Geschichte und Gegenwart* [3] 1:347–348. J. DEDIEU, *Dictionnaire d'histoire et de géographie ecclésiastiques* 2:1380–81.

[J. T. MCNEILL]

AN-XING, ANNA, AND COMPANIONS, SS.

Female lay martyrs; b. Anping County, Hebei (Hopeh) Province; d. Hebei Province, China, July 11, 1900. This subgrouping of the Martyrs of China incorporates three generations of the An family: The matriarch Anna An-Xing (also called An Hsin-shih, An Hsin-shih, Nan-Sinn-Cheu, or Nan-Sinn-Cheu; b. 1828); her daughter-in-law Mary An-Guo (also called An-Keo or Nan-Kouo-Cheu; b. 1836); her granddaughter Mary An Linghua (also called Nan Ling-Hoa, b. 1871); and her grandson's wife Anna An-Jiao (also called Nan-Tsiao-

Cheu, b. 1874). They were arrested by the Boxers as they sought refuge from the persecutions, and were killed outside the village for refusing to apostatize. They were among the 2,072, killed between June and August 1900, whose causes were submitted to the Vatican, of which 56 were beatified by Pope Pius XII (April 17, 1955) and canonized (Oct. 1, 2000) by Pope John Paul II with Augustine Zhao Rong and companions.

Feast: July 20.

Bibliography: L. MINER, *China's Book of Martyrs: A Record of Heroic Martyrdoms and Marvelous Deliverances of Chinese Christians during the Summer of 1900* (Ann Arbor 1994). J. SIMON, *Sous le sabre des Boxers* (Lille 1955). C. TESTORE, *Sangue e palme sul fiume giallo. I beati martiri cinesi nella persecuzione della Boxe Celi Sud-Est, 1900* (Rome 1955). *L'Osservatore Romano*, Eng. Ed. 40 (2000): 1–2, 10.

[K. I. RABENSTEIN]

ANABAPTISTS

The term Anabaptist, meaning literally "rebaptizer," occurs from the fourth century onward and was first used to designate those who insisted on the rebaptism of persons baptized by heretics or by clergy who had fallen away from the faith under persecution.

In the sixteenth-century it was applied to those elements in the Reformation movement who denied the validity of infant baptism. It became a pejorative term, used by their Catholic and Protestant opponents to associate them with a heresy condemned for centuries by both ecclesiastical and civil law and incurring the death penalty according to the Justinian Code, and was applied indiscriminately to a heterogeneous group of the "left wing" of the Reformation. The association with DONATISM was inaccurate, since the sixteenth-century Anabaptists were not concerned with the validity of the administration of the Sacrament of Baptism but rather denied its sacramental character. Their attitude toward baptism with water ranged from seeing it as an important act of public confession (e.g., Swiss Brethren) to the denial of the necessity of any physical baptism (e.g., Schwenckfeld). Thus the Schleitheim Confession of the Swiss Brethren (1527) states: "Baptism shall be given to all those who have learned repentance and amendment of life, and who believe truly that their sins are taken away by Christ and to all those who walk in the resurrection of Jesus Christ." By contrast, Caspar Schwenckfeld asserts summarily: "God does not tie his grace to water." Since the differences among those who rejected infant baptism are vast, it is advisable to divide the so-called Anabaptists into four separate but related groups: (1) New Testament-oriented pacifists, (2) Old Testament-oriented revolution-

aries, (3) spiritualists, and (4) rationalists. It should be noted, however, that in the 16th century the lines between these groups were somewhat fluid and that they exerted considerable influence upon each other.

New Testament-oriented Pacificists. This segment had its origin in lay Bible study groups in Zürich, Switzerland (1523–25). The movement was led by men close to ZWINGLI (Conrad GREBEL, Felix Manz, Georg Blaurock, and later Balthasar HUBMAIER), impatient with Zwingli's hesitation and vacillation in his interpretation and administration of the sacraments, his attitude toward political authority, and the nature of the church. On Jan. 21, 1525, Grebel baptized Blaurock, and "believer's baptism" became the outward mark of the movement. When those rebaptized were soon expelled from Zürich, they spread their new teaching all over central Europe. Later some, following the example of the early Christian community in Jerusalem (Acts 4.32–35), organized Christian communist communities that have survived to the present (*see* HUTTERITES). In northern Europe the New Testament-oriented pacifist Anabaptists eventually found an eloquent leader in Menno Simons (1496–1561) (*see* MENNONITES).

The theology of the group was expressed in the Schleitheim Confession. Besides condemning infant baptism and favoring adult baptism as confession of faith, it advocated the "ban" (the strict discipline of the community of the baptized), a memorial view of Holy Communion, complete separation from all who did not share their views, and the refusal to bear arms and participate in political life.

Old Testament-oriented Revolutionaries. This group originated in Zwickau in Saxony (c. 1520) among the impoverished weavers of that town. Led by Nicholas Storch, they were soon joined by Thomas MÜNZER, who became one of their most voluble spokesmen, and participated actively in the Peasant War. While they also opposed infant baptism, they distinguished themselves from the pacifist Anabaptists by their emphasis upon the Old Testament call to war against the "Canaanites," their stress upon direct revelations from God independent of the Bible, and their elaborate millennial speculations based on an allegorical interpretation of the Book of Daniel and the Apocalypse. Although Münzer perished (1525) in the fiasco of the Peasant War, views similar to his own were later expressed by the Münster Anabaptists, who, influenced by the millennial hopes of Melchior HOFFMANN and under the leadership of Anabaptist refugees from the Netherlands, the "prophet" John Mathijs and his successor "king" John Beukels (John of Leiden), attempted to establish a communist and polygamous "kingdom of God" in this Westphalian city by force of arms (1533–35). After the utter collapse of this "kingdom" the surviving Anabaptist elements were absorbed in the New Testament-oriented pacifist Anabaptists under the leadership of Menno Simons.

Spiritualist Anabaptists. This group, whose rejection of infant baptism was not accompanied by an equally clear endorsement of baptism for adults, saw in the organizational structures of the church, as well as the sacraments and even the Bible, regulations applicable only to the infancy of God's people. Thus Sebastian Franck (1499–1542) suggested that in its childhood the church could not dispense with such crutches, but when it discarded them in its maturity, the Father would be pleased rather than angered. Similarly Caspar Schwenckfeld (1489–1561) advocated the suspension of infant baptism, since he considered it so utterly immersed in superstition and abuses as to be worthless (*see* SCHWENCKFELDERS).

Central in the thought of Spiritualist Anabaptists such as Franck and Schwenkfeld was the denial of the absolute claims of all the contending religious movements of the time, from the Roman Catholics and Lutherans to the pacifist and revolutionary Anabaptists. They believed in an invisible church, which might well include not only sincere Christians but also good Muslims and pagans obedient to the "inner Word" wherever they might be. Such emphasis upon the inner Word of the Spirit distinguished the Spiritualist Anabaptists from the other groups and their Biblical literalism.

Rationalist Anabaptists. This last body had its roots primarily in the Romance lands. The Spaniard Michael SERVETUS (1511–53) as well as the Italians Laelius (1525–62) and his nephew Faustus Socinius (1539–1604) were not only opposed to infant baptism but rejected the Trinitarian theology of the ancient Church as well (*see* SOCINIANISM). In this they were influenced by the Arianizing tendencies of Renaissance humanism (e.g., Florentine Academy under Marsilio FICINO), by the Biblical literalism and the rejection of non-Biblical language typical of Anabaptists, which brought the complex Christological formulations of Nicaea and Chalcedon into disrepute, and by the confidence in the God-given ability of human reason to comprehend and follow the council of God. The rationalist Anabaptists tended to identify "spirit" with "reason" and saw Biblical truth as that which contributed to the moral improvement of humanity. Thus they tended to depreciate the confession of Christ as God and Savior, considering Him the great ethical teacher and example.

Anabaptists have survived in some contemporary denominations. Mennonites, Amish, and Hutterites carry on the tradition of the New Testament-oriented pacifists. The Schwenckfelder Church originated in the spiritualist tradition, and the Society of Friends (Quaker) has incorporated many of its teachings. Unitarians are loosely related to the rationalists. Only the Old Testament-oriented revolutionaries have found no permanent institutional expression although some of their millennial claims can be found in groups at the fringe of Protestantism. In the scholarly investigation of the Anabaptist movement, the following questions have been debated: (1) the influence of medieval sects on Anabaptists (e.g., L. Keller); (2) the place of origin in Switzerland (e.g., E. Troeltsch) or Saxony (e.g., K. Holl); (3) the definition of Anabaptism restricting it to the New Testament-oriented pacifists (e.g., H. Bender); (4) Anabaptist contributions to the doctrine of the church (e.g., F. Littell); (5) Anabaptist contributions to concept of separation of Church and State (e.g., G. H. Williams).

While the influence of medieval sectarianism is vague, the origin of the 16th-century movement can be considered settled if the distinction between the various groups of Anabaptists is maintained. Switzerland applies to the New Testament-oriented pacifists, and Saxony, to the Old Testament-oriented revolutionaries. The attempt to restrict the term Anabaptist to the pacifists is not accurate. Some groups of Anabaptists like the Münster prophets did stage armed rebellions. Others refused to take up the sword. The Anabaptists did make a major contribution to the voluntaristic view of the church and their impact on the development of notions of the separation of Church and state was important, too. During the sixteenth and seventeenth century the numbers of all those involved in these groups was extremely small. It was in eighteenth- and nineteenth-century North America that groups like the Hutterites, Mennonites, and Amish were able to flourish. And as a result, the religious beliefs of these groups came to exert an influence on Christian thinking in general out of proportion to their numbers.

Bibliography: H. E. FOSDICK, ed., *Great Voices of the Reformation* (New York 1952). H. J. HILLERBRAND, *A Bibliography of Anabaptism 1520–1630,* (Elkhart, IN 1962). MENNO SIMONS, *Complete Writings,* tr. L. VERDUIN, ed. J. C. WENGER (Scottdale, PA 1956). G. H. WILLIAMS, *The Radical Reformation* (Philadelphia 1962); ed., *Spiritual and Anabaptist Writers* (Philadelphia 1957). *The Mennonite Encyclopedia,* 4 v. (Scottdale, PA 1955–60). K. HOLL, "Luther und die Schwärmer," *Gesammelte Aufsätze zur Kirchengeschichte,* 3 v. (Tübingen 1927–28) 1:420–467. F. H. LITTELL, *The Origins of Sectarian Protestantism* (New York 1964). J. LORTZ, *Die Reformation in Deutschland,* 2 v. (Freiburg 1949). E. TROELTSCH, *The Social Teaching of the Christian Churches,* tr. O. WYON, 2 v. (New York 1931; repr. 1956). A. L. E. VERHEYDEN, *Anabaptism in Flanders,* 1530–1650, tr. M. KUITSE et al. (Scottdale, PA 1961). H. FAST, *Die Religion in Geschichte und Gegenwart,* 7 v. (3d ed. Tübingen 1957–65) 6:601–604, bibliog. A. BAUDRILLART, *Dictionnaire de théologie catholique,* ed. A. VACANT, 15 v. (Paris 1903–50; Tables générales 1951–) 1.1:1128–34. Y. CONGAR, *Catholicisme* 1:500–501. P. BERNARD, *Dictionnaire d'histoire et de géographie ecclésiastiques,* ed. A. BAUDRILLART (Paris 1912–)

2:1383–1405, bibliog. P. J. KLASSEN, *The Economics of Anabaptism, 1525–1560* (The Hague 1964). E. GRITSCH, *Thomas Müntzer* (Minneapolis 1989). L. GROSS, *The Golden Years of the Hutterites* (Scottdale Penn. 1980). H. J. GOERTZ, *Die Täufer* (Munich 1980). W. E. KEENEY, *The Development of Dutch Anabaptist Thought and Practice from 1539 to 1564* (Nieuwkoop 1968). M. LIENHARD, ed., *The Origins and Characteristics of Anabaptism* (The Hague 1977). P. MATHESON, ed. *The Collected Works of Thomas Muentzer* (Edinburgh 1988). T. SCOTT, *Thomas Müntzer* (London 1989). J. M. STAYER, *Anabaptists and the Sword* (Lawrence KS 1972).

[G. W. FORELL]

ANACLETUS (CLETUS), ST. POPE

Pontificate, *c.* 80 to 92. Anacletus appears in the *Liber pontificalis* and the Roman martyrology as two popes, both martyrs, with feasts on April 26 and July 13. St. Irenaeus (*Adv. haer.* 3.3) and the liturgy of the Mass make him the second successor of Peter. The Greek form of his name, Anencletus, was common for slaves and may point to his social status. The third form of his name Cletus, was simply a shortened form of the other two but is the one found in the ancient canon of the mass. (*see* POPES, LIST OF). Eusebius (*Hist.* 3.13, 15, 21; 5.6) says that he died in the 12th year of Domitian's reign after a 12-year episcopate. The *Liber pontificalis* probably mistakes Anacletus for ANICETUS as the builder of a burial monument for Peter. Modern excavations show that Anacletus was not buried near Peter in the Vatican.

Bibliography: *Liber pontificalis*, ed. L. DUCHESNE (Paris 1886–92) 1:xix–xx, 52–53. J. P. KIRSCH, *Dictionnaire d'histoire et de géographie ecclésiastiques* 2:1407–08. E. CASPAR, *Geschichte de Papsttums von den Anfängen bis zur Höhe der Weltherrschaft* (Tübingen 1930–33) 1:8–16. L. KOEP, *Reallexikon für Antike Christentum*, ed. T. KLAUSER [Stuttgart 1941 (1950)] 2: 410–415. E. KIRSCHBAUM, *Tombs of St. Peter and St. Paul*, tr. J. MURRAY (New York 1959). G. SCHWAIGER, *Lexikon für Theologie und Kirche*, ed. J. HOFER and K. RAHNER (Freiberg 1957–65) 1:524. J. N. D. KELLY, *Oxford Dictionary of Popes*, p.7

[E. G. WELTIN]

ANACLETUS II, ANTIPOPE

Pontificate: Feb. 14, 1130–Jan. 25, 1138. Born around 1090 into one of the richest and most powerful Roman families, Peter Pierleoni was a student in Paris and a monk of Cluny. In 1111 or 1112 he was made cardinal deacon of SS. Cosmas and Damian by Paschal II (1099–1118). Peter was a leader among the cardinals who elected Callistus II (1119–24) at Cluny, and was promoted to cardinal priest of St. Maria in Trastevere in 1120. In 1121 he was papal legate to England and in 1122 and 1123 to France. A strong opponent of imperial involvement in questions of investiture, nothing else is heard of

him until the disputed election that would make him antipope.

Pope Honorius (1124–30) was gravely ill and had been moved by the papal chancellor, Aimeric, from the Lateran to the monastery of St. Gregory on the Caelian hill. This part of the city was controlled by the Frangipani family. During the night of February 13, Honorius died and was quickly buried so an election could be held immediately. By morning a minority of 16 cardinals, led by Aimeric, had elected and consecrated Gregorio Papareschi as Pope Innocent II (1130–43). In response to what they perceived as treachery, the majority of cardinals met later that day in St. Mark's (February 14) and elected Peter Pierleoni, who took the name Anacletus II, a reference to a martyr-pope of the early church. These two irregular elections began an eight-year schism. In addition to the old rivalry between the Frangipani and the Pierleoni, most of Innocent's supporters were younger cardinals from northern Italy and France, while most of Anacletus' cardinals represented an older generation within the Curia and came from Rome and southern Italy. There was also the memory of Aimeric's support of Leo Frangipani and his troops, who compelled the previous papal conclave to elect Honorius by force of arms.

Initially, it appeared that Anacletus would prevail. He sent letters appealing for support to the German and French kings. Anacletus was in a strong position since he had the support of the majority of the cardinals and the Roman people. It even appears that the Frangipani temporarily joined his side. Soon Rome became too dangerous for Innocent. He left with Aimeric for France, where the two appealed to major European figures with letters of their own. Innocent was recognized by most western kings and the emperor Lothair (1125–37) largely because of the support of Bernard of Clairvaux (1090–1153), who had exchanged letters with Aimeric for many years. Also both Aimeric and Innocent were early supporters of the Cistercians and Premonstratensians, new but influential orders. Soon only Scotland, Aquitaine, Milan, and southern Italy recognized Anacletus. He secured the obedience of southern Italy when he recognized Duke Roger II of Sicily (1095–1154) as king of Sicily, Calabria, and Apulia overlord of Capua, Naples, and Benevento; in effect making Roger the first King of the Two Sicilies (September 27).

After 1133 Anacletus lost even this support. In that year Lothair came to Italy with Innocent, but they lacked the troops to oust Anacletus, who remained secure in the Castel Sant' Angelo. Soon Lothair left the city and Innocent was forced to flee to Pisa. Anacletus held out in Rome for the next five years. However, he lost Milan in 1136 through the influence of Bernard of Clairvaux, and many of his leading supporters (including Peter of Pisa, an important canonist) abandoned his defense in a series of debates sponsored by Roger in Salerno during November and December 1137. This again was largely due to Bernard's influence. Anacletus died not long afterward in Rome, Jan. 25, 1338. His followers elected Victor IV (1138) to a brief reign as successor. While Peter Pierleoni continues to be seen as having been quite willing to use his family's considerable wealth to secure position, there is an increasing consensus that he has been unfairly branded a reprobate by his enemies. Recognizing the bitter divisions within the college of cardinals at the time and the irregular nature of both elections in 1130, recent scholarship has in some respects restored his reputation.

Bibliography: L. DUCHESNE, ed. *Liber Pontificalis* (Paris 1886–92; repr. 1955–57) 2.313, 317, 322–28, 379–83, 410, 449, 543. P. JAFFÉ, *Regesta pontificum Romanorum* (Leipzig 1885–88; repr. Graz 1956) 1.911–19. J. P. MIGNE, ed. *Patrologia Latina* (Paris 1844–64) 179.687–732. PETER THE DEACON, *Chronica monasterii Cassinensis* 4.103–29 in *Monumenta Germaniae historica, Scriptores* 34.564–607 passim (also in older MGH SS edition, 7.816–44 passim). L. DUCHESNE, *The Beginnings of the Temporal Sovereignty of the Popes* (London 1908). E. VACANDARD, *Dictionnaire d'histoire et de géographie ecclésiastiques* (Paris 1914) 2.1408–19. H. W. KLEWITZ, ''Das Ende des Reformpapstums,'' *Deutsches Archiv für Erforschung des Mittelalters* 3 (1939) 371–412. P. F. PALUMBO, ''La cancelleria d'Anacleto II,'' *Scritti di paleografia e diplomatica in onore di Vincenzo Federici* (Florence 1945). F. J. SCHMALE, *Studien zum Schisma des Jahres 1130* (Cologne 1961). M. DA BERGAMO, ''La duplice elezione papale del 1130,'' *Contributi dell'istituto de storia medievale* 1 (1968) 265–302. S. CHODOROW, *Christian Political Theory and Church Politics in the Mid-Twelfth Century* (Berkeley 1972). W. ULLMANN, *The Papacy and Political Ideas in the Middle Ages* (London 1976). R. HÜLS, *Kardinäle, Klerus und Kirchen Roms, 1049–1130* (Tübingen 1977) 189–91, 225. H. DITTMANN, *Lexikon des Mittelalters* (Munich 1977) 1.568–69 for additional bibliography. H. FUHRMANN, *Germany in the High Middle Ages, c. 1050–1200* (Cambridge 1986) 105, 117–22. J.N.D. KELLY, *The Oxford Dictionary of Popes* (New York 1986) 169–170. M. STROLL, *The Jewish Pope: Ideology and Politics in the Papal Schism of 1139* (Leiden 1987). I. S. ROBINSON, *The Papacy 1073–1198: Continuity and Innovation* (Cambridge 1990). P. KERBRAT, *Encyclopedia of the Middle Ages*, ed. A. VAUCHEZ (Chicago and London 2000) 1.53.

[P. M. SAVAGE]

ANALOGY

Analogy, a technical, philosophical and theological term, commonly designates a kind of predication midway between univocation and equivocation. Thus it denotes a perfection (the ''analogon'') that, though found similar in two or more subjects called ''analogates,'' is neither simply the same nor simply different. As a technical notion, analogy must be distinguished from ''argument by analogy.'' The latter has the following structure: if a given perfection *a* is possessed by two individuals, *B* and *C*, and if *a* is accompanied by another perfection *d* in *B*, then *d* will also be found in *C*. This argument is heuristic, or suggestive; of itself it is not and cannot be certain.

History of the Concept of Analogy

The term analogy was first used by Greek mathematicians in the sense of proportion. PLATO is generally conceded to have been the first to use it philosophically to designate proportions between the elements of the world and between kinds of knowledge and types of reality. Plato also applies it to similarities of function in different things, and occasionally to a likeness between two things that is not an identity.

These uses were expanded and developed by ARISTOTLE. In biology, the ''analogy'' between different organs that perform similar functions became an important concept. In his ethical writings, Aristotle uses the term analogy in a similar way. Thus, there is no single ''idea of the good''; ''the good'' designates something found in unequal degrees in different subjects. In the *Metaphysics* the principles, elements and causes of things are said to be common ''analogously,'' that is, proportionately common. In his logical writings, analogy is sometimes used in the sense of similar proportions. However, when Aristotle says that the most common classes of terms are analogous, he refers rather to a general similarity which cannot be further analyzed into common genera and specific differences. In his psychological works he notes that actual knowledge is analogous to the object known. This is a type of proportion in the sense of suitability, ''adaptation to'' rather than similarity. Although these uses of analogy are clearly not identical, Aristotle does not explain how they are related, probably because he has no explicit theory of analogy.

One other discussion is important in Aristotle for the doctrine of analogy (though here he himself does not use the term): *being* is a word with many meanings, but all the meanings are somehow reduced to a primary one. Aristotle explains this by saying that all the things that are called being are so called by reference to one subject that is being in the primary sense; this is the so-called πρὸς ἕν equivocity.

The Greek and Arabian commentators on Aristotle gathered these comments together, but did not develop a full theory of analogy. In the same way the later Platonists, especially Pseudo-Dionysius, extended Plato's use of analogy and adopted some of the Aristotelian terminology.

MEDIEVAL DEVELOPMENT

In the Augustinian tradition, no formal, explicit doctrine of analogy is to be found; since intellectual knowledge does not arise from the sensible world, such a doctrine is not necessary. But prominent among St. Augustine's themes are the inability of our language to express the perfection of God, and the similarity-in-dissimilarity of creatures in relation to God.

The doctrine of St. THOMAS AQUINAS will be considered in great detail below. He used analogy more than any of his predecessors and made a number of formal analyses of it. There is, however, no single, adequate summary. Some of his uses reflect the original meaning of proportion; one usage (analogy of Scripture) is derived from the grammatical meaning of agreement. Such usage is irrelevant to analogy as a philosophical doctrine.

St. Thomas's immediate predecessors, like his teacher St. Albert the Great and his contemporaries, used analogy only incidentally. In St. Bonaventure we find instead a highly developed doctrine of creatures as vestiges and images of God. Even such authors as Henry of Ghent do not elaborate a doctrine of analogy; he, for example, is content to say that there are two types of being.

John DUNS SCOTUS is aware of Aquinas's doctrine of analogy as well as of equivalents like that of Henry of Ghent's double notion of being. His arguments for the univocity of being rest on his view of metaphysics (univocal being is its object), the possibility of a proof for the existence of God (only from being as being can the existence of a transcendent God be proved), and the principle of contradiction and the laws of logic (if being is not univocal, formal contradictions are impossible; arguments employing "being" would have four terms). However, along with the univocity of being, Scotus holds an analogy of beings in themselves insofar as they are related and ordered.

In the hands of WILLIAM OF OCKHAM, the univocity of being becomes the logical univocity of a name or a sign. A word is "common" to many things; if it is not univocal, it must be equivocal. In addition to words, there are also signs, and signs are very like the words which conventionally express them. But there can be no question of any analogy of beings in themselves, since things are radically singular and unrelated to each other.

THOMISTIC COMMENTATORS

Against this background, the great commentators on St. Thomas Aquinas, such as John Capreolus excepted, systematized and developed the doctrine of their master. In the 15th century, Cardinal Tommaso de Vio CAJETAN wrote his famous *On the Analogy of Names.* Cajetan holds that there are three basic types of analogy, according to the division of analogy given by St. Thomas in *In 1 sent.* 19.5.2 ad 1. These are analogy (1) according to being alone and not according to intention, (2) according to intention alone and not according to being, (3) according to both being and intention. Analogy according to being alone and not according to intention is also called analogy of inequality and analogy of genus. In St. Thomas, the example is the term "body," predicated of terrestrial and celestial bodies. A logician always defines this term in the same way, but the philosopher of nature and the metaphysician define the two kinds of bodies differently. Cajetan considers that a similar difference can be found in all generic predicates; he therefore concludes that such predication is not really analogy at all. The second analogy, according to intention and not according to being, is called analogy of attribution. In it, the perfection exists only in one analogate, the *primary* analogate, but is attributed to other things, the *secondary* analogates, which have some relation to the primary one (cause, effect, sign, exemplar and so on).

The third kind of analogy, according to both being and intention, is the most important for metaphysics. According to Cajetan, this analogy is the analogy of proportionality, discussed by St. Thomas in *De ver.* 2.11. In this analogy there is no direct relation between the two analogates; instead, there is a relation within each of the analogates, and it is these relations that are similar and are the bases for analogical predication. In the two analogates which are unlike, there are four *relata* which are also unlike, but the two relations, or proportions, are similar (schematically: *A:B: C:D*). The analogon thus seems at first sight to be a similar function, or relation, but it is sometimes also called a common perfection. This analogy can be of two types: proper (intrinsic) and improper (extrinsic, metaphorical). Cajetan also asks whether there is one concept (*una ratio*) corresponding to the single analogous term. He answers with a distinction: first, there is a clear concept that perfectly represents the relation in one of the analogates and imperfectly represents the others; this concept is simply many concepts and only proportionately one concept. Secondly, there is a "confused" concept which only imperfectly represents the relation in the analogates and so is simply one concept, though it is proportionately many. The clear multiple concepts become the common concept by a special abstraction in which the particular modes are run together (con-fused); the single, common but confused concept becomes one of the clear concepts by way of fuller expression.

Cajetan considers two objections against analogy from the viewpoint of his own systematization. One is that analogy leads to agnosticism. He answers that only in the analogy of proper proportionality is the perfection intrinsic to both analogates and yet not in such a way as to destroy the inequality of the analogates. His other objection is that the use of an analogous term in reasoning makes that reasoning formally invalid. He answers that the term, when confusedly conceived, does have a true unity and so is not used equivocally.

JOHN OF ST. THOMAS, the third of the great commentators, is principally concerned with defending the doctrine of Cajetan. He does, however, differ on one point: it seems to him that individuals in the same species are univocal, for example, that many men are univocally beings.

Sylvester of Ferrara (FERRARIENSIS), the fourth great commentator, takes exception to one of Cajetan's statements about the analogy of proper proportionality. Because many texts of St. Thomas assert that there is a primary analogate in every analogy, he holds that even in the analogy of proper proportionality there is a first analogate, though Cajetan had denied this.

LATER SCHOLASTICS

The next major writer on analogy is Francisco SUÁREZ. He is not usually considered among the commentators of St. Thomas, though he does regard his theory of analogy as that of the Angelic Doctor. Suárez disagrees on many counts with Cajetan. He holds, first, that attribution is not necessarily extrinsic; in an intrinsic analogy the perfection exists perfectly and independently in one analogate, and imperfectly and dependently on the first in the secondary analogates. Secondly, he holds that proportionality is always extrinsic. He therefore holds that the relation between God and creatures cannot properly be expressed by the analogy of proportionality except in metaphorical language. Suárez considers the same objections which Cajetan had considered; these objections seem to him to require a strict unity of the objective concept which abstracts from the differences of the modes.

Later scholastic writers on analogy fall into three categories. There are followers of both Cajetan and Suárez; in addition, many Thomists and some Suarezians have adopted elements of both theories. In particular, these Thomists make use of an idea already mentioned by Cajetan: that a single pair of real beings may be related by several analogies; thus, God and a creature are analogously beings by both analogy of attribution and of proportionality. God is prior to the creature inasmuch as the analogy of attribution is made use of; both are intrinsically beings because of the analogy of proper proportionality.

Apart from Suárez and the Suarezians, most scholastics could be considered followers of Cajetan. Not until the 1920s were there signs that any Thomist began to question Cajetan's interpretation. Since then, a number of writers have tried to work out anew the actual texts of St. Thomas. Here several views have been stressed. Some

authors have emphasized the so-called Platonic strains in St. Thomas, and in the light of this new point of view the doctrine of PARTICIPATION has been stressed. Participation is a real, intrinsic analogy, which is not proportionality because it does not involve four terms. Similarly, the analogy of proportion has reappeared in many authors and this too, is a direct, intrinsic analogy. Finally, several authors depart from Cajetan in another direction; they assert that analogy is an affair of language, not of conceptions nor of being, and therefore pertains to logic, not to metaphysics.

RECENT THOUGHT

The historical movement has been considered as staying within the scope of scholastic thought. Analogy for many years was of no interest to nonscholastic thinkers; rationalists, idealists, and their followers restricted scientific language to univocal terms. Kierkegaard here represents a break; he considered univocal language, as belonging to science whose proper field is that of objects. But persons, and especially God, cannot be known objectively; the only valid knowledge here is "subjective." In the Danish thinker himself there is no theory of predication or of knowledge which systematically considers this difference. Karl Barth and after him, Paul Tillich, consider the possibilities of analogy in solving this problem. It seems to both that any real analogy reduces God to the category of finite things. We can speak about God only through symbols.

The notions of symbol and of myth have been exploited by many writers who feel, on the one hand, that abstractive organized knowledge is not the only kind of knowledge man has, and on the other, that any direct, purely intellectual knowledge is necessarily abstractive. Knowledge through symbol and myth is direct, profound, and vitally moving, but it is not a grasp of the intrinsic reality of the thing known. Thomistic criticism of this theory generally centers on the issue of intrinsic vs. extrinsic knowledge. A being that is known only through symbol, myth, or metaphor is not known in itself; hence we can never make any statement about that being in itself, but only statements about ourselves and objects of direct experience. While this is not sufficient for religious language, it must be recognized as playing some partial role.

Something similar to analogy has been reached by an altogether different road. The movement called POSITIVISM considered that only scientific language was worthy of analysis, and so all non-univocal terms that deserved consideration had to be reducible to univocal ones. Moreover, univocal terms were restricted to things of immediate experience or to logical and mathematical terms. In the last decade or so, linguistic analysis began to consider common language rather than scientific language. In common language, there are of course many univocal terms; but a great number of terms are found to have many meanings, and in some of their usages no single meaning can be pinned down. This usage has been called systematic ambiguity. Several Thomistic writers have seen in the theory of systematic ambiguity a contemporary approach to the same problem that St. Thomas and his followers handled through the notion of analogy. A few think that the modern approach is better than the traditional one. For they point out, traditional discussions of analogy, at least since Cajetan, have been metaphysical. They think, however, that this is a mistake; analogy is and remains a matter of terms. Properly, therefore, analogy is to be treated by logic. There has been as yet no general and sharply focused Thomistic critique of this theory, but it would seem to raise serious difficulties with the traditional notion of logic as a science of second intentions, as well as to question the possibility of sciences other than logic, such as theology, to attain valid knowledge of the real. In the last analysis, ambiguous terms may serve to confuse or to persuade, perhaps even to suggest; but they would seem to have no place in anything like a science whose object is to know. Only if analogy reaches into our knowledge and even into the objects of our knowledge can analogical predication be admitted as scientific.

Doctrine of St. Thomas on Analogy

For St. Thomas analogy is a kind of predication midway between univocation and equivocation. Since analogy is the use of a term to designate a perfection found in a similar way in two or more subjects in which it is found partly the same and partly different, the first step is to clarify what is meant by the words "partly the same, partly different." (*Summa theologiae* 1a, 13.5; *In 4 meta.* 1.534–539; *In 1 eth.* 7.95–96.) In univocal predication, predicates have an absolute meaning and can be accurately and distinctly defined in themselves. But strictly analogous predicates cannot be so defined; their meaning is proportional to the subjects of which they are predicated. The reason for this difference is that univocal terms arise by abstraction from the particular subjects in which the perfection is present, so that the difference in the subjects does not enter into their meaning. Analogous terms do not arise by abstraction but rather by "separation," or negation (*In Boeth. de Trin.* 5.3–4), and so retain a relation to a concrete subject. A consequence of this is that there is no single clear meaning for an analogous predicate (ST 1a, 13.5 ad 1). Nevertheless, analogous terms can be validly used in argumentation on condition that they are not mistaken for univocal concepts of essences. Even if we cannot judge the conclusion of a univocal argumentation

without considering the premises from which it was derived, we can use that conclusion without keeping the original premises in mind as a premise for further argumentation. But in an argument using an analogous term, the conclusion cannot be abstracted from its premises, because the secondary analogate arrived at by the argument must include the primary in its definition (ST 1a, 13.6). That is why our statements concerning the existence and nature of God are limited in scope (ST 1a, 2.2 ad 3; 3.4 ad 2) and why St. Thomas made no concessions to rationalism, whether heterodox or Christian in intent, Averroistic or Anselmian.

The kind of abstraction called separation arrives at terms which in all their major uses are analogous and which can therefore be considered primarily analogous terms. In addition, some terms are first univocal but become analogous in other applications; these are secondarily analogous terms. Thus, some qualities of sensible things can be simply abstracted and are therefore univocal; but they can also be used to signify something that is primarily analogous. "Life," for instance, is a primarily univocal term. But in a second use, it can signify the kind of being that lives, and thus we use the term analogously when we speak of intellectual life.

KINDS OF ANALOGY

Analogical predication therefore involves a relation to, and between, the analogates themselves. The most fundamental division of analogy is into intrinsic, or proper, and extrinsic, or improper (*De prin. nat.* 6; *In 1 sent.* 19.5.2 ad 1; *De ver.* 21.4 ad 2). An analogy is intrinsic when the perfection which is predicated is really found in both of the analogates; it is extrinsic when it is really found in only one but imposed by the mind on others. Thus the term "living" is analogously applied to angels and animals by an intrinsic analogy, for both live but in an irreducibly different way. But when it is applied to the language of Shakespeare, it is applied by an extrinsic analogy; for life is only attributed, it is not found there in reality (cf. ST 1a, 18.1).

Various relationships. The second way of dividing analogy is based on the relation between the analogates themselves (*De pot.* 7.7; ST 1a, 13.5; *De ver.* 2.11; *In 5 eth.* 5.939–945). This relation can be directly between the two analogates, a "one-to-one," two-term analogy, as substance and accident are related to each other. Again, it can be a relation, not between the analogates themselves but between the analogates and some third object, as two accidents of a thing may be unrelated to each other but both be related to the same substance; this is a "many-to-one," three-term analogy. Finally, there may be no direct relationships of the analogates at all, but each of them may contain a relation that is similar to the relation in the other, a "many-to-many," four-term analogy, also called "proportionality." For example, when one understands something immediately, he says that he *sees* it. What he means is that as vision is to the power of sight, so direct understanding is to the intellect, not that the intellect is similar to the eye or vision to understanding.

Two-, Three- and Four-Term Analogies. In two- and three-term analogies there is necessarily an inequality between the terms, so that the terms can always be compared to each other as greater and lesser (*De prin. nat.* 6; *De subs. sep.* 8). Consequently one of the analogates will be "prior" to the other or others in time, in understanding, in perfection, in causality (*In 3 meta.* 8.4374–38; *In 4 meta.* 1.534–539; *In 5 meta.* 1.749). Moreover, when there is a direct order between the terms, one of them will be defined by the other; that is, all the posterior analogates will be defined through the first. But since definition is relative to knowledge (*In 5 meta.* 5.824), the first analogate will be the one which is first in our knowledge, not necessarily the first in reality. Thus we define accidents through their dependence on substance, for we know substance as prior; but we "define" God through the creatures' dependence on Him, for creatures are first in our knowledge and we know God only through them (*ST* 1a, 13.6).

In four-term analogies, on the other hand, there is no direct relationship between the analogates; hence, priority of one over the other is not necessary and one is not defined through the other (*De ver.* 2.11).

Mutual determination and eminence. Two- and three-term analogies can be further divided according to the kind of relation that is in question. Two-term analogies are sometimes definite proportions which are mutually determining (*In 1 sent.* prol., 1.2 ad 2; *In Boeth. de Trin.* 1.2 ad 3; *De ver.* 2.11). For example, knowledge can be possessed habitually or actually exercised. In the former case, "knowing" is predicated as in potency (and potency is always proportioned to the act of which it is the potency); in the latter, as in act (in creatures, an act is always the act of some potency). So, too, analogous causes are often strictly proportioned to their effects (*In 4 meta.* 1.534–538).

A direct relationship, however, need not be understood as a definite, interdetermining proportion. Indeed, the term "proportion" itself is often used by St. Thomas to indicate an indefinitely greater perfection in the prior analogate (*In 3 sent.* 1.1.1 ad 3; *ST* 1a, 12.1 ad 4). In such cases, the prior analogate possesses a perfection eminently, in a higher degree, more perfectly; whereas the others possess it deficiently, in a lesser degree, less perfectly (*C. gent.* 2.98; *De pot.* 7.5; *De ver.* 4.6; *In 1 sent.* 8.1.2; *ST* 1a, 13.2, 104.1; *Comp. theol.* 2.8). This language must

not be allowed to mislead us. The expression "degree of difference" may refer to a difference that is directly quantitative or at least based on a directly quantitative one; and then there is no analogy, but univocation, for the perfection in question is reducible to a single one (*ST* 1a, 42.1 ad 1). But at other times we speak of degrees of difference when the differences are greater than merely specific ones and cannot be reduced to univocal genera and differences (*De pot.* 7.7 ad 3). Similarly, we sometimes use the terms "perfect" and "imperfect" to refer to stages of one and the same perfection, as when we say that a baby has only an imperfect control of his limbs, whereas the grown man has perfect control; this also is univocation. On the other hand, we might say that animals have an imperfect spontaneity because they are not merely passive to outside influences; whereas the spontaneity of a man is perfect, in the sense that his spontaneity is truly a freedom, not only from external violence, but also from other predeterminations (cf. *ST* 1a, 4.1, 2; *Comp. theol.* 1.101; *De ver.* 8.1).

Participation. One kind of analogy of eminence has additional characteristics. For the prior analogate can be more eminent because it is the analogous perfection by its essence, whereas the imperfect analogates are such because they possess that perfection as distinct from themselves, as received, and so as limited by their own proper nature. The primary analogate, then, is identically its perfection and so is unlimited in its order; if we are talking about being and the properties of being, the being by essence is simply infinite. The secondary analogates, which have the perfections as received and limited, are being good and so on, by participation (*De pot.* 3.5, 7.7 ad 2; *C. gent.* 2.15, 53; 3.66, 97; *ST* 1a, 3.8, 44.1, 47.1, 75.5 ad 1 and 4; 79.4; *In Ioann.* prol.; *Quodl.* 2.2.1). In other perfections, too, a similar relation can be found. Thus, the acts of reason itself are reasonable by their essence, whereas the desires of a virtuous man are reasonable— truly enough and intrinsically—only by participation, inasmuch as through obedience to reason they possess some order, structure, and so forth, that is derived from reason (*De virt. in comm.* 12 ad 16).

Three-term analogies are sometimes a set of two-term analogies with a common primary analogate which is numerically one and the same, as medicine, health, food and complexion are each called "healthy" by their various relations to the health of the animal (*C. gent.* 1.34). Such a form of analogy is not really distinctive, since it can be simply reduced to the two-term analogies which make it up. At other times, however, the common term is not itself one of the analogates that are immediately understood but is entirely outside the predication or is a whole made up of all the analogates (*In 1 sent.* prol. 1.2 ad 2, 35.1.4; *De nat. gen.* 1). In the latter case, evidently, the parts cannot be equal or quantitative parts; otherwise there would simply be univocation.

CHIEF APPLICATIONS OF ANALOGY

For St. Thomas, analogy is not simply a formal structure of predication to be treated in logic. When analogy is "applied" to a particular case, the content or matter of what is said must be taken into account. For this reason, analogy is properly treated in metaphysics.

Being. The analogon most often and most fully discussed by St. Thomas is BEING. But there is no single analogy of being; rather, the various beings have different relations to each other. Following the lead of Aristotle, St. Thomas finds in each being a set of internal components. Of these, the most thoroughly discussed principles are substance and accident. Substance is being in the primary sense, and the act of being (*esse,* existence) properly pertains to it. Accident is proportioned to substance, and its being consists in its actual inherence in substance (*In 4 meta.* 1.534–539; *In 7 meta.* 4.1334–38; *De ver.* 2.11; *In 1 eth.* 7.95–96). Thus, substance and accident stand in a one-to-one, two-term analogy, the analogy of proportion. However, we can also consider that accidents are not beings by themselves but rather by their relation or reference to substance, and that the being attributed to them is the being of substance; we would then call this an analogy of reference or attribution (*De prin. nat.* 6; *In 4 meta.* 1.543; *In 11 meta.* 3.2197). The various internal principles of being and substance are similar pairs of proportioned analogates and so can all be understood as act and potency; the act-potency correlation is itself the proportional relationship (*In 5 meta.* 9.897; *In 9 meta.* 7–10.1844–94). The act-potency correlation itself is first discovered in motion; it is again found in substance (potency) and accident (act), in matter (potency) and form (act), faculty (potency) and operation (act) and essence (potency) and the act of being, esse (act).

Causality. Beings are also related to each other as cause and effect. Though many causes are univocal, having the same perfection as their effects, these are only the proximate causes of beings. More ultimate causes are not specifically the same as their effects; nevertheless, they can be denominated extrinsically from these effects by causal reference (ST 1a, 6.4, 16.6). In addition, these equivocal causes must be in some sense "more perfect" than their effects (ST 1a, 4.2). This is the analogy of eminence—but merely by knowing this we are unable to determine whether the perfection of the effect is intrinsically in the equivocal cause or whether the equivocal cause is more perfect inasmuch as its perfection is simply different. After the existence of God is known and His nature as pure act is apprehended, then His causal eminence in regard to His creatures is seen to consist in

this, that He is being, goodness and other similar perfections by His essence and therefore infinitely; whereas creatures both are and are *what* they are by participation (ST 1a, 14.6, 25.2 ad 2, 45.5, 57.2, 79.4, 93.2 ad 1 and 4; *In Dion. de div. nom.* 1.3, 2.4). Inasmuch as the being-by-essence is simple and self-identical, the analogy of participation in being is necessarily an intrinsic analogy. Hence, whatever is predicated of God according to this analogy is truly a knowledge of God, even though it remains a knowledge of Him through His creatures. Because God is the cause of the world through intellect and will (ST 1a, 44.3), He is the exemplar of all things; and created things are related to Him as images (ST 1a, 3.3 ad 2, 35.1 ad 1, 93.1; *In 1 Cor.* 11.1), as representations (ST 1a, 45.7), and as similar to Him (*De pot.* 7.7 ad 4 *in contrarium;* ST 1a, 4.3 ad 4). At the same time, created beings as individuals are seen to be related to each other as diverse participants in the One Being that is being by essence.

Good. The good that is convertible with being is predicated according to the analogy of participation, as is being (ST 1a, 6.1, 2); this transcendental good is, however, only a qualified good and as such, a secondary analogate (in an analogy of proportion) to the unqualified good, which is the "proper" good (ST 1a, 5.1 ad 1). The proper good is itself divided into the moral good, the pleasurable and the useful (ST 1a, 5.6 ad 3). Whereas the good is in things, truth is primarily in the intellect and only secondarily in things (ST 1a, 16.1). As it is in things, it is analogous according to their intrinsic perfection (ST 1a, 16.3); as it is in the mind, it is dependently and imperfectly in created minds, absolutely and perfectly in the divine mind (ST 1a, 16.5). Perfections such as life and wisdom (ST 1a, 18.3, 14.1, 9.1 ad 2, 13.9 ad 3, 41.3 ad 4) are also predicated by essence and by participation.

God. The transcendentals and those perfections which are called pure perfections (which do not necessarily include a mode of participation, ST 1a, 13.3 ad 1), are the concern of both natural theology and revealed theology. Negative statements about God are no problem. But affirmative statements can also be made about God (ST 1a, 13.12), both on the basis of the perfections of creatures and on the basis of revelation. A theory of analogy is the only way in which we can be sure of the *meaning* (not the truth) of these statements. St. Thomas's fullest explanation is given in regard to the predicate "living" (ST 1a, 18.3). Living can mean (1) a kind of substance capable of certain activities, (2) the activities themselves, (3) the way of existing proportioned to such a nature and such activities. The first two senses are univocal; only the third is analogous. In the richest sense the phrase "God is living" means: being the cause of life as we know it and having the perfection of life intrinsically, not as a limiting essence, but as identical with an unlimited existence and as expressing what we conceive as a mode of being. Surely we can form no simple concept of this or any other perfection that is drawn into the analogy of being (ST 1a, 13.1), yet we can understand what we mean by saying "God is living," and "God is life"; we can also show why we make such a statement.

On the other hand, *what* we can say significantly about God is often metaphorical. St. Thomas shows us how we can determine the abstract philosophically analyzed meaning of metaphorical statements (ST 1a, 4.2), and his commentaries on Sacred Scripture provide many instances of such analysis. But he does not engage in an investigation of the psychological, or subjective, meaning of these metaphors. For such analysis, fruitful recourse can be had to phenomenological and existentialist as well as to psychological, and literary studies of metaphor and symbol. Many modern writers on Sacred Scripture are successfully doing this.

See Also: ANALOGY, THEOLOGICAL USE OF; BEING; ACT; SUBSTANCE; ACCIDENT; GOOD; PARTICIPATION; CAUSALITY; TRANSCENDENTALS; GOD

Bibliography: History. J. F. ANDERSON, *The Bond of Being* (St. Louis 1949). H. LYTTKENS, *The Analogy between God and the World* (Uppsala 1952). J. OWENS, *The Doctrine of Being in the Aristotelian Metaphysics* (Toronto 1951) 58–60. Doctrine. CAJETAN, *The Analogy of Names and the Concept of Being,* tr. E. BUSHINSKI and H. KOREN (Pittsburgh 1953). T. M. FLANAGAN, "The Use of Analogy in the Summa Contra Gentiles," *The Modern Schoolman,* 35 (1957) 21–37. JOHN OF ST. THOMAS, *The Material Logic,* tr. Y. R. SIMON et al. (Chicago 1955) 152–208. G. P. KLUBERTANZ, *St. Thomas Aquinas on Analogy* (Chicago 1960). E. L. MASCALL, *Existence and Analogy* (New York 1949). R. MASIELLO, "The Analogy of Proportion in the Metaphysics of St. Thomas," *The Modern Schoolman,* 35 (1958) 91–105. A. MAURER, "St. Thomas and the Analogy of Genus," *The New Scholasticism,* 29 (1955) 127–144. R. MCINERNY, *The Logic of Analogy* (The Hague 1961). M. T.-L. PENIDO, *Le Rôle de l'analogie en théologie dogmatique* (Bibliothèque Thomiste 15; Paris 1931). G. PHELAN, *St. Thomas and Analogy* (Milwaukee 1941). J. M. RAMIREZ, "De analogia secundum doctrinam aristotelico-thomisticam," *La Ciencia Tomista,* 24 (1921) 20–40, 195–214, 337–357; 25 (1922) 17–38.

[G. P. KLUBERTANZ]

ANALOGY, THEOLOGICAL USE OF

Analogy is a word that stands for many different meanings. The most important are: (1) a form of reasoning, i.e., reasoning by analogy, also called argument from CONVENIENCE; (2) a mode of explanation (the parable); and (3) a mode of predication, i.e., analogous predication. The present article is concerned with analogy as a form of predication and with the use of analogy in THEOLOGY.

Aristotle. Called by some scholars the father of analogy [see A. Goergen, *Kardinal Cajetans Lehre von der*

Analogie (Speyer 1938) 86], ARISTOTLE was the first to deal systematically with analogy as a form of predication. In the *Organon* (106a–108b) he divides the predicates, according to their modes of signification, into three classes. To the first class belong the terms that are predicated of many subjects according to the same meaning, to the second the terms that are predicated of many subjects according to meanings that are entirely different, and to the third the terms that are predicated of many subjects according to a meaning that is partly the same and partly different. Aristotle calls the terms of the first class univocal and the terms of the second class equivocal. Then one would expect him to call analogous the terms of the third class. But this use of the term analogy does not go back to Aristotle, who defines this class of words as terms that do not differ by way of equivocalness. It is only later, in the Middle Ages, that the word analogy is used for this form of predication.

Aristotle did not content himself with elaborating a perfect logical theory of analogy: in his metaphysical and ethical works he applies this theory to metaphysical and ethical language, and says that terms such as being, substance, cause, good, etc., are predicated neither univocally, nor equivocally, but according to a certain analogy (κατ᾽ ἀναλογίαν). However, he did not go so far as to elaborate a systematic theory of theological language. But from what he said about metaphysical language (of which theological language is the most conspicuous part) and about God's transcendence it is necessary to draw the conclusion that the words used when one talks about God have, according to Aristotle, an analogous meaning.

Aquinas. ST. THOMAS AQUINAS distinguishes three kinds of predicative analogy. There is (1) attributive analogy, e.g., when "healthy" is predicated of Peter, medicine, food, climate, color, etc. In attributive analogy a quality is predicated properly and intrinsically of the first analogate, and it is predicated of the other analogates because of the relation that they have to the first analogate. There is also (2) metaphorical analogy, e.g., when "to smile" is predicated of Peter and of the meadow. In metaphorical analogy a quality is predicated properly only of the first analogate; of the others it is predicated only because of some similarity between their situations and the situation of the first analogate. There is, finally, (3) proportional analogy, e.g., when "substance," "nature," "being," "cause" are predicated of man, animals, trees, stones, etc. In proportional analogy a perfection is predicated properly and intrinsically of each analogate.

According to Aquinas all three kinds of analogy may be used in theology. Attributive and metaphorical analogies help one to talk about God's dynamic perfections. Proportional (and also attributive) analogy enables one to talk about God's entitative perfections, i.e., about God's nature as it is in itself (see *C. gent.* 1.30–34; ST 1a, 13).

Bonaventure and Scotus. The other great scholastics, also, especially BONAVENTURE and John DUNS SCOTUS, have made careful studies of analogy, the former more from an ontological, the latter more from a logical standpoint.

According to Bonaventure every creature bears some analogy to God because every creature is an imitation of God inasmuch as it is caused by God and is conformed to Him through the divine idea. Bonaventure distinguishes between two main levels of likeness: the vestige and the image. The vestige is the likeness that irrational creatures bear to God. The image is the likeness of rational creatures to God.

Duns Scotus, in his study of theological language, recognized that it is essentially analogical, but he insisted that analogy presupposes univocity since one could not compare creatures with God unless he had a common concept of both. God is knowable by man in this life only by means of concepts drawn from creatures, and unless these concepts were common to God and creatures one would never be able to compare the imperfect creatures to the perfect God: there would be no bridge between creatures and God.

After the Middle Ages analogy tends to disappear from philosophy but continues to be used by both Catholics and Protestants in theology. The main effort of Catholic theologians is to interpret and systematize Aquinas's teaching, whereas the aim of Protestant theologians is to elaborate a theory of theological language consistent with their views of the relationship between God and man, nature and grace.

Cajetan, Suárez, and the Modern Thomists. The official interpretation of Aquinas's teaching has been for centuries that of Thomas de Vio, better known as Cardinal CAJETAN (d. 1534), who in his famous little book *De nominum analogia* "solved the more metaphysical difficulties concerning analogy so thoroughly and subtly that no room is left to find out anything further" [John of St. Thomas, *Cursus philosophicus thomisticus* (Marietti ed. 1:481)]. Cajetan's interpretation (an interpretation based on an isolated text of St. Thomas—*In 1 sent.* 19.5.2 ad 1) starts out with a threefold division of analogy: attributive, metaphorical, and proportional. He then goes on to show that attributive and metaphorical analogies can be of little use in metaphysics (and in theology): the first because it is always extrinsic, the second because it is always improper. Therefore the only analogy capable of saving metaphysics (and theology) is analogy of proportionality, since it is the only analogy apt to express the true being of something.

Although this interpretation of Aquinas's doctrine of analogy became for centuries the official interpretation, there was from the very beginning a powerful dissenting voice, the voice of SUÁREZ, who was not willing to grant to Cajetan either that attribution is only extrinsic or that proportionality is the safeguard of metaphysics and theology. In his *Disputationes metaphysicae* (Vivès ed. 26:13–21) Suárez attempts to prove that Cajetan misinterprets Aquinas's doctrine of analogy on two main points. The first misinterpretation, according to Suárez, is of his doctrine on analogy of proportionality, since this analogy includes an element of metaphor and of impropriety, just as "smiling" is said of a meadow through metaphorical reference. Therefore Cajetan would be wrong in giving such prominence to the analogy of proportionality. And he is wrong, claims Suárez, also on another point: his identification of Aquinas's analogy of attribution with analogy of extrinsic attribution. Now, shows Suárez, analogy of attribution can be intrinsic and extrinsic, and Aquinas teaches both of them. Besides analogy of extrinsic attribution (i.e., the analogy where the denominating form exists only in the primary analogate), Aquinas teaches also analogy of intrinsic attribution, i.e., the analogy where the denominating form exists in all the terms, in one absolutely and in the others relatively, through a relation of efficient and exemplary causality of the latter to the former. The analogy between God and creatures is of this type. Therefore, to leave it out, as Cajetan did, is a fatal blow for theology.

For centuries Suárez's view was an isolated one. But in recent years many students of St. Thomas have joined him in his criticism of Cajetan's version of analogy. The reaction was led by É. Gilson's important essay, "Cajétan et l'existence" [*Tijdschrift voor Phil.* 15 (1953) 267–286], in which he attacked Cajetan's Aristotelian and essentialist interpretation of Aquinas, as well as the "minor" problem of Cajetan's version of analogy. This interpretation of the philosophy of St. Thomas, says Gilson, has been "the main obstacle to the diffusion of Thomism." By explaining Aquinas in the light of, and according to, Aristotle, Cajetan misses the great novelty of his philosophy, the discovery of being (*esse*). To Cajetan the supreme perfection continues to be essence, not existence. He is an essentialist, not an existentialist.

Encouraged by GILSON's authority, more and more Thomists have denounced Cajetan's version of analogy and have propounded some new interpretation of Aquinas's teaching. The interpretation that is now receiving almost universal consent (it is supported by É. Gilson, C. Fabro, J. Nicolas, B. Montagnes, A. Hayen, and many other scholars, as well as the present writer) can be summarized as follows: Aquinas teaches both analogy of intrinsic attribution and proper proportionality. At the beginning of his theological career he seems to emphasize proportionality more than attribution, but toward the end of his life his preference is for attribution, although he never rejects proportionality. He prefers attribution, because proportionality is inadequate to express at the same time God's transcendence and immanence. Proportionality is certainly able to express God's transcendence, but fails to express His immanence adequately, since it cannot express the dependence of the finite on divine causality. In analogy of proper proportionality there are no primary and secondary analogates. All analogates are primary. For this reason Aquinas came to the conclusion that analogy of proper proportionality cannot give an adequate interpretation of the God-creature relationship, and dropped it in theology but kept it in metaphysics.

Aquinas believes that an adequate interpretation of the God-creature relationship can be provided by analogy of intrinsic attribution. Analogy of intrinsic attribution is able to signify both that there is a likeness between primary and secondary analogates, and that the secondary analogates are imperfect imitations of the primary. Intrinsic attribution is able to stress the likeness between analogates as much as their difference. It says that the analogous perfection is predicated of the primary analogate essentially and of the secondary analogate by participation.

Analogy in Protestant Theology. Up to 1965 no systematic historical study of the doctrine of analogy in Protestant theology has been made [although there is an outline drawn up by the author of the present article in *The Principle of Analogy in Protestant and Catholic Theology* (The Hague 1963)]. However, it is probable that a good history of analogy in Protestant theology could be written by distinguishing three periods: (1) the period of the reformers and orthodoxy, during which Protestant theologians were still attached to Catholic tradition and considered analogy as the only proper way of talking about God; (2) the period of Hegelian and Kierkegaardian theology, during which analogy was replaced by dialectic; and (3) the period of the great modern theologians, K. BARTH, P. TILLICH, and R. BULTMANN, during which a remarkable revival of analogy has taken place. These theologians recognize that analogy is the only proper way of talking about God, but do not agree about its nature: Tillich conceives it as symbolic, Barth as an analogy of faith (*analogia fidei*), and Bultmann as an existential analogy.

Both classical and modern Protestant theologians have tried to elaborate a theory of analogy coherent with their doctrine of the relationship between nature and grace, which are conceived as opposites that can never be reconciled. Sin has caused in human nature a corruption that cannot be healed; it has raised between God and man an infinite qualitative difference that will last forever. This principle of the infinite qualitative difference is reflected in the Protestant theories of theological language: in the theory of analogy of extrinsic attribution of classical theology, in the Hegelian theory of dialectic, in Tillich's theory of symbolic analogy, in Barth's theory of analogy of faith, and in Bultmann's theory of existential analogy. While in the Catholic theory of analogy it is legitimate to use human concepts and human language when one talks about God because of a permanent analogy existing between God's being and man's being, according to the Protestant theories of analogy any such use is condemned, because after the Fall there is no longer an analogy of being between God and man. Therefore men's words are such that they can never, of themselves, be properly predicated of God. They can express divine reality either by a purely extrinsic attribution, or dialectically, or symbolically, or mythically, or by a divine choice.

What should one say of these Protestant theories of theological language? Are they satisfactory? Are they such as to give one some knowledge of God? Catholic and Protestant theologians generally agree that the very possibility of any knowledge of God, both natural and revealed, rests on analogy: in the natural knowledge it is man who takes some concepts from nature and applies them to God; whereas in the supernatural knowledge it is God Himself who chooses some of the concepts used by man in order to tell him something about Himself. The first kind of analogy is called *analogia entis,* the second, *analogia fidei.* According to the Catholic doctrine on the relationship between GRACE AND NATURE, there is no conflict, but harmony, between the two analogies: grace does not destroy analogy, but, by raising it into analogy of faith, fulfills it. On the contrary, according to the Protestant doctrine on the relationships between nature and grace, there can be no harmony between the two analogies but only conflict: analogy of being cannot be redeemed and therefore it cannot be raised into analogy of faith. Between analogy of being and analogy of faith there is a permanent "ontological" conflict.

From the Catholic point of view such a conflict is inadmissible: "to separate the supernatural from the natural knowledge of God in this radical way is to render the former unintelligible and impossible, since revelation, and this is clear, does not change our natural mode of knowing, but utilizes the natural instruments of our knowledge, our acquired concepts, and our mental constructions" [J. H. Nicolas, "Affirmation de Dieu et connaissance," *Revue thomiste* 64 (1964) 201].

See Also: ANALOGY; ANALOGY OF FAITH; ANTHROPOMORPHISM (IN THEOLOGY);

METHODOLOGY (THEOLOGY); REASONING, THEOLOGICAL; THEOLOGICAL CONCLUSION; THEOLOGICAL TERMINOLOGY; THEOLOGY, HISTORY OF; THEOLOGY, INFLUENCE OF GREEK PHILOSOPHY ON.

Bibliography: The use of analogy in theology. G. P. KLUBERTANZ, *St. Thomas Aquinas on Analogy* (Chicago 1960), full bibliog. A. CHOLLET, *Dictionnaire de théologie catholique,* ed. A. VACANT, 15 v. (Paris 1903–50; Tables générales 1951–) 1.1:1142–54. Y. M. J. CONGAR, *ibid.* 15.1:382–386, 389–390, 452–453. E. CORETH and E. PRZYWARA, *Lexikon für Theologie und Kirche,* ed. J. HOFER and K. RAHNER, 10 v. (2d, new ed. Freiburg 1957–65); suppl., *Das Zweite Vatikanische Konzil: Dokumente und kommentare,* ed. H. S. BRECHTER et al., pt. 1 (1966) 1:468–473. E. PRZYWARA, *ibid.* 473–476. K. BARTH, *Anselm: Fides quaerens intellectum,* tr. I. W. ROBERTSON (London 1960); *Nein! Antwort an Emil Brunner* (Munich 1934); *Church Dogmatics* (New York 1955–). J. BITTREMIEUX, *De analogica nostra Dei cognitione* (Louvain 1913). Y. M. J. CONGAR, *La Foi et la théologie* (Tournai 1962). M. T. L. PENIDO, *Le Rôle de l'analogie en théologie dogmatique* (*Bibliothèque Thomiste* 15; Paris 1931). I. T. RAMSEY, *Religious Language* (New York 1963). G. SÖHNGEN, *Analogie und Metapher: Kleine Philosophie und Theologie der Sprache* (Freiburg 1962). V. BRUSOTTI, "L'analogia di attribuzione e la conoscenza della natura di Dio," *Rivista di filosofia neoscolastica* 27 (1935) 31–66. K. FECKES, "Die Analogie in unserem Gotteskennen," in *Probleme der Gotteserkenntnis,* ed. A. DYROFF et al. (Münster 1928). L. LE ROHELLEC, "Cognitio nostra analogica de Deo," *Divus Thomas* 30 (1927) 298–319. G. M. MANSER, "Die analoge Erkenntnis Gottes," *Divus Thomas* 6 (1928) 385–403. J. F. ROSS, "Analogy as a Rule of Meaning for Religious Language," *International Philosophical Quarterly* 1 (1961) 468–502. A. D. SERTILLANGES, "Agnosticisme ou anthropomorphisme," *Revue de philosophie* 8 (1906) 129–165. Aquinas's theory of analogy. J. F. ANDERSON, *The Bond of Being* (St. Louis 1949). B. M. BELLERATE, *L'analogia Tomista nei grandi commentatori di S. Tommaso* (Rome 1960). C. FABRO, *Partecipazione e causalità secondo S. Tommaso d'Aquino* (Turin 1960). J. FEHR, *Das Offenbarungsproblem in dialektischer und thomistischer Theologie* (Fribourg 1939). J. HABBEL, *Die Analogie zwischen Gott und Welt nach Thomas von Aquin* (Berlin 1928). H. LYTTKENS, *The Analogy between God and the World* (Uppsala 1952). R. M. MCINERNY, *The Logic of Analogy* (The Hague 1961). B. MONTAGNES, *La Doctrine de l'analogie de l'être d'après saint Thomas d'Aquin* (Louvain 1963). G. PHELAN, *St. Thomas and Analogy* (Milwaukee 1941). O. A. VARANGOT, *Analogia de atribución intrinseca y analogia del ente segun Santo Tomas* (Buenos Aires 1957). F. A. BLANCHE, "La Notion d'analogie dans la philosophie de S. Thomas d'Aquin," *Revue des sciences philosophiques et théologiques* 10 (1921) 170–193. B. LANDRY, "L'Analogie de proportion chez S. Thomas d'Aquin," *Revue néo-scolastique de philosophie* (1922) 257–280. A. MARC, "L'Idée thomiste de l'être et les analogies d'attribution et de proportionnalité," *ibid.* 35 (1933) 157–189. E. WINANCE, "L'Essence divine et la connaissance humaine dans le Commentaire sur les Sentences de S. Thomas," *Revue philosophique de Louvain* 55 (1957) 171–215. H. A. WOLFSON, "St. Thomas on Divine Attributes," in *Mélanges offerts à Étienne Gilson de l'Academie française* (Toronto 1959) 673–700.

[B. MONDIN]

ANALOGY OF FAITH

Originally a mathematical term, the Greek word for ANALOGY means "proportion" and was borrowed by philosophers to refer to the relationship between concepts of things that are partly the same and partly different. It took on special importance in the concept of analogy of being (*analogia entis*). The analogy of faith (*analogia fidei*) must not be confused with this more philosophic concept. The phrase analogy of faith is Biblical: Rom 12.6 speaks of the charism of prophecy, along with such similar gifts as ministering, teaching, exhorting. Prophets exercised one of several "offices" within the primitive church (Acts 11.27; 13.1); guided by the Spirit, they gained insight into the faith or recognized tasks to be undertaken. The Pauline injunction is given that this gift of prophecy must be exercised "according to the proportion [ἀναλογίαν] of faith." No prophet is to be accepted who proclaims anything opposed to the "one faith" proper to the "one body in Christ." Such preaching would be out of proportion to, or beyond, the objective truth entrusted to the Christian community.

The analogy of faith, therefore, has always been associated with the one unchanging faith of the Church; it is closely related to the notion of TRADITION and soon became a norm for the early Christian writers. They saw a "proportion" in the manner in which the New Testament complements the Old Testament, and in which each particular truth contributes to the inner unity of the entire Christian revelation. Thus the phrase came to indicate a rule or guide for the exegesis of Scripture (*see* HERMENEUTICS, BIBLICAL). In difficult texts, the teachings of tradition and the analogy of faith must lead the way. The Catholic exegete, conscious of his faith, recognizes the intimate relationship between Scripture and tradition; he strives to explain Scriptural passages in such a way that the sacred writers will not be set in opposition to one another or to the faith and teaching of the Church (cf. Leo XIII, *Enchiridion symbolorum,* 3283; Pius X, *Enchiridion symbolorum,* 3546; Pius XII, *Enchiridion symbolorum,* 3887).

Karl Barth's violent rejection of the *analogia entis* "as the invention of Antichrist" and his insistence that in questions of revelation only the *analogia fidei* is acceptable occasioned further study of this problem. In its reaction against the extremes of liberal Protestantism, DIALECTICAL THEOLOGY (or crisis theology) built upon KIERKEGAARD's notion of God as "completely other" than man, and as totally transcendent. *Analogia fidei* means for Barth that we possess a "theological language" in which God and not man gives meaning to the words. His great fear is that philosophy (represented by *analogia entis*) will sit in judgment on the Word of God.

Söhngen points out that Barth misunderstands the Catholic notion of *analogia entis,* and that it does not make philosophy master over faith [*Catholica,* three (1934) 113–136, 176–208; four (1935) 38–42]. Though not convinced, Barth admits the pertinence of Söhngen's remarks. Barth's fear of rationalistic "proofs" for the mysteries of faith may indicate here an identification of the Catholic doctrine with the admittedly too rationalistic theories of faith of the post-Cartesian era; a clearer grasp of the Thomist-Suarezian approaches might remove this fear. Barth seems to be more concerned here with certitude, so that he looks upon the *analogia entis* as something on the level of knowledge rather than being—noetic rather than ontic. The Catholic will not hesitate to admit that it is God who gives His meaning to the human words used to express the divine; an *analogia fidei* in this sense is essential. The Christian vocabulary has only gradually been formed throughout the life of the divinely guided Church. To reject the *analogia entis* entirely, however, cuts man off so radically from God that, as Emil Brunner points out, the end result can be nothing but the most advanced form of Nominalism, in which human words take on divine meanings that are purely arbitrary and are in no way reflected in a reality already existing in the midst of creatures.

Bibliography: K. BARTH, *Church Dogmatics,* tr. G. T. THOMSON (New York 1955–). H. U. VON BALTHASAR, *Karl Barth: Darstellung und Deutung seiner Theologie* (2d ed. Cologne 1962). H. BOUILLARD, *Karl Barth,* 3 v. (Paris 1957) 2:190–217. J. L. MURPHY, *With the Eyes of Faith* (Milwaukee 1965). B. NEUNHEUSER, "La teologia protestante in Germania," in *Problemi e orientamenti di teologia dommatica,* 2 v. (Milan 1957) v.1. E. PRZYWARA, *Lexikon für Theologie und Kirche,* ed. J. HOFER and K. RAHNER, 10 v. (2d new ed. Freiburg 1957–65) 1:473–476.

[J. L. MURPHY]

ANALYSIS AND SYNTHESIS

Transcriptions of the Greek ἀνάλυσις, from ἀνά and λύω, meaning resolution, and σύνθεσις, from σύν and τίθημι, meaning composition. Analysis and synthesis are methods of inquiry and processes of things. Logical statements of analysis and synthesis, therefore, reflect basic metaphysical and epistemological theories.

Greek Thought. EPICURUS, building on the atomic philosophy of DEMOCRITUS, rejected dialectic for a canonic of sensations, preconceptions, and passions. All man's notions are derived from sensations by contact, analogy, likeness, and synthesis (Diogenes Laertius, 10.31–32). PLATO distinguished two methods in dialectic: division (διαίρεσις) and bringing together (συναγωγέ); and later commentators, such as Ammonius, PROCLUS, and Diogenes Laertius, enumerate three or four dialectical methods that include "analysis" but not "synthesis."

Aristotle, who frequently contrasted the methods of Democritus and Plato, made use of both analysis (but not in the sense of dichotomous division) and of synthesis (but not in the sense of combination of atomic parts). Aristotle distinguishes between a mixture, or composition (σύνθεσις), and a compound, or combination (μίξις; *Gen. et cor.* 328a 5–17); but he also uses "synthesis" more broadly to include three kinds: compositions of elements in simple substances, compositions of simple substances in homoeomerous substances (bones, flesh, etc.), and compositions of these in more complex organic and inorganic bodies (*Part. animal.* 646a 12–24; *Topica* 151a 20–31). Thinking is true or false by a synthesis (or division) of objects of thought (*Anim.* 430a 26-b 4); synthesis and division are essential to truth and falsity, and nouns and verbs are related by synthesis and division in propositions (*Interp.* 16a 9–18). In general, a synthesis is a combination of parts in a whole, and its opposite is division rather than analysis. Analysis is resolution in two senses for Aristotle. In the *Prior Analytics* it is the resolution of all syllogisms to the perfect, or universal, syllogisms of the first figure (47a 2–5). In the *Posterior Analytics* it is the resolution of demonstrative syllogisms to true premises (78a 6–8). In the latter sense practical deliberation, like mathematical inquiry, is an analysis: what is sought is assumed and the means of achieving it are sought. What is last in the order of analysis is first in the order of genesis (*Eth. Nic.* 1112b 11–24).

Commentators. Mathematical analysis is presented by Euclid, Pappus, and Proclus as Aristotle formulated it. Analysis is the method of assuming what is sought and tracing its consequences to something admitted to be true. These thinkers added, however, that synthesis is the contrary method of assuming that which is admitted to be true and tracing its consequences. Alexander of Aphrodisias attributes this geometrical conception of analysis and synthesis to Aristotle in his commentary on the *Prior Analytics.* Synthesis is the way from principles to that which is derived from the principles, and analysis is the return from the ends to the principles. Greek commentators tended to accept this interpretation, and it was reinforced by Galen's inclusion of analysis and synthesis among the methods of medicine. Cicero, on the other hand, distinguished two methods, "invention" and "judgment" and since the method of invention is developed in the *Topics,* the method of judgment was sought in the *Analytics.* After the translation of the *Analytics* and the *Topics* in the 12th century, the terms *resolutio* (analysis) and *compositio* (synthesis) took their places beside *inventio* and *judicium* in the interpretation of Aristotle's logic. THOMAS AQUINAS distinguishes three applications of these terms: (1) nouns and verbs are related in propositions by composition and division; (2) inferences involving certainty depend on judgment and are treated in the *Analytics,* those short of certainty depend on invention, and inventions concerned with probabilities are treated in the *Topics;* and (3) inference from experienced composites to simple principles is resolution, and inference from principles or simples to conclusions or composites is composition.

Renaissance and Modern Thought. During the Renaissance, problems of method assumed a central place in the arts and sciences and in logic. All the varieties of classifications of methods in logic and rhetoric, mathematics and medicine, science, practice, and the arts were brought into complex opposition. Two pairs of distinctions—analysis and synthesis, and judgment and invention (or discovery)—emerged as dominant, sometimes in opposition, sometimes merging. Peter RAMUS held that there is a single method and that invention and judgment are phases of its employment. His opponents, e.g., J. Schegk (1511–87) and J. ZABARELLA, differentiated analysis and synthesis, resolution and composition. Basic issues of philosophy and scientific method were involved in the oppositions. Analysis and synthesis may be conceived in terms of parts and wholes or in terms of principles and conclusions. By the first approach analysis proceeds from wholes to parts, and synthesis arranges parts in wholes; by the second approach analysis proceeds from effects to causes, and synthesis from principles to conclusions. The first constitutes a single method in which discovery is a synthesis of elements analyzed, and knowledge is conceived as empirical and a posteriori; the second distinguishes two processes, the analytic discovery of causes and principles and the synthetic derivation of conclusions; knowledge is conceived as universal and a priori. These differences emerged in formulations of scientific method when F. BACON sought a method of discovery in topics or tables of observations and a synthesis in the increase and organization of the sciences, while R. DESCARTES sought a method of discovery in the methods of mathematical analysis and a synthesis in mathematical deduction.

Differences of method underlie the treatment of simple, clear, and distinct ideas by the philosophers of the 17th and 18th centuries. I. Kant abandoned dogmatic philosophy for the methods of critical philosophy and emphasized the need to distinguish (as many philosophers beginning with Aristotle had) between analytic and synthetic as applied to propositions or judgments and analytic and synthetic methods. He argued against D. HUME that significant, and therefore true, judgments must be synthetic and that mathematical truths are synthetic, not analytic; he also sought to establish synthetic judgments a priori in mathematics, physics, and ethics by deriving them from principles synthetically.

Contemporary Usage. The oppositions of analytic and synthetic in contemporary philosophy apply the same distinctions to experience, nature, phenomena, and language; and the prominence of ''analysis'' in many 20th-century philosophies is conditioned by the same contradictory oppositions of definition. The truths of mathematics are analytic in an ''analysis'' related to the language of the *Principia Mathematica,* and they are derived, as the truths of any formalized science can be, from logical primitives. The analysis of language may be of formal languages or of actual languages, and it may proceed by constructing operational rules of use and of interpretation or by uncovering meanings of basic terms and of their coherences and incoherences. Phenomenological and existential analysis, on the other hand, seeks to avoid deduction and returns at each point to direct experience of phenomena without abstract separation of language, thought, and thing. Mathematics, psychology, and all the special sciences are subject to the same phenomenological analysis, but for that reason analysis does not depend on the conclusions of any of the sciences. The analysis of the phenomenologically given may adumbrate a transcendent ontological reality, or it may proceed creatively and operationally to the discovery of ontological essences emergent from existences. In both forms of analysis there is a tendency to refute or destroy the errors of past philosophers. Error is a mistaken synthesis, but there are many forms of analysis and, therefore, many errors of analysis owing to the fact that by one analysis other analyses are frequently seen to be undetected syntheses.

See Also: DEDUCTION; INDUCTION.

Bibliography: S. CARAMELLA, *Enciclopedia filosofica,* 4 v. (Venice-Rome 1957) 1:185–90. R. EISLER, *Wörterbuch der philosophischen Begriffle,* 3 v. (4th ed. Berlin 1927–30) 1:45–46, 3:201–04. S. E. DOLAN, ''Resolution and Composition in Speculative and Practical Discourse,'' *Laval Théologique et Philosophique* 6 (1950) 9–62. L. M. RÉGIS, ''Analyse et synthèse dans l'oeuvre de saint Thomas,'' *Studia Mediaevalia in honorem A. R. P. Martin* (Bruges 1948) 303–30.

[R. MCKEON]

ANAMNESIS

From the Greek ἀνάμνησις, meaning remembrance, commemoration, memorial, re-presentation in the sense of ''making present'' once again in the here and now. It takes up Christ's injunction, ''Do this in remembrance of me'' (1 Cor 11.24), and recalls the purpose of the Eucharistic rites as a commemoration of Christ and His salvific work.

History of the Term. It is not easy to render the word accurately in English, since it implies both a subjective and an objective element. Greek versions of the Bible use the word to translate various forms of the Hebrew root *zkr*. Such passages as Prv 10.7, Jb 18.17, and Ps 134 (135).13 show that memory and memorial are closely connected with the Hebrew conception of the "name," which connotes the personality and power of God. From Nm 15.40 and Ps 103.18 it is clear that remembering is inseparably linked with action of some kind. A memorial sacrifice is suggested by *'azkārâ* in Lv 24.7 and *zikkārôn* in Nm 10.10. Anamnesis and its cognate verb have the sense not merely of remembering something absent but of recalling or representing before God an event of the past so that it becomes present and operative in the here and now. Thus the sacrifice of a wife accused of adultery (Nm 5.15) is an ordeal that recalls her fault to God's remembrance, and the widow in 1 Kgs 17.18 complains that Elijah had come only to recall to God's remembrance the record of her sin. Finally, remembering is further related to the covenant (1 Chr 16.17–18; Ex 6.5–6) and to the theme of the Passover feast (Ex 12.14; Dt 16.1–3); but we cannot deduce much from this association.

St. Paul may have been influenced by the use of *zikkārôn* in Ex 13.9, when in 1 Cor 5.7–8 he declares: "Christ our passover has been sacrificed. Let us celebrate . . . with the unleavened bread of sincerity and truth."

Function in the Eucharist. The anamnesis interprets the mystery of the Mass, tying it to the events of salvation history; it serves to bring out a basic aspect of the Mass, that it is a memorial of Christ and His salvific acts. Because it is a relative sacrifice, the Eucharist not only recalls by reflection the personal relationship God established by Christ's death and Resurrection, but also represents these acts sacramentally, so that the worshiping community enters effectively into the everlasting sacrifice of the risen Lord, which is thus made present on earth. St. John Chrysostom is typical of early writers and subsequent tradition alike in his emphasis on the relation of Christ's sacrificial death and Resurrection: "We offer even now what was done then, for we perform the anamnesis of His death" (*In Hebr. Hom.* 17.3; *Patrologia Graeca*, ed. J. P. Migne, 63:131). The anamnesis in the Roman Canon makes clear, too, the role of the Church: "We thy servants and thy holy people" join in offering Christ's sacrifice.

In the light of OT and early Christian usage, it is evident that the celebration of the Eucharist is certainly more than a mere recollection or subjective memory (μνεάτα or μνήμη; cf. Rom 1.9–10); the Lord's Supper was not continued as a sort of funeral banquet, implying a mere mental commemoration. Nor is it some pale and powerless imitation of the *dromena* of the pagan mysteries, for it is the memorial that proclaims the Lord's sacrificial death (1 Cor 11.26). It is rather an anamnesis, an objective memorial directed Godward, releasing Christ's personality and power afresh; it is the experience of a fellowship with Christ in His eternal sacrifice. Since Christianity is a historical religion, based on the Incarnation of the Son of God and His redemptive death and Resurrection, it is these paschal mysteries that are sacramentally perpetuated in the Mass, the sign of Christ's new covenant with the whole of humanity.

Liturgical Use. The anamnesis follows the Consecration and is found in almost all liturgies (Serapion's is a marked exception). The oldest extant text is in the 3d-century *Apostolic Tradition* of Hippolytus: "Memores igitur mortis et resurrectionis eius offerimus tibi panem et calicem" (4; B. Botte, ed., *La Tradition apostolique de saint Hippolyte: Essai de reconstitution*, 16). In Gallican and Mozarabic liturgies this prayer is called *post pridie, post mysteria*, or *post secreta*. The Gallican liturgies generally limit themselves to an anamnesis of Christ's death; the Resurrection is already mentioned in Hippolytus; and the Ascension is cited in the 4th-century *De Sacramentis*. Eastern liturgical rites often add other mysteries.

Bibliography: J. A. JUNGMANN, *The Eucharistic Prayer: A Study of the Canon Missae*, tr. R. L. BATLEY (Notre Dame, Ind. 1956) 1–14. P. L. MALLOY, "Christian Anamnesis and Popular Religion," *Liturgical Ministry* 7 (1998) 121–28. P. SCHÄFER, "Eucharist: Memorial of the Death and Resurrection of Jesus," in *The Meaning of the Liturgy*, ed. A. A. HÄUSSLING (Collegeville, Minn. 1994) 56–78. R. L. BRAWLEY, "Anamnesis and Absence in the Lord's Supper," *Biblical Theology Bulletin* 20 (1990) 139–46. D. N. POWER, "The Anamnesis: Remembering, We Offer," in *New Eucharistic prayers*, ed. F. SENN (Mahwah, N.J. 1987) 146–168.

[F. A. BRUNNER/EDS.]

ANARCHISM

A doctrine that teaches the necessity to eliminate political authority in order to realize social justice and individual freedom. It is usually accompanied by opposition to private property and organized religion. Anarchism is rooted in these assumptions: (1) that man is good and essentially altruistic by nature; (2) that he is free only when he follows his powers and prescribes a rule to himself; (3) that he has been corrupted by the STATE and by LAW, which are always instruments of class or personal exploitation and oppression; and (4) that a natural, interpersonal harmony of interests exists in the economic and the moral order in the absence of the state. These assumptions lead to the following conclusions: (1) that social injustice and moral evil can neither be cured nor diminished by state action; (2) that the division of labor should always be on a voluntary basis; (3) that the state should be replaced by voluntary cooperation arising from below, that is, proceeding from individuals to groups, and, on the federal principle, to higher forms of human association; and (4) that voluntary association implies the right of secession.

History. Anarchist ideas extend back at least as far as Zeno (*c.* 320–*c.* 250 B.C.), the founder of STOICISM. Building on the principle of self-sufficiency, Zeno prescribed an ideal society wherein men would live without family, property, or courts of law. In medieval Europe the pantheistic BROTHERS AND SISTERS OF THE FREE SPIRIT rejected all authority and advocated communism of goods and women. During the Hussite wars, Petr Chelčický (*c.* 1390–*c.* 1460) taught that since all compulsion is from the devil, the state is evil and must disappear along with class distinctions. ANABAPTISTS of the 16th century believed themselves freed from all law by Christ's grace, refused to pay taxes or tithes, and held wives and property in common. The French writers Rabelais (*c.* 1495–1553) and FÉNELON (1651–1715) expressed anarchist ideas that were later shared by some 18th-century *philosophes*. A couplet of Diderot is typical: "La nature n'a fait ni serviteurs ni maitres/Je ne veux ni donner ni recevoir des lois."

Systematic Anarchism. Modern anarchist thought draws on the classical liberal belief in a natural economic order and on the philosophy of Ludwig FEUERBACH (1804–72), which emphasizes the need to eliminate man's alienation from his true self by a reduction of all barriers and a reclamation of the material world. William Godwin (1756–1836), in his *Enquiry Concerning the Principles of Political Justice* (1793), considered government and property acquired by exploitation as basic evils, and he advocated a stateless society of self-governing communities with goods in common. He conceded that if the most natural and just associations were established, the conduct of some men would need to be restrained for a lengthy period until their corrupted instincts were corrected. The left-wing Hegelian Max Stirner (1806–56), in his *Der Einziger und sein Eigentum* (1844), argued that only the individual is real and that restraints such as the state, property, religion, and philosophical abstractions are detrimental to his self-realization. He advocated replacing the state with a voluntary association of egoists. The term anarchism was used for the first time by a systematic anarchist thinker, Pierre Joseph Proudhon (1809–65), in his *Qu'est-ce que la propriété?* (1840). He defined property, in the sense of goods obtained by usurpation and monopoly, as theft. He urged its elimination not by expropriation but by the establishment of banks of exchange that would operate on a basis of mutuality of individual services calculated in units of labor. He thought that such banks would lead to further free associations of persons having the same interests, which would ultimately eliminate the exploitative economic order and the state. Proudhon recognized that a complete removal of the state could not be readily realized, and he argued that the practical aim should be a minimization of coercion and decentralization, and the encouragement of voluntary groups.

Collectivist Form. With Michael Bakunin (1814–76), anarchism assumed a decidedly collectivist form. He argued that political authority, private property, and religion are natural institutions in the lower stages of human evolution, and proclaimed: "L'Eglise et l'Etat sont mes deux bête noires." The state is harmful because it supports an exploitative economic order and acts by coercion. Bakunin held that society should be built on voluntary association and cooperation, with common ownership in land and the means of production—"there will be a free union of individuals into communes, of communes into provinces, of provinces into nations, and finally of nations into the United States of Europe, and later of the whole world." Bakunin introduced into the anarchist movement an emphasis on terroristic violence that was brought to Russia and merged with NIHILISM by his pupil Sergei Netschayev. Prince Peter Kropotkin (1842–1921) wedded anarchism to a communism based on the commune, an autonomous unit owning all means of production and consumption. He believed coercive authority unnecessary because the new society would accord with the natural cooperative impulse in man and because free agreements need not be enforced. That modern anarchist thought is not uniformly antithetical to religion is evidenced in the thought of Count Leo TOLSTOI (1828–1910). Although he rejected the divinity of Christ and personal immortality, Tolstoi taught that the Gospels indicate that religion means altruistic love of neighbor and that this is negated by political authority, which proceeds from egoism and violence.

Contemporary Significance. Proponents of anarchism have differed over means of implementation. Godwin rejected violence and advocated education; Proudhon did not preach violence but believed outbreaks to be inevitable; the collectivists Bakunin and Kropotkin preached its necessity while Tolstoi repudiated it, emphasizing noncooperation with the state. With the spread of the ideas of Bakunin and Kropotkin, propaganda by the deed of terroristic violence was accepted by many and rationalized as a proper means to capture the imagination of the masses. Unquestionably the invidious connotation given the term anarchist in the popular mind is due principally to acts of terror, such as the assassination of Pres. William McKinley. Generally speaking, violence (and atheism) has been most associated with anarchism in the Latin countries. Allied with syndicalism as a mass movement, it reached a high point for a short period in the

Spanish Civil War in Catalonia when anarchosyndicalists assumed authority. In the contemporary world, however, anarchism has little significance as a political movement. It survives principally in intellectual circles as an ideal to be approximated, if not realized, and as a means of protest against the mass society and centralized economic and political order.

Critique. Anarchism's fundamental assumption of man's natural goodness is contradicted not only by the theological doctrine of original sin but also by historical experience. Although the antagonistic tendencies in men may be less strong than the cooperative, it is unwarranted to attribute the former solely to the institutional environment while deeming the latter completely natural. Further, legal power subserving the common good is not an avoidable hindrance to, but a necessary precondition of, the full development of human freedom and the attainment of social justice. Finally, it is inconceivable that the state can be destroyed without violence; if violence is used, a new coercive state will necessarily succeed.

Bibliography: M. NETTLAU, *Bibliographie de l'anarchie* (Brussels 1897); *Der Anarchism von Proudhon zu Kropotkin* (Berlin 1927). E. V. ZENKER, *Anarchism* (New York 1897). E. H. CARR, *Michael Bakunin* (London 1937). R. ROCKER, *Anarcho-Syndicalism* (London 1938). H. READ, *The Philosophy of Anarchism* (London 1940). G. D. H. COLE, *Socialist Thought: Marxism and Anarchism* (London 1954). J. JOLL, *The Anarchists* (London 1964). I. L. HOROWITZ, ed., *The Anarchists* (New York 1964). D. NOVAK, "Place of Anarchism in the History of Political Thought," *Review of Politics* 20 (1958) 307–29.

[A. J. BEITZINGER]

ANASTASIA, SS.

Anastasia is the name of a martyr saint commemorated in the Canon of the Roman Mass and in the second Mass of Christmas. The only known fact regarding Anastasia is that during the persecution by DIOCLETIAN a woman of that name suffered martyrdom at SIRMIUM, where the faithful constructed a church in her honor. Gennadius, Patriarch of Constantinople (458–471), had her body translated to a sanctuary in the Byzantine capital. Various theories have arisen to explain her connection with Rome. In the fourth century Pope Damasus decorated a Roman basilica known under the title of "Anastasia," which apparently served the Palatine and imperial palace. Thus, the Church of Anastasia is an important Roman edifice having some connection with the emperor and the pope. Since the word "Anastasia" means Resurrection, H. GRISAR suggested that the church may have been built to commemorate that Christian mystery.

But P. Whitehead believes it took its name from the founder, probably the Emperor Constantine's sister, An-

astasia. The name Anastasia was added to the Canon of the Mass late in the fifth century, and in the sixth century the basilica is referred to as a title church. The basilica, constructed between the Circus Maximus and the Palatine palace, seems to have originally been cruciform in style. It underwent various reconstructions and is an imposing structure with three aisles.

Feast: Dec. 25.

The Roman Martyrology cites another Anastasia, on April 15, who, with Basilissa, supposedly buried the bodies of SS. Peter and Paul and was beheaded by NERO. No evidence supports the existence of Anastasia and Basilissa.

Bibliography: H. GRISAR, *Analecta Romana* 1 (Rome 1899) 595–610. L. DUCHESNE, *Mélanges d'archéologie et d'histoire* 7 (1887) 387–413. P. B. WHITEHEAD, "The Church of S. Anastasia in Rome," *American Journal of Archaeology* 2d ser. 31 (1927) 405–420. R. KRAUTHEIMER, *Corpus basilicarum christianarum Romae* (Vatican City 1937–) 1:42–61. A. BUTLER, *The Lives of the Saints*, ed. H. THURSTON and D. ATTWATER (New York 1956) 2:98; 4:613–614.

[E. G. RYAN]

ANASTASIUS, ST.

Hungarian archbishop; d. Nov. 12 *c.* 1036–39. A German disciple of Bishop ADALBERT OF PRAGUE, Anastasius (or Ascherich; Ascrick; Astericus; Astrik; Radla-Astericus) became abbot of Adalbert's newly founded monasteries at Brevnov, near Prague (993), and then at Miedzyrzecz, Poland. He later undertook a mission to Hungary at the request of King STEPHEN I of Hungary, according to Stephen's vita (Monumenta Germaniae Historica: Scriptores 11:232–33). There Anastasius became abbot of St. Stephen's foundation at Pannonhalma, and later archbishop of Esztergom, possibly the only Hungarian metropolitan see (K. Schünemann). In 1007 Anastasius attended the Synod of Frankfurt, and in 1012 he was at the consecration of the church of St. Peter in Bamberg. His possible German origin and his certain presence at German synods is witness to the continued close links between Germany and the Christianization of Hungary under Duke Geza and Stephen I.

Feast: Nov. 12.

Bibliography: K. SCHÜNEMANN, *Die Deutschen in Ungarn bis zum 12. Jahrhundert* (Berlin-Leipzig 1923) 35–37, 46–48. A. BRACKMANN, *Kaiser Otto III und die staatliche Umgestaltung Polens und Ungarns* (Abhandlungen der Deutschen 1939) 23–26; *Zur Entstehung des ungarischen Staates* (ibid. 1940) 17–19. R. BÄUMER, *Lexicon für Theologie und Kirche*, ed. J. HOFER and K. RAHNER (Freiburg 1957–65) 1:494. A. BUTLER, *The Lives of the Saints*, ed. H. THURSTON and D. ATTWATER (New York 1956)

Martyrdom of St. Anastasia, miniature in the 11th-century "Menologion of Basil II" (Vat. Cod. gr. 1613, fol. 110).

4:325–326. F. DVORNIK, *The Making of Central and Eastern Europe* (London 1949).

[V. I. J. FLINT]

ANASTASIUS I, BYZANTINE EMPEROR

491 to 518; b. Epidamnus, modern Durrës, Albania, 431; d. Constantinople, July 9, 518. He married the widowed Empress Ariadne and was named emperor after a successful administrative career. At heart he was a Monophysite, who as a layman had engaged in preaching and had exhibited traits of religious scrupulosity. Before being crowned emperor, he was forced to sign a profession of faith in the Council of Chalcedon by the patriarch of Constantinople, Euphemius. His reign was troubled by the strife wrought by the HENOTICON. An able administrator, he did much to reorganize the interior administration and settle the external problems of the empire. He attempted to impose MONOPHYSITISM on the Eastern bishops, aided mainly by SEVERUS OF ANTIOCH and PHILOXENUS OF MABBUGH. In 496 he succeeded in deposing Euphemius, the patriarch of Constantinople, on

surreptitious charges that stemmed from his intransigent support of the Council of Chalcedon; he deposed also Patriarch Macedonius (511), as well as Flavian of Antioch (512) and Elias of Jerusalem (516). The imposition in the liturgy of the Monophysite Trisagion brought strong reactions in Constantinople, and one of the imperial officers on the Danube, Vitalian, revolted (513–515). His attempts at reconciliation with Rome did not put an end to the ACACIAN SCHISM; and only in Syria and Egypt were the religious policies of Anastasius temporarily successful. However, he proved to be one of the most efficient and remarkable Byzantine emperors, despite the failure of his religious policy.

Bibliography: L. BRÉHIER, *Dictionnaire d'histoire et de géographie ecclésiastiques* 2:1447–57. P. CHARANIS, *Church and State in the Later Roman Empire: The Religious Policy of Anastasius* (Madison, Wis. 1939). E. STEIN, *Histoire du Bas-Empire* (Paris 1949–59) 2: 77–217.

[P. ROCHE]

ANASTASIUS I, ST. POPE

Pontificate: Nov. 27, 399 to Dec. 19, 401. Anastasius was apparently a Roman. St. Paulinus of Nola, whom he received in Rome and invited to attend his anniversary in 400, praised his charity and zeal. Jerome likewise held him in high esteem, particularly as he favored the anti-Origenist group of Jerome's friends in Rome.

After Rufinus of Aquileia translated Origen's *Peri Archon* in 398, omitting or correcting heterodox doctrines ascribed to Origen, Jerome was encouraged to make a literal translation, thus renewing the controversy over the orthodoxy of Origen, a theologian about whom Anastasius knew very little. Rufinus had enjoyed the confidence of Pope Siricius, but evidently Jerome's friends in Rome, particularly Marcella, and Eusebius of Cremona alerted Anastasius to the perceived dangers of Origen's teachings. When he received a cautionary letter from THEOPHILUS OF ALEXANDRIA, probably instigated by Jerome, he convened a Roman synod to condemn Origenism and then wrote to Simplicianus, Bishop of Milan, and to his successor, Venerius, proscribing Origenistic heresies. Rufinus, feeling himself implicated, wrote an *Apologia* addressed to Anastasius in which he gives an orthodox explanation of his faith and justifies his translations of Origen. Anastasius further wrote to JOHN OF JERUSALEM, and in mentioning Rufinus declared himself disinterested in the latter's fate, as long as he did not propagate Origenism.

Anastasius had also written to the Council of Carthage, which convened on Sept. 13, 401, to urge the African bishops to continue the battle against the Donatists (J. D. Mansi, *Sacrorum Conciliorum nova et amplissima collectio* 3:1023; 4:491). The Africans ignored his advice, however, and negotiated with the Donatists. He died on Dec. 19, 401 (*Liber pontificalis*, ed. L. Duchesne, 1:219) and was buried "ad ursum pileatum."

Bibliography: P. JAFFÉ, *Regesta pontificum romanorum ab condita ecclesia ad annum post Christum natum 1198*, ed. S. LÖWENFELD et al. (Graz 1956). J. P. KIRSCH, *Dictionnaire d'histoire et de géographie ecclésiastiques*, ed. A. BAUDRILLART, et al. (Paris 1912–) 2:1471–73. *Liber pontificalis*, ed. L. DUCHESNE (Paris 1886–92, 1958) 1:218–219. F. CAVALLERA, *Saint Jérôme*, 2 v. (Spicilegium sacrum Lovaniense 1, 2; 1922). E. CASPAR, *Geschichte de Papsttums von den Anfängen bis zur Höhe der Weltherrschaft* (Tübingen 1930–33) 1:285–287, 291. E. FERGUSON, ed., *Encyclopedia of Early Christianity* (New York 1997), 1:49. H. JEDIN, *History of the Church* (New York 1980), 2:126–128, 250–254. J. N. D. KELLY, *Oxford Dictionary of Popes* (New York 1986), 36–37; *Jerome* (London 1975), 246–253. E. CLARK, *Origenist Controversy* (Princeton 1992), 171–173. A. DIBERARDINO, *Patrology* (Westminster, Md. 1986), 4:581–582

[P. T. CAMELOT]

ANASTASIUS II, POPE

Pontificate: Nov. 24, 496, to Nov. 19, 498. When GELASIUS I was succeeded by the conciliatory Anastasius II, hopes were raised that the ACACIAN SCHISM could be brought to an end. Papal legates were dispatched to Constantinople to announce the pope's election and to sound out the Emperor ANASTASIUS I. The pope was prepared to make a notable concession by recognizing the baptisms and ordinations performed by Acacius, but required that Acacius' name be removed from the diptychs. He made no mention of Peter Mongos. The success of the mission was compromised by the senator Faustus, the emissary of the Gothic King Theodoric, who led the emperor to believe that Rome could be won over to acceptance of the HENOTICON if the emperor recognized Theodoric's rule in Italy.

The pope's conciliatory efforts in his friendly reception of the deacon Photinus, sent to Rome by the archbishop of Thessalonica, who had been one of the most determined supporters of Acacius, displeased some of the Roman clergy and they renounced communion with Anastasius II, thus creating a schism within Rome itself. The pope died at this juncture, "struck dead by the divine will" according to the *Liber pontificalis*. This statement perpetuated the legend of the pope's "apostasy" during the Middle Ages. Dante placed him among the heretics in the sixth circle of hell. Pope Anastasius II wrote a letter to the bishops of Gaul condemning traducianism. A letter to King CLOVIS I congratulating him on his conversion is apocryphal, as Clovis was not baptized until after the pope's death. Anastasius II was buried in the portico of St. Peter's.

Bibliography: A. THIEL, ed., *Epistolae Romanorum pontificum* (Braunsberg 1868) 1.615–639. *Liber pontificalis*, ed. L. DUCHESNE (Paris 1886–92, 1958) 1:258–259; 3:87. W. ULLMANN, *The Growth of Papal Government in the Middle Ages,* 2nd ed. (New York 1962). R. U. MONTINI, *Le tombe dei papi* (Rome 1957) 105. E. FERGUSON, ed., *Encyclopedia of Early Christianity* (New York 1997), 1:49. H. JEDIN, *History of the Church* (New York 1980), 2:430. J. N. D. KELLY, *Oxford Dictionary of Popes* (New York 1986), 49–50. J. RICHARDS, *Popes and Papacy the Early Middle Ages* (London 1979), 67–68.

[J. CHAPIN]

ANASTASIUS III, POPE

Pontificate: *c.* June 911 to *c.* October 913; b. Rome; d. there. He was the son of Lucian, but little is known of him, except that he was a man of good repute. He succeeded SERGIUS III and ruled in a time of turmoil when the government of Rome was dominated by THEOPHYLACTUS, *consul et senator,* and his energetic wife, THEODORA. The papal throne was at that time entirely in the control of this powerful family (*see* TUSCULANI). There is extant only one authentic document of Anastasius' reign, a bull granting the PALLIUM to Ragembert,

Bishop of Vercelli. Another bull, purporting to grant extensive jurisdiction to the bishop of Hamburg, is spurious. Anastasius was buried in ST. PETER'S BASILICA.

Bibliography: A. CLERVAL, *Dictionnaire d'histoire et de géographie ecclésiastiques*, ed. A. BAUDRILLART et al. (Paris 1912) 2:1475. F. X. SEPPELT, *Geschichte der Päpste von den Anfängen bis zur Mitte des 20. Jh.* (Munic 1954–59) 2:350. G. HOCQUARD, *Catholicisme* 1:510–511. R. BENERICETTI, *La cronologia dei Papi dei secoli IX–XI secondo le carte di Ravenna*, (1999) 34–35. S. SCHOLZ, *Lexikon für Theologie und Kirche*, 3d. ed. (1995). J. N. D. KELLY, *Oxford Dictionary of Popes* (New York 1986) 120–121.

[A. J. ENNIS]

ANASTASIUS IV, POPE

Pontificate: July 12, 1153, to Dec. 3, 1154; b. Conrad de Suburra, Rome. As cardinal bishop of Sabina (named probably 1126), he actively supported the election of Innocent II in 1130 and served as his vicar in Rome when that pope was absent in France. Already old and experienced, he was elected pope without opposition on the day of Eugene III's death and consecrated on July 12, 1153. Anastasius was charitable to the Romans during famine, and he built a papal residence near the Pantheon. During his pontificate, WILLIAM FITZHERBERT was reinstated and Sweden began to pay PETER'S PENCE. When his legate to Germany failed to settle the matter of Frederick I Barbarossa's translation of WICHMANN from Naumburg to the See of Magdeburg, a move already denounced by Eugene, Anastasius accepted Wichmann and bestowed the *pallium* on him in Rome. He was criticized for his overly compliant attitude.

Bibliography: *Patrologia Latina*, ed. J. P. MIGNE (Paris 1878–90) 188:989–1088. P. JAFFÉ, *Regesta pontificum romanorum ab condita ecclesia ad annum post Christum natum 1198*, ed. S. LÖWENFELD (2d ed. Leipzig 1881–88; repr. Graz 1956) 2:89–102. *Liber pontificalis*, ed. L. DUCHESNE ((Paris 1886–92) 2:388. H. K. MANN, *The Lives of the Popes in the Early Middle Ages from 590 to 1304* (London 1902–32) 9:221–231. J. HALLER, *Das Papsttum* (2d rev. ed. Stuttgart 1950–53) 3:116–120. F. X. SEPPELT, *Geschichte der Päpste von den Anfängen bis zur Mitte des 20. Jh.* (Munich 1956) 3:212, 606ff. J. LAUDAGE, *Lexikon für Theologie und Kirche* (3d ed. Freiburg 1995). J.N.D. KELLY, *Oxford Dictionary of Popes* (New York 1986) 173.

[M. W. BALDWIN]

ANASTASIUS, PATRIARCH OF CONSTANTINOPLE

Patriarch, 730 to 753. At the dismissal of Germanus as patriarch of Constantinople because of his opposition to ICONOCLASM, the Emperor LEO III appointed the syncellus Anastasius as patriarch (Jan. 22, 730). Anastasius was excommunicated by Pope GREGORY III as a heretic and intruder, and the emperor in turn detached the Hellenized provinces of Sicily, Calabria, and the Balkan Peninsula from Roman allegiance, attaching them to the Patriarchate of Constantinople. Thus a further step was taken in the rupture between Rome and Byzantium. In 741 Anastasius supported the revolt of usurper Artabasdus, crowned him emperor, and agreed to the restoration of the holy icons in the city's churches. On suppression of the rebellion by the Emperor CONSTANTINE V Anastasius was severely punished and humiliated publicly, but retained the patriarchal throne. His subsequent reign was marked by an intensification of iconoclastic propaganda directed by the emperor himself. The patriarch died while preparations were being made for the Iconoclast council of 754.

Bibliography: B. KOTTER, *Lexikon für Theologie und Kirche*, ed. J. HOFER and K. RAHNER (Freiburg 1957–65) 1:491. G. OSTROGORSKY, *History of the Byzantine State* (Oxford 1956)145–147, 152–153. V. GRUMEL, *Les Regestes des actes du patriarcat de Constantinople* (Kadikoi-Bucharest 1932) 1.2:8–9.

[F. DE SA]

ANASTASIUS, PATRIARCHS OF ANTIOCH, SS.

Anastasius I, Patriarch of Antioch; d. *c.* 599. He was *apocrisiarius* of the See of Alexandria at Antioch and was elected patriarch in 559. He showed himself an intrepid defender of orthodoxy, opposing strenuously Emperor JUSTINIAN I's edict on Aphthartodocetism (565), and was exiled to Jerusalem in 570 by Emperor JUSTIN II. Pope GREGORY I, then *apocrisiarius* of Pope PELAGIUS II at Constantinople, sent several consoling letters to the exile, and on becoming pope interceded with Emperor Maurice for Anastasius' reinstatement (593). In exile Anastasius wrote much against heresy; five of his philosophical works are available in Latin translations. Because of the diversity of his argumentation, he is considered a precursor of scholasticism. He exercised great influence on later Greek theologians.

Feast: April 21.

Anastasius II, Patriarch of Antioch; d. *c.* 609. His letter to Pope Gregory I announcing his election and profession of faith is lost, but Gregory's reply exists (*Monumenta Germaniae Historica: Epistolae* 7:48). His Greek translation of Gregory's *Liber regulae pastoralis* also has disappeared. He was killed during an insurrection of the Jews when Emperor Phocas attempted to convert them by force.

Feast: Dec. 21.

Bibliography: Anastasius I. *Patrologia Greaeca* 89:1293–1308. A. RAES, *Bibliotheca sanctorum* (Rome 1961) 1:1064–65. E. STOMMEL, *Lexicon für Theologie und Kirche,* ed. J. HOFER and K. RAHNER (Freiburg 1957–65) 1:490–491. S. VAILHÉ, *Dictionnaire de théologie catholique,* ed. A. VACANT et al. (Paris 1903–50) 1.1:1166. R. JANIN, *Dictionnaire d'histoire et de géographie ecclésiastiques,* ed. A. BAUDRILLART et al. (Paris 1912) 2:1460. B. ALTANER, *Patrology* (New York 1960) 619. L. DUCHESNE, *L'Église au VI e siècle* (Paris 1925). R. DEVREESSE, *Le Patriarcat d'Antioche* (Paris 1945) 81, 83, 99, 118, 119. Anastasius II. A. RAES, *Bibliotheca sanctorum* (Rome 1961) 1:1052–53. H. RAHNER, *Lexicon für Theologie und Kirche,* ed. J. HOFER and K. RAHNER (Freiburg 1957–65) 1:491. R. JANIN, *Dictionnaire d'histoire et de géographie ecclésiastiques,* ed. A. BAUDRILLART et al. (Paris 1912) 2:1460.

[F. DE SA]

ANASTASIUS SINAITA, ST.

Seventh-century Palestinian monk, theological controversialist, and exegete revered as a saint by the Byzantine Church and included in the Roman Martyrology; d. Mt. Sinai, *c.* 700. He is of unknown origin and is confused with other authors. Anastasius was a monk on Mt. Sinai who left the monastery to dispute with heretics in Egypt and Syria and became known as the New Moses. His writings are edited uncritically and do not permit a fair judgment. The *Hodegos,* or *Viae Dux,* in 24 chapters, was composed in the desert against the monophysites (*c.* 685). The arguments on which it is based are buttressed by Aristotelian definitions and citations from the Fathers and the councils that are frequently faulty, indicating that he quoted from memory. In the *Hodegos* he mentions four other works: a Dogmatic Tome, the Apologetic Tome, the Treatise against Nestorius, and a Treatise against the Jews, which are now lost. A *Quaestiones et Responsiones* (*Eratopokriseis*) is in substance the work of Anastasius, but in its present form it shows signs of later additions. It deals with the whole gamut of monastic life and secular culture, and answers objections to the faith with Biblical and patristic texts. Eleven books of an exegetical work, Commentary on the Hexameron, are preserved in Latin, and only the twelfth is in the original Greek. The author depends on Pseudo-Dionysius and engages in exaggerated allegorism. A Dialogue on the Jews (*Patrologia Graeca* 89:1203–72) is not authentic.

Feast: April 21 (Orthodox Church).

Bibliography: *Patrologia Graeca,* ed. J. P. MIGNE (Paris 1857–66) 89:35–1288. B. ALTANER, *Patrology* (New York 1960) 633, 644. G. BARDY, *Revue biblique* 42 (1933) 339–343; *Dictionnaire de spiritualité ascétique et mystique,* ed. M. VILLER et al. (Paris 1932–) 1:546–547. J. D. BAGGARLY, *The Conjugates Christ-Church in the Hexaemeron of Ps.-Anastasius of Sinai* (Rome 1974). J. B. PITRA, *Iuris ecclesiastici Graecorum historia et monumenta,* 2 v. (Rome 1868) 2:238–294. R. JANIN, *Dictionnaire d'histoire et de géographie ecclésiastiques,* ed. A. BAUDRILLART et al. (Paris 1912) 2:1482–83. U. RIEDINGER, *Lexicon für Theologie und Kirche,* ed. J. HOFER and K. RAHNER (Freiburg 1957–65) 1:492. H.G. BECK, *Kirche und theologische Literatur im byzantinischen Reich* (Munich 1959) 442–446. M. SALSANO, *Bibliotheca sanctorum* (Rome 1961) 1:1059–61.

[F. DE SA]

ANASTASIUS THE LIBRARIAN

Enigmatic personality, very influential behind the scenes in Rome from the 840s to 870s; b. probably Rome, *c.* 810–817; d. *c.* 878. By his own account he was the nephew of Arsenius, the influential bishop of Orte, rather than his son, as HINCMAR OF REIMS held (*Annales Bertiniani,* ann. 868). His knowledge of Greek, which he learned at an early age, brought him into prominence. The beginning of his career was stormy and even scandalous. Created cardinal priest of St. Marcellus by LEO IV in 847 or 848, Anastasius soon abandoned his church for motives still obscure but in which ambition must have played a part; he was excommunicated (Dec. 16, 850), anathematized (May 29, and June 19, 853), and deposed (Dec. 8, 853). Between the election and the consecration (Sept. 29, 855) of BENEDICT III, successor to Leo IV (d. July 17, 855), Anastasius attempted to secure the pontifical throne by force and for a few days stood as antipope. Benedict III later admitted him again to lay communion. Anastasius henceforth altered his whole attitude, becoming a zealous defender of the succeeding popes. It is this change that explains why, up to the time of HERGENRÖTHER, Lapôtre, and Perels, the existence of two men named Anastasius (Anastasius the cardinal and Anastasius the librarian) was admitted. Anastasius became abbot of S. Maria in Trastevere under NICHOLAS I, was freed from his suspension on the day of the consecration of ADRIAN II (Dec. 14, 867), and immediately afterward was named librarian of the Holy Roman Church, a post he retained under JOHN VIII until his death (the last official mention of him is May 29, 877, the first allusion to his successor, Zacharias of Anagni, March 29, 879).

It is hard to exaggerate the part Anastasius played from 861 onward in drawing up papal letters, especially those dealing with the Byzantine Church and the Patriarch PHOTIUS, whose determined opponent he was. At the beginning of 868 Anastasius was acting patron to SS. CYRIL (CONSTANTINE) and Methodius on their arrival in Rome with the Slavonic liturgy. When Eleutherius, the son of Arsenius, shortly afterward (March 10, 868) ravished the daughter of Adrian II and a few months later killed her and her mother, Stephania, Anastasius was accused of complicity in the murder, whereupon the previous condemnations were at once reimposed. After being rehabilitated, probably before the middle of 869, he was sent by Emperor LOUIS II to Constantinople, on the occasion of the eighth ecumenical council, CONSTANTINOPLE IV, to arrange a marriage between Louis's daughter, Ermengard, and the eldest son of the Byzantine Emperor Basil I. The project did not succeed, but Anastasius made good use of his stay, now in questioning METROPHANES OF SMYRNA, the bishop whom Photius had once exiled to Cherson, about the discovery there of the relics of Pope St. CLEMENT I by Cyril (Constantine), now by helping the official delegates of the Holy See to the Council, at whose last session (Feb. 28, 870) he also assisted. As the *acta* of the official delegates perished, it was his personal copy that was accepted in Rome; in 871 Anastasius offered Adrian his Latin translation of these *acta*, preceded by a long dedicatory epistle. He was to do precisely the same thing, at the beginning of the pontificate of the new Pope John VIII, with the *acta* of the seventh ecumenical Council (NICAEA II, 787). During John's pontificate Anastasius' literary activity was particularly intense, consisting mainly of translations (of unequal value) from Greek into Latin. Thus, he composed for John the Deacon of Rome (Hymmonides) a *Chronographia tripertita* out of extracts from the Byzantine chronicles of Patriarch NICEPHORUS I, GEORGE SYNCELLUS, and THEOPHANES and a *Collectanea* relating to the history of MONOTHELITISM. For Emperor Charles II the Bald, both before and after his coronation (Christmas 875), he translated the *Scholia* of St. MAXIMUS THE CONFESSOR and of Patriarch JOHN III Scholasticus to the works of PSEUDO-DIONYSIUS and the life of the latter by Patriarch METHODIUS OF CONSTANTINOPLE (*Bibliotheca hagiographica latina antiquae et mediae aetatis* 554d), as well as summaries of liturgical treatises attributed to Maximus and to Patriarch GERMANUS I OF CONSTANTINOPLE and a *passio* of St. DEMETRIUS. His hagiographical work over 20 years included versions of lives, miracles, or translations relative to SS. JOHN THE ALMSGIVER, Patriarch of Alexandria, Basil of Caesarea, John Calybites, Bartholomew the Apostle, Pope Martin I, Stephen the protomartyr, Peter of Alexandria, Cyrus and John, and the 10,000 martyrs of Mt. Ararat. His translations of two short works of Cyril (Constantine) and his letter to Photius when he was restored to favor by John VIII are lost. Of the LIBER PONTIFICALIS, the composition of which was once gratuitously attributed to Anastasius, probably only the notice on Pope Adrian II is from his hand.

Bibliography: ANASTASIUS THE LIBRARIAN, *Epistolae sive praefationes*, ed. E. PERELS and G. LAEHR, *Monumenta Germaniae Historica: Epistolae* 7:395–442. U. WESTERBERGH, *Anastasius Bibliothecarius. Sermo Theodori Studitae de sancto Bartholomaeo apostolo* (Stockholm 1963). J. HERGENRÖTHER, *Photius Patriarch von Konstantinopel*, 3 v. (Regensburg 1867–69). A. LAPÔTRE, *De Anastasio bibliothecario sedis apostolicae* (Paris 1885). E. PERELS,

Papst Nikolaus I und Anastasius Bibliothecarius (Berlin 1920). G. LAEHR, "Die Briefe und Prologe des Bibliothekars Anastasius," *Neues Archiv der Gesellschaft für ältere deutsche Geschichtskunde* 47 (1928) 416–468. F. DVORNIK, *The Photian Schism: History and Legend* (Cambridge, Eng. 1948). P. DEVOS, "Anastase le bibliothécaire: Sa Contribution à la correspondance pontificale. La date de sa mort," *Byzantion* 32 (1962) 97–115; "Une Passion grecque inédite de S. Pierre d'Alexandrie et sa traduction par Anastase le bibliothécaire," *Analecta Bollandiana* 83 (1965) 157–187.

[P. DEVOS]

ANATHEMA

A Greek term (ἀνάθεμα) found in the sense of accursed or separated from the fold in Rom 9.3 or 1 Cor 16.22. Theologically, the anathema in the canons of councils generally means that the doctrine so condemned is heretical and it's contradictory defined as revealed truth (*see* DEFINITION, DOGMATIC). Such is the case for the canons of Vatican I. However, P. Fransen's study of the anathema as used in Trent has shown that not only revealed doctrine but also DOGMATIC FACTS or disciplinary laws can be covered by a condemnation under anathema of their denial. In such a case, the anathema expresses repudiation of an inadmissible doctrine or practice.

Bibliography: A. VACANT, 1.1:1168–71. A. BRIDE, *Catholicisme* 1:516–517. H. VORGRIMLER, *Lexikon für Theologie und Kirche*, ed. J. HOFER and K. RAHNER, 10 v. (2d, new ed. Freiburg 1957–65) 1:494–495. P. FRANSEN, "Réflexions sur l'anathegrave;me au concile de Trente," *Ephemerides theologicae Lovanienses* (Bruges 1924–) 29 (1953) 657–672.

[P. DE LETTER/EDS.]

ANATHEMAS OF CYRIL

A summary under 12 heads (hence the alternative names, κεφάλαια, *capitula*) of St. CYRIL OF ALEXANDRIA's teaching against NESTORIUS. They were worded in such a way that refusal to accept any of them is to be regarded as a denial of the Catholic faith. "If anyone does not confess . . . let him be anathema."

Nestorius was condemned in Rome in 430, and Pope Celestine commissioned St. Cyril of Alexandria to obtain from him a retraction of his errors. On receiving the papal instructions, Cyril took it upon himself to draw up 12 propositions and send them with a covering letter to Nestorius. This action was unfortunate. He went beyond his brief in drawing up what amounted to a new profession of faith, and the way he formulated his doctrine was misunderstood in Antioch and Constantinople. At this time the use of certain terms in Christology was not yet stabilized. Moreover, there were two different current approaches to the theology of the Word Incarnate. Both were legitimate, both were based on scripture; but whereas Alexandria stressed the unity of Christ and thence proceeded to consider the divine and human elements, Antioch began with the humanity and then turned attention to the mystery that this man was also God. Cyril seems to have been unaware of the difference in terminology and emphasis of the two schools. What is more, the sources of some of his phrases were suspect. Both the μίαφύσιζ (one *physis*) and the analogy between the human and divine nature in Christ and the union of body and soul in man were taken from Apollinarist works on the mistaken assumption that they were Athanasius'. It was not surprising then, that the Anathemas met with opposition. Theodoret of Cyr and Andrew of Samosata wrote refutations, and Cyril was obliged to defend his views in three apologies: *Against the Eastern Bishops* (*Patrologia Graeca* 76:315–386); *Letter to Eutropius* (*Patrologia Graeca* 76:385–452); *Explanation of Twelve Chapters Pronounced at Ephesus* (*Patrologia Graeca* 76:293–312). The text of the Anathemas can be found in *Enchiridion symbolorum* 252–263.

Contents. The first Anathema deals with the chief objection to Nestorius, since it defends Mary's title of THEOTOKOS, Mother of God. The second and third show the inadequacy of Cyril's vocabulary. In describing the unity of Christ he speaks indiscriminately of a physical or hypostatic union. For him the terms *physis* and HYPOSTASIS are interchangeable, and they are used to stress the fact that Christ is truly one, that there is a real union, not a mere association or harmony of two distinct realities. At Antioch the terms *physis* and hypostasis were also interchangeable, but there they were applied to the humanity and to the divinity to convey the idea that Christ is not only truly man but truly God as well. And so whereas Cyril maintained there was but one *physis* or hypostasis, Antioch maintained that there were two. Yet both views were within the realm of orthodoxy.

Some of the Anathemas have to do with predication. Both divine and human attributes are to be referred to the same Christ (4). The divine Word really suffered and died (12). St. Cyril later allowed that it was lawful to distinguish between statements concerning the human nature and those concerning the divine. The Nestorian heresy meant the need for caution in the use of certain titles and expressions in reference to Christ. He would not allow Christ to be called Theophoros, God-bearer. Some of the Fathers did use this name, but it does not sufficiently indicate the intimate union of the divine and human in Christ (5). Although scripture speaks of Christ as a servant, one cannot allow the Word of God to be called the master of Christ as Nestorius had done (6). Similarly, Nestorius had misconstrued Heb 3.1. The High Priest of men is not a man, but the Incarnate Word Himself (10). Neither is Christ an instrument of the Word; He is the Word (7). And so there is to be a single adoration of Christ, the Word Incarnate, not a coadoration of the man and the Word (8). Cyril brings out the fact that the Holy Spirit is not an alien power but the very Spirit of Christ (9). In the eleventh Cyril states that the flesh of the Lord has power to vivify, since it is the flesh of the divine Word. Antioch suspected such sentiments of APOLLINARIANISM, not recognizing that by flesh was meant the living, animated flesh.

Subsequent History. At the Council of EPHESUS in 431 approval was given to Cyril's letter to Nestorius (no. 4 in collected letters; *Patrologia Graeca* 77:44–49), and this was accepted as the authentic interpretation of Nicaea I. But the other letter of Cyril (no. 17; *Patrologia Graeca* 77:105–121) to which the 12 Anathemas were appended did not receive such formal recognition. Later, at the time of Pope Vigilius, there was to be confusion as to which of the letters was solemnly approved. As Galtier has shown, the Anathemas are not to be taken as the solemn dogmatic teaching of the Council of Ephesus, although they are to be found in the acts of the Council. This is not to say that one can disregard the Anathemas. The first one with its defense of Theotokos was certainly accepted, and even the others reflect the mind of the Council. But the true meaning of these propositions was clouded by the lack of terminological precision; and when MONOPHYSITISM arose, the Church defended its position without recourse to the Anathemas. Cyril himself recognized their inadequacy in the discussions after Ephesus; and when union was achieved in 433 with John of Antioch, there was no mention of them. The contention that Monophysitism was a natural outcome of Cyril's teaching cannot be maintained; and if certain less happy terms of his were dropped at Chalcedon, it is incorrect to say that there was an abandonment of his theology.

In the changed conditions of the 6th century there was an attempt to incorporate into the Church's teaching certain formulas of Cyril that had been omitted at Chalcedon, including the Anathemas. But much of this stemmed from a desire to find agreement among the various contending parties. When the good name and traditions of ALEXANDRIA and ANTIOCH were at stake, much depended on the official recognition of the orthodoxy of the great figures in these churches. Consequently, the mention of the Anathemas in subsequent documents is often motivated by reasons other than theology. Now that the terminology has been stabilized, it is only the Monophysite churches that keep to the Cyrilline way of speaking.

See Also: JESUS CHRIST, II (IN THEOLOGY); CHRISTOLOGY, CONTROVERSIES ON; JESUS CHRIST, ARTICLES ON.

Bibliography: *Dictionnaire de théologie catholique,* ed. A. VACANT et al., 15 v. (Paris 1903–50; Tables générales 1951–), Tables générales 2:2642–43. G. JOUSSARD, *Lexikon für Theologie und Kirche,* ed. J. HOFER and K. RAHNER, 10 v. (2d, new ed. Freiburg 1957–65); suppl. *Das Zweite Vatikanische Konzil: Dokumente und Kommentare,* ed. H. S. BRECHTER et al., pt. 1 (1966) 1:495–496. J. QUASTEN, *Patrology,* 3 v. (Westminster, Md. 1950–53), 3:116–142. J. N. D. KELLY, *Early Christian Doctrines* (2d ed. New York 1960). H. DU MANOIR DE JUAYE, *Dogme et spiritualité chez saint Cyrille d'Alexandrie* (Paris 1944) 491–523. E. L. MASCALL, *Via Media: An Essay in Theological Synthesis* (Greenwich, Conn. 1957) 79–120. J. H. NEWMAN, *Historical Sketches,* 3 v. (New York 1903–06) 2:307–362 (Theodoret). P. T. CAMELOT, *Éphèse et Chalcédoine* (Histoire des conciles oecuméniques 2; Paris 1962). H. M. DIEPEN, ''Les Douze anathématismes au concile d'Éphèse et jusqu'en 519,'' *Revue Thomiste* 55 (1955) 300–338. P. GALTIER, ''Les Anathématismes de saint Cyrille et le concile de Chalcédoine,'' *Recherches de science religieuse* 23 (1933) 45–57; ''L'unio secundum hypostasim chez saint Cyrille,'' *Gregorianum* 33 (1952) 351–398. J. LEBON, ''Autour de le définition de la foi au concile d'Éphèse,'' *Ephemerides theologicae Lovanienses* 8 (1931) 393–412. L. R. WICKHAM, ''Cyril of Alexandria and the Apple of Discord,'' *Studia Patristica,* vol 15, pt 1 (Berlin 1984): 379–392.

[M. E. WILLIAMS]

ANATOLIUS OF CONSTANTINOPLE

Patriarch; b. Alexandria *c.* 400; d. Constantinople July 3, 458. He was a disciple of St. Cyril, who ordained him deacon and sent him to Constantinople as his apocrisiary. Anatolius was chosen by Dioscorus of Alexandria and the eunuch Chrysaphius to succeed Flavian as bishop of Constantinople after the Robber Synod of Ephesus in August of 449. His good faith was challenged by Pope Leo I, who sent legates to Constantinople, demanding that he condemn Eutyches and Nestorius explicitly and subscribe to Leo's *Tome to Flavian* (Leo, *Ep.* 80, 85).

On the accession of Marcian and Pulcheria as emperors in late August of 450, Anatolius accepted Leo's conditions, agreed to the rehabilitation of the bishops deposed at Ephesus in 449, and exhumed the body of Flavian for burial in the Church of the Holy Apostles in Constantinople. He encouraged Emperor Marcian to call the Council of Chalcedon in 451 and played a critical part in its decisions, taking his position immediately after the papal legate. In agreeing to the condemnation of Dioscorus for his unjust activity at the Robber Synod, not for doctrine, he was instrumental both in convincing the Illyrian and Egyptian bishops of the orthodoxy of Leo's *Tome* and in formulating the statement of faith that became the council's decision. Anatolius, accused by Pope Leo of ambition in promoting canon 28 of the council, which declared the See of CONSTANTINOPLE second after Rome, protested his innocence but eventually wrote a letter of submission and entered into full communion with Rome. He was rebuked by Leo for exceeding his authority in consecrating Maximus successor to Domnus of Antioch, but in general he cooperated with the Pope in pursuing an anti-Monophysite policy, particularly after the accession of Emperor Leo I in 457. His part in the coronation of Marcian as emperor is not clear, but the ceremony for Emperor Leo set the precedent for all subsequent Byzantine coronations.

Bibliography: M. JUGIE, *Dictionnaire d'histoire et de géographie ecclésiastiques* 2:1497–1500. LEO I, *Epistularum Collectiones, Acta Conciliarum Occumenicorum* 2.4. P. JAFFÉ, *Regeste pontificum romanorum ab condita ecclesia ad annum post Christum natum 1198* (Graz 1956) K 452–540. S. LE NAIN DE TILLEMONT, *Mémoires pour servir à l'histoire ecclésiastique des six premiers siècles* (Paris 1693–1712) 15:588–832.

[P. T. CAMELOT]

ANATOLIUS OF LAODICEA, ST.

Third-century bishop; d. Alexandria, *c.* 282. Founder of a school for Aristotelian philosophy, Anatolius achieved public honors in his native city. Consecrated coadjutor bishop by Theotecnus of Caesarea in Palestine, he became bishop of Laodicea in 268. He was the author of a work on the dating of Easter, a manual of arithmetic in ten books, and one of theology (Eusebius, *Hist. eccl.* 7.32).

Feast: July 3 (Byzantines).

Bibliography: ANATOLIUS OF LAODICEA, *Fragmenta ex libris arithmetic, Patrologia Graeca* 10:231–236. *Acta Sanctorum* July 1:571–585. O. BARDENHEWER, *Geschichte der altkirchlichen Literatur* (Freiburg 1913–32) 2:227–230. J. QUASTEN, *Lexicon für Theologie und Kirche,* ed. J. HOFER and K. RAHNER (Freiburg 1957–65) 1:497. M. ANDRIEU, *Dictionnaire d'histoire et de géographie ecclésiastiques,* ed. A. BAUDRILLART et al. (Paris 1912) 2:1493–94.

[F. X. MURPHY]

ANAXAGORAS

Greek philosopher; b. Clazomenae in Asia Minor, *c.* 500 B.C.; d. Lampsacus in Ionia, *c.* 428 B.C. As a young man, he was probably acquainted with the work of Anaximenes. During the Persian invasion of Ionia, he settled at Athens, where he engaged in scientific inquiry, wrote, and taught such personages as Pericles and Euripedes. He appears to have been the first thinker to bring the scientifico-philosophical spirit from Ionia to Athens. He was celebrated for his astronomical investigations, especially his discovery of the true cause of eclipses, and respected for his high moral character. In middle life, after 30 years at Athens, he was indicted by Pericles's political foes on a charge of impiety, namely, claiming the sun was but an incandescent stone. Through the persuasive influence of Pericles, he was released. However, having been compelled to leave Athens, he retired to Lampsacus, a Milesian colony, where he may have founded a school.

Teaching. Anaxagoras most likely wrote only one book, probably under the customary title *On Nature*. It was composed in an attractive and lofty style and was sold at Athens for one drachma during the time of Socrates's trial. From a critical examination and interpretation of the extant fragments, a rather self–consistent cosmological system can be constructed.

In his study of the physical universe, Anaxagoras was confronted with two interrelated problems: stability and change, unity and plurality. Among his predecessors and contemporaries, the Milesians, Pythagoreans, and HERACLITUS emphasized becoming and multiplicity, whereas PARMENIDES, ZENO OF ELEA, and Melissus stressed permanency and oneness. Anaxagoras attempted to bridge the gulf between these extremes with a compromise solution.

Stability and Change. In his explanation of the special qualities of individual things, Anaxagoras assumed the existence of as many original qualitative principles as there are qualitative determinations in perceptible things. On the empirical ground of innumerable phenomena, he pluralized the Parmenidean being into an unlimited number of seeds (H. Diels, *Die Fragmente der Vorsokratiker. Griechisch und Deutsch* 4 59A). Each seed is infinitesimal, infinitely divisible, eternal, qualitatively unchangeable, stable, and homogeneous, for this simple principle, however much it is divided, always separates into parts qualitatively the same as its whole; accordingly, Aristotle called them "ὁμοιομερῆ" or "like things" (Phys. 187a 25). Agreeing with Parmenides that coming-to-be and ceasing-to-be are only apparent, Anaxagoras explained the generation and corruption of complex things as simply the mixing and unmixing of seeds (*Fragmente* 17).

Unity and Plurality. Anaxagoras's account of unity and plurality logically develops from his theory of stability and change in accordance with Parmenides's two canons: the exclusion of real change and the impossibility of deriving plurality from unity. Anaxagoras reasoned that the manifold different sense objects can be adequately explained only by a plurality of originally different seeds, each a qualitative unit. Although all the primordial seeds—e.g., flesh, bone, and hair—are mixed in individual things, there being "a portion of everything in everything" (*Fragmente* 6), yet each complex thing is (and is called) whatever preponderates. Anaxagoras theorized that in the far distant past all the seeds co-existed in the unity of a primeval agglomerate, and that, through the powerful forces of vortex motion, they were separated and then organized to form the present visible cosmos (*Fragmente* 2, 9, 15).

Mind. Although the seeds are movable in space, they are not in motion of themselves. Rather they require an ultimate, universal principle of their orderly movement—Nous or Mind (*Fragmente* 12, 13). Alone in motion of itself, Mind communicates orderly movement to the seeds, separating them from the pristine conglomerate. Mind is no less illimitable than the chaotic congeries. Like the seeds, it is eternal (*Fragmente* 14); simple, "mixed with no thing" (*Fragmente* 12), homogeneous; quantitatively divisible, yet qualitatively unchangeable; participated by some things, yet remaining essentially identical with itself. Unlike other things, however, Mind is the finest and purest being; it is independent, since it is self-ruling and self-moving, the first principle of motion and order in the cosmos, with "complete understanding of everything" and it "has the greatest power" (*Fragmente* 12).

Influence and Critique. Anaxagoras's conception of Mind represents a major contribution in the history of philosophy. For his supreme psychophysical principle, transcendent being of beings and unifying cause of all becoming, he was justly commended by ARISTOTLE as "a sober man in contrast with the random talk of his predecessors" (*Meta.* 984b 15–18). Both PLATO (*Phadeo* 98) and Aristotle (*ibid.* 985a 18), however, criticized Anaxagoras for failing to go beyond the function of Mind as the initiator of cosmic motion to its subsequent causal influence in the production of natural phenomena. Once Mind originates movement, its causality—somewhat suggestive of teleology—becomes less direct and rather obscure, and then purely mechanical factors seem to assume hegemony.

Nevertheless, in Anaxagoras's thought there is the emergence of a dualism between Mind and nonmental reality. Although Mind is still conceived as something material, it is a distinct, independent, universal, primary cause of orderly motion in the cosmos. This notion is given a central role and greatly enriched in the natural theology of subsequent Greek and Christian philosophers.

Bibliography: K. FREEMAN, *The Pre-Socratic Philosophers: A Companion to Diels, Fragmente der Vorsokratiker* (2d ed. Cambridge, Mass. 1959); *Ancilla to the Pre-Socratic Philosophers* (Cambridge, Mass. 1957). G. S. KIRK and J. E. RAVEN, *The Pre-Socratic Philosophers: A Critical History with a Selection of Texts in Greek and English* (Cambridge, Eng. 1957). J. BURNET, *Early Greek Philosophy* (4th ed. London 1930; reprint 1957). W. W. JAEGER, *The Theology of the Early Greek Philosophers*, tr. E. S. ROBINSON (Oxford 1960). J. OWENS, *A History of Ancient Western Philosophy* (New York 1959). F.C. COPLESTON, *History of Philosopy* (Westminster, MD 1946—) 1:66–71.

[P. J. ASPELL]

ANCESTOR WORSHIP

An important special form of worship of the dead found in certain cultures. It is concerned with dead relatives, particularly blood relatives. Although ancestors of the larger kinship groups are also included, the cult involves especially the immediate members of the family to the third generation. Families and clansmen, through their veneration of ancestors, maintain solidarity and a sacred dignity. Although the cult of ancestors is, for the most part, characteristic of the primitive religions of the matriarchal agricultural peoples, and is connected especially with planting and harvesting, in general it is the patriarchal feature that is dominant in it.

Of the early higher cultures, the Chinese was the one in which ancestor worship attained its greatest development. It exercised influence on Japanese Shintoism, although in Japan, as in Peru, ancestor worship had its own root in the existing clan system. Among the Finns, a corner in the house was regarded sacred to ancestors. The pagan Scandinavians set out barley and beer on fixed days for their farmer ancestors. The "cult of the fathers," i.e., the worship of male forbears, was widely practised not only among the ancient Germans but also in Aryan India; in fact it is so well attested for other Indo-European peoples that it must go back to the age of primitive Indo-European unity. In Greece, the dead were believed to become incarnate in snakes, and if these creatures appeared in a house, they inspired a feeling of special awe.

H. SPENCER (1820–1903) held that manism was the primitive form of religion, but his theory has received no corroboration from investigations of even the lowest and simplest cultures. Mythical ancestors or more or less mythical forbears were given the status of heroes. However, historical members of families were not raised immediately to divine status by their people. On the other hand, it is known that even higher cosmic beings, like Amaterasu, the Japanese sun-goddess in the imperial palace, became ancestor divinities.

Images of ancestors were especially significant in ancestor worship. The ancestor tablets of the Chinese probably go back to such representations. In rites at the grave, these were marked with sacrificial blood by the son of the dead man. They had their place at the domestic altar, before which all significant family happenings were reported. The chief place of cult was the grave, but the temple dedicated to ancestors was important also. The priestly function in the ancestor cult was performed originally by the head of the house.

The Feast of All Souls, celebrated among the ancient Germans in the Yule Festival, the Feast of Lights held in July in the Far East, and the Urabon Feast of the Japanese are all connected with the reception and entertainment of the spirits of ancestors.

Bibliography: F. HAMPL et al., F. KÖNIG, *Religionswissenschaftliches Wörterbuch* (Freiburg 1956) 25–30. W. CROOKE et al., J. HASTINGS, ed., *Encyclopedia of Religion & Ethics,* 13 v. (Edinburgh 1908–27) 1:425–467. C. M. EDSMAN, *Die Religion in Geschichte und Gegenwart,* 7 v. (3d ed. Tübingen 1957–65) 6:959–961. J. HAEKEL, *Lexikon für Theologie und Kirche,* ed. J. HOFER and K. RAHNER, 10 v. (2d, new ed. Freiburg 1957–65) 1:222–223. W. SCHMIDT, *The Origin and Growth of Religion,* tr. H. J. ROSE (2d ed. London 1935) 61–72. W. OTTO, *Die Manen* (Berlin 1923). F. KRAUSE, *Maske und Ahnenfigur: Ethnologische Studien* (Leipzig 1931). H. FINDEISEN, *Das Tier als Gott: Dämon und Ahne* (Stuttgart 1956). A. E. JENSEN, *Myth and Cult among Primitive Peoples,* tr. M. T. CHOLDIN and W. WEISSLEDER (Chicago 1963). F. HERRMANN, *Symbolik in den Religionen der Naturvölker* (Stuttgart 1961) 109–111.

[A. CLOSS]

ANCHIETA, JOSÉ (JOSEPH) DE, BL.

Jesuit priest, "Apostle of Brazil" cofounder of São Paolo and Rio de Janeiro; b. San Cristobál de la Laguna, northern end of Tenerife, Canary Islands, Spain, March 19, 1534; d. Reitiba (now Anchieta), Espíritu Santo, Brazil, June 9, 1597. Anchieta was born into a noble family related to St. IGNATIUS OF LOYOLA. After studying for a year in the Jesuit college at Coimbra, Portugal, he entered the Society of Jesus on May 1, 1551. Following his novitiate the 19-year-old Anchieta was sent to Brazil (1553) where he worked in the missions until his death 44 years later.

At first, Anchieta was in the captaincy of São Vicente and was one of the founders of the village of São Paulo de Pirtatininga and the Jesuit school there. He learned Tupi, the language in general use on the coast, and prepared a grammar for it.

In 1567, Anchieta was appointed superior of the Jesuits in the captaincy of São Vicente. During his ten years (1577–1587) as the fifth provincial of Brazil, he was the major architect of a plan later used elsewhere to liberate the indigenous people from brutal slavery under the colonists. He gathered the natives into *aldeias,* communities similar to the *pueblas* in Mexico and the *reducciones* in the Spanish colonies of South America, where they could be instructed in the faith, protected from exploitation, and taught the arts and letters. Much of the indigenous culture was preserved because he encouraged native crafts and music. He also possessed a fair knowledge of medicine, which he employed to help the natives. The last years of his life he spent in the captaincy of Espíritu Santo.

Anchieta was, above all, a man of action and a missionary of the first rank. During his life he was the object of popular veneration because of his apostolic work, his lofty ideals, and a certain untenable and unsubstantiated reputation for heroic deeds. He was said to have suppressed cannibalism practiced on enemy captives, who were eaten at ritual banquets, and to have protected the chastity of Christian native women, who were often raped in local wars. His fame as a miracle-worker added to his effectiveness as a missionary. No one has been so openly termed a saint, apostle, and father of Christianity in colonial Brazil as has Anchieta. Two biographers, Sebastián Beretario, who wrote in Latin, and Simão de Vasconcellos, who wrote in Portuguese, reflected in their writings the sincere feeling of veneration toward him then current in seventeenth-century Brazil. This devotion continues to be strong today among Brazilian Catholics. Pilgrimages are still made to the house of his birth in Tenerife, and a bronze statue of him was erected in La Laguna in 1960. It is said that he baptized two million natives. Although so high a number may be apocryphal, it assuredly testifies to his reputation for numerous baptisms.

Anchieta was an excellent writer, using both Portuguese and Tupi-Guaraní. In addition to two catechetical texts, he attempted to teach the faith to the native people by composing many canticles, dialogues, and religious plays. One of his morality plays, the three-hour *Auto de Pregacão Universal,* performed in the open-air at Bahia, may have been the first acted in the New World. His other important theatrical venture was the allegorical *Na Festa de S. Lourenco* or *Misterio de Jesus.* He compiled the first Tupi-Guaraní grammar (1555) and later a Tupi dictionary. His medieval-style poetry combined religious images with native customs.

After his death his body was buried in the Jesuit chapel at Espírito Santo where local tribes came in vast numbers to honor him. The bishop of Bahia preached at his funeral and named Anchieta the ''Apostle of Brazil.'' Although Anchieta's cause was introduced by the petition of the Brazilian Jesuits in 1615 and he was declared venerable on Aug. 10, 1736, it was forgotten during the suppression of the Society of Jesus in the second half of the eighteenth century. Pope John Paul II beatified Anchieta on June 22, 1980.

Feast: June 9 (Jesuits).

Bibliography: *Acta Apostolicae Sedis* 73 (1981): 253–258. *Cartas: correspondência ativa e passiva,* ed. H. A. VIOTTI (São Paulo 1984); *Cartas: informações, fragmentos históricos e sermões* (Belo Horizonte 1988). *Compendio de la vida del apóstol de el Brazil, V.P. J. de Anchieta,* tr. B. ANCHIETA (Xeres de la Fr. 1677). *José de Anchieta: vida y obra,* eds. M. RODRÍGUEZ-PANTOJA MÁRQUEZ and F. GONZÁLEZ LUIS (La Laguna, Tenerife 1988). *L'Osservatore Romano,* English edition 26 (1980): 10–11. S. BERETARIO, *Josephi Anchietae Societatis Jesu sacerdotis . . . vita* (Lyons 1617). A. M. DE B. CARVALHO, *Anchieta* (Rio de Janeiro 1989). CRÉTINEAU-

Bl. José Anchieta.

JOLLY, *History of the Society of Jesus,* II, 119 (Paris 1851). H. G. DOMINIAN, *Apostle of Brazil: The Biography of Padre José de Anchieta, S.J. 1534–1597* (New York 1958). P. DE FUENTES Y DE VALBUENA, *El beato Padre José de Anchieta* (León 1982), poetry. A. KISIL, *Anchieta, doutor dos índios* (São Paulo 1996). D. M. V. MINDLIN, *José de Anchieta* (Goiânia, Brazil 1997). F. NOBRE, *Anchieta, apóstolo do novo mundo* (2d ed. São Paulo 1974). J. PONTES, *Teatro de Anchieta* (Rio de Janeiro 1978). A. DE QUEIROZ FILHO, *A vida heróica de José de Anchieta* (São Paulo 1988). G. ROMEIRO, *São José de Anchieta* (São Paulo 1987). J. THOMAZ, *Anchieta* (Rio de Janeiro 1981). S. DE VASCONCELLOS, *Vida do veneravel padre José de Anchieta,* 2 v. (Rio de Janeiro 1943). C. VIEIRA, *El padre Anchieta* (Buenos Aires 1945). H. A. VIOTTI, *Anchieta nas artes* (2d. ed. São Paulo 1991); *O anel e a pedra* (Belo Horizonte 1993).

[F. MATEOS]

ANCHIN, ABBEY OF

Near Douai, Flanders, north France; a Benedictine foundation (1079) by two (later nine) local noblemen on land donated by several persons, including the bishop of CAMBRAI, the suzerain lord, who confirmed the donation, and the cantor of Cambrai. To teach the monastic rule, Bishop Gerard II sent two monks from Hasnon, one of whom he made abbot. After a fire (1083), Hugh, dean of Cambrai and a skilled architect, used his wealth to rebuild the abbey. The church, consecrated in 1086, was soon too small and was rebuilt (1182–1230) with four towers and a magnificent interior (350 by 85 by 85 feet); 14 columns enclosed a choir 43 feet wide. Conventual buildings and an abbot's house also were built. Abbots Pierre Toulet (1449–64) and Hugh of Lobbes (1464–90) enriched the church with marble statues, alabaster, paintings, organs, sacred vessels, and a miter and cross of great value. Divine services were of unusual splendor in the 15th century. Abbot Charles Coguin (1511–46) began a new cloister which was decorated with sculpture, stained glass, and Biblical frescoes—one of the most beautiful in Europe.

Abbot Alvisus (1120–30, d. 1148), once prior of SAINT-VAAST in Arras, devoted himself to the Cluniac reform and to temporal affairs. Callistus II confirmed new donations (1123), and the abbey came under papal protection. The virtuous and learned GOSWIN (1130–65) fostered an active scriptorium and continued Alvisus's work after the latter became bishop of Cambrai. Jean de Batheries (1414–48) and Charles Coguin acquired many MSS. Jean Letailleur (1555–74) established a school of theology where Greek and Hebrew were taught, furnishing professors for the new University of DOUAI (1562). Gaspard de Bovincourt (d. 1577), François de Bar (d. 1606), and Jean Despierres (d. 1664) were prominent authors.

Powerful and rich, Anchin had pontifical privileges from 1219; it was under the bishop of Arras but also was a member of the estates of Flanders and the Netherlands. It held many properties and houses, received tithes, and named pastors to 53 churches. It contested abbatial rights and privileges with lords and the bishop of Arras (1252–54). Philip II of Spain appointed Warnier de Daure abbot (1574–1610), and the kings of France appointed commendatory abbots from 1681 (*see* COMMENDATION). The zeal of the abbots offset the effects of disasters and wars. At the time of the FRENCH REVOLUTION monastic observance was good. Despite the desire of the 30 monks to remain at Anchin, the abbey was razed, gold and silver work and bells were melted down, and the community was dispersed.

Bibliography: A. ESCALLIER, *L'Abbaye d'Anchin, 1079–1790* (Lille 1852). M. G. BLAYO, *Dictionnaire d'histoire et de géographie ecclésiastiques*, ed. A. BAUDRILLART et al. (Paris 1912–) 2:1516–24. P. HELIOT, ''Quelques monuments disparus de la Flandre wallonne: L'Abbaye d'Anchin,'' in *Revue belge d'archéologie et d'histoire de l'art* 28 (Brussels 1959) 129–173.

[P. COUSIN]

ANCHOR

A symbol of safety, so regarded because of its importance in navigation. The Christians, in using the anchor on funeral monuments, jewels, and rings as a symbol of hope in a future existence, gave a loftier signification to an already familiar sign. In early Christian thought, hope in the salvation assured by Christ was of paramount importance. The author of the Epistle to the Hebrews is the first to connect the idea of hope with the symbol of the anchor: ''We have hope set before us as an anchor of the soul, sure and firm'' (Hebrew 6.19–20). CLEMENT OF ALEXANDRIA mentions its use on jewels and rings (*Patrologia Graeca*, ed. J. P. Migne 8:633). The anchor, appearing in the epitaphs of the catacombs and the cemeteries of SS. Priscilla, Domitilla, and Callistus during the second and third centuries, was an expression of confidence that those departed had arrived at the port of eternal peace. Seldom used as a symbol in medieval ornamentation, the anchor reappeared in the baroque period associated with the patrons of sailors, with ports, and particularly with representations of Pope St. CLEMENT I. In the sepulchral ornamentation of the late baroque and the classical periods, it reassumed its original Christian character as the symbol of hope in life eternal.

Bibliography: C. A. KENNEDY, ''Early Christians and the Anchor,'' *Biblical Archaeologist* 38 (September–December 1975) 115–124.

[M. A. BECKMANN/EDS.]

ANCHORAGE, ARCHDIOCESE OF

The Archdiocese of Anchorage (*Ancoragiensis*) in Alaska was established Feb. 9, 1966, from territory taken from the Dioceses of Fairbanks and Juneau; these sees, previously included in the ecclesiastical Province of Seattle, Washington were made suffragans of Anchorage. The Right Rev. Joseph T. Ryan, National Secretary of the Catholic Near East Welfare Association, was named the first bishop of the newly created archdiocese and was consecrated in his native city of Albany, N.Y., on March 25, 1966. At the time of its creation, the see had a population of 130,000, of whom 17,000 were Catholics. Upon Archbishop Ryan's transfer to the Military Ordinariate in 1975, Bishop Francis T. Hurley, who since 1971 had been bishop of Juneau was installed as the second archbishop of Anchorage in 1976. In order to reach the distant reaches of the archdiocese (138,985 sq. miles) Archbishop Hurley piloted his own plane. In 1990, he initiated a mission outreach to Magadan, in the Russian Far East, establishing the Nativity of Jesus Parish, the first and only Catholic parish in that city. In 2001, Archbishop Hurley was succeeded by Roger L. Schwietz, OMI, the Coadjutor Archbishop of Anchorage. Before going to Anchorage Archbishop Schweitz had been bishop of Duluth, Minn.

At the beginning of the 21st century, Catholics numbered 32,376, about nine percent of the total population.

[M. P. CARTHY/EDS.]

ANCHORITES

Persons who have retired into solitude to live the religious life. The term is derived through the Latin and French from the Greek ἀναχωρητής, from ἀναχωρεῆ (to withdraw, to retire). In practice the Latin words *anachorita* and *eremita* have been used synonymously, and the same holds for the modern language derivatives of these two words. If a slight nuance of distinction is discernible, however, it is that HERMIT refers to one who has retired into a place far from human habitation, whereas anchorite refers to one living in a cell adjacent to a community. In both East and West, this latter kind of solitary has been more numerous than the former kind. With the Justinian reforms of the 6th century, the Eastern solitaries were gathered in to dwell near a community, although other and more dramatic forms of eremitical life continued to exist by way of exception. In the Eastern Christian tradition, all anchorites live adjacent to a community and in some way are dependent upon it, although a few non-canonical hermits continue to exist. In the West, the medieval anchors and anchoresses, solitaries who lived usually in cells built against the walls of churches, have ceased to exist; but the anchoritic life has been preserved by congregations such as the Carthusians and the Camaldolese.

Bibliography: R. M. CLAY, *The Hermits and Anchorites of England* (London 1914). A. K. WARREN, *Anchorites and Their Patrons in Medieval England* (Berkeley, CA 1985) V. ARNONE, *La valle degli anacoreti: viaggio nella solitudine agli albori del cristianesimo* (Casale Monferrato 1999).

[A. DONAHUE/EDS.]

ANCRENE RIWLE

A medieval code of rules for the life of anchoresses or recluses. The *Ancrene Riwle*, or *Ancrene Wisse*, was written specifically for three sisters (not nuns) who had retired to a life of prayer and penance. Seven copies of the text are extant in English. The best-known is the British Museum Cotton Manuscript Nero A.xiv, which furnished the basis of James Morton's original edition for the Camden Society in 1853. Two French versions, several Latin versions, and some adaptations of material taken from the Rule show the popularity of this much-read classic of Middle English prose. The Early English Text Society is well on its way toward offering reliable texts of all manuscripts of the Rule, along with critical apparatus. Once these editions are available, a full investigation of the relationships between the manuscripts can be begun, and a solution of problems connected with the Rule may be possible. Date, authorship, place of composition, and names of the women for whom the Rule was written are unknown. The general approach to these questions, particularly that of date, is being made through a study of the theological background of the work. Scholars agree generally that the original text (probably not extant) existed in English not long after 1200.

The *Ancrene Riwle* contains interesting details of domestic arrangements and the daily horarium of medieval recluses. Commonly an anchoress lived alone, but the three sisters addressed here lived within a single enclosure in separate cells. Each had a window looking into the sanctuary of the adjoining church so that she could see the Blessed Sacrament exposed over the altar. The parlor window, through which she spoke to visitors, was to be heavily draped. The author warns his spiritual charges against possible abuses from outside their cloister. Daily life consisted of prayer (chiefly oral), spiritual reading, and plain sewing. The two meals permitted were to be eaten in silence. Each anchoress had a "maiden" to look after her material needs. She was responsible for instructing her servant in religion and general behavior.

The *Ancrene Riwle* is divided into eight parts: Divine Service, Keeping the Heart, Moral Lessons and Examples, Temptation, Confession, Penance, Love, and Domestic Matters. The first and last parts form the "outer rule"; and the other parts, the "inner rule."

The style and tone show that the author had rather wide scholarly interests. He refers to the Bible, Lives of the Fathers, Cassian, Gregory the Great, works of Anselm and Bernard; he quotes Ovid and Seneca; he appears to know Geoffrey of Monmouth's *History*. He seems, moreover, from the practical, moral aim of the work, to have been kindly and devout. His prose is easy, lively, and concrete, with imagery suggestive of the world of feudalism. He stresses the inner life that the outer rule is to foster. The *Ancrene Riwle* throws light on the religious aspirations of late 12th-century England, and reflects indirectly much secular life of the time.

The *Ancrene Riwle* is one of six prose treatises in the Katherine Group, so-called from a work in the group, *Lifode of Seint Katheryn*. The Katherine Group is evidence that after the Conquest a "school" of Middle English prose writing continued the Old English homiletic prose tradition. The works in the Katherine Group are in the same dialect and are somewhat uniform in style. The *Ancrene Riwle* is the outstanding member of the group.

Bibliography: *Ancrene Wisse: Parts 6 and 7*, ed. G. SHEPHERD (London 1959–60). J. E. WELLS, ed., *Manual of the Writings* *in Middle English*, and supplements 1–8 (New Haven 1916–41). F. W. BATESON, ed., *Cambridge Bibliography of English Literature*, 5 v. (Cambridge, Eng. 1940–57). Modern Humanities Research Association, *Annual Bibliography of English Language and Literature* (Cambridge, Eng. 1921—), see v. for 1938.

[M. M. BARRY]

ANCYRA

Two ancient cities of Asia Minor, important for early Church history.Ancyra in Galatia is the modern city of Ankara, Turkey. St. Paul visited Galatia twice, in 51 or 52 (Acts 15:30–18:1) and 54 or 55 (Acts 18:23) and addressed an Epistle to the GALATIANS from Corinth in 57. Crescens, its first known bishop, founded the church of Vienne in Gaul. Ancyra had a number of early martyrs, including Theodotus, the brothers Plato and Antiochus, and Clement, to whom a 6th-century church with cupola was dedicated. Its temple of Augustus was converted into a Christian church, and the city served as a monastic center (Palladius, *Hist. Laus.*66–68). It was early troubled by heretical movements, as St. Paul testifies (Epistle to the Galatians), and MONTANISM and other sects spread from there (Council of Constantinople I, c.7; In Trullo, c.95). Synods were conducted in 273 and 277. The acts of the synod in 314 deal mainly with apostates, or *lapsi,* and moral discipline (Mansi 2:513–540); that of 358, called by George of Iconium and presided over by BASIL OF ANCYRA, adopted the homoiousian formula against the Anomeans, avoiding the HOMOOUSIOS for fear that it favored SABELLIANISM, while the semi-Arians opposed the formula ''similar in all things'' (Mansi 3:265–290). The synod of 375 deposed the Catholic Bp. Hypsis of Parnassus and attempted to arrest GREGORY OF NYSSA. As a metropolitan see of Constantinople, Ancyra in the 7th century had seven or eight suffragans and was considered fourth in rank. It lost importance after the Arab invasions, and its Greek population became Turkish-speaking. It was colonized by the Armenians in the 13th century. In the 19th century Pius IX created a bishopric for the Armenians, who had been united to Rome since 1735. The massacre of the Armenians in 1917 and the treaty of Lausanne following the Greco-Turkish war in1923 put an end to Christianity in the region.

Ancyra in Phrygia (known also as *Ancyra ferrea* or Ancyra of Synaos), originally in the province of Lydia, formed part of Laodicea in the 6th century and*c.* 900 was suffragan of Hierapolis. Florentius, its first known bishop, participated in the Council of Nicaea I (325). Philip of Ancyra was at Chalcedon (451); Cyricus, atConstantinople III (680–681) and in Trullo (692); Constans, at Nicaea III (787); and Michael, at the Photian Council of Constantinople (879). Ancyra had two Latinbishops in the 15th century: Francis (d. 1434) and Gonsalvus of Curiola. Its ruins were discovered by Hamilton near the modern village of Klisse-Keuï not far from Synaos (modern Simaoul); they include a theater and temple.

Bibliography: K. GROSS, *Lexikon für Theologie und Kirche,* 1:568. C. KARALEVSKY, *Dictionnaire d'histoire et de géographie ecclésiastiques* 2:1538–43. C. J. VON HEFELE, *Histoire des conciles d'après les documents originaux,* tr. and continued by H. LECLERCQ, 1.1:298–326; 1.2:903–908. P. JOANNOU, *Discipline générale antique (IIe-IXe s.)* (Sacra Congregazione Orientale, *Codificazione orientale, Fonti*; 1962) 1.2:54–73.H. GROTZ, *Die Hauptkirchen des Ostens (Orientalia Christiana Analecta* 169; 1964) 126–133, 158–159. G. DE VRIES, *Cattolicismo e problemi religiosinel prossimo oriente* (Rome 1944) 131–138. L. ROBERT, *Hellenica* 9 (1950) 67–77.S. VAILHÉ, *Dictionnaire d'histoire et de géographie ecclésiastiques* 2:1546–48. M. LE QUIEN, *Oriens Christianus* 1:799–802. T. WIEGAND, ''Reisen in Mysien'' *Mitteilungen des kaiserlichen deutschen archaeologischen Instituts: Athenische Abteilung* 24 (1904) 311–339. For Ancyra, Armenian Catholicbishopric, see F. TOURNEBIZE, *Dictionnaire d'histoire et de géographie ecclésiastiques* 2:1543–46.

[P. JOANNOU]

ANDECHS, ABBEY OF

Former Benedictine abbey in the Diocese of AUGSBURG, Bavaria, south Germany. It was founded by Duke Albrecht III of Bavaria (1455–56) during the reform of his friend NICHOLAS OF CUSA and dedicated to St. Nicholas; monks from TEGERNSEE settled it. Originally Andechs was a castle of the powerful Counts of Diessen-Wolfratshausen (of Andechs after 1130), who had extensive holdings in Bavaria, Main-Franconia, the Tyrol, Istria, and Burgundy, and who produced many saints and bishops before becoming extinct in 1248. The relics the counts had collected in the Holy Land and Italy were kept in a chapel, cared for by Benedictines, which in 1248 came under the bishop of Augsburg. Chapel and relics survived the destruction of the castle (1248), and the relics, after discovery, were exhibited (1388). Many illustrious monks lived in Andechs before it was suppressed (1803); as a rule, there were 25 to 30 monks (1750–1802). In 1846 Louis I of Bavaria gave Andechs to the newly founded St. Boniface Abbey in Munich, to which it still belongs. The 15th-century Gothic hall church has furnishings of 1755. Among the famous relics, a host consecrated by Pope Gregory I (d. 604) attracts many pilgrims.

Bibliography: L. H. COTTINEAU, *Répertoire topobibliographique des abbayes et prieurés,* 2 v. (Mâcon 1935–39) 1:94–95. A. BAYOL, *Dictionnaire d'histoire et de géographie ecclésiastiques,* ed. A. BAUDRILLART et al. (Paris 1912–) 2:1552–56. R. BAUERREISS, *Lexikon für Theologie und Kirche,* ed. J. HOFER and K. RAHNER, 10 v. (2d, new ed. Freiburg 1957–65) 1:505–506. O. L.

KAPSNER, *A Benedictine Bibliography: An Author-Subject Union List,* 2 v. (2d ed. Collegeville, Minn. 1962) 2:185–186.

[W. FINK]

ANDERSON, LARS (LAURENTIUS ANDREAE)

Founder of a national Protestant ecclesiastical polity in Sweden; b. Strängnäs, *c.* 1480; d. there, April 29, 1552. He studied at Rostock, Leipzig, and Greifswald and made several trips to Rome. A canon of Strängnäs, he became the secretary of Bishop Mathias, received the title of apostolic notary, and finally became head of the cathedral chapter in Strängnäs. He was converted to Lutheran views under the influence of the deacon Olaus PETRI. Anderson, a talented administrator, became King Gustavus Vasa's chancellor in 1523 and aided Olaus and Laurentius Petri in their reforming endeavors, working for a break with Rome and for a Swedish national church, and fully establishing the Reformation at the Council of Oerebro in 1529. In 1540 he opposed Vasa's effort to transform the Swedish church in the direction of Presbyterianism; he was sentenced to death, was pardoned, and lived out his days in retirement. He wrote one theological treatise on *Faith and Good Works.*

Bibliography: H. HOLMQUIST, *Die Schwedische Reformation 1523–1531* (Leipzig 1925) 24–27, 32 and *passim.* H. SANDBERG, *Kring Konflikten mellan Gustav Vasa och reformatorerna* (Uppsala 1941) 127–146. P. B. WATSON, *The Swedish Revolution under Gustavus Vasa* (Boston 1889). J. WORDSWORTH, *The National Church of Sweden* (Milwaukee 1911).

[L. W. SPITZ]

ANDERTON, ROBERT, BL.

Priest, martyr; b. Isle of Man; hanged, drawn, and quartered on the Isle of Wight, April 25, 1586. After completing his studies at Rivington grammar school and Brasenose College, Oxford, Anderton traveled abroad. He converted to Catholicism and entered the seminary at Rheims in 1580, where he began a lifelong friendship with Bl. William Marsden. Following their ordination, they set sail for England, where they were immediately captured after a storm forced the ship ashore. They pled after conviction that they had not transgressed the statute because they did not willingly land in England but were forced by nature to do so. This led to their being summoned to London, where they were examined upon the celebrated "bloody question," whether they would fight against the pope, even if the quarrel were for purely religious causes. Though they acknowledged Elizabeth as their lawful queen in all temporal matters, they would not consent to the required test. The sentence was then confirmed, and a proclamation was published to explain their guilt. They were taken back and executed near the place where they had been cast ashore. Anderton was beatified by Pius XI on Dec. 15, 1929.

Feast of the English Martyrs: May 4 (England).

See Also: ENGLAND, SCOTLAND, AND WALES, MARTYRS OF.

Bibliography: R. CHALLONER, *Memoirs of Missionary Priests,* ed. J. H. POLLEN (rev. ed. London 1924; repr. Farnborough 1969), 66–82. J. H. POLLEN, *Acts of English Martyrs* (London 1891).

[K. I. RABENSTEIN]

ANDERTON, ROGER AND LAWRENCE

Seventeenth-century English Catholic writers and controversialists.

Roger, son of Christopher Anderton of Lostock and cousin of Lawrence; b. place and date unknown; d. 1640? Roger came into possession of Birchley Hall near Preston, *c.* 1615, and was probably the patron of the Catholic secret press in Lancashire, later called the Birchley Hall press. It operated from 1615 to 1621, when it was discovered and seized by the government. Several of the books printed at this press were issued under the pseudonym "John Brereley, Priest," who has sometimes been identified with Lawrence Anderton, though the evidence is far from conclusive.

Lawrence, Jesuit controversialist; b. County of Lancashire, England, *c.* 1575–76; d. there, April 17, 1643. He was the son of Thomas Anderton of Chorely, Lancashire, and was educated at Blackburn Grammar School and Christ's College, Cambridge, where he earned a reputation for intellectual brilliance and received his B.A. in 1596 or 1597. Anderton went abroad, probably on becoming a Catholic, and apparently returned to England in 1602 as a priest. He joined the Society of Jesus in 1604. Anderton spent much of his missionary life in his native Lancashire and was superior of the Lancashire district for several years after 1621. He labored principally in London and the South *c.* 1627 to 1642. He wrote several notable works of controversy against the English Protestants.

Bibliography: T. COOPER, *The Dictionary of National Biography from the Earliest Times to 1900,* 63 v. (London 1885–1900; repr. with corrections, 21 v., 1908–09, 1921–22, 1938; suppl. 1901–) 1:396–397. J. GILLOW, *A Literary and Biographical History or Bibliographical Dictionary of the English Catholics from 1534 to the Present Time,* 5 v. (London-New York 1885–1902; repr.

New York 1961) 1:34–38, 39–41. A. F. ALLISON and D. M. ROGERS, *A Catalogue of Catholic Books in English . . . 1558–1640,* 2 v. (London 1956).

[A. F. ALLISON]

ANDLAUER, MODESTE, ST.

Martyr, Jesuit (SJ) priest; b. May 22, 1847, Rosheim, Bas Rhin, Alsace, France; d. July 19, 1900, Wuyi, Hopeh (Hebei) Province, China. Modeste Andlauer studied in the minor seminary in his home town for seven years before beginning his year of philosophy and three years of theology in the major seminary. He entered the Jesuit novitiate at Saint-Acheul on Oct. 8, 1872, studied theology for two more years at Arras after his novitiate, then was ordained on Sept. 22, 1877, at Laval, France. Thereafter he taught German in Amiens, Lille, and Brest.

In 1881, he was sent to China, where he arrived the following year. He studied Chinese with his fellow martyrs Leon Mangin and Remi ISORÉ at Zhangjiazhuang, before beginning his mission in Wuqizo and Wuyi, where he continued to preach and teach after the uprising of the Boxers in early 1899.

On June 18, 1900, Fr. Isoré arrived in Wuyi after a retreat to visit Fr. Andlauer. The Boxers had already arrived at the village to obtain the release of some of their fellows who had been imprisoned the previous winter. They delayed their departure upon hearing that a foreign priest was resident.

Realizing that probable martyrdom was at hand, the priests spent that night in prayer. About 6:00 P.M. the following afternoon the Boxers broke into the chapel where the priests were praying. The two were stabbed with swords and lances before being decapitated. Their heads were posted at the village gate as a warning to others. They were beatified by Pius XII (Apr. 17, 1956) and canonized (Oct. 1, 2000) by Pope John Paul II with Augustine Zhao Rong and companions.

Feast: July 20; Feb. 4 (Jesuits).

Bibliography: P. X. MERTENS, *Du sang chrétien sur le fleuve jaune. Actes de martyrs dans la Chine contemporaine* (Paris 1937). J. SIMON, *Sous le sabre des Boxers* (Lille 1955). C. TESTORE, *Sangue e palme sul fiume giallo. I beati martiri cinesi nella persecuzione della Boxe Celi Sud-Est, 1900* (Rome 1955). J. N. TYLENDA, *Jesuit Saints & Martyrs* (Chicago 1998), 173–75. L'Osservatore Romano, Eng. Ed. 40 (2000): 1–2, 10.

[K. I. RABENSTEIN]

ANDLEBY, WILLIAM, BL.

Priest, martyr; b. Etton near Beverley, East Riding, Yorkshire, England; hanged, drawn, and quartered at York, July 4, 1597. At age 25, the well-born Andleby left England to participate in the Dutch war. He visited Douai to debate Dr. Allen, but found that Allen's arguments made sense. Thereafter he converted to Catholicism and eventually was ordained. He labored for 20 years in Yorkshire and Lincolnshire. Bp. Challoner recorded of him: "His zeal for souls was such as to spare no pains and to fear no dangers. For the first four years of his mission he traveled always on foot, meanly attired, and carrying with him usually in a bag his vestments and other things for saying Mass; for his labors lay chiefly among the poor, who were not shocked with such things. Afterwards, humbly yielding to the advice of his brethren, he used a horse and went somewhat better clad. Wonderful was the austerity of his life in frequent watchings, fastings, and continual prayer, his soul so absorbed in God that he often took no notice of those he met; by which means he was sometimes exposed to suspicions and dangers from the enemies of his faith, into whose hands he at last fell after twenty years' labor in the vineyard of the Lord." He was condemned for his priesthood and was executed with three laymen: BB. Henry ABBOT, Thomas Warcop, and Edward Fulthrop. He was beatified by Pius XI on Dec. 15, 1929.

Feast of the English Martyrs: May 4 (England).

See Also: ENGLAND, SCOTLAND, AND WALES, MARTYRS OF.

Bibliography: R. CHALLONER, *Memoirs of Missionary Priests,* ed. J. H. POLLEN (rev. ed. London 1924; repr. Farnborough 1969). J. H. POLLEN, *Acts of English Martyrs* (London 1891).

[K. I. RABENSTEIN]

ANDORRA, THE CATHOLIC CHURCH IN

A landlocked region, the Principality of Andorra is located in the east Pyrenees of Europe, and is bordered on the north and east by France, and on the south and west by Spain. A mountainous region, with peaks rising 6,000 feet above narrow valley regions, Andorra has a temperate climate, although snow slides and avalanches are common in the winter months. Natural resources include mineral water, timber, iron ore and lead, while agricultural products consist of rye, wheat, barley, oats and sheep.

Made a co-principality following a dispute over the region between Spain and France during the 13th century, Andorra adopted a democratic constitution in 1993. Under the constitutional heads of state—co-princes are the president of France and the Bishop of Urgel in

Spain—true governmental power lies in a General Council of 28 members. The region's population, of predominately Spanish ancestry, is supplemented by numerous immigrants, attracted by Andorra's thriving tourism-based economy and the country's lack of an income tax. Actual citizens of Andorra comprise only 20 percent of the total population.

History. Part of the Roman Empire and of the Visigothic kingdom, Andorra, like the rest of the Pyrenees, was little affected by the Arab invasion. With the creation of the Spanish March it came under Carolingians as part of the country of Urgell. Bishops of Urgell from the ninth century gained feudal lands and rights in Andorra, where they established, with the consent of the counts of Urgell, an ecclesiastical domain based around the town of La Seau d'Urgell. From the 11th century it was a fief of the Caboet family, which transmitted it by marriages to the Castellbó and then to the Foix family (1208). Henry of Navarre, Count of Foix and Viscount of Bearn, brought his rights to the crown of France when he became king in 1589. The indivisible co-dominion over Andorra exercised by the French president and the Spanish bishop of Urgell was based on the agreement (*Pareatges*) of Bishop Pedro de Urg of Urgell and Count Roger Bernard III of Foix (1278, 1288) after a long and bitter dispute.

Its isolated location high in the Pyrenees allowed Andorra to keep its political constitution and traditional institutions from the Middle Ages, notwithstanding economic progress resulting from immigration and tourism during the 20th century. Its laws and customs were codified in the *Manual Digest* (1748) of A. Fiter Rosell and the *Politar* (1763) of A. Puig.

There are pre-Romanesque (9th–11th century) and Romanesque (11th–12th century) churches of archaeological interest; most of the murals have disappeared or are in museums and private collections. Our Lady of Meritxell, proclaimed principal patroness of Andorra in 1873, has a shrine with a 12th-century Romanesque image, probably the oldest from the Pyrenees.

Into the 21st Century. By the year 2000, there were 19 priests tending to the nation's Catholics, 13 diocesan and six religious. In addition, 13 Holy Family sisters tend to students at the two Catholic schools—one Spanish-, one French-language—in Andorra. Upon reaching university level, students have the option of going to Spain or France for higher studies. Andorra had no higher school of religious studies or charitable and social work apart from parochial institutions. Religious education in the Catholic faith was also available through public schools as an after-school elective option, with those teachers being paid by the government. Andorra established diplomatic relations with the Holy See in 1995.

Capital: Andorra la Vella.
Size: 179 sq. miles.
Population: 66,825 in 2000.
Languages: Catalan, French, Castilian.
Religions: 60,250 Catholics (90%), 2,000 Muslims, 4,575 Protestants.
Parishes: seven, all of which are included in the diocese of Urgell, suffragan to the archdiocese of Tarragona, Spain.

The more than 50 scattered churches and chapels testified to the strong religious tradition in the region. Under the constitution, Catholicism remained the official religion, and a special relationship with the state was endorsed, although the Church did not receive direct state subsidies. An increase in the activity of religious sects in the late 20th century prompted a system of registration that was endorsed by Catholic leaders. The Church remained cordial with other religious groups, with the church at La Massana lending its sanctuary to the small Anglican community of English-speaking immigrants on a monthly basis. In 2001, Andorra was the focus of a United Nations effort to adopt a pro-abortion policy throughout Europe. Andorran law supports the rights of the unborn and abortion was treated as a criminal act. Concerns were also raised by U.N. representatives regarding the availability of sex education in the country's private schools.

Bibliography: C. BAUDON DE MONY, *Relations politiques des comtes de Foix aves la Catalogne jusq'au commencement du XIVe siècle,* 2 v. (Paris 1896). J. A. BRUTAILS, *La Coutume d'Andorre* (Paris 1904). F. PALLEROLA Y GABRIEL, *El Principado de Andorra y su constitución política* (Lérida 1912). P. PUJOL, "L'acta de consagració i dotació de la catedral d'Urgell," *Estudis romàncis,* 2 (1917) 1–28. F. VALLS TABERNER, *Privilegis i ordinacions de les valls pirinenques,* v. 3, *Vall d'Andorra* (Barcelona 1920). J. M. VIDAL, *Instituciones políticas y sociales de Andorra* (Madrid 1949). J. M. FONT I RIUS, "Els origens del co-senyoriu andorrà," *Pirineos,* 11 (1955) 77–108. J. M. GUILERA, *Una història d'Andorra* (Barcelona 1960). J. CAPEILLE, *Dictionnaire d'histoire et de géographie ecclésiastiques,* ed. A. BAUDRILLART et al. (Paris 1912) 2: 1585–87. *Bilan du Monde,* 2:70.

[C. BARAUT]

ANDRADE, ANTONIO DE

Portuguese missionary; b. Oleiros, Portugal, 1580; d. Goa, India, March 19, 1634. He entered the Society of Jesus in 1596, went to India in 1600, and became rector of the colleges at Goa, and in 1621 superior of the Mogul mission at Agra. Lured by reports of Christian communities to the north, he became the first European to cross the Himalayas into Tibet in 1624, and in 1625, with six other Jesuits, five Portuguese and one French, he estab-

ANDORRA

0 2 4 6 8 10 Miles

0 2 4 6 8 10 Kilometers

FRANCE

El Serrat

Pic de Coma Pedrosa 9,652 ft. 2942 m.

Llorts

PYRENEES

Valira del Nord

Arinsal

Ordino

Valira d'Orient

Soldeu

Pal

La Massána

Anyos

Encamp

Pas de la Casa

Andorra la Vella

Estany d'Engolasters

Les Escaldes

Santa Coloma

Sant Juliá de Lòria

Valira

Farga de Moles

Arcabell

SPAIN

Segre

Valira

Andorra

---

lished a mission at Tsaparang, on the Sutlej River. The accounts of his two trips were quickly translated into several European languages. In 1629 he returned to Goa as provincial superior. The Tsaparang mission was destroyed in 1631 during a revolt inspired by hostile lamas; the Christian community had numbered about 400. Andrade was preparing to return to Tibet when he died, probably from poison.

Bibliography: C. WESSELS, *Early Jesuit Travelers in Central Asia* (The Hague 1924) 43–91. *Archivum historicum Societatis Jesu*, Index generalis (1953) 299.

[M. B. MARTIN]

ANDRÉ, BERNARD ANDREAS

AUGUSTINIAN poet and historiographer; b. Toulouse, France, *c.* 1450; d. London, England, after 1521. Although he was a doctor of civil and canon law, his fame was that of a poet and humanist. He went to England, perhaps *c.* 1485, and came under the patronage of Richard FOXE, later bishop of Winchester. It was probably Foxe

who introduced André to the court, where HENRY VII appointed him poet laureate and royal historiographer. André directed the education of Arthur, Prince of Wales, and possibly also that of the future HENRY VIII. He wrote a life of Henry VII, begun in 1500 but never fully completed (ed. J. Gairdner, London 1858). Most of his writings are in Latin, although he has left a few French poems. His work, most of which is unedited, has value chiefly as a source of contemporary information, for its literary value is disputed. In official records André is frequently referred to as "the blind poet."

Bibliography: J. GAIRDNER, *The Dictionary of National Biography from the Earliest Times to 1900* 1:398–399. F. ROTH, *History of English Austin Friars 1249–1538* (New York 1961), v.2 *Sources*. A. PALMIERI, *Dictionnaire d'histoire et de géographie ecclésiastiques* 2:1722–23.

[A. J. ENNIS]

ANDREW, APOSTLE, ST.

The name Ἀνδρέας is Greek in origin (perhaps related to the Greek word for "courage") and has no apparent Aramaic or Hebrew equivalent, although the name was used among Jews at the time of Jesus (Str. B. I, 535). For the most part Andrew remains an enigmatic figure in the New Testament. Matthew, Luke, and John all agree that he was the brother of Simon PETER, but beyond this there is little information that could be of historical value.

The Synoptic tradition consistently groups Andrew with Peter, JAMES, and JOHN in the list of the Twelve (Mk 3.18; Mt 10.2; Lk 6.14; Acts 1.13). Occasionally Andrew is also included in this "inner circle" apart from the catalogue of the Twelve (Mk 13.3). In the Gospel of Mark, Andrew first appears in a scene whose literary form resembles that of the calling of Elisha in 1 Kgs 19.19–21. A commission is received and this commission entails a radical change of life. ELISHA, as well as Andrew and Simon, abandon their respective occupations to receive the divine call—Elisha to become a prophet and Andrew and Simon to become "fishers of men" (Mk 1.16–18). Andrew is also mentioned, along with others, as one of those present when Jesus heals Simon's mother-in-law (Mk 1.29). Matthew and Luke both preserve the Marcan material, but omit the name of Andrew from Mk 1.29, Mt 8.14, 4.38–41 and Mk 13.3, Mt 24.3, Lk 21.5. Acts also fails to mention Andrew apart from the catalogue of the eleven in Acts 1.13.

Andrew enjoys a more significant place in the Fourth Gospel. Though John does not contain a catalogue of the Twelve, Andrew does play a role in the development of two important episodes. In Jn 1.35–40, Andrew is the first of the disciples to follow Jesus. He is counted as one of two disciples of JOHN THE BAPTIST who hear John identify Jesus as "the Lamb of God" (1.35–6) and then pursue Jesus. It is only after they remain (Greek: μένω) with Jesus some time that Andrew finds his brother, Simon Peter, and declares, "We have found the Messiah" (1.41). In the Fourth Gospel Andrew is the first to make this declaration, and he makes it at the beginning of Jesus' ministry. This stands in contrast to the Synoptic tradition, where Peter is the first to make this declaration of faith after a lengthy period of following Jesus in his ministry. In Jn 6.8 Andrew appears again, this time with Philip, as both disciples express their incredulity at the prospect of feeding the multitude with the five barley loaves and two fish presented by a young man. As in the case with Mk 1 and 1 Kgs 19, Andrew plays a part in an episode that evokes the memory of the prophet Elisha who multiplies barley loaves in 2 Kgs 4.42–44. In Jn 12.20–22, Andrew again appears along side Philip, and together they present Jesus with Greek proselytes who have come "to see" (believe in?) him. Since both Philip and Andrew have Greek names and hail from a Gentile region of Palestine (i.e., Bethsaida in Galilee), they become the appropriated intermediaries to bring the Gentiles to Jesus, and help provide the transition to the Fourth Gospel's "Book of Glory."

Many of the traditions about Andrew emerge from the late second century *Acts of Andrew*, the complete Greek text of which does not survive except in fragments, most of which contain the account of Andrew's martyrdom. The sixth-century historian and hagiographer Gregory of Tours made an abstract of the *Acts of Andrew* in his *Liber de miraculum* and helped contribute to Andrew's popularity in the West. In the *Acts* Andrew is portrayed as a zealous missionary who evangelized the region around the Black Sea (Scythia), and this tradition is picked up by Origen and Eusebius (*Histoire ecclesiastique* III, 1), while other ancient writers suggest that Andrew was active in and around Greece and Asia Minor. According to the *Acts of Andrew*, the Roman Governor Aegeas (or Aegeates), crucified him by tying him to a cross.

In the early Middle Ages Andrew became a politically significant figure in the struggle between Rome and Constantinople. The See of Constantinople, owing its prominence and indeed its existence to the Emperor Constantine, used the legends of Andrew in an effort to demonstrate its apostolic origin. The figure of Andrew was well suited for these polemics given the account in Jn 1:37 where he was the "first called" (πρωτοκλήτος), i.e. before Peter, and on account of the legends that placed his missionary activity in the area of the Black Sea.

In iconography, Andrew is sometimes depicted with a long beard and fishing net, or other symbol of his life as a fisherman. He is also represented with the implements of his death, including, beginning in the Middle Ages, a saltire (X-shaped) cross and a rope. Andrew is celebrated as the patron saint of Scotland and Russia.

Feast: Nov. 30.

Bibliography: R. E. BROWN, *The Gospel According to John*, (*Anchor Bible* 29, 29A; Garden City, NJ, 1966, 1970). D. MACDONALD, "Andrew," ABD 1:242–244. P. M. PETERSON, *Andrew, Brother of Simon Peter: His History and Legends* (Nov. Test. Suppl. 1; Leiden, 1958).

[C. MCMAHON]

ANDREW ABELLON, BL.

Dominican teacher, reformer, and artist; b. Saint-Maximin-la-Saint-Baume, France, *c.* 1375; d. Aix, France, May 15, 1450. He joined the DOMINICAN order in his native village and taught philosophy and theology in various Dominican priories until 1408, when he became master of theology. From 1408 to 1419 he devoted himself exclusively to preaching in southern France, but found time to minister to the victims of the plague that broke out at Aix in 1415. While prior of SAINT-MAXIMIN (1419–22 and 1425–29), he restored observance in that house and completed and embellished its buildings. As vicar of observance appointed by Master General Bartholomew Texier (d. 1449), Abellon introduced reform in the priories of Aix, where he was prior from 1438 to 1442, and Marseilles, where he was prior from 1444 to 1448. An artist, he used his talents to teach the eternal truths by paintings. He was beatified in 1902.

Feast: May 17.

Bibliography: H. M. CORMIER, *Le Bienheureux André Abellon* (2d ed. Rome 1902). D. A. MORTIER, *Histoire des maîtres généraux de l'ordre des Frères Prêcheurs*, 8 v. (Paris 1903–20) 4:145, 193–210. G. GIERATHS, *Lexikon für Theologie und Kirche*, ed. J. HOFER and K. RAHNER, 10 v. (2d, new ed. Freiburg 1957–65) 1:513.

[A. H. CAMACHO]

ANDREW CACCIOLI, BL.

Franciscan, early companion of St. Francis; b. Spello, near Assisi, Italy, 1194; d. there, June 3, 1254. These dates (*Acta sanctorum*, 1869, June 1:356–362) are to be preferred to those (1181–1264) suggested by WADDING (*Scriptores Ordinis Minorum* 1256, n. 50 and 1264, n. 11). The name Caccioli is puzzling as it can scarcely have been a family name, for at that time it was not usual to use surnames, especially in the case of MENDICANTS. In 1223, after the death of his parents and sister, Andrew

(Italian: Andrea) received the habit at the hands of FRANCIS OF ASSISI. He was thus one of his early companions, and we are informed that he was the first priest to join the group (*inter quos fuit primus sacerdos*). He received permission in writing from Francis to win souls for Christ by preaching, and in 1226 he was present at the founder's death. His interpretation of the rule, which he shared with many of the saint's early companions, twice earned for him imprisonment under ELIAS OF CORTONA. On the first occasion he was set free by GREGORY IX on the intercession of ANTHONY OF PADUA and the second time by JOHN OF PARMA; thus, there seem to be no grounds for asserting that he died in prison. He was present at the general chapter held at Soria in Spain in 1233. His remains lie under the altar of the chapel dedicated to his honor in the church of Saint Andrew the Apostle in Spello and his cult was confirmed by Pope CLEMENT XII in 1738.

Feast: June 9 (formerly June 3).

Bibliography: *Acta sanctorum* June 1:356–362. *Martyrologium Franciscanum,* ed. ARTURUS A MONASTERIO, rev. I. BESCHIN and J. PALAZZOLO (Rome 1939). *Il beato Andrea Caccioli da Spello,* ed. E. MENESTÒ (Spoleto 1997). O. BONMANN, *Lexikon für Theologie und Kirche*, 10 v. (2d, new ed. Freiburg 1957–65) 1:514. *Acta Ordinis Fratrum Minorum* 69 (1950) 129. A. BUTLER, *The Lives of the Saints* 2: 466–467.

[T. C. CROWLEY]

ANDREW CORSINI, ST.

Bishop of Fiesole; b. Florence, Italy, Nov. 30, 1302; d. Fiesole, Italy, Jan. 6, 1373. After a misspent childhood he donned the Carmelite habit *c.* 1317. He was sent to study at the University of Paris in 1329 and was named provincial of his order for Tuscany in 1348. He was most active in this office both during the plague that struck Florence and later in undertaking an extensive campaign to rebuild the hard-hit religious communities and restore their spiritual fervor and monastic discipline. He was nominated as bishop by the cathedral chapter at Fiesole, and the election was confirmed by Clement V in a bull of Oct. 13, 1349. Andrew Corsini was an able and wise administrator; he visited the parishes of his diocese, founded confraternities of priests in honor of the Trinity, and provided for restoration and construction of churches. He also mediated quarrels between the families of the Florentine nobility. His cult became popular shortly after his death; and papal approval, several times requested, was finally granted by Urban VIII on April 22, 1629, and the bull of canonization was promulgated June 4, 1724, by Benedict XIII. Alexander VII extended his veneration to the whole Church, although he is especially honored in Florence, where he is buried and where his intercession

is credited with the repulse of Filippo Maria Visconti's attack on Pope Eugene IV and the fathers of the Council of Florence in 1440.

Feast: Feb. 4.

Bibliography: *Acta Sanctorum* Jan. 2:1061–77. S. MATTEI, *Vita di Santo Andrea Corsini* (Florence 1872). P. CAIOLI, *S. Andrea Corsini carmelitano* (Florence 1929). F. CARAFFA and S. ORIENTI, *Bibliotheca sanctorum* 1:1158–69. A. BUTLER, *The Lives of the Saints,* ed. H. THURSTON and D. ATTWATER (New York 1956) 1:246–247. P. MARIE-JOSEPH, *Dictionnaire d'histoire et de géographie ecclésiastiques*, ed. A. BAUDRILLART et al. (Paris 1912) 2:1655–59. *Analecta Bollandiana* 48 (1930) 432–434. ANASTASIO DIS. PAOLO, *Analecta Ordinis Carmelitarum Discalceatorum* 4 (1930) 232–250.

[M. MONACO]

ANDREW DE COMITIBUS, BL.

Franciscan brother; b. Anagni, Italy, *c.* 1240; d. convent of San Lorenzo al Piglio, Rome, Feb. 1, 1302. He was a member of the noble family of the Conti (de Comitibus) and a close relative of Popes INNOCENT III, GREGORY IX, ALEXANDER IV, and BONIFACE VIII. Pope Boniface wished to create him cardinal, but Andrew's humility and holiness of life led him to refuse the proffered dignity; some chronicles suggest that he was actually created cardinal and renounced the office.

Andrew is said to have been the author of the treatise *De partu Beatae Mariae Virginis,* which has since been lost. Andrew was famous during his lifetime for his many miracles, and Boniface VIII is quoted as saying that, had Andrew died during his reign, he would have canonized him. He was eventually beatified by INNOCENT XIII in 1724, and his cause is still under consideration. He is buried in the church of San Lorenzo al Piglio.

Feast: Feb. 15; Feb. 1 (Franciscans).

Bibliography: *Compendium chronicarum Fratrum Minorum scriptum a patre Mariano de Florentia, Archivum Franciscanum historicum* 2 (1901) 457–472. B. MARINANGELI, "Memorie del convento di S. Lorenzo al Piglio (Roma)," *Miscellanea Franciscana* 20 (1919) 148–154. S. PELLEGRINI, *Il beato Andrea Conti, 1250–1302* (Piglio 1959). M. BIHL, *Dictionnaire d'histoire et de géographie ecclésiastique,* ed. A. BAUDRILLART (Paris 1912–) 2:1654–55. W. FORSTER, *Lexikon für Theologie und Kirche,* ed. J. HOFER and K. RAHNER, 10 v. (2d, new ed. Freiburg 1957–65) 1:514–515. A. MERCATI and A. PELZER, *Dizionario ecclesiastico,* 3 v. (Turin 1954–58) 1:139.

[T. C. CROWLEY]

ANDREW DOTTI, BL.

Servite preacher; b. San Sepolcro, Tuscany, Italy, 1256; d. Vallucola, Italy, Aug. 31, 1315. He belonged to the noble Italian family of Dotti, and he received an excellent education. Touched by a sermon of PHILIP BENIZI, he entered the SERVITE order in 1278 at Florence, where Alexis FALCONIERI, one of the seven founders, was superior. His progress in religious virtue was rapid, and after his ordination he was sent to a convent near San Sepolcro, where his zeal manifested itself in preaching, prayer, and penance. He received permission to join a group of hermits at Vallucola, whom he united with the Servites in 1294. Between 1297 and 1310 Andrew preached with extraordinary results throughout Italy. After the death of Alexis Falconieri he returned to the hermitage of Vallucola, where he led a life of charity, mortification, and contemplation. He was buried in a church in his native town. Pope PIUS VII approved his cult on Nov. 29, 1806.

Feast: Sept. 3.

Bibliography: M. POCCIANTI, *Chronicon rerum totius sacri ordinis servorum beatae Mariae virginis* (Florence 1567). C. BATTINI, *Vita del beato Andrea Dotti dei Servi di Maria* (Bologna 1866). P. SOULIER, *Vie de saint Philippe Benizi* (Paris 1886); P. SOULIER et al., eds., *Monumenta servorum sanctae Mariae*, 20 v. (Brussels 1897–1930) v.2. S. M. LEDOUX, *Histoire des sept saints fondateurs* (Paris 1888). T. ORTOLAN, *Dictionnaire d'histoire et de géographie ecclésiastiques*, ed. A. BAUDRILLART (Paris 1912–) 2:1663–64.

[M. B. MORRIS]

ANDREW FRANCHI, BL.

Preacher and bishop; b. 1335, Pistoia, Italy; d. there May 26, 1401. He was born of the noble family of Franchi-Boccagni, took the DOMINICAN habit *c.* 1351 and graduated as doctor in theology at Rome. He was successively prior (1370–75) at Pistoia, Orvieto, and twice at Lucca, and was noted as a teacher, preacher, and spiritual director. Exceptionally austere, Franchi was devoted to Christ Crucified, the Madonna and Infant, and the Magi. As bishop of Pistoia from about 1380 to his resignation in 1400, he lived as a religious, preached, spent his income on the poor and on pious causes, converted many sinners, and healed factional strife. His body, buried in San Domenico, Pistoia, was found incorrupt in 1911. BENEDICT XV (1921) and PIUS XI (1922) approved his cult.

Feast: May 26 (Pistoia); May 30 (Dominicans).

Bibliography: J. QUÉTIF and J. ÉCHARD, *Scriptores Ordinis Praedicatorum*, 5v. (Paris 1719–23); continued by R. COULON (Paris 1909—); repr. 2 v. in 4 (New York 1959) 1.2:717–718. *Acta Apostolicae Sedis* 13 (1921) 549; 14 (1922) 16–19. I. TAURISANO, *Beato Andrea Franchi* (Rome 1922).

[W. A. HINNEBUSCH]

ANDREW OF CRETE (OF JERUSALEM), ST.

Archbishop; b. Damasus, *c.* 660; d. Erissos, July 4, 740. A monk in Jerusalem (678), he became a deacon in Constantinople (*c.* 685) and head of a refuge for orphans and the aged. He later became archbishop of Gortyna in Crete (692). At the Monothelite Synod of Constantinople (712), he subscribed to the repudiation of two wills in Christ defined by the Council of Constantinople III. In 713 he retracted, explaining his doctrine in a metrical confession, and participated in the quarrels over ICONOCLASM. He was remarkable as an orator; 22 of his homilies and panegyrics have been published, while some are still unedited. He furthered the development of the Byzantine Liturgy, inaugurating a type of penitential hymn or Great Canon still in use, and he is respected as one of the principal hymnographers of the Oriental Church.

Feast: July 4.

Bibliography: ANDREW OF CRETE, *Opera Omnia, Patrologia Graeca* 97:805–1443. S. VAILHÉ, *Échos d'Orient* 5 (1901–02) 378–387. O. CLÉMENT, *Le chant des larmes: essai sur le repentir* (Paris 1982). V. NECHAEV, *Uroki pokaianiia v Velikom Kanone Sviatogo Andreia Kritskogo, zaimstvovannye iz bibleiskikh skazanii* (Moscow 1995; originally published in 1891). E. MERCENIER, *A propos d'Andrée de Créte* (Alexandria 1953). O. BARDENHEWER, *Geschichte der altkirchlichen Literatur* (Freiburg 1913–32) 5:152–157. B. ALTANER, *Patrology* (New York 1960) 645. H. RAHNER, *Lexicon für Theologie und Kirche*, ed. J. HOFER and K. RAHNER (Freiburg 1957–65) 1:516–517. H. G. BECK, *Kirche und theologische Literatur im byzantinischen Reich* (Munich 1959) 500–502.

[L. VEREECKE]

ANDREW OF FIESOLE, ST.

Archdeacon of Fiesole, Italy; of Scottish or possibly Irish birth; d. *c.* 877. He accompanied (St.) Donatus to Rome on a pilgrimage. On their return they passed through the town of Fiesole near Florence, where the episcopal see was vacant. The clergy and people were assembled in the cathedral praying for a pious and worthy bishop when Andrew and Donatus entered. At once, reportedly, the bells began to ring and candles and lights were illumined by superhuman power. Donatus was elected bishop, and he ordained Andrew as his archdeacon. Andrew restored the church of San Martino di Mensola at Fiesole and built a monastery there. In 1284 his relics were found in the church where they are still preserved. His *acta* of the fourteenth or fifteenth century are too late to be of any value.

Feast: Aug. 22.

Bibliography: A. M. TOMMASINI, *Irish Saints in Italy*, tr. J. F. SCANLAN (London 1937). S. AMMIRATO, *Vescovi di Fiesole, di Vol-*

terra e d'Arezzo (Florence 1637; reprinted Bologna 1976). *Acta Sanctorum* Feb. 1:245–248; Aug. 4:539–548. A. M. ZIMMERMANN, *Lexicon für Theologie und Kirche*, ed. J. HOFER and K. RAHNER (Freiburg 1957–65) 1:515–516. A. BUTLER, *The Lives of the Saints*, ed. H. THURSTON and D. ATTWATER (New York 1956) 3:382.

[R. T. MEYER]

ANDREW OF LONGJUMEAU

Dominican missionary and papal ambassador; b. Longjumeau, France, early 13th century; d. France, *c.* 1270. In 1238 King LOUIS IX commissioned him to bring the Crown of Thorns back to France from Constantinople. Innocent IV made use of his proficiency in Oriental languages and sent him to negotiate the return of the Jacobite and Nestorian churches to unity with Rome. While on the Crusades with King Louis (1248–54) he went on a mission to the Great Khan at Karakorum to investigate his reported conversion to the Faith. In 1256 he was in Tunis working for the conversion of the Sultan, but sometime before 1270 he returned to France, where he died.

Bibliography: P. PELLIOT, "Les Mongols et la papauté," *Revue de l'Orient Chrétien* 23 (1922–23) 1–30; 24 (1924) 225–335; 28 (1931–32) 3–84. J. S. DE JOINVILLE, *The History of St. Louis*, ed. N. DE WAILLY, tr. J. EVANS (New York 1938) 39–41, 142–148. J. QUÉTIF and J. ÉCHARD, *Scriptores Ordinis Praedicatorum*, 5 v. (Paris 1719–23); continued by R. COULON (Paris 1909—); repr. 2 v. in 4 (New York 1959) 1.1:140–141. A. DUVAL, *Catholicisme* 1: 530–531.

[J. D. CAMPBELL]

ANDREW OF PESCHIERA, BL.

Dominican; b. Peschiera on Lake Garda, Italy, *c.* 1400; d. Morbegno, Switzerland, Jan. 17–18, 1485. At an early age Andrew Grego entered the DOMINICANS at Brescia and was sent to San Marco, Florence, for his studies. He had a special attraction for the virtue of obedience. His life work was the evangelization of Vatellina, a district in southern Switzerland, where he labored so zealously for 45 years that he became known as its apostle. He assisted in the foundation of two Dominican houses, in Morbegno (1457) and in Coire. At times he acted as inquisitor at Como. He was especially solicitous for the poor. Solemn veneration was accorded him at the translation of his remains to the chapel of St. Roch in 1497. His cult was approved Sept. 23, 1820, by Pius VII.

Feast: Jan. 19.

Bibliography: R. COULON, *Dictionnaire d'histoire et de géographie ecclésiastiques* 2:1690–91. J. L. BAUDOT and L. CHAUSSIN, *Vies des saints et des bienheureux selon l'ordre du calendrier avec l'historique des fêtes* 1:392. A. BUTLER, *The Lives of the Saints* 1:123–124.

[M. G. MCNEIL]

ANDREW OF RINN, BL.

Also known as Anderl, peasant child, alleged martyr; b. Nov. 16, 1459; d. Rinn, near Innsbruck, Austria, July 12, 1462. At his father Simon Oxner's death, his mother Maria entrusted Andrew, then two years old, to the care of his uncle Meyer, an innkeeper. Andrew disappeared July 12, 1462, and his mother found his body hanging from a tree in a nearby forest. The uncle claimed he had sold the child to Jews returning from a fair. The child's body was buried in a cemetery of Ampass without any extant evidence of a juridical investigation. Veneration was first given to the remains when the inhabitants of Rinn, imitating the citizens of Trent who honored a boy, SIMON OF TRENT, murdered by Jews in 1475, solemnly transferred Andrew's body to Rinn *c.* 1677–85. His cult spread through northern Tyrol and a commemoration Mass first celebrated in his honor in 1722. Upon the petition of the bishop of Brixen and the abbot of the prémontrés of Wilten, Benedict XIV approved his equivalent beatification Dec. 25, 1752 because of the pre-existing cultus, but refused canonization Feb. 22, 1755. In 1985 Bp. Reinhold Stecher of Innsbruck ordered the body transferred from the church to the parish cemetery. His cultus was officially forbidden in 1994.

See Also: MEDIEVAL BOY MARTYRS.

Bibliography: A. KEMBTER, *Acta pro ueritate martyrri corporis el cultus publici B. Andreae Rinnensis* (Innsbruck 1745). BENOÂT XIV, *Constitutio XLIV: Beatus Andreas, dans Bullarium romanum magnam sue ejusdem Continuatio* (Luxembourg 1758) 120–136. J. DECKERT, *Vier Tiroler Kinder, Opfer des chassidischen Fanatismus* (Vienne 1893). W. KUNZEMANN, *Judenstein: Das Ende einer Legende* (Innsbruck 1995). E. VACANDARD, *Dictionnaire d'histoire et de géographie ecclésiastiques*, ed. A. BAUDRILLART et al. (Paris 1912) 2:1700–02. A. BUTLER, *The Lives of the Saints*, ed. H. THURSTON and D. ATTWATER (New York 1956) 3:86–87. M. MAYER, *Lexikon für Theologie und Kirche*, ed. J. HOFER and K. RAHNER (Freiburg 1957–65) 1:519. J. L. BAUDOT and L. CHAUSSIN, *Vies des saints et des bienhereux selon l'ordre du calendrier avec l'historique des fêtes* (Paris 1935–56) 7:282.

[M. G. MCNEIL]

ANDREW OF SAINT-VICTOR

Canon regular of the Abbey of Saint-Victor, Paris, and on two occasions, abbot of Wigmore Abbey in Hereforshire, England. Andrew is most remembered for his dedication to the literal exegesis of Scripture and his use of Jewish traditions in pursuing the literal/historical sense of the biblical text. Born in England, *c.* 1110, he died at Wigmore, Oct. 19, 1175. He entered the Abbey of Saint-Victor in 1130 and studied under Hugh of Saint-Victor (d. 1141), whose interest in the literal sense of Scripture was a fundamental influence on Andrew. In 1147, Andrew went to England as the first abbot of Wigmore. At one point he returned to Saint-Victor, but then returned to England as abbot at Wigmore again *c.* 1161–63, remaining there until his death. Unlike Hugh, who was interested in the allegorical and moral senses as well as the literal, Andrew devoted himself only to the literal sense, and only to exegesis of the Hebrew Bible. He commentaries on the Octateuch, the Books of Kings and Chronicles, Proverbs, Ecclesiastes, the Minor Prophets, Isaiah, Jeremiah, Ezekiel and Daniel are extant. It appears that Andrew discussed points of interpretation with rabbis in the vernacular and then presented their ideas in his Latin commentaries, indicating such materials by referring to "the Jews" and using in some places not only the Latin but also the Hebrew biblical text. His interest in and focus on the literal meaning of the Scripture text drew him to the Jewish exegetical tradition stemming from the work of Rashi (Rabbi Solomon ben Isaac of Troyes). In a treatise entitled *De Emmanuele*, Richard of Saint-Victor entered into a dispute with Andrew over the interpretation of Isaiah 7:14, criticizing what Richard considered Andrew's acceptance of Jewish teaching about this major text for Christian Messianic prophecy. Andrew's influence in stressing the fundamental place of the literal exegesis of the biblical text (and the use of Jewish learning and Hebrew language study in that exegesis) can be traced in the work of many later medieval exegetes, including Herbert of Bosham (Thomas Becket's guide in theology and exegesis), Peter Comestor, Peter the Chanter, Stephen Langton, Hugh of Saint-Cher, and Nicholas of Lyra.

Bibliography: ANDREAS DE SANCTO VICTORE, *Expositio in Ezechielem*, ed. M. A. SIGNER, *Corpus Christianorum Continuatio Mediaevalis* 53E (Turnhout 1991). *Expositio super Danielem*, ed. M. ZIER, *Corpus Christianorum Continuatio Mediaevalis* 53F (Turnhout 1990). *Expositio super heptateuchum*, ed. C. LOHR and R. BERNDT, *Corpus Christianorum Continuatio Mediaevalis* 53 (Turnhout 1986). R. BERNDT, *Expositiones historicae in Libros Salomonis, Corpus Christianorum Continuatio Mediaevalis* 53B (Turnhout); *André de Saint-Victor (1175) Exégète et théologien* (Turnhout 1992). M. A. SIGNER, "Peshat, Sensus Litteralis and Sequential Narrative: Jewish Exegesis and the School of St. Victor in the 12th Century," in *The Frank Talmage Memorial Volume*, ed. B. WALFISH (Haifa 1993) 1:203–16. B. SMALLEY, *The Study of the Bible in the Middle Ages* (Oxford 1983) ch. 4. "Andrew of St. Victor, Abbot of Wigmore: A Twelfth-Century Hebraist," *Recherches de théologie ancienne et médiévale* 10 (1938) 358–373. "The School of Andrew of St. Victor," *Recherches de théologie ancienne et médiévale* 11 (1939) 145–167. J. W. M. ZWEITEN, "Jewish Exegesis within Christian Bounds: Richard of St. Victor's De Emmanuele and Victorine Hermeneutics," *Bijdragen* 48 (1987) 327–35.

[G. ZINN]

ANDREW OF STRUMI, BL.

Abbot and church reformer; b. Parma, Italy, first half of the 11th century; d. Parma, March 10, 1097. A disciple of the deacon ARIALDO, he took part in the church reform movement at Milan, and at great personal risk he recovered the body of his master who had been slain at the instigation of the simoniacal archbishop Guido of Velate (d. 1071). About 1069, while still in his 40s, Andrew joined the VALLOMBROSANS and was in close contact with their founder, JOHN GUALBERT, for some years. He became abbot of STRUMI *c.* 1085, when the Vallombrosans replaced the BENEDICTINE community there. He was called upon to mediate between FLORENCE, which was supporting URBAN II, and AREZZO, partisan of Emperor HENRY IV. Andrew wrote a life of Arialdo (*Patrologia Latina,* 143:1437–86) and also one of John Gualbert (*Patrologia Latina,* 146:765–960). There is in the latter work a reference to one of the saint's miracles that could have been performed only after 1106, and this has cast some doubt on the date usually given for Andrew's death. In the late 13th century Andrew's relics were enshrined in the church of S. Fedele at Strumi.

Feast: March 10.

Bibliography: Sources. *Acta Sanctorum* March 2:47–49. **Literature.** B. ALBERS, "Die aeltesten Consuetudines von Vallumbrosa," *Revue Bénédictine* 28 (1911) 432–436. G. DOMENICI, "La badia di S. Fedele di Strumi presso Poppi," *Rivista storica benedettina* 10 (1915) 72–92, esp. 87–89. U. ROUZIÈS, *Dictionnaire d'histoire et de géographie ecclésiastiques*, ed. A. BAUDRILLART (Paris 1912–) 2:1716. A. M. ZIMMERMANN, *Kalendarium Benedictinum: Die Heiligen und Seligen des Benediktinerorderns und seiner Zweige,* 4 v. (Metten 1933–38) 1:309–310. A. BUTLER, *The Lives of the Saints*, ed. H. THURSTON and D. ATTWATER, 4 v. (New York 1956) 1:549–550. A. M. ZIMMERMANN, *Lexikon für Theologie und Kirche*, ed. J. HOFER and K. RAHNER, 10 v. (2d, new ed. Freiburg 1957–65) 1:520.

[B. J. COMASKEY]

ANDREW THE CATECHIST, BL.

Also known as André de Phú Yên, lay catechist and protomartyr of Vietnam; b. Ran Ran, Annam (Vietnam), 1625; d. Ke Cham, Annam, July 27, 1644. A fervent Vietnamese Christian woman named Joanne convinced the Jesuit missionary Alexandre de Rhodes to accept her sickly, youngest son, Andrew, as his student, and Rhodes later baptized him when he was 15 or 16. About 1641 Andrew joined the *Maison Dieu* (God's House) association of catechists and, in 1643, vowed with other catechists to serve the Church throughout his life. Despite a prohibition against Christianity, Andrew continued to spread the Gospel and as a result was beaten, tortured, and placed under house arrest in July 1644. Mandarin Ong Nghè Bo offered Andrew an opportunity to recant the faith, but he refused. Condemned to death, Andrew was publicly hanged and then decapitated. Fr. de Rhodes, who witnessed Andrew's martyrdom and retrieved the body, recorded the circumstances of his death; Andrew's remains were taken to Macau for burial. Although many other Vietnamese martyrs, including 125 from the nineteenth century, were previously beatified, Andrew has been remembered by Vietnamese Catholics as the country's first martyr. He was beatified in St. Peter's Square on March 5, 2000 by Pope John Paul II.

Feast: July 27.

Bibliography: *L'Osservatore Romano,* English edition, 10 (8 March 2000). PHAM DINH KHIEM, *The First Witness* (Saigon 1959).

[K. I. RABENSTEIN]

ANDREWE, RICHARD

Dean of York, English royal servant; b. Adderbury, Oxfordshire; d. 1477. He was educated at Winchester and New College, Oxford, where he was a fellow (1421–33). A doctor of civil law in 1432, he practiced as a canon lawyer, becoming an official of the court of Canterbury (1439 and 1441), and chancellor of Abp. Henry CHICHELE. He was a king's clerk as early as 1433. His reputation with King HENRY VI and the archbishop led to his nomination on May 20, 1438, as first warden of Chichele's new College of All Souls, Oxford, an office he held until 1442. He then became a king's secretary (1443–55). He served on many diplomatic missions, including the negotiations, in 1444, for Henry's marriage. His services were rewarded with appropriate preferment: he held several canonries at York, Salisbury, and Saint David's, and became archdeacon of Salisbury (1441–44) and of Buckingham (1447–49). Imposed on a reluctant chapter by king and pope, he became dean of York, serving from 1452 until June 2, 1477. His political career ended with the fall of Henry VI, but in his later years he acted as vicar-general of the archbishop of York. He founded chantries at Deddington, Oxfordshire, and Chipping Sodbury, Gloucestershire, and gave a number of Canon Law books to All Souls and New College, Oxford.

Bibliography: *Testamenta Eboracensia*, 6 v. (Surtees Society 4, 30, 45, 53) v.3 (1865). A. J. OTWAY-RUTHVEN, *The King's Secretary . . . in the XV Century* (Cambridge, Eng. 1939). A. B. EMDEN, *A Biographical Register of the University of Oxford to A.D. 1500* 1:34–35.

[C. D. ROSS]

ANDREWES, LANCELOT

Anglican bishop of Winchester, prominent prelate, preacher, and apologist for the Church of England as reformed yet still Catholic, equally opposed to the extremes of Romanism and Puritanism; b. London, 1555; d. Winchester, 1626. He was the son of a master mariner. Andrewes's early promise showed rapid development at Cambridge, where he acquired a critical knowledge of 15 languages that he later used to good purpose as a principal translator of the Authorized Version (King James) of the Bible (1611). He was ordained in 1580, and withstood the influence at Cambridge University of the strong Puritan party eager to win his support. His attraction to Calvinism was only to the devotional side and he showed himself a conservative in Church affairs, appealing in his *Catechetical Lectures* for "apostolic handsomeness and order." Although he retained altar, candles, and incense, then despised as "popish furniture," he yet toured the north (1586) with the Puritan Earl of Huntingdon to win over Catholic recusants. Having been appointed canon penitentiary at St. Paul's, London, in 1589, he began the series of sermons that won him the title "an angel of the pulpit." Andrewes refused two offers of bishoprics from Elizabeth in protest against the policy of alienating episcopal revenues to the crown, but was persuaded by King James to accept the See of Chichester (1605), whence he moved to Ely (1609) and to Winchester (1613). He took no umbrage at being passed over for Canterbury, probably realizing, as did others, that he had no bent for the ecclesiastical politics necessary in the primatial see. When James I was involved in controversy with Cardinal (St.) Robert Bellarmine over the divine right of kings and the oath of allegiance imposed on English papists after the Gunpowder Plot (1605), Andrewes rallied to his king's support in *Tortura Torti* (1609) and *Responsio ad Apologiam Cardinalis Bellarmini* (1610), upholding the orthodoxy of the reformed Church of England and ridiculing the term Roman Catholic as a contradiction in terms, serving only "to distinguish your Catholic Church from another Catholic Church which is not Roman." His equal dislike of Calvinism explains his absence from the Anglican delegation to the Synod of the Dutch Reformed Church at Dort (1618), though the previous year he had gone with James I to Scotland to try to persuade the Presbyterians to accept episcopacy. Andrewes himself was a dedicated bishop, intervening in public affairs only when he thought it necessary. He remained a bachelor, and was a lifelong student, acquiring a profound knowledge of patristic theology. His charming delivery and classical style made him a popular and famous preacher. He was a saintly man with a gift for composing prayers, and his *Preces Privatae* have retained their appeal. His importance in the theological development of the Anglican Church is as a forerunner, with his friends Richard Hooker and George Herbert, of the CAROLINE DIVINES.

Bibliography: *Works,* ed. J. P. WILSON and J. BLISS, 11 v. (*Library of Anglo-Catholic Theology*; Oxford 1841–54). A. T. RUSSELL, *Memoirs of the Life and Works of Lancelot Andrewes* (London 1863). T. S. ELIOT, *For Lancelot Andrewes* (London 1928). J. H. OVERTON, *The Dictionary of National Biography from the Earliest Times to 1900* 1:401–405. M. SCHMIDT, *Die Religion in Geschichte und Gegenwart* ³ 1:369.

[G. ALBION]

ANDRIEU, MICHEL

Liturgist; b. Millau, May 28, 1886; d. Strasbourg, Oct. 2, 1956. He took his theology as an Oratorian in Fribourg from 1907 until ordination, July 18, 1910. Studies in Christian archeology in Rome and literature in Paris fitted him for his more than 30–year career of liturgical scholarship. L. Duchesne, his first master, opened to him the virginal field of the Ordinals. Invited to the faculty of Catholic theology at Strasbourg in 1918, he remained there until his forced retirement in 1956, his 70th year. At the University while patiently pursuing research in the manuscript traditions of the Ordinals, he poured into the faculty review (*Revue des sciences religieuses*) the stream of his monumental essays on Roman liturgy, by-products of his main investigation. He brought to his work an exacting scientific method and an awareness that the liturgy of the past, once restored critically, would be a vital source of theology. He also feared that the fast-growing liturgical movement would bypass the heritage of the past centuries. His method, spirit, and fears were contagiously transmitted, personally to his associates, and by his writings to his careful readers. His two great works, *Ordines Romani,* 5 v. (Louvain 1931–61) and *Pontifical Romain,* 5 v. (Vatican City 1938–63), map out the course taken by the Roman liturgy in its growth from the 6th to the 15th century.

Bibliography: C. VOGEL, *Lexikon für Theologie und Kirche*² 1:522; ''L'Oeuvre liturgique de Mgr. M. Andrieu,'' *Revue des sciences religieuses* 31 (1957) 7–19. B. CAPELLE, ''L'Oeuvre liturgique de Mgr. Andrieu et la théologie,'' *Nouvelle revue théologique* 79 (1957) 169–177. *Mélanges en l'honneur de Monseigneur Michel Andrieu* (Strasbourg 1956).

[R. T. CALLAHAN]

ANDRONICUS II PALAEOLOGUS, BYZANTINE EMPEROR

Patriarchate 1282 to 1328; b. Constantinople, 1256; d. May 24, 1332. He was the son of Michael VIII Palaeologus and Theodora Ducas. At 15 he was married

to the daughter of Stephen V of Hungary and associated in the Emperorship (1271). Breaking with his father's conciliatory policy toward Rome after the Sicilian Vespers had destroyed the Anti-Constantinopolitan designs of Charles of Anjou, he deposed JOHN XI BECCUS and restored the deposed anti-union Patriarch, Joseph. On Joseph's death (March 1283), he imposed Gregory of Cyprus (d. 1289) in the patriarchate, forcing his mother Theodora to renounce communion with Rome.

Because of his devotion to theology and ecclesiastical politics, he tried to pacify the followers of the deceased Patriarch Arsenius, deposed by MICHAEL VIII, and to institute a reform of clergy and monasteries under the hermit Athanasius, who became patriarch in 1289 but abdicated in 1293. Under the patriarch John (Comus) in 1295 the emperor convoked a reform synod; when he attempted an alliance with the Serbs and espoused his daughter to the already married Kral Stephen Urosh II; he was reproached in a synod (1300) and ceded. He restored Athanasius as patriarch (1304–12) and deposed Niphon of Cyzicus as patriarch in 1315 for simony, replacing him with a layman, John XIII Glycas (1315–19), then with Gerasimus (1320–21), and then with the monk Isaac (1323).

The reign of Andronicus was accompanied by a series of disasters including interior religious quarrels, the continual threat of western crusading attacks, Italian colonizing enterprises, and Turkish invasions. The attempt to exclude his grandson, ANDRONICUS III, from the throne resulted in civil war and on May 24, 1328, he was deposed and finished his life in a monastery.

Bibliography: L. BRÉHIER, *Dictionnaire d'histoire et de géographie ecclésiastiques,* ed. A. BAUDRILLART et al. (Paris 1912—) 2:1782–92. *Cambridge Medieval History,* 8 v., (1923) 4: 613–614. F. DÖLGER, *Lexikon für Theologie und Kirche,* ed. J. HOFER and K. RAHNER, 10 v. (2d, new ed. Freiburg 1957–65) 1:523. I. SYKUTRES, *Hellenika,* 2 (1929) 267–333; 3 (1930) 15–44, on the Schism of Arsenius (in Greek). G. OSTROGORSKY, *History of the Byzantine State,* tr. J. HUSSEY from 2d German ed. (Oxford 1956) 426–444.

[J. GEIGER]

ANDRONICUS III PALAEOLOGUS, BYZANTINE EMPEROR

May 5, 1328, to June 15, 1341; b. Constantinople, 1296?; d. Constantinople. He was the eldest son of Michael IX Palaeologus, and was coemperor with his grandfather ANDRONICUS II, who on Michael's death in 1320 attempted to exclude Andronicus III from the succession. He joined John Cantacuzenus against the government at Constantinople, and in a civil war forced the abdication of Andronicus II. He married Irene of Brunswick (d.

1324), then Jeanne (later Anne) of Savoy (1326). Andronicus was an outstanding military leader who sought the assistance of Pope BENEDICT XII against the Turks, promising to join a crusade. In 1339 he dispatched Stephen Dandolo and BARLAAM the Calabrian to Avignon for aid. There, in regard to the question of Church reunion, the Latin hatred for the Greeks, rather than dogmatic differences, was cited as the obstacle, and the question of an ecumenical council was raised. Andronicus increased the influence of the Church in the juridical system of the empire by the establishment of an ecclesiastical law court under the patriarch, and in the disputes over HESYCHASM he attempted to act as pacifier but accepted the judgment of Cantacuzenus in favor of PALAMAS.

Bibliography: F. DÖLGER, *Lexikon für Theologie und Kirche*, ed. J. HOFER and K. RAHNER, 10 v. (2d, new ed. Freiburg 1957–65) 1:523–524. L. BRÉHIER, *Dictionnaire d'histoire et de géographie ecclésiastiques*, ed. A. BAUDRILLART et al. (Paris 1912—) 2:1792–97. BARLAAM CALABRO, *Epistole greche*, ed. G. SCHIRÒ (Palermo 1954). G. OSTROGORSKY, *History of the Byzantine State*, tr. J. HUSSEY from 2d German ed. (Oxford 1956) 444–454.

[J. H. GEIGER]

ANEIROS, LEÓN FEDERICO

18th bishop, and 2d archbishop of Buenos Aires; b. Buenos Aires, Aug. 28, 1828; d. there, Sept. 4, 1894. He was appointed bishop of Aulon *in partibus* in 1870, and chosen archbishop on July 24, 1873; he remained in that capacity until his death. He was educated at the San Ignacio College when it was directed by the Jesuits. In 1848 he received his doctorate in theology and civil and Canon Law. After having taught at the University of Buenos Aires, he was simultaneously a delegate for the province of Buenos Aires and the secretary of Bishop Escalada. One of his major concerns was to foster the Catholic press. In 1853 he founded the newspaper *La Religión* and in 1855, *El Orden*, both directed by Félix Frias. Aneiros contributed to them until 1858 and 1861, when they ceased publication. From the time he occupied the See of Buenos Aires, he was obliged to combat secularism, which was gaining ground. His need of clergy led him to be lenient in receiving unworthy priests from France, Italy, and especially Spain who in the end did more harm than good. He fostered Catholic education and facilitated the establishment of the colleges of San José and of El Salvador. In 1878, because he wished to return the church of San Ignacio to the Jesuits, a mob led by a renegade Spanish priest tried to set fire to the archiepiscopal curia, and did in fact burn El Salvador College. When a persecution against the Church and its institutions was initiated in 1883–84, Archbishop Aneiros endorsed the brave and determined action of the Catholic delegates, who personally upheld Christian interests in the Parliament, but he did little himself. It was said that he did not wish to offend the men who governed the country at that time. He was a holy man but rather short–sighted and not very energetic.

Bibliography: R. D. CARBIA, *Mons. León Federico Aneiros* (Buenos Aires 1905). E. LAMAREA, "Mons. León F. Aneiros," *Archivum: Revista de la Junta de Historia Ecclesiástica Argentina* 2 (1944) 165–173.

[G. FURLONG]

ANFREDUS GONTERI

Also known as Alfredus, Aufredus, or Gaufredus Gontier; Franciscan theologian, *Doctor Providus*; b. *c.* 1270 in Brittany. He studied at Paris between 1302 and 1307, and while there was a disciple of DUNS SCOTUS, whom he repeatedly calls "my master." A contemporary document records him, in 1303, as a signatory of an appeal to the council against Pope BONIFACE VIII in the latter's conflict with Philip the Fair. He twice commented on the *Sentences*, in 1322 at Barcelona and in 1325 at Paris, where he became a master in theology. There is no further information about his life.

Only Book 2 of his first commentary on the *Sentences* has been identified, while of his Paris commentary Books 1–3 are extant. In addition, there exists a *Quaestio de paupertate Christi*, written at Barcelona *c.* 1322 [*Studi Francescani* 33 (1936) 240–291]. His *Quaestiones quodlibetales* is cited by WILLIAM OF VAUROUILLON. Anfredus himself mentions his *Quaestiones ordinariae* and his *Quaestiones disputatae de beatitudine, super IVm,* but these have not been discovered.

Vaurouillon (*In 4 sent.* 45.1) calls Anfredus "an outstanding disciple of Scotus." He himself confesses in his commentary on the *Sentences:* "I am not quite willing to contradict the *Doctor Subtilis*," but in fact depends substantially on the anti-Scotist, HENRY OF HARCLAY, in the same work. In Anfredus's first book, the more than 200 questions utilize almost exclusively the first book of Harclay. His borrowings, here as in the second book, are for the most part as good as literal; even when he contests Harclay's opinions, he depends upon him in literary and technical matters. In addition there are indications that Anfredus utilized the first book of John of Reading. He often cites PETER AUREOLI, as well as the work of a friend, a certain "Frater Franciscus"—probably Francis of Marchia or Francis of Meyronnes. (*See* SCOTISM.)

Bibliography: J. DUNS SCOTUS, *Opera Omnia*, ed. C. BALIĆ (Vatican City 1956) 4:15*–28*. J. ALFARO, "La Inmaculada Concepción en los escritos inéditos de un discipulo de Duns Escoto, Aufredo Gontier," *Gregorianum* 36 (1955) 590–617.

[A. EMMEN]

ANGEL OF THE LORD

A theophanic messenger of God, mentioned mainly in ancient texts of the Pentateuch and the Historical Books of the OT, distinct from, and posing a different problem than, the angels in general.

Summary of Usage. The Hebrew word *mal'āk* (messenger) may be used of human messengers (Gn 32.4), prophets as spokesmen for God (2 Chr 36.15–16), or God's superhuman envoys (Gn 19.1, 15), but its use in the phrase *mal'ak yahweh* or *'elohim* (the messenger of Yahweh or God) has a more specific meaning that has not yet been satisfactorily explained.

In a series of passages taken from the Yahwistic and Elohistic traditions that formed the nucleus of the Pentateuch and in other early texts, the messenger of the Lord is presented not as a created heavenly envoy, distinct from God, but as Yahweh or God appearing to humans in sensible form (Gn 16.7–13; 21.17–20; 22.11–18; 31.11–13; Ex 3.2–6; 14.19, 24–25; Nm 22.22–35; Jgs 2.1–5; See also Jos 5.13–15; Jgs 6.11–24; 13.3–23). In a few other passages (Ex 23.20–23; Gn 24.7; 48.16; Nm 20.16) a messenger sent by God and apparently distinct from Him performs salvation acts that are attributed directly to God in other places. Other passages ascribe vengeance to messengers from God, who are distinct from Him, e.g., the Exterminator of Ex 12.23 (See also 1 Cor 10.10 Heb 11.28; Gn 19.1; 2 Sm 24.16; 2 Kgs 19.35). Finally, David is compared to an angel of the Lord because of his goodness and wisdom (1 Sm 29.9; 2 Sm 14.17–20; 19.27). The burden of the rest of this article is to determine what the angel of the Lord in the first series of texts means.

Original Meaning of Yahweh's Messenger. There are three theories that attempt to explain the origin and meaning of these texts: (1) the messenger is one who represents the Lord, transmits His will and promises, and therefore speaks God's message in the first person singular as the Prophets also did (Jerome and Augustine); (2) the messenger is the ubiquitous God Himself who directly but in human form manifests His message to His chosen leaders (see the Greek and early Latin Fathers of the Church who affirmed that the angel was a manifestation of the Logos); and (3) the messenger is the result of later theological speculation and was interpolated into ancient, naïve traditions relating direct, nonmediated appearances of God to humans that clashed with the evolved concept of God's transcendence and the angels' mediation.

Each theory has valid elements that aid in the understanding of the individual passages, but none of them solves all the problems concerned with the messenger of the Lord wherever it appears. The third theory mentioned above (interpolation) cannot by itself explain why vestiges of the direct intervention of God were left uninterpolated. But it does explain how postexilic Jews must have understood the passages into which they did not interpolate the angel of the Lord. The first theory mentioned above (representation) is certainly Biblical and is to be applied to the second and third series of texts cited above, and perhaps even to the fourth where David is praised as God's representative; but in the first series the messenger is certainly not distinct from God Himself.

The second theory mentioned above (identity) appears to offer more solutions than the other two, especially when one considers that the original meaning of *mal'āk* may not have been messenger but a sending or a message. Certainly in other ancient passages no mediation whatsoever is found when God communicates with His elect (Gn 12.1–3, *passim*). "The angel of the Lord is therefore a form in which Yahweh appears . . . . He is God himself in human form" [G. Von Rad, *Genesis*, tr. J. H. Marks (Philadelphia 1961) 188]. God appearing in human form then is a type of the Logos, Christ, who fulfills the directness and mediation of this mysterious "message" of Yahweh. In Mal 3.1 the messenger of the Lord and messenger of the covenant appear to be both Yahweh Himself and the messenger sent before Him.

In the NT (Lk 1.11; 2.9; Jn 5.4; Acts 5.19; etc.) the angel of the Lord is distinct from God, "sent from God" (Lk 1.26).

Bibliography: W. G. HEIDT, *Angelology of the Old Testament* (Washington 1949). W. G. MACDONALD, "Christology and 'the Angel of the Lord'," in *Current Issues in Biblical and Patristic Interpretation: Studies in Honor of Merrill C. Tenney Presented by His Former Students*, ed. G. F. HAWTHORNE (Grand Rapids 1975) 324–335. D. SLAGER, "Who Is the 'Angel of the Lord'?" *Bible Translator* 39 (1988) 436–438.

[T. L. FALLON/EDS.]

ANGELA OF FOLIGNO, BL.

Mystic; b. Foligno, Italy, *c.* 1248; d. Jan. 4, 1309. Almost nothing is known about the details and external circumstances of Angela's life. Except for the date of her death, virtually all the information we have about her must be deduced or inferred from her *Book*. The first part of this *Book*, the *Memorial*, was dictated to a Franciscan friar whom we only know as Bro. A. He was to serve as Angela's confessor, scribe, and protagonist of her communications from God. Bro. A. not only translated into

Latin what Angela dictated to him in her Umbrian dialect (she was unlettered), but also, and in spite of repeated affirmations to the contrary he, and perhaps other unnamed scribes or subsequent copyists, organized and reworked the text. The *Memorial* contains the thirty steps, told by Angela to Bro. A. and her companion (referred to as M.), that delineate the itinerary of her passionate love affair with the "suffering God-man," how she was transformed and led into the deep abysses of the Trinitarian life. The second part of the *Book*, the *Instructions*, portions likely redacted by Bro. A., but mostly by anonymous disciples, shows us Angela's role as a spiritual mother. It contains her teachings in the form of letters, exhortations, summaries of her spirituality, further visionary accounts, a testament, and an epilogue.

From the scant information that can be gleaned from her *Book* about the external context of her life, we do know that before her conversion Angela was a married woman with children and lived a well-to-do and, likely, a conventional life—even if in her eyes it was a very sinful one. What triggered her mid-life conversion in about 1285 is unknown. Certainly, it was aided by a dream in which St. Francis appeared to her. The Poverello was to become her spiritual guide, appearing to her several times and even, at one point, making the stunning declaration: "You are the only one born of me."

The first nineteen steps of the *Memorial* describe Angela's entrance into the way of penance, a season of purification through suffering. Set ablaze by the fire and intensity of Christ's love as revealed to her through increasingly vivid and focused visions of his passion and crucifixion, her one desire was to grow in amorous response by aligning her life with his, and, following the example of her model St. Francis, stripping herself of all her possessions and taking steps to become truly poor. Very early on in her conversion, her mother, husband, and sons died, which she experienced as a relief. During this period, covering about six years, "Christ's faithful one" (as she is habitually referred to) also entered the Third Order of St. Francis and made a pilgrimage to Assisi during which she experienced a numinous and decisive experience of God.

The final eleven steps, condensed into seven so-called supplementary ones because of Bro. A.'s inability to accurately distinguish them from one another, describe the deepening of Angela's perception and mystical ("from within") experience of Christ's passion. A number of stunning Eucharistic visions are also recorded, one in which she sees the world "as pregnant with God." Even more striking and indicative of the mystical heights which Angela had attained are the formless visions in which she perceived the attributes of God such as his

beauty and goodness. What elevates Angela, to the ranks of the greatest mystics of the Christian Tradition, however, is what takes place in the final steps of the *Memorial*. The sixth supplementary step describes the "horrible darkness" of sharing in Christ's abandonment on the cross, and the seventh describes her almost simultaneous propulsion to the summit of her spiritual journey—the great apophatic visions of God in, with, and beyond the divine darkness (*via negativa*) and her "in abyssation" in the depths of the Trinitarian life. As the oft-quoted locution from one of the *Instruction XXIII* declares: "God's love for her had not been a hoax." The *Memorial* contains some of the most excessive and volcanic pages in all of Christian mystical literature.

Likely because of its role in the internecine quarrel taking place at the time between the Franciscan Spirituals, of which she was set up as a champion, and those referred to as belonging to the Community, Angela's *Book* was initially viewed with suspicion and went underground. The only early mention occurs in the prologue to Ubertino of Casale's *Arbor vitae crucifixae Jesu*. This early eclipse notwithstanding, down through the ages various editions of the *Book* surfaced, merited the esteem, and served as inspiration to an impressive number of saints, spiritual writers, theologians, and thinkers both inside and outside ecclesiastical circles. In the fifteenth century, for instance, Angela's writings enjoyed considerable success in the circles linked to the Observant Franciscans. It is likely that a translation of her *Book* ordered by Cardinal Francis Ximenes, an Observant Franciscan, found its way into the hands of St. Teresa of Avila, who uses Angela's language to describe the trials of the sixth mansion in her *Interior Castle*.

In the seventeenth century, others who were influenced and refer to Angela include St. Francis de Sales, St. Alphonsus Liguori, Pope Benedict XIV, Fenelon, Bossuet, and Jean Jacques Olier. In the late nineteenth century, the brilliant, even if faulty, translation of the French philosopher Ernest Hello—*Le livre desvisions et instructions de la bienheureuse Angèle de Foligno*—catapulted Angela's *Book* (75,000 copies, ten editions) into the consciousness of contemporary French culture. The novelist George Bernanos, the poet-philosopher George Bataille, and the visionary theologian Teilhard de Chardin, as well as prominent French feminists such as Simone de Beauvoir, Julia Kristeva, and Luce Irigaray, quote her in their writings. Furthermore a new, even if contested, critical edition, translations in all the major languages, a number of scientific congresses held in Italy, a flurry of anthologies, biographies, articles, and references in various publications have placed Angela at the forefront of contemporary interest in mysticism. Angela was beatified on July 11, 1701 and her feast day is celebrated on January 4. Although often referred to as a saint, Angela has never been canonized. A commission is currently working on this project.

Feast: Jan. 4.

Bibliography: G. BARONE and J. DALARUN, ed., *Angèle de Foligno: Le Dossier.* (Rome, 1999). L. THIER and A. CALUFETTI, ed., *Il libro della beata Angela da Foligno.* (Grottaferrata, 1986). P. LA-CHANCE, O. F. M., ed. and tr., *Angela of Foligno: Complete Works.* (New York, 1993). S. ANDREOLI and F. SANTI, ''Bibliografia sulla Beata Angela da Foligno,'' (Fondazione Ezio Francescini, Florence, 2001).

[P. LACHANCE]

ANGELINA, ST.

Serbian princess; b. fifteenth century; d. Fruška Gora (Yugoslavia), *c.* 1510. She was the daughter of Ivan Tsrnoievič, prince of the independent state of Zeta. From her marriage to the despot Stephen Branović she had two sons, Jörg and Hanns. After the death of the despot Vonk, she ruled the Zetans (1497–99) and fought against the Turks to preserve Zetan independence. She became a heroine to the Serbians, who called her the mother and queen of Montenegro. Her piety and devotion attracted much admiration, and her cult is still popular in Yugoslavia, where folk poems and songs commemorate her holiness and her patriotism. She was buried in the monastery of Krusedol in the Fruška Gora Mts., where her son Jörg had become a monk. He was later metropolitan of Belgrade (d. 1516).

Feast: June 30.

Bibliography: Z. KOSTELSKI, *The Yugoslavs* (New York 1952). J. MATL, *Lexicon für Theologie und Kirche,* ed. J. HOFER and K. RAHNER (Freiburg 1957–65) 1:532–533.

[F. J. LADOWICZ]

ANGELINA OF MARSCIANO, BL.

Founder of a congregation of Third Order Regular FRANCISCANS; b. Angelina Angioballi in Montegiove near Orvieto, 1377; d. Foligno, July 14, 1435; known also as Angelina of Corbara or of Foligno. She was married to John of Terni, Count of Civitella, at 15 and was a widow at 17. She became a Franciscan tertiary and converted her castle in the Abruzzi into a home for a community of tertiaries. She was so successful in persuading young girls of the area to choose a state of virginity and to enter the convent that she was denounced as a sorcerer and a Manichaean to Ladislaus of Durazzo, King of Naples. He dismissed the charges against her, but in 1395

he exiled her. She and her companions went to Assisi and then to Foligno, where they formed a community of which she became the abbess; in 1398 they made solemn profession and set up strict enclosure. Pope Martin V united her 16 foundations into one congregation, making her superior general in 1428. Evidences of her sanctity were noted at her death, and her body was found incorrupt in 1492. Pope Leo XII approved her cult in 1825.

Feast: July 21; July 13 (Franciscans).

Bibliography: A. BUTLER, *The Lives of the Saints,* ed. H. THURSTON and D. ATTWATER (New York 1956) 3:160–161. O. BON-MANN, *Lexikon für Theologie und Kirche,* ed. J. HOFER and K. RAHNER (Freiburg 1957–65) 1:532.

[N. G. WOLF]

ANGELO CARLETTI DI CHIVASSO, BL.

Franciscan moral theologian and canonist; b. Chivasso, Piedmont, Italy, probably in 1411; d. Cuneo, Italy, April 12, 1495. He came of a wealthy and distinguished family and studied at the University of Bologna. After receiving his doctorate in civil and canon law, the youth was soon entrusted with responsibilities that gave promise of a distinguished career in civil government. But at the age of 30 he gave up his worldly expectations and entered the Franciscans of the Cismontane Observance, taking the name Angelo in place of that of Antonio, which he had been called at Baptism. His learning and holiness quickly won the confidence of his brethren. He was four times chosen vicar general of his order and was held in great esteem outside the order. In 1450 SIXTUS IV commissioned him to preach the crusade against the Turkish invaders of Otranto, and in 1491 he was appointed by INNOCENT VIII to work against the spread of the Waldensian heresy in Savoy and Piedmont. He was a zealous champion of the poor and the oppressed, doing much by his preaching and writing to promote the *MONTES PIETATIS.*

Chivasso's reputation as a moralist rests chiefly on his *Summa casuum conscientiae,* which was first published by Chivasso himself at Venice in 1486. A second edition followed in 1488, and thereafter for the rest of the century republications appeared almost annually. Many new editions throughout the following century are evidence of its continuing popularity. The work came to be known as the *Summa angelica* because of the author's name. Its doctrine, sound and exact, was expressed with rare perspicuity. The arrangement and presentation of topics in alphabetical sequence made it, in effect, a kind of dictionary or encyclopedia of practical moral theology and Canon Law, which proved most helpful to confessors. Luther detested the work and consigned it to the flames at Wittenburg, along with the bull of his excommunication, a collection of the decretals, and the *Summa theologiae* of St. THOMAS AQUINAS (Dec. 10, 1520).

Chivasso enjoys the title Blessed, his cult, which began shortly after his death, having been confirmed by BENEDICT XIV in 1753.

Feast: April 19.

Bibliography: A. L. GABRIEL, *Description of the Summa Angelica* (Notre Dame, Ind. 1991). *Nomenclator literarius theologiae catholicae* 2:1072–73. L. WADDING, *Scriptores Ordinis Minorum* (3d ed. Rome 1906) 19. L. WADDING, *Scriptores Ordinis Minorum* (3d ed. Quaracchi-Florence 1931) 13, 14, 15 *passim.* A. BEUGNET, *Dictionnaire de théologie catholique* 1.1:1271–72.

[P. K. MEAGHER]

ANGELO OF ACRI, BL.

Famous Capuchin preacher; b. Luke Anthony Falcone, Acri, Calabria, Italy, Oct. 19, 1669; d. there, Oct. 30, 1739. He was born of poor parents. After two attempts and two failures, he was invested a third time in the Capuchin Order in 1690; this time he persevered and was ordained in 1702. While Leonard of Port Maurice won fame by his preaching in northern Italy, Angelo did the same in southern Italy. Until his death, he preached home missions and at Forty Hours Devotions. His confreres elected him provincial of the Capuchin province of Cosenze in 1717. In Acritania he founded a convent of Capuchinesses (1725), for whom he wrote his only work, a book of prayers on Christ's sufferings. On Oct. 24, 1739, he became ill of a fever; he died a few days later. He was beatified by Pope Leo XII on Dec. 18, 1825. His cause of canonization was reintroduced in 1853 and is still active.

Feast: July 30.

Bibliography: *Lexikon Capuccinum* (Rome 1951) 71–72. A. RANGE, ''Angelus of Acri,'' *Round Table of Franciscan Research* 24 (1959) 42–48; ''Makings of a Saint,'' *ibid.* 13–19. *Acta Sanctorum* Oct. 13:658–682. *Analecta Ordinis Fratrum Minorum Cappucinorum* 1–70, see index.

[C. KRONZER]

ANGELOLOGY

The theology of angels is a science that studies in the light of divine revelation the invisible world of spiritual intelligences (good angels) created by God who assist man in the attainment of his salvation and share with him the divine call to supernatural grace and glory.

It is a true science: it (1) is based on the certainty that angels exist (H. Denzinger, *Enchiridion symbolorum*, ed. A. Schönmetzer, 800, 3891); (2) attains through an intellectual study of the causal influence exercised by angels upon corporeal beings a knowledge of angelic nature; and (3) is established under the precise modality whereby angels realize substance, i.e., immateriality (St. Thomas, *In meta.*, prooem.; *In 7 meta.* 11.1536). It is a systematic science which, by means of theological and philosophical reflection, has developed and coordinated into a coherent system the divinely revealed data. The theology of angels is not merely a metaphysics of angels; it also shows the relationship of angels to the government of the universe (*Summa theologiae* 1a, 110.1) and the Christian economy. Although angelology is a kind of microtheology which pays special attention to Christ's employment of angels in His Redemption of mankind, it properly sees a continuity in the role of the angels in both the Old and New Testaments, a role that is continuously salvific. Indeed, in the Bible the world of angels appears as tangential to the world of the Jewish people, of Christ, and of His Church. It may be added that angelology implicitly refutes opinions that reject existing reality beyond the empirically scientific.

Patristic Tradition. The Fathers Christianized angelology by subordinating angelic ministry to Christ's unique mediation. In their concepts they went beyond the Judaic notion of the angelic mediator of God and messenger of God. They decidedly opposed syncretistic efforts to identify angels with the pagan messengers of gods or impersonal protective deities. In addition, they developed important points of doctrine related to the angels: their existence and nature, call to grace and glory, society, missions, and functions in the government of the world.

The *Celestial Hierarchy* of PSEUDO-DIONYSIUS proffered the first complete systematic theory of an angelic society (*c.* A.D. 600). Before that time the Fathers did not approach an angelology. They were slow to arrive at an exact concept of the true spirituality of angels, particularly because they lacked a clear philosophical distinction between body and spirit. In this question the Latins lagged behind the Greeks. In general it may be said that there was no apparent progress in systematized angelology from the 7th to the 13th centuries.

Scholastics. The interest of early scholastics, largely of theological import, centered on the place of angels in the divine plan of creation and Redemption. In the West, theological *summae* of the 12th century affirmed the personal character of angels, their knowledge and liberty, but failed to develop these notions. The 13th century witnessed a more philosophical treatment of the being and operations of angels. St. Thomas Aquinas, with his genius and the advantage of the Greek, Arabian, Jewish, and Christian philosophical studies upon the existence of separated substances, offered an extensive synthesis of thought in his angelology; in his system, angels are pure spirits, subsistent separated substances, forms not joined with body (*Summa theologiae* 1a, 50.2, 4, 5; *C. gent.* 2.45–56). Scotus, holding an opposite view, considered angels as incorporeal but composed of matter and form (see *Dictionnaire de théologie catholique,* ed. A. Vacant, 15 v. 1.2:1230–48 for a comparative study of three systems of angelology, i.e., of St. Thomas, Suárez, and Scotus).

Contemporary Angelology. Since the 17th century angelology has not been limited to the studies of the scholastics; it has come into its own positive theology. Treatises on the angels are normally found in dogmatic treatments of God the Creator. Of particular note are the contributions of Cardinal A. LÉPICIER, R. GARRIGOU-LAGRANGE, Jean DANIÉLOU, and Karl RAHNER. Synthesis has advanced but there is need for additional study to understand better the relationship of angelic mediation and intervention with Christ's unique mediation. Further studies have already determined a specific distinction between the patronages of angels and saints (human), based on a ''movement'' peculiarly angelic. This ''movement,'' involving operations of the angelic will and intellect whereby inferior creatures are moved toward their respective ends, is ordinary to angels but extraordinary to the nonangelic beings.

Magisterium of the Church. The basic truths about angels are accepted on faith; their existence, creation, and spirituality (H. Denzinger, *Enchiridion symbolorum,* ed. A. Schönmetzer 800, 3002, 3021, 3025); their personal nature (*ibid.* 3891); their not emanating from the divine substance (*ibid.* 3024). For an extensive account of conciliar teaching on angels, see *Dictionnaire de théologie catholique,* ed. A. Vacant, 15 v. (Paris 1903–50) 1.2: 1264–71. The Church's teaching is shown best on the practical level in the liturgy. Here especially it is made clear that the role of angels in man's salvation is not of prime importance, that Christ is the one Mediator.

See Also: ANGELS; ANGELS, GUARDIAN (IN THE BIBLE); ANGELS OF THE CHURCHES; DEMON (IN THE BIBLE); DEMON (THEOLOGY OF); DEMONOLOGY.

Bibliography: A. VACANT et al., *Dictionnaire de théologie catholique,* ed. A. VACANT, 15 v. (Paris 1903–50); Tables générales 1951–)1.1:1189–1271. *ibid.* Tables générales 1:153–165. K. RAHNER, *Lexikon für Theologie und Kirche,* ed. J. HOFER and K. RAHNER, 10 v. (2d, new ed. Freiburg 1957–65) 1:533–538. R. HAUBST, *ibid.* 3:867–872. J. DUHR, *Dictionnaire de spiritualité ascétique et mystique. Doctrine et histoire,* ed., M. VILLER et al. (Paris 1932) 1:580–625. H. LECLERCQ, *Dictionnaire d'archéologie chrétienne et de liturgie,* ed. F. CABROL, H. LECLERCQ and H. I. MARROU, 15 v.

Madonna and child with angels, c. 1500, marble relief sculpture, Tuscany.

(Paris 1907–53) 1.2:2080–2161. A. A. BIALAS, *The Patronage of Saint Michael the Archangel* (Chicago 1954). J. D. COLLINS, *The Thomistic Philosophy of the Angels* (Washington 1947). J. DANIÉLOU, *The Angels and Their Mission* . . . , tr. D. HEIMANN (Westminster, Md. 1957). P. P. PARENTE, *The Angels* (St. Meinrad, Ind. 1958) also pub. as *Beyond Space* (New York 1961). P. DE LETTER, ''Trends in Angelology,'' *Clergy Monthly* 24 (1960) 209–220. P. MILWARD, ''Angels in Theology,'' *Irish Theological Quarterly* 21 (1954) 213–225.

[A. A. BIALAS]

ANGELS

Celestial spirits who serve God in various capacities. This article treats of (1) the angels in the Bible, (2) theology of the angels, (3) devotion to the angels, and (4) iconography of the angels.

IN THE BIBLE

The word ''angel'' ultimately is derived from the Greek ἄγγελος, which is the translation of Hebrew *māl'āk,* messenger. The primary significance of angel,

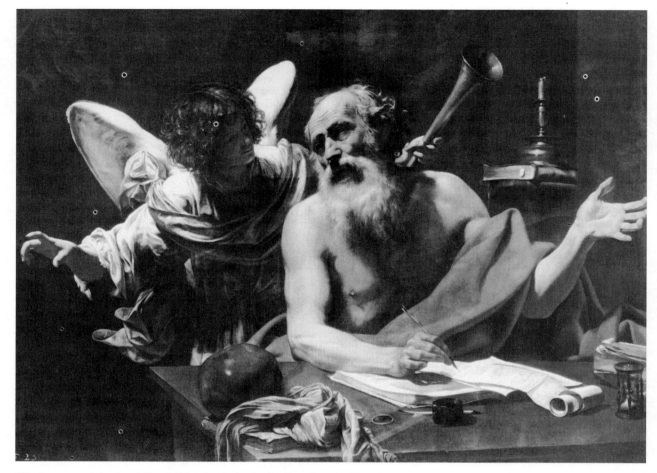

"St. Jerome and the Angel," c. 1625, *oil painting by the French artist Simon Vouet.*

therefore, is messenger from God, a significance describing function rather than being or nature. A few other Hebrew words sometimes signify angels, and some of these are more indicative of being, e.g.: *'abbîrîm,* the mighty [Ps 77(78).25]; *'ĕlohîm* (gods) of Ps 8.6, which is still translated angels, but as such is questionable; *bᵉnē 'ĕlohîm* of Jb 1.6; 2.1 and *bᵉne 'ēlîm* (SONS OF GOD) of Ps 88(89).7; 28(29).1, which surely mean angels in Job and probably in the Psalms, but the designation "sons" is one of association and identity of wills rather than similarity of natures; *mᵉšārᵉtîm* [Ps 102(103).21], ministers, which refers to the heavenly spirits or angels; *'ăbādîm* (Jb 4.18), servants, which is used in parallel with angels; the Aramaic *'îr,* watchers, of Dn 4.10, 14, 20, which is interpreted by the Septuagint (LXX) as angels; *ṣābā'* (1 Kgs 22.19; 2 Chr 18.18; Neh 9.6; Ps 148.2), host(s), which indicates the ordered service of the angels; *qᵉdōšîm* [Ps 88(89).6, 8; Jb 5.1; 15.15; Dn 8.13], holy ones, the angels as "set apart" for the service of God.

Angels in the Old Testament. The angel is an object of divine faith. Knowledge of their existence must come from God. Therefore, the intelligence concerning angels that one may garner from Hebrew Scripture is not a human fabrication or an evolution of religious thought resulting in the projection upon human consciousness of images not truly extramental. The angels are real, possessors of real objective natures, whose appearances and functions are real.

It is true that in the Scriptures, to some degree in the OT, more noticeably in the NT, a development can be discerned in the way man comprehends the angelic world. It is true also that God undoubtedly used the cultural and religious content of man's knowledge as a screen on which to project knowledge of His messengers and their work. Thus, the disturbed course of Israel through eras and empires was influenced by foreign ideas that God willed to use, as catalysts and elements, to communicate His truth of beings superior to man, instruments of His government of His people. To classify Israel's angels merely as the residue of former polytheism, the extravagances of religious élan, or the Jewish expropriations of Persian ideas is to deny Judaeo-Christian belief in them. Polytheism, devout speculation, and Persia were all present, but as catalysts speeding the development of the essential relationship of God's people to Himself and His heavenly court.

Nature of Angels. Hebrew mentality paid little heed to the abstract and did not advert to the spiritual defined as nonmaterial. The Israelite never thought of God as being philosophically supernatural. Hence one does not find in the OT a sophisticated theological definition of the nature of angel or a formally developed angelology. Angels are mentioned frequently, however, and on the whole are understood to be superhuman, heavenly beings whose normal habitat is Yahweh's court (Jb 1.6; 2.1), where they enter into divine counsels (1 Kgs 22.19–22) yet always in subordination to God [Tb 12.18; Ps 102(103).20–21]. Like Yahweh they are normally invisible, unapproachable, and unaffected by human needs (Tb 12.19). Thus, without philosophical advertence to them, angels are assigned to God's extramundane place and manner of being (Gn 28.12). Though there is no explicit mention of their creation, they belong to God (Ex 23.23; 32.34). In the OT there is no mention of fallen angels or of battles in heaven, although Satan, the adversary of Job, is gradually thought of as an evil force (Jb 1.6–12; 2.1–7; Zec 3.1–2; 1 Chr 21.1).

Appearance of Angels. For the most part, the angels sent by God to intervene in men's lives appeared to them in human form (Gn 18.2; 19.1; Dn 8.15). Because of the editorial layers of Genesis chapters 18 and 19, it is difficult to determine whether there was something in the appearance of the ''three men'' that revealed them to be angels (19.1). In Gn 18.2 Abraham saw three men, yet Yahweh alone appeared to him in 18.1, and again Yahweh spoke alone in 18.13, 17, 20, etc. Samson's mother, however, asserted that a man of God, who appeared to her, had the ''appearance'' of an angel of God (Jgs 13.6), as though there was a standard way to recognize an angel in human guise, but Manoe does not know him to be the Angel of the Lord who is later identified as Yahweh Himself (Jgs 13.3–23). Only one angel is said to be able to fly (Dn 9.21).

Function of Angels. The primary function of angels is to do God's will (Tb 12.18). They serve and praise God and are closer to Him than men [Ps 102(103).20–21; Dn 7.10]. Yet God's will has them also intervene in human affairs, by the exercise of power over nature without any apparent material energy (Gn ch. 19), by communicating God's messages (Gn 31.11; Zec ch. 4), by destroying and punishing (2 Kgs 19.35; 2 Sm 24.16), and by helping and saving [1 Kgs 19.5–8; Ps 33(34).8; 90(91).11–12; Dn 6.23].

Angels in the New Testament. With the advent of the Son of God into the world, the prime office of the angel, mediation between God and men, was overshadowed by Our Lord's perfect mediation. Whereas the Old Law came through the ministry of God's angels (Gal 3.19; Heb 2.2), the new dispensation came through His Son, superior to the angels and adored by them (Heb 1.1–8). The Christian dispensation is not subject to angels but to the Lord Jesus (Heb 2.5–18). Also, a greater knowledge of angels and their functions in God's government has been revealed to Christians, which has led to the development of the more elaborate doctrine of Christian angelology.

Nature of Angels. Angels are spirits (Heb 1.14). Their spirituality is not simply immateriality but is totally above human experience so that a worthy man's spiritualization at the resurrection will make him the angel's equal, i.e., unmarried, immortal, and the son of God and of the resurrection (Lk 20.36; Mt 22.30; Mk 12.25). Angels see, praise, and worship God in His presence (Mt 18.10; Rv 5.11–13; 7.11–12; 8.2). They experience joy (Lk 15.10); they desire to bend over and get a better look at the mysteries of salvation (1 Pt 1.12)—obvious anthropomorphic expressions applied to angelic activity. They are stronger and more powerful than men (2 Pt 2.11) and instill fear by reflecting God's glory (Acts 10.4). Yet, at some time they were capable of rebelling against God, for some sinned (2 Pt 2.4; Jude 6). The consequence of the evil angels' defection is described in a mysterious battle won by Michael and his angels over SATAN and his angels (Rv 12.7–9; cf. Mt 25.41). The NT texts suppose that the evil angels are unalterably opposed to God and incapable of redemption.

The notion of angelic rank and gradation, adopted from Jewish literature, also began to crystallize (Jude 8–9; Lk 1.19; Eph 1.21; Col 1.16; see section 2, below). As to the number, Christ speaks of 12 legions (Mt 26.53); the author of Hebrews, of many thousands (Heb 12.22); and John, of thousands of thousands of angels (Rv 5.11). The actual multitude of the angels is vast, therefore, but beyond that nothing else is known.

Appearance of Angels. Of themselves, spiritual beings are invisible and intangible to men. Hence when angels communicate with men, they ordinarily assume a human form that is either indicated or presumed in the text, e.g., the angelic appearances to Zachary (Lk 1.11), to Mary (Lk 1.26, 28), to the shepherds (Lk 2.9, 13), to the witnesses at the tomb (Mt 28.2–7; Mk 16.5; Jn 20.12; Lk 24.4), and to Peter (Acts 12.7). In some of these appearances there is an aura of glory, i.e., light, radiance, and whiteness. The angels mentioned so frequently in the Revelation are described with the imagery of the OT apocalypses, adapted to the author's purposes (Rv 10.1). These descriptions of angelic appearances to men are anthropomorphic accounts of supernatural experiences, and as a result, it is impossible to determine their material objectivity in detail.

Functions of Angels. "Are they not all ministering spirits, sent for service, for the sake of those who shall inherit salvation?" (Heb 1.14). The angels are subject to Christ (Eph 1.20–22; 1 Pt 3.22), and their prime role is to minister to Jesus and His kingdom. They announce its preparation and its actual commencement (Lk 1.11, 19, 26–37). They obviate obstacles to the King's advent (Mt 1.20; 2.13, 19–20); they are the first heralds of the gospel of peace (Lk 2.9–13); and they minister to and strengthen the King (Mt 4.11; 26.53; Lk 22.43). As harbingers of glory, they roll back the stone from the tomb's mouth (Mt 28.2–4), wait for those who would seek the living among the dead, and give them the first news of the victory of the light over darkness (Mt 28.5–7; Mk 16.5–7; Lk 24.4–7; Jn 20.12–13). For the children of light, the little ones, they are advocates before God (Mt 18.10; Acts 12.11) and bearers of prayers to God (Rv 8.3). Through the good offices of angels, the Prophets of the new and eternal Covenant are delivered from bondage (Acts 5.19; 12.7–11). The vital force of God's Kingdom, the grace of its King, is spread through angels' instrumentality to new peoples and in new directions (Acts 8.26; 10.3, 22; 27.23–24).

They avenge God's honor (Acts 12.23), and on the day of judgment the angels of His power (2 Thes 1.7) will accompany the King in His PAROUSIA (Mk 8.38), when they will be part of Christ's and His Father's glory and gather together the elect (Lk 9.26; Mt 25.31). They will gather also the workers of evil and cast them into the fire (Mt 13.41), thus separating the wicked from the just (Mt 13.49). Jesus will acknowledge before the angels those who in their lives have acknowledged Him before men (Lk 12.8–9), and Christians will enter the heavenly Jerusalem in the company of myriads of angels (Heb 12.22). They are not, however, to be worshiped by the citizens of God's Kingdom (Col 2.18); rather, the saints, who belong to Jesus, will judge the angels (1 Cor 6.3).

The angelic panoply of the Revelation deserves special mention, but it is much too intricate for detailed treatment here. Since almost everything in Apocalyptic literature is symbolic, undoubtedly the angels of many of this book's visions are also symbolic, e.g., the seven ANGELS OF THE CHURCHES (Rv 2.1–3.14, *passim*). At least this much may be said of the angels of Revelation: they are servitors of God's power, glory, and judgment and are constantly active in God's government of apocalyptical and eschatological battle.

See Also: CHERUBIM; SERAPHIM; ANGELS, GUARDIAN; MICHAEL, ARCHANGEL; GABRIEL, ARCHANGEL; RAPHAEL, ARCHANGEL.

Bibliography: *Catholic Commentary on Holy Scripture,* ed. B. ORCHARD et al. (London–New York 1957). A. LEMONNYER, *Dictionnaire de la Bible,* suppl., ed. L. PIROT, et al. (Paris 1928) 1:255–262. J. BONSIRVEN, *ibid.* 4:1161–66. *Encyclopedic Dictionary of the Bible* (New York 1963) 81–87. K. RAHNER, *Lexikon für Theologie und Kirche,* ed. J. HOFER and K. RAHNER (Freiburg 1957–65) 1:533–538. J. MICHL, *ibid.* 3:863–867. W. G. HEIDT, *Angelology of the Old Testament* (Washington, D.C. 1949). J. L. MCKENZIE, "The Divine Sonship of the Angels," *Catholic Bible Quarterly* 5 (1943) 293–300.

[T. L. FALLON]

THEOLOGY

Christian theology drew on Holy Scripture, both the Old and the New Testament, for its angelology, but in the beginning it was also guided by extra-biblical, Judaic ideas as well as by prevailing views on nature-spirits. In this way opinions about the angels that were contemporary and popular gained, at times, wide circulation. Gradually, however, in the course of a long development and refinement, theology time and again pared away these accretions, until finally, through speculative elaboration of the concepts contained in Holy Scripture, there evolved an angelology that, with varying degrees of certitude, has become the doctrine of the Church.

Nature of the angels. In pre-Christian Judaism there already existed the conviction that angels were spiritual beings without bodies (*First Book of Enoch* 15.6; Philo, *De sacrif. Abelis et Caini* 5), and that, consequently, they were visible to men only as apparitions and did not appear in material bodies (Tb 12.19). For this reason, angels were always known in Christendom as spiritual beings (Irenaeus, *Adversus haereses* 2.30.6–7; Pseudo-Dionysius, *Hierarchia coelestis* 1.3; *Eccl. hier* 1.2; Gregory the Great, *Moralia* 2.8;4.8), and were called simply "spirits" (Tertullian, *Apologeticum* 22.8; Clement of Alexandria, *Str.* 5.36.3; 7.82.5; Origen, *Contra Celsus* 4.24–25; 6.18; cf. Heb 1.14). They were said not to have a body of flesh (Irenaeus, *Adversus haereses* 3.20.4; Eusebius *Praeparatio evangelica* 4.3.18), which did not mean, however, that they had no body of any kind, i.e., absolute spirituality as opposed to some sort of corporeality. It was said rather that angels had an immaterial body corresponding to their nature (Tertullian, *De carne Christi* 6.9: "constat angelos . . . substantiae spiritalis, etsi corporis alicuius, sui tamen generis"; see also Gregory of Nazianzus, Orat. 28.31; Ambrose, De Abrahamo 2.58; Augustine, Lib. Arb. 3.11.33; Gen. Ad Litt. 3.10). These bodies were considered to be in some way vaporous or firelike (Basil, *Spir.* 38: ἡ μὲν οὐσία αὐτῶν ἀέριον πνεῦμα, εἰ τύχοι, ἢπῦρ ἄϋλον; Fulgentius, *Trin.* 9: the good angels have a *corpus aethereum, id est igneum,* the bad a *corpus aerium*). This was not to say, however, that they were material in any sense known to man's experience (Gregory of Nazianzus, *Orat.* 38.9). At that time the view prevailed that everything created was corporeal; the angels, then, could be no exception (cf. Gennadius, *Liber ecclesiasticorum dogmatum* 12: "creatura omnis corporea est: angeli et omnes caelestes virtutes corporeae, licet non carne subsistant; ex eo autem corporeas esse credimus intellectuales naturas, quod localitate circumscribuntur"). Augustine, to be sure, already knew of the opinion concerning the pure spirituality of angels, but he did not think that it could be accepted inasmuch as occasionally they became visible in visions (*Epistolae* 95.8). Pseudo-Dionysius was the first to teach the complete spirituality of angels (*Hierarchia coelestis* 2.2–3; 4.2–3; *Eccl. hier.* 1.2; *Div. nom.* 7.2) and following him was Gregory the Great (*Moralia* 2.8; 4.8; 7.50; cf. *Dialogues* 4.3.29). But this doctrine still encountered long opposition because of the contrary views of many Fathers in the East as well as in the West, where it was opposed by the authority of Augustine. Then, Rupert of Deutz espoused the notion that the bodies of angels were vaporous (*De victoria Verbi Dei* 1.28, *Patrologia Latina* 169:1241–42; *In Gen.* 1.11; *Patrologia Latina* 167, 208–209), while Bernard of Clairvaux took no stand on the question (*De consideratione* 5.4.7; cf. *In Cant. sermo* 5.7). It was first in the period of high scholasticism (e.g., Thomas Aquinas, *Summa theologiae* 1a, 50.1) and then, subsequently, that a spirituality of angels, no longer burdened by any corporeality, was generally taught.

Holy Scripture and the history of the Church tell of the appearances of angels. This led to the question of how spiritual beings could be seen. It was thought that an angel was perceived in an ethereal body that was proper to it (Augustine, *Trin.* 3.5; *Enchir.* 59; Fulgentius, *Trin.* 9), or that he assumed a material body for the apparition (Augustine, *Trin.* 3.5; Augustine took this possibility into consideration but avoided making a decision on the question), perhaps a body from air (Gregory the Great, *Moralia* 28.3: "ad tempus ex aere corpora sumerent", so also Thomas Aquinas, *Summa theologiae* 1a, 51.2), all of which were inadequate hypotheses. In any case, so it was said, an angel never showed himself in a body of flesh (John Chrysostom, *C. Anom.* 7.6), nor in his true form, but in a special form suited to the apparition (ἐν μετασχηματισμῷ: John Damascene, *Fide orth.* 2.3; *Patrologia Graeca*: 94, 869).

Angels as moral beings. The doctrine that God had created the angels was, in general, firmly held from the beginning [Justin, *Dialogues* 88.5; 141.1; Athenagoras, *Leg.* 24.3; Irenaeus, *Adversus haereses* 2.2.3; Clement of Alexandria, *Prot.* 63.2; Augustine, *Civ.* 9.23; 12.26(25)],

and, in fact, through the power of the preexisting Christ (Tatian, *Orat.* 7.1–2; Irenaeus, *Adversus haereses* 2.2.4; 3.8.3; Origen, *Princ.* 1.7.1; Athanasius, *C. Ar.* 1.62; cf. Col 1.16). The angels, moreover, came into being before any other creature [Basil, *Hex.* 1.5; Augustine, *Conf.* 12.13 (according to these explanations the concept of heaven in Gn 1.1 would include the creation of the angels); *Civ.* 11.9, 32; Gregory the Great, *Moralia* 28.34] as beings gifted with reason and given freedom for forming personal, moral decisions (Justin, *Dialogues* 102.4; Tatian, *Orat.* 7.3; Athenagoras, *Leg.* 24.4; Irenaeus, *Adversus haereses* 4.37.1, 6; Augustine, *Civ.* 22.1; Gregory the Great, *Moralia* 6.20).

The angels, therefore, could also sin (Augustine, *Enchir.* 15). Origen was of the opinion that all the heavenly spirits had sinned, and, according to the gravity of the offense, they had then become demons, souls of men, or angels (*Princ.* 1.8.1). Other sources supposed that only a part of the angels had sinned. For the most part, in the beginning, their sin was considered in conjunction with a Judaic opinion (*Book of Jubilees* 4.22; 5.1, 6, 10; *First Book of Enoch* 6–7 and frequently; *Syriac Apocalypse of Baruch* 56.12–13; Philo, *De gigantibus* 6; Flavius Josephus, *Ant.* 1.3.1.73) to be one of sexual union with human women [Justin, 2 *Apol.* 4(5).3; Athenagoras, *Leg.* 24.5; Irenaeus, *Adversus haereses* 4.36.4; Clement of Alexandria, *Str.* 3.59.2; 5.10.2; Tertullian, *De cultu fem.* 1.2.1–4; 1.4.1; Cyprian, *De hab. virg.* 14; Ambrose, *De virginibus* 1.52–53; *De Noe et Arca* 4; cf. Jude 6; 2 Pt 2.4]. This opinion was based on a specific interpretation of the "Sons of God" in Gn 6.2, 4, but there were also other interpretations assigned to the passage (Origen, *Contra Celsus* 5.55; Augustine, *Civ.* 15.22–23; John Chrysostom, *Homily 22 in Gen.* 2). The sin of the angels was then connected with abuse of the service that God had intrusted to them (Origen, *Homily 4 in Ezech.* 1; *In Jo.* 13.59.412), and especially with pride (Athenagoras, *Leg.* 24.4; John Chrysostom, *Homily 22 in Gen.* 2; Augustine, *Gen. ad litt.* 11.15; *Enchir.* 28; Gregory the Great, *Moralia* 4.8; 27.65). According to those who held for a sexual transgression, the sin of the angels occurred in the course of human history, namely, before the flood; according to those who presumed a sin of a different kind, it had already occurred at the beginning of the world (Augustine, *Civ.* 15.23). This view then prevailed generally. The sin of Satan and the sin of the bad angels had to be considered different things as long as the sin of the angels was presumed to be sexual, because the devil existed, as the seducer, in Paradise (Gn 3.1–5, 13–14) long before the fall of the angels. Already from the second century, however, the two offenses were linked in such a way that the other angels were thought to have been taken up in the sin of the one angel who through pride became Satan (Tatian, *Orat.* 7.5; Augustine, *Enchir.* 28; Gregory the Great, *Moralia* 4.15). It also continued to be the view of later times (e.g., Thomas Aquinas, *Summa theologiae* 1a, 63.8; Suárez, *De angelis* 5.12.13).

According to an early opinion, the rest of the angels, who had not sinned the previous time, did not yet experience the full beatitude of heaven, but they had first to undergo a period of trial like humans on earth (cf. Ignatius, *Smyrn.* 6.1; Clement of Alexandria, *Str.* 7.5.2). They were not without guilt (Ambrose, *Expos.* Ps 118.8.29; *De Spir. Sancto* 3.134; Jerome, *In Micheam* 2 at 6.1–2, concerning the angels of the Churches in Rv ch. 2 and 3, who are praised and reprimanded) and required the forgiveness of God (Cyril of Jerusalem, *Catech.* 2.10). Gradually, however, another opinion prevailed according to which the angels were absolutely spotless and happy beings (Methodius, *Symp.* 3.6; Gregory of Nazianzus, *Orat.* 38.9; Augustine, *Civ.* 10.26; *Enchir.* 57; Pseudo-Dionysius, *Hierarchia coelestis* 7.2; *Eccl. hier.* 6.3, 6; Gregory the Great, *Moralia* 18.71; 27.65); they were sanctified by the Holy Spirit from their creation (Basil, *Hom. in Ps.* 32.4; John Damascene, *Fide Orth.* 2.3, *Patrologia Graeca* 94:869); they had never been involved in sin (Gregory the Great, *Moralia* 18.71), and they live in blessed communion with God [Gregory of Nazianzus, *Orat.* 28.31; Augustine, *Civ.* 7.30; 11.13; *Doct. christ.* 1.31(30); Pseudo-Dionysius, *Hierarchia coelestis* 4.2].

Service of the angels. According to the general view, the angels serve God (Clement of Rome, 1 *Clem.* 34.5–6; Clement of Alexandria, *Str.* 7.3.4; Origen, *Contra Celsus* 8.13, 25; Athanasius, *C.Ar.* 1.55, 62; Augustine, *Civ.* 10.26), who works in creation through them (Tertullian, *De anima* 37.1; Origen, *Contra Celsus* 8.47; Augustine, *Civ.* 7.30; 10.12). The angels, however, also serve men, especially Christians [Hermas, *Vis.* 4.2.4; *Sim.* 5.4.4; Clement of Alexandria, *Str.* 5.91.3; Origen, *Contra Celsus* 1.60; Athanasius, *C.Ar.* 1.61; Augustine, *Civ.* 7.30; *Doctr. christ.* 1.33(30); cf. Heb 1.14]. It was believed that God even appointed a guardian angel for every man (Clement of Alexandria, *Str.* 6.157.5; Origen, *Orat.* 11.5; *Contra Celsus* 5.57; *Princ.* 1.8.1; Ambrose. *Explan. Ps.* 38.32; Jerome, *In Matth.* 3 at 18.10; John Chrysostom, *Hom. 59 in Mt.* 4; cf. Mt 18.10; Acts 12.15) or, according to another explanation, at least for the baptized (Origen, *Contra Celsus* 6.41; *Princ.* 2.10.7; Basil, *Adv. Eun.* 3.1; John Chrysostom, *Hom. 59 in Mt.* 4). While Pseudo-Dionysius and Gregory the Great, theologians very influential in angelology, never mention a personal guardian angel, in the Middle Ages the view prevailed that every man had such a spirit at his side (e.g., Thomas Aquinas, *Summa theologia* 1a, 113.2–5). An echo of a prior Judaic view (Qumran, *Manual of Discipline*

3.18–19) was the opinion that every man had at his side an angel of justice and an angel of wickedness (Hermas, *Mand.* 6.2.1–10; Origen, *Princ.* 3.2.4; Cassian, *Conl.* 7.13; 8.17 13.12).

According to an early Christian view, nations also have their angels (Irenaeus, *Adversus haereses* 3.12.9; Clement of Alexandria, *Str.* 6.157.5; Origen, *Contra Celsus* 5.29–32; *Princ.* 1.5.2; 3.3.3; John Chrysostom, *Hom. 59 in Mt* 4; Jerome, *In Dan.* at 10.13; Augustine, *In ps. 88 sermo* 1.3; Pseudo-Dionysius, *Hierarchia coelestis* 9.2–4; Gregory the Great, *Moralia* 17.17; cf. Dn 10.13, 20–21; 12.1), cities likewise (Clement of Alexandria, *Str.* 6.157.5; Origen, *Hom. 12 in Luc.*, Rauer 87; Jerome, *In Ierem.* 6.7 at Jer 30.12) and the Christian communities (Hermas, *Sim.* 5.3; Tertullian, *De pudicitia* 14.28; Origen, *Orat.* 11.3; 31.6–7; *Princ.* 1.8.1; Ambrose, *In Luc.* 2.50; cf. Rv 1.20; ch. 2–3).

Various duties in creation were attributed to the angels (Justin, 2 *Apol.* 4(5).2; Athenagoras, *Leg.* 10.3–4; 24.3; Origen, *Contra Celsus* 8.31–32, 36; Gregory of Nazianzus, *Orat.* 28.31; Augustine, *Civ.* 7.30; *Gen. ad litt.* 8.24: "sublimibus angelis . . . subdita est omnis natura corporea, omnis inrationalis vita, omnis voluntas vel infirma vel prava, ut hoc de subditis vel cum subditis agant, quod naturae ordo poscit in omnibus iubente illo, cui subiecta sunt omnia"; *ibid.* 8.45, 47). They were said to move the stars (Clement of Alexandria, *Str.* 5.37.2), and to be placed over the four elements: earth, water, air, and fire (Origen, *Hom. 10 in Jer.* 6; cf. Rv 7.1–2; 14.18; 16.5), over plants (Origen, *Hom. 10 in Jer.* 6) and animals (Hermas, *Vis.* 4.2.4; Origen, *Hom. 10 in Jer.* 6; *Hom. 14 in Num.* 2). But this concept of nature-angels also met with rejection because it was thought unworthy in the Christian view of their contemplation of God (Jerome, *In Hab.* at 1.14). In refined form, however, it still perdured in the Middle Ages and even in Thomas Aquinas, according to whose doctrine all things corporeal were governed by angels (*Summa theologiae* 1a, 110.1–3).

What is more, it was thought that the procreation of living creatures could not be explained except by the participation of angels (Origen, *Contra Celssus* 8.57; *Hom. 14 in Num.* 2); even human beings were said to originate with their help [Tertullian, *De anima* 37.1; Clement of Alexandria, *Excerpta ex Theo.* 53.3; Origen, *In Jo.* 13.50 (49).326–327, 329, 335]. They were, indeed, not considered for this reason to be creators of life (Augustine, *Civ.* 12.25–26(24–25); *Trin.* 3.8.13], but to be helpers in a manner that men were not capable of discerning (Augustine, *Gen. ad litt.* 9.16).

Angels punish men (Hermas, *Sim.* 6.2.5–7; Clement of Alexandria, *Str.* 7.12.5; Cyprian, *Ad Demetrianum* 22; Ambrose, *De Abraham* 2; Gregory the Great, *Hom. in evang.* 38.5; *Moralia* 19.46); these angels were thought by some to be evil spirits (Jerome, *In Is.* 6 at 13.3), by others good spirits (Eusebius, *Ecclesiastical History* 5.28.12; Ambrose, *Epist.* 34.10; Augustine, *Civ.* 9.5).

Angels take part in the Divine Service with Christians (Origen, *Orat.* 31.5–6; Ambrose, *In Luc.* 1.12; *Const. App.* 8.4.5; Gregory the Great, *Dialogues* 4.58) and celebrate with the Church on earth the feasts of Christendom (Gregory of Nazianzus, *Orat.* 38.17; John Chrysostom, *Sermo de resurrectione* 3). The angels also bring the prayers of men before God (Clement of Alexandria, *Str.* 7.39.3; Origen, *Orat.* 11.1, 5; *Contra Celsus* 5.4; 8.36; Ambrose, *In Luc.* 8.61; Augustine, *In psalm.* 78.1) and watch over men from heaven (Clement of Alexandria, *Str.* 7.20.4; Tertullian, *De spectaculis* 27.3; Basil, *Hom. de ieiunio* 2.2).

Finally, it was expected that at men's death angels would come and lead the souls of the deceased into the next world (Tertullian, *De anima* 53.6; Origen, *Hom. 5 in Num.* 3; John Chrysostom, *Laz.* 2.2; Gregory the Great, *Hom. in evang.* 35.8; *Moralia* 8.30; *Dial.* 2.35; 4.7, 19; in the Roman rite, the "Ordo commendationis animae" and the Offertory of the Mass for the dead; cf. Lk 16.22).

Groupings of angels. From Judaic tradition (Tb 12.15; *First Book of Enoch* 20.2–7; 61.10; *Testament of Levi* 3.2–8) and from the New Testament (Rom 8.38; 1 Cor 15.24; Eph 1.21; Col 1.16) the view was taken that there were various orders of angels. The princes of the angels, who are usually called ἀρχάγγελοι, archangels, command a leading role [*Epistula Apostolorum* 13(24); Irenaeus *Adversus haereses* 5.25.5; Clement of Alexandria, *Str.* 6.41.2; Pseudo-Dionysius, *Hierarchia coelestis* 9.2]. As was already true in Judaism, so also at this time their numbers fluctuated. Four such angels are mentioned (*Orac. Sib.* 2.215), six (Hermas, *Vis.* 3.1.6–7), or seven (Clement of Alexandria, *Str.* 6.143.1). Under the influence of the Book of Tobit (12.15) and Revelation (ch. 8 and 9; cf. 1.4), the number was finally fixed at seven, and they have been revered, especially in the religion of the common people, throughout the entire Middle Ages in the East and West and even down into modern times. It was, however, only the three archangels mentioned in Holy Scripture, MICHAEL, GABRIEL, and RAPHAEL, who received attention in theology and who were also gradually honored in the liturgy (Gregory the Great, *Hom. in evang.* 34.9; Lateran Synod of 745, J. D. Mansi *Sacrorum Conciliorum nova et amplissima collectio* [Paris 1889–1927] 12:380A).

Since the 4th century the choirs of angels have been reckoned at nine both in the East (Cyril of Jerusalem, *Catech. mystag.* 5.6; Chrysostom, *Hom. 4 in Gen.* 5) and in the West (Ambrose, *De apologia prophetae David*

5.20). This number prevailed because the five groups named in the Pauline Epistles (δυνάμεις, *virtutes,* virtues; ἐξουσίαι *potestates,* powers; ἀρχα, *principatus,* principalities; κυριότητες, *dominationes,* dominations; θρόνοι, *throni,* thrones) were looked upon as good heavenly spirits, and they were placed together with the angels and archangels [their numbers were estimated at a gradually increasing figure (*Const. Ap.* 8.12.27: a million archangels)] along with the cherubim and seraphim. This series, somewhat schematic and not fully in accord with the Bible, was speculatively developed under Neoplatonic influence by Pseudo-Dionysius into a hierarchical structure of three triads (*HIerarchia coelestis* 6.2; 7–9; *Eccl. hier.* 1.2). Thus elaborated, this doctrine of nine choirs of angels was commonly held in the West from the time of Gregory the Great (*Hom. in evang.* 34.7; *Moralia* 32.48; *Epist.* 5.54). It received widespread attention chiefly from John Scotus Erigena's Latin translation of the writings of Pseudo-Dionysius in the 9th century (see, e.g., Thomas Aquinas, *Summa theologiae* 1a, 108.5–6; a vision and description of the nine choirs by Hildegard of Bingen, *Scivias* 1.6; and a poetical description by Dante, *Paradiso* 28.88–129).

Names of angels. Most frequently mentioned are the names that occur in Holy Scripture: Michael, Gabriel, and Raphael (Origen, *Contra Celsus* 1.25; Gregory the Great, *Hom. in evang.* 34.9). People were especially fond of linking the names of Michael and Gabriel (Tertullian, *De carne Christi* 14.3; Origen, *Contra Celsus* 8.15). In Syria the sign XMT—usually rendered Christ, Michael, Gabriel (see *Reallexikon für Antike und Christentum* [Stuttgart 1941] 5:182)—was frequently found on tombs, doorframes, and rings. Another name for one of the princes of the angels that is encountered with relative frequency is Uriel. It comes from the Judaic angelology [*Orac. Sib.* 2.215; *Epist. Apost.* 13(24); Ambrose, *De fide* 3.20]. Over and above the names found in the Bible, popular belief, and particularly superstition, attributed still further names to the princes of angels and other angels. These were names borrowed from the Jews, or even invented arbitrarily or out of ridicule. The Church, however, condemned these tendencies in the Lateran Synod of 745 (J. D. Mansi *Sacrorum Conciliorum nova et amplissima collectio* [Paris 1889–1927] 12:379–380) and in further decrees of the 8th and 9th centuries. When similar attempts were made in the 15th century and again later, the Church once more took steps against them (see *Reallexikon für Antike und Christentum* [Stuttgart 1941] 5:188).

Teaching of the Church. The Church has defined as dogma that besides the visible world God also created a kingdom of invisible spirits, called angels, and that He created them before the creation of the world (Lateran

Council IV, 1215, ch. 1, H. Denzinger *Enchiridion symbolorum* [Freiburg 1963] 800; repeated at Vatican Council I, 1870, *ibid.* 3002; cf., earlier, the Nicene Creed of 325, *ibid.* 125: Πιστεύομεν εἰς ἕνα θεόν . . . πάντων ὁρατῶν τε καὶ ἀοράτων ποιητήν). In conformity with Holy Scripture and with the whole Christian tradition, these angels must be regarded as personal beings and not as mere powers or the like. Pius XII rejected a contrary opinion as being opposed to Catholic doctrine (encyclical *Humani generis,* Aug. 12, 1950; 3891). Only those three names for angels that occur in the Bible may be used.

The Church has further declared as dogma that God created the devil and the demons good by nature, and that they became bad through a fault of their own (Lateran Council IV, ch. 1; H. Denzinger *Enchiridion symbolorum* [Freiburg 1963] 800). The Church, however, has never declared authoritatively the way in which the angels sinned to become the devil and demons.

Moreover, in evaluating the accounts taken from the Bible and from Christian tradition, two extremes are to be avoided: on the one hand, not everything that is therein contained can be taken as fact because much of it belongs simply to the philosophy of life in antiquity and must be discarded; so, too, the existence and efficacy of angels cannot be denied out of hand simply because it is possible today, because of more accurate knowledge, to explain by natural causes what was once attributed to the angels. In the interpretation of biblical passages, the literary type must be taken into consideration, that is, whether it intends simply the communication of a fact, e.g., that angels are helpers of the Christians (Heb 1.14); or a narrative that popular imagination has embellished (e.g., the Book of Tobit); or symbolic visions whose true message must first be discovered through the veil of symbolic experiences that are presented in images proper to the period (e.g., in Revelation). In expressions drawn from tradition, however, one must take into consideration that in the course of time theology has purified the obscurity and error contained in traditional views about angels. In this way theology has now come to a point of distinguishing exactly among angels, stars, and the powers of nature, and specifies that the nature of angels is completely spiritual and no longer merely a very fine material, firelike and vaporous. Up to now it has not yet been defined as dogma that every man has a guardian angel. This opinion does, however, have a basis in Holy Scripture and has been maintained in the Church since ancient times, despite the uncertainty of the question in the first 1,000 years. The Church has never declared itself on whether the angels are divided into orders, nor has it said what kinds of orders there might be. Still, it can be drawn from the New Testament that angels exist and are effective in various ways, as can be detected there within certain limits. Many questions, however, that are raised in Scripture and tradition relating to the angels, cannot be answered or, at least, cannot be answered convincingly, because the necessarily certain knowledge is not possible.

Modern attitudes toward the belief in angels. In the modern mind, angels are considered to be tenuous creatures who, with the passage of time, are more and more being relegated to the sphere of legend, fairy tale, and child's fancy. Then, of course, there was rationalism, which thought that all belief in the existence of angels should be repudiated. Inasmuch as they are considered to be products of the imagination, their existence is widely denied. The believing Christian, however, will even today maintain that there are angels because the Bible and the Church teach it. What is more, he is convinced that the assertions of the Bible must be understood and evaluated in terms of the basic principles laid down in the previous section. Some reservations are also required in regard to many of the expressed views of the Fathers or other theologians. The old opinion that events in the world were caused by spiritual beings has been replaced in favor of a mechanical explanation arising from insight into the play of cause and effect. Therefore, the Christian can no longer postulate angelic activity where he knows that impersonal forces are at work. Furthermore, he will reject each and every embellishment of the concept of angels. He also believes that the angels, inasmuch as they are pure spirits, can never appear in a real body; that as spiritual beings they act on earth as causes in a manner that is unknown to men but verified in Scripture and in the experience of the Christian life of grace. Such spiritual beings can evoke in the phantasms of men a vision structured in accordance with the concepts of the times (a similar explanation was already attempted in the Middle Ages and was rejected by Thomas Aquinas, *Summa theologiae* 1a 51.2 by an appeal to Scripture, but clearly from an outdated exegesis). Finally, one must be aware that the profane sciences can never prove either the existence or the activity of angels. One knows that angels exist, as St. Augustine once said, through faith [''esse angelos novimus ex fide'' (*In psalm. 103 serm.* 1.15)].

See Also: ANGELOLOGY; ANGELS, GUARDIAN; ANGELS OF THE CHURCHES; CHERUBIM; DEMON (IN THE BIBLE); DEMON (THEOLOGY OF); ORIGINAL SIN; SERAPHIM.

Bibliography: See tracts on the angels in the manuals of dogma. J. TURMEL, ''Histoire de l'angélologie des temps apostoliques à la fin du Ve siècle,'' *Revue d'histoire et de littérature religieuses* 3 (1898) 289–308, 407–434, 533–552, ''L'Angélologie depuis le faux Denys l'Aréopagite,'' *ibid.* 4 (1899) 217–238; 289–309, 414–434, 537–562; *Histoire des dogmes,* 6 v. (Paris 1931–36) 4:45–119. W. LUEKEN, *Michael: Eine Darstellung und Vergleichung der jüdischen und der morgenländisch-christlichen Tradition vom Erzengel Michael* (Göttingen 1898). G. BAREILLE et al., *Dictionnaire de théologie catholique,* ed. A. VACANT et al. (Paris 1903–50) 1:1192–1271. P. PERDRIZET, "L'Archange Ouriel," *Seminarium Kondakovianum* 2 (Prague 1928) 241–276. J. DUHR, *Dictionnaire de spiritualité ascétique et mystique,* 1:580–598, 622–625. E. PETERSON, *Das Buch von den Engeln: Stellung und Bedeutung der hl. Engel im Kultus* (2d ed. Munich 1955). O. HOPHAN, *Die Engel* (Luzern 1956). J. DANIÉLOU, *The Angels and Their Mission,* tr. D. HEIMANN (Westminster, Md. 1957). A. WINKLHOFER, *Die Welt der Engel* (Ettal 1958). R. HAUBST, *Lexikon für Theologie und Kirche,* ed. J. HOFER and K. RAHNER (Freiburg 1957–65) 3:867–872. C. D. G. MUELLER, *Die Engellehre der koptischen Kirche* (Wiesbaden 1959). P. GLORIEUX, ed., *Autour de la spiritualité des anges: Dossier scripturaire et patristique* (Tournai 1959). B. NEUNHEUSER, "Die Engel im Zeugnis der Liturgie," *Archiv für Liturgiewissenschalft* (1959) 4–27. J. MICHL, *Reallexikon für Antike und Christentum,* ed. T. KLAUSER [Stuttgart 1941 (1950)—] 5:115–258.

[J. MICHL]

DEVOTION

In the strict sense, cult of (devotion to) angels denotes a religious practice flowing from the virtue of RELIGION (St. Thomas Aquinas, *Summa theologiae* 2a2ae, 82.2) and constituting an external manifestation of honor and reverence to angels in recognition of their excellence and of one's own reasonable dependence on them. It is an act of secondary veneration (dulia). In general, any religious act of venerating angels can be termed angelic devotion; however, where such an act possesses the required internal (intellect and will) and external (reverence and subjection) elements, it will coincide with angelic cult as defined above. When associated with divine faith, cult of the angels belongs to the supernatural order and has its place in the spiritual life.

Sacred scripture. The Christian concept of angelic cult is verified only in practices of genuine, divinely revealed, religion and has no equivalent in pagan cults associated with "angels." Assyrians, Persians, and Egyptians paid honor to protective deities, in Accadian *kāribu,* but there is no identity between these pagan deities and the Hebrew *kᵉrûbîm.*

The OT offers some manifestations of angelic cult, e.g., by Balaam (Nm 22.21–35), Tobit (Tb 12.16), and Daniel (Dn 10.9), but such practices did not constitute the principal object of prophetic teaching; nor did people, though conscious of angels, consider their existence relevant. In the NT, the Gospels mention angels but do not specifically recommend or reject devotion to them; St. Paul implicitly teaches veneration of angels (1 Cor 11.10; Gal 4.14), but such cult is to be given in a manner that does not derogate from Christ, the one and unique mediator; he shows displeasure at false or exaggerated cult to angels. In Rv 22.8–9 St. John is rebuked and corrected for offering excessive veneration to an angel but not for venerating him.

Patristic era. Fathers of the East and West showed their approval of angelic cult and testified to its early existence. They warned against idolatrous cult of angels (see Aristides, *Apol.* 14; *Patrologia Graeca* 96:1121), condemned latreutic acts of worship toward angels (see Origen, *Contr Celsus* 8.13, 57; *Patrologia Graeca* 11:1533, 1601), defended angelic cult as distinct from adoration reserved to God alone, latria (see Eusebius, *Praeparatio evangelica* 7.15; *Patrologia Graeca* 21:553). There was a period when reserve and restriction had to be urged especially because of false cults and charges of "atheism" against Christians for not worshiping pagan deities [Justin Martyr, 1 *Apol.* 6, *Patrologia Graeca* 6:336; Athenagoras, *Leg.* 10, *Ante-Nicene Fathers* (New York 1903) 2:133]. St. Augustine deserves credit for the excellent formula of honor and love as proper cultic dispositions for venerating angels, distinct from the worship given to God: "[W]e honor them out of charity not out of servitude" (*Vera relig.* 55.110; *Patrologia Latina* 34:170). The acceptance of the angelology of Pseudo-Dionysius (5th–6th century), taught especially in his *Hierarchia coelestis* (*Patrologia Graeca* 3:119–370), is largely responsible for angelic cult becoming firmly and universally established in the Church.

The earliest known devotion to angels was principally centered on the Archangel MICHAEL, the only individual angel honored in liturgical feasts in the Church before the 9th century. In the East, Michaeline devotion was evidenced by the 4th century in the churches and sanctuaries in and near Constantinople. It then spread to Italy and to the rest of Europe.

In the West, the feast of St. Michael and the angels was celebrated as early as the 5th century in the church of the same name outside Rome (*see* LEONINE SACRAMENTARY, 7th century; Masses and prayers in honor of St. Michael are also mentioned). Devotion at two presently active Michaeline sanctuaries began with separate apparitions of St. Michael in the early centuries: one at Monte Gargano (*c.* 490), near Foggia, Italy, and the other at Mont-Saint-Michel (708), Manche, France.

Beginning with St. Benedict (543) in the West, there was a steadily growing tradition of angelic cult of faith, love, and devotion from the time of Pope Gregory the Great to St. Bernard of Clairvaux (d. 1153). The latter was the principal and most eloquent exponent of cult of the guardian angels; with him angelic cult assumed that form which has continued unchanged in the Church.

Scholasticism. Theologians of the school were less occupied with devotion to angels and more with a study of their nature, intelligence, and will. Even so, angelic cult was not dormant. The scholastic period was noted for prayers to the guardian angels (13th century), growth of associations and confraternities formed to honor the angels (15–16th centuries), development and popularization of angelic devotion—in which religious orders (Dominican, Franciscan, Jesuit) and individuals [Pierre Caton (d. 1626), Johannes Tauler, Ludolph of Saxony] played prominent roles. Of particular note, also, were a popular treatise on angels by Fra Francesco Eiximenis (d. 1409) and a collection of the practical counsels of mystics on angels by Denis the Carthusian (d. 1471). By 1630 the cult of angels was widespread.

Nineteenth and twentieth centuries. Devotion to the angels has been perpetuated in various ways in the last two centuries but in particular through: (1) associations and societies, such as the Archconfraternity of St. Michael Archangel (formally erected by Leo XIII, 1878), and the episcopally approved association of Philangeli (''Friends of Angels,'' founded in England, 1950, by Mary Angela Jeeves—hqs., 1212 E. Euclid, Arlington Heights, IL); (2) patronages under the titles of holy and guardian angels in general, and of SS. Michael, GABRIEL, and RAPHAEL in particular; (3) publications, such as the two currently (1965) published— *L'Ange gardien* (Clerics of St. Viator, 28 rue du Bon-Pasteur, Lyons, France) and *Les Annales du Mont-Saint-Michel* (Mont-Saint-Michel, Manche, France); and (4) a variety of liturgical and nonliturgical rites or practices—Masses and Divine Offices in honor of guardian angels and the Archangels Michael, Gabriel, and Raphael; prayers in the Mass, e.g., Preface, *Supplices te rogamus, Per intercessionem, Domine Jesu Christe;* the prayer in the Communion of the Sick, *Exaudi nos;* in the burial service of adults, *In paradisum;* in the blessing of homes, *Exaudi nos;* the Litany of All Saints and novenas [see *The Raccolta* (New York 1957) 440–455 and *The Roman Martyrology*].

Magisterium of the Church. Whatever had contributed to the original establishment and development of angelic cult, however it was associated with the beliefs of the faithful and even subjected to Jewish-Gnostic influence, it is evident that the Church, through its official magisterium, unified and clarified belief in the angels and guided this cult (see J. Michl, *Reallexikon für Antike und Christentum* [Stuttgart 1941] 5:199–200). The positive teaching of the Church treats of veneration due to angels, the benefits of angelic intervention, and the man-angel relationships in the communion of the saints (blessed). It encourages the faithful to love, respect, and invoke the angels (see Nicaea II, H. Denzinger *Enchiridion symbolorum* [Freiburg 1963] 600; Benedict XIV, *ibid.* 2532; *The Raccolta*); on the other hand, the Church guards its subjects against false and dangerous practices, e.g., by rejecting all names of individual angels except Michael, Gabriel, and Raphael [see the Council of Rome under Pope St. Zachary (745); c.35 of the Council of Laodicea

(4th century); the Synod of Aachen (789); the Council of Trent, *ibid.* 1821–25].

Orthodox churches. The devotion to angels among the Orthodox is found particularly in their Liturgy (Mass and Divine Office) and their observance of special feasts; it is directed especially to Michael, Gabriel, and Raphael.

Bibliography: J. MICHL and T. KLAUSER, *Reallexikon für Antike und Christentum,* ed. T. KLAUSER [Stuttgart 1941 (1950)—] 5:53–322. A. VACANT et al., *Dictionnaire de théologie catholique* (Paris 1903–50) 1.2:1189–1271. K. RAHNER, *Lexikon für Theologie und Kirche,* ed. J. HOFER and K. RAHNER (Freiburg 1957–65) 1:533–538. R. HAUBST, *ibid.* 3:867–872. J. DUHR, *Dictionnaire de spiritualité ascétique et mystique,* ed. M. VILLER et al. (Paris 1932) 1:580–625. H. LECLERCQ, *Dictionnaire d'archéologie chrétienne et de liturgie,* ed. F. CABROL, H. LECLERQ, and H. I. MARROU (Paris 1907–53) 1.2:2144–59, bibliog. 2159–61. *Encyclopedic Dictionary of the Bible* (New York 1963) 81–87. C. J. VON HEFELE, *Histoire des conciles d'après les documents originaux* (Paris 1907–38) v. 1, 4, 5. A. A. BIALAS, *The Patronage of Saint Michael the Archangel* (Chicago, Ill. 1954). J. DANIÉLOU, *The Angels and Their Mission . . .*, tr. D. HEIMANN (Westminster, Md. 1957). J. DANIÉLOU, *Theology of Jewish Christianity,* ed. and tr. J. A. BAKER (Chicago, Ill. 1964) 147–187. L. M. O. DUCHESNE, *Christian Worship: Its Origin and Evolution,* tr. M. L. MCCLURE (5th ed. repr. New York 1949). W. G. HEIDT, *Angelology of the Old Testament* (Washington, D.C. 1949). P. P. PARENTE, *The Angels* (St. Meinrad, Ind. 1958), also pub. as *Beyond Space* (New York 1961). J. W. MORAN, ''St. Paul's Doctrine on Angels,'' *American Ecclesiastical Review* 132 (1955) 374–384. M. A. JEEVES, ''The Friends of Angels,'' *Life of the Spirit* 8 (1953–54) 159–163.

[A. A. BIALAS]

ICONOGRAPHY

The concept of angels originated in the Orient, but the figural type of the Christian angel was derived from the winged Greek goddess of Victory, or Nike. During and after the Italian Renaissance, pagan putti, cupids, or amors served as models for new types of Christian angels. (Illustrations on following pages.)

Gender, garments, and wings. According to Scripture, angels are masculine, youthfulness and virility being their general attributes. It was only in the late Gothic period that artists began to depict angels of an ideal beauty; this development led to the invention of the purely feminine angel in the Renaissance. The infant angel, also created in the late Gothic period, was used widely during the Italian Renaissance. In early Christian times angels were represented in long white tunics and palliums, which symbolized both the divine light emanating from angels and the purity of angels. At times they were represented in togas with the chlamys of the Roman senator to give them an air of dignity. During the Byzantine period the influence of imperial ceremony increased; often they were represented in the guise of imperial court guards, i.e., in loro and military chlamys and holding standards. In the West, the early Christian type was used continuously during the Middle Ages, often with additions such as a diadem, a scepter, a codex or roll, or taenia, all symbolic of divine power. From the 13th century the influence of the liturgy and mystery plays became stronger, and their garments imitated various liturgical costumes according to their liturgical functions. At the beginning of the early Christian period angels were represented as wingless youths; it was only in the 4th century that they were depicted with wings. The earliest Christian example of a winged human figure is found in S. Pudenziana in Rome as the symbol of St. Matthew. In St. Mary Major in Rome winged angels are represented hovering in the air.

Functions. As the original Greek word indicates, the most important function of angels is to bring messages from God to men. In scenes from the life of Christ and the life of the Virgin, angels come to assist or to serve them. Angels appear also in scenes of the martyrdom of saints to give them strength and to deliver them a palm branch or a crown as a symbol of their martyrdom. They are shown, like ancient muses, inspiring an Evangelist or a Church Father, such as St. Jerome, engaged in writing. As the liturgical system developed and became more complex in the late Middle Ages, angels were regarded as participants in the heavenly liturgy, and many liturgical functions were attributed to them, such as those performed by deacons, acolytes, etc.

Angelic choir. The concept of a celestial hierarchy is derived from the order of Oriental monarchism. It was the *Hierarchia coelestis* by Pseudo-Dionysius the Areopagite that inspired the artistic representation of the heavenly hierarchy. Three orders are recognized, each order consisting of three choirs: seraphim, cherubim, and thrones (first order); dominations, virtues, and powers (second order); principalities, archangels, and angels (third order). Often the Virgin Mary is brought into the center of this hierarchy. Seraphim and cherubim are to be distinguished from other messenger angels in that they alone guard the thrones of the Holy of Holies, sometimes hiding them with their wings from human eyes. The seraph is characterized by six wings covered with eyes, whereas the cherub has only four wings. The former is represented in the red color of fire, the latter, in the blue color of sky. The origin of the type is Oriental, and the biblical statement of the vision of Isaiah (Is 6.21) provided the basis for the iconography. In scenes of the stigmatization of St. Francis, the crucifix appears in the guise of a Seraph.

Archangels. Among archangels, seven (and at times nine) are given names as well as various functions based on relevant biblical testimony. Three of them, MICHAEL, GABRIEL, and Raphael, have been most popularly vener-

ated. Among them Michael is the most popular as the militant angel and as the guard of the faithful— *Princeps militiae angelorum.* In Byzantine art he is represented in the purple chlamys or in the loro of the imperial court. In the West he is represented in a long tunic or in the coat of mail and helmet of a medieval knight. He appears in scenes of the Last Judgment combating the dragon of the apocalypse (Rv 12.7) or battling the hordes of Satan. This iconography is not to be confused with that of St. George. Michael is represented also weighing the souls of the dead. In the iconography of the heavenly hierarchy, he is shown as the guard of the celestial domain, hurling the rebellious angels, or demons, into the abyss. Gabriel is familiar to us as the bringer of glad tidings from God to men, as in the Annunciation to the Virgin and the annunciation to Zachariah. Raphael is represented most frequently in association with the story of Tobit.

Bibliography: G. STUHLFAUTH, *Die Engel in der altchristlichen Kunst* (Fribourg 1897). C. E. CLEMENT, *Angels in Art* (London 1901). K. KÜNSTLE, *Ikonographie der christlichen Kunst* (Freiburg 1926–28) 1:239–264. H. LECLERCQ, *Dictionnaire d'archéologie chrétienne,* ed. F. CABROL, H. LECLERQ, and H. I. MARROU (Paris 1907) 1:2080–2161. R. P. RÉGAMEY, *Anges* (Paris 1946). L. RÉAU, *Iconographie de l'art chrétien* (Paris 1955–59) 2.1:30–55. K. A. WIRTH, *Reallexikon zur deutschen Kunstgeschichte,* ed. O. SCHMITT (Stuttgart 1937–) 5:342–602.

[S. TSUJI]

ANGELS, GUARDIAN (IN THE BIBLE)

Guardian angels are intelligent spiritual creatures divinely deputed to exercise individual care and protection over men on this earth and assist them in their attainment of eternal salvation. Most frequently, guardian angel is taken to mean a single angel assisting an individual person or groups of persons or a single nation, parish, etc.

The term ANGEL, as presently used in Catholic theology, indicates a spiritual minion of the divine court. Guardian indicates a protective function, not an entitative grade. The concept of guardian angel as a distinct spiritual being sent by God to protect every individual person is a development of Catholic theology and piety not literally contained in the Bible, but fostered by it.

Scattered references to angelic guardianship of individuals or small groups in the Old Testament [Gn 19.10–14, 16; 24.7, 40; 1 Kgs 19.5, 7; Tb 5.6 and *passim;* Dn 3.49–50, 95; Ps 33(34).8; 90(91).11–12] cannot be interpreted as presenting Israelite belief in a universal protective ministry of angels. The angelology of the Old Testament is so unclear that it precludes any such well-defined conclusion. G. von Rad observes that the angels had little significance in the Israelite life of faith because

Two guardian angels, with St. Joseph at far right, protecting the Child Jesus as He is received in the Egyptian city of Sotinen—according to an Apocryphal Gospel. Mosaic of the 5th century on the apse of S. Maria Maggiore, Rome.

their consciousness was of Yahweh's direct and pervasive action in nature and history without the help of intermediaries [*Genesis* (London 1961) 110]. Again, each instance of angelic custody (excluding those in the Psalms) is presented as special mission rather than customary office. Finally, the Israelites' pride in being Yahweh's chosen people and their concept of such exclusiveness would hardly be conducive to a universal extension of individual guardianship of angels over all people.

Nevertheless, the proximity of Israel to the extravagant Persian angelology and the increasingly emphasized transcendence of Yahweh in postexilic Judaism formed the consciousness into which God communicated deeper knowledge of the instruments of His government, as witnessed by the divine tenderness exercised by RAPHAEL, in Tobit, the angel interpreter of Zachariah ch. 2 and 3, and the national tutelary angels of Daniel ch. 10. This led to an exaggerated proliferation of protecting angels' functions in intertestamental literature.

Thus, the way was prepared for the Christian angelology delineated in New Testament writings (*see* Gal 1.8; Acts 10.3–7; 12.15; Heb 1.13–14). Jesus' good news of the universality of God's love germinated the Catholic doctrine of the guardian angel from such sources as Jesus' saying, "See that you do not despise one of these little ones [members of His kingdom]; for I tell you their angels in heaven always behold the face of my Father in heaven" (Mt 18.10).

Bibliography: *Encyclopedic Dictionary of the Bible*, tr. and adap. by L. HARTMAN (New York 1963) 911–912. P. R. RÉGAMEY, *What Is an Angel?*, tr. M. PONTIFEX (New York 1960). P. HEINISCH, *Theology of the Old Testament*, tr. W. G. HEIDT (Collegeville, Minn. 1955).

[T. L. FALLON]

ANGELS OF THE CHURCHES

Term used in the Book of REVELATION to designate the heavenly counterpart of the seven churches of the Roman province of ASIA. John sees the glorified Christ holding seven stars, perhaps in the form of a scepter, as He walks among the seven lampstands (Rv 1.20). His presence in the churches on earth is thus indicated. The stars are said to symbolize the "angels" of the churches; this is in keeping with the close relationship between stars and angels in ancient Semitic thought. Each of the seven letters that follow is addressed to its respective angel, who is praised, blamed, or warned, as the situation requires (2.1, 8, 12, 18; 3.1, 7, 14). Many Latin Fathers and modern commentators think that by angel here John means the bishop of the particular church. Nowhere in

Revelation, however, or in the rest of the NT does "angel" mean anything but a superterrestrial being. St. Jerome, the Greek Fathers, and many other modern commentators think that the guardian angel of each church is the recipient of the letter. But can one suppose that John would be told to reprimand the guardian angel for disorders in the church? Here, as frequently in Revelation, the author depends upon the Book of DANIEL, where heavenly beings are called "princes" of the kingdoms of Persia, Greece, and Israel, respectively (Dn 10.13, 20, 21). From the context it is clear that they are not guardian angels, as one would now think of them. That they are called princes rather than angels suggests that they were regarded as a kind of heavenly corporate personality, summing up the characteristics and history of the earthly realm with which they were related. John calls them angels to underline their heavenly character, since the earthly reality was considered less real than its heavenly counterpart (see Heb 9.11, 23; 10.1). Because they are the heavenly reality of the respective church with, certainly, its bishop as the earthly corporate personality, they can be praised or reprimanded, as the case may be, for the merits or failings of their particular church.

Bibliography: J. MICHL, *Die Engelvorstellungen in der Apokalypse des hl. Johannes* (Munich 1937). *Encyclopedic Dictionary of the Bible* 81–87.

[E. F. SIEGMAN]

ANGELUS

The practice of commemorating the mystery of the Incarnation by reciting certain versicles, three Hail Marys, and a special prayer while a bell is being rung at 6 A.M., 12 noon, and 6 P.M. Although the origin is obscure, it is certain that the morning, midday, and evening Angelus did not develop simultaneously. While no direct connection can be claimed between the evening Angelus and the ringing of the curfew bell in the 11th century, Gregory IX is said to have prescribed the daily ringing of the evening bell to remind the faithful to pray for the Crusades. In 1269 St. Bonaventure admonished his friars to exhort the faithful to imitate the Franciscan custom of reciting three Hail Marys when the bell rang in the evening. John XXII attached an indulgence to this practice in 1318 and 1327. The morning Angelus again seems to be a 14th-century outgrowth of the monastic custom of reciting three Hail Marys at the sound of the bell during Prime. The noon Angelus originated in a devotion to the Passion that occasioned the ringing of the bell at noon on Fridays; it also came to be associated with praying for peace. The practice is first mentioned by the Synod of Prague in 1386 and was extended to the whole week when Callistus III in 1456 invited the whole world to pray for victory over the Turks. The 16th century saw a unification of the three customs.

Bibliography: W. HENRY, *Dictionnaire d'archéologie chrétienne et de liturgie,* ed. F. CABROL, H. LECLERCQ, and H. I. MARROU, 15 v. (Paris 1907–53) 1:2069–78. H. THURSTON, *Dictionnaire de spiritualité ascétique et mystique. Doctrine et histoire,* ed. M. VILLER et al. (Paris 1932–) 1:1164–65.

[A. A. DE MARCO]

ANGELUS CLARENUS

Franciscan author, co-founder of the Clareni; b. Peter, at Fossombrone (Pesaro), March of Ancona, Italy; d. S. Maria d'Aspro, Basilicata, Italy, June 15, 1337. After joining the FRANCISCANS at Cingoli, Italy, *c.* 1270, he became a partisan of the Franciscan SPIRITUALS, and after the Council of LYONS (1274) was on this account condemned to life imprisonment in 1275. When freed *c.* 1289 by the minister general Raymond Gaufridi, he and other Franciscan Spirituals from Ancona went to Lesser Armenia, but the hostility of the Franciscans of the Syrian province forced the group back to Ancona (early 1294), where they were not welcome. Consequently, Friar Peter of Macerata, together with Peter, went to Pope CELESTINE V and obtained permission for their group to leave the Franciscan First Order and become CELESTINES. Peter of Macerata took the name of Liberatus: Peter of Fossombrone, that of Angelus (the Clarenus or Chiarino was added later). BONIFACE VIII, however, voided the authorization granted these Franciscan Celestines, or more properly CLARENI, and they migrated to one of the islands of Achaia, to southern Thessaly, and back to Italy in 1304–05. When Liberatus died, Angelus succeeded him (1307) as head of the group. In 1311 he attempted to obtain papal recognition for the Clareni, but he was received by the pope only in 1317. JOHN XXII acknowledged Angelus's personal innocence, but the Franciscan minister general, MICHAEL OF CESENA, would not tolerate a separate group in the order, and Angelus agreed to receive the habit of the Benedictine Celestines—despite their opposition—under Abbot Bartholomew II of Subiaco. Angelus moved to the lands of Subiaco and devoted himself to his followers. His main writings date from this time. His extremist *Apologia* reached Friar Alvaro Paez in October 1331 and on November 22, John XXII ordered inquisitorial proceedings against Angelus, but the inquisitor died. In February 1334 came new pontifical orders; Angelus fled to Basilicata where he died. His cause for beatification was studied *c.* 1808 but rejected. His works included translations from the Greek of the Rule of St. Basil and of the *Scala* of John Climacus. He wrote an Expositio of the Franciscan Rule *c.* 1321, *Historia sep-*

tem tribulationum in 1323, and two ascetical treatises. His abundant correspondence, almost entirely unedited, is at Florence (B. N. Magliab. xxxix, 75).

Bibliography: L. VON AUW, ed., *Epistole* (Rome 1980). G. L. POTESTÀ, *Angelo Clareno: dai poveri eremiti ai fraticelli* (Rome 1990). B. MCGINN, ''Apocalyptic Traditions and Spiritual Identity in Thirteenth-Century Religious Life,'' in *Spirituality of Western Christendom,* II (Kalamazoo, MI 1984), 1–26. L. VON AUW, *Angelo Clareno et les spirituels italiens* (Rome 1979). E. R. DANIEL, ''Spirituality and Poverty: Angelo da Clareno and Ubertino da Casale,'' in *Medieval et Humanistica* (Denton, TX 1973), 89–98.

[J. CAMPBELL]

ANGELUS DE SCARPETIS, BL.

Augustinian; b. Borgo San Sepolcro, Umbria, Italy, date unknown; d. there, 1306. Angelus's surname has, in the past, been taken more often from his town (Angelus of Borgo San Sepolcro) or region (Angelus of Hetruria) than from his noble family. He became a hermit of St. Augustine *c.* 1254. The virtues for which he was most noted were humility, a childlike innocence, the spirit of poverty, and apostolic zeal. He supposedly went to England and established a number of houses of his order there; but the source for this tradition cannot be ascertained. He reputedly worked miracles even during his lifetime. His cult was confirmed July 27, 1921.

Feast: Feb. 15 or Oct. 1.

Bibliography: F. ROTH, *The English Austin Friars, 1249–1538* 2 v. (New York 1961–), v.1 *History,* v.2 *Sources* (1961). *Acta Apostolicae Sedis* 13 (1921) 443–446. J. LANTERI, *Postrema saecula sex religionis Augustinianae* 3 v. (Tolentino-Rome 1858–60) 1:60–61. A. BUTLER, *The Lives of the Saints* 1:345.

[J. E. BRESNAHAN]

ANGELUS SILESIUS

German mystic and religious poet of the baroque period; b. Breslau, December 1624; d. there, July 9, 1677. He was born Johannes Scheffler, the son of a Protestant landowner who had emigrated from Poland for religious reasons. Johannes studied philosophy and medicine at the Universities of Strassburg, Leyden, and Padua and was appointed court physician by Duke Sylvius Nimrod of Württemburg in 1649. Disgusted by the court chaplain's religious intolerance, Johannes resigned his post in 1652 and became a Catholic in 1653, taking the name Angelus Silesius; the conversion made him the target of vicious attacks and ridicule. After six years in Vienna, where he was court physician to Emperor Ferdinand III, he returned to Breslau, entered the Franciscans, and was ordained in 1661. From 1664 until his retirement in 1671, he held high positions in the service of his friend Sebastian Rostock, the prince-bishop of Breslau. Angelus then lived in ascetic seclusion until his death at St. Matthias monastery.

While studying in Holland, Angelus had read and admired the writings of another Silesian mystic, Jakob BÖHME, the cobbler of Görlitz. But while Böhme, though uneducated, approached the object of his quest through intuition and an impressive poetic talent, Angelus founded his ideas on a continuation of early Christian MYSTICISM. In 1657 Angelus published the five-volume *Geistreiche Sinn- und Schlussreime.* For his aphorisms (1665) he used the verse form of the contemporary French drama, the Alexandrine, in which another Silesian, Daniel Von Czepko (1605–60), had written his mystical-theosophical *Monodisticha sescenta sapientium.* With extraordinary creative power Angelus molded the experience of God in mystical absorption into the pointed and often paradoxical form of the epigram, in which he fused antitheses of *visio* and *ratio,* the mystical and the conceptual, since, to him, antithesis was the most significant expression of the deity who reconciles and resolves all contradictions. Angelus' theme was not meditation on or adoration of the suffering Christ or the ascent of the soul to God, but rather God's descent to the soul: "I am as great as God, He is as small as I am"; "I know that God cannot live a moment without me; if I perish, He must needs give up the ghost."

Such ambiguous expressions made Angelus suspect of pantheism, which probably accounts for the esteem in which he was held by romantics and such moderns as R. M. Rilke. But Angelus' spiritual-intellectual epigrams must be understood as a new variety of Christian mysticism, as the continuation of a tradition that cannot be interpreted by more recent concepts. His censor, the Jesuit N. Avancini, dean of the faculty of theology at the University of Vienna, not only gave permission for publication but wrote a highly commendatory preface to the work, which in its second edition (1674) and with the added sixth volume became known as *Cherubinischer Wandersmann. Heilige Seelenlust oder Geistliche Hirtenlieder der in ihren Jesum verliebten Psyche,* a collection of 205 songs (1657), revealed the zealous convert who, in the spirit of the Song of Songs and of contemporary bucolic poems, wanted to testify to his love for Jesus. Some of these poems are profoundly moving and have become favorites in both Protestant and Catholic churches.

Apart from a number of apologetic writings or "Lehrtraktätlein," as he called them, Angelus engaged also in spiteful religious polemics. Spurred on by his

"Anger," mid-19th century drawing by Louis Boilly. (©Historical Picture Archive/CORBIS)

friend, the prince-bishop of Breslau, who was very active in the COUNTER REFORMATION movement, and constantly provoked by his own detractors, Angelus published 55 pamphlets in which he battled with Protestant theologians, such as Chemnitz, Strauch, Scherzer, and Alberti. Two years before his death he published *Sinnliche Beschreibung der vier Letzten Dinge* (1675), a phantasmagoria on the four last things, meant to terrify men into abjuring sin. But he is best remembered for *Cherubinischer Wandersmann* and a few beautiful religious songs.

Bibliography: W. KOSCH, *Deutsches Literatur-Lexikon,* v.3 (2d ed. Bern 1956), 2431, with bibliog. H. GIES, "Ein Dichter und Mystiker des Barock," in *Literaturwissenschaftliches Jahrbuch der Görresgesellschaft* 4 (1929), 129–142. M. H. GODECKER, *Angelus Silesius' Personality through His Ecclesiologia* (Washington, D.C. 1938). W. STAMMLER, *Von der Mystik zum Barock: 1400–1600* (Stuttgart 1927; 2d ed. 1950), with extensive bibliog.

[S. A. SCHULZ]

ANGER

A strong feeling of vexation, an antagonistic emotion usually aroused by a sense of injury. In animals this biological response serves the useful purpose of preservation. Among humans, anger is usually considered as capable of having an ethical rating inasmuch as it can lead to vengeful actions that are disproportionate to the injury suffered or simply unlawful, e.g., murdering a man for an insulting remark. From this point of view an excessive experience of wrath, the misguided discharge of vengeance, or the objectionable damage done in rage to persons or property could result in sins that would be seriously opposed to charity and justice.

Obviously, the forementioned expressions of resentment might be of such inconsequential proportions as to be merely slightly sinful, or even not sinful at all if the subject has not yet reached an age at which the habitual control of his emotions is to be expected as part of human maturity. Even the most violent and disproportionate discharges of anger can be considered to be of little or no ethical import from the subjective point of view, if the outrageous assault is normally beyond ordinary human endurance, or if the psychological reaction is of such abrupt emergence that rational control becomes humanly improbable. Even in those who are of an age when emotional maturity is fairly well established, it is not uncommon that intense feelings of indignation will be experienced on the sense level, without in any way being made externally manifest in serious violations of justice and charity. Even from the most cautious and critical point of view, such feelings ought to be considered as of slight moral consequence.

Many vexations and the resultant expressions of emotion are entirely without moral objection, or are even morally laudable. Such a situation may occur when only a vigorous display of emotion will secure attention and obedience. Sometimes, as in the classical case of Jesus' driving the buyers and sellers from the Temple, deliberately achieved and discharged rage can be virtuous and worthy of praise.

Different personality types experience anger differently. Some find that the emotion arises quickly and subsides with equal rapidity; others find that anger is more slowly stimulated and only with difficulty dissipated. Accordingly, there are different approaches to the rational control of this human emotion. Granted that psychological understanding of self and others is a basic factor in conditioning one to bear vexations with tranquillity of spirit, various vicarious discharges of energy, e.g., golf or rail-splitting, frequently assist in the dissipation of pent-up rage. Some forms of entertainment that include a degree of violence also serve this same wholesome purpose.

Ancient Christian moralists incorporated anger along with the other six in their list of capital sins. This classification indicates merely that anger is related causally to other sins, and does not imply that it is per se grievous. The anger that St. Paul describes as excluding one from the kingdom of heaven would of necessity have to be seriously sinful.

See Also: ANGER (IN THE BIBLE); EMOTION (MORAL ASPECT); DEADLY SINS.

Bibliography: THOMAS AQUINAS, *Summa theologiae* 1a2ae, 74.3; 2a2ae, 157–158. D. M. PRÜMMER, *Manuale theologiae moralis*, ed. E. M. MÜNCH (Freiburg-Barcelona 1955) 2:709–710.

[J. D. FEARON]

ANGER (IN THE BIBLE)

Human anger is generally frowned upon in the Bible. Jacob curses the anger of Simeon and Levi (Gn 49:5–7; see also ch. 34). The wisdom literature sees anger as a source of harm for the one angered; it is folly, a source of sins, and a cause of discord (Ps 36[37].8; Prv 14.17, 29; 15.18; 29.22; see also 15.1; 19.11). To be the object of anger could be disastrous (Gn 4.5; 27.43–44; 1 Sm 18.8–9; Prv 16.14; 20.2; Eccl 10.4; see also Lk 4.28; Acts 7.54–58). The NT sees anger and its consequences as things to be avoided in the Christian community (Mt 5.21–22; 1 Cor 13.5; Eph 4.31; 6.4; Col 3.8; 1 Tm 2.8; Ti 1.7). "The wrath of man does not work the justice of God" (Jas 1.19–20). Eph 4.26 (cf. Ps 4.5) recognizes the uncontrollable movements of anger and admonishes the faithful not to remain in an angry state. Yet anger ordered to divine justice is just (Ex 16.20; 32.19–20; Is 13.5; 1 Sm 15.33). This is certainly true of Christ's anger (Mk 3.5; 10.14; Mt 12.34; 15.7; 16.23; 23.13–36; Jn 2.15–17.)

Divine anger in the Bible is an anthropomorphical expression of divine retributive justice. It brings out the personal element in God's dealings with men. His anger is provoked by Israel's unresponsiveness to divine love offered in the COVENANT (Ex 32.1–10; Dt 11.16–17; Jgs 2.11–15; Is 65.1–7; Ez 7.1–27; Hos ch. 13). God's anger, however, is balanced by His love (Ex 32.12–14; Is 54.7–10; 63.9–15; Hos 11.8–9; Mi 7.18–20). Divine anger is aroused by the wickedness of nations (Ps 2) or by the rebellion of men against their Creator (Gn 4.10–14; 6.5–8; Sir 5.7). Often inexplicable, God's wrath is never satanical or a matter of divine caprice, though a few texts present difficulty in interpretation (Ex 4.24; 2 Sm 6.7; 24.1). Already an active force (Gn 6.17; Nm 11.33; 16.25–35; Ps 105[106].13–18; Is 30.30; 10.5–6; Jer 21.14; 22.1–6; Jgs 2.11–15; 1 Sm 5.9), it is being stored up for the DAY OF THE LORD (Am 5.18–20; Is 13.9; Zep 1.15–18). God's final wrath also is a prominent theme in the NT (Mt 3.7; 18.23–35; Lk 14.16–24; Rom 2.5; Col 3.5–6; 1 Pt 4.17–18; Jude 14–15). The last day

St-Jean Hospital, now a museum, on the banks of the River Maine, Angers, France. (© Adam Woolfitt/CORBIS)

is still the day of wrath, but the redeemed in Christ will be delivered from it (Jn 3.36; Rom 5.9; Eph 5.1–7; 1 Thes 1.9–10; 2 Tm 1.12, 18). Christ Himself will be the executor of divine anger (Mt 25.31–46; Jn 5.22; Rv 6.15–17; 22.12–13).

Bibliography: M. ALOYSIA, ''The God of Wrath?'' *Catholic Biblical Quarterly* 8 (1946) 407–415. L. BOUYER, ''The Servant of Yahveh,'' *The Paschal Mystery,* tr. M. BENOIT (Chicago 1950) 181–191. W. EICHRODT, *Theology of the O.T.,* tr. J. A. BAKER (Philadelphia 1961–) 1:250–258. A. RICHARDSON, *An Introduction to the Theology of the N.T.* (New York 1958) 75–79. W. EICHRODT and H. CONZELMANN, *Die Religion in Geschichte und Gegenwart,* 7 v. (3d ed. Tübingen 1957–65) 6:1930–32. *Encyclopedic Dictionary of the Bible,* tr. and adap. by L. HARTMAN (New York 1963), from A. VAN DEN BORN, *Bijbels Woordenboek* 90–91.

[J. A. FALLON]

ANGERS

City of the Maine River near its confluence with the Loire, in western France. The Diocese of Angers (*Andegavensis*), suffragan of TOURS, comprises the Maine-et-Loire Department (2,787 square miles), of which Angers is the capital. The Plantagenet kings of England were descended from the original counts of Anjou; and from Charles of Anjou, brother of LOUIS IX OF FRANCE, descended a house that had ties with several European dynasties.

Caesar made the residence of the Gallic *Andes* or *Andegavi* a town called *Juliomagus*. Christianity was probably introduced rather early, and after the first known bishop, Defensor (372), the episcopal succession was regular. The rebuilding of a circus in honor of Minerva in 347 showed pagan strength, but the evangelization of the countryside, especially along the Loire, made progress under the bishops Saints Maurilius (d. 453), ALBINUS, LICINIUS and MAGNOBOD. In Merovingian times many richly endowed abbeys such as Saint-Aubin (chapter founded *c.* 530, monastery in 966) and Saint-Serge (in existence in the seventh century) flourished; of which SAINT-MAUR-SUR-LOIRE and SAINT-FLORENT-LE-VIEIL are located near Angers. Angers was a strong point in CHARLES MARTEL's time and a Carolingian frontier post against the Bretons. THEODULF OF ORLÉANS composed his hymn *GLORIA, LAUS ET HONOR* while imprisoned in Angers, in order to gain a pardon from Louis the Pious (818). Bretons and Normans ruined ecclesiastical establishments in the ninth century. Thereafter the bishops were dominated by the counts, who restored monasteries and built many churches and buildings in Plantagenet Gothic. Bishop Ulger (1125–48) defended episcopal rights, especially against monasteries such as FONTEVRAULT. His reorganization of the episcopal school (where BERENGARIUS OF TOURS, BAUDRY of BOURGUEIL-EN-VALLÉE, MARBOD OF RENNES and ROBERT OF ARBRISSEL studied or taught) made it famous enough to attract an exodus of the English nation from the University of Paris in 1229 (when the University of Toulouse was founded). Bulls of Urban V made the school a university (1366, 1373), which, however, was suppressed in 1793.

Henry II, Count of Anjou, became king of England and duke of Normandy in 1154, but LOUIS VIII restored Anjou to France. Louis IX had the present castle built during an expedition against Brittany and gave Anjou as an appanage to his brother Charles (1246). The Hundred Years' War ruined Anjou, which Louis XI returned to France on the death of ''King René'' (1480), who had left Angevin Sicily to return to Anjou. Protestant pamphlets circulated from 1525, and Huguenots sacked the cathedral in 1562. The Edict of Nantes gave the Protestants a refuge in Saumur, where they organized a university of sorts. Many religious houses were founded in the Counter Reformation and Jansenism gained influence under Bishop Henri ARNAULD (1649–92). In the French Revolution, Bishop Michel de Lorry (1782–1802) refused the oath of the CIVIL CONSTITUTION OF THE CLERGY, as did most of his clergy, 204 of whom were deported to Spain (1792) while others were drowned in the Loire at Nantes. The Vendée rising broke out at Saint-Florent in 1793 and revolutionary tribunals claimed at least 3,000 victims, including the Blessed Noël PINOT. Count Frédéric de FALLOUX, from Angers, gave his name to the law of freedom of instruction that was passed in 1850. Bishop Charles E. FREPPEL (1870–91) restored many high schools and was responsible for the founding of the Catholic University of the West in Angers (1875). Bishop François MATHIEU (1893–95), of the French Academy, was transferred to Toulouse after which he became a cardinal in the Curia.

The first cathedral was burned when Childeric's Franks sacked the town in 471. Originally dedicated to Our Lady, it was dedicated to St. Maurice after St. Martin supposedly gave it a vial of the blood of the martyrs of Agaune in the fourth century. Bishop Ulger rebuilt it in Plantagenet Gothic with one nave; the choir is 13th-century. The church of Saint-Nicholas Abbey, founded by Fulk Nerra (1010–20), was consecrated by Urban II, who visited Angers in 1096. Fulk Nerra also added a convent of nuns to the sixth-century chapel at Ronceray. Angers had six collegiate chapters besides that of the cathedral. The abbots of the Augustinian Toussaint Abbey date from 1118; in 1635 it joined the reform of

Sainte-Geneviève. The Dominican convent was one of the first in France (1219).

Angers' traditional procession (13th century) was a protest against Berengarius's heresy concerning the Real Presence even before the Feast of CORPUS ET SANGUINIS CHRISTI was instituted. Jehan Michel's beautiful dramatic *Passion* was performed in front of the cathedral (1486). The tapestry of the Apocalypse (1380), restored and retouched, still adorns the castle hall. Louis XIV founded a literary academy in Angers (1685). David of Angers was a painter and sculptor in the early 19th century. René Bazin (1853–1932), a novelist known for purity of language, freshness of feeling and his vigorous Christian tradition, was from Angers.

Bibliography: F. UZUREAU, *Dictionnaire d'histoire et de géographie ecclésiastiques,* ed. A. BAUDRILLART et al., (Paris 1912–) 3:85–114. E. JARRY, *Catholicisme,* 1:556–559. G. H. FORSYTH, *The Church of St. Martin at Angers* (Princeton 1953). J. MCMANNERS, *French Ecclesiastical Society under the Old Régime: A Study of Angers in the 18th century* (Manchester, Eng. 1961). C. PORT, *Dictionnaire historique et biographique de Maine-et-Loire et de l'ancienne provence d'Anjou,* ed. J. LEVRON and P. D'HERBÉCOURT, v.1 (Angers 1965) 31–170.

[E. CATTA]

ANGILBERT, ST.

Carolingian poet and courtier, abbot; b. *c.* 750; d. Feb. 18, 814. He was an official in the court of CHARLEMAGNE for more than 20 years. He was a figure in the CAROLINGIAN RENAISSANCE, a student of ALCUIN in the PALACE SCHOOL, the head of the court chapel, and tutor of the young Pepin. He fathered two sons out of wedlock, Nithard and Harnid, by Charles's daughter Bertha. Between 792 and 796, he took part in three embassies to Rome, taking the *LIBRI CAROLINI* to Adrian I in 794. He was present at Charlemagne's coronation in 800. In 811, he was one of the witnesses to Charlemagne's will. In 781, he was appointed lay abbot of Saint-Riquier (*Centula*). Sometime between 796 and 802, he retired to his abbey to live an austere life. As abbot, he was an able administrator and builder. He wrote two treatises about his monastic work. He greatly increased the library holdings and introduced the uninterrupted recital of the Hours, the *laus perennis,* for his 300 monks. His poems have no exceptional literary merit but they do give interesting insight into life at Charlemagne's court. St. Angilbert's cult began at Saint-Riquier in the twelfth century.

Feast: Feb. 18.

Bibliography: *Monumenta Germaniae Historica: Poetae* 1:355–381. *Monumenta Germaniae Historica: Scriptores* 15.1:173–190. *Acta Sanctorum* Feb. 3:91–107. HARIULPHE,

Chronique de l'abbaye de Saint-Riquier, ed. F. LOT (Paris 1894). S. A. RABE, *Faith, Art, and Politics at Saint-Riquier: The Symbolic Vision of Angilbert* (Philadelphia 1995). W. WATTENBACH, *Deutschlands Geschichtsquellen im Mittelalter*, ed. W. LEVISON and H. LÖWE (Weimar 1952–63) 2 235–241. R. AIGRAIN, *Catholicisme* 1:559–560. A. BUTLER, *The Lives of the Saints*, ed. H. THURSTON and D. ATTWATER (New York 1956) 1:371. *Bibliotheca sanctorum* (Rome 1961–) 1:1249–50. M. MANITIUS, *Geschichte der lateinische Literatur des Mittelalters* (Munich 1911–31) 1:543–547. P. RICHARD, *Dictionnaire d'histoire et de géographie ecclésiastiques*, ed. A. BAUDRILLART et al. (Paris 1912) 3:120–123.

[V. GELLHAUS]

ANGILRAMNUS OF METZ

Bishop and canonist; d. 791. He was at one time abbot of the BENEDICTINE monastery of Sens and was consecrated bishop of METZ on Sept. 25, 768. He was chaplain at the court of CHARLEMAGNE from 784. Angilramnus seems to owe his place in history almost entirely to the accidental circumstance of being named author of that part of the pseudo-Isidorian decretals called the *Capitula* or *Capitularia Angilramni* (*see* FALSE DECRETALS). This collection of canons, which represents one stage in the gradual build-up of the celebrated *pseudo-corpus*, concerns itself chiefly with the defense of bishops against encroachments and molestations of civil tribunals and with establishment of the *privilegium fori*. Ostensibly Angilramnus sent the collection to Pope ADRIAN II (*Capitularia Hadriani*) as part of his defense against accusations impugning his episcopal administration at Metz. Evidently, the sketchily known facts of his episcopate illustrate the evils that the pseudo-Isidorian decretals were designed to counter. The long-acclaimed text of P. Hinschius, *Decretals pseudo-Isidorianae et capitula Angilramni*, has recently come under severe criticism on scientific and paleographical grounds, but the continuing debate at least preserves for Angilramnus his anomalous place in history.

Bibliography: G. HOCQUARD, *Catholicisme* 1:560–561. A. AMANIEU, *Dictionnaire de droit canonique* 1:522–526. P. FOURNIER and G. LEBRAS, *Histoire des collections canoniques en occident depuis les fausses décrétales jusqu'au Décret de Gratien* 1:142–145. *Decretales Pseudo–Isidorianae et Capitula Angilramni*, ed. P. HINSCHIUS, (Leipzig 1863; repr. 1963) 757–769. J. P. MIGNE, *Patrologia latina* 96:1031–1102. A. M. STICKLER, *Historia iuris canonici latini* 1:128. S. WILLIAMS, ''The Pseudo–Isidorian Problem Today,'' *Speculum* 29 (1954) 702–707. A. HUMBERT, *Dictionnaire d'histoire et de géographie ecclésiastiques* 3:125–127.

[P. L. HUG]

ANGLESEY, PRIORY OF

Cambridgeshire, England, Ely Diocese (patrons, SS. Mary and Nicholas). It was of unknown origin, served as a hospital in the 12th century, and was refounded for the CANONS REGULAR OF ST. AUGUSTINE, probably when it was endowed by Richard de Clare (*c.* 1212). It was further endowed and its buildings provided (1217–36) by Master Lawrence of St. Nicholas, papal chaplain. It undertook many chantry services for small benefactions in the 13th century. It was also enriched (1331–60) under the patronage of Elizabeth de Burgh, Lady Clare. The community numbered usually nine members. Its 1535 income was £125; it was suppressed in 1536.

Bibliography: *A Descriptive Catalogue of Ancient Deeds in the Public Records Office* (London 1890). No known chronicle or cartulary. W. DUGDALE, *Monasticon Anglicanum* (London 1655–73); best ed. by J. CALEY et al., 6 v. (1817–30) 6:394–396. E. HAILSTONE, *The History and Antiquities of . . . the Priory of Anglesey* (Cambridge, Eng. 1873). *The Victoria History of the Counties of England: Cambridge and the Isle of Ely*, v. 2 (London 1948) 229–234.

[S. WOOD]

ANGLICAN COMMUNION

As defined by the LAMBETH CONFERENCE of 1930, the Anglican Communion is ''a fellowship, within the One Holy Catholic and Apostolic Church, of those duly constituted Dioceses, Provinces or Regional Churches in communion with the See of Canterbury.'' They ''uphold and propagate the Catholic and Apostolic faith and order as set forth in the Book of Common Prayer,'' and are ''bound together not by central legislative and executive authority, but by mutual loyalty sustained through the common counsel of the Bishops in conference.'' The latter is a reference to the decennial Lambeth Conference of all the bishops of the Communion. As at the beginning of the 21st century, the Anglican communion comprised 37 autonomous provinces in more than 160 countries, with some 70 million Anglicans.

Churches of the Anglican Communion also subscribe to the LAMBETH QUADRILATERAL of 1888, which affirms as the essential elements of faith and order in the quest for Christian unity:

1. The Holy Scriptures of the Old and New Testament as the revealed Word of God
2. The Nicene Creed as the sufficient statement of the Christian Faith
3. The two Sacraments instituted by Christ: Baptism and the Eucharist
4. The historic Episcopate

Other elements which unite the Anglican Communion include the celebration of Holy Eucharist, and the BOOK OF COMMON PRAYER in its various recensions throughout the Communion.

The 37 provinces of the Anglican Communion are:

GREAT BRITAIN
The Church of England
The Church of Ireland
The Scottish Episcopal Church
The Church in Wales

ASIA
The Church of Bangladesh
The Church of the Province of the Indian Ocean
The Holy Catholic Church in Japan (Nippon Seikokai)
The Episcopal Church in Jerusalem and the Middle East
The Anglican Church of Korea
The Church of the Province of Myanmar (Burma)
The Church of Pakistan
The Philippine Episcopal Church
The Church of the Province of South East Asia

AFRICA
The Church of the Province of Burundi
The Church of the Province of Central Africa
The Province of the Anglican Church of the Congo
The Anglican Church of Kenya
The Church of the Province of Nigeria
The Province of the Episcopal Church of Rwanda
The Church of the Province of Southern Africa
The Episcopal Church of the Sudan
The Church of the Province of Tanzania
The Church of the Province of Uganda
The Church of the Province of West Africa

NORTH AMERICA
The Anglican Church of Canada
The Episcopal Church in the United States of America

CENTRAL/SOUTH AMERICA
The Episcopal Anglican Church of Brazil (Episcopal Church of Brazil)
The Anglican Church of the Central American Region
The Anglican Church of Mexico
The Anglican Church of the Southern Cone of America
The Church in the Province of the West Indies

EUROPE
The Lusitanian Church of Portugal
The Spanish Reformed Episcopal Church

OCEANIA
The Anglican Church in Aotearoa, New Zealand and Polynesia
The Anglican Church of Australia
The Church of the Province of Melanesia
The Anglican Church of Papua New Guinea

In addition to the foregoing, the Anglican Communion also comprises the Extra Provincial Dioceses of Bermuda, Cuba, Hong Kong and Macau, Puerto Rico, and Venezuela, and the Church of Ceylon (Sri Lanka) Extra Provincial.

The following are churches which are in full communion with the See of Canterbury, as defined by the 1958 Lambeth Conference, but which are not denominationally Anglican:

Die Alt-Katholiken in Deutschland (Old Catholic Church of Germany)
Old Catholic Church of the Netherlands
Church of North India
Church of South India
Mar Thoma Syrian Church of India
The Philippine Independent Church

A move to give Anglicanism greater cohesion without providing it with a central governing head was proposed by the Lambeth Conference of 1968 and subsequently adopted by unanimous approval of the member churches. This is the Anglican Consultative Council, a representative advisory body of bishops, clergy, and laity. The objective of the Anglican Consultative Council council is to supply a continuity of consultation and guidance on policy. Like the Lambeth Conference, the council has only advisory power, with no coercive authority.

Bibliography: *The Episcopal Church Annual* (New York). C. E. SIMCOX, *The Historical Road of Anglicanism* (Chicago 1968). F. L. CROSS, ed., *The Oxford Dictionary of the Christian Church* (Oxford, New York 1957). J. S. HIGGINS, *One Faith and Fellowship* (New York 1958).

[E. MCDERMOTT/C. E. SIMCOX/EDS.]

ANGLICAN ORDERS

The problem of the validity of Anglican orders arose in the Catholic Church during the reign of the Catholic Queen MARY (1553–1558), when Cardinal Reginald POLE as papal legate governed the reconciliation of the Church in England with the Holy See. The English Church had been schismatic under HENRY VIII (1509–1547) since the Act of Supremacy adopted in 1534. Under EDWARD VI (1547–1553) it had officially endorsed and enforced Protestant doctrines with a Calvinist orientation, yet without modifying the episcopal organization. The validity of its ordinations became a problem because of the liturgical reforms of Archbishop Thomas CRANMER (1489–1557). Edward's government, bent on reformation on a continental model, successively adopted the BOOK OF COMMON PRAYER in 1549 (revised in a more Protestant direction in 1552), the Ordinal in 1550, and Forty-two Articles of Religion in 1552 (reduced to Thirty-nine under Queen Elizabeth). From 1550 on, the ritual of ordination departed from the rite that had been traditional in the English Church from time immemorial.

Due to the circumstances of the times the theological question was inextricably bound with politics. Upon the

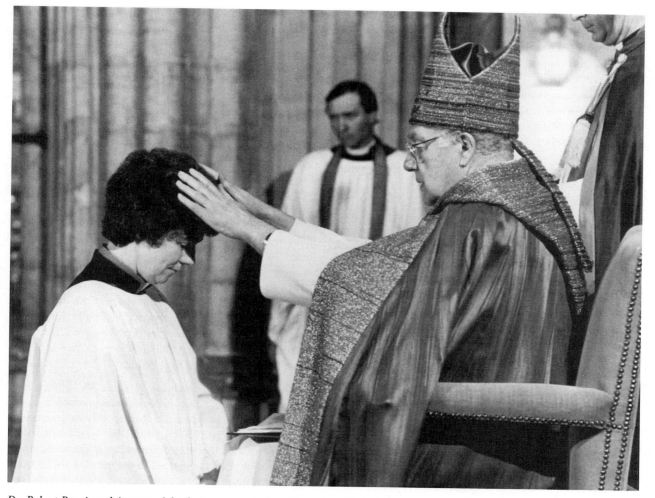

Dr. Robert Runcie ordains one of the first woman priests in Canterbury Cathedral, Kent, England. (Hulton/Archive Photos)

death of Edward on July 6, 1553, the attempt to place the young Lady Jane Grey (1537–1554) on the throne was in keeping with an Act of Succession signed by the king. It was somewhat reluctantly agreed to by Archbishop Cranmer and enthusiastically supported by Nicholas Ridley (*c.* 1503–1555), bishop of London. The Catholic Queen Mary, however, daughter of Henry VIII and Catherine of Aragon, got enough support to conquer the crown some two weeks later, and the pious Protestant Queen Jane was beheaded on Feb. 1, 1554. Mary wished to have the entire kingdom reconciled with the Holy See and the old liturgy restored. At her request this task was entrusted by Pope JULIUS III (1550–1555) to the queen's relative, Reginald Pole (1500–1558), the first prelate who faced Anglican ordinations as a problem.

From time to time during the next three centuries, the question was raised again, until Pope LEO XIII (1878–1903) appointed a special commission with a view to settling the matter once for all. He reached his conclu-

sion in the apostolic letter *Apostolicae curae,* issued in 1896.

The Question in the Sixteenth Century

A cardinal and a deacon since December of 1536, Reginald Pole had been named papal legate to England by Paul III on Feb. 15, 1537, but, Henry VIII having ordered his assassination, he had not gone to England at the time. His legatine commission was renewed by Julius III (*Si ullo unquam tempore,* on Aug. 5, 1553) and the extent of his powers determined on August 6 (*Post nuntium nobis*). Having finally landed in England on Nov. 20, 1554, the cardinal officially absolved the kingdom of England from schism ten days later, and Parliament passed an Act of Reconciliation on Jan. 4, 1555, thus repealing the ecclesiastical legislation of both Henry and Edward.

The situation that faced Pole was extremely complex. Under Edward VI and his Protestant advisers, priests and bishops had been ordained at first with the old Pontifical, then with the Ordinal. Most of those who opted for the Reformation had time to flee to the Continent. A few bishops, notably Nicholas Ridley and Cranmer, were arrested for high treason because of their support of Jane Grey. Hugh Latimer (*c.* 1483–1555), bishop of Worcester, was arrested on suspicion of heresy. He was burnt on Oct. 15, 1555, together with Nicholas Ridley. Archbishop Cranmer was eventually tried for heresy. Deprived of his see by Paul IV (1555–1559) on Dec. 4, 1555, he was burnt on March 21, 1556, while Pole, promoted to the see of Canterbury as soon as it was officially vacant, was hurriedly ordained a priest on March 20 and a bishop two days later. The remaining clergy of Edward VI were generally willing, and some were eager, to be reconciled with the Holy See. Many of the priests, however, were now married and the status of their wives raised difficult questions.

The history of the reconciliation begins in uncertainty, for one cannot know what happened before the arrival of Cardinal Pole in England in November of 1554. It is inconceivable that no reintegration of the clergy had taken place. Many of the priests, including those ordained under Edward, simply changed their liturgy of Holy Communion and picked it up where it had been in the last years of the reign of Henry VIII. Instructions sent by the queen to Bishop Edward Bonner on March 4, 1554 specified that no heretic may now be admitted to ecclesiastical functions, that priests who refuse to separate from their wives must be deprived while those who, with their wife's consent, promise to abstain from matrimony may be assigned ecclesiastical functions, and that all former religious who have attempted marriage must be divorced without exception. These instructions do not question the validity of the priests' orders.

Meanwhile, the papal bull of Julius III *Dudum dum charissima* (March 8, 1554) gave Cardinal Pole, though he was not a priest, and was not yet in England, unlimited power of absolution for all those (even ''in patriarchal dignity'') who ''ask to be received in the orthodox faith.'' The papal instructions regarding the reconciliation of the clergy, however, were far from clear. Some, the bull noted, had been properly ordained (with the old Pontifical). Others were never ordained at all: they must now be ordained if they wish to remain in ministry and if they are otherwise qualified. A third category includes priests who are in ''orders that they never or badly received,'' and also bishops who received their orders ''from other heretical or schismatic bishops or archbishops, or otherwise less properly [*minus rite*] and the usual form of the Church not being followed.'' The bull does not specify what the legate should do in regard to their ordination. A fourth category is that of bishops who were

promoted by the king or the metropolitan, and thus without the proper papal bulls; the legate has full authority to confirm them, with the queen's agreement, in their see or place them in another one. There is no suggestion that these illegitimate bishops are not in valid orders or that they should now be ordained.

Paul IV. Three bulls of PAUL IV, composed during Queen Mary's reign, touch on the question of Anglican orders. *Praeclara charissimi* (June 20, 1555) approves generally the rulings that have been made by the legate, including his decisions and dispensations regarding those who had obtained indults ''concerning orders'' by virtue of ''the pretended authority of the Supremacy of the Church of England'' so that these men could ''remain in their orders or benefices.'' The bull specifies that only the orders conferred by bishops who had been ordained *rite et recte* (with the Pontifical) are to be honored. The pope does not mention the ritual specifically; one may infer from this that Paul IV's concern was not with the rite, but with the lack of proper jurisdiction of the Edwardian bishops, since neither the metropolitans (of Canterbury and of York) nor the king had the canonical power to give spiritual jurisdiction to new bishops.

Dudum ecclesiae eboracensis (Oct. 30, 1555), a brief addressed to the Church in York, was composed to explain a mistake made in the Roman offices concerning Nicholas Heath (d. 1572), whom the queen wanted to transfer from the diocese of Worcester to the archdiocese of York. The pope had agreed to the transfer but had said that Heath must now be consecrated. He had, however, already been consecrated in 1540, with the Pontifical. Pole asked for further instructions. *Dudum ecclesiae* blamed the mistake on the insufficient information provided by England. It went on to declare that the three bishops who had consecrated Heath were lacking in *executione ordinis episcopalis*. In other words, they were true bishops, who nonetheless lacked the proper jurisdiction since they were functioning under the king's usurped supremacy.

The bull *Regimini universalis ecclesiae* bears the same date and was composed on the same occasion. Addressed to the papal legate, it is more general in scope. It formulates the question well: Which bishops, ''during the schism of the kingdom, could be said to be licitly and rightly [*rite et recte*] ordained?'' The answer, however, cast in the form of a double negation, is unclear: ''Only those cannot be said to have been ordained *rite et recte* who were not ordained and consecrated in the form of the Church; and therefore the persons whom they promoted to these orders did not receive the orders, but must receive them again. . . . The others to whom these orders were given by bishops and archbishops who had been ordained and consecrated in the form of the Church, even though these bishops and archbishops were schismatic and received the churches over which they presided from Henry VIII and Edward VI, pretended kings of England . . . did receive the character of the orders given to them and were only lacking in regard to the fullness of the same orders.'' The text does not specify if the form of the Church is the rite of the Pontifical (which would rule out ordinations according to the Ordinal) or the canonical confirmation of their election by the bishop of Rome (which would deny these bishops' power of jurisdiction, but not the validity of their ordination). Since the bull, however, shows no intent of introducing a new principle in the legate's extended authority, one must assume that, like Julius III, Paul IV denies the validity of episcopal jurisdiction received *nulliter et de facto* from the royal supremacy, but says nothing about the rite of ordination. In fact, the researches that have been made into the episcopal registers of Queen Mary's time, especially by W. H. Frere, indicate that only about fifteen reordinations took place under Cardinal Pole's authority (Hughes, *Absolutely Null*, 253–254).

Pius V. After Elizabeth ascended the throne on Nov. 17, 1558, she reversed the Catholic measures taken by her sister, though she did not share the Calvinist principles of her brother. She selected a scholar from Cambridge, Matthew Parker (1504–1575), to succeed Cardinal Pole in Canterbury. Parker was consecrated on Dec. 17, 1559 by four bishops, two of whom had been ordained according to the Pontifical, two according to the Ordinal. The queen also issued a decree, *Supplentes*, to the effect that by virtue of the Royal Supremacy she "supplied" whatever could happen to be defective in the proceedings. The queen's ability to do this was precisely what the papal policy toward England was determined to deny. While Pius IV (1555–1565) did not interfere in English affairs, it was under Elizabeth, during the "Great Controversy" between the Anglican John Jewel and the Catholic Thomas Harding, that the validity of Anglican orders was openly denied for the first time. The main reason given by Harding when he refused the title of bishop to Jewel was that he had been made bishop (of Salisbury) by the queen, who had no authority to do this. Finally, in 1571 (*Regnans in excelsis*) Pius V accused the "pretended queen" of destroying the Church and giving "ecclesiastical possessions" to heretics, and he declared her excommunicate, thereby inviting her subjects to rebel. While Julius III had dealt chiefly with the problem of married priests, and Paul IV with the Royal Supremacy and bishops who had no ecclesiastical jurisdiction, Pius V approached the Anglican problem politically, and his wish to unseat the queen was frustrated.

The Council of Trent. The lack of precision as to the meaning of *rite et recte* in the papal documents of the sixteenth century is not surprising. The Council of Trent gave no more information in the decree of its 23d session on the sacrament of orders (July 15, 1563). Neither the four chapters of the decree nor the following eight canons specify what rites are adequate. Chapter 3 says simply that sacred ordination "is done with words and external signs" (*quae verbis et signis exterioribus perficitur*: DS 1766), and canon 3 anathematizes anyone who says that ordination is "only a rite [*ritum quemdam*] for selecting ministers of the word of God and the sacraments" (DS 1773). A few words of the ritual appear in canon 4, which says that the bishops do not say "Accipe Spiritum Sanctum" in vain (DS 1774). These words also begin the formula that accompanies the laying on of hands in the Ordinal. Canon 5 condemns those who say that "the sacred unction used by the Church in holy ordination not only is not needed, but is contemptible and pernicious, and likewise the other ceremonies" (DS 1775). Canon 7 rejects the idea that "those who are not *rite* ordained and sent by ecclesiastical and canonical authority, but come from somewhere else, are legitimate ministers of word and sacraments" (DS 1777). By implication this denies that the Royal Supremacy can be a legitimate source of ministerial authority, but it says nothing about any specific rite. In all the decree there is not even an allusion to the scholastic theology of the form and matter of a sacrament.

This lack of interest in the rite of ordination is confirmed by the *Catechism of the Council of Trent*, or *Roman Catechism*, that was issued by Pius V. The twenty-three sections of its long treatment of the sacrament of orders (pt. II, ch. VII) allude to the rite of all the minor and major orders, the priesthood included (XXV), drawing attention to the porrection of instruments and the accompanying words. Within the priesthood it places the ranks of bishop, archbishop, and patriarchs (XXVI–XXVII), of whom the pope is the principal, *episcopus maximus* by divine law, successor of Peter and vicar of Christ (XXVIII). The bishop is the only minister of the major orders (XXIX). In keeping with "the tradition of the Apostles," he is himself consecrated by three bishops. But there is no reference to the words and gestures of the rite. The most likely explanation for this silence is that legitimate episcopal authority did not depend on the rite of episcopal consecration but on the source of episcopal jurisdiction. The question was not: How was he consecrated? It was: By whom was he ordained a priest, and by what authority was he made a bishop?

The Question in the Seventeenth and Eighteenth Centuries

The Ordinal was slightly modified in 1662 in order to pull the rug out from under a Puritan interpretation that argued that the bishops of the Church of England had only a title without substance because the rite of ordination did not specify that its purpose was precisely the making of a bishop. Though the intent of the rite was already formulated in the preface to the Ordinal, the formula of ordination was henceforth: "Receive the Holy Ghost for the office of a Bishop in the Church of God now committed unto thee by the imposition of our hands." The opinion of the Recusants on the value of Anglican ordination was not a factor in the process.

In 1684 a former French Calvinist, who had been ordained a priest by an Anglican bishop and had entered the Catholic Church later as layman, asked the apostolic nuncio in Paris if he was free to marry or if he was bound by the law of clerical celibacy. The problem went to Cardinal Jerome Casanate, prefect of the Holy Office under Pope Innocent XI (1676–1689). Casanate, who was unacquainted with the bulls of the sixteenth century, focused his attention on episcopal succession at the time of the Reformation, on the Ordinal, and on the "form and matter" of the rite. He consulted with the apostolic nuncio in the Netherlands and with the internuncio in Flanders, who journeyed to England before taking his position. The nuncio argued that the ordinations were invalid because the Ordinal does not mention the priest's sacrificial function. The internuncio reached the same negative conclusion on the general opinion of English Recusants that Matthew Parker was not a true bishop, and the belief that the Catholic "form" of ordination had been sufficiently altered in the Ordinal to warrant a negative judgment. A similar conclusion was therefore reached by the Holy Office on Aug. 13, 1685, to the effect that the petitioner was not a priest and was therefore free to marry. The decision, however, "delayed" in order not to increase the political difficulties of the Catholic King James II (king, 1665–1689), was never officially promulgated.

Clement XI (1700–1721) faced a somewhat similar question in 1704, when John Clement Gordon (1644–1726), a bishop ordained in the Scottish Episcopal Church in 1688, was received in the Roman Catholic Church. What rite was used at his consecration, the English rite of 1662 being illegal in Scotland at the time, has not been ascertained. In fact, no new investigation was made. The Holy Office declared that Gordon was not in ecclesiastical orders.

During this period, Catholic scholars in France studied the problem of Anglican orders in learned publications, and, as would be expected, they reached divergent verdicts. In 1720 the liturgiologist Eusèbe Renaudot concluded to their invalidity (*Mémoire sur les ordinations des Anglais*). In 1723 the theologian Pierre François Le Courayer reached the opposite conclusion (*Dissertation sur la validité des ordinations des Anglais*). In 1725 Michel Le Quien denied their validity (*La Nullité des ordinations anglicanes*), and the two of them argued back and forth without reaching agreement (Le Courayer in 1726, Le Quien in 1730, and again Le Courayer in 1732). Although the controversy was inconclusive, it did refocus the question, which now became whether the essence of the sacrament of Orders had been preserved in the rite of the Ordinal and the consecration of Matthew Parker.

The Question in the Nineteenth century

Pope Leo XIII (1878–1908) would have had no reason to study the Ordinal if, in 1894, the Vincentian Fernand Portal (1885–1926) and the distinguished Anglican layman Lord Halifax (1839–1834) had not asked him to recognize the validity of Anglican orders. There had been a new flurry of writing pro and con, with books or memoranda by Peter Kenrick (1841), E. E. Estcourt (1873), Johann Baptist Franzelin (1875), F. Dalbus (penname of Fernand Portal, 1894), Sydney Smith (1894), Auguste Boudinhon (1895), among others. A pontifical commission was created, the work of which is now well known thanks to the opening of the Vatican archives for the period and the subsequent publication of the documentation. Although the commission (Adrian Gasquet, James Moyes, David Fleming, known to favor the negative opinion; Duchesne, Pietro Gasparri, Emilio De Augustinis, known to be more or less favorable; plus, added after the first meeting, Calasanzio de Llaveneras, T. B. Scannell) was chaired by Cardinal Marcello Mazzella, and Rafael Merry del Val acted as its secretary. Although it met twelve times betweem March 24, and May 5, 1896, it made no recommendation, for it was suddenly disbanded by Pope Leo, who ordered the documentation to be handed over to the master of the sacred palace, Rafaele Pierotti. His negative conclusion passed into Leo's apostolic letter, written under Mazzella's supervision. The apostolic letter, *Apostolicae curae*, was dated Sept. 13, 1896, and it said that ordinations (of bishops) according to the Ordinal are invalid for defect of form and defect of intention. The argumentation was based on the text of the Ordinal and what was deemed to be its "native character and spirit" (*nativa indoles ac spiritus*). (*See* APOSTOLICAE CURAE.)

The Emergence of a "New Context"

The ecumenical dialogue between the Catholic Church and the Anglican Communion that followed Vatican Council II was bound to bring up the question of Anglican orders again. ARCIC-I (ANGLICAN/ROMAN CATHOLIC INTERNATIONAL COMMISSION) felt that the time was not ripe for an attempt to solve the impasse created by Leo XIII's rejection of their validity. In 1973 it nevertheless recorded its agreement as to the nature of ordination (Canterbury statement, n. 14) and declared that "the development of the thinking in our two communions regarding the nature of the Church and of the ordained ministry, as represented by our statement, has put these issues in a new context" (n. 17). On July 13, 1985 Cardinal Jan Willebrands, in a letter to the co-chairs of ARCIC-II, recognized the existence of this new context and suggested that the doctrinal agreements reached between the two Churches should eventually remove what Leo XIII considered to be unacceptable in the "native character and spirit" of the Ordinal. This topic was taken up by the American dialogue between the Catholic Church and the Episcopal Church (ARC-USA), which issued its findings in 1994: *Anglican Orders: A Report on the Evolving Context of Their Evaluation in the Roman Catholic Church.*

The situation is still ambiguous. On the one hand, the ordination of women to the presbyterate and the episcopate in parts of the Anglican Communion has suggested that Anglicans may not exactly share the sacramental doctrine of the Orthodox and Roman Catholic Churches. In addition, the hypothesis has been raised that the condemnation of Anglican orders might belong in the undefined category of doctrines that could be infallible by virtue of being universally taught in the ordinary magisterium of the episcopal college. On the other hand, it is not without significance that on Jan. 6, 2001, as he closed the Great Jubilee of the new millennium, John Paul II made a sharp distinction between "the Anglican Communion and the Ecclesial Communities issued from the Reformation" (*Novo millennio ineunte*, 48).

Bibliography: G. DIX, *The Question of Anglican Orders* (London 1944). F. CLARK, *Anglican Orders and Defect of Intention* (London 1956); *Eucharistic Sacrifice and the Reformation* (Oxford 1967). J. J. HUGHES, *Absolutely Null and Utterly Void: An Account of the 1896 Papal Condemnation of Anglican Orders* (Washington 1968); *Stewards of the Lord: A Reappraisal of Anglican Orders* (London 1970). E. P. ECHLIN, *The Story of Anglican Ministry* (Slough 1974). C. F. SCHREINER, *The Christian Priesthood of the Anglican Communion and Apostolicae Curae* (Pelham Manor 1974). E. YARNOLD, *Anglican Orders: A Way Forward?* (London 1977). G. H. TAVARD, *A Review of Anglican Orders: The Problem and the Solution* (Collegeville, Minn. 1990). R. W. FRANKLIN, ed., *Anglican Orders: Essays on the Centenary of Apostolicae Curae, 1896–1996* (New York 1996). J. GROS et al., eds., *Common Witness to the Gospel: Documents on Anglican-Roman Catholic Relations, 1983–1995* (Washington 1997).

[G. TAVARD]

ANGLICAN/ROMAN CATHOLIC CONSULTATION IN THE UNITED STATES (ARC-USA)

The Anglican/Roman Catholic Consultation in the United States (ARC-USA) is the official dialogue on the national level seeking full communion between the Roman Catholic Church and the Episcopal Church. ARC-USA is jointly sponsored by and reports to the Bishops' Committee on Ecumenical and Interreligious Affairs (BCEIA) of the UNITED STATES CONFERENCE OF CATHOLIC BISHOPS (USCCB) and the Standing Commission on Ecumenical Relations (SCER) of the House of Bishops and the House of (Clerical and Lay) Deputies of the General Convention of the Episcopal Church. By March 2001, the consultation had met 51 times since its initial meeting in Washington, D.C. in June 1965. Meetings include periods of shared prayer, theological discussion, and reports.

During its first few years, the theological dialogue focused on the Eucharist and its liturgical celebration, the nature of doctrinal agreements, and practical and methodological considerations and produced several agreed statements: *Eucharist* (1967), *Progress and Practical Cooperation* (1969), *Doctrinal Agreement and Christian Unity: Methodological Considerations* (1972), *Agreed Statement on the Purpose of the Church* (1975), and *Where We Are: A Challenge for the Future* (1977), a 12-year report. When the General Convention of the Episcopal Church was expected to consider the question of the ordination of women in 1976, ARC-USA addressed this development and related theological topics with *Statement on the Ordination of Women* (1975) and *Images of God: Reflections on Christian Anthropology* (1983). Anticipating the 100th anniversary of Pope Leo XIII's apostolic letter on Anglican orders (*Apostolicae Curae*) and taking into account the considerable progress of the Anglican/Roman Catholic International Commission (ARCIC) on eucharist and ministry, ARC-USA produced *Anglican Orders: A Report on the Evolving Context for their Evaluation in the Roman Catholic Church* (1990). Faced with the need to reconsider certain aspects of the agreements already reached between Anglicans and Catholics by this national dialogue and ARCIC, ARC-USA issued: *A Recommitment to Full Communion* (1992), *How Can We Recognize "Substantial Agreement"?* (1993), and *Five Affirmations on the Eucharist as Sacrifice* (1994). ARC-USA also turned its attention to a topic on the ongoing agenda of ARCIC by issuing *Christian Ethics in the Ecumenical Dialogue: Anglican Roman Catholic International Commission II and Recent Papal* (1995). At the turn of the millennium ARC-USA was engaged in the study of ecclesiology with emphasis on the exercise of authority within the Church. The first step of this project was *Agreed Report on the Local/Universal Church* (1999). In the ''Introduction'' this report is described as ''a contribution to the healing of wounds and the sharing of gifts'' so that both churches will ''reach a more profound understanding of authority and will embody it more faithfully'' and ''will learn better how to learn from the other.''

Bibliography: J. W. WITMER and J. R. WRIGHT, eds., *Called to Full Unity* (USCCB Publication No. 937; Washington, D.C. 1986), includes ARC-USA's first 7 statements in chronological order. J. GROS, E. R. ELDER, and E. K. WONDRA, eds., *Common Witness to the Gospel* (USCCB Publication No. 5-060; Washington, D.C. 1997), includes ARC- USA's next 5 statements. ''An Agreed Report on the Local/Universal Church,'' *Origins, Catholic News Service Documentary Service* 30, 6 (June 22, 2000): 85–95. E. R. FALARDEAU, *ARC Soundings* (NADEO, 1990). *Receiving the Vision* (Collegeville, Minn. 1995). J. BORELLI, ''Renewal for Anglican-Roman Catholic Relations,'' *America* (Aug 26–Sept. 2, 2000): 12–15. G. H. TAVARD, ''The Work of ARC-USA: Reflections post-factum,'' *One in Christ* (1993) 247–59; ''Communion in a Time of Estrangement,'' *Ecumenical Trends* 22, 5 (May 1993) 1, 10–13. J. R. WRIGHT. ''The Reception of ARCIC I in the USA [by ARC-USA] Latest Developments,'' in *Communion et Reunion: Mélanges Jean Marie Roger Tillard*, ed. G. R. EVANS and M. GOURGUES (*Bibliotheca Ephemeridum Theologicarum Lovaniensium* 121; Leuven 1995) 217–230.

[J. BORELLI]

ANGLICAN/ROMAN CATHOLIC INTERNATIONAL COMMISSION (ARCIC)

On March 24, 1966, Archbishop Michael Ramsey of Canterbury and Pope Paul VI issued a *Common Declaration* in which they set forth their determination to inaugurate between the Anglican Communion and the Roman Catholic Church ''a serious dialogue which, founded on the Gospels and on the ancient common traditions, may lead to the unity in truth for which Christ prayed.'' Thus, building upon earlier conversations (1960) between Archbishop Geoffrey Fisher and Pope John XXIII, the foundations were laid upon which a new and extensive program of Anglican/Roman Catholic consultations would be built.

An Anglican/Roman Catholic Joint Preparatory Commission began to meet in January of 1967 and issued its ''Malta Report'' by January 1968. The report contained an extensive list of recommendations to the respective church authorities: preparation of a common declaration of the faith; the issuance of parallel statements on international, national, and local issues; regular joint meetings of bishops; and that a ''permanent'' international commission be set up to carry forward the work

begun in the preparatory phase. This was done, and in January of 1970 the Anglican/Roman Catholic International Commission (ARCIC) held its first session at Windsor, England. Its members, consultants, and secretaries were bishops, priests, and lay persons jointly appointed by the archbishop of Canterbury and the pope to promote and coordinate the restoration of complete communion in faith and sacramental life between the self-governing provinces (churches) constituting the Anglican Communion and the Roman Catholic Church. The chairmen were the Most Rev. Henry McAddo, Anglican archbishop of Dublin, and the Rt. Rev. Alan Clark, Catholic bishop of East Anglia. At its initial session ARCIC set as its task the exploration of agreement and disagreement in three areas: 1) the church and the eucharist, 2) the church and the ministry, and 3) the church and authority.

ARCIC continued to meet annually for a ten-day period of shared prayer and research issuing a statement (1971) and an elucidation (1979) on eucharistic doctrine, a statement (1973) and an elucidation (1979) on ministry and ordination, and two statements (1976 and 1981) and an elucidation (1981) on authority in the church. These were collected in a single volume and released by ARCIC under the title *The Final Report* (1981). Various joint commissions of Anglicans and Catholics around the world and individual church officials and scholars had offered their comments on different statements as they were released, one by one. Some comments were addressed in the three elucidations as ARCIC's work proceeded. Now with all seven items under one title, the work of ARCIC as a whole was assessed. The ''Introduction'' to *The Final Report* states that ''in producing these statements, we have been concerned, not to evade the difficulties, but rather to avoid the controversial language in which they have often been discussed.'' To stress the importance of the topics addressed in the report, the introduction concludes: ''Full visible communion between our two Churches cannot be achieved without mutual recognition of sacraments and ministry, together with the common acceptance of a universal primacy, at one with the episcopal college in the service of *koinonia* [communion].'' It concludes optimistically: ''There are high expectations that significant initiatives will be boldly undertaken to deepen our reconciliation and lead us forward in the quest for the full common to which we have been committed, in obedience to God, from the beginning of our dialogue.''

Various national Anglican/Roman Catholic dialogues, Catholic episcopal conferences, and member churches of the Anglican Communion responded to the report. The first church-wide response came in the form of a resolution from the Lambeth Conference (1988). The resolution had to do with whether or not the statements were consonant with Anglican faith and enabled further steps forward; it also referred to responses from the provinces. With regard to eucharist and ministry and ordination, the response was a clear "yes." On authority in the church, the resolution said that the two statements and elucidation gave "real grounds" for believing fuller agreement can be reached "especially on primacy, jurisdiction and infallibility, collegiality, and the role of the laity." Thus from a highly influential point of view in the Anglican Communion, the substantial agreement in the first two areas was seen as sufficient and agreement in the third area was viewed as a good step, but incomplete. ARCIC itself had recognized the speculative condition of some of its work on authority and stated that all differences have not been eliminated. *The Official Roman Catholic Response to the Final Report of ARCIC I* came three years later, in 1991. Produced in collaboration with the Congregation for the Doctrine of the Faith, it was issued by the Pontifical Council for Promoting Christian Unity (PCPCU). Although the response was laudatory of doctrinal convergence in *The Final Report*, it called for further clarifications on eucharist and ministry and ordination before substantial agreement could be recognized and additional work on certain aspects of authority in the church for complete agreement on some and even convergence on the others.

In the meantime, a second international commission (ARCIC-II) was appointed, as was announced in the *Common Declaration* (1982) of Archbishop Robert Runcie of Canterbury and Pope John Paul II. Although the second commission was chaired by two Englishmen, the Rt. Rev. Michael Santer, anglican bishop of Kensington (and later of Birmingham), and the Most Rev. Cormac Murphy-O'Connor, Catholic bishop of Arundel and Brighton (later, after his role on ARCIC-II, cardinal and archbishop of Westminister), an effort was made to form a slightly larger commission with wider geographical representation. ARCIC-II issued statements on the doctrine of justification (*Salvation and the Church*, 1987), the meaning of ecclesial communion (*Church as Communion*, 1991), and moral teaching (*Life in Christ: Morals, Communion, and the Church*, 1994).

In 1993, ARCIC-II issued a list of clarifications answering the queries raised in the 1991 response of the Catholic Church to *The Final Report*. With regard to eucharist, the clarifications addressed: the link of the eucharistic memorial with the once-for-all sacrifice of Calvary, which it makes sacramentally present; the propitiatory nature of the eucharist sacrifice, which can be applied also to the deceased; Christ's substantial and sacramental presence in the eucharistic species of bread and wine; and adoration of Christ in the reserved sacrament. With regard to ministry and ordination, the clarifications also ad-

dressed four points: only a validly ordained priest, acting in the person of Christ, can be the minister of the eucharist; the institution of the sacrament of orders, conferring the priesthood, comes from Christ and orders are not a simple ecclesiastical institution; the character of priestly ordination implying configuration to the priesthood of Christ; and apostolic succession in which the unbroken lines of episcopal succession and apostolic teaching stand in causal relationship to each other. In 1994, Cardinal Edward Cassidy (PCPCU President), replying to ARCIC-II's chairmen, wrote that "the said clarifications have indeed thrown new light on the questions concerning eucharist and ministry" in the report and "the agreement reached on eucharist and ministry by ARCIC-I is thus greatly strengthened and no further study would seem to be required at this stage."

The Final Report noted in its elucidation (1979) rapid developments leading to the ordination of women and offered "that the principles upon which its doctrinal agreement rests are not affected by such ordinations; for it [ARCIC] was concerned with the origin and nature of the ordained ministry and not with the question who can and cannot be ordained." *A Common Declaration* (1989) by Archbishop Runcie and Pope John Paul II recognized that "the admission of women to the ministerial priesthood in some provinces of the Anglican Communion prevents reconciliation between us even where there is otherwise progress towards agreement in faith on the meaning of the eucharist and the ordained ministry." The Lambeth resolution (1988) mentioned the ordination of women in two places: among the issues, acknowledged with assurance, that ARCIC-II would explore "within an understanding of the church as communion" and imposing serious responsibility on Anglican bishops "to weigh the possible implications of action on this matter for the unity of the Anglican Communion and for the universal Church." A paragraph in the Catholic Church's response (1991) stated that in the view of the Catholic Church "the question of the subject of ordination is linked with the nature of the sacrament of holy orders." Then in its clarifications (1993) ARCIC-II stated that the issue of who can or cannot be ordained "involves far more than the question of ministry" and "raises profound questions of ecclesiology and authority in relation to tradition."

ARCIC-II has also issued *The Gift of Authority* (1999), also known as "Authority in the Church-III" because the report already had two statements on authority. Because a major Anglican study on the exercise of authority and the structures of communion (*The Virginia Report*, 1998) was being prepared for the Lambeth Conference (1998), ARCIC-II waited for its completion and presentation to Lambeth before releasing its statement on authority. *The Gift of Authority* seeks to restate the consensus thus far and to come to consensus on the remaining issues on the exercise of authority. It suggests it has made advances on 11 points of doctrinal agreement, calls attention to significant developments in both communions, names issues facing Anglicans and those facing Catholics, and recommends "that Anglicans be open to and desire a recovery and re-reception under certain conditions of the exercise of universal primacy by the Bishop of Rome" and "that Roman Catholics be open to and desire a re-reception of the exercise of primacy by the bishop of Rome and the offering of such a ministry to the whole Church of God."

Lambeth (1998) recommended ARCIC-II's statements of 1987, 1991, and 1994, and the one to appear later (*GA*, 1999) for referral "to the provinces for study and response." Already in a *Common Declaration* (1996), Pope John Paul II and Archbishop George Carey of Canterbury affirmed "the signs of progress provided in the statements of ARCIC-I on the eucharist and on the understanding of ministry and ordination, which have received an authoritative response from both partners of the dialogue." They declared that the statements of ARCIC-II "require analysis, reflection, and response," and then they referred to "a new situation" caused by the ordination of women as an "obstacle to reconciliation." In view of all these developments over the past 25 years, they suggested that "it may be opportune at this stage in our journey to consult further about how the relationship between the Anglican Communion and the Catholic Church is to progress." This started a process of church-wide consultation within both communions leading to a special international meeting of Anglican and Roman Catholic bishops (2000), chaired by Archbishop Carey and Cardinal Cassidy, which produced *Communion in Mission* and an action plan. It asserts that communion between Anglicans and Catholics "is no longer to be viewed in minimal terms," "is even now a rich and life-giving, multifaceted communion," is "closer to the goal of full visible communion than we first dared to believe," and that "a sense of mutual interdependence in the Body of Christ has been reached, in which the churches of the Anglican Communion and the Roman Catholic Church are able to bring shared gifts to their joint mission in the world." The plan called for a new high-level working group to "monitor the reception of ARCIC agreements." Appointment of the Anglican–Roman Catholic Working Group was announced in January of 2001 with a first meeting expected to take place late in the same year.

For a new topic, the 1999 meeting included "preliminary discussion of the ecumenical problems surrounding the Virgin Mary," and the 2000 and 2001 meetings referred to the topic as "Mary in the life and doctrine of the Church."

Bibliography: J. W. WITMER and J. R. WRIGHT, eds., *Called to Full Unity* (USCCB Publication No. 937; Washington, D.C. 1986), includes documents related to ARCIC up through 1983. J. GROS, E. R. ELDER, and E. K. WONDRA, eds., *Common Witness to the Gospel*, (USCCB Publication No. 5-060; Washington, D.C. 1997), includes documents up through 1995. *The Gift of Authority* (New York 1999). All ARCIC documents have appeared in the PCPCU's *Information Service* as well as meeting reports and most documents in *Origins*. C. HILL and E. J. YARNOLD, S. J., eds., *Anglicans and Roman Catholics: The Search for Unity* (London 1994). W. PURDY, *The Search for Unity* (London 1995). M. RICHARDS, "Twenty-five Years of Anglican-Roman Catholic Dialogue—Where Do We Go from Here?" *One in Christ* 18 (1992): 126–35.

[J. BORELLI]

ANGLICANISM

This entry surveys the origin, establishment, and history of the Church of England.

Origins. The Church of England was established and given its powers by the English crown in Parliament in 1559. The first Parliament of Queen Elizabeth I during the Easter of that year promulgated two acts concerning religion: by the Act of Supremacy the Queen was declared to be "the only supreme governor of this realm . . . as well in all spiritual or ecclesiastical things or causes, as temporal," and the authority of the pope was wholly repudiated; by the Act of Uniformity, though all the bishops in the House of Lords voted against it, the BOOK OF COMMON PRAYER was made the sole service book to be used in all English churches on and after the forthcoming feast day of St. John the Baptist. All existing service books, missals, pontificals, and the like, were henceforth forbidden to be used. Any priest, for example, who said Mass in England was to lose his income for one year and go to prison for six months. A second conviction was to bring one year's imprisonment and loss of his benefice and clerical dignities. A third conviction was to bring life imprisonment. An act passed later in Elizabeth's reign ordered all priests to leave the country within 40 days under pain of death for high treason.

The movement toward the establishment of a state church in England had been begun by Henry VIII, the father of Elizabeth I. It had been continued during the reign of his youthful successor, Edward VI, when Thomas CRANMER, Archbishop of CANTERBURY, had produced his first edition of the Book of Common Prayer in 1549. This book contained an outline of the Mass service in English with Communion under both kinds. In 1552 Cranmer's second edition, showing the significant influence of Continental Protestants. It was thoroughly Protestant in word and attitude. After Edward VI's death in 1553, his sister, Queen Mary, restored Catholicism; but her

Bishop Misaeri Kauma (left), Bishop Festo Kivengere (center left), Archbishop of Canterbury Robert Runcie (center right), Reverend John Wilson (right). (Archive Photos)

death and the accession of her sister, Elizabeth, repudiated that whole process. Elizabeth herself, or her ministers, wished to impose the first Book of Common Prayer as the standard text for all church services. Parliament, however, was dominated by a group of erstwhile Marian exiles and their sympathizers who were pressing hard to impose Calvinistic views on the English Church. The upshot was a compromise on the second Book of Common Prayer. This was further than Elizabeth's government had wished to go, but it was not Protestant enough for the agitators in Parliament. This Elizabethan settlement of religion, therefore, had no body of supporters for at least a generation, until those who had been brought up under its aegis gradually worked out its defense. Among the most notable of these was Richard HOOKER.

A series of THIRTY-NINE ARTICLES of religion, similar to those of Cranmer in Edward VI's reign, were promulgated in 1563. These articles, while not a complete statement of Anglican belief, have remained authoritative to such an extent that all ordinands were henceforward required to subscribe to them and likewise all OXFORD and Cambridge graduates until 1871. The articles contained many fundamental Christian teachings, an assertion of Elizabeth's power in Church and State, a

statement that general councils of the Church were not necessarily infallible, a recognition of only two Sacraments, namely, Baptism and the Lord's Supper, and a declaration that what Catholics believed about the Mass was "a blasphemous fable and dangerous deceit." This last assertion was included in the 1571 edition of the Thirty-Nine Articles when it was clear that there could be no hope of reconciling convinced Catholics to the Elizabethan settlement of religion after the pope's excommunication of the queen (*Regnans in Excelsis*) and his order to her subjects (1570) to cease to obey her government. This decree encouraged on the one hand a more thorough persecution of Catholics on the ground that they must be traitors, and on the other, renewed efforts of many Catholics to overthrow Elizabeth's government; a few preferred exile. In contrast, the PURITANS, as the more extreme Protestants of Elizabeth's reign were called, sought to overthrow the compromise in favor of PRESBYTERIANISM. While the government steadily opposed both Catholic and Puritan efforts to change the religious settlement, it did little or nothing to help the archbishop of Canterbury to foster Anglicanism. A major problem was to find Anglican preachers; another was to ensure uniformity of ritual. Puritanism, however, continued to grow both in numbers and in political influence by uniting itself with the increasing numbers of opponents to royal policy in the Elizabethan and Stuart Parliaments.

Historical Development. In 1604 the Hampton Court Conference set up by King James I emphasized the irreconcilability of Anglicanism and Puritanism. Meanwhile, a number of vigorous and intellectually gifted churchmen, generally known as the Caroline divines, among them Lancelot ANDREWES, Bishop of Winchester, and William LAUD, Archbishop of Canterbury, were giving an example of churchmanship that would have more than ensured Anglicanism's supremacy over Puritanism if the monarchy had not become financially dependent on Parliament. The political consequences of the Civil War and the events culminating in the REVOLUTION OF 1688 made it clear that Puritanism, once divested of its political supporters, could not supplant Anglicanism as the established religion; that uniformity of religious belief and practice could not be enforced by the State; and that, as a consequence, England must accept the presence of numerous religious sects. As a result of the refusal of many Anglicans to recognize the supersession of the Stuart dynasty by the Hanoverian, and partly because of the close, political control exercised by the Whigs over Anglican prelates, the Established Church came, in the 18th century, to take on the appearance of a major department of state. One important group in the Church adopted a religious outlook known as LATITUDINARIANISM. This group endeavored so to ally itself with what were thought to be the requirements of scientific thought as to accept beliefs that to many seemed non-Christian.

The general decline of the spiritual health of Anglicanism in the 18th century was partly halted by the rise of EVANGELICALISM. This movement stressed the importance of personal religion and paid little heed to ritualism and church organization. Its greatest exponents were John WESLEY and George WHITEFIELD. Evangelicalism became a great influence for social reform, and one of its achievements was the abolition of slavery throughout the British Empire in the first half of the 19th century. One group of Evangelicals, however, left the Church of England and formed the various sects of Methodism that became a powerful religious and social force in the industrial areas of 19th-century England to which the Church of England was slow to penetrate.

Benthamism, which exerted so much power over the political, legal, and social life of England, was not without effect on the religious life of the nation. This was seen in the demands for reform of the financial structure of the Established Church and, chiefly, for the reduction of the immense incomes of prelates and an increase in the small stipends of the lower clergy. There was also much dissat-

isfaction with the notorious pluralism and nepotism. In 1827, for example, three-fifths of all Anglican incumbents were nonresident.

Tractarians. Contemporary with this reforming spirit appeared the ANGLO-CATHOLICS, a group that sprang from the TRACTARIAN movement led by John KEBLE, John Henry NEWMAN, and Edward PUSEY. These Tractarians, affected by the Romanticism of the time, with its idealization of the Gothic ages, took a growing interest in the Catholic, as distinguished from the Evangelical or Protestant, view of Anglicanism. That is, they stressed the Anglican links with the medieval Church in belief, ritual, and organization. Their ideas were spread in a long series of tracts published in the face of mounting opposition from Anglican Church leaders, who forbade the continuance of the tracts. One effect of this opposition was to cause many of the Tractarians, led by John Henry Newman, to enter the Catholic Church. The increasing campaign of the Anglican bishops against the ritualism of these HIGH CHURCH clergy, as the Tractarians were called, culminated in the passage by Parliament with the encouragement of Archbishop Archibald Tait of Canterbury, of the Public Worship Regulation Act of 1874, whereby those Anglican clergymen who in their services diverged too far from the prescriptions of the Book of Common Prayer could be more easily punished in the ecclesiastical courts. The High Church continued, however, its slow growth; and it now represents a major grouping in the Church of England, though the crown has shown a steady reluctance to advance its adherents to the episcopate. The other major group in the modern Church consists in the successors to the Evangelicals, the LOW CHURCH group, whose outlook has not changed much in the last century, though some of them have continued the Latitudinarian ideas of a past age and have become known as BROAD CHURCH group.

The Anglican Church has always taken pride in its comprehensiveness and has sought to make little inquiry into the beliefs of its members as long as they were prepared to worship publicly in the forms prescribed by the Book of Common Prayer. However, the growth of unauthorized ritualistic practices and the desire to reform the Prayer Book led to the production of a new Book after 20 years of effort and with the authority of the bishops. Parliament, however, rejected it in 1927. A somewhat revised Book was submitted to Parliament in the following year and again vetoed. Much chagrined by its evident subjection to Parliament, many members of the Church of England make use of the 1928 Book.

Two 19th-century events had important consequences for the Church of England. In 1853 John William Colenso became the first bishop of the See of Natal. Biblical studies in which he denied traditional Christian doctrines concerning hell, the Sacraments, and the Pentateuch appeared under his name; and he was, in consequence, deposed by his metropolitan, Robert Gray of Capetown. Colenso repudiated Capetown's jurisdiction and appealed to the Judicial Committee of the Privy Council in England, which declared in his favor. Though his metropolitan consecrated another bishop of Natal, Colenso refused to yield and by means of the civil courts kept possession of his cathedral and his episcopal income. Backed by members of his diocese, Colenso never gave way and the schism continued long after his death, despite the efforts of successive archbishops of Canterbury to end it.

As a result of the publication in 1860 of *Essays and Reviews*, advocating freedom of inquiry into religious beliefs, two of the seven authors were officially condemned by the archbishop and bishops of the Province of Canterbury. However, the two defendants had the judgment quashed by the Judicial Committee of the Privy Council. The opposition to the book was so strong, nevertheless, that 11,000 clergymen of the Church of England joined in a declaration of their belief in the divine inspiration of the Bible and in the existence of hell. As a result of these events in the English Church, a synod of the Anglican Church in Canada in 1865 appealed for the holding of a general council of the Anglican Churches to issue an official statement of belief. Though agreement on such a statement proved impossible, such a council did meet at Lambeth Palace, the official home in London of the archbishop of Canterbury, under the archbishop's presidency. Similar meetings have been held at more or less 10-year intervals ever since. At the first LAMBETH CONFERENCE in 1867, there were 76 bishops present; in 1908, there were 242; in 1920 there were 252; and in 1958 there were 310 bishops in attendance. The conferences have no executive authority and their resolutions have no binding force on Anglicans, but they enjoy great moral prestige and are obvious expressions of some contemporary Anglican thought and teaching.

Anglican Doctrine. In 1888 a series of four propositions, originally adopted at a general convention of the Protestant Episcopal Church in Chicago in 1886, were promulgated by the Lambeth Conference of that year as a statement of basic Anglican beliefs. These propositions subsequently known as the LAMBETH QUADRILATERAL, represented an official declaration of fundamental Anglicanism. They were as follows: The Holy Scriptures of the Old and New Testaments contain all things necessary to salvation and are the rule and ultimate standard of faith. The Apostles' Creed and the Nicene Creed are a sufficient statement of the Christian faith. The two Sacraments ordained by Christ Himself, namely, Baptism and

the Supper of the Lord, ministered with unfailing use of Christ's words of institution and of the elements ordained by Him are a necessary part of the Christian life. The historic episcopate, locally adapted in the methods of its administration to the varying needs of the nations and peoples called of God into the unity of His church, is also a necessary part of Christian life.

This Lambeth Quadrilateral was issued primarily to provide a basis for discussion on reunion with the other Protestant Churches of England and elsewhere. In 1897 it was again declared to represent the mind of the Anglican Communion and to it was added the statement: "we believe that we have been Providentially entrusted with our part of the Catholic and Apostolic inheritance bequeathed by our Lord."

This Quadrilateral together with the report of the Archbishops' (of Canterbury and York) Committee on Doctrine in the Church of England, published in 1938, represent two major statements of Anglican belief in modern times.

The fact of establishment has come to mean less and less in the effective religious life of England. The sovereign, who must be a member of the Church of England and must swear at the coronation ceremony to uphold it, receives the title of DEFENDER OF THE FAITH, originally bestowed on Henry VIII by the pope but assumed by subsequent monarchs by parliamentary grant. The archbishop of Canterbury has the right of anointing and crowning the monarch. All diocesan bishops are appointed by the sovereign on the advice of the prime minister and all clergy take an oath of allegiance to the monarch. The bishops take precedence over the peerage and the 24 senior bishops and the two archbishops have a right to a seat in the House of Lords. (Anglican clergymen and Catholic priests are legally disqualified from sitting in the House of Commons.)

To many Anglicans the advantages of establishment are outweighed by the benefits that would follow a complete break with the State and it is likely that support for disestablishment will continue to grow. Many Anglicans regard their Church as continuing the ancient Catholic Church of England, differing only in a substitution of State authority for papal authority since the 16th century.

Ecclesiastical Organization. The Church of England is organized into 2 provinces, Canterbury and York, and their suffragan dioceses. Authority in matters of belief and practice is exercised, under the supreme jurisdiction of Parliament, by the Convocations of Canterbury and York. A convocation comprises the archbishop, an upper house of bishops, and a lower house of representatives of each cathedral chapter, archdeacons, and elected clergy. There is also the Church Assembly established in 1919 at the request of the two Convocations and composed of three houses of bishops, clergy, and laity to propose ecclesiastical legislation for parliamentary approval. The Church Assembly has a general supervisory authority over the bodies dealing with the Church's work in education, the training of ministers and general Church work in England and abroad. The costs and expenses are shared between the Church and the State.

The Church of England has a system of ecclesiastical courts chiefly concerned with maintaining discipline among its clergy. Until the second half of the 19th century, the Church so dominated the ancient Oxford and Cambridge Universities that they were, in effect, Anglican seminaries. This atmosphere has gone and only certain professorships are still reserved to Anglican clerics.

Anglican Societies. In 1698 a group of Anglicans set up The SOCIETY FOR PROMOTING CHRISTIAN KNOWLEDGE, which has worked with much success to promote education and missionary work. It built many Church primary schools and teachers' training colleges both in England and in missionary lands. It is also widely known for its extensive publishing of religious literature. While the SOCIETY FOR THE PROPAGATION OF THE GOSPEL was to share its work abroad, the National Society for the Education of the Poor in the Principles of the Established Church, founded in 1811, was a chief agent in the provision of primary schools in England and Wales before the State began its own national program in 1870. They received government grants from 1833 onward. The National Society also set up training colleges for teachers. After 1870 these Church schools remained independent, but they received State aid after 1902. As a consequence of the Act of 1944, the schools came increasingly under local government control though the teaching of Anglicanism was not interfered with.

The year 1701 saw the foundation of the Society for the Propagation of the Gospel in Foreign Parts. This Anglican organization sought not only to evangelize native peoples but also to minister to British people living abroad.

Bibliography: H. H. HENSON, *The Church of England* (Cambridge 1939). C. F. GARBETT, *Church and State in England* (London 1950). P. E. MORE and F. L. CROSS, eds. *Anglicanism* (Milwaukee 1935). S. NEILL, *Anglicanism* (New York 1977). A. M. STEPHENSON, *Anglicanism and the Lambeth Conferences* (London 1978). G. ROWELL, *The Vision Glorious: Themes and Personalities of the Catholic revival in Anglicanism* (Oxford 1983). J. WHALE, *The Anglican Church Today: The Future of Anglicanism* (London 1988). J. DAVIES, *The Caroline Captivity of the Church: Charles I and the Remoulding of Anglicanism, 1625–1641* (Oxford 1992). W.L. SACHS, *The Transformation of Anglicanism: From State Church to Global Communion* (Cambridge 1993). A.E. MCGRATH, *The Renewal of Anglicanism* (Harrisburg, Pa. 1993). V. STRUDWICK, *Is the Anglican Church Catholic?: The Catholicity of Anglicanism* (London 1994). G. ROWELL, *The English Religious Tradition and the Genius of Anglicanism* (Nashville, Tenn. 1992). S. R. WHITE, *Authority and Anglicanism* (London 1996). S. SYKES and J. E. BOOTY, eds., *The Study of Anglicanism* (London 1998). A. WINGATE, *Anglicanism: A Global Communion* (London 1998). I. T. DOUGLAS and P. L. KWOK, *Beyond Colonial Anglicanism: The Anglican Communion in the Twenty-first Century* (New York 2001). D.W. HARDY, *Finding the Church: The Dynamic Truth of Anglicanism* (London 2001).

[E. MCDERMOTT/EDS.]

ANGLO-CATHOLICS

Since the OXFORD MOVEMENT, this term has been commonly used to designate the Catholic wing of the HIGH CHURCH Movement within the Anglican Communion. Somewhat ambiguously, the term's use covers two movements within modern ANGLICANISM that, although evidently related, do not always coincide: the revival of Catholic dogmatic, sacramental and liturgical tenets, and the Ritualist movement. The outstanding figures in the Oxford Movement were not liturgical innovators but faithful adherents of the prescriptions of the BOOK OF COMMON PRAYER interpreted according to what was perceived as the Catholicism of pre-Reformation England. In this regard, the 19th century Anglo-Catholics were in the forefront to revive the pre-Reformation SARUM USE as a genuine liturgical rite of pre-Reformation Catholic England.

In its origins, the Ritualist movement was the natural outgrowth of TRACTARIANISM. It was inevitable that the revival within the Church of England of Catholic doctrines concerning the Sacraments and public worship should result in a desire to express these beliefs outwardly through appropriate religious symbolism. This natural consequence was reinforced in the years immediately following the Oxford Movement by a growing appreciation of aesthetic values in England, a movement that, although not religious in its origins, led to a reaction against the Puritanism that characterized contemporary liturgical practice.

Doctrinal Positions and Ritualist Practices. The basic doctrinal commitment of the Oxford Movement to the principle of apostolic succession, besides constituting a protest against the protestantizing of the Church of England and the inroads of religious LIBERALISM, was also, at least implicitly, an assertion of the Church's freedom from unwarranted interference by the state. As such, it encountered many challenges during the years immediately after the Oxford Movement. In 1850, in the Gorham case, the Privy Council decided in favor of a clergyman, whose views on Baptism had been found unorthodox by his bishop, and permitted him to teach that the doctrine of baptismal regeneration was an open question. In 1853 the Privy Council passed judgment on the Eucharist, sustaining the acquittal by the Court of Arches of Archdeacon George Denison of Taunton, who had denied the doctrine of the Real Presence.

In addition to such opposition to the doctrinal positions of Anglo-Catholicism, its Ritualist practices also came under fire. The ornaments rubric of the 1559 Book of Common Prayer was sufficiently ambiguous to permit the Anglo-Catholic clergy to introduce the use of Eucharistic vestments. After unsuccessful efforts to get the rubric changed, Abp. Archibald Tait obtained the passage of the Public Worship Regulation Act (1874), which was subsequently made more drastic by the amendments of Lord Anthony Shaftesbury. Four clergymen were imprisoned for contumacious violation of this act. The practice of confession by the Anglo-Catholic clergy also aroused bitter opposition. In this case, however, the practice had the explicit sanction of the Prayer Book, so that its opponents were forced to press for revision of the formula of absolution in the Visitation of the Sick.

By the mid-20th century, most of the practices for which the Anglo-Catholics suffered in the 19th century were taken as a matter of course, and the major concern of their spiritual descendants arose from the desire of Protestant elements within the Church of England to unite with Nonconformist bodies. The 1955 Convocations of Canterbury and York, concerned with relations between the Church of South India and the Church of England, produced a crisis of conscience for some Anglo-Catholics who believed that the Anglican episcopate, in declaring the orders of the new church to be equivalent to its own, had defined the intention of the Anglican ordination rite in a clearly heretical sense. Further crisis of conscience arose in the latter part of the 20th century, when the U.S. Episcopal Church, followed by most of the members of the Anglican Communion, including the Church of England, began to ordain women. Many Anglo-Catholics, while not rejecting in principle the possibility of women ordination, felt that it was not a decision that could be taken by the Anglo-Catholic unilaterally. Rather, if there were to be any change, it had to be made at the level of an ecumenical council promulgating a common position for all churches professing to be part of the ancient catholic, apostolic, faith. As a result of this, as well as other disappointments with what was being perceived as doctrinal and theological liberalism within Anglicanism, many Anglo-Catholics left Anglicanism to embrace Roman Catholicism, Old Catholicism and Byzantine Orthodoxy. Others have chosen to remain to work for change within the Anglican Communion. In the Church of England, a system of episcopal visitors (affectionately known as ''flying bishops'') was put in place

in the 1990s for those Anglo-Catholics who could not, in good conscience, accept the decision of their local bishops to participate in women ordination.

On a different issue, the Ritualist movement within the Church of England has recently been affected by currents of liturgical change brought about by the Second Vatican Council. The effort to be more Roman than the Romans, which has sometimes led Anglo-Catholics to adopt liturgical practices deplored by Catholic liturgists, has become rather pointless in the light of the constitution on the liturgy enacted by VATICAN COUNCIL II. While some Anglo-Catholics chose to ally themselves with Catholic traditionalists fighting against the liturgical renewal of Vatican II, other Anglo-Catholics have adopted the principles of liturgical reform of Vatican II.

Bibliography: G. E. DEMILLE, *The Catholic Movement in the American Episcopal Church* (Philadelphia 1941). W. L. KNOX, *The Catholic Movement in the Church of England* (New York 1924). W. J. S. SIMPSON, *The History of the Anglo-Catholic Revival from 1845* (London 1932). G. ROWELL, *The Vision Glorious: Themes and Personalities of the Catholic Revival in Anglicanism* (Oxford 1983). C.G. BUCHANAN, *Anglo-Catholic Worship: An Evangelical Appreciation after 150 Years* (Bramcote, Eng 1983). V. STRUDWICK, *Is the Anglican Church Catholic?: The Catholicity of Anglicanism* (London 1994). F. PENHALE, *The Anglican Church Today: Catholics in Crisis* (London 1986). G. ROWELL, ed., *Tradition Renewed: the Oxford Movement Conference Papers* (Allison Park, Pa. 1986). W. S. F. PICKERING, *Anglo-Catholicism: A Study in Religious Ambiguity* (London 1989). J. JEFFREY, *Living Tradition: Affirming Catholicism in the Anglican Church* (Cambridge, Mass. 1992). J. JEFFREY, *Living the Mystery: Affirming Catholicism and the Future of Anglicanism* (London 1992). P. B. NOCKLES, *The Oxford Movement in Context: Anglican High Churchmanship, 1760–1857* (Cambridge, England 1994). J. S. REED, *Glorious Battle: The Cultural Politics of Victorian Anglo-Catholicism* (Nashville, Tenn. 1996).

[S. BROWN/EDS.]

ANGLO-SAXON ART

Anglo-Saxon art embraces both the pre-Christian idiom of Scandinavian and Germanic provenance, and, following the conversion of the British Isles, its Christian transformation. The Christian Anglo-Saxon style in turn pervaded Continental Europe by way of Irish and Anglo-Saxon missionary foundations, to enrich Carolingian art and constitute an essential element in the development of Romanesque and subsequent medieval art.

Pagan Period. Pagan Anglo-Saxon art (fifth-seventh centuries) is seen in the decoration of arms, jewelry, pottery, and other small personal belongings or home decorations. There is nothing monumental, no large sculpture or painting. The metalwork, however, is often of great splendor, fashioned in gold, silver, or gilt, and boldly jeweled with garnets, colored glass, and shell. Where the cloisonné technique was used, Anglo-Saxon jewelers attained a skill unsurpassed in the pagan Germanic world and made dexterous use of filigree and niello. Metalworkers of the pagan period produced accurate enameling in the Celtic style deriving from Celtic influences that preceded or existed along with Saxon conquests.

The first Germanic invasions brought "chip-carving" metalwork preserving vestiges of foliate scrolls and animals that are Roman and naturalistic in origin, but the favorite Anglo-Saxon animal styles reject naturalism and adopt instead a tightly jumbled pattern of separate heads, limbs, and bodies, covering the surface without background space (Style I), or a sinuous openwork treatment of an entire animal twisting itself into S's and loose knots (Ribbon Style). Occasionally the two styles are found in a single object, such as the rim of a seventh-century drinking horn from Taplow, Buckinghamshire (British Museum), but in general Style I, the earlier of the two, is characteristic of the fifth and sixth centuries. The fine polychrome jewelry with Ribbon Style animals dates from the seventh century, and the most spectacular examples are to be seen among the treasure of an East Anglian king, found in a ship burial in 1939 at Sutton Hoo, near Woodbridge, Suffolk (British Museum).

Christian Period. The Anglo-Saxon conversion began with the arrival of St. Augustine at Kent (597), survived difficulties with the Irish at the Synod of Whitby (664), and after 669 found reorganization through a number of remarkable men, such as Theodore of Tarsus and BENEDICT BISCOP. The period yields illuminated manuscripts and sculpture in stone, besides fine metalwork, such as the golden "Alfred Jewel," that displays an enameled portrait under crystal (Ashmolean Museum, Oxford). The earliest manuscript painting, from late seventh-century Northumbria, decorates the Book of DURROW (Trinity College, Dublin); its style is hard and metallic, and embodies millefiori panels, Ribbon Style animals, and Celtic spiral scrolls. On the other hand, the Codex Amiatinus (Laurentian Library, Florence), a Northumbrian work of c. 700, includes paintings of the Evangelists done in a naturalistic Italian manner. The Lindisfarne Gospels (British Museum), also c. 700, is illustrated with Evangelist portraits of Italian origin (changed in a hard, insular way) and magnificent full pages of minutely intricate, carpetlike abstract ornament of Celtic and Saxon origin. The eighth- and ninth-century manuscripts of the Canterbury School, though under Carolingian influence, are also of insular design imitating enameled or engraved metalwork.

In the early tenth century, Carolingian art of Byzantine origin is reflected in figures of Prophets and saints on the embroidered stole and maniple given to the shrine of St. Cuthbert by King Athelstan (Durham Cathedral Library). Under the Benedictines brought to Winchester by Bishop Aethelwold (963–984), a new style of illumination evolved with the introduction of the Carolingian minuscule. The Winchester school made figure drawings in Continental classical form, sometimes in the light, impressionistic style of the School of Rheims, but sometimes in more substantial form. They appeared on daringly colored decorative pages with lavish scrollwork frames, figure and frame composing a single openwork design.

Anglo-Saxon sculpture has few works of merit, and the appeal of the stone crosses in churchyards and carvings in early churches lies chiefly in their settings. The Ruthwell cross in Dumfrieshire of c. 700 is heavily carved with figures and displays a pretty, inhabited scroll; the Bewcastle cross in Cumberland has these same features, treated in a harder, insular manner and combined with a checker pattern and interlacings. There are many crosses in Northumbria, some later ones showing Viking influence, although the best known cross with Scandinavian elements is the round shaft at Gosforth, Cumberland, on which both Christian and pagan figure subjects appear. In the south there are some 20 carvings of the late Saxon period, with figure sculpture in the Winchester style. The "Harrowing of Hell" panel in Bristol Cathedral and the angels at Bradford-on-Avon, Wiltshire, are the best known of these.

See Also: CAROLINGIAN ART; MANUSCRIPT ILLUMINATION.

Bibliography: G. B. BROWN, *The Arts in Early England*, 6 v. in 7 (London 1903–37). T. KENDRICK, *Anglo-Saxon Art to A. D. 900* (London 1938); *Late Saxon and Viking Art* (London 1949). D. T. RICE, *English Art, 871–1100* (Oxford 1952). F. WORMALD, *English Drawings of the Tenth and Eleventh Centuries* (New York 1953). D. M. WILSON, *The Anglo-Saxons* (New York 1960). T. KENDRICK et al., eds., *Codex Lindisfarnensis*, 2 v. (Lausanne 1956–60). R. L. S. BRUCE-MITFORD, *Encyclopedia of World Art* (New York 1959–) 1:446–463.

[T. KENDRICK]

ANGLO-SAXONS

Christianity came to Britain about A.D. 200. Britain was an ordinary part of the Church, organized on diocesan lines; it sent three bishops to the Council of Arles in 314, from London, York, and probably Lincoln. Between the middle of the fifth and the end of the sixth century, Christianity in eastern and southern England was almost completely wiped out by the invasion of the heathen Angles and Saxons. The remnant of British Christianity, centering in Devon and Cornwall, Wales, and Strathclyde, remained in isolation after Augustine of Canterbury failed to establish communication with them.

In A.D. 597 the Roman mission sent by Pope GREGORY I and led by Augustine landed in Kent where it began the conversion of the English and the organization of the English Church according to the directions sent by the Pope in 601. The growth of the English mission is the story of the conversion of one heathen people after another and the establishment of dioceses for them. The earliest of these dioceses were Canterbury, London, Rochester, and York. The mission to York, under Paulinus, collapsed with the defeat of King Edwin at Hatfield in 632, but the work was begun again within a few years by Irish monks who came from Iona to LINDISFARNE on the coast of Northumbria. At the Synod of WHITBY in 663, King Oswiu settled in favor of Rome the conflict between the Irish and Roman missions over the date of Easter and certain ecclesiastical customs. In May of 669 Theodore of Tarsus, a Greek monk consecrated in Rome for the vacant see, arrived at Canterbury. Between then and his death in 690 he established dioceses, appointed bishops, held councils, founded monasteries for both men and women, and greatly fostered learning and culture.

Theodore began a quarrel with Wilfrid, Bishop of York, that lasted for many years, over the erection of new sees in Northumbria. However, Gregory, Theodore's successor, virtually completed his own plan with the appointment of the twelfth suffragan bishop of Canterbury. Although the projected 12 suffragans for York never materialized, the work begun by Augustine came to a successful conclusion in 735 with the conferral of the pallium on Egbert, Archbishop of York.

Monasticism had been a strong element in the Anglo-Saxon Church from the beginning. Canterbury, Glastonbury, Malmesbury, Melrose, Lindisfarne, Monkwearmouth, Jarrow, and the nunneries at Whitby, Ely, and Barking were but a few of the foundations. Augustine and his companions and Theodore and his companion, Hadrian, were monks; Aidan, Colman, Fursey, and countless others were Irish monks; SS. Cedd and Chad, brothers educated by Aidan at Lindisfarne, as well as Cuthbert, Ceolfrith, Benedict Biscop, and Bede, shed luster on Northumbria. No less famous were the Abbesses Hilda at Whitby, Ethelburga at Barking, and Etheldreda at Ely.

The monasteries provided a refuge where the holiness could grow what once made England an island of saints, but they did more. They spread civilization and learning, gathered books, provided schools, and produced literary works in both Latin and the vernacular. Though

---

Capital: Luanda.
Size: 481,351 sq. miles.
Population: 10,145,267 in 2000.
Languages: Portuguese; Bantu and other tribal languages are spoken in various regions.
Religions: 5,147,400 Catholics (51%), 1,531,785 Protestants (15%), 3,384,793 practice indigenous beliefs (33%), 81,289 without religious affiliation.

---

none of the monks reached the greatness of BEDE, who rose to a true conception of history and preserved much of what is known of early England, Aldhelm of Malmesbury, a great teacher and writer, could claim at the beginning of the eighth century that it was no longer necessary to go to Ireland to get an education.

Art flourished along with letters, especially in Northumbria, and in the eighth century, Anglo-Saxon monks, missionaries, and teachers went to the Continent in the footsteps of the Irish to advance the cause of religion and learning. The most famous of the teachers was ALCUIN of York; the greatest of the missionaries was St. BONIFACE, the apostle of Germany, who returned to convert the land of his fathers.

With the burning of Lindisfarne in 793, the Viking raids began, causing great damage to the Church, especially in eastern England. King ALFRED began the work of recovery; the invaders accepted the faith, and in the tenth century, St. DUNSTAN initiated a reform that eliminated abuses and brought the English Church into closer contact with the Continent. In 1066, with the coming of the Normans, the Anglo-Saxon era came to a close.

Bibliography: F. BARLOW, *The English Church, 1000–1066: A Constitutional History* (Hamden, Conn. 1963). C. J. GODFREY, *The Church in Anglo-Saxon England* (New York 1962). E. A. FISHER, *The Greater Anglo-Saxon Churches* (London 1962). M. DEANESLY, *The Pre-Conquest Church in England* (New York 1961). D. M. WILSON, *The Anglo-Saxons* (New York 1960). P. H. BLAIR, *An Introduction to Anglo-Saxon England* (Cambridge, Eng. 1959). BEDE, *A History of the English Church and People,* tr. L. SHERLEY-PRICE (Baltimore 1955). D. WHITELOCK, *The Beginnings of English Society* (Baltimore 1952). F. M. STENTON, *Anglo-Saxon England* (*Oxford History of England,* ed. G. N. CLARK [Oxford 1934–] 2; 2d ed. 1947). W. LEVISON, *England and the Continent in the Eighth Century* (Oxford 1946).

[C. P. LOUGHRAN]

ANGOLA, THE CATHOLIC CHURCH IN

Located in southwestern Africa, the Republic of Angola borders the Democratic Republic of the Congo (for-

Sees	Suffragans
Huambo	Benguela, Kwito-Bié, Lwena
Luanda	Cabinda, Malanje, Mbanza Congo, Ndalatando, Novo Redondo, Saurímo, Uíe
Lubango	Menongue, Ondjiv

merly Zaire) on the north and northwest, Zambia on the southeast, Namibia on the south and the Atlantic Ocean on the west. It also includes an exclave to the north of the Congo river that comprises Cabinda Province. Angola's coastal plains, marked by a semi-arid climate, rise sharply to a vast plateau region in the east. The climate in the north ranges from cool and dry during the summer months to rainy and hot during the winter. The Congo serves as the northern boundary, and other rivers flow through the country to empty into the Atlantic. Agricultural products include coffee, corn, sisal, peanuts, cotton, sugarcane and timber from extensive forested areas, while hidden beneath the land surface are diamonds, iron ore, copper, bauxite and petroleum.

Once known as Portuguese West Africa, Angola ceased being a colony and became an oversees province of Portugal in 1951. African nationalist sentiment arose later in the decade and led to bitter fighting in 1961. Decades of civil war followed Angolan independence, leaving its economy in disarray and 75 percent of its population surviving by means of subsistence agriculture, despite the proliferation of land mines in farming areas. The average life expectancy for an Angolan is 38.1 years, and only 42 percent of the population is literate.

History. The Portuguese explored the coast beginning in 1483, bringing the first Catholic missionaries to the region in 1491. The first permanent settlement was at Luanda in 1575. As Portugal extended its rule over the region between 1575 and 1680, Jesuits, Franciscans, Dominicans and a few secular priests, inaugurated effective Catholic missionary activity. While their efforts were seriously hampered by the slave trade, the region had about 20,000 Catholics in 1590. The Diocese of São Salvador was erected in 1596 and transferred to Luanda in 1676. Dutch Calvinists occupied the coastal area from 1641 to 1648; that region would provide large numbers of slaves for Brazil until 1875, when slavery was finally abolished.

In 1640, the Prefecture of the Congo was created and entrusted to Italian Capuchins, who labored in the interior of northern Angola. The mission was the most flourishing in Africa in the 17th and early 18th centuries; it then de-

clined for a century. Portugal expelled the Jesuits in 1759 and suppressed all orders in 1834. From 1826 to 1852, the diocese was without a bishop.

Revival of Catholic influence in Angola began in 1866 with the arrival of French Holy Ghost Fathers. Despite difficulties between the Portuguese government and the French missionaries, the Prefecture Apostolic of Cimbebasia was created in 1879, whose jurisdiction extended over the southern half of Angola and included southwestern Africa. In the late 19th century, the boundaries of Angola were defined by diplomatic agreements with surrounding colonial governments, and the enclave of Cabinda annexed to Angola in 1886. Following a series of native uprisings from 1902–1907, Portuguese colonial authorities seriously hampered the mission, closing mission stations in 1910 and replacing them with lay missions based on the belief that missionaries were supporting pro-independence activities. Improvement in the Church's situation became noticeable after the arrival of Benedictines in 1933.

After a concordat between Portugal and the Holy See was signed in 1940, the Church grew in strength, its missions entrusted by the government with the responsibility for primary education. That same year Luanda became an archdiocese and metropolitan see for the country. The archbishop of Luanda administered the suffragan see comprising the islands of SÃO TOMÉ AND PRINCIPE until it was transferred to the Holy See. Meanwhile, Protestant evangelical activity increased in Angola's interior.

Tensions between Portuguese military forces in the region and nationalist agitators erupted in 1961, resulting in over a decade of violence before Angola gained independence from Portugal on Nov. 11, 1975. Independence under the one-party Marxist regime of President Jose Eduarto Dos Santos prompted followers of the National Union for the Total Independence of Angola (UNITA) to begin a civil war that would last into the next century. Meanwhile, under Marxist doctrine, Church schools and clinics were soon nationalized, Catholic leaders were persecuted, and most foreign missionaries were expelled from the country. Despite such actions, the government tolerated the practice of religion, and in 1978 created a registration of all "legitimate" religions, including Catholicism. Government policies relaxed in the 1980s, when it became apparent that religious leaders did not direct political opposition. In the wake of peace accords signed in 1991, missionaries were once again allowed into Angola's coastal region, and the Church became a major force for continued political stability. Fighting resumed following multi-part elections held under a revised constitution dated Aug. 26, 1992 that restored Dos Santos to power amid charges of election fraud. A second peace,

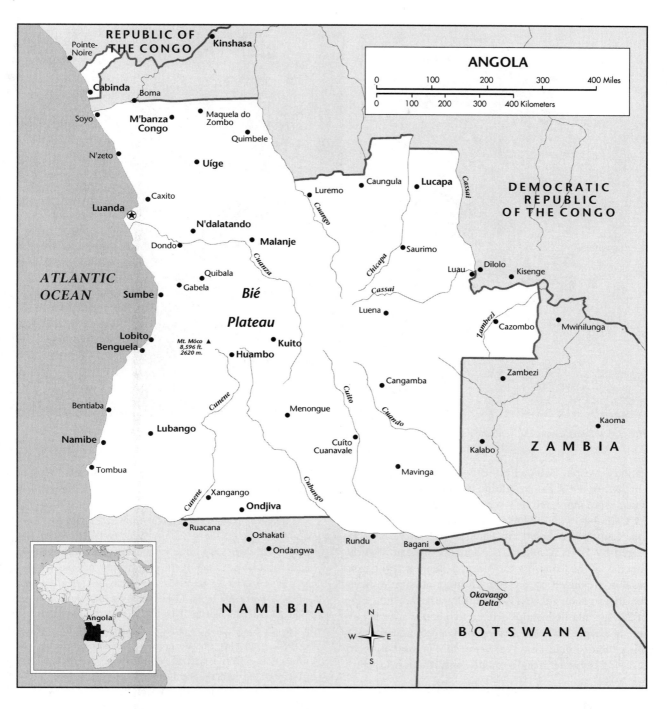

signed in 1994, failed to bring an end to the fighting, and Church leaders and lay members became the target of intermittent violence as the civil war continued. A third effort, in December 1998, also failed.

Into the 21st Century. During the 1990s the Angolan government continued to relax some of its policies toward religion, reinstating religious holidays and ending other atheistic policies. However, continued harassment from the government focused on Church leaders who criticized policies that harmed the social fabric of Angola, and in 1996 a German missionary was charged with subversion. In an effort to bring an end to the continuing violence, the Vatican established formal diplomatic relations with Angola in 1997, following a 1992 request by President Dos Santos. In 1999 Pope John Paul II spoke out against the war in Angola, and the Holy See called for all nations to suspend arms traffic to warring African

The city of Luanda, Angola. (©Francoise de Mulder/CORBIS)

nations. Despite Vatican efforts, the fighting continued. On Jan. 6, 1999 Father Albino Saluhaku and two catechists were murdered in Huambo, while in July of 2000, 34 Catholics were abducted from the Swiss mission of Our Lady of La Salette in Dunde—they were later released by UNITA rebels. The kidnapping came on the first day of the Congress for Peace, a planned negotiating session organized by the Church in an attempt to bring the government and UNITA rebels together. In the spring of 2001, Catholic bishops offered to mediate a further effort at peace, with the Bishop of Uíe commenting, ''I think there should be a cease-fire; that is the only way. It should be bilateral and simultaneous. And it is urgent.''

By the year 2000, Angola contained 246 parishes, its faithful tended by 220 diocesan and 283 religious priests. Brothers working in the missions numbered 85, while 1,538 sisters attended to the country's educational, medical and other social welfare needs, including 177 primary and 55 secondary schools. A Catholic radio station, Radio Ecclesia, aired weekly Church services and other religious programming. Protestant denominations in Angola included Methodists, Baptists and Congregationalists, while syncretic groups, animists and adherents to indigenous faiths were also active. As a result of the civil war, ten percent of the nation's population was living in refugee camps by 2001.

Bibliography: F. DE ALMEIDA, *História da Igreja em Portugal,* v. 3 (Coimbra 1912). E. A. DA SILVA CORREIA, *História de Angola,* 2 v. (Lisbon 1940). J. ALVES CORREIA, *Les Missionnaires français en Angola* (Lisbon 1940). G. LEFEBVRE, *Angola: Son Histoire, son économie* (Liège 1947). M. DE OLIVEIRA, *História eclesiástica de Portugal* (2d ed. Lisbon 1948). R. DELGADO, *História de Angola,* 3 v. (Benguela 1948–53). J. CUVELIER and L. JADIN, *L'Ancien Congo, d'après les archives romaines, 1518–1640* (Brussels 1954). A. BRÁSIO, ed., *Monumenta missionária africana,* 8 v. (Lisbon 1952–55). B. J. WENZEL, *Portugal und der Heilige Stuhl* (Lisbon 1958). R. PATTEE, *Portugal na África centemporânea* (Coimbra 1959), with full bibliog. J. DUFFY, *Portuguese Africa* (Cambridge, MA 1959); *Portugal in Africa* (Cambridge, MA 1962). A. DA SILVA REGO, *Lições de missionologia* (Estudos de ciências políticas e sociais 56; Lisbon 1961). A. MENDES PEDRO, *Anuário Católico do Ultramar Português (1960): Annuaire Catholique de l'Outre-Mer Portugais* (ibid. 57; 1962). *Bilan du Monde,* 2:71–77. Centro de Estudos Políticos e Sociais, Lisbon. Missão para o Estudo da Missionologia Africana, *Atlas missionário português* (Lisbon 1962). *Annuario Pontificio* has annual data on all dioceses.

[R. PATTEE]

ANI

Medieval Armenian city, 20 miles east of Kars, Turkey; the capital of Armenia under the Bagratuni dynasty (885–1079) and the seat of the Armenian patriarchs between 992 and 1072. The city, which is now in ruins, was built on a triangular promontory between mountain crags and surrounded by the Aladja-Tchaï (Akhourian) and Arpa-Tchaï Rivers. It was acquired by the satrap family of Kamsarakans from the King of Armenia, Ashot Mesaker (806–826); and its fortifications were built by Ashot III the Merciful (952–977), who transferred his residence there from Erazgavor. Smpat II (977–989) enlarged and beautified the city, had himself crowned there, and used it as his capital. Before his death the foundations for the cathedral were laid by the architect Tiridates.

A synod was held in Ani (c. 969) in which Bishop Ter Khatchik Archaruni and Abbot Stephen of Sevan, along with many bishops, abbots and priests, condemned the legitimate catholicos, Vahan (967–969), and with the assent of the king replaced him with Stephen of Sevan (969–971). Vahan was accused of Western and Catholic sympathies in his attempt to achieve a union with the Greeks by favoring the faith of the Council of Chalcedon.

Catholicos Ter Khatchik I Archaruni (971–992) prepared Ani to be the patriarchal see. He had been elected to replace Stephen in 971 and proved a strict Monophysite in controversy with Sion, the Armenian bishop of Sebaste and John of Larissa. However, Khatchik I seems to have mitigated his Monophysite doctrine, despite his acerbity, in an exchange of controversial views with Theodore, the Greek metropolitan of Sebaste. His successor, Sargis I (992–1019), transported his residence from Arkina to Ani (993) and consecrated Peter Guetadartz (1019–54) as his successor. Both Peter and Khatchik II of Ani (10547–60) resided there intermittently.

A second synod was held at Ani in 1039 under the leadership of Joseph, Catholicos of the Aghovans. He reestablished Peter Guetadartz in the Armenian Patriarchate and deposed the Abbot Dioscorus of Sanahin, whom King John Bagratuni had imposed on the see. Ani was used as a residence by Basil I (1105–13), the nephew and coadjutor of Catholicos Gregory II. Basil is considered to have been a legitimate catholicos in contradistinction to Basil II, who had proclaimed himself patriarch in 1195, when Gregory VI Apirat established his residence at Hromcla on the Euphrates. After the transfer of the catholicate from Ani, the resident priests and monks became intransigent opponents of the Chalcedonian doctrine and refused every effort at achieving religious unity.

After being sacked several times, Ani suffered an earthquake in 1319 and was practically abandoned. Although the city had been magnificently adorned, ancient descriptions of its beauty and the number of its inhabitants were greatly exaggerated; this is true likewise of the oath by which its citizens swore on its 1,001 churches (Matthew of Edessa, *Chron.* 2.88). However, excavations at the beginning of the 20th century revealed a splendid collection of monuments, particularly the royal palace and numerous chapels and churches. As a commercial center on the route between the Orient and Asia Minor, the city had achieved the height of prosperity under King Gagik I (989–1020) and was celebrated in legends and chronicles of the Armenian historians.

The Armenian historians Agathangelus, Phaustus and M. Khorenensis speak of a second Ani (Ani-Gamakh), the fortress situated to the southwest of Eriza on the Euphrates River, where Artaxias I collected his treasures and where many of the Arsacid kings were buried. GREGORY the Illuminator destroyed a statue of Jove there and burned many books connected with Armenian mythology. In 681 George the Bishop of Ani-Gamakh subscribed the acts of the Council of Constantinople III, and he also took part in the Council in Trullo (692).

Bibliography: F. TOURNEBIZE, *Histoire politique et religieuse de l'Arménie,* v.1 (Paris 1910) 126–139; *Dictionnaire d'histoire et de géographie ecclésiastiques,* ed., A. BAUDRILLART et al., (Paris 1912–) 3:270–271. H. F. B. LYNCH, *Armenia: Travels and Studies,* 2 v. (London 1901) 1:354–392. J. J. M. DE MORGAN, *Histoire du peuple arménien* (Paris 1919) 121–123. N. and M. THIERRY, *Jardin des Arts,* 65 (1960) 132–145. L. M. ALISHAN, *Description of Shirak* (Venice 1881), in Armenian. A. VROUIR, *The Labors and Excavations of Professor N. Mar in Ani, 1905–1906* (Houscharar 6; Tiflis). STEPHANUS OF TARON, *Armenische Geschichte,* tr. H. GELZER and A. BURCKHARDT (Leipzig 1907). A. TER-MIKELIAN, *Die armenische Kirche in ihren Beziehungen zur Byzantinischen (vom IV. bis zum XIII. Jahrhundert)* (Leipzig 1892). S. LYONNET, *Recherches de science religieuse,* 25 (1935) 170–187.

[N. M. SETIAN]

ANIANE, ABBEY OF

Benedictine abbey of the Holy Savior, in lower Languedoc, France; in the former Diocese of Maguelone (today Montpellier). It was founded by WITIZA (BENEDICT OF ANIANE), son of the Count of Maguelone, in 782 and was favored by Charlemagne, friend of Benedict, immunity being granted in 787. It soon prospered and spread the Benedictine rule to nearby Gellone (SAINT-GUILHEM-DU-DÉSERT, founded in 806 by Duke William Short Nose, hero of *chansons de geste*), and also to Cormery (Touraine), Île-Barbe (Lyons), MICY (Orléans), Sainte-Colombe-lès-Sens, and SAINT-SAVIN-SUR-GARTEMPE (Poitou). The Council of Aachen (817) imposed Aniane's monastic customs on all monasteries of the Empire. Archbishop Rostaing of Arles occupied the rich abbey

(890), leaving it to his successor; it later went to the bishops of Béziers. In the 11th century the Holy See recognized Gellone's independence, which was disputed by Aniane. Conflict with CHAISE-DIEU over a priory was settled by compromise (13th century). Aniane's abbots were important in general chapters, in Narbonne province, and at the papal court in Avignon (14th century); several became bishops of Béziers, Nîmes, Saint-Papoul, and Montpellier. Decline in the 16th century (COMMENDATION was begun in 1542) was followed by the pillaging of Calvinists, who burned the archives and furnishings and razed the church and buildings (1561–62). The Bonzi bishops of Béziers acquired the abbey's goods (1616–1703), redeeming the irregularity of their acquisition by charitable zeal. Clement de Bonzi (1621–59) instituted the MAURIST reform in 1633. His nephew, Cardinal Pierre de Bonzi (1660–1703), rebuilt (1679) and consecrated the church (1688). The 300 monks of 800 declined to ten by 1768. Aniane was suppressed in the Revolution (1790); the abbey church became the parish church for the village of Aniane, and the buildings (now a house of detention) became a textile mill. Both Smaragdus Ardon (d. 843?), biographer of the founder (*Monumenta Germaniae Historica: Scriptores* 14.1:178–200), and an anonymous chronicler of Charlemagne's reign were monks of Aniane.

Bibliography: *Cartulaires des abbayes d'Aniane et de Gellone,* ed. P. ALAUS et al., 2 v. (Montpellier 1898–1910). R. THOMASSY, "Critique des deux chartes de fondation de l'abbaye de St-Guillem-du-Désert," *Bibliothèque de l'École des Chartres* (Paris 1839–) 2:177–187. A. DU BOURG, "L'Abbaye d'Aniane, son rôle, son influence, sa destinée," *Mélanges de littérature et d'histoire religieuses pour jubilé de Mgr de Cabrières (1874–1899)* (Paris 1899) 1:165–193. A. WILMART, "Le Lectionnaire d'Aniane," *Revue Mabillon* 13 (1923) 40–53, study of the only Visigothic liturgical text in France. R. GAZEAU, *Catholicisme. Hier, aujourd'hui et demain,* ed. G. JACQUEMET (Paris 1947–) 1:573–574. A. RASTOUL, *Dictionnaire d'histoire et de géographie ecclésiastiques,* ed. A. BAUDRILLART et al. (Paris 1912–) 3:277–279. L. H. COTTINEAU, *Répertoire topobibliographique des abbayes et prieurés,* 2 v. (Mâcon 1935–39) 1:115–117.

[P. COUSIN]

ANIANUS OF CHARTRES, ST.

Bishop of Chartres at the beginning of the fifth century. Medieval accounts name Anianus (Agnan) as the fifth bishop of Chartres, but no early source mentions him. The church under his patronage and in which his relics are enshrined, burned in 1134. At Chartres his feast is commemorated on December 7, the date on which his relics were returned to the reconstructed church in 1136. A similar event in 1262 resulted in a second feast day, but this has not been retained.

Feast: Dec. 7.

Bibliography: *Bibliotheca hagiograpica latina antiquae et mediae aetatis* (Brussels 1898–1901) 1:80 suppl. 321. A. CLERVAL, "Translationes S. Aniani," *Analecta Bollandiana* 7 (1888) 321–335; *Dictionnaire d'histoire et de géographie ecclésiastiques,* ed. A. BAUDRILLART et al. (Paris 1912) 1:1111–14. J. L. BAUDOT and L. CHAUSSIN, *Vies des saints et des bienhereux selon l'ordre du calendrier avec l'historique des fêtes* (Paris 1935–56) 12:228.

[B. L. MARTHALER]

ANIANUS (AIGNAN) OF ORLÉANS, ST.

Bishop; b. Vienne, France; d. Orléans, *c.* 453. In a letter to Bishop Prosper of Orléans, Sidonius Apollinaris confirmed that Orléans was saved from Attila and his Huns in 451 by the intervention of Anianus (*Monumenta Germaniae Historica: Auctores Antiquissimi* 8:147). A century later GREGORY OF TOURS gave a more detailed and picturesque account (*Monumenta Germaniae Historica: Scriptores rerum Merovingicarum* 3:108–117). It seems that Anianus's contribution to saving Orléans lay in his organization of the defenses and in rallying the townsmen to resistance. The military defeat of Attila must be attributed to the Roman general, Aetius. The relics of Anianus are venerated in Orléans in the church that bears his name. F. Dupanloup founded a teaching and nursing congregation in Orléans, the Sisters of St. Anianus, which was approved in 1852.

Feast: Nov. 17.

Bibliography: P. BARBIER, *Vie de S. Aignan* (1912). J. L. BAUDOT and L. CHAUSSIN, *Vies des saints et des bienhereux selon l'ordre du calendrier avec l'historique des fêtes* (Paris 1935–56) 11:559–562. A. BUTLER, *The Lives of the Saints,* ed. H. THURSTON and D. ATTWATER (New York 1956) 4:367. E. EWIG, *Lexicon für Theologie und Kirche,* ed. J. HOFER and K. RAHNER (Freiburg 1957–65) 1:561–562.

[B. L. MARTHALER]

ANIANUS AND MARINUS, SS.

Hermits of the seventh century. Anianus, a deacon, and Marinus, a bishop, established themselves as hermits at Wilparting in the Bavarian Alps. They were of either Irish or West Frankish origin, and their vita (in two manuscripts, twelfth and fifteenth centuries) goes back to the work of Bp. Arbeo of Freising (eighth century). They were martyred by a band of Vandals or Wends and their cult, which is still active, derives historical support from an entry in the Sacramentary of Emperor Henry II, the patron of Rott (on the Inn River) in the twelfth century. Discoveries in the eighteenth century settled the dispute between Rott and Wilparting over who had the relics of the saints in favor of Wilparting.

Feast: Nov. 15.

Bibliography: B. SEPP, ed., *Vita SS. Marini et Anniani* (Regensburg 1892). R. BAUERREISS, "Die *Vita SS. M. et A.* und Bischof Arbeo von Freising," *Studien und Mitteilungen zur Geschichte des Benediktinerordens und seiner Zweige* 51 (1933) 37–49; *Kirchengeschichte Bayerns* (2d ed. Munich 1958–) 1:47–48. G. BAESECKE, "Bischof Arbeo von Freising," *Beiträge zur Geschichte der deutschen Sprache und Literatur* 68 (1945–46) 75–134. *Bibliotheca hagiograpica latina antiquae et mediae aetatis* (Brussels 1898–1901) 2:5531–35.

[C. P. LOUGHRAN]

ANICETUS, ST. POPE

Pontificate: 150 or 157 to 153 or 168. Eusebius says Anicetus ruled for 11 years, placing his death in 168, the eighth year of Marcus Aurelius (*Hist.* 4.11, 14, 19, 22; 5.6, 24; Irenaeus 3.3). Jerome (*Chron.*) dates his accession in the eighteenth year of Antoninus Pius (155 or 156). POLYCARP came from Smyrna to discuss with Anicetus variations in the date of Easter according to the QUARTODECIMAN and Roman systems. The discussions ended amicably, but both Rome and the Orient continued their separate, traditional observance of the feast. In fact, at that time Rome did not have a special Easter feast, but observed the resurrection every Sunday. Polycarp's martyrdom on his return to Smyrna in 155 fixes the beginning of Anicetus's episcopacy as 155 or earlier.

Eusebius records that the Gnostic VALENTINUS remained in Rome until Anicetus's pontificate, and that the great Syrian scholar, HEGESIPPUS, and JUSTIN MARTYR were there. The *Liber pontificalis* says Anicetus was from EMESA (Homs) in Syria and that he was a martyr, but this is uncertain. It also reports that he forbade clerics to wear long hair and gives two accounts of his burial: one in the Vatican and the other in the cemetery of Calixtus, which did not exist, at least in name, until 50 years later. It reports that ANACLETUS (79?–92?) built a sepulchral monument for Peter but probably mistakes that pope for Anicetus since it refers to the tropaion mentioned by the Roman priest Gaius in the second century; recent excavations under St. Peter's have shown this monument to be a late, second-century structure.

Feast: April 17.

Bibliography: EUSEBIUS, *Historia Ecclesiastica* 4.11, 14, 19. E. KIRSCHBAUM, *Tombs of St. Peter and St. Paul*, tr. J. MURRAY (New York 1959). E. FERGUSON, *Encyclopedia of Early Christianity* (New York 1997), 1:56. J. N. D. KELLY, *Oxford Dictionary of Popes* (New York 1986), 10–11. G. QUISPEL, "Valentinus and the Gnostikoi," *Vigiliae Christiane* 50: 1–4.

[E. G. WELTIN]

ANIMA CHRISTI

Also known as *Aspirationes Sancti Ignatii,* by virtue of St. IGNATIUS OF LOYOLA's frequent recommendations of this prayer in his *Spiritual Exercises.* But, since he always quoted only the opening words, the *Anima Christi* must have been already quite well known in his time. That it was known as early as the 14th century is evident from several sources: a manuscript (now in the British Museum) written in England *c.* 1370 states that John XXII granted 3,000 days indulgence for the saying of this prayer under certain conditions; the text of the prayer is carved on the wall of the palace of the Alcazar in Andalusia, done probably about 1364; it is known that Margaret Ebner (d. 1351), a mystic of Swabia, was familiar with the prayer. That it was quite well known throughout Europe by the 15th century is evident from its frequent appearance in books of hours and other devotional books of that century (*see* PRAYER BOOKS). The author of the prayer is unknown. It has been attributed to Pope John XXII because of the many extraordinary indulgences he attached to it, and also to Bl. Bernardine of Fletre, OFM (1439–94), although the prayer was well known before his time. The suggestion that St. Thomas Aquinas composed the *Anima Christi* seems unlikely, since no 13th-century manuscript containing it has been found, and it has no special place in Dominican devotion, as has, for example, the *Lauda Sion* and the *Adoro te,* the former composed by St. Thomas and the latter frequently attributed to him. The existing manuscripts have interesting variations, the invocations *Sudor vultus Christi, defende me* and *Sapientia Christi, doce me* occurring in some.

Bibliography: H. THURSTON, "The *Anima Christi,*" *The Month* 125 (1915) 493–505; *Dictionnaire de spiritualité ascétique et mystique. Doctrine et histoire,* ed. M. VILLER et al. (Paris 1932–) 1:670–672. M. VILLER, "Aux Origines de la prière *Anima Christi,*" *Revue d'ascétique et de mystique* 11 (1930) 208–209. P. SCHEPENS, "Pour l'histoire de la prière *Anima Christi,*" *Nouvelle revue théologique* 62 (1935) 699–710.

[M. J. BARRY]

ANIMA NATURALITER CHRISTIANA

A phrase used by TERTULLIAN (*Apol.* 17.6; *Patrologia Latina* 1:377). Like Hellenistic philosophers, Tertullian looks for knowledge of God from the world outside of man and from the world within man's soul. Thus he appeals even to the witness of the pagan, a witness that he terms the "testimony of the soul naturally Christian" (*testimonium animae naturaliter christianae*). Even the pagan, he says, by different exclamations ("Great God!" "Good God!") spontaneously testifies to his knowledge of God (one and unique) and of those Christian truths which belong to the sphere of natural knowledge (*De test. animae*).

As used by theologians, this axiom came to mean: (1) the possibility of a knowledge of God and of the natural moral law belongs to the very essence of man (Rom 1.20; 2.14–15) and predisposes him to Christianity; (2) a cult (even false and atheistic) is an essential anthropologic element; as a tendency towards transcendence it belongs necessarily to a real individual and collective human existence and thus witnesses to the *anima naturaliter christiana;* (3) man is naturally open to a possible divine word-revelation; (4) man as a creature of the Trinity and redeemed by Christ is a carrier of Trinitarian and Christologic seals and has an OBEDIENTIAL POTENCY that is actualized by a SUPERNATURAL GRACE in at least the lowest degree of intensity.

See Also: GOD, NATURAL LAW; SUPERNATURAL EXISTENTIAL.

Bibliography: K. RAHNER, *Lexikon für Theologie und Kirche,* 10 v. (2d, new ed. Freiburg 1957–65) 1:564–565 with bibliog. J. QUASTEN, *Patrology* 2:264–266. B. ALTANER, *Patrology* 166–177 with bibliog. M. SCHMAUS and K. FORSTER, eds., *Der Kult und der heutige Mensch* (Munich 1961).

[P. B. T. BILANIUK]

ANIMALS, RIGHTS OF

Catholic tradition distinguishes between positive or legal rights and natural or moral rights. While the former are properly the concern of jurists, the latter—rights grounded in the natural order—fall within the sphere of moral theology. Human rights are moral rights of this sort: according to the Second Vatican Council, in virtue of their unique nature humans possess "universal and inviolable" rights to everything necessary "for leading a life that is truly human, such as food, clothing, and shelter; the right to choose a state of life freely and to found a family, the right to education, to employment, to a good reputation, to respect, to appropriate information, to activity in accord with the upright norm of one's own conscience, to protection of privacy and to rightful freedom in matters religious" [*Gaudium et spes* 26].

Proponents of animal rights have prompted consideration of the extent to which similar moral claims might be made on behalf of animals. At issue is the morality of human practices ranging from meat-eating and animal experimentation to recreational hunting, blood sports, and the marketing of furs. From the standpoint of Catholic tradition, the question posed by these practices is, strictly speaking, not so much whether animals have rights per se; it is rather what, if any, moral constraints apply to humans in their treatment of animals. This question turns on a deeper issue regarding the nature and ontological basis of the distinction between humans and animals.

Moral philosophers defending strong human obligations toward animals argue that the radical moral distinction traditionally assumed to exist between humans and animals is ultimately without warrant. Inspired by the utilitarianism of Bentham, Peter Singer (1975), a prominent activist on behalf of animals, holds that the capacity of sentient animals to experience suffering and enjoyment entitles them to equal consideration of their interests. Tom Regan (1983), following the lead of H. S. Salt's classic *Animals' Rights* (1894), couches his argument in the language of rights: because some animals possess consciousness, they, like the very young or deranged, should be considered moral "patients" (as distinct from agents) who have inherent value and hence a valid claim, i.e., a right, to respectful treatment. An Aristotelian conception of the good life as one based on the virtue of sharing in the lives of other beings, including animals, is commended by Stephen Clark (1977). These philosophers are united in their endeavor to include at least some animals within the sphere of moral community.

Catholic teaching conjoins an affirmation of the distinctive worth of humans with an endorsement of the need to treat animals with respect. Pope John Paul II's encyclical *Evangelium vitae* (EV) describes the human being as "a manifestation of God in the world, a sign of his presence, a trace of his glory" (34). The Vatican II statement that the human person is endowed with a "spiritual and immortal" soul and is "the only creature on earth that God has willed for its own sake" (GS 23) is echoed in the CATECHISM OF THE CATHOLIC CHURCH (CCC) number 1703. CCC adds that in the "hierarchy of creatures" humans represent "the summit of the Creator's work" (342–43). Animals, for their part, are "by nature destined for the common good of past, present, and future humanity" (2415). Accordingly, as set forth in Genesis 1.28, humans enjoy "dominion over the earth and over every living creature" (EV 42).

This dominion, however, "is not an absolute power, nor can one speak of a freedom to 'use and misuse,' or to dispose of things as one pleases" [*Sollicitudo rei socialis* 34]. It is limited by a "specific responsibility" toward the "creation which God has put at the service" of human dignity (EV 42); indeed it "requires a religious respect for the integrity of creation" (CCC 2415). It follows that each animal, as a creature which, "willed in its own being, reflects in its own way a ray of God's infinite wisdom and goodness," deserves kindness and respect (CCC 339). In light of the fact that creatures "exist only in dependence on each other, to complete each other, in the service of each other," humans are enjoined to exercise their dominion in terms of "stewardship" (CCC 340; 2417). This notion allows for the use of animals for food and clothing, for the domestication of animals, and,

"Saint Elijah Heals a Lame Horse," "Book of Veterinary," manuscript illumination, Biblioteca Malatestiana, Cesena, Italy, 15th century, photograph. (© Archivo Iconografico, S.A./Corbis)

within limits, for experimentation on animals in the interest of caring for or saving human lives. However, "it is contrary to human dignity to cause animals to suffer or die needlessly" (CCC 2418). By spelling out the obligations of humans toward their fellow creatures in this way, Catholic tradition, without endorsing the notion that animals possess rights, nonetheless provides a basis for moral constraints on the treatment of animals.

Bibliography: J. M. JASPER and D. NELKIN, *The Animal Rights Crusade: The Growth of a Moral Protest* (New York 1992). A. LINZEY, *Animal Rights: A Christian Assessment of Man's Treatment of Animals* (London 1976). M. MIDGLEY, *Animals and Why They Matter* (Athens, GA 1984). C. MURPHY, *At Home on Earth: Foundations for a Catholic Ethic of the Environment* (New York 1989). J. PASSMORE, *Man's Responsibility for Nature* (New York 1974). P. SINGER, *Animal Liberation* (New York 1975). T. REGAN, *The Case for Animal Rights* (Berkeley 1983). L. G. REGENSTEIN, *Replenish the Earth: A History of Organized Religion's Treatment of Animals and Nature* (New York 1991). B. E. ROLLIN, *Animal Rights and Human Morality* (rev. ed. Buffalo, NY 1992). S. R. L. CLARK, *Animals and Their Moral Standing* (London 1997). D. DEGRAZIA, *Taking Animals Seriously: Mental Life and Moral Status* (Cambridge 1996). R. SORABJI, *Animal Minds and Human Morals: The Origins of the Western Debate* (London 1993).

[W. A. BARBIERI]

ANIMALS, SYMBOLISM OF

In Christian symbolism, animals as well as plants, monograms, and other objects have often been used as religious symbols. The early Church preferred to use the animals mentioned in Sacred Scripture. In the Bible as well as in the liturgy, so-called clean animals are clearly distinguished from those that are unclean. As regards the virtues, the lion symbolizes courage and the services of a powerful protector. The lamb represents Christ, and the meekness of the Christian. The bull represents strength; the dog, fidelity; the snake, caution and prudence; the

Dove released by Khajag Barsamin during culmination of Easter celebrations, on steps of St. Vartan Cathedral; photograph by Steve Chernin. (AP/Wide World Photos)

dove, the Holy Spirit; the swallow, innocence; the lark, the singing of the praises of God; the deer, the longing of the Christian for salvation; the peacock, immortality. Certain animals are regularly used to represent the various vices. The chameleon symbolizes hypocrisy; the hyena, impurity; the wolf, greed; the fox, cunning; the owl, darkness; the ass, self-will; the serpent, the devil. In early Christian literature animals are borrowed also from the ancient fables together with their connotative symbolism. For example, the PELICAN is used to represent redemption, and also Christ's giving of Himself in the Eucharist. The many-headed hydra is often used to represent heresy. The FISH is one of the earliest and most important of Christian symbols. The five letters of the word for fish in Greek form an acrostic, signifying Jesus, Christ, Son of God, Savior (see ICHTHUS). The fish is used also as a symbol of Baptism and of Christ in the Eucharist. The Church still encourages the use of animal symbols in her churches and schools as an easy means of symbolizing virtue and vice.

See Also: SYMBOLISM, EARLY CHRISTIAN; BESTIARY; PHYSIOLOGUS.

Bibliography: K. KÜNSTLE, *Ikonographie der christlichen Kunst* (Freiburg 1926–28) 1:119–132. B. KÖTTING, ''Tier und Heiligtum,'' in *Mullus: Festschrift Theodor Klauser,* ed. A. STUIBER and A. HERMANN (*Jahrbuch für Antike und Christentum* suppl. 1; 1964) 209–214. L. RÉAU, *Iconographie de l'art chrétien* (Paris 1955–59) 1:76–132, bibliog. 138–140.

[T. J. ALLEN]

ANIMISM

''Animism'' is the name given to a complex of primitive beliefs that imputes a soul or spirit (Latin: *anima*) to all things both animate and inanimate. The idea was important in one of the earliest anthropological accounts of the origin of religion.

Tylor's Theory. This theory, as formulated by Edward B. Tylor (1832–1917) in his book *Primitive Culture* (1871), states that the first really religious thought that primitive humans ever had came from their experience of dreams. A person dreams that he or she goes to a distant place and meets other people, and upon waking, concludes that in some sense such a meeting actually happened. Not distinguishing between the world seen while waking and that seen in dreams, the dream-meeting seems as ''objectively real'' as any that might happen in the daytime. In addition, people sometimes dream of departed relatives or friends, and this meeting too is considered to have really taken place.

The ''savage'' (Tylor's word) thus reasons that there is within himself or herself some part that is conscious and physical, but which can travel long distances instantaneously and even survives after death. They then impute the existence of such a soul or spirit to all people. Furthermore, since their mental abilities are like children's, they do not clearly distinguish animals from humans, or even animate from inanimate objects; all are alike in their minds. Thus, from a primitive cult of the dead, savages eventually come to recognize souls or spirits in everything. They develop rituals to propitiate them or induce their cooperation, and taboos to keep from unintentionally offending them. Thus, from the simple experience of traveling and seeing others in dreams, the rudimentary forms of primal religion take shape.

Having thus identified the earliest form of religion, Tylor then elaborated an evolutionary view of religious history. Using as his model an understanding of Darwin's theory prevalent in his day, which saw a necessary progression over time from simpler (or ''lower'') forms of life to more complex (or ''higher''), Tylor saw the religious landscape of his day as the latest development in an evolutionary progression from crude animism to higher contemporary religions. However, in putting this theory forth he did not mean to ascribe any value to religion. In fact, he asserted that all religion must eventually be superseded by science.

Frazer's Elaboration. This theory was accepted and extended by others, notably Herbert Spencer (1820-1903) and James G. Frazer (1854–1941). The latter, whose massive work *The Golden Bough* was highly influential in the first half of the twentieth century, extended Tylor's work, showing, for instance, that in many myths and rituals it was apparent that certain people or animals could keep their souls somewhere other than their own body, and providing much more ethnographic evidence for shamanistic and medicinal practices that aimed at bringing a sick patient's soul back to them to restore vitality.

Not all scholars accepted this theory as explaining the origin of religion. Among the most influential of its detractors was Emile Durkheim (1858–1917). In his *Elementary Forms of the Religious Life*, he critiqued this theory for its thin ethnographic base and analytical deficiency. He asserted that, for any conclusion about the religious life of any primitive tribe to be valid, it must be very carefully documented and contextualized in the overall life of the tribe. Tylor, Frazer, and company had merely pieced together a patchwork of ethnographies, traveler's tales, and missionaries' accounts, taking elements from each to prove a point about humanity as a whole without bothering to understand any particular people in detail.

The analytical defects were even more serious. Why should one assume that religion, which has endured through all of recorded history, is based on a blatant, easily detected error? (One need only ask the person with whom one conversed in a dream whether they recall the conversation to find that it never actually happened.) Also, why should we assume that primitive peoples took dreaming as the primary datum for their religious reflections? Based on these and other criticisms, Durkheim suggested that other avenues of enquiry, namely the sociological, would prove more fruitful in explaining the genesis of religion.

Useful as a Descriptor. Even if animism no longer serves as a general explanation for the origins of human religion, it is useful as a descriptor of certain religious modes of thought and conduct within anthropology. For example, traditional Japanese scholars of Shintō such as Motoori Norinaga (1730–1801) understood the spiritual beings known as *kami* to be reifications of natural phenomena based on the sense of awe they evoked in human

beings. The feeling of numinous presence led people to venerate mountains, waterfalls, boulders, and other impressive natural formations, set apart sacred precincts around them, and conduct rituals before them. In addition, there were rituals directed at the *kami* of agriculture, fishing, and hunting that guaranteed a community's economic well-being.

A more contemporary account by a western anthropologist, Richard K. Nelson, working among the Koyukon Athapaskans of northern Alaska, sets forth the animist viewpoint this way (though without labeling it as such):

> Traditional Koyukon people live in a world that watches, in a forest of eyes. A person moving through nature—however wild, remote, even desolate the place may be—is never truly alone. The surroundings are aware, sensate, personified. They feel. They can be offended. And they must, at every moment, be treated with proper respect. All things in nature have a special kind of life, something unknown to contemporary Euro-Americans, something powerful. (*Make Prayers to the Raven*, University of Chicago Press, 1983, p. 14.)

In their broad outlines, the beliefs and practices described above with respect to Japanese and Koyukon societies holds true for other cultures as well, and we can see that animism serves to situate human beings and their activities within the natural world in such a way that they are required to attend to nature, deal with it respectfully, and maintain a level of humility at their own accomplishments and abilities. It encourages an attitude of cooperation with nature, rather than domination and exploitation.

Bibliography: E. DURKHEIM, *The Elementary Forms of the Religious Life* (trans. J. W. SWAIN; London 1915); J. G. FRAZER, *The Golden Bough* (3rd ed., London 1911–1915; R. K. NELSON, *Make Prayers to the Raven* (Chicago 1983); D. L. PALS, *Seven Theories of Religion* (Oxford, 1996); J. S. PREUS, *Explaining Religion* (New Haven 1987); E. B. TYLOR, *Primitive Culture* (New York 1958).

[C. B. JONES]

ANNALS AND CHRONICLES

Along with HAGIOGRAPHY, annals and chronicles constitute the typical forms of medieval historical literature. In practice, annals and chronicles often overlap in content and form, but they are theoretically distinct. Annals may be described as brief chronological listings of events regarded as important in the history of a kingdom, bishopric, or monastery, etc., by contemporary compilers who are usually anonymous. Chronicles list such events in chronological order also, but they furnish more detail, deal with the past, even the remote past, as well as with the contemporary period, and their authors are frequently known. Annals as described give way to chronicles in the later Middle Ages, but the term annals continues to be used to designate what may properly be considered chronicles, and the later chronicles themselves in part assume the character of "history" in the strict sense, since their authors tend to indicate causal relations between events and to inject formally their own judgments or evaluations.

Annals to the 7th Century A.D. As a literary genre, annals go back to the Hittites and Assyrians, who left records of their military campaigns in annalistic form. The Greeks apparently did not compose annals as distinct from chronicles. However, the early Roman historians were more properly annalists, as they presented historical events in a bald, annalistic fashion. The Romans adopted the practice also of recording contemporary historical events on their calendars, a procedure that anticipated the Christian usage, which is the foundation of all medieval annals.

The pattern for medieval annals was set by the CHRONOGRAPHER OF 354. This work contains an official Roman calendar, a long list of consuls, Paschal Tables for 100 years beginning with the year 312, a list of popes from PONTIANUS (230–235) to LIBERIUS, and a brief chronicle to the year 338. The Paschal Tables took on a new significance in CHRONOLOGY in the West after the disintegration of the Western Roman Empire and the abandonment of the consular system of dating. The EASTER CONTROVERSY between the Irish and the Anglo-Saxons, which was finally settled at the Synod of Whitby (664), indicates the special importance of the Paschal Tables in early Christian Britain. Anglo-Saxon missionaries carried their Paschal Tables to the Continent during the 7th century, and in the early 8th they were equipped with the invaluable *De temporum ratione* of BEDE, which, in addition to Paschal Tables, contained a brief chronicle of the Six Ages of the world from Creation to A.D. 729. It had already become customary in England to make marginal notes of historical or other events thought worthy of record opposite the given years in the Paschal Tables. These notes were at first very short, occupying not more than a single line, but as they necessarily had a chronological sequence, they were annals in embryo. The practice was likewise introduced on the Continent. Annals proper were created when the notations mentioned were detached from the Paschal Tables and assembled and circulated in an independent form. This final stage in the development of annals was reached in the course of the 7th century in Merovingian Gaul.

Chronicles to the 7th Century A.D. The so-called *Babylonian Chronicle* (a cuneiform document now in the British Museum, No. 21946) is an annalistic record rather than a chronicle in the strict sense. The chronicle proper was a creation of the Greeks. The *Atthis,* or *Chronicle of Athens,* and especially the *Marmor Parium,* or *Parian Chronicle,* covering a period from the 13th to the middle of the 3d century B.C., may be cited as typical examples. Pagan histories and chronicles could not satisfy the early Christians, preoccupied as they were with SALVATION history as contained in the Old and New Testaments and as reflecting the universal power of God, the Father of all mankind. Furthermore, it was of the greatest importance for Christian apologetics to show that the history of the people of God, particularly their religious history, began long before that of the Greeks and Romans. Hence the Christian chronicle was created to meet a twofold Christian need by Sextus JULIUS AFRICANUS, whose *Chronicles* (preserved only in fragments) furnished a synchronized record of profane and Biblical events from Creation (5500 B.C.) to A.D. 221. A few years later (A.D. 234), HIPPOLYTUS OF ROME published a somewhat similar *Chronicle* of world history which is preserved only in fragments and in Latin translation. It was based in part on Africanus, but relied most heavily on the Bible itself. Africanus and, especially, Hippolytus were millenarians. *See* MILLENARIANISM.

The *Chronicle of Eusebius-Jerome.* The greatest and most influential of all Christian chronicles was compiled by EUSEBIUS OF CAESAREA. His *Chronicle* (first published in 303, but later brought down by him to 325) contains a brief survey of universal history as it was then known, followed by elaborate synchronistic tables of sacred and profane history. He begins his chronology with the birth of Abraham (2016–2015 B.C.), maintaining that no certain dates could be established for the period from Adam and the Fall to Abraham. He wished to demonstrate that the religion of the Hebrews was the oldest of all religions and that Christianity was its continuation and fulfillment. He used much better profane sources than his Christian predecessors and abandoned their millenarian ideas. The Greek original is lost except for fragments, but an Armenian translation of the whole work made in the 6th century is extant. The second part is preserved also in the free translation (*c.* 380) of St. JEROME, who introduced much new material, especially from Roman history, and added a section covering the years from 325 to 378. The *Chronicle* of Eusebius or of Eusebius-Jerome became the immediate source of almost all subsequent universal Christian chronicles and histories in East and West until early modern times.

Post-Eusebian Chronicles. Among the other chronicles compiled before the 7th century, in part as supplements or continuations of Eusebius or Eusebius-Jerome, some in particular deserve mention. As already noted, the

Chronographer of 354 included a world chronicle to A.D. 334, which was essentially a Latin translation and continuation of the *Chronicle* of Hippolytus of Rome. The African Bishop Quintus Iulius Hilarianus (second half of the 4th century) compiled a chronicle, *De cursu temporum,* recounting events from Creation to A.D. 397. A pronounced chiliast, he set the end of the world for A.D. 470. *The World Chronicle (Chronicorum libri duo)* of SULPICIUS SEVERUS, which runs from Creation to A.D. 400, is well organized and is especially valuable for the history of the 4th century A.D. Reference must be made also to St. AUGUSTINE'S *De civitate Dei* and to OROSIUS'S *Historiae adversus paganos.* In dealing with the past, and especially the remoter past, they present their material in chronicle fashion, and by their division of world history, beginning with Creation, into six and four periods respectively, both exercised an enormous influence on all later Western HISTORIOGRAPHY down to the 17th century. PROSPER OF AQUITAINE compiled a World Chronicle (*Epitoma chronicon*) from Creation to A.D. 455. For the period before 412, he took his material from Eusebius-Jerome and other sources, but the coverage of the years from 412 to 455 is his own. The *Chronicon* of the Spanish bishop HYDATIUS may be described as a continuation of the *Chronicle* of Eusebius-Jerome to 468. Marcellinus Comes compiled a *Chronicon* in Latin for the years 379 to 534. He restricted it almost exclusively to the Eastern Empire. The *Chronica* of CASSIODORUS, which goes down to 519, is based directly on Eusebius-Jerome and other sources, having independent value only for the last 20 years. Of the *Chronicle* of the African bishop VICTOR OF TUNNUNA, only the second part, which covers the years 444 to 566, is extant. ISIDORE OF SEVILLE compiled a short World Chronicle (*Chronicon*) from Julius Africanus, Eusebius-Jerome, and Victor of Tunnuna, continuing the work of the last to 615. He followed St. Augustine in dividing world history into six periods. The first book of the *Historia Francorum* of GREGORY OF TOURS must be included among the Latin chronicles of this period, because it is actually a brief chronicle of world history from Creation to the death of St. Martin of Tours (397).

Of the post-Eusebian chronicles compiled in the East and written in Greek or Syriac before the middle of the 7th century, it will suffice to mention the following. About 400 an anonymous Greek writer composed a World Chronicle down to the year 387. The work is extant only in a Latin translation made in the Merovingian period, the so-called *Excerpta Latina Barbari.* JOHN MALALAS (d. 577) compiled an elaborate and influential—but uncritical—*Chronographia* in 18 books. The extant text breaks off at the year 563. An anonymous Syrian writer composed, after 540, the *Chronicle of Edessa* covering the period from 133 to 132 B.C. to A.D. 540, in which

he made good use of the archives of his native city. The most important and most valuable of the Eastern chronicles from this period is the so-called *Chronicon Paschale,* the name given to it by DU CANGE because of the preoccupation of its anonymous author with the dating of Easter. Written most probably at Constantinople before the middle of the 7th century, it runs from Adam to A.D. 629.

Annals and Chronicles, c. 650–1100. The period down to 900 was a golden age of annals; historical works of the high quality of Bede's *Ecclesiastical History* and EINHARD'S *Life of Charlemagne* must be regarded as rare and isolated phenomena. The annals fall into two major categories, monastic and royal, although their authors were all monks or clerics. The older type of annals appearing as notes in Paschal Tables continued to flourish also, especially locally in monasteries somewhat removed from the main centers of ecclesiastical and political life. Chronicles became increasingly important in the 10th, 11th, and early 12th century. In this period one notes also the rise of a third type of historical work that is closely related to annals and chronicles and that was to have a wide development in the Middle Ages, namely, the *Gesta* of kings, bishops, abbots, etc., in which emphasis was placed on achievements and events rather than on biographical details. The LIBER PONTIFICALIS served as a model. The *Gesta episcoporum Mettensium* of PAUL THE DEACON (*c.* 784) and the *Gesta abbatum Fontanellensium* (*c.* 833) may be cited as early and typical medieval examples. The gradual adoption of the birth of Christ as a starting point in chronologies is evident in both annals and chronicles. Finally, it is of interest that the *Anglo-Saxon Chronicle,* and the early Irish annals in part, were composed in the vernacular.

Annals. Among the earlier and rather sketchy annals produced in these four centuries may be mentioned the *Annales S. Amandi* (708–810), *Annales Mosellani* (703–98), *Annales Guelferbytani* (741–90), and the *Annales Mettenses priores* (late 7th and early 8th century). The *Royal Annals* are represented by the collection formerly called *Annales Laurissenses maiores* (741–829). Considering their central interest in the Carolingian kings, royal campaigns, and government, they could hardly have been composed at LORSCH or any other monastery. The *Annales Bertiniani* continue the *Royal Annals* to 882. In this case it is certain that PRUDENTIUS OF TROYES compiled the section for 835 to 861, and HINCMAR OF REIMS, that for 862 to 882. For the 9th century, in part continuing the *Royal Annals,* of special note are the *Annales Xantenses* (831–73); the *Annales Fuldenses,* more properly called *Magontiacenses* (680–901, especially in its last sections); and the *Annales Vedastini,* or of *SAINT-VAAST* (875–900). The so-called *Annales Einhardi* is merely a worked over and extended portion of the

Royal Annals. After long controversy it has been almost definitely established that the *Royal Annals* derived some material from earlier and shorter annals and that the latter must be given priority.

Among the annals dealing with the Saxon House, particular value attaches to the *Annales* of FLODOARD OF REIMS for the years 919 to 968; the *Annales Quedlinburgenses,* beginning with Creation and exhibiting a fuller form from 708 on, and especially from 913 to 1025; and the *Annales Hildesheimenses,* likewise beginning with Creation, but becoming a valuable independent historical source for the years from 818 to 1137. The Salian House is better covered in the chronicles than in the annals. Lambert of Hersfeld, for example, incorporated much material from the lost *Annales Altahenses maiores* and from other annals into his own *Annales,* which, despite the name, should be classified as a chronicle or even a history.

The annals compiled in Italy during this period were relatively few and poor in quality. Although England was the land of origin of annals based on the historical notations in Paschal Tables, no significant annals or chronicles in Latin—apart from the work of BEDE—were produced in that country before the Norman conquest. One collection provides an exception, namely, the *Annales Cambriae,* covering the years 444 to 954. The Irish were very fond of annals and compiled them in the vernacular as well as in Latin. The annalistic material from these early annals was incorporated into the much more elaborate Latin and Irish annals of the late Middle Ages and early modern times.

Chronicles. Although few chronicles were produced in the Carolingian Age and the decades immediately following, three are important because they are world chronicles modeled on Bede. Freculf, Bishop of Lisieux (d. *c.* 853), compiled a *Historia*—a chronicle, despite its name—beginning with Creation and coming down to his own time. The fifth and last book, especially, indicates an effort to write a connected narrative. ADO, Bishop of Vienne (859–75), wrote a *Breviarium chronicorum,* beginning with Adam and closing with the year 869. In dealing with events of his own time, and especially with his own episcopal see, he did not scruple to introduce his own forgeries or falsifications. Regino of Prüm, Abbot of Prüm in Lotharingia (892–99) and then of St. Martin's in Trier (to his death in 915), composed a chronicle, *Chronica,* beginning with the birth of Christ and ending at the year 905. Book one covers the period to 740, and book two, from 741 through 905. He was interested primarily in the events of the western half of the Frankish Empire. Despite their shortcomings, these works reveal the awareness of their authors that they belonged to a new

age and that it was important to have an understanding of the past and of its relation to the present.

In the 10th and 11th centuries numerous chronicles, universal, regional, or local, were composed on the Continent north of the Alps. Several were typical and at the same time of major importance. THIETMAR OF MERSEBURG (975–1018) composed a *Chronicle of the Kings of Saxony.* Lambert of Hersfeld (d. 1077) wrote a work called *Annales,* which was really a world chronicle. MARIANUS SCOTUS (1028–83), one of the last of the significant Irish scholars on the Continent, compiled a *World Chronicle* exhibiting a number of personal ideas and contributions. HERMANNUS CONTRACTUS (1013–54) produced a similar work, *Chronicon,* extending from the birth of Christ to 1054 and distinguished for its remarkable accuracy and objectivity. The *World Chronicle,* once assigned to Ekkehard of Aura (d. 1225), who revised and continued the work, was actually written by FRUTOLF OF MICHELSBERG. In content and arrangement it is one of the superior works of its kind. Much of its material for the period down to the middle of the 11th century was taken from the *Chronicon Wirziburgense* composed in 1045 or 1054. SIGEBERT OF GEMBLOUX (1030–1112) produced a universal chronicle, *Chronographia,* which begins with the year 381. It is one of the best of the universal chronicles of the Middle Ages and probably the most influential of all such works in subsequent medieval historiography. Hugh of Flavigny (d. after 1112) wrote a *Chronicon Virdunense seu Flaviniacense,* which begins with the birth of Christ and ends at 1102. It is not strictly a universal chronicle, although it is often so designated, or it is concerned almost exclusively with Church history and more specifically with northern France in the 10th and 11th centuries. Among the *Gesta*—which are closely related to chronicles—composed in the German area in this period, was the *Gesta Hammaburgensis ecclesiae pontificum* of Adam of Bremen (d. 1076), one of the major historical works of the Middle Ages. All seven chronicles listed, especially those of the 11th century, reveal a greater concern for the immediate past and for contemporary events than do the earlier chronicles, and their writers often indicate their own convictions about events. This is true in particular in matters pertaining to the INVESTITURE struggle.

Historical events of England in this period are recorded in the *Anglo-Saxon Chronicle,* more properly the *Old English Annals.* All extant versions stem from the compilation made in 891. Successive annalists carried the record down, in the E text, even to the middle of the 12th century (1154). These *Annals,* written in the vernacular, are of primary importance for the early history of England and for the history of the English language. Typical of Italy in the same period is the *Chronicon Salernitanum* (ed. U. Westerbergh, Stockholm 1956), which, after listing the Lombard kings from 574, begins its narrative in some detail with the year 775, ending at 964. This should, perhaps, be regarded as a history rather than as a chronicle in the strict sense.

Chronicles of the 12th Century. The distinction between annals and chronicles largely disappeared in the 12th century. The rather sparse, annalistic material was confined mainly to the earlier and unoriginal portions of chronicles as they became much more preoccupied with their own age and its immediate backgrounds. Their increasing fullness of treatment, and their interpretations, however embryonic, of historical events justify the classification of at least some chronicles as histories. The chronicles from the 12th century on, thanks to the Norman conquests, the Crusades, and the entry of northern Europe into the full life of Christendom, reveal much wider horizons of knowledge and interests. They exhibit the new intellectual depth and maturity and the greater mastery of Latin expression that are characteristic features of the renaissance of the 12th century. Furthermore, in the universal chronicles especially, alongside the traditional division of world history into six or four ages, a new tripartite division was introduced: *ante legem, sub lege, sub gratia* (before the Mosaic Law, under the Law, in the Age of Grace).

Universal Chronicles. The *Chronicon ex chronicis* of FLORENCE OF WORCESTER (d. 1118) is the first attempt in England after the time of Bede to compile a universal chronicle. It is independent only from 1030 on, but is valuable for its record of events from that date to 1117. It was continued by John of Worcester to 1141, and by other writers to 1295. Five universal chronicles written on the Continent are more important. The Norman ROBERT OF TORIGNY, Abbot of Mont-Saint-Michel (d. 1186), continued the Chronicle of Sigebert of Gembloux. His work is especially valuable for the period from 1150 to 1186. It was continued by later chroniclers to 1272. Robert of Auxerre (1156–1212) composed a universal chronicle, *Chronologia*, divided according to the six ages of the world. Its geographical data, lists of rulers, the critical spirit displayed in the handling of legends, and the selection of material from the better earlier works ensured its success and its employment as a model by later chroniclers. It is one of the best historical contributions of the Middle Ages. VINCENT OF BEAUVAIS put it to good use in his *Speculum historiale.* Guy of Bazoches (d. 1203) wrote a *Chronographia* in seven books, covering the time from Creation to 1199; this too has independent value for its contemporary age. HÉLINAND OF FROIDMONT (d. after 1230) was the author of a universal *Chronicle* (634–1204) in 49 books made up largely of extracts from other authors and arranged in the manner later adopted

by Vincent of Beauvais. OTTO OF FREISING (c. 1112–58) shares with JOHN OF SALISBURY the distinction of being the most personal and original writer of the 12th century. His universal chronicle *Historia de duabus civitatibus* deliberately echoes in its title the *De civitate Dei* of Augustine. It is unique in that it is permeated throughout with philosophico-theological ideas and interpretations, which have as their immediate background, not paganism, but the history of the Christian centuries from Augustine to his own time. Romuald II of Salerno (d. c. 1182) compiled *Annales ab ortu Christi usque ad 1178,* for which sources now lost were employed; it has independent value especially for the years 1125 to 1178. Romuald compares the six ages of Augustine to the six ages of man, adding two others: a seventh, that of the elect before the Resurrection, and an eighth, that after the Last Judgment. In many respects the *Historia ecclesiastica* of ORDERICUS VITALIS (1075–1142) is notable because, although the work was projected as a history of the Abbey of SAINT-ÉVROULT, it was transformed in the course of composition into a kind of universal chronicle that is of the greatest value for the period from 1125 to 1140.

Regional and Local Chronicles Composed on the Continent. A few of the more important and typical regional chroniclers in France were: SUGER OF SAINT-DENIS (d. 1151), *Liber de rebus in administratione sua gestis* (begun in 1144–45); Rigord of Saint-Denis (d. c. 1209), *Gesta Philippi II Augusti;* Geoffrey of Vigeois, *Chronicon,* covering Limousin and La Marche (1184). Those from Italy were: Falco of Benevento, *Chronicon* (1140); Caffaro of Caschifelone (d. 1166) et al., *Annales Genuenses* (1099–1294); Bernard Marangon (fl. 1175) et al., *Annales Pisani* (1004–1178); LEO MARSICANUS (d. c. 1114–18) and Peter the Deacon of Monte Cassino (first half of 12th century), *Chronica monasterii Cassinensis* (1098–1138). Germany and the Low Countries had: *Annales Erphesfurdenses* (1125–57); Gislebert of Mons (second half of 12th cent.), *Chronicon Hanoniense* (1050–1195); Reiner, monk of the Abbey of St. Lawrence at Liège (d. after 1182), *De ineptiis cuiusdam idiotae* (in part a history of important abbots and monks of his monastery). Eastern and northern Europe include: Helmold of Bosau (c. 1120–77), *Chronica Slavorum* [to 1172; continued by Arnold of Lübeck (d. c. 1211–14) to 1209]; *Chronica Polonorum* (written between 1109 and 1113); Cosmas of Prague (1045–1125), *Chronica Bohemorum,* continued by successive writers to 1283; Saxo Grammaticus (d. c. 1220), *Gesta Danorum,* in prose and verse; *Kaiserchronik,* a German chronicle in verse running from the time of Caesar to the Crusade of Conrad III in 1147. (It was written at Regensburg after 1160 by several ecclesiastics and continued in Bavaria to Frederick II, and in Swabia to Rudolph of Hapsburg.)

Anglo-Norman Chronicles. The chronicles produced in the Anglo-Norman world deserve special attention. Through the Norman conquest of 1066 England was brought into the full current of European affairs and into active participation in religious reform, in the new intellectual movement of the 11th and 12th centuries, and in the Crusades. A series of Anglo-Norman writers produced a number of outstanding chronicles and related works in a fluent Latin style. The universal chronicle of Florence of Worcester was mentioned above. WILLIAM OF MALMESBURY (d. 1143) wrote *Gesta regum Anglorum* in 1125, *Historia novella* as a continuation to 1142, *Gesta pontificum Anglorum,* and *De antiquitate ecclesiae Glastoniensis.* He was much admired centuries later by Milton. HENRY OF HUNTINGDON (1084–1159) wrote a *Historia Anglorum,* divided into four periods: Roman, Saxon, Danish, and Norman. He revised the work five times. However, as a historian he was inferior to William of Malmesbury. John of Salisbury (d. 1180) wrote the *Historia pontificalis* (1162), preserved in part only, but an excellent work intended especially to correct Sigebert of Gembloux and his continuators. Roger of Hoveden (d. 1201) compiled his *Chronica* in two parts, running from 732 to 1201. His chronicle was much read and used well into the 15th century. The Cistercian Ralph of Coggeshall (d. *c.* 1228) compiled a *Chronicon Anglicanum* covering the years from 1066 to 1224. GEOFFREY OF MONMOUTH (*c.* 1100–55), with his *Historia regum Britanniae,* produced a work of little historical value but one that from the first exercised an enormous influence on all the European literatures. Typical 12th-century monastic chronicles were: Jocelin of Brakelond (d. *c.* 1215), *Chronica,* recording the events in BURY-ST.-EDMUNDS for the years 1173 to 1202; GERVASE OF CANTERBURY (d. 1210), *Chronica* of the Abbey of Christ Church, Canterbury (1105–99).

Chronicles and Annals of the 13th, 14th, and 15th Centuries.

The last years of the 12th century and all of the 13th were the golden age of monastic chronicles (often anonymous) and related works. The FRANCISCANS and DOMINICANS gave a new impetus to the writing of such narratives. The universal chronicle enjoyed a revival, and the rise of towns encouraged the production of city-chronicles. The Crusades and the rapidly developing national literatures led to the composition of chronicles in vernacular prose and verse, as well as in Latin. The volume of chronicle literature from the early 13th century is especially large, and all parts of Europe are represented. Therefore, a few of the more important and typical chronicles are indicated here and further guidance is given in the bibliography to complete lists and detailed descriptions.

England and Ireland. Roger of Wendover (d. 1236), a monk of SAINT ALBANS, compiled a universal chronicle, *Flores historiarum,* which has independent value only from 1188 and especially from 1202 to 1235. MATTHEW PARIS, his successor at Saint Albans, the greatest of the Anglo-Norman chroniclers, wrote an elaborate universal chronicle, *Chronica majora,* which depends essentially on Roger of Wendover up to 1235 but from then to 1259 is an independent work of special interest because of the author's personal outlook and observations; his *Historia Anglorum (Historia minor)* is his revision and abridgment of the larger work. Bartholomew Cotton, monk of Norwich (d. *c.* 1298), wrote a *Historia Anglicana* (449–1298); Geoffrey Baker (d. *c.* 1358–60), a Chronicon (1303–56) and a *Chroniculum* (from Creation to 1336); RALPH HIGDEN, a Benedictine monk (d. 1364), a universal chronicle, *Polychronicon,* to 1342 (translated by John TREVISA in 1387, printed by Caxton in 1482, and by Wynkyn de Worde in 1495); NICHOLAS TREVET (*c.* 1258–1328), *Annales sex regum Angliae* (1135–328); Walter of Hemingburgh, prior of St. Mary's, Gisborn (d. after 1313), *Chronicon* (1048–1364); Thomas WALSINGHAM, monk of Saint Albans (d. 1422), *Chronicon Angliae* (1328–88); and William Worcester (Botoner; d. *c.* 1480), *Annales rerum Anglicarum* (1324–1468).

Ireland exhibits among its chronicles: *Annals of Innisfallen* (to 1215, and later continued to 1318), in Irish and Latin; *Annals of Ulster* (from 444), compiled by Cathal Maguire (d. 1498) and continued first to 1541 and then to 1604; *Annals of Boyle* (from earliest times to 1253), in Irish and Latin; *Annals of Clonmacnois* (to 1408), written originally in Irish but preserved only in the English translation of 1627.

France. The wide use of the vernacular in what may be regarded as national chronicles of France is noteworthy. The Dominican VINCENT OF BEAUVAIS (*c.* 1190–1264) wrote a universal chronicle on a vast scale with copious citations from his sources, the *Speculum historiale* (from the beginning of the world to 1250). Albéric of Trois Fontaines, a Cistercian (d. after 1251), composed a universal chronicle, *Chronicon* (to 1251). The *Grandes chroniques de France,* or *Chronique de Saint-Denis* (from the beginnings of the monarchy to the end of the 15th century), is based in large part on earlier Latin chronicles and related works. *Les Gestes des Chiprois* is a collection of French chronicles written in the East in the 13th and 14th centuries. Jean Froissart (d. after 1404) wrote *Chroniques de France, d'Angleterre, d'Ecosse, de Bretagne, de Gascogne, de Flandre et lieux circonvoisins* (1328–1400), one of the greatest of medieval historical works.

Germany and the Low Countries. Eike von Repkow wrote *Sächsische Weltchronik* (*c.* 1230), the first German historical work in prose; the Dominican MARTIN OF TROPPAU, or Polonus (d. 1278), the *Chronicon pontificum et imperatorum* (to 1277), one of the most widely disseminated historical works of the Middle Ages. The *Chronicon Austriacum* (973–1327) is very valuable from the last part of the 13th century; the *Chronica S. Petri Erfordensis moderna* (1–1334) has copious information on the early 14th century. C. Kuchimeister produced *Niiwe Casus Monasterii Sancti Galli* (1228–1329); John of Thilrode, a monk of Saint-Bavon in Ghent, a *Universal Chronicle* (to 1298); William Procurator, a monk of EGMOND in Holland from 1324 to 1333, *Chronicon* (647–1332).

Italy and Spain. The Franciscan SALIMBENE of Parma (1221–c. 89) wrote a *Chronica* (1167–1287), in which the record of historical events is spiced with anecdotes, satire, and humor; the Dominican BARTHOLOMEW OF LUCCA (1236–1326), an *Annales* (1063–1303) of great value for the history of the Church in the 13th century. The *Chronicon Estense* is especially valuable for the period from 1241 to 1354. The *Historie Fiorentine,* or *Chronica universale* (from Creation to 1348) by Giovanni Villani (*c.* 1275–1348) is a work of the greatest value for the history of Florence because of its exact and detailed information on all aspects of Florentine life; it is one of the best historical works of the Middle Ages. The *Chronicae* or *Summa historialis* of ANTONINUS (1389–1459), Archbishop of Florence, is a universal chronicle that enjoyed a great vogue for two centuries, but which has independent value only for the late 13th and the 14th century. It should be remarked that Italy in the late Middle Ages is especially rich in city-chronicles.

Spain produced Lucas of Túy (d. 1249), *Chronicon mundi* (to 1236); Rodrigo-Jiménez de Rada (1170–1247), *Historia Gothica,* or *De rebus Hispaniae* (to 1212); *La crónica general,* a vast universal chronicle on the Spanish kings, inspired by Alfonso X of Castile, the Wise (1252–84), covering history from the time of the Flood to his own time; Pero López de Ayala (1332–1407), compiler of chronicles of the reigns of Peter the Cruel, Henry II, John I, and Henry III; Gutierre Díez de Games (1379–1450), *Crónica de Don Pedro Niño, o El victorial;* Bernat Dezcoll (d. *c.* 1390), *Crónica* of Pedro IV, King of Aragon (1336–87).

General Evaluation. Annals, chronicles, and the related genre, *gesta,* constitute a huge mass of historical source material from the end of antiquity to the beginning of modern times. They continued to exercise an influence on the form, at least, of 16th-century historiography, for BARONIUS, the CENTURIATORS OF MAGDEBURG, and, at a lower level, Holinshed reflect the annalistic or chronicle tradition. The medieval annals, chronicles, and *gesta*

dealt with world history, secular rulers, popes, peoples, cities, bishops, abbots, and monasteries. In a large number of cases they are anonymous. In general, it may be said that all these works take on real historical value only as they approach periods contemporary with or immediately preceding those of their writers. Many of those extant have gone through repeated reworkings and enlargement by addition of later continuations, so that the original form is not always easy or even possible to establish. The material covering world history before the 5th century A.D. is based essentially on the Bible, Eusebius-Jerome, Augustine's *De civitate Dei,* and Orosius. This material is usually not taken directly from these sources in the later annals and chronicles, but is simply incorporated from earlier medieval works of the same kind.

The vast majority of the authors of annals, chronicles, and *gesta* were monks, friars, or members of the secular clergy. All regarded history in a religious sense, that is, as the working out of the history of salvation. With a small number of important exceptions, writers were more or less uncritical or even credulous in dealing with secular as well as religious themes. Furthermore, the horizons of writers of local or regional chronicles, and especially of annals, are very limited. Almost all are preoccupied not only with ecclesiastical affairs, but primarily with the special interests of the religious orders and the diocesan clergy. The monastic writers constituted the larger and more influential group.

Given the handicap that beset the obtaining, using, and disseminating of knowledge before the invention of printing, it is surprising to note that so many works, relatively speaking, were so widely known and employed. Latin was the international language, and French became a second international language in the course of the Norman expansion and the Crusades. The monks and friars played a very important role in the spread of annals and chronicles of a general nature. Medieval authors of annals, chronicles, and *gesta* were not trained historians nor could they be expected to be critical before the rise of genuine historical criticism centuries later. Their works contain precious metal, but the percentage shows wide variation, and the separation of the precious metal from the low grade ore is often a complicated and difficult process.

See Also: HISTORIOGRAPHY, ECCLESIASTICAL; BYZANTINE LITERATURE.

Bibliography: B. ALTANER, *Patrology,* tr. H. GRAEF from 5th German ed. (New York 1960) 278–84. R. L. POOLE, *Chronicles and Annnals: A Brief Outline of Their Origin and Growth* (Oxford 1926). C. W. JONES, *Saints' Lives and Chronicles in Early England* (Ithaca 1947) 16–30. M. L. W. LAISTENER, *Thought and Letters in Western Europe, A.D. 500 to 900* (2d ed. New York 1957) 261–65. W. WATTENBACH, *Deutschlands Geschichtsquellen im Mittelalter.*

Vorzeit und Karolinger, Hefte 1–4, ed. W. LEVINSON and H. LÖWE (Weimar 1952–63) 1:50–108. "Anhang: Quellenkunde für die Geschichte der europäischen Staaten während des Mittelalters," in A. POTTHAST, *Bibliotheca historica medii aevi* (2d ed. 1896; repr. Graz 1954) 2:1647–1735, a comprehensive survey of each country or people of Europe with the names and dates of all annals and chronicles listed among the sources in each case. K. H. QUIRIN, *Einführung in das Studium der mittelalterlichen Geschichte* (2d ed. Braunschweig 1961) 251–64, annals and chronicles among the sources with dates and eds. "Die Chronisten," in K. KRUMBACHER, *Geschichte der byzantinischen Literatur* (Munich 1890; 2d ed. 1897) 319–408, a comprehensive treatment of Byzantine chronicles to 1453. *Repertorium fontium Historiae medii aevii primum ab Augusto Potthast digestum, nunc cura collegii historicorum e pluribus nationum emendatum et anctum*; v.1, Series collectionum, Instituto Storico Italiano per il Medio Evo (Rome 1957–), annals and chronicles listed among the sources described in the analyses of the contents of the *Rerum Britannicarum medii avei scriptores, Recueil des historiens des Gaules et de la France, Rerum italicarum scriptores, España sagrada*, and other collections. T. MOMMSEN, *Chronica Minora, Monumenta Germaniae Historica: Auctores antiquissimi* (Berlin 1826–) v.9, 11, 13. C. GROSS, "Chronicles and Royal Biographies," *Sources and Literature of English History* (2d ed. New York 1915; repr. 1952) 326–99, includes Ireland, Scotland, and Wales; "Collections Privately Edited: Chroniclers, etc.," *ibid.* 105–12, with lists of English chronicles printed in the *Rerum Britannicarum medii avei scriptores, Monumenta Germaniae Historica*, etc. A. E. MOLINIER et al., *Les Sources de l'histoire de France*, 6 v. (Paris 1901–06) v.2–4, chronicles—including those outside of France that are pertinent—among the sources listed in the *Table de Matières* at the end of each v. J. F. KENNEY, *The Sources for the Early History of Ireland: v. 1, Ecclesiastical* (New York 1929) 1–90, 103–04. M. MANITIUS, *Geschichte der lateinischen Literatur des Mittelalters*, 3 v. (Munich 1911–31) v.1–3, treatment of annals, chronicles, and their writers when known, easily controlled through indexes under *Annales, Chronica, Chronicon,* and pertinent personal names. J. DE GHELLINICK, *L'Essor de la littérature latine au XIIᵉ siècle*, 2 v. (Brussels-Paris 1946) 2:93–114, 135–63, with excellent bibliog. M. SCHULZ, *Die Lehre von der historischen Methode bei den Geschichtsschreibern des Mittelalters, 6.–13. Jahrhundert* (Berlin 1909). J. SPÖRL, *Grundformen hochmittelalterlicher Geschichtsanschauung: Studien zum Weltbild der Geschichtsschreiber des 12. Jahrhunderts* (Munich 1935). H. ZIMMERMAN, *Ecclesia als Objekt der Historiographie: Studien zur Kirchengeschichtsschreibung im Mittelalter und in der frühen Neuzeit* (Vienna 1960). A. D. VON DEN BRINCKEN, *Studien zur lateinischen Weltchronistik bis in das Zeitalter Ottos von Freising* (Düsseldorf 1957). V. H. GALBRAITH, *Historical Research in Medieval England* (London 1951). H. GRUNDMANN, "Geschichtsschreibung im Mittelalter," in *Deutsche Philologie im Aufriss*, ed. W. STAMMLER, v.3 (Berlin 1957) 1273–1335; v.3 (2d ed. 1961) 2221–. J. W. THOMPSON and B. J. HOLM, *A History of Historical Writing*, 2 v. (New York 1942) 1:143–469.

[M. R. P. MCGUIRE]

ANNATES

Annates was a tax on the first year's income of an ecclesiastical benefice paid to the papal treasury. By the 11th century it had become customary for some bishops and ecclesiastical corporations to appropriate the income of a benefice for a year or more after collation (*see* COLLATIO). This revenue, known as *fructus primi anni, annalia* or *annualia,* was sometimes collected with papal permission by bishops and kings in special need. Financially embarrassed in 1306, Pope CLEMENT V asserted a similar claim for the Holy See, appropriating the first fruits of all minor benefices in the British Isles for three years. The levy was repeated and extended to most of the Church by JOHN XXII in 1318. Beginning in 1326 the application of the tax became narrower but virtually continuous: it was paid on all minor benefices becoming vacant at the Holy See or reserved to it. As this was the period during which the number of papal collations and confirmations increased rapidly (*see* PROVISION), the income from the tax assumed considerable importance. Details touching EXEMPTIONS and the amount and manner of payment were worked out during the remainder of the century, a period that witnessed the first use of the word *annata* for this tax. John XXII had exempted benefices with an income less than six silver marks, but BENEDICT IX set the minimum at 24 gold florins in 1389. The tax usually amounted to about one-half the gross annual income.

From the end of the 14th century the payment of annates received more and more opposition. Though it was defended in principle in the agreements between the papacy and the national churches after the Council of CONSTANCE, income declined sharply because the papacy resigned many appointments and because payment was usually limited to 24 florins. The Council of BASEL (1435) sought to suppress annates entirely, and the Council of TRENT (sess. 24, c.13) restricted them considerably. In 1728 BENEDICT XIII imposed a similar payment in favor of cathedral or capitular churches on minor benefices in Italy and adjacent islands not reserved to the Holy See. In the 15th and following centuries annates came to mean all taxes paid to the papacy on the reception of a benefice, whether major or minor.

Bibliography: C. SAMARAN and G. MOLLAT, *La Fiscalité pontificale en France au XIVᵉ siècle* (Paris 1905) 23–34, 87–96. Studies. J. P. KIRSCH, ed., *Die päpstlichen Annaten in Deutschland während des XIV. Jahrhunderts* (Paderborn 1903). E. GÖLLER, *Die Einnahmen der apostolischen Kammer unter Johann XXII* (Paderborn 1910); *Die Einnahmen . . . Benedikt XII* (Paderborn 1920). W. E. LUNT, "The First Levy of Papal Annates," *American Historical Review* 18 (1912–13) 48–64; *Financial Relations of the Papacy with England to 1327* (Cambridge, Mass. 1939); *Financial Relations of England with the Papacy, 1327–1354* (Cambridge, Mass. 1962). A. PUGLIESE, *Annate e mezz'annate nel diritto canonico* (Milan 1939). J. P. KIRSCH, *Dictionnaire d'histoire et de géographie ecclésiastiques*, ed. A. BAUDRILLART et al. (Paris 1912–) 3:307–315. K. HONSELMANN, *Lexikon für Theologie und Kirche*, ed. J. HOFER and K. RAHNER, 10 v. (2d, new ed. Freiburg 1957–65) 1:575. For a general orientation on papal finances, see G. LEBRAS, *Institutions ecclésiastiques de la chrétienté médiévale*, 2 pts. *His-*

toire de l'église depuis les origines jusqu'à nos jours 12; (1959–64) 2:351–353.

[M. M. SHEEHAN]

ANNE OF DENMARK

Queen consort of King James I of Great Britain; b. Skanderborg, Jutland, Dec. 12, 1574; d. Hampton Court, England, March 2, 1619. Anne, whose parents were King Frederick II of Denmark and Norway and Queen Sophia of Mecklenburg, was brought up in a traditional Lutheran household, and was the second of four daughters in a family of seven children. Anne was sought in marriage by James VI of Scotland as a means of settling in Scotland's favor a dispute with Denmark over the Orkney Islands. The marriage was solemnized at Oslo, Nov. 24, 1589. Of an indolent, but tolerant and amiable nature, the young bride showed little interest in anything more serious than rich clothes, court balls, and masques, which remained her chief delight throughout her life. She was the mother of six children: her eldest son, and favorite, Henry Frederick, was born at Stirling, Feb. 19, 1594, and his premature death in 1612 left her inconsolable; Elizabeth (b. 1596) became Princess of Bohemia; Margaret (b. 1598) died in infancy; Charles, the future King Charles I of England, was born in 1600; Robert (b. 1601) died in infancy, as did Mary (b. at Greenwich, England, 1605; d. 1607).

Anne preferred Lutheranism to the Calvinism of Scotland. The deprivation of Lutheran services seems to have led to her interest in Catholicism. In 1600, at Holyroodhouse Palace, she received Robert ABERCROMBY, SJ: "After a long conversation with the father, she earnestly entreated him to stay with her three days that he might instruct her fully in Catholic doctrines and ceremonies. . . . On the fourth day, full of holy joy she made her general confession and having heard Mass twice, she received the most holy sacrament with joy in the presence of only a few persons of rank." Not only did James know of her conversion, he utilized it in negotiations with CLEMENT VIII for recognition of James's right to the throne of England at Elizabeth's death. The negotiations were carried on through Sir James Lindsay, the pope's messenger.

During Anne's reign as Queen of England (1603–19), it is known that Alexander MacQuhirrie, SJ, was her chaplain and that Richard Blount, English Jesuit provincial, visited her secretly on a number of occasions before and after the birth of her daughter Mary at Greenwich. He reprimanded her severely for attending her infant daughter's baptism according to the Protestant form. Anne's light and frivolous nature has caused many historians to regard her Catholicism as a passing fancy and fad. Certainly her conversion seemingly did nothing to make her serious and devout, or to offer strength of character. Nonetheless, her refusal to receive the Sacrament according to the rites of the Church of England at her coronation with James, July 24, 1603, showed some courage and raised the hopes of Catholic England. She urged a Catholic marriage for Prince Henry and sought to obtain office for her co-religionists. She corresponded with the Spanish infanta and dared to employ Sir Anthony Standen, James's ambassador to Italy, as her private agent in Rome. Undoubtedly the storm over the Gunpowder Plot and the pressures of James, who then found his wife's Catholicism awkward for him, did much to weaken her resolution, at least publicly. Although James made a point of choosing only those favorites first accepted by his wife, it was always actually a manipulated affair, and Anne was known to have little political influence, as, e.g., in the case of Sir Walter Raleigh. Her correspondence with Ottaviano Lotti, the opinions of Philip III and Francisco Gómez de Sandoval y Rojas, Duke of Lerma, and ambassador's reports, all indicate continued knowledge and acceptance of her Catholicism throughout the years 1605 to 1618. Don Diego de Sarmiento de Acuna, Count Gondomar, Spanish Ambassador, attests to the fact that though Anne attended the services of the Church of England with James, she never took Communion at these services, and that at Denmark House, her London residence, she frequently heard Mass secretly in the garret from recusant priests. At her country residence at Oatlands she had two priests and while there she heard Mass daily.

Anne, frustrated in any powerful public influence, seems to have resorted to extravagant expenditures for masques and building, utilizing the genius of Inigo Jones at Greenwich House and Denmark House especially. After 1612 Anne suffered for many years from dropsy, which eventually caused her mortal illness. She was attended at her deathbed by George Abbot, Archbishop of Canterbury, and the bishop of London. Her deathbed renunciation of "the mediation of all saints and her own merits" is taken as a denial of her Roman Catholicism, a position most recently accepted by Philip Caraman, SJ, who felt she was "persuaded vs. her true conviction." A virtuous wife, affectionate mother, and good friend, generous and compassionate, Anne was well liked by the English people.

Bibliography: D. H. WILLSON, *King James VI and I* (New York 1956). G. P. V. AKRIGG, *Jacobean Pageant* (Cambridge, Mass. 1962). L. HICKS, "The Embassy of Sir Anthony Standen in 1603," *Recusant History* 5 (1959–60) 91–127, 194–222; 6 (1961–62) 163–194; 7 (1963–64) 50–81. A. W. WARD, *The Dictionary of National Biography from the Earliest Times to 1900* 1:431–441, bibliog. S. R. GARDINER, *History of England*, 10 v. (2d rev. ed. London 1883–84) v.1–3. A. STRICKLAND, *Lives of the Queens of England*, 12 v. (London 1840–48) v.7.

[J. D. HANLON]

ANNE OF JESUS, VEN.

Spanish Discalced Carmelite; b. Medina del Campo, Léon, Nov. 25, 1545; d. Brussels, Mar. 4, 1621. Her parents, Diego de Lobera and Francisca de Torrès, were from prominent families of Spain. When 15 she rejected the prospect of a rich marriage because of a vow of chastity. She cut off her hair, wore a penitential gown, and under the guidance of a Jesuit, Pedro Rodriguez, sought admission into the reformed Carmel at Salamanca. There she took the habit, Aug. 1, 1570, and was professed Oct. 22, 1571. She assisted St. Teresa of Avila in the foundation of convents in Andalusia (1575), where she was prioress for three years, and in Granada (1581). After the death of Teresa (1582), she became prioress in Madrid (1586) and began the edition of Teresa's writings. When Anne of Jesus obtained a brief from Sixtus V on June 5, 1590, confirming the constitutions of the Discalced Carmelites, she displeased the Carmelite Vicar-General, Nicolò Doria, and the *Consulta* (his six advisers), and was deprived of jurisdiction for three years (*see* CARMELITES, DISCALCED). In 1596 she was again prioress at Salamanca. At the invitation of Cardinal Pierre de Bérulle, she and Anne of St. Bartholomew established houses at Paris (1604), and Pontoise (1605), but opposed the cardinal's aim to associate the Reformed Carmelites with his French Oratory. She left France, founded a convent at Brussels (1607), and then returned to Spain, where she worked on further editions of St. Teresa's works, translated them into Latin and Flemish, and wrote a biography of the saint. She also concurred in the establishment of communities in Cracow, Galicia, and Antwerp.

Bibliography: BERTHOLD-IGNACE DE SAINTE ANNE, *Vie de la mère Anne de Jésus*, 2 v. (Mechlin, Belgium 1877–83). P. MARIE JOSEPH, *Dictionnaire d'histoire et de géographie ecclésiastiques*, ed. A. BAUDRILLAT et al. (Paris 1912–) 3:340–343, bibliog. G. MARSOT, *Catholicisme* 1:588.

[E. D. MCSHANE]

ANNE OF ST. BARTHOLOMEW, BL.

Spanish Discalced Carmelite; b. Almendral, near Ávila, Oct. 1, 1549; d. Antwerp, June 7, 1626. Anne, the daughter of Ferdinand Garcia and Maria Manzanas, entered the Carmelite convent of St. Joseph at Ávila, Nov. 7, 1570, and was professed as the first lay sister of the Reform, Aug. 15, 1572. She was constantly with St. TERESA

of Avila until the latter's death in her arms, Oct. 4, 1582. She accompanied ANNE OF JESUS in 1604, when the Reformed Carmelites were invited by Cardinal Pierre de BÉRULLE to found convents in France. There she was unwillingly promoted to a choir sister on Jan. 6, 1605, and became prioress at the convent of Pontoise, and then of Tours in 1608. Against the opposition of Bérulle, she left Paris on Oct. 5, 1611, to join Anne of Jesus in the Spanish Netherlands. She founded a convent at Antwerp (1612), and because of her prayers, she is credited with saving the city from the hands of the Calvinists (1622 and 1624). For this she is acclaimed "Liberator of Antwerp." There she wrote her autobiography and her instructions for superiors and mistresses of novices. She was declared venerable June 29, 1735 by Clement XII, and proclaimed blessed May 6, 1917 by Benedict XV.

Feast: June 7.

Bibliography: *Anne de Saint-Barthélemy: lettres d'Anvers*, ed. P. SÉROUET (Paris 1981). *Autobiography of the Blessed Mother Anne of Saint Bartholomew. . .*, ed. M. BOUIX (St. Louis 1917). M. BOUIX, *Vie de la vén. mère Anne de Saint-Barthélemy* (2d ed. Paris 1872), the second edition is based on the autobiography. P. MARIE-JOSEPH, *Dictionnaire d'histoire et de géographie ecclésiastiques*, ed. A. BAUDRILLART (Paris 1912–) 3:346–349, bibliog. *Acta Apostolicae Sedis* 9:257–261. R. AIGRAIN, *Catholicisme* 1:589. A. BUTLER, *The Lives of the Saints*, ed. H. THURSTON and D. ATTWATER, 4 v. (New York 1956) 2:499–500.

[E. D. MC SHANE]

ANNE AND JOACHIM, SS.

Traditional names of the mother and father of the Blessed Virgin Mary. Since Sacred Scripture makes no mention of Mary's parents, one may rightly wonder about the basis for the devotion to St. Anne and St. Joachim. Does this devotion rest merely on a late invention of popular piety? Be that as it may, the Blessed Virgin surely had parents, no matter what their names may have been. The assumption that they were sanctified by God in view of their election by Him to bring the immaculate Mother of God into the world is entirely reasonable; otherwise it would be unreasonable to assume that Mary, Joseph, and John the Baptist had been sanctified in view of their participation in the Redemption.

There is not, however, a total lack of information about the lives of Mary's parents. The apocryphal Gospel known as the Protoevangelium Jacobi, written *c.* A.D. 170–180, offers some interesting information on this matter. This work, which tells of Mary's infancy, is undoubtedly one of the most famous of the apocryphal writings, not only because of its antiquity and wide diffusion, but also because of the unparalleled influence that it had on devotion to Mary. It would be a sad mistake to class this work with the heretical writings that were circulated in the early Christian centuries, even though everything in it cannot be taken, without further ado, as historical. In any case, the story that it tells of Mary's parents is worth summarizing here.

Joachim and Anne According to the Protoevangelium. It happened one day that Joachim, who was rich and respected in Israel, met with reproaches because of his sterility. Feeling downcast, he left his wife Anne and retired to the desert to pray and fast. Meanwhile Anne, too, now that she was left alone, wept and lamented before the Lord, bewailing her seeming widowhood and actual childlessness, which she regarded as a punishment from God. Finally, the prayers of both spouses were answered. An angel appeared to Anne and announced that she would conceive and bear a child who would become famous throughout the world. Anne thereupon promised to offer to the Lord the fruit of her womb. At the same time Joachim in the desert had a similar vision. Full of joy, he returned home. When his wife was told of his coming by messengers, she went out to meet him at the city gate. At the sight of Joachim, she ran and embraced him. "Now I know," she said, "that the Lord has wondrously heard my prayer. I who was a widow am a widow no longer; I who was once sterile have conceived in my womb."

The account of Mary's birth is then given, followed by the story of how the little girl was later presented to the Lord in the Temple by her parents. In the rest of the account Mary's parents no longer appear.

Diffusion of the Story. The Christians of the early centuries were fascinated by the Protoevangelium. "In the original Greek text, or in the Latin, Syriac, Coptic, Armenian, Georgian, Arabic, and Ethiopic translations, or in more or less complete paraphrases in seven different languages, it spread at an early date in every part of Christendom. . . . It gave rise to a series of liturgical feasts: the feasts of Mary's Conception, her Nativity, and her Presentation in the Temple, as well as the feast of her parents, St. Joachim and St. Anne" (De Strycker, v). Numerous Fathers cited or commented on the story told in the Protoevangelium, among them St. Epiphanius, Andrew of Crete, the Patriarch Germanus I of Constantinople, St. John Damascene, Photius and his friend George of Nicomedia, St. Sophronius.

Popular Devotion. Churches in honor of St. Anne began to be erected in the sixth century. According to Procopius, there was a church dedicated to her in Constantinople c. A.D. 550. At about the same time a church in her honor was built in Jerusalem at the traditional site of her birthplace. These two churches were very influen-

tial in spreading the cult of Mary's parents, especially that of St. Anne. In the later Middle Ages, after her cult had spread to Europe, there were numerous churches, chapels, and confraternities dedicated to her.

The feast in honor of both St. Anne and St. Joachim on September 9, for which selections or paraphrases of the stories from the Protoevangelium were used as liturgical texts, was introduced first in the East, probably at the church of St. Anne in Constantinople or at her church in Jerusalem toward the end of the sixth century. In the West the cult of St. Anne was introduced at Rome in the eighth century; it was not until the fourteenth century that it became widespread in Europe. In 1584 Gregory XIII extended her feast, celebrated on July 26, to the whole Latin Church. Thereafter St. Anne became extraordinarily popular, especially in France. Her two greatest shrines are still those of Ste. Anne d'Auray in Brittany and Ste. Anne de Beaupré near Quebec in French-speaking Canada. The feast of St. Joachim was not introduced in the West until the fifteenth century. After being suppressed by St. Pius V, it was restored by Paul V (1621) and raised to a higher rank by Leo XIII.

One of the reasons for the popularity of the cult of SS. Joachim and Anne is its close connection with the cult of the Blessed Virgin Mary. At the same time, Christian married couples find in the parents of Mary a model of conjugal life such as they do not find in Joseph and Mary, at least on the level of conjugal relations. In this regard it is significant that, until the sixteenth century, the conception of Mary was represented in iconography by showing the meeting of Joachim and Anne at the Golden Gate of Jerusalem. The embrace (*osculum*) of the two spouses suggesting the conception of Mary is the sole example known in iconography. It seemed entirely normal that the faithful should see in this a glorification of Christian marriage.

Another reason for the popularity of their cult is the fact that the family, especially in former days, could not be thought of without the grandparents. If Mary is the mother of Jesus, her parents are His grandparents and belong, in a certain sense, to the "Holy Family." Finally, Joachim and Anne are becoming symbols of the messianic expectations of the Old Testament, while they introduce the New Testament. With Mary, they form the point in history where divinity entered into humanity.

Iconography. Christian iconography abounds in treatments of Mary's parents, especially in the cycles of the infancy of the Virgin. After Jesus and Mary, St. Anne is one of the subjects that appears most frequently in iconography, whether alone or with others in various scenes of her life. Extremely popular in the Middle Ages was the portrayal of Anne with the infant Jesus as well as the

Blessed Virgin. She is represented most often as a venerable matron wearing a long robe, with cincture, mantle, and veil. Around A.D. 1500 artists added the headdress that was worn by the ladies of their time. St. Joachim is usually represented together with St. Anne. He is sometimes shown carrying the infant Mary or bringing two turtledoves (cf. Lk 2.24) as the offering for her presentation in the Temple.

Feast: July 26.

Bibliography: É. AMANN, *Le Protévangile de Jacques et ses remainiements latins* (Paris 1910). É. DE STRYCKER, *La Forme la plus ancienne du Protévangile de Jacques* (Brussels 1961). B. KLEINSCHMIDT, *Die Heilige Anna: Ihre Verehrung in Geschichte, Kunst und Volkstum* (Düsseldorf 1930). P. C. BOEREN, *La légende de Passecrate et la Sainte Parenté* (New York 1976). P. V. CHARLAND, *Madame Saincte Anne et son culte au moyen âge*, 2 v. (Paris 1911–13); *Les Trois légendes de Madame Saincte Anne* (Montreal 1898). G. CINQUE, *Le glorie di s. Gioacchino* (Naples 1970). A. DÖRFLER-DIERKEN, *Die Verehrung der heiligen Anna in Spätmittelalter und früher Neuzeit* (Göttingen 1992). K. ALGERMISSEN et al., eds., *Lexicon der Marienkunde* (Regensburg 1957–) 1:230–257. *Interpreting cultural symbols: Saint Anne in Late Medieval Society*, ed. K. ASHLEY and P. SHEINGORN (Athens, Ga. 1990). H. LECLERCQ, *Dictionnaire d'archéologie chrétienne et de liturgie*, ed. F. CABROL, H. LECLERCQ, and H. I. MARROU (Paris 1907–53) 1.2:2162–74. H. SCHAUERTE, *Lexikon für Theologie und Kirche*, ed. J. HOFER and K. RAHNER (Freiburg 1957–65) 1:570–571. B. KRAFT, *ibid.* 5:973. A. AMORE, *ibid.* 6:403–404. J. VON BEHR, *Die Pisaner Marientafel des Meisters von San Martino und die zyklischen Darstellungen der Annenlegende in Italien von 700 bis 1350* (Frankfurt am Main 1996). E. CAMPAGNA, ''Iconografia dell' Immacolata,'' *Arte Cristiana* 15 (1915) 354–368. H. AURENHAMMER, *Lexikon der christlichen Ikonographie* (Vienna 1959—) 1:139–149. K. KÜNSTLE, *Ikonographie der Christlichen Kunst* 1:321–332. L. RÉAU, *Iconographie de l'art chrétien* 2.2:155–161; 3.1:90–96; 3.2:751.

[J. P. ASSELIN]

ANNECY, MONASTERY OF

A priory of the Canons Regular of the Holy Sepulchre, founded in the 12th century in the town of Annecy, eastern France. Its members were authorized by Pope Celestine III (1191–98) to beg for their support and that of the pilgrims they received in their hospice; the surplus was to go for the Holy Land. In the 14th century, the monastery had 18 members. About mid-14th century the canons built a Gothic church, which still stands in great part, though invisible under later construction. Bl. Andrew of Antioch was probably prior of the community when the church was built, and his tomb was venerated there until 1792. In 1484 Innocent VIII united the houses of the order in France and elsewhere to the Knights of Malta, but the monastery at Annecy was excluded from the decree. The priory was destroyed by fire in 1590 and was not rebuilt. The canons did not live in community thereafter, and the decline in religious spirit that had preceded this event continued its course and led to their secularization in the 17th century and their suppression in the 18th.

Bibliography: A. GAVARD, *Dictionnaire d'histoire et de géographie ecclésiastiques*, ed. A. BAUDRILLART et al. (Paris 1912–) 3:363. G. LETONNELIER, *Annecy au XVe et XVIe siècles* (Annecy 1911).

[C. FALK]

ANNIBALE, GIUSEPPE D'

Cardinal, canonist, and moral theologian; b. Borbona (Aquila), Italy, Sept. 22, 1815; d. Rieti, July 18, 1892. Ordained at Rieti in 1839, he became professor of moral theology and Canon Law in the local seminary. Later he was named vicar-general of Rieti. In 1873 he published his commentary on the constitution *Apostolicae Sedis*, issued by Pius IX in 1869, abrogating, changing, and establishing a new list of censures. D'Annibale's commentary is renowned for its combination of conciseness and accuracy, and it won him the title *Commentator Reatinus*. Leo XIII named him titular bishop of Caristo Aug. 12, 1881, when he was appointed assessor of the Holy Office. And in 1889 Leo XIII created him a cardinal with the title of SS. Boniface and Alexis; he then became prefect of the Congregation of Indulgences. In addition to his commentary on the *Apostolicae Sedis*, he wrote a manual of moral theology, *Summula theologiae moralis* (3 v. Milan 1881–83).

Bibliography: P. DE SANCTIS, *Biografia del cardinale Giuseppe d'Annibale* (Rome 1898). J. J. A'BECKET, *The Catholic Encyclopedia* 1:540–541. A. BEUGNET, *Dictionnaire de théologie catholique* 1.2:1322. T. ORTOLAN, *Dictionnaire d'histoire et de géographie ecclésiastiques* 3:390–393. H. HURTER, *Nomenclator literarius theologiae catholicae* [3] 5.2:1797.

[P. F. MULHERN]

ANNIHILATION

Hypothetically considered in theology, annihilation is the total reduction of the whole being from existence to nonexistence. Whereas CREATION in the active causal sense is the act whereby the entire supposit (the individual being as such) is brought from nonexistence to existence, the act of annihilation is the reduction of the supposit in its entirety from existence to nonexistence (St. Thomas Aquinas, *Summa theologiae* 1a, 41.3; 45.4, 8; 104.1, 3, 4; *De potentia Dei* 3.3; 5.1, 4).

Comparison with Creation. Annihilation, theologically considered, is used in the proper sense and can be understood only by comparison with the concept of creation. God's causality of a being effects the production of the total creature from absolute nonexistence. The divine causality of the existence of being is not distinct as the principle of its being and as the principle of its conservation in being. Creation is the continuous conservation of the being in existence by the First Cause of its existence. The First Cause as the essential proper cause of being remains the proper direct cause as long as being, the proper effect, continues to exist (*see* CONSERVATION, DIVINE).

To say that God could create a being that would not need to be conserved in existence involves a contradiction in terms. Only that which has no proper cause needs not to be kept in existence by its proper cause. The withdrawal of the proper cause of existent being would constitute annihilation of being.

While science, philosophy, and theology deny annihilation in the real order, speculative theology, nevertheless, asks the question whether or not God could annihilate creatures. Since God is the cause of all being by His absolute will and not by intrinsic or extrinsic necessity, He could withdraw His creative act and thereby annihilate created being (*Summa theologiae* 1a, 9.2). As before He caused its existence, without prejudice to His goodness He could have abstained from bringing it into existence, so He could withdraw His act and as He did so creatures would cease to exist. An act may be said to be impossible to God either because the very act involves a contradiction, or because the opposite of the act would be necessary. But absolute nonexistence of creatures does not involve a contradiction, otherwise they would be necessary and not contingent. Moreover, God's power is not determined to the existence of creatures by any necessity. His goodness does not depend on their existence and gains nothing therefrom. He who is their First Cause is not necessitated to give them being unless He has divinely decreed their being. Therefore, it is not impossible for God to reduce being to nonexistence by the simple withdrawal of His conserving power.

The Fate of the Sinner. Although God could annihilate creatures who sin against Him, yet it is more fitting that He conserve them in existence. Sin involves the rebellion of the will against the will of the Creator; it does not involve rebellion of the created nature as such; for despite the moral state of the sinner, his nature observes the order assigned it by God. Since sin is both aversion from the ultimate Good and conversion to an apparent, but not real, transient good, fitting punishment involves, therefore, the pain of loss proportionate to the sinner's aversion from the ultimate Good, and the pain of sense proportionate to the conversion to the apparent transient good. But if the sinner were annihilated, there could be no such fitting punishment, since the whole being would be reduced to nonexistence (*Summa theologiae* 1a2ae, 87.4; 87.1).

Failing to find in reason or revelation any support for the erroneous supposition that there should be an ultimate conversion of all sinners, and considering immortality of the soul to be a grace rather than its natural attribute, some persons who came to be known as annihilationists proposed annihilation as the ultimate end of the finally impenitent, and maintained that God would be compelled thereby to confess failure of His purpose and His power.

In Eucharistic Theology. In the history of theological speculation relative to the nature and effects of the act of Consecration in the Holy Sacrifice of the Mass, certain theologians of the Scotist and nominalist schools came to advance the theory of annihilation as an explanation for what St. Thomas and his followers described to be "the disappearance" of the bread and wine after the words of the separate consecrations. As a result of long profound argumentation between the adherents of the respective positions, there gradually emerged the theological clarification of the doctrine of TRANSUBSTANTIATION. Ultimately, theologians came to distinguish the concept of *change* in which one of the two terms, the *terminus a quo*, or the *terminus ad quem*, may be expressed *negatively,* from that of *substantial conversion* in which two *positive extremes* are involved, each of which is related to the other by such an intimate connection that the last extreme (*terminus ad quem*) begins to exist only as the first extreme (*terminus a quo*) ceases to exist, while a third element (*commune tertium*) unites the two extremes with each other, and continues to exist after the conversion of the substances has taken place (*De veritate* 28.1; *De potentia Dei* 3.2). This unique conversion was defined by the Council of Trent as transubstantiation (H. Denzinger, *Enchiridion* 1642). In the use of the phrase, "disappearance of the bread and wine," St. Thomas had consistently refused to equate annihilation simply and properly; and while at first Scotus was inclined to accept annihilation as identified with "disappearance," the speculations that his position induced ultimately led to the clarification of the meaning of the Consecration of the Mass as the positive action of God effecting a total conversion of the *terminus a quo* into the *terminus ad quem* with the *commune tertium* of the accidents of the bread and wine remaining (*Summa theologiae* 3a, 75.3; 77.5; Denzinger 1642, 1652).

See Also: CHANGE; ELEMENTARY PARTICLES; GENERATION-CORRUPTION.

Bibliography: K. JÜSSEN, *Lexikon für Theologie und Kirche,* ed. J. HOFER and K. RAHNER, 10 v. (2d new ed. Freiburg 1957–65) 1:576–577. A. MICHEL, *Dictionnaire de théologie catholique*

15.1:1396–1406. P. RAYMOND, *Dictionnaire de théologie catholique* 4.2: 1916–18. A. PIOLANTI, *The Holy Eucharist,* tr. L. PENZO (New York 1961) 54–77. E. DORONZO, *De eucharistia* (Milwaukee 1947) 1:224–367.

[M. R. E. MASTERMAN]

ANNIUS, JOHN (NANNI)

Dominican humanist; b. Viterbo, Italy, *c.* 1432; d. Rome, Nov. 13, 1502. He is noted also as a theologian, historian, archeologist, preacher, and student of Oriental languages. His fame led ALEXANDER VI to appoint him master of the sacred palace in 1499, for in the previous year Annius had begun his *Antiquitatum variarum volumina* (Rome 1498), later completed in 17 volumes. The work was designed to throw new light on ancient history by containing the writings and fragments of several pre-Christian Greek and Latin authors. Annius's work created an immediate controversy, especially among his contemporaries who questioned the authenticity of his texts of Berosus and Cato. Modern scholars regard Annius's work with some skepticism and charge him with naïveté in the acceptance of the authenticity of some of his sources. He is the author also of *De futuris Christianorum triumphis in Saracenos,* a commentary on the Apocalypse (Genoa 1480), *Tractatus de imperio Turcorum* (Genoa 1480), and *Chronologia nova* (unpub.), which was designed to correct the historical errors of EUSEBIUS OF CAESAREA.

Bibliography: J. QUÉTIF and J. ÉCHARD, *Scriptores Ordinis Praedicatorum* (New York 1959) 2.1:4–7. L. PASTOR, *The History of the Popes from the Close of the Middle Ages* 6:491.

[C. L. HOHL, JR.]

ANNO OF COLOGNE, ST.

Archbishop of Cologne; b. Swabia, Germany, *c.* 1010; d. Abbey of Siegburg, Germany, Dec. 4, 1075. He came of a noble Swabian family and was educated probably at Bamberg. He was named a canon of Goslar by Emperor Henry III and became archbishop of Cologne and chancellor of the Empire in 1056. To avoid confusion with an earlier archbishop, he is sometimes designated as Anno II. Dissatisfied with the regency of Agnes of Poitou (d. 1077), Anno connived in the kidnaping of the minor Henry IV at Kaiserswerth and made himself guardian and regent for the boy in 1062. Because of his severe discipline, he was dismissed by Henry in 1063 in favor of the more lenient Adalbert of Bremen, but was recalled in 1072.

At Augsburg, in 1062, during the struggle between ALEXANDER II and the antipope Cadalus, Bishop of Parma (d. *c.* 1071), Anno supported Alexander. Despite his holy and penitential life, he was unpopular with the citizens of Cologne, who drove him from the city in 1074. Quickly restored through the help of the peasants, he retired shortly thereafter to the monastery of Siegburg, where he spent his last days, and where he was buried. He was canonized by Pope Lucius III *c.* 1183. His episcopacy was noteworthy both for the reform of existing monasteries and the establishment of new ones: Sankt George and Sankt Maria zu den Stufen (*ad gradus*), both in Cologne, as well as Saalfeld, Grafschaft, and Siegburg. The vita of Anno, composed about 1106 by a monk of Siegburg, is the basis of the Middle High German *Annolied* (*Monumenta Germaniae Historica: Scriptores* 11:462–464 and *Monumenta Germaniae Historica: Dt Chron* 1:2), but neither has historical value.

Feast: Dec. 4.

Bibliography: W. NEUSS, ed., *Geschichte des Erzbistums Köln* (Cologne 1964–) 1:184–200. P. RICHARD, *Dictionnaire d'histoire et de géographie ecclésiastiques,* ed. A. BAUDRILLART et al. (Paris 1912) 3:396–398. A. HAUCK, *Kirchengeschichte Deutschlands* (Berlin-Leipzig 1958) 3:712–730. T. LINDNER, *Anno II., der Heilige, Erzbischof von Köln, 1056–1075* (Leipzig 1869). G. BAUERNFEIND, *Anno II., Erzbischof von Köln* (Munich 1929). *Sankt Anno und seine viel liebe statt,* ed. G. BUSCH (Siegburg, Germany 1975) M. MITTLER, ed., *Siegburger Vorträge zum Annojahr 1983* (Siegburg 1984); *Vita Annonis minor=Die jüngere Annovita* (Siegburg 1975); *Libellus de translatione Sancti Annonis archiepiscopi et miracula Sancti Annonis. Liber primus et secundus* (Siegburg 1966). G. JENAL, *Erzbischof Anno II von Köln und sein politisches Wirken,* 2 v. (Stuttgart 1974–1975). A. HAVERKAMP, *Typik und Politik im Annolied* (Stuttgart 1979).

[M. F. MCCARTHY]

ANNUARIO PONTIFICIO

The ''pontifical yearbook'' is the official directory of the Roman Catholic Church throughout the world. Published annually by the Libreria Editrice Vaticana, the *Annuario* is a reference tool that lists the members of the College of Cardinals, patriarchates, residential and titular bishoprics, abbeys and prelatures *nullius dioeceses,* apostolic administrations *ad nutum S. Sedis,* eastern rite prelates with ordinary jurisdiction, apostolic vicariates and prefectures, missions *sui juris,* and the custody of the Holy Land. It includes the Orders, Congregations and Religious and Secular Institutes, the Sacred Congregations, the tribunals and offices that make up the Roman Curia, the diplomatic representatives of the Holy See and the diplomatic corps accredited to the Holy See, as well the members of the papal household, the administration of the Vatican State, and the vicariate of Rome. It has historical notes on many offices and agencies, addresses and telephone numbers, and a lengthy appendix containing statistics and other useful information.

Origins. Although the title, *Annuario Pontificio,* dates only from 1860 its origins are traceable to the printers Luca and Giovanni Cracas who in 1716 published *Notizie per l'anno.* Although it varied in completeness, the *Notizie* served as a directory of the hierarchy, the Curia, and the papal court; it appeared annually with some interruptions between 1798 and 1817, until 1859. In addition, Cracas published in 1802–1803 the *Elenco degli eminentissimi signori Cardinali, delle Congregazioni e Tribunali e della Famiglia pontificia.* Beginning in 1851 the Camera Apostolica annually published the *Gerarchia della Santa Chiesa cattolica apostolica romana in tutto l'orbe ed in ogni rito con cenni storici (1851–59).* In 1860 this became the *Annuario Pontificio,* whose publication was suspended in 1870 with the loss of the papal states. In 1872, however, a new directory, which was to continue until 1911, appeared. Originally entitled *La Gerarchia Cattolica e la Famiglia Pontificia per l'anno con appendice di altre norizie riguardanti la S. Sede,* it began under the direction of a family of printers, the Monaldi brothers. In 1885 the Typographia Vaticana took over this publication. From 1899 to 1904 the annual volume was designated as the *edizione ufficiale.* In 1912 the name *Annuario Pontificio* was revived, and from 1912 to 1924 some brief notes were added on the offices of the Curia. The present format dates from 1940. Since 1967 the *Annuario Pontificio* has been under the direction of the Ufficio Centrale di Statistica della Chiesa. During the pontificate of John Paul II the publication has shown an increasing awareness of the importance of women in the Church's ministry and governance. Since the 1996 edition of the *Annuario,* the names of mothers general of women's orders and congregations are now included. Previously it mentioned the names of all male generals but not those of the women.

Bibliography: L. N. LORENZONI, "The *Annuario Pontificio:* The Vatican's Pontifical Year Book and a Recent Editorial Decision," *Review for Religious* 58, no. 3 (1999) 261–265.

[R. B. MILLER]

ANNUNCIATION

The message by which God revealed to Mary that she would be the virgin mother of the Messiah; or, in a broader sense, the entire account of Lk 1.26–38, that contains later reflections upon the mystery of the Incarnation. The New Testament (in Mt 1.18–25) contains another account of an annunciation according to which Joseph is informed of Mary's virginal and miraculous conception of the Messiah. This latter section, however, seems to represent an official report of the Jerusalem church, for it is more concerned with scriptural fulfillment than Luke ch.

1–2 and more careful to present a summary of Christian beliefs, including the royal Davidic prerogatives of Jesus through His foster father Joseph. Interest here is limited to the Lukan account. After investigating the authorship of Luke ch. 1–2, this article considers some of the important doctrinal questions raised by the Annunciation narrative.

Authorship of the Account. The origin and literary style of the entire INFANCY NARRATIVE of Lk 1.5–2.52 must be appreciated in order to look with proper focus upon all other questions, such as those that inquire about the nature of the angel's appearance and the meaning of the message to Mary. In brief, according to the hypothesis proposed here, the Greek text of the Lukan infancy narrative reflects an earlier Hebrew form that circulated in a group dominated by St. JOHN THE APOSTLE. John, in turn, derived the salient ideas from Mary herself in the early days after Pentecost. One must trace this development with more precision.

Hebrew Background. A Hebrew original frequently appears beneath the surface of the present Greek text, not only in the continual use of parallelism, but also in many other literary details. Parallelism is a balancing of ideas, so that the second member repeats the first but with some new or different insight; such an ebb and flow of thought moves through almost every sentence of Luke ch. 1–2. A careful study of the Greek text reveals other Hebraic features, different from the classical Greek style of the prologue (Lk 1.1–4) and from the Septuagint form of Luke ch. 3–24. By translating the Greek back into Hebrew, one can discover examples of assonance, alliteration, and onomatopoeia typical of Hebrew poetry: e.g., "He shall go before him [*lipnê*]. . . to prepare [*l*e*pannôt*] for the Lord. . . (1.17; cf. Mal 3.1); "Mary remained [*wattēšeb*]. . . and returned [*wattāšob,*] to her own house" (1.56).

Another indication of Hebrew background, evident in the larger development of these chapters, is the prevailing style of HAGGADAH. Whereas the midrashic style quotes Scripture and sees its interpretation in terms of present events (cf. Mt ch. 1–2), the haggadic presentation simply alludes to Biblical passages and penetrates into a contemporary act of salvation by continual but indirect appeal to the ancient Scriptures. Later some of these allusions will be cited, but the following instances in Luke's Gospel can be noted at present: 1.12–13 (Dn 10.7, 12); 1.16–17 (Mal 3.1, 23); 1.19 (Dn 9.20–21); 1.28–32 (Zep 3.14–17); 1.35 (Ex 40.35). Haggadah, like MIDRASH, begins with history—with the great redemptive acts of God in the present as well as in the past—but it never delays over, nor is it primarily interested in, details of chronology, geography, or history. It seeks to bring the reader into

The Annunciation, detail of the mosaic executed c. 432–440 on the arch of the apse of the Basilica of S. Maria Maggiore, Rome.

close contact with the mysterious work of salvation contained within and beneath events and continuing into the present moment.

Marian and Johannine Influence. The first two chapters of Luke's Gospel, moreover, move in the quiet, rhythmic meter of personal reflection and humble simplicity. They reveal an intuitive, subjective, feminine approach. The heart in which these verses were originally formed seems to have been Mary's, for they reveal the secrets of her soul at that moment when God chose her to be His mother as well as during that long time afterward when she pondered God's goodness toward her. One also senses in the infancy narrative the calm, joyful spirit of the Christian assembly during the first years after Pentecost (Acts 2.42–47): the expectation of the messianic triumph any moment; the assiduous study and the careful observance of the Mosaic Law; Jerusalem as the center of hopes; the special place accorded the poor and lowly (Acts 1.12; 4.23–37; 1 and 2 Thes). The atmosphere is not troubled by any of the controversies that soon began to disturb the Church: quarrels about the care of Hellenists and the reception of Gentiles (Acts 6.1; 11.1–3; Gal 2.11–14). During the first years of the Church Mary shared, especially with John, her contem-

plative appreciation of the Incarnation (cf. Jn 19.26–27; Acts 1.14).

John, for his part, made his own contribution to the infancy narrative, or at least one can say that, as Mary's story was sung or recited in the Johannine circle of Christians, ideas typical of John's theology acquired a prominent place in the narrative: e.g., the delight in number symbolism; the overarching presence of the Jerusalem Temple; the overshadowing of the divine presence; the analogies with the Book of Revelation in schematization, scenes, lyrics and Old Testament imitation.

Diptych Arrangement. It is difficult to determine whether John or Luke was ultimately responsible for the carefully wrought literary structure of these chapters. They are arranged like a sacred drama in two diptychs: one of the annunciations of John the Baptist and of Jesus; the other, of their births. Each section is divided into a series of seven scenes, including: introduction of time and place; appearance of actors; canticle or dialogue; departure of actors. That the two annunciation scenes carefully follow a literary pattern becomes evident in the following outline, borrowed in part from René Laurentin's studies:

Annunciation of John the Baptist (1.5–25)

"The Annunciation," tempera painting on wood panel by Fra Filippo Lippi, c. 1440, National Gallery of Art, Washington D.C. (©Francis G. Mayer/CORBIS)

Presentation of the parents
Apparition of the angel
Anxiety of Zachariah
"Do not fear"
Announcement of the birth
Question: "How shall I know this?"
Answer: the angel's reprimand
Sign: "Behold, thou shalt be dumb"
Silence of Zachariah
Departure of Zachariah

Annunciation of Jesus (1.26–38)

Presentation of the parents
Entrance of the angel
Anxiety of Mary
"Do not fear"
Announcement of the birth
Question: "How shall this happen?"
Answer: the angel's revelation
Sign: "Behold, thy kinswoman has conceived"
Response of Mary
Departure of the angel

Luke, in any case, put the infancy narrative into final shape when he included it in his Gospel. This study of literary origins has important conclusions for the Annunciation account. In such an intricate, artificial arrange-ment as found in Luke ch. 1–2, one must admit that the author(s) took liberty with historical details in order to highlight the religious significance of these details. The chapters contain far more than what Mary understood at the moment of the Annunciation; they are the fruit of her long, meditative prayer and the appreciation of her intu-ition by John, Luke, and others. Here, as elsewhere in the Gospels, God is not giving us a biography of Mary and Joseph, not even of Jesus, but the good news of salvation in Christ Jesus. Many details, therefore, which our curios-ity finds important, are passed over in silence.

Doctrinal Question. Some doctrinal questions de-serve attention. First, what, precisely, was God asking of Mary? In other words, did Mary understand that she was consenting to be the Mother of God or simply the Mother of the Messiah?

Mary's Knowledge of the Divinity of Her Son. From her Old Testament background, Mary had no clear reason to think that the Messiah would also be personally and substantially divine. The Scriptures spoke of a royal Mes-siah born of the family of David [2 Sm ch. 7; Ps 2; 88(89); 109(110); Isaiah ch. 7–11; Mi 5.1–5], of some kind of priestly Messiah in the line of Aaron (Ez 44.15–31; Zec ch. 3–4; Dn 9.24–27; Joel), and possibly of a prophetic Messiah (Dt 18.15–19). Each of the messianic figures, although God's special representative, was expected to be thoroughly human. True, the Annunciation account describes Mary's child with Biblical phrases proclaiming God's presence among His people. Mary's child would be: great [Ps 48.1; 86.10; 96.4], the Son of the Most High (Gn 14.19–20; Sir 24.2), the Holy One (Is 1.4; 5.24; 41.14), the everlasting King of all the earth (Ex 15.18; Is 24.23; 40.10; Za 14.9); and the Savior, as implied in the name Jesus [Ps 24.5; Is 43.3; Dn 6.27]. In Old Testament times, however, all these phrases were understood of God's personal intervention through human mediators, but not of the mediators' being personally divine. From the Biblical texts woven into the Annunciation account, one can never establish a clear awareness on Mary's part of Jesus' divinity. If God accorded Mary a special revelation about the divine nature of her son, Mary's approach toward the Incarnation would have remained thoroughly Biblical, that is, more implicit than explicit, more experiential than notional, and more intuitive than rational.

Even Pentecost, which brought new light to Mary's understanding, did not direct attention primarily to the distinction of person and nature in Jesus, but rather to God's presence in Jesus, dynamically saving His people in the Messiah, even to the extent of placing Him as an equal at His side in bestowing the Spirit (cf. Acts 2.32–36; 3.20–26; Rom 1.3–7). Mary certainly agreed to be the mother of the promised Messiah; how much more she knew about her son at the moment of the Annunciation cannot be clearly established from the Biblical text.

Mary's Resolution to Remain a Virgin. Another, perhaps insoluble, question centers on Mary's resolution to remain a virgin. When asked to be the mother of the Messiah, Mary replied: "How shall this happen, since I do not know man [as a wife does her husband for the procreation of children]?" (Lk 1.34; cf. Gn 4.1; Jgs 16.26; 1 Sm 1.19). Various interpretations are given to this answer: Mary is not yet married but only espoused to Joseph and therefore not able to conceive immediately (P. Gaechter); Mary is intending to be Joseph's wife and, therefore, unable to bear the Messiah who must be virginally conceived (J. P. Audet; T. W. Auer). The latter interpretation adds an elliptic phrase: "How can this be since I ought not to know man if I am to be mother of the Messiah, when, as a matter of fact, I am already bound to a man?" Both of these opinions seem to circumvent the obvious meaning of 1.34. Against the first, one can object that solemn espousals granted marital privileges, although at that time in Galilee it was considered improper to enjoy them; against the second opinion, the proposed interpretation cannot be supported by Greek grammar. The meaning, then, of Mary's words would seem to imply a resolve to

maintain virginity and to follow a way of life intended to prepare one for the great eschatological victory of God. Such a vocation was known in the Bible (Jer 16.2) and especially among the members of the QUMRAN community. Why, then, it is asked, did Mary consent to the solemn espousals with Joseph? Did she and Joseph have a private agreement between them? These confidences, understandably enough, remained locked within Mary's heart.

Mary's Holiness. The Annunciation account presents a rich theology of Mary's holiness. Aside from God, no one in the entire Bible is the recipient of such beautiful salutations as Mary: Lk 1.18, 30, 35, 45, 49; 2.19, 34. Mary is presented also as the new Temple and the new ark of the covenant, for God's spirit overshadows her (1.35) as it did Moses' Tent of Meeting and Solomon's Temple (Ex 40.35; Hg. 2.6–9). She represents God's people at prayer, in pilgrimage to the Temple, struggling with the evil one and witnessing the promised salvation (1.35, 46–55; 2.21–50). Because of God's generosity in her regard, she already possesses what the rest of the world still anticipates. She receives in advance what other men will be given after the death and Resurrection of Jesus.

Appearance of the Angel. Finally, the question is asked, "Did an angel actually appear to Mary?" Some have raised a doubt because a number of Old Testament passages actually refer to God under the metaphor of the ANGEL of the Lord (Gn 16.11–14; 48.15–16; Ex 3.2–4). There is little doubt, however, in late Old Testament books, such as Daniel and Tobit, or in apocryphal works of the last century B.C., or in the New Testament that Palestinian Jews believed in angels and accorded them great veneration. In any case, the Annunciation account does not speak of any bodily appearance of the Angel. The best Greek MSS do not say that Mary saw the angel; even the words found in a few MSS, "when she heard him [the angel]" are not part of the original text. If God sent the angel Gabriel to communicate His message to Mary, the angel mediated some kind of interior locution within the silence of Mary's soul.

[C. STUHLMUELLER/P. ROUILLARD/EDS.]

Liturgical Feast. Of Eastern origin, the liturgical Feast of the Annunciation (March 25) was introduced at Rome between 660 and 680. Strictly speaking, it is a feast of our Lord and the oldest liturgical books entitled it *Adnuntiatio Domini.* The date, March 25, was chosen in relation to that of Christmas, but also in virtue of an old tradition according to which the creation of the world, the Incarnation, and the Passion of Christ occurred on that date. These historical data, as well as the prayers of the Mass and the readings from St. Leo in the Office of Matins, placed the feast in the general framework of the plan of salvation. In the Middle Ages, popular piety resulted in the Feast of the Annunciation being celebrated as a Marian feast. The 1969 revision of the Roman liturgical calendar restored the feast as primarily a Solemnity of the Lord in which Mary, his mother, is intimately associated. The full title of the feast indicates its christological focus—the Annunciation of the Lord—restoring its ancient name.

Bibliography: E. BURROWS, *The Gospel of the Infancy, and Other Biblical Essays,* ed. E. F. SUTCLIFFE (London 1940). R. LAURENTIN, *Structure et théologie de Luc I–II* (*Études Biblique*; 1957), with ample bibliog. A. MEDÉBIELLE, *Dictionnaire de la Bible,* suppl. ed. L. PIROT, et al. (Paris 1928–) 1:262–297. T. MAERTENS, *Le Messie est là: Lc 1–2* (Bruges 1954). P. GAECHTER, *Maria im Erdenleben* (Innsbruck 1953). M. J. LAGRANGE, "Le Récit de l'enfance de Jésus-Christ dans Saint-Luc," *Revue Biblique,* 4 (1895) 160–185; "La Conception surnaturelle du Christ d'après Saint-Luc," *ibid.* 11 (1914) 60–71, 188–208. K. BORNHAUSER, *Die Geburts- und Kindheitsgeschichte Jesu* (Gütersloh 1930). H. SAHLIN, *Der Messias und das Gottesvolk: Studien zur proto-Lukanischen Theologie* (Uppsala 1945).

[C. W. FIELDS/EDS.]

ANOINTING

The smearing or pouring of an unctuous substance, especially olive oil, on a person, both as a utilitarian practice and as a symbolic ceremony. It was an ancient custom among various peoples, particularly in the Near East. Of special interest here is the custom of anointing as described in the Bible and the medieval ceremony of anointing high dignitaries in Church and State when they entered upon their offices. (For the religious ceremony of anointing as an essential or a secondary part in the administration of the Christian Sacraments, *see* ANOINTING OF THE SICK, I, II.)

In the Bible. The anointing of persons and objects with oil or an unctuous substance was a frequent occurrence in the Bible. It had both a secular use and a religious use and significance.

Secular Use. Anointing had many uses in biblical times. Its sanitary and therapeutic benefits were recognized at an early date. Palestine, with its semitropical and dry climate in the summer, made the smearing of oil on one's body almost a necessity, if not for health at least for comfort. Because of exposure to the sun and wind people used olive oil, sometimes scented, as a body lubricant after bathing (Ru 3.3; Ez 16.9; Dn 13.17; Ps 103[104].15). Mourners abstained from ointment (2 Sm 14.2; Dn 10.3) since it was a sign of joy (Is 61.3; Mt 6.7). Oil bases were used for perfumed cosmetics (Dt 28.40; Jdt 10.3; 2 Sm 14.2). As a sign of respect a host anointed the head of a guest (Mt 26.7; Lk 7.46; Ps 22[23]).5). The anointing of the feet of a guest had a special significance of humble devotion and respect (Lk 7.28, 46; Jn 12.3). Released captives were clothed, fed, and anointed (2 Chr 28.15). Various ointments were used for curing wounds and bruises (Is 1.6; Mk 6.13; Lk 10.34). Corpses were anointed in preparation for burial (Mk 16.1; Lk 23.56; Jn 19.39; *see* BURIAL, II).

Religious Use. Both persons and objects were anointed for religious purposes. It would appear that the notion of a constitutive blessing was basic to this custom, which belonged to the process of setting apart either a person or thing for religious use. Jacob thus anointed the memorial pillar that he erected at Bethel (Gn 28.18; 35.14; *see* STONES, SACRED [IN THE BIBLE]). The TENT OF MEETING and its sacred furniture and utensils were anointed with an expertly prepared ointment (Ex 30.22–33; 40.10–11). There seems, however, to be no reason to believe that implements of war were anointed with sacred oil, though they were apparently smeared with oil or fat as a preservative (2 Sm 1.21; Is 21.5).

The practice of anointing persons was a ceremony usually performed on only priests and kings. The consecration of priests was prescribed in the rather late texts of Ex 28.40–42; 29.1–46; 30.30–33, where the evidence points to the limitation of consecration by anointing to the class from which the high priests came, while there was no anointing for the ordinary members of the priestly tribe of LEVI. The anointing of prophets is generally interpreted as analogical to that of kings (1 Kgs 19.16; Is 61.1). In poetry the whole people are called Yahweh's anointed (Ps 104[105].15).

Among the laypeople only the kings on their ascendance to the throne were consecrated by an anointing. A high priest or prophet anointed the head of the king, who henceforth was regarded as the anointed (māšiāh, whence Messiah) of the Lord (1 Sm 10.1; 16.13; 1 Kgs 1.39). The right of succession to the throne was assured by the ceremony of anointing (2 Kgs 9.3; 11.12; 23.30; 2 Chr 23.11). The consecration of Israelite kings was similar to that of their neighbors, but its significance rested in its particular Yahwistic religious meaning rather than in any borrowed elements of the rite. The kings of Israel were inviolable because they were the "anointed of Yahweh" (1 Sm 24.7; 26.9, 11, 16, 23; 2 Sm 1.14, 16; 9.22). (*See* MESSIAH; MESSIANISM.)

Religious Significance. The peculiar significance of the anointing of persons rested in their consecration to the service of the Lord. The Bible took this point for granted and did not dwell on it at length. The anointed was separated from others and placed directly under the authority of God. Among the few certain parallels in extra-biblical literature, the Amarna Letters (51.6–9; 34.51) record two ceremonies of religious investiture. The anointing of

Hazael as king of Damascus by the prophet ELISHA might not have been a strictly religious rite despite the fact that the king became an instrument for the visitation of divine wrath upon unfaithful Israelites (1 Kgs 19.15). Although the enthronement of the king was a religious ceremony, the voice of, at least, the tribal leaders of the people had great weight in the selection or acceptance of a king (2 Sm 2.4, 7; 5.3; 1 Kgs 12.2–19; 2 Kgs 23.30). Some scholars have presumed that the original ceremony of the anointing of kings was at first secular in nature and then given a religious form. Israelite enthronement, however, always had a religious character. Its particular significance rested in the fact that the king became God's chosen one invested with His spirit and guarded by His special providence (1 Sm 10.1; 16.13). The king was thus a leader divinely endowed to carry out the wishes of Yahweh.

See Also: KINGSHIP IN THE ANCIENT NEAR EAST.

Bibliography: E. COTHENET, *Dictionnaire de la Bible,* suppl. ed. L. PIROT et al. (Paris 1928–) 6:701–732. E. KUTSCH and G. DELLING, *Die Religion in Geschichte und Gegenwart,* 7 v. (3d ed. Tübingen 1957–65) 5:1330–32. *Encyclopedic Dictionary of the Bible,* tr. and adap. by L. HARTMAN (New York 1963), from A. VAN DEN BORN, *Bijbels Woordenboek* 92–95. R. DE VAUX, *Ancient Israel, Its Life and Institutions,* tr. J. MCHUGH (New York 1961) 103–106, 398–400. J. DE FRAINE, *L'Aspect religieux de la royauté Israélite* (Rome 1954). A. R. JOHNSON, *Sacral Kingship in Ancient Israel* (Cardiff 1955). D. LYS, ''L'Onction dans la Bible,'' *Études théologiques et religieuses* 29 (1954) 3–54. C. R. NORTH, ''The Religious Aspects of Hebrew Kingship,'' *Zeitschrift für die alttestamentliche Wissenschaft* 50 (1932) 8–38. R. PATAI, ''Hebrew Installation Rites,'' *Hebrew Union College Annual* 20 (1947) 143–255.

[G. T. KENNEDY]

Anointing in the Middle Ages. The practice of anointing, derived from biblical tradition (1 Sm 10.6), which was in turn perhaps inspired by Egyptian and Canaanite practices (E. Kutsch, *Salbung als Rechtsakt im alten Testament u. im alten Orient* [Berlin 1963]), became an integral part of the enthronement ceremonies of kings, popes, and emperors during the high Middle Ages. Anointing was in effect the traditional procedure for transferring a man or object from a profane to a sacred status. Used in the first centuries of Christianity for the confirmation of catechumens and for ordination of priests and bishops, it was employed by the VISIGOTHS (M. Ferotin, ''Le liber ordinum en usage dans l'église wisigothique,'' *Monumenta ecclesiae liturgica,* 5 [1904]) and the FRANKS in ceremonies relating to their sovereigns.

Anointing in France. When, with papal approval PEPIN III superseded the MEROVINGIANS and was elected king of the Franks in 751, he had himself anointed by St. BONIFACE to set the seal of legitimacy on his rule; this anointing was renewed by Pope STEPHEN II in 754 at SAINT-DENIS. Pope LEO III added coronation to this anointing for CHARLEMAGNE in 800. Anointing and coronation were again combined in the ceremony performed at Reims in 816 for Emperor Louis the Pious. The head of the emperor was anointed with holy oil to indicate his status as protector of the Church. This rite was retained by the Carolingians and was renewed by the Capetians. As a consecrated person, *gratia Dei Rex,* the king of France exercised a thaumaturgic power; Charles X in 1825 was the last to claim its use. The Plantagenets exercised an analogous power in England, patterned upon the French example. The author of the *Songe du Verger,* however, was anxious to assert the independence of the king from the clergy and contended that the miracle-working power of kings was not derived from anointing. Anointing exalts the king above the laity and grants him status approximating that of priests (i.e., makes them *sacerdotalis ministerii participes,* said Guido of Osnabrück [*De controversia inter Hildebrandum et Heinricum, Monumenta Germaniae Historica: Libelli de lite* (Berlin 1826–) 1:467]). Enhanced as the custom was by legendary tales, it furnished a weighty argument in favor of the pretensions of the Capetians in Church affairs and bolstered the prestige of the French monarchy not only in France but even among foreign princes. For, according to legend, the holy oil used was of divine origin. Kept in the Abbey of SAINT-REMI in Reims, it assured this city the privilege of being the site of all royal anointing and coronation, with the exceptions of King HENRY IV at Chartres, and NAPOLEON I at Paris. The ritual followed in the coronation ceremonies is known from liturgical manuals, the *Ordines ad consecrandum et coronandum regem.* One of these ceremonials, drawn up at Reims toward the end of the reign of King LOUIS IX (*Ordo ad inungendum regem*) is particularly explicit (de Pange, *Le roi,* 374–378). The coronation book of Charles V (1364) likewise gives a detailed description. The unction took place during combined anointing-coronation ceremonies in the cathedral. The king knelt, and the archbishop of Reims anointed him on the head, breast, shoulders, and elbows. The *Traité du sacre,* drawn up by the Carmelite Jean Golein in the entourage of Charles V (extracts, M. Bloch, *Les rois,* 478–488), described the ritual and simultaneously explained its symbolism, stressing the religious character of royal power. The anointing ceremony in France generally enjoyed high political significance. It served to bolster the tenets of GALLICANISM, and even when critics challenged the basic concepts of anointing, it was to remain, as Étienne Pasquier stated, ''most fitting for every good citizen to accept them, for the sake of the majesty of Empire.'' Eager to stress the anointing of bishops as a rite superior to the anointing of princes, Pope INNOCENT III, in a letter (*Patrologia Latina,* ed. J. P. Migne, 271 v., indexes 4 v. [Paris 1878–90] 213:284) reproduced in the

Compilatio III and in the Decretals of GREGORY IX (*Corpus iuris canonici*, ed. E. Friedberg [Leipzig 1879–81; repr. Graz 1955] X 1.15.1.5), declared that only bishops should be anointed on the head with chrism, while kings were to be anointed with holy oil on shoulders and arms only.

Anointing in England. The ritual dates at least from the time of King Egbert of Mercia at the Council of Chelsea (787). His anointing, doubtless patterned after Frankish practice, became normal for the whole of Anglo-Saxon England and became part of the coronation ceremony (see the Egbert Pontifical, 9th century; ed. Publications of the Surtees Society 27 [1853]). In the course of time certain variations were introduced into the rite. Thus, in the reign of King Henry I only the head of the king was anointed. The unction of shoulders and arms appeared at the end of the 12th century, but already in 1154 HENRY II had been anointed on the head, breast, and arms. In the 13th century, Henry III adopted the Reims ceremony as a pattern for the coronation of the English sovereign at WESTMINSTER ABBEY (Richardson, 136–150).

Anointing in the Empire. The Carolingian tradition was maintained both for the German king and for the emperor, and although both offices were most often held by one and the same person, a distinction was maintained between royal and imperial anointing.

Royal Anointing. In conformity with biblical and Carolingian tradition the German king required anointing, the ceremony that conferred on him supernatural graces for the exercise of his functions, and that, according to the theology of the 12th century, possessed a sacramental character. The king was exalted above the laity; he was *rex et sacerdos.* Anointing imprinted upon the king a quasi-indelible character, which, during the INVESTITURE STRUGGLE, was set forward as the reason no king could be deposed. Although Henry I (r. 919–936) refused anointing, his son OTTO I received it (936), and the tradition was respected thereafter (Sachsenspiegel, Ldr. III, 52.1). It was united to the coronation ceremony that was held at AACHEN. Until 1028 the archbishop of Mainz had the privilege of crowning and anointing; after this it became the right of the archbishop of Cologne, on whom the diocese of Aachen depended (C. Vogel, *Ephemerides liturgicae* [1960], 153, n.25, 155; *Pontifical romano-germanique,* 1:252–254). After the Great Interregnum (1250–73) anointing and coronation of the king lost their importance.

Imperial Anointing. Imperial coronation and anointing were reintroduced when Otto I, already king of Germany (936), became emperor (962). From this time forward the two ceremonies were performed at St. Peter's in Rome, even during the period of the AVIGNON PAPACY,

when Emperors Henry VII (1312) and Charles IV (1355) were anointed and crowned in Rome by cardinals. It was this twin ceremony that created the emperor and introduced him into the *ordo clericalis.* At first the imperial anointing closely imitated episcopal anointing, but the imperial ceremony was gradually modified to eliminate any confusion between the two and to circumvent any unfounded pretensions on the part of the emperor with respect to the Church. The 12th-century Roman PONTIFICAL (Andrieu, *Pontifical romain* 1:251, 253; 2:383, 389) describes the anointing ceremony thus: "using blessed oil, the bishop of Ostia is to anoint him on the right arm and between the shoulder blades." While performing the anointing the bishop is to recite the consecration prayer in which he declares that the emperor has been *constitutus ad regendam ecclesiam* (on the ritual, see Andrieu, *Ordines romani,* 4:459, 503; and C. Vogel, *Pontifical romano-germanique,* 1:263–266). The anointing between the shoulder blades instead of on the head, and with merely blessed oil instead of chrism, which was used for bishops, underscored the inferiority of the imperial anointing, while the increasing precision of sacramental theology denied sacramental character to imperial anointing. For their part, the theorists treating of imperial power were at pains to assert their independence of the pope and declared that imperial power was acquired prior to the coronation ceremony, that the anointing conferred only the name and not the imperial power (GERHOH OF REICHERSBERG, *De investigatione Antechristi* 1:40; *Braunschweiger Reichsweistum* of 1252). The *Sachsenspiegel,* however, (Ldr. III, 52.1) and the GOLDEN BULL of 1356 still made imperial power depend on pontifical anointing, and imperial coronations continued to be held in Rome until 1452.

Anointing and Consecration of the Pope. In the Middle Ages anointing was only one of the ceremonies marking the enthronement of a pope; in fact, it was required only in order to confer on him episcopal consecration. Consequently, anointing was part of the enthronement ceremonies only when the pope-elect was not already a bishop. This was the case with each new pope during the period in which the law, forbidding the transfer of bishops from one see to another, was strictly observed (Roman Synod of 769; *Ordo Romanus IX,* c. 5). But from the 11th century the pope was usually chosen from among the bishops, and thus the episcopal consecration was rarely a necessary part of the enthronement.

It was, however, the example of the episcopal consecration of the new pope that had inspired the imperial ritual, and the symmetry of imperial and papal enthronement was to symbolize and justify an equality of powers. The description of the papal rite given by the *LIBER DIURNUS* (no. 57) probably goes back to the 6th century, and this text remained the basis of the *ordinatio pontificis* until the 13th century. The *Ordo Romanus IX*, c. 5 (first half of 9th century, reproduced with slight variations in the Collection of DEUSDEDIT 2.13 [ed. W. von Glanvell, 240]), described a similar ceremony, and though it is not an official document, it probably represents the practice followed from the 10th to the 11th centuries. The *Romano-German Pontifical* no. 71, composed shortly after 950 by a monk of St. Alban in Mainz (cf. *Ordo XL* B in C. Vogel, *Pontifical romano-germanique* 1:245), kept the formula of the *Liber diurnus* 57, with a few additions. The Roman Pontifical of the 12th century, ch. 33 (Andrieu, *ibid.* 1:249) remains faithful to that of the 10th century. The *Ordo Romanus XIV* (*ibid.* 2:380–382) gives a description of the rite as it was observed between approximately the 7th and the end of the 13th century: prior to consecration the new pope was merely the *electus*. Consecration took place at St. Peter's the Sunday following the election. As was necessary prior to the 11th century, the new pope was consecrated bishop during the Mass, between the Kyrie and the Gloria, by the bishop of Ostia (L. Duchesne, ed., *Liber pontificalis*, v. 1–2 [Paris 1886–92] 1:202, 360; 2:175). After prostrating himself before the *confessio* of St. Peter and then at the altar, the pope-elect was helped to his feet by the consecrating bishops, who placed the open gospel book on his head and shoulders and then recited the prayer of consecration while laying their hands upon his head. The prayer preserved in the Romano-German Pontifical (Andrieu, *Pontifical romain* 1:147) refers to a "heavenly" anointing; but texts prior to the 10th century fail to indicate a physical anointing of the pope-elect. The consecration was effected simply by the laying-on of hands and reciting the appropriate prayer.

The break between Rome and Byzantium and the concurrently growing influence of the Franks in the 9th and 10th centuries explain the introduction of anointing at Rome in the first half of the 10th century. Anointing was in fact unknown to the Oriental liturgy, while in the Frankish liturgy it was employed for bishops, priests, and princes. Inspired by imperial practice, papal anointing took place immediately after the consecration prayer, which had previously alluded to a celestial anointing. Holy chrism was used in anointing the head of the pope, whereas the emperor was thence-forth anointed only on the arms and neck with oil used in exorcism. The rite of papal consecration, however, never developed beyond this point, because the disappearance of the ban on episcopal translation in the 11th century generally brought an end to the rite of anointing in the ceremony of papal enthronement (see L. Duchesne, ed., *Liber pontificalis,* 2:296– ; *Ordo Romanus XII* [*Census,* c. 1192] in J. Mabillon, *Musaeum italicum* 2:165– ; and *Ordines Romani XIII* [1275] and *XIV* [1311]).

Bibliography: T. GODEFROY, *Le Cérémonial de France,* 2 v. (Paris 1649). R. POUPARDIN, ''L'Onction impériale,'' *Moyen âge* 18 (1905) 113–126. M. BLOCH, *Les Rois thaumaturges* (Strasbourg 1924). P. E. SCHRAMM, ''Die Krönung bei den Westfranken und Angelsachsen von 878 bis um 1000.'' *Zeitschrift der Savigny-Stiftung für Rechtsgeschichte, Kanonistische Abteilung* 23 (1934) 117–242; ''Die Krönung in Deutschland bis zu Beginn des salischen Hauses (1028),'' *ibid.* 24 (1935) 184–332; ''Der König von Frankreich: Wahl, Krönung, Erbfolge und Königsidee vom Anfang der Kapetinger (987) bis zum Ausgang des MAs,'' *ibid.* 25 (1936) 222–354; 26 (1937) 161–284; *Der König von Frankreich,* 2 v. (2d ed. Weimar 1960). H. W. KLEWITZ, ''Die Krönung des Papstes,'' *Zeitschrift der Savigny-Stiftung für Rechtsgeschichte, Kanonistische Abteilung* 61 (1941) 96–130. J. DE PANGE, *Le Roi très chrétien* (Paris 1949). E. EICHMANN, *Die Kaiserkrönung im Abendland,* 2 v. (Würzburg 1942); *Weihe und Krönung des Papstes im Mittelalter* (Munich 1951). C. A. BOUMAN, *Sacring and Crowning . . . Anointing of Kings and the Coronation of the Emperor before the 11th Century* (Groningen 1957). *Ordines coronationis imperialis,* ed. R. ELZE, *Monumenta Germaniae Historica: Fontes Iuris Germanici* 9 (1960). H. G. RICHARDSON, ''The Coronation in Medieval England,'' *Traditio* 16 (1960) 111–202. M. ANDRIEU, *Les ''Ordines Romani'' du haut moyen-âge,* 5 v. (Louvain 1931–61). M. ANDRIEU, *Le Pontifical Romain au moyen-âge,* 4 v. (Rome 1938–41). C. VOGEL, ''Précisions sur la date et l'ordonnance primitive du Pontifical romano-germanique,'' *Ephemerides liturgicae* 74 (1960) 145–162. C. VOGEL and R. ELZE, eds., *Le Pontifical romanogermanique du dixième siècle,* 2 v. (*Studi e Testi* 226, 227; 1963). Also profitable are the articles in *Sacral Kingship* (*Studies in the History of Religions* 4; Leiden 1959).

[J. GAUDEMET]

ANOINTING OF THE SICK, I: THEOLOGY OF

Formerly called Extreme Unction, this sacrament is conferred upon Christians in serious illness or in old age. This article discusses the existence of the sacrament: its history, effects, and administration.

EXISTENCE OF THE SACRAMENT

That Jesus exercised a ministry of healing is recorded (Mt 9.35) and that He enjoined this ministry on the Apostles is recorded (Mt 10.1, Mk 6.7, and Lk 9.1). In speaking of their fulfillment of it, Mark alone adds the significant detail: ''And they . . . anointed with oil many sick people, and healed them'' (6.13). Mark does not explicitly state that the employment of this rite was at Jesus' command. There is certainly no question here of a Christian sacrament, but the Council of Trent sees in the text a foreshadowing of the sacrament of Anointing of the Sick (H. Denzinger, *Enchiridion symbolorum* [Freiburg 1963] 1695).

Scriptural evidence. Since anointing with oil had a recognized therapeutic value among the Jews, and oil was staple for many domestic and medicinal purposes in Antique Mediterranean cultures, it is entirely plausible that the Apostles should have elected this as the sign ready-at-hand to signify the conferring of a special grace on those in a state of sickness just as an ablution was made a "new Baptism" when it was constituted a sign of Christian regeneration by the annexing to it of Christian grace. In ch. five of his Epistle, St. James, in a context of counseling norms of Christian conduct in several life situations, recommends a special remedy in time of sickness. "Is any among you sick? Let him bring in the presbyters of the Church, and let them pray over him, anointing him with oil in the name of the Lord. And the prayer of faith will save the sick man, and the Lord will raise him up, and if he be in sins, they shall be forgiven him. Confess your sins, therefore, to one another, that you may be saved" (14–16).

The subject of this rite described by James is a Christian who is not moribund, but seriously ill (ἀσθενεῖ; cf. Jn 4.46; 11.1–6; Acts 9.37). The presbyters of the Church are not the miracle-workers of 1 Cor 12.10, but the official leaders of the local Church, for the rite is not charismatic but hierarchic; the use of the plural need not designate that many presbyters be summoned, for it is a categorical plural. The rite itself is one of prayer accompanied, as the aorist participle ἀλείψαντες implies, by anointing with oil. This is performed "in the name of the Lord," an expression that scarcely implies a command of the Lord, but rather ascribed the efficacy of this rite to His power of healing (Lk 10.17; Mk 9.38; Acts 3.6, 16; 4.7–10; 9.34). The Christian is anointed in the name in which he was baptized (Acts 2.38; 8.16; 10.48). The explicit invocation of the powerful name of Jesus excludes any notion of a magical healing power.

The "prayer of faith" spoken in verse 15 may mean prayer said in confidence or prayer inspired by faith. In this second acceptation, which in the context is the more probable, the ritual prayer of the community is designated. The effect of this rite is expressed by three verbs, all in the future tense. There is a parallelism between the first two "will save" (σώσει) and "will raise up" (ἐγερεῖ). Though σώσει can refer to spiritual healing and does so in Jas 1.21; 2.14; 4.12; 5.20, it never in New Testament usage bears this meaning in contexts of sickness, death, or their danger. Because of the above parallelism, it should be here accepted in the sense of restoration to bodily health, as the meaning of ἐγερεῖ suggests. The notion of spiritual healing need not be excluded; indeed, it is expressly, although conditionally, stated as the third effect of this rite, but it is the physical effect that is emphasized. The purpose of the rite looks principally to the physical sickness that is certainly present and only secondarily to the sin that may possibly be present. ἁμαρτία implies grave sin, and the conditional reference to its forgiveness may be interpreted in three ways: (1) that not only those

who are now in sin may receive this anointing; (2) that there is no necessary connection between sin and sickness; (3) that the eschatological effect of the rite is related to the forgiveness of sin.

HISTORY

The monuments of tradition witnessing to this sacrament fall into three categories: patristic references to the ministry for the sick; texts of the liturgy employed in the blessing of the oil; mentions, in the biographies of saints, of the actual use of this oil.

The Fathers. Some of the earliest references to the ministry for the sick are so brief or their historical context so obscure that we cannot invoke them as certain witnesses to this sacrament (Tertullian, *De praescriptione haereticorum* 41 [*Patrologia Latina* 2:56] Aphraates the Syrian (*Demonstrationes* 23.3 [*Patrologia syriaca*] 2.6); Athanasius (*Epistola ad episcopos encyclica* 5 [*Patrologia Graeca* 25:234]). Other references imply a rite of anointing and invoke James as authority, but in a context suggesting penance and reconciliation rather than sickness (Origen, *Hom. 2 in Leviticum* 4 [*Patrologia Graeca* 12:419]); John Chrysostom (*De sacerdotio* 3.6 [*Patrologia Graeca* 48:644]). Still others speak clearly of anointing the sick in fulfillment of James' command (Cyril of Alexandria, *De adoratione et cultu in spiritu et veritate* 6 [*Patrologia Graeca* 68:472]; Victor of Antioch, *Catena in evang. S. Marcae* 6.13, ed. J. Cramer, *Catenae Graecorum Patrum* [Oxford 1840] 1:340). A letter of Innocent I (d. 417) to Decentius (*Epist.* 25.8 [*Patrologia Latina* 20:559–60]) is a further witness to the evolving anointing of the sick. Innocent cites the Epistle of James and explains that it refers to the faithful who are sick and make use of the oil blessed by the bishop. This oil is used "not only by priests, but also by all Christians for their own need or the need of their families." Innocent further explains to Decentius that ministry to the sick should not be reserved just to presbyters but also includes the bishop. He also advises Decentius that the anointing is *genus sacramenti* and thus is reserved for those in full communion with the Church; those in the order of penitents may not be anointed.

That pastors urged the practice of anointing the sick with oil we know (Caesarius of Arles, *Sermones* 50.1, 52.5 [CCL 103:225, 232]; Eligius of Noyon, *De rectitudine Catholicae conversationis* 5, among the works of Augustine *Patrologia Latina* 40:1172–73]). Possidius (d. after 437), the contemporary and first biographer of St. Augustine (d. 430), informs us that the saint "was accustomed to visit the sick who desired it in order to lay his hands on them and pray at their bedside" (*Vita S.* Aug. 27; *Patrologia Latina* 32:56). Since Augustine incorporated Jas 5.14–16 into his *Speculum* (*Patrologia Latina*

34:1036) as one of the counsels of Christian life, it is probable that on such occasions he personally anointed them with oil.

Liturgical books. Significant witness to this sacrament is found in the early rituals containing formulas for consecrating the oil for the sick. Their inclusion in these rituals manifests that the oil had to be blessed before it was used and offers the presumption that its use was widespread. The earliest extant formula that clearly applies to oil of the sick is found in the *Apostolic Tradition* (5; B. Botte, *La Tradition apostolique de saint Hippolyte: Essai de reconstitution* [1963] 18–19). It is noteworthy that in this liturgy the blessing of oil takes place toward the end of the Eucharistic prayer (anaphora), a position it retains in the present Roman liturgy of Holy Thursday. In the *Euchologian of Serapion* (d. after 362), we find a blessing entitled ''Prayer for the Oil of the Sick or for Bread or for Water.'' Despite the ambiguity of the title, the prayer is almost exclusively concerned with oil, upon which God is entreated to bestow a curative power ''so that it may become a means of removing every disease and sickness . . . unto health and soundness of soul and body and spirit, unto perfect well-being'' (29 F. X. Funk, *Didascalia et constitutiones apostolorum* 2:191–193). Another blessing is found in the *GELASIAN SACRAMENTARY* (1.40; ed. K. Mohlberg 61). This formula remains substantially unchanged in the present Roman Pontifical.

Biographies of saints. In the *Dialogues* (3.3; *Patrologia Latina* 20:213), Sulpicius Severus (d. 430?) tells of the wife of a certain Count Avitus who asked St. Martin of Tours to bless ''as is the custom'' a vessel of oil intended as a remedy in illness. A similar, but more revealing incident, is related of St. Genevieve (*Vita b. Genovefae;* in *Monumenta Germaniae Historica: Scriptores rerum Merovingicarum* [Berlin 1926–] 3:236). She was accustomed to anoint with blessed oil the sick for whom she cared. One day, when the oil was urgently needed, the vessel containing it was found empty. The saint was deeply disturbed at this ''because there was no bishop within reach to bless it [the oil].''

Lay anointing. It was always the rule, although one does find exceptions, that the oil for this sacrament had to be consecrated by a bishop. It is important to note that the intervention of the Church was indispensable in the blessing of this oil. The oil itself appears to have been regarded as a permanent sacrament, in much the same way as the Eucharist today, and so its confection could be separated from the administration of the sacrament. If this is so, the practice of lay anointing is easily understood. The use of the oil, either by drinking it or applying it to the sick was a religious gesture that invoked the healing power of God over whatever ailment, evil, or sin afflicted

the person. The practice of lay anointing gradually fell into disuse from about the beginning of the 8th century in the Frankish kingdom and probably at an earlier date in Celtic lands. The reform councils of the Carolingian era witness to this, while at the same time encouraging the clergy to provide greater ministerial care for the sick and the dying.

During the Carolingian period, the anointing of the sick became increasingly associated with spiritual healing and the forgiveness of sin. The clergy took further responsibility for the sacrament, and people increasingly put the sacrament off until they were close to death.

Scholastic era. With the rise of the scholastics in the 12th century, two views of the purpose of this sacrament become evident. The first of these continues the early view and regards it as a sacrament of the sick. The proper effect, therefore, is the cure of the body even though its more noble effect is the forgiveness of sins. This tradition is represented by Hugh of Saint-Victor (d. 1141), Roland Bandinelli (later Alexander III, d. 1181), Omnebene (d. 1185), and William of Auxerre (d. 1231). The second view stresses the spiritual effect of the anointing, the forgiveness of sin, and tends to see it as a Sacrament of the dying. This view is represented by the unknown author of the *Epitome theologiae christianae* and the author of the *Summa sententiarum*. It is the view adopted by Peter Lombard (d. 1160), who was among the first to employ the term Extreme Unction. The first to speak of this anointing as a preparation for the beatific vision was Master Simon, author of the *De septem sacramentis*. This opinion was further developed by William of Auvergne (d. 1249) and is the one adopted by the great scholastic doctors, including St. Albert the Great (d. 1280), St. Thomas Aquinas (d. 1274), St. Bonaventure (d. 1274), and Duns Scotus (d. 1308).

Although the Franciscan and Dominican schools agreed in viewing this sacrament as a preparation for glory, the former saw this effected by the remission of venial sins, while the latter regarded the reality of this sacrament as the purification of the soul of those remnants of sin that impeded its transit to glory. In either view, however, the sick person was only to be anointed when death was imminent and recovery despaired of. In this period, Anointing displaces Viaticum as the final sacrament. In the older rituals the order of administering the sacraments to the dying was Penance, Anointing, and Viaticum. The rituals of this period give the order as Penance, Viaticum, and Anointing. In our own time the Holy See has restored the earlier order of administration.

Responsible for this changed attitude toward the purpose of this sacrament was an inability to appreciate how a physical effect, the recovery of health, could be the effect of a sacrament. Sacraments are means of grace, and grace is a supernatural perfection of man. Again, if sacraments always produce their effect in a disposed subject, how could the recovery of health, an effect so seldom realized, be the effect of this sacrament? These difficulties were obviated by concluding that the remission of sin was the sacrament's principal effect. But since two sacraments, Penance, and Baptism, already had this purpose, it was logical to see this one as destined for the removal of sin's last remnants, to delay its reception to the last moments of life, to see it as Extreme Unction. Several non-theological factors abetted the popular acceptance of the view that this sacrament was to be delayed until life's final moments (e.g., that one who had received it and recovered could never again enjoy marriage.)

Council of Trent. There is no evidence of change in the theological attitude toward the effect of this sacrament in the period leading to the Council of Trent. Indeed, the first draft of the schema on Extreme Unction presented at this council might well stand as its epitome. It is to be administered "only to those who are in their final struggle and have come to grips with death and are about to go forth to the Lord" (*Acta genuina ss. oecumenici concilii Tridentini*, ed. Theiner 1:590). The statement of the decree that was finally adopted states: "This anointing is to be used for the sick, but especially for those who are dangerously ill as to seem at the point of departing this life" (H. Denzinger, *Enchiridion symbolorum* [Freiburg 1963] 1698). While this is not a forthright recapture of the primitive view, it is certainly an amelioration of the medieval position. In coming to this conclusion, the Council of Trent did not endorse one school over the other, but left open the question of the effects (DS 1696), including bodily health.

Post-Tridentine era. From the Council of Trent to the Second Vatican Council, one notes a progressive leniency in the theologians' interpretation of the danger of death required for anointing and a consequent reassertion of Extreme Unction as a sacrament of the sick. Theologians suggested that the danger of death need not be proximate, but remote; that a probable judgment of danger of death, even if an objective and real danger is not actually present, sufficed for both validity and licitness. This view received support from the Apostolic Letter *Explorata Res* of Feb. 2, 1923 [*Acta Apostolicae Sedis* 15 (Rome 1923) 105], which says: "It is not necessary either for the validity or lawfulness of the Sacrament that death should be feared as something proximate; it is enough that there should be a prudent or probable judgment of danger." The Second Vatican Council marks the culmination of the movement to restore this sacrament as a sacrament of the sick. *Sacrosanctum concilium*, nos. 72 through 74, providing directives for the reform, instructed that this

sacrament "may also and more fittingly" be called "Anointing of the Sick." The emergence of the reformed rite of the anointing of the sick, as it appears in the *Pastoral Care of the Sick: Rites of Anointing and Viaticum* (1983), is the result of adaptations made by the INTERNATIONAL COMMISSION ON ENGLISH IN THE LITURGY (ICEL) to the 1972 Latin *editio typica* of *Ordo Unctionis infirmorum eorumque pastoralis curae*, which itself was a revision of the *Ordo ministrandi sacramentum extremae unctionis*, found in Title VI, chapter ii of the *Rituale Romanum* (1614).

Pastoral care of the sick, 1983. For its part, the General Introduction to the *Pastoral Care of the Sick* indicates that this sacrament is provided for the seriously ill who need the special help of God's grace in their time of anxiety, lest they be broken in spirit, and under the pressure of temptation, perhaps become weakened in their faith (no. 5). Detailing the effects of the sacrament, the General Introduction (no. 6) maintains that the sacrament gives the grace of the Holy Spirit to those who are sick: "By this grace the whole person is helped and saved, sustained by trust in God, and strengthened against the temptations of the Evil One and against anxiety over death. Thus the sick person is able not only to bear suffering bravely, but also to fight against it. A return to physical health may follow the reception of this sacrament if it will be beneficial to the sick person's salvation. If necessary, the sacrament also provides the sick person with the forgiveness of sins and the completion of Christian penance."

ADMINISTRATION

While the priest is recognized as the only proper minister of this sacrament (no. 16), all baptized Christians share in this ministry to the sick by helping the sick return to health, by showing love for the sick, and by celebrating the sacraments with them. In particular, family members and friends of the sick person, and those who take care of the sick, share in this special ministry of comfort and mutual charity (nos. 33–34).

The rite of anointing, proper, contains three distinct and integral aspects: the prayer of faith, the laying on of hands, and the anointing with oil (no. 104). Through the prayer of faith, the Church, which is made present in this community of at least the sick person, the priest, and the family, friends, and others, responds to God's word and, in a spirit of trust, asks for God's help for the sick person (no. 105). Restored to major significance in the reformed rite, the laying on of hands has several meanings. In the first place, it indicates that this person is the object of the Church's prayer of faith. Second, it is a clear sign of blessing that by the power of God's healing grace, the sick person may be restored to health, or at least strengthened in time of illness. Third, the laying on of hands is also an invocation through which the Church prays for the coming of the Holy Spirit upon the sick person. Finally, it is a biblical gesture of healing that recalls Jesus' own manner of healing (no. 106). For its part, the practice of anointing with oil signifies: (1) healing, through comfort and restoration of the tired and the weak; (2) strengthening to fight against the physically and spiritually debilitating effects of illness; and (3) the presence, power, and grace of the Spirit (no. 107). In light of these significations, the rite specifies that a generous amount of oil should be used so it will be seen and felt as a clear sign of the Spirit's healing and strengthening presence (no. 107).

In the *Apostolic Constitution on the Sacrament of the Anointing of the Sick* (Nov. 30, 1972), Paul VI noted that olive oil, which had been prescribed until this date for the valid celebration of the sacrament, is unobtainable or difficult to obtain in some parts of the world. Hence, at the request of a number of bishops, Paul VI indicates that, according to circumstance, another kind of oil can also be used, provided it is derived from plants, and is thus similar to olive oil. While ordinarily the priest uses the oil blessed by the bishop on Holy Thursday, the priest may, in case of necessity, bless oil to be used within the celebration of the sacrament (no. 21).

The General Introduction to the *Pastoral Care of the Sick* holds that ''great care should be taken to see that those of the faithful whose health is seriously impaired by sickness or old age receive this sacrament'' (no. 8). In a footnote, it states that the Latin word *periculose* has been carefully studied and rendered as ''seriously,'' rather than as ''gravely,'' ''dangerously,'' or ''perilously.'' Such a rendering serves to avoid restrictions upon the celebration of the sacrament, which may and should be given to anyone whose health is seriously impaired. Further, the General Introduction specifies the following subjects for anointing: a sick person, before surgery whenever a serious illness is the reason for surgery (no. 10); elderly people, if they become notably weakened even though no serious illness is present (no. 11); sick children, if they have sufficient use of reason to be strengthened by this sacrament (no. 12); sick people who, although they have lost consciousness or the use of reason, have, as Christian believers, at least implicitly asked for anointing when they were in control of their faculties (no. 14); and a sick person whose death is in doubt (no. 15). Canon 844 in the 1983 *Code of Canon Law* also indicates that members of the Eastern Churches, which do not have full communion with the Catholic Church, and members of other Churches, which in the judgment of the Apostolic See are in the same condition in regard to the sacraments, may receive Anointing of the Sick if they

seek it on their own accord and are properly disposed. Further, if in danger of death or if, in the judgment of the diocesan bishop or conference of bishops, some other grave necessity urges it, the sacrament may be ministered to Protestants, who cannot approach their own minister and who seek Anointing of the Sick on their own accord, provided they manifest Catholic faith in respect to this sacrament and are properly disposed. The sacrament of the Anointing of the Sick may be repeated: when a sick person recovers after being anointed and, at a later time, becomes sick again; when during the same illness the condition of the sick person becomes serious; and when, in the case of a person who is chronically ill, or elderly and in a weakened condition, the priest judges it to be pastorally warranted (nos. 102–103). Finally, the General Introduction specifies that the priest should not administer the sacrament to anyone who remains obdurately in open and serious sin or to one who is already dead. In the case of the latter, the priest and gathered community should pray for the dead person, asking God to forgive the deceased person's sins and to welcome him or her into the kingdom (no. 15).

Bibliography: Sources. *Pastoral Care of the Sick: Rites of Anointing and Viaticum.* The Roman Ritual Revised by Decree of the Second Vatican Ecumenical Council and Published by Authority of Pope Paul VI, Approved for Use in the Diocese of the United States of America by the National Conference of Catholic Bishops and Confirmed by the Apostolic See, Prepared by the International Commission on English in the Liturgy—A Joint Commission of Catholic Bishops' Conferences (New York 1983). **Literature.** A. CHAVASSE, *Étude sur l'onction des infirmes dans L'Église Latine du IIIe au XIe siècle,* v. 1 *Du IIIe siècle à la Réforme Carolingienne* (Lyons 1942). P. MURRAY, ''The Liturgical History of Extreme Unction,'' *Furrow* 11 (1960) 572–593; this article has special importance because the author saw, in MS, the unpub. 2d v. of Chavasse. J. L. EMPEREUR, *Prophetic Anointing: God's Call to the Sick, the Elderly, and the Dying,* Message of the Sacraments, v. 7 (Wilmington, Del. 1982). C. GUSMER, *And You Visited Me: Sacramental Ministry to the Sick and the Dying,* Studies in the Reformed Rites of the Catholic Church, v. 5, rev. ed. (New York 1984, 1989). J. M. HUELS, ''Who May Be Anointed,'' in *Disputed Questions in the Liturgy Today* (Chicago, Ill. 1988). *The Pastoral Care of the Sick,* ed. M. COLLINS and D. N. POWER, *Concilium* 1991/92 (Philadelphia, Pa. 1991). K. RAHNER, *The Church and the Sacraments* (New York 1963). J. J. ZEIGLER, *Let Them Anoint the Sick* (Collegeville, Minn. 1987).

[J. P. MCCLAIN/J. M. DONOHUE]

ANOINTING OF THE SICK, II: LITURGY OF

Prior to the ninth century, all of the earliest liturgical sources that provide fixed formulas have to do with the preparation or blessing of the oil used in anointing, rather than its application. Hagiographic writings, patristic letters, and sermons indicate that, in addition to presbyteral anointing, lay people took the blessed oil home and either drank it or rubbed themselves with it as needed. However, several factors contributed to the ritualizing of anointing. Due to the severity of the penances imposed, people began to postpone reconciliation until they were close to death, after which they would be anointed *in extremis*. This is evident in several eighth-century Gelasian sacramentaries, which move the death-bed reconciliation prayers from their original position in the *Old Gelasian Sacramentary* (mid-seventh century), where they are located among the prayers for the general reconciliation of penitents on Holy Thursday, to their new position before the rites for death and burial. With the emergence of private penance, however, some of the rites formerly associated with death-bed penitence became attached to the ritual for the anointing of the sick, which had by now become a sacrament for the dying. In addition, the ninth-century Carolingian reforms confirmed the trend toward clericalization, reserving anointing exclusively to priests, while at the same time encouraging clergy to have greater care for the sick and the dying.

A Carolingian reform rite for anointing the sick appeared in the ninth century, of which, according to Frederick Paxton, the *Sacramentary of Rodradus* (found in Jean Deshusses' *Le sacramentaire grégorien*), written at the monastery of Corbie shortly after 853, is its earliest and best witness. This rite, which Paxton ascribes to Benedict of Aniane, is essentially the seventh-century Visigothic rite for the anointing of the sick, to which Roman and Frankish elements have been added. The rite opened with water being blessed and sprinkled over the sick person and the house, to the accompaniment of an antiphon and the prayer *Domine Deus, qui per apostolorum.* Surviving in some form even in the post-conciliar rite, this Carolingian prayer is a proclamation of the apostolic authority for the rite and a declaration of its effects. After genuflecting, the sick person stands to the right of the priest, at which point all the priests and their ministers lay hands, followed by a verse, two prayers, and two antiphons, all of which are from Visigothic sources. Then the sick person is anointed by making the sign of the cross with the oil on the back of the neck, the throat, between the shoulders, the chest, and the focal point of the pain, accompanied by the following words: "I anoint you in the name of the Father and the Son and the Holy Spirit so that no unclean spirit may remain either in your limbs, marrow, or joints, but that the power of Christ the most high and the Holy Spirit may live in you, so that through the operation of this mystery, and through the anointing with holy oil and our prayer, cured or comforted by the power of the Holy Trinity, you will merit the restoration and improvement of your health" (trans. Paxton). Fol-

lowing the anointing are two Visigothic prayers, a Visigothic benediction and a rubric indicating that the sick person should receive the Body and Blood of the Lord, and that the rite should be repeated for seven days if necessary.

This *Sacramentary of Rodradus* containing a full Hadrianum, a complete text of the Supplement, and Benedict of Aniane's rite of anointing of the sick, which was written sometime after the Supplement and not contained in it, includes a gloss added to the final rubric: "Many priests, however, anoint the sick over the five senses of the body, that is on the eyebrows, the inside of the ears, on the end of or within the nostrils, on the outside of the lips, and on the backs of the hands. . . . They do this so that if any impurity of the soul or body adheres to the five senses, the medicine of God will wipe it away" (trans. Paxton). According to Paxton, this gloss is noteworthy for two reasons: (1) it reveals a variety of practices among Frankish clerics in the middle of the ninth century, and (2) the anointing of the five senses, instead of the place where the sickness was concentrated, denotes a shift in emphasis away from physical healing and toward spiritual purification.

Paxton's insights are verified through the examination of another ritual, the *Capitulary of Theodulph of Orleans* (*Patrologia Latina*, ed. J. P. Migne [Paris 1878–90] 105: 220–222). Although attributed to Theodulf (d. 821), this rite is probably descriptive of late tenth or early eleventh-century procedures. After Penance was administered, the sick person, if the state of sickness would allow it, was washed, clothed in white garments in remembrance of baptism, and carried to the church, where the sick person was laid on sack-cloth sprinkled with ashes. Three priests administered the sacrament that began by sprinkling the sick person with holy water while the antiphon *Pax huic domui* was recited. The sick person was then signed with ashes in the form of a cross on the head and chest while the formula of Ash Wednesday was recited. The seven PENITENTIAL PSALMS and the litany were prayed, followed by the anointing. Fifteen anointings were prescribed, and the possibility of many more was approved. The sick person and the priest jointly prayed the Lord's Prayer and the Creed, after which the sick person's soul was commended to God. Armed with the sign of the cross, the sick person takes leave of the living. Then the priest gives the sick person the kiss of peace and communion. The rite concluded with the directive that the priest should visit the person, if life persists, for seven days to provide communion and to repeat this prescribed rite. Evidence to a variety of practices of anointing, this rite is clearly a rite for the dying, not the sick.

As a sacrament for the dying, the prayers associated with Anointing ceased to speak of physical healing and stressed spiritual healing through the forgiveness of sins as a preparation for death. Over time, these rites for the dying became increasingly elaborate, and if the Sacrament was not to fall into desuetude, a reform of simplification was inevitable. This reform asserted itself in some areas while the rite was still developing in other areas. The rite adopted by the Benedictines of Cluny contributed greatly to the movement toward simplification. This rite appears to have influenced, at least indirectly, the *Ordo compendiosus*, an abridged rite of Anointing, found in the thirteenth-century *Pontifical of the Roman Curia*. This Pontifical, itself influenced by the *Romano-Germanic Pontifical* of the tenth century, contained five rites connected with Christian death and burial. The first of these was a rite for the visitation of the sick (*Ordo ad visitandum infirmum*), while the second was the rite of Anointing (*Ordo compendiosus et consequens ad ungendum*). In the *Franciscan Regula Breviary* of 1230, these two rites were combined under the title *Ordo minorum ad visitandum infirmum*, and were followed by the rite for communion to the sick, which included Viaticum (*Ordo ad communicandum infirmum*) and the rite to commend the dying (*Ordo commendationis animae*). However, the revisions of the 1260 *Franciscan Breviary* inverted the first two orders so that the rite of Anointing, and not Viaticum, stood in the closest proximity to the rite of the Commendation of the Soul. The most notable point of all, however, is that the Franciscan ritual, because of its wide use, served to spread and perpetuate this separation of Viaticum from the hour of death, as well as the insertion of Extreme Unction between Viaticum and the commendation rite. On the journey through sickness to death, the more proximate acts of preparation for death in the Franciscan ritual are now Extreme Unction and the Commendation of the Soul and not, as is the case in the ancient Roman order, Viaticum.

Alberto Castellani's *Liber Sacerdotalis* (1523) and Julius Santori's *Rituale Sacramentorum Romanum* (1602), two important sixteenth-century liturgical predecessors to the 1614 *Rituale Romanum*, follow the Franciscan pattern, giving witness to the fact that Viaticum continued to be separated from the moment of death by the rites of Extreme Unction and the Commendation of the Soul. Entrenched in practice, this pattern is taken up and continued in the 1614 *Rituale Romanum*.

The 1614 rite, used until the reforms of the Second Vatican Council (1962–65), bears witness to its evolution. Its matrix was a rite for the visitation of the sick. The opening greeting, *Pax huic domui*, and the three prayers that follow it, *Introeat* (from a ninth-century *Ordinal*), *Oremus et deprecemur* (from *Roman Ordinal X*), and *Exaudi nos* (from a prayer for blessing water in the mid-seventh-century *Gelasian Sacramentary*), none of which

mentions anointing, manifest this origin. The provision for Confession and the *Confiteor* that follows these prayers, and the mention of the Penitential Psalms and the litany that may be recited by the bystanders, show the imprint left on this rite by Penance. The prayer *In nomine Patris* was originally a formula for anointing the head. Later this anointing was dropped and replaced in 1925 by an imposition of hands. The 1614 *Rituale Romanum* admits two types of anointing. The First, the usual one, involves an unction of the five senses with a corresponding form for each sense: "Through this holy anointing and through his tender mercy may the Lord forgive you whatever sins you have committed by the sense of sight (hearing, smell, taste, and power of speech, touch). Amen." The second, to be used in the case of emergency, calls for an anointing of the forehead, using the same form without reference to any sense. The rite concludes with three prayers, the first of which (*Domine Deus*) is found in the *Gregorian Sacramentary*, the second (*Respice*) in the *Hadrianum*, and the third (*Domine sancte*) in the *Gelasian Sacramentary*.

The Sacrament of the Anointing of the Sick was revised within the post-conciliar liturgical reform of the rites of the sick, the dying, and burial. In *Sacrosanctum concilium*, nos. 73–75, the Second Vatican Council provided directives for the reform of "*Sacramentum Extremae Unctionis*," suggesting: that it may also, and more fittingly, be called "anointing of the sick;" that separate rites for anointing of the sick and for Viaticum, as well as continuous rites involving penance, anointing of the sick, and Viaticum, be prepared; and that the number of anointings be adapted and the prayers accompanying the rite of anointing be revised to correspond to the varying conditions of the sick person. This resulted in the publication in 1972 of the Latin *editio typica of Ordo Unctionis infirmorum eorumque pastoralis curae*, which was a revision of the *Ordo ministrandi sacramentum extremae unctionis*, found in Title VI, chapter ii of the 1614 *Rituale Romanum*. The English translation and adaptation by the International Commission on English in the Liturgy (ICEL) appeared in 1983 under the title *Pastoral Care of the Sick: Rites of Anointing and Viaticum*.

Restored as a sacrament for Christians "whose health is seriously impaired by sickness or old age" (no. 8), the 1983 *Pastoral Care of the Sick* provides three rites for anointing—Anointing outside Mass, Anointing within Mass, and Anointing in a Hospital or Institution—as well as a Continuous Rite of Penance, Anointing, and Viaticum, to be used in exceptional circumstances. The outline of the rite for Anointing outside Mass and within Mass are similar, including: introductory rites (greeting with optional sprinkling with holy water, instruction/reception of the sick, penitential rite, and opening prayer), liturgy of the word, liturgy of anointing, optional communion rite if outside Mass, and concluding rites (blessing and dismissal). The structure of the liturgy of the anointing includes: a litany, a laying on of hands, a prayer over the oil, the anointing, and the prayer after anointing, which includes the Lord's Prayer in the rite outside Mass. The anointing on the forehead and the hands of the sick person is accompanied by a prayer (no. 25), which is drawn from the earlier anointing prayer in the 1614 *Rituale Romanum*, the teaching of the Council of Trent, and the letter of James (5:14–16). While anointing the forehead, the priest prays, ''Through this holy anointing may the Lord in his love and mercy help you with the grace of the Holy Spirit. Amen.'' While anointing the hands, the priest prays, ''May the Lord who frees you from sin save you and raise you up. Amen.'' Following the anointing, there is a choice of seven prayers, adapted to the sick person's condition: two are of a general nature, while the others are for extreme or terminal illness, for advanced age, before surgery, for a child, and for a young person.

There are several noteworthy aspects of the reformed rite. In the first place, scriptural readings, which are totally absent in the 1614 *Rituale Romanum*, are to be chosen in light of the sick person's condition. The readings and the homily are to assist those present to reach a deeper understanding of the mystery of human suffering in relation to the paschal mystery of Christ (no. 100). Secondly, since the celebration of the sacrament is to take place while the sick person is capable of actively participating, the priest is cautioned not to delay the sacrament (no. 99). Thirdly, because of its very nature as a sign, the sacrament should be celebrated in the midst of family and representatives of the Christian community whenever possible, for then it will more clearly signify this experience as the prayer of the Church and an encounter with the Lord (no. 99). Finally, while the priest is recognized as the only proper minister of this sacrament (no.16), all baptized Christians share in the ministry to the sick by helping the sick return to health, by showing love for the sick, and by celebrating the sacraments with them. In particular, family and friends of the sick and those who take care of them share in this special ministry of comfort and mutual charity (nos. 33–34).

Bibliography: Sources. *Liber sacramentorium romanae aeclesiae ordinis anni circuli (Cod. Vat. Reg. Lat. 316, Sacramentarium Gelasiansum)*, ed. L. CUNIBERT MOHLBERG, with L. EIZENHÖFER and P. SIFFRIN, RED, series maior, fontes 4 (Rome 1960). *Le sacramentaire grégorien: Ses principales formes d'après les plus anciens manuscrits*, ed. J. DESHUSSES, SF 16, 24, 28 (Fribourg, 1971, 1979, 1982). M. ANDRIEU, *Le pontifical de la curie romaine au XIIIᵉ siècle*, vol. 2, Studi e Testi 87 (Vatican City 1940). *Sources of the Modern Roman Liturgy: The Ordinals by Haymo of Faversham and Related Documents (1243–1307)*, ed. S. J. P. VAN DIJK, Studia et documenta Franciscana, 2 vols (Leiden 1963). A. CASTELLANO, *Liber Sacerdotalis* (Venice 1523; Paris 1973). J. A. CARDINAL SANTORI, *Rituale Sacramentorum Romanum Gregorii Papae XIII Pont. Max. iussu editum* (Rome: 1584–1602; Paris 1973). *Rituale Romanum Pauli V. Pont. Max. iussu editem* (Rome 1614; Paris 1973). *Ordo Unctionis infirmorum eorumque pastoralis curae*, Rituale Romanum ex decreto sacrosancti oecumenici Concilii Vaticani II instauratum auctoritate Pauli PP. VI promulgatum, editio typica (Rome 1972). *Pastoral Care of the Sick: Rites of Anointing and Viaticum. The Roman Ritual Revised by Decree of the Second Vatican Ecumenical Council and Published by Authority of Pope Paul VI, Approved for Use in the Dioceses of the United States of America by the National Conference of Catholic Bishops and Confirmed by the Apostolic See, Prepared by the International Commission on English in the Liturgy: A Joint Commission of Catholic Bishops' Conferences* (New York 1983). **Literature.** J. L. EMPEREUR, *Prophetic Anointing: God's Call to the Sick, the Elderly, and the Dying*, Message of the Sacraments, vol. 7 (Wilmington, Delaware 1982). C. W. GUSMER, *And You Visited Me: Sacramental Ministry to the Sick and the Dying*, Studies in the Reformed Rites of the Catholic Church, vol. 5, rev. ed. (New York 1984, 1989.) F. S. PAXTON, *Christianizing Death: The Creation of a Ritual Process in Early Medieval Europe* (Ithaca, New York 1990). H. B. PORTER, ''The Origin of the Medieval Rite for Anointing the Sick or Dying,'' *Journal of Theological Studies* 7 (1956): 211–225. H. B. PORTER, ''The Rites of the Dying in the Early Middle Ages, I: St. Theodulf of Orleans,'' *Journal of Theological Studies* 10 (1959): 43–62.

[J. M. DONOHUE]

ANONYMITY AND PSEUDONYMITY

Many ancient literatures displayed a strong preference for anonymity and pseudonymity, literary techniques whereby a writer either withheld his identity or published under an assumed name. Authenticity (publication under the true author's name) was admittedly frequent in Chinese and Roman writing, but gave way to anonymity and pseudonymity in the literatures of Egypt, Mesopotamia, Syria, Asia Minor, and Hellenistic Greece at a time when these cultures were providing literary models for the writers of the Jewish and Christian Scriptures.

Concealment of authorship could occur in a variety of ways, some of which were never exemplified in the Bible. For instance, many works of antiquity were anonymous only because the author's name, originally given, was later lost. Some pseudonymous productions appeared, not under the name of a celebrated personage of the past, but under a fictitious nom de plume. Still other pseudonyms were intended to deceive the reading public; thus, Jewish apologists in the Hellenistic Diaspora (*see* DIASPORA, JEWISH) published tracts purporting to be written by Sophocles, Euripides, Aristotle, and the like, in praise of monotheism; similarly, heterodox Christian groups often published their sectarian doctrines under the guise of apostolic authorship, such as the Gospel of Thomas and the Acts of John. But anonymity and pseudonymity in Scripture were neither accidental, nor casual, nor fraudulent.

In the Old Testament. The name of the author of only a single book of the OT is known with certainty—Jesus ben Elezar ben Sirach, whose *Wisdom* is commonly called the Book of SIRACH (for "ben Sirach"). Yet most of the books of prophecy, although later edited by others, are so integrally the work of the Prophets whose names they bear that they are best considered as authentic, for example, Ezekiel and most of the MINOR PROPHETS. Some prophetic books, such as the Books of Isaiah, Jeremiah, and Zachariah, have basic nuclei of oracular sayings deriving from the titular authors, plus large blocks of supplemental material inserted later; they are thus partly authentic and partly pseudonymous. Books of historical or fictional narrative, on the other hand, tend to be uniformly anonymous.

Not all anonymous works remained so, however. Since Solomon enjoyed the reputation of being a sage, many of the sapiential books came to be pseudonymously attributed to him, although they were compilations of materials originally anonymous (Proverbs, Ecclesiastes, Song of Songs, and Wisdom). By a similar process Moses, the lawgiver, became in tradition (not in the text itself) the putative author of the PENTATEUCH; David, the bard, was thought to have composed the entire collection of Psalms; and Lamentations passed as Jeremiah's elegy over fallen Jerusalem. Finally, a few books alternated between anonymous passages in the third person and pseudonymous passages in the first person, such as Ezra, Tobit, and Daniel.

In the New Testament. The bulk of the Pauline corpus of letters is generally acknowledged as authentic. If one agrees that the hints in the Fourth Gospel point intentionally to John the Apostle as author, then this Gospel may be considered substantially authentic too. The Apocalypse claims to have been written by a certain John on Patmos, a claim one need not disallow despite later attempts to identify him with the Apostle. The authenticity of some NT books (Ephesians, Pastoral Epistles, and 1 Peter) is presently disputed. Eight were published anonymously (the three Synoptic Gospels, Acts, 1–3 John, and Hebrews). Nearly all critics agree that James, 2 Peter, and Jude are pseudonymous.

Most of the Biblical writings underwent considerable re-editing and interpolation before final publication. Thus authorship was more of a group activity than was once thought. Yet among the hundreds of men who lent their pens to this literary endeavor, certain individuals—or, rather, classes—stood out clearly as direct spokesmen for God. The Prophets and the Apostles generally did not conceal themselves behind anonymity or pseudonymity, but spoke or wrote in their own right and name. Other writers, on the contrary, conceived of themselves as collaborators in a group effort, rather than as men with a personal message to deliver. They compiled legal statutes, liturgical hymnody, moral aphorisms, royal chronicles, theological summaries of history, edifying fiction, homilies, and reinterpreted prophecy. They tended to publish these works anonymously, considering that they were transmitting, rather than shaping, a tradition. They sometimes pseudonymously attributed their own or others' writings to one or more of the recognized ancient, charismatic authors.

It has been conjectured that such pseudonymity was a device for endowing one's own works with authority, gaining for the authors a hearing they might otherwise not have enjoyed and lending their works enough antiquity to have them classified as sacred books. Such motives may possibly have been behind pseudonymous heretical literature, but fails to account for Biblical pseudonymity. Such intentions seem to be deceptive; and besides, a writer's contemporaries would likely be incredulous enough to reject such pious fraud. In actual fact, when unknown writers published under the names of Isaiah, Ezra, or Paul, they were asserting their solidarity with the tradition that they traced back to their fathers in the faith. Just as they were anxious in their preaching to preserve the "faith once delivered to the saints," so in their writing they resorted to this accepted cachet of orthodoxy, pseudonymity, which was why the heretics so assiduously imitated it. Far from being a devious ploy to shore up an author's deficient personal authority, pseudonymity signified his intention to convey the same authoritative message of Isaiah, Ezra, or Paul.

Bibliography: J. A. SINT, *Pseudonymität in Altertum* (Innsbruck 1960); *Lexikon für Theologie und Kirche*, ed. J. HOFER and K. RAHNER (Freiberg 1957–65) 8:867. K. ALAND, "The Problem of Anonymity and Pseudonymity in Christian Literature of the First Two Centuries," *Journal of Theological Studies* 12 (1961) 39–49; et al., *The Authorship and Integrity of the NT* (London 1965). F. TORM, *Die Psychologie der Pseudonymität im Hinblick auf die Literatur des Urchristentums* (Gütersloh 1932). D. S. RUSSELL, *The Method and Message of Jewish Apocalyptic, 200 B.C. to 100 A.D.* (Philadelphia 1964). G. BARDY, "Faux et fraudes littéraires dans l'antiquité chrétienne," *Revue d'histoire ecclésiastique* 32 (1936) 5–23, 275–302.

[J. T. BURTCHAELL]

ANONYMOUS CHRISTIAN

A notion of contemporary theology usually connected with the name of Karl RAHNER, who proffered it as a way to maintain the universalism of Christianity within the present context of heightened consciousness of religious pluralism. Since Christians believe not only that God wills the salvation of all men (1 Tm 2.4) but also that no man is saved except through Christ (1 Tm 2.5–6), it follows that all men must be affected by God through Christ. For most men this grace is real but hidden; it constitutes the possibility of an authentic though implicit faith without which salvation is impossible (Heb 11.6). This implicit faith, this personal *fides qua creditur,* is genuine whenever a man does the will of the Father even if he has never really heard of the Lord. Since Christ is the effective paradigm of the *de facto* salvific significance of human self-transcendence, wherever true humanity is realized Christians celebrate the hidden dynamism of the grace of Christ. Correlative to the universality of grace is general revelation, through which every man can acknowledge the unfathomable thrust of existence toward the infinite.

This notion presupposes a broad Christian anthropocentrism which intrinsically connects creation (nature) and redemption (grace) as two moments of God's self-communication to man. As such it recalls the lofty Christocentric streams of the tradition: the cosmic Christ texts of the New Testament, the Logos doctrine of the Apologists (cf. Justin, *Apology* 1.46), Irenaeus's theory of recapitulation, the *anima naturaliter christiana* theme of Tertullian, and, among the scholastics, the Scotist thesis on the finality of the Incarnation. Rahner presented this doctrine as a ''comfort of objectivity'' for anxious Christians in a secular and pluralistic situation.

Bibliography: H. OTT, ''Existentiale Interpretation und anonyme Christlichkeit,'' *Zeit und Geschichte: Festgabe R. Bultmann,* ed. E. DINKLER (Tübingen 1964) 367–379. K. RAHNER, ''Christianity and the non-Christian Religions,'' *Theological Investigations* 5 (Baltimore 1966) 115–134; ''Anonymous Christians,'' *Theological Investigations* 6.390–398. A. RÖPER, *The Anonymous Christian* (New York 1966).

[M. J. SCANLON/EDS.]

ANONYMOUS OF YORK

Referred to also as the Norman Anonymous, is the title given by H. Böhmer to a series of 31 tractates found in the Cambridge, Corpus Christi, MS 415, written in several hands in the early 12th century. Some historians (H. Böhmer and N. F. Cantor) have proposed that they were composed by a single author, *viz,* the Norman Archbishop GERARD OF YORK (1101–08), and that York was the place of composition. Others have accepted the idea of single authorship but changed the person and location to Abp. William Bona Anima of Rouen (1079–1110).

Multiple authorship also is suggested. Böhmer's thesis has generally prevailed. Although six tracts (nos. 8, 9, 10, 18, 21, and 31) present ideals of GREGORIAN reform, the majority attack papal authority and defend royal and episcopal rights; canonical election is rejected, lay INVESTITURE and clerical marriage are vindicated. The most important tract is no. 24a *De consecratione pontificum et regum (Monumenta Germaniae Historica: Libelli de lite* 3:662–679) on lay investiture and theocratic monarchy. Apart from the novelty and extremism of its political and theological ideology, of interest to historians of political theory, the collection has had no influence. It probably was never published.

Bibliography: *Monumenta Germaniae Historica: Libelli de lite* 3:642–687. H. BÖHMER, *Kirche und Staat in England und in der Normandie im XI. und XII. Jahrhundert* (Leipzig 1899). H. SCHERRINSKY, *Untersuchungen zum sogenannten Anonymus von York* (Würzburg 1940). G. H. WILLIAMS, *The Norman Anonymous of 1100 A.D.* (Cambridge, MA 1951). N. F. CANTOR, *Church, Kingship, and Lay Investiture in England, 1089–1135* (Princeton 1958).

[J. GILCHRIST]

ANOVULANTS (MORAL ASPECT)

An anovulant is a hormonal steroid derivative that suppresses ovulation by acting upon the hypothalmo-pituitary system to suppress the secretion of LH (luteinizing hormone) and FSH (follicle stimulating hormone). These actions eliminate follicular development and/or the LH surge without which ovulation cannot take place (see Goldzieher 1989, 34). During the early 20th century a number of scientists investigated the properties of the hormones estrogen and progesterone, and in 1921 the idea of a hormonal contraceptive pill was first proposed (see Marks 2001, 41–48). The development of synthetic forms of estrogen (ethynyl estradiol) and progesterone (progestins) led to the development of pills that combine synthetic progestins and estrogens for a synergistic and more efficient suppression of follicular development and/or ovulation (combined oral contraceptives). At the same time, progestin-only oral contraceptives (mini-pill) were also developed.

Mechanisms of Action. The primary mechanism of combined oral contraceptives as reported in the medical literature is the inhibition of follicular development and ovulation. Other, secondary mechanisms are also recognized with varying degrees of evidence (see, for example, Rivera, Yacobson, and Grimes; Larimore and Sanford). These mechanisms include: alterations of cervical mucus which interferes with sperm penetration of the ovum; alterations of the endometrium (uterine lining) which might prevent implantation of the embryo; and changes to the

Fallopian tubes which might interfere with sperm, ovum, and embryo transport (in the latter case possibly preventing implantation or causing an ectopic pregnancy). Progestin-only pills prevent ovulation less consistently than combined oral contraceptives and have similar secondary mechanisms.

Roman Catholic Moral Teaching. The Second Vatican Council reaffirmed the constant teaching of the Church that ''God himself is the author of marriage and has endowed it with various benefits and with various ends in view. . . . By its very nature the institution of marriage and married love is ordered to the procreation and education of the offspring. . .'' (*Gaudium et spes*, n. 48). The ordering of married love toward procreation is rooted in the very nature of the reproductive powers and in the nature of the conjugal act between the spouses. The complete, mutual self-surrender of the spouses to each other in their conjugal act necessarily includes the sharing of their reproductive capacity with each other (see *Familiaris consortio*, n. 32). In this sense the Church teaches that the procreative and unitive meanings of the conjugal act are inseparable because they are fulfilled in and through each other (see HUMANE VITAE, n. 12). ''This connection,'' *Humane vitae* teaches, ''was established by God, and Man is not permitted to break it through his own volition'' (*Humanae vitae*, n. 12). The moral obligation to respect the procreative ordination of the conjugal act is stated in this norm of *Humanae vitae*: ''But the Church, which interprets natural law through its unchanging doctrine, reminds men and women that the teachings based on natural law must be obeyed and teaches that it is necessary that each conjugal act remain ordained in itself to the procreating of human life'' (n. 11).

Based upon these principles Catholic teaching has formulated prohibitions against contraceptive acts. Any action deliberately taken to thwart the procreative ordination of the conjugal act either as an end in itself or as a means to an end that is otherwise morally good is fundamentally contrary to married love and the dignity of the human person, and is, therefore, morally impermissible without exception. This prohibition applies to contraceptive acts before, during, or after the conjugal act (*Humanae vitae*, n. 14; see *Catechism of the Catholic Church*, n. 2370; and *Veritatis splendor*, ns. 79–82) and applies to the contraceptive use of anovulants which are taken prior to the conjugal act, but which are also operative before, during, and after any given conjugal act they are intended to impede.

Non-Therapeutic and Therapeutic Uses. There may be morally justified therapeutic uses of anovulants, but their use for the purpose of preventing a future pregnancy that would threaten the physical or mental health of the woman should not be confused as a therapeutic use. The preservation of physical or mental health in this way is not the direct and immediate effect of using anovulants. Rather, these ends are achieved as the result of the prevention of pregnancy brought about by the action of anovulants. For example, the end of preventing the aggravation of a woman's underlying renal or cardiovascular disease is attained not from the anovulatory effect of the drug, but from the resulting prevention of pregnancy. The Church considers such acts to be direct sterilization: ''Any sterilization which of itself, that is, of its own nature and condition, has the sole immediate effect of rendering the generative faculty incapable of procreation, is to be considered direct sterilization, as the term is understood in the declarations of the pontifical magisterium, especially of Pius XII. Therefore, notwithstanding any subjectively right intention of those whose actions are prompted by the care or prevention of physical or mental illness which is foreseen or feared as a result of pregnancy, such sterilization remains absolutely forbidden according to the doctrine of the Church'' (*Quaecumque sterilizatio*, n.1).

The use of anovulants can have a direct therapeutic effect in the treatment of several conditions, such as dysmenorrhea, chronic anovulatory disorders, dysfunctional uterine bleeding, and endometriosis (see *Merck Manual*, 1792; 1801–1805; 1808; 1810–1811). Cases in which the use of an anovulant has a direct therapeutic effect and is intended as such can be morally justified even though there is also a sterilizing effect. Pope Pius XII addressed this issue in 1958 concluding that the inhibition of ovulation by the use of pills would be morally licit as a necessary remedy of a ''condition of the uterus or the organism'' (Pope Pius XII, 395). Pope Paul VI reiterated this teaching in *Humanae vitae*: ''The Church, moreover, does allow the use of medical treatment necessary for curing diseases of the body although this treatment may thwart one's ability to procreate. Such treatment is permissible even if the reduction of fertility is foreseen, as long as the infertility is not directly intended for any reason whatsoever'' (*Humanae vitae*, n. 15). The teaching of the Church on the distinction between direct sterilization and directly therapeutic actions with foreseen but unintended sterilizing effects is also represented in the document from the United States Conference of Catholic Bishops, *Ethical and Religious Directives for Catholic Health Care Services (ERDs)*, n. 53.

The Church teaches that the human zygote is an actual human individual from the moment it is formed and must be ''respected and treated as a person'' from that first moment (*Donum vitae*, I, 1; see *Evangelium vitae*, n. 60). If, therefore, a human zygote or embryo does not implant in the uterus because of the secondary mechanisms of an anovulant, the effect of the drug would be abortifacient. The use of anovulants for contraceptive purposes is intrinsically immoral, but also to sustain a risk of an abortifacient effect over an extend period of time only compounds the serious moral gravity of the act.

Pregnancy Prevention after Sexual Assault. Anovulants are also used for pregnancy prevention in the treatment of survivors of sexual assault. A commonly used method, known as the Yuzpe regimen, involves the administration of two doses of an increased combined formulation of estrogen/progestin pills. The first dose is given within 72 hours of the sexual assault, and the second dose is taken 12 hours following the first. There are differing reports in the medical literature about the various possible mechanisms of these pills in this regimen. Studies show a range of possibilities, from the inhibition of ovulation as the primary mechanism to a greater prominence of other mechanisms such as prevention of implantation (see Swahn et al. 1996; Trussell and Raymond 1999). Clinically, this regimen can be provided at any time during the woman's menstrual cycle.

The Catholic moral tradition has recognized that a woman may licitly take actions in self-defense against the unjust aggression of sexual assault before, during, and after an assault (see Bayer 1985; Noonan 1965). Lingering effects of the assault such as the attacker's semen and the risk of fertilization are considered a part of the aggression. Thus, measures may be taken to prevent fertilization in self-defense. According to the *ERDs*, Catholic health facilities may provide hormonal intervention that would prevent ovulation only if, after appropriate testing, there is no evidence that conception has occurred. No interventions are permissible that "have as their purpose or direct effect the removal, destruction, or interference with the implantation of a fertilized ovum" (*ERDs*, n. 36). Catholic health facilities have developed hormonal intervention protocols that include tests and other criteria for identifying the ovulatory phase of the woman so that anovulants are administered only during a phase in which a possible abortifacient effect can be avoided with moral certitude. Because absolute certitude is not attainable in this matter, and because it is not a question of already knowing that some entity is present which might be a human being, no certitude greater than moral certitude is required (see McShane et al. 2001, 11/11–11/17).

Bibliography: E. J. BAYER, *Rape Within Marriage: A Moral Analysis Delayed* (Lanham, Md. 1985). G. J. MCSHANE, et al., "Pregnancy Prevention after Sexual Assault," in *Catholic Health Care Ethics: A Manual for Ethics Committees*, ed. P. J. CATALDO and A. S. MORACZEWSKI (Boston 2001), 11/1–11/22. J. W. GOLDZIEHER, *Hormonal Contraception: Pills, Injections & Implants* (San Antonio 1989). W. L. LARIMORE and J. B. STANFORD, "Postfertilization Effects of Oral Contraceptives and Their Relationship to Informed Consent," *Archives of Family Medicine 9* (February 2000): 126–133. L. V. MARKS, *Sexual Chemistry: A History or the Contraceptive Pill* (New Haven 2001). National Conference of Catholic Bishops, *Ethical and Religious Directives for Catholic Health Care Services*, 4th ed. (Washington, D.C. 2001). J. T. NOONAN, JR., *Contraception: A History of Its Treatment by the Catholic Theologians and Canonists* (New York 1965). POPE PIUS XII, "An Address to the Seventh International Hematological Congress in Rome, September 12, 1958," *The Pope Speaks* 6, 4 (December 1960): 392–400. R. RIVERA, I. YACOBSON, and D. GRIMES. "The Mechanism of Action of Hormonal Contraceptives and Intrauterine Contraceptive Devices," *American Journal of Obstetrics and Gynecology* 181 (November 1999): 1263–1269. M.-L. SWAHN, et al. "Effect of Post-Coital Contraceptive Methods on the Endometrium and the Menstrual Cycle," *Acta Obstetrica et Gynecologica Scandinavica* 75 (1996): 738–744. *The Merck Manual*, 16th ed., ed. R. BERKOW (Rahway, N.J. 1992). J. TRUSSELL and E. G. RAYMOND, "Statistical Evidence About the Mechanism of Action of the Yuzpe Regimen of Emergency Contraception." *Obstetrics and Gynecology* 93 (May 1999): 872–876.

[P. J. CATALDO]

ANSBALD, ST.

Abbot; d. July 12, 886. Very little is known about his early life, but after Eigil resigned as abbot of Prüm (860), Ansbald was elected to succeed him. He is regarded as one of the outstanding men who held this office, and under his leadership the abbey gained great renown for its flourishing religious observance. From letters written by LUPUS OF FERRIÈRES, a close friend of the abbot of Prüm, it is clear that Ansbald was interested in collating the monastery's manuscripts of various classical authors, especially the manuscripts of the *Letters* of Cicero. After the havoc wrought by the raids of the Normans, Ansbald was able rapidly to restore the abbey to its once flourishing condition with the help of Charles III the Fat. He died with a reputation for great sanctity, and his name was inserted in several monastic MARTYROLOGIES.

Feast: July 12.

Bibliography: J. MABILLON, *Acta sanctorum ordinis S. Benedicti* (Venice 1733–40) 6:475–477. R. AIGRAIN, *Dictionnaire d'histoire et de géographie ecclésiastiques*, ed. A. BAUDRILLART et al. (Paris 1912) 3:429–430. J. L. BAUDOT and L. CHAUSSIN, *Vies des saints et des bienheureux selon l'ordre du calendrier avec l'historique des fêtes* (Paris 1935–56) 7:270–272. A. M. ZIMMERMANN, *Kalendarium Benedictinum* (Metten 1933–38) 2:439, 441. A. ZIMMERMANN, *Lexicon für Theologie und Kirche*, ed. J. HOFER and K. RAHNER (Freiburg 1957–65) 1:583; *Bibliotheca sanctorum* (Rome 1961–) 1:1336. LUPUS OF FERRIÈRES, *Correspondance*, ed. and tr. L. LEVILLAIN, 2 v. (Paris 1927–35) 2:4.

[H. DRESSLER]

ANSBERT OF ROUEN, ST.

Archbishop of Rouen; b. Chaussy, France, *c.* mid-seventh century; d. Hautmont, France, Feb. 9, 693. He came from a distinguished family of Chaussy and rose to be *referendarius* in the court of Chlotar III (d. 673). In 673 he entered the BENEDICTINE Order at Fontenelle under Abbot WANDRILLE, and in 679 he was himself made abbot. He succeeded Ouen in the See of Rouen in 684. He had dedicated a poem to his saintly predecessor, and he promoted his cult. About 689 he secured for Fontenelle the right to elect its abbot free from royal and episcopal interference. Soon after, he was for political reasons confined by Pepin of Heristal (d. 714) to a monastery at Hautmont, where he died. His body was returned to Rouen and buried in the abbey church, where the translation of his relics took place early in the eighth century. He is mentioned in the Roman Martyrology, and his biography, written *c*. 800, is fairly trustworthy.

Feast: Feb. 9.

Bibliography: *Vita Ansberti, Monumenta Germaniae Historica: Scriptores rerum Merovingicarum* 5:613–643, critical ed. W. LEVISON; uncritical ed. *Acta Sanctorum* 2 (1863) 348–357. His poem pub. by W. WATTENBACH, *Neues Archiv der Gesellschaft für ältere deutsche Geschichtskunde* 14:171–172. According to S. LOEVENFELD, ed., *Gesta abbatum Fontenellensium, Monumenta Germaniae Historica: Scriptores rerum Germanicarum* 28 (1886) 48, A. wrote *Quaestiones ad Siwinum reclausum,* but this has been lost. E. VACANDARD, *Dictionnaire d'histoire et de géographie ecclésiastiques,* ed. A. BAUDRILLART et al. (Paris 1912) 3:431–433; "Les Deux vies de saint A.," *Revue des questions historiques* 67 (1900) 600–612. R. AIGRAIN, *Catholicisme* 1:611–612. A. M. ZIMMERMANN, *Kalendarium Benedictinum* (Metten 1933–38) 1:189–191.

[M. C. MCCARTHY]

ANSCOMBE, GERTRUDE ELIZABETH MARGARET

British philosopher, b. March 18, 1919; d. Jan. 5, 2001. G. E. M. ("Elizabeth") Anscombe was the youngest of three children of Alan Wells and Gertrude Elizabeth Anscombe; her father taught science at Dulwich College. She attended Oxford University and was received into the Roman Catholic Church in her first year there. In 1941, after her graduation from Oxford with first-class honors in classics, ancient history, and philosophy, she married Peter Geach, who was also a convert and who himself became a prominent philosopher. They had seven children.

A year after graduation, Anscombe became a student fellow at Newnham College, Cambridge and eventually a full fellow at Somerville College, Oxford. In 1970 she was appointed to a chair in philosophy at Cambridge, where she continued until her retirement in 1986. She was elected a Fellow of the British Academy in 1967 and, with Peter Geach, she received the papal medal Pro Ecclesia et Pontifice in 1999.

After the ancients, the main influence on Anscombe's thought was Ludwig WITTGENSTEIN. Anscombe first met Wittgenstein in the 1940s at Cambridge and later translated many of his works. She used the rigorous philosophical methods of the analytical school in a wide range of fields, including logic, causality, action theory, and ethics.

Her essay "Modern Moral Philosophy" (1958) and her book *Intention* (1957, revised 1963) constitute the hallmark of her philosophy. Anscombe pursues three arguments in "Modern Moral Philosophy." First, she contends that moral philosophy should cease until philosophers have developed a workable philosophy of psychology. Until philosophers are clear about what they mean by such terms as "intention," "wanting," and "virtue," she believes, they cannot offer any moral guidance. Second, she holds that moral philosophers should avoid using the language of moral obligation because they have abandoned the notion of divine law that gave this language meaning. Without a divine legislator, arguments about "right" and "wrong" can only appeal to personal or societal dispositions, even as they retain an unfounded connotation of special urgency because of their lost roots in divine providence. Anscombe devotes most of her essay to her third thesis, that "the differences between the well-known English writers on moral philosophy from [Henry] Sidgwick [d. 1900] to the present day are of little importance." Against all the major thinkers who preceded them, these philosophers hold that it is impossible to exclude any course of action as a means to some end. Anscombe coined the term "consequentialism" to name this moral philosophy.

In her short monograph 'Intention,' Anscombe illustrates what she means by a philosophy of psychology. She begins by noting that the word "intention" seems to have divergent meanings, depending on whether it refers to wishing, acting, or making a plan. After she has revealed the complexities of these basic notions, Anscombe offers a new and more precise interpretation of practical reasoning, building on Aristotle's discussion in the *Nicomachean Ethics*. The notion of intention, she believes, helps to explain how referring actions to the desires of those performing them shows the meaning of the actions. For example, Aristotle would explain the action of pumping water by starting with the good one achieves by pumping, then showing the causal chain that links the choice to pump with the good of having water. Anscombe, however, begins with the question of how the man using the pump might describe what he is doing, then relates this to what he might in fact bring about by this action.

A commitment to protect innocent human lives united her life with her philosophical work. In 1939 she and her fellow Oxford student Norman Daniel wrote and privately published a pamphlet, "The War and the Moral Law," in which they examined Britain's participation in World War II in the light of traditional just-war theory and argued that Britain was failing to meet several of the conditions (each of them necessary) for waging war. Anscombe's opposition to the modern practice of war, especially its denial of noncombatant immunity, continued throughout her life. She opposed (unsuccessfully) Oxford University's conferral of an honorary degree on former President Truman in 1957, on the grounds that his authorization of the attacks on Hiroshima and Nagasaki had been grossly immoral. Later, Anscombe became an active opponent of legalized abortion.

Anscombe's work has significantly influenced modern philosophy in a number of ways. Her book *Intention* is foundational for the contemporary field of action theory. In moral philosophy, she deserves much of the credit for the contemporary interest in virtue theory. Her sensitive translations and creative interpretations of Wittgenstein have made this great philosopher's thought more readily available to a wide readership.

Bibliography: C. R. PIGDEN, "Anscombe on 'Ought,'" *The Philosophical Quarterly* 38 (1988) 20–41. D. RICHTER, "The Incoherence of the Moral 'Ought,'" *Philosophy* 70 (1995) 69–85; "Ethics after Anscombe—Post 'Modern Moral Philosophy,'" *Library of Ethics and Applied Philosophy* 5 (Dordrecht 1999). R. TEICHMANN, ed. *Logic, Cause and Action: Essays in Honour of Elizabeth Anscombe,* Royal Institute of Philosophy Supplements, v. 46 (Cambridge 2000).

[R. KENNEDY]

ANSE, COUNCILS OF

A number of provincial councils held at the small town of Anse (Ansa, Asa) in the Diocese of Lyons.

In 994 the archbishops of Lyons, Vienne, and Tarantaise, meeting with many bishops and abbots, confirmed the possessions of the Abbey of CLUNY at the request of St. ODILO, its abbot, and provided for canons in the church of Saint-Romain. Among other things, its nine disciplinary canons directed that consecrated hosts reserved in churches were to be renewed every Sunday, that only priests could and must take Viaticum to the sick, that there be no servile labor after three P.M. on Saturday.

In 1025 a council of prelates from the provinces of Lyons and Vienne heard the bishop of Mâcon protest against the archbishop of Vienne's having ordained monks at Cluny, an abbey located in the Diocese of Mâcon. Abbot Odilo exhibited a papal privilege exempting Cluny from diocesan authority, authorizing its abbot to choose any bishop to ordain his monks. Citing the an-

cient canons, notably canon four of the Council of CHALCEDON, which said that abbots and monks everywhere must be subject to their bishop, the council rejected any privilege to the contrary. Cluny's privilege was suspended, but restored when Odilo obtained a papal bull confirming it (Rome, 1027).

At a council in 1070, the bishop of Chalon-sur-Saône gave the cloister of Saint-Laurent to a monastery near Lyons.

In 1076 HUGH OF DIE, the papal vicar, held at Anse one of the several councils called to promote GREGORY VII's reforms, especially the prohibition of lay INVESTITURES.

In 1100 a council excommunicated those who broke their vow to go on the Crusade. The papal vicar, Hugh, now archbishop of Lyons, requested money for a trip to the Holy Land.

In 1112 the archbishop of Lyons, claiming primatial authority in France, tried unsuccessfully to convoke a national council concerning investitures. His authority was contested; a provincial synod, however, may have actually been held.

In 1300 the archbishop of Lyons held a synod in Anse designed to restore or modify ancient ordinances.

Bibliography: C. J. VON HEFELE, *Histoire des conciles d'après les documents originaux,* tr. and continued by H. LECLERCQ, 10 v. in 19 (Paris 1907–38) 4:871–872, 938–939, 1272; 5:219, 467, 535. J. D. MANSI, *Sacrorum Conciliorum nova et amplissima collectio,* 31 v. (Florence-Venice 1757–98) 19:177–180, 423–424, 1077–80; 20:481–482, 1127–28; 21:77–84; 24:1217–32. A. REGNIER, *Dictionnaire d'histoire et de géographie ecclésiastiques,* ed. A. BAUDRILLART (Paris 1912–) 3:443.

[A. CONDIT]

ANSEGIS OF FONTENELLE, ST.

Abbot, collector of Carolingian CAPITULARIES; b. Lyonnais, France, *c.* 770; d. Fontenelle, July 20, 833. After being educated in a Lyonnaise monastery, he became a monk at Fontenelle (Saint-Wandrille) in Normandy, as advised by BENEDICT OF ANIANE. His abbot Gervold presented him to Charlemagne, who entrusted him with various political missions. He was named abbot at Saint-Germer-de Fly (Diocese of Beauvais), which he restored to prosperity. The emperor called him to the imperial court at Aachen, and sent him to the Spanish March (Catalonia). He was a friend and correspondent of EINHARD. Louis the Pious made him abbot of two more abbeys: Luxeuil (817) and Fontenelle (823), where he restored the observance of the BENEDICTINE RULE, enriched the libraries, and encouraged education (at Luxeuil, Angelomus was his disciple). In 827, for the convenience of the emperors and in order to safeguard the goods of the Church, he undertook to make a collection of the imperial laws from 789 to 826, divided into four books: (one) *Capitularia Caroli Magni ad ordinem pertinentia ecclesiasticum,* 176 chapters; (two) *Capitularia Ludovici Pii ad ordinem pertinentia ecclesiasticum,* 46 chapters; (three) *Capitularia Caroli Magni ad mundanam pertinentia legem,* 90 chapters; (four) *Capitularia Ludovici Pii ad mundanum pertinentia legem,* 74 chapters. All these capitularies are authentic—even those that are preserved only in this collection of Ansegis. The collection (*Monumenta Germaniae Historica: Leges* 2: Capitularia regum Franc. 1:382–450) enjoyed great authority from the time it first appeared. Louis the Pious referred to it already in 829 (cf. the capitulary of Worms, 829). It was one of the principal sources for the similar work of BENEDICT THE LEVITE in 845. Several chapters passed into the *Decretum* of GRATIAN, but through the intermediary of canonical collections. The collection is not without minor errors in chronological order, transcription of names, etc. (It was E. Baluze who correctly reattributed this edition to Ansegis of Fontenelle rather than to the nonexistent ''Ansegis of Lobbes.'') Ansegis is inscribed in the catalogue of saints at Luxeuil.

Feast: July 20.

Bibliography: *Gesta abbatum Fontanellensium, Monumenta Germaniae Historica: Scriptores* 2:293–300. *Gallia Christiana* 11:173–174. M. BUCHNER, ''Zum Briefwechsel Einhards und des hl. Ansegis von Fontanelle,'' *Historische Vierteljahrschrift* 18 (1918) 353–385. P. FOURNIER, *Dictionnaire d'histoire et de géographie ecclésiastiques,* ed. A. BAUDRILLART et al. (Paris 1912) 447–448. A. AMANIEU, *Dictionnaire de droit canonique,* ed. R. NAZ (Paris 1935–65) 1:564–567. A. J. KLEINCLAUSZ, *Eginhard* (Paris 1942) 47, 160.

[P. COUSIN]

ANSELM II OF LUCCA, ST.

Bishop; b. Mantua, Italy, 1036; d. there 1086. Anselm came from a noble Milanese family and was a nephew and successor of Anselm I, who became Pope Alexander II. Anselm, who was consecrated bishop in 1073, was a firm supporter of Pope St. Gregory VII and of the movement to reform the Church. His efforts to reform the Diocese of Lucca, especially to force the cathedral canons to live the common life, caused opposition. He also opposed the Emperor Henry IV and the antipope Clement III. Having been forced to leave his see, he spent his last years as spiritual director to Countess Matilda of Tuscany, and vicar apostolic in Lombardy.

His main works were the *Liber contra Wibertum* and the *Collectio canonum.* The collection, compiled in about

1083 for Gregory VII, exists in two forms, called A and B. Form A is regarded as the original. The number of *capitula* varies from manuscript to manuscript but is between 1,150 and 1,281. These are divided into 13 books of unequal length. The contents of the books include the Roman primacy (one), appeals and clerical trials (two, three), ecclesiastical privileges (four), status of churches (five), episcopal elections (six), the priesthood (seven), lapsed clergy (eight), Sacraments (nine), Marriage (ten), Penance (11), excommunication (12), and lawful coercive power (13). The main formal sources were the *Hadriana, Hispana, Pseudo-Isidore, Anselmo dicata,* Burchard, and especially the SEVENTY-FOUR TITLES. A number of other miscellaneous sources provided texts, e.g., of Roman law. The majority of the *capitula* were from papal decretals (about 300 false; about 420 genuine). A rubric title introduces each *capitulum.* These enable us to determine the author's own views. Pre-Gratian collections had no glosses as such, and the texts were open to interpretation. Thus the rubrics play a part in bringing about the concordance of texts that triumphed with Gratian.

As an instrument of papal reform Anselm's collection ranks with the *Seventy-four Titles* in importance. It was a carefully constructed collection that enjoyed wide popularity, being used in later collections as well as in polemical writings during the investiture struggle. The main problems of the reform—simony, clerical celibacy, monastic freedom, lay investiture, the superiority of the spiritual power—inspired Anselm. Thus the collection is an important source for the history of the Gregorian reform, and as well for dogmatic and moral theology. Some 14 manuscripts of the collection are extant. Collections that used Anselm include the *Liber Tarraconensis, Caesaraugustana,* Alger of Liége, *Ashburnham,* and Gratian. The collection was also a main source through which the False Decretals were popularized in Italy and beyond.

Feast: March 18.

Bibliography: ANSELM OF LUCCA, *Liber contra Wibertum,* ed. E. BERNHEIM, *Monumenta Germaniae Historica: Libelli de lite* 1:517–528, *Patrologia Latina* 149:435–634, *Anselmi episcopi Lucensis collectio canonum una cum collectione minore,* ed. F. THANER 2 v. (Innsbruck 1906 and 1915). P. FOURNIER and G. LEBRAS, *Histoire des collections canoniques en occident depuis les fausses décrétals jusqu'au Décret de Gratien* (Paris 1931–32) 2:25–37. R. MONTANARI, *La ''Collectio canonum'' de S. Anselmo di Lucca e la riforma Gregoriana* (Mantua 1941). A. M. STICKLER, *Historia iuris canonici latini: vol. 1, Historia fontium* (Turin 1950) 170–172, 187. G. B. BORINO, ''Il monacato e l'investitura di Anselmo vescovo di Lucca,'' *Studi Gregoriani* 5 (1956) 361–374. K. G. CUSHING, *Papacy and Law in the Gregorian Revolution: The Canonistic Work of Anselm of Lucca* (Oxford 1998). *Sant'Anselmo, Mantova e la lotta per le investiture,* ed. P. GOLINELLI (Bologna 1987). *Sant'Anselmo vescovo di Lucca nel quadro delle trasformazioni sociali e della riforma ecclesiastica,* ed. C. VIOLANTE (Rome

1992). F. KEMPF, *Lexicon für Theologie und Kirche*, ed. J. HOFER and K. RAHNER (Freiburg 1957–65) 1:596. *Acta Sanctorum* March 2:647–663. A. BUTLER, *The Lives of the Saints*, ed. H. THURSTON and D. ATTWATER (New York 1956) 1:628–629.

[J. T. GILCHRIST]

ANSELM OF CANTERBURY, ST.

Doctor of the Church; b. Aosta, Val d'Aosta (formerly Piedmont), *c.* 1033–34; d. (possibly in Canterbury), April 21, 1109. His parents were of the nobility. After the death of his mother, he went to France to further his education.

Life as a Churchman. In 1060 Anselm entered the newly formed Abbey of Bec in Normandy, and three years later he succeeded Lanfranc of Pavia as prior. Herluin, the founding abbot of Bec, died in 1078, and Anselm was unanimously elected abbot.

Although reluctant to accept this office, Anselm submitted to the wishes of the community and proved an excellent abbot. His skill as a teacher and his great virtue were assets in developing the abbey into a monastic school influential in philosophical and theological studies. At the behest of the community at Bec, Anselm began publishing his theological works, writings comparable to those of St. AUGUSTINE in quality and respected even in modern times.

In March 1093 Anselm was again called upon to succeed Lanfranc, this time as archbishop of Canterbury. The See of Canterbury, like many other bishoprics and abbeys, had been purposely left vacant after Lanfranc's death in 1089 so that the revenues might be appropriated by King WILLIAM II (William Rufus). Not until he was seriously ill did this king appoint Anselm archbishop. Anselm, realizing it would be impossible to cooperate with William Rufus, refused to accept the appointment; he was forced to yield, however, by moral pressure from all sides. The consecration took place on December 4.

As an energetic defender of Church reform, particularly that associated with Gregory VII, he foresaw the almost hopeless task with which he would be confronted because of Rufus's opposition. The king refused any cooperation in reforming morals or organizing a reform council. He denied Anselm permission to visit Rome to receive the pallium from URBAN II (d. 1099) on the grounds that Urban had not been recognized in England as the rightful pope. Anselm, however, had recognized Urban, and now proposed a council of bishops and nobility to decide whether he could reconcile his obedience to the Holy See and his loyalty to the king. In the council, which met at Rockingham in March 1095, the bishops,

fearing the king, sided against Anselm; it was the secular princes who prevented his immediate removal. The king's proposal after his recognition of Urban, to request the pallium himself in order to confer it on another, failed because the Cardinal-legate Walter, who had brought the pallium, would not consent to it. Finally, Anselm realized he must yield and leave England (Oct. 15, 1097); the king immediately took possession of the See of Canterbury.

The pope received Anselm with dignity and declined to accept his proposed resignation from Canterbury. At Bari, Anselm took part in the council (Oct. 1, 1098) that sought reunion with the Greek church. Through his profound theological proof that the Holy Spirit also proceeds from the Son, Anselm played a prominent role in this council. Moreover, he effectively sought postponement of the council's planned excommunication of the English king. At the Easter Synod in the Lateran (April 24, 1099), he again participated, and again heard excommunication pronounced against kings and princes who awarded ecclesiastical offices through presentation of ring and crosier (lay-investiture), against recipients of such offices, and all who became vassals of laymen for the sake of ecclesiastical dignities. At the close of the council Anselm accepted the hospitality of the archbishop of Lyons. It was at Lyons that he received the news of the king of England's death in a hunting accident (Aug. 2, 1100).

Rufus's brother and successor, HENRY I, immediately recalled Anselm to England. Even before Anselm called his council in London (1102), he had been in conflict with Henry, who, reluctant to relinquish his ancient "right," had insisted on Anselm's taking an oath of allegiance to the king. Anselm's refusal, based on the decree of the Council of Bari, led both sides to send envoys to Rome. When no solution to the difficulty was forthcoming, the king asked Anselm to go to Rome. This was tantamount to another three years in exile.

Finally, in 1106, an agreement was reached through compromise: the king renounced the right of investiture by means of ring and crosier; on the other hand, the archbishop would not refuse consecration to anyone who had taken the oath of allegiance. The last years of Anselm's life were saddened by York's claiming the primacy that had always belonged to Canterbury. Anselm died on Wednesday of Holy Week. He was canonized in 1163 (though this is disputed) and declared a Doctor of the Church in 1720.

Teaching. Before Anselm's time the study of theology had been a collecting and systematic arranging of the authorities (Sacred Scripture and Doctors of the Church). Anselm strove to analyze and prove the truths of faith by reason alone (*sola ratione*). His goal was to go beyond mere faith and arrive at an insight into faith. In the scale of values that he constructed, faith is in the lowest place; in the middle is the insight into faith that is attainable in this life, and that brings us closer to the beatific vision; the beatific vision is at the top of the scale. Anselm expected from insight into faith joy in the spiritual beauty of the truths of faith for the believer; furthermore, he believed that when he showed the reasonableness and necessity of truths of faith, he also defended them against all those who denied or argued against them.

In this, however, Anselm did not stop at the so-called natural truths, but extended his arguments to include specifically revealed doctrines, such as those of the Trinity, the Incarnation, and the Redemption. In so doing he went beyond the boundaries taken for granted by us today but not yet clearly defined in his time. Disregarding all authority in inquiry was for Anselm only a methodological means to demonstrate the reasonableness of faith. Subjectively, Anselm was far from being an unchristian rationalist. In the event that Sacred Scripture and proofs from reason seemed to clash, he emphatically held the former to be correct; he submitted certain works to the judgment of the pope; he was prepared in every respect to retract anything in which he had been proven in error. Moreover, he was the most unyielding adversary of such rationalists of his time as Roscelin of Compiègne (d. *c.* 1120). Anselm demanded firmness in faith and philosophical preparation in everyone who approached theological issues. He himself had the best philosophical preparation of his time; he was a master of grammar, logic, and dialectics, although only a few writings on logic by Aristotle were known to him through Boethius. In addition he was well acquainted with the writings of the Fathers of the Church, especially St. Augustine. Anselm was rightfully called *"Augustinus redivivus."* However, the more or less generally held opinion that he accepted, without question, Augustine's Neoplatonic line of reasoning must be revised. He remained independent of Augustine and took issue with him on more than one occasion, e.g., in the definition of free will and the doctrine of Redemption. Anselm let himself be governed by principles of logic as well as by common sense. These simple tools never failed him in his explorations of new theological lands.

Writings. The works Anselm left behind [recent ed. F. S. Schmitt, 5 v. and index (Edinburgh 1942)] are divided into systematic works, prayers and meditations, and letters.

Systematic Works. The *Monologion* presents a kind of theodicy. Anselm, with precision and unprecedented skill in speculation, shows the existence of a Supreme Being to be the causal origin of everything good and great, and of all being and its essential properties. The word, love, and the Trinity are examined in their turn.

Being is considered to be the object of reason, love, and future happiness. The last chapter states that this is what is signified by the name "God." Although in his speculation Anselm relies on Augustine, especially in what pertains to the analogy with the human psyche, he is independent in his method. Anselm is convinced that a nonbeliever could concede all this without the help of revelation.

The *Proslogion* is better known. In it Anselm seeks to replace the many proofs of the *Monologion* with a single argument. This argument consists in the concept of God as "that beyond which nothing greater can be conceived" (*id, quo maius cogitari nequit*). Here he seeks an *a priori* proof of the existence of God by analyzing the concept of God. He argues that such a being is greater when it exists in reality than when it exists merely in the mind. Consequently it must exist in reality, because if it were only in the mind it would not be that beyond which nothing greater can be conceived. Anselm's proof, known since the time of Kant as the "ontological proof" of the existence of God, had already been challenged by one of his contemporaries, Gaunilo of Marmoutiers, and later by Thomas Aquinas and others, on the grounds that it implied an invalid step from the sphere of logic to that of ontology. Others, such as Bonaventure, Descartes, Leibniz, and Hegel, incorporated this proof, with certain ramifications, into their systems. Today, men like Karl Barth, in attempting to explain the proof as a theological one, overlook the fact that it was designed for the benefit of atheists to whom revelation is meaningless (*see* ONTOLOGICAL ARGUMENT).

Following the proof are four dialogues between teacher and students. The first is an astute dialectical exercise on the question whether the word "grammarian" is a substance or a quality; *On Truth* and *On Free Will* give Anselm's own definitions of truth, free will, and justification; and *On the Fall of the Devil* goes deeply into the doctrine on the angels.

Because of Roscelin's tritheism (according to which Father, Son, and Holy Spirit are not the same from the standpoint of essence), Anselm wrote a letter dedicated to Urban II entitled "Letter on the Incarnation of the Word," in which he clearly presents and rationally defends the Catholic doctrine on the three Persons in one essence. His remarks on universal ideas are usually evaluated as expressions of extreme realism, which is perhaps an overstatement.

Anselm's main work is the dialogue *Cur Deus Homo* (*Why God Became Man*). In it he takes a stand in opposition to a theory of redemption widely held up to that time, namely, that the devil had a claim on man. Anselm denies any such right on Satan's part and works out the so-called "satisfaction doctrine." According to it, sin is an infinite offense against God, which demands adequate atonement. Mere pardon cannot be reconciled with the justice of God. So the God-Man had to atone, since on the one hand man was obliged to do so, but on the other only God could do so adequately. From this situation, Anselm deduced the necessity of the Incarnation of God and the Redemption through Christ, and all other Christological dogmas so that God's plan for man—to make man happy—might not be frustrated. The main points of this theory were adopted by subsequent theologians, prescinding from the necessity of the Redemption's taking place exactly as it did. Anselm's partner in conversation here was a non-Christian, whom it was necessary to convince.

In the work *On the Virginal Conception and Original Sin* Anselm examines the question how Christ, although descended from the sinful mass (*massa damnatrix*), remained without sin. In this writing as well as in *Cur Deus Homo* it is evident that Anselm did not accept the Immaculate Conception of Mary. The work *On the Procession of the Holy Spirit* is a reworking of the speech Anselm delivered in Bari before the Fathers of the Council; it is an important advance in the doctrine on the Trinity. The last work of significance, *De concordia*, handles the difficult problem of reconciling God's prescience, predestination, and grace with the free will of man.

Although Anselm left behind no complete system of doctrine in the form of a *summa*, his individual treatises, complete in themselves, cover a large portion of Catholic doctrine. For his outstanding initiative in using reason for the examination of questions of faith he had earned the honorary title "Father of Scholasticism"; however, since he did not found a school, scholasticism cannot be regarded as direct outgrowth of his work.

Prayers and Meditations. The 19 meditations are creations of his own individual art. The prayers, written at special requests, are short, brilliantly executed rhetorical masterpieces, with the classical six parts of a discourse, in which God or a saint is to be moved to render help. The thing that is most striking in the artistic style employed is the use of parallelism in the sentences. *On the Redemption of Mankind* stands out above the rest of the meditations. In it Anselm summarizes the thought developed at greater length in his *Cur Deus Homo.* The meditation is not only shorter; it is in a purely theological form and has dispensed with the supplementary apologetics.

Letters. His correspondence (475 letters, 100 of which are from others) gives invaluable insight into Anselm's personality and is at the same time the most significant source for the history of the Church in England during his time. The addressees are popes, royalty, monks, nuns, and laity, living in all parts of the Christian world of that time. Anselm's letters to friends, particularly his early letters, illuminate his Germanic temperament and the richness of his spiritual character. In them the saint's views on Christian and monastic asceticism are aired.

Many ascetical works have been erroneously attributed to Anselm. Notes of his students concerning his oral method of teaching, based on parables from life, are available to us in *De similitudinibus* (*Patrologia Latina*, ed. J. P. Migne (Paris 1878–90) 159:605–708). Eadmer recorded also Anselm's famous speech at Cluny on the 14 happinesses of heaven (*ibid.* 587–606).

Feast: April 21.

Bibliography: *The Letters of Saint Anselm of Canterbury*, tr. W. FRÖHLICH, 3 v. (Kalamazoo, Mich. 1990–1994). *Cur deus homo: atti del Congresso anselmiano internazionale*, ed. P. GILBERT, H. KOHLENBERGER and E. SALMANN (Rome 1999). J. HOPKINS, *A New, Interpretive Translation of St. Anselm's Monologion and Proslogion* (Minneapolis 1986). M. RULE, *The Life and Times of St. Anselm*, 2 v. (London 1883). J. CLAYTON, *Saint Anselm* (Milwaukee 1933). R. W. CHURCH, *Saint Anselm* (London 1937). J. BAINVEL, *Dictionnaire de théologie catholique*, ed. A. VACANT, et al. 15 v. (Paris 1903–50; Tables générales 1951–) 1.2:1327–60. F. UEBERWEG, *Grundriss der Geschichte der Philosophie*, ed. K. PRAECHTER et al., 5 v. (11th, 12th ed. Berlin 1923–28) 2:192–203, 698–700. E. GILSON, "Sens et nature de l'argument de saint Anselme," *Archives d'histoire doctrinale et littéraire du moyen-âge* 9 (1934) 5–51. J. BAYART, "The Concept of Mystery According to St. Anselm of Canterbury," *Recherches de théologie ancienne et médiévale* 9 (1937) 125–166. R. W. SOUTHERN, "St. Anselm and His English Pupils," *Mediaeval and Renaissance Studies* 1 (1941–43) 3–34; *Saint Anselm and His Biographer* (New York 1963); *Saint Anselm: A Portrait in a Landscape* (Cambridge 1990). EADMER, *The Life of St. Anselm: Archbishop of Canterbury*, ed. and tr. R. W. SOUTHERN (New York 1962); *Eadmer's History of Recent Events in England. Historia novorum in Anglia*, tr. G. BOSANQUET (London 1964). E. J. BUTTERWORTH, *The Identity of Anselm's Proslogion Argument for the Existence of God with the Via quarta of Thomas Aquinas* (Lewiston, N.Y. 1990). G. GÄDE, *Eine andere Barmherzigkeit: zum Verständnis der Erlösungslehre Anselms von Canterbury* (Würzburg 1989). L. GIRARD, *L'argument ontologique chez Saint Anselme et chez Hegel* (Amsterdam 1995). M. GRANDJEAN, *Laïcs dans l'Eglise* (Paris 1994). J. MCINTYRE, *St. Anselm and His Critics: A Reinterpretation of the Cur Deus Homo* (Edinburgh 1954). International Anselm Committee, *Anselm Studies*, 3 v., (v. 1–2, Millwood, N.Y. 1983; v. 3, Lewiston, N.Y. 1996). K. A. ROGERS, *The Anselmian Approach to God and Creation* (Lewiston, N.Y. 1997); *The Neoplatonic Metaphysics and Epistemology of Anselm of Canterbury* (Lewiston, N.Y. 1997). W. H. SHANNON, *Anselm: The Joy of Faith* (New York 1999). *Filosofia e mistica*, ed. A. MOLIARO and E. SALMANN (Rome 1997). *Twenty-Five Years (1969–1994) of Anselm Studies*, ed. F. VAN FLETEREN and J. C. SCHNAUBELT (Lewiston, N.Y. 1996). G. R. EVANS, *Anselm and Talking About God* (Oxford 1978); *Anselm and a New Generation* (Oxford 1980); *Anselm* (London 1989). J. HOPKINS, *A Companion to the Study of St. Anselm* (Minneapolis 1972).

[F. S. SCHMITT]

ANSELM OF LAON

Theologian; b. Laon, date unknown; d. Laon, 1117. After receiving his training at the school of Bec, he sojourned in Paris in 1089. There he met Bernard of Chartres, who brought him to his city for a brief stay. On his return to Laon, he directed the illustrious school of Laon with his brother Raoul. Anselm—his real name was Ansellus (Anseau)—was a brilliant teacher, the "Teacher of teachers," who attracted many pupils. Some of these became famous: WILLIAM OF CHAMPEAUX (1068–1122), GILBERT DE LA PORRÉE (d. 1154), Peter ABELARD (c. 1113). This last ridiculed him, comparing him to the fig tree of the Gospel that, while covered with leaves, remained fruitless. In reality, Anselm was one of the best teachers of the 12th century.

Works. Despite the fact that some works attributed to him remain doubtful, the *Sentences* are considered authentic. This is a particularly important work, for it is an example of the first attempts to systematize theological thought. Other works of the time manifested this tendency, which led to PETER LOMBARD's *Book of Sentences,* and through it, to the great *Summas* of the end of the 12th and 13th centuries. Anselm's *Sentences* are collected according to a plan inspired—like many works of those times—by Scotus Erigena: creation, the Fall of the angels and of men (original sin), the necessity of Redemption, Redemption and the Sacraments. It is rather difficult to find texts that present Anselm's thought in continuity. More often than not, one must be content with small pieces or the *Liber Pancrisis de Troyes,* a neighbor if not a cousin of the *Sentences.* One of Anselm's innovations is to name the authors whom he quotes. Of his scriptural work, we possess commentaries on the Psalms, the Song of Songs, the Revelation, fragments on Matthew's Gospel, lengthier ones on the Pauline Epistles, and Genesis.

Thought. It is impossible to give a complete exposition of Anselm's thought here. He is mainly attracted to problems connected with creation and original sin. His treatment is moral rather than dogmatic. Concerning the problem of the nature of the soul, however, he is more precise than others, i.e., for him the soul is less subject to the body, and even though it is weak like Adam toward Eve, its freedom is certain. Contrary to some of his contemporaries, Anselm considers the gifts of the Holy Spirit as transient graces.

If Anselm remained somewhat apart from the renaissance movement that, because of the originality of its discoveries, was to be the glory of the next century, he was nonetheless a remarkable school director to whom this century owed a great deal.

Bibliography: F. CAVALLERA, "D'Anselme de Laon à Pierre Lombard," *Bulletin de littérature ecclésiastique* 41 (1940) 40–54, 103–114. F. BLIEMETZRIEDER, "Trente-trois pièces inédites de l'oeuvre théologique d'Anselme de Laon," *Recherches de théologie ancienne et médiévale* 2 (1930) 54–79. A. M. LANDGRAF, *Lexikon für Theologie und Kirche,* ed. J. HOFER and K. RAHNER (Freiburg 1957–65) 1:595–596.

[P. ROUSSEAU]

ANSELM OF LIÈGE

Chronicler; b. near Cologne, probably late 10th century; d. after March 3, 1056. Anselm, the chronicler of the bishops of LIÈGE, went to study at Liège through POPPO OF STAVELOT. He became a canon there in 1041, then dean of St. Lambert's Cathedral. He was esteemed by Bishops WAZO OF LIÈGE (1042–48) and Theoduin (1048–75) for his integrity, holiness, and knowledge. In 1053–54 he accompanied Theoduin to Rome. Before that date he had written, at the request of his aunt, Abbess Ida of St. Cecilia in Cologne, his two-volume *Gesta Episcoporum Tungrensium, Trajectensium et Leodiensium,* which is the principal source for the history of the Diocese of Liège to 1048. In a second version of the *Gesta* dedicated to Archbishop ANNO OF COLOGNE in 1056, he substituted the newly discovered chronicle of HERIGER OF LOBBES for his first volume, since it was closer to the source and more accurate. Anselm's second volume is most original and complete in its section on Bishop Wazo. In the documents reproduced (mostly liturgical and religious), and in the use of sources, Anselm showed himself to be well read and, by the standards of his age, critical.

Bibliography: *Monumenta Germaniae Historica: Scriptores* 7:161–234; 14:107–120. E. MARTÈNE, *Veterum scriptorum et monumentorum ecclesiasticorum et dogmaticorum amplissima collectio* 4:837–911. J. P. MIGNE, *Patrologia latina* 139:957–1102. W. WATTENBACH, *Deutschlands Geschichtsquellen im Mittelalter. Deutsche Kaiserzeit* 1.1:143–148. R. GORGAS, *Über den kürzeren Text von Anselms "Gesta . . ."* (Halle 1890). J. DE GHELLINCK, *Dictionnaire d'histoire et de géographie ecclésiastiques* 3:487–489. R. H. A. HUYSMANS, *Wazo van Luik* (Nijmegen 1932). F. J. SCHMALE, *Lexikon für Theologie und Kirche* 2 1:596–597.

[T. A. CARROLL]

ANSELM OF NONANTOLA, ST.

Duke, abbot; d. March 3, 803. Anselm, who was the Duke of Friuli in the Lombard Kingdom and brother of Giseltrudis, the wife of King Aistulf, founded the Benedictine abbeys of Fanano in 750 and Nonantola c. 752. He withdrew from the world, entered Nonantola, and in 753 was appointed its first abbot by Pope Stephen II. In 756 the relics of Pope St. Sylvester I were translated from Rome to Nonantola. Presumably, this was a "pious theft,'' because at the time King Aistulf was pillaging the Via Salaria, the former location of the relics. Anselm founded a number of hospices for the poor and for pilgrims. For a time he was *persona non grata* to Aistulf's successor, King DESIDERIUS, and spent several years in exile at Monte Cassino.

Feast: March 3.

Bibliography: *Monumenta Germaniae Historica: Scriptores rerum Langobardicarum* 208–209, 503, 566–571. P. F. KEHR, *Regesta Pontificum Romanorum. Italia Pontifica.* (Berlin 1906–35) 5:330–362. R. AIGRAIN, *Dictionnaire d'histoire et de géographie ecclésiastiques,* ed. A. BAUDRILLART et al. (Paris 1912) 451–452. A. BUTLER, *The Lives of the Saints,* ed. H. THURSTON and D. ATTWATER (New York 1956) 1:470.

[A. G. BIGGS]

ANSELMO DEDICATA, COLLECTIO

Toward the end of the 9th century in Milan, a canonical collection came to light, which the unknown author had dedicated to Anselm, Archbishop of Milan (II, 882–896), and which was to have considerable importance both in Italy and in Germany.

The scheme of this collection was new, since it was aimed at the distribution of a large number of matters, primarily but not exclusively of canonical origin, into a systematic form. However, this was done by using a method different from that which appeared in previous works—perhaps unknown to the author himself—such as the *DACHERIANA COLLECTIO.*

The subject matter was divided into 12 books of different lengths, containing three sections: works strictly canonical (canons and pontifical decretals); works derived from the letters of St. Gregory the Great; and works of Roman sources, from which came also the ''Lex romana canonice compta'' and the ''Regulae ecclesiasticae'' (called also ''Excerpta bobiensia'').

The contents of the work are as follows: book 1: high ecclesiastical hierarchy (pope, patriarchs, and metropolitans); book 2: bishops; book 3: councils; book 4: priests and deacons; book 5: minor clergy; book 6: regulars and widows; book 7: the laity; book 8: the practice of virtues; book 9: Baptism; book 10: worship, ecclesiastical benefices; book 11: feasts; and book 12: heretics, schismatics, and non-Catholics.

A plan so formulated was suitable for placing at hand, in an organic form, a number of works that were not easy to consult otherwise. This explains the great diffusion of the work and its direct or indirect influence on all the canonical collections until the time of Gregory

VII. The sources the author used included the FALSE DECRETALS, in the so-called A² edition. The part dealing with the conciliar canons and the post-Damasian authentic decretals was taken from the *HADRIANA COLLECTIO.* Many norms were taken also from the Collection of the manuscript of Novara (an edition of the *Hadriana Collectio* with many additions) and from other minor works of various origin.

Because of the form and scope of the *Anselmo Dedicata,* the texts are not always reproduced in their entirety but are split into several chapters and which are inserted into their proper places. Consequently, some texts are repeated more than once.

The diffusion of this collection was quite extensive for more than a century, and one may say that it governed the Italian as well as German canonical life until the publication of the *Decretum* of BURCHARD OF WORMS. Indeed, some manuscripts in Germany prove that a certain influence was exercised by the collection until the first quarter of the 11th century, while in Italy its effects were felt until the time of ANSELM II OF LUCCA.

Bibliography: P. FOURNIER and G. LEBRAS, *Histoire des collections canoniques en occident depuis les fausses décrétales jusqu'au Décret de Gratien,* 2 v. (Paris 131–32) 1:235–243. C. G. MOR, ''Diritto romano e diritto canonico nell'età pregrazianea,'' in v. 1 of *L'Europa e il diritto romano: Studi in memoria di Paolo Koschaker,* 2 v. (Milan 1954). A. AMANIEU, *Dictionnaire de droit canonique,* ed. R. NAZ, 7 v. (Paris 1935–5) 1:578–583.

[C. G. MOR]

ANSFRID, BL.

Duke of Brabant, Benedictine, bishop of Utrecht; d. May 3, 1010. Ansfrid (Aufrid, Anfroi) was educated at the imperial school at Cologne. As duke, he vigorously suppressed brigandage. In 992 Ansfrid founded at Thorn a convent which his wife and daughter entered, and he himself became a monk at Heiligen, a monastery that he established. In 994 Emperor OTTO III persuaded the reluctant Ansfrid to accept the bishopric of Utrecht, where he served until 1006, when he became blind. He withdrew again to Heiligen. He died there but his relics were later stolen and now repose in St. Peter's Church in Utrecht.

Feast: May 3.

Bibliography: *Acta Sanctorum* May 1:433–435. THIETMAR VON MERSEBERG, *Monumenta Germaniae Historica: Scriptores rerum Germanicarum* 4:31 NS 9. A. M. ZIMMERMANN, *Lexikon für Theologie und Kirche*² 1:597. A. BUTLER, *The Lives of the Saints* 2:273.

[R. BALCH]

ANSGAR, ST.

Abbot, archbishop, "Apostle of the North;" b. near Corbie, Picardy, France, *c.* 801; d. Bremen, Germany, Feb. 3, 865. Ansgar (Anskar, Anschaire, Anschar, Scharies) entered the BENEDICTINES (814?) at Corbie, where he had been educated. After 823, he was a teacher and preacher at Corvey. After the conversion of the Danish King Harold at the court of Louis the Pious, Ansgar went to Denmark as a missionary; but three years later (829) he returned without having achieved any remarkable success. When a Swedish embassy asked for Christian missionaries, he immediately set out for that country with Witmar, another monk from Corvey. The ship on which they sailed fell into the hands of pirates, and only after great hardships did the two priests arrive at Björkö, where King Björn received them well. Among Ansgar's converts was Heriger, governor and councilor to the King. Emperor Louis recalled Ansgar 18 months later and designated him abbot of Corvey and bishop of Hamburg, a new diocese planned earlier by Charlemagne and decreed by the Reichstag at Thionville (Nov. 10, 831). Consecrated in 832 by DROGO OF METZ, Ansgar proceeded to Rome, where Pope GREGORY IV made him archbishop and the papal legate for the Scandinavian and remaining Slavic missions. In 834 Louis assigned Turholt monastery as Ansgar's training center and source of financial support for the Nordic mission, but Louis's death (840) and the Treaty of Verdun (843), which divided the empire, deprived Ansgar of this source of income. After 13 years of work in Hamburg, Ansgar suffered his gravest setback when Northmen (845) burned Hamburg to the ground. Sweden and Denmark returned to paganism. In 847, Emperor Louis the German appointed Ansgar to the vacant See of Bremen, which was to be united with Hamburg, although the pope and the archbishop of Cologne actually refused to recognize this amalgamation. From his see in Bremen, Ansgar directed new missionary activities in the North. His associates, Gautbert, Bishop of Sweden, and Nithard, who had been working in Denmark and Sweden since 832, were caught in the pagan rebellion, and so it was Ansgar who traveled to Denmark, converted King Haarik, and, having obtained Louis the German's authorization and a letter of introduction from Haarik, set out for Sweden (852–853). There King Olaf cast lots to determine whether Christian missionaries should be allowed to return or not. The verdict was favorable, and the king himself was eventually won over to the Christian faith. Nithard had been killed during the persecutions, and Bishop Gautbert, a close friend, refused to return to his see. He was replaced by REMBERT, Ansgar's successor at Bremen-Hamburg. Contrary to his wish, Ansgar was not to become a martyr; he died peacefully in Bremen and was buried in the cathedral. He was an ex-traordinary preacher, a modest, self-effacing priest and ascetic, a benefactor of the poor and sick, and a brilliant administrator, whom his biographer, Bishop Rembert, named a saint. Pope Nicholas I confirmed the canonization. St. Ansgar is usually depicted with a fur collar on his episcopal robes and with a model church held in his hand.

Feast: Feb 3.

Bibliography: *Monumenta Germaniae Historica: Scriptores* 2:683–725. *Monumenta Germaniae Historica: Scriptores rerum Germanicarum* v.51. REMBERT, *Anskar,* tr. C. H. ROBINSON (London 1921); tr. G. WAITZ (Hannover 1977); *Das Leben des heiligen Ansgar von seinem Nachfolger Rimbert,* ed. W. SCHAMONI (Düsseldorf 1965). W. LÜDTKE, "Die Verehrung des hl. Anschar," *Schriften des Vereins für Schleswigholsteinische Kirchengeschichte* 8.2 (1926) 123–162. É. DE MOREAU, *Saint Anschaire* (Louvain 1930). H. DÖRRIES, *Ansgar; seine Bedeutung für die Mission* (Hamburg 1965). H. GAMILLSCHEG, *Ich kenne keine Angst: Ansgar, Missionar bei den Wikingern* (Mödling 1979). A. M. ZIMMERMANN, *Kalendarium Benedictinum* (Metten 1933–38) 1:159–165. A. HAUCK, *Kirchengeschichte Deutschlands* (Berlin-Leipzig 1958) 2:693–707. J. L. BAUDOT and L. CHAUSSIN, *Vies des saints et des bienhereux selon l'ordre du calendrier avec l'historique des fêtes* (Paris 1935–56) 2:73–78. A. BUTLER, *The Lives of the Saints,* ed. H. THURSTON and D. ATTWATER (New York 1956) 1:242–243. S. HILPISCH, *Lexicon für Theologie und Kirche,* ed. J. HOFER and K. RAHNER (Freiburg 1957–65) 1:597–598. ADAM OF BREMEN, *History of the Archbishops of Hamburg-Bremen,* tr. F. J. TSCHAN (New York 1959).

[S. A. SCHULZ]

ANSTRUDIS, ST.

b. *c.* 645; d. *c.* 709. Anstrudis (Austru, Austrude) was the daughter of SS. Blandinus and Salaberga. At the age of 12, when a certain Laudrannus claimed her in marriage, she sought refuge in the monastery of Notre Dame (later Saint-Jean) of Laon, where her mother was abbess (*c.* 657). At the age of 20 she succeeded her mother. The death of her brother Baldwin, deacon of Laon (*c.* 679), marked the beginning of serious difficulties in her life. She was accused of a liaison with the mayor of the palace, Ebroin, and the Bishop of Laon, Madelgarius, tried to take the abbey from her. More than once her life was in danger. At her death she was buried in one of seven churches built around her convent, and numerous miracles have been attributed to her. Her cult began soon after her death; her relics, transferred to Saint-Jean of Laon, were venerated there until the French Revolution.

Feast: Oct. 17.

Bibliography: *Acta Sanctorum* Oct. 8:108–117. *Monumenta Germaniae Historica: Scriptores rerum Merovingicarum* 6:64–78. M. MELLEVILLE, *Histoire de la ville de Laon,* 2 v. (Laon 1846) v.2. P. FOURNIER, *Dictionnaire d'histoire et de géographie ecclésiastiques,* ed. A. BAUDRILLART et al. (Paris 1912) 5:798. G. JACQUE-

MET, *Catholicisme* 1:622. E. EWIG, *Lexicon für Theologie und Kirche*, ed. J. HOFER and K. RAHNER (Freiburg 1957–65)1:601. J. L. BAUDOT and L. CHAUSSIN, *Vies des saints et des bienhereux selon l'ordre du calendrier avec l'historique des fêtes* (Paris 1935–56) 10:548–549. M. A. CALABRESE, *Bibliotheca sanctorum* 2: 44–45.

[É. BROUETTE]

ANSUERUS, ST.

Abbot and martyr; b. Mecklenburg, Germany, *c.* 1040; d. Ratzeburg, Germany, July 15, 1066. He entered the BENEDICTINE monastery of Sankt Georg in Ratzeburg, where he was noted for his learning and piety and became abbot while still young. He devoted himself to the conversion of the Slavs and preached the gospel to the pagans still living around Ratzeburg. In 1066, together with about 30 companions, he was stoned by pagan Wends. He begged his executioners to kill him last so that his companions would not apostatize and so that he could comfort them. His body was first interred in the crypt at Sankt Georg; but when a blind man was restored to sight at the tomb, Bishop Evermond (d. 1178) had the martyr's remains translated to the cathedral of Ratzeburg. The relics perished during the disorders of the Reformation period. Canonization was granted with papal approval by Abp. ADALBERT OF BREMEN. Ansuerus was included in the Schleswig and Ratzeburg Breviaries, but since the Reformation he is remembered only in monastic martyrologies. His memorials are a cross near Ratzeburg and a painting in the cathedral there.

Feast: July 15.

Bibliography: F. CASTAGNE, *Der Mönch Ansverus und die Heidenmission in Holstein und Lauenburg* (Hannover 1966). *Acta Sanctorum* July 4:97–108. A. M. ZIMMERMANN, *Kalendarium Benedictinum* (Metten 1933–38) 2:456–458. A. M. ZIMMERMANN, *Lexicon für Theologie und Kirche*, ed. J. HOFER and K. RAHNER (Freiburg 1957–65) 1:602. A. TAYLOR, *Dictionnaire d'histoire et de géographie ecclésiastiques*, ed. A. BAUDRILLART et al. (Paris 1912) 3:509.

[G. SPAHR]

ANTEPENDIUM

A piece of precious material, richly ornamented, that was historically used to cover the entire front of an altar. The use of the antependium is probably derived from the practice of the early Church of covering the table-altar with a colored fabric. The antependium became an element in the decoration of the altar from the 4th century in the East and the 5th in the West. It used to be prescribed by a rubric of the Roman Missal, but the 1960 revision of the Code of Rubrics dropped all references to it in dealing with the preparation of the altar for Mass (526). Until the 13th century the color for the antependium was not determined, but since then it was fixed as the liturgical color of the day. There were two exceptions to this rule: at an altar where the Blessed Sacrament was exposed the frontal was to be white; for a Requiem Mass at an altar where the Blessed Sacrament was reserved the frontal was to be violet.

Bibliography: J. B. O'CONNELL, *Church Building and Furnishing* (Notre Dame, IN 1955) 192–196. J. BRAUN, *I Paramenti sacri*, tr. G. ALLIOD (Turin 1914) 171–176. P. RADÓ, *Enchiridion liturgicum*, 2 v. (Rome 1961) 2:1410.

[J. B. O'CONNELL/EDS.]

ANTERUS, POPE, ST.

Pontificate: Nov. 21, 235 to Jan. 3, 236. The *Libe pontificalis* says Anterus was a Greek, son of a Romulus, and that he was interested in collecting acts of martyrs. Its report that he was a martyr is untrustworthy. The Liberian catalogue says that he "fell asleep," and he does not appear in lists of martyrs. Little is known of his pontificate. He was the first pope buried in the bishops' crypt of the Cemetery of Callistus; apparently the body of PONTIANUS, his predecessor, was buried there later. His feast does not appear in ancient calendars or Roman books of the liturgy before the ninth century.

Feast: Jan. 3.

Bibliography: EUSEBIUS, *Ecclesiastical History* 6.29 G. SCHWAIGER, *Lexikon für Theologie und Kirche*, ed. J. HOFER and K. RAHNER (Freiberg 1957–65) 1:602–603. J. P. KIRSCH, *Dictionnaire d'histoire et de géographie ecclésiastiques*, ed. A. BAUDRILLART, et al. (Paris 1912–) 3:520–521. E. FERGUSON, ed., *Encyclopedia of Early Christianity* (New York 1997), 1.415. J. N. D. KELLY, *Oxford Dictionary of Popes* (New York 1986), 16. A. CALABRIA, *S. Antero Papa e Martire, Patrono di Casalbuono* (Salerno), *Storia e leggenda* (Salerno 1994).

[E. G. WELTIN]

ANTHELM OF CHIGNIN, ST.

Carthusian reformer; b. Chignin, Savoie, France, 1107; d. June 26, 1178. Having become a Carthusian at the charterhouse of Portes, 1136–37, he was sent to rebuild the damaged La Grande-Chartreuse. He became its seventh prior (1139) and the first minister-general of the Carthusian Order (1142). He revived discipline and restored prosperity, creating five new charterhouses; but encountering difficulties with Pope Eugene III, he resigned in 1151. Anthelm served as prior at Portes from 1152 to 1154, and then was made bishop of Belley,

France, in 1163 by ALEXANDER III, whom he had supported against the emperor's papal candidate. He was appointed legate to Henry II of England in the hope that he might reconcile the king with Thomas BECKET, but Anthelm was unable to go. In 1175 Frederick BARBAROSSA bestowed on him and his bishop successors the title of Prince of the Holy Roman Empire. His cult has been observed by the CARTHUSIANS since 1607. The elevation of his relics took place at Belley in 1630.

Feast: June 26.

Bibliography: *Acta Sanctorum* June 7:201–219. GUILLAUME, CHARTREUX DE PORTES, *Vita Sancti Antelmi Bellicensis Episcopi Ordinis Cartusiensis = Vie de saint Antelme, évêque de Belley, chartreux*, Latin and French text, tr. J. PICARD (Lagnieu, France 1978). L. MARCHAL, *Vie de Saint Anthelme* (Paris 1878). S. AUTORE, *Dictionnaire d'histoire et de géographie ecclésiastiques*, ed. A. BAUDRILLART et al. (Paris 1912) 3:523–525. J. L. BAUDOT and L. CHAUSSIN, *Vies des saints et des bienhereux selon l'ordre du calendrier avec l'historique des fêtes* (Paris 1935–56) 6:444–447. R. AIGRAIN, *Catholicisme* 1:625–626. H. WOLTER, *Lexicon für Theologie und Kirche*, ed. J. HOFER and K. RAHNER (Freiburg 1957–65) 1:603. A. BUTLER, *The Lives of the Saints*, ed. H. THURSTON and D. ATTWATER (New York 1956) 2:650–652. L. RÉAU, *Iconographie de l'art chrétien* (Paris 1955–59) 3.1:99–100. C. VENS, *Bibliotheca sanctorum* 2:48–50.

[É. BROUETTE]

ANTHELMI, JOSEPH

Learned ecclesiastical historian, whose works are still highly regarded; b. Fréjus, France, July 27, 1648; d. there, June 21, 1697. A theology student of François de LA CHAIZE at Lyons, Anthelmi received his doctorate in theology in Paris (1688). After his ordination in Fréjus in 1673, he preferred the life of a scholar to that of church administrator. Accordingly, he devoted his life to the history of the Church, particularly of his province. Within a few years he published *De initiis ecclesiae Forojuliensis* (1680). His next few works were in local hagiography (St. Antiolus and St. Tropez). For the next few years he became involved in polemics with P. Quesnel over the authorship of several religious works, among which was the Athanasian Creed. In 1693 Anthelmi published a study of St. Martin of Tours. His scholarly activity was interrupted in 1694 by three years of fruitful conciliation as vicar-general of the diocese of Pamiers. In 1697, exhausted by years of work and apparently ill from tuberculosis, Anthelmi returned to Fréjus. In addition to his many works, Anthelmi left manuscripts and notes, several of which were published as late as 1872.

Bibliography: R. D'AMAT, *Dictionnaire de biographie française* 2:1467. F. BONNARD, *Dictionnaire d'histoire et de géographie ecclésiastiques* 3:515–516, contains list of works. H. HURTER, *Nomenclatur literarius theologiae catholicae* 2:540.

[R. J. MARION]

ANTHEMIUS

The name of many saints, ecclesiastics, and statesmen in the Church. The following are significant:

(1) Anthemius (Anthemus, Attenius, Aptemius) of Poitiers, St., is named as 13th in the Episcopal List, which according to L. Duchesne is subject to great caution during this period. Nothing is known of his life, but his feast has been celebrated in the dioceses of Poitiers and Saintes since the 17th century. There is no authentic document supporting the claim that he died in Jonzac *c.* 400.

Feast: Dec. 3.

(2) Anthemius, prefect of the Orient under Arcadius (fl. 400–414), undertook a successful embassy to the Persians, served as *magister officiorum* and patrician (406), and directed the government of the empire when Theodosius II became emperor in 408 at the age of seven. He was praised by St. JOHN CHRYSOSTOM for his rectitude (*Patrologia Graeca* 52:699). He pushed the Huns beyond the Danube, organized a fleet, furnished Constantinople with a protective wall (413), and erected the Baths of Honorius and the church of St. Thomas. In 414 he ceded the government to Empress Pulcheria and disappeared from history.

(3) Anthemius of Constantia, Cyprus (fl. end of 5th century), is renowned for having discovered the body of St. Barnabas in 488. He used the occasion as a support for the claim of apostolicity, and therefore independence from Antioch, for the Church in Cyprus. The account of this miraculous event, written by Alexander, a 6th century monk of Cyprus, in his encomium of St. Barnabas describes the finding as a result of a dream and states that a copy of the Gospel of Matthew was found on Barnabas's chest. Emperor Zeno exempted Cyprus from the ecclesiastical jurisdiction of Antioch, and Anthemius built a basilica and established the feast of St. Barnabas on June 11.

Bibliography: (1) P. DE MONSABERT, *Dictionnaire d'histoire et de géographie ecclésiastiques*, ed. A. BAUDRILLART et al. (Paris 1912) 525. R. AIGRAIN, *Catholicisme* 1:626. (2) L. BRÉHIER, *Dictionnaire d'histoire et de géographie ecclésiastiques*, ed. A. BAUDRILLART et al. (Paris 1912) 525–526. (3) *Acta Sanctorum* June 2:444–446. R. AIGRAIN, *Dictionnaire d'histoire et de géographie ecclésiastiques*, ed. A. BAUDRILLART et al. (Paris 1912) 526–527.

[F. X. MURPHY]

ANTHIMUS

The name of many saints, ecclesiastics, and statesmen in the Church. The following are significant:

(1) Anthimus, St., bishop of Nicomedia, martyr, beheaded in the Diocletian persecution of 303. Emperor

Justinian I built a church in his honor, and the legend of SS. Domna and Indes (*Patrologia Graeca* 116: 1073–76) credits him with a letter written to his community during the persecution of Diocletian.

Feast: April 27; Greek, Sept. 13.

(2) Anthimus, St., priest and martyr during the Diocletian persecution. His *Acta* recount a series of conversions among Roman officials because of his courage.

Feast: May 11.

(3) Anthimus of Tyana, 4th-century bishop, adversary and friend of St. BASIL OF CAESAREA, supported Basil's anti-Arian offensive, but opposed his jurisdictional arrangements, particularly in reference to the Church in ARMENIA.

(4) Anthimus, St., hymnographer, member of a pious association of laymen called the Spoudaioi, was given to keeping vigils in the church of St. Irene in Constantinople. He became a priest (after 457) and the leader of the Chalcedonian party and was celebrated as the author of liturgical tropes or hymns for popular chanting

Feast: June 7, Synaxary of Constantinople.

(5) Anthimus I, patriarch of Constantinople (535–536). Named bishop of Trebizond in 533, he was transferred to Constantinople at the instance of Empress THEODORA in June of 535. Because of his Monophysite leanings and epistolary relations with SEVERUS OF ANTIOCH and THEODOSIUS OF ALEXANDRIA, he was deposed by a synod of Constantinople under Pope AGAPETUS I, and the decision was implemented by JUSTINIAN I, who exiled him. His profession of faith is preserved by ZACHARY THE RHETOR (*Corpus scriptorum Christianorum orientalium* 2:96–117).

(6) Anthimus, a 14th-century anti-Latin Bulgarian archbishop, was a theologian.

(7) Anthimus II to VII were patriarchs of Constantinople. *Anthimus II* (June to October 1623) was supported by French policy in his opposition to Cyril Lucaris. He died at Mt. Athos, 1628. *Anthimus III* (1822–24); b. Naxos, c. 1760; d. Smyrna, 1842. He was exiled in 1824. *Anthimus IV*, Bambakis (1840–41 and 1848–52); b. Constantinople, c. 1788; d. Isle of Princes, 1878. He became metropolitan of Iconium (1825), of Larissa (1835), and of Nicomedia (1837). Elected patriarch in February of 1840, he was deposed in 1841, but reelected in 1848 and deposed again on Nov. 11, 1852, when he retired to the Isle of Princes, where he died a nonagenarian. *Anthimus V* (1841–42); b. Neochorion, Turkey; d. Constantinople, June of 1842. He was metropolitan of Agathopolis (1815), Anchialos (1821), and Cyzicus (1831) and was

elected patriarch of Constantinople in May of 1841. *Anthimus VI*, Joannides (1845–48; 1853–55; 1871–73); b. Isle of Koutali, c. 1790; d. Candili, 1878. A monk on Mt. Athos, he was elected and deposed three times. A decisive opponent of Bulgarian orthodoxy, he retired to Candili in 1873 and died there almost a nonagenarian. *Anthimus VII*, Tsatsos (1895–96); b. Janina, c. 1835; d. Halki, December of 1913. He was a renowned preacher and theologian. Bishop of Paramythia (1869), metropolitan of Ainos (1878), then of Korytsa, Leros, and Kalymnos, he served 22 months as patriarch and retired to Halki. He rejected the ecumenical efforts of Pope Leo XIII's encyclical *Praeclara gratulationes* (June 20, 1894) in a letter published in September of 1895 (*see* BYZANTINE THEOLOGY, II).

Bibliography: (1) H. RAHNER, *Lexikon für Theologie und Kirche* (Freiburg 1957–65) 1:603–604. B. ALTANER, *Patrology*, tr. GRAEF (New York 1960) 248. R. JANIN, *Dictionnaire d'histoire et de géographie ecclésiastiques* 3:530. G. MERCATI, *Studi e Testi* 5 (1901) 87–98. M. RICHARD, *Mélanges de science religieuse* 6 (1949) 5–28. (2) R. JANIN, *Dictionnaire d'histoire et de géographie ecclésiastiques* 3:529–530. *Acta Sanctorum* May 2:612–614. (3) R. JANIN, *Dictionnaire d'histoire et de géographie ecclésiastiques* 3:534. J. B. LIGHTFOOT, *A Dictionary of Christian Biography* 1:119. (4) S. PÉTRIDÈS, *Échos d'Orient* 4 (1900) 228; 7 (1904) 341–342; *Dictionnaire d'histoire et de géographie ecclésiastiques* 3:531. K. GROSS, *Lexikon für Theologie und Kirche* 1:604. (5) E. STEIN, *Histoire du Bas–Empire*, tr. J. R. PALANQUE (Paris 1949–50) 2:381–388. R. JANIN, *Dictionnaire d'histoire et de géographie ecclésiastiques* 3:531. H. RAHNER, *Lexikon für Theologie und Kirche* 1:603. (6) K. KRUMBACHER *Geschichte der byzantinischen Literatur* (Munich 1897) 110. S. SALAVILLE, *Dictionnaire d'histoire et de géograhpie ecclésiastiques* 3:532. (7) R. JANIN *Dictionnaire d'histoire et de géographie ecclésiastiques* 3:532–534.

[F. X. MURPHY]

ANTHIMUS OF TREBIZOND

Monophysite bishop of Trebizond, named patriarch of Constantinople in 535, and deposed in 536; d. after 548. As bishop of Trebizond he participated in the Colloquy of Constantinople (532) in which JUSTINIAN I attempted to achieve agreement between the orthodox and the Monophysite bishops. Although he participated on the Catholic side, Anthimus leaned toward the party of Severus of Antioch, and Empress THEODORA who had him named patriarch of Constantinople to succeed Epiphanius (d. June 5, 535) despite the canons that forbade transfer from one see to another. Anthimus promised to stay in communion with Rome, but sent an encyclical letter to the two Monophysite patriarchs, SEVERUS OF ANTIOCH in exile, and THEODOSIUS OF ALEXANDRIA. Pope AGAPETUS I, who arrived in Constantinople in early March of 536, refused to communicate with Anthimus and demanded his deposition. In a synod held by the pope, Anthimus was declared contumacious and deprived of his powers as priest and bishop. He was replaced by Mennas as patriarch on March 13, 536, and lived an ascetical life for at least 12 more years in Constantinople under the protection of Empress Theodora. Of his writings, fragments of a tract sent to Justinian I concerning the doctrine of one energy and one will in Christ and his synodal letter to Severus have been preserved. His profession of faith is recorded by Zachary Rhetor (*Hist. Eccl.* 9.21; 25: *Corpus scriptorum Christianorum Orientalium* 2:96–117).

Bibliography: H. RAHNER, *Lexikon für Theologie und Kirche* 1:603. E. CASPAR, *Geschichte des Papsttums von den Anfängen bis zur Höhe der Weltherrschaft* (Tübingen 1930–33) 2:222–223. A. GRILLMEIER and H. BACHT, *Das Konzil von Chalkedon: Geschichte und Gegenwart* (Würzburg 1951–54) 2:159–162. C. J. HEFELE, *Histoire des conciles d'après les documents originaux* (Paris 1907–38) 2.2:1142–55. H. G. BECK, *Kirche und theologische Literatur im byzantinischen Reich* (Munich 1959) 392–393. E. STEIN, *Histoire du Bas-Empire,* tr. J. R. PALANQUE (Paris 1949–59) 2:381–385, 388.

[P. ROCHE]

ANTHONY, PATRIARCHS OF CONSTANTINOPLE (I-IV)

Anthony I, Kassimatas, iconoclast and patriarch, January 821 to *c.* Jan. 21, 837. As the son of a priest shoemaker, he became a teacher, then a monk, probably hegumen (abbot) of the Monastery of the Metropolitou in Petrion before 815, and later, apparently bishop of Sylaion. An iconoclast because of ambition, he aided Emperor LEO V (813–820) against Patriarch NICEPHORAS I, took part in the Iconoclastic Synod of 815 under Theodotus Melissenus, and became patriarch in 821. He excommunicated Job, Patriarch of Antioch, because he had crowned the usurping Emperor Thomas, who was supported by the Arab Emir Mamun.

Anthony II, Kauleas, patriarch, August 893 to Feb. 12, 901. At 12 he followed his father as a monk and later as hegumen in the Monastery of the Mother of God, whose title was later changed to Kalliou Kauleos (*Patrologia Graeca,* ed. J. P. Migne, 117:308d). He instigated the canonization of the Athonite monk St. Blasius of Amorion (*c.* 894), and in the synod of September 899 received opponents of PHOTIUS into communion with the Church in the presence of two papal legates. He also strengthened the power of the Byzantine patriarchate over the Church in Dalmatia.

Anthony III, the Studite, patriarch, March 974, to *c.* April 979; d. Studiu, Mt. Athos, 983. A monk in the Studiu monastery, he became Syncellus to Patriarch Basil I and after the latter's deposition by Emperor John I

Tzimisces, patriarch. He supported the anti-pope Boniface VII against Pope BENEDICT VII and was forced into retirement (979), possibly for having sided with Bardas Sclerus in his conflict with Emperor Basil II. He left a *Monitum* to his monks on confession and the monastic account of conscience, and fought against the simoniacal activity connected with taxes for HAGIA SOPHIA.

Anthony IV, patriarch, 1389 to 1390, and 1391 to 1397; d. Constantinople, May 1397. Named patriarch in January 1389, he was deposed in July 1390, but he managed to regain imperial favor and returned to power in March 1391. He played a primary role in supporting the Byzantine sovereignty, despite the fact that Constantinople had become a vassal of the Turks under Bajezid. He controverted the statement of Basil I, Grand Duke of Russia, ''We have a Church but no emperor,'' with the claim that the Apostle Peter's admonition, ''Fear God, honor the emperor'' (1 Pt 2.13) referred specifically to the ecumenical ruler of Byzantium. He tried to regulate the conflict between the various Byzantine-rite churches; held the Patriarchate of Alexandria in obedience to Constantinople despite the divisive efforts of the Sultan of Egypt; and not only wrote to King Jagellon of Poland (January 1397), the Hungarian monarch, and the Metropolitan of Kiev, begging their assistance against the Turks, but encouraged Manual II to make a journey to the West in 1399 for this purpose. He also laid down regulations for the conduct of monks, particularly in regard to their novitiate and their clothing.

Bibliography: P. JOANNOU, *Lexikon für Theologie und Kirche,* ed. J. HOFER and K. RAHNER (2d, new ed. Freiburg 1957–65) 1:669–670. V. GRUMEL, ed., *Les Regestes des Actes du Patriarcat de Constantinople* (Istanbul 1932–) 1.2:412, 594–597, 798–799; *Échos d'Orient* 33 (1934) 257–288; 35 (1936) 5–42. R. JANIN, *La Géographie ecclésiastique de l'Empire byzantin,* v.1.3 (Paris 1953); *Dictionnaire d'histoire et de géographie ecclésiastiques,* ed. A. BAUDRILLART et al. (Paris 1912–) 3:746, 796–797. H. G. BECK, *Kirche und theologische Literatur im byzantinischen Reich* (Munich 1959) 584. F. MIKLOSICH and J. MÜLLER, eds., *Acta et diplomata graeca medii aevi,* 6 v. (Vienna 1860–90) 2:112–291. G. OSTROGORSKY, *History of the Byzantine State,* tr. J. HUSSEY from 2d German ed. (Oxford 1956); American ed. by P. CHARANIS (New Brunswick, N.J. 1957) 181–186, 491–493.

[P. JOANNOU]

ANTHONY BONFADINI, BL.

Franciscan preacher; b. Ferrara, Italy, *c.* 1402; d. Cotignola, Romagna, Dec. 1, 1482. He left a noble family to become a FRANCISCAN at the friary of the Holy Spirit, Ferrara, in 1439. Having obtained a doctorate in theology, he became a renowned preacher in Italy and a missionary in the Holy Land. On his return he preached at Cotignola, where he died at a pilgrim's hospice. Mariano of Florence praised his kindness and peacemaking spirit. One miracle was attributed to him during his lifetime, several others after his death. He protected Cotignola from calamities in 1630, 1688, and 1696. His body was transferred (1495) into the church of the Observant friary founded by Bl. Angelo Carletti di Chivasso. A tomb (1631) and a special chapel were erected (1666). The diocesan process was held at Faenza (1894), and Leo XIII confirmed his cult (1901). The recognition of his intact body took place in 1902.

Feast: Dec. 1 (Diocese of Faenza and among Franciscans).

Bibliography: L. N. CITTADELLA, *Vita del beato Antonio Bonfadini da Ferrara* (Ferrara 1838). L. OLIGER, *Dictionnaire d'histoire et de géographie ecclésiastiques,* ed. A. BAUDRILLART (Paris 1912–) 3:763. W. FORSTER, *Lexikon für Theologie und Kirche,* ed. J. HOFER and K. RAHNER, 10 v. (2d, new ed. Freiburg 1957–65); suppl., *Das Zweite Vatikanische Konzil: Dokumente und kommentare,* ed. H. S. BRECHTER, pt. 1 (1966)[2] 1:672. A. BUTLER, *The Lives of the Saints,* ed. H. THURSTON and D. ATTWATER, 4 v. (New York 1956) 4:460–461.

[J. CAMBELL]

ANTHONY NEYROT, BL.

Dominican martyr; b. Rivoli, Italy; d. Tunis, April 10, 1460. Contrary to the advice of St. ANTONINUS, under whom he had been professed several years earlier, Neyrot went to Sicily to preach; but growing tired of the island, he embarked for Naples. Pirates captured the ship (Aug. 1458) and took its passengers to Tunis. After a prison term Neyrot was released, but while waiting ransom he succumbed to temptation (April 1459), publicly denied Christ, became a Muslim, and contracted marriage. Four months later he repented, undertook a life of penance, and was reconciled to the Church. On Palm Sunday 1460 he publicly rejected Islam, renounced his apostasy, and preached Christ before the Sultan, who had him executed. His body was sent to Genoa and thence to Rivoli (1469). Clement XIII beatified him on Feb. 21, 1767.

Feast: April 10.

Bibliography: *Acta Sanctorum* Aug. 6:530–541. I. TAURISANO, *Catalogus hagiographicus ordinis praedicatorum* (Rome 1918) 1:41. P. ALVAREZ, *Santos Bienaventurados venerables O.P.,* 4 v. (Vergara 1920–23) 2:195–200.

[F. C. RYAN]

ANTHONY OF EGYPT, ST.

Primitive Egyptian hermit; b. Comus, Egypt, 250; d. Egyptian Desert, 356. Anthony (or Antony Abbot) found

"St. Anthony of Egypt Distributing His Wealth to the Poor," painting by Sassetta, c. 1440.

school distasteful and shunned the companionship of other children. His well-to-do parents died when he was about 20, and he was left in charge of a younger sister. He gave himself over to prayer, and on hearing the Gospel message in church, he divided his property, keeping only enough to support his sister, whom he entrusted to a community of pious women. He practiced the religious life close to home and attached himself to an aged solitary, from whom he had the first lessons in the ascetic life. Later he went off in solitude to some empty tombs at a distance from the village. Here he remained some 12 or 15 years and was tempted by the devil. Then he moved to the desert and lived in an abandoned fort, where he was visited by people who had heard stories of his holiness and power over demons. He became their director in the spiritual life and gave them a long discourse, probably in the Coptic tongue since he knew no Greek.

This discourse on ascetic theology deals with the means of overcoming temptation and with the gift of the discernment of good and evil spirits. Later Anthony offered himself as a victim for martyrdom during the persecution of the Emperor Maximin Daja. He assisted the Christians in prison with material and spiritual solace, but was not called upon to suffer and recognized later that it took great spiritual courage to be a daily martyr to the flesh and one's own conscience.

He left his mountain retreat to combat the Arian heresy in Alexandria, and he spent his life partly in solitude, partly in journeys to his brethren to exhort them in the religious life. When he felt his end drawing near, he took two companions and retired into solitude. He died at the age of about 105 years.

The *Vita Antonii* was written by St. Athanasius one year after Anthony's death and influenced the whole Christian world. A Latin translation made by Evagrius, bishop of Antioch (d. 392), spread through the Roman Empire, and both St. JEROME and St. AUGUSTINE knew of it. It was modeled on Greek biography, which had sought to idealize an important figure in public life.

Athanasius saw in Anthony the ideal monk, who could prove his divine vocation by discerning spirits and by performing miracles—which he never claimed for himself but always attributed to God. Though illustrated with preternatural and, to modern tastes, bizarre incidents, the biographical data appear authentic. This vita influenced subsequent hagiography and literary and pictorial art as well.

Feast: Jan. 17.

Bibliography: ATHANASIUS, *Vita Antonii, Patrologia Graeca* 26:835–978; *The Coptic Life of Antony,* tr. T. VIVIAN (San Francisco 1995); *La vie primitive de S. Antoine: conservée en syriaque,* ed. R. DRAGUET (Louvain 1980); S. RUBENSON, *The Letters of St. Antony: Monasticism and the Making of a Saint* (Minneapolis 1995). *The Paradise or Garden of the Holy Fathers,* tr. E. A. WALLIS BUDGE of *Vita Antonii* and other texts from Syriac (New York 1972). M. ALEXANDRE, *Saint-Antoine entre mythe et légende,* ed. P. WALTER (Grenoble 1996). R. ABT-BAECHI, *Der Heilige und das Schwein* (Zurich 1983). A. KLAUS, *Lexikon für Theologie und Kirche,* ed. J. HOFER and K. RAHNER (Freiburg 1957–65) 1:667–669. L. BOUYER, *La Vie de Saint Antoine* (Paris 1950). J. QUASTEN, *Patrology* (Westminster, MD 1950) 3:39–45. H. DÖRRIES, "Die *Vita Antonii* als Geschichtsquelle," *Nachrichten der Akademie der Wissenschaften in Göttingen* 14 (1949) 359–410. G. BARDY, *Dictionnaire de spiritualité ascétique et mystique,* ed. M. VILLER et al. (Paris 1932) 1:702–708.

[R. T. MEYER]

ANTHONY OF PADUA, ST.

Franciscan Doctor of the Church; b. Lisbon, Portugal, Aug. 15?, 1195; d. Arcella, near Padua, Italy, June 13, 1231.

Life. At the age of 15, Anthony, the son of noble parents, entered the monastery of the CANONS Regular of São Vicente in Lisbon. After two years he came to S. Cruz in Coimbra, the study house of the Augustinian Canons, and there became expert in Sacred Scripture. Disappointed with the religious spirit of his monastery, which was under the patronage of the Portuguese court, and inspired by the news of the first Franciscan martyrs in Morocco, Anthony joined the FRANCISCANS at the friary of San Antonio in Coimbra (1220). At his own request, he was sent as a missionary to Morocco, but he was forced by illness to return; his boat, however, was driven off course, and he landed in Sicily. Arriving in Italy as an unknown, he took part in the famous chapter of the Mats at the Portiuncula (1221) and was affiliated to the Franciscan province of Romagna. For a time he resided in solitude and penance in the hermitage of Monte Paolo near Forlì. At his ordination he was recognized as an inspiring preacher and was commissioned to preach against the heretics in northern Italy (1222–24) and against the ALBIGENSES in southern France (1224). From 1227 to 1230 his preaching activity brought him back to Italy, and during the Lent of 1231 he preached daily in Padua.

In 1223 FRANCIS OF ASSISI appointed Anthony the first professor of theology for the friars; he is credited with introducing the theology of St. AUGUSTINE into the Franciscan Order. During his brief career Anthony was guardian in Le Puy, custos in Limoges, and provincial in the Romagna. The furious pace of his activities completely mined his feeble health; he died at the age of 36. At his canonization, May 30, 1232, Gregory IX declared him to be a "teacher of the Church," and Pius XII (Jan. 16, 1946) made him a Doctor of the Church with the title *Doctor evangelicus.*

Cultus. In popular devotion Anthony is venerated as the apostle of charity, invoked in both spiritual and temporal needs (the finder of lost objects; patron of lovers, of marriage, of pregnant women; as a helper against diabolic obsession, fever, animal diseases; as the patron of miners). The blessing of St. Anthony has become popular in all the above instances. His veneration as an effective preacher, added to his other titles of respect, have to a great extent caused the saint of Padua to displace St. ANTHONY OF EGYPT in popular esteem. Special forms of veneration are the St. Anthony Bread (alms given to the poor in his name to beg his intercession) and the Prayer League of St. Anthony (both in vogue since the end of the 19th century); the Tuesday devotion to St. Anthony (since the 17th century), because his burial day (June 17, 1231) fell on a Tuesday; his veneration as an admiral by the Portuguese (because of their victory over the French in 1710) and by the Spanish (because of the expulsion of the Moors from Oran in 1732).

In iconography he is variously symbolized according to his many activities: with book or cross for the teacher or preacher, a flame or a burning heart for the former Augustinian or the apostle of charity, and with a lily or the Christ Child for the saint. From the 13th century the liturgy for the Mass and Office of his feast was that of the common of a Doctor of the Church, still employed within the Franciscan Order. In the 16th-century liturgical reform of Pius V, the feast was suppressed, except within the order and in Portugal and Brazil. In 1585, however, Sixtus V restored the feast to the universal Church, with the liturgy taken from the common of a confessor.

Feast: June 13.

Bibliography: S. CLASEN, ed., *Antonius Patavinus: Lehrer des Evangeliums* (Werl 1954). C. JARMAK, *If You Seek Miracles: Reflections of Saint Anthony of Padua* (Padua 1998). C. JARMAK, *Saint Anthony: Herald Of The Good News* (Ellicot City, MD 1995). B. PRZEWOSNY, tr. *Life of St. Anthony: Assidua 1232* (Padua 1984). L. POLONIATO, ed., C. JARMAK, L. FRASSON, B. PRZEWOSNY, tr., *Anthony of Padua. Seek First His Kingdom* (Padua 1988). G. MARCIL, *Anthony of Padua: Sermons for the Easter Cycle* (St. Bonaventure, NY 1994). C. JARMAK, tr. *Anthony of Padua. Praise To You Lord: Prayers Of St. Anthony* (Padua 1986).

[S. CLASEN]

ANTHONY OF STRONCONE, BL.

Franciscan laybrother; b. Stroncone (Umbria), Italy, 1381; d. at San Damiano in Assisi, Feb. 7, 1461, *not* 1471. Antony Vici was reared by fervent Franciscan tertiary (*see* THIRD ORDERS) parents of a prominent family that gave several outstanding priests to the FRANCISCANS. Anthony was only 12 when he joined the Observant Friars Minor. He served as assistant novicemaster in Fiesole (1411–20) under the saintly Thomas Bellacci. From 1420 to 1435 he helped Bellacci convert and repress the FRATICELLI in Tuscany and Corsica. He spent his last decades as questing brother at the Carceri hermitage above Assisi and died in San Damiano friary there; he was revered for his humility, mortification, prophecies, and contemplative prayer. More than a score of major favors were reported at his tomb between the years 1461 and 1475. He was beatified by Pope INNOCENT XI in 1687. In 1809 his well-preserved body was forcibly translated to Stroncone by 20 armed citizens.

Feast: Feb. 7.

Bibliography: G. ODDI, *La Franceschina,* ed. N. CAVANNA, 2. v. (Florence 1931) 1:397–410. A. BUTLER, *The Lives of the Saints,* ed. H. THURSTON and D. ATTWATER, 4 v. (New York 1956) 1:272–273. L. CANONICI, *Antonio Vici, principe conteso* (Assisi 1961), with extensive bibliog. *Il beato Antonio da Stroncone,* ed. M. SENSI (Porziuncola 1993).

[R. BROWN]

"High Altar of St. Anthony," marble and bronze sculpture group by Donatello, Padua, Italy, 15th century. (©Elio Ciol/CORBIS)

ANTHONY OF THE HOLY GHOST

Discalced Carmelite, moral theologian, canonist, spiritual writer, and bishop; b. Monte Moro Velho (Coimbra), Portugal, 1618 (baptismal date, June 20); d. Loandra, Jan. 27, 1674. He took the habit of the Discalced Carmelites in Lisbon, and after studying at the college of the order in Coimbra, he was ordained and became a lector in theology. He won some reputation for himself as a preacher, and held various offices of responsibility in his order, being successively prior of the Lisbon house, provincial definitor, and definitor for Spain. Nominated bishop of Angola by Peter II of Portugal, he took possession of his see Dec. 11, 1673, but died the following month. His works included: *Directorium regularium* (Lyons 1661), consisting of case studies in the law for regulars; *Directorium confessariorum* (Lyons 1668), a work for the guidance of confessors, with case studies on the Sacraments, censures, the Commandments, justice, law, and contracts; and *Directorium mysticum* (Lyons 1677, Paris 1904), a treatise on the spiritual life tracing the three ways in the Fathers, St. Thomas Aquinas, and St. Teresa of Avila.

Bibliography: *Bibliotheca carmelitico-Lusitana* (Rome 1754) 28–30. SILVERIO DI SANTA TERESA, *Historia del Carmen De-*

scalzo en España, Portugal, y América, 15 v. (Burgos 1935–52) 10: 665–666. ELISÉE DE LA NATIVITÉ, *Dictionnaire de spiritualité des lettres françaises* 1:717–718.

[B. CAVANAUGH]

ANTHONY PAVONIUS, BL.

DOMINICAN inquisitor and martyr; b. Savigliano, Piedmont, Italy, *c.* 1326; d. Bricherasio, April 9, 1374. Born of noble stock, Anthony entered the Dominican priory at Savigliano in 1341 and made his novitiate there. In later years he was twice prior of this community. Ordained in 1351, he became a master in theology and in 1365 was appointed inquisitor general (*see* INQUISITION) for Liguria, Piedmont, and upper Lombardy. In the course of these duties he had to contend principally with the WALDENSIANS, some of whom became so infuriated with his persistence and success that they brutally murdered him as he left the church after preaching. He was beatified Dec. 4, 1856.

Feast: April 9.

Bibliography: *Acta Sanctorum* April 1:844–846. *Archivio-storico italiano* 3d ser., 1.2 (1865) 28–30. *Année dominicaine,* 23 v. (new ed. Lyons 1883–1909) April 1:295–301. I. TAURISANO, *Catalogus hagiographicus ordinis praedicatorum* 30.

[J. E. BRESNAHAN]

ANTHROPOCENTRISM

This article discusses the notion and refers to historical forms of anthropocentrism in Christian thought.

Notion. As the name implies, anthropocentrism makes the dimensions of human existence (the supreme reality of the world of man's experience) a central term of reference in the orders of intelligibility and value. Anthropocentrism is only fully intelligible as a correlative of THEOCENTRISM on the one hand and a dehumanized naturalism on the other.

Two basic tendencies have constantly manifested themselves in human culture. One is preoccupied with realities immanent to this world, and especially with the supreme among them, man. (Protagoras: "Man is the measure of all things.") The other is preoccupied with the Transcendent. (Plato: "God is the measure of all things.") The supreme achievement of human culture is an integration of what is valid in both of these insights. Such an integration is essential to Christianity, founded as it is upon the Divine Word's presence in the world in human flesh (*see* INCARNATION). The Christ event at once canonizes anthropocentrism and subordinates it to theo-

centrism: the intelligibility and values of human existence are safeguarded by their subordination to the divine reality, through Christ.

Historical Review. The reconciliation of anthropocentrism with theocentrism cannot remove the tension that exists between these two terms of reference in man's world-view. It is with reference to this tension that historical forms of anthropocentrism within Christian thought should be understood. Broadly, it seems true to say that thought in the Western Church (which has its beginnings against the background of the anthropocen the world-view of Stoicism) has been characteristically anthropocentric, while that of Eastern Christianity (which developed in a confrontation with a theocentric Gnosticism) has been more markedly theocentric. Thus the great theological controversies of Western Christianity have concerned man's condition under God's grace (Pelagianism, Lutheranism); while those of the East have concerned the supreme mysteries of God (Trinity, Incarnation). In the theological traditions that are the background to the early councils, the anthropocentric tendency was most evident in the school of ANTIOCH. It provided a healthy corrective to the theocentric tendency of the school of ALEXANDRIA.

In reaction to the unbalanced theocentrism of the early Middle Ages, the late medieval period in the West saw the emergence of a new anthropocentrism that progressively obscured the recognition of the Transcendent. It is typified in a concern with the human sufferings of Christ in the Passion that loses sight of the essentials of the Paschal mystery (*see* RESURRECTION OF CHRIST). This tendency emerged as the humanism of the Renaissance and the modern period, more and more emancipated from religious connotations.

With EXISTENTIALISM and PERSONALISM a new form of anthropocentrism has emerged in Western thought in recent decades and has had a profound influence upon Christian theology. Its essential correlative is not theocentrism but a positivistic naturalism that would neglect the unique ontological status and value of the human person in a world of things.

Bibliography: C. H. DAWSON, *The Dynamics of World History,* ed. J. J. MULLOY (New York 1956) e.g., 458–459. K. RAHNER, *Lexikon für Theologie und Kirche,* ed. J. HOFER and K. RAHNER, 10 v. (2d, new ed. Freiburg 1957–65); suppl., *Das Zweite Vatikanische Konzil: Dokumente und Kommentare,* ed. H. S. BRECHTER et al., pt. 1 (1966) 1:632–634.

[J. THORNHILL]

ANTHROPOLOGY, THEOLOGICAL

In its most generic sense, anthropology may be considered as man's explanation of himself. As an empirical science, anthropology is usually divided into cultural and physical: the study of human beings' social behavior, languages, world views, family life, and communal organizations as distinguished from the investigation into the physical evolution of human beings, the functional capacities of the human body, the development of races, etc. But anthropology may also be considered, especially in European terminology, as a sector of philosophy and theology. Man is the one being who is a problem to himself and philosophers have continually striven to explain the human situation. Within the theological enterprise, anthropology would be the study of human beings insofar as they are related to God. Christian anthropology seeks to explain man in the light of revelation, particularly the Christ event. It asks how man can relate to God's word, and hence inquires into his understanding of the world and himself. This aspect of theology has received considerable attention in recent times, and will constitute the basis for this article.

There are two significantly different approaches for constructing a theological anthropology. The first approach, which has been characteristic of Roman Catholic theology since the 17th century and theology's dependence upon philosophical idealism, would be an abstract anthropology of man's "essential" nature. The distinction between nature and grace, between an autonomous natural order and a more or less extrinsic supernatural vocation, would be sharply drawn. In this schema, human beings are regarded as having at most a passive obediential potency—little more than a lack of intrinsic contradiction—for participation in the life of God. Contemporary theology, however, has generally followed a much more existential method. Rather than an abstract concept of man's nature as such, theologians have begun with the concrete unity of man as he appears within history, situated within the one, actual and supernatural existential order. In accepting this direction, theology has been clearly indebted to philosophical existentialism and phenomenology.

Contemporary Theology. In choosing the latter approach, theology must also accept the need to be in open dialogue with the social sciences and history as well as with the types of philosophy mentioned above. Although it is impossible to discuss or even fully list the contributions of these disciplines as they have had a bearing on a contemporary theological anthropology, some can be emphasized. (1) Man is a being-in-time in the sense that he experiences his own radical finitude; bounded by death, he perceives that he does not have any hold upon existence. He faces this realization with anxiety, and seeks to make sense of it in the light of his orientation toward the fullness of being or (within the category of time) eternity. (2) Man is historical or social. His awareness of

reality is not achieved in isolation from the cultural forces that variously shape his perspectives. Language, even though culturally conditioned and limited, is the necessary embodiment of truth. (3) Freedom is an essential prerequisite for human fulfillment, without which cultural advance is an illusory veneer. (4) Man is future oriented. As Marxists stress, the future is the dominant mode of time and a vision of an authentic although yet-to-be-achieved model supplies the hope out of which a nonalienated society can be achieved.

Thus influenced by the data of the phenomenologists and social scientists, theology reflects upon man within the ambit of revelation. In one sense, this reflection has always been the business of theology and anthropology may be said to be one with the whole of theology. What distinguishes the contemporary approach is that it is explicit and systematic, rather than fragmented into the broad spectrum of theological tracts or divisions—each one dealing with some aspect of man—which characterized medieval theology. In addition, contemporary Christian anthropology perceives the need for a conscious principle or formal object according to which its study can proceed. Tentatively at least, such an organizing principle emerges as the dynamic orientation toward the Absolute as the term of all human tendency. In precise contradistinction to God as man's "over-against," the Absolute is perceived as the metaphysical ground of man's limitless receptivity toward being-itself. Man is a being of finite resources oriented to the infinite. The accepting acknowledgement of this tension and its implications for man as both limited and transcendent is the foundation for the open-ended anthropology without which religion and revelation become totally extrinsic to the human spirit. The final fulfillment of this tendency becomes explicit for the Christian in the mystery of the incarnate Word, the ultimate union of God and man who is the paradigm for all humankind. Christology becomes, therefore, the culmination of theological anthropology.

Other Components. In addition to this fundamental principle, three other significant components of a Christian anthropology can be identified. If man precisely in and through his finitude is ordered to the Absolute as the culmination of all human dynamism, then this Absolute will be manifest within the social-historical process and not centrally in some individualistic religious experience. Thus what Vatican Council II called the process of socialization (Constitution on the Church in the Modern World, 25) is not a "merely" secular, spiritually inconsequential development. Any dichotomy, either between soul and body or the material and spiritual realms, is regarded as a contradiction to the fundamental unity which is man. Secondly, man is radically free to respond to or reject God. The unique supernatural existential order wherein

God draws all men to himself does not forestall the sin of unbelief or the acceptance of this divine self-communication as totally gratuitous. Indeed, only insofar as man's free response to God's word is recognized as self-realization can this response be fully human. Finally, an adequate Christian anthropology must also form the basis for a relevant eschatology according to which death (understood within the biblical message of resurrection) is an opening to the world rather than a flight from the prison of corporeality.

Bibliography: E. CORETH, *Metaphysics* (New York 1968). J. METZ, *Theology of the World* (New York 1971). O. MUCK, *The Transcendental Method* (New York 1968). P. MCSHANE, *Foundations of Theology* (Notre Dame 1972). K. RAHNER, ''Man (Anthropology) III,'' *Sacramentum Mundi* 3.365–370. R. SHINN, *Man: The New Humanism* (Philadelphia 1968).

[T. M. MCFADDEN]

ANTHROPOMORPHISM

The representation of God or gods under human form and with human attributes. In a broader sense it may be applied to the practice of assigning human characteristics or attributes to nonhuman beings or objects. It is a common phenomenon in primitive religion and has a practically worldwide distribution. The two forms of anthropomorphism are well illustrated by Greek and early Roman religion, respectively.

In Greek religion, the sky and earth are represented as gods, 'Ουρανός and Γαῖα, and creation as a generation and a birth (cf. Hesiod, *Theog.*). The Greeks always sought to get closer to their gods or to bring their gods closer to themselves. However, when Homer calls Zeus ''father of gods and men,'' he does not mean necessarily that he considers the two races identical. The distinction is clear, e.g., in the *Iliad* 5.441–442, where Apollo in addressing Diomedes says: ''since in no wise of the same kind is the race of immortal gods and that of men who walk upon the earth.'' Pindar uses almost identical language: ''One is the race of men, one is the race of gods'' (*Nem.* 6.1). Divine power is especially manifest in Apollo, but most of the other gods in Homer are almost too human to be gods in a strict sense. This ''humanization'' of the gods made man familiar with them. The Greek, accordingly, was without fear of his gods, and opposed to any magical conception of terror or restraint; he was able to study the nature and order of the world and to create science.

But ''humanization'' had other results also. In its extreme form, it set up a contrast between the gods fashioned in the image of man, with all their weaknesses and even their crimes, and the sublimity and omnipotence attributed to them by earlier faith. This contrast was exploited by the comic poets, and, in particular, by Aristophanes (*Clouds, Birds, Frogs*), yet he remained strongly attached to traditional beliefs. The logic of anthropomorphism finally worked against religion. The philosophers repeatedly protested against such a gross anthropomorphic conception of the gods; e.g., Xenophon of Colophon in the 6th century, the philosopher and dramatist Euripides in the 5th, and Plato in the 4th century.

Animism, the second form of anthropomorphism, peopled all nature with *numina* (powers) or *daemones* (spirits). A formula, although one too brief perhaps, has been proposed for the religion of the Greeks, namely, that it was the resultant of a clash between two attitudes or outlooks: the dynamic animism of the Indo-Europeans, which might be defined as ''anthropopsychic,'' and the ''Aegean'' and subsequent Hellenic demand for divine generating presences, which was anthropomorphism proper.

If this formula is applied to the Romans, it must be recognized that ''anthropopsychism'' lasted much longer among them than among the Greeks. In fact, it left marked traces of its vitality in the course of an evolution spread over 1,000 years and exercised an influence on the concept of the anthropomorphic gods themselves. The history of Vesta is a case in point. She was not given anthropomorphic form until late in Roman religion.

Anthropomorphism did not spare the basic cult of the Mother-Goddess and her male companion, whether husband or son. Even in the case of Mithras, who personified Heaven, and later the sun and light, personification signified the progress of anthropomorphism at the same time, for Mithras thus becomes an intermediary (μεσίτη) between man and the Supreme Being.

See Also: GREEK RELIGION; ROMAN RELIGION.

Bibliography: F. B. JEVONS, J. HASTINGS, ed., *Encyclopedia of Religion and Ethics*, 13 v. (Edinburgh 1908–27) 1:573–578. G. VAN DER LEEUW, ''Anthropomorphismus, nichtchristlich,'' *Reallexikon für Antike und Christentum*, ed. T. KLAUSER [Stuttgart 1941 (1950)–] 1:446–448. G. MENSCHING, *Die Religion in Geschichte und Gegenwart*, 7 v. (3d ed. Tübingen 1957–65) 1:424. K. PRÜMM, *Religionsgeschichtliches Handbuch für den Raum der altchristlichen Umwelt* (2d ed. Rome 1954), esp. 42–46. C. BAILEY, ''Roman Religion,'' *The Cambridge Ancient History*, 12 v. (London and New York 1923–39) 8:423–453. J. BAYET, *Histoire politique et psychologique de la religion romaine* (Paris 1957).

[É. DES PLACES]

Incised anthropomorphic petroglyphs, Butler Wash, Utah. (© David Muench/CORBIS)

ANTHROPOMORPHISM (IN THE BIBLE)

The attribution of human characteristics, emotions, and situations to God. Israel's faith in God found concrete expression in anthropomorphic language. Anthropomorphisms occur in all parts of the OT. God is described as having eyes (Am 9.3; Sir 11.12), ears (Dn 9.18), hands (Is 5.25), and feet (Gn 3.8; Is 63.3). He molds man out of the dust, plants a garden, takes His rest (Gn 2.3, 7–8). He speaks (Gn 1.3; Lv 4.1), listens (Ex 16.12), and closes the door of Noah's ark (Gn 7.16); He even whistles (Is 7.18). Other expressions credit God with human emotions: He laughs (Ps 2.4), rejoices (Zep 3.17), becomes angry (1 Chr 13.10), disgusted (Lv 20.23), regretful (Jer 42.10), and revengeful (Is 1.24). Very frequently He is declared to be a jealous God (Ex 20.5; Dt 5.9).

Such language reflects the Semitic belief that the spiritual and physical realms are not mutually exclusive. The Hebrews, little inclined toward philosophical abstraction, were helped by anthropomorphisms better to understand God's living presence among them.

To speak so familiarly of God entailed some risk, but no widespread misunderstanding of the bold imagery of anthropomorphic language seems to have arisen. Periodically, however (Hos 11.9; Jb 10.4; Nm 23.19), warnings were issued lest anyone take the graphic images literally. Yahweh was consistently understood to be divine, holy, entirely different from creatures, and utterly unique. No man-made image of Him was ever permitted (Dt 4.12; 5.8), lest it be thought to imprison Him or to place Him under man's control. Unlike the pagan gods, Yahweh had no visible shape or form, and was clearly known to be all-holy, transcendent, self-sufficient, and spiritual.

Bibliography: W. EICHRODT, *Theology of the Old Testament,* tr. J. A. BAKER (London 1961). P. VAN IMSCHOOT, *Théologie de* *l'Ancien Testament,* 2 v. (Tournai 1954–56). E. JACOB, *Theology of the Old Testament,* tr. A. W. HEATHCOTE and P. J. ALLCOCK (New York 1958).

[R. T. A. MURPHY]

ANTHROPOMORPHISM (IN THEOLOGY)

From the two Greek words ἄνθρωπος (man) and μορφή (form). The term designates in THEOLOGY the tendency to conceive God in human terms. To think of God, for instance, as literally shaking His fist, would be anthropomorphic. For God is pure spirit; before His Incarnation, even the Son, the eternal Word, was exclusively spirit. Since God as God, then, is pure spirit, He has no body, and so no fist.

Such an example may be quite obvious. A much more subtle and problematical anthropomorphism, however, has lain at the base of some of theology's greatest controversies. Thus, to cite a single but very important example, the various attempts to explain Christ's sacrificial death on the cross as satisfying the Father's vindictiveness have been motivated, at least in part, by a subconscious anthropomorphism. For, in the final analysis, they picture the heavenly Father as subject to a strictly human sort of passion and reaction.

In a brief article, it is possible to touch only on selected aspects of this total question: first, the pedagogical anthropomorphism of which God Himself made use; second, the successful elimination of anthropomorphism through theological analogy; and, third, the psychological inevitability of at least an element and degree of anthropomorphism in theology despite man's best efforts.

Any reader of the OT is aware of the extent to which God tolerated provisionally anthropomorphic ideas about Himself in His slow, step-by-step instruction of His chosen people. He had walked with Adam in the garden, spoken with him as one man with another. He was moved to anger and then placated, all in a manner that sounded very much human.

But in the same divine plan, there would come a time, in the new dispensation, when theological understanding—the effort of human intelligence illuminated by faith—would see rather clearly that nothing material can be said of God, unless in metaphor, but only what is purely spiritual. More than this, not even what is purely spiritual can be said of God, unless by ANALOGY. If God is called a lion, this is metaphor. If God is said to see, and hear, and vent emotion, this also is metaphor. On the other hand, when God is said to know and, in the strictly spiritual sense, to love, this is not metaphor. For God really does know and love—just as human beings do; *just as,* yet *differently.* And this is analogy. Man's knowing and loving is imperfect; God's is infinite. What separates analogy from metaphor is the dropping out of the "as it were." One says that God shouts, "as it were." For God cannot really shout. To take out the "as it were" at this point is anthropomorphism. But one says that God knows—period. The "as it were" drops out, and must drop out; because God really does know, even though His knowing is infinitely more perfect than man's.

There is still, however, a psychological problem. Under the influence of imagination, even the sharpest theological mind can avoid only with difficulty the almost inevitable inclination to invest the divine object, which in this life man can know but dimly, with the qualities of the human object, which man knows quite well, and upon which he bases his analogical understanding of the infinite. Unless attention to the true nature of analogical predication along with exercise of theological judgment supply, so to speak, a constant corrective, an element or degree of unsuspected anthropomorphism will always be just around the corner.

See Also: ANALOGY, THEOLOGICAL USE OF; METHODOLOGY (THEOLOGY); REASONING, THEOLOGICAL; THEOLOGICAL TERMINOLOGY.

Bibliography: A serious study of anthropomorphism, and in the context of theological analogy, courses through several of the writings of B. LONERGAN, e.g., *Insight: A Study of Human Understanding* (New York 1957), ch. 17 and 19, nos. 9, 10; *De Deo trino,* 2 v. (v.1 2d ed., v.2 3d ed. Rome 1964) 1:15–112; 2:7–64. Cognate ideas are reflected also by J. C. MURRAY, *The Problem of God* (New Haven 1964), pt. 2. There are likewise the excellent studies, with more attention to linguistics, of E. L. MASCALL, *Words and Images: A Study in Theological Discourse* (New York 1957); *Existence and Analogy* (New York 1949); *He Who Is* (New York 1948).

[R. L. RICHARD]

ANTHROPOSOPHY

A religious system developed by Rudolf STEINER (1861–1925) from THEOSOPHY as a means of arriving at true knowledge and of final liberation from enslavement to the material world. Anthroposophy, as a theory of knowledge, claims that man originally shared in the spiritual consciousness of the cosmos and that his present mode of knowledge is only a dreamlike vestige of a primordial cognitive state. Through various disciplines it is possible to regain more or less of this innate intuition. In its metaphysical aspect, Anthroposophy holds to the existence of spiritual worlds that are more real than matter and knowable through direct vision by the higher but latent powers of man.

As the name implies, Anthroposophy postulates a "wisdom of man" that calls for two selves in each person: a lower self that knows and a higher ego that is known. In this sense, it is not unlike philosophic HINDUISM, in which Brahman, or the impersonal Absolute, is identified with Athman, or the inner Self; and all human striving after the divine is a quest for self-knowledge in the deepest ontological terms. Similar to Hinduism, Anthroposophy requires certain physical, mental, and spiritual exercises to arrive at final wisdom. The enlightened one thus becomes a *Hellscher*, or master of clear vision, gaining supersensible means of perception that are familiar in Buddhist psychology.

Theosophy teaches that besides the material world there are six invisible worlds of subtle matter, which interpenetrate the visible world as water permeates a sponge. Man possesses three bodies, a physical body of motion, an astral body of feeling, and a mental body of thought. Anthroposophy adopts the same premises, but considers the invisible world immaterial and gives man seven corporeities in addition to body, soul, and spirit that correspond to the common triad of the physical, astral, and mental Theosophy. The seer of Anthroposophy gradually comes to understand these seven "bodies" and especially the most intimate "I" that forms the human personality. The same septet obtains in the world outside man. There are seven colors to the spectrum and seven planets to the universe—Saturn, Sun, Moon, Earth, Jupiter, Venus, and Vulcan. As the clairvoyant penetrates into the recesses of his own ego, he also learns the secrets of the world around him, always in greater depth as one after another the elements of the cosmic septet unfold.

Steiner elaborated on this higher knowledge in all his major writings, but mainly in the *Akaska Chronicle*. He differed further from the Theosophists in assigning a leading role to Christ in his system. Whereas Theosophy makes Christ to be merely one of many *arhats* (master teachers) or *avatars* (incarnations), Anthroposophy holds that Christ is the one *avatar*, or divine manifestation, yet only in the sense of a greater solar being who appeared among men to rescue the human race from its own destruction. The merger of Christianity and Anthroposophy was due largely to the efforts of Friedrich Rittelmeyer (1872–1938), former Evangelical pastor, who organized the existing societies into Christian Fellowships and promoted the establishment of a sacerdotal class of priests and priestesses to care for the ritual aspect of the movement.

Furthermore, Christ is claimed to possess the full revelation of the supersensible world. Contact with him affords deeper penetration into his own profound vision of reality. Accordingly, celebration of the Sacrament of the Eucharist is considered the highest act of worship in the Christian religion. Anthroposophy teaches that the bread and wine are changed with the spirit and body of Christ, through which the communicant becomes truly human, whereas before he was only an image distorted by hostile powers. The service is called Act of Consecration of Man, and has a liturgy filled with Steiner's teachings, yet modeled on the Catholic Mass.

Anthroposophists are found mainly in Germany, Britain, and the United States, especially among those in search of religious experience outside the normal channels of church life. Anthroposophy was condemned by the Roman Catholic Church in 1919.

Bibliography: G. A. KAUFMANN, comp. and ed., *Fruits of Anthroposophy* (London 1922). R. STEINER, *The Story of My Life*, ed. A. FREEMAN (London 1928); *World History in the Light of Anthroposophy*, tr. G. and M. ADAMS (New York 1951). F. RITTELMEYER, *Reincarnation* (New York n.d.).

[J. A. HARDON]

ANTICHRIST

One opposed to the work of God, especially that accomplished in Jesus the Messiah (Christ).

In the Bible

Some passages suggest that this hostile figure attempts to work by usurping divine and messianic prerogatives, and thus winning over followers by deceiving them concerning his (or its) true nature. The Greek prefix ἀντί the first element of ἀντίχριστος can express the idea of substitution or replacement, as well as that of hostility. The term Antichrist is found only in 1 Jn 2.18, 22; 4.3; 2 Jn 7; but the concept is present in 2 Thes 2.3–12, in certain passages in the Revelation, and possibly in other NT texts. In some of these passages the figure is referred to in personal terms, and Christian interpretation has traditionally regarded the Antichrist as a person; it is, however, far from certain that the personification is intended to point to an individual at all, much less to any specific person. Before attempting to appraise the NT teaching, it will be useful to look for the roots of this idea in the OT.

Old Testament Roots of Antichrist Concept. In certain OT passages, largely apocalyptic in nature, there is the expectation of a final great struggle between the forces of good and evil, between those faithful to God (the true Israel) and those hostile to Him (mainly identified with the pagan nations). The struggle is to culminate in the eschatological battle in which the victory will be won by God Himself intervening on behalf of His people to the accompaniment of cosmic signs and disturbances.

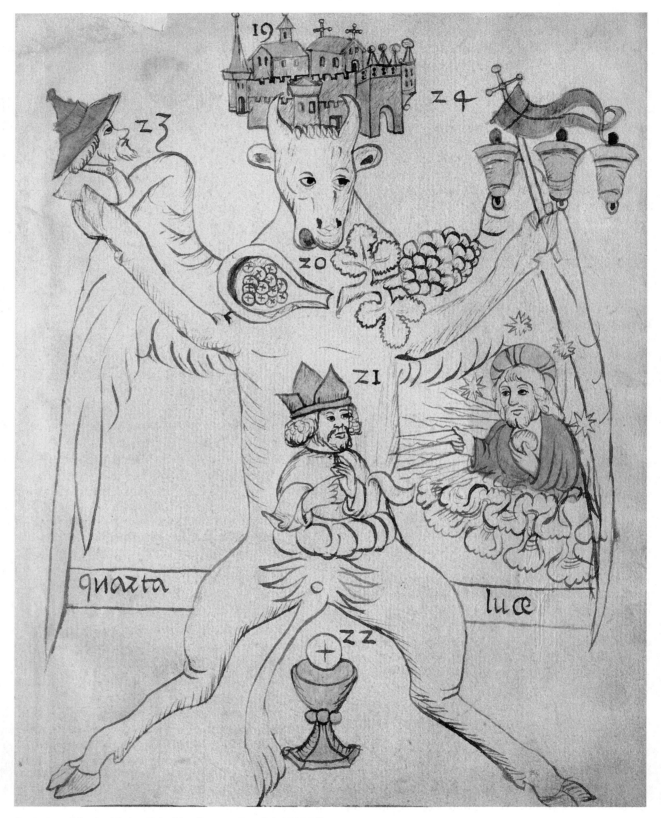

Depiction of the Antichrist. (©Archivo Iconografico, S.A./CORBIS)

The clearest example of this picture is found in Ez 38.1–39.29, a passage usually conceded to be later than Ezekiel himself. The nations of the earth assemble under the leadership of Gog, chief prince of Meshach and Tubal, in order to attack and plunder the land of Israel. But God will strike the bow and arrows from their hands, the invaders will be slaughtered on the mountains of Israel, and the birds and beasts will feast on their flesh (39.3–5, 17–20). It is to be noted that, while Gog is an individual, he is not a historical figure but simply the embodiment of the leadership of those forces hostile to God's people (*see* EZEKIEL, BOOK OF).

The four beasts of Daniel ch. 7 represent the great world kingdoms; special attention is given to the fourth beast, which represents the Greek Empire, under which the Israelites were suffering at the time of the composition of Daniel. The "little horn" (v. 8, 21–22, 24) of the fourth beast represents ANTIOCHUS IV EPIPHANES, desecrator of the Temple and dreaded persecutor. The vision describes God's intervention in the form of judgment upon the beasts and the end of their power to harm. Antiochus IV is given special attention again in 11.21–45, where his campaigns and victories are described; but the section concludes with the note that "he shall come to his end with none to help him." There is little doubt that the author of this apocalyptic composition expected that God's intervention to end this crisis would be the definitive intervention and would usher in the final age. But the final struggle had not yet come. History was to vindicate the author's expectation of God's delivering intervention, but other crises would be known. Antiochus IV, so closely connected with a particular persecution, was to become a type of those who lead the anti-God forces, and elements of the descriptions of him in Daniel are to be found in later writings (*see* DANIEL, BOOK OF).

Antichrist in the New Testament. The closest link between the OT passages just reviewed and the NT is found in the Revelation. Imagery taken from Daniel is freely used, and the struggle between the Church and the wicked persecutors is an important part of the concern of the book. Chapter 13 describes a "beast of the sea," which is a composite of the four beasts of Daniel ch. 7. Many commentators identify it with the Roman Empire, the power persecuting the Christian Church during much of the late 1st century at any rate, it is an instrument of Satan (the Dragon of 12.3–18) in his war against the Church. The beast of the sea is also aided by the "beast of the earth" (13.11–17), possibly to be identified with the pagan priesthood of Rome. These two together sum up, in this section of the book, the forces on earth utilized by Satan in the struggle against the people of God. Elements of these visions have been referred to historical Roman emperors, but the personal aspect is not stressed.

God's victory over the forces hostile to Him is described in the latter part of the book; see especially ch. 17–18, where the beast described is probably the same as the beast of the sea; see also 19.17–21, where Christ effortlessly overcomes the beast and the false prophet (probably the beast of the earth) and their armies, and the birds of the air are invited to feast on their flesh. Although the term Antichrist does not appear, the concept is present. The struggle now has specifically Christian features, not only in that it is the Christian Church that is being persecuted and Christ who overcomes, but also in that the hostile forces are in many ways a blasphemous parody of elements in the Christian dispensation (note the "unholy trinity" in 12.3–13.17; and cf. 7.3 with 13.16–17, and 5.9–10 with 13.7) (*see* REVELATION, BOOK OF).

The same picture of the final violent struggle of the anti-God forces with the people of God lies at the base of St. Paul's thought in 2 Thes 2.3–12. Paul is attempting to allay the fears of the Thessalonians, who seem to believe that the final day has already arrived, by insisting on certain recognizable signs, not yet in evidence, that must precede it. The principal one of these is the ἀποστασία (apostasy, rebellion), which probably refers to the eschatological struggle. St. Paul sees the hostile forces led by "the man of sin . . . the son of perdition . . . the wicked one," whom "the Lord Jesus will slay with the breath of his mouth." Again there is the parody of true religion: the adversary will "be revealed," will assume divine prerogatives, and his coming is connected with the "mystery of iniquity" that is already at work.

Certainly the manner of speaking in this passage seems highly personalistic, but it must be remembered that St. Paul is using apocalyptic language; the details need not be considered to have been revealed to him, for obscure events of the last day are habitually presented in stereotyped imagery. Some of the descriptive details of the "man of sin" are taken from earlier presentations of the wicked men (Ez 28.2; Dn 11.36). The fact that the "man of sin" is presented as already in existence but held in check by someone or something (the Thessalonians knew what Paul was referring to, but the modern reader can only guess) tells against a specific person. Yet it would not be false to Paul's thought to see here an expectation that, when the final assault of evil does materialize, it will be headed by an individual who incarnates, so to speak, the power of evil in his person.

There is no clear reference to the cosmic struggle in the allusions to Antichrist in St. John's Epistles, although the evidences of Antichrist's activity are seen to indicate that the "last hour" is at hand (1 Jn 2.18). Yet St. John can also speak of "many antichrists," referring to apostate Christians, and can label as "the liar . . . the Antichrist'' the one who denies that ''Jesus is the Christ'' (v. 22; see also 2 Jn 7). Thus the author thinks of a person or a power hostile to God whose influence and activity are seen in and inferred from the rejection of God's revelation in Christ by some.

Bibliography: D. BUZY, *Dictionnaire de la Bible,* suppl. ed. L. PIROT, et al. (Paris 1928–) 1:297–305. *Encyclopedic Dictionary of the Bible,* tr. And adap. By L. HARTMAN (New York 1963), from A. VAN DEN BORN, *Bijbels Woordenboek* 96–98. E. B. ALLO, *L'Apocalypse* (Paris 1921) cxi–cxxi. W. BOUSSET, *Der Antichrist in der Überlieferung des Judentums, des N. T. und der alten Kirche* (Göttingen 1895). P. H. FURFEY, ''The Mystery of Lawlessness,'' *The Catholic Biblical Quarterly* (Washington 1939–) 8 (1946) 179–91.

[M. RODRIGUEZ]

Comment of Fathers, Theologians

Like other prophecies, that of the Antichrist will be clearly understood only in its fulfillment. Understandably, then, there is little on the subject in the documents of the Church's magisterium other than in its condemnations of Wyclif and the Fraticelli (H. Denzinger, *Enchiridion symbolorum,* ed. A. Schönmetzer (32d ed. Freiburg 1963) 916, 1156, 1180). This section, therefore, confines itself to a sketch of the patristic and theological speculation that has surrounded the Antichrist.

Patrology. The comment of the Fathers on the Antichrist, which begins with the DIDACHE, is complete in all its essential features by the First Council of Nicaea (325). According to the Didache, the final days of the world will be marked by the advent of the ''world-tempter,'' appearing as though he were the Son of God and doing ''signs and wonders.'' The earth, it is said, will be given into his hands (Didache 16.3–5).

Preceded by false prophets speaking in the name of Christ, he will appear with the whole panoply of diabolic power (Justin, *Dial.* 51, 110). ''Sinner, murderer, robber,'' says Irenaeus, he will make incarnate in himself the entire diabolic apostasy. Of Jewish origin, sprung from the tribe of Dan, he will establish himself in Jerusalem and reign for three-and-a-half years (*Haer.* 5.30.2; 5.25.3; 5.30.4). The unhappy privilege of fathering the Antichrist is assigned to the tribe of Dan by many of the ancient writers, who deduce it from Gn 49.17 and from the omission of the name of Dan in Rv 7.5–8.

The antithetic character of ''the man of sin'' is developed by Hippolytus, who sees in the Antichrist a perfect caricature of Christ Himself. Like Christ, he will be of Jewish ancestry; as Christ is from the tribe of Judah, his adversary will be from Dan. Claiming the scriptural titles of lion, lamb, and man, the Antichrist will have his own apostles and will dedicate himself to the persecution of the saints; his assault on the work of Christ will culminate in an apotheosis of himself (*Antichr.* 5–19; 29–41; 48–58). Commenting on Daniel's prophecy of the four kingdoms, Hippolytus says that the Antichrist will appear at the END OF THE WORLD after the Babylonian, Persian, Greek, and Roman empires (*Com. in Dan.* 4.1–10).

Tertullian added a new dimension to patristic thought when he applied the term Antichrist to any heretic or rebel against Christ (*Adv. Marcion.* 5.16: *De praescr. haer.* 4.4). The African author, however, clearly distinguished these forerunners of the Antichrist from the eschatological personality who would appear at the end of time.

Neither Cyprian nor Origen denied the eschatological character of the Antichrist but, like Tertullian they found an application of the idea in their own times. Origen described what might be termed the principle of the Antichrist: ''Invenimus omnes veras virtutes esse Christum, et omnes simulatas virtutes esse Antichristum'' (*Comm. ser. 33 in Mt.*). The principle of the Antichrist, he said, has many proponents, but from among these many antichrists, there will come one who will deserve the name in its proper sense, one whose types and forerunners the others are. This true Antichrist will appear at the end of the world, while the others, in some measure, are already in the world (*Comm. ser. 47 in Mt.; Cels.* 6.79). Among the antichrists already present Cyprian lists the heretics and schismatics (*Ep.* 69.5, 70.3). They deserve the name, he says, because they are imbued with the spirit of the Antichrist who will be the complete antithesis of Christ (*Ep.* 73.15; 71.2).

The figure of the Antichrist, as it emerges from patristic speculation, has both a contemporary and an eschatological dimension. There is, first of all, the individual who will appear at time's end to launch a final assault on the work of Christ. In a second, but by no means contradictory, perspective, the Antichrist is seen to be embodied in the archenemies of God and his Church. This dual dimensionality of the patristic Antichrist seems an adequate premise for K. Rahner's remark in this regard that Christians have the right not only to abhor ungodly ideas but to recognize and to flee from the individual men who champion evil (*Lexikon für Theologie und Kirche,* ed. J. Hofer and K. Rahner 1:635).

Extension of Term. The patristic license to concretize unholy ideas and forces in individuals and organizations and to label them Antichrist has been exercised by innumerable writers over the centuries. Countless political figures and institutions from Nero to Stalin have been identified with the ''man of sin'' (see W. Bornemann). Indeed, the popular interest in the Antichrist and the ''signs of the times'' that were to precede his coming was so played upon by the preachers of the 14th and 15th centuries that Lateran Council V forbade preachers to describe as imminent the coming of the Antichrist.

The polemic possibilities of the Antichrist idea escaped neither the Church's friends nor its foes. Thus it became quite common in the Middle Ages for opponents—popes and emperors, Guelfs and Ghibellines—to hurl this epithet at one another. While Catholic writers denounced as Antichrist those who dissented from the doctrines of the Church or attacked its liberty, their antagonists saw the Antichrist in the institution of the papacy itself. As Cardinal J. H. Newman observed, the papal Antichrist theory was developed gradually from the 11th to 16th centuries by the ALBIGENSES, the WALDENSES, and the FRATICELLI ["The Protestant Idea of Antichrist," *Essays Critical and Historical*, v.2 (London 1897)]. A terrifying weapon during the great religious controversies of the 16th century, the idea of the papal Antichrist had been used effectively by John Wyclif in England and John Hus in Bohemia. One of the dynamisms of Martin Luther's thinking, the idea was even incorporated into the Schmalkaldic Articles. St. Robert Bellarmine refuted the exegesis by which the beast of the Apocalypse was identified with the papacy; and it was also rejected by the Protestant H. Grotius. Nevertheless, papal Antichrist theory persisted into the 19th century and accounted for Newman's two essays on the subject, "The Protestant Idea of the Antichrist" and "The Patristic Idea of the Antichrist," the latter in *Discussions and Arguments on Various Subjects* (London 1899).

Theologians. Catholic theologians have been nearly unanimous in maintaining that the Antichrist will be an individual person. Those, however, who prefer a collective interpretation can point out quite correctly, it seems, that in this matter there is no real doctrinal tradition. And even in this latter interpretation, the eschatological character of the Antichrist is preserved, for the "last times" commence with the first coming of Christ and extend to the PAROUSIA.

Bibliography: A. GELIN, *Dictionnaire de théologie catholique,* ed. A. VACANT, 15 v. (Paris 1903–50; Tables générales 1951–), Tables générales 1:179–180. R. SCHÜTZ et al., *Die Religion in Geschichte und Gegenwart,* 7 v. (3d ed. Tübingen 1957–65) 1:431–436. W. BOUSSET, J. HASTINGS, ed., *Encyclopedia of Religion & Ethics,* 13 v. (Edinburgh 1908–27) 1:578–581. L. ATZBERGER, *Geschichte der christlichen Eschatologie* (Freiburg 1896). W. BORNEMANN, *Die Thessalonicher-briefe,* v.10 of *Kritisch-exegetischer Kommentar über das Neue Testament,* ed. H. A. MEYER (Göttingen 1891–). V. DECHAMPS, *Christus und die Antichristen nach dem Zeugnisse der Schrift, der Geschichte und des Gewissens* (Mainz 1859). T. MALVENDA, *De antichristo libri undecim* (Rome 1604). B. RIGAUX, *L'Antéchrist et l'opposition au royaume messianique dans l'Ancien et le Nouveau Testament* (Gembloux 1932).

[G. J. DYER]

ANTICLERICALISM

This is a term whose prefix and suffix render it equivocal. "Anti" indicates that the word is the contrary of CLERICALISM. Clericalism, however, has two principal meanings very different from one another; sometimes it is considered as an abuse and is reproved by the ecclesiastical magisterium; at other times it is identified with the Church itself. "Ism," the suffix, intimates that the term deals with a doctrine. But the best-known type of anticlericalism, that which is opposed to the Church and generally to other religions, is much less a doctrine than a practical attitude, whose aims and themes vary according to circumstances. To avoid confusion it is preferable to distinguish two kinds of anticlericalism. The first is that of Catholics, anxious to maintain the dignity of the clergy and the abstention of the Church from state affairs. The second is that of adversaries of religion, which is sometimes so ardent that it resembles a religious faith that revolves around belief in humanity, in reason, and in liberty.

Catholic Anticlericalism. An anticlericalism that seeks to remain Catholic obviously cannot be destructive of the Church's hierarchical order. Theories claiming to suppress differences between clerics and laymen pertain, properly speaking, to LAICISM. Catholic anticlericalism presents itself under a double guise in two epochs far distant from one another.

Medieval. During the Middle Ages secular and regular clergy were very numerous in western Europe, but their quality was much inferior to their quantity. Clerics were recruited from all classes of society and mixed intimately with all classes. When clerics deviated from their obligations, their ecclesiastical confreres, and laymen too, constituted themselves censors and thereby practiced a kind of fraternal correction. Not all of them were as severe in criticism as St. Bernard; many preferred a comic tone: *Castigat ridendo mores.* Pleasantries against lazy, greedy, ribald monks developed into almost a literary genre, in which the Latin language in particular ventured to defy what is nowadays regarded as propriety. ERASMUS in his *Praise of Folly* and RABELAIS in *Gargantua* and *Pantagruel* prolonged a medieval tradition into the Renaissance with a sense of opportuneness that was, to say the least, questionable. Critics who practiced this rather smirking type of anticlericalism did not do so without peril, even in the Middle Ages. No doubt they acted from a praiseworthy desire to possess a clergy worthy of its vocation and of its ministry; but they risked scandalizing the weak, who inclined to form generalizations as hasty as they were unjust.

20th Century. Catholics before the Second Vatican Council ran the same risk by openly calling themselves anticlerical. They often preferred to take this stance in another fashion, by posing as adversaries of a certain type of clericalism and by repeating with Cardinal Saliège that "the Church is not clerical." They mistrusted the distinction between a country that is supposedly unanimous in its Catholic belief and a religiously divided (pluralistic) country in which the State must allow each citizen to practice his religion freely. These Catholics were aware of the unwarranted conclusion drawn from this distinction, namely, that wherever Catholics were in the majority their consciences obliged them to oppress those who disagree with them, but wherever Catholics were relatively few and powerless to impose their doctrines, only there did they consent to religious liberty. These anticlerical Catholics asked themselves if unanimity of belief was not a figment of the imagination, and if any Catholic country existed without free thinkers. It is not by religious indifference, they said, but by respect for persons and for the complete liberty of the act of faith (1917 CIC c.1351) that the Church must preserve itself from becoming servile to the State, which will be more tempted to promote its own interests than to serve the Church. Fear of clericalism did not lead necessarily to a regime of separation of Church from State; it was compatible with a concordat such as that of Portugal (see Maritain, 140–149).

Antireligious Anticlericalism. This type of anticlericalism, as the words indicate clearly, is aggressive. It is not to be confused with simple irreligion, which skeptics, atheists, and merely tolerant persons can profess. Antireligious anticlericalism regards religion as an error and an evil, something that must be extirpated. Nothing prevents it from sparing the faithful in order to strike harder at the clergy who guide them, or from flattering the secular clergy by picturing the regular clergy as competitors who are harmful to the influence and well-being of the seculars. This kind of anticlericalism gives little heed to religions with few adherents and directs its blows at the strongest, particularly at the Catholic Church in countries where the majority is Catholic. It has preceded, prepared, and accompanied laicism. Since the 19th-century anticlericals of this type have venerated as their ancestors the rationalists of the 16th century, the libertines of the 17th, and especially the philosophers of the Enlightenment of the 18th, whose actions and writings continue to inspire them. Although the term "anticlericalism" was not part of the 18th-century vocabulary, it was then that the phenomenon took shape.

18th Century. The 16th and 17th centuries supplied the themes destined to undermine religion, but it was the 18th century that discovered the art of popularizing them and placing them within reach of wide circles of readers, even those deprived of philosophical formation. The 18th

century began by using irony to sow doubts; it imagined Chinese, Persians, Congolese, Hurons, and other "good savages" who came to Europe, only to meet there Christians who massacred in the name of religion, while recommending to others charity and pardon for injuries. Another tactic was to mock at mysteries as offensive to reason and at biblical accounts as contrary to scientific discoveries. Still another strategy was to interpret current events in a manner injurious to religion. Thus divine providence was denied because Lisbon, with all its churches and convents, was leveled by an earthquake (Nov. 1, 1755). Suspicion was directed at the faith of priests, because a pastor who had been very exact in the fulfilment of his ministry had left a will that was a profession of atheism. VOLTAIRE declared war c. 1760 on the infamous thing (*l'infâme*), by which he meant Christianity. St. Francis of Assisi and Dante, as he pictured them, were fools. From Voltaire's literary mill in Ferney flowed an endless stream of pamphlets that were more dangerous to believers than the productions of Amsterdam, London, Paris, or Berlin. The same negation appeared under a thousand guises, according to Paul Hazard. This century prided itself on being the age of light (ENLIGHTENMENT, *Aufklärung*), in which experience and reason would expel faith and its obscurities. To speed this process Denis Diderot launched a voluminous *Encyclopédie,* among whose mass of notions about history, geography, physics, and other subjects the essential concept, a "firm, audacious philosophy," was adroitly distributed, a tactic that Diderot himself admitted in a letter to his publisher (1764). After sowing the wind, these men reaped the whirlwind. During the FRENCH REVOLUTION, c. 1793, everything that tended to discredit priests and religion became acceptable, including the filth in which the journal *Le Père Duchesne,* published by Jacques Hébert, specialized. Despite the Reign of Terror, the faithful churchgoers (*calotins*) and the "papists" were not annihilated. In vain did the Directory attack "the infernal empire of priests." For many decades afterward, however, this style remained in fashion among anticlericals.

19th Century. NAPOLEON I, although a free-thinker, ended this odious and sterile combat by concluding with Pius VII the CONCORDAT OF 1801. Priests were placed on the payroll of the State and were directed to teach Frenchmen their duties toward their emperor (*see* CATECHISM, IMPERIAL). It sufficed, however, for the clergy to be "grenadiers in long vestments and short ideas," a role that was anything but enviable. After Napoleon's downfall, the *bourgeoisie,* which remained Voltairean, profited from its liberty to ridicule the clergy, who were rendered still more unpopular by the royal government's maladroit measures, such as the law regarding sacrileges (1825). Caricatures, songs, novels, and theatrical productions did not spare clerics. Anticlericalism of the most violent type was at times furnished with weapons by Catholics such as Count François de Montlosier, whose famous *Mémoire* (1826; placed on the Index June 12, 1826) denounced Jesuitism, ULTRAMONTANISM, and the ''priest party,'' which was ''composed of those who will brave any risk or peril to hand over society to the priesthood.''

The ''tyranny'' of the JESUITS became, between 1830 and 1848, the theme preferred by anticlericalism. At the Collège de France in Paris, Edgar Quinet and Jules Michelet presented the Revolution of 1789 as the new revelation, denigrated the Church, and thundered against the Jesuits. The publication of a collaborative work, *Des Jésuites* (1843), did nothing to moderate the irritation of these two professors against the Society of Jesus, according to the testimony of a student who audited their lectures (M. Minghetti, *Miei ricordi* [2d ed. Turin n.d.] 2:131–132). Eugène Sue increased the circulation of the journal *Le Constitutionnel* by publishing in serial form *The Wandering Jew* (*Le Juif errant*). When these episodes were collected, they formed a 10-volume novel, which went through many editions and translations into English and several other languages; it concentrated on the dark intrigues and infamies attributed to the sons of Loyola.

In Italy, the struggle for political unification provoked a rash of anticlericalism that supposedly revealed the imprisonments, hangings, and other atrocities practiced by the clergy in collusion with the Austrian army (see V. Gorresio, *Risorgimento scomunicato*, Florence 1958). Francesco Crispi, president of the Chamber of Deputies (1876) and premier (1887–91, 1893–96), was considered the ''high priest of anticlericalism'' in Italy and in Europe. At a meeting in 1877 with Léon Gambetta and Otto von Bismarck, the inaugurator of the KULTURKAMPF, Crispi persuaded them that the peace of Europe was menaced by only one man, the pope, who aspired to the reestablishment of the States of the Church. The renewal of the Senate in 1879 permitted French anticlerical opinion to take root in a body of laic laws. Until World War I, anticlericalism permeated the government of the Third Republic.

20th Century. Other countries copied France and Italy, notably Portugal (1910–18) and Mexico (1911–20). In the Union of Soviet Socialist Republics the government forbade all religious propaganda and established the Union of the Militant Godless, which claimed in 1930 a membership exceeding two million. National Socialism in Germany combined anticlericalism with anti-Semitism. In Spain during the civil war (1936–39), 4,184 priests or seminarians were executed, along with 2,635 religious.

Bibliography: G. DE BERTIER DE SAUVIGNY, ''French Anticlericalism since the Great Revolution: A Tentative Interpretation,'' *Historical Records and Studies of the U.S. Catholic Historical Society of New York* 42 (1954) 3–21. L. L. RUMMEL, ''The Anticlerical Program as a Disruptive Factor in the Solidarity of the Late French Republics,'' *American Catholic Historical Review* 34 (1948–49) 1–19. C. A. WHITTUCK, *Encyclopedia of Religion and Ethics*, ed. J. HASTINGS, 13 v. (Edinburgh 1908–27) 3:689–693. C. J. H. HAYES, *A Generation of Materialism, 1871–1900* (New York 1941). P. HAZARD, *European Thought in the Eighteenth Century: From Montesquieu to Lessing*, tr. J. L. MAY (New Haven 1954). J. MARITAIN, *Man and the State* (Chicago 1951; repr. 1956). V. GIRAUD, *Anticléricalisme et catholicisme* (Paris 1906). É. FAGUET, *L'Anticléricalisme* (Paris 1906), liberal viewpoint by an agnostic. B. EMONET, *Dictionnaire apologétique de la foi catholique*, ed. A. D'ALÈS, 4 v. (Paris 1911–22; Table analytique 1931) 2:1771–81. J. LECLER, ''Origines et évolution de l'anticléricalisme,'' *Études* 253 (1947) 145–164; *Catholicisme. Hier, aujourd'hui et demain*, ed. G. JACQUEMET 1:633–638. L. CAPÉRAN, *L'Anticléricalisme et l'affaire Dreyfus, 1897–1899* (Toulouse 1948); *Histoire contemporaine de la laïcité française*, 3 v. (Paris 1957–61). *Dictionnaire de sociologie*, ed. G. JACQUEMET (Paris 1933–) 1:936–951. I. MARTÍN MARTÍNEZ, *El desarrollo de la Iglesia Española y sus relaciones con el Estado* (Madrid 1963). B. DUHR, *Jesuiten-Fabeln* (4th ed. Freiburg 1904). A. BROU, *Les Jésuites de la légende*, 2 v. (Paris 1906–07). E. M. ACOMB, *The French Laic Laws, 1879–1889* (New York 1941).

[C. BERTHELOT DU CHESNAY/EDS.]

ANTINOMY

An antinomy is a real or apparent contradiction between equally well-based assumptions or conclusions. Contradiction is a generic term for both paradox and antinomy, which are roughly synonymous. However, many recent writers employ PARADOX as an informal catchall for interesting contradictions of any sort, and antinomy as a technical term for contradictions derivable by sound rules of reasoning from accepted axioms within a science. Antinomies may for convenience be gathered under three headings, depending on whether they arise: (1) in ordinary language; (2) in metaphysics or cosmology; or (3) in logic, mathematics, and kindred formal disciplines.

Ordinary Language. Paradoxes arising in ordinary language have been pondered from early Greek times (cf. Plato, *Parm.*). The Megaric philosophers about 400 B.C. studied the well-known Liar Paradox, one version of which runs as follows: If a man says ''I always lie,'' how are we to understand his statement? In a puzzling way it seems to be both true and false, since the truth of his confession conflicts with the fact that it is a confession of never telling the truth. Among the main suggestions offered to resolve the Liar Paradox are: (1) that the man's remark can be called both true and false, but in different respects (Aristotle); (2) that it makes no sense at all (Chrysippus); (3) that in a covert manner it embodies two statements having different levels of reference, and when these are kept separate no paradox arises (Bertrand RUSSELL); and (4) that the offending sentence would normally be used as an outpouring of remorse or self-disgust, not as an occasion for drawing inferences, and its paradoxical aspect troubles us only when we fail to notice its normal use (Ludwig WITTGENSTEIN). The Liar Paradox and numerous other *insolubilia,* i.e., statements whose assertion or denial leads to the opposite, were discussed in great detail by medieval logicians (*see* LOGIC, HISTORY OF).

Kantian Antinomies. In his *Critique of Pure Reason* Immanuel Kant claimed to expose four serious antinomies in the then prevailing COSMOLOGY. Using valid steps of reasoning, he said, a philosopher can demonstrate on the one hand that the universe is infinite in size and duration, and on the other that it is finite. He constructed similar pairs of rival proofs for and against the infinite divisibility of matter, the possibility of freedom, and the world's ultimate dependence upon a necessary being. The scandal of these antinomies, Kant believed, spelled the doom of metaphysics as a science. He regarded them as a species of "transcendental illusion," the result of a natural and unavoidable human urge to apply the categories of the understanding beyond their safe reach, the realm of sensible experience.

Kant's notion that nature should have built into man a disposition toward illusion has tended to strain his readers' comprehension as much as the antinomies themselves. Part, at least, of the blame can be laid to an obscurity in the tradition Kant criticized, dominated by the philosophy of LEIBNIZ and C. WOLFF. That tradition spoke of the physical universe and everything in it "as appearance," i.e., in terms of the perceiver's mental content. This habit of thought, shared by Kant himself, left unsettled the primary issue between IDEALISM and REALISM: whether what we call the material world is mind-dependent, like the domain of mathematical inventions, or exists independently of minds. Where that issue is unresolved, the inadvertent risk of thinking about the world in both ways at once is also left open, and with it the possibility of antinomous proofs.

Antinomies in Formal Systems. At the turn of the 20th century, antinomies of a different sort forced logicians and mathematicians to reconsider certain accepted fundamentals, chiefly in the foundations of arithmetic. Russell's antinomy, discovered in 1901, was derived from the efforts of Gottlob Frege to develop number theory in terms of the theory of classes. It can be paraphrased in nontechnical terms as follows: The class of all classes is itself a class, but the class of all lions is not a lion. Some classes, then, appear to be members of themselves while others do not. Now consider the whole class of classes

which are not members of themselves. Call it *C.* Is *C* a member of itself or not? Let us suppose that it is. That would make *C* a member of a class that is by definition made up of classes that are not members of themselves. Therefore *C* is not a member of itself, which contradicts the original supposition. On the other hand, if we now suppose it is not, then on second look *C* must be included in the membership it was defined as having, and so must be counted a member of itself. Whether we call *C* a member of itself or not, the result leads to the opposite position.

At one time Russell suggested that expressions of the form "*C* is either a member of itself or not" be struck out of the theory of classes as meaningless. A more popular solution, his "simple theory of types," instead lays down restrictions on the ways in which references to classes of different levels may be combined in a single assertion. Alternative solutions pioneered by Ernst Zermelo in 1904 can be found in certain axiomatizations of set theory.

Semantical Antinomies. It is now common practice to distinguish between antinomies containing reference to natural language, and those involving no metalinguistic expressions. The first kind are called semantical, the second logical. One example of the former, called Grelling's paradox, runs as follows: Work up two lists of adjectives, the first titled self-describing and containing words that apply to themselves, such as "mispelled," "short," "four-syllabled" the second titled non-self-describing and containing words that do not, such as "long," "misspelled," "five-syllabled." Into which list shall we put the term "non-self-describing"? If it is a non-self-describing word, as "short" is a short word, then it belongs under self-describing. But in order to go there, "non-self-describing" would have to be non-self-describing, as "short" is short. Put into either list, it switches into the other. This antinomy, like that of Russell, can be solved by employing suitable type restrictions.

Logical Antinomies. Among the second group are certain contradictions arising in theories of ordinal and cardinal number series. In the years from 1895 to 1897, Georg Cantor and C. Burali-Forti independently hit upon a contradiction involving ordinals, i.e., numbers defined in terms of their relations to neighbors in a series. If we suppose the series to be well ordered, which roughly means surveyable in the way that segments of it are, then we can speak of the type of the greatest ordinal. At the same time, as we know, any ordinal can be increased by adding one, so there can be no greatest. As a result of holding to both claims, one is forced to allow the possibility of two different ordinals neither of which is greater.

This runs counter to the accepted role of "greater than" in numerical relations. The question of removing this contradiction turns upon the permissibility of assuming that the whole series resembles well-ordered classes within itself.

About 1900, Russell pointed out contradictions arising in connection with Cantor's proofs that there is no greatest cardinal number. Cantor argues, for example, that the number of classes in any class is larger than the number of terms in the class. The contradictions appear, according to Russell, when we assume that Cantor's proofs hold good for nonnumerical classes, such as the class of propositions. If we correlate every class of propositions with its own logical product, and then apply Cantor's argument, we notice something wrong with the phrase "every class" as used here. It fails to include the class of propositions that are logical products but are not members of the class they are products of. Where does the product of that excluded class belong? It can be shown, by the kind of reasoning used in Russell's antinomy above, to be both a member and not a member of the excluded class.

See Also: LOGIC, SYMBOLIC; MATHEMATICS, PHILOSOPHY OF.

Bibliography: I. M. BOCHEŃSKI, *A History of Formal Logic,* tr. I. THOMAS (Notre Dame, Ind. 1961). B. RUSSELL, *Introduction to Mathematical Philosophy* (London 1919); *Principles of Mathematics* (2d ed. New York 1938). A. N. WHITEHEAD and B. RUSSELL, *Principia Mathematica,* 3 v. (2d ed. Cambridge, Eng. 1925) v. 1.

[H. A. NIELSEN]

St. Ignatius of Antioch. (Archive Photos)

ANTIOCH

The ancient city situated on the Orontes in what is now Syria. The word comes from the Greek Ἀντιόχεια (Latin *Antiochia*). It was "the first place in which the disciples were called Christians" (Acts 11.26), and was especially fitted to be the center of the mission to the Gentiles.

The Apostles. Founded in 300 B.C. by Seleucus, a general of Alexander the Great, Antioch was a center of communications by land and also by sea through its port, Seleucia Pieria. The population was cosmopolitan and JUDAISM was familiar to some of the people because of the presence of an important Jewish colony, which provided an opportunity for Gentiles to hear the Old Testament read in Greek at synagogue services. Nicholas, one of the seven deacons in Jerusalem, was a proselyte from Antioch (Acts 6.5). Thus when some Greek-speaking Christians fled to Antioch from persecution in Jerusalem, they were able to preach to Greeks (Acts 11.19–21), some

of whom may have already been acquainted with Judaism. Barnabas and Paul converted "a great multitude," and there were five "prophets and teachers" at the head of the local community—Barnabas, Simon Niger, Lucius of Cyrene, Manahen, and Paul (Acts 13.1). The presence of both Jewish and Gentile Christians raised the question of whether the Jewish law (e.g., concerning food and circumcision) should be extended to Gentile converts. The famous dispute between Peter and Paul (Galatians 2) resulted, and Paul devoted himself to the Gentile mission, using Antioch as the base for his journeys. The ultimate fate of the Jewish Christian community is not known. According to tradition, Peter was the founder of the Church at Antioch and its first bishop. Luke the Evangelist was said to be from Antioch. The Gnostic teachers Menander, Basilides, and Satornilus were active there.

Pagans and Arians. The first figure in the post-Apostolic Church at Antioch known in any detail is Bishop IGNATIUS OF ANTIOCH, martyred at Rome under Trajan (98–117). His letters are important evidence for the development and emergence of the episcopate, showing

St. Simeon Stylites, 10th-century illumination from "Menology of Basil II."

the function and authority of the bishop at the head of the threefold ministry of bishop, presbyters, and deacons. Prominent figures in the early Church at Antioch were Babylas, a bishop martyred in the persecution of Decius (249–51), and PAUL OF SAMOSATA (260–72), a heretical bishop deposed by a local council for his Christological doctrine. By the time of the persecution of Diocletian, the Christian community at Antioch was sufficiently large to have a number of martyrs, including Saint ROMANUS, one of the most important local saints. In the Arian controversy, local councils (325, 341) formulated anti-Arian creeds, but Antiochene theologians were inclined to accept Arian ideas; Arian or crypto-Arian bishops came into power and a council in 361 issued an extreme Arian creed. Often during this period there were two rival bishops of Antioch: one Arian, supported by the local congregation; the other orthodox, supported by the imperial government. In addition, there was for a time a schism within the orthodox, "Nicene," party, so that at times there were two "Nicene" bishops.

The Emperor JULIAN THE APOSTATE (361–63) made Antioch the headquarters of his campaign to suppress Christianity and restore paganism, and a number of Christians, especially in the army, were martyred at Antioch. Julian's efforts, though unsuccessful, made such an impression on the Christians that they joined to seek a solution of their doctrinal differences. The Arian emperor Valens in 365 inaugurated a persecution of the orthodox Christians at Antioch which continued until 376. Peace was made within the Church at Antioch when Valens's successor, Gratianus, in 378 issued a rescript of toleration. The restoration of orthodoxy was celebrated by a council in 379 and by the construction of the cruciform church of Saint Babylas, which was found in the excavations. Saint Jerome visited Antioch in 374 to 375. After a period of retirement in the desert east of Chalcis, he returned to Antioch and was ordained there. The latter part of the 4th century is one of the best-known periods of the Christian history of Antioch, thanks to the writings of Saint JOHN CHRYSOSTOM, a leading figure in the local community from his ordination as deacon in 381 until his departure in 398 to become archbishop of Constantinople. Like many Christians, Chrysostom studied Greek literature and rhetoric under Libanius, the celebrated pagan teacher who at this time was the leading citizen of the city. The simultaneous careers of teacher and pupil exemplify the interaction between paganism and Christianity at Antioch at this period.

Patriarchate Rivalry, Nestorius. The status of Antioch among the great churches was altered by the Council of Constantinople in 381. Since Nicaea (325) Antioch and Alexandria had been recognized as preeminent in the East. Now Constantinople sought recognition for its see corresponding to its political prestige as imperial capital, and in 381 the Church of Constantinople was given first place after that of Rome. One purpose of the pronouncement was to put down the pretensions of Alexandria, but it also had the effect of reducing the prestige of Antioch.

In the time of Chrysostom, Christians were being attracted to the Jewish cult at Antioch. The ceremonial, the fasts, the monotheistic teaching, and the reputed healing powers of the relics of Jewish martyrs, all drew Christians, especially women, to the synagogues. During the reign of Theodosius II (408–50) Saint Simeon Stylites was a popular and influential figure in all the region of Antioch. On his death (459) his body was buried in a church built for the purpose at Antioch. Under Theodosius a council at Antioch (424) condemned Pelagius (*see* PELAGIUS AND PELAGIANISM). Theodore of Mopsuestia, who had been trained at Antioch, continued his important Christological studies along the lines indicated by DIODORE OF TARSUS. Theodore's pupil at Antioch, NESTORIUS, who became archbishop of Constantinople, carried the same line of investigation further, and a major controversy was precipitated, in which Antioch, supporting Nestorius's views that there were two separate Persons in the Incarnate Christ, came into conflict with ALEXANDRIA, whose patriarch CYRIL became Nestorius's chief opponent. A council at Antioch in 430 warned Nestorius to avoid excess. At the Council of Ephesus in 431 Nestorius was deposed, the Antiochene party was defeated by Cyril of Alexandria, and the territorial jurisdiction of the Antiochene See was reduced in favor of the See of Jerusalem. At the end of the council Nestorius by imperial order was confined in his old monastery outside Antioch. Two synods were later held at Antioch at which peace with Alexandria was restored. The Nestorians remained influential in Syria and another council at Ephesus in 449 took such measures against them that it became known as the Latrocinium or Robber Council. Though the Council of Chalcedon (451) convened in order to undo the injustices of the Latrocinium, its definition of the faith only produced further dissension. Syria and Egypt, in reaction against the Chalcedonian formula for the nature of Christ, became predominantly Monophysite.

Monophysitism. The whole history of Antioch until the Arab conquest was colored by its being one of the strongholds of MONOPHYSITISM. Some scholars have considered that the Monophysite heresy combined with Syrian and Egyptian nationalism to produce a heightened opposition to the imperial government as the representative of Chalcedonian orthodoxy. This hostility developed into a separatist movement which in time facilitated the conquest of Syria and Egypt by the Persians and the Arabs, who were welcomed by the dissident Monophysites as being less oppressive than the Constantinopolitan government.

The story of the remainder of the 5th and 6th century is dominated by the struggle between Chalcedonians and Monophysites for control of the Church at Antioch and in the rest of Syria. One of the prominent Monophysites, Peter the Fuller, was bishop of Antioch on four separate occasions. In 488 he brought to a head the old dispute about the ecclesiastical supremacy of Antioch over Cyprus. Antioch, as an apostolic foundation, claimed ecclesiastical jurisdiction over Cyprus, whose Church (Antioch asserted) was not of apostolic origin. However, the alleged discovery in Cyprus of the perfectly preserved body of Saint BARNABAS, holding on his chest a copy of the Gospel of Matthew written in Barnabas's own hand, was taken as proof that the Church in Cyprus was apostolic, and the Emperor Zeno pronounced it to be ecclesiastically autonomous. The accession of the Emperor Anastasius (491–518), who favored the Monophysites, brought heightened disorders in Antioch, culminating in the election of the prominent Monophysite Severus as bishop. In addition to a permanent resident synod which Severus established, special synods convened at Antioch in 513 and 515 to enforce Severus's policies; but he had to flee when the orthodox Justin I (518–27) succeeded Anastasius. The ecclesiastical fortunes of the Monophysites were reversed. The circus factions, which had become powerful political influences in all large cities, continued the street fighting which kept cities such as Antioch and Constantinople in continual unrest. The Green faction had been Monophysite; the Blue faction, orthodox. The government began a veritable persecution of the Monophysites, which continued with increased severity under Justinian (527–565). All this time, however, the Monophysites managed to maintain an organized church, with a complete hierarchy, throughout Syria. This was a national Syrian church, known as the Jacobite Church from its leader, James BARADAI. Justinian's reign witnessed the remarkable series of disasters which marked the end of ancient Antioch. A devastating fire (525) was followed by two severe earthquakes (526, 528), all resulting in serious losses in population and economic activity. The culmination was the capture and sack of the city by the Persians (540). Antioch continued to exist until it was taken by the Persians (611) and the Arabs (638), but it never recovered its ancient greatness. Under the Arabs it soon shrank to a village.

Pagan Survivals. Reports of Justinian's vigorous persecution of pagans and heretics indicate that paganism survived to some extent at Antioch, as at other old pagan centers, such as Athens. Even after Justinian's death a number of pagan priests were discovered in Antioch and in 578 a bishop of Antioch was accused of taking part, with another Christian priest, in the sacrifice of a boy. He was able to clear himself before a court in Constantinople, but the fact that the charge could be made is significant of the strength of paganism.

Theological School. As an ancient center of Greek learning, Antioch offered excellent facilities for the study of Greek philosophy and rhetoric, and the terms of Greek philosophy and the methods of Greek speculation had an important influence on the thought of the Antiochene theologians. A regular "school" of theology was flourishing under LUCIAN OF ANTIOCH (martyred 312), if not earlier. Theologians trained in this school followed Aristotelian, historical, and philological methods, in contrast to the Platonic, mystical approach of the great rival school of Alexandria. Lucian's scientific study of the text of the Bible was the examplar of the famous Antiochene Biblical scholarship, which combined meticulous textual criticism with literal exegesis, as against the allegorical method popular at Alexandria. Prominent representatives of Antiochene theology were MARCELLUS OF ANCYRA; Chrysostom; Diodore, later bishop of Tarsus; Theodore of Mopsuestia; Nestorius; and THEODORET OF CYR. Beginning with the heretical teaching of Paul of Samosata on the Person of Christ, Antioch tended toward an insistence on the oneness of God, which in time made the city a stronghold of Arianism. In the Christological controversies of the 5th century, the Antiochene emphasis on the humanity of Christ clashed with the Alexandrian tendency to stress the Divine Nature of the Incarnate Christ.

Art and Archeology. Excavations conducted at Antioch, the suburb Daphne, and the seaport Seleucia Pieria (1932–39) obtained important results, but time did not allow extensive exploration and much remains to be excavated. Objects found in the excavations are preserved in the museum at Antioch, in the Louvre, and in museums in the United States. The city plan can be restored in its main features from surface indications, archeological evidence, literary testimonia, and air photography. Along with topographical evidence, many fine mosaic floors were found in houses, public baths, churches, and luxurious suburban villas. A unique discovery was the topographical border of a large mosaic floor in a villa at Daphne depicting a tour of Antioch and Daphne (late 5th century). The route illustrated corresponds with the itinerary described by Libanius in his encomium of Antioch (356). The scenes in the border are a precious source for contemporary architecture and daily life, illustrating dress, food, occupations, social life, recreations, and worship. This mosaic and Libanius's description of Antioch

offer a view of Antiochene life that is not available for other cities in this epoch.

The city having suffered from frequent natural disasters and pillage, Christian archeological remains found in the excavations were not extensive, but the style of the local church architecture and liturgical silver is known from discoveries made elsewhere. Antioch and Constantinople were centers for the manufacture of gold and silver liturgical vessels and church ornaments, and numerous examples of silversmith work, both secular and religious, found in Syria illustrate the style and craftsmanship of the Antiochene workshops. The celebrated Chalice of Antioch is a fine example of 4th-century work.

No early house churches such as those at Ostia and DURA-EUROPOS were found, but later Antiochene structures had an important influence on church architecture. The famous octagonal church of Constantine the Great, the Domus Aurea or Golden House, was the prototype of the great pilgrimage church of Saint Simeon Stylites in the mountains east of Antioch, and the Church of Saint Babylas was an important early example of the cruciform plan. Names of a number of churches are preserved in literary texts and the topographical border at Daphne illustrates "the *ergasterion* of the martyrium," evidently the workshop at the shrine of Saint Babylas at Daphne where religious objects and souvenirs for pilgrims were manufactured. The Greek and Latin inscriptions of Antioch and its vicinity contain a number of Christian texts recording the building of churches, dedications and offerings, and names of bishops, priests, and church officials. A number of Christian epitaphs also have been found.

Bibliography: G. DOWNEY, *A History of Antioch in Syria from Seleucus to the Arab Conquest* (Princeton 1961), bibliography; *Ancient Antioch* (Princeton 1963). L. A. JALABERT and R. MOUTERDE, eds., *Inscriptions grecques et latines de la Syrie* (Paris 1929–), v.3 contains the inscriptions from Antioch, Daphne, and vicinity. C. H. KRAELING, "The Jewish Community at Antioch," *Journal of Biblical Literature* 51 (1932) 130–60. G. DOWNEY, tr., "Libanius' Oration in Praise of Antioch (Oration XI)," *Proceedings of the American Philosophical Society* 103 (1959) 652–86. A. J. FESTUGIÈRE, *Antioche païenne et chrétienne* (Paris 1959). R. DEVREESSE, *Le Patriarcat d'Antioche* (Paris 1945). M. H. SHEPERD, JR., "The Formation and Influence of the Antiochene Liturgy," *Dumbarton Oaks Papers* 15 (1961) 25–44. *Antioch-on-the-Orontes*, v.1–4 (Princeton 1934–52), reports on the excavations. D. LEVI, *Antioch Mosaic Pavements* (Princeton 1947), complete publication and study of all floors discovered. H. H. ARNASON, "The History of the Chalice of Antioch," *The Biblical Archaelogist* 4 (1941) 49–64; 5 (1942) 10–16. G. DOWNEY, *Antioch in the Age of Theodosius the Great* (Norman, Okla. 1962). B. M. METZGER, "The Lucianic Recension of the Greek Bible," *Chapters in the History of New Testament Textual Criticism* (Leiden 1963). E. C. DODD, *Byzantine Silver Stamps* (Washington 1961), on hallmarks used at Antioch and elsewhere.

[G. DOWNEY/EDS.]

ANTIOCH, PATRIARCHATE OF

According to ancient tradition, the Christian community of ANTIOCH was founded by St. Peter, and with the destruction of Jerusalem in A.D. 70 it became the chief radial point of Christianity in the East. Its authority spread over Syria, Phoenicia, Arabia, Palestine, Cilicia, Cyprus, and Mesopotamia.

Formation of the Patriarchate. In the Ecumenical Council of NICAEA I (325), Antioch was recognized after Rome and Alexandria as one of the ancient apostolic patriarchates. However, its authority was gradually decentralized in the 5th century. At the Ecumenical Council of EPHESUS (431), Cyprus obtained its autonomy. At the Council of CHALCEDON (451) the Patriarchate of Antioch suffered even greater losses by the formation of the Patriarchate of Jerusalem with 58 bishoprics formerly under Antiochene jurisdiction. The council condemned the heresy of Eutyches (*see* MONOPHYSITISM), and the Patriarchate of Antioch split into two factions concerned with this Christological dogma. Orthodox predominated in the Hellenized cities along the coast, while the Monophysites occupied the country and the towns of inner Syria, such as Edessa and northern Mesopotamia, where the Jacobite Syrian Church emerged. The Christians faithful to the Chalcedonian Christology became known at first as the Melkites, a term that eventually came to refer to those Antiochene Christians who recognized papal oversight.

Melkites and Jacobites. The first Monophysite to rule as patriarch of Antioch was Peter the Fuller (468–470; 485–488), but SEVERUS OF ANTIOCH (512–518), as a theological writer, was the true founder of Monophysitism, although his doctrine was unorthodox more by expression than in fact. He was deposed by the Byzantine emperor, and under JUSTINIAN I, the Orthodox faction prevailed. When Severus died in exile (538), his followers were unable to elect a successor. However, James BARADAI (*c.* 543), with the cooperation of Empress Theodora (1), consecrated a Monophysite hierarchy, whose members were called JACOBITES in his honor. In 550, the Patriarchate of Antioch was split between the Melkites, faithful to Chalcedon, and the Jacobites.

The Melkite Church remained powerful even after the Arab invasion. The Muslim conquerors preserved the *status quo* as regards the Church's position, while the Melkite Patriarch of Antioch continued to exercise jurisdiction over his see from the imperial court at Constantinople until the end of the 7th century.

Break with Rome. When the Byzantines recaptured part of Syria in 960, the Melkite Patriarchs in Antioch gradually accepted Byzantine liturgical rite and church canons, thereby becoming more dependent upon the Pa-

triarchate of Constantinople. Until then the Melkites had used the West Syrian rite in both the Antioch and Jerusalem patriarchates. Between the 10th and 12th centuries the Antiochene rite was replaced by the Byzantine liturgical rite of Constantinople. The Melkite Patriarchate of Antioch chose to remain in communion with the Patriarch of Constantinople after the schism of 1054.

The Latin Crusaders fomented division by regarding the Antiochene Melkites as schismatics and heretics. Rival Latin patriarchates were set up in Antioch and Jerusalem. During the Latin occupation the Melkite Patriarch of Antioch resided in Constantinople. After the fall of the Crusaders' kingdom of Antioch in 1268, the Melkite patriarch returned to his native see. But the city of Antioch had suffered greatly under the siege of the Mameluke Turks; its glory was gone; hence the Melkite patriarch changed his see to Damascus (1366). This patriarchate was more strictly controlled by the Muslims than was that of the Maronites, and the sultans of Egypt, on whom Syria depended during this time, forbade all contact with the West.

Catholic Patriarchate. Work to reestablish communion between the Patriarchate of Antioch and the See of Rome began with the arrival of the Capuchins, Jesuits, and Carmelites after the foundation of the Congregation for the PROPAGATION OF THE FAITH in Rome in 1622. These missionaries slowly infiltrated a community with Catholic elements so that eventually a Catholic hierarchy could be introduced, in the beginning allowing Catholics to receive the Sacraments from the Orthodox clergy. For a time no true distinction was made between Catholic and Orthodox communities. Gradually one or another patriarch or bishop and many faithful recognized the primacy of Rome. The amalgamation of the entire patriarchate, however, was premature. The two rival patriarchs, Athanasius III (1686–1724) and Cyril V (1672–1720), were recognized as Catholics by Rome at different times but still governed mixed Catholic and Orthodox communities. Archbishop Euthymius Saifi of Tyre and Sidon played an important role in the reunion when in 1701 he was accepted by Rome as bishop of all the Melkite Catholics who did not have their own bishop.

Cyril Tanus. On the death of Athanasius III (*c.* 1724, as a Catholic), it seemed to the Catholics of Antioch that the moment had come to make the patriarchate unmistakably Catholic, and they chose an unequivocal Catholic for the patriarchal see. This was CYRIL (SERAPHIM) OF TURIV, the nephew of Archbishop Euthymius, who took the name of Cyril VI. His election, in which the Orthodox also participated, was made according to ancient custom by the clergy and people of Damascus. The intention of the voters to give the whole patriarchate a Catholic bishop was nullified when Sylvester of Cyprus, consecrated by Jeremias III, Patriarch of Constantinople, obtained the support of the Sultan and Cyrus VI had to flee into exile. He took up residence in the mountainous monastery of the Redeemer near Sidon. The patriarch of Constantinople excommunicated Cyril Tanus as an apostate. The Holy See at first delayed its recognition since Cyril, like his uncle, had been denounced in Rome for his tendency to change customs, and also because there were doubts concerning the validity of his election. In 1729 he received recognition, and in 1744, the pallium.

With the election of Cyril, the Antiochene Patriarchate was actually, but against Rome's intention, split into two communities: one was unmistakably Catholic, while the other was acknowledged as Orthodox. In 1759 Cyril VI retired and named his young nephew Ignatius Gohar as his successor; this led to complications because some of the bishops rejected the nephew and appealed to Rome. Rome named Archbishop Maximus Hakim of Alep as patriarch. This was a difficult test for the still new union, but it soon proved a happy solution.

Melkite Catholics. At first the authority of the Catholic patriarch was confined to Antioch, but on July 13, 1772, the Holy See gave the patriarch jurisdiction over the Melkite Catholics in the territories of Jerusalem and Alexandria [J. D. Mansi, *Sacorum Concilliorum nova et amplissima collectio,* 31 v. (Florence-Venice 1757–98); repr. and cont. by L. Petit and J. B. Martin 53 v. in 60 (Paris 1889–1927; repr. Graz 1960–) 46.581–582].

There have been conflicts in the course of history between the Holy See and the Melkite hierarchy caused by an assertion of rights claimed by each side. The Synods of Qarqafel (1806) and of Jerusalem (1849), whose aim was to make of the Melkite community an independent law-making body, were not acknowledged by Rome. The renowned Patriarch MAXIMOS III MAZLŪM (1833–55) had many difficulties with Rome, but in 1838 the Holy See gave him as a personal privilege the right to assume the threefold title of patriarch of Antioch, Alexandria, and Jerusalem; this right has been uninterruptedly renewed by all his successors. Maximos was able to set up a residence in Damascus in 1834, and he received full civil recognition from the Sultan in 1848.

Gregory II Jusof (1864–97) appeared at VATICAN COUNCIL I as an opponent of the definition of the Primacy because he saw in it an obstacle to reunion. He accepted the definition only on condition of the acknowledgement of the rights accorded the patriarchs by a clause in the acts of the Council of FLORENCE (1439), which Pius IX took amiss. Under Leo XIII, who valued him greatly, Gregory played a leading role in the Conference of Oriental Patriarchs held under the presidency of the pope in

1894. Patriarch MAXIMOS IV SAYEGH proved himself an energetic assertor of the traditions of the Oriental churches and the rights of the patriarchs at Vatican Council II.

In 1662 Andrew Akidgean was consecrated Syrian Catholic Patriarch of Antioch, thus creating an even more confused picture of an ancient apostolic patriarchate broken up into five distinct patriarchates. Today, these five patriarchs continue to claim the ancient patriarchal See of Antioch as their legitimate heritage: the Antiochene Orthodox and the Eastern Catholic Melkite patriarchs, the Maronite Catholic Patriarch, the Jacobite Syrian Patriarch, and the Syrian Catholic Patriarch.

Bibliography: D. ATTWATER, *The Christian Churches of the East,* 2 v. (rev. ed. Milwaukee 1961–62). R. DEVREESSE, *Le Patriarcat d'Antioche* (Paris 1945). C. KARALEVSKIJ (Charon), *Dictionnaire d'histoire et de géographie ecclésiastiques,* ed. A. BAUDRILLART et al. (Paris 1912–) 3:563–703; *Histoire des Patriarcats Melkites,* 3 v. in 2 (Rome 1909–10). A. A. KING, *The Rites of Eastern Christendom,* 2 v. (London 1950). J. NASRALLAH, *Sa Beatitude Maximos IV et la succession apostolique* (Paris 1963). W. DE VRIES et al., eds., *Rom und die Patriarchate des Ostens* (Freiburg 1963). R. ROBERSON, *The Eastern Christian Churches: A Brief Survey,* 6th ed. (Rome 1999).

[G. A. MALONEY/EDS.]

ANTIOCH, SCHOOL OF

The common doctrinal tendencies, particularly in exegesis and Christology, that characterized the theological thinkers and writers who represented the Antiochian tradition. There is no record of a formal school such as apparently existed at ALEXANDRIA, although LUCIAN OF ANTIOCH directed his *didascalion* and Diodore of Tarsus his *asceterion* in Antioch. The school of Antioch represented a group of theologians exhibiting common doctrinal characteristics; these theologians were not necessarily from Antioch, although they had undergone the influence of Antiochene masters. The problems posed to the theologians of Antioch in the third century and at the beginning of the fourth century differed from those dealt with at the end of the fourth century and during the fifth century. Hence there were two distinct periods in the history of the school of Antioch.

First Period. Eusebius of Caesarea mentioned the literary activity of Bishop Serapion of Antioch at the beginning of the third century, and Jerome spoke of a priest, Geminus of Antioch (d. *c.* 230), as a writer of theology. At the Synod of Antioch in 268, two Antiochene theologians, PAUL OF SAMOSATA and the Sophist Malchion, held discussions on the Trinity and Christ. The true founder of the school, however, was Lucian of Antioch. From about 270 he conducted an important *didascalion;* he died a martyr in 312. During this time a certain Dorotheus also served as a theologian and exegete. The relationship between him and Lucian, as between the latter and Paul of Samosata, is not clear. Little is known of the doctine of Lucian himself. He labored at scriptural exegesis and composed a version of the text after the example of ORIGEN. He had many disciples, who were called Collucianites or followers of Lucian, among whom PHILOSTORGIUS named: Eusebius of Nicomedia, Maris of Chalcedon, Theognis of Nicaea, Leontius of Antioch, Anthony of Tarsus, Menophantes of Ephesus, Noominus, Eudoxius, Alexander, and ASTERIUS THE SOPHIST.

These authors defended ARIUS, who was also a disciple of Lucian. Lucian is, as a consequence, properly considered the father of ARIANISM. This does not exclude the possibility that Lucian actually found inspiration in the thought of Origen. One of Arius's most rabid opponents was EUSTATHIUS, Bishop of Antioch. He made a clear distinction between the divinity and the humanity of Christ. This caused him to be considered a precursor of the Christology defended against the school of Alexandria by the theologians of the school of Antioch in its second period. With them, he attacked the allegorical exegesis of Origen.

Second Period. The problem of Christology dominated the controversies that began with APOLLINARIS OF LAODICEA (fl. *c.* 362). This period was inaugurated with DIODORE OF TARSUS, who was primarly an exegete; but Diodore developed a dualistic Christology that remained characteristic of the school of Antioch. As disciples, Diodore had JOHN CHRYSOSTOM and THEODORE OF MOPSUESTIA; NESTORIUS and THEODORET OF CYR also belonged to this lineage. Finally, the school of EDESSA was influenced by Antioch. It is through this school that Theodore of Mopsuestia became the official exegete of the Persian Church. The consequence of this was the "Nestorianization" of Mesopotamian Christianity.

Doctrine. The schools of Antioch and Alexandria developed opposing theologies in the spheres of exegesis and Christology. Explicitly, the teachers of Antioch adhered to a literal understanding of Scripture as opposed to the allegorical interpretation of their Egyptian colleagues. They did not repudiate typology as such when the employment of it was justified by the text, but they were opposed to the arbitrary manner in which the Alexandrian exegetes discovered typological meaning in the Bible.

Opposition of the Antioch school to the school of Alexandria was more marked in its approach to Christology, and this difference dominated the controversies of the fifth century. Against Apollinaris, who was regarded as a representative of Alexandria, Diodore strongly defended the immutability and eternity of the Logos. This led

him to insist on the duality of the natures in Christ, as Eustathius of Antioch had already done. However, Diodore did not succeed in explaining the unity in the person of Christ with the same exactitude. He spoke of Him as at once "Son of God" and "Son of Mary," a distinction that was too readily accepted as stemming from a doctrine of two persons in Christ. Diodore preferred to speak of the indwelling of the Word in the Flesh, rather than of the Incarnation. Mary, he said, is the mother of a man (*anthropotokos*); she is not the mother of God (*theotokos*); and he cautioned against saying that God suffered. The Word of God and the Son of Mary are both Sons of God, the one by nature, the other by grace. These are characteristic formulas of the Antiochene Christology and can be found in the writings of Theodore of Mopsuestia, Theodoret of Cyr, and other theologians of the Antiochene Patriarchate who rallied to the defense of Nestorius.

Bibliography: G. BARDY, *Recherches sur S. Lucien d' Antioche et son école* (Paris 1936). H. DE RIEDMATTEN, *Les Actes du procès de Paul de Samosate* (Fribourg 1952). L. ABRAMOWSKI, *Dictionnaire d'histoire et de géographie ecclésiastiques* 14:496–504; "Zur Theologie Theodors von Mopsuestia," *Zeitschrift für Kirchengeschicte* 72 (1961) 263–293. F. A. SULLIVAN, *The Christology of Theodore of Mopsuestia* (Analecta Gregoriana 82; Rome 1956); "Further Notes on Theodore of Mopsuestia," *Theological Studies* 20 (1959) 264–279. J. L. MCKENZIE, "Annotations on the Christology of Theodore of Mopsuestia," *ibid.* 19 (1958) 345–373. R. V. SELLERS, *Two Ancient Christologies* (London 1940). J. GUILLET, "Les Exègétes d'Alexandrie et d'Antioche," *Recherches de science religieuse* 34 (1947) 257–302. V. ERMONI, *Dictionnaire de théologie catholique.* ed. A. VACANT et al., (Paris 1903–50) 1.2:1435–39. F. L. CROSS, *The Oxford Dictionary of the Christian Church* (London 1957) 63–64. H. RAHNER, *Lexikon für Theologie und Kirche,* ed. J. HOFER and K. RAHNER (Freiberg 1957–65) 1:650–652. W. ELTESTER, *Die Religion in Geschichte und Gegenwart* (Tübingen 1957–65) 1:452–453.

[A. VAN ROEY]

ANTIOCHENE LITURGY

The manner of celebrating Christ's redemptive mystery in the Patriarchate of Antioch and, in a modified form, among some Syrians today.

Origins. The tradition is that the liturgical formula of "offering thanks" as observed at Antioch of Syria, an important early Christian community (Acts 8 to 11), spread to Jerusalem, where it was translated from Greek to Aramaic. The Antioch usage, further modified at Jerusalem, thereafter became the model of almost all the other Eastern rites.

Liturgical customs radiating from Antioch left their mark on the Church life of the surrounding area. The rapid growth of Christianity in this region (Antioch itself counted 150 suffragan bishops at Nicaea in 325) demanded a close surveillance over the prayers of the liturgy lest nonapproved forms be adopted. As a consequence, prayer texts came to be written, and in this manner, rather than orally, they were transmitted from one community to another; the smaller communities of Christians borrowed the written texts from those that were larger and more influential. In due time, then, the liturgical practices carried out in the city of Antioch were found in use throughout the area known as the Patriarchate of ANTIOCH. Thus, the Antiochene Liturgy came into existence.

It is not surprising to discern in the somewhat fixed 4th-century Antioch usage described below the outlines of various other Eastern rites. Such a resemblance was inevitable in the Liturgy of Byzantium or Constantinople, by tradition the handiwork of St. John Chrysostom, who before he became bishop of Constantinople (370–397) was a priest of the city of Antioch. At a much earlier date, St. Mark is said to have introduced the Antiochene usage into Egypt, where it developed into the Alexandrian rite (*see* ALEXANDRIAN LITURGY).

Order of the Divine Liturgy. There follows in outline form, based on quotations taken from book eight of the *Apostolic Constitutions,* a 4th-century Syrian Christian writing, a description of the early Antioch usage: (1) reading from the Old Testament, (2) reading from the Epistles and Acts and the Gospels, (3) homily by the bishop, (4) dismissal of nonmembers, those preparing for Baptism, and public penitents, (5) prayer for all the faithful, (6) kiss of peace and greetings by the bishop, (7) washing of hands, (8) bringing in of the gifts, (9) Eucharistic Prayer, Preface, Sanctus, (10) words of institution, (11) Anamnesis, (12) Epiclesis, (13) intercessory prayers for the Church, the living, the dead, (14) prayers in preparation for Communion (''Holy things for the holy''), (15) Communion, (16) post-Communion prayer of thanks, and (17) final blessing by the bishop. Of note in this usage at this time are: (1) the prominent role played by the deacon as intermediary between bishop and people; (2) the frequent petitions made in litany form by the deacons to which the faithful responded ''Kyrie eleison''; (3) the position of the Epiclesis after the Consecration (see Quasten *Monumenta eucharista et liturgica vetustissima* 198–233).

Later Developments. From the time of the Council of Chalcedon (451) until the 7th-century Arab conquest of Syria, the Antiochene Liturgy was used by both Orthodox and Jacobite Syrians. However, with the rise of Constantinople to a position of ecclesiastical supremacy in the East came the widespread use of the BYZANTINE LITURGY. The Antiochene Liturgy, except for its use in a modified form by the Jacobites, simply ceased to exist (*see* JACOBITES [SYRIAN]).

The Antiochene Liturgy is sometimes called the West Syrian Liturgy to distinguish it from the East Syrian Liturgy, a liturgy usually identified with the Christian churches of Mesopotamia and Chaldea. These Christians, originally dependent on Antioch, dwelt beyond the borders of the Roman Empire, where because of their isolated position they gradually acquired an ecclesiastical semi-independent status, a condition that favored the development of a distinct liturgical rite. The liturgy that evolved in that region is the one we know today as the East Syrian Liturgy. Christians of this liturgical rite who have reestablished full union with Rome are today known as the CHALDEAN CATHOLIC CHURCH.

Today, the Antiochene Liturgy is celebrated by only a small body of Christians, divided almost equally between Syrian Catholics and Syrian Jacobites.

Bibliography: D. ATTWATER, *The Christian Churches of the East,* 2 v. (Milwaukee 1961). J. A. JUNGMANN, *The Mass of the Roman Rite* (New York 1959). N. LIESEL, *The Eucharistic Liturgies of the Eastern Churches,* tr. D. HEIMANN (Collegeville, Minn. 1963). R. ROBERSON, *The Eastern Christian Churches: A Brief Survey,* 6th ed (Rome 1999).

[E. E. FINN/EDS.]

ANTIOCHUS IV EPIPHANES

King of the Seleucian Kingdom of Syria (175–163 B.C.). He pursued a policy aimed at Hellenizing the Jewish religion that brought on the Machabean revolt; occupied by revolts in the eastern part of his empire and strongly opposed by the nationalism and religion of the Jews, Antiochus IV was unable to implement his Hellenizing decrees in Palestine.

Aggressive Hellenism of Antiochus IV. After the Battle of Magnesia (190 B.C.), Epiphanes was taken hostage and held in Rome for about 15 years. Upon his release, though not in a position to succeed immediately to the throne, he was able to eliminate his older brother's rightful heir, Demetrius. Antiochus made extravagant efforts to live up to his surname Epiphanes, which means ''(God) Manifest''; his enemies punned on it, calling him Epimanes, ''crazy.'' His relationship with the Jews and Jerusalem was unhappy and turbulent. Early in his reign he intervened to settle the dispute between the high priest ONIAS III and his brother Jason. Since Jason showed Hellenizing sympathies and came forward with a substantial bribe, Antiochus deposed Onias and made Jason high priest. Three years later one Menelaus, not of the lineage of the high priests, successfully bribed Antiochus to depose Jason and make him high priest. A subsequent, ill-advised revolt led by Jason in the absence of Antiochus was severely punished; Antiochus stripped the Temple of its treasures and put Jerusalem under a despotic governor named Philip (1 Mc 1.21–29). Frustrated in Egypt by Roman interference, Antiochus vented his anger on the Jews. His edict (1 Mc 1.43–53) that all peoples within his kingdom must be one in law, custom, and religion brought his relationship with the Jews to the worst possible climax, that of general persecution. Antiochus decreed the sternest measures against the Sabbath observance, circumcision, and food laws (1 Mc 1.48, 51). Any Jew discovered in possession of a copy of the Law was executed. The unforgiveable desecration, however, was the erection of an altar to the Olympian Zeus in the Temple, the ''horrible abomination'' (Dn 11.31; 1 Mc 1.57; *see* ABOMINATION OF DESOLATION).

Maccabean Revolt. In 167 B.C. Antiochus's policy, aimed at Hellenizing the Jews, brought open revolt, first under the leadership of the priest Mattathias (1 Mc 2.1–2.69), and then under his famous son Judas Machabee. The latter, aided by the Jews faithful to the Law, especially the HASIDAEANS (1 Mc 2.42), drove the Syrians out of Judea through a swift succession of victories (3.1–4.35). The enraged Antiochus was powerless to do anything about it. He was distracted and concerned by serious insurrections in Parthia and Armenia. Eventually he lost his life in leading an expedition against the Parthians (1 Mc 6.1–16). Tradition adds the ironic note of tragedy that, shortly before his death, Antiochus really became insane. The Book of Daniel, in its last four chapters, tells in veiled symbolism the story of Antiochus IV.

See Also: DANIEL, BOOK OF; MACCABEES, HISTORY OF THE; SELEUCID DYNASTY.

Bibliography: F. M. ABEL, ''Antiochus Épiphane,'' *Revue biblique* 50 (1941) 231–254. A. AYMARD, ''Autour de l'avènement d'Antiochos IV,'' *Historia* 2 (Wiesbaden 1953–54) 49–73. M. NOTH, *The History of Israel,* tr. P. R. ACKROYD (2d ed. New York 1960). J. BRIGHT, *A History of Israel* (Philadelphia 1959) 401–412. G. DOWNEY, *A History of Antioch in Syria from Seleucus to the Arab Conquest* (Princeton 1961) 95–111. M. WELLMANN, *Paulys Realencyklopädie der klassischen Altertumswissenschaft* 1.2 (1894) 2470–76.

[J. F. DEVINE]

ANTIPATHY

An emotional reaction of an individual who experiences aversion, repugnance, or dislike. It is a fixed attitude and may be based on either rational or irrational foundations. In the former case, the individual is usually aware of his or her feelings and the reason for them; in the latter case, the individual simply experiences an aversion for the object or person without any recognized justifiable reason. Whenever the individual finds himself or herself confronted with the object, he or she involuntarily shrinks from it. Antipathy usually includes some degree of hostility, inasmuch as it involves feelings of opposition.

[R. P. VAUGHAN]

ANTIPHON

In Western liturgical practice, a refrain sung before and after a Psalm or canticle. In Byzantine liturgical usage it means several verses of a Psalm, a complete Psalm, or even several Psalms followed by a doxology. Although the original meaning seems to have referred to an alternation of groups in Psalm singing (*see* PSALMODY), by the 6th century it had come to mean in the West a refrain that accompanied such alternation. It forms the largest category of chants found in the Office and in the Mass. Later medieval pieces with alternating choruses but not with accompanying psalmody are also called antiphons (processional antiphons and MARIAN ANTIPHONS).

Bibliography: O. STRUNK, ''The Antiphons of the Oktoechos,'' *Journal of the American Musicological Society* 13 (1960) 50–67. A. GEVAERT, *Le Mélopée antique dans le chant de l'église latine* (Gand 1895).

[R. G. WEAKLAND]

ANTIPODES

This term was used to designate either the opposite sides of the earth or the people who dwelt there. The problem of whether there were people living on the opposite sides of the earth was of great interest to ancient and medieval scientists, philosophers, and theologians. While the question was mainly a geographical one, and the Fathers of the Church considered it open as regards the faith, St. Augustine questioned whether such inhabitants, if they existed, would be descendants of Adam. He concluded they would not be. This gave a theological cast to the problem and led to a situation frequently cited by the enemies of the Church as a conflict between the Church and science.

Following the Augustinian line of thought, Pope Zachary on May 1, 748, asked St. Boniface to inquire about Virgilius (or Fergal), who perhaps believed in another world and other men existing beneath the earth, or in another sun and moon there, and to excommunicate him if he held these ''perverse'' tenets (*Patrologia Latina* 89:946). Virgilius was an Irish monk who had become abbot of St. Peter's in Salzburg and who for many years (746–784) administered that episcopal see, though he was not consecrated bishop until 767. He was also a geographer and, as Lowe has proved, he wrote (under the pseudonym of Ethicus Istes) a *Cosmographia* (Clavis Patrum; no. 2548), a mixture of ancient geographical doctrines and curious stories. He did not mention the antipodes in this book, but perhaps in another he had quoted or commented on MARTIANUS CAPELLA.

The outcome of this case is not known, but surely Virgilius was not condemned since he remained abbot-bishop of Salzburg (*see* VIRGILIUS, [FERGAL FEIRGIL] OF SALZBURG, ST). Because of the subsequent furor, it is important to emphasize that the pope did not pass canonical sentence. Further, the pope was interested in the question from a theological point of view and, following Augustine, objected to the antipodes on account of the unity of mankind. Once writers began postulating the ability of reaching the antipodes by navigation, the theological aspect of the problem disappeared.

By the 13th century writers were beginning to see the antipodes as a scientific question, and many argued that it could be settled only by experiment—that all that transpired before experimental verifications was pure speculation and no more. There is a possibility that Christopher Columbus had read PETER OF AILLY's *Imago Mundi* before his voyage and was influenced by its insistence on experimental inquiry.

The conflict with Virgilius and the letter of Pope Zachary were used by Kepler and Descartes against the theologians who did not accept the Copernician system, while the Encyclopedists employed the incident to attack the Church and the papacy. These objections were answered by the Jesuits in the *Mémoires de Trévoux* (1708).

Bibliography: F. S. BETTEN, *St. Boniface and St. Virgil* (Washington 1927). G. BOFFITO, "Cosmografia primitiva: Classica e patristica," *Pontifica accademia delle scienze: Memorie* 19 (1901) 301–353; 20 (1902) 113–146. P. DELHAYE, "La Théorie des antipodes et ses incidences théologiques," in *Le Microcosmus de Godefroy de St-Victor: Étude théologique*, ed. P. DELHAYE (Lille 1951). H. LÖWE, *Ein literarischer Widersacher des Bonifatius: Virgil Von Salsburg und die Kosmographie des Aethicus Ister* (Wiesbaden 1952). G. MARINELLI, "La Geografia ed i Padri della Chiesa," *Scritti minori* (Florence 1908) 1:281–381. J. O. THOMSON, *History of Ancient Geography* (Cambridge, Eng. 1948).

[P. DELHAYE]

ANTIPOPE

One who uncanonically claims or exercises the office of Roman pontiff. Historically this situation has occurred as the result of various causes, not all of which imply bad faith. Antipopes have risen by violent usurpation (Constantine II, 767); by election following a prior selection falsely judged as invalid (Clement VII, 1378);

accession after an unwarranted deposition or deportation of the previous pope (Felix II, 355); or double election (Anacletus II, Innocent II, 1130). Yet not all antipopes emerged because of malfeasance or bad faith. Because of the lack of a readily accessible electoral code, there could be confusion as to the requirements for a valid choice. Instances occurred where a pontificate, uncanonical in its beginnings, was validated by subsequent acceptance on the part of the electors (Vigilius, after Silverius's resignation or death, 537). It must be frankly admitted that bias or deficiencies in the sources make it impossible to determine in certain cases whether the claimants were popes or antipopes.

The term "antipope" can be traced to *c.* 1192 [J. H. Baxter and C. Johnson, *Medieval Latin Word-List* (1950) 22], although other names appear earlier, e.g., *perturbator* (370; *Corpus scriptorum ecclesiasticorum latinorum* 35:52), *pervasor* (506; Thiel, *Epist. Rom. pont.* 1:697). Authors variously calculate the number of antipopes: Baümer counts 33 with three others bracketed with legitimate popes: Amanieu, 34; Frutaz, 36 plus seven doubtful and nine improperly designated; Moroni, 39. Since 1947 the Vatican *Annuario Pontificio* has printed Mercati's list of popes that includes 37 antipopes in the text. All lists are subject to reservations, and the Mercati catalogue has provoked dissent. Biographies of the 37 antipopes can be found in this encyclopedia under their pontifical names, except for Anastasius the Librarian, who can be found under that name.

Bibliography: *Annuario Pontificio* (2001) 7*–22*, cf. A. MERCATI, "The New List of the Popes," *Mediaeval Studies* 9 (1947) 71–80. L. DUCHESNE, *Liber pontificalis* (Paris 1886–92; 1958). P. JAFFÉ, *Regista pontificum romanorum ab condita ecclesia ad annum post Christum natum 1198* (2d ed. Leipzig 1881–88; repr. 1956). L. A. ANASTASIO, *Istoria degli antipapi*, 2 v. (Naples 1754). G. MORONI, *Dizionario de erudizione storico-ecclesiastica* (Venice 1840–61) 2:181–215. A. AMANIEU, *Dictionnaire de droit canonique* ((Paris 1935–65) 1:598–622. G. JACQUEMET, *Catholicisme* 1:653–658. *Lexikon für Theologie und Kirche*, ed. J. HOFER and K. RAHNER (Freiberg 1957–65) 4:583–585. R. BÄUMER, *ibid.* 8:54–59.

[H. G. J. BECK/EDS.]

ANTOINE, PAUL GABRIEL

Jesuit theologian; b. Lunéville, Lorraine, Jan. 10, 1678; d. Pont-à-Mousson, Jan. 22, 1743. He entered the Jesuits on Oct. 9, 1693, and after his studies he taught humanities for several years. He became professor of philosophy at Pont-à-Mousson and then professor of theology. Eventually he became rector of the college there.

His *Theologia universa, speculativa et dogmatica*, published in 1723, immediately established his reputation

Devils crowning an Antipope, 15th-century illustration (©Archivo Iconografico, S.A./CORBIS)

as one of the foremost theologians of his time and went through nine editions during his lifetime and ten editions after his death. His *Theologia moralis universa* (1726) brought him even greater acclaim and was published in 60 editions in different countries. In the judgment of St. Alphonsus Liguori and also of Jean Pierre Gury, Antoine's doctrine was overly severe, but its excellence as a textbook in moral theology recommended its wide use. The Roman edition of 1746, published with several additions by Philip Carbognano, was prescribed by Benedict XIV for use by the students of the College of Propaganda and was widely encouraged also by many bishops in France and Italy.

Bibliography: C. SOMMERVOGEL, *Bibliothèque de la Compagnie de Jésus* 1:419–427. H. HURTER, *Nomenclator Literarius theologiae catholicae* 4:1351–52.

[J. C. WILLKE]

ANTOLÍNEZ, AGUSTÍN

Augustinian theologian; b. Valladolid, Castile, Dec. 6, 1554; d. June 19, 1626. Antolínez was a professor of theology at Valladolid and at Salamanca and became bishop-elect of Ciudad Rodrigo in 1623 and archbishop of Santiago de Compostela in 1624. He left a number of theological treatises in manuscript and published lives of St. John of Sahagún and St. Clare of Montefalco. His pious commentary on the strophes of the *Spiritual Canticle* of St. JOHN OF THE CROSS—*Amores de Dios y el Alma*—has in recent times emerged from oblivion because of its bearing on the critical problem of the works of the Mystical Doctor.

In 1922 P. Chevallier, OSB, arguing against the authenticity of the second redaction of the *Spiritual Canticle,* stated that it made use of the commentary by Antolínez. In 1948 J. Krynen published a voluminous study in support of this position. Neither author, however, established the contention, for a careful comparison of the two redactions of the *Spiritual Canticle* with the *Amores* provides evidence that Antolínez had before his eyes the text of the second *Canticle* in the form of a transcription revised by John of the Cross himself. It is probable that this text had been left to Antolínez by his equally distinguished confrere, Luis de León.

The possession by the Augustinians of an unquestionably authentic text of St. John of the Cross, quite different from that which the Carmelites, for good reasons, intended to edit, and the transmission to the Carmelites of this text and that of the *Amores* after the death of Antolínez suggest answers to a number of vexing questions in the history of the works of John of the Cross. In particular

this helps to explain why Antolínez and later the Carmelites did not wish the *Amores* to be published and why the Augustinians were willing to make no claim on behalf of Antolínez.

Bibliography: A. C. VEGA, *Fray A. Antolínez: Amores de Dios y el Alma* (Madrid 1956), with app. by M. LEDRUS, ''L'Incidence de l'*Exposición* d'Antolínez sur le problème textuel johannicrucien.'' P. CHEVALLIER, ''Le Cantique spirituel a-t-il été interpolé?'' *Bulletin Hispanique* 24 (1922) 307–342. J. KRYNEN, *Le Cantique spirituel de s. Jean de la Croix commenté et refondu au XVIIe siècle* (Salamanca 1948). J. DE JESÚS-MARIA, ''El 'Cantico espiritual' de San Juan de la Cruz y 'Amores de Dios y el Alma' de A. Antolinez, O.S.A.,'' *Ephemerides Carmeliticae* 3 (1949) 443–542. I. GONZALEZ MARCOS, ''Datos para una biografía de Agustín Antolínez OSA,'' *Revista Agostiniana* 30 (1989).

[M. LEDRUS]

ANTONELLI, GIACOMO

Cardinal, secretary of state to Pius IX; b. Sonnino, near Terracina (Latium), Italy, April 2, 1806; d. Rome, Nov. 6, 1876. His sharp mind, practical sense, and elegant manners favored his rapid progress in the papal administration, despite his lowly birth. After being attached to a tribunal from 1830 he became successively delegate to Orvieto (1835), Viterbo (1837), and Macerata (1839). He returned to Rome (December 1840) as assistant to Cardinal Mattei in the department of the interior (*dicastero dell' interno*). At this time he received the diaconate; he never advanced to the priesthood. As head of the financial administration (1845), he proved very capable.

PIUS IX (1846–78) named him cardinal (June 11, 1847). During the first two years of this pontificate Antonelli pleased the moderate liberals by favoring a policy less reliant on alliance with Austria. He became president of the *Consulta di Stato* (November 1847) and played an important role in the elaboration of the new constitution (*Statuto*). Antonelli's first term as secretary of state lasted from March 10 to May 3, 1848. At this time Pius IX placed him at the head of the first ministry charged with applying the new constitution. When this ministry resigned after the papal allocation of April 29, Antonelli temporarily receded into obscurity, although he remained a highly regarded counselor of the pope. He returned as prosecretary of state (Dec. 6, 1848) and as secretary (March 18, 1852), holding office until death. Largely because of him Pius IX decided first to flee Rome (Nov. 24, 1848) and then to remain at Gaeta, despite the contrary advice of ROSMINI-SERBATI, whose influence Antonelli knew well how to undermine. Antonelli was made head of the papal government in exile (November 26). Convinced that it would be impossible to make the government of the STATES OF THE CHURCH partially a lay one, he decided to practice a severe policy toward the Roman liberals by refusing all contact with them and appealing to the Catholic powers to restore papal temporal power by arms. After the fall of the Roman Republic, Antonelli was the source of the *motu proprio* (Sept. 12, 1849) that promised administrative and judicial reforms and immunities to municipalities, but no specific political liberty. As secretary of state he was the one mainly responsible for putting it into effect. Although his policy had become frankly reactionary, his government, which lasted until 1870, did not lack merit, but neither did it progress beyond the outlook characteristic of 18th-century enlightened despotism.

The ROMAN QUESTION came to the forefront with the war in Italy (1859). Antonelli had no faith in direct negotiations with Piedmont and regarded the policy of armed independence advocated by Monsignor de MERODE as chimerical. Instead he relied, as in 1849, on the support of the conservative powers to save the States of the Church, not realizing how much ideas and political conditions had changed in the interim. Believing that the young kingdom of Italy would soon disintegrate, he supported the Neapolitan guerrillas. Monsignor de Merode could not support the concessions to the France of NAPOLEON III implicit in this policy of passive resistance and sought to utilize his ascendancy over Pius IX to undermine the influence of Antonelli, who was also being attacked by all who reproached him with replacing the nepotism of the popes with the nepotism of the secretary of state. The pope, however, judged Antonelli "without equal for the defense" and refused to part with his secretary, who, moreover, was conscious that he had no title to involve himself in the spiritual government of the Church and very carefully refrained from doing so. After 1870 Antonelli, who had advised the pontiff against leaving Rome, as some wished, successfully reorganized the new situation of the Holy See on solid financial bases.

Antonelli was severely criticized as a morally lax man, avid for money, who strove by authoritarian means to concentrate all power in his own hands, and did not hesitate to break those who opposed him. Although his concepts were lacking in breadth and his actions in grandeur, he possessed admirable qualities. He was diligent and competent in economic and administrative matters, energetic, invariably amiable, and master of himself. His clear, subtle mind permitted him to adapt himself to circumstances with dexterity and to find a ready solution to difficulties that arose daily. His defects and limitations were undeniable; yet he was a conscientious servant of Pius IX and managed affairs with great skill under the circumstances, whatever the exalted ultramontanes grouped around Monsignor de Merode may have thought.

Bibliography: M. ROSI in *Dizionario del Risorgimento nazionale*, ed. M. ROSI et al., 4 v. (Milan 1930–37) 2:85–87. P. RICHARD, *Dictionnaire d'histoire et de géographie ecclésiastiques*, ed. A. BAUDRILLART et al. (Paris 1912) 3:832–837. P. PIRRI, "Il cardinale Antonelli tra il mito e la storia," *Rivista di storia della Chiesa in Italia* 12 (1958) 81–120; ed., *Pio IX e Vittorio Emanuele dal loro carteggio privato*, 5 v. (Rome 1944–61). A. LODOLINI, "Un archivo segreto del cardinale Antonelli," *Studi romani* 1 (1953) 410–424, 510–520. A. OMODEO, *Rassegna storica del Risorgimento* 47 (1960) 319–324. A. M. GHISALBERTI, *Roma da Mazzini a Pio IX* (Milan 1958). F. ENGEL-JANOSI, *Österreich und der Vatikan, 1846–1918*, 2 v. (Graz 1958–60) v.1. *The Roman Question: Extracts from the Despatches of Odo Russell from Rome, 1858–1870*, ed. N. BLAKISTON (London 1962). M. GABRIELE, *Il carteggio Antonelli-Sacconi, 1858–1860*, 2 v. (Rome 1962). N. MIKO, *Das Ende des Kirchenstaates* v.2 (Vienna 1961). R. AUBERT, *Le Pontificat die Pie IX* (2d ed. Paris 1964). E. E. Y. HALES, *Pio Nono* (New York 1954).

[R. AUBERT]

ANTONIA OF FLORENCE, BL.

Poor Clare; d. Aquila, Italy, Feb. 29, 1472. As a young widow she entered the convent of Third Order sisters founded in Florence by ANGELINA OF MARSCIANO (1429), and later went on to Foligno. In 1432 she was made prioress at Aquila, an office she held for 13 years. Moved by the desire for a stricter rule of life, she consulted (St.) JOHN CAPISTRAN, and through his intercession was placed in charge of a cloister of POOR CLARES. She was an example of patience under the trials of long, painful illness and of family difficulties, caused by a spendthrift son and other relatives. Her cult was approved in 1847.

Feast: Feb. 28.

Bibliography: LÉON DE CLARY, *Lives of the Saints and Blessed of the Three Orders of St. Francis* 2 (Taunton, Eng. 1885–87). A. BUTLER, *The Lives of the Saints* 1:446–447.

[N. G. WOLF]

ANTONIĬ (ALEKSEĬ PAVLOVICH KHRAPOVITSKIĬ)

Outstanding metropolitan and controversial theologian of the Russian Orthodox Church; b. March 17, 1863; d. Karlovci, Yugoslavia, Aug. 10, 1936. He graduated from St. Petersburg Theological Academy, entered a monastery, and was ordained in 1885. He was a professor at St. Petersburg Academy and Kholm Seminary, and rector of theological academies in Moscow and Kazan and of St. Petersburg Seminary. Consecrated in 1897 and appointed bishop of Volhynia, Ukraine, in 1902, he suppressed remnants of the Ukrainian Catholic Church and national aspirations of the Ukrainian Orthodox Church.

He was archbishop of Kharkiv (1914–17) and in 1918 became metropolitan of Kiev. When the Ukraine won its independence, he was exiled to Buczacz because of his anti-Ukrainian activities. The Bolshevik occupation of the Ukraine forced him to flee to Yugoslavia, where he became head of the Russian Synod. He was strongly anti-Catholic and very radical in his dogmatic teachings, which caused conservative Orthodox theologians to accuse him of heresy. He wrote many ascetic and dogmatic works, the most controversial of which are *Dogma of Redemption* (Kharkiv 1917) and *Catechism* (Karlovci 1924).

Bibliography: *Opera*, 4 v. (St. Petersburg 1911; v.4, 2d ed. Kharkiv 1917). NIKON RKLITSKIĬ, *Biography of His Beatitude Antony Metropolitan of Kiev and Halych*, 10 v. (New York 1956—), in Russ. A. M. AMMANN, *Abriss der ostslawischen Kirchengeschichte* (Vienna 1950). M. JUGIE, *Theologia dogmatica christianorum orientalium ab ecclesia catholica dissidentium* v.1, 3–4. M. D'HERBIGNY and A. DEUBNER, *Evêques Russes en exil, 1918–1930* (Orientalia Christiana 21; Rome 1931).

[W. LENCYK]

ANTONINES (ANTONIANS)

Under this title are included several religious orders of the Eastern Churches that have taken as their guide and inspiration St. ANTHONY OF EGYPT. Anthony did not leave a written rule; his followers were united only by a common spirit and the observance of similar ascetic practices. What is known as the Rule of St. Anthony is of later origin and was published in Arabic (1646) by ABRAHAM ECCHELLENSIS and in Latin (1661) by Lukas Holste (Holstenius); it is based on the life of Anthony, his authentic and apocryphal writings, and a compilation known as the *Apophthegmata patrum.* The influence of Anthony over Oriental monachism is universally recognized, but the systematic application of his rule to a religious order dates only from 1695, when it was adopted by a group of Maronite monks. Only the first part of their monastic legislation was based on the Rule of St. Anthony; the second part was patterned according to the constitutions of the Order of St. Paul the First Hermit, a community founded in Hungary in 1250 (*see* HERMITS OF ST. PAUL). Following the occupation of Hungary by the Turks and the subsequent decline of the order, a thorough reform was made in the 17th century by means of new constitutions that were devised at Rome in 1643. These constitutions became the prototype not only for the Antonines, but also for other Oriental orders.

Lebanese Maronite Order of St. Anthony. Monasticism flourished among the Maronite people who lived in the neighborhood of the great monastery of St. Maro, located near the source of the Orontes River (*see* MARO OF

CYR, ST.). When the monks of St. Maro migrated to Lebanon, they were already accustomed to the cenobitic life, but they were forced, by lack of means for building monasteries, to return to a more heremitic form of monastic life. The valley called Qadisha, with its numerous natural caves, lent itself to this type of life and became for centuries the abode of holy hermits. At that time there were no explicit vows made in a juridical form. According to the traditional custom of the East, the embracing of the religious life was manifested by the taking of a religious habit and by the celebration of a special rite.

Patriarch Stephan Al-Douaihi (1671–1704), who had studied at Rome, introduced among the Maronite monks the Western system of religious congregations in order to unite the separate and independent monasteries. He began with three young men from Aleppo who, on Nov. 10, 1695, received from his hands the monastic habit. Soon a group of disciples gathered around them. In 1698 a first draft of constitutions was adopted along with the Rule of St. Anthony. The constitutions, approved by the patriarch in 1700, were later revised and approved by Clement XII in 1732.

The new order was known at first as the Aleppian congregation after the name of the city of the founders. This name was changed to that of Lebanese in 1706. At certain periods the Lebanese monks were known also as Baladites, that is, "natives," from the Arabic word *balad.* At first the contemplative life prevailed in the congregation, but in time the monks began to dedicate themselves to parish work and teaching. This new role was officially recognized by the Holy See in the motu proprio *Postquam apostolicis litteris* (1952), and on Dec. 16, 1955, the Lebanese Antonine congregation was declared a nonmonastic (active) order. Associated with the order is a branch for religious women, comprising five autonomous monasteries of ancient origin.

Aleppian Maronite Order of St. Anthony. Tensions that existed in the original Maronite congregation between the Aleppian and Lebanese (Baladite) factions were not resolved. At a meeting held at Louaizé, Lebanon, on April 1, 1758, the order split into two independent congregations, one called Aleppian, and the other Lebanese. The successive attempts of Rome to reconcile the two groups failed. Finally Clement XIV, in the brief *Ex iniuncto* (July 19, 1770), approved officially the split in the order. The Aleppian congregation retained the same constitutions and the same form of government as the Lebanese. It too was declared a nonmonastic order in 1955.

Maronite Antonine Order of St. Isaia. In 1700 the Maronite bishop of Aleppo, Gabriel Blouzawi, gathered some of the remaining independent monasteries, those that had not joined the Lebanese congregation, to form the Antonine Order of St. Isaia, named after the principal monastery, Mar Isaya. He gave them the Rule of St. Anthony and constitutions that were approved by Patriarch Al-Douaihi in 1703. Clement XII granted papal approval in the brief *Misericordiarum Pater* (Jan. 17, 1740). The constitutions and way of life are practically identical to those of the other Antonines, and, like them, the congregation of St. Isaia also was declared a nonmonastic order in 1955. The headquarters are located near Beirut. From the beginning there existed also a feminine branch of the order, dedicated to the contemplative life. In 1953 the religious women of the Antonine Order of St. Isaia were constituted as an independent congregation with an active apostolate.

Chaldean Antonines of St. Hormisdas. The ancient Chaldean monachism, which flourished in Persia from early Christian times until the invasion of the Mongols (12th century), became extinct at the beginning of the 19th century. Around that time a Catholic Chaldean merchant, Gabriel Dembo, founded the Chaldean Antonines. He embraced the monastic life in the novitiate of the Maronite Antonines in Lebanon. After returning to his own country (Iraq), he established a monastery on the ruins of the ancient monastery of Rabban Hormizd (7th century) near Alqosh in 1808. There he gathered a few followers to whom he gave the Rule of St. Anthony and constitutions borrowed from the Maronite Lebanese Antonines. These constitutions, with some modifications, were approved by Rome in 1830 and 1845. Dembo spent the rest of his life working for the conversion of the Assyrian Christians. He was assassinated by the pasha of Ravanduz in 1834. The Chaldean Antonines, are found principally in Iraq

Other Antonines. Several groups that no longer exist, some of them Oriental and others Latin, are included under the term Antonines.

Armenian Antonines. Four brothers, Armenian Catholics who lived in Aleppo, established a monastic institute in 1705 and founded the monastery of St. Salvator at Creim, near Beirut, Lebanon. An attempt to join their group to the MECHITARISTS of Venice failed, and the congregation adopted (1752) the Rule of St. Anthony after the manner of the Maronite Antonines. Clement XIII approved the constitutions in 1761 and transferred the novitiate to Rome. The monks never exceeded 60, and their number declined after they went into schism during the politico-religious troubles (1869–80) under the rule of the Armenian Patriarch and Cardinal Anthony Hassoun (1809–84). The former library of these Antonines is conserved in the Armenian institute at Bzommar, Lebanon.

Ethiopian-Coptic Antonines. Although there has never been a congregation of Antonines among the Ethio-

"St. Anthony Leaving His Monastery," painting by Sassetta, c. 1440.

pians of either the Monophysite or the Catholic tradition, there is a fictional "Order of St. Anthony" associated with the hospice San Stefano dei Mori in Vatican City. San Stefano was designated for the use of Ethiopian pilgrim monks by Sixtus IV in the 15th century. The so-called rule of the hospice dates from 1551, but it is only a set of regulations for the discipline of the house. In a brief of Clement XII (Jan. 15, 1731) the care of the hospice was handed over to the Coptic and Ethiopian monks of the "Order of St. Anthony," although no such order existed. Much later, in 1919, San Stefano dei Mori was converted into the Ethiopian College and placed under the direction of the Capuchins.

Antonines of the Latin Rite. The Antonine Hospitallers, or Canons Regular of St. Anthony of Vienne, began in France in 1095, and the Antonines of Flanders, founded in 1615, did not follow the Rule of St. Anthony, but rather that of St. Augustine. Neither group is extant.

See Also: MONASTICISM.

Bibliography: *Oreinte Cattolico* (Vatican City 1962) 560–565, 606–608. P. J. KHAIRALLAH, *Histoire résumée de l'ordre Antonin Maronite de la Congrégation de s. Isaie* (Beirut 1939). C. KARALEVSKIJ and F. TOURNEBIZE, *Dictionnaire d'histoire et de géographie ecclésiastiques,* ed. A. BAUDRILLART et al. (Paris 1912–) 3:861–873. R. JANIN and K. HOFMANN, *Lexikon für Theolo-*

St. Antoninus, bust in the Church of S. Maria Novella, Florence, Italy. (Alinari-Art Reference/Art Resource, NY)

gie und Kirche, ed. J. HOFER and K. RAHNER (Freiburg 1957–65) 1:676–677. H. HEIMBUCHER *Die Orden und Kongregationen der Katholischen Kirche* (Paderborn 1932–34) 1:67–76. V. ADVIELLLE, *Histoire de l'ordre hospitalier de s. Antoine* (Paris 1883).

[E. EL-HAYEK]

ANTONINUS, ST.

Archbishop of Florence, founder of the Convent of San Marco in that city, 15th century reformer, pastoral theologian, economist, sociologist, historian; b. Florence, March 1389; d. May 2, 1459.

Life. When but a delicate youth of 15 years, Antoninus Pierozzi was inspired by the preaching of Bl. John Dominici to apply for admission to the Dominican Order. For several years Dominici had been the idol of his native Florence and for 15 years the leader in Italy of the reform movement within his Order initiated by Bl. Raymond of Capua, Master General (1380–99) and former director of St. Catherine of Siena (d. 1380). Dominici accepted the frail youth a year later and sent him to Cortona for his novitiate. There Antoninus made profession in February 1406. In that same year he became the first religious to be assigned to a convent of strict observance, dedicated

to St. Dominic and erected by Dominici in Fiesole. In his formative years Antoninus was grievously troubled by the general corruption in the Church and society, but especially by the turbulent events in the closing years of the Western Schism. Dominici was called to Rome shortly after the election of Gregory XII (1406) to become cardinal archbishop of Ragusa. Then the friars at Fiesole lost their convent and fled to Foligno because they refused obedience to Alexander V elected in the pseudo-Council of Pisa (1409). In consequence of these disturbances, Antoninus had a teacher for but a short time and in logic only. He was dependent upon his own inclinations and industry in pursuing his studies. He was ordained at Cortona in 1413.

He quickly became prominent. He was prior at Cortona in 1418, at Fiesole in 1421 when the friars there recovered their convent, at Naples in 1428, and at the Convent of S. Maria sopra Minerva in Rome in 1430. After the election of Eugene IV (1431) Antoninus became auditor general of the Rota, a tribunal that in his day had jurisdiction over all ecclesiastical trials in Christendom and all civil cases in the Papal States. He was also vicar-general of Dominican convents of strict observance in Italy from 1432 to 1445. Since this office was under the immediate jurisdiction of the master general of the Order, it served a twofold purpose: it gave protection and sanction to the reform, and it preserved the unity of the Order.

Antoninus returned to Florence in 1436 or 1437, and with the aid of the despotic but munificent Cosimo di Medici, he established the Convent of San Marco. Even after the lapse of centuries, San Marco is one of the artistic glories of Florence. As theologian, Antoninus took part in the Council of Florence (1439), and as prior conjointly of San Marco's and of San Domenico's in Fiesole, he was host to other Dominican theologians summoned to the council by Eugene IV. As a token of esteem, the pope with the whole college of cardinals assisted at the consecration of the Church of San Marco in 1443. The following year the famed library of San Marco was made available to scholars. It was probably the first public library in Europe.

The austere simplicity of the buildings, illuminated by the delicate frescoes of Bl. Fra Angelico in the convent, is a fitting monument to the spirit of Antoninus and his influence on Florentine society. He had no interest in the new learning, but by word and example he raised the hearts of his brethren to the heights of the Dominican ideal. The office of preaching raised him above and beyond the narrow horizons of those immersed in the study of ancient pagan lore. He deserved to be called "Antoninus the Counselor," for he was sought by all classes as confessor and director of souls. Though a simple friar, he was commissioned by Eugene IV to supervise the creation of societies to bring children together for instruction in Christian doctrine. His compassion for the degraded poor, for the victims of political strife, of the forces of nature, of plague, and of pestilence, inspired him to form an association of charitable citizens, known as the *Buonomini di San Martino*. It was somewhat similar to the Society of St. Vincent de Paul in modern times but had a more extensive field of action. It is still in existence.

Antoninus's nomination by Eugene IV to the archiepiscopal See of Florence brought joy to his native city. He was consecrated in the Church of San Domenico in Fiesole on March 12, 1446, and took possession of his see the next day in utmost simplicity. From the episcopal palace he removed all that smacked of luxury and pomp, for he was determined to continue living as a poor friar. The revenues of his see were spent upon the poor. By his visitation of parishes, he remedied abuses of long standing: he insisted upon the preaching of the Gospel, services in the churches, ministrations to the faithful, observance of Canon Law. He had the churches repaired and made worthy of divine worship. His reputation for prudence and justice made him arbiter in party strife, and his tact brought him papal commissions to institute reforms in religious communities canonically exempt from his jurisdiction.

His pastoral labors were frequently interrupted. He was summoned to Rome by Eugene IV to take part in the negotiations terminating in the Concordat of Princes, and he assisted at the deathbed of that pontiff. In the conclave that followed, in which the humanist Tommaso Parentucelli was elected, Antoninus received several votes. The new pope, Nicholas V, desired to retain him in the Roman Curia, but Antoninus was able to evade what might have led to the cardinalate. He headed the Florentine embassies to the papal court of Calixtus III and Pius II, and by the latter pontiff he was appointed to serve on the committee of cardinals charged with the proposed reform of the Roman Court. When Antoninus died, Pius II, then in the vicinity, came to Florence to preside at the obsequies. His native city gave testimony of the veneration in which he was held by placing his statue in her exclusive hall of fame—the only statue of a priest in the Uffizi Palace.

Writings. Reform had been the keynote of his life and labors; it was also the motive that inspired him to write. He humbly claimed to be only a compiler, not an author; yet he was proclaimed to be among the Doctors of the Church in the bull of his canonization (1523), though the title has never been conferred upon him.

His first work, which really consists of three distinct treatises, has been called the *Confessionale* (1472, 1473,

1475). The 102 incunabula editions attest its importance and practicality. The *Omnium mortalium cura* (1475), written in Italian to help the faithful in approaching the tribunal of Penance, was a guide to Christian living. The *Defecerunt* (1473) and the *Curam illius habe* (1472) constituted manuals for priests in the administration of the Sacrament of Penance.

The *Summa Theologica* (1477), more properly called the *Summa Moralis,* is the work upon which his theological fame chiefly rests. There were no less than 20 complete editions in four large folio volumes, excluding the reprint in 1958 of the 1740 Verona edition. The first part, reflecting the doctrine of St. Thomas Aquinas, treats of the soul and its faculties, the passions, sin, law; the second deals with the various kinds of sin; the third is concerned with the different states and professions in life whether social, political, religious, or ecclesiastical; and it has added treatises on the pope, the councils, and censures. The fourth part is devoted to the cardinal and theological virtues and to the gifts of the Holy Spirit. This *Summa* is probably the first—certainly the most comprehensive—treatment from a practical point of view of Christian ethics, asceticism, and sociology in the Middle Ages. It gives to Antoninus the place of honor in moral theology between St. Thomas and St. Alphonsus Ligouri.

The *Chronicon* (1440–59)—an episodical history of the world in three folio volumes—was designed to illustrate from the past how men should live in this world. It is filled with borrowings from the Scriptures, lives of the saints, extracts from the writings of the Fathers and Doctors of the Church, and decrees of popes and councils—the whole forming a practical library for preachers and pastors of souls.

The *Sermones* of Antoninus remain unpublished. The *Opera a ben vivere,* a treatise on the Christian life, was not printed until 1858.

Feast: May 10.

Bibliography: R. MORÇAY, *Saint Antonin, fondateur du Couvent de Saint-Marc, archevêque de Florence, 1389–1459* (Paris 1914). B. JARRETT, *S. Antonino and Medieval Economics* (St. Louis 1914). J. B. WALKER, *The "Chronicles" of Saint Antoninus: A Study in Historiography* (CUA Stud. in Med. Hist. 6; Washington 1933). W. T. GAUGHAN, *Social Theories of Saint Antoninus from His Summa Theologica* (CUA Stud. in Sociol. 35; Washington 1951). R. DE ROOVER, *San Bernardino of Siena and Sant'Antonino of Florence; the Two Great Economic Thinkers of the Middle Ages* (Boston 1967). G. AGRESTI, *L'arcivescovo dei ronzini: vita di S. Antonino da Firenze* (Genoa 1989). E. MAURRI, *Un fiorentino tra Medioevo e Rinascimento: Sant'Antonino* (Turin 1989). P. F. HOWARD, *Beyond the Written Word: Preaching and Theology in the Florence of Archbishop Antoninus* (Florence 1995).

[J. B. WALKER]

ANTONIUS ANDREAS

Franciscan scholastic, known as *Doctor dulcifluus* and *Scotellus;* b. Tauste, Saragossa, *c.* 1280; d. *c.* 1320. A member of the province of Aragon, Antonius studied at the newly founded University of Lérida, then under DUNS SCOTUS at Paris. An ardent advocate of the Subtle Doctor, he promulgated his master's teaching in numerous writings, notably commentaries. Although he wrote a commentary on the *Sentences* (ed. Venice 1572), it is not certain that he ever became a master in theology. Nevertheless, his works were widely read and frequently printed in the 15th and 16th centuries. Although not an original thinker, he substantially influenced the development of SCOTISM. The *Quaestiones de anima* commonly attributed to Scotus were probably written by him. Among his better-known writings are *Tractatus formalitatum ad mentem Scoti* (ed. Padua 1475); *Quaestiones super libros 12 metaphysicae* (ed. Venice *c.* 1475); *Expositio in libros metaphysicae* (ed. Venice 1482); *De tribus principiis rerum naturalium* (ed. Padua 1475); *Commentaria in artem veterem* (ed. Bologna 1481); and the *Compendiosum principium in libros sententiarum* (ed. Strassburg 1495), formerly attributed to St. Bonaventure.

Bibliography: É. GILSON, *History of Christian Philosophy in the Middle Ages* (New York 1955) 466, 765, 768. M. BIHL, *Dictionnaire d'histoire et de géographie ecclésiastiques*, ed. A. BAUDRILLART, et al. (Paris 1912–). 2:1633–34. H. HURTER, *Nomenclator literarius theologiae catholicae* (Innsbruck 1926) 2:466–467. L. AMORÓS, *Lexikon für Theologie und Kirche*, ed. J. HOFER and K. RAHNER (Freiberg 1957–65) 1:671–672. T. CARRERAS ARTAU, *Historia de la filosofia española*, v.2 (Madrid 1943) 458–571. M. DE BARCELONA in *Criterion* 5 (1929) 321–346.

[M. J. GRAJEWSKI]

ANTONIUS DE BUTRIO

Lay canonist, decretalist, and teacher; b. Butrio, near Bologna, 1338; d. Bologna, Oct. 4, 1408. He received his degrees in civil law (1384) and canon law (1387) in Bologna. He periodically taught in Bologna, Florence, Ferrara, and Perugia. In 1407 he was sent by Gregory XII to Marseilles to negotiate the end of the schism with Benedict XIII. After helping bring about the treaty of April 21, 1407, he returned to Bologna where he died. His works, which were noted for their practicality and wide diffusion, included *Commentaria in quinque libris Decretalium* (2 v. Rome 1473, 1474; Milan 1488, etc.), *Commentaria in Sextum* (Venice 1479, 1575), *Consilia* (Rome 1472, 1744; Pavia 1492; Venice 1493, etc.). He also produced other works designed to remedy the evils in the Church and to bring about Christian unity.

Bibliography: A. AMANIEU, *Dictionnaire de droit canonique*, ed. R. NAZ, 7 v. (Paris 1935–65) 1:630–631. H. HURTER, *Nomenclator literarius theologiae catholicae*, 5 v. in 6 (3rd ed. Innsbruck 1903–13) 2: 771–772. A. VAN HOVE, *Commentarium Lovaniense in Codicem iuris canonici* (Mechlin 1945) 1:496–497. J. G. VON SCHULTE, *Die Geschichte der Quellen und der Literatur des kanonischen Rechts* (Stuttgart 1875–80, repr. Graz 1956) 2:289–294.

[H. A. LARROQUE]

ANTWERP

Capital of Antwerp province, Belgium, on the Schelde River, 55 miles from the North Sea. It revived as a port when France reopened the Schelde to navigation in 1795, which had been closed since the Peace of WESTPHALIA (1648). The Diocese of Antwerp (created 1559, suppressed 1801–1961), suffragan to Mechelen-Brussels, is 985 square miles in area.

History. Christianity was first preached there by Saints ELIGIUS (647), AMANDUS (650) and WILLIBRORD (697 and after). From the 7th to the 11th centuries there was a parish inside the bourg of Antwerp, which was part of the See of CAMBRAI. The chapter of canons moved to the Church of Our Lady and left St. Michael Church, Antwerp's first church, to St. NORBERT'S PREMONSTRATENSIANS (1124).

In the 13th century the port of Antwerp began to develop; but annexation by the county of Flanders, which favored the port of Bruges, hampered its growth. Only in the late 15th century did Antwerp develop commercially to become the largest Atlantic port and the most important banking center of Europe in the 16th century. New parishes were added: St. Willibrord (1441), St. George (1477), St. Walburga and St. James (1477–79), and St. Andrew (1529).

This international commercial center, with an important German colony, was the first Lutheran center in the Low Countries. The first Protestants to be burned at the stake in the Low Countries were two Augustinians of Antwerp (1523). In vain did Charles V issue condemnations of heretics; Antwerp, concerned only with commercial prosperity, was quite tolerant in religion and invariably moderated governmental intervention in religious matters and the enforcement of Charles' condemnations. After Lutherans and Anabaptists, Calvinists became the important religious group in Antwerp (from 1560).

In 1559 Paul IV made Antwerp a see suffragan to Mechelen; but Antwerp, not wishing an Inquisitor bishop inside its walls, sent an embassy to Philip II in Madrid and the installation of a bishop was suspended *sine die*. Only under the duke of Alva could the first bishop obtain his see (1570). After the Spanish Fury, which destroyed 600 houses and massacred thousands of people in Antwerp (1576), Protestants held the city until they were expelled by Alexander Farnese (1585). The city of 100,000 (14,000 foreigners) was cut off from the sea by the Sea Beggars for more than 200 years and not until the 19th century did Antwerp revive as a world port. Its first bishops, F. Sonnius (1570–76), L. Torrentius (1586–95) and J. Miraeus (1603–11), with the aid of Jesuits and Capuchins especially, obtained the triumph of the Catholic Reformation. Its last bishop, C. F. Nelis (1785–98), opposed JOSEPHINISM. The CONCORDAT OF 1801 suppressed the see, which was not restored until 1961.

Art. Antwerp was a center of famous painters. In the 16th century Quinten Massys and the Brueghels prepared the way for the great school of Peter Paul Rubens, which included Anthony Van Dyck, Caspar de Crayer, Jacob Jordaens, Adriaen Brouwer and others, almost all of whom endowed churches with magnificent religious paintings. The Cathedral of Our Lady (1352–1606), with seven naves, is 384 feet long and 213 feet wide and has a tower 403 feet high; it is the largest church in Belgium. Although it was badly damaged by iconoclasts in 1566, it still has famous paintings by Rubens (*Crucifixion, Descent from the Cross, the Assumption*) and statues by Artus Quellinus (1609–68). St. James Church (1491–1656), with many artistic masterpieces, and St. Paul's Church (1533–1621), with paintings by Rubens, Jordaens and David Teniers (1582–1649), are Gothic. The Jesuit St. Charles, a famous baroque church with many paintings by Rubens, was damaged in a fire in 1718. The hôtel de ville by Cornelius Floris de Vriendt stands on one side of the main square, which is bordered by other admirable buildings dating from the 16th century.

Monasteries. The Norbertine Abbey of St. Michael (1124), a double monastery for 30 years, was ruined by iconoclasts (1566, 1576) but flourished under J. C. Van der Sterre (d. 1652); confiscated by JOSEPH II in 1789 and suppressed in 1796, it was sold and demolished in 1831. It founded other famous abbeys, such as TONGERLOO (*c.* 1130) and Averbode (1134–35). Antwerp also had a Victorine priory (Sainte-Margrietendal), a charterhouse for men (Sainte-Cathérine-au-Mont-Sinaï, 1320), the Cistercian Peeter-Pots or St. Salvator (1446, an abbey in 1652), a BEGUINE HOUSE (*c.* 1250), and other religious houses. The BOLLANDIST editors of the *Acta Sanctorum* lived in Antwerp from *c.* 1650 until the suppression of the Jesuits in 1773.

Bibliography: P. F. X. DE RAM, *Synopsis actorum eccelesiae Antverpiensis* (Brussels 1856); *Synodicum belgicum*, 3 (Louvain 1858). J. DE WIT, *De kerken van Antwerpen* (Antwerp 1910). É. DE MOREAU, *Dictionnaire d'histoire et de géographie ecclésiastiques,* ed. A. BAUDRILLART et al., (Paris 1912–) 3:885–908; *Histoire de l'Église en Belgique,* 5 v. (Brussels 1945–52; 2 suppl.). J. A. GORIS, *Lof van Antwerpen* (Brussels 1940). A. VAN DE VELDE, *Antwerpen de Stoute* (Bruges 1942). F. PRIMS, *Antwerpen door de eeuwen heen* (Antwerp 1951); *Antwerpen in de XVIIIe eeuw* (Antwerp 1951); *Bouwstoffen voor de geschiedenis van Antwerpen in de nouveaux diocèses aux Pays-Bas, 1559–1570* (Brussels 1966). *XIXe eeuw* (Antwerp 1964). M. DIERICKX, *L'Érection des, Annuario Pontificio* (1965) 34.

[M. DIERICKX]

Cathedral of Antwerp. (©Vanni Archive/CORBIS)

ANUNCIACIÓN, DOMINGO DE LA

Dominican missionary and explorer; b. Fuente-Ojejuna (Vejuna), Estremadura, Spain, 1510; d. Mexico City, 1591. He was baptized Juan de Paz. His father, Ferdinando de Ecija, had five other sons and three daughters. In 1528 Juan and Alonso, his oldest brother, went to Mexico. Juan entered the Dominican Order in 1531 or 1532. He received a brief education in the Dominican convent and was ordained in 1534, sometime before October, by Julian Garcés, the Dominican bishop of Tlaxcala. He then apparently did missionary work among the Amerindians, probably at Tepetloaxtac, and learned native dialects. As a result, in 1544 or 1545 he wrote a *Doctrina Cristiana* for use in native catechetic work. (*See*

CATECHISMS IN COLONIAL SPANISH AMERICA.) The history of his province, begun by Andrés de Moguer, was continued by Domingo de la Anunciación down to 1580, and later completed by DÁVILA Y PADILLA. During a number of epidemics among the indigenous tribes, particularly in 1545 and again in 1577, Fray Domingo worked among the sick and dying. This may help to explain the fact that over 100,000 baptisms are attributed to him. He accompanied Governor Tristán de Luna y Arellano on the expedition of 1559–61 to the port of Ochuse (Pensacola Bay) and northwest Florida. He went out with scouting parties which, in search of food, explored parts of Alabama. The hardships he underwent on these expeditions undermined his health, but it improved after his return to Mexico. The last years of his life were spent in missionary work in Mexico.

Bibliography: V. F. O'DANIEL, *Dominicans in Early Florida* (New York 1930). H. I. PRIESTLEY, ed. and tr., *The Luna Papers,* 2 v. (De Land Fla., 1928).

[A. B. NIESER]

ANXIETY

An emotional state of fearfulness or of uneasiness. The concept has recurred throughout the history of philosophy but has taken on special meaning in existentialist thought; it has been discussed also in traditional psychology, and here too has received new emphasis owing to developments in psychiatry. This article is thus divided into two parts; the first considers anxiety in philosophy; the second, anxiety in psychiatry.

Anxiety in Philosophy. The notions of anxiety, fear, and dread are as old as human nature itself. Not only did Homer and Vergil dramatize them in the lives of their heroes, but both Plato and Aristotle gave their genius to an analysis of their basic meanings. Summarizing what the important philosophers and theologians had written, St. THOMAS AQUINAS defines FEAR as the sadness that arises in man from his awareness of an approaching misfortune, evil, or suffering (*see* APPETITE). But for modern thought, especially that of the existential variety, fear, anxiety, and dread have taken on added significance.

Kierkegaard. S. A. KIERKEGAARD is the source of this contemporary interest. In his work *The Concept of Dread,* Kierkegaard distinguishes between ordinary fear and dread (the usual translation of his term *Angst*). The various fears of men have determinate and specifiable objects, whereas dread is an apprehension that, though very real, is an anxiety about "nothing in particular," since one cannot indicate just what it is that is making him so profoundly uneasy and alarmed. What is at the root of this deep-seated uneasiness, according to Kierkegaard, is the note of possibility that is inherent in human FREEDOM. One is in the grip of dread because he is beginning to appreciate the awesome expanse of the POSSIBILITY that is the meaning of human freedom. It is beginning to dawn on him that freedom entails the possibility of willing an infinity of things in an infinity of ways, and he is both fascinated and horrified at the prospect. Hence Kierkegaard sees dread as an antipathetic sympathy in relation to the good and as sympathetic antipathy as regards evil. In either case the individual undergoes a dialectic of contrary emotions, for he loves the possibility of freedom and yet flees from it. This profound uneasiness, this elemental disquietude at the alarming possibility of "being able" is what Kierkegaard calls dread.

Since dread arises from the awareness of freedom, it is the mark of a man who is beginning to exist as a true human being. In the past it has manifested itself in the thoughtful Greek as dread of fate; in the observant Jew it is a dread of guilt before the Law; in the Christian context it can appear as the dread of sin. It is this dread that, according to Kierkegaard, is the only true way to faith in Christ. But dread in any case is the sign of the awakening spirit in man.

Heidegger. Aware of Kierkegaard's distinction between fear and dread, M. HEIDEGGER in his *Being and Time* carries on the analysis, but he uses the term dread or anxiety (both are used in translating his term *Angst*) with a somewhat different meaning (*see* EXISTENTIALISM). Fear again designates the feeling that is aroused by the approach of a determinate threatening object, and anxiety still signifies an apprehensiveness brought about by an object that is indeterminate, indefinite, and "nothing in particular." But this "nothing in particular" is not so much the possibility that is inherent in freedom as it is the possibility of a human being to become himself in all his unique individuality, that is, the possibility to become his true and authentic self. Man, or *Dasein* as he is called by Heidegger, easily becomes involved in a mode of existence that, although less demanding of him, is not truly his own. This happens when *Dasein,* forgetting its own individuality and selfhood, allows itself to become absorbed into the many, into "the crowd." Accepting the judgment of "they say" and conforming all its activity to the pattern of "they all do," *Dasein* has not yet achieved its true selfhood; anxiety can be the means by which this might be attained.

While in anxiety, *Dasein* feels threatened, not in any particular and relative facet of its existence as happens in fear, but in the very roots of its being, its very possibility of being. Because *Dasein* has been existing in an inauthentic mode, it has been fleeing from its innermost self to find shelter in "the many." But while in the state of anxiety, this inauthentic existence begins to disintegrate. *Dasein* can find no help in the various entities in the world that until now have absorbed its attention, nor can it receive support in the clichés of the "they say." *Dasein* is thus thrown back upon its own resources. For the first time it is face to face with itself; it can recognize itself in its own unique individuality; it can now see that it must depend upon itself.

Anxiety thus opens up to a man the possibility of becoming what he should be; for it takes away all the extrinsic props on which he has been leaning. *Dasein* can now become really free; for it can turn to its innermost, or in Heidegger's terms, its "ownmost" possibility; the possibility of becoming its own self. This possibility of becoming his authentic self means that man must choose himself in all his individualized being. As in Kierkegaard, so in Heidegger, anxiety or dread can bring man to his true being; for it makes man aware of his freedom, which is his only authentic existence.

Sartre and Others. In this question as in many others, J. P. SARTRE has been greatly influenced by Heidegger. Sartre teaches that man's existence becomes truly human only when he freely begins to make himself the man he has freely decided to become; for Sartre maintains that each man forms his own essence by the morality he pursues. Since there is no God, in Sartre's opinion, he insists that there are no objective standards of morality, so that each individual man becomes the supreme arbiter of values. This total and complete responsibility for creating goods and values brings with it the feeling of anguish (*angoisse*). A man can run away from this anguish or try to conceal it, but the existential man, the man of good faith, is the man who recognizes that anguish is the very quality of human freedom. Sartre's work *Being and Nothingness* examines in great detail the meaning and responsibility of human freedom, and his many plays are concerned with portrayals of men either accepting or shirking the anguish of freedom's responsibility. In all his writings Sartre makes it clear that though the anguish of responsibility is burdensome, it is the crowning point of human existence; for freedom means that each man is the supreme legislator of morality—man is the being whose existence is to make his own essence.

Similar to Sartre's position is that of the artists of the nonobjective school, the authors of the literature of despair, and the dramatists of the theater of the absurd, all of whom depict man as struggling in anguish and dread to grasp at some semblance of freedom in a world that has no God, is without any ultimate truth and lacks any objective moral standard (*see* ABSURDITY).

The concept of dread has thus taken a full and complete turn in its meaning. Kierkegaard saw in it a fruitful theme that could recall men to a rich existence lived in the presence of God thanks to their faith in Christ. Because they lack belief in Christ, many contemporary thinkers use the concept to remind men of the agony of existence in a world from which God is absent.

Bibliography: F. BERTHOLD, *The Fear of God: The Role of Anxiety in Contemporary Thought* (New York 1959). M. HEIDEGGER, *Being and Time,* tr. J. MACQUARRIE and E. ROBINSON (New York 1962). S. KIERKEGAARD, *The Concept of Dread,* tr. W. LOWRIE (Princeton 1944). J. P. SARTRE, *Being and Nothingness,* tr. H. E. BARNES (New York 1956); *Existentialism and Humanism,* tr. P. MAIRET (London 1948).

[V. M. MARTIN]

APAMEA

Apamea is the name of several ancient cities. Modern Mudanya was once the bishopric of Apamea in Bithynia originally called Myrleia and located in southeast Propontis on the Sea of Marmara. The city was founded by colonists from Colophon, and taken by Philip V of Macedonia (221–179 B.C.) and given to Prusias I of Bithynia (*c.* 230–183 B.C.), who changed its name to Apamea in honor of his wife. Julius Caesar called it colonia Julia Concordia Augusta Apamea. There were many Christians in Bithynia in the early 2nd century as a letter of Pliny the Younger (A.D. 62–113) to Trajan proves; but there is little information on the early bishops of Apamea. It was a suffragan see of Nicomedia; but by 536 it had become a metropolitan see. Since the middle of the 14th century it has been only a titular see.

In Phrygia, Apamea is known to have had a bishop during the 4th or 5th century; but the exact site is not known, and it is not mentioned in the Byzantine lists of bishoprics.

Apamea in Pisidia is known from the ruins found near modern Dinar at the source of the Maeander River. The original city, built on a hill, was called Kelainai. At the foot of this hill the Syrian King Antiochus III (223–187 B.C.) built a new town and gave it the name of his mother, Apamea. It was known in history as Apamea ad Meandrum, Apamea Kelainai, and Apamea of the Ark (Cibotus), since legend made it the landing site of Noah's ark. After Ephesus, it was the most renowned see in Asia Minor. Under the Romans it was a trade center, but it was destroyed in the 11th century by the Seljuk Turks.

Apamea, metropolitan see in Syria, was first called Pharnake, and then Pella by the Macedonians. Seleucus I Nicator named it Apamea for his wife. It was sacked under the Persian Chosroes II in 611 and, though rebuilt, was destroyed in an earthquake in 1152. Its ruins can be

541

seen near modern Qal'at al-Mudiq northeast of Hama. It is possible that Apamea in Syria had a bishop in apostolic times. Under Theodosius II (408–450) it was a metropolitan see that disappeared under Arab occupation after 650. Tancred captured it in 1111 and erected a Latin archbishopric that continued in existence till 1238; since then it has served as a titular archbishopric.

Bibliography: R. JANIN, *Dictionnaire d'histoire et de géographie ecclésiastique,* ed. A. BAUDRILLART et al. (Paris 1912–) 3:916–920. R. NORTH, *Lexikon für Theologie und Kirche,* ed. J. HOFER and K. RAHNER, 10 v. (2d, new ed. Freiburg 1957–65) suppl., *Das Zweite Vatikanische Konzil: Dokumente und Kommentare* 1:684. W. M. RAMSAY, *Cities and Bishoprics of Phrygia,* 2 v. (Oxford 1895–97) 2:396–483. V. SCHULTZE, *Altchristliche Städte* 4 v. (Leipzig 1913–37) 2.1:450–461. R. DUSSAUD, *Topographie de la Syrie* (Paris 1927) 194–198. F. MAYENCE, *L'Antiquite classique* 1 (1932) 233–242; 4 (1935) 199–204; 5 (1936) 405–411.

[A. NEUWIRTH]

APARICIO, SEBASTIÁN DE, BL.

Pioneer colonist in New Spain; b. Gudiña, Galicia, Spain, Jan. 20, 1502; d. Puebla, Mexico, Feb. 25, 1600. The son of poor peasants, Sebastián de Aparicio worked as a field hand during his adolescent years. In 1533 he sailed to Mexico and established his residence in Puebla de los Angeles. He worked there as a farmer, a road builder, and a trainer of young bulls, and he taught all those trades to the Indians. In 1542 he started the construction of the highway that later linked Mexico City and Zacatecas. He was married twice, but neither marriage was consummated. When his second wife died, he sold all his possessions and gave the proceeds to the poor.

At the age of 72 he received the friar's habit at the convent of San Francisco in Mexico City. He made his profession in 1575 and was assigned by his superiors to procure the daily bread by asking for charity at various convents. He carried out this task, a burdensome one for his old age, with great efficiency. He was noted for his extraordinary health and strong will; his humility and charity were outstanding. He was assigned to serve at the Franciscan house of studies in the convent of Puebla, and for 20 consecutive years he provided it with all the needed material goods. In like manner, he gave extensive help to all sorts of poor and needy people. Granted the grace to work miracles, he performed so many toward the end of his life that the bishop of Puebla, Diego Romano, determined to begin at once the canonical process for his beatification. Despite the fact that his miracles continued after his death, the process lasted for two centuries; his two marriages were among the main causes for the delay. Finally he was solemnly beatified by PIUS VI on May 17, 1787.

Feast: Feb. 25.

Bibliography: E. ESCOBAR, *Vida del B. Sebastián de Aparicio* (Mexico City 1958). C. ESPINOSA, *Fray Sebastián de Aparicio* (Mexico City 1959). B. SÁNCHEZ PAREJO, *Vida y milagros del glorioso confesor de Cristo, el Padre Fray Sebastián de Aparicio, fraile lego de la Orden de San Francisco, de la Regular Observancia,* ed. F. DE J. CHAUVET (Mexico 1965). G. CALVO MORALEJO, *Emigrante . . .* (Madrid 1973). J. GALLEGO FERNÁNDEZ, *Beato Sebastián de Aparicio . . .* (Orense 1974).

[F. DE J. CHAUVET]

APER OF TOUL, ST.

Also called Aprus, Apre, Epvre, Evre, bishop; b. Trancault, Diocese of Troyes, in the fifth century; d. *c.* 507. Aper was the seventh bishop of Toul. A late, formalized vita gives his birthplace and states that he served seven years as bishop. The only positive information furnished by this life (aside from the account of his miraculous liberation of three prisoners of the common law of Chalon-sur-Saône) is his construction of a basilica in honor of St. Maurice at the gates of Toul. Aper was buried in this basilica, which bore his name as early as 626 or 627 and which later became famous as the Abbey of Saint-Aper. The cult of the bishop is widespread in the ancient See of Toul and in several neighboring dioceses.

Feast: Sept. 15.

Bibliography: *Bibliotheca hagiograpica latina antiquae et mediae aetatis* (Brussels 1898–1901) 1:616–618. *Acta Sanctorum* Sept. 5:55–79. *Monumenta Germaniae Historica: Scriptores* 4: 515–520. E. MARTIN, *Histoire des diocèses de Toul, de Nancy et de Saint-Dié,* 3 v. (Nancy 1900–03) v.1. L. DUCHESNE, *Fastes épiscopaux de l'ancienne Gaule* (Paris 1907–15) 3:62.

[J. CHOUX]

APHRAATES

The earliest-known Christian writer in Persia; fl. first half of the 4th century. He was an ascetic and high-ranking cleric, but it is not clear whether he was a bishop. Manuscripts of the 5th and 6th centuries preserve 23 of his sermons or homilies, the first 10 composed in 337, the following 12 in 344, the last in 345, at the beginning of the persecution of Sapor II. The homilies are preceded by a letter falsely ascribed to Gregory the Illuminator.

Sermons 1 to 10 are hortatory and ascetical in tone and content: 1, on faith, contains an ancient Trinitarian creed; 2 to 4 deal with charity, fasting, and prayer; 5, written when war was imminent, hopes subtly for Roman victory in the interests of Christianity; 6 to 10 cover Christian perfection, Penance (against rigorism in forgiving sins), resurrection of the dead, humility, and the shepherds of souls. The remainder are frequently polemics against the Jews, who were numerous and learned in Northern Mesopotamia, and treat of circumcision, Easter, the Sabbath, distinction of foods, Gentiles supplanting the chosen people, Jesus' divine sonship, virginity, impossibility of restoring the kingdom of the Jews, and the saving blessing that lay hidden on the vine of Israel and came to flower in the Gentiles. Sermon 14 castigates clerical morals; 20 is concerned with the poor and needy; 21, with impending persecution; 22, with the last things.

Doctrinal elements in Aphraates include a profession of the Trinity, salvation through Christ-God, who invaded Sheol and conquered the devil in his own domain, and the Real Presence. His works bear no trace of Hellenistic influence; rather, he reveals a mentality discoverable in contemporary rabbinic literature and Judeo-Christian thought. His grasp of Scripture is remarkable, his use of it felicitous, especially in his constant recourse to the Old Testament, which he regards as intimately linked to the New. His theology, while genuinely Christian, is quite primitive; the Bible may well have been his only written source.

Bibliography: J. PARISOT, ed., *Demonstrationes* (*Patrologia syriaca,* ed. R. GRAFFIN et al., 1–2; 1894–1907). I. ORTIZ DE URBINA, *Patrologia syriaca,* 43–47, with bibliog. E. J. DUNCAN, *Baptism in the Demonstrations of Aphraates, the Persian Sage* (Washington 1945). A. VÖÖBUS, "Methodologisches zum Studium der Anweisungen Aphrahats," *Oriens Christianus* 46 (Leipzig-Wiesbaden 1962) 25–32. E. BECK, "Symbolum-Mysterium bei Aphraat und Ephräm," *ibid.* 42 (1958) 19–40.

[I. ORTIZ DE URBINA]

APOCALYPSE, ICONOGRAPHY OF

The Apocalypse of St. John the Apostle, now commonly known as the Book of REVELATION, has been a rich source of subjects for art, especially in the early Christian and medieval periods. The abundant symbolism has yielded, through commentary and interpretation, such major themes as the Christ in Majesty (*Majestas Domini*) and the Adoration of the Lamb, in addition to a large number of other figural subjects. Verse by verse, the Apocalypse is one of the most thoroughly illustrated books of the Bible.

Early Christian. The visions of the Apocalypse appeared on the triumphal arches of the basilicas of Rome to exalt the triumph of Christ and His Church after the persecutions (432–440, S. Maria Maggiore). The theophany of the adoration of the Lamb by the 24 Elders was represented (5th-century mosaic, St. Paul-Outside-the-Walls), as well as that of the Lamb enthroned between the seven lamps "which are the seven Spirits of God" (Rv 4.5). These important themes were repeated in Caro-

lingian illumination (the Elders in the Evangeliary of St. Médard of Soissons and the Codex aureus of 870) and in later periods of Christian art. The Venerable Bede tells in the *Lives of the Abbots* (ch. 6) that Benedict Biscop brought back from Rome images from the Apocalypse of St. John for the decoration of the abbey church of St. Peter at Wearmouth. These images were copies made after Roman frescoes.

Early Medieval. In North Africa the visions of St. John found early commentators, such as Tertullian and St. Cyprian. The enthusiasm for the Apocalypse, rendered more pathetic by the persecutions of the Christians under the Vandal occupation, reached Visigothic Spain. There it became sanctioned by the 17th canon of the Council of Toledo (633). The 12 books of commentaries on the Apocalypse written by Beatus of Liébana (d. 798) were recopied until the 15th century. Twenty-four manuscripts of the illustrated text still bear witness to their fame (MSS 429 and 644; Pierpont Morgan Library, New York City). Three capitals in the church of St. Mary at Fleury were inspired by Spanish models in an illuminated Beatus commentary. They show the Son of Man in the midst of the seven candlesticks, the Four Horsemen, and the Dragon put in chains and thrust down to the abyss.

Romanesque. The influences of the Beatus manuscripts is detectible on Romanesque sculpture of southern France. In the tympanum of the porch of St. Peter at Moissac, the 24 Elders raise their crowned heads toward the vision of a colossal Christ. He is crowned (Rv 12.10) and enthroned amidst a complex pattern of the Four Animals and two six-winged Seraphs. The tympanum of Moissac represents essentially the diffusion of the *Majestas Domini*. The theopathy of the *Majestas*, a theme first created for the decoration of the apses, was transferred in the 11th century to the front of the churches, as a sign of holiness and salvation. The façade of the church, being turned toward the setting sun, designated the place where the assize of the Last Judgement was anticipated.

As a revival of the Carolingian style within a Romanesque environment, an outstanding series of frescoes was painted at the end of the 11th century in the porch under the western tower of the church of Saint-Savin-sur-Gartempe, accompanied by the Apostles and adored by angels, who bend in the attitude of the proskynesis. Twelve scenes encompass the *Majestas*, illustrating: the swarm of locusts appearing like battle horses (Rv 9.7); the release of the four angels imprisoned by the Euphrates (9:14–15); the Woman attacked by the Dragon; the war fought by Michael and the Angels against the Dragon (12); and the new Jerusalem sent down by God from heaven, clothed like a bride adorned to meet her husband (21.2).

In the *Hortus Deliciarum* of Herrade de Landsberg (*c.* 1180) we find the unique representation of God wiping away the tears from the eyes of His own people and emphasis laid on the deeds of antichrist in nine illustrations, an emphasis derived from St. Augustine's *de Civitate Dei*. The influence of the Byzantine iconography of the Last Judgement and of Greek art is obvious in the *Hortus Deliciarum*. The dragon with seven heads is named *eptazephalus* after the Greek. The throne prepared for the judgement—the Etimasia of Byzantine art—was interpreted as the altar above "the souls of those who had been slain for the word of God" (6.9).

Gothic. In the monumental art of the High Gothic period, the representations of the Apocalypse disappeared from the tympanum of the portals. The radiant vision of the 24 Elders occupies the rose window in the south transept of Chartres cathedral. Apocalyptic cycles were carved in the voussoirs of the archivolts of the Last Judgment portals of the cathedrals of Paris and Amiens, where the Four Horsemen and the torments in hell are prominent.

The inexhaustible attraction that the Apocalypse exerted as a source of grandiose imagery is exemplified in a series of English or Franco-English manuscripts of the 13th and the early 14th century. They continue the early Christian tradition of manuscript illustration that was transmitted by Italy to Gaul. The earliest and perhaps most beautiful English Gothic Apocalypse is that of Trinity College, illustrated around 1230 at St. Albans. This and other manuscripts of its type were decorated splendidly for royal and aristocratic patrons, most of them English. A few are only picture books, with legends in Latin and French accompanying the illuminations; they include a sequence of illustrations picturing the miracles and final overthrow of the antichrist. The importance granted to the antichrist was later to be echoed in the frescoes of the Last Judgment with apocalyptic overtones, painted after 1500 by Signorelli in the cathedral of Orvieto.

The monumentality inherent in the Apocalyptic visions was fully realized in the tapestries woven in Paris on the looms of Nicolas Bataille from 1375 to 1381 for Duke Louis of Anjou. The cartoons provided by Jean Bondol of Bruges copied the illuminations of various manuscripts of the Channel school. The original tapestry for the chateau of Angers was made up of seven pieces, each divided into 14 subjects arranged in seven pairs, with backgrounds alternately blue and red and introduced by an enraptured reader, sitting under a canopy. The seven readers, who are as tall as the height of the tapestry, may symbolize the seven Churches of Asia (1.11). The gigantic cycle of Angers included 98 scenes and was 800 square meters when intact.

Only faded remains of Cimabue's frescoes—the opening of the seals, the angels holding the winds, and the fall of Babylon—remain in the upper church at Assisi. But the Apocalyptic frescoes incorporated by Giusto de' Menabuoi in the encyclopedic program of paintings in the baptistery at Padua (1375–78) are particularly important because they are related to the Pentecost in the choir and also to the "great multitude which no man could number" (7.9) displayed in the cupola, illustrating the theme of All Saints. In the oldest Italian tradition, Rv 7.9 was read on Pentecost, but the evocation of the Great Multitude was shifted to All Saint's Day. The immense east window in the choir of York Minster was filled by John Thornton of Coventry (1405–08) with 1,700 square feet of painted glass that developed a program second in scope only to that of Padua, since it includes 27 panels illustrating the Old Testament and 81 depicting 90 scenes of the Apocalypse.

In the polyptych by Jan van EYCK at St. Bavon, Ghent (1432), the vision of the Heavenly Jerusalem descended in the form of a reredos upon the altar itself. Open, it shows in the upper section the world of transcendence: a Deesis, in which the Virgin and St. John are enthroned in glory as Christ's first elect, and musicians, who are symbols of the 44,000, singing and playing on their harps (Rv 14). Below, a flowering meadow introduces the world of immanence in the Adoration of the Lamb. Around the Lamb, who sheds His blood on the altar amidst angels proffering the trophies of the death and Resurrection of Christ, are assembled eight groups: the martyrs and the virgins nearest to the altar; in the foreground, the patriarchs and Prophets, the Apostles and confessors, to the left and right of the fountain of life; on the wings, the just judges, the knights, the hermits and, finally, the pilgrims. These eight groups represent the Beatitudes, in keeping with the Gospel read on All Saint's Day. The core of the iconography, which is the "choir of the blessed in the sacrifice of the Lamb," as the painting is entitled in a document of 1458, corresponds to the reading of Rv 9.2–12 on November 1. The adoration of the Lamb by all the saints received its visual expression as a result of the liturgy adopted in 835 for All Saint's Day.

Renaissance and Modern. From the 15th century on, the chief medium of the illustration of the Apocalypse was the woodcut. Albrecht DÜRER published his Apocalypse himself, both in Latin and German, in 1948. This great artist condensed the Apocalypse into 14 woodcuts. What was fundamentally new in Dürer's Apocalypse was the individual and polemical approach, the material aspect of the pamphlet that he conveyed through his work. This was soon to inspire the Protestant iconography of the Apocalypse originated in Wittenberg by Luther and Cranach in 1522. Through the Wittenberg New Testament the imagery of Dürer was carried to Lutheran Bibles illustrated by Burgkmair, Schaufelein, Hans HOLBEIN the Younger (1523), Erhard Altdorfer (1533–34), and Martin Schaffner (1534). On the Catholic side, his influence was felt in Bibles edited by Martin l'Empereur (Antwerp 1530) and Sebastian Gryphius (Lyons 1541). The woodcuts of Dürer, reinterpreted in the formal idiom of the school of Fontainebleau, gave birth to the magnificent series of Apocalyptic windows in the chapel of the chateau of Vincennes (1558).

Paradoxically enough, Dürer's Apocalypse, or a set of illustrations inspired by him, was used as a model book in the first apocalyptic cycle painted in Byzantine art at the Dionysiou monastery on Mt. Athos in 1547. In Byzantium the Apocalypse was not accepted as a canonical book before the 12th century. The contribution of Byzantine art to the iconography of the Apocalypse is late and remained derivative. The Elizabeth Day McCormick Apocalypse in Chicago illustrates 69 subjects of an early 17th-century translation of the Apocalypse into vernacular Greek.

The tragic events of the mid-20th century surrounding World War II have inspired moving interpretations of the Apocalypse in the graphic arts by E. Georg (1943), G. de Pogedaïeff (1947–50), A. Collot (1952), G. de Chirico (1952), and H. de Waroquier (1955). The medieval cycle of Angers was emulated by Jean Lurçat in the great tapestry that decorates the apse of Notre-Dame-de-Toute-Grâce at ASSY (1947–48), showing the vision of the Dragon pursuing the "Woman that wore the sun for her mantel" and bore a Son (Rv 12).

Bibliography: For an essential treatment see F. VAN DER MEER, *Maiestas Domini: Theophanies de l'Apocalypse dans l'art chrétien* (Paris 1928), extensive bibliog. H. L. RAMSAY, "Manuscripts of the Commentary of Beaatus of Liébana on the Apocalypse," *Revue des bibliothèques* 12 (1902) 74–103. C. SCHELENBERG, *Dürers Apokalypse* (Munich 1923). H. C. HOSKIER, *Concerning the Text of the Apocalypse*, 2 v. (London 1929). M. R. JAMES, ed., *The Dublin Apocalypse* (Cambridge, Mass. 1932). I. YOSHIKAWA, *L'Apocalypse de Saint-Savin* (Paris 1939). H. R. WILLOUGHBY, and E. C. COLWELL, *The Elizabeth Day McCormick Apocalypse*, 2 v. (Chicago 1940). E. A. VAN MOE, *L'Apocalypse de Saint-Sever* (Paris 1943). J. CROQUISON, "Une Vision eschatologique carolingienne," *Cahiers archeologiques* 4 (1949) 105–129. R. PLANCHENAULT, "L'Apocalypse d'Angers: Éléments pour un nouvel esssai de restitution," *Bulletin monumental* 111 (193) 209–262. P. CORMANS, *Van Eyck: L'Adoration de l'Agneau* (new ed. Anvers 1951). J. LURCAT, *L'Apocalypse d'Angers* (Angers 1955). L. RÉAU, *Iconographie de l'art chrétien* 2.2:663–726. H. AURENHAMMER, *Lexikon der christlichen Ikonographie* (Vienna 1959).

[P. VERDIER]

"Four Horsemen of the Apocalypse," in a miniature from a manuscript of "Beatus' Commentary on the Apocalypse," produced for the Abbey of Santo Domingo de Silos, Spain, c. 1091–1109.

APOCALYPTIC

A biblical style of writing that developed during the Exile (587–538 B.C.) and especially the postexilic age. The term is derived from the Greek verb ἀποκαλύπτω, meaning to unveil. The apocalyptists wrote as though they had received a vision involving God's cosmic kingdom and His eschatological battle to establish it. Almost every earthly element acquired symbolic value—parts of the human body, animals, colors, clothing, and numbers— for God was utilizing everything for His world triumph. Angels acted as mediators not only of the revelation, but particularly of its explanation. Finally, the authors usually wrote in the name of personages of the distant past; thus, under the literary form of a vision granted centuries earlier, they actually described contemporary scenes.

Apocalyptic evolved out of an earlier prophetic style of preaching. A historical study of the development of prophecy into apocalyptic not only explains the origin but also the dominant features of apocalyptic. The development can be observed in the three periods of OT history: (1) the late preexilic, (2) the exilic, and (3) the postexilic age.

Late Preexilic Age. The weird symbolism of apocalyptic had its roots in the events and reactions of the last 60 years before the Babylonian exile, which began in 587 B.C. The colossal Assyrian empire was collapsing. In 22 years it plunged from a peak of extravagant glory and terrifying ruthlessness to the depths of total destruction. Nations shuddered at such swift reversals. They began to write official documents, as in Babylon, in ancient scripts and long-forgotten languages, and in many ways people revived religious traditions and practices of hoary origin.

This almost haunting return to ancient customs and accounts showed up in Jerusalem in the Deuteronomic reform of King Josia (c. 640–609 B.C.). The biblical books of Joshua, Judges, Samuel, and Kings were redacted, and their Deuteronomist author recognized in the accumulation of early stories, folklore, and liturgy a pattern of action repeated over and over again in history: sin brings suffering; suffering induces compunction; compunction moves God to send deliverance (Jgs 2.6–3.6). Deuteronomy used these early traditions to actualize faith in the present moment (Dt 5.1–5).

In a somewhat different way the Prophets of this final period before the exile thundered doom and destruction upon sin. Zephaniah and Nehemiah both cried out that a DAY OF THE LORD was to strike Israel with almost annihilating force (Zep) and to sweep aside all opposition from foreigners (Neh). The Prophet JEREMIAH stressed the cosmic impact of Israel's sins (Jer 2.12; 4.23–36; 5.22–23). In this account of preexilic Israel only those details are highlighted that later become united in apocalyptic: reappearance of ancient personages and events; cosmic and agonizing battles between God and wickedness; and victory's emerging out of the sorrowful effects of sin.

Exilic Age. The Babylonian Exile (587–538 B.C.) destroyed all the external forms of religious and civil life, almost everything that seemed of utmost importance to Israel. Two prophets—EZEKIEL and Deutero-Isaiah (author of Isaiah ch. 40–55)—then pointed out what was truly at the heart of existence: faith in God, who is personally interested in His chosen people, who is adamant against evil, and who will secure His world kingdom.

Ezekiel is of special interest here in the development of prophecy into apocalyptic. He made a free, extravagant use of symbolism (ch. 1–3; 40–48); his word pictures defy imagination, just as the explosive destruction of the Exile did (see EZEKIEL, BOOK OF). The mystery of God's promised kingdom breaks the bonds of reasoning and picturing. Ezekiel not only spoke but acted apocalyptically (5.1–5; 12.6, 11; 24.24, 27). By his concern over the priestly traditions within the Pentateuch (see PRIESTLY WRITERS, PENTATEUCHAL) Ezekiel may have been responsible for preserving accounts that later apocalyptists generously used, such as the creation story, Enoch and other patriarchal figures, and Noah and the Flood.

Postexilic Age. During the postexilic age, from the return of the first Jewish exiles to the first half of the 2d Christian century, apocalyptic writing completely replaced the older prophetic style. There are only a few exceptions, such as parts of Zechariah (ch. 7–8) and of Malachi [see ZECHARIAH, BOOK OF; MALACHI, BOOK OF]; but even in these cases the Prophets were subservient to the priest, a situation that had hardly been true of the preexilic Prophets. In Joel, for instance, trumpet blasts and locust plague proclaim the Day of the Lord, but the writer calls not for social reform but for fasting and liturgical prayer (ch. 1–2; see JOEL, BOOK OF). The liturgy suddenly expands into the outpouring of the Spirit with "blood, fire and columns of smoke" (ch. 3) and a terrifying judgment upon the nations of the world (ch. 4).

The great persecution of 167 to 164 B.C., when ANTIOCHUS IV EPIPHANES, the Seleucid king of Antioch, attempted to suppress Jewish national identity in Palestine, brought forth the most complete form of OT apocalyptic, the Book of DANIEL. The first six chapters of the book are probably a haggadic reediting of early stories (see HAGGADAH), some of which originated as far back as the Exile. Chapters 7 to 12 show all the major trends of apocalyptic: visions explained by the angel Gabriel; a pseudonym of a hero of the Babylonian Exile; a flamboyant concoction of clashing and fearful images; catastrophic suffering; and the sudden appearance of a glorious cosmic victory for Yahweh. The author seeks to sustain the faith of his persecuted coreligionists by assuring them that God will quickly reverse their sorrows with eschatological triumph.

Apocalyptic continued in Judaism among the PHARISEES and the members of the QUMRAN community. It seems, however, that after the devastation of Jerusalem in A.D. 70 and again after the suppression of the revolt of BAR KOKHBA in A.D. 136, JUDAISM gave up its apocalyptic hopes and settled down as the people of the Torah, devoted to the careful study and punctilious fulfillment of the Law.

Christianity inherited the apocalyptic; and, in fact, the last NT book, the Book of REVELATION, like the Book of Daniel, is one of the finest examples of this literary form. Jesus used the apocalyptic style (Mk ch. 15), and the Apostles after the Resurrection did likewise (1 and 2 Thess). Soon, however, the tendency set in of seeing apocalyptic hopes already realized in Jesus' presence, in the gift of the Spirit, and in the liturgy (Rom and Gospel of St. John). Christians, however, still looked forward to a new heaven and a new earth (2 Pt), when sorrow would be totally removed (Rom ch. 8) and the fullness of the Godhead revealed (Eph and Col). Then would apocalyptic hopes be satisfied, and vision and symbol be turned into reality.

Bibliography: S. B. FROST, *O.T. Apocalyptic: Its Origin and Growth* (London 1952). H. H. ROWLEY, *The Relevance of Apocalyptic* (3d ed. New York 1964). R. H. CHARLES et al., eds., *The Apocrypha and Pseudepigrapha of the O.T. in English,* 2 v. (Oxford 1913); *Religious Development Between the Old and the New Testaments* (New York 1914). M. J. LAGRANGE, *Le Judaïsme avant Jésus-Christ* (*Études bibliques* 1931). D. S. RUSSELL, *Between the Testaments* (Philadelphia 1960). O. PLÖGER, *Theokratie und Eschatologie* (2d ed. Neukirchen 1962). J. BLOCH, *On the Apocalyptic in Judaism* (Philadelphia 1952). J. B. FREY, *Dictionnaire de la Bible,* suppl. ed. L. PIROT, et al. (Paris 1928–) 1:326–354. F. J. SCHIERSE, *Lexikon für Theologie und Kirche,* ed. J. HOFER and K. RAHNER (Freiburg 1957–65) 1:704–705. H. RINGGREN and R. SCHÜTZ, *Die Religion in Geschichte und Gegenwart,* 7 v. (3d ed. Tübingen 1957–65) 1:464–469. J. SICKENBERGER, *Reallexikon für Antike Christentum,* ed. T. KLAUSER (Stuttgart 1950–) 1:504–510. *Encyclopedic Dictionary of the Bible,* tr. and adap. by L. HARTMAN (New York 1963) from A. VAN DEN BORN, *Bijbels Woordenboek,* 110–111. J. H. CHARLESWORTH, *The Old Testament Pseudepigrapha* (Garden City, N. Y. 1983). J. J. COLLINS, *The Apocalyptic Imagination. An Introduction to the Jewish Matrix of Christianity* (New York 1984). B. MCGINN, *Visions of the End* (New York 1979). C. ROWLAND, *The Open Heaven. A Study of Apocalyptic in Judaism and Christianity* (New York 1982).

[C. STUHLMUELLER/EDS.]

APOCALYPTIC MOVEMENTS

Trends toward revolutionary eschatology, which foresee the return of Christ as imminent. Deriving sustenance from Ezekiel, Daniel, and the Book of Revelation, these movements keep alive messianic hopes and emphasize the prophetic note. Often vigorously individualistic in character, they attempt to identify the ANTICHRIST, prepare through militant asceticism for the impending end of the world and the PAROUSIA, or second coming of Christ, and indulge in visionary expectation. Socioeconomic grievances may often guide such chiliastic exaltation (*see* CHILIASM) and sharpen an ethic built on penitence and voluntary poverty.

It is convenient to treat these movements in three periods: early Christian, high and late Middle Ages, and modern. The emergence of the visible church was accompanied by the formation of such Judeo-Christian sects as the EBIONITES (Poor Men). As a protest against growing

Commentary on the Apocalypse of Beatus: The Harvest of the World, 10th century. (©Archivo Iconografico, S.A./CORBIS)

institutionalism and secularization of the Church, the MONTANISTS appeared in Phrygia in the second half of the 2d century and spread to North Africa, where they attracted the sympathetic attention of TERTULLIAN. While reaction to relaxed discipline and externalism fostered the primitivism of the apostolic Church, political failure fed millenarian hopes (*see* MILLENARIANISM). By the 4th century this eschatological and chiliastic stream receded, only to reappear in periods of religious and social unrest. In the medieval period crusades, war, pestilence, social instability, and clerical delinquency created the environment from which the flagellants (*see* FLAGELLATION) sprang in the 13th and 14th centuries. Apocalyptic literature was given fresh impetus by JOACHIM OF FIORE (1130–1202), Cistercian abbot, hermit, and founder of the stricter Cistercian monastery of S. Giovanni in Fiore (Calabria). He proclaimed the imminent coming of the kingdom of the Spirit. Essential to Joachimism was the unfolding of history through three successive stages: the Age of the Father (Old Testament), the Age of the Son (New Testament to 1260), and the Age of the Holy Spirit (since 1260). This ascent leads to a vision that can be identified with the "everlasting gospel" to be preached to all peoples in the Last Days. Although hierarchy and Sacraments will disappear, monasticism as the essence of the primitive Church will become the vehicle of the new age. Such ideas were especially potent among the Franciscan SPIRITUALS, the Fraticelli, and the disciples of Fra DOLCINO. In 1254 Gerard of Borgo San Donnino completed Joachim's blueprint by proclaiming the *Evangelium aeternum* which would supersede both Testaments. If Emperor FREDERICK II served as the object of eschatological expectation in the 13th century, this apocalyptic literature found, in the political and religious scene, conditions congenial to the later visions of COLA DI RIENZO, the Bohemian TABORITES, and SAVONAROLA. Since the 16th century the apocalyptic stream has been represented chiefly by a segment of the Radical Reformation: ANABAPTISTS and SEVENTH-DAY ADVENTISTS. In the English civil war of the mid-17th century, Fifth Monarchy Men kept alive chiliastic dreams.

Bibliography: N. R. C. COHN, *The Pursuit of the Millennium* (London 1957). A. DEMPF, *Sacrum Imperium* (2d ed. Darmstadt 1954). D. L. DOUIE, *The Nature and the Effect of the Heresy of the Fraticelli* (Manchester, England 1932). H. GRUNDMANN, *Studien über Joachim von Floris* (Leipzig 1927). R. M. JONES, *Spiritual Reformers in the 16th and 17th Centuries* (Boston 1914; repr. pa. 1959). E. ANAGNINE, *Dolcino e il movimento ereticale al-l'inizio del trecento* (Florence 1964).

[E. W. MCDONNELL]

APOCATASTASIS

The only place the Greek term apocatastasis (restoration) in the New Testament in Acts 3.21 (ἀποκατάστασις) where universal restoration to the original state of bliss is linked with the coming of the messianic age. Some individual theologians, ancient and modern, expanded it to mean the ultimate salvation of all rational creatures. As it is expounded in the *De Principiis* by Origen, its most influential early exponent, the doctrine implies that all rational creatures, including sinners, the damned, and devil, will be reconciled. According to Origen all punishment, whether in this world or in the next, is educative and is therefore not eternal. Other ancient writers who held a similar view were St. Gregory of Nazianzus, St. Gregory of Nyssa, Didymus the Blind, Evagrius Ponticus, Diodore of Tarsus, and Theodore of Mopsuetia. Apocatastasis was condemned by the Synod of Constantinople in 543 (H. Denzinger, *Enchiridion symbolorum* 409, 411). Since the Reformation it has had supporters among Anabaptists, Moravians, Christadelphians, and Universalists. In modern times followers of Friedrich SCHLEIERMACHER (1768–1834) have given a renewed emphasis to the doctrine.

Bibliography: F. L. CROSS, *The Oxford Dictionary of the Christian Church* 67 (London 1957). H. CROUZEL, *Sacramentum Mundi* 1:51–52. C. ANDRESEN and P. ALTHAUS, *Die Religion in Geschichte und Gegenwart* (Tübingen 1957–65) 6:1693–96. J. DANIÉLOU, *Origen*, tr. W. MITCHELL (New York 1955).

[A. D. TURNEY/EDS.]

APOCRISIARIUS

A Byzantine diplomatic term for the representative of a civil, military, or ecclesiastical governor at another headquarters or court. The Latin term was *responsalis,* or one bringing an answer; and the word referred primarily to the representatives of the pope, metropolitan bishoprics, or monasteries in Constantinople, although it was employed also of ecclesiastical representatives at other patriarchates or metropolitan sees. Bishop Julian of Cos served as an *apocrisiarius* at Constantinople, for Pope Leo I (440–461); while the patriarch of Alexandria had had an official representative there since the beginning of the 5th century. ANATOLIUS became patriarch of Constantinople (449–458) after serving as the Alexandrian *apocrisiarius* for the Patriarch Dioscorus. John the Scholastic had served as *apocrisiarius* for Antioch before being selected patriarch of Constantinople (565–577) by Justinian I. Rome recalled its *apocrisiarius* from Constantinople at the beginning of the Acacian Schism (484), but was represented intermittently during the reign of Emperor ANASTASIUS I. A permanent *apocrisiarius* seems to have taken office with the appointment of the deacon (543), later Pope Pelagius I. Pope GREGORY I, while a deacon, had served in Constantinople as the papal *apocrisiarius* (579–585). The representative of the patriarch at the imperial court in Constantinople was known as the *referendarius.* At the court of CHARLEMAGNE, the term was applied to the ecclesiastic who served as spiritual adviser to the king, and not infrequently it was applied also to the papal representative.

Bibliography: J. PARGOIRE, *Dictionnaire d'archéologie chrétienne et de liturgie* 1.2:2537–55. A. EMEREAU, *Échos d'Orient* 17 (1914) 289–297, 542–548. R. GUILLAND, *Revue des études byzantines* 5 (1947) 90–100. H. G. BECK, *Kirche und theologische Literatur im byzantinischen Reich* 103. A. BAUS, *Lexikon für Theologie und Kirche,* 10 v. (2d, new ed. Freiburg 1957–65) 1:712. O. TREITINGER, *Reallexikon für Antike und Christentum* 1:501–504. M. JUGIE, *Catholicisme* 1:694.

[F. X. MURPHY]

APOCRYPHA

Under this term are included those books that were written by Jews for the purpose of continuing their sacred tradition. Many of the compositions contain several Christian additions, and a few of them, according to some scholars, may even be completely Christian in their extant form (e.g., the Odes of Solomon and the Testament of the Twelve Patriarchs). The style, however, is closely modeled upon that of the OT, and the thought represents the religious currents circulating among the Jews during the intertestamental period, the two or three centuries before the NT writings appeared. The apocrypha can be conveniently arranged according to the threefold Septuagint (LXX) division of the OT: historical books, prophetic books, and didactic or sapiential books. From ancient catalogs of books and from quotations in early Church Fathers it is certain that many more apocrypha existed than are now extant.

The pseudohistorical apocrypha are Jubilees, 3 Esdras, 3 Maccabees, Life of Adam and Eve, Ascension of Isaiah, and Lives of the Prophets. (*See* ARISTEAS, LETTER OF.)

The prophetic-apocalyptic apocrypha are the Books of Henoch, or Enoch (i.e., the 1 or Ethiopic, 2 or Greek, and 3 or Hebrew), Assumption of Moses, 4 Esdras, Baruch (Syriac), Baruch (Greek), and Sibylline Oracles (Jewish).

The moral-didactic apocrypha are the Testament of the Twelve Patriarchs, Psalms of Solomon, Odes of Solomon, Prayer of Manasseh, and 4 Maccabees. (*See* DEAD SEA SCROLLS.)

PSEUDOHISTORICAL APOCRYPHA

Works patterned after the historical books of the OT but only in a very loose way have been so designated. They try to recapture and relive the glorious stages in the history of salvation.

Book of Jubilees. Other names for the Book of Jubilees are Little Genesis, because it retells the stories and laws of Gn 1.1–Ex 12.36, and the Apocalypse of Moses, because it claims that God revealed its contents during Moses' 40 days and 40 nights on Mt. Sinai. The name Jubilees is the most appropriate, not only because the book divides history into 49 jubilee periods of 49 years each (Lv 25.8–22), beginning with creation and concluding with the revelation of the Mosaic Law, but also because it places great importance upon the sacred, solar calendar, the fixation of feast days, and the certainty with which history is striding forward to the messianic millennium or jubilee. The author had still other purposes in writing his book: to expand and clarify the law, which he claims was kept before Moses' time by every great personage; to defend Judaism against the corroding influence of pagan Hellenism; and to exalt the privileged place of the Levitical priests. Also worth noting in the content of the book are these details: silence about any personal, royal Messiah; well-developed angelology and demonology; and expectation of a messianic period of 1,000 years,

after which the just will enjoy immortality in the spirit world.

The style is best described as that of an enlarged Targum (R. H. Charles), like the HAGGADAH in the narratives and the HALAKAH in the legal sections. It was most probably written first in Hebrew, but until the discovery of the Dead Sea Scrolls there existed only an Ethiopic text, some Syriac and Latin fragments, and a few Greek citations in the Fathers. There is sufficient manuscript evidence, however, testifying to the popularity of Jubilees in ancient Jewish and Christian circles.

The author seems to have been a Palestinian Jew, scrupulously observant of the law, devoted to the Maccabees and the priestly tribe of Levi, cool toward any messianic aspirations in the tribe of Judah, and hostile toward Hellenistic influences. These facts help to locate him in the Maccabean period, before the Pharisaic rupture with King John Hyrcanus (r. 135–104 B.C.) and possibly even before Jonathan assumed the high priestly office in 152 B.C. The author's determined views on the calendar associate him with a Jewish sect such as the ESSENES. His book was very popular in the QUMRAN COMMUNITY.

Third Esdras. Four books are attributed to Esdras (Ezra in the Hebrew spelling). The distinction between these books is confusing because of manuscript and denominational differences.

Third Esdras (in Vulgate) chronicles events from the time of King Josiah (r. 640–609 B.C.) through the Exile and into the postexilic period up to and including the ministry of Ezra. For the most part it simply repeats, with some minor revision and transposition, what already exists in the canonical books of Chronicles, Nehemiah, and especially Ezra. Third Esdras, however, expunges any mention of Nehemiah, and in 3.1–5.6 it adds a legend of Hebrew or Aramaic origin about a battle of wits among Darius's bodyguard, who contended the relative strength of wine, women, kings, and truth. Zorobabel, who championed truth, won the contest and as a reward was allowed to rebuild the Temple of Jerusalem (*see* TEMPLES [IN THE BIBLE]). Most scholars have noticed that 3 Esdras ends very abruptly, in the middle of a sentence quoted from Neh 8.13, but O. Eissfeldt claims that 3 Esdras has a normal conclusion since the second part of Neh 8.13 and the succeeding verses are secondary to the latter text.

The origin of 3 Esdras cannot be adequately explained. Third Esdras could actually be the original LXX version of the canonical books, while the current Greek translation of Chronicles, Ezra, and Nehemiah could represent the work of Theodotion. The case of 3 Esdras would then be very similar to that of Jeremiah. Or it is possible, but not generally held, that 3 Esdras is a compilation taken from the present Greek translation. Finally, it may trace its independent way to a Hebrew text or tradition noticeably different from the Masoretic reading.

The book was certainly compiled before A.D. 90, for the Jewish historian Josephus quoted from it (*Ant.* 11); but its exclusive concern with Jewish interests puts its composition before the Christian era, closer to 100 B.C. Until the 5th century, Christians very frequently ranked 3 Esdras with the canonical books; it is found in many LXX MSS and in the Latin Vulgate (Vulg) of St. Jerome. Protestants therefore include 3 Esdras with other apocrypha (deuterocanonical) books such as Tobit or Judith. The Council of Trent definitively removed it from the canon.

Third Maccabees. This is a fantastic novel about a persecution of Jews in Alexandria, Egypt. It can make very little claim to literature, and it has nothing whatever to do with the Maccabees, except that many LXX MSS, including A and V, place it immediately after 2 Maccabees. The story is a succession of quick reversals. Ptolemy IV Philopator, Pharaoh of Egypt (r. 221–204 B.C.), is victorious in a battle fought in northern Palestine. In thanksgiving he sacrifices at the Jerusalem Temple, but when he attempts to enter the HOLY OF HOLIES, God strikes him dumb (cf. Heliodorus in 2 Mc 3.8–40). Returning to Egypt, Philopator determines upon a pogrom, to have drunken elephants trample the Jews to death in the hippodrome. When heavenly visitors appear, the elephants turn upon the soldiers; the Jews are then granted many favors. These events are reminiscent of the Book of Esther and the origin of the feast of PURIM. It is possible that some major misfortune may have been the cause for the writing of the book, perhaps the persecution by Ptolemy VII Physcon (r. 146–117 B.C.) or the revoking of Jewish civil rights in 25–24 B.C. Josephus, in *Contra Apionem* 2.5.53–55, recorded a plan to drive a herd of elephants against a mass of Jews during Physcon's reign. The author may have combined facts drawn from the lost memoirs of Philopator with other events spun out of his own imagination.

The style of 3 Maccabees is mouthy and declamatory; the plot, artificial and forced. In this regard there are many points of similarity with 2 Maccabees and especially with the letter of Aristeas.

The book was written in Alexandria, Egypt, c. 100 B.C.; the latest date would be A.D. 70, when the Jerusalem Temple was destroyed by Titus. Third Maccabees presumes that Jerusalem and its temple are still in the possession of the Jews.

Life of Adam and Eve (Apocalypse of Moses). A large group of legends about man's first parents that once circulated among the Jews and the early Christians was collected and entitled the Life of Adam and Eve. It is extant only in Latin, although a Greek version often appears beneath the surface. The Apocalypse of Moses, wrongly so named by its discoverer K. von Tischendorf, exists in a Greek text. Scholars generally agree, however, that both forms were originally written in Hebrew or Aramaic, somewhere between 20 B.C. and A.D. 70, because of references to the Herodian Temple (cf. Jn 2.20). The two books frequently run parallel to one another, as each tells the story of the first parents: their fall and repentance; new temptations and sorrows; dreams and predictions about the Jewish race up to the last judgment; the death, and finally the burial of Adam and Eve by angels. There seem to be Christian interpolations, especially in the prophecies. The story is told with pathos, often with literary finesse; at times it emphasizes penance and ascetical practices.

Ascension of Isaiah. This is a compilation, according to most scholars, of three separate works, put together between the 3d and the 5th Christian centuries, when it became very popular among heretical Christians. The first section, "The Martyrdom of Isaiah" (ch. 1–5), expands upon a brief reference in 2 Kgs 21.1–8 and recounts the events, including the intrigues of the apostate King Manasseh, a Samaritan, and a false prophet Belchira, that led up to Isaiah's martyrdom. The prophet is said to have been cut in two by a wood saw. The story, reflected in Heb 11.37 and in the Jewish TALMUD and TARGUMS has its literary origins in Palestinian Judaism of the 1st century B.C. The second section (3.13b–4.18) is a "Christian apocalypse," originating around A.D. 100 and only later placed within the martyrdom story as a reason for Isaiah's violent death. It proposes to be the prophet's "predictions" of Jesus' life and work, the mission of the 12 Apostles, the faults of the early Church, the Antichrist and Beliar (identified with Nero), and the Second Coming (PAROUSIA). Such details probably account for the work's appeal to heretical and splinter groups of Christians. The final section (ch. 6–11) of the 2d Christian century recounts the "Vision [or Ascension] of Isaiah" in the seventh heaven and his discovery of celestial secrets. This revelation of Christian GNOSIS, or mysterious knowledge, also fitted appropriately into the religious system of the early heretics. The complete book has survived only in an Ethiopian version; scattered fragments exist in Greek, Latin, Coptic, and Old Slavonic.

Lives of the Prophets. Biographies were written, not only of the 4 Major and the 12 Minor Prophets, but also of other prophetic figures such as ELIJAH, ELISHA, Nathan (David's adviser), Ahijah (1 Kgs 14.1–18), Joed (Neh 11.7, said to be the same as Addo the seer in 2 Chr 9.29 and the anonymous prophet in 1 Kings ch. 13),

Azariah (2 Chr 15.1–8), and Zechariah (2 Chr 24.20–24, mentioned in Mt 23.35 and Lk 11.51). The author draws upon legendary stories and popular traditions in order to supplement the biblical account. The work was composed in Hebrew by a Palestinian Jew during the 1st Christian century. There is a large Christian addition to the life of Jeremiah, referring to Jesus' virginal birth and the flight into Egypt. For the most part, however, Christian interpolations are scarce. Little historical value is attached to the events narrated in the work. (See C. C. Torrey, *The Lives of the Prophets* [*Journal of Biblical Literature* Monograph Series 1; Philadelphia 1946].)

PROPHETIC-APOCALYPTIC APOCRYPHA

The apocryphal books classified under this heading imitate the PROPHETIC BOOKS OF THE OLD TESTAMENT and the apocalyptic literature of late JUDAISM.

Books of Enoch. These represent the remnants of an extensive Enoch literature, circulating between 200 B.C. and A.D. 300. There are three rather divergent books, which are usually distinguished by the language in which they were transmitted: 1 or Ethiopic Enoch: 2 or Slavonic Enoch (called also the Secrets of Enoch): and 3 Enoch, preserved in the original Hebrew.

Ethiopic Enoch. The longest and certainly the most important Book of Henoch was the Ethiopic, used by the authors of Jubilees, Testament of the Twelve Patriarchs, and the Apocalypse of Baruch. It is quoted in Jude 14 and cited as a divine authority by Pseudo-Barnabas and Tertullian. Except for a few Latin fragments the book was known only in the Ethiopic version that was brought to Europe in 1773 by James Bruce; but recently there have turned up in cave 4 along the Dead Sea 10 Aramaic MSS of ch. 1–36 and ch. 83–90, besides 4 additional Aramaic MSS of ch. 72–82 (following R. H. Charles's chapter division). These discoveries not only establish the original language to be Aramaic rather than Hebrew and supply a very early text, but they also reveal the popularity of the Henoch literature among the Palestinian Jews (see Gn 5.21–24; Sir 44.16; 49.14; Heb 11.5).

The earliest collection of 1 Enoch found among the Dead Sea Scrolls consists of ch. 1–36 and ch. 83–90. The first section describes Enoch's journey through the celestial spheres and discusses the origin and spread of sin through the fall of the angels, the punishment of sinners, the eschatological blessedness of the just, and the bodily resurrection. The second part comprises apocalyptic stories, similar to those in Daniel ch. 7–12, in which there is presented a history of Israel from the Deluge to the messianic reign. Since the last historical reference is to Judas Maccabee, who died in 160 B.C., the book was probably composed sometime between the period 167 to

164 B.C., the date for the great persecution and the Book of Daniel, and 160 B.C. From the Qumran evidence it is apparent that ch. 72–82 circulated as a separate piece; it reflects the astronomical and meteorological beliefs of the Palestinian Jews, and, among other important details, it agrees with the Book of Jubilees in favoring the solar year calendar.

Another major division is ch. 91–105 (plus the conclusion, ch. 106–108), which consists principally of "Admonitions" and the "Apocalypse of Weeks." The author is preoccupied with the doom awaiting the unjust and the final glorification of the elect. The "Admonitions" was composed *c.* 160 B.C., i.e., very soon after the death of Judas Maccabee, while the "Apocalypse of Weeks" appeared sometime before the Roman conquest of Palestine in 63 B.C.

The fifth major portion of 1 Enoch is the very important series of "Similitudes," or "Parables," pronouncing judgment upon men and angels (ch. 37–71). In these chapters occur the repeated references to the "SON OF MAN," who seems to be some kind of suprahuman person, combining in himself all the hopes and triumphs of Israel. If these chapters are pre-Christian, then the concept of "Son of Man" represents a stage of development, slightly beyond the symbolic usage in Dn 7.13 and closer to the personal messianic meaning on the lips of Jesus (Mk 14.62). The absence of these chapters at Qumran does not disprove but only throws doubt upon their pre-Christian origin; in any case, the absence of definitely Christian ideas certainly indicates a Jewish author.

When the five major sections were gathered into one book—possibly in imitation of the five books of Moses in the Torah and the five books of Davidic Psalms—a few other minor selections, such as the Book of Noah, were interspersed among the chapters. The author of the final, edited book seems to have belonged to an eschatological circle, similar to the Pharisees or the Qumran covenanters; he accepted the final triumph of the just, the complete damnation of the wicked, the resurrection of the body, and the belief in angels. The messianic joys are frequently described in terms quite earthly and sensuous (10.17; 25.4); the solar religious calendar is preferred to the lunar.

Second or Slavonic Enoch. This book, also called the "Secrets of Enoch," presents a fanciful apocalypse of Enoch's assumption to the 10th heaven, his visions, and admonitions. As he journeys through the heavens, he views the rewards and punishments of the future life and the various movements of the Sun, Moon, and stars (ch. 1–21), in the 10th heaven he sees the appearance of the Lord (ch. 22) and is told many secrets, especially an elaborate account of how the universe was created in six days (ch. 23–30). The last part of the book consists mostly of a long series of admonitions by Enoch to his sons (ch. 31–68).

The book now exists in two Slavonic recensions of very unequal length. It is very difficult to account for the relationship of these two versions to one another, but there is no doubt that both go back to an original Greek text, now lost. An acrostic explanation of Adam's name in 30.13 is intelligible only in Greek. This Greek composition is usually attributed to a Jewish author, living in Egypt, before the destruction of the Temple of Jerusalem (A.D. 70). This last detail is based upon his references to sacrifice (51.4; 59.1–2; 61.4; 62.1). His work was very influential and seems to be responsible for statements in other apocryphal literature such as the Books of Adam and Eve, the Apocalypses of Moses and Paul, and the Ascension of Isaiah. A few scholars, however, e.g., F. C. Burkitt and J. K. Fotheringham, argue for a much later authorship, the 7th century A.D. at the earliest.

Third Enoch. This is an amalgam of disparate Hebrew parts, treating of angels, the divine chariot or throne (Ez 1.14), and the destinies of a rather illusive figure called Metatron (perhaps, the Son of Man or the Elect One of 1 Enoch). The title ascribes the work "to Rabbi Ishmael ben Elisha, high priest" and dates it at the beginning of the 2d Christian century; but Hugo Odeberg, who first edited the Hebrew manuscripts in 1928, traces individual parts to a period immediately after the revolt of Bar Kokhba (A.D. 132–135). Before the book reached its present form in the 3d century, it had felt the impact of Gnosticism and various religious movements within Judaism.

Fourth Esdras. What is sometimes called 2 Esdras by non-Catholics is called 4 Esdras in the Vulgate. It was one of the most popular and most frequently translated books of all the apocrypha. Although written originally in Hebrew and subsequently translated into Greek, both of which texts are lost, the book has survived in Christian editions in Latin, Syriac, Ethiopic, Arabic, Armenian, Sahidic, and Georgian. It has supplied several liturgical passages: the reproaches (*improperia*) of Good Friday (ch. 1.13, 14–24); the Easter antiphon for martyrs (ch. 2.35); and the *requiem aeternam* in the prayer for the deceased (ch. 2.34–35). In their attachment to this book, Christians not only made slight modifications in the text (ch. 7.28–35[?]; 8.3; 13.29–32[?]), but they also wrote a new introduction and conclusion (ch. 1–2, sometimes called "5 Esdras," and ch. 15–16, sometimes called "6 Esdras"). The newer chapters (1–2 and 15–16) are missing in the Syriac, Ethiopic, Arabic, and Armenian versions.

The Jewish original can be dated *c.* A.D. 100, i.e., "thirty years after the downfall of the city [Jerusalem, in A.D. 70]" (ch. 3.1) and a few years after A.D. 96, the end of the reign of "the three heads," i.e., the Flavian Roman emperors, Vespatian, Titus, and Domitian (11.1). The author drew his material from preexisting sources and put together a mosaic of ideas. Composing in an apocalyptic style, he assumed an ancient name, Ezra, and pretended to be writing from Babylon. He was, however, a devout Jew, perhaps a Pharisee, living in Rome (see 1 Pt 5.13). He was crushed by the destruction of the Holy City and was continually obsessed with the mystery of sin, human misery, the trials of the just, the prosperity of the wicked, and the large number of the reprobate. Pessimistic is the evaluation usually attached to his character. He firmly expected a divine judgment upon Israel's enemies, once the number of the elect was complete, and he hoped for a general resurrection and a new creation.

Chapters 3–14 present an account of seven visions. The third vision (6.35–9.25) describes the death of the Messiah, but in the succeeding judgment scene the Messiah does not appear—in opposition to the Gospel story about Jesus. In the sixth vision (ch. 13) there are many parallels to the Son of Man image in Daniel ch. 7. The last vision (ch. 14) is important for the study of the formation of the canon. Ezra is said to have dictated the sacred books to five secretaries who wrote "in letters they did not know"; Ezra spoke around the clock, and at the end of 40 days, 94 books had been transcribed: 24 open to the worthy and the unworthy; 70 reserved for the initiated. The number 24 accorded with one of the more common Jewish ways of combining and numbering the canonical books (5 in the Torah, 8 in the earlier and later Prophets, and 11 in the Writings).

Syriac or Second Baruch. Several works were attributed to Jeremiah's secretary, Baruch. First Baruch belongs to the list of deuterocanonical books received into the LXX, the Vulgate, and the canon as formulated at the Council of Trent, but rejected by Jews and Protestants from their canonical list. Second Baruch has survived in a single Syriac copy. Third Baruch, the least important, was written originally in Greek.

Second Baruch is an apocalyptic work that reveals a marked dependency upon 4 Esdras. A pious Jew, drawing upon the latter and other disparate sources, describes a vision that, he pretended, was granted to Jeremiah's secretary about Israel's future after the destruction of Jerusalem in 587 B.C. Not only did some of the facts in the vision disagree with biblical history, but the author was actually writing about another devastation of the Holy City, that by Titus in A.D. 70, and the concomitant frustrating condition of his people. The author is ignorant of the revolt of Simon BAR KOKHBA (Bar Cocheba) in A.D. 132–135, nor does he know anything of the events that followed the revolt and the expulsion of all Jews from the Jerusalem area of Palestine. He must have written, therefore, before A.D. 130.

A summation of 2 Baruch follows. The opening 12 chapters present Baruch's announcement of the destruction of Jerusalem, its collapse before the power of four angels, and the Babylonian possession of the city. Contrary to the Bible, Jeremiah withdraws to Babylon, there to comfort the exiles (see Jer 40.1–6 and the LXX and Vulgate introduction to Lamentations), while Baruch remains to chant a lamentation over the ruins of Jerusalem. After his seven-day fast, divine revelation comes to Baruch's tortured mind, assuring him that the godless will eventually be punished and that ZION was ravaged in order to hasten the day of judgment and the dawn of a new age for the righteous. Baruch is then told to "seal it [the message] in the recesses of your mind" and "sanctify [another] seven days" of fast. In ch. 21–34 God consoles Baruch by allowing him to peer into the heavens and see that everything must be judged in the light of the appointed end of all creation. Twelve woes must first scourge the earth, and only then will the Messiah appear, the manna drop down from heaven, and the dead arise from their sleep. In an important section (ch. 35–46) Baruch uses an image from Daniel, the four world empires of wickedness; the Messiah will be revealed to capture and execute the last world leader and to establish a kingdom that will endure as long as the world. Baruch then announces his own death and encourages the people to maintain their hope in God. Chapters 47–52 repeat familiar themes—fasting, revelation of the future, the resurrection of the just and the damned to the identical bodies that they once possessed on Earth, and the final judgment. After a mysterious vision of black and clear water rained upon the earth, Baruch receives an explanation that spans world history from Adam to the appearance of the Messiah in the form of lightning (ch. 53–76). A golden age follows. Finally, in ch. 77–87, two letters are introduced, but only the first is preserved. It announces the catastrophe of Jerusalem (that of A.D. 70) and future happiness, and it provides suitable advice.

The book, written in apocalyptic style, is full of visions and symbols that attempt to make vivid sacred history, Israel's great calamities, the resurrection, and the final victory. The work would have been lost except for a single Syriac manuscript, translated from a no longer extant Greek version, and a few Greek fragments (ch. 12–14). The original language was Aramaic.

Greek or Third Baruch. This is a Jewish work, highly apocalyptic in style with a free blending of visions, symbols, astronomical details, and eschatological facts. In places, e.g., ch. 6–8, the book attains an extreme-

ly poetical style. The author was dependent upon 2 Baruch and, therefore, wrote sometime after A.D. 130. Origen (d. 254) seems to have had this composition in mind when he referred to a book of the Prophet Baruch and the latter's evidence of seven worlds or heavens. A Greek text, speaking of but five heavens, was discovered only in 1896. Until then there existed only a Slavonic version, much shorter and envisaging only two heavens. Upon investigation the Greek text of 3 Baruch was found colored with heretical Gnostic ideas adapted to Christian truths. In ch. 4, for instance, Baruch sees the tree or vine that Adam was forbidden even to touch (Gn 3.3); but after the Deluge the angel Sarasael instructs Noah to plant a twig of this vine for "its bitterness shall be changed into sweetness and . . . it shall become the blood of God" (4.15).

The book opens with Baruch's weeping over the ruins of Jerusalem. An angel approaches to calm his questioning and anxious mind (ch. 1). Baruch is led through five successive heavens and is initiated into many mysteries of sacred history. (A similar idea of seven heavens occurs in the Testament of the Twelve Patriarchs and the Ascension of Isaiah, while the notion of many heavens is reflected in Dt 10.14; 1 Kgs 8.27; 2 Cor 12.2.) Baruch sees the builder and designer of the TOWER OF BABEL in the first and second heavens, the serpent, the forbidden tree, Hades (the huge belly of the serpent), the bird Phoenix, who is the guardian of the earth and who feeds on the manna, in the third heaven, the souls of the just in the stately form of beautifully singing birds in the fourth heaven, and the angel Michael, who alone can open the fifth heaven and who holds an immense vessel that other angels fill with the good works of the righteous, in the fifth heaven (see Rv 5.8). Baruch is then "restored . . . to the place where I was in the beginning" (17.2).

Jewish Sibylline Oracles. This is a Jewish-Christian adaptation of the Greco-Roman oracles; it was composed between 160 B.C. and A.D. 240. The collection consists of 12 books (bks. 1–8, 11–14; bks. 9, 10, and 15 are lost) and scattered fragments among other writers. Sibylla, or Sibyl (Counsel of God), was the name of a Greek prophetess, very advanced in years, who lived at least before the 5th century B.C. and therefore before the great classical period. She uttered prophecies, mostly of doom and tragedy, in Greek hexameter; tradition even claims that Homer copied his style from her. The Sibyl's prophecies consisted of past history written in the future tense (*vaticinia ex eventu*). When the oracles became increasingly popular, other Sibyls appeared and the birthplace of the original one became a center of controversy. The popularity of the Sibyl appears in the reverential way in which Aristophanes and Plato speak of her.

SIBYLLINE ORACLES were preserved at Rome until the great fire of 82 B.C. destroyed them. Rome sent agents through the empire to recopy the sayings; the demand created such a proliferation of false oracles that Augustus ordered 2,000 volumes of them to be destroyed. The oracles were frequently consulted by the Roman government.

In order to gain a hearing and to win respect with their non-Hebrew neighbors, Hellenistic Jews of Alexandria, Egypt, proceeded to adapt some of the Sibylline oracles to Israelite history and to compose some new ones of their own. They boldly pretended that the Sibyl was the daughter-in-law of Noah. What they produced, however, amounted to a weak parroting of the prophetic oracles against the nations (Isaiah ch. 13–23; Jeremiah ch.46–51; Ezekiel ch. 25–32). Themes of doom and terror are continually repeated, even to the point of monotony, as in one way or another cataclysmic forces of water, fire, earthquake, pestilence, and war sweep through the universe. Idols are overturned, and Israel alone survives to enjoy the messianic prosperity.

These Jewish Sibylline oracles became very popular among the Christians down to the 5th century, especially among Gnostic sects, who may have been responsible for books 6–7. They were edited in their present form in the 6th Christian century. An echo of them is still heard in the *DIES IRAE*, where doomsday is spoken of as *teste David cum Sibylla*.

The rambling, repetitious style is apparent from a survey of book 3. This tells of Beliar, from the stock of Sebaste in Palestine (i.e., Simon Magus; see Acts 8.9–24), and of a lawless widow, both of whom manage to lead even the Jews astray, till God rains destruction upon everything (ll. 63–92). A short Christian interlude prays for the return of the Savior (ll. 93–96). Other lines describe the prosperity of the Jews, which incites the envious Gentiles to attack (see Ps 2.1–3; Ezekiel ch. 38–39). God destroys the enemy in a wondrous way and grants great favors to His people. The Gentiles consequently seek conversion, study the law, and embrace Judaism. The Messiah has an important part in the war of deliverance but disappears from the scene in the victory celebration. No word is heard of a bodily resurrection. The kingdom is described in very earthly tones. In the midst of book 3 occur indirect references to Alexander the Great, Ptolemy VII Physcon, and other notables; the historical sequence is rather chaotic.

MORAL-DIDACTIC APOCRYPHA

These works imitate the style and content of the didactic books of the OT, i.e., the Wisdom Books and the Psalms.

Testament of the Twelve Patriarchs. One such work purports to give the farewell discourses spoken by the 12 sons of Jacob at their deathbeds. It follows a literary pattern fairly common during the century before and the century after the birth of Christ. The origin can be traced to such biblical passages as Jacob's final words in Genesis ch. 49 and Moses' last message in Deuteronomy ch. 33 and is found also in intertestamental literature, such as Ethiopic Enoch (i.e., the book of admonition in 92.1–5; 91.1–11, 18–19), Jubilees (discourse by Isaiah in 31.4–22 and by Jacob in 45.14–16), and the Assumption of Moses. Jesus' parting discourse in John ch. 13–17 may have been composed according to this literary style.

Each of the 12 testaments follows a tripartite division: first, a pseudohistorical narrative of the Patriarch's life with particular attention to some major fault of his; then, the moral lessons to be learned from his experience; finally, a messianic-apocalyptic view of each tribe's future. The first part especially is embellished with legendary and popular traditions, while the third section reflects a tense messianic expectation. The suggestion has been made, not without good reason, that these 12 testaments constitute an anthology of liturgical sermons in which the preacher applied scriptural readings to contemporary problems and needs.

The testaments do not always follow the order of births in Genesis ch. 29–30, but the four eldest sons of Jacob speak first. Ruben (Reuben), of course, shamefully remembers his act of incest with his father's wife Bala (Gn 35.22; 49.4) and repeatedly warns his own sons against fornication. Great caution is necessary, because of the seven evil spirits, the hostile Beliar, and the fickleness of all women. The author shares the SAPIENTIAL BOOKS' suspicion of womankind. The messianic section is practically nonexistent in this, the first testament. Simeon, because of his part in the betrayal and selling of Joseph into slavery, speaks against jealousy and envy. The messianic lines are again very few, and, like Ruben, Simeon expresses loyalty to the priestly tribe of Levi and the kingly tribe of Judah. The testament of Levi is one of the longer and more developed pieces; it reveals a strongly apocalyptic style of visions and heavenly secrets, of past history recounted in the future tense, and of keen eschatological concern. The slaughtering of the Shechemites is justified as an order placed upon Levi and Simeon by an angel, when Levi stood in the divine throne room. Although an eternal right to the priesthood is granted to Levi, he is told nonetheless that a new priest shall arise from the tribe of Judah, who will assist Gentiles as well as Jews, remove sin forever, bind Beliar, open the gates of Paradise, and show the way to the tree of life. Apocalypticism dominates over moralism in the testament of Levi. Because the royalty became Judah's prerogative, his testament begins with a grandiose account of his extraordinary feats of valor and strength. The incident of Judah's relations with his daughter-in-law Tamar provides the preacher with an opportunity to speak forcefully against the dangers of wine and women. After a quick summary of the destruction of Jerusalem in 587 B.C. and the return from the Exile, Judah foresees the Messiah to arise from his offspring, a man who will be meek, without sin, filled with the Spirit, a life-giving fountain, a judge, and a savior of all who call upon the Lord. The eight other testaments, of Issachar, Zabulon, Dan, Nephthali, Gad, Aser, Joseph, and Benjamin, proceed more or less in this same style.

Doctrinal teaching and moral ideals reach a very high quality in this apocryphon. Its authors preferred honest morality to liturgical ceremonies; they kept apocalyptic interests under control, so that hopes in any imminent, divine breakthrough never confused immediate moral demands. Sin is resolutely condemned, but the sinner is always offered the possibility of repentance. Fasting is seen as a mighty weapon against the evil spirits. Besides the seven principal spirits of depravity, the testaments refer also to the leader, Beliar (the word is derived from the biblical Belial; see Dt 13.13; Jgs 19. 22; 1 Sm 1.6). Beliar is an individual person (testaments of Joseph 20.2; of Simeon 5.3; of Nephthali 2.6). The resurrection of the body is clearly taught (testament of Benjamin 10.6–8), and, in fact, the future age is filled with all kinds of earthly delights. The place of the messiahs and their special qualities have already been mentioned. The testaments expect two messiahs, the one a religious leader, a priestly messiah from the tribe of Levi, by far the more important, and the other a royal messiah of the tribe of Judah. A few scholars (e.g., M. J. Lagrange) deny that the references add up to a belief in any personal messiahs; the authors, instead, look forward to messianic, redemptive movements in which the tribes of Levi and Judah will take the lead. Most scholars, however, especially with the evidence of the Dead Sea Scrolls at hand, recognize the expectation of individual messiahs.

Until research was made on the Dead Sea Scrolls, questions about the authorship of the testaments were generally settled in favor of a Jewish origin, with later Christian interpolations. The bulk of the 12 testaments were said to have been composed by a Jew, who may have belonged to the Essene sect, sometime after 200 B.C., perhaps during the reign of the worldly Hasmonean king Alexander Jannaeus (r. 103–76 B.C.). This age accounts for the antagonism to the royalty (testaments of Judah 21.6–23.5; of Levi 14.5–16.5). Christian additions were inserted into the text c. A.D. 100 in order to sharpen the messianic references in favor of Jesus Christ (testaments of Joseph 19.11; of Benjamin 3.8, 9.3–5). Repre-

sentative scholars (e.g., O. Eissfeldt) still prefer this explanation; but others (e.g., J. T. Milik) hold a different opinion on this question. The sections of the testaments found at Qumran (an Aramaic fragment of Levi; a Hebrew fragment of Nephthali) are longer, and, especially in the case of Nephthali, they are considerably different. They represent the source from which a Jewish Christian of the 1st or 2d Christian century prepared a set of testaments for all 12 Patriarchs. The original Hebrew or Aramaic texts no longer exist, except for the Dead Sea Scrolls and a Hebrew fragment of Nephthali that was found in the Cairo Geniza at the end of the 19th century. There are extant 10 Greek MSS, of two basic forms, besides two translations from the Greek, one in Slavonic and a more important one in Armenian.

Psalms of Solomon. These are 18 hymns, composed originally in Hebrew but existing now only in Greek and in a Syriac version derived from the Greek. These psalms (hereafter *Ps. Sol.*) must be kept distinct, not only from the Book of Psalms in the Bible, but also from another collection, *The Odes of Solomon,* 42 hymns by a 2d-century Christian (see next section).

Because of cryptic historical references in *Ps. Sol.,* it is usually stated that the author(s) wrote a little after the violent death of Pompey, who, in 48 B.C., was slain, left unburied, and finally cremated on an improvised pyre in Egypt. The second psalm seems to refer to the manner in which the Jewish leaders, Aristobulus II and John Hyrcanus II, first welcomed the approaching army of Pompey; then, when Aristobulus's group resisted, Pompey fought back, razed the walls around the temple enclosure, and sacrilegiously entered the Holy of Holies (*Ps. Sol.* 2.2, 29–31; 8.15–20). At least the second and eighth psalms can be traced back to the middle of the 1st century B.C.; but a further question is still not completely solved, whether the same poet composed all the psalms or whether the collection grew over a long time. Because the psalms breathe a certain peace, at least in not expecting any violent changes, their composition must have been completed before the great unrest of the 1st Christian century.

Another open question is the identity or character of the author(s). The name Solomon was adopted because this king was the model of a glorious, wise, and peaceful monarch; in *Ps. Sol.* faith is expressed in a new king of the line of Judah who will receive wisdom from God and will conquer the world not by the sword but "with the word of his mouth forever" (*Ps. Sol.* 17.39). It was the customary style, ever since the emergence of apocalyptic literature in the postexilic age, for authors to use pseudonyms (as in Daniel, Jonah, Wisdom, and Ecclesiastes). Not only because of the messianic interests of the writer but also because *Ps. Sol.* ch. 17 argues very vigorously against the Hasmonean kings, it is often presumed that the poet belonged to the sect of the Pharisees. Toward the end of his reign the Hasmonean king Alexander Jannaeus ordered a large number of Pharisees to be impaled before his very eyes. But this evidence does not suffice to establish the author as a Pharisee; many of the common people hated the Hasmoneans. Nor were messianic interests in a king of the line of Judah confined to the Pharisees. Such a key Pharisaic doctrine as the resurrection of the body is found in *Ps. Sol.* 3.16 but not in the important *Ps. Sol.* 17–18. Finally, *Ps. Sol.* 4, according to M. J. Lagrange, seems directed against Pharisaic hypocrisy. It is better to conclude, with O. Eissfeldt, that the author of *Ps. Sol.* was not necessarily a Pharisee; he may have belonged to the Essenes. He was a layman, very devoted to his religion, feeling deeply its abuses, and firmly confident in God's deliverance.

The principal purpose of the poet(s) was to sustain hope in divine promises by assuring the people that God would replace the depraved Hasmoneans with a worthy king of the house of David. The Messiah of the tribe of Levi is passed over in silence, and here one notes quite a change from the Testament of the Twelve Patriarchs and the Qumran Scrolls. (No copy of *Ps. Sol* has yet turned up among the Dead Sea Scrolls.) The Davidic Messiah will not be a suffering redeemer or a priest or a warrior. He will cleanse Jerusalem and make the Holy City a world capital "with the word of his mouth." All members will become "SONS OF GOD." The messianic picture, it will be noted, is peaceful but very nationalistic. An exalted moral ideal is constantly to the fore, including personal freedom and responsibility, the righteous fear of God, patience and long-suffering, and the expectation of a reward after death.

The style is what one would expect in songs that arose within the Israelite liturgy. Compared to the biblical Book of Psalms, *Ps. Sol.* sometimes has similar titles (for the leader in *Ps. Sol.* 8.1) and identical liturgical rubrics (the *selâ* in 17.31; 18.10). The same general types are found in both cases: hymns (*Ps. Sol.* 2.20, 33–37; 3.1–2); collective or individual plaints (2.19–25; 7; 8.22–34; 16.6–15); thanksgiving songs (13.1–4; 15.1–6; 16.1–5); didactic songs (3.3–12; 6). These various kinds of songs, however, now freely intermingle, so that a single psalm, such as canonical Psalm 2, shifts from one type to another. *Ps. Sol.* also manifest a greater precision in historical references than one is accustomed to meet in the biblical Psalms. One last feature about *Ps. Sol.* is noteworthy: the apocalyptic imagery is held in restraint. One senses no imminent cataclysm to break up the present age and suddenly inaugurate the new. The Messiah will conquer, but peacefully and mysteriously.

Odes of Solomon. These are 42 hymns, known principally through a Syriac translation discovered in 1908 by J. Rendel Harris, but written originally in Greek in the early 2d Christian century for liturgical usage in the Eastern Church. These songs are not to be confused with the previously mentioned apocryphon, the *Psalms of Solomon*. The odes reveal a strong Jewish influence: the parallelism of the biblical Psalms, references to Christ in the form of prophecy rather than of history, and a strong monotheism. Christian references, however, are almost everywhere present, and they are too intimate a part of the text to be considered additions to an earlier Jewish work. The author never quotes any single word of Jesus from the Gospels; in fact, he never uses the proper name Jesus, but he prefers the common Jewish form Christ (i.e., the Messiah, the Anointed One). An exalted mysticism, derived from the writings of St. John and especially of St. Paul, spreads a contemplative spirit throughout the hymns.

The poet is particularly interested in the illumination that proceeds from the resurrected Christ (ode 42 is one of the oldest Christian poems on the Resurrection). He shies away from the humiliating details of Jesus' earthly life. Baptism, the Sacrament of initiation and enlightenment, is the only rite of the Christian Church to receive special attention. The author's Christology is not heretical, but it could become very compatible with Docetist Gnosticism, especially in odes 19 and 35. It is not surprising that five of the odes were included in the Gnostic book *Pistis Sophia*. (See J. Labourt and P. Batiffol, *Les Odes de Salomon* [Paris 1911]; J. R. Harris and A. Mingana, *The Odes and Psalms of Solomon* [2 v. Manchester 1916–20]; J. Quasten, *Patrology* [v. 1 Westminster, Md. 1950] 160–168.)

Prayer of Manasseh. This is a penitential psalm of Jewish origin, consisting of only 15 verses (from 37 to 42 lines in the Greek text), composed around the beginning of the Christian era. The Greek style is very impressive, with its flowing rhythm and rich vocabulary. Most scholars, therefore, deny the possibility of a translation from the Hebrew. R. H. Pfeiffer and R. H. Charles consider that at least in verse 7 one can detect traces of an original Hebrew text beneath the surface of the Greek language. They have found only a limited number of supporters for this position.

The prayer pretends to express the contrite spirit of Manasseh (r. 687–642 B.C.). This king of Judah had reversed the fervent religious policy of his father, King Hezekiah (r. 716–687 B.C.), introduced pagan rites into the temple compound (idols, child sacrifice, and fertility cult), and violently removed all opposition among the Prophets and people (2 Kgs 21.1–18). Manasseh's apostasy may have been forced on him by a resurgent Assyria, who expected vassal countries to worship its gods. It is not clear whether or not Manasseh finally decided to resist Assyrian pressure, but it is stated in 2 Chr 33.11–12 that the Assyrians took Manasseh in chains to Babylon, where the Judean king humbled himself and did penance before the God of his fathers. According to 2 Chr 33.18 a prayer uttered by Manasseh on this occasion was preserved in the ''Chronicle of the Kings of Israel'' and the ''Chronicle of the Seers,'' records that are no longer extant. This apocryphon fills in the lacuna and in doing so makes the ancient past meaningful for a later age.

The Prayer of Manasseh was rejected by St. Jerome along with all deuterocanonical and apocryphal works, and the Council of Trent did not include it in the Church's official list of inspired books. Its presence, however, among 14 canticles or odes in the 5th-century MS Alexandrinus and in many other Greek, Latin, Syriac, Ethiopic, Arabic, Armenian, and Coptic MSS indicates that it was a popular liturgical piece in the Eastern Church. The religious doctrine of the prayer is very encouraging: God is infinitely compassionate, and sincere repentance obtains forgiveness for the worst sins.

Fourth Maccabees. This is a philosophical sermon or disquisition demonstrating the Mosaic Law as the supreme example of reason's triumph over the passions (1.1). Its present title dates back to LXX MSS Sinaiticus (4th century) and Alexandrinus (5th century), in which the book follows immediately upon the other three Books of Maccabees. It has, however, very little in common with any of them. Unlike 1 and 2 Maccabees, it does not feature the Maccabean wars of independence, and it is unlike 3 Maccabees in that it does not follow a narrative style. The book is found also among the collected works of Flavius Josephus, where it is entitled more appropriately, ''On the Supremacy of Reason.''

The 18 chapters of 4 Maccabees can be divided into four principal sections. (1) The introduction (1.1–12) states the theme and gives a general plan of development. Here it is plainly admitted that ''inspired reason is supreme ruler over the passions, and . . . the greatest virtue . . . [is] self-control'' (1.1–2). (2) In the philosophical exposition (1.13–3.18) an attempt is made to ''define what the reason is and what passion is.'' Wisdom is ''the knowledge of things, divine and human, and of their causes, . . . the culture acquired under the [Mosaic] Law'' (1.14–17). (3) The third section (3.19–17.24) establishes and illustrates these statements, especially the one on the importance of the law, by drawing upon the events narrated in 2 Maccabees ch. 3; 6.18–7.42, namely, Heliodorus's futile attempt to rob the temple treasury, the martyrdom of Eleazar, and the agonizing death of a moth-er and her seven sons (called the Maccabean martyrs in the Christian liturgy). The gruesome and graphic account of their tortures are frequently interrupted with speeches in praise of the law and its wisdom. (4) The final section (ch. 18) presents a peroration on obedience to the law, addressed like the entire book to ''Israelites, children born of the seed of Abraham.''

The style and vocabulary of the book is thoroughly Greek, following the literary form of the diatribe as known among the Cynics and Stoics, i.e., a popular discourse on philosophical or religious matters. The author shows himself superior to the epitomizer of 2 Maccabees and far more capable than the composer of 3 Maccabees. The subject matter, however, is Jewish through and through, so that some scholars think that the book may have originated as a synagogal sermon.

Four Maccabees drew freely upon Jewish tradition. The author mentions the paradise in which he claims that Eve was beguiled into a sexual sin by the serpent; Cain, Abel, and the sacrifice of Isaac; David the psalmist; the Prophet Ezekiel; and the deuterocanonical stories of Daniel. The expiatory suffering of the innocent for the sinful is clearly taught, a rare example of the influence of the Suffering Servant of the Songs of the SUFFERING SERVANT (Is 52.13–53.12) on later Jewish thought (4 Maccabees 1.11; 6.28–29; 17.21–22). Retribution after the death of the just and the wicked is presumed throughout the work, but, contrary to 2 Mc 7.11, 14, 19, 22–23, the resurrection of the body is not taught. Immortality is presented in a more Platonic fashion (4 Maccabees 5.37; 9.8; 10.11; 12.13).

Eusebius of Caesarea (A.D. 270–340) and St. Jerome (A.D. 342–420) identified the author with the Jewish historian Flavius Josephus (A.D. 37–100), but this opinion is not accepted today. The author's name, therefore, remains unknown, but from his book one can deduce that he was a fervent Jew, well versed in the Hebrew Scriptures and in later traditions. He shows himself very favorable to Greek philosophical influences, the Platonic, the Cynic, and particularly the Stoic. For these reasons he must have lived in the Jewish DIASPORA, either in Syria, birthplace of the Stoic philosopher Zeno and possibly the home of the Jewish author of 2 Maccabees, or Alexandria, Egypt, where the LXX originated and where the MSS Sinaiticus and Alexandrinus were written. He composed his work sometime after 2 Maccabees but before the spread of Christianity—therefore, in the two or three decades before or after the beginning of the Christian Era.

Bibliography: R. H. CHARLES et al., eds., *The Apocrypha and Pseudepigrapha of the O.T. in English,* 2 v. (Oxford 1913), the standard book for Eng. tr. and the longest commentaries. O. EIS-SFELDT, *Einleitung in das A.T.* (3d ed. Tübingen 1964) 777–864, the most incisive and up-to-date introd. R. H. PFEIFFER, *The Interpreters' Bible,* ed. G. A. BUTTRICK et al., 12 v. (New York 1951–57) 1:391–436. H. H. ROWLEY, *The Relevance of Apocalyptic* (2d ed. London 1952). A. BENTZEN, *Introduction to the O.T.,* 2 v. in 1 (2d ed. Copenhagen 1952) 2:218–252. J. B. FREY, *Dictionnaire de la Bible,* suppl. ed. L. PIROT et al. (Paris 1928–) 1:354–460. I. M. PRICE et al., *Dictionary of the Bible,* ed. J. HASTINGS and J. A. SELBIA, rev. in 1 v. ed. F. C. GRANT and H. H. ROWLEY (New York 1963) 39–41, 820–823. R. J. FOSTER, "The Apocrypha of the O.T. and N.T.," *Catholic Commentary on Holy Scripture,* ed. B. ORCHARD et al. (London, New York 1957) 92–94. D. S. RUSSELL, *The Method and Message of Jewish Apocalyptic* (Philadelphia 1964).

[C. STUHLMUELLER]

APOCRYPHA OF THE NEW TESTAMENT

The NT Apocrypha, as the term is used here, are the early Christian writings that more or less resemble the books of the NT but have not been received as canonical Scriptures by the Church. The beginnings of the NT apocryphal literature coincide with the slow crystallization of the NT canon. Most of the Apocryphal books are known only by title because their existence was mentioned by the Fathers of the Church in their struggle against heresy. Origen, Irenaeus, Jerome, Eusebius, and especially Epiphanius in his comprehensive *Panarion,* or Refutation, of all heresies (*Patrologia Graeca,* ed. J. P. Migne, 161 v. [Paris 1857–66] v. 41) are the main sources of information on the NT Apocrypha; some information is found also in the Stichometry of Nicephor (*ibid.* 100:1060) and the Pseudo-Gelasian Decree (*Patrologia Latina,* ed. J. P. Migne, 271 v., indexes 4 v. [Paris 1878–90] 59:162–164; *Texte und Untersuchungen zur Geschichte der altchristlichen Literatur* [Berlin 1882–] 3.8.4).

The main characteristics of the NT Apocrypha are not only their pseudonymous use of the names of the Apostles or other personages who were supposed to know something of the life and teachings of Our Lord, but also their general imitation of the four kinds of the NT canonical writings—the Gospels, Acts, Epistles, and Revelation. They differ, however, from the canonical writings by the excess of the miraculous element in their stories and by the esoteric aspect of their teachings. In regard to their doctrinal contents one can distinguish those that are heretical (mostly Gnostic, but later at times purged by orthodox editors) from those that are merely fictitious and can be considered as the beginnings of Christian devotional literature or even as the first attempts at dogmatic development (e.g., in regard to the Assumption of Mary). They had a great influence on the liturgy (e.g., the Feasts of the Presentation, of St. Joachim, and of St. Anne), the iconography, and Christian symbolism. Their greatest value consists in the witness they offer in proof on the one hand, of the first daring movements of Christian thinking and imagination, and on

the other, of the sure discriminatory power of the Church in distinguishing them from the canonical writings.

Bibliography: J. A. FABRICIUS, *Codex Apocryphus Novi Testamenti,* 3 v. (Hamburg 1719–43). J. C. THILO, *Codex Apocryphus Novi Testamenti* (Leipzig 1832). S. SZÉKELY, *Bibliotheca Apocrypha* (Freiburg 1913). J. BOUSQUET and É. AMANN, *Les Apocryphes du Nouveau Testament* (Paris 1910; 3d ed. 1922). E. KLOSTERMANN and A. HARNACK, *Apokrypha,* 4 v. (Kleine Texte 3, 8, 11, 12; v. 1, 3d ed. Bonn 1921; v. 2–4, 2d ed. 1910–12). B. ALTANER, *Patrology,* tr. H. GRAEF from 5th German ed. (New York 1960) 51–73. J. QUASTEN, *Patrology,* 4 v. (Westminster, Md. 1950–86) 1:106–157. O. BARDENHEWER, *Geschichte der altkirchlichen Literatur,* 5 v. (Freiburg 1913–32). E. HENNECKE, *Neutestamentliche Apokryphen,* 2 v. (3d ed. Tübingen 1959–64), Eng. tr. of v. 1 (London 1963); references below to v. 1 are to the Eng. ed. M. R. JAMES, *The Apocryphal New Testament* (Oxford 1924; corrected repr. 1953). A. WALKER and B. P. PATTERN, *Ante-Nicene Christian Library,* 24 v. (Edinburgh 1866–72; additional v. 1897); new impression, ed. A. COXE, 8 v. (Buffalo 1884–86) 8:349–644, 657–665. W. MICHAELIS, *Die apokryphen Schriften zum Neuen Testament* (Bremen 1956). R. H. PFEIFFER, *History of NT Times with an Introduction to the Apocrypha* (New York 1949). C. C. TORREY, *The Apocryphal Literature* (New Haven, Conn.1945). É. AMANN, *Dictionnaire de la Bible,* suppl. ed. L. PIROT et al. (Paris 1928–) 1:1217–33. L. VAGANEY, *Catholicisme. Hier, aujourd'hui et demain,* ed. G. JACQUEMET 1:699–704. J. MICHL, *Lexikon für Theologie und Kirche,* ed. J. HOFER and K. RAHNER, 10 v. (2d, new ed. Freiburg 1957–65) 1:698–704, 712–713, 747–754; 2:688–693; 3:1217–33. B. M. METZGER, *Die Religion in Geschichte und Gegenwart,* 7 v. (3d ed. Tübingen 1957–65) 1:473–474.

[C. H. HENKEY]

APOCRYPHA, ICONOGRAPHY OF THE

From late Hellenistic times through the medieval period, apocryphal literature constantly provided artists with rich sources of iconography. As a source of iconography the apocrypha of the New Testament is of much greater importance than that of the Old Testament. Of the Old Testament apocrypha, *Ascensio Jesaiae* is the only book known today to have been used as an iconographical source. It is assumed that there existed a certain number of narrative cycles on deuterocanonical literature of Hellenistic Jewish origin from the late Hellenistic period.

In early Christianity artists used the apocryphal New Testament literature to complete narrative cycles of the lives of Christ, the Virgin Mary, the Apostles and other saints, since canonical books gave artists only imperfect information about the lives of these important figures. The influence of apocryphal New Testament literature is most conspicuous in the following cycles: (1) The life of Christ. For the Nativity and the Infancy, the *Protoevangelium Jacobi* and the *Evangelium Pseudo-Matthaei* are the main sources for themes such as the Birth in the Mountain Cave, Two Midwives, the Animals by the

558

Manger, etc. The *Evangelium Infantiae Salvatoris arabicum* as well as the *Gospel of St. Thomas* provide supplementary information about the Nativity and the Infancy, such as the Star of Angels and the occurrence of early miracles. The Bathing of the Infant Christ in the Nativity scene is a borrowing from pagan birth scenes. There are two sources for the apocryphal details of the Passion and the DESCENT OF CHRIST INTO HELL: the *Gospel of Bartholomew* and the *Gospel of Nicodemus* (*Acta Pilati*). (2) The life of the Virgin. The *Protoevangelium Jacobi* is again the most important source for the life of the Virgin in reference to Joachim and Anna, the Nativity of the Virgin, the Presentation of the Virgin, the Engagement, and the Annunciation. For the last part of her life, the *De transitu Beatae Mariae Virginis* attributed to Melito of Sardis is the main source. (3) The lives of Apostles. There are several apocryphal books of the Acts of the Apostles, e.g., *Acts of Paul, Acts of Peter, Acts of Andreas,* etc. They are the principal sources of the miraculous deeds and martyrdoms of the Apostles as well as the source of their portraits [Peter and Simon Magnus, Martyrdom of Peter (*Quo vadis, Domine*), etc.].

Bibliography: E. B. SMITH, *Early Christian Iconography* (Princeton 1918). *Reallexikon zur deutschen Kunstgeschichte*, ed. O. SCHMITT, v.1 (Stuttgart 1937) 781–801. K. WESSEL, ed., *Reallexikon zur byzantinischen Kunst*, v.1 (Stuttgart 1963) 1: 209–218.

[S. TSUJI]

APOLLINARIANISM

A fourth-century Christological heresy that denied the human soul in Christ. It received its name from Apollinaris, Bishop of Laodicea, who had been a champion of Nicene orthodoxy and a friend of St. ATHANASIUS OF ALEXANDRIA. Apollinarianism signalized the point of transition from the Trinitarian to the Christological heresies.

Its principal thesis was a result of the anti-Arian polemic of Apollinaris, but in attempting to defend the divinity of the Word, he actually accepted the Arian postulate minimizing the human nature in Christ (*c.* 352). In his zeal to preserve the humanity of Christ, and his lack of a distinction between the concept of nature and person, Apollinaris relied on the Platonic trichotomy of the human being: body, sensitive soul, and rationality (σάρξ, ψυχή σαρκική, and ψυχή λογική).

In his literal interpretation of the Johannine text "The Word became Flesh," Apollinaris believed that he had found the key to the solution of the Christological problem. He taught that (1) if one does not admit a diminution of the human nature in Christ, the unity of Christ cannot be explained since two complete natures cannot constitute one unique entity; (2) where there exists a complete man, sin exists since sin resides in the will, that is, in man's spirit, for free will and sin are interdependent; hence Christ's being exempt from sin cannot be explained if he had a human spirit in the Incarnate Word; and (3) the Word of God did not assume a complete human nature, but only a body (σάρξ) and what is strictly connected with the body, the sensitive soul. The Word itself has taken the part of the spirit of man, or the rational soul (νοῦς). Only thus can one speak of "one sole nature incarnate of the Word of God" (μία φύσις τοῦ λόγου τοῦ θεοῦ σεσαρκωμένη). This formula is found in Apollinaris' *Incarnation of the Word of God,* which is frequently interpolated among the works of St. Athanasius.

As intended by Apollinaris, the sentence cannot have an orthodox meaning, but because it was reputedly accepted by St. Athanasius, St. CYRIL OF ALEXANDRIA, in his polemic against NESTORIANISM, gave it an orthodox interpretation. After the Council of EPHESUS, however, it was accepted by EUTYCHES and DIOSCORUS OF ALEXANDRIA in a strictly Monophysitic sense, and by Sergius of Constantinople with a Monoenergetic and Monothelite meaning. Apollinarianism appears in the history of Christian dogma as a heresy more disturbing in its consequences in the long perspective than in its immediate effects.

Examined first in the Synod of Alexandria in 362, the doctrine of Apollinaris was condemned on the principle common in Oriental theology that "that which is not assumed [by the Divine word] is not healed." Hence if the Logos had not assumed a rational soul, the redemption would be inefficacious as regards human souls. This condemnation was formulated in a delicate manner, not mentioning the name of Apollinaris, but his position was definitively compromised when his disciple Vitalis, after the MELETIAN SCHISM (362), founded an Apollinarian party at Antioch (375). Vitalis at first deceived Pope DAMASUS I, but in a Synod of 377, on the basis of further information, the pope admonished Vitalis to reject Apollinarianism and called for the deposition of Apollinaris and the bishops infected with his heresy.

Apollinaris gave final definition to his ideas in his *Demonstration of the Divine Incarnation* (376), answered the papal condemnation by consecrating Vitalis a bishop for his sect in Antioch, and helped his follower Timotheus to become bishop of Berytus. However, neither these measures nor the attempt to spread his teaching among the Egyptian bishops exiled by the Emperor Valens to Diocaesarea succeeded.

The Roman Synod's decision was confirmed by Synods of Alexandria (378) and Antioch (379) and by the General Council of CONSTANTINOPLE I (381). It was reconfirmed by Damasus' Roman Council in 382. Thereupon the Emperor THEODOSIUS I intervened with decrees in 383, 384, and 388, outlawing the Apollinarists and sending their major representatives into exile. The imperial decrees did not succeed, however, and the heresy was well received among many Orientals, but it did not long survive its originator, who died in 390.

Toward 420 the schismatic community was reabsorbed into the Catholic Church, although a group of intransigents, called Sinusiati, finished later by joining the Monophysite movement, with whom they had a theological affinity.

The dogmatic writings in which Apollinaris exposed his doctrine have been handed down as having other authorship than his: *Profession of Faith,* among the works of St. Athanasius, and a letter to the presbyter Dionysius, under the name of Pope JULIUS I. His principal work *Demonstratio Incarnationis divinae* is known mainly through its refutation in the writings of St. GREGORY OF NYSSA (*Antirrheticus adv. Apollinarem*). St. GREGORY OF NAZIANZUS, DIODORE OF TARSUS, and THEODORET OF CYR also wrote against Apollinarianism, but their works have not been preserved. The work *Adv. fraudes Apollinaristarum* is probably to be attributed to LEONTIUS OF BYZANTIUM.

Bibliography: H. LIETZMANN, *Apollinaris von Laodicea und seine Schule* (Tübingen 1904). G. VOISIN, *L' Apollinarisme* (Louvain 1901). C. E. RAVEN, *Apollinarianism* (Cambridge, Eng. 1923). H. DE RIEDMATTEN, ''Some Neglected Aspects of Apollinarist Christology,'' *Dominican Studies* 1 (1948) 239–260; A. GRILLMEIER and H. BACHT, *Das Konzil von Chalkedon: Geschichte und Gegenwart* (Würzburg 1951–54) 1:102–117, 203–212. B. ALTANER, *Patrology,* tr. H. GRAEF (New York 1960) 363–365. J. QUASTEN, *Patrology* (Westminster, Maryland 1950–) 3:377–383. A. GESCHÉ, *Revue d'histoire ecclésiastique* 54 (1959) 403–406.

[F. CHIOVARO]

APOLLINARIS OF HIERAPOLIS, ST.

Bishop in Phrygia who received his see in the second half of the second century during the reign of Marcus Aurelius (161–180). In the early days of MONTANISM Apollinaris the Apologist, also called Claudius Apollinaris, was an outstanding champion of orthodoxy whose writings served to counteract the heresy. Though none of his works is extant, he wrote much, including an apology of the Christian faith addressed to the Emperor Marcus Aurelius. Apollinaris wrote also five books: *Against the Greeks,* two *On the Truth,* and two *Against the Jews.* There is no serious reason to attribute to Apollinaris the *Cohortatio ad Graecos,* nor is he the author of the long anti-Montanist fragments cited by Eusebius (*Hist. Eccl.*

5.16–19). Since Apollinaris wrote against the early Montanists and these fragments were written 14 years after Maximilla's death, they could not have been written by Apollinaris.

Feast: Jan. 8.

Bibliography: P. DE LABRIOLLE, *Dictionnaire d'histoire et de géographie ecclésiastiques,* ed. A. BAUDRILLART et al. (Paris 1912) 3:959–960. J. QUASTEN, *Patrology* (Westminster, MD 1950) 1:228–229. H. RAHNER, *Lexikon für Theologie und Kirche,* ed. J. HOFER and K. RAHNER (Freiburg 1957–65) 1:713–714.

[E. DAY]

APOLLINARIS OF LAODICEA, THE YOUNGER

Fourth-century theologian and heretic; b. Laodicea in Syria *c.* 300; d. *c.* 390. Apollinaris, the son of grammarian and priest Apollinaris the elder, received an excellent profane and religious education. He served as lector in the church of Laodicea under Bishop Theodotus (d. 333) and taught rhetoric. Although he was excommunicated by the bishop for participating in a pagan ceremony conducted by the rhetorician Epiphanius, he was subsequently readmitted to communion. He was excommunicated a second time, by the Arian Bishop George in 346, for giving hospitality to ATHANASIUS OF ALEXANDRIA, but was elected bishop (*c.* 361) by the Nicene community of Laodicea.

Apollinaris the Younger lectured at Antioch (*c.* 374) where St. Jerome was one of his auditors (Jerome, *Epist.,* 84.3), and was renowned for his support of Trinitarian doctrine against the Arians, his opposition to Julian the Apostate, and his logical mind and knowledge of Hebrew. He had opposed the doctrine of DIODORE OF TARSUS, who apparently taught that in Christ the union of the divine and human natures was purely moral. In his opposition Apollinaris denied that Christ had a soul, thinking that His divine personality supplied the assumed human nature with that function. This error was condemned at a synod of Alexandria, which did not mention Apollinaris by name because of his strong opposition to Arianism, and he modified his teaching.

Accepting the Semitic trichotomy of body-soul-spirit, he admitted that Christ had a soul, but denied He had a human spirit. This doctrine was opposed in 374 by BASIL OF CAESAREA, who asked Pope DAMASUS I to condemn it as heresy. In 377 Rome censured Apollinaris's teaching, and he was condemned at the Council of CONSTANTINOPLE I (381). In 385 GREGORY OF NYSSA wrote a refutation of Apollinaris called the *Antirrheticus contra Apollinarem,* that was directed against Apollinaris's *Proof of the Incarnation.*

Most of Apollinaris's writings have disappeared. However, his disciples camouflaged several under pseudonyms, such as the letter of the Pseudo-Athanasius to the Emperor Jovian, letters under the name of Pope Julius, and a *Profession of Faith in Detail,* attributed to GREGORY THAUMATURGUS. Fragments of his writings have been discovered in Gregory of Nyssa's *Antirrheticus* and in the *Contra fraudes Apollinaristarum,* attributed to Anastasius of Sinai. His 30 books against Porphyry, his *De veriate* against Julian the Apostate, and his Biblical commentaries are represented by citations in the scriptural chains or testimonia. The full extent of Apollinarist frauds and interpolations came to be understood only in the 6th century, during the later Monophysite controversy. However, early orthodox writers were aware that St. CYRIL's famous phrase ''one nature of the Logos incarnate'' was actually a definition created by Apollinaris.

Bibliography: H. LIETZMANN, *Apollinaris von Laodicea und seine Schule* (Tübingen 1904). H. DERIEDMATTEN, A. GRILLMEIER and H. BACHT, *Das Konzil von Chalkedon: Geschichte und Gegenwart* (Würzburg 1951–54) 1:203–212, fragments; *Lexikon für Theologie und Kirche,* ed. J. HOFER and K. RAHNER (Freiberg 1957–65) 1:714. C. RAVEN, *Apollinarianism* (Cambridge, Eng. 1923). A. AIGRAIN, *Dictionnaire d'histoire et de géographie ecclésiastiques,* 3:962–982. G. L. PRESTIGE, *St. Basil the Great and Apollinaris of Laodicea,* ed. H. CHADWICK (Society for Promoting Christian Knowledge 1956). R. WEIJENBERG, *Antonianum* 33 (1958) 197–240, 371–414; 34 (1959) 246–298, Basil. J. QUASTEN, *Patrology* (Westminster, Maryland 1950–) 3:377–383. B. ALTANER, *Patrology,* tr. H. GRAEF (New York 1960) 363–365.

[J. BENTIVEGNA]

APOLLINARIS OF MONTE CASSINO, ST.

Benedictine abbot; d. Nov. 27, 828. Having been given as an oblate to Monte Cassino by his parents when he was still very young, he was ordained deacon and priest under Abbot Gisulfus, whom he succeeded (817–828). During his reign, the monastery received many endowments. He was famous for the sanctity of his life, and he is said to have crossed the Liri River dryshod. His remains were interred first near the church of St. John and were transferred by Abbot Desiderius (VICTOR III) to the same church and honored with an epitaph in verse. In 1592 the relics of Apollinaris were placed under an altar in the chapel dedicated to him, decorated with paintings by Luca Giordano. The relics survived the destruction of World War II and were replaced in the same chapel after its restoration.

Feast: Nov. 27.

Bibliography: *Bibliotheca hagiographica latina antiquae et mediae aetatis* (Brussels 1898–1901) 1:622. DESIDERIUS, *Dialogi*

1.1–2. G. FALCO, ''Lineamenti di storia cassinese . . . ,'' *Casinensia* (Monte Cassino 1929) 2:510. *Monumenta Germaniae Historica: Scriptores* 30.2:1118. *Chronicon Casinense* 1.19–21, *Monumenta Germaniae Historica: Scriptores* 7: 594–596. PETER THE DEACON, *De ortu et obitu iustorum Casinensium,* ch. 26 in *Patrologia Latina* (Paris 1878–90) 173:1081–90. L. TOSTI, *Storia della badia di Montecassino,* 4 v. (Rome 1880–90) 1:46. A. M. ZIMMERMANN, *Kalendarium Benedictinum: Die Heiligen und Seligen des Benediktinerordens und seiner Zweige* (Metten 1933–38) 3:363–365.

[A. LENTINI]

APOLLINARIS OF VALENCE, ST.

Bishop; b. Vienne, France, *c.* 453; d. Valence, France, *c.* 520. Apollinaris (or Aplonay) was the son of (St.) Hesychius (Isicius) and the brother of (St.) AVITUS, successively bishops of Vienne. When elected to the See of Valence (*c.* 490), vacant for some years and in dire need of reform, Apollinaris successfully labored to reestablish discipline in his diocese and to restore the Catholic faith to the Burgundian kingdom, which had fallen into ARIANISM. He assisted at the synods of Epaon (517) and Lyons (516–523). Shortly after Epaon he was exiled by King Sigismund, angered (according to a vita of questionable historical value) by the excommunication of a royal official on charges of incest, but he was restored to his see the following year. His correspondence with Avitus, together with the acts of the councils, are the best sources for his biography. He is the principal patron of the Diocese of Valence.

Feast: Oct. 5.

Bibliography: *Monumenta Germaniae Historica: Scriptores rerum Merovingicarum* 3:197–203. Correspondence with Avitus, *Patrologia Latina,* ed. J. P. MIGNE (Paris 1878–90) 59:231–232, 273. *Monumenta Germaniae Historica: Concilia* 1:29, 32–34. P. CHAPUIS, *S. Apollinaire, évêque, principal patron de tout le diocèse de Valence* (Paris 1898). R. AIGRAIN, *Dictionnaire d'histoire et de géographie ecclésiastiques,* ed. A. BAUDRILLART et al. (Paris 1912) 982–986; *Catholicisme* 1:705–706. H. LECLERCQ, *Dictionnaire d'archéologie chrétienne et de liturgie,* ed. F. CABROL, H. LECLERCQ, and H. I. MARROU (Paris 1907–53) 15.2:2901. A. BUTLER, *The Lives of the Saints,* ed. H. THURSTON and D. ATTWATER (New York 1956) 4:36. G. MATHON, *Bibliotheca sanctorum* 2:249–250.

[G. M. COOK]

APOLLONIA OF ALEXANDRIA, ST.

Also called Appolline, virgin and martyr, died in a popular uprising preceding the persecution of DECIUS. Her martyrdom is described in a letter of Dionysius, Bishop of Alexandria, to Fabius, Bishop of Antioch (Eusebius, *Eccl. Hist.* 6.41.7). According to Dionysius, a

St. Apollonia of Alexandria, portion of predella, early 16th century, by Andrea del Sarto.

mob seized "the marvelous aged virgin Apollonia," broke her teeth, and threatened to burn her alive. Having been given a brief respite, she leaped into a fire and was consumed. The morality of such acts was discussed by St. Augustine (*Civ.* 1.26). Despite the fact that Dionysius explicitly mentions her age, Apollonia is usually represented in the late Middle Ages and Renaissance as a young woman, generally holding a forceps and a tooth. She is venerated as the patroness of dentists.

Feast: Feb. 7.

Bibliography: J. DE P. BOLÉO, *O Martírio de Santa Apolónia* (Porto 1968) includes a summary in Eng. W. BULK, *St. Apollonia, Patronin der Zahnkranken; ihr Kult und Bild im Wandel der Zeit* (Bielefeld 1967). C. A. MENA SERRA, *Santa Apolonia: patrona dental* (Miami, FL 1986). F. QUADRI, *Sant'Apollonia nella Svizzera italiana: studio storico e iconografico* (Lugano 1984). G. D. GORDINI, *Bibliotheca sanctorum* 2:258–262.

[M. J. COSTELLOE]

APOLLONIUS OF TYANA

Neopythagorean philosopher and alleged wonderworker; b. Tyana in Cappadocia; fl. first century A.D. The chief source for his career is the *Life of Apollonius,* written in Greek, by Philostratus II (b. *c.* A.D. 170), a typical representative of the SECOND SOPHISTIC, who enjoyed the patronage of the Emperor Septimius Severus (A.D. 193–211) and his wife Julia Domna. Apollonius is described as a wandering ascetic and teacher, a miracle-worker, who traveled as far East as India and who barely escaped death under Nero and Domitian. As a clairvoyant he foretold the death of the latter. Philostratus apparently wished to present his hero as an ideal representative of Pythagoreanism and to refute charges that Apollonius was a common magician or charlatan. It is quite possible, as De Labriolle suggests, that Philostratus became acquainted with the Gospel narrative and utilized some of its elements to transform Apollonius into a kind of pagan Christ.

In spite of the unreliability of the *Life,* Apollonius should be regarded as a historical person and as a Neopythagorean teacher, although there is no precise information extant on his doctrine. The *Life* was very popular among pagans in the third and fourth centuries. Sossianus Hierocles, a high official under Diocletian, wrote a book against the Christians in which he employed the work of Philostratus to make an unfavorable comparison between the life and miracles of Christ and those of Apollonius. The great Church historian, Eusebius, refuted this attack on Christianity in his *Contra Hieraclem.*

Bibliography: A. BIGELMAIR, *Lexikon für Theologie und Kirche,* ed. J. HOFER and K. RAHNER, 10 v. (2d, new ed. Freiburg 1957–65) 1:718–720. K. GROSS, *Reallexikon für Antike und Christentum,* ed. T. KLAUSER (Stuttgart 1950) 1:529–533, with bibliography. P. DE LABRIOLLE, *La Réaction païenne: Étude sur la polémique antichrétienne du Ier au VIe siècle* (6th ed. Paris 1942) 175–189.

[M. R. P. MCGUIRE]

APOLLOS

A pious Jew whose name (Gk. Ἀπολλῶς) is a contracted form of Apollonius (of Apollo), mentioned by St. Paul and in Acts. Expert in Scripture, eloquent and with an ardent temperament, he was perhaps a traveling lecturer or professional orator. Apollos was a native of Alexandria, the center of Jewish Hellenism, which boasted of its exegetical Scripture schools and also of the Jewish philosopher PHILO JUDAEUS. While not yet fully instructed in Christianity, Apollos met PRISCA (PRISCILLA) AND AQUILA in Ephesus; they completed his instruction, baptized him, and sent him with recommendations to Achaia and Corinth (Acts 18.24–27). A clever apologist, he refuted the Jews at Corinth and deeply impressed Jews and Christians by his eloquence (Acts 18.28). One of the cliques formed at Corinth gave him special allegiance (1 Cor 1.10–13). He joined Paul in Ephesus and did not want to return to Corinth (1 Cor 16.12). The only other mention of this loyal friend of Paul is in Ti 3.13. A tradition (*Menolog. Graec.* 2b.17) places him later as bishop of Caesarea. He has been suggested as the author of Hebrews (*see* HEBREWS, EPISTLE TO THE).

Bibliography: E. B. ALLO, *Saint Paul: Première épître aux Corinthiens* (*Études Bibliques* 2d ed. 1956) xix-xxi. *Encyclopedic Dictionary of the Bible,* tr. and adap. by L. HARTMAN (New York 1963), from A. VAN DEN BORN, *Bijbels Woordenboek* 114–115.

[R. G. BOUCHER]

APOLOGETICS, HISTORY OF

The term apologetics is an almost exact transliteration of the adjective ἀπολογητικός used substantively.
The root verb, ἀπολογεῖοθαι, meaning to answer, to account for, to defend, or to justify, gives an indication of
what apologetics has actually been and what one may expect it to be, no matter what the technical definition. In
the large sense of giving an answer, accounting for, or defending, the Judeo-Christian tradition has a rich apologetic history reaching back to the very earliest records of
God's intervention in human history.

Old Testament. To give an account of Yahweh's
great deeds is the purpose of the Old Testament itself. As
has been so often noted, the narration is not simply the
detached recital of past acts, though the Old Testament
is sometimes this, but rather the theologically interpreted
account of Yahweh's activity in relation to His chosen
people. Thus there is, in the broad sense of the term, an
''accounting for'' God's actions, or what might be described as an apologetic concern. To cite an instance,
Yahweh's covenant relation with the Israelites is central
to the OT experience. ''I will be your God and you shall
be my people'' (Jer 7.23). This covenant bond literally
founds the religious experience of Israel. [*See* COVENANT
(IN THE BIBLE)]. Obedience to the Mosaic LAW, loyalty to
the covenant relationship, is always related to the history
of Yahweh's choice of Israel. The apologetic element that
one finds in most of the OT and especially in covenant
history is precisely the attempt of the authors and of those
who stood behind the tradition to render Yahweh's activity in history both comprehensible and credible. The activity and demands of Yahweh are not presented primarily
for study but for acceptance. Thus when the Israelites
find themselves in exile and their temple destroyed, the
Deuteronomist explores various explanations—the WORD
OF GOD as a promise to the Patriarchs, the Word considered in the covenant, which allows the possibility of a
curse, the Word as prophetic and therefore giving hope
for the future. In 2 Kings ch. 17 the Deuteronomist reflects mournfully on the exile, for he has not solved the
problem of the exile except to affirm that the ways of
Yahweh toward men are just. He is thus giving ''an account of,'' or ''answering for,'' or ''justifying'' Yahweh's activity in history, an activity that man is to
embrace and accept in faith. In this type of event and in
its portrayal by the Deuteronomist one sees an essential
demand for FAITH.

New Testament. The historical evidence of the NT
indicates that Jesus worked miracles and that His words
and deeds led His disciples to believe that He was the
Christ, the Son of God. Hardly anyone would deny that
the tradition of the above occurrence was formed and
written with some, in the large sense of the term, apologetic intent. Hence the very structure of the gospel may
be considered to be apologetic in the sense that the thinking from within faith from which the Holy GOSPELS
emerged was again a thinking and a witnessing that directed itself to religious persuasion, to giving an account
of God's activity in Christ (*see* WITNESS, CHRISIAN). Very
clear indications of apologetic intent can be seen in
Mark—probably the least apologetic of the four Gospels—which apparently intends to answer evident questions that would occur to early Christian readers. If Jesus
performed so very many miracles, how is it that the Jews
refused to believe in Him? If Jesus were the Son of God,
could He not have saved Himself from the Crucifixion?
To these questions Mark proposes the fact that people in
general did accept Jesus, and in Jerusalem people listened
gladly to Jesus. In fact, Mark narrates, it is this very success with the people that induced the leaders to arrest
Jesus by stealth and have Him crucified very shortly after.
And in ch. 8, 9, and 10 Mark gives the three prophecies
of the Passion, death, and Resurrection in which Jesus affirmed the necessity of His suffering and dying. Thus the
Passion and death did not come on Jesus by surprise but
rather as part of His redemptive task.

This same general notion of apologetics in the NT
is found in 1 Pt 3.15, where the writer asks that the believer be able to give a reason for the faith that is in him, a
procedure that is exemplified in the Lukan accounts of the
very first preaching. In an analysis of this first preaching
in Acts, one sees OT quotations used apologetically. An
analysis of Acts on the basis of form criticism discloses
a further apologetic intent in the very structure of the
speeches and of the narrative material, e.g., the account
of Cornelius. Thus an apologetic concern is deeply involved in the intention, the structure, and the contents of
the NT.

Early Apologetics. The Greek APOLOGISTS of the 2d
century defended Christianity through four arguments.
The first argument was from the moral effects of Christianity, especially from the exercise of Christian charity.
Justin Martyr, writing about 150, pointed out how Christianity made men change from the practice of magic to
the worship of the good God, changed a craving after
wealth to a common possession of goods and a sharing
of wealth with the poor and needy, altered hatred to charity, self-gratification to self-restraint, selfishness to generosity. Second, the apologists argued from the predictions
of both Christ and the Prophets. The third argument was

the proof from antiquity. This argument emphasized the coherence and unity of the Old and New Testaments, for the prophetical books of the OT received their highest fulfillment in the NT. Thus, Christianity was not a new religion, one that had come on the scene only lately, but a religion that went back to Moses, who lived before the Greek poets and sages. The fourth argument, the one least used, was the proof from the miracles of Christ. Miracles were not widely used as apologetic proofs because at that time there were wandering magicians and pseudo-Christs, who seemed able to perform wonders, apparently through demonic assistance.

The high point of 2d- and 3d-century apologetics was probably reached by Origen (c. 185–c. 254) in his *Contra Celsum* (246–248). Origen used all the four arguments listed above. But he went on to point out that the greatest miracle is that of the Resurrection, and he stressed the demonstration of the Spirit, the power of the Spirit to demonstrate and persuade one of the credibility of Scripture and its contents. In general, the highly gifted Origen employed a tremendous variety of arguments sufficient to answer the individual difficulties brought up by Celsus. Particular arguments for Christianity were virtually unlimited, especially in the hands of skillful dialecticians. Tertullian, for example, on occasion used the argument that Christian teachings were quite similar to those of pagan poets and philosophers. The effort was to relate the Christian demand for faith to the concrete man as he existed in a well-determined set of historical circumstances.

Medieval Period. In the *Summa contra gentiles* Aquinas began with principles that he knew his opponents would acknowledge, the principles of Aristotelian philosophy. In the light of these mutually acknowledged principles Aquinas sought to answer objections to the faith. Aquinas further evolved the argument of the superiority of Christianity over another religion that would win its adherents by promising carnal delights, for instead of carnal delights Christianity offered only spiritual benefits and, indeed, suffering. Thus the enigmatic fact that Christianity existed at all was a proof, really, that miracles did take place and did, therefore, guarantee the truth of Christian revelation. On the other hand, a fully developed apologetic in the modern sense of the term did not really exist in the medieval period because people born into a Christian community assumed that faith was the normal status of man and was a communal possession. Thus the medievals did not grapple with the problem of the nonbeliever coming to the faith, for the medieval community was a social entity in which it was connatural to believe.

Reformation. The Reformation generated a polemic apologetics largely limited to an apologetic of the Church. Bellarmine, de Sales, and others explained the necessity of the Church in opposition to the reformers, who believed in Scripture but not in the external Church as it existed in the 16th century. The treatise on the Church that emerged at the end of the 16th and the beginning of the 17th century proceeded from the marks of the Church to a proof that the Roman Catholic Church was the true Church, and as the true Church had the right and the authority to judge controversies. The 16th century was the period when apologies abounded. Religious divisions and the antipathies aroused among the contenders turned the apologetic arguments into a form of attack and counterattack. The argument from authority remained basic. Scripture was a quarry from which theologians and apologists could hew quotations to use against each other. In general, because of the climate of controversy, polemic intruded into the area of theological understanding.

After the Reformation. DESCARTES (1596–1650) greatly, though unintentionally and unknowingly, influenced apologetics. His scientific criterion of not accepting anything as true unless it is perceived to be evident by the knowing subject was transferred to theology. And Descartes's basic principle was that all nature is intelligible through a disciplined scientific method and the proper use of reason. True in itself, this principle was incorporated into a book, *Forma verae religionis quaerendae et inveniendae* (Naples 1662), written by Miguel de Elizalde. [Some writers find the beginning of the manual form of apologetics in Hugo Grotius (1583–1645) and his book *De veritate religionis christianae*, published in 1627.] The basic premise of the work was that Christian faith should be justified by a speculative, articulated, and antecedent knowledge of the fact of divine revelation. At this point a new factor enters Christian apologetics—some anterior certification for the future commitment and knowledge of faith. After de Elizalde, treatises on *De vera religione* multiplied and were dominated by the Cartesian mentality, viz, that there must be a clear, precise, and ascertainable reason for everything, as is so in mathematical procedure.

DEISM, which began with J. Toland in 1696, is largely a consequence of the use of Cartesian method in the sphere of the religious. The 18th-century Encyclopedists in France, the *Aufklärung* in Germany, and an atmosphere somewhat less acrimonious than that of Reformation days continued and developed an increasingly rationalistic apologetic.

In the 19th century, Christian apologetics was directed to the defense of the supernatural and the historical reliability of Scripture against those who denied the supernatural and held that both the Bible and tradition were unreliable sources of historical truth. When David

F. Strauss (1808–74) said Scripture was predominantly myth, and Joseph Ernest RENAN (1823–92) sought to diminish the mysterious and supernatural element in Christianity, apologists directed their attention to showing that supernatural revelation was possible, suitable, necessary (if God destines man for a supernatural end), and actually took place. The same emphasis was placed on showing that the Gospels are true historical documents and thus are to be believed. In the mid-19th century the general form of apologetics as it would be known for the next 100 years became fairly well settled. The pattern appeared in G. PERRONE's *Praelectiones theologicae* (1835–42), a series that went through 30 editions. His tract *De vera religione* determined the tone, content, and method of nearly all Catholic apologetics for the next century. From Perrone's time on, apologetic treatises began with the possibility of revelation, the necessity of revelation, the criteria of revelation, and the existence of revelation in the OT, in Christ and in the Church.

In the latter half of the 19th century Christian apologetics centered about the historical reliability of the Gospels, especially their testimony to the Resurrection and divinity of Christ. The divinity of Christ was, at times, established from the OT. After verifying the authenticity and veracity of the canonical Gospels in the historicist sense, the divinity of Christ was attested by His preaching, His miracles, and His prophecies.

During exactly this same period John Henry NEWMAN (1801–90) was writing about the primacy of conscience and its first principle that the world is governed by a providential Creator. From providence and creation Newman proceeded to the fact that all nature manifests both the intention and design of God. From this Newman went to the principle of analogy, primarily to refute objections to the supernatural. The accumulation of probabilities and the use of the illative sense made Newman's apologetic different from the one common in his day. Because Newman was well aware of the depths of the human mind, and the tortuous route it follows to religious truth, Newman's writings treat the human mind with great reverence. Nonetheless, Newman continually proposed the perennial problems: the existence of God, the relation of God to contemporary man, the development of DOCTRINE, the identification of the Church of his time with the apostolic Church.

M. BLONDEL (1861–1949) based his immanentist apologetic on the theory that Christianity does not come exclusively from the outside (*see* IMMANENCE APOLOGETICS). Some few other apologists paralleled the apologetic of Newman, as, for example, Jean Guitton, who considered the divinity of Jesus and the Resurrection of Jesus in the light of the rationalist, Protestant, and Catholic approaches and asked which opinion best explains all the data.

Modern apologetics is in a state of flux and tends toward versatility of approach. Most Catholic apologists feel that the modern option is between belief or nonbelief. Thus apologetics is tending to ask questions about the basic orientation involved in either position. Modern apologetics is also attempting to formulate an ontology of the principles of natural and supernatural revelation. Theologians such as Karl RAHNER have attempted to exploit the openness of man, since he is spirit, to all being. Because revelation is essentially relational, both terms in the relation are undergoing scrutiny, and apologetics is becoming more subjective to offset the overly objective and extrinsicist apologetics of the mid-20th century. Apologists are likewise tending to view Scripture in the light of the latest research and as religious witness and testimony. Modern apologetics is emphasizing that since man exists in the temporal order, the apologetic approach must be in categories and patterns taken from that order. Because man is open to all being, the transcendent God can perpetually and permanently give stability within a very variable and volatile temporal order.

Bibliography: L. MAISONNEUVE, *Dictionnaire de théologie catholique,* ed. A. VACANT et al. (Paris 1903–50; Tables générales 1950–)1.2: 1511–80. A. MICHEL, *ibid.,* Tables générales 1: 196–206. H. LAIS and W. LOHFF, *Lexikon für Theologie und Kirche,* ed. J. HOFER and K. RAHNER (Freiburg 1957–65) 1: 723–731. J. H. CREHAN, *A Catholic Dictionary of Theology,* ed. H. F. DAVIS et al. (London 1962) 1: 113–122. R. AUBERT, *Le Probléme de l'acte de foi* (3d ed. Louvain 1958); "Le Caractére raisonnable de l'acte de foi," *Revue d'histoire ecclésiastique* 39 (1943) 22–99. A. DULLES, *Apologetics and the Biblical Christ* (Westminster, Md. 1963). C. DONAHUE, "Roman Catholicism," in *Patterns of Faith in America Today,* ed. F. E. JOHNSON (New York 1957). R. KNOX, *In Soft Garments* (2d ed. New York 1953). J. LEVIE, *Sous les yeux de l'incroyant* (2d ed. Paris 1946). B. LINDRAS, *N.T. Apologetic* (Philadelphia 1961). A. RICHARDSON, *Christian Apologetics* (London 1947; repr. 1960). H. BOUILLARD et al., "Le Christ envoyé de Dieu," *Bulletin du Comité des Études* 35 (1961) 303–456. J. M. LEBLOND, "Le Chrétien devant l'athéism actuel," *Études* 231 (1954) 289–304, condensed in *Theology Digest* 3 (1955) 139–143. R. X. REDMOND, "How Should *De Ecclesia* Be Treated in Scientific Theology," *Catholic Theological Society of America. Proceedings* 17 (1962) 139–160. F. TAYMANS, "Le Miracle, signe du surnaturel," *Nouvelle revue théologique* 77 (1955) 225–245, condensed in *Theology Digest* 5 (1957) 18–23.

[P. J. CAHILL]

Contemporary Apologetics. Vatican Council II, reaping the fruits of a long theological renewal, has given (especially in its Constitution on Divine Revelation, *Dei Verbum,* ch. 1–2) a deep and rich understanding of revelation, its transmission, authentic interpretation, and acceptance in personal faith than any previous document of the magisterium. It thus has helped apologetics to discard certain one-sidedly rationalistic and individualistic models of the past and to ask the question of the credibility of revelation in all its dimensions.

Contemporary apologetics addresses itself primarily to the believer (or the believing community), reflecting on the reasons and motives that render faith intellectually honest, morally responsible, and existentially authentic. The believer, however, shares the insights and aspirations as well as the difficulties and anxieties of the men of today. Thus his reflection is at the same time an honest invitation to all men to seek and find the ground of their existence in that faith which he has responsibly embraced.

Since today there is no universally accepted philosophy (except where politically imposed), apologetics cannot take a philosophical system for granted but has to work out, in the light of faith and with a truly open and critical use of all available resources of reason, its own philosophical foundations.

Contemporary human beings, for all their (available) historical knowledge, are often skeptical and indifferent toward history (historical relativism). Thus apologetics has to awake man to his indebtedness to historic traditions and the peculiar nature and value of historical knowledge in order that he may realize the uniqueness of the historical revelation culminating in Jesus Christ. In this task a critical assimilation of contemporary hermeneutic philosophy, as for instance that of H. G. GADAMER, could make a valuable contribution.

In the face of a new humanism preoccupied with the future of the human community in this world, apologetics has to show the relevance of Christianity for founding those ultimate values and hopes which alone can render all human decisions and endeavors meaningful. Thus the various theologies of hope and political theology are important elements in contemporary apologetics.

Parallel to and in reaction against the modern secularization process there are also signs of a new mystic quest, evident in such varied phenomena as interest in Oriental wisdom, drug mysticism, and the Pentecostal movement. Thus apologetics should not only make man aware of the ''supernatural'' implied in his everyday life (P. Berger), but also show how Christianity can fulfill his transcendent aspirations.

The ''method of immanence,'' originally connected with the name of Maurice Blondel, has dominated recent apologetic reflection. Its most influential contemporary exponent has been Karl Rahner (*Hearers of the Word*). According to the perspective, man is conceived as dynamically inclined toward the absolute horizon of being itself and the Christian message is presented as the ultimate word of God in Christ, demonstrating to man the de facto finality of all human tendency.

This existentialistically inspired transcendental Thomism has been criticized, however, from several points of view: that of a more traditional Thomism (E. L. Mascall), of a radical and problematic program of de-Hellenizing Christianity (L. Dewart), of a political theology striving to overcome its alleged individualism (J. B. Metz), and in the name of a theology of ''the self-authenticating glory of God's utterly free gift of love'' (H. U. von Balthasar).

Bibliography: J. B. METZ, ''Apologetics,'' *Sacramentum Mundi* 1.66–70. P. HENRICI, ''II. Immanence Apologetics,'' *Sacramentum Mundi* 1.70–72. H. U. VON BALTHASAR, *Herrlichkeit, Eine Theologische Aesthetik* I ff (Einsiedeln 1961); *Love Alone* (New York 1969). J. ALFARO, H. BROUILLARD, et al., ''La théologie fondamentale à la recherche de son identité: Un carrefour,'' *Gregorianum* 50.3–4 (1969) 757–776. G. BAUM, *Faith and Doctrine: A Contemporary View* (Paramus, N.J. 1969). P. BERGER, *A Rumor of Angels* (Garden City, N.Y. 1969). L. DEWART, *The Foundations of Belief* (New York 1969). H. FRIES, *Faith under Challenge* (New York 1969). J. B. METZ ed., ''The Development of Fundamental Theology,'' *Concilium* 46 (New York 1969). K. RAHNER, *Do You Believe in God?* (Paramus, N.J. 1969); ''Reflections on the Contemporary Intellectual Formation of Future Priests,'' *Theological Investigations* 6 (Baltimore 1969) 113–138. J. SCHMITZ, ''Die Fundamentaltheologie im 20. Jahrhundert,'' *Bilanz der Theologie im 20. Jahrhundert* 2 (Freiburg 1969) 197–245. A. DULLES, *A History of Apologetics* (New York 1971). R. LATOURELLE, *Christ and the Church Signs of Salvation* (New York 1972). B. LONERGAN, *Method in Theology* (New York 1972). E. L. MASCALL, *The Openness of Being: Natural Theology Today* (Philadelphia 1971).

[D. L. BALAS]

APOLOGIES, LITURGICAL

A liturgical apology is an acknowledgment of personal unworthiness, generally on the part of the celebrant, to take part in the celebration of the Mass. An apology evinces therefore, at least implicitly, a consciousness of personal sin; and it is often conjoined to a prayer begging God's merciful forgiveness.

The apology was not much employed in the ancient Christian liturgy. However, for various reasons, apologies began to appear with greater frequency within the GALLICAN RITES in the 6th and 7th centuries (cf. the Mone Masses, *Patrologia Latina*, ed. J. P. Migne, 138:863–882, *passim*); and they reached the peak of their development between the 9th and 11th centuries, finding their way into numerous Mass formulas. The *Missa Illyrica* (*c.* 1030), for example, contains apologies after vesting, before entering the house of God, after kissing the altar, during the Gloria and the chants between the readings, during the Offertory singing and the preparation of the offerings, after the Orate fratres, during the Sanctus, and during the Communion of the faithful (E. Martène, *De antiquis ecclesiae ritibus* 1.4.4:490–518). In the Orient, apologies that serve as prayers of preparation for the priest are found in the 6th century.

Some authors maintain that apologies were adopted in the Celtic-Gallican liturgical tradition in imitation of Eastern practices (L. Eisenhofer and J. Lechner, *The Liturgy of the Roman Rite*, tr. A. J. and E. F. Peeler from the 6th German ed., ed. H. E. Winstone, 83). Others attribute the apologies in the East and West to a common cause, namely, the fact that the concept of the mediatorship of Christ had receded into the background as a result of the Arian controversy. In opposition to ARIANISM, the Catholic camp stressed the divinity of Christ rather than his humanity and mediatorship. Such a tendency impressed upon sinful man the awesome majesty of the Almighty, without reminding him of the Mediator between God and man. Thus the celebrant was led to insert into the liturgy admissions of his own unworthiness to celebrate the divine mysteries. Moreover, until the 11th century, sacramental Penance was an infrequent matter, and greater emphasis was placed upon extrasacramental confession of sins as a means of forgiveness; hence the celebrant lessened his unworthiness by frequent apologies in the course of the liturgical service.

In the medieval Roman Rite of the Mass, the Confiteor and the two prayers that follow it, the *Aufer a nobis* and the *Oramus*, were apologies that served to prepare the celebrant for the celebration of Mass. These began originally as silent prayers recited by the celebrant as he approached the altar. Traditionally, the *Munda cor meum* was an apology that prepared the minister for the reading or chanting of the Gospel, and the *Per evangelica dicta* was a plea for forgiveness through the efficacy of the Gospel. Under Innocent III (d. 1216), the Offertory rite in Rome was accomplished in silence on the part of the celebrant (*De sacro altari mysterio* 29; *Patrologia Latina* 217:831), but in 1570 Pope Pius V inserted apologies into the Offertory Rite of the Mass. Historically, the two apologies *Domine Jesu Christe* and *Perceptio Corporis tui* prepared the celebrant for the reception of Communion. The *Placeat* which preceded the blessing was found in the Sacramentary of Amiens in the 9th century [V. Leroquais, "Ordo Missae du sacramentaire d'Amiens," *Ephemerides liturgicae* 41 (1927) 444].

Bibliography: J. A. JUNGMANN, *The Mass of the Roman Rite*, tr. F. BRUNNER, 2 v. (New York 1951–55) 1:78–80; *Die Stellung Christi im Liturgischen Gebet* (Liturgiegeschichtliche Forschungen 19; Münster 1925) 223–225.

[E. J. GRATSCH/EDS.]

APOLOGISTS, GREEK

Greek Apologists were Greek Christian writers of the 2nd century who presented an account of their faith for outsiders. The term is not ancient, for the Greek word *apologia* meant a speech from the dock made by one about to suffer martyrdom. JUSTIN MARTYR was an apologist who suffered martyrdom, but not all the apologists did. After the close of the apostolic age Christians became conscious that they were a third race, neither Jewish nor Hellene, and two kinds of apology began to appear, aimed at either of these groups. Justin's *Dialogue with Trypho* and the dialogues of Jason and Papiscus, of Timothy and Aquila, of Athanasius and Zacchaeus, or of Simon and Theophilus are specimens of the dialogue with Jews. The better-known works addressed to Greeks, and most educated Romans had some Greek, were prompted mainly by the desire to remove from Christianity what the Emperor TRAJAN had called the *flagitia cohaerentia nomini*, i.e., crimes associated with the (Christian) name; these were cannibalism, promiscuity, and the worship of many gods, including animals (*see* ATHENAGORAS). The spur to the writing of apologies was the knowledge that it was imperial policy to give Christians a fair hearing. A rescript of HADRIAN, now generally accepted as genuine, to Minucius Fundanus in 124 and 125 had ordered governors not to listen to popular clamor against Christians but only to evidence of crimes. QUADRATUS, the first apologist, was contemporary with this rescript, and he was soon followed by ARISTIDES, Aristo of Pella, and in midcentury by Justin. MELITO OF SARDES is credited with an apology (now lost) presented to Marcus Aurelius. The *Embassy* of Athenagoras to the same emperor (c. 176–180) is fortunately preserved. CLEMENT OF ALEXANDRIA'S *Protrepticus* and Origen's reply to Celsus are apologies; and the *Logos alethes* of Celsus (c. 178) and satire of Lucian on the *Death of Peregrinus* (c. 167) show that a pagan reaction was beginning. The only apology that is a speech from the dock is that of Apollonius, delivered c. 180–185; it is extant in an Armenian version, having been recovered by F. C. Conybeare in 1894, and part of a Greek version has survived also. Attacks on Greek culture, such as those of TATIAN AND HERMIAS, cannot be considered apologies for Christianity. Knowledge of the apologies is in large part attributable to Bishop ARETHAS, who in 914 had a copy made of many of them. It is from this codex that present texts are derived.

Bibliography: J. QUASTEN, *Patrology*, 3 v. (Westminster, Md. 1950–) 1:186–252. M. PELLEGRINO, *Studi sul'antica apologetica* (Rome 1947). P. C. DE LABRIOLLE, *La Réaction païenne: Étude sur la polémique antichrétienne du Ier au VIe siècle* (6th ed. Paris 1942). A. L. WILLIAMS, *Adversus Iudaeos* (Cambridge, Eng. 1935). E. J. GOODSPEED, *Die ältesten Apologeten* (Leipzig 1914); *Index Apologeticus* (Leipzig 1912). F. C. CONYBEARE, ed. and tr., *The Apology and Acts of Apollonius* (New York 1894). E. GROAG, *Paulys Realenzyklopädie der klassischen altertumswissenschaft*, ed. G. WISSOWA et al. 13.1 (1926) 461–462, rescript of Hadrian. R. M. GRANT, *Greek Apologists of the Second Century* (London 1988). F. M. YOUNG, "Greek Apologists of the Second Century," in *Apolo-*

getics in the Roman Empire, ed. M. EDWARDS et al. (Oxford 1999) 81–104.

[J. H. CREHAN]

APOPHATIC THEOLOGY

Apophatic theology (from the Greek, *apophanai*, to speak out, to deny) developed within the Christian tradition as a reaction to EUNOMIUS in the 4th century and to other thinkers who overstressed *cataphatic* theology (from the Greek, *kataphasis*, to speak positively or in an affirmative manner) and exaggerated the ability of human beings to form rational concepts—as though they exhausted the reality of God.

The key thinkers who evolved apophatic theology were the Cappadocian Fathers, St. BASIL, St. GREGORY OF NAZIANZUS, and St. GREGORY OF NYSSA. This teaching must be distinguished from St. THOMAS AQUINAS' *via negativa* which is a corrective to an affirming theologizing about God and His qualities. Whatever we affirm of God must be somehow also denied in the way it pertains to God in His essence. True apophatic theology will always contain such a strictly so-called *via negativa* in order to remove the limitations of human thinking about God.

The essence, however, of apophatic theology, as evolved by Gregory of Nyssa, has a very positive aspect and provides the basis for true mystical theology. It embraces a positive statement covering an experiential knowledge of God that goes beyond anything that the mere power of human beings can attain outside of God's gift.

Gregory of Nyssa's mystical writings, especially his *Commentary on the Song of Songs* and his *Life of Moses*, form the basis of this dialectical, mystical experience of God, a knowing by not knowing, that Pseudo-Dionysius in his 6th-century classic, *Mystical Theology*, would bequeath to Maximus the Confessor of the 7th, to Scotus Erigena and the 14th-century Rhenish and Flemish mystics, such as Meister Eckart, Tauler, Suso and Jan Ruysbroeck, to the anonymous writer of the 14th-century English classic, *The Cloud of Unknowing*, as well as to St. John of the Cross of the 16th.

Gregory describes this apophatic presence without seeing through intellectual knowledge: "The Bride is surrounded with the divine night in which the Bridegroom comes near without showing Himself . . . but by giving the soul a certain sense of His presence while fleeing from clear knowledge" (*Commentary on the Song of Songs*).

Knowledge in Loving Union. The very transcendence of the infinite God brings darkness to one's own reasoning powers, but offers a more sublime way of knowing God through loving union, a sheer gift of God to the pure of heart. In paradoxical fashion, the closer one comes to union with God, the more blinding God becomes to human reasoning. This is not a matter of the knowledge of God becoming more abstruse, but of the nature of God itself becoming more immediately present. Such a presence brings to the human individual the realization of the absolute awesomeness of the goal of one's earthly existence.

The apophatic approach is found also in Far Eastern religious traditions, such as Hinduism, Buddhism, and Taoism. Such apophatic terms of negation, common to all true mystical traditions, especially Eastern Christianity and the Far Eastern religions, such as emptiness, void, darkness, and nothingness, are paradoxically positive. Such terms are symbols pointing to God who remains completely "other." God is not known by him who knows Him, not understood by him who understands. He alone contemplates Him who has ceased to contemplate Him. In all knowledge, as though by intuition, the wise man discovers and experiences God.

Bibliography: GREGORY OF NYSSA, *The Life of Moses*, tr. A. J. MALHERBE and E. FERGUSON (New York 1978). DIONYSIUS THE AREOPAGITE, *On the Divine Names and the Mystical Theology*, tr. C. E. ROLT (New York 1940). NICHOLAS OF CUSA, *On Learned Ignorance*, tr. J. HOPKINS (Minneapolis 1981).

[G. A. MALONEY]

APOPHTHEGMATA PATRUM

In its primitive state an *apophthegma* is a terse reply or statement made by an elderly monk to a young candidate whom he is instructing in the ways and principles of the monastic life. The word is based on the Greek ἀποφθέγγομαι—I speak my mind plainly, I make a statement—and the axiomatic type of counseling, whether spontaneous or requested, could develop into a short dialogue, a parable in words or actions, or more rarely, into the discussion of a Scripture passage. Eventually collections of such axioms were called in monastic circles "The Sayings of the Fathers."

Such an utterance was looked upon as inspired, a charism, and was treasured by the recipient as a gift from heaven. In terse and vivid terms, without rhetorical development or philosophical grounding, it set forth some principle of the spiritual life or its application from the elementary repelling of vice to the highest type of contemplation.

The second stage of the *apophthegma* came when the saying was repeated by the monks and commented upon. The point at issue was noted and the name of the author preserved as the saying became common property.

Eventually some literate monk wrote these statements down, and they became material for the collections of later days.

The *apophthegmata* of the fathers first appeared at the beginning of the 4th century among the monks and solitaries of Egypt, seemingly in Nitria, the Cellia, and especially in the Scetis Valley. The gift belonged mainly to the unlettered Copts, and it was in their language that the oral tradition was active. The written recording was done for the most part in Greek by educated Hellenes from the Greek settlements in Egypt. Yet much of the vigor of the popular tongue was kept in the Greek translations, and the form of life presented is the semianchoritic. After the mid-5th century, with the spread of education and monastic rules, the authentic type of *apophthegmata* disappeared, although new forms of expression came under this name: excerpts from the lives of the saints and from homilies, miracle stories, and so on.

The *apophthegmata patrum* are of importance for understanding the beginnings of monastic life and the development of religious centers. In the opinion of W. Bousset, they can be compared to the primitive life of St. PACHOMIUS and his rule as a source for the history of Christian piety.

Bibliography: F. CAVALLERA, *Dictionnaire de spiritualité ascétique et mystique. Doctrine et histoire,* ed. M. VILLER et al. (Paris 1932–) 1:766–770. W. BOUSSET, *Apophthegmata: Studien zur Geschichte des ältesten Mönchtums,* ed. T. HERMANN and G. KRÜGER (Tübingen 1923); J. C. GUY, *Recherches sur la tradition grecque des Apophthegmata Patrum* (Brussels 1962). J. QUASTEN, *Patrology,* 3 v. (Westminster, Md. 1950–53) 3:187–189.

[A. C. WAND]

Tapestry of Hungarian bishop Vilmos Apor, hanging from the central balcony on the facade of St. Peter's Basilica. (Associated Press/AP)

APOR, VILMOS, BL.

Martyr, bishop of Györ in northwest Hungary; b. Segesvar, Hungary (now Romania), Feb. 29, 1892; d. Györ, April 2, 1945. By birth, Apor was a baron, the sixth child of a noble family. He received his early education from the Jesuits and began his theological studies at their college in Innsbruck, Austria (1910), where he earned a doctorate. After his ordination (Aug. 24, 1915), he was incardinated in the diocese of Nagyvárad, becoming a parish priest in Gyula. He served as a military chaplain during World War I, then returned to Hungary to assume the duties of prefect of Nagyvárad's seminary and curate in Gyula. He also founded a theological college. In 1941 Pope Pius XII appointed him bishop to the diocese of Györ because of his zeal for catechesis, his charity toward the poor, his ecumenical sensitivity, and his encouragement of fellow priests.

Apor condemned the racist laws introduced into Hungary (May 1939) in his writings and his sermons.

Through his efforts and those of others, such as Blessed József MINDSZENTY, the majority of the Jews in Budapest were spared from Nazi extermination camps. He was shot by Soviet soldiers on Good Friday 1945 while trying to protect about 100 women to whom he had given refuge in the episcopal residence; he died of his wounds on Easter Monday. He was originally buried in the Carmelite church, but is now enshrined in the cathedral of Györ. Apor was beatified in St. Peter's Square by John Paul II on Nov. 9, 1997.

Feast: July 13 (Györ), May 23 (Knights of Malta, for whom he was conventual chaplain).

Bibliography: L. BALÁSSY, *Apor Vilmos, a vértanú püspök* (Budapest 1989). S. CSEH, *Apor püspök vértanúhalála: ahogy a szemtanú átélte* (Budapest 1997). E. HULESCH, *Gyóori nagypéntek 1945: a koronatanú így látta* (Györ 1990). *L'Osservatore Romano,* English edition, 37 (1996): 6; 46 (1997): 1–2. E. SZOLNOKY, *Fellebbezés helyett: Apor Vilmos püspök élete és vértanúsága* (Szeged, Hungary 1990).

[K. I. RABENSTEIN]

APORIA

A transliteration of the Greek ἀπορία, meaning without passage, is used to signify the mental state of DOUBT arising from consideration of a vexing problem or difficulty that causes anxiety and is apt to urge further inquiry or investigation. Aporia or mental impasse can arise from any set of difficult circumstances or considerations regarding either thought or action. It can also be aroused artfully by the dialectician who desires to make someone aware of a problem and perhaps help toward solving it. The Socratic method of question and answer, of argument and counter argument, was aimed at bringing attention to bear on a problem so that an aporia would result, which would stimulate further inquiry and lead to clarification. An aporia is thus a kind of methodical doubt that may be both real and positive, with probable arguments pro and con.

Aristotle approved and regularly employed the method of raising aporia while teaching. In the *Metaphysics,* he says that philosophical investigation should begin with consideration of the aporias that arise from the conflicting statements of other philosophers or from matters they have not treated (995a 22). An aporia does not spring from nowhere, but from imperfect knowledge of things and from the natural curiosity or drive of the mind. It urges one to consider carefully what is doubtful and what is not doubtful, and to find out why it is or is not so. Just as a hard knot can be untied only after one knows how it was tied in the first place, so also in the investigation of truth it is necessary to know beforehand the various reasons or causes of aporia. Otherwise in study or research one would not know what to look for and whether to stop or to continue the investigation. But this is manifest to one who knows his previous doubts and the reasons for them; he is thus better able to judge of the TRUTH when it appears.

Thus aporia is not a skeptical doubt, nor does it lead to SKEPTICISM, because it presupposes that one already knows something and hopes to know something more or better. It does not take away all CERTITUDE, nor does it commit one to an aimless search; rather it urges him to proceed hopefully in the light of what he already knows toward the solution of a clearly formulated question or problem.

See Also: EPISTEMOLOGY; KNOWLEDGE

Bibliography: R. EISLER, *Wörterbuch der philosophischen Begriffe* (4th ed. Berlin 1927–30) 1:77. G. FAGGIN, *Enciclopedia filosofica* (Venice-Rome 1957) 1:302. L. M. RÉGIS, *Epistemology,* tr. I. C. BRYNE (New York 1959) 21–26.

[W. H. KANE]

APOSTASY

In the strict, traditional sense of the word, is the gravely sinful act by which one totally abandons, inwardly and outwardly (both *corde* and *ore,* in a kind of perversion of Rom 10.10), the Catholic faith in which he has been baptized and which he has heretofore professed (*see* St. Thomas Aquinas, *Summa theologiae* 2a2ae, 12.1; 10.1; 10.5; *Codex iuris canonici* c. 1325.2; 188.4; 646.1; 1065.1). Complete and massive disbelief is the immediate term of such an apostasy from the Christian faith. In order to have the sin of apostasy it is not required that the defector find a surrogate for the Christian faith, which he has entirely forsworn, in a non-Christian religion, such as Judaism, Islam, or paganism, much less that he start a new non-Christian religion of his own devising. Even if he remain alienated from religious belief of any kind, and lead a wholly areligious life, he is an apostate from the faith.

It is commonly held that the sin of apostasy differs not in kind but only in degree from the sin of HERESY, with apostasy accidentally aggravating heresy's malice by the totality of its rupture with God's word and of its rebellion against His authority (*Summa theologiae* 2a2ae, 12.1 ad 3). However, in the concrete pastoral sense, an apostate differs notably from a heretic in that (1) unlike the heretic who ''retains the name of Christian'' (1917 *Codex iuris canonici* c. 1325.2), he abjures and discards that name completely; and (2) while he may pass over to a non-Christian religion, he does not form a rival Christian communion, as heretics often have done.

See Also: FAITHFUL; INFIDEL; SCHISM; UNITY OF FAITH.

Bibliography: A. BEUGNET, *Dictionnaire de théologie catholique,* ed. A. VACANT, 15 v. (Paris 1903–50) 1.2:1602–12. J. BOUCHÉ, *Dictionnaire de droit canonique,* ed. R. NAZ, 7 v. (Paris 1935–64) 1:640–652. P. DE LABRIOLLE, *Reallexikon für Antike und Christenum,* ed. T. KLAUSER (Stuttgart 1941) 1:550–551. G.W.H. LAMPE, ed., *A Patristic Greek Lexikon* (Oxford 1961–) fasc. 1:208.

[F. X. LAWLOR]

APOSTLE

One of the 12 intimate followers of Jesus who were commissioned by Him to preach His gospel. This article will first treat of the Biblical data on the Apostles and then consider the theological significance of their office in the Church that Christ founded.

1. In the Bible

In classical Greek the word ἀπόστολος (from the verb ἀποστέλλω, to send away, to send out) is used sev-

Jesus Christ the Redeemer, in glory, attended by His 12 Apostles and 2 angels, detail of a 9th-century mosaic commissioned by Pope Paschal I, on the arch above the apse of the Church of S. Maria in Dominica, Rome.

eral times in the meaning of a naval "expedition," but seldom in the meaning of "one sent," a messenger, an envoy. In the Greek New Testament, besides being used to designate a messenger in general (Jn 13.16; 2 Cor 8.23; Phil 2.25) and a messenger from God in particular (Lk 11.49; Heb 3.1—in this case of Christ as God's messenger), it is most frequently used in a special sense to designate the TWELVE whom Jesus chose from among His DISCIPLES to assist Him in His earthly mission and to be its continuators under the leadership of Saint PETER, His vicar.

The Greek word as used in the New Testament is no doubt a translation of the Aramaic word šelîḥā', "one sent." But its change of meaning from a term connoting a temporary function of anyone sent on any mission to a title of a permanent office is strictly a New Testament development. The Talmudic use of the Hebrew word šlîaḥ in a similar sense for the Jewish officials who acted as contact men between the Jews of Palestine and those of the Diaspora is post-Christian and perhaps due to Christian influence. In the New Testament the broader usage that includes any Christian missionary (e.g., Barnabas in Acts 14.13; 1 Cor 9.6) is older than its technical usage as limited to the Twelve and Paul, who puts himself on a par with them. In the latter sense it is used only once in Matthew (10.2) and Mark (6.30) and never in John, but it is common in the Epistles, Acts, and Luke, who ascribes to Jesus Himself the attribution of this title to the Twelve: "He chose twelve, whom he also named apostles" (Lk 6.13). Treatment will be made here of the call of the Apostles by Jesus, the lists of their names, and their office.

Call of the Apostles. Andrew, John, Simon (Peter), Philip, and Nathaniel (Bartholomew) were on intimate terms with Jesus before He formally chose the Twelve. They first met Him at the Jordan, where they had been disciples of John the Baptist (Jn 1.35–51). They were witnesses of His first public miracle at Cana (Jn 2.1–11), and they stayed in His company when He made His headquarters at Capharnaum (Jn 2.12). Where the other Apostles first met Jesus is not known, except for Matthew (Levi), who, as he was sitting in his tax collector's place, received from Jesus the simple call, "Follow me" (Mk 2.13–14 and parallels).

Later, after spending a night in prayer, Jesus summoned all His Disciples and from among them selected twelve (Mt 10.1; Mk 3.13–14; Lk 6.12–13). Mark and

Luke situate the event on "a mountain," but Matthew does not connect it with his Sermon on the Mount. From then on the Twelve formed a special inner circle within the general group of Jesus' Disciples, preparing for an unexampled work, to be Christ's envoys as He was the envoy of His Father (Jn 17.18; 20.21).

Scriptural Lists of the Apostles. The names of the twelve Apostles are listed four times in the New Testament, once in each of the three Synoptic Gospels and once in Acts. The relatively fixed nature of the lists, with minor variations in each one, shows that they represent four variant forms of a single early oral tradition. The need that was felt for a knowledge of the names of the Twelve among the early Christians is an indication of the reverence in which the early Church held them.

In each of the four lists the names fall into three groups of four names each, the first name in each group being constant. On the assumption that Jude, the brother of James, is the same as Thaddeus, the same men are mentioned in each of the three groups of the four lists (see JUDE THADDEUS, ST.). But the order of the names varies somewhat in each group, with the exception that Judas Iscariot is named last by all three Synoptics (and naturally is missing from the list of Acts). The greatest variation occurs in the third group, where the lists distinguish between an Apostle already mentioned and another with a similar name. (For the epithet of St. SIMON the Apostle, see ZEALOTS.)

Apostolic Office. The essence of the apostolic office lies in the sending or commission of the Apostles by Christ. As one who is sent (the meaning of the Greek term for Apostle), an Apostle is Christ's envoy ambassador, or vicar, with full power to act in His name. Hence the stress that is laid in the New Testament on the sending by Christ of His Apostles (Mt 28.19: Mk 3.14 and parallels); He sends them just as He has been sent by His Father (Mt 10.40; Jn 13.20). Matthias cannot take the place of Judas among the Apostles until God has designated him by lot for this commission (Acts 1.21–26). The Apostles do not receive their commission from the Church (Gal 1.1), and therefore they are above the Church and not subject to its tribunal (1 Cor 4.3). They are the official witnesses of Christ, especially of His Resurrection (Lk 24.48; Acts 1.8, 21–22; 13.31); Paul can rank as Apostle because he too saw the risen Lord (Acts 9.3–5; 1 Cor 15.8). Yet the mere fact of having seen Christ risen from the dead does not make a man an Apostle (1 Cor 15.5–6).

As God's envoys and spokesmen, the Apostles have the right to be heard (2 Cor 5.20; 1 Thes 2.13) and to be received as if they were Christ Himself (Gal 4.14). In the same capacity they perform the liturgical functions of the Church—baptizing (Acts 2.41), celebrating the Eucharist (Acts 20.7–11), and laying their hands on other men in Confirmation and Ordination (Acts 6.6; 8.15–17). In God's name they can forgive sins (Mt 18.18; Jn 20.23). With the fullness of Christ's power they can work miracles (Mk 3.15; 6.7 and parallels; Acts 2.43; 5.12; Rom 15.19; 2 Cor 12.12; Heb 2.4).

The Apostles are thus the ministers and fellow workers of God and of Christ (Rom 1.9; 15.15–16; 1 Cor 3.9; 2 Cor 6.1; Col 1.23; 1 Thes 3.2). As such, they can demand the obedience of the community (Rom 15.18; 1 Cor 14.37; 2 Cor 10.8; 13.1–3). Yet they must be willing to forego their personal privileges (1 Cor 9.12–19; 1 Thes 2.7), for they are not the lords but the servants of the Church (Mk 10.42–45; Mt 24.45–51; 2 Cor 1.24; 4.5), its shepherds or pastors (Jn 21.15–17; Acts 20.28; Eph 4.11; 1 Pt 5.2–4), and its fathers (1 Cor 4.15). Theirs is a ministry of service (Acts 20.24; Rom 11.13; 12.7). They preside over the faithful, not as rulers over subjects, but as fellow members of the same community (Acts 15.22; 1 Cor 5.4; 2 Cor 2.5–10). They serve as models for them (1 Cor 4.16; 1 Thes 1.6; 2 Thes 3.9; 1 Pt 5.3), and the Church is built upon the Apostles as an edifice on its foundation (Mt 16.18; Eph 2.20; Rv 21.14).

Bibliography: A. MÉDEBIELLE, *Dictionnaire de la Bible* suppl. ed. L. PIROT et al. (Paris 1928–) 1:533–88. *Encyclopedic Dictionary of the Bible*, tr. and adap. by L. HARTMAN (New York 1963), from A. VAN DEN BORN *Bijbels Woordenboek* 115–20. K. H. RENGSTORF, G. KITTEL, *Theologisches Wörterbuch zum Neuen Testament* (Stuttgart 1935–) 1:397–448. K. E. KIRK, ed., *The Apostolic Ministry* (London 1957). K. H. SCHELKLE, *Jüngerschaft und Apostelamt* (Freiburg 1957).

[M. L. HELD]

2. In Theology

The Twelve. According to Catholic tradition the college of the Twelve is an institution of Jesus historically significant in the economy of SALVATION for the Church, for office in the Church, and for the DEPOSIT OF FAITH entrusted to the Church.

While alive the Twelve were first witnesses of the RESURRECTION OF CHRIST (Acts 1.21–22; 10.41; Lk 1.2; 24.36–43; Jn 20.24–29; 1 Jn 1.1–3) and guarantors of "the continuity between the risen and historical Jesus" (O. Cullmann), who authorized them (Acts 1.8, 24–26; Mt 28.18–20; Mk 16.15–18; Lk 24.47–49; Jn 21.15–17). They were the nucleus of the primitive Church in Jerusalem under the guidance of Peter (Acts 1–6; 9–12; 15; 1 Cor 15.5; Gal 1.18–19). Their missionary activity hardly extended beyond Judea, Galilee, and Samaria according to Acts 8–11. Because of persecution Peter "went into another place" (Acts 12.17). After the "council of JERU-

SALEM'' (Acts 15.30; 16.4) further details are lacking. The first mention of the missionary journeys is in the apocrypha.

Even after death the Twelve, apart from their eschatological significance (Mt 19.28; Lk 22.30; Rv 7.4–8; 21.12–14), are "the foundation and origin of the Church" (P. Gaechter; ct. Eph 2.20; Rv 21.14; H. Denzinger, *Enchiridion symbolorum*, ed. A. Schönmetzer 468–69, 2886–88). From the Apostles it receives doctrine and fundamental structure (Acts 2.42; 5.28; Gal 2.2); to them are referred CREEDS (Apostles' Creed; cf. Rufinus, *Expositio symb*. 2.10–15, *Corpus Christianorum. Series latina* 20:134) and Church regulations; even heretics appeal to them. Hence the care for reliable apostolic tradition (2 Thessalonians 2.15) and the κοινωνία of the Churches among themselves.

It is thus that the Twelve stand between Jesus and the Church. They preach what they have received from the Lord by revelation, not by tradition; the Church preaches what has been entrusted to it by the preaching of the Apostles (1 Tm 6.20; 2 Tm 1.12, 14; 2.2; 3.14; Ti 2.1). Despite the difference between "Age of the Apostles" and "Age of the Church," between apostolic and postapostolic (ecclesiastical) tradition, the latter tradition also can be normative, even infallible, because of the presence of the Lord (Mt 28.20; Jn 16.8–15; cf. Cullmann).

Bibliography: A. MICHEL, *Dictionnaire de théologie catholique*, ed. A. VACANT et al., 15 v. (Paris 1903–50) 16:216–18. H. BACHT, *Lexikon für Theologie und Kirche*, ed. J. HOFER and K. RAHNER, 10 v. (2d, new ed. Freiburg 1957–65) 1:736–38. E. M. KREDEL, *Bibeltheologisches Wörterbuch*, ed. J. B. BAUER, 2 v. (2d ed. enL. Graz 1962) 1:61–69. A. KOLPING, H. FRIES, ed., *Handbuch theologischer Grundbegriffe*, 2 v. (Munich 1962–63) 1:68–74. J. BROSCH, *Charismen und Amter in der Urkirche* (Bonn 1951). G. SÖHNGEN, *Die Einheit in der Theologie* (Munich 1952) 305–22. H. VON CAMPENHAUSEN, *Kirchliches Amt und geistliche Vollmacht in den ersten drei Jahrhunderten* (Tübingen 1953), bibliography. O. CULLMANN, *Die Tradition als exegetisches, historisches und theologisches Problem*, tr. P. SCHÖNENBEGER (Zürich 1954). T. ZAPELENA, *De ecclesia Christi*, 2 v. (5th ed. Rome 1950–54). P. GAECHTER, *Petrus und seine Zeit* (Innsbruck 1958). G. KLEIN, *Die zwölf Apostel* (Göttingen 1961), bibliography. K. RAHNER and J. RATZINGER, *The Episcopate and the Primacy*, tr. K. BARKER et al. (New York 1962). W. SCHMITHALS, *Das kirchliche Apostelamt* (Göttingen 1961), bibliography. F. KLOSTERMANN, *Das Christliche Apostolat* (Innsbruck 1962), bibliography. H. KüNG, *Strukturen der Kirche* (Freiburg 1962), bibliography.

[F. KLOSTERMANN]

APOSTLES, ICONOGRAPHY OF

The 12 disciples of Christ were called "apostles," because they were sent out (Gr. ἀποστέλλειν, to send

forth) by Him to spread the gospel through the world. Thus one of the characteristics of the Church is its apostolicity; an indispensable element in its foundation was the preaching, holiness, and martyrdom of the Apostles. This article treats the development in Christian art of the full group, or college of the Apostles, in symbolic representations and in narrative scenes from the New Testament. (For additional information on the Apostles in art, *see* LAST SUPPER, ICONOGRAPHY OF; PENTECOST, ICONOGRAPHY OF; *and* SAINTS, ICONOGRAPHY OF.)

Traditio Legis. The establishment of the Church is shown in early Christian art by the seating of the Apostles to the left and right of Christ. The idea of the *Traditio Legis* or expansion of the Church is conveyed by standing Apostles converging in a double line toward Christ (4th-century sarcophagus; S. Ambrogio, Milan). The establishment of the Church by the teaching of Christ to the Apostles was painted in the Roman catacombs. In the fresco of the "cripta dei fornai" (Domitilla), St. Peter and St. Paul are sitting on folding stools, while the other ten Apostles are standing. Christ was shown enthroned twice amidst ten Apostles making the gesture of "adclamatio" (5th-century silver chalice from Antioch, The Cloisters, New York). He appears as the teaching Logos and as the Apocalyptic Christ, accompanied by the lamb.

The hillock represented in the early Christian sarcophagi, on which Christ teaches, sitting, or delivers the Law, standing, was interpreted as Mt. Zion on which Jerusalem is built. The mountain in Galilee where Christ appointed the "eleven disciples" to meet him before He delegated to them His authority and vanished from their view (Mt 28.16–20) was equated by St. Jerome with the mountain, exalted above the mountaintops, toward which a multitude of people will climb to hear the teaching of the Lord (Is 2.2–3). Thus, Christ stands on the mountain, "giving the law" to the Apostles and presenting St. Peter with the rotulus of the New Dispensation (Borghese sarcophagus, probably of the 4th century, Louvre).

Sometimes the college of the Apostles is gathered around Christ resurrected and holding the victorious "crux gemmata" (Probus sarcophagus, Museo Petriano). In a "star and wreath" sarcophagus in the Museum of Arles, the Resurrection was rendered symbolically present by a cross topped by a wreath of victory encompassing the monogram of Christ. On a beautiful fragment of a sarcophagus in the S. Sebastiano catacomb, the crowns, which in the Arles sarcophagus are held by the hand of God above the head of each Apostle against a starry sky, are now presented by the Apostles to Christ. The latter theme was taken from the Roman practice of having the provinces send the *aurum coronarium* to the head of state and according to which on solemn occasions the senators offered to the emperor the *aurum oblaticium*.

"Death of Ananias," painting by Raphael. (Victoria & Albert Museum, Crown Copyright/Art Resource, NY)

The key motif of the *Traditio Legis* was made explicit by the words "Dominus legem dat" inscribed on the rotulus proffered by Christ to Peter (sarcophagus, Arles Museum). According to St. Irenaeus and to the Fathers, the *Traditio Legis* consisted in the authority delegated to the Apostles to redeem through Baptism (Mk 16.16; Mt 28.19). That connection is made manifest in the mosaics of the early Christian baptisteries (S. Giovanni in Fonte and Baptistery of the Arians, Ravenna).

The *Traditio Legis* received its official recognition at the Roman synod of 382. Christ stands on the mountain, Mt. Zion and Paradise, uplifting His right hand with the gesture of *Sol Salutis* (Sun of Salvation), inherited from the Roman monuments of *Sol Invictus.* St. Paul hails Him and St. Peter takes in his veiled hands the rotulus of the new law. In this way the doctrine of the priority of the See of Rome, based on the double apostolicity of Peter and Paul in Rome and their martyrdom there, was confirmed in the circle of Pope Damasus. In the apse of the Cluniac priory of Berzé-la-Ville, the early 12th-century fresco developing the theme of the *Traditio Legis,* complete with 12 Apostles, signified the direct allegiance of the order of Cluny to the Holy See under the patronage of St. Peter and St. Paul, whose relics had been

deposited in the main altar of the abbey church consecrated in 1095. In Rome the tradition of the modified *Traditio Legis* was continued until the 9th century (mosaics in SS. Cosmas and Damian, S. Prassede, and S. Cecilia).

Animal Symbols. As early as the time of Pope Damasus the *Traditio Legis* theme developed into the introduction into Paradise of saints whom St. Peter and St. Paul presented to Christ. After the saints, a new symbol appears. Twelve lambs representing the Apostles are shown going out of the symbolical cities of Bethlehem and Jerusalem; they converge toward the *Agnus Dei* standing on the mount. The Apostles are symbolized by lambs also in the presence of the Transfiguration (mid-6th-century mosaic, S. Apollinare in Classe, Ravenna).

In the apse of the 5th-century baptistery at Albenga, 12 doves, symbolizing the 12 Apostles, surround a triple halo bearing the triple monogram of Christ as well as the letters alpha and omega repeated three times, which is a threefold anti-Arian reference to the Trinity.

Narrative Scenes. In the primitive liturgy the Ascension was celebrated on the afternoon of the Feast of the Pentecost. In the church of the Apostles in Constantinople, as it had been rebuilt by Justinian I (546), the cupola with the mosaic of the Ascension was located above the southern arm of the cross-shaped building—a plan that was copied in the church of the Apostles in Milan— and the cupola with the mosaic of the Pentecost was located above the western arm. The Ascension cupola was separated from the central cupola, reserved to the Pantocrator, by an arch the mosaics of which illustrated the appearance of Christ before His Disciples in the cenacle before the Ascension. The Pentecost cupola was separated from the Pantocrator cupola by an arch illustrating the mission of the Apostles. Mosaics on the three wall arches supporting the Pentecost cupola showed the Apostles administering Baptism. In a 9th-century manuscript of the sermons of St. Gregory of Nazianzus, the scene of the mission given to the 11 Apostles (Mt 28.19) tops a composition divided into 12 compartments in each of which an Apostle is painted performing the rite of Baptism. Together with the 46 illuminations representing the Passions of the Apostles, they constitute a cycle illustrating the common feast of the Apostles which, in the Greek East, was celebrated on June 13. The Greek iconography of the Apostles' Passion, revived in the 9th century after preiconoclastic models, was transmitted to the illustrators of the Western medieval Passionalia; their works, in their own turn, were used as the sources of the martyrdom of the Apostles in Gothic sculpture (portals of the cathedral of Strasbourg, Holy Cross in Gmünd, and Saint-Thiébaut in Thann).

Although the feast of the *Divisio Apostolorum,* which in the West occurs on July 15, was not celebrated until the end of the 11th century, a long tradition prepared it. It was initiated by Eusebius's *Historia Ecclesiastica* (*Patrologia Graeca,* ed. J. P. Migne 20:213–216) and the apocryphal Acts of the Apostles and iconographically anticipated in illuminated codices of the commentary on the Apocalypse by Beatus of Liébana (*c.* 776). The names of the nations allotted to the Apostles are written above the head of each, that of ''Spania,'' inscribed above St. James, bearing testimony to the belief in the apostolicity of his mission in Spain and to the fame of the pilgrimage to Santiago de Compostela. The separation of the Apostles, departing toward their respective assignments, appears in the lunettes of the 12th-century façade of the cathedral of Angoulême. Peculiar to Byzantine iconography is the blessing of His Apostles by Christ in Bethany, before ''He parted from them and was carried up into heaven'' (Lk 24.50–51). The ceremonious bowing down of the Apostles worshiping Christ is treated in an awe-inspiring way in a splendid mural painting in the choir of Hagia Sophia at Trebizund (13th century).

Romanesque art, with its propensity for synthesis, achieved the fusion of the iconography of the mission of the Apostles and that of Pentecost. In the Pentecost image

Procession of Apostles, and Baptism of Christ with St. John the Baptist, 5th-century mosaic in the dome of the baptistery of the Arians, Ravenna, Italy.

in a lectionary from Cluny, Christ proffers a scroll with the inscription: ''Ecce mitto promissum Patris mei in vos.'' The first word ''Et'' of Lk 24.49 was significantly changed to ''Ecce.'' On the main tympanum of the Magdalene church at Vézelay, a gigantic Christ, flattened against the mandorla that circumscribes Him, darts shafts of light onto the Apostles. On His proper right the clear sky and the books held open by the Apostles proclaim in the words of Mk 16.16: ''He who believes and is baptized shall be saved.'' On the left side the closed books and the waves of thunder, billowing above the Apostles, warn that ''he who does not believe shall be condemned.''

The renewal of the early Christian and Byzantine association between the Ascension and the mission of the Apostles is exemplified in a relief by Donatello (*c.* 1427). Christ enthroned on a mountain between clouds beyond which He is about to vanish, gives the keys to St. Peter in the presence of the Virgin and the other Apostles. The tapestry cartoons designed by Raphael in 1514, however, broke with every allegorizing trend as well as with the apocryphal tradition. Following the literal straightforwardness first exhibited by Giotto in the Arena Chapel of Padua, Raphael conceived his cycle of the life of the Apostles as ''istorie'' in the sense of Alberti. The first series of the tapestries for the Sistine Chapel was begun in Brussels in 1516 (cartoons, Victoria and Albert Museum).

The Mystical Mill. At the opposite aesthetic and intellectual pole of the compositions by Raphael, the dying spirit of the Middle Ages invented the mystical mill or host mill. The theme assumed an extraordinary development in the visionary and surrealistic art of the end of the Middle Ages and was used for the purpose of putting double emphasis on the "Corpus Mysticum" both as the Eucharist and as the Church. In a miniature of a Gradual, the Apostles turn the crank of the host mill, *molendarium hostiae* (Zentralbibliothek, Lucerne).

Apocalyptic Themes. The Apostles embody the walls of the heavenly Jerusalem in keeping with Rv 21.14: "The wall of the city has twelve foundation stones, and on them twelve names of the twelve apostles of the Lamb" (Romanesque fresco; San Pietro al Monte, Civate). The 24 Elders (Rv 4.4) are interpreted as the double college of the Prophets and Apostles in early medieval illustrated apocalypses and in Romanesque portals. As a rule, the 24 Elders accompany the *Majestas Domini,* but in the transept of the cathedral of Lausanne (13th century) they gyrate around the coronation of the Virgin. In the final phase of Romanesque art, the theophany of the Last Judgment according to Matthew (24.27–31) progressively replaced the Apocalyptic *Majestas Domini.* In an intermediate period, the *Majestas Domini* became more and more imbued with connotations of the Last Judgment. The Apostles, enthroned on globes, accompany Christ enthroned as a judge (Mt 19.28): "You shall sit on twelve thrones and shall be judges over the twelve tribes of Israel" (early 12th-century fresco, church of Saint-Savin-sur-Gartempe).

Architectural Symbolism. On account of the very number 12, the college of the Apostles sustained a special relationship with architectural symbolism. Realizing the will of Emperor Constantine the Great, Emperor Constantius II (337–361) buried him in a mausoleum joining the church of the Apostles. Because of relics deposited there of St. Peter, St. Paul, St. John, and St. Thomas, with those of St. Timothy added in 356 and those of St. Andrew and St. Luke in 357, the church became the shrine of the apostolic founders of the church. The mausoleum was in the form of a rotunda surrounded on the inside by 12 columns which were surmounted by as many bust reliefs of the Apostles as *imagines clipeatae* (Medallions of the Apostles, Ottoman Museum, Istanbul). As we see on an ivory plaque representing the Resurrection (*c.* 400, Bayerisches Nationalmuseum, Munich), the rotunda built above the tomb of Christ in the Anastasis church in Jerusalem was decorated with similar busts of the Apostles. The formula of the college of Apostles, carved on both sides in the splays of a Last Judgment portal, prevailed in the cathedrals of Chartres and Amiens between 1215 and 1230. There, as "bases" and "columns" of the church of which Christ standing against the trumeau of the portal is the "doorway," they continued the tradition

of statue-columns of the ancestors of Christ on façades of cathedrals and abbey churches of western and northern France of the mid-12th century. Apostle portals descended from French models are found in the German Gothic cathedrals at Strasbourg, Münster, Erfurt, and Augsburg.

Symbol of the Creed. According to early tradition, before they scattered toward the countries assigned to them (Rufinus, *Patrologia Latina,* 21:337), on the very day of the Pentecost (Pseudo-Augustine, *Patrologia Latina,* 39:2188–91), the Holy Spirit inspired the Apostles to speak, each in his turn, one article of the creed. Ottonian art seized upon that tradition and dramatized it by building the concordance of the articles of faith and the prophecies, perching the Apostles on the shoulders of the Prophets (fresco, S. Sebastiano in Pallara, Rome). This caryatidal pattern of concordance struck deep roots in Germany (12th-century baptismal font, cathedral of Merseburg; 13th-century "Fürstenportal," Bamberg Cathedral). The iconographical scheme of the concordance of the Prophets and Apostles became very popular in the 12th century in the Cologne and Mosan workshops (enameled portable altar, made by Eilbertus of Cologne, *c.* 1130, Berlin Museum). In France, Suger had laid out symbolically the choir of his abbey church—"raised aloft by columns representing the number of the twelve Apostles and, on the second hand, by as many columns in the ambulatory that signified the number of the prophets" (*De Consecratione* 5, with reference to Eph 2.20). From the end of 14th to the 16th century the credo tapestries continued the tradition of presenting the Apostles and Prophets in pairs.

Apostle Glasses and Spoons. Some early Christian sense of the mysterium of the Church embodied in the college of the Apostles was salvaged in the decorative arts of the Renaissance and 17th century, illustrating the Apostles. On enameled glasses produced in Silesia, Franconia, and Bohemia, the 12 Apostles distributed into two tiers under arches surround the *Salvator Mundi.* The Apostle silver spoons were first made as separate baptism gifts, and later ordered as complete iconographical series. They are recorded from 1494 to 1686 in England, Holland, Germany, Switzerland, and Italy.

Bibliography: D. T. B. WOOD, "Credo Tapestries," *Burlington Magazine* 24 (1914) 247–254, 309–316. A. FABRE, "L'Iconographie de la Pentecôte," *Gazette des beaux-arts,* 5th ser., 8 (1923) 33–42. C. G. RUPERT, *Apostle Spoons* (New York 1929). A. KATZENELLENBOGEN, in *Reallexikon zur deutschen Kunstgeschichte,* ed. O. SCHMITT (Stuttgart 1937–) 1:811–829, bibliog.; "The Separation of the Apostles," *Gazette des beaux-arts,* 6th ser. 35 (1949) 81–98. J. POPE-HENNESSY, *Donatello's Relief of the Ascension with Christ Giving the Keys to Saint Peter* (London 1949). G. DOWNEY, "The Builder of the Original Church of the Apostles at Constantinople," *Dumbarton Oaks Papers,* Harvard University 6 (1951) 53–82. F. SALET, "Les Statues d'apôtres de la Sainte Chapelle conservées au musée de Cluny,'' *Bulletin monumental* 109 (1951) 135–156; 112 (1954) 357–363. E. MÂLE, *Les Saints compagnons du Christ* (Paris 1958), iconography of individual apostles. C. DAVID-WEYER, ''Das Tradito Legis und seine Nachfolge,'' *Münchner Jahrbuch der bildenden Kunst,* 3d ser., 12 (1961) 7–45. A. E. M. KATZENELLENBOGEN, ''The Sarcophagus in S. Ambrogio and St. Ambrose,'' *Art Bulletin* 29 (1947) 249–259.

[P. VERDIER]

APOSTLES' CREED

The creedal statements used in the Western Churches for instructing catechumens had been almost invariably versions of the old Roman Creed. Rufinus of Aquileia had given evidence of the existence of a creed attributed to the Apostles at Rome and Aquileia in the late 4th century. An almost identical creed was used at Milan in catechetical instruction; its text can be reconstructed from three sermons of Augustine (212; 213; and 214) and from the *Explanatio Symboli* attributed to Ambrose. Six sermons (57 to 62) of PETER CHRYSOLOGUS, Bishop of Ravenna (431 to 450), and a homily of MAXIMUS OF TURIN (*Hom.* 83 *de trad. symb.*) make reference to the creeds used in their respective sees. NICETAS OF REMESIANA (*c.* 335 to 414) provided the formula of faith used in the Balkan area (*Patrologia Latina*, ed. J. P. Migne, 52: 847–76). Quodvultdeus of Carthage (*c.* 437) is credited with the sermon preserving the African creedal formulary [G. Morin, *Revue Bénédictine* 31 (1914) 156–35 (1923) 233–]. Priscillian (d. 385) quotes the creed used at Avila in Spain (*Tract.* 2), and a 6th-century Spanish creed has been reconstructed from the works of Martin of Braga (*De correct. rust.*), Ildefonsus of Toledo (*De cognit. bapt.* 36), and the *Ad Elipandum epistula* (1.22). Finally, three Gallic creeds are attributed to Faustus of Riez (*c.* 458 to 477), Caesarius of Arles (502 to 542), and Cyprian of Toulon (516 to 546). All these creeds have the Roman Creed as foundation and differ from it only in minor variations.

The so-called *textus receptus* of the Apostles' Creed is provided by Pirminius of Reichenau in his *Scarap sus* (chapter 10; 12; 28), or handbook of Christian doctrine, written between 710 and 724. It is likewise preserved in the 7th- or 8th-century Missal of Bobbio; in the Antiphonary of Bangor, written by Comgall between 680 and 689; and in the so-called *Missale Gallicanum Vetus* of the early 8th century, written probably in Auxerre, Gaul. St. Fructuosus of Braga (d. 665) assigned the Apostles' Creed a place in Compline; Benedict of Aniane (d. 821) and Amalarius of Metz ordered it to be said before Matins and Prime and after Compline. These considerations lead to the conclusion that the *textus receptus* had its origin in southern Gaul rather than at Rome.

The Carolingian reforms centered on the religious instruction of both clergy and laity, and at the basis was a knowledge of the Apostles' Creed and an ability to explain it. The text of this creed was likewise incorporated into the Carolingian psalters. However, it did not replace the Constantinopolitan Creed in Rome until the late 10th or early 11th century, when, as GREGORY VII said, ''Teutonicis concessum est regimen nostrae ecclesiae'' (The government of our Church has been surrendered to the Germans''; G. Morin, *Anecd. Mared.* 2.1:460), testifying to the reforms introduced into the liturgy as well as administration of the Roman Church by the northern Europeans. By the pontificate of INNOCENT III (d. 1216) the *textus receptus* of the Apostles' Creed was universally acknowledged in the West as the official creed of the Church and was commented on as such by Thomas Aquinas (*Exp. super symb. Apost.*). At the Council of Florence in 1438, however, Mark EUGENICUS shocked the Western prelates by claiming that he had never heard of it (Harduin, *Act. conc.* 9.842E–843A). But it was recognized as a basic statement of Christian belief by Luther, Calvin, and Zwingli during the Reformation. It was put forward by the Anglicans at the Lambeth Conference of 1920, and at the World Conference of Faith and Order in 1927 as a basis on which the unity of the Church might be erected.

Bibliography: H. DENZINGER and A. SCHÖNMETZER, *Enchiridion Symbolorum* (36d ed. Herder, 1976).

[F. X. MURPHY/EDS.]

APOSTLES OF JESUS

The Apostles of Jesus (AJ) is an order of men founded in 1968 for the express purpose of the evangelization of Africa and the world. The founders were two Italian Comboni missionaries, Bishop Sixtus Mazzoldi (d. 1987) and the Reverend John Marengoni (MCCJ), working in Uganda. They shared the conviction that for it to survive in Africa as elsewhere in the world, the Catholic Church needs indigenous diocesan clergy as well as missionaries. The mission statement of the Apostles of Jesus gives priority to the work of evangelization and emphasizes the spiritual, pastoral, and social ministry to all people with preference to the poor. Their work is carried out by founding parishes and helps existing parishes to become self-supporting. The Apostles of Jesus promote vocations to the priesthood, religious life, and lay ministry. Within a few decades after their founding, the Apostles of Jesus were ministering in Kenya, Ethiopia, Sudan, Tanzania, and South Africa, and later in the United States in the dioceses of New York and Allentown, PA. They have minor seminaries in Tanzania, Uganda, and Kenya where they also have a major seminary for the study of philosophy and theology.

[P. O. GAGGAWALA]

APOSTLESHIP OF PRAYER

A spiritual association of Catholics who are not only concerned for their own salvation but also intent on spreading the Kingdom of Christ. They work for this by prayer and sacrifice in the spirit of apostles, mainly through three practices: (1) the daily offering of all their prayers, works, joys, and sufferings to the Sacred Heart of Jesus, or to God the Father through Him, (2) the uniting of their offering with the sacrifice of Christ renewed in the Mass and reception of Communion in reparation at least once a month, (3) the daily recitation of the Rosary, or at least one decade of it.

Although it was started in 1844 by Francis X. Gautrelet, SJ, in Vals, France, Henri Ramière, SJ, is credited with making it a world movement by giving it a definite structure; by publishing in 1861 his book, *The Apostleship of Prayer, the Holy League of Hearts United to the Heart of Jesus;* and the *Messenger of the Sacred Heart.*

Theological Basis. The Apostleship of Prayer strives to enroll and continually remind all Catholics, as members of Christ's Mystical Body enjoined to love others as He has loved them, that they should make everything they do every day a prayer and sacrifice for the salvation of souls. It promotes devotion to the Sacred Heart, the soul of the Apostleship, through consecration, reparation, and other practices.

Organization. The head of the Apostleship of Prayer is the father general of the JESUITS. His delegate directs it from Rome with the assistance of national, regional, and diocesan directors. He appoints the diocesan directors nominated by their bishops. Diocesan directors establish local centers in parishes, schools, institutions, and societies and appoint pastors, chaplains, or other priests to serve as local directors of these centers. The faithful who have the intention of making the daily offering may become members for life by enrolling in any center. The national office of the Apostleship of Prayer is in New York.

Bibliography: P. ARRUPE, *The Apostleship of Prayer in the Church and in the World of Today* (Rome 1974); *The Apostleship of Prayer Twenty Years after the Council: Documents of the World Congress of the National Secretaries of the Apostleship of Prayer, Rome, 8–14 April 1985* (Rome 1985).

[F. SCHOBERG/EDS.]

APOSTLESHIP OF THE SEA

Opus Apostolatus Maris, an international association for the spiritual care of seafarers, was founded by a priest and two lay Catholics, Rev. Donald Macintosh, Arthur Gannon, and Peter Anson in Glasgow, Scotland, in 1920. Two years later Archbishop Mackintosh of Glasgow secured the blessing of Pius XI and a letter of approval for the society dedicated to prayer and good works for seafarers. By 1927, 200 churches in various ports of the world were designated as centers for seafarers. In 1942 the Consistorial Congregation assumed jurisdiction over both the port and ship chaplains, and in 1952 the apostolic constitution *Exsul familia* established the general secretariate in Rome. In 1957 Pius XII promulgated a series of laws and statutes for the organization and guidance of the movement. John XXIII granted special supplementary faculties to chaplains in 1961. In the United States the office of episcopal moderator of the Apostleship of the Sea was established in 1951. The apostleship chaplain has the care of souls of maritime personnel both ashore and at sea. He serves seafarers aboard ship and in port, at navigational academies and in maritime hospitals; he is responsible for arrangements necessary for the proper liturgical celebration of Mass by all priests making a sea voyage. His faculties include the administration of the sacraments to seafarers under special conditions. Traditionally the Apostleship of the Sea ministers to all seafarers, with special concern for foreign seafarers of all faiths. The Apostleship of the Sea comes under general supervision of the Pontifical Council for Migrants & Itinerant People in Rome. The general headquarters of the apostleship is in Rome.

Bibliography: PIUS XII, ''Exsul familia'' (Apostolic Constitution, August 1, 1952) *Acta Apostolicae Sedis* 44 (1952) 649–704. V. A. YZERMANS, *American Catholic Seafarers' Church: A Narrative History of the Apostleship of the Sea and the National Catholic Conference for Seafarers in the United States* (Washington, DC 1995). D. ZIMMERMAN, *A Guide to the Archives: Records of the Catholic Maritime Clubs and the National Conference of the Apostleship of the Sea* (Staten Island 1989).

[M. F. CONNOLLY/EDS.]

APOSTOLATE AND SPIRITUAL LIFE

From the Greek ἀποστολή, a sending, commission, or expedition. The Greek term is more indefinite than the Latin *apostolatus,* which refers more to the condition and office of the messenger than to his action. The Koine (NT) is of course greatly influenced by the Latin. The word came to signify in particular the active mission of the Church in the world. The normal relationship between the apostolate and the spiritual life is a mean standing between the various species of activism, on the one hand, and another extreme less easily denominated, the main feature of which would be solicitude about the "disturbances" consequent upon the exercise of the apostolate, on the other. This article provides a brief introduction to the question of how the two complement one another and how, under some conditions, the apostolate is apparently opposed to the spiritual life.

The Church has been in a mission status from the very beginning of its existence. Those who first constituted the new people of God were given the title "apostles." The community founded upon them is essentially apostolic, not merely in the sense of being in historical continuity with that small group through the apostolic succession of episcopal consecration but also in the sense of having the mission, at the present time, of preaching the gospel to the whole of creation (Mk 16.15).

The Church, however, is a community in whose members the word of the Gospel has borne fruit in various degrees, and it is also a community that is organized hierarchically. Both these factors determine the exercise of the apostolate—the former because it is assumed that apostolic works are somewhat the overflow of communion with God in the Church, the latter because the whole apostolate of the Church is under the direction of the episcopal hierarchy, who stand in place of the Apostles.

The exercise of the apostolate, by those who share in this mission of the Church, normally bears fruit in the interior life of the apostle himself. Experience witnesses to the fact, and that it should be so is to be expected because such activity is in the likeness of trinitarian life. In God, the Father unceasingly generates the Son without losing anything of Himself. Rather, the Son abides in the bosom of the Father and gives Himself to Him in love, so that from their mutual embrace proceeds the Holy Spirit. The apostle exercises, in one degree or another, a spiritual paternity, through which real relations are established between himself and those to whom he is sent. "I became your Father in Christ Jesus through the Gospel," says St. Paul (1 Cor 4.15b). This does not mean that the persons brought forth "in Christ Jesus" remain in some infantile way dependent upon the Father-Apostle, for "through the Gospel" they receive a share not in his life but in God's. Nonetheless, if the exercise of the apostolate is authentic, those who are spiritually engendered thereby, as they grow up in Christ Jesus, remain united to their apostle-father by love and piety. The communion thus established must obviously bear fruit in his interior life.

What, then, in this context, is an authentic apostolate? Reference here is not primarily to the so-called canonical mission, which gives a certain juridical authenticity to the work of the apostle who receives such a mandate, even though the canonical mission should normally be the sign and guarantee of the overall authenticity of a given work. Here the word "authentic" refers more to the moral quality of the apostolate, its genuineness as an exterior and visible expression of the apostle's interior life.

St. John provides the best possible description of this authenticity: "[T]hat which we have seen and heard we proclaim also to you, so that you may have fellowship with us; and our fellowship is with the Father and with his Son, Jesus Christ" (1 Jn 1.3). The order is clear: seeing and hearing come first, then proclamation, and this in turn is for the sake of fellowship, i.e., deeper communion with God in the Church. An authentic apostolate, therefore, in terms of the spiritual life, is one that is based upon a measure of "seeing and hearing" and is motivated by a desire for sharing. Of course, St. John refers to an experience wherein Jesus was physically present to those whom he chose as Apostles, but the sensible contact scarcely exhausts what he means. The Apostles saw and heard by faith what the Father revealed in Jesus, especially through his "enactment" of the paschal mysteries. Living faith, then, is the heart of the apostolate, together with that work of charity called mercy. The interior life of any apostle is constituted by an acceptance and assimilation of the living truth of God's love for mankind in Christ Jesus, together with the urge to share the joy that is the normal fruit of being "in the truth." "The love of Christ urges us on" (2 Cor 5.14a).

Bibliography: J. B. CHAUTARD, *The Soul of the Apostolate,* tr. J. A. MORAN (Trappist, Ky. 1941). F. CUTTAZ, *Dictionnaire de spiritualité ascétique et mystique,* ed. M. VILLIER et al. (Paris 1932—) 1:773–790. THOMAS AQUINAS, *Summa theologiae* 2a2ae, 32.2–3; 182, 188.2.

[M. B. SCHEPERS/F. KLOSTERMANN]

APOSTOLIC

The adjective affirming a relation of people, activities, or objects to the APOSTLES, their mission, their actions. It is first found in Ignatius of Antioch (*Trall.*) and the *Martyrdom of Polycarp.* In the patristic age the word serves to represent the relation of origin and similarity of the Church to the TWELVE and PAUL (apostolicity). It is applied to the immediate disciples and successors of the Twelve and Paul; from the 3rd and 4th centuries to BISHOPS; from the Middle Ages, religious, missionaries, priests, and lay people are called *viri apostolici. Ecclesia apostolica* is a Church established by one of the Twelve or their immediate successors; from the 4th century it designates every episcopal see and the whole Church (H.

Denzinger, *Enchiridion symbolorum* 3, 43—as a property and a note). In the 6th century, particularly in the West, apostolic is restricted to the papal sphere (cf. 1917 *Codex iuris canonici* cc.3, 4, 7 etc.). *Vita apostolica* is, from the 2nd and 3rd centuries on, a life like that of the Apostles, i.e., an ascetic life (Nilus of Ancyra, *Ep.* 3.26; *Patrologia Graeca* 79:384), the monastic life (Socrates, *Hist. eccl.* 4.23; *Patrologia Graeca* 67:512), from the 6th century on rather the active pastoral life; so also among the sects.

As a noun *apostolicus* means bishop (Tertullian), in the 6th century pope, and later the receiver of certain papal letters. As early as the 4th and 5th centuries *apostolici* are heretics; *apostolicum,* the word of an Apostle (Augustine); later the designation was connected with a creed, a lectionary, letters and decrees of the popes. *Apostolica* were the official vestments of bishops.

See Also: APOSTOLATE.

Bibliography: H. BACHT, *Lexikon für Theologie und Kirche,* 10 v. (2d, new ed. Freiburg 1957–65) 1:758–759, bibliog. K. G. STECK, *Die Religion in Geschichte und Gegenwart* 1:516, bibliog. W. NAGEL, *Der Begriff des Apostolischen in der christlichen Frühzeit bis zur Kanonsbildung* (Habilitationsschrift, typescript; Leipzig 1958).

[F. KLOSTERMANN]

APOSTOLIC BLESSING

A blessing was usually given at Mass by a bishop, in the Gallican rite after the fraction, but in the Roman rite at the end of the eucharist. When the pope gave this blessing, it was known as an apostolic blessing. The custom developed of its being given solemnly after Mass on certain occasions, e.g., at St. Peter's on Maundy Thursday and Easter Sunday, at St. John Lateran's on Ascension Thursday, at St. Mary Major's on the Assumption. Historically, a plenary indulgence was attached to it. Sometimes it was also given outside Mass, e.g., the papal blessing *Urbi et orbi* from the balcony of St. Peter's.

[B. FORSHAW/EDS.]

APOSTOLIC CAMERA

The Apostolic Camera administers the property and guards the temporal rights of the Holy See during its vacancy (*Pastor bonus,* art. 171). It is presided over by the Cardinal Camerlengo (Chamberlain) of the Holy Roman Church, and assisted by the Vice-Camerlengo together with other prelates (art. 171 §1). Art. 171 §2 of the apostolic constitution, *Pastor bonus* directs the Cardinal Camerlengo, upon the vacancy of the Apostolic See, to ascertain the financial and economic status of the various administrative units and dependencies of the Apostolic See, and report his findings to the College of Cardinals. He also has such other duties and responsibilities as may be assigned to him by special law.

History. The *camerarius* (chamberlain, camerlengo) dates from the end of the 11th century, when he appears as the chief financial administrator of papal properties and revenues. In the 13th and 14th centuries he acquired also judicial functions not only in fiscal matters but also in other civil and penal cases. The Camera thus became an extremely important administrative office and judicial tribunal. The senior assistants of the *camerarius* were the *clerici Camerae.* Several special assignments, branching off from the office of the chamberlain, subsequently developed into independent offices. The vice chamberlain became the *gubernator urbis* or governor of Rome; the general treasurer remained in charge of financial administration; the auditor general was a strictly judicial officer with a tribunal of prelates and doctors of laws at his disposal. The highest court was the *Tribunal plenae Camerae,* with appellate jurisdiction; its judges were the *clerici Camerae* already mentioned. Since the events of 1870 and the end of the Papal States, there remains only a trace of all this activity.

Bibliography: E. HESTON, *The Holy See at Work* (Milwaukee 1950). B. OJETTI, *De Romana Curia: Commentarium in constitutionem apostolicam ''Sapienti consilio''* (Rome 1910). John Paul II, apostolic constitution, *Pastor bonus* (June 28, 1988).

[T. L. BOUSCAREN/EDS.]

APOSTOLIC CHURCH ORDER

A small treatise that claims to have been written at the command of the Lord by the 12 Apostles. The first half (4–14) sets forth moral precepts in the form of a description of the two ways, that of good and that of evil, based on DIDACHE (1–4). The author adapts the two-way device to the more developed ecclesiastical situation of the 4th century. The second part (15–29) contains canonical legislation and issues regulations for the election of a bishop, priests, readers, deacons, and widows and for the subordination of the laymen. The author, and the time and place of origin are unknown. There are indications that it might have been composed in Egypt *c.* 300; but some scholars point to Syria as its place of origin. The high authority in which it was held in Egypt speaks perhaps more for Egyptian provenance.

J. Bickel was the first to publish (1843) the Greek original from a 12th-century Vienna manuscript, the only one containing the entire text. He named it the *Apostolic*

Church Order. There is reason to assume that its real title was *Ecclesiastical Canons of the Holy Apostles.* These canons are attributed to the various Apostles who spoke at a reputed council at which Mary and Martha were present. The ignorant compiler ranked Peter and Cephas as two different Apostles. The extant Latin, Syriac, Coptic, Arabic, and Ethiopic versions testify to the reputation this *Church Order* enjoyed.

Bibliography: J. W. BICKEL, *Geschichte des Kirchenrechts,* 2 v. in 1 (Giessen 1843–49) 1:107–132, Gr. text. T. SCHERMANN, *Die allgemeine Kirchenordnung,* v.1 (Paderborn 1914) 12–34. G. HORNER, ed. and tr., *The Statutes of the Apostles or Canones ecclesiastici* (London 1904), gives Eng. tr. of the Coptic-Sahidic version and the Arabic and Ethiopic text with Eng. tr. E. HAULER, ed., *Didascaliae apostolorum fragmenta Veronensia Latina* (Leipzig 1900) 92–101, fragment of Lat. version. A. HARNACK, *Texte und Untersuchungen zur Geschichte der altchristlichen Literatur* 2.5 (1886). F. X. FUNK, ed., *Didascalia et constitutiones apostolorum.* J. QUASTEN, *Patrology* 2:119–120.

[J. QUASTEN]

APOSTOLIC CONSTITUTION

A form of papal decree dealing with matters of faith and affairs of the universal Church or a sizable portion of it. It is usually written according to the formal style of a papal bull, beginning with the words *Constitutio Apostolica,* followed by a statement of the subject matter. Then is inscribed the name of the pope, to which is added the title *Episcopus, Servus Servorum Dei* and the expression *Ad perpetuam rei memoriam.* If the apostolic constitution deals with a dogmatic definition it is signed only by the pope as the Bishop of the Catholic Church. Otherwise, this kind of letter is signed by the cardinal chancellor, the prefect or secretary of that Congregation to whose jurisdiction the subject matter pertains, and then the protonotaries. Apostolic constitutions are published in the ACTA APOSTOLICAE SEDIS.

[J. A. FORGAC/EDS.]

APOSTOLIC CONSTITUTIONS

A church order written in Syria about 380. The full title, *Ordinances of the Holy Apostles through Clement,* suggests that these canons had been drawn up by the Apostles and transmitted to the Church by CLEMENT I of Rome. In reality they are the work of an Arian, who seems to be identical with the fourth-century interpolator of the Epistles of St. IGNATIUS. The first six of its eight books are an adaptation of the *DIDASCALIA APOSTOLORUM,* a Church Order composed in the first half of the third century in Syria.

The Constitutions contain canonical legislation for the clergy and deal with Christian ethics, the penitential discipline and Eucharistic Liturgy, fasts and feasts, schism, heresy, and Christian burial. Book 7, 1–32, is based on the DIDACHE; book 7, 33–38, contains a very interesting collection of Jewish prayers; 39–45, the Antiochene rites of Baptism and Confirmation; and 46–49, other liturgical material, especially (47) the *Gloria in excelsis* as the liturgical morning prayer.

Book 8 is the most important. Its first two chapters probably used a lost work of HIPPOLYTUS of Rome, *Concerning Spiritual Gifts;* ch. 3–22 adapt the *Apostolic Tradition,* formerly called the *Egyptian Church Order.* Book 8, 3–27, is an elaborate version of the Antiochene Liturgy. This section contains (5–15) the so-called Clementine Liturgy for use in the consecration of a bishop. Its completeness renders it a valuable source for the history of the Mass. Chapters 16 to 46 describe the duties of the members of the community. Chapter 47 comprises the so-called Apostolic Canons, a collection of 85 canons, derived in part from the preceding Constitutions, in part from the canons of the Councils of Antioch (341) and Laodicea (363). The first 50 of these were transmitted by DIONYSIUS EXIGUUS and were used in later canonical collections of the West. The last of the 85 canons contains a list of Biblical books that omits the Book of Revelation, but adds the Apostolic Constitutions and the two epistles of Clement to the canon of Scripture.

An "Epitome" of book 8 of the Constitutions draws independently on the *Apostolic Tradition.* The title "Epitome" is misleading because it is not an abbreviation or condensation, but a series of excerpts. In some of the manuscripts this "Epitome" is called "Constitutions through Hippolytus." Time and place of origin are unknown and difficult to determine but the excellence of its readings suggests that these extracts must have been made at a fairly early date after the composition of the Constitutions.

Bibliography: *Patrologia Graeca,* ed J. P. MIGNE (Paris 1857–66) 1:555–1156. F. X. FUNK, ed., *Didascalia et constitutiones apostolorum* (Paderborn 1905). J. QUASTEN, ed., *Monumenta eucharista et liturgica vetustissima* (Bonn 1935–37) 178–233, liturgical texts. F. E. BRIGHTMAN, *Liturgies Eastern and Western,* 2 v. (Oxford 1896) 1:3–30. J. QUASTEN, *Patrology* (Westminster, Maryland 1950–) 2:183–185 M. METZGER, *Les constitutions apostoliques,* 3 v. (Paris 1985–86).

[J. QUASTEN/EDS.]

APOSTOLIC DELEGATION IN THE U.S.

Although the Holy See prefers to be represented in most countries by an apostolic nuncio (accredited to the civil government as well as to the episcopate) rather than by an apostolic delegate (having only an internal or religious and not also an external or political mission), an apostolic delegation was established in the United States because a nunciature was found to be impossible.

Preliminary steps. In 1853, five years after Pius IX had received an American minister in Rome, he sent Gaetano BEDINI, titular archbishop of Thebes and apostolic nuncio to Brazil, to the United States in the hope of preparing the way for a nuncio in Washington and of solving certain purely ecclesiastical problems. When John Hughes, archbishop of New York, addressed an inquiry to a Catholic in the Cabinet, James Campbell, postmaster general, the reply stated that President Franklin Pierce would receive a chargé or minister but only as the pope's political representative, and would prefer a layman. The U.S. government, under pressure from nativists and European exiles, did not deem it opportune to increase its diplomatic relations with the reactionary Papal States (*see* NATIVISM, AMERICAN). Nevertheless, Bedini's July 12, 1854, report advised the Holy See to establish a nunciature in Washington at once in order to effect complete unity among the U.S. bishops, to ensure uniformity of discipline, to safeguard the Church's interests in the newly acquired lands of Texas and New Mexico, and to provide a substitute for the primate desired by the First Plenary Council of Baltimore (1852). The U.S. bishops, however, feared that if diplomatic representatives were exchanged mutually, the government might meddle in spiritual affairs and that KNOW-NOTHINGISM might assail the Church even more violently. In view of the riots and demonstrations staged against Bedini in Cincinnati, Ohio; Wheeling, W.Va.; and elsewhere, and of the government's failure to accord him the promised protection, the Holy See wisely declined to risk the possibly disastrous consequences involved in any such unilateral action as Bedini recommended. If the U.S. government refused to receive a nuncio who would be an ecclesiastic at this time, it would be even less likely to agree to such a proposal after it ceased, in 1868, to maintain its own minister in Rome and after the pope ceased in 1870 to be *de facto* a temporal sovereign. Overtures were still made occasionally and secretly, however, on the part of the Holy See; for example, a minor Roman prelate, Paolo Mori, on a visit to the United States in 1886, tried to persuade the government to accredit an envoy to the Holy See, and the bishop of Fort Wayne, Ind., Joseph Dwenger, apparently used his insufficient influence both in Rome and in Washington to have himself appointed first nuncio or delegate.

Apostolic visitators and temporary delegates. In the course of the 19th century, several ecclesiastics were commissioned by the Holy See to act as apostolic visitators or delegates to the United States for specific purposes. In 1820 Joseph Octave Plessis, bishop of Quebec, Canada, at the request of the Congregation for the Propagation of the Faith (the Propaganda), investigated the troubles caused by obstreperous trustees in New York. In 1852, 1866, and 1884 the successive archbishops of Baltimore, Francis Patrick Kenrick, Martin John Spalding, and James GIBBONS, were appointed apostolic delegates by the Holy See to preside over the First, Second, and Third Plenary Councils of Baltimore, respectively. From time to time, moreover, foreign churchmen were sent to the United States to handle particular cases.

Petitions and recommendations for a permanent delegation. Petitions for an apostolic delegate were sent to Rome mainly by priests who looked to the Holy See for support in their quarrels with their bishops. Thus around 1819, Robert Browne, OSA, who had resisted the legitimate authority of the archbishop of Baltimore, Ambrose Maréchal (and his two predecessors), in his undated report to the Propaganda concerning the Church in the United States, requested the establishment of an apostolic delegation in Washington for the purpose of settling the controversies existing in many U.S. dioceses. Similarly, in 1883 Rev. William Mahoney in a 385-page book entitled *Jura Sacerdotum Vindicata. The Rights of the Clergy Vindicated; or, A Plea for Canon Law in the United States,* which he published anonymously in New York, asserted with moderation and respect that the necessary remedy for the widespread abuse and "monstrous evil" "of priests being uncanonically dismissed from their dioceses and thrown helplessly on the world, to the infinite degradation of the sacerdotal character . . . and to the great scandal of the faithful" was the appointment by the Holy See of an apostolic delegate who would enforce a just and uniform discipline and insist on the observance of the then unheeded laws. Furthermore, Rev. Edward MCGLYNN, who had been suspended in 1886 by Michael Corrigan, Archbishop of New York, for supporting Henry George and had been excommunicated for not obeying a summons to Rome, publicly welcomed and vaunted the report of the Holy See's endeavors to send a representative to Washington.

Advice of a similar nature was first offered to the Holy See in 1817, when Jean Lefebvre de Cheverus, bishop of Boston, suggested to the Propaganda that Archbishop Maréchal be appointed apostolic delegate for the United States with power to settle in the first instance all conflicts between the lay trustees and the bishops.

After the First Plenary Council of Baltimore, Rev. Thomas Heyden, of Bedford, Pa., wrote to the Propaganda (Nov. 12, 1852): "What we need is not more bishops and more councils but an apostolic nuncio so that we may speak more often with the Holy Father." In 1857 the Propaganda asked Pius IX to appoint an apostolic delegate to the United States without diplomatic character in order to promote uniformity in the petitions presented to the Holy See and to provide a source of information; the cardinals of the congregation proposed to give the office to a resident American, Archbishop Kenrick of Baltimore, who was practically serving in that capacity already. But the pope feared that the appointment would revive the desire for an American primate and preferred to choose a non-American. In the end nothing was done during his pontificate.

In 1878 George Conroy, bishop of Ardagh, Ireland, and temporary apostolic delegate to Canada, after visiting the United States, expressed the opinion that a delegate should be appointed for that country too, but only for a time, according to need; and not with residence in Washington, where he might be slighted by the U.S. government and the foreign diplomatic corps, but rather in New York. In the same year Francis X. Weninger, the famous Jesuit missionary among the German immigrants, urged the Propaganda to appoint a permanent delegate, "a solid and moderate Italian," not an Irishman—in view of the serious disorders in the U.S. Church and of the caprice with which so many bishops treated their clergy.

Reasons for and against a delegation. In the last quarter of the 19th century, more and more priests turned to the Holy See for the redress of their real or imagined grievances against their ecclesiastical superiors. On the whole, both bishops and priests were extremely ignorant of canon law and, consequently they were unaware of their respective and reciprocal rights and duties. Most of the dioceses lacked a regularly organized tribunal or court, or even a regularly appointed quasi-judicial counsel; hence, the cases were not properly handled in the first instance, and this lack of a proper trial often made it difficult in Rome to evaluate the conflicting testimony and to render a definitive judgment. In a considerable number of cases, the Holy See gave a decision favorable to the priest, because the bishop had failed to furnish the requisite evidence. Some bishops maintained that they were not bound by various provisions of the general law of the Church because of the missionary status of this country. Some priests, acting in good faith, availed themselves of Roman justice and impartiality in order to protect themselves against the arbitrary dispositions of their bishops; others, acting in bad faith, took advantage of Roman leniency and slowness in order to evade due punishment and to prolong their refractory conduct. The Holy See believed that a delegate with his auditor could hear such appeals much nearer the scene of the disagreement, weigh the arguments on either side more judiciously, and pronounce a verdict more promptly.

Another reason for establishing an apostolic delegation was the Holy See's desire to bring the U.S. episcopate into closer union and greater concord with itself. Roman officials had the impression that the Americans were jealous and distrustful of them, were eager to remain as independent as possible in administrative affairs, and were suspicious of a highly centralized government of the Church. The proximate reason, however, was the need to restore harmony among the American bishops themselves. In the last two decades of the 19th century, they were divided on several vital issues: on the rights of national groups, especially of the German Americans; on the founding, location, and support of The Catholic University of America; on the toleration of secret societies that were essentially benevolent associations; and most of all, on the question of parochial or public schools. Only a disinterested observer on the scene could ascertain which of the contrary views were objectively based on fact.

All the bishops, however, with the single exception of John IRELAND, archbishop of St. Paul, who expected a delegate to sustain his singular position in the school controversy, were as united in their rejection of the proposal of establishing an apostolic delegation in the United States as their predecessors had been in regard to a nunciature. Probably the chief motive for their opposition was the fear that the presence of a delegate (or nuncio) would limit the power and diminish the dignity of the individual bishops and decrease the esteem with which the faithful regarded them. The bishops resented the prospect of having their actions reported to Rome; moreover, they had been annoyed by minor Roman prelates who had visited the United States from time to time without any particular mission but had conducted themselves in an imprudent and officious manner, especially by commenting for the newspapers on problems they did not understand. Not unnaturally, the bishops dreaded the thought of their coming to this country a stranger who would immediately be besieged by a crowd of malcontents and would be unable to appreciate the circumstances or implications of the cases laid before him. They believed that the appointment of a delegate would harm their precarious relations with non-Catholics by confirming their enemies' allegation that the Catholic Church was a foreign religion and paid homage to a foreign power; that it would arouse latent prejudices; and, especially in the 1890s, would pour fuel on the flames of bigotry being fanned by the American Protective Association (APA). In the political sphere, the sending of a delegate, they felt, would embarrass the Democratic party, to which a majority of the Catholics belonged, and thus would help the Republicans. They knew that there was no apostolic delegate in the United Kingdom and perceived no greater need of one in the United States; in fact, there were only seven apostolic delegates in the whole world at that time, and all of them were in predominantly Orthodox or Muslim countries. Hence, the American bishops, individually and collectively, repeatedly endeavored, up to the last minute, to dissuade the pope and his officials from sending a delegate to this country.

As an alternative, many of the American bishops favored the proposal of engaging an American prelate who would reside in Rome and represent them before the Holy See. Such an agent, they believed, could wield more influence on behalf of the U.S. Church than any individual bishop in his own diocese; moreover, he could supply authentic information on American problems and prevent inept legislation. The Roman officials, however, thought that the American bishops envisioned a plenipotentiary such as no other national episcopate had and desired to tie Rome's hands. Hence, when in 1882, Gibbons in his own name and in that of other bishops requested of the Propaganda that an American prelate be established in Rome, no affirmative response was given. Then, after Denis J. O'CONNELL was named rector of the American College in Rome in 1885, he was employed by the bishops who trusted him as an intermediary with the Holy See, but he never received an official appointment from the American episcopate as a whole or any official recognition from the Holy See, even though Gibbons formally asked Leo XIII to appoint him a counselor of the Propaganda. The greatest concession that the American bishops would willingly have made was that one of their own number be appointed delegate, although they could not easily have agreed on the choice of the individual; if the appointee were an American, said Gibbons, the principal objection would be removed. The Holy See, nevertheless, thought that only an Italian could be impartial among the rival national factions in the American Church.

Establishment of the delegation. At last Leo XIII decided to overrule the objections of the American hierarchy. He found a convenient occasion for sending the future delegate when the Holy See was invited by the U.S. government to lend some 15th-century maps from the Vatican Library for the World's Columbian Exposition in Chicago. The pope not only complied with this request but also appointed a personal representative to bring the historic materials for the exhibit. This was Francesco SATOLLI, titular archbishop of Lepanto, who also had been ablegate at the celebrations for the centennial of the American hierarchy and the opening of The Catholic University of America, Washington, D.C., in November of 1889, and who had afterward told the pope that more direct means of communication between the Holy See and the U.S. Church were desirable. He arrived in New York on Oct. 12, 1892 and in the following month announced to the archbishops assembled in that city the pope's desire to establish with their concurrence a permanent apostolic delegation in the United States. All the archbishops but Ireland were unwilling to give their consent because of the "serious difficulties connected with the subject." Throughout that autumn, Satolli was not only attacked mendaciously in the APA press but also treated disrespectfully in certain Catholic quarters. On Jan. 3, 1893, Gibbons in the name of the archbishops signed a letter to Leo XIII in which he declared that a permanent delegate "would not serve the best interests of the Church." In the next few days many U.S. newspapers carried false reports about the ablegate's mission and sensational stories of ecclesiastical intrigue and conspiracy, and the journalists were abetted in creating this confusion by deplorable breaches of confidence among the bishops themselves. Satolli believed that the Jesuits also opposed him because of his approval of Ireland's plan for elementary education (*see* FARIBAULT PLAN).

On January 10, in the midst of all this discord, the pope ordered the establishment of the delegation and appointed Satolli first delegate; the official documents were dated a fortnight later. On January 21 the prefect of the Propaganda, cardinal Miecislaus Ledochowski, informed the bishops in a circular letter that the decision was made both because it was customary to provide a delegate for countries in which the Church had reached a certain stage of maturity and because the peculiar situation in the United States required special attention. In the instructions drawn up for Satolli, the chief purpose of the delegation was said to be the fostering of a more intimate union of the American bishops among themselves and with the Holy See. He was also directed to see to the organization of episcopal courts and the due observances of juridical procedure in the various dioceses, to settle disputes between bishops and priests in the second or third instance without the right of further appeal, to study the reasons for the existence of so many "tramp-priests" in the United States, to induce the bishops to adopt uniform regulations regarding schools, and to gather information on episcopal candidates.

Confronted with this *fait accompli,* the American bishops for the most part acquiesced to the pope's will; some even wrote letters of thanks to the pope for the great joy and immense benefit just conferred on the U.S. Church. James Ryan, bishop of Alton, Ill., however, sent three cablegrams of vehement protest to Cardinal Ledochowski, who in reply sternly rebuked him for his "irreverence" toward the pope and demanded "condign satisfaction" under threat of canonical penalties; the bishop made adequate amends but did not change his mind. Gradually the bishops reconciled themselves to the presence of the delegate in the United States. Nevertheless, in the following year John Lancaster Spalding, bishop of Peoria, Ill., published an article entitled

"Catholicism and Apaism" in the *North American Review* [159 (September 1894) 278–287], in which he asserted that the delegate was "a source of strength to the Apaists," because this so-called "American Pope . . . though a foreigner, with no intention of becoming a citizen, ignorant alike of our language and our traditions, was supposed to have supreme authority in the church in America." Thereupon Satolli not only reprimanded Spalding directly but also reported him to Rome, and Leo XIII ordered the cardinal prefect to remonstrate with him for his hostile attitude toward the apostolic delegation.

In the apostolic letter *Longinqua oceani* of Jan. 6, 1895, Leo XIII averred that the apostolic delegation fittingly crowned the work of the Third Plenary Council of Baltimore, denied that the powers conferred on the delegate would be an obstacle to the authority of the bishops, and asserted that the ultimate aim of the delegation was to strengthen and perfect the constitution of the Church in the United States.

FUNCTIONS AND RESIDENCES

In addition to the functions mentioned in Satolli's original instructions, he and his successors have discharged all the usual duties of an apostolic delegate, including the furnishing of advice to the Holy See on the division of existing dioceses and the erection of new ones, the oversight of religious orders, and the granting of dispensations, and they have exercised certain special powers (faculties) bestowed on them by the pope. They have also consecrated many bishops of American birth and for American sees. Until 1908 the successive delegates were dependent upon the Propaganda; since that year they have been dependent upon the Consistorial Congregation, but have dealt directly with all the proper organs of the Roman Curia; at all times they have remained in close contact with the papal secretariate of state. As the representative of the Consistorial Congregation, the delegate is the ordinary of the Pontifical College Josephinum at Worthington (near Columbus), Ohio, and he assigns its students to the various dioceses at the request of the bishops. The first delegate was assisted by one auditor and one secretary, both Italians; in 1964 the delegate had a staff of five Italian and three American priests.

Satolli was ordered to fix his residence in the national capital. At first he resided at The Catholic University of America, and then on Nov. 16, 1893, he moved to a house in northwest Washington, which had been purchased with money collected by the American bishops and priests. In 1906 and 1907 a new building was erected for the delegation, again through the generosity of U.S. Catholics. The next home of the delegation, a stately edifice on Massachusetts Avenue, N.W., was paid for with similar contributions and was occupied in the spring of 1939.

List of delegates. By 1984 ten ecclesiastics had served as apostolic delegates to the United States. All titular archbishops during their term of office, the first eight were created cardinals at the end of it, and were appointed to various offices in the Roman Curia. Thus the delegation is practically equivalent to a first-class nunciature in the Vatican diplomatic service. From the date of their elevation to the Sacred College until their departure the incumbents are called pro-delegates. The ten delegates included: Francesco Satolli, delegate from 1893 to 1896; Sebastiano Martinelli, OSA, delegate from 1896 to 1902; Diomede Falconio, OFM, delegate from 1902 to 1911, who had been ordained in the United States in 1866, had been rector of the seminary of Allegany, N.Y., and had been naturalized as a citizen; Giovanni Bonzano, delegate from 1911 to 1922, who returned as papal legate to the International Eucharistic Congress held in Chicago in 1926; Pietro Fumasoni-Biondi, delegate from 1922 to 1933; Amleto Cicognani, delegate from 1933 to 1958, who returned as papal legate to the Inter-American Congress of the Confraternity of Christian Doctrine held in Dallas in 1961; Egidio Vagnozzi, delegate from 1958 to 1967, who was secretary and then auditor of the delegation from 1932 to 1942; Luigi Raimondi, delegate from 1967 to 1973; Jean Jadot, delegate from 1973 to 1980; and Pio Laghi, delegate from 1980 to 1984. Several of the other auditors and secretaries eventually became cardinals, e.g., Donato Sbarretti, Francesco Marchetti-Selvaggiani, and Paolo Marella.

Archbishop Pio Laghi was the last to serve as apostolic delegate. In 1984, when the United States established formal diplomatic relations with the Holy See, he was appointed pro-nuncio, and the apostolic delegation headquarters on Massachusetts Avenue in Washington, D.C. became the apostolic nunciature.

Bibliography: J. T. ELLIS, *Life of James Cardinal Gibbons: Archbishop of Baltimore, 1834–1921,* 2 v. (Milwaukee, Wisc. 1952). W. J. LALLOU, *The Fifty Years of the Apostolic Delegation, Washington, D.C.* (Paterson 1943); "The Apostolic Delegation at Washington," *American Ecclesiastical Revue* 65 (1921) 447–462; rev. *ibid.* 95 (1936) 576–592. T. T. MCAVOY, *The Great Crisis in American Catholic History, 1895–1900* (Chicago, Ill. 1957). F. J. ZWIERLEIN, *The Life and Letters of Bishop McQuaid,* 3 v. (Rochester, N.Y. 1925–27).

[R. TRISCO]

APOSTOLIC EXHORTATION

In modern times, the form of "exhortation" was apparently first used by Pope Pius XII on Dec. 8, 1939 (*As-*

persis commitis anxietatibus) on the occasion of the beginning of hostilities in World War II. It was an address to priests involved in the armed forces. Since then, the Roman pontiffs have used this form regularly to exhort various categories of persons to seek for greater perfection. For instance, the exhortation *Menti Nostrae* of 1950 on the holiness of priests (*AAS*, 42 [1950], 657–702) was one of the first texts to make this form of document commonly known. As the name implies, exhortations are not legislative. Although not juridically binding, they are a significant expression of the magisterium of the Church, and are morally persuasive and quite influential because they are frequently the product of consensus. In the exhortation *Redemptoris custos* on the person and mission of St. Joseph (Aug. 15, 1989), Pope John Paul II speaks of this document as a means of fulfilling a "pastoral duty." More recently, a distinct form, the postsynodal apostolic exhortation, has been used to issue the papal document presenting the results of an ordinary general assembly of the Synod of Bishops; for instance, *Vita consecrata* (March 25, 1996) follows upon the synod on consecrated life. An exhortation can also be the base for further study and for special norms putting its teaching into effect. Thus, for instance, in *Vita consecrata,* no. 59, the pope calls for careful consideration of the norms regulating papal cloister; this led to the publication of the instruction *Verbi sponsa* (13 May 1999) which revised such norms and stated that the document was a direct consequence of the provisions of *Vita consecrata.*

See Also: PRONOUNCEMENTS, PAPAL AND CURIAL.

Bibliography: J. HUELS, "A Theory of Juridical Documents Based on Canons 29–34," *Studia canonica* 32 (1998) 337–370. F. G. MORRISEY, *Papal and Curial Pronouncements: Their Canonical Significance in Light of the Code of Canon Law* (Ottawa 1995), 13.

[F. G. MORRISEY]

APOSTOLIC FAITH

New ecclesial perspectives, combined with ecumenical projects, have placed the notion of apostolic faith at the forefront of theological research. Indeed, the ecclesiology of communion (*koinônia*) makes communion with that which has always been, lived, and proclaimed itself the apostolic community *the* fundamental theme of the ecclesial mystery. Also, following the publication of the LIMA TEXT on Baptism-Eucharist-Ministry (BEM), the diverse churches have become more and more aware of the profound tie which exists between faith and sacrament. It is not possible to think of communities united by sacramental life if they do not live in a common confession of faith. The measure and source of that common faith, however, cannot be understood to be anything other than apostolic faith itself.

Nature of Apostolic Faith. According to the language of the World Council of Churches Assembly at Nairobi (1975), apostolic faith is that which has been "delivered through the Apostles and handed down through the centuries" [*Breaking Barriers* (Nairobi 1975)]. This formula, which is very synthetic, hides the complexity of the problem. There is today an awareness that the notion of apostolic faith is not nearly so simple— that it implies many diverse elements. What is the true meaning and origin of this apostolic faith?

The authority of the Apostles derives not only from the fact that they have been the witness of the preaching and the life of Christ Jesus, but also from the fact that they have been the sole authentic interpreters of the Resurrection. Their preaching has essentially consisted in a rereading, through the Holy Spirit, of the entire life and preaching of Jesus in the light of their own faith in the Resurrection. The message they preached is therefore both conditioned and marked by their faith. In this sense all that we know of Jesus *derives from* the faith of the apostolic community, that is, from the apostolic faith.

This apostolic preaching is communicated to us in documents themselves profoundly marked by the manner in which apostolic faith was "received" and lived out in the first Christian communities. Paul himself is attentive to this link of faith to the other apostolic communities. Apostolic faith thus reunites us with the apostolic traditions, each one of which already possesses an ecclesial life, in the diversity with which that life appears according to its sociological, cultural, and religious context. Once again, at this level, the faith of the Church precedes the documents through which the truths of the faith are transmitted.

Not every text that the first generation of Christians attributed to the Apostles has been recognized by the tradition as an authentic and reliable expression of apostolic faith. From the first to the fourth century the Church gradually discerned which documents (already "received" in the local churches) were to constitute the scriptural canon, that is to say, the supreme rule of faith insofar as it contains the authentic witness of the Revelation that was given in Christ Jesus. The texts so chosen have not all been composed in the same epoch; some documents which were accepted as important for a time by certain local churches were later eliminated from the normative ensemble. In this manner, the experience of three centuries of faith and ecclesial life mark the determination of the official *corpus* of Scriptures recognized as the authentic witness of the apostolic faith.

From the very beginning this authentic canon of Scriptures, which transmits the apostolic faith, has appeared profoundly pluralistic and diversified. Views as different as those of Paul and James on the relation between faith and work are found here; the christological perspective of the Johannine tradition does not coincide exactly with the vision of Paul; the place of the apostolic mission in the ecclesial structure is not the same according to Luke and the author of the Johannine Gospel (who insists on the quality of discipleship). Thus, apostolic faith has been, since the beginning, transmitted in a manner which shows respect for the different readings of the common *depositum fidei*, that is, the common truth received through the Apostles.

"Recognition" of the Apostolic Faith. Most of the churches—even those which do not make use of it in their own liturgy and in the great manifestations of their faith—are in agreement in seeing in the symbol of Nicea-Constantinople the articulation *par excellence* of the apostolic faith such as it has been explicated and understood in the first centuries of the Church. The official ecumenical milieu—thus *Faith and Constitution*—thinks therefore that the only means of acquiring certitude that on the essential points the churches agree in their faith, while safeguarding a healthy and necessary diversity of theologies and of interpretations, is for them to agree officially that they "recognize" in this creed at least the fundamental articles of their faith.

Nevertheless, the language in which the "Nicene faith" is expressed [cf. P. CAMELOT, "Symbole de Nicée ou Foi de Nicée?" *Orientalia Christinana periodica* 12 (Rome 1947) 425–438], and the technical terms in which the most decisive points have been formulated, today require a common "official" interpretation; otherwise there may be the risk of *apparent* rather than *true* agreement. Many difficulties arise with such an interpretation. Should one search within the Scripture itself for the principle of its proper interpretation, or will one clarify the most complex points by recourse to other important aspects of Church life, in particular to sacramental and liturgical life according to the axiom *lex orandi lex credendi*? Should one take into account the evolution of the human sciences or of the social contexts (today for instance many contest the biblical usage of uniquely masculine names in speaking of God)? The concerns of the theological milieu are not yet in accord on these thorny problems. Moreover, in some areas there unfortunately reappears precisely the same confessional oppositions that one seeks to overcome through this common interpretation. Is it a vicious circle?

With regards this project, the Catholic Church for its part is especially anxious that what concerns the foundation, nature, and mission of the Church shall be adequately expressed. The third article of the Nicene Creed is crucial for its understanding of the whole design of God.

It is this, for its most lucid representatives, which will probably be the stumbling block, as it is already, in the whole ecumenical venture.

Bibliography: J.M.R. TILLARD, "Introduction," *Faith and Order* (Bangalore 1978); "Towards a Common Confession of Apostolic Faith," *Faith and Order Paper* 100. "Baptism, Eucharist and Ministry," *Faith and Order Paper* 111. H. KÜNG and J. MOLTMANN, eds., *An Ecumenical Confession of Faith?* (New York 1979).

[J. M. R. TILLARD]

APOSTOLIC FATHERS

The term employed for a collection of the earliest Christian writings contemporary with and succeeding the later New Testament documents. The Monophysites already used it, but its precise denotation is still disputed. In 1672 J. B. Cotelier published works by Pseudo-Barnabas, the Shepherd of Hermas, Clement I of Rome, Ignatius of Antioch and Polycarp of Smyrna under the name *Patres aevi apostolici*. In a second edition in 1698, J. Clericus used the expression Apostolic Fathers (*Patres apostolici*); but L. Ittig restricted the term to Clement, Ignatius and Polycarp in 1699. However the name was extended later to include the *Ad Diognetum,* fragments of Papias of Hierapolis, Quadratus, the Presbyter fragments in Irenaeus and the Didache.

Apostolic Tradition. Pieces of different types and times of composition were thus bound together as a whole, but the term Apostolic in a strict sense used as a historical and traditional qualification was not applicable to each of the authors included. It would seem proper to limit the term Apostolic Fathers to those non-New Testament early Christian authors who were disciples or hearers of the Apostles (in a strict sense) or, even though without personal contact with the Apostles, demonstrate their particular respect for them, and in a comparatively truer sense are carriers and witnesses of Apostolic tradition.

Inclusion. These attributes belong to St. Clement of Rome's letter to the Corinthians, the seven letters of St. Ignatius of Antioch and the two letters of St. Polycarp of Smyrna; Quadratus, though actually an apologist, should also be added (Eusebius *Hist. eccl.* 4.3). All the writings falsely attributed to these men, such as the so-called Second Letter of Clement, should be excluded, as well as the reports of their martyrdom, which do not come from their works. Neither the so-called Letter of Barnabas, nor the work of the Shepherd of Hermas, qualify as Apostolic Fathers under the criteria in the sense described above. The *Ad Diognetum* was scarcely written by Quadratus and is of later authorship, while Papias was probably not an immediate disciple of the Apostles, but hands down an at least partially confused tradition. The Didache, recently studied as a collection of instructions given by Apostles in a generic sense, probably stands closest in time and content to the Twelve and thus could be added as an appendix to the Apostolic Fathers. Finally there are sayings of the Apostolic Fathers in the Presbyter sections of IRENAEUS.

Literary Form. With regard to literary form, the Apostolic Fathers imitate the Epistles of the Apostles. Their language in general, the Greek *Koine,* is influenced by the Septuagint and gives signs of the formation of a Christian *Sondersprache* or idiom. Yet there are stylistic differences among them: they extend from simple and uncontrived narrative as in Polycarp, through changes of format (Clement of Rome), to the passionately mystic expressions of Ignatius of Antioch. The classical rules of rhetoric and letter writing were not unknown to the Apostolic Fathers, and the authors are related to one another in literary dependence.

Theological Witness. In the ancient Church these writings received a high, partially canonical evaluation. They possess an uncommon significance as the oldest testimonies to the development of the CHRISTIAN way of life alongside and after the New Testament.

For Biblical theology, they show the way from an extraordinary consideration of the Old Testament (Clement of Rome and partly the Didache) to the formation of the New Testament canon; and in Polycarp there is all but clear certification of the Pauline Corpus.

The scriptural inspiration of the Holy Spirit is clearly taught, and doctrinally the Apostolic Fathers are the oldest witnesses for the CREED tradition. Their declarations concerning the three divine Persons, and particularly their witnesses to Christology and the Redemption as the midpoint of the new faith, are a reflective and clarifying theology, in part mystical, particularly in Ignatius, and based primarily on the foundation of the Scripture and the earlier Apostolic preaching.

The concept of the church exhibited by the Apostolic Fathers is stamped with the battle against schisms and primitive heresies. Hence the essential and necessary oneness of the Catholic Church (καθολικὴ ἐκκλεσία, first used by Ignatius: *Smyr.* 8.2), as an organism and the Body of Christ, is signified by a unified community whose character is demonstrated in unity with the bishop and in a common celebration of the liturgy.

In Ignatius there is a development of the theology and mystique of ecclesiastical offices, particularly that of the bishop. Besides the idea of spiritual unity, a God-willed hierarchy differentiated into clergy and laity

(λαϊκός, first used by Clement 40.5) is given prominence. The Didache describes a collegial hierarchy in the community, and a definite teaching authority of the charismatically gifted; meanwhile there is evidence in the other documents for a transition from a collegiate to a monarchical episcopate without loss of the benefit of extraordinary charisms. Ignatius is the first witness to the threefold order: bishop, priests, and deacons; and the commanding position of the Roman church is indicated early on (Clement of Rome and Ignatius). There is likewise evidence for the ecclesiastical position of widows and virgins. In the contribution of Ignatius one finds beginnings of patristic sacramental theology (particularly in regard to the Eucharist).

The writings of the Apostolic Fathers state the faith with regard to sin, justification and grace, as well as the possibility of cooperation in salvation, and they offer numerous examples for it. Abstracting from the ''one Penance'' doctrine of the Shepherd of Hermas, who does not properly belong to the Apostolic Fathers, the theology and practice of Penance is developed beyond the foundation appearing in the New Testament.

In eschatological thought the authentic Apostolic Fathers are sober, but filled with the hope of the nearness of the Lord. Finally, the letter of Clement affords an insight into contemporary preaching on the resurrection of the flesh (ch. 24–26).

In their writings, the Apostolic Fathers desire above all else to serve the divinely willed order in the Church, and directions in moral, ascetical and pastoral theology play an important role. The call to faith, fraternal charity and ecclesiastical obedience is clear and notable. Whereas in the letter of Clement and the Didache, great Old Testament influence appears, in Ignatius the imitation of and union with Christ becomes an essential motive. Stimulated also by his mysticism, Ignatius likewise elaborates an early Christian theology of martyrdom. The Apostolic Fathers approach the pagan state with express loyalty. Finally these writings are sources for the Church history of their time, especially for the history of the liturgy: the Didache records the earliest texts for the performance of Baptism and the celebration of the Eucharist; the letter of Clement gives the oldest form of prayer of the community (Ch. 59–61); and Ignatius' letters are likewise rich in liturgical allusions.

Certain Hellenistic elements from philosophy, Gnosticism and an insight into the mystery religions in the writings of the Apostolic Fathers attest the education and spiritual predilection of the authors; an example of this is the obvious Stoic influence on the letter of Clement.

Bibliography: Editions and translations. K. BIHLMEYER and W. SCHNEEMELCHER, *Die Apostolischen Väter* (Tübingen 1956–).

J. A. FISCHER, *Die Apostolischen Väter* (Munich 1956). L. T. LEFORT, *Les Pères Apostoliques en copte*, 2 v. [*Corpus scriptorum ecclesiasticorum latinorum* (Vienna 1866–) 135–136, Scriptores Coptici 17–18; 1952]. E. J. GOODSPEED, *The Apostolic Fathers* (New York 1950). J. A. KLEIST, *Ancient Christian Writers* 6 (1948). Literature. H. KRAFT, *Clavis Patrum Apostolicorum* (Munich 1964). B. ALTANER, *Patrology*, tr. H. GRAEF from 5th German ed. (New York 1960) 50–54, 80–88, 97–113, 117–118. J. QUASTEN, *Patrology*, 3 v. (Westminister, Md. 1950–) 1:29–105. G. JOUASSARD, "Le Groupement des Pères dits Apostoliques," *Mélanges de science religieuse*, 14 (1957) 129–134. H. PIESIK, *Bildersprache der Apostolischen Väter* (Bonn 1961). J. LAWSON, *A Theological and Historical Introduction to the Apostolic Fathers* (New York 1961). G. KITTEL, "Der Jakobusbrief und die Apostolischen Väter," *Zeitschrift für die neutestamentliche Wissenschaft und die Kunde der älteren Kirche*, 43 (1950–51) 54–112. F. X. GOKEY, *The Terminology for the Devil and Evil Spirits in the Apostolic Fathers* (Washington 1961). *The Apostolic Fathers*, ed. R. M. GRANT, v.1 (New York 1964). S. TUGWELL, *The Apostolic Fathers* (Harrisburg, Pa. 1990). C. N. JEFFORD, *Reading the Apostolic Fathers: An Introduction* (Peabody, Mass. 1996).

[J. A. FISCHER]

APOSTOLIC SEE

The noun see, meaning seat, is now used only of the seat of a bishop, in the sense of the place where he presides, or the church over which he rules. In early Christian literature the term apostolic was applied to those churches that had been founded by one of the Apostles and hence were looked upon as primary witnesses of the apostolic tradition, agreement with which was a norm of orthodoxy for the other churches. In this sense, Tertullian appealed to Corinth, Philippi, Ephesus, and Rome as "Apostolic Churches, in which the seats of the Apostles still preside" (*De praescr. haer.* 36; *Corpus Christianorum* 1:216). While in the eastern part of the Roman Empire there were many apostolic sees, the most prominent of which were Jerusalem, Antioch, and Alexandria, the only church in the West recognized as an apostolic see was Rome.

See of Rome. One finds Rome referred to as the "see of Peter" in the writings of St. Cyprian (*Epist.* 59.14; *Corpus scriptorum ecclesiasticorum latinorum* 3.2:683), Optatus (*Contra Parm.* 23.2.; *Corpus scriptorum ecclesiasticorum latinorum* 54:63–64), as also in the synodical letter of the Council of Sardica to Pope Julius (Denz 136). It is in the writings of Pope Damasus I (366–384) that one first finds the term Apostolic See used consistently of Rome. From this time onward it was a characteristic of papal letters, and it was similarly used in the acts of western synods and in the writings of the Latin Fathers, for whom Rome was *the* Apostolic See. While the Greek Fathers recognized Rome to be the see of Peter, and thus the first among apostolic sees, examples are rare of their adopting the Latin usage of referring to Rome simply as *the* Apostolic See.

The Code of Canon Law gives a working definition of Apostolic See in these words: "the term Apostolic See or Holy See refers not only to the Roman Pontiff, but also to the Secretariat of State, the Council for the public affairs of the Church, and other Institutes of the Roman Curia, unless it is otherwise apparent from the nature of the matter or context of the words" (*Codex iuris canonici* c. 361). Canon 360 adds a more specific listing of the Roman Curia by stating that: "The Roman Curia consists of the Secretariat of State of the Papal Secretariat, the Council for the Public Affairs of the Church, congregations, tribunals, and other institutes."

The term Apostolic See was in constant use during the Middle Ages to designate the pope together with his Curia. However, such a concept only gradually entered the written law, and the designation given in the Code is the most general and absolute use of this term. In international diplomacy the term Holy See, and not Vatican City, is the proper nomenclature. In 1957 the United Nations, as a result of an agreement with the Holy See, discontinued the use of the term Vatican City in international conferences.

The composition of the Roman Curia changed as a result of the 1988 apostolic constitution of John Paul II, *Pastor bonus* [*Acta Apostolicae Sedis* 80 (1988) 841–934]. The Curia now consists of the Secretariat of State, nine congregations, three tribunals, twelve pontifical councils, several commissions, three offices, and a number of institutes (*New Commentary on the Code of Canon Law* [New York and Mahwah 2000] 481–489.).

Bibliography: H. LECLERCQ, *Dictionnaire d'archéologie chrétienne et de liturgie* 15, 1:1427–31. P. BATIFFOL, "Papa, sedes apostolica, apostolatus," *Rivista di archelogia cristiana* 2 (1925) 99–116; *Cathedra Petri* (Paris 1938) 151–168. M. MACCARRONE, "'Sedes Apostolica' et 'Sedes Apostolicae': de titulo et ratione apostolicitatis in aetate patristica et in altiore Medio Aevo," *Acta Congressus Internationalis de Theologia Concilii Vaticani II* (Vatican City 1968) 146–162; "'Sedes Apostolica-Vicarius Petri.' La perpetuità del Primato di Pietro nella Sede e nel Vescovo di Roma," in *Romana Ecclesia Cathedra Petri* (Rome 1991) 1:1–101.

[F. A. SULLIVAN/J. F. DEDE/G. CARIE]

APOSTOLIC SUCCESSION

While there is general agreement among Christians that the Church of Christ is and must be apostolic in its doctrine and its ministry, the doctrine of apostolic succession on which the Christian Churches remain divided is expressed in the statement of Vatican II that "by divine institution the bishops have succeeded to the place of the apostles as shepherds of the Church'' (*Lumen gentium* 20). Catholics, Orthodox and most Anglicans believe that the episcopate is a divinely willed element of the structure of the Church; Protestants see it as the result of a purely human, historical development in the post-New Testament period. At the same time there is a broad consensus among scholars, both Catholic and Protestant, that in the New Testament one does not find evidence to support the theory that before the apostles died they appointed a bishop in charge of each of the churches which they had founded. Rather, it is generally agreed that with the exception of Jerusalem, where James the brother of the Lord exercised leadership, at the close of the New Testament period each local church was being led by a group of men, called ''elders'' (*presbuteroi*) or ''overseers'' (*episkopoi*). Most Catholic scholars agree that the historic episcopate is the result of a development that took place in the post-New Testament period, and that a satisfactory argument for the doctrine that bishops are the successors of the apostles by divine institution cannot be drawn from the New Testament or from early Church history alone, but must be based on a combination of historical evidence and theological reflection. Such an argument can be developed in the following steps: (1) The post-New Testament development of the episcopate is homogeneous with the development of the presbyterate that took place during the New Testament period. (2) By the end of the second century, the Christian churches were being led by bishops whom they recognized as the successors to the apostles, and as transmitters of the genuine apostolic tradition. (3) As the churches received certain writings as the written norm of their faith, so they received the teaching of their bishops as the living norm of their faith. The Holy Spirit, who maintains the Church in the true faith, must have guided the Church in its reception of these norms of its faith, since error about the norms would have led to untold errors in faith. Therefore the Holy Spirit must have guided the development of the episcopate as it guided the development of the New Testament canon. Such guidance of the Spirit justifies the belief that bishops are the successors of the apostles by divine institution.

Homogeneous Development. When we look to the parts of the New Testament that were written during the sub-apostolic period (from about 67 to the end of the first century), we see that as the Church came to realize that it had to think in terms of future generations, it also developed a form of local leadership that would provide for continuity in doctrine and practice. 1 Peter 5, Acts 20 and the Pastorals all witness to the fact that by the 80s, each local church, including those of the Pauline tradition, had a group of leaders who were called ''elders'' or ''overseers.'' 1 Peter and the Pastorals also witness to the con-

tinuation of the pastoral care exercised over a number of churches by co-workers of an apostle, as in the Pastorals, or by one who writes in the name of the apostle himself, as in 1 Peter. Furthermore, Acts 20:17–35 and 2 Tim 4:1–8 witness to the conviction of Christians of the sub-apostolic period that it was Paul himself who, when foreseeing his own death, had entrusted the ongoing care of the church of Ephesus to its presbyters, and had bequeathed his own ministry of evangelization to Timothy. The Pastorals also witness to the concern of the sub-apostolic Church for the safeguarding and faithful handing on of the ''deposit,'' which was to be provided by the careful selection of leaders who would be ''apt teachers'' (1 Tim 3:2) and would ''hold to the true message as taught so as to be able both to exhort with sound doctrine and to refute opponents'' (Tit 1:9). In these letters it is also clear that it was an important task of the apostolic co-workers to select the right persons for ministry in the local churches, and to ordain them by the laying on of hands.

The development of ministry that took place in mainline Christian churches during the sub-apostolic period was a response to the realization that provision had to be made for the continued life of the Church into future generations, and that this called for a stable structure of ministry that would guarantee the faithful handing on of all that the Church had received from the apostles. While this did not mean the end of charismatic ministry (cf. 1 Peter 4:10–11), it did call for the choice and ordination of responsible pastors and teachers: ''faithful people who would have the ability to teach others as well'' (2 Tim 2:2). The choice and ordination of such people was in the hands of individuals like Timothy and Titus, but the local leadership was entrusted to a group of presbyters, among whom some ''presided well'' and some ''toiled in preaching and teaching'' (1 Tim 5:17).

The post-apostolic development of ministry was consistent with what took place during the period of the New Testament. Just as during the sub-apostolic period the need was recognized for a structure that would provide stable and continuing leadership in the churches, and that need was met by the development of the presbyterate, so also in the post-apostolic period the growing threats to unity and the need for a form of leadership that could more effectively maintain unity in the face of those threats, led to the development and general acceptance of the episcopate. The episcopate provided the instrument which the post-NT Church needed to be able to maintain its unity and orthodoxy in the face of the dangers that threatened it. The greatest threat to the unity of the Church in the second century came from the spread of Gnosticism. This danger was particularly evident in the church of Rome, where various exponents of this heresy established themselves, and formed communities of their followers, claiming to possess a secret apostolic tradition that surpassed what was being taught in the ordinary Christian communities. Most modern scholars are agreed that the development of the episcopate was the Church's answer to this threat to its unity, but they differ in their assessment of its significance. Protestants judge it to have been a merely natural response to the need for stronger leadership, while Catholics believe they have good reason to recognize it as guided by the Holy Spirit.

Bishops as Successors to the Apostles. The few extant Christian writings from the late first and early second century do not allow us to reconstruct the process by which the Christian churches moved from the leadership of a group of presbyters to the leadership of a single bishop. The Letter of the Romans to the Corinthians, known as 1 Clement, which dates from about 96, attributes to the apostles the appointment of the first generation of local church leaders, with the directive that when these died, other ''approved men'' should be appointed to succeed them. But it is clear from 1 Clement that in the last years of the first century the church of Corinth was still being led by a group of presbyters, with no one bishop in charge. Most scholars think the same would have been the case in Rome at that time. On the other hand, the Letters of Ignatius of Antioch witness to the fact that by the second decade of the second century the churches of Antioch and Ephesus, and some others in the vicinity of Ephesus, were being led by a single bishop, assisted by presbyters and deacons. However, Ignatius sheds no light on our question as to how the transition to episcopal leadership had taken place, nor does he speak of himself or those other bishops as ''successors to the apostles.'' A few years later, one of them, Polycarp, bishop of Smyrna, wrote a letter to the church of Philippi, in which he mentioned the presbyters and deacons, but said nothing about a bishop in that church. Similarly, the *Shepherd of Hermas*, written in Rome sometime around 130, speaks of ''the elders who preside over the church,'' with no reference to a bishop there.

The few extant documents of the period suggest that the development of the episcopate took place at varying rates of speed in various regions of the church, but do not reveal exactly how it took place. However, one may affirm on solid historical ground that by the end of the second century, every Christian church about which information has come down to the present was being led by a single bishop, that these churches recognized their bishops as the rightful successors to the apostles, and that they received their teaching as normative for their faith. For these facts there is clear evidence in the writings of Hegesippus, Irenaeus, and Tertullian. The move from these facts to the conclusion that the development of the episcopate was guided by the Spirit calls for reflection on the theological significance of the reception by the Church of the norms for its faith.

Reception of the Norms of Faith. It was the consensus to which the Christian churches arrived during the second and third centuries concerning the reception of four Gospels, the letters of St. Paul, the Acts of the Apostles, and the Catholic Epistles, that substantially fixed the canon of the New Testament. By virtue of this consensus the Church recognized this collection of writings as normative for Christian faith. It is obvious that an erroneous decision about the norm of its faith would have led the Church into incalculable errors on particular matters of faith. If one believes that the Holy Spirit maintains the Church in the true faith, one must also believe that the Holy Spirit guided the Church in its discernment of the books that would constitute a written norm for its faith.

The fact that in the course of the second century the Gnostics also appealed to these writings makes it evident that the Church needed another norm by which to be able to judge which interpretation of the New Testament corresponded to the authentic apostolic faith. The Gnostics claimed that their interpretation was based on a secret tradition originating from one of the apostles, and handed down by a succession of their teachers. The response of Christian writers, such as Hegesippus, Irenaeus, and Tertullian, was to appeal to the tradition handed down from the apostles by the succession of bishops in the churches. The fact that in all those churches one found the same ''rule of faith,'' in contrast to the great diversity of Gnostic teachings, proved that the churches that were led by bishops had maintained the genuine apostolic doctrine. These writers, from different regions of the Church, witness to the recognition of the bishops as the authoritative bearers of the apostolic tradition, and to the reception of their teaching as normative for Christian faith.

It would have been just as disastrous for the Church to have made the wrong decision about the living norm of faith by which it countered the threat of Gnosticism, as it would have been to make a wrong decision about the reception of the New Testament as its written norm. There is as good reason to believe that the Church was guided by the Spirit in the recognition of its bishops as successors of the apostles and authoritative teachers of the faith, as there is to believe that it was guided by the Spirit in its discernment of the books that make up the New Testament.

From this it follows that there is also good reason to believe that the development of the episcopate itself was guided by the Spirit, since it was to play such a primary role in maintaining the Church in the true faith. Without the leadership of its bishops, the early Church could hardly have achieved a consensus on the canon of Scripture, nor could it have overcome the very real threat which Gnosticism posed to its unity and orthodoxy. The structure of the Church was in the process of development through the period of the New Testament, but at the close of that period the Church did not yet have a structure that would have been adequate to meet the challenges it would face during the second century. Catholics see no reason to think that the Holy Spirit who guided the Church during the period of the New Testament, would have ceased to guide it as it developed the basic structure it needed for its long-term survival.

Bibliography: F. PRAT, *Dictionnaire de théologie catholique*, ed. A. VACANT et al., (Paris 1903–50; Tables générales 1951–) 5:1656–1701. A. EHRHARDT, *The Apostolic Succession in the First Two Centuries of the Church* (London 1953). E. MOLLAND, "Le développement de l'idée de succession apostolique," *Revue d'histoire et de philosophie religieuses* 34 (Strasbourg-Paris 1954) 1–29. Semana Española de Teologia, 16, 1956, *Problemas de actualidad sobre la sucesión apostolica* (Madrid 1957). A. M. JAVIERRE, "Le thème de la succession des Apôtres dans la littérature chrétienne primitive," *L'Épiscopat et l'Église universelle*, ed. Y. CONGAR, B-D. DUPUY (Paris 1962) 171–221. J. RATZINGER, "Primacy, Episcopate and Apostolic Succession," *The Episcopate and the Primacy*, ed. K. RAHNER, J. RATZINGER (New York 1962) 37–63. Y. CONGAR, "Composantes et idée de la succession apostolique," *Oecumenica* 1 (1966) 61–80. J. F. MCCUE, "Apostles and Apostolic Succession in the Patristic Era," *Lutherans and Catholics in Dialogue IV, Eucharist and Ministry* (New York 1971) 138–171. INTERNATIONAL THEOLOGICAL COMMISSION, "Apostolic Succession: A Clarification," *Origins* 4 (1974) 193–200. "Apostolic Continuity of the Church and Apostolic Succession," *Louvian Studies* 21 (1996) 109–200. T. M KOCIK, *Apostolic Succession in an Ecumenical Context* (Staten Island 1996). W. KASPER, "Apostolic Succession in the Office of Bishop as an Ecumenical Problem," *Theology Digest* 47 (Kansas City, Mo. 2000) 203–10. F. A. SULLIVAN, *From Apostles to Bishops* (Mahwah 2001).

[F. A. SULLIVAN]

APOSTOLICAE CURAE

Apostolic letter of LEO XIII on the question of the validity of Anglican ordinations, issued Sept. 13, 1896. It embodies the pope's conclusion that ordinations made according to the Anglican Ordinal are null and void. Although it calls itself an apostolic letter, it is sent in the name of Leo XIII (*Leo episcopus, servus servorum Dei, ad perpetuam rei memoriam*), and the conclusion is formulated in the first person plural commonly used by the pope. The document was not signed personally by Leo, but by Cardinals Bianchi and De Ruggiero. For the historical background of the question and the history of the apostolic letter, *see* ANGLICAN ORDERS; *see also* SATIS COGNITUM, Leo XIII's encyclical on the unity of the Church, published less than three months before *Apostolicae curae*, which sets the condemnation of Anglican ordinations in the horizon of Pope Leo's "unionism."

While no divisions other than unnumbered paragraphs appear in the text, it can be conveniently divided into an introduction and four parts. The introduction reviews the pope's benevolent regard toward the people of England, the "common view" that the sacrament of Order lapsed under Edward VI because of the new rite that was then introduced, and the fact that in recent times many Anglicans have judged their orders valid because they believed in "the excellence of the Christian priesthood." It notes that a few Catholics, "the majority of them not English," have wished to remove an obstacle in the way of the Anglicans' return to unity by having the bishop of Rome declare Anglican ordinations valid. The pope therefore agreed to reexamine the question and remove every doubt. Recalling that a special commission had been formed, the text goes on: "We finally directed the findings of these sessions, together with other documents," to be placed before the cardinals of the Holy Office. Following the introduction, part one gives the history of the question before the present pontificate. Part two studies the Ordinal, which it finds inadequate for the validity of ordination because of a defect of form, which is then interpreted as pointing to a defect of intention. Part three formulates Leo XIII's negative decision regarding the value of the ordinations given with this ritual. Part four is a pious exhortation to "those who sincerely desire and seek the blessings of Orders and Hierarchy: May they return to the one fold of Christ!"

There are three historical mistakes in the letter. First, it declares that there has been a constant practice of reordaining those Anglican ministers who have joined the Catholic Church and wished to function in the clergy; it then argues from the canonical principle, "Custom is the best interpreter of the law," that the question is already settled by custom. In reality, the instructions given by the popes to Cardinal Pole for the reconciliation of the Edwardian clergy stated a general principle and left the application to him. The practice of the cardinal included no systematic reordination. Second, as it speaks of the Gordon case the letter assumes that in 1704 Gordon was ordained according to the Edwardian ritual, whereas his ordination took place in Scotland, where the Ordinal of Edward VI was not legal. Third, it assumes, in part two, that an addition to the "form" that was made in 1662 was intended to remedy a perceived inadequacy of the Edwardian form in light of Catholic criticisms, whereas it was in fact made to respond to Puritan critics.

Drawing on the neo-scholastic theology that Leo XIII had strongly advocated in the encyclical *AETERNI PATRIS* (1879), the letter explains the Catholic doctrine on the essentials of a sacrament. It distinguishes between the ceremonial and the essential part, which includes "matter and form," and must "signify the grace that they cause."

The "matter" of ordination is the imposition of hands, which needs to be supported by a "form" to make its meaning clear. The letter finds the Anglican form, "Receive the Holy Ghost . . . ," insufficient because it does not "signify definitely the order of the priesthood or its grace and power." The addition of 1662, it says, came too late, since Anglican orders derive historically from Matthew PARKER, the Elizabethan archbishop of Canterbury who was consecrated in 1559.

Defect of form. Pope Leo's judgment flows from his exclusive focus on the words of the form, where he expects the order or its essential purpose to be explicitly stated. This purpose is indeed mentioned in a general way by reference to the sacraments ("Receive the Holy Ghost; whose sins thou dost forgive they are forgiven, and whose sins thou dost retain, they are retained; and be thou a faithful dispenser of the Word of God and his holy sacraments"), but there is no explicit mention of the eucharistic sacrifice. If, however, the form is understood in light of the preface to the Ordinal, its purpose is clear: It is intended to continue "the Orders of Ministers in Christ's Church, Bishops, Priests, and Deacons," as "from the Apostles' times . . . they have been in Christ's Church." The reference to the apostolic tradition and its continuity implies the fullness of this tradition, even if the sacraments are not itemized and no allusion is made to the sacrificial dimension of the Eucharist as it was understood in sixteenth-century theology. *Apostolicae curae*, however, takes no account of the preface.

The letter applies the same requirement of explicit mention to episcopal consecration: "Take the Holy Ghost for the office and work of a Bishop in the Church of God [added in 1662], and remember that thou stir up the grace of God which is in thee by imposition of hands, for God has not given us the spirit of fear, but of power, and love, and of soberness." Since references to the Episcopal Order are abundant in previous and subsequent prayers, the formula cannot be taken as meaning anything other than episcopal consecration, even without the addition of 1662. The apostolic letter, however, declares this context irrelevant because, in its estimation, "from them has been deliberately removed whatever sets forth the dignity and office of the priesthood in the Catholic rite." The preface that is included in the ritual of episcopal ordination "has been stripped of the words which denote the *summum sacerdotium*."

Defect of intention. Having established that the form of ordination in the Ordinal is defective, the pope argues from the axiom *lex credendi lex supplicandi* that the Anglican liturgy of ordination betrays a basic theology of Orders that is not compatible with the Catholic view of the sacrament. There is, on the contrary, a *nativa Ordi-nalis indoles ac spiritus*, a "natural character and spirit of the Ordinal," that is fundamentally opposed to the Catholic doctrine. The pope infers from this that the intention of the ordaining ministers is necessarily defective. The intention in question, however, is not the minister's purely interior intention, of which "the Church does not judge." It is the intention as externally expressed through the ritual, the intention of the Church which devised and chose the Ordinal, which the pope esteems to be contrary to the intention of the Catholic Church.

The exact scope of the defect of intention that the pope had in mind was the object of debate in the twentieth century among Catholic theologians who were persuaded of the invalidity of Anglican ordinations, yet disagreed as to the nature of the intention that would be required for validity. The general principle, explicitly cited in *Apostolicae curae*, is that the minister must intend "to do what the Church does." The faith and the doctrine of the minister is irrelevant, since, as Leo XIII points out, an unbeliever gives a valid baptism if he uses the proper matter and form, which express the intention to do what the Church does. The change of form in the Ordinal, however, denotes an intention to reject what the Church does, a point which Leo XIII has established by referring to the sacramental theology of the authors of the Ordinal and the ensuing *nativa indoles* of the text. One may then argue that the defect of intention lies in the theology of Thomas CRANMER, the chief author of the Ordinal, or else in the ritual itself, or in the general intention of the Church of England or the Anglican Communion, which would be manifest in the imprecision of its doctrines and the tolerance of opposite interpretations (HIGH-CHURCH, LOW-CHURCH, BROAD-CHURCH, etc.).

If, however, what Leo XIII had in mind was the intention of the minister to do what the Church does, this could be either the "external intention," identical with the exact meaning of the words used in the rite (a position defended in the sixteenth century by Ambrose Catharinus), or the "internal intention" by which the minister understands his own actions. Thus an Anglican minister will spontaneously intend either what the Church of Christ in general does or what the Church of England or the Anglican Communion or his own Province of the Anglican Communion does. It is evident that the pope demands that the Anglican minister intend what the Roman Catholic Church does in the sacrament. His decision is based on the assumption that the Ordinal includes a "positive exclusion" of the Catholic priesthood, and that those who used it endorsed this denial of the tradition regarding the sacrament of Orders, whatever their own personal conviction might have been as to the nature and purpose of the priesthood. In the circumstances of the ordination of Matthew Parker to the episcopate, however, when a growing conflict was brewing between Queen Elizabeth and the pope, the consecrating bishops could hardly have intended to do what the Roman Catholic Church did. Their intention was stated in the preface to the Ordinal: to continue in England the Orders that had always been in the Church since the Apostles. There is no reason to think that such an intention was based on the personal theology of Thomas Cranmer.

The Decision. Given the papal interpretation of the form of ordination in the Ordinal and of the intention objectively expressed by the rite and its context, along with the general impression that the Ordinal is of a piece with the Protestant doctrines that were enforced under Edward VI, the pope's decision was unavoidable: "We pronounce and declare that ordinations performed according to the Anglican rite have been and are completely null and void." While the negative conclusion was absolute, a degree of confusion was caused by the printed texts of *Apostolicae curae*. In the apostolic letter as it was printed by itself in Rome in 1896, the decision was called a *caput disciplinae jure jam definitum*, a matter of discipline already defined in law. The text that was printed in the *Acta Leonis XIII* in 1897, however, did not contain the word *disciplinae*, with the result that what was simply a matter of the discipline of the sacraments could now be considered a matter of unchangeable doctrine.

The last lines of the letter embody Leo's firm intention to give a final and definitive judgment that cannot be assailed at any time "on the ground of obreption, subreption, or defect in our intention, or any defect whatsoever." This was confirmed in a letter to the archbishop of Paris, Cardinal Francis Richard, on Nov. 5, 1896: "It was our intention to deliver a final judgment and to settle the question completely. . . . All Catholics are bound to receive the decision with the utmost respect as being fixed, ratified, and irrevocable." The pope did not hint at infallibility, even though there were theologians who would have placed the question of the validity of Orders among possible secondary objects of infallibility.

The archbishops of Canterbury and of York, Frederick Temple and William Maclagan, published a Latin response, *Saepius officio*, addressed "to the whole body of the bishops of the Catholic Church," dated Feb. 19, 1897. The tone is more hurt than angry. Leo XIII is called "our venerable brother," "our revered brother in Christ," and the Roman Church "a Sister Church of Christ." The most telling point of their reply is that "Pope Leo demands a form unknown to previous bishops of Rome and an intention which is defective in the catechisms of the Oriental Church" (13).

Bibliography: *Leonis XIII Acta*, XVI, 258–275 (Latin text). R. W. FRANKLIN, ed., *Anglican Orders: Essays on the Centenary of*

Apostolicae curae, 1896–1996 (New York 1996): English text of *Apostolicae curae*, 127–137; abridged English text of *Saepius officio*, 138–149.

[G. H. TAVARD]

APOSTOLICI

Apostolici is a term applied at various times, generally in a pejorative sense, to reformers wishing to return to the primitive Church, poor, humble, simple, and penitential, through close imitation of the Apostles. Some Gnostic communities (*see* GNOSTICISM) in Asia Minor from the 2nd to the 4th centuries were called "*apostolici*" by EPIPHANIUS (*Panarion* 2.1,61; *Patrologia Graeca* ed. J. P. MIGNE, 161 v. (Paris 1857–66) 41: 1040–52). Extremely austere, they renounced property, marriage, and religious practices, which they considered mere outward forms. In the 12th century, alongside such *Wanderprediger* as Robert of Arbrissel and NORBERT OF XANTEN, whose orthodoxy was never impugned, were other itinerant barefoot preachers, near Cologne, in Périgueux, and in Brittany, who were infected with the spreading Manichaeism. Their presence in the Rhineland about 1143 induced Everwin, prior of Steinfeld (*Patrologia Latina* 182:676–680), to enlist the services of BERNARD OF CLAIRVAUX in combatting them. In refutation Bernard wrote his *Sermones in Canticum Canticorum 65–66* (*Patrologia Latina* 183:1088–110). Sharper identification may be found in the sect begun at Parma in 1260 by Gerard Segarelli, who emphasized penance and apostolic poverty (*see* POVERTY MOVEMENT), and was indebted to Joachimite ideas (*see* JOACHIM OF FIORE) and Franciscan example. These *apostolici* (*ordo apostolorum*), described by contemporaries as pseudo-apostles or hypocrites, were condemned by Pope Honorius IV in 1286 (A. POTTHAST, *Regesta pontinficum romanorum inde ab a. 1198 ad a. 1304* 22391) and by Nicholas IV in 1291 for violating the decree of the Second Council of LYONS (1274) regulating the mendicant orders. In 1287 the council of Würzburg proscribed them as vagabonds (c.34; J. D. MANSI, *Sacrorum Conciliorum nova et amplissima collectio* 24:863). But shortly after Segarelli was sent to the stake in 1300, the movement was revived by Fra DOLCINO, who elaborated apocalyptic doctrines (*see* APOCALYPTIC MOVEMENTS) and a theology of history derived from Joachimism. Imitation of apostolic life and absolute poverty, mitigated only by alms, constituted the basis of the new order. In the early modern period the term was assigned to branches of ANABAPTISTS who observed poverty and interpreted Scripture literally.

Bibliography: SALIMBENE, *Cronica fratris Salimbene de Adam*, ed. O. HOLDER-EGGER in *Monumenta Germaniae Historica Scriptores* 32 (Berlin 1905–13) 255–293, 389, 563, 619. *Historia* *fratris Dulcini haeresiarchae,* in L. A. MURATORI, *Rerum italicarum scriptores, 500–1500,* 25 v. in 28, ed. G. GARDUCCI and V. FIORINI (2d, new ed. Città di Castello 1900–) 9:427–460. B. GUI, *Manuel de l'inquisiteur,* ed. and tr. G. MOLLAT, 2 v. (Paris 1926–27). E. VACANDARD, *Vie de saint Bernard* (4th ed. Paris 1910). M. BODET and J. M. VIDAL, *Dictionnaire d'histoire et de géographie ecclésiastiques,* ed. A. BAUDRILLART et al. (Paris 1912–) 3:1037–48. A. MENS, *Oorsprong en betekenis van de Nederlandse Begijnen en Begardenbeweging* (Louvain 1947) 23–36. L. SPÄTLING, *De apostolicis, pseudoapostolicis, apostolinis* (Munich 1947). E. ANAGNINE, *Dolcino e il movimento ereticale all'inizio del trecento* (Florence 1964).

[E. W. MCDONNELL]

APOSTOLICI REGIMINIS

A bull published Dec. 19, 1513, by Leo X in the eighth session of the Fifth Lateran Council. Three propositions were designated heretical: that the soul is mortal; that all humanity shares a common soul; and that truth may be double, i.e., that a certain proposition may be true in terms of rationalistic philosophy even if it is not in accord with truth as disclosed by revelation. The bull expressly affirms that each man has an individual and immortal soul. The condemned propositions concerning the soul were conspicuously defended by Pietro POMPONAZZI in his *De immortalitate animi* in 1516. The notion of a DOUBLE TRUTH, associated with nominalism, had been suggested by NICHOLAS OF CUSA in his *De docta ignorantia* in 1440. To offset paganistic ideas derived from classical studies, the bull stipulated that clergy intending to pursue advanced philosophical and literary studies should first devote five years to theology and canon law.

Bibliography: W. BETZENDÖRFER, *Die Lehre von der zweifachen Wahrheit* (Tübingen 1924). F. VERNET, *Dictionnaire de théologie catholique,* ed. A. VACANT et al., 15 v. (Paris 1903–50; Tables générales 1951–) 8.2:2681–83.

[D. R. CAMPBELL]

APOSTOLICITY

The first creed to mention the "apostolic Church" comes from Salamis and is dated 374 (DS 42). The creed of the Council of Constantinople in 381 follows this practice (DS 150), and henceforth mention of the apostolic Church is general practice. The adjective had been developed earlier in the vocabulary of Christians, first appearing in IGNATIUS OF ANTIOCH (*Trall,* intro.). In the course of the controversies with MARCION and GNOSTICISM, it appeared more frequently. IRENAEUS of Lyons in particular was at pains to define the faith as apostolic, by which he meant to indicate that its content and normative writings derive from the public teaching of the apostles in contrast to a purported hidden or secret revelation from the apostles in gnostic Christianity. But the term was never fixed definitively and was used in various controversies to address neuralgic issues, sometimes of faith-statements, Christian writings, ecclesial practices, or Church institutions.

Meaning. Some of the fluidity of the term can be attributed to the multivalence of the term "apostle" in the early Church. Modern biblical scholarship indicates that apostleship began in the period after Easter, that there was a broader use of the term than just the Twelve and Paul, and that the term included a wide range of persons: missionary, Church-founding figures such as Paul, Peter, Apollos, Andronicus, and Junia; coworkers in missionary activity such as Timothy, Titus, and Silvanus, who were also accorded the title of apostle; resident figures such as James of Jerusalem; such delegates of local churches as Epaphroditus (Phil 2.25); and wandering preachers well into the second century (see *Didache* 11.3–6) who are sometimes mentioned with "prophets" (see Lk 11.49 and Rv 2.2). Even Christ is given the title of *apostolos* (Heb 3.1). Other scholars have pointed out the different conceptions of an apostle in Luke and Paul, uses that apparently cannot be harmonized. Also, the group of the Twelve and the broader group of apostles are not interchangeable.

Apostolicity Has Many Dimensions. First, one can point to the apostolic *origin* of the local churches. Apostles were responsible for founding churches. In the early centuries, Christians distinguished between communities clearly established by an apostle—primary apostolic churches, e.g., Antioch, Alexandria, Ephesus, etc.—and those that were founded by primary apostolic churches (*see* TERTULLIAN). According to this usage, not all churches were of apostolic origin in the same sense. In resolving disagreements among the churches, recourse was had first of all to the primary apostolic churches as depositories of the apostles' teaching (J. McCue calls them "norm churches"). In most instances, such recourse would settle the matter. Thus, communion among all the churches fostered their apostolicity. Second, a church is apostolic because of its beliefs and practices. One looks to the concrete *life* of a Christian community to determine its genuineness—its doctrines, its sacred writings, its sacramental practices, its style of discipleship, its exercise of charity, its moral principles, its internal discipline, its leadership structure, etc. This aspect of apostolicity today is called "substantive apostolicity." It is the living *traditio apostolica,* and is more than purely doctrinal since it is also based on right praxis. Since Vatican II, this dimension has received increased attention. It is based on the importance of apostolic witness to the

Christian mystery in the early Church. The accent has also shifted away from the isolated authoritative witness of the leadership of the local church to the authentic witness of that church as such. Substantive apostolicity points to the Church as a communion of churches. Third, there is apostolicity of the ordained ministry. Apostolic succession of the bishops is not an affair of a historically unbroken chain of episcopal leaders, but of proper, sacramental succession to the leadership of an apostolic community. This leadership is equipped with its own ministry of symbolizing, defending, and confirming that church's internal apostolic character. Apostolic succession points to the very sacramentality of the Church, i.e., the Church as the Fundamental Sacrament (*Grundsakrament*). Apostolicity in the full meaning is found only when all three senses are operative and interacting.

Theological Reflection. The meaning of apostolicity is dictated by the Church's historical circumstances. From a hermeneutical point of view, the term's formal content demands interpretation. When an ahistorical cognitional theory is operative, apostolicity tends to be envisioned as sameness. The Church's beliefs, practices, and offices are identical throughout time. Until Vatican II, under the dominance of a scholastically inspired epistemology, apostolicity was often identified with such a historically naive theory of identity. The Council, opening itself up to more contemporary philosophical influences, encouraged greater historical consciousness. Change and development are a part of reality. Thought and language are theory laden and methodologically directed. The understanding of reality is never without presuppositions, and reality must be approached by a critical understanding. Increasingly, theologians reject a theory of the simple identity over time of substantive apostolicity and ecclesial structures in favor of theories of continuity in the course of change and development. Past meanings of teachings and the stages of the exercise of structures are not simply discarded but are organically incorporated into newly emerging expressions and forms. Revelation and the gospel are not superseded by novelty but are critically rethought and receive new life. G. Thils gave an admirably flexible definition of apostolicity as the Church's character of being "in perfect reference to the Apostles." This phrase both refuses to claim too much and demonstrates an openness to inevitable change. A more hermeneutically conscious epistemology positively forces us to rethink the Church's apostolicity.

Historicity is not an accident but a constitutive dimension of what it is to be human, both as an individual person and corporately. The apostolicity of the Church points to this gift and task. It points to the fact that the Church must be located in history and not in timeless myth or immaterial idealism. Apostolicity emerged out of the ministry of Jesus and the encounter of the apostles with the risen Christ. The experience of having been commissioned by the Lord to bring the gospel to humankind and the empowerment of the Holy Spirit led Christians to treasure the unrepeatable ministry of the apostles as well as the unfulfilled apostolic mission throughout history, in all of the unavoidable tension that unrepeatability and genuine open-endedness include. Apostolicity points, Janus-like, both to its historical past in Jesus and the earliest community of disciples, as well as to its future goal, the salvation of all humankind in accord with God's universal salvific will (1 Tm 2.4). God's will to save can be worked out only as history unfolds, both under the positive lure of Christ from the future fulfillment that the resurrection represents and the real burden of human freedom to achieve itself in time. In Christ, God has once again and definitively announced the dialogic structure of revelation. In a word, only the mystery of the Trinity helps us understand and realize the Church's apostolicity. Apostolicity, then, is an expression of the Church's experience of God as Trinity, and so founds the Church's understanding of itself as missionary.

Because the Church experiences its apostolicity in freedom, it is conscious of its burden of ever realizing itself in history. While always remaining true to the gospel, it is free to realize its faith-expressions, its practice of the faith, and its governing structures in forms appropriate both to the historical moment and to its transcendent mission. For the human being as spirit and history, or spirit in the world, particularity and transcendence are not antithetical to one another but mutually related. Contemporary Catholic ecclesiology struggles to keep in balance an eschatological view of apostolicity and one that takes the data of historical origins and historical growth seriously. At the same time, it seeks to strike a balance between its christological and its pneumatological dimensions. Not everything in the Church can be determined from a purported will of the historical Jesus as the Church's founder, for christology also includes the paschal existence of Christ. Moreover, the risen Lord continues to enrich the Church with the ever new and creative outpouring of the Spirit, and so to endow the Church with a certain unpredictability.

Finally, theologians have been at pains to show how apostolicity needs to be considered in relation to the catholicity of the Church. The latter opens the Church in its extension in time and space to the multiplicity of cultures. As the Church becomes more aware of its character as world church (K. RAHNER) and not primarily as culturally Eurocentric, it is challenged to interpret its apostolicity as open to inculturated expressions and governance structures. Here, again, greater advertence to the Church as *communio,* while not forgetting that it is also *sacramen-*

tum, can underscore more forcefully the relationship between the Church's apostolicity and its catholicity.

In Ecumenism. Apostolicity has been treated in *extenso* in the various bilateral and multilateral national and international dialogues between the churches. The "Ministry" section of the World Council of Churches (WCC) Faith and Order Commission's *Baptism, Eucharist and Ministry* (1982) ranks among the most important. The document prefers to speak about "apostolic tradition" rather than "apostolicity," and defines it as "witness to the apostolic faith, proclamation and fresh interpretation of the Gospel, celebration of baptism and the Eucharist, the transmission of ministerial responsibilities, communion in prayer, love, joy and suffering, service to the sick and the needy, unity among the local churches and sharing the gifts which the Lord has given to each" (art. 34). It stresses the role of the Spirit as well as that of Christ. On the matter of apostolic ministry, the document states that "the primary manifestation of apostolic succession is to be found in the apostolic tradition of the Church as a whole" and it shows a deep appreciation of the Church's ministry by indicating that "the ordained ministry has a particular task of preserving and actualizing the apostolic faith. The orderly transmission of the ordained ministry is therefore a powerful expression of the continuity of the Church throughout history" (art. 35). "Ministry" challenges the non-episcopal churches to consider restoring the episcopacy as a service to the apostolic faith and the episcopal churches to purify the concrete exercise of the ordained apostolic ministry (see art. 38). The WCC's *Baptism, Eucharist and Ministry, 1982–1990: Report on the Process and Responses* indicates the persistence of problems in the area of apostolic ministry and apostolic succession (see D. 26–27). Some progress is noted in the openness of the churches to accept a distinction, not a separation, between apostolic tradition and apostolic succession. In its document *The Nature and Purpose of the Church: A Stage on the Way to a Common Statement* (1998), the WCC's Faith and Order Commission notes the progress made in the course of the various dialogues and indicates a possible way out of the impasses that have resulted from the different historical contexts of the churches. The document stresses the notion of *koinonia* or communion as a possible way of reconciling differences that are seen to be legitimate and not church dividing. The New Testament itself and early church practices indicate a legitimate variety in the ministry. If there is fundamental unity on apostolic faith and life, how far can the churches go in recognizing a diversity of ministries in service of apostolicity?

Progress has also been made in Roman Catholic dialogues with the Lutheran Church, the Anglican Communion, the World Methodist Council, the World Alliance of Reformed Churches, and the Orthodox Church. In all of these, one notes the introduction of broader theological categories for rethinking apostolicity. One of these is *communio.* Another is *mission,* which introduces important ideas of dynamism, historicity, and the mystery of the Trinity into the ecclesiological discussion of apostolicity and apostolic succession. Promising ground, too, has been broken between the British and Irish Anglican Churches and the Nordic and Baltic Lutheran Churches in *The Porvoo Common Statement* (1992). Though the Catholic Church was not directly involved in the discussions, the matter concerns it, since the agreement between the Catholic Church and the Lutheran Church and the Anglican Communion is so advanced. Porvoo continues to stress the apostolicity of the whole Church without compromising the importance of the ordained episcopal ministry, which it sees as abidingly constitutive for the Church. Thus, it is more successful than earlier reports in maintaining the delicate balance between these two dimensions of apostolicity. In fact, it looks to the intention and action of the ordaining church and judges the apostolic character of ministry by the total life of a church and the ministry. Porvoo does not dispense with concerns of validity with respect to ordained ministry, but places these concerns in the broader context of the underlying apostolicity of any given church.

The Catholic Church still struggles with finding a formula that can maintain the right balance between the apostolicity of the whole Church and episcopal apostolic succession, between the validity of ordained ministries in the churches and the signs of apostolicity of these churches, and finally between the rightful concerns for the Church's unity and a desirable diversity of structures given to the Church by the continuing presence of the Spirit in the churches.

Bibliography: W. BEINERT, "Die Apostolizität der Kirche als Kategorie der Theologie," *Theologie und Philosophie* 52 (1977) 161–81; "The Picture of the Apostle in Early Christian Tradition," in E. HENNECKE and W. SCHNEEMELCHER, eds., *New Testament Apocrypha,* rev. ed. (Louisville 1992) 2:5–27. Y. CONGAR, "Composantes et idée de la succession apostolique," in *Oecumenica: Jahrbuch für ökumenische Forschung* (Minneapolis/Neuchâtel 1966) 61–80; "Apostolicité de ministère et apostolicité de doctrine: Essai d'explication de la réaction protestante et de la tradition catholique," *Ministères et communion ecclésiale* (Paris 1971) 51–94. L. M. DEWAILLY, "Note sur l'histoire de l'adjectif Apostolique," *Mélanges de Science Religieuse* 5 (1948) 141–52. W. KASPER, "Die apostolische Sukzession als ökumenisches Problem," *Theologie und Kirche* (Mainz 1999) 2:163–82. J. N. D. KELLY, "'Catholic and Apostolic' in the Early Centuries," *One in Christ* 6 (1970) 274–87. J. F. MCCUE, "Apostles and Apostolic Succession in the Patristic Era," in *Eucharist and Ministry,* Lutherans and Catholics in Dialogue 4 (Washington, D.C. 1970) 138–71. M. O'GARA, "Apostolicity in Ecumenical Dialogue," *Mid-Stream* 37 (1998) 175–212. W. PANNENBERG, "The Significance of Eschatology for an Understanding of the Apostolicity and Catholicity of the

The Apotheosis of Antoninus and Faustina, relief on the base of the Antonine Column (A.D. 161–169) in the Cortile della Pigna of the Vatican. (Anderson-Art Reference/Art Resource, NY)

Church,'' in *The Church,* tr. K. CRIM (Philadelphia 1983) 44–68. J. ROLOFF, G. G. BLUM, and F. MILDENBERGER, ''Apostel/Apostolat/ Apostolizität,'' in *Theologische Realenzyklopädie,* 3:430–477. F. J. SULLIVAN, ''The Church Is Apostolic,'' in *The Church We Believe In: One, Holy, Catholic and Apostolic* (New York 1988) 152–84; ''Apostolicity in Ecumenical Dialogue,'' in *ibid.,* 185–209. G. THILS, ''Apostolicity,'' in *New Catholic Encyclopedia,* 1:699f. J. M. R. TILLARD, ''Ministry and Apostolic Tradition,'' *One in Christ* 25 (1989) 14–22. O. TJØRHOM, ''The Porvoo Statement—A Possible Ecumenical Breakthrough?'' *One in Christ* 29 (1993) 302–309. J. WICKS, ''Ecclesial Apostolicity Confessed in the Creed,'' *Pro Ecclesia* 9 (2000) 150–64. J. D. ZIZIOULAS, ''Apostolic Continuity and Succession,'' in *Being as Communion: Studies in Personhood and the Church* (Crestwood, N.Y. 1985) 171–208.

[J. J. BURKHARD]

APOTHEOSIS

In the ancient Greek world it was believed that divinity was everywhere, but in a special way in great men. The legendary founders of cities were thought to have been gods in disguise or at least the offspring of gods. They were worshiped by the official cult of the city. Contrasting with this ''descending'' theology was an ''ascending'' point of view expressed in the idea that exceptional men escaped the common fate of mortals and were transported beyond the stars to share in the eternal blessedness of the gods. Hercules is the classical case in mythology of the hero who by his exploits on earth achieved divine status. Within historical times Alexander the Great and later Hellenistic kings were apotheosized. An Athenian memorial to the heroes fallen at Potidaea (432 B.C.) goes so far as to ascribe this blessedness even to ordinary soldiers: ''The ether has received their souls, the earth their bodies'' (Cumont, 146). The apotheosis of the first two Caesars may be said to have been, to some extent at least, the result of a genuine religious feeling that a divine hand was at work in the reestablishment of peace and order in a ravaged world. In accordance with the scientific picture of the world at that time, apotheosis was conceived of in strictly spatial terms. A Roman relief represents Julius Caesar standing in a chariot that four winged horses are carrying toward the heavens.

Some historians of the early 20th century tried to explain Christianity's faith in the divinity of Christ as a derivation from the apotheosis of heroes and emperors. W. Bousset, in his *Kyrios Christos* (Göttingen 1913), advanced the hypothesis that the title LORD was first given to Jesus by gentile converts at Antioch and other centers of gentile Christianity under the influence of the mystery cults (*see* MYSTERY RELIGIONS, GRECO-ORIENTAL). St. Paul would have introduced the title and the divine worship paid to Christ into the Judeo-Christian Churches. E. Lohmeyer [*Christuskult und Kaiserkult* (Tübingen 1919)] held that the title SON OF GOD was commonplace in ancient times and expressed man's need for a concrete embodiment of the divine on earth. The term was used of political saviors and of religious saviors. It was given, according to Lohmeyer, to Jesus under the influence of the apotheosis of Augustus some decades earlier.

Contemporary scholars are agreed that these titles arose, not within gentile Christianity, but in the Judeo-Christian Churches. The title Lord is found in the oldest passages of the New Testament (e.g., Mk 12.35–37; Acts 2.36; Gal 4.1), and the passage in which Christ is given the divine ''name that is above every name'' (Phil 2.9) is clearly inspired by passages in Isaiah. The title Son of God probably originated with, or at least was popularized by, St. Paul, for whose gentile hearers Our Lord's own designation of Himself, Son of Man, would be meaningless.

Bibliography: K. PRÜMM, *Lexikon für Theologie und Kirche*, ed. J. HOFER and K. RAHNER (2d, new ed. Freiburg 1957–65) 1:766–767. L. CERFAUX, *Christ in the Theology of St. Paul*, tr. G. WEBB and A. WALKER (New York 1959). O. CULLMANN, *The Christology of the New Testament*, tr. S. C. GUTHRIE and C. A. M. HALL (rev. ed. Philadelphia 1963). F. CUMONT, *Lux perpetua* (Paris 1949) 171–. G. DIX, *Jew and Greek* (Westminster, Eng. 1953).

[J. M. CARMODY]

APPEAL TO A FUTURE COUNCIL

Appeal to a future council is a complaint by a physical or juridic person against a papal act, in order to have this act examined by the next ecumenical council (*see* COUNCILS, GENERAL). An appeal of this kind implies a belief in the superiority of a general council over the pope. Two opinions are current concerning the origin of this appeal. However, according to Victor MARTIN this term did not always have the above significance. After studying the earliest of these appeals—those made by the Colonna cardinals (1297), by King PHILIP IV OF FRANCE and his counselors (1303), and by Emperor LOUIS IV THE BAVARIAN (1334)—Martin concluded that these early appeals were based on two traditional principles: (1) the pope cannot be judged by anyone (*Corpus iuris canonici*, ed. E. Friedberg [repr. Graz 1955] C.9 q.3, c.16) and (2) a heretical pope, by deviating from the faith, is already judged and lacks authority (*ibid.*, D.40 c.6). Martin was all the more certain that these first appellants were orthodox, because, in his view, the doctrine of the superiority of a council over a pope arose between 1409 and 1415 and not before. Brian Tierney, on the other hand, has found it curious that a pope could be already judged without the existence of a judge to pronounce on his culpability. He has established that from the end of the 12th century different opinions existed among canonists and that one of these opinions asserted the superiority of a council over a pope (*see* CONCILIARISM). According to Tierney, when the Council of CONSTANCE in its fifth session issued the decree *Sacrosancta* (April 6, 1415) it was not ratifying a recently formed opinion but one that had been in existence for more than two centuries without being condemned. Whatever may be said of Martin's and Tierney's interpretations, it is certain that appeals to a future council were numerous in France, especially during the 15th century. The supporters of GALLICANISM claimed constantly that one could appeal from a pope to a council; they affirmed this claim in the PRAGMATIC SANCTION of Bourges (1438), in the quasi-official book in 1594 by Pierre PITHOU, *Les Libertez de l'Église gallicane* (art. 78), and in the DECLARATION OF THE FRENCH CLERGY in 1682 (art. 2). LOUIS XIV appealed to a future council in 1688, and the French Jansenists did so in 1717.

Pius II (1458–64) was the first pope to denounce this appeal as an ''execrable abuse'' and ridiculed it by asking how anyone could appeal ''to a tribunal that does not yet exist, and, for all anyone knows, may never sit.'' The same pope also excommunicated appellants (*Execrabilis*, Jan. 18, 1460) and later repeated his condemnation (Nov. 2, 1460). His example was followed by Sixtus IV (1483), Julius II (1509), Leo X (1520), Benedict XIV (1745), and Pius IX (1869). The Latin and Eastern codes condemn such an appeal [*Codex iuris canonici* (repr. Graz 1955) c. 333 §3; *Codex canonum ecclesiarum orientalium, c.* 45 37]. Furthermore, the Latin code provides for a censure for a person who would make such an appeal (*Codex iuris canonici* [repr. Graz 1955] c. 1372).

Bibliography: V. MARTIN, *Les Origines du gallicanisme*, 2 v. (Paris 1939). B. TIERNEY, *Foundations of the Conciliar Theory* (Cambridge, Eng. 1955); ''Pope and Council: Some New Decretist Texts,'' *Mediaeval Studies* 19 (1957) 197–218. P. G. CARON, *L'Appello per abuso* (Milan 1954). A. AMANIEU, *Dictionnaire de droit canonique*, ed. R. NAZ, 7 v. (Paris 1935–65) 1:807–818. H.

KÜNG, *Structures of the Church,* tr. S. ATTANASIO (New York 1964).

[C. BERTHELOT DU CHESNAY]

APPELLANTS

A name given to opponents of the bull *UNIGENITUS,* who appealed against the papal decree to a general council; they thus logically applied the Gallican doctrine of the Four Articles of 1682 that affirmed the superiority of a general council over a pope. The first act of appeal was presented under the form of a notarized act lodged at the Sorbonne on the morning of March 5, 1717 by four bishops: Jean Soanen, of Senez; Joachim Colbert, of Montpellier; Pierre de la Broue, of Mirepoix; and Pierre de Langle, of Boulogne. Many members of the secular and regular clergy, an important segment of the faithful, as well as several corporate societies, among them the Sorbonne, adhered to the Appeal, which finally united 12 bishops and a little more than 3,000 priests and religious of the approximately 100,000 that made up the French clergy.

The Appellants thought that the bull condemned some authentic Christian truths, that consequently the pope had erred in faith, and that only a general council could remedy the situation. On Sept. 8, 1718 (day of publication), by the brief *Pastoralis officii,* Clement XI excommunicated the Appellants. In view of the opposition from the Gallican parliamentaries, this measure produced no practical effect. To guarantee the failure of any attempt at a compromise, the four bishops renewed their appeal on Sept. 10, 1720, and the "Reappellants" who joined them were numerous. The regent then embarked on a veritable campaign of police persecution against the Appellants, and their number decreased year by year; many of them, however, maintained their attitude until death.

See Also: JANSENISM; ACCEPTANTS.

Bibliography: The most complete selection of the acts of appeal is that of G. N. NIVELLE, *La Constitution "Unigenitus" déférée à l'église universelle,* 3 v. in 4 (Cologne 1757).

[L. J. COGNET]

APPETITE

In normal usage the term appetite designates a desire for food and the capacity to enjoy it. Without straining its meaning, however, it can signify almost any desire, for example, an appetite for hard work or for pleasure. The word derives from the Latin *appetitus,* which means a seeking for something. As used in scholastic philosophy, appetite is defined as the inclination and order of a thing toward the GOOD, and designates the element in the nature of things whereby they have or develop tendencies toward objects that benefit them.

Thomistic Concept of Appetite

In Thomistic philosophy, appetite in the strict sense specifies the capacity of a thing to seek its good; when used more broadly, it includes the actual seeking as well. Appetite thus is both the fundamental power to seek and the actual exercise of that power. Psychologically, this concept is closely connected with a number of other concepts, for example, orexis, conation, urge, drive, feeling, emotion, affectivity and passion. Orexis is the Aristotelian term for appetite, sometimes signifying appetite in general and at other times the power of the will. Conation, urge and drive are terms that are used almost interchangeably to indicate the forceful or impulsive aspect of appetites. FEELING and affectivity are generally used to indicate the felt quality connected with appetitive activity. Emotion and passion can be used for both the feeling aspect and the drive aspect of appetites. Passion in current usage often signifies a more intense emotion; in scholastic use, it did not have this connotation.

In the philosophy of St. THOMAS AQUINAS and among scholastics generally, appetite is attributed to all beings, from God, who has Will, to primary matter, which has an appetite for substantial form. The classical expression of this idea is: An inclination follows every form (*Summa theologiae* 1a2ae, 8.1), for everything is either on account of itself or on account of another and what is on account of itself seeks itself, while what is on account of another seeks that other. Otherwise the parts of the universe are absurd, as being ordered to purposes but not effectively equipped to attain them (*see* FINAL CAUSALITY; TELEOLOGY).

DIVISION OF APPETITE

The first division of appetite is into natural and elicited appetites. Because things exist as they are and tend to continue in existence for a while and because they operate as they ought to operate, they are said to have a natural appetite to exist and to operate. Such a natural appetite is not conceived as a reality in a thing distinct from its NATURE; it is rather the nature itself conceived in terms of tendency to be and to operate.

Elicited appetites are the appetites aroused by cognitive acts and they are considered to be distinct parts of the nature of a cognitive being. The evidence for elicited appetites is firstly our human experience and secondly our observation of other animals. We feel impulses and affects aroused in ourselves by cognitive acts toward various objects and these impel us to action toward these objects; we see, moreover, that animals seem to act the same way and are furnished with the same kind of organs that serve us. We conclude, then, that cognitive beings are in fact equipped with appetites. Moreover, it would be absurd if the case were otherwise, for a knowing being who was absolutely unable to be moved by what he came to know would be frustrated; his knowledge would be futile. Therefore knowing beings ought to have the capacity to be moved by objects as known and such a capacity would be, by definition, an elicited appetite.

Therefore, since there are appetites aroused by cognitive acts, there will be at least as many distinct kinds of elicited appetite as there are distinct orders of KNOWLEDGE (ST 1a, 80.1). Scholastics, dividing knowledge basically into SENSE knowledge and intellectual knowledge, divide appetite into sensitive appetites and the will, which is the appetite of the intellective part.

SENSITIVE APPETITES

By definition, a sensitive appetite is a capacity to be aroused by a concrete object perceived through the SENSES. It is, therefore, an operative power, that is, a power to respond and to react. This response or reaction on the part of the possessor of the appetite has a twofold moment. First of all, it is a kind of passivity, by which the possessor is changed or moved by the impact of the object sensed. Secondly, since this change is of the nature of a tension produced in the possessor, an inclination to action follows, for the purpose of relieving the tension. Hence appetites tend to provoke action. The actions are designed to obtain or avoid the object that originally aroused the appetite: to obtain it if it is good, or to avoid it if it is evil. Since avoiding evil is itself good, one can define the appetite as ordered simply to the good, either directly or indirectly.

Organic changes. Hence the sense appetites arise from the sense knowledge that elicits them, involve a physical change in the organism, and result in action. The physical change may be greater or less, but it is always present. Medieval scholastics spoke of such changes as the rising of the blood around the heart in anger, the withdrawal of the blood toward the bowels in fear and so on. Modern physiology recognizes changes in the circulatory, respiratory, glandular and other systems, as component parts of emotional changes. The basic organs of appetitive movement seem to be the hypothalamus in the brain and perhaps parts of the rhinencephalon, for experiments stimulating these organs of the brain with electric currents result in reaction patterns of the emotive or motivational order [see J. Olds, "Pleasure Centers in the Brain," *Scientific American* 195 (October 1956)

105–116]. The autonomic nervous system that stimulates visceral, glandular and other somatic changes in emotional reactions is the connecting link between the brain centers of sensitive appetite and the other corporeal reactions involved.

Concupiscible vs. irascible appetites. Thomistic psychology posits two sensitive appetites, the concupiscible and the irascible. The arguments for this division run thus: Some passions in the organism are aroused on the basis of simple PLEASURE and pain, as it seeks out what is pleasing physically and avoids what feels injurious. These reactions constitute the operations of one appetite, the concupiscible, whose ultimate object is defined as the simple, sensitive good. But other emotional reactions are based not simply on pleasure and pain. Thus we experience inclinations impelling us toward things that are hard or difficult to attain, or we find emotional responses impelling us to reject or despair of good objects. These appetitive activities are assigned to a second sensitive appetite, called the irascible appetite, whose object is the difficult or arduous sense good.

Of the two, the basic appetite is the concupiscible. The irascible appetite is an emergency appetite, aroused when simple movements toward a sensible good or away from a sensible evil are impeded by some obstacle. The irascible appetite is aroused precisely to overcome the obstacle. When it is overcome, the irascible appetite subsides and the simple concupiscible appetite functions alone. For example, love is a simple concupiscible movement toward a good or pleasant object and when the object is here and now attainable, the love for it generates an actual desire. If the object can be obtained, the desire comes to fruition in joy or delight. This all occurs in the concupiscible appetite. But if, when desire is aroused, a sudden obstacle impedes the attainment of the good, then anger, an irascible passion, will perhaps be stirred up against the impediment. Anger urges toward overcoming or destroying it; once this is done, nothing prevents obtaining the object and so there is a return to delight or joy. Or again, one might be faced with an object he dislikes, feel an aversion toward it and hence avoid it—all movements of the concupiscible appetite. If he can avoid it, he feels contentment or joy. But if some circumstance suddenly appears making it seem impossible to avoid the disliked object, his aversion takes on an emergency quality; it turns into fear, another irascible passion and under the stimulus of fear he reacts more energetically to escape the evil. If he does escape it, he again feels joy.

Acts of the sense appetites. The various actions of the sense appetites, which are called the PASSIONS or EMOTIONS, are divided in Thomistic psychology into 11 general categories, six in the concupiscible appetite and five in the irascible appetite. LOVE, the first passion of the concupiscible appetite, is the fundamental passion underlying all others. Love is defined, in an abstract way, as the simple tendency toward a good thing. DESIRE, which arises from love, is a tendency toward a good thing that is not yet possessed but is presently possessible. JOY follows from desire when the good thing is actually possessed. Hate, the opposite of love, is the turning away from an evil thing. Aversion arises from hate, as an actual repugnance to an evil thing presenting itself. Sorrow follows after aversion, if the evil thing actually afflicts us. HOPE is the name given to the first of the irascible appetites. It is the vehement seeking of a good object that is hard to obtain. COURAGE is the energetic attack on an evil that is hard to overcome. Despair is the giving up of a good object because of difficulties, and FEAR is the urgent avoidance of an evil that is hard to escape. Anger, finally, is the movement toward an evil that is hard to overcome for the sake of destroying it. All movements of passion, with their various modalities and mixtures and shades of difference, can be comprised without great difficulty under these 11 basic categories.

HUMAN WILL

The WILL is the rational or intellectual appetite in man, that is, the appetite that seeks goods as they are perceived by the power of INTELLECT. As the intellect is the supreme cognitive power in man, so the will is the supreme appetite in man, controlling all human behavior; and as the intellect is a spiritual power, so is the will. Thus all purely spiritual or rational goods are sought by the will alone and rational and spiritual evils are rejected by the will. It is the will that desires justice, truth, order, immortality, the service of God and the like, and hates injustice, deceit, chaos, and death. However, the will's objects are not limited to spiritual things—it seeks also to obtain or avoid physical goods sought by the sensitive appetites; but when the will acts in this sphere, it is because it sees reasonableness in these physical goods. Thus, the sight of food might arouse a person's concupiscible appetite because food is pleasant to eat but he wills to eat it only if he sees that it is reasonable here and now to do so. Hence a man can also starve himself in spite of a contrary urging from the sensitive appetites, if in the circumstances he judges this is a reasonable thing to do. The will ultimately controls all behavior, as long as man is conscious and sane; even behavior motivated primarily by the sense appetites is not carried out unless the will consents.

Free Will. The will is a free power in man, because it is the appetite that follows reason (*see* FREE WILL). Because reason can see several alternatives equally feasible as means of reaching one end, the will has freedom to elect from among them.

Acts of the Will. The acts of the will are often called by the same names as the passions of the sense appetites, namely, love, hate, desire, fear, anger and so on. These, however, are not the names of the will's proper acts. The principal proper acts of the will are to intend an end or purpose, to elect the means to accomplish it, to command the actions that execute it, and to rest content in the purpose accomplished (*see* HUMAN ACT). If the purpose is to attain a good, we call the acts of intention, election and command, acts of love; if they are aimed at destroying evil, we call them anger; if at escaping an evil, we call them fear and so on.

Relationship to sense appetites. The relationships between the will and the sense appetites are complex. One can arouse the sensitive appetites deliberately by willing to think about and imagine the objects that stir them. Moreover, it often happens that a particularly strong act of the will produces a similar passion in the sense appetites, by a kind of overflow or redundance. So, for instance, some people feel fright physically when called on suddenly to address a large audience, although there is nothing physically threatening. In their turn, the sense appetites can exert considerable influence on the will. The freedom of the will, for instance, depends on the power of reason to judge a situation calmly, taking into account all possibilities. But when the passions are strongly aroused, the power of reason often fails to judge carefully and a man is precipitated into actions he would not otherwise have performed. The passions fix the attention of the mind on the things that stir them and limit its capacity to reflect and thus indirectly limit the freedom of the will. Moreover, to act contrary to strong passions produces strong feelings of pain and sorrow and rather than endure these, men often consent to things they would otherwise reject. Thus, although the will is free and in supreme command in theory, in practice it is often limited by the sense appetites.

Other Theories of Appetition

Many philosophers and psychologists have disagreed with one element or another of the theory of appetition outlined above. Some have denied that appetition is a force consequent and subordinate to cognition. Others have questioned its precise relationship to action. Still others deny the distinction between sense appetites and will, or introduce a dichotomy between affectivity and conation or drive. A summary of representative views along these lines follows.

SCOTUS, SCHOPENHAUER AND FREUD

John DUNS SCOTUS in the 14th century placed appetite above cognition in the ordering of faculties, arguing that the will is the supreme power in man, against the

Thomistic position that intellect is the highest power, eliciting, governing and regulating the acts of the will (*see* VOLUNTARISM; INTELLECTUALISM).

Arthur SCHOPENHAUER (1788–1860) made will not only the supreme power in man's psychological equipment, but the fundamental reality in all of nature. He argued that the will leads the intellect to its judgments; governs memory, imagination, logic and reflection; drives men in all their actions; and in short, constitutes the essence of man. Moreover, will governs all movements in nature, in animals, in plants and in inanimate bodies—will is the ultimate reality. "The world is wide in space and old in time and of an inexhaustible multiplicity of forms. Yet all this is only the manifestation of the will to live" [*The World as Will and Idea,* tr. R. B. Haldane and J. Kemp (London 1906) 3:379].

Sigmund Freud (1856–1939) made drive the major element in human nature and denied that it was elicited by cognition. For him, drives are basically the psychological manifestations of biological processes, arise spontaneously and inexorably in the mind and only subsequently attach themselves to cognitive elements or objects that represent actions and things peculiarly fitted to provide satisfaction ["Instincts and their Vicissitudes," *Collected Papers* (London 1956) 4:60–67].

LEIBNIZ, JAMES AND DEWEY

Other theories of appetition differ regarding its relation to action. G. W. LEIBNIZ (1644–1716) gave his monads two basic activities, perception and appetition, but appetition did not give rise to action, it merely effected the transition from one perception to another within the MONAD. Since Leibniz did not hold that the mind could efficiently move the physical world, he could not make appetition the cause of action. In higher organisms, appetition is called will, which is an effort or tendency toward good and away from evil. Will results from consciousness of good and evil and is guided by reason, which propose images of the greater goods and evils that will follow from different courses of action [*New Essays Concerning Human Understanding,* tr. A. G. Langley (La Salle, Ill. 1916) 177, 195].

The so-called James-Lange theory of emotions, proposed by William JAMES in 1884 and Carl Lange in 1885, also realigns emotion and action. According to this theory, objects arouse instinctive reactions that in turn produce bodily changes, which are then perceived as emotions. The instinctive reaction results directly from the perception of the exciting fact, whereas the emotion is the felt result of the bodily alteration. "Common-sense says, we lose our fortune and weep . . . the more rational statement is that we feel sorry because we cry" [James

Principles of Psychology (New York 1913) 2:449–450]. Experimental evidence does not give unqualified support to this theory, but the element of truth it expresses may perhaps be accounted for by the fact that man becomes conscious of his emotions as a consequence of feeling the bodily commotions they cause [M. Stock, "Sense Consciousness according to St. Thomas," *The Thomist,* 21 (1958) 460–466].

John Dewey (1859–1952) proposed a theory of emotions that made them the effects of impeded action rather than a spur to effective action. He held that emotions are felt as physical disturbances that arise when a strong urge to act is impeded; as long as actions are carried out uninhibitedly, emotions do not occur.

MATERIALIST VIEWS

Philosophers of materialist schools deny the scholastic distinction between sense appetites and will. Herbert SPENCER (1820–1903) thought of the will and all the higher powers in man as products of materialistic evolution, whereby simpler psychic responses such as reflexes and tropisms are gradually developed into the more complex operative patterns we name intelligence and will [*Principles of Psychology* (New York 1883) 1:495].

Freud also denied the will as a distinct and higher faculty in man and attributed all drive in human nature to instinctual urges. He did, however, believe that men could control their drives reasonably, and contemporary psychoanalysis often accepts will as a power in man distinct from instinctual drives [for example H. Hartmann, *Ego Psychology and the Problem of Adaptation,* tr. D. Rapaport (New York 1958) 74–75].

HAMILTON, LOTZE AND CANNON

Modern psychological theory, both philosophical and empirical, usually makes a dichotomy between affectivity, or the felt quality of emotion and conation or drive. This distinction is at least as old as William HAMILTON (1788–1856) who posits cognition, feeling and conation as the three elemental phenomena of consciousness.

R. H. LOTZE (1817–1881) makes the division of ideation, feeling and volition. Feelings arise from pleasure and pain, which are caused by circumstances that are either harmonious to or disturbing to the body. Impulses arise from these feelings, but as distinct from them. Volition also is distinct from impulse [*Microcosmus,* tr. E. Jones and E. Hamilton (Edinburgh 1888) 1.2.2.3]. Although there is a basis in felt experience and in the functional role for a distinction between affect and drive, the intimate connection between these two aspects of appetitive activity is lost by positing two distinct powers or capacities. An affect, for example, guilt feeling, can motivate a conation, for example, the urge to confess. An action motivated by a drive, for example, eating when hungry, terminates in an affect, namely, contentment. The interplay of drive and feeling is obscured and rendered difficult to explain if the two aspects of appetite are not seen in their organic relationship.

The physiological researches of W. B. Cannon (1871–1945) have contributed useful information to theories of appetite. Cannon investigated the physiological changes produced in the body by situations that demand vigorous action. He traced the patterns of discharge in the involuntary nervous system, the glandular reactions and the alterations in respiration, circulation and muscular tension, etc., and noted how they were all ordained to the exigencies of a body about to be engaged in violent action. These patterns of response did not correlate with specific emotional categories, but were generalized reactions to an emergency. In a scholastic theory of appetite, they would suggest the physiological changes involved in the arousing of the irascible appetite [see *Bodily Changes in Pain, Hunger, Fear and Rage* (New York 1929)].

See Also: PASSION; WILL

Bibliography: G. P. KLUBERTANZ, *The Philosophy of Human Nature* (New York 1953). T. V. MOORE, *The Driving Forces of Human Nature* (New York 1948). J. WILD, *Introduction to Realistic Philosophy* (New York 1948). J. F. DASHIELL, *Fundamentals of General Psychology* (New York 1937). R. S. WOODWORTH, *Experimental Psychology* (rev. ed. New York 1954). W. MCDOUGALL, *Body and Mind* (7th ed. London 1928).

[E. M. STOCK]

APPREHENSION, SIMPLE

The operation by which the INTELLECT apprehends a QUIDDITY without affirming or denying anything of it. In this operation the intellect simply grasps what a thing is, that is, its ESSENCE, without attributing any predicate to it. THOMAS AQUINAS described this activity as an *indivisibilium intelligentia,* understanding of indivisibles or of essences (*In 1 perih.* 3.3).

Explanation. Three things should be noted in the definition of simple apprehension. (1) It is an operation, that is, the second act or activity of an operative power. As in most creatural activities, four really distinct factors must be recognized: the operative power itself, its operation, its internal product, and the external SIGN of that product. The operative power or faculty involved in simple apprehension is the possible intellect; the first activity the possible intellect performs is that of simply apprehending a quiddity; its internal product is a formal CON-CEPT or mental word; the external sign of that concept is an oral or written TERM. (2) It apprehends a quiddity, an essence. Simple apprehension knows merely what man, or white, or learned is. Such ''whatnesses'' or quiddities are called indivisibles in the sense that a definite group of notes is required for their comprehension—if any of these is missing, the quiddity is not attained. For example, the quiddity of man requires the inclusion of the notes of substance, body, living, sentient, and rational; none can be eliminated and still leave as remainder the quiddity of man. Furthermore, simple apprehension is not limited to merely substantial and accidental essences, formal acts; even when it knows something that is not itself a quiddity, it knows this as if it were one (*per modum quidditatis*). (3) It does so without affirming or denying. This feature distinguishes simple apprehension from JUDGMENT. This first act rests in the knowledge of what man, or white, or learned is; it does not go on, as judgment does, to assert the existential identity or non-identity of two notions, such as ''man *is* white'' or ''this man *is not* learned.''

The act of simple apprehension is not simple, for it involves three prerequisite steps and then the act itself. The first step is the operation of the external SENSES, since nothing comes to be in the intellect that was not first in some way in the senses. The external senses supply various unrelated bits of information about the external thing and thus supply the material for intellection and its bridge of contact with extramental reality. The second step involves the activities of the internal senses. The CENTRAL SENSE combines the data received from the external senses into a common sensible image or percept. The other internal senses either estimate the thing thus perceived or reproduce the thing's image in its absence. The common sensible image of the internal senses is, in general, called a PHANTASM. Then begins the third step in the process, the functioning of the active intellect; this gives a dematerializing illumination to the phantasm, rather like an X-ray. Using the phantasm as its instrument, the active intellect produces a determinate immaterial impression on the possible intellect, called the impressed intelligible species (*see* SPECIES, INTENTIONAL). At this stage comes the act of simple apprehension itself. Thus determined and specified by the reception of the impressed species, the possible intellect actually knows by producing an expressed species or mental WORD in which it attains its abstracted object (*see* ABSTRACTION).

When the possible intellect moves on to its second type of operation, forming judgments, simple apprehension is required to present the concepts of the possible subject and predicate. Likewise, simple apprehension is required in REASONING, which basically is only a special coordination of judgments.

How Effected. The perfection of human knowledge is a gradual process; it is not fully accomplished in one swoop. Simple apprehension does not grasp an object in all its richness at first thrust. It attains it first in its most general aspects, then gradually proceeds through the more proximate genera and differences, down to its most special species, and finally its individuality. St. Thomas illustrates this by an analogy: "When a thing is seen afar off it is seen to be a body before it is seen to be an animal; and to be an animal before it is seen to be a man; and to be a man before it is seen to be Socrates or Plato" (*Summa Theologiae* 1a, 85.3). Similarly, human knowledge proceeds from confused notions, wherein an object is known only generically, to distinct notions, wherein it is known in its proper and specific features. It must be recognized, however, that even if man does succeed in attaining an explicit knowledge of the inmost constitution of some few things, in most instances he has to be content with imperfect knowledge through external signs.

Apprehension of Singulars. The above description of the process of simple apprehension indicates that the human intellect directly proceeds by abstracting from the individuating conditions with which an object is represented in the phantasm. Consequently, in its state of union with the body the intellect directly knows only UNIVERSALS. However, since the universal has been drawn from the sensed singular, the intellect can, as it were, retrace its steps and through reflection see an essence as it is individualized in the phantasm. This dependence of intellect on phantasm precludes the possibility of imageless thought in such knowledge. Yet the intellect is only one of the instruments by which man knows. As Aquinas observes, "Man knows singulars through the imagination and sense; and therefore he can apply the universal knowledge which is in the intellect, to the particular: for, properly speaking, it is not the senses or the intellect that know, but man through both" (*De ver.* 2.6 ad 3). Ordinarily, human knowledge of a singular material thing is, therefore, a complex of contributions: man's knowing through what is contributed by both the intellect and the senses.

Apprehension of Self. In the light of the abstractive process, how does man know himself and his spiritual aspects? First of all, he knows himself and his acts through the act of knowing something other than himself. When, in signified act (*in actu signato*), he knows something extramental, such as a tree, he is concomitantly aware of himself and of his activity in knowing the tree. Such concomitant knowledge is called by scholastics exercised knowledge (*in actu exercito*) and, by psychoanalysts, coconsciousness.

Likewise, man knows the existence of his soul experimentally and immediately through its activities. When he perceives that he is exercising any vital operation, such as intellection or sensation, he vaguely perceives that he has a principle of intellection, of sensation, and so on, which is his soul. In knowing the existence of the soul, he has an obscure and confused knowledge of its essence. However, a clear and distinct knowledge of the essence of the soul is arrived at only after a careful and diligent inquiry based on the objects and acts of the vital principle (*see* SOUL, HUMAN).

Moreover, man has a rational appetite called a WILL. He is vaguely aware of its existence and essence in the exercise of its acts. This knowledge becomes clarified and perfected by inferences from activities that indicate the nature of the principle from which they spring. It is in the same manner that man gains a knowledge of habits, for these are but further determinations of operative powers, disposing them to act easily and stably in a certain manner.

Apprehension of Spiritual Entities. The proper object of the human intellect while united to the body is the abstracted essences of material things as represented in a phantasm. Since pure spirits, such as angels and God, are by definition immaterial beings, man can rise to a knowledge of them only by ANALOGY. He affirms of such spirits some positive perfections (called pure perfections) noticed in inferior beings; these perfections he affirms of them in a higher degree, while denying the imperfections involved in "mixed" perfections. Thus the presence of intellection is affirmed of such spirits in an eminent degree, for this involves no imperfection in its proper concept. On the other hand, sensation is denied of pure spirits, for this is a mixed perfection that involves organicity, an imperfection, in its proper concept.

Relation to Intuition. Some contemporary thinkers, especially under the influence of H. BERGSON, tend to devalue conceptual knowledge as gained through simple apprehension in comparison with that gained through INTUITION. Such antipathy is better directed against Kant than Aquinas. Aquinas frequently used intuition in the broad sense of understanding anything whatsoever. He also used the term analogously with reference to the omniscience of God, the nonabstractive knowledge of angels, and human abstractive knowledge. Concepts arrived at through abstraction are called intuitive if they represent a thing that is present precisely as it is present. Conceptual knowledge gained through abstraction does not necessarily distort or falsify; it can well be thoroughly accurate as far as it goes, even though it does not grasp the full richness of the object. In this regard, St. Thomas noted that "the understanding of mathematical notions is not false, although no line is abstracted from matter in reality" (*In 1 sent.* 30, 1.3 ad 1). Abstraction and conceptualization is simply the lot of a human intellect while united to a body.

See Also: KNOWLEDGE, PROCESS OF; UNDERSTANDING; INSIGHT.

Bibliography: J. MARITAIN, *The Degrees of Knowledge,* tr. G. B. PHELAN et al. (New York 1959); *Bergsonian Philosophy and Thomism,* tr. M. L. and J. G. ANDISON (New York 1955). J. F. PEIFER, *The Concept in Thomism* (New York 1952); *The Mystery of Knowledge* (Albany 1964). É. H. GILSON, *The Christian Philosophy of St. Thomas Aquinas,* tr. L. K. SHOOK (New York 1956); *Réalisme thomiste et critique de la connaissance* (Paris 1947). G. P. KLUBERTANZ, *The Philosophy of Human Nature* (New York 1953). J. DE TONQUÉDEC, *La Critique de la connaissance* (3d ed. Paris 1961). R. GARRIGOU-LAGRANGE, *God: His Existence and His Nature,* 2 v., tr. B. ROSE (St. Louis 1934–36). R. ALLERS, ''On Intellectual Operations,'' *New Scholasticism* 26 (1952) 1–36. B. J. F. LONERGAN, ''The Concept of *Verbum* in the Writings of St. Thomas Aquinas,'' *Theological Studies* 10 (1949) 3–40, 359–393. M. DE MUNNYNCK, ''Notes on Intuition,'' *Thomist* 1 (1939) 143–168.

[J. F. PEIFER]

APPROPRIATION

Appropriation is a more or less spontaneous way of thinking and speaking about the Triune God relative to creatures. In appropriation some divine characteristic, activity, or effect that belongs equally to all three Persons is thought and spoken of as belonging to one of the three. This manner of thinking and speaking is not merely an invention of men but is sanctioned by God Himself, who inspired the writers of the New Testament in their use of appropriation, and who providentially safeguards the creeds and liturgy of the Church in their use of appropriation. By means of appropriation God reveals to men the otherwise unknowable depths of the divine being and life and the truly distinct characters of the Father, the Son, and the Holy Spirit, who live it.

Scripture, Creeds, Liturgy. St. Paul offers an example of appropriation in the New Testament. He sometimes speaks of God (and by God, Paul generally means the Father) dwelling in the Christian community: ''. . . in him [the Lord] you too are being built together into a dwelling place for God in the Spirit'' (Eph 2.22). Another time he says the Holy Spirit dwells in the community: ''Or do you not know that your members are the temple of the Holy Spirit, who is in you, whom you have from God, and that you are not your own?'' (1 Cor 6.19). It should be noted that ''you'' in this passage is, in the Greek, plural, referring to the Corinthian community. Thus the divine presence in the Christian community is appropriated in one instance to the Father, in another to the Holy Spirit; yet one knows that wherever one of the Divine Persons is present, the other two must also be present as well.

The early creeds also use appropriation. One professes belief, for example, in God, the Father almighty, creator of heaven and earth . . ., in the Holy Ghost, the holy Catholic Church, the communion of saints, etc. Thus creative power and activity are attributed to the Father and the effects of unifying Christian love, forgiveness of sins, resurrection, eternal life—in a word, sanctification—are attributed to the Holy Spirit.

A similar manner of expression is found in the liturgy, where prayers are usually addressed to the Father, who is considered as having the power to grant man's request, through the Son (though the mediation of the Son in virtue of His human nature is not appropriation, but truly the unique possession of the Word incarnate), and in the Holy Spirit, who is conceived as the source of the love that binds Christians together with one another and with Christ and God in the liturgical assembly.

Theology of Appropriation. In the Scriptures the Father is associated with creation and power (Mt 3.9; Acts 4.24). Thus one begins to see the Father more clearly as the source of all and realizes more what is implied in His fatherhood within the Trinity, e.g., His being without a principle. The Son is viewed as the Word of God through whom God creates (Jn 1.3; Col 1.15–17); He gives meaning, order, and intelligibility to chaos. Hence the Son is associated with wisdom, and is understood to proceed from the Father by a generation akin to the generation of an idea in knowing. The Holy Spirit is given to Christians as a gift to sanctify, to aid, to comfort them (Rom 5.5; 2 Cor 1.22; Jn 14.26; 16.13); thus one is led to understand His position in the Trinity as the bond of love between Father and Son.

The basis for attribution usually is a similarity between a divine perfection, action, or effect and a characteristic proper to one of the Persons. Something in the Person Himself calls for the appropriation. The appropriations fall into a pattern with certain things seen usually in relation to one Person, as, for example, goodness, peace, joy to the Holy Spirit. There should be a mutual clarification between the quality, action, or effect appropriated and the Divine Person. Gradually one discovers in these relationships what God wishes to tell man about Himself, not so much with regard to His absolute nature as in His Trinitarian being—the character of the Persons involved and their intra-Trinitarian dialogue.

The divine nature, however, is one and possessed completely by all three Persons, so that what is not relatively opposed in the Trinity is really something belonging to all three Persons (*see* TRINITY, HOLY; PERSON, DIVINE). Because divine power, divine wisdom, divine love, mercy, etc. are associated with one Person, it does not mean that they belong exclusively to that Person. Divine power, for example, is connected with the Father, but not only the Father is powerful. The various divine qualities and activities do not cease to be essential and common by the fact of appropriation. All of God's external works proceed from divine omnipotence under the direction of His wisdom inspired by love, and are actions of the Trinity as a whole, not of this or that Person. Although Sacred Scripture does associate creation with the Father, wisdom with the Son, sanctification with the Holy Spirit, nevertheless, as exercises of the divine power these activities and their effects have their effective source in all three Divine Persons functioning through the one power and the one activity.

This does not mean that appropriation is useless or a mere playing with words. It is one of the ways for God to reveal His inner self and the uniqueness of Persons. Furthermore, there is a basis in the Trinity itself for appropriation, in the proper characteristics of each Person; that is, creation is associated with the Father as generator of the Word; the unity of the soul with God and of Christians with one another is associated with the Holy Spirit as bond of unity. That which is common to all, at least as one conceives it, has a greater likeness to what is proper to one Person than to what is proper to another.

Insofar as any one of the Divine Persons can be considered from several aspects, a number of things may be appropriated to Him. For example, depending on the aspect considered, eternity, power, or unity may be seen in relationship to the Father; or wisdom, beauty, or truth to the Son; or goodness, love, or joy to the Holy Spirit. Furthermore, one and the same divine quality or action might be associated with different Persons depending on the aspect of the Person or quality considered. The revelation of the mysteries of God to men might be connected with the Son as the Word of God and with the Holy Spirit as manifesting or communicating goodness or aiding men (Heb 1.1–4; Jn 16.12–14).

See Also: TRINITY, HOLY, ARTICLES ON.

Bibliography: A. CHOLLET, *Dictionnaire de théologie catholique,* ed. A. VACANT et al., 15 v. (Paris 1903–50) 1.2:1708–17. M. SCHMAUS, *Lexikon für Theologie und Kirche,* ed. J. HOFER and K. RAHNER, 10 v. (2d, new ed. Freiburg 1957–65) 1:773–75. I. M. DALMAU, *Sacrae theologiae summa,* ed. FATHERS OF THE SOCIETY OF JESUS, PROFESSORS OF THE THEOLOGICAL FACULTIES IN SPAIN, 4 v. (Madrid), v.2 (3d ed. 1958) 2.1:544–53.

[J. B. ENDRES]

AQUILEIA

Former patriarchate and metropolitan see on the Natissa River in Friuli (Udine), Italy. Having been founded

"Deposition of Christ and Saints" from "Passion of Christ Fresco Cycle," 9th-century Early Medieval ceiling fresco in the crypt of Basilica of Aquileia, Italy. (© Elio Ciol/CORBIS)

as a Roman military colony *c.* 180 B.C., Aquileia was greatly prized by the Caesars as a port and bastion against the Illyrians. A 5th-century legend traces its Christianity to St. Mark and names St. Hermagoras its first bishop, though its beginnings were in the mid-3d century. In the 5th century it exercised metropolitan rights over Venice, Istria, West Illyricum, Rhaetia, and Noricum; and its bishops claimed the title of patriarch in the mid-6th century (Pelagius I, *Epist.*). When the Huns destroyed Sirmium in 452, they besieged Aquileia, which thereafter extended its jurisdictional claims to the Pannonian borderlands.

After the condemnation of the THREE CHAPTERS in 553 by the Council of CONSTANTINOPLE II and Pope VIGILIUS, Patriarch Paulinus I rejected the condemnation in a provincial council (554); the schism thus created lasted until 607, when Bishop Candidianus restored communion. However, Paulinus had fled to the isle of Grado in Byzantine territory before the Lombards in 568; hence the Lombards elected their own patriarch for ancient Aquileia with its see at Cividale, and this territory remained in schism until Patriarch Peter, with the consent of King Cunibert, made peace with Rome in a synod at Pavia (*c.* 700).

In 716 two dioceses were recognized: Aquileia and Grado. Grado's line of patriarchs continued until the 15th century. Under Paulinus II (*c.* 785–804), a friend of CHARLEMAGNE, missioners were sent among the Avars and Slovenes, and the Drava River was made the boundary between Aquileia and the See of Salzburg in 811. Patriarch Maxentius attempted vainly to reunite Aquileia with Grado in a synod at Mantua (827), when the patriarchate was granted immunity and free election.

The present cathedral was begun by Poppo (1019–42), and in 1077 Henry IV granted suzerainty to Patriarch Sigehard (1068–77) as Count of Friuli and Istria. Berthold of Andechs changed the see to Udine in 1238, and Gregory of Montelongo (1251–69) was the first Italian to become patriarch. Beset by its neighbors, particularly Venice, the patriarchate functioned only partially; but Marquard of Randech (1365–81) issued a civil and penal code (*Constitutiones patriae Foriiulii*) with the consent of the city's parliament. Louis of Tech (1412–39) joined the king of Hungary in war against Venice, and the territory was then taken over by the Venetians. When the Hapsburgs assumed jurisdiction over Aquileia, the patriarchate was absorbed by Venice; leaders such as Marco Barbo (1465–91), Ermolao Barbaro (1491–93), Giovanni and Daniello Delfino (1658–99, 1734–51) subsequently ruled as patriarchs.

Under Austrian pressure, BENEDICT XIV suppressed the Patriarchate of Aquileia (July 6, 1751) and erected the archbishoprics of Udine and Gorizia, and the former patriarchate was made a parish church depending immediately on the Holy See.

Archeological excavations have uncovered an imperial villa under the foundations of the ancient church, which after the peace of Constantine was enlarged and decorated with mosaics of the Good Shepherd, Jonas, etc. A stone pavement (lithostratos) was uncovered. The baptistery was on one side and surrounded an octagonal basin. In the 5th century a large basilica with three naves and a decorated pavement was destroyed by fire. New constructions were made under JUSTINIAN I and at that time a polygonal baptistery was added. The present campanile tower dates from the patriarchate of Poppo.

Bibliography: P. PASCHINI, *Storia del Friuli*, 3 v. (Udine 1934–36). G. BRUSIN, *Aquileia e Grado* (2d ed. Padua 1952). M. M. ROBERTI, G. BOVINI, G. CUSCITO, eds., *Aquileia e l'alto Adriatico Vol. 2: Aquileia e l'Istria* (Udine 1972). S. TAVANO, J. LEMARIÉ, M. M. ROBERTI, *Aquileia e l'alto Adriatico Vol. 1: Aquileia e Grado* (Udine 1972). Y.-M. DUVAL, E. CATTANEO, J. LEMARIÉ, eds., *Aquileia e Milano* (Udine 1973). G. C. MENIS, E. JASTRZEBOWSKA, G. RINALDI, eds., *Mosaici in Aquileia e nell'alto Adriatico* (Udine 1975). J. NORDHAGEN, G. CUSCITO, J. LEMARIÉ, eds., *Aquileia e Ravenna* (Udine 1978). C. JÄGGI, "Aspekte der städtebaulichen Entwicklung Aquileias in frühchristlicher Zeit," *Jahrbuch für Antike und Christentum, Jahrgang 33 1990* (Münster 1991) 158–196. G. CUSCITO, "Alle origini della storiografia critica sul primo cristianesimo aquileiese," *Quaeritur inventus colitur* (Vatican City 1989) 161–175. G. C. WATAGHIN, "Problemi e ipotesi sulla basilica della Beligna di Aquileia," *Quaeritur inventus colitur* (Vatican City 1989) 71–90.

[F. X. MURPHY/EDS.]

AQUILEIAN RITE

Little is known about the primitive liturgical rite of Aquileia that emerged in the 7th century, but it was used in such distant places as Verona, Trent, and Pola. Much of the manuscript evidence is of a late date. Very few manuscripts have preserved the state of the liturgical rite before the introduction of the Roman Rite by the Aquileian Patriarch Paulinus II (787–802). The oldest extant document pertaining to the rite is a fragmentary 7th- or 8th-century Lectionary (*Capitulare evangeliorum*), added by a Lombard hand to the earlier Codex Richdigeranus; its characteristics resemble the Ambrosian Rite more than the Roman Rite. In evidence of this, Advent has five Sundays, with the Gospel for the fifth Sunday commemorating the Annunciation, and there are three baptismal scrutinies and the *Traditio Symboli* on the Sunday before Easter. The feast of St. Stephen is kept on the Antiochene date, December 27. Ambrosian usages are found in the marginal notes of the Codex Forojuliensis of the Gospels, in which the rubric "In triduanas" precedes the Rogation Days (P. Borella, "L'anno liturgico Ambrosiano," M. Righetti, *Manuale di storia liturgica* 2:288). The treatise of the Aquileian Patriarch Massentius (811–33) and the *Ordo scrutinii* by Lupus I (*c.* 870) both mentioned the Aquileian baptismal rites.

Whatever form this primitive rite may have taken, it was slowly superseded in the Carolingian period by the Roman Rite that Patriarch Paulinus II had introduced in the 9th century. Although the Roman Rite became the norm for liturgical celebrations, the later manuscript tradition suggests that the Aquileian Church retained some of its distinctive features: "secundum morem et consuetudinem aquilegensis ecclesiae" ("following the practice and custom of the church of Aquileia"), "iuxta consuetudinem aquilegensis ecclesiae" ("according to the custom of the Church of Aquileia"), "in hoc non observamus romanum ordinem"("in this [practice] we do not observe the Roman ordo"), "sed aquilegiensis ecclesia hoc non utitur"("but the Church of Aquileia does not use this [practice]").

The last Aquileian Missal (1519) had retained few distinctive characteristics. The liturgical rite, such as it was, is now extinct, having been suppressed at Trieste (1586), Monza (1578), Aquileia (1596), and Como (1596 or 1597).

Bibliography: A. A. KING, *Liturgies of the Past* (Milwaukee 1959). G. VALE, "La liturgia nella chiesa patriarcale di Aquileia," *La Basilica di Aquileia*, ed. N. ZANICHELLI (Bologna 1933) 367–81. M. HUGLO, "Liturgia e musica sacra aquileiese," *Storia della cultura veneta, i: Dalle origini al Trecento*, ed. A. GIROLAMO, M. PASTORE STOCCHI and G. FOLENA (Vicenza 1976) 312–25. M. HUGLO, "Les manuscrits notés du diocèse d'Aquilée," *Scriptorium* 38 (1984) 313–17. G. PRESSACCO, "La tradizione liturgico-musicale di

Aquileia," *International Musicological Society: Congress Report* 14 (1987) 119–29. G. PRESSACCO, *Tropi, prosule e sequenze del messale Aquileiese: un primo censimento* (Udine 1995). R. CAMILOT-OSWALD, *Die liturgischen Musikhandschriften aus dem mittelalterlichen Patriarchat Aquileia* (Kassel 1997).

[A. A. KING/EDS.]

AQUILINUS OF MILAN, ST.

Martyr; b. Würzburg, Germany, *c.* 970; d. Milan, Italy, *c.* 1015 (?). There is uncertainty regarding the period during which Aquilinus (Aquilino) lived. He went to Cologne in order to pursue his studies but left when his fellow canons attempted to make him bishop. Leaving Paris for the same reason, he crossed the Alps, stayed a short while at Pavia, and finally joined the canons of the church of S. Lorenzo at Milan. Early in the eleventh century he was martyred because of his outspoken opposition to the spread of Manichaeism. His body rests in a chapel of the church of S. Lorenzo that bears his name and is decorated with 24 scenes from his life. He seems to have enjoyed a continuous cult, and he is honored by the churches of Cologne, Würzburg, and Milan and by the canons of the Lateran. Ancient Breviary lessons, the martyrologies, and the Bollandist critique of the sources all indicate that he was martyred in conflict with ARIANISM and lived probably during the sixth century.

Feast: Jan. 29.

Bibliography: *Acta Sanctorum* Jan. 3:585–586. G. DORIO, *Memoria sul culto del martire Santo Aquilino* (Milan 1856), basic study. G. ALLMANG, *Dictionnaire d'histoire et de géographie ecclésiastiques*, ed. A. BAUDRILLART et al. (Paris 1912) 1147–48. A. WENDEHORST, *Lexikon für Theologie und Kirche*, ed. J. HOFER and K. RAHNER (Freiburg 1957–65) 1:782.

[N. M. RIEHLE]

AQUINAS, PHILIPPUS

Hebrew scholar and convert to Christianity; b. Carpentras, southern France, *c.* 1575; d. Paris, 1650. His Jewish name was Juda Mordechai. Little is known of his early years, but while occupying the position of rabbi at Avignon he showed great sympathy for Christianity. Because of this, he was forced to resign his position in 1610. He subsequently entered the Church at Aquino in the Kingdom of Naples, taking the name Philip Aquinas (of Aquin). In later years he was engaged in teaching Hebrew in Paris, where he was named professor at the College of France by Louis XIII. Some indication of his position in French court life may be drawn from the fact that his grandson, Anthony of Aquin (d. 1696), became the chief physician of Louis XIV. Philippus worked on the Paris

Polyglot (*see* POLYGLOT BIBLES), but his principal publications were *Radices breves linguae Sanctae* (Paris 1620) and *Dictionarium Hebraeo-Chaldaeotalmudico-rabbinicum* (Paris 1629), in which he made the Hebrew dictionaries of Nathan ben Jehiel of Rome (d. 1106) and J. Buxtorf more complete.

Bibliography: A. STROBEL, *Lexikon für Theologie und Kirche*, ed. J. HOFER and K. RAHNER, 10 v. (2d ed. Freiburg 1957–65) 1:782. *Nouvelle biographie générale*, ed. J. C. HOEFER, v. 2 (Paris 1859) 946.

[S. M. POLAN]

ARABIA

A large triangular peninsula lying between Asia and Africa. Classified by geographers as a part of Asia, although connected to Africa by the Sinai Peninsula and in many respects more properly a part of the African land mass, its size of approximately one million square miles entitles it to be considered as a subcontinent. The following entry discusses Arabia in that geographical and historical context; for information on Catholicism in the modern states of Oman, Saudi Arabia, the United Arab Emirates, and Yemen, which now occupy the peninsula, see those individual entries.

1. HISTORY

Before treating of the Islamic and pre-Islamic history of Arabia, this article will give a brief description of the geography and ethnology of the Arabian peninsula.

Geography. Arabia is bounded on three sides by water (the Red Sea on the west, the Gulf of Aden and the Arabian Sea on the south, the Gulf of Oman and the Persian Gulf on the east) and has from early times been called *Jazīrat al-'Arab* (Island of the Arabs) by its inhabitants. There is no natural northern boundary; a vast steppe leads into Jordan, Iraq, and Syria. There are many islands off the southern coasts and a few shallow bays along those coasts. A chain of mountains (in some regions two chains) called al-Sarah runs close and parallel to the coastline of the Red Sea, with many plateaus along their eastern slopes. The mountains are highest in the Yemen and reappear again in the southeast in Dhufar and Oman. There are coastal plains and hills, mesas, and buttes, especially in the north. Most of the peninsula, however, is a sandy desert. The principal desert areas are the Great Nufud and the Empty Quarter (*al-Rub' al-Khâlî*), the latter constituting the largest continuous body of sand in the world.

Climate and Rainfall. Arabia, bisected by the Tropic of Cancer, generally enjoys a temperate climate, although the lowlands are semitropical. The summer heat is intense, with temperatures as high as 122° F, but winter in the highlands can be proportionately bitter. The inlands are dry and subject to severe sandstorms. Limited eastern parts are affected by the monsoons, but, in general, rainfall is scarce throughout the peninsula. In the desert regions, in fact, no rain may fall for periods of 8 or 10 years, though in some places sudden torrential rains caught in a stream channel (wâdī) cause flashfloods. There are no large rivers (a few small ones flow along the southern and eastern coasts) and no lakes. In fact, human life is made possible in much of the peninsula only by the presence of springs, pools, and wells, around which oasis settlements have grown up. Some of these oases are hundreds of square miles in area, large enough to permit several separate villages and large camping areas within them; others are merely watering places where the water is too salty for human consumption but generally satisfactory for camels. There is some evidence of ancient irrigation systems and dams, which very probably made fertile some regions that are no longer so.

Produce. Since there are no prairies or forests and many inimical migrating dunes, cultivation in Arabia is necessarily limited and requires much skill. The date palm is the principal tree and is put to many uses. Some wheat, barley, and alfalfa are grown, as well as coffee, introduced by Europeans, and qat, with its slightly narcotic leaves, in Yemen and the south. Plants yielding frankincense, myrrh, and other aromatics, as well as dyes such as indigo, have been grown there since ancient times. In a few isolated regions roses, pomegranates, mangoes, figs, grapes, peaches, and bananas can be grown. In general, milk and dates provide the staple foods, supplemented by bush fruit and truffles, for man and beast alike. The camel is the most important animal, since it is well adapted to desert conditions, and there are many sheep and goats. Arabian horses and gazelles are rapidly dying out. There is a wide variety of small animals, birds, and insects.

Ethnology. Much more archeological and anthropological research will have to be done before the ethnology of Arabia is reliably clear. Tribal traditions are mostly legendary and unreliable, although they are not to be dismissed for more recent Arabian history. Nearly all Arabians are of the Mediterranean race, but there is a distinct Veddoid strain in the south. The modern Arabs themselves accept a descent from two ancestors, Qahtan and Adnan, the descendants of the former being supposed to be the southern Arabs and those of the latter the northern Arabs. Naturally such a scheme is open to serious question. There are strong indications that the earliest southern Arabians had migrated from the northern and central parts of the peninsula. Many tribes retain no tradition of

ever having belonged to either group, while others are known to have moved or changed their allegiance by alliances. Nevertheless, the tradition expresses something utterly real: a cultural difference and a spirit of rivalry between northern and southern Arabians, which remained a factor of notable importance in Islamic history well into modern times and as far away from Arabia as Spain and Transoxiana. Today there are a few immigrants, mostly in the coastal regions. Slavery of Africans apparently still exists, although it is said to be minimal. There has been no type of color bar in Arabia since Islamic times. Significant migrations of peoples have taken place within the peninsula in recent times, but few Arabians have emigrated, and those few to adjacent Iran, India, and East Africa.

Pre-Islamic history. Arabia is still one of the lesser-known parts of the world, and a great amount of basic scientific exploration remains to be done before its history can be made precise.

Modern Exploration. Such investigation began with Carsten Niebuhr and the Danish expedition of 1761 to 1764. A century later Joseph Halevy and Eduard Glaser explored several south Arabian sites and were able to copy many Sabaean inscriptions. [*See* SABA (SHEBA)]. The interior of Arabia was penetrated during the 19th century by J. L. Burckhardt, Richard Burton, and W. G. Palgrave; British officers of the Indian government completed technical surveys of the southeastern regions, and Charles Doughty wrote his invaluable study of northern Arabia. The studies preparatory to the building of the Hejaz railway and the work of Alois Musil, K. S. Twitchell, and H. St. John B. Philby have added immeasurably to knowledge of the peninsula. The Empty Quarter was crossed and documented by Bertram Thomas in 1931 and 1932. More recently oil companies have sponsored illuminating surveys of eastern Arabian territories.

Dawn of History in Arabia. Future investigations will doubtless improve the state of knowledge of early Arabia, but as yet it has only the most shadowy history before the 1st millennium B.C. A few chance finds have proved that the peninsula was inhabited in Palaeolithic and Neolithic times. Some of those who believe in the existence of a Semitic race have speculated that Arabia might have been the original home of that race. It is quite solidly established, at any rate, that nomads from the Arabian deserts began infiltrating the Iraqi and Syrian portions of the Fertile Crescent about the middle of the 4th millennium B.C. and made substantial incursions thereafter at intervals of approximately a millennium until the Moslem conquest. Early in the 2d millennium B.C. a system of alphabetic writing was invented and about the same time the camel was domesticated. Soon afterward there were considerable migrations of peoples within

Arabia, perhaps originating the traditional division between northern and southern tribes, and about 1500 B.C. the Aramaeans entered the Fertile Crescent in large numbers.

Assyro-Babylonian, Egyptian, and Hebrew (notably Gn 10.26–30; see under 2. below) records mention some place names and tribes that are almost certainly to be identified within Arabia. The "Aribi" in Assyro-Babylonian texts are thought by some scholars to denote the Arabs. Strong organized states came into being in South Arabia during the second half of the first millennium B.C., while in North Arabia the Persians were succeeding the Assyrians and Neo-Babylonians in bringing substantial portions of that area under their influence. Evidently there was a rapid development of commerce and trade at this time, and Arabia—particularly South Arabia—merged and flourished on that account. The Neo-Babylonian king Nabu-Na'id (Nabonidus; 556–539 B.C.), as a recent discovery indicates, had extended his influence as far south as Yathrib, and the presence of Jewish colonies in Arabia may date from this time.

Early Kingdoms. The kingdom of Ma'in existed in Yemen from about 1200 to 650 B.C. Scholars are at variance as to how long it continued to coexist with the Sabaean kingdom, which was newly founded, after a three-century rule of priest-kings, about 650. A queen of the Sabaeans (the Queen of Sheba) is reported in 1 Kgs 10.1–13 to have visited Solomon. Saba was more or less constantly at war with the younger kingdoms of Hadramaut and Qataban, but appears to have maintained the upper hand. Its rule lasted until 115 B.C., when it was conquered by the Himyarites. Qataban fell at about the same time. The Himyarite kingdom lasted until A.D. 525. In the meantime the Nabataean kingdom rose in the north, from its famous capital at Petra, and prospered as an entrepot and from later cooperation with the Romans. Rome launched its single attempt to conquer Arabia in 24 B.C. under Aelius Gallus, but the expedition ended in failure. The height of Nabataean influence occurred during the reign of Harithath (or Aretas) IV, who ruled from 9 B.C. to A.D. 40. In 106 the Emperor Trajan incorporated the state into the Roman Empire.

There is mention of Arabs at Pentecost (Acts 2.11) and St. Paul visited Arabia, although that may only mean some region south of Damascus, after his conversion (Gal 1.17). Some Arab *shaykhs* whose identity is now impossible to determine are known to have accepted the Christian faith in the 3d century, and Arab bishoprics are noted thereafter by historians of the times (see under 5. below). In the mid-4th century the (Christian, later Monophysite) Abyssinians succeeded in occupying Himyarite territory in South Arabia. The ensuing struggle became an open quarrel between Judaism, accepted by the Himyarites, and Christianity. Abyssinia, supported by Byzantium, assumed a spacious colony in Arabia in 525, but 50 years later was effectively defeated by Persian forces. In the meantime the political arrangements in North Arabia had come to reflect this important power-struggle. Client kingdoms had been established: Hīra, the Lakhmids, dependent upon Persia, and the Ghassanids, dependent upon Byzantium. After 583 the Ghassanids themselves split, and in the later years of the century the tribe of Kindah began to assume power in Central Arabia as a type of vassal state of Yemen. There was thus a condition of political confusion on the eve of the foundation of Islam.

Islamic History. About 570 MUHAMMAD was born in MECCA, a center of trade and religious pilgrimage in west Central Arabia. His career as founder of the religion of ISLAM fundamentally changed the entire course of Arabian history. In his youth Muhammad was a poor orphan, but later he married a wealthy woman. About the age of 40 he received his "prophetic call" to unite the Arabs under a monotheism, which he came to insist was a reaffirmation of pure Judaism and Christianity. His "revelations" were collected after his death in the QUR'ĀN. But the Meccans did not welcome Muhammad's message, and he was obliged to flee with his followers to Yathrib (known thereafter as MEDINA) in 622, the HIJRA (Arabic *hijrah*, "flight") from which Muslims date their era. At Medina Muhammad's fortunes took a sharp turn for the better and he found himself directing a political community, which gradually gained ascendancy in Central Arabia and was ready, at the time of his death in 632, to consolidate its territories and prepare to conquer other lands.

In the Middle Ages. Muhammad's immediate successors, the "Orthodox" caliphs, superintended a series of successful invasions to the north, east, and west of the Arabian peninsula. During the reign of the caliph ALI, Muhammad's cousin and son-in-law, there ensued a dispute over the caliphate that resulted in the establishment of the dynasty of the UMAYYADS, which ruled over the still-expanding Islamic empire for almost a century (661–750) from its capital in DAMASCUS, but resulted also in the most important and enduring division among Muslims, that between the SUNNITES and the SHĪ'ITES. A carefully planned revolution put the dynasty of the 'ABBĀSIDS in power in 750, and the capital of the empire was moved to BAGHDAD. The 'Abbāsid caliphs continued nominally to rule the Islamic empire until the capture of Baghdad by the MONGOLS in 1258, though in point of fact the empire was already hopelessly fragmented after the first century of their rule. Arabia, in particular, provided favorable conditions for the further growth of Shiism, and by the end of the 9th century two revolutionary branches of Shī'ites, the ISMAILIS and the Carmathians held large portions of the peninsula. The success of the Ismaili Fatimid caliphate in Egypt prolonged the dominance of Shī'ites rule of Arabia, but Salah-al-Din (SALADIN) restored Sunnite control toward the end of the 12th century.

Arabia generally shared the fortunes and misfortunes of neighboring Egypt and Syria during the period of the Mamelukes (1250–1517), but in some respects and more particularly in its southern and eastern regions was able to follow an independent course. Early in the 16th century Portuguese explorers reached Arabia, and at the same time the OTTOMAN TURKS wrested Egypt from Mameluke rule. Under the impact of European trading activity in south and east Asia, Yemen, Hadramaut, and Oman in South Arabia entered upon a new period of prosperity. In the 18th century the reforming movement of the WAHHĀBIS took root in Najd and won over the Saud tribe to its tenets. But its expanding state ran into powerful opposition from the sherifs of Mecca and the newly vitalized Sayyid dynasty in Oman, which eventually extended its authority to the coastal areas of East Africa. Later technological advances enabled the Ottomans to strengthen their hold over parts of Arabia.

In Modern Times. The Arab Revolt under Sharif Husayn of Mecca, with British assistance, brought about the end of Ottoman rule during World War I. Sharif Husayn was recognized as king of Arabia (and later, briefly, as CALIPH), but was soon at war with the Saud tribal confederacy under Abd-al-Aziz ibn-Saud. Ibn-Saud defeated Husayn, conquered the Hejaz, and proceeded to unify the peninsula under his own rule; in 1932 he assumed the title of king of Saudi Arabia. His conquest stopped short at the boundaries that have been maintained since, separating Saudi Arabia from the surrounding states. The discovery of enormous deposits of oil in eastern Arabia and their subsequent exploitation very markedly changed the fortunes of this country and brought it increasingly forward into world affairs.

Bibliography: D. G. HOGARTH, *Arabia* (Oxford 1922). C. M. DOUGHTY, *Travels in Arabia Deserts,* 2 v. (new ed. New York 1937). A. MUSIL, *In the Arabian Desert* (New York 1930). B. THOMAS, *Arabia Felix* (New York 1932). J. A. MONTGOMERY, *Arabia and the Bible* (Philadelphia 1934). H. R. P. DICKSON, *The Arab of the Desert* (London 1949). R. H. SANGER, *The Arabian Peninsula* (Ithaca 1954). H. ST. J. B. PHILBY, *Saudi Arabia* (London 1955). P. K. HITTI, *History of the Arabs* (6th ed. New York 1956). K. S. TWITCHELL, *Saudi Arabia* (3d ed. Princeton 1958). G. A. LIPSKY et al., *Saudi Arabia* (New Haven 1959).

[J. KRITZECK]

2. ARABIA IN THE BIBLE

The Hebrew word *'ărab* is used in Is 21.13 to designate the steppe countries where the nomads, the desert dwellers (Jer 25.24), lived, regardless of the dialect spoken by each individual ethnic group. Therefore, Arabia (in the contemporary meaning of the Arabian peninsula inhabited by Arabic-speaking populations) is an entity foreign to the Israelites of the OT period. The generic name Arabian(s) (Heb. collective *'ărab;* gentilic *'ărābî,* pl. *'ărābîm;* the *Aribu* of the cuneiform inscriptions), refers to the tent-dwelling (Is 13.20) Bedouins of the desert (Jer 3.2) east of Palestine; hence they are known also as the Cedemites or Easterners (*benê-qedem,* the children of the East, e.g., in Is 11.14). The generic name, however, is used rather seldom compared with the proper names of the various Arabian populations neighboring Palestine, as they are found, for instance, in the ethnic genealogical lists of Genesis ch. 10, 11, and 25. Although the ancestors of the Israelites originated about the 19th century B.C. in northwestern Mesopotamia, where they had been in contact with and influenced by Semitic as well as non-Semitic populations, their conviction of being close kinsfolk of the peoples living in northern and southern Arabia is stressed in these lists. Among the descendants of Eber (Heb. *'ēber*), a descendant of Sem, several names are mentioned in Gn 10.25–29 that are similar to those of peoples in South Arabia, such as *yoqṭān* (Qaḥṭān; mentioned in Jamme 635.27 [about 60 B.C.] as forming a kingdom along with Kindat); *ḥăsarmāwet* (Ḥadramawt); *šebā'* (Saba'); and *ḥăwîlâ* (Ḥawlân). It is noteworthy that the names of Ma'în and Qatabân are not found, and that Saba' is listed as the brother of Dedan in the Bible (in Gn 10.7 as a grandson *kûs*— Chus; in Gn 25.3 as a grandson of Abraham and *qetûrâ*—Cetura; see also Ez 38.13). The city of Dedan, at the present time al-'Ulá, was an important Minaean (not Sabaean) trading center. The mention of faraway Ḥadramawt is explained by actual commercial contacts, as illustrated by the Ḥadrami clay stamp (probably of the 9th century B.C.) discovered by J. L. Kelso during the 1957 excavations at Beitin, biblical Bethel. The Sabaeans, whose country is said to be far off (Jl 4.8), are described as merchants (Ez 25.23; 27.22–23) trading in gold, frankincense (Is 60.6; Jer 6.20; Ps 71 [72]. 15], the best spices, and precious stones (Ez 27.22), but also as raiders (Jb 1.15) and slave traders (Jl 4.8).

During the monarchical period of the Israelite history, the Arabians intervened in Jewish affairs on several occasions. For instance, the Queen of SABA (Sheba) visited Solomon; King Josaphat of Juda received a large tribute of sheep and goats from the Arabians (2 Chr 17.11); South Arabians raided the realm and even the capital of Judah at the time of King Jehoram (2 Chr 21.16–17; 22.1). After the return from exile, Geshem the Arabian (Neh 2.19) and his band of Arabs (Neh 4.1) joined the coalition that tried unsuccessfully to prevent the reconstruction of the walls of Jerusalem.

Among the descendants of Ismael (Ishmael), the son of Abraham and HAGAR the Egyptian (Gn 25.12), the most famous were the Nabataeans, known also as Arabians (2 Mc 5.8; Acts 2.11). Finally, it was in the northern end of Arabia, i.e., in the Syro-Arabian desert east of Damascus, that Paul withdrew after his conversion to Christianity (Gal 1.17).

Bibliography: R. P. DOUGHERTY, *The Sealand of Ancient Arabia* (New Haven, CT 1932). J. A. MONTGOMERY, *Arabia and the Bible* (Philadelphia 1934). A. JAMME and G. W. VAN BEEK, "The South-Arabian Clay Stamp from Bethel Again," *Bulletin of the American Schools of Oriental Research* 163 (1961) 15–18. *Encyclopedic Dictionary of the Bible,* tr. and adap. by L. HARTMAN (New York 1963), from A. VAN DEN BORN, *Bijbels Woordenboek,* 122. J. ASSFALG, *Lexikon für Theologie und Kirche,* ed. J. HOFER and K. RAHNER (Freiburg 1957–65) 1:786–787.

[A. JAMME]

3. PAGANISM IN NORTH ARABIA

Before Islam and the religious beliefs of the Nabataeans and Palmyrenes, there existed among the tribes of the central and northern portions of the Arabian Peninsula a pantheon and cult that assumed growing importance. Being more or less nomadic, these northern tribes retained certain primitive traits found also in the religion of the Hebrews of the patriarchal era.

Early North Arabians. The earliest firsthand information on North Arabia is from Assyrian annals. For the Neo-Babylonian period we have a few proto-Arabic graffiti. Their consonant script is related to that of South Arabic inscriptions. The most ancient are those of Dedan (Is 21.13–14); but those of Tema follow closely and constitute Thamudic A (6th and 5th centuries B.C.). The tribe of Thamud was already mentioned in the annals of Sargon II for the year 714 B.C.; but in the proto-Arabic graffiti its name does not appear until the end of the Persian era and during the Hellenistic era. (Thamudic B, in the Nejd). At Dedan the tribe of Liḥyan was in control during this time. Its script (Liḥyanite A and B) derives from Dedanite. At the Roman epoch and in the early Byzantine era, the proto-Arabic alphabet continued to be used, with increasingly cursive forms: Thamudic C and D in the Dedan region, E in the regions of Tebuq and Petra, and the so-called Ṣafaitic script in the eastern and southeastern Hauran. The explorations of H. St. John B. Philby and of G. and J. Ryckmans show that the more southerly routes also, which lead from MECCA or Ryad to YEMEN, are covered with proto-Arabic graffiti. Studies of these indicate that they should not be attributed to the Thamudeans, inasmuch as classical and Arabic sources situate this tribe only in the northwestern portion of the peninsula. The Aramaean sources are represented by the famous stele of Tema (6th century B.C.), by the Nabataean and Palmyrene inscriptions (1st century B.C. to 3d century

A.D.), and by a few passages of Syriac literature. It has been possible to glean precious information from Greek Byzantine writings and Arabic authors. In fact, the Book of Idols of Ibn al-Kalbi (*c.* A.D. 800) deals exclusively with this subject.

The Pantheon. A description of the gods of ancient North Arabia can best be made by considering separately the inscriptions, according to their provenance, that mention these gods.

The Cuneiform Texts. The annals of Esarhaddon (680–669) contain a list of the Arabic gods of Adumatu, the Duma of Gn 25.14 (Pritchard ANET 291b). At the head of the list is Atar-samain, i.e., Atar-of-the-heavens. It is the god 'Athtar of Ugarit (15th century) and of the southern Arabs. But here it is a goddess, like the Babylonian Ishtar and the Phoenician Astarte (1 Kgs 11.5). 'Athtar (this seems to be the primitive form of these four names) is above all the personification of the planet Venus, whence the vagueness in the attribution of sex. The brilliant star of morning and evening, so familiar to the nomad, thus supplemented El, the ancestral deity of the Semites. ("El" appears also under the augmentative form "Ilah," whose plural of majesty is the Hebrew "Elohim.") The fourth god in the list is Ruldaiu, who is also mentioned by Ibn al-Kalbi under the form of Ruḍa. The corresponding root signifies "to satisfy," and various indices lead one to think that Ruḍa is the name of Mercury, the beneficent planet.

Dedan and *Liḥyan, Thamud* and *Ṣafa.* The proto-Arabic inscriptions of Dedan give little information on the autochthonous gods of the Neo-Babylonian era. The name of the supreme god El is found only in personal names. Thus a "king of Dedan" was named Kabir'el, son of Mati'el. The names ending in *'ēl* and in *'ilah* are more numerous in the various proto-Arabic dialects than those in honor of any other deity. Taken as a whole, they are to be considered as survivals, for it has been proved that they were preponderant in ancient Akkadian and in proto-Aramaic. Since the word *'ēl* corresponds to the word god, it has been rightly concluded that the proto-Semites invoked only El. In fact, if the word god had applied to various deities, the personal names in *'ēl* would have had an equivocal meaning. It is legitimate to translate El as God, but this practical monotheism does not imply a clear awareness that the gods adored by neighboring peoples did not exist. The reason that the primitive Dedanite and Thamudic texts now known contain no direct invocation to El or Ilah is perhaps because of the rarity of these graffiti. In Thamudic B several examples have been found that cannot be interpreted as innovations or said to have been borrowed. The authors of the graffiti in Thamudic A gave first place to Ṣalam. His name, which signifies

Image, was actually accompanied by the image of the ox-head; in South Arabia this was generally the symbol of the lunar god, who was almost as important as the god 'Athtar. The Aramaic stele of Tema also names Ṣalam, with the same representation of an oxhead. The moon regularly accompanies Venus; 20 kilometers east of Tema, Philby discovered a Thamudic graffito in which a "king of Duma" invokes 'Atarsam and Ṣalam.'' The first name is a shortened form of Atar-samain. Venus seems also to have been designated by the appellation al-Ilat, the Goddess, in a contemporary graffito, an appellation that was afterward widely accepted. We find this name also in Herodotus in the mid-5th century. The Arabs of Sinai invoked Orotal and Alilat in their oath, names they gave to Dionysus and heavenly Aphrodite (*Histories,* 3.8; 1.131). The form Orotal is the approximate pronunciation of Ruḍa by a Greek, the *ḍ* giving rise to a light "l" sound. Ruḍa was identified with Dionysus as the god of renewed vegetation. The explorations of N. Glueck have shown that the Sinai Peninsula has almost always been partly under cultivation. As for the heavenly Goddess, she is also attested to by the Aramaic dedication of a silver bowl ''offered by Qainu, son of Geshem, king of Qedar [see Is 21.16] to han-Ilat'' (*han* is an ancient form of the Arabic article *al*). The tribe of Qedar lived nomadically in the north of Dedan, and our Geshem was doubtless the same ''Geshem the Arab'' of Nehemia 2.19, thus bringing us back to the mid-5th century B.C. At Dedan the Liḥyanites also adored Ilat, and this goddess first appeared under the name of 'Uzzai, the very strong one, in a text in Liḥyanite A. In South Arabia 'Athtar was given similar epithets, no doubt as the Morning Star. Other inscriptions in Liḥyanite A name han-Aktab, i.e., the scribe, the Arabic counterpart of the god-scribe Nebo, whose planet was Mercury. Thus han-Aktab could very well be identical with Ruḍa, frequently invoked in the Thamudic B graffiti, which were in part contemporaneous. The Liḥyanite texts name Dhu-Ghabat even oftener, i.e., the One from Ghabat, an oasis north of Medina. Dhu-Ghabat is an anonymous appellation in truly Arabic manner, referring perhaps to han-Aktab himself. The Thamudic B graffiti are addressed also to 'Atarsam. Thus in the Persian era, the North Arabic pantheon is consistently astral. One qualification to this must be made by those who agree that the mysterious NHY (Nahay), the divine name that appears most frequently in Thamudic B, is merely a phonetic variation of LHY or 'LHY (Lahay, Ilahay), elongated forms of Ilah. In this case, the important tribe of Thamud would have reserved first place for the ancestral deity. But if we come down to the Greco-Roman era, we see that Ilah (sometimes elided to Lah) is mentioned far less often than Ruḍa, and especially than Ilat (or Lat).

The Nabataeans. At the end of the Persian era the Nabataeans, who had come from central or southern Arabia, displaced the Qedarites in the area extending from Dedan to Petra. They soon controlled all of Transjordania and even southern Syria. At Gaia (modern Wadi Musa), a village close to which flowed the spring that also watered Petra, a god of anonymous appellation was venerated: Dushara, the One of the Shara. This Arabic word signifies region and even to this day designates the mountain range on whose western slopes Gaia was nestled. Two inscriptions described Dushara as the ''god of Gaia.'' According to the Alexandrian lexicographer Hesychios, Dusares (the Greek form of Dushara) was identified with Dionysus, as the god of vegetation and vineyards. The equation Orotal-Dionysus (made by Herodotus) thus suggests that the real Master of the Shara was none other than Ruḍa, which would explain the curious absence of this divine name in Nabataean texts. Besides, several dedications lend support to this identification, as well as to that of Ruḍa with the scribe-god Mercury. Thus the chief gods of the Nabataeans appear to have been Venus and Mercury. Venus was invoked also under the name of Allatu (the Goddess), in particular at Iram (modern Ramm) and Boṣra. Among the other Arabic deities named in the Nabataean inscriptions, the mysterious Hubalu and the goddess of fate Manawatu may be cited; both were invoked at Hegra.

Palmyra. Allat, Shamash (Shams), and Raḥim (the Merciful, likewise discovered in the Ṣafaitic graffiti) are Arabic gods who were adopted at Palmyra. To these may be added Arṣu, whose name represents another form of Ruḍa and who seems to have been invoked in a special way by the caravaneers. One relief shows him mounted on a camel before 'Azizu on horseback. The latter name is simply a masculine form of 'Uzza. Pairs of masculine deities are characteristic of the Palmyrene pantheon. Ma'an and Sha'ar, or Shalman and Abgal, should also be mentioned. They are the ''Ginnaye'' (whence the Arabic word *jinn*), i.e., ''protective'' gods. The name Gad, Fortune, expresses the same need of protection. Veneration was given the Gad of the village, the Gad of the gardens or of the olive tree, the Gad of Palmyra, the Gad of Taimay (the ancestor of a tribe). But the Arabic deities had been preceded by those of Babylon. The largest temple of the city was dedicated to Bel, the Master, whom Greek dedications called Zeus. He replaced the indigenous god Bol, whose goddess-consort was called 'Ashtor, the local pronunciation of 'Athtar (just as Bol equates with Bel, or rather with Baal). Bel was the great cosmic god, and by virtue of this title, the Sun and the Moon were associated with him, they being represented by Yarḥi-Bol and 'Agli-Bol. The second divine name signifies Bull-of-Bol, the horns symbolizing the crescent. Originally Yarḥi-Bol, i.e., Moon-of-Bol, also was represented by the crescent, but he was later transmuted into a solar god. 'Agli-Bol is often paired with another solar deity, Malak-Bel, and these two represent the two heavenly luminaries in the second triad, the triad of Be'el-Shemin, the Master-of-the-heavens, dispenser of fecundating rain. The inscriptions describe him as "master of the world," and as the "kind and remunerating" god. In the 2d and 3d Christian centuries the cult of Be'el-Shemin became anonymous. The many pyres dedicated to him were then offered "to the one whose name is blessed forever, the kind and remunerating one," a formula that translated an almost monotheistic attitude. The Jewish colony that resided in Palmyra or the philosophers who had been attracted to the princely court influenced this movement, but its origins were Semitic. The name of Ilahay is attested to on a relief in the Palmyrene region, the name of El or Ilah has been preserved in the onomastic (Rabbel, Zabdilah). Finally, several inscriptions attest to the cult of El-qōne-ra', i.e., of El-Creator-of-the-Earth, one of the Phoenician aspects of El. In the Nabataean region, there was no analogous purification of worship, but the numerous personal names ending in El or in Ilahay, e.g., Wahbilahay, "God has given," reveal an ancient heritage that was certainly related to the cult of Ilah among the Thamudeans.

The Arabs on the Eve of Islam. In the 7th century of our era, Thamud had disappeared, but the preaching of Muḥammad assumed faith in Ilah on the part of the Meccans, or rather faith in Allah (al-Ilah), the Creator of heaven and earth, the provider of fecundating rain and the savior from danger. When they were out in their boats they all prayed to Allah, but once back on land they "associated" other gods to him (Qur'ān, 29. 61–65). To the mind of Ibn al-Kalbi, the principal god of the Qa'ba, the sanctuary of Mecca, was Hubal, an anthropomorphous idol who was consulted by means of arrows. The prophet first set up Allah in opposition to him and then substituted Allah for him, holding Allah to be the Lord of the Qa'ba, which had been founded by Abraham and his son Ishmael (Qur'ān, 96.3, and 2.121).

The Jewish colonies of Tema, Khaibar, and Medina, as well as the colony of San'a in South Arabia, and the Christian community of Najran on the borders of Yemen, had created a climate of opinion favorable to the *ḥanifs,* or devout Arabs who were becoming aware of the impossibility of associating other gods to the supreme deity Ilah. Before the triumph of Muḥammad's efforts, there were certainly many idols on the peninsula. Ibn al-Kalbi enumerates 24; but most of these belonged to a particular ethnic group. In addition to Hubal, the Qoraish invoked al-Lat, al-'Uzza and Manāt (Manawat), a triad that is likewise mentioned in the Qur'ān. The cult of the goddess 'Uzza persisted even after the coming of Islam, for the

ritual of abjuration dating from the 9th century anathematized "worshippers of the Morning Star, i.e., Lucifer and Aphrodite, who is called Chabar in Arabic, i.e., the Great One." This ritual mentions also the great stone of the Ka'ba, "bearing a representation of Aphrodite." Is this betyl of 'Uzza the famous Black Stone of the Ka'ba, through which certain poorly Islamized Arabs continued to venerate Venus?

Cult. Pagan religion in ancient North Arabia had its own kind of idols and sanctuaries, its proper priests and rites, and its special funeral customs.

Betyls and Sanctuaries. The idols of the Arabs were often sacred STONES, considered as abodes of the gods, whence the word betyl (*bet-'el,* "house of the god"). The idol of Atar-samain mentioned by Esarhaddon as having a golden star adorned with precious stones, the symbol of Venus-Ishtar (Pritchard ANET 301a), was probably a betyl. Several South Arabic texts describe 'Athtar as Ḥagar, i.e., stone. We know other betyls of the goddess, under the name of 'Uzza, Allat, or Kokabta (Star). The betyl of Dushara was "a black stone, quadrangular and aniconic, four feet high and two feet wide, resting on a gold base" (Suidas, s.v. "Theusares"). Philo of Byblos says that the betyls were "animates," and the Arabs did not escape the danger of litholatry. The people who lived on the banks of the Orontes river venerated a "Zeus-Betyl, ancestral god," and the North Syrians venerated "the ancestral gods Symbetylos and Leōn" (the associated gods Betyl and Lion). Another degradation of the divine was the worship of the "seat" of the deity, i.e., of the throne or base beneath the betyl, sometimes even when the betyl was not there. The Nabataean inscriptions introduce us to the god Motaba (seat). An analogous phenomenon was the deification of the altar. In North Syria, which was strongly Arabized, dedications to Zeus-Altar have been found; and the Nabataean stone pyres, which the inscriptions call *masgida,* might first have been betyl altars. Porphyry says likewise that the Arabs of Duma used their altars as if they were idols (*De Abstinentia,* 2.56). By extension, the word *masgida* designates the sanctuary and has been borrowed by Islam with this particular signification (MOSQUE).

The cult of betyls did not exclude the cult of divine effigies. In Palmyra the sacred stones of the Arabs never supplanted cultural beliefs. And temples in the strict sense were not unknown in Arabia, especially in Palmyra, where the temples of Bel and of Be'el-shemin are still standing. Within the cella of the temple of Bel two large cult niches face each other, both described by the name "Holy" in an inscription (cf. the Holy of Holies of the Temple of Jerusalem). The rear of the principal temple of Petra has three compartments, according to a plan well known in Syria; the central one was no doubt occupied by the betyl of Dushara described by Suidas. In the Nabataean region, there are also sanctuaries with small cellae, sometimes designated by the word *rab'ata* (square), which corresponds to the Arabic *ka'ba*, "cubic" chapel. The Black Stone, of volcanic origin, is immured in the Ka'ba of Mecca. Nabataean chapels were sometimes encased inside a second wall, with a stairway between the two. This is the plan of the Iranian fire temples. The *ḥammana* mentioned in certain Palmyrene and Nabataean dedications is perhaps a fire temple.

Priests and Rites. Priests were designated by various terms, such as the Aramaic *kumra* (in the Bible: priest of the idols); the Akkadian *apkal,* which signifies wise man in that language, but which in the Arabic cults alludes to a category of priests; or the Arabic *kāhin,* diviner. This last was used in Hebrew also, but to refer to Jewish priests. In the Assyrian era there were priestesses as well (*kumirtu, apkalatu*). And even at the time of the birth of Islam, women could be guardians of the *qobba* (the betyl tent). Divination with arrows (Ez 21.21) played an important role, and Ibn al Kalbi mentions an idol who was consulted by means of three arrows: the imperative, the prohibitive, and the expectative. The Arabs had communion sacrifices (1 Sm 20.4–6), but the Palmyrenes had holocausts as well. The essential rite was the pouring of the victim's blood against the altar (Ex 24.6) or against the betyl. At Boṣra the god A'ra was venerated, whose name signifies betyl "anointed" with blood. He was identified with Dushara. The sacrifice was followed by a sacred meal, in which the deity was supposed to take part. The existence of cult associations is attested to also by Nabataean inscriptions (the term is *marzeḥa,* cf. Jer 16.5). The ceremony of sacrifice was often preceded by processions or, more precisely, by circumambulations: the one around the Ka'ba of Mecca is still observed, obviously with a new significance. There are no Arabic liturgical anthologies in existence, but the proto-Arabic graffiti give us ample information on what the nomads asked of their gods. Thus Lat was invoked for security, but also for vengeance. There is little evidence of prayers of thanksgiving except those that are found in the Palmyrene dedications to the unnamed god.

The Dead. The Arabs shared the Semitic belief in the survival of the *nepeš* (i.e., the vital principle), which, being deprived of its body, was thought to lead a very reduced existence. The stone or stele erected on the tomb was supposed to localize the presence of the deceased one; in funerary texts it too is called *nepš,* a term that was ultimately applied even to mausoleums. At Palmyra the *nepš* was often a tower with several stories of sepulchers. The funerary temples and the hypogea were equally common. Elsewhere, and in particular in Petra, the word *nepš*

referred above all to the monument built of a square block of stone and surmounted with a pyramid. However, the majority of tombs in this city were hewn out of the rock, the façade being sculpted in the form of an edifice with merlons. The central room of these hypogea was sometimes used for the funeral banquet. According to a Hellenistic custom, the kings of the Nabataeans were divinized after their death. We know of a festival of Obodat the god. And on the Petra-Gaza route, the city of Eboda (modern Avdat) owed its name to the same Obodat I of the early 1st century, where the deceased king had his mausoleum (Stephen of Byzantium). We do not know how widely the Greek concept of the immortality of the soul had penetrated Arabia. Funerary paintings attest to such a belief in Palmyra, where a few inscriptions have been found that envisaged the survival of the soul in the Sun, in the Pythagorean manner. On the eve of the coming of Islam, Judaism and Christianity had made great inroads against Saracen paganism, certain tribes having even been converted to one or the other of these religions. But it is established that the Arabs in all epochs invoked Ilah (God), even when they associated idols with Him.

See Also: PALMYRA.

Bibliography: G. RYCKMANS, "Les Religions arabes préislamiques" in M. GORCE and R. MORTIER, *Histoire générale des religions,* 4 v. (rev. ed. Paris 1960) 4:201–228, 593–605. J. STARCKY, "Palmyréniens, Nabatéens et Arabes du Nord avant l'Islam," *Histoire des religions,* ed. M. BRILLIANT and R. AIGRAIN, 5 v. (Paris 1953–56) v.4. *Dictionnaire de la Bible* supplement, ed. L. PIROT et al. (Paris 1928–) 6:1088–1101; 7:951–1016. R. DUSSAUD, *La Pénétration des Arabes en Syrie avant l'Islam* (Paris 1955). H. LAMMENS, *L'Arabie occidentale avant l'Hégire* (Beirut 1928). H. SEYRIG, *Antiquités syriennes,* ser. 1–5 (Paris 1934–58) offprints from *Syria* (1931–57). M. HÖFNER, "Nord- und Central-arabien," in *Wörterbuch der Mythologie,* ed. H. W. HAUSSIG (Stuttgart 1961–) 1.1:407–481.

[J. STARCKY]

4. PAGANISM IN SOUTH ARABIA

South Arabic pre-Islamic religions are still in a rudimentary stage of investigation; no mythological or ritual text or important temple has been discovered, and the inscriptions that have been found need further study. Many interpretations offered by the Dane D. Nielsen, are definitive; others, though inaccurate, survive, viz, the identification of 'Il with the moon-god, the restriction of the South Arabic pantheon to the three astral deities, and the primacy of 'Attar in the pantheon (this last was maintained especially by J. Plessis).

Deities. The three great deities are the astral triad composed of the moon, Venus ('Attar), and the sun. Only these had official cults in the several kingdoms.

The Moon-god. The most important of the three great deities is the moon-god. His name as the national god varies in each kingdom, and the populations call themselves his children: the children of *Wadd* (Minaeans), of *'Ilumquh* (Sabaeans), and of *'Amm* (Qatabanians). The moon-god is also the protective deity of the main cities, where his most important temples existed, and he is represented as the owner of Qataban and Saba. In Saba, his chief name is *'Ilumquh* (*'Il* is power), often qualified by *Tahwan* [he who speaks (through his oracle)]; three other names allude to the phases of the moon. In Ḥadhramaut his principal name is *Sin*. In *Ma'in* his national name is *Wadd* (love). In Qataban his principal designation is *'Amman* or *'Ammum* (uncle); the epithets *ray'an* or *ray-'um* (he who grows) and *ray'an waṣaḥrum* (he who grows and rises), as well as the two names *Waraḥ* (month) and *Rub' Šahr* (the lunar quarter), refer to the phases of *Wadd*.

The Stellar God. The name of *'Attar* seems best explained by the Arabic adjective *'attār* (strong, brave, courageous); the name is often accompanied by the epithet *'izzān* or *'izzum* (strength). Other names of the stellar god mentioned in Sabaean texts are *Ḥagar* (stone), *Mutibnaṭiyan* (he who secures humidity), *Nawraw* (light), and *Saḥar* (dawn).

The Sun-Goddess. Unique in some ways is the sun-goddess. Like *'Atar*, she has a proper name, *Šams,* which is used in all the kingdoms, though sometimes treated as a dual, *Šamsay,* or plural, *'Ašams.* Like the moon-god, she also has diverse names. These are ordinarily given in antithetic pairs and do not characterize the sun-goddess as a national deity. In Saba, the two antithetic names *Ḏāt-Ḥimyām* (she who darts forth her rays) and *Ḏāt-Ba'dān* (she who is remote) refer respectively to the summer and winter sun. Other names are *Samayhat* (celestial), *Tadūn* (despised), and *Tanūf* (sublime). She is also described as *'Umm 'Attar* (the mother of *'Attar*). In Qataban, she is called *Ḏāt-Ẓahrān* (she who appears in her splendor) and *Ḏāt-Ṣantim* (she who fixes); a third name, *Ḏāt-Raḥbīn* (she who is broad), is sometimes added. The main phases of the sun's course are given in the names *Mašraqītān* (she who rises), *'Aṯirat* (bright), and *Maḥrudāwu* (she who declines). In *Ma'in,* the most common name is *Nakraḥ*. In Ḥadhramaut, her antithetic names are *Ḏāt-Ḥusūl* (she who is rejected) and *Ḏāt-Ḥimyām* as in Saba. In a few cases in the inscriptions all three of the deities are mentioned together, under an aspect of kindness or strength.

Lesser Gods. Minor deities protect persons, clans, families, and places; they are often referred to under the titles *'l* (god of . . .) and *b'l* (patron of . . .). We know of *Warafu,* the Qatabanian god of boundaries, and *Mundiḥ,* the god of irrigation. Other gods are named only by their attributes. Such in *Ma'in* are *Ḏū-'Awdān* (he

who preserves), *Madhuwāwū* (he who brings calamity), and *Muṭībqabṭ* (he who secures the harvest). In Saba there are *Balw,* a god connected with burial who is known also in Qataban; *Bašīr* (announcer of good tidings); *Halīm* (kind); *Halfān* (the oath); *Yiṯa'um* (savior); *Mutībmadgad* (he who guards the house); *Nasrum* (eagle); *Qaynān* (artisan); *Raḥīm* (gentle); *Rā'at* (frightening); and *Ta'lab* (he who collects, that is, the clouds). Several North Arabic, Syrian (*Rummān*), and Egyptian (*Osarapis*) deities also appear. Four deified persons also known are the Sabaean *'Azizlat, Hawf'il,* and *Yada'sumhu,* and the Awsanite king *Yaṣduq'il.*

Divine Attributes and Activities. Attributes and activities of the deities are described in detail in theophonic names. The divinity in general (*'il,* god) is generous, jealous, large of stature, and handsome; he speaks, orders, helps, and rewards; he also overwhelms and lacerates. He is considered as father, brother, king, lord, savior, protector, and lover of justice. Individuals are called his sons, servants, friends, etc. Theophoric names related to the three principal deities describe these same relationships. *'Ilumquh* is attested only once, in the name *'Amat'ilumquh* (the maid-servant of *'Ilumquh*); it is usually replaced by *'Awwām,* the name of the great moon temple near Mārib. Known inscriptions abound in data on the relations of the deities with one another, with men, and with things. Gods are sometimes represented as unequal and sometimes as equal to one another. *Wadd* orders sacrifices to be offered to *'Attar,* who commands the Sabaeans to build a temple for *'Ilumquh*. At times, offerings are presented to two different deities (e.g., *Tadūn* and *Sin*), or to three (e.g., *'Attar, Nakraḥ,* and *Wadd*), or to several (e.g., *'Amm, Ḏāt-Raḥān,* and the deities of the clan Rawyān); similarly, temples and altars are built and sacrifices offered to several deities at once. The deities command their worshipers to undertake particular work and sometimes help them to accomplish it. The gods are invoked as witnesses, guarantee possessions, and are owners of land.

Cult. Places of worship are both public and private. The exteriors of five of the larger temples have been described by travelers. Excavations have been made in five less important temples: in Yeḥa, Ethiopia; at Ḥureida and Ḥōr Rōrī, both in Ḥadhramaut; at Ḥeid bin 'Aqīl, Qataban; and at Ḥugga in Saba. At each site the three requirements for a temple were found: a cella with an altar, a reservoir or well with a drainage canal, and one additional room. The principal temples, such as 'Awwām in Mārib, doubtless were more complicated and included the *mdqnt* (oratory for prostrations), the *mśwd* (place for burning incense), and the *mḥtn/mlkn* (ceremonial place of the king). In addition to these, there probably was at least another place where either the originals or copies of various juridical protocols were kept under the protection of a god. There was a great variety of altars for incense (*mśwd* and *mqṭr*), libations (*mslm*), burnt offerings (*mṣrb*), and sacrifices (*mdbḥt*). Idols were doubtless used in the temples. The location of the idols in a temple is probably indicated by the inscriptions *tbt/'l'ltn* (the seat of the deities). Ceremonial utensils are probably indicated by the noun *ṣrf* in a text from al-'Amāyid at Mārib, and benches were discovered in the temple at Ḥōr Rōrī.

Temple Personnel. There were three classes of temple personnel: priests, superintendents, and assistants. The common noun for priest is *ršw* (fem. *ršwt*). While the specific difference between *ršw, šw'*, and *'fkl* (a loanword from Sumerian) is unknown, the *šhr* was probably a kind of priest-magician who gyrated around the altar or offering. The Qatabanian temple was administered by a group (*'rby;* sing. *rby*) of which a priest might eventually become a member. They had charge of the temple and the gifts it received, whether in money or in kind. There were also regular revenues from estates and properties, first fruits of the harvest, and tithes on individuals and clans. Some persons were oblates for various reasons; they probably assisted the priests in the maintenance of the temple. There is no evidence of the existence of sacred prostitution; expressions such as "son of *Wadd*" and "firstborn of *'Amm* and *Ḥawkum*," referring to an Awsanite king and a Qatabanian *mukarrib* respectively, are to be understood as metaphorical. The existence of private sanctuaries for household gods is indicated by expressions such as "his god," "his patron," and "the patron of their house." A sanctuary where incense was burned is represented as belonging to three courtiers of a Sabaean king.

Religious Customs. Private devotions included the use of a geometric symbol or of a symbolic animal along with an inscription, astral worship on the terraces of homes, and the cult rendered to the household gods. On the other hand, observances during pilgrimage were a part of the public cult. Religious solemnities are known only through ritual prescriptions for public worship: an ordinance prescribing purity for the feast of *Ḥalfān,* stipulations for offerings and ritual purity during pilgrimages, etc. Sexual relations were forbidden during certain periods of the year. Known texts do not establish the existence of a ritual hunt. Ablutions were required before entering the temple, and during ceremonies or acts of devotion it was forbidden to sit. For sacrificial banquets in the temple, however, when devotees partook of an animal victim cooked, as in *'Awwām,* with "onions and stinking herbs," they sat on benches, sometimes before a statue representing a deceased associate. Offerings to the deities frequently were outright gifts: persons made slaves or oblates, temple buildings and their appurtenances, statues, animals, all kinds of incense and spices, libations, and other tangible objects.

The texts commemorating these offerings ordinarily specify the reasons for the ritual act, the petitions addressed to the deities, and the occasions for thanksgiving. Personal, public, military, and historical considerations were involved, and the material dealing with these makes up the most detailed section of the inscriptions. Several texts refer to faults and sanctions of an unknown nature. Other acts of expiation were performed to atone for transgressions or precepts imposed by a god, violations of regulations on sexual purity, and violations of a god's property or of the immunity of the temple and of the documents it contained. Consultation of the deities doubtless took many forms. Only a few of them are known, among which are dice (*m'rb*, pl. *m'rbt*) and sorcery (*rqt*). The divine answer was immediate in the first case. In the second, however, the divinity had to make his decision known in some way; the texts speak of oracles (*ms'l*), dreams (*ḥlm*), and omens (*r'y* and *hr'yt*). The wearing of amulets was a common practice; many of them were inscribed with the magic formula "*Waddum* is father." Incantations (*'r'b*) were probably connected with the hunt, and there are indications of bewitching through an image (*ḥtt*). The invocation *'ynm/n'm* concerns the "good eye"; however, *šṣy,* which is commonly translated "evil eye," means "wickedness." Geometric and quasi-alphabetic forms in rock carvings are most probably emblems of clans, caravans, or individuals.

The astral character of the three main divinities must be seen as connected with the importance of the stars to communities whose wealth depended to a large extent on the caravan trade. Moreover, the rigors of the climate helped to produce an acute sense of helplessness and an anxiety for divine aid. The great diversity of deities matches a complexity of needs, and the frequency of recourse to the gods shows the people's desire to involve the divinity in every aspect of their lives; yet their devotion is strongly characterized by materialistic egocentricity.

Incipient Monotheism. None of the inscriptions tells us about the beginnings of monotheism in South Arabia; the so-called "Sabaean era," mentioned only in monotheistic texts, began roughly about 110 B.C. The texts with the monotheistic name of God number about 20 and date from the 4th or 5th centuries A.D. Their vocabulary, phraseology, and contents do not in any way differ from those of the polytheistic texts. In some inscriptions the use of a symbol and two monograms intimately connected with the moon-god suggests that the authors of these monotheistic texts indulged in syncretism. The one God is called *'lhn* (the God), *mr'* (Lord), or more often *rḥmnn* (the Merciful); and His name is normally followed by the epithet *b'l/smyn* or *smyn/w'rḍn* [Patron of heaven (and of earth)]. One expression is certainly Jewish: *rḥmn/ḏbsmyn/* . . . / *w'/lhhmw/rbyd* [the Merciful, He (who is) in heaven . . . and their God, master of Judah]; two others are Christian: *rḥhmnn/wmsḥhw/wrḥqds* (the Merciful and His Messiah and the Holy Spirit) and *rḥmnn/wbnhw/ krśtś/ǧbln* (the Merciful and His Son Christ the Victorious).

Bibliography: A. JAMME, "Le Panthéon sud-arabe préislamique d'après sources épigraphiques," *Muséon* 60 (1947) 57–147; "La Religion sud-arabe pré-islamique," *Histoire des religions,* ed. M. BRILLANT and R. AIGRAIN, 5 v. (Paris 1953–56) 4:239–307. D. NIELSEN, "Zur altarabischen Religion," *Handbuch der altarabischen Altertumskunde* (Copenhagen 1927) 1:177–250. G. RYCKMANS, "Les Religions arabes préislamiques," *Histoire générale des religions,* v.2 (Paris 1960) 200–228, 593–605.

[A. J. JAMME]

5. CHRISTIANITY IN ARABIA

Arabia here is taken to include the Arabian peninsula and, to the north of it, the desert and sown land adjacent to the territories of Rome and Persia. The period studied runs from the 1st to the 7th Christian century. Sources of evidence include lists of bishops at Church councils and inscriptions and writings in Greek, Syriac, Arabic, and South Arabic.

Northwest. The origins of Christianity in the northwest sector of this area are obscure. Among its bearers may have been "Arabs" of Pentecost (Acts 2.11) and Jewish Christians of Pella. Christian development here can be followed only partially. In the 3d century mention must be made of Origen, who intervened so fruitfully; of Philip the Arab, the officially pagan and privately Christian roman emperor; and of the martyrs of Philadelphia. Church organization in the region was marked by many small sees. The change from the patriarchate of Antioch to that of Jerusalem was evidenced at Chalcedon (451). It is interesting to note that, in the mounting conflict with the Monophysites, the Chalcedonians seemed to have clung to the churches of the small towns and villages. Arab phylarchs emerged from legend in the 4th century, but the first Ghassanid phylarch belonged to the early 6th century. Al-Ḥārith ibn Jabala (528–569), the second of this line, was something of a pious Monophysite Constantine. The picture of this late Arab Christianity includes the traits of monastic zeal and austerity; of rulers at times polygamous, who protected the Church, visited shrines, and yet projected through the pagan Arabic poetry the image of the pleasant life of wine, flowers, music, and women. The vigorous persecution of the Monophysites by the Melkites and the imperial distrust and treachery have their part in explaining the warm reception given by these Arab Christians to their Muslim brothers.

Northeast. Christian origins in the northeast sector also are poorly known. At Pentecost "Parthians, and Medes, and Elamites, and inhabitants of Mesopotamia" (Acts 2.9) were present. Toward the middle of the 3d century there were Christians in Hatra, and toward the end of the century Roman Christian captives in Babylonia. Ḥīra, the Lakhmid capital and a settled Arab town, was the earliest but not the only see among the Christian Arabs of this territory. Other sees lay north along the Euphrates and south along the western shore of the Persian Gulf. Even in Ḥīra not all the Arabs were Christian. The bishops of the Arab sees had their part in cutting the Persian Church off from Antioch (424) and orienting it into the path of Nestorianism (486). In the 6th century, Monophysites from the Roman zone were active and initiated the continuing Monophysite-Nestorian conflict. Lakhmid phylarchs, like their Ghassanid counterparts, emerge from legend in the 4th century. Of the 15 Lakhmid rulers, one was married to a Christian; two may have been Christian; one, al-Nu'man, the last of the line (d. 602), became a Christian. The quality of his Christianity, however, has to be appreciated in the light of his polygamy, his marriage to his stepmother, and his imprisonment and execution of the Christian to whom he owed his throne. Ḥīra was the principal center of the wine trade and naturally an inspiration of Bacchic poetry. The Christians of Ḥīra and al-Anbār (to the north on the Euphrates), through their Syriac alphabet, shared in creating the Arabic alphabet (early 6th century). The Arab Christians of this zone exercised a religious influence through the work of certain pagan and Christian poets. The extent of that influence is felt to have been reduced by the fact that Syriac, not Arabic, was their religious language, and also by a certain weakness in their Christian life.

Southwest. In the southwest or Ḥimyarite sector the rulers were polytheistic pagans until the late 4th century. Monotheistic terms, particularly *al-raḥmān* (the merciful), then began to be found in inscriptions. Far though this region was from Persia and Byzantium, both these empires sought to dominate it. Christianity came from Alexandria and directly from the emperor. The account of Christian origins mentions the names of SS. Bartholomew and Pantaenus. There was an Arian mission in the mid-4th century. A more influential mission was sent under Emperor Anastasius (491–518). It resulted in conversions and the ordination of a bishop. There were churches at Taphar, Aden, and Najrān. In 523, probably after an Abyssinian conquest and more conversions, Christianity was felt to wear the appearance of something protected by foreigners. A persecution followed under Masruḳ ḎHŪ NUWĀS (Dunaan of the Roman Martyrology), a member of the old ruling family and a Jew by religion. After the persecution the Abyssinians returned.

Abraha, a governor of the Abyssinian viceroy, revolted and achieved independence. Under his reign the number of priests dwindled while he vainly insisted that the Emperor Justinian should send a Monophysite bishop to ordain more. Abraha's expedition in the late 6th century against the Hijaz (al-Ḥijāz) may have been due to rivalry between his church at Sanʿāʾ and the Kaʿba of Mecca or to the desire to move against Persophile Jews in the Hijaz.

The Hijaz. In speaking of Christians in the Hijaz one must limit the term to mean Mecca, Taymāʾ, Khaibar, al-Ṭāʾif, and Medina. The existing evidence refers to the time just before or during the lifetime of Muḥammad. The Hijaz had not been touched by Christian preaching. Hence organization of a Christian church was neither to be expected nor found. What Christians resided there were principally individuals from other countries who retained some Christianity. Such were African (mainly Coptic) slaves; tradespeople who came to the fairs from Syria, from Yemen, and from among the Christian Arabs under the Ghassanids or Lakhmids; Abyssinian mercenary soldiers; and miscellaneous others whose Christianity was evidenced only by their names. The few native Christians whose names have come down to us furnish us with more questions than answers. This Christianity had the marks that go with want of organization. It lacked instruction and fervor. It is therefore not surprising that it offered no opposition to Islam. Finally it is to be borne in mind that it was the Christianity in Arabia, here briefly sketched, that projected the image of Christianity seen in the Qurʾān.

Bibliography: R. AIGRAIN, *Dictionnaire d'histoire et de géographie ecclésiastiques*, ed. A. BAUDRILLART et al. (Paris 1912) 3:1158–1339, with detailed bibliog.; scholars still find the essentials on this subject in this masterly study. J. ASSFALG, *Lexikon für Theologie und Kirche*, ed. J. HOFER and K. RAHNER (Freiburg 1957–65) 1:788–789. P. GOUBERT, *Byzance avant l'Islam*, 2 v. (Paris 1951–55) v.1. G. RENTZ, *Encyclopedia of Islam*, ed. B. LEWIS et al. (Leiden 1954) 1:533–556. S. SMITH, "Events in Arabia in the 6th Century A.D.," *Bulletin of the School of Oriental and African Studies* 16 (1954) 425–468; facing 426, detailed and helpful map. J. RYCKMANS, *La Persécution des chrétiens himyarites au sixième siècle* (Istanbul 1956).

[J. A. DEVENNY]

ARABIAN PHILOSOPHY

"Arabian philosophy" usually denotes the philosophical thought of those inhabitants of the Islamic world who were influenced by Greek learning but used the Arabic language as their medium of expression. An Arabian philosopher, therefore, was not necessarily a native of the Arabian peninsula but perhaps a native of Persia, like Avicenna, or of Spain, like Averroës, or of any of the lands conquered by the followers of Muḥammad. Since the Arabic word for philosopher, *failasūf,* referred to one who made use of Greek learning, this account of Arabian philosophy begins with the transmission of Greek culture to the Arabic-speaking world, continues with an introduction to the thought of the major Arabian philosophers and the problems they discuss, and concludes with an indication of their influence on the Christian philosophers of the Middle Ages.

Greek and Arab background. The Arab world was introduced to Greek culture between the eighth and tenth centuries by the Syrian Christians. Having learned Greek to read theological works, the Syrians had also studied philosophical and scientific writings of the Greeks. They translated some of these into Syriac and, for the caliphs who employed them, especially for al-Mansur and al-Mamun, made Arabic translations either directly from the Greek or by way of Syriac translations. Notable among the Syrian Christian translators were Ḥunayn ibn Isḥāq (JOHANNITIUS) of Baghdad (809–873) and COSTA BEN LUCA (864–923), author of a work translated into Latin in the twelfth century as *De differentia spiritus et animae.* Among the works that the translators made available in Arabic were Plato's *Republic, Laws, Timaeus, Sophist; Aristotle's Organon, Physics, Metaphysics, De anima, Nicomachean Ethics;* and two pseudo-Aristotelian treatises with a Neoplatonic content, the so-called *Theology of Aristotle* and the LIBER DE CAUSIS.

Some of the theologians of Islam saw in Greek thought a danger to their religion. Influenced by the Jews and the Christians, whom he respected as "People of the Scripture," the Prophet Muḥammad had taught the unity of God, creation, the divine knowledge of individual things, and the resurrection of the body. These and other teachings expressed in the holy book of Islam, the QURʾĀN seemed to be challenged by the views of Greek thinkers.

Among the theologians, one group—the MUʿTAZILITES, the so-called people of unity and justice who were known as opponents of fatalism—began to use reason and argument, KALĀM, in their work as apologists of the Koranic teachings. Although they were regarded as too liberal and rationalistic by orthodox theologians, the latter group also began to use *kalām* against the *kalām* of the Muʿtazilites. Thus the orthodox theologians became the *Mutakallimun* (*Loquentes,* to the Latins), and the scholastic theology of Islam was founded.

One of the most influential of the early theologians was a man who renounced the Muʿtazilite views and became a Mutakallim, al-ASHʿARĪ (873–935). In an effort to exalt the power and the arbitrary will of God, he taught a cosmology of atomism. He held that matter was composed of separate and distinct atoms continually being recreated by God, with their accidents, in each instant of time. According to his view, fire does not cause burning, but God creates a being that is burned when fire touches a body. There are no secondary causes; the sole cause of all change is God.

A contrast to this attempt at a rational defense of a dogmatic position was the movement of SUFISM, or Islamic mysticism. The Sufis, or those clothed in wool (*sūf*), sought to achieve union with God through asceticism and prayer, first singly, and in the later history of the movement, through religious communities. Their early stress on religious practices was later combined with more speculative interests. Among the more famous Sufis was Rabi'a, the woman mystic of Basra (d. 801); al-Hallaj, a Persian who was tortured and executed for heresy in 922; and JALĀL AL-DĪN AL-RŪMĪ (d. 1273), a Persian mystical poet.

Arabian philosophers in the East. The religious movements of Islam influenced Arabian thinkers, but the first outstanding Arabian philosopher, the only one of Arabic descent, undertook the task of presenting Greek thought to the Muslims. Abū Yūsuf al-KINDĪ (*c.* 805–873), called "the first Peripatetic in Islam," translated and commented on some of Aristotle's works. His acceptance as a genuine work of Aristotle of the so-called *Theology of Aristotle,* an abridged paraphrase of the last three books of the *Enneads* of PLOTINUS, was to give a Neoplatonic tinge to the Arabs' interpretation of Aristotle. A prolific writer with a wide range of interests, al-Kindī wrote more than 260 treatises on such varied subjects as mathematics, music, astronomy, optics, meteorology, medicine, politics, logic, and psychology. His treatise on the intellect, circulated in Latin translation during the Middle Ages, shows his interest in the problems of Aristotle's *De anima* and the influence of Alexander of Aphrodisias, the Greek commentator on Aristotle. al-Kindī's teachings concerning the "first intelligence that is always in act," distinct from and superior to the soul, marks the beginning of the Arabian doctrine of one agent intellect for all men.

Alfarabi (*c.* 870–950) was born in Turkistan and studied at Baghdad. Known as "the second master" (Aristotle being the first), he wrote commentaries on Aristotle, and in his treatise *The Harmonization of the Opinions of Plato and Aristotle* tried to show a basic agreement in the thought of "the two founders of philosophy." Platonic influences are evident in his works on political theory, which include *Political Regime* and *Aphorisms of the Statesman.* Regarded as the founder of political philosophy among the Arabs, Alfarabi also had a great interest in metaphysics and anticipated Avicenna in the presentation of a Neoplatonic doctrine of emanation together with a distinction of essence and existence in creatures. His treatise on the intellect, known to medieval Europe in Latin translation, posits, like the treatise of al-Kindī, an agent intellect or intelligence that is a separated spiritual substance. This agent intelligence, by abstracting sensible forms, enables man's possible intellect to pass from potency to act and become first an "intellect in act" and, when in possession of knowledge, an "acquired intellect" (*intellectus adeptus*). When the human intellect has acquired almost every abstracted intelligible, then the intelligible forms that never did, do not, and never will exist in matter can become objects of direct human intellection. On man's abstractive knowledge of sensible being, Alfarabi thus seems to superimpose a non-Aristotelian intuitive knowledge of separated intelligible forms. His theory of intellect has been described as Aristotelian at its base and Neoplatonic at its summit.

Ibn Sina or, to the Latins, AVICENNA (980–1037) was born in Persia. Of his many works, one of the best known is his *Canon of Medicine;* its Latin translation was used as a standard textbook of medicine through the seventeenth century. His chief philosophical work was the *al-Shifa* (*The Cure*), which included sections on logic, mathematics, physics, and metaphysics. The last section sets forth a theory of emanation similar to that of Alfarabi. At the summit of Avicenna's universe is a Necessary Being, who is one, incorporeal, and the source of all other beings. Through this Being's act of self-reflection, the first effect, a Pure Intelligence, necessarily proceeds. This effect must be one, for from one simple thing, only one can proceed. When this First Intelligence thinks of the Necessary Being, it gives rise to a Second Intelligence. When the First Intelligence thinks of itself as necessary by the First Being, it gives rise to the soul of the outermost celestial sphere; when it thinks of itself as possible in itself, it gives rise to the body of this same sphere. Then the Second Intelligence, in similar fashion, gives rise to a Third Intelligence, and to the soul and body of the second sphere. This emanation of intelligences is halted only with the production of the sphere of the moon and the tenth or last intelligence, which is called the agent intellect. The agent intellect, instead of begetting the soul and body of a sphere, begets human souls and the four elements (*Meta.* 9.4, fol. 104v–105r).

This theory is primarily a description, in temporal imagery, of the eternal relation of the world to God. It is meant to safeguard the unity of the Necessary Being and to stress that creatures that are "possible in themselves but necessary through another" depend for their actual existence upon that Being. In addition to its metaphysical implications, as for example, the real distinction of essence and existence, the theory also has implications for a doctrine of intellect and the nature of man. Here the agent intellect, the last of the separated intelligences, is a spiritual substance and one for all men. From it intelligible forms or species are infused into the possible intellects belonging to individual human souls (*De anima* 5.5–6). Each human soul, although a form in its function of animating the body, is in itself an immortal spiritual substance, for a man could know himself to be, even without knowing whether he had a body (*De anima* 1.1, 5.4 and 7). Some of the views expressed by Avicenna seem consistent with the teachings of Islam, but an eminent theologian, Algazel, opposed him.

Al-Ghazzālī or ALGAZEL (1058–1111), a Persian, is regarded as one of the great theologians of Islam for his work, the *Iḥyā' 'Ulūm ad-Dīn,* on the renewal of religious knowledge. Called "the Muslim St. Augustine," he tells in his spiritual autobiography, *Deliverance from Error,* about his painful doubts concerning the basis of certitude, his search for truth among the theologians and philosophers, and his surrender of wealth and position to lead for ten years the life of a Sufi. One of his later achievements was to incorporate the values of Sufism into the orthodox Muslim tradition. Although he knew the positions of the philosophers, as is clear from his summary in the *Maqāṣid al-falāsifah* of the views of Alfarabi and Avicenna, he strongly opposed them. In his *Tahāfut al-Falācifah* he tried to show the limits of reason by exposing incoherence in the philosophers' handling of 20 important problems. Because many medieval Christians, including Albert the Great and Thomas Aquinas, knew only the *Maqāṣid* in Latin translation, and not the *Tahāfut,* they thought Algazel was a follower rather than an opponent of Avicenna.

Thought in the West. The Arabian philosophers mentioned so far belonged to the eastern part of the Arabian empire, but after the Arab conquest of Spain there was also an Arabian philosophy of the west. Ibn Baddja or, to the Latins, AVEMPACE (d. 1138), one of the first outstanding philosophers among the Arabs in Spain, wrote commentaries on Aristotle and some original works. In his *Regime of the Solitary* he discussed the philosophical means by which man could achieve union with the agent intellect. A younger contemporary, Abū Bakr ibn Ṭufail or, to the Latins, Abubacer (*c.* 1105–85), is famous for his novel, *Hayy ibn-Yaqẓan,* an allegorical statement of the author's position on faith and reason. It was also Ibn Ṭufail who introduced Ibn Rushd at the court of the caliphs in Spain.

Ibn Rushd or, to the Latins, AVERROËS (1126–98), was born at Cordova, Spain. He studied theology, law, medicine, and philosophy. He wrote a work on medicine

that was known to Christian thinkers as *Colliget* and used by them as a textbook. He wrote a paraphrase of Plato's *Republic* and commentaries on many of the works of Aristotle, including the *Metaphysics, Physics, On Generation and Corruption, Nicomachean Ethics,* and *De anima.* For him, Aristotle was "the Master," and any attack on him or his followers had to be answered. In the *Tahāfut al-Tahāfut (The Incoherence of the Incoherence),* Averroës attempts to destroy Algazel's "destruction" of the philosophers. Averroës implies, in *The Accord between Religion and Philosophy,* that the philosopher sees truth as it is; the ordinary believer attains only a symbolic representation of the truth. The troublemakers of Islam are not the philosophers, he claimed, but the theologians who arouse the people against each other by openly teaching different interpretations of the Qur'ān.

On the question of the world's relation to God, philosophy might seem to oppose religion. Religion teaches that the world had a beginning and was created *ex nihilo;* for Aristotle and Averroës the world existed necessarily and eternally. Averroës rejected Avicenna's "concessions" to the theologians (*In 4 meta.* 3). He rejected the principle that from one only one can proceed, the type of emanation theory that Avicenna developed from that principle, and the Avicennian distinction between existence and essence (*Tahāfut al-Tahāfut,* disp. 3.182; *In 4 meta.* 2–3). For Averroës being is substance, and God may be called a cause of being insofar as "the bestower of the conjunction of matter and form is the bestower of existence" (*In 4 meta.* 3; *Tahāfut al-Tahāfut,* disp. 3.180). Thus both the philosopher and the simple believer may say that the world is dependent upon an eternal "Creator," but the philosopher, in Averroës's view, gives a more exact statement of this truth.

On the intellect Averroës held not only that the agent intellect is a separated substance and one for all men, but that this is true also of the possible intellect. The highest powers of the individual human soul are the COGITATIVE POWER, IMAGINATION, and memory, and their task is to prepare phantasms for the separated intellects to use. When the separated agent intellect has made the intelligible species potentially present in these phantasms actually intelligible, the separated possible intellect is put in act (*In 3 de anima,* comm. 4–6, 32–33). Averroës's doctrine was meant to ensure the spirituality of the possible intellect and the universality of its knowledge, but by denying to man a spiritual power of knowing, it seemed to destroy the philosophical basis for maintaining the immortality of the individual human soul.

The intellect and knowledge, the relation of the world to God, and the relation of philosophy and religion are topics that were often discussed by Arabian philosophers. They were also interested in science, but for the Arabs' accomplishments in this field one would have to consult the work of such astronomers as al-Battani (Al-batani, *c.* 900), al-Farghani (Alfraganus, *c.* 860), al-Biṭrūjī (Alpetragius, *c.* 1180), and such mathematicians as Alkwarizmi (*c.* 830) and Alhazen (*c.* 1000). All these men were known to medieval Christians through Latin translations of some of their writings.

Influence on Christian philosophy. One of the main channels by which Arabian works were transmitted to Christian Europe was the school of translators founded during the first half of the twelfth century by Archbishop Raymond at Toledo, Spain. As these works became available in Latin translation, the names of their authors began to be cited by Christian thinkers. The influence of Avicenna and Averroës on Christian thought is especially notable. DOMINIC GUNDISALVI, ROGER BACON, and JOHN PECKHAM identified Avicenna's agent intelligence with the Christian God. Other thinkers, including WILLIAM OF AUVERGNE, HENRY OF GHENT, Duns Scotus, and THOMAS AQUINAS, although critical of Avicenna's teachings, were favorably impressed by some aspects of his metaphysics.

Averroës was known to Christian thinkers as "the Commentator" on Aristotle. Those who, like SIGER OF BRABANT, had read his commentaries in Latin translation and accepted as necessary conclusions of human reason such teachings as the eternity of the world and unity of the intellect for all men, were called Latin Averroists (*see* AVERROISM, LATIN). Because they refrained from asserting that these teachings were true, they thought they could still be good Christians. But seeing in such views a source of error, Bishop Tempier of Paris condemned these and related propositions in 1270 and 1277. Three of the leading thinkers of the thirteenth century attacked the errors of Averroës: St. Albert in *De unitate intellectus contra Averroem;* St. Bonaventure, especially in the *Collationes in Hexaemeron,* Sermo VI; St. Thomas Aquinas, especially in *De aeternitate mundi contra murmurantes* and *De unitate intellectus contra Averroistas.* Because these refutations were not always understood or accepted, Averroism continued to flourish, especially in Italy, during the fourteenth, fifteenth, and sixteenth centuries. The history of western philosophy from the twelfth to the sixteenth centuries is, in part, an account of the influence of Arabian thought on Christian philosophers.

See Also: DOUBLE TRUTH, THEORY OF; INTELLECT, UNITY OF; NEOPLATONISM; SCHOLASTICISM; ISLAM.

Bibliography: É. H. GILSON, *History of Christian Philosophy in the Middle Ages* (New York 1955). W. M. WATT, *Islamic Philosophy and Theology* (Edinburgh 1962). T. J. DE BOER, *The History of Philosophy in Islam,* tr. E. R. JONES (London 1933). M. FAKHRY, *Islamic Occasionalism and Its Critique by Averroës and Aquinas* (London 1958). D. O'LEARY, *How Greek Science Passed to the Arabs* (London 1949); *Arabic Thought and Its Place in History* (New York 1939). É. H. GILSON, "Les Sources gréco-arabes de l'augustinisme avicennisant," *Archives d'histoire doctrinale et littéraire du moyen-âge* 4 (1929) 5–149.

[B. H. ZEDLER]

ARAMAEANS

An ancient northwest Semitic people who inhabited the area between the Taurus Mountains and the Arabian Peninsula, east of the Lebanon and principally in Upper Mesopotamia about the Tigris, Euphrates, Habur, and Balih Rivers. This region was called Aram, or Paddan-Aram, or Aram-Naharaim ("Aram of the two rivers"). This article will discuss the folkloric origins and historical emergence of this ancient people, the development of the Aramaean states, their religion and language, and the Nabataean and Palmyrene kingdoms.

Folkloric Origins and Historical Emergence. The Old Testament made Aram, the descendant of Shem (Gn 10.22–23; 1 Chr 1.17), the son of Noah, the progenitor of the Aramaeans, thus relating them to the Semitic peoples. Kemuel, "the father of Aram" (Gn 22.21), was born to Nahor, brother of Abraham; Laban, Rebekah's brother, was "the son of the Aramean Bethuel," another son of Kemuel (Gn 28.5). Israel thus remembered that its patriarchs were Aramaeans (Dt 26.5) who first learned Hebrew, the language of Canaan, when they arrived in Palestine. According to Amos 9.7, the Aramaeans came from Kir (see also Am 1.5), a place not identified with certainty, but associated with Elam in Isaiah 22.6.

Unsuccessful attempts have been made to trace the Aramaeans back to the beginning of the third millennium; the first certain appearance of this people is found in historical records of the twelfth century B.C. From the early second millennium B.C., however, there is evidence of a people in northern Mesopotamia with west-Semitic names who may be the forebears of the Aramaeans later found in Syria and Palestine. Moreover, a nomadic people, called Aḥlame, appear in Assyrian records [of the time of King Arikden-ilu (1325–1311 B.C.)], emerging from the Syrian-Arabian Desert, attacking Assyrian lands and towns, and gradually settling down in the northern Mesopotamian area. The specific "Aramaean" type of Aḥlame appears only in the late twelfth century. In the fourth regnal year of Tiglath-Pileser I (1115–1076 B.C.) a major campaign was first recorded against "Aramaean Aḥlame" in the area about the confluence of the Ḥabur and Euphrates Rivers. Their invasion of Assyrian territory was persistent, and Tiglath-Pileser I eventually had to conduct 28 campaigns against them. Soon thereafter an Aramaean usurper, Adad-apil-iddin (1079–1058 B.C.), mounted the throne of Babylon. To this wave of Aramaean invaders belongs also the origin of the Chaldeans, who settled in southern Babylonia probably in the tenth century. But the most important area penetrated by the Aramaeans was Syria, on both sides of the Upper Euphrates; it became known as Aram (Nm 23.7; 22.5). The Aramaeans never formed one great empire to rival the empires of the Assyrians or the Babylonians, but lived, instead, in small federated states.

Aramaean States. Although historical data about the Aramaean states at the beginning of the first millennium B.C. are scarce, the eventual emergence of these must have been the result of their importance, which fluctuated constantly as certain areas were dominated now by one, now by another of their more powerful neighbors. Eleventh-century cuneiform texts reveal Bit-Adini (Beth-Eden in Am 1.5) in north Syria, with its capital at Til-Barsip, as the most important Aramaean state of that time. In the ninth and eighth centuries B.C. the prominent states were Arpad (2 Kgs 18.34) in northern Syria, with such places as Aleppo and Nerab its vassal kingdoms; Hamath (2 Kgs 18.34) in central Syria, with 19 vassal districts; and DAMASCUS in southern Syria. Damascus (often called simply Aram) figured prominently in the history of Israel. Rezon I, who had rebelled against Hadadezer, king of Zobah (1 Kgs 11.23–25), set up the Damascene dynasty during Solomon's reign.

Four other Aramaean states are mentioned in the Old Testament. Zobah (2 Sm 8.3–8) was a state north of Damascus in the Beqa', rich in silver and copper. At a time when it outranked Damascus, David defeated its king, Hadadezer, son of Rehob. Beth-Rehob (2 Sm 10.6) was a small state east of the Jordan and north of Ammon, whose armies the AMMONITES hired to fight David. Maacah (2 Sm 10.6), a small state at the southern ends of the Lebanon and Anti-Lebanon ranges, west of Dan, had once belonged to Israel, but was conquered by Ben-hadad I of Damascus. Geshur (2 Sm 3.3; 13.37–38) was a small state east of the Sea of Galilee. Other Aramaean states are known from inscriptions, such as Sam'al (Ya'di), 'Umq, Lu'ath.

Ben-Hadad I had 32 vassal kings in his Damascene army (1 Kgs 20.1, 24)—an indication of the multiplicity of Aramaean states in his time. The independence of these states came to an end with the campaigns of Tiglath-Pileser III, who subjugated most of them between 740 and 732 B.C. Little is known about the political history of the Aramaeans after they were incorporated into the Persian Empire in the sixth century. They continued to appear as traders and traveling merchants. Aramaean ethnic groups were found throughout the empire, even at Elephantine in Egypt, where they served along with Jews in a fifth-century military colony.

Religion and Language. The Aramaeans were not monotheistic, but rather venerated a pantheon headed by Hadad, the storm god, whose principal temple was in Aleppo (Ḥalab). His consort was apparently 'Attar (Ishtar—but 'Attar sometimes appears as a god!). In 2 Kings 5.18 Hadad is mentioned under the local Damascene epithet Rimmon ("Thunderer"; Zec 12.11); he was apparently also called *Ilu-wer* ("the god Wer") and *Be'elshamayn* ("Lord of the heavens") in the states of Hamath and Lu'ath (Zakur inscription a1, b20, 23; see J. B. Pritchard, *Ancient Near Eastern Texts Relating to the Old Testament* [2d rev. ed. Princeton 1955] 501–502). The Sefîre treaty between Bar-Ga'yah, king of *Ktk*, and Mati'el, king of the Aramaean state of Arpad (see *ibid.*), reveals that the Aramaeans admitted many Babylonian and Canaanite deities to their pantheon. Among the gods who are called to bear witness to the treaty are MARDUK and Zarpanit, Nabu (*see* NEBO) and Tashmet, Nergal and Laṣ, Shamash and Nur, Sin and Nikkal, Sibitti, El and 'Elyân (these last two Canaanite names eventually became epithets of the Old Testament Yahweh in Gn 14.22), Heaven and Earth, Abyss and Springs, and Day and Night (the last three pairs are personifications).

The early Aramaeans spoke a northwest Semitic language called Aramaic, cognate to the Hebrew and Canaanite dialects. Though derived from a common Proto-Semitic parent stock, it developed independently as a sister language of Hebrew and Phoenician, and constantly underwent influence from the languages spoken by the peoples who adopted it as a secondary language. It was widely used for international communication from *c.* 700 to 200 B.C., until it was superseded by Greek. (*See* ARAMAIC LANGUAGE.)

Nabataeans and Palmyrenes. Two later Aramaean kingdoms came to prominence at Petra in southern Transjordan and at PALMYRA in the Syrian Desert. The Nabataeans were originally nomads of obscure origins, perhaps connected with Nebaioth, the first-born of Ishmael (Gn 25.13; Is 60.7), or with the Nabate of eighth-to seventh-century Assyrian inscriptions (*ibid.*). They first clearly emerged near Petra *c.* 312 B.C., when they refused allegiance to Antigonus, a successor of Alexander the Great. As prosperous caravan traders, they conducted a flourishing commerce along the caravan route from the Persian Gulf across the Arabian Desert to the Palestinian and Syrian coasts. Though they spoke Aramaic, it was influenced by early Arabic, as was their religion and culture; indeed, their rulers sometimes bore the title, "King of the Arabs" (ὁ τῶν Ἀράβων τύραννος). Some of the chief names of the Nabataean dynasty are Aretas I (*c.* 169 B.C.), associated with the flight of the Jewish high priest Jason (2 Mc 5.8); Aretas III, the conqueror of Damascus *c.* 85 B.C.; Aretas IV (9 B.C. to A.D. 40), whose daughter was married to Herod Antipas, but was later repudiated by him in favor of Herodias (Mt 14.3–4). The ethnarch of Aretas IV controlled Damascus at the time of Paul's escape (2 Cor 11.32). The Nabataeans were conquered by the Romans in A.D. 106, and the Nabataean town, Bostra, became the capital of the Roman province, Arabia.

With the decline of the Nabataeans, the rich caravan trade passed into the hands of the Palmyrene Aramaeans. Palmyra was the Greek name used by the Romans for ancient Tadmor, a fertile oasis in the Syrian Desert. An amalgamation of Aramaean tribes settled there and dominated the caravan route from Babylon to Damascus. Though Tadmor had been inhabited much earlier (built by Solomon according to 2 Chr 8.4), it emerged into political importance only in the first century as a somewhat Hellenized kingdom. From that day until its final defeat in A.D. 272 by the Emperor Aurelian, it passed through various periods of Roman colonization and independent rule, a fact that reflected the unstable conditions of Mesopotamia in those centuries. The Aramaeans who settled there were considerably influenced by the spread of Hellenistic and Roman culture to that part of the world; many bilingual inscriptions (Aramaic and Greek) witness to this influence. Palmyra's heyday, which occurred during the reign of Odaenathus and Queen Zenobia (c. A.D. 260), immediately preceded its downfall.

Bibliography: R. T. O'CALLAGHAN, *Aram Naharaim: A Contribution to the History of Upper Mesopotamia in the Second Millennium B.C.* (Rome 1948). S. C. LAYTON, ''Old Aramaic Inscriptions,'' *Biblical Archaeologist* 51 (1988) 172–189. P. E. DION, *Les Araméens à l'âge du fer: Histoire politique et structures sociales* (*Études bibliques* 34; Paris 1997). A. DUPONT-SOMMER, *Les Araméens* (Paris 1949). A. ALT, ''Die syrische Staatenwelt vor dem Einbruch des Assyrer,'' *Kleine Schriften zur Geschichte des Volkes Israel*, 3 v. (Munich 1953–59) 3:214–232. W. T. PITARD, *Ancient Damascus: A Historical Study of the Syrian City-State from the Earliest Times until Its Fall to the Assyrians in 732 B.C.E.* (Winona Lake, Ind. 1987); ''Arameans,'' *The Oxford Encyclopedia of Archaeology in the Near East,* 5 v. (Oxford-New York 1997), 1.184–187. J. STARCKY, *Palmyre* (Paris 1952); ''The Nabateans: A Historical Sketch,'' *Biblical Archaeologist* 18 (1955) 84–106. I. BROWNING, *Palmyra* (Park Ridge, N.J. 1979). R. STONEMAN, *Palmyra and Its Empire* (Ann Arbor, Mich. 1992). S. ABOU ZAYD, ed., ''Palmyra and the Aramaeans,'' ARAM 7 (1995 [whole issue]).

[J. A. FITZMYER]

ARAMAIC LANGUAGE

One of the SEMITIC LANGUAGES, belonging, together with Ugaritic, Phoenician, HEBREW, and other Canaanite dialects, to the Northwest Semitic group. Originally spoken by ARAMAEANS in northern Syria and Mesopotamia, it gradually became the lingua franca of the ancient Near East from India to Egypt. In importance it rivaled Phoenician and far surpassed Hebrew. It is the general name for various dialects often difficult to classify.

Four main phases of ancient Aramaic are distinguishable: Old Aramaic, Official Aramaic, Middle Aramaic, and Late Aramaic. For the sake of completeness, a few words will be added concerning its survival in the dialects of Modern Aramaic.

One of the features that make Aramaic distinct from all the other Semitic languages is the phonetic shift whereby the Proto-Semitic fricative interdentals, which were largely retained in Arabic and South Arabic and which became sibilants in Akkadian and Canaanite (Hebrew), became simple dentals in Aramaic; thus, Proto-Semitic $d, t, \underline{t}$ became respectively $z, š, ṣ$ in Akkadian and Canaanite, but $d, t, ṭ$ in Aramaic. But in Old Aramaic this shift had apparently not yet taken place in all local dialects. Old Aramaic was written in a script borrowed from the Phoenician script of only 22 consonants, which had no letters for fricative interdentals. The indiscriminate writing of the demonstrative particle as both d and z in Official Aramaic documents seems to show that this particle was still pronounced as $\underline{d}$ (as in Proto-Semitic). The phoneme that was $\underline{d}$ Proto-Semitic (voiced emphatic interdental), which shifted to $ṣ$ in Canaanite, became in Aramaic first q (*qoph*) and then ' (*'ayin*).

Another characteristic of Aramaic is its means of expressing determination (the definite article). Proto-Semitic had no article; Akkadian did not develop one. In Canaanite (e.g., Hebrew) the article was expressed by prefixing *ha*'- to the substantive; in Aramaic it was expressed by suffixing -a at the end of the substantive. Finally, at least in the later periods of the language, Aramaic reduced to zero grade unaccented short vowels much more than the other Semitic languages did, especially in the pretonic syllable (syllable before the accented syllable).

Old Aramaic. The earliest attested phase of Aramaic extends from *c.* 925 to *c.* 700 B.C. Inscriptions from northern Syria, written in the borrowed Canaanite (Phoenician) alphabet, preserve dedications and treaties in a language that is basically Aramaic, but distinct from its later phases by the retention of Canaanite phonetic and syntactic features. Probably not many centuries earlier both Aramaic and Canaanite developed from a common mother-language (Proto-Northwest-Semitic). Except for two inscriptions from Zinjirli, *Hadad* and *Panammu,* the rest (e.g., *Ben-Hadad, Zakur, Sefire I–II–III, Nerab I–II;* see J. B. Pritchard, *Ancient Near Eastern Texts Relating to the Old Testament* 501–05) present a fairly homogeneous picture of this early Aramaic.

Official Aramaic. During the Assyrian domination of the 7th century, Aramaic developed a characteristic form and came to be used widely in the Levant as a means of international communication, probably due to traveling Aramaean merchants. The name "Imperial" was given to this form of Aramaic, which lasted from *c.* 700 to *c.* 200 B.C., in the belief that its standardization was due to the Persian imperial chanceries' use of it for communication in their far-flung administration. Though its international use clearly antedated that empire (see 2 Kgs 18.26; Asshur Ostracon, dated *c.* 650, in which an Assyrian official writes to a colleague in Aramaic), the Persian imperial administration certainly furthered its use and standardization. Documents from 5th-century Egypt show how it was used for contracts, letters, and notes about household affairs between Jews and Egyptians or other Jews (Pritchard, *Ancient Near Eastern Texts Relating to the Old Testament* 427–30, 491–92). The largest group of Official-Aramaic texts has come from Egypt (Elephantine, Saqqarah, Hermopolis West, etc.). The correspondence of the satrap, Arsames, was found in Egypt, but written apparently in Babylon. To this phase also belongs Biblical Aramaic (see below).

Likewise from this period come the Aramaic ideographs in Middle Persian (i.e., words written as Aramaic but read as Persian) and inscriptions from such places as Arabia, Persia, Asia Minor, India, and Afghanistan. It is also during this period that Aramaic gradually supplanted Hebrew in Palestine, although small areas or levels of society always remained where Hebrew too was used. With the fall of the Persian Empire, Aramaic was replaced gradually by Greek as the international language, but it persisted in wide use among Semitic peoples.

Middle Aramaic. This phase of Aramaic is a slight development of the former, when Aramaic, lacking the normative control of royal chanceries, began to break down into dialects. To be grouped here is the Aramaic used between roughly 200 B.C. and A.D. 200. To this phase belong (1) in Palestine: the Nabataean inscriptions of PETRA (Aramaic with early Arabic influence), Qumran Aramaic, Murabba'at Aramaic (*see* DEAD SEA SCROLLS), the beginnings of Rabbinical literature, inscriptions on Jewish OSSUARIES and tombstones, the Aramaic words in the NT and Josephus; and (2) in Syria and Mesopotamia: the inscriptions found at PALMYRA, Hatra, etc. Local dialects now appear, especially Palestinian, Nabataean, and Palmyrene, but they are still a closely related development of Official Aramaic. The discovery of Qumran-Aramaic texts fills in a gap in our knowledge of Palestinian Aramaic that previously existed between the final redaction of Daniel (*c.* 165 B.C.) and the first of the Rabbinical writings (*Megillat Ta'anit* or "Scroll of Fasting," *c.* A.D. 100). Whereas Palestinian Aramaic of this period was previously known almost exclusively from short funerary inscriptions, there are now about 125 literary texts, which reveal the type of Aramaic in use in Palestine at the time of Jesus Christ. Moreover, several scraps of Tar-

gums have also been found there, which suggest that some of the Targums that are extant only from a later date (Yerushalmi I–II, Neofiti) may possibly preserve older translations belonging to this period.

Late Aramaic. In this phase, which extends from about A.D. 200 to 700 mainly, but in certain areas lasted even longer (into the Middle Ages), a clear distinction can be made between Western Aramaic, which includes Syro-Palestinian Christian Aramaic, Samaritan Aramaic, and Palestinian Jewish Aramaic on the one hand, and Syriac, Babylonian Talmudic Aramaic, and Mandaic on the other. (Mandaic is the language of the Gnostic sect of Mandaeans in southern Mesopotamia; *see* MANDAEAN RELIGION.)

Syriac, the dialect of Edessa (modern Urfa in Turkey), became the most important dialect of Late Aramaic; it developed two chief forms, Eastern or Nestorian at Nisibis, Western or Jacobite at Edessa. This form of Aramaic, Syriac, persists as the liturgical language of several Eastern churches, among them the Chaldean, Malabar, Malankarese, Maronite, and Syrian Jacobite churches. (*See* SYRIAC LANGUAGE AND LITERATURE.)

Modern Aramaic. Aramaic has persisted into modern times, being spoken in the west in isolated villages of the Anti-Lebanon regions north of Damascus in Syria (by Christians in Ma'lūla, by Muslims in Jubba'dīn and Bakh'a); and in the east in three areas [by Jacobite Christians in Tur 'Abdīn, by Jews and Nestorian Christians ("Assyrians") between the Lakes Urmia and Van in Kurdistan and Azerbaijan, by Chaldean Christians in the region about Mosul]. Modern Aramaic is quite corrupt, having been heavily influenced by Kurdish, Turkish, and Arabic.

Bibliography: F. ROSENTHAL, *Die aramaistische Forschung seit Th. Nöldekes Veröffentlichungen* (Leiden 1939), basic. C. BROCKELMANN et al., "Aramäisch und Syrisch," *Handbuch der Orientalistik*, 3.2–3 (Leiden 1954) 135–204. E. Y. KUTSCHER, "Aramaic," in *Linguistics in South West Asia and North Africa* (Current Trends in Linguistics 6; The Hague 1971). K. BEYER, *The Aramaic Language,* tr. J. F. HEALEY, (Göttingen 1986). J. C. GREENFIELD, "Aramaic in the Achaemenian Empire," *Cambridge Ancient History* 2 (1985) 698–713. S. A. KAUFMAN, "Languages (Aramaic)," *Anchor Bible Dictionary* 4 (1992) 173–78. E. M. COOK, "Aramaic Language and Literature," *The Oxford Encyclopedia of Archaeology in the Near East* 5 v. (Oxford-New York 1997), 1:178–84. J. A. FITZMYER, "The Phases of the Aramaic Language," in *A Wandering Aramean: Collected Aramaic Essays* (SBLMS 25; Missoula, MT 1979); "Aramaic," *Encyclopedia of the Dead Sea Scrolls*, ed. L. H. SCHIFFMAN and J. C. VANDERKAM, 2 v. (Oxford 2000) 2:48–51; *The Aramaic Inscriptions of Sefire: Revised Edition* (*Bibliotheca orientalis* 19A; Rome 1995). A. LEMAIRE and J. M. DURAND, *Les inscriptions araméennes de Sfiré et l'Assyrie de Shamshi-Ilu* (Ecole Pratique des Hautes Etudes 2, Hautes Etudes Orientales 20; Paris-Geneva 1984). J. A. FITZMYER and S. A. KAUFMAN, *An Aramaic Bibliography: Part I, Old, Official, and Biblical Aramaic* (Baltimore,

MD 1992). M. BLACK, "The Recovery of the Language of Jesus," *New Testament Studies* 3 (1956–57) 305–13.

[J. A. FITZMYER]

ARAMAIC LANGUAGE, BIBLICAL

The term Biblical Aramaic refers to the form of Aramaic, once called Chaldaic, that is used in certain passages of the original text of the OT. These passages, written in general between the second half of the 5th century B.C. (if the Ezra passages were composed at that time, as is commonly accepted) and the second quarter of the 2d century B.C. (the Daniel passages), are: Gn 31.47 (two words); Jer 10.11; Ezr 4.8–6.18; 7.12–26; and Dn 2.44–7.28.

Older Term. It had been the custom to speak of the Aramaic of the Bible and the Targums as "Chaldaic." Strictly speaking, this would be the correct term for the Aramaic used in the first millennium B.C. by the Chaldeans of Mesopotamia. St. Jerome used it for the Aramaic of the Bible and the Targums, partly because it is said to be the language used by the "Chaldeans" in Dn 2.5 (where, however, the word Chaldeans means merely soothsayers) and partly because he thought that the Jews who returned to Palestine from the Babylonian Exile had brought this language back with them from Mesopotamia, which was at that time largely inhabited by Aramaic-speaking Chaldeans. Actually, the fact that certain passages of the OT are composed in Aramaic is merely a manifestation of the widespread process whereby in the second half of the first millennium B.C. Aramaic supplanted, not only Hebrew in Palestine, but also the remnants of other older languages in Syria and Mesopotamia, while it was used as the lingua franca throughout the ancient Near East and the official chancery language of the Persian Empire. Biblical Aramaic, however, represents a somewhat late stage of this Official or Imperial Aramaic, as it is called, standing in general about midway between the Aramaic of the Elephantine papyri of the late 5th century B.C. and the Aramaic of the Dead Sea Scrolls from about the time of Christ.

Characteristics. There are some slight differences between the Aramaic of the Book of Ezra and that of the Book of Daniel. The former is more archaic and closer to the language of the Elephantine papyri, while the latter has traits in common with Middle Aramaic. Thus, with one exception, the suffix of the second person masculine plural is -*kōm* (as in the Elephantine papyri), whereas it is -*kōn* in Daniel (as in the Targums). The suffix of the third person masculine plural, -*hōm,* is found in Ezra, as it is in older Aramaic, but it is no longer used in Daniel.

The Aramaic passages of the OT are important from a linguistic viewpoint, inasmuch as their traditional vocalization, as preserved in the Masoretic Text, casts light on the pronunciation of the unvocalized texts written in Official Aramaic. Some of the more striking features of Biblical Aramaic, as contrasted with Biblical Hebrew, are: the absence of the reflexive-passive form of the verb, *nif'al,* for which a *hithpeʿēl* form is substituted; the existence of a verbal form *hithpaʾal* in place of the passive *puʾal;* the absence, on the other hand, of the *hithpaʾēl* form; and traces of a causative form of the verb in *š-* (in a few words borrowed from Akkadian), which is used in both an active and a passive sense. The normal causative form appears both as an ʾ*afʿēl* (the later form) and as a *hafʿel* (the older form, corresponding to the Hebrew *hifʿîl*). The active participle is used very frequently in Biblical Aramaic, where it is employed to form both an imperfect and a present tense. Finally, the preposition *l* is used not only to express the dative relationship, but also as the so-called sign of the accusative.

As distinct from general Official Aramaic, Biblical Aramaic has been considerably affected by Biblical Hebrew, not only in its vocabulary (particularly in religious terminology), but also, to some extent, in its vocalization. Together with general Official Aramaic, it contains many words borrowed from Akkadian and Persian (particularly terms used in political and legal administration) and a few words from Greek (names of musical instruments).

Bibliography: F. ROSENTHAL, *A Grammar of Biblical Aramaic* (Wiesbaden 1961). L. PALACIOS, *Grammatica aramaico-biblica* (Rome 1953). H. BAUER and P. LEANDER, *Grammatik des Biblisch-Aramäischen* (Halle 1927); *Kurzgefasste biblischaramäische Grammatik* (Halle 1929). H. L. STRACK, *Grammatik des Biblisch-Aramäischen* (6th ed. Munich 1921). H. H. ROWLEY, *The Aramaic of the O.T.* (Oxford 1929). G. R. DRIVER, "The Aramaic of the Book of Daniel," *Journal of Biblical Literature* 45 (1926) 110–119, 323–325. H. L. GINSBERG, *Studies in Daniel* (New York 1948).

[J. M. SOLA-SOLE]

ARATOR

A 6th-century Christian poet; b. Liguria, before 500; d. *c.* 550. He was an orphan and was educated by Bp. Lawrence of Milan and the poet ENNODIUS. He studied classical literature and rhetoric with Parthenius and became an advocate and careerist at the court of THEODORIC THE GREAT in Ravenna. With the collapse of the Ostrogothic kingdom in Italy *c.* 540, Arator retired and was ordained subdeacon in Rome under Pope VIGILIUS. In 544 he published an epic poem, *De Actibus Apostolorum,* in 2,326 hexameters, modeled on the *Carmen Paschale* of SEDULIUS, with three metric letters of dedication to Vigilius, an Abbot Florian, and his friend Parthenius, respectively. The poem was originally read to an audience in St. Peter-in-Chains and was popular during the Middle

Ages; it is an amalgam of faulty prosody, uninspired rhetoric, excessive allegory, and the mystical interpretation of numbers. There are editions in *Patrilogia Latina*, ed. J. P. Migne, 217 vol., 68:45–252 and in *Corpus scriptorum ecclesiasticorum latinorum*, 72 (1951) by A. P. McKinlay.

Bibliography: P. DE LABRIOLLE, *Dictionnaire d'histoire et de géographie ecclésiastique*, ed. A. BAUDRILLART et al. (Paris 1912–), 3:1443–45. F. J. E. RABY, *A History of Christian-Latin Poetry from the Beginnings to the Close of the Middle Ages* (2d ed., Oxford 1953) 117–120. B. ALTANER, *Patrology*, (New York 1960) 600–601. *Clavis Patrum latinorum*, ed. E. DEKKERS (2d ed. Streenbrugge 1961) 1504–05.

[V. C. DE CLERCO]

ARAÚJO, ANTÔNIO DE

Jesuit missionary in Brazil, linguist, and historian; b. São Miguel, Azores, 1566; d. Espíritu Santo, Brazil, 1632. He had already obtained the master's degree when in 1582 he entered the novitiate of the Society of Jesus at Bahia, Brazil. After ordination, he taught briefly in Bahia and was then assigned to missionary work among the Tupí people. Noteworthy were Araújo's apostolic zeal and his ability to master the native tongue. He was admired by his contemporaries also for the facility with which he adapted himself to living conditions among the native Brazilians. In spite of an extremely active apostolic life, he found time to write his famed *Catecismo na lingoa brasilica no qual se contem a summa da doctrina christã* (Lisbon 1618; 2d ed. 1686; new ed. Leipzig, 1898), a catechetical work written in Tupí and later translated into other native languages. Araújo wrote also two historical treatises. The *Informação da entrada que se pode fazer da vila de São Paulo ao Grande Rio Pará* treats of one of the *bandeirante* expeditions led by Pero Domingues out of São Paulo through Brazil's northern hinterland to the Pará River. Written about 1625, it is considered one of the period's valuable historiographical works. A few years later, Araújo wrote the shorter *Relação dada perlo mesmo [Pero Domingues] sobre a viagem que de São Paulo fez ao Rio de S. Francisco* describing with more precision the route of the expedition and certain ethnographical details. These were first published in Brazil in 1937 by Serafim Leite.

Bibliography: S. LEITE, *Páginas da história do Brasil* (São Paulo 1937).

[N. F. MARTIN]

ARAÚJO, FRANCISCO DE

Dominican bishop and theologian; b. Vérin, Spain, 1580; d. Madrid, March 19, 1664. Born of a noble family, he entered the Order of Friars Preachers at Salamanca and was professed in 1601. He taught in various houses of the order, including that of Burgos until 1617, when he became assistant to Pedro de Herrera at the University of Salamanca. In 1623 he succeeded Herrera in the chair of moral theology, a position that he held for 25 years. In 1648 he was consecrated bishop of Segovia, and he governed the see until 1656, when he retired to a Dominican house in Madrid. His writings include *Commentarii in universam Aristotelis metaphysicam* (2 v. Burgos 1617; Salamanca 1631); *Opuscula tripartita* (Douai 1633); *Commentarii in primam, secundam et tertiam partem d. Thomae* (7 v. Salamanca 1635–47); and *Variae et selectae decisiones morales ad statum ecclesiasticum et civilem pertinentes* (Lyons 1664).

Bibliography: QUÉTIF–ÉCHARD, *Ordinis Praedicatorum*, 5 v. (Paris 1719–23) 2:609–611. H. HURTER, *Nomenclator literarius theologiae catholicae*, 5 v. in 6, (3d ed. Innsbruck 1903–13) 2:5–7. P. MANDONNET, *Dictionnaire de théologie catholique*, ed. A. VACANT et al., 15 v. (Paris 1903–50) 1.2:1729–30.

[J. C. WILKE]

ARBELA, CHRONICLE OF

The ancient city of Arbela in Mesopotamia was renowned for its temple to Astarte, which became world famous after Alexander's victory over the Persian Darius in 331 B.C. Having been converted to Christianity under the martyrs Bps. John (d. November 343) and (St.) Abraham II (martyred Feb. 4 or, according to the Armenians, 7 or 8 344), its Christians were savagely persecuted by the Persian King Shapur II (309–379). It was originally the metropolitan See of Adiabene, but was united to NISIBIS AND MOSUL in the late fourth century and became a Nestorian center before the Arab domination.

The *Chronicle of Arbela* is a Syrian Acts of the Martyrs discovered and published by A. Mingana in 1907. It was written by Měšiḥā-Zěkā, probably at Adiabene in the mid-sixth century and covers the history of Christianity in Persia between 100 and 550. Recent scholarly investigation indicates that much of its information is legendary.

Bibliography: A. MINGANA, ed. and tr., *Sources syriaques* (Leipzig 1908) v.1. F. ZORELL, ed., "Chronica ecclesiae Arbelensis," *Orientalia Christiana* 8 (1926–27) 145–204, Lat. tr. E. SACHAU, *Die Chronik von Arbela* (Abhandlungen der Deutschen [Preussischen, to 1944] Akademie der Wissenschaften zu Berlin [1815] 6; 1915). I. ORTIZ DE URBINA, "Intorno al valore storico della cronaca di Arbela," *Oriens Christianus* Per 2 (1936) 5–32. E. STOMMEL, *Lexikon für Theologie und Kirche*, ed. J. HOFER and K. RAHNER (Freiberg 1957–65) 1:820.

[F. X. MURPHY]

ARBEZ, EDWARD PHILIP

Biblical scholar and Orientalist; b. Paris, May 16, 1881; d. Washington, D.C., Dec. 27, 1967. Arbez began his studies for the priesthood at l'Argentière and for philosophy at Alix (Rhône). He began studying theology at Issy (1900–01), but came to Washington, D.C., as a candidate for the Society of St. Sulpice on the "American mission" (1901–03). Studies in Near Eastern languages with Henri Hyvernat at The Catholic University of America ran parallel to his theological formation. Ordained subdeacon by Cardinal Gibbons in May 1903, Arbez returned to Issy where he was ordained priest and formally received as a Sulpician on May 28, 1904.

For a year Arbez taught apologetics at St. Patrick's Seminary, Menlo Park, California; then from 1905 to 1928, he regularly taught Old and New Testament and Hebrew courses at St. Patrick's, giving history and other language courses on the side. The year 1917–18 marked his only break; he spent it in Washington, at the Department of Semitic Languages of Catholic University. Recalled to Washington in 1928, he taught both seminary courses in Sacred Scripture (as late as 1945) and graduate courses in Old Testament (1933–38). His old associations with the Semitic language program were renewed, informally at first, then with a full-time appointment from 1938 until his retirement in 1951 as ordinary professor and head of the department (from 1943). During his years in California, he had developed an excellent library for his expanding scholarly interests; by long-standing arrangement this eventually went to St. Mary's Seminary in Baltimore, from which he held an S.T.D. (1938).

Arbez keenly felt the strictures placed against Catholic biblical scholarship (Brassac, Dennefeld, Touzard) in the wake of the Modernist ferment. Although he had contributed early to the original *Catholic Encyclopedia,* the incentive to write came only gradually with his university associations, and most of the scholarly works with which he was connected were published after his 60th birthday. Meanwhile, his critical judgment, humor, and candor, along with his scholarly control of sources, encouraged his students to be ready for and work toward the new era inaugurated by *Divino afflante Spiritu.* In 1936 he was cofounder, with R. F. Butin, of the Catholic Biblical Association of America. From then until 1951, as chairman of the editorial board, he was a leading figure in the translation work which culminated in the *New American Bible.*

In the 1950s with M. R. P. McGuire, and in the 1960s, he oversaw the adaptation of the Robert-Tricot and Robert-Feuillet biblical manuals into English. As an associate trustee of the American Schools of Oriental Research, he laid the groundwork for more active Catholic participation in its scholarly undertakings. His talent for language study embraced a variety of modern, as well as ancient, languages (Turkish, the Scandinavian languages, Maltese). He was devoted to his adopted country, working for the Near Eastern affairs section of the Department of State and for the Federal Bureau of Investigation. In the years 1951 to 1961, he was a consultant for the Bureau and a popular figure with its personnel. He is buried at St. Charles College, Catonsville, Maryland.

Bibliography: W. F. HILL, "Rev. Edward P. Arbez, S.S.," *The Catholic Biblical Quarterly* 23 (1961) 113–124, with picture and bibliography to 1960; obituary notice, *The Catholic Biblical Quarterly* 31 (1969) 72–75.

[P. W. SKEHAN]

ARBIOL Y DIEZ, ANTONIO

Franciscan spiritual writer; b. Torellas (Spain), 1651; d. Saragossa, Jan. 31, 1726. Arbiol, who entered the Franciscans at Saragossa, was a brilliant teacher of philosophy and of theology, a celebrated preacher, and a prolific writer. He held various offices within as well as outside the order. In 1720 Philip V offered him the bishopric of Ciudad Rodrigo, but he refused. He died with a reputation for holiness. His writings are in the fields of theology, homiletics, asceticism, and mysticism. He defended the Ven. Mary of AGREDA, but was a strenuous adversary of the ALUMBRADOS and of Miguel de MOLINOS. The list of his published works includes 33 items, some of which had as many as 10 editions, e.g., *Desengaños misticos* (Saragossa 1706), *Novenarios espirituales* (published posthumously, Saragossa 1928), and *La familia regulada* (Saragossa 1715). Other works worth mentioning are: *Manuale sacerdotum* (Saragossa 1693), *Certamen Marianum Parisiense* (Saragossa 1698), and *Mistica Fundamental* (Saragossa 1723). Some of his works, such as *Contra insanias de Molinos,* have never been edited. His mystical theology was inspired by SS. BONAVENTURE, TERESA OF AVILA, and especially JOHN OF THE CROSS.

Bibliography: J. HEERINCKX, "Les Écrits d'Antoine Arbiol, O.F.M.," *Archivum Franciscanum historicum* 26 (1933) 315–342; *Dictionnaire de spiritualité ascétique et mystique. Doctrine et histoire,* ed. M. VILLER et al. (Paris 1932–)1:834–836.

[G. GÁL]

ARBOGAST OF STRASBOURG, ST.

Bishop; b. probably Aquitaine; d. near Strasbourg, mid-sixth century. It was his original intention to live as a hermit, and to that end he settled in a forest in Alsace. According to a later tradition, he was made bishop of

Strasbourg *c.* 673 through the influence of King DAGO-BERT II, who seems to have been his patron. As bishop, Arbogast was known for his simplicity and humility, and before his death he asked to be buried in a cemetery where only criminals had previously been interred. In the eleventh century a magnificent church was erected on the site, but it was destroyed in the sixteenth century and the relics of the saint were lost. He is the patron of the Diocese of Strasbourg. It should be noted that the ancient episcopal catalogues of the diocese, as well as inscriptions on parts of the cathedral built in the sixth century, assign his episcopate to *c.* 550. In art he is represented as walking dry-shod over a river.

Feast: July 21.

Bibliography: *Acta Sanctorum* July 5:168–179. UTO III, *Vita* in A. POSTINA, *Sankt Arbogast, Bischof von Strassburg* (2d ed. Strasbourg 1929). A. BUTLER, *The Lives of the Saints*, ed. H. THURSTON and D. ATTWATER (New York 1956) 3:158–159. A. MERCATI and A. PELZER, *Dizionario ecclesiastico* (Turin 1954–58) 1:203. G. ALLMANG, *Dictionnaire d'histoire et de géographie ecclésiastiques*, ed. A. BAUDRILLART et al. (Paris 1912) 3:1462–63. A. M. ZIMMERMANN, *Kalendarium Benedictinum*, (Metten 1933–38) 2:484–485.

[J. F. FAHEY]

ARBROATH, ABBEY OF

Former Benedictine abbey of the Tironian congregation (*see* TIRON, ABBEY OF) situated in Angus, Scotland, within the ancient Diocese of Brechin, and now a ruin. It was founded by King William the Lion, Aug. 9, 1178, from the Abbey of Kelso, and dedicated to St. Thomas BECKET, whom the king may well have known in his younger days. Arbroath was richly endowed at its foundation, and later it became one of the wealthiest abbeys in Scotland. Among its many distinguished abbots were Bernard de Linton, who may have drafted the Scottish Declaration of Independence dispatched to Pope JOHN XXII from Arbroath, April 1320; John Gedy (1370–95); and Cardinal David Beaton, its last resident abbot (1524–36). After a series of commendatory abbots (*see* COMMENDATION) Arbroath was erected into a temporal lordship for the Marquis of Hamilton in 1608.

Bibliography: C. INNES and P. CHALMERS, eds., *Liber S. Thome de Aberbrothoc*, 2 v. (Edinburgh 1848–56). R. L. MACKIE and S. CRUDEN, *Arbroath Abbey* (Edinburgh 1954). D. E. EASSON, *Medieval Religious Houses: Scotland* (London 1957) 58.

[L. MACFARLANE]

ARCADELT, JAKOB

Renaissance composer, master of the madrigal (also Arkadelt, Archadet, Harcadelt); b. Liège?, Belgium, *c.*

1504; d. Paris?, between 1562 and 1572. His Flemish nationality is attested in the 1539 records of the Julian Chapel at the Vatican (*Jacobus Flandrus magister Capellae*). By 1540 he was appointed to the Sistine Chapel, and he remained there until at least 1549. During the 1550s he was perhaps in Paris, where his chansons, earlier published only sporadically, were issued as collections after 1553. In his book of Masses (1557) he is called choirmaster of Cardinal Charles Lorraine (Duc de Guise), as well as *regius musicus* to the king of France. Since he is in the royal chapel records for 1562, but not in the next extant list, 1572, he probably died between these dates. Although Arcadelt composed motets, Lamentations, and Masses, his greatest importance rests with his chansons and madrigals, whose four-part species he brought to perfection. The madrigals are essentially diatonic works, displaying a sensitive awareness of the text, and are written in a judicious alternation of imitative and note-against-note polyphony. In them he first successfully infused the simple Italian forms with the artistic polyphony of his homeland.

Bibliography: A. EINSTEIN, *The Italian Madrigal*, tr. A. H. KRAPPE et al., 3 v. (Princeton 1949). W. KLEFISCH, *Arcadelt als Madrigalist* (Cologne 1938). G. REESE, *Music in the Renaissance* (rev. ed. New York 1959). T. W. BRIDGES, "The Publishing of Arcadelt's First Book of Madrigals" (Ph.D. diss. Harvard University, 1982). B. BUJIC, "Palestrina, Willaert, Arcadelt, and the Art of Imitation," *Recercare* 10 (1998) 105–131. K. VAN ORDEN, "*Les Vers lascifs d'Horace*: Arcadelt's Latin Chansons," *The Journal of Musicology* 14 (1996): 338–369. D. M. RANDEL, ed., *The Harvard Biographical Dictionary of Music* (Cambridge, Massachusetts 1996). B. V. RIVERA, "The Two-Voice Framework and Its Harmonization in Arcadelt's First Book of Madrigals," *Music Analysis* 6 (1987) 59–88. A. SEAY, "Jacques Arcadelt" in *The New Grove Dictionary of Music and Musicians, v.1*, ed. S. SADIE 546–550, (New York 1980). N. SLONIMSKY, ed. *Baker's Biographical Dictionary of Musicians, Eighth Edition* (New York 1992).

[E. R. LERNER]

ARCADIUS, ROMAN EMPEROR

Ruled from 383 to 408; b. *c.* 377; d. Constantinople, 408. Flavius Arcadius was the eldest son of Emperor THEODOSIUS I and Aelia Flaccilla. Proclaimed Augustus by his father in 383, he was left in Constantinople as sole ruler in the East in 394. Upon the death of Theodosius I (395), the administration of the empire was shared by Arcadius, who retained the East, and his younger brother, HONORIUS I, in the West. Lacking both energy and judgment, Arcadius submitted to the schemes of his wife, Eudoxia (d. 404), whom he had married in 395, and those of two ministers, the prefect Rufinus (murdered in 395) and the eunuch Eutropius (executed in 399). Growing friction with the Western imperial administration and increasing difficulties with the barbarians troubled his reign. From 395 to 396 the Visigoth Alaric devastated Greece, while Gothic troops led by Gainas were in open revolt from 399 to 400 in support of the Arians in Constantinople.

Orthodox in his ecclesiastical policies, Arcadius prohibited assemblies of heretics, ordered the confiscation of pagan temples, and banished Apollinarians, (*see* APPOLLINARIANISM); however, his religious zeal was motivated by caesaropapism. When the Patriarch of Constantinople, JOHN CHRYSOSTOM, denounced the frivolity of the court and of the empress, the quarrel led to the disgrace and banishment of the patriarch and to a temporary success of Eudoxia's Arian policies. The banishment furthered the subordination of the patriarch to the emperor in the East. Arcadius was succeeded by his only son, THEODOSIUS II.

Bibliography: E. STEIN, *Histoire du Bas-Empire*, tr. J. R. PALANQUE 1:225–253. A. FLICHE and V. MARTIN, *Histoire de l'église depuis les origines jusqu'á nos jours* 4:145–159. J. B. BURY, *A History of the Later Roman Empire* 2 v. (London 1923; repr. New York 1957) v.1. E. DEMOUGEOT, *De l'unité à la division de l'Empire romain 395–410* (Paris 1950). C. BAUR, *John Chrysostom and His Time*, tr. M. GONZAGA 2 v. (Westminster, Md. 1960–61).

[J. BRÜCKMANN]

ARCANUM

An encyclical letter of LEO XIII (Feb. 10, 1880) occasioned by the increasingly vehement demands that civil legislation be enacted even in Christian countries to loosen the bond of marriage. This pope restated the Church's position that by divine law marriage is one and indissoluble, as manifested by the design of the Creator in uniting the first man and woman "in one flesh" (Gn 2.24). These necessary properties of the marriage bond were reaffirmed by Christ in all their pristine vigor. Men had always recognized the sacred and religious character of matrimony by reason of its divine institution. Christ not only deepened this conviction by blessing this union, but elevated it to the supernatural order by making of it a Sacrament of the New Covenant. Since it is the very contract between man and woman that constitutes the Sacrament, only the religious authority established by Christ to continue His mission, the Church, has a right to enact laws regulating marriage. Civil authority may issue only such decrees as affect the civil order without prejudice to the nuptial bond, and even in these limited areas the State must bow to the prior rights of the Church in the event of conflict. While their marital status grants the partners many privileges, it imposes corresponding duties—to each other and to the fruit of their union. Relations be-

tween husband and wife must ever be founded upon true conjugal love that will never deprive their children of the love and care that is their right. Children will in turn be moved to render their duties of filial respect and obedience gladly. The Church's marriage laws have ever been intended to be and have in fact been a boon to both the individual and to society. She has always safeguarded the sanctity of marriage despite all opposition. It is clear that all bishops must instruct the faithful committed to their care, concerning the sacredness of the marriage bond. Moreover the faithful must be warned of the dangers inherent in mixed marriages. Lastly, no pastor of souls may abandon those involved in illicit unions but should encourage them to obtain the graces of the Sacrament.

Bibliography: LEO XIII, "Arcanum" (Encyclical, Feb. 10, 1880) *Acta Sanctae Sedis* 12 (1879) 385–402, Eng. *The Church Speaks to the Modern World*, ed. H. GILSON (Garden City, NY 1954) 86–113. J. HUSSLEIN, comp., *Social Wellsprings*, 2 v. (Milwaukee 1940–42) 1:24–46.

[S. KARDOS]

ARCHANGELA GIRLANI, BL.

Carmelite; b. Eleanora, at Trino, 1460; d. Mantua, Jan. 25, 1494. Her father resisted her desire to become a religious but finally agreed to allow her to enter a Benedictine convent of relaxed observance near Trino. This plan having been thwarted, she eventually joined the CARMELITES at Parma (1477), who led the stricter life she desired. Soon after she was made prioress, the GONZAGA family requested that she be sent to Mantua to found a new convent. She was noted for her austerity, charity, and spirit of prayer and for reputed mystical experiences. Her body was found to be incorrupt three years after her death. Her cult was confirmed in 1864.

Feast: Feb. 13

Bibliography: ALBAREI, *Notice sur la vie de la bse. Archangela Girlani* (Poitiers 1865). A. BUTLER, *The Lives of the Saints*, rev. ed. H. THURSTON and D. ATTWATER (New York, 1956) 1:327–328.

[N. G. WOLF]

ARCHANGELO OF CALATAFIMI, BL.

Hermit, Franciscan observant, b. Archangelo Placenza, Calatafimi, Sicily, 1380; d. Alcamo, July 26, 1460. Desirous of a hermit's life, he sought solitude as a young man but his reputation for sanctity and the miracles attributed to him attracted many seeking advice. He fled to Alcamo where he revived and organized a hospice for the poor. When MARTIN V required all hermits in Sicily to re-

Newly appointed Archbishop Norberto Rivera blessing woman in Mexico City. (AP/Wide World Photos)

turn to the world or to accept religious life in an approved order he became a Franciscan of the Observance at Palermo. He was sent back to the hospice at Alcamo to make it a house of his order, and later was made provincial of the Sicilian Observants. His cult was approved in 1836.

Feast: July 30

Bibliography: A. GIOIA, *Il beato Arcangelo Placenza da Calatafimi* (Palermo 1926). LÉON DE CLARY, *Lives of the Saints and Blessed of the Three Orders of St. Francis*, 4 v. (Taunton, Eng. 1885–87) v.2. A. BUTLER, *The Lives of the Saints*, rev. ed. H. THURSTON and D. ATTWATER (New York, 1956) 3:214–215.

[N. G. WOLF]

ARCHBISHOP

This ancient designation for certain major ecclesiastics has undergone, in the course of centuries, changes of meaning in the East and West that make it difficult to ex-

plain. Originally, as its etymology suggests, it designated a superior or chief bishop and was applied to bishops who presided over the greater sees. It was not infrequently in the East a title for those who later were called more technically PATRIARCHS.

In the West (Latin Church) at the present time the title is closely allied to that of metropolitan, the head of an ecclesiastical Province (or regional group of dioceses), and it may be said that today in the West every metropolitan is an archbishop. It is by no means true, however, that everyone with the title of archbishop is a metropolitan. We may distinguish three other uses of the term ''archbishop.'' It has been used (1) for the diocesan bishop of a diocese that is outside any ecclesiastical province but itself is not a metropolitan see and hence has no suffragan dioceses. Such for instance was the Archdiocese of Washington, D.C., from 1947, when it was severed from the Province of Baltimore, to 1965, when it was made a metropolitan see. The reason for this somewhat unusual disposition is sought in the civil importance of the place or in its former ecclesiastical prestige. The term is used (2) for an ordinary who personally has been given the title by the Holy See. In this case the diocese itself does not change its ecclesiastical status; i.e., it remains within the province to which it already belongs and the successors in that see do not succeed to the title of archbishop. Finally, the term is used (3) for titular bishops who are raised to the dignity because of their special functions as members of the Roman Curia or of the papal diplomatic corps (e.g., apostolic delegates) or because of exceptional service as coadjutor or auxiliary bishops.

With regard to the powers and rights of an archbishop who is a metropolitan *see* ARCHDIOCESE. For archbishops who head archdioceses that are not metropolitan sees, the dignity is one of a certain immediate dependence on the Holy See. In the case of ordinaries who are "personal" archbishops and of titular archbishops, the title confers a special honor rather than any ecclesiastical power.

See Also: BISHOP (IN THE BIBLE); BISHOP (IN THE CHURCH); BISHOP, AUXILIARY; ORDINARIES, ECCLESIASTICAL.

Bibliography: E. RÖSSER, *Lexikon für Theologie und Kirche,* ed. J. HOFER and K. RAHNER, 10 v. (2d, new ed. Freiburg 1957–65) 3:1066–67. K. MÖRSDORF, *ibid.* 7:373–375. E. VALTON, *Dictionnaire de théologie catholique,* ed. A. VACANT, 15 v. (Paris 1903–50) 5.2:1704–05. A. S. POPEK, *The Rights and Obligations of Metropolitans* (Catholic University of America Canon Law Studies 260; Washington 1947).

[S. E. DONLON]

ARCHCHANCELLOR

The title given in the Middle Ages to a high ecclesiastical official who also directed the royal chancery. The Merovingian Franks continued the late Roman practice of having lay persons, *referendarii,* prepare royal documents and letters. In Carolingian times, when the educated were predominantly clerics, and when civil and religious administration were closely related, priest members of the court chapel also prepared the royal documents. At their head was the first chaplain, called (after 825) archchaplain, who was the highest church dignitary at the court of the Franks. At the time of CHARLEMAGNE and LOUIS the Pious, an untitled chief chancellor oversaw the actual writing of documents. In 856 LOUIS the German put the document-preparing organization directly under the archchaplain. The combined office was given to Abp. Liudhard of Mainz in 870. Under the Ottonian emperors, the office was attached to the see of Mainz and the title archchancellor commonly applied to it. After 1031 the archchancellor was the archbishop of Cologne,

who also fulfilled this office for the Roman Church during the 11th century. Under HENRY III (1039–56) the archbishop of Besançon was archchancellor; after 1157 under the Hohenstaufen, the archbishop of Vienne; after 1308, the archbishop of Trier. As the office of archchaplain disappeared in the 11th century, a distinction was made between the chancellor, who directed the work of chancery personnel, and the chaplain, who directed clerics attached to the royal CHAPEL in their spiritual functions. In the 12th century the chancery became an independent institution. As archchancellor in the 9th century, the archbishop of Mainz had a definite influence on chancery procedure, as did the archbishop of Cologne to some extent during the 11th and 12th centuries. The title archchancellor was applied analogously to a position established for the three spiritual electors of the empire by Charles IV in the Golden Bull of 1356. The abbot of Fulda was designated archchancellor of the empress. The position remained in later years only as a title that accorded its possessor certain honors in court ceremonial.

Bibliography: L. PERRICHET, *La Grande chancellerie de France des origines à 1328* (Paris 1912). P. F. KEHR, "Die Kanzlei Ludwigs des Deutschen," *Abhandlungen der Akademie (Gesellschaft, to 1940) der Wissenschaften* (Göttingen 1941–) (1932) fasc. 1. L. GROSS, *Die Geschichte der Reichshofkanzlei von 1559 bis 1806* (Vienna 1933). H. W. KLEWITZ, "Cancellaria," *Deutsches Archiv für Geschichte des Mittelalters* 1 (1937) 44–79. F. HAUSMANN, *Reichskanzlei und Hofkapelle unter Heinrich V und Konrad III* (Stuttgart 1956). J. FLECKENSTEIN, *Die Hofkapelle der deutschen Könige* (Stuttgart 1959–).

[W. H. WALLAIK]

ARCHDEACON

Although the title of archdeacon is first referred to by St. Optatus of Milevis (4th century), from the 3d century the bishop would select one of the deacons (not necessarily the senior) to assist him in both the liturgy and administration of the diocese. The office grew in importance as the amount of administration grew, so that by the 5th century the archdeacon was next in importance to the bishop, whom he frequently succeeded. Although at first there was only one, from the 9th century additional archdeacons were appointed (first in France, later elsewhere) within a diocese; they were delegates of the bishop in the areas into which the diocese was divided for administrative purposes. They gradually increased in power and obtained first a share in the bishop's jurisdiction, then independent jurisdiction in courts of their own. Their heyday was in the 12th century; thereafter a succession of councils, culminating in Trent, restricted their power, while as a counterblast to it, bishops appointed their own vicars-general. After the Reformation the English Church did not revive this institution, although it continues to exist in the Anglican Church. In Ireland, archdeacon is the honorific title of the second dignitary of the diocesan chapter.

See Also: DEACON.

Bibliography: A. AMANIEU, *Dictionnaire de droit canonique* 1:948–1004. G. W. O. ADDLESHAW, *The Beginnings of the Parochial System* (St. Anthony's Hall Publications 3; London 1953); *The Development of the Parochial System from Charlemagne (768–814) to Urban II (1088–1099)* (*ibid.* 6; London 1954).

[B. FORSHAW]

ARCHDIOCESE

In the Latin Church the archdiocese is generally a DIOCESE whose bishop exercises metropolitan authority within a province composed of the archdiocese and several suffragan dioceses; occasionally such a diocese stands by itself outside the provincial structure.

This article confines its attention to the metropolitan see in its relationship to the province and to the suffragan dioceses, and to the reasons for this structural form in the Church.

The relationship to the province and to the individual suffragan dioceses is most easily treated by citing the rights and duties that the ARCHBISHOP has in the present canon law. It may be noted that there is no uniformity in the number of dioceses grouped within a province.

In regard to the province as a whole, the archbishop's principal duties are found in *Codex iuris canonici* (Rome 1918; repr. Graz 1955) *c.* 442 or *Codex Canonum Ecclesiarium Orientalium c.* 133. The metropolitan is to choose the place for the sessions of a provincial council. It is the archbishop's right also to convoke the council and to preside at its sessions.

In regard to the individual dioceses and bishops of his province, the archbishop's functions are listed in *Codex iuris canonici* (Rome 1918; repr. Graz 1955) *c.* 436 or *Codex Canonum Ecclesiarium Orientalium c.* 133. The principal ones are: (1) to observe the faith and discipline of the suffragan dioceses and in case he notes any abuses to report these to superior authority; and (2) if a suffragan has neglected to do so, to conduct a canonical VISITATION of the suffragan diocese.

From this it is clear that the archdiocese and its bishop have little right to interfere in the ordinary pastoral direction of the local bishop; in fact there is little that the archbishop can do ex officio except report abuses to superior authority. Outside the time of a visitation, he cannot exercise doctrinal or disciplinary functions within the territory of a suffragan. The Church has for centuries found this grouping of dioceses within provinces under the leadership of one designated archdiocese a useful instrument for safeguarding order and preventing fragmentation that might ensue were all dioceses subjected only and immediately to the Holy See.

In the Eastern patriarchal churches the prestige of the PATRIARCH throughout the region subject to him historically tended to absorb the metropolitan structure, though in recent times there has been a move to restore the province as a functioning unit. In these churches the metropolitan is subject to his patriarch and does not, as in the Latin Church, immediately depend on the one who is at the same time Patriarch of the West and supreme pontiff.

The origins of the archdiocese and the metropolitan arrangement are hard to fix in time. It would seem that such intermediate groupings—between the individual local Churches or dioceses and the Church universal—emerged as recognized units at least in the 3d century, and many trace the metropolitan (as well as the patriarchal) divisions back to the special prestige enjoyed by certain Churches from the first postapostolic generations. Thus the grouping arises out of a combination of factors: some embedded in the Church's own nature, some in the historical development from apostolic times of the Church in a given area, some in the politico-geographical conditions that prevailed in the world in which the Church began its corporate life.

See Also: BISHOP (IN THE BIBLE); BISHOP (IN THE CHURCH) ORDINARIES, ECCLESIASTICAL.

Bibliography: K. MÖRSDORF, *Lexikon für Theologie und Kirche,* ed. J. HOFER and K. RAHNER, 10 v. (2d, new ed. Freiburg 1957–65) 7:373–375. E. RÖSSER, *ibid.* 3:1066–67. E. VALTON, *Dictionnaire de théologie catholique,* ed. A. VACANT, 15 v. (Paris 1903–50; Tables générales 1951–) 5.2:1704–05. A. S. POPEK, *The Rights and Obligations of Metropolitans* (Catholic University of America Canon Law Studies 260; Washington 1947).

[S. E. DONLON]

ARCHE INTERNATIONAL, L'

L'Arche International is a federation of faith communities in which people with disabilities and their assistants choose to live and work together. The mission of L'Arche is to welcome people with disabilities and give them a valid place in society. L'Arche fosters the particular gifts and value of people with disabilities, seeking to show that people of differing intellectual capacity, social origin, religion, and culture can come together in unity, faithfulness, and reconciliation (L'Arche International, 1998). There are more than 113 L'Arche communities in 30 countries throughout the world, including 13 in the United States.

L'Arche began in France in 1964 when Jean Vanier and Father Thomas Philippe, a Dominican, invited two men with disabilities, Philippe Simi and Raphael Seux, to share a home together near Trosly-Breuil, France. Having first met Philippe and Raphael in an institution, Jean believed that a warm and loving home would have a significant impact on the lives of these two men. They all soon learned that the impact of sharing life together in a simple way lead to mutual transformation of heart.

From the desire of two people with disabilities to have a home and share life with Vanier and Father Thomas, L'Arche has grown into an international network of communities. While the founding roots of L'Arche are in the Roman Catholic tradition, it has now developed in various cultures and religious traditions throughout the world. It is recognized as one of the most significant Christian ministries of the twentieth century.

Jean Vanier was born in Canada in 1928, the son of Georges and Pauline Vanier. He was educated in England and Canada. After serving several years in the British Navy and Canadian Royal Navy, he earned a Doctorate in Philosophy from Institut Catholique de Paris, France. He continues to live in the first L'Arche Community in Trosly-Breuil. Vanier also inspired ''Faith and Sharing'' communities that meet once a month for scripture reflection, and with Marie Hélène Mathieu he founded the ''Faith and Light'' communities of disabled people, their families, and friends that meet regularly. Vanier received the Paul VI International Prize for his lay ministry work. Vanier has promoted L'Arche through lectures and interviews and has written more than twenty books. His *Becoming Human* (Mahwah, N.J. 1999) was derived from a series of lectures aired on public broadcasting in Canada. Recognizing Vanier's work, Pope John Paul II stated, ''Over the past 30 years, L'Arche has grown to become a dynamic and providential sign of the civilization of love.''

Bibliography: J. VANIER, *An Ark for the Poor: The Story of L'Arche* (New York 1995).

[J. EADS]

ARCHES, COURT OF

The Court of Arches is the ecclesiastical court of appeal for the Ecclesiastical Province of CANTERBURY. From as early as the end of the 13th century it sat in St. Mary of the Arches (*de arcubus*), so called for its arched crypt. St. Mary was an exempt deanery within the city of London. This court dealt with the provincial appeals of the archbishop, and presiding over its sessions was the archbishop's official, who later frequently combined that

office with the deanship of the Arches. The Court continued after the Reformation and has also been known as the Arches Court. It is still the Provincial Court of the Archbishop of Canterbury, the corresponding institution for York being the Chancery Court of York. Woodcock has an illuminating discussion of the medieval practice; there is much further material in the *Black Books of the Arches* (partially printed in D. Wilkins, *Concilia,* 2, London 1737, and described by Churchill, 2:206).

Bibliography: W. LYNDWOOD, *Provinciale* (Oxford 1679). J. AYCLIFFE, *Parergon juris canonici anglicani* (London 1726). W. S. HOLDSWORTH, *A History of English Law,* 13 v. (London 1903–38; rev. ed. 1956–) 3 369–. I. J. CHURCHILL, *Canterbury Administration,* 2 v. (New York 1933) 1:422. *Canon Law of the Church of England* (London 1947) 48, 89, 198. B. L. WOODCOCK, *Medieval Ecclesiastical Courts in the Diocese of Canterbury* (New York 1952). C. R. CHAPMAN, *Ecclesiastical Courts, Their Officials and Their Records* (Dursley, England 1992).

[R. J. SCHOECK/EDS.]

ARCHIEREUS

Greek, ἀρχιερεύς, equivalent of the Russian *arkhierei,* a term used in the Christian East for bishop in its theological and liturgical meaning: one possessing the fullness of the power of the priesthood. It is applicable to any consecrated bishop. The term is frequently used in the liturgical books of the Greek Orthodox, Greek Catholic, and Byzantine churches. Without any special jurisdiction, his position was to represent the hierarchy of Order in solemnizing divine services. The title enhanced the dignity of those holding the office of rector of certain theological establishments or of archpriest of historic basilicas and was a mark of personal privilege. Conferred frequently on major religious superiors, it was a mark of special honor to their communities. This term is not to be confused with *protoiereus,* the highest rank to which married clergy could aspire, in contrast to the celibate episcopacy. In the rubrics of the Byzantine liturgies, a bishop is frequently referred to as archpriest, but he is distinguished as *archiereus* from the *protoiereus,* as above indicated.

Bibliography: J. BJERRING, *Offices of the Oriental Church* (New York 1884). A. MICHIELS, *Les Origines de l'épiscopat* (Louvain 1900). N. MILASH, *Pravoslavno Crkveno pravo* (3d ed. Belgrade 1926). R. JANIN, *Les églises orientales et les rites orienteaux* (Paris 1955).

[L. NEMEC/EDS.]

ARCHIVES, ECCLESIASTICAL

The necessity of archives was recognized very early in history, and we find them in use among the most ancient peoples. Assyria, Babylon, Israel, Phoenicia, Egypt, Greece, and Rome appreciated the value of preserving important documents and usually reserved a part of the temple for the archives. The sacredness of the holy place was expected to be an additional guarantee against violation.

Ecclesiastical archives are as old as the organization of the earliest churches, for these produced records that required preservation and storage.

History. As early as 367 B.C. Roman law saw the need of an archivist. The norms of Roman law undoubtedly served as guides in the development of administrative procedures of the early Christian Church.

The Liber pontificalis claims that Pope St. Clement (*c.* 88–97) divided the Church at Rome into seven regions, and assigned to these regions notaries who were to compile accurate and diligent accounts of the history of the martyrs. Most likely the procedure followed by these notaries was patterned after that of the civil government except that the Liber pontificalis adds that these accounts were kept ''in ecclesias,'' that is, in the church itself or one of its buildings. Pope St. Fabian (236–250) is said to have appointed seven subdeacons who were to supervise the notaries and transcribe the *acta* in full from the *notae* or shorthand methods of the notaries.

In the Middle Ages episcopal sees, collegiate and cathedral chapters, and monasteries continued to be important archival centers, preserving not only records of their own land holdings, contracts, etc., but also important documents that civil officials might want to deposit there.

At the beginning of the modern era the Council of TRENT promulgated brief regulations on the preservation of important documents. Subsequently Popes SIXTUS V (who planned a central Roman Archives and the Notarial Archives for the States of the Church), CLEMENT VIII, and PAUL V initiated important archival reforms. Pope BENEDICT XIII issued his constitution on Italian ecclesiastical archives *Maxima vigilantia,* dated June 14, 1727 [*Bullarium Romanum* 12 (Rome 1736) 221–225, entitled: ''A constitution on archives to be erected in Italy for the preservation of legal papers and documents pertaining to cathedral churches both collegiate and noncollegiate, to seminaries, monasteries of both men and of women, guilds, confraternities, hospitals and to all other pious institutions legally instituted.

To further and coordinate archival activities in the Church, the Associazione Archivistica Ecclesiastica was founded in Rome in 1956. Membership is open to all ecclesiastical archivists. Since 1958 it has published *Archiva Ecclesiae,* with important articles on church archives in all countries.

Common and Secret Archives. The rules for the erection, contents, custody, and use of both common and secret archives is contained in *Codex Iuris Canonicis* (CIC) cc. 486–491 and *Codex Canonum Ecclesiarium Orientalium* (CCEO) cc. 256–261. It is impossible to give an exhaustive list of all the documents that should be kept in the archives but the law gives an indication of what type of material ought to be preserved there: e.g., records of ordinations (CIC c.1053; CCEO c. 774), and authentic documents regarding church property ownership and rights (CIC c. 1284 §2, 9°; CCEO c. 1028 §2, 8°).

The obligation of some practical and orderly arrangement of the archives is indicated by CIC c. 486 and CCEO c. 256. A chronological filing may be preferable for certain types of documents whereas an alphabetical system might be more practical for other types. The diocesan CHANCELLOR is the legal custodian of the archives (CIC c. 482 §1; CCEO c. 252 §1) and therefore he or she, together with the bishop, should determine their arrangement.

Custody of the archives is a serious matter, and an inventory of archive documents is required as a safeguard (CIC c. 486 §3; CCEO c. 256 §2). The law requires also that permission be obtained to enter the archives (CIC c. 487 §1; CCEO c. 257 §1) and to borrow or remove any document (CIC c. 488; CCEO c. 258).

The secret archives are governed by similar norms. The 1917 Code of Canon Law made universal laws regarding secret archives for the first time, although such archives were in existence in many areas prior to the 1917 Code. The types of documents contained in this special archive are cited in various canons, e.g., notations of marriages secretly celebrated (CIC c. 1133), and documents of criminal cases in matters of morals (CIC c. 489 §2; CCEO c. 259 §2). The custody of these secret archives is particularly important if the see is vacant (cf. CIC c. 490 §2; CCEO c. 260 §2).

Ecclesiastical Archives in the United States. Church archives formally developed in the United States after the publication of the 1917 Code of Canon Law. Prior to 1918 many documents disappeared or were dispersed, out of carelessness, ignorance, lack of adequate facilities, or an unwillingness to preserve them for posterity. However, some dioceses, like those of Baltimore and St. Louis, succeeded in preserving archival materials intact. On Nov. 22, 1974 the NCCB Committee for the Bicentennial issued ''A Document on Ecclesiastical Archives,'' stressing their importance:

> At the same time we regret that our Church's singular role in the development of our country has not been presented as fully as it deserves to be. Al-

though books, monographs, articles, and essays on the subject of American Catholicism abound and many of them are of high scholarly and literary quality, church historians have still not penetrated to the heart of the peculiarly American experience in all too many cases, because they have not had access to the pertinent documents of bishops, dioceses, religious orders, and institutions. The difficulty is not so much that such papers are not extant, although it is true, unfortunately, that in certain known cases large holdings of important documents have been destroyed because they were mistakenly judged to be "outdated" or "useless" or "trash." The problem is rather that in many places the papers which do exist in abundance have not yet been organized for preservation and research. Consequently, on the one hand, they are not easily accessible to church historians and, on the other, they are in danger of being lost, dispersed, or damaged through lack of proper care, fire or flood, or inadvertent disposal.

The documents urged that all bishops appoint a diocesan archivist. Access to ecclesiastical papers and records was encouraged:

> Finally, we express our sincere hope that the residential bishops may be disposed to grant access to the diocesan archives without undue limitations when properly accredited ecclesiastical historians request it. The past products of such research support, we believe, the contention that serious historians, even graduate students and doctoral candidates, have, with very rare exceptions, used such permission with honesty, fairness, responsibility, respect for the documents, and true Christian charity. Catholic historians have characteristically evinced a distinct pride in the persons and institutions of their Church of past generations, and, in our judgment, no bishop need fear that by opening his archives to scholarly examination, he will expose the Church's past to deliberate attempts at embarrassment.

Notable Depositories in the United States. To check the frequent loss of church papers the University of Notre Dame, through its Archives, has been active in collecting personal papers of bishops, priests and Catholic laypersons, as well as transcripts of American missionary letters sent to Europe. The collections include copies of letters from the United States to the Congregation for the Propagation of the Faith in Rome from 1622 to 1865. The American Catholic Historical Society Archives, housed on the campus of St. Charles Seminary in Philadelphia, are a mine of early Catholic Americana, including newspapers and serials. Georgetown University contains early Catholic Americana, notably the papers of John Gilmary Shea, the first scholarly historian of the Catholic Church in the United States. Between 1872 and

1927, Bishops Gibbons, Keane, and O'Connor, exercised leadership on a national level, and thus their papers take on added significance. Many are now preserved at the Richmond Diocesan Archives. The Archives of the Archdiocese of Santa Fe has published a listing of its holdings that encompasses Franciscan missionary activities and the career of Archbishop John Lamy (made famous by Willa Cather in *Death Comes for the Archbishop*). The Archives of the Catholic University of America, Washington, D.C., has noteworthy collections on labor relations and labor unions. In addition, it has assembled copies of the papers of John Carroll (1735–1815), the first bishop of Baltimore, and other materials on the early American Church. Marquette University, Milwaukee, Wisconsin, has an archival center for Catholic journalism in the United States.

A unique collection of approximately 30,000 bound manuscripts or codices representing the holdings of fifty monastic libraries in Europe is now available on microfilm at St. John's University, Collegeville, Minnesota. A major portion of the manuscript holdings of the Vatican Library on microfilm is now on deposit at St. Louis University, St. Louis, Missouri.

Valuable collections have been assembled through the interests of religious communities and orders, like that on Franciscan history now available at the Academy of American Franciscan History, Berkeley, California; the collection of Dominicana at the Dominican House of Studies, Washington, D.C.; and the Jesuit collections at Georgetown University, Washington, D.C., St. Louis University, St. Louis, Missouri, and at Gonzaga University, Spokane, Washington.

Though there is no current standard guide to Catholic church archives nor an inventory of unpublished material on the history of the American Catholic Church, those interested in doing further research on specific topics will want to consult *The National Union Catalog of Manuscript Collections*, a continuing series published by the Library of Congress since 1959. Here appear many entries on collections of Catholic church archives, plus valuable annual indexes and a cumulative index for reports from 1959 to 1963. Occasional articles on Catholic church records and depositories appear in the *American Archivist*, a journal sponsored by the Society of American Archivists.

Specific Subject Collections. The following is a compilation of the main depositories of church history materials and sources primarily located in the United States. *Abbey of St. Martin, 1077–1780*: Huntington Library, San Marino, Calif.; *Alaska Missions*: Gonzaga University, Spokane, Wash.; *American Catholicism before 1842*: Catholic University Archives, Washington,

D.C.; *Benedictines:* St. John's University Archives, Collegeville, Minn. and St. Vincent's Archabbey Archives, Latrobe, Pa.; *Bureau of Catholic Indian Missions Archives*: Marquette University, Milwaukee, Wisc.; *California Church History and Missions, 1770–1955*: University of San Francisco Archives, San Francisco, Calif.; *Catholic Charities*: Catholic University Archives, Washington, D.C.; *Catholic Newspapers*: American Catholic Historical Society, Philadelphia, Pa.; *Catholic Order of Foresters, St. Paul, 1894–1928*: Minnesota Historical Society, St. Paul, Minn.; *Church in Michigan*: Detroit Public Library, Detroit, Mich.; *Church in the Mississippi Valley and in the West*: St. Louis University Archives, St. Louis, Mo.; *Church in Missouri and the Dakotas*: Conception Abbey Archives, Conception, Mo.; *Church in Texas*: Texas Catholic Historical Society, Austin, Texas; *Church in the United States*: American Catholic Historical Society, Philadelphia, Pa.; *Church in Western Pennsylvania*: Duquesne University Archives, Pittsburgh, Pa.; *Church in Wisconsin, 1695–1944*: State Historical Society of Wisconsin, Madison, Wisc.

Dominicans: Dominican House of Studies, Washington, D.C.; *Dublin, Ireland Mission Society*: University of Notre Dame Archives, South Bend, Ind.; *Franciscans*: Bancroft Library, University of California, Berkeley, Calif.; St. Bonaventure University Archives, St. Bonaventure, N.Y.; John Carter Brown Library, Brown University, Providence, R.I.; Academy of American Franciscan History, Berkeley, Calif.; and Santa Fe Archdiocesan Archives, Santa Fe, N.M.; *Gambell Missionaries, 1898–1906*: Alaska Historical Society, Anchorage, Alaska; *German Settlements*: St. Vincent's Archabbey Archives, Latrobe, Pa.; *German Jesuits in America, 1611–1760*: Library of Congress, Washington, D.C.; *Irish and Home Rule*: American Irish Historical Society, New York, N.Y.; *Jesuits in Alaska*: Gonzaga University Archives, Spokane, Wash.

Jesuits in California, 1768: Oscott College, Birmingham, England; *Jesuit Missions among Kickapoo and Potawami Indians*: St. Louis University Archives, St. Louis, Mo.; *Jesuits in North America, 1612–1685*: State Historical Society of Wisconsin, Madison, Wisc.; *Jesuit Missions in the Northwest, 1843–1947*: Gonzaga University Archives, Spokane, Wash. and University of Alaska Museum, Fairbanks, Alaska; *Jesuits in Oregon*: Gonzaga University Archives, Spokane, Wash.; *Jesuit Papers, Copies from Germany, Mexico, Rome, and Spain, "Jesuit Americana"*: St. Louis University Archives, St. Louis, Mo.; *Latin-American Church*: Bancroft Library, University of California, Berkeley, Calif.; Museum of New Mexico, Santa Fe, N.M.; and Academy of American Franciscan History, Berkeley, Calif.; *Lyons* (France) *Mission Society*: University of Notre Dame Archives, South

Bend, Ind.; *Missions in Missouri and the Dakotas, 1873–1923*: Conception Abbey Archives, Conception, Mo. *Munich (Germany) Mission Society*: University of Notre Dame Archives, South Bend, Ind.

Oregon Missions: Oregon Historical Society, Portland, Oreg. *Paris (France) Mission Society*: University of Notre Dame Archives, Notre Dame, Ind.; *Phillipines*: Newberry Library, Chicago, Ill.; University of Michigan Library, Ann Arbor, Mich.; Duke University Library, Durham, N.C; and Princeton University Library, Princeton, N.J.; *Representatives of the American Hierarchy in Rome, 1832–1903*: Catholic University Archives, Washington, D.C.; *Society for the Propagation of the Faith, 1822–1900*: University of Notre Dame Archives, South Bend, Ind.; *Spaniards in Florida and West Indies, 1783–1795*: Huntington Library, San Marino, Calif.; *Spanish-American War Papers*: St. Joseph Central House, Emmitsburg, Md.; *Spanish Missions, 1776–1955*: Bowers Museum, Santa Ana, Calif.; *Sulpicians in the United States*: St. Mary's Seminary Archives, Roland Park, Md.; *Texas and Southwest Missions*: University of Notre Dame Archives, South Bend, Ind.; *Vienna (Austria) Mission Society*: University of Notre Dame Archives, Notre Dame, Ind.

See Also: VATICAN ARCHIVES.

Bibliography: R. NAZ, *Dictionnaire de droit canonique*, 7 v. (Paris 1935–65) 1:1026–36. E. LOEVINSON, "La costituzione di papa Benedetto XIII sugli archivi ecclesiastici: Un papa archivista," *Gli archivi Italiani* 3 (1916) 159–206. G. BATTELLI, "Il censimento degli archivi ecclesiastici d'Italia e la loro tutela durante la guerra," *Rivista di storia della Chiesa iri Italia* (Rome 1947–) 1:113–116; "Gli archivi ecclesiastici d'Italia danneggiati dalla guerra," *ibid.* 306–308. A. CICOGNANI, *Canon Law* (2d ed. rev. Westminster, Md. 1947) 141. H. J. WOLFF, *Roman Law* (Norman, Okla. 1951) 34. A. TOSO, *Ad codicem iuris canonici commentaria minora* (Rome 1925) 2.3.1:22. W. F. LOUIS, *Diocesan Archives* (Catholic University of America Canon Law Studies, 137; Washington 1941). J. E. PRINCE, The Diocesan Chancellor (Catholic University of America Canon Law Studies, 167; Washington 1942). C. A. KEKUMANO, *The Secret Archives of the Diocesan Curia* (Catholic University of America Canon Law Studies, 350; Washington 1954). H. HOFFMANN, "De codificatione iuris archivistici per jus novissimum Codicis Iuris Canonici," *Periodica* 49 (1960) 204–236. H. L. HOFFMANN, *De archivis ecclesiasticis, imprimis dioecesanis secundum iuris canonici codicem* (Rome 1962). J. GRISAR, "Notare und Notariats-archive im Kirchenstaat des 16. Jahrhunderts," *Studi e Testi* 234 (1964) 251–300.

[C. A. KEKUMANO/K. A. FINK/R. A. BURKE]

ARCHIVES, U.S. CATHOLIC

This article presents the history of the development of Catholic manuscript centers in the U.S., and then describes some of the more important centers, categorized by their connection with archdiocesan and diocesan sees, educational institutions, and religious orders and congregations.

History. Before the 1960s, almost no dioceses had more than part-time archivists, only a few Catholic colleges and universities devoted much attention or resources to the collection and preservation of Catholic documents, and most religious orders had hardly even considered the need to create archives. Professional training among archivists in Catholic institutions was virtually unheard of and standards of professional practice nonexistent. Since 1960, the increased public interest in history (reflected in the formation of new history museums, the popularity of historic preservation, and the increase in the numbers and professionalism of public history personnel) has been mirrored by the development of archives within the Church. In 1974, in preparation for the nation's Bicentennial celebration and after effective lobbying by several historians, the National Conference of Catholic Bishops issued "A Document for Ecclesiastical Archives." The bishops noted the general neglect of Catholics in the writing of American history and conceded that that neglect had been caused, at least in part, by historians' lack of "access to the pertinent documents of bishops, dioceses, religious orders." The document urged all bishops who did not have an archivist to appoint one quickly. More recently, in 1997, the Vatican's Pontifical Commission for the Cultural Heritage of the Church contended that "Archives are places of memory which must be preserved, transmitted, renewed, appreciated, because they represent the most direct connection with the heritage of the Church community." The Commission went on to encourage professional training of archival staffs.

In the late 1970s the Leadership Conference of Women Religious launched an archival development program, led by Sr. Evangeline Thomas, C.S.J. This eight-year project provided professional training for nearly 400 archivists of women religious orders and produced a rich and extensive survey of the holdings of over 500 archives of congregations of women religious in 1983. Picking up on this effort, a group of archivists from congregations of women religious began meeting in the late 1980s to form a permanent organization where they could discuss common problems and work together for common solutions. In 1992, they organized formally into the Archivists of Congregations of Women Religious (ACWR). Through the work of the first officers the ACWR established a relationship with the Society of American Archivists (SAA), meeting annually at the SAA's convention. ACWR members also began to meet together on their own every three years for a more extensive program of workshops and forums directly related to their own problems.

Inspired by the bishops' 1974 *Document on Ecclesiastical Archives* and growing out of discussions held as part of the meetings of the SAA in 1979–1980, the Association of Catholic Diocesan Archivists (ACDA) was formally established, with a constitution and bylaws, in 1982, to promote professionalization and standards among diocesan archivists. Early on ACDA addressed the important issue of access to sacramental records with a 1982 *Statement on Access and Use of Sacramental Records* which recognized the sensitivity of these records as well as the legitimacy of genealogical research therein and urged diocesan archivists to make them available under controlled conditions. In 1991, the ACDA tackled the issue of access to church records generally with its *Guideline for Access to Diocesan Archives*, which recommended equality of access within the demands of canon law and generally following the procedures of broader archival world in general.

There has been no equivalent for the ACDA or the ACWR for Catholic college and university archivists. Nonetheless, they have been very active in encouraging the professionalization of Catholic archives as well. In the late 1980s and early 1990s and again in the late 1990s, for example, Catholic University has offered training for archivists through a Religious Archives Institute cosponsored by the University's Archives and Library School.

The following survey will highlight some of the more important archives among the three main groups, diocesan, college and university, and religious order archives, which make up the world of Catholic archives today.

Diocesan Archives. Because of the fundamental importance of diocesan units in the church's ecclesial structure, diocesan archives are necessarily the foundation for the documentation of Catholic religious life in the nation. The following is but a brief survey of some of the major Archdiocesan archives. As might be expected given their greater resources, the nation's archdioceses have many of the best endowed and well-staffed archival programs. Yet there are numerous excellent programs among smaller dioceses, such as in Galveston, Texas; Harrisburg and Pittsburgh, Pennsylvania; and Brooklyn, New York.

Baltimore is the mother see of the American church. Founded in 1789, all other dioceses in the nation descend from it. The Baltimore Diocesan Archives, known until 1974 as the Baltimore Cathedral Archives, is particularly rich in the papers of such leaders like James Cardinal Gibbons and Bishop John Carroll and the records of the Plenary Councils of American bishops held there in 1866 and 1884.

Several dioceses were created from Baltimore in 1808 as the American church grew in size. The sees of three of the dioceses were major cities of the northeast coast: Boston, New York, and Philadelphia. Boston's archives were largely administered informally until the late 1970s when they were completely reorganized under the leadership of James O'Toole. O'Toole, a force in the formation of the ACDA, helped establish in Boston a model of professional practice for other diocesan archives through the professional processing of papers, development of quality finding aids and guides, and codification of rules of access. Whereas Baltimore's collections are heavy in the papers of its distinguished prelates, Boston's are more diverse. Boston's collections include bishops' papers, thin in the nineteenth century apart from a remarkable journal kept by Bishops Fenwick and Fitzpatrick, but generally richer in the twentieth century. More important may be the very extensive collection of correspondence between chancery officials and parishes, charitable agencies and religious orders beginning with the O'Connell administration in 1907. Boston has also collected parish announcement books and bulletins from selected parishes and pre-1920 sacramental records from every parish in the diocese.

Philadelphia's collections are more diverse than Boston's and Baltimore's, since they include not only the archival records of the archdiocese but the manuscripts acquired by the American Catholic Historical Society. Thus at Philadelphia one can not only find papers of nineteenth-century Archbishops Wood and Ryan but also their notable contemporary, the Catholic lay activist and Irish American nationalist, Martin Ignatius Griffin, as well as a very extensive collection of Catholic newspapers from around the nation. New York's Archdiocesan Archives also has rich collections, that, like Baltimore's appear to be especially rich in the papers of bishops like Archbishop John Hughes, Michael Corrigan and Francis Cardinal Spellman.

The Chicago Archdiocesan Archives includes the papers of the archdiocese's many notable leaders, Cardinals Mundelein, Stritch, Meyer, Cody, and Bernardin. The Archives also has extensive chancery correspondence files, records of scores of schools, and microfilm copies of all pre-1916 sacramental registers from all of the Archdiocese's parishes. Since 1966, the Archive has been located in newly renovated, fully climate-controlled facility in downtown Chicago.

New Orleans has a long tradition of Catholic settlement that predates its incorporation into the United States. The Archdiocesan Archives there has rich collections of correspondence from Louisiana pastors in the late eighteenth and early nineteenth century documenting the material and spiritual life of their parishes. It also holds the pre-1900 sacramental records for all the Archdiocese's parishes.

Long before there was a United States of America and a diocese of Baltimore, Catholicism had been established in the Spanish colonies of what today has become New Mexico and Texas. The Archives of the Archdiocese of Santa Fe are especially strong in regard to both Hispanic and Native Americans and include documents dating from 1678, account books from 1736, and sacramental records from 1694 are housed since 1993 in a facility combining offices, storage, and a museum. The Catholic Archives of Texas is a unique institution serving as the only state Catholic archives in the United States. Founded in 1923 under the auspices of the Texas Knights of Columbus Historical Commission, it cooperates closely with the Diocese of Austin, where it is located, other dioceses in Texas, and with cultural and historical institutions in the area to achieve historical preservation of catholic history. Holdings include records of the Texas Catholic Conference and the Texas Knights of Columbus and its Historical Commission, Texas Catholic Historical Society, and religious associations, societies and Catholic clubs in Texas, personal papers and biographical files of the bishops and clergy in Texas, and documents dealing with various religious orders. Like Santa Fe the Catholic Archives of Texas has a rich collection of records dating back to the Spanish colonial era, with holdings documenting Catholic life in eighteenth-century San Antonio and El Paso.

On the West Coast the three principal archives are in Los Angeles, San Francisco and Seattle. Housed in the beautiful old San Fernando mission in Mission Hills, California, the Los Angeles Archives is particularly rich in the papers of Los Angeles' bishops, such as Thomas J. Conaty and John J. Cantwell. The Archives has indexed the papers of many of these men in detailed item-level calendars. The San Francisco Archdiocesan Archives contains documents extending back to the region's mission history but the collections are strongest in the Archdiocese' administrative records of the twentieth century. The Archives also has sacramental records for every parish in the diocese and has conducted a very ambitious oral history program since 1986 that has produced over 150 interviews. Seattle's collections include early sacramental records and diocesan administrative files.

Catholic College and University Archives. Beyond the records they keep of their own institutions, the archives and special collections departments at Catholic colleges and universities range widely in the kinds of records and papers they have collected to document the American Catholic experience. As a rule they are further advanced in professional practice and particularly in the use of computer technology than diocesan or religious order archives. The largest Catholic college archives are those at Catholic University, University of Notre Dame, and Marquette University. Other schools such as Boston College, Holy Cross, Seton Hall, St. John's (New York), and St. John's (Minnesota), also have critically important collections documenting American Catholic history and most, like Boston College and St. John's (New York) have professionally sophisticated programs.

Catholic University's archives date to 1949. The strengths of its collections are Catholic organizational records and personal papers from the twentieth century. The University Archives, for example, holds the records of the three most important national Catholic organizations in the country: the United States Catholic Conference of Bishops (formerly the United States Catholic Conference-National Conference of Catholic Bishops and before that the National Catholic Welfare Conference); the National Catholic Education Association, and Catholic Charities USA (formerly the National Conference of Catholic Charities). The Catholic University Archives also includes the personal papers of a number of important twentieth-century Catholic intellectuals and social activists such as Monsignors John Ryan, George Higgins, John Montgomery Cooper and John Tracy Ellis, who were connected to the above organizations or were members of the University's faculty or both. The University Archives and Manuscripts department has centralized its operations by moving into a single renovated facility, with up-to-date climate-controlled storage rooms and a refurbished reading room and offices.

Father Edward Sorin, the founder of the University of Notre Dame, also founded the University's archives. Not long thereafter, Professor James Fenwick Edwards established a repository at the school entitled the Catholic Archives of America project and began collecting the early diocesan records of Detroit, New Orleans, and Cincinnati; personal papers of Catholic lay leaders like Orestes Brownson and William Onahan; and records relating to Catholic participation in the Civil War. The Archives has continued to collect papers and records of critical importance in American Catholic history, including the papers of Monsignor Reynold Hillenbrand, a leading figure in the liturgical movement; the Christian Family Movement; and Archbishop John F. Dearden of Detroit, the first president of the National Conference of Catholic Bishops. Of special note are collections of the records of two of the most important Catholic journals in America, *Commonweal* magazine and the *National Catholic Reporter*. Together the archives of the University and the manuscripts collections at Notre Dame make up about 19,000 feet of records and papers, making it the largest single Catholic repository in the United States.

Marquette University's Department of Archives and Special Collections was established in 1961 and now houses more than 15,000 feet of records. In addition to maintaining the University's own institutional archives, the department has rich resources in its manuscript collections documenting the American Catholic experience. It includes, for example, some 150 feet of the papers of Dorothy Day and Catholic Worker houses in New York City and other cities around the country; collections in Catholic Women's history comprising the records and papers of the Institute of Women Today, the National Coalition of American Nuns and the Women's Ordination Conference; and 16 collections documenting Christianity among the native peoples of the Americas. These last include the 500 feet of records of the Bureau of Catholic Indian Missions.

Archives of Congregations of Women and Men Religious. Many communities of men religious have been able to deposit their community or provincial records at colleges or universities founded by their orders, and many such colleges and universities have established archival or special collections programs to take care of those records or to assist the establishment of order archives. Some of the Jesuit provinces, for example, have deposited their records at Georgetown, Holy Cross, and St. Louis University, among other institutions, while Marianists and Augustinians have set up congregational archives at the University of Dayton and Villanova respectively. Women religious, who have smaller colleges with more limited library resources and have been largely involved in primary or secondary education or health or charitable work, have not had the same options. Yet women's congregations have generally been better organized and more active in attending to their records and the preservation of their history. Congregations like the Visitation sisters in Washington and the Discalced Carmelites in Baltimore have sought and received funds from the National Historical Publications and Records Commission, a federal funding agency, to organize their archives. Several other communities, most notably the Immaculate Heart of Mary Sisters in Michigan, Felician Sisters in Connecticut, Sisters of Mercy in Pittsburgh, Pennsylvania, Ursuline congregations in Missouri and Kentucky, Discalced Carmelites in Albany, New York, Daughters of Charity in Emmitsburg, Maryland and Sisters of St. Joseph in Massachusetts have created professional archives, preserving, arranging and describing collections according to archival principles and working with computer technology.

Unlike the colleges and universities, and, perhaps more so even than for the dioceses, collecting for religious congregations is more focused, for they are in the truest sense strictly archives, repositories with a precise institutional role to preserve the records of their order, province, or community. Records thus often include, as in the archives of the Ursuline nuns of Crystal Heights of Missouri: papers of provincial superiors; rules, constitutions and chronicles of the order, province or community; formation records; and personal papers, diaries, journals and correspondence of sisters. Many, too, like the Missouri Ursulines often include records of the order's closed hospitals, schools or charitable institutions.

Such a description hardly does justice to the importance of these archives for the study of American Catholic history. The Jesuit Maryland provincial records deposited at Georgetown, for example, are one of the richest single sources in the nation for research into seventeenth century American Catholicism. Among other things, they extensively document Jesuit plantations and slave holding in that era. The records of Baltimore's Discalced Carmelites are a rich resource for Maryland Catholicism in the later years of the early Republic when their community was established at Port Tobacco in Maryland. Missionary society archives like those of the Maryknoll fathers and sisters include correspondence and diaries rich with observations on cultures and societies in Asia and Africa.

Bibliography: C. E. NOLAN, ''Historians and Diocesan Archives: A View from New Orleans,'' *U.S. Catholic Historian* 16, 1 (Winter 1998), 73–83. M. J. OATES, ''Religious Archives Undo Stereotypes about the Role of Sisters,'' *Catholic Library World* (July/August/September 1991), 47–53. J. M. O'TOOLE, ''Catholic Diocesan Archives: A Renaissance in Progress,'' *The American Archivist* (Summer 1980), 284–293; ''Twenty-Five Years of Preserving American Catholic History,'' *U.S. Catholic Historian* 16, 1 (Winter 1998), 1–13. M. B. OCHOA, ''Archives of the Archdiocese of Santa Fe and 400 Years of Church History in New Mexico,'' *U.S. Catholic Historian* 16, 1 (Winter 1998), 23–34. K. F. PERZYNSKA, ''Catholic Archives of Texas: Sense and Sensibility of Catholic History Preservation and Research,'' *U.S. Catholic Historian* 16, 1 (Winter 1998), 35–46. F. POWERS, ''Archives of the Archdiocese of Baltimore: History and Content,'' *U.S. Catholic Historian* 16, 1 (Winter 1998), 47–56. E. THOMAS, ed., *Women Religious History Sources: A Guide to Repositories in the United States* (New York and London 1983).

[T. J. MEAGHER/W. J. SHEPHERD]

ARCHPRIEST

This title dates from the 4th century; it was given, usually, to the senior priest attached to a cathedral. He was empowered to take the bishop's place at liturgical functions. Later, rural archpriests also were appointed who were superior to the local clergy as was the cathedral archpriest to the cathedral clergy. The cathedral archpriest became known as the dean; his rural counterparts, as rural deans; vicars forane are the modern equivalent of rural archpriests. Today the title archpriest, as at St.

Peter's, Rome, Notre Dame, Paris, and elsewhere is honorific. In England from 1598 to 1623 the Church was ruled by an archpriest as superior of the English mission; when in 1623 persecution had abated sufficiently to make it probable that the presence there of a bishop would not provoke worse persecution, the third and last archpriest was replaced by a vicar apostolic.

Bibliography: A. AMANIEU, *Dictionnaire de droit canonique* 1:1004–26. P. HUGHES, *Rome and the Counter-Reformation in England* (London 1942) 287–306. 1917 *Codex iuris canonici* c. 217.

[B. FORSHAW]

ARCHPRIEST CONTROVERSY

The archpriest controversy (1598–1602) grew out of the opposition of a few English seminary priests to the institution of the archpriest and to the authority of George BLACKWELL, first to be appointed to this office in March 1598. During Cardinal William ALLEN'S lifetime the weakness of having no superior over the clergy in England was obscured by his own great prestige and by that of Henry GARNET, the Jesuit superior, who dealt with urgent practical problems.

After Allen's death in October 1594, Clement VIII, thinking the time yet unripe for a bishop, appointed Blackwell through Cajetan, the Cardinal Protector, as archpriest with 12 assistants to rule the seminary priests on the mission. Over Blackwell with appellate powers was the papal nuncio to Flanders. For years there had been a combined move on the part of the rebellious students in the English College, the faction in Flanders, and a few priests in England, mostly prisoners in Wisbech Castle, to have the Jesuits recalled from England and removed from the government of the seminaries. One clause of the Protector's Instructions to Blackwell provided for consultation with the Jesuits. This later caused contention. The new appointment was warmly welcomed in England by more than 300 priests. Some 15, however, at first refused to recognize their new superior. Two of them, William Bishop and Robert Charnock, left for Rome in late summer 1598 to appeal, while those remaining enlisted the support of the persecuting government, a ploy later so characteristic of the group. Blackwell's appointment, however, was but the occasion for the journey, for the trouble-makers in England and abroad had been planning an embassy to Rome some months before it had been made; they now pursued these plans, adding thereto dislike of the new office and personal complaints against Blackwell.

Their embassy caused great displeasure in Rome. They were examined individually, and a papal brief on

April 6, 1599, confirmed both the institution of archpriest and the appointment of Blackwell. Hostilities against Blackwell were resumed, and for two years letters, manifestoes, and polemical pamphlets, printed with the connivance of the bishop of London, developed the grievances of the dissidents. They alleged canonical objections to Blackwell and his office, and even questioned the pope's power to make such an appointment. The appellants charged that Blackwell was a tool of the Jesuits, who, according to the appellants, were interested chiefly in their own aggrandizement on the English mission. Exasperation at their insolent tone and their protection by the persecutors drove Blackwell to denounce them in sharp language and to issue edicts and suspensions against them somewhat indiscriminately, thus providing ostensible justification for their second appeal, Nov. 17, 1600. A second brief reconfirmed the appointment and forbade prosecution of the appeal, but the appellants, having left England late in 1601, with passports and covert government backing, saw the brief in Flanders and ignored it. In France they were favorably received by the court, for reasons of its anti-Spanish policy, and in Rome they were protected by the French ambassador. The documents reveal the latter's skillful intervention, as well as the impudence and inveracity of the appellants.

Hearings were terminated by a brief, Oct. 5, 1602, addressed to Blackwell, *ipso facto* confirming his authority, but severely reproving aspects of his conduct. It restricted his powers and ordered him to appoint appellants among his assistants. Though the Jesuits were praised, all official consultation with them was, with their agreement, forbidden. All controversial writings, and collusion with heretics *in praejudicium Catholicorum,* were forbidden under censures. Because it broke unity among mission workers, the brief was a disastrous turning point for English Catholicism.

Bibliography: T. G. LAW, ed., *The Archpriest Controversy,* 2 v. (Camden Society 56, 58; London 1896–98). J. H. POLLEN, *The Institution of the Archpriest Blackwell* (New York 1916). R. PERSONS, *A Briefe Apologie . . .* (London 1602). P. RENOLD, ed., *The Wisbech Stirs, 1595–1598* (*Proceedings of the Catholic Record Society* 51; 1958).

[P. RENOLD]

ARCIMBOLDI, GIOVANNANGELO

Archbishop of Milan and papal nuncio to the Scandinavian countries; b. in Milan, 1485; d. there, April 6, 1555. After traveling in the Low Lands and Germany, he purchased (for 1,100 guldens) the right to preach in Scandinavia the indulgence for the building of St. Peters. When he arrived in Denmark in 1516, he was well received by King Christian II. Two years later Arcimboldi went to Sweden to preach, and while there he associated and sympathized with those forces plotting rebellion against Denmark. He even negotiated with Sten Sture on behalf of Pope LEO X, implying papal sympathy with the rebel cause. Christian II, who believed the papal nuncio was working on his behalf in Sweden, was furious upon learning the contrary. He immediately confiscated all of the property and money Arcimboldi had left in Denmark and imprisoned his brother and servants. The nuncio fled to Lübeck, from whence he was recalled by LEO X as soon as news of his activities reached Rome. However, the damage was done, and Christian II invited Lutheran theologians to the Danish court—thus paving the way for the conversion of Scandinavia to LUTHERANISM. In 1522 Arcimboldi was sent to Spain to meet the pope-elect, ADRIAN VI. In 1526 he was named bishop of Novara by CLEMENT VII. In 1550 he became archbishop of Milan.

Bibliography: E. SANTOVITO, G. M. MAZZUCHELLI, *Gli scrittori d'Italia,* 2 v. (Brescia 1753–63). C. M. BUTLER, *The Reformation in Sweden* (New York 1883). J. LENZENWEGER, *Lexikon für Theologie und Kirche,* ed. J. HOFER and K. RAHNER, 10 v. (2d, new ed. Freiburg 1957–65). L. PASTOR, *The History of the Popes from the Close of the Middle Ages* (London-St. Louis 1938–61) 1:827–828.

[J. G. GALLAHER]

ARCOSOLIUM

An elaborate *loculus,* or catacomb grave. The word may owe its origin to *arcus* (arch) or *arca* (coffin) and *solium* (throne). The processional litter used in antiquity in the burial rites of important personages was called a *solium.* By extension, the tomb itself came to be called a *solium,* and the term was used in this sense by certain ancient writers (Curtius, *Hist.* 10.10; Suetonius, *Nero.* 50). The *arcosolium* was formed by excavating in the wall a space similar to that of an ordinary *loculus* and surmounting the space by an arch. The arch facilitated the opening of the downward cavity where the corpse was to be laid. *Arcosolia* differed from *loculi* in elegance and in the mode of closing. *Loculi* were closed vertically by a marble slab fixed to the wall, whereas *arcosolia* were closed horizontally. Above the horizontal slab was an arch or vault of stucco, frequently ornamented with frescoes. A more ancient form of *arcosolium* was the arched niche excavated to floor level; sarcophagi were placed in this earlier type. Although some *arcosolia* are found along the passages of the catacombs, the greater number are located in the *cubicula. Arcosolia* were used everywhere in Rome during the 3d century, and many later martyrs were interred in them.

Bibliography: Centre de Pastorale Liturgique, *Le Mystère de la mort et sa célébration* (Le Orandi 12; Paris 1956). H. LECLERCQ,

Dictionnaire d'archéologie chrétienne et de liturgie 1.2:2774–87. O. MARUCCHI, *Le Catacombe romane* (Rome 1932) 312–336. J. KOLLWITZ, *Reallexikon für Antike und Christentum* 1: 643–645; 3:231–235. P. TESTINI, *Archeologia cristiana* (Rome 1958) 75–326. F. DE VISSCHER, *Analecta Bollandiana* 69 (1951) 39–54.

[M. C. HILFERTY]

ARCOVERDE DE ALBUQUERQUE CAVALCANTI, JOAQUIM

First cardinal of Rio de Janeiro and of Latin America; b. Pernambuco, Jan. 17, 1850; d. Rio de Janeiro, April 18, 1930. He was ordained on April 4, 1874. Although elected bishop of Goias in 1890 and consecrated in Rome, he renounced that office before taking power and was named coadjutor bishop of the Diocese of São Paulo in 1892. In 1894 he became bishop of São Paulo, and then strove to stimulate the rather lifeless Brazilian Catholicism of the period, coordinating the labors of Catholic associations and attracting to the diocese such religious congregations as that of the Immaculate Heart of Mary, the Premonstratensians, and the Redemptorists.

In 1897 he was transferred to Rio de Janeiro as the second archbishop of the archdiocese created there in 1892. In this position Dom Joaquim gave his greatest contribution to the Church of Brazil, which at the time not only failed to influence national life—though Catholics formed an absolute majority—but also lacked sufficient organized political support. He actively participated in the Latin American Plenary Council held in Rome in 1899. The better to put the decisions of the council into practice, he assembled his suffragan bishops annually after 1901. The fruits of these reunions were published in *Pastorais colectivas* (1901, 1909, 1915). These episcopal meetings were necessary antecedents for the important Brazilian Plenary Council held in Rio de Janeiro in June 1939.

In Rio de Janeiro Dom Joaquim constructed the Palácio S. Joaquim, the archiepiscopal headquarters. A series of difficulties forced him to close the diocesan seminary in 1907, but he sent his more intelligent clerical students to Europe to complete their studies. He reaped the fruits of closer contact between the Church and the new republic when, in 1905, he was named cardinal of Rio de Janeiro, the first Latin American cardinal in history. In 1921 D. Arcoverde's mental and physical health began to fail. From that date until his death, he was merely a figurehead as the archdiocese was administered by coadjutor Abp. D. Sebastião LEME DE SILVEIRA CINTRA, who succeeded the cardinal in 1930.

Bibliography: M. ALVARENGA, *O Episcopado Brasileiro* (São Paulo 1915). L. CASTANHO DE ALMEIDA, *São Paulo, filho da Igreja*

(Patrópolis, Brazil 1955). G. SCHUBERT, ed., *A província eclesiástica do Rio de Janeiro* (Rio de Janeiro 1948).

[I. SILVEIRA]

ARDBRACCAN, ABBEY OF

Former Celtic monastery of Áird Breccáin near Navan, in Meath, Ireland. It was distinguished by its bishop and abbot, Ultan moccu Conchobuir, who seems to have been the first scholar to collect, or have collected, into one volume the historical material dealing with the work of St. PATRICK in Ireland. It was this *Liber apud Ultanum* that was used by Bishop Tírechán *c.* 670, when he compiled the Memoir, which is the earliest account now extant of St. Patrick's life. The deaths of various abbots who headed this abbey were recorded in the Irish annals of the 8th, 9th, and 10th centuries. Maelruba, e.g., anchorite, bishop and abbot of Ardbraccan died in 825. Like every other Irish monastery, it was plundered and burnt on many occasions by the Northmen: as late as 1031 its chief church was set on fire by the Norse of Dublin, and the 200 people who had taken refuge within its walls were burned to death. Maelbrigte, head of the monastic school, died in 1054. By the end of the 12th century the monastery had ceased to function, and its lands had passed to the bishopric of east Meath.

Bibliography: *The Annals of Ulster,* ed. and tr. W. M. HENNESSY and B. MACCARTHY, 4 v. (Dublin 1887–1901). *The Annals of Inisfallen,* ed. and tr. S. MACAIRT (Dublin 1951). *Chronicum Scotorum,* ed. W. M. HENNESSY (Rerum Britannicarum medii aevi scriptores 46; 1866). "Annals of Tigernach," ed. W. STOKES, *Revue celtique* 17–18 (1896–97). *Annals of the Four Masters,* ed. and tr. J. O'DONOVAN, 7 v. (Dublin 1851). *The Martyrology of Tallaght,* ed. R. I. BEST and H. J. LAWLOR (Henry Bradshaw Society 68; London 1931). *The Martyrology of Oengus the Culdee,* ed. W. STOKES (*ibid.* 29; 1905). *The Martyrology of Gorman,* ed. W. STOKES (*ibid.* 9; 1895).

[J. RYAN]

ARDCHATTAN, PRIORY OF

A former VALLISCAULIAN house on the shores of Loch Etive, Argyllshire, Scotland, founded by Duncan Mackoull, or Macdougall, in 1230, and dedicated to St. Mary and St. John the Baptist. Its name was derived from the Gaelic, meaning "hill of Cattan," which probably refers to Cailtan, an early Scottish saint of the district. The priory's early history is obscure: it is known to have sworn fealty to Edward I in 1296, although Robert the Bruce held a parliament there in 1308. In 1506 James, the prior general of the order, commissioned the prior of Beauly to visit Ardchattan and to make such reform regulations as he should find necessary. By 1538 only six monks appear to have been left at Ardchattan, and in 1602 James VI dissolved the monastery and erected it into a temporal lordship for Alexander Campbell, its former prior. It is now a ruin.

Bibliography: Edinburgh Bannatyne Club, *Origines parochiales Scotiae,* ed. C. INNES, 2 v. (Edinburgh 1850–55) v. 2.1. M. BARRETT, *The Scottish Monasteries of Old* (Edinburgh 1913). D. E. EASSON, *Medieval Religious Houses: Scotland* (London 1957) 70. S. CRUDEN, *Scottish Abbeys* (Edinburgh 1960).

[L. MACFARLANE]

ARDEN, EDWARD

High sheriff of Warwickshire; b. Warwickshire, 1542?; d. Smithfield, Dec. 30, 1583. Arden succeeded as heir to his grandfather Thomas's estates in 1563. A devout Catholic, he maintained a priest disguised as a gardener at Park Hall, his residence. Under the influence of Father Hugh Hall, members of the Arden household, especially John Somerville, Arden's son-in-law, began to conspire and intrigue against Queen Elizabeth I. Somerville's recklessness soon led to his arrest. Under torture, Somerville implicated Hall and the Arden family. Unfortunately, Arden had also cast aspersions on the character of Robert Dudley, Earl of Leicester, who soon took a personal hand in prosecuting Arden. Hall, Somerville, and Arden were tried, convicted, and sentenced to death. Somerville strangled himself in his cell. Mrs. Arden and Hall, who aided the prosecution, were pardoned; but Arden was hanged for treason, protesting until the end that his only crimes were those of being a devout Catholic and of having incurred Leicester's wrath.

Bibliography: R. HARRISON, *The Dictionary of National Biography from the Earliest Times to 1900,* 63 v. (London 1885–1900) 1:546. J. GILLOW, *A Literary and Biographical History or Bibliographical Dictionary of the English Catholics from 1534 to the Present time,* 5 v. (London–New York, 1885–1902) 1:57–58.

[P. S. MCGARRY]

ARDENNE, MONASTERY OF

Abbey of PREMONSTRATENSIANS near Caen, Normandy, Diocese of BAYEUX, dedicated to the Blessed Virgin. Founded as a cell of hermits by a certain Gilbert (1138) and endowed by Aiulph du Four, it was traded to the Premonstratensian abbey of La Luzerne by Bp. Philip de Harcourt of Bayeux (1144). In 1150 it became an abbey, with 16 churches and chapels eventually, receiving papal confirmation in 1161. One of the richest Premonstratensian houses in France, it received, after 1507, commendatory abbots. Wars and the rapacity of abbots afflicted it in the 17th century, when its annual revenue was 17,800 livres. In 1629 it joined the Reformed Congregation of Lorraine. When it was suppressed (1790), its abbot was an Englishman, Edward Booth. Its many buildings were standing a century ago, but the destruction of World War II left only the Gothic church (14th–15th century), a 13th-century tithe barn, a Gothic gatehouse, and parts of the monastery. The church, which was used as a barn in 1944, is in the process of being restored.

Bibliography: E. RINGARD, ''Les Origines de l'Ordre de Prémontré en Normandie: Recherches sur la filiation des abbayes de la Luzerne et d'Ardenne,'' *Analecta Praemonstratensia* 2 (1926) 159–177. L. H. COTTINEAU, *Répertoire topobibliographique des abbayes et prieurés,* 2 v. (Mâcon 1935–39) 1:893. M. PREVOST, *Dictionnaire d'histoire et de géographie ecclésiastiques,* ed. A. BAUDRILLART et al. (Paris 1912–) 3:1602–04. N. BACKMUND, *Monasticon Praemonstratense,* 3 v. (Straubing 1949–56) 3:33–36.

[N. BACKMUND]

AREDIUS, ST.

Abbot, also known as Aridius, Arigius, Yrieix, Yriel, Yriez, Ysary, Ysère, Yséry; b. Limoges, France, early sixth century; d. Aug. 25, 591. He came from an important family and grew up at the court of King THEUDEBERT I. Attracted by the sanctity and eloquence of Bishop NICETIUS OF TRIER, he went to study under him, subsequently becoming one of his clergy and showing signs of holiness. He returned to Limoges after the death of his father and used his patrimony to build churches and, some time before 572, to found the Abbey of Attane, later named St. Yrieix in his honor. Aredius became first abbot, and he and his monks followed the teachings of the monastic fathers, especially those of BASIL and John CASSIAN. He was also a friend of the poet Fortunatus, who mentions him in his poems. He was buried in the abbey, and his relics were translated when a new church was built *c.* 1180. GREGORY OF TOURS reported many miracles worked through his intercession.

Feast: Aug. 25.

Bibliography: GREGORY OF TOURS, *Historia Francorum* 10.29, *Monumenta Germaniae Historica: Scriptores rerum Merovingicarum* 1:440–442. *Bibliotheca hagiograpica latina antiquae et mediae aetatis* (Brussels 1898–1901) 1:664–668, lists other refs. in Gregory. *Vita, Acta Sanctorum* Aug. 5:178–194 and *Monumenta Germaniae Historica: Scriptores rerum Merovingicarum* 3:581–609. F. ARBELLOT, *Vie de saint Yrieix* (Limoges 1900). R. AIGRAIN, *Dictionnaire d'histoire et de géographie ecclésiastiques,* ed. A. BAUDRILLART et al. (Paris 1912) 1632–36; *Catholicisme* 1:806. J. L. BAUDOT and L. CHAUSSIN, *Vies des saints et des bienhereux selon l'ordre du calendrier avec l'historique des fêtes* (Paris 1935–56) 8:475–478. A. M. ZIMMERMANN, *Kalendarium Benedictinum* (Metten 1933–38) 2:622–623.

[M. C. MCCARTHY]

AREOPAGUS

A rocky height in Athens west of the Acropolis, from which it is separated by a narrow depression bears the name Areopagus [hill of Ares (Mars)]. In antiquity it was the meeting place of the oldest Council of Athens, also called the Areopagus, made up of the king's chief men and having special authority to try murder cases. Its competence varied with the times, but its authority was very great until the democratic reforms of the early 5th century B.C. Thereafter it remained an honorable remnant of antiquity but without political power. At the time St. Paul was summoned before this Council it probably met in the agora and no longer on Mars Hill.

Paul's Arraignment before the Areopagus. When Paul arrived in ATHENS, although he had been fleeing from the Jews in Thessalonica and Boroea, he nevertheless first went to the synagogue of the Jews and to others favorable to monotheism. He also preached in the market place every day, debating with Epicurean and Stoic philosophers without much success. His audience either did not understand him at all or they misinterpreted his teaching as propaganda for two new gods, Jesus and Anastasis (Resurrection). This confusion led to a more formal inquiry about his doctrine before the Areopagus. There was nothing particularly hostile about the hearing as some have thought; it was called to gather information about a doctrine new to the Athenians' jaded ears. Something entirely new and unheard of had come to the center of human wisdom and learning (Acts 17.16–21).

Paul's Speech before the Areopagus. A literary problem is connected with Paul's exposition of his new doctrine (Acts 17.22–31). Is it really Paul's speech or St. Luke's invention put into Paul's mouth to break the narrative's monotony and add greater vividness? It is universally agreed that Greek and Roman historians invented speeches that they attributed to various historical persons. Furthermore, Luke did not accompany Paul from Philippi and he rejoined him only during his last journey, as may be surmised from the long hiatus between the "we sections" of the Acts (16:17; 20.5). Apart from the possibility of a written source, then, Luke had to rely on only Paul himself for knowledge of the Athenian sojourn and the discourse—unless Timothy had not yet returned to Thessalonica (1 Thes 3.1–2). Whatever his source, the author of the Acts had ample means to learn of the substance of Paul's discourse; and there is no need to demand a verbatim account of it. The speech has an authentic ring to it, when one considers that it is a type of Paul's customary KERYGMA to polytheistic pagans. Moreover, the citation of a Greek poet and philosopher (Acts 17.28) to an Athenian audience is especially appropriate. The judgment of the world by Jesus—established as judge by His Resur-

rection—brings out the specifically Christian character of this kerygma (Acts 17.31). Finally, if the writer were a forger, he would certainly have represented the result of the speech quite differently (Acts 17.32–34).

Paul's mission in Athens, although it was apparently frustrated, fulfilled nevertheless his principle: he became all things to all men, even a poet-quoting Greek, that he might save at least some (1 Cor 9.22, in the Greek text). Later, however, in Corinth, having learned his lesson from the Athenians' scorn, he would no longer speak in the words of human wisdom but in those of divine wisdom and the Cross—and with much more success (1 Cor 1.17–31).

Bibliography: *Encyclopedic Dictionary of the Bible,* tr. and adap. by L. HARTMAN (New York 1963), from A. VAN DEN BORN, *Bijbels Woordenboek* 129–130. *The Oxford Classical Dictinary,* ed. M. CARY et al. (Oxford 1949) 85. A. WIKENHAUSER, *Lexikon für Theologie und Kirche,* ed. J. HOFER and K. RAHNER, 10 v. (2d, new ed. Freiburg 1957–65); suppl., *Das Zweite Vatikanische Konzil: Dokumente und Kommentare,* ed. H. S. BRECHTER et al., pt. 1 (1966) 1:830–831. I. C. T. HILL, *The Ancient City of Athens: Its Topography and Monuments* (Cambridge, Mass. 1953).

[P. P. SAYDON]

ARETHAS, ARCHBISHOP OF CAESAREA

Exegete; b. Patras, *c.* 850; d. *c.* 944. Possibly he was a pupil of the Patriarch of Constantinople PHOTIUS; Arethas was prominent in the revival of classical and patristic letters at Constantinople during the latter part of the 9th century. He procured several classical manuscripts, of which the *Cod. Clarkianus* of Plato is the best-known survivor, and he is responsible for the preservation of many excerpts from the works of the early Church Fathers, particularly the Greek text of the Apologists. The Arethas codex (Paris gk. 451) testifies to his scholarship. He was ordained deacon *c.* 895 and became court orator to the Byzantine Emperor LEO VI in 900. After his appointment to the See of Caesarea (*c.* 903), he produced a series of tracts and letters in opposition to the Emperor Leo's fourth marriage, for which the Patriarch of Constantinople NICHOLAS I wished to grant a dispensation (906–907). Arethas wrote a treatise on polygamy, quoting patristic authors; a diatribe; and an elenchus against Nicholas's position. But later he seems to have acquiesced in the dispensation granted by the next patriarch, EUTHYMIUS I. The most famous of Arethas's exegetical writings is his commentary on the Johannine Apocalypse (*c.* 913) based on that of Andrew of Caesarea (between 563 and 614). He wrote a commentary and gloss on the Pauline letters, attempted to complete the homilies of St.

Basil of Caesarea on the Old Testament, and provided scholia for the writings of the earliest Church Fathers, such as CLEMENT OF ALEXANDRIA and JUSTIN. He fought for the right of asylum and against the translation of bishops. His pastoral interests brought him into contact with the theological problems of the day, and he wrote letters and sermons for the consecration of bishops and churches. Many of his writings are still unpublished.

Bibliography: *Kirche und theologische Literatur im byzantinischen Reich* 591–595. U. RIEDINGER, *Lexikon für Theologie und Kirche,* 10 v. (2d, new ed. Freiburg 1957–65) 1:832. O. VON GEBHARDT, ''Der Arethascodex Paris Gr. 451'' *Texte und Untersuchungen zur Geschichte der altchristlichen Literatur* 1.3 (Berlin 1883) 154–196. F. DIEKAM, *Analecta patristica* (*Orientalia Christiana Analecta* 117 (Rome 1938) 230–236. G. HEINRICI, J. J. HERZOG and A. HAUCK, eds., *Realencyklopädie für protestantische Theologie* 2:1–5. R. J. JENKINS and B. LAOURDAS, ''Eight Letters of Arethas,'' *Hellenika* 14 (1956), 293–372. R. J. JENKINS et al., *Byzantinische Zeitschrift* 47 (1954), 1–40, Photius Scholia. J. SCHMID, *Biblische Zeitschrift* 19 (1931), 228–254, Apocalypse. J. COMPERNASS, *Studi bizantine* 1–44, psalms; 4 (1935), 87–125, translation of bishops.

[F. X. MURPHY]

ARÉVALO, RODRIGO SÁNCHEZ DE

Spanish bishop and canonist-theologian; b. Santa María de Nieva, 1404; d. Rome, Oct. 4, 1470. His diplomatic career as well as his writings defended the papacy against conciliarist attacks after the Council of CONSTANCE, promoted supreme spiritual and temporal papal primacy, and urged ecclesiastical reforms. Arévalo graduated from Salamanca (1428–29) with doctorates in civil and canon law. Between 1434 and 1439 he served as a member of the Castilian delegation to the Council of BASEL. By June 16, 1439, when that delegation under the leadership of Alfonso of Cartagena withdrew from Basel in protest over the council's attempt to depose Pope Eugene IV, Arévalo's anticonciliarist ideas had fully matured (*see* CONCILIARISM). These he expressed in his *De remediis schismatis,* a tract resulting from diplomatic missions undertaken for his sovereign, John II of Castile. The tract promoted adherence to Eugene IV (d. 1447) in the courts of France, Germany, and Italy. Four similar works, written between 1447 and 1470, apply his basic attitudes to recurring instances of conciliarist agitation. On April 22, 1457, Pope Callistus III raised Arévalo to the Spanish bishopric of Oviedo. Later Pope Paul II made him bishop successively of Zamora, Calahorra, and Palencia. As royal procurator for King Henry IV, and then as adviser to Paul II, he resided in Rome, from 1460 to 1470, serving also as papal castellan of Castel San Angelo.

His ideas on the PRIMACY of the pope were best formulated in his *Libellus de libera et irrefragabili auctori-*

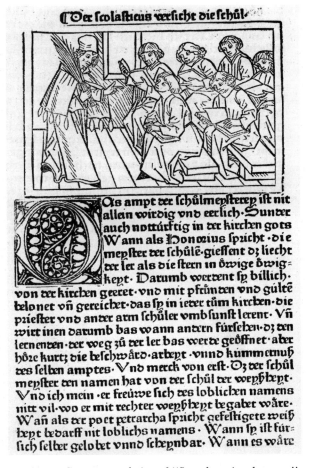

Page from a German translation of ''Speculum vitae humane,'' written by Rodrigo Sánchez De Arévalo.

tate Romani Pontificis and *De monarchia orbis;* his ideas on REFORM IN THE CHURCH, in *Defensorium ecclesiae et status ecclesiastici.* His Latin letters to contemporary Italian humanists place Arévalo among Spain's foremost humanists (*see* HUMANISM); his Castilian essays rank him first among his country's 15th-century writers in the vernacular. His writings are mostly unedited.

Bibliography: T. TONI, *Don Rodrigo Sánchez de Arévalo . . . su personalidad y actividades . . .* (Madrid 1941). R. H. TRAME, *R. S. de A., 1404–1470* (Washington 1958). R. B. TATE, ''R. S. de A. (1404–1470) and his *Compendiosa Historia Hispanica,*'' *Nottingham Mediaeval Studies* 4 (1960) 58–80.

[R. H. TRAME]

ARGENTEUIL, ABBEY OF

Benedictine monastery near Versailles, founded for religious women, between 650 and 675, by Erminric and his wife, Numana, courtiers at the Neustrian court. Its

Capital: Buenos Aires.
Size: 1,079,965 sq. miles.
Population: 36,955,182 in 2000.
Languages: Spanish; English, Italian, German, and French are also spoken.
Religions: 33,259,662 Catholics (90%), 739,105 Protestants (2%), 719,500 Jews (2%), 2,236,915 other (6%).

early history is obscure. In the 9th century, Theotrade, a daughter of Charlemagne, and Judith, a daughter of Charles the Bald, were abbesses; but their role was probably limited to receiving the revenues and giving protection from afar. It was destroyed *c.* 1000 by the Normans and restored again under Robert the Pious. Héloïse made her first studies there *c.* 1115 before becoming a pupil of ABELARD in Paris and took the veil there (1118–20) after the tragic sequel to her marriage. She became superior soon afterward. In 1129 she and the nuns were replaced by monks, and the monastery became a dependent priory of St. Denis. A very austere regime was introduced, but a gradual decline set in. A reform took place in 1646 under the Maurists. Of the four monks living there at its suppression in 1791, only one left the religious life. The holy cloak of Argenteuil, thought to be the seamless garment woven for Christ by his mother, was venerated at the priory; it is first mentioned in a 12th-century document of uncertain value.

Bibliography: A. LESORT, *Dictionnaire d'histoire et de géographie ecclésiastiques,* ed. A. BAUDRILLART et al. (Paris 1912–) 4:22–39. L. H. COTTINEAU *Repertoire topobibliographique des abbayes et prieurés* (Mâcon 1935–39) v. 1. H. GLASER, *Lexikon für Theologie und Kirche,* ed. J. HOFER and K. RAHNER, 10 v. (2d, new ed. Freiburg 1957–65) 1:833–834.

[C. FALK]

ARGENTINA, THE CATHOLIC CHURCH IN

The Argentine Republic, the second largest country in South America, is bounded on the north by Bolivia and Paraguay, on the east by Brazil, Uruguay, and the Atlantic Ocean, and on the west by Chile, which separates Argentina from the Pacific Ocean. The country's northern Pampas region is characterized by fertile lowland plains, its climate subtropical, while the land rises to fertile plains in the central region, and the uneven plateau of Patagonia to the south. The Andes mountains to the west provide a natural boundary between Argentina and Chile, and the range contains several volcanos. Argentina's highly literate population is largely of Spanish or Italian origin, with ethnic Amerindians, mestizos, and Africans comprising less than five percent of its citizens.

While Argentina is highly urbanized, it still derives much of its national income from agriculture. Natural resources include deposits of oil, natural gas, zinc, uranium, and lead; the nation's agricultural production includes wheat, corn, cotton, rice, and sugarcane. In a strategic position due to its location near the Strait of Magellan and other sea lanes connecting the Atlantic and Pacific oceans, Argentina remained under control of Spain until 1816. After achieving independence, it spent the rest of the 19th century resolving border disputes with its neighbors. Its constitutional government was overthrown in 1943 by a military coup led by Juan Perón, whose dictatorship lasted for several decades. In the years following Perón's ouster, the country was controlled by a military junta. Since 1983 democratic elections have been held in Argentina.

Early Christianization. On April 1, 1519, several priests came ashore at San Julián, Patagonia, as part of Ferdinand Magellan's expedition to Argentina. In February 1536 the colonizing expedition of Pedro de Mendoza arrived at the site of Buenos Aires. Three churches or provisional chapels were built, and the same was done a few months later in Asunción, Paraguay. One of the priests, Juan Gabriel de Lezcano, opened a school for the indigenous people, teaching them catechism, chant, reading, and writing, while trying to instill in them Christian values.

The first settlement at Buenos Aires was soon depopulated, its inhabitants moving to other, more recently established towns such as Corpus Christi (1536) and Asunción, Paraguay (1537). Years later, settlers from Chile founded the city of Mendoza (1560) and San Juan (1561); others from Peru founded Tucumán in 1565, Córdoba in 1579, Santa Fe in 1578, and resuscitated Buenos Aires in 1583. All of these settlements and most of the military expeditions were attended by regular or secular clergy, Franciscans and Dominicans predominating at first. For the Spaniards at that time, founding a city meant establishing a *cabildo,* and a church and school entrusted to the priest. The CONQUISTADORES were predominantly men of profound and deep-rooted faith, loyal to religious and pious practices, even if the habits of some were not always in accordance with moral standards. Some priests, fleeing from the peninsular Inquisition or in search of freedom for their licentiousness, went to Río de la Plata and became a corrupting influence.

The Spanish Period. On July 1, 1547, Pope Paul III created the Diocese of Río de la Plata, which encompassed the Spanish Viceroyalty of La Plata (present-day Argentina, Uruguay, Paraguay north to the Paranapanema River, and the southern part of present-day Brazil). The see was in Asunción, and the first bishop to actually serve in the position was Pedro Fernández de la Torre (1555–73), a Franciscan. With the creation of the Diocese of Tucumán (sometimes called Córdoba de Tucumán) in 1570, including the central and northwest sections of the country, and the appointment of Francisco de Victoria as bishop, effective episcopal action began. While Victoria had difficulties because of his mercantilist enterprises and his pro-Portuguese attitude (he was a native of Portugal), to him is owed the ecclesiastical organization of the Argentine territory. Both he and his successor, Fernando de TREJO Y SANABRIA (1595–1614), made much use of the religious orders, especially the Jesuits, brought in by Bishop Victoria.

Bishop Sanabria organized his diocesan church in conformity with the decisions of the Council of Trent. To better prepare his clergy he established the Colegio Seminario de Santa Catalina, which eventually found a home in Córdoba and was called Loreto. Later he founded the Colegio Convictorio de San Javier in Córdoba, and in 1613 he took the first steps toward the creation of the University of Córdoba, founded in 1622. At the end of the 17th century this initial work, implemented by the Jesuits, would be completed by Ignacio Duarte y Quirós with the foundation of the Convictorio de Monserrat, which fostered many priestly vocations.

For the next 400 years there would be a steady increase in the number of dioceses in Argentina, a reflection of the slow but constant progress of Catholicism and evidence of the success of the conversion of the region's native peoples. Franciscans such as Alonso de Buenaventura and Luis de Bolaños (c. 1578), and the Jesuits Alonso Barzana and Pedro de Añasco (1586), approached their work in an organized and systematic manner: the Franciscans worked in the prosperous Reductions in present-day Paraguay and in San José del Bagual, Santiago del Baradero, Isla de Santiago, and Tumbichaminí, while the Jesuits worked in the 30 Reductions they established, beginning in 1610, in what is now the Province of Misiones and in adjacent regions, both Paraguayan and Brazilian. In addition to these Reductions the Jesuits founded in the 18th century those of Abipones in the Chaco, the Mocobíes in Santa Fe, the Vilelas in Salta, the Lules in Tucumán, and those of the Pampas in the Province of Buenos Aires.

After their expulsion in 1767, the Jesuits were replaced in their 30 Reductions by Franciscans, Dominicans, and Mercedarians. These towns were destroyed in the battles that took place between 1810 and 1818 by Paraguayans, Uruguayans, and Brazilians. The other Jesuit Reductions ceased to exist after the expulsion of the

Archdioceses	Suffragans
Bahía Blanca	Alto Valle del Río Negro, Comodoro Rivadavia, Río Gallegos, San Carlos de Bariloche, Santa Rosa, Viedma
Buenos Aires	Avellaneda, Gregorio de Laferrere, Lomas de Zamora, Merlo-Moreno, Morón, San Isidro, San Justo, San Martín, San Miguel
Córdoba	Cruz del Eje, San Francisco, Villa de la Concepción del Río Cuarto, Villa María (and a prelature at Deán Funes)
Corrientes	Goya, Posadas, Puerto Iguazú, Santo Tomé
La Plata	Azul, Chascomús, Mar del Plata, Nueve de Julio, Quilmes, Zárete-Campana
Mendoza	Nequén San Rafael
Paraná	Concordia Gualeguaychú
Rosario	San Nicolás de los Arroyos, Venado Tuerto
Salta	Catamarca, Jujuy, Orán (and prelatures at Cafayate and Humahuaca)
San Juan de Cuyo	La Rioja, San Luis
Santa Fe de la Vera Cruz	Rafaela, Reconquista
Tucumán	Añatuya, Concepción, Santiago del Estero

Mercedes Luján is immediately subject to the Holy See

order. At the end of the 18th century Franciscan fathers from the Propaganda Fide, and after 1876 the Salesians, again undertook conversion efforts in the extreme north and the extreme south of the country. Their numbers did not exceed 30,000.

Although the Jesuit professors at the University of Córdoba and in the Convictorio de Monserrat had been Cartesian, as were the Franciscans who succeeded them after 1767, Catholic doctrine suffered no impairment, nor was it affected by the liberal ideas dominant in Spain. This was not the case at the Colegio de San Ignacio in Buenos Aires, directed by the secular clergy since 1773, among them Julián Fernández de Agüero, a priest of agnostic doctrines and lax morality.

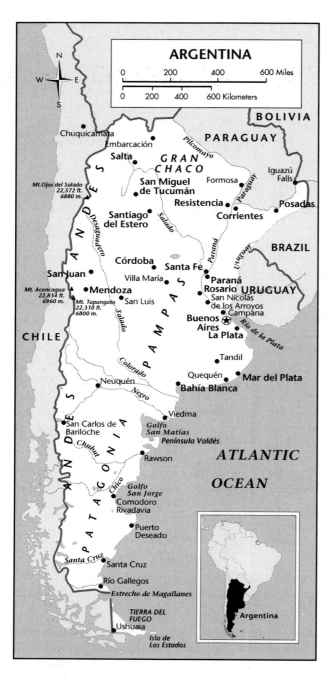

ARGENTINA

Political Independence. Since the more radical ideas of the Enlightenment were not widespread in the area, the Revolution of 1810, which broke the ties with Spain, was completely Catholic and orthodox. Cornelio Saavedra, leader of the revolt, was a thorough and even pious Catholic, as was the priest Manuel Alberti, who was one of the spokesmen of the revolutionary government. While the bishops of Buenos Aires, Córdoba, and Salta did not sympathize with the separatist movement, most of the clergy and many of the religious supported the new political regime. While almost all the Mercedarian fathers were separatist, most Franciscans were against or only tolerated the revolution. Since ties between religious orders and their superiors in Europe had been broken, the new government created the Commission for Religious, an illegitimate instrument of the antireligious assembly. The nature of the revolution soon changed under the leadership of misguided and immoral men such as Juan José Castelli and Bernardo Monteagudo. However, the movement was corrected at the Congress of Tucumán, which proclaimed the independence of the United Provinces of South America (present-day Argentina) on July 9, 1816. Eleven of the twenty-nine representatives who signed this declaration were priests.

While independence had been declared, the form of government for La Plata was a matter of dispute. Buenos Aires wanted to hold control of all the provinces, and this attitude provoked a civil war lasting from 1818 to 1820. Waging such a prolonged conflict necessitated a strong government, and RIVADAVIA aspired to be that government. However, he could count on the support only of the Province of Buenos Aires, and even there he had committed serious errors. A presumptuous man, dazzled by what he had seen in France, Rivadavia was imbued with the ideas of Joseph of Austria and Febronius, particularly the concept of patronage that national and provincial governments each believed they had inherited from Spain. Wishing to legislate ecclesiastical as well as civil affairs and influenced by enlightened priests who wished to end completely Christian preaching, Rivadavia attempted to carry out the ill-named Reform of the Clergy. In 1824, when the papal delegate arrived in Buenos Aires on his way to Chile, Rivadavia refused to let him administer the Sacrament of Confirmation and ordered him to leave the city as soon as possible. In this Rivadavia was supported by the high clergy in Buenos Aires. The next year Rivadavia made a treaty with England by which Protestantism was officially permitted, and with it toleration of all religions. His government proved disastrous for Argentina.

In 1829, during one of many short-lived governments, Buenos Aires governor Juan José Viamonte initiated the restoration of relations with Rome that had been suspended since 1810. Pope Pius VII appointed Mariano MEDRANO bishop of Buenos Aires, and Medrano served until 1832, to the great satisfaction of the Argentine people and the great opposition of some jurists and many priests.

The Liberal Constitution of 1853. From 1835 to 1852 Juan Manuel Rosas governed the whole of Argentina through its capital in Buenos Aires and, through force, brought a measure of peace and order to the region. A firm supporter of patronage, he interfered in clearly eccle-

Interior of the cathedral at the Plaza de Mayo, Buenos Aires, Argentina. (©Susan D. Rock)

siastical matters, supporting the Church in spiritual and apostolic work but expelling from the country priests and religious whom he considered too involved in politics. His relations with Bishop Medrano were always of a very cordial nature.

After Rosas was overthrown in February 1852, the government fell under the control of men of heterodox views, such as Juan María Gutiérrez; or of ambition, such as Bartolomé Mitre; or of flexible ideology, such as Domingo Sarmiento. Such men dominated the preparation of the Constitution of 1853, a document little in keeping with the doctrine and spirit of Catholicism. Among the members of the congress drawing up this constitution was a priest, Benjamín Lavaisse; and another, Mamerto ESQUIÚ, spoke in favor of its adoption.

Catholicism waned appreciably among intellectuals during the period 1853 to 1880. At the same time Masonry became more and more prevalent, its followers believing that the time had arrived to do away with the decadent Argentine Church. By 1880 the effects of the constitution of 1853 upon the Church had become evident, some resulting from specific provisions within its articles, others the consequence of erroneous interpretation. President Julio A. Roca, detested in Buenos Aires because he was

from Tucumán, allowed Masons to attack the Church openly and thus began a struggle that lasted throughout his term of office (1880–86). In and out of parliament battles were fought over education and civil marriage, the enemies of the Church winning on both counts.

To oppose these liberal tendencies, José Manuel Estrada, a former liberal who had become a militant Catholic, formed the Unión Católica and became the moving force behind the First Argentine Catholic Assembly, which met in 1884. Estrada founded the newspaper *La Unión,* and, above all, motivated others with his heroic spirit. Pedro Goyena, Tristán Achaval Rodríguez, Emilio de Alvear, Aureliano Argento, Mariano Demaría, Emilio Lamarca, Dámaso Centeno, and many others were inspired by Estrada to fight boldly for the interests of Christ. If the ecclesiastical authority of Buenos Aires proved less than valiant, the Franciscan Bishop of Salta, Buenaventura Risso Patron and the vicars of Córdoba, Santiago del Estero, and Jujuy acted so valiantly that they were either arrested and jailed or removed from their ecclesiastical posts.

The Early 20th Century. As Argentina entered the 20th century, it was believed that the de-Christianizing process begun by left-leaning liberals in 1880 could be

Jerónimo Emiliano Clara, Argentine defender of the rights of the Church.

completed by introducing divorce. While it seemed that everything favored this project in the Argentine Congress, the calm and effective speech of a young deputy from Tucumán, Ernesto E. Padilla, brought about its spectacular failure. Padilla was part of a Catholic revival led by German Redemptorist Federico GROTE and others. Grote's work was in accordance with the necessities of the age: He started the Workingmen's Groups, founded the Catholic newspaper *El Pueblo,* and inspired a new generation of men, among them Emilio Lamarca, Miguel de Andrea, Alejandro Bunge, Gustavo J. FRANCESCHI, and José M. Samperio.

The International Eucharistic Congress of 1934 was a success that exceeded even the hopes of the most optimistic. The entire nation took part, with many in attendance converting or returning to God. In 1943, after the military government of Gen. Pedro Pablo Ramírez ordered that elective courses in religion or morals be offered in all public schools, 92 percent elected religion. Even in cosmopolitan cities, such as Buenos Aires, the majority remained Catholic. From 1934 through the middle of the century, the Church advanced in many areas: the number of dioceses increased; the Argentine Catholic Action Movement, founded in 1931, gained membership; the number of parishes and of parochial schools grew;

secondary schools were founded and directed by the Jesuits, the Missionaries of Our Lady of Lourdes, the Betharram Fathers, Salesians, Order of the Divine Word, Brothers of the Pious Schools, Christian Brothers, and Marist Brothers, as well as other male and female congregations.

The Perón Era. When the populist government of Juan Domingo Perón stressed its totalitarian tendencies in 1952, it provoked a serious conflict with the Church. The official press began to mock everything Catholic; Catholic gatherings were prohibited; Catholic organizations, such as the university athenaeums of Santa Fe and of Córdoba, were abolished; crucifixes were removed from government offices; religious teaching in schools was suppressed; the divorce law was approved; and houses of prostitution were again authorized. While the episcopate remained firm and energetic, and the faithful supported their pastors, priests and laymen were jailed and mistreated on many occasions, and every expedient was used to harass Catholics. Persecution reached its high point on June 11, 1955, when a huge crowd gathered in the cathedral in Buenos Aires and in the adjacent plaza to hear Mass and afterward, in absolute silence, passed through the center of the city to the congressional building. Five days later, after an attempt to overthrow the government had been thwarted, the government instigated mobs to take revenge by burning local churches and the episcopal curia, the contents of which, including the historical archives, were reduced to ashes. The sacking and burning of churches raised a great reaction throughout the country and even abroad. Never had anything like this occurred in Argentina.

After the fall of the Perón government in September 1955 the new revolutionary junta began to reestablish justice. Unfortunately, this government was soon infiltrated by anti-Catholic elements, and although the divorce law passed in the time of Perón was suspended, the pre-Perón religious education law was not reinstated.

Bibliography: J. C. ZURETTI, *Historia eclesiástica argentina* (Buenos Aires 1945). G. FURLONG, *Diócesis y obispos de la iglesia argentina, 1570–1942* (Buenos Aires 1942). *Anuario eclesiástico de la República Argentina* (Buenos Aires 1961–). A. DONINI, "Un análisis para el futuro del catolicismo argentino," *Estudios* 549 (Buenos Aires 1963) 651–657. A. P. WHITAKER, *Argentina* (Englewood Cliffs, NJ 1964).

[G. FURLONG/EDS.]

Vatican II and Beyond. On the eve of the Second Vatican Council (1962–65), the Church held the spiritual allegiance of the vast majority of Argentinians, despite a century of attacks waged by liberalism and secularism, not to mention the terrible confrontation with Perón's populist dictatorship. The Catholic hierarchy projected a

Exterior of the cathedral at the Plaza de Mayo, Buenos Aires. (©Pablo Corral Vega/CORBIS)

conservative, sternly authoritarian, and reactionary image as it presided over what was seen as a closed, intolerant, and elitist institution anxious to retain its strong political presence in the country. Religious traditions and rituals survived as major elements in Argentine public and private life, while Catholic educational and charitable institutions contributed an indispensable part of the nation's academic and welfare services. A renewed spirit resulted from Vatican II that gradually found its flowering in the quincentennial celebration of the European discovery of the New World (1992) and the launching of a new program of evangelization of the Americas inspired by Pope John Paul II.

In Argentina, the 1960s was characterized by strife and turmoil. Old forms of Church life were dying out. The Argentine Catholic Action (ACA) movement, inspired by papal social teaching, had inspired great social change during the 1930s and 1940s, but by the 1960s was in rapid decline as it lost its former youthful energy and purposefulness. The days of truly outstanding lay leadership were over. At the same time, the chronic shortage of priests and religious became more acute, reaching critical proportions by the middle of the decade.

In 1962 the radical Frondizi government, which had been well disposed toward the Church, fell to a military coup aimed at halting the unchecked resurgence of Peronism. The next year Arturo Illia, with only 25 percent of the vote, became president and provided honest but weak leadership in a land torn by irreconcilable divisions. Peronist labor leaders refused to compromise or collaborate with Illia, while the military watched over his government with a menacing vigilance. A major development for the Church occurred in 1962 with the promotion of Catholic private education led by Tomás Walsh, FSC (Hermano Septimio). Together with the religious and lay members of the Superior Council of Catholic Education, Walsh spearheaded a successful crusade for equality of rights and privileges with state education throughout Argentina. That same year over 4,000 people attended the First National Catechetical Conference in Buenos Aires that gave a fresh start to religious instruction.

New categories of thought, attitudes, and action were urgently needed for the Church remain relevant in a rapidly modernizing world. Being a Christian was now more a matter of personal choice than a result of birth and national identity. As Argentina alternated between rudderless civilian governments and repressive military regimes, her society was on the verge of a rupture with its Catholic foundations. It had become a society in the grip of traumatic political conflict and confrontation, of confusion and rebellion set within the context of revolutions led by Fidel Castro and the Argentine Ernesto ''Che'' Guevara in Cuba and fast spreading to Brazil, Chile, and the rest of South America.

In 1966 the military struck once again in an attempt to check and purge the persistent and growing Peronist movement, naming General Juan Carlos Onganía president. An admirer of Spanish dictator Francisco Franco, Onganía established a conservative, pro-Catholic, anti-communist regime which initially enjoyed a broad base of popular support. Business, industry, and even labor looked to the military to put an end to the economic chaos, crime, and corruption that now permeated society and politics. Over a four-year period Onganía's government pushed ahead with economic and industrial development, but it could not cope with the emerging guerrilla and urban terrorist movements.

During Onganía's presidency several major events took place in the Church: the end of the Patronato Regio (union of church and state) in a bilateral accord signed in 1966 by the Argentine government and the Holy See; the emergence of the Argentine-based Priests for the Third World movement; and 1968's CELAM (Latin American Bishops Conference) meeting in Medellín, Colombia, for the implementation of Vatican II in Latin America. In 1969 the Argentine Bishops' Conference issued its ''Document of San Miguel'' calling for sweeping Church reforms based on the conclusions of Medellín and emphasizing the need for lay leadership and active participation in the work of the Church. This document, an oft-cited and highly praised source of Catholic teaching, bore little practical fruit in a country caught up in a whirlwind of political and economic troubles that culminated in May 1969 in the bloody *Cordobazo*, a series of labor strikes and rebellions that brought death and destruction on an unheard-of scale.

In 1970 terrorists in Buenos Aires kidnaped and murdered General Pedro Aramburu, who had overthrown Perón in 1955. Kidnaping for ransom and political murder soon became commonplace strategies of fanatics intent upon driving the country to armed revolution. Onganía's comrades-in-arms lost faith in his ability to govern, and they replaced him eventually with General Alejandro Agustín Lanusse. Adopting a policy of compromise and dialogue, Lanusse was able in some measure to create a climate of hope despite the ongoing violence and assassinations masterminded and executed by rival groups of radicals such as the Montoneros, mostly young guerrillas of communist or Peronist ideology.

Perón's Return and a Divided Church. In September 1973, Perón and his third wife, María Estela ''Isabelita'' Martínez de Perón, were elected president and vice president respectively. The octogenarian Perón could not deliver on his promises of unity and progress for the nation. When he died the following year he was succeeded by his wife who, inexperienced in politics, suffered from unfavorable comparisons with the glorified memory of Perón's second wife, the beloved Evita, who had died in 1952.

The brief presidency of Perón and his wife was marked by a profound national crisis which gave rise to struggles within the Church, especially between the relatively small membership—about 400 priest supporters and 140 active members at most—of Priests for the Third World and the hierarchy. Led by the charismatic Carlos Mujica, the Priests' movement had run head-on into conflict with Church and state authorities over the proper mission and role of the clergy in politics. With its aim the rapid and radical application of the teachings of Medellín and the ''Document of San Miguel,'' the movement sought political means of implementing social justice. Its members were mostly Peronists who supported the return of their leader from his long exile in Spain. The Episcopal Conference insisted that priests stay out of politics, and that they promote no specific party or ideology but instead dedicate themselves to their religious and spiritual mission. After the ill and aging Perón returned to power, the movement began to fragment due to ideological and tactical disputes. In May 1974, Mujica was shot down as he left his church in the working-class parish of San Francisco Solano in Buenos Aires. He was instantly transformed into an heroic martyr for the Priests of the Third World and for others who struggled for social justice and the cause of the preferential option for the poor. The movement as such, however, was censured by the conservative hierarchy and its members were persecuted by the military government that seized power in 1976.

To many the Argentine political scene appeared to be on the path to ruin. Paradoxically, during those years of wrenching political conflicts in the Church, there appeared a strong reaffirmation of the once-despised religion of the people, a religion characterized by spontaneous pious practices and individual expressions of faith by the masses rather than the sacramental and structured spirituality controlled and regulated by the clergy. In this world of sacramentals, of votive candles, of favors asked of God and the saints, and of pilgrimages to holy places, many Argentinians found a sacred space for inward retreat and spiritual growth and consolation. In 1974 the first organized pilgrimage specifically for Catholic youth to Luján, the national Marian shrine about 50 miles from central Buenos Aires, proved successful.

This annual pilgrimage soon grew to become the major expression of popular religious devotion in Argentina, and it provided a sense of community and identity for Catholics throughout the land.

On the political front, however, there was no letup in the wave of violence, conflict, and confrontation. As the economy collapsed, institutional corruption respected no boundaries, and the country became ungovernable. General Jorge Rafael Videla headed the new military regime that ousted Isabelita Perón in March 1976. Anticipated by all and welcomed by broad sectors of society, Videla resorted to fierce repression in order to blot out insurgency by warring factions. According to many responsible sources, the use of excessive force, and of kidnapping, torture, and murder as norms of action in what was dubbed the "dirty war" left at least 10,000 known dead and "disappeared". Among the victims were three priests in Buenos Aires, two in La Rioja, and one in Bahía Blanca. Of the few bishops who spoke up boldly and publicly against the abuses of the military regime, perhaps the most respected was a former supporter of Priests for the Third World, Enrique Angelelli. When Angelelli died mysteriously in July 1976 in a car accident on a lonely road in his diocese, many believed he too had fallen victim of "The Process," as the military regime called its program.

The Church and the "Dirty War." A thorny controversy soon arose about the role played by the Church hierarchy during "The Process." The point at issue was whether or not the Episcopal Conference as an institution, and bishops individually, lived up to their obligations as Christian witnesses and protested against violations of human rights during the Videla government's war against subversion. One thing was clear: the hierarchy was not silent on these issues, as was evident from the documentation published by the Episcopal Conference between 1976 and 1982. The bishops also claimed they did considerable work in favor of victims through both personal contacts and behind-the-scenes negotiations with the military. Many critics, however, found the "voice of those who have no voice," as Latin American bishops styled themselves, far too tentative, artful, diplomatic, and conciliatory in Argentina when viewed in comparison with bishops of Chile and Brazil who, at the same time, spoke out valiantly under equally repressive military regimes. Many critics claimed that what was reported in Church documents was not voiced strongly enough, and such documentation was not supported by pastoral action on the local level where high-sounding principles could have been translated into deeds of justice and Christian service. For example, there was no Argentinian parallel to Solidaridad, the Chilean Church organization set up for the defense of political prisoners of the infamous Pino-

chet regime and for the support of families of the disappeared. Some noted writers went so far as to accuse the Argentine Church of complicity with Videla dictatorship. While the record did not appear to support such a sweeping judgment, some bishops, especially the military vicar, and a few reactionary priests publicly supported "The Process." In 1997 Cardinal Pio Laghi, who served as papal nuncio in Argentina during the Videla years, was formally charged with "intimate knowledge" of government concentration camps. A year earlier, the country's bishops had released a document of confession that stated that the Church's actions were insufficient. The document was sent to the Vatican.

A bright spot in the bleak panorama of torture and oppression under the Videla regime was the courageous role of small groups of lay people, nuns, and priests who, in ecumenical efforts with Protestant colleagues, worked tirelessly for the promotion of social justice for the poor and the cause of human rights. They labored for the most part independently of the hierarchy and were inspired by ideas from other Latin American countries concerning liberation theology and from Comunidades Eclesiales de Base (CEB), Christian grassroots communities basing their lives and social action upon reflection on the Bible. These groups disappeared for the most part with the collapse of "The Process" and the continued coldness of the hierarchy towards them. The most outstanding Catholic defender of human rights during "The Process" was Adolfo Pérez Esquivel, a militant critic and prisoner of the military government who won the Nobel Prize for Peace in 1980.

With time, healing took place. The feared conservative counter-attack on liberation theology at the 1979 CELAM conference with Pope John Paul II in Puebla, Mexico, never materialized. Instead, Puebla reaffirmed Medellín and its preferential option for the poor. Meanwhile, the Church in Argentina and Chile gained considerable sympathy and support for its role in arbitrating border disputes in the extreme south of the continent that brought the two countries to the edge of war in late 1978. Asked to mediate the issue, the pope designated Antonio Cardinal Samoré, an experienced, patient, and skillful Vatican diplomat, as his personal representative in the protracted negotiations. Samoré managed to avoid an outbreak of war by postponing matters until the dispute could be settled peacefully in 1985 following a 1984 plebiscite overwhelmingly in favor of the accords.

By 1981 the military regime in Argentina had lost all popular support, and the nation was ruined economically. In this context the Episcopal Conference published its collective pastoral letter "Church and National Community." In strong and authoritative language the bishops called for the restoration of democracy and listed immediate steps to promote national reconciliation, starting with the government's respect for and protection of the fundamental human rights of all citizens. This document put an end to the hierarchy's policy of delicately phrased admonition in the face of government abuses; instead they spoke out prophetically, voicing their Christian conviction. Unfortunately, such strong statements came too late to save the thousands of innocent victims of the "dirty war." In April 1982 General Leopoldo Galtieri, the new military president, launched an ill-advised and catastrophic attack on the British-controlled Falkland Islands in the South Atlantic, a desperate ploy to rally Argentina to support a war of territorial vindication. In May, a British expeditionary force handed the Argentines a bitter and ignominious defeat which left the nation in turmoil. In June, Pope John Paul II paid a two-day visit to Buenos Aires, the very first papal visit to Argentina, to promote peace and reconciliation. His visit was met with massive outpourings of gratitude and religious fervor in support of the papal mission.

The Church and Democracy. The defeat in the Falklands brought down the Galtieri regime. In October 1982, the Argentine Episcopal Conference published guidelines urging lay people to become actively involved in politics, to form their political opinions on the basis of serious study of the issues, and to vote their conscience enlightened by the moral teaching of the Church. Responsible participation in politics thus became a constant theme in the bishops' statements. After a one-year transition period, Raúl Alfonsín won the presidency with 52 percent of the vote in the first Radical Party victory over the Peronists in an open and free election. With democracy restored, the major military culprits in the "dirty war" were called to justice by the new civilian government.

In 1987 Pope John Paul II returned to Argentina, this time for a six-day visit during which his central theme was once again forgiveness and national reconciliation. The pope also spoke energetically against divorce, abortion, and the country's increasing drug abuse, and voiced his support for social justice, fair wages, and workers rights. The presence of the Holy Father and the emotional fervor of the multitudes bolstered a sense of national solidarity with the Church and stimulated the promotion and consolidation of democracy.

Severe economic problems led to the May 1989 election victory of Peronist candidate Carlos Saúl Menem. The Church hierarchy worked for harmony and peace with the new government. Menem, a man of enormous charisma, managed to close the door on "dirty war" reprisals and assured the nation unparalleled freedom of the press. He turned to capitalism and the United States to lift

Argentina out of the pit of hyperinflation and economic chaos, and in the process transformed Peronism into Menemism, in many ways its ideological and practical opposite.

The 1994 Assembly drafted a new constitution aimed at allowing the re-election of Menem in 1995. Among the changes were several that weakened the traditional influence of the Church. The president of the Republic would no longer have to be a Catholic, and strict anti-abortion laws would be modified. The separation between church and state was now increasing in fact, whereas it had previously only increased in theory. However, the Catholic Church continued to remain the state religion, sustained through a variety of government subsidies. Showing both personal support for Church teachings and political courage in the face of increasing liberalism internationally, in 1999 President Menem proclaimed March 25 as "The Day of the Unborn Child." Applauded by the Vatican, Menem's pronouncement drew worldwide attention and was emulated by leaders in other predominately Catholic nations.

The Church Faces New Challenges. With the stabilization of democracy in Argentina, the Church was once again able to focus on the quality of life. In 1996 Catholic physicians throughout the country joined a government effort to fight the increasing incidence of AIDS in Argentina. Public schools once again made religious instruction available to all students, and by 2000 the Church operated seven Catholic universities within Argentina. Ecumenical efforts by the Church included conferences to discuss current issues and an open invitation to leaders of all faiths to attend the Te Deum Mass on national holidays. Gestures of openness to Argentine' Jewish population were considered particularly important because of a trend toward increasing anti-Semitic activity during the late 1990s.

With modernization and increasing economic stability came complex moral questions regarding social policy, the same questions that prompted liberal legislation in much of the world. The Church engaged fully with these questions, in many cases speaking out with vigor. With the highest rate of in vitro fertilization in Latin America, Argentina was confronted with what to do with the thousands of human embryos frozen and stored in medical facilities. Unlike nations such as Great Britain which routinely destroyed such embryos, Argentinian legislators reflected the Church's hopes in determining in 1996 that such embryos would not be destroyed. While Catholic bishops condemned government economic policies decreasing financial aid to poor, pregnant women, they were also confronted, in August 2000, with a new law that allowed the dispensation of abortifacient drugs and birth control devices to all women. Buenos Aires became a particular cause for concern in 1996 when, due to a change in the capital city's legal status, the liberal local government was able to pass legislation guaranteeing reproductive rights that threatened to undercut national pro-life laws. The country's high unemployment rate prompted the government, in 1997, to propose anti-immigration legislation until the bishops called the proposal "a shame and a stain on Argentina's tradition of openness and human sensibility." Church leaders also expressed increasing concern about the spiritual laxness of society, and encouraged families to work toward a moral conversion.

By the end of the 20th century, Protestant and sectarian missionary groups, along with national evangelical and Pentecostal churches had become active in Argentina, and were zealously winning over adherents among neglected Catholics, especially the marginalized poor living in the slums and shanty towns surrounding all the major cities. In response to such aggressive anti-Catholic proselytism, in 1990 the Episcopal Conference published an elaborate plan for the "New Evangelization" of Argentina, to be launched in conjunction with the quincentennial celebration of the evangelization of the Americas begun in 1492. The document emphasized greater lay participation in the spiritual enterprise of preaching the good news of the gospel, and called for vigorous steps urgently needed to hold the line on Catholic Church membership. The Conference, led by the politically astute Antonio Cardinal Guarracino, archbishop of Buenos Aires, was certainly on the right track two years later when, after a respectful look back on the 500 years of evangelization in the Americas, it insisted that the task at hand was to look forward into the third Christian millennium and to prepare for it with a faith that does justice for all Argentines, but especially for the poor who need it most.

By 2000 Catholic sentiment and cultural identity remained strong, despite the fact that many Catholics no longer regularly attended church. The country's 2,596 parishes, 3,532 secular and 2,345 religious priests, 848 brothers, and 10,773 sisters attested to the fact that the majority of Argentinians continued to look to the Catholic rites of baptism, first communion, confirmation, marriage, and Christian burial to give spiritual meaning to major moments in their lives. In a survey taken in 1996, 94 percent of all Argentinians professed a belief in God, while 78 percent regularly dedicated time to some form of spiritual contemplation. At the dawn of the 21st century, despite the concern of Argentina's bishops that the nation was experiencing a moral crisis of values, such responses showed that the Church remained a potent factor in the creation of a sense of national cohesion, identi-

ty, and unity in a land seemingly destined for unending political strife and economic upheaval.

Bibliography: AGENCIA INFORMATIVA CATÓLICA ARGENTINA, *Argentina* (Buenos Aires 1992). COMISIÓN DE ESTUDIOS DE HISTORIA DE LA IGLESIA EN AMÉRICA LATINA, *500 años de cristianismo en Argentina* (Buenos Aires 1992). CONFERENCIA EPISCOPAL ARGENTINA, *La Iglesia y los derechos humanos* (Buenos Aires 1988). E. DUSSEL, ed., *The Church in Latin America, 1492–1992* (Maryknoll, NY 1992). T. FARRELL, *Iglesia y pueblo en Argentina* (Buenos Aires 1988). E. F. MIGNONE, *Witness to the Truth: The Complicity of the Church and Dictatorship in Argentina* (1976–83) (Maryknoll, NY 1988). P. SIWAK, *500 años de evangelización americana,* vol. 3 (Buenos Aires 1992). A. J. SONEIRA, *Iglesia y nación* (Buenos Aires 1986).

[E. S. SWEENEY/EDS.]

ARGENTRÉ, CHARLES DU PLESSIS D'

Theologian; b. near Vitré, France, May 16, 1673; d. Tulle, Nov. 27, 1740. After he became a socius of the Sorbonne in 1698, he was ordained in 1699 and obtained a doctorate in theology the next year. In 1707 he was named vicar-general of Tréguiers and in 1725 was consecrated bishop of Tulle. Among his scholarly works are the anonymous *Apologie de l'amour* (Amsterdam 1698) written against F. FÉNELON in the controversy over QUIETISM, and his edition of *Martini Grandini opera theologica* (6 v. Paris 1710–12), to which he added some valuable works of his own as appendices. His most important contribution is, however, his *Collectio de novis erroribus* (3 v. Paris 1724–36). This work contains many documents (decisions of Roman congregations, papal *acta,* judgments of famous universities) on erroneous doctrines and controverted theological questions from the 12th century onward.

Bibliography: J. BALTEAU, *Dictionnaire de biographie française* (Paris 1929–) 3:575–576. F. STEGMÜLLER, *Lexikon für Theologie und Kirche,* ed. J. HOFER and K. RAHNER, 10 v. (2d ed. Freiburg 1957–65) 1:837.

[M. A. ROCHE]

ARGIMIR, ST.

Martyr; b. *c.* 785, Cabra, Spain; d. June 28, 856, Córdoba. Argimir was an elderly nobleman who had earlier held the office of *censor* in the Muslim government of Córdoba. He had retired from the administration of justice and withdrawn to a monastery when certain Muslims accused him of scurrilous derision of their prophet and profession of the divinity of Christ. Argimir admitted the charges before the *qadi* and was hung on the *eculeus* while still alive and finally slain by the sword. Christians buried his relics in the basilica of St. Acisclus in Córdoba. He was included in the Roman martyrology in 1586.

Feast: July 7.

Bibliography: EULOGIUS, *Memoriale sanctorum, Patrologia Latina*, ed. J. P. MIGNE (Paris 1878–90). 115:815–818. E. P. COLBERT, *The Martyrs of Córdoba, 850–859* (Washington 1962) 262–264.

[E. P. COLBERT]

ARGUMENTATION

An argumentation is defined as an expression signifying the inference of one TRUTH from another truth. Just as a TERM is the SIGN of a CONCEPT, and a PROPOSITION the sign of a JUDGMENT, so argumentation is the sign of the act of the mind known as REASONING. As a sign, it is expressed primarily in spoken words and secondarily in written words. An example of the latter would be: "Everything white reflects light, and snow is white; hence snow reflects light."

Elements of Argumentation. Every argumentation consists of three elements: the antecedent, the conclusion, and the inference. The antecedent is the truth or truths already known as a starting point; the conclusion, sometimes called the consequent, is the truth newly arrived at; the inference, also called the illation or consequence, is the mental act involved in drawing the conclusion from the antecedent. The first two elements are found explicitly in an argumentation, while the third is indicated implicitly by a "therefore," "so," or "hence." Of the three inference is the most important element, because it gives unity and meaning to the other two, fashioning them into a logical unit. Thus, an argumentation is not merely a list of truths connected by a "therefore"; rather it signifies a growth of truth. And just as a growing organism has parts that are unified by its soul or vital principle, so argumentation has parts that are unified by the act of inference.

One difficulty in understanding argumentation comes from the inadequacy of examples. A teacher can communicate antecedent and conclusion to a student, but he cannot communicate or exemplify the inference. The act of inferring must take place in the student's mind, and there alone. As a result, examples of argumentation given in standard logic texts can be meaningless to the reader. Unless he proceeds step by step and sees the conclusion as a new truth drawn from the old, there is for him no argumentation. Inference, therefore, is not to be confused with mere succession. In argumentation one truth does not follow another; rather it follows *from* another. There must be a causal dependence of the conclusion on the antecedent, and precisely this is difficult to convey by means of examples.

Valid Inference. The rules or laws of argumentation are phrased as follows: (1) from a true antecedent there always follows a true conclusion; (2) from a false antecedent there sometimes follows a true conclusion; and (3) the conclusion always follows the weaker part, i.e., if the antecedent is negative or particular, the conclusion will correspondingly be negative or particular. These rules govern the inferences made in a reasoning process.

Another type of inference is found in judgment, when, from the truth or falsity of a given proposition, one infers the truth and falsity of related propositions. This is done in the matrices of symbolic LOGIC and in the traditional square of OPPOSITION. Such a procedure is improperly called immediate inference by some writers. Mediate inference, which is said to be employed in argumentation, requires, on the other hand, that the conclusion be a new truth and not merely the rephrasing of a truth already known.

Because of the role of inference, argumentation is not said to be true or false (although obviously the conclusion can be so called), but rather argumentation is valid if it observes the necessary dependence of the conclusion on the antecedent, and invalid if it does not. Some authors speak of good and bad argumentation. Thus a geometrical proof that leads to a true conclusion through the observance of proper method is known as a good or valid argumentation.

Kinds of Argumentation. Argumentation can be divided on the basis of either its form or its matter. The division on the basis of form or structure has two principal members: argumentation that is good, and argumentation that is only apparently good. The latter is called FALLACY or sophistry. Although it has the appearance, at least to the neophyte, of valid argumentation, some fault hidden in its structure or content renders it invalid.

Argumentations that are good or valid are of two types: inductive and deductive (*see* INDUCTION; DEDUCTION). The inductive process is one whose antecedent is less general than the conclusion; the deductive process, on the other hand, is one whose antecedent is more general than its conclusion. Both induction and deduction are equally argumentations. When arranged artificially by the logician, deduction is formulated in the SYLLOGISM. The argumentation already given as an example can be cast in syllogistic form as follows:

Everything white reflects light. But snow is white. Therefore snow reflects light.

Another division is that on the basis of matter or content. Argumentation is apodictic when the matter involved is necessary, i.e., the various terms of the antecedent cannot be related other than they are. When this obtains within the deductive process the argumentation is a DEMONSTRATION. When the matter is only contingent or probable, the argumentation is dialectical (*see* DIALECTICS). When the matter is such that it involves the emotions, but in a hidden way, the argumentation is rhetorical (*see* RHETORIC). Finally, when open appeal is made to the emotions, the argumentation may be called poetic [*see* POETICS (ARISTOTELIAN)]. Thus argumentation can express a reasoning process in a variety of ways, ranging from the strictest scientific reasoning to the subtle intimations of poetry. It embraces inductive and deductive processes, and often combines both.

The universal scope of argumentation is often lost on the rationalist, who overemphasizes deduction, and on the empiricist, who stresses induction to an extreme. Neither the rationalist nor the empiricist considers rhetorical and poetical forms of argument as legitimate forms of reasoning. This is in sharp contrast to the cultural and scientific appreciation accorded this means of attaining truth by the ancient Greeks and medieval schoolmen.

See Also: LOGIC; PROOF.

Bibliography: S. J. HARTMAN, *Fundamentals of Logic* (St. Louis 1949). J. A. OESTERLE, *Logic: The Art of Defining and Reasoning* (2d ed. Englewood Cliffs, N.J. 1963), V. E. SMITH, *The Elements of Logic* (Milwaukee 1957). E. D. SIMMONS, *The Scientific Art of Logic* (Milwaukee 1961).

[E. BONDI]

ARGYROPOULOS, JOHN

Byzantine scholar teaching in the West; b. Constantinople, 1415; d. Rome, June 26, 1487. One of the most celebrated Byzantine scholars to appear in Italy during the years immediately preceding and following the fall of Constantinople to the Turks in 1453, Argyropoulos was a member of the Greek delegation to the Council of FLORENCE (1438–39) and seems to have remained in Italy after the close of the council, studying and subsequently teaching Greek privately at Venice and Padua. After returning to Byzantium a few years later, he taught Greek literature at Constantinople's higher school, the Mouseion of Xenon, and took the side of the pro-unionists in the conflict over the union with Rome. Upon the capture of Constantinople by the Turks, he fled to the Peloponnesus, whence, in 1456, he was summoned to Florence by Cosimo de' MEDICI to occupy Chrysoloras's old chair of Greek studies at the University of Florence. During the epidemic of 1471 he moved to Rome, where he continued teaching Greek until his death.

Argyropoulos made major contributions to the transmission of Greek learning to the West, particularly of Ar-

istotelianism. His translations of many of the works of Aristotle (among them the *Physics,* the *Metaphysics,* and the *Nicomachean Ethics*) facilitated the study of that author among Western humanists. Equally important, Argyropoulos numbered among his students in Florence and Rome some of the most influential Western intellectuals of the age: Politian, REUCHLIN, Palla Strozzi, Donato ACCIAIOLI, and even Lorenzo de' Medici. Lorenzo the Magnificent and Acciajuoli were later to become admirers of Plato. However, Argyropoulos's translations and teaching were signally to help in the diffusion of the philosophy of Aristotle, especially north of the Alps, at a time when it appeared that Aristotelianism might be completely overshadowed by the Quattrocento's concentration on Platonism.

Bibliography: S. LAMPROS, *Argyropouleia* (in Greek) (Athens 1910), for his minor works. G. CAMMELLI, *Giovanni Argiropulo,* v.2 of *I dotti bizantini e le origini dell'umanesimo* (Florence 1941–), for biog. and writings. D. J. GEANAKOPLOS, *Greek Scholars in Venice: Studies in the Dissemination of Greek Learning from Byzantium to Western Europe* (Cambridge, Mass. 1962), for the problem of the transmission of Greek learning to the West.

[D. J. GEANAKOPLOS]

ARGYROS, ISAAC

Antipalamite, Greek monk, theologian, and astronomer; d. *c.* 1375. Although Argyros followed the inspiration of Theodore Metochites and Gregoras in pursuit of astronomy and mathematics, he also proved himself to be a theologian and powerful polemist. Argyros ranged himself with Nicephorus Gregoras against GREGORY PALAMAS and Emperor John VI Cantacuzenus in the controversy over HESYCHASM. He seems to have accepted the theological method of BARLAAM OF CALABRIA in his principal treatise against Palamism, written probably after 1360. He is also credited with a monograph on the teaching of Barlaam against Theodore DEXIOS and is probably the author of a tome published by the patriarch of Antioch (*c.* 1370). Two further opuscules against Palamism are also attributed to him.

Besides theological treatises, Argyros wrote numerous scientific tracts that are still in manuscript: *Apparatus astrolabii* (Vatican), *De reducendis triangulis* (Oxford), *De reducendo calculo astronomicorum* (Vienna), *Methodus Geodesiae* (Escorial), *Methodus solarium et lunarium* (Leyden), and *Geometriae aliquot problemata* (Paris). His chief scientific works concern the sun and the moon cycles and the 12 winds. It is probable that Argyros wrote a short commentary on the works of Ptolemy relating in particular to the defective chapter of the *Harmonics,* a work to which Nicephorus had also given attention.

Bibliography: G. MERCATI, *Notizie di Procoro e Demetrio Cidone* (*Studi e Testi* 56; 1931) 229–242, 270–275. J. F. MOUNTFORD,

"The Harmonics of Ptolemy and the Lacuna in II, 14," *Transaction and Proceedings of the American Philological Association* 57 (1926) 71–95, esp. 95. *Kirche und theologische Literatur im byzantinischen Reich* 729–730. M. CANDAL, "Un escrito trinitario de Isaac Argiro en la contienda palamítica del siglo XIV," *Orientalia Christiana periodica* 22 (1956) 92–137; "Argiro contra Dexio," *ibid.* 23 (1957) 80–113. M. JUGIE, *Dictionnaire de théologie catholique* 11.2:1806. E. VON IVÁNKA, "Die philosophische und geistesgeschichtliche Bedeutung des Palamismus," *Studi bizantini* 7 (1953) 124–129.

[G. LUZNYCKY]

ARIALDO, ST.

Reformer, and martyr; b. Cantu, Italy, *c.* 1000; d. on an island in Lake Maggiore, Italy, June 27, 1066. Although he had never been elevated beyond the rank of deacon, he was chosen by Henry III to lead the reform of the Milanese clergy, a movement assisted by the Milanese Cardinal Anselm II of Lucca and the noted clerical historian Landulph Cotta (fl. 1085). Reform was already a leading demand of the PATARINES, but Guido of Velate (d. 1071), archbishop of Milan, led the forces that opposed it. Soon after Arialdo began preaching at Varese, a provincial synod with Guido presiding excommunicated Arialdo and Landulph, both of whom appealed to Rome. Thereupon the Roman legates, Anselm of Baggio and Hildebrand, who became popes as ALEXANDER II and GREGORY VII respectively, reached Milan and encouraged the reformers to persevere. When Landulph died, his brother ERLEMBALD led the cause, associating his name and sanctity with Arialdo, whose feast he shares. A bull of excommunication against Guido prompted his associates to capture Arialdo and isolate him on an island in Lake Maggiore. There he was assassinated by two priests; his body was later brought to Milan by Erlembald. In 1068 Alexander II declared Arialdo a martyr, and his ancient cult was confirmed by Pius X in 1904.

Feast: June 27.

Bibliography: *Acta Sanctorum* June 7:250–272. C. PELLEGRINI, *I santi Arialdo ed Erlembaldo* (Milan 1897). C. CASTIGLIONI, *I santi Arialdo ed Erlembaldo e la Pataría* (Milan 1944).

[N. M. RIEHLE]

ARIANISM

Major 4th-century Trinitarian heresy, originated by the teachings of the Alexandrian priest ARIUS (d. 336). The basic tenet of Arianism was a negation of the divinity of Christ and, subsequently, of the Holy Spirit. Arius reduced the Christian Trinity to a descending triad, of whom the Father alone is true God.

The key to the theology of Arius is the doctrine of *agennèsia* (the unbegotten) as the essential attribute of the Godhead: God is by necessity not only uncreated, but unbegotten and unoriginate. Hence God is absolutely incommunicable and unique. As a result the Logos, whom the Scriptures designate clearly as begotten from the Father, cannot be true God. Even though He is adored by all Christians, He is God and Son of God only by participation in grace or by adoption. Since the Godhead is indivisible and incommunicable and the Logos has His being from the Father, there remains but the affirmation that He is a creature, "alien and dissimilar in all things from the Father"; a perfect creature and immensely above all other created beings, but a creature nevertheless.

Since Arius did not accept the opinion of ORIGEN, which postulated an eternal creation, he asserted that the Son had a beginning: "There was when He was not." This assertion was considered blasphemous by the faithful, and it was condemned as such by the Council of NICAEA I (325). Since He was not true God, the Logos had but an imperfect knowledge of the Father; He was also subject to change and peccable by nature, if not in fact.

The main arguments used by the Arians were scriptural texts such as "The Lord created me a beginning of his ways" (Prv 8:22); "The Father is greater than I" (Jn 14.28); "the first-born of all creation" (Col 1.15). Moreover, all through the controversy with the defenders of the Nicene Creed, the Arians consistently rejected nonscriptural words and expressions.

Part of the Arian system was the Word-flesh CHRISTOLOGY, which denied the existence of a human soul in the Incarnate Word; its place was taken by the Logos Himself. Although Arius said little about the Holy Spirit, his followers, true to the logic of their system, considered the third person, or hypostasis, of the Trinity as the highest creature produced by the Son, but inferior to and dissimilar from both the Father and the Son.

Doctrinal Antecedents. The problem of the doctrinal antecedents of Arianism has not yet been fully elucidated. Although Arius claimed to be a disciple of LUCIAN OF ANTIOCH, much of his theology points to the Origenistic tradition, which was dominant in Alexandrian circles: an insistence on the Father as the only God; an emphasis on distinction rather than unity in the Trinity; and the subordinate position of the Son and the Spirit. But neither Origen nor any other pre-Nicene writer offered support for Arius's teaching that the Logos had a beginning of existence. The influence of Aristotle, for which Arians were often blamed by their adversaries, seems to have consisted more in the rationalistic method of argument than in the ideas themselves. Certainly, the cosmological conception of the Logos as a demigod, produced by the Father of all as an intermediary being between the Godhead and the universe, appeared as an adaptation of Christiani-

The priest Arius of Alexandria prostrate before the emperor and the archbishops at the Council of Nicaea I. Miniature in the 10th-century "Menologion of Emperor Basil II," Vatican Library (Cod. Vat. Gr. 1613, fol. 108).

ty to the Hellenistic philosophy of the time. As H. Gwatkin justly remarked, Arianism, scarcely disguised by the traditional terminology and the addition of scriptural quotations, was pagan to the core.

Historically, the controversy concerning the theology of Arius broke into the open in Alexandria about 320, when a local synod under Bishop Alexander condemned his views. When he refused to submit and gained more followers, Alexander summoned a council of the entire Egyptian episcopate, which again condemned Arius and excommunicated him. As a result he left Alexandria and journeyed through Palestine, Syria, and Asia Minor, gaining support from such influential bishops as EUSEBIUS OF CAESAREA and EUSEBIUS OF NICOMEDIA. They sent out numerous letters to fellow bishops and organized synods to uphold Arius's position, while Alexander, in turn, wrote to Eastern and Western bishops to express the true nature of the conflict. Thus, what started as a local dispute soon caused division in the entire Eastern Church.

Constantinian Intervention. When CONSTANTINE I conquered the East in 324, he sent his ecclesiastical adviser Bishop Hosius of Córdoba (more properly Ossius) to Alexandria with a letter to Bishop Alexander and Arius

exhorting them to make peace. But this mission failed; and Hosius on his return to the court presided at a Council of the Orient in Antioch (early 325). Arianism was condemned, and a profession of faith was promulgated that closely resembled the Alexandrian creed. Three bishops were provisorily excommunicated for their refusal to sign it. Meanwhile Constantine, probably at the suggestion of Hosius, had summoned a general council of the Church, first at Ancyra in Galatia, then at Nicaea in Bithynia for the summer of 325.

Council of Nicaea I. Having heard an exposition of the teachings of Arius, the Council of Nicaea I condemned them as blasphemous; from this condemnation radical Arianism never recovered. The Council, apparently led by Hosius, also promulgated the famous NICENE CREED, defining once and for all the true relation of the Son to the Father as *HOMOOUSIOS.*

Eusebius of Caesarea, ATHANASIUS of Alexandria, and PHILOSTORGIUS have given divergent accounts of how this creed was drafted; what follows is only the most probable reconstruction of events at Nicaea. Some bishops, Hosius and probably Alexander among others, persuaded Constantine that the promulgation of a unique creed would be the surest way to achieve lasting unity in the Church. They selected a local creed, probably that of Syro-Palestinian origin, and inserted into it several clauses intended to exclude the typically Arian opinions. Thus they added "from the substance of the Father"; "true God from true God, begotten not made"; and the key word of the creed, which was to become so controversial for many decades, *homoousion tōi Patri,* that is, "of one substance with the Father." In the end the redactors added the anathemas and explicitly rejected the shocking Arian expression "there was when He was not." Significant in this connection was the fact that *hypostasis* (person) was identified with *ousia* (substance), against the dominant Origenist tradition in the East that affirmed three *hypostaseis* in the Godhead. But Constantine crushed the opposition among the bishops and demanded the signature of all present under the penalty of banishment. Only two bishops from Libya refused; together with Arius and the priests who remained faithful to him, they were exiled to Illyricum.

Anti-Nicene Reaction. Ostensibly, the Arian crisis had been resolved, and unity had been restored among the churches. But a few years later a strong anti-Nicene reaction arose, in which two tendencies seem to have been at work. There was a small but active group of Arian sympathizers who had signed the Nicene Creed for fear of exile but had renounced none of their convictions. The other group comprised a large number of Eastern bishops whose beliefs were basically orthodox but whose fear of MONARCHIANISM inspired them with a marked distrust of the *homoousios.* These sentiments were shrewdly exploited by the first group, to which the real leaders of the reaction belonged, including both Eusebius of Nicomedia and Eusebius of Caesarea, Paulinus of Tyre, and Menophantes of Ephesus. Knowing how strongly Constantine was attached to the Nicene faith, they at first avoided a direct attack against it and concentrated their efforts on eliminating the most influential defenders of the *homoousios.* Thus, from 328 on Eustathius of Antioch, Marcellus of Ancyra, Asclepas of Gaza, and finally the foremost leader of all, Athanasius of Alexandria, fell victim to this war of persons: all were deposed by synodical sentence and replaced by members of the anti-Nicene party. After the death of Constantine (337) all exiled bishops were allowed to return to their sees; but the division of the Empire between Constans, who ruled in the West and favored the Nicene party, and Constantius II, who ruled the East and favored the anti-Nicene reaction, soon was reflected on the ecclesiastical level.

Athanasius, Marcellus, and others were recognized as legitimate bishops by the West at the Council in Rome (340–41) but were considered deposed and excommunicated by the East at the Dedication Council of Antioch (341). At the Antioch meeting Eusebius of Nicomedia and his supporters for the first time dared to attack the Nicene faith directly: they promulgated the so-called Second Creed of Antioch, known also as the creed of Lucian of Antioch, which, while condemning several Arian doctrines, omitted the characteristic Nicene phrases "from the essence of the Father" and *homoousios.*

Synods at Sardica and Sirmium. The Council of SARDICA, summoned in 343 by both emperors to restore unity, failed to heal the breach between the Eastern and Western episcopates, as the former refused to sit in a joint meeting with Athanasius and his fellow exiles. Nevertheless the dominant position of Emperor Constans and a general desire for *rapprochement* produced a precarious peace; Athanasius returned to Alexandria in 346 and remained in possession of his see until 356. But the deaths of Constans in 350 and Pope JULIUS I in 352, and the accession of Constantius II as sole ruler of the Empire, gave rise to a renewed offensive on the part of the Arians.

As early as the winter of 351 a group of Eastern bishops held a synod in the imperial residence at SIRMIUM. After deposing the local bishop, Photinus, a disciple of MARCELLUS OF ANCYRA, they promulgated what is known as the First Formulary of Sirmium, consisting of the Fourth Creed of Antioch and a series of anathemas directed partly against radical Arianism and partly against the doctrines of Marcellus and Photinus. Except for the omission of *homoousios* and a few traces of subordinationism, this formulary was susceptible of an orthodox interpretation. The leaders of the anti-Nicene party, especially two Arian court bishops, Valens of Mursa and Ursacius of Singidunum, then staged an all-out attack against the undisputed leader of Nicene orthodoxy, Athanasius. Under strong pressure by Emperor Constantius, two Western councils agreed to the condemnation of Athanasius: Arles in October 353 and Milan in the spring of 355. The few bishops who refused, including Pope Liberius and HILARY OF POITIERS, were exiled to the East, and the centenarian Hosius of Cordova was detained for a year at the court of Sirmium.

Arian Triumph and Downfall. Having forced the Western churches into submission, Constantius and his Arianizing counselors then turned to the East. In February 356 Athanasius was forced to flee to the desert, where he hid for six years; and an Arian intruder, George of Cappadocia, was installed in his place. Thus all voices raised in defense of the Nicene faith were silenced, and all bishoprics were occupied by the opposition.

This apparent triumph caused the downfall of the anti-Nicene coalition: united in the battle against Athanasius and the faith of Nicaea, they fell out with each other when trying to impose a definitive substitute for the *Ni-*

caenum. Three main factions emerged, vying for the favor of Constantius and supremacy in the Church. Each had its own formulary; each held a council dominated by its leaders; each knew its hour of triumph. Since the doctrinal position of each was characterized by a proposed substitute for the Nicene *homoousios,* they have been named after their favorite theological expression: the radical Anomoeans, who held that the Son was *anomoios* (unlike) the Father; the moderate Homoeousians, who preferred the term *homoiousios* (of like substance) with the Father; and the devious Homoeans, whose password *homoios* (similar to, like) covered any and all opinions.

The first to bid for power were the radical Arians, led by Valens and Ursacius in the West and by Eudoxius and Eunomius in the East. In the summer of 357 they held a synod at Sirmium that, with the approval of Constantius, promulgated the Second Formulary of Sirmium. This stressed the inferiority of the Son to the Father; and since their doctrine was of unmistakingly Arian inspiration, it provoked violent indignation both in the West and in the East. BASIL OF ANCYRA and George of Laodicea organized the opposition among the moderates of the anti-Nicene party. In the synods of Ancyra (spring 358) and Sirmium (summer 358) they strongly condemned anomoeism and defined their own position in the Third Formulary of Sirmium, the key word of which was *homoiousios,* that is, "the Son is of like substance with the Father." Basil of Ancyra even planned another general council to be held at Nicomedia, but an earthquake forced postponement and gave his enemies time to gain the emperor's favor for a third group, the Homoeans, led by ACACIUS OF CAESAREA. He persuaded Constantius to summon not one but two meetings, one for the West at Rimini and the other for the East at Seleucia.

To prepare for these meetings, Marcus of Arethusa drew up yet another creed, the Fourth Formulary of Sirmium, better known as the Dated Creed, which proclaimed the Son *homoios,* like the Father in all things that the Scriptures declare. With a few variations—the most important of which was the final omission from the text of the clause "in all things"—this creed was forced on the bishopric of the entire Church at the councils of Rimini (October 359), Seleucia (winter 359), and Constantinople (January 360).

This triumph of homoeism was deceptive, however, since it was based solely on imperial support: it collapsed immediately after the death of Constantius in 361. Moreover, by persecuting Homoousians and Homoeousians alike, it brought about better understanding and, ultimately, reconciliation between the two groups. Beneficial in this aspect were also the wise decisions of Athanasius at the Synod of Alexandria in 362; the peacemaking efforts of Basil of Caesarea; and the theological writings of all three Cappadocian Fathers.

Under VALENS (364–78) homoeism regained imperial favor in the East; but it collapsed again after his death. Both Gratianus and THEODOSIUS I were strong defenders of the Nicene faith: by official decrees of 380 and 381 Catholic orthodoxy was imposed on all Christians and the Arians were deprived of their offices and churches. In 381 the Council of CONSTANTINOPLE I for the East and that of Aquileia for the West sealed the final adoption of the faith of Nicaea by the entire Church and completed it by proclaiming the full divinity of the Holy Spirit against the so-called Macedonians, or Semi-Arians as they are known also.

Later Revival. Utterly defeated in the Roman Empire, Arianism received new life through its implantation among the Germanic tribes and, with them, reentered the Western Empire. The conversion of these peoples was initiated by the missionary activity of Wulfila, apostle of the Goths, who were established on both banks of the lower Danube. This grandson of Christian captives from Cappadocia had been consecrated bishop by Eusebius of Nicomedia at the Dedication Council of Antioch in 341; and upon his return north, he succeeded in converting a good many of his people. He invented a Gothic alphabet and translated the Bible; but the creed he gave his people was the Homoean Creed of the Council of Constantinople of 360, at which he was present. Thus the Germanic Christians were known as Arians. Despite some persecution, Christianity in this form spread with remarkable vigor from the Goths to the neighboring tribes, such as the Gepides, Herules, Vandals, Suevi, Alamanni, and Burgundians. When they invaded the West and established the various Germanic kingdoms, most of these tribes professed homoeism as their national religion and in some instances persecuted those among the Roman population who professed Catholic orthodoxy.

This religious division, added to the ethnic antagonism, retarded the unification of the Roman and barbarian peoples; but gradually the Catholic Church succeeded in eliminating Arianism. In some instances this was achieved by military action that all but wiped out the Germanic element: in 553 the VANDALS in Africa were utterly destroyed by the armies of Justinian I; and in 552 the Ostrogothic kingdom of Italy suffered a similar fate. By peaceful means and through the action of Bp. AVITUS OF VIENNE, the Burgundians in southwestern Gaul had accepted Catholicism in 517, under King Sigismund.

In Spain the Suevi turned to Catholicism *c.* 450 but were soon afterward absorbed by the strong Visigothic kingdom, which remained Arian until 587, when its king, Reccared, became Catholic under the guidance of LEAN-

DER OF SEVILLE. The LOMBARDS, the last tribe to enter the former Roman Empire, were partly pagan and partly Arian. Their conversion to Catholicism, prepared by queens Theodolinda and Gondeberga, took place under kings Aribert and Perctarit toward the end of the 7th century.

Bibliography: J. R. PALANQUE et al., *The Church in the Christian Roman Empire,* tr. E. C. MESSENGER, 2 v. in 1 (New York 1953) 396–408. A. D'ALÈS, *Le Dogme de Nicée* (Paris 1926). J. N. D. KELLY, *Early Christian Creeds* (2d ed. New York 1960); *Early Christian Doctrines* (2d ed. New York 1960) 223–79. G. L. PRESTIGE, *God in Patristic Thought* (Society for Promoting Christian Knowledge; 1935; repr. 1959). T. E. POLLARD, "The Origins of Arianism," *Journal of Theological Studies* (new series 1950–) 9 (1958) 103–11. H. A. WOLFSON, *Dumbarton Oaks Papers,* Harvard Univ. 12 (1958) 3–28. W. HAUGAARD, "Arius Twice a Heretic?," *Church History* 29 (1960) 251–63. H. GWATKIN, *Studies of Arianism* (2d ed. Cambridge 1900). E. SCHWARTZ, *Zur Geschichte des Athanasius* (Gesammelte Schriften 3; Berlin 1959); "Zur Kirchengeschichte des 4. Jahrhunderts," *Zeitschrift für die neutestamentliche Wissenschaft und die Kunde der älteren Kirche* 34 (1935) 129–213. H. G. OPITZ, ed., *Urkunden zur Geschichte des arianischen Streites* (Athanasius' Werke v.3.1; Berlin 1934). J. ZEILLER, *Les Origines chrétiennes dans les provinces danubiennes* (Paris 1918). K. D. SCHMIDT, *Die Bekehrung der Germanen zum Christentum,* 2 v. (Göttingen 1939–40). M. R. BARNES and D. H. WILLIAMS, eds., *Arianism after Arius: Essays on the Development of the Fourth Century Trinitarian Conflicts* (Edinburgh 1993). R. C. GREGG and D. E. GROH, *Early Arianism—A View of Salvation* (Philadelphia 1981). R. P. C. HANSON, *The Search for the Christian Doctrine of God: The Arian Controversy 318–381* (Edinburgh 1988). G. S. STEAD, *Divine Substance* (Oxford 1977). R. GREGG, *Arianism, Historical and Theological Reassessments* (Cambridge, Mass. 1985). R. WILLIAMS, *Arius: Heresy and Tradition* (London 1987).

[V. C. DE CLERCQ]

ARIAS, FRANCIS

Jesuit theologian and spiritual writer; b. Seville, 1533; d. there, May 15, 1605. His work as a Jesuit included a four-year professorship in theology at the University of Cordoba and two successive terms as rector of the colleges at Triguero and Cadiz. Among his contemporaries Arias was known for his rigorous discipline and observance. In a letter to C. ACQUAVIVA in 1594, a fellow Jesuit described him as a holy man, exemplary, devout, and spiritual. Renown has come to him primarily because of his spiritual writings. In 1588 he wrote *Exhortación al aprovechamiento espiritual,* in which he discussed spiritual progress, mistrust of self, and mental prayer. The work was later translated into other languages. *Libro de la imitación de Cristo nuestro Señor* and *Contemptus Mundi,* among his other works, gave him a reputation as another Thomas à Kempis, despite the fact that his style lacked the simplicity and brevity of à Kempis. St. Francis de Sales admired his works.

Bibliography: A. ASTRAIN, *Historia de la Compañía de Jesús en la Asistencia de España,* 7 v. (Madrid 1902–25) v. 4. J. DE GUIBERT, *Dictionnaire de spiritualité ascétique et mystique. Doctrine et histoire,* ed. M. VILLER et al. (Paris 1932–) 1:844–855. C. SOMMERVOGEL et al., *Bibliothèque de la Compagnie de Jésus,* (Brussels-Paris 1890–1932) 1:540–549. *Enciclopedia universal ilustrada Europeo-Americana,* 70 v. (Barcelona 1908–30) 6:174.

[D. M. BARRY]

ARIBO OF MAINZ

Archbishop of Mainz, a member of the noble Aribo family; b. *c.* 990; d. Como, April 6, 1031. He was buried in the Mainz cathedral, which he rebuilt. He founded (1020) the Styrian convent of Göss and later the church at Hasungen. Already an imperial chaplain, he became in 1021 archbishop of Mainz and thereby archchaplain of the empire. In 1025, through CONRAD II, whose imperial election he had effected, he also became the chancellor of Italy. Gifted, learned, and a prodigious writer, he succeeded in obtaining EKKEHARD IV of Sankt Gallen as director of the cathedral school at Mainz. In several synods he strengthened the ecclesiastical discipline of his province. His domineering character and intolerance of the rights of others involved him in numerous disputes. He revived the controversy regarding metropolitan jurisdiction over GANDERSHEIM with Bp. Godehard of Hildesheim, a struggle that the latter's tact and goodness brought to an end in 1030. His harsh attitude toward Otto and Irmgard of Hammerstein, whose marriage had already been contested by his predecessor, became so offensive that BENEDICT VIII withdrew his faculties when he rejected Irmgard's appeal to the Holy See (Synod of Seligenstadt, in 1023; cc. 16, 18; J. C. von Hefele *Histoire des conciles d'après les documents originaux* [Paris 1907–38] 4:921–924). Thus he is said, though unjustly, to have been an opponent of the CLUNIAC reform. Because, among other reasons, he doubted the validity of Conrad's marriage, he refused to permit the coronation of the Empress Gisela in Mainz and thus relinquished an ancient privilege of his see. In 1027 he attended the coronation of Conrad II and also a Lateran council in Rome. He died returning from a later trip to Rome.

Bibliography: *Monumenta Germaniae Scriptores rerum Germanicarum* (Berlin 1825–) 11:684. N. BISCHOFF, *Mitteilungen des Instituts für österreichische Geschichtsforschung* 58 (1950) 285–309. P. ACHT, *Neue deutsche Biographie* (Berlin 1953–) 1:351. A. HAUCK, *Kirchengeschichte Deutschlands,* 5 v. (9th ed. Berlin-Leipzig 1958) v. 3, *passim.* A. BRÜCK, *Lexikon für Theologie und Kirche,* ed. J. HOFER and K. RAHNER, 10 v. (2d, new ed. Freiburg 1957–65); suppl., *Das Zweite Vatikanische Konzil: Dokumente und kommentare,* ed. H. S. BRECHTER, pt. 1 (1966) 1:849–850.

[H. WOLFRAM]

ARIDITY, SPIRITUAL

Spiritual aridity is a condition of soul in which a person derives no consolation or satisfaction from prayer. This absence of spiritual gratification makes it very difficult for one to produce the intellectual and affective acts of prayer. According to spiritual writers, aridity may be due to different causes. It may be caused by such infidelity to God's grace as lukewarmness in the service of God, habitual venial sin, habits of sensuality, vain curiosity, inconstancy, superficiality, lack of esteem for spiritual goods, or excessive activism.

Aridity may result also from the physical discomfort caused by sickness, by heat or cold, or by the lack of sufficient sleep. Or it may be the effect of the mental uneasiness caused by worry, family problems, absorbing occupations, overwork, or a lack of the natural ability for a particular method of prayer. Certain mental or emotional problems also may cause aridity in the spiritual life.

Finally, aridity may be sent by God to humble the soul and purify it of its excessive attachment to consolation in prayer. But if this aridity is accompanied by the signs of purgative contemplation, by an inability to meditate upon the things of God, a disinclination to fix the mind on other objects, and an anxious solicitude about backsliding and not serving the Lord, then the dryness is an indication of a more accentuated divine influence. In this case, aridity manifests a divine call to enter upon a new, more simplified form of prayer—a contemplative loving attentiveness to God.

When the aridity is caused by infidelity, a person may find the remedy in a greater diligence in his practices of the spiritual life and in a more careful effort to correct his defects. In the case of the aridity caused by physical discomfort or mental uneasiness, a person should seek the means for alleviating the causes of these ills. If this alleviation is not attainable, the endurance of the aridity can then be the occasion for the practice of greater virtue, especially patience. When purgative contemplation is the cause of the dryness, a person should not continue to try to meditate or force particular acts, but he should remain at peace, in a simple, loving attentiveness to God in pure faith and love, without the desire to experience or feel anything.

See Also: PURIFICATION, SPIRITUAL.

Bibliography: FRANCIS DE SALES, *Introduction to the Devout Life,* ed. and tr. J. K. RYAN (New York 1950) 2.9; 4.14–15. JOHN OF THE CROSS, *The Dark Night of the Soul,* in *Collected Works,* tr. K. KAVANAUGH and O. RODRIGUEZ (Garden City, N.Y. 1964). A. F. POULAIN, *The Graces of Interior Prayer,* tr. L. L. YORKE SMITH, ed. J. V. BAINVEL (St. Louis 1950). J. DE GUIBERT, *The Theology of the Spiritual Life,* tr. P. BARRETT (New York 1953). R. DAESCHLER, *Dictionnaire de spiritualité ascétique et mystique. Doctrine et histoire,* ed. M. VILLER et al. (Paris 1932–) 1: 845–855.

[K. KAVANAUGH]

ARINTERO, JUAN GONZÁLEZ

Spiritual writer; b. Lugueros (Province of León), Spain, June 24, 1860; d. Salamanca, Feb. 20, 1928. He entered the Dominican Order at Corias in 1875. From 1881 to 1886 he studied at Salamanca. As a specialist in the natural sciences, he taught at colleges in Vergara, Corias, and Valladolid from 1886 to 1898. During this period he published works on topics of scientific and religious interest. In 1900 he inaugurated at Valladolid the Academía de Santo Tomás, dedicated to the study of natural science in relation to philosophy and theology. In 1903 he was recalled to Salamanca as professor of apologetics, and except for one year (1909–10), which he spent as a professor at the Angelicum in Rome, he remained for the rest of his life in that city. The title of master in sacred theology was conferred upon him in 1908. At this period, he abandoned the study of the natural sciences and apologetics in order to give himself completely to ascetical and mystical theology. At the age of 45 Arintero projected the four-volume work that was to be his masterpiece, *Desenvolvimiento y vitalidad de la Iglesia.* As a result of his teaching regarding the call of all Christians to perfection and the normal development of the life of grace into contemplative prayer, and as a result of his denial of such a thing as acquired contemplation, Arintero became embroiled in controversies with Jesuits and Carmelites and with some of his Dominican brethren. In 1920 he founded the Spanish Dominican review of spirituality, *La Vida sobrenatural,* after having collaborated with the French Dominicans the previous year in the inauguration of *La Vie spirituelle.*

Bibliography: *The Mystical Evolution in the Development and Vitality of the Church,* tr. J. AUMANN, 2 v. (St. Louis 1949–51); *Stages in Prayer,* tr. K. POND (St. Louis 1957); *Cuestiones místicas* (Biblioteca de autores cristianos 154; 1956). A. SUÁREZ, *Vida del M. R. P. Juan de Arintero . . .* (Cádiz 1936). J. AUMANN, "Mystic of San Esteban," *Cross and Crown* 1 (1949) 198–207. J. L. CALLAHAN, "Fire on Earth," *ibid.,* 225–234. M. M. GORCE, *Dictionnaire de spiritualité ascétique et mystique* 1: 855–859.

[J. AUMANN]

ARISTEAS, LETTER OF

The *Letter of Aristeas* is a narrative that, under the guise of a letter, purports to tell how a Greek translation of the Law of Moses was made during the reign of Ptolemy II Philadelphus (285–247 B.C.). Recounted by a Gentile courtier named Aristeas for his brother Philocrates, the narrative may be summarized as follows. Demetrius of Phalerum, the royal librarian, informs Ptolemy that the Jewish Law is worthy of inclusion in the royal library, but that manuscripts and translators are needed (9–11; 28–32). Aristeas, a pious and influential courtier, first persuades Ptolemy to emancipate all Jewish slaves as a gesture of good will, and then leads a delegation to the high priest in Jerusalem (12–27; 33–40). Aristeas's delegation requests a team of 72 translators, to which the high priest Eleazar readily agrees (41–46). Elaborate details follow, such as the names of the translators (47–50), the gifts sent by Philadelphus (51–82), descriptions of the temple, the temple service and the holy city (83–120), and a disquisition on the logic of the Jewish dietary laws (128–71). The translators receive a royal welcome upon their arrival in Egypt (173–86), and display their wisdom at a series of seven banquets hosted by Philadelphus (187–294). They then set about their task and produce a consensus translation in exactly 72 days (301–7). The new translation is approved by the Jewish community, and a curse is pronounced against anyone who would alter it (308–11). Philadelphus marvels at the wisdom of the Law and sends the translators back to Jerusalem with lavish gifts (312–21).

The *Letter of Aristeas* has attracted scholarly interest primarily for its relevance to the origin of the Septuagint. The document was known to Josephus, who cites it in his *Jewish Antiquities* (12.2.1–15 §11–118), and possibly to Philo, who recounts a similar version of LXX origins (*De vita Mosis* 2.25–44). Previous generations of scholars have viewed the narrative as motivated by apologetic concerns, either for the LXX or for a Jewish cultural ethos. Because of its sympathetic portrayal of the Ptolemaic ruler and its cosmopolitan outlook, recent assessments view the document as a product of a Jewish community open to a principled rapprochement with Hellenism. Many scholars have dated the work to the 2d century B.C., though both earlier (3d century B.C.) and later dates (1st century B.C.) have been suggested.

Bibliography: *Anchor Bible Dictionary* 1.380–82. *The Old Testament Pseudepigrapha*, ed. J. H. CHARLESWORTH, 2.7–34. M. HADAS, *Aristeas to Philocrates (Letter of Aristeas)* (New York 1951). G. BOCCACCINI, "The Letter of Aristeas: A Dialogical Judaism Facing Greek Paideia," in *Middle Judaism: Jewish Thought 300 b.c.e. to 200 c.e.* (Minneapolis 1991), 161–85. L. J. GREENSPOON, "Mission to Alexandria: Truth and Legend about the Creation of the Septuagint," *Bible Review* 5 (1989) 34–41. V. A. TCHERIKOVER, "The Ideology of the Letter of Aristeas," *Harvard Theological Review* 51 (1958) 59–85.

[J. N. RHODES]

ARISTIDES

Second-century Athenian philosopher and Christian apologist. Aristides, known primarily through a notice in Eusebius (*Hist. Eccl.* 4.3.2), was the author of an Apology for the Christian faith addressed to the Emperor Hadrian (117–138). In 1878 the Mechitarist monks of San Lazzaro in Venice published an Armenian fragment of an Apology discovered in their monastery; its title indicated that it was the lost Apology of Aristides. The authenticity of this claim was substantiated by J. R. Harris, who found a fourth-century Syrian version of the full text at Mt. Sinai in 1889. This discovery led J. A. Robinson to conclude that most of the Greek text was embodied in the legendary vita of BARLAAM and Joasaph (ch. 26–27) found among the writings of JOHN DAMASCENE. In the vita, the author presents the Apology as made by a pagan philosopher in favor of Christianity. Papyri in the British Museum also contain several chapters of the Greek text (5.4; 6.1–2; 15.6–16.1).

The Apology begins with a discussion of the harmony in creation using stoic concepts. This harmony, the author claims, led him to a knowledge of the Divine Being who created and preserves the universe (ch. 1). The author divides mankind into three categories in accordance with their religious beliefs: the barbarians, the Greeks, and the Jews. He describes as inadequate the barbarian (Chaldean) worship of the elements of the universe (ch. 3–7), the Greek cult of anthropomorphic deities, including Egyptian animal worship (ch. 8–13), and the Jewish devotion to angels and external ceremonies instead of adoration of the true God whom their prophets served. He acknowledges, however, a nobility in the Jewish concept of spirituality (ch. 14).

Aristides viewed the Christians as a "new nation" who alone have a true idea of God, the creator of all things, in His only begotten Son and in the Holy Spirit. Their worship of God consists in purity of life based upon the commandments of the Lord Jesus Christ, to whom they look for the resurrection of the dead and life in the world to come (ch. 15–17). Together with a well-developed Christology (2.6–9), Aristides stressed the charity of the Christian community (15.7–9) and insisted that it is due to the supplications of the Christians that God allows the world to continues to exist. His Apology is close in sentiment to that of QUADRATUS and the letter to DIOGNETUS. While he acknowledged the small number of Christian faithful, he believed that as a new people they were to reanimate the world and save it from the corruption of contemporary immorality. The claim that Aristides is the author of the letter to Diognetus and possibly also identical with Quadratus has not met with the assent of most patristic scholars.

Bibliography: J. R. HARRIS and J. A. ROBINSON, eds., *The Apology of Aristides* (Texts and Studies 1; 2d ed. Cambridge, Eng. 1893). R. SEEBERG, ed., *Der Apologet Aristides* (Erlangen 1894). J. R. HARRIS, *The Newly Recovered Apology of Aristides* (London 1891). J. GEFFCKEN, *Zwei griechische Apologeten* (Leipzig 1907). B. ALTANER, *Reallexikon für Antike und Christentum.* ed. T. KLAUSER [Stuttgart 1941 (1950)–] 1:652–654. P. FRIEDRICH, *Zeitschrift für katholische Theologie* 43 (1919) 31–77, doctrine. B. ALTANER, *Patrology,* tr. H. GRAEF (New York 1960) 118–119. K. RAHNER, *Lexikon für Theologie und Kirche,* ed. J. HOFER and K. RAHNER (Freiberg 1957–65) 1:852–853. J. QUASTEN, *Patrology* (Westminster, Maryland 1950–) 1:191–195, 247–248.

[F. X. MURPHY]

ARISTOCRACY

The rule by a few by reason of their wealth, nobility, or virtue.

Early Concepts. For PLATO (*c.* 427–347 B.C.) the perfect state was the aristocratic state. This ideal was given its best expression in the *Republic:* "Unless philosophers become kings, or those now called kings become philosophers, there will be no end of evils for mankind" (473). Plato describes a state in which social justice would be fully realized as embracing three classes of men: the king-philosophers, or the ruling class, who constitute the legislative and executive power; the soldiers or guardians of the state; and the workers. The rulers must be intensely trained to become true philosopher-kings and must be subjected to a rigid process of selection that will bring the best philosophic minds to the top. Rulers and soldiers must be supported by the state; they cannot hold private property or enjoy normal family life because these are incompatible with full devotion to their duties. This system is proposed as a "model fixed in the heavens for human imitations, but not attainment" (592). Aristotle (384–322) attempted to describe the existent state. To discover an ideal state, he observed in the *Politics,* it is necessary to begin by examining both the best states of history and the best that the theorists have imagined. The best practical policy is aristocracy, the rule of the informed and capable few; this is nowhere described realistically, however.

St. THOMAS AQUINAS (*c.* 1225–74) also insisted that the state should be governed by the ablest. Right order among men demands naturally that the more intelligent should rule (*C. gent.* 3.81). Later St. Thomas MORE (1478–1535) revived Plato's conception in his *Utopia,* describing an imaginary communist state so governed as to secure universal happiness. *The City of the Sun* of Tommaso CAMPANELLA (1568–1639) substituted wise priests to rule instead of philosophers. In the *New Atlantis,* Francis BACON (1561–1626) placed scientists at the head of the state.

Modern Forms. An imitation of an aristocracy might have been the appropriate political form under FEUDALISM, in which ownership of land was accompanied by special duties of armed defense. In modern circumstances, aristocracy can be described as the dominance of a single, well-organized interest group over other community groupings. Perhaps the most obvious examples are the hereditary aristocracies that alternated in power with absolute monarchies in European history until the time of the French Revolution and even later. Also, merchant groups ruled many prosperous European states, such as Venice and the states of the Hanseatic League.

Plato's *Republic* has also been the source of inspiration for modern and contemporary theorists, such as Charles de MONTESQUIEU, G. W. F. HEGEL, J. F. RENAN, Thomas Carlyle, Ralph Waldo EMERSON, Edmund BURKE, Friedrich NIETZSCHE, and George SANTAYANA. These theorists generally claim that men have always been governed by aristocratic institutions; that political power has changed its shape but not its nature; that every people is governed by an ELITE, by a chosen element in the population; that aristocracies have been more favorable to literature, arts, and sciences; and, in a phrase that summarizes their theory, that all civilization is the work of aristocracies.

The managerial aristocracy of business corporations corresponds to the members of a mediocre state bureaucracy. It is an aristocracy of wealth. In 1933 President F. D. Roosevelt enlisted a so-called brain trust to cure national ills. Some theorists advocate an aristocracy of talent and the reconstruction of the federal and state system to arm the executive branch with great and immediate power. They find traditional DEMOCRACY dangerously unworkable when faced by the challenge of the cold war. They fear collapse and defeat by default for the democratic Western world unless something along this line is attempted.

Democratic theorists, on the other hand, such as K. R. Popper or D. Spitz, deny the above allegations, and indict Plato and his followers as forerunners of modern totalitarianism. Plato's ideal state is not regarded as a means to an end, but becomes an end in itself. Such a view militates against sound philosophy and Christian belief. Plato held that each individual and family exists for the state; Christianity holds that each individual and family possesses certain natural rights that every government must respect and protect. Among these rights are the right to life and to a reasonable amount of liberty of movement, of self-assertion, and association.

Bibliography: R. H. CROSSMAN, *Plato Today* (London 1937). H. W. ELDREDGE, *The Second American Revolution* (New York

1964). *The Works of Plato,* tr. B. JOWETT (New York 1936). D. GRENE, *Man in His Pride* (Chicago 1950). K. R. POPPER, *The Open Society* (Princeton 1963). B. F. SKINNER, *Walden Two* (New York 1948). D. SPITZ, *Patterns of Anti-democratic Thought* (New York 1949). J. WILD, *Plato's Theory of Man* (Cambridge, Mass. 1946).

[A. J. OSGNIACH]

ARISTOTELIANISM

The effect of the philosophical and scientific teachings of ARISTOTLE upon subsequent intellectual history through the transmission of his writings, terminology, ideas and influence. To trace the history of Aristotelianism is to unravel one of the major strands in the evolution of Western and Near Eastern civilization. In the ancient and medieval periods especially, its history has been intimately bound up with that of PLATONISM, NEOPLATONISM and STOICISM and with the theological development of the three monotheistic religions Christianity, Islam and Judaism.

Greek Aristotelianism

Beginning with the death of Aristotle (322 B.C.), this section discusses the Aristotelianism of the early Peripatetic, the Hellenistic and the Byzantine periods.

PERIPATETIC PERIOD

After Aristotle's death, his disciple Theophrastus of Eresos (d. *c.* 288 B.C.) became scholarch or head of his school, called the Peripatos or the Lyceum. The older representatives of this school were of varying fidelity to the balanced synthesis of the empirical and the ideal that had been achieved by their founder; most tended toward more empirical researches in the natural sciences, popular considerations in psychology, ethics and politics, philosophical doxography, studies in the history of literature and institutions stemming from Aristotle's *Rhetoric, Poetics* and *Politics* and constitutional researches. Theophrastus was exceptional in that, besides researches in biology and characterology (the latter of relevance to rhetoric), he wrote a small treatise of *Metaphysica* that seems to be an introduction to a more complete work (ed. W. D. Ross and F. H. Fobes, Oxford 1929). His most significant contribution to theoretical thought, his logic, has been reconstructed from fragments by I. M. Bocheński. Developing modal argument and propositional logic, it shows an effort at a higher synthesis of Megaric and peripatetic logic. His Opinions of the Philosophers of Nature was the source for much of the doxography concerning the first centuries of Greek thought. For the most part the writings of the early Peripatos survive only in fragments.

Dicaearchus of Sicilian Messene (b. before 341) and Aristoxenus of Tarentum, immediate followers of Aristotle, were associated in their theory of the soul as a mortal harmony of the elements but as sharing in the divine. Dicaearchus is typical of this early school. He held the eternity of the human species (a dubious point in Aristotle; confer, *Pol.* 1269a 5) and a cyclical theory of history that he attempted to reconcile with a doctrine of cultural development. Besides a treatise On the Soul, he wrote on prophecy, on the cultural history of Greece, on geography, and on Homeric literary problems. Aristoxenus, who wrote a life of Plato, made lasting contributions to the theory of music.

Eudemus of Rhodes seems to have edited Aristotle's *Physics.* He devoted attention to the history of mathematics and astronomy and worked with Theophrastus in logic. Substantial parts of his history of geometry were transmitted by Proclus in his commentary on Euclid. Demetrius of Phaleron was engaged mainly in the study of politics. He brought the Aristotelian spirit of empirical research to Alexandria. Strato of Lampsacus (d. 269), who followed Theophrastus as scholarch, was interested chiefly in the philosophy of nature; his views are quite materialist. The *De coloribus* and *De lineis insecabilibus,* included in the *Corpus Aristotelicum,* can be ascribed to him or to Theophrastus; the *De audibilibus* is Strato's; and the *Mechanica* comes from him or his school. In the *Mechanica* and *On Motion* he discussed the acceleration of falling bodies, the law of the lever, inertia and the parallelogram of velocities and controverted Aristotle's theory of projectile motion. His mathematical formulations are accurate but his ultimate explanations are more qualitative, that is, physical. One of his students was the astronomer Aristarchus of Samos (fl. 280), who anticipated the Copernican system. Strato's brother Lyco (d. 225) succeeded him in the Lyceum and made contributions to pedagogy and *paideia* (general education; confer, *Part.animal.* 639a 1–15). Other early members of the school are of importance mainly for their doxographical or biographical contributions, largely fragmentary, for example, Hieronymus of Rhodes, Aristo of Ceos, and Hermippus.

HELLENISTIC PERIOD

Philosophical polemics with the Skeptics and with other doctrinal schools (*c.* 100 B.C.–A.D. 100) resulted in the widespread use of Aristotelian dialectic and logic in the clarification of their positions and their absorption of Aristotelian natural philosophy and psychology, for example, Carneades' mastery of the *Topics* and the Stoic discussions on the internal senses. By the same process, the materialistic tendency of the Peripatetics was reinforced by Middle Stoicism, though in a strangely theological way. The Middle Stoic school centering on Rhodes—Panaetius, Posidonius and especially the Stoic-Platonist

Antiochus of Ascalon—seems to have reinforced the immanentist factor present in Aristotle's dialogue *On Philosophy,* where stars and souls both are said to be of ether and in parts of the *De caelo* (for example, 279a 30–b 3), where the God seems to be the immanent form of the outermost heaven. The apocryphal *De mundo,* included in the *Corpus Aristotelicum,* bespeaks this tendency. In reaction to the polemics of the other schools, this group and Antiochus in particular, began the harmonization of Aristotle with Stoicism and especially with Platonism. (Only the Epicurean tradition remained obdurately anti-Aristotelian.) Through Cicero it is known that Antiochus considered the difference between Plato and Aristotle to be one merely of vocabulary.

The peripatetic historico-philological interest continued with Diodorus of Tyre and eventually effected its own cure with the edition of Aristotle's works by Andronicus of Rhodes (fl. 50–40 B.C.) and his collaborator Boethus of Sidon. This invited the first extensive philosophical commentary, the paraphrases On The Philosophy of Aristotle in five books by Nicolaus of Damascus, fragments of which survived among the Arabians along with his *De Plantis,* falsely ascribed to Aristotle and included in the *Corpus Aristotelicum.* Though Boethus insisted on the Aristotelian methodic dictum that one must proceed from the more familiar toward the more intelligible in itself, which would indicate starting with natural philosophy, Andronicus seems to have organized the philosophical works of his edition in a descending order: God, the world, the celestial phenomena; the soul, nature and the natural phenomena (I. Düring). He probably coined the term metaphysics, which first appears in Nicolaus and certainly assigned the term Organon to Aristotle's collected logical treatises. He prefaced the whole with a critical essay On Aristotle's Writings, parts of which were cited by later commentators, particularly Simplicius.

2d to 4th Centuries. There is a gap until the 2d century A.D. and Aspasius, who commented on the *Ethics* and is said to have taught Galen's teacher. Both PTOLEMY (fl. 150) and Galen (129–c. 199) must be loosely accounted, by their education and participation in the peripatetic logical and scientific interest, as Aristotelian. Ptolemy attempted a brilliant mediation between Eudoxus and Aristotle, but the element of the Academy dominates that of the Lyceum in his work. His astronomy thus stood somewhat in opposition to the physicotheological astronomy of Aristotle and was a remote prototype of mathematical physics. Galen wrote an important Introduction to Logic that combined Aristotelian and Stoic elements.

Herminus (c. 130–190), a highly independent commentator on the *Prior Analytics,* taught Alexander of Aphrodisias (c. 160–220), the first commentator whose stature is evident, since many of his works survive. He directed the Peripatos at Athens and was called by later generations the Exegete, or Commentator and the Second Aristotle. He had a sharp awareness of the distinction between the form and the matter of the logical art and appears to have been the first to comment extensively on the *Posterior Analytics,* an indication of his intention to proceed throughout his expositions in accordance with the scientific canons of Aristotle. He commented on nearly all of Aristotle's major works and in addition wrote important Questions on problems arising from his philosophy. (As a literary form this is a remote ancestor of the scholastic *quaestiones.*) There are Platonic elements in his interpretation, but he does not intentionally attempt harmonization of Aristotle with Plato. On the contrary, he is materialistic in his psychology, reducing the individual human intellect to little more than an especially gifted animal imagination (νοῦς ὑλικός, the scholastic *intellectus materialis,* or *intellectus passivus*) and exalting the separate agent intellect by identifying it as the First Cause. Aristotle had expressed his noetic theory, both human and divine, somewhat indeterminately (*Anim.* 424b 20–435b 26; *Meta.* 1074b 15–1075a 11), but its problems as focused by Alexander's commentary were to remain central to Aristotelian interpretation down through the Renaissance. Alexander's work is essential for understanding the original texts and also contains precious fragments taken from Aristotle's youthful exoteric writings. His treatise On Fate was used in Muhammadan debates on determinism and free will.

In this late Hellenistic period the attempt to systematize the Aristotelian corpus was paralleled by the efforts of Plotinus and Porphyry to give a unified exegesis of the Platonic writings. PLOTINUS opposed as two extremes the current GNOSTICISM and the naturalism of the Aristotelian materialists and advanced his combination of rationalism and his own private mysticism. He severely attacked the Aristotelian categories, yet he incorporated Aristotle's act and potency and the separate intellect. He freed act and potency from confinement within the physical principles of matter and form and developed the doctrine of the limitation of act by potency, harmonizing it with Platonic participation theory; and he attempted a unified metaphysics of knowledge by locating the Platonic Ideas in the Aristotelian separate Intellect. He was able to take these steps by drawing upon that element in Aristotle himself that had always remained Platonist, the ultimate primacy of FINAL CAUSALITY.

PORPHYRY moved closer to Aristotle with a commentary on the *Ethics* and his important harmonization, On the Unity of the Doctrine (αἵρεσιν) of Plato and Aristotle, works known through Arabic channels but lost in the original. He developed the theme that their apparent disharmony stems from the fact that Aristotle began with sense knowledge and physics, whereas Plato started higher, with the mind of man and went further in divine matters. In weakened form this harmonization became a commonplace of the tradition of *philosophia perennis,* for example, the prologues of Aquinas and Albert the Great to their commentaries *In de divinis nominibus* (and recently, J. Wild's defenses of classical philosophy against K. Popper). Porphyry regarded the Aristotelian categories more favorably than had Plotinus. His chief legacy to the Aristotelian tradition was his treatise On the Five Predicables, or the *Isagoge.* It was later used as an integral part of the Organon, though some avowed Aristotelian logical purists, notably William of Ockham, have claimed that it obscures the realistic beginnings in the matter of Aristotelian logic by substituting as initial the Neoplatonic dialectical form—that is, the context of logical relations, the PREDICABLES, which are second intentions—for the original starting point in first intentions, the CATEGORIES OF BEING.

In the 4th century, IAMBLICHUS preserved most of Aristotle's early introduction to philosophy, the *Protrepticus,* by quoting almost all of it, in his own work of the same name. Themistius (fl. *c.* 387), who wrote incisive paraphrases of most of Aristotle's chief theoretical works, enkindled Aristotelian studies in Constantinople. His commentary on the *De anima* was of great value to Thomas Aquinas in arguing against its Averroist interpretation.

5th and 6th Centuries. Members of the 5th-century Neoplatonic school at Athens stemming from Porphyry and Iamblichus were PROCLUS and Syrianus (fl. *c.* 430); Syrianus is often cited by Boethius. Among them Platonic convictions replaced Aristotle's critical suspension of judgment on certain transcendental matters, for example, life after death, prophecy and divine inspiration. In contrast the more economical Alexandrian school of the late 5th and 6th centuries advocated rationalism in natural theology and regarded the various religious revelations as symbolic manifestations of the one transcendent truth evidentially accessible only through the rigors of philosophical discipline. This notion of levels of communication was articulated by considerable reflection upon the so-called Aristotelian modes of discourse: demonstrative, dialectical, rhetorical and poetic. *The Rhetoric* and *Poetics* were relocated as extensions of the *Topics* and *Sophistical Refutations* and therefore as parts of the Organon. Simplicius explained them Neoplatonically as degrees of participation in the maximal type, absolute demonstration. This Alexandrian idea of an expanded Organon, passing westward via the Arabs, became another commonplace of perennial philosophy (see Thomas Aquinas,

In 1 perih. 1, *In 1 anal. post.* 1). This development of a theory of symbolic forms was an important work of the Alexandrian philosophers. Alfarabi continued this line of inquiry among the Arabs.

The moving spirit of this late Alexandrian school was the Aristotelian commentator Ammonius Hermeae (fl. 485), who is said to have studied under Proclus in the Athenian Academy. Upon returning to Alexandria, he taught John Philoponus, Simplicius (fl. *c.* 533), and Olympiodorus (fl. *c.* 535). Simplicius, in his prologues and his commentaries on the *Physics* and the *De caelo,* shows himself the master doxographer of this school. He followed courses in the Academy of Athens and taught there until it was closed in 529 by decree of the Emperor Justinian. Then he and the scholarch Damascius sought refuge at the court of the Persian Emperor Chosroes, bringing with them the teachings of the Alexandrian school.

Some of Ammonius's disciples had become Christian, notably JOHN PHILOPONUS, who holds a central place in the long history of the interpenetration of Christianity and Aristotelianism. Upon his conversion, Philoponus took independent positions against the Aristotelian doctrine of the eternity of the world and Alexander's doctrine of a separate agent intellect and he taught the creation of matter and the immortality of the personal soul. His commentary on the *Physics* advanced, in dynamics, the theory of IMPETUS, which was destined to play an important role among the Latins of the 14th century. Remotely preparing the way for both the Muslim dialectical theologians and the Latin scholastics, John entered the Christological dispute. Though his solution tended to MONOPHYSITISM, theological controversy was henceforth inseparable from the technical equipment of Aristotelian logic and metaphysics.

BYZANTINE PERIOD

The Latin Church Fathers generally distrusted Aristotle, of whom they knew little more than the *Categories.* Typically, Jerome said that it is characteristic of heretics to quote Aristotle. Laymen such as MARIUS VICTORINUS and Boethius were exceptions. But in the East the theologians were forced by the learned climate of controversy to use Aristotle more and more. This tendency is already present in NEMESIUS (fl. 400), Bishop of Emesa, whose treatment of the soul and human acts shows study of the *De anima* and *Ethics.* But it was the full theology of St. JOHN DAMASCENE that became a channel for the importation of Aristotelian ideas and terms into Latin theology, counterbalancing the earlier importation of theological Neoplatonism via PSEUDO-DIONYSIUS. In the Byzantine Church the tradition of a sort of Aristotelian scholasticism, side by side with a stronger Platonism continued, following the authority of the Damascene and the educational reform of the patriarchal academy by PHOTIUS, through Michael Psellus and his pupil Michael of Ephesus (fl. 1090), down to the controversies at the Council of Florence and during the Renaissance. During these centuries the defensive military position of the Byzantines against the Muslim advance did not dispose them to be receptive to developments in Islamic Aristotelianism; the openness of the West explains in large part the superior growth of Latin scholasticism. (*See* GREEK PHILOSOPHY; PLATONISM; NEOPLATONISM.)

Semitic Aristotelianism

This section discusses the influence of the ideas of Aristotle on Syrian, Arabian and Hebrew philosophies.

SYRIAC TRANSLATION

The relatively small but formative Roman absorption of Greek philosophical literature and thought, particularly Stoic, in the late Republic and the Augustan empire was far exceeded by the Syriac, which took place from the 5th to the 8th century. It divided itself along religious and linguistic lines into the East Syriac and Armenian absorption by the Nestorian academic centers of Mesopotamia and northward, chief among them Edessa and Jundi-Shapur (Gandisapora); and the West Syriac and Coptic absorption by the Jacobite and smaller Orthodox or Catholic centers in the great cities of the Levant and Egypt. When Simplicius and Damascius were at the court of the Emperor Chosroes, *c.* 529, the Persians and the Syrians within their empire had shown considerable interest in Greek philosophy and their school at Jundi-Shapur was already in existence. The Nestorian Probus (fl. 480) and the Monophysite physician Sergei of Reshaina (fl. 530) had done early translations and commentaries on Aristotle in Syriac. Sergei, along with many other early Syrian scholars, had studied in Alexandria. Paul of Persia (fl. 570) dedicated to the same Emperor Chosroes, a still extant treatise on the Organon. Thus the entire Syriac tradition bears the impress of Ammonius and his Alexandrian disciples at the end of the pagan period.

But with the fall of this whole area to Islam, the Arab reception of Greek philosophy took place on a scale dwarfing both of the earlier cultural absorptions and remains unsurpassed, at least in range and quantity, even by the Latin West of the 12th and 13th centuries. The beginnings of the reception of Greek philosophy can be traced back as early as 150 years after the HIJRA (622); it took place full scale between 800 and 1000. It bears three features: (1) a motivation that is strongly theoretical and scientific, but even more strongly political and religious; (2) a powerful Neoplatonic impetus toward the One—toward seeing Aristotle as the thoroughly method-

ic teacher of a nearly complete system, which yet is open at the top and in doctrinal continuity with the transcendental philosophy of Plato and Plotinus; (3) the order in which the books of Aristotle came into Arabic: (*a*) what the Latins were to call the *logica vetus,* namely, the *Categories, On Interpretation,* and schematic digests of the beginning of the *Prior Analytics,* appeared first; (*b*) next was the *logica nova,* the full *Prior Analytics* and the books on the degrees of proof as grouped together by the Alexandrians, namely, *Posterior Analytics* through *Poetics;* (*c*) the translation of the rest of Aristotle did not begin until the founding of the Beit al-Hikma, or House of Wisdom, in 830 under the Caliph of Baghdad, al-Mamun. Here certain scientific and theoretical works seem to precede the practical.

ARABIAN DEVELOPMENT

The medical, astrological and transcendental interests of the first major Muslim philosopher, al-KINDI, ibn-Ishāq, court philosopher of the Baghdad caliphate, are shown by the works made available to him in Arabic: the main zoological writings, *On the Heavens, Meteorology, Metaphysics,* and the so-called *Theology of Aristotle;* the last two works expressly translated for his use. The last is one of two mistaken ascriptions that bedeviled the medieval philosophical interpretation of Aristotle in both Islam and Christendom. The Arabs generally so take for granted the Neoplatonic harmonization of the Stagirite with Plato that they credit him with Neoplatonic works. The *Theology of Aristotle* is a reedited selection from Proclus's *Elements of Theology.* (The other false ascription, a paraphrase of Plotinus's *Enneads,* is the LIBER DE CAUSIS, whose authority was not questioned until St. Thomas Aquinas.)

The work of translating became highly organized under the Nestorian Hunayn ibn-Ishāq (the scholastic Johannitius) and his son Ishaq ibn-Hunayn. They showed a scholarly prudence by their care to establish critical Greek and Syriac texts before translating into Arabic.

ALFARABI began his studies with Nestorians in Khorasan, then continued in Baghdad with teachers in filiation from the Alexandrian academy. He taught in Baghdad and Aleppo. His propaedeutic works, the Introduction to the Philosophy of Plato and Aristotle and the Enumeration of the Sciences, were the highroads to philosophy for generations in Islam. He was a master of the liberal arts in the broad sense, ranging from Arabic grammar to the mode of communication of divine law, all seen in the light of the Aristotelian modes of discourse. He was accomplished even in the quadrivial arts, having written a major commentary on the *Almagest* of Ptolemy. He was more Aristotelian than Platonic, except in the domain of political philosophy. His scholastic associates, Abu Bishr

Matta ibn-Yunus (*c.* 870–940) and the Jacobite Yahya ibn-'Adi, also are interesting. The former did treatises on the *Prior Analytics* and on conditional syllogisms. The latter proposed a rationalistic Aristotelian ''trinity'' as the philosophical way of stating what Christians express symbolically as the Triune God.

In regard to his sources in practical philosophy, Alfarabi is typical of the Islamic philosophers. Though there are occasional references and even quotations from the *Politics,* no Arab ever wrote a commentary on it. In the late 12th century, AVERROËS sought in vain for a copy. All this points to the likelihood that the Arabs had only a digest of its chief sentences. In this respect Islam was in just the reverse position to that of Latin Christendom, which possessed the *Politics* but lacked the *Republic* and the *Laws* until the Renaissance. The Arab world lacked also the *Eudemian Ethics,* the *Magna Moralia* and the dialogues, except for fragments cited mainly by Alexander, Iamblichus and Simplicius.

The two greatest Islamic philosophers, who became most thoroughly known to the Latin West, were the Persian Avicenna and the Spanish Moor Averroës. The logic of AVICENNA is like that of Al-kindi, that is, it shows the Stoic preference for the hypothetical syllogism. Avicenna attempted a systematic harmonization of Aristotle, Neoplatonism and Muslim belief. He made substantial contributions to psychology and wrote a *Metaphysics* that is both Neoplatonic and Aristotelian in inspiration but is not a commentary on Aristotle's *Metaphysics.* He accepted the Aristotelian definition of the soul as first act and form of the body but maintained also that the individual human soul is an incorporeal substance and hence, as the Qur'ān teaches, immortal. He anticipated Descartes with his mental experiment of the ''flying man,'' that is, thinking away one's body until one is simply thinking that one is thinking. He elaborated a theory of the internal senses that was in large part taken over by St. Albert the Great and Aquinas and that culminated in his theory of imagination as elevated by prophetic inspiration.

In metaphysics Avicenna is more the Platonist and Averroës the Aristotelian, although Averroës rejected Avicenna's distinction between the *forma partis* and *forma totius,* thus making it necessary to affirm that the soul of man and the species man are one and the same (*see* QUIDDITY). Moreover, Avicenna tried to balance necessary and contingent aspects of the natural world, preparing the way for the Thomistic real distinction between ESSENCE AND EXISTENCE; whereas Averroës is more immanentist and necessitarian in his view of the relationship between God and the world. Their metaphysical influence increased with the Renaissance, when they were frequently reprinted.

With respect to the agent intellect, Avicenna maintained a separate agent intellect less than God and identifiable more with the demiurge of the *Timaeus* and a personal possible intellect proper to each individual man; Averroës maintained a separate agent intellect that is, in a sense, a separate possible intellect as well. This is the human species, identified as the intelligence of the lunar sphere. Such a doctrine seems to leave individual men with nothing more than acutely receptive animal imaginations. It appeared again in the late Latin AVERROISM of Italy. Avicenna favored a hypothetico-mathematical astronomy in the tradition of Eudoxus, the *Timaeus* and Ptolemy, which Averroës rejected for a physical astronomy that is a celestial physics and a star theology, similar to that of the *De caelo.* Echoes of this controversy were heard in the opposition between Adelard of Bath and the Mertonians at Oxford, on the one hand, and the Parisian Aristotelians, on the other; and later in the Galileo-Bellarmine controversy.

In logic Averroës emphasized the *Posterior Analytics* and, accordingly, attacked Avicenna's preference for the hypothetical syllogism. This was a renewal of Alfarabi's criticism of al-Kindi and the Stoic logic of the Kalam: unlike Aristotelian demonstration the hypothetical syllogism lacks terminal resolution since it fails to display through an explicitly defined middle term the causal force of the nature under discussion.

Like Alexander and Alfarabi, Averroës was also known as the Commentator and became a model for the scholastic art of commenting. He brought to perfection three types of exposition that reflect forms of teaching current in the late Hellenistic Empire. The short commentary, or epitome, seeks to give the student guidance to an intelligent first reading of the text. The middle commentary is a paraphrase, a close second reading and reexpression of the text, accompanied by fresh and effective examples. The long commentary is a thorough reading of the text, which has been broken down into small passages, each of which is thoroughly analyzed and related structurally to the whole of the work. Other texts of the author are correlated with it; controversies over special passages are examined and solutions proposed. This last is the genre in which Thomas Aquinas wrote his commentaries on Aristotle.

Other notable Arabian thinkers of Aristotelian inspiration were the sociological philosophers al-Baruni, who analyzed Indian religion and culture and Ibn Khaldun, who analyzed world culture. ALGAZEL objectively summarized philosophical views, particularly those of Alfarabi and Avicenna, in On the Intentions of the Philosophers. As doxography this had wide circulation among the Latins; however, they lacked his sequel of refutation, the Destruction of the Philosophers. Averroës's Spanish predecessors, AVEMPACE and Ibn Tufail, are also significant. (*See* ARABIAN PHILOSOPHY.)

HEBREW PHILOSOPHY

Medieval Hebrew philosophy benefited from both Islamic and Christian speculation, but it benefited Christian philosophy even more by serving as the conveyor of texts and ideas. CRESCAS was a strong critic of Aristotelian physics; of more significance to the West was AVICEBRON, whose *Fons Vitae*, translated at Toledo by DOMINIC GUNDISALVI with either Abraham ibn Daoud or JOHN OF SPAIN or both, was influential especially among the 13th-century Franciscans. It is important for its anti-Aristotelian doctrines of spiritual matter and plurality of forms and for the scriptural inspiration of its assigning a powerful role of efficient causality to these forms and their divine author. Most important was MAIMONIDES, whose *Guide for the Perplexed* influenced Albert the Great and Thomas Aquinas. (*See* JEWISH PHILOSOPHY; FORMS, UNICITY AND PLURALITY OF.)

Latin Aristotelianism

The absorption of the Aristotelian corpus by the Latins extended over a much longer period than that of the Arabs, that is, from the 4th to the 13th century.

THE CLASSICAL PERIOD

The Romans of the first centuries B.C. and A.D., for example, CICERO, Varro and SENECA, read Aristotle in the original, mainly his exoteric writings; their understanding of him was colored by the syncretism of the Middle Stoa. Cicero is significant for his enrichment of Latin philosophical language through his invention of Latin parallels to Greek technical terms and for his *Topics,* destined to play a central role in the long and confusing history of rhetoric and dialectic in the Latin West.

With the decline of Greek cultural dominance at the extremities of the Roman Empire a period of translation into Latin set in, from the 4th to the 6th century. MARIUS VICTORINUS, who had become a Christian *c.* 355, translated the *Categories* (lost) and Porphyry's *Isagoge* (partly preserved). Adaptations into Latin of Themistius's paraphrases of the *Analytics* (also lost) were made by Agorius Praetextatus at Rome. AUGUSTINE mentions having studied the *Categories;* and a paraphrase of it, also made about this time, was later incorrectly ascribed to him. Toward the close of the 4th century, Martianus Capella digested the *Categories* and *On Interpretation* in book 4 of his *De nuptiis philologiae et mercurii.* A hundred years later BOETHIUS set himself the task of rendering all of Plato and Aristotle into Latin, of interpreting them, and in the spirit of Porphyry, of showing their continuity with each other.

Of these four early translators, the two Christians, Victorinus and Boethius, were Aristotelianizing Neoplatonists in the more intellectual tradition of Porphyry and Proclus, rather than in the mystical tradition of Iamblichus. Boethius's ambitious project, far from finished at his death, was well begun with the *Isagoge* and *Categories,* each with a commentary, *On Interpretation* with two large commentaries, *Prior Analytics, Posterior Analytics, Topics,* and *Sophistical Refutations.* All this he completed with a highly significant personal treatment of argument in three works: *De categoricis syllogismis, De hypotheticis syllogismis,* and *De differentiis topicis.* In them the Aristotelian syllogistic laws are reformulated in Stoic rules; the treatment of the hypothetical syllogism shows the influence of Theophrastus and the Stoics; and the *Topics* shows study of both Cicero's and Aristotle's *Topics.* His posing of the problem of UNIVERSALS in his commentary on Porphyry's *Isagoge* is the *locus classicus* for the many-sided medieval debate on their ontological status.

Though laymen, Victorinus and Boethius each wrote a *De Trinitate* against the Arian heresy. In Boethius's treatise, his combination of Aristotelian and Neoplatonic terminology and definitions became a source within Latin Christian theology for Aristotelian theorizing. Noteworthy in this regard are his definitions of ETERNITY and PERSON, his definitions and divisions of NATURE and his briefly sketched division and methodology of the sciences commented on by Thomas Aquinas (*In Boeth. de Trin.* 5, 6) and later scholastics. On the whole, however, Boethius's influence in theology was that of a dialectical theologian, one who seeks to clarify and show the implications of theological positions but does not demonstrate.

12TH CENTURY

The fulfillment of the Latin aspiration toward scientific theology became possible with the translation of the *Posterior Analytics* by James of Venice. The *Physics, De anima, Metaphysics* 1–4, and the *Parva Naturalia* first came to the Latins through his hands. His translations, though revised in the next century by William of Moerbeke, remained the received texts until the Renaissance.

Besides translating into Latin two of the three Platonic dialogues known to the scholastics, the *Meno* and the *Phaedo* (the *Timaeus* had been done by Calcidius *c.* 300 and revived at Chartres), HENRICUS Aristippus translated book 4 of the *Meteorologica* and possibly the *De generatione et corruptione.* About this time anonymous renditions were made from Greek of the *De generatione et corruptione, De sensu et sensato,* and the *Nicomachean Ethics;* the *Posterior Analytics* and *Physics* were retranslated.

Translation of Aristotle from Arabic began slightly later, in Spain and in England. GERARD OF CREMONA at Toledo rendered into Latin the *Physics, De caelo, De Generatione et Corruptione, Meteorologica, Metaphysics* 1–3, and the *Posterior Analytics* accompanied by Themistius's paraphrase. ALFRED OF SARESHEL commented on the *Meteorologica* that he translated from Arabic and commented on the *De plantis* of Nicolaus of Damascus, believed then to be by Aristotle. Associated with Alfred was ADELARD OF BATH, the translator of Euclid, first among the scholastics to make current the Arabian commonplace that Aristotle represents science while Plato represents wisdom. At this time the works of the Arabian philosophers, largely commentaries on Aristotle, began to come into Europe through the Spanish translation centers.

13TH CENTURY

The frequent retranslation of the *Posterior Analytics* testifies to the intellectual effort being made during the course of the 12th century to capture the spirit of Aristotelian scientific explanation. At the beginning of the 13th century this key work received its first major Latin commentary from the hand of ROBERT GROSSETESTE; his was a somewhat Neoplatonizing interpretation influential throughout the Middle Ages, which continued to be reprinted even in the Renaissance. He gathered and translated from Greek the erroneously ascribed *De mundo* and the *De caelo* and *Nicomachean Ethics.* Chronologically, the scholastics distinguished among the Greco-Latin translations between an *Ethica vetus,* comprising books 2 and 3 and the first complete *Ethics,* that of Grosseteste. Likewise they spoke of a *Metaphysica vetustissima,* comprising books 1 to 4, the work of James of Venice; a *Metaphysica media,* comprising all but book 11; and finally the complete *Metaphysics,* done at Thomas Aquinas's request by William of Moerbeke.

An event of major importance for the subsequent evolution of philosophical thought was the introduction of Averroës into the Latin West in the second quarter of the 13th century. WILLIAM OF AUVERGNE and PHILIP the Chancellor were the first to quote the Arabian Commentator. Albert the Great used him about equally with Avicenna, being more Averroist in logic and natural philosophy but more Avicennian on the deeper problems of human psychology and metaphysics. St. Thomas was exposed to Averroës at the University of Naples. The principal translator of Averroës was Michael Scot at the court of Frederick II in Sicily between 1228 and 1235. Averroës's infiltration into the Western world was virtually complete by 1240, and the extent of his challenge to Christian faith had become evident. The chief points of conflict were three: (1) his doctrine of the eternity and ne-

cessity of the world opposed the Christian doctrine of creation; (2) the unity of the separate intellect, both agent and possible, conflicted with the immortality of the personal soul; and (3) his Latin interpreters' understanding that he taught a theory of DOUBLE TRUTH and the primacy of the philosophical over the theological mode of knowledge ran counter to the primacy accorded revelation by Christianity.

The vigor and originality of the scholastic intellectual response was in proportion to the profundity of the Averroist challenge. Members of the arts faculty at Paris, such as SIGER OF BRABANT and BOETHIUS OF SWEDEN, favored the Commentator's interpretations, whereas champions of theology, chiefly ALBERT THE GREAT and THOMAS AQUINAS, advanced their own resolutions of the problems. The challenge forced them to acquire more accurate translations of Aristotle, which were provided by their confrere WILLIAM OF MOERBEKE. He translated in their entirety and for the first time the *Poetics, Rhetoric,* and zoölogical books, though the first two works were almost totally neglected by scholastics. He also translated books 3 and 4 of the *De caelo;* books 1 to 3 of the *Meteorologica,* and retranslated book 4; books 3 to 8 of the *Politics;* and the theretofore missing book 11 of the *Metaphysics.* He also translated once again the *Categories* and *On Interpretation* and thoroughly revised the existing Greco-Latin translations, chiefly those of James of Venice.

During the 13th century, Aristotelianism was the object of several prohibitions by ecclesiastical authorities. But in 1255 a statute was enacted by the University of Paris legalizing the study of all the known works of Aristotle. Then in 1270 E. TEMPIER, Bishop of Paris, condemned the chief doctrines of Averroist Aristotelianism; on March 7, 1277, he summed up in a brutal, haphazard, pell-mell fashion (F. van Steenberghen) under 219 headings the doctrines to be rejected. Similar but less rash prohibitions were imposed on the philosophy of Aristotle at Oxford by ROBERT KILWARDBY and JOHN PECKHAM. With the more mature study of Thomas Aquinas's writings, the difficult but successful defense of Thomas by the early Thomistic school, notably by JOHN (QUIDORT) OF PARIS, and the canonization of St. Thomas (1323), the cause of Christian Aristotelianism was assured. Then the pendulous weight of authority swung the other way. The inceptor in arts at Paris was sworn during the 14th century to teach nothing inconsistent with Aristotle, and as late as 1624 the French Parlement threatened with death all who taught anything contrary to his doctrines. This was renewed by the University of Paris in 1687. Among the colleges of the New World there were some restrictions against Copernican astronomy and in support of the traditions of Aristotle and PTOLEMY. The surviving Dominican oath to teach according to the mind of St. Thomas is in this paradoxically voluntaristic tradition.

Thomas Aquinas distinguished between theology and philosophy, according to both the dignity of science; and in analogous fashion he distinguished between Church and State, according to each the dignity of being a perfect society. His commentaries on the *Ethics* and *Politics* won a lasting place for them in civil and ecclesiastical governmental theory. John of Paris, in *De potestate regia et papali*, championed the Aristotelian and Thomistic principles of natural law and the integrity and natural character of the State against the theory of absolute papal monarchy in temporal matters propounded by GILES OF ROME. The relevance of the *Ethics* and *Politics* to civil life was sufficiently appreciated by the middle of the 14th century for NICHOLAS ORESME, Bishop of Lisieux, to translate them into the vernacular. On the opposite side from Giles of Rome there soon appeared the *De Monarchia* of DANTE, who insisted on a world-state centering in the independent and supreme power of the emperor against the claims of the pope, and capable of achieving human happiness on earth. The imperial unity and world-state theme seems to owe something to the Arabian interpretations of Aristotle regarding the common agent and possible intellect.

Both the 13th and the 14th centuries saw advances in the empirical scientific side of Aristotelianism made principally at Merton College, Oxford, in the tradition of Robert Grosseteste; in France by JOHN BURIDAN, Oresme and others; and by the German Dominicans, for example, THEODORIC OF FREIBERG, in the tradition of St. Albert. (*See* THOMISM, 1; SCHOLASTICISM, 1.)

The Renaissance, Reformation and Enlightenment

The 14th to the 18th century was a period characterized by four developments respecting the authority of Aristotle: (1) the humanist movement; (2) psychological and methodological controversies; (3) naturalistic and scientific movements; and (4) development of political theory. The first and third are understood to be largely revolts against the Aristotle of scholasticism, the second is, by intention at least, in part pro-Aristotelian, and the third and fourth have both aspects. They began or centered in Italy.

HUMANISM, PLATONISM AND SECOND AVERROISM

The humanist revolt was a vengeance taken on the demonstrative logic and dialectic of the late scholastics by the practitioners of the so-called lesser modes of discourse, rhetoric and poetics, for scholasticism's neglect

since the 12th century of these modes of communication in favor of what appeared to be the sterility of Aristotelian logic and methods. Though a late expression, Stefano Guazzo's *La Civil Conversazione* (Venice 1586) sums up this reaction. Already in the 14th century the humanist followers of the medieval *ars dictaminis* had begun to unearth unsuspected treasures of classical Roman history and literature, and the mid-15th century saw Greek letters come alive again in Italy. That the humanists were not unfriendly to Aristotle as such is shown by their continued interest in the ethical writings and the *Politics,* and by their studies and editions of the long neglected *Rhetoric* and *Poetics,* which the famous Aldine press in Venice first published in 1498 in the *Rhetores Graeci,* edited by Giorgio Valla. The influence of the *Poetics,* rightly or wrongly understood, is a whole chapter in early modern literature, culminating in the French classical theater.

Closely associated with humanism was the Platonic revival. A Christian Platonism flourished in the Platonic Academy at Florence. Its founder, Marsilio FICINO, was particularly concerned about defending the immortality of the soul against the Averroist Aristotelians. The humanists underestimated the degree to which Aquinas was able to master Aristotle while remaining, in a profound sense, a good Augustinian theologian. On substantive matters such as defense of the natural freedom of man, which had been attacked by LUTHER, ERASMUS quickly fell back upon the moral theology of St. Thomas and its philosophical base in the Aristotelian *Ethics.*

The humanist movement took place to a large extent outside the university framework. The revived Averroist tradition that began early in the 14th century was scholastic in the broad sense of the term. It arose within and came to dominate, the Italian universities, chiefly Bologna in the early period and Padua later. Remote inspiration came from the natural philosopher JOHN OF JANDUN and the political theorist MARSILIUS OF PADUA at the court of Ludwig of Bavaria. At Bologna were Gentile da Cingoli, his pupil Angelo of Arezzo and Thaddeus of Parma, who worked in the allied fields, for an Averroist, of astronomy and psychology. At Padua, Peter of Abano was more of a Galenian medical methodologist than an Averroist. In the 15th century the distinguished logician Paolo VENETO, an Averroist, taught at Padua. Sharing the scholarship of the Paduan school and well acquainted with its Averroism, was the celebrated Thomist philosopher and theologian Tommaso de Vio CAJETAN, who also commented on Aristotle.

The humanist appetite for belles-lettres and the university study of Aristotle were the primary and secondary conditions preparing the ground for the reception of Byzantine learning. The 15th-century Greek contribution to

Aristotelian scholarship was a substantial and permanent acquisition for all subsequent ages. The Council of Florence and the fall of Constantinople (1453) brought to Italy many learned Greeks, among them George of Trebizond, who, in a comparative study of Plato and Aristotle, opts for the latter; Theodore of Gaza; John ARGYROPOULOS, Bishop of Florence, who commented on the *Ethics* and translated Aquinas's *De ente et essentia* into Greek; and Cardinal BESSARION, who translated the *Metaphysics* into Latin, moderated Gemistos Plethon's criticisms of Aristotle and attempted anew the conciliation of Aristotle with Plato. Philosophical Greek was taught, new translations were made and many theretofore unknown Greek commentaries were printed and translated; finally in 1495 the Aldine press produced the *Editio princeps* of most of the Aristotelian works. Textual criticism, developed first by Lorenzo VALLA on historical documents, began to be applied to Aristotle and his commentators. In 1549 Robertellus produced the important second edition of the *Poetics* with Latin translation and commentary, and Fasolo translated Simplicius's commentary on the *De anima*.

PSYCHOLOGICAL AND METHODOLOGICAL CONTROVERSIES

All this sharpened the quest for an authentic interpretation of Aristotle and led to controversy in two chief areas: (1) psychology, centering on *De anima* 3, *Metaphysics* 12, and *De caelo;* and (2) methodology, centering on the opening chapters of the natural works and the prologue literature of the Greek and Arabian commentators.

The first controversy involved rival supporters of the interpretations of Alexander of Aphrodisias and Averroës, who differed over whether the separate agent intellect discussed in the *De anima* is in any sense human. According to the Averroists an impersonal but human immortality is attached to the separate intelligence of the species man, a sort of immortal overmind, or ''noosphere''; the Alexandrists denied human immortality, holding that the only overmind, or separate intellect, was God. Some historians regard the Averroists as attempting to de-Christianize the Aristotle of Thomistic interpretation, and the Alexandrists as attempting to demetaphysicize Aristotle in himself.

In 1516 Pietro POMPONAZZI, drawing support from Alexander, wrote a treatise against the immortality of the soul. The more important of the Averroists were Nicoletto Vernia, who taught at Padua from 1471 to 1499, Agostino NIFO, Leonicus Thomaeus, Alexander Achillini and Marco Antonio ZIMARA. J. ZABARELLA, who had studied Greek with Robertellus, developed Pomponazzi's position in psychology but in other parts of philosophy was much influenced by Averroës, as well as by Themistius

and Simplicius. He made his chief contribution in methodology where, as a logician and natural philosopher, he opposed the moralist and metaphysician Francesco Piccolomini (1520–1604). His works and commentaries and those of his student Julius Pacius continue to influence modern scholarship on Aristotle. Pacius (1550–1635) edited and translated Aristotle's Organon and *Physics* (Frankfurt 1592, 1596) and edited the whole *Corpus Aristotelicum* (Lyons 1597). His *Institutiones logicae* (Sedan 1595) marks him as an extreme methodological pluralist, a humanist inclined to see the differences in texts, whereas Zabarella, a logician, had seen their structural similarities.

In the Protestant north, particularly in Calvinist circles, the anti-Aristotelian logic and methodology of the Huguenot martyr Peter RAMUS had great vogue. In his *Dialecticae institutiones* and *Aristotelicae animadversiones* (Paris 1543) and his two books on the *Posterior Analytics* (1553) he fused logic and rhetoric and reduced all methods to one. Historical Aristotelianism had begun in France with J. Lefèvre d'Étaples and was carried on after Ramus's attacks by Pacius. Ramus was opposed by J. Carpentarius (or Charpentier, 1524–74), a student of Greek mathematics who wrote a Comparison of Plato and Aristotle (Paris 1573) in the ancient tradition of their harmonization.

The controversy between Aristotelians and Ramists was continued in England and Germany. Oxford tended to be more Aristotelian, Cambridge more Ramist and later, Platonist. At Oxford the study of Aristotle remained an integral part of the university curriculum until the middle of the 17th century; particular attention was given to the reading and explication of the logical, ethical, and political works. Thomas HOBBES wrote a digest of the *Rhetoric* and was a keen student of its theory of the passions. Of varying strength among the representatives of declining Aristotelianism in this period were John Sanderson, John Case (d. 1600), whose Roman Catholic leanings forced him to teach privately, Richard Crackenthorpe, Thomas Wilson, Ralph Lever, Jacobus Martinus Scotus and the extraordinary Everard DIGBY. In 1620 Francis BACON published his *Novum Organum*, a work stressing induction and intended to replace the Organon of Aristotle. Nonetheless, an impressive strand of Aristotelian and Thomistic learning, tempered with humanism, continued in the clergy of the Anglican Church, particulary in matters of logic, ethics and politics. It flowered in Richard HOOKER (1554–1600), author of *Ecclesiastical Polity;* in the 18th century, in the ethics and natural theology of Joseph BUTLER (1692–1752) and the Bishop of Durham; as late as the 19th century in the logic of H. L. Mansel (1820–71); and in the 20th-century metaphysics of E. L. Mascall (1905–93). Especially worthy of mention is a member of the dissenting ministry, Thomas Taylor (1758–1835), who single handedly translated nearly the whole Aristotelian corpus between the years 1801 (*Metaphysics*) and 1818 (*Nicomachean Ethics*). To these he added *Copious Elucidations from the Best of his Greek Commentators.* He was devoted to a Neoplatonism that, in the Alexandrian fashion, he regarded as capable of taking into its higher synthesis of wisdom all that is scientifically positive in Aristotle.

In Germany, despite Luther's opposition, the scholarly conciliator P. MELANCHTHON worked to ensure the continuance of Aristotelian learning, particularly the logic, where his authority prevailed over that of Ramus. However, the Aristotelianism he had in mind contained Stoic elements. A branch of early Lutheran theology, following Melanchthon, has been called Lutheran scholasticism. Jacob Schegk (1511–87), professor of logic and medicine at Tübingen, was an able Greek scholar and student of the *Analytics* who refuted Ramus. Others undergoing Aristotelian influence were J. Jungius, his student G. W. LEIBNIZ, who corrected the excessive attacks of the Italian Renaissance rhetorician M. Nizolio (1498–1576) on Aristotelian logic and theoretical philosophy and the systematizer Christian WOLFF. The decisive critic of Ramus was the progressive Aristotelian Bartholomew Keckermann (*c.* 1572–1609), whose work gained wide circulation on the Continent and in England. With the Germans must be mentioned the Dutch professor of theology at Utrecht, G. Voëtius, who, though Calvinist, was far from being a Ramist. He based himself on Aristotle in order to attack the new methodical monist R. DESCARTES. In the 16th and 17th centuries the German universities began the double tradition of metaphysical and philological penetration of Aristotle that was to flower in the 19th-century work of the Berlin Academy.

SECOND SCHOLASTICISM

This movement began mainly in Italy with the Dominican resurgence prior to and during the Council of Trent. The expositors of Aquinas commented also on Aristotle, for example, DOMINIC OF FLANDERS wrote on the *Metaphysics*; FERRARIENSIS on the *Posterior Analytics, Physics,* and *De anima;* G. C. JAVELLI on Aristotle's chief works (he also refuted Pomponazzi); and Cajetan on the *Categories, Posterior Analytics, De anima* and on Porphyry's *Praedicabilia.*

Soon the center of the second scholasticism became Spain and Portugal. At Salamanca F. de VITORIA revived and developed the Aristotelian-Stoic heritage of natural law and Domingo de SOTO commented on the Organon, *Physics* and *De anima.* The COMPLUTENSES, Carmelite professors at Alcalá, and the Conimbricenses, the Jesuits of Coimbra, did collective works on Aristotle's logic and

physical philosophy. F. de TOLEDO, who had studied under Soto at Salamanca, taught there and in Rome and commented on Aristotle. In 1585, Benedict Pereira wrote a vast and free commentary on the *Physics,* showing study of contemporary Italian humanist and naturalist work as well as a slight Scotist influence. The chief scholarly contributions to Aristotelian studies were made on the *Metaphysics* by P. da FONSECA and F. SUÁREZ. Fonseca's work is considered the first erudite edition of the *Metaphysics* in the modern age by reason of its vast critical apparatus: collation of codices, discussion of the authenticity of texts, evaluation of variants and comparison of translations. Suárez' *Disputationes metaphysicae* (1597), not a commentary as such, develops according to his own outline but is doxographically helpful for all prior, particularly scholastic, views on Aristotelian metaphysics. To these should be added the useful paraphrases of Sylvester MAURUS on the chief works of Aristotle (1668). As a whole, however, the second scholasticism has been judged to have been too drawn in upon itself, too exclusively clerical and to have lacked the dialectical engagement with contemporary thought and science and the appreciation for empirical research that characterized the historical Aristotle and marks vital philosophizing in any age (F. Copleston).

NATURALISM AND SCIENCE

In Italy there arose a kind of natural philosophy, which conceived of nature as a more or less self-sufficient system, either independent of God once it had been created (*see* DEISM), or tending to be identified with God (*see* IMMANENTISM; PANTHEISM). To the Aristotelian HYLOMORPHISM it opposed ATOMISM and HYLOZOISM; to the Aristotelian intentionality of cognition, a mechanical theory of perception and even of intellection; to the Aristotelian view of the universe as finite, its extensive infinity. From the Aristotle of Averroës and Alexander it took a necessitarian view of the existence of the universe. Chief among these natural philosophers were G. Fracastoro (1478–1553), G. Cardano, B. TELESIO, G. BRUNO and T. CAMPANELLA. Using Aristotelian terms to oppose Aristotle, Bruno revived David of Dinant's identification of pure matter with pure act. G. C. Vanini (1584–1619), much influenced by Pomponazzi, also used Aristotelian language to maintain that Nature, which he divinized, is the prime mover and needs no prime moving principle outside itself. Two thinkers loosely associated with the Italian natural philosophy who explicitly attacked Aristotle were F. PATRIZI, in *Discussionum Peripateticarum Libri XV* (1571), and P. GASSENDI, in *Exercitationes Paradoxicae adversus Aristoteleos . . .* (1624).

The influence of these philosophers on the development of modern science was overshadowed by that of the

Aristotelian methodologists of Padua. However, it was chiefly the revival of pure Greek mathematics, mathematical physics and the tradition of hypothetico-mathematical astronomy, which in the Alexandrian and Arabic worlds had constantly rivaled Aristotle's *De caelo,* that set the stage for classical modern physics and astronomy. This revival began the refutation of Aristotle on falling bodies, the movement of the planets, the aether, or so-called crystalline quintessence, the speed of light, etc. Among its chief figures were COPERNICUS, G. GALILEI and S. Stevin.

Modern and Contemporary Aristotelianism

Aristotelian scholarship declined in the 18th century, was revived in the 19th century under the influence of the Berlin Academy, and flourished with the third scholasticism of the 20th century.

18TH CENTURY

The victory of classical modern physics had been interpreted to be so crushing that there was little activity in Aristotelian studies during this period. In epistemology some idea of the Aristotelian-scholastic theory of intentionality managed to survive the Enlightenment and the rise of idealism, through B. Bolzano. Only logic and to a greater degree, political philosophy received much attention.

No part of Aristotle's writings has a more extensive history of study than the *Politics.* From Aquinas and Moerbeke there is a continuous line through John of Paris, Cajetan, Bellarmine, Suárez, the founders of international law, Vitoria and GROTIUS, to the English common and natural law traditions of Blackstone (1723–80) and to others in the 20th century. The idea of division of powers found in MONTESQUIEU (1689–1755) is traceable to Aristotle and it appeared also in Thomas Jefferson (1743–1826). The direct influence of Aristotle and Aquinas on R. HOOKER, of Aristotle and Hooker on J. LOCKE and of all these on E. BURKE, J. ACTON and J. Bryce (1838–1922) is certain. The discovery of Aristotle's *Constitution of Athens* in 1890 intensified interest in his philosophy of the state.

19TH CENTURY

During the 19th century in France, Italy and especially Germany, the philosophical climate of nationalism and IDEALISM and the consequent interest in philology and the history of ideas and institutions combined with the continuity, maintained chiefly in England, of Aristotelian philosophical studies and a more traditional humanistic philology to bring about a revival of Aristotelian scholarship, with emphasis on the literary style of the treatises, their chronological order, the youthful frag-

ments and the evolution of Aristotle's thought. The Berlin Academy sponsored a definitive edition of the *Corpus Aristotelicum* (1831) under the supervision of J. Bekker, who edited Aristotle's treatises (v.1, 2) and the Latin versions of the Renaissance (v.3); C. A. Brandis and H. Usener edited the scholia (v.4); and H. Bonitz edited the *Index Aristotelicus* (v.5, 1870). V. Rose's edition of the fragments in the *Corpus* was superseded by his third edition, *Aristotelis qui ferebantur librorum fragmenta* (Teubner 1886). Theodor Waitz edited the Organon with commentary in 1844–46. The Berlin Academy also sponsored the *Commentaria in Aristotelem Graeca,* completed in 1909 and a *Supplementum Aristotelicum* (1882–1903).

A. Trendelenburg along with his students C. Heider, F. Brentano and R. Eucken placed Aristotle at the base of their philosophical teaching as a result of their researches showing his formative role through Roman and scholastic translators in the whole history of Western philosophical vocabulary. Trained in scholasticism and by Trendelenburg, BRENTANO maintained that the true method of philosophizing is continuous with that of the science of nature, meaning by the latter to include both the Aristotelian organic and the modern positive approaches to nature. He tried to demonstrate this in the field of psychology, to which he introduced the Aristotelian and scholastic notion of INTENTIONALITY. This was continued in various ways by his followers in PHENOMENOLOGY, C. Ehrenfels, A. Meinong, E. HUSSERL, M. SCHELER and their existentialist successors. Other Germans who have studied the thought of Aristotle are H. DRIESCH, E. Zeller and H. Maier.

Aristotle's reception in France was less sympathetic. F. Ravaisson-Mollien (1813–1900) found that the Aristotelian characterization of being as ACT complemented his dynamic spiritualism. He influenced a whole generation of French philosophers, such as L. BRUNSCHVICG, O. Hamelin (1856–1907) and L. Robin (1866–1947), but their idealist and rationalist positions caused them to regard Aristotle merely as a rather prosaic follower of Plato. However, the appreciative work of the great French historians of science, P. Tannery (1843–1904) and especially P. Duhem, is indispensable for an understanding of the scientific role of Aristotle and his successors. A Platonic and idealistic judgment of Aristotle is present also in the work of the Englishmen J. Burnet, A. E. Taylor and A. N. WHITEHEAD, though less sharply than in that of their French counterparts.

20TH CENTURY

The neoscholastic movement, or preferably, the third scholasticism, was already underway at the time of Leo XIII's encyclical *AETERNI PATRIS* (1879), formally directed to revitalizing the teaching of Thomas Aquinas. But, by its admonition to return to the sources of Aquinas's teaching, the encyclical did much to direct the attention of scholars to Aristotle and to the problems of Aristotelian transmission, especially in the Latin, Arabic and Syriac periods. Especially noteworthy in this regard is the ambitious project of editing and publishing, with studies, the whole corpus of extant Latin translations of Aristotle made during the Middle Ages—*Aristoteles Latinus.*

The dominant problem of 20th-century Aristotelian studies, however, is not the place of Aristotle in the grand scale of development of human thought, but the personal evolution of his doctrines. W. Jaeger, in his monumental *Aristotle: Fundamentals of the History of His Development* (1923, Eng. tr. 1934), offered a creative solution and formulated problems for subsequent students. He concluded that Aristotle's development was a sort of fall from grace: from a wholly transcendental young Platonist, an extreme realist committed to the existence of the Forms and the immortality of the soul, through a stage of abandonment of the Forms and divinization of the visible heavens, to an old naturalist, empiricist and nominalist who regarded astral theology and metaphysics as ''conjecture'' (τὸ φαινόμενον ἡμῖν, *Part. animal.* 645a 5). The developmental hypotheses of the Jaeger school were received cordially but critically, by the more conservative Oxford scholars, such as W. D. Ross, G. R. Mure, E. Barker and in general the group that under the general editorship of Ross and J. A. Smith, has succeeded in translating the whole of the *Corpus Aristotelicum* into English. The difference between the Jaeger and the Oxford schools is not unlike that in English literature between the historical critics and the new or Aristotelian critics of the Chicago school.

The work of I. Düring has indicated that after an early and brief adherence to Plato's doctrine of Forms, Aristotle opposed his master with the thesis that οὐσία (substance, entity) is concrete; then, through the biological, psychological, and astronomical researches of his middle period, he found his way to a philosophical position much nearer to Plato's metaphysical doctrine, but on his own terms and out of, rather than in place of, his own sense of concretion and immanent final causality. The later works of the *Metaphysics,* particularly books 7 to 9, belong to this last period.

A recent characteristic of 20th-century textual study of Aristotle has been teamwork. The central organ of this is the *Symposium Aristotelicum.* One was held at Oxford in August 1957, and its papers were published by the University of Göteborg, *Aristotle and Plato in the Mid-Fourth Century,* ed. I. Düring and G. E. L. Owen (1960); the work of the second symposium, held at Louvain in August 1960, was published there in 1961, *Aristotle et les problèmes de méthode,* ed. S. Mansion.

See Also: PLATONISM; NEOPLATONISM; SCHOLASTICISM, 1, 2, 3; THOMISM, 1; NEOSCHOLASTICISM AND NEOTHOMISM

Bibliography: General. L. MINIO-PALUELLO, *A Catholic Dictionary of Theology,* 1 (1962) 142–145. R. WALZER, *Encyclopedia of Islam,* ed. B. LEWIS et al. (2d ed. Leiden 1954—) 1:630–633. G. DI NAPOLI, *Enciclopedia filosofica,* 4 v. (Venice-Rome 1957) 1:369–375. G. PATZIG, *Die Religion in Geschichte und Gegenwart,* 7 v. (3d ed. Tübingen 1957–65) 1:602–606. E. GILSON, *History of Christian Philosophy.* F. C. COPLESTON, *History of Philosophy* (Westminster, Md 1946—) v.3. K. O. BRINK, *Paulys Realenzyklopädie der klassischen Altertumswissenschaft,* ed. G. WISSOWA et al., Suppl. 7 (1940). Special. E. ZELLER, *Aristotle and the Earlier Peripatetics,* tr. B. F. C. COSTELLOE and J. H. MUIRHEAD, 2 v. (New York 1897). F. R. WEHRLI, ed. *Die Schule des Aristoteles,* 10 v. (Basel 1944–59), texts and notes. P. MORAUX, *Alexandre d'Aphrodise: Exégète de la noétique d'Aristote* (Paris 1942). E. F. CRANZ, *Alexander of Aphrodisias: Genuine and Spurious Works and Their Translations, History, Description, Bibliography,* v.1 of *Catalogus translationum et commentariorum: Mediaeval and Renaissance Latin Translations and Commentaries: Annotated Lists and Guides,* ed. P. O. KRISTELLER et al. (Washington 1960—). R. WALZER, *Greek into Arabic: Essays on Islamic Philosophy* (Oriental Studies 1; Cambridge, Mass. 1962). M. GRABMANN, *Methoden und Hilfsmittel des Aristotelesstudiums im Mittelalter* (Munich 1939). G. LACOMBE and M. DULONG, *Aristoteles Latinus,* cod. 1 (Rome 1939). *Aristoteles Latinus,* ed. L. MINIO-PALUELLO, codex 2— (Cambridge, Eng. 1953). F. VAN STEENBERGHEN, *Aristotle in the West* (Louvain 1955); *Siger dans l'histoire de l'aristotelisme* (Louvain 1942). R. P. MCKEON, *Aristotelianism in Western Christianity* (Chicago 1939). S. D. WINGATE, *The Mediaeval Latin Versions of the Aristotelian Scientific Corpus* (London 1931). D. A. CALLUS, ''Introduction of Aristotelian Learning to Oxford,'' *Proceedings of the British Academy,* 29 (1943). P. MORAUX et al., *Aristote et Saint Thomas d'Aquin* (Paris 1957). *Medieval Political Philosophy: A Sourcebook,* eds. R. LERNER and M. MAHDI (New York 1963). N. W. GILBERT, *Renaissance Concepts of Method* (New York 1960). J. H. RANDALL, *The School of Padua and the Emergence of Modern Science* (Padua 1961), repr., with original texts added, of ''The Development of Scientific Method in the School of Padua,'' *Journal of the History of Ideas,* 1 (1940) 177–206. P. PETERSEN, *Geschichte der aristotelischen Philosophie im protestantischen Deutschland* (Leipzig 1921). I. DÜRING, *Aristotle in the Ancient Biographical Tradition* (Göteborg 1957); ''Von Aristoteles bis Leibniz,'' *Antike und Abendland,* 4 (1954) 118–154.

[J. J. GLANVILLE]

ARISTOTLE

Philosopher of Stagira, a Greek colony in the Chalcidic Peninsula, and hence referred to as the Stagirite; b. summer of 384 B.C.; d. Chalcis in Euboea, autumn of 322 B.C. For 20 years a student of PLATO, Aristotle broke with Plato's successors in the Academy and founded his own school, later known as the Peripatetics. Very influential in the whole of Western philosophy, especially with the scholastics of the 13th century, his thought is notable for its development of logic; its elucidation of the four causes and the related doctrines of matter and form, and potency and act; its ethical teaching on the moral virtues; and the political notion of the common good. His writings are important also in the history of literature and of the natural sciences.

Biography

Nothing is known directly of Aristotle's boyhood, though his ancestry was thoroughly Greek. His father, Nicomachus, was described as a descendant of the Machaon Asclepiadae, thus indicating aristocratic birth and medical interests. As physician and personal friend of Amyntas (II or III), father of Philip of Macedon, Nicomachus lived at the Macedonian court. Aristotle's mother, Phaestis, of a colonizing family from Chalcis in Euboea, was also represented as of Aesculapian lineage.

Early Life. Both parents died while Aristotle was a minor, and the charge of his education devolved upon a certain Proxenus, probably a close relative. At about 17 Aristotle arrived at Athens. During the next 20 years, his "first Athenian period," he associated with the great philosopher Plato, head of the already highly organized and well-known Academy. His writings show that he acquired a deep and solid background in Platonic philosophy during his formative days. He engaged in teaching, and at a certain time he is reported to have suddenly changed his method of instruction to emphasize rhetorical training, in order to compete with the rival school of Isocrates. His prolific career as a writer began with *Gryllus,* a work on rhetoric named after Xenophon's son, which may be dated about 361 B.C., when Aristotle was about 23. Another work, *Eudemus,* suggests dating about 353, when he was about 30.

Early in 347, possibly before Plato's death in the first half of that year, Aristotle left Athens, perhaps because of a surge of anti-Macedonian sentiment, and spent the next three years at the court of Hermias, ruler of Atarneus and Assos, coastal towns of Asia Minor facing the island of Lesbos. Hermias had been interested in Plato's work and was most cordial in his hospitality to Aristotle, giving him in marriage Pythias, his niece and adopted daughter. Of this marriage was born a daughter, named Pythias. Aristotle had a son also, called Nicomachus. In his will the two children are viewed in the same legal status. A later report, claiming that Nicomachus was Aristotle's son by Herpyllis, one of his domestics, was taken from the noted but adversely disposed historian Timaeus and has the earmarks of a calumny circulated in a program of defamation after the Stagirite's death. Sometime during 345-344 B.C. Aristotle left the court of Hermias for Mytilene on

nearby Lesbos. In 343-342 he was summoned to Macedon to tutor Alexander. His stay there lasted until a short time after Alexander's succession to the throne at about 20 in the summer of 336. Geographical indications suggest that Aristotle conducted his extensive research in natural history mainly during these years in Asia Minor and Macedon.

Aristotle's School. In 335 or 334, probably in the spring of 334, Aristotle returned to Athens and remained there until near the end of 323 or early 322. These years are known as his "second Athenian period," or *Meisterjahre.* During this remarkably short span of about 12 years he gave definite shape to a philosophical tradition that was to carry his name and intellectual seal through the subsequent centuries. While absent in Macedon, he had been proposed for election as head of the Platonic school after the death of its second scholarch, Speusippus, but Xenocrates received a plurality of votes over two other members. The two withdrew from the Platonic circle, and Aristotle, on his return to Athens, began to teach in the Lyceum, another public park. From the Lyceum gatherings an organized philosophical school developed. By the next century it was known as the *peripatos;* its adherents, as Peripatetics. The original force of *peripatos* as its designation is obscure. Etymologically signifying a "walking about," the word had come to mean a place for walking about, a discussion carried on during a stroll, school discussions or lectures in general, or a place in which school activity was conducted. As applied to the Peripatetic school, it most likely came from the place where the gatherings were held. Theophrastus, Aristotle's successor, left in his will "the garden and the *peripatos,*" with houses adjoining the garden, to the common possession of a group of associates for use in philosophic pursuits. He likewise provided for the upkeep of the *peripatos,* showing that a place was meant. Theophrastus had drawn exceptionally large numbers of hearers to his own discussions, so it is not surprising that the place in which his discussions were conducted should have become known as "the" *peripatos,* outstanding among centers referred to at Athens as *peripatoi.* Privately owned by Theophrastus, it could hardly have been located in the Lyceum. The explanation that Aristotle and his associates walked up and down while engaged in philosophical discussions, though circulated about 200 B.C., appears in an unreliable context and seems to have been a guess based on the etymology of the term Peripatetic. Though connection with a *peripatos* is traceable to Theophrastus rather than to Aristotle, a comparison of the writings of the two men shows that the structure and methods of thought and the teachings characteristic of the Peripatetics are attributable to Aristotle himself. The immense amount of work that he accomplished and the influence apparent in his followers mark these years as a period of indefatigable, penetrating, well-organized intellectual labor carried on in common with a closely associated group of companions and disciples.

Retirement. After the death of Alexander in June 323 B.C., Aristotle was exposed to a wave of anti-Macedonian feeling, possibly for a second time. A charge of impiety, reported to have been based on a hymn and inscription written in memory of his deceased father-in-law, Hermias, was laid against him. By the early spring of 322 he had retired to Chalcis; and by October, just past 62, he had died of what was vaguely called a stomach illness. In his will, Aristotle makes arrangements for disposing of slaves and goods that imply considerable family wealth, making possible his life of cultural and scholarly pursuits. The warm, high-minded, urbane, and understanding personality manifested in the will shines on occasion through his usually objective writings. Derogatory views of his character stem from a deliberate campaign to belittle his reputation during the decades following his death. Some later reports about unattractiveness in physical appearance, though handed down only as hearsay, possibly stem from reliable sources. Other adverse reports, for instance that he spoke with a lisp, that he was ungrateful and disloyal to his teacher, that he was profligate, that he turned to philosophy too late in life, and that he ended his life by drinking poison, have by careful criticism of their origins been shown to be without foundation.

Philosophical Teaching

Philosophy had for Aristotle a much wider ambit than it has today. It included rhetoric, poetics, mathematics, natural science, and political science, as well as LOGIC, PHILOSOPHY OF NATURE, METAPHYSICS, and ETHICS. Aristotle himself was a pioneer in making a systematic classification of all fields of knowledge. Though he called logic a science, Aristotle did not list it in his formal classification but regarded it as a preparation and instrument for science proper. SCIENCE (*scientia*) itself meant for Aristotle universal and necessary knowledge through causes. Metaphysics, natural philosophy, and ethics were accordingly sciences as he understood the term. His division of the sciences was based on their purposes and starting points (*see* SCIENCES, CLASSIFICATION OF). One broad type, proceeding from starting points in the things known, aimed at knowledge alone. As a scrutiny or contemplation (*theoria*) of things it was called theoretical science, either natural, mathematical, or theological. The other type had its starting point in the knower, and it aimed at action or at production. If the starting point was free choice, the aim was confined to human conduct and Aristotle called the science practical. If the starting point

was a conception of something to be made, the aim was a product different from the action itself, and he called the science productive. Practical and productive sciences, accordingly, aimed at something over and above knowledge.

Logic. Aristotle may be called the founder of logic, as logic was handed down to later Christian culture, although the Megarians before him had already inaugurated a tradition in logic (*see* LOGIC, HISTORY OF). One of their leaders, Eubulides of Miletus, is reported to have kept up controversial attacks on the Stagirite. In such a milieu, against the background of Platonic dialectic, a scientific logic achieved full development in Aristotle. He called it "analytics"—an unraveling, as it were, of the complicated processes of human thought. It regarded particular sensible things, in which all human cognition originates, as knowable under universal aspects. The proximate universal is the SPECIES. Continually widening generic aspects follow, until the most universal, those that cannot be divided into further genera, are reached. Individual horses, for instance, are seen; they are known specifically as horses, generically as animals, and so on to wider generalizations. Aristotle called this process INDUCTION (ἐπαγωγή), meaning that by a consideration of particulars the mind is "led to" the universal content present in the particular or the less general. Under each supreme GENUS the inferior genera are arranged in columns named categories. As supreme logical genera Aristotle lists substance and nine accidents (*see* CATEGORIES OF BEING). He also catalogues some features that are not confined to any one category. Often a notion appears as belonging immediately to a subject and is at once predicated of it, for instance that an ox is an animal or that a man is running. In this immediate intuition (*nous*) the basic premises for reasoning are grasped.

Because of their relatively increasing degrees of universality, two notions that do not immediately show connection may each be seen as related to a third in a way that involves relationships with each other. Three such notions form the basis of reasoning, or the SYLLOGISM. The three notions, called the terms, are arranged in three propositions, two of which are known as the premises and the third as the conclusion. Exact rules are elaborated for arranging the terms so that their varying degrees of universality allow a conclusion to be drawn. Affirmative and negative premises make possible different types of reasoning, or figures of the syllogism. Particular premises, and the notes of possibility or necessity, add complications. If reasoning proceeds according to a correct figure from true and immediately known premises, it is called DEMONSTRATION and yields scientific knowledge. If demonstrative reasoning is based on the proximate cause of what is concluded, it gives the most perfect type of science, "knowledge of the reasoned fact" (Gr. ἐπιστήμη διότι, Lat. *scientia propter quid*). If demonstrative reasoning is based on an effect, or in negative demonstration upon a remote cause (e.g., a wall does not breathe because it is not an animal), it gives only "knowledge of the fact" (Gr. επιστήμη ὅτι, Lat. *scientia quia*). If reasoning proceeds from premises that are merely probable, it is called dialectical. DIALECTICS is important for the inductive process by which the mind gradually focuses attention on universal aspects of things and so comes to grasp the immediate indemonstrable premises of scientific reasoning. All truths cannot be demonstrated, since demonstration itself requires indemonstrable premises.

This logic, very evidently, has as its operative unit the universal (*see* UNIVERSALS). It is therefore labeled today a "class logic," in contrast to propositional logics. It was consistently viewed by Aristotle not as self-sufficient but as meant to guarantee scientific procedure in other branches of knowledge. Although pedagogically it came before the other sciences, it was not given any commanding rank over them. Their proper intelligibility was already constituted in priority to any logical activity of the human mind.

Philosophy of Nature. One type of theoretical science deals with things that are mobile and that have their intelligible content or FORM inseparable from MATTER. These things constitute the sensible universe. They may be approached from the standpoint of their changeableness, or mobility. CHANGE, or MOTION, requires a subject that loses one form (understood as an intelligible aspect) and acquires another. If the forms lost and acquired are accidents, such as QUANTITY, QUALITY, or PLACE, the change is accidental. Change in the category of SUBSTANCE, called SUBSTANTIAL CHANGE or GENERATION-CORRUPTION, correspondingly involves a subject that loses one form and acquires another. Since form in the category of substance is the basic form in the thing, its subject as such has no form or intelligibility whatever. This subject, because able to receive form, is potency, or primary matter (*see* MATTER AND FORM). In contrast, the intelligible aspect, or form, is actuality (ἐνέργεια) and perfection, or ENTELECHY (ἐντελέχεια). Change, or motion, is defined as the actuality of something existent in potency precisely as it is in potency. The actuality, or intelligible aspect, present in the changing thing is there in the status of POTENCY to further ACT. The notions of potency and act, taken originally from analysis of change, run through all of Aristotelian philosophy (*see* POTENCY AND ACT).

Nature. Since sensible things are changeable, they are composed of matter and form. Each of these components is called NATURE, and things formed by their com-

position are natural. Nature is itself defined, from the viewpoint of sensible change, as a primary principle of motion and rest. Matter and form are two of a natural thing's causes. The other two causes are the AGENT and the END, or purpose. In later Peripatetic tradition the four causes are named, respectively, material, formal, efficient, and final. On the basis of these causes Aristotle investigates themes such as CHANCE, place, TIME, the void, and the infinite. Motion and time emerge as eternal of their very nature. They exist in an indivisible, but are unable to start or end in an indivisible, and so always require both previous and subsequent parts. An examination of the nature of motion and a survey of its instances show that everything in motion is being moved by something else; therefore an infinite regress in moved movers cannot account for any motion (*see* MOTION, FIRST CAUSE OF). In a self-mover, one part has to remain unmoved while moving the whole. Most unmoved movers are perishable; but since motion is eternal, the primary mover of the sensible universe will have to be eternal. Located at the circumference of the universe, such a mover imparts rotatory motion only, the one motion that is unchangeable in direction. The heavens are regarded as animated. They are imperishable, because their one observable motion, the circular, leaves no room for alteration or perishing. Their matter is accordingly distinguished from the traditional sublunar elements (earth, water, air, and fire) and is characterized as a further nature called ether (αἰθήρ).

Soul. SOUL is the basic actuality of a natural organic body. In sentient things soul is the principle not only of movement and growth, but also of SENSATION and APPETITE. In man it is also the principle of intellection and volition. Actual KNOWLEDGE, both of sense and of INTELLECT, consists in a peculiarly cognitional identity of knowing subject and thing known. From this viewpoint "the soul is in a certain way all things." In man the intellect is called a part of the soul and is divided into passive intellect and agent intellect, or intellect that produces. The passive intellect perishes in death. The agent intellect is not only imperishable but is "separate" from matter; as a form separate from matter it is not a subject for natural philosophy. Such teaching on the human soul is brief and somewhat obscure. It does not seem to allow the imperishable intellect, after death, any recollection of happenings in the body, and if so, precludes personal immortality.

Other Sciences. For Aristotle, natural philosophy included qualitative procedures that are now assigned to botany, zoology, experimental psychology, and other such studies. These qualitative procedures he regarded as giving only "knowledge of the fact." Knowledge through the basic causes, matter and form, was in contrast the most scientific of physical knowledge. If there were no immaterial beings, it would constitute for Aristotle the absolutely highest type of science, higher than any mathematical procedure.

Mathematics. Mathematics in the Aristotelian explanation was a theoretical science dealing with objects immobile but not existent outside mobile things, for instance numbers, lines, surfaces, and mathematical solids. By a process called ABSTRACTION, the mathematician may, without falsification, consider these as though they had existence separate from sensible bodies. Since there could be many individual instances of the same mathematical form, some kind of matter was required to explain the multiplicity. It was called intelligible matter, in contradistinction to sensible matter in real bodies. Sciences such as optics, harmonics, astronomy, and mechanics he regarded as essentially mathematical sciences, though as the "more physical" of those sciences. In contrast to qualitative procedures, they explained bodies through "knowledge of the reasoned fact." For further details of Aristotle's teaching on mathematics, see H. G. Apostle, *Aristotle's Philosophy of Mathematics* (Chicago 1952).

Metaphysics. Things entirely immobile and in their existence completely separate from matter Aristotle regarded as divine, hence coming under theological science. He based his proof of their real existence on the eternity of motion established in natural philosophy. Since the unmoved physical movers impart motion eternally, the ultimate ground of that eternity must be a substance entirely actual and so without matter. Any potency in it would mean that motion could in some way cease to be. Such substance is real form without matter, real actuality without potency. It causes motion only by being desired. It is so completely self-contained that it cannot know anything outside itself, since any dependence whatsoever on something outside itself would mean imperfection and so potentiality. It is a plurality, because there has to be one such substance for every original astronomical movement. It is a thinking that has itself as its object, and so may be described as a "thinking on thinking." It is the highest and most divine life. The science treating it is "first philosophy," and so is universal in scope, the science of being as being. Accidents are beings only in reference to prior, relatively permanent substance, while in sensible substance itself form is primary substance and the cause of being to both matter and composite. But the primary instance of substance without qualification is simple substance. According to the movement of Aristotle's metaphysics in relating secondary to primary instances, and against a background in which being meant permanence in contrast to becoming, theological science as first philosophy could readily be understood as the science that treats universally of beings as beings. Among

modern commentators, however, there is much disagreement on the way Aristotle conceived metaphysics and on the nature of the unmoved movers dealt with respectively in natural and first philosophy.

The title "metaphysics" does not appear in Aristotle's writings, but seems to date back to his immediate disciples. In the Aristotelian setting it meant that the things "beyond" the physical were investigated "after" natural philosophy (Reiner). The proposal that the term "metaphysics" was merely editorial in origin (Buhle) is an unsupported conjecture of the late 18th century.

Ethics and Politics. Moral philosophy is called political by Aristotle on the ground that the supreme human good is the same for individual and for city-state. Its subject matter is human conduct, and its aim is to achieve the GOOD. This good, continually fluctuating, always consists in a mean between two ever-varying extremes of excess and defect. The mean is determined in each individual case by a judgment of the prudent man. Since the good is always a mean, it can serve as a universal that makes possible the type of reasoning proper to practical science. To be prudent, a man needs the moral virtues, of which the three basic are temperance, fortitude, and justice. Yet to have these one must have the intellectual virtue of prudence (φρόνησις) for determining their mean.

These four virtues have to be inculcated simultaneously by correct education from earliest youth. Good laws and customs are therefore all-important in the formation of the correct ethical starting points. If accompanied by bodily welfare, good fortune, sufficient riches, and friends—all spread through a complete lifetime—the virtues make possible a life of contemplation. Contemplation is the highest human activity, thinking on the highest knowable objects. It is felicity (εὐδαιμονία), the chief good (*see* EUDAEMONISM). To its attainment all other activity, individual and social, is to be orientated. It is self-sufficient and in its own way divine, and gives the greatest of pleasure. Other ways of virtuous living give only secondary degrees of happiness. Some men are fashioned by nature itself to work with their bodies, as instruments under the guidance of others; slavery for such men is therefore natural. True forms of government aim at the common good, instead of at the good of a particular class.

Poetics and Rhetoric. Aristotle develops the "productive" sciences in his treatises on poetics and RHETORIC. *See* POETICS (ARISTOTELIAN). In his poetics he makes "re-presenting" (*mimesis*) the basis of fine art. Concentrating on tragedy, he exploits this view especially in regard to the elaboration of plot. To tragedy he assigns the much-debated function of catharsis, variously interpreted as a purification either of the tragic events (G. F. Else) or of the spectators' emotions. In his rhetoric he investigates persuasive arguments and their use through proper delivery, style, and composition.

Development, Works, and Influence

In Aristotle's philosophy a number of items may easily be characterized as Platonic, in contrast to distinctively Peripatetic thought. In the 19th century Platonic passages were at times excised as unauthentic or labeled as inherent contradictions in Aristotle's basic thought. In the first half of the 20th century a development theory, outlined by Thomas Case and elaborated in detail by Werner Jaeger, represented the Stagirite's thought as noticeably Platonic in the earliest writings, then gradually changing until it culminated during his mature period in a philosophy characteristically his own. Shadings and changes were added to this theory by other interpreters. It was carried to its extreme in the stand that Aristotle's own thought always remained Platonic, with all the characteristically Peripatetic philosophy coming from Theophrastus (Zürcher). A later reaction has explained the development in the opposite direction—Aristotle began strongly in his own characteristic way of thinking, then strove through the years to become a Platonist (I. Düring). No development theory has proved satisfactory, nor has any adherence of Aristotle to Platonic elements inconsistent with his own proper thought been sufficiently established.

Writings. In later antiquity Aristotle's writings, filling several hundred rolls, were distinguished in three broad classes: hypomnematic, exoteric, and acroamatic. The hypomnematic were notes to aid the memory and prepare for further work. The exoteric, written in dialogue and other current literary forms, were meant for the general reading public. Only fragments of them are extant. No reason why they ceased to be copied has been handed down in Greek tradition. Outstanding titles were *On Philosophy, Protrepticus, Eudemus, On Justice,* and *On Ideas.* The third class consisted of treatises (λόγοι, μέθοδοι, πραγματείαι) meant for school use and written in a concise style peculiar to their own literary genre. To this class belong the surviving works of Aristotle.

The *Categories, On Interpretation, Prior Analytics, Posterior Analytics, Topics,* and *Sophistical Refutations* contain the Aristotelian logic. In later Greek tradition they became known as the *Organon,* or instrument for learning. The general topics of natural philosophy are investigated in the *Physics,* and more particular phases in *On the Heavens, On Generation and Corruption, Meteorology, On the Soul,* and in a group of shorter treatises known since the Middle Ages as *Parva Naturalia.* The

animal kingdom is studied in five works: *History of Animals, Parts of Animals, Generation of Animals, Progression of Animals,* and *Movement of Animals.* The collection later known as the *Metaphysics* contains the treatises on first philosophy. The Aristotelian ethics has come down in three redactions, the *Nicomachean Ethics* (seemingly named from some unknown connection with Aristotle's son, Nicomachus), the *Eudemian Ethics* (seemingly named from Eudemus of Rhodes or, as Dirlmeier suggests, from Eudemus of Cyprus), and though of still disputed authenticity, the *Magna Moralia.* The treatment in the *Nicomachean Ethics* is continued in the *Politics.* A study of constitutions of various cities intervened; of these only the *Constitution of Athens,* recovered from Egyptian papyruses during the last quarter of the 19th century, is extant. The *Rhetoric* and the *Poetics* round out the list of surviving works.

A number of these treatises, missing in the earliest catalogue, seem to have been recovered only with the finding of Theophrastus's personal library, buried for nearly 200 years in a cellar at Scepsis in Asia Minor. A few works that would come under Aristotle's notion of mathematics were listed in the ancient catalogues, but none has survived.

Since the acroamatic writings were school λόγοι, they were open to additions and to change in arrangement as long as Aristotle continued his teaching career. This circumstance renders dating difficult and uncertain. As yet no satisfactory overall chronology has been established. For scholarly use the fragments, edited traditionally according to the order given them by Rose under the pseudepigrapha, should be divided into three classes: (1) those ascribed with sufficient certainty to a definite work, followed by fragments that may be attached to these; (2) those attributed with sufficient certainty to Aristotle but not to any definite work; and (3) those whose attribution to Aristotle has been alleged but remains doubtful (Wilpert).

Influence. Aristotle's philosophy continued to be taught at Athens under a succession of scholarchs that can be traced quite definitely into the 1st century B.C., and nebulously into the 3rd century A.D. After the death of Theophrastus the school seems to have had less widespread influence than its rivals. Upon the edition of the Stagirite's works by Andronicus of Rhodes in the 1st century B.C., the extensive Greek commentaries began; and they continued down to the 14th century A.D. Among the Christian Church Fathers, the attitude toward Aristotle was not favorable. His logic became influential in the early Middle Ages through BOETHIUS. His metaphysics and natural philosophy (in spite of several ecclesiastical prohibitions) and his ethical and political doctrines came to provide the framework for philosophical thought during the 13th century. They earned for Aristotle his rank as "The Philosopher," and with Dante the title of "the master of those who know." His doctrines were made to fit into various Christian interpretations. The Renaissance and the Reformation reacted violently against the scholastic Aristotle, although since the Renaissance the *Poetics* has served as a fundamental text in literary criticism. The rapidly developing quantitative physics and chemistry struggled bitterly to throw off the yoke of qualitative methods that had become traditional in the wake of Aristotelian doctrine, even though the Stagirite's teaching, if it had been rightly understood, could have provided a welcome abode for these new sciences under its mathematical divisions, as it had done for the ancient astronomy, optics, harmonics, and mechanics. Early in the 19th century, a keen philological interest in Aristotle took hold, and it developed increasingly in the 20th century. Along with the revival of interest in scholasticism, this has led to renewed philosophical appreciation of the Stagirite's doctrines, giving assurance that Aristotle's wisdom will continue to be digested with increasing profit by Western culture. Its outstanding importance for the Church lies in the help its fundamental principles can give to the structure of Christian philosophy and theology, even though Aristotle himself developed these principles in a thoroughly pagan atmosphere.

See Also: ARISTOTELIANISM; GREEK PHILOSOPHY; SCHOLASTICISM.

Bibliography: Sources. *Opera,* ed. I. BEKKER, 5 v. (Berlin 1831–70); in scholarly works Aristotle is cited by page, column, and line of v. 1–2; v. 5 contains the invaluable *Index Aristotelicus* by H. BONITZ. There are more recent critical texts of most individual treatises. *The Works of Aristotle Translated into English,* ed. W. D. ROSS, 12 v. (Oxford 1908–52), standard Eng. tr. T. W. ORGAN, *An Index to Aristotle in English Translation* (Princeton 1949). For translations of individual works see *Loeb Classical Library* (London-New York-Cambridge, Mass. 1912–) and others. F. R. WEHRLI, ed., *Die Schule des Aristoteles,* 10 v. (Basel 1944–59), fragments of the Peripatetics up to the beginning of the 1st century B.C. Preussische Akademie der Wissenschaften, *Commentaria in Aristotelem Graeca,* 23 v. (Berlin 1882–1909); *Supplementum Aristotelicum,* 3 v. (Berlin 1885–1903), Greek commentaries. Literature. I. DÜRING, *Aristotle in the Ancient Biographical Tradition* (Göteborg 1957). I. DÜRING and G. E. L. OWEN, eds., *Aristotle and Plato in the Mid-Fourth Century* (Göteborg 1960). M. SCHWAB, *Bibliographie d'Aristote* (Paris 1896). M. D. PHILIPPE, *Aristoteles* (Bern 1948), a bibliographical study. A. H. ARMSTRONG, *An Introduction to Ancient Philosophy* (3d ed. London 1957). W. W. JAEGER, *Aristotle: Fundamentals of the History of His Development,* tr. R. ROBINSON (2d ed. New York 1948). W. D. ROSS, *Aristotle* (5th rev. ed. New York 1953). G. R. G. MURE, *Aristotle* (London 1932). J. H. RANDALL, JR., *Aristotle* (New York 1960). D. J. ALLAN, *The Philosophy of Aristotle* (New York 1952). J. OWENS, *The Doctrine of Being in the Aristotelian Metaphysics* (Toronto 1951). C. GIACON, *Enciclopedia filosofica,* 4 v. (Venice-Rome 1957) 1:339–365. F.C. COPLESTON, *History of Philosophy,* v. 1 (Westminster, Md 1946)

[J. OWENS]

ARIUS

Alexandrian priest and heresiarch; b. Libya, *c.* 250; d. 336. Arius probably studied under LUCIAN OF ANTIOCH and joined the Alexandrian clergy. While still a minor cleric, he took part in the MELETIAN schism against Bp. Peter of Alexandria, but afterward he made his peace and was promoted to deacon and priest. Bishop Alexander held him in high repute and gave him charge of the important parish of Baucalis. His learning, grave manners, and ascetical life gained him a large following, but his unorthodox views on the divinity of Christ came under attack; *c.* 318—or 323, according to others—the conflict with Alexander broke into the open.

Arius was first rebuked at a local synod, and when he refused to submit he was excommunicated by a provincial council of all Egypt. He went to Palestine and Bithynia, where he received support from EUSEBIUS OF CAESAREA and EUSEBIUS OF NICOMEDIA, who sent out numerous letters to fellow bishops and convened synods in his defense. Macarius of Jerusalem and Marcellus of Ancyra opposed his doctrine and, as a result, the Church in the East was divided on his account. This caused the intervention of CONSTANTINE I, who conquered the East in 324. He sent Hosius of Córdoba with a letter to Alexander and Arius, urging them to cease fighting over what he called "a trifling and foolish verbal difference." Hosius' efforts to restore peace failed and, upon his recommendation, Constantine summoned a general council of the Church.

Hosius presided at a council of Antioch (324) that condemned Arius's doctrine. At the Council of NICAEA I (325), some of his writings were read and rejected as blasphemous by a vast majority of the fathers. The NICENE CREED, with the HOMOOUSIOS and the anathemas, was drawn up to exclude his errors.

After the council Arius was banished to Illyricum. When and how he was recalled and rehabilitated is a matter of dispute. Some historians connect this with an alleged second session of the Nicene Council in 327; others, with the Council of Tyre and Jerusalem in 335. It is certain that the assembly of Jerusalem (335) decided to readmit him into the Church. Constantine ordered a solemn reinstatement in Constantinople, but Arius died suddenly on the eve of the appointed day, early in 336. Of his writings there exist only three letters and fragments of the *Thalia,* or versified condensation of his teaching chanted by his followers in the church and streets.

See Also: ARIANISM.

Bibliography: H. G. OPITZ, ed., *Athanasius' Werke,* v.3.1 (Berlin 1934) 1–3, 12–13, 64, letters. G. BARDY, *Recherches sur St.*

Mission Tumacacori, partially in ruins, Mission Tumacori National Historic Park, Arizona. (©David Muench/CORBIS)

Lucien d'Antioche et son école (Paris 1936) 246–274, Thalia. H. GWATKIN, *Studies of Arianism* (2d ed. Cambridge, Eng. 1900). X. LE BACHELET, *Dictionnaire de théologie catholique.* ed. A. VACANT et al., (Paris 1903–50) 1.2:1779–1806. E. SCHWARTZ, *Zur Geschichte des Athanasius* (Gesammelte Schriften 3; Berlin 1959); *Kaiser Constantin und die christliche Kirche* (2d ed. Leipzig 1936). N. H. BAYNES, *Constantine the Great and the Christian Church* (London 1930). G. BARDY in J. R. PALANQUE et al., *The Church in the Christian Roman Empire,* tr. E. C. MESSENGER, 2 v. in 1 (New York 1953) 1:73–132. J. QUASTEN, *Patrology* (Westminster, Maryland 1950–) 3:7–13. E. BOULARAND, ''Les Débuts d'Arius,'' *Bulletin de littérature ecclésiastique* 75 (1964) 175–203.

[V. C. DE CLERCQ]

ARIZONA, CATHOLIC CHURCH IN

A state in the southwest U.S., one of the Rocky Mountain states, admitted (1912) to the Union as the 48th state, bounded on the north by Utah; on the west by the Colorado River, Nevada, and California; on the south by Mexico; and on the east by New Mexico. The capital and largest city is Phoenix. The two dioceses within its boundaries, Tucson and Phoenix, are suffragans of the Metropolitan See of Santa Fe, NM. In 2001, Catholics comprised approximately 23 percent of the total population.

The Missions Era. The Roman Catholic historical heritage of Arizona dates back to 1539, when a small expedition under the leadership of Franciscan Fray Marcos de Niza (of Nice), provincial of the Franciscans of New Spain arrived in the land of Pimería Alta. Spanish viceroy of Mexico, Antonio de Mendoza, had dispatched Fray Marcos north into the region from the Valley of Mexico. Fray Marcos, with Estevan, the Moor companion of Álvar Nuñez Cabeza de Baca on the latter's earlier return to Mexico from Florida in 1536 serving as a guide at the vanguard of the expedition, made his way as far northeast as the land of the Zuñi-Cibola. The 1540–1542 Spanish expedition of Francisco Vâsquez de Coronado brought additional missioners into the area, traveling even farther east to what would be present-day Kansas.

A more concerted evangelization effort among the natives of Arizona began later with the appearance of other Franciscans, venturing west to the land of the Zuni from New Mexico, and Jesuits, with Father Eusebio Francisco Kino as their leader. In April of 1598 Juan de Oñate crossed the Rio Grande into what was then called the Kingdom of New Mexico, after having stopped his expedition for *un día de dar gracias* (a day of thanksgiving). The Franciscans who came to New Mexico as a part of the Oñate *entrada*, missioned into the northern reaches of the land at least as far as Santa Fe. There they erected, possibly as early as 1610, what is today recognized universally as the oldest church still in use in the present-day United States, Mission San Miguel. Eventually, the Franciscans made their way west to the land of the Zuñi in future Arizona. Laboring among the Zuñi for some time, the Franciscans saw their endeavors interrupted with the Pueblo Revolt at Santa Fe, NM in 1680. Even though the Spanish Catholic presence returned to Santa Fe in 1692 under the devout Catholic leadership of Don Diego De Vargas, governor of New Mexico twice, from 1692 to 1697 and again from 1703 to 1704, further Franciscan evangelization of the Zuñi from New Mexico failed to materialize.

In the meantime, the work of Jesuit missionary Eusebio Francisco KINO began in the southern part of the region, south of the Gila River. Kino was born in the small Italian mountain hamlet of Segno near the border of Switzerland on Aug. 10, 1645. Completing his studies and religious formation as a Jesuit, Kino was ordained and from Oettingen University in Germany was selected to venture to Mexico as a missionary, departing the Spanish port city of Cádiz in January 1681. Eventually arriving in Mexico City, Father Kino missioned in Baja, CA, for a period of time before ultimately being dispatched to the vast lands of New Spain's (that part of the territory referred to as Nueva Navara) Primería Alta. There he was to peacefully promote the economic and social well being of countless natives while catechizing among them.

In that work he founded 22 churches and missions for the natives' sacramental lives, the best known of which was San Xavier del Bac Church in Tucson, AZ. Father Kino never remained permanently at Mission San Xavier del Bac. Instead, he spent some 24 years headquartered at the first major church that he founded back in 1687, that of Nuestra Señora de los Dolores de Cosari, more than 100 miles south of San Xavier del Bac in Sonora's valley of the Rio de San Miguel. Father Kino continued in his labors and other missionaries increasingly came to assist him in evangelizing the peoples of Sonora-

Arizona, the Primería Alta. Outstanding among those missionaries extraordinary was Father Augutin de Campos, who was by Kino's side when the Jesuit from Italy died on March 15, 1711 in Magdalena, Sonora, Mexico.

Catholic evangelizing among the natives south of the Gila River continued after the death of Father Kino. Beyond the region where an imaginary line might be drawn from Tucson in the south to present-day Flagstaff in the north all the way west to Kingman and the Mojave Desert, the land was mostly parched and difficult to settle. The Spanish royal government discouraged migrants (the Irish, for example) from entering the land, who were neither Catholic nor loyal to Spain. Because of their centuries-long struggle with the English and the latter's occupation and attempted Anglicization of Ireland, many Irish left their homeland and resided in Spain before venturing to the Americas. Some of those immigrants eventually came to Arizona. One such Irishman was Hugo Oconór. Born in Dublin, Ireland in 1734 with the Gaelic name, Hugh O'Connor, he became a resister to the English presence in Ireland and eventually was forced to flee to Spain. He entered the Volunteer Regiment of Aragón and was sent to New Spain, serving first in Cuba and then in Mexico. The Spanish began to refer to him as Hugo Oconor. Because of his prominent red hair he also became known as "Capitán Colorado." From 1767 to 1770 he served the Spanish government as governor of Texas.

In 1772, the viceroy of New Spain named Oconor "Comandante Inspector," and assigned him the task of establishing order and security along the northern frontier of Spain's territory from Texas to California. While serving the Spanish Crown in that capacity, Oconor established the presido at Tucson near Mission San Xavier del Bac (1775). Later transferred to the Yucatán as governor, Oconor died there in 1779. Like Oconor, the last Viceroy of New Spain that the Spanish government dispatched to Mexico was Irish—Don Juan O'Donojú, more accurately known as Sean O'Donohugh. It was O'Donohugh who signed the Aug. 23, 1821 Treaty of Córdoba with Augustín Iturbide, granting Mexican independence and ensuring that the Catholic Church would be "established" in the new nation of Mexico.

Diocesan Foundations. Acting upon the request of Bishop Benito Crespo of Durango, Mexico, the Spanish Crown began to focus more attention on sending missionaries into the northern region of the Primeriá Alta. As had happened earlier to missionaries in other areas of New Spain, wherein indigenous peoples' revolts against the Spanish erupted (the Land of the Guale north of Las Floridas in the late 17th century, for example), priests were killed. In the case of the future Arizona, priests died in the Piman revolt of 1751. And then, in 1767, a final blow came to the Sons of Saint Ignatius and their dedication to Catholic evangelization of the Primeria Alta, when King Charles III of Spain, acting upon misguided advice from his liberal ministers, expelled the Jesuits from all Spanish lands. A year later, in 1768, Franciscans appeared in the Primería Alta to continue the work of missioning until a more hierarchically structured Church could be put into place.

From 1779 to the Treaty of Gudalupe Hidalgo, signed between the United States and Mexico in 1848, following the American annexation of much of northern Mexico after their invasion of that country in 1846, the land that was to become Arizona fell under the ecclesiastical jurisdiction of the bishop of Sonora, Mexico. In 1850, Arizona became identified as part of the newly-established U.S. Territory of New Mexico. In 1868, Arizona became a vicariate apostolic, and a French priest from Clermont, Jean Baptiste Salpointe, was named vicar apostolic. Salpointe labored dedicatedly for 15 years to build up the Catholic presence in Arizona. In April 1884 he was named coadjutor archbishop of Santa Fe, but served as apostolic administrator of Arizona until May 1, 1885. On Aug. 18, 1885, Salpointe succeeded former Archbishop John Baptist Lamy as head of the archdiocese. Back in Arizona on that same day of May 1, 1885, Father Peter Bourgarde, also from the Diocese of Clermont, was consecrated a bishop and vicar apostolic of Arizona. Several years later, on May 10, 1897, he became the first bishop of Tucson. In June 1900, another French priest, Henri Granjon of the Archdiocese of Lyon, assumed ecclesiastical authority over the Diocese of Tucson. Granjon would emerge as one of the Tucson diocese's longest serving and most dedicated ordinaries, focusing especially on the needs of the poor Hispanic Catholics of his diocese.

The first American-born bishop of Tucson, and the ordinary who headed the diocese for almost 37 years, was Bishop Daniel James Gercke of Philadelphia, PA. Gercke was ordained bishop of Tucson on Nov. 6, 1923, and served until his retirement in September 1960 at the age of 80. He passed away in Tucson, March 19, 1964. Gercke's coadjutor, Francis J. Green, assumed leadership of the diocese before retiring in July 1981. Green was succeeded by Manuel D. Moreno, the auxiliary bishop of Los Angeles, who was appointed to Tucson in 1982.

With the steady growth of Arizona' population, a second Catholic diocese (Phoenix), was established on Dec. 2, 1969. The Most Reverend Edward Anthony McCarthy became the new diocese's first bishop. He served until July 5, 1976, when he was named archbishop of Miami. The second bishop of Phoenix, James S. Rausch, was installed in March 1977 and administered the diocese until his death in May 1981. He was succeeded by Thomas J. O'Brien who was installed in January 1982.

The two dioceses, together with the Diocese of Gallup, New Mexico, whose territory extends across the border, form the Arizona Catholic Conference. This organization enables the various dioceses to collaborate in applying Catholic social teachings to public policy that affect issues like education, family life and immigration.

Bibliography: H. E. BOLTON, *Spanish Exploration In The Southwest, 1542–1706: Original Narratives of Early American History* (New York 1963); *Rim of Christendom: A Biography of Eusebio Francisco Kino* (New York 1936). E. J. BURRUS, ed. *Kino and Manje: Explorers of Sonora and Arizona* (St. Louis 1971). P. FOLEY, "From Linares to Galveston: Texas in the Diocesan Scheme of the Roman Catholic Church to the Mid-Nineteenth Century," *Catholic Southwest: A Journal of History and Culture* v. 8 (1997) 25–44. R. E. NORDMEYER, K. MCCARTHY and C. POLZER, *Shepherds in the Desert: A Sequel to Salpointe* (Tucson 1978). C. POLZER, *A Kino Guide: His Missions-His Monuments* (Tucson 1976). J. B. SALPOINTE, *Soldiers of the Cross: Notes on the Ecclesiastical History of New Mexico, Arizona and Colorado* (Banning, CA 1898). D. TEJADA, *The San Miguel Chapel: Oldest Church in the U.S.* (Santa Fe 1968).

[P. FOLEY/EDS.]

ARK OF THE COVENANT

The sacred chest of ancient Israel. The ark (Heb 'ărôn) of the covenant is described in Ex 25.10–22 and 37.1–9 as a chest of acacia wood, about 4 feet long, 2.5 feet wide and 2.5 feet high; it was covered with gold plates and fitted with rings, through which poles for carrying it could be passed. Over the ark was a gold plate, the same size as the ark, called in Hebrew the *kappōret.* This word is usually translated either as propitiatory (Douay-Calloner and Confraternity of Christian Doctrine versions, through the Vulgate's *propitiatorium* from the Septuagint's ἱλαστήριον—means or place of propitiation) or as mercy seat (AV,RSV, from the influence of Luther's rendering, *Gnadenstuhl*) in accordance with the meaning of the Hebrew root *kpr* (to cover) in the transferred sense "to atone" (*kippēr*) and with the role of the *kappōret* in certain ceremonies (Lv ch. 16) on the Day of ATONEMENT (Yom Kippur). Two golden CHERUBIM rested on the *kappōret,* one at one end and one at the other, and covered it with their outspread wings. According to Ex 25.16; and 40.20; and Dt 10.1–5, the tablets on which the Ten Commandments were written were placed in the ark. In Dt 31.25; Ex 16.33; and Nm 17.10, mention is made of other objects beside or in front of it.

In Dt 10.8 it is stated that the ark was carried by Levites; and in Nm 10.33–36, that when the Israelites left

Third panel from top depicts the Ark of the Covenant carried on the shoulders of the Israelites of the Exodus, detail of a miniature in a 12th-century Bible from S. Maria ad Martyres, Rome. (Cod. Vat. Lat. 12958, fol. 60v.)

Sinai, it went before them and indicated the resting places. In these desert wanderings the ark was probably sheltered in the tent sanctuary, called the TENT OF MEETING by the Pentateuchal PRIESTLY WRITERS. At the Jordan the ark led the way into the Promised Land (Jos ch. 3–6). Then the ark, without the tent sanctuary of the desert, stood in the camp at Gilgal (Jos 7.6). It is next mentioned at BETHEL (Jgs 20.27) and then in a more permanent sanctuary at Shiloh (1 Sm 3.3). In 1 Sm 4.3–7.2 it is stated that it was carried into battle at Aphec, captured by the Philistines, and then returned to the Israelites at Beth-Sames (Beth-shemesh) and housed for a while at Cariath-Jarim. David finally brought it to Jerusalem and installed it in a tent (2 Sm ch. 6). After Solomon built the Temple, the ark was placed in its Holy of Holies (2 Kgs 6.19; 8.1–9). It was probably destroyed with the Temple in 587 B.C. (despite 2 Mc 2.4–5).

Of all the aspects about the ark, the one most easily understood is that of a container for the stone tablets from Sinai, which explains why the ark was called ''the ark of the covenant.'' But it is also the visible sign or extension or even the embodiment of the presence of God, as can be seen in Nm 10.35–36; 1 Sm ch. 4–6; 2 Sm ch. 6; and 2 Kgs ch. 8. Many extra-biblical parallels show that there is no contradiction between the idea of the ark symbolizing God's presence and of the ark as a receptacle. (*See* SHEKINAH.) It is also a war palladium according to Nm 10.35–36; 1 Sm ch. 4; and 2 Sm 11.11. Its formidable power is seen also in 1 Sm ch. 5; 6.19; and 2 Sm 6.7. From the period at Silo onward the ark was called ''the ark of Yahweh Sabaoth who sits above the Cherubim.'' This idea of the ark as the throne of God is not necessarily contradicted by references to the ark as the ''footstool'' of God in 1 Chr 28.2; the ark, the cherubim, and eventually even the *kappōret* were all symbols of God's providential presence with His chosen people. Posture hardly makes a difference in symbolic presence. In this as well as in the various explanations of the purpose of the ark, there are several ideas that overlap to some extent, and different aspects are emphasized in different traditions.

The late tradition of Lv ch. 16, confirmed by 1 Chr 28.11, indicates that after the Exile the *kappōret* had been substituted for the ark. As for the antiquity of the ark itself, it seems from the old tradition of Nm 10.35–36 to extend in some form back into the desert period. In fact, the conception of a deity standing or enthroned on an animal or mythical creature was common in the Near East for centuries before the Exodus. It is not strange to find Israel using a similar symbol—but without an image of Yahweh Himself. (*See* IMAGES, BIBLICAL PROHIBITION OF.)

Bibliography: R. DE VAUX, *Ancient Israel, Its Life and Institutions* (New York 1961) 297–302, 540. A. MILLER, *Lexikon für Theologie und Kirche*, ed. J. HOFER (Freiburg 1957–65) 2:780. *Encyclopedic Dictionary of the Bible* (New York 1963) 133–136. T. WORDEN, ''The Ark of the Covenant,'' *Scripture* 5 (1952) 82–90. M. HARAN, ''The Ark and the Cherubim: Their Symbolic Significance in Biblical Ritual,'' *Israel Exploration Journal* 9 (1959) 30–38. E. NIELSEN, ''Some Reflections on the History of the Ark,'' *Congress Volume, Oxford 1959*, Vetus Testamentum Suppl. 7 (1960) 61–74.

[E. J. CROWLEY]

ARKANSAS, CATHOLIC CHURCH IN

In the year 2000 the Roman Catholic Church in Arkansas numbered 93,480 members, about 3.4% of the total population of the state. The growth of the Church was slow but steady from the colonial period. There had been a small Catholic presence in Arkansas during the days of the French and Spanish, but the acquisition of the territory by the United States dramatically changed the demographics of the region. The Native Americans had been driven out of Arkansas by 1840, while the people who displaced them, both Anglo-Americans and African Americans, were overwhelmingly Protestant. In 1850 Catholics made up only 1% of the white population.

The first Catholics arrived in the territory that would become the state of Arkansas less than a half-century after Columbus first entered the western hemisphere, and some 66 years before the English established their first permanent settlement in North America. Hernando De Soto, the first European actually to see the Mississippi River, crossed the ''Father of Waters'' on June 18, 1541 and then erected a cross on its western bank. Seven days after arriving in the land that became Arkansas, he led his men in a religious ceremony, kneeling before the cross and singing a Te Deum, a traditional Catholic hymn of praise. That date, June 25, 1541 was the date of the first Christian religious event ever recorded within the future state of Arkansas. While De Soto stayed in the area for another year, Spain was too preoccupied with its holdings elsewhere to colonize much of North America. Brief as this encounter was, it was Arkansas's first experience with Catholic Christianity.

More than a century passed before another Catholic missionary visited Arkansas. Jesuit missionary Fr. Jacques MARQUETTE and fur trapper Louis Joliet journeyed southward from French Canada, where they entered the northern section of the Mississippi River. Using that watery thoroughfare, they made it to the mouth of the Arkansas River, staying for two weeks in the area in July of 1673 before returning to Canada. Robert Cavalier De La Salle followed the same path of Marquette and Joliet nine years later, yet followed the Great River to its mouth and claimed all lands that touch this river and its tributaries. De La Salle designated the region Louisiana in honor of his earthly sovereign, Louis XIV. The French explorer also gave his Italian lieutenant Henri de Tonti, a grant of land to start a colony. Tonti returned in 1686 to found the first European settlement in Arkansas near the juncture of the Arkansas and Mississippi Rivers. Named the Arkansas Post, it was abandoned a decade later and there would be no further European settlement in the area for a quarter century. Fr. Jacques Gravier, SJ, a French missionary traveling down the Mississippi said the first recorded Catholic Mass in Arkansas on Nov. 1, 1700.

Colonial era. France re-founded the Arkansas Post in August of 1721, and this settlement would be the center of European activity in Arkansas for the rest of the 18th century. Little effort was made, however, to colonize the area or convert the natives. Fr. Paul du Poisson, SJ, worked as a missionary for two years in Arkansas, suffering martyrdom near what is now Natchez, Mississippi on Nov. 28, 1729. (This was exactly 114 years to the day before the establishment of a Catholic Diocese in Arkansas.) Few Catholic missionaries came to Arkansas during the 18th century or even during the first 40 years of the 19th century. Until the diocese came into existence in 1843, the longest time a priest had been in Arkansas was Jesuit missionary Fr. Louis Carette, SJ (1750–1758).

The Spanish assumed control over the western half of the old Louisiana Territory after 1763, and this included Arkansas. The Spanish eventually placed their Louisiana and Florida holdings under a newly created Diocese of New Orleans in 1793. After decades of being a mission outpost, Arkansas got its first resident Catholic priest in almost 40 years in 1796. Fr. Pierre Janin, a French diocesan priest fleeing the French Revolution, stayed in Arkansas for three and a half years. Janin failed to actually gather the funds to build a church and so he abandoned Arkansas forever in late 1799. After Napoleon pressured Spain to give him Louisiana in 1800, the crafty Frenchman turned around and sold it to the United States three years later.

Ecclesiastical changes. Arkansas remained part of the New Orleans diocese until 1826, when the Holy See created the Diocese of St. Louis, covering the Louisiana Purchase north of the state of Louisiana, with Joseph M. ROSATI named as its first bishop. Bishop Rosati sent some missionaries to Arkansas and one was so disgusted with Arkansas in 1832 that he referred to it as the "suburb of Hell" in a letter to a St. Louis prelate. Despite the rough goings on, the Sisters of LORETTO from Kentucky opened Arkansas's first Catholic school, St. Mary's Academy, on the southern shore of the Arkansas River, just south of what is now Pine Bluff on Nov. 19, 1838. Three years

later, the sisters started St. Joseph's Catholic School in Little Rock. In 1842, they closed the school near Pine Bluff and began another school at the Arkansas Post called St. Ambrose Female Academy. Both of these schools were closed in 1845 due to lack of funds and the Sisters of Loretto left Arkansas.

At the fifth provincial council of Baltimore in May of 1843, the Holy See was petitioned to erect four new dioceses: Chicago, Pittsburgh, Milwaukee, and Little Rock. Responding to this request, Pope Gregory XVI erected the Diocese of Little Rock on Nov. 28, 1843. The papal document stated that its boundaries would correspond to that of the state of Arkansas, boundaries that have not been altered after more than a century and a half.

Infant diocese and Civil War. Irish-born Andrew BYRNE (1802–1862), Arkansas's Catholic bishop, arrived in Arkansas in 1844 and labored for 18 years in this frontier diocese. While he never had more than ten priests working under him, he founded Arkansas's first Catholic college, St. Andrew's, in 1849. He recruited Irish Sisters of Mercy to come to Arkansas in 1851 and in that year, they opened St. Mary's Academy in Little Rock, the oldest continuous academic institution in the state. Over the next decade, the Mercy Sisters opened additional schools in Fort Smith and Helena, but only the academy in Little Rock survives to this day. Byrne never owned any slaves, but if he had any opinion on slavery, he never recorded it. During the Know-Nothing uproar in the 1850s, Byrne judiciously avoided political disputes and concentrated on building up the Catholic population by promoting Irish migration to Arkansas. His efforts, however, met with little success. By 1860, the Catholics only numbered about 1% of the white population of the state, less than 1% of the general population. Byrne died on June 10, 1862 in Helena, Arkansas, and was buried in the courtyard of St. Catherine's Mercy convent. His successor moved his body to Little Rock and placed it under the newly constructed Cathedral of St. Andrew in 1881.

Arkansas joined the southern Confederacy in 1861, and the war closed St. Andrew's College that same year. When the competing armies finally made it to Little Rock in September of 1863, the Sisters of Mercy ministered to the sick and wounded of both the Confederate and Union armies. As the Union blockade disrupted communication between the struggling southern nation and the outside world, it took four years for the Holy See to name a successor to the Arkansas diocese, and that came after the war ended in 1865. No other American diocese was without a successor for such a long time. In the interim, Bishop Byrne's last vicar general, Irish-born Fr. Patrick Reilly served as apostolic administrator.

In the summer of 1866, Rome appointed Irish native Fr. Edward M. FITZGERALD, a pastor in Columbus, Ohio, and a priest with the Archdiocese of Cincinnati, to be Arkansas's next Catholic prelate. Fitzgerald initially rejected the appointment in September, causing the Vatican to issue the young priest a mandamus, a command under holy obedience to accept the Arkansas position. By the time he received this news in December, however, Fitzgerald had changed his mind about accepting the Little Rock bishopric. Consecrated at his home parish by Archbishop John Purcell of Cincinnati, Fitzgerald arrived in Little Rock on St. Patrick's Day in 1867.

Bishop Edward M. Fitzgerald. Fitzgerald proved to be a unique Catholic bishop for his time and the most significant prelate in the history of Arkansas Catholicism. Only 33 years old at the time of his appointment, he was the youngest bishop in the United States, if not the world. He distinguished himself in the annals of the universal Church by being one of two bishops in the world, and the only English-speaking prelate, to cast his vote against the declaration of papal infallibility at the First Vatican Council in 1870. This vote, together with his opposition to the setting up of Catholic schools in every parish at the Third Plenary Council in 1884, plus his sympathy with the early labor movement, marks him as one of the most interesting and overlooked 19th-century American Catholic bishops. He consistently defended papal infallibility and worked to establish Catholic parish schools, positions with which he had publicly disagreed. Pope Leo XIII offered him at least two archbishoprics (Cincinnati and New Orleans) and several other dioceses, yet the maverick Irish prelate rejected all of them, preferring to remain in Arkansas.

Like his predecessor, Fitzgerald sought to bolster the Catholic population by bringing his fellow religionists from Europe. Some Irish continued to migrate to the state, yet more German, Swiss German, and Polish Catholics came between 1870 and 1890. They mainly inhabited land along the Little Rock–Fort Smith railroad and in northeastern Arkansas. Italian immigrants came to Sunnyside Plantation in southeast Arkansas, yet three years later many of them moved to the Ozarks in the northwestern part of the state to found a community called Tontitown. Other Italians moved from Chicago to land about 40 miles west of Little Rock in 1915. There were also small pockets of Slovaks, Czechs, and Austrians scattered around the state. Despite his efforts, Fitzgerald was no more successful than his predecessor in luring Catholic immigrants to Arkansas. By 1900, only about 1% of the white population of the state was foreign born. In contrast to his predecessor, however, Fitzgerald sponsored an aggressive outreach to the African Americans in Arkansas, but this too met with only limited success. St. Peter's, an African American church in Pine Bluff, became the first Catholic parish in U.S. history to have a black Catho-

lic pastor and a school staffed by the black Sisters of the Holy Family based in New Orleans in 1905.

New religious orders, both men and women, arrived during Fitzgerald's tenure. The Order of St. Benedict (BENEDICTINES) and the Congregation of the Holy Ghost (Spiritans), both men's orders, came in 1878. That same year, four sisters from the Order of St. Benedict also came to Arkansas and became the nucleus of a group of women religious based now in Fort Smith, Arkansas. In northeastern Arkansas, women religious came to the state in 1887, and six years later they aligned themselves with an order in Switzerland to become the Olivetan Benedictine sisters of Arkansas based in Jonesboro. St. Vincent's Infirmary, Arkansas's oldest medical facility, opened in Little Rock in 1888 and was staffed by the Sisters of Charity of Nazareth, Kentucky. Even though Arkansas Catholics were still only about 1% of the population, they started Arkansas's oldest educational institution, Mount St. Mary's, and its oldest medical hospital, St. Vincent's, both in Little Rock.

Bishop Fitzgerald's active career ended in January of 1900, when the aging prelate suffered a stroke and eventually died at St. Joseph's Hospital in Hot Springs in February of 1907. For six years, the diocese operated under the direction of Fitzgerald's last vicar general, German-born Fr. Fintan Kraemer, OSB.

Twentieth-century developments. During most of the 20th century, the Catholic Diocese of Little Rock had only three prelates. Two of the three bishops were of Irish-American ancestry and were born outside the state, John B. Morris (1866–1946) and Andrew J. McDonald (1923–). Only Albert L. Fletcher (1896–1979) was an Arkansas native of parents who had converted to the faith.

A native of Tennessee, Bishop Morris became coadjutor bishop for Little Rock in the summer of 1906. Once Fitzgerald died, Morris automatically became Arkansas's third Catholic shepherd. Over the next four decades that he was bishop, Morris oversaw tremendous institutional growth. Within five years of becoming bishop, Morris started Arkansas's second Catholic institution of higher education, Little Rock College, and St. John's Home Mission Seminary, and St. Joseph's Orphanage near North Little Rock. The second Catholic college in Arkansas closed in 1930, the seminary shut down in 1967, and the Ophanage closed in 1970. The diocesan newspaper, called the *Guardian*, begun in 1911, continues to this day, though its name was changed to the Arkansas Catholic in 1986.

Between 1910 and 1930 there was a strong rise in anti-Catholic feeling within the South, fed by a bitter, agrarian-populist Georgian named Tom Watson. Watson's own magazine sold well in the South and, after 1910, he launched a major attack on Catholicism. Watson soon had imitators, including a weekly published in Missouri called *The Menace*, which had 1 million subscribers by 1914. A version of this paper, named *The Liberator*, appeared briefly in Magnolia, Arkansas, where it was edited by a Baptist minister. In 1915, the Arkansas General Assembly became one of several southern states to pass the Convent Inspection Act, allowing local law enforcement authorities to inspect Catholic convents and rectories at different occasions. This act remained law until repealed rather quietly in 1937. During the 1920s the Ku Klux Klan became a potent political force in the South, West, and Midwest, yet the ''Invisible Empire'' was not as strong in Arkansas as in other states. Arkansas even voted for Alfred E. Smith, the first Roman Catholic nominated by a major party for the presidency of the United States. (A major factor in the vote may have been that Smith's Vice Presidential running mate was Senator Joseph T. Robinson of Arkansas.)

Bishop Morris vigorously attempted to both convert and educate African Americas during his episcopacy. There were only two black Catholic churches and schools when he arrived; by his death there were nine black parishes and all but two had Catholic schools. Near Pine Bluff, a black Catholic orphanage opened in the fall of 1932, but this facility closed five years later. Ultimately, blacks were reluctant to place their children in an orphanage run by whites and operated by a church of which most of them were not members. By 1940, Arkansas Catholics made up just over 2% of the white population and 1.7% of the total population.

When Bishop Morris died in 1946, he was succeeded by his auxiliary, an Arkansas native, Albert L. Fletcher. It was Bishop Fletcher's lot to serve the diocese during its most turbulent years. In 1957, the eyes of the nation and the world focused on the attempted racial integration of Little Rock public schools. Throughout the turmoil, Bishop Fletcher counseled calm and supported peaceful integration in his public pronouncements. He published a local catechism in 1960, stating that racial hatred and legal segregation were morally wrong. When integration did occur during the 1960s in all the diocesan Catholic schools, it greatly reduced the number of black Catholic parishes and schools. In 1961 there were eleven black Catholic parishes and seven schools, while a decade later there were only three black Catholic schools and parishes in operation. The racial turmoil in Little Rock caused Bishop Fletcher to move the cloistered Carmelite sisters from Pennsylvania who had come to the diocese in 1950 from downtown Little Rock to a safer area in the city.

In the decades from 1940 to 1960, Arkansas Catholicism continued to experience real growth. Bishop Fletcher attended all four sessions of the Second Vatican Council (1962–1965). Nine of the thirteen suggestions he made found their way into the final documents. Although the Catholics were only 2.8% of the state's population, Arkansas residents voted for John F. Kennedy in the presidential election of 1960.

Three years prior to his resignation, Bishop Fletcher asked Rome for an auxiliary bishop. He was Lawrence P. Graves (1916–1994), a native of Texarkana, Arkansas, who went on to become bishop of Alexandria-Shreveport in Louisiana in 1973. Bishop Fletcher's successor in Little Rock was the Reverend Andrew J. McDonald, a native of Savannah, Georgia, who was to head the Church in Arkansas for almost three decades. Consecrated in Savannah, Bishop McDonald moved to Arkansas in early September of 1972. He led the Arkansas church at a time when the American Catholic Church as a whole suffered a massive decline in religious vocations and the closing of many schools and hospitals. While the Catholic population declined in many parts of the country, it grew in Arkansas. In 1980 there were only 59,911 Catholics in the state, but by the year 2000 there were 93,480. In 1990 Catholics made up only 2.5% of the total population; ten years later Catholics made up more than 3% of the total population, 3.4%. Much of the growth in the number of Catholics stemmed from immigration from southeast Asia and, even more significantly, from Mexico, the Caribbean, and Central America. In addition, there was an influx of Catholics into the booming areas of northwestern and central Arkansas from elsewhere in the United States, as well a modest increase in individual conversions. The Church in Arkansas, despite a leveling off in the number of priests and religious, struggled earnestly to minister to the new immigrant population, building new facilities and expanding existing facilities across the state.

Bibliography: Diocesan Historical Commission, *The History of Catholicity in Arkansas* (Little Rock, AR 1925). F. S. GUY, ''The Catholic Church in Arkansas, 1541–1843.'' M.A. thesis (Catholic University of America, 1932). J. M. WOODS, ''To the Suburb of Hell: Catholic Missionaries in Arkansas, 1803–1843.'' *Arkansas Historical Quarterly* 48 (autumn 1989) 217–242. J. M. WOODS, *Mission and Memory: A History of the Catholic Church in Arkansas Little Rock*, (Little Rock, AR 1993).

[J. M. WOODS]

ARLEGUI, JOSÉ

Franciscan chronicler; b. Laguardia, Navarre, Spain, 1685; d. place unknown, 1750? He was the son of José Arleguiz and Ana San Martín and joined the Franciscans at San Francisco de Vitoria in 1701. He taught arts and theology at the convent of Aránzazu. Then he went to Zacatecas, Mexico, where he was lector in theology, regent of studies, guardian (1721), provincial (1725), and chronicler of the province. He was also an officer and commissary of the Inquisition. As an administrator he walked 900 miles visiting his provincial area. He promoted education and built (and actively helped build—since he himself cut trees in the sierra to get wood for church floors) convents and churches. He was a noted preacher, and many of his sermons were printed in Mexico City, Guatemala, and Madrid; they have been catalogued by the bibliographer Beristain. Arlegui's most important work is *Crónica de la santa provincia de nuestro P. San Francisco de Zacatecas* (Mexico City 1737; repr. 1851). It is divided into five parts: part one, the origin of the custody of Zacatecas; part two, the founding of monasteries; part three, Amerindian customs and the conflicts with native peoples; part four, biographies of martyred friars; part five, biographies of famous Franciscans. The chronicle is inaccurate for the early period but becomes more exact for the late 17th and the early 18th century. It closes with 1733. Arlegui stated that his order then had in New Spain ten provinces with 3,200 religious, 397 convents, 122 missionary centers among the natives, four apostolic colleges, and 187 professorships of theology, grammar, rhetoric, and the various native languages.

Bibliography: J. M. BERISTAIN DE SOUZA, *Biblioteca hispanoamericana septentrional,* 5 v. in 2 (3d ed. Mexico City 1947).

[E. GÓMEZ-TAGLE]

ARLES

A city on the Rhône, department of Bouches-du-Rhône, France, 55 miles northwest of Marseilles, formerly the seat of an archbishopric.

Secular History. There is no knowledge of a settlement on the site by the native Ligurians, but by the sixth century B.C. a trading post by the name of Theline had been established by the Ionians from Marseilles, and by the fourth century B.C. the port was being designated as Arelate. In 46 B.C. Julius Caesar gave his name to the community of veterans located there and they came to be known as the *colonia Julia Paterna Arelate Sextanorum.* The Romans, under Caius Marius (*c.* 104 B.C.) had linked Arles to the Mediterranean by canal, and the city came to exercise a monopoly over the river traffic of lower Provence. Impressive ruins—an amphitheater, forum and theater (all of the Augustan Age), baths (Constantinian) and the city walls (late Empire)—were witness to Arles's splendor in this period. After A.D. 353 the city was named *Constantia* in honor of Constantius II (350–361) who re-

sided there. The prefecture of the Gauls was transferred from Trier to Arles *c.* 395, and in 418 the city was made the seat of the assembly of the seven Gallic provinces.

Arles was controlled by the Visigoths from *c.* 480 to 508–510, then by the Ostrogoths to 536, and thereafter by the Franks. When the Carolingian empire broke up in 879, the city was incorporated into the kingdom of Provence-Vienne. In 947 the kingdom of Burgundy-Provence was constituted, and this in turn passed under the titular control of the Holy Roman Empire in 1032. Arles was held by the counts of Barcelona from 1113 to 1245 and, through marriage, by the house of Anjou-Naples from 1246 to 1481. On the death of Charles III of Anjou, Dec. 11, 1481, Arles and Provence were ceded to Louis XI of France.

Church History. The presence of Christianity at Arles before the middle of the third century cannot be documented. GREGORY OF TOURS (*Franc.* 1.30) attributes its evangelization to Bishop Trophimus in 250. By the year 254, Bishop Marcianus of Arles had embraced the teachings of NOVATIAN (Cyprian, *Epist.* 68) and a see was soon established. In connection with the Donatist question (*see* DONATISM) a council of Western bishops was held at Arles in 314 under the presidency of its bishop, Marinus. In the long list of Arles's prelates (probably 94 in all) eminent names appear: Saints HONORATUS (d. 429?), HILARY (d. 449), CAESARIUS (d. 542) and AURELIAN (d. 551); Archbishops Rotlandus (d. 869) and Rostagnus (d. after 904); Blessed LOUIS D'ALEMAN (d. 1450) and its last archbishop, Jean Marie Dulau, a victim of the Paris massacre of Sept. 2, 1792.

The council of Turin *c.* 398 (can. 2) was prepared to recognize Arles' metropolitan authority over neighboring dioceses within the civil *provincia Viennensis.* On March 22, 417, Pope ZOSIMUS extended Arles' prerogative to all the sees of the civil provinces of Vienne and Narbonne I and II (*Regesta pontificum*, 328), but in 422 Boniface I withdrew Narbonne I from the metropolitan authority of Arles (*Regesta pontificum*, 362). LEO I abolished this metropolitanate altogether on July 8, 445, only to reestablish it in 450, over all but four of the dioceses in the Vienne province, as well as over the dioceses of Narbonne II and, probably, of Alpes-Maritime (*Regesta pontificum*, 407, 450). The erection of Aix and Embrun as archdioceses in 794 limited Arles' jurisdiction to eight sees stretching from Marseilles to Trois-Châteaux, though by the 10th or 11th century the dioceses of Antibes and Vence were also subject to Arles. The erection of Avignon as an archbishopric in 1475 withdrew four suffragans from Arles, which itself was abolished as an episcopal see by the Concordat of 1801.

Arles has been the scene of numerous diocesan synods (the series between 1410 and 1570 is unique in its documentation) and of many broader councils: in 314, 353, 443–452, 451, 455, 475–480, 524, 554, 813, 1211, 1234, 1263 and 1275. The archbishop of Arles has served as papal vicar for France several times, a dignity that can be documented for 417, 514, 545, 546, 557, 595 and 878 (Jaffé K, 328, 769, 913, 918, 944, 1374 and 3148).

Architecture. The paleochristian archeology of the city is not without difficulties. That the cathedral (probably the site of the council of 314) was known as St. Stephen's by 449 appears from the *Vita s. Hilarii* (28). Originally it seems to have stood at the inner angle of the southeast corner of the city walls, where the Asile de Saint-Césaire now stands on the Rue Vauban. During the pontificate of St. Caesarius (502–542) the female monastery of St. John was transferred to this place from its first site at Aliscamps and by 524 had been provided with the basilica S. Mariae. It is F. Benoît's contention (*Villes*, 18) that this monastic church was but a reworking of the ancient cathedral, and that this (the ancient cathedral) had already (before 449) been relocated at the center of the city, at the site of today's Saint-Trophime's on the Place de la Republique. The present writer has argued against this view, contending that the cathedral continued at the original location all through the episcopate of St. Caesarius and that the nuns' church was thus a flanking edifice (Beck, 363–368); and that the ancient pavement underlying Saint-Trophime's (the oldest portions of the present church date from the eighth century) probably belonged to the basilica Constantia, mentioned in the *Vita s. Hilarii* (13).

There is no contemporary evidence for the claim made by an inscription in the vestibule of the church of Notre Dame de La Major that it was dedicated in 453. Its most ancient sections date from the 12th century, yet it does stand on the site of a pagan temple. The basilica Apostolorum et Martyrum connected with the men's monastery founded by St. AURELIAN in 546 or 548 (*Regula ad monachos, Patrologia Latina* 68:395) is later localized by GREGORY I (*Reg.* 9.216) as within the city walls. This cannot, therefore, be identified with the basilica Saints Petri et Pauli, founded by 530, which corresponds with the actual S. Pierre des Mouleirés, just to the east of the city's modern cemetery (Benoît, *Provence historique*, Jan.–March 1957, 8–21). However, the basilica S. Crucis to which the Abbot Florentinus's remains were removed *c.* 588 (*Corpus inscriptionum latinarum* 12.944) would seem to fit the church of Sainte-Croix on the Rue de la Roquette.

There are two ancient Arlesian cemeteries: that on the west bank of the Rhône at Trinquetaille, attached to the 12th century church of Saint-Genest de la Colonne, which probably marks the site of the martyrdom of St.

Portico of Church of St. Trophime, tympanum sculpture shows "Christ in Majesty with the Four Evangelists," Arles, France. (© Diego Lezama Orezzoli/CORBIS)

GENESIUS (d. 303?); and the famed Aliscamps (southeast of Arles) with its avenue of Merovingian stone sepulchres and the church of St. Honoratus, which, though rebuilt in the 9th and 12th centuries, still contains a monolithic threshold of the basilica Beati Genesii where St. Honoratus was interred in 429 or 430.

Bibliography: L. ROYER, *Dictionnaire d'histoire et de géographie ecclésiastiques*, ed., A. BAUDRILLART et al., (Paris 1912–) 4:231–243. J. GILBERT, *Arles gréco-romaine* (Aix-en-Provence 1949). H. G. J. BECK, *The Pastoral Care of Souls in South-East France During the Sixth Century* (Analecta Gregoriana; Rome 1950). *Villes épiscopales de Provence*, ed. F. BENOÎT, et al., (Paris 1954). R. BUSQUET, *Histoire de Provence* (Monaco 1955). G. BAADER, *Lexikon für Theologie und Kirche²*, eds., J. HOFER and K. RAHNER, 10 v. (2d, new ed. Freiburg 1957–65) 1:864–865. M. C. MCCARTHY, *The Rule for Nuns of St. Caesarius of Arles* (Washington 1960). *Corpus inscriptionum latinarum* (Berlin 1863–). P. JAFFÉ, *Regesta pontificum romanorum ab condita ecclesia ad annum post Christum natum 1198*, ed. F. KALTENBRUNNER, ?–590, 2 v. (2d ed. Leipzig 1881–88; repr. Graz 1956). *Patrologia Latina*, ed., J. P. MIGNE, 217 V., indexes 4 v. (Paris 1878–90).

[H. G. J. BECK]

Original draft, dated Aug. 1, 1588 (O.S.), of an English council of war held immediately after the defeat of the Spanish Armada. Signatures include the Earls of Cumberland and Sheffield, Francis Drake, and John Hawkins.

ARMADA, THE SPANISH

A naval expedition sent in 1588 by PHILIP II, KING OF SPAIN to rendezvous with the Spanish army in the Netherlands and to escort it across the English Channel in order to effect the conquest of England. Philip II embarked on this enterprise against Queen Elizabeth I after the execution of Mary, Queen of Scots, on Feb. 18, 1587. Mary's failure to accede to the English throne had removed the threat of strong alliance between England and France that might have effectively closed the English Channel to Spain, thereby rendering Philip's position in the Spanish Netherlands intolerable. Until 1587 many cogent economic, strategic, and diplomatic reasons favored peace between Philip and Elizabeth. Since 1567, however, seamen such as John Hawkins and Francis Drake had encroached on Spain's trade monopoly with her American colonies, and had acted as privateers against Spanish ports and shipping. Elizabeth, moreover, fearing the ef-

fects that a victorious Spanish suppression of the Dutch revolt would have on the Protestant cause and on England's national security and commerce, had supplied the Dutch with men, money, and material.

Preparation of the Fleet. In 1587 Philip II began to fit out the expedition against England, but was delayed by Drake's pillaging of Cadiz harbor and his blockading operations off the Portuguese coast. His destruction of available supplies of seasoned barrel staves destined for the preservation of the Armada's provisions further jeopardized its success. In February 1588, Philip II placed Alonzo Pérez de Guzmán, Duke of Medina Sidonia, in command. Although he was inexperienced as an admiral, Medina Sidonia nevertheless quickly organized the fleet; by May 30, there were 130 assorted ships carrying 30,000 men at Lisbon, led by a fighting core of 20 galleons. It was forced by storms to put into Coruña for refitting and reprovisioning. On July 22, a fair wind for England blew the Armada northward, forcing at the same time the fortuitous turnabout of an English fleet that had been sailing to engage the Spaniards in their home waters.

To prevent any landing on the English coast and to destroy the Armada were the objectives of the English fleet, comprising 21 of the fastest, most modern, and best-armed galleons in Europe, equal to and often larger than their Spanish counterparts. These warships, commanded by the experienced Admirals John Hawkins, Martin Frobisher, and Francis Drake under First Lord Howard of Effingham, were supported by 151 other armed vessels.

The Encounter. As the Armada, arrayed in an impregnable crescentlike formation slowly plodded up the Channel between July 31 and August 6, two concepts of naval warfare clashed in the greatest sea battle in history to that time. The Spanish with their high forecastled and pooped galleons filled with soldiers strove to lure the English ships within grappling distance and capture them. The English with their more seaworthy and faster galleons hoped to sink their opponents with long-range culverin cannon. When the Armada anchored at Calais roads, both sides had practically exhausted their supply of shot without having inflicted significant damage on each other.

Medina Sidonia had up to this point succeeded according to the royal plan, but the Spanish general, Alexander Farnese, Prince of Parma, was not prepared to embark his troops at the rendezvous near Dunkirk. He considered the venture impossible from a military point of view and had so advised Philip II several times. Heavily armed Dutch flyboats controlled the intervening waters between the Armada's anchorage and the coast, so that before Parma's troop barges could have reached the protection of the galleons' guns, these flyboats would have decimated them.

Defeat. On the night of August 7, five English fireships threw the anchored Spaniards into a panic, causing them to slip their cables and scatter. Medina Sidonia again reassembled his fleet and on August 8 the last battle began. The English finally realized that if they were to destroy the enemy they must move in close to deliver really damaging broadsides. Having exhausted their supply of large shot, the Spanish sustained serious damage, which ended short of complete destruction when the English also ran out of cannon balls. On August 9, after escaping destruction again on the Zeeland sandbars, the Armada sailed into the North Sea. The English pursued the Spanish northward until on August 12, they turned wearily into the Firth of Forth, satisfied that the immediate danger of invasion was past.

Medina Sidonia now issued orders that the desperate fleet would sail north around the Shetland Islands and southward into the Atlantic, giving wide berth to the inhospitable western coast of Ireland. Sixty-four battered hulks, which had followed the Admiral's instructions, limped into northern Spanish ports at the end of September carrying 9,000 sick and dying men.

Bibliography: G. MATTINGLY, *The Armada* (Boston 1959); *The "Invincible" Armada and Elizabethan England* (Ithaca, NY 1963). M. A. LEWIS, *Armada Guns, A Comparative Study of English and Spanish Armaments* (London 1961). T. WOODROOFFE, *The Enterprise of England* (London 1958). J. A. WILLIAMSON, *The Age of Drake* (London 1938); *Hawkins of Plymouth* (London 1949). J. S. CORBETT, *Drake and the Tudor Navy*, 2 v. (New York 1898). A. L. ROWSE, *The Expansion of Elizabethan England* (New York 1955). R. B. MERRIMAN, *The Rise of the Spanish Empire in the Old World and in the New*, 4 v. (New York 1934). L. VAN DER ESSEN, *Alexandre Farnèse*, 5 v. (Brussels 1933–37). A. MCKEE, *From Merciless Invaders: An Eye-Witness Account of the Spanish Armada* (London 1963). C. MARTIN and G. PARKER, *The Spanish Armada* (New York 1988). R. WHITING, *The Enterprise of England* (Gloucester, UK 1988).

[R. H. TRAME]

ARMAGH, PRIMATIAL SEE OF

Located in the southern region of Northern Ireland, the See of Armagh (Armachanus) has been the primatial see of All-Ireland since 1152. Founded by St. PATRICK *c.* 450, Armagh developed on Irish monastic lines; its abbots were also bishops until *c.* 750. The school was famous both in Great Britain and on the Continent. Armagh's ecclesiastical preeminence appears in documents from 640 and in periodic visitations of other provinces carried on from the eighth century by its head, a cleric who bore the title of *Comharba Phádraig* (successor of Patrick).

Despite a CULDEE foundation (8th–16th century), Armagh declined with the coming of Danish raids and

The Cross of Muiredach at Monasterboice, in the See of Armagh.

local warfare (9th–10th centuries). The way was thus opened for the intrusion of lay abbots from a local family, the Clann Sínaigh (965–1129), one of whom, Ceallach (St. Celsus), ended the abuse by having himself consecrated bishop (1106).

At the Synod of Rathbreasail (1111), which assigned jurisdictions to Irish sees, Armagh received what is roughly its present territory in the counties of Armagh, Tyrone, and Derry (Northern Ireland) and in Louth and Meath (Irish Republic). Ceallach chose as his successor St. MALACHY, who resigned the see after much opposition. Gelasius (1137–74) received the pallium at the Synod of Kells (1152); Concord (1174–75) is still venerated at Chambéry, where he died.

The Anglo-Norman invasion brought a struggle between Irish and English for the see and prepared the ground for conflicts with Dublin about the primacy. Maolpadraig O'Scanlan (1261–70) built a larger cathedral, of which the present Protestant cathedral is an 18th-century rebuilding. Nicholas Mac Maolíosa (1272–1303) was the last Irish prelate till the Reformation. Of the Norman prelates, the most noteworthy was RICHARD FITZRALPH (1346–60), known for his contests with the mendicant orders. In these years the see was virtually partitioned between the Irish in Armagh, Tyrone, and Derry under an Irish dean and the English in Louth, where the archbishop resided. At the Reformation, George Cromer (1521–42) and George DOWDALL (1553–58) opposed doctrinal changes, but failed to provide the leadership of their successors.

Outstanding prelates under the penal laws were Richard Creagh (1564–85), who spent 18 years in the Tower of London before his death, Hugh O'Reilly (1628–53), who played a prominent part in the Confederation of Kilkenny, Edmund O'REILLY (1657–69), Oliver PLUNKET (1669–81), and Hugh McMahon (1714–37), who defended Armagh's primatial rights against Dublin. Peter Lombard (1601–25) and Hugh McCaughwell (1626), two of Armagh's distinguished scholars, spent their lives in exile. In 1731 the see still had 26 places of worship served by 77 secular priests and 22 friars.

The easing of persecution in the late 18th century allowed many small churches to be built. Discipline was restored by Richard O'Reilly (1787–1818). William Crolly (1835–49) took up residence in Armagh and began the building of the neo-Gothic St. Patrick Cathedral (dedicated in 1873). Paul CULLEN (1849–52) transferred to Dublin after the national synod of Thurles (1850). Within the ecclesial territory of Armagh, the shrines of St. BRIGID (Faughart) and Bl. Oliver Plunket (Drogheda) continue to attract many pilgrims.

Bibliography: J. STUART, *Historical Memoirs of . . . Armagh,* ed. A. COLEMAN (Dublin 1900). H. J. LAWLOR and R. I. BEST, *The Ancient List of the Coarbs of Patrick* (Dublin 1919). J. B. LESLIE, *Armagh Clergy and Parishes* (Dundalk 1911, suppl. 1948). A. GWYNN, *The Medieval Province of Armagh,* 1470–1545 (Dundalk 1946). *Seanchas Ardmhacha* (Armagh 1954–), annual journal of the Armagh Diocesan Historical Society, ed. T. Ó FIAICH.

[T. Ó FIAICH/EDS.]

ARMELLINI, MARIANO

Benedictine historian; b. Ancona, Dec. 10, 1662; d. Foligno, May 4, 1737. He entered the monastery of St. Paul in Rome in 1682. After completing his studies at Monte Cassino, he taught at various Cassinese monasteries from 1687 to 1695. He preached with great success throughout Italy and was appointed abbot of the monastery at Siena by Pope Innocent XIII (1722). He was sent to the monastery of St. Peter at Assisi (1729) and to the monastery of St. Felician, near Foligno (1734). He is an eminent historian of the Cassinese congregation and wrote the well-known *Bibliotheca Benedictino-Cassinesis* (2 v. Assisi 1731–32), *Appendix de viris literis illustribus a congregatione Casinensi* (Foligno 1732), *Additiones et correctiones bibliothecae Benedictino-Casinensis* (Foligno 1735–36), *Catologi tres episco-*

porum, reformatorum et virorum sanctitate illustrium e congregatione Casinensi (Assisi 1755).

Bibliography: H. HURTER, *Nomenclator literarius theologiae catholicae,* 5 v. (3d ed. Innsbruck 1903–13) 2:1212. M. ZIEGEL-BAUER, *Historia rei literariae ordinis S. Benedicti. . . ,* 4 v. (Augsburg 1754) v. 3. A. PRÉVOST, *Dictionnaire d'histoire et de géographie ecclésiastiques,* ed. A. BAUDRILLART et al. (Paris 1912) 4: 283. O. L. KAPSNER, *A Benedictine Bibliography: An Author-Subject Union List,* 2 v. (2d ed. Collegeville, Minn. 1962) 1:29.

[N. R. SKVARLA]

ARMENIA, MARTYRS OF, BB.

Also known as Salvatore Lilli of Cappadocia and companions, martyrs; d. Nov. 22, 1895, near Mujuk-Deresi, Cappadocia, Armenia (now eastern Turkey). Among the 100,000 civilians of Armenia slaughtered by the Turkish Army in 1895–96 were Franciscan Father Salvatore Lilli and seven of his parishioners.

Salvatore of Cappadocia (b. June 19, 1853 in Cappadocia) was the son of Vincenzo and Annunziata Lilli. He joined the Franciscans (1870), completed his studies in Bethlehem following the suppression of religious orders in Italy (1873), received presbyteral ordination in Jerusalem (April 16, 1878), and was sent to Marasco, Lesser Armenia (1880), where he was named pastor (1890). He diligently cared for the sick during a cholera epidemic (1890). In an effort to improve living conditions, Lilli established schools, clinics, and other social services.

In 1894, he was transferred to the mission at Mujuk-Deresi. When the violent persecution of Christians began the following year, Lilli's superiors twice urged him to leave, but he refused to abandon his flock. The following month Turkish soldiers invaded the convent, injuring many including Lilli as he tried to help others. The Christians were confined to a convent cell, where they were alternately abused and cajoled in an effort to convert them to Islam. Lilli urged the farmers imprisoned with him to remain steadfast. En route under guard to Marasco, they were ordered to apostatize; they refused and were killed.

Killed with Father Salvatore were seven of his parishioners: Jeremias (Ieremias) Ouglou Boghos, Lilli's assistant; David Oghlou David and his brother Toros Oghlou David; Khodianin Oghlou Kadir (Khodeanin Khadjir); Baldji (or Baldju) Oghlu Ohannès; Dimbalac Ouglou Wartavar; and Kouradji Oghlou Zirou (also spelled Tzeroum, Ziroun, Zirun).

The ordinary process for their beatification was begun in 1930–32 and initiated in Rome in 1959 by Pope John XXIII. The apostolic process in Aleppo, Syria, (1962–64) investigated the veracity of the claim of martyrdom, which was testified by an eyewitness, an eleven-year-old girl who survived. The eight martyrs were beatified at Rome by Pope John Paul II on Oct. 3, 1982.

Feast: Nov. 19.

Bibliography: *L'Osservatore Romano,* English edition, 42 (1982): 9–10.

[K. I. RABENSTEIN]

Capital: Yerevan.
Size: 11,506 sq. miles.
Population: 3,344,336 in 2000.
Languages: Armenian; Russian is spoken by 2% of the population.
Religions: 145,260 Latin-rite Catholics (4%), 3,143,600 Armenian Apostolic (94%), 50,076 Yezidi (a Kurdish, Islamic-based sect; 1%), 5,400 other.

ARMENIA, THE CATHOLIC CHURCH IN

Part of the USSR until 1991, the modern nation of Armenia is located in southwestern Asia. A mountainous region, it is bordered on the north by Georgia, on the east by Azerbaijan, on the south by Azerbaijan and Iran, and on the west by Turkey. Although historically Armenia once covered much of western Turkey and northern Iran, political divisions from the 17th through the 19th centuries divided its area between the Ottoman Empire (now Turkey), Persia (now Iran), and Russia; the plight of ethnic Armenians in diaspora continued to be problematic throughout the 20th century.

Politically joined to Russia in 1828, modern Armenia built its economy on the rich soil of the Aras river valley as well as from industry. A major producer of grapes, vegetables, and livestock, the country also worked to privatize formerly communist-run machine, textile, and other industries following the end of socialist rule. After gaining its independence from the Soviet Union, the predominately Christian country entered into a dispute with neighboring Azerbaijan over Nagorno-Karabakh, a region largely populated by ethnic Armenians that was made part of Islamic Azerbaijan at the break-up of the USSR. Instability caused by such political disputes as well as the decay of the economy during Soviet rule left almost half Armenia's population living below the poverty level by 2000.

Ecclesiastically, Armenia is predominately Oriental Orthodox, with the ordinariate for the Armenian Apostolic Church located at the monastery of Echmiadzin, near Yerevan. The Latin-rite Church has an apostolic administration covering the entire Caucasus region (Georgia, Armenia, and Azerbaijan), with its seat in the Georgian capital of Tbilisi. The Armenian Catholic Church, with its apostolic center in Beirut, Lebanon, is a minority religion in modern Armenia, most of its membership existing in Syria and Lebanon. The historic region known as Armenia is considered the first Christian nation.

The essay that follows, in relating the development of the Church in Armenia, includes the history of the Ottoman Empire (Turkey) and Persia (Iran); for modern histories of the Church in these countries see entries on Turkey and Iran.

Early History. According to recovered Assyrian and Urartian cuneiform monuments, ancient Armenia was inhabited by the 13th century B.C. During the 6th century B.C. Indogermanic tribes from the Thrasic-Phrygian Tsaph invaded the area and eventually blended with the native Assyrians; eventually these Armenians fell under the domination of first the Medes (612–549 B.C.) and then the Persians (549–331 B.C.).

Artaxias, or Artashēs, was appointed governor by Antiochus the Great (223–187) and is said to have founded Artaxata, or Artashat, on the advice of Hannibal. Tigranes II, after extending his reign over the whole of southwestern Asia, was defeated by Pompey in 66 B.C. A pact with their new Roman rulers made the Armenian kings dependent on the Parthians. Under Marcus Aurelius (161–180) Artaxata was destroyed and a new capital erected at Valarshapat. Tiridates III of the Arsacid dynasty was recognized by Rome (*c.* 296), and Armenia became a Roman protectorate.

Christianity. The Christianization of Armenia began with the missionary efforts of GREGORY THE ILLUMINATOR, who received episcopal consecration in Cappadocia and converted King Tiridates III at the end of the 3d century. By 303 Christianity had been adopted as the national religion, and under King Chosroes III (330–339) efforts were made to evangelize the neighboring Georgians and Albanians. The Church, with its see at Valarshapat, was a suffragan of Cappadocia, but the bishopric remained in the possession of Gregory's family; his son Aristaces attended the Council of Nicaea in 325. Despite the conversion of the king, Christianity received opposition from pagan priests as well as several princes. King Arsaces (Arshak) II (350–367) named NERSES the Great as bishop in 353. Consecrated in Cappadocia, Nerses held a synod at Ashtishat that legislated regarding matrimonial impediments for the nobles, the abolition of pagan funeral customs, and the establishment of hospitals and leprosaria. Nerses was eventually assassinated by King Pap (367–374).

ARMENIA

0   25   50   75 Miles

0   25   50   75 Kilometers

GEORGIA

Kalinino   Alaverdi
Akstafa

LESSER CAUCASUS MTS.

Step'anavan   Ijevan   Tovuz

Kumayri   Kirovakan

Dilijan

Akhta

AZERBAIJAN

Mt. Aragats
13,419 ft.
4090 m.

Kamo   Sevana
Lich

Nagorno-Karabakh
boundary

Ejmiatsin   Arzni   Zod

Hoktemberyan   Aras   Yerevan   Basargech'ar

Garni   Martuni   Kälbäjär

Igdir   Artashat

Ararat   Arpa

TURKEY   Vorotan

Sisian
Goris

Shakhbus   Ghap'an

AZERBAIJAN

Meghri
Aras

IRAN

Armenia

During the 4th and 5th centuries, the Church would lose its political support. Christians were persecuted under King Yazdgard I (399–420), but through the intervention of Emperor Theodosius II they obtained toleration from King Vahrām V (*c.* 421–439). King Chosroes selected ISAAC the Great as bishop (*c.* 390–438), and with the aid of MESROP, the calligrapher Rufinus, and a group of young monks educated in the West established an alphabet and translated the Bible as well as Greek and Syrian works of the Church Fathers, thereby originating an Armenian Christian literature. When the see was brought under the control of Constantinople, schools and missionaries were provided with Byzantine support. After the Council of EPHESUS (431) the Armenian bishops requested information regarding Nestorianism and received the renowned Tome of Proclus to the Armenians. A council was held at Ashtishat (435) accepting the THEOTOKOS.

In the 5th century the term *CATHOLICOS* came into use as the official title for the metropolitan. In 444 Catholicos Joseph (441–453) held a synod of 20 bishops that condemned the Messalians, or PAULICIANS, in 444, while in 450 at Artashat 17 bishops refused the invitation of the Persian king to embrace the cult of the god Aramazd. A persecution followed, and in 454 Archbishop Gevund and a number of clerics were martyred. With Byzantine assistance peace was restored in 506.

Prevented from attending the Council of Chalcedon (451) by internal troubles, the Armenian bishops had developed a faulty understanding of the problems posed by MONOPHYSITISM, and in 506 they accepted the HENOTICON of Zeno. Catholicos Nerses II (548–557) and 17 bishops came under the influence of followers of JULIAN OF HALICARNASSUS and repudiated the doctrines of the Council of Chalcedon.

Religious division continued. In 572, after a revolt against the Persians, Catholicos John II fled to Constantinople and accepted the Chalcedonian doctrine. Emperor MAURICE, after acquiring western Armenia to the river Ozal from King Chosroes Abharvēz II (590–628), held a council in Constantinople for its 21 bishops. Catholicos Moses II (574–604) of Dwin refused to attend and was replaced by John III (592–610). Iberian Catholics accepted the teachings of the Council of Chalcedon, and Kyrion, Archbishop of Mts'khet'a, entered into communion with Pope Gregory I (590–604). While the Syro-Armenian Synod at Ctesiphon (*c.* 614) rejected Chalcedon, the synod held by Catholicos Eger under Emperor HERACLIUS (632) at Karin (Erzurum) accepted it. In 649 the third Council of Dwin accepted Monophysitism under Catholicos Nerses II at the insistence of Arab conquerors anxious to separate the Armenians from the Byzantines. When Emperor Constans II (653) dominated the region the catholicos returned to Dyophysite doctrine.

Arab Rule. Arab invaders conquered Armenia in 653. Although Arab conquerors at first were lenient, Catholics were eventually intimidated and persecuted because of their revolts. Governors in Dwin were appointed from among Armenian nobles, but after a rebellion at Vardanakert power was transferred to Muslim rulers. An uprising in 772 resulted in the burning of churches, convents, and the wiping out of a large portion of the aristocracy.

Several 8th-century synods at Manzikert dealt with the Christological doctrines in dispute in Byzantium, and the catholicos found it necessary to leave the see of Dwin because of the hostility of the Muslims. Under the 'Abbāsids the lot of the Christians became almost intolerable, and frequent revolts were put down with intensified persecutions.

In 859 Caliph Motawakel-Billah named Ashot Bagratuni governor with the title prince of princes, and for

Statue of Lenin, Yerevan, Armenia. (©Dave Bartruff/CORBIS)

two centuries this new dynasty worked to rebuild the country and the Church, despite continual wars with the Byzantines, the Arabs, and the Armenian dynasty of the Artsruni. Under a succession of Bagatid rulers from 855–1020, Ani became one of the principal cities of the Orient, while commerce and literature flourished. Catholicos Peter I (1019–54) of Ani was suspected of treason for his voyages among the Greeks and in 1045 delivered his cathedral to Emperor Constantine Monomachus, who tried to force Chalcedonian doctrine on the Armenian clergy. When King Gagik II (d. 1079) repudiated this doctrine and broke the agreement reached with the Byzantines, he was imprisoned and deposed. Catholicos Gregory (Vahrām Pahlav) communicated with Pope Gregory VII (1073–85) and received the pallium as well as instructions to subscribe to the Council of Chalcedon.

Kingdom of Cilicia provides Refuge. While warring among noble families prevented the unification of Armenia, Seljuk Turks invaded the Euphrates Valley (1048–54) and sacked Sebaste (1059). With the defeat of Byzantine Emperor Romanus IV at Manzikert in 1071 the Seljuks were free to conquer Armenia. Many of the aristocracy fled west to Constantinople and Europe; others escaped into the Taurus Mountains.

During the persecutions of the 4th century a number of Armenians had taken refuge in Cilicia (in south-central Turkey); they were now joined by other compatriots. Armenian prince Ruben (1080–95) took the fortress of Partzpert and proclaimed the independence of Cilicia in 1080. His son Constantine (1095–99) enlarged the territory and made contact with the Roman Catholic leaders of the Second CRUSADE.

In 1113 Catholicos Basil was succeeded by Gregory III (1113–66), who took part in the Latin-rite synod at Antioch. Pope Innocent II sent him the pallium, and he in turn assured Pope Eugene III of his willingness to accept Roman stipulations regarding the sacrifice of the Mass. Catholicos Nersēs IV (1166–73), called the Gracious for his theological disquisitions, entered discussions with the representatives of the Greek Church at Hromcla, and his successor Gregory IV pursued reunion efforts with the Greek Church at the synod of Hromcla in 1179. Gregory was also in contact with Pope Lucius III, whom he assured of his filial submission in 1184 and from whom he received the pallium with a miter and ring.

Cilicia's aid to the Third Crusade was rewarded by Pope Celestine III, who acknowledged King Leo I the Magnificent (1196–1219) as the monarch of the Arme-

Keghart Church and monastery, walls hewn from solid rock, shown by Jordanian monk, Keghart, Armenia. (Hulton/Archive Photos)

nians. Leo adopted many Western customs and passed the custody of his principal fortresses to the Knights Templars. HET'UM I (1226–70) personally visited the court of the Mongol Khan Mangou and arranged a treaty of peace. However, the Mamelukes of Egypt invaded Cilicia, and Het'um retired to a monastery in 1270. Under Leo II (1270–89) the kingdom enjoyed a minor renaissance of culture, commerce, and religious life, despite a temporary alienation from Rome over the Templars. Leo's successor Het'um II (1289–1305) and Catholicos Constantine I protested to Pope Gregory IX against the crusaders' attempt to extend the jurisdiction of the Latin Patriarchate of Antioch over Armenia.

Het'um II sent JOHN OF MONTE CORVINO to Pope Nicholas IV with his testimony of submission (1289), and despite the pope's attempt to send aid, the Mamelukes captured Hromcla (1292), took Catholicos Stephen prisoner, and carried off the relic of the right arm of St. Gregory the Illuminator. A synod at Sis in 1307 undertook dogmatic and disciplinary reforms in accord with Roman prescriptions, and despite violent opposition from some clergymen King Oshin held a council at Adana in 1316 that received encouragement from Pope JOHN XXII (1316–34). In 1356, Innocent IV approved the constitu-

tion of an order of Friars Unifiers, who exercised a fruitful apostolate near Nakhichevan (1440–1766).

Despite continued appeals of the popes, Western princes failed to aid the kingdom of Cilicia; its last king, Leo of Lusignan (d. 1393), was captured by the Emir Ischqtimur, and on being ransomed from the Caliph of Egypt became the guest of Charles VI of France until he died and was buried in the Abbey of St. Denis outside Paris. Cilicia then fell under the power of the Tartars and was given up to persecution and plunder. Despite the disarray of the region's Armenian church its catholicos Constantine VI was represented at the Council of Ferrara-Florence and on Nov. 22, 1439, accepted decrees of the council. Pope Eugene IV sent a letter of gratitude that was received by the Catholicos Gregory IX (1440–53).

Division within Armenian Church Widens. Although supported by the Church in Cilicia, opposition to the Council of Florence came from the monks of Oriental Armenia. Four bishops demanding the change of the catholicate to Valarshapat (modern Echmiadzin) were excommunicated by Gregory X. In a reactionary synod at Valarshapat 12 bishops elected the monk Cyriacos, who immediately won the support of 12 other bishops and their people. After the fall of Constantinople (1453) Muḥammad II recognized the Armenian bishop Joachim (Hovakim) as patriarch with his palace at Psammathia (1461), and entrusted him with ruling the domestic affairs of all the Armenians in his vast realm.

The catholicos of Sis was restricted to spiritual functions; in 1587 it had 12 chapels and the catholicate counted 24 dioceses, 300 priests, 20 convents, and hundreds of monks. Catholicos Khach'atur (1560–84) wrote to Pope Gregory XIII; and his successor, Catholicos Azaria, accepted a profession of Catholic faith. In 1683 another Azaria died in Rome, where he had taken refuge; so too did his successor Gregory Pidzak (1683–91).

Catholicos Stephen V had made a profession of faith in Rome (1548–50), and his successor Michael sent an envoy to the court of Paul IV, who helped found an Armenian printing press in Rome. Pius V gave the Armenians the church of St. Mary of Egypt, and Gregory XIII, in his bull *Romana Ecclesia,* praised the faith of the Armenians. But Armenia itself was continually attacked by Turks, then Persians, leaving its bishops and people in continual ferment, at times in union with Rome, and at times in schism.

Meanwhile, religious priests remained active. In 1583 the Dominicans established a province in Trans-Caucasia; and in 1626 the Jesuits opened a house in Alep. They started a mission at Isfahan in 1653 and carried on successful work at Erzurum (1685–91) and Yerevan toward the end of the century despite the outbreak of persecution. The Capuchins arrived in Alep in 1627; and the Carmelites were sent into Persia in 1705. Augustinians and Theatines also worked in Persia and Georgia. Between 1694 and 1764 the constant struggle between Catholics and Orthodox Armenians for predominance would be fueled by civil rulers, and many Armenians left the area for the Holy Land.

Birth of Modern Nation of Armenia. In 1828 Russia gained control of the northeastern portion of Armenia, which had been under the control of the Ottoman Turks for over 300 years. A systematic attempt was made to incorporate the Armenians into both the Russian state and the Russian Orthodox church. While in 1866 the Armenian and the Russian branches of the Church were united under Patriarch Peter IX Hassun, this effort masked difficulties that would be renewed half a century later, in 1911, when a synod was held in Rome to deal with the reorganization of the Church's governance.

Meanwhile, at the close of the 19th century a group of Turkish-Armenian intellectuals educated in the West formed resistance groups in the remainder of Armenia, hoping to enlist the aid of Western powers in preserving their culture. They joined the Young Turks in their 1908 revolt, but their goal of uniting Armenians backfired under the Young Turk government. Amid an outbreak of ethnic violence, all Turkish Armenians were deported to Syria and Palestine, resulting in a million deaths; the date of April 24th thereafter served to commemorate those who died in concentration camps or of disease and starvation during their forced relocation east of Turkey between 1915 and 1918. Ottoman persecutions during and after World War I reduced the Armenian clergy by more than half and exterminated up to two million of the region's Christian inhabitants before the Treaty of Lausanne incorporated Turkish Armenia into the republic of Turkey in 1923.

Meanwhile, Russian-controlled Armenia, Azerbaijan, and Georgia joined together in 1917 to form the Transcaucasian Federal Republic. Unfortunately, the new nation would last only a short while before falling victim to further Turkish aggression. On May 28, 1918, Armenia declared its independence, but by 1922 was once again joined with its Transcaucasian partners as one of 15 Soviet Socialist Republics, with Yerevan as its capital. In 1936 the region split again, with the Soviet Socialist Republic of Armenia the result. Some 150,000 ethnic Armenians moved to this new homeland following World War II, but many more resided in Istanbul, Lebanon, and other parts of the world. The city of Jerusalem had an Armenian quarter, in addition to quarters for Jews, Christians, and Muslims.

Ethnic Divisions Characterize 20th Century. As was the case with other nations while under Soviet rule, from the 1950s through the 1980s Armenia's Apostolic and Latin-rite churches suffered both materially and spiritually under communist domination. Monasteries and other church buildings were closed, and clergy were forced either underground or out of the country as communist leaders sought to eradicate all vestiges of the Armenian Christian heritage.

During the 1970s the Armenian Secret Army for the Liberation of Armenia began a campaign of terror against Turkish officials as a way to balance the scales of justice against the atrocities perpetrated upon the Armenian people during the late 19th and early 20th centuries. In 1989 a second wave of violence erupted in Nagorno-Karabakh, a region of Muslim-dominated Azerbaijan that was home to a predominately Armenian Catholic population. When Armenia declared independence from the USSR on Sept. 23, 1991, violence on the part of Armenian separatists in Nagorno-Karabakh increased, forcing Islamic Azeri populations from Armenia and Catholic populations from the Nagorno region. This violence, supported by the Armenian government, was halted by a cease-fire in 1994 from which permanent political resolutions had yet to be made by 2000. Political crises continued to haunt Armenia following a constitutional referendum in the mid-1990s, with the election of a strongly nationalist president 1998 suggesting that the region's long history of religious and ethnic instability might easily be revisited. The region's increasing poverty did little to allay fears of political upheaval.

While political changes were marked by division, the Church Armenian Apostolic moved toward closer relations with the See of Rome following the overthrow of communism. On Dec. 10, 1996, Catholicos Karekin I (d. 1999) joined with Pope John Paul II in a joint declaration of faith that helped bridge the theological gap between the two churches. This declaration would be mirrored in a similar reconciliation of faith between the pope and Armenian Apostolic Catholicos Aram I of Antelias. Both church leaders were also assured of Vatican support of their efforts toward rebuilding Armenian society following communism. In addition, the pope offered words of encouragement to the leaders of the Armenian Catholic Church (*see* ARMENIAN CHRISTIANITY).

The Church Moves into the 21st Century. The Armenian Apostolic Church was granted the status of national church of Armenia by the 1991 constitutional Law on Freedom of Conscience. While Armenia's constitution also proclaimed religious freedom, ''proselytizing'' was prohibited by all but the national church, all minority religions being required to register with the government.

Because of the separatist efforts in the Nagorno-Karabakh region, followers of Islam were treated in a discriminatory manner and many continued to leave Armenia.

In 2001, Armenians celebrated the country's 1,700 years of Christianity. As was characteristic within many former Soviet republics, the Armenian Apostolic Church had several claims against the government for land and other properties confiscated by the communist administration. In April 2000 negotiations between church and state began, the Church's goal to settle those disputes prior to the anniversary celebration. Another goal of the Armenian Apostolic Church was to begin a dialogue with the state regarding taking its role in education as well as in the moral guidance of Armenian society.

The preeminent Catholicos of Echmiadzin was led by Catholicos Karekin II Nersissian, former archbishop of Yerevan, beginning in October 1999, following Karekin I's death. Among the new Church leader's first actions was the creation of a new department of Christian outreach, designed to begin a dialogue between the Apostolic Church and other Armenian faiths. Such a dialogue would help bolster the Church's weakened resources in the wake of communism, as well as combat the sagging spiritual fervor of many Armenians. Indeed, by the millennium Christianity had become less a faith than an ethnic marker separating the majority population from Azeri Muslims. Karekin II also met with Pope John Paul II in November 2000 to continue efforts at reconciling the Armenian Apostolic Church with the Holy See. During that visit the pope presented the catholicos with relics of St. Gregory the Illuminator for placement in a cathedral in the Armenian saint's honor then under construction in Erevan.

In 2000 Armenia contained 29 parishes administered to by one secular and 16 religious priests, the scarcity of clergy a consequence of Soviet government. The Latin-rite church shared a papal nuncio with Georgia and Azerbaijan. The Armenian Catholic Church, which counted close to 345,000 members worldwide in 2000, was headed by Patriarch Nerses Bedros XIX of Cilicia, who was based in Beirut, Lebanon. During a Jubilee celebration in Rome in September, the pope spoke to a group of Rome-based Armenian Catholics, urging them not to abandon those who remained in Armenia due to poverty. He also sent a message to members of the Armenian Apostolic Church, letting them know that ''the Pope of Rome is carefully following [your] efforts to be 'the salt of the earlth and light of the world.'.''

Bibliography: V. INGLISIAN, *Armenien in der Bibel* (Vienna 1935). F. KÖNIG, *Handbuch der chaldischen Inschriften*, v.1 (Graz 1955). H. F. TOURNEBIZE, *Histoire politique et religieuse de l'Arménie* (Paris 1910). M. ORMANIAN, *The Church of Armenia*, ed. T. POLADIAN, tr. G. M. GREGORY (2d Eng. ed. London 1955). W. DE VRIES, *Der christliche Osten in Geschichte und Gegenwart* (Würzburg 1951). M. J. TERZIAN, *Le Patriarcat de Cilicie et les Arméniens cath.* (Beirut 1955). M. VAN DEN OUDENRIJN, *Oriens Christianus* 40 (1956) 94–112. N. ADONTZ, *Histoire de l'Arménie* (Paris 1946). J. SANDALGIAN, *Les Inscriptions cunéiforms urartiques* (Venice 1900). R. KHERUMIAN, *Les Arméniens* (Paris 1941). S. WEBER, *Die katholische Kirche in Armenien* (Freiburg 1903). H. HAGOPIAN, *The Relations of the Armenians and the Franks* (Boston 1905).

[N. M. SETIAN/EDS.]

ARMENIAN CHRISTIANITY

ARMENIAN APOSTOLIC CHURCH (ORIENTAL ORTHODOX)

Although an ancient national tradition places the origins of Christianity in Armenia as far back as apostolic times, it is certain that until the end of the 3d century the doctrine of Christ had made little progress and the country had no ecclesiastical hierarchy in the strict sense. Christianity became the state religion *c.* A.D. 300, when the great apostle of Armenia, St. GREGORY THE ILLUMINATOR preached the gospel there. This noble descendant of the royal family, who had been trained in Christian doctrine from childhood and was consecrated by the bishop of Caesarea in Cappadocia, quickly won over King Tiridates III to Christianity, as well as a large portion of the population. He was helped in his work of evangelization by Greek and Syrian missionaries whom he had invited to Armenia from Asia Minor (Cappadocia) and Syria (Edessa), respectively.

The invention of the Armenian alphabet at the beginning of the 5th century by St. Mesrop (d. 439), Doctor of the Armenian Church, resulted in the substitution of the national language for two foreign languages, Greek and Syrian. Holy Scripture and the most important works of the Fathers of the above-mentioned Churches, as well as the liturgies then in existence in Armenia, were translated into the Armenian language. This was done during the reign of the Catholicos Sahag the Great (387–438).

The Armenian Church was suspected, at least nominally, of MONOPHYSITISM by unfortunate political circumstances. Caught as a political pawn between the opposing armies of the Byzantine and Persian Empires, the Armenians were unable to attend the Councils of EPHESUS (431) and CHALCEDON (451). The decrees were translated into their new but undeveloped national language, and they saw only heretical teachings as the result of the Councils' acts. It was an easy step for the Synod of Dvin (506–507) to accept the *Henoticon* of Emperor ZENO and condemn formally the Council of Chalcedon in order to receive political protection from the Monophysite-tainted Byzantine emperor. Attempts by the Byzantine Church under the emperors Heraclius (610–641) and Justinian II (685–695, 705–711) failed to convince the Armenian Church to accept Chalcedon.

The kingdom of Armenia had been for centuries the victim of attacks by the Byzantines, the Persians, and later by the Turks. It dissolved with the destruction of its capital, Ani. The catholicoi (comparable to a patriarch) moved their see of residence first to Ashtishat, then finally in 1293 to Sis, CILICIA (Turkey), to set up New Armenia. Here, near the Holy Lands fought for by the Latin Crusaders, the Armenians came into close contact with Roman Catholicism and a communion with the See of Rome was actually effected that lasted from 1198 until 1375. Internal strifes within the Armenian Church of Cilicia then split the Church into many factions and dissolved the union with Rome. From the 15th century it had four competitors for the legitimate Armenian lineage. In 1113 the bishop of Aghtamar, on an island in Lake Van (Armenia), declared himself the legitimate successor of the ancient See of Etchmiadzin and took the title of catholicos. An Armenian bishop of Jerusalem in 1311 took the title of patriarch. A rival group in 1441 moved back to former Armenia from Cilicia and set up the seat of a catholicate at Etchmiadzin while the legitimate catholicos remained in the See of Sis in Cilicia. In 1461 Muḥammad II recognized at Constantinople a new Armenian patriarchate. Thus in the 15th century there were three catholicates: the one at Etchmiadzin enjoying the greatest authority and largest following, and two others at Sis and Aghtamar. Two other patriarchates split the Armenian Church further, one at Constantinople and the other at Jerusalem.

The collapse of the Soviet Union resulted in a renaissance of the Armenian Apostolic Church in its homeland, the independent Republic of Armenia. Today, the Armenian Apostolic Church is divided into four jurisdiction: two catholicosates — Etchmiadzin and Cilicia — that are juridically independent but in full communion with each other, and two patriarchates — Jerusalem and Constantinople — that are dependent on Etchmiadzin on spiritual matters. As the Supreme Patriarch and Catholicos of All Armenians, the Armenian Catholicos of Etchmiadzin is the principal spiritual and temporal leader of the Church. The catholicos of Etchmiadzin has a primacy of honor over the other ruling prelates but jurisdiction only in his own catholicate. His jurisdiction covers the Republic of Armenia, as well as much of the former Soviet Union and the Armenian diaspora, which includes Iraq, India, Egypt, Syria, Sudan, Ethiopia, Europe, Oceania, Southeast Asia, and the Americas. The Catholicos of Cilicia is based in Antelias, Lebanon and has jurisdiction over Armenians in Lebanon, Syria, Cyprus, Iran, Syria and Greece. The Patriarchate of Jerusalem is responsible for the churches and other holy shrines belonging to the Armenian Church in Jerusalem. The Patriarchate of Constantinople covers modern-day Turkey and the Greek island of Crete. The tiny catholicate of Aghtamar was dissolved in 1915 and is no longer extant.

Canonical Sources. After the monk Mesrop invented the Armenian written language, scholars busied themselves in the 5th century translating the Bible and liturgical and canonical books into Armenian. The acts of the Councils of NICAEA I (325) and Ephesus (431) were thus introduced as a basic canonical source for the growing Armenian Church. A series of early canons proper to the Armenian Church is attributed to Sahag the Great, a 4th-century catholicos; in it attention is given to the office of chorbishop, an inspector sent by the bishop to visit the far-distant places of the diocese. Two important, early councils, Chahapivan (447) and Vagarshapat (491), are significant for Armenian Christianity. The first legislated 20 canons setting the catholicate on a solid foundation of independence, and the second rejected the Council of Chalcedon (451) and made the rift from the Byzantine Church definitive. Gradually the canons of Council of CONSTANTINOPLE I (381) and those of the local synods accepted by the Byzantine Church in general, such as Ancyra, Neocaesarea, Antioch, Gangres, Sardis, and Laodicea, were translated from the Greek and incorporated as a basis of the Armenian canon law. Other traditional sources, such as the *85 Canons of the Apostles,* the *90 Canons of St. Athanasius,* and the *50 Canons of St. Basil,* were incorporated; so also were certain canons proper to the Armenian Church, such as the *39 Canons* attributed to the catholicos Narses Achtarak (548–577), those of the Councils of Dvin (645) (719), and those of Partav (771).

Byzantine influence was felt in the field of canonical sources, depending on the political events at any given period. At one time even the canons of the Council of Chalcedon were accepted along with the 22 canons of NICAEA II (787). Historians claim that Catholicos John Otznetzi (717–728) was the first to collect all the canons then in force into one volume. It is certain at least that these became fixed in some sort of a compendium in the 8th century. The canonical sources from then until the Crusades did not change radically.

Influence from the Crusades. With the establishment of New Armenia in Cilicia (Turkey) and the arrival of the Latin Crusaders in the Holy Land, new contact was made with Rome and a new influence entered into the canonical legislation of the Armenian Church. An important work at this time was compiled by the monk Mechitar Goch at the end of the 12th century. He strove to compile a book on jurisprudence, but succeeded only in collecting and commenting on canonical texts that seemed to him useful. His *Book of Judicial Cases* was a standard work for all Armenian canonists. In 1198, when Rome recognized the Catholicos Gregory VI, the door was opened both to a religious renaissance and to radical changes in canonical legislation. The Councils of Sis (1204, 1246, 1307, 1342) and of Adana (1316) inaugurated many Latinizations into the liturgy. This was the basic reason for the hostility of the Armenian monks of Jerusalem, who elected their own patriarch in 1311. After the schism in 1441, when a group left Sis to establish a seat at Etchmiadzin and the two principal catholicates and two patriarchates were formed, no new canonical additions were added to the ancient sources.

ARMENIAN CATHOLIC CHURCH (EASTERN CATHOLIC)

The reunion with Rome of the Armenians in Cilicia, lasted from 1198 until 1375. The Dominican Order was engaged in keeping alive the union when it began to flounder in the 14th century. A native Armenian order, the Friars of Unity, founded in 1320, was a peculiar adaptation of Armenian monasticism to the Dominican rule, but was gradually absorbed entirely into the Dominican Order. The bull of reunion of the Council of Florence (1439), *Exsultate Deo,* did not effect a lasting union but did lay down norms of discipline and liturgical practices that later were put into effect by the Armenian Catholics. There had always been an occasional catholicos united with Rome; but after the union of 1375 was dissolved, there was no Catholic Armenian Church until the Armenian Catholic bishop of Alep, Abraham Ardzivean, was elected Catholicos of Cilicia (Sis). However, he was unable to return as catholicos to Cilicia (Sis) after Benedict XIV confirmed him in Rome in 1742 because a rival was appointed in his stead. He moved his seat to Kraim in Lebanon, and his successor transferred the see to Bzommar, which then became the center for the Armenian Catholics, who were scattered throughout Syria, Mesopotamia, Palestine, and Egypt.

The Armenian Catholics in various parts of the Ottoman Empire were subject to the Latin apostolic vicar, but under the Ottoman millet system, that provided for the administrative autonomy of minorities under their religious leaders, all Armenians were place under the jurisdiction of the Armenian Patriarch of Constantinople. This caused friction and even bitter persecution of the Armenian Catholics from 1700 until 1830. The Ottoman government, through French insistence, granted the Catholics in Turkey civil and religious freedom under the single leadership of the Catholic archbishop of Constantinople, whom the Turks wanted as patriarch. Since there could hardly be two simultaneous Catholic Armenian pa-

triarchs, the problem was solved in the Synod of Bzommar through the election of the primate of Constantinople as Catholicos of Cilicia in 1867. Pope Pius IX confirmed the union of the two Catholic Armenian sees in his bull *Reversurus,* but this only led to a schism of several bishops and many monks of St. Anthony under the leadership of Father Malachy Ormanian. Further internal disputes and persecutions by the Turks almost completely dissolved the Catholic Armenian Church. A decree from Rome in 1928 transferred the patriarchal seat from Constantinople to Beirut, and Constantinople (Istanbul) became an archbishopric.

From the 14th century there had already existed an Armenian bishopric in Galicia (Ukraine) with residence at Lvov. In 1635 Abp. Nicholas Torosowicz became a Catholic, and thus this archbishopric continued to be Catholic until 1944. During World War II the faithful were dispersed, many having gone to Silesia, in East Germany.

The Armenian Catholic Church suffered severe losses during World War I, especially in the dioceses of Turkey, where great numbers of Catholics were put to death for the faith by the Turks. The Church was reorganized in 1928 through a synod held in Rome. The Patriarch of Cilicia of the Armenians became the supreme leader of the Armenian Catholic Church. The patriarchal seat is located in Beirut, Lebanon. Constantinople (Istanbul) became a simple archbishopric.

As was the case with the other Eastern Catholic Churches, the Armenian Catholic Church was suppressed under Soviet rule. When the Republic of Armenia regained its independence in 1991 after the collapse of the Soviet Union, the Armenian Catholic Church re-emerged in its homeland.

Bibliography: *Acta et decreta concilii nationalis Armenorum Romae habiti anno Domini MDCCCCXI* (Rome 1914). A. BALGY, *Historia doctrinae catholicae inter Armenos . . .* (Vienna 1878), in Armenian and Lat. V. HATZUNI, *Cenno storico e culturale sulla nazione Armena* (Venice 1940). R. JANIN, *Les Églises Orientales et les Rites Orientaux* (Paris 1955). A. A. KING, *The Rites of Eastern Christendom,* 2 v. (London 1950). G. ZANANIRI, *Pape et patriarches* (Paris 1962). G. AMADUNI, ed., *Disciplina Armena: Testi vari di diritto canonico armeno* (Fonti CICO, ser. 1, fasc. 7; 1932). P. HATZUNI, "Disciplina Armena" in *Studi storici sulle fonti del diritto canonico orientale* (ibid. fasc. 8; 1932) 139–168. C. DE CLERCQ, "Notae historicae circa fontes iuris particularis Orientalium Catholicorum," *Apollinaris* 4 (1931) 409–427; T. E. DOWLING, *The Armenian Church* (The Society for Promoting Christian Knowledge. 1910). R. ROBERSON, *The Eastern Christian Churches: A Brief Survey*, 6th ed (Rome 1999).

[J. KAFTANDJIAN/EDS.]

ARMENIAN LITURGY

The liturgical usages and practices indigenous to the Church of Armenia, which is sometimes referred to as the Armenian Apostolic Church, the Armenian Orthodox Church, or simply the Armenian Church. Along with the Coptic, Ethiopian, Syriac (Jacobite), and Malankara Orthodox Churches, the Armenian Church is one of the so-called Oriental Orthodox Churches, united by their rejection of the Council of Chalcedon, but in liturgical rite, history, and spirituality quite distinct from one another. Today the Armenian Liturgy is used by an estimated 6,000,000 faithful of the Armenian Church, as well as approximately 344,000 members of the Armenian Catholic Church in communion with Rome. Officially, the liturgical language is Classical Armenian (Grabar), which differs decidedly from the eastern and western modern Armenian dialects. The vernacular is increasingly used in the celebration of the sacraments, but not habitually in the Divine Liturgy or the Daily Office.

The Armenian Liturgy is one of the five liturgical families of the Christian East. Although scholars long considered the Armenian Liturgy to be but a branch of the Byzantine liturgical family, recent scholarship has demonstrated beyond doubt the independence and distinctiveness of the ancient liturgical tradition of the Armenian Church.

Compared with other liturgical rites east and west, several remarkable features characterize Armenian Liturgy. The christological controversies of the fifth and subsequent centuries embroiled the Armenians in polemics with the Greeks, who wrongly accused them of confessing Eutychian monophysitism. For centuries the Armenians became absorbed in christological apologetics and speculation, which left its mark on the liturgy. The high Alexandrian christology promulgated by the Armenian Church is reflected in many facets of its liturgical expression. The Armenian anaphora of St. Athanasius, while addressed to the Father, is christological from the outset. The opening discourse on God's creation found in conventional Antiochene Eucharistic prayers is reduced in Armenian Athanasius to a mere mention. Other christological emphases include a christological doxology that always precedes the Lord's Prayer, and the perpetuation in Armenia of the unified celebration of Christ's birth and baptism on January 6, which became for the Armenians a symbol of the perfect divinity and perfect humanity of Christ in one nature.

The Armenian Church's preservation of the original eastern date of Christmas (January 6) is but one manifestation of the remarkable protective tendency of the Armenian Liturgy. The Armenian Liturgy often preserves ancient structures and usages long since supplanted in other rites. In Armenian Sunday Matins, to cite one example, the Cathedral Vigil exhibits today the same lucid structure that the Spanish pilgrim Egeria described toward the end of the fourth century. Scholars are increasingly turning to the Armenian Liturgy as an important witness for the historical reconstruction of early liturgical structures and practices.

Origin and Historical Evolution of the Armenian Liturgy. The Gospel was brought to Armenia from two ancient Christian centers: Edessa and Caesarea in Cappadocia. These two cultural poles, one semitic, the other hellenistic, shaped the Armenian Liturgy in its formative stage. Philologists have confirmed the Armenian patristic claim that the early fifth-century Armenian translation of the Bible was based on Syriac texts imported from Edessa and Greek prototypes brought in from Caesarea. Much early Armenian ecclesiastical terminology derives from Iranian or Syriac, and Armenian initiation rites share a striking resemblence to East Syrian paradigms. These examples attest to early influence from Edessa. From the other cultural pole came the Armenian Eucharistic Prayers, which are all of the West Syrian type, and several seem to be translations or reworkings of Greek originals. The Caesarean connection is to be explained not only by its proximity to historical Armenia in eastern Asia Minor, but also because St. Gregory the Illuminator, who converted the Armenian King Trdat [Tiridates III] (298–330) to Christianity, received his episcopal consecration by the hand of Metropolitan Leontius of Caesarea, probably in 314 A.D.. Thus Armenia fell under the general jurisdiction of the great Cappadocian see. In the wake of the partition of Armenia between Persia and Rome in 387 A.D., the authority of Caesarea over the affairs of the Armenian Church waned, and by 389 A.D., Catholicos Sahak I acceded to the patriarchal throne of St. Gregory without reference to Caesarea.

During the fifth century, the nascent Armenian Liturgy was strongly influenced by the liturgy of Jerusalem. Already in the fourth century Armenian pilgrims and monks began traveling to the Holy Land. St. Euthymius (377–473), founder of an important fifth-century lavra on the Dead Sea, and teacher of St. Sabas, was an Armenian by birth. A sixth-century source counts seventy Armenian churches and monasteries in the Holy Land. The Armenians' fascination with the Church in Jerusalem led them to translate into Armenian the lectionary of the Holy City, which contained not only the scripture readings to be read at liturgical synaxes throughout the year, but also detailed rubrical information regarding the litugical life of the Holy City. The Armenian Lectionary (Čašoc') maintains the contours of the fifth-century Jerusalem lectionary. Similarly, the shape of the Armenian liturgical year and the system of feasts evolved, with little adaptation initially, from that of Jerusalem.

A long period of byzantinization of the Armenian Liturgy reached its apex early in the second millennium. Conspicuous Byzantine influence is to be found in the Armenian Divine Liturgy, including the Liturgy of the Word, in some of the daily offices, especially Vespers, and in other ceremonies such as the Rite of the Dedication of a Church. It cannot be ruled out, however, that some liturgical usages common to the Armenian and Byzantine Liturgies may go back to a common Cappadocian root.

Beginning in the twelfth century, crusading Latin and Frankish armies passed through the Armenian Kingdom of Cilicia on their way to the Holy Land. This, for the first time, brought the Armenians into sustained contact with the Christian West. In 1318 Pope John XXII (1316–1334) created a Latin metropolitan see in Armenian Nakhijevan and ordered the establishment of Latin schools, which he entrusted to the Dominican missionaries. The encounter proved fruitful for the Armenians as, with remarkable openness, they adapted certain western liturgical traditions to their own use. While Rome was rarely reluctant to coerce other churches, including the Armenian, to reform their liturgical rites along Roman lines, it has been demonstrated that a number of Latin features in the Armenian Liturgy were not the result of an imposed ''latinization,'' but were integrated by the Armenian hierarchy with great discretion. Latin influence is palpable in Armenian ordination rites, penance, the beginning and end of the Divine Liturgy, and in some liturgical vestments. The calculated integration of Latin usages into the Armenian Liturgy reveals both a sensitivity to liturgical structure and an openness to outside influence which are unusual among the eastern rites.

As in all rites, the steady development of the Armenian Liturgy essentially ceased with the emergence of printed editions of the liturgical books. The first edition of the Armenian Divine Liturgy (Pataragamadoyc') was published in Venice in 1513, with editions of the Ritual (Maštoc'), Hymnal (Šarakan) and Book of Hours (Žamagirk') appearing by mid-century.

The Armenians boast a singularly rich tradition of liturgical commentaries on their church services. Besides explanations of the Divine Liturgy, no less than eight authors between the seventh and fourteenth centuries penned commentaries on the Daily Office, a literary genre apparently unknown in Greek literature. There are even allegorical commentaries on the Lectionary (Čašoc') and on occasional rites such as the Foundation and Dedication of a Church. Most of these liturgical-exegetical works have yet to be edited and studied.

Divine Liturgy. Like all ancient churches the Divine Liturgy of the Armenian Church (Patarag) comprises two main components: the Liturgy of the Word or Synaxis, and the Eucharist proper. To these a preparatory introduction and a final blessing, gospel reading, and dismissal were added fairly late, both under Latin influence.

Since at least the tenth century the only Eucharistic Prayer used in the Armenian Liturgy is attributed to St. Athanasius, probably because the elegant depiction of Christ's incarnation in its preface is strikingly reminiscent of Athanasian christology. The Anaphora of St. Athanasius has a traditional Antiochene or West Syrian shape: the Preface leads to the Sanctus, with Christ's Words of Institution embedded within the Anamnesis, followed by the Oblation. The Epiclesis comes next, from which flow the anaphoral Intercessions, accompanied by the DIPTYCHS.

Four other Armenian anaphoras survive in medieval manuscripts, all of them apparently early translations from Greek. These anaphoras seem to have been used in Armenia during the first millennium. The most important of them is ascribed to St. Gregory the Illuminator, but is actually an early form of the Anaphora St. Basil of Caesarea. Armenian-Basil closely resembles the most primitive known form of this prayer, preserved in Coptic. The anaphoras attributed to St. Sahak Part'ew and St. Cyril of Alexandria are close derivatives of Armenian-Basil. The Armenian anaphora ascribed to St. Gregory Nazianzus (the Theologian) is addressed to the Son. Other anaphoras translated by the Armenians include the Byzantine recension of Basil's anaphora, and the anaphoras of St. John Chrysostom, St. James, St. Ignatius of Antioch (a Syriac anaphora), and the Roman Canon.

The early eighth-century commentary on the Daily Office by Bishop Step'anos of Siwnik' (†c. 735) depicts the outline of the present Armenian Liturgy of the Word, before successive waves of Byzantine influence. The Synaxis opened with Ps 93, evidently accompanying an introit procession. This was followed by a procession with the gospel book while the people sang the Trisagion. A litany precedes Scripture readings from the Old and New Testaments. Unlike the Byzantine Liturgy, where the Old Testament lesson was supplanted very early by new developments in the structure of the Enarxis, in the Armenian Liturgy a lesson from the Old Testament is always read during the Armenian Liturgy of the Word. Scripture readings are followed by the recitation of the Nicene Creed, recited by the people in the plural form, ''We believe in one God . . .'' Only the Armenian and Roman liturgies recite the Creed immediately following the Gospel, though the Armenian usage predates the Roman by three centuries at least.

To this skeleton, several Byzantine elements were added later, including the three antiphons and their prayers (only remnants of which remain today), and some other prayers. It seems that the Synaxis maintained a degree of autonomy in Armenia, conducted apart from the Eucharist in certain circumstances. This is probably yet another remnant of the liturgical life of early Jerusalem, where the Liturgy of the Word and the Eucharist sometimes took place at different shrines in the city, the faithful processing from one stational church to the next.

As a result of contact with the Crusaders, the Armenians prefaced the Synaxis with an introduction comprising a new entrance procession of the priest and ministers, the confession and absolution of the celebrant using Armenian renderings of the *Confiteor* and the *Misereatur*, and the celebrant's ascent of the altar accompanied by Psalm 43, as found in the Dominican and other western rites.

Likewise, a new conclusion was appended to the liturgy including the reading of the Prologue of the Gospel according to John. It is noteworthy that the Dominicans, too, concluded the Mass with the Prologue of John. The new introduction and conclusion of the Divine Liturgy very gradually took hold in Armenia, but did not become universal for centuries thereafter. As late as the middle of the seventeenth century, some manuscript euchologies still did not contain the innovations.

The two most important commentaries on the Armenian Divine Liturgy are by Xosrov Anjewac'i (†c. 963), who scrupulously interprets the prayers phrase by phrase. In so doing, he provides our earliest extant text of the anaphora of St. Athanasius. The commentary of Nersēs Lampronac'i (†1198) is unabashedly allegorical but invaluable in its attention to the details of the ritual.

Since at least the sixth century, the Armenians use unleavened bread and pure wine (without the addition of water) for the Eucharist. These distinctive usages provoked centuries of hostility by the Greeks and Latins, who time and again set the abrogation of these usages as the condition for ecumenical relations. Only the Armenians and Latins use unleavened bread for the Eucharist. Yet an historical connection cannot be made because unleavened bread came into widespread use in the West only in the eleventh century. By contrast, the earliest probable reference to the use of unleavened bread in the Armenian Eucharist dates to the late sixth century. While the origins of the usage are unknown, there is no evidence that the Armenians ever used leavened bread in the Eucharist. Nor is there any evidence that they ever mixed water in the chalice. The age-old Christian custom of consecrating a mixed chalice at the Eucharist originally had no theological pretensions. From time immemorial

it was customary in many areas to cut table wine with water, a domestic custom that inevitably found its way into the liturgy, and in time inspired various theological interpretations.

Daily Office. The Armenian Book of Hours [*Žamagirk'*] contains The Office of the Night [*Gišerayin žam*], Morning [*Arawōtean žam*], Sunrise [*Arewagali žam*], the Third, Sixth, and Ninth, so-called "Little Hours"; the Evening [*Erekoyan žam*], and two compline offices: Peace [*Xałałakan žam*], and Rest [*Hangstean žam*]. Apart from the gradual accretion of variable diaconal proclamations and prayers, and the proliferation of ecclesiastical poetry, the basic shape of the daily offices has changed little since the 7th and 8th centuries, when Armenian theologians began to compose allegorical commentaries on them. Catholicos Nersēs IV of Glayec'i (†1173), called Šnorhali ("the Grace-filled"), greatly enriched the Night, Morning, Sunrise and Peace offices by adding hymns that are as elegant poetically and musically as they are profound theologically.

The Armenian hours are predominantly cathedral in character, featuring fixed psalms appropriate for the hour of the day, effusive hymnody, processions and other rituals. The prominent exception is the Night Hour, which, after an invitatory of fixed psalms (3, 87, 102, 142), features the recitation of the psalms in numerical order, an ancient trait of monastic worship. The Armenians divide Psalms 1–148 into eight "canons," one of which is sung each night. Each canon is associated with an Old Testament canticle.

Monasteries in Armenia, Jerusalem, and Lebanon conduct the daily cursus in full, although the Night Office is often delayed until early morning and conducted together with Matins. Many parish churches in Armenia conduct Matins and Vespers every day, with the Sunrise Office and compline offices used primarily in Lent. This is also the practice in Armenian parishes in the Middle East, Europe, and America. Given that most people in the diaspora live quite a distance from an Armenian Church, liturgical services there tend to be concentrated on Saturdays and Sundays.

Sacraments. The limitation of the number of sacraments [*Xorhurt'*] to seven is a late development in Armenia, under Latin influence. As late as the mid-tenth century, the Armenian liturgical commentator Xosrov Anjewac'i could still consider funerals, erecting an altar, and blessing church vessels on the same level as baptism, ordination, and marriage.

Baptism. Armenian initiation rites are characterized by their ancient structure and theology. The ritual envisions baptism as a rebirth "of water and the Spirit" (Jn

3:5) to become the sons and daughters of God, and as an imitation of Christ's baptism in the Jordan. The Pauline theology of dying and rising with Christ in baptism (Rom 6) is marginal, as is its apotropaic aspect. The Armenians no longer have a pre-baptismal anointing. Baptism is by triple immersion in the name of the Holy Trinity. The newly baptized are then sealed on nine parts of the body with holy chrism and then led to the altar where they will worship and receive holy communion for the first time.

Ordination. Armenian ordination rites diverge sharply from those of any other eastern church. In 1185, the Armenian bishop Nersēs Lampronac'i (†1198) translated the new *Pontificale romanum seculi XII*, incorporating its Franco-germanic ordination rites into the ancient Armenian ceremony. The result is an elaborate ritual (*Jernadrut'iwn*) comprising the quadruple repetition of the ancient ordination hymn, "The divine and heavenly grace," the laying on of hands, anointing of the forehead and hands, and the *traditio instrumentorum*. Immediately following ordination, the new priest spends forty days in seclusion and spiritual preparation. Only then does he celebrate his first Divine Liturgy.

The Armenian rite of episcopal ordination blends Byzantine, Latin, and indigenous Armenian elements. There is also an elaborate ceremony of enthroning and anointing a Catholicos.

To the minor and major orders are added the ten monastic orders of *Vardapet*, or teacher, unique to the Armenian Church.

Reconciliation. Like all eastern churches, the Armenians consider reconciliation to be a continual process not limited to confession and absolution. The Daily Office incorporates specific penitential prayers and hymns, most notably Ps 51, the penitential prayer *par excellence*. The Armenian Church has two ancient offices of public reconciliation. The first is a one-time reconciliation following a grave sin, and is modeled after baptism. The other is an elaborate synaxis of psalmody, lections, and prayers on Holy Thursday to reconcile sinners to God before Easter. This office includes the splendid deuterocanonical Prayer of King Manasseh, to which the Armenians added a christological appendix, proclamation, and priestly prayer of reconciliation.

In the late middle ages, Armenian penitential practice came increasingly under Latin scholastic influence. Today a brief office of public confession and absolution hailing from this late period has become widespread in parish churches. Private confession is also practiced.

Matrimony. Following Eastern practice, Armenians refer to the sacrament of marriage as "Blessing of the Crown" [*Psak ōrhnel*]. The ceremony originally took place during the Eucharistic Liturgy of the Word. The crowning of the bride and groom is accompanied by a long benediction which, like the Old Testament lections appointed for the ceremony, recalls the blessed unions of the patriarchs and their wives. In recent times, the exchange of vows and rings has been added to the ceremony, as well as the sharing of a cup of wine, a symbol of bounty.

Anointing of the Sick. Since ancient times the Armenians have anointed the sick with oil blessed by the priest. At various times, the Armenians translated and used both the elaborate Greek ritual, as well as a Latin form. In addition, they composed prayers of their own. In current usage, the anointing has fallen out of use, having given way to the prayer alone.

Liturgical Year and Sanctoral. The liturgical year of the Armenian Liturgy is characterized by the mobility of its feasts, by the emphasis on Sunday, and by the celebration of Christmas on January 6. The liturgical year revolves around the two principal Christian feasts of Theophany [*Asduacyaytnut'iwn*] and Pascha [*Zatik*].

The Armenian calendar preserves the shape of the liturgical year as presented in the fifth-century lectionary of Jerusalem. After the Bible, this document was among the first writings to be translated into Armenian from Greek by St. Mesrop Maštoc' (†439) and his school, shortly after the invention of the Armenian alphabet.

The Armenians celebrate Christ's nativity and his baptism together on January 6. This is the original date of Christmas in the East, before it was transferred to December 25. The Presentation of the Lord to the Temple is celebrated forty days later, on February 14, and the Annunciation to Mary is nine months before Christmas, on April 7. The Armenian calendar has only three other fixed feasts, all pertaining to the Mother of God: her birth (September 8), her Presentation to the Temple (November 21) and her Conception to Joachim and Anna (December 9).

All other feasts and saints' commemorations are moveable and depend upon the day of the week. Major feast days must be celebrated on Sunday, the *dies dominica*. The Assumption of the Mother of God (*Verap'oxum*) and the Exaltation of the Holy Cross (*Xač'verac'*) are celebrated on the Sundays falling closest to August 15 and September 14 respectively. Wednesdays and Fridays are days of abstinence, and have a penitential theme (unless one of the six fixed feasts above falls on them). Saints' commemorations are celebrated exclusively on Mondays, Tuesdays, Thursdays, and Saturdays, the latter reserved for the most important saints. Accordingly, saints' days are not attached to a particular date, but are defined in relation to the closest major feast and a day of the week. For example, the feast of St. Constantine the Emperor and his mother, Helena, is always celebrated on Tuesday of the fourth week after Pentecost, the precise date changing from year to year. Every feast day of the liturgical year except for the six fixed feasts is determined in this way, making the Armenian liturgical year highly variable from year to year.

The Armenians calculate Easter according to the Nicene definition. The Gregorian calendar was adopted in 1923 for civil and liturgical use, making the Armenian Church one of the few eastern churches to celebrate Easter on the same date as the Catholic and Protestant world. Only the Armenian Patriarchate of Jerusalem follows the Julian calendar because of the *status quo* of the Holy Places.

Lent begins on the seventh Monday before Easter. It is preceded by a one-week Anterior Fast (*Arajaworac' pahk'*) beginning on the third Monday before Lent.

Advent (*Yisnak*) begins on the day after the Sunday nearest November 18. It lasts between six and seven weeks, depending each year on the duration of the period between Assumption (Sunday closest to August 15) and Theophany (January 6).

The Armenians celebrate four feasts of the Cross: Exaltation (Sunday nearest September 14); Apparition (commemorates the appearance of the cross in the sky over Jerusalem on May 7, 351; celebrated on the Sunday closest to May 7); Discovery of the Cross (seventh Sunday after Exaltation); and the Apparition of the Cross on Mount Varak, commemorating the miraculous 7th-century discovery of a fragment of Christ's cross in Armenia (third Sunday after Exaltation).

Bibliography: (a) **Armenian Liturgy in General.** M. D. FINDIKYAN, "L'Influence latine sur la liturgie arménienne," in *Roma-Armenia*, CLAUDE MUTAFIAN, ed. (Rome, 1999) 340–344. K. MAKSOUDIAN, "The Religion of Armenia," in *Treasures in Heaven: Armenian Illuminated Manuscripts*, T. F. MATHEWS and R. S. WIECK, eds. (New York, 1994) 24–37. M. ORMANIAN, *The Church of Armenia: Her History, Rule, Discipline, Literature and Existing Condition* (London, 1955). C. RENOUX, "Liturgie arménienne et liturgie hiérosolymitaine," in *Liturgie de l'église particulière, liturgie de l'église universelle* (Bibliotheca Ephemerides Liturgicae Subsidia 7) (Rome, 1976) 275–288. R. TAFT, "The Armenian Liturgy: Its Origins and Characteristics," in *Treasures in Heaven: Armenian Art, Religion, and Society*, Papers delivered at the Pierpont Morgan Library at a Symposium Organized by T. F. MATHEWS and R. S. WIECK, May 21–22, 1994 (New York, 1998) 13–30. (b) **Divine Liturgy.** S. P. COWE, ed. *Commentary on the Divine Liturgy by Xosrov AnjewaÉi* (New York, 1991). *Divine Liturgy of the Armenian Apostolic Orthodox Church with Variables, Complete Rubrics and Commentary*, T. NERSOYAN, trans., rev. 5th ed. (London, 1984). M. FINDIKYAN, "Bishop Step'anos Siwnec'i: A Source for the Study of Medieval Armenian Liturgy," OKS 44/2–3 (1995) 171–196. C. RENOUX, "L'Anaphore arménienne de Saint Grégoire l'Illuminateur," in *Lex Orandi* 47 (Paris, 1970) 83–108. R. TAFT, "The Armenian 'Holy Sacrifice' (*Surp Patarag*) as a Mirror of Armenian Liturgical History," in *The Armenian Christian Tradition: Scholarly Symposium in Honor of the Visit to the Pontifical Oriental Institute, Rome of His Holiness Karekin I Supreme Patriarch and Catholicos of All Armenians, December 12, 1996*, ed. R. F. TAFT, S.J. (OCA 254) (Rome, 1997) 176–197. (c) **Daily Office.** *The Book of Hours or the Order of Common Prayers of the Armenian Apostolic Orthodox Church: Matins, Prime, Vespers and Occasional Offices* (Evanston, Ill., 1964). *Breviarium Armenium sive dispositio communium Armeniacae Ecclesiae* (Venice, 1908). M. D. FINDIKYAN, "On the Origins and Early Evolution of the Armenian Office of Sunrise" in *Crossroad of Cultures: Studies in Liturgy and Patristics in Honor of Gabriele Winkler*, H-J FEULNER, E. VELKOVSKA, R. F. TAFT, S.J., eds. (OCA 260) (Rome, 2000) 283–314. T. NERSOYAN, "The Structure of the Canonical Hours of the Armenian Church," in Idem, *Armenian Church Historical Studies: Matters of Doctrine and Administration*, V. N. NERSESSIAN, ed. (New York, 1996) 315–325. R. TAFT, *The Liturgy of the Hours in East and West: The Origins of the Divine Office and Its Meaning for Today* (Collegeville, Minn., 1985) 219–224. G. WINKLER, "The Armenian Night Office II: The Unit of Psalmody, Canticles, and Hymns with Particular Emphasis on the Origins and Early Evolution of Armenia's Hymnography," REArm 17 (1983) 471–551. G. WINKLER, "Über die Kathedralvesper in den verschiedenen Riten des Ostens und Westens," *Archiv für Liturgiewissenschaft* 16 (1974) 53–102. (d) **Sacraments.** F. C. CONYBEARE, *Rituale Armenorum: Being the Administration of the Sacraments and the Breviary Rites of the Armenian Church together with the Greek Rites of Baptism and Epiphany [and the East Syrian Rites]* (Oxford, 1905). C. GUGEROTTI, "Valori etnici e scambi interculturali nella liturgia armena delle ordinazioni," in *The Armenian Christian Tradition: Scholarly Symposium in Honor of the Visit to the Pontifical Oriental Institute, Rome of His Holiness Karekin I Supreme Patriarch and Catholicos of All Armenians, December 12, 1996*, ed. R. F. TAFT, S.J. (Rome, 1997) 57–69. G. KOCHAKIAN, *The Sacraments: The Symbols of Our Faith* (New York, 1983). A. RAES, "Les rites de la Pénitence chez les arméniens," OCP 13 (1947) 648–655. C. RENOUX, "Le Mariage arménien dans les plus anciens rituels," in *Le Mariage*, Conférences Saint-Serge LXe Semaine d'Etudes Liturgiques (Rome, 1994) 289–305. C. RENOUX, *Initiation chrétienne I: Rituels arméniens du baptême. Traduit, introduit et annoté* (Paris, 1997). G. WINKLER, *Das armenische Initiationsrituale: Entwicklungsgeschichtliche und liturgie-vergleichende Untersuchung der Quellen des 3. bis 10. Jahrhunderts* (OCA 217) (Rome, 1982). (e) **Liturgical Year.** K. BARSAMIAN, *The Calendar of the Armenian Church* (New York, 1995). C. RENOUX, *Le codex arménien Jérusalem 121. Édition comparée du texte et de deux autres manuscrits. Introduction, textes, traduction et notes*, 2 vols. Patrologia orientalis 35/1 (1969), *Patrologia orientalis* 36/2 (1970). C. RENOUX, "Les Fêtes et les Saints de l'Église arménienne de N. Adontz," REArm 14 (1980) 287–305; 15 (1981) 103–114. C. RENOUX, "L'Epiphanie à Jérusalem au IVe et au Ve siècle d'après le Lectionnaire arménien de Jérusalem," REArm 2 (1965) 343–359. C. RENOUX, "Liturgie de Jéusalem et lectionnaires arméniens. Vigiles et anée liturgique" in Cassien-Botte, *La prière des heures* (Lex orandi 38) (Paris, 1963) 167–200.

[M. D. FINDIKYAN]

ARMENIANS, DECREE FOR

The decree *Exsultate Deo,* published in the Council of Florence on Nov. 22, 1439, by Pope Eugene IV, in an attempt to bring about the union of the Armenian Church with the See of Rome. The decree constitutes a compendium of Christian doctrine concerning especially the unity of the divine essence and the Trinity of Divine Persons, the humanity of Christ, and the nature of the seven Sacraments. It contains the Constantinople Creed, the definitions made at the Council of Chalcedon about the two natures in Christ and at Constantinople III about the two wills and operations of Christ, a decree about accepting the authority of Chalcedon and the Letter of Pope Leo I, an instruction concerning the Sacraments, the Athanasian Creed, the decree of union with the Greeks, and a decree about the common celebration of certain feasts.

It is best known for the lengthy instruction on the Sacraments that constitutes its fifth section, taken almost verbatim from the opusculum of St. Thomas Aquinas entitled *De articulis fidei et ecclesiae sacramentis*. This instruction enumerates the seven Sacraments and indicates how they differ from the sacraments of the Old Law. The distinction between Sacraments for the individual and social Sacraments is made, and the essential elements of matter, form, and intention in the Sacraments are treated. Mention is made of the indelible character of the Sacraments of Baptism, Confirmation, and Orders. Each Sacrament is then taken up in particular, with a consideration of its form, matter, and minister.

Bibliography: J. GILL, *The Council of Florence* (Cambridge, England 1959). N. VALOIS, *Le Pape et le concile, 1418–1450*, 2 v. (Paris 1909). A. BALGY, *Historia doctrinae Catholicae inter Armenos unionisque eorum cum Ecclesia Romana in Concilio Florentino* (Vienna 1878). Z. OBERTYNSKI, . . . *Die Florentiner union der polnischen Armenier und ihr bischofskatalog* (Rome 1934). L. S. KOGIAN, *Hayots' ekeghets'in mindzeio P'lorentian zhoghoue* [=L'Église Armenienne, jusqu'au concile de Florence] (Beirut 1961).

[W. F. HOGAN/EDS.]

ARMENTIA, NICOLÁS

Franciscan missionary, explorer, and bishop; b. in a small town in the Spanish Basque country, 1845; d. La Paz, Bolivia, November, 1909. He entered the Franciscan Order while still a boy and was sent to La Recoleta in La Paz where he was ordained. Between 1870 and 1883 he worked in the missions of Covendo, Ixiamas, and Tumupasa, on the western shore of the Beni River. In addition to serving the neophytes there, he made many expeditions through the neighboring jungles in search of aborigines to attract to the missions. He explored unknown regions, with the idea of converting new groups of the forest tribes and founding new missions.

During 1884 and 1885 he made an expedition down the Beni River to the Madre de Dios River, at the behest of the Bolivian government. He toured the hinterland of both rivers extensively, establishing relations with the Araona and Toromona tribes, among which he founded a mission. The following year he entered those regions again and reached the Purus River and later the Amazon. As a result of these and other travels he wrote several books, among which were *Exploración del Madre de Dios, Diario de viaje a las tribus comprendidas entre el río Beni y el arroyo Ibon, Límite de Bolivia con el Perú por la parte de Caupolicán*, and *Navegación del Madre de Dios*. The last-mentioned work contains valuable information for ethnography and observations of the flora and fauna of the area that reveal the soundness of his knowledge of zoology and botany. He wrote also a grammar and vocabulary of the Chipibo language spoken by a jungle tribe of the High Beni. He translated and published the curious work of the Jesuit Father Eder, *Descripción de los Moxos*.

He was consecrated Bishop of La Paz in Sucre early in 1902. As prelate he was distinguished by his dedication in instructing the native population, his careful attention to religious services, and, principally, his reorganization of the seminary.

[H. SANABRIA FERNÁNDEZ]

ARMINIANISM

A system of belief that takes its name from ARMINIUS (Jacobus Hermandszoon). During the 16th century much theological discussion centered in Holland. In their efforts toward attaining national independence, the people of Holland had been attracted to CALVINISM. Although they eventually accepted it as their national religion, in those early days many expressed dissatisfaction with rigid Calvinist principles, especially the teaching that God had predestined some to be saved and others to be lost even before the Fall (SUPRALAPSARIANS). These held the milder doctrine that while God foresaw the Fall, the formal decree was not made until after Adam's transgression (INFRALAPSARIANS). Some professors at Leyden University who were opposed to strict Calvinism sought for tolerance of all religions, believing that persuasion, not persecution, should be the policy; they met with strong opposition. It was in such an atmosphere that Arminius made his studies. After he began his ministry he defended the strict Calvinist doctrine, but was later repelled by its harshness, and participated in a number of discussions that resulted in the formulation of his own doctrine. Appointed at Leyden, he found himself involved in controversy, especially with a fellow professor, Franciscus GOMARUS, who upheld the rigid Calvinist principles of absolute predestination with strong feelings and bitter antipathy toward his adversaries.

As a religious system, the teaching of Arminius was stated in the Remonstrance of 1610. The major points of departure from stricter Calvinism were contained there: (1) atonement was intended for all men, (2) man needs grace, yet is able to resist it and can even lose it. This denial of absolute predestination and admission of the concurrence of free will and grace were strongly condemned by Gomarus, who feared that such a view would undermine the Protestant teaching on salvation. Dutch Protestants were divided; the general populace inclined toward Gomarus, while many of the learned and a number of high public officials favored Arminius. The discussions became so heated that there was fear of a civil war in some of the Dutch provinces. The professors debated even before the States General in 1608 and 1609. Though Arminius seemingly won the arguments and appeared in a favorable light to those who followed the discussions, Gomarus gave the impression that Arminian doctrines would disrupt the national unity that was being accomplished through strict Calvinist belief. Maurice of Orange, impressed with Gomarus's argument, and believing that the Arminians favored the pro-Spanish party in politics, attacked the group. After their condemnation at the Synod of Dort (1618–19), they were persecuted and banished by the prince. Arminianism was tolerated in Holland after the death of its founder, but it was not until 1795 that it was able to gain official recognition (*see* CONFESSIONS OF FAITH).

The Arminians are one of the smaller religious sects in Holland. Yet their teachings have been taken over by some Methodists, by many individuals who belong to churches that are Calvinist in name, by some Baptists, and by members of other religions.

Bibliography: G. O. MCCULLOH, ed., *Man's Faith and Freedom* (New York 1962), contains addresses of the Arminius symposium held in Holland 1960. R. L. COLIE, *Light and Enlightenment: A Study of the Cambridge Platonists and the Dutch Arminians* (Cambridge, Eng. 1957). F. A. CHRISTIE, "The Beginnings of Arminianism in New England," *American Society of Church History. Papers,* Ser. 2, v.3 (1912) 151–172. W. F. DANKBAAR, *Die Religion in Geschichte und Gegenwart.* 1:620–622. Y. CONGAR, *Catholicisme* 1:845.

[L. F. RUSKOWSKI]

ARMINIUS, JACOBUS

Called also Jakob Hermandszoon, Dutch Reformed theologian; b. Oudewater, South Holland, Oct. 10, 1560; d. Leiden, Oct. 19, 1609. Aided by friends, Arminius, after his father's death, studied at Utrecht and at Marburg (only briefly, since he was called home when most of his family was slain during the Spanish siege of Oudewater); he later attended the University of Leiden to study theolo-

Jacobus Arminius.

gy (1576–82). He went to Geneva, at that time under Theodore Beza, where he studied for three years (interrupted by a brief stay in Basel); he then went to the University of Padua, made a short visit to Rome, and spent a few more months in Geneva. In 1587 he was called to Amsterdam and in the following year became a minister. For 15 years he served as a kind and devoted pastor, showing his love for his people especially at the time that the plague struck so devastatingly (1602). He was a gifted preacher who possessed a thorough knowledge of the Scriptures. A few years after his arrival in Amsterdam he married and became the father of nine children. In 1603 he was invited to become professor of theology at the University of Leiden, where he remained until his death. By nature a peace-loving man, Arminius nevertheless became involved in many disputes over the Calvinist teaching of unconditional predestination, since his studies in St. Paul's Epistle to the Romans had led him to doubt so harsh a doctrine and inspired him to promote the milder form of a conditional predestination. The disputes continued until the time of his death.

Bibliography: *Opera theologica* (Leiden 1629); Eng. ed. and tr. J. NICHOLS, 3 v. (London 1825–75). C. BRANDT, *The Life of James Arminius,* tr. J. GUTHRIE (Glasgow 1854). N. BANGS, *Life of James Arminius,* ed. J. NICHOLS (New York 1843). J. H. MARONIER, *Jacobus Arminius* (Amsterdam 1905). A. H. W. HARRISON, *The Beginnings of Arminianism to the Synod of Dort* (London 1926);

Arminianism (London 1937). W. F. DANKBAAR, *Die Religion in Geschichte und Gegenwart* [3] 1:622.

[L. F. RUSKOWSKI]

ARNÁIZ BARÓN, RAFAEL, BL.

Trappist Oblate mystic; b. Burgos, Spain, April 9, 1911; d. San Isidro de Dueños, Palencia, Spain, April 26, 1938. Rafael Arnáiz, the eldest of four children in a socially prominent family, was educated by the JESUITS, then studied architecture in Madrid. Following the completion of his military service, he joined the TRAPPISTS at San Isidro de Dueños in Palencia (1933). Almost immediately *diabetes mellitus* forced him to return home. When he was better, Rafael returned to San Isidro, but was never able to become a monk because of his health. Another attack brought about his death at age twenty-seven. He is remembered both for his continual search for unity with God and for his spiritual writings, which attracted pilgrims to his grave at San Isidro. He was beatified by John Paul II, Sept. 27, 1992.

Bibliography: R. ARNÁIZ BARÓN, *Vida y escritos de Fray María Rafael Arnáiz Barón*, ed. M. BARÓN, 10th ed. (Madrid 1974). J. ALVAREZ, *Rafael* (Burgos 1952). A. COBOS SOTO, *La "pintura mensaje" del hermano Rafael: estudio crítico de la obra pictórica del venerable Rafael Arnáiz Barón, "monje trapense"* (Burgos 1989). L. MAQUEDA, *Un secreto de la Trapa,* 2d. ed. (Burgos 1993).

[K. I. RABENSTEIN]

ARNALDUS AMALRICI

Called also Arnaud-Amaury, archbishop of Narbonne; b. southern France, *c.* 1160; d. Cistercian abbey of Fontfroide, Sept. 26, 1225. He was from Languedoc nobility, and his cousin was vice count of Narbonne; he was buried at Cîteaux. He entered the monastery of Cîteaux, became abbot of Poblet, in Catalonia (*Gallia Christiana* 6:61); and, in 1199, of Grandselve, in Languedoc. Finally, in 1201 at Cîteaux, he was elected abbot general of the order, which, since the days of St. Bernard, had been involved in the intellectual controversy with the ALBIGENSES. Toward the end of 1203, Pope Innocent III appointed the Fontfroide monks Raoul and PETER OF CASTELNAU as missionaries and papal legates for Languedoc, which was threatened by heresy. On May 31, 1204, Arnaldus was commissioned to join them (A. Potthast, *Bibliotheca historica medii aevi* n.2229), but he could not begin his mission until March 1207, after the general chapter of 1206 at Cîteaux, in which his order gave the enterprise its strong support. The failure of their efforts because of the opposition of the southern clergy and the nobility, led by Raymond VI of Toulouse, culmi-

nated in the murder of Peter of Castelnau on Jan. 14, 1208, for which Raymond was believed to have been responsible. With a papal commission, Arnaldus began a crusade against the Albigenses, mustering an army at Lyons in June 1209; they captured Béziers on July 22 and perpetrated a bloody massacre. It was there that Arnaldus is said to have uttered the infamous words: "Kill them all. God knows his children." The authenticity of this statement is questionable; none of the chroniclers (e.g., Pierre de Vaux-Cernay) or accounts (*Chanson de la Croisade*) mention it, although they did not shrink from horrors (e.g., they report a genuine statement of Arnaldus, encouraging the crusaders with: "Do not worry. I believe very few will be converted."). Pope Innocent tried to change the course of events by reprimanding his legate and by negotiating personally with Raymond VI in 1209; but ultimately (1211) Innocent excommunicated Raymond. On March 12, 1212, Arnaldus replaced Archbishop Berenger II of Narbonne (who either resigned or was deposed); but then, because he also ruled the duchy of Narbonne, Arnaldus came into conflict with SIMON DE MONTFORT l'Amaury, who claimed Narbonne on March 21, 1215. Against Simon's bid for power Arnaldus defended even his former enemy Raymond VI at the Lateran Council of 1215 and excommunicated Montfort in 1216. As papal legate, Arnaldus had led the French troops into the battle of Navas de Tolosa, in which the three united Spanish kings defeated the Moors (July 16, 1212). He succeeded in separating Raymond VII and his knights from the Albigenses at the Synod of Montpellier (Aug. 25, 1224); nevertheless, under pressure by the French king, the agreements resulting from the negotiations were rejected by Honorius III.

Bibliography: PETRUS DE VAULX-CERNAY, *Hystoria Albigensis*, ed. P. GUÉBIN and E. LYON, 3 v. (Paris 1926–39). Literature. A. LUCHAIRE, *Innocent III: La Croisade des Albigeois* (3d ed. Paris 1911). C. J. VON HEFELE, *Histoire des conciles d'après les documents originaux* (Paris 1907–38) 5.2:1260–1303. P. BELPERRON, *La Croisade contre les Albigeois* (Paris 1942). A. BORST, *Die Katharer* (Stuttgart 1953). F. NIEL, *Albigeois et Cathares* (Paris 1956). A. SABARTHÈS, *Dictionnaire d'histoire et de géographie ecclésiastiques,* ed. A. BAUDRILLART et al. (Paris 1912) 4:420. A. POSCH, *Lexikon für Theologie und Kirche,* ed. J. HOFER and K. RAHNER (Freiburg 1957–65) 1:888.

[H. WOLFRAM]

ARNAULD

The name of a family whose many members were involved in the French Jansenist movement. The Arnaulds came of middle-class stock from Herment in Auvergne. Their rise to political power began with *Henri Arnauld* (1485–1564), who served Pierre de Bourbon and his nephew the constable, who owed much, possibly his life,

Mother Catherine Agnès Arnauld (Mother Agnès de Saint-Paul) and Sister Catherine of St. Susan (daughter of the artist), votive painting by Philippe de Champaigne, 1662, painted upon his daughter's recovery from illness.

to Henri's loyalty. This connection assisted the brilliant career of his son, *Antoine de la Mothe-Arnauld* (?–1585), who moved to Paris, where he reached high legal office at the Parlement and was ennobled in 1577. A Huguenot, he had converted back to Catholicism after the ST. BARTHOLOMEW DAY MASSACRE (1572). Several of his children and their families remained Protestants. His son, *Antoine II* (1560–1619), surpassed his father's reputation at the bar, while leaving his descendants the so-called "original sin of the Arnaulds." This was the *Plaidoyer pour l'Université de Paris contre les jesuites* (Paris 1594–95), which started the quarrel with the Jesuits that Jansenist theologians, particularly his own children, continued with untiring relish. Antoine is remembered chiefly as the father of almost all the first leaders of the French Jansenist party. Ten of the twenty children whom he had by Catherine Marion, his wife, reached maturity. The six girls entered the Cistercian convent of PORT-ROYAL. Jacqueline (Mother Angélique) and Jeanne Catherine Agnès (Mother Agnès) were most prominent in making Port-Royal the center of French Jansenism. Their eldest sister, *Catherine* (1590–1651), as the wife of Antoine Le Maistre before entering Port-Royal, bore two famous Jansenist theologians, Antoine Le Maistre and Le Maistre de

Saci (*see* LE MAISTRE). The three other sisters were *Anne de Sainte Eugénie de l'Incarnation* (1594–1653), *Madeleine de Sainte-Christine* (1607–49), and *Marie de Sainte-Claire* (1600–42), who for a short time threatened to upset the peace of Port-Royal by heading an opposition to Jean Duvergier de Hauranne, Abbé Saint Cyran. The sons, apart from *Simon* (1603–39), a lieutenant in the French army, were distinguished in the story of JANSENISM: Antoine, the "Great Arnauld," became the chief theologian of the sect in France; Henri was Bishop of Angers; Robert Arnauld d'Andilly was the influential *solitaire.*

This distinguished legal family continued to produce several lawyers during the 17th century, and there is much to suggest that some of the theologians and ascetics in the family remained lawyers at heart. This is apparent particularly in the "Great Arnauld's" theological distinctions and argumentations. With their legalistic outlook the Arnaulds seemed to thrive on controversy. The Arnaulds' very prominence as theologians and spiritual leaders hurt the young Jansenist party by making it seem the possession of a family clique.

Jacqueline Marie Angélique. Mother Angélique, abbess and reformer of Port-Royal; b. Paris, Sept. 8,

1591; d. Port-Royal, Aug. 6, 1661. At the age of seven she was named coadjutrix with the right of succession to Jeanne Boulehart, Abbess of Port-Royal, and she assumed government of the convent at Jeanne's death in 1602. She shared the worldly life of her spiritual charges until converted by a Capuchin friar in 1608. Ruthless reforms followed, culminating in the famous "day of the grating," when her father and brothers were turned away from the convent cloister. Reform was carried to many other foundations, beginning with Maubuisson, where Mother Angélique spent five years from 1618. The following year Saint FRANCIS DE SALES influenced her so strongly that she tried impetuously, but unsuccessfully, to join his Visitation nuns. After she was replaced as abbess in 1630, she remained influential and was instrumental in introducing the abbot of Saint-Cyran as the convent's spiritual director from about 1636. In 1633, under the guidance of Sebastian Zamet, Bishop of Langres, she established the Institute of the Blessed Sacrament, whose orthodoxy was questioned because of the writings of Mother Agnès. As abbess from 1642 to 1655, Mother Angélique ensured the permanence of Saint-Cyran's work. Mother Angélique's spiritual teaching can be studied in papers that were written either by her or under her immediate inspiration. They include: *Mémoires pour servir à l'histoire de Port-Royal* . . . , 3 v. (Utrecht 1742–44); *Entretiens ou conférences de la Révérende Mère Angélique Arnauld* . . . , 3 v. (Utrecht 1757); *Mémoire et relations sur ce qui s'est passé à Port-Royal des Champs* . . . (Utrecht 1716); and *Lettres de la Rév. Mère Marie-Angélique*, 3 v. (Utrecht 1742).

Jeanne Catherine Agnès. Mother Agnès de Saint-Paul, Abbess of Port-Royal; b. Paris, Dec. 31, 1593; d. Port-Royal, Feb. 19, 1672. At the age of six she was nominated abbess of Saint-Cyr. In 1608 she joined her sister, Mother Angélique, at Port-Royal, where she gave valuable help in carrying out reforms. She was abbess of Tard at Dijon from 1630 to 1636, of Port-Royal from 1636 to 1642, and again at Port-Royal from 1658 to 1661. After refusing repeatedly to accept the "Formulary" of Alexander VII against Jansenism, she was banished to the Visitation Convent in 1664, but returned to Port-Royal the next year. Although Agnès lived in the shadow of her sister Angélique, her own deep spirituality greatly impressed contemporaries. Her manuscript work of 1627, *Le Chapelet secret du Saint Sacrement,* which was championed by Saint-Cyran in a lively debate, was her most important writing. It interjected into traditional Augustinianism what Jean Orcibal in *Les Origines* . . . described as "the negative theology of the mystics" (2.311). Many other of her spiritual writings, mainly in manuscript, are summarized in C. J. Goujet's *Mémoires* (3.241–250). Her *Lettres* (ed. A. P. Faugère, 2 v. Paris 1858) are a useful source for the history of Port-Royal.

Antoine. Called the "Great Arnauld"; b. Feb. 5, 1612; d. Brussels, Aug. 2, 1694. He came increasingly under the influence of his mother after his father's death (1619), and through her, of Saint-Cyran. After studying law, he entered the Sorbonne and in 1635 presented his Bachelor's theses on the doctrine of grace. Force of argument and lyrical eloquence, together with the fortuitous attendance of many bishops, gave it a brilliant success. This success, despite the fact that Arnauld's views were essentially those that Jansen developed five years later in his *AUGUSTINUS*, shows the prevalence of AUGUSTINIANISM among French theologians. That Jansenist ideas had already made headway before they were branded as heretical explains much of the bitterness and confusion of Jansenist controversy.

A new phase in Arnauld's life began in 1638 when he put himself completely under the spiritual direction of Saint-Cyran, who insisted on his ordination in 1641 and inspired him to write *De la Fréquente communion* (Paris 1643). This became probably the most influential of all the Jansenist writings. It established Arnauld after Saint-Cyran's death (1643) as the undisputed head of the Jansenist sect in France. While Jansen himself had written almost exclusively about predestination and grace, Arnauld elaborated the Jansenist position on the Sacraments, particularly Penance and the Eucharist, on the ecclesiastical hierarchy, and on papal infallibility. His defense of Jansenius's *Augustinus*, his resistance to papal condemnations lead to his expulsion from the faculty of theology (1656) and self exile in 1679, after a period of intense intellectual activity following the "Peace of the Church" (1669). Most of his writings are collected in *Oeuvres de Messire Antoine Arnauld* (43 tomes, ed. G. Dupac and J. Hautefage, 38 v. Lausanne 1775–83). These show that, although Arnauld's chief interest lay in theology, he wrote also important works on mathematics, science, and philosophy.

Henri. Bishop of Angers; b. Paris, October 1597; d. Angers, June 8, 1692. To please his father, Henri practiced at the bar until his parent's death in 1619. The Papal Nuncio Cardinal Guido Bentivoglio took Henri with him to Rome in 1621. Meanwhile, Louis XIII appointed Henri Abbot of Saint-Nicolas d'Angers in 1622; later, Henri was ordained in 1624. On his return from Rome in 1625, Henri would certainly have had a fine career but for Richelieu's implacable hostility toward the Arnauld family. For about 20 years Henri lived in retirement, following a life of prayer and austerity in the shadow of Port-Royal, while taking a leading part at the literary *salons* of the Hôtel Rambouillet. In 1645 Mazarin charged him with the delicate task of reconciling the Barberini, clients of France, with Clement X. His great skill as a diplomat emerged from his *Négotiations à la cour de Rome*

(1645–48; 5 v. Paris 1748). In 1649 he was rewarded for his services by nomination to the See of Angers. Henri was a devoted pastor, tireless in carrying out visitations and in raising standards among the clergy. His codified *Statuts de l'évêché d'Angers* (1680) became a model for the French episcopate. Henri's position made him one of the most prominent French Jansenists. He was among the 11 bishops to protest that the five propositions condemned by Innocent X in the bull CUM OCCASIONE (1653) were not in the works of Jansen. Together with bishops Caulet of Pamiers, Buzenval of Beauvais, and Pavillon of Alet, he refused for several years to accept the ''Formulary.'' Henri's Jansenist sympathies involved him in protracted disputes, particularly with the University of Angers. Nonetheless, this saint of the Jansenist calendar disliked controversy and, with age, cooled in his affections toward Jansenism.

Robert Arnauld d'Andilly. Celebrated *solitaire* of Port-Royal; b. Paris, 1588; d. Port-Royal, Sept. 17, 1674. Andilly married Catherine Le Fèvre de la Boderie (1613). Of his 15 children the most famous were: *Mother Angélique de Saint-Jean* (1624–84), Abbess of Port-Royal, and considered by Sainte-Beuve the most brilliant after Pascal of Port-Royal's second generation; and *Simon, Marquis de Pomponne* (1618–99), who was Secretary of State for Foreign Affairs to Louis XIV at the height of his power. Five others, *Catherine de Sainte-Agnès* (1615–43); *Marie Charlotte de Sainte-Claire* (1627–78); *Marie Angélique de Sainte-Thérèse* (1630–1700); *Anne Marie* (1631–60); and *Charles Henri* (1623–84), a *solitaire* under the name of M. de Luzancy, were associated with Port-Royal. Andilly's own political career under Gaston d'Orleans was ended by Richelieu's rise to power. Nonetheless, his likeable nature won him many influential friends, including the Queen Mother (Anne of Austria) and Mazarin. It appears that only his Jansenistic connections decided them against making him tutor to Louis XIV. In 1643, after much indecision, Andilly went into semiretirement at Port-Royal. In addition to tending the convent's gardens, he showed himself to be an industrious and talented writer. Besides his chief writings that appear in the three folio volumes of *Oeuvres diverses* . . . (Paris 1675) are several translations that include *The Confessions of Saint Augustine, The Lives of the Desert Fathers, The Meditations of Saint Teresa,* and *Josephus's History of the Jews.*

Bibliography: J. BRUCKER, *Dictionnaire de théologie catholique,* ed. A. VACANT et al., 15 v. (Paris 1903–50) 1.2:1978–83. J. OSWALD, *Lexikon für Theologie und Kirche,* ed. J. HOFER and K. RAHNER, 10 v. (2d, new ed. Freiburg 1957–65) 1:889–90. F. L. CROSS, *The Oxford Dictionary of the Christian Church* (London 1957) 88–89. R. P. DU PAGE, *Dictionnaire de biographie française* (Paris 1929–) 1:760–64. J. DEDIEU, *ibid.* 2:1061–71. J. BALTEAU et al., *ibid.* 3:849–97. L. PICHARD et al., G. GRENTE et al., *Dictionnaire des lettres françaises:* v.2, Le XVIIIᵉ siècle (Paris 1954–60) 2:64; 84–85; 98–103. A. VOGT et al., *Dictionnaire d'histoire et de géographie ecclésiastiques* ed. A. BAUDRILLART et al. (Paris 1912–) 4:444–500. J. ORCIBAL, *Les Origines du jansénisme,* 5 v. (Louvain 1947–62). P. J. VARIN, *La Vérité sur les Arnaulds,* 2 v. (Paris 1847). J. LAPORTE, *La Doctrine de Port-Royal,* 2 v. in 4 (Paris 1923–51). C. A. SAINTE-BEUVE, *Port-Royal,* ed. M. LEROY, 3 v. (Bibliothèque de la Pléiade 98, 99, 107; Paris 1952–55). A. DE MEYER, *Les Premières controverses Jansénistes en France, 1640–1649* (Louvain 1919). A. GAZIER, *Histoire générale du mouvement janséniste . . . ,* 2 v. (Paris 1922); *Jeanne de Chantal et Angélique Arnauld d'après leur correspondance, 1620–1641* (Paris 1915). C. P. GOUJET, ed., *Mémoires pour servir à l'histoire de Port–Royal,* 3 v. (n.p. 1734–37). J. PANNIER, . . . *La Mère Angélique* (Issy-les-Moulineaux 1930). L. COGNET, *La Mère Angélique et saint François de Sales, 1618–1626* (Paris 1951). P. BUGNION SECRETAN, *Mère Angélique Arnauld* (Paris 1991); *Mère Agnès Arnauld, 1593–1672. Abbesse de Port-Royal* (Paris 1996). A. SEGWICK, *The Travails of Conscience: The Arnauld Family and the Ancien Régime* (Cambridge, Mass. 1998). L. COGNET, *La Réforme de Port-Royal, 1591–1618* (Paris 1950). F. ELLEN WEAVER, *The Evolution of the Reform of Port-Royal* (Paris 1978). I. BONNOT, *Hérétique ou Saint? Henri Arnauld, évêque janséniste d'Angers au XVIIe siècle* (Paris 1984). E. JACQUES, *Les années d'exil d'A. Arnauld* (Louvain 1976). H. BOUCHILLOUX and A. MCKENNA, ed., *Antoine Arnauld (1612–1694): Philosophe, Écrivain, Théologien* (Paris 1995). L. DELAVAUD, *Le Marquis de Pomponne* (Paris 1911).

[J. Q. C. MACKRELL/J. M. GRES-GAYER]

ARNOBIUS THE ELDER

Fourth-century Christian apologist; d. *c.* 327. According to St. JEROME (*Chron.* ad ann. A.D. 253–327), Arnobius, a distinguished rhetorician at Sicca in proconsular Africa, who numbered Lactantius among his pupils (*De vir. ill.* 80), was a pagan who vigorously combated Christianity. Arnobius, however, was converted by dreams (*Chron. loc. cit.*), although he himself did not mention his motives. To prove his sincerity, he composed the *Adversus nationes* sometime before 311. More an attack on paganism than a defense of Christianity, the *Adversus nationes* is classed among the apologies on the strength of the first two of its seven books. In the fourth century only Jerome knew of it; by the sixth century it was grouped with the apocrypha. It is extant in only one ninth-century manuscript. The work was greatly influenced by non-Christian writers, although it gives evidence that Arnobius was familiar with Clement of Alexandria, Tertullian, and Minucius Felix. Arnobius made no use of the New Testament, and openly repudiated the Old (*Adv. nat.* 3.12). Though a poor source for Christian teaching, the work is useful for information about contemporary pagan religions. Book 1 defends Christianity against the calumnies of the pagans. Book 2 treats Christ's salvific acts, the final destiny of mankind, and the essence of Christianity. Books 3 to 5 attack the pagans, their deification of abstractions, and the mystery cults. Books 6 to 7 demonstrate that the pagans offend the divinity by their false cults and pagan sacrifices.

Bibliography: A. REIFFERSCHEID, ed., *Corpus scriptorum ecclesiasticorum latinorum* v.4 (1875). J. P. MIGNE, *Patrologia latina* 5:350–1372. O. BARDENHEWER, *Geschichte der Altkirchlichen Literatur* 2:517–525. P. MONCEAUX, *Histoire littéraire de l'Afrique chrétienne*, 7 v. (Paris 1901–23; repr. Brussels 1963) 2:135–197. E. RAPISARDA, *Arnobio* (Catania 1946). J. QUASTEN, *Patrology* 2:383–392. J. MARTIN, *Lexikon für Theologie und Kirche*, ed. J. HOFER and K. RAHNER (Freiburg 1957–65) 1:891–892.

[R. K. POETZEL]

ARNOBIUS THE YOUNGER

Fifth-century Christian writer; d. after 451. Arnobius was probably an African who lived as a monk in Rome. The list of his writings is equally uncertain, but modern critics, especially Dom G. Morin, have tried to establish them.

Arnobius wrote *Commentarii in Psalmos* (*Patrologia latina* 53:486–552), which contains brief and pointed, but uncritical comments on the Psalms as well as an attack on the Augustinian theory of predestination. He probably wrote also *Expositiunculae in Evangelium*, a poorly constructed commentary on the Gospels of Matthew, Luke, and John, and *Conflictus Arnobii catholici cum Serapione Aegyptio* (*Patrologia latina* 73:569–580), a dialogue attacking the Monophysites (*see* MONOPHYSITISM). Morin attributed two other works to him: *Liber ad Gregoriam*, a spiritual treatise addressed to an unhappily married woman, formerly attributed to JOHN CHRYSOSTOM; and *Praedestinatus* (*Patrologia latina* 73:587–672), a tract in three books that surveys the heresies listed in Augustine's *De haeresibus*, outlines the doctrine on grace and predestination wrongly attributed to Augustine, and refutes these latter doctrines.

In Morin's attribution of these works to Arnobius, one problem remains unexplained: how can the man who attacked Augustinian teachings in both *Commentarii* and *Praedestinatus* be also the author of *Conflictus*, which defends Augustine's writings on Pelagianism almost as if they were the writings of an Apostle. Arnobius is considered a semi-Pelagian who approached orthodoxy in *Commentarii* with his recognition of the evils that befell mankind as a result of original sin.

Bibliography: G. MORIN, *Anecdota maredsolana*, v.3.3 (Maredsous 1903) 129–151; *Études, textes, découvertes*, v.1 (Maredsous 1913) 383–439. P. DE LABRIOLLE, *Dictionnaire d'histoire et de géographie ecclésiastiques* 4:547–549. H. KEYSER, *Die Schriften des sogenannten Arnobius* (Gütersloh 1912). M. MONACHESI, *Bolletino del circolo universitario di studi storico–religiosi*, 1 (1921) 96, 2 (1922) 18. A. PINCHERLE, *Enciclopedia Italiana di scienze, littere ed arti* 4:551.

[R. K. POETZEL]

ARNOLD, GOTTFRIED

Evangelical mystic and Church historian; b. Annaberg, Saxony, Sept. 5, 1666; d. Perleberg, May 30, 1714. After absorbing PIETISM from Philipp SPENER in Dresden, he drifted toward radical spiritualism. In line with the teaching of Abbot Joachim of Floris and Sebastian Franck, his *Die erste Liebe* (1696) depicted the early Church as a golden period from which subsequent ages fell. His controversial, richly documented *Unpartheyischen Kirchen- und Ketzerhistorie* (1699), though announcing the principle of impartiality, virtually presented the heretics, especially the mystics, as the true Christians. In it Church and piety, dogma and experience are considered incompatible; Church history becomes the history of regenerate men. This subjective emphasis anticipated the idealistic principle that history is the education of mankind; it influenced the historiography of the Enlightenment (Johann Semler, Johann Lorenz von Mosheim), of Johann Gottfried von Herder, Johann Wolfgang von Goethe, Wilhelm Dilthey, and Walther Koehler. Subsequently moderating his religious views, he settled down as a pastor in Allstedt (1702) and Werben (1704), and as superintendent in Perleberg (1707). He was a prolific author of historical works, devotional treatises, and hymns; translator of Miguel de Molinos and Mme. Jeanne Guyon; and editor of Angelus Silesius.

Bibliography: *Gottfried Arnold*, ed. E. SEEBERG (Munich 1934), excerpts. E. SEEBERG, *G. Arnold, die Wissenschaft und die Mystik seiner Zeit* (Meerane, Germany 1923). W. NIGG, *Das Buch der Ketzer* (Zurich 1949). E. HIRSCH, *Geschichte der neuern evangelischen Theologie*, 5 v. (Gütersloh 1949–54; rep. 1960) v.2. B. HEURTEBIZE, *Dictionnaire de théologie catholique*, ed. A. VACANT, 15 v. (Paris 1903–50; Tables générales 1951–) 1.2:1987. M. SCHMIDT, *Die Religion in Geschichte und Gegenwart*, 7 v. (3rd ed. Tübingen 1957–65) 1:633–634. E. W. ZEEDEN, *Lexikon für Theologie und Kirche*, ed. J. HOFER and K. RAHNER, 10 v. (2d, new ed. Freiburg 1957–65) 1:896.

[R. H. FISCHER]

ARNOLD OF BONNEVAL (MARMOUTIER)

Abbot, writer, and friend and biographer of St. Bernard of Clairvaux; d. after 1156. Few facts about his life are available, but he is known by his writings and for the esteem in which he was held by St. Bernard. He was a monk of Marmoutier in 1138 and was made abbot of Bonneval in the Diocese of Chartres, probably c. 1144. Because of internal troubles in his monastery, he journeyed to Rome, where he received papal approval for his policies. He resigned his abbatial office sometime before 1156 and possibly died at Marmoutier. He was recognized for his learning and piety, and many important personages were numbered among his friends and correspondents. At the request of the monks of Clairvaux, he undertook the writing of the life of St. Bernard begun by WILLIAM OF SAINT-THIERRY. His writings include discourses on the gifts of the Holy Spirit, on the seven last words of Our Lord, a sermon in praise of Our Lady, a commentary on Psalm 132, and a variety of meditations and spiritual treatises.

Bibliography: A. PRÉVOST, *Dictionnaire d'histoire et de géographie ecclésiastiques,* ed. A. BAUDRILLART et al. (Paris 1912—) 4:421–423. P. POURRAT, *Catholicisme. Hier, aujourd'hui et demain,* ed. G. Jacquemet (Paris 1947—) 1:849.

[J. C. WILLKE]

ARNOLD OF BRESCIA

Radical Church reformer; b. Brescia, Italy, *c.* 1100; d. Rome, 1155. Arnold studied at Paris under PETER ABELARD and later joined the CANONS REGULAR OF ST. AUGUSTINE, becoming prior of the monastery in Brescia. There he advocated a radical reform of the Church, emphasizing the necessity of absolute clerical poverty and the abandonment of wealth and temporal power by the Church. In 1139, when his reform proposals were condemned by the second LATERAN COUNCIL, Arnold was banished from Italy. He took refuge in France and helped his former master, Abelard, defend himself at the Council of Sens in 1141. They were unsuccessful, for by a decree of July 16, 1141, INNOCENT II upheld the Council's condemnation of Arnold and Abelard and ordered them to be confined in separate monasteries. Soon after this, however, Arnold was teaching in the schools of Mont Sainte-Geneviève in Paris. When BERNARD OF CLAIRVAUX persuaded the French king to expel him from France, Arnold took refuge in Zurich and later in Bohemia. In 1145 he was reconciled with Pope EUGENE III, but the reconciliation was short-lived. Arnold soon broke with the pope and allied himself with a rebel political party in Rome that sought to abolish the pope's temporal power. Arnold was excommunicated once more on July 15, 1148. Pope ADRIAN IV continued the struggle against Arnold and his allies. In 1155 Arnold was finally expelled from Rome and fell into the hands of the Emperor FREDERICK I BARBAROSSA, who committed him to the prefect of Rome for trial as a rebel. The prefect condemned Arnold to be hanged, his body to be burned, and his ashes to be thrown into the Tiber. Arnold was executed in 1155.

The Arnoldist movement, which survived Arnold's death and which became overtly heretical, stressed apostolic poverty for the clergy, as did other heretical movements of the 12th century. The Arnoldists went further, however, and repudiated the power of the hierarchy entirely, denied the jurisdictional powers of the Church, and held as invalid the Sacraments administered by clerics possessed of any worldly goods. They were condemned by the Council of Verona in 1184.

Bibliography: OTTO OF FREISING, *The Deeds of Frederick Barbarossa,* ed. and tr. C. C. MIEROW and R. EMERY (New York 1953). JOHN OF SALISBURY, *Memoirs of the Papal Court,* ed. and tr. M. CHIBNALL (New York 1956). A. FRUGONI, *Arnaldo da Brescia nelle fonti del secolo XII.* (Rome 1954). A. FLICHE, *Catholicisme* 1: 849–850.

[J. A. BRUNDAGE]

ARNOLD OF HILTENSWEILER, BL.

Monastic founder; fl. first quarter of the 12th century. He was a layman who founded a convent at Langnau, near Bern. Few details of his life are known. He appears to have been a member of the First CRUSADE from 1099 to 1100 and is usually represented with a banner on which there is a cross inscribed. Although married, he was childless, and in 1122, by a grant confirmed by the Emperor HENRY V, he left all his property to the house of All Saints at Schaffhausen on the Rhine. The date of his death is unknown but was after 1127, when his name last appears in the records. He was buried in the oratory that he had founded at Hiltensweiler.

Feast: May 1.

Bibliography: W. MÜLLER, *Lexikon für Theologie und Kirche*[2] 1:893. P. VOLK, *Dictionnaire d'histoire et de géographic ecclésiastiques* 4:565. *Schriften des Vereins für Geschichte des Bodensees* 13 (1884) 133–148.

[J. L. GRASSI]

ARNOLDI, BARTHOLOMAEUS

Augustinian, Luther's teacher, later opponent; b. Usingen near Frankfort, 1465; d. Würzburg, Sept. 9, 1532. Arnoldi (commonly called Usingen) entered the University of Erfurt in 1484 and received a master of arts (1491) and a doctorate in theology (1514). As a professor of philosophy there he expounded the nominalist viewpoint (*via moderna*) of Ockham and Biel, which Luther (studying there, 1501–05) later reflected in his theology. Around 1512 Luther persuaded him to join the Augustinians, for whom Usingen later taught theology. Always firmly Catholic, although he attacked abuses, Usingen rejected Luther's 95 theses and broke with him in 1520. He feared the consequences of the new doctrines, especially that on good works. Luther tried persuasion, but after Usingen's sermons at Erfurt in 1521, his violent reply provoked a war of letters. Although weak as theologian and Latinist, Usingen answered Luther's ideas on their own ground after thorough study. He believed that Luther had gone wrong in theology by rejecting philosophy. In 1526 he left Erfurt to join the Augustinians at Würzburg. There he assisted the bishop (Conrad von Thungen), took charge of several monasteries, and preached against Luther. At the diet of Augsburg (1530) he helped examine the Augsburg Confession.

Bibliography: N. HÄRING, *Die Theologie des. . .B. A. v. Usingen* (Limburg 1939). A. GODDU, ''The use of Dialectical Topica in the 16th and 17th Centuries,'' *Medioevo* 24 (1989) 301–355. A. ZUMKELLER, ''Die Antwort des Erfurter Universitätsprofessor und Augustiners Bartholomaeus von Usingen auf die 'Apologie' des Philipp Melanchthon der 'Confessio Augustana' von 1530,'' *Cor Unum* 58 (2000) 24–31.

[J. T. GRAHAM]

ARNULF OF GAP, ST.

Bishop; b. Vendôme, France; d. Sept. 19, 1070–79, Gap, France. Only fragments of information about Arnulf have been preserved. While a monk of Sainte-Trinité at Vendôme, he accompanied his abbot, Oderic, to Rome (*c.* 1061) to secure for Sainte-Trinité papal confirmation of the Roman church of St. Prisca and for its abbot the dignity of cardinal priest. Pope ALEXANDER II detained Arnulf as an adviser until *c.* 1066, when he consecrated him and installed him as bishop of Gap, where he is principal patron. There he was an able administrator and defender of the Church during the tumultuous Gregorian Reform of the late eleventh century.

Feast: Sept. 19.

Bibliography: *Acta Sanctorum* Sept. 6:95–101. A. M. ZIMMERMANN, *Kalendarium Benedictinum* (Metten 1933–38) 3:77–79. A. M. ZIMMERMANN, *Lexikon für Theologie und Kirche*, ed. J. HOFER and K. RAHNER (Freiburg 1957–65) 1:899–900. R. AIGRAIN, *Catholicisme* 1:855.

[S. WILLIAMS]

ARNULF OF LISIEUX

Bishop; b. possibly Rouen, Normandy, France; d. monastery of Saint-Victor, Paris, France, Oct. 31, 1184. He was born of a well-known family in Normandy, and under the tutelage of his uncle John (fl. *c.* 1150), who was bishop of Sées, he began intensive literary studies. He became an archdeacon and subsequently went to Rome, where he remained for some time engaged in the study of Canon Law. While in Rome he was a witness to the difficulties caused by the antipope Anacletus II (*see* PIERLEONI), who opposed the election of INNOCENT II, and in

1134 he wrote a violent letter in defense of the pope against Gerard, bishop of Angoulême (d. 1136). Elected bishop of Lisieux in 1141, he was for some time prevented from taking possession of his see until BERNARD OF CLAIRVAUX interceded with Pope Innocent to prevail upon Geoffrey, count of Anjou (d. 1151), to withdraw his objections. In 1147 he accompanied LOUIS VII on his crusade. Arnulf was an important figure and was deeply involved in the political events of his time. In the schism that followed the election of Pope ALEXANDER III he was faithful to the pope and encouraged his fellow bishops in France, as well as HENRY II and the English bishops, to remain loyal. Arnulf became involved in the Thomas BECKET affair and attempted to arbitrate the difficulties although he has often been accused of being motivated by personal interests. In spite of serving the cause of the Plantagenet kings he was disgraced by the king, but successfully defended himself against his charges. He resigned his episcopacy in 1181 and spent his final years in the monastery of SAINT-VICTOR in Paris. His works included the treatise on the schism of Anacletus and 130 letters to important personages of his time, as well as a collection of sermons and poems (*Patrologia latina* 201:5–200).

Bibliography: H. WOLTER, *Lexikon für Theologie und Kirche* 2 1:900. A. NOYON, *Dictionnaire d'histoire et de géographie eccléiastiques* 4:609–611. M. MANITIUS *Geschichte der lateinischen Literatur des Mittelalters* 3:59–60, 903–905. *Histoire Littéraire de la France* 14:304–334; 16:655–679.

[V. A. SCHAEFER]

ARNULF OF METZ, ST.

Bishop; b. near Nancy, France, *c.* 582; d. Remiremont (*Habendum*), July 18, *c.* 641. A member of a prominent Austrasian family, Arnulf was reared at the court of Metz and entered the administration of King Theodebert II (d. 612), possibly as mayor of the palace. He was the father of two sons, Ansegis (Ansegisellus; d. *c.* 685) and (St.) CHLODULF (Cloud), the first of whom married (St.) BEGGA, the daughter of (Bl.) Pepin of Landen (d. 640), and became the father of Pepin of Heristal (d. 714). Arnulf was thus the progenitor of the CAROLINGIAN dynasty. The second son, Chlodulf, became his father's third successor in the See of Metz. After the fall of Brunhilde in 613, Arnulf assisted Pepin of Landen in reuniting the Frankish kingdoms; the following year his wife entered a convent in Trier, and Arnulf, still a layman, was promoted to the bishopric of Metz. He took part in the synods of Clichy (626–27) and Reims (627–30), and after serving both church and state for 15 years, he retired with his friend (St.) Romaric (d. 653) to the solitude of *Habendum* (REMIREMONT), where he passed his remaining years. His successor, Abbo (d. 642), brought Arnulf's relics back to Metz.

Feast: July 18.

Bibliography: *Vita,* ed. B. KRUSCH, *Monumenta Germaniae Historica: Scriptores rerum Merovingicarum* 2:426–446. PSEUDO-FREDEGARIUS, *Chronicon (ibid.* 2:140, 146–147, 150). PAUL THE DEACON, *Liber de episcopis Mettensibus, Monumenta Germaniae Historica: Scriptores* 2:264–265. E. HATTON, *Dictionnaire d'histoire et de géographie ecclésiastiques,* ed. A. BAUDRILLART et al. (Paris 1912) 4:612–615. R. AIGRAIN, *Catholicisme* 1:855–857. J. DEPOIN, ''Grandes figures monacales des temps mérovingiens: Saint Arnoul de Metz,'' *Revue Mabillon* 11 (1921) 245–258; 12 (1922) 13–25, 105–118. O. ABEL, *Die Chronik Fredegars und der Frankenkönige, die Lebensbeschreibungen des Abtes Columban, der Bischöfe Arnulf, Leodegar und Eligius, der Königin Bathilde* (third ed. Leipzig 1888).

[O. J. BLUM]

ARNULF OF MILAN

Historian of the archbishops of Milan; d. 1077. He was the great-grandson of the brother of an earlier archbishop of Milan, Arnulf I (d. 974), but very little is known of his life; what is known about him is derived from his writings. He was a member of the aristocratic class of the Capitani and was a notable person in his day. He was probably a cleric and perhaps even a subdeacon, for his writings contain many Biblical allusions and his style is Biblical. In the struggle for supremacy, in spite of his aristocratic background, he remained faithful to the discipline of the Church and to Pope GREGORY VII, although he frequently spoke out sharply against other ecclesiastics for their fraud and deceit, and he even resisted the appointment of Abp. ATTO OF MILAN. After the submission of HENRY IV at Canossa (*see* INVESTITURE STRUGGLE), Arnulf submitted to Atto and was a member of the diplomatic mission sent by the Milanese to promise loyalty to the archbishop. Arnulf is famed for his authorship of the *Gesta archiepiscoporum Mediolanensium.* In his history he related the events in which he participated, or based his account on the testimony of those whom he considered credible. The chronicle begins with King Hugo of Italy (d. 947) in 925 and concludes with the election of Rudolf of Rheinfelden (d. 1080) as king through the year 1077, though without a formal conclusion. The work is a source of first rank, and it is of great value for the study of the period.

Bibliography: *Patrologia Latina,* ed. J. P. MIGNE, 217 v. (Paris 1878–90) 147:279–332. *Monumenta Germaniae Scriptores* (Berlin 1825–) 8:1–13. L. BOEHM, *Lexikon für Theologie und Kirche,* ed. J. HOFER and K. RAHNER, 10 v. (2d, new ed. Freiburg 1957–65) 1:900–901. M. MANITIUS, *Geschichte der lateinischen Literatur des Mittelalters,* 3 v. (Munich 1911–31) 3:507–509. A. FLICHE, *Dictionnaire d'histoire et de géographie ecclésiastiques,* ed.

A. BAUDRILLART (Paris 1912–) 4:599; *La Réforme grégorienne,* 3 v. (Louvain 1924–37) v.2, *passim.*

[V. A. SCHAEFER]

ARNULF OF SOISSONS, ST.

Reforming bishop; b. Pamel, Brabant, Belgium, *c.* 1040; d. Oudenbourg, Belgium, Aug. 15, 1087. His life admirably illustrates both the piety and the irregularity of ecclesiastical life in Europe before the Gregorian Reform. He devoted himself to personal asceticism and to an unsuccessful effort at ecclesiastical reform. After a brief military career, Arnulf entered the monastery of Saint-Médard at Soissons *c.* 1020. His rigorous asceticism won the admiration of his fellow monks, and they elected him to replace Raymond, then abbot of the monastery, a worldly man and guilty of simony. In the year 1080 or 1081 he was elected bishop of Soissons, again to replace an ecclesiastic of bad repute, Bishop Ursio. However, Arnulf's efforts to reform the diocesan clergy were stoutly and successfully resisted, and within a few years he was compelled to leave the diocese. He resigned the bishopric and again took up the monastic life, this time at Oudenbourg in Flanders, where he founded a monastery and lived out his days. He was buried in the church there, and in 1121 his body was translated and a public cult was declared. His life was written by Lizard, Bishop of Soissons, in the same century. Another account was written by Hariulf (d. 1143), who was abbot of Saint-Médard at Oudenbourg.

Feast: Aug. 15.

Bibliography: *Bibliotheca hagiograpica latina antiquae et mediae aetatis* (Brussels 1898–1901) 1:703–705a. *Monumenta Germaniae Historica: Scriptores* 15.2:872–904. A. PRÉVOST, *Dictionnaire d'histoire et de géographie ecclésiastiques,* ed. A. BAUDRILLART et al. (Paris 1912) 4:617–618. A. M. ZIMMERMANN, *Kalendarium Benedictinum* (Metten 1933–38) 2:576–578. F. RAMON, *Drie vlaamsche sinten in een kerkraam* (second ed. Tielt, Flanders 1945). É. DE MOREAU, *Histoire de l'Église en Belgique* (second ed. Brussels 1945–). O. ENGLEBERT, *The Lives of the Saints,* tr. C. and A. FREMANTLE (New York 1951). A. BUTLER, *The Lives of the Saints,* ed. H. THURSTON and D. ATTWATER (New York 1956) 3:335–336. A. M. ZIMMERMANN, *Lexikon für Theologie und Kirche,* ed. J. HOFER and K. RAHNER (Freiburg 1957–65) 1:901.

[H. MACKINNON]

ARRAS, COUNCILS OF

Episcopal succession at Arras (*Atrebatum*) dates from St. VEDAST (VAAST), *c.* 500– *c.* 540, though in the pontificate of either St. Vedulph (*c.* 545– *c.* 580) or St. GÉRY (Gaugericus, 584 or 590–624 or 627) the diocesan seat was moved to Cambrai, where it remained until Pope Urban II (Dec. 2, 1092, and March 23, 1094; *see* L. Jaffé, *Regesta pontificum romanorum ab condita ecclesia ad annum post Christum natum 1198,* ed. S. Löwenfeld 5472, 5512) decreed that Arras be a diocese distinct from Cambrai. On a Sunday early in 1025 the first known synod at Arras was summoned by Bp. GERARD OF CAMBRAI (1013–51). The extant acts (J. D. Mansi, *Sacrorum Conciliorum nova et amplissima collectio,* 31 v.; reprinted and continued by L. Petit and J. B. Martin, 53 v. in 60, 460) show it to have dealt with the disciples of an Italian Manichee, Gundulph, who relied upon works for justification and rejected Baptism, the Eucharist, Matrimony, Penance, and Holy Orders, as well as sacred images and ecclesiastical burial. Gerard expounded a solid theology of the Church, of the Sacraments, and of justification and won a recantation from the heretics. Subsequent to Arras's reestablishment as a see, Bishop Lambert (1094–1115) held two synods in the city, one on February 5, the other on Oct. 21, 1097 (*Sacrorum Conciliorum nova et amplissima collectio* 20:941–948). In February he granted a privilege to St. Denis monastery, Rheims; and in October, exemptions to religious houses at Saint-Amand-les-Eaux, Mont-Saint-Eloi, and Arrouaise. One of these assemblies threatened the chatelain Gonfrid with excommunication for his occupancy of church lands. A provincial council at Arras on May 10, 1128 (*Sacrorum Conciliorum nova et amplissima collectio* 21:371–374), transferred the church of the Virgin and St. John, Laon, from the control of canonesses who were in poor repute to that of monks. Later synods took place at Arras in 1442, 1490, and 1501 (C. J. von Hefele, *Histoire des conciles d'après les documents originaux,* tr. and continued by H. Leclercq, 10 v. in 19, 7:1151; 8:142, 219). In 1570 at Arras Bp. Francis Richardot (1561–74) published a collection of synodal statutes; between 1604 and 1616 eight diocesan synods were held, and another was convened in 1678 (J. Lestocquoy, *La Vie religieuse d'une province: Le Diocèse d'Arras* 102, 130, 147).

Bibliography: Sources. T. M. J. GOUSSET, *Les Actes de la province ecclésiastique de Reims,* 4 v. (Reims 1842–44). Literature. R. RODIÈRE, *Dictionnaire d'histoire et de géographie ecclésiastiques,* ed. A. BAUDRILLART (Paris 1912–) 4:688–706. F. VERCAUTEREN, *Étude sur les civitates de la Belgique seconde* (Brussels 1934). H. LANCELIN, *Histoire du diocèse de Cambrai* (Valenciennes 1946). S. RUNCIMAN, *The Medieval Manichee* (Cambridge, England 1947). J. LESTOCQUOY, *La Vie religieuse d'une province: Le Diocèse d'Arras* (Arras 1949). O. ENGELS, *Lexikon für Theologie und Kirche,* ed. J. HOFER and K. RAHNER, 10 v. (2d, new ed. Freiburg 1957–65) 1:903.

[H. G. J. BECK]

ARRAS, MARTYRS OF, BB.

A group of four beatified Daughters of Charity of St. Vincent de Paul who were martyred in 1794 during the French Revolution. They were Marie Madeleine Fontaine (b. Etrépagny, Eure, France, 1723), superior of the community in Arras (Pas-de-Calais), Marie Françoise Lanel (b. Eu near Rouen, 1745), Marie Thérèse Fontou (b. 1747), and Jeanne Gérard (b. 1752). The Daughters of Charity, who had been in Arras since 1656, were conducting a school for girls and aiding the sick in the town in 1789 and had seven sisters in their convent. Their work continued as usual until 1793 when Joseph Lebon, an apostate priest and government official, imposed a lay director on the house, whose name was changed to *La Maison de l'Humanité,* and seized the community's goods, but permitted the sisters to remain and care for the sick, while dressed in secular attire. At this time the superior sent the two youngest sisters to Belgium, disguised as peasants, to preserve them from danger. A third sister returned to her family when her temporary vows expired (July 1792). When the four remaining sisters persisted in their refusal to take the oath of *Liberté-Égalité,* they were imprisoned (Feb. 14, 1794). On June 26 they were brought to Cambrai, placed on trial, condemned, and guillotined. They were beatified, together with the Martyrs of Valenciennes, June 13, 1920.

Feast: June 26.

Bibliography: A. LOVAT, *The Sisters of Charity Martyred at Arras in 1794* (London 1920). J. L. BAUDOT and L. CHAUSSIN, *Vies des saints et des bienhereux selon l'ordre du calendrier avec l'historique des fêtes* (Paris 1935–56) 6:448–455.

[M. LAWLOR]

ARREGUI, ANTONIO MARÍA

Spanish Jesuit theologian; b. Pamplona, Navarre, Jan. 17, 1863; d. Barcelona, Oct. 10, 1942. After teaching for 13 years before World War I in the Jesuit theologate at Oña, he published *Summarium theologiae moralis* (Bilbao 1918), a convenient handbook of moral theology used by Jesuit students of theology ever since. His 20 years as tertian master at Manresa brought him fame as an expert director in Jesuit spirituality. His second major work was on the constitution and rules of the Society of Jesus, *Annotationes ad epitomen Instituti Societatis Jesu* (Rome 1934).

Bibliography: M. ZALBA, ''Un moralista español de nuestros días,'' *Estudios eclesiásticos* 19 (1945) 247–257.

[J. M. UPTON]

ARRIAGA, PABLO JOSÉ DE

Jesuit missionary and author; b. Vergara, Guipúzcoa, Spain, 1564; d. in a shipwreck near Cuba, Sept. 6, 1622. Arriaga had been a student in Madrid before he entered the Jesuit novitiate at Ocaña Feb. 24, 1579. He taught rhetoric there and at Belmonte before going to Peru in 1585. He became a professor of rhetoric in Lima and made his profession in the society March 19, 1594. With the exception of a few intervals, he served as rector of the Colegio de San Martin in Lima and the Colegio in Arequipa for 24 years. He made a trip to Spain in 1601 and was on his way there again as a representative of his province when he died. Arriaga was a man of action as well as of study. Much concerned with the apostleship to the unfortunate native Peruvians in both urban and rural areas, he worked particularly in the cities where they were mixed with Europeans. In Lima he supervised the building of a school for the children of the neighboring caciques. He was the author and translator of many spiritual books, including *La retórica cristiana* and some works of Mariology. His experiences as official visitor of the native people resulted in his most important work, *Extirpación de la idolatría del Perú* (Lima 1621). José Toribio Medina felt that this volume, of all such books printed in Lima in colonial times, was worthy of being reprinted because of the information it contained on the history and ethnology of the Quechua area and especially of the Inca religion.

Bibliography: J. E. DE URIARTE and M. LECINA, *Biblioteca de escritores de la Compañía de Jesús pertenecientes a la antigua asistencia de España desde sus orígenes hasta el año de 1773*, 2 v. (Madrid 1925–30).

[A. DE EGAÑA]

ARRIAGA, RODRIGO DE

Spanish Jesuit philosopher and theologian; b. Logroño, Spain, Jan. 17, 1592; d. Prague, June 7, 1667. He entered the Society of Jesus in 1606 and taught philosophy at Valladolid and theology at Salamanca. In 1625 he was sent to the University of Prague, where he remained for the rest of his life. There he became professor of theology, then chancellor, and finally prefect of studies. His important works were *Cursus philosophicus* (Antwerp 1632, and other editions) and *Disputationes theologicae* (8 v. Antwerp 1643–55) based on St. Thomas Aquinas. He is known as one of the foremost Spanish Jesuits of his day and as a leading representative of the school of Suárez.

Bibliography: A. ASTRAIN, *Historia de la Compañía de Jesús en la Asistencia de España*, 7 v. (Madrid 1902–25) 6:4–5, 49–53.

C. SOMMERVOGEL et al., *Bibliothèque de la Compagnie de Jésus*, 11 v. (Brussels-Paris 1890–1932) 1:578–581.

[J. C. WILLKE]

ARRICIVITA, JUAN DOMINGO

Franciscan missionary and historian; b. Toluca, Mexico, 1720; d. Querétaro, Mexico, April 16, 1794. He entered the Franciscan Order at the Mission College of the Holy Cross in Querétaro in 1735. A reliable friar and a good priest, he spent most of his years in posts of secondary importance: as missionary in the San Sabá region of Texas (1748–50) and procurator of the missions of his college from 1757 to 1767, when he helped make arrangements for the Franciscans to replace the expelled Jesuits in their former missions in Sonora and lower Arizona. As part of this plan, he went to Spain in 1768 to recruit more missionaries. In 1770 the Inquisition named him censor of books for the Querétaro region and in 1778 his friend, Juan Ignacio de la Rocha, Bishop of Michoacán, requested him to head a group of friars to give missions in Colima and its environs. On Oct. 29, 1787, Arricivita was named official historian of Querétaro College to continue the work of Isidro ESPINOSA, who had published the first part of the history of the college in 1746. The work had been neglected by the official historians in favor of other books, so Querétaro's achievements were sometimes bypassed as the chroniclers of the other colleges in Mexico published their accounts. Arricivita worked rapidly and his *Crónica seráfica y apostólica del colegio de Propaganda fide de la Santa Cruz de Querétaro* was sent to the press in 1791. Historians have generally considered Arricivita's work inferior to that of Espinosa even though its merits are substantial, chiefly because Arricivita knew the mission area so well and had taken an active part in many of the enterprises he described.

[L. G. CANEDO]

ARRIETA, FRANCISO SALES DE

Peruvian FRANCISCAN, archbishop of Lima; b. Lima, Jan. 29, 1768; d. there, May 4, 1843. He joined the Discalced Franciscans in Lima. He was named director of the Franciscan house of exercises in 1813, and later served as inspector of convents of the Lima province and as rector of the Third Order. In 1839 President Gamarra nominated him for archiepiscopal to the See of Lima. Arrieta's secret letter to Gregory XVI asking that he be excused from serving in this post was to no avail. On Jan. 24, 1841, he was consecrated archbishop. Arrieta worked to reform monastic life in Peru, becoming the confessor of many of the regular clergy. Owing to the reorganization he initiated in 1842, the Seminary of San Toribio began gradually to reacquire intellectual influence. Arrieta was indefatigable in his efforts to improve the religious instruction of children. The most serious challenge to Archbishop Arrieta was the shifting attack of Peruvian liberalism against the Church, manifested particularly in the actions of Manuel Lorenzo Vidaurre (1773–1841). As a young man Vidaurre showed a tendency to dismiss the spiritual beliefs of Catholicism, boasting deism and confidence in reason and science. In 1839 he published the *Vidaurre contra Vidaurre*, allegedly disavowing his own theological errors. The book, however, reflected the new position of Peruvian liberalism, insisting that the Church democratize its organizational structure, questioning papal supremacy, arguing that councils represented the voice of ultimate truth in church affairs, demanding the suppression of ecclesiastical privileges such as private law courts, and affirming the absolute right of the state to supervise the church in all temporal activities. Archbishop Arrieta condemned the widely read book. Thus, were clearly established the main battle lines that Peruvian churchmen and anticlerical liberals defended for the next half century.

Bibliography: J. A. DE LAVALLE, *Galería de retratos de los arzobispos de Lima* (Lima 1892).

[F. B. PIKE]

ARRILLAGA, BASILIO

Jesuit defender of the Church in Mexico; b. Mexico City, June 1, 1791; d. there, July 28, 1867. After completing his studies in the humanities, philosophy, and law, and being ordained, Arrillaga joined the Jesuits (July 28, 1816). He was first appointed assistant to the master of novices, and from then on he held various important offices in the order, including dean of the college in Puebla and in Mexico City and later Jesuit provincial. During much of his life the Jesuits lived a precarious existence in Mexico, for the order was dissolved on occasion and persecuted frequently. Arrillaga was a dynamic and competent protagonist in the political-religious debates between the Church and the State. In 1821 he was named an alternate deputy to the Cortes and in December of that year he was one of the supporters of ITURBIDE. From 1822 to 1825 he was rector of the Colegio Carolino in Puebla, but left there to go to Mexico City. He served briefly as a pastor, but even while carrying on pastoral duties he engaged actively in political discussion. He represented the Federal District in the congress in the mid-1830s and was president of the congress several times.

He worked on a commission to plan a new educational system and was one of the founders of the Academia Mexicana de la Lengua and the Academia Nacional de la Historia. Santa Anna included him in a national legislative junta in 1842. From 1844 to 1849 he was rector of the University of Mexico. He was an honorary councilor of state under Maximilian, for which he was briefly imprisoned on the restoration of the republic. Arrillaga was a militant defender of the Church against liberal Catholicism and against the antireligious actions of those in charge of the government. He spoke and wrote vehemently and frequently, publishing in books and periodicals. He collected a library of thousands of volumes principally in philosophy, law, and history, which he used in writing his books, refuting his critics, and preparing his polemics.

Bibliography: G. DECORME, *Historia de la Compañía de Jesús en la República mexicana durante el siglo XIX,* 3 v. (Guadalajara, Mex. 1914–21; Chihuahua City 1959). E. VALVERDE TÉLLEZ, *Biobibliografía eclesiástica mexicana, 1821–1943,* 3 v. (Mexico City 1949).

[F. ZUBILLAGA]

ARROWSMITH, EDMUND, ST.

Jesuit priest and martyr; b. Haydock, near St. Helens, England, 1585; hanged, drawn, and quartered at Lancaster, Aug. 28, 1628. This son of Robert Arrowsmith, a yeoman farmer of Lancashire, and Margery Gerard of Bryn, both of whom had been imprisoned for their faith, was christened Brian and in Confirmation took the name Edmund, by which he was henceforth known. After his father's death he was educated by an old priest, who in December 1605 sent him to the English College, Douai. There, after delays caused by ill health, he was ordained in 1612; the following year he returned to Lancashire. His forthright speech and fearlessness put his life in such constant danger that a friend recommended in jest that he should always carry salt in his pocket to season his actions. About 1622 he was caught and examined before the Anglican bishop of Chester, but he was released; for at this time James I, interested in a Spanish match for his son, was anxious that his officials should show clemency to Catholics. Later Arrowsmith entered the Society of Jesus in the London novitiate at Clerkenwell, where his name appears on the lists of the house when it was raided in 1628. Shortly after his return to Lancashire, he was betrayed by Holden, a young man whom he had reproved for his immoral life. At Lancaster assizes in August 1628 Arrowsmith came before Sir Henry Yelverton and was indicted for being a priest. Although the evidence against him was inadequate, he was sentenced to death and for two days was left without food and heavily manacled in a cell so narrow that he was unable to lie down. In the prison yard on his way to execution he received absolution from St. John SOUTHWORTH, who was also confined in Lancaster castle. Until his last moment Arrowsmith was heckled by ministers with the promise of his life if he would renounce his faith. He pleaded: "Tempt me no more. I will not do it, in no case, on no condition." His last words were "Bone Jesu." His hand is preserved in the Catholic Church of St. Oswald at Ashton-in-Makerfield, near Wigan, and has been the source of many remarkable cures. He was beatified by Pius XI on Dec. 15, 1929 and canonized by Paul VI on Oct. 25, 1970 as one of the Forty Martyrs of England and Wales.

Feast: Aug. 28; Oct. 25 (Feast of the 40 Martyrs of England and Wales); May 4 (Feast of the English Martyrs in England); Dec. 1 (Jesuits).

See Also: ENGLAND, SCOTLAND, AND WALES, MARTYRS OF.

Bibliography: *A True and Exact Relation of Two Catholicks Who Suffered for Their Religion at Lancaster in 1628* (London 1737), repr. and modernized in *Bl. Edmund Arrowsmith* (Postulation pamphlet; London 1960). G. BURNS, *Gibbets and Gallows* (London 1944). B. CAMM, *Forgotten Shrines* (St. Louis 1910). H. FOLEY, ed., *Records of the English Province of the Society of Jesus,* 7 v. (London 1877–82) 7.1:18–19. R. CHALLONER, *Memoirs of Missionary Priests,* ed. J. H. POLLEN (rev. ed. London 1924; repr. Farnborough 1969). J. N. TYLENDA, *Jesuit Saints & Martyrs* (Chicago 1998) 268–70. A. BUTLER, *The Lives of the Saints* (New York 1956) 3:439–440.

[G. FITZHERBERT]

ARRUPE, PEDRO

Twenty-eighth Superior General (1965–1983) of the Society of Jesus (JESUITS); b. Bilbao, Spain, Nov. 14, 1907; d. Rome, Feb. 5, 1991.

Early Years. The only boy among five children, Pedro Arrupe was the son of a well-to-do architect, who enabled him to receive a good education. He decided to become a physician, but in 1927, just before completing medical studies in Madrid, he felt the call to religious life and entered the Society of Jesus. When the Spanish Republic expelled all Jesuits in 1932, Arrupe studied for the priesthood in Holland and in Belgium, where he was ordained in 1936. Afterwards he continued his education in the United States.

In answer to his frequent requests Arrupe was assigned to Japan in 1938. After the Japanese attack on Pearl Harbor in 1941, he was imprisoned for thirty-three days on false charges of spying. At the time that the first atomic bomb exploded on Aug. 6, 1945, he was director of novices in Nagatsuka, on the outskirts of Hiroshima.

St. Edmund Arrowsmith.

Arrupe rushed into the ruins to treat the wounded, and turning the Jesuit residence into a hospital, he supervised the care of more than 200 survivors for six months. In 1958 the Japanese mission was raised to a province, and Arrupe was named the first provincial superior.

Superior General. On May 22, 1965 Arrupe was elected superior general by the Thirty-first General Congregation, the legislative body of the Society of Jesus. The first Basque to lead the Jesuits since their founder, St. IGNATIUS OF LOYOLA, he was eminently suited to lead the Society in the era following VATICAN COUNCIL II. Arrupe was a man of international experience and vision, who could bridge East and West because he had lived and worked in both areas, spoke the languages, and appreciated different cultures. He realized that the center of gravity of worldwide Christianity was moving toward Asia and Africa. As a veteran and well-traveled missionary he had learned to adapt the Christian message and the ways of the Church to different cultures.

As superior general, Arrupe felt his mandate was to promote the renewal of Jesuit life in accord with the norms set down by Vatican II: a continuous return to the Gospel and the original inspiration of the founder and at the same time an adaptation to the changed conditions of the times. Arrupe was the first Jesuit general to travel extensively. He visited six continents, enabling him to meet and speak with thousands of Jesuits. His simplicity, warmth, vigor, candor, and obvious expertise made him an instant hit with his brother Jesuits, who referred to him affectionately as "Don Pedro."

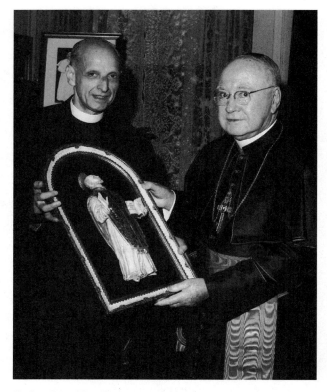

Father General Pedro Arrupe (left) of the Society of Jesus presents Francis Cardinal Spellman of New York with a ceramic of St. Ignatius of Loyola, founder of the Jesuit Order. (AP/Wide World Photos)

Having come face-to-face with the dehumanizing poverty that afflicts a vast part of the human race, Arrupe had by 1970 reached a strong conviction that never left him: religious faith, to be truly evangelical, had to be vigorous in promoting justice and in opposing injustice, oppression, and social evils such as poverty, hunger, and all forms of racial discrimination. One of his earliest letters as superior general was written in 1967 to the Jesuits in the United States on racial discrimination and the interracial apostolate. The letter had wide repercussions and served the Society as a kind of "Magna Carta" for the interracial aspects of its work all over the world.

Arrupe's influence went far beyond Jesuit circles. He attended the last session of the Second Vatican Council, speaking twice before the general assembly. In 1967 he was elected to the first of five consecutive terms as president of the Union of Superior Generals, which represented some 300,000 male religious throughout the world. He participated in and spoke at all the international synods of bishops from 1967 to 1980. Arrupe took part in the great meetings of Latin American bishops in Medellín, Colombia (1968) and in Puebla, Mexico (1979), and in episcopal symposia in Europe and Africa. Quick to sense the magnitude of the worldwide refugee problem, he launched a program in 1980 throughout the Society to meet the desperate needs of millions of displaced persons, particularly in Southeast Asia and Africa.

Relations with the Holy See. Arrupe confessed that he had three great loves: Jesus Christ, the Church, and the Society of Jesus. For him the central figure in the Church was the pope, to whom he pledged himself and the Society, fostering the special bond of love and service that has linked the Society to the pope since its very beginning. He served under three popes: PAUL VI, JOHN PAUL I, and JOHN PAUL II. Two of his favorite photographs showed him kneeling and receiving the blessings of Paul VI and John Paul II as he pledged the service of the Society to them.

No one was superior to Pedro Arrupe in loyalty and dedication to the Holy Father, and any meeting with the pope was a very special moment in his life. That is why moments of tension and of misunderstandings with the popes caused him so much pain. In certain Vatican circles, Arrupe was categorized as somewhat naive, an incurable optimist, and more a charismatic and inspirational leader than a strong administrator who could control his men.

During the Thirty-second General Congregation a conflict arose between Paul VI and the participants, with Arrupe in the eye of the storm. The main issue was a possible change in who would be eligible to pronounce the fourth vow of special obedience to the pope. Led by Arrupe's example, the Congregation exercised an act of obedience to the wishes of Paul VI, who was also concerned lest a spirit of social and political activism should undermine the Society's priestly ministries. Peaceful relations were restored and remained warm and friendly until Paul VI's death in 1978.

A more critical period began in April 1980 when Arrupe informed Pope John Paul II of his plans to resign as superior general and to convoke a General Congregation to elect his successor. Disconcerted by this information, the pope wrote to Arrupe on May 1, 1980, and asked him to postpone this step for the good of the Church and of the Society. The pope discussed the situation at a meeting with Arrupe in January 1981. Meanwhile the press carried reports and rumors of a rift between the Holy Father and the Society, stressing of the Holy See's apparent loss of confidence in Jesuit leadership. A second meeting took place in April 1981. The discussions were interrupted, first by the attempt to assassinate John Paul II on May 13, 1981, and then by a severe and permanently disabling stroke that Arrupe suffered when he returned Aug. 7, 1981 from a long trip to the Philippines and the refugee camps in Bangkok. After consulting with his doctors, on

August 10 Arrupe named one of his assistants vicar general for the duration of his illness, in accord with the Constitutions of the Society.

On Oct. 5, 1981, Pope John Paul II intervened. He appointed Paolo Dezza as his personal delegate to govern the Society. At the same time the pope also appointed Giuseppe Pittau, SJ, to be Dezza's coadjutor with the right of succession. Arrupe remained the superior general but was unable to function. John Paul II clarified the unusual situation by stating that, in postponing the General Congregation and naming his own delegate, he had suspended the Jesuit Constitutions on these two points only.

Dezza convoked a meeting in Rome of all the Jesuit provincials and assistants and counsellors of the General Curia from Feb. 23 to March 3, 1982. In a series of conferences Dezza informed the participants of the concerns and hopes of the pope for the Society. The highlight of the meeting was the audience with John Paul II and his address to the participants. The pope greeted the superior general with great affection: "To Father Arrupe, present here in the eloquent silence of his infirmity, offered to God for the good of the Society, I wish to express, on this occasion particularly solemn for the life and history of your Order, the thanks of the Pope and of the Church!" John Paul II expressed gratitude for the way his decision had been accepted, and after mentioning his concern for the order, he asked the Society to help him and all the bishops implement the Second Vatican Council, just as Paul III had asked Ignatius and his companions to help the Church to implement the Council of Trent. At the end of his address, the pope invited the order to convoke a General Congregation.

A Spiritual and Apostolic Legacy. The Thirty-third General Congregation assembled in Rome in September 1983. Arrupe offered his resignation, and Peter-Hans Kolvenbach was elected to succeed him. After his resignation as superior general, Arrupe's life was one of silent and patient prayer and suffering. In the end Arrupe left a rich spiritual and apostolic legacy in his addresses and writings. Among these are: *Challenge to Religious Life Today* (1979); *Justice With Faith Today* (1980); *Other Apostolates Today* (1981); and *In Him Alone Is Our Hope: Texts On The Heart of Christ* (1984). Always a faithful Jesuit, Arrupe articulated ideas that were developed in the Thirty-third General Congregation, which emphasized "a spiritual doctrine at once profoundly rooted in the Gospel and our tradition and yet one which responds to the challenges of our times."

During Arrupe's final illness John Paul II came to visit him in the Jesuit Curia, regretting that Arrupe's condition prevented them from conversing. After several days in a comatose state, Pedro Arrupe died peacefully in the Jesuit infirmary, surrounded by his Jesuit brothers.

Bibliography: P. ARRUPE, *One Jesuit's Spiritual Journey. Autobiographical Conversations with Jean-Claude Dietsch, S.J.* (St. Louis 1986). J.-Y. CALVEZ, *Le Père Arrupe: L'Église apès le Concile.* (Paris 1997). Y. T. DEMOLA, trans. *Recollections and Reflections of Pedro Arrupe, S.J.* (Wilmington 1986). G. HUNT, ed. "Pedro Arrupe, S.J. 1907–1991." *America* 164:6 (1991) 138–188. P. M. LAMET, *Arrupe Una Explosión En La Iglesia.* (Madrid 1989).

[V.T. O'KEEFE]

ARS MORIENDI

Definitions. The term *ars moriendi* (the art of dying) has three interrelated meanings: (1) any extended theological or spiritual discussion designed to prepare Christians to die; (2) a genre of works originating in the fifteenth century whose titles generally (but not always) include words like "art" or "method" suggesting their special identity as a guide to the management of the final period of one's life; and (3) two closely related anonymous works whose popularity in print in the fifteenth century was exceeded only by the *Imitation of Christ*. Following the practice of Sister Mary Catharine O'Connor's learned monograph (still the most valuable work on the subject) this article will distinguish the two versions by the initials of their *"incipits"* (beginning words): the earlier, longer and more widely published version as the "CP Ars" (it begins "Cum de presentis"); and the later, shorter, usually illustrated version (a carefully revised extract from the CP) as the "QS Ars" (it begins "Quamvis secundum"). Some authors refer to the CP as the "Speculum" (from *Speculum artis bene moriendi,* a frequently used title) and to the QS as the "Picture Ars."

In its late-medieval context "art" means "skill": the ability to apply the principles of a specific body of knowledge to concrete situations. The choice of the word "art" conveyed its practical nature to a world familiar with a variety of such works: for example, the *ars dictaminis,* the art of hunting, the notarial art, the art of chess, or the art of being a good confessor. The most complete modern catalog of fifteenth-century books lists 132 editions of various arts, including a dozen expounding the fundamentals of rhetoric. Of those 132, 75 are editions in Latin and various vernaculars of the longer CP Ars (39) and the illustrated QS Ars (26).

The Spiritual Logic of Holy Dying. Discussion of preparation for a holy death may appear in a sermon, treatise, catechism, or devotional work and is a problem in moral, pastoral, and sacramental theology. Whatever the literary form, however, there are two divergent emphases. (1) The *ars vivendi* (art of living), is the special province of preaching and devotional literature; it teaches about sin and exhorts Christians to lead a virtuous life so that they will be prepared for death whenever and in whatever form it comes. (2) The *ars moriendi* is expressed liturgically in prayers and rites for the dying—especially the last sacraments of confession, Viaticum, and Extreme Unction—and in that literary genre that is the subject of this article—manuals of the fifteenth century and later that teach Christians how to manage the last days or hours of their lives so that they can be saved in that final crisis.

Indispensable to the psychology of the *ars moriendi* is the assumption that every individual's eternal destiny is determined by the state of soul as it leaves the body. That idea developed almost imperceptibly in the first centuries of Christian history as the expectation of an imminent Second Coming diminished and the dominant eschatology shifted from the Last Judgment to the particular judgment of every soul immediately after death. The decline of martyrdom and the rejection of the custom of delaying Baptism until the end of life also influenced speculation on the form and meaning of a Christian death.

Ars vivendi and *ars moriendi* are not mutually exclusive, and no author can deny the spiritual logic underlying either emphasis. Nor is it possible to avoid the negative consequences of too heavy an emphasis in either direction. Too much stress on the life of virtue and the uncertainty of late repentance can imply limitations on divine mercy and act as a discouragement to sinners whose repentance is a fundamental goal of Christian parenesis. Too heavy a stress on the possibility of last-minute repentance endangers the equally fundamental Christian belief in divine justice and the correlative seriousness of the call to live according to the Gospel. In the traditional vocabulary, the first can lead to despair, the second to presumption. The *ars moriendi* emphasis focuses on the final hour, stimulates interest in the circumstances of death, and produces prayers and invocations of saints offering protection against a sudden and unprepared-for death. The *ars vivendi* emphasis reaches back to a Stoic maxim—given Christian meaning by the Fathers of the Church and special prominence by Renaissance humanists—which declares that no death is evil if it is preceded by a good life. The history of the art of dying finds authors seeking a mean between those extremes, with some drifting in one direction, others in the other. At the extremes are a warning attributed to St. JEROME that scarcely one in a million deathbed penitents escapes damnation, and a fourteenth-century scholastic theologian's speculation that suicides might be saved if they fully repented in the moments between the commission of the act and their actual death.

Three general influences helped to mold the literature of the *ars moriendi*. First, liturgical practice looms over all reflection on the subject. Nowhere is the rule "lex orandi, lex credendi" more aptly applied, and liturgical practice—along with magisterial directives about it—consistently affirmed the possibility of deathbed repentance and the obligation of priests to behave as if it were indeed possible by administering sacraments to the dying. That long history—dating to at least the third century—influences all treatments of the final hour.

Second, theology, reflecting on practice, began laying the doctrinal foundations of a personal ESCHATOLOGY in the age of the fathers. In the eleventh and twelfth centuries, theologians routinely addressed the question of whether God would accept repentance at the end, and a series of positive responses (symbolized most poignantly by the good thief of Lk 23.43) gave authoritative support to the *ars moriendi*. At the same time sinners were warned about the difficulty of repentance at death. The examples of a JUDAS or an ANTIOCHUS IV EPIPHANES (2 Mc 9.13) and a popular Augustinian sermon of CAESARIUS OF ARLES (*c.* 470 to 542) cast doubt on the effectiveness of late repentance, encouraged the *ars vivendi* tendencies of sermons and devotional literature, and might even be invoked in ars moriendi manuals to temper the enthusiasm for last-minute forgiveness. Peter Lombard took wellworn citations and forged an artfully balanced and authoritative treatment of this problem in Sentences 4.20.1.

Finally, pastoral theology contributed one of the most distinctive features of the ars moriendi after 1400: the exhortation to the laity to take an active part in the preparation for death—not only their own death, but, more and more insistently in the late middle ages, at the deathbed of a friend. In the first two areas the borrowing from earlier traditions is everywhere evident. The evangelization of the laity into an active role at the deathbed, however, is a distinctively new feature of the late medieval *ars moriendi* that virtually every historian of the subject has stressed.

The Anselm Questions. Among the medieval sources of the fifteenth-century genre a set of questions originally designed for monastic houses was especially influential. Attributed to ANSELM of Canterbury (*c.* 1033 to 1109)—with foreshadowings in the early medieval Council of Nantes (between 656 and 850) and the *Decretum* of BURCHARD OF WORMS (d. 1125)—the work is commonly titled "Admonition of St. Anselm to Someone Dying and Fearing Excessively for his Sins." Each question guides the dying to affirm the morally and doctrinally correct opinion. German translations appeared in the thirteenth century and contain, like many later Latin manuscripts, eight questions for religious followed by a slightly revised set of six for the laity. In close paraphrase the latter read: Do you believe in the elements of the Christian faith as they have been defined by the Church? Do you rejoice that you die in the Christian faith? Do you recognize that you have seriously offended God? Are you sorry you have offended your Creator? Do you intend to avoid offending God if He should prolong your life? Do you hope and do you believe that you will come to eternal salvation not by your merits but by the merits of Jesus Christ? Then the dying person is urged to place all his faith in the death of Christ and to respond to all temptations to despair over life's sins by interposing that death and His merits between the judgment of God and the dying person's unworthiness. The dying person is then directed to say traditional prayers including the universally invoked *"In manus tuas, Domine, commendo spiritum meum"* (Ps 30.6; Lk 23.46), and one to Mary to intercede in the hour of death. In some versions Anselm is said to have given assurance of salvation to all who complete this exercise sincerely. In the tradition of *ars vivendi*, however, the last paragraph urges everyone to avoid offending God and to think daily on the shortness of life, the uncertainty of one's death, the rewards of the just, and the suffering of the damned.

The Anselm Questions, and the prayers and exhortations attached to them, were clearly intended as the principal component of a medieval ars moriendi. Like the Last Sacraments, and sacramentals such as holy water, the cross, holy pictures, and candles, they were specifically intended for use at death. They directly influenced the late medieval genre, and striking echoes are discernible in Lutheranism, Calvinism, and the Catholic Reformation.

The ars moriendi as a Literary Genre. Jean GERSON (1363 to 1429) initiated this literary form with a work written in French before 1403 that was translated into Latin as *De arte moriendi* (or variations on that title). It was incorporated (with Latin translations of two other French works on the Ten Commandments and confession) as the third and last section of his immensely popular *Opus tripartitum* (1404/8). Gerson envisioned the widest imaginable audience for this work—from priests and prelates to the simple laity.

The first two treatises in Gerson's Opus tripartitum represent the *ars vivendi*, without connecting it to preparation for death. They summarize basic Christian doctrine, explain the Ten Commandments and the seven DEADLY SINS, and describe the proper disposition for and conduct of confession, the sacrament that had been deemed necessary for forgiveness since at least the eleventh century. (Gerson calls hearing confession the "art of arts"—the same phrase customarily applied to an *ars moriendi*.) Then Gerson turns to the art of dying. In at least a dozen other sermons, letters, or treatises Gerson confronted the problem of how to prepare for and manage the final months, weeks, days, or hours of a believer's life, but the third part of the *Opus tripartitum*, the *De arte moriendi*, remained by far his most influential contribution to the subject. Between 1400 and the Reformation, numerous works or parts of works were written on this perennial personal and pastoral problem. In addition to the CP and QS Ars, Rainer Rudolf lists more than 20 works in manuscript and print between 1400 and 1520 that address the twin arts of living and dying and that inventory is not exhaustive. Known authors include Johann NIDER, Stephan von Landskron, Johann GEILER VON KAYSERSBERG, Jacobus de Clusa (von Jüterborg), Jean MOMBAER, DENIS THE CARTHUSIAN, Johann von Paltz, and Girolamo SAVONAROLA. All of them were influenced in one way or another by Gerson.

In organization and content, Gerson's work was seminal. It consists of an introduction and four parts: (1) four exhortations emphasizing complete acceptance of death and renunciation of worldly attachments; (2) six interrogations modeled on the Anselm Questions; (3) prayers to be said by the dying person; and (4) general observations on the whole process. In the first three sections the dying person is addressed directly as "friend" or "beloved friend" in masculine and feminine forms: "mon amy ou amye" in French, "amice dilecte aut dilecta" in Latin. In succinct, simple language Gerson commends traditional virtues, gratitude to God (including the mercy not to have been cut down by sudden death), admission of guilt, and patient acceptance of suffering. He expands Anselm's questions, adding a special emphasis on the confession of all remembered sins, the obligation to make restitution, and the practice of mutual forgiveness. A set of brief prayers include "in manus tuas," a petition to the Father for protection from evil spirits, an expression of trust in the saving passion of the Son, and invocations for the intercession of Mary and a favorite saint. The concluding observations again mention the Last Sacraments, especially confession. Alternatives for those who have lost speech or reason are intimated, the Crucifix commended, distracting contact with friends and family discouraged. Gerson warns that encouraging hope of recovery is a spurious kindness that can lead to eternal damnation. The treatise as a whole balances a sensitivity to the anxiety of dying and the dangers of a scrupulous conscience against a conscientious concern that at least minimal standards of belief and sincere repentance be met. Its direct influence endured for over a century—not the least on the CP and QS Ars.

Manuscripts, Xylographs, and Printings of the CP and the Illustrated QS Texts. The current consensus among historians is that the longer CP Ars was written first, by an anonymous author, almost certainly a German, as Sister O'Connor had argued in 1942. By her count over 300 manuscripts of the CP have survived and only six of the QS. The QS also appeared in 13 xylographic editions—"block books" made from woodcuts—a form of printing that existed briefly alongside movable type in the fifteenth century. The *ars moriendi* was the most popular among the block books: 61 of 300 surviving copies contain the Picture Ars (none before 1460).

The 75 editions of both versions (39 CP, 26 QS) place them among the most popular of fifteenth-century books printed from movable type. The first printed Latin CP was published in Cologne in 1474; the first Latin QS in Cologne, *c.* 1475. A German translation of the CP had already appeared in Strasbourg in 1468 (or earlier) and a German translation of the QS was printed at the monastery of Saints Ulrich and Afra in Augsburg (bound with the Dialogs of Gregory I) in 1473. Fifteenth-century France's Latin and French editions actually outnumber the German, and they include five printings (Paris, 1492 to 1498) by Antoine Vérard of the famous and much expanded *L'art de bien vivre et bien mourir*. In England William Caxton made a translation (from French) and published it as the *Arte and Crafte to Know Well to Dye* in 1490. And Italy produced 16 incunabular editions, 13 of them in the vernacular, between 1476 and 1500.

The CP Text (Speculum artis bene moriendi). The CP Ars draws on commonplaces from pagan moral philosophy, Scripture, the Fathers, and a variety of medieval sources. Its eclectic nature and lack of clear organization challenge the reader to select and order the material presented. Its immense popularity indicates that its readers understood that it was composed with practical, not literary, qualities in mind. Historians who disparage it for not measuring up to high compositional standards have misjudged its purpose.

The CP Ars consists of six parts: (1) a short introduction praising death and exhorting Christians to die willingly; (2) a description of five temptations (to unbelief, despair, impatience, vainglory, and avarice) with their remedies; (3) a set of questions, modeled on Anselm and Gerson; (4) prayers to be said by the dying, introduced by brief instructions on the proper attitude to death; (5) instructions to be given to the dying person on the virtues necessary to remain steadfast; (6) a set of prayers to be said by those in attendance as death approaches. The two most striking sections are the questions and the temptations.

The interrogations expand on Gerson's clarifications of the Anselm Questions. Revealing the double purpose of the CP as an *ars vivendi* and an *ars moriendi*, they combine the didacticism of devotional literature with the consolatory impulse of rituals for the dying. Some historians (Peter Neher, most judiciously) believe that the CP Ars overemphasizes doctrine and catechesis to the detriment of consolation, but that judgment seems to anticipate the debate over certitude of forgiveness during the Reformation.

The five temptations and contrary remedies are the most original feature of the CP. They portray the deathbed as a struggle in which the Devil tries to seduce the dying person to doubt, despair, impatience, false pride, and love of this world. Exhortations to resist are built out of Scripture, the Fathers, and commonplace spiritual wisdom. The text asserts repeatedly that the believer has it in the power of his free will to reject the Devil's temptations. The confrontation between good and evil underscores medieval Christianity's insistence that every soul counts in the divine economy and hence every death is an eschatological drama. A sense of urgency prevails. Thus the CP author commends to all Christians the monastic custom of gathering at the deathbed, recalling that the Rule permits running in only two situations: from a fire and to a dying brother or sister. But the mood here and throughout the CP is optimistic, confident of the possibility of success.

The consolation of the CP Ars is primarily Christocentric. In its exhortations, prayers, and imagery there is a constant return to the sole efficacy of the sacrifice of Christ, whose merits alone can win the forgiveness all humans require. The recurrent image of the interposition of Christ's merits between the sinner and the Father's judgment echoes the Anselm Questions and foreshadows remarkably similar language in Luther.

The QS or "Picture Ars." The shorter version is almost always supplied with woodcuts or engravings that depict a battleground. "Moriens," the dying man, is beset by devils busily promoting the five temptations, then comforted by angels, saints, and the Trinity urging the five contrasting inspirations. An eleventh picture shows the death of Moriens, whose soul is received by angels, to the consternation of the defeated devils.

The Picture Ars begins by borrowing from the CP Aristotle's assertion that the death of the body is the greatest of all terrors, but immediately contradicts it with St. Augustine's pronouncement that it is rather the death of the soul. That defining thought is part of a very brief introduction (typically fitted onto a single page) that distills some of the main points of the longer treatise. Bernard attests that one soul is worth more than the whole world. The author laments that it is rare to find anyone who prepares for death since no one can bring himself to believe that he will soon die. Gerson's six questions are tersely phrased, and Moriens is instructed to recite them himself if there is no one to assist in this office. The reverent reception of the sacraments is urged—especially a "true, whole, and contrite confession"—as well as total commitment to and constant meditation on the Passion of Christ. It is to prepare everyone for that final struggle—lay and clerical, literate and illiterate—that the most memorable *ars moriendi* of the age was composed, in succinct texts and vivid drawings. In the block books alone there are eleven distinct versions of the illustrations, and despite variations in detail, the basic iconography is remarkably stable.

The illustrations depict a man lying in a bed placed diagonally across the page with his head at the upper right. He is unclothed and partially covered by a sheet. Although Moriens is always a man, it is a well-established feature of the genre that a man or a woman might be the subject of these instructions. The five temptations and five inspirations almost always appear in the order fixed in the CP version (disbelief, despair, impatience, vainglory, and avarice). Block-book and printed editions almost always place the illustration of a temptation on one page and the textual description of that temptation on the facing page.

The first two temptations are by common consent of medieval spiritual authorities the most dangerous: faith is the indispensable foundation for every good, and final despair is, by anyone's definition, an unforgivable sin. But the iconography of the temptation to disbelief—an idolatrous worshipper, a frankly pagan incitement to suicide, a denial of the existence of hell—gives more prominence to paganism than seems relevant to late-medieval religious experience. The illustration to the third temptation, however, in which the impatient Moriens kicks over a table and creates a mild disorder among the attendants, is an entirely credible representation of a deathbed scene. Many have commented on the odd positioning of the fifth temptation, and the weakness of the original text in the CP, which comprises three sentences on avarice and a one-sentence transition to the concluding exhortation. The QS text is much more substantial, however, and the details of its illustration bring it psychologically to life. As for the somewhat anticlimactic order, the author of the CP Ars had already pointed out that the fourth and fifth temptations speak to the twin audiences of religious and laity: monks being more prone to the temptation to presumption and the laity to avarice. A very brief conclusion faces an eleventh woodcut—the only picture in which the head of Moriens is at the left—showing the death of Moriens. Cross and candle occupy central places. A tiny naked soul issues from his mouth and is received above the head of the bed by an angel. A crowd of saints looks on—preserving the sense the artist conveys throughout

that Moriens is not alone, that he has friendly spirits to assist him in his ordeal.

In later editions, other illustrations were occasionally added to the original eleven. The most common, placed after the death of Moriens, shows St. Michael the Archangel holding a scale with a soul on one side. A bug-like devil tries to weigh down the other side, which contains symbols of the sins of the soul being judged. Lost souls appear beneath St. Michael's feet, undergoing various forms of torture. But one soul is being carried aloft, and the soul in the balance—though in the familiar form of the naked childlike figure—weighs more than the material objects the devil has amassed and will presumably find an angel to accompany him to paradise as well. At the end of the fifteenth century the Leipzig printer Kachelofen added two frontispiece illustrations to his editions. In the first a priest hears confession, and as a devil tries to lure away the man next in line an angel urges him to stay. Next to it is an illustration of a dying man receiving the Last Sacraments.

That the illustrations are easy to grasp and didactically effective is evident from the sequence on despair. Six lurid devils assault Moriens by recalling his sins. Intermingled with them are human figures representing scenes of his sinful life. Banderoles above the devils accuse Moriens of fornication, murder, and perjury. One says "behold your sins" as a devil points at a manuscript written with rows of illegible lines. The contrary inspiration is no less transparent in meaning. The New Testament's greatest repentant sinners are at the bedside: St. Peter with his keys and rooster; the Magdalen, with her penitent's tresses and jar of ointment; the good thief of Luke 23.42–44; and Saul (soon to be Paul) knocked from his horse on the road to Damascus. An angel exhorts "never despair" while a devil on the floor cries "no victory for me."

The QS Ars (even more than the CP) was undoubtedly intended as a devotional work that would encourage the meditation on death and detachment that Christians were constantly urged to practice. Yet both versions offer practical directions—to Moriens and the attendants—for the management of the deathbed experience itself. The five temptations also seem chosen for that crisis. Whereas the author might have simply opted for an organization around the seven deadly sins, the selectivity here arguably draws on actual pastoral experience with dying persons. Perhaps the most telling evidence that the *ars moriendi* of either version is not just the repackaging of standard themes of devotional and ascetic literature is the absence of a temptation to lust.

The ars moriendi in its Late Medieval Context. Almost every historian who writes about the *ars moriendi* has asserted that the genre is the product of an obsession with death, characteristic of late medieval art and literature and directly attributable to the Black Death of 1348 to 1349. There is little evidence, however, to support that link.

It took a half-century after the first and most devastating onslaught of the plague before Gerson wrote the French treatise that became the *De arte moriendi* of the *Opus tripartitum.* Gerson refers to the plague in that work, but not to provide a motivation for its composition: he simply compares his "craft" with those practical medical works designed to teach people how to avoid or treat it. Nor are references to plague a distinctive feature of subsequent works in the genre. Indeed, the premise of every guide to holy dying is that the work is necessary precisely because Christians of all classes and states are not sufficiently concerned about their own death. The CP Ars complains that even pious members of third orders have little experience with witnessing death. When, to convince its audience that life is short, the CP Ars lists illnesses that unexpectedly shorten life, it does not mention the plague. Even more decisive, a genre calling on true friends to be present in the final hours does not bother to address the predictable reluctance of this audience to expose themselves to the plague. In sermons, tracts, and even fiction, one finds speculation on the morality of flight from the plague, or on the precautions one should exercise in contact with those stricken with the disease. Europeans everywhere (in contrast to Muslims in the Ottoman Empire) were familiar with quarantines and other measures taken to prevent the spread of the plague. But fear of contagion is not prominent in any fifteenth-century *ars moriendi.*

On the contrary, the *ars* genre is based on traditional sources and assumptions that long antedate the mid-fourteenth century. Christians had heard for centuries that they were mortal and that they would be judged as they exited this life. The early development of a ritual for the dying reinforced that message constantly. The *ars moriendi*'s preparation for death was expressed in late medieval cultural language—depiction of personal devils and intense scrutiny of conscience and motivation. It is not unreasonable to imagine that demographic calamities gave added urgency to the spiritual logic of this response to human mortality. But Christians had understood and tried to ignore that same logic long before 1348, continued both to internalize and deny it as the plague raged, and could not forget it (as they kept trying to) long after the seventeenth century, when that specific epidemic ended.

Because of inordinately high mortality rates among the clergy the Black Death has also been invoked to explain the prominence of the laity and the surprisingly small place allotted in the CP and QS Ars to priests and the Last Sacraments, especially confession. But Gerson's *De arte moriendi* also devotes few words to confession, and it would be impossible to find a more ardent exponent of confession than he. In all three of these texts, sacramental ritual is seen as a given, something commanded by church law. At the same time, every theologically knowledgeable writer understood that the efficacy of the rite of confession depends on the will of the penitent and that perseverance to the end—after a last confession—is essential. Thus the active participation of the laity is better understood as one of the varied fruits of over a century of intensive pastoral efforts to bring monastic standards into the world—an effort especially nurtured by mendicant preachers.

Protestant Reformation and Early Modern Catholicism. Roger Chartier and Daniel Roche have documented the decline in printing and listings by booksellers of the *ars moriendi* genre between about 1520 and 1560, followed by the period of its greatest popularity between about 1560 and 1800 (achieving a peak around 1675 to 1700). When books identifiable as an art of dying regained popularity in this later period, it was under titles by other authors, Protestant and Catholic. Catholic books place priests and sacraments at the center of the art, Protestant books rely on justification by faith. Historians have discerned in both an increased emphasis on the *ars vivendi*. Nevertheless, the Reformation initiated a polemic in which apologists insisted that their theologies provided the most authentically Christian and therefore the most effectively consoling way to die.

For LUTHER the promise of salvation by faith guaranteed comfort and certainty of forgiveness to the dying. His extremely popular "Sermon on Preparation for Death" of 1519 was decidedly in the *ars* tradition, a fact that underscores the fideistic elements of the late medieval genre and its influence on him. But Lutheranism soon rejected the synergistic elements of the Catholic tradition. Forgiveness of sin through unmerited grace alone, passive righteousness, and certitude of salvation became the core of "Christian liberty." In that form it was eagerly applied to the deathbed, and the consolation of an evangelical death was proclaimed in plays, poetry, hymns, sermons, and tracts. The printing press contributed heavily to this campaign. By the late sixteenth century it was routine for Protestant pastors in Germany to write catechisms for their own parishes that unfailingly contained an evangelical discourse on preparation for death (Luise Klein asserts that it was the primary concern of Lutheran teaching on justification). Thousands of Lutheran funeral orations replicated that message. If the Protestant art became increasingly oriented to the *ars vivendi*, it did not abandon what Luther believed had been a liberating and consoling provision for the blessed little hour that everyone, especially he, hoped might be granted at the end. In the Table Talk he occasionally recalled persecutors of the Gospel who (in demotic Latin) died "sine crux et sine lux," without the cross and candle that had been for centuries basic accompaniments of deathbed practice. When Luther said that he meant, of course, without the opportunity to declare their trusting faith.

Christian humanism's art of dying has been correctly characterized as encouraging the pursuit of virtue and life-long meditation on death in the Platonic as well as the Christian ascetic tradition. The most illustrious exponent of this approach was Desiderius ERASMUS, who attacked what he deemed a religion of externals—improper invocation of saints, repetitive recourse to auricular confession, and, in his most acerbic moods, a hypocritical bargaining designed to assuage divine wrath without having to make a change of heart. The *ars-vivendi* principle that there is no bad death if it is preceded by a good life was explicitly directed against "superstitious" fears of a sudden death without the Last Sacraments. The colloquies "Shipwreck" and "Funeral" parody those mentalities. But his *De Praepartione ad mortem* (1533) brought to the *ars moriendi* a new literary voice, a more sophisticated use of Biblical citations (especially Paul), and a distinctive, intensely personal Christology. Printed in 29 Latin and vernacular editions, it was one of his most popular works before his writings were condemned in the Counter Reformation. Erasmus's preparation again disparages fear of sudden death and obsession with the circumstances of death, yet it accepts much of the medieval tradition. He begins with the same quotation from Aristotle that had been used in the CP and QS Ars, and he writes about death as a final combat with eternal consequences. Sacraments are at least commended, the Devil is seen at his most active and dangerous, and fear of hell is exploited. Erasmus's exhortations to trust in the mercy of Christ are eloquent, but he rejects a recognizably Lutheran formula for justification by faith. Most traditional of all, when Satan assails his faith the Christian is instructed not to argue, but simply to affirm, repeatedly, that he dies believing whatever the church believes.

A similarly balanced theological approach is evident in one of most successful works in the later genre, *Holy Living* (1650) and *Holy Dying* (1651) by the Anglican bishop Jeremy TAYLOR.

Calvin accepted the evangelical doctrine of forgiveness, and a dramatic colloquy pitting that understanding of holy dying against Catholic "superstition" was printed in Geneva in the early years of that city's Reformation. Calvin's draft of the Genevan Ecclesiastical Ordinances contains instructions to pastors for the visitation of the sick and prisoners in which he affirms that death is the most salutary occasion for ministry to believers. He also warns against delay, lest fear of death render pastoral comfort impossible. But Calvinism added new accents: the importance of explicit faith, the purity of ritual observances, and the godly virtue of the dying saints (especially belief in election and submission to divine providence). These elements—evident in Calvin's own accounts of deathbed scenes, including that of his wife—characterize one of the most famous of the Reformed treatments of dying, Thomas Becon's lengthy and heavily didactic *Sicke Mannes Salve* (17 editions between *c.* 1560 and 1620). Becon's art of dying exemplifies the Reformed tradition's commitment to certitude of salvation (N. L. Beaty estimates that fully one-fourth or 17,000 words are devoted to despair). The art of dying remained a theological battlefield as evidenced by *Bunny's Resolutions* (1584), the puritan author's polemical revision of the English Jesuit Robert Parsons's *Christian Directory*.

Between 1575 and 1800 Jesuits produced more than 200 works dealing with the art of dying. Two popular examples, by Juan Polanco and Robert BELLARMINE, reveal both continuities and changes in the pastoral style of post-Tridentine Catholicism. Both differ from the late medieval genre most obviously in their intense focus on the sacraments and the office of the priest. The 20 chapters of Polanco's *Methodus ad aiuvandos eos qui moriuntur* (1575) recycle Christian commonplaces. But Polanco's main interest is to prepare the priest for the variety of dying believers he might meet—those who suffer doctrinal doubt, fear of death, moral uncertainty, impatience, and despair. The longest chapter by far discusses help for those who have been condemned to death and await execution. In every case the goal is the proper reception of the Last Sacraments, especially the making of a good confession, and perseverance in the intentions those works imply.

One-half of Bellarmine's *De arte bene moriendi* is devoted to the life-long preparation for death that every prudent Christian should practice. But traditional ideas and tactics for the management of the final days or hours are just as prominent—including exposition of temptations and their remedies, and interrogations to ensure the proper disposition of the dying. A remarkable chapter deals with death "not from ordinary illness" but rather from events like heart attack or lightning; war or shipwreck; and, finally, execution for capital crimes. The last of these, St. Robert declares, are by far the most fortunate because their suffering is less likely to impair their free will, and they can apply themselves with full consciousness to prayer, confession, and communion. Condemned prisoners have the added advantage of help from those Christians who devote themselves to the instruction of the condemned as a pious work and who know how to teach them to die in a holy way. It was just such a confraternity of "Bianchi" that guided the condemned to die in Palermo from 1541 to 1820. The process of conversion centered on confession, with ritual displays of willing submission by the convicts to their sentence. Lay opinion apparently drew the same conclusion about the chances of the condemned as had Bellarmine, for the historian of the Bianchi, Maria Pia di Bella, reports that those executed prisoners who conformed to the confraternity's exemplary pattern were popularly thought to be saints. The path to that paradoxical conclusion stretches back to Christian antiquity, but the most important contributions to its development were made in the century before the Reformation, first by Gerson, and then by two anonymous works either one of which might deservedly be called "the" *ars moriendi.*

Bibliography: Primary Sources. ANSELM OF CANTERBURY, "Admonitio morienti et de peccatis suis nimium formidanti," *Patrologia Latina,* ed. J. P. MIGNE (Paris 1878–90) 158, 685–88. A. TENENTI, "Ars Moriendi" (xylographic QS version, *c.* 1470), *La Vie et la mort à travers l'art du XVe siècle* (Paris 1952), 97–120. *Ars moriendi (1492), ou, L'Art de bien mourir: suivi de L'aiguillon de la crainte divine pour bien mourir, Peines de l'enfer et du purgatoire et des joies du paradis* (Paris 1986). T. BECON, "The Sick Man's Salve in Prayers and Other Pieces," ed. JOHN AYRE, Parker Society, *The Works of Thomas Becon,* 4 (Cambridge 1844) 88–191. R. BELLARMINE, "The Art of Dying Well," *Spiritual Writings,* tr. and ed. J. P. DONNELLY, S.J. and R. J. TESKE, S.J. (New York and Mahwah 1989). F. COMPER, M. M., ed. and trans., *The Book of the Craft of Dying and Other Early English Tracts Concerning Death* (New York, Bombay, and Calcutta 1917; reprint New York 1977). D. ERASMUS, "Preparing for Death. De praeparatione ad mortem," tr. J. N. GRANT, *Spiritualia and Pastoralia,* ed. J. W. O'MALLEY, *Collected Works of Erasmus 70* (Toronto, Buffalo, and London 1998). J. GERSON, "La Médicine de l'ame," *Oeuvres complètes,* ed. PALÉMON GLORIEUX, 10 v. (Paris 1960–73) 7, 404–07; "Opusculum tripartitum," *Opera Omnia,* ed. E. DUPIN (Antwerp 1706) 1, 425–50. Secondary Sources: R. A. ANSELMENT, *The Realms of Apollo* (Newark, Delaware and London 1995). H. APPEL, *Anfechtung und Trost im Spätmittelalter und bei Luther, Schriften des Vereins für Reformationsgeschichte,* 165 (Leipzig 1938). F. BAYARD, *L'art du bien mourir au XVe siècle: étude sur les arts du bien mourir au bas moyen âge à la lumière d'un "Ars moriendi" allemand du XVe siècle* (Paris 2000). N. L. BEATY, *The Craft of Dying: A Study in the Literary Tradition of the Ars Moriendi in England* (New Haven, London 1970). R. CHARTIER, "Les arts de mourir, 1450–1600," *Annales E.S.C.,* 31, no. 1 (January–February 1976) 51–75. M. P. DI BELLA, *La pura verità: Discarichi di coscienza intesi dai 'Bianchi'* (Palermo 1541–1820, 1999). F. FALK, *Die deutschen Sterbebüchlein von der ältesten Zeit des Buchdruckes bis zum Jahre 1520* (Cologne 1890). L. KLEIN, "Die Bereitung zum Sterben: Studien zu den frühen reformatorischen Sterbebüchern," *Dissertation in Theology,* Georg-August-Universität (Göttingen 1958). G. W. MCCLURE, *Sorrow and Consolation in Italian Humanism* (Princeton 1991) chapter 3. R. MOHR, "Ars Moriendi, 16.–18, Jahrhundert" *Theologische Realenzyklopädie* 4 (Berlin and New York 1979) 149–54. P. NEHER, *Ars Moriendi—Sterbebeistand durch Laien. Eine historisch-pastoraltheologische Analyse, Dissertationen Theologische Reihe,* ed. B. SIRCH, 34 (St. Ottilien 1989). SISTER M.

C. O'CONNOR, *The Art of Dying Well: The Development of the Ars moriendi Columbia University Studies in English and Comparative Literature,* 156 (New York 1942; repr. 1967). J. W. O'MALLEY, "Introduction, Spiritualia and Pastoralia," *Collected Works of Erasmus 70* (Toronto, Buffalo, and London 1998). C. C. OLDS, "Ars Moriendi: A Study of the Form and Content of Fifteenth-Century Illustrations of the Art of Dying," University of Pennsylvania Dissertation in Fine Arts (1966). S. E. OZMENT, *The Reformation in the Cities: The Appeal of Protestantism to Sixteenth-Century Germany and Switzerland* (New Haven and London 1975) esp. chapter 3. F. S. PAXTON, *Christianizing Death: The Creation of a Ritual Process in Early Medieval Europe* (Ithaca and London 1990). D. ROCHE, "La Mémoire de la Mort: recherche sur la place des arts de mourir dans la Librairie et la lecture en France aux XVIIe et XVIIIe siècles," *Annales E.S.C.,* 31, no. 1 (January–February 1976) 76–119. R. RUDOLF, "Ars moriendi: Mittelalter," *Theologische Realenzyklopädie* 4 (Berlin and New York 1979) 143–49. R. RUDOLF et al., "Ars moriendi" *Lexikon des Mittelalters* 1 (Munich and Zurich 1980) 1039–44. D. SCHÄFER, "Texte vom Tod. Zur Darstellung und Sinngebung des Todes," *Spätmittelalter, Göppinger Arbeiten zur Germanistik,* eds. U. MÜLLER, F. HUNDSNURSCHER, and C. SOMMER, Number 620 (Göppinger 1995). P. SLACK, *The Impact of the Plague in Tudor and Stuart England* (Oxford 1985, repr. with corrections, 1990). A. TENENTI, "Ars Moriendi: Quelques notes sur le problème de la mort à la fin du XVe siècle," *Annales. E.S.C.,* 6, no. 4 (October–December 1951) 433–46. T. N. TENTLER, "Peter Lombard's 'On Those Who Repent at the End': Theological Motives and Pastoral Perspectives in the Redaction of Sentences 4.20.1," *Studi e Testi in Archivio Italiano per la Storia della Pietà* 9 (1996) 281–318; "Forgiveness and Consolation in the Religious Thought of Erasmus," *Studies in the Renaissance,* 12 (1965) 110–33; *The Problem of Anxiety and Preparation for Death in Luther, Calvin, and Erasmus* (Harvard University Dissertation in History, 1961). C. VOGEL, *La Discipline pénitentielle en Gaule des origines à la fin du VIIe siècle* (Paris, 1952) 24–120. M. VOVELLE, *La mort et l'occident de 1300 à nos jours* (Paris 1983), especially chapters 3 and 7. D. WEINSTEIN, "The Art of Dying Well and Popular Piety in the Preaching and Thought of Girolamo Savonarola," *Life and Death in Fifteenth-Century Florence,* M. TETEL, R. WITT, and R. GOFFEN, eds. (Durham and London 1989) 88–104.

[T. TENTLER]

ARS PRAEDICANDI

A literary genre comprising manuals on the art of preaching. In the period from 1200 to 1500, with the rise of the great preaching orders and the spread of scholasticism, preaching flourished both in practice and in theory. Special manuals proliferated; well over 200 are known, although most of them are still in manuscript form, unpublished. Many are anonymous. These systematic treatises are quite different from the sketchy and rudimentary attempts of the earlier period to give outline to the art, a period when the direct and uncomplicated homily was the common type of preaching.

The professed aim of the preacher was to win souls to God, to provide instruction in faith and morals. He was advised to feed the mind rather than charm the ear, to confer profit rather than delight, and not to make a vainglorious display of his powers. Yet eloquence could be the handmaid of Christian truth and secular learning could be made use of by the preacher. Several of the best treatises on the *ars praedicandi* were devoted to sermons to be delivered to the clergy and students in the theological schools of the great universities, and they therefore reflect the taste of learned audiences.

The influence of classical rhetoric on the *ars praedicandi* is in some degree apparent, but the scholastic foundation goes even deeper—dialectical *topoi* abound in the method of developing the sermon. The most common method of sermon development in this period was the thematic, and this embraced a variety of types.

The thematic sermon was generally constructed of the following parts: the theme, drawn from the Bible; the protheme (or antetheme), likewise from the Bible, which should render the hearers attentive, receptive, and well disposed, and lead to a prayer invoking God's aid; the reintroduction of the theme, beginning with a citation from Scripture, the Fathers, or a moral philosopher, and then proving by scriptural authorities the terms present in the theme, employing for the purpose argument, narration, example, or other means of explication; finally, the development, in which the parts of the theme are divided and subdivided and the process is carried out with application of a great variety of hermeneutical principles. Recourse to the concordant points in the authorities is constant. The sermon was often compared to a tree, the theme corresponding to the root, the protheme to the trunk, the main divisions to the larger branches, the subdivisions to the smaller, and the development to the rich foliage, flowers, and fruit.

Development by expansion was an important feature of preaching theory. Among the numerous means are maxims, the *EXEMPLUM*, etymology, the four senses of scriptural interpretation, rhythm, metrical consonance, and cadence (the last three serving also a mnemonic purpose), multiplication of synonyms, interpretation of a name, the logical categories, cause and effect, syllogisms and enthymemes, and opportune humor. The preacher's ethical qualities, personality, and deportment, and the psychology of many different kinds of audience are often considered, and advice of practical value is offered for the delivery of the sermon. Occasionally homiletical aids are recommended, such as biblical commentaries, glosses, concordances, tracts on vices and virtues, collections of *exempla*, homiletic lexica, and text-materials—all storehouses on which the preacher could draw.

The highly schematized nature of the *artes*, with their serrated tissue of texts and divisions and their tendency to encourage mechanical artifice, verbal dexterity, and often false subtleties, induced an adverse reaction on the part of some critics both at the time and later. Others, however, praised the ingenuity of the inventional scheme, the adherence to good order, the firm foundation in Scripture, and the shrewd and sound observations. When allied to talent, the rules doubtless trained many effective preachers in their day.

See Also: PREACHING, I (HISTORY OF); PREACHING, II (HOMILETIC THEORY).

Bibliography: É. GILSON, "Michel Menot et la technique du sermon médiéval," *Revue d'histoire franciscaine* 2 (1925) 301–350. G. R. OWST, *Preaching in Medieval England* (Cambridge, Eng. 1926). T. M. CHARLAND, *Artes praedicandi* (Ottawa, Canada 1936). W. O. ROSS, ed., *Middle English Sermons* (London 1940). C. H. E. SMYTH, *The Art of Preaching: A Practical Survey of Preaching in the Church of England, 747–1939* (New York 1940) 1998. D. ROTH, *Die mittelalterliche Predigttheorie und das Manuale Curatorum des Johann Ulrich Surgant* (Basel 1956). H. CAPLAN, "Classical Rhetoric and the Mediaeval Theory of Preaching," in *Historical Studies of Rhetoric and Rhetoricians*, ed. R. F. HOWES (Ithaca, NY 1961) 71–89, 387–391; "Rhetorical Invention in Some Mediaeval Tractates on Preaching," *Speculum* 2 (1927) 284–295; "The Four Senses of Scriptural Interpretation and the Medieval Theory of Preaching," *ibid.* 4 (1929) 282–290; *Mediaeval Artes praedicandi: A Hand-List* (Ithaca, NY 1934); *Mediaeval Artes praedicandi: A Supplementary Hand-List* (Ithaca, NY 1936).

[H. CAPLAN]

ARSENIUS AUTORIANUS, PATRIARCH OF CONSTANTINOPLE

Patriarch 1255 to 1259 and 1261 to 1266, surnamed Autoreianos; b. probably Constantinople, *c.* 1200; d. 1273. He was baptized George, but changed his name to Gennadius as a monk; he became abbot of the monastery of Oxeia on the island of Prinkipo. As Arsenius, he was chosen by Theodore II Lascaris as an emissary to Rome (1254) and on his return was named patriarch of Nicaea (1255). Despite his distrust of the emperor, he permitted himself to be used by the latter to crown (1259) MICHAEL VIII PALAEOLOGUS emperor of Byzantium disregarding claims of the legitimate heir to the throne, John IV Lascaris. Tormented by his conscience, he resigned as patriarch of Nicaea; but under the prompting of Michael VIII he accepted the patriarchate of Constantinople (1261). When Michael VIII had John IV, the legitimate heir to the throne, blinded, Arsenius excommunicated the emperor; and when Michael refused to abdicate, Arsenius was dethroned and exiled to the island of Proconnesus. Arsenius declared his deposition and the nomination of the new Patriarch Joseph (1267–75), and spoke out against misdeeds that were bringing about the ruin of the Church. His many followers among the clergy and laity caused a crisis in the Byzantine Church by provoking the

Schism of the Arsenites. Arsenius was exonerated and given a pension of 300 byzants, but he spent the remaining years of his life in exile on Proconnesus. Of his writing, a number of Patriarchal Acts and a Testament have been preserved. He is credited with a Euchelaion Liturgy (last anointing), which is probably the result of a MS misunderstanding. He seems to have been the author of an Easter Sunday song and several poetic canons.

Bibliography: H. G. BECK, *Kirche und theologische Literatur im byzantinischen Reich* 702–703. G. OSTROGORSKY, *History of the Byzantine State*, tr. J. HUSSEY 395, 411, 435. L. PETIT, *Dictionnaire de théologie catholique* 1.2:1992–94. L. BRÉHIER, *Dictionnaire d'histoire et de géographie ecclésiastiques* 4:750–751. A. A. VASILIEV, *History of the Byzantine Empire* (2d Eng. ed. Madison, WI 1952) 544–661. V. LAURENT, *Byzantinische Zeitschrift* 30 (1929–30) 489–496. M. JUGIE, *Échos d'Orient* 26 (1927) 416–419, Extreme Unction. V. GRUMEL, *ibid.* 33 (1934) 269–270.

[G. LUZNYCKY]

ART

This article discusses art and religion as well as art and Christianity.

1. ART AND RELIGION

The historic beginnings of religion, magic, and art are irrevocably lost, although it may be assumed that all three belong to the cultural heritage of homosapiens from the earliest times of their existence. Prehistoric finds clearly demonstrate the existence of art in Paleolithic times. There is no such incontrovertible evidence for the very early existence of religion and magic, although this existence can be deduced with a fair degree of probability from certain prehistoric data. However, it must be noted at once that our knowledge of religion and magic in prehistoric times never goes further than more or less plausible conclusions based on analogy. Direct knowledge concerning the manifestations of the human spirit begins with the invention and development of writing, that is, from the last part of the 4th millennium B.C. Hence, while the history of art may well start with Paleolithic art, as long as it is confined to stylistic and aesthetic studies and does not attempt to interpret the spiritual content of prehistoric art forms, a comparable history of prehistoric religion and magic is not possible. Prehistoric finds furnish at best only indirect knowledge of prehistoric religion and magic, as all finds have to be interpreted in the light of religions known through history or modern observation.

The foregoing preliminary remarks must be kept in mind in discussing the connections between art, religion, and magic. In this section, magic and religion will be considered as one complex whole. There is no sharp dividing line between magic and religion, although a progressive differentiation in both directions may be observed. There is, however, a clear difference between religion and sorcery in its many forms, but the facts do not justify the view that primitive or archaic religions are made up wholly or mainly of elements of magic—the word magic being taken here in its usual and popular sense.

Distinction between Art and Religion. In most cultures art and religion are closely connected. Nevertheless, unlike religion and magic, which are interwoven and interdependent, art and religion form two clearly differentiated manifestations of the human spirit. Both transcend the rational limits of the human mind, and both depend heavily on the possibilities of symbolic representation of a spiritual reality envisioned in, behind, or above the material world of the senses. Without the possibility of symbolic representation, art can be nothing more than a duplication of material forms, and religion has to be silent. In both art and religion man can feel himself to be in communication with the inexpressible infinite. In both, humanity tries to break through the frontiers of existence.

Even though in recent times art has more than once been proposed as a substitute for religion, it can never replace religion—except perhaps in the case of a few exceptional individuals. Art, even when it serves religion, is essentially concerned with beauty and with beauty only. It is self-evident that beauty in this context is not meant to be identified with any historic ideal of beauty, as, e.g., the Greek, but is meant to express the specific concern of art, the truth of art. Art as such is autonomous. Religion, on the contrary, in one way or another always offers a coherent whole on which man can base his present existence and, if necessary, his hereafter.

Although there may be ethics without religion, there is certainly no religion without ethics. A work of art may be completely without ethics, for instance, a landscape, a flower piece, a still life. The quest of art is the quest for beauty; religion is always concerned with God or gods and the reality of the divine in whatever form this conception may be symbolized. Looked at in this way, religion is autonomous. Although art and religion may collaborate, and have done so extensively in fact, both are to be regarded as autonomous fields of human spiritual endeavor. A work of art as such is not to be judged by any religious or ethical standards, nor is religion to be judged by criteria of beauty. It is clear, in practice, that other considerations may intervene, since art and religion both must function in a community and in a society that cannot be atomized or divided into a number of watertight compartments. The secondary character of such considerations, however ought to be clearly understood.

Art and Magic. Many elements of religion have been misinterpreted as magic. Elements such as hunting rites, fertility ceremonies, and many others, are here considered to be religious and not magical. With this in mind, it may be said that the relations between art and magic are far less close than those between art and religion. This is not difficult to understand, for, while religion is a social as well as an individual phenomenon, magic is in nearly all instances strictly personal, or at the most is practiced by a small minority group. It may perhaps be better described by the terms sorcery and witchcraft. On this point E. Durkheim is right in his sociological distinction between religion and magic: there is no *église magique*.

In every culture art is produced by artists—even though they need not be professional artists—and they often serve their society by serving religion. In many cultures, in fact, the production of art is connected mainly with religious purposes. Artists seldom have reason, however, for putting their gifts at the service of magic. Hence, the paraphernalia of sorcery are usually the home products of the performers of magic themselves, irrespective of their artistic talents, as can be demonstrated in any ethnographic or folkloristic museum. The waxen images of European sorcery, to mention one convincing instance, were not fashioned by professional sculptors but by sorcerers, lay or professional, themselves. Moreover, art is generally meant to be seen, and art in the service of religion can, as a rule, be seen by the religious group as a whole and not merely by a restricted number of persons. Magical art, on the other hand, is not meant to be observed and inspected but is often kept hidden or secret. Hence, magical figurines, for example, are usually much poorer artistically than religious ones. All great art in primitive cultures is religious art; or, if it is not religious in the full sense of the word, it has a social function as a mark of status. In any case, it may be considered as participating in religions values.

Religion and Art in Primitive Cultures. In primitive societies most art has either a religious or a social function. Art for art's sake does not exist. When a work of art has a social function, there may be indirect connections with religion. Accordingly, royal insignia are more than merely symbols of status; they belong to the sphere of religion as participating in the sacred position of the king. Other insignia, too, may have a religious value, e.g., the ceremonial adzes from Mangaia (Polynesia), which are shaped in such a way that they are useless for any real work, but serve to indicate the special place of the skilled craftsmen in the service of the god Tane. Among the Dan tribes (West Africa) masks have a religious function, but masks may be used also to implement the power of a chief. Utensils, weapons, and other objects may be ornamented with sacred motives that remind the user of religious concepts. Most utensils from the Geelvinkbay area (northwest New Guinea) are ornamented, in the local

"Christ Crucified," oil on panel by Antonello da Messina, signed and dated 1475.

Korwar style, with a small human figure representing an ancestor and, in this way, rendering the ancestor present in the daily life of his descendants. Practically everything made by the Dogon (western Sudan) and related tribes bears an ornamentation consisting of religious symbols. A zigzag line signifies the principle of duality that pervades the whole universe and is, at the same time, a reminder of the spiral movement of the unfolding of creation. By such ornamentation even the humble tools of everyday life are placed in the context of the sacred.

In primitive art there is no clear dividing line between the sacred and the profane. Only a few objects, if any, are completely free from connections with religion. This should not be interpreted to mean, as is often done, that all primitive art is religious art.

Art Objects in Their Functional Relations. For a better understanding of the religious art of the nonliterate peoples it is necessary to study the function and significance of the individual objects in the context of their own

Stone sculpture of the Virgin Mary, French Romanesque, 12th century, Isabella Stewart Gardner Museum, Boston. (©Burstein/ CORBIS)

cultures. While it is possible to arrive at an aesthetic appreciation of primitive art without possessing specialized knowledge, it is clear that religious understanding is not possible without a thorough study of the whole cultural background. A people of hunters has a type of religion that differs from that of an agricultural tribe; the culture of an island in Melanesia is far different from that of an Inuit tribe in the high North or from that of a West African monarchical state. All these differences in cultures and religions are reflected in their art. It is impossible to mistake a mask from New Ireland (Melanesia) for one of the Yoruba (Nigeria) or to confuse it with an Inuit mask from Alaska. Nor is the function and significance of the mask in all three cases exactly the same.

Within a given culture it is of importance to know whether an object may be part of anyone's private possessions, such as an amulet or some kinds of oracles; or whether it belongs to the sacred possessions of the whole community, as is, for instance, a mask used and shown in a ceremony that is generally accessible to all; or whether it is the prerogative of some person or group of persons to have and use such objects, as is the case with the paraphernalia of the priest and of the shaman and objects that are the exclusive possession of a secret society. Among the Azande (southern Sudan) the rubbing oracle is generally in use, but only their Mani secret society possesses the small figurines, called *yanda*, that preside over the oracles of this society.

It is important, too, to know whether a given object is meant to be used and kept for as long a time as possible, as, e.g., the image of a deity, often made from stone or hardwood for that purpose, or whether it has been produced to serve only for a short period. In that case it is often made of more perishable material, such as light wood or even less permanent materials. This is true of many masks, dance ornaments, and other ceremonial paraphernalia that are made for use in one ceremony and must be replaced by new ones the next time the same ceremony is to be performed. In some cases the term of life is not fixed in advance. The Korwar ancestor figures from the Geelvinkbay area are used and preserved as long as the ancestor represented through the medium of the Korwar manifests himself as helpful, but may be thrown away or sold without much ado as soon as the ancestor shows himself unwilling to help his descendants.

It is likewise important to know under what kind of conditions a work of sacred art is shown and observed. It makes a difference whether a statue or mask is meant to be seen clearly in the full light of day or only vaguely in the flickering light of the fire, or whether it is meant to be seen from nearby, to be touched, perhaps, or to be viewed only from afar. To judge a mask, it is necessary to know to what kind of full costume it belongs. The form of some statues can be understood only if it is known that they are kept partly wrapped up and that the shape is adapted to that purpose.

Importance of Attitudes and Attributes. Knowledge of attitudes, attributes, and symbolic ornamentation is indispensable for the understanding of primitive religious art. The Dogon have figures with the hands raised to indicate the attitude of praying to the powers of heaven. Many African statues show a woman pressing her breasts, a gesture of loving motherhood. One type of canoe ornament of the Solomon Islands (Melanesia) consists of a prognathic head and a pair of arms. Such figures, which were fastened to the prow of the large war canoes, represent the protecting spirit of the headhunting expedition. These figures sometimes hold a head in their hands. This signifies that the head they go out to hunt has already been cut off by the protecting spirit of the expedition. In a few cases, the figure holds a bird instead of a

"Christ in the House of Mary and Martha," painting by Diego Velasquez, c. 1620, National Gallery, London. (©National Gallery Collection; By kind permission of the Trustees of the National Gallery, London/CORBIS)

head, but the meaning is the same, for the bird is the soul bird and can thus substitute for the head. A few statues from the Bapende (Kwango region, Congo) have been found that represent a woman, the so-called "woman of power," and were originally placed on the hut of the chief of the village. They represent the first wife of the chief. In her right hand the woman holds an ax, in the left one, a bowl. The ax is a deviation from the original meaning, as it is the misrepresentation of an agricultural tool for hacking open the ground, an attribute serving as a symbol of the fertility of the fields. This change probably took place under the influence of the significance of the bowl. At the ceremony of the installation of a new chief a human sacrifice was made and the bowl was used for holding the blood.

Significance of Symbolism. Symbolism is one of the most prominent features of primitive religious art, and it can be present in various ways. In some instances it is indicated by a combination of heterogeneous elements that are held together by an underlying idea. Knowledge of the religious conceptions behind such combinations—which are often strange to us—is the only key to their understanding. There is a type of mask from the Inuit of Alaska representing an animal and its *inua* (soul). A seal

and its *inua*, for instance are represented by the combination of a recognizably realistic figure of a seal combined with a human face because the *inua* of a seal, being a spirit, is thought to be of a more or less anthropomorphic shape. There are comparable masks of other animals, of birds, and even fish, such as the salmon. A large type of mask in use among the Senufo (Ivory Coast) is often called a firespitter because burning tinder may be placed in the open mouth. It is emphasized in the ceremonies of the Korubla anti-sorcery society and combines the characteristics of various animals, such as the hyena, wart hog, antelope, and sometimes other elements. All species represented in this type of mask are of importance in the mythology of the Senufo.

Symbolism in Morphological Characteristics. Symbolism may be found in morphological characteristics. A type of mask in use among the Bambara (western Sudan) during the initiation ceremonies for boys of the Ndomo society has a very large nose and an extremely small mouth or no mouth at all. In the symbolism of this people the nose is the organ of social contact. A large nose symbolizes full participation in the social life of the community. The mouth, the organ of speaking, on the contrary, is made as small as possible, for in the mouth lies danger

Martyrdom of St. Sebastian, marble sculpture, Santa Maria sopra Minerva church, Rome. (©Andrea Jemolo/CORBIS)

for a man: ''The mouth is the enemy of the man'' is an utterance found in a Bambara sacred chant.

Symbolism in Ornamentation. Many examples from native North American tribes have been collected by F. Boas in his well-known book *Primitive Art*. He describes, e.g., the hood of a cradle board of the Cheyenne on which, in various colors and ornamental forms, the life of the child has been symbolically expressed. The white background designates the sky and life. A strip, bounded by blue lines, running down the middle of the hood is meant to represent the path of life of the child lying in the cradle. Here, again, use is made of color symbolism: green for growth and development; yellow for maturity and perfection; red for blood, life, and good fortune.

The Inuit of Alaska have masks surrounded by a number of rings, each of which designates one of the spheres of the universe that encompass our world.

A very rich symbolism is connected with masks of the Dogon. One type, the *kanaga* mask is characterized by a double-armed cross (Lorraine cross) on the top, the symbolism of which is explained by M. Griaule in a number of publications. The esoteric meaning is that it represents a species of bird in flight, and this is what is told to the young members of the *Awa*, the community of all

those who are entitled to wear a mask and to participate in the masked ceremonies. In the esoteric meaning the double-armed cross is connected with the myths of creation that play a prominent role in all religious speculations of the Dogon. This symbolism is explained to the members of the *Awa* only in a later stage of their membership. They are then told that the double-armed cross is derived from a half swastika, which symbolizes the creator pointing upward to heaven with one arm and downward to earth with the other, thus indicating that he has created heaven and earth. The statues from this tribe exhibiting the same attitude ought perhaps to be interpreted in the same way. The half swastika is still at rest, but to bring forth order out of chaos the creator had to move. This movement is conceived as rotary, the spiral movement described in another version of the creation myth. Thus the half swastika is duplicated and now assumes a completed form, the symbol of a rotary or spiral movement.

The development of the swastika into the Lorraine double-armed cross remains unexplained, but it may be surmised that the resemblance to a human being in the fully developed form is the main source of this development. The supposition is supported by the further symbolism connected with this type of mask, for the double-armed cross is interpreted also as a representation of the world. The world, according to the religious philosophy of the Dogon, is said to be in the shape of a man, as is made clear in another part of their myths of creation.

Symbolism of Numbers. Number symbolism is also present in primitive religious art. Among the Bambara, horned masks are in use during ceremonies of initiation. The horns themselves, as in African art generally, symbolize force and fertility. Horns may be compared to vegetation: they push up from the head as the vegetation rises from the earth. The growth of plants and trees is a sign of the forces of fertility residing in the earth; in the same way, horns demonstrate the force innate in many animals. D. Zahan has found in the Ndomo society of the Bambara masks with two to eight horns. Two is the number of duality. It also reminds human beings of their dual nature: in body they are animals, but they possesses also reason and intelligence. Three is the number of masculinity, spirit, activity, etc. Four is that of femininity, the material nature of humanity, passivity, and suffering. Five reminds humanity, because of the five fingers of the hand, of the need to work. Six is the symbolic number of knowledge and instruction. According to the Bambara, human beings have six senses: hearing, sight, smell, taste, feeling and the sense of orientation. Seven designates the integrity of the human personality: each is partly male and partly female (the same conception and the same symbolism is found among the Dogon) but is integrated into one indivisible whole. Seven symbolizes humanity also as created to live in community in a society, and the smallest cell of society, marriage, is symbolized by this number as well. Eight, the highest number employed in this series of symbolic numbers, expresses the principle of renewal embodied in humanity: as an individual destined to die but who may rise immortal from death, as is taught by the Kore society and represented dramatically in its rites.

Arbitrary Character of Symbols. Some symbols in primitive religions and art can best be explained psychologically, as has been shown by the researches of Freud, Jung, and many others; but most of these symbols can be understood only as more or less arbitrarily chosen or invented signs. They must be interpreted in the context of the religion and culture of which they constitute a part. A symbol of the first type, to give one instance, is that of the mother goddess among the Ibo (southern Nigeria); it consists of a pot filled with water. Symbols of the second type, consciously chosen images, are often combined into complexes of interrelated symbols that can be read, once one possesses the necessary data, in a way comparable to that in which the solution of an allegory, or sometimes even a rebus, is worked out. This can be demonstrated convincingly by a concrete example from the culture of the Asmat Papuans (southwest New Guinea). The Papuans of the Asmat area live in a country of extensive swamps. Their world consists mainly of water and mud, and of trees. In their religious world view, human being and tree are closely related: a human is a tree, and a tree is a human. Human and tree are not completely identified, but they are so closely related that they can stand as symbols, the one for the other. If one now starts by comparing a man to a tree, it is reasonable to compare the fruit of a tree to the head of a man; the shape of the coconut especially is well adapted for this comparison. Then, again, one can compare the eating of fruit to the ritual act of head-hunting as practiced among these tribes. When the comparison has gone as far as this, one may employ also the black, fruit-eating birds, like the black cockatoo and the hornbill, as symbols of the Asmat head-hunters, who are black as well, and this is what is actually done.

Rules Governing the Production of Religious Objects. The person who fashions the objects for religious purposes must often submit to special rules. He may have to practice sexual abstinence for a time, and certain kinds of food may be prohibited. The rule is practically universal that sacred objects must be made in secret. On the Ivory Coast the sculptor retires into the bush when making a mask, because women and uninitiated children are strictly prohibited from seeing his work—in any case before it has been finished. Their viewing of his work would

cause failure on his part or would be an evil omen generally.

Other rites, too, may be performed. Small sacrifices are offered and ceremonies performed when cutting down a tree. In Hawaii a human being was sacrificed when a divine image was to be made. Special values may be attached to certain materials and special demands may be made concerning the materials used. In West Africa gold was sacred. Certain species of trees may be regarded as sacred, as, e.g., in Indonesia, and their wood may be considered as especially well adapted for religious purposes. Among the Iroquois (colonial New York) masks were worn for certain ceremonies. The wood for these masks had to be cut out of a living tree in such a way that the tree did not die afterward. Thus, the vital force of the wood was kept intact.

Religion and Art in Myths. The close connections between religion and art may receive explicit mention in myths regarding the origins of sculpturing, painting, or other forms or techniques of art. As a rule, the myth tells that some divine being was the first to practice the particular art and that he then taught it to human beings or, in the case of a deified ancestor, to his descendants. A myth of the Baluba (Katanga, Congo) narrates how Nkulu teaches the making of the small figurines in use in this tribe to ward off illness and other kinds of ill luck.

In summary it may be stated that any view of the relations between religion and art in prehistoric times rests on assumptions, some rather plausible, some very tenuous. The theories on the relation of prehistoric religion and art reflect for the most part the theories on primitive religion and art in force at the same time and in the same school.

Separation of Religion and Art. The close relations between religion and art in some cultures tend to become less close as the progressive differentiation within a culture takes place. In less complex cultures religion is the main client of the artist. Chiefs and other persons of authority come second, but their power and dignity are still intimately connected with religious values. Utensils, tools, weapons, and other objects of everyday life may attain the beauty of an object of art, and this beauty may be considered very important, but no need is felt, in either the house or the village, for objects serving merely the purpose of decoration. The situation changes when further development results in social and economic changes through which religion as patron of the arts becomes less important. Religious changes, too, may have the same result, as in those parts of Europe that became Protestant. Authority, too, became gradually more secularized.

Art under New Patronage. On the other hand, a new class of patrons comes forward, demanding the services of the artist to decorate its houses, gardens, cities etc. While some of this decoration may still be of a religious character, much of it is bound to be completely secular: portraits painted or carved, sculptures and paintings commemorating special events of family life or of the life of the nation, etc. Through this development the purpose of a work of art becomes less clearly circumscribed than it once was, and the way is opened to a purely aesthetic appreciation of art for art's sake. This aesthetic tendency is evidenced, for example, in the collecting of art objects, first the pastime of princes, then that of the rich, and now in part an activity of the state. In a collection or museum the objects of art are completely divorced from their original practical purposes. Except for some forms of modern art, they are completely divorced also from their original function and stripped of all values except the aesthetic. This process is now spreading very quickly throughout the world. In a comparable way religion has been driven away or excluded from many fields that in the past it could consider its own, and it has been compelled to concentrate more on its own specific values and categories.

Opposition between Art and Religion. While usually art and religion go together, history reveals instances also of enmity between art and religion, as, on the one hand, ICONOCLASM, and on the other, the propagation of art and beauty, as such, as rivals of religion. These clashes, however are of less real significance than the relations between both. They are not so much conflicts between art and religion as such but are based rather on disagreement between a specific type of religion and a specific type of art.

Bibliography: C. H. RATSCHOW, *Die Religion in Geschichte und Gegenwart* (3d ed. Tübingen 1957–65) 4: 126–131. K. DITTMER et al., *ibid.* 131–161. H. G. GEYER, *ibid.* 161–165. A. HALDER et al., *Lexikon für Theologie und Kirche,* ed. J. HOFER and K. RAHNER (Freiburg 1957–65) 6: 682–687, with bibliog. F. BOAS, *Primitive Art* (New York 1955). G. VAN DER LEEUW, *Sacred and Profane Beauty: The Holy in Art,* tr. D. E. GREEN (New York 1963), with bibliog. H. READ, *Icon and Idea* (Cambridge, Mass., 1955). A. LEROI-GOURHAN, ''Préhistoire,'' *Histoire de l'art 1* (Encyclopédie de la Pléiade; Paris 1961) 1–92. J. GUIART, ''Océanie,'' *ibid.* 1587–1635. G. BALANDIER, ''Afrique noire et Madagascar,'' *ibid.* 1743–1829. M. GRIAULE, *Folk Art of Black Africa,* tr. M. HERON (New York 1950); *Masques dogons* (Paris 1938), with bibliog. D. ZAHAN, *Sociétés d'initiation Bombara* (Paris 1960). T. P. VAN BAAREN, *Bezielend Beelden: Inleiding tot de beeldende Kunst der primitieve Volken* (Amsterdam 1962). A. MALRAUX, *Psychology of Art,* tr. S. GILBERT, 2 v. (Bollingen Ser. 24; New York 1949–51).

[T. P. VAN BAAREN]

2. ART AND CHRISTIANITY

The relationship between art and Christianity has had profound influences on the development of painting, architecture, sculpture, and the minor arts. It has produced a vast deposit of iconographic schemes and influ-

enced both the theories of aesthetics and the artistic procedures of artists themselves. This article considers only the general relationship of Christianity to the artist and his artistic production; it attempts to present some of the more important ways in which Christianity is related to the arts.

Christianity and Art in General. The artistic production of humanity preceded Christianity by many thousands of years, and, since the beginnings of Christianity, it has existed alongside of and, for the most part, independent of Christian influence in large geographic areas of the world, e.g., countries of the Far East, such as China, Japan, India, and Malaya; all the regions of North and South America up to the time of modern history; and the larger parts of Africa. The first Christian influences on art occurred during the early Christian period in northern Egypt, and in and around Rome and Constantinople. During the Middle Ages this influence gradually spread throughout Byzantium, western and central Europe, and the British Isles. A high sophistication of art under Christian influence was achieved in Europe during the late Middle Ages and the Renaissance; following the Counter Reformation and baroque art this influence gradually waned and, by the 19th century, had lost its inner vitality. Modern efforts at renewal on the part of Christians began in the late 19th century in Europe and spread to North America in the 20th century.

In order to examine the relationship of Christianity to art as manifested in this development, art is taken first in its most general meaning in Western thought as an intellectual virtue directive of the skilled making of things [*See* ART (PHILOSOPHY)]. The influence of Christianity on the practice of art may be examined then under two aspects: the actual making and the maker himself.

The Making of Things. Human making (both of tools and of things) is rooted in the desire to satisfy human needs, which are determined by the urge to survive and by the will toward perfection. Such needs are dictated and evaluated by the aims that humanity consciously sets for itself and that give meaning to human existence. The virtue of art is the developed aptitude of making things properly; and, insofar as human existence is recognized as being dependent on God and ordered to union with Him, art is at once endowed with religious significance.

Christianity with its clear teaching on creation and on the ultimate purpose of human activity as the glory of God, as well as on the immortal destiny of man, emphasized the intimate and natural relation of art to religion. In common with other religions it helped humanity to see nature as the language and instrument of God, as full of His presence and as sharing in His power and beauty. To this it added the realization that humanity was participating in the work of creation and enabling it to attain its end. Art could thus be seen as endowed with cosmic purpose and with a dignity exceeding that of the object made.

The Maker or Artist. The sense of dependence on and of union with God, which is so central to the great world religions, was presented by Christianity as a dependence based on creation rather than myth; this implied that at every moment all things and all actions continue to depend on God for their existence. The Christian could view all productive activity as a certain cooperating with God "in whom we live and move and have our being" (Acts 17.28). Human making could thus be seen as sacred and significant not only in its object and end but in its source, the human person as sustained and moved by God. However, the artist's view of himself in Christianity may not be isolated to a single concept; it was colored in the East and the West with shifting theological and philosophical speculation. By the time of the Renaissance art was profoundly influenced by the Christian insistence on the dignity of man. The human being was seen as a creature, made in the image of God, intellectual and free, with an immortal soul directly created by God and destined for eternal union with Him. Thus the Renaissance artist was able to produce an image of the Christian world and its beliefs that was permeated with the light of reason and carried the imprint of the dignity of Christians.

Christianity and the Concept of Art. Concepts of art emerge reflectively through the interest of philosophers, artists themselves, and in modern times through the work of art historians and critics. Contemporary concepts of art in Western thought vary considerably and often bear the influence of concepts inherited from Christian tradition. In order to examine some influences Christianity has wielded on theories of art, considerations are presented here first under the aspect of beauty and then under the aspect of the art process.

Beauty. A Christian synthesis of Jewish thought and of Greek thought from Plato to Plotinus on beauty in relation to God is already found in St. Augustine and the Pseudo-Dionysius. It formed a tradition that had a profound influence on the art of the Middle Ages and was clearly formulated in the 12th-century school of Chartres (see de Bruyne). Its speculation on number, light, proportion, and order was realized especially in the Gothic cathedral. This tradition saw beauty, in its formal elements, as verified most fully in God, and as shared from God to creatures, so that the beauty of finite things was seen as stemming from God and as apt to raise the mind of the beholder to the contemplation of God. To see beauty as a divine perfection is to stress its spiritual nature, or at least to ensure that it will not be identified entirely with

its sensible forms. The transcendent character of beauty was thus strongly affirmed by Christian thought, all the more so since created beauty was seen as sharing in the perfection of the Creator.

The humanity of Christ was, moreover, exalted as the supreme beauty of the created order, and that beauty was regarded as shared and manifest to varying degrees in the sensible realities of the world. Beauty was thus more closely linked with God and valued because of that link. The Incarnation was seen as an exemplar that elevated all created and visible forms of beauty.

This Christian teaching on beauty strengthened and helped deepen the vision and enhance the function of the artist. It implied that to make a beautiful thing is to make something sacred; "every good painting is noble and devout of itself, for it is nothing more than a copy of the perfections of God and reminiscence of His own painting" (Michelangelo, as recorded by Francis of Holland in his *Four Dialogues on Painting;* Fr. tr. L. Rouanet, 1911, 29–30).

The Art Process. The Greek and Neoplatonic notion of the formation of things from an eternal matter by a demiurge looked to subsistent ideas as prototypes to serve as an illustration of the human process of artistic making. The demiurge, however, was conceived as being inferior to God, to whom action could not be attributed. It was St. Augustine who, on lines suggested by Philo and Plotinus, identified the eternal exemplars with ideas in the divine mind, and thus conceived of God's activity as supremely artistic. It was possible to conceive of God in this way only when the notion of creation had been accepted from revelation.

The Christian concept of God's creative activity, while affirming a great difference between divine creation and human making, drew attention to the intellectual side of the artistic process, to the stage now known as conception or idealization. By attributing art in its supreme form to the creation of the universe by God it ennobled and enhanced the analogous human activity of artistic creation and the status of those who exercised it.

Speculation on intra-Trinitarian life and the Incarnation also served to deepen the analogy between God as Creator and artist as creator. The Son of God was seen as the revealed word, the Idea born from all eternity in the mind of the Father, by which and in which all things were created. He was thus seen as the Supreme Art or the Perfect Image of the Father, the Idea by which all things were made (Aquinas, *In 2 sent.* 16.1. ad 2; *De ver.* 1.7). The Incarnation gave a supreme exemplar of what the work of art can be. Not only is the Word made flesh, the Idea given a visible form, but the flesh is spiritualized and made the outward sign of the invisible Godhead. From this point of view the art process was seen as analogous to the Incarnation, and at the same time the symbolical character of art was thrown into relief. Considerations such as these permitted Dante to sum up the Christian notion of art in his immortal words: "sì che vostr' arte a Dio quasi è nipote" (so that your art is to God, as it were, a grandchild, *Inferno* 11.105).

Christianity and the Content of Art. In any consideration of content in art it is important to distinguish between the subject matter and the content of a work. A subject treated by an artist in the Renaissance may be quite the same as that treated by a Byzantine artist. However, the manner of conception deriving from different social, theological, geographical, and technical factors produces a content in one somewhat different from that in the other. Thus the person of Christ may be conceived by the Byzantine artist theocentrically in terms of hieratic power and executed in an otherworldly planal structure with a strict symbolical hierarchy of organization. The Renaissance artist, on the other hand, may interest himself more in the humanity of Christ divinized through dramatic heroic power and thus present Him as a believable figure in a rationalized space displaying active moral concern and emotional force. The manner of conceptualization employed by the artist enters the content of the work. Throughout Christian cultures in different geographic areas and at different times, shifting theological emphases have colored the content of Christian themes as they are presented in Christian art.

That Christianity has provided art with new and specific subjects is obvious in the vast deposit of Christian iconography. The primary source of such subjects was the Bible, especially the Gospels, in the presentation of the life, death, and Resurrection of Christ. The events of the life of Mary, her sorrows and her assumption and glorification, were favorite subjects of art in all its forms; so too were the lives, and especially the miracles and martyrdoms, of the saints; the Church herself, usually through some symbol; the Sacraments; the Last Judgment; heaven; and hell (*see* MARY, BLESSED VIRGIN, ICONOGRAPHY OF; JESUS CHRIST, ICONOGRAPHY OF; SAINTS, ICONOGRAPHY OF).

Christian art represented humanity in the light of its supernatural destiny, showing human life as guided by the New Law and as consisting essentially in the exercise of the virtues. The various states of life and the different vocations of humanity in the Christian order were frequent subjects for artistic presentation, just as the main human activities were shown in their religious significance, usually through connection with a patron saint.

This does not imply that visible nature was excluded from Christian art, as though such art were concerned with a spiritual reality divorced from the sensible world. The Augustinian tendency in theology, with its Neoplatonic heritage, invited man to turn away from bodily manifestations of beauty in order to gaze on spiritual beauty and thus to gain almost an intuition of God (see St. Augustine, *Trin.*, *Patrologia Latina* 42:949, 950; St. Anselm, *Proslogion,* PL 158:225). But the insistence of Christian realism, as formulated by St. Thomas on the ground of Aristotelian thought, on the sense origin of all knowledge, taught men rather to find beauty first among finite things and then to rise to a purified knowledge of the beauty of the spirit and of God. The more severe and purely symbolic forms of early Christian art gradually gave way to more realistic and naturalistic forms (e.g., the introduction of landscape into painting), which opened up the whole of nature for artistic use.

Christian Art. Art within Christianity has been a vital part of the mainstream of Western culture and, like other areas of human endeavor, is in process. As such, its characterizing qualities and its aims are subject to continuing discussion. Questions of whether or not there is a Christian art in a strict and proper sense of the term have been raised in the context of the modern renewal in sacred art. The problem has been sharpened by the use within the Church of purely abstract art that is not distinguishable from certain works one might see in museums far removed from the immediate interests of formal religion. The attitude one takes in regard to the nature of Christian art depends largely on the angle from which one approaches the question and on the philosophical framework within which it is considered.

The scholastic philosopher will presumably approach the question of Christian art by asking first of all whether there is any such thing, for it can well be maintained that art remains just art whoever may happen to practice it, whether Jew or Hindu or Christian or otherwise. It can be argued that art is essentially the same, whatever the beliefs or conduct of the artist. One does not speak of a Christian mathematics or medicine. The arts and sciences have their own laws and standards; to qualify them or restrict them in any way would seem to interfere with their essence, to spoil their purity and to limit their freedom.

On the other hand we do in fact speak of Christian art, though not of Christian geometry. We speak of a Christian literature, of Christian painting, sculpture, architecture, and music that are recognized as such.

The common assumption that art can be called specifically Christian when its subject matter is drawn from Christianity is narrow and derives from an inadequate understanding of content in art. On this assumption, the difference between Christian and other forms of art would be purely external (iconographic). Much less can one define Christian art in terms of technique or style, except perhaps in the historical sense that certain styles have in fact evolved in a Christian context. To limit Christian art to fixed forms, as PUGIN, who would lodge the Christian ideal only in a Gothic-styled architecture, is to stifle art and to relegate it to stylism.

If we regard art, insofar as it is art, in the scholastic sense of a naturally acquired intellectual virtue of the practical order, it is one and the same in all men whatever their creed or culture. Art, in its formal constituents, is as unaffected by one's belief as it is by one's conduct.

Art, however, should not be viewed only in relation to its own proper object and in its formal elements, but as placed in the stream of activity issuing from the person of the artist, as a vital power at the service of that person, and as affected by the status or manner of being of the artist. Art is more affected than philosophy and the sciences by this influence. The sciences, in search of truth, are determined by their object, and seek to conform to things as they are; hence they are predetermined in their very nature. Art is practical, and rather than conform itself to what is, it seeks to mold reality to its inner form. Art begets its own form, which it molds in conjunction with existing elements; its object is partly within the artist himself so that art is much more free than science. It will, to a far greater extent, be the expression of the inner life of the artist, communicate his vision, glow with his feeling and embody his ideals. Where art and architecture have been molded from a Christian vision of the world as distinct, for example, from a primitive vision of the world, we can speak of that art as Christian. The science of iconology, which attempts to interpret the meanings underlying structure and iconographic motifs, is best equipped to determine the formative Christian elements in a specific work.

Insofar then as art bears the imprint and shows the influence of its existential Christian setting it can be regarded as a distinctive kind of art with a modality proper to itself. The question has been raised whether this Christian modality may be present in the work of the non-Christian artist who executes a work of art for specific Christian use, or who selects Christian themes. One thinks, for instance, of Matisse and the Stations of the Cross in the chapel at VENCE. To the extent that such artists effect the Christian conceptions attempted in such works one can speak of their art as Christian.

See Also: LITURGICAL ART, HISTORY OF; CHURCH ARCHITECTURE.

Bibliography: General. F. A. R. DE CHATEAUBRIAND, *Génie du christianisme,* 2 v. (new ed. Paris 1885; repr. 1936), Eng. *Genius of Christianity,* tr. C. I. WHITE (7th ed. Philadelphia 1868). A. GHIGNONI, *Il pensiero cristiano nell' arte* (Rome 1903). A. FABRE, *Pages d'art chrétien* (new ed. Paris 1920). J. SAUER, *Wesen und Wollen der christlichen Kunst* (Freiburg 1926). P. GARDNER, *The Principles of Christian Art* (London 1928). L. BRÉHIER, *L'Art chrétien* (2d ed. Paris 1928). E. GILL, "Christianity and Art," in *Art-Nonsense* (London 1929). M. S. GILLET, *Le Credo des artistes* (Paris 1929). *Atti delle Settimana d'arte sacra per il clero,* 5 v. (Vatican City 1933–38). C. COSTANTINI, *L'istruzione del S. uffizio sull' arte sacra* (Vatican City 1952). E. I. WATKIN, *Catholic Art and Culture* (rev. ed. London 1947). B. CHAMPIGNEULLE et al., *Problèmes de l'art sacré* (Paris 1951). J. MONCHANIN, *De l'esthétique à la mystique* (Tournai 1955). M. A. COUTURIER, *Se garder libre: Journal, 1947–54* (Paris 1962). **Particular.** J. AUMANN, *De pulchritudine, inquisitio philosophico-theologica* (Valencia 1951). J. CAMÓN AZNAR, *El tiempo en el arte* (Madrid 1958). C. BELL, *Art* (New York 1958). W. G. COLLINGWOOD, *The Art Teaching of John Ruskin* (London 1900). E. DE BRUYNE, *Étude d'esthétique médiévale,* 3 v. (Bruges 1946); *L'Esthétique du Moyen Âge* (Louvain 1947). M. ELIADE, *The Sacred and the Profane,* tr. W. R. TRASK (New York 1959). É. H. GILSON, *Painting and Reality* (Bollingen Ser. 35.4; New York 1957). A. LITTLE, *The Nature of Art* (New York 1946). J. B. LOTZ, "Christliche Inkarnation und heidnischer Mythos als Wurzel sakraler Kunst," *Archivio di filosofia* 3 (1957) 55–78. J. MARITAIN, *Art and Scholasticism,* tr. J. W. EVANS (New York 1962); *Creative Intuition in Art and Poetry* (Bollingen Ser. 35.1; New York 1953); *The Responsibility of the Artist* (New York 1960). A. M. MONETTE, *La Beauté de Dieu* (Montreal 1950). F. PIEMONTESE, *Problemi di filosofia dell'arte* (Turin 1962). F. VON SCHLEGEL, *Ansichten und Ideen von der christlichen Kunst,* v.6 of *Sämtliche Werke,* 15 v. (2d ed. Vienna 1846).

[A. MCNICHOLL]

ART (PHILOSOPHY)

There is no simple yet comprehensive definition of art; the word has in fact many meanings. The Greek and Latin equivalents (τέχνη, *ars*) can broadly include everything customarily grouped under the label of fine art as well as servile and liberal arts. Even when narrowed to fine art, the word retains ambiguity in at least two important respects. First, whatever community of meaning the various fine arts share, distinctive differences among them prevent the name's remaining exactly the same in meaning; poetry and painting, for example, are not art in a wholly identical sense. Current usage tends to limit the meaning of art to painting and sculpturing. Second, within the context of fine art, art may signify the product of art, the creative process itself, or the experience of appreciating a work of art, sometimes referred to as the aesthetic experience.

This article deals with art from a broad, philosophical point of view, considering its definition and division, the notion of fine art and problems associated with the latter's finality.

Notion of Art

In the Western tradition, the original meaning of art is skill in making; the word was used by the ancient

Greeks to refer, first of all, to the crafts that satisfy basic human needs. Throughout the dialogues of PLATO and the writings of ARISTOTLE, this meaning of art is the basic one employed to explain all other skills, whether physical or mental. Art was also early on recognized as a sign of a certain excellence, testifying to man's progress beyond what nature can provide. Aristotle accordingly points out that he who invented any art was naturally admired by men as being wise and superior to the rest. "But as more arts were invented, and some were directed to the needs of life, others to recreation, the inventors of the latter were naturally always regarded as wiser than those of the former, because their branches of knowledge did not aim at mere utility" (*Meta.* 981b 16–19). Art as "the capacity to make, according to sound reason" (*Eth. Nic.* 1140a 20) was accordingly extended to what we now call liberal and fine art. The history of the meaning of art is the history of man's progress from making products immediately necessary for living to making things ordered to knowledge or enjoyment. This Greek conception of art dominated the Middle Ages and persists in modern times.

ART AND NATURE

Craftsmanship enabled man to attain a grasp of the operations of nature, for he soon noted strong resemblances between the way he produces something and the way in which nature works. Much of Plato's *Timaeus* seeks to render the pattern of the universe intelligible by comparison with man's own making, while still viewing nature as a work of divine art. In the *Physics,* Aristotle appeals to the making of a statue or a bed to help understand how natural CHANGE takes place. It is in this context of making as resembling natural processes that Aristotle's often misunderstood dictum, "art imitates nature," should first be grasped before it is applied to fine art. In another area, medicine, the understanding of nature in terms of art has been fruitfully pursued, as the writings of Galen and Harvey show. Nevertheless, however much art and nature resemble each other, and however much the understanding of one leads to an understanding of the other, they remain quite distinct. The likeness of the work of art exists first in the mind of the maker; the FORM of a living natural object, existing independently of the human mind, preexists in some other natural object. A chair comes from a man's mind, but the man himself comes from another man, from nature.

ART AND SCIENCE

The common notion of art as skill also distinguishes art from SCIENCE, even though both arise from the human mind. Both art and science are KNOWLEDGE, but art is ordered to something apart from knowledge itself, namely, the work produced. In art, therefore, knowing is for the sake of producing. In science, we seek to understand that

something is so or why it is so. This distinction does not prevent some disciplines from being both art and science. For example, figures are constructed in MATHEMATICS, and thus there is both knowledge and production; at the same time what is produced is a subject of DEMONSTRATION, and thus pertains to a science.

ART AND PRUDENCE

Art also differs from prudence or practical wisdom, for although both involve reason, they are concerned with distinct kinds of activity: work and behavior. Art uses knowledge to produce a work; prudence uses knowledge to deliberate well and to arrive at decisions regarding what is to be done to ensure right behavior. Prudence therefore involves the moral order in a way that art does not; consequently, prudence is a moral as well as an intellectual quality in man.

ART AND AESTHETICS

The narrowing of the meaning of art to fine art and the corresponding resolution of a theory of art to AESTHETICS is a relatively modern contribution. The development of art in the Renaissance undoubtedly accelerated this tendency. Alexander Baumgarten, in the middle of the 18th century, is generally regarded as the first to try to construct a systematic aesthetics in the modern sense. True enough, Plato and Aristotle in ancient times, and various writers in the Middle Ages, made major contributions to what is now regarded as a philosophy of fine art. But in the last 200 years the fine arts have been approached in quite different spirit, emphasizing an association of art with BEAUTY and stressing the autonomy of fine art. In such a view, there is a distinct world of fine art and aesthetic experience; a special CREATIVE IMAGINATION and sensibility are thus required to appreciate the distinctive values found in such works.

Kinds of Art

Art has been traditionally divided into liberal and servile arts. This division is basic, referring as it does to a difference in the work to be made. The most obvious type of makeable object is one that exists in external physical matter, for such matter is susceptible to receiving an artificial form; wood, for example, readily lends itself to being shaped into a table, a chair or a bed. It is equally evident that such making, initially at least, is the result of bodily effort on the part of the maker and this feature characterizes such art as servile. Further, the action involved in such making is transitive, that is, an activity which though originating in an agent, terminates outside the agent in some product that comes to exist in physical matter. These characteristics of servile art indicate, as suggested earlier, that the name "art" refers primarily to servile art; this priority is in the order of naming, not a priority of perfection.

LIBERAL ART

Liberal art, therefore, is art in a less obvious sense. We are nonetheless familiar with the extension of the name to liberal art; we are also familiar with the traditional division of the liberal arts into the *trivium* (logic, grammar and rhetoric) and the *quadrivium* (arithmetic, geometry, music and astronomy). Liberal art is less evidently art because the making involved is not a transitive action, but immanent, activity that both originates and terminates within the agent, forming the agent rather than some external physical object. The object of a wholly liberal art, therefore, is immaterial, found primarily in the mind or imagination of the artist. Such an object does not involve making in the original sense, yet proportionally, there is an indetermination in the mind of man requiring that he set in order his means of knowing; for example, order is brought into man's thinking when he establishes what a PROPOSITION is or how we reason in a valid way. A SYLLOGISM, for example, is something we construct deliberately, in the manner of a mathematical figure and not just spontaneously. Such constructions enjoy existence in the mind and imagination. We thus see the reason for calling such arts liberal, since the subjects and purposes of these arts pertain to the mind of man whereby he is set free from lack of ORDER. We see also that although the name ''art'' first signifies manual craft, nevertheless, considering the work produced, liberal art is primary. (*See* LIBERAL ARTS.)

FINE ART

Though the distinction of servile and liberal is basic, it is not particularly revealing in regard to fine art which, in fact, cuts across that division. Some fine arts are liberal; poetry and music, for example, would fall within the liberal division, for the poet and the composer produce their works primarily by immanent action and their works exist chiefly in the imagination. Other fine arts are servile in the sense that the objects made require external physical matter and labor for their existence; thus the painting is embodied on canvas and paint, the statue in stone and the church in stone or brick. To appreciate the distinctive character of fine art, another division must be considered.

From the standpoint of purpose, art is further divided into useful and fine. The useful arts produce things to be enjoyed not in and for themselves, but for some other good. The servile arts would here be classed as useful. Liberal arts such as LOGIC, grammar and RHETORIC could be termed useful in the sense they are not ends in themselves but are sought as indispensable aids for bringing about knowledge, adequate expression or persuasion.

The productions of fine art are contemplated and enjoyed for their own sake (which does not preclude their also being ordered to another extrinsic end). The reason for this division can be shown in a painting, for example, that has a kind of significance inciting enjoyment of a form wholly lacking to a merely useful product, such as a shovel. The painting is viewed primarily for itself; any functional value it might have, such as its location in a particular area, is secondary. There is, moreover, a distinctive and unique type of enjoyment that arises in the viewing or hearing of a work of fine art consequent upon the equally distinctive type of CONTEMPLATION realized in appreciating the work. Some prefer to make this point by saying that the end sought in the work of fine art is the contemplation and enjoyment of beauty, provided that beauty is taken in a properly aesthetic sense.

It is worth noting that man's preoccupation with beauty, pleasing form, design and so on, carries over into many useful products of art and hence the division into useful and fine should not be understood too rigidly. A shoe is clearly a product of useful art, yet we find it both necessary and desirable that a shoe look good. As human beings, we project our desire for beauty of form into objects around us as much as possible; in fact, very few products of human art, no matter how utilitarian they are, escape our passion for artistic enjoyment. We humanize our environment in precisely this way.

Analysis of fine art. From an Aristotelian point of view, what sets off fine art from either liberal or servile is imitation. We have already noted that in a sense all art imitates nature, sometimes in appearance, sometimes in operation. What is peculiar to fine art is that imitation (and delight in the imitation) is the immediate end sought in fine art, whereas imitation serves only as a means in liberal or servile art.

The word ''imitation'' is subject to easy misunderstanding (''representation'' might serve better for a modern reader). In any event, it is not to be identified with more or less literal copying. The tendency to identify them may originate in the fact that the most evident instances of artistic imitation occur in the visual arts, where imitation is associated too readily with natural or photographic likeness. Artistic imitation by no means rests upon a complete dependence of the image upon some original in nature from which it proceeds. It always involves some degree of abstraction. There is equal, if not more, dependence of the image upon man's creative imagination and understanding. Such imitation should therefore be understood as creative. It is imitative in the sense that a work of art represents something other than itself, being some sort of SIGN or SYMBOL; it thus has reference to some aspect of reality as we experience it. It is creative as well, for the mind and IMAGINATION of the artist is also a source and indeed a more significant one. Hence no artist merely reproduces some aspect of reality; on the other hand, no matter how "abstract" or "nonobjective" the work of art, it cannot wholly escape reference to human experience of reality.

Artistic imitation, therefore, is a broad notion ranging from the one extreme of approaching a somewhat literal representation of reality to the opposite extreme of retaining only a tenuous but still significant representation of some quality detected in reality. The history of painting and sculpturing reflects this movement within these extremes. It is realized also in proportionately different ways in other arts. In the poetic arts the object of imitation is the action and passion of men as reflected variously in the poem, the novel or the drama. One could say that the common object of all fine art is human action and passion; the differences among the fine arts come from the manner and means of imitation. Though music is sometimes regarded as a non-imitative art, the facts of musical history belie this observation. Music, of course, does not represent in a visual manner nor is it imitative in the sense that it copies natural sounds. Music represents the flow of passion, originally expressed in the intonation of the human voice, by means of tonal and properly musical progressions. The use of music to accompany drama or motion pictures obviously manifests this; more serious works, even the most "abstract" forms of musical composition, do so more subtly and with more elaborate technique. Even 20th-century music bears witness to such primal representational principles as tension and release, the expected and the unexpected, arousal and resolution. [See MUSIC (PHILOSOPHY)].

Finality of Art

Finality refers to a good or purpose; in art, this refers both to the purpose of the artist and to the work of art itself. The two may coincide, but the artist can also order the work of art to something extrinsic to the work itself. Thus the artist can intend the work for propaganda or some other foreign end. The artist then acts as man rather than as artist and this is one way art and morality may be related. In other words, over and beyond the good of art itself, the artist may be working for a morally good or bad cause; this consideration falls under the scope of prudence.

MORALITY OF ART

Art and morality may also be related within the work itself. Any work of art is an idea expressed by an image in the artist's mind and in an appropriate sense medium. The power of art lies in its simultaneous appeal to SENSES and UNDERSTANDING. What is universal in art is realized in this sense medium; the tragic hero, for example, is a type of man exemplified individually by his action and with whom the spectators can identify themselves. Such a work of art images human nature in its various manifestations and chiefly in its moral character. The artistic image, while not itself of a moral nature, can thus express man in some way acting as a moral agent. This is primarily so in poetic art and proportionately so in other arts.

Consequently, an intrinsic relation between art and morality is evident in the following way. Whenever the work of art creatively represents something of human action and passion, the moral order enters into the work of art as a formal constituent, for human action and passion are voluntary, and voluntary acts are moral acts. Moreover, the moral order contributes to the delight, intelligibility and beauty of much art. For example, the intelligibility and delight we find in a tragedy depend in great measure on grasping some moral grandeur in the action of the hero; the development of a musical composition images in tonal progression the movement of human passion at its finest, whether noble, tragic or joyful. Hence it can be maintained that when a moral dimension enters into the construction of a work of art, the artist, as artist, has an obligation to represent as morally right what is morally right or as morally wrong what is morally wrong. As far as the relation of art and the moral order is concerned, then, what should be excluded from good art is the artist's representing what is morally good as evil and what is morally evil as good; otherwise, he will be unconvincing as an artist and will fail to move us in the manner that is appropriate to art.

At the same time, the intrinsic end of art cannot be overtly moral; art suffers when used merely to propagandize morality. It is one thing for a moral dimension to enter into the artistic representation; it is quite another to make the work of art specifically moral in its aim. We are thus led to recognize a finality of art, which in fact, is twofold. One end is the arousal and release of the emotions wherein lies the great appeal art has for man, for art represents the flow of emotional tension and release more skillfully than our normal experience usually permits. Aristotle's notion of catharsis manifests this point in relation to tragedy. The cathartic end in art is instrumental, however, in that it disposes us for the ulterior end of artistic contemplation and delight. [See POETICS (ARISTOTELIAN)].

ART AND CONTEMPLATION

Artistic contemplation is a distinct kind of knowing, accompanied by a distinct type of delight, realized proportionately in the different arts. So far as this can be summarized generally, it is a knowledge of what need not be, rather than of what must be, and yet the work has its self-contained inevitability; it is an imaginative reconstruction of some aspect of reality and life we are familiar with; it is more intuitive than discursive; it bears on the singular, but in such a way that something universal is realized in it; it must be both concrete and abstract. It is knowledge especially appropriate to the human mode of knowing: an intimate union of sense and intellect, image and concept, imagination and understanding. Therein lies the source of the special delight that accompanies this contemplation, which is at once an action of sense and intellectual APPETITE. There is the initial sense delight accompanying the grasp of such qualities as color, tone, line and sound. There is the intellectual delight attendant upon the grasp of the order entering into the rhythmic, melodic and harmonic construction of a musical composition, or of the order of elements in a work of sculpture or a drama. Most of all, however, such delight arises from seeing in a work of creative representation an object that is more expressly formed and more intelligible than the original referent. The action of the play is more intelligible and more significant than human action ordinarily is. The sound of music is better formed and more discerning than the sound of speech as normally expressive of passion.

Artistic contemplation, constantly fluctuating between an image and an original, never exhausts the significance set in motion by the initial experience of the work of art. The unterminating character of this contemplation is the main reason we enjoy the same work over and over again, for new significance and vitality always emerge in enduring works of art, tantalizing the mind with promises of hidden meaning waiting to be uncovered. Such artistic finality, contemplation with its ensuing delight, constitutes the primary worth of art. For in the final analysis, the work of art is simply the worth of man himself as mirrored in his creative representations.

See Also: LIBERAL ARTS; AESTHETICS; BEAUTY; SYMBOL; PRUDENCE

Bibliography: J. DEWEY, *Art as Experience* (New York 1934). E. GILL, *Art* (New York 1950). T. M. GREENE, *The Arts and the Art of Criticism* (Princeton 1940). S. K. LANGER, *Philosophy in a New Key* (3rd ed. Cambridge, Mass. 1957). J. MARITAIN, *Art and Scholasticism and the Frontiers of Poetry,* tr. J. W. EVANS (New York 1962). T. MUNRO, *The Arts and Their Interrelations* (New York 1949). R. WELLEK and A. WARREN, *Theory of Literature* (New York 1956). H. READ, *Meaning of Art* (new ed. London 1956).

[J. A. OESTERLE]

ART, EARLY CHRISTIAN

Early Christian art comprises the architecture, painting and mosaic, sculpture, and minor arts of the first four centuries of Christianity. After the fifth century, it was re-

placed by Byzantine art. In this article early Christian art is treated under its three geographical manifestations: (1) in the West, (2) in the East, and, because of special conditions prevailing there, (3) in Egypt.

See CHURCH ARCHITECTURE, 2; SYMBOLISM, EARLY CHRISTIAN.

1. In the West

The limits in time and space of early Christian art in the West are somewhat a matter of convention. Nevertheless, as far as time is concerned, the flowering of Byzantine art in the sixth century at Constantinople under Justinian establishes a convenient *terminus ad quem* for all early Christian art. With regard to extent in space, the works of Christian art produced in the areas under Roman domination can be considered as belonging to early Christian art of the West. However, the monuments and objects produced in the Byzantine enclaves in the West, notably at RAVENNA, and above all the monuments that were direct forerunners of Byzantine art, must be excluded. With its limits thus defined, early Christian art in the West is seen to be the continuation of Roman art under new social conditions as well as in a new spirit, that of Christianity.

Actually, one cannot speak of a Christian art in a strict sense. The essential of any art is not the subjects it treats so much as the forms in which they are arrayed, the latter issuing on one hand from the physical and social milieu and on the other hand from the moral climate, which is often even religious and mystical. It is in this sense that one can speak of an art that is Christian. Situated within the orbit of imperial Rome, the Christian ideal was clothed from its very beginnings in the forms offered to it by Roman art.

From the technical point of view, the West offered unusually propitious conditions for the formation of a Christian art. Among these was a certain richness of means available even to the less wealthy classes. These means included: solid and varied materials for construction, architectural knowledge that was constantly employed, a pictorial tradition inherited from the Etruscans, a craft that handled the difficulties of sculpture with great ease, and a whole range of possibilities in the minor arts, including mosaic work. Because of these factors, it is easier to follow the various stages of early Christian art in the West than in the East. Moreover, it is quite possible that the West furnished to Christian art as a whole its first expressive forms.

The evolution of early Christian art is not, however, an unbroken progression. A definite date—the official recognition of Christianity by the Edict of Milan in 313—

Diptych of Boethius, depicting the Roman consuls Boethius (left) and Lampadio (seated), holding staffs of office, ivory, 5th century.
(Alinari-Art Reference/Art Resource, NY)

"The Fall of Jericho," mosaic panel, c. 432–440, basilica of S. Maria Maggiore.

separates it into two stages. Before 313, Christian art was clandestine; after that date, it was openly established.

Clandestine Period. Christianity is in large part rooted in Judaism, but unlike Judaism it is not hostile to the use of images. Even though Christianity emphasizes the importance of the invisible, it is nevertheless the religion of an incarnate God and consequently recognizes the full value of the visible. The use of works of art is therefore in complete accord with its teaching. But Christianity was born in a milieu and in circumstances far from favorable to this concept.

In early apostolic times, those who preached did so in the synagogues. At that period, and especially throughout the regions of the Diaspora, the synagogues were less rigid in their opposition to the representation of sacred objects. This is borne out particularly by the presence of the paintings at DURA-EUROPOS and of others in Palestine itself. The evidence, however, dates from a period later than the beginning of the third century and is scanty. In Rome the decoration of Jewish catacombs is confined almost exclusively to ornamental motifs or reproductions of liturgical furnishings. It is therefore quite probable that at first in the Christian communities the converts from paganism had to combat a current of opinion somewhat opposed to the representation of religious scenes. But the doctrine of the Church was on the side of the converted pagans, and they won their case.

Very soon both in Rome and throughout the empire, Christianity was faced with persecution. The Jewish communities were accused of atheism, exclusiveness, and hatred of the human race. The Christian faith aroused the same prejudices, since it appeared to be linked with the Jewish faith. A decree of Nero after the burning of Rome made the profession of Christianity a legal offence. Under Decius the profession of Christianity was counted as an attack against the Roman religion (which in fact it was) and by that very fact, an attack against the imperial authority. Persecution was undertaken as a measure of public safety and would often be cruel and violent, except under the reign of tolerant emperors such as Alexander Severus, Philip the Arab, and Gallienus. Throughout this whole period, therefore, the Christians were forced into the practice of covert worship.

They nevertheless took advantage of all the available possibilities to construct and decorate what they needed for worship or for the burial of their dead. Under these conditions Christian art began, and the circumstances and milieu of the time played a large role in shaping it.

Architecture. The first Christian churches were modest and unobtrusive. As the Acts of the Apostles indicate, the first churches were in private homes. It is probable that, especially in Rome, the richer Christians offered their palaces for the reunions of the faithful, since these were buildings particularly suited to the celebration of divine services. Doubtless the first churches in the real sense of the term were constructed under the reign of Alexander Severus (222–235); at least, according to Origen, his successor Maximinus had them burned. In any case, at the beginning of the third century, Pope Callistus arranged for the purchase of meeting places (*tituli*) in the different quarters of Rome. In 260 Gallienus issued a decree ordering the restitution to the Christians of their places of worship. During the period of peace lasting from that date until 300, churches were permitted to be built.

These churches were in the form of BASILICAS, a type of structure whose origin is uncertain. Unlike the ceremonies in the pagan temples or in the Temple of Jerusalem, in the Christian ceremonies the faithful participated in the drama taking place in the sanctuary. The Roman civil basilica, like the *tablinum* adjoined by the *triclinium* in the palaces, permitted this participation, though there were other possible architectural arrangements that could have been used.

The CATACOMBS also formed part of Christian architecture; they represent an authentic Christian innovation. In various sections of Rome, taking advantage of the laws applicable to groups, the Christians acquired ground for burial and then used it to dig catacombs. Such burial places are most numerous in Rome, but they exist also in Naples, Syracuse, and even outside of Italy.

Roman underground burial areas (hypogeums) consisted of only two or three subterranean rooms containing tombs (sarcophagi) or cinerary urns. Cremation was rejected by the first Christians as a practice opposed to the preservation of the body for the resurrection and lacking in respect for those sanctified members whose fidelity to Christ had been carried often to the point of martyrdom. To find sufficient space for the burial of the constantly increasing number of Christians became a problem. It was resolved by constructing something resembling the modern skyscraper in reverse. Subterranean galleries at various levels were dug out. In the walls of the galleries, niches were hollowed out to serve as tombs, either in the form of an arch (ARCOSOLIUM) or cubicles that were placed one above the other (LOCULUS).

One must classify also as catacombs the underground burial places (hypogeums) of such families as the Aurelii, who were heretical Christians of Rome. The catacomb on which the basilica of St. Peter now stands is one of the most ancient. It is the probable burial place of Peter the Apostle and is surrounded by a number of pagan and Christian tombs, all of which are decorated like the catacombs.

Painting. In the hypogeums, the walls and the *arcosolia* were decorated with paintings. In the catacombs, such paintings are scattered. At regular intervals along the passageways of the catacombs, either *arcosolia* or square rooms were dug out and sometimes provided with *loculi.* The walls of the rooms were further excavated to form *arcosolia*; it is there that the paintings are found on each side of the arch or vault: at the back of the *arcosolium,* on the area below the *arcosolium,* or on the ceilings of the rooms. In these rooms, squares and lozenges in imitation of marble designs cover the lower part of the walls, while the ceilings are divided into sections by geometric lines. In these sections there are decorative motifs taken from Roman art (heads, busts, and animals) and especially figures of people either singly or in groups. The latter adorn also the various parts of the *arcosolia.*

In general, the subjects in the catacomb paintings are taken from the Bible, and the same ones occur repeatedly. The subjects most frequently treated include: the Good Shepherd or Orpheus with the animals, the story of Jonah, the resurrection of Lazarus, Daniel in the lions' den, the Multiplication of the Loaves, Noah's ark, the sacrifice of Abraham, the paralytic of Bethsaida, the three youths in the fiery furnace, Adam and Eve, the Adoration of the Magi, the story of Job, the Baptism of Jesus, the man born blind, Moses and the burning bush, Susannah and the elders, the Good Samaritan, and the Wedding Feast of Cana. To these may be added a few mythological subjects, such as Eros and Psyche and the seasons. It is remarkable that Christ is shown only under the symbol of the Good Shepherd or Orpheus, or in the working of a miracle, but never in a scene showing His Crucifixion or His Resurrection.

Various hypotheses have been offered to explain the choice of these subjects. J. WILPERT has tried to link them with the Christian idea of death and, in particular, to the episodes from the Old Testament and the Gospels mentioned in the ancient prayer commending a soul to God. The archeologist P. Styger believes that these subjects were used to adorn both the catacombs and the Christian homes, and that they have therefore no symbolical value. Neither of these theories takes into account all the facts. The symbolism of these subjects cannot be denied, as the painting showing Susannah as a lamb between two wolves proves, but the symbolism is more general than Wilpert believes. The symbolism may also be related to the CATECHESIS and the liturgy of the period, though it is safer to say that it is related to the ancient Jewish rituals and to Jewish and early Christian ''summaries.'' The latter were canonical or apocryphal enumerations of outstanding deeds of the heroes of the faith and of the miracles worked by God. In any event, the symbolism is essentially related to the general idea of the economy of the salvation of human souls.

The oldest examples of these paintings date from the beginning of the third century. In this first period of early Christian art, the paintings either express a certain blitheness to be found in pagan art, or they are symbolical in nature and in accord with millennialist, other-worldly ideas. The earliest style closely resembled the elegant Roman style, as in the catacomb of Domitilla, but it later became more impressionistic. At the end of the third century, relief was replaced by contrasting tones, as in the group of Adam and Eve in the catacomb of SS. Peter and Marcellus. These changes in style indicate an acceptance of the contemporary tendencies toward allegory and symbolism, and an evolutionary process in which classical naturalism was gradually replaced by abstraction and simplification.

Sculpture. In the third century the wealthier pagans and Christians interred their dead in tombs, and the walls of the tombs were decorated with reliefs. On the Christian tombs frequent use was made of decorative motifs, particularly strigils and other motifs carrying Christian symbolism, e.g., the fish (*see* FISH, SYMBOLISM OF). But quite early other decorative motifs, such as the masks employed in ancient art, were combined with these.

The decorated lamps used in the catacombs to light the passageways and the places of burial first appeared probably in this period. The subjects used on them are in most cases conventional; fish, laurel leaves, cross, shell, and rosette (*see* LAMPS AND LIGHTING, EARLY CHRISTIAN).

In the beginning, different Christian subjects were juxtaposed or combined with others of pagan origin without much concern for blending the subjects into a unified whole. This can be seen in the tomb of Livia Primitiva, where the Good Shepherd with his sheep is seen between strigils, flanked by a fish and an anchor; or in the tomb at La Gayolle in Provence, where the Good Shepherd is shown with a fisherman, an orante, and a seated figure. A fragment depicting the story of Jonah shows the attempt to use the classical style to express Christian content. As the century progresses, the Christian subject becomes the central or dominant element of the whole composition, which is generally pastoral in nature. Though derived from pagan sources, the Good Shepherd is represented in the light of the imagination of Christian artists intent on their own religious symbolism.

In this first period, then, Christian art developed by borrowing forms, by introducing new themes into them, and by transforming the whole in the direction of symbolic abstraction. The tendency toward symbolic abstraction is evident in all the art of the time, but Christian inspiration was one of the most active forces producing it.

Period of Open Development. The ordinance of 313 issued by Licinius in agreement with Constantine granted official recognition to Christianity and, by so doing, afforded conditions favorable to the fuller development of Christian art. The support given to religion by the emperors—except during the brief reign of Julian the Apostate (361–363)—improved these conditions still further. As a result, the erection of religious edifices became widespread. The art of mosaic, used to decorate the buildings, received new impetus, as increasingly its use in the catacombs was abandoned. The spirit of artistic productions also changed. The gracious charm of the classical style gave way to a more serious tone, eventually yielding a hieratic style more suited to the exaltation of the Supreme Sovereign, and modeled after the respectful images demanded by the emperor.

Church Architecture. The number of churches increased, and from the very beginning they were of large dimensions. The form most frequently employed was that of the basilica. Constantine probably took an active part in the erection of the following churches of this type in Rome: St. John Lateran, St. Peter, St. Paul-Outside-the-Walls, SS. Peter and Marcellinus, and St. Agnes. The basilicas of St. Pudentiana and St. Mary Major were also begun in the fourth century, and St. Sabina in the fifth. St. John Lateran is evidently the prototype of the Christian basilica; it is the first church mentioned in the records of the Holy See and the one in which the heads of St. Peter and St. Paul were deposited. It seems to have been the first official church of the bishops of Rome and was without doubt built at the same period as the triumphal arch of Constantine (315).

In Rome the basilica of the period of Constantine had five naves, with a projecting transept and apse at the east end of the building; in the provinces it was built with one or three naves without a transept and with a recessed apse. Unlike the ancient temples, which did not provide for the participation of the faithful in the important ceremonies, the Christian churches had their chief decorative work on the interior. The high-pitched wooden roof of the principal nave was gilded; the effect of depth was accentuated by the long rows of columns and by the austere appearance of the walls, relieved only by mosaics of a didactic nature. In addition, bays or bay windows in the walls lit the major interior area. Attention was thus drawn toward the altar, the center of worship. The transept itself was a passageway that permitted the faithful to approach directly. On the exterior there were no longer any of the groups of pillars typical of ancient buildings. On the façade the pediment remained to emphasize the sacred character of the edifice. In North Africa the Western type of basilica grew more complicated, as at Damus el-Carita, where it is divided into nine naves, or at Orléansville, where a new apse was added facing the west.

The circular plan of construction was taken from the Eastern basilica. It was employed particularly for commemorative monuments and persisted in the West in the form of BAPTISTERIES. The circular plan was used for the octagonal church of St. Constance, which was built in the first third of the fourth century and transformed into a baptistery in the fifth.

Painting. Painting was confined almost entirely to the decoration of the catacombs, where it served the cause of decoration along with mosaics. In the fourth century the character of painting remained the same as before until 350, when there was a sudden shift to the classic style. This can be seen in the decoration of the New Catacomb on the Via Latina. However, the quality of painting declined increasingly, and in the fifth century it wavered between conventionalism and mechanical execution. The decline of painting in the catacombs was due to the fact that the attention of artists was turned to the decoration of the buildings in which Christian life was then being carried on. At the same time, the subjects assumed a less symbolical and more profane aspect as the life of the Christians became more involved in the temporal world (e.g., tomb of Maximus and hypogeum of Trebius Justus).

Mosaics. As a result of the exuberance of this period of open development, wall surfaces blazed with the beauty of a technique richer than painting. Mosaic work took on a new life, which would reach its highest peak of expression in the Byzantine world. (*See* MOSAICS.) Up to this point, mosaic work had been confined to the vaulting, to the apses, and to the upper friezes. In the fourth century in St. Constance it was still strongly classic in style with a mixture of picturesque tendencies. The ceiling of the vaulted aisles of this church is divided into eight sections, on either side of which there are agricultural scenes related to the Eucharist, geometric and natural motifs, and portraits. In the fifth century the style changed. It evolved toward the hieratic Byzantine style, as in the representation of Christ enthroned among Apostles and holy women in the apse of St. Pudentiana. Narrative cycles with a didactic content appear also, as on the upper frieze of the nave of St. Mary Major, where in 44 panels the whole story of Genesis is told in a very compact and rigid style.

In fifth-century North Africa, mosaic work still retained many of its classical tendencies, as in the decoration of a tomb in a church near Kelibia in which birds and flowers are depicted near the plaque bearing the name of the deceased. Mosaic work also took on a more popular and abstract aspect, as on the tomb stones of Tabarka, where the deceased is represented in a full-face portrait with the features greatly simplified.

Certain features of the evolution that affected both mosaic and painting can be seen in the reliefs on tombs. Orderly structuring in composition disappears; different episodes are ranged next to one another in little pictures, sometimes in a disorderly fashion, in an effort to use all the available space. Artistry was still very flexible and strong in the fourth century, as is demonstrated by the tomb of Junius Bassus in 359 (*see* SARCOPHAGUS); but it became increasingly less skillful in the handling of planes and of figures. The human body became thicker and postures more stiff. Symbolism, such as the representation of the faithful by sheep, was progressively replaced by the use of historical figures in hieratic poses.

Minor Arts. In this period the minor arts assume more importance than they had during the period of clandestine Christian life. Notable examples of work in glass, gold, silver, and ivory survive. There is a fifth-century cup of engraved glass in the Louvre Museum that shows the monogram of Christ surrounded by scenes from the Old Testament. Fine examples of goldsmith's work include a gold buckle bearing portraits of saints and another in filigreed gold showing birds facing each other. A silver box for liturgical use bears scenes from the Scriptures: the three youths in the fiery furnace, the Adoration of the Magi, and the resurrection of Lazarus. Numerous examples of an art peculiar to this period have been found, especially in the catacombs. Glasses depicting Biblical scenes similar to those on the walls of the catacombs were made by placing a sheet of cut gold between two layers of glass. Another art form that developed and became more widespread was that of ivory carving, in the round or, more commonly, on diptychs, pyxes, and combs. Christian subjects are used along with profane subjects from mythology. Classical forms are employed, as on a diptych from the north of Italy (Brescia Museum) that depicts Diana and Endymion and on a panel showing Christ's Ascension (Munich Museum; *see* ASCENSION OF JESUS CHRIST). There occur forms tightly compressed within the frames, as on the diptych of Boethius in the Brescia Museum. Several ivory statuettes of the Good Shepherd are still in existence; one is in the Louvre.

Early Christian art in the West thus shows two fundamental tendencies, one toward mysticism and the other toward an acceptance of the secular. Their respective force depends on the circumstances, but between them an equilibrium is established in accord with Christian ideas. In the first period, mystical symbolism is preponderant and closely corresponds to the tendency of the time. It is expressed in the choice of subjects and in its spiritual overtone, even though it does not at first reject the classical style. In the second period, when Christianity became more involved in daily life, the use of symbolism diminishes to permit a more direct representation of the divine. However, the divine is exalted so that the world in which Christianity is henceforth involved may be submitted to it.

2. In the East

Early Christian art of the East, like that of the West, consists in general of the Christian art previous to the appearance of Byzantine art. Actually, only a few examples remain, and those are too scattered to permit the formation of an idea of the whole.

In no city of the East are there Christian funerary monuments comparable to those of Rome. As in the West, persecution in the East was intermittent; but the religious edifices built during the lulls in persecution were either destroyed by wars and invasions or replaced by Byzantine-style churches. Because of the paucity of exemplars, the major tendencies of the period cannot be easily discerned. The difficulty is increased by the fact that each center of art was quite different from the others and by the fact that the influence of Roman art entered subtly into local art. Documentation on the subject is too incomplete to permit tracing a systematic picture of early Christian art in the East. To supplement the lack of objects and monuments, one is forced to draw up instead a sort of nomenclature and to have recourse to contemporary or later written documents.

Early Christian art in the East reached a dividing point at the beginning of the fourth century, as had Christian art during the imperial era in the West. Just as in the West, two periods are apparent: a period of semiclandestine activity and a period of open, officially sanctioned life.

Period of Semiclandestine Activity. The use of private homes for gatherings of the faithful, following the example of Christ in the Cenacle, is attested to from apostolic times. As proof of this one need only refer to the Acts of the Apostles (8.3) and to the Acts of the Martyrs. This custom continued for quite a long time and resulted in the transformation of private homes into "church homes." This was the case at Dura-Europos, a caravan stop between northern Syria and Mesopotamia, dating beyond any doubt from the first third of the third century.

The house at Dura-Europos was built around a court and consisted of several rooms, one of which was arranged and decorated as a chapel, probably with the additional use of one or two other rooms as the community grew. At the back of the chapel was a sort of receptacle in front of which there was an arch on two columns; the back wall was ornamented with two superimposed frescoes. The upper fresco depicted the Good Shepherd and the lower one Adam and Eve in the Garden of Eden. On the walls beginning at the north side of the arch were the story of Peter saved from the waters of Genesareth, followed by the episode of the paralytic of Capharnaum, and underneath that the three Marys at the sepulcher; on the south side, the story of David and Goliath; on the west, the Good Samaritan.

The first two paintings show clear evidence of Roman influence. The others bear traces of Roman influence, yet something of the Oriental style is also apparent, notably in the hieratic quality of certain poses. The style is more marked in numerous paintings depicting scenes from the Old Testament that adorn a synagogue (of a slightly later date), which is located quite close to the chapel.

According to the Chronicle of Edessa, the great flood of 201 destroyed a church of Edessa, and if it is recalled that under Abgar IX the Great, Christianity was established in 202 as the state religion, there is every reason to suppose that numerous churches were then constructed in this independent kingdom. In Apamea in Phrygia, traces of a small, square church with an apse, called the church of the Ark, can still be seen in the location of the acropolis of Celaenae. The church was doubtless anterior to the persecution of Diocletian in 303.

The numerous square churches in Asia Minor, notably the group known under the name of Bin-bir-Kilissé (the thousand and one churches) and the basilicas of central Syria built in the fourth century, lead one to believe that they had been preceded by churches of the same style, especially if one reads the letter of St. Irenaeus to Florinus (190) in which he speaks of Polycarp of Smyrna teaching in a *Basilichê aulê*. In the middle of the third century, because of his crimes, the Emperor Philip was forbidden access to the *Palaia Ecclesia* (Ancient Church) of Antioch.

It seems quite certain that there were numerous Constantinian churches in Palestine and Syria. This can be surmised from several works written in the fourth century by Gregory of Nyssa, and also from the writings of Origen. According to the latter, in the middle of the third century the churches of Caesarea of Palestine were burned by the pagans. Eusebius also recorded that a large number of churches were destroyed by the persecution of Diocletian, though they had been officially tolerated by Gallienus.

Very little can be learned either from literature or archeology about the funerary architecture. Dating certain-ly from this period are tombs in Palestine and Arabia (Khefa Amer, Haifa, Nâblus, and Nazareth), in Mesopotamia (Edessa and Dara), and in Asia Minor (Ephesus, Seleucia, and Sardis). On the whole, except for Dura-Europos, whose Western characteristics have been noted, recourse must be had to written documentation for information about this period. It is from texts that one learns of the transformation of the ''church home'' into a church in the real sense of the word.

Period of Open Development. When they had received full liberty to practice their religion, the first concern of the Eastern Christians, like those of the West, was to erect places of worship. The destroyed churches were rebuilt; the written records of about the same date, and in particular the *Ecclesiastical History* of Eusebius, are explicit on this point. A great number of new churches were built. Starting in the fourth century, the greater part of them were built on the plan of a basilica, which was so common in the fifth century; but the octagonal plan was used also, as described in a letter of St. Gregory of Nyssa to Amphilochus, Bishop of Iconium. Among the various forms of decoration, painting was frequently employed; at the end of the fourth century St. Nilus wrote a letter about a church that an eparch wished to have decorated with hunting scenes. Relief work on the capitals and friezes was certainly employed, since a link must have been established in this period between the elongated and pointed acanthus leaves of Leptis Magna of the third century in North Africa and those of the same type used in the sixth century throughout the East.

The birth of Byzantine art may be attributed to a new spirit that substituted aulic directions for local initiative and provided an environment of Oriental richness. Artistic techniques, however, had developed before the sixth century and later were only transformed.

Influences on Church Architecture. The art of the early Christian period, especially in regard to the basilicas, can be distinguished by geographical areas, i.e., Constantinople, Greece and the Balkans, Palestine, and Syria and Asia Minor; and by influences, i.e., Roman, Hellenistic, Constantinopolitan, and Oriental.

The Roman influence is seen in the basilica type of construction with its three or five naves, transept, apse to the east, wooden roof, and preference for brick. The Roman influence was evident in Constantinople in the first church of Hagia Sophia (415) and the church of John Studios (463); in Greece at Epidaurus (end of the fourth century), Nicopolis (end of the fifth century), Corinth (fifth century), and at Salonika in the basilica of Demetrius, which in its original state dates from 412; in northern Syria, in the church of Kalat Siman (end of the fifth century) and at Tafna in the Hauran, where the buildings were close to the square type; and in Asia Minor in the group of churches known as the Bin-bir-Kilissé (fifth–sixth centuries). The Hellenistic influence contributed the ornamental arcades on the façade and along the interior walls, as well as the arches with ceiling beams on the inside, to the church of Kalat Siman and the buildings at Tafna. Constantinople's main architectural contribution was to provide Asia Minor with the Roman type of construction, to which was added the façade with columns, but without any decoration in relief which was forbidden by the formal austerity of Constantinople. Examples can be seen at Perga, at Sagalassos, and in the group of Bin-bir-Kilissé.

The Oriental tendencies appear under four combined or separate aspects: the absence of the transept or the prolongation of the naves into the transept with a widening of the choir, the commemorative function of the sanctuary, and the triumphal arches on the pillars. Basilicas without a transept are found also in Greece at Salona (early fifth century), in Palestine in the basilica of the Nativity at Bethlehem (326), and in the basilica of the Holy Sepulcher at Jerusalem (323–335).

The prolongation of the naves into the transept together with the broadening of the choir to meet the needs of the liturgy can be seen in Greece in the basilica of Demetrius at Salonika. The sanctuary is most frequently octagonal in form and honors a monument of sacred history: in Palestine, the basilica of the Nativity at Bethlehem and the basilica of the Holy Sepulcher at Jerusalem; and in Asia Minor, the original church of St. John at Ephesus, which consisted of four basilicas adjoining the MARTYRIUM OF THE SAINT. This latter type of construction on a larger scale is found at Kalat Siman. There four buildings of the basilica type, one of which has an apse at its east end, are arranged in a cross around an octagonal court whose center is occupied by the pillar of St. Simeon.

The triumphal arches with pillars originated in central Syria at the end of the fourth century at Idjaz in the church of the Apostles. They appeared again in the same region at the end of the fifth century at Kalb Lauzeh and Ruweha, and in Hauran at Umm Idj-Djimal in the churches of Julianos and of Masechot.

In ancient Mesopotamia the use of unfired brick as well as a fondness for display resulted in the technique of applying facings to buildings. The Christian Orient shared the same tastes, joined with a predilection for fired brick, which, though not used in Syria, was the most commonly employed material in Roman architecture. Under the reign of Constantine, several churches were decorated at Constantinople, and doubtless also at Bethlehem, with facings of marble and mosaic. Where mural paintings existed, they were repeated in the floor mosaics,

as St. Gregory of Nyssa attested in his description of the representation of the martyrdom of St. Theodore. The same sumptuous technique was used also in secular edifices. The mosaics of the pavement of the Grand Palace or those found while the foundations were being dug for the City Hall at Constantinople, all dating from the fifth century, are justly celebrated.

Mosaic and Mirror Arts. In the fifth century, mosaic work covered the walls of churches and apses and appeared in the ornamentation of the cupolas; regrettably, very few examples remain. There is outstanding work in several churches in Palestine, especially in the church of the Multiplication of the Loaves at Et-Tabgah on Lake Genesareth. In Syria, the celebrated mosaic of the Phoenix of Antioch was probably Christian in origin.

Some famous buildings and important objects can be dated from the fourth and fifth centuries: the baptistery of the Orthodox or the mausoleum of Galla Placidia at Ravenna (fifth century); the Rothschild Cameo (middle of the fourth century); the numerous consular diptychs or pyxes in ivory; golden objects such as buckles, of which one bearing the name of Constantine is in the Louvre; illuminated manuscripts such as the Itala (Berlin), Homer's *Iliad* (Ambrosian Library, Milan), and the Vaticanus and Romanus Virgils (Vatican Library). All these are objects belonging to court art and therefore essentially pre-Byzantine. For this reason they perhaps should not be assigned to the period of early Christian art.

Sculpture. The same holds true for sculpture in Byzantium, where statues of the emperors and functionaries and the triumphal columns were erected by imperial or official order. Unlike the West, tombs with figures are rare and of the triumphal type, such as the tomb found at Constantinople (now in Berlin) on which Christ is shown between two Apostles.

Objects that sprang from individual or local initiative are also of considerable interest. There is, for example, a head of the fourth or fifth century (Louvre), which came from Tartus in Syria. It shows some Oriental characteristics in the treatment of the eyes and hair, and there is a Greek cast to the outline of the face, indicating that studios were set up in the vicinity of the court. A Syrian relief depicts St. Simeon Stylites praying on his pillar. Its decidedly local origin is indicated by the stiff style employed. A fragment of a parapet from Crimea (fourth or fifth century) has a clearly designed and finely cut picture of Christ. There is also a small gold box of the fifth century from Syria, decorated with repoussé work of a rather primitive style. The fragment remaining bears two medallions, one of which contains a picture of the Virgin and the other a figure who perhaps is Christ. The eyes, the stylization of the hair, and the beard of the male figure are all of a very definite Oriental style.

It is regrettable for the history of early Christian art that examples are so rare in the East. The few that do remain illustrate some of the techniques adopted by Byzantine art, but they can give no true notion of the interpenetration of ancient aesthetics and Christian ideas, which must have been greater in the East than in the West.

3. In Egypt

During the Christian period and long after the country came under Muslim domination, Egypt had an indigenous Christian art, known as Coptic art. Before the distinguishing characteristics of Coptic art developed, and parallel to its development up to the sixth century, there was a certain amount of artistic production that cannot be called Coptic and belongs to an early Christian art linked to the art that appeared in the area covered by the expansion of Christianity. Much of this art has disappeared, and nothing is known of some works but the bare mention by contemporary or later writers. Celsus speaks of the "great church" of Alexandria, ruled by Bishop Demetrius (189–231). A papyrus of Oxyrhyncus (third century) mentions churches located in the upper and lower valleys of the Nile, which undoubtedly were destroyed during the persecution of Diocletian. In Alexandria, before the peace of Constantine, a martyrium of St. Mark and a church built by the bishop Theonas are known to have existed. It is also possible that during this period the back portion of the columned agora of Ashmunein in Middle Egypt was transformed into a trefoiled apse.

Catacombs. The catacombs of Abu el-Akhem, Mustapha, and Qabbary, all near Alexandria, belong also to this first period. To these must be added the hypogeums of Qabbary, of Kom al-Kugafa, and of the eastern necropolis. There are *loculi,* or small chambers, hollowed out in their rooms. The inscriptions and the ampullae found there prove they are Christian. At some distance, but unfortunately destroyed, is the subterranean cemetery of Karmuz, behind the Serapeum; the arrangement would lead one to believe that it originally served as a sanctuary. The gallery containing the *loculi* was entered through a square chamber lengthened by an apse, and on the side was another square chamber in which *arcosolia* were dug. The frieze of the apse, from the third century but altered during the Byzantine period, presented successively the Wedding Feast of Cana, the Multiplication of the Loaves and Fishes, and a Eucharistic banquet. It is possible that this painting should be listed among the very rare examples of the union of a Biblical scene and its symbolical interpretation. Some of its details were unusual: the presence in the farthest scenes of a half-nude seated woman seen from the back; the movement of the Apostle

Andrew carrying the fish to Christ; and especially the triangular composition formed by Christ between the Apostles Peter and Andrew. The *arcosolia* of the lateral room were also decorated with paintings: angels standing erect, the Marys at the Tomb, Christ with a lion and a dragon under His feet, the Apostles, St. John the Baptist, and others.

Churches. Of the churches erected by imperial order in Egypt, the best known are the four basilicas that constituted the center of pilgrimage of Apa Menas, near Lake Mariut, west of Alexandria. The basilica of the crypt, with three naves, a projecting apse, and a baptistery, was constructed probably by Constantine. The basilica was intended for pilgrims, but it proved too small. At the end of the fourth century, therefore, Arcadius constructed a longer basilica with a protruding transept. The sick gathered in the basilica of the Baths (fifth century); this basilica terminated in two facing apses. A funerary basilica with two apses, an atrium, a baptistery, and funeral chapels on the sides (fifth century) was joined to the north cemetery. These basilicas are in ruins, but enough remains to indicate how rich they were in decoration: marble columns, marble facings, beautiful capitals, and sometimes mosaics.

At the other extreme of Egypt, as far south as Luxor, a group of 10th-century chapels is found in the oasis of Khargeh, where Nestorius died in exile (c. 451). In the midst of the chapels are two little sanctuaries in the form of square mausoleums (fourth and fifth centuries). One is called the chapel of the Exodus because the principal painting on the ceiling, which is in the form of a cupola, depicts soldiers pursuing the Hebrews. Other figures and scenes from the Old and New Testaments include: Adam and Eve, Noah, Jonah, Job and his friends, Daniel in the lions' den, the sacrifice of Isaac, St. Thecla and her followers, a shepherd with his flock, the suffering of Isaiah, and Susannah and the elders. Some subjects are of special interest because they are unknown in other early Christian monuments: Jeremiah weeping over the ruin of Jerusalem, Jethro rejoining Moses on Sinai, and the meeting of Rebecca and Eliezer. The painting in the other chapel, called the chapel of Peace, contains several hieratic figures grouped around a center decorated with plant motifs: Adam and Eve, the sacrifice of Isaac, an allegory of peace, Daniel in the lions' den, allegories of justice and of prayer, Jacob, Noah's ark, the Annunciation, and St. Paul with his disciple St. Thecla. Certain elements are clearly Egyptian, notably the costumes in the allegory of peace and the shape of the boat representing the ark.

These are the principal Egyptian early Christian monuments that are not typically Coptic. Unlike the products of Coptic art, on the whole these monuments show a direct Alexandrian or imperial influence.

Bibliography: *Dictionnaire d'archéologie chrétienne et de liturgie.* R. GARRUCCI, *Storia dell'arte cristiana,* 6 v. (Prato 1872–81). J. WILPERT, *Die Malereien der Katakomben Roms.* 2 v. (Freiburg i.Br. 1903). H. LECLERCQ, *Manuel d'archéologie chrétienne,* 2 v. (Paris 1907). W. LOWRIE, *Monuments of the Early Church* (New York 1923). P. STYGER, *Die römischen Katakomben* (Berlin 1933). E. W. ANTHONY, *A History of Mosaic* (Boston 1935). WALTERS ART GALLERY, *Early Christian and Byzantine Art* (Baltimore 1947). F. W. DEICHMANN, *Frühchristliche Kirchen im Rom* (Basel 1948). E. H. SWIFT, *Roman Sources of Christian Art* (New York 1951). C. R. MOREY, *Early Christian Art* (2d ed. Princeton 1953). D. T. RICE, *The Beginnings of Christian Art* (Nashville 1957). E. COCHE DE LA FORTÉ, *L'Antiquité chrétienne au Musée du Louvre* (Paris 1958). L. HERTLING and E. KIRSCHBAUM, *The Roman Catacombs and Their Martyrs,* tr. M. J. COSTELLOE (2d ed. London 1960). W. F. VOLBACH, *Early Christian Art,* tr. C. LIGOTA (New York 1962). W. SAS-ZALOZIECKY, *L'Art paléochrétien* (Paris 1964). P. DU BOURGUET, *La Peinture paléochrétienne* (Paris 1965). R. KRAUTHEIMER, *Early Christian and Byzantine Architecture* (Pelican History of Art, ed. N. PEVSNER) (Baltimore 1965), a good survey in English.

[P. DU BOURGUET]

ARTHURIAN AND CAROLINGIAN LEGENDS

Of all the legends that flourished in the Middle Ages, the two major cycles clustered around the figures of Arthur and Charlemagne. Both cycles were widely known throughout Western Christendom, and their literary influence has extended even into modern times. Arthur and Charlemagne were historical personages, though Arthur is known almost exclusively through the legendary material. Reliable historical sources tell us much more about CHARLEMAGNE (742–814), his conquests, his interests in education and government and the revival of learning he fostered in an age of barbarism. The legends of Arthur and Charlemagne, in the course of time, followed paths of development so different that in spirit they seem to have little in common. The romances about Arthur and his knights of the Round Table deal with a world of chivalry, love, and adventure, in which marvels occur with astonishing frequency. The *chansons de geste* about Charlemagne and his paladins, on the other hand, exalt French nationalism in the struggle against the infidel and stress the conflicts arising between feudal obligations to the suzerain and personal concepts of honor.

ARTHURIAN LEGENDS

Historically, Arthur is the earlier figure. During the Saxon invasions of Britain in the late 5th century, Arthur led the British forces in a series of battles that ended with a decisive victory at Mt. Badon, somewhere in southern England, about A.D. 500. Despite the eventual triumph of the Saxons, Arthur's fame lived long in the memory of the defeated British and their descendants. St. GILDAS, a Briton, writes (*c.* 540) about the battle of Mt. Badon as a British victory that halted the advance of the Saxons and initiated a period of peace, although he does not mention Arthur. The earliest extant reference to Arthur by name occurs in a Welsh poem, *The Gododdin* (*c.* 600), which extols the valor of a fallen warrior by comparing him with Arthur. About 800, the Welsh priest NENNIUS, in the *Historia Britonum,* lists Arthur's 12 victories over the Saxons, concluding with that at Mt. Badon, and in an account of the natural wonders of Britain, he records two local legends connected with Arthur. The *Annales Cambriae,* another Latin compilation of Welsh origin (*c.* 950), also mentions the victory at Badon and another battle at Camlann, in which Arthur and Medraut (Modred) fell.

Early Welsh literature independent of the chronicles and historical annals presents Arthur as the hero of adventures derived from Celtic myth and the leader of a company endowed with preternatural powers. In a Welsh poem of the 10th century, *The Spoils of Annwn,* Arthur sets out with three shiploads of men to capture the magic cauldron of Annwn, the Celtic Otherworld. Although the vessel is taken, only seven men, including Arthur, return from the disastrous raid. In another early Welsh poem, a fragmentary dialogue between Arthur and a gatekeeper, Arthur lists among his companions not only Kay and Bedivere but also many figures derived from Welsh myth, with references to their accomplishments as slayers of monsters. The Welsh prose romance *Kulhwch and Olwen* (*c.* 1100) includes a rationalized version of Arthur's raid upon the Otherworld and recounts his hunting of a preternatural boar.

Origin and Diffusion. The legend of Arthur, according to the earliest documents, originated in Wales, where the memory of the historic military leader was preserved and later drawn into the orbit of native Welsh mythological tradition. Arthur's fame was cultivated also among the Cornish and the Bretons, linguistically and culturally allied with the Welsh. Traditions of Arthur's birth and death were localized in Cornwall, and the Cornish, like the Bretons, believed in the survival of Arthur and his inevitable return to his people. The wide diffusion of the Arthurian legends on the Continent, beginning in the 11th century, was chiefly the work of the Bretons, whose fluency in French and whose professional skill in exploiting their Celtic heritage of legend to entertain French-speaking patrons spread the stories wherever the language was understood—not only in France, but also in England, Italy, and the crusader states.

Another major contribution to Arthur's international fame was the appearance about 1136 of GEOFFREY OF MONMOUTH'S Latin *Historia Regum Britanniae,* a work intended to give the British a full-scale history like those

King Arthur being transported to Avalon after his death. (©Bettmann/CORBIS)

of the Normans, the Saxons, and the French. Geoffrey purports to be merely a translator of an ancient book in the British tongue, but no trace of such a source has ever been discovered. Geoffrey's book is primarily his own invention, based upon material derived from Nennius, Welsh genealogies, and the usual historical sources accessible to a cleric. Geoffrey's history begins with the first king of Britain, Brutus, who, as a descendant of Aeneas, links Britain with Rome. Among the early figures are King Lear, Cymbeline, and Sabrina, whose legends later influenced Shakespeare, Spenser, and Milton.

Arthur as Central Interest. The Arthurian story is naturally the center of interest. Arthur in his youth was supervised and protected by the wizard Merlin. After his coronation and marriage, he subjugated not only the Saxons but other Continental peoples and established his empire even over Gaul. When the Roman emperor challenged him, he set out to conquer Rome, leaving his kingdom in charge of his nephew Modred. Modred's at-

tempt to usurp the throne and to seize Arthur's queen brought the king home before he could complete the conquest. At a battle on the River Camel in Cornwall, Modred was slain and Arthur, though mortally wounded, was borne to the isle of Avalon to be healed. After the reign of Arthur, the British kingdom declined until it was finally overwhelmed by the Saxons in the 7th century.

Geoffrey presents Arthur as a 12th-century king presiding over a magnificent court and accepting the homage of royal vassals. The emphasis upon the theme of empire and the independence of Britain agrees with the political aspirations of the Anglo-Norman kings of the time. Although some of Geoffrey's contemporaries doubted his veracity, the *Historia* was generally accepted as the standard history of early Britain until the 16th century, when historical scholarship revealed it to be largely fiction.

In 1155 the *Historia* was translated into French as *Le Roman de Brut* by the Norman poet Wace, evidently in response to a demand from courtly patrons. Wace follows his original faithfully and adapts the story to courtly interests chiefly by expanding descriptive passages. His most significant addition is the story of Arthur's Round Table, of which, he writes, Bretons tell many tales, and which was founded to prevent quarrels over precedence. About 1200, the first English version was composed by a parish priest in Worcestershire named Layamon. Although an expanded paraphrase of Wace, Layamon's *Brut* is a recreation of the story in the alliterative meter and style typical of the Old English epic, ironically the literary style of Arthur's historic foes, the Saxons.

The account of Arthur's career in Geoffrey's *Historia* remains substantially unchanged in these and later versions, but its influence is negligible on the French Arthurian romances that began to appear in the second half of the 12th century. These stories were derived from the oral legends circulated by Breton storytellers, and they deal with a variety of heroes unknown in the pseudohistorical tradition of Geoffrey. Many of these tales, though originally independent, were absorbed into the Arthurian legend because of the great king's prestige. Sometimes the process began before the story reached the Continent. When the Tristan legend, for example, migrated from northern Scotland to Wales, the Welsh linked Arthur to the originally Pictish hero, and in some Continental versions of the Tristan legend, Arthur plays a minor role that is evidently derived from this tradition.

Heroes other than Arthur; the Grail. In general, Arthur and his court become in the French romances of the 12th century the background for the adventures of the hero of the story. In the four romances of Chrétien de Troyes that are based on traditional sources, the interest is centered not on Arthur himself but on the individual heroes—Erec, Yvain, Lancelot, and Perceval—and the role of Arthur varies according to the story. In *Erec* and *Yvain,* in which Chrétien delicately balances the claims of love and chivalry, the hero's adventures begin at Arthur's court and the happy outcome of his trials and suffering in each romance is explicitly connected with Arthur and his knights. In the unfinished *Lancelot,* on the contrary, Arthur's role is ignominious: he allows his queen to be abducted, and her rescue is accomplished by her devoted but adulterous lover Lancelot. In the story of Perceval (*Li Contes del Graal*), which Chrétien also left unfinished, the hero is at first an uncouth lad whose gradual education in chivalry prepares him for the adventures of the Grail; Arthur's court clearly represents the standards of chivalry that test the hero's worth, although the king himself suffers without resistance a humiliating insult that is avenged by the young Perceval.

Other French romancers attempted to continue Chrétien's unfinished works, especially the *Graal;* and his in-

Woodcut of a battle scene in the epic poem "Orlando Furioso," written by Ludovico Ariosto, printed in Venice by V. Valgrisi, 1562.

fluence penetrated fruitfully into Germany, where Hartmann von Aue adapted *Erec* and *Yvain,* and where Wolfram von Eschenbach composed *Parzival,* a profoundly spiritual yet realistic reworking and expansion of Chrétien's story, stressing humility and compassion as the noblest virtues of chivalry.

Prose Cycles. Although the Grail stories were derived from the same reservoir of Celtic tradition as other parts of the Arthurian legend, the mysterious vessel called the Grail inevitably suggested Christian interpretation, which became a prominent feature of 13th-century versions (*see* HOLY GRAIL, THE). Two other major trends distinguish the development of the French Arthurian legends in the 13th century: the use of prose rather than verse and the effort to assemble all the legends into one immense compilation. The so-called Vulgate prose cycle consists of five long romances, written at various times and by different authors whose identity remains unknown. The earliest part, composed between 1215 and

Ludovico Ariosto.

1230, is the trilogy of the prose *Lancelot, La Queste del Saint Graal,* and *La Mort Artu.* The prose *Lancelot* is a long biographical romance about Lancelot, his devotion to the Queen, his supremacy as a knight, and his begetting of Galahad, the destined Grail hero. The *Queste* is a religious allegory, the work of a Cistercian, the hero of which is the sinless Galahad, who achieves the perfect mystical vision of the Grail denied to his father Lancelot because of adultery with Guenevere. Inexorable doom dominates the *Mort Artu,* causing the sequence of disasters resulting from that sin: Arthur's discovery of his queen's infidelity with Lancelot, the feud between Gawain and Lancelot, and the final battle between Arthur and his incestuously begotten son Modred. To this trilogy two other romances were added: the *Estoire del Saint Graal,* a prelude relating the early history of the Grail and its role in the evangelization of Britain, and the prose *Merlin,* which carries the narrative through the period of the pre-Arthurian kings to the coronation of Arthur, the establishment of the Round Table, and the Saxon wars.

The Vulgate cycle spread the concept of CHIVALRY as a noble, ideal way of life through its powerful influence upon later romances in France, Italy, Spain, the Netherlands, Ireland, Wales, and England. It was the principal source of Sir Thomas Malory's *Le Morte d'Arthur* (1469–70). Although Malory used other sources, French and English, he followed the Vulgate in presenting Lancelot as the embodiment of chivalry and the hero of the Arthuriad. Malory condensed and abridged freely; and he deliberately unraveled stories that were carefully interwoven in his French sources, narrating them as self-contained units. Caxton edited and printed (1485) Malory's work and gave it the title by which it is generally known.

In the English Renaissance, the Arthurian legend became the center of political controversy over the authenticity of Geoffrey's *Historia,* which was used to support Tudor claims to the throne; and moralists like Roger Ascham condemned Malory's tales for their bawdry and manslaughter. Yet Caxton's edition of Malory was reprinted five times before the 18th century, and such poets as Spenser and Milton were attracted to the legends. As a result of the renewed interest in medieval legends during the Romantic revival, Arthurian themes became important in the 19th century. The most notable achievements are Tennyson's *Idylls of the King* and Richard WAGNER'S music dramas *Tristan und Isolde* and *Parsifal.*

CAROLINGIAN LEGENDS

If the romance is the characteristic genre of the Arthurian legend, the epic, or *chanson de geste,* is the natural form for the legends about Charlemagne. Unlike Arthur, there was never any question about Charlemagne's historicity, and his conquests of most of western Europe were real, not fictional. The actual Charlemagne was a Frank, whose native language was German, and whose principal residence was Aix-la-Chapelle, the German Aachen. Yet he became the national hero of the French, who developed the earliest epics about his exploits.

Legends about Charlemagne seem to have circulated even in his lifetime. Court poets composed Latin panegyrics about him in a rhetorical style that made him a majestic, almost superhuman figure, and even EINHARD'S generally trustworthy biography, modeled upon Suetonius's life of Augustus, contributed to this idealization by associating him with the great Roman emperor and by recording the preternatural portents that preceded his death. Oral traditions about Charlemagne were compiled by a monk of St. Gall about 885, for example, the anecdote about King Desiderius of Lombardy and Otker the Frank awaiting Charles's arrival at Pavia, and Otker's swoon at the awesome sight of the Iron Emperor. Charlemagne's glorious memory was fostered by the clergy partly because from the beginning he was regarded as the defender of Christendom against its enemies and partly because of his benefactions to numerous churches. There can be little doubt that the clerical tradition encouraged the spread of the Carolingian legends along the great pilgrimage routes of the Middle Ages, but there is also evidence of a vigorous vernacular tradition of songs and tales about Charlemagne that prepared the way for the later epics.

Transformation of the Historical Figure. The legendary Charlemagne differs, of course, from the historic original. Although the historic Charlemagne waged long and successful wars against the Saxons, the Slavs, the Huns, and the Danes, legend made his chief enemy the Saracens, transforming a minor engagement in Spain into a major threat to Christian civilization. Another legend recounts his journey to Jerusalem and Constantinople and his return with relics of Christ's Passion. Although Charlemagne never visited the Orient, his friendly relations with Harun al-Rashid (764?–809), the Caliph of Baghdad, with whom he exchanged gifts, and with the Greek emperors of Constantinople may well have inspired the invention of such a legend. Since no historical records survive of Charlemagne's childhood and youth, a legend was invented to fill the gap, relating his exile in Spain to escape from his two evil bastard brothers. Under the assumed name of Mainet, he offers his services to the Saracen king and delivers him from a dangerous foe. The king's daughter falls in love with him, becomes a Christian, and marries him after Charlemagne regains his throne and punishes the wicked brothers. Although Charlemagne is a youth in this story, he is usually depicted as an aged man with a flowing white beard, yet vigorous and commanding—a majestic, patriarchal figure.

Defender of Christendom. So he is presented in the stories dealing with the wars against the infidel. In this cycle he is the leader of France, the people chosen by God to defend all of Christendom. The mutation of history into legend can be observed in the *Song of Roland* (c. 1100), the earliest, the best, and the most famous of these epics. Earlier versions seem to have been reshaped under the powerful impetus of the Crusades to emphasize the urgency of military action against the infidel and the spiritual rewards awaiting those martyred for the faith.

The only defeat of Charlemagne recorded by Einhard was the result of a surprise attack by Basques in a pass of the Pyrenees on the rearguard of Charlemagne's army, an assault that destroyed all the men, among them Roland, Count of Brittany. The Basques plundered the baggage train and fled under cover of nightfall. Their dispersal, we are told, made immediate vengeance impossible. The event, dated in 778, was an interruption of the Saxon wars that Charlemagne undertook to assist Saracen princes in Spain who had appealed for his aid against foes of their faith. The defeat occurred after Charlemagne's recall from Spain to meet a renewed attack by the Saxons.

At the time Charlemagne was 38, but in the *Song of Roland* he is 200 years old; the Basques are metamorphosed into a horde of treacherous Saracens, greatly outnumbering the French rearguard; and Charlemagne exacts a mighty vengeance (although the historical sources are careful to explain why he could not do so). The ambush in the poem is initiated by a conspiracy between Roland's stepfather Ganelon and the Saracens in order to destroy Roland, who is here represented as Charlemagne's nephew and the mightiest of the 12 peers. The central episode is the heroic defense led by Roland and the peers in the Battle of Roncevaux, ending in death for them and the 20,000 who would never again see France. Charlemagne himself is the hero of the rest of the poem, destroying the infidels, leveling Saragossa, and converting the queen to Christianity. Ganelon's fate is decided not by Charlemagne but by God in a judicial combat. His terrible punishment for his treason follows, and the poem ends, not with a celebration of victory but with Charlemagne's weary acceptance of the angel Gabriel's summons to yet another war in defense of Christendom.

The wars in Spain became the center of the early Carolingian legend since they presented Charlemagne as the divinely ordained defender of Christianity against the infidel and as a king of justice and piety. A far smaller number of *chansons de geste* deal with Charlemagne's wars against foes in Italy and against the Saxons, though historically these conquests were more significant than the Spanish expedition. Later, other legends developed about his relationship with his vassals and these offer a less idealized image of Charlemagne. Since the narrator's sympathy is usually with the rebellious vassal, Charlemagne is often presented as harsh, vindictive, and cruel in stories that probably reflect the struggles in the 9th and 10th centuries between the ruling monarchs who succeeded Charlemagne and their recalcitrant but powerful vassals. Even in the *Song of Roland* there is a hint of this theme in the hostile attitudes and actions of Ganelon, which, though directed against Roland rather than Charlemagne, nevertheless endanger the emperor's cause. Such *chansons de geste* as *Ogier the Dane, The Four Sons of Aimon,* and *Doon de Mayence* relate at great length the feuds between the rebel vassals, aided by their families and allies, against the authority of Charlemagne. There were intermittent reconciliations and renewals of hostilities, but the foes generally united if Christendom was threatened.

In the 13th century the Carolingian legends, like the Arthurian, were combined into cycles, but there was no influential re-creation of the stories comparable to the Arthurian Vulgate. Such Carolingian compilations as those of Philippe Mouskés and the monk Alberic of Trois-Fontaines are valuable because they preserve legendary material that has since disappeared from the extant versions; and the Old Norse prose *Karlamagnús saga* is important because its compilers had access to texts that are often superior to those that have survived.

Spread of the Legends. The legendary fame of Charlemagne spread into Germany, the Low Countries, Scandinavia, England, Italy, and Spain. Knowledge of Carolingian legends can be documented in England over a long period. One of the earliest allusions tells of the minstrel Taillefer at the Battle of Hastings in 1066 who sang of Charlemagne, Roland, and those who died at Roncevaux. Though his song could not have been the extant epic, it is significant that the earliest MS was written in Anglo-Norman about 1170 and that it was preserved at Oxford. The Carolingian legends in Middle English are late and inferior versions, but in the 15th century interest was still strong enough to persuade Caxton to publish *Charles the Great* in 1485 and four years later *The Four Sons of Aymon.*

In the Italian Renaissance, the Carolingian legends experienced a literary rebirth in the narrative poems of L. Pulci (1432–84), M. Boiardo (1441–94), and Ariosto. The work of their 14th-century predecessors, the Franco-Italian compilations and the Italian prose *Reali di Francia* (c. 1400), by Andrea da Barberino (c. 1370–c. 1432), had already established the distinctive features of the Italian tradition: the reduction of the complicated relationships into a feud between two great families, the houses of Clermont and Mayence. Charlemagne became a background figure, and the heroes of Clermont were Roland (Orlando) and Renaud de Montauban (Rinaldo). The head of the enemy house, of course, was Ganelon.

Professional minstrels popularized these stories orally in the streets of Italian cities and along the pilgrimage routes to Rome. They reached literary eminence when Pulci, poet of the household of Lorenzo de Medici, used them as the basis of his comic epic *Il Morgante Maggiore* (1482). Boiardo's *Orland Innamorato* (1494) inaugurated a new phase with the introduction into the Carolingian epic of chivalric and romantic themes derived from the Arthurian cycle. The invincible Roland of earlier tradition becomes Orlando, vanquished by love for a pagan princess who plans to destroy Christendom by seducing Charlemagne's paladins. In this romantic epic, Boiardo invents a world of knight-errantry, surprises, enchantments, and magic, blended with the wars of Christian against Saracen. With a spirit of ironic detachment, Ariosto continued Boiardo's unfinished poem in *Orlando Furioso,* the central theme of which is Orlando's madness induced by love and jealousy. Thus transformed, the old Carolingian tradition contributed to one of the most brillant and polished narrative poems of the Italian Renaissance.

Except for the influence of Ariosto's masterpiece on Spenser's *Faerie Queen* in the 16th century in England and Byron's delighted discovery of Pulci in the 19th, the Carolingian legends have been less important in modern times than the Arthurian. In different ways, however, the two cycles of legends have significantly enriched the culture of western Europe.

Bibliography: R. S. LOOMIS, ed., *Arthurian Literature in the Middle Ages* (Oxford 1959); *The Development of Arthurian Romance* (London 1963); *The Grail: From Celtic Myth to Christian Symbol* (New York 1963). J. S. P. TATLOCK, *The Legendary History of Britain: Geoffrey of Monmouth's Historia Regum Britanniae and Its Early Vernacular Versions* (Berkeley 1950). J. FRAPPIER, *Chrétien de Troyes: L'Homme et l'oeuvre* (Paris 1957); *Étude sur La Mort le Roi Artu* (2d ed. Paris 1961). T. MALORY, *Works,* ed. E. VINAVER, 3 v. (Oxford 1947). J. A. BENNETT, ed., *Essays on Malory* (Oxford 1963). R. S. and L. A. H. LOOMIS, *Arthurian Legends in Medieval Art* (New York 1938). G. PARIS, *Histoire poétique de Charlemagne,* ed. P. MEYER (new ed. Paris 1905). J. BÉDIER, *Les Légendes épiques,* 4 v. (2d ed. Paris 1914–21). H. G. LEACH, *Angevin Britain and Scandinavia* (Cambridge, Mass. 1921). J. E. WELLS, *A Manual of the Writings in Middle English, 1050–1400* (New Haven 1916; 9 suppl. 1919–52). J. B. FLETCHER, *Literature of the Italian Renaissance* (New York 1934). L. A. H. LOOMIS, *Adventures in the Middle Ages* (New York 1962).

[H. NEWSTEAD]

ARTICLE OF FAITH

The term was unknown in the age of the Fathers. Though it came into use before the time of St. Thomas Aquinas, it was he who apparently first gave it precise meaning. For him an article of faith has three qualities: it is a formally revealed doctrine (that is, its meaning is made known by God in a SUPERNATURAL way) conceptually distinct from other doctrines; it embodies a truth of salvific importance; and it is incorporated into an official Church CREED.

The articles of faith are the basic expressions of Christian belief. They are interrelated in the organically unified body of Church teaching. Some are more fundamental than others, the less fundamental being amplifications of the more fundamental. Thus, the articles of faith are the building blocks of THEOLOGY, which is the science of first revealed principles. In the course of the centuries the Church makes explicit the doctrines implicitly contained in them, and it strives to show ever more clearly the interrelationships existing among them, and between them and the doctrines derived from them.

See Also: DEPOSIT OF FAITH; DOGMA.

Bibliography: R. RUCH, *Dictionnaire de théologie catholique* 1.2:2023–25. H. BACHT, *Lexikon für Theologie und Kirche*, ed. J. HOFER and K. RAHNER, 10 v. (2d new ed. Freiburg 1957–65), 4:934–935.

[P. F. CHIRICO]

ARTIFICIAL INTELLIGENCE

Artificial intelligence (AI) is that division of science, particularly of computer science, which attempts to emulate and extend with programmed and fabricated elements the cognitive and affective functions of animals and human beings. AI can be viewed as a division of "artificial life" (AL) whose principal findings come from biology, psychology, and sociology. The definition and history of artificial intelligence, the principal divisions of the field, its tools, influential persons and overall significance, along with sources for further information, are considered in this article.

The phrase "artificial intelligence" first gained general acceptance after John McCarthy used it as the title of a summer 1956 Dartmouth College computer conference. It eventually replaced other terms such as "machine intelligence," "complex information processing," and "heuristic programming," each of which indicated a particular emphasis or approach to the field.

The somewhat amorphous character of AI research is a result of its shifting frontiers, which continually redefine AI's major focus. In any given period fundamental problems and processes that extend beyond the then better understood and more structured forms of information handling are discovered. In general these are problems whose formalized descriptions do not indicate the implementation of simple algorithmic methods for their solution. They are therefore said to call for "intelligence." For example Arthur Samuel's Checker Player, a pioneering computer program (proposed 1947, master level play 1961) that was among the first to "learn" from its mistakes, has in time been supplanted as a paradigm for a stream of AI research by backgammon and chess-playing programs and machines. These are yielding in turn to "games" of greater combinatorial complexity and logical ambiguity or probability.

In these AI research areas the common and what have proven to be difficult tasks include the identification and in some sense formalized articulation of the underlying "intelligence" problems. Despite, and to an extent because of, major technological advances, the obstacles encountered have led to a more sophisticated appreciation of the richness of intelligence and its subtle possibilities. This appreciation stands in marked contrast to earlier optimism regarding near-term "thinking machines" and "mechanical brains" (cf. Perceptron). Consequently, cognate disciplines such as cognitive and animal psychologies, neurology, various kinds of material or semantic logics as well as "fuzzy set" and other theories in mathematics and philosophy are increasingly being drawn upon for the light they might cast on the generalized problematic of intelligence. Consciousness, particularly human subjective or self-reflexive consciousness of relations of second or higher degree, represents one of AI's major hurdles.

Chief Topics. The principal sub-topics of current AI research include continuous-speech recognition and synthesis, natural language interpretation, generation, and translation, the processing of stereoscopic visual patterns, the extension of such sensory receptors and effectors as tactile and auditory elements in robots, signal and symbol processing, machine learning and reasoning, inductive logic programming, neural networks with parallel processing, aspects of computer-assisted instruction (CAI) and computer-assisted design and manufacture (CAD/CAM) especially in the computer field itself, automatic programming, and more generally expert or knowledge-based systems.

Expert systems usually consist of an extensive database of facts and rules about some domain such as diesel-locomotive repair (Delta), emergency room medical diagnosis (Internist, Caduceus), mineral exploration (Prospector), the structure of organic molecules (Dendral) or world-class chess-playing (Deep Blue). The facts are incorporated via a "knowledge representation" into a model of the system in question or, alternatively, with a series of heuristic rules which attempt to capture the expertise of accomplished human practitioners in that domain.

Besides such particularized efforts, the overall process of creating expert systems in any field is undergoing automation. "Knowledge engineering" topics such as generalized inference engines, problem solving in a large search space, subgoaling, abstraction, forms of knowledge representation involving the predicate calculus, semantic primitives and networks, frames and scripts all contribute to the building and use of expert systems in many domains; these broader considerations in turn clarify the more general AI "intelligence" tasks described above.

In a reciprocal almost symbiotic manner the HUMAN GENOME Project, genomics, and proteomics use AI to reproduce the evolutionary history of human beings, thus displaying the brain's "blueprint" which in conjunction with its past environments reveals to cognitive science more of the nervous system's physiological capacities, more challenges for AI.

Programming languages and environments developed for AI work include John McCarthy's LISP and Alain Colmerauer's PROLOG (1973)—with important French, British, and Japanese developments. Progress is being made in supercomputer and LISP machines and parallel processing with not only electromechanical and electronic but also optical and experimental biological computing machines in the offing. Somewhat more speculative are the varieties of quantum computing that have been proposed.

In addition to the classical contributions of the Greek logicians, of Ramon Lull, G. Leibnitz, B. Pascal, G. Boole, and K. Goedel, leading figures in recent AI work have included Alan Turing, Claude Shannon, Allen Newell, Herbert Simon, Hubert Dreyfus, and Roger Penrose.

Scientific advances in AI can be viewed in the context of philosophy's mind-body problematic and religious assertions regarding the unique dignity and immortal destiny of the human person. Recent efforts have helped clarify such assertions and indicated the shortcomings of earlier somewhat simplistic reductionist claims. For the short-term at least, man-machine interactions via "agents" and "bots" (software robots) appear to offer the most promising ways of enhancing human activities.

For ongoing developments cf. *AI Magazine*, a serial publication of AAAI, *The American Association for Artificial Intelligence*, founded in late 1979 (first annual conference 1980) and the major professional society of the discipline, as well as *Artificial Intelligence: An International Journal* (Amsterdam: North-Holland).

Bibliography: S. B. TORRANCE, ed., *The Mind and the Machine: Philosophical Aspects of Artificial Intelligence* (New York 1984). S. SHAPIRO, *Encyclopedia of Artificial Intelligence* (New York 1992). J. CHANGEUX and P. RICOEUR, *What Makes Us Think?* (Princeton 2000).

[J. F. SMOLKO]

ARTUSI, GIOVANNI MARIA

Music theorist of the Roman conservative circle; b. Bologna, Italy, 1540 (1545?); d. Bologna, 1613. By 1562 he was a canon of the Congregation of the Saviour. Though his polemics against MONTEVERDI put him in the early Italian baroque, it is difficult not to classify him with the Renaissance. He took exception not only to the *seconda prattica* of Monteverdi, but also wrote against Gesualdo, Vincentino, Rore, and A. Gabrieli, showing how they had strayed from classical Renaissance traditions. In *L'Arte del contrapunto* (1586–89; microprint, Rochester, N.Y. 1954) he showed himself a conservative student of Zarlino, but later attacked even him. Other writings were *L'Artusi, overo delle imperfettioni della moderna musica* (1600) and *Considerazioni musicali* (1603). He remained a defender of the old styles until the end, but in later life he softened with regard to Monteverdi's music, which he even professed to admire. Of his compositions a book of four-voiced *Canzonette* is well known (1598).

Bibliography: O. STRUNK, ed., *Source Readings in Music History* (New York 1950). R. H. F. REDLICH, *Die Musik in Geschichte und Gegenwart*, ed. F. BLUME (Kassel-Basel 1949–) 1:747–749. G. REESE, *Music in the Renaissance* (rev. ed. New York 1959). R. L. SCHRADE, *Monteverdi: Creator of Modern Music* (New York 1950). G. GASPARI, *Dei musicisti bolognesi al XVI secolo* (Bologna 1876). G. B. MARTINI, *Esemplare ossia saggio fondamentale di contrapunto*, 2 v. (Bologna 1774–75). G. M. ARTUSI, "Of the Imperfections of Modern Music" in *Strunk's Source Readings in Music History, vol. 4: The Baroque Era*, rev. ed. L. TREITLER, (New York 1998). D. M. RANDEL, ed., *The Harvard Biographical Dictionary of Music* 28 (Cambridge, Massachusetts 1996). P. P. SCATTOLIN, "Giovanni Maria Artusi" in *The New Grove Dictionary of Music and Musicians, v.1*, ed. S. SADIE (New York 1980) 646–648. N. SLONIMSKY, ed. *Baker's Biographical Dictionary of Musicians, Eighth Edition* (New York 1992).

[F. J. SMITH]

ARUNDEL, THOMAS

Archbishop, chancellor of England, foe of Lollards; b. 1352; d. Feb. 19, 1414. He was the son of Richard Fitzalan, Earl of Arundel, whose title he used as a surname; his mother, Eleanor, his father's second wife, was daughter and coheiress of Henry, Earl of Lancaster. His studies at Oriel College, Oxford, were terminated by his exceptionally early promotion to the bishopric of ELY, to which he was provided by the pope (Aug. 13, 1373) in opposition to both King Edward III and the cathedral chapter. On the same day that he was consecrated bishop (April 9, 1374) he was ordained both deacon and priest. During the turbulent reign of RICHARD II, Arundel joined his brother Richard, Earl of Arundel, in opposition to the king. He supported the Lords' Appellant (1386–88) and served as Lord Chancellor (1386–89). When Abp. ALEXANDER NEVILLE of York was translated *in partibus* to the schismatic See of Saint Andrews, Scotland (*see* WESTERN SCHISM), Arundel was translated to YORK (April 3, 1388). In May 1389 he relinquished the great seal to William of WYKEHAM, but he resumed the chancellorship in 1391 and held it until his translation to the Archbishopric of CANTERBURY (Sept. 25, 1397). However, the Commons impeached and banished him as Richard II's former adversary at the same time that his brother, the Earl of Arundel, was appealed of treason, summarily condemned, and executed (Sept. 1397). Arundel fled to Rome, but Richard II's will prevailed, and Pope BONIFACE IX translated him, as his predecessor at York, Neville, *in partibus* to Saint Andrews. After he had traveled widely on the Continent, visiting among others the great Florentine humanist Coluccio Salutati, Arundel joined Henry Plantagenet, with whom he returned to England in July 1399; restored to his see, he crowned Henry IV (Oct. 13, 1399). Subsequently Arundel proved an efficient and vigorous administrator: he made a visitation of his entire province, successfully maintained his right to visit Oxford University, and provided new statutes for the Court of ARCHES. Most important he became a vigorous opponent of LOLLARDS, whom he fought through provincial councils at London (1397) and at Oxford (1408) and through constitutions regulating preaching and forbidding the translation of the Bible into the vernacular; above all he worked in cooperation with the secular authority through parliament. In 1401 he was instrumental in securing the passage of the statute *De heretico comburendo,* after which he presided at the trials of Lollard sympathizers John PURVEY and William Sawtry (1401), John Badby (1410), and Sir John Oldcastle (1413). In addition, he vigorously opposed the Commons's demand for disendowment of the Church, especially in 1404 and 1410. He served Henry IV as chancellor (1407–10 and 1412–13). Because of his exercise of authority during Henry's illness, he earned the resentment of Henry V, who replaced Arundel as chancellor with Henry BEAUFORT upon his accession in 1413. Arundel was buried in a tomb, since destroyed, in Canterbury cathedral.

Bibliography: Arundel's registers are extant in MS: Ely at the Ely Diocesan Registry; York, Borthwick Institute of Historical Research; Canterbury, Lambeth Palace Library, London. J. GAIRDNER, *The Dictionary of National Biography from the Earliest Times to 1900,* 63 v. (London 1885–1900; repr. with corrections, 21 v., 1908–09, 1921–22, 1938; suppl. 1901–) 1:609–613. A. STEEL, *Richard II* (Cambridge, Eng. 1941; repr. 1963). K. B. MCFARLANE, *John Wycliffe and the Beginnings of English Nonconformity* (New York 1953). A. B. EMDEN, *A Biographical Register of the University of Oxford to A.D. 1500,* 3 v. (Oxford 1957–59) 1:51–53. J. LENEVE, *Fasti Ecclesiae Anglicanae 1300–1541* (1716). Corrected and continued from 1215 by T. D. HARDY, 3 v. (Oxford 1854). New ed. by H. P. F. KING et al. (London 1962–) 4:4, 14 for Canterbury and Ely; 6:4.

[H. S. REINMUTH, JR.]

ÅS (ASYLUM), ABBEY OF

A former CISTERCIAN monastery located at the mouth of the Viska River, Halland, Sweden, in the former Archdiocese of Lund (also known as *Aos, Aas, Asylum*). It was founded in 1194, probably by Waldemar (d. *c.* 1237), a son of King Canute V of Denmark and Bishop of Schleswig, and placed in the care of Cistercian monks who had been encouraged to come to the area by Abp. ESKIL OF LUND. It was affiliated to the abbey of Sorö, near Copenhagen, which was in turn a daughterhouse of Esrom, founded directly from CLAIRVAUX. Very little is known of the history of the abbey. Two daughters of the Swedish king Magnus Eriksson were buried there *c.* 1340, and Queen Margaret of Denmark gave the monastery a gilded table with relics, asking the community for remembrance in its prayers; in return, her deceased father, King Waldemar, was affiliated with the order. During the last decades of the 14th century two of the abbots later became abbots of Sorö. The records show that the abbey was devastated by fire in 1397, and a document of 1441 notes that the church of the monastery was damaged and had no roof. In 1535 the last abbot, Mats Eriksson, was appointed as the first Protestant rector of the parishes of Veddige and Ås. The abbey was later destroyed.

Bibliography: P. VON MÖLLER, *Bidrag till Hallands historia* (Lund 1874), v. 1. J. M. CANIVEZ, *Dictionnaire d'histoire et de géographie ecclésiastiques,* ed. A. BAUDRILLART et al. (Paris 1912–) 4:865–867. L. H. COTTINEAU, *Répertoire topobibliographique des abbayes et prieurés,* 2 v. (Mâcon 1935–39) 1:168–169.

[O. ODENIUS]

ASBURY, FRANCIS

First Methodist bishop in America; b. Handsworth, England, Aug. 21, 1745; d. Spotsylvania, Va., March 31, 1816. His parents were poor, and after a scanty common school education, he was apprenticed to a blacksmith. In 1763 he was converted and became a lay preacher, while continuing to work at the forge. In 1766 he was asked to take the place of an ailing Methodist itinerant and thereafter devoted himself entirely to preaching. At the Bristol Conference in 1771, he volunteered for America; he arrived at Philadelphia, Pa., on Oct. 27, 1771. He set out at once on a preaching tour of New Jersey and southern New York, forming new congregations and strengthening old ones. Devoted to John WESLEY'S principle of itinerancy, he never again had a home and, with one brief exception, continued these missionary journeys until his death. Between 1772 and 1776 he preached in Pennsylvania, Maryland, Virginia, and West Virginia. Because of war conditions, he was in partial retirement in Maryland and Delaware until 1780; in the ensuing years he continued preaching from North Carolina to New York.

In November of 1784 Thomas Coke and Richard Whatcoat arrived from England to discuss proposals for the organization of an independent Episcopal Church. At the Christmas conference in Baltimore, Asbury was chosen superintendent with Dr. Coke and on three successive days was ordained deacon, elder, and finally superintendent on Dec. 27, 1784. Asbury later used the title bishop, although this was repugnant to Wesley. The *Form of Discipline* was adopted in 1785 and the *Arminian Magazine* was begun in 1789. Throughout this period, Asbury continued his itinerant ministry, visiting existing congregations and penetrating South Carolina (1785), Georgia and Tennessee (1788), and New England (1791). He was able to block Coke's efforts at reunion with the Protestant Episcopal Church in 1791; his insistence on itinerancy made the remarkable growth of Methodism possible. He was less successful in his efforts against slavery. In 1785 he petitioned the Virginia Assembly in favor of general emancipation and sought to make abolitionism a principle of the Methodist Church. He ordained Richard Allen as the first African-American Methodist minister in 1799 but was unable to prevent the change from separate black congregations (1793–95) to a wholly independent African Methodist Episcopal Church. He was an early advocate of camp meetings and made them a fixture of American Methodism. Despite his continual journeys, his health was always precarious, and in 1800 Bishop Whatcoat was chosen to assist him. He continued his missionary labors, however, and died on a preaching tour.

Bibliography: F. ASBURY, *Journal and Letters,* ed. E. T. CLARK et al., 3 v. (Nashville 1958). H. K. CARROLL, *Francis Asbury in the Making of American Methodism* (New York 1923). W. L. DUREN, *Francis Asbury* (New York 1928). W. C. LARRABEE, *Asbury and His Coadjutors,* ed. D. W. CLARK, 2 v. (Cincinnati 1853). W. P. STRICKLAND, *The Pioneer Bishop* (New York 1858). E. S. TIPPLE, *Francis Asbury: The Prophet of the Long Road* (New York 1916).

[R. K. MACMASTER]

ASCELLINO

Also known as Asselino, Anselmo. Dominican from Lombardy; papal envoy to the Tartars. His antecedents and the dates of his birth and death are not known. In 1245 he headed one of four missions that Innocent IV sent by different routes to the Tartars, who were exhorted to cease their depredations and become Christians. Apparently, he was also commissioned to treat with the dissidents and Moslem sultans of the Near East with regard to reunion and conversion. These tasks occupied him and his Dominican staff of four until the fall of 1246. Going from Acre, the friars contacted the Tartar general Batschu in the Transcaucasus (or middle Persia) on May 24, 1247, 59 days after leaving Tiflis. Ascellino's undiplomatic re-

fusal to follow Oriental protocol endangered the lives of the envoys and led to great discomfort, hunger, and insults. Finally Batschu accepted the papal letters but forced Ascellino to await a reply from the Grand Khan. He departed for Europe on July 25, 1247, accompanied by two Tartar envoys to the pope. The letters from the khan and Batschu were arrogant, demanding papal submission to the Tartars. Ascellino reached Lyons in the autumn of 1248. His later career is unknown. The story of his martyrdom in Asia is pure speculation.

Bibliography: B. ALTANER, *Die Dominikanermissionen des 13. Jh.: Forschungen zur Geschichte der kirchlichen Unionen unter den Mohammedanern* (Breslauer Studien zur historischen Theologie 3; Habelschwerdt 1924). P. PELLIOT, "Les Mongols et le papauté," *Revue de l'Orient Chrétien* 24 (1924) 265–335.

[W. A. HINNEBUSCH]

ASCENSION OF JESUS CHRIST

The Church believes that the risen Jesus "ascended into heaven" in body and soul (H. Denzinger, *Enchiridion symbolorum,* ed. A. Schönmetzer [32d ed. Freiburg 1963] 11, and in the creeds generally).

Biblical

In its widest sense the Ascension includes three moments: the final historical departure of Jesus from His disciples, the metahistorical passage and entry into heaven, and the exaltation, also metahistorical, "at the right hand of the Father." Three groups of NT texts describe these three moments: those that narrate the visible departure of Jesus as a *terminus a quo;* those that treat of the Ascension from a primarily theological aspect, more or less explicitly referring to the witnessed departure while concentrating on the metahistorical victory; and, finally, those texts that refer to the exaltation of Jesus as a *terminus ad quem* without explicit mention of the previous moments. This article under the heading "Biblical" treats the first two moments.

Visible Departure. The primitive kerygma recorded in 1 Cor 15.3–8 mentions no final leave-taking of the risen Jesus. The early Jerusalem preaching (see below) refers to Jesus' departure only in as far as it is theologically significant and never turns to the material details of when, where, and how that are the indispensable data for the historian. The early preaching, for which the continual presence of the risen Jesus with believers (Mt 28.20) was the all important datum, may well have considered such details irrelevant. The departure of Jesus did not alter essentially the relation of the believer to his Lord. He had been seen, and He would be seen again—soon, they hoped; meanwhile, His invisible presence perdured.

The Ascension of Jesus, early-14th-century fresco by Giotto in the Scrovegni Chapel at Padua, Italy.

As years lengthened into decades and fervent hope for the PAROUSIA was tempered by the full realization that no one knew the exact time of the future return (Mk 13.32; Acts 1.6–7, 11), the second generation of Christians desired to know further details about the final visible departure of Jesus. Luke responded by gleaning from the first-generation preaching and its documentary precipitate (Lk 1.1–4) such details as he could concerning the when, where, and how of Jesus' departure.

The final chapter of St. Luke's Gospel describes appearances of the risen Jesus to the disciples at Emmaus (24.13–33, 35), to Peter (24.34), and to the Eleven (24.36–43). The narrative seems to place these events on the day of the Resurrection (24.13), and the following discourse (24.44–49) is not distinguished in time from the preceding meal. The notice of the Ascension then occurs with no indication of its being separated from the preceding materials. "He then [Gr. δέ] led them out towards Bethany, and lifting up his hands, he blessed them. While he blessed them, he parted [aorist] from them *and was carried up* [imperfect] *into heaven*" (24.50–51). The italicized words are found in P75, B, A, W, and Θ, but they are omitted by S, D, and the Western tradition, perhaps because of the difficulty of harmonizing these verses with Acts 1.1–12. The form and the language of this notice are filled with cultic connotations. Certain data are, however, of a primarily historical nature. At first glance, since the day of the Resurrection frames all the other events in this chapter, it seems that Luke has placed the Ascension during Easter night (see 24.29). Yet there are no indications of time in this chapter after 24.33, and their absence might well be deliberate and theologically motivated. Luke depicts Jesus' departure as occurring after He had led His disciples out of Jerusalem up the western slope and over the crest of Mt. Olivet to Bethany (15 stadia from Jerusalem, according to Jn 11.18, or about 1 5/8 miles). There, in the very act of blessing them, He made His final departure (verb in the aorist). The next action is presented as a progressive movement that takes time (verb in the imperfect), as the risen Jesus is borne into the sky. Even here the simply physical movement is described with the theologically evocative ἀναφέρειν, usually used in the NT for an offering of sacrifice.

The Ascension also figures in the canonical conclusion of Mark (Mk 16.19), which is the Gospel reading for the Feast of the Ascension in the Roman rite. The text is certainly canonical and inspired (H. Denzinger, *Enchiridion symbolorum* 1502), and the verse in question may even belong to a very archaic creed, but historically speaking the notice is dependent upon the traditions recorded in Luke and John and thus cannot be treated as a primary witness.

The only lengthy description of Jesus' Ascension in the NT is Acts 1.1–11 (the epistle for the feast in the Roman Missal). Luke begins by recapitulating his Gospel, noting that his first volume had extended "until the day that . . . [Jesus] was taken up" (Acts 1.2.—the original Western tradition may have omitted the verb). The events that were framed as a miniature within the "day" of the Resurrection Luke now sketches on a broader temporal canvas. The appearances of the risen Lord are now said to have occurred "during 40 days" (1.3), a number that need not be taken as exact (cf. Acts 13.30–31; Mk 1.13) but simply as referring to a rather lengthy period. After noting Jesus' final instructions (1.4–5, 7–8; cf. Lk 24.47–49), Luke begins his description of the Ascension itself with the words, "he was lifted up before their eyes, and a cloud took him from their sight" (1.9). The narrative unmistakably emphasizes that the departure had been witnessed. The language, however, is highly charged theologically. The verb of v. 9a is usually used in the NT of gestures associated with prayer and hope (cf. Lk 18.13; 21.28; 24.50); in v. 9b the cloud (cf. Lk 9.34–35) is represented as bearing Jesus off as on a chariot (cf. 2 Kgs 2.10–12; Ps 103[104].3). The witnesses did not grasp the full significance of this leave-taking. But while "they were still staring after him into the sky," a revelation given by "two men in white garments" (1.10; cf. Lk 24.4) enabled them to begin to penetrate what they had seen. This last glimpse of the risen Jesus borne into heaven on a cloud was a sign and promise of how He would appear again (cf. Mk 13.26; 14.62 and parallels). Luke's narrative then closes with a reference to Mt. Olivet as the scene of the departure (cf. Lk 24.50).

Entrance into Glory. The next question concerning the Ascension moves from the area of the historically verifiable to the metahistorical. No passage says that the disciples understood that this was the last appearance of Jesus to them in their lifetime. Ever since His Resurrection His visible presence had not been continuous, but He

had appeared to His disciples only to vanish again (Lk 24.31). Where was He at other times? The answer (implicit in the arrangement of the materials in Luke ch. 24) is explicit in Jn 20.17. On the morning of the Resurrection, Jesus, appearing to Mary Magdalene, says: "Do not cling to me, for I have not yet ascended to the Father. Rather go to my brothers and tell them 'I am ascending to my Father and your Father, to my God and your God.'" The disciples first saw Jesus on that evening (Jn 20.19). Evidently, in John's thought, when the risen Jesus left Mary Magdalene, He ascended to heaven. Thence He returned for each later appearance. Thus an "ascension," a return to the Father's glory (*see* GLORY [IN THE BIBLE]), is implied after every appearance of the risen Jesus. He was no longer earthbound, and the Ascension was linked immediately with His Resurrection as part of a single movement from the grave to glory. Eventually the term "Ascension" was reserved for what had proved to be the final leave-taking of Jesus.

What happened to Jesus after His departure? An answer to this can be had only from revelation. The archaic Jerusalem kerygma presumed the fact of the Ascension (Acts 5.30–31) and probed its metahistorical aspect by applying the words and concepts of the OT to what the disciples had witnessed (Acts 2.33–35, using Ps 109[110].1). The Pauline didache of Eph 4.7–10, in like fashion, uses Ps 67(68).19 to show that "he ascended far above all the heavens, that he might fill all things." Thus the Ascension brought everything in the universe into contact with the risen Jesus. The ancient Christian hymn quoted in 1 Tm 3.16 links "taken up in glory" with "seen by angels" and thus specifies those who witnessed the Ascension victory. The baptismal didache of 1 Pt 3.18–22 specifies still further that "the spirits that were in prison" (i.e., fallen angels, conceived as imprisoned in the lower "heavens"; cf. Eph 1.20–21; 2.2; Col 2.15) became subject to the risen Jesus as He ascended. The Ascension is used in the Epistle to the HEBREWS as a theological fact linked to the priesthood of Jesus, who passed through the heavens as a great high priest (Heb 4.14) to enter the heavenly sanctuary (6.19–20; 9.24).

Ascension in Early Christian Literature. The writings of the Apostolic Fathers contain no reference to the Ascension, but Judeo-Christian literature, with its distinctive theological methodology, exploited it fully. These writers added Psalm 23 (24) to those already used in the NT as loci for the Ascension. Their central interest was the manifestation of Jesus' victory in the realm of the angels, both good and bad; but the details they give are patently nonhistorical.

In the writings of Justin the perils inherent in using the Jewish Ascension imagery appear, for he was compelled to defend the fact of Jesus' Ascension (1 *Apology* 50) as something quite different from the "ascensions" of Dionysus, Bellerophon (1 *Apology* 54), and Heracles (*Dialogue* 69). Irenaeus reaffirmed the basic fact of the Ascension (*Demonstration of the Apostolic Teaching,* 83–85), evidently depending upon Acts 1.9–12, and he used Psalms 23(24) and 67(68) to develop the theological aspects of the event.

The centrality of the Ascension in the faith of the Church is witnessed not only by the most archaic creeds but also by the Roman canon, where it figures with the Passion and Resurrection in a summary of Jesus' whole redemptive work.

Bibliography: *Encyclopedic Dictionary of the Bible,* tr. and adap. by L. HARTMAN (New York 1963), from A. VAN DEN BORN, *Bijbels Woordenboek* 144–150. F. J. SCHIERSE, *Lexikon für Theologie und Kirche,* ed. J. HOFER and K. RAHNER, 10 v. (2d, new ed. Freiburg 1957–65) 5:358–360. E. LUCCHESI-PALLI, *ibid.* 362–363. P. BENOIT, "L'Ascension," *Revue biblique* 56 (1949) 161–203, repr. in *Exégèse et théologie,* 2 v. (Paris 1961) 1:363–411. J. DANIÉLOU, *The Theology of Jewish Christianity,* ed. and tr. J. A. BAKER (Chicago 1964) 248–263. E. H. SCHILLEBEECKX, "Ascension and Pentecost," *Worship* 35 (1961) 336–363.

[J. D. QUINN]

Theological

The Ascension of Jesus Christ, theologically speaking, is first a mystery of faith; second, it is an event that has a meaning in God's plan to save mankind because it concerns the human nature of Christ; and, third, it has, as an essential element in the mystery of salvation, a meaning in the life of each Christian now and for eternity.

Mystery of Faith. As an object of FAITH the Ascension is not something the contemporary believer can see or sense in any way (*see* MYSTERY [IN THEOLOGY]). The reality one believes is that the human nature of the risen Christ has been taken into the sphere of divine life with the Father, Son, and Holy Spirit in power and majesty. This reality of Christ's bodily entry into a new order of existence transcends the experience of one's human senses and imagination and as a result can only be inadequately represented in the human expressions used to describe it. One must be careful, therefore, not to mistake the total reality of faith with the presentation that is used in Scripture to express it. One uses the word "Ascension" for either or both the invisible aspect, or theological fact of Christ's exaltation and glorification with the Father in heaven that in this area is the principal object of faith; and the visible aspect, or historical fact (also object of faith) of Christ's manifestation of His glory that was incorporated in His last farewell on Mt. Olivet (Acts 1.3, 9–11). The latter is also a sign of the divine reality contained in the former.

Salvation Event. The role of theology is to investigate the meaning of this event, as an object of faith, and to examine and elucidate its meaning in relation to the other mysteries of faith and the final goal of mankind. What then is the theological significance of this exaltation of Christ's manhood? The dogmatic definition of Chalcedon, that Christ is one Person in two natures, implies that one and the same Person, the Son of God, also took on a visible human nature. In His humanity Christ is the Son of God. Therefore Christ is God in a human way and man in a divine way. Everything Christ does as man is therefore an act of the Son of God; His acts then are a penetration of a divine activity into a human activity (*see* THEANDRIC ACTS OF CHRIST). His human love is the embodiment of the redeeming love of God. Now it is precisely because the human acts of Christ are divine acts of the Son of God that He can fulfill God's promise of SALVATION in the concrete way intended by God. As divine acts in visible human form they possess a divine saving power and are therefore causes of man's salvation, accomplished in time and space but transcending the limits of time and space. Although this is true of every human action of Christ, it is especially true of those actions that, though enacted in His human nature, are by nature acts of God (because actions are done by persons) bringing man back to Himself. This truth is realized in a special way in the great mysteries of Christ's life: His Passion, death, Resurrection, and exaltation to the side of His Father.

St. John and St. Paul (each in his own way) link the Ascension with Christ's death and Resurrection and point out its relationship in the total picture of salvation. John's Gospel gives a central place to the redemptive work of Christ in His death and Resurrection. It must be remembered, however, that for John "glory" and "lifted up" refer to all the aspects of salvation: Passion, Resurrection, and Ascension (Jn 12.32–33; 3.13; 6.63). For John the Resurrection and Ascension are but two aspects of the same mystery (Jn 13.1). Exalted in glory at the right hand of the Father (Jn 12.23; 17.5), Christ sends the Holy Spirit (Jn 7.39) and through Him extends His dominion over the world (Jn 16.14).

For Paul the Ascension takes on a value in terms of man's salvation because Jesus was not only a man among men, but a new Adam (Rom 5.18). Hence each event of Christ's life modifies the condition of our own life to the very depths of our being. The mystery of man's salvation, accomplished by Christ, is not simply paying a debt or a buying back, but rather it is a mysterious but very real transformation of mankind in Christ. Salvation, in its most profound reality, is for Paul the God-Man in the Person of the Son incarnate, agreeing to succumb to the power of death but soon snatching His victory from it by

His Resurrection. His Ascension renders this victory definitive. Mankind thus enters into the sphere of the Trinity once and for all in the Person of the Word incarnate as the Epistle to the Hebrews insists (Heb 9.26; 10.10). Nothing henceforth will be able to separate from God the human nature that has entered into heaven. The Ascension of Christ, then, is the ascension of man, united to the divinity, arriving substantially at its goal, substantially served forever. "But God . . . even when we were dead by reason of our sins, brought us to life together with Christ . . . and raised us up together, and seated us together in heaven in Christ Jesus" (Eph 2.4–6). This passage is especially interesting because it shows how the mysteries of Christ's death, Resurrection, and Ascension were linked in Paul's mind as one great mystery of salvation. For the formulas used here—"to be given life together with Christ," "to be raised up from death together with Christ," and "to be seated together with Christ in heaven"—have the same meaning in Paul's mind, the salvation of mankind in Christ Jesus Our Lord.

Christian Meaning. The fact that Christ's Ascension has vital meaning for each Christian was forcefully pointed out in Christ's words: "It is expedient for you that I depart. For if I do not go, the Advocate will not come to you; but if I go, I will send him to you" (Jn 16.7). Hence the departure of Christ in His physical humanity was to be the inauguration of a new presence of Jesus, more profound and fruitful, for the Father, Son, and Holy Spirit would now come to live in a new way in the individual Christian. St. Paul makes it clear in the above text from the Ephesians that Christ's exaltation was the beginning of our own glory by reason of the mysterious living unity that we have with the physical Christ, who is now with the Father. St. Thomas, following Paul, maintains that our contact with Christ in glory is not merely something in the future, but now, in the present, and is indeed a marvelous basis for hope (*Summa theologiae* 3a, 57.6 and ad 2; cf. 2 Cor 5.16–18).

Though Christ possessed the fullness of the Spirit throughout His life, He could communicate it to others only by His death, that is, by His death, glorification, and Ascension, which taken together form the unity of mysteries that conditioned the coming of the Holy Spirit. In departing physically by His Ascension, Christ promises a far richer presence in the Spirit. In promising His Apostles that He would not leave them orphans, Christ indicates that only after His return to the Father would they discover His enduring presence with them that is modeled after the presence of the Father and the Son to one another in the Trinity (Jn 14.18–21). St. Augustine compares the presence of Christ with us after His Ascension to His presence with the Father after His Incarnation.

Pope St. Leo says that Christ became more fully present as God on the day He became less present as man.

As a pledge of our own glory, the mystery of the Ascension points out clearly that human nature in its totality, the embodied human person, is now glorified with Christ. In Christ Jesus the final effect of our grace of adoption is attained, the Redemption of our body. In Him, too, the yearning of all creation toward its full achievement is resolved at the same time. What this means for the Christian in his practical everyday life is beautifully expressed in ch. 4 of St. Paul's Epistle to the Ephesians. By means of Christ's Ascension the individual Christian is enabled to mature to the full stature of Christ his head. He is drawn by the gift of the Spirit toward his own personal fulfillment, and that of the whole universe, in Christ in one simultaneous movement of faith, hope, and love.

See Also: RESURRECTION OF CHRIST.

Bibliography: B. VAWTER and J. HEUSCHEN, "Ascension of Jesus," *Catholicisme. Hier, aujourd'hui et demain,* ed. G. JACQUE-MET 1:887–888. J. H. BERNARD, *Encyclopedia of Religion and Ethics,* ed. J. HASTINGS, 13 v. (Edinburgh 1908–27) 2:151–157. L. CERFAUX, *Christ in the Theology of St. Paul,* tr. G. WEBB and A. WALKER (New York 1959). F. X. DURRWELL, *The Resurrection: A Biblical Study,* tr. R. SHEED (New York 1960). W. K. M. GROSSOUW, *Revelation and Redemption,* ed. and tr. M. W. SCHOENBERG (Westminster, Md. 1955). E. H. SCHILLEBEECKX, *Christ: The Sacrament of the Encounter with God,* tr. P. BARRETT et al. (New York 1963); "Ascension and Pentecost," *Worship* 35 (May 1961) 336–363. R. SCHNACKENBURG, *New Testament Theology Today,* tr. D. ASKEW (New York 1963). P. BENOIT, "L'Ascension," *Revue biblique* 56 (1949) 161–203, repr. in *Exégèse et théologie,* 2 v. (Paris 1961) 1:363–411. C. DAVIS, *Theology for Today* (New York 1962). P. MIQUEL, "Christ's Ascension and Our Glorification," *Theology Digest* 9 (1961) 67–73.

[J. C. MURRAY]

ASCETICISM

The Greek noun ἄσκησις from which "asceticism" is derived means "exercise," "practice," or "training" for the purpose of obtaining something that is worth aspiring to, that represents an ideal.

TERMINOLOGY AND CONCEPT

Displaying an extraordinary flexibility in their application, ἄσκησις and its cognates (the verb ἀσκεῖν, "to practice," and the noun ἀσκητής, "one who practices") are related to a fourfold ideal in ancient literature.

Association with Training. In connection with the ideal of bodily excellence, the word and its cognates denote the strenuous training and the whole mode of life that leads to the highest possible degree of physical fitness either of the athlete (Aristophanes, *Plut.* 585; Plato,

Republic 403E; Xenophon, *Mem.* 1.2.24; Plutarch, *De gen. Socr.* 24.593D) or the soldier (Thucydides, 2.39; 5.67; Xenophon, *Cyr.* 8.1.34). The ἀσκητής, "the man who is trained," is contrasted with the ἰδιώτης, "the one who is untrained" (Xenophon, *Mem.* 3.7.7; *Eq. Mag.* 8.1).

With the development of philosophy came the training of the mind. To the ideal of the athlete and soldier there was added the ideal of the man who by exercising his intellectual faculties acquired wisdom. Heraclitus [Frg. 129 (H. Diels, *Die Fragmente der Vorsokratiker: Griesch und Deutsch,* ed. W. Kranz, 3 v.)] says that Pythagoras "practiced research" (ἱστορίην ἤσκησεν) and, by using an eclectic method, "created for himself a wisdom that was his own." Isocrates (*Bus.* 22) points to the benefit derived from "philosophy's training," namely, its power "to establish laws and to inquire into the nature of the universe." He contrasts the training of the mind with that of the body and recommends a liberal education and "a training of this sort" (τὴν ἄσκησιν τὴν τοιαύτην) for young men (*Antid.* 302; 304). Elsewhere (*Ad. Demon.* 40) he gives the advice: "But above all train (ἄσκει) your intellect; for the greatest thing in the smallest compass is a good mind in a human body." With this the word ἄσκησις and its synonym μελετή entered the field of education and, together with two other terms—φύσις (natural endowment) and μάθησις (acquisition of knowledge), or ἐπιστήμη (knowledge)—has an important place in Greek philosophical thought, but especially in the pedagogical system of the Sophists. The three terms occur frequently in ancient literature. They are mentioned by Plato (*Phaedrus* 269D) as the necessary requirements for a good orator.

Association with Ethics. The idea of the body's requiring strenuous training in preparation for an athletic contest or for warfare was easily extended to the areas of mental culture and ethics. The ideal aspired to was that of καλὸς κἀγαθός, the "good and worthy man." As early as Herodotus (1.96; 7.209) the verb ἀσκεῖν is found in such combinations as "to practice justice" or "veracity." In the sense of a systematic and comprehensive training as a self-preparation for a virtuous course of conduct it is used by Xenophon (*Mem.* 1.2.19–). Comparing those who do not "train" the body with those who neglect the "training" of the soul, he observes that, as the former cannot perform the functions proper to the body, so the latter cannot perform those proper to the soul, because they are not able to control their will with regard to what they ought and ought not to do. Hence one should cultivate the association with good men, because it is an ἄσκησις τῆς ἀρετῆς, a "training for virtue" (cf. same idea in Aristotle, *Eth. Nic.* 1170a 11). The training for virtue is then expounded especially by Epictetus. A chapter

in his *Dissertationes* (3.12), entitled περὶ ἀσκήσεως, is devoted to this subject. The object of this training, according to Epictetus, is the freedom of the sage who acts without hindrance in choice and in refusal. It is, therefore, principally a training of the will. If one is fond of pleasure, loath to work, or hot-tempered, he must, "to train himself" (ἀσκήσεως ἕνεκα), turn to a behavior directly contrary to the dictates of those urges. Similarly, indulgence in drinking, eating, and sensual love must be counteracted by a training in the opposite direction (*Dissertation* 3.12.7–12). Moreover, whatever is outside the moral purpose—be it women's beauty, compassion, or fame—is of no concern to the sage (*ibid.* 3.3.14–19; cf. 4.1.81).

Association with Religion. With the growth of a stronger sense of personal religion, in the history of Greek religious life, ἄσκησις assumed a final meaning, denoting an act of religious devotion or an exercise of piety. In this sense ἄσκησις is probably first used by Isocrates (*Bus.* 26) who describes Busiris, a legendary king of Egypt, as establishing for his subjects "numerous and varied exercises of piety" (ἀσκήσεις τῆς ὁσιότητος), convinced that this would accustom them to obeying the commands of those in authority. Religious asceticism, in the form of purificatory observances such as fasting and refraining from sexual intercourse, was practiced especially by sects of a religio-mystic temper like the Orphics and Pythagoreans. It continued to gain ground with the spread of the Oriental mystery religions, especially those of Attis-Cybele and Isis, that followed an elaborate system of ascetical exercises as cathartic measures before certain celebrations, and, through the proselytizing efforts of mendicant preachers of the Cynic school, it exhorted men to combat their appetites and to practice virtue.

In Cynic-Stoic popular philosophy the concept of ἄσκησις grew narrower and assumed a negative character, not in the sense that the ideal aspired to had ceased to be positive, but in that the main stress was laid on a complete detachment from the comforts and enticements of the world, on a radical suppression of the appetites, and on a predisposition to accept every hardship in the pursuit of this ideal, in accordance with the Epictetian precept: ἀνέχου καὶ ἀπέχου, "endure and renounce" (Favorinus *apud* Gell., *Noct. Att.* 17.19.6). This negative attitude is prominent also in Orphic-Pythagorean asceticism: the soul was to be purified by the denial and inhibition of the body and its impulses. Because of this strong negative emphasis, the notion of ἄσκησις as "practice" or "training" receded into the background. The influence of Cynic-Stoic philosophy and Orphic-Pythagorean thought is still discernible in the notion of the modern word "asceticism," which has eluded a generally accepted definition. In common usage it refers ordinarily to all those phenomena in the history of religion that are characterized by a methodical, and often minutely regulated, practice of a varied amount of austerities, ranging from the denial of comforts, emotions, desires, and activities to the actual self-infliction of pain.

Most frequently asceticism is conceived as the product of a more or less developed system of dualism, its basic motive being the endeavor to free the spiritual part of man from the defiling corruption of the body. This one-sided conception is no doubt too narrow. Although dualism is most conducive to asceticism, not all asceticism is dualistic. The two weekly fasts of the Pharisee (Lk 18.12) can unhesitatingly be termed ascetical practices. Yet, in observing them, the Pharisee was not motivated by any kind of dualistic speculation but considered them simply an especially meritorious work and a self-understood expression of his piety. Dualistic ideas no doubt were a powerful impulse toward asceticism, but, besides them, many other factors were active in its birth and development: the fear of hostile influences from demons, the conception of asceticism as a potent means to enter into communion with the supernatural, the sense of sin with the concomitant urge for atonement, the idea of earning salvation by merit, a radical otherworldliness of interest in view of the instability and transitoriness of all things earthly, and an ethical rigorism provoked by weariness with exaggerated cultural refinement and hope for a realization of the ascetic ideal in simple social environments.

MEANS AND METHODS

Both may be grouped into acts of self-discipline passing over into the outward life on the one hand and exercises of an inward kind on the other. To the former belong fasting, sexual continence, renunciation of bodily comforts, and actual infliction of pain.

Fasting. The history of religion reveals a widespread belief among primitive peoples that taking food is dangerous because demoniac forces may enter and harm the body. As a precaution, primitive man fasted or avoided certain foods that he considered dangerous because they were attractive to such pernicious forces. This originally negative aim to avert evil can, by the natural development of the same idea, be changed into a positive one. To be free from disturbing demoniac influences means also to be in a state of ritual purity, a necessary condition, it seems, for one who wants to enter into communion with the supernatural. This purity is supposed to bring man nearer to the divine, to endow him with extraordinary, superhuman powers. It is, therefore, required in the sacred rites of initiation. It is demanded also of the seer or proph-

et, to free his soul from any possible obstruction so that the god can take full possession of him during the ecstasy. In the same sense, the ascetic of religio-mystic temper hopes that such a state of purity will aid him in surmounting the barrier separating man from god, lift him up into the spiritual, and lead him to his final goal, the union with the divine. Finally, fasting is practiced as an act of devotion and morality. In its religio-ethical aspect it aims especially at controlling the lower appetites and promoting the cultivation of virtues.

Sexual Continence. As in fasting, the aim of sexual continence originally is apotropaic, or evil-averting. Cohabitation is regarded as producing ceremonial uncleanness. Ritual purity, on the other hand, is considered a necessary condition for approaching the divine. Hence Greek inscriptions, dealing with regulations concerning the ritual purity of lay worshippers entering sacred precincts, put great stress on their freedom from the defilements of sexual intercourse. Continence was a requisite also for participation in certain religious celebrations such as the Eleusinian Mysteries or the festival of the Thesmophoria. Connected with the same idea was a custom according to which a number of ancient Greek priesthoods were held by a boy or a girl until the age of puberty, but not after, or by old women. Sometimes priestly functions were performed by priestesses who were obliged to remain virgins during their tenure of office, either for a certain period or for life. Chastity was made one of the rules also of Buddhist monasticism.

Isolation and Self-infliction of Pain. Other external acts of self-discipline, practiced especially among primitive peoples in the training preparatory to admission to the mysteries of their tribal religions, and practiced also by Buddhist monks, include retirement from the world or solitary confinement, utmost simplicity in dwelling and clothing, sleeping on the bare ground or in an uncomfortable position, privation of sleep, and general neglect of the body. These austerities are sometimes increased by the infliction of pain, a method used by the fakirs of India. To this category belong immobility in diverse postures of the body, self-laceration, and other kinds of self-torture. The highest expression of non-Christian asceticism is found in spiritual exercises. They include such observances as silence, the examination of conscience, the study of sacred writings, prayer, mental concentration, and meditation. Buddhism provides remarkable examples of this kind.

ASCETICISM IN THE HISTORY OF RELIGION

Hardly any religion is without at least some traces of asceticism. Ascetical practices, rooted in magical or crude religious beliefs and belonging to a rigorously enforced set of purificatory rites for males at the age of puberty, or at a time previous to their admission to the tribal community, are found among the more advanced agricultural, herding, and higher hunting tribes that constitute most of the uncivilized population of the world. While the boys undergoing initiation are introduced into the religious lore and the moral code of the tribe, they must live in seclusion, submit to a harsh discipline with regard to the quantity and quality of their food, and bear with fortitude tests of endurance and actual torment. The purificatory rites to be observed by pubescent girls correspond in character to those imposed on boys at initiation. Moreover, in the mind of primitive man childbirth and death are phenomena that, because of their mysteriousness and therefore dangerousness, require certain precautions and abstentions such as seclusion, fasting, and cessation of customary activities. The medicine man also must be an ascetic, lean from fasting, because it is only through severe and constant self-discipline that he is able to acquire and retain occult powers.

Primitive Survivals in Higher Religions. Survivals of this primitive asceticism, which aims simply at averting a polluting evil that might threaten man from without, occur even in such highly developed religions as that of the Hebrews. Thus the rule requiring sexual abstinence of priests as preparation for liturgical functions is rooted ultimately in the belief that sexual phenomena, especially intercourse, produce ceremonial uncleanness and thus disqualify for worship (cf. Ex 19.15; Lv 15. 16–18; 1 Sm 21.5–; 2 Sm 11.5–13). A similar notion is at the root of the widespread custom in later Judaism to abstain from sexual intercourse on the Sabbath. To the same category belongs, apart from the extraordinarily complicated system of dietary laws, the abstention from wine observed by the priest before offering sacrifice (Lv 10.9; Ez 44.21), by the Nazirite for the period of his vow (Nm 6.3–; Am 2.11–; cf. Jgs 13.4, 7, 14), and by the Rechabites for life (Ez 35). The traditional ritual of mourning after a death also included restrictions such as fasting, abstaining from sexual intercourse, and avoidance of bathing and anointing.

Ascetical Aspects of Hebrew Practices. There are religions in which asceticism does not figure as an essential feature. Among the Hebrews the Old Testament concept of man and the world as the handiwork of an infinitely perfect God, precludes a dualistic view of the world. Married life and earthly possessions are thought of as having their foundation in a divine order and being God's gifts to man. What God in turn demands of man is not renunciation of these gifts, but the fulfillment of certain obligations laid down by the Mosaic Law in cult and in the moral and social spheres. Despite its essentially nonascetic character, however, the religion of the He-

brews contained seeds from which ascetical practices in the strict sense of the word could later develop.

The doctrine of reconciliation or atonement, always set forth by the teachers of Israel as their peculiar faith, led to the custom of penitential fasting. While at first the only fast day strictly enjoined in the Law (Lv 16.29–; 23.27–; Nm 29.7) was the Day of Atonement (Tishri 10), four more fast days were introduced into the Jewish calendar of the fourth, fifth, seventh, and tenth months during the Babylonian Exile (Zec 7.3, 5; 8.19) to commemorate disasters in the history of the Jewish people. How long the fast days of the fourth, seventh, and tenth months were kept after Zechariah, was no longer known in later rabbinic tradition. Only the fast day of the fifth month (Ab 9) seems to have continued as a national day of mourning in the post-Exilic period; it grew in importance after the Romans captured Jerusalem A.D. 70, since on this day, according to rabbinic tradition, both the first and the second temple were destroyed by fire.

On what day the so-called Fast of Esther (Est 9.31), now kept on the eve (Adar 13) of the Feast of Purim, was observed in antiquity, is not known. Many other fast days were later introduced; the *Megillat Ta'anit* (Scroll of Fasting) lists as many as 24. They were, however, not considered obligatory and were never accepted universally. In times of national emergencies, such as war, and imminent danger of extermination or public calamities, such as drought or locusts devouring the harvest, extraordinary general fasts were ordered by the authorities (Jgs 20.26; 1 Sm 7.6; 2 Chr 20.3; Jdt 4.9; Est 4.16; Jer 14.12; 36.6; Jl 1.14; 2.12, 15; Jon 3.5–; 1 Mc 3.47; 2 Mc 13.12; *Syr. Bar Ap* 86.1–; Josephus, *Ant. Jud.* 11, 134; *id., Vita* 290).

The more vigorous way of fasting consisted in abstaining from food and drink and in avoiding other physical pleasures such as bathing, anointing, and sexual intercourse; and in donning penitential garments, sprinkling the head with dust and ashes, and performing acts of self-humiliation. Since fasting on these days was accompanied by prayer and almsgiving, it was considered meritorious and pleasing to God. A certain measure of asceticism was then generally regarded as a sign of virtuous and holy living (Jdt 8.6; *Testament of Joseph* 9; *Henoch* 108.7; Lk 2.36–; 18.12; Josephus *Vita* 2). Fasting was used also to strengthen the prayer of the prophet and to prepare him for the reception of divine revelations (Dn 9.3; 10.2, 3, 12). As with other ascetical exercises, it is characteristic of the prophet in a number of late Jewish apocalypses (4 Ezr 5.13, 19f–; 6.31, 35; 9.23–25; 12.51; *Syriac Apocalypse of Baruch* 9.2; 12.5; 20.5; 21.1–; 43.3; 47.2; cf. *Apocalypse of Abraham* 9.7; *Ascension of Isaia* 2.7–11).

A fully developed ascetical system, however, remained a foreign thing in Jewish thought. As in ancient

Greece, it found a home only in such closed and exclusive societies of spiritualistic enthusiasts as the Essenes who lived outside of the broad current of Jewish piety and formed a kind of religious order, following an established mode of life with vows of celibacy, poverty, and obedience. An idealized picture of asceticism is given by Philo of Alexandria in his treatise *De vita contemplativa*, in which he describes the mystic-contemplative life of the Therapeutae, a colony of Jewish ascetics in Egypt.

See Also: RELIGION (IN PRIMITIVE CULTURE); BUDDHISM; HINDUISM; JAINISM; YOGA; MYSTERY RELIGIONS, GRECO-ORIENTAL.

Bibliography: E. D'ASCOLI, *La spiritualità precristiana* (Brescia 1952). G. VAN DER LEEUW, *Phänomenologie der Religion* (2d ed. Tübingen 1956). F. PFISTER, "Lanx Satura," no. 2, Ασκησις, *Festgabe für A. Deissmann* (Tübingen 1927) 76–81. H. STRATHMANN, *Geschichte der frühchristlichen Askese,* v.1 *Die Askese in der Umgebung des werdenden Christentums* (Leipzig 1914). J. DE GUIBERT and M. OLPHE-GALLARD, *Dictionnaire de spiritualité ascétique et mystique. Doctrine et histoire,* ed., M. VILLER et al. (Paris 1932) 1:936–960. J. HASTINGS, ed., *Encyclopedia of Religion & Ethics,* 13 v. (Edinburgh 1908–27) 1:63–111, introduction and separate articles by a number of specialists on Buddhist, Greek, Hindu, Japanese, Jewish, Islamic, Persian, Roman, Semitic and Egyptian asceticism. H. WINDISCH, G. KITTEL, *Theologisches Wörterbuch zum Neuen Testament* (Stuttgart 1935–) 1:492–494. R. MOHR and R. SCHNACKENBURG, *Lexikon für Theologie und Kirche,* ed. J. HOFER and K. RAHNER, 10 v. (2d, new ed. Freiburg 1957–65) 1:928–932. H. STRATHMANN, *Reallexikon für Antike und Christenum,* ed. T. KLAUSER (Stuttgart 1941–) 1:749–758. R. MENSCHING et al., *Die Religion in Geschichte und Gegenwart,* 7 v. (3d ed. Tübingen 1957–65) 1:639–642. H. DRESSLER, *The Usage of ἀσκήω and Its Cognates in Greek Documents to 100 A.D.* (Washington 1947).

[R. ARBESMANN]

ASCETICISM (IN THE NEW TESTAMENT)

In the Gospels asceticism is presented under the concrete theme of following the historical Christ and thus sharing the hardships, dangers, and penalties that loyal discipleship to Him exact; in the Epistles of St. Paul asceticism is described principally in the image of the spiritual athlete who consciously and constantly disciplines himself in a strong effort to live more fully in docile obedience to the Spirit of Christ, to attain not only his own salvation but also that of the community.

In the Gospels. The relationship between the disciples and Jesus, described in the Gospels as following Jesus, implies an ascetic self-renunciation by the disciple. Those invited by Jesus to follow Him must sacrifice their feelings and former ties, give absolute priority to the work of the kingdom, and be animated by a singleness of purpose. His call was: "If any man wishes to come after me, let him deny himself and take up his cross and follow me. For whoever would save his life will lose it; and whosoever loses his life for my sake and the gospel's will save it" (Mk 8:34–35; Mt 16:24–25; Lk 9:23–24). Following Jesus is difficult for human nature because it requires total self-commitment and entails contempt and danger from others. Yet following the historical Christ is a special gift of God (Jn 6:65), not granted the wise of this world (Mt 11:25). In the Gospels, following Christ does not mean merely imitating what Jesus does, but actually sharing His experiences with Him. It means discipleship and participation in His fate. For later Christians the lesson of the Gospels is that they, as Jesus' disciples, must deny themselves all that separates them from Christ and be ready to sacrifice even their life in loyalty to Him. Another ascetic theme of the Gospels is that of humility, so well exemplified in the poor of spirit ('ănāwîm; Mt 5:3; cf. Lk 6:20). The 'ănāwîm are those pious and humble persons who, conscious of their spiritual need, look to God for strength and help. Often enough they are also the economically poor, oppressed and trodden upon by the rich and powerful. To them Christ addresses the first beatitude, "Blessed are the poor in spirit for theirs is the kingdom of heaven" (Mt 5:3). Christ, in describing Himself as "meek and humble of heart" (Mt 11:29), is probably referring to Himself as an 'ănāw (a poor one).

In the Epistles of St. Paul. In St. Paul the asceticism necessary for the Christian life is expressed by diverse images, especially that of the spiritual athlete: the Christian is like the athlete who must constantly train and practice self-control in order to win the race (1 Cor 9:24–27; 1 Tm 4:7); his fight is against the old man (Eph 4:22), the flesh and its weaknesses (Rom 8:12–13; Eph 6:8), and the demonic world rulers (Eph 6:12). The Christian thus must practice humility and self-discipline in emptying himself of selfishness (Phil 2:5–8) in order to live in communion with Christ (Rom 6:1–3, 12–14). St. Paul himself has made strenuous efforts in the manner of the disciplined athlete in striving for the goal (Acts 24:16; see also Heb 5:14; 12:11; 2 Pt 2:14), and he is aware that he must strive to the end (Phil 3:13).

Another prominent feature of Paul's asceticism is its corporate significance. The Christian lives and acts in and with his glorified Lord and His Spirit. He has a mystical relationship to Christ (Gal 2:19–20) and to all who are baptized into Christ (Rom 6:3–14); thus what he does either helps or hurts the total body of Christ. The individual's strivings, like those of Paul, have communal significance; he "fills up what is lacking in the sufferings of Christ for His body, which is the Church" (Col 1:24).

See Also: FAST AND ABSTINENCE; FOLLOWING OF CHRIST.

Bibliography: R. SCHNACKENBURG, *Lexikon für Theologie und Kirche,* 1:930–932. T. W. MANSON, "The Sayings of Jesus," *The Mission and Message of Jesus,* ed. H. D. A. MAJOR and C. J. WRIGHT (New York 1938) 301–639. G. T. MONTAGUE, *Growth in Christ: A Study in Saint Paul's Theology of Progress* (Kirkwood, Mo. 1961). L. BOUYER, *Introduction to Spirituality,* tr. M. P. RYAN (New York 1961). A. GELIN, *Les Pauvres de Yahvé* (Paris 1953). J. KREMER, *Was an den Leiden Christi noch mangelt* (Bonn 1956). 4:38 PM 3/15/02

[J. LACHOWSKI]

ASCETICISM (THEOLOGICAL ASPECT)

For the Christian, asceticism is an aspect of the following of Christ, the price that must be paid daily for increasing assimilation to Christ. Certainly, asceticism is not itself the aim and substance of the following of Christ but only a means thereto, an expression for resoluteness of will. Asceticism means conscious self-control and systematic exercise of the Christian life.

Eschatological View. Asceticism is not merely an exercise of self-mastery or a struggle against the passions; neither is it a mere subjection of the body to the spirit. Granted, the struggle is against human weakness and instability; yet when the Scriptures speak of the war against "the flesh" (σάρξ) they do not mean against bodiliness, but against the existential condition of fallen man, proud and self-centered. Implied in this are all the forces of perdition: original sin, the burden of personal sins for which one is still insufficiently repentant and for which he has not yet sufficiently atoned, the social milieu formed by one's sins and the sins of others that tends to draw one downward, and the fallen angels, who exercise their powers in the world. "For our wrestling is not against flesh and blood, but against the Principalities and the Powers, against the world-rulers of this darkness, against the spiritual forces of wickedness on high. Therefore take up the armor of God. . ." (Ephesians 6.12–18). On the opposite side stand Christ and the community of saints.

When Christian asceticism is considered thus at the level of the history of salvation and the sacred-social order, it is clear that the important thing should not be a rigidly patterned routine. Asceticism must rather be—and this above all—*true to life,* suited to the necessities and contingencies of the battle. The Apostle admonishes us to this effect when he says, "Therein be vigilant in all perseverance" (Eph 6.18). Vigilance is one of the typical Christian eschatological virtues. When Paul claims that "he chastises his body" he actually refers to the notion taken from boxing jargon (ὑποπιάξειν), to strike decisively at the right moment. The context makes this still clearer: "I, therefore, so run as not without a purpose; I so fight as not beating the air. . ." (1 Cor 9.26–27). Here the chief enemy is not the inertia of the body but pride of spirit and ambition, which are responsible for the disorder of the passions. The driving power of the passions ought not be weakened, but must be systematically guided toward the good—above all through attention to purity of motive.

Asceticism within the Order of Love. Asceticism must help to overcome all that stands in the way of fulfilling the chief commandment: love of God and love of neighbor. From this point of view it is likewise clear that Catholic moral theology—no less than evangelical theology—must reject that form of asceticism that is chosen for motives of vainglory. Asceticism ought never be practiced at the expense of service to the kingdom of God and to one's neighbor; for the central notion of Christian morality is not self-perfection—definitely not self-perfection conceived egoistically—but true fulfillment of the general and particular call received from God. An asceticism that is true to life is thus a conscious exercise of service. In case of doubt, mere exercise must yield to the service of love. Augustine says of the virtue of temperance that "discipline and moderation is that love which keeps itself unsullied and undiminished for God" (*De Moribus Ecclesiæ Catholicæ et de Moribus Manichæorum Patrologia Latina,* ed. J. P. Migne, 217 v., indexes 4 v. (Paris 1878–90) 32:1322). This is true also of asceticism, which is allied with the Christian virtue of temperance.

Legal Prescription as Secondary. A Catholic understanding of asceticism ought not to lay emphasis one-sidedly on legally prescribed action, as if, for example, the purely external fulfillment of abstaining from meat on Friday implied ascetical perfection. The intent of the law is rather education to genuine abstinence, indeed likewise to humble obedience through which pride is put in check. More important than the exact fulfillment of an act positively prescribed by the Church is the fulfillment of the intent of the law. Still more important—and this is the ultimate purpose of the Church—is the ever-ready submission to every renunciation and sacrifice imposed by divine providence (the best school of suffering) and demanded by the love of neighbor.

For the most part, asceticism is a "work of supererogation." Actually, that implies no arbitrary self-righteousness. It means only that most forms and exercises of asceticism are not universal legal impositions to which all can and should conform. It implies a call suited to the situation, a call of service for the kingdom of God and for neighbor, a call that goes beyond the legal obligations affecting all men. It is a responsive fulfillment of the call of grace. Christian asceticism is distinguished from most non-Christian forms precisely by this humble openness for the καιρός for each individual opportunity with its offer of grace.

Asceticism as a Universal Requirement. Asceticism is not a concern peculiar to the monastic state. It belongs to the Christian living in the midst of the world as well as to the monk, though the forms and emphases differ. The monks—sometimes simply called ascetics—should bear witness through their state and their example to the fact that "this world as we see it is passing away" (1 Cor 7.32). Yet if the entire people of God (and especially the laity living in the midst of the world) must attempt that brave encounter with the world of which Vatican II speaks in the schema *On the Church and the World Today*, then the spirit of evangelical poverty, i.e., renunciation of the egoistic desire to possess and to rule, is an absolute prerequisite. The Christian who is aware of the groaning of creation, of its longing to partake more and more in the blessed freedom of the children of God (cf. Rom 8.19–23), must follow this admonition: ". . . it remains that . . . those who use this world [be] as though not using it, for this world as we see it is passing away" (1 Cor 7.29–31). Without a definite, though flexible, measure of self-control, discipline and systematic struggle, the Christian cannot attain to this freedom.

Asceticism: A Way of the Joyful to Joy. Christian asceticism must be ultimately understood in terms of the paschal mystery. It is an affirmation of the cross as the path to resurrection. The ability to bear the cross, of which asceticism is indeed only one aspect, comes from the joy of being redeemed. "Joy in the Lord is your strength" (Neh 8.10): this is true also with regard to asceticism. The aim of the exercise that at times is found painful is a purified love of God, of neighbor, and of the whole of creation. But that also means an increase of joy.

Bibliography: *Christian Asceticism and Modern Man,* tr. W. MITCHELL and the CARISBROOKE DOMINICANS (New York 1955). R. EGENTER, *Die Aszese des Christen in der Welt* (Ettal 1956). H. FICHTENAU, *Askese und Laster in der Anschauung des Mittelalters* (Vienna 1948). B. HÄRING, *The Law of Christ: Moral Theology for Priests and Laity,* tr. E. G. KAISER (Westminster, Md. 1961–) 1:528–562. H. E. HENGSTENBERG, *Christliche Askese* (Regensburg 1936). J. LINDWORSKY, *The Psychology of Asceticism,* tr. E. A. HEIRING (London 1936). H. SCHMIDT, *Organische Aszese* (6th ed. Paderborn 1952).

[B. HÄRING]

ASEITY (ASEITAS)

A term used in scholastic philosophy and theology to express one of the primary attributes of God. Aseity comes from the Latin *a se* (*aseitas*), and signifies the attribute of God whereby He possesses His existence of or from Himself, in virtue of His own essence, and not from any other being outside Himself as cause. It is best understood by contrast with its opposite, that is, the attribute whereby a being receives its existence from another (*ab alio*) or is a caused or contingent being. It is thus one of the primary marks distinguishing God from creatures.

Meaning. Aseity has two aspects, one positive and one negative. In its negative meaning, which emerged first in the history of thought, it affirms that God is uncaused, depending on no other being for the source of His existence. In its positive meaning, it affirms that God is completely self-sufficient, having within Himself the sufficient reason for His own existence. The technical analysis of this in terms of essence and existence, which took longer to develop in Christian thought, affirms that God possesses existence per se, that is, through, or in virtue of, His own essence. This does not mean that God is literally the cause of Himself in the strict sense of cause, since this would imply some kind of real distinction between God as causing and God as effect. Such a teaching, as St. Thomas Aquinas has pointed out (*C. gent.* 1.22), would be absurd. What it does mean is that God's existence is absolutely identical with His essence, that His essence necessarily includes existence itself, so that God cannot not exist: He is the Necessary Being par excellence.

This identity of essence and existence, although held by all Christian thinkers, has been explained in different ways. The following account traces the development of the notion in Catholic thought from the Greek and Latin Fathers to the late scholastics and then concludes with some observations on the meaning of aseity as understood by certain modern philosophers.

Patristic Writers. The notion appears first clearly in the Apologists of the second century, expressed in the negative terms ἀγένητος (uncaused, unoriginated) and ἀγέννητος (ungenerated). St. JUSTIN MARTYR is a typical witness: "For God alone is unoriginated and incorruptible, and it is for this reason that He is God. Everything else after Him is originated and corruptible" (*Dialogue with Trypho,* 5.4–6). The same idea, in one form or another, quickly became the primary attribute of God among the Greek Fathers: He alone is uncaused, unoriginated, underived and ultimate.

The early Latin writers repeated this doctrine. But LACTANTIUS (early fourth century) adds a more positive analysis of his own, describing God as "self-originated (*ex se ipso est*) and therefore of such a nature as He wanted Himself to be" (*Div. instit.* 2.8, *Corpus scriptorum ecclesiasticorum latinorum,* 19:137). At times he slips into such philosophically unsound and theologically unorthodox language as the following: "Since it is impossible for anything that exists not to have at some time begun to exist, it follows that, when nothing else existed before Him, He was procreated from Himself before all things (*ex se ipso sit procreatus*)," and again, repeating the words of SENECA, "God made Himself (*Deus ipse se fecit*)"—*Div. instit.* 1.7, *Corpus scriptorum ecclesiasticorum latinorum,* 19:28. The same positive notion of self-causality, but without the note of temporal beginning, appears in MARIUS VICTORINUS, the convert who so deeply influenced St. Augustine. He speaks of God in one place as "*a se, per se,* without any beginning of existence" (*Contra Arium,* 4.5 ed. P. Henry and P. Hadot, *Sources Chétiennes,* 68). In another context, not very consistently, he says that God is "the original cause both of Himself and all others," who "makes Himself to be (*se esse efficit*)" (*ibid.,* 1.3; 4.27). This incautious interpretation of *a se* as self-caused, taken over from pagan philosophers like Seneca or PLOTINUS (God "made Himself . . . is cause of Himself"— *Enneads* 6.8.13–14), was later rejected by Latin Fathers such as St. AUGUSTINE (*Trin.* 1.1.1). Neither Lactantius nor Marius Victorinus, it should be noted, is a Father of the Church.

Saints Hilary and Jerome. The next important step is the linking of the notion of God as *a se* with the Biblical text in which God declares His name to Moses: "I am who am" (Exodus, 3.14). The result is the identification of being itself with the very essence of God. This appears first in St. HILARY OF POITIERS, who describes his sudden realization, while meditating on the text of Exodus, that the essential nature of God and the source of all his attributes was revealed therein (*Trin.* 1.5–6, *Patrologia Latina,* 10:28; cf., *In psalm.* 2.13, *Corpus scriptorum ecclesiasticorum latinorum,* 22:46).

St. JEROME also appeals to the Exodus text. The strong expressions he uses to explain it, such as, God is "the origin of Himself and cause of His own substance," are interpreted quite traditionally by him as meaning that God has no cause or origin outside of Himself (*In Eph.* 2.3.14; *Patrologia Latina,* 26:488).

From Hilary on, the text of Exodus 3.14 is central in the West for the analysis of the essence and attributes of God. The official Vulgate translation of St. Jerome, commonly used in the Latin Church, was: "*Ego sum qui sum*" (I am Who am). This was universally interpreted as identifying the very essence of God (since the name for the Hebrews signified the essence) with being itself. This interpretation endured and continued to deeply nourish the thought of Christian theologians and philosophers, until the revival of Biblical scholarship in the 20th century. Contemporary Biblical studies have however shown, that the original Hebrew text does not in fact offer any positive metaphysical description of the essence of God,

but most probably means simply, "I am Who I am," that is, My name (and therefore My essence) is My own secret, hidden from men. It is an affirmation of the mystery, incomprehensibility and ineffability of the divine nature with respect to the human mind. Another possible but less favored meaning is: "I am the one Who gives, or is the source of, being." Thus theologians no longer hold that the identity of God's essence and existence is directly revealed in this text. This does not alter the fact that the older interpretation exerted a decisive influence on Christian thought about God for many centuries, especially on St. Thomas Aquinas and the whole tradition of SCHOLASTICISM in the West.

St. Anselm. St. ANSELM OF CANTERBURY is responsible for firmly imbedding the notion of aseity in the rising scholastic tradition as a primary attribute of God, thus summing up the whole patristic tradition. He expresses the negative aspect by *a se,* the positive by *per se* (*Monologion,* 6). Anselm also introduces a more technical analysis of the identity of essence and existence. He explains existence as an attribute or perfection flowing necessarily from the very concept of the divine essence as the infinitely perfect Being; thus, for him, it is impossible even to think of God, that is, of "that than which nothing greater can be conceived," save as actually existing. This notion is basic to his famous ONTOLOGICAL ARGUMENT (*Proslogion,* 1–4).

St. Thomas. The next decisive step, marking a new orientation in the interpretation of the identity of the divine essence and existence, was taken by St. THOMAS AQUINAS. In terms of his central thesis of existence as act, the fundamental perfection of all things that is participated only in limited modes by finite essences, Aquinas teaches that the very essence of God is a pure subsistent act of existence (*Ipsum Esse Subsistens*). This has no admixture of potency or limit of any kind, and thus contains within it the plenitude of all possible perfection (*C. gent.* 1.26, 28; *Summa Theologiae* 1a, 3.4; 8.1). The Exodus text is his central authority from revelation (ST 1a, 13.11). In view of his radical reduction of essence to existence in the divine nature, St. Thomas carefully avoids the Anselmian way of speaking of the divine existence as though it were an attribute flowing necessarily from the divine essence, with its hint of a conceptual priority of essence. In fact, the term itself, *a se* (or *aseitas*), traditional though it be, is never actually used by Aquinas in speaking of God, possibly because of its faintly ambiguous suggestion of some causal relation between the divine essence and its existence. The closest he comes is when he speaks of God as the per se necessary being (ST 1a, 2.3; *C. gent.* 1.15), or as being by essence (*ens per essentiam*), in contrast to creatures, which are beings by participation (ST 1a, 3.4; 6.3). Later Thomists resume the use of the older term aseity, but continue to explain the identity between essence and existence in the same way as St. Thomas.

Franciscan School. The Franciscan school parted company with St. Thomas on his doctrine of existence as the basic perfection of all things limited by essence, and preferred to explain the perfection of things as rooted in their essences or forms. In agreement on this point with all non-Thomist scholastics, they analyzed all the attributes of God, including existence itself, in terms of His infinitely perfect essence, to which, precisely because of its infinite perfection, existence necessarily belongs. Hence it is not surprising that in all these schools aseity should retain a central place among the divine attributes.

Not yet clear-cut in St. BONAVENTURE (*Itinerarium*, 5.5), the difference of approach becomes fully explicit in the teaching of John DUNS SCOTUS. For him, though the divine existence is, of course, absolutely identical with the divine essence, it is conceived by man as an intrinsic mode of the latter following logically after the primary mode of infinity. This, for Scotus, is the proper defining note of the metaphysical essence of God (*Opus Oxon.* 1.2.1–2.1.4; 1.8.3.3.28; for God as *ex se,* see *De primo principio,* 3).

Suárez. Founder of the school of Suarezian Thomism that had been widely influential, F. SUÁREZ sought to make a synthesis of Thomism and Scotism. His *Disputationes Metaphysicae,* the first systematic treatise of metaphysics in the West, did much to render classic the primary division of all beings into *ens a se* (God) and *ens ab alio* (creatures) and to establish aseity as the primary attribute of God. Although in explaining the positive meaning of aseity Suárez often uses the Thomistic description of the divine essence as the subsistent act of existence, his own metaphysical doctrine of existence led to a more Scotistic interpretation. For Suárez, existence is reducible to actual essence—hence his denial of their real distinction in creatures; this made it inevitable that he should interpret God's existence more as a necessary attribute of the infinitely perfect divine essence than as the very core of all its perfection. (*Disp. Meta.* 28.1.6–7; 30.1.2–23; *Tract. de Div. Subst.* 1.2; 1.3.1; 1.5–9.) In Suárez's teaching, *ens a se* becomes practically synonymous with Necessary Being.

Modern Philosophy. The Suarezian notion of aseity seems to have passed into modern philosophy through the teaching of C. WOLFF and influenced the development of the branch of philosophy known as THEODICY. Other thinkers gave different interpretations of aseity in the modern period, notably R. DESCARTES and certain rationalist, idealist and spiritualist philosophers.

Descartes initiated the rationalist tradition that restored to honor Anselm's ontological argument and deduced the existence of God from the concept of His essence as an infinitely perfect being (*Medit.* 3 and 5). He also revived the ancient term *causa sui,* abandoned since Augustine. When taken to task for this, he explained, that he did not mean cause in the strict sense of producing an effect distinct from itself. But he insisted that it did mean some positive power in God that is responsible for constantly maintaining Him in existence. This is none other than the infinite power of God's essence, conceived as eternally positing His own existence (*Resp. to 1st and 4th Obj.*).

The same basic conception, understood in an even more rigorously rationalistic way, is found in the notion of God as *causa sui* advanced by B. SPINOZA (*Eth.* 1, Def. 1). A similar notion of God as somehow self-causing keeps recurring in various forms down through the German idealist philosophers, as, for example, in F. W. J. Schelling's conception of a procession of the conscious divine being from a deep, irrational, groundless abyss within Himself, or in A. Schopenhauer's notion of an autogenesis of God by absolute will, or in the self-positing, self-unfolding Absolute Spirit of G. W. F. HEGEL. The primary defect in all these positions, when they are to be taken literally, is that they all imply either some ultimate priority of essence, or will, or power over actual existence, or some kind of distinction (contrary to the absolute divine simplicity) between the ultimate source or ground of God and His actual completed being.

A more subtly qualified and acceptable notion of God as *causa sui* has reappeared among some French spiritualist philosophers of the 20th century, such as M. BLONDEL (*L'Etre et les êtres,* Paris 1935, 176–181, 342, 520) and L. LAVELLE (*De l'Acte,* Paris 1937, 111–126). Despite their sometimes obscure and ambiguous language, especially Lavelle's, there is a profound and mysterious truth hidden behind their descriptions of God as pure spiritual act, pure ''cause'' without effect, as though somehow giving Himself to Himself in a pure spontaneous eternal act of consciously loving self-position or self-affirmation.

See Also: GOD; ESSENCE AND EXISTENCE; PURE ACT; SUFFICIENT REASON, PRINCIPLE OF.

Bibliography: G. L. PRESTIGE, *God In Patristic Thought (Society for Promoting Christian Knowledge,* London 1959). C. TOUSSAINT, *Dictionnaire de théologie catholique,* ed. A. VACANT et al., 15 v. (Paris 1903–50) 1.2:2077–80, 2223–35. M. CHOSSAT et al., ibid. 4.1:756–1300. P. DESCOQS, *Praelectiones theologiae naturalis,* 2 v. (Paris 1932–38). R. GARRIGOU-LAGRANGE, *God, His Existence and His Nature,* 2 v. (St. Louis 1934–36). J. D. COLLINS, *God in Modern Philosophy* (Chicago 1959). M. BOURKE, ''Yahweh the Divine Name,'' *The Bridge,* 3 (1958–59) 271–287. J. ÉCOLE, ''La

Notion de 'Deus causa sui' dans la philosophie française contempo- raine,'' *Revue thomiste*, 54 (1954) 374–384. S. CARAMELLA, *Enciclopedia filosofica*, 4 v. (Venice-Rome 1957) 1:393–394. *Sources Chétiennes*, ed. H. DE LUBAC, et al. (Paris 1941–) 68. *Corpus scriptorum ecclesiasticorum latinorum* (Vienna 1866–). *Patrologia Latina*, ed. J. P. MIGNE, 217 V., indexes 4 v. (Paris 1878–90).

[W. N. CLARKE]

ASENSIO BARROSO, FLORENTINO, BL.

Bishop of Barbastro (Spain), martyr; b. Villasexmir, Valladolid, Spain, Oct. 16, 1877; d. near Barbastro in the central Pyrenees, Spain, Aug. 9, 1936. Although born into a poor family, Florentino attended seminary and was ordained (1901). After earning the licentiate and doctorate in theology from the Pontifical University of Valladolid, he taught there, but illness forced him to give up teaching. Upon recovery Asensio was assigned to Valladolid cathedral. His serenity and piety resulted from his devotion to the Blessed Sacrament, and his inspired homilies gained him renown as a zealous preacher and spiritual director. He was consecrated bishop of Barbastro on Jan. 26, 1936 despite civil disturbance. Even though he had initially hesitated to accept the position, he ministered with fervor, introducing reform, caring for the poor and the sick, and writing a pastoral letter that appealed for unity in Christ.

Soon after his consecration, he was put under observation by the Communist authorities, and on July 20, 1936, he was placed under house arrest. He was later imprisoned, then placed in solitary confinement, tortured, and mutilated for ''collaborating with the enemies of the people.'' Before being shot to death in a cemetery, he serenely told his executioners: 'I am going to heaven.' His mortal remains were recovered from the common grave of the twelve shot with him and placed in a cathedral crypt. Bp. Asensio was beatified by John Paul II on May 4, 1997.

Feast: Aug. 2.

Bibliography: V. CÁRCEL ORTÍ, *Martires españoles del siglo XX* (Madrid 1995). W. H. CARROLL, *The Last Crusade* (Front Royal, Va. 1996).

[K. I. RABENSTEIN]

ASH'ARĪ, AL-(ABŪ AL-ḤASAN) 'ALĪ

Eponym of the Ash'arite school of Islamic theology; b. Basra, 873; d. Baghdad, *c.* 924.

Life. Very little is certain about al-Ash'arī's life. For a long time he was a pupil of the famous Mu'tazilite, Abū 'Alī al-Jubbā'ī. Tradition gives six different accounts of his conversion from the MU'TAZILITES to ''orthodoxy,'' i.e., to traditional Islamic doctrine. After his conversion, al-Ash'arī championed the traditionist approach, which was finally to triumph over Mu'tazilism. Later in life he moved to Baghdad, where he lectured and wrote until his death. More than 100 titles are attributed to him in the various sources. With the exception of a few short treatises, only three important works seem to be extant: *Kitāb al-Luma'*, *al-Ibāna 'an Usūl al-Diyāna*, and *Maqālāt al-Islāmiyyīn*. The first two are dogmatic treatises and exist in English translations. The third is an objective and immensely important heresiography, edited by H. Ritter in 1929.

Doctrine. Al-Ash'arī owed much to his Mu'tazilite training. It is difficult from the extant sources to form a clear and complete synthesis of his own teaching. Much of the doctrine attributed to him by subsequent writers may well have been the work of later Ash'arites.

It has been affirmed that al-Ash'arī's chief contribution to Islamic theology was his introduction of a *via media* between the two extremes of the Mu'tazilites (and others) and the traditionists. But I. Goldziher insists that Ash'arism, not al-Ash'arī, was the *via media*. Some idea of his teaching may be had from his *Ibāna,* written from an extremely traditionist point of view with an admixture of rational argument, and from the *Luma',* which contains more rational argument, but remains quite traditionist. It seems to have been intended as a brief handbook of polemics for use against the Mu'tazilites, and its structure follows the five basic Mu'tazilite principles.

Al-Ash'arī's doctrines are presumably those summed up in the creeds inserted in the *Maqālāt* and the *Ibāna,* both strongly traditionist. On the problem of man's responsibility for his acts, al-Ash'arī is quite deterministic. He made some effort to save free will by the doctrine of acquisition (*kasb*), but this doctrine was not originated by him, and it is not clear precisely what he, or anyone else, meant by it.

Among the works attributed to al-Ash'arī is a short treatise containing a vindication of *kalām*, that is, of the use of rational argument in dogmatic discussions. While it may not be the actual work of al-Ash'arī, it is an interesting document which underlines a certain tension that was long felt in Muslim theological circles. It appears that al-Ash'arī himself was rather reserved in this use of rational argument. Certainly he was far removed from the long and subtle philosophical discussions of the much later theologians who were called Ash'arites.

Influence. Whatever the immediate personal influence of al-Ash'arī may have been, his name is associated with the theological synthesis that ultimately came to be the "orthodox" theology of the vast majority of Muslims. Yet it is not clear why al-Ash'arī came to be regarded as its founder; sources close to his time give no indication of the prominence his name was to enjoy. Nevertheless, the work of al-Ash'arī himself, and of those whom he did influence, may well have given rise to the currents developed and enriched by the genius of later "Ash'arite" theologians.

The earliest complete Ash'arite treatise at our disposal is the *Tamhīd* of al-Bāqillānī (d. 1013). In this dogmatic and apologetic compendium are discussed, or at least adumbrated, practically all the questions with which Muslim theology would ever deal. It is possible that much of what al-Bāqillānī wrote was simply a restatement of views and arguments already put forth by al-Ash'arī. The next important Ash'arite theologian was al-Juwaynī (d. 1085). His work shows considerable advances in reasoning over that of al-Bāqillānī. ALGAZEL (Ghazzālī, al-; d. 1111) was a disciple of al-Juwaynī and an Ash'arite, but his work marked a new departure in theology, and his *Iqtisād* is far removed from al-Ash'arī's *Luma'*. Ibn Khaldūn calls him the first of the "modern" theologians.

The most prominent Ash'arites after Algazel were Shahrastānī (d. 1153), Fakhr al-Dīn al-Rāzī (d. 1210), Isfahānī (d. 1348), Ījī (d. 1355), and Jurjānī (d. 1413). But no real theological advances were made. More emphasis was given to questions now regarded as purely philosophical. Ash'arism as a theology was no longer a living system, but a kind of fixed dogmatic conservatism. It ended, as W. M. Watt put it aptly, in a blaze of philosophy. This was a consummation very far from the essentially religious spirit of its eponym.

See Also: KALĀM.

Bibliography: AL-ASH'ARĪ, *Al-Ibānah 'an Usūl ad-Diyānah,* tr. W. C. KLEIN, *The Elucidation of Islam's Foundation,* in *American Oriental Series 19* (New Haven 1940). *The Theology of al-Ash'arī,* ed. R. J. MCCARTHY (Beirut 1953), the *Luma',* the vindication of Kalām, and other texts in Arabic and English. G. MAKDISI, "Ash-'ari, and the Ash'arites in Islamic Religious History," *Studia Islamica,* 17 (1962) 37–80; 18 (1963) 19–39.

[R. J. MCCARTHY]

ASHES, LITURGICAL USE OF

The ashes of burned objects (plants, animals, human bodies) and dust are commonly found in use among ancient peoples for religious, magical, and medical purposes; opinions regarding the import of these uses are diverse (cf. Cabrol and Schneider). The two principal meanings are that certain ashes have a sacred character and power and that dust and ashes signify mortality, mourning, and penance. In the OT one finds ashes ('ēper) and dust ('āpār) used only as signs of mortality and worthlessness, sorrow and repentance. One finds such practices as sprinkling them on the head, covering the body, sitting or lying in them, and eating them. A sacrificed cow's ashes mixed with water are used with a purificatory significance (Nm 19.9). Christian liturgical usage and symbolism seem clearly to have been taken from the Jewish tradition.

In the Roman Rite, the practice of the faithful receiving ashes on Ash Wednesday has been universal since the Synod of Benevento in 1091 (J. D. Mansi, *Sacrorum Conciliorum nova et amplissima collectio* 20:739); however, this was known by the Anglo-Saxons a century earlier (Jungmann, 58–60). Originally ashes were used as signs of private penance; then they became a part of the official ritual for public penitents and were given to them only. Another important dimension of this action is that the ashes on the penitent were to arouse prayerful sympathy for him within his fellow Christians.

Historically, ashes were employed in the medieval period in the dedication of a church. The so-called Gregorian water used for sprinkling the interior of the church was a mixture of water, wine, salt, and ashes; the addition of salt and ashes was already found in the 8th-century Roman Ordinal 41, perhaps a biblicism from Nm 19.9. After the bishop entered the church, he wrote in ashes strewn on the floor with the Latin and Greek alphabets crossing each other diagonally to form the Greek letter "chi" (X for Christ). The symbolism seemed to indicate that Christ, the beginning and the end, has taken possession of the new church. This seems to be an Irish custom, which came through Roman Ordinal 41 (M. Andrieu, *Les 'Ordines Romani' du haut moyen-âge,* 4:319–320).

Formerly, in some places, ashes were imposed on Rogation days and used also for catechumens. In the Middle Ages one finds the custom of laying a dying person in ashes before he was anointed. Popular, nonliturgical uses also arose attributing special powers to the ashes of the Easter fire and to the dust of saints' remains (see Cabrol, 3043–44, 3039).

Bibliography: J. A. JUNGMANN, *Die lateinischen Bussriten in ihrer geschichtlichen Entwicklung* (Innsbruck 1932).

[E. J. JOHNSON/EDS.]

ASHLEY, RALPH, BL.

Jesuit lay brother, martyr; b. unknown; hanged at Red Hill near Worcester, England, April 7, 1606. On

A Franciscan priest sprinkles ashes on the head of a worshiper during an Ash Wednesday Mass, at the Church of the Holy Sepulchre in Jerusalem, photograph by Ruth Fremson. (AP/Wide World Photos)

April 28, 1590, Br. Ralph Ashley left his position as cook at the English College, Rheims, France, to take up that same position at the new English College of Valladolid, Spain, where he was accepted into the Jesuits. In 1598 he returned to England because of illness. En route he fell into the hands of the Dutch Protestants, among whom he displayed courage and eventually won release. After serving the English Jesuit superior, St. Henry GARNET, he was assigned to assist (Bl.) Fr. Edward Oldcorne in his ministry at Hinlip Hall, Worcestershire, for the next eight years. At the outset of the Gunpowder Plot, Brs. Ashley and (St.) Nicholas OWEN hid in the priest-hole at Hinlip Hall until thirst forced them out on the fourth day (Jan. 23, 1606). The lay brothers were arrested immediately; Fr. Garnet and Oldcorne were captured on Jan. 27. All were taken to the Tower of London, on Feb. 3, and subjected to torture, which killed Owen. Ashley and Oldcorne were returned to Worcester, March 21, for trial. Ashley was condemned for assisting an illegal priest. Fr.

Oldcorne was executed first. As he hanged Br. Ashley kissed his feet, saying: "Happy I am to follow in the steps of my sweet Father." He was beatified by Pius XI on Dec. 15, 1929.

Feast of the English Martyrs: May 4 (England); Dec. 1 (Jesuits).

See Also: ENGLAND, SCOTLAND, AND WALES, MARTYRS OF.

Bibliography: R. CHALLONER, *Memoirs of Missionary Priests,* ed. J. H. POLLEN (rev. ed. London 1924; repr. Farnborough 1969). J. H. POLLEN, *Acts of English Martyrs* (London 1891). J. N. TYLENDA, *Jesuit Saints & Martyrs* (Chicago 1998) 94–95.

[K. I. RABENSTEIN]

ASIA, ROMAN PROVINCE OF

The Roman province of Asia, a region comprising the western section of Asia Minor (modern Turkey), constituted a Roman province in the late 2nd century B.C. During the Apostolic period it included the territory from GALATIA to the sea, with the offshore islands of Ionia, and was bounded on the north by Bithynia and on the south by Lycia. A senatorial province, it was governed by a proconsul who resided at Ephesus. It was a rich agricultural and pastoral land, famous for the fabrication of colorful woolen cloth and was much subject to the exploitation of Roman capitalists. Its ports connected the hinterland of Asia Minor and the East with Greece and Rome through the opulent Hermus and Maeander valleys. Besides Ephesus the most important ports were Cos, Miletus, Smyrna, Pergamum, and Troas, while farther inland, along the valley routes, were Thyatira, SARDIS, Philadelphia on the Hermus, and Laodicea, Colossae, and Hierapolis on the Maeander.

ST. PAUL first passed through Asia on his second missionary journey when he traveled through Mysia and set sail from Troas for Neopolis in the Roman Province of MACEDONIA (Acts 16.6–10). He spent most of his third missionary journey in Ephesus (Acts 19.1–20.1), where his disciples evangelized the hinterland and where he could have easy access to his churches in the Roman Province of Achaia. He gave his pastoral sermon to the elders of the Church of Ephesus at Miletus on his last trip to Jerusalem with the collection for the poor from the Greek communities (Acts 20.17–38). Two of his so-called CAPTIVITY EPISTLES were sent to the churches of Asia to combat the incipient heresies that were taking root there. (*See* COLOSSIANS, EPISTLE TO THE; EPHESIANS, EPISTLE TO THE.) That such heresies were commonplace in this region at the crossroads of the Eastern and Western worlds is clear also from the letters sent by John, the author of the book of Apocalypse, to the seven churches of Asia from his exile on the island of Patmos (Rv 1.9–3.22).

In the books of the MACCABEES the term Asia (e.g., 1 Mc 8.6) refers to the empire of the SELEUCID DYNASTY, which included, at the time of its greatest expansion, the modern countries of Turkey, Syria, Iraq, Iran, and Afghanistan. By the Maccabean period, however, the Seleucids had forfeited Asia Minor to the Romans at the battle of Magnesia, near Ephesus, a fact that led them to concentrate their military efforts on holding their eastern territories (1 Mc 6.1–5).

Bibliography: *Encyclopedic Dictionary of the Bible,* tr. and adap. by L. HARTMAN (New York 1963), from A. VAN DEN BORN, *Bijbels Woordenboek,* 152. F. DÖLGER, *Lexikon für Theologie und Kirche,* ed. J. HOFER and K. RAHNER, 10 v. (2d, new ed. Freiburg 1957–65) 6:327–329. G. BARDY, *Dictionnaire d'histoire et de géographie ecclésiastiques,* ed. A. BAUDRILLART et al. (Paris 1912–) 4:966–989.

[P. P. SAYDON]

ASIA MINOR, EARLY CHURCH IN

In extant documents, the fifth-century author OROSIUS (*Patrologia Latina.* ed. J. P. Migne [Paris 1878–90.] 31:679A) is the first to use the term Asia Minor. The name Asia occurred earlier and designated the Roman Province that developed from the kingdom of Pergamum bequeathed to Rome by Attalus III (d. 133 B.C.). To the Attalid legacy were subsequently added Mysia, Lydia, Caria, Phrygia, Cappadocia, Bithynia, Galatia, and Pontus. At the beginning of the Christian era the territory thus augmented was coextensive with the Asiatic peninsula of which Ephesus was the administrative center. In the late third century, Diocletian and his immediate successors reorganized the territory into the Diocese of Asia in seven separate provinces along the lines of the older boundaries: Proconsular Asia, the islands of Lesbos, Chios, Rhodes, and Cyprus, the Hellespont and Cyzicus, Lydia, Caria, Phrygia I Pacatiana, and Phrygia II Salutaris. To the Byzantines this area was known as *mikrà Asía* or *Anatolé,* and still later it was called the Levant.

Culture and Religion. Asia Minor, the bridge between East and West, felt the impact of many cultures, some dating back to the third millennium B.C. More important for the early Church, however, were the contacts established there with Hellenistic civilization, the Hellenized Jews of the Diaspora, the Roman imperial administration, and the mystery religions. The great temple of Diana at Ephesus and the cult image of the Mother Goddess and her mysteries were factors that left traces of influence on the manner in which the Christian gospel was proclaimed. Well-organized Jewish communities in all the large cities, though frequently hostile to Christianity (see Acts 13.45; 14.2), disposed many for accepting its message. The presence of diverse ethnic groups seems to have minimized any national resistance to Christianity, such as the Syro-Phoenician sun-worship at Emesa.

Knowledge of the spread of Christianity in apostolic times is limited to the information gathered from the books of the New Testament. The record of Paul's activity in Asia Minor is found in Acts ch. 13–16 and 18 or can be inferred from his Epistles to the Ephesians, Colossians, and Galatians. The messages directed by John to the seven Churches in Asia (Rv 1.11; ch. 2, 3), each located in a capital city with a *conventus juridicus*—Ephesus, the largest market west of the Taurus, Smyrna, Pergamum, Thyatira, Sardis, Philadelphia, Laodicea—all point to an urban-centered Church in the region that was to become the land of Christianity par excellence.

The Post-apostolic Age. Evidence of the growth of Christianity centers in important places, as is indicated by the letters of IGNATIUS OF ANTIOCH to the Churches in Asia Minor. It tends to become slightly more detailed in regard to specific persons. Smyrna gained renown through its Bishop Polycarp, the spokesman with Pope Anicetus for the Church in Asia Minor in the EASTER CONTROVERSY. The account of his martyrdom (*Martyrium Polycarpi*), written, in its earliest form, immediately after his death, continued to focus attention on the Church of that city. Laodicea is known for its Bishop Sagaris, who died as a martyr (Eusebius, *Hist. eccl.* 4.26.3), and Eumenia in Phrygia is famous for its martyr Bishop Thraseas (*ibid.* 5.24.4). Ephesus took on a preeminence that it held for many years; it is known in this period for its Bishop Polycrates, who presided at a synod *c.* 190 attended by numerous bishops (*ibid.* 5.24). Hierapolis in Phrygia is especially remembered for two of its bishops, Papias, author of an *Explanation of the Sayings of the Lord,* and Apollinaris, an apologist and strenuous opponent of MONTANISM. Sardis merits specific mention because its Bishop Melito was distinguished as an apologist and author of numerous treatises (*ibid.* 5.28.5).

The Church in Asia Minor was disturbed by the rigoristic errors and the so-called ''new prophecy'' of Montanus in Phrygia and by the Monarchian teachings of Noëtus of Smyrna. From the closing years of this period comes the earliest extant nonliterary evidence concerning the spread of Christianity, recorded in the inscription of ABERCIUS, Bishop of Hierapolis in Phrygia Salutaris.

Only a few place names are known as early centers of Christianity. CAESAREA IN CAPPADOCIA, under the leadership of its Bishop FIRMILIAN, was a thriving center of missionary activity. Between 230 and 235 two important councils were held, one at Iconium, the other at Synnada, attended by bishops from Galatia, Phrygia, Cappadocia, and Cilicia. On both occasions the bishops of Asia Minor denied the validity of heretical baptism, thus anticipating the decision of the African bishops in the Council of CARTHAGE of 256 under the leadership of CYPRIAN (*Epistula* 75.7).

The tragic event for the Church in this period was the Decian persecution and the serious problem it caused in dealing with LAPSI. Only two authentic contemporary accounts of the martyrs in Asia Minor are extant. The *Acta Pionii* relate the martyrdom of the presbyter Pionius of Smyrna and the apostasy of his bishop, Euctemon, a successor of Polycarp (*Acta Pionii* 15; 16). The *Passio SS. Carpi et sociorum* gives the details of the trial and death of Carpus, Papylus, and Agathonice at Pergamum [see

Analecta Bollandiana 58 (1940) 142–176]. Later information coming from Gregory of Nyssa (*Patrologia Graeca.* ed J. P. Migne [Paris 1857–66] 46:944–953) tells of the ravages of this persecution in Pontus and the flight of Gregory Thaumaturgus. Legendary accounts of martyrdoms purporting to date from this persecution are numerous; among them is the account of the SEVEN SLEEPERS OF EPHESUS walled up in a cave during the Decian persecution; their alleged tomb was a famous place of pilgrimage till the days of the Turkish conquest of Asia Minor. Toward the end of the third century, METHODIUS OF OLYMPUS, an early opponent of Origen, defended Christianity against the attacks of Porphyry. Of his voluminous writings, only one, the *Symposium* or *Banquet of the Ten Virgins,* has survived in its entirety.

The Diocletian Persecution. While the Church in Asia Minor suffered greatly during this period, surviving documents yield little detailed information. It is recorded that ''armed soldiers surrounded a little town in Phrygia, of which the inhabitants were all Christians, every man of them, and setting fire to it burnt them all, along with young children and women'' (Eusebius, *Hist. eccl.* 8.11.1). The little town is probably Eumeneia. Pontus felt the terror of persecution in which judges are said to have vied with one another, ''ever inventing novel tortures, as if contending for prizes in a contest'' (*ibid.* 8.12.1). A third place in Asia Minor afflicted by this persecution was Cappadocia (*ibid.* 8.12.1).

With the accession of Constantine I a new era began for the Church. Local councils dealing with doctrinal and disciplinary matters became frequent, and great ecumenical councils met in this region to deal with fundamental Christian teachings. From the great urban centers, Christianity spread to the outlying districts, thus increasing the number of the chorepiscopi or bishops (*see* CHORBISHOP) of rural areas, 50 of whom are said to have been assisting the bishop of Caesarea by the end of the fourth century. The pattern for the administrative organization of the Church into metropolitan sees with suffragan bishops was set in Asia Minor.

Bibliography: W. M. RAMSAY, *The Historical Geography of Asia Minor* (London 1890). C. BRANDIS, *Paulys Realencyklopädie für protestantische Theologie und Kirche* 2 (1896) 1533–62. H. LECLERCQ, *Dictionnaire d'archéologie chrétienne et de liturgie.* ed. F. CABROL, H. LECLERCQ and H. I. MARROU (Paris 1907–53) 5.1:1013. H. GELZER, ''Ungedruckte und ungenügend veröffentlichte Texte der *Notitiae Episcopatuum,*'' *Abhandlungen der Bayerischen Akademie der Wissenschaften. Philosophisch-philologische Klasse* 21 (1901) 529–641. G. BARDY, *Dictionnaire d'histoire et de géographie ecclésiastiques* 4:966–988; *Catholicisme* 1:896. J. KEIL, *Reallexikon für Antike und Christentum,* ed. T. KLAUSER (Stuttgart 1941 [1950]–) 1:740–750. B. KÖTTING, *ibid.* 2:1144–47. E. KIRSTEN, *ibid.* 2:1105–14. H. JEDIN, *Handbuch der Kirchengeschichte* (Freiburg 1962–). J. DANIÉLOU and H. I. MARROU, *The First Six Hundred Years,* tr. V. CRONIN, v. 1 of *The Chris-*

tian Centuries (New York 1964–). A. VON HARNACK, *The Mission and Expansion of Christianity in the First Three Centuries*, ed. and tr. J. MOFFATT, 2 v. (2d ed. New York 1908). J. LEBRETON and J. ZEILLER, *The History of the Primitive Church*, tr. E. C. MESSENGER, 2 v. (New York 1949).

[H. DRESSLER]

ASKE, ROBERT

Leader in Yorkshire insurrection during the PILGRIMAGE OF GRACE, 1536–37; b. place and date unknown; d. York, England, (June–July?) 1537. Little is known of his early life, except that he was a lawyer with a good London practice. Restrictive enactments of Parliament (1536) brought about an uprising of squires, knights, and commons in Lincolnshire. By October 30,000 Yorkshiremen, wearing the badge of the ''Five Wounds,'' also were in arms; Aske was their leader. Objectives of the pilgrimage were complex; the pilgrims' motives were not always clear and distinct; and religious and social elements were inextricably combined in the revolt. Aske issued a proclamation opposing Thomas Cromwell and ''other evil counsellors'' of Henry VIII, demanding repeal of the Statute of Uses, and calling for an end to the suppression of monasteries. The pilgrims proclaimed loyalty ''to Holy Church militant . . . and to the preservation of the King's person and his issue.'' Aske advocated moderation and restraint. Only if all petitions to the king failed was the sword to be used. Under the command of Thomas Howard, Earl of Surrey and second Duke of Norfolk, a royal force of some 8,000 was sent to quell the revolt. On December 5 Aske, falling on his knees, confronted Norfolk at Doncaster and petitioned the king's pardon. Invited to court, Aske received Henry's promises of pardon and assurance that a parliament would shortly be held at York. In January 1537 a new outbreak in East Yorkshire provided Henry with a pretext for breaking his pledge. Treachery and brutality marked his treatment of the leading insurgents. Aske, again summoned to London, was imprisoned in the Tower. He insisted that the Supremacy Act ''could not stand with God's law,'' and that belief in the pope's authority was the touchstone of orthodoxy; he maintained that Thomas Cranmer and other bishops were heretics because they had been the cause of the breach of unity in the Church and were supporters of the new learning and of the opinions of Luther and Tyndale. Aske was sentenced and condemned to be drawn on a hurdle through the city of York and hanged in chains.

Bibliography: M. H. and R. DODDS, *The Pilgrimage of Grace, 1536–1537, and the Exeter Conspiracy, 1538*, 2 v. (Cambridge, Eng. 1915). P. HUGHES, *The Reformation in England* (New York 1963) A. TAYLOR, *Dictionnaire d'histoire et de géographie ecclésiastiques* 4:1048–49. J. GAIRDNER, *The Dictionary of National Bi-*

ography from the Earliest Times to 1900 (London 1908–09), 1:661–664.

[J. G. DWYER]

ASPERGES

The liturgical rite of sprinkling altar, clergy, and people with holy water on Sundays, so-named after the antiphon *Asperges me* (but during Paschal time, *Vidi aquam*) which accompanies the sprinkling. Pope Leo IV (d. 885) decreed that each priest should bless water every Sunday in his own church and sprinkle the people with it (*Patrologia Latina,* ed. J. P. Migne 115:679). At the same time Hincmar (d. 882), Archbishop of Reims, made a similar disposition for his diocese:

> Every Sunday, before the celebration of Mass, the priest shall bless water in his church; and, for this holy purpose, he shall use a clean and suitable vessel. The people, when entering the church, are to be sprinkled with this water; and those who desire may carry some away in clean vessels so as to sprinkle their houses, fields, vineyards, and cattle, and the provender with which these last are fed, as also to throw over their own food (*Capitula synodica* 5; *Patrologia Latina* 125:774).

Bibliography: For bibliography and further discussion, *see* WATER, LITURGICAL USE OF.

[E. J. GRATSCH/EDS.]

ASPILCUETA, MARTIN (DOCTOR NAVARRUS)

Canonist and moral theologian; b. Barasoain, Navarre, May 13, 1493; d. Rome, June 21, 1586. A cousin of St. Francis Xavier, he became a doctor of canon law and taught at the Universities of Toulouse, Salamanca, and Coimbra (1524–38). Three popes, Pius V, Gregory XIII, and Sixtus V, honored him with their friendship and made him consultor to the Sacred Penitentiary. The high point of his juridical career was his acting as lawyer for the defense of the Dominican Archbishop of Toledo, Bartolomé de CARRANZA. Because of Spanish prejudice, he demanded that the case be transferred to Rome and thus incurred the enmity of King Philip II, who later prevented his becoming a cardinal. His chief work, *Manuale sive Enchiridion confessariorum et paenitentium* (Rome 1588), was long considered a classic. The best complete edition of his numerous writings is *Doctoris Navarri . . . opera* (5 v. Cologne 1609).

Bibliography: A. LAMBERT, *Dictionnaire d'histoire et de géographie ecclésiastiques,* ed. A. BAUDRILLART et al. (Paris 1912—)

5:1368–74, with extensive bibliog.; *Dictionnaire de droit canonique,* ed. R. NAZ, 7 v. (Paris 1935–65) 1:1579–83. H. HURTER, *Nomenclator literarius theologiae catholicae,* 5 v. (Innsbruck 1903–13) 3:344–348.

[M. J. BARRY]

ASSAULT

Understood in moral theology as the unjust infliction of bodily harm on another. It is equivalent not to simple assault but to the assault-and-battery of civil law, for in civil law simple assault may be committed by menacing words and actions, even though no physical harm is actually done. Assault as here understood is distinguished from the ''criminal assault'' of newspaper euphemism, which is assault with the specific injury of sexual violation. It also differs from the infliction of bodily harm in legitimate self-defense and from the reasonable infliction of punishment by one having the authority to do so.

In inflicting bodily injury and pain on another, the assailant usurps to himself an unlawful control over another, thus affronting his victim's human dignity and autonomy and depriving him of his well-being, comfort, and security—goods of which presumably he is reasonably and seriously unwilling to be dispossessed. Assault is therefore a violation of commutative JUSTICE, and as such it is per se gravely sinful, although subjective considerations such as imperfect responsibility or the triviality of the injury can make it less than a grave sin in particular cases. In sports involving physical contact and in good-natured roughhouse and horseplay among the young, actions that would in other circumstances constitute assault may be free of any moral fault whatever.

As an offense against commutative justice, assault subjects the assailant to an obligation to RESTITUTION for the damage he has done. Evidently he is bound in justice to make amends for what the victim is out of pocket by reason of medical expenses, loss of income, etc., in consequence of injuries received. What restitution is owed for other elements in the injury is more difficult to estimate. Strictly speaking there is no equivalence between monetary damages and the pain or humiliation the victim may have suffered, but if legitimate authority imposes indemnification of this kind, justice demands that it be made.

See Also: INJURY, MORAL

Bibliography: T. AQUINAS, *Summa theologiae* 2a2ae, 65. J. A. MCHUGH and C. J. CALLAN, *Moral Theology,* rev. E. P. FARRELL, 2 v. (New York 1958).

[T. J. HAYES]

ASSEMANI, JOSEPH ALOYSIUS

Theologian and canonist; b. Syria, 1710; d. Rome, 1782; one of the pioneers in modern Oriental studies. Following his theological studies in Rome under his uncle, Joseph Simon ASSEMANI, he was appointed by the pope as professor of Syriac at the Sapienza in Rome. Benedict XIV named him professor of liturgy at the same institute and a member of the newly formed academy of research. His principal works are the *Codex liturgicus ecclesiae universae in XV libros distributus* (Rome 1749–66); *De sacris ritibus dissertatio* (Rome 1757); *Commentarius theologicocanonicus criticus de ecclesiis, earum reverentia et asylo atque concordia Sacerdotii et Imperii* (Rome 1766); *Dissertatio de unione et communione ecclesastica* (Rome 1770); *Dissertatio de canonibus poenitentialibus* (Rome 1770); *De Catholicis seu Patriarchis Chaldaeorum et Nestorianorum commentarius historicochronologicus* (Rome 1775); and the *De Synodo Diocesana dissertatio* (Rome 1776); a Latin version of Ebedjesus' *Collectio Canonum,* published by Cardinal Mai.

Bibliography: A. MAI, *Scriptorum veterum nova collectio e Vaticanis codicibus edita,* 10 v. (Rome 1825–38). A. VAN HOVE, *Commentarium Lovaniense in Codicem iuris canonici I,* 5 v. (Mechlin 1928—) 1:563.

[T. F. DONOVAN]

ASSEMBLIES OF FRENCH CLERGY

Convocations of representatives of the clergy called by the French king during the 16th, 17th, and 18th centuries.

Origins. The first such assembly is usually considered to have been the Colloquy of Poissy convened in 1561 by Michel de L'HÔPITAL, Chancellor for Charles IX. Catholic and Protestant theologians were invited to attend in an effort to work out a formula for religious agreement that would satisfy both reformers and Catholics. The Protestant reformer Theodore BEZA attended and refused to accept the doctrine of the Real Presence in the Eucharist. On the other side, the Catholic leaders refused to accept any form of compromise, insisting that only the pope had authority to arbitrate on such religious matters. From the time of the Assembly of Melun (1579) the assemblies became an established institution, and eventually they met every five years. In due time procedures for representation and the conduct of business were developed. Each French province was represented by two bishops and two members of the inferior clergy, usually abbots and canons. A president was elected and members were divided into committees to carry on the detailed business of the meeting.

Evolution. One of the regular features of the assemblies, introduced at Poissy, was the approval of the *don gratuit,* an annual free gift to the king. In 1561 the amount of the *don gratuit* was fixed at 1,600,000 livres per year for six years. Additional grants were made on special occasions. In 1641, for example, the assembly was virtually coerced into approving an additional 4,000,000 livres to be contributed within three years. The regular annual grant was gradually increased to a maximum of 16,000,000 livres by 1755. Attempts by the crown to make the *don gratuit* compulsory were successfully resisted.

One of the most famous of the assemblies was held in 1682. It was called by Louis XIV as a means of resisting papal pressure to end the *régale,* the right of the French kings to appropriate the revenues of a vacant see and to make appointments to its benefices. It was at this time that Jacques BOSSUET, Bishop of Meaux, delivered an eloquent oration at the opening of the session, emphasizing the unity of the Church. The assembly supported the position of the king on the *régale* and also approved the Four Articles: (1) the temporal sovereignty of monarchs is independent of the pope; (2) the supremacy of the General Council over the pope as affirmed at the Council of CONSTANCE is to be upheld; (3) the ancient liberties of the Gallican church are inviolate; (4) the infallibility of the *magisterium* belongs to pope and bishop jointly. These had been drawn up by Bossuet and represented an expression of GALLICANISM. Although Innocent XI was offended by the Four Articles, he took no action against them. He did, however, demonstrate his opposition by refusing to approve members of this assembly as appointees for vacant sees. In 1693 the Four Articles were withdrawn on the insistence of Innocent XII and with the approval of Louis XIV.

The last struggle between the Assembly of French Clergy and the government occurred in 1785 when the finance minister, Charles de Calonne, demanded an increase in the *don gratuit.* The clergy refused, and no further action was taken.

The meetings were concerned as much with religious as with temporal matters. In many of the sessions the question of Protestantism was considered. One of the important issues was JANSENISM. In general, the clergy supported the proclamations of the popes against Jansenism. In effect, the assemblies assigned the French clergy an important role in maintaining the purity of French Catholicism and a voice in determining the extent of secular influence in the Church.

The beginning of the French Revolution brought the institution of the assemblies to an end. To a significant degree they had represented the independence of the French clergy in their relations with the crown. Unlike the nobles who had lost most of their rights and privileges, the clergy had maintained their immunities and privileges; the institution through which this was successfully accomplished had been the Assembly of French Clergy.

Bibliography: R. CHALUMEAU, *Catholicisme* 1:916–918. L. SERBAT, *Les Assemblées du clergé de France . . . 1561–1615* (Paris 1906). P. BLET, *Le Clergé de France et la monarchie: Étude sur les assemblées générales du clergé de 1615 à 1666,* 2 v. (Rome 1959). A. SICARD, *L'Ancien clergé de France,* 3 v. (Paris 1893–1903). I. BOURLON, *Les Assemblées du clergé sous l'ancien régime,* 2 v. (Paris 1907).

[W. J. STEINER]

ASSEMBLIES OF GOD

The largest organized church in the pentecostal movement. Its origins may be found in the holiness revival within the Methodist Church in the decades immediately following the Civil War. It grew out of the broader Pentecostal movement of the early 20th century, which reflected influences of the Holiness and Fundamentalist (biblicism) movements. The main distinction between the pentecostal groups and the other denominations that grew from the same source lies in their belief that, after the religious experience of conversion and of the baptism by the Holy Spirit that sanctifies and cleanses from inner sin, it is part of the divine dispensation that the same charismatic signs that marked the Apostles after the first Pentecost should reappear in the Christian community. Thus, the "second blessing" of the holiness sects is made manifest among the pentecostals by the healing of the sick and speaking with tongues. Baptist influence is seen in the practice of immersion and in the rejection of infant baptism.

The Apostolic Faith Movement, the immediate precursor of the Assemblies of God, began (1901) at Bethel Bible College, Topeka, Kans. Charles F. Parham, a holiness revival preacher, had organized this small institution the previous year to offer courses in Scripture study and to prepare men and women for the evangelistic ministry. Speaking in unknown tongues became common among the Topeka students, and this form of the "second blessing" began to manifest itself in revival meetings. Pentecostal congregations developed in Kansas, Missouri, and Oklahoma in a loose fellowship. William J. Seymour experienced a similar outpouring of the Holy Spirit in Texas and founded a holiness mission (1906) in Los Angeles, Calif. One of his converts, G. B. Cashwell, conducted similar revivals in North Carolina. The same type of pentecostal movement sprang up elsewhere, with such lead-

Jimmy Swaggart, a televangelist of the Assemblies of God, broadcasts from his World Ministry Center in Baton Rouge, Louisiana. (©Philip Gould/CORBIS)

ers as A. J. Tomlinson gathering (1908) the Church of God at Cleveland, Tenn., and Elder C. H. Mason forming the Church of God in Christ the same year.

In the Dec. 20, 1913, issue of *Word and Witness* published in Malvern, Ark., editor E. N. Bell called ''saints who believe in the baptism with the Holy Ghost, with signs following'' to a meeting in Hot Springs, Ark. In 1914 a general convention of Pentecostal Saints and Churches of God in Christ was held at Hot Springs, Ark. Endorus N. Bell, pastor of a Baptist church in Texas and editor of the pentecostal *Word and Witness,* and J. Roswell Flower, editor of the *Christian Evangel,* were the prime movers of the meeting. Its aim was to recognize the need for a standard in the ministry and preaching of the pentecostal movement, for fellowship between the congregations, and for a centralized agency for foreign missionary work. A missionary board, the Home and Foreign Mission Committee, was set up and a general council was incorporated legally. The highly democratic movement had little interest in denominational machinery, loosely organizing itself under an annual general council, with state and district councils, and local assemblies. The ministry of women was recognized and a central publishing house set up in St. Louis, Mo.

Originally conceived as an informal fellowship to facilitate cooperative work and provide such services as ministerial certification, the simple structure formed in 1914 evolved into a large organization administering extensive programs. The General Council, which meets every two years, includes all ministers and a delegate from each local church. The 240-member General Presbytery meets annually, and governance between its sessions is in the hands of the 13-member Executive Presbytery, consisting of the four-member Administrative Board, a director of foreign missions and eight regional representatives. Local churches retain a high degree of autonomy.

In 1916, the new body adopted ''A Statement of Fundamental Truths,'' including assertion of a trinitarian position and rejection of the quasi-unitarian shift of some pentecostals to baptism in the name of ''Jesus only.'' In 1918, the denomination declared it would not accept those who considered optional ''our distinctive testimony'' of speaking in tongues. The constitution now says baptism in the Holy Spirit is an experience ''distinct from and subsequent to the experience of the new birth,'' is ''witnessed by the initial physical sign of speaking with other tongues,'' and produces an ''enduement of power for life and service.'' The gift of tongues is also seen as a sign of the imminent return of Christ.

Although the Assemblies of God have increasingly come to resemble the older Protestant denominations and belong to the National Association of Evangelicals, they continue their distinctive emphases on tongues and divine healing, though without rejecting modern medicine. Informal in worship, they are aggressive in evangelism and missionary work.

The Assemblies of God are avowedly fundamentalist in their theological views, emphasizing the unity and Trinity of God, the Incarnation and atoning death of Christ, humanity's fallen nature, the need for repentance and sanctification by faith, and the inspiration and sufficiency of the Scriptures. They stress the work of the Holy Spirit in the process of conversion and the outpouring of the Spirit cleansing from inner sins. The movement known as the New Order of the Latter Rain, beginning in 1947, placed even greater stress on pentecostal manifestations, but this group has gradually died out. In addition, the Assemblies of God condemn the use of liquor, tobacco, cosmetics, and worldly adornment. A great deal of freedom is allowed in both worship and evangelistic services for spontaneous demonstrations of praise or zeal. Services center on sermons and hymns and are often of long duration.

Bibliography: C. BRUMBACK, *Suddenly From Heaven* (Springfield, Mo. 1961). I. WINEHOUSE, *The Assemblies of God* (New York 1959). R. M. RIGGS, *We Believe* (Springfield, Mo. 1954). R. M. ANDERSON, *Vision of the Disinherited: The Making of American Pentecostalism* (New York 1979). W. W. MENZIES, *Anointed to Serve: The Story of the Assemblies of God* (Springfield, Ill. 1971).

[R. K. MACMASTER/T. EARLY/EDS.]

ASSISI

Located in central Italy in the Umbrian valley on the slopes of Monte Subasio, Assisi gained fame as the home of SS. FRANCIS and CLARE (both of whom are buried there) and came to be a major pilgrimage center. In the 20th century many artists and writers made it their home.

History. In ancient times the site was inhabited by the *umbri*, a local population with Etruscan ties, and later under the Romans *Assisium* it acquired the status of a municipium. Although Assisi became a diocese probably in the 3d century, the first recorded bishop, Aventius, was a legate of the Ostrogoths of Justinian after Totila took the town (*c.* 545). The passions of SS. Victorinus, Felicianus, Sabinus, and Ruffinus (early martyr bishops) are late and unreliable. St. Ruffinus, whose cult is mentioned by St. PETER DAMIAN, became Assisi's first patron.

From the late 8th to the 12th century, Assisi was subject to the Lombard Duchy of Spoleto. Bishop Ugo

(1036–52) was a civic leader of the newly independent Ghibelline commune. The first of Assisi's numerous wars with its belligerent Guelf neighbor Perugia occurred in 1054. Assisi was dominated by the Hohenstaufens from 1160 to 1198 when the citizens revolted against the German rulers and razed their fortress (rebuilt by Cardinal Albornoz in 1367). Under the litigious Bishop Guido II (1204–28), who approved the foundation of the first and second orders of Franciscans, the prosperous diocese owned half the area of the commune. In the 14th and 15th centuries Assisi fell under the Visconti, Montefeltro, and Sforza families, suffered internal conflicts, was sacked several times, and gradually lapsed into three relatively uneventful centuries (1535–1860) as part of the States of the Church. St. Gabriel POSSENTI was born there in 1838.

The communal library is rich in medieval MSS from religious houses suppressed in 1866. Since 1902 Assisi has been the headquarters of the International Society of Franciscan Studies and since 1939 of the pious society Pro Civitate Christiana. The First International Congress on Pastoral Liturgy met there in 1956.

Before and after his election to the papacy, JOHN PAUL II visited Assisi several times. He joined Christian and other religious leaders for the World Day of Prayer for Peace held there Oct. 27, 1986, and again in 1999.

Architecture and Paintings. In the center of the city there are the remains of an amphitheater from Roman times and the hexastyle Corinthian pronaos of the Temple of Minerva (1st century B.C.). Among the medieval secular buildings the Piazza del Comune, the Palazzo del Capitano del Popolo (1212–1305) and the Palazzo dei Priori (1337) are notable, but Assisi's architectural glories are its major Romanesque and Gothic churches: (1) S. Maria Maggiore, or Vescovado, the first cathedral, rebuilt in 1163 by Giovanni da Gubbio, who also enlarged (2) the second cathedral, S. Rufino, with its striking Lombard Romanesque facade; (3) the Benedictine Abbey of S. Pietro, rebuilt in 1253; (4) the Basilica of S. Chiara, erected in 1257 in place of the earlier S. Giorgio over the tomb of St. Clare; and (5) the Gothic Basilica of S. Francesco (1228–53) designed by Brother ELIAS OF CORTONA which includes the single-naved upper and lower churches, the crypt tomb of St. Francis (reopened in 1818 and restored in 1925), a sacristy rich in the saint's relics, and the vast Sacro Convento and papal residence, with portico (1300), cloister (1476), and 18th century refectory. Outside the city are the modest 11th century oratory of S. Damiano and the 13th century convent where St. Clare lived. On the hillside above the city is the Eremo delle Carceri (Hermitage), given to St. Francis by Benedictine monks and enlarged by St. BERNARDINE OF SIENA; and in the valley below the city, Basilica of S. Maria degli

Angeli (1569–1676, rebuilt in 1836) which encloses the Portiuncula Chapel, sometimes described as the "cradle of the Franciscan Order." It was a place of retreat and prayer much favored by St. Francis.

The frescoes in the upper and lower churches of the Basilica of S. Francesco provide an invaluable record of the fresco styles of the 13th and 14th centuries in central Italy. Each level of the basilica consists of a simple nave, transept, and a sanctuary. During the 14th century, chapels were added to the nave of the lower church. Faded remnants of the earliest frescoes, episodes from the life of Christ and of St. Francis, are in the nave of the lower church. In the right transept, frescoes of the 14th century hem in an earlier painting by Cimabue depicting an enthroned Madonna with St. Francis. The juxtaposition of Christ and St. Francis occurs again in frescoes painted by Giotto's workshop and Pietro Lorenzetti in the transepts and the crossing vault. The frescoes in the St. Nicholas and the Magdalen chapels, added in the 14th century, are the work of pupils of Giotto. The St. Martin chapel was decorated by Simone Martini.

The walls of the upper church are divided into two registers. The upper register is covered with frescoes begun during the late 13th century. The earliest, in the sanctuary and transepts, are by Cimabue and assistants. On the upper half of the nave walls in two registers are stories from the Old and New Testaments. These are chiefly the work of artists of the Roman school, Torriti and Rusuti and their assistants, the anonymous Isaac Master, and the young Giotto.

The crowing decoration in the upper church are the 28 scenes from the life of St. Francis in the lower register. Framed by a painted colonnade, a *stoa pictile*, they have been variously attributed to Giotto and assistants, to the St. Cecilia Master, and to a 14th century Umbrian.

Preservation and Restoration. In 1944 the Germans designated Assisi a hospital town at the request of the Holy See, and thus it escaped damage during World War II. At the end of September 1997, a series of earthquakes, the first on September 27, devastated the city, causing extensive damage to homes and public monuments. The Basilica of San Francesco, the Church of Santa Chiara and other buildings were closed for two years and more while repairs were made and the paintings restored.

Bibliography: F. S. ATTAL, "Assisi città santa: Come fu salvata: dagli orrori della guerra," *Miscellanea francescana* 48 (1948) 3–32. A. CRISTOFANI, *Le storie di Assisi* (4th ed. Venice 1959). A. FORTINI, *Assisi nel media evo* (Rome 1940). W. HUGO, *Studying the Life of St. Francis of Assisi* (Quincy, Ill. 1996). B. KLEINSCHMIDT, *Die Basilika San Francesco in Assisi*, 3 v. (Berlin 1915–28); *Die Wandmalereien der Basilika San Francesco in Assisi* (Berlin 1930). F. LANZONI, *Le diocesi d'Italia dalle origini al principio del secolo VII (an. 604)*, 2 v. (2d ed. Faenza 1927), 1:461–480. F. J. MATHER, *The Isaac Master* (New York 1932). M. MEISS, *Giotto and Assisi* (New York 1960). E. RYMOND, *In the Steps of Saint Francis* (Chicago 1975). I. B. SUPINO, *La Basilica di San Francesco d'Assisi* (Bologna 1924). L. TINTORI and M. MEISS, *The Painting of the Life of St. Francis in Assisi* (New York 1962). P. URBANI, *Patriarchal Basilica in Assisi, Saint Francis, Artistic Testimony, Evangelical Message*, ed. ENEL (Milan 1991). G. WEIGEL, *Witness to Hope* (New York 1999).

[R. BROWN/E. T. DE WALD/EDS.]

Convent of Basilica of San Francesco, Assisi, Italy. (© Elio Ciol/CORBIS)

ASSOCIATION

As a social entity, an association is a durable union between men to attain a common goal. It is thus an expression of the human sociality that is manifested in many ways, from occasional and fortuitous encounters or more or less stable interrelations between persons, to lasting structures that can extend from the family or clan to worldwide pluralities. In every time and place that men have lived in SOCIETY, human existence is social coexistence. Human personality cannot develop or express itself except within and through society; personal life has a social end just as social life has a personal end. The "life within the self" of the human person cannot be conceived without "living for others." Thus, human sociality is commonly expressed in the formation of an association to attain a COMMON GOOD that is beyond individual capabilities. In short, since man cannot live adequately or attain the goals of his life outside of society, his sociality must be regarded as a requisite of his human nature and the right of association must be respected as a right based on the natural law.

Classification. Given the complexity of human life and its needs, human sociality gives rise to a great variety of groupings whose names are to be found in all modern languages; one needs only to peruse any dictionary to note the richness of terminology that points to the fundamental tendency of man to associate with others. Scholastic philosophers customarily distinguish the different forms of associations according to their (1) end, (2) origin, (3) legal status, and (4) degree of perfection. According to their end associations are religious, scientific, cultural, social, sporting, commercial, etc. They are further classified as natural or voluntary in origin. Thus natural societies are those that are indispensable for the attainment of man's existential ends. Traditionally these have been regarded as the family (or clan) and the STATE in the natural order and the Church in the supernatural order (*see* CHURCH, II), but the international society must now be included among the former. Societies that are not necessary to attain human existential ends are called voluntary or free. Reminiscent of this distinction are sociological typologies such as that of Ferdinand Tönnies, for whom *Gemeinschaft* (community) is based on a common love arising from natural affinity; and *Gesellschaft* (association), on a common interest pursued by deliberate choice. According to their legal status, public societies, regulated by public law, are distinguished from private societies arising from private rights. Last, social philosophy distinguishes between perfect and imperfect societies. Perfect societies are those possessing all the necessary means to procure their final good for their members. Traditionally the sovereign state in the natural order and the Church in the supernatural order have been regarded as perfect societies.

The development of international society makes necessary some modification of this view of the state. As Pope John XXIII remarked in *PACEM IN TERRIS,* "at the present day no political community is able to pursue its own interests and develop itself in isolation, because the degree of its prosperity and development is a reflection and a component of the degree of prosperity and development of all the other political communities" [*Acta Apostolicae Sedis, 55* (1963) 292; cf. *Mater et Magistra, ibid.* 53 (1961) 449]. It follows that no contemporary state can be considered a perfect society in the scholastic sense of the word. The inclusion of the international community, politically organized, is necessary to ensure to men the totality of temporal goods to which they may quite rightly aspire.

Recognition of the right of association. Although it is a natural right, the right of association is not absolute,

nor has it been or is it now guaranteed by law everywhere. In the history of ideas this right is associated with individual rights, but in fact it safeguards collective interests as well; moreover, it is intimately linked with other civil liberties, such as FREEDOM OF RELIGION, freedom of the press, FREEDOM OF SPEECH and the right of petition. The Bill of Rights added to the Constitution of the United States in 1791 was one of the first guarantees of the right of association as well as of other liberties. In the same year in France the Le Chapelier law forbade the reestablishment under any pretext or form of the corporations (or guilds) that were dissolved by its provisions. Interestingly, it was in the name of individual liberty that the right of association and of coalition was outlawed. In the mind of the law's authors an association, as the organ and voice of a collective interest, had no reason for existence; for it was believed that there was no interest intermediate between the particular interest of the individual and the general interest of the state. Freedom to associate, by grouping collective interests, was held to constitute a hindrance to individual goals as well as a menace to the general welfare of the state, the trustee of individual welfare. In other nations also certain forms of association were forbidden in the name of the public interest. Otto von Bismarck's KULTURKAMPF in Germany, for example, excluded the Society of Jesus (1871) and socialist groups (1878); later, the right of association recognized by the Weimar constitution of 1918 was abolished by the National Socialist regime in 1933 and reestablished in the constitution of the Federal Republic in 1952.

It is impossible to summarize the varied legal provisions dealing with the right of association in individual countries. In general this right is recognized in most and is usually made explicit as one of the personal rights of citizens. It is legally acknowledged even in Communist countries, where it is sometimes more clearly formulated statutorily than in democratic nations. But there always exists some discrepancy between the law and the spirit, between theory and practice. The right of association is required in the name of liberty; yet in every instance it is limited by the needs of the public order and the public good. To understand its real meaning one must understand the meaning of freedom and of the public interest in each case. Thus the right of association in the "peoples' democracies" is not seen as the guarantee of personal or collective liberty but as the right of a so-called socialist personality at the service of the Communist system in force.

The right of association has been affirmed constantly by the popes since Leo XIII, who insisted in particular on the right of workers to form unions at a time when this right was often denied. In *RERUM NOVARUM* he wrote: "Although private societies exist within the state and are, as it were, so many parts of it, still it is not within the authority of the state universally and *per se* to forbid them to exist as such. For man is permitted by a right of nature to form private societies; the state, on the other hand, has been instituted to protect and not to destroy natural right, and if it should forbid its citizens to enter into associations, it would clearly do something contradictory to itself because both the state itself and private associations are begotten of one and the same principle, namely, that men are by nature inclined to associate" [*Acta Sanctae Sedis,* 23 (1891) 665; cf. Pius XII, *Sertum laetitiae, Acta Apostolicae Sedis,* 31 (1939) 643]. In MATER ET MAGISTRA John XXIII stressed the importance of associations or intermediary bodies between the state and individuals (*loc. cit.* 417). In *Pacem in terris* he declared: "From the fact that human beings are by nature social, there arises the right of assembly and association. They have also the right to give the societies of which they are members the form they consider most suitable for the aim they have in view and to act within such societies on their own initiative and on their own responsibility in order to achieve their desired objectives" (*loc. cit.* 262–263).

The Declaration of the Rights of Man of 1948 includes the right of association (art. 20), as does the European Convention of the Rights of Man of 1950 (art. 11).

Moral right of association. It is natural for every being to seek its good. Man also has a natural tendency toward his own good, toward the development of his being. This development can be realized only with the help of his fellows and by collaboration with others. To attain his own good, man not only has the right but also the duty to associate with others for common purposes that are genuine and useful. This right and duty extend to association not only with contemporaries but also with successive generations, since human progress is a sacred task confided to all men and transmitted from age to age.

Man must seek in social life not only an individual profit that supplies for his personal deficiencies, but a field of action for his devotion to the common good; to fulfill himself he must surpass himself. Society is not an agglomeration of individual egos but a cluster of reciprocal attachments. To live for himself alone is one of the worst sins that man can commit. Moreover, his personal good can be realized only in and by the common good. It is necessary therefore to keep in mind the duty as well as the right to associate.

This duty, however, is not absolute and unlimited. Although there exists among all men a community of nature, of origin and of natural and supernatural destiny, one cannot conclude that a given man is bound to associate with all men. He has this duty only toward those with whom he interacts in concrete situations of life and

with whom he can collaborate for common goals. Similarly, the right of association is neither absolute nor unlimited. It proceeds from human nature and provides for the normal development of man. It follows that this right exists only to serve man's true welfare, that is, a personal or common good. It is the prerogative of public authority to recognize the right of association within the limits of the common good and to respect the autonomy of associations and enact statutes permitting them to survive and develop.

Associations in contemporary society. Responding to their needs, men of all ages have united with others to form associations. Primitive man lived in such intimate dependence on his social group that his own personality was often submerged or at least diminished; he was above all a member of the clan or tribe. The modern era, beginning with the Renaissance, has given rise to the cult of the individual and of the rights of the individual and of the human person. It is the era of both individualism and PERSONALISM, the latter transcending the limitations of the former. Personalism, while proclaiming the primacy of the human person, recognizes his social dimension and social end. "One of the principal characteristics of our times is the multiplication of social relationships," wrote John XXIII in *Mater et Magistra,* referring to "a daily more complex interdependence of citizens, introducing into their lives and activities many and varied forms of association, recognized for the most part in private and even in public law" (*loc. cit.* 415–416). The increase in number and influence of associations is at the same time a cause and an effect of the socialization to which Pope John referred. It is explained by scientific and technical progress, the proliferation of needs, the increase of productivity and the growth of civilization; it is at the same time the index and the cause of increasing government intervention, even in the intimate spheres of personal life.

In the last analysis the phenomenon of increasing social complexity is traceable to natural human sociality and is therefore almost irresistible. In effect "men are impelled voluntarily to enter into association in order to attain objectives which each one desires, but which exceed the capacity of single individuals. This tendency has given rise, especially in recent years, to organizations and institutes on both national and international levels, which relate to economic and social goals, to cultural and recreational activities, to athletics, to various professions, and to political affairs" (*ibid.* 416). The benefits derived from associations are incontestable: they facilitate the realization of a great number of personal rights, especially those dealing with the means of subsistence, medical care, cultural values, professional formation, lodging, work and recreation. They permit individuals and groups to defend and promote their particular interests, which, although subordinate to the public good, constitute an important part of it. They contribute to the maintenance, among their members, of a sense of social responsibility, a spirit of devotion and a willingness to collaborate with public authority and other groups. They also contribute to the structuring of society by creating intermediary groups between the state and the individual, thus avoiding the two extremes of social atomism and state collectivism.

Unfortunately the proliferation of social bonds also presents problems, such as the restriction of individual liberty, the diminution of initiative and personal responsibility—in one word, depersonalization. To prevent these problems from arising or at least to ameliorate them and attain the maximum advantages from the development of social bonds in associations, it is necessary (1) that public authority be guided by a precise notion of the common good that consists in the creation of that ensemble of social conditions necessary to promote the full development of the human person, for in the last analysis the common good is the personal good of each member of the collectivity (*Mater et Magistra, loc. cit.* 417; *Pacem in terris, loc. cit.* 262); (2) that the associations or intermediary bodies enjoy real autonomy and instead of hindering or replacing the personal activity of their members associate them with organized action and treat them as responsible persons; and (3) that every effort be made through education to form men convinced of their dignity and their personal responsibility as well as of their social duty.

Bibliography: L. JANSSENS, *Personne et société: Théories actuelles et essai doctrinal* (Gembloux 1939). J. LECLERCQ, *Leçons de droit naturel,* v.1 *Le Fondement du droit et de la société* (3d ed. Namur 1947). W. MALLMAN, *Staatslexikon,* ed. GÖRRES-GESELLSCHAFT, 8 v. (6th new and enl. ed. Freiburg 1957–63) 8:106–109. A. VERDOODT, *Naissance et signification de la Déclaration universelle des droits de l'homme* (Doctoral diss. Louvain 1964). E. WELTY, *Gemeinschaft und Einzelmensch . . . nach Thomas v. Aquin* (Salzburg 1935). M. WULLAERT, *Maatschappelijke Ordening en Toegang tot het beroepsen bedrijfsleven (Organization sociale et accès à la vie professionnelle et industrielle)* (Doctoral diss. Louvain 1964). ''L'État et les associations'' in Union internationale d'études sociales, *Code de morale politique: Synthèse doctrinale* (Paris 1957) 124–130. D. FELLMAN, *The Constitutional Right of Association* (Chicago 1963). *Acta Apostolicae Sedis,* 31 (1939) 643, 55 (1963) 292; cf, *Mater et Magistra, ibid.* 53 (1961) 449. *Acta Sanctae Sedis,* 23 (1891) 665; cf, PIUS XII, *Sertum laetitiae.*

[C. VAN GESTEL]

ASSOCIATION OF PROFESSORS OF MISSIONS

The Association of Professors of Missions (APM) brings together the teachers of missions throughout the United States and Canada to promote the development of the field of mission studies and the personal growth of the members themselves. Organized in 1952 in Louisville, KY, the Association built on a previously established Fellowship of Professors of Missions from the Atlantic seaboard area. A similar Midwest Fellowship of Professors of Missions also developed at the same time. Both regional groups continue to meet annually.

From 1952 to 1972 the APM met biennially, normally at the same location and just after or prior to the meeting of the American Association of Theological Schools. Membership in the APM was initially open only to those professors of missions from institutions accredited with the American ASSOCIATION OF THEOLOGICAL SCHOOLS and to other qualified persons by invitation of the executive committee. In a growing effort to be more ecumenical, the reference to institutional relationship with the Association of Theological Schools was removed from the membership requirement in 1972. That same year at the time and place of the APM's biennial meeting (June 1972, in Nashville), the AMERICAN SOCIETY OF MISSIOLOGY (ASM) came into being with the help of the Association. Since 1972 the two organizations meet at the same time and place, with the APM meetings focusing more sharply on issues related to the teaching of missions. The Proceedings of the biennial meetings of the Association of Professors of Missions were published from 1952 to 1974. The publication of the Proceedings was suspended when the ASM began in 1973 to publish the journal *Missiology* (135 North Oakland Street, Pasadena, CA 91101).

Bibliography: J. T. BOBERG, ed., *Proceedings: Association of Professors of Missions* (Chicago 1972 and 1974).

[J. T. BOBERG]

ASSOCIATION OF THEOLOGICAL SCHOOLS

The Association of Theological Schools in the United States and Canada (ATS) is a voluntary association of graduate level theological schools committed to promoting the improvement of theological education. Membership is open to schools that offer graduate theological degrees, that are demonstratively engaged in educating professional leadership for communities of the Jewish and Christian faiths, that meet the standards and criteria of the Association, and that have been elected in accordance with stipulated procedures.

Origins. ATS has its origins in the Conference of Theological Seminaries and Colleges that met biannually to address the special needs of churches for ministry after World War I. In 1936 it became a formal association and adopted standards and procedures for judging quality. In 1938 it adopted the name of the American Association of Theological Schools and established a list of accredited schools. In 1956 it incorporated and secured full-time staff and offices in Dayton, OH, before moving to Pittsburgh, PA, in 1990. In the early 1970s the name was changed to the Association of Theological Schools in the United States and Canada to emphasize its original binational character.

Until 1966, the membership was composed entirely of Protestant schools. In 1966 four Roman Catholic Schools were admitted: Maryknoll School of Theology, Weston Jesuit School of Theology, Mount Saint Alphonsus Seminary, and Woodstock College. Within a decade most of the Catholic theological schools had joined, expanding the base of the Association and the scope of the dialogue among them. Roman Catholic schools were moved to seek membership by the statement in the original edition of the Program of Priestly Formation (1971) of the National Conference of Catholic Bishops, which encouraged theological schools to seek accreditation from appropriate accrediting agencies [no. 92]. Other groups whose membership developed at the same time were the Evangelical schools, the Eastern Orthodox schools, and some Jewish theological schools. With this ATS became representative of the full range of theological schools in the U.S. and Canada. In accordance with the guidelines of ATS, Roman Catholics are represented on all major commissions and committees as well on the professional staff. The first Catholic to serve as ATS president was Vincent Cushing, OFM, (1980–84), president of the WASHINGTON THEOLOGICAL UNION.

Policy. ATS respects the denominational differences and relations of its member schools and does not address doctrinal isues proper to any tradition. In 1990 the members approved a Policy Statement that described as clearly as possible the relationship between theological schools and the churches [''The Accreditation of Theological Schools and Ecclesiastical Assessment of Schools,'' ATS Bulletin 41 (1994) 45–49]. The purposes of ATS as stated in the ATS Constitution are:

1. To provide a continuing forum and entity for its members to confer concerning matters of common interest in the area of theological education;

2. To consider issues that may arise as to the relations of such institutions to one another, to other educational institutions or associations, or to ecclesiastical or governmental authorities;

3. To establish standards of theological education and to maintain a list of institutions on the basis of such standards;

4. In general, without limitation as to the foregoing, to promote the improvement of theological education in such ways as it may deem appropriate.

The third purpose was added in 1936 to accommodate accreditation as the principal means for supporting and monitoring the quality of degree programs.

The Association is recognized by the Commission on Recognition of Post Secondary Accreditation for the accreditation of graduate professional theological education. It is also a recognized accrediting agency for the U.S. Department of Education and works cooperatively with regional accrediting associations, other professional associations, state departments of education, the National Catholic Education Association, and other allied organizations in Canada and the United States. The Association also maintains relationships with various ecclesiastical boards and committees dealing with ministry and higher education.

The several sections of the ATS Bulletin published biannually provide detailed information about the Association, its requirements for membership, its members and officers, its constitutional structures, its policy statements about the work of theological education and its list of accredited institutions.

Bibliography: ATS Bulletin 41: Part 1, Constitution; Part 3, Procedures, Standards and Criteria; Part 5, Policy Statements; Part 7, Membership List (Pittsburgh 1994). NATIONAL CONFERENCE OF CATHOLIC BISHOPS, Program of Priestly Formation (Washington, D.C. 1971; 4th. ed. 1992). J. H. ZIEGLER, ATS Through Two Decades 1960–1980 (Dayton 1984).

[W. BAUMGAERTNER/EDS.]

ASSOCIATIONISM

A theory contending that the entire conscious life of man can be explained on the basis of associative processes. It teaches that the mind consists of mental elements and compounds thereof. When one perceives an object, he has a sensation; but even when the object is no longer actually present, he may retain an idea, meaning by this a faint copy of a sensation or sensory image. Sensations and their copies are the sole elements of mind, and they are compounded or synthesized into larger mental structures, like complex perceptions and thoughts, by the mechanism of association. Conversely, any complex mental content can be reduced into its elemental components by mental analysis.

Hence the assumptions underlying associationistic psychology are those of elementarism and SENSISM. Since its method is introspective, it is a form of mentalism. It has also been called content psychology, because of its concerning itself solely with contents that the mind passively receives; strictly speaking, its advocates maintained that there is no mind apart from its contents. At times associationism was referred to as the "brick-and-mortar theory," the bricks being the sensory impressions and their copies, and the mortar the associations connecting them.

Historical Development. Associationist theory, being a continuation of British EMPIRICISM, has as its forerunners John LOCKE and David HUME. Its founder, however, was David Harley (1705–57), a physician who gave the theory a physiological reference. For him, sensations occur parallel with vibrations in the nerves, and ideas run parallel with minute vibrations in the brain. When the vibratiuncles form clusters, the corresponding simple ideas coalesce into complex ideas by means of simultaneous association.

British Associationists. James MILL (1773–1836) further elucidated the process of coalescence: the mental elements are connected by mechanical synthesis but remain what they are in the associative whole. This is the brick-and-mortar theory in its purest form. His son, John Stuart MILL (1806–73), tempered the explanation by replacing mental mechanics with the concept of mental chemistry: the whole is not merely the sum of its elements, but something new, just as water is more than the sum of hydrogen and oxygen.

Other British associationists were Alexander Bain (1818–1903), who combined associationism with physiological psychology, and Herbert SPENCER (1820–1903), who introduced a new class of mental elements—feelings—previously thought of as mere attributes of sensations. Spencer also taught evolutionary associationism: when associations are often repeated, they create a hereditary predisposition. The last orthodox British associationist was E. B. Titchener (1867–1927), who brought the theory to the U.S. via Germany.

German Associationists. The outstanding proponent of associationism in Germany was Wilhelm Wundt (1832–1920), whose doctrine of content psychology was mitigated from the British form in two ways. First, Wundt introduced the concept of apperception: whereas association is passive, apperception is an active process that focuses attention upon certain features of a perception. Second, Wundt's system broke with the mentalist method underlying other types of associationism. According to Wundt, introspection and mental analysis can be applied only to lower mental processes, viz, sensory perceptions and feelings; the method is inadequate for the study of higher processes of mind, such as thinking, reasoning, and problem solving. These can be studied only by examining what Wundt called the natural history of mankind,

i.e., by observing what these higher processes have produced: language; customs; moral habits; works of science, art, and culture; social and economic systems; and religion. These cultural goods are objectivations of the human mind and, therefore, reveal its abilities. Wundt called this branch of psychology *Völkerpsychologie* (ethnic psychology).

Other psychologists, especially George Elias Miller (1850–1934) and his school, continued the associationist trend, but the movement has faltered in more recent times under the attacks of its critics.

Critique. The crux of associationist psychology has always been the problem of meaning. Many associationists attempted to solve the problem with what Titchener named the context theory: one perception or idea has no meaning, at least in the case of new ideas, but meaning arises from the context of related images that gather about the original presentation. How this came about was never satisfactorily explained. Since, according to the fundamental presupposition of associationism, there is no other mental mechanism, meaning presumably becomes attached to a perception or image by association. But if this is so, is meaning to be considered another mental element or a free-floating entity?

Another objection to associationist psychology was its limitations. Though it claimed to cover the whole of mental life, it confined itself to cognitive aspects alone, and was deficient in its consideration of the dynamic, motivational features of psychology. The Würzburg school, dissatisfied with the associationist contention that all conscious data of a cognitive order could be reduced to sensations and images, introduced a new kind of mental element, namely, imageless thought—a position strongly criticized by Titchener, who maintained that even thought processes are of a sensory and imaginal nature.

The art psychology of F. BRENTANO and his followers was a partial return to Aristotelian-scholastic psychology; it taught that the mind is not simply a kind of receptacle passively receiving impressions, but is itself active in reacting to the presentations of sense.

The Gestalt school—preceeded, if not influenced, by the Graz school with its form qualities—denied the very notion of mental elements and mental analysis. Perception, in Gestalt psychology, is not a mosaic of elementary sensations and feelings, but the resultant of the total sensory impression: one perceives a unitary whole immediately, and not as a sum of its parts. Phenomenological psychology also rejected INTROSPECTION, in the sense of mental analysis, and insisted upon the total description of immediate experience.

The most radical opposition to associationist and content psychology came from American functionalists, who were no longer interested in the theoretical problem posed by CONSCIOUSNESS and concentrated on the practical question of its use. Finally, behaviorism gave associationism the *coup de grâce* by repudiating all mentalism as irrelevant or useless, and by concentrating exclusively on the observation of human behavior.

Bibliography: H. C. WARREN, *A History of the Association Psychology* (New York 1921). E. G. BORING, *History of Experimental Psychology* (2d ed. New York 1950). W. DENNIS, ed., *Readings in the History of Psychology* (New York 1948).

[J. H. VAN DER VELDT]

ASSUMPTION, RELIGIOUS OF THE

The Religious of the Assumption (Religieuses de l'Assomption, R.A.; OCD #3390) is a congregation of teaching sisters with papal approbation (1888), founded in 1839 by Mother Marie Eugénie de Jésus (Anne Eugénie Milleret de Brou, d. 1898, beatified Feb. 9, 1975 by Pope Paul VI) at Paris, France, where the Generalate is located. The congregation is semicontemplative, combining elements of prayer with an active ministry of the transformation of society through Christian education, catechetical, and mission work. In the lifetime of the founder, the congregation established itself in France, England, Spain, Italy, the Philippines, Nicaragua, and El Salvador. By the end of 2000, the congregation had thriving communities in 35 countries in Europe, Africa, Asia, and the Americas. The sisters arrived in the U.S. in 1919, establishing the first community in Pennsylvania, where the provincialate is located. In the U.S., the congregation is engaged in education, spiritual direction, youth formation, counseling, campus ministry, and pastoral and social outreach.

Bibliography: G. BERNOVILLE, *Les Religieuses de l'Assomption* (Paris 1948). C. C. MARTINDALE, *The Foundress of the Sisters of the Assumption* (London 1936). A. M. F. LOVAT, *Life of Mère Marie Eugénie Milleret de Brou* (London 1925).

[M. D. BLACHÈRE/EDS.]

ASSUMPTION, SISTERS OF THE

A congregation whose full title is Sisters of the Assumption of the Blessed Virgin Mary (SASV; OCD #0150). It was founded in 1853 by Rev. J. Harper, pastor of Saint-Grégoire, Quebec, Canada, to provide teachers for his school. The community was canonically erected as a diocesan institute in 1856, received the decree of praise from the Holy See in 1923, and became a pontifical institute in 1944, with final approbation of the constitutions in 1957. The motherhouse and novitiate were

"Assumption of the Virgin," painting by Titian, 1518.

transferred to Nicolet, Quebec, in 1872. A foundation in Western Canada and one in the U. S. at Southbridge, Mass., were made in 1891. Missions were begun in Japan in 1934 and in Brazil in 1956.

The Sisters of the Assumption are engaged in a diverse range of ministries, including education, parish administration, religious education, campus ministries, retreat and spiritual direction, chaplains, and caregivers. In addition to Canada and the United States, communities have also been established in Brazil, Ecuador, Haiti, and Japan.

[A. O. BAILLARGEON/EDS.]

ASSUMPTION OF MARY

"The Immaculate Mother of God, the ever-Virgin Mary, having completed the course of her earthly life, was assumed body and soul into heavenly glory." In these words of the apostolic constitution

The Death of the Virgin, 12th-century mosaic in the church of the Martorana at Palèrmo. This motif is the Eastern counterpart of the Western iconography of the Assumption.

MUNIFICENTISSIMUS DEUS (MD) Pope Pius XII, on Nov. 1, 1950, most solemnly described the crowning event of the life of the Blessed Virgin. Thus defining the dogma of Mary's Assumption, he wrote the final chapter of the centuries-long tradition of belief in this mystery.

This article considers mainly the scriptural basis, taking as its guide the apostolic constitution, the theological explanation of the Assumption, and, finally, the question of the death of Mary.

Scripture. There is no explicit reference to the Assumption in the Bible, yet the pope insists in the decree of promulgation that the Scriptures are the ultimate foundation of this truth. Our Lord Himself, the Evangelists, and the Fathers repeatedly emphasize the capital importance of the RESURRECTION OF CHRIST as proof of His divinity, as promise of man's victory over sin, Satan, and death. "If Christ has not risen," wrote St. Paul (1 Cor 15.14–22), "vain then is our preaching, vain too is your faith. . . . For if the dead do not rise, neither has Christ risen. . . . If with this life only in view we have had hope in Christ, we are of all men the most to be pitied. But as it is, Christ has risen from the dead, the first-fruits of those who have fallen asleep. For since by a man came death, by a man also comes resurrection of the dead. For as in Adam all die, so in Christ all will be made to live." The new life brought by Christ is a life transforming man totally, body and soul, so that man's body too is meant to share in the victory of Christ over death, just as the whole of man, body and soul, suffers the consequences of Adam's sin. "When this mortal body puts on immortality, then . . . 'Death is swallowed up in victory.' . . . Now the sting of death is sin. . . . But thanks be to God who has given us the victory through our Lord Jesus Christ" (1 Cor 15.53–57). If these texts are part of the scriptural basis for the resurrection of the Christian, there remains the need to justify the anticipated resurrection that he attributes to the Virgin Mary. Pius XII himself extends the relevance of Lk 1.28 and 42 (which Pius IX had carefully analyzed in the bull of definition of the IMMACULATE CONCEPTION, *Ineffabilis Deus,* in 1854) to the Assumption: "Hail, [thou who art] full of grace, the Lord is with thee. Blessed art thou among women." That fulness of grace bestowed on the Blessed Virgin was, according to Pius XII, only achieved by her Assumption (MD 27).

It is not theology, but the evidence of Scripture that shows Mary "as most intimately joined to her divine Son and as always sharing His lot" (MD 38). St. Paul assures the Romans (6.4–13) that through Baptism they are joined to Christ and share in His victory over sin. Mary's unique similarity to Christ began with her conception. Since it is sin and its consequent punishment in death and corruption that delay the final triumph of the ordinary Christian, it is implicit that anyone perfectly free from sin, like Christ, would be free from the deferment of the resurrection of the body, as Christ was. Mary is surely an exception to the rule (MD 5), portrayed perhaps (MD 27) in the Revelation (12.1) as the great sign in the heavens, a woman clothed with the sun, the moon under her feet, her head crowned with 12 stars. That St. John was primarily here describing the Church in ultimate victory is generally agreed, but that he was also describing the personification of the Church in Mary, the eschatological image of the Church, a prototype already enjoying the glory that the Church will eventually share, has been seriously proposed and defended.

New Eve. However, the most pregnant idea, implied in Scripture and specific already in patristic writings, for accepting and understanding something of the mystery of the Assumption, is that of Mary as the New Eve. Three times in the bull of definition (MD 27, 30, 39) the Holy Father alludes to this telling comparison, without defending or explaining it, accepting it as an obvious deduction from Scripture and a logical development of tradition. Holy Writ says that "as from the offense of the one man the result was unto condemnation to all men, so from the justice of the one the result is unto justification of life to all men. For just as by the disobedience of the one man the many were constituted sinners, so also by the obedience of the one the many will be constituted just" (Rom 5.18–19). The first Eve proved not to be the helpmate God had intended her to be for Adam, proved not to be the "mother of the living" but rather, in a sense, mother of the dead, for she led Adam into sin and thus was his accomplice in bringing all men to the punishment of death and the dominion of Satan.

In contrast, Mary, the New Eve, by her obedience to the Annunciation of the angel, brought life to men in having conceived the person of the New Adam and in having united herself to the principal acts of His redemptive mission. Just as Eve cooperated not only in the original sin but also shared with Adam his subsequent life, parenthood, and the sufferings that were sin's punishment, so Mary cooperated with Christ not only in giving Him birth, but she cooperated with Him, evidently in a secondary and unessential—but actually necessary and important—role, in the significant events of His life, the Presentation, one of His first miracles, the Crucifixion, the Ascension, and, later, in the beginnings of His Church (His members) at Pentecost. More truly than Eve ever would have been, Mary became—at Nazareth, at Bethlehem, at Calvary—in an ever fuller sense, the mother of all the members of the Mystical Body. Hence as things said of Adam apply also, but proportionately, to Eve, so things said of Christ apply also, but proportionately, to

Mary. The author of the Epistle to the Hebrews (2.14) had said "that through death He [Christ] might destroy him who had the empire of death, that is, the devil." Christian intuition, guided by the Holy Spirit, gradually came to see that Mary's share in Christ's victory over sin began with her conception in a state free from all sin (the state in which Eve was created), and ended with her miraculous Assumption (an immunity from death and corruption which Eve enjoyed until the Fall).

The union of Mary with Jesus, so obvious in the scriptural record of their earthly lives, is just as true of their respective roles in the Redemption. Holy Scripture, the Fathers, the medieval theologians, and Pius XII in this most solemn pronouncement, tell of one enmity between God and the devil; one evil—embodied in Adam, Eve, Satan, and his seed—confronting one power of good—God, the Woman, and her Seed; an enmity that will end in a single triumph—of the Woman and her Seed; and of the New Adam one with the New Eve. As Adam's love for Eve led him into sin, so Christ's love for Mary led Him to have her "share in the conflict [and] share in its conclusion" (MD 39)—like Him, a complete victory in body and soul over sin and death.

Mother of God. Pius XII repeatedly refers to Mary's being the Mother of God as the theological reason (for Christ's unique love for and union with Mary and) for the Assumption (MD 6, 14, 21, 22, 25), like a superlative application of the text, "His father's honor is a man's glory; disgrace for her children, a mother's shame" (Sir 3.11). For Mary was united to all three Persons of the Blessed Trinity in a unique relationship—as privileged daughter, mother, and spouse, privileges that involved her body and soul, that implicated her in extraordinary sufferings and joys (MD 14). From earliest times the Fathers defended her perpetual virginity as a proof of the divinity of her offspring, as evidence of her exemption from painful parturition, which is the punishment for sin (cf. Gn 3.16), as the effect of a sinlessness that, negatively, preempts her from the curse of death and that, positively, merits for her the immediate contemplation (after this life), in body and soul, of God. God's justice would not inflict punishment (pain, death, corruption) on one innocent of the crime (sin) being punished: "For all lives are mine; the life of the father is like the life of the son, both are mine; only the one who sins shall die" (Ez 18.4). Briefly—and less weightily than the two previous explanations—the propriety of the Assumption is indicated: The fact that Christ loved Mary and united her in His mysteries makes it proper that the woman He had created sinless, that the virgin whom He had chosen for His mother, be, like Him, completely triumphant over death in her Assumption as He had triumphed over sin and death in His Resurrection.

Death of the Virgin. One final question: Did the Blessed Virgin die? In the climactic paragraph of definition, the pope chose to say, "Mary, having completed the course of her earthly life, was assumed body and soul into heavenly glory" (MD 44). The crucial phrase *expleto terrestris vitae cursu* offers support neither to those who argue that Mary died (the "mortalists") nor to those who say that she did not die (the "immortalists"). While most of the faithful and most of the writers on the subject accept without debate the fact of the death of Mary, it is a subject of controversy among theologians.

Patristic writers cannot be called as support for either side. Before the Council of Nicaea (325) the only overt reference to the close of Mary's life is a phrase attributed to Origen: "With respect to the brethren of Jesus, there are many who ask how He had them, seeing that Mary remained a virgin until her death." But this and a phrase in a hymn of St. Ephraem are praises of the perpetual virginity of Mary; her death is taken for granted, affirmed but not explained. The only writer before the Council of Ephesus (431) to treat the problem *ex professo* was St. Epiphanius, and he concludes that Mary could have enjoyed immortality or could have suffered either martyrdom or natural death. The ambiguity of SS. Augustine, Ambrose, and Jerome point rather to the assumption by Christians that Mary had died than that she was an exception to the law of death to which even Christ had submitted. As history, the apocryphal accounts of *transitus Mariae* are ambivalent, but they are respectable evidence of a conviction among Christians of the fifth century that Mary had died. And the feast of the Dormition of Mary, documented from the second half of the sixth century in the East (Syrian Jacobite Church) and from the seventh century in the West (in Rome under Pope Sergius I), was in its beginnings a tribute to the anniversary of the death of Mary—only later to become a commemoration of the Assumption as such. For patristic writers the reasons for Mary's death were: (1) she belonged to a fallen human nature (even though sinless herself) and inherited a mortal human body; and (2) she was conformable in all things to Christ, who had chosen the humiliation of death despite His divine holiness.

Scholastic theologians such as St. Bonaventure were to accept these explanations for Mary's death and add: (1) the pertinence of virginity, i.e., that Mary's body, which had maintained its integrity even in childbirth, and which was always in harmony with reason and grace, would have merited assumption after death (e.g., St. Bernardine of Siena); (2) the advantage of Mary's meriting herself, by her own death, the resurrection and glorification, as Christ had done (e.g., St. Thomas Aquinas and Dun Scotus).

Most theologians of our day are mortalists and find that the Holy Father, while not taking an ex officio position on the question of the death of Mary, repeatedly used texts from tradition that refer to or imply Mary's death; but a few writers (Balić, Carol, Coyle, Filograssi) have expressed the opinion that the Pope's not favoring either side has left the question in the same state as it was before the definition.

See Also: MARY, BLESSED VIRGIN I, II; MARIAN FEASTS; DORMITION OF THE VIRGIN.

Bibliography: PIUS XIII, "Munificentissimus Deus" (Apostolic Constitution, Nov. 1, 1950) *Acta Apostolicae Sedis* (Rome 1909–) 42 (1950) 753–771. *Catholic Mind* (Eng.) 49 (Jan. 1951) 65–78. *Thomist* 14.1 (1951); the entire issue is on the Assumption. W. BURGHARDT, "The Testimony of the Patristic Age Concerning Mary's Death," *Marian Studies* 8 (1957) 58–99. J. M. EGAN, "The Doctrine of Mary's Death During the Scholastic Period," *ibid.,* 100–124. T. W. COYLE, "The Thesis of Mary's Death in the Light of *Munificentissimus Deus,*" *ibid.,* 143–166. J. B. CAROL, ed, *Mariology* (Milwaukee 1954–61) 2:461–492. F. M. BRAUN, *La Mère des fidèles: Essai de théologie johannique* (Tournai 1953) 134–176. C. X. FRIETHOFF, *A Complete Mariology,* tr. Religious of the Retreat of the Sacred Heart (Westminster, Md. 1958) 143–164. M. JUGIE, "Assomption de la Sainte Vierge," *Maria,* ed. H. DU MANOIR (Paris 1959) 1:621–658. R. LAURENTIN, *Queen of Heaven,* tr. G. SMITH (London 1956) 114–125. S. MATHEWS, ed., *Queen of the Universe* (St. Meinrad, Ind. 1957). K. RAHNER, "The Interpretation of the Dogma of the Assumption," *Theological Investigations,* tr. C. ERNST (Baltimore 1961) 215–227.

[J. W. LANGLINAIS]

ASSUMPTIONISTS

(AA; Official Catholic Directory #0130); the Augustinians of the Assumption (AA) is an apostolic community of priests and brothers with simple vows, who live "the common life according to the Rule and the spirit of St. Augustine, for the sake of the Kingdom." It was founded in 1845 by Emmanuel Daudé d'Alzon (1810–1880), vicar-general of the Diocese of Nîmes, France, with several professors of a school that bore the name, College of the Assumption. It is not a specifically Marian congregation. The first members pronounced their vows on Christmas Day 1850. A pontifical brief of Nov. 26, 1864, encouraged the foundation. The constitutions were approved on Jan. 30, 1923. Following Vatican Council II, a new *Rule of Life* was approved by the Congregation for Religious on Dec. 8, 1983.

The founder, a staunch supporter of ULTRAMONTANISM, was strongly influenced by the thought of Félicité de LAMENNAIS. The purpose assigned to the institute was "to restore higher education according to the mind of St. Augustine and St. Thomas; to fight the Church's enemies enlisted in secret societies under the revolutionary flag; to fight for the unity of the Church." D'Alzon's spiritual doctrine was essentially Trinitarian, tending to a contemplation of the Three Divine Persons and a participation in the mysteries of Jesus, in the spirit of the French school of spirituality of the 17th century. This spirituality was expressed in the founder's *Directory* (1859–65), *Instructions, Circular Letters* (1868–75), as well as in many *Sermons* and *Meditations* (1879–80). Under Emmanuel d'Alzon, the Priests of the Assumption, in keeping with the threefold purpose of the institute, established three kinds of activities: teaching, the Catholic press (in Paris they created and are still responsible for the Catholic daily, *La Croix*), pilgrimages to the Holy Land, to La Salette and Lourdes, as a form of popular education. They opened houses in Bulgaria—later in Turkey, Rumania, and Russia—and welcomed members of the Byzantine Catholic Church. A mission in Queensland (Australia) was short-lived.

Expelled from France at the end of the nineteenth century by the anticlerical government, the congregation temporarily closed most of itshouses there, and it migrated to Spain, the Netherlands, Belgium, England, Chile, and the United States. One of their first American settlements was in Louisiana, where they stayed only a short time. In 1891 they settled in New York City, where they opened the first Hispanic parish, Our Lady of Guadalupe. In 1903 they founded Assumption Preparatory School in Worcester, MA, from which the contemporary Assumption College derives. In the meantime, they consolidated their work in Eastern Europe. One of their members. Pie Neveu, was made a bishop in Russia and remained in Moscow after the Soviet Revolution. In Jerusalem they built the first major hostel for pilgrims, Notre Dame de France, at the end of the nineteenth century. This was abandoned after major damage was caused to the building by the fighting between the armies of Israel and of Jordan after the creation of the State of Israel. It now belongs to the Holy See in its restored form, under the name, Notre Dame of Jerusalem. Under Gervais Quenard, fourth superior general (1923–51), the congregation was divided into provinces.

Before 1939 Assumption missionaries were in the Congo, Brazil, Tunisia, and Manchuria. After 1945 they entered the Ivory Coast, Madagascar, Algeria, and New Zealand. Their province of Central Africa, centered in Butembo (Nord-Kivu, Democratic Republic of the Congo), has extended to Kenya and Tanzania. After World War II the Assumptionists greatly suffered from the communist regimes, as they were expelled from China and three of their Bulgarian priests were condemned to death and executed by firing squad as "spies of the Vatican." In spite of this, one of their American members remained in Moscow through the Second

World War, looking after Latin Catholics in the city. The congregation is still in charge of the oldest Latin parish in Moscow.

The spirit of the founder inspired an intellectual apostolate focused on Byzantine studies (begun in 1897, successively located in Istanbul, Bucarest, and Paris), and later on Augustinian studies in Paris (founded in 1939). For lack of recruits and volunteers these institutes were turned over to the Catholic Institute of Paris in the 1960s. Concern for the unity of the Church was responsible for the foundation of reviews devoted to ecumenical questions, *Echos d'Orient* in 1897 (renamed *Revue des Études Byzantines* when it moved to Paris in 1945), *L'Union des Églises* (published from 1922 to 1938, in Lyon, France), and, in Nijmegen, Netherlands, a quarterly dealing with the Eastern Churches, *Het Christelijk Oosten en Herenining*. In Athens, Greece, they opened an ecumenical library.

The irenic attention that was paid at first to Orthodoxy later included the Anglican and Protestant Churches and the ecumenical movement in the World Council of Churches. When John XXIII created the Secretariat for the Unity of Christians, an Assumption priest was among the consultants; he was appointed later a *peritus* of Vatican II and became an active member of several of the major ecumenical dialogues.

The headquarters of the American province moved in 1982 from New York City to Boston. The province maintains houses in Massachusetts, in the province of Quebec, and in Mexico. Its most active center is at Assumption College in Worcester, MA. The generalate is in Rome.

Several communities of religious sisters are connected, by their origin and their spirituality, with the Augustinians of the Assumption: the Religious of the Assumption, who were actually founded before the Agustinians, by Eugénie Milleret de Brou (Blessed Marie-Eugénie de Jésus, beatified in 1975) with the help of Abbé Combalot, the Oblates of the Assumption (founded by Emmanuel d'Alzon, with Marie Correnson as the first Mother general), the Little Sisters of the Assumption (founded by Étienne Pernet and Marie-Antoinette Fage), and a contemplative community, the "Orantes" of the Assumption (founded by François Picard and Isabelle de Clermont-Tonnerre). Other members of the Congregation founded the Sisters of Joan of Arc in Massachusetts and Quebec, and the Little Sisters of the Presentation in Beni, Democratic Republic of the Congo.

Bibliography: S. VAILHÉ, *Vie du Père Emmanuel d'Alton* (Paris 1926–34); *Lettres du P. Emmanuel d'Alzon, 1822–1835*, 3 v. (Paris 1923, 1925, 1926). P. TOUVENERAUD, ed., *Lettres du P. Emmanuel d'Alzon, 1861–1880*, 13 v. (Rome 1978–1996). A. SAGE, *Un Maître spirituel du XIXᵉ siècle* (Rome 1958). G. H. TAVARD, *The Weight of God. The Spiritual Doctrine of Emmanuel d'Alzon* (Rome 1980); *Le Père d'Alzon et la Croix de Jésus: Les lettres aux Adoratrices* (Rome 1992). A. SÈVE, *Christ Is My Life* (New York, 1988). W. DUFAULT, *The Spiritual Legacy of Emmanuel d'Alzon* (Milton, MA 1988).

[G. H. TAVARD]

ASSUMPTUS-HOMO THEOLOGY

"Assumptus homo" is the name given to the first of the three main trends Peter Lombard identified in theological attempts to explain the INCARNATION. It is not a particular theory, but a line of thought that can be traced back to the Patristic period when many of the Fathers described the Incarnation in terms of the Word assuming humanity in its entirety. It can also claim to find roots in such scriptures as the baptismal account in Mark and Peter's sermon in Acts of the Apostles 2, both of which could be read to say that an already existing human being, Jesus of Nazareth, has been made Lord and Messiah either at the baptism or the resurrection.

Christologies of this sort seek to protect the full humanity of Christ. However, they do so by means that tend toward such heresies as ADOPTIONISM and NESTORIANISM. The term used, *assumptus homo*, could be read as "the man the Word assumed to himself," suggesting the existence of an already-existing man. Further, some medieval thinkers assumed that the full humanity of Christ, composed of body and soul, must constitute a human person. They lacked a more technically sophisticated language that would enable them to hold the full humanity of Christ without claiming that it must be a human person. This line of thought was never condemned, but Thomas, Scotus and other scholastics express serious reservations about it.

Recent theology has seen many attempts to recover the full humanity of Christ, including a fully human psychological autonomy. Some have returned to the *assumptus homo* line of thought to accomplish this. D. M. de Basly (d. 1937) claimed that his view was in the tradition of the Antioch school and of Scotus. L. Seiller went so far as to say that Christ in His manhood was a "somebody" and this opinion was condemned by the Holy Office [*Acta Apostolicae Sedis* 43 (1951) 561]. The encyclical *Sempiternus rex* (H. Denzinger, *Enchiridion symbolorum*, ed. A. Schönmetzer, 3905) does not reject the term *assumptus homo*, but says it has to be used with discernment as it can easily lead to adoptionism. Other theologians simply discuss the full humanity of Christ without getting involved in the technical scholastic issues concerning the term "person." Karl Rahner claimed that the word "person" has undergone great shifts in the modern period and that any future Christology must begin by rethinking the terminology.

Bibliography: K. RAHNER, "Current Problems in Christology," *Theological Investigations* 1 (Baltimore 1961), 149–200; "On the Theology of the Incarnation," *Theological Investigations* 4 (Baltimore 1964), 105–20. J. PELIKAN, *The Christian Tradition: A History of the Development of Doctrine*, v. 1 (Chicago 1971), 175–76. W. KASPER, *Jesus the Christ* (New York 1976), 238–45. W. PANNENBERG, *Jesus, God and Man* (Philadelphia 1968), 295–96.

[M. E. WILLIAMS/M. B. RASCHKO]

ASSY, NOTRE-DAME-DE-TOUTE-GRÂCE

A parish church, consecrated in August of 1950 to service Catholics in the French Alps where tubercular patients and sanatoria convalescent services increased considerably between 1930 and 1950. The church, designed by Maurice Novarina, is not particularly distinguished architecturally; however, the appointment of its decoration served as a focal point of the postwar controversies surrounding the Dominican-led art *sacré* movement in France.

In March of 1939, at the request of the Canon Jean Devémy and the architect M. Novarina, Pierre M. A. COUTURIER, OP, agreed to assist in the planning and execution of the church. The subsequent evolution of this plan in its iconographic program and its relationship to the specific convictions and abilities of the artists engaged, as well as the kind and quality of contemporary art employed, served to sharpen questions on contemporary religious art. The problems posed were consequent to the employment of outstanding artists from the secular art world in an effort to initiate a notable renascence within the area of religious art. The majority of artists engaged were chosen not on the basis of their faith, but on the basis of the quality of their work; most were non-Catholics. The art work itself was, for that time, unusually advanced and seemed foreign to what was considered religious art by reactionary Catholics in France and elsewhere.

The iconographic program unfolded gradually and was partly adjusted to afford a suitable conjunction of the temperament and ability of a particular artist with the subject and its location in relation to the sanctuary. Works for the church included: a façade mosaic by F. LÉGER, "Virgin of the Litany"; baptistery mosaic and reliefs by Marc Chagall, "Crossing of the Red Sea," "Psalm 42," and "Psalm 124"; stained glass designed by G. ROUAULT, notably his "Christ aux outrages"; a large tapestry based on Revelation, ch. 12, by Jean Lur-çat; altar pieces representing St. Dominic (ceramic tile) by H. Matisse and St. Francis de Sales (oil) by P. Bonnard; a bronze statue by J. Lipchitz, "Notre-Dame-de-Liesse"; tabernacle door relief by G. Braque; and stained-glass windows by J. Bazaine, P. Bony, P. Berçot, M. Brianchon, A. Hébert-Stevens, and Father Couturier. The controversial bronze crucifix was designed by Germaine Richier for placement on the main altar.

Although brilliant in individual qualities and somewhat appropriately appointed iconographically, the works as an artistic ensemble show a disparity of styles that has been criticized as an exhibition of talent more suitable for a museum. The controversies that followed the dedication of the church were precipitated by the wide attention given to the church through illustrated articles in magazines such as *France Illustration* and *Life*. A public lecture given by the Canon Devémy on Jan. 4, 1951, for the Friends of Art at Angers received cries of "insult" and "outrage" from a band of Integrists when the crucifix by Germaine Richier appeared in the slides. The Integrists distributed a tract (known as "The Tract of Angers"), that attacked the Richier crucifix. It indicted artists belonging to a "school" led by the "communist Picasso" and asserted that it was time to "unmask the trickery of this spurious art." During February and March the bishop of Annecy was pressured by letters and by a drive led by Charles du Mont in the *Observateur de Genève;* in April, Bishop Cesbron ordered that the crucifix be removed. Reactions to this move were rapid and received wide attention in the press. The art critics Jean Cassou and Bernard Dorival defended the Richier work and saw the move as an imposition on what is properly the domain of art; G. Marcel responded to Dorival noting that an art critic may not contest ecclesiastical authority. F. Mauriac asked whether art can be heretical, and Gaston Bardet answered by proposing that there be created an "index" for artistic works. Celso COSTANTINI issued the most provoking censure in the *Osservatore Romano* (June 10, 1951) in an article *"Dell'arte sacra deformatrice,"* which referred to the crucifix as an "indecent (*sconcio*) pastiche" and attacked the so-called modern movement in art as a Protestant plot against figurative art.

The debates over sacred art were met by an official 11-point directive issued in May of 1952 by an episcopal commission for pastoral and liturgical matters and approved by the cardinals and archbishops of France. The document avoided mentioning any specific works and provided a sufficiently general basis to pacify both sides. The first article recognized that sacred art like all other art is a living art and must correspond to the spirit of its times in its techniques as well as in its use of available materials.

Carchemish city wall relief from Assyrian period, Ankara, Turkey. (©Nik Wheeler/CORBIS)

The Assy controversies, by sharpening questions surrounding contemporary art, the artist, and the Church, provided practical precedents and a spirit of inquiry that contributed considerably to the growing modern renewal in liturgical art.

See Also: CHURCH ARCHITECTURE.

Bibliography: W. S. RUBIN, *Modern Sacred Art and the Church of Assy* (New York 1961), illus., extensive bibliog.; for critical evaluation see R. SOWERS, *Stained Glass: An Architectural Art* (New York 1965), n. 39, p. 126–127, *passim.* A. CHRIST-JANER and M. M. FOLEY, *Modern Church Architecture* (New York 1962).

[R. J. VEROSTKO]

ASSYRIA

Ancient country in northeastern Mesopotamia (*see* MESOPOTAMIA, ANCIENT). Its heartland was the area of the middle Tigris, the site of the cities of Assur (from which the land takes its name), NINEVEH, and Calah (see Gn 10.11). Shut off by mountain ranges on the north and east, the land has a rugged aspect throughout much of its extent; this factor encouraged the yearly military campaigns by which, from the 14th century B.C., the kings of Assyria sought to gain control of neighboring and more richly endowed lands. Their greatest successes were obtained from the 9th to the 7th centuries B.C., with the subjugation of Syria, northern Palestine, and parts of Egypt and Asia Minor (see 2 Kgs 15.27; 17.3–6; 18.13–19.37). At the zenith of its power, Assyria was overcome by a coalition of its Chaldean and Median enemies, who captured the capital city of Nineveh in 612 B.C. (see Neh 2.2–14).

Bibliography: B. MEISSNER, *Babylonien und Assyrien,* 2 v. (Heidelberg 1920–25). *Reallexikon der Assyriologie,* ed. E. EBELING and B. MEISSNER (Berlin 1928) 228–303. M. A. BEEK, *Atlas of Mesopotamia,* tr. D. R. WELSH (London 1962).

[R. I. CAPLICE]

ASSYRIAN CHURCH OF THE EAST

Historically known by the derogatory term "Nestorian Church." The Holy Synod of the Assyrian Church of the East has requested that the term "Nestorian Church" not be used, because of its historically negative connotations. Strictly speaking, The Assyrian Church holds the moderate Antiochene christological position, and the 1994 Common Christological Delaration signed between Mar Dinkha IV and Pope John Paul II recognizes the Assyrian Church's *de facto* acceptance of the substance of Chalcedonian christology.

Origins. Very little is known about the introduction of Christianity into Persia. Later Greek, Syrian, and Persian legends variously maintain that the Apostles Peter and Thomas preached to the Parthians and that Thaddaeus, Bartholomew, and Addaeus (ADDAI), one of the 72 Disciples, evangelized Mesopotamia and Persia. An ancient chronicle notes the destruction of a Christian church by a flood at Edessa in 201. It is quite possible that the first real Christian communities were founded in 260, when, after the defeat of Valerian, many Christians with their priests and bishops were carried off from Coelesyria into Mesopotamia. The inner organization of the Persian Church was effected by Papa bar Aggai, who was bishop of the royal city Seleucia-Ctesiphon in the last decades of the 3d century and the first decades of the 4th.

Under the relatively weak Arsacids (c. 247 B.C.–A.D. 224) Christianity was largely tolerated; but when the Sassanids (224–651) came to power, conversions from Zoroastrianism were regarded as a capital offense. This opposition to Christianity was sharpened in the 4th century, when it became the official religion of the Roman Empire. The Christians were subject to intermittent and, at times, violent persecutions. For 40 years (348–88) no patriarch, or catholicos, could be elected to the See of Seleucia-Ctesiphon. Since no theological school could be erected in Persian territory and the schools of Antioch, Alexandria, and Constantinople were so far distant, it was extremely difficult to provide instruction for future priests.

The problem was partially solved by James, Bishop of NISIBIS, a Roman city near the Persian frontier. On his return from the Council of Nicaea in 325 he founded a theological school at Nisibis and entrusted its direction to the future saint and Doctor of the Church EPHREM THE SYRIAN. The school flourished until 363, when Nisibis was handed over to the Persians by the Emperor Jovian after Julian's disastrous campaign against Ctesiphon. Transferred to Edessa, the school became famous for its adaptation of Aristotelian philosophy to theology and for its translations of Greek works into Syriac.

In 399, when Yazdgard I became King of Persia, Emperor Arcadius sent Bishop Maruthas of Martyropolis to congratulate him on his accession. Maruthas, a Mesopotamian and a skilled physician, was able to win the monarch's favor for the Christians. With the help of his governors, Yazdgard (also Yazdagrid) in 410 convoked a synod at Seleucia under the direction of the Catholicos Isaac. The plenary session that was held February 1 with 40 bishops in attendance adopted the Nicene Creed and the principal disciplinary decrees of Nicaea and of the provincial synods that completed it. Toward the end of his reign Yazdgard was influenced by the MAGI, who were alarmed by the spread of Christianity; and he ordered the destruction of Christian churches and the exile of Christians themselves. Though he died soon after giving this order, the persecution was continued by his son, Vahrām V (421–38). When the Persians demanded the return of Christians who had fled into Roman territories, war broke out. In the treaty of peace that followed, THEODOSIUS II obtained from Vahrām (also Vaharam, Bahram) a promise of freedom of conscience for Christians in Persian lands, and at the same time he guaranteed a similar liberty for Mazdakites living within the Roman Empire.

A synod held in 424 under Patriarch Dadisho' with 36 bishops present decreed that the Persian catholicos was subject only to the tribunal of Christ. This implicit declaration of independence from the Church of the West was followed in later years by the adoption of the radical Christological doctrines of Theodore of Mopsuestia and Nestorius. In its teaching on Christ the school of EDESSA, where the Persian clergy were educated, was essentially Antiochene; that is, it so stressed the distinction between the two natures in Christ as to give the impression, albeit unintentional, that there was no really personal union but only one that was moral or accidental. At the time of Nestorius's condemnation, RABBULA, a violent opponent of Nestorius, was bishop of Edessa. On his death in 435 he was succeeded by Ibas, head of the school at Edessa and staunch defender of Theodore of Mopsuestia. In 449 at the "Robber Synod" of EPHESUS Ibas was deposed on the basis of a letter that he had written to the Persian Bishop Mari of Seleucia-Ctesiphon (433 or 436), in which he defended Diodore of Tarsus and Theodore of Mopsuestia while strenuously rejecting Nestorius. Though Ibas was reinstated at Chalcedon (451) after anathematizing Nestorius, his letter was condemned at the Council of CONSTANTINOPLE II (553) as one of the "Three Chapters." On the death of Ibas in 457 Narses, who had succeeded him as head of the school of Edessa, was driven from the city by the Monophysites. Going to Nisibis, he founded a school there that continued to keep alive the teachings of Theodore and Nestorius on the two natures in Christ.

The college eventually accommodated some 800 students and became so famous that Pope AGAPETUS I and CASSIODORUS thought of founding a similar one in Italy.

When the Catholicos Dadisho' died in 456, he was succeeded by Bâbôe (457–84). His position was sought by Bar Sauma, Metropolitan of Nisibis, patron of Narses, and friend of King Peroz. At court Bar Sauma urged the advantages of a married Christian clergy, a project favored by the Magi, and a Christian teaching or doctrine that would be different from that of Byzantium. In 484 Bâbôe was arrested because of a letter he had written to Constantinople that was intercepted at Nisibis. When he refused to "prove" his loyalty to the king by worshiping the sun, he was cruelly executed. Bar Sauma's hopes of obtaining the catholicate were, however, shattered by the death of King Peroz shortly after that of Bâbôe.

In 485 Acacius was elected patriarch, and in February of the following year he held a synod at Seleucia in which the Antiochene formula for the dogma of the two natures in Christ was adopted and permission was granted to deacons and priests to marry even after ordination. In 497 a synod held by the Catholicos Bābai extended this permission to bishops and the catholicos.

During the 6th century the Assyrian Church was torn by a long schism (521 or 522–37 or 539), a violent persecution (540–545) under Chosroes (Khusro) I (531–79), and by various ecclesiastical scandals. Order was restored through the reforms of the great Patriarch Mar Aba (540–52), but his successor, Joseph, was deposed for simony and oppressing his subject priests and bishops. When the Catholicos Gregory I died in 609, Chosroes II ordered the confiscation of his goods and forbade the election of a successor. The see was vacant until 628. At a synod held by the Assyrian bishops in 612 without the presidency of a patriarch, the Christology of the energetic monk Bābai the Great was adopted. Unlike other earlier Assyrian formulas of the Antiochene position, that of Bābai can in no sense be interpreted in a way that would make it harmonize with the decrees of the Council of Chalcedon.

In 628 Chosroes was assassinated, and his son Kavādh II came to the throne. A secret convert to Christianity, the new king permitted the Assyrians to elect a catholicos, Ishojabh (also Ishō'jab; 628–44 or 646), but he died after six or eight months of a troubled reign. Yazdgard III (631–51), the last of the Sassanids, was unable to muster sufficient forces to ward off the attacks of Islam and in 637 saw the fall of his capital city Seleucia-Ctesiphon.

Monasticism and Missionary Endeavors. Despite the frequent persecutions from without and the scandals,

schisms, and dissensions from within, the Assyrian Church showed a remarkable vitality under the Sassanids, especially in the growth of monastic institutions and in the founding of numerous missions. Already in the 3d century there were hermits in Persia leading ascetical lives in solitude. In the writings of APHRAATES in the following century mention is made of the "sons" and "daughters of the covenant," men and women dedicated to study and prayer, leading celibate lives in a community. This native monastic movement was influenced by the ideals and practices of immigrant monks from Egypt. The great organizer and reformer of monasticism among the Assyrians was Abraham of Kashkar (501–86). After traveling in Egypt and spending some time in Nisibis, he established a retreat on Mount Izlā. Numerous other monasteries were founded by his disciples. A distinctive characteristic of Assyrian monasticism was the active interest that the monks took in the physical and spiritual needs of their peoples.

The missionary labors of the Assyrians were partially due to the persecutions to which they were subject. Driven from their homes, they established new centers of Christianity in remote parts of the kingdom or in foreign lands. But they also engaged in active missionary activities along the great trade routes leading to the north, south, and east. Before the Arab conquest of Persia they had brought Christianity to Yemen and the eastern coasts of Arabia. Other missionaries were active on the islands of Socotra and Ceylon (modern-day Sri Lanka) and in South India, as is evidenced by Pahlavi inscriptions of the 6th and 7th centuries on stone crosses found at Saint Thomas's Mount near Madras and at Kottayam in Travancore. During this period there were Assyrian churches, bishops, and even metropolitans in the great caravan cities of Central Asia, including Merv, Herat, and Samarkand.

The first Assyrian missionaries reached China in 631. Four years later one of them, Aluoben (Alopen) visited Emperor Taizong (T'ai Tsung) in his capital of Changan, more recently known as Xi'an (Sian). He received permission to preach the "Luminous Doctrine," as Christianity was then known in China. During the course of the next century several monasteries and a metropolitanate were established. The early history of this mission has been recorded on the so-called "Nestorian Monument" of Xi'anfu erected in February 781 and discovered in 1625. The imperial edict of 845 primarily against the Buddhists caused serious harm to the Assyrian Church in China, and by the 10th century Christianity had completely disappeared from the empire.

Assyrian Church under Islamic Rule. The conquest of Persia by the Arabs brought two centuries of relative peace and prosperity to the Assyrian Church. The Muslims granted the Christians, who were monotheists and to a great extent Semites like themselves, freedom of worship and the right to make converts among the Persians. Realizing their own cultural inferiority, they employed Christian scholars to translate the writings of the ancient Greek philosophers into Arabic and were thus able to acquire the Hellenic culture that they later communicated to the Christians of the West. But Islamic rule also had its disadvantages. Ordinary Christians were forced to accept a lower position in society and to pay a special tax. The Assyrian catholicos came to be regarded as the civil head of his community, especially after the patriarchate was moved to Baghdad, and this increased the rivalry for election. But, despite these difficulties, the missionary activities of the Assyrians continued to flourish, especially under Timotheus I (780–823). Missionaries sent out by him made numerous converts in Tibet and Chinese Turkestan, who were to be of great importance because of the connections these peoples had with the Mongols.

One of the sons of Genghis Khan (1162–1227) married a Christian princess of the Keraits, and she became the mother of his two most famous grandsons, Kublai (1216–94) and Hulagu Khan (1217–65). Hulagu's favorite wife was a Christian, and Mangu, grand khan from 1251 to 1259, is said to have been baptized by an Armenian bishop. Under Mongol rule Christian missionaries were again able to enter China, and the Assyrians had an archbishop in the Mongol capital of Kambaluk (modern-day Beijing).

After falling into the hands of the Seljuk Turks in the 10th century and then passing through a period of political anarchy, Persia was subjected to the Mongols by Hulagu Khan in 1258. In 1281 Mark, a Mongolian monk and son of an archbishop, who had come to Baghdad to visit the center of Assyrian Church, was named catholicos and took the name of Yabhalaha III. Of a kindly disposition, he ruled the Assyrian Church through a stormy period under seven Mongol kings and had the consolation of baptizing some of them. His hope that the Mongols would join forces with the Christians of the West to crush Islam was doomed to failure. After a period of vacillation the Mongols turned to Islam rather than to Christianity, finding it more compatible with their temperament. Under the Muslim Timurlane (1379–1405) the Assyrian Church suffered a terrible persecution. All those who failed to escape to the mountains were put to the sword, and very little is heard of the Assyrian Christians in these areas until the accession of 'Abbas the Great in 1582.

Attempts at union with Rome. The Latin Crusades provided various contacts between the Churches of the East and the West, and these in turn led to more or less successful attempts at reunion with Rome. Negotiations were frequently conducted through Franciscan, Dominican, and, in later centuries, Jesuit missionaries, but not always with sufficient understanding and prudence. In the spring of 1235 the Dominican William of Montferrat was sent by Gregory IX to the Catholicos Sabrīshō' V, who had shown some interest in a reunion. This embassy proved to be fruitless, but soon after it an Assyrian archbishop, probably from Damascus, on the occasion of a pilgrimage to Jerusalem made his submission to the Holy See and was congratulated by Pope Gregory IX in a letter dated July 29, 1237. In 1304 the Catholicos Yabhalaha sent to Rome from Maragha a profession of faith through a Dominican returning to Italy, but his desire for reunion was frustrated by the Assyrian clergy and faithful. In 1340 Elias, Archbishop of Nicosia in Cyprus, made a profession of faith in which he upheld the authority of the Holy See, but it was only in 1445 that a reunion of the Assyrian Church in Cyprus was officially recorded in Rome. This is to be found in a bull of EUGENE IV, which he promulgated after the Metropolitan Timotheus had made his profession of faith before the archbishop of Colossae.

In 1551 a group of Assyrian Christians eager for reunion met at Mosul and delegated Sullāqā, superior of the monastery of Rabbān Hormizd, near Alkōsh, to go to Rome. There he made his profession of faith and on April 28, 1553, received the pallium and the title of Chaldean patriarch. He returned to the East with two Maltese Dominicans to help him with the work of reunion. After taking up residence at Diárbekr, he was imprisoned and executed at the beginning of 1555. The united Chaldeans chose as his successor 'Abdīshō, the metropolitan of Jeziret ibn-Omar (Beit-Zabdaï), who went to Rome and received the pallium from Pius IV.

During the 17th and 18th centuries reconciliations with various Assyrian groups continued to be made. By the 19th century the Assyrian Church was greatly diminished in numbers. Their chief center was around Lake Urmia in the mountainous regions of northwestern Persia. In the 1830s and 1840s they were frequently attacked and massacred by the neighboring Kurds. During these same decades they were visited by English and American Protestant missionaries, and toward the close of the century, by Russian missionaries as well. During World War I their numbers were further diminished by marauding bands of Turks, Kurds, and Muslim Persians. Many fled from the mountains of Kurdistan to the plains of Mesopotamia, then under English colonial rule. In 1933, after Iraq's declaration of independence, many Assyrian Christians fled to Syria. In that year, the Assyrian Patriarch Mar Simon XXIII was sent into exile in the United

States. Since then, the Assyrian patriarchs have resided in exile in the United States.

The 1990s was a period of significant ecumenical developments. On Nov. 11, 1994, Mar Dinkha IV of the Assyrian Church and Pope John Paul II signed a Common Christological Declaration in the Vatican, recognizing that the Assyrians and Catholics are united in a common christology. In 1996, Mar Dinkha IV met his Chaldean Catholic counterpart, Patriarch Raphael I Bidawid and signed a joint patriarchal statement on joint collaboration between the two churches. The Holy Synods of both churches subsequently ratified a ''Joint Synodal Decree for Promoting Unity'' in 1997. At the beginning of the 21st century, the Assyrian Church is not in formal communion with any church.

Bibliography: A. ATIYA, *A History of Eastern Christianity* (London 1968). H. HILL, ed., *Light from the East: A Symposium on the Oriental Orthodox and Assyrian Churches* (Toronto 1988). R. ROBERSON, *The Eastern Christian Churches: A Brief Survey* (6th ed. Rome 1999).

[M. J. COSTELLOE/EDS.]

ASTARTE

A Canaanite goddess. In the texts of UGARIT she plays the subordinate role of introducing adorers to BAAL. In the OT, however, she is interchanged repeatedly with Asera (Asherah), frequently associated with Baal, and is probably taken to be Baal's wife. There is no agreement as to which goddess—Asera, Anath, or Astarte—was Baal's consort. Astarte is the Greek form of the Hebrew ʻaštōret (see below), often used in the plural ʻaštārōt as referring to her various local manifestations. She was called Ištar in Babylonia, where her cult originated and where she was identified with the planet Venus. Venerated as the goddess of fertility and war throughout the ancient Semitic world, she began to be worshiped by the Israelites after their arrival in Palestine (Jgs 2.13; 10.6). Although Samuel opposed her cult (1 Sm 7.3–4;12.10), King SOLOMON adopted it and erected in Jerusalem an altar in her honor, which was later destroyed by Josia (1 Kgs 11.1–13; 2 Kgs 23.13). That her cult was popular is shown by numerous statues and plaques of the ''naked goddess'' type found even in Israelite levels of archeological sites. The deliberate misvocalization in the Hebrew OT of original ʻaštart into ʻaštōret by taking the vowels from the word bōršēt (shame), indicates a later attempt to ridicule the cult.

Bibliography: *Encyclopedic Dictionary of the Bible* 162–163. T. KLAUSER, *Reallexikon für Antike und Christentum* 1:806–810. J. B. PRITCHARD, *Palestinian Figurines in Relation to Certain Goddesses Known through Literature* (Philadelphia 1943).

[H. MUELLER]

ASTERIUS OF AMASEA, ST.

Bishop and preacher; b. Cappadocia, *c.* 350; d. Amasea, *c.* 410. Asterius, having specialized in rhetoric and the practice of law, abandoned this profession to enter the clergy, and subsequently became metropolitan of Amasea in Pontus between 380 and 390. His extant writings consist of 16 homilies and panegyrics of the martyrs (*Patrologia Graeca* 40:155–480). PHOTIUS supplies quotations from ten other sermons that have disappeared (PG 104:201–204). Some works formerly attributed to him belong to his namesake, ASTERIUS THE SOPHIST (d. 341). His style is elegant, vigorous, and vivid, as in his description of a hunting scene in a sermon on Lazarus. His sermons show the high esteem in which the martyrs were held and throw light upon contemporary events, such as the persecution under Julian the Apostate and the pagan customs still in vogue at the beginning of the year. A sermon on St. EUPHEMIA is important in the history of art, because a painting of this saint is compared with the works of Euphranor and Timomachus. The Second Council of Nicaea (787) twice referred to this picture as a proof that sacred images were venerated in the ancient Church. This council also speaks of Asterius as a saint, and he is honored as such by the Greek church.

Feast: Oct. 30.

Bibliography: ASTERIUS OF AMASEA, *Ancient Sermons for Modern Times*, tr. G. ANDERSON and E. J. GOODSPEED (New York 1904). J. QUASTEN, *Patrology* (Westminster MD 1950) 3:300–301. A. BRETZ, *Studien und Texte zu Asterios von Amasea* (Leipzig 1914). M. RAUER, *Lexikon für Theologie und Kirche*, ed. J. HOFER and K. RAHNER (Freiburg 1957–65) 1:958.

[S. J. MCKENNA]

ASTERIUS THE SOPHIST

Born in Cappadocia; died *c.* A.D. 341. He was a pupil of Lucian of Antioch, but unlike his teacher, who died a martyr, Asterius apostatized in the persecution of Maximinus. St. ATHANASIUS, who is the chief source for his life, calls him the ''sacrificer'' because of his apostasy, and, on his return to the faith, the ''advocate'' of Arian doctrines. As a well-trained sophist—St. Athanasius calls him ''the many-headed sophist''—he was a persuasive speaker and a voluminous writer. He exercised considerable influence as he traveled from place to place, participating even in synodal discussions. He has been characterized as perhaps the first Arian writer. At any rate, Arius employed his works in his polemic against the Nicene teachings, and by his own example encouraged their circulation. The *Syntagmation* of Asterius, known only through excerpts quoted by Athanasius and Marcellus of Ancyra, is Arian in its treatment of the Son. According to Marcellus, Asterius drew copiously on the writings or official pronouncements of Eusebius of Nicomedia and other Arian-minded bishops to support his position. His *Refutation of Marcellus* is lost. The church historian Socrates (*Hist. eccl.* 1.36) stated that Asterius accused Marcellus of SABELLIANISM; St. Jerome (*De vir. ill.* 94), that he wrote commentaries on the Epistle to the Romans, on the Gospels, and on the Psalms, and many other works, all of which were long regarded as lost. Since the 1930s, however, M. Richard and E. Skard have discovered 31 homilies, of which 29 are on the Psalms, and 27 fairly large fragments of the Commentary on the Psalms. Nine of the homilies were preached in Easter Week. These finds not only reveal the ability of Asterius as a preacher and theologian, but also furnish valuable information on Antiochene exegesis. It is now clear that Asterius represented a moderate form of Arianism.

Bibliography: J. QUASTEN, *Patrology* 3:194–197, with copious bibliog. G. BARDY, *Recherches sur St. Lucien d'Antioche et son école* (Paris 1936). E. SKARD, ''Asterios von Amaseia und Amasios der Sophist,'' *Symbolae Osloenses* 20 (1940) 86–132.

[M. R. P. MCGUIRE]

ASTORCH, MARÍA ANGELA, BL.

Mystic, virgin of the Poor Clare Capuchins; b. Barcelona, Spain, Sept. 1, 1592; d. Murcia, Spain, Dec. 2, 1665. María Angela was professed as a POOR CLARE in Barcelona. Because of her spiritual maturity she was appointed novice mistress and formation director for her sisters. She was especially successful in these positions because she readily accepted the individuality of those in her care. Later she was elected abbess of the community. Blessed María Angela is often called the ''Mystic of the Breviary'' because her identification with the liturgical life of the Church led her to mystical union with God. Pope John Paul II beatified her at Rome, May 23, 1982.

Feast: Dec. 9 (Capuchins).

Bibliography: M. A. ASTORCH, *Mi camino interior*, ed. L. IRIARTE (Madrid 1985). L. DE ASPURZ, *Beata María Angela Astorch, Clarisa Capuchina, (1592–1665): la mística del breviario* (Valencia 1982). *Acta Apostolicae Sedis* (Rome 1982) 607. *L'Osservatore Romano* (Rome 1849–) English edition, 24 (1982) 6–7.

[K. I. RABENSTEIN]

ASTRAIN, ANTONIO

Spanish Jesuit historian; b. Undiano, Navarre, Nov. 17, 1857; d. Loyola, Spain, Jan. 4, 1928. After joining the JESUITS (1871) and completing his priestly studies, he taught humanities and history to Jesuit scholastics for several years. In 1891 he became editor of the *Mensajero del Sagrado Corazón*. During his editorship he contributed important historical and literary studies to the *Mensajero* on the Spain of Loyola, Spaniards at the Council of Trent, the works of Menéndez y Pelayo and other such topics. Next he joined the staff of the *Monumenta historica Societatis Iesu*. This labor oriented him toward the great work that preoccupied his life after 1895, the principal one on which his scholarly reputation stands, *Historia de la Compañia de Jesús en la asistencia de España*. Seven volumes appeared (1902–25) detailing the Spanish Jesuit story from its origins to the mid-18th century. Illness and death prevented him from completing the history to the Jesuit expulsion from Spanish dominions (1767). The first volume is largely a life of St. IGNATIUS OF LOYOLA, later reworked and published separately. The last four volumes devote half their pages to the work of Spanish Jesuits in the Americas, the Pacific Islands, and the Philippines. Astrain was greatly aided in preparing these sections by the prodigious archival researches of his fellow Jesuit, Pablo Pastells, although Astrain was no stranger in the great document depositories of Spain and Mexico.

[J. F. BANNON]

ASTRAL RELIGION

Worship of the stars, which long antedated ASTROLOGY. It was an underlying element in many ancient cults, more conspicuously in some than in others. The observable combination of change and variety with fixed and undeviating regularity (i.e., the motions of the sun, moon, and planets as contrasted with that of the ''fixed'' stars and constellations) deeply impressed even the profoundest thinkers, such as Aristotle (see *Frag.* 10, found in Sextus Empiricus, *Adv. Mathematicos* 3.20–22), Plato (*Phaedrus* 246F), the Stoics, Immanuel Kant (*Critique of Practical Reason ad fin.*), and even the Biblical poet (Psalm 19). Some writers, both ancient and modern, have held that astral religion was the beginning of true worship as distinct from magic, and have interpreted the Greek and Egyptian mythology as parables or allegories of the heavenly constellations. More probably, however, the constellations were interpreted from current mythology, and so received their names. One cannot fail to see here the poetic instinct at work, endeavoring to describe the harmony of the heavens in personal terms. Some of this poetry was religious, some merely secular—as Plutarch assumed in his meteorological interpretation of Isis and Osiris.

Babylonian Star Worship. The ancient Babylonian religion was the classic development of star worship.

Here the stars were all gods, animate beings of a divine, or at least supernatural, rank. The earliest cuneiform sign for "god" was a star (*). Thus the sun, moon, and planet Venus were identified with Shamash, Sin, and Ishtar; Jupiter was Marduk; Saturn (not Mars) was the war god; Mercury was Nebo, the herald; Mars was Nergal, god of the dead. This system of identification was taken over and modified by the Greeks and Romans, using the names of their own deities.

Among Other Peoples. People in a variety of areas of the world, including the East African Masai and some of the Native North Americans, worshipped the stars. Often the sun was the chief god of the pantheon and the other heavenly bodies were his family of servants. This primeval cult not only influenced many others, both Semitic and Western as well as Egyptian, but even survived them, as when the cult of *Sol Invictus* (the Unconquerable Sun) supplanted many others under the dynasty of the Severi in the Roman Empire of the third century. The god Mithras, originally a friend of the Sun, was finally identified with him. The Egyptian Pharoah Akhnaton (Amenhotep IV) tried to establish the Sun God (Aton) at Heliopolis as the center of the whole Egyptian cult, but he was unsuccessful; the entrenched priesthoods of the old deities rejected this revolution in the direction of monotheism. In pre-Islamic Arabia there was a whole pantheon of astral deities; astral rites and beliefs were found also in ancient China, so widespread was this primitive cult. Among the Indo-Iranian peoples the same phenomenon was found, but in a modified form. The "Heaven God" (or gods) was only the personification of heaven—a usage still reflected, in reverse, in the Jewish religion (e.g., "Let the fear of Heaven [i.e., God] be upon you," Mishnah, Pirke Aboth 1.3). The immense influence of this ancient terminology survived in the Roman imperial and early Christian designation of the first day of the week as "Sun-day" (the very earliest Christian designation was "first day of the week," as in 1 Cor 16.2, or "the Lord's day," Rv 1.10).

Stars in the Bible. Among the Greeks, even in Plato's later writings (*Tim.* 40B), the stars were thought to be animate beings or "visible gods." Among the Hebrews and the Biblical writers, however, the references to stars either were figurative or stressed the sovereignty of the one and only God, their Creator (Is 14.12; Sir 50.6; Rv 22.16; and see Gn 1 and Ps 19). The "seven stars" in Am 5.8 are the Pleiades; in Rv 1.20 they are the seven churches in the Province of Asia. Only in connection with pagan religion and rites are the stars referred to as deities (Am 5.26; cf. Jer 7.18; 19.13; 44.17, 19, 25; Acts 7.43).

Relation of Star Worship and Astrology. It is easy to see how the Greek and Roman inheritance of astral worship led directly to astrology. It had originated in Babylonia and was combined with Iranian influence to enter the West during the two centuries of the Persian Empire (538–330 B.C.) and later. Eudoxus and Theophrastus were the first to show acquaintance with it, and both rejected it (Cicero, *Div.* 2.87; Proclus, *In Tim.* 285f). But with Eudemus of Rhodes a contrast began to be drawn between the baleful and the beneficent stellar beings—a theory derived from Zoroastrian dualism (Damascius, *De princ.* 125). The rest followed easily; star worship had opened the gate to astrology, and even some of the best minds cultivated it henceforth, for it was regarded as a science. *Fata regunt orbem, certa stant omnia lege*, "Fates rule the world, and everything stands firm by law" (Manilius, *Astronomicon* 4.14). Any religious sentiments retained by astrology were derived from the earlier star worship; however, many later writers viewed astrology exclusively as a science with no reference to religion. Thus, Melanchthon the German reformer was an expert astrologer, but would have denied *in toto* astral religion. In passing on the torch to astrology, astral religion met its end, and thus itself reflected the further principle of Manilius (4.16): *Nascentes morimur; finisque ab origine pendet*, "Being born, we begin to die; and the end depends upon the beginning."

In Christian theology and philosophy the Biblical conception naturally prevailed: the stars are "divine" only in a poetic or figurative sense; they are God's creation, His "handiwork," and manifest His glory. Yet they shall fade, or fall from heaven, or be supplanted by other stars in a new heaven, after the Judgment. Nevertheless, the old usage still survived. In the Roman catacombs there are inscriptions that imply that the Christian soul is now *super astra* ("above the stars"), and the beautiful passage in Dn 12.3 is not forgotten: "They shall shine as the stars for ever and ever."

See Also: ASTROLOGY.

Bibliography: F. VON OEFELE et al., J. HASTINGS, ed., *Encyclopedia of Religion and Ethics* (Edinburgh 1908–27) 12:48–101, a series of 12 articles. W. GUNDEL, *Reallexikon für Antike und Christentum*, ed. T. KLAUSER (Stuttgart 1941 [1950]–) 1:810–817. G. R. DRIVER, J. HASTINGS and J. A. SELBIA, eds., *Dictionary of the Bible* (Edinburgh 1942–50) rev. in 1 v. ed. F. C. GRANT and H. H. ROWLEY (New York 1963) 936–938. F. J. BOLL, *Kleine Schriften zur Sternkunde des Altertums,* ed. V. STEGMANN (Leipzig 1950). H. GRESSMANN, *Die hellenistische Gestirnreligion* (Leipzig 1925). E. W. MAUNDER, *The Astronomy of the Bible* (4th ed. London 1923). O. RÜHLE, *Sonne und Mond im primitiven Mythus* (Tübingen 1925); *Die Religion in Geschichte und Gegenwart* (Tübingen 1957–65) 1:662–664. E. ZINNER, *Sternglaube und Sternforschung* (Freiburg 1953).

[F. C. GRANT]

ASTROLOGY

Although the study of astrology has been pursued in many cultures and continues to have an important role in the Far East, this article deals only with Babylonian astrology and its subsequent development in the Greco-Roman world and in Europe. It is important to note that astrology, in many aspects at least, was recognized as a science—not as a pseudoscience—until the 18th century.

Babylonian Astrology. The chief source for information about Babylonian astrology is the library of King Assurbanipal (668–626 B.C.) at Nineveh, from which many thousands of astrological documents and fragments, embodying a simple type of astrology that did not distinguish celestial from terrestrial phenomena, have been recovered. Babylonian HOROSCOPES were applied to the royal family and the land; the earliest known prediction for a private person dates from 263 B.C. The following example is typical: ''If an eclipse of the moon occurs on 14 Sivan and the fourth [east] wind is blowing, enmity will prevail; there will be deaths.''

It is not surprising that astrology arose in Mesopotamia, with its extremely clear atmosphere and a religion that identified various gods with particular heavenly bodies. Babylonian astrology rests ultimately on a single large work of unknown date written in about 70 large tablets, fragmentarily preserved in several recensions. This system, unlike that of the Greeks later, made the Moon more important than the Sun (probably because of its easy observability and conspicuous phases) and arranged the planets in the so-called Babylonian order: Moon, Sun, Jupiter, Venus, Saturn, Mercury, Mars. More than 200 constellations were distinguished, as well as 12 signs of the zodiac, and attention was paid also to comets, meteors, winds, storms, earthquakes, clouds, thunder, and lightning. Although the documents are in Old Babylonian and Assyrian, traces of Sumerian usage suggest that some of this material is earlier than 2000 B.C.

In Classical Greece. Though the early Greeks practiced various forms of DIVINATION, they had no astrology. Minoan art shows little concern with the heavens, and few early Greek myths deal with the stars. Even an author as late as Aristophanes (*Peace* 406–413; 421 B.C.) can refer to the Sun and Moon as barbarian gods. Zeus, despite the etymology of his name, was far more to the Greeks than a sky-god; and this broader conception accords with the fact that the major Greek gods, unlike the Semitic, were not closely bound to nature. The stars were observed for purposes of navigation, but there is hardly a trace of astral religion. Thales of Miletus (6th-century B.C.) and his successors derived much, directly or indirectly, from Babylonian sources (e.g., the rough prediction of solar eclipses, celestial equator, ecliptic, planets,

''The Victory of Christendom over Heathen Stargazing,'' woodcut from an edition of Paul of Middleburg's *''De recta Paschae celebratione,''* published in 1513.

constellations, the 12-hour day), but they used these data to construct a scientific cosmology. Typical of classical Greek rationalism is the story of Pericles (Plutarch, *Pericles* 35), who calmed a frightened sailor by holding up his cloak to show how an eclipse occurs. Among the classical Greeks prophecy based on such phenomena as eclipses and lightning was on the same footing as prophecy from the flight of birds, the entrails of sacrificial animals, and dreams. There were no special astrological techniques.

Greek reason, however, provided a potentially hospitable environment for the introduction of astrology: if the world is governed by unchanging (scientific) laws, then fatalism becomes easy. The early Pythagoreans illustrate the possibilities. They discovered the oldest known scientific laws by experiments with the strings of musical instruments, but they also developed numerical and geometrical symbolisms involving astral elements, such as the harmony of the spheres.

Plato and even Aristotle (who was no mystic) believed the stars to be divine, no doubt under Oriental influence. The planets play an important role in the myth of Er, son of Armenius (an Oriental name), at the end of the *Republic*, and Plato emphasizes the relationship between souls and stars in *Timaeus* (41D). The appendix to the *Laws* by Plato's nephew and successor, Philip of Opus, is full of astral lore. Such developments prepared the way for astrology, though so distinguished an astronomer as Eudoxus of Cnidus (*c.* 350 B.C.) was opposed to it.

Rise of Astrology in the Hellenistic Age. Between Alexander and Augustus the Greek world was altered by world-shaking political, economic, and cultural upheavals. Reason (*logos*) gave way to esoteric knowledge (*gnosis*). Imperturbability (*ataraxia*) before the buffetings of FORTUNE became the great desideratum, and chance was deified (*see* FATE AND FATALISM). Carneades (214–128 B.C.) and Panaetius (*c.* 185–109 B.C.) might oppose astrology, but Posidonius (*c.* 135–50 B.C.) and Hipparchus of Nicaea (*c.* 190–*c.* 126 B.C.), the greatest Greek astronomer, both accepted its validity.

It was in Hellenistic Egypt, where all races and cultures mingled, that Greek astrology finally developed. There is no evidence of astrology in Egypt under the old Kingdom, but Babylonian lore reached there under the Ptolemies and was combined with the exact data of Greek astronomy to produce the strange two-headed monster of astrology, partly religious and mystical and partly scientific. There can be no doubt about the importance of Greek astronomy in this development, for the standard order of the planets was the so-called Greek, which is based on the observed periods of revolution: Moon, Mercury, Venus, Sun, Mars, Jupiter, Saturn. The Sun was most important, not the Moon as in Babylonian astrology. Some Egyptian star lore also entered the system: for example, the decans, a series of 36 constellations, each ruled a ten-day week. The earliest authoritative handbook now known, called *Nechepso-Petosiris* (*c.* 170–150 B.C.) after the names of its supposed authors, remained the astrological bible until the publication of Ptolemy's *Tetrabiblos.*

Dominance of Astrology in the Greco-Roman World. Astrology swept the Greco-Roman world, reaching all races, nations, and types of men: rulers, scholars (such as Varro), philosophers (*see* NEOPYTHAGOREANISM), and also the well-to-do, both aristocrats and *nouveaux riches* (such as Trimalchio in Petronius's *Cena Trimalchionis* 39, 77). It invaded the sciences of medicine, botany, chemistry (via alchemy), and mineralogy. It had a central place also in the mystery religions, especially that of Mithras, whose votaries invoked the

planet ruling the day of the week. In the end, only the skeptics and Epicureans held out against astrology.

At first it was available only to the rich; the necessary computations were complicated and difficult, and consequently astrologers were often called *mathematici*. But the Julian calendar reform of 46 B.C., introduced later in outlying parts of the empire, changed this. The Sun now entered a new sign of the zodiac, usually on the 25th of the month, the Moon was easily observable, and the planets were assigned each to a day of the week (first evidence is found in Tibullus, 1.3.18). With the new calendar the poorest persons, even slaves, could afford astrology, and its use became almost universal. The popularity of talismans and amulets shows that astrology was often combined with belief in MAGIC, while the educated resorted to it because it contributed to apathy by removing the unexpected. Stoicism was its natural home. The final, complete victory of astrology is well illustrated by the emperor Aurelian's introduction of the worship of *Sol invictus* into the state cult after his victory over Palmyra in A.D. 273.

Astrology's success is hard for the Western mind to comprehend, but it doubtless came about because astrology offered a causal explanation, based on the most advanced science, of everything that occurs. Since people of antiquity often thought "in myths," no one attacked the mythological foundation of astrology. It could, and sometimes did, lead to atheism, as in the case of the emperor Tiberius; but to most men it was a cosmology that was also a religion, and a universal religion in contrast with belief in the Greek and Roman gods, who were essentially local.

Astrology and Christianity. Christianity is fundamentally opposed to astrology; yet the earliest Christian documents contain references to it, partly in opposition (Gal 4.9–11; Rom 8.38; Col 1.16; 2.8, 20), but partly because astrology permeated the entire culture. The Church, by calling Christ "the sun of justice" (a phrase derived from Mal 3.20), substituted Him for Sol; and in the 4th century it deliberately put His Nativity on December 25, the birthday of the Sun, when "lux crescit." Christ was now "the light of the world" in a symbolic sense, but His day was still called *dies solis* (Sunday) in the West, as contrasted with *Kyriake* (the Lord's Day) in the East. The Gospels speak of the eclipse at Christ's death and of the wonderful star seen by the Magi, a phenomenon that Christian defenders of astrology always cited. Astrology must have continued or even begun to revive among Christians, for Tertullian found it necessary to state that God tolerated it only until Christ's birth. Lactantius and St. Augustine believed that demons were at work in the stars and in astrology, but that their influence could be overcome through God's grace. It should be observed that astrology is logically compatible with a belief in predestination.

Astrology among the Byzantines and in Islam. The Church Fathers were not completely successful in rooting astrology out, since it pervaded all ancient culture, and it revived during the Byzantine renaissance of the 9th century along with Greek astronomy, which was rediscovered partly in original Greek documents and partly in Arabic translations. The Byzantine emperor Manuel Comnenus (A.D. 1143–80) relied on astrology and defended it on the basis of natural science, the Gospels, and the Fathers. Greek translations of Arabic and Persian astrological treatises became common, though some leading Byzantine astronomers and Churchmen condemned the art. The revived Greek doctrines spread from Byzantium to the West long before the fall of Constantinople.

Astrology flourished under Arabic influence, for Islam is essentially fatalistic, and it spread to the West from Arabic sources as well as from the Greek East. While Avicenna and ibn-Khaldun condemned it, such influential thinkers as al-Kindi and Averroës supported it. As late as 1909 the sultan Abdul-Hamid II still had a court astrologer. Christians came in contact with Arabs not only during the Crusades but also in Spain and Sicily, so that scholastic philosophy was brought face to face with the problem of astrology. The scholastic philosopher, Michael Scotus (d. *c.* 1235) was court astrologer to Frederick II of Sicily, whose son-in-law Ezzelino also kept astrologers about him, including some Saracens. Roger Bacon also recognized astrology as a science. Many Italian cities, dynasties, and prelates resorted to astrologers; and since medieval culture was international, astrology spread rapidly throughout Europe as early as the 13th century.

Astrology in the Renaissance and Later. Astrology was used by Pope Julius II to set the day of his coronation and by Paul III to determine the proper hour for every Consistory. Leo X founded a chair of astrology at the Sapienza, for by that time no respectable university could ignore the subject. Down to the 18th century many literary works, buildings, and works of plastic art were unintelligible without a knowledge of astrological doctrines.

Astrology pervaded European culture just as it had the culture of the Roman Empire, and, though official Church doctrine opposed it, no one attacked the whole manner of thinking that lay behind it. Even St. Thomas Aquinas had attributed physique, sex, and general character to the stars, and was followed by Dante ("Purg." 17.73). "Inclinant astra, non necessitant" (the stars influ-

ence, they do not compel) was the most that Christian thinkers would allow. The humanists, inspired by later antiquity, only strengthened the movement, and the Reformation made no difference. Melanchthon, for example, lectured on astrology at Wittenberg and published a standard Latin translation of Ptolemy's *Tetrabiblos*. The leading astronomers, including Kepler, Tycho Brahe, and (later) Newton, were usually astrologers also.

The invention of the telescope damaged astrology seriously. The seven Pleiades, of which most people can see but six, were discovered to include scores. Two more planets, Uranus and Neptune, were presently discovered, as well as hundreds of planetoids between Mars and Jupiter, and thousands of stars whose very existence destroyed the apparent primacy of the traditional constellations. Astrology's neat system, which had never been really neat or systematic, broke down. As a pseudoscience astrology survives only among the uneducated and the credulous, while the influence of the heavenly bodies upon Earth and man has become the subject of various strictly scientific studies without occult implication.

See Also: ASTRAL RELIGION.

Bibliography: M. VERENO and J. C. PILZ, *Lexikon für Theologie und Kirche,* ed. J. HOFER and K. RAHNER, 10 v. (2d, new ed. Freiburg 1957–65) suppl., *Das Zweite Vatikanische Konzil: Dokumente und Kommentare,* ed. H. S. BRECHTER et al., pt. 1 (1966) 1:964–967. J. H. CREHAN, H. F. DAVIS et al., *A Catholic Dictionary of Theology* (London 1962–) 1:179–182, with bibliog. F. VON OEFELE et al., *Encyclopedia of Religion and Ethics,* ed. J. HASTINGS, 13 v. (Edinburgh 1908–27) 12:48–103, a comprehensive world coverage. F. J. BOLL, *Sternglaube und Sterndeutung,* ed. W. GUNDEL (4th ed. Leipzig 1931).

[H. S. LONG]

ASTROS, PAUL THÉRÈSE DAVID D'

French cardinal, archbishop; b. Tourvès (Var), Oct. 15, 1772; d. Toulouse, Sept. 29, 1851. He was ordained in 1797. In 1802 he was named a canon in the Cathedral of Notre Dame in Paris. He was assigned in 1806 to draw up the Imperial Catechism. When the Archdiocese of Paris fell vacant in 1808, D'Astros was appointed vicar capitular. In this position he opposed the ecclesiastical pretensions of NAPOLEON I and withstood the efforts of Cardinal MAURY, the Emperor's appointee, to take possession of the see without the approval of Pope PIUS VII. As a result D'Astros was imprisoned (1811–14). While bishop of Bayonne (1820–30) and archbishop of Toulouse (1830–51) and cardinal (1850) he was a zealous and capable pastor and administrator. D'Astros, a conservative, was a supporter of GALLICANISM. He denounced Hugues Félicité de LAMENNAIS to Rome and composed a censure of 56 propositions drawn from the latter's writings. The archbishop asserted his independence of the July Monarchy and upheld vigorously liberty of education for Catholic schools. As a champion of the diversities in the traditional Gallican liturgy he opposed Dom Prosper GUÉRANGER.

Bibliography: P. DROULERS, *Action pastorale et problèmes sociaux. . .chez Mgr. d'Astros* (Paris 1954). J. BELLAMY, *Dictionnaire de théologie catholique,* ed. A. VACANT, 15 v. (Paris 1903–50; Tables générales 1951–) 1.2:2142–43. J. DEDIEU, *Dictionnaire d'histoire et de géographie ecclésiastiques,* ed. A. BAUDRILLART (Paris 1912–) 4:1253–55. G. LAZARE, *Dictionnaire de biographie française* (Paris 1929–) 3:1383–88. R. C HALUMEAU, *Catholicisme* 1:970–971.

[M. H. QUINLAN]

ASTRUC, JEAN

French physician of the 18th century who played an important role in the history of biblical criticism; b. Suave (Tarn), France, March 19, 1684; d. Paris, May 5, 1766. Though his father was a Protestant at the time of Jean's birth, and though the latter was baptized in the Protestant church at Suave, the elder Astruc was soon after converted to Catholicism, and his son was raised and always lived as a Catholic. Jean Astruc received his higher education at Montpellier, France, where he became a doctor of medicine in 1703. He succeeded his former master, Pierre Chirac, in teaching medicine at Montpellier (1707–10) and then obtained the chair of anatomy at the University of Toulouse. After a year in Paris and a year as physician to King Augustus II of Poland, he was appointed medical consultant to Louis XV of France and later (1731) professor at the College of France. Besides publishing several works on medical topics, he took a side interest in philosophy, theology, and biblical exegesis. He is best known for a work that he published anonymously, *Conjectures sur les mémoires originaux dont il paraît que Moise s'est servi pour composer le livre de la Genèse* (Brussels 1753). Noticing that in certain parts of Genesis, God is designated by the Hebrew word "Elohim" and in other parts by the Hebrew word "Yahweh" he strung the Elohim parts together and the Yahweh parts together and thus obtained two fairly coherent parallel accounts. From this he concluded that Moses had used two principal documents, an Elohistic one and a Yahwistic one, in addition to ten smaller documents (from Moab, Edom, etc.); Moses would have placed the documents one parallel to the other, but later copyists jumbled them together. Thus, was born the so–called documentary hypothesis, which Astruc proposed as merely probable and expressly subject to the judgment of the church. This hypothesis as applied to the other books of the PENTATEUCH by J. G. Eichhorn and K. D. Ilgen won favor, especially in Germany. Although Astruc was not correct in most of the points of his theory about the composition of Genesis, his acute observation about the Elohistic and the Yahwistic documents used in the composition of this book laid the foundation for the modern, much more elaborated documentary hypothesis on the composition of the Pentateuch.

Bibliography: A. LODS and P. ALPHANDÉRY, *Jean Astruc et la critique biblique au XVIIIe siècle* (Paris 1924). A. M. LAUTOUR, *Dictionnaire de biographie française* 3:1391–94. E. O'DOHERTY, "The Conjectures of Jean Astruc, 1753," *The Catholic Biblical Quarterly* 15 (1953) 300–304. J. DE SAVIGNAC, "L'oeuvre et la personnalité de Jean Astruc," *La Nouvelle Clio* 5 (1953) 138–147. A. STROBEL, *Lexikon für Theologie und Kirche* 2 1:967. E. KUTSCH, *Die Religion in Geschichte und Gegenwart* 3 1:666. P. AUVRAY, *Catholicisme* 1:971.

[A. M. MALO]

ASYLUM, CITIES OF

Designated sanctuary cities in Israel that took the place of local altars in offering protection to the involuntary manslayer who fled for his life from the blood avenger. Among many ancient peoples, the inviolable right of asylum at a designated sanctuary for the fugitive was a common institution (Tacitus, *Ann.* 3.60; Strabo, 16.2.6; 1 Mc 10.43; 2 Mc 4.33). As part of their culture, the Israelites inherited the ancient nomadic custom of BLOOD VENGEANCE, imposed as a duty on the nearest of kin, the *gōʾēl*. He was held responsible to execute the capital punishment by killing the murderer in retribution and avenging the blood of his slain kinsman. As a means of preventing undue blood vengeance, the law provided six cities of refuge to be administered by the Levites (Nm 35.6). The place of refuge took the manslayer from the personal police action of the avenger (*gōʾēl*) and gave him an opportunity for an orderly trial. Such a sanctuary was meant only for the unintentional or accidental manslayer (Dt 4.42; 19.4). He was safe in the city of refuge as long as he stayed there, but outside of it, he could be put to death by the avenger. Once the prevailing high priest died, the manslayer could return home and have no further anxieties (Nm 35.25–28). Of these six cities, Deuteronomy represents Moses himself selecting three in Transjordan, namely, Bosor in the tribe of Reuben, Ramoth in the tribe of Gad, and Golan in the tribe of eastern Manasse (Dt 4.43). On the western side of the Jordan, three other cities were chosen, namely, Cedes in Nephthali, SHECHEM in Ephraim, and HEBRON in Juda (Jos 20.1–9).

Bibliography: R. DE VAUX, *Ancient Israel, Its Life and Institutions* (New York 1961) 160–163, 276, 414. *Encyclopedic Dictio-*

nary of the Bible 164–165. N. M. NICOLSKY, "Das Asylrecht in Israel," *Zeitschrift für die alttestamentliche Wissenschaft* 48 (1930) 146–175. J. P. E. PEDERSEN, *Israel: Its Life and Culture,* 4 v. in 2 (New York 1926–40; repr. 1959) 1:396–397, 425. M. GREENBERG, "City of Refuge," in G. A. BUTTRICK, ed., *The Interpreters' Dictionary of the Bible* 1:638–639; "The Biblical Conception of Asylum," *Journal of Biblical Literature* 78 (1959) 125–132. M. HARAN, "Studies in the Account of the Levitical Cities," *ibid.* 80 (1961) 45–54.

[J. E. STEINMUELLER]

ASYLUM, RIGHT OF

The custom or privilege by which certain inviolable places become a recognized refuge for persons in danger. Asylum may take a secular form, such as an immunity granted to a locality (i.e., a city of refuge or an embassy with extraterritorial rights), or a religious form, when it is attached to a consecrated place.

Religious asylum, or "sanctuary," with which the present article is concerned, is found at some stage in the history of most religions. It assumes special prominence when the maintenance of justice by public authority is weak, for it limits the excesses of private vengeance. Asylum was honored by the Jews (Ex 21.12–14; Nm 35.11–29; Dt 19.1–13), by the Egyptians, by the Greeks, and to a lesser extent by the Romans. As Christianity became the religion of the Roman Empire, a right of asylum became attached to churches, though at first it was simply a delay of pursuit while the clergy made intercession for the refugee.

In medieval Europe asylum attached to a sacred place was usually independent of intercession. It assumed an important place in the peace movement of the 11th century, protecting not only those accused of crime, but also peasants, merchants, and others threatened by the violence of the time (*see* PEACE OF GOD). During the 12th century the canon law of asylum was elaborated (e.g., *Corpus Iuris Canonicis,* c.17 q.4).

As civil society extended its authority late in the Middle Ages, asylum declined in importance, a fact recognized by the popes since Gregory XIV (*Cum alias,* May 24, 1591).

Bibliography: J. C. COX, *The Sanctuary and Sanctuary Seekers of Medieval England* (London 1911). P. TIMBAL DUCLAUX DE MARTIN, *Le Droit d'aisle* (Paris 1939). L. R. MISSEREY, *Dictionnaire de droit canonique,* ed. R. NAZ (Paris 1935–65) 1:1084–1104. J. LECLER, *Catholicisme* 1:909–913.

[M. M. SHEEHAN]

ATHALA OF BOBBIO, ST.

Abbot; b. Burgundy, *c.* 570; d. March 10, 627. His life was written by his contemporary JONAS OF BOBBIO. After having been educated at Lyons and having become a monk at Lérins, Athala (or Attalas) sought the stricter observance of Luxeuil. Though nominated to replace COLUMBAN, who had been exiled by Brunhilde (610), he followed the Irish ascetic into northern Italy, where they established the monastery of Bobbio. Here he succeeded Columban as abbot (*c.* 615), combatted ARIANISM among the LOMBARDS, and sided with the pope in the schism of Aquileia over the condemnation of the THREE CHAPTERS.

Feast: March 10.

Bibliography: B. KRUSCH, *Monumenta Germaniae Historica: Scriptores rerum Merovingicarum* 4:113–119. *Bibliotheca hagiograpica latina antiquae et mediae aetatis* (Brussels 1898–1901) 1:742–744. J. L. BAUDOT and L. CHAUSSIN, *Vies des saints et des bienhereux selon l'ordre du calendrier avec l'historique des fêtes* (Paris 1935–56) 3:232–233. A. BUTLER, *The Lives of the Saints,* ed. H. THURSTON and D. ATTWATER (New York 1956) 1:547–548. *Bibliotheca Sanctorum* 2:565–567.

[J. E. LYNCH]

ATHANASIAN CREED

Also called the *Quicumque-vult* ("Whoever wills [to be saved]") or for short, *Quicumque* from its opening words; a profession of the Christian faith in 40 rhythmical sentences. Although originally private and non-liturgical, it gradually found its way into the liturgy of the Western Church in the early Middle Ages. It achieved quasi-ecumenical standing in Carolingian times, and the scholastics of the 13th century placed it on a par with the Apostles' and Nicene Creeds.

Content. The *Quicumque* deals mainly with the Trinity and the Incarnation. It reflects a doctrinal development corresponding to the era after the Council of CHALCEDON (451). The divine nature is expressed by the term "substance," and the term "person" is used to describe the three in the Trinity. Hypostasis is not used. The distinction of the Persons and their equality are strongly emphasized. The unity of the three Persons in common attributes, such as eternity and omnipotence, is expressed by stating that there is "one omnipotent"—*unus omnipotens non tres omnipotentes*—a usage that St. THOMAS AQUINAS justifies but does not prefer (*Summa theologiae* 1a, 39.3). The Holy Spirit is said to be "from" the Father "and" the Son.

In the theology of the Incarnation, Christ's full and perfect divinity and full and perfect humanity are vindicated. Christ was born by eternal generation from the

Illumination, beginning of Athanasian Creed, from English, "Saint Alban Psalter," 12th century, preserved at Cathedral Treasury, Hildesheim, Germany.

substance of the Father, by temporal generation from the substance of Mary. Christ's humanity is composed of a rational soul and human flesh. In a characteristically Western expression, Christ is said to be equal to the Father in His divinity and less than the Father according to His humanity. EUTYCHIANISM is excluded by the denial of any conversion or confusion of natures and by the affirmation of the assumption of a human nature in the divine Person. The comparison of union of body and soul is used to illustrate the union of the divine and human natures in the person of Christ. The concluding portion of the Athanasian Creed deals with the Passion of Christ, his descent into hell, Resurrection, Ascension, enthronement at the right hand of the Father, the Second Coming, general resurrection, Judgment, and the sanctions of eternal life and eternal fire. The Creed begins and ends with the necessity of so believing for salvation under pain of eternal loss.

Problem of authorship. Attribution of the formula to ATHANASIUS, the 4th-century patriarch of Alexandria, seems to have been a gradual process beginning in the 7th century and continuing uncontested until the 17th century. This attribution is now generally abandoned. Except for a few Eastern scholars, most hold that the original lan-

guage of the Creed was Latin and that the Greek forms are later translations. The content and style of expression as well as the documentary evidence indicate that Athanasius was not its author. The first certain witness to its existence as a creed is CAESARIUS OF ARLES (c. 542) but the first manuscripts in which it occurs are from the 7th and 8th centuries. From southern Gaul or, more exactly, the region around Arles, it seems to have spread to Spain and to the Carolingian Empire. A document of Autun (670) obliging clerics to memorize it attests to its penetration into the liturgy and clerical training.

It may be that the *Quicumque* is the work of several authors and is perhaps a compilation of the decrees of several synods, but most probably it was composed by St. Caesarius, a great admirer of St. Augustine. It is suggested that he built the text from a series of quotations from Augustine's work on the Trinity and other writings. The time of composition may be placed sometime between 434 and 440 (date of *Excerpta Vincentii Lirinensis,* discovered in 1940, which suggest a source for some of the expressions in the Creed), with a terminal date of 542, the year of the death of Caesarius of Arles.

Liturgical use. In Germany the *Quicumque* had penetrated into the liturgy by the 9th century. It was recited on Sunday after the sermon. Later it was used in the Office at Prime. It entered the Roman liturgy somewhat later. It found a place in the service books of a number of Protestant Churches, notably the Anglican BOOK OF COMMON PRAYER and the Lutheran Prayer Book. It formed part of the ordinary Sunday Office for Prime in the Roman liturgy until 1955 when its use was restricted to Prime on the feast of the Most Blessed. Subsequently it was dropped from the breviary altogether.

Quicumque in the Christian Eastern Church. The earliest manuscripts are from the 14th century, but it seems that the Western monks in Jerusalem in the 9th century confronted the Eastern monks with the *Quicumque* in support of the FILIOQUE, since it read ''from the Father and the Son.'' The Eastern theologians at first paid no attention to the claim that attributed the Creed to Athanasius and simply rejected its authority in the matter of the filioque. At a later date, when manuscript evidence showed that the Creed enjoyed some support in Eastern tradition, the filioque text was regarded as an interpolation and deleted. The *Quicumque* was adopted into the Russian liturgy in the 17th century, and into the Greek liturgy beginning in 1780 for a short period.

Bibliography: J. QUASTEN, *Patrology* (Westminster, Md. 1950—) 3:32–33. H. DENZINGER and A. SCHÖNMETZER, *Enchiridion symbolorum* (36d ed. Herder, 1976). J. N. D. KELLY, *The Athanasian Creed* (New York 1964). E. HILL, *The Mystery of the Trinity* (London 1985).

[G. OWENS/EDS.]

ATHANASIUS, ST.

Bishop of Alexandria from 328 to 373, dominant 4th-century churchman, and theologian in the battle for orthodoxy against ARIANISM; b. Alexandria, *c.* 295; d. Alexandria, May 2, 373 (feast, May 2).

Life. Athanasius was born apparently of a Christian family and received a good classical education that was followed by a solid scriptural and theological formation. At an early age (*c.* 312) he entered the ranks of the Alexandrian clergy and was ordained a deacon (*c.* 318) by Bishop Alexander, whom he served as secretary. Contemporary sources say little about his role in the earliest stages of the Arian dispute; undoubtedly not he but Bishop Alexander was the leading figure. Athanasius accompanied Alexander to the Council of NICAEA I (325) and supported his actions but did not occupy the predominant position in this assembly attributed to him in later panegyrics.

Before his death in 328, Alexander designated Athanasius as his successor, and this choice was confirmed by

St. Athanasius.

the Egyptian bishops, despite the opposition on the part of Arians and Meletians. Athanasius first made extensive pastoral visits to the entire Egyptian province, but soon had to face vicious attacks from various enemies. In 331, the partisans of the MELETIAN SCHISM accused him at the court of Constantine I, but Athanasius was able to vindicate himself, and on his return to Alexandria he took severe measures against the Meletians. Next, he became the target of the anti-Nicene reaction, led by the Arian-minded EUSEBIUS OF NICOMEDIA, who had already succeeded in deposing EUSTATHIUS OF ANTIOCH and other bishops for their pro-Nicene stand.

First Exile and Exoneration. With the approval of Constantine, Athanasius was summoned to the Council of Tyre (335), composed almost exclusively of his enemies. Seeing no hope of obtaining a fair judgment, he left for the imperial court to present his case directly to the emperor. There are conflicting reports on what happened in Constantinople; however, Constantine exiled him to Treves in Northern Gaul. On the emperor's death (May 337), his son Constantine II gave Athanasius permission to resume his episcopal duties. Soon afterward, however, the Eusebian bishops deposed him again at the Synod of Antioch (337 or 338) and established first Pistus, then Gregory as bishop in Alexandria. Athanasius protested this violence in an encyclical letter to all Catholic bishops and took his case to Rome, where he found MARCELLUS OF ANCYRA, Asclepas of Gaza, and other victims of the anti-Nicene reaction. Pope Julius I (337–352) convened a Roman synod attended by some 50 bishops in the fall of 340 or spring of 341. The charges brought forth at the Council of Tyre were fully examined, and Athanasius and Marcellus were declared innocent.

The Eastern bishops refused to accept this verdict, and Athanasius remained in the West, where he promoted the monastic ideal in his travels through Italy and Gaul. With Bishop Hosius of Córdoba he traveled to SARDICA, where a general council had been summoned by the emperors Constans and Constantius II (343). The council proved a failure because the Eastern bishops refused to sit in joint session with their Western colleagues, who had Athanasius and Marcellus in their midst. The Western assembly proceeded to examine anew the case of the accused bishops and again fully exonerated them. On the death of the Alexandrian usurper Gregory of Cappadocia, Constantius allowed Athanasius to return to his see, where he arrived in October 346. There followed 10 years of relative peace, which he used to renew Christian life in Egypt, to promote monasticism, and to compose some of his writings, including his *On the Decrees of the Nicene Synod* and *On the Opinion of Dionysius of Alexandria.*

Subsequent Exiles. On the death of Constans in 350, Constantius became sole emperor, and the enemies of Athanasius resumed their agitation against him. Concentrating their efforts in the West, they had him condemned at the Council of Arles in 353 and at the Council of Milan in 355. Later, imperial emissaries were sent to collect signatures from the bishops absent from these councils; the few who resisted, among whom were Pope LIBERIUS (352–366) and HILARY OF POITIERS, were banished to the East, while the centenarian Hosius of Córdoba was detained for a year in the imperial court at Sirmium. Abandoned by the West, Athanasius was attacked at home. In February 356 a military detachment invaded the church where he was celebrating a vigil service; he managed to escape and went into hiding in the Libyan Desert, while an Arian bishop, George of Cappadocia (357–361), was installed in his place. For the next six years, eluding pursuit by moving from one hiding place to another and supported by the loyalty of his clergy and monks, Athanasius managed to govern his flock and even made several secret visits to Alexandria. During this period he composed some of his major writings, including the three *Discourses against the Arians,* the *Life of St. Antony,* the *History of the Arians,* and the *Letters to Serapion* and *to Epictetus.* He kept himself well informed about events in the Christian world, and particularly about the many synods held during these years, each of which proclaimed a

different creed according to the faction of the anti-Nicene coalition enjoying the momentary favor of Emperor Constantius. Like Hilary of Poitiers exiled in Phrygia, Athanasius in his *De Synodis* ridiculed this multiplication of creeds and, powerless, watched the defeat of orthodoxy at the councils of Rimini, Seleucia, and Constantinople.

A reaction set in with the death of Constantius, on Nov. 3, 361. George of Cappadocia was murdered by the rabble (Dec. 24, 361), and the new emperor, JULIAN the Apostate, set the exiled bishops free. In February 362 Athanasius made his triumphant reentry into Alexandria. Immediately he convened a synod, attended mostly by bishops who had suffered for the orthodox faith. Its decisions, contained in the *Tomus ad Antiochenos,* had far-reaching effects and contributed greatly to the restoration of unity in the Eastern Church. The Synod anathematized Arianism and made special note of the heresy's application to the Holy Spirit (so-called Semi-Arianism), and also condemned the first traces of the Christological heresies. It dealt leniently with bishops who had signed the Arian, Homoean formulary under duress, provided they now adhered to the Nicene Creed. By admitting that the Origenistic formula of ''three hypostases'' could have an orthodox meaning, it paved the way for the reconciliation of many Homoiousians. Julian, however, who promoted a revival of paganism, did not desire a strong and united Christianity. In October 362 Athanasius was exiled once more, but the death of the emperor in June 363 set him free. Before regaining his see, Athanasius tried without success to solve the Antiochian schism.

On the death of Jovian in February 364, the new emperor, Valentinian, made his brother Valens coemperor and entrusted him with the government of the Eastern Empire. Valens favored a return to the Homoean (Arian) formulary and resumed the persecution of all who rejected it. For the fifth time, Athanasius went into hiding. Four months later the mutinous attitude of the Alexandrians forced Valens to rescind the exile. Athanasius spent the last years of his life in peace, continuing by his actions and writings to prepare the ultimate triumph of orthodoxy. Before his death, he designated his brother Peter as his successor.

Writings. Athanasius was a prolific author whose literary production was intimately linked with his life and, as such, part of his unceasing battle against the enemies of Christ, as he designated Arianism in any form. This explains the predominantly polemical nature of most of his dogmatic works, the biased selection of documents in his historical compositions, the lack of serenity in his argumentation, and the public character of his letters. Even the *Life of St. Antony* contains an attack against Arianism. For the same reason he cared more for clarity and persuasiveness than for literary excellence.

Dogmatic Writings. The major work in this section is constituted by his three *Discourses against the Arians;* they contain a summary of the Arian doctrine, a defense of the Nicene definition, and a comprehensive discussion of scriptural arguments. The discourses were written, in all probability, during his third exile (*c.* 358). A fourth *Discourse,* added in the Benedictine and Migne editions, is now considered as definitely spurious. The *Oration against the Pagans* and the *Oration on the Incarnation of the Word,* although often edited as separate works, are one treatise mentioned by Jerome as the *Two Books against the Pagans.* Since this work contains no reference to Arianism or to Nicaea, the date of composition is commonly assigned to *c.* 318. A third work *On the Incarnation and against the Arians* deals with the divinity of Christ and of the Holy Spirit. It dates probably from a later period of his life; but its authenticity has been challenged. To this category belong also several letters that are, in fact, short dogmatic treatises: the *Four Letters to Serapion,* written between 359 and 360, in which Athanasius set forth his admirable doctrine on the divinity and procession of the Holy Spirit; the *Letter to Epictetus,* often quoted in later Christological controversies; the *Letter to Adelphus,* on the same theme; and the *Letter to Maximus the Philosopher.* His *Letter concerning the Decrees of the Nicene Council* (*c.* 350 or 351) presents a defense from Scripture and the Fathers of the nonscriptural expressions in the Nicene Creed. The *Letter on the Teaching of Dionysius the Alexandrian* is probably a later addition to the letter on the decrees of Nicaea. Among the dogmatic writings attributed to Athanasius but definitely spurious, the following should be mentioned: *On the Incarnation against Apollinaris;* the *Sermo Maior de Fide;* the *Expositio Fidei;* and the *Athanasian Creed* called the *Quicumque,* the date and authorship of which is still debated.

Historical-Polemical Writings. Athanasius composed several apologies during his third exile from 356 to 362; they include: the *Apology against the Arians,* particularly valuable for its collection of documents pertaining to the councils of Tyre and Sardica; the *Apology to Constantius,* important for its doctrine on Church and State; the *Apology for His Flight;* and the *History of the Arians,* written at the request of the monks with whom he was living in 358. This last book covers events from 335 to 357. To this category belong also his *Letter on the Synods of Rimini and Seleucia* of 359, which contains valuable data on the texts of the various Arian creeds; the *Encyclical Letter to the Bishops,* protesting his expulsion from Alexandria in 339; and the *Encyclical Letter to the Bishops of Egypt and Libya,* written on his expulsion in 356.

Ascetical Writings. Of paramount importance is the *Life of St. Antony,* founder of Christian monasticism. Written *c.* 357 at the request of the Egyptian monks and intended to provide "an ideal pattern of the ascetical life," it enjoyed astonishing popularity and was soon translated into various languages. Particularly in the Latin translation of Evagrius of Antioch, this biographical tract contributed greatly to the establishment of monastic life throughout the Western Christian world. From the literary point of view, it created a new, Christian genre, and set the pattern for countless later lives of monks and saints. The *Letter to the Monk Amun* and the *Letter to Dracontius* also belong in this category. According to Jerome, Athanasius wrote several treatises on virginity; because of this statement, many similar treatises have been attributed to him, creating problems of authenticity that contemporary scholars have only begun to solve. The treatise *On Virginity,* for example, edited among his works (*Patrologia Graeca,* 28:251–282), is defended as authentic by E. von der Goltz but rejected by M. Aubineau. In recent years several other treatises and fragments of works on virginity have been discovered and edited, some in the original Greek, others in Coptic, Syriac, or Armenian translations. Not all of these are genuine writings of Athanasius, but some of them will undoubtedly in time be recognized as his. Noteworthy among these is a *Letter on Love and Self-control* that may well be an original Athanasian Coptic writing.

Homiletic and Exegetical Works. Much remains to be done to determine the authenticity of sermons attributed to Athanasius, either in the collection published in *Patrologia Graeca,* v. 28 or in newly discovered Syriac and Coptic manuscripts. As to his Biblical commentaries, none has survived in full, but numerous fragments are found in ancient CATENAE. Many of these pertain to a *Commentary on the Psalms,* a few, to Genesis or to Ecclesiastes and the Song of Songs. There is also a *Letter to Marcellinus on the Interpretation of the Psalms* that serves as a general introduction on their meaning and use.

Letters. Besides the letters mentioned in the preceding groups, there is a collection of annual Lenten messages, the so-called *Festal Letters.* Thirteen of these have been preserved in a Syriac translation; 17 others, in a recently published Coptic manuscript. Of major importance among these is the festal letter of 367 for its enumeration of the canonical books of the Old and New Testaments. Three other letters were written at the request of Alexandrian synods: *Tome to the Antiochians* (362), *To the Emperor Jovian* (363), and *To the African Bishops* (369). The *Letter to Bishop Rufianus* gives directives for the reconciliation of the Arians; while the *Letter to the Monks* contains a warning against the heretics.

Doctrine. Because Athanasius's life and writings were one long battle against Arianism, his doctrinal horizon is dominated by Trinitarian and Christological controversies; there is little to glean in his writings on other tenets of the Christian faith. His doctrine is eminently traditional; he created no new synthesis of his own, but clarified and defended the central mysteries of the Trinity and the Incarnation by means of revealed concepts rather than philosophical constructions. While not opposed to philosophy in principle, Athanasius had little use for it. The key to his theological thinking is the dogma of Redemption. Like Justin Martyr and Irenaeus of Lyon, he stressed the identity of the Logos with the Son of God become man. He saw the Logos as the mediator of divine salvation rather than as the agent of divine creativity; hence the predominantly soteriological nature of his argumentation.

Against the Arians, Athanasius argued that if Christ were not truly God, He could not have imparted divine life and resemblance to man. Similarly, against the Pneumatomachians, he argued that, since men are divinized and sanctified by partaking of the Holy Spirit, He must have the nature of God. Again, against the incipient Christological errors, Athanasius stressed the reality of the Incarnation and the personal unity of Christ as indispensable conditions for the effectiveness of His redeeming death. In his spiritual doctrine, asceticism and virginity are but means to achieve in man the divine image through the Divine Word, who is the substantial image of the Father.

Bibliography: *Patrologia Graeca*, ed. J. P. MIGNE, 161 v. (Paris 1857–66) v.25–28. H. G. OPITZ, *Untersuchungen zur Überlieferung der Schriften des Athanasius* (Berlin 1935). G. MÜLLER, *Lexicon Athanasianum*, 10 pts. (Berlin 1944–52). X. LE BACHELET, *Dictionnaire de théologie catholique*, ed. A. VACANT et al., (Paris 1903–50; Tables générales 1951–) 1.2:2143–78. J. QUASTEN, *Patrology*, 3v. (Westminster, Md. 1950–) 3:20–79, editions and bibliog. *Bibliographia patristica*, ed. W. SCHNEEMELCHER (Berlin 1956–). H. M. GWATKIN, *Studies in Arianism* (2d ed. Cambridge, Eng. 1900). E. SCHWARTZ, *Zur Geschichte des Athanasius* (Gesammelte Schriften 3; Berlin 1959). H. VON CAMPENHAUSEN, *The Fathers of the Greek Church*, tr. S. GODMAN (New York 1959) 67–79. *Athanasius, Contra Gentes and De Incarnatione*, ed. R. W. THOMSON (Oxford 1971). **Doctrine.** F. LAUCHERT, *Der Lehre des hl. Athanasius* (Leipzig 1895). E. WEIGL, *Untersuchungen zur Christologie des hl. Athanasius* (Mainz 1914). A. GAUDEL, "La Théorie du Logos chez S. Athanase," *Revue des sciences religieuses* 9 (Strasbourg 1929) 524–539; 11 (1931) 1–26. C. HAURET, *Comment le "Défenseur de Nicée" a-t-il compris le dogme de Nicée?* (Rome 1936). L. BOUYER, *L'Incarnation et l'Église-Corps du Christ dans la théologie de S. Athanase* (Paris 1943). F. L. CROSS, *The Study of St. Athanasius* (Oxford 1945). M. RICHARD, "S. Athanase et la psychologie du Christ selon les Ariens," *Mélanges de science religieuse* 4 (Lille 1947) 5–54. A. GRILLMEIER and H. BACHT, *Das Konsil von Chalkedon: Geschichte und Gegenwart*, 3 v. (Würzburg 1951–54) 1:77–102. J. LEBON, "Le Sort du 'consubstantiel' nicéen," *Revue d'histoire ecclésiastique* 48 (Louvain 1953) 632–682. R. BERNARD, *L'Image de Dieu d'après S. Athanase* (Paris 1952). P. GALTIER, "S. Athanase et l'âme humaine du Christ," *Gregorianum* 36 (Rome 1955) 553–589. T. E. POLLARD, "Logos and Son in Origen, Arius and Athanasius," *Studia patristica* 2 (*Texte und Untersuchungen zur Geschichte der altchristlichen Literatur* 64; Berlin 1957) 282–287. G. FLOROVSKY, "The Concept of Creation in Saint Athanasius," *ibid.* 6 (*Texte und Untersuchungen zur Geschichte der altchristlichen Literatur* 81; Rome 1962) 36–57. K. ANATOLIOS, *Athanasius: The Coherence of His Thought* (London; New York 1998). D. BRAKKE, *Athanasius and the Politics of Asceticism* (Oxford; New York 1995). P. WIDDICOMBE, *The Fatherhood of God from Origen to Athanasius* (Oxford; New York 1994). E. P. MEIJERING, *Orthodoxy and Platonism in Athenasius, Synthesis or Antithesis?* (Leiden, 1968); *Athanasius, Contra Gentiles: Introduction, Translation and Commentary* (Philosophia Patrum 7; Leiden 1984). L. W. BARNARD, *Studies in Athanasius Apologia Secunda* (Louvain 1986). T. D. BARNES, *Athanasius and Constantius: Theology and Politics in the Constantinian Empire* (Cambridge, Mass. 1993). C. KANNENGIESSER, *Arius and Athanasius: Two Alexandrian Theologians* ([Aldershot], Hampshire, UK; Brookfield, VT 1991).

[V. C. DE CLERCQ]

ATHANASIUS I, PATRIARCH OF CONSTANTINOPLE

Patriarch 1289 to 1293, 1304 to 1310; b. Adrianople, 1230; d. Constantinople, Oct. 28, 1310. He was baptized Alexius and took the name Athanasius on becoming a monk at Thessalonica, whence he immigrated to the monastery of Esphigmenou on Mt. ATHOS. He undertook a journey to the Holy Land and became a hermit at St. Lazarus on Mt. Galesios, but he soon returned to Mt. Athos. His opposition to the reunion Council of Lyons (1274) and to John Beccus forced him to return to Mt. Galesios and later to go to Ganos in Thrace, where he founded a monastery. Probably during his stay at Mt. Galesios he was ordained; he was selected patriarch of Constantinople by Emperor ANDRONICUS II (1289), and set about stabilizing ecclesiastical discipline. He passed severe measures for the reform of the clergy; despite his own travels, he restrained wandering monks and bound the bishops to residence in their own dioceses. In 1293 reaction against the severity of Athanasius was such that the emperor had to accept his resignation (October 13). Athanasius retired to a monastery of Xerolophus, but he had to be recalled because of the demands of the people. He expelled the Franciscans from Constantinople in 1307 and early in 1310 resigned a second time. He died a short while later in the monastery of Xerolophos. Most of the writings of Athanasius are unedited; 126 letters concerned with the ecclesiastical discipline are known, and he is credited with two catechetical lectures and a canon or hymn in honor of the Mother of God (*Theotokaria*).

Bibliography: *Patrologia Graeca*, ed. J. P. MIGNE (Paris 1857–66) 142:471–528. *Acta Sanctorum* Aug 1:169–175. H. G.

BECK, *Kirche und theologische Literatur im byzantinischen Reich* (Munich 1959) 692. K. BAUS, *Lexikon für Theologie und Kirche,* ed. J. HOFER and K. RAHNER, 10 v. (2d, new ed. Freiburg 1957–65) 1:981. H. DELEHAYE, *Mélanges d'archéologie et d'histoire* 17 (1897) 47–74. R. GUILLAND, *Études sur l'histoire et sur l'art de Byzance. Mélanges Charles Diehl,* v.1 (Paris 1930) 121–140.

[F. CHIOVARO]

ATHANASIUS OF NAPLES, ST.

Bishop; b. 832; d. Veroli, Italy, July 15, 872. He was a pastor of great compassion for the needs of his flock, a competent administrator, and a staunch champion of the Church against the political freebooters of the age. Rather precise details of his life may be gathered from two contemporary works: a vita by JOHN THE DEACON of Naples and another more complete version by an anonymous Neapolitan, who provides also an account of the translation of his remains. His father, Sergius, came from a powerful Neapolitan family, and as defender of his city against Lombard incursions, was elected duke by his fellow citizens; Athanasius' mother, Drusa, was a noble lady.

Athanasius, destined for the clerical life from early youth, came under the tutelage of priests at the church of Santa Maria and of the saintly bishop John IV (d. 849). After the death of John, Athanasius, a deacon only eighteen years of age, was elected bishop and consecrated in Rome by Pope Gregory IV. Personally austere of life, he poured himself out in service to his flock, especially the poor, orphans, and Saracen prisoners. He rebuilt churches, reunited communities of priests and monks, and represented the interests of Naples before the emperor, who esteemed him both for holiness and for his practical conduct of affairs.

After the death of his father and his brother, Duke Gregory, Athanasius suffered the relentless persecution of his ambitious nephew, the younger Duke Sergius, who held Athanasius and other relatives prisoner despite courageous protests of the clergy of both the Latin and the Greek rites. Sergius tried to force him to renounce his episcopacy and retire into a monastery, but, rescued by Louis I the Pious, Athanasius came with honor to Benevento. Sergius's pillaging of Church property and the rebellion of the people against their bishop brought down upon the city of Naples the excommunication of ADRIAN II.

From 867 to 872 Athanasius sought refuge with his brother Stephen, Bishop of Sorrento, and worked indefatigably for a lifting of the ban on Naples and a return to his see. To this end he traveled to Rome and approached the emperor, who was then engaged in freeing southern Italy from Saracen incursions, but on the return trip he died at Veroli, near Monte Cassino. He was 40 years old and had governed the Church of Naples for 22 years. First buried at Monte Cassino, his body was translated to Naples five years later by his nephew Bishop Athanasius II (d. 895) and interred at the church of San Gennaro. Later, probably during the thirteenth century, his relics were translated into the cathedral church, where they are venerated in Saint Savior's chapel.

Feast: July 15.

Bibliography: *Acta Sanctorum* July 4 (1867) 72–89. *Monumenta Germaniae Historica: Scriptores rerum Langobardicarum* 433–435, 439–452, 1065–76. F. BONNARD, *Dictionnaire d'histoire et de géographie ecclésiastiques,* ed. A. BAUDRILLART et al. (Paris 1912) 4:1388–90. *Bibliotheca hagiograpica latina antiquae et mediae aetatis* (Brussels 1898–1901) 1:734–739.

[P. L. HUG]

ATHANASIUS THE ATHONITE, ST.

Byzantine founder of cenobitic monasticism on Mt. Athos; b. Trebizond, *c.* 920; d. Mt. Athos, *c.* 1000. His well-to-do family had him baptized Abraham. He studied at Constantinople and became a monk at Mount Kiminas under Abbot Michael Maleinos, uncle of NICEPHORUS PHOCAS (later emperor). While still a general, Nicephorus employed Abraham as his spiritual director. Abraham changed his name to Athanasius and retired to Mt. Athos as a hermit to escape court honors; however, he was persuaded to accompany the general during his campaign against the Saracens in Crete. With imperial support he founded the Great Lavra on Mt. Athos in 963 and introduced a *Typicon,* or rule, for cenobites based on the common-life ideals of St. BASIL THE GREAT and THEODORE THE STUDITE. Opposition to this innovation developed on the death of the emperor (969) and was combined with the accusation that the success of Athanasius's experiment was a result of imperial influence. But the new emperor, John I Tzimisces, rallied in favor of Athanasius, who had fled to Cyprus. Strengthened by a vision as well as by financial support, Athanasius returned to Mt. Athos, where he was killed *c.* 1000 when the masonry collapsed as he was laying the keystone of a dome. The Athanasian *Hypotyposis* was based upon the Studite rule but shows strong traces of Benedictine influence. A third document, the *Diatyposis,* deals with the succession and station of superiors and the rights of the *epitropos,* or adminstrator, and provides a directory for the Easter Liturgy and other rites. A factual life of Athanasius was written by a younger Athanasius who seems to have obtained most of his information from the founder's disciple, Anthony, and a John Hexapteryos. A second anonymous *Bios,* or life, seems to have been based on the first. Athanasius is named in the preparatory part of the Byzantine Eucharistic Liturgy.

Noted American atheist Madalyn Murray O'Hair leaves court after urging a federal judge to block Pope John Paul II from celebrating Mass on Washington's Mall, arguing it would violate constitutional guarantees separating church and state, Washington, D.C., Oct. 1, 1979. (©Bettmann/CORBIS)

Feast: July 5.

Bibliography: K. BAUS, *Lexicon für Theologie und Kirche,* ed. J. HOFER and K. RAHNER (Freiburg 1957–65) 1:976. P. MEYER, *Die Haupturkunden für die Geschichte der Athosklöster* (Leipzig 1894). L. PETIT, ''Vie de Saint Athanase l'Athonite,'' *Analecta Bollandiana* 25 (1906) 5–89. J. LEROY, ''S. Athanase L'Athonite et la règle S. Benoît,'' *Revue d'ascétique et de mystique* 29 (1953) 108–122. E. AMAND DE MENDIETA, *La Presqu'île des Caloyers: Le Mont-Athos* (Paris 1955). H. G. BECK, *Kirche und theologische Literatur im byzantinischen Reich* (Munich 1959) 578, 588–589. P. LEMERLE, ''La Vie ancienne de S. Athanase l'Athonite,'' *Le Millénaire du Mont Athos* (Chevetogne 1963–) 1:59–100.

[G. A. MALONEY]

ATHEISM

An atheist is a man who lives without God. If he persists in this state, atheism truly becomes a way of life. It is not possible to formulate a single, comprehensive definition of atheism that will cover all cases equally and adequately. The very term is analogical and the notion is realized in actual historical instances only with important variations. After presenting an historical survey, this article discusses three principal types of atheism, and various theological responses to atheism in the distinctively modern situation.

Historical Survey. Statements of an atheistic character are traceable as far back as the pre–Socratic philosophers, while there are indications of at least a practical atheism in primitive tribes discovered by European explorers in Brazil in the 16th century. It was not until the 18th century, however, that explicit and energetic formulations of atheistic doctrine were attempted, as part of a general attack on Christianity and the sociocultural order with which it had become identified.

Greco-Roman antiquity. If there were expressions of atheism in Greco-Roman antiquity, these were for the most part directed against the prevailing civic religions or the popular polytheistic superstitions of the masses. The earliest philosophers did not clearly distinguish matter and spirit, so that it is somewhat inappropriate to accuse them of a MATERIALISM that would be incompatible with belief in divinity, in unequivocal terms. After Socrates it was not uncommon for philosophers, and especially poets, to be suspected of atheism and impiety, but this generally meant a skeptical or critical attitude toward the debased religious practices and fantastic myths on which the populace thrived. Alongside a proliferation of magical and superstitious creeds and rites, there actually developed among the Stoics a purer and more refined notion of a supreme Deity. Pantheism was prominent well into the imperial era of Rome, but there were some signs of a personal approach to a God who was regarded as benign and providential.

It seems clear that ancient proponents of atheism were more concerned with overthrowing moral principles and conventional ideas of right and wrong based on a belief in the gods than with denying absolutely the reality of the divine. The Epicureans in particular, who are most commonly regarded as atheists, did not reject the gods as nonexistent, but taught that men should not fear them and that moral standards must be derived from considerations of man's welfare and happiness and not from the alleged decrees of divine beings. Lucretius' *De rerum natura* may be atheistic in tone and inspiration, but it was intended to be primarily a treatise of a new, radically immanentist humanism. The note struck at this early date, many centuries later signaled the arrival of an unabashed atheism, the sweeping away of every vestige of belief in an order not imposed or controlled by and for mankind itself.

Sources of Modern Atheism. The traces of atheism in the Middle Ages are too faint and uncertain to merit consideration. It may be noted that as early as the 13th century forces of irreligion were in evidence in the intellectual as well as in the political and social orders. When atheism made its unequivocal appearance, it had behind it several centuries of a falling away from the Christian faith and the gradual construction of a way of life from which religion was increasingly excluded. The 16th century witnessed for the first time in the history of Christendom men who openly professed contempt for the faith of Jesus Christ and still maintained positions of public respect and trust, at least in some parts of Europe. Contemporary documents, including citizens' petitions and reports of official commissions, indicate that the 17th century saw the diffusion of anti-Christian ideas and irreligious movements and societies in England, France, the territories of Spain, and Italy. It was not until the 19th century that atheism managed to capture the allegiance of leaders in public life as well as in the arts and sciences. For this full-blown atheism the way was cleared in three stages: (1) libertinism or freethinking, in the 17th century; (2) deistic and anti–Christian naturalism, in the 18th century; and (3) materialistic scientism, after 1750 and well into the 19th century.

The self-styled FREETHINKERS or *libertins* appeared first in France, hard upon a period of ideological strife and chaos that covered the closing decades of the 16th century with a pall of SKEPTICISM. There was a concrete effort to "liberate" reason from faith and morals from the influence of religion. In England the freethinkers were even more outspoken and published numerous works calculated to undermine Christian belief and to substitute for it a cult of humanity and a thoroughly laicized social order. Throughout the 18th century, atheism attracted adherents and fervent supporters among the *philosophes* and advocates of revolutionary upheaval, as well as the champions of a materialistic view of man and of the universe. The French ENCYCLOPEDISTS counted several atheists in their number; but in some instances it is not easy to distinguish outright atheism from other positions, ranging from virulent rejection of the supernatural to pantheism, deism, and agnosticism. The 18th century closed with Kant's attack on metaphysics and the power of natural reason to attain an objective and certain knowledge of God. Concomitant with this, there developed a heightened sensitivity to the misery and suffering of mankind and a corresponding desire for man to find, by his own efforts and here in this life, satisfaction of all his needs and an existence free of all pain and want.

Modern Atheists. At the head of the 19th century stands the figure of G. W. F. HEGEL. To his intellectual posterity Hegel bequeathed a vision of human history caught in the snares of an impersonal ABSOLUTE that would subsequently be misapprehended as the Living God of Christianity. The vision was intolerable, and, to some, atheism seemed the only viable alternative. They

were trapped in this impasse by their rejection of Christian faith. Henceforth atheism was embraced as the only way to preserve men's rights and liberties: enlightenment had to be godless, in opposition to the forces of reaction and ignorance in league with the old religion (*see* HEGELIANISM AND NEO–HEGELIANISM).

In the mid-19th century Karl MARX declared religion to be the "opium of the people" and proposed atheism as the cornerstone of a brave new edifice of humanity transformed by total revolution. His was a war cry, in the name of the downtrodden proletariat, against belief in a God who provides for His creatures and in behalf of a new order in which individuals would provide for themselves (*see* MATERIALISM, DIALECTICAL AND HISTORICAL).

Marx's atheism was scientistic, at least in part, and materialistic; Nietzsche's was lyrical and romantic, a paean of praise of the superman of the future. F. W. NIETZSCHE lashed out against the "slave morality" of Christianity and exhorted whoever could to go beyond the distinction between good and evil and to decide his own future for himself in complete autonomy. Nietzsche left to the 20th century the twofold boast that God is dead and that hereafter man is completely free; for him, the possibilities for human achievement were unlimited.

Both scientistic and romantic atheism continued in the 20th century, but a new and profoundly disturbing voice was heard as well. J. P. Sartre was representative of a new brand of atheism that was deeply skeptical and pessimistic and at times collapsed into sheer NIHILISM. Existentialist atheism agreed that God is dead, but doubted seriously that this liberates man in any sense other than that of leaving him alone and overwhelmed in an absurd universe filled with peril and dread (*see* EXISTENTIALISM).

Vatican II and Atheism. The problem of atheism was faced several times by the popes of the 20th century, especially by Pius XI (*Divini Redemptoris*), Pius XII (*Ad Apostolorum Principis*), John XXIII (*Mater et magistra*) and Paul VI (*Ecclesiam suam*). Quite naturally the problem of atheism was also brought to the attention of the Fathers of Vatican II, who dedicated an important section of the Pastoral Constitution on the Church in the Modern World to the study of the different types of atheism, to their causes, and to the answers the Church should give to them (*Gaudium et spes* 19–21). The Council does not provide a systematic division of the different species of atheism. It speaks of two forms of atheism which take "a systematic expression": the humanistic atheism of the Western world, grounded on the assumption of the incompatibility of man's freedom and dignity with religious belief; and the materialistic atheism associated with communism, grounded on economic and social criteria (ibid. 20). But it is clear that not all the forms of systematic or theoretical atheism can be reduced to these two. As a matter of fact there are many more; and almost all the species of atheism mentioned by the Council (skeptical, agnostic, scientific, positivistic etc., ibid. 19) belong to the systematic or theoretical type.

Vatican II identified several causes of modern atheism. (1) The mystery of God: this leads some people "to believe that man can assert absolutely nothing about him." (2) Fallacious methodologies: "Others use such a method so to scrutinize the question of God as to make it seem devoid of meaning. Many, unduly transgressing the limits of the positive sciences, contend that everything can be explained by this kind of scientific reasoning alone." (3) False humanism: "Some laud man so extravagantly that their faith in God lapses into a kind of anemia, though they seem more inclined to affirm man than to deny God. . . . They claim that this [human] freedom cannot be reconciled with the affirmation of a Lord who is author and purpose of all things." (4) Religious deviations: "Some form for themselves such a fallacious idea of God that when they repudiate this figment they are by no means rejecting the God of the Gospel." (5) The problem of evil: "Atheism results not rarely from a violent protest against the evil of this world." (6) Hedonism and materialism: "Modern civilization itself often complicates the approach to God . . . because it is excessively engrossed in earthly affairs." (7) The scandals of the believers: "To the extent that they neglect their own training in the faith, or teach erroneous doctrines, or are deficient in their religious, moral or social life, they must be said to conceal rather than reveal the authentic face of God and religion" (ibid.).

Types of Atheism. The man for whom atheism is a way of life may be found to (1) deny in fact, by the way he lives, the God in whom he professes to believe, or (2) believe, in spite of himself, in the God in whom he thinks he does not believe, or (3) deny, knowingly and in reality, the true God. These three types may, in J. Maritain's terminology, be designated respectively as (1) the practical atheist, (2) the pseudo–atheist, and (3) the absolute atheist.

Practical Atheism. The practical atheist is perhaps the most common and certainly the most curious, because he is not only unaware of his atheism but would almost infallibly deny it if it were called to his attention. For this type of atheism is grounded in lifestyle: it is as significant of character and personality as any other single physical or mental trait. What is true of every atheist as such—that he lives without God—is verified in a striking manner in the practical atheist. Practical atheism evidently entails a

set of moral standards, a code of ethics that flatly ignores the force of the precepts of the divine and natural moral law. A completely naturalistic moral code guides the practical atheist in his actions only to the extent that he finds in the code a ready justification. Every sinner may be acutely and even painfully aware of his terrible isolation. The practical atheist is neither conscious of, nor disturbed by, the absence of God from his life.

Pseudo-Atheism. The pseudo-atheist is willing to be called an atheist because he denies and repudiates the gods he knows other men worship. He knows of no other god, none he finds understandable or is willing to love and serve. Yet in his heart he yearns for the presence of the God of life; he may even search for years, drawing ever closer to the Unknown God, while continuing to proclaim his unbelief in the ghosts and shadows other men take for God. Life must be lived without God, because God is nowhere to be found. At least He is unrecognizable in these absurd substitutes and surrogates that men falsely endow with His sacred name. The pseudo-atheist has never sufficiently known the true God, whereas the practical atheist has chosen to ignore God and to eject Him effectively from his thoughts and his way of life. In his contacts with the practical atheist, the pseudo-atheist may be chagrined and scandalized by the contradiction between lip service to divinity and the flouting of standards of human decency.

Absolute Atheism. Radical and absolute atheism, that of a life from which God has been consciously and consistently excluded, is not only possible, it is actual. For the absolute atheist the denial of God is the natural and indispensable corollary of the positive affirmation of himself, of humanity focused and concentrated in his own person as his solitary concern and ultimate end. The absolute atheist has much in common with the practical atheist, but the two types should not be confused. The practical atheist almost never thinks of God, and when he does, his thoughts are characteristically fleeting and vague, without personal impact. The absolute atheist, however, may think of God often, but only the more firmly and resolutely to shut Him out of his life and to deepen his attachment to the values that have usurped the place of God.

Christian Response. Atheism has been recognized as a phenomenon that requires a response from all believers. The Church's pastoral concern for the growing phenomenon of world atheism prompted Paul VI to establish the Vatican Secretariat for Non-Believers in 1965. John Paul II in 1993 joined this official body with the Pontifical Council for Culture. The council, composed of bishops and experts in various fields, is charged with establishing dialogue with those who do not believe in

God, provided that they are sincerely open to cooperation. For the problem of the evangelization of the atheists, the main positions taken by Christian philosophers and theologians can be reduced to four.

Adaptation. According to a small group of authors who received great publicity immediately after Vatican II, under the name of theologians of "the death of God" (*see* DEATH OF GOD THEOLOGY), atheism is to be taken very seriously, since in modern culture there is no longer any rational motivation for believing in God. Modern man is honestly an atheist. Therefore, according to these theologians, the best strategy in the present situation is to adapt the Gospel to his atheistic understanding of reality, by eliminating from the Christian message and from Christian life in general, the whole religious, supernatural, and divine aspect, and by stressing on the contrary its content on a humanist level, showing, at this level, how Christianity is superior to any other interpretation of reality. As St. Paul became a Jew with the Jews and a Greek with the Greeks, so the preachers of the 20th century must become atheists with atheists, abandoning "the religious hypothesis." Even when this hypothesis is dropped, Jesus has sufficient prerogatives (his love for others, his complete dedication to his neighbor, his perfect freedom etc.) to win man's confidence, obedience, faith, and complete surrender. He has still sufficient claims to be considered the savior of mankind. This strategy of an "atheistic" (nonreligious) proclamation of the Gospel to an atheistic and secularized world was initially proposed by the Lutheran theologian and martyr of Nazi persecution, Dietrich Bonhoeffer. It was then followed and promoted by such "death of God" theologians as Altizer, van Buren, and Robinson. After a short, passing success it was recognized that the strategy of "historical compromise" between Christianity and atheism is a failure and extremely self-defeating. In the concern (certainly a legitimate one) to make the Gospel intelligible to modern man, this compromise mutilates it in its most essential element—precisely in the religious, ultramundane, transcendent, sacred, divine element. The originality of Christ and the quality that rendered him capable of being the savior of mankind is not just that of being a supremely free man, or a man completely dedicated to others (man-for-others), but his identity of being the Son of God.

Confrontation. According to some authors the only valid strategy of the Church in the face of atheism is frontal counterposition. Atheism is seen as the extreme expression of man's pride, the most detestable aberration of reason and heart, since only a madman or a fool can proclaim that God does not exist or that "God is dead." Therefore for a believer it is impossible to come to an agreement with atheism; it is impossible even to start a dialogue for the atheist's motivations cannot be justified nor his perspectives and language accepted. Atheism is the number-one enemy of mankind. The first condition for mankind to be able to receive the message of salvation is to abandon atheism and the human idolatry which is masked under the attractive mantle of secular humanism. Salvation is possible for the atheist only on the condition that he is converted and professes the most complete and unconditional submission to God. Among the most authoritative assertors of this strategy were Barth and Brunner, two of the major exponents of 20th-century Protestant theology, and such Catholic thinkers as Maritain, Molnar, and Del Noce.

This strategy seems too drastic to many people. It forgets that every error contains at least a kernel of truth that must be patiently picked out and carefully preserved. In the second place, while admitting that to embrace the Gospel a deep conversion is always necessary, it must be clarified that this conversion does not entail sacrifice of everything human, as Barth claims. Humanity is living today under the sign of the Cross and many human achievements are in conformity with God's plan. Finally, it is necessary to distinguish between atheists and atheism. While atheism must be criticized and rejected with firm resolution, it is necessary to show the greatest understanding for atheists.

Integration. According to other theologians the most effective and appropriate strategy is that which does not eliminate either the originality of the Gospel or the reality of atheism, but tries on the contrary to preserve them both by integrating atheism into Christianity. The attempt to reach this goal consists in reducing the significance of atheism: by showing the atheist that his own view of the world, of history, of society, of man, of science, of politics etc., if developed consistently, does not exclude God at all, but, on the contrary, logically, leads to Him, to His plan of salvation, to the liberation, the love, the divinization that Jesus Christ alone makes possible. There are three main versions of this strategy of *integration:* the scientific one of TEILHARD DE CHARDIN, the political one of the theologians of Latin America (Gutierrez, Assmann, Boff, etc.), and the metaphysical one of Tillich and Rahner. The first version tries to integrate into the Gospel the scientific doctrine of evolution (generally professed by scientific atheism). The second adopts the political doctrines of Marxism. The third tries to make the Gospel emerge from the idealistic metaphysics of man, conceived as an infinite capacity for self-transcendence.

The positive aspects of this strategy are obvious. It is capable of entering into dialogue with scientists, philosophers, artists, politicians who do not share a religious belief; it manages to appreciate their ways of understanding and explaining things, their social, economic, and political initiatives, their dynamism, their determination to improve our society, to change the world. But the strategy also raises serious reservations: it seems too optimistic, since it establishes a natural bridge between metaphysics, science, and politics on the one hand, and the Gospel on the other hand, ignoring the absolute qualitative difference that distinguishes God from man. In the second place, by establishing a natural, logical connection between science, politics, metaphysics, and the Gospel, it eliminates the perfectly gratuitous, absolutely new and unforeseeable character of God's plans and His intervention for the salvation of mankind by grace.

Double Conversion. According to some authors atheism implies a double distortion, namely, of the natural order and of the supernatural order. Consequently, of an atheist they require a double CONVERSION: (1) on the natural level, a conversion of mentality, which will cause him to embrace a more open view of things, so as to make room for a transcendent reality; (2) on the supernatural level, a conversion to the work of salvation that God accomplishes in Jesus Christ. A first conversion at a natural level is required because the Gospel is the proclamation of the Good News that God has saved mankind in Jesus Christ. Now, this proclamation will continue to seem absurd, aberrant, and stupid as long as the convert remains completely shut up in himself and does not recognize any other reality except the "this-wordly" one or any other action except one that man himself carries out in history. So, a conversion of viewpoint, a change of mentality is required in the first place, to lead man to confess his own finiteness and, at the same time, to recognize his capacity for overcoming it not only horizontally but also vertically. Then he will be ready to enter into dialogue not only with his fellowmen but also with other beings superior to him, should he perceive their existence.

At this point, with the help of God's grace, the phase of the second conversion will begin: the phase in which the Gospel will no longer be considered as a fairy tale, an absurd story or mere myth, but as the truth that brings freedom and the restoration of interior health, and fills his heart with joy, since "only in the mystery of the Incarnate Word does the mystery of man take on light" (*Gaudium et spes* 22). Among the most brilliant supporters are J. Miguez Bonino, H. urs von BALTHASAR, Richard NIEBUHR, and Henri de LUBAC.

This theory is apt to safeguard both the originality of the Gospel and the necessity of a rational basis for Christian faith. It is also fully consistent with the teachings of *Gaudium et spes,* which does not simply invite the atheist "to examine the Gospel of Christ with an open mind" and to gladly accept it (*second conversion*) but also requires from him to reject all those prejudices and fallacious methodologies that prevent him from seeing that the recognition of the reality of God does not cause any damage to the nobility and greatness of man (*first conversion*).

Bibliography: E. BORNE, *Atheism,* tr. S. J. TESTER (New York 1961). H. DE LUBAC, *The Drama of Atheist Humanism,* tr. E. M. RILEY (New York 1949). I. LEPP, *Atheist in Our Time,* tr. B. MURCHLAND (New York 1963). J. MARITAIN, *The Range of Reason* (New York 1952) 103–117. J. D. COLLINS, *God in Modern Philosophy* (Chicago 1959). A. J. FESTUGIERE, *Epicurus and His Gods,* tr. C. W. CHILTON (Cambridge, MA 1956). C. FABRO, *God in Exile, Modern Atheism* (New York 1968). P. HEBBLETHWAITE, *The Council Fathers and Atheism* (New York 1967). K. RAHNER, ed., *Pastoral Approach to Atheism* (New York 1967). J. P. REID, *Man without God* (New York 1971). T. ALTIZER, *The Gospel of Christian Atheism* (Philadelphia 1966). H. U. VON BALTHASAR, *The God Question and Modern Man,* tr. H. Graef (New York 1967). E. BLOCH, *Atheismus im Christentum* (Frankfurt 1969). P. TEILHARD DE CHARDIN, *The Phenomenon of Man,* tr. B. WALL (New York 1959). A. DEL NOCE, *Il problema dell'ateismo* (Bologna 1965). G. GUTIERREZ *Theology of Liberation,* tr., ed., E. INDA and J. EAGLESON (Maryknoll, NY 1973). B. MONDIN, *Cultura, marxismo, cristianesimo* (Rome 1978). K. RAHNER, "Atheism and Implicit Christianity," *Theological Investigations* 9, tr. G. Harrison (London 1972) 145–164. J. A. T. ROBINSON, *Honest to God* (London 1963), B. WELTE, *Nietzsches Atheismus und das Christentum* (Darmstadt 1958). M. J. BUCKLEY, *At the Origins of Modern Atheism* (New Haven 1987). W. KASPER, *The God of Jesus Christ,* tr. M. J. O'CONNELL (New York 1984).

[J. P. REID/B. MONDIN/EDS.]

ATHELNEY, ABBEY OF

Former Benedictine monastery established by King ALFRED in 888, on an island site amid marshes in the county of Somerset and in the ancient Diocese of BATH AND WELLS, England. The original foundation, made by foreign monks under John the Scot, was a failure. It was refounded *c.* 960 with a Saxon community under the BENEDICTINE RULE. There were insufficient resources for great development and the house was little more than a satellite of GLASTONBURY. The monks were few and poor, but content with their poverty and solitude. The church, dedicated to SS. Peter and Paul, rested on piles and was built on the round continental plan. It was rebuilt in 1321. The abbey was dissolved in 1539 when the abbot and six monks were pensioned. Chancellor Audley sold the buildings.

Bibliography: Somerset Record Society, *Two Cartularies of the Benedictine Abbeys of Muchelney and Athelney in the County of Somerset,* ed. E. H. BATES (London 1899). *The Victoria History of the County of Somerset,* ed. W. PAGE (London 1906–) v. 2. D. KNOWLES, *The Monastic Order in England, 943–1216* (2d ed. Cambridge, Eng. 1962). D. KNOWLES and R. N. HADCOCK, *Medieval Religious Houses: England and Wales* (New York 1953).

[F. R. JOHNSTON]

ATHELSTAN, KING OF ENGLAND

Reigned from 925 to 939. Athelstan was the grandson of Alfred the Great (871–899) and the son of Edward the Elder (899–925). In his reign of fourteen years he became a man of immense power and prestige. The *Anglo-Saxon Chronicle* refers to him as "lord of warriors, Ring-giver of men" who "won undying glory with the edges of swords in warfare. . . ." As evidenced by the *Chronicle*, charters, and other contemporary documents, Athelstan was the first English king to successfully unite the various peoples of England; he also subdued the Scots, forcing them to accept his overlordship, and reaffirmed English suzerainty over the Welsh. He never married, and, as far as is known, had no children.

There are very few contemporary sources about Athelstan; his actions were mostly recorded in the *Anglo-Saxon Chronicle*, in his charters, in the chronicles of religious houses, and in several Welsh, Norse, and Continental sources. On the death of Edward the Elder, his son, Athelstan, was accepted as king by the Mercians as well as the men of Wessex, and he was consecrated at Kingston. Athelstan's first official act as king was probably the manumission of a slave, one Eadhelm; the act was recorded in a book of the Gospels owned at the time by St. Augustine's, Canterbury. Shortly thereafter he began a series of dynastic alliances, beginning with the marriage of his sister to Hugh, duke of the Franks. That same year, Athelstan met Sihtric, the Danish king of Northumbria, at Tamworth and gave him another sister in marriage. Sihtric died soon after, however, and Athelstan annexed the kingdom of Northumbria. He then went on to bring into submission all of the kings in Britain, beginning with Hwyel Dda, king of the West Welsh, and then Constantine, king of the Scots, Owain, king of Gwent, and Ealdred Ealdulfing from Bamburh. In July of 926, the kings gave Athelstan pledges and oaths to keep the peace, after which they departed.

Athelstan then faced Sihtric's brother, Guthfrith, king of the Danes at Dublin, who was probably in York, and drove him out of England. Shortly thereafter, Athelstan met with the Welsh kings near Hereford and created the *Dunsæte*, a legal document that was intended to peacefully settle disputes between Welsh and English on both sides of the Wye. According to William of Malmesbury, Athelstan then fiercely attacked the Cornish, who were living in Exeter, and cleansed the city "by purging it of its contaminated race, he fortified [the city] with towers, and surrounded [it] with a wall of squared stone. . . ." Afterward, Athelstan penned the Cornish up on the other side of the Tamar, which he fixed as the boundary of their province and also as the boundary of British territory. A letter from Archbishop Dunstan to King Ethelred stated that "Then it happened that King Athelstan gave to Cunan the bishopric as far as the Tamar flowed."

Athelstan's actions created discontent within Britain; in *The Great Prophecy of Britain*, written by a monk living in Hwyel's kingdom, there is a poem that calls upon the Britons to throw off the yoke of the *mechteryn*, the great king, and stresses unification of all Celts against Wessex. Despite the Welsh malcontents, Hwyel supported Athelstan wholeheartedly and was often at his court. Athelstan apparently had a firm hold on his kingdom, and after 927 he began to use the inscription *Rex to Brit*, most likely translated as "King of all Britain" on his coinage. At some time he fostered the son of the Norwegian king, Harold Fair Hair, in the Norse sources Hakon was known as "*Athalsteins fostri*." He also sent a sister to the Continent to be married, this time to the son of Otto the Great, emperor and king of Germany.

Shortly after his coronation, Athelstan began to issue laws that covered almost every aspect of society. His legislation consisted of seven codes, some of which reinstated legislation from his father's and grandfather's reigns. The first code was ecclesiastical in nature, and dealt primarily with tithing. Others cover many aspects of life, including theft, coinage, the *burh*, and the relationship between a lord and his man. The last code is a report to the king regarding enforcement of earlier legislation.

Athelstan also issued many charters. Beginning with the Easter Court of 928, Hwyel and the other Welsh kings were often at court, where they sometimes served as witnesses to his charters. They were present on at least two occasions in 931, and attended at least twice in 932, once in 933, three times in 934, and once again in 937. Many of the charters they witnessed concerned land grants to religious houses; religion was a subject that appears to have been very important to Athelstan.

It was recorded at Athelstan's coronation that he was a collector of relics. They most often consisted of bits of various saints, or items that had personal contact with either Jesus or Mary. Relics were used in a variety of ways, all of which designed to provide protection as well as political power and prestige for the king. They were often kept in the king's *haligdom*, a place where the king's treasures were housed, but he also bestowed them on many religious institutions. The Old English Relic list, written at Exeter in the late tenth century, includes many relics that Athelstan gave to the cathedral.

Athelstan also bestowed relics upon the abbeys and monasteries of Exeter, Glastonbury, Milton Abbas, Muchelney, Wilton, Winchester, Westminster, Canterbury, Bury St. Edmunds, Beverly, York, Durham, Worcester,

Malmesbury, and Bath. Other religious houses received books, land, and grants of money, but the relics seem to have been reserved for the above-mentioned abbeys and monasteries. Athelstan placed relics in these strategic locations to create a boundary around his kingdom in the belief that they would protect England by their spiritual power. If those abbeys and monasteries are located on a map, and if a line is drawn connecting them, they form a perimeter around most of the country with the exception of the northwest. However, years earlier, Athelstan's aunt, Æthelflaed, Lady of the Mercians, translated the bones of St. Werburg from Hanbury to Chester, St. Ealhmund from Derby to Shrewsbury, and St. Oswald from Bardney to Gloucester, all out of Danish lands and into English territory. If Chester, Shrewsbury and Gloucester are added to the map, the boundary of England is complete.

In 934, the peace in England ended. Athelstan invaded Scotland with both land and naval forces, and "harried much of the country." The war lasted until 937, when the famous Battle of Brunanburh occurred. The *Chronicle* records that Athelstan and his brother, Edmund, led levies to Brunanburh and fought Anlaf, Sihtric's son, who had apparently allied with Constantine, king of Scotland. Five kings were killed that day, along with seven of Anlaf's jarls, and a "countless host of seamen and Scots." Anlaf and Constantine were forced to retreat. This battle, the *Chronicle* tells us, was the greatest fought since the Anglo-Saxons first invaded Britain from the east.

At the end of the year 937, Athelstan held his Christmas Court at Dorchester, and Hwyel Dda was again in attendance, as evidenced by three charters from December 21. The contemporary sources tell us little more until 940, when the *Chronicle* mentions the passing of Athelstan, at Gloucester, on October 27. He was about 45 years old. The *Chronicle* recorded Athelstan's death a year too late; Athelstan actually died in October 939.

King Athelstan reigned little more than fourteen years; yet in that short time he became what J. Armitage Robinson calls "one of the makers of England," in company with only Alfred and St. Dunstan.

Bibliography: J. A. ROBINSON, *The Times of St. Dunstan* (Oxford 1923). G. N. GARMONSWAY, ed. *The Anglo-Saxon Chronicle* (London 1992). F. STENTON, *Anglo-Saxon England* (Oxford 1989). F. HARMER, *Select English Historical Documents of the Ninth and Tenth Centuries* (Cambridge 1914). *Rerum Britannicarum Medii Aevi Scriptores: Chronicon Monasterii de Abingdon I*, Rolls Series 2. R. M. THOMSON and M. WINTERBOTTOM, ed. and tr. *William of Malmesbury; Gesta Regum Anglorum* (London 1999). F. L. ATTENBOROUGH, ed. *The Laws of the Earliest English Kings* (Cambridge 1922). P. SAWYER, *Anglo-Saxon Charters, An Annotated List and Bibliography* (London 1968). D. W. ROLLASON, "Relic Cults as an Instrument of Royal Policy, c. 900–1050," *Anglo-Saxon England* 15 (1986) 96.

[L. A. LEHTOLA]

ATHENAGORAS

Apologist of the 2d century. By the report of PHILIP SIDETES he was founder of a Christian philosophical school at Alexandria. Between 176 and 180 he wrote an *Embassy for the Christians* for presentation to Marcus Aurelius and a treatise on *Resurrection of the Dead*. Before his conversion to Christianity he was a Platonist, and he used Plato's strictures on the ancient poets with great effect in his attack on paganism. The wealth of detail that Athenagoras supplied concerning pagan worship makes him a principal source for knowledge of ancient Greek cults. He defended Christians against the three charges of atheism, cannibalism, and promiscuity. In answering the first charge he had to show that the doctrine of the Trinity does not involve Christians in polytheism, and thus he became one of the first Christian writers to philosophize about the Trinity. In reply to the third charge, Athenagoras set out contemporary Christian teaching on sexual morality in these words: "The begetting of children is the limit of our indulging our passions." To answer the charge of cannibalism, Athenagoras appealed to the fact that Christians were not allowed to be present at public shows involving loss of human lives; hence they could certainly not be guilty of eating human flesh. Furthermore, Christians had their own slaves, and these had never accused their masters; he was thus the first author to advert to the widespread ownership of slaves by Christians.

Athenagoras's two works have survived in a single manuscript; and though the second work is in slightly more formal language, there is no reason for assigning the two works to different authors.

The quality of the work of Athenagoras is higher than that of the other 2d-century apologists. He was better versed in Greek philosophy, and more moderate in tone, and he tried to find new technical terms in which to express the concepts of his faith.

Bibliography: ATHENAGORAS, *Libellus pro christianis* and *Oratio de resurrectione cadaverum*, tr. J. H. CREHAN (Ancient Christian Writers 23; 1956); tr. C. C. RICHARDSON in *Early Christian Fathers* (Philadelphia 1953) 290–340. H. H. LUCKS, *The Philosophy of Athenagoras* (Washington 1936). R. M. GRANT, *Harvard Theological Review* 47 (1954) 121–129.

[J. H. CREHAN]

ATHENAGORAS I

Orthodox patriarch of Constantinople (Istanbul); b. Vassilikon, Epirus, Greece, March 25, 1886; d. Istanbul, July 6, 1972. The son of a prominent physician and civic leader in what was then a Turkish-ruled area, Aristokles Spirou had his primary and secondary education in Joannina, capital of Epirus, and then attended the Patriarchal Theological School on the island of Halki, near Istanbul. Upon graduation in 1910, he took the name Athenagoras. After serving as archdeacon in the diocese of Pelagonia, in Eastern Europe, he became associate to Archbishop Meleties of Athens in 1919, and in 1922 was raised to the hierarchy as metropolitan of Corfu and Paxos. In 1931 he became archbishop of the Greek Orthodox Archdiocese of North and South America, taking U.S. citizenship in 1938. When Maximos V retired for health reasons, the Holy Synod of Constantinople elected Athenagoras to the position of spiritual leader of the world Orthodoxy, with the titles archbishop of Constantinople, and new Rome and ecumenical patriarch (1948). Outspokenly anticommunist, he was said to have been supported for the post by U.S. president Truman, who provided the plane that took him to Istanbul.

Athenagoras led his see into active participation in the World Council of Churches, formed the year of his election, and into closer relations with the Catholic Church. In events of historic importance, he sent observers to Vatican II, exchanged the kiss of peace with Pope Paul VI at the Mount of Olives in 1964, joined with the pope the following year in simultaneously nullifying the anathemas pronounced by their predecessors in 1054, received Paul at the Phanar in July 1967, and visited him at the Vatican the following October. Seeking to advance unity among the Orthodox churches also, Athenagoras convened a pan-Orthodox conference at Rhodes in 1961 to begin preparations of an ecumenical council that would be the first in the Orthodox world since the 11-century division between East and West.

[T. EARLY]

ATHENS, SCHOOLS OF

The Athenian schools in the early Christian period never formed a corporate university. However, from the time of the Antonine emperors (A.D. 86–180) there were imperial endowments for chairs in each of the four schools of philosophy, and one for Sophism. During the 2nd- to 4th-century sophistic revival (*see* SECOND SOPHISTIC) several Christians came to Athens. CLEMENT OF ALEXANDRIA may have received an Athenian education; BASIL OF CAESAREA and GREGORY OF NAZIANZUS studied rhetoric there (A.D. 351–357); and DIODORE OF TARSUS imbibed the wisdom of Athens. When SYNESIUS OF CYRENE visited the city, the schools were dormant, for the Goths had overrun the city's outer precincts in 396. The founding of the Neoplatonic school by Plutarch of Athens (*c.* 400) made the city again a famous center. BOETHIUS studied the systematic curriculum of this school (*c.* 500). Striking evidence of the later school's influence on a Christian appears in the works of PSEUDO-DIONYSIUS THE AREOPAGITE. An edict of JUSTINIAN I forbidding the "teaching of philosophy and interpretation of law at Athens" caused the Athenian schools to close in A.D. 529.

Bibliography: J. W. H. WALDEN, *The Universities of Ancient Greece* (New York 1909). T. WHITTAKER, *The Neo-Platonists* (2d ed. Cambridge, Eng. 1928). F. SCHEMMEL, "Die Hochschule von Athens im IV. und V. Jahrhundert," *Neue Jahrbücher für Pädagogik* 22 (1908) 494–513. L. G. WESTERINK, ed. and tr., *Anonymous Prolegomena to Platonic Philosophy* (Amsterdam 1962) xxv–xli, curriculum. E. ÉVRARD, "Le Maître de Plutarque d'Athènes et les origines du néoplatonisme athénien," *L'Antiquité classique* 29 (1960) 108–133, 391–406. H. D. SAFFREY, *Revue des études grecques* 67 (1954) 396–410, curriculum. F. FUCHS, *Die höheren Schulen von Konstantinopel im Mittelalter* (Leipzig 1926).

[R. F. HATHAWAY]

ATIENZA, JUAN DE

Jesuit educator and collaborator with Toribio de MOGROVEJO; b. Valladolid or possibly Tordehumos, 1544; d. Lima, 1592. He studied Canon Law for two years and entered the Society of Jesus at Salamanca on May 1, 1564. He made his profession of three vows on September 14, 1570, and of four vows on June 5, 1580. He was professor of philosophy in Avila, rector of San Ambrosio at Valladolid, and rector and master of novices at Villagarcía de Campos (Valladolid). In 1581 he went to Peru, where he founded the Colegio de San Martín in Lima and wrote its constitution. He was rector of the major seminary of San Pablo in Lima and participated in the third and fourth provincial councils of Lima. During his term as provincial, beginning in 1585, the society spread itself through Tucumán, the Chaco, and Paraguay. The Archbishop of Lima, Toribio de Mogrovejo, greatly esteemed him for his prudence and his knowledge of ecclesiastical law. Atienza was concerned during his term as provincial with two main questions of government: the internal discipline of the province, and the organization of the missions already established and expansion to new areas. Acting little for public acclaim, he concentrated on creating and directing significant works, guided by his knowledge and his experience of the South American situation.

Bibliography: A. ASTRAIN, *Historia de la Compañía de Jesús en la asistencia de España,* 7 v. (Madrid 1902–25).

[A. DE EGAÑA]

ATKINSON, MATTHEW (PAUL OF ST. FRANCIS)

English Franciscan who was imprisoned for more than 30 years under the anti-Catholic penal laws of his time; b. Yorkshire, 1656; d. Hurst Castle, Hampshire, 1729. Father Paul, who had served for 12 years on the English mission and was at one time definitor of the English province of Franciscans, was betrayed to the authorities for £100. In 1698 he was condemned to life imprisonment for the offense of being a Catholic priest, and most of the long years of his incarceration were spent at the prison of Hurst Castle on the Solent. Gentle and amiable, he soon gained the trust and regard of his keeper, and was allowed for a time to walk outside the prison walls and to enter into friendly relations with many of the people of the area. Eventually, however, a complaint was made about his warder's leniency, and for the last 30 years of his life he voluntarily confined himself to the narrow limits of his cell to avoid causing difficulties for his keeper.

Bibliography: J. GILLOW, *A Literary and Biographical History or Bibliographical Dictionary of the English Catholics from 1534 to the Present time,* 5 v. (London–New York 1885–1902) 1:84. J. COOPER, *The Dictionary of National Biography from the Earliest Times to 1900,* 63 v. (London 1885–1900) 1:697.

[H. F. GRETSCH]

ATKINSON, THOMAS, BL.

Priest, martyr; b. ca. 1546 in the East Riding, Yorkshire, England; d. March 11, 1616, hanged, drawn and quartered at York under James I. After his studies and ordination to the priesthood at Rheims (1588), he immediately returned to his native England. For 28 years he went about mostly on foot, ministering to his flock, especially the poor, and became so well known that he could not safely travel by day. At age 70 he was betrayed and taken to York with his host, Mr. Vavasour of Willitoft, and some members of the family. A pair of beads and the form of an indulgence found upon him confirmed his religion. He suffered "with wonderful patience, courage, and constancy, and signs of great comfort." Atkinson was beatified by Pope John Paul II on Nov. 22, 1987 with George HAYDOCK and Companions.

Feast of the English Martyrs: May 4 (England).

See Also: ENGLAND, SCOTLAND, AND WALES, MARTYRS OF.

Bibliography: R. CHALLONER, *Memoirs of Missionary Priests,* ed. J. H. POLLEN (rev. ed. London 1924). J. H. POLLEN, *Acts of English Martyrs* (London 1891).

[K. I. RABENSTEIN]

ATLANTA, ARCHDIOCESE OF

The Archdiocese of Atlanta (*Atlantensis* embraces 69 counties in the northern part of Georgia. The area was part of the Diocese of SAVANNAH (1850–1937), then Savannah-Atlanta (1937–56), and was established as an independent diocese July 2, 1956. Created an archdiocese Feb. 21, 1962, its suffragans include the Dioceses of Charleston, SC, Charlotte, NC, Raleigh, NC, and Savannah, GA. In 2000 the Catholic population of the diocese numbered about 320,000 in a total population of about 5,000,000. Catholicism in the area centered principally in the vicinity of the city of Atlanta.

The city of Atlanta, founded in 1836, was originally called "Terminus," because it was the point at which five railway lines converged on northern Georgia. Its first Catholic parish, the Shrine of the Immaculate Conception, was established in 1848. Father Thomas O'Reilly, who became pastor of the shrine in 1861, was instrumental in saving five downtown churches of various denominations, including Immaculate Conception, from the fire set at General William T. Sherman's orders in 1864. A second parish, Sacred Heart, was established in 1880. Saint Anthony's Church opened in 1903 and added a school in 1912, the same year in which Our Lady of Lourdes Church opened.

The first Sisters of Mercy arrived in Atlanta in 1866 to teach. Additional SISTERS OF MERCY opened an infirmary, which later became Saint Joseph's Hospital, in 1880. The Sisters of SAINT JOSEPH first came to what is now the Archdiocese of Atlanta in 1876, when they moved their orphanage, later known as the Village of Saint Joseph, from Savannah to Washington, GA. The Village closed as a residential treatment center in 1998 and now offers counseling services to families.

Although Savannah Bishop Thomas A. Becker petitioned Rome to transfer the see to faster-growing Atlanta in 1896, his petition was denied as "inopportune." By the time Gerald P. O'Hara became Bishop of Savannah (1935), Atlanta's continued growth could no longer be ignored. He petitioned Pope Pius XI to designate the diocese "Savannah-Atlanta." According to the terms of the decree, authorized on January 5, 1937, the bishop would reside part-time in Atlanta and would minister to his metropolitan flocks on alternate Holy Weeks. The new church of Christ the King (built on land originally owned by the Ku Klux Klan) was designated a "co-cathedral *ad honorem.*" In 1944 the Trappist monks established the Abbey of Our Lady of the Holy Ghost near Atlanta at Conyers, GA.

When Atlanta was established a diocese in its own right in 1956, Francis E. Hyland, a native of Philadelphia,

PA, and auxiliary bishop of the Savannah-Atlanta diocese since 1949, became its first bishop. Hyland resigned on October 11, 1961 (and retired to St. Charles Seminary where he died, January 31, 1968). The following February, Pope John XXIII created Atlanta an archdiocese and appointed Bishop Paul J. HALLINAN, of Charleston, SC, the first archbishop. Hallinan, a rising star in the American hierarchy, contracted hepatitis while in Rome for the Second Vatican Council and died on March 27, 1968. His successor, Joseph L. BERNARDIN (d. 1996), who since 1966 had been auxiliary bishop, served only a brief time before being appointed General Secretary of the United States Catholic Conference, April 5, 1968. Ogdensburg Bishop Thomas A. Donnellan, installed as Atlanta's third bishop (second archbishop) on May 29, 1968, served until his death on October 15, 1987. His successor, Archbishop Eugene A. Marino, SSJ, was the first African American appointed a residential archbishop in the United States (March 14, 1988). He resigned for personal reasons in 1990 and died in 2000. Cleveland's auxiliary bishop James P. Lyke, OFM, served as Apostolic Administrator from July 10, 1990 until his appointment as archbishop on April 30, 1991. Lyke, the nation's second African-American archbishop, died of cancer on December 27, 1992.

Lyke was succeeded by John Francis Donoghue, who had served as Bishop of Charlotte from 1984 until his appointment to Atlanta on June 22, 1993.

Although the industrialization of the diocese in the latter half of the 20th century had attracted many Catholics, they still constituted only 6% of the overall population in 2000. The diocese publishes a weekly newspaper, *The Georgia Bulletin*, whose origins lie in *The Bulletin* of the Georgia Catholic Laymen's Association, founded in Augusta in 1916 at the urging of Savannah Bishop Benjamin J. Keiley.

Bibliography: J. J. O'CONNELL, *Catholicity in the Carolinas and Georgia 1820–1878* (New York 1879). T. J. SHELLEY, *Paul J. Hallinan. First Archbishop of Atlanta* (Wilmington, DE, 1989).

[D. K. CLARK]

Archbishop Eugene A. Marino of Atlanta, the first African American appointed a residential archbishop in the U.S. (©Bettmann/CORBIS)

ATOMISM

A term deriving from the Greek ἄτομον, meaning indivisible, and usually applied to systems maintaining that everything is composed of unchanging and indivisible elements or atoms, whose movements and arrangements account for the changing appearances of reality. In a broader sense, the term is applied also to any systematic explanation that attempts to reduce complex phenomena to invariant unit factors. Thus one may speak of logical atomism, as elaborated in the philosophy of Bertrand RUSSELL, which regards the logical proposition as an ultimate unit; psychological atomism, which attempts to reduce all mental phenomena to combinations of simple elements, along lines proposed by J. LOCKE, D. HUME and the advocates of ASSOCIATIONISM; and biological atomism, which attempts to explain vital phenomena in terms of discrete units such as genes, cells, etc. (*see* MECHANISM, BIOLOGICAL). The historically more important type of atomism may be described as physical atomism to distinguish it from these other forms. From its beginnings in Greek philosophy it has consistently lent its support to the philosophies of MATERIALISM and MECHANISM and has been used by proponents of ATHEISM to combat belief in the world of SPIRIT. Physical atomism is not to be completely identified with materialism, however, for many thinkers have subscribed to atomistic hypotheses without regarding atoms as the sole reality and while admitting the existence of spiritual entities. Again, physical atomism permits of many different views regarding the nature of the ultimate units, ranging from the mathematical points of the Pythagoreans, the force centers of R. Boscovich and the monads of G. W. Leibniz to the solid particles of Democritus and the qualitatively similar parts (Gr. ὁμοιομερῆ) of Anaxagoras. Yet most forms of atom-

Robert Boyle.

ism maintain that there is a quantitative limit to the division of bodies, that small ultimate units exist and that all large-scale phenomena are to be accounted for in terms of these.

This article treats physical atomism chronologically under the headings of Greek atomism, other early forms, medieval conceptions, developments from the Renaissance to the 17th century, the classical atomism of the 18th and 19th centuries and the status of atomism in the 20th century.

Greek Atomism

The first atomistic theories to arise among the Greeks were speculative in nature. The forerunners of Greek atomist concepts are to be found among the Milesian naturalists, such as Thales, Anaximenes and HERACLITUS, who successively conceived water, air and fire as the primary matter of which all things are made. The solutions these thinkers proffered to the problem of change prompted PARMENIDES, a philosopher of the Eleatic school in Italy, to argue that change itself is an illusion: in his view, being is one and unchangeable, for apart from it, there is only nothing. The metaphysical speculations of Parmenides gave birth to the first atomist school at Abdera in Thrace, where atomism was proposed by Leu-

cippus (fl. 450 B.C.) and his pupil DEMOCRITUS. Democritus argued against Parmenides, that being is not one, but is divided into a number of beings, themselves unchangeable and indivisible, which he called atoms (Gr. ἄτομα). He also conceived of nothing as differently from Parmenides, assigning it a type of reality that he described as the VOID. By admitting the void Democritus thought he could explain the motion of atoms and through this motion all types of change. He postulated that atoms were infinite in number, qualitatively identical and distinct only in shape and size; he also endowed his atoms with motion, which he conceived as ceaseless and eternal like the atoms themselves (*see* MATERIALISM).

At approximately the same time as Democritus was elaborating his atomic theory, rival theories were being proposed by EMPEDOCLES and ANAXAGORAS. According to Empedocles, the primordial beings are four qualitatively different elements, namely, fire, air, water and earth; he explained change in terms of the commingling and separation of these four elements, which themselves remain unchanged. Anaxagoras accented Empedocles's notion of commingling, but held that the primitive constituents of matter are an unlimited number of qualitatively different substances, themselves eternal and incorruptible, which he referred to as seeds (Gr. σπέρματα). In his view, every composed substance contains all possible kinds of seeds and is named after the type of seed that predominates in it.

In the classical period of Greek philosophy, PLATO, influenced by the ideas of PYTHAGORAS and the Pythagoreans, who held that number is the essence of things and likewise influenced by Democritus, proposed a geometrical theory of the basic particles of the universe. He regarded these as fire, earth, air and water and associated them with the four regular solids, namely, the tetrahedron, the cube, the octahedron and the icosahedron. ARISTOTLE, less partial to Democritean ideas than his teacher, explained change by a fourfold causal analysis that placed accent on substance and primary matter as substrates underlying accidental and SUBSTANTIAL CHANGE respectively (*see* MATTER AND FORM). In this context, he adapted Empedocles's theory of the four elements and taught that all bodies are continuous but composed of natural *minima,* that is, smallest particles of various kinds (*see* CONTINUUM).

Later Greek thought centered on the theories of Democritus and of Aristotle and thereby provided two influential currents that have persisted down to recent times. The notions of Democritus were taken up by EPICURUS, who reformulated them and used them as a method of inference from the visible to the invisible. The school of EPICUREANISM that he founded kept atomistic notions alive long after the decline of Greek philosophy and can be said to have laid the remote foundations for the atomic theories of modern chemistry. The views of Aristotle, on the other hand, were taken up by his Greek commentators, Alexander of Aphrodisias, Themistius and JOHN PHILOPONUS, all of whom contributed to a more systematic explanation of Aristotle's theory of natural *minima*. They spoke of the smallest particles of particular kinds of matter as ἐλάχιστα, a term with somewhat the same connotation as the modern word molecule. The concept was further developed in the Middle Ages and in the Renaissance; it was eclipsed somewhat with the rise of modern chemistry, only to take on new significance in 20th-century discussions of elementary particles.

Other Early Forms

A type of atomism is also to be found in INDIAN PHILOSOPHY, where it is associated with the system of Vaiśésika Sūtra, attributed to a mythical Kanāda but probably recorded during the first two centuries A.D. Little is known of its origins, although it is possible that it was influenced by Greek thought. Indian atomism is relativistic; both the small (*anu*) and the very small (*paramānu*) are denied any absolute value. In the system of Vaiśésika the very small is described as an elementary form; in an earlier type of atomism associated with JAINISM, it is regarded as lacking in any forms that would make it perceptible but still as endowed with qualities. Both systems deny the existence of a void and do not regard the atom as the unique principle of reality, admitting that the soul is a spiritual substance and not atomic in character. Where materialism does appear in Indian philosophy, it does not assume an atomistic form.

In Rome, the Greek physician Asclepiades (*c.* 124–40 B.C.) ascribed diseases to alterations in the size, arrangement and motion of the atoms that make up the human body. More influential was the teaching of the Roman poet and philosopher LUCRETIUS, who gave eloquent expression to the ideas of Democritus in his poem *De rerum natura*. This was a systematic account of an atomist theory of nature, describing in detail the formation of the universe, the origins of life and thought, the nature of human sensation and sexual attraction and the development of human society. Preserved in monastic libraries during the Dark Ages, this became the principal channel through which interest in Greek atomism was preserved to modern times.

Largely because of the materialistic atheism endorsed by Lucretius, Christian writers, such as DIONYSIUS OF ALEXANDRIA, attacked the atomists' doctrine as being based on CHANCE and denying a principle of order within the universe (*see* UNIVERSE, ORDER OF). The Fathers of the Church were likewise unfavorable to atomistic concepts because these seemed to form the basis for a materialistic Epicurean ethics. Through their polemics and through the efforts of encyclopedists such as ISIDORE OF SEVILLE, basic atomic concepts continued to be discussed. Isidore likened atoms to points, since they were indivisible and distinguished atoms of matter, time, number and language [*Etymol.*, 13.3; *Patrologia Latina,* ed. J. P. Migne, 217 V., indexes 4 v. (Paris 1878–90) 82: 472–473].

Medieval Conceptions

Atomistic theories did not enjoy great popularity during the Middle Ages, the main line of development taking place in a thought context that was predominantly Aristotelian. In the 9th century, an Arab alchemist and physician named Rhazes (al-Rāzī, 865?–924) taught a type of atomism and other Islamic thinkers developed atomic ideas not unlike the earlier Indian concepts (*see* ARABIAN PHILOSOPHY). In the 14th century NICHOLAS OF AUTRECOURT defended a Democritean type of atomism, speculating over the motions of atoms and their mutual attractions. Some historians list WILLIAM OF CONCHES, HUGH OF SAINT-VICTOR and ADELARD OF BATH as atomists also, but the basis for this ascription is debatable (Van Melsen, *Van atomos naar atoom; de geschiedenis van het begrip atoom* 77).

The main concern in the Middle Ages regarding theories of matter was one of reconciling how material substance could be composed (*compositum*) of primary matter and substantial form and at the same time be a compound (*mixtum*) formed from the four elements. The problem this posed is referred to as that of the presence of elements in compounds; this was strenuously debated because of its intimate connection with the problem of the unicity of substantial forms (*see* FORMS, UNICITY AND PLURALITY OF). AVICENNA taught that the essential form of the element remains unchanged in the compound, although the qualities that characterize the element, undergo a remission of intensity. AVERROËS disagreed with this teaching, maintaining that not only the qualities of the element, but its substantial form also, undergo remission, and thus the element is not present in all its perfection within the compound. St. ALBERT THE GREAT minimized the differences between Avicenna and Averroës, while associating the minimum elemental parts present in a compound with the atoms of Democritus (*In 1 de gen.* 1.12; ed. Borgnet, 4:354b). St. THOMAS AQUINAS rejected both Avicenna's view, that the elements are actually present in compounds, and Averroës's view, that they are present only potentially, to propose an intermediate position, namely, that elements are present virtually in compounds, in the sense that their forces or powers (*virtutes*) are there conserved. Most other medieval thinkers, as A.

Maier has shown, adopted either the Averroist solution (*see* ROGER BACON; HENRY OF GHENT; PETER JOHN OLIVI; THEODORIC OF FREIBURG; JOHN OF JANDUN) or that proposed by Aquinas (*see* PETER OF AUVERGNE; GILES OF ROME; DUNS SCOTUS; WILLIAM OF OCKHAM; JOHN BURIDAN; Nicolas Oresme).

The controversy over the presence of elements in compounds was related to Aristotle's theory of natural *minima.* 14th-century thinkers generally did not identify such *minima* with atoms, as Albert the Great had been tempted to do. They distinguished between *minima inexistentia,* that is, as these might exist within a body and *minima per se existentia,* that is, as these exist when separated from a body. It was generally taught that separated *minima* could exist, but that *minima inexistentia* were not present within a body. The elaboration of a theory of natural *minima* that could be reconciled with atomistic concepts had thus to await the developments of later centuries.

Renaissance to 17th Century

The Italian Averroist movement of the 16th century, in the person of such thinkers as A. NIFO, continued to develop Aristotelian doctrine and to apply this to speculation concerning the physical universe. Natural *minima* were conceived as parts of substance with a more independent existence than heretofore and were ascribed certain functions in physical and chemical processes. A. Achillini (1463–1512) spoke of the *minima* as reacting upon each other and J. ZABARELLA worked out a more explicit theory concerning the forms of the *minima* and that of the bodies constituted from them. Perhaps the most complete theory of natural *minima* that shows affinities with atomic theories was that of J. C. Scaliger, who taught that the *minima* of different substances vary in size and who used this to explain their different properties, such as density. Scaliger defined chemical composition as "the motion of *minima* toward mutual contact so that a union is effected."

Other Renaissance thinkers, such as G. BRUNO and F. BACON, revived the notions of Democritus as transmitted through Lucretius and began to explain physical phenomena in terms of the motion of the ultimate particles of bodies. From about 1550 onward, increased interest manifested itself in Greek atomism and in the relation of atomic concepts to the newly forming sciences of mechanics and chemistry. In 1575 F. Commandino published a translation of the writings of Hero of Alexandria (1st century A.D.), who emphasized the importance of the size and shape of the empty space between the particles of bodies. G. GALILEI read Democritus and Hero, and used their notions to propose a distinction between primary and secondary qualities: the first are those associated with the motions of atoms and are objectively real; the second are sensations produced in a knowing subject and are merely subjective (*see* QUALITY).

The first systematic application of atomic notions to chemistry was made by a German physician, D. Sennert (1572–1644), who developed the ideas of Scaliger and attempted to reconcile the *minima* theory with Democritean concepts. He taught that in chemical compositions the reagents are divided into their smallest parts, which subsequently unite through their *minima* and then act upon each other through their contrary properties. Perhaps the most influential atomist of the early 17th century was P. GASSENDI, a French priest and mathematician, who expurgated materialistic connotations from Democritean atomism. According to Gassendi, atoms are not eternal but are created by God; they are not infinite in number; and their motion is not eternal but has been impressed upon them by God for a definite purpose. R. DESCARTES rejected the Democritean concept of the void and conceived all physical processes as taking place in a medium composed of infinitely small particles in motion. Although not an atomist in the strict sense, Descartes contributed to the growth of atomism by his highly influential mechanical philosophy. T. HOBBES, the English mechanist, held for the existence of atoms but taught that the spaces between them were filled with some kind of fluid. Rejection of empty space in this and later periods was usually prompted by a philosophical recognition of the impossibility of ACTION AT A DISTANCE.

The most influential atomists of the later 17th century were R. Boyle, R. Hooke, C. Huygens and I. Newton. Boyle made use of both medieval and modern concepts to clarify the notion of a chemical element. He regarded heat as a type of atomic vibration and explained alteration as well as generation and corruption mechanically, that is, in terms of the motions and rearrangements of atoms. Boyle proposed a complex hierarchy of particles (primary, secondary, etc.), but shared the alchemists' conviction of the unity of matter and the transformability of one type of atoms into another. Hooke suggested that the regular forms of bodies, particularly of crystals, could be explained in terms of arrangements of "globular particles." He taught that all particles are in vibration and explained heat as an oscillatory motion of the smaller particles. Huygens further developed Gassendi's notions while attempting to work out a consistent kinetic theory that would explain the phenomena of gravitation, atmospheric pressure, light and cohesion. Newton also subscribed to the atomistic views of Gassendi, as well as those of Lucretius and attempted to elaborate these quantitatively in terms of his laws of mechanics. He showed that Boyle's law for gases could be derived on the assumption that these consist of hard particles repelling each other inversely as the distance. He also considered both attractive and repulsive forces and used them to replace the hooks postulated in more naïve explanations of atomic combination. From optical studies of the thickness of soap bubbles, he calculated an upper limit of about 10^{-5} cm for the size of soap particles.

Classical Atomism

Quantitative atomism thus had its tentative beginnings in the second half of the 17th century. The 18th century saw an accumulation of experimental data and the proposal of theoretical concepts that would lay the groundwork for the full-blown development of classical atomism in the 19th century.

18TH CENTURY

G. W. LEIBNIZ, G. VICO, E. SWEDENBORG, R. G. Boscovich, J. Priestley, R. J. Haüy and J. L. Proust figured most prominently in this period. At first a materialistic atomist, Leibniz later developed his theory of the MONAD, which he conceived as a simple substance without extension, shape, position, or movement but with the power of perception. Somewhat similar was the view of Vico, who held that the universe is constituted of point centers of action; unlike Leibniz's ''metaphysical points,'' however, these had location and a tendency to movement and were not endowed with perception. Swedenborg proposed a theory of natural points similar to Vico's to explain all geometrical and mechanical phenomena.

These dynamistic notions reached their culmination in the mathematical theory of atomism proposed by the Jesuit mathematician Boscovich. This theory postulated the existence of a finite number of quasi-material point centers of action, all with identical properties and all obeying an alternately repulsive and attractive force of interaction whose magnitude depended on the distance between each pair. In proposing it, Boscovich substituted a monism of special relations for the earlier dualism of occupied vs. empty space, and gave meaning to the concept of physical structure in terms of a three-dimensional array of point centers. His ideas were viewed favorably by I. KANT, who developed a similar theory shortly after Boscovich. Priestley also was aware of Boscovich's theory and called it to the attention of English scientists (see DYNAMISM).

While these theoretical considerations were being proposed, the French chemist Proust was gathering proof that true compounds contain chemical elements in constant proportions. His countryman C. A. Coulomb at about the same time established his law of the attraction and repulsion of electrical charges; and Haüy, a French priest and mineralogist, proposed that a crystal of any type could be subdivided into ultimate solid units of the same shape as the crystal.

19TH CENTURY

Such contributions prepared for the serious experimental work that provided the empirical base for 19th-century theories of classical atomism. Although many distinguished scientists collaborated in this development, J. Dalton, J. L. Gay-Lussac, A. Avogadro, D. I. Mendeleev and M. Faraday may be singled out for comment.

Dalton is generally credited with having placed the atomic theory, for the first time, on an exact quantitative basis. Building on the experimental findings of A. L. Lavoisier and assuming the law of conservation of weight in chemical reactions, he first formulated the law of multiple proportions. With its aid and using measurements of the weights in which chemical elements combine, he was able to calculate the relative weights of their constituent atoms; in this way he reasoned to the existence of about 20 kinds of atoms or elements. Gay-Lussac, experimenting with gases entering into chemical combination, concluded that gases combine in very simple ratios by volume; in his analysis, the law of combining volumes was more accurate than the law of combining weights proposed by Dalton. The oversimplified conceptual schemes used by both Dalton and Gay-Lussac in analyzing their data thereupon led Avogadro to adumbrate the distinction between atoms and molecules. Avogadro assumed that the constituent molecules of any simple gas are made up of half-molecules or third-molecules, etc., later identified with atoms and proposed as a hypothesis that the number of integral molecules in any gas is always the same for equal volumes, or is always proportional to the volumes. With the aid of this hypothesis, he was able to reconcile apparently contradictory experimental data obtained by Dalton and Gay-Lussac.

Building on the work of Avogadro and of S. Cannizzaro, Mendeleev noted regularities in the properties of the then-known elements, by this time 63 in number. He argued that since the mass of a substance is its most fundamental property, a periodicity of its other properties should be expected when the elements are arranged in the order of their atomic weights. He then proposed conclusions following from the periodic law that would be useful for discovering and correcting data on the elements. Meanwhile, Faraday's work on electrolysis led directly to the conception of units of electricity and to estimates of the value of charge that were later to be identified with the electron.

Despite vocal opposition from the empiricist E. Mach and from the energeticist W. Ostwald, the cumulative effect of these discoveries convinced most scientists, toward the close of the 19th century, of the atomic structure of matter. Almost all of the data of chemistry were then capable of explanation in terms of atomic concepts. It seemed only a matter of time that the more complex electromagnetic phenomena of physics would yield to their explanatory power.

20TH-CENTURY STATUS

Such confidence, however, was doomed to be short-lived. The even more rapid development of atomic physics in the first part of the 20th century led quickly to the abandonment of attempts to explain all physical phenomena in terms of the mechanical motion of Democritean atoms. The details of this development are quite complex and are treated elsewhere. For present purposes, it suffices to mention only the major conceptual developments as these are relevant to the present state of atomistic thought.

No sooner had fairly conclusive evidence for the existence of atoms and molecules been made available than a series of investigators, including J. J. Thomson, E. Rutherford, F. W. Aston and G. H. J. Moseley, produced a theory of atomic structure that viewed the atom as composed of subatomic particles. In the process, it was shown that the atom was divisible, that is, that electrons could be removed from it and that its nucleus could be disintegrated. Attempts to explain electromagnetic radiation and absorption in terms of this atomic structure led to the development of the quantum theory but produced no clear-cut mechanical conception of the motion of atomic parts. L. de Broglie, noting parallels between the dynamics of bodies and wave propagation, showed how electrons and other subatomic particles also have a wave or undulatory aspect. This led to the introduction of wave mechanics by E. Schrödinger and others, wherein the planetary motion of electrons was replaced by the interference of systems of stationary waves. More elaborate mathematical theories were then developed, which have been subjected to various physical interpretations but provide no easily imaginable picture of the structure of the atom. W. Heisenberg has pointed out how these conceptual advances forced physicists to adopt the UNCERTAINTY PRINCIPLE, to abandon their commitment to physical determinism and to seek only statistical laws when investigating the microcosm. In 1958 he suggested that ''all particles are basically nothing but different stationary states of one and the same stuff'' (*The Physicist's Concept of Nature,* 46), and urged the return to the Aristotelian concept of potency as an ontological basis for the indeterminism that seems to characterize the realm of the very small (*Physics and Philosophy,* 41, 53, 59–62, 69–72, 160, 166).

The status of atomism in 20th-century thought must be evaluated in the context of continuing research in the theory of elementary particles. While atomistic concepts have proved most fruitful in exploring the structure of matter, physicists have generally abandoned hope of attaining the indivisibles Democritus regarded as the ultimate building blocks of the universe. Their researches have accented, rather, elements of truth in competing theories, such as those of Aristotle and his medieval commentators. At the same time, philosophers of science have become more critical of conceptual schemes elaborated by physicists and are more prone to question the ontological status of theoretical entities than heretofore.

In light of these trends, atomism has ceased to play the central role in speculation about the physical universe that it played in the 19th century. This notwithstanding, and granted the oversimplifications that it involves when attempting to account for the wealth of detail in the microcosm, it still stands as one of the most fruitful conceptualizations in the history of scientific thought.

See Also: HYLOSYSTEMISM; ELEMENT; SPACE.

Bibliography: L. L. WHYTE, *Essay on Atomism* (New York 1960). A. G. VAN MELSEN, *From Atomos to Atom,* tr. H. J. KOREN (Pittsburgh 1952; 1960). K. LASSWITZ, *Geschichte der Atomistik vom Mittelalter bis Newton* (Hamburg 1890). R. EISLER, *Wörterbuch der philosophischen Begriffe,* 3 v. (4th ed. Berlin 1927–30) 1:132–137. V. E. ALFIERI, *Enciclopedia filosofica,* 4 v. (Venice-Rome 1957) 1:447–455. F. C. COPLESTON, *History of Philosophy* (Westminster, Md 1946—) v.1. S. SAMBURSKY, *The Physical World of the Greeks,* tr. M. DAGUT (New York 1962). C. BAILEY, *The Greek Atomists and Epicurus* (Oxford 1928). A. MAIER, *Die Vorläufer Galileis im 14. Jahrhundert* (Rome 1949); *An der Grenze von Scholastik und Naturwissenschaft* (2d ed. Rome 1952). *Readings in the Literature of Science,* eds. W. C. and M. D. DAMPIER (Cambridge, Eng. 1924; 1959), classical contributions to atomic theory. L. K. NASH, ''The Atomic Molecular Theory'' in *Harvard Case Histories in Experimental Science,* ed. J. B. CONANT, 2 v. (Cambridge, Mass. 1957) 1:215–321. M. BOAS, ''The Establishment of the Mechanical Philosophy,'' *Osiris,* 10 (1952) 412–541. C. NING YANG, *Elementary Particles* (Princeton 1962). W. HEISENBERG, *The Physicist's Concept of Nature,* tr. A. J. POMERANS (New York 1958); *Physics and Philosophy* (New York 1958). P. SOCCORSI, *Quaestiones scientificae cum philosophia coniunctae: De vi cognitionis humanae in scientia physica* (Rome 1958); *Quaestiones scientificae cum philosophia coniunctae: De physica quantica* (Rome 1956). W. A. WALLACE, ''The Reality of Elementary Particles,'' *American Catholic Philosophical Association. Proceedings of the Annual Meeting,* 38 (1964) 154–166.

[W. A. WALLACE]

ATONEMENT

The word atonement is of special interest in the fields of philology, literature, theology, and Scripture. It is the only word of Anglo-Saxon origin that signifies a theological doctrine. It indicates a setting ''at one'' of two parties that were estranged.

History of the Word. The verb "atone" existed in Middle English prior to the substantive "atonement." "Atone" was coined from "at" and "one" and signifies to set at one, to reconcile. It originated in the phrase "to be at one," a translation of the Anglo-French phrase *être à un*, to agree. In *Le Livre de reis* we read of Henry II and St. Thomas Becket: "Ils ne peusent être à un"— They could not agree.

Wyclif already used the noun "onement" for reconciliation. From frequent use of the phrases "set at one" or "at onement," the combined *atonement* began to take the place of *onement* early in the 16th century. St. Thomas More is the earliest known author to use the word atonement, in his English work the *History of King Richard III*. William Rastell, More's nephew, edited a strictly correct text in 1557. Rastell claimed that More wrote this incomplete history in 1513. Referring to the discord of the nobles at the time of Richard's coronation, More observed their lack of regard for their new atonement. *Atonement* was used here to signify reconciliation.

The Anglican Bibles—Tyndale (1525 or 1526), Coverdale (1535), Matthew (1537), Taverner (1539), Geneva (1557). King James (1611)—made ample use of the word atonement in the sense of reconciliation and expiation. C. S. Lewis, an Oxford authority on Tudor English, observed that the use of this word of Anglo-Saxon origin was probably no more than a case of stylistic preference. The King James Version was substantially Tyndale corrected and improved by Coverdale, Geneva, Rheims, and Cranmer, almost in collaboration [C. S. Lewis, *English Literature in the Sixteenth Century, Excluding Drama* (Oxford 1954) 214]. This was reflected in the use of the word atonement to translate καταλλαγή in Rom 5.11, as evidenced in the English Hexapla (Bodleian Library, Oxford MS Mason H H. 168, p. 88), which used later editions of the Tyndale and Geneva Bibles.

Theology. Since reconciliation is generally between one who has been offended and one who offends, atonement receives the ordinary meaning of satisfactory reparation or expiation for an offense. In the Old Testament, atonement is the reestablishment of Yahweh's communion with His people, who had offended Him by sin. It is a work of mercy on the part of God and on the part of man the fulfilling of certain things prescribed by God.

The Hebrew verb *kippēr*, pi'el of the root *kpr*, is translated as atone. It probably meant to cover, especially with a liquid. In the priestly documents it signifies mainly "to make atonement for sin by an expiatory rite" (Lv 4.31–35; 6.17–23). The LXX regularly translates *kippēr* by ἐξιλάσκομαι, which means to propitiate, also to atone. The highest spiritual sense of atonement in the Old Testament is found in Is 52.13–53.12. The placation con-

cept of atonement seems to have disappeared, and the passage concentrates on expiation. Sin is atoned for with a life, the life of the Suffering Servant of Yahweh, as a guilt offering. The personal deeds of this innocent mediator take the place of sinners. He suffers for them and effects atonement with a personal God moved by pity for them. The ideas of reconciliation and vicarious expiation permeate the passage.

In the New Testament, atonement does not play a primary role. In Heb 2.17 Christ has "become a merciful and faithful high priest before God to expiate [ἱλάσκεσθαι] the sins of the people." Paul presents atonement as an act of divine love that effects a new state of things, the peaceful relationship between God and man. Man is reconciled to God (2 Cor 5.18–19; Eph 2.15–16). In the second phase man acts: "be reconciled to God" (2 Cor 5.20). Paul develops these ideas out of the Old Testament background: e.g., the Old Testament notion of sacrifice, when he speaks of the SACRIFICE OF THE CROSS, of which atonement is an effect. Thus atonement is effected through the blood of the cross (Rom 5.9; Eph 2.13–16). The Pauline concept of atonement is related to the idea of justification, which forms the basis of atonement. Man is placed in a new relation to God. We live with God in peace (Rom 5.1–2; Eph 2.17–18).

Among the Christian writers atonement in the sense of satisfaction for sin, as applied to Christ's work, is found in its early development in the works of SS. Irenaeus, Ambrose, and Peter Damien. It assumed greater importance in the *Cur Deus Homo* of St. Anselm of Canterbury. Anselm made the atonement the basis of his explanation of the INCARNATION and the REDEMPTION, in place of earlier notions of sacrifice and payment for sin. The great scholastic theologians of the 13th century, notably, St. Thomas Aquinas, perfected the Anselmian doctrine. In place of Anselm's teaching on the quasi-necessity of the atonement, St. Thomas holds that it was a work of the free choice of God that vicarious satisfaction for sin was effected by the God-Man.

While the Council of Trent treats of the all-sufficient atonement of Our Lord, it also takes into account man's personal cooperation in the work of satisfaction for sin under the influence of Christ's grace. Trends in contemporary Lutheran theology of justification show remarkable agreement with this position. Excessive stress on man's personal cooperation in the work of atonement is evidenced in the long and arduous penances for remission of sin demanded by the Jansenists. In the present stance of Catholic and Protestant Biblical studies, there is a common stress on the atonement as a work of divine mercy rather than a juridical placation of divine wrath.

See Also: EXPIATION (IN THEOLOGY); REPARATION; SATISFACTION OF CHRIST.

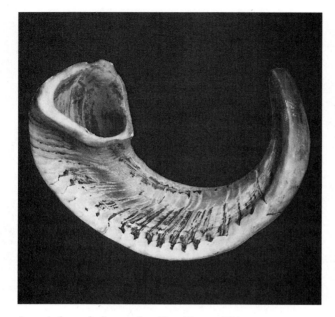

A ram's horn shofar, used on Yom Kippur, 20th century.

Bibliography: A. C. BAUGH, *A History of the English Language* (2d ed. New York 1957) 245. W. W. SKEAT, *Principles of English Etymology* (2d ed. Oxford 1892) 56. A. MÉDEBIELLE, *Dictionnaire de la Bible,* suppl. ed. L. PIROT, et al. (Paris 1928–) 3:1–262. G. KITTEL, *Theologisches Wörterbuch zum Neuen Testament* (Stuttgart 1935–) 1:252–260; 3:301–318; 4:330–337. H. F. DAVIS, CDT 1:189–198. J. BONSIRVEN, "Le Péché et son expiation selon la théologie du judaisme palestinien au temps de Jésus-Christ," *Biblica* 15 (1934) 213–236. S. LYONNET, *De peccato et redemptione* (Rome 1957–), 4 v. planned. J. DUPONT, *La Réconciliation dans la théologie de St. Paul* (Paris 1953).

[K. F. DOUGHERTY]

ATONEMENT, DAY OF (YOM KIPPUR)

An annual fast and day of expiation, observed on 10 Tishri (September or October), the most widely observed of all Jewish holy days. The term *yôm kippûr* is late rabbinical Hebrew for Biblical Hebrew *yôm hakkippûrîm,* both terms meaning Day of Atonement.

In the Bible. The only explicit references to this day in the Old Testament are found in the most recent stratum of the Pentateuch: Lv 16.1–34; 23.26–32; 25.9; Nm 29.7–11. In this source the prescriptions for Temple worship are projected historically to the TENT OF MEETING in the desert where Aaron ministered. The day is described as one of most solemn rest from work as on the Sabbath. There is a convocation at the Temple and special sacrifices are ordained. All must "afflict themselves," i.e., fast and perform acts of penance for their sins and those

of the whole nation. The JUBILEE YEAR is to be heralded by the blowing of the ceremonial ram's horn, the Shofar, on the Day of Atonement.

The unusual Temple ceremonies are described in detail in Lv 16.1–34. The high priest, wearing special vestments, first sacrificed a bull for his own sins and those of the priests. On this occasion only, he was permitted to enter the Holy of Holies, behind the sanctuary veil, with incense and the blood of the sacrificial animal to sprinkle the mercy seat as an act of expiation. Then he repeated this ritual, the second time sacrificing a male goat in expiation for the sins of the people and for the sanctuary itself. Finally the priest made atonement also for the outer sanctuary by sprinkling blood upon the altar (Ex 30.10).

In addition there was quite a different kind of rite often referred to as that of the SCAPEGOAT. The high priest selected two goats and cast lots upon them, "one lot for Yahweh and one lot for Azazel" (Lv 16.8). The goat "for Yahweh" was sacrificed as described above; the other had all the sins of the people placed upon its head by the symbolic imposition of the high priest's hands and was released in the wilderness to carry away the burden of guilt. The name scapegoat (Lat. *caper emissarius*) reflects a misunderstanding of some of the ancient versions in translating the phrase "for Azazel." A modern theory, that the word identifies the place where the goat was released, is not generally accepted. Azazel was in fact thought by the Jews to be an evil spirit or devil that dwelt in the wilderness (a fallen angel according to 1 Enoch 10.4–8). The Israelites did not sacrifice a goat to him, but they presented it before Yahweh and then sent it and their sins "into the wilderness to Azazel" (Lv 16.10). A number of parallels to this ritual have been pointed out in Babylonian and other ancient religions, and it is very probable that the Israelites here adopted an ancient popular custom and interpreted it in the light of their own religious observance.

The origin of the Day of Atonement itself remains obscure. The fact that it is not mentioned in any pre-exilic text of the Old Testament, nor even in the oldest postexilic texts, establishes a probability that it was instituted very late, but more precise information is not available. It is possible, however, that the practice of expiatory rites among the Hebrews was itself very ancient. The ritual of the Day of Atonement is alluded to in the New Testament (e.g., Heb 6.19; 9.7), but it did not persist in Christian observance. A tractate of the Mishnah (*Yômâ,* The Day) is devoted to details of the ritual.

Modern Customs. After the destruction of the Temple, prayers and synagogue services replaced the sacrifices and rites described above, but the essential motifs of self-affliction, confession, and expiation have always remained the heart of Yom Kippur observance. In the modern celebration there is a preliminary ritual on the eve, for which tradition prescribes a festive meal before sundown, the kindling of the festival lights, the settling of debts and disputes, and reconciliation with relatives and neighbors. The evening penitential services that follow in the synagogue begin with the *Kol Nidrê* (All vows . . .), a formula of absolution from all ceremonial or ritual vows intended to provide the worshiper with a new beginning and release him from any unfulfilled or forgotten promises of cult or custom. In the Ashkenazic (German-Jewish) ritual the *Kol Nidrê* is adapted to a distinctive and beautiful melody characteristic of the emotions of Yom Kippur. Since in history this formula has been the occasion of much misunderstanding outside Judaism, Jewish writers have been careful to insist that it does not refer to obligations to one's fellowmen or one's country.

On the Day of Atonement itself observance prohibits, even more solemnly than on the Sabbath, not only all business transactions or manual labor, but also, throughout the holy day, eating and drinking, bathing and anointing, the wearing of shoes, especially during services, and sexual relations. Custom has also associated almsgiving with Yom Kippur, and also the burning of candles in the synagogue in memory of the deceased, and the visiting of their graves. In keeping with the ancient idea of substitution or transference, it was once customary for an individual to swing a fowl over his head in symbolic sacrifice for some other person deserving of death for his sins. Other men, as an additional form of self-affliction, submitted to 39 lashes to be administered in the synagogue.

The essence, however, of the observance is the series of synagogue services, consisting of prayers, hymns, readings, and the confession of sins, which have been so much expanded that from sunrise to sunset on Yom Kippur they constitute one continual service. The Morning Service (*šaḥărît*) contains a memorial ceremony for the dead, including the prayer *yizkōr* (may he remember). The passages of Lv 16.1–34, Nm 29.7–11, and Is 57.15–58.14 are read at this time. In the Additional Service (*mûsāp*), there is a long description of the Temple ceremony on the Day of Atonement. The Afternoon Service (*minḥâ*) contains the reading of Leviticus ch. 18 and the Book of Jona. In the evening again there is a service peculiar to this day called the Neilah (*neʿîlâ*, conclusion), which concludes with the recital of the liturgical prayer *Shema* (Hear, O Israel . . .) and a single blast on the Shofar. The public confession of sins, which recurs throughout the day, is a general formula recited in unison, and not an individual confession. In the Ashkenazic, Sephardic (Spanish-Jewish), and other rituals there are many more prayers and readings that have been adopted into the liturgy. These rituals also contain many minor variations in the services themselves.

Bibliography: *Encyclopedic Dictionary of the Bible*, translated and adapted by L. HARTMAN (New York, 1963) 175–178. R. DE-VAUX, *Ancient Israel, Its Life and Institutions*, tr. J. MCHUGH (New York 1961) 507–510. H. DANBY, tr., ''Yoma,'' *The Mishnah* (Oxford 1933). K. KOHLER and M. L. MARGOLIS, *The Jewish Encyclopedia*, J. SINGER (New York 1901–06) 2:275–289. G. F. MOORE, *Judaism in the First Centuries of the Christian Era: The Age of the Tannaim*, 3 v. (Cambridge, MA 1927–30) v.2. S. LANDERSDORFER, *Studien zum biblischen Versöhnungstag (Alttestamentliche Abhandlungen* 10.1; Münster 1924). J. MORGENSTERN, ''Two Prophecies of the 4th Century B.C. and the Evolution of Yom Kippur,'' *Hebrew Union College Annual* 24 (1952–53) 1–74. A. Z. IDELSOHN, *Jewish Liturgy and Its Development* (New York 1932) 223–248.

[G. W. MACRAE]

ATTICUS OF CONSTANTINOPLE, ST.

Patriarch 406 to 425; b. Sebaste, Armenia; d. Constantinople, Oct. 10, 425. Atticus became a monk and an admirer of EUSTATHIUS OF SEBASTE, and ''though of mediocre talent, was endowed with sagacity'' (Sozomen, *Hist. eccl.* 8.27). After his ordination in Constantinople, although not a great orator, he gained a reputation as a facile speaker despite his Armenian accent. He served as one of the seven accusers of St. JOHN CHRYSOSTOM at the Synod of the OAK (Palladius, *Vita John Chrysos.* 11), and succeeded Arsacius as patriarch in 406. He increased the episcopal authority of his see through a law, sanctioned by Theodosius II, that prohibited episcopal consecrations in Hellespont, Bithynia, and Asia Minor without his consent (Nicephorus Callistus, *Hist. eccl.* 14.29). An imperial decree of 421 directing appeals from Illyricum to Constantinople instead of Rome, although canceled because of the protest of Pope Boniface I, was incorporated in the Justinian code. Atticus's orthodoxy was acknowledged by the councils of Ephesus (431) and Chalcedon (451). Having avenged himself on the followers of John Chrysostom, he sought reunion with Rome, inscribed Chrysostom's name in the diptychs, forcing (St.) Cyril of Alexandria to do likewise (V. Grumel, *Les Regestes des actes du patriarcat de Constantinople* 1.1:37, 40, 41), and attacked the Pelagian Celestius and the Messalians. His sanctity was acknowledged by the Bollandists but challenged by L. de TILLEMONT. Of his writings, letters to St. Cyril, Bishop Sahak of Armenia, Calliopes of Nicaea, and others, and fragments of a *Treatise against Nestorius* have been preserved. The Latin version of the Canons of Nicaea, which he sent to the Synod of Carthage (419), is preserved under his name.

Feast: Jan. 8.

Bibliography: A. BIGELMAIR, *Lexikon für Theologie und Kirche*, ed. J. HOFER and K. RAHNER (Freiburg 1957–65) 1:1016–17. O.

BARDENHEWER, *Geschichte der altkirchlichen Literatur* (Freiburg 1913–32) 3:361–363. M. T. DISDIER, *Dictionnaire d'histoire et de géographie ecclésiastiques*, ed. A. BAUDRILLART et al. (Paris 1912) 5:161–166. G. BARDY, *Histoire de l'église depuis les origines jusqu'à nos jours*, ed. A. FLICHE and V. MARTIN (Paris 1935) 4:149–162. V. GRUMEL, *Les Regestes des actes du patriarcat de Constantinople* (Kadikoi-Bucharest 1932) 1.1:35–48. M. BRIÈRE, "Une Homélie inédite d'Atticus," *Revue de l'orient chrétien* 34 (1933–34) 160–186. J. LEBON, "Discours d'Atticus de Constantinople," *Muséon* 46 (1933) 167–202. C. H. TURNER ed., *Ecclesiae occidentalis monumenta iuris antiquissima* (Oxford 1899–1939) 1.1:104–142.

[P. JOANNOU]

ATTIGNY, COUNCILS OF

A number of Church councils held at Attigny, near Vouziers, France, in the Diocese of Reims, where there were both an episcopal residence and an important residence of the Carolingian kings.

In 765 about 25 bishops, 17 abbots, and other clerics met there; all that is now known of their transactions is that they promised that when one of them died the others would offer as suffrages a certain number of Masses and Psalms.

In 785 or 786, CHARLEMAGNE attended the council at which two conquered Saxon princes, WIDUKIND and Albuin, were baptized.

In 822, at an assembly of bishops and princes, Emperor Louis the Pious was reconciled with his three brothers, including DROGO OF METZ, and did public penance for blinding his nephew Bernard, King of Italy. He promised to correct abuses and to restore ecclesiastical and civil order. He commended the Rule of St. CHRODEGANG OF METZ for every chapter of CANONS. The bishops promised a program of reform, including the foundation and improvement of schools for future clerics.

At a council held in 834, Louis again promised to correct abuses and ordered his son Pepin to return certain Church properties.

There may have been a council at Attigny in 847, confirming decisions of the council of Paris of 846 or 847, which denied the claims of EBBO OF REIMS and confirmed the nomination of HINCMAR as archbishop of Reims.

In 865 a council decreed that King LOTHAIR II must leave his concubine and take back his wife. The papal legate promulgated two papal excommunications.

In 870, 30 bishops from ten provinces and six archbishops participated in a council that found Carloman guilty of conspiracy against his father, Emperor Charles II the Bald. HINCMAR, Bishop of Laon, had to promise obedience to Charles and to his metropolitan.

Bibliography: C. J. VON HEFELE, *Histoire des conciles d'après les documents originaux*, tr. and continued by H. LECLERCQ, 10 v. in 19 (Paris 1907–38) 3:951–952, 994; 4:34–36, 88–89, 363–364, 1306–07, 1344. A. PRÉVOST, *Dictionnaire d'histoire et de géographie ecclésiastiques*, ed. A. BAUDRILLART (Paris 1912–) 5:168.

[A. CONDIT]

ATTILANUS, ST.

Patron and probably first bishop of Zamora; place and date of birth unknown (sometimes given as Tarazona, Spain, *c.* 939); d. Zamora(?), Oct. 5, 916. He was the colleague of St. FROILÁN in the organizing of monastic life in northwestern Spain. His name appears in the cartularies of Sahagun and Santiago. Zamora was destroyed by the Moors at the end of the tenth century, but, when the diocese was restored in the twelfth, the cult of St. Attilanus spread widely. In 1260, thanks to a miraculous revelation, a shepherd discovered his relics in Zamora; his head was later stolen and taken to Toledo. A twelfth-century vita that ascribes his origin to Tarragona lacks authenticity; and the claim that Urban II canonized him is false. He was included in the Roman martyrology in 1583.

Feast: Oct. 3; Aug. 28 (in Tarragona).

Bibliography: A. LAMBERT, *Dictionnaire d'histoire et de géographie ecclésiastiques*, ed. A. BAUDRILLART et al. (Paris 1912) 5:169–173. B. DE GAIFFIER, "Les Notices hispaniques du martyrologe romain," *Analecta Bollandiana* 58 (1940) 80–89. E. FERNÁNDEZ-PRIETO DOMINGUEZ, *Actas de visitas reales y otras realizadas por acontecimientos extraordinarios a los cuerpos santos de San Ildefonso y San Atilano . . .* (Zamora 1973).

[E. P. COLBERT]

ATTITUDES

Predispositions to react in a certain way in response to certain kinds of stimuli. Attitudes are accompanied by positive or negative feelings associated with a specific psychological object, i.e., a habitual way of thinking and feeling about a group, person, situation, or object.

Attitudes are complex; they are composed of elements that fall into three categories—cognitive, affective, and behavioral. Attitude structure tends to be hierarchical; specific attitudes tend to be subsidiary to general attitudes; e.g., one prejudiced against a religious minority group will more than likely be found prejudiced against other minority groups whether religious, racial, or national.

In most adults attitudes are moderately well integrated and generally resistant to change. People tend to seek out persons and situations reflecting attitudes consistent with their own. It is unclear, however, as to whether consistency or attitudes is a cause or a reflection of certain personality characteristics.

Social environment is the principal determinant of the kinds of attitudes acquired and held. A child tends to acquire the attitudes he sees and hears expressed within the home. Where there is attitude uniformity in the environment, attitudes take shape readily. Generally accepted attitudes become stable and enduring. They can be changed through altering a person's perception of the significance of the attitude object as a means for obtaining cherished goals.

In principle, an attitude cannot be measured directly but rather by inference from what a person says or does. In general, what one says is the more direct measure of attitude since what is said is affected principally by one's habitual way of thinking and feeling about a given object or situation.

Attitude scales, consisting of 15 to 25 statements, fairly equally spaced along the continuum from very favorable to very unfavorable, ask the respondent for expressions of opinion on specifics of a given attitude. Each attitude statement is assigned by a group of "judges" a value on a 1-to-11 point scale according to degree of attitude expressed. An individual's score is the median value of items checked.

Attitude measures can evaluate the extent to which educational aims are achieved, e.g., the effect of a school program in achieving attitudinal objectives. Attitude evaluation likewise assists in the understanding of the dynamics of behavior.

Attitudes are effective determinants of behavior that can be influenced through education and measured. Current techniques, while being improved, are sufficiently valid and reliable to warrant their use.

Bibliography: H. J. LAUSMEIER, *Learning and Human Abilities* (New York 1961). R. E. RIPPLE, ed., *Readings in Learning and Human Abilities* (New York 1964). L. L. THURSTONE, *The Measurement of Values* (Chicago 1959), pt. 3; *Multiple Factor Analysis* (Chicago 1947). M. J. ROSENBERG et al., *Attitude, Organization and Change* (New Haven 1960). B. F. GREEN, "Attitude Measurement," in *Handbook of Social Psychology*, ed. G. LINDZEY, 2 v. (Reading Mass. 1954).

[U. H. FLEEGE]

ATTO, COLLECTION OF

A compendium of Canon Law, *Breviarium,* in 500 unnumbered Chapters, compiled in Rome *c.* 1075 by ATTO OF MILAN, cardinal priest of St. Mark, to supply the needs of the clergy of his titular church. It stands among the first such works inspired by the program of Pope Gregory VII, to which the author was devoted, at least in its early stage. He aimed to present in brief the norms of law and morality that represented the discipline of the Roman Church, as found in the ancient papal decretals and conciliar canons, and constituted the basis of the GREGORIAN reform. His chief sources were the FALSE DECRETALS, DIONYSIUS EXIGUUS (for Oriental and African councils), and Pope Gregory I's letters (more than 100 excerpts). Material not previously in circulation came notably from Pope Gelasius I. The first series of texts embraces the decretals; the second, the councils—each in chronological order. Its influence was very limited, but it was used in the Collection of DEUSDEDIT and by Anselm of Lucca. The title *Capitulare* is a modern misnomer.

See Also: CANONICAL COLLECTIONS BEFORE GRATIAN.

Bibliography: A. MAI, *Scriptorum veterum noval collectio e Vaticanis codicibus edita* (Rome 1825–38) 6.2:60–120, from the one known MS, now identified as Codex Vaticanus latinus 586. P. FOURNIER and G. LEBRAS, *Histoire des collections canoniques en occident depuis les fausses décrétales jusqu'au Dét de Gratien* (Paris 1931–32) 2:20–25. P. FOURNIER, "Les Collections canoniques romaines de l'époque de Grégoire VII," *Mémoires de l'Académie des inscriptions et belles-lettres* 41 (1918) 271–395, also pub. sep. (Paris 1918). A. M. STICKLER, *Historia iuris canonici latini* (Turin 1950) 166–167. R. NAZ, ed., *Dictionnaire de droit canonique* (Paris 1935–65) 1:1330–31.

[J. J. RYAN]

ATTO OF MILAN

Cardinal and canonist; birthplace and date unknown; d. 1085 or 1086. A Milanese cleric of noble birth, he was elected to succeed Archbishop Wido on Jan. 6, 1072, in the presence of Pope Alexander II's legate and with the support of the PATARINE reformers. Ensuing disorders prevented enthronement, and Atto took refuge in Rome under Pope Gregory VII when a rival candidate was consecrated with King Henry IV's approval. Despite recognition of Atto as bishop-elect by Roman synods in 1072 and 1074 and efforts to secure his rights by Pope Gregory (*Registrum* 2.30; 3.8, 9), he never occupied the see. He was created cardinal priest of the title of St. Mark, but little is known of his Roman career. He was among those who deserted Gregory in 1084, as Cardinal Beno and Hugh of Lyons both testified, and he was eulogized after death by the moderate Pope Victor III. His fame rests on his *Breviarium* (*see* ATTO, COLLECTION OF). The title cardinal of Milan is a modern misnomer.

Bibliography: BONZIO OF SUTRI, *Liber ad amicum,* lib. 6, *Monumenta Germaniae Historica, Libelli de lite,* (Berlin 1826—)

1:599–600. ARNULF OF MILAN, *Gesta archiepiscoporum Medio-lanensium,* lib. 3–4, *Monumenta Germaniae Historica, Scriptores,* (Berlin 1826—) 8:22–31. A. FLICHE, *Dictionnaire d'histoire et de géographie ecclésiastiques,* ed. A. BAUDRILLART et al. (Paris 1912—) 5:184–185.

[J. J. RYAN]

ATTO OF VERCELLI

Bishop, theologian, and canonist; b. *c.* 885; d. Dec. 31, 961. He is called also Atto II, to distinguish him from an earlier bishop of Vercelli of the same name who lived about the middle of the 8th century. Born of a distinguished Lombard family, the son of the Viscount Aldegarius, he became a figure of outstanding importance in the Church and state of his day. Details of his education are not known, but it must have been considerable, for his works indicate a knowledge of Greek. The year 924 was the turning point in his career; the Hungarians, during their incursion into Italy, ravaged the city of Pavia on March 12, and Ragembert, Bishop of Vercelli, died in the attack. Atto was made his successor, and his office brought him into association with the leading figures of his day: Hugh of Provence, king of Italy (d. 947), whose grand chancellor he became; LOTHAIR II (d. 950), Hugh's son, whom he served in a like capacity; and the Margrave Berengar II (d. 966). Yet his activities did not prevent him from devoting considerable time to writing. The three books of his *De pressuris ecclesiasticis* (*c.* 940) are the earliest of his major works and deal with such subjects as the refutation of charges against the clergy, the filling of clerical posts (especially bishoprics), and the unjust seizure of Church property by the laity after the death of the bishop. His *Commentary on the Epistles of Paul* considered the question of why the Roman Epistles stand first. There are also *Letters and Sermons,* as well as a work titled *Canones statutaque Vercellensis ecclesiae,* which is a recapitulation of past ecclesiastical legislation in the diocese and includes the FALSE DECRETALS. His somewhat remarkable *Polipticum* (*Polypticum, Perpendiculum*), an abridgment of moral philosophy [ed. G. Goetz, *Abhandlungen der Sächischen Akademie (Gesellschaft, to 1920) der Wissenschaften* 1922, 37.2], seems to have been completed in the last months of Atto's life and to have been sent to a friend, who in turn composed a foreword to the work, using the same distinctive Latinity that Atto had employed. Atto himself stands as a valuable index to his age and as a person of notable endowments and achievements.

Bibliography: Works. *Patrologia Latina,* ed. J. P. MIGNE, 217 v., indexes 4 v. (Paris 1878–90) 134:9–916. C. BURONZO DEL SIGNORE, ed., 2 v. (Vercelli 1768). **Literature.** J. SCHULTZ, *Atto von Vercelli* (Göttingen 1885). E. PASTERIS, *Attone di Vercelli ossiail*

più grande vescovo e scrittore italiano del secolo X (Milan 1925). P. PIRRI, "Attone di Vercelli," *La civiltà cattolica* 1 (1927) 27–42. A. FLICHE, *La Réforme grégorienne,* v.1 (Paris 1924) 61–74. M. MANITIUS, *Geschichte der lateinischen Literatur des Mittelalters,* 3 v. (Munich 1911–31) 2:27–34. W. WATTENBACH, *Deutschlands Geschichtsquellen im Mittelalter. Deutsche Kaiserzeit,* ed. R. HOLTZMANN, v.1.1–4 (3d ed. Tübingen 1948) 1.2:317. P. MIKAT, *Lexikon für Theologie und Kirche,* ed. J. HOFER and K. RAHNER, 10 v. (2d, new ed. Freiburg 1957–65) 1:1019.

[W. C. KORFMACHER]

ATTRITION AND ATTRITIONISM

Attrition or imperfect contrition is sorrow and detestation of sin motivated by sin's malice or the fear of hell and God's punishments. The term was first employed by Alan of Lille (d. 1202) to express a certain displeasure for sin, but one not deep enough to prompt the sinner to a firm purpose of amendment. According to Alan, those who are attrite "become less evil, but they do not cease to be evil until they are perfectly contrite" [*Regulae de sacra theologia,* 85 (*Patrologia Latina.* ed. J. P. Migne [Paris 1878–90] 210:665)]. A more positive approach to attrition was taken by William of Auvergne (d. 1249). Having more regard for the etymology of the word (Latin *attero,* p. part. *attritus,* to wear away by rubbing), William regarded attrition as the first step in the removal of sin. Attrition is not merely the natural displeasure that is consequent upon sin, it is the result of God's gratuitous grace (*gratia gratis data*) by which the destruction of sin is begun, whereas CONTRITION is the result of God's sanctifying grace (*gratia gratum faciens*) by which the process is completed. Hence, contrition presupposes the gift of charity, whereas attrition is a preparation for the grace of charity that elicits the act of contrition. Although William is not the author of the adage *"ex attrito fit contritus"* (a person who is attrite becomes contrite), William regarded attrition as a sufficient preparation for the Sacrament of Penance, in and through which the sinner becomes contrite [cf. *De sacramento paenitentiae,* 4; *Opera Omnia* (Venice 1591) 441].

William of Auvergne's distinction between attrition and contrition became the common property of the great scholastic doctors of the 13th century, including St. Bonaventure and St. Thomas Aquinas. Out of deference, however, to Peter Lombard (d. *c.* 1160), the Master of the *Sentences,* who held that sorrow prompted by perfect love of God was the only proper disposition for the remission of sins, both Thomas and Bonaventure held that contrition informed by charity should be the normal disposition in one approaching the power of the keys. Both admitted, however, that putative contrition (actually attrition), when informed by the priest's absolution, would result in perfect contrition and the remission of sins, the position of William of Auvergne (cf. Bonaventure, *In 4 Sent.* 17.2.2.3; Thomas, *Summa Theologiae* Suppl 3a, 18.1).

Council of Trent. In the 14th session of the Council of Trent (1551) attrition was distinguished from contrition not so much by the eliciting principle, the virtue of charity, but by the motive that prompted the act. Thus, against Luther, who held that attrition made man a hypocrite and a greater sinner, Trent defined attrition as a gift of God and a prompting of the Holy Spirit, since "it is ordinarily conceived from a consideration of sin's malice or from fear of hell and punishment" [Sess. 14, ch. 4 (H. Denzinger, *Enchiridion symbolorum*, ed. A. Schönmetzer, Freiburg, 1963; 1678)]. True, such attrition does not of itself justify the sinner apart from the Sacrament of Penance, "yet it disposes him for the attainment of God's grace in the Sacrament" (*ibid.*). Trent also insists that such attrition must exclude the will to sin and be accompanied by hope of pardon (*ibid.*).

Controversies after Trent. The basic issue after Trent concerned attrition from the motive of fear (*attritio formidolosa*). According to the Jansenists "fear of hell is not supernatural" nor a sufficient motive for attrition [cf. *Propositions,* 14, 15, condemned by Alexander VIII, 1690 (Denzinger 2314, 2315)]. According to the Jansenist Quesnel, "Fear merely restrains the hand, while the heart is attached to sin so long as one is not motivated by love of justice" [*Proposition* 61, condemned by Clement XI, 1713 (Denzinger 2461)]. The Jansenist Synod of Pistoia (1794) insisted that sorrow for sin even in the Sacrament of Penance must be prompted by the most perfect love of God, the "fervor of charity" (cf. Denzinger 2636). Against the Jansenists, Catholic theologians appealed to the Old and the New Testament to show that God repeatedly urges the motive of fear as the first step in the repentance of the sinner and as an incentive for avoiding sin in the future. Typical of such exhortations is Christ's own warning: "And do not be afraid of those who kill the body but cannot kill the soul. But rather be afraid of him who is able to destroy both soul and body in hell" (Mt 10.28). Again, to demand perfect contrition as the motive of sorrow in the Sacrament of Penance is to deny that the priest's absolution is in any way directed to the remission of sin.

Unlike the Jansenists, the Contritionists of the 17th century admitted that fear of God was both good and salutary. They denied that attrition from the motive of fear was a sufficient preparation for obtaining pardon in the Sacrament of Penance. Without going to the extremes of the Jansenists who demanded the fervor of charity, the Contritionists demanded some love of God or love of benevolence for pardon even in the Sacrament of Penance. Attrition from the motive of fear disposes the sinner for the grace of pardon in the Sacrament of Penance, but only remotely. The proximate disposition must be love or charity towards God.

The Attritionists, many of whom were Jesuits and suspicious of anything that seemed to be Jansenistic, insisted that attrition from the motive of fear, so long as it was coupled with hope of divine pardon, was a proximate disposition for forgiveness in and through the Sacrament of Penance. For Attritionists, love of God for His own sake, no matter at what state of development, or how lacking in emotional fervor, was sufficient of itself to justify the sinner even before the actual reception of the Sacrament of Penance. Hence, it could not be demanded in the Sacrament of Penance without undermining the sacramental efficacy of the priest's absolution. Many Attritionists, however, did speak of "love," but it was a love of concupiscence or the love of hope (*amor concupiscentiae vel spei*), an initial love of God as the source of all justice, of which Trent speaks in its decree on justification (cf. Denzinger 1526).

The controversy between the Contritionists and the Attritionists waxed so warm, particularly in Belgium, the homeland of Jansenism, that Alexander VII sponsored a decree of the Holy Office which warned both parties to the controversy under the severest of penalties "not to dare to affix a note of theological censure" to either opinion. The decree, however, does note in passing that the view of the Attritionists "appears to be more common among scholastics" [*Decree of the Holy Office,* May 6, 1667 (Denzinger 2070)].

See Also: PENANCE, SACRAMENT OF.

Bibliography: P. F. PALMER, ed., *Sacraments and Forgiveness* (Sources of Christian Theology 2; Westminster, Md. 1960). J. PÉRINELLE, *L'Attrition d'après le Concile de Trente et d'après Saint Thomas d'Aquin* (Kain, Belg. 1927). H. DONDAINE, *L'Attrition suffisante* (Paris 1943). H. DENZINGER, *Enchiridion symbolorum*, ed. A. SCHÖNMETZER (Freiburg 1963).

[P. F. PALMER]

ATTWATER, DONALD

Writer and editor; b. Dec. 24, 1892, Forest Garte, Co. Essex, England; d. Feb. 3, 1977, Storington. Of devout, Wesleyan parentage, in his youth Attwater became, with his family, an Anglican and at 18, on his own, a Catholic. After schooling in private and public institutions, he studied law, but did not earn a degree. He was in Egypt and Palestine with the Royal Artillery during World War I (1916–1919). While there, he began to take an interest in

Eastern Christianity, an interest that would lead him into becoming a writer and a specialist on the Christian Orient. Among his works in this field are *The Dissident Eastern Churches* (Milwaukee 1937), *The Golden Book of Eastern Saints* (Milwaukee 1938), *Life of St. John Chrysostom* (Milwaukee 1939), *Eastern Catholic Worship* (Milwaukee 1945), *The Christian Church of the East* (Milwaukee 1947), and *Saints of the East* (New York 1963).

After the war, Attwater settled on the Isle of Caldey where he came under the influence of the Benedictines and of Eric Gill, both of whom were to mold his life. He took over the editorship of the Benedictines' quarterly review, *Pax*. He also edited a popular review on the liturgy, contributing many articles to it. This led to his becoming, in 1925, associate editor for England of the American review *Orate Fratres* (later to become *Worship*). For a time, he was also contributing editor of the American weekly *Commonweal*. He was on the staff of the *Catholic Herald*, London, from its inception, and served as its editor from 1935 to 1936. He was assistant editor of a daughter paper, *The Glasgow Observer,* from 1939 on.

Prior to his work on *The Glasgow Observer*, he founded the Society for the Vernacular in English. The liturgy became one of his absorbing interests, and he was a strong voice in the liturgical movement. He wrote liturgical pieces for Catholic reviews both in England and the U.S. and, in 1961, published his *Layman's Missal*.

Attwater also authored several dictionary-type works. In 1931, e.g., he published *A Catholic Dictionary* (issued in England as *A Catholic Encyclopedic Dictionary*). His *Dictionary of Saints*, published in 1938, was later reissued as the *Penguin Dictionary of Saints* (Baltimore 1965), a continuing best seller. Earlier he published an edition of the monumental Alban Butler-Herbert Thurston, SJ, *Lives of the Saints* (4 v., with notes and commentaries, New York 1956).

During World War II, Attwater was employed by the British Military Forces as a lecturer on current affairs. At war's end, he went on three lecture tours of the United States and became a visiting lecturer at Notre Dame University.

Attwater's other works include *The Catholic Church in Modern Wales* (London 1935), *The White Fathers in Africa* (London 1937), *Names and Name Days* (Milwaukee 1939), *A Dictionary of Mary* (New York 1956), and *Dictionary of the Popes* (London 1965). Among his translations are V. Solov'ev, *God, Man, and the Church*; N. A. Berdiaev, *The End of Our Time; Dostoievsky* (New York 1934); and *Christianity and Class War* (London 1932). His last book *The Cell of Good Living* (London

1969) is a study of the life and views of Eric Gill, the artist who deeply influenced the renaissance of English letters, of which Attwater was a part.

Bibliography: The London *Tablet* (Feb. 12, 1977) 161. *The Times* of London (Feb. 5. 1977) 18.

[P. F. MULHERN]

ATWATER, WILLIAM

Bishop of Lincoln; b. according to his epitaph *c.* 1440; d. February 4, 1520 or 1521. He was probably a fellow of Magdalen College, Oxford, in 1480. In 1492 and 1493 he took the degree doctor of theology and in 1497 became vice chancellor of the university. He held this office in conjunction with others until 1502, for a time filling the post of chancellor left vacant by the death of Abp. John Morton. On June 21, 1504, he became canon of Windsor and registrar of the Order of the Garter. From 1506 to 1512 he was chancellor of the cathedral of Lincoln, exchanging the chancellorship on Oct. 30, 1512, for a prebend in the cathedral. In July of 1509 Atwater secured the prebendary of Ruscomb in Salisbury cathedral along with a coat of arms, and in September of the same year he obtained the appointment of dean of Salisbury. For a short time from 1509 to 1512 he was archdeacon of Lewes. From June 3 until November of 1514 he was archdeacon of Huntington. He was elevated to the bishopric of Lincoln in September of 1514 in succession to Wolsey and was consecrated at Lambeth on Nov. 12, 1514. His rise in the Church was due probably to the favor of Wolsey. On Oct. 22, 1514, he resigned the canonry of Windsor, but continued in the deanery of the chapel royal. He was buried in Lincoln Cathedral; an inscription above his grave states that at the time of his death he was 81 years old.

Bibliography: A. B. EMDEN, *A Biographical Register of the University of Oxford to A.D. 1500*, 3 v. (Oxford 1957–59). 1:73–74. P. GAMS, *Series episcaporum ecclesiae catholicae* (Regensburg 1873; suppl. 1879–86; repr. Graz 1957) 192. S. LEE, *The Dictionary of National Biography from the Earliest Times to 1900*, 63 v. (London 1885–1900) 1:713. R. VAN DOREN, *Dictionnaire d'histoire et de géographie ecclésiastiques*, ed. A. BAUDRILLART (Paris 1912—) 5:199.

[V. PONKO, JR.]

AUBENAS, MARTYRS OF, BB.

Jesuits slain Feb. 7, 1593, by Huguenots in Aubenas, Diocese of Viviers, France. They were beatified June 6, 1926, and are honored as "Martyrs of the Eucharist." James Salès, b. Lezoux in Auvergne, March 21, 1556;

studied at Billom and Paris. He entered the novitiate at Verdun and taught philosophy at Pont-à-Mousson and theology in Tournon. Ordained in 1585, he preached in Lorraine. In November of 1592 on the request of the mayor for a Jesuit to preach the Advent series, he was sent to Aubenas, recently retaken from the Huguenots. A lay brother, William Saultemouche, b. St. Germain d'Herm, Clermont, 1556, was his companion. On Feb. 6, 1593, the Huguenots attacked Aubenas and seized the Jesuits. Salès defended the faith at length before a court of Calvinists. When he refused to renounce articles of the faith, especially with regard to the Eucharist, he was shot, stabbed, and beaten. Saultemouche remained with him rather than attempt to escape. Their relics are in Avignon.

Feast: Feb. 7.

Bibliography: G. WAGNER, *Catholicisme* 1:1008–09. B. SCHNEIDER, *Lexikon für Theologie und Kirche*, ed. J. HOFER and K. RAHNER (Freiburg 1957–65) 1:1022.

[F. D. S. BORAN]

AUBERT OF AVRANCHES, ST.

Bishop; d. Avranches, 725. According to the accounts of the foundation of Mont-Saint-Michel, Aubert (or Autbert), Bishop of Avranches (704?–725), had retreated to Mont Tombe to pray. Having fallen asleep, he was told three times in a dream to build a church on the site and dedicate it to St. Michael the Archangel. The records report that the church was so dedicated on October 16, 709. Aubert is supposed also to be the founder of the pilgrimage to the famous spot, henceforth called Mont-Saint-Michel. The chapter of canons was later replaced by Benedictines; Aubert's body was translated to the abbey June 18, *c.* 1009. Since the French Revolution, the only relic extant is in Saint-Gervais in Avranches. A fifteenth-century vita of St. Aubert is of little value.

Feast: Sept. 10.

Bibliography: *Acta Sanctorum* Sept. 8:76–78. *Bibliotheca hagiograpica latina antiquae et mediae aetatis* (Brussels 1898–1901) 1:858–860; 2:5951. E. DUPONT, *Dictionnaire d'histoire et de géographie ecclésiastiques*, ed. A. BAUDRILLART et al. (Paris 1912) 5:222. R. AIGRAIN, *Catholicisme* 1:1009–10. A. BUTLER, *The Lives of the Saints*, ed. H. THURSTON and D. ATTWATER (New York 1956) 3:533.

[G. J. DONNELLY]

AUBIGNÉ, JEAN HENRI MERLE D'

Swiss Protestant ecclesiastical historian, preacher, and founder of the College of Geneva, whose thinking and achievement influenced Genevan Calvinism, b. Eaux Vives, Geneva, Aug. 8, 1794; d. there, Oct. 21, 1872. D'Aubigné's paternal ancestors were French Huguenot refugees, the name *d'Aubigné* being added to the family name of *Merle* by his maternal grandmother. He was educated in Geneva, where he imbibed the influence of the Scottish missionary preacher, Robert Haldane, and in Berlin, where he profited from the scholarship of William Neander and W. M. L. de Wette. After ordination he was appointed in 1819 pastor of the Protestant French church in Hamburg. From 1823 to 1830 he served as court preacher to King William I of the Netherlands in Brussels and also became president of the consistory of the French and German Protestant churches. The Belgian revolution of 1830 decided his return to Geneva, where he served as professor of church history until his death. He became an outstanding promoter of "evangelical alliance," founding, with others, the Evangelical Society for the promotion of evangelical Christianity. Calvinistic in its main doctrines, under d'Aubigné's guidance this society staunchly opposed Church-State union and aimed boldly at establishing an all-Protestant church relationship. Thus he helped to break that inflexible exclusiveness hitherto characteristic of Genevan Calvinism. As a counterpoise to the Genevan Academy, and to meet the need for theologically trained ministers capable of pursuing the necessary Protestant colloquy and union, as well as to encourage a missionary spirit, he founded the College of Geneva and was its president. He remained very anti-Catholic.

In addition to preaching and instructing, he labored indefatigably in writing ecclesiastical history. His most notable works are: *Histoire de la réformation du XVIe siècle* (5 v. Paris 1835–53, tr. into most European languages), *Histoire de la réformation en Europe du temps de Calvin* (8 v. Paris 1862–77, tr. into English), and a historical monograph on Oliver Cromwell. He visited Britain frequently and was honored both by Oxford University and by the city of Edinburgh.

Bibliography: V. ROSSEL, *Histoire littéraire de la Suisse romande des origines à nos jours*, 2 v. (Geneva 1889–91), v.2. H. HOHLWEIN, *Die Religion in Geschichte und Gegenwart* 4:879.

[F. D. S. BORAN]

AUBRAC, ORDER OF

Community of hospitallers founded in 1120 by Adalard, Viscount of Flanders, as he was returning from SANTIAGO DE COMPOSTELA. At the same time he established the hospital (*see* HOSPITALS, HISTORY OF) of Sainte-Marie at Aubrac, on a mountain in Rouergue, 22 km from Espalion, France. In 1162, Peter II, Bishop of Rodez, gave the community a rule based on the Rule of St. AUGUSTINE; it was confirmed by Pope Alexander III. The community was composed of five groups: priests, knights, lay brothers, oblates, and the women assistants of high birth. Aubrac founded a number of dependent hospitals. Attempts to amalgamate with the Order of St. John of Jerusalem (KNIGHTS OF MALTA) or with the TEMPLARS were unsuccessful. In 1477 the monastery was placed in COMMENDATION. By 1697 such laxity had set in that the Congregation of France (canons of SAINTE-GENEVIÈVE OF PARIS) was sent to take over the hospital. The harsh climate forced the canons to withdraw, and in 1699 they were replaced by the Reformed Canons of Chancelade. Aubrac was suppressed by the French Revolution. The religious at Aubrac wore a black cassock with an eight-pointed blue cross at the left side; in choir, they wore a black cowl that bore the same cross.

Bibliography: C. DE VIC and J. VAISSETE, *Histoire générale de Languedoc,* ed. E. DULAURIER et al., 16 v. in 17 (2d ed. Toulouse 1872–1904) 4:888–898. P. HÉLYOT, *Histoire des ordres monastiques, religieux et militaires,* 8 v. (Paris 1714–19) 3:169–174. C. BELMON, *Dictionnaire d'histoire et de géographie ecclésiastiques* 5:256–258. R. CHALUMEAU, *Catholicisme* 1:1013–14. Archives of Department of Aveyron, ser. G. and H.; Collection Doat.

[J. CAMBELL]

AUBUSSON, PIERRE D'

Cardinal and grand master of the Order of St. John of Jerusalem; b. 1423; d. July 3, 1503. He belonged to the noble family who ruled the town of Aubusson, the Viscounts de la Marche. He served with Emperor SIGISMUND and with Albert VI, Archduke of Austria (d. 1463), before joining the Order of St. John (*see* KNIGHTS OF MALTA), where he rose rapidly through the various offices until he was selected grand master, June 8, 1476. The main problem during his administration was to prevent the Turks from conquering Rhodes. The knights fought off an all-out attempt in 1480 in an engagement in which Aubusson was wounded. His success against the Turks made him widely known in Europe. The island was temporarily saved from further attack by the death in 1481 of Mohammad II, the Turkish leader. During the struggle for succession, one of Mohammad's sons, Jem, sought asylum with the grand master. Aubusson sent him to France and then, for reasons that are not exactly clear, accepted an annuity of 45,000 ducats from Sultan Bajazet (d. 1513), the captive's brother, on condition that he prevent Jem from appealing to Christian Europe for aid. Jem, in effect, became a prisoner of the knights in France until 1489, when he was handed over to Pope INNOCENT VIII. In that same year Aubusson was made a cardinal and given the power to confer all benefices connected with

the order without the sanction of the papacy. The knights received also the wealth of the suppressed orders of the Holy Sepulcher and the HOSPITALLERS OF ST. LAZARUS. Aubusson spent the last years of his life trying to organize a crusade against the Turks, but the death of Jem in 1495 removed the most formidable weapon that could be used against the Sultan. Aubusson's last efforts were handicapped also by dissension among his own troops. Aubusson was an able soldier and an effective diplomat, but his reputation has been somewhat clouded by his acceptance of money from the Sultan for the neutralization of Jem and his efforts, in his last years, at stamping out JUDAISM on Rhodes by expelling all adult Jews and forcibly baptizing their children. The letters and documents of Aubusson are to be found in the second volume of the *Codice diplomatico del sacro militare ordine Gerosolimitano,* ed. S. Paoli (Lucca 1737).

Bibliography: R. A. DE VERTOT, *Histoire des chevaliers hospitaliers de S. Jean de Jerusalem,* 7 v. (Paris 1778) v.3. D. BAUHOURS, *Histoire de P. d'Aubusson* (4th ed. Paris 1806). G. E. STRECK, *Pierre d'Aubusson* (Chemnitz 1872). A. GABRIEL, *La Cité de Rhodes, 1310–1522* (Paris 1923). G. MOLLAT, *Dictionnaire d'histoire et de géographie ecclésiastiques,* ed. A. BAUDRILLART et al. (Paris 1912–) 5:270–274.

[V. L. BULLOUGH]

AUCTOR OF METZ, ST.

Bishop; fl. *c.* 451. Auctor, thirteenth bishop of Metz, was apparently a contemporary of Attila the Hun, who ravaged the region in 451. In the time of Louis the Pious, Bp. Drogo of Metz transferred the relics of Auctor to Maursmünster. Although there are distinct traditions surrounding an Auctor, bishop of Trier, whose feast was formerly kept on August 20, he is an unhistorical personage whose vita (*Acta Sanctorum* Aug. 4:37–53) perhaps derives from that of Auctor of Metz (*Acta Sanctorum* Aug. 2:536–538). There is extant a life of Auctor of Metz written by PAUL THE DEACON.

Feast: Aug. 10 (Maursmünster).

Bibliography: *Bibliotheca hagiograpica latina antiquae et mediae aetatis* (Brussels 1898–1901) 1:746 (A. of Metz); 747–749 (A. of Trier). A. M. BURG and A. HEINTZ, *Lexikon für Theologie und Kirche,* ed. J. HOFER and K. RAHNER (Freiburg 1957–65) 1:1024–25.

[W. A. JURGENS]

AUCTOREM FIDEI

A bull of Pius VI, dated Aug. 28, 1794, condemning the errors of the Synod of Pistoia. This synod was held in the autumn of 1786 on the initiative of Scipione de'

RICCI, Bishop of Pistoia-Prato, a protégé of Peter Leopold, the Grand Duke of Tuscany and brother of Emperor Joseph II. Ricci, imbued with the Gallican, Richerist, and Jansenist ideas of the French APPELLANTS, which at the time were widespread in Italy, from 1780 on attempted to introduce these ideas into his diocese. The decrees of the synod that he held at Pistoia clearly reflect his thought, but at the same time they give evidence of a very real concern for the moral improvement of the faithful and the formation of the clergy. The council held at Florence in April-June 1787 sharply criticized a number of the decisions made at Pistoia. The acts of the synod were nevertheless published in October 1788. Pius VI had them examined by a commission, and Ricci had to resign in June 1791. Numerous translations of the acts, however, spread his ideas everywhere, particularly among the constitutional French clergy. The bull *Auctorem fidei* condemned the 85 propositions extracted exactly from the acts of Pistoia, while giving to each one a formal theological note. The condemned errors referred mainly to the Church and the hierarchy, grace, the Sacraments, and the liturgy. All aspects of JANSENISM had already been censured, but never in such a precise and consistent manner. Appearing during the troubled times of the Revolution, the bull *Auctorem fidei,* although remarkably well drawn up, did not produce the reaction that one could expect. It nevertheless reflected Roman resolve to resist Enlightened Catholicism in asserting the full authority of the Holy See.

Bibliography: H. DENZINGER, *Enchiridion symbolorum* (Freiburg 1963) 2600–2700. A. C. JEMOLO, *Il giansenismo in Italia prima della rivoluzione* (Bari 1928). E. CODIGNOLA, *Illuministi, giansenisti e giacobini nell'Italia del settecento* (Florence 1947). PIETRO STELLA, *Il giansenismo in Italia, V 2, pt 1: Roma: La bolla Auctorem fidei, 1794, nella storia dell'ultramontanismo: Saggio introduttivo e documenti* (Rome 1995). C. LAMIONI, ed., *Il Sinodia di Pistoia del 1796* (Rome 1991). L. PAZTOR, "La Curia romana e il Giansenismo," *Actes du Colloque sur le Jansénisme organisé par l'Academia belgica* (Louvain 1977) 89–104.

[L. J. COGNET/J. M. GRES-GAYER]

AUDI BENIGNE CONDITOR

A Lenten hymn formerly attributed to Pope Gregory the Great (Migne), but now dated as late as the early ninth century (Szövérffy). It was composed either in Italy (Raby) or in Gaul (Blume) and appears in many tenth century MSS from those areas, as well as in numerous German and English MSS of the following century. The hymn consists of five strophes of octosyllabic iambic dimeter. Half of its 20 lines are rhymed, in the unschematic manner characteristic of pre-Carolingian prosody. The first four strophes each contain a reference to human infirmity and a request for divine assistance; the fifth concludes this simple theme with a prayer that the Trinity will make our fasting fruitful. Assigned in the Roman Breviary of 1632 to Vespers between the Saturday after Ash Wednesday and Passiontide, it had been sung also at Lauds in many places before the Reformation. Its English translators include W. Drummond ("O merciful Creator!, hear our prayer," 1619), J. M. Neale ("O Maker of the world, give ear," 1852), and E. Caswall ("Thou loving Maker of mankind," *Lyra Catholica,* 1849).

Bibliography: *Analecta Hymnica* (Leipzig 1866–1922) 51:53–55. *Patrologia Latina* 78:849–850. A. S. WALPOLE, ed., *Early Latin Hymns* (Cambridge, Eng. 1922) 320–321. M. BRITT, ed., *The Hymns of the Breviary and Missal* (new ed. New York 1948). J. CONNELLY, *Hymns of the Roman Liturgy* (Westminster MD 1957). F. J. E. RABY, *A History of Christian-Latin Poetry from the Beginnings to the Close of the Middle Ages* (Oxford 1953) 124. J. JULIAN, ed., *A Dictionary of Hymnology* (New York 1957) 91.

[J. DU Q. ADAMS]

AUGER, EDMOND

Jesuit preacher and confessor of Henry III, effective in stemming Calvinist influence; b. Alleman, near Sézanne in Champagne in 1530; d. Como, Lombardy, Jan. 19, 1591. In 1550 St. Ignatius himself admitted Auger to the novitiate and formed him in the religious life. Auger was made professor of Latin, first at the Roman College and then at Perugia and Padua. Even before his ordination he began to manifest great talent for preaching. In 1559 Auger returned to France where with others he founded a college at Pamier and later another college at Toulouse. He taught at Pamier and Tournon. He preached with great naturalness, vigorously and cheerfully, in the most varied circumstances. He was hailed as the "Chrysostom of France," and was so able and gracious a preacher that he attracted even the Calvinists, whose heresy was then spreading in southern France. He had ardently and successfully devoted himself to counteract their influence. Having been captured by the Huguenots in Valence in 1562 and sentenced to death by burning, he addressed the onlookers while standing at what was intended to be his pyre and so won them that they demanded his release. To his preaching he added works of charity, visiting the sick, and comforting the prisoners. He was tireless in administering the Sacraments.

His French catechisms earned him the title of the "French Canisius." The first, a larger work, a summary of Catholic doctrine, appeared in 1563; the second, a smaller catechism published in 1568, was translated even into Greek. Both catechisms were reprinted and translated several times. Since they were written in the form of

NEW CATHOLIC ENCYCLOPEDIA

847

a dialogue and showed less erudition than the Canisius Catechism, they were useful for instructing children and uneducated adults. The catechisms confuted Calvinist doctrine without entering into polemics.

Auger became the first provincial of Aquitaine in 1564. He preached to King Charles. He became the chaplain of the Duke of Anjou. In 1574 when the duke became Henry III, Auger was made his confessor and preacher. Henry III appealed to the pope to have Auger remain at court, and only in 1587 was Auger authorized to leave. His attachment to Henry III aroused the hostility of the Leaguists. After the assassination of the king, Auger had to take refuge in Lyons and Tournon before leaving for Como where he died.

Bibliography: J. DORIGNY, *La Vie du P. Emond Auger* (new ed. Avignon 1828). F. J. BRAND, *P. Edmundus Augerius, S.J.* (Cleve 1903); *Die Katechismen des Edmundus Augerius* (Freiburg 1917). C. SOMMERVOGEL et al., *Bibliothèque de la Compagnie de Jésus*, 11 v. (Brussels-Paris 1890–1932; v.12, suppl. 1960) 1:632–642; 8:1706. P. DESLANDRES, ''Le Pére Emond Auger,'' *Revue des études historiques* 104 (1937) 28–38. H. JOLY, *Dictionnaire de biographie française* (Paris 1929–) 4:504–511. J. DUTILLEUL, *Dictionnaire d'histoire et de géographie ecclésiastiques*, ed. A. BAUDRILLART et al. (Paris 1912–) 5:378–383.

[R. B. MEAGHER]

AUGSBURG

City in Swabia, Bavaria, Germany, at the confluence of the Wertach and Lech Rivers. The diocese is named *Augustanus Vindelicorum*. The city, of ancient origin, was a site of significant events during the Reformation.

Founded by Rome *c.* A.D. 30, Augsburg, as the capital of Raetia, thrived culturally and economically. The martyrdom of St. AFRA (*c.* 304) and archeological findings show that Christians were there before the time of Constantine, and in such an important city there was probably a bishop. The Romans withdrew *c.* 400 and Alamanni destroyed the city *c.* 450, but Christianity survived, the tomb and chapel of St. Afra being a pilgrimage center in the sixth century. In 536 the Franks took Augsburg, which became a bishopric *c.* 600. Wikterp (738) is the first bishop known with certainty. Invested by the Carolingians as counts, the bishops were able to encompass merchant settlements south of Augsburg as late as the 12th century. In the 10th century Bishop ULRIC (923–973) defended the city against the Magyars until Otto I won the battle of the Lechfeld in 955. An episcopal schism (1077–88) followed the investiture struggle. In the 11th and 12th centuries the burghers, abetted by the German kings, began to seek independence of the bishop. In 1316 Emperor LOUIS IV made Augsburg an imperial city, and in the 15th century the split between bishop and city became so bad that the chancery, and at times the bishop moved to Dillingen. Jews were banned from Augsburg from 1439 to 1805, while from the late 15th century the city became world famous for its extensive trade and riches, which did not benefit the lower classes.

Humanism, introduced to Augsburg through trade relations with Italy, was taken up in ecclesiastical circles. The split between bishop and city, social agitation and the worldliness of the higher clergy prepared for the Reformation of Luther, who was in Augsburg in 1518. Zwinglianism replaced Lutheranism in 1526, and even Anabaptists became prominent. In 1537 Catholic services were banned by law, images were forbidden and the clergy was forced to leave the city. After Charles V's victory over the Schmalkaldic League in 1547, the city had to agree in the Interim of Augsburg (1548) to the return of the clergy, the restoration of church goods and the continuation of Catholic services. In 1555 the Peace of AUGSBURG, ratified by the Augsburg Diet, specified the equality of Catholicism and Lutheranism in Augsburg; apart from passing disturbances, it was strictly observed, as the Peace of Westphalia (1648) witnesses. The restoration of Catholicism after 1548 was the work of the bishops, especially Cardinal Otto TRUCHSESS VON WALDBURG and Heinrich von Knöringen, with the help of the FUGGERS and new religious houses.

In 1809, when Augsburg ceased to be an imperial city, it was again predominantly Catholic (16,944 Catholics and 11,534 Evangelicals). The secularization of 1802–03 suppressed religious institutions (12 men's and five women's), deprived the bishop of his principality and chapter, and incorporated the city into Bavaria (1805). Romanticism in the early 19th century favored the Catholic revival. Religious orders returned after 1820. Rapid industrialization after 1835, with increases in population density and the incorporation of heavily Catholic fringe communities, posed difficult problems for the Church. New parishes were built, social and charitable institutions founded, and associations developed. World War II destroyed several churches, but Bishop Joseph Freundorfer (d. 1963) and the city, with help from abroad, repaired the damages and overcame post-war problems.

Augsburg has had noteworthy ecclesiastics: David of Augsburg (*c.* 1200–72); Johannes Fabri (1504–58); St. PETER CANISIUS (1521–97); Placidus Braun (1756–1829); canon Antonius Steichele (1816–89), historian and archbishop of Munich-Freising; and Bishop Pancratius von Dinkel (1858–94).

The 11th-century Romanesque cathedral was modified with Gothic in the early 14th century. St. Gall Church dates from the 11th, and St. Peter am Perlach from the

12th century. Several churches were built in the 15th and 16th centuries. In the Middle Ages there were three collegiate cloisters (founded 1020, 1060, 1071) apart from the cathedral chapter, two Augustinian cloisters (1135, 1160), a Benedictine (1012), a Dominican (1225), a Conventual Franciscan (1221), and a Carmelite (1321); a cloister of canonesses (968) and a Benedictine (1262); three Franciscan (1258?, *c.* 1315, before 1366) and three Dominican (1235, *c.* 1250, 1298) convents. A number of others were founded during and after the Reformation, including the Jesuits (1579), the Capuchins (1601) and the English Ladies (1662), who dedicated themselves to educating young girls.

Augsburg has been famous for religious art and artists, including Burkhard Engelberger, Gregor Erhardt, Hans Holbein the Elder, Hans Burgkmair, Johann Georg Bergmüller, Matthew Günther, Christopher Thomas Scheffler, Francis Xavier and Johann Michael Feuchtmayr. Goldsmiths Jörg Seld, Johann Zeckel, Franz Ignaz Berthold and others supplied liturgical equipment far and wide from the 15th to the 18th century. The holy pictures of the Klauber press in the 18th century had worldwide distribution. Erhard Ratdolt printed liturgical books (1486–1528) and the Benedictines of St. Ulrich managed a press (1472–74). The cathedral choir was known for its music and organists (Jacobus de Kerle, Gregor Aichinger and Christian Erbach).

The Latin schools of the cathedral chapter and four cloisters, suspended 1537–48, were surpassed by the Jesuit school founded in 1582. The cloister schools were suppressed with the secularization of 1802–03, but in 1828 the state opened a Catholic *Gymnasium* under the Benedictines.

In the tenth century Bishop Ulrich founded a hospital (*hospitium*) for the poor. Another appeared in 1143, and a third by 1239. A house for lepers was founded *c.* 1250. St. Jacob's Hospital (1348) also cared for pilgrims. In 1514 the Fuggers built a model settlement for poor families that still exists.

Bibliography: W. ZORN, *Augsburg: Geschichte einer Stadt* (Munich 1955). C. BAUER et al., *Augusta 955-1955* (Munich 1955). T. BREUER, *Die Stadt Augsburg* (Munich 1958). A. HORN, *Dome, Kirchen, und Klöster in Bayr. Schwaben* (Frankfurt A.M. 1963). F. ZOEPEL, *Das Bistum Augsburg und seine Bischöfe im Mittelalter* (Munich 1956); *Lexikon für Theologie und Kirche*, eds., J. HOFER and K. RAHNER, 10 v. (2d, new ed. Freiburg 1957–65) 1:1076–79. A. SCHRÖDER, *Dictionnaire d'histoire et de géographie ecclésiastiques*, ed. A. BAUDRILLART et al., (Paris 1912–) 5:389–406. *Annuario Pontificio* (1964) 43.

[F. ZOEPFL]

AUGSBURG, PEACE OF

An agreement between the Catholics and Lutherans of Germany giving recognition in imperial to the AUGSBURG CONFESSION (1530) as well as to the Catholic faith. Embodied in a decree delivered at the Diet of Augsburg on Sept. 25, 1555, it definitively registered the failure of Emperor CHARLES V's efforts to repair the broken religious unity of Germany (*see* INTERIMS). The emperor's military pacification of Germany was wrecked by the political ambitions of the princes who rose in rebellion under Maurice of Saxony in 1552. This second Schmalkaldic war resulted in the defeat of Charles V by Maurice, who was aided by his French allies (*see* SCHMALKALDIC LEAGUE). Charles's subsequent failure to recapture Metz after his treaty with Maurice completed his discouragement. Charles appointed his brother Ferdinand (later Emperor Ferdinand I) to preside over the negotiations that arranged a political settlement of the religions strife. The treaty stipulated that the religion of the ruler was to determine whether a state was to be exclusively Catholic or Lutheran. In the Holy Roman Empire's more than eighty "imperial cities" (towns that owed political obedience solely to the emperor), both religions—Lutheranism and Catholicism—were to be tolerated. Lutheran's legal title to church property they had appropriated before 1552 was also upheld. A private declaration of Ferdinand conceded religious freedom to certain subjects of ecclsiastical princes. Ecclesiastical princes who turned Protestant were obliged to resign their sees according to a clause inserted by Ferdinand. The conversion of several high-ranking princes to Calvinism in the 1560s and 1570s, strained the terms of the Peace, since the treaty had recognized only Lutheranism and Catholicism as licit religions. Despite that and other challenges, the treaty's solution to the imperial religious crisis proved long lasting, persisting until the outbreak of the Thirty Year's War in 1618. The treaty that concluded that conflict in 1648—the Peace of Westphalia—granted legal recognition to Calvinism within the Empire, but in most other respects it merely repeated many of the compromises that had first been worked out in the Peace of Augsburg.

Bibliography: M. SIMON, *Der Augsburger Religionsfriede* (Augsburg 1955). H. HOLBORN, *A History of Modern Germany* (New York 1959–) v.1 *The Reformation*. J. HECKEL *Die Religion in Geschichte und Gegenwart*, 7 v. (3d ed. Tübingen 1957–65) 1:736–737. E. W. ZEEDEN, *Lexikon für Theologie und Kirche*, ed. J. HOFER and K. RAHNER, 10 v. (2d, new ed. Freiburg 1957–65) 1:1081–83. H. TÜLCHE, "The Peace of Augsburg: New Order or Lull in the Fighting" *Government in Reformation Europe, 1520–1560*, H. J. COHN, ed. (New York 1972). P. WARMBRUNN, *Zwei Konfessionen in einer Stadt* (Wiesbaden 1983).

[T. S. BOKENKOTTER]

AUGSBURG CONFESSION

So called from its presentation (in slightly divergent but equally authoritative German and Latin versions) at the Diet of Augsburg on June 25, 1530, to Holy Roman Emperor CHARLES V in response to his invitation to the parties in the theological debate to present their "opinions and views." The Augsburg Confession (*Confessio Augustana*) is the primary particular symbol of the Lutheran Church. Although signed by seven imperial princes and representatives of two imperial free cities, it is primarily the work of Philipp MELANCHTHON, who drew it up in its present form (chiefly on the basis of the Schwabach, Marburg, and Torgau Articles) to counter the charge of Johann ECK in his *404 Articles* that the Lutheran party was reviving ancient heresies.

Deliberately irenic in character, it consists of 21 articles (on God, original sin, Christ, justification through faith, the sacred ministry and the channels of the Holy Spirit; the new obedience, the Church, the Sacraments, ecclesiastical order, humanly instituted rites, civil affairs, Christ's return to Judgment, free will, the cause of sin, faith and good works, and the veneration of the saints) explicitly designed to show that the Lutherans did not depart at any point from Scripture, the Catholic Church, or the Roman Church (Epilogue to pt. 1.1), plus seven concluding articles on Communion under both species, the marriage of priests, the abrogation of private Masses, confession, humanly instituted traditions, monastic vows, and the authority of bishops. The imperial reply, commonly called the Papalist Confutation because it was drawn up by a panel of theologians at the Diet, approved nine articles without exception, approved six with qualifications or in part, and condemned thirteen. The Lutheran theologians under Melanchthon's leadership readied the first draft of a Defense (Apology) and submitted it on September 22, but the emperor refused to receive it. Back at Wittenberg, Melanchthon reworked it into the Apology of the Augsburg Confession, first printed (along with the *editio princeps* of the Confession itself) in 1531. It repeats and defends the positions taken by the Confession, but goes beyond it in its definition of the Sacraments and in its exposition of the sacrificial aspects of the Holy Eucharist. The official German version of the Apology is a paraphrase by Justus JONAS. The Apology formally received symbolical status as a commentary on the Augsburg Confession in 1537. A revised edition (Variata) of the Augsburg Confession, which Melanchthon published in 1540, was less explicit in its Eucharistic doctrine than the 1530 edition and gained extensive acceptance in German Reformed circles; the Lutherans rejected it in the Preface to the Book of Concord (1580) and committed themselves to the 1530 edition (see CONCORD, FORMULA AND BOOK OF).

In varying degrees the Augsburg Confession influenced other 16th-century confessions, including the THIRTY-NINE ARTICLES of the Church of England and through them John WESLEY's Methodist Articles of Religion. An effort of Samuel S. Schmucker (1799–1873) to accommodate the Augsburg Confession to the prevailing Protestantism of the U.S. in the *Definite Platform* (1855), by omitting all characteristically Lutheran elements, was vigorously rejected. The original manuscripts of the Augsburg Confession submitted to Charles V appear to have perished in the 16th century, but 54 copies surviving from 1530 alone adequately secure the text of both the Latin and the German version.

See Also: CONFESSIONS OF FAITH, PROTESTANT.

Bibliography: H. LIETZMANN, ed., *Die Bekenntnisschriften der evangelisch-lutherischen Kirche*, 5th ed. by E. WOLF (Göttingen 1963) 44–404, critical Lat. and Ger. text of both documents. Eng. T. G. TAPPERT, ed. and tr., *The Book of Concord: The Confessions of the Evangelical Lutheran Church* (Philadelphia 1959) 24–285. Text of the Papalist Confutation in *Corpus reformatorum* 27 (1859) 81–244. J. M. REU, *The Augsburg Confession* (Chicago 1930), contains Eng. tr. of many of the pertinent documents. W. D. ALLBECK, *Studies in the Lutheran Confessions* (Philadelphia 1952). M. LACKMANN, *The Augsburg Confession and Catholic Unity*, tr. W. R. BOUMAN (New York 1963). W. MAURER. *Historical Commentary on the Augburg Confession* (Philadelphia 1986).

[A. C. PIEPKORN]

AUGURY

A term deriving its name from the fact that the officials of the Roman state who were legally and constitutionally empowered to practice the art of divination for official purposes were called Augurs. The Roman College of Augurs, consisting eventually of 16 members, had as its function not to foretell the future but to discover by observation of signs (the flight of birds, the behavior of chickens, etc.) whether the gods did or did not approve a proposed action. Such signs could be accidental, such as the flight or cry of birds, or could be carefully studied, such as the manner in which domestic fowls pecked at their food.

See Also: DIVINATION.

Bibliography: H. J. ROSE, *The Oxford Classical Dictionary* 120. F. MÜLLER, *Reallexikon für Antike und Christentum* 1:975–980.

[T. A. BRADY]

AUGUSTINE, ST.

Bishop and Doctor of the Church, b. Thagaste in Numidia, North Africa, Nov. 13, 354; d. Hippo, Aug. 28,

Saint Augustine, detail from the "Apse Mosaic of San Paolo duori le Mura," by Edward Burne–Jones. (©Araldo de Luca/CORBIS)

Saint Augustine.

430. By the power of his language and the depth of his thought Augustine became the dominant figure and force in Western Christianity and continues to be a very powerful influence up to the present. Even in his own lifetime Augustine was described by Saint Jerome, a man hardly given to flattery, as ''the second founder of the faith'' (*Ep.* 149). In an apostolic letter commemorating the 1600th anniversary of Augustine's conversion Pope John Paul II described him as ''an incomparable man'' and added that ''almost all in the Church and in the West think of themselves as'' his ''disciples and children.''

LIFE

Augustine was born to Patricius, a pagan, and MONICA, a Christian. He had at least one brother and one sister. Monica delayed Augustine's baptism, as was customary at the time. His parents sacrificed to provide him with a classical Roman education in Thagaste and in neighboring Madaura. Patricius died in 370, having been baptized on his deathbed. With financial help from his wealthy patron and fellow townsman, Romanianus, Augustine was able to go to Carthage in 371 to continue his education. There he studied rhetoric, lived a somewhat wild student life, and took a companion, whose name he never mentions, but with whom he lived faithfully for 15 years and fathered a son, Adeodatus, who died in 390.

In 372–3 he read Cicero's *Hortensius*, an exhortation to the life of philosophy, which is no longer extant; it kindled in him a burning love for wisdom, from which he was held back only by the fact that he did not find there Christ's name (*Conf.* iii, 4, 8). Augustine turned to the Christian Scriptures, but found that the style of the Old Latin Bible was crude, especially in comparison with the Roman classics, and he was repelled by the anthropomorphism of the Scriptures and the immoral conduct of the patriarchs (*Conf.* iii, 4, 7–5, 9). Hence, he turned to the Manichees who always had the name of Christ on their lips and who promised him a wisdom without the yoke of an authority that demanded a blind faith. In 375 he returned from Carthage to Thagaste to teach, only to return again to Carthage in 376 in search of better students. In 380 he wrote a work on aesthetics, *The Beautiful and the Fitting* (*De pulchro et apto*), which was lost even during his lifetime.

Augustine's conversion to MANICHEISM was largely the result of a strong anti-intellectualism on the part of the African Church, which seems to have demanded a blind faith that Augustine looked upon as a yoke and a terror. The Church of North Africa lacked a well-educated clergy able to provide intelligent answers to the questions of the young man who was to become the greatest doctor of the Western church. He explains that he fell in with the Manichees ''for no other reason than that they said that they would set aside the terror of authority and would bring to God by pure reason those who were willing to listen to them and thus set them free from all error'' (*Util. cred.* 1, 2). Hence, he spurned the religion of his childhood like old wives' tales and thirsted to drink in the pure truth from the Manichees.

The Manichean account of the cosmic battle in the beginning, in which particles of the good principle wound up captive in the power of the evil principle, provided the young Augustine with an answer to the question of the origin of evil and the comforting doctrine that it was not he himself who committed sin, but the evil principle within him. He said, ''I still thought that it is not we who sin, but that some other nature sins in us, and it pleased my pride to be above all guilt'' (*Conf.* v, 10, 18). For nine years Augustine remained as a hearer in their sect (a second-class member, who unlike the ''elect'' did not have to observe all the rules of abstinence, in terms of food and sex, that were imposed on the latter), awaiting the enlightenment he had been promised, especially from the Manichean bishop, Faustus, whom he finally met in Carthage in 383 and whom he found to be a charming man of letters, but without the answers he had hoped for (*Conf.* v, 6, 10–7, 13). Faustus proved to be a disappointment, but the decisive argument against Manicheism was provided by Augustine's friend, Nebridius, when he and

Date	Works	Principal Editions			English Translations		
		PL	CCL	CSEL	FathCh	WSA	Other
386-87	*Contra Academicos (Answer to the Skeptics) c. Acad.*	32	29	63	5		AnChrWr 12
386-87	*De beata vita (The Happy Life) b. vita*	32	29	63	5		
386-87	*De ordine (Order) ord.*	32	29	63	5		
386-87	*Soliloquia (Soliloquies) sol.*	32		89	5		LCC 6, NPNF 7
387	*De immortalitate animae (Immortality of the Soul) imm. an.*	32		89	4		
386-430	*Epistulae (Letters) ep. (epp.)*	33		34, 44, 57-58		II, 1-3	NPNF 1
	Epistulae nuper in lucem prolatae (Recently Discovered Letters)			88		II, 4	
387	*De dialectica (Dialectic) dial.*	32					
387-88	*De moribus ecclesiae catholicae et de moribus Manichaeorum (The Morals of the Catholic Church and the Morals of the Manichees) mor.*	32		90	56		NPNF 4
387-88	*De animae quantitate (The Greatness of the Soul).quant.*	32		89	4		AnChrWr 9
387-91	*De musica (Music) mus.*	32	4				
387-88; 395	*De libero arbitrio (Free Choice) lib. arb.*	32	29	74	59		AnChrWr 22
388-89	*De Genesi contra Manichaeos (Genesis against the Manichees) Gen. c. Man.*	34		91	84		
388-96	*De diversis quaestionibus octoginta tribus (Eighty Three Different Questions) div. qu.*	40	44A		70		
389	*De magistro (The Teacher) mag.*	32	29	77	59		AnChrWr 9
390-391	*De vera religione (The True Religion) vera rel.*	34	32	77			LCC 6
391-92	*De utilitate credendi (Usefulness of Believing) util. cred.*	42		25			LCC 6, NPNF 3
391-430	*Sermones (Sermons) s. (ss.)*	38-39	41		81 (*ss.* 184-265)	III, 1-10	
	Sermones nuper in lucem prolatae (Recently Discovered Sermons) Dolbeau, 1996					III, 11	
392-422	*Enarrationes in Psalmos (Homilies on the Psalms) en. Ps.*	36-37	38-40			III, 14–15	AnChrWr 29-30, NPNF 8
392	*Acta contra Fortunatum Manichaeum (Proceedings against Fortunatus the Manichee) c. Fort*	42		25.1			NPNF 4
392-93	*De duabus animabus (The Two Souls) duabus an.*	42		25			NPNF 4
393	*De fide et symbolo (Faith and the Creed) f. et symb.*	40	46	41	27		LCC 6, NPNF 3
393-94	*Psalmus contra partem Donati (A Psalm against the Sect of Donatus) ps. c. Don*	43		51			
393-94; 426-27	*De Genesi ad litteram liber imperfectus (Genesis Literally Interpreted: An Unfinished Book) Gen. lit. imp*	34		28.1	84		
393-95	*De sermone Domini in monte (The Lord's Sermon on the Mount) s. Dom. mon*	34	35		11		AnChrWr 5, NPNF 6
394	*Contra Adimantum Manichaei discipulum (Answer to Adimantum, Mani's Disciple) c. Adim*	42		25.1			
394-95	*Expositio quarumdam propositionum ex epistula ad Romanos (An Explanation of Some Propositions from the Letter to the Romans) ex. prop. Rom.*	35		84			
394-95	*Expositio in epistulam ad Galatas (Explanation of the Letter to the Galatians) ex. Gal.*	35		84			
394-95	*Epistulae ad Romanos inchoata expositio (The Beginning of an Explanation of the Letter to the Romans) ex. Rom. inch.*	35		84			
394-95	*De mendacio (Lying) mend.*	40		41	16		

Date	Works	Principal Editions			English Translations		
		PL	CCL	CSEL	FathCh	WSA	Other
396	*De agone christiano (Struggle of a Christian) agon.*	40		41	2		
396-98	*De diversis quaestionibus ad Simplicianum (Various Questions for Simplicianus) Simpl.*	40	44				LLC 6
396; 426-27	*De doctrina christiana (Christian Doctrine) doc. Chr.*	34	32	80	2	I,11	
397	*Contra epistulam quam vocant Fundamenti (Answer to the Letter Called "The Foundation") c. ep. Man.*	42		25			NPNF 4
397-99	*Contra Faustum Manichaeum (Answer to Faustus the Manichee) c. Faust.*	42		25			NPNF 4
397-99	*Regula: Objurgatio (The Rule: A Rebuke) reg. 1*	32					Lawless, 1987
397-99	*Regula: Ordo Monasterii (Monastic Order) reg. 2*	32					Lawless, 1987
397-99	*Regula: Praeceptum (The Rule: Precepts) reg. 3*	32					Lawless, 1987
397-401	*Confessiones (Confessions) conf.*	32	27	33		I,1	NPNF 1
398	*De disciplina christiana (Christian Discipline) disc. Chr.*	40	46			III, 10	
399	*De natura boni (Nature of the Good) nat. b.*	42		25			LCC 6, NPNF 4
399	*Contra Secundinum Manichaeum (Answer to Secundinus the Manichee) c. Sec*	42		25			
399	*Adnotationes in Iob (Comments on Job) adn. Job*	34		28.2			
399	*De catechizandis rudibus (Catechizing the Uneducated) cat. rud.*	40	46				AnChrWr 2, NPNF 3
399-400	*De consensu evangelistarum (The Agreement of the Evangelists) cons. Ev.*	34		43			NPNF 6
399-400	*Quaestiones evangeliorum (Questions on the Gospel) qu. Ev.*	35	44B				
399-400	*Quaestiones XVII in Matthaeum (Seventeen Questions on Matthew) qu. Mt.*	35	44B				
399-422/426	*De trinitate (The Trinity) Trin.*	42	50, 50A	45		I, 5	NPNF 3
400	*De fide rerum quae non videntur (Faith in Things Not Seen) f. rerum*	40	46		2		PS 84, NPNF 3
400	*Contra epistulam Parmeniani (Answer to the Letter of Parmenian) c. ep. Parm.*	43		51			
400	*Ad inquisitiones Ianuarii (= epp. 54-55) (Replies to the Questions of Januarius) inq. Jan.*	33		34.2	12	II, 1	
400-01	*De baptismo contra Donatistas (Baptism: An Answer to the Donatists) bapt.*	43		51			NPNF 4
400- 03	*Contra litteras Petiliani (Answer to the Letter of Petilian) c. litt. Pet.*	43		52			NPNF 4
401	*De opere monachorum (Work of Monks) op. mon.*	40		41	16		NPNF 3
401	*De bono coniugali (Good of Marriage) b. conjug.*	40		41	27	I, 9	NPNF 4
401	*De sancta virginitate (Holy Virginity) virg.*	40		41	27	I, 9	NPNF 3
401-15	*De Genesi ad litteram (The Literal Meaning of Genesis) Gen. litt.*	34		28.1			AnChrWr 41-2
402-05	*Ad Catholicos de secta Donatistarum (Answers for Catholics on the Sect of the Donatists) cath.*	43		52			
404	*Contra Felicem Manichaeum (Answer to Felix the Manichee) c. Fel.*	42		25.2			
405-06	*Contra Cresconium (Answer to Cresconius) Cresc.*	43		52			
406	*De divinatione daemonum (Divination by Demons) divin. daem.*	40		41	27		

Date	Works	Principal Editions			English Translations		
		PL	CCL	CSEL	FathCh	WSA	Other
406-07	*In epistulam Johannis ad Parthos tractatus (Homilies on John's First Letter) ep. Joh.*	35			92		LCC 8, NPNF 7
406-21	*In Evangelium Johannis tractatus (Homilies on John's Gospel) Jo. ev. tr.*	35		36	78, 79, 88, 90,92		NPNF 4
408	*Contra paganos (= ep. 102) (Answer to the Pagans) c. pag.*	33		34	18	II, 2	
408	*De utilitate ieiunii (The Usefulness of Fasting) util. jejun.*	40	46		16		PS 85
411	*De excidio urbis (Destruction of the City) exc. urb.*	40	46				PS 89
411	*Breviculus collationis contra Donatistas (A Summary of the Debate with the Donatists) brev.*	43		53			
411	*De unico baptismo (The Singleness of Baptism) un. bapt.*	43		53			
411	*Ad Donatistas post collationem (Answer to the Donatists after the Debate) c. Don.*	43		53			
411-12	*De peccatorum meritis et remissione et de baptismo parvulorum (The Punishment and Forgiveness of Sins and the Baptism of Little Ones) pecc. mer.*	44		60		I, 23	NPNF 5
412	*De gratia novi testamenti (= ep. 140) (The Grace of the New Testament) gr. nov. t.*	33		44	20	II, 2	
412	*De spiritu et littera (The Spirit and the Letter) spir. et litt.*	44		60		I, 23	LCC 8, NPNF 5
413	*De fide et operibus (Faith and Works) f. et op.*	40		41	27		AnChrWr 48
413	*De videndo Deo (Seeing God) (= ep. 147) vid. Deo*	33		44	20	II, 2	
413	*Commonitorium ad Fortunatianum (= Ep. 148) (Memorandum for Fortunatian) com. Fort.*	33		44	20	II, 2	
413-27	*De civitate Dei (The City of God) civ. Dei*	41	47-48	40	8, 14, 24		NPNF 2
414	*De bono viduitatis (The Good of Widowhood) b. vid.*	40		41	16	I, 9	NPNF 3
415	*De natura et gratia (Nature and Grace) nat. et gr.*	44		60	86	I, 23	NPNF 5
415	*De perfectione iustitiae hominis (The Perfection of Human Righteousness) perf. just.*	44		42		I, 23	NPNF 5
415	*Contra Priscillianistas et Origenistas (Answer to the Priscillianists and Origenists) c. Prisc.*	42	49			I, 18	
415	*De origine animae (= ep. 166) (The Origin of the Soul)*	33		44	30	II, 3	
415	*De sententia Iacobi (= ep. 167) (A Statement of James) sent. Jac.)*	33		44	30	II, 3	
416-17	*De gestis Pelagii (The Deeds of Pelagius)*	44		42	86	I, 23	NPNF 5
417	*De correctione Donatistarum (= ep. 185) (The Correction of the Donatists) correct.*	33		57	30	II, 3	
417	*De praesentia Dei (= ep. 187) (The Presence of God) praes. Dei*	33		57	30	II, 3	
417-18	*De patientia (Patience) pat.*	40		41	16		NPNF 3
418	*De gratia Christi et de peccato originali (The Grace of Christ and Original Sin) gr. et pecc. or.*	44		42		I, 23	NPNF 5
418	*Sermo ad Caesareensis ecclesiae plebem (Sermon to the People of the Church of Caesarea) s. Caes.*	43		53			
418	*Gesta cum Emerito Donatista (Debate with Emeritus) Emer. (The Proceedings with Emeritus the Donatist)*	43		53			

Date	Works	Principal Editions			English Translations		
		PL	CCL	CSEL	FathCh	WSA	Other
418	*Contra sermonem Arianorum (Answer to the Arian Sermon) c. s. Ar.*	42				I, 18	
418-20	*De continentia (Continence) cont.*	40		41	16	I, 9	NPNF 3
419	*Contra Gaudentium (Answer to Gaudentius) c. Gaud.*	43		53			
419	*De VIII quaestionibus ex Vetere Testamento (Eight Questions from the Old Testament) qu. vet. T.*	35	33				
419-20	*Locutionum in heptateuchum (Discussions of the Heptateuch) loc. in Hept.*	34	33	28.1			
419-20	*Quaestionum in heptateuchum (Questions on the Heptateuch) qu.*	34	33	28.2			
419-20	*De natura et origine animae (The Nature and Origin of the Soul) nat. an. et or.*	44		60		I, 23	NPNF 5
419-20	*De adulterinis coniugiis (Adulterous Marriages) adul. conj.*	40		41	27	I, 9	
419-20	*Contra adversarium legis et prophetarum (Answer to an Opponent of the Law and the Prophets) c. adv. leg.*	42	49			I, 18	
419-20	*Contra duas epistulas Pelagianorum (Answer to Two Letters of the Pelagians) c. ep. Pel.*	44		60		I, 24	NPNF 5
419-421	*De nuptiis et concupiscentia (Marriage and Desire) nupt. et conc.*	44		42		I, 24	NPNF 5
420	*Contra mendacium (Against Lying) c. mend.*	40		41	16		NPNF 3
421-22	*Contra Iulianum (Answer to Julian) c. Jul.*	44			35	I, 24	
421-22	*Enchiridion ad Laurentium (Handbook for Laurentius) ench.*	40	46		3		AnChrWr 3, LCC 7, NPNF 3
422	*De cura pro mortuis gerenda (Proper Care for the Dead) cura mort.*	40		41	27		NPNF 3
424	*De octo Dulcitii quaestionibus (Eight Questions of Dulcitius) Dulc. qu.*	40	44A		16		
425	*De symbolo ad catechumenos (The Creed for Catechumens) symb. cat.*	40	46		27	III, 10	
426-27	*De gratia et libero arbitrio (Grace and Free Choice) gr. et lib. arb.*	44			59	I, 26	NPNF 5
426-27	*De correptione et gratia (Rebuke and Grace) corrept.*	44		86	2	I, 26	NPNF 5
426-427	*Retractationum (Revisions) retr.*	32	57	36	60		
427	*Speculum (The Mirror) spec.*	34		12			
427-28	*Collatio cum Maximino (Debate with Maximinus) conl. Max.*	42				I, 18	
427-28	*Contra Maximinum Arianum (Answer to Maximinus the Arian) c. Max.*	42				I, 18	
428-29	*De haeresibus (Heresies) haer.*	42	46			I, 18	PS 90
428-29	*Adversus Judaeos (Answer to the Jews) adv. Jud.*	42					
428-29	*De praedestinatione sanctorum (The Predestination of the Saints) praed. sanct.*	44			86	I, 26	NPNF 5
428-29	*De dono perseverantiae (The Gift of Perseverance) persev.*	45			86	I, 26	PS 91, NPNF 5
428-430	*Contra Iulianum opus imperfectum (Unfinished Work in Answer to Julian) c. Jul. imp.*	45		85.1 (books I-III)		I, 25	

Augustine were still in Carthage. Nebridius asked what the nation of darkness, the Manichean evil principle, would have done to God, the good principle, if God had in the beginning times refused to do battle with it. If the Manichees claimed that the evil principle would injure the good, then God would be violable and corruptible, something Augustine clearly saw to be impossible. If, however, the evil principle could not injure the good, then God had no reason to do battle with it, a battle in which, according to the Manichean myth, particles of the good were captured by the nation of darkness. Hence, Nebridius argued, if the Manichees contend that God is incorruptible, their whole myth is false; if, however, they say God is corruptible, this too is seen to be false (*Conf.* vii, 2, 3).

In 383 Augustine left Carthage for Rome where he hoped to find better students, leaving Monica behind and lying to her about his departure. After a year in Rome where he stayed with influential Manichean friends, he was appointed professor of rhetoric in Milan. There he encountered Bishop AMBROSE, whose eloquent preaching introduced him to a spiritual interpretation of the Scriptures that allowed him to think that the faith of the Church might be maintained against the Manichees without having to be ashamed of it, though at this point both positions seemed to him equal in their defenses (*Conf.* v, 14, 24–25). Hence, he found himself attracted to the skeptical view that truth could not be found (*Conf.* v, 10, 19). In 385 Monica arrived in Milan and set about arranging a marriage for her son. The mother of Adeodatus was sent back to Africa, since Augustine could not by Roman law marry her. Monica's candidate for her son's wife was, however, two years under the legal age; Augustine, not yet a model of chastity, therefore took a mistress to tide him over until he, a man in his thirties, could marry the eight-year-old bride Monica had chosen for him (Conf. vi, 13, 23–15, 25).

Before reading in the summer of 386 "certain books of the Platonists" (*Conf.* vii, 9, 13) or "a very few books of Plotinus" (*B. vita* 1, 4), Augustine had no concept of God or the soul as incorporeal beings. In retrospect he recognized that his inability to think of anything that was not a body was "the greatest and almost the sole cause of his unavoidable error" (*Conf.* v, 10, 20), since it forced him to think that evil was such a substance and to hold that it was a mass opposed to the good God, who, of course, could not have created it. With regard to the Manichean arguments he says, "If I were only able to conceive a spiritual substance, then all their stratagems would be destroyed and driven from my mind, but this I could not do" (*Conf.* v, 14, 25).

To his astonishment he found that, when Ambrose and others in the Milanese circle of Platonists spoke about God and the soul, they were not thinking of anything bodily (*B. vita* 1, 4). Through hearing Ambrose preach, he at last discovered that the spiritual men in the Church did not interpret man's being made in the image of God (Gn 1.26) in the sense that God was limited by the shape of the human body. He was pleased to find out that he had for years argued, "not against the Catholic faith, but against the fantasies of his carnal imagination"(*Conf.* vi, 3, 4). In the central seventh book of *The*

Confessions, he spells out the fruit of his encounter with Plotinian thought. He found that the books of the Platonists contained the truth about God and his Word, but knew nothing about the Word becoming flesh. He sums up in book seven his appropriation of Platonism as he grasped it, not in the days prior to his baptism, but from the perspective of the time of the composition of the work, when he had some ten years to read more extensively in the *Enneads* and to absorb their metaphysical ideas.

In the summer of 386, Augustine, still hesitant about committing himself to the Catholic faith, visited Simplicianus, Ambrose's father in the faith, who would in 397 succeed Ambrose as bishop of Milan. Simplicianus congratulated Augustine on his discovery of the writings of the Platonists because of their emphasis upon God and his Word and recounted the story of the conversion of Marius Victorinus, the translator into Latin of the *Enneads* of PLOTINUS, in order to exhort Augustine to accept the humility of Christ (*Conf.* viii, 2, 9). Also in that summer Ponticianus, a high official at the imperial court, a fellow African, and a Christian, visited Augustine and found him with a copy of the writings of Paul. He, too, congratulated Augustine and told him of the life of St. ANTHONY, who sold all his possessions and became a monk, and of the conversion of two special agents of the emperor who likewise became monks. The stories served to thrust Augustine before his own eyes and make him realize to his shame how long he had dallied after being first set afire with the love of wisdom and that he still held back from giving himself fully to its search (*Conf.* viii, 6, 13–7, 19). Shortly thereafter, he heard in the garden of the house the words, "Take up and read." He picked St. PAUL where he read from the Letter to the Romans a passage that served as the decisive admonition that led to his finally becoming a Christian and a servant of God (*Conf.* viii, 12, 29).

In September he resigned his teaching position and withdrew to the villa of his friend, Verecundus, which was situated outside of Milan at Cassiciacum. There along with Alypius, his friend from boyhood and the future bishop of Thagaste, he tutored some youngsters, including his own son, Adeodatus, and Licentius, the son of Romanianus. At Cassiciacum he composed four works in dialogue form, *Answer to the Academics, The Happy Life, Order,* and *The Soliloquies,* the last a dialogue between Augustine and reason. At the beginning of Lent in 387 he returned from Cassiciacum to Milan to become a candidate for baptism; he was baptized along with his son, Adeodatus, and his friend, Alypius, during the Easter vigil on April 24 at the hands of Ambrose. In Milan he wrote *The Immortality of the Soul* and began *Music.* Soon he arranged to return to Africa with his mother and son, but was forced by the outbreak of war to spend a year in Rome, where he wrote *The Greatness of the Soul*, the first two books of *Free Choice*, and *The Morals of the Catholic Church and the Morals of the Manichees*. As they were waiting for a ship to Africa at the port of Ostia, Monica died and was buried there (*Conf.* ix, 11, 27–12, 32). Shortly before Monica's death Augustine and his mother shared a mystical vision of the life to come, which Augustine describes in language that is both Plotinian and Pauline (*Conf.* ix, 10, 23–26).

Back in Africa Augustine established a monastic community of sorts at Thagaste where he aimed at "growing godlike in leisure" (*Ep.* 10, 2), continued his correspondence with his friend Nebridius, who was soon to die in Carthage, and wrote his first commentary on Genesis, *Genesis against the Manichees*, as well as *Diverse Questions*, *The Teacher*, and *True Religion*. During these years Adeodatus also died. Though Augustine carefully avoided cities where the episcopal see was vacant for fear that he would be made bishop and lose his life of prayerful leisure, he came to Hippo in the spring of 391 to found a monastery. He was present at a sermon of Bishop Valerius who was speaking of the need of a priest for the city. The congregation saw Augustine and chose him by acclamation (*S.* 355, 2); Valerius ordained him, provided him with a place for a monastery, and insisted contrary to the custom of the time that as a mere priest Augustine should preach to the people. In fact, at the Council of Hippo in 391, Valerius had him explain the Creed in simple terms to the assembled bishops, men who apparently needed rudimentary instruction in the basics of their faith.

Once ordained, Augustine pleaded with Valerius for time off in order that he might study the Scripture, not for his personal needs and his own salvation, but in order to be able to minister effectively to the people (*Ep.* 21). As a priest at Hippo Augustine wrote *The Usefulness of Believing* and *Two Souls against the Manichees*. In August 392 he debated the Manichean priest Fortunatus, of which *Answer to Fortunatus* is a record; in the same year he began *Homilies on the Psalms*. In 393 he undertook a literal commentary on Genesis, which he left unfinished, and in 394 he lectured on and discussed Romans at Carthage and began commentaries on Romans and Galatians as well as a treatise on lying and a commentary on the Lord's Prayer. In 395 Valerius shrewdly connived with Aurelius, the recently consecrated bishop of Carthage and primate of Africa, to have Augustine ordained as his coadjutor in order to assure that Augustine would remain in Hippo after Valerius's death, though neither of them knew at the time that it technically violated the canons of the Council of Nicaea to have two bishops in one city (*Ep.* 213, 4).

During the early years of the 35 that Augustine spent as bishop of Hippo, his pen was directed principally against the heretical sect of which he had himself been a member and to which he had converted a number of his friends, such as Romanianus, his wealthy patron. From the African coastal city of Hippo Augustine's literary reputation spread to the Italian mainland, and by 394 Paulinus, a priest and the future bishop of Nola in Campagnia, had received from Alypius five books written by Augustine against the Manichees, which Paulinus labeled Augustine's "Pentateuch against the Manichees" (*Ep.* 25, 2). Since the Manichees rejected the Old Testament and especially the creation narratives in Genesis, Augustine had to show that Genesis could be interpreted without the problems that the Manichees found in it and that the world God created was good. He also had to defend the holiness of the morality preached by the Catholic Church against Manichaean attacks and uphold Catholicism as the true religion. His fight with the Manichees continued well into the years of his episcopacy and is a dominant theme in most of his writings prior to 400.

Already as a priest, Augustine began the struggle to bring the Donatists (*see* DONATISM) back into the Catholic unity, writing an abecedarian piece of doggerel, *Psalm against the Sect of Donatus*, and appealing by letter to the Donatist bishop of Siniti in Numidia (*Ep.* 23). After his consecration as bishop, however, the conflict with the Donatists became, along with the Manichean heresy, a principal focus of his pastoral work and writing until well after the Conference of Carthage in 411, where the schism was officially ended. Valerius died in 396 leaving Augustine as bishop of Hippo. In that year, while responding to a set of questions on Paul's Letter to the Romans sent to him by Simplicianus, who had by that time succeeded Ambrose as bishop of Milan, Augustine underwent his third conversion (the first being to Manicheism and the second to Catholic Christianity). He tells us that God revealed to him as he was replying to Simplicianus that, contrary to what he had earlier claimed in his commentaries on Romans, faith, even the beginning of faith, is a gift of God. Though he "fought hard in defense of the free choice of the will, the grace of God conquered" (*Praed. sanct.* 4, 8) so that all human pride was banished and the grace of God was seen to have the absolute initiative in our salvation.

The Struggle with Donatism. The Donatist schism arose in Africa after the persecution of DIOCLETIAN early in the 4th century; it centered around the validity of sacraments conferred by clergy who were allegedly guilty of the sin of surrendering the sacred books or vessels (*traditio*). In 313 a rigorist group of Christians charged that Caecilian, the newly elected bishop of Carthage, had been ordained by a bishop guilty of *traditio*, and they ordained Majorinus as a rival bishop. Majorinus died shortly thereafter and was succeeded by Donatus, from whom the sect took its name. By the time of Augustine's return to Africa the schism had been established for over 75 years and grown in size and strength to the point that there were in Africa and Numidia as many Donatist as Catholic churches. When Augustine became bishop of Hippo, the Donatists probably outnumbered the Catholics there. Over the years the coexistence of the two churches in Africa and Numidia was anything but peaceful; roving bands of Donatists, the Circumcellions, wandered between shrines of the martyrs, often wreaking havoc on Catholic property as they injured, maimed, and even killed Catholic clergy and laity.

In 313 Donatus himself appealed to the emperor, Constantine, against his Catholic rival, Caecilian, though his case repeatedly met with defeat before episcopal courts in Rome and in Arles and before the emperor himself. Augustine first wanted to use only persuasion in trying to bring the schismatics back to the Catholic unity for fear that, if force were used, Donatists would be reconciled only as a pretense and the Church would be filled with people who were Catholics only in name. But the Donatists proved themselves singularly resistant to reasoned appeals. Despite his initial opposition to the use of force, Augustine allowed himself to be convinced by the arguments of his fellow bishops and by the results of the implementation of the imperial laws of February 405 that the use of force was not merely justified, but successful. Many Donatists returned to the Catholic unity, some willingly and gladly; others did so against their will, but were soon won over (*Ep.* 93, 16–19).

Among his many anti-Donatist writings Augustine produced four that rank as great works of theology: *Answer to the Letter of Parmenian, Baptism in Answer to the Donatists, Answer to the Letters of Petilian*, and *Answer to Gaudentius*. He insists against the Donatists that the Catholic Church is spread throughout the whole world, as Scripture had promised, not just in Africa, where the sect of Donatist is found; that it is Christ who baptizes, not the human minister, so that the validity of a sacrament does not depend upon the holiness of the minister; that the repetition of the rite of baptism subjects the standard of Christ the King to the insult of exorcism and exsufflation; and, that the Donatist schism has torn members from the very body of Christ, the Church. Under pressure from the imperial authorities, the Donatists finally agreed to hold a conference with their Catholic counterparts at Carthage in 411; the conference was attended by over 280 bishops from each side and terminated in a decision against the Donatists. On Jan. 30, 412, the emperor Honorius issued an edict that proscribed Donatism and imposed penalties of fines, exile, and the confiscation of church property. In the wake of the Conference of Carthage, which was a personal triumph for Augustine and his friend Marcellinus, the imperial commissioner, Augustine wrote two follow-up works, *Summary of the Conference* and *Appeal to the Donatists after the Conference*.

During the years between his consecration as bishop and the Conference of Carthage Augustine began *Teaching Christianity*, continued to write against the Manichees and on aspects of Christian life, and began two of his great works: *The Trinity*, whose composition stretched over twenty years and was complicated by the theft and premature publication of the first twelve books, and *The Literal Meaning of Genesis*, whose composition lasted until 414. Beginning in 396, he also wrote his most popular work, *The Confessions*, the first ten books of which recount, from the perspective of a Catholic bishop some ten years later, his life up to his conversion to Catholic Christianity and the death of Monica. In books 11 to 13 he turns to a commentary on the six days of creation and the Sabbath of God's rest, in which he presents his understanding, highly influenced by the thought of Plotinus, of the Christian faith concerning the origin, life, and destiny of human beings.

In August of 410 Alaric's vandals sacked the city of Rome, an event that shook the ancient world. Subsequent to Rome's fall there arrived in Africa a stream of the Roman nobility and their entourages, among whom were found the British ascetic PELAGIUS and his disciple Caelestius, who spread about ideas on the purpose of BAPTISM, especially the baptism of children. Their teaching came to the attention of Marcellinus, who in turn reported it to Augustine so that the bishop of Hippo became involved in the long struggle in defense of the grace of God, the struggle that was to earn for him the title "Teacher of Grace." At the same time many of the pagans declared that Rome's fall was due to the abandonment of the old gods of Rome and the acceptance of the Christian religion. Again at Marcellinus' instigation Augustine undertook to write another work, the 22 books of *The City of God*, the composition of which was completed only in 427. In the first ten he argued that the gods of Rome were not to be worshiped either for happiness in this life or for happiness in the life to come; in the last 12 books he described the origin, course, and destiny of the city of God and the city of man, the one founded upon love of God to the point of contempt for oneself, the other founded upon love of oneself to the contempt of God.

The Pelagian Controversy. From the Conference of Carthage in 411 until the end of his life in 430 Augustine was involved in a controversy on grace, first with Pelagius and Caelestius, and after 418 with Julian, bishop of

Eclanum in Italy. Pelagius and Caelestius were condemned in the summer of 418 by Pope ZOSIMUS in his letter ''Tractoria,'' which has been lost, as well as by the Council of CARTHAGE, and sent into exile by the emperor Honorius. Along with 18 other bishops, Julian refused to accept the condemnation of Pelagius's teaching, and he subsequently wrote extensively against Augustine's teaching on ORIGINAL SIN and the need for GRACE.

Pelagius and Caelestius had for a number of years been teaching in Rome a rigorous Christian asceticism that emphasized the need for willpower and belittled excuses based on human frailty. As early as 405 Pelagius heard in Rome the passage from *The Confessions* in which Augustine prayed to God, ''Give what you command, and command what you will'' (*Conf.* x, 29, 40). These words so upset Pelagius that he nearly came to blows with the bishop who was reading them, for in his eyes they typified the spiritual passivity and laxity that excused sin as the result of human weakness. Though Pelagius and Augustine never met, they exchanged greetings by letter before Pelagius left Africa for the East (*Ep.* 146).

Caelestius, however, remained in Africa. He was condemned at the Council of Carthage in 411 after he had sought to be ordained a priest and was charged with heresy. Soon afterwards Caelestius too left Africa for the East. Augustine wrote his first work against the Pelagian heresy in the fall of 411 or early in 412, *The Punishment and Forgiveness of Sins and the Baptism of Little Ones.* His friend Marcellinus had asked him to answer those who held ''that, even if he had not sinned, Adam would have died, that nothing passed to his descendants as the result of his sin by the process of generation,'' and ''that in this life there are and have been and will be human beings who have absolutely no sin'' (*Pecc. merit.* iii, 1, 1). Late in 412 or early in 413 Augustine wrote *The Spirit and the Letter*, again at the request of Marcellinus, to explain how it can be possible that there be human beings without sin in this life, though no one has ever lived a life of such righteousness. In 414 or 415 two disciples of Pelagius gave Augustine a copy of Pelagius' *Nature*, a work probably written in Rome between 406 and 410, after Augustine convinced them of the errors of Pelagius and won them over to his side. Through it Augustine for the first time realized the full danger of Pelagius's teaching and wrote in response *Nature and Grace*, in which he mentions Pelagius and Caelestius by name for the first time. In 415 Augustine also wrote *The Perfection of Human Righteousness* in order to refute a work of Caelestius, entitled *Definitions*, in which Caelestius tried to show that it is both possible and obligatory for people to live sinless lives.

In the winter of 415 an episcopal council held in Diospolis in Palestine acquitted Pelagius of heresy. Augustine was astounded to hear reports of this outcome and eventually managed to obtain a record of the trial. In *The Deeds of Pelagius* he commented point by point on the record of the trial, showing that the Eastern bishops who acquitted Pelagius did not have sufficient evidence to find him guilty and that Pelagius would have been condemned if he had not condemned points of his own and of Caelestius's teaching. In the summer of 418 Augustine wrote *The Grace of Christ and Original Sin* for three Roman aristocrats who, after fleeing from Rome to Africa, left Africa in 417 for the East where they met and befriended Pelagius. They had written to Augustine that Pelagius had, they believed, embraced the full Catholic teaching on the necessity of grace. Augustine, however, warned them to pay careful attention to what Pelagius meant by grace. Pelagius had no problem in acknowledging the importance of grace, provided that grace meant no more than the human nature that God gave us in creating us, the teaching of Scripture, the example of Christ, or the forgiveness of sins.

The second phase of the Pelagian controversy began when Julian, bishop of Eclanum in Apulia, and 18 other bishops refused to accept Pope Zosimus's encyclical letter ''Tractoria,'' with its condemnation of Pelagius and Caelestius. After Julian was in turn condemned by the pope, he appealed to Count Valerius at the imperial court in Ravenna for competent judges to hear his case and complained that Augustine was condemning marriage as the work of the devil. Warned by Valerius, Augustine wrote the first book of *Marriage and Desire*; later he received various excerpts from Julian's *To Turbantius*, a work written for one of the 18 other bishops who rejected ''Tractoria.'' In reply to these excepts, Augustine wrote the second book of *Marriage and Desire*. When he finally received, probably in 421, the full text of *To Turbantius*, Augustine wrote in reply to it the four books of his *Answer to Julian*, which Julian most probably never saw, exiled as he was in the East. Meanwhile, Julian wrote a letter to Pope Boniface and wrote along with his fellow dissidents another letter to Bishop Rufus of Thessalonica; when Augustine received copies of these letters, he wrote and dedicated to Pope Boniface *Answer to Two Letters of the Pelagians*. Finally, Julian wrote *To Florus*, an attack on the second book of *Marriage and Desire*, to which Augustine replied with six books of his *Unfinished Work in Answer to Julian*, in which he so meticulously quotes Julian's work that the first six books of *To Florus* are fully preserved, though the last two have been lost. Augustine died in 430 before he was able to complete his answer.

The controversy on grace took another turn in 426 or 427 when some Catholic monks of Hadrumetum in Africa and of southern France near Marseilles objected to aspects of Augustine's teaching on grace. Post-Reformation theologians have anachronistically called them heretics and misleadingly labeled them Semi-Pelagians. The Catholic monks at Hadrumetum exploited Augustine's theory of grace to their advantage and claimed that superiors ought not to rebuke monks who misbehave, but should simply pray that God may give the monks the grace to act correctly. After all, the monks claimed, according to Augustine, no one can do good actions without God's grace; hence, it was not their fault if they sinned. In *Rebuke and Grace* Augustine explained to them how his teaching on grace did not remove the meaningfulness of rebukes, but he needed another work, *Grace and Free Choice*, to show how Scripture teaches the necessity of both grace and of free choice.

The monks of Provence, under the influence of John CASSIAN, also resisted Augustine's teaching that the very beginning of faith (*initium fidei*) is a gift of God and pointed out that Augustine himself had earlier agreed with them, as he in fact had prior to his third conversion in 396. They also resisted Augustine's teaching on the grace of perseverance and on predestination. In opposition to their teaching, which was reported to Augustine by letters from two layman, a certain Hilary and Prosper of Aquitaine, Augustine wrote *The Gift of Perseverance* and *The Predestination of the Saints*, in which he explained the necessity of God's grace for the very beginning of faith and for perseverance up to the end of one's life and defended the grace of predestination without which no one can be saved and with which one cannot fail to be saved.

At the age of 72, in 426, Augustine had the clergy and people of Hippo approve Heraclius as his successor. Augustine transferred much of the work of the diocese to him, though he was not consecrated bishop until Augustine's death. Meanwhile, Augustine continued to write, undertaking the *Revisions*, a work in which he reexamined, corrected at times, and at times defended his books. He wrote for Quodvultdeus, a deacon of Carthage, *Heresies*, a work in which he listed and briefly described all the 88 heresies that had arisen from the time of Christ to the present. Moreover, in 428 Maximinus, an Homoian Arian bishop, arrived in Hippo in the company of the army of the Goth, Segisvult. Maximinus challenged the Catholics to a debate and, though Maximinus began the debate with Heraclius, Augustine was quickly summoned to take over; a verbatim record is given in the *Debate with Maximinus*. After the Arian bishop departed from Hippo, Augustine wrote the two books of his *Answer to Maximinus* to refute what Maximinus said in his long final intervention that kept Augustine from answering him on the date of the debate. Along with his earlier *Answer to an Arian Sermon* the works confronting Maximinus's teaching provide valuable insight into Homoian Arian theology and its vigorous survival, well into the fifth century, as well as into Augustine's CHRISTOLOGY.

An account of Augustine's life that mentions his theological controversies and principal works is bound to give the picture of a scholar who spent most of his time in writing, but the days of a Catholic bishop in North Africa at Augustine's time were filled with other work and problems. For example, as bishop, Augustine heard court cases between Christian as well as non- Christian parties; he traveled on over 50 journeys about his diocese, to Carthage, and even to Mauretania on a mission from the pope; preached countless sermons, of which we have almost 500; and wrote letters, of which we have close to three hundred and by which he carried on an extensive correspondence that reached Palestine in the East, Rome and Milan to the north, and Spain to the West.

At the end of his long life, as the Vandals plundered Africa and besieged Hippo Augustine, as Possidius, his first biographer reports, consoled himself with the words of Plotinus, ''He is not a great man who thinks it something great that sticks and stones fall and that mortals die'' (*Vita Augustine* 28, 11). During his final days, after being stricken with a fever, Augustine had the penitential Psalms written out on parchment and hung on the wall near his bed. On Aug. 28, 430, he died at the age of 76, almost 40 years after his ordination.

WORKS

There are modern critical editions of nearly all of Augustine's work in either *Corpus Christianorum*, Series latina (CCL) or *Corpus scriptorum ecclesiasticorum latinorum* (CSEL), though for a few works scholars must still rely on *Patrologia Latina* (PL). In some cases the text in the *Bibliothèque Augustinienne* volumes is an improvement over the critical edition, for example, for *De Genesi ad litteram* and for the letters recently discovered by J. Divjak, but the *Bibliothèque Augustinienne* volumes are always worth consulting for their rich annotation. The list contained within this essay puts Augustine's works in chronological order, though in many cases the dating is only an approximation. The translation of the *Works of Saint Augustine* (WSA) being published by the Augustinian Fathers in the United States will be the first complete English translation of Augustine's works; volumes in the series that have already been published or are in press are indicated. Translations in other series, *Ancient Christian Writers*, *Fathers of the Church*, and *Nicene and Post-Nicene Church Fathers* (NPNF) are also listed as well as works translated in the *Library of Christian Clas-*

sics (LCC) and in the series *Patristic Studies* (PS). The electronic version of PL published by Chadwick-Healey and the CETEDOC CD-ROM disks allow electronic searches of the works of the Fathers. The *Corpus Augustinianum Gissense* on CD-ROM contains not merely the text of Augustine's works, but a very valuable bibliography of secondary sources. The discoveries in 1976 by Johannes Divjak of 29 new letters in Marseilles and in 1990 by François Dolbeau of 26 new sermons in Mainz have opened up important new perspectives on Augustine's extensive collections of letters and sermons.

AUGUSTINE'S PHILOSOPHY AND THEOLOGY

Augustine's thought underwent dramatic development in the 50 years of his writing career from 380, when he penned a work on aesthetics, which is now lost, until his death as an old man with hundreds of books, sermons, and letters to his credit. He himself admits that he made progress as he wrote (*Retr.* prol.); hence, in attempting to present an overview of his philosophy and theology, one is not merely faced with the vast sweep of his thought, but must try to situate his ideas within their context, paying attention to the development of his thought, not merely from before his conversion to Catholic Christianity until afterwards, but also during the whole of his life as a priest and bishop.

Philosophy. Augustine was not a philosopher in the modern sense in which philosophy is viewed as a discipline independent of faith or theology. He did, however, describe himself as a philosopher in the sense of a lover of wisdom (*Sol.* i, 11, 22) and used the term "theology" only to refer to the accounts of the gods of the pagan religions (*Civ. Dei* vi, 5). Augustine's encounter with the books of the Platonists during his stay in Milan played a decisive role in his conversion. From the books of Plotinus Augustine learned to think of God and the soul as non-bodily and to think of God as non-temporal. As a result, he was able effectively to answer the Manichean objections that the God in whose image human beings were made according to Genesis must have hair, teeth, and organs like us and that evil, if real, must be a body. He learned that evil was a privation of good and, hence, did not need an evil cause (*Conf.* iii, 7, 12). So too, his ability to conceive of God as eternal, having neither past nor future, but only a present, permitted him to answer the further Manichean or Gnostic question about what God was doing before he created heaven and earth (*Conf.* xi, 10, 12).

In the Platonists, whom he read at Cassiciacum and whose thought he pondered during the years ahead and used to come to an understanding of the Christian faith, Augustine found philosophers who, he said, "agree with us about the one God who is the author of this universe, who is not only above all bodies insofar as he is incorporeal, but is also above all souls insofar as he is incorruptible, who is our principle, our light, our good" (*Civ. Dei* viii, 10). In the eyes of Augustine the Platonists had brought philosophy to its perfection, dividing it into three parts: moral, natural, and rational, and each of these parts dealt with God "the end of all actions, the cause of all natures, and the light of every reason" (*Civ. Dei* viii, 5). And yet, though the Platonists saw God and even saw that God had an only-begotten Son, they refused to accept that the Word became flesh (*Conf.* vii, 21, 27). Soon after his conversion, he said that, if the Platonists of the past could live again, they would "with the change of a few ideas and thoughts, have become Christians, as many Platonists of recent times have done" (*Vera rel.* 4, 7). But his enthusiasm for the truth he found in the books of the Platonists began to wane somewhat, as he came to realize how their pride kept them from accepting the humble Christ. "Many," he says, "saw where to go, but did not see the way. They loved the fatherland with its height, but did not know the way with its humility" (*S.* 140, 4). The Platonists "were able to see that which is, but they saw it from a distance; they refused to hold onto the humility of Christ, the ship by which they would have reached that which they were able to see from afar" (*Joh. ev. tr.* 2, 4).

When Augustine spoke of "our philosophy" (*C. Iul.* iv, 14, 72), he meant Christian wisdom, whose sole task, he said, "is nothing else than to teach what is the principle without principle of all things and what a great intellect abides in it and what flows from it for our salvation without any deterioration. This principle is the one, almighty God, Father, Son, and Holy Spirit, as our venerable mysteries teach" (*Ord.* ii, 5, 16). Hence, even in his early dialogues he had a grasp of the Christian Trinity as one God, Father, Son, and Holy Spirit, without any subordination of the Son and Spirit to the Father.

Faith and Reason. Though Augustine was lured into the Manichean sect by their promises of the pure truth and was repelled from the Catholic Church by the demand for a blind faith, he came to see the need to believe the word of God prior to understanding it and adopted as his motto the words of Isaiah, "Unless you believe, you will not understand" (Is 7.9 LXX). Soon after his conversion he saw two parallel paths to the truth: reason and authority. "Authority is prior in time, but reason is prior in reality" (*Ord.* ii, 9, 26). "Philosophy promises reason and scarcely sets free a very few" (*Ord.* ii, 5, 16), but the few whom it does set free attain a knowledge in this life beyond which one cannot go even hereafter (*Ord.* ii, 9, 26), and those few whom reason sets free need to follow the path of faith and authority only to avoid setting a bad example for those who cannot fly (*Util. cred.* 10, 24). In his early view reason was for the few an independent way to the truth, while believing was useful for those unable to follow the path of reason.

Later he held that, with a mystery of faith or a difficult passage of Scripture, one should first believe in order to understand. ''Understanding is the reward for believing. Do not, therefore, seek to understand in order that you may believe, but believe in order that you may understand'' (*Joh Ev. tr.* 29, 6). The faith that must come before understanding is not, however, an utterly blind faith, since Augustine insists that one must understand the words in some way if one is to believe them. As he puts it, ''Understand in order that you may believe my words; believe in order that you may understand the word of God'' (*S.* 43, 7, 9). Later, when a young Spaniard, Consentius, wrote him, claiming that one ought to seek the truth from faith rather than from reason, since otherwise only philosophers would attain happiness, Augustine wrote back, ''God forbid that we should believe in such a way that we do not accept or seek a reason. . . . In certain matters, then, pertaining to the doctrine of salvation that we cannot as yet perceive by reason, but that we will at some point see, faith precedes reason. . . . If, then, it is reasonable that faith precedes reason for certain important ideas that cannot yet be grasped, a slight reason that persuades us of this undoubtedly precedes faith'' (*Ep.* 120, 1, 3). In fact, Augustine urges Consentius, ''Love understanding very much,'' and explains that even the holy Scriptures are useless if one does not understand them (*Ep.* 120, 3, 13).

God, One and Triune. The movement to God is in Augustine's thought always from the external world through the inner self and up to God: ''from the exterior to the interior and from the inferior to the superior'' (*En. Ps.* 145, 5). God, he says, is ''more inward than my inmost self and higher than my highest being'' (*Conf.* iii, 6, 11). Though he presents what many have taken to be a demonstration of God's existence, his concern in his ascent to God aims at least as much to show the incorporeal and eternal being of God as to establish his existence (*Lib. arb.* ii, 3, 7–15, 39). The God to whom Augustine comes is Being itself, the Truth, absolutely immutable, eternal, and omnipresent, and yet a personal God, whose name is not only ''I am,'' but ''the God of Abraham, the God of Isaac, and the God of Jacob.'' God told Moses that his name was ''He Who Is,'' and Augustine interprets this name, putting words in God's mouth: ''I am called 'Is.' What does it mean that I am called 'Is.' That I remain for eternity, that I cannot change'' (*S.* 6, 3, 4). But because ''He Is'' was perhaps too much for Moses to understand, as it is too much for us, God immediately went on to say to Moses, ''I am the God of Abraham, the God of Isaac, and the God of Jacob. This you can grasp.

For what mind can grasp, 'I am who am'?'' (*Joh. Ev. tr.* 36, 8).

God is the source of everything other than himself, originally making heaven and earth out of nothing, not out of his own substance, freely, not from any necessity, by his eternal Word, not by any external instrument. Even if God made something from something else, ''he did not make it from something that he himself had not made'' (*F. et symb.* 2, 2). Hence, if he created heaven and earth out of unformed matter, he, of course, made the matter out of which he formed the world (*Conf.* xii, 8, 8). Since time is a creature, there was no time before God created heaven and earth (*Conf.* xi, 13, 15–16). God made everything with measure, number, and order (*Gen Man.* i, 16, 26). He made each thing good, and all things together are not merely good, but very good (*Conf.* vii, 12, 18). By their changing creatures cry out that they have been made; by their beauty, goodness, and wisdom they testify to the beauty, goodness, and wisdom of their creator (*Conf.* xi, 4, 6). God not only creates all things in accord with what Plato called ''ideas'' (*Div. qu.* 46, 1–2), but has foreknowledge or rather knowledge of all that happens in the world (*Simpl.* ii, 2, 2).

In the Cassiciacum dialogues Augustine already articulated his faith in the Trinity, avoiding any subordinationism (*Ord.* ii, 5, 16). In his great work, *The Trinity*, Augustine advanced the speculative understanding of the Trinity by distinguishing absolute and relative predication of God, setting forth rules for speaking of the one God and the three persons. He held that whatever is said of God non-relatively is said of God according to substance, that is, to signify the substance of God common to the three (*Trin.* v, 6, 7). Nothing, however, is said of God according to accident, that is, to signify anything mutable in God. But things are said of God according to relation, for the Father is said to be in relation to the Son and the Son is said to be in relation to the Father, just as the Holy Spirit is said to be in relation to the Father and the Son (*Trin.* v, 5, 6). Hence, whatever is said properly of the individual persons in the Trinity is not said absolutely, but relatively to one another (*Trin.* vii, 9, 2). The Father, Son, and Holy Spirit are consubstantial or of one substance, and ''the force of 'the same substance' in the Father, Son, and Holy Spirit is so great that whatever is said of them non-relatively, is not said in the plural, but in the singular'' (*Trin.* vii, 8, 9). Augustine prefers to speak of one essence and three persons rather than to follow the Greek usage of three ''hypostases,'' which to Latin ears implies three substances (*Trin.* vii, 5, 10), though he admits that we say, ''persons,'' only to have something to call the three (*Trin.* viii, *prooem.* 1). Even in his early correspondence with Nebridius Augustine maintained that the external operations of the three were common to all, though he struggled to explain to his friend how only the Son assumed a human nature (*Ep*. 11, 2).

In his *Confessions* Augustine had offered a single faltering example of trinity in unity, namely, the being, knowing, and willing of one mind, in order to understand somehow "that immutable being that is above all these, which is immutably, knows immutably, and wills immutably" (*Conf*. xiii, 11, 12). But in *The Trinity* he developed more than 20 examples of trinities, each attempting to illustrate in some way the Trinity that is God. With the trinity of memory, understanding, and will in one mind, he was able to offer an illustration of the generation of the Son from the Father and of the procession the Spirit from the Father and the Son (*Trin*. xv, 21, 40–41). In his account of our the inner word, Augustine developed an image of the generation of the eternal Word from the Father (*Trin*. xv, 10, 17–19), and in the expression of our mental word in a spoken word he found a likeness of the eternal Word's becoming flesh.

Christology and Redemption. In his earliest reference to Christ Augustine says in highly Plotinian language that "out of a certain compassion for the masses God most high bent down and subjected the authority of the divine intellect even to the human body itself" in order to recall "to the intelligible world souls blinded by the darkness of error and befouled by the slime of the body" (*C. Acad*. iii, 19, 42). In another Cassiciacum dialogue he clearly maintains that Christ is the Son of God sent to us by the Father (*Ord*. i, 10, 29); he again speaks of Christ as the great intellect that abides in the Father and emphasizes the great mercy and humility involved in the fact that "so great a God has on our account deigned to assume and move about a body of our kind" (*Ord*. ii, 5, 16). In retrospect, he says in his *Confessions* that, at the time when he read the books of the Platonists, he considered "Christ as only a man of excellent wisdom whom no one could equal, especially because he was miraculously born of a virgin" (*Conf*. vii, 19, 25). He later admitted that at that point he had no idea of the mystery involved in the Word's becoming flesh, but insisted that he had learned that the Word was not joined to the flesh without a human soul. His friend, Alypius, on the other hand, had thought that Catholics held the Apollinarian view, one also shared by the Homoian Arians who were present in Milan, that Christ lacked a human soul and mind, though only later did Augustine learn of these heresies or of his own Photinianism, which may have actually been derived from Porphyry. During his Manichean years, of course, Augustine thought of the Savior as "something extruded from" God's "bright substance" and did not believe that he was born of Mary in the flesh for fear that he would have to believe that he was defiled by the flesh (*Conf*. v, 10, 20). Hence, as a Manichee he did not believe that either his death or his resurrection was real.

Clearly by 391 Augustine held a fully orthodox view of Christ. He preached on Easter that the whole of the Word and man "is the Son of God the Father in terms of the Word and Son of Man in terms of the man. . . . not only man, but Son of God . . . and not only the Word but the Son of Man" (*S*. 214, 6). The following year he preached on the two births of Christ, his eternal birth from the Father and his temporal birth in our human nature, and taught that "the Word of God assumed" this man "so that God and he are one" (*En. Ps*. ii, 7 and iii, 3).

Because in Adam our nature was wounded by sin and left in ignorance and weakness, Augustine often describes the redemptive work of Christ as deliverance from the power of sin or of the devil and a healing of our wounded nature. Christ is a physician who came to heal those who are ill. "The human race lies ill, not with diseases of the body, but with sin. . . . To heal this huge patient the omnipotent physician descended from heaven. He lowered himself to mortal flesh, as if to the bedside of ailing humanity" (*S*. 87, 9, 13). Christ is himself the good Samaritan, and we are all the man left half dead on the road. "The passing Samaritan did not scorn us; he cared for us, put us on his animal, and on his own flesh brought us to the inn, that is, the Church" (*En. Ps*. 125, 15). In other texts Christ's work is seen as mediating between the righteousness of God and our sinfulness. "Temporal sinfulness separated us from eternal righteousness; there was need of an intervening temporal righteousness, a midpoint that would be temporal from below and righteous from above and thus, in breaking away from the highest and conforming to the lowest, he might restore the lowest to the highest" (*Cons. ev*. i, 35, 53). But there are also passages in which he stresses Christ's work as making us divine. He says, "In order to make us gods, he who was God became man" (*S*. 192, 1), and, "God wants to make you god, not by nature, as the Son is whom he begot, but by his gift and adoption" (*S*. 166, 4, 4). Similarly, he speaks of the Word's mission as liberating us from time, "He was God before all time and man in time in order to set us free from time" (*S*. Guel. 32, 5). Again, he describes Christ as "calling us who are temporal and making us eternal" (*En. Ps*. 101, s. ii, 11). Christ is also the counter type to Adam. Augustine says that the Christian faith consists in the influence of these two men. "By one of them we are sold under the power of sin; by the other we are redeemed from sin. By the one we were cast down to death; by the other we are set free for life" (*Gr. et pecc. or*. ii, 24, 28).

Scripture. When Augustine first seriously turned to the Scriptures after reading *Hortensius* he found them repulsive (*Conf.* iii, 5, 9 and 7, 12–13). As a Manichee, he certainly had some familiarity with the Old and New Testaments, for, even though the Manichees rejected the former entirely and the latter in parts, they used as objections against the Catholics passages that they themselves rejected as the word of God. The creation narratives of Genesis were especially the target of Manichean attack since these passages taught the goodness of all of creation. A literal interpretation of the text all too often led to baffling conundrums, such as the passing of day and night before the creation of the sun or the making of man to God's image and likeness with its implication of gross anthropomorphism. The preaching of Ambrose allowed Augustine to see that "the spiritual people" in the Church did not always understand the text of Scripture in a literal fashion, but often understood the text spiritually (*Conf.* v, 14, 24 and vi, 3, 4). Twice Augustine lists four senses of Scripture: historical, aetiological, analogical, and allegorical. The historical sense tells us what was said or done; the aetiological sense gives the cause of its being said or done; the analogical sense shows the harmony of the two testaments; the allegorical sense shows that some passages must be interpreted figuratively, not literally (*Util. cred.* 3, 5 and *Gen. imp.* 2, 5). Elsewhere he says that "in all the holy books we must look at the eternal truths that we are taught in them, the deeds that are reported, the future events that are foretold, and what we are commanded or admonished to do" (*Gen. litt.* i, 1, 1).

Augustine has at least two criteria for resorting to a non-literal interpretation of a passage. A literal reading that leads to blasphemy or absurdity requires a figurative interpretation (*Gen. Man.* ii, 2, 3). But besides this more moderate criterion he also claimed, "Whatever in the word of God cannot in the proper sense be referred to the goodness of morals or the truth of the faith is figurative" (*Doc. chr.* iii, 10, 14). In accord with the latter criterion, for example, the precise number of fishes caught according to Jn 21.11 must have a figurative meaning, since it clearly does not refer to faith or morals (*Joh. ev. tr.* 122, 9).

What the Scriptures state is true because what they say God himself says (*Conf.* xiii, 29, 44). Augustine sharply reprimanded Jerome of Bethlehem for his interpretation of Gal 2.14 in the sense that Paul was telling a useful lie when he said that he saw that Peter was not acting correctly in relation to the truth of the Gospel. "For, if so-called useful lies are admitted into the holy scriptures, what authority will be left in them?" (*Ep.* 40, 3, 3). The authority of the Scriptures "is confirmed by the agreement of so many nations through the succession of apostles, bishops, and councils" (*C. Faust.* 13, 5) and must be believed without hesitation, though such immediate assent is only due to the canonical books (*Nat. et grat.* 61, 71). The whole text of the Scriptures, both Old and New Testaments, speak of Christ (*Ep. Joh,* 2, 1). "The Old Testament is revealed in the New; the New is veiled in the Old" (*En. Ps.* 105, 36). And the key to the unveiling of the Old Testament is the cross of Christ (*En. Ps.* 45, 1).

Despite all the authority of the canonical Scriptures, they are only needed by fallen human beings as part of our dependence upon signs for communication, signs that were not needed in paradise (*Gen. Man.* ii, 4, 5) and will not, of course, be needed in heaven (*Conf.* xiii, 15, 16). Furthermore, the whole purpose of the Scriptures is development in faith, hope, and charity, and persons who have acquired these virtues no longer need the Scriptures for themselves, though they may still need them for the instruction of others (*Doct. chr.* i, 34, 43). Augustine held that many true senses could be found in a passage of Scripture; even if the human author did not intend all of them, the divine author might very well have intended them and put them there for our mental exercise and discovery (*Conf.* xii, 31, 42–32, 43).

Souls: Origin and Destiny. From early on Augustine claimed that he wanted to know only God and the soul (*Sol.* 2, 7). From the Platonists he learned to conceive of the soul as incorporeal, and in the early years after his conversion he struggled to prove the immortality of the rational soul in his *Soliloquies and The Immortality of the Soul.* Though very early he speaks of the soul as divine (*C. Acad.* i, 1, 1 and 4, 11), he was soon convinced that the soul is mutable and, therefore, not divine (*Ep.* 166. 2, 3), though he continued to hold that, "though the human soul is not what God is, . . . there is nothing closer to God" (*Quant.* 34, 77). The human soul is equal to an angel in nature, but not in its function (*Lib. arb.* iii, 11, 32). He defines the human soul in Platonic language as "a certain substance partaking in reason and suited to rule the body" (*Quant.* 13, 22) and elsewhere speaks of a human being as "a rational soul using a mortal and earthly body" (*Mor.* i, 27, 52). Augustine compares the union of soul to the body in one person to the union of the Word with the man in the one person of Christ and finds the latter easier to believe (*Ep.* 137, 3, 11).

The question of the origin of human souls subsequent to those of Adam and Eve troubled Augustine throughout his life, and he insisted, when reviewing his books, that he did not know at Cassiciacum and that he did not know in his old age whether souls come by generation from Adam's soul or are created individually for each person who is born (*Retr.* i, 1, 3). He did, however, present four hypotheses regarding the origin of souls: that they come by propagation from Adam's soul (TRADU-CIANISM), that individual souls are created for each infant born (creationism), that souls are created outside their bodies and sent by God to rule bodies, and that souls are created elsewhere and fall into bodies of their own accord (*Lib. arb.* iii, 20, 56–58). When he formulated these hypotheses, his principal concern was to defend the justice of God, no matter which one of them might be true, but it seems clear that in his early writings he held that souls existed before their embodiment and fell into these mortal bodies by sin (*Ep.* 7, 1, 2). He clearly held that a soul brought with it into this life all the arts and that "what is called learning is nothing other than remembering and recalling" (*Quant.* 20, 34). It seems likely that as late as the time of *The Confessions* he held the view that the soul fell into the body, but at least by 411 he came to realize that Rom 9.11 excluded any prenatal sin (*Pecc. mer.* ii, 36, 59). While traducianism seemed more compatible with the transmission of original sin, the generation of souls seemed to implied that they were bodily, and while creationism was certainly compatible with the spirituality of souls, it both left the transmission of original sin puzzling and had no clear support in the Scriptures.

Though Augustine early was concerned with proving the soul's immortality, he later drops any concern with such proofs and focuses his attention almost entirely upon the Christian doctrine of the resurrection of the body, something that he was slow to mention in his early writings (*Quant.* 33, 76), perhaps due to his fondness for Platonism. But soon he saw the resurrection as central to the Christian faith and says that the body will enjoy full health without any need or weariness after the resurrection of the flesh (*Vera rel.* 53, 103).

Knowledge. Augustine, of course, recognized the five bodily senses as well as an interior sense by which we become aware of our sensing and by which we picture to ourselves what we have previously sensed or imagine other things by combining, separating, enlarging, or reducing images of things we have previously sensed (*Lib. arb.* ii, 3, 8). He defined sensation in Plotinian language as "a modification of the body that of itself does not escape the soul's awareness" (*Quant.* 25, 48), thus making sensing an act of the soul and excluding any action of the body upon the soul (*Mus* vi, 5, 10). He thought of intellectual knowing on the model of seeing with the eyes. "To understand is to the mind what to see is to the sense" (*Ord.* ii, 3, 10) Hence, just as in order to see, we need such eyes that are open, healthy, and clean that turned toward something made visible by the light, so we need a mind that is healthy and whose gaze, reason (*Quant.* 27, 53), is turned toward something intelligible that has been illumined by God, who is "the light of minds" (*Sol.* i, 13, 23), "the intelligible light in whom and from whom

and through whom all things are intelligibly bright that anywhere are intelligibly bright" (*Sol.* i, 1, 3). The theory of divine ILLUMINATION clearly makes human intellectual knowing dependent upon God in some way, but it is not clear precisely what divine illumination contributes to human knowing.

Nature, Freedom, and Grace. In his opposition to Manicheism Augustine defended the goodness of every nature. He wrote to Celestine, the future pope, that there is a nature mutable in place and time such as a body, and a nature mutable only in time, such as a soul, and a nature wholly immutable whether in time or in place, namely, God (*Ep.* 18, 2). The absolutely immutable nature of God is obviously a great good since it is incorruptible, that is, cannot lose any goodness. Bodies and souls, though corruptible, are still good since, unless they had some goodness to lose, they would be incorruptible and, hence, very good (*Conf.* vii, 12, 18). So too, when his focus was directed to the refutation of the Manichees, Augustine emphasized the freedom of the will, claiming that nothing is so in the power of the will as the will itself and that, in order to have a good will, one only needs to will it (*Lib. arb.* i, 12, 26). In his early commentary on Romans Augustine claimed that God did not choose the works of anyone, but chose in his foreknowledge those whom he foreknew were going to believe. He explicitly stated, "That we believe, then, comes from us, but that we do good comes from him who gives the Holy Spirit to those who believe" (*Ex. prop. Rm.* 52). In that way he left the initiative in the salvation of human beings with human beings. But by the time he wrote to Simplicianus in order to answer his questions on Romans, Augustine claimed that God made it clear to him that we have nothing of our own over which we might boast, not even faith (*Praed. sanct.* 4, 8). He also came to see that the human nature with which each of us is born suffers under ignorance of what we ought to do and difficulty in doing the good, even when we know it (*Lib. arb.* iii, 20, 55). Our present nature is, therefore, damaged or vitiated in comparison with the nature with which human beings were originally created (*Lib. arb.* iii, 19, 54). Hence, though our will remains free, our present free choice without the help of grace is capable only of sin (*Sp. et litt.* 3, 5). Our will, which is free to sin, is not free for good actions unless it has been set free by the grace of God (*C. ep. Pel.* 3, 7). And God grants his grace gratuitously to those he chooses without any preceding merits on our part (*C. ep. Pel.* 6, 11); even the very beginning of faith is a gift of God, not due to any merit on our part (*Praed. sanct.* 41, 43).

Church. The Donatists claimed that the Church of Christ survived only in Africa and in their sect because of the invalidity of the sacraments administered by sinful ministers in the Church who had surrendered the sacred books during the persecution under Diocletian. Against their position Augustine emphasized the unity and peace of Christ from which the Donatists had torn themselves away (*Ep.* 61, 1). He also stressed the catholicity of the Church that had spread throughout the whole world, as the Scriptures had foretold, while the sect of Donatus was confined to Africa and only to a part of it (*S.* 19, 7). He pointed out that the Catholic Church in Africa was in communion with all those churches founded by the apostles, and in the bishops of Rome he traced the apostolic succession step by step from St. Peter to the current bishop (*Ep.* 53, 1, 2). Though the Donatists insisted that all they wanted was holiness (*Ep.* 93, 10, 43), Augustine argued that without being united to the body of Christ, the Church, they were also separated from Christ, its head, and claimed that, though they had the sacraments of Christ, they were not useful or salutary for them as long as they remained in their schism (*C. Cresc.* 29, 35).

The Church is the body of Christ and Christ himself is the head of the Church so that together Christ and the Church form the whole Christ (*totus Christus*). "For without him we are nothing, but in him we too are Christ. Why? Because the whole Christ is the head and the body. The head is the body's savior who has already ascended into heaven, but the body is the Church that labors on earth" (*En. Ps.* 30, ii, 1, 3). Augustine appeals to Christ's words, "Saul, Saul, why are you persecuting me" (*Acts* 9.4), as evidence of the unity of Christ as head with his body, the Church (*En. Ps.* 30, ii, 1, 3). The Church is, nonetheless, a Church of sinners. All in the Church have to pray daily both for the forgiveness of their own sins and for help to avoid sins in the future (*Nat. et gr.* 67, 80). Against the Donatist insistence upon holiness Augustine repeatedly appeals to the gospel parables of the wheat and the weeds in the field, the grain and the chaff on the threshing floor, and the good and bad fishes in the net, insisting that we cannot separate the saints from the sinners until we come to the harvest, the final winnowing, or the shore (*Ep.* 105, 5, 16). After all, we do not know who will be saved and who will not be saved, for that must be left to the judgment of God (*Corrept.* 8, 17).

Sacraments. Augustine uses the term "sacrament" in a wide sense as a sacred sign. He speaks of the sacraments of the Old Testament (*Ep.* 82, 3, 28) and sees sacraments as constitutive of a people (*C. Faust.* 19, 11). But he also uses the term in a narrower liturgical sense to refer to Baptism, especially in the controversies with the Donatists and with the Pelagians, and to the Eucharist, "the sacrament of the Lord's table" (*S.* 227). Though he does speak of the "the Holy Spirit, whose sacrament is found in a visible anointing" (*In ep. Joh.* 3, 5), it is not clear whether he is referring to the anointing administered in Baptism or perhaps in Orders. In contrast with the many sacraments of the Jewish people, the Christian people have only a few most salutary sacraments (*Vera rel.* 17, 33). For the celebration of the sacraments Christians uses only a few creatures, such as bread, wine, water, and oil (*Ep.* 55, 7, 13). Baptism and the Eucharist alone receive extensive theological discussion, though there is also some treatment of anointing, penance, orders, and marriage as sacraments.

Last Things. Augustine firmly rejected the Platonic or Pythagorean theory of a repeated reincarnation of the soul in human or other bodies (*S.* 241, 5). He saw death as the end of our being able to sin (*Civ. Dei* xxii, 30, 3) or to repent of our sins (*S.* 18, 5, 5), though he thought that prayers for the dead were beneficial to them (*Ench.* 29, 110) and prayed for his mother who on her deathbed had asked to be remembered at the altar (*Conf.* ix, 11, 27 and 12, 32). Between death and the last judgment the soul "enjoys rest or suffers affliction in accord with its merits in its life in the body"(*Enchr.* 29, 109). But the final reward and condemnation will occur only after the resurrection of the body (*Civ. Dei* xxi, 26, 4). Though infants who die without baptism will have the mildest condemnation of all (*Pecc. merit.* i, 16, 21), Augustine saw no possibility for some third place for them between reward and punishment (*C. Jul. imp.* i, 50, 1). The punishment of the damned will be eternal along with the devil (*C. Prisc.* 5, 5–6, 7), and the reward of the blessed with Christ will be life that is truly eternal, where they will be at rest, see, love, and praise God "in the end without end" (*Civ. Dei* xxii, 10).

Influence. In philosophy and theology Augustine had no rival in the Western world at least until Thomas Aquinas. His thought and writings literally formed the mind of the Christian West. He has been credited with much that is good in the Western world and Church and blamed, unjustly, for many of their evils. His language has molded the way people speak of themselves, their destiny, and of their God and will very likely continue to do so. The Church has not accepted all of his teachings, even on grace, but his language and thought have so influenced ours over the past 1600 years that it is hard to imagine what the West would have been like without him. Almost all parties at the time of the Reformation claimed him as their own, and he continues to be read and to be a source of inspiration for Christians of every denomination, at least in the West.

Feast: Aug. 28

Bibliography: General. G. BONNER, *St. Augustine of Hippo: Life and Controversies* (London 1963; rev. ed. Philadelphia 1986). P. R. L. BROWN, *Augustine of Hippo: A Biography* (London 1967; repr., with an epilogue, Berkeley and Los Angeles 2000). H. CHADWICK, *Augustine* (Oxford 1986). M. T. CLARK, *Augustine* (London 1994). *Congesso internazionale su s. Agostino nel XVI centenario* *della conversione. Roma*, 15–20 settembre 1986, 3 v. (Rome 1987). A. FITZGERALD et al., eds. *Augustine through the Ages: An Encyclopedia* (Grand Rapids, Mich. 1999). C. KIRWAN, *Augustine, The Arguments of the Philosophers* (London 1989). S. LANCEL, *Saint Augustin* (Paris 1999). J. M. RIST, *Augustine: Ancient Thought Baptized* (Cambridge 1994). E. TESELLE, *Augustine the Theologian* (New York 1970). G. WILLS, *Saint Augustine* (New York 1999). **Studies.** *The Rule of St. Augustine*, intro. and comm. T. J. VAN BAVEL, tr. R. CANNING (Garden City 1986). D. W. H. ARNOLD and P. BRIGHT, eds. *De doctrina christiana: A Classic of Western Culture* (Christianity and Judaism in Antiquity 9; Notre Dame 1995). W. S. BABCOCK, ed. *The Ethics of St. Augustine* (Atlanta 1991). G. BONNER, *God's Decree and Man's Destiny: Studies in the Thought of Augustine of Hippo* (London 1987). K. E. BÖRRESEN, *Subordination and Equivalence: The Nature and Role of Woman in Augustine and Thomas Aquinas* (Washington 1981). V. J. BOURKE, *Augustine's Love of Wisdom: An Introspective Philosophy* (West Lafayette, Ind. 1992). P. BROWN, *The Body and Society: Men, Women and Sexual Renunciation in Early Christianity* (New York 1988); *Society and the Holy in Late Antiquity* (Berkeley and Los Angeles 1982). J. P. BURNS, *The Development of Augustine's Doctrine of Operative Grace* (Paris 1980). D. X. BURT, *Augustine's World: An Introduction to His Speculative Philosophy* (Lanham, Md. 1996); *Friendship and Society: An Introduction to Augustine's Practical Philosophy* (Grand Rapids, Mich. 1999). R. CANNING, *The Unity of Love for God and Neighbour in St. Augustine* (Heverlee-Louvian 1993). P. CARY, *Augustine's Invention of the Inner Self: The Legacy of a Christian Platonist* (Oxford 2000). H. CHADWICK, "New Sermons of St. Augustine," *Journal of Theological Studies* n.s. 47 (1996) 69–91. F. DOLBEAU, ed., *Augustin d'Hippone: Vingt-six sermons au peuple d'Afrique* (Paris 1996). G. R. EVANS, *Augustine on Evil* (Cambridge 1982). L. C. FERRARI, *The Conversions of Saint Augustine* (Villanova 1984). K. FLASCH and D. DE COURCELLES, eds., *Augustinus in der Neuzeit* (Turnhout 1998). K. FLASCH, *Was Ist Zeit? Augustinus von Hippo. Das XI. Buch der Confessiones. Historisch-philosophische Studie. Text-Übersetzung-Kommentar* (Frankfurt am Main 1993). W. H. C. FREND, "Augustine and Orosius: On the End of the Ancient World," *Augustinian Studies* 20 (1989) 1–38. W. J. HARMLESS, *Augustine and the Catechumenate* (Collegeville, Minn. 1995). C. HARRISON, *Augustine: Christian Truth and Fractured Humanity* (Christian Theology in Context; Oxford 2000); *Beauty and Revelation in the Thought of St. Augustine* (Oxford 1992). L. HÖLSCHER, *The Reality of Mind: Augustine's Philosophical Arguments for the Human Soul as a Spiritual Substance* (London and New York 1986). G. A. LAWLESS, *Augustine of Hippo and His Monastic Rule* (Oxford 1987). J. T. LIENHARD, E. C. MULLER, and R. J. TESKE, eds., *Augustine: Presbyter Factus Sum* (Collectanea Augustiniana 2; New York 1993). J. T. LIENHARD, "Reading the Bible and Learning to Read: The Influence of Education on St. Augustine's Exegesis," *Augustinian Studies* 27 (1996): 7–25. G. MADEC, *La patrie et la voie: Le Christ dans la vie et la pensée de Saint Augustin* (Paris 1989); *Saint Augustin et la philosophie: Notes critiques* (Paris 1996). J. E. MERDINGER, *Rome and the African Church in the Time of Augustine* (New Haven 1997). M. MILES, *Desire and Delight: A New Reading of Augustine's Confessions* (New York 1992). R. J. O'CONNELL, *Images of Conversion in St. Augustine's Confessions* (New York 1996); *The Origin of the Soul in St. Augustine's Later Works* (New York 1987); *Soundings in St. Augustine's Imagination* (New York 1994). G. O'DALY, *Augustine's "City of God:" A Reader's Guide* (Oxford 1999); *Augustine's Philosophy of Mind* (Berkeley and Los Angeles 1987). J. J. O'DONNELL, "The Authority of Augustine," *Augustinian Studies* 22 (1991): 7–35. J. J. O'DONNELL, ed., *Augustine: Confessions*, 3 v. (Oxford 1992). J. PELIKAN, *The Mystery of Continuity: Time and History, Memory and Eternity in the Thought of Saint Augustine* (Charlottesville 1986). C. STARNES, *Augustine's Conversion: A Guide to the Argument of Confessions I–IX* (Waterloo 1990). B. STOCK, *Augustine the Reader: Meditation, Self-Knowledge, and the Ethics of Interpretation* (Cambridge, Mass. 1996). B. STUDER, *The Grace of Christ and the Grace of God in Augustine of Hippo: Christocentrism or Theocentrism*, tr. M. J. O'CONNELL (Collegeville, Minn. 1997). R. J. TESKE, *Paradoxes of Time in Saint Augustine* (Milwaukee 1996). T. J. VAN BAVEL, "De la raison à la foi: La conversion d'Augustin," *Augustiniana* 36 (1986) 5–27. F. VAN FLETEREN and J. SCHNAUBELT, eds., *Augustine: "Second Founder of the Faith"* (Collectanea Augustiniana; New York 1990); *Augustine: Mystic and Mystagogue* (Collectanea Augustiniana 3; New York 1994); *Augustine in Iconography: History and Legend* (Collectanea Augustiniana; New York 1999). J. VAN OORT, *Jerusalem and Babylon: A Study into Augustine's City of God and the Sources of His Doctrine of the Two Cities* (Leiden and New York 1991). J. WETZEL, *Augustine and the Limits of Virtue* (Cambridge 1992).

[R. J. TESKE]

AUGUSTINE, RULE OF ST.

AUGUSTINE of Hippo lived as a monk from the time of his return to Africa from Italy in 388 and, as bishop of Hippo, required his cathedral clergy to imitate his monastic way of life. There is, however, no claim in his writings to have composed a rule. His biographer, Possidius of Calama, although stating that Augustine founded a monastery at Hippo "according to the manner and rule of the apostles" (*Life*, 5), does not say that he composed a rule for it or list one in the bibliography of Augustine's writings which he compiled. Nevertheless, from the 6th century onwards, a number of rules ascribed to Augustine for both men and women have been found in manuscripts, sometimes singly, sometimes in combination. These have engaged the attention of scholars from Erasmus to C. Lambot, but the major contribution to scholarship has been by Luc Verheijen, who devoted the greater part of his life to the study of the rule and its transmission. It must, however, be accepted that absolute certainty in this matter is impossible and that our judgments are primarily determined by the dating of manuscripts.

Four monastic documents are principally associated with Augustine (their Latin names are not traditional but were bestowed by Verheijen). They are (1) the *Ordo Monasterii* (Monastic Order) known in the Middle Ages as the *Regula secunda,* a short document of fewer than 400 words, giving general directions for the life of a masculine community. (2) The *Praeceptum,* or *Regula tertia,* the traditional *Rule of St. Augustine.* (The medieval *Regula prima,* or *Regula consensoria,* is today recognized as a forgery.) (3) The *Obiurgatio,* or *Reprimand,* Augustine's Letter 211, sections 1–4, a rebuke addressed to a community of nuns, who had revolted against their superior and asked Augustine to intervene. (4) The *Regularis*

Informatio, or feminine version of the *Praeceptum,* was long considered by many scholars as the original Augustinian rule, from which the masculine version was thought to have been adapted in the 12th century to provide a form of religious life permitting a wider field of action than the Benedictine rule. This supposition was strengthened by the fact that in some manuscripts the *Obiurgatio* and the *Regularis Informatio* were joined together and so appeared to form a single letter, being so printed as Augustine's Letter 211 by the Benedictine editors and by A. Goldbacher in the *Corpus Scriptorum Ecclesiasticorum Latinorum* edition in 1911. It now appears that only a few manuscripts of later date have *Ep.* 211 in this form, while earlier copies have an *explicit* after the *Obiurgatio,* separating it from the text of the *Regularis Informatio.*

The earliest witness ascribing the *Ordo Monasterii* and the *Praeceptum* to Augustine is the late 6th–early 7th century Paris manuscript. They are also found in the Bibliothèque Nationale 12,634, a collection of monastic rules formed by Eugippius of Lucullanum, an admirer of Augustine, less than a century after Augustine's death. There is no manuscript witness for the *Regularis Informatio* before the incomplete 10th-century Madrid manuscript Escorial aI13, while the oldest complete text is the Codex Turicensis, Zurich, manuscript, Rheinau 89, of the 11th–12th century. Since a number of manuscripts antedating the 10th century specifically ascribe the *Praeceptum* to Augustine, the codicological evidence supports the priority of the masculine rule. Furthermore, when St. Caesarius of Arles composed his *Rule for Nuns* in about 512, he drew upon the *Praeceptum,* not the *Regularis Informatio.*

There is no reason why Augustine should not be the author of the *Praeceptum* and there are good arguments for his authorship, since the psychology of the *Praeceptum* differs from that of later Western rules like the Rule of the Master and the Benedictine Rule. These stand in a tradition which ultimately looks back to the Egyptian desert, in which the monastery was a school and the abbot the teacher, a ''master and disciple'' relationship. Augustine, in contrast, characteristically starts from a bond of friendship between Christian souls, united by love of God and one's neighbor. Verheijen has drawn attention to the influence of Acts 4:32 on Augustine's thinking: ''Now the company of those who believed were of one heart and soul, and no one said that any of the things which he possessed was his own, but they had everything in common.'' This is the thought underlying the opening of the *Ordo Monasterii,* which is now prefaced to the *Praeceptum* in the *Regula recepta,* the official version of the rule used by the Augustinian order: ''Before all else, dearest brethren, let God be loved and then your neighbor, be-cause these are the chief commandments which have been given us.''

The authorship of the *Ordo Monasterii,* which passed out of use in the Middle Ages as being no longer liturgically and administratively appropriate, has been the subject of much speculation. Verheijen suggested Augustine's friend Alypius, but the document is too short to permit any stylistic comparisons. It must suffice to say that the *Ordo* clearly comes from Augustine's milieu and could conceivably have been composed by him. It could, hypothetically, have been used at Augustine's first monastic settlement at Thagaste, and later at Hippo. The *Praeceptum,* equally hypothetically, could have been composed when Augustine had to leave his monastery for the bishop's house at Hippo and sought to commend a pattern of monastic life to his brethren; but these can only be conjectures.

We know little of the history of the rule for six centuries after Augustine's death, apart from what can be deduced from the various surviving codices. Then, in the later 11th century, there occurred a sudden flowering of interest, no doubt due to the influence of the Gregorian reform movement, which sought to bring about a renewal of religious life in the Western Church by reforms, including the requirement of common living and renunciation of private property on the part of canons of cathedral and collegiate churches. To this end a number of communities adopted the Augustinian Rule. Reforming bishops founded new Augustinian houses. The Premonstratensians, founded by St. Norbert (*c.* 1080–1134), called after their parent monastery at Prémontré, near Laon, became a regular Augustinian order, and the rule was adopted by the Knights of St. John of Jerusalem. The Fourth Lateran Council approved the rule, and it was adopted by St. Dominic for his friars.

Bibliography: Editions. Of *Praeceptum,* L. VERHEIJEN, *Règle de Saint Augustin,* 2 v. (Paris 1967) 1:417–437. G. P. LAWLESS, *Augustine of Hippo and His Monastic Rule* (Oxford 1987) 80–103, with Eng. tr.; *Patrologia Latina,* ed. J. P. MIGNE, 217 v., indexes 4 v. (Paris 1878–90) 32:1387–84. Of *Ordo Monasterii,* VERHEIJEN, 1:148–52; LAWLESS, 74–79, with Eng. tr., *Patrologia Latina,* ed. J. P. MIGNE 217 v., indexes 4 v. (Paris 1878–90) 32:1449–52. Of *Obiurgatio,* VERHEIJEN, 1:49–53; LAWLESS, 104–109, with Eng. tr. Of *Regularis Informatio,* VERHEIJEN, 1:53–66. LAWLESS gives only a translation 110–118. Aug., *Ep.* 21 1. *Corpus scriptorum ecclesiasticorum latinorum* (Vienna 1866–) 57:359–71; *Patrologia Latina,* ed. J. P. MIGNE 33, 958–965. *Regula recepta. Constitutiones Ordinis Fratrum S. Augustini* (Rome 1968), tr. by R. P. RUSSELL, *The Rule of Our Holy Father St. Augustine* (Villanova, Penn. 1976). For the collected documents, VERHEIJEN, *La Règle de Saint Augustin,* 2 v. (Paris 1967); LAWLESS, *Augustine of Hippo and His Monastic Rule* (Oxford 1987). AGATHA MARY, *The Rule of St. Augustine: An Essay in Understanding* (Villanova, Penn. 1992). R. ARBESMANN, ''The Question-of-the Regula Sancti Auctustini,'' *Augustinian Studies* 1 (1970) 237–261. J. J. GAVIGAN, *De vita monastica, in Africa Septentrionali inde a temporibus S. Augustini usque ad invasiones Ara-*

bum (Turin 1962). C. LAMBOT, "Saint Augustin a-t-il rédigé la règle pour moines?" *Revue Bénédictine* 136n. 53 (1941) 41–58. P. MANDONNET, *St. Dominique,* 2 v. (Paris 1937). T. VAN BAVEL, *The Rule of Saint Augustine: Masculine and Feminine Versions,* tr. R. CANNING (London 1996). A. ZUMKELLER, *Augustine's Ideal of the Religious Life,* tr. E. COLLEDGE (New York 1986); *Augustine's Rule: A Commentary,* tr. M. J. O'CONNELL (Villanova, Penn. 1987).

[G. BONNER]

AUGUSTINE KAŽOTIĆ, BL.

Dominican bishop; b. Trogir, Dalmatia, *c.* 1260; d. Lucera, Apulia, Aug. 3, 1323. He entered the Order of Preachers at an early age and in 1286 was studying at the University of Paris. On returning to Dalmatia he founded several convents and undertook missions in Italy, Bosnia, and Hungary. BENEDICT XI consecrated him bishop of Zagreb, Croatia (1303). He restored discipline in his diocese and fostered learning, particularly in Biblical studies. Miladin, governor of Dalmatia, against whose tyranny he had protested, defied and persecuted him. In 1317 JOHN XXII transferred him to the See of Lucera in Apulia, where he died in the Dominican convent he had founded. He was venerated for his charity to the poor and for his gift of healing, and was accorded public honor soon after his death; in 1702 Clement XI confirmed his cult.

Feast: Aug. 3 (Dominicans).

Bibliography: J. QUÉTIF and J. ÉCHARD, *Scriptores Ordinis Praedicatorum,* 5v. (Paris 1719–23); continued by R. COULON (Paris 1909–); repr. 2v. in 4 (New York 1959) 1.2:553. A. BUTLER, *The Lives of the Saints* 3:255–256. A. WALZ, *Lexikon für Theologie und Kirche*² 1:1103.

[M. J. FINNEGAN]

AUGUSTINE NOVELLUS, BL.

Jurist and Augustinian prior general; b. Tarano, in Sabina, Italy, date unknown; d. near Siena, May 19, 1309. He studied law at the University of BOLOGNA and became chancellor to Manfred, King of Sicily. After the death of the king (1266) he entered the AUGUSTINIAN Order as a brother and took the name Augustine. According to the traditional account, he was ordained a priest after his identity as a famed jurist became known among his fellow religious. He was appointed papal confessor by NICHOLAS IV and served as papal legate in Siena under BONIFACE VIII. Together with Bl. Clement of Sant'Elpidio (d. 1291) he revised the early constitutions of his order and in 1298 was elected prior general. After resigning in 1300, he retired to the hermitage of San Leonardo near Siena. The designation "Novellus" was added in the 15th century, when his cult became widespread, in order to distinguish him from St. AUGUSTINE of Hippo. The cult was confirmed by CLEMENT XIII in 1759, and his relics are preserved in a church dedicated to him at Siena, where there is also an early 14th-century portrait.

Feast: May 19.

Bibliography: *Acta Sanctorum* May 4:614–626. *Analecta Augustiniana* 6 (1915–16) 120–133. A. CORRAO, *Sopra la patria del beato Agostino Novello* (3d ed. Palermo 1922). JORDAN OF QUEDLINBURG, *Liber vitasfratrum,* ed. R. ARBESMANN and W. HÜMPFNER (New York 1943), *passim.* M. NICOLOSI, "Il codice senese della vita di Matteo Novelli. Codice Senese (K.VII,36). Annotazioni codicologiche" *Analecta Augustiniana* 54 (1991) 303–319.

[A. J. ENNIS]

AUGUSTINE (TRIUMPHUS) OF ANCONA

Augustinian philosopher; b. Ancona, *c.* 1241; d. Naples, April 2, 1328. In 1297 he was made lector in his order. He read the *Sentences* for two years in Paris and became master of theology *c.* 1314. Assigned to Naples in 1321, he served also as counselor to King Robert. In 1326 Augustine published his celebrated treatise *Summa de ecclesiastica potestate,* reputed to be the earliest work of its kind on the Roman pontiff. He was called "the most encyclopedic and prolific theologian of the school of Giles" (M. Grabmann), though many of his works, including treatises on philosophy, Scripture, and Canon Law, remain unpublished. He undertook the earliest concordance of the writings of St. AUGUSTINE, the *Milleloquium veritatis,* which was completed by his pupil BARTHOLOMEW OF URBINO. Although medieval historians acknowledge his merits as an exegete and Aristotelian commentator, Augustine remains best known for his political doctrines on the nature and extent of papal authority. Carrying the theocratic principles of his predecessors, GILES OF ROME and JAMES OF VITERBO, to their extreme conclusions, Augustine contended that all power, spiritual and temporal, resides in the pope, and that through him alone (*mediante ipso*) other rulers, both religious and lay, derive their authority. Thus, for example, the grant of Constantine to Pope Silverius was in no sense a donation but rather the restoration of alienated property to its lawful possessor.

See Also: AUGUSTINIANISM.

Bibliography: Works. *Summa de potestate ecclesiastica* (Rome 1584); *Tractatus brevis de duplici potestate praelatarum et laicorum,* ed. N. SCHOLZ in *Die Publizistik zur Zeit Philipps des Schönen und Bonifaz VIII* (Stuttgart 1903) 486–501. Literature. B. MINISTERI, "De A. de A. vita et operibus," *Analecta Augustiniana* 7 (1952) 7–56, the only modern critical study on Augustine's life and works. M. J. WILKS, *The Problem of Sovereignty in the Latin Middle Ages: The Papal Monarchy with Augustinus Triumphus and the Publicists* (New York 1963). U. MARIANI, *Chiesa e Stato nei teologi Agostiniani del secolo XIV* (Rome 1957). A. MCGRADE, ''William of Ockham and Augustinus de Ancona on the Righteousness of Dissent,'' *Franciscan Studies* 54.

[R. P. RUSSELL]

AUGUSTINE OF CANTERBURY, ST.

Apostle of England, first archbishop of Canterbury; d. May 26, 604. Augustine (Austin) was prior at St. Andrew's on the Coelian Hill, Rome, when GREGORY I (the Great) sent him with 30 monks to evangelize the Anglo-Saxons. After difficulties in Gaul and his return to Rome, he was consecrated bishop and landed at Ebbsfleet in 597. There the king, ETHELBERT OF KENT, who was married to a Christian, allowed the monks to preach, giving them a house and an old church in Canterbury. Eventually Ethelbert and many of his people became Christian. In 601, reinforcements of personnel, books, relics, and sacred vessels arrived from Rome.

Augustine was given a PALLIUM and made a metropolitan, independent of the bishops in Gaul but without authority over them. Surviving letters from Gregory instructed him on principles and procedure: he was left free to adopt Gallican or other liturgical uses; he was to live a common life with his monks, although married clerks in minor orders also had a place in his household. He was not to destroy pagan temples, only the idols. Pagan rites, if innocent, could be taken over for the Christian feasts. Relying on Roman documents, Gregory decided that he should establish his see at London, with 12 suffragans, and another see at York, also with 12 suffragans. Instead, Augustine founded his see at Canterbury, the capital of Kent, the most cultured and the only Christian Anglo-Saxon kingdom. There he built the Cathedral of Christ Church, and just outside the city wall Ethelbert erected the abbey of SS. Peter and Paul, later called St. Augustine. Augustine established a bishopric at London, with MELLITUS as its bishop, having already set up Rochester as a kind of suburban see to Canterbury. Shortly before his death he consecrated Lawrence of Canterbury as his successor.

In his seven-year apostolate, Augustine failed to win any cooperation from the Christian Britons in the West Country because of their hatred for the Anglo-Saxon race and their attachment to provincial Celtic customs. Meeting with real but limited success in his lifetime, Augustine's mission bore fruit long after in the conversion of the rest of England, in the Synod of Whitby, and in the missionary work of Anglo-Saxons on the Continent. He was buried at SS. Peter and Paul, Canterbury.

Feast: May 27 (Roman Calendar), May 26 (England).

Bibliography: *Gregorii I Papae registrum epistolarum,* ed. P. EWALD and L. M. HARTMANN, *Monumenta Germaniae Historica: Epistolae* v.1, 2. BEDE, *Historia ecclesiastica,* ed. C. PLUMMER (Oxford 1896; reprint 1956) 1:23; 2:3. A. BROU, *St. Augustine and His Companions,* tr. from the French (London 1897). M. DEANESLY, *Augustine of Canterbury* (London 1964). F. A. GASQUET, *Mission of St. Augustine* (London 1924). M. A. GREEN, *St. Augustine of Canterbury* (London 1997). C. DONALDSON, *The Great English Pilgrimage: In the Footsteps of Saint Augustine* (Norwich 1995). F. M. STENTON, *Anglo-Saxon England* (Oxford History of England 2; Oxford 1943) 103–112. S. BRECHTER, *Die Quellen zur Angelsachsenmission Gregors des Grossen* (Münster 1941). P. MEYVAERT, ''Les 'Responsiones' de S. Gregoire le Grand a S. A. de Cantorbéry,'' *Revue d'histoire ecclésiastique* 54 (1959) 879–894.

[H. FARMER]

AUGUSTINIAN HERITAGE INSTITUTE

The Augustinian Heritage Institute, Inc., was founded in 1986 by John E. Rotelle, O.S.A. The purpose of the institute is to render into English translation the works of St. AUGUSTINE. Aside from his many books and treatises, about 300 of his letters and almost 500 of his homilies are also extant. To date the entire corpus of Augustine's works has never been rendered into English. The institute is dedicated to filling that gap with more than 40 volumes, 23 of which had been published by 2001. Each work has its own introduction plus notes and other scientific data. In 1999 the institute was formally incorporated. It is served by a board that oversees the work, as well as a translation advisory board that recommends translators for particular works. After the completion of the series of Augustine's works in English, the board of directors will outline a program for supplementary works, such as the many works attributed to Augustine, the writings of the medieval Augustinian school, and other works of the Augustinian tradition. The headquarters of the institute are in Villanova, Pennsylvania.

Bibliography: J. E. ROTELLE, ed. *The Works of St. Augustine: A Translation for the 21st Century* (Hyde Park, N.Y. 1990).

[J. ROTELLE]

AUGUSTINIAN NUNS AND SISTERS

In the lifetime of St. Augustine of Hippo, his monastic spirituality, especially as embodied in his Rule, was embraced by both male and female religious (*see* AUGUSTINIAN SPIRITUALITY). The Rule of St. Augustine (*see* AUGUSTINE, THE RULE OF) has also served in later times as the basis for the religious ideals of many women's orders and congregations, such as the Augustinian Canonesses and Dominican nuns and sisters. Only those nuns and sisters who are affiliated with the Augustinian Order (O.S.A.) are considered here.

Augustinian Nuns. After the Hermits of St. Augustine, asthey were then known, were organized into the present Augustinian Order in 1256 (*see* AUGUSTINIANS), certain convents of nuns, who already followed St. Augustine's Rule, wished to associate themselves with the Augustinian Order. The first convent was that of Oberndorf am Neckar, Germany, in 1264. Seven other convents in Germany followed suit. In Italy, the first convent to come under the jurisdiction of the order was that of St. Mary Magdalene in Orvieto by 1295. In some instances Augustinian friars founded convents of nuns, such as Bl. SIMON FIDATI OF CASCIA (d. 1348), who founded two convents in Florence. While the exact numbers remain problematic, by *c.* 1516 convents had been established in the area embraced by the German Provinces (20), France (6), Ireland (2), Italy (80), Portugal (1), and Spain (11). Where the Protestant Reformation prevailed, many were closed soon afterwards, but the number of convents increased elsewhere. By 1566 there were 125 convents in Italy, 24 in the Iberian peninsula (60 in the seventeenth century). During the colonial period in the New World, convents were established in Argentina, Boliva, Chile, Mexico and Peru.

Since each convent was independent, the formal relationship of the nuns to the male branch differed from time to time and convent to convent. In general, the nuns followed the style of life, discipline, and practice of the Augustinian Order. In some instances, the nuns adopted a modified version of the order's constitutions. The prior general was the superior of the nuns. The friars were expected to serve as confessors and celebrants of the liturgy for the nuns. As a result of the suppressions in the course of the 19th century, the convents of nuns associated with regulars were placed under the jurisdiction of the local bishops. This arrangement endures to the present, although in the case of a few convents, the prior general shares jurisdiction with the local bishop.

At the beginning of the third millennium, there are just over 1,000 cloistered nuns in 79 convents. In Italy, 27 convents form the Federation of the Blessed Virgin Mary of Good Counsel, which also embraces two convents in the Philippines and a new house in Romania. Of the two Spanish federations, one consists of 24 convents, including one in the United States at New Lenox, Illinois, and another in Panama, while the other federation has 21 convents, including one in Chile and two in Ecuador. In addition, seven convents in Boliva, Kenya, Malta, Mexi-

co, Peru, the Philippines, and Switzerland do not form part of any federation.

In their lives, the nuns, strive to practice the ideals of charity and community set forth in the teachings of St. Augustine within the context of the cloistered, contemplative style of life. Two canonized saints pertaining this branch of the Augustinian Order are St. CLARE OF MONTEFALCO and St. RITA OF CASCIA. Of those nuns accorded the title Blessed by the Church, the most recent, Maria Teresa Fasce (1881–1947), superior of the convent at Cascia, Italy, was beatified in 1997.

Augustinian Sisters. Augustinian Sisters of Apostolic Life are those congregations of religious women who have been aggregated to the Augustinian Order. This second type of affiliation with the order originated in 1399 when Pope Boniface IX granted the use of the habit and a share in the privileges of the order to groups of women, known as oblates or *mantellate*. In general, their relationship with the order was less formal and structured than that of the cloistered nuns. The prior general was not the superior of these groups.

With the evolution in religious life, various groups of sisters of active life were united to the order, especially in the 20th century. In 1683 the Sisters of St. Thomas of Villanova, founded by Angel Le Proust, O.S.A., were the first to be formally aggregated to the Augustinian Order by a decree of the prior general. At the present time over 80 congregations of women are aggregated to the order. The congregations have their headquarters in Belgium, England, France, Germany, Holland, Italy, Poland, Switzerland, the Congo, Indonesia, the Philippines, Benin, Chile, Mexico, Peru, Canada, and the United States.

The sisters accept the Rule of St. Augustine as the fundamental norm of their religious congregations and seek to integrate the spirituality of St. Augustine with their own proper charism. The presence of so many groups of sisters in the Augustinian Family testifies to the continuing vitality and adaptability of Augustine's Rule and spirituality to many forms of religious life.

Bibliography: ''Bibliographie historique de l'ordre de Saint Augustin,'' (for years 1945–75) Augustiniana 26 (1976), 39–340; (for 1970–75) ibid. 28 (1978), 448–516; (for 1975–80) ibid. 31 (1981), 5–159; (for 1980–84) ibid. 35 (1985), 5–192; (for 1985–89) ibid. 39 (1989), 189–392; (for 1989–93) ibid. 43 (1993), 171–407; (for 1993–1996) ibid. 47 (1997), 1–242. *Catalogus Ordinis Sancti Augustini: Status Ordinis die I Ianuarii* 2000 (Rome 2000). J. GAVIGAN, O.S.A. *The Augustinians from the French Revolution to Modern Times. Vol. 4 of History of the Order of St. Augustine* (Villanova 1989). D. GUTIERREZ, O.S.A. *The Augustinians in the Middle Ages 1256–1356.* Vol. 1: Part 1 of *History of the Order of St. Augustine* (Villanova 1984). *The Augustinians in the Middle Ages 1357–1517.* Vol. 1: Part 2 of *History of the Order of St. Augustine* (Villanova 1983). *The Augustinians from the Protestant Reformation to the Peace of Westphalia 1518–1648.* Vol. 2 of *His-*

tory of the Order of St. Augustine (Villanova 1979). B. RANO, O.S.A., "Agostiniane, Monache" in *Dizionario degli istituti di perfezione*, 1:155–90 (Rome 1973). "Agostiniane, Suore" in *Dizionario degli istituti di perfezione*, 1:190–92 (Rome 1973).

[K. A. GERSBACH]

AUGUSTINIAN RECOLLECTS

Origins and Early Development. The Order of the Augustinian Recollects grew out of the Order of St. Augustine. Two movements prompted the founding of the Recollects: one was the Council of Trent that called for a renewal of the religious spirit of the Augustinian Order; the second was the spiritual fervor found in the Spanish houses of the Order of St. Augustine at the end of the sixteenth century. The document of foundation was signed on Dec. 5, 1588 at a provincial chapter in Toledo: "In order not to put obstacles in the way of the Holy Spirit, having previously consulted our very Reverend Father General and having requested his consent, we determine that in our province there are to be designated or established three monasteries of men and the same number for women, in which a more austere form of life will be practiced, as will be defined by the Father Provincial and his Council after sufficient reflection."

Fray Luis de LEON developed this declaration into a longer text approved by the Province of Castilla on Sept. 20, 1589. Its 14 chapters deal with three ideas: spirit of prayer, fraternal equality, and asceticism. The Eucharist, the liturgy of the hours, and mental prayer were to enrich the daily life of the community. There was to be no room for exemptions or privileges, because all professed religious were equal by virtue of their vows. Asceticism, necessary for disciplining the passions and facilitating prayer, called for simple and rustic buildings, for small and austere rooms, and for fasts and frequent discipline.

This style of living began to be practiced on Oct. 19, 1589 in Talavera de la Reina, from which it was extended to El Portillo (1590), Nava del Rey (1591), Madrid (1596), and El Toboso (1600). In 1602 Rome formed those five convents into a Recollect Province of the Augustinian Order. In subsequent years this province was extended to other regions of Spain and to a foundation in Rome (1619). It then absorbed a similar movement that had begun in Colombia in 1604, and began its missionary history by sending fourteen missionaries to the Philippines. In 1621 the Holy See raised the province to a Congregation and entrusted its governance to a vicar general with ample autonomy from the general of the Order of St. Augustine.

Within a few years the Recollects became 1,500 religious, distributed among five provinces, 43 convents, and

20 missionary sites. Three provinces had all their convents in Spain. The other two provinces were overseas and had their houses in the Philippines, Guam, Colombia, and Panama. During the 18th century, few changes took place in the number of friars and convents, or in their location and activities.

Conventuals and Missionaries. During two centuries the Spanish provinces and, to a lesser degree, the Colombian province, in accord with their legislation, maintained a contemplative character. Their friars lived in convents dedicated to divine worship, study, and the apostolate. Divine worship had a eucharistic and Marian orientation. The entire community gathered daily for the conventual Mass. Individual priests celebrated private Mass each day, and the lay brothers received communion with a frequency that was unusual in the Church of the time (130 days each year). On the day of profession, they consecrated themselves to Mary and they promised perpetual service. Almost all of their churches were dedicated to the Virgin. All of the Recollect convents maintained public churches and almost all were obliged by foundational agreements to preach the Word of God, administer the sacraments, and take care of the sick of the region (area). Their contribution to popular missions was notable.

In the Philippines, the missionary life prevailed. Over three centuries, some one thousand religious evangelized the most remote islands of the archipelago (Mindanao, Palawan, Romblon, Mindoro, etc.). From the Philippines they went to Japan, where in 1632 four Recollects crowned their labors with martyrdom, along with more than 300 neophytes. One of them, Magdalena de Nagasaki, was canonized in 1989. From 1768 to 1908, about 70 religious worked in the Pacific islands.

The Crisis of the 19th Century. In 1835 the government of Spain confiscated 32 of the 33 Spanish monasteries and evicted their inhabitants. In 1861 Mosquera did the same in Colombia. The congregation's loss of 38 convents reduced their influence to the Philippine missions and to the one remaining convent of Monteaguado (Spain) that provided them with missionaries. This plundering of the congregation's monasteries modified the spiritual orientation of the group, forcing it to adopt a more apostolic life. For 70 years the Recollects were obliged to live in parishes, separated from one another.

In 1898 a new challenge put the congregation to the test. In just a few months, 34 religious were killed at the hands of the Filipino patriots, 80 were arrested, and 300 evacuated and left without resources. The survivors managed to overcome these difficulties and opened up new possibilities for the congregation. By mid-1899 about 100 religious were traveling through South America to explore new horizons, and new possibilities were opening in Spain. In 1904 the novitiate was reopened, and in 1908, after 79 years of interruption, the General Chapters of the congregation were resumed. In September of 1912, Pius X abrogated any ties still linking the Recollects to the original Order of St. Augustine.

Houses were established in the United States (1917), Argentina (1925), Puerto Rico and the Dominican Republic (1927), England (1932), and Mexico (1941). In response to the call of Pius XI, the order increased its missionary presence in the Philippines and Colombia and took responsibility for the new territories in China and Brazil, and later in Peru, Panama, Mexico, and Sierra Leone. In 1941 the Recollects entered into the field of education. In 2000 the order had 1,250 religious in 17 countries, dedicated to the missionary, parochial, and educational apostolates.

Bibliography: Á. MARTÍNEZ CUESTA, *Historia de los Agustinos Recoletos,* vol. 1, *Desde sus orígenes hasta el siglo XIX* (Madrid 1995); *La orden de agustinos recoletos: Evolución carismática* (Madrid 1988). J. GRUBEN, *History of the Province of St. Augustine of the Order of Augustinian Recollects* (West Orange, N.J. 1997).

[Á. MARTÍNEZ CUESTA]

AUGUSTINIAN SPIRITUALITY

The spiritual legacy associated with AUGUSTINE of Hippo can be considered from a twofold perspective: the actual thought and teaching of St. Augustine, and subsequent traditions of spirituality associated with and based upon the figure and thought of Augustine. The saint himself represents an approach to what will subsequently be called spirituality that is thematic rather than systematic. Subsequent traditions associated with Augustine will highlight, emphasize, and accordingly systematize aspects of his spirituality.

THE SPIRITUALITY OF AUGUSTINE OF HIPPO

There are a variety of specific characteristics associated with Augustine of Hippo which, when taken together, constitute his distinctive spiritual vision. They find expression in all his writings, but are particularly noteworthy in the *Confessions,* his preaching on John's Gospel and the Psalms, the *Trinity,* and his *Sermons.* The following are considered the most important.

Christological. Christ as the Way, Christ as the Homeland (*Via* and *Patria*)—this is one of many Christological titles used by Augustine both to affirm and to explore the central place and role of Jesus Christ in the Christian life. To affirm the centrality of Christ is likewise to affirm the centrality of the Trinity for Augustine's spirituality, since it is Christ who reveals the Father and promises the Spirit, it is the Father who sends the Son, it is the Spirit who inflames the hearts of the followers of the Son. Every dimension of Augustine's vision of the spiritual life is vitally linked to and grounded in his profound sense of the identity and work of the Son of God, expressed in key affirmations such as Christ-Physician (*medicus*), Teacher (*magister*), Word (*Verbum*), and the uniquely rich *Christus totus*—the whole Christ.

Grace-centered. From his earliest writings to his final work Augustine provocatively placed God's gratuitous initiative (GRACE) at the center of the divine-human relationship. This emphasis on grace is both profoundly Christological and deeply anthropological, since it reveals both God's gracious initiative in Christ and total human dependence upon this initiative. ''Without me you can do nothing'' is equally, for Augustine, an affirmation of God's absolute sovereignty in the process of salvation and a confirmation of the total incapacity of human nature without this sovereign initiative.

Inner-directed. Drawing upon the affirmation of Genesis that humans are created in God's image (*imago Dei*), Augustine continually calls the Christian to turn within to discover that divine presence, seal, and identity. The heart (*cor*) becomes for Augustine a key term and symbol for the profound and challenging depths every human being finds and faces within. However, ''Return to yourself'' is never for Augustine a selfish movement of escapism but a true opening to and discovery of authentic human identity.

Scriptural. The New and Old Testaments provide the vocabulary, ideas, and content of Augustine's spirituality. Sharing with all patristic authors a profound sense of the centrality of the Word of God for worship, prayer, and daily living, Augustine's spiritual writings are so filled with Scripture that it is often difficult to know when Augustine ends and Scripture begins. Key texts occur over and over again in Augustine's writings and provide his thought with coherence and continuity (e.g., Gn 1:27; Jb 7:1; Is 7:9 [LXX]; Jn 1:14; Rom 5:5; 7:24–25a; 11:33–36; 1 Cor 1:31; 3:6–7; 4:7; Gal 5:6; etc.). This profoundly scriptural spirituality finds its apex in the *Confessions,* where scripture text and Augustine's voice are blended together indistinguishably.

Communal. The community of Adam and Eve in the garden of Paradise is profoundly emblematic for Augustine of humanity's communal nature. ''You have made *us* for yourself, O Lord, and *our* heart is restless until it rests in you.'' Augustine's own human make-up was decidedly social, poignantly portrayed in the *Confessions* as he shares both grace and sin. Augustine took a communal key text from Acts 4:32, describing the early apostolic community in Jerusalem, as a guidepost for not only his monastic community but the church as a whole.

Love-motivated. Both enthralled and terrified with the scriptural affirmations that "God is love" (1 Jn 4:16) and Christ's own description of the Final Judgment in terms of love of the poor Christ (Mt 25), Augustine saw love as the central command of Jesus that summed up the whole Christian life. "Love and do what you will" was, for Augustine, an affirmation not only of the centrality of love but of its nature as guarantor of the Christian life.

Progressive. The "restless heart" that Augustine places within every true Christian marks his spirituality with a fundamental dynamism and vitality that is expressed in his frequent use of the word "pilgrimage" to describe the life of the Christian. Following Christ is always a matter of ongoing CONVERSION, taking up new challenges in response to God's call. Conversion, progress, ascent—Augustine's model for the Christian life demands an ongoing journey of transformation.

In the Augustinian monastic-religious tradition these characteristics find principal expression in the *Rule of St. Augustine.* Augustine's teaching on prayer, especially noteworthy in his *Letter 130* to Proba, embodies all of these characteristics. His preaching turns again and again to these themes.

AUGUSTINIAN SPIRITUALITY

Though a number of particular groups and movements have explicitly considered themselves Augustinian in character, the spirituality associated with the Order of St. Augustine (the Augustinian Order) will be highlighted here. Despite medieval attempts to prove direct descent from Augustine, it is clear that the Augustinian Order's links to the bishop of Hippo are best seen as a deliberate embrace of his spirituality and an explicit attempt to embody his monastic vision. These efforts begin to emerge most clearly in the 14th century, in the writings of HENRY OF FRIEMAR and even more particularly in the *Liber Vitasfratrum* of JORDAN OF SAXONY. Jordan's highlighting of the common life as what is most distinctive about Augustine's vision of religious life ensured that the *Rule of St. Augustine* would remain the charter document of the Augustinian Order's understanding of Augustine's spiritual vision. This understanding prompted a centuries-long tradition of Rule commentaries, with the 16th-century commentary of Bl. Alfonso de OROZCO emerging as a key guide down to the 20th century for the efforts of Augustinian communities to live the spirituality of Augustine. This commentary tradition has seen a particularly fruitful expansion in the years since the Second Vatican Council, as the Augustinian Order's embrace of the council's call to rediscover their charism placed a great deal of emphasis on the foundational character of the Rule for a vision of Augustine's spirituality.

The Augustinian Order has likewise sought since the 14th century to spread knowledge of and devotion to St. Augustine. The *Milleloquium S. Augustini* (Lyons 1555) of BARTHOLOMEW OF URBINO (d. 1350), accompanied by numerous medieval *Vitae Augustini* that highlighted the miracles attributed to devotion to Augustine, found a strong artistic complement in iconography. Botticelli, Gozzoli, Carpaccio, Mantegna, Nelli, and Piero della Francesca are just a few of the masters called upon to portray and present in painted form the spiritual ideals of the bishop of Hippo.

The Augustinian Order throughout the ages seemed well aware that the spirituality of Augustine flowed from a distinctive theological understanding of Christ and the Christian life and accordingly sought to give specific attention to an articulation of Augustine's theology. Beginning with GILES OF ROME (d. 1316), continuing with figures such as THOMAS OF STRASSBURG (d. 1357), GILES OF VITERBO (1532), Jerome SERIPANDO (d. 1563), HENRY NORIS (d. 1704), and Giovanni L. BERTI (d. 1766), the Augustinian Order saw emerge from its ranks leading theologians who both synthesized and defended the distinctive theological vision of Augustine which the order saw as the wellspring of its own spirituality. This continued in the twentieth century in the writings of recognized Augustinologists such as L. Verheijen, A. Trape, T. van Bavel, and A. Zumkeller.

Contemporary revival of Augustinian spirituality has laid great emphasis on Augustine's image of the restless heart and the importance of the first apostolic community in Jerusalem as a continuing model for true Christian community: one mind and one heart on the way to God.

[T. MARTIN]

AUGUSTINIANISM

The particular philosophical and theological doctrines identified with the Order of St. Augustine, as well as the entire intellectual tradition stemming from Augustine and continuing, in various forms, to the 20th century. This article outlines the history of Augustinianism, discussing its doctrinal origins with St. Augustine, its development in the Middle Ages, and its status in the modern and contemporary periods.

General Doctrines

For its founder, St. AUGUSTINE, Augustinianism represented an attempt to reach an ever fuller understanding of revealed truth through supernatural graces and gifts, aided by the principles of philosophical inquiry. The various doctrines presented in this section express the more characteristic features of Augustinianism.

The Primacy of Faith. The esteem of Augustine for the role of UNDERSTANDING (*intellectum valde ama—Epist.* 120.3.13; *Patrologia Latina* 33:458–459) was to exercise a decisive influence not only on the destiny of Augustinianism but also on the whole intellectual history of the West. The roles of faith and reason, as distinct but inseparable sources of learning, constitute a point of departure already clearly formulated in the earliest of Augustine's works (cf. *C. acad.* 3.20.43). The basis for faith is the supreme authority of Christ; for reason, the philosophy of PLATO and PLOTINUS, but only to the extent that it is not at variance with revealed truth. The emphasis on the primacy of faith and on the necessary function of reason permanently determined the Augustinian view of philosophy, which appears to exclude the possibility of a philosophy autonomous in its own right or completely independent of theology. Accordingly, Augustine anticipated by some five centuries the celebrated formula of Anselm of Canterbury, *credo ut intelligam.* Intimately connected with this relation between faith and reason is the entire Augustinian anthropology, which, neglecting a purely abstract or purely natural view of man, considers him in his full historical situation—a creature destined to share in the life of God, redeemed after his fall by Christ, who thereby becomes the central and unifying factor in any ''philosophy'' of history. This constant and compelling consciousness of God imparts to Augustinianism its preeminently theocentric character and leads Augustine to view God as the source of man's total life (*causa, subsistendi, ratio, cognoscendi, ordo vivendi—Civ.* 8.4).

The Soul. Again, because speculation is so strongly focused on God, knowledge of the soul takes on a unique importance for Augustine and his successors (*see* SOUL, HUMAN). In two of his earliest works, composed before his baptism in April 387, he had declared God and the soul the two principal objects of philosophic inquiry (*Ordine* 2.18.47; *Soliloq.* 1.15.27). But to know the soul is, in some measure, to know God, since no other creature approaches Him so closely in perfection (*nihil . . . Deo esse propinquus—Quant. anim.* 34.77). Here is the basis for the important doctrine of image, termed ''the cornerstone of Augustinian anthropology,'' which underlies and inspires the psychological doctrine of the TRINITY as well as the discovery of its manifold analogies in the soul. Such concentration on the soul also gives Augustinianism its character of ''interiority,'' which stems from Augustine's conviction that it is within the soul itself that man must search for truth and certitude (*in interiore homine habitat veritas—Vera relig.* 39.72). Deserving of special mention here is Augustine's refutation of universal doubt by the compelling and infallible fact of personal existence implied in acts of the thinking subject (*scio me cogitare—Soliloq.* 2.1.1; *si fallor, sum—Civ.* 11.26),

which anticipates the Cartesian ''cogito'' and leads further to the soul's direct knowledge of itself (*semetipsam per semetipsam novit—Trin.* 9.3.3), which was a controversial doctrine for the Augustinians of the 13th century.

Divine Illumination. The doctrine of divine ILLUMINATION is so central as to be almost identified with the very substance and spirit of Augustinianism. By reason of its spiritual nature, the soul enjoys a continuous and connatural union with the world of intelligible reality, which it is able to perceive in a kind of incorporeal light akin to its own nature (*in quadam luce sui generis incorporea—Trin.* 12.15.24). The soul, however, is not the source of its light but is a derived light (*lumen quod illuminatur*) participating in the light of God (*Deus intelligibilis lux*). It is the Truth itself, present within, that alone instructs man (*Mag.* 11.38), so as to exclude learning by any mere human agency (*nusquam igitur discere—ibid.* 12.40). From the presence of truth in the soul Augustine develops his most characteristic proof for the existence of God as ''the unchangeable Truth containing all those things that are unchangeably true'' (*Lib. arb.* 2.12.33). Truth is not so much an object of intellectual contemplation for man as it is a good conferring joy and happiness (*gaudium de veritate—Conf.* 10.23.33). This doctrine was to oppose the INTELLECTUALISM of the Aristotelian-Thomistic position in the 13th century. From the primacy of love Augustine distinguished between what must be loved (*fruenda*) and what should merely be used (*utenda*); he concluded that God alone, as man's true end, is to be loved for His own sake, whereas creatures are to be used only as means toward this good (cf. *Doctr. christ.* 1.3–5); hence, too, the Augustinian notion of virtue as the right ordering of love (*ordo amoris, Civ.* 15.22).

Seminal Reasons. Augustine's teaching on the SEMINAL REASONS (*rationes seminales*), sometimes regarded as a forerunner of modern evolutionary theory, is, essentially, an attempt to reconcile the simultaneity and uniqueness of God's creative act with the progressive appearance of new living things throughout the course of time. According to Augustine's notion of a virtual creation, newly emerging forms of life were already present from the moment of creation, not in their actual state but in a seminal, potential, and causal condition (*invisibiliter, potentialiter, causaliter—Gen. ad litt.* 5.23.45). Although it would be an exaggeration to deny Augustine a notion of efficient causality in physical nature, it is undeniable that in the Augustinian universe the role of secondary causes is reduced to a relatively minimal status.

Grace. In the realm of moral activity the Augustinian conception of God's sovereignty and man's dependence finds its most profound and perennial expression in the saint's teaching on GRACE. His doctrines on ORIGI-

NAL SIN and on the necessity and gratuity of grace, developed during his extended polemic with Pelagianism and SEMI-PELAGIANISM, have dominated the whole theology of grace (*see* PELAGIUS AND PELAGIANISM). In a letter to Vitalis of Carthage, *c.* 427, Augustine formulates in 12 propositions his entire anti-Pelagian teaching on grace and FREE WILL, assuring Vitalis that these doctrines "belong to the right and Catholic rule of faith" (*Epist.* 217.5.16–17). However, Augustine's treatment of certain aspects of these doctrines and his views on predestination seem to have influenced later Augustinians to exalt divine action and minimize the role of created causality.

Origins and Transmission to 13th Century

Although Augustine founded no school or system, properly speaking, even before his death the influence of his thought had won him a position of eminence and authority that remained unique and unchallenged for more than 800 years. In tracing the course of Augustinianism to the 13th century, a review is here made of writers, or compilers, whose familiarity with the Augustinian corpus made them influential vehicles of his thought, and this not only in theology but also in the apostolate of preaching and in the foundation and development of the first Christian schools in the West. Next, mention must be made of several important controversies in which recourse to St. Augustine served to transmit and formalize his teaching.

Compilers. Paul OROSIUS was a friend of Augustine and author of the *Liber apologeticus contra Pelagium de arbitrii libertate,* written in defense of his own orthodoxy, in which he presented the saint's teaching on the necessity of grace for every salutary and meritorious act. He also composed, at Augustine's suggestion, a compendium of universal history in seven books, *Historiarum adversus paganos,* which resumed a central thesis of Augustine's *City of God,* viz, that temporal calamities had afflicted the world long before the advent of Christianity.

Prosper of Aquitaine defended Augustine against attacks by John CASSIAN and the Semi-Pelagians and composed the *Book of 392 Sentences,* excerpted from works of Augustine. Prosper is important as a faithful exponent of Augustine's teaching. By way of exception, he mitigated Augustine's view on the predestination of reprobates by substituting the notion of a condemnation subsequent to God's foreknowledge of their sins (*post praevisa demerita*).

CAESARIUS OF ARLES (470–542) played a dominant role in the condemnation of Semi-Pelagianism by the Council of Orange (529) and in the vindication of Augustine's essential teaching on original sin and on the necessity and absolute gratuity of grace. Besides his treatise *De gratia,* he composed a rule for monastic foundations that follows closely Augustine's ideas and even his expressions.

FULGENTIUS OF RUSPE was known in the Middle Ages as *Augustinus breviatus* because of his brief and concise presentations of Augustine's doctrine. His Manual, modeled after Augustine's *Enchiridion,* contains an excellent summary of the principal beliefs of faith. He has been called "Augustine of the strict observance" (F. Cayré) because of his rigid interpretations of Augustine's teaching on predestination. He composed three works against Semi-Pelagianism, including one against FAUSTUS OF RIEZ. In imitation of Augustine's "abecedary" poem against the Donatists (*Psalmus contra partem Donati*), Fulgentius wrote a *Psalmus abecedarius* against the Arians.

The unfinished *Complexio in psalmos* of CASSIODORUS is patterned after Augustine's *Ennarationes in psalmos.* Cassiodorus is best known for his celebrated *Institutiones,* a detailed program of studies for Christian schools, inspired in large part by Augustine's *De doctrina christiana* and later developed by ALCUIN and RABANUS MAURUS.

St. ISIDORE OF SEVILLE wrote *Tres libri sententiarum,* the forerunner of similar works in the 12th century, drawn for the most part from Augustine and Gregory the Great. He reproduced, in substance, the prevailing Augustinian theology of the period.

St. ANSELM OF CANTERBURY was one of the most authentic and influential representatives of Augustinianism in the early Middle Ages. He defended such basic Augustinian tenets as ontological truth, divine exemplarism, and divine illumination and preferred the Platonic-Augustinian argument for God's existence from the diverse levels of perfection in nature. In his effort to reconcile divine foreknowledge, predestination, and grace with free will, he emphasized the absolute mastery and sovereignty of God.

HUGH OF SAINT-VICTOR was a representative of the school of Saint-Victor, "the school perhaps most directly and intimately inspired by St. Augustine's thought" (Marrou). In keeping with Augustine's principle of interiority, outlined in the *Soliloquies,* Hugh stressed the necessity of inner experience, not only as the ground of certitude for personal existence but also as valid evidence for the spiritual nature of the soul. He composed an important commentary on the Rule of St. Augustine.

PETER LOMBARD, also of the school of Saint-Victor, wrote four books of the *Sentences,* drawn mainly from the teachings of Augustine, which reproduced copious passages from his works in a systematized presentation. Commentaries on the *Sentences* continued to appear until the end of the 16th century.

Controversies. The controversies that recurred intermittently within the Church from the 10th to the 12th centuries dealt with the validity of simoniacal ordinations and the related problem of the lawfulness of reordaining, and with the politicotheological doctrines underlying the conflicts between the Church and civil authority. Regarding ordinations, the anti-Donatist writings of Augustine provided the principal source of arguments for defenders of the orthodox position. The validity of the Sacraments, for Augustine, did not depend on the faith of the minister (vs. CYPRIAN) or on his moral dispositions (vs. DONATISM). Augustine's views gradually prevailed and, with their acceptance by the theologians of the 13th century, secured a permanent place in sacramental theology. Similarly, from various interpretations of such notions as peace, justice, and kingdom, drawn from Augustine's *City of God,* political theories were formulated for the new Christian society and for resolving the conflicts between papal and imperial claims. It remained, however, for theologians of the Augustinian school, such as Giles of Rome and Augustine of Ancona, to expound a politicotheological theory in support of a theocratic view of papal authority.

Medieval and Scholastic Augustinianism

Although the intellectual influence of Augustine dominated the West until the 13th century, it must be acknowledged, with F. van Steenberghen that "the synthesis achieved by the Bishop of Hippo was wholly theological in character." On the other hand, this theological synthesis had assimilated much of the prevailing NEOPLATONISM of his age and, quite possibly, in an already Christianized form. Because many 13th-century theologians viewed with alarm an ARISTOTELIANISM that was clearly incompatible with a number of revealed truths, a new Augustinian synthesis began to emerge, containing, besides its theological component, philosophical notions taken from St. Augustine or, at least, reputed to be Augustinian in origin. This resulting doctrinal amalgam, championed mainly within the Franciscan Order, is what has come to be known as medieval or scholastic Augustinianism.

Characteristic Theses. The following summary embodies the more characteristic theses of this intellectual movement: (1) No strict formal distinction between rational and revealed truths, with a denial, at least implicit, of an autonomous philosophy completely independent of theology. (2) A primacy of the will and of the affective powers over the intellectual. (3) A real identity between the essence of the soul and its powers. (4) The soul as a complete substance, composed of spiritual matter and form and therefore individuated by its own principles without reference to the body. (5) Necessity of divine illumination, together with the complementary notion of EXEMPLARISM, which makes the divine ideas the guarantee of certitude for the mind. (6) Direct and immediate knowledge of the soul's nature by the soul itself. (7) A universal HYLOMORPHISM, embracing all created reality. (8) The doctrine of SEMINAL REASONS. (9) A pluralism allowing for several substantial forms in the concrete structure of every created composite (*see* FORMS, UNICITY AND PLURALITY OF). (10) The impossibility of creation *ab aeterno.*

Opinions concerning the authenticity of this doctrinal corpus attributed to St. Augustine range from the view that all these theses have a foundation in Augustine (Mariani) to the opposite position, which denies their Augustinian authenticity *in toto* (Boyer). Accordingly, some historians have rejected the term medieval Augustinianism, preferring instead to describe the movement as early scholasticism, pre-Thomistic school (De Wulf), or eclectic Aristotelianism (Van Steenberghen).

Dominican and Franciscan Proponents. Opposition on the part of medieval Augustinians to Aristotelianism, culminating in the ecclesiastical condemnation of 1277, came from Dominican as well as Franciscan theologians. The Dominicans included Peter of Tarentaise (later INNOCENT V), who denied the possibility of creation *ab aeterno* and defended the doctrine of seminal reasons, and RICHARD FISHACRE, who subscribed to such notions as seminal reasons, illumination, and universal hylomorphism. Since the Franciscans were far more numerous, it is convenient to identify them according to the following doctrinal schema:

1. Primacy of will: JOHN PECKHAM, ROGER MARSTON, RICHARD OF MIDDLETON, and WILLIAM OF WARE

2. Identity of soul with its powers: ALEXANDER OF HALES, JOHN OF LA ROCHELLE, John Peckham, and William of Ware

3. Illumination: Alexander of Hales, John of La Rochelle, BONAVENTURE, THOMAS OF YORK, MATTHEW OF AQUASPARTA, John Peckham, and Roger Marston

4. Universal hylomorphism: Alexander of Hales, Bonaventure, Thomas of York, John Peckham, WILLIAM DE LA MARE, Roger Marston, and Richard of Middleton (except for four elements)

5. Seminal reasons: Bonaventure, Thomas of York, Matthew of Aquasparta, and Roger Marston

6. Pluralism (substantial): Thomas of York, William de la Mare, and Roger Marston

7. Impossibility of eternal creation: Bonaventure, Thomas of York, Matthew of Aquasparta, John Peckham, William de la Mare, Roger Marston, and Richard of Middleton

The condemnation of 1277, which included several theses of Thomas Aquinas, was followed by a gradual adaptation and fusion of Augustinianism with the main body of SCHOLASTICISM, both Thomistic and non-Thomistic. Such a doctrinal assimilation was possible because of the eclectic character of these schools and the influence of Aristotelian notions present within the Augustinian synthesis itself.

Within the Augustinian Order. The origin of the Augustinian school is commonly identified with the decree of the general chapter of 1287, which made the works of Giles of Rome, present and future (*scripta et scribenda*), mandatory upon all members of his order (*see* AUGUSTINIANS). Liberal interpretations of the decree were promoted by Giles himself, founder of the school, for whom "our intellect has been made subject, not to the service of man, but to Christ" (*De gradibus formarum* 2.6). The spirit of independence and adaptation within the school is evident in its relation to Augustinianism and is exemplified by its founder, himself an immediate disciple of Thomas Aquinas.

Foundations and Development. GILES OF ROME followed, in general, the basic metaphysical positions of Aquinas, although he occasionally blended them with Augustinian elements. Thus, while accepting the peripatetic notion of matter and form as a "more complete" explanation for the origin of new substances, he also insisted that the doctrine of seminal reasons is complementary to the hylomorphic thesis rather than opposed to it. The seminal reasons are described as "certain capacities implanted in nature which produce things like themselves" (*In 2 sent.* 18.2). At first a defender of the plurality of substantial forms, he gradually accepted the Thomistic view of the unicity of the substantial form, even going so far as to brand his former position as contrary to Catholic teaching. In political philosophy he passed from the Aristotelian-Thomistic view of society and civil authority to a doctrine of papal theocracy, based on an interpretation of notions drawn from Augustine's *City of God.* He retained the Augustinian teaching on the primacy of the will against the intellectualism of St. Thomas, arguing that the "good" is more excellent than the "true" (*see* VOLUNTARISM).

JAMES OF VITERBO also accepted the voluntarist teaching because, for him, the notion of the "good" derives immediately from the "one" and, being prior to the "true," is thereby superior to it. He assigned to seminal reasons an intermediate place between primary matter—which is pure POTENCY, excluding forms, even in potency—and substantial form itself. He equated seminal reasons with the forms present in potency.

Augustine of Ancona indirectly influenced the wider acceptance of Augustine's teachings within the order by his *Milleloquium S. Augustini,* the first concordance of the saint's works, which was completed by his pupil Bartholomew of Urbino.

The politicotheological views of Augustine of Ancona are reflected in his famous treatise on papal authority, *Summa de potestate ecclesiastica.* He went beyond Giles in formulating a strict theocratic conception of the papacy. Alexander of St. Elpidio (d. 1326) also wrote political treatises in defense of papal authority, notably his *De potestate ecclesiastica ad Joannem XXII.* BARTHOLOMEW OF URBINO defended political teachings of the Augustinian school against MARSILIUS OF PADUA and WILLIAM OF OCKHAM.

THOMAS OF STRASSBURG upheld the primacy of the will, adducing, in addition to St. Augustine, the authority of Anselm and Bernard. Alphonsus Vargas maintained a voluntarist position and used the Augustinian argument for God's existence from diverse grades of perfections manifested in the world.

GREGORY OF RIMINI, despite nominalist tendencies in philosophy, remained faithful to the main body of the theological doctrine of his school. Because of his success in reproducing the theology of Augustine in the language of his own time, he has been called "the true author of Augustinianism in the 14th century."

Council of Trent. The order was represented among the fathers of the Council of TRENT by four bishops and two generals, assisted by some 50 theologians. Besides Girolamo SERIPANDO, who was present successively as prior general, cardinal president, and papal legate, the fathers included Christopher of Padua (1500–69), prior general, and Bps. John Barba of Teramo (d. 1564), Gaspar of Coimbra (1512–84), Juan Suárez of Portugal (d. 1572), and Juan de Muñatones of Segarbe (d. 1571). Seripando was unquestionably the principal spokesman of the Augustinians at Trent; according to H. Jedin, his name is "inseparable from the story of the Decree on original sin and justification."

To understand properly Seripando's teaching on original sin and justification, it is necessary to examine his view on CONCUPISCENCE, which he describes as the sum total of forces of the lower appetite opposed to the law of God; consequently, something displeasing in His sight and therefore somehow sinful (*aliquam pecati rationem*). The impact of this view of concupiscence upon the notion of justification is clear. First, Baptism of itself is insufficient for justification and must be joined with faith in the death and Resurrection of Christ. But concupiscence remains in the baptized and continues somehow to be sinful, not merely as the penal consequence of original sin but also as a dynamic source of personal sins and a positive obstacle to the perfect observation of God's law. Accordingly, the Augustinians tried unsuccessfully to have removed from the decree on justification statements that Baptism removes "whatever has the true and proper character of sin," that in the baptized the "old man is put off," and that "God finds nothing hateful in the reborn."

The same view of concupiscence underlies Seripando's doctrine of "double justice," a critical thesis within his description of the total process of JUSTIFICATION (*see* JUSTICE, DOUBLE). In relating double justice to the MYSTICAL BODY OF CHRIST, Seripando was convinced that he was following faithfully the teaching of Augustine himself. And although the Council did not accept his views, his influence was positive as well as negative, since his theory "furnished the occasion for reexamining the fundamental problems of the dogma with unprecedented care" (Jedin, 391).

Modern and Contemporary Augustinianism

This section discusses the revival within the Augustinian school during the 17th and 18th centuries occasioned by controversies growing out of the Protestant and Jansenist theologies, including the theology of grace and its most outstanding representatives of this period, and the later influence of Augustinianism in the 20th century.

17th and 18th Centuries. This period is characterized by (1) a gradual lessening of Thomistic influence; (2) the appearance of numerous tracts composed "ad mentem Aegidii"; and (3) the adaptation and interpretations of St. Augustine's teaching on grace in a manner already delineated by GREGORY OF RIMINI.

Lesser Figures. Before an outlining of the theology of grace of the so-called Augustinians, viz, Noris, Bellelli, and Berti, mention should be made of the following representatives of the period.

Federico Gavardi (1640–1715), teacher of Henry Noris, was the principal influence in the revival of the Augustinian school. He wrote a voluminous tract, *Theologia exantiquata juxta B. Augustini doctrinam ab Aegidio Columna expositam.* A compendium of this work, *Hecatombe theologica,* was written by Anselm Hormannseder (d. 1740). Nicholas Straforelli composed in 1679 a compendium, *Theoremata theologica Aegidianae scholae conformia.* Agostina Arpe (d. 1704) wrote a manual, *Summa totus Aegidii Columnae . . .ex doctrina eiusdem collecta.* Benignus Sichrowski (d. 1737) was a disciple of Gavardi and author of the manual *Theologia scholastica Aegidio-Augustiniana.* Pedro Manso (d. 1736) wrote philosophical and theological works marked by a return to the teaching of Giles of

Rome and Gregory of Rimini. A staunch defender of Noris, he wrote tracts against Jansenist interpretations of St. Augustine, including a masterful treatise, *Augustinus sui interpres.*

Theology of Grace. Of more significance than the foregoing are those Augustinians of the period who gave distinctive interpretations of St. Augustine's doctrines on grace. Since their teachings evidence a basic doctrinal continuity with the earlier Augustinian school, it is inaccurate to represent them as having founded a "new" school. Their teachings, in fact, occupy an important place in the history of Augustinianism.

The writings of Henry NORIS aim at refuting the Protestant and Jansenistic interpretations of Augustine by an authentic presentation of his teaching accommodated to the doctrinal demands of the period. They include *Historia Pelagiana, Dissertati de Synodo V Oecumenica,* and *Vindiciae Augustinianae.* Later, Fulgentius Bellelli (1675–1742), a general of the order, wrote two important polemical works against BAIUS and JANSEN, dealing with the states of man before and after the FALL respectively: *Mens Augustini de statu naturae rationalis ante peccatum . . .* and *Mens Augustini de modo reparationis humanae naturae Post lapsum.* Finally, Lorenzo BERTI composed a theological compendium in six volumes, *De theologicis disciplinis,* described by M. Grabmann as "the best manual of the school."

The more characteristic doctrines of these theologians may be reduced to the following: First, the entire economy of grace rests on a concrete and historical conception of man before and after the Fall rather than on any purely metaphysical or abstract consideration of man's nature. In fact, the denial of a state of pure nature is a capital and decisive doctrine in this theology of grace. Having distinguished between God's absolute and ordered power, they maintain that while such a state of pure nature is possible according to God's absolute power, it is impossible by reason of His ordered power, i.e., viewed in the light of His goodness or wisdom, or from a certain fittingness on His part (*ex decentia Creatoris*). Consequently, the gifts of immortality, knowledge, and even sanctifying grace itself were conferred on Adam not as strictly owing to his nature, but as called for by God's goodness (*ex decentia bonitatis suae*). Hence, man's fallen state is envisaged as the loss of all those qualities given him *ex decentia Creatoris,* leaving him, as Noris put it, "despoiled of the gratuitous gifts and impaired in his natural endowments" (*expoliatus gratuitis et laesus insuper in naturalibus*). The latter privation accounts for concupiscence, which, for these theologians, is meaningless apart from original sin. Again, the distinction between the "innocent" and "fallen" states explains the two kinds of grace conferred respectively, namely, "indifferent grace" (*gratia versatilis*) and "efficacious grace" (*gratia efficax*). In the state of innocence, man's will was able to determine itself either for good or evil, whereas, since the Fall, it lacks sufficient power to do the good and must be determined by efficacious grace. Similarly, before the Fall, predestination to glory (and reprobation) was subsequent to God's foreknowledge of man's merits (*post praevisa merita*). To explain the nature of efficacious grace, Augustinians adduced the notion of a *delectatio victrix,* a doctrine developed by St. Augustine that had been interpreted by Jansenists to support their theology of grace. For Noris and his followers, the role of this *delectatio* is described as follows: the human will is beset by two opposing forces, or attractions, grace (charity) and cupidity. Since, in his fallen state, man's will follows the stronger attraction, it is only when grace is the more powerful that it efficaciously produces its effect. Yet as Berti insists, the will responds to this attraction not from necessity, but with complete freedom (*liberima voluntate*). Otherwise, grace remains inefficacious and, as Augustine had pointed out, leaves the will weak, *parva,* and feeble, *invalida* (*Grat. et lib. arb.* 17). Again, though admitting the salvific will of God, Augustinians claimed that sufficient grace is not bestowed on all, as evidenced, e.g., in infants who die without Baptism and pagans unenlightened by the Christian revelation.

A final feature of this theology of grace is its somewhat rigorous teaching on the role of charity in human acts. Since the precept to love God obliges at all times (*semper et pro semper*), these theologians maintain that man's every act must be directed to God, either actually or, at least, by a virtual intention. Further, man is bound to love God above all things not only *appretiative,* i.e., in preference to everything else, but also *intensive,* with a maximum intensity of love.

Contemporary Influence. Although Augustine founded no school, properly speaking, he remains in the 20th century a source and inspiration for many and diversified currents of thought. In general, these represent reactions to earlier mechanistic and materialistic systems, as well as to schools of rationalism and idealism. Contemporary thinkers whose orientation reveals certain affinities to, or dependence on, the doctrines and spirit of Augustine include Bergson, Scheler, Lavelle, Sciacca, Carlini, Kierkegaard, and Jaspers.

Bergson. The insistence of Henri BERGSON on the primacy of a concrete apprehension of reality, his preference for intuitive cognition and the method of "interiority," and his theory of intuition of duration reveal striking analogies with corresponding doctrines in Augustine. However, in view of Bergson's disavowal of any conscious Augustinian influence, such similarities can, at best, be ascribed to a common source, viz, Plotinianism, with which Bergson was well acquainted.

Scheler. No philosopher of the 20th century professed so great a dependence on Augustine as Max SCHELER, who regarded Augustine as the true founder and sole representative of Christian philosophy. Augustine alone produced, though only tentatively, a philosophy directly inspired by the Christian "living-experience" (*Erlebnis*). In Scheler's view, other thinkers, e.g., Aquinas, merely gave a Christian coloring to preexisting forms of Greek philosophy. Scheler undertook to correct Augustine's imperfect realization of this ideal by the complete removal of all Neoplatonic vestiges, with the help of later Augustinians such as N. MALEBRANCHE, B. PASCAL, J. H. NEWMAN, and A. GRATRY. The primacy of love, prior even to the will, is the focal point in Scheler's attempt to reconstruct Augustine's thought, replacing Neoplatonism with modern PHENOMENOLOGY and its *Wesenerfarung.* However, Scheler's highly personal interpretations of Augustine, as well as his later tendency toward pantheism, raised serious doubts concerning the validity of his professed Augustinianism.

Lavelle. The spiritualistic philosophy of Louis LAVELLE reflects certain characteristic positions of Augustine, although the influence is mainly indirect, stemming from the writings of Malebranche. The influence of Augustine is discernible in Lavelle's point of departure, his basic scope of philosophy, and his analysis of time. His notions of *présence total* and *expérience métaphysique fondamentale,* as primordial intuitions, recall the twofold object of speculation, God and the soul, outlined in Augustine's early dialogue *On Order* and the *Soliloquies.* In Augustinian fashion, Lavelle attempts to elaborate his whole philosophy by the "dialectic of PARTICIPATION"; but whereas Augustine is always careful to safeguard the divine TRANSCENDENCE, Lavelle's language, if not his thought, lends itself possibly to pantheistic interpretations.

Sciacca. M. F. Sciacca is an exponent of the Italian "philosophy of the spirit." For him, Augustine's doctrine of divine illumination is the central problem of metaphysics, revealing the essential dependence of man's spiritual nature on God, whose transcendent and necessary existence is the absolute source of certitude. Consequently, the certitude of personal existence follows from the intuition of truth ultimately identified with God in a manner reminiscent of Augustine's dictum: "I could more easily doubt my own existence than that Truth exists" (*Conf.* 7.10.6).

Carlini. Armando Carlini, also of the Italian spiritualist school, evidences even more of Augustine's influence. For Carlini, the central and crucial problem for philosophy is the nature and destiny of the human PERSON; any solution must follow Augustine's method of introspection and interiority. But since philosophy can do no more than discover and formulate this problem, man must turn to faith, specifically the Catholic faith, which alone can satisfy the demands of reason.

Kierkegaard. Since existentialist philosophers recognize the influence of S. A. KIERKEGAARD in the development of their movement, it is important to consider Augustine's influence on him. He possessed the complete works of Augustine and regarded him as the one writer who used the "dialectic of existence" to solve the problem of human existence by recourse to faith rather than to reason. The conflict between the abstract religion of reason and that of faith and the eventual triumph of the latter have, according to Kierkegaard, been dramatically portrayed in the *Confessions,* in the case of Augustine himself, and in *The City of God,* with respect to the human race as a whole.

Jaspers. While existentialists such as M. HEIDEGGER, G. MARCEL, and J. P. SARTRE show a certain affinity with Augustinianism by their concentration on the problem of human existence, only K. JASPERS reveals any real dependence on Augustine (*see* EXISTENTIALISM). His insistence, for example, on the necessity of faith to discover reality itself, including one's personal existence and God, since reason cannot reach beyond phenomena, derives from his understanding of Augustine's injunction *credo ut intelligam.* And though he calls Augustine the founder of true philosophy, Jaspers contends that this philosophy, being specifically Christian and tentative, must be transformed and perfected by an inner and "fundamental revelation" to achieve a philosophy of absolute validity and value.

Bibliography: Doctrines and origins. E. PORTALIÉ *Dictionnaire de théologie catholique,* (Paris 1903–50) 1:2501–61. A. VACANT et al, ed. *Dictionnaire de théologie catholique* (Paris 1903–50), tables générales 1:314–324. É. H. GILSON, *The Christian Philosophy of St. Augustine,* tr. L. E. M. LYNCH (New York 1960); *Spirit of Medieval Philosophy* (New York 1950). É. H. GILSON, *History of Christian Philosophy in the Middle Ages* (New York 1955). H. I. MARROU, *St. Augustine and His Influence through the Ages,* tr. P. HEPBURNE-SCOTT (New York 1958). E. PORTALIÉ, *A Guide to the Thought of Saint Augustine* (Chicago 1960). F. CAYRÉ, "The Great Augustinism," *Theology Digest* 2 (1954) 169–173; *Patrologie et histoire de théologie,* v.3 (2d ed. Paris 1950). M. GRABMANN, *Die Geschichte der scholastischen Methode,* 2 v. (Freiburg 1909–11). G. A. LEFF, *Medieval Thought: St. Augustine to Ockham* (Chicago 1960). **Medieval and Scholastic.** F. EHRLE, "Der Augustinimus und der Aristotelismus in der Scholastik gegen Ende des Jhs.," *Archiv für Literatur- und Kirchengeschichte des Mittelalters,* ed. H. DENIFLE and F. EHRLE [(Berlin) Freiburg 1885–1900] 5:605–635. "L'Agostinismo e L'Aristotelismo nella scolastica del sec. XIII," *Xenia Thomistica* 3 (1925) 517–588. A. FOREST et al., *Le Mouvement doctrinal du XIe au XIVe sièle* [*Histoire de l'église depuis les origines jusqu'à nos jours* (Paris 1951) 13] 179–305. L. DE SIMONE, "S. Agostino e l'agostinianismo medievale," *Sapientia* 8 (1955) 5–17. F. J. THONNARD, "Augustinisme et Aristotélisme au XIIIe siècle," *L'Année théologique augustinienne* 5 (1944) 442–466. F. VAN STEENBERGHEN, *The Philosophical Movement in the 13th Century* (Edinburgh 1955). K. WERNER, *Der Augustinimus des späteren Mittelalters* (Vienna 1833). D. A. PERINI, *Bibliographia Augustiniana: Scriptores Itali,* 4 v. (Florence 1929–38). L. FERNENDEZ, *Trajectoria Historica de la Escuela Agustiniana* (Bogotá 1963). G. LEFF, *Gregory of Rimini* (New York 1961). J. L. SHANNON, *Good Works and Predestination according to Thomas of Strassburg* (Westminster, Md. 1940). R. KUITERS, "The Development of the Theological School of Aegidius Romanus. . . ," *Augustiniana* 4 (1954) 157–177. D. TRAPP, "Augustinian Theology of the 14th Century," *ibid.* 6 (1956) 146–274. A. ZUMKELLER, "Die Augustinerschule des Mittelalters," *Analecta Augustiniana* 27 (1964) 167–262. M. WILKS, *The Problem of Sovereignty in the Later Middle Ages: The Papal Monarchy with Augustinus Triumphus and the Publicists* (Cambridge, Mass. 1963). H. JEDIN, *Papal Legate at the Council of Trent: Cardinal Seripando,* tr. F. C. ECKHOFF (St. Louis 1947). E. STAKEMEIER, *Der Kampf um Augustinus: Augustinus und die Augustiner auf dem Tridentinum* (Paderborn 1937). D. GUTTIÉRREZ, "Los Agostinos en el Concilio de Trento," *La Ciudad de Dios* 158 (1946) 385–491. Modern and contemporary. F. ROJO, "Ensaya bibliográfica de Noris, Bellelli y Berti," *Analecta Augustiniana* 26 (1963) 294–363. A. TRAPÈ, "De gratuitate ordinis supernaturalis apud theologos Augustinienses," *ibid.* 21 (1950) 217–265. L. RENWART, *Augustiniens du XVIIIe siècle et "Nature Pure"* (Paris 1948). H. DE LUBAC, *Surnaturel: Études historiques* (Paris 1946). B. HWANG, "The Nature and Destiny of Man according to F. Bellelli," *Augustiniana* 3 (1953) 224–259. *S. Agostino e le grandi correnti della filosofia contemporanea* (Atti del Congresso Ital. di Filos. agostiniana; Rome 1954). F. THONNARD, "Saint Augustin et les grands courants de la philosophie contemporaine," *Revue des Études Augustiniennes* 1.1 (1955) 69–80. J. GUITTON, *The Modernity of St. Augustine,* tr. A. V. LITTLEDALE (Baltimore 1959). *Augustinus Magister,* 3 v. (Études Augustiniennes; Paris 1955), *passim.*

[R. P. RUSSELL]

AUGUSTINIANISM, THEOLOGICAL SCHOOL OF

The school arose toward the end of the thirteenth century and includes theologians of the Order of Hermits of St. Augustine (*see* AUGUSTINIANS), beginning with GILES OF ROME (Aegidius Romanus, *c.* 1243–1316), its foremost representative. At the general chapter of Florence in 1287, Giles's teachings were made mandatory upon all the members of the order. That the decree came to be liberally interpreted, despite its rigid formulation, is largely due to Giles's own conviction that freedom should be enjoyed wherever there is no danger to faith, since man's intellect is subject only to Christ (cf. *De gradibus formarum* 2.6).

For convenience, the history of the school may be divided into two periods: the early period, from Giles to the end of the sixteenth century; and the later period, comprising the seventeenth and eighteenth centuries. Members of the school in the later period are described in theological literature as the *Augustinenses.* That the theologians of the later period do not constitute a new or distinct school will be seen from an examination of their most characteristic teachings, which reflect a clear dependence upon those of their predecessors.

Early period. Besides Giles, the most important representatives include the following: JAMES OF VITERBO (d. 1307 or 1308), Alexander of San Elpidio (d. *c.* 1326), AUGUSTINE (TRIUMPHUS) OF ANCONA (d. 1328), Gerard of Siena (d. 1336), Michael de Massa (d. 1337), HENRY OF FRIEMAR (d. 1340), BARTHOLOMEW OF URBINO (d. 1350), WILLIAM OF CREMONA (d. 1356), THOMAS OF STRASSBURG (d. 1357), Alfonsus of Toledo (d. 1366), GREGORY OF RIMINI (d. 1358), UGOLINO OF ORVIETO (d. 1373), JOHN KLENKOK (d. 1374), Augustine Favaroni (d. 1443), John Hiltalinger (d. 1392), GILES OF VITERBO (d. 1532), Gerolamo SERIPANDO (d. 1563), and Luis de LEÓN (d. 1591).

Representative Doctrine. Allowing for occasional differences, the following doctrinal summary may be taken as representative of this period, as well as of the Augustinian school in general.

(1) It is characterized by an eclecticism based on fundamental Thomistic doctrines and Augustinian teachings wherein the latter are given interpretations proper to this school. After Giles, however, and beginning with Gregory of Rimini, there is a gradual lessening of Thomistic influence and a corresponding stronger emphasis on St. Augustine in developing a more positive theology. Augustinian houses of study accumulated and copied St. Augustine's writings, notably in Paris, Siena, and Padua.

(2) It is distinguished by a consistent orientation toward holy Scripture and the church fathers, especially St. Augustine, as theological sources. In addition, there is a distinct awareness of the historical origin and context of sources, evident in a frequency and accuracy of quotations, even from contemporary authors, unusual for the times.

(3) There is an insistence upon the primacy of the will over the intellect, together with the corollary that beatitude is essentially and primarily achieved through love rather than knowledge. This pivotal position is reflected in several teachings of the school, particularly on grace and the kind of obligation attached to the precept of charity.

(4) Inspired by Augustine's familiar dictum, ". . . our heart is restless until it rests in Thee" (*Conf.* 1.1), as well as by the Augustinian notion of image, which accounts for the soul's radical capacity for possessing God (*Trin.* 14.8.11), the school defends man's natural DESIRE TO SEE GOD. Against the objection of a disproportion between natural powers and BEATIFIC VISION, Augustinians reply with Gerard of Siena that, while the tendency is natural, the actual attainment requires GRACE (*In 1 sent.* 3.2.).

(5) The end of THEOLOGY, according to the school, is neither speculative nor practical, but affective, since this science directs man to beatitude that consists essentially in love. Similarly, the central consideration in theology is not God in Himself, *sub ratione deitatis,* or in His infinity but, as Giles teaches, God as the source of glory and beatitude, *Deus glorificator et beatificator* (*In 2 sent.* 1.1.1.).

(6) The school holds the impossibility of a state of PURE nature for man, not from any strict exigency on the part of his nature but by reason of the divine wisdom and goodness and a fittingness on the part of the Creator (*ex quadam decentia Creatoris*). This notion, already found in Giles, received further development and importance with the Augustinian theologians of the seventeenth and eighteenth centuries.

(7) It stresses the necessity for medicinal grace (*gratia sanans*) consequent upon original sin, by which man is deprived not only of SUPERNATURAL goods but also suffers impairment in his natural endowments (*vulneratus in naturalibus*), with the further result that he is incapable without this grace of observing the natural law or of performing acts possessed of a natural morality (Giles, *In 2 sent.* 28.1.2).

(8) The school emphasizes the primacy of grace over free will in salutary and meritorious works [". . . magis agimur quam agamus" (Giles, *In 2 sent.* 38.1.3)], as further reflected in the Augustinian teaching on the nature of predestination. Consequent upon original sin, PREDESTINATION to glory is absolutely gratuitous and is antecedent to God's foreknowledge of man's merits (*ante praevisa merita*); REPROBATION (negative), on the other hand, an effect of God's justice, and likewise consequent upon original sin, is the lot of those left unrescued from what Augustine had called the "massa perditionis" (*Persev.* 19.35). In explaining the efficacy of grace, Augustinians of the period introduce the notion of an attraction to good ["non movetur voluntas . . . nisi per amorem" (Giles, *In 2 sent.* 41.1.2)]. This notion of a *delectatio victrix,* already formulated by St. Augustine (cf. *Pecc. merit.* 2.19), was more fully developed by the Augustinians of Salamanca during the celebrated controversy *de auxiliis* and, even to a greater degree, by theologians of the so-called school of Noris.

(9) A strict theocratic position is held by the Augustinian school on the nature and scope of papal authority.

The position is inspired by an interpretation of Augustine's notion of the state (*res publica*) and its foundation upon "justice," namely, that "true justice is not to be found except in that commonwealth [*res publica*] whose founder and ruler is Christ" (*Civ.* 2.21). First enunciated by Giles, this theory of direct power (*potestas directa*) in the temporal order is mitigated by James of Viterbo under the influence of Aristotle's teaching on the natural origin of the state. From man's social nature the state comes to an "inchoative" existence ("inchoative habet esse"), whereas in its full and formal condition ("perfective autem et formaliter") it exists for the spiritual power in somewhat the same way that grace does not destroy nature but perfects it. The *De regimine christiano* of James has been called the earliest treatise on the Church. The most extreme proponent of the Augustinian theory, Augustine of Ancona, holds that both powers, spiritual and temporal, reside solely in the pope, through whom ("mediante ipso") all others, clerical and lay, receive their authority (*see* CHURCH AND STATE).

Beginning with Gregory of Rimini and extending to the sixteenth century, the Augustinian school takes on a somewhat new direction characterized by the following trends: an increasing dependence upon the teachings and authority of St. Augustine, a vigorous anti-Pelagian polemic occasioned by the nominalist influence, and the development of a more positive theology based upon an extensive study of the Fathers of the Church, particularly St. Augustine.

During the Tridentine period, the Augustinian theologians naturally focused their attention upon doctrines relative to the controversies of the times, such as original sin, concupiscence, and the nature of justification.

Gerolamo Seripando. Since Cardinal Seripando, one-time president of the council, is unquestionably the most important representative of the period, a summary of his teachings will serve to outline the broad doctrinal positions of the Augustinian theologians of the sixteenth century.

Seripando's entire notion of JUSTIFICATION is developed from his definitive teaching on CONCUPISCENCE, understood as the cumulative impact of man's lower appetite in conflict with God's law. Concupiscence, being displeasing to God, is thereby somehow sinful in His sight. Following Baptism, which requires the complement of faith, personal or at least vicarious, concupiscence, while no longer imputed, remains an active source of personal sins, a hindrance to the perfect observance of God's law. It is therefore denominated as sinful. This understanding of concupiscence is essential to Seripando's theory of the double JUSTICE, the culminating point in his theory of justification, which includes the following

steps: (1) first grace, or call to faith (*gratia praeveniens*), (2) an additional grace (*adjutorium*) to accept the former, enabling man to abandon sin through penance, (3) incorporation into the Mystical Body by faith and trust in Christ, resulting in the remission of sin, (4) infusion of charity and the gifts of the Holy Spirit, whereby man is able to observe the commandments, and (5) the justice of Christ, which must still be applied to His members, since, owing to the active and sinful influence of concupiscence, man's justice remains otherwise incomplete and cannot merit eternal life.

Further Development. Related doctrines on original justice, grace, predestination, and the law of charity were later developed and systematized by the Augustinians of the seventeenth and eighteenth centuries. For a complete list of Augustinians, fathers and theologians, at Trent, see D. Gutiérrez, *Analecta augustiniana* 22 (1949) 55–157.

Finally, toward the end of this earlier period, there was a notable resurgence of interest in Giles, as evidenced by a number of systematic summaries of his teaching. Most important were F. Gavardi (d. 1715), *Theologica exantiquata juxta b. Augustini doctrinam ab Aegidio expositam,* in six volumes, and A. Hormannseder (d. 1740), *Hecatombe theologica,* a compendium in two volumes of Gavardi's work. P. Manso (d. 1736), author of a *Cursus philosophicus ad mentem Aegidii Romani* and an important treatise on Augustine's teaching on grace, *Augustinus sui interpres,* was a link between the early and later periods of Augustinianism. A pioneer in adapting Augustinianism to the doctrinal exigencies of the period, against JANSENISM, he was also a defender of Cardinal Henry NORIS.

Later period. Augustinianism of the later period is sometimes known as the school of Noris, after its most important representative; the theologians of this school are also known as the *Augustinenses* in various theological tracts and histories. They attempt to remove the authority of St. Augustine from the teachings of Calvin, BAIUS, and JANSEN on grace and to present a new synthesis of the saint's theology on grace conformable to Catholic teaching and accommodated to the doctrinal exigencies of the time. Principal theologians of the period are Cardinal Henry Noris (1631–1704), whose more important works include *Historia pelagiana, Dissertatio de synodo V oecumenica* and *Vindiciae augustinianae;* Fulgenzio Bellelli (1675–1742), general of his order and author of two works against doctrines of Baius and Jansen, namely, *Mens Augustini de statu naturae rationalis ante peccatum* and *Mens Augustini de modo reparationis humanae naturae post lapsum;* Giovanni Lorenzo Berti (1696–1766), author of *De theologicis disciplinis,* a systematic, six-volume synthesis of St. Augustine's theology, particularly on grace and free will. A compendium of the work by Buzio appeared in 1767. For a complete listing of works by these theologians, see D. Perini, *Bibliographia augustiniana: Scriptores itali* (Florence 1929–38).

Representative Doctrine. Undoubtedly, the central and controlling doctrine underlying the Augustinian theology of this period is that of man's natural desire to see God in beatific vision and its corollary of the impossibility of a state of pure nature for man. Continuing St. Augustine's doctrine of image, already elaborated in the earlier period, the later theologians of the school conclude that without the beatific vision man's state would be one of utmost misery. Similarly, since the soul, by reason of its inborn tendency to inform the body, would be in a violent state unless permanently united with the body, in which, in turn, concupiscence is an active force to sin, immortality and immunity from concupiscence are qualities eminently suited to man's true nature. Consequently, while these gifts are in no manner strictly due to man's nature itself and are, therefore, gratuitous, they are due to it by reason of God's goodness and wisdom, that is, by a kind of fittingness on the part of God Himself (*ex decentia Creatoris*). Hence the conclusion that, though a state of pure nature is possible from God's absolute power, it is impossible from His ordered power—whence comes the insistence upon the necessity of a medicinal grace (*gratia sanans*) or, better, upon the medicinal aspect of grace to remedy man's nature following the loss of gifts due him by God's goodness and wisdom. Concupiscence, consequent upon the loss of this integrity, remains inconceivable, therefore, apart from original sin and constitutes its material element.

In explaining the divine economy of grace, Augustinians proceed historically and concretely in distinguishing the two states of man, that of innocence and fallen nature. To the former, God granted an indifferent grace (*gratia versatilis*), giving the will the power (*posse*) to do good, which Adam could resist, but not the grace of actual volition (*velle*) and of the performance (*perficere*) of the good. After the Fall man has need of efficacious grace, which infallibly produces its effect without detriment to man's freedom. Similarly, in the state of innocence predestination and reprobation were subsequent upon God's foreknowledge of man's merits (*post praevisa merita*), while after the Fall predestination to glory is absolutely gratuitous and previous to any merit (*ante praevisa merita*); reprobation (negative), consequent upon original sin, is the lot of those comprising the "massa perditionis," in keeping with God's "just judgment," as Augustine had expressed it (*Persev.* 19.35).

To explain the nature of efficacious grace, Augustinians develop the notion already adumbrated in Giles of

the *delectatio victrix*, the most crucial and controversial point in their theology of grace. According to Noris, for example, man's will is beset by two opposing forces or attractions: concupiscence (*cupiditas mali*) and grace (*caritas—cupiditas boni*). Since, in his fallen state, man's will follows the stronger attraction, it is only when grace is the more powerful that it efficaciously produces its effect; however, as Berti points out, the will responds to this attraction not from necessity but with complete freedom (*liberrima voluntate*). Otherwise grace remains inefficacious or sufficient, bestowing the power (*posse*) but not the actual accomplishment of good since it fails to overcome the stronger attraction of evil. These graces differ in degree rather than in kind, so that the efficacy of grace is not absolute but relative, that is, measured by the intensity of the evil attraction to be overcome and the moral condition of the individual subject. In other words, a grace efficacious for one may be inefficacious for another.

Finally, reacting in part against the laxism of the period, Augustinians propose a strict interpretation of the divine precept of charity and of the role of love in human acts. Since the commandment obliges man to love God always, he must, at least frequently and in particular instances, do so actually; at all other times, by a virtual disposition of soul. Furthermore, in the performance of acts morally good in every respect, he must refer them to God by at least a virtual intention. Finally, even in the Sacrament of Penance, fear alone of punishment does not justify the sinner unless there is present a kind of initial love.

Opposition. The teachings of Noris and his followers were violently attacked because of their alleged affinity or even identity with the errors of Baius and Jansen, for example, by the Franciscans Neusser in Germany and F. de Macedo in Italy, by the Jesuit J. Hardouin in France, and by the Benedictine Navarro in Spain. Although Noris's works were favorably reviewed by the Roman Inquisition, his *Historia pelagiana* was placed on the Index of the Spanish Inquisition in 1742. In a brief of July 31, 1748, Benedict XIV protested this action (H. Denzinger, *Enchiridion symbolorum* [Freiburg 1963] 2564) and, in a later brief, of Feb. 19, 1749, ordered the book removed from the Index. In the first brief, the pope significantly granted the same status to the Augustinian system as that enjoyed by Bañezianism (*see* BÁÑEZ AND BAÑEZIANISM) and MOLINISM on the question of grace and free will. Favorable judgment was also passed upon the teachings of Berti by a papal commission appointed by Benedict XIV.

See Also: AUGUSTINIANISM; AUGUSTINE, ST.; THEOLOGY, HISTORY OF.

Bibliography: E. PORTALIÉ, *Dictionnaire de théologie catholique*, 15 v. (Paris 1903–50) 1.2:2485–2561. L. HÖDL, *Lexikon* *für Theologie und Kirche,* 10 v. (Freiburg 1957–65) 1:1089–1092. W. BOCXE, *Introduction to the Teaching of the Italian Augustinians of the 18th Century on the Nature of Actual Grace* (Héverlé-Louvain 1958). L. FERNANDEZ, *Trayectoria historica de la escuela agustiniana* (Bogotá 1963). H. JEDIN, *Papal Legate at the Council of Trent: Cardinal Seripando,* tr. F. C. ECKHOFF (St. Louis 1947). G. LEFF, *Gregory of Rimini* (New York 1961). L. RENWART, *Augustiniens du XVIIIᵉ siècle et "nature pure"* (Paris 1945). J. L. SHANNON, *Good Works and Predestination according to Thomas of Strassburg* (Westminster, Md. 1940). M. WILKS, *The Problem of Sovereignty in the Later Middle Ages: The Papal Monarchy with Augustinus Triumphus and the Publicists* (Cambridge, Eng. 1963). D. GUTIÉRREZ, "Los agustinos en el concilio de Trento," *La Ciudad de Dios* 158 (1946) 385–491, B. HWANG, "The Nature and Destiny of Man according to F. Bellelli," *Augustiniana* 3 (1953) 224–259. R. KUITERS, "The Development of the Theological School of Aegidius Romanus in the Order of St. Augustine," *ibid.* 4 (1954) 157–177. F. ROJO, "Ensayo bibliográfico de Noris, Bellelli y Berti," *Analecta Augustiniana* 26 (1963) 294–383. D. TRAPP, "Augustinian Theology of the 14th Century," *Augustiniana* 6 (1956) 146–222. A. ZUMKELLER, *Theology and History of the Augustinian School in the Middle Ages* (Villanova 1996). GILES OF ROME, *Commentary on the Song of Songs and Other Writings,* ed. J. ROTELLE (Villanova 1998). F. MARTIN and J. O'MALLEY, *Friar, Reformer, and Renaissance Scholar: Life and Work of Giles of Viterbo 1469–1532,* ed. J. ROTELLE (Villanova 1993). B. HACKETT, *William Flete, O.S.A., and Catherine of Siena: Masters of Fourteenth-Century Spirituality,* ed. J. ROTELLE (Villanova 1993). *A Shepherd in Their Midst: The Episcopacy of Girolamo Seripando— 1554–1563,* ed. J. ROTELLE (Villanova 1995).

[R. P. RUSSELL]

AUGUSTINIANS

Since 1969 the order's official title has been the Order of Brothers of St. Augustine or the Order of St. Augustine (O.S.A.). The order was formerly known as the Order of Hermits of St. Augustine (O.E.S.A.). The term *hermits* refers to the origins of the order, which arose out of the eremitical movement of the 11th and 12th centuries. In contrast to the large monastic establishments, groups of hermits living in small houses sought to live a more evangelical style of life. At the request of hermits near Siena and Pisa, Pope Innocent IV began a process of unification under the guidance of Cardinal Richard Annibaldi in December of 1243. In the Little Union, achieved in March of 1244, the hermits in Tuscany were organized into a single order that came to be known as the Hermits of St. Augustine, under a prior general were directed to adopt the rule and style of life of St. AUGUSTINE.

In 1256 the Tuscan hermits were united by papal directive with several other orders: (1) the Williamites, who were followers of St. William of Malavalle (d. 1157); (2) the *Gianboniti,* followers of Blessed John Bono (d. 1249); (3) the hermits of Monte Favale; and (4) the hermits of Brettino. After an initial meeting at Santa Maria del Popolo in Rome, Pope Alexander IV issued the bull *Licet ecclesiae catholicae* on April 9, establishing the "Order of Hermits of St. Augustine." This unification of the several religious orders is known as the Great Union of 1256. Although the Williamites subsequently withdrew from the union, as did the hermits of Monte Favale, most of the Williamite houses in Germany and Hungary passed to the Augustinian Order. Of the three remaining groups, the Tuscan hermits numbered some 70 monasteries, including houses in Spain, Germany, France and England. The *Gianboniti* had three provinces in Lombardy and the Romagna. The hermits of Brettino were settled mostly in the Marches of Ancona. The total number of houses of the new order was between 150 and 200.

While the individual orders that came together in the Great Union had their own constitutions, no record of the initial constitutions of the combined order survives. The order followed the general structures of the mendicant orders. The entire order, governed by a prior general and assisted by his curia in Rome, was divided into provinces and directed by prior's provincial. Each province was comprised of houses, each headed by a local prior. All superiors except the local prior were elected. Supreme legislative power rested in the general and provincial chapters respectively for the entire order or province. This structure is reflected in the first extant constitutions, dating from the general chapter of 1290 in Ratisbon. The constitutions were frequently modified in subsequent general chapters, with major revisions in 1551, 1581, 1686, 1895, 1926 and 1968. The basic structures, however, have remained the same.

Pope Alexander IV and subsequent popes enriched the order with many favors, such as exemption from episcopal jurisdiction. In establishing the order as a mendicant order, the pope directed the hermits, now become friars, to works of the active apostolate, such as preaching, hearing confessions and teaching. The enduring desire for a more contemplative dimension found expression in the reform movements of the 14th, 15th and 16th centuries and in less organized ways in later periods.

Relationship to St. Augustine. The ideal proposed for unifying the groups that constituted the order was the observance of the *Rule of St. Augustine* (*see* AUGUSTINE, THE RULE OF). While other orders, such as the Dominicans, also followed the *Rule,* they had a more immediate figure to whom they looked as the inspiration or founder of their order. Gradually, the Hermits of St. Augustine became more identified as the followers of St. Augustine and came to be known simply as the Augustinians. In England, they were called Austin Friars. The popes also recognized the close connection of the order with Augustine. Thus in 1327 the Augustinian Hermits were given joint

Facade of the Church of Santa Maria del Popolo, Rome; scene of the "Great Union" of the Augustinians in 1256. (Alinari-Art Reference/Art Resource, NY)

custody of the tomb of St. Augustine in Pavia, where the CANONS REGULAR OF ST. AUGUSTINE were already established.

In their desire to establish a closer link with St. Augustine, the friars began to look for historical connections between Augustine and the predecessors of the order, especially in Tuscany. Within a few generations legends arose that Augustine had visited groups of Tuscan hermits on his way from Milan to Rome after his conversion. An alternative version of the story stated that Augustinians had come to Italy from monasteries of hermits established by St. Augustine in North Africa. Such legends found literary expression in the works of HENRY OF FRIEMAR the Elder (d. 1340) and JORDAN OF SAXONY (d. 1380) and were reflected in artistic depictions in Augustinian churches where Augustine is portrayed wearing the black tunic, cincture and capuche of the order's habit.

Besides following the Augustinian *Rule*, the order looked to the theological and spiritual thought of St. Augustine for guidance (*see* AUGUSTINIAN SPIRITUALITY). Though colored by the erroneous historical connection, the work of Jordan of Saxony, entitled *Vitasfratrum* (*Life of the Brethren*), published in 1357, presents a synthesis of Augustine's monastic thought and the manner in which the vows of poverty, chastity and obedience are to be observed within the order. In accord with Augustine's emphasis on common life, Jordan structures his work on a fourfold communion: living together, oneness of spirit, sharing of temporal possessions and proportional distribution. Later commentaries on the *Rule* were written by Ambrose Massari of Cori (d. 1485) and Blessed Alfonso de OROZCO (d. 1591).

In the Middle Ages Augustinian libraries often had manuscripts of Augustine's works. Today Augustinians in Spain, Italy and the United States are publishing the entire corpus of Augustine's writings in translation. Since the Second Vatican Council the Augustinians have sponsored many seminars and lectures on St. Augustine as well as publishing studies on his teaching. Recent popes have indicated that they consider the Augustinians as entrusted with task of representing Augustine's thought and spirituality in the Church.

Because Augustine's spirituality in general and the *Rule* in particular are directed to the heart of religious living, namely, the love of God and neighbor, rather than to the details, Augustinians have enjoyed a certain flexibility in adapting to changing historical circumstances. The order has thus been able to incorporate or to abandon practices linked to a particular age. The order is not identified with any particular apostolate but remains available to serve the needs of the Church.

Saints and Beati. The Church has accorded the title of blessed to more than 50 Augustinians, professed friars, nuns or affiliates. Fourteen were martyrs in Japan between 1622 and 1632. St. NICHOLAS OF TOLENTINE (d. 1305) was the first member of the order to be formally canonized (1446). St. CLARE OF MONTEFALCO (d. 1308) was canonized in 1881. St. RITA OF CASCIA (d. 1457 and canonized 1900) is the most popular saint of the order. Others include St. John of SAHAGUN (d. 1479 and canonized 1691); St. John STONE, martyr in the reign of Henry VIII (d. 1539 and canonized in 1970); and St. THOMAS OF VILLANOVA (d. 1555 and canonized 1658). The most recently beatified are Anselmo POLANCO (1881–1939), martyred in the Spanish civil war; Elias NIEVES (1882–1928), martyred in the Mexican persecution; and Maria Teresa FASCE (1881–1947), superior of the monastery at Cascia. The Blessed Virgin Mary is venerated under the titles of Mother of Consolation, Our Lady of Grace, and Mother of Good Counsel. Augustinians have extended their devotion to St. Augustine to include his mother, St. MONICA, and others associated with him, such as St. POSSIDIUS, his biographer and St. ALIPIUS, his close friend.

Scholars and Authors. From the earliest days, the order showed great concern for the intellectual development of its members. Lanfranc of Milan (d. 1264), the first prior general, established the first general house of study at Paris in 1259. Others followed at university sites such as Oxford, Cambridge, Bologna, Padua, Rome, Naples, Salamanca and Cologne. Lanfranc sent GILES OF ROME (*c.* 1243–1316) to study at Paris under St. Thomas Aquinas. Though he generally followed his master, Giles differed from St. Thomas on several points. Giles was so highly regarded in the order that the general chapter of Florence in 1287 declared that Augustinians were to follow his teachings, past and future. He thus became the

founder of the medieval Augustinian school within the order (*see* AUGUSTINIANISM and AUGUSTINIANISM, THEOLOGICAL SCHOOL OF). Other important Augustinian theologians of the first period of the Augustinian school include Blessed JAMES OF VITERBO (d. 1308), AUGUSTINE OF ANCONA (d. 1328) and THOMAS OF STRASSBURG (d. 1357). A new period began in the mid-fourteenth century with GREGORY OF RIMINI (d. 1358). Others of this second period include Alonso Vargas (d. 1366), HUGOLINO OF ORVIETO (d. 1373), John Hiltalingen (d. 1378) and Augustino Favaroni (d. 1443). The Augustinians were known as defenders of the papacy. Giles of Rome, James of Viterbo, Augustine of Ancona and Augustine Favaroni wrote treatises supporting papal supremacy. Paul of Venice (d. 1429) made important contributions in logic and philosophy.

In the area of Sacred Scripture, more than 80 authors wrote commentaries on books of the Bible over a period of 300 years. In his *De gestis Domini Salvatoris (The Deeds of Our Lord and Savior)*, Blessed SIMON FIDATI OF CASCIA (d. 1348) presented an original treatment of the life of Christ in a manner that differed from the usual style of commentary. Blessed Simon had forsaken the pursuit of an academic career to give himself to contemplation. In a similar spirit, William FLETE (d. *c.* 1390), declined the degree of *magister* in his native England and withdrew to Lecceto near Siena.

Augustinians were among the first orders to embrace the Renaissance. The first humanist of the Italian Renaissance, Petrarch (d. 1374), counted Augustinians among his closest friends. Dionysius of Borgo San Sepulchro (d. 1342) presented Petrarch with a copy of Augustine's *Confessions* and was himself the author of a commentary on Valerius Maximus. Another of the same circle, BARTHOLOMEW OF URBINO (d. 1350), composed the *Milleloquium sancti Augustini*, in which he gathered nearly 15,000 citations of Augustine under key words. Bonaventure of Peraga (d. 1385) gave the funeral oration for Petrarch. At Santo Spirito in Florence were found Luigi Marsili (1394) and Martin of Signa (d. 1387), friend of Boccaccio. In his *Rerum Mediolanensium historia (History of Milan)* Andrea Biglia (d. 1435) offers an excellent example of humanist historiography. In France Jacques LeGrand (d. 1415) combined humanism and Christian faith in his *Sophilogium*. In England John CAPGRAVE (d. 1464) gained renown for his *Chronicle of England and Book of the Illustrious Henries*. The name of Ambrogio Calepino (d. 1511) became synonymous with the word *dictionary*, through his lexicon. Giles of Viterbo (d. 1532) sought to interpret Platonism along Christian lines and also produced studies on Hebrew philology with a special interest in mystical cabalistic interpretations. In the 16th century Onofrio PANVINIO (d. 1568) composed numerous studies on Roman antiquity and the history of the Church.

In Spain Luis de LEON (d. 1591), theologian and significant figure in Spanish literature, is remembered for *Los nombres de Cristo* (*The Names of Christ*). The Portuguese THOMAS OF JESUS (d. 1582) wrote the *Os trabalhos de Jesus* (*The Sufferings of Our Lord Jesus Christ*), while a prisoner of the Moors in North Africa. Blessed Alonso de Orozco (d. 1591) composed many treatises of a devotional nature.

An important contribution to intellectual life in Rome was made by Angelo ROCCA (1545–1620), who opened the first public library, the Biblioteca Angelica, in 1614. During his years of teaching at Erfurt in Germany, the Irish friar, Augustine Gibbon (d. 1676), composed his massive *Speculum Theologicum* and four disputations concerning the doctrines of Luther and Calvin. The later Augustinian school, which developed in the 17th and 18th centuries amid the controversies over the teaching of St. Augustine on grace, is best represented in the works of Henry Cardinal NORIS (1631–1704), custodian of the Vatican Library, Fulgentius Bellelli (1675–1741) and Gianlorenzo BERTI (1696–1766). Because of the political and social disturbances of the later 18th and early 19th centuries, a decline in studies ensued. Many valuable libraries were lost in the suppressions ordered by civil governments.

Through his experiments on peas in the monastery garden at Brno, Gregor MENDEL (1822–1884) discovered basic laws of genetics, though his contribution was not fully recognized during his lifetime. Among many fine scholars in the 20th century, one can cite Cardinal Augustine Ciasca (d. 1902), an outstanding orientalist; Angel Vega (d. 1972), historian and patrologist; Anthony Casamassa (d. 1955) and Agostino Trapé (d. 1987), patrologists. Damasus Trapp (d. 1996) is credited with having awakened a new appreciation of 14th century theologians such as Gregory of Rimini. With the establishment of the Augustinianum in Rome in 1969, the order committed itself in a special way to the study of patristics.

History

The first hundred years saw the consolidation of the order particularly through the work of Blessed Clement of Osimo (d. 1291) and Blessed Augustine of Tarano (d. 1309), who prepared the constitutions adopted at Ratisbon in 1290. At that time the order possessed ten provinces in Italy and one each in England, France, Provence, Germany, Hungary and Spain. By 1329 the provinces had increased to 24 through the division of some provinces and the addition of Sicily and the Oltremarina, which embraced the islands of the eastern Mediterranean. From

around the mid-fourteenth century until the Reformation and Counter-Reformation the order underwent a period of decline in numbers and in observance. A important factor was the Black Death, which killed more than 5,000 friars in 1347–1350. During the same period, however, the order saw the rise of movements of strict observance, the first of which began at Lecceto near Siena in 1387. From these movements several congregations developed within the order during the next two centuries. Two observant groups, the Recollects in Spain and the Discalced in Italy, eventually became fully independent orders in 1912 and 1931 (*see* AUGUSTINIAN RECOLLECTS).

In 1517 Martin LUTHER (1483–1546), a member of the observant congregation of Saxony, began the Protestant Reformation. While some of his fellow friars followed him, he was opposed by others, such as Bartholomaeus Arnoldi von Usingen (d. 1532), Konrad Treger (d. 1542) and Johannes Hoffmeister (d. 1547). The Saxon-Thuringian province and the observant congregation of Saxony collapsed during the religious and political upheaval of the 16th century. The English province was completely destroyed by Henry VIII and the Irish vicariate suffered suppressions and persecutions. A period of great renewal, however, began under the leadership of Jerome SERIPANDO, prior general (1538–1551). The reforms of the Council of Trent brought greater stability to the Church and the order.

The 16th century marked the beginning of extensive missionary outreach by the Spanish and Portuguese Augustinians. In 1533 the first group of Augustinians arrived in Mexico and began to work with great success among the Spanish and native populations. In 1568 an independent province was established, followed by another in 1602. The first Augustinian house in Peru was founded in 1551 and soon the order was established in other regions of the country. In the course of evangelization, some friars were killed, including Diego Ortiz, the protomartyr of Peru. From Peru the Augustinians extended their work to other areas. The Ecuadorian province was established in 1537; the Colombian in 1601; the Chilean in 1627. Augustinian friars also served other areas in Latin America and the Caribbean. The popes gave permission for pontifical universities in Quito, Ecuador in 1586; in Lima, Peru in 1608; and in Bogotá, Columbia in 1694. Alonso de la Vera Cruz (d. 1584) made important contributions to the newly founded university of Mexico. The Augustinian missionaries first arrived in the Philippines in 1543, but a permanent mission was not established until 1565. The latter expedition from Mexico was directed by Andres de URDANETA (1498–1568), who charted the return route that was later used by the Manila fleet. The Philippine province was founded in 1575. In the islands the Augustinians composed dictionaries and grammars as well as catechisms in the native languages. Missions in Japan began in 1602, but as a result of the persecution in which both missionaries and Japanese affiliates were martyred, the mission effort ended in 1637. From the Philippines too the Augustinians established their first house in China in 1681 and remained there until 1800. From the last quarter of the sixteenth century the Portuguese Augustinians labored in Africa in areas with Portuguese connections such as Guinea. At the mission at Mombasa, begun in 1598, three Augustinians were martyred along with a number of other Christians in 1631. Portuguese Augustinians began missionary endeavors in India as early as 1573. Missions were established in Persia (1602), Sri Lanka (1606) and Iraq (1623).

In the 17th and early 18th centuries, the order experienced a period of stability and growth. It is estimated that by 1753 the order had around 20,000 members in 1,500 houses, divided among 43 provinces and 13 congregations. But beginning with the last part of the 18th century and through much of the 19th century, suppressions by various governments greatly weakened the order in Europe. In the wake of the French Revolution, the order's five French provinces completely disappeared. The Napoleonic wars and subsequent invasions and revolutions did much to reduce the order in Italy. No general chapter was held between 1792 and 1822 or between 1865 and 1889. In Germany only two houses were left after 1803 and the Austrian province disappeared in 1812. The Portuguese province was suppressed in several stages with the definitive suppression coming in 1834. By reason of restrictive laws the major orders in Spanish lands were governed by an independent superior subject to the Spanish government. This measure affected 11 Augustinian provinces in Spain and the New World. Moreover, in Spain a series of repressive measures culminated in the suppression of all the Spanish provinces except the Philippine. In Latin America independence from Spain brought various secularizations of religious houses. This period marked the end of the Augustinian universities in Latin America: Bogotá (1773), Quito (1791) and Lima (1826).

Gradually, in the later part of the 19th century, the order recovered in Europe. Pope Leo XIII appointed Pacifico Neno first as commissary general (1881–1886) and then as prior general (1887–1889). Under his vigorous leadership and that of his successor, Sebastian Martinelli, who was later named cardinal and apostolic delegate to the United States, the Italian provinces began a long process of recovery from the suppressions and confiscations inflicted on them. In Spain the province of Castile was restored in 1881. The Spanish provinces were also completely reunited to the order in 1893. The Escorial province was founded in 1895; the province of Spain in 1926.

The growth of the Spanish provinces resulted in renewed missionary effort in Latin America and in China. The Irish province, which had already sent friars to the American mission as early as 1794, began working in Australia in 1837, but a province was not founded there until 1952. In 1864 the Irish Augustinians began the restoration of the order in England. In Germany Pius Keller (1825–1904) brought about the establishment of the German province in 1895. Growth in Holland led to the founding of an independent province in 1895.

During the Spanish civil war a number of Spanish Augustinians were killed by the Communists. World War II caused disruptions in the life of the other continental provinces of Europe, and the ensuing political conditions of the Iron Curtain all but destroyed the order in Poland and Czechoslovakia. One unforeseen result was the renewal of the presence of the order in Austria through friars who were expelled by the Communist government in Czechoslovakia.

The Dutch Augustinians established missions in Bolivia in 1930 and in Irian, Jaya in 1953. The Irish Augustinians began working in Nigeria in 1940. From Nigeria, favored with many native vocations, a mission has now been established in Kenya. The Irish have also sent friars to Ecuador in recent decades. Before World War II, German Augustinians had begun laboring in the United States and Canada, where the Canadian province of St. Joseph was established in 1967. The Belgian province began missions in the Congo in 1952 where the German Augustinians later joined them. In 1977 the province of England and Scotland was established. The Italian provinces, which began a mission in Peru in 1968, were united into one province by the general chapter of 1995. Members of the Spanish Philippine province founded a house of formation in Tanzania in 1976 and a seminary in Cochin, India, in 1987. The Korean mission, now supported by the Australian and Cebu provinces, was begun in 1984 by friars from England and Australia.

The American Provinces. The American provinces trace their origin to the arrival of Thomas Matthew CARR (1755–1820) in Philadelphia in 1796. Though he had been preceded by John Rosseter (1751–1812) two years earlier, Carr brought with him the authorization to establish a new province. The focus of activity was Philadelphia where the St. Augustine church opened in 1801 and the St. Augustine Academy in 1811. Michael HURLEY (c. 1780–1837) was the first candidate for the order from the United States. After training in Italy, he returned to the United States in 1803 and spent all but two years in Philadelphia. A few other Irish Augustinians came, but growth was very slow and the friars' efforts were dispersed in various places. Robert Brown (1770–1839) labored in the southern states without any connection to the other Augustinians in the country while others served in New York. During the Nativist riots the St. Augustine church was burnt in 1844, but within four years a new and larger church was rebuilt. The establishment of Villanova College near Philadelphia in 1842 brought more friars together and attracted vocations. In 1874 the American province of St. Thomas of Villanova was established. The Augustinians accepted further parish commitments in the diocese of Philadelphia in the 1850s and in Lawrence, Massachusetts beginning in 1848. Other parishes followed in the sees of Albany (1858), Ogdensburg (1874), Havana, Cuba (1899), New York (1905), Chicago (1905), Los Angeles (1924) and Detroit (1926). In 1941 the new province of Our Mother of Good Counsel was formed from the order's houses in the Midwest. The Augustinian houses in California became the province of St. Augustine in 1968. The Villanova province made further commitments to higher education with the establishment of Santo Tomás de Villanueva in Havana (1946), Biscayne College (now St. Thomas of Villanova University) in Miami (1961) and Merrimack College, Andover, Massachusetts (1947). Villanova College became VILLANOVA UNIVERSITY in 1953. In 1952 the Villanova province began a mission in Nagasaki, Japan. The Midwest province accepted responsibility to serve in the prelature of Chulucanas, Peru, in 1964. Both of these missions, which have been enriched with native vocations, are now vicariates within the order.

The American provinces have given four bishops to the Church. Thomas GALBERRY, first provincial of the American province in 1874, was bishop of Hartford, Connecticut (1876–1878). William Jones served as bishop of San Juan, Puerto Rico (1907–1921). John McNabb, named prelate of Chulucanas, Peru, in 1964 and consecrated as bishop in 1967, became the first ordinary of Chulucanas when it attained the status of a diocese. Upon his retirement in 2000, Daniel Turley, coadjutor, became ordinary of Chulucanas. Joseph HICKEY was the first American to serve as prior general (1947–1953) and Theodore Tack the second (1971–1983).

Present State of the Order. At the beginning of the third millennium the Augustinian Order is divided into 25 provinces, one abbey, three vice-provinces and 14 vicariates and eight regions while 2,868 friars live in 465 houses. In Europe, the order is established in England, Scotland, Ireland, France, Holland, Belgium, Germany, Austria, Poland, the Czech Republic, Slovakia, Italy, Malta, Spain and Portugal. In Africa, Augustinians are present in the Congo, Nigeria, Algeria, Kenya, Tanzania and South Africa. In Asia and the Pacific, the order is represented in India, the Philippines, Korea, Japan, Indonesia and Australia. The Americas have Augustinians in Canada, the United States, Mexico, Puerto Rico, the Dominican Republic, Nicaragua, Costa Rica, Panama, Columbia, Venezuela, Brasil, Argentina, Chile, Bolivia, Peru and Ecuador.

In addition to Villanova and Merrimack in the United States, Augustinian provinces sponsor the following institutes of higher learning: the University of San Agustin in Iloilo City, Philippines; Maria Cristina, Escorial, Spain; and the Real Colegio de Agustinos Filipinos, Valladolid, Spain. The Augustinianum in Rome is supported by the entire order and is esteemed in the scholarly world for the quality of its conferences and publications in the field of patristic studies.

The Augustinian family. The entire Augustinian Family includes cloistered nuns (*see* AUGUSTINIAN NUNS AND SISTERS), 100 aggregated congregations of men and women, religious lay fraternities and societies of St. Augustine. The order also grants individual affiliations, which include a sharing in all of the spiritual benefits of the order, to persons who have participated in the works of the Augustinians in a special manner. While preserving the traditional pious societies, the order has sought to involve the laity in the spirit and work of the order in new ways. Lay observers have been invited to attend general and provincial chapters and special congresses for the laity have been offered in Rome and in various provinces. In recent years International Youth Congresses have been held periodically with representation from many parts of the world.

Bibliography: Sources. *Analecta Augustiniana* (Rome 1905ff.). *Augustiniana* (Louvain 1951ff.). *Augustinianum* (Rome 1961ff.). *Archivo histórico hispano-agustiniano* (Madrid 1914-27); replaced by *Archivo Agustiniano* (El Escorial and Valladolid 1929ff.). *Fontes Historiae Ordinis Sancti Augustini*; prima series, *Registra Priorum Generalium* (Rome 1976ff.); series altera, *Epistolaria aliique fontes* (Rome 1990ff.); tertia series, *Bullarium Ordinis Sancti Augustini Regesta*, ed. C. ALONSO (Rome 1997ff.). T. DE HERRERA, *Alphabetum Augustinianum* (Madrid 1644; repr. Rome 1990). JORDAN OF SAXONY, *The Life of the Brethren*, tr. G. DEIGHAN (Villanova 1993). Studies. S. ARNEIL, *Out Where the Dead Men Lie: The Augustinians in Australia 1838–1992* (Brookvale, N.S.W. 1992). *Agustinos en América y Filipinas: Actas del Congreso Internacional, Valladolid, 16–21 de abril de 1990*, 2 v., ed. I. RODRÍGUEZ (Valladolid-Madrid, 1990). A. J. ENNIS, *No Easy Road: The Early Years of the Augustinians in the United States, 1796–1874* (New York 1993); *The Augustinians: A Brief Sketch of Their American History from 1796 to the Present* (Villanova 1985). J. GAVIGAN, *The Augustinians from the French Revolution to Modern Times*, v. 4 of *History of the Order of St. Augustine* (Villanova 1989). D. GUTIERREZ, *The Augustinians in the Middle Ages 1256–1356*, vol. 1, part 1 of *History of the Order of St. Augustine* (Villanova 1984); *The Augustinians in the Middle Ages 1357–1517*, v. 1, part 2 of *History of the Order of St. Augustine* (Villanova 1983); *The Augustinians from the Protestant Reformation to the Peace of Westphalia 1518–1648*, v. 2 of *History of the Order of St. Augustine* (Villanova 1979). A. KUNZELMANN, *Geschichte der Deutschen Augustiner-Eremiten*, 7 v. (Würzburg 1969–1976). R. LAZ-

CANO, *Generales de la orden de San Agustín: Biografías-Documentacion-Retratos* (Rome 1995). B. VAN LUIJK, *L'ordine Agostiniano e la riforma monastica dal cinquecento alla vigilia della rivoluzione Francese* (Herverlee-Leuven 1973). *Men of Heart: I Pioneering Augustinians: Province of Saint Thomas of Villanova*, ed. J. E. ROTELLE (Villanova 1983). *Men of Heart: II Noteworthy Augustinians: Province of Saint Thomas of Villanova*, ed. J. E. ROTELLE (Villanova 1986). N. NAVARRETE, *Historia de la Provincia Agustiniana de San Nicolás de Tolentino de Michoacán*, 2 v. (Mexico 1978). B. RANO, *Augustinian Origins, Charism, and Spirituality* (Villanova 1994). F. ROTH, *The English Austin Friars 1249–1538*, 2 v. (New York 1966, 1961). A. RUIZ ZAVALA, *Historia de la Provincia Agustiniana del Santisimo Nombre de Jesus de Mexico*, 2 v. (Mexico 1984). J. R. SANDERS, *Before All Else: the History of the Augustinians in the Western United States* (Villanova 1987). A. ZUMKELLER, *Theology and History of the Augustinian School in the Middle Ages* (Villanova 1996).

[K. A. GERSBACH]

AUGUSTINIS, AEMILIO DE

Theologian and educator; b. Naples, Italy, Dec. 28, 1829; d. Rome, Jan. 17, 1899. Service in the army interrupted his legal studies at the Royal University in Naples. After briefly resuming the study of law, he entered the novitiate of the Society of Jesus at Conocchia, near Naples, Jan. 24, 1855. Garibaldi's revolution disrupted his theological studies, and he was transferred to the theologate at Laval, France, where he remained until his ordination, 1861. Two years later he left to spend a year in the Jesuit province of Champagne, France, after which he returned to Laval, where he served as professor of dogma, prefect of studies, and director of the library. In 1869 De Augustinis joined the faculty of the Jesuits' new scholasticate in Woodstock, Maryland, as professor of Sacred Scripture and librarian. During his tenure at Woodstock he served also as professor of ethics and dogma, and was one of the founders and editors of the *Woodstock Letters,* a news publication for Jesuits. In 1885 De Augustinis, who had been cited by Leo XIII for his contributions as a theologian, was assigned to the commission revising Jesuit theological studies. When the commission completed its work, he succeeded his former Woodstock colleague, Cardinal Camillo Mazzella, as professor of dogma at the Gregorian University in Rome. De Augustinis served also as rector of the Gregorian University from September 1891 to October 1895. In October 1897 he became ill and was forced to give up teaching, but he held certain minor positions until his death.

Bibliography: P. J. DOOLEY, *Woodstock and Its Makers* (Woodstock, Md. 1927). ''Two of Woodstock's Founders,'' *Woodstock Letters* 29 (1900) 309–315.

[F. G. MCMANAMIN]

AUGUSTINUS

A posthumous work by Cornelius JANSEN, Bishop of Ypres, published in Louvain, Belgium, in October 1640, which is the source of the Jansenist controversies. The work, the result of many years of research, intended to be an accurate exposition of the thought of St. AUGUSTINE on the disputed issues of salvation and grace. Since Jansen claimed to be only the interpreter of St. Augustine, the enormous folio volume was simply entitled *Augustinus.*

The first tome is devoted to the study of the opinions held by the Pelagians and Semi-Pelagians, according to St. Augustine. The second is preceded by a very interesting *Liber proemialis,* in which Jansen studied what the relationship between philosophy and theology ought to be and, using notes furnished by Saint-Cyran, affirmed that the Church had given to St. Augustine an absolute authority in questions pertaining to grace. Jansen then studied the state of the angels and man after the Fall, assuming a very pessimistic standpoint in which he presented as absolute the power of CONCUPISCENCE over free will, thenceforth inclined to sin. Finally, Jansen proved the impossibility of a state of PURE NATURE, thus attacking a thesis defended by the Molinists. The third tome goes to the core of the problem by studying the healing of human nature and its restoration by the grace of Christ the Redeemer. Vigorously affirmed are the Augustinian theses concerning the necessity of grace for every GOOD WORK, the infallibility of grace without nevertheless suppressing freedom, and the absolute gratuity of predestination. On all these points, Jansen adopted in their entirety the most rigid of St. Augustine's formulas and adhered especially to the last, the most rigid, in which he had expressed his thought. He spurned the Thomist idea that liberty is capable of opposites, is a *potestas ad opposita,* and maintained that an act is free when it is in accord with the profound spontaneity of nature, to which he gives the name of will, even if this nature cannot act otherwise; in his eyes, free and voluntary are identical. This will is moved only by delectation. In the state of corrupt nature, it is invincibly drawn to seek this delectation in the love of self and in creatures, and grace is necessary to put it right. Grace is an inclination of love that enters the will and there diffuses charity, inclining the will toward a completely spiritual delectation, which renders it conformable to the will of God. These two delectations, therefore, are the true principles of men's acts; that which leads the will to assent is called *delectatio victrix,* victorious delectation. Finally, in order that there be no misunderstanding regarding his intentions, Jansen added to his work an appendix called the *Parallelon,* which had the purpose of establishing the consistency of thought between the Pelagians and the Molinists, thus giving *Augustinus* a very controversial turn.

The work was finished just before the author's premature death on May 6, 1638. In his will Jansen had entrusted its publication to his friends and disciples Henri Calenus and Liber Froidmont and at the same time had submitted the work to the judgment of the Holy See. Despite the precautions taken by Jansen, his project became known, especially by the Jesuits, who endeavored to prevent the publication of the work. At their intervention Stravius, the Internuncio of Brussels, opposed the publishers with the decrees of Paul V (1611) and Urban VIII (1623), which forbade any publication on the subject of grace. But these decrees had never been officially served at the University of Louvain, which consequently attached no importance to them. Since they had already gone to considerable expense in the printing, Calenus and Froidmont used this as an argument to obtain permission in September 1640 to put the work up for sale. However, in view of the difficulties that they had encountered, they did not include at the beginning of the work the dedicatory letter to Urban VIII that Jansen had composed. Despite its considerable bulk—nearly 1,300 folio pages in two columns of close printing—copies of *Augustinus* were disseminated rapidly across Europe, especially in France. In 1641 it was reprinted in Paris with the approval of six Parisian doctors; other editions followed in Rouen in 1642 and 1643. The French editions added to *Augustinus* an austere treatise by the Franciscan F. Conrius that condemned to hell children who died without Baptism. There were no further editions. It remained however at the center of the Jansenist controversy. The bull *In Eminenti* (1643) censured it with other works for not respecting the papal restrictions. *CUM OCCASIONE* (1653) condemned as heretical five propositions "on the occasion" of its publication: 1. Some of God's commandments are impossible for the just who wish and endeavor to obey them, considering the forces they possess; the grace that would make their fulfillment possible is also lacking. 2. In the state of fallen nature, no one ever resists interior grace. 3. To merit or demerit in the state of fallen nature, it is not necessary that man be free from internal necessity; it is sufficient that he be free from external constraint. 4. The Semi-Pelagians admitted the necessity of an interior prevenient grace for every action, but they were heretical in that they held that this grace was such that man could either obey or resist it. 5. To hold that Jesus Christ died or shed His blood for all men, without excepting anyone, is Semi-Pelagianism.

AD SANCTAM BEATI PETRI SEDEM (1656) precised the presence of the propositions in the book and their condemnation in the sense given to them by Jansenius.

See Also: JANSENISM.

Bibliography: L. CEYSSENS, *Sources relatives aux débuts du jansénisme et de l'antijansénisme, 1640–1643* (Louvain 1957); "Les cinq propositions de Jansenius à Rome," *Revue d'histoire ecclésiastique* 66 (Rome) 449–501; 821–886; "L'authenticité des cinq propositions condamnées de Jansenius," *Antonianum* 50 (Rome) 368–424. J. ORCIBAL, *Jansenius d'Ypres* (1585–1638) (Paris 1989)

[L. J. COGNET/J. M. GRES-GAYER]

AULNE-SUR-SAMBRE, ABBEY OF

Former Cistercian monastery, on the Sambre River, former Diocese of Liège, present Diocese of Tournai, Belgium (also Alna, Alne, Aune). Founded as a BENEDICTINE abbey in the 7th century, it came briefly under the Rule of St. AUGUSTINE in 1144, but in 1147 became a CISTERCIAN abbey, daughterhouse of CLAIRVAUX. It continued as a flourishing monastery until it was burned by the French revolutionary armies in 1794. Its extensive ruins include the church (13th- and 16th-century Gothic) and several monastic buildings dating from the 18th century when the entire monastery was restored in the baroque manner, except for the earlier church. Hagiography records several names from Aulne: Bl. Walter and Bl. Wéry (d. 1217), priors; Bl. Simon (d. 1229), a conversus. Jean de Gesves (d. 1420) was an effective reformer of monks and nuns. Outstanding in the intellectual sphere was Reginald de la Buissière (d. after 1400), master at Paris, Heidelberg, and Cologne. The abbey library, before it was burned, was especially noteworthy. In 1629, Aulne erected a university college in Louvain which in 1857 became the American College for clergy from the U.S.

Bibliography: *Statuta capitulorum generalium ordinis cisterciensis,* ed. J. M. CANIVEZ, 8 v. (Louvain 1933–41), *passim.* L. JANAUSCHEK, *Origines cistercienses,* v.1 (Vienna 1877) 108. U. BERLIÈRE, *Monasticon belge* (Bruges 1890–) 1:329–342. E. REUSENS, "Collège de l'abbaye d'Alne," *Analectes pour servir à l'histoire ecclésiastique de la Belgique* 23 (1892) 106–124. G. BOULMONT, *Les Fastes de l'abbaye d'Aulne* (Ghent n.d., c. 1907). P. CLEMEN and C. GURLITT, *Die Klosterbauten der Cistercienser in Belgien* (Berlin 1916). J. M. CANIVEZ, *L'Ordre de Cîteaux en Belgique* (Forges-lez-Chimay, Belg. 1926) 94–103; *Dictionnaire d'histoire et de géographie ecclésiastiques,* ed. A. BAUDRILLART et al. (Paris 1912–) 5:667–669. L. H. COTTINEAU, *Répertoire topobibliographique des abbayes et prieurés,* 2 v. (Mâcon 1935–39) 1:202–203.

[M. STANDAERT]

AUNARIUS OF AUXERRE, ST.

Bishop of Auxerre; b. near Orlèanais, date unknown; d. Auxerre, France, Sept. 25, 601. As a youth of noble birth, Aunarius (Anacharius, Aunachaire, Aunacharius, Aunaire) was sent to the royal court of Burgundy, which he soon left in order to become a priest. Trained by (St.) Syagrius (Siacre, d. 600), Bishop of Autun, he was later elected and consecrated bishop of Auxerre (July 31, 561), participating in the councils of Paris (573) and Mâcon (583, 585). He is famous for the 45 canons of a diocesan synod of Auxerre (578?, 588?), some of which discuss marriage and superstitions. Concerned for the cult of the saints, Aunarius arranged for a transcription of the martyrology attributed to St. Jerome (592), and from that MS all extant copies are derived. He also provided vitae of his predecessors, AMATOR (390–418) and GERMAIN (418–448), and organized liturgical prayer in the diocese. He received two letters from Pope Pelagius II announcing the sending of relics. Aunarius was buried in the abbatial church of Saint-Germain. His relics, transferred to the crypt in 859 and stolen by the Calvinists in 1567, were recovered and are recognized as authentic.

Feast: Sept. 25.

Bibliography: *Acta Sanctorum* Sept. 7:79–102. HERICUS, "De gestis episcoporum Antissiodorensium," *Patrologia Latina*, ed. J. P. MIGNE (Paris 1878–90) 138:231–236. *Monumenta Germaniae Historica: Concilia* 1.1: 178–184. J. LEBEUF, *Mémoires concernant l'histoire civile et ecclésiastique d'Auxerre*, ed. A. CHALLE and M. QUANTIN, 4 v. (Auxerre 1848–55) v.1. G. LE BRAS, "L'Organisation du diocèse d'Auxerre à l'époque mérovingienne," *Études de sociologie religieuse* (Paris 1950—) 1:27–38.

[P. COUSIN]

AUNEMUND OF LYONS, ST.

Bishop; d. Mâcon, France, Sept. 28, 658. He was reared at the court of Dagobert I and Clovis II and probably held an official position there before his appointment to the archbishopric of Lyons. According to Bede (*Eccl. Hist.* 5.19), in 653 BENEDICT BISCOP and WILFRID stopped at Lyons during their journey to Rome and were hospitably received by Aunemund, who is called Dalfinus in Bede's narrative. The archbishop of Lyons was so favorably impressed by Wilfrid that he offered him "the government of a large part of France" (*ibid.*) and his niece as wife. Determined upon a different course of life, Wilfrid declined and went on to Rome, but after his visit there he returned to Lyons and remained for three years, received the tonsure from Aunemund, and was present when Queen BATHILDIS, a second Jezebel in the opinion of Wilfrid's biographer Stephen Eddi, sent soldiers and "commanded that the bishop be put to death" (*ibid.*). Most modern scholars, however, put the blame for Aunemund's murder on Ebroin (d. 681), Mayor of the Palace of Neustria. His body was returned to Lyons, and his name appears in the martyrologies of that city at the beginning of the ninth century.

Feast: Sept. 28.

Bibliography: *Monumenta Germaniae Historica: Scriptores rerum Merovingicarum* 6:197, 199–200. *Acta Sanctorum* Sept. 7:673–698. J. L. BAUDOT and L. CHAUSSIN, *Vies des saints et des bienhereux selon l'ordre du calendrier avec l'historique des fêtes* (Paris 1935–56) 9:579–581. A. M. ZIMMERMANN, *Lexikon für Theologie und Kirche*, ed. J. HOFER and K. RAHNER (Freiburg 1957–65) 1:1106. H. LECLERCQ, *Dictionnaire d'archéologie chrétienne et de liturgie*, ed. F. CABROL, H. LECLERCQ, and H. I. MARROU (Paris 1907–53)10.1:219–226. C. LEFEBVRE, *Bibliotheca sanctorum* 1:1311. R. AIGRAIN, *Catholicisme* 1:1064–65.

[H. DRESSLER]

AURAEUS, ST.

Fifth-century bishop of Mainz, Germany. RABANUS MAURUS and the oldest sources link Auraeus and his sister, (St.) Justina, as martyrs in the time of Attila (*c.* 451). GAMS places Auraeus's martyrdom at the time of the destruction of Mainz by the Vandals (406). The monk Sigehard (thirteenth century) wrote of SS. Auraeus and Justinus as the patron saints of Heiligenstadt. Justinus is called a deacon in a Heiligenstadt MS printed by the Bollandists, and he is sometimes called a subdeacon. Some would recognize in Justina and Justinus two persons, but such a coincidence of names in the circumstances of our information on Auraeus is unlikely.

Feast: June16.

Bibliography: *Acta Sanctorum* June 4:37–79. P. GAMS, *Series episcoporum ecclesiae catholicae* (Graz 1957) 289. H. LECLERCQ, *Dictionnaire d'archéologie chrétienne et de liturgie*, ed. F. CABROL, H. LECLERCQ, and H. I. MARROU (Paris 1907–53) 11.1:26.

[W. A. JURGENS]

AUREA OF CÓRDOBA, ST.

Widow martyr; b. Córdoba or Seville, *c.* 810; d. Córdoba, July 19, 856. An Arab of noble descent, Aurea (or Aura) lived as a Christian with her mother Artemia in the monastery of Cuteclara for more than 30 years after the martyrdom of her brothers Adulfus and John in Córdoba. When her own relatives from Seville brought her before the *cadi*, also related to her, Aurea agreed to abandon Christianity but immediately returned to the practice of her faith. Persecuted a second time, she denied that her previous lapse had been genuine and, constant in her faith, was imprisoned and executed by decree of the emir. Her body was thrown into the Guadalquivir with the bodies of thieves and was never recovered. She was included in the Roman martyrology in 1583.

Feast: July 19.

Bibliography: EULOGIUS, *Memoriale sanctorum, Patrologia Latina*, ed. J. P. MIGNE (Paris 1878–90) 115:815–818. A. LAMBERT,

Dictionnaire d'histoire et de géographie ecclésiastiques, ed. A. BAUDRILLART et al. (Paris 1912) 5:706–707. E. P. COLBERT, *The Martyrs of Córdoba, 850–859* (Washington 1962) 263–264.

[E. P. COLBERT]

AURELIAN OF ARLES, ST.

Archbishop; d. Lyons, France, June 16, 551. He was elected to the See of Arles to succeed Auxanius in 546. Pope VIGILIUS wrote four letters to him between 546 and 550, the first of which (Aug. 23, 546) named him papal vicar for Gaul, i.e., for the kingdom of Childebert I (d. 558), son of CLOVIS, and granted him the PALLIUM. On Oct. 28, 549, Aurelian signed the *acta* of the Fifth Synod of Orléans; his signature appears in the second place, immediately after that of the archbishop of Lyons.

In its first canon the synod condemned EUTYCHES and NESTORIUS; it discussed further the matter of the THREE CHAPTERS. This problem concerned three bishops, THEODORE OF MOPSUESTIA, Ibas of Edessa, and THEODORET OF CYR, whom the Monophysites particularly detested and whom Emperor JUSTINIAN I felt should be condemned by papal approval of the Three Chapters. Consulted on this subject by Aurelian, Vigilius, who was not disposed to give in to the emperor and anxious to avoid weakening the authority of the Council of CHALCEDON of 451, replied in vague terms on April 29, 558. He made a special point of begging the bishop of Arles to use his influence with Childebert to prevent Totila, the Arian King of the Ostrogoths, who had captured Rome, from harming the Catholics living there.

Showered with endowments by Childebert, Aurelian founded a monastery and a convent at Arles. His rule for the former, consisting of a prologue, 55 chapters, and an appendix, was based on that of St. BENEDICT and of his predecessor CAESARIUS OF ARLES; it later entered the collection of BENEDICT OF ANIANE. Aurelian wished the monks to be educated, imposed a strict cloister, and went beyond the Benedictine rule in prescribing additional Psalms for the hours. The rule for the nuns of Saint Mary of Arles, in 40 articles, was, with variations, modeled on the rule for the monks. The archbishop was interred in the basilica of the Holy Apostles (Saint-Nizier), where his epitaph was discovered in 1308.

Feast: June 16.

Bibliography: *Regula, Patrologia Latina,* ed. J. P. MIGNE (Paris 1878–90) 68:385–408. *Monumenta Germaniae Historica: Epitolae* 3:124–126, letter to Théodebert. *Acta Sanctorum* June 4:91–94. *Gallia Christiana* 1:537–539. P. JAFFE, *Regesta pontificum romanorum ab condita ecclesia ad annum post Christum natum 1198,* ed. F. KALTENBRUNNER (Graz 1956) 1:119–122. C. J. VON HEFELE, *Histoire des conciles d'après les documents originaux*

(Paris 1907–38) 3.1:157–164, synod of Orléans of 549. L. ROYER, *Dictionnaire d'histoire et de géographie ecclésiastiques,* ed. A. BAUDRILLART et al. (Paris 1912) 4:231–243, esp. 235–236, 242. S. BOSQ, *ibid.* 5:741. H. FUHRMANN, *Lexikon für Theologie und Kirche,* ed. J. HOFER and K. RAHNER (Freiburg 1957–65) 2 1:1107.

[J. DAOUST]

AURELIAN OF RÉOMÉ

First theorist of GREGORIAN chant, flourished in mid-ninth-century France. His importance rests upon his treatise, *Musica disciplina,* (c. 830; reproduced in *Scriptores ecclesiastici de musica potissimum* 1:27–63). In the introduction he mentions his name and that of his monastery and Bernard to whom the treatise is dedicated (*Bernardo, futuro nostro Archiepiscopo*). No other facts about his life can be ascertained. His treatise is divided into two parts: chapters one to seven, which transmit the theories of music inherited from Greek authors through Boethius, Cassiodorus, and Isidore; and chapters eight to twenty, which deal with the chant repertory of his day. In the second part he reveals his familiarity with the practical performance of chant, treating at great length how antiphons are to be intercalated into psalm singing, both at Mass and at Office. In this context he speaks for the first time of modes, using the terminology *protus, deuterus, tritus,* and *tetrardus* in authentic and plagal forms. Several passages show his knowledge of a primitive notation and chironomy. The treatise is, thus, a juxaposition of ancient theory and contemporary practice without achieving a synthesis of the two.

Bibliography: A. GASTOUÉ, *Dictionnaire d'archéologie chrétienne et de liturgie* 1.2:3150–51. H. HÜSCHEN, *Die Musik in Geschichte und Gegenwart,* ed. F. BLUME (Kassel-Basel 1949–) 1:858–859. J. P. PONTE, *The "Musica disciplina" of Aurelianus Reomensis,* 3 v. (Unpub. doctoral diss., Brandeis U. 1961), a rev. text, tr. and commentary. L. A. GUSHEE, "The *Musica disciplina* of Aurelian of Réomé: A Critical Text and Commentary" (Ph.D. diss. Yale University, 1963); "Aurelian of Réomé" in *The New Grove Dictionary of Music and Musicians, v.1,* ed. S. SADIE (New York 1980) 702–704. J. P. PONTE III, "The *Musica disciplina* of Aurelianus Reomensis" (Ph.D. diss. Brandeis University, 1961). D. M. RANDEL, ed., *The Harvard Biographical Dictionary of Music* (Cambridge, Massachusetts 1996).

[R. G. WEAKLAND]

AURELIUS OF ARMENIA, ST.

Bishop in Armenia; d. Milan, 475. Nothing is known of his early life. He is said to have brought from Cappadocia to Milan the relics of St. DIONYSIUS, Bishop of Milan (355) who had died in exile, and who was to have been buried in Milan beside Aurelius. In 830 Bishop Noting of Vercelli removed his body to Hirsau, where he founded a church of which Aurelius is patron. The earliest vita, now lost, was written in the ninth century, probably at Reichenau. The extant life is an eleventh-century revision by Abbot Williram of Ebersberg.

Feast: Nov. 9; formerly Sept. 13.

Bibliography: *Act Sanctorum* Nov. 4:128–142. *Bibliotheca hagiograpica latina antiquae et mediae aetatis* (Brussels 1898–1901) 1:819–822. F. LUTZ, *Württemberger Vierteljahrbücher,* NS 33 (1939) 29–72. M. MILLER, *Lexikon für Theologie und Kirche,* ed. J. HOFER and K. RAHNER (Freiburg 1957–65) 1: 1108.

[R. BROWNING]

AURELIUS AND SABIGOTONA, SS.

Martyrs; b. Córdoba, *c.* 820; d. Córdoba, July 27, 852. From Christian-Moslem homes, they lived as Christians in secret before and after their marriage. When the persecution of Christians began in 851, they devoted themselves to asceticism and chastity. They placed their two young daughters in the care of a monastery, and with their relatives Felix and Liliosa, let their faith be known publicly. Both couples were tried before the *cadi* and imprisoned before execution. At the same time George, a monk from Jerusalem, was slain for his denunciation of the prophet Mohammed. The relics of the five martyrs were buried in and near Córdoba. In 858 USUARD and Odilard translated relics of Aurelius, Sabigotona (or Natalia), and George to Paris. Usuard included the five martyrs in his martyrology on August 27, but they are included in the Roman Martyrology on October 20 (translation) and July 27.

Bibliography: EULOGIUS, *Memoriale sanctorum* 2.10, and Aimoin, *Translatio* in *Patrologia Latina,* ed. J. P. MIGNE (Paris 1878–90) 115:772–792, 939–960. E. P. COLBERT, *The Martyrs of Córdoba, 850–859* (Washington 1962).

[E. P. COLBERT]

AUREOLE (NIMBUS)

Latin, *aureolus* (of gold, golden), one of a number of symbols or devices used in pagan and Christian art and archeology to suggest or represent divinity, holiness, or eminence in the person portrayed. Closely related are the halo, *mandorla,* and glory. Such symbols antedate the Christian era; in Greek and Roman art the heads of gods, heroes, and distinguished citizens were often portrayed with a circle of light or a rayed fillet about the head.

In Christian art the aureole is the symbol of divinity and has therefore been reserved for representing the Holy Trinity and Christ. It has been extended only to representations of the Virgin Mary. The aureole consists essentially in a radiant field of light that appears to surround the whole body of the person represented and to emerge from it. The rays of light may be attached directly to the body, or they may be separated from it. If the rays are not attached directly to the body, they give the impression of emerging from a central point, such as the head. The rays of light depicted in the aureole terminate in pointed flames, which may be white in color, or may be tinted with the colors of the rainbow. Early examples of the aureole are usually white, but in Renaissance art gold and blue are often used.

The Italian name for the aureole is *mandorla,* since the symbol was often enclosed in an almond-shaped framework. In some instances, instead of a framework, seven doves are used to frame the *mandorla,* denoting the seven gifts of the Holy Spirit. Other examples show a group of angels as a framework, although this form is less frequent. The *mandorla* is often used to depict certain mysteries of the life of Christ and the Blessed Virgin Mary, such as the Last Judgment or the Assumption into heaven.

The distinction between an aureole and a halo is somewhat vague, but the word "halo" refers most often to the symbol of divinity or holiness, which is placed about the head of the one represented, and which is enclosed in a geometrical figure. The shape and the form of the halo differ according to the degree of divinity, holiness, or eminence of the person depicted. The type of geometrical figure used to enclose the halo suggests also the degree of eminence in the person for whom it is used. The triangle, for example, is used exclusively for representations of the Holy Trinity, and particularly for the Father, the three sides of the triangle suggesting the Trinity. The halo used to portray Christ, the Blessed Virgin Mary, and the saints is circular. The cross within the circle is used only for Christ, and suggests the redemption through the cross. To indicate her eminence among the saints, the halo of the Virgin is elaborately decorated, while those of the saints are less ornate.

The square halo is used to distinguish eminent persons from canonized saints, and often for persons who may still be living. Thus for example, a square halo may be used to depict a living person such as the founder of a religious order, or of a great monastery, or a great benefactor. Since the square is thought to be a less perfect geometrical figure than the circle, it suggests Earth, while the circle suggests heaven. Polygons are also used, the hexagon being preferred; the sides of the polygon suggest the virtues or have some other allegorical meaning. The glory is merely a luminous glow that combines the halo surrounding the head and the aureole surrounding the whole body. This combination is used to suggest the most exalted state of being, and therefore it is reserved for God as the lord of heaven, or for Christ as the judge of mankind, or for some other function associated closely with divinity.

See Also: HALO.

Bibliography: J. H. EMMINGHAUS, *Lexikon für Theologie und Kirche,* ed. J. HOFER and K. RAHNER, 10 v. (2d, new ed. Freiburg 1957–65) 7:1004–05, with bibliog. H. LECLERCQ, *Dictionnaire d'archéologie chrétienne et de liturgie,* ed. F. CABROL, H. LECLERCQ, and H. I. MARROU, 15 v. (Paris 1907–53) 12.1:1272–1312, with list of illus. K. KEYSSNER, *Paulys Realenzyklopädie der klassischen Altertumswissenschaft,* ed. G. WISSOWA et al. (Stuttgart 1893–) 17.1 (1936) 591–624. M. COLLINET-GUÉRIN, *Histoire du nimbe* (Paris 1961). L. RÉAU, *Iconographie de l'art chrétien,* 6 v. (Paris 1955–59) 1:423–425. K. KÜNSTLE, *Ikonographie der christlichen Kunst,* 2 v. (Freiburg 1926–28) 1:25–29.

[E. E. MALONE]

AURILLAC, ABBEY OF

Former Benedictine monastery of Saint-Pierre (later Saint-Gèraud), founded *c.* 890 by Count GERALD OF AURILLAC in a valley where the present town of Aurillac was later to develop. Very early an integral part of the Cluniac Reform, the abbey flourished in the 10th century, numbering among its monks Gerbert, the future Pope SYLVESTER II. Aurillac remained a powerful BENEDICTINE abbey to the end of the 16th century, holding as many as 74 dependent priories scattered over various provinces of France. But decline set in with the practice of COMMENDATION and culminated in the secularization of 1561, which transformed the abbey into a collegiate church of secular priests. It was ruined during the WARS OF RELIGION (1569), and the church was not restored until 1642. Since the suppression of its college of priests in 1790 during the French Revolution, the church, which has undergone modifications, has been the main church of Aurillac in the Diocese of Saint-Flour.

Bibliography: G. SITWELL, ed. and tr., *St. Odo of Cluny . . . St. Gerald of Aurillac* (New York 1958). *Gallia Christiana,* v. 1–13 (Paris 1715–85), v. 14–16 (Paris 1856–65) 2:438–447. G. M. BOUANGE, *Histoire de l'abbaye d'Aurillac,* 2 v. (Paris 1899). P. FONTAINE, *Dictionnaire d'histoire et de géographie ecclésiastiques,* ed. A. BAUDRILLART et al. (Paris 1912–) 5:757–760.

[L. GAILLARD]

AURORA IAM SPARGIT POLUM

A hymn once ascribed to St. Ambrose, but now generally considered to be the work either of Pope GREGORY THE GREAT (Blume) or of an anonymous author as late as the eighth century (Szövérffy). Its four "Ambrosian" strophes are in octosyllabic iambic dimeter. In vigorous but rather obscure language, the hymn greets the dawn and prays for the shadows of night and evil to disappear so that its singers may be fit to welcome both this and the last day. Appearing in the ninth century "Later Hymnal" (which Blume considers Irish in origin, though Wilmart and others call it "Old Benedictine"), it spread widely throughout Carolingian Europe as a hymn for Lauds on Saturdays. Closely following earlier usage, the Roman Breviary (1632) assigned it to the Saturday office from the Octave of Epiphany to the first Sunday in Lent, and from the Octave of Corpus Christi to the first Sunday of Advent. The MOZARABIC Breviary of 1775 assigned it to Matins for Saturdays in Lent. Among its English translators are E. Caswall ("The dawn is sprinkling in the East," *Lyra Catholica,* 1849) and R. Campbell ("The morn has spread its crimson rays," *St. Andrew's Hymnal,* 1850).

Bibliography: B. STÄBLEIN, ed., *Monumenta monodica medii aevi* (Kassel-Basel 1956–) 1.1:665. *Analecta hymnica* 51:xiii–xxi, 34. C. BLUME, *Unsere liturgischen Lieder* (Regensburg 1932) 149–152. M. BRITT, ed., *The Hymns of the Breviary and Missal* (new ed. New York 1948). J. CONNELLY, *Hymns of the Latin Liturgy* (Westminster MD 1957). A. WILMART, "Le Psautier de la reine," *Revue Bénédictine* 28 (1911) 341–376. J. JULIAN, ed. *A Dictionary of Hymnology* (New York 1957) 93–94. A. S. WALPOLE, ed., *Early Latin Hymns* (Cambridge, Eng. 1922) 279–280. F. J. E. RABY, *A History of Christian-Latin Poetry from the beginnings to the Close of the Middle Ages* (Oxford 1953) 36–40. J. SZÖVÉRFFY, *Die Annalen der lateinischen Hymnendichtung* (Berlin 1964–65)

[J. DU Q. ADAMS]

AURORA LUCIS RUTILAT

An Easter hymn consisting of eleven 4-line strophes of somewhat loose iambic dimeter, unusually rich in end-rhyme and internal alliteration, which is strikingly exemplified in the first strophe. The theme is one of joy at the Lord's triumphant Resurrection, successive incidents of which banish fear among His disciples. Vivid and extremely visual in development despite a simple vocabulary, this hymn may be a stylistic ancestor of late Carolingian rhythms and Easter TROPES. It was admired by Abelard. Once attributed to St. Ambrose, it is now thought to be of Gallican origin (Wilmart); it was composed sometime between the sixth and the early eighth centuries (Bulst, Szövérffy). Besides St. Ambrose's authentic works, this and *Christe, qui lux es et dies* are the only pieces common to the two hymnal traditions most widespread before the Carolingian liturgical reforms (Blume, Raby, Walpole).

The hymn was traditionally sung at Matins or Lauds daily from Low Sunday to the Ascension—although the

MOZARABIC Breviary of 1502 assigns it to Prime in Paschaltide. It was divided and drastically altered by the compilers of the Roman Breviary of 1632. Lines 1 to 16, scarcely recognizable as *Aurora caelum purpurat,* were left at Lauds between Low Sunday and Ascension (and in the Dominican rite, at Matins during Paschaltide); lines 17 to 32 (*Tristes erant Apostoli*) were assigned to Vespers and Matins of Apostles and Evangelists during Paschaltide; and lines 32 to 44 (*Paschale mundo gaudium,* originally *Claro paschali gaudio*), to Lauds of that Office. Pope PIUS V was responsible for the division at line 32 and for the association with the Common of Apostles. The best known English translations of both versions of this hymn, whole and divided, are those by E. Caswall (1849) and J. M. Neale (1852 and later).

Bibliography: B. STÄBLEIN, ed., *Monumenta monodica medii aevi* (Kassel-Basel 1956–) 1.1:665, melodies. *Analecta hymnica* 51:89–90. M. BRITT, ed., *The Hymns of the Breviary and Missal* (new ed. New York 1948). C. BLUME, *Unsere liturgischen Lieder* (Regensburg 1932) 53–59, 188–190. A. BYRNES, ed., *Hymns of the Dominican Missal and Breviary* (St. Louis 1943), nos. 27, 28. W. BULST, ed., *Hymni Latini antiquissimi LXXV* (Heidelberg 1956) 114–115. J. CONNELLY, *Hymns of the Roman Liturgy* (Westminster MD 1957) No. 59, A. WILMART "Le Psautier de la reine," *Revue Bénédictine* 28 (1911) 341–376. J. JULIAN, ed., *A Dictionary of Hymnology* (New York 1957) 94–96. A. S. WALPOLE, ed., *Early Latin Hymns* (Cambridge, Eng. 1922) xi–xx, 356–359. F. J. E. RABY, *A History of Christian-Latin Poetry from the Beginnings to the Close of the Middle Ages* (Oxford 1953) 36–40. J. SZÖVÉRFFY, *Die Annalen der lateinischen Hymnendichtung* (Berlin 1964–65).

[J. DU Q. ADAMS]

AUSCULTA FILI

A bull of Pope BONIFACE VIII indicting King Philip IV the Fair of France and announcing a synod for the reform of the Church in France. It was written Dec. 5, 1301. It is the most striking example in practice of Boniface's theory of the direct power of the papacy over the secular order. "Wherefore, dearest son," Boniface wrote, "let no one persuade you that you have not a superior or that you are not subordinate to the head of the ecclesiastical hierarchy. For he is a fool who so thinks, and whosoever pertinaciously affirms it brands himself an unbeliever." Philip burned the letter publicly in Paris. He circulated an emended version, together with a pretended answer to Boniface that started "your great fatuousness . . . in temporalities we are subject to no one." There followed two years of bitter controversy culminating at Anagni, in September 1303. Though the original bull was burned, copies are extant in Boniface's *Register* in the Vatican Archives. The register copy is mutilated, since CLEMENT V had the more forceful passages erased.

Bibliography: J. RIVIÈRE, *Dictionnaire d'histoire et de géographie ecclésiastiques,* ed. A. BAUDRILLART et al. (Paris 1912)

5:767–768; *Le Problème de l'Église et de l'État au temps de Philippe le Bel* (Paris 1926). T. S. R. BOASE, *Boniface VIII* (London 1933).

[L. E. BOYLE]

AUSTIN, JOHN

Controversialist and hymnodist; b. Walpole, Norfolk, England, 1613; d. London, 1669. Austin (pseudonym, William Birchley) was educated at St. John's College, Cambridge, where he was contemporary with John SERGEANT. He became a Catholic *c.* 1640 and left the university for Lincoln's Inn. For some time he was tutor to Walter Fowler of St. Thomas's, Staffordshire, a noted recusant literary center. He probably visited the English Hospice at Rome in 1640 and 1646. During the Interregnum Austin belonged to the group of Catholics (White, Sergeant, Holden, Belson, Keightley) who advocated allegiance to the Cromwellian government and hoped for a degree of toleration and sympathy from the Independents. Austin's *Christian Moderator* (1651–53) advocated toleration for recusants from an Independent viewpoint and was quick to use T. Hobbes's *Leviathan* (1651) in support of its arguments. When the question of toleration arose again at the Restoration, Austin published *Reflexions upon the Oathes of Supremacy and Allegiance* (1661). He published also *Devotions in the Ancient Way of Offices* (1668), a version of the primer with original hymn versions, which ran through several editions. There had been several recusant primer versions before this, but Austin's was adapted for non-Catholic use by Theophilus Dorrington (*Reform'd Devotions,* 1686) and Susanna Hopton (*Devotions in the Ancient Way of Offices,* ed. G. Hickes, 1700); both these works were often reedited. The hymns in Austin's book also found their way separately into other non-Catholic collections, most notably S. Speed's *Prison Pietie* (1677), John Wesley's *Collection of Psalms and Hymns* (Charlestown 1737), and Roundell Palmer's Book of Praise (1862).

Bibliography: O. SHIPLEY, *Annus Sanctus* (New York 1884). J. JULIAN, ed., *A Dictionary of Hymnology,* 2 v. (2d ed. London 1907; repr. New York 1957) E. HOSKINS, *Horae Beatae Mariae Virginis* (London 1901). J. GILLOW, *A Literary and Biographical History or Bibliographical Dictionary of the English Catholics from 1534 to the Present Time,* 5 v. (London-New York 1885–1902; repr. New York 1961) 1:87–90.

[T. A. BIRRELL]

AUSTRALIA, THE CATHOLIC CHURCH IN

An account of Australian developments invites a comparison with the United States. The two nations occupy roughly the same area, and each had its beginnings as a group of New World colonies of the British crown. Geographically and historically, however, there are great contrasts. The immensely fertile territory occupied by the United States promised a spectacular extension of European experience in the midst of familiar seasons and natural surroundings. The weathered and largely barren land mass of the Australian continent—geologically, the oldest of our planet—with flora and fauna which defied European expectations, promised a very different and challenging experience. Shortly before European settlement commenced in Australia, the American colonies had formed a federation, as they declared themselves independent of British rule. It would be more than a century before the Australian colonies formed a federation under the British crown as constitutional monarch. Although this arrangement gave Australia complete independence in the shaping of national life and policy, most Australians see the symbolic step of severing the nation's link with the British crown as inevitable. The details of appropriate constitutional arrangements for an Australian republic, however, are the subject of ongoing debate.

Another important difference affects directly the life of the Christian church. The American colonies were established by Christian communities wishing to safeguard their religious freedom. As a consequence, the American psyche has an enduring respect for religious institutions. The culture of white Australia had its origins at the time when the Enlightenment was bringing widespread disillusionment with religious traditions. As a consequence, religious concerns have never had a prominent place in the nation's psyche. As Australia's best known historian has put it, for most Australians the Christian faith has become "a whisper in the mind and a shy hope in the heart."

Ambiguous Beginnings. From ancient times it was taken for granted that a Great South Land must exist to balance the land masses of the northern hemisphere. Spanish and Portuguese mariners based in Peru came close to discovering the Australian continent in the 16th and 17th centuries. One of them, Pedro Fernandez de Quiros—who believed himself providentially destined to discover the elusive land for Christ and set out with the blessing of Pope Clement VIII—thought he had discovered the coast of the unknown continent when he reached a cluster of islands known today as Vanuatu. He named the cluster Austrialia del Espiritu Santo. In the 17th century seamen of the Dutch East India Company explored

Capital: Canberra.
Size: 2,967,909 sq. miles.
Population: 19,169,083; about 92% of the population are Caucasians, 7% Asians, and 1% Aboriginals and others.
Languages: English and a variety of native languages.
Religions: Christianity is the predominant religion in Australia. The two largest Christian denominations are the Roman Catholic Church (26% of total population) and the Anglican Church of Australia (also 26% of total population). Other Christian denominations include Uniting Church, Presbyterian, Methodist and Orthodox communities, collectively comprising about 25% of the total population. There are small but significant Jewish, Muslim and Buddhist communities.

the western coast of the continent, but were repelled by its barren, inhospitable character. In the end, it was the English navigator Captain James Cook who discovered the rich east coast of the continent, which he claimed for the British crown (Botany Bay, April 1770). White settlement of the Australian continent had a direct link with the Declaration of Independence of the American colonies. During the 18th century, the British government sent convicted felons to North America as cheap labor on the plantations of the colonies. When this was no longer possible, another destination had to be found if British prisons were not be become overcrowded. Captain Cook's discovery gave rise to a plan to establish a penal colony on the Australian east coast. On January 26, 1788, a fleet finally arrived in Port Jackson, the site of Sydney, Australia's largest city, to establish the new colony. About a thousand souls disembarked, of whom over 700 were prisoners of the crown.

Although lawbreakers formed by far the greater part of the convict group, under the draconian property laws of the time the majority were transported for crimes which today would be considered minor offences. Social and political reformers were a significant group, and of these the largest contingent came from Ireland. The statistics now available make clear the challenge faced by the church in ministering to the needs of Catholics transported to New South Wales, as the new colony was called. When transportation finally ended in 1853, a total of 168,000 convicts had been transported to Australia. Of these, about 40,000 had been sent directly from Ireland. Of those sent from England it is estimated that about 8,000 were Irish born and probably a similar number were of Irish descent. Between 1795 and 1804 nearly 6,000 Irishmen were transported to New South Wales, many of them persons of ability and education who had been involved in the Irish struggle for independence. During the period of transportation, the number of free settlers who came to Australia was roughly the equivalent of the number transported as convicts.

Metropolitan Sees	Suffragans
Adelaide	Darwin, Port Pirie
Brisbane	Cairns, Rockhampton, Toowoomba, Townsville
Melbourne	Ballarat, Sale, Sanhurst, Ukrainian eparchy of Ss. Peter & Paul of Melbourne
Perth	Broome, Bunbury, Geraldton
Sydney	Armidale, Bathurst, Broken Bay, Lismore, Maitland-Newcastle, Parramatta, Wagga Wagga, Wilcannia-Forbes, Wollongong
Exempt Sees	Canberra, Hobart, Greek-Melkite Eparchy of St. Michael of Sydney, Maronite Eparchy of St. Maron of Sydney.

Arrival of the First Catholic Priests. The religious welfare of the convicts was overlooked in the first official instructions prepared for the governor of the colony. Later he was directed ''to enforce a due observance of religion.'' The religion to be observed, of course, was that of the Church of England; and nothing was done by the colonial authorities to provide for the religious needs of Catholics. Three Catholic priests were among the early convicts, convicted for alleged complicity in the 1898 rebellion. Although all three returned to Ireland some years later, one, Rev. James Dixon, was allowed for a time to exercise his ministry (1803–04). An uprising of 400 Irishmen in 1804, however, caused Governor Phillip to withdraw Dixon's authorization and salary. He remained in Sydney for four more years, ministering privately to Catholics, with several Protestants contributing to his support. Brought to Australia by the laity, the Catholic faith was kept alive by the laity, who, in 1816, took the initiative of petitioning the Holy See for the services of a priest in their midst.

The clergy who played an important part in the early history of the Australian Church were a colorful group. Many were dedicated missionaries from various European countries, drawn by the needs of a penal colony on the other side of the world. They also included a number of restless souls who were happy to leave behind them the constraints of the old world. Jeremiah O'Flynn, who had himself appointed prefect apostolic as a result of the New South Wales petition, was one of the latter. Although neither the colonial office nor the vicar apostolic of London endorsed his appointment, he set out for the colony at his own expense, hoping that proper authorization would follow. He arrived in November 1817. When it became clear to the governor that he had no official authorization, a warrant was issued for his arrest. He evaded the authorities for several months, eventually being deported in 1818. O'Flynn's escapade had an unexpected consequence. The matter of his deportation was raised in the House of Commons, and a Catholic mission in Australia was eventually authorized.

Canonical Establishment. The first canonical status of the Catholic Church on the Australian continent placed it under the jurisdiction of Dom. Edward Slater OSB, vicar apostolic of the Cape of Good Hope with jurisdiction over an immense territory including Madagascar, Mauritius, New Holland (as the Australian continent was still called) and a large portion of the Pacific Ocean. Two Irish priests volunteered their services and arrived in Sydney in May 1820: John Joseph Therry, who is remembered as the founding father of the church in many regions of New South Wales, and Phillip Conolly, who went to a second penal colony at Hobart in Van Dieman's Land (later renamed Tasmania, Australia's only island state).

Some years later, the affairs of the church were entrusted to an English Benedictine, William ULLATHORNE, who arrived as vicar-general in 1833. This remarkable priest later became bishop of the English diocese of Birmingham, where he was John Henry NEWMAN's ordinary; he participated in the First Vatican Council, leaving in his correspondence a valuable source of information concerning its debates. Although only 27 years of age when he arrived in Sydney, Ullathorne provided vigorous leadership for the struggling Catholic community. He studied closely the social effects of the convict system, and during a visit to England campaigned brilliantly for its suppression. The Holy See accepted Ullathorne's recommendation that the Australian mission be separated from Mauritius. In May 1834, New Holland became a vicariate in its own right, and in September 1835 Ullathorne's friend and teacher at DOWNSIDE ABBEY, John Bede POLDING OSB arrived at Australia's first bishop.

In 1841, when convict transportation to eastern Australia officially ended, the total population was 211,000 of whom 40,000 were Catholics. There were 15 churches, several chapels, 31 schools, 24 priests and a community of nuns. In 1842 two new sees (Hobart in Tasmania and Adelaide in South Australia) were established and Dr. Polding became an archbishop. Despite unpromising beginnings, the Australian colonies had evolved a relatively prosperous society relying heavily upon the wool industry. The character and bearing of its people surprised and impressed visitors from overseas. In the 1850s, shortly

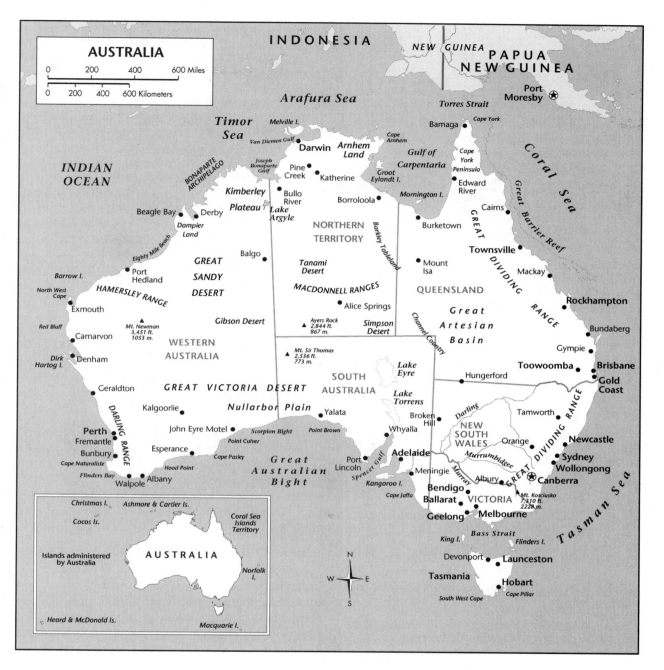

after the close of the convict era, major discoveries of gold attracted large numbers of immigrants, and within a decade the white population trebled. Between 1841 and 1891, the Catholic population increased from 40,000 to 713,000.

Before the federation of the various colonies in 1901, dioceses were established in their various capitals, and by the end of the 19th century most had become archdioceses with suffragan dioceses (Adelaide established in 1842, an archdiocese in 1887; Hobart established in 1842, an archdiocese in 1887; Perth established in 1845, an archdiocese in 1913; Melbourne established in 1847, an archdiocese in 1874; Brisbane established in 1859, an archdiocese in 1887). An Apostolic Delegation representing the Holy See was established in 1914, and an Apostolic Nunciature was established in 1973. There were six synods of Australian bishops—two provincial synods, Sydney (1844) and Melbourne (1859), and four plenary synods held in Sydney (1885, 1895, 1905, 1937). On the occasion of visits to Australia by Pope Paul VI and Pope John Paul II, Australia has hosted consultations of bish-

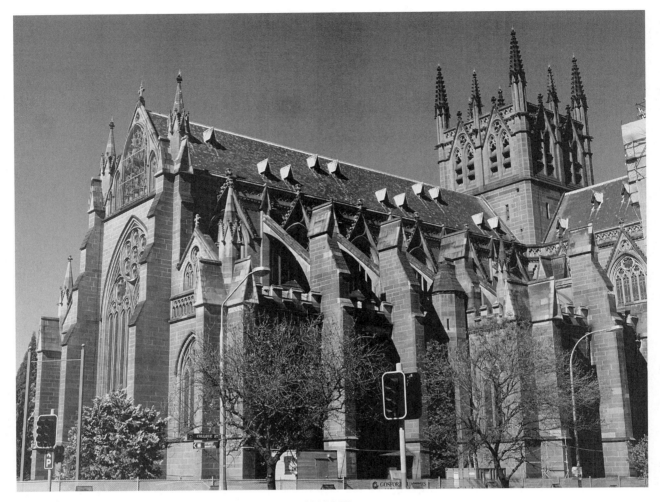

St. Mary's Cathedral, Sydney, Australia. (©Christine Osborne/CORBIS)

ops of the region. Australian bishops participated in the Synod of the Church in Oceania, held in Rome in 1999. In 1928 the 29th International Eucharistic Congress was held in Sydney.

Influences Shaping a Local Church. Since the vast majority of Catholics in the Australian colonies were of Irish descent, it was inevitable that the Irish connection should prove an important factor in the development of the Catholic Church. Australia's first bishop had other ideas, however. John Bede Polding was a remarkable pioneering bishop. Usually traveling on horseback, sometimes undertaking precarious sea journeys along the treacherous coastline, Polding undertook heroic missionary journeys caring for his flock across the length and breadth of the continent. In his pastoral letters he gave expression to a rich theological vision and expressed farsighted hopes for his new land, stressing themes uncommon in 19th century Catholicism such as the domestic ''church'' of the family and frequent reception of the sac-

raments. Whenever he could, he met ships bringing convicts to Sydney, ministering personally to their needs and championing their interests. Called before a Royal Commission inquiring into the tragic situation of indigenous Australians, Polding affirmed in memorable terms their human dignity and rights, and condemned the injustices to which they were being subjected. Formed in the Benedictine tradition, so important in the history of the English Church, this idealist envisaged a future for the Australian Church nurtured by the monastic tradition. He worked to foster a Benedictine community associated with his cathedral church in Sydney and with the early developments of the local church. He became the founder of an Australian institute of religious sisters in the Benedictine tradition which has made an important contribution to the history of Australian Catholicism.

Inevitably, as the population of the colonies expanded rapidly and the majority of the clergy who ministered to them came from Ireland, the march of history left Pold-

A Roman Catholic church in Australia. (©E.O.Hoppe/CORBIS)

ing's Benedictine dream behind. Polding's successor as archbishop of Sydney, Roger Bede Vaughan, also an English Benedictine, recognized the signs of the times and made plans for the formation of a local clergy.

The Irish Church, which was to prove so influential in the formation of the Australian Church, was itself undergoing a transformation under the leadership of Paul Cardinal Cullen. A former rector of the Irish College in Rome, Cullen became a trusted advisor to the Holy See, and one of the most influential figures in the English speaking world of 19th century Catholicism. Cullen's leadership—he eventually became the cardinal archbishop of Dublin—put a strong Counter-Reformation stamp on the Irish Church as it emerged from centuries of oppression and persecution. Several of Cullen's kinsmen and proteges were appointed bishops in Australia and New Zealand, the most important of whom was Patrick Francis MORAN, who succeeded Vaughan as archbishop of Sydney (1884–1911) and was to become Australia's first cardinal.

Sectarian discrimination was very real in colonial Australia, and it was inevitable that Catholic awareness should be colored by the struggles of the Irish people. As a derivative of Paul Cullen's Irish Church, the Australian

Church came to share in the strengths and weaknesses of its Irish counterpart—triumphalistic in mood, with the shamrock and the harp much in evidence at the opening of its ever increasing numbers of churches and presbyteries. At least one Australian bishop, however, was unhappy with the prevailing mood. Robert Dunne, an Irishman like his fellow bishops, succeeded James O'Quinn, a protege of Cardinal Cullen, as bishop of Brisbane (1882-1917, appointed archbishop in 1887). The church, Dunne declared, should be building up families and community, not erecting impressive churches and presbyteries; it should be finding common cause with Protestant neighbors to build a healthy nation, rather than adopting the confronting and intolerant stance that was developing. The later situation of the Australian Church would probably have been very different if Dunne had been able to persuade his fellow bishops to his views.

Penal and Social Reform. The life of the Australian Church has been influenced by the developments in the country's cultural and political life. Mention has already been made of the impressive stand taken by Australia's first bishop on behalf of the indigenous population. Like Ullathorne, his predecessor in Sydney, and Bishop Wilson, his suffragan in Hobart, Polding also concerned himself with the reform of the penal system. With the increase in population brought by the gold rushes, Australian bishops concerned themselves with immigration, some of them setting up schemes of sponsorship which were not always appreciated in the sectarian climate of the times—Bishop Quinn of Brisbane was accused of trying to transform Queensland into "Quinn's land." Caroline Chisholm, a Catholic laywoman, did much to assist migrant women who were easily victimized upon their arrival in colonies. Her work has been commemorated by the printing of her portrait on Australian currency. The men and women of the St. Vincent de Paul Society, in parish conferences throughout the nation, have come to constitute by far the largest organisation extending charity to the needy of Australian society.

Church and Politics. With the majority of Catholics belonging to the working class, and often discriminated against by an unfriendly establishment, it is not surprising that Catholics were prominent in the struggle for social justice in Australian political life. Cardinal Moran gave his encouragement to the foundation of the Australian Labour Party (ALP), initiating an association which has often been significant in Australian politics. When the Australian colonies were entering into federation as a single nation governed by a national House of Representatives and a Senate house of review, controversy broke out when it was learned that the possibility of Cardinal Moran's standing as a candidate for the senate was being considered.

During the First World War, Daniel MANNIX, the charismatic leader and orator who had come some years before as coadjutor to the archbishop of Melbourne (he was ordinary 1917–1963, dying at the age of 99) became a national figure when he campaigned against a referendum promoted by Australia's wartime prime minister, which would have opened the way to the conscription of Australians for the European conflict. The fact that the proposal was twice rejected by the majority of citizens was due in no small measure to the efforts of Archbishop Mannix—efforts, he made clear, which he undertook, not as a Catholic bishop, but as a concerned citizen.

Catholic Action. Under the leadership of Mannix, Melbourne was to become an important center of Catholic Action initiatives, modelled on the Jocist Movement in Europe. Many thousands of Australian Catholics joined the Young Christian Workers, the National Catholic Girls Movement, the Young Christian Students and the National Catholic Rural Movement. Archbishop Mannix encouraged talented young Catholics to involve themselves in the intellectual and political life of the nation, setting the stage for one of the most dramatic developments in Australian church-state relations. The vigor

and successes of Catholic Action organizations led to the setting up of the National Secretariate of Catholic Action (NSCA) under the direction of a gifted young Melbourne lawyer, B.A. Santamaria. One of the most widely known activities of the NSCA was the publication of social justice statements authorized by the bishops of Australia. These annual statements applied the principles of papal social encyclicals to current challenges faced by Australian society. Inaugurated in 1940, the series ended in 1962 with a pastoral letter of the hierarchy concerning the recently convened Second Vatican Council.

Church and Communism. As the Cold War developed in the aftermath of World War II, the NSCA became involved in initiatives to counter the influence of the Communist party. The war had provided a climate in which every major industrial union in Australia except one was controlled by communists or was in the process of coming under their control. The NSCA organized groups of concerned citizens, mainly Catholics, who worked in Australian cities to counter communist infiltration tactics. The organization became known as The Movement. It cooperated with the Australian Labour Party with considerable success between 1948 and 1953. But its growing influence was seen as a threat by elements of the leadership of the ALP, and a split developed within the old party, leading to the formation of a breakaway Democratic Labour Party. As a consequence, the ALP was denied the possibility of office for several successive elections. Catholics found themselves deeply divided by the issue. There was a division of opinion among Australia's Catholic bishops as to the appropriateness of the strategies of The Movement as a form of Catholic Action. A ruling of the Holy See was sought. As a result a restructuring took place. Official church groups were given exclusively to the promotion of adult education under the direction of the local bishop. To carry on the fight against communism in the political sphere, those involved created an independent National Civic Council in 1957.

Catholic Education. Perhaps the most significant initiative of the Australian Church was its role in establishing a comprehensive system of elementary and high school education. By the 1930s it had virtually achieved its goal of providing a Catholic school for every Catholic child. This remarkable effort, which was to leave its mark on the ethos of the Catholic community, was the outcome of a complex history. Education began in the Australian colonies as a makeshift system of schools, largely administered by the churches. The government provided grants of land and financial assistance for the construction of buildings and teacher salaries. It was an uneven system with many shortcomings. During the decade from 1870 to 1880 the governments of the colonies assumed more direct control of public education. It was unfortunate that the architects of state educational programs were strongly influenced by the tendencies of Enlightenment liberalism. "Free, compulsory and secular education" became the avowed goal of the new state systems.

The Catholic bishops saw this development as constituting a danger to Catholic youth. Against all odds, they mobilized the Catholic community to build a separate school system without any help from public funds. Catholics shouldered the burden; by the 1930s it was normal for every Catholic parish to have its own primary school, and the number of secondary schools was increasing rapidly. Religious orders took up the cause and made a truly heroic contribution. Between 1870 and 1890 ten more religious orders entered the Australian Catholic educational system. By the mid-20th century their membership was predominantly Australian by birth.

After the Second World War, however, an increase in the birth rate, a huge influx of Catholic migrants from Europe, and the steady increase in numbers seeking higher education, confronted the Catholic education system with a crisis of survival. Catholic protests at the injustice of their taxes being used to maintain the public system while they financed their own independent system began to be heard, as old sectarian prejudices diminished. Political realism recognized that the collapse of the Catholic system would constitute national disaster, and the government began to give direct assistance. In 1963 a national election made it clear that the Australian public was not opposed to so-called "state aid" to Catholic schools. Today, although the bulk of funds necessary to maintain the Catholic system comes from the government through a commission set up by the bishops, a significant segment of funding still comes from school fees and parochial revenues.

Until the recent past, the only institutes offering tertiary education established by the Catholic Church in Australia were seminaries for the education of the clergy (diocesan and regular), and colleges preparing religious and lay persons for work as teachers. Building upon preparations made by his predecessor Roger Vaughan, one of the first initiatives of Patrick Moran when he arrived from Ireland as archbishop of Sydney was the establishment, within his diocese, of St Patrick's College Manly (1885) for the education of local clergy. Dedicated in 1888, this seminary served the dioceses of the whole country until the 1920s, when the establishing of provincial seminaries began in all the mainland states of the commonwealth—Victoria in 1923, Queensland in 1941, South Australia and Western Australia in 1942. Priests from Irish seminaries continued coming to Australia after World War II, but by the mid-1960s, the vast majority of Australian priests were local-born and trained in the 40 ecclesiastical colleges and seminaries. Since the Second Vatican Council Catholic, colleges of theology have opened their doors to non-clerical students, and many hundreds of whom have gained degrees.

In 1991, the Australian Catholic University, an independent institution funded by the Australian government, was established through the amalgamation of four colleges of advanced education occupying eight campuses originally established as training colleges for teachers and nurses, in the Australian Capital Territory, New South Wales, Queensland and Victoria. In 1992, Notre Dame University Australia, affiliated with the famous university of the same name in Indiana, was established in West Australia.

Religious Communities. Twelve congregations of Sisters were founded in Australia: six in the 19th century, and six in the 20th century. Blessed Mary MACKILLOP, who founded the Sisters of St. Joseph of the Sacred Heart, was beatified in Sydney by Pope John Paul II (1995), the first Australian to be so honored. There were five institutes of Brothers. While the vast majority of Australian religious at that time were engaged in the education apostolate, women and men were also working in Australia's 80 Catholic hospitals, which made an important contribution to the life of the nation.

The Challenge of Renewal. The distinctive mood of the Australian derivative Counter-Reformation Church did not prepare Australian Catholics for the challenges of implementing Vatican II's program of renewal. At the time the council was convoked, the Australian Church, like that of most of the developed world, was in the midst of a period of building and expansion made possible by postwar prosperity. It inevitably proved difficult for the Australian Church to make the transition from the self-confident institutional emphasis which it had so long taken for granted to one reflecting the gospel call to discipleship and service. The internal cultural upheaval was further aggravated by external cultural dislocation arising from massive immigration and pervasive undercurrent of secularism in the wider society.

The period of institutional changes initiated by the Second Vatican Council coincided with the far-reaching demographic changes that were taking place in Australia. At the same time the fragile new-world culture of Australia began to be profoundly affected by the upheaval taking place in the contemporary Western world. Since World War II the Australian population has grown from 7.5 to over 18 million. Australian immigration has no parallel in relative terms in this period apart from the state of Israel. In 1981, one-fifth of the population had been born overseas, constituting with its offspring a significant segment of the population. Immigrants have come from the British Isles and northern Europe, and in increasing numbers from Mediterranean countries, from the Middle East and from Asia. In the 1980s, 3.6 percent of the population of Sydney were of Asian extraction, and the percentage continues to grow each year. With the influx of immigrants, Catholics have come to constitute the largest denomination in Australia.

The attitudes of ordinary Australians have helped to form a welcoming and relatively tolerant multicultural society. As this demographic change called for policy decisions, the Australian hierarchy set its face against the establishing of national parishes after the earlier U.S. model. The main burden of ministry for immigrant Catholics fell to a dedicated corps of migrant chaplains, most of them from overseas. If people from other cultural backgrounds have sometimes found the undemonstrative style of worship of Australian congregations discouraging, early evidence would seem to indicate that integration into the local church has been relatively successful.

The Challenge of Secularism. As a new world culture, Australia's way of life has been profoundly affected by the crisis through which the Western world is passing. Permissiveness and hedonism have made great inroads into the nation's traditional value system in the period since the Second Vatican Council. In 1901, almost all (98 percent) of Australians declared themselves to be Christians; in the 1991 census 12.9 percent described themselves as having no religion. Australia has been described as the most secularized country in the contemporary world. There is an innocence, however, to the secularity of Australians: sacralization is absent, not because it has been rejected, but because it was never present as a significant aspect of Australia's national psyche.

Liturgical Renewal. It was especially in the reform of liturgical worship that Catholics experienced the impact of the changes brought by the council. By and large, Australian parishes have been relatively successful in their efforts to renew liturgical life, producing a liturgy that combines broad participation and local self-expression with the dignity of the Church's great liturgical tradition. The nostalgia of older Catholics for the popular devotions which were so much a part of the culture of the Counter-Reformation may well indicate that the new liturgical forms have not yet succeeded in giving worshipers an effective access to the divine mystery in its transcendence. The increasing cultural and linguistic diversity of the Australian Church resulting from immigration continues to challenge efforts at creating cohesive liturgical celebrations, and integration of immigrants with older Catholic communities.

Pastoral Renewal. Vatican II has given dedicated Australian Catholics access to a far more inspiring life of Christian faith. A greater familiarity with the Scriptures and a liturgy that elicits a more active participation in the sacramental mysteries have fostered a number of grassroots renewal movements that would have been out of place in the institutionalized Catholicism of yesteryear: parish faith sharing groups, the CURSILLO MOVEMENT, MARRIAGE ENCOUNTER, groups concerned with the study of the Scriptures and with issues of social justice, etc. Among these, Charismatic Renewal groups have proved a help to many Catholics who sensed the need to embark upon a more personalized faith journey. An increasing number of women have concerned themselves with the rights of women in society and in the church, and women are making many creative contributions to Church life. The Rite of Christian Initiation for Adults, in which the baptized play a fundamental part in preparing candidates for reception into full communion with the Church, has come to be accepted as an important part of the life of the local community.

Increasing Lay Involvement. As in other parts of the Western world, the Australian Church has witnessed a dramatic decline in the number of clergy and religious in the wake of Vatican II. On the eve of the council, in 1963, there were 1463 candidates in Australian seminaries; in 1994 there were 287; in 2000 they number no more than a few dozen. The mean age of the clergy has increased by 25 years. Many parish communities are being deprived of the leadership which has so long been provided by the ordained and religious. While many of the clergy have recognized the need for more lay involvement and collaborative style of leadership, the hierarchical clerical mindset of the Church is still influential, even among some of the younger clergy. As reflective Catholics ask themselves who will lead their communities when ordained ministers are no longer available, it is being recalled that the Catholic Church was brought to Australia by the a pioneering laity. The laity will once again have to take up the task of responsibility for the growth of the Church.

One area where the laity has taken on greater responsibility is the field of Catholic education. As Australia enters the third Christian millennium very few religious remain on the teaching staff of Australian Catholic schools. Lay administration has become the norm. The Catholic education system faces a challenging future. Its establishment forged closely knit parish communities committed to the assumption that no sacrifice was too great in the cause of Catholic education. The number of Catholic children passing through church schools, however, has continued to diminish: 80 percent in 1950; 70 percent in 1965; 55 percent in the early 1980s. The pluralism of the nation's value systems makes it increasingly difficult to find effective ways of promoting the distinctive ethos for which the church schools came into existence.

The Church and Indigenous Australians. While the genius of Catholicism found an early expression in the championing of the dignity and rights of the indigenous people who inhabited the continent for tens of thousands of years before white colonization, until the recent past Catholics by and large shared in an outlook which turned a blind eye to their tragic history of oppression and exploitation. There is a growing appreciation of the profound accord that is possible between the wisdom of the traditional lore of Australia's aboriginal people and the truth of Christian faith. Speaking to indigenous Australians in Alice Springs in 1986, of the ''dreaming'' of their traditional mythologies, Pope John Paul II said: ''For thousands of years you have lived in this land and fashioned a culture that endures to this day. And during all this time, the Spirit of God has been with you. Your 'Dreaming' which influences your lives so strongly that, no matter what happens, you remain forever people of your culture, is your own way of touching the mystery of God's Spirit in you and in creation.''

Bibliography: E. CAMPION, *Australian Catholics* (Ringwood Vic. 1987). H. N. BIRT, *Benedictine Pioneers in Australia*, 2v (London 1911). N. J. BYRNE, *Robert Dunne: Archbishop of Brisbane* (St. Lucia Q 1991). R. FOGARTY, *Catholic Education in Australia 1806–1950*, 2v (Melbourne 1959). C. HALLY, *Migrants and the Australian Catholic Church* (Melbourne 1980). R. M. MACGINLEY and T. KELLY, *The Church's Mission in Australia* (Blackburn Vic. 1988). J. N. MOLONY, *The Roman Mould of the Australian Catholic Church* (Melbourne 1969). J. G. MURTAGH, *Australia: The Catholic Chapter* (Sydney 1959). E. M. O'BRIEN, *Life and Letters of Archpriest John Therry: The Foundation of Catholicism in Australia*, 2 v (Sydney 1922); *The Dawn of Catholicism in Australia*, 2 v (Sydney 1928). P. O'FARRELL, *The Catholic Church and Community: An Australian History* (3rd ed. Kensington N.S.W. 1992). J. THORNHILL, *Making Australia: Exploring Our National Conversation* (Newtown N.S.W. 1992). N. TURNER, *Catholics in Australia: A Social History* (Blackburn Vic. 1992).

[J. THORNHILL]

AUSTREBERTA, ST.

Benedictine abbess; b. Thérouanne, Artois, France *c.* 635; d. Abbey of Pavilly, Normandy, France, Feb. 10, 704. Her father, Badefridus, was apparently a member of the Merovingian royal family; her mother, Framehilda (d. *c.* 680), of German royal blood, was later honored as a saint and had a feast celebrated on May 17 at the Abbey of Sainte-Austreberta at Montreuil-sur-Mer. While Austreberta (Eustreberta) was still a young girl, her parents contracted her marriage, but she secretly took the veil in 655–656 under the spiritual direction of Omer, Bishop of Thérouanne. Shortly thereafter, with parental

permission, she entered the abbey of Port-le-Grand in Ponthieu. She was prioress there for 14 years until Philibert, founder of Jumièges, persuaded her to become abbess of his foundation at Pavilly. Her relics were transferred to Montreuil-sur-Mer in the ninth century and were venerated also at the cathedral of Saint-Omer, but they were burned in 1793.

Feast: Feb. 10.

Bibliography: J. MABILLON, *Acta sanctorum ordinis S. Benedicti* (Venice 1733–40) 3:23–38. *Bibliotheca hagiograpica latina antiquae et mediae aetatis* (Brussels 1898–1901) 1:831–838. L. VAN DER ESSEN, *Dictionnaire d'histoire et de géographie ecclésiastiques*, ed. A. BAUDRILLART et al. (Paris 1912) 5:790–792. *Analecta Bollandiana* 54 (1936) 9. A. M. ZIMMERMANN, *Lexikon für Theologie und Kirche*, ed. J. HOFER and K. RAHNER (Freiburg 1957–65) 1:1122. A. M. ZIMMERMANN, *Kalendarium Benedictinum* (Metten 1933–38) 1:194–197. R. AIGRAIN, *Catholicisme* 1:1077–78.

[P. BLECKER]

AUSTREGISILUS (OUTRIL), ST.

Abbot and bishop; b. Bourges, France, November 29, 551; d. there, May 20, 624. It seems that Austregisilus (Aoustrille, Outril, Outrille) was born of noble but not very wealthy parents; and when he was about 24, he was sent to live at the court of King (St.) Guntram (d. 593). There, according to his vita, he was falsely accused of forging an authorization for one of the courtiers and was ordered to fight a duel to prove his innocence. By divine intervention, it is reported, his traducer was kicked to death by his horse on the morning of the day appointed for the ordeal. Austregisilus then left the court, became a priest, and was appointed abbot of St. Nicetius. He was consecrated bishop of Bourges on Feb. 13, 612. In October 614 he attended a synod that met at Paris, and his name appears eighth in the list of 79 bishops who signed the decrees (*Monumenta Germaniae Historica: Concilia* 1:191). He is reported to have granted a hermitage at Bourges to AMANDUS, later the apostle of Belgium.

Feast: May 20.

Bibliography: *Bibliotheca hagiograpica latina antiquae et mediae aetatis* (Brussels 1898–1901) 1:835–843. *Acta Sanctorum* May 5:60–69. *Monumenta Germaniae Historica: Scriptores rerum Merovingicarum* 4:188–200. L. BOURNET, *Dictionnaire d'histoire et de géographie ecclésiastiques*, ed. A. BAUDRILLART et al. (Paris 1912) 5:792–793. A. M. ZIMMERMANN, *Kalendarium Benedictinum* (Metten 1933–38) 2:207. R. AIGRAIN, *Catholicisme* 1:1078. H. PLATELLE, *Bibliotheca sanctorum* 2:630. A. ZIMMERMANN, *Lexicon für Theologie und Kirche*, ed. J. HOFER and K. RAHNER (Freiburg 1957–65) 1:1122.

[H. DRESSLER]

Capital: Vienna.
Size: 32,366 sq. miles.
Population: 8,131,111 in 2000.
Languages: German.
Religions: 6,342,266 Catholics (78%), 40,664 Protestants (5%), 34,998 other (4.5%), and 1,713,183 with no religious affiliation.
Archdioceses: Vienna, with suffragans St. Pölten, Linz, and Eisenstadt; Salzburg, with suffragans Gurk-Klagenfurt, Graz-Sechau, Innsbruck, and Feldkirch. Wettingen-Mehrerau is an abbey nullius. There is also an ordinariate for the Byzantine-rite Church in Austria.

AUSTRIA, THE CATHOLIC CHURCH IN

Because of its location along the Danube, Austria has long been considered at the crossroads of Europe. Also known as Österreich, the Republic of Austria is bordered on the south by the Alps, Italy and Slovenia, on the west by Switzerland and Liechtenstein, on the north by Germany and the Czech Republic, and on the east by Hungary and Slovakia. Located in a temperate climatic zone, Austria possesses a landscape that ranges from alpine peaks to river valleys; most of its settlement occurred at the foothills of the Alps and the Carpathian mountains. It is one of the most heavily wooded countries in Europe.

Modern Austria is a remnant of the Austro-Hungarian empire that was dissolved after World War I. From the Middle Ages onwards, its history was dominated by the house of Hapsburg. After World War I, the country suffered economic depression and political instability. In 1938, while occupied by German troops, the region became a province of the Third Reich and was known as Ostmark. Following World War II, it was occupied by Allied forces and divided into four zones. The modern Republic of Austria dates from Oct. 26, 1955 when the Allies agreed to leave Austria in exchange for a promise of perpetual neutrality. A federal state consisting of nine independent regions, Austria joined the European Union in 1995 and adopted the Euro monetary system in 1999.

The essay that follows is divided into four parts. Part one deals with the early history of Austria; part two covers the Church from 1500 to 1848; part three covers the history of Austria through World War II; and part four follows the Church into 2000.

Christianity to 1500

The Christianization of Austria was an irregular process that developed in three phases stretching over several centuries. Christian origins date from Roman times and produced several martyrs. St. Florian, who held an administrative post in the Danubian province of Noricum, hastened to Lauriacum (Lorch, near Enns), the capital of the province during Diocletian's persecution and there suffered a martyr's death in 304. St. SEVERIN, the apostle of Noricum, died at Favianis (Mautern, near Krems) on Jan. 8, 482, after working among the Roman population, which was suffering from the invasion of the Germanic Rugieri. Ecclesiastical organization developed early. Bishoprics existed at Lauriacum, Virunum (Zollfeld near Klagenfurt), Teurnia (St. Peter im Holz near Spittal on the Drau) and Aguntum (near Lienz in eastern Tyrol). The bishopric established in Sabiona (Säben, in southern Tyrol) during the 6th century was a forerunner of the medieval bishopric of Brixen (Bressanone); St. INGENUIN was bishop there c. 590.

The second period of Christianization coincides with the conversion of Bavarians during the 6th century. St. COLUMBAN and his disciples Saints GALL and EUSTACE were active among the Alamannians in Bregenz c. 600. A century later St. RUPERT founded the bishopric of Salzburg. A descendant of Rhenish-Franconian counts related to the Carolingians, Rupert came to Bavaria as part of the missionary efforts of the Frankish Empire in the early 8th century. He founded the Abbey of St. PETER, the oldest monastery still existing in Austria, as well as the Abbey of NONNBERG, where he installed his niece as abbess. When St. BONIFACE organized the Church in Bavaria, Salzburg became a diocese, evolving into the principle see in Bavaria with St. VIRGILIUS as bishop. A prominent exemplar of Irish-Scottish MONASTICISM on the Continent, Virgilius consecrated the cathedral of St. Rupert in 774. The monastery of Maria Saal was founded to serve the mission to the Slavonians. Among the other new foundations were the monasteries of Mondsee (748), KREMSMÜNSTER (777) and the collegiate monastery of Innichen, San Candido, (769).

The third period of Christianization began with CHARLEMAGNE's establishment of an empire and his expansion eastward. After the fall of Duke Tassilo III, Bishop Arno became Charlemagne's trusted adviser for ecclesiastical matters in the east. At the king's command he received the PALLIUM from Pope Leo III (798), and Salzburg became the head of the ecclesiastical province of Bavaria until its secularization (1803). Gaining the area between the Drau, Raab and Danube Rivers after the defeat of the Avatars, Salzburg, followed by Passau and Regensburg, extended its mission activity eastward to Moravia, where it encountered the apostles of the Slavs, Saints CYRIL and Methodius, who had come westward from Constantinople. In the early Carolingian period the monastery of St. FLORIAN was established in Lorch; and

St. Pölten was established as a daughter-house of the Bavarian monastery of TEGERNSEE.

Medieval Growth. The victory of OTTO I over the Magyars and the erection of a fortified frontier along the Danube made the Church more secure against invasions from the east. The frontier district was entrusted in 976 to the counts of Babenberg; it was called Ostarrichi in 996. About that time Bishop PILGRIM OF PASSAU (971–991), whose name is immortalized in the *Nibelungenlied*, undertook a mission to the Hungarians that led to the conversion of Grand Duke Geza and to the baptism of his son St. STEPHEN I. Pilgrim failed to secure metropolitan jurisdiction over Moravia and Hungary for the See of Passau, though he forged charters to support his claim that Passau should be independent of Salzburg, and his diocese became one of the largest in Germany. The vigorous missionary activity of the Austrian bishops was crowned by the consecration of St. Stephen's Cathedral in Vienna by Bishop Reginbert, who died in 1147. The most eminent bishop of Passau was St. ALTMANN (1065–91), a firm supporter of the popes during the INVESTITURE struggle. He founded St. Nikola in Passau as

well as the Benedictine Abbey of GÖTTWEIG (1094), and reformed the monasteries of St. Florian and St. Pölten. Conrad I (1106–47), a leading reform bishop, made 14 foundations of canons in his diocese and introduced their reforms into his own chapter.

Monastic Life. Benedictine foundations and reforms were characterized by the spirit of monastic renewal emanating from GORZE and CLUNY. LAMBACH ABBEY, established in 1056 by Adalbero of Würzburg on his family estate, was immediately affected by the Gorze reform. Next was Kremsmünster, where Bishop Altmann installed the monk Theodorich de Gorze as a reforming abbot. After that came MELK, where in 1089 Abbot Sigibold organized a monastic community that was richly endowed by Margrave Leopold III and placed under papal protection in 1110. St. COLOMAN, Austria's first patron saint, was interred at Melk in 1014. The CLUNIAC REFORM came to Austria through the abbeys of St. BLASIEN, Siegburg, near Cologne and HIRSAU in Swabia. In 1094 Bishop Udalrich of Passau brought some Benedictines to Göttweig from St. Blasien in the Black Forest. The main support for Hirsau reform in Austria was ADMONT

Franz II (Francis II) (1768–1835), Emperor of Austria, last Holy Roman Emperor.

Abbey, built in 1074 on the property of Blessed HEMMA of Gurk (d. 1045) and peopled with monks from St. Peter. Under the reforming abbots Wolfhold (1115–37) and Gottfried (1137–65) it influenced most religious houses in Bavaria and Austria. During the 11th century the Benedictines established St. Lambrecht, St. Paul, Ossiach (before 1028) and Millstatt (*c.* 1070).

The Margrave St. Leopold III (1095–1136), patron saint of Austria, transformed a frontier district into a territorial duchy. He gave his residence of Klosterneuburg near Vienna to Canons Regular of St. Augustine. He also brought CISTERCIANS from MORIMOND to HEILIGENKREUZ, where his son OTTO, later bishop of Freising, had become a monk. From Heiligenkreuz, St. Bernard's monks went to ZWETTL (1138), Baumgartenberg (1142) and LILIENFELD (1202). Cistercian monasteries also arose in VIKTRING (Carinthia, 1142) and WILHERING in Upper Austria (1146). The monasteries of the old orders, joined by the MENDICANT ORDERS (DOMINICANS in 1217 at Friesach, FRANCISCANS in 1230 in Vienna), established a firm structure lasting until the dissolution of religious houses by Emperor Joseph II. In the 14th century, the House of HAPSBURG favored the AUGUSTINIANS and CARTHUSIANS.

Austria's frontier position prevented the creation of a regular bishopric. Unsuccessful attempts in this direction were later made by the dukes of Babenberg, the Bohemian King Premysl Ottokar and Duke Rudolph IV, the last-named a founder of the University of Vienna (1365) and of a collegiate chapter at St. Stephen's Cathedral. Emperor Frederic III established Vienna (1469) and Wiener Neustadt as bishoprics. Within the Diocese of Salzburg private bishoprics appeared at Gurk (1072), Seckau (1218) and Lavant (1225). Some of the prominent bishops of Brixen were St. ALBUIN (975–1005); Poppo, who became Pope DAMASUS II (1048); Reginbert, who, before 1138, brought PRAEMONSTRATENSIANS to Wilten and Benedictines to St. Georgenberg; and Hartmann (1140–64), who sent Augustinian canons from Klosterneuburg to Neustift. Together with the bishops of TRENT, the bishops of Brixen exercised sovereign rights in Tyrol until the local counts of Andechs-Meranien, Tyrol and Görz contested those rights.

1500 to 1848

The crises of the Protestant revolt and the energetic policies of Catholic reform led the Church in Austria into its Baroque age, when it displayed a distinctive piety in its devotional practices and its religious art forms. In the subsequent period of JOSEPHINISM it experienced the good and evil effects of the ENLIGHTENMENT, surrendering, under force, much of its internal government to state controls.

Reformation and Counter Reformation. Rivalry for power between the Hapsburg rulers and their subject nobles was a prominent factor in the rise of Protestantism within Austria. Thus the growth of Protestantism was promoted by the nobles, who as lords of their estates could encroach upon the administration of parishes, confiscate Church property and replace Catholic pastors with Evangelical preachers. The towns and marketplaces were influenced by the example of the nobles, so that at the time of its widest spread, the REFORMATION would claim three-quarters of the Austrian population. The alliance between the nobles and LUTHERANISM was cemented by the continuing threat of Turkish invasion. The cost of protecting the frontier against Turkish forces could not be met by the contributions of the churches and monasteries alone. The emperor relied upon taxes within the states of the empire that were often exchanged for religious concessions. Furthermore, the condition of the clergy did not provide a strong weapon of defense against the spread of Protestantism and spiritual indifference and moral breakdown continued to increase. The Bishop of Salzburg, Cardinal Matthäus LANG (1519–40), was more successful than others at fighting the new faith, despite his unclerical private life. As sovereign and bishop, he was able to prevent local peasant uprisings and thus hinder the victory of Lutheranism. Protestantism was like-

Innsbruck, Austria. (Wolfgang Kaehler)

wise aided by the favor of Maximilian II (1564–76), who throughout his reign remained in sympathy with creedal innovation and allowed his lords to accept the Confession of AUGSBURG, until finally, for dynastic reasons, he withstood the power of the Protestant states. His son Rudolph II (1576–1612) pursued a policy of Catholic support.

Of particular importance in withstanding Lutheranism in Austria were the JESUITS, who were invited by King Ferdinand I (emperor 1556–64). Peter CANISIUS arrived in Vienna in 1552, where he taught theology in the newly founded Jesuit college, preached in the cathedral of St. Stephen and administered to many of the abandoned parishes of Lower Austria. Other Jesuits lectured at the universities, served as confessors and advisers of Hapsburg princes and founded colleges and spiritual gymnasia at Innsbruck (1562), Graz (1573), Hall, Leoben, Linz, Klagenfurt, Krems, Judenburg and Steyr. They were joined by the Capuchins *c.* 1600. St. LAWRENCE OF BRINDISI served as an army chaplain with the imperial troops in Hungary and founded Capuchin convents in Vienna and Graz.

The year 1580 marked the beginning of substantial Catholic recovery in Vienna and Lower Austria. Arch-

duke Ernest governed Upper and Lower Austria for his brother Emperor Rudolph II, while the latter resided in Prague. Ernest was aided by the gifted Cardinal Melchior KLESL, who had been converted from Protestantism by the Jesuit court chaplain George Scherer, and assumed the role of leader of the COUNTER REFORMATION. He became the provost of St. Stephen's Cathedral and chancellor of the University of Vienna (1579), councilor of the bishop of Passau in Lower Austria (1580), imperial councilor of Rudolph II (1585), court chaplain and administrator of the Diocese of Wiener Neustadt (1588) and bishop of Vienna (1598). Melchior's diplomatic skill and firmly rooted Catholicism prepared him to confront the political and religious problems of the period. With much personal risk he won back the cities of Baden, Krems and Stein and restored organization to the dioceses under his control.

In Styria and Carinthia the champion of reform was Archduke Charles, who was aided in his reform schemes by the capable bishops Martin Brenner of Seckau and George Stobäus of Lavant. In the Tyrol and neighboring territories, not so touched by Evangelicalism, Archduke Ferdinand and his successor, Archduke Maximilian, enacted comprehensive policies of reform. Maximilian en-

Otto of Freising, Austrian bishop and historian, stained glass window, probably 12th century, Abbey of Heiligenkreuz, Vienna.

couraged the regular visitations of parishes enacted by the reform synod of 1603, built a school for Jesuits at Innsbruck, established one Capuchin convent at Meran (1616) and assisted in founding another at Neumarkt. The court provided good example by the conduct of its household and the foundation of a house at Hall for gentlewomen interested in works of charity. Archduke Ferdinand's second wife, Anna Caterina de Medici, established convents for the Servites at Innsbruck and later became a Servite Tertiary under the name of Anna Juliana. From 1621 the Servites of Innsbruck spread over most of the crown lands of the Hapsburgs as far as the Rhine.

In the Archdiocese of Salzburg, Catholic restoration dates from the provincial synod of 1569, the work of the Dominican Feliciano NINGUARDA. His work was continued by archbishops Wolfdietrich of Reitenau (1587–1612), Mark Sittich of Hohenems (1612–19) and Paris, Count of Lodron (1619–53), who made Salzburg a cultural center. During the tenure of Archbishop Leopold Anton FIRMIAN (1724–44), Lutherans throughout Salzburg formed into a league. In 1731 he responded by publishing an edict demanding their recantation or emigration, and within ten years over 30,000 had immigrated to East Prussia, Hanover and the North American colony of Georgia.

The major source of Protestant strength in Austria was concentrated in the land along the Enns River, where the hard-fought struggle of the Protestant states for religious liberty took place. The principal combatants were the noble families of Jörger and Starhemberg, and especially George Erasmus of Tschernemble, who abandoned Lutheranism for Calvinism. The fraternal discord within the House of Hapsburg aided Protestantism and kept it a threat in Upper Austria. Burckhard Furtenbacher (d. 1598) at Lambach, Alexander of Lacu (d. 1612) at Wilhering, Anthony Wolfrat (d. 1639) at Kremsmünster and other prelates continued the work of Church renovation, while in Passau Archduke-bishops Leopold (1597–1626) and Leopold Wilhelm (1626–62) kept Catholicism strong. However, it was in FERDINAND II of Inner Austria (emperor 1619–37) that the Counter Reformation would have its most sincere and consistent leader. His Catholicism alienated the Bohemians, who rebelled in 1618 under Frederick V, ruler of the Palatinate and leader of the Protestant Union. Their forceful protests occasioned the Thirty Years' War, which terminated any compromise between the two. Ferdinand's forceful reign drove the nobles of Upper Austria into open revolt and into alliance with the Calvinists. The victory of the Catholic League in the battle of the White Mountain (Nov. 8, 1620) decided the fate of Protestantism in Austria by forcing the rebellious nobles to accept Catholicism or emigrate.

The Baroque Age. As a result of the Counter Reformation, Austria remained Catholic and the Hapsburgs became Catholicism's chief defenders in the Thirty Years' War and in the struggle against Western Christendom that ended with the defeat of the Turks before the walls of Vienna (Sept. 2, 1683). This heroic period in Austria's history was characterized by a strong religious zeal.

The 18th century was a time of enthusiasm for the renewed ancient faith, when Church and State joined in close union against the dangers of the Crescent. The baroque piety that flourished (*pietas Austriaca*) affected the devotion to the Trinity, the Eucharist and the veneration of the cross, Our Lady and the saints (*see* BAROQUE CULTURE). The Forty Hours devotion, general Communions, formation of pious confraternities and congregations, processions and PILGRIMAGES became popular. Besides visiting places of pilgrimage such as the Sonntagsberg, near Waidhofen on Ybbs and Stadlpaura, near Lambach, Austrians covered the land with Calvaries, Ways of the

Cross, columns in honor of the Trinity and Mary, wayside chapels and memorials, and statues of St. John of Nepomuc erected on bridges. They listened with pleasure to impressive musical services and to ornate baroque sermons, best represented by the Discalced Augustinian friar ABRAHAM OF SANCTA CLARA (Ulrich Megerle) in Vienna.

Although Saints Joseph, Charles Borromeo, Teresa of Avila, Ignatius of Loyola, Francis Xavier, Leopold and John of Nepomuc had a wide popularity, this was preeminently Mary's century. The Jesuits and various Marian congregations cultivated her devotion and sought her intercession in times of danger from plague or Turk. The numerous sanctuaries to the *Mater dolorosa,* recall these times of distressed Christianity. The oldest of the Marian SHRINES, at Mariazell, had attracted pilgrims since the late Middle Ages. There were sanctuaries also at Maria-Taferl and Maria-Dreieichen. In the environs of Vienna were erected the shrines of Mariabrunn, Maria-Lanzendorf and Maria-Enzersdorf; in Upper Austria, Pöstlingberg near Linz; in Styria, Maria-Trost, near Graz; in Salzburg, Maria-Plain and Maria-Kirchental; in Carinthia, Maria-Saal, Maria-Wörth and the baroque sanctuaries of Maria-Rain, Maria-Loretto (St. Andrä) and Maria-Luggau.

The revival of religious life and monastic discipline introduced a lustrous period of church ornamentation, in which a display of outward pomp was joined to the practice of the monastic ideal. The baroque church followed a pattern of an amply articulate façade, double spire and cupola; its uniform, spacious interior was well lighted, richly decorated with frescoes on ceiling and dome, and pompously ornamented. The most illustrious Austrian baroque architects were Johann Bernhard Fischer of Erlach (1656–1723), whose masterpiece is the Charles's Church in Vienna, begun on behalf of Emperor Charles VI; Lucas of Hildebrand (1668–1745), who created the Vienna Belvedere; and Jakob Prandtauer (1660–1726), who designed the church at Melk and the shrine on Sonntagsberg. Among the baroque architects of monasteries were Carlo Antonio Carlone (d. 1708), whose spirit breathes in the Upper Austrian monasteries of St. Florian, Garsten, Kremsmünster and Schlierbach; Donato Felice d'Allio (d. 1761), creator of the huge monastic building of Klosterneuburg; and Joseph Mungenast (d. 1741), who erected or completed several monasteries in Lower Austria.

Josephinism. While the Hapsburgs had rescued the Church from Protestantism and the threats of Turkish invasion, they gradually attempted to control ecclesiastical government. When the empire evolved into a centralized, utilitarian and materialistic state under the influence of enlightened absolutism, it no longer tolerated the Church as an equal, much less as a superior partner. As a result it took measures to subordinate the Church and fit it into its own apparatus of jurisdiction. During the reign of MARIA THERESA (1740–80), Prince Wenzel Anton von Kaunitz took the preliminary steps toward the system of Church-State relations that came to be known as JOSEPHINISM that brought hardship to the Church.

Josephinism represented a mixture of JANSENISM and the principles of the Enlightenment matured in the soil of Austrian Catholicism. Emperor JOSEPH II (1765–90) wanted to isolate the Austrian Church from Rome and subject it to his control. The Clerical Court Commission became the state office for Church affairs, generating as many as 6,000 Josephinist decrees *in publico-ecclesiasticis.* Cutting deeply into the clerical sphere was the marriage decree (Jan. 17, 1783), which regarded marriage as a civil contract, the privileges and obligations of which were enforced entirely by civil law. In 1783 episcopal and monastic schools for training the clergy were abolished and replaced by general seminaries at Vienna, Louvain, Budapest, Pavia, Graz, Olmütz, Innsbruck, Freiburg, Pressburg (Bratislava) and Prague. By the Patent of Tolerance (Oct. 13, 1784) Lutherans and Calvinists were permitted the private practice of their religion. Of special concern was the dissolution of all monasteries and convents not engaged in pastoral, educational, or social activities. All revenue gained from the sale of such confiscated properties was used to create new parishes and to provide salaries for the clergy.

The emperor's attempt to align diocesan and political boundaries resulted in several changes. In 1785 the Diocese of Wiener Neustadt was incorporated into the Archdiocese of Vienna. The newly instituted Dioceses of St. Pölten (S. Hippolyti) and Linz became suffragans to Vienna. The archbishopric of Salzburg gained as suffragans the enlarged Dioceses of Seckau-Graz and Gurk-Klagenfurt. The Upper Styrian Diocese of Leoben, with its seat at Göss, was united to Sechau. Several bishoprics were incorporated in the Diocese of Lavant, including the district of Völkermarkt in Carinthia, which was detached and given to Gurk in 1859; Lavant itself was transferred to the South Styrian bishopric of Marburg in 1859. The Vicariate of Feldkirch was established for the Diocese of Brixen. In addition, 600 new parishes were founded.

Josephinist Austria also commanded a firm state control of schools and educational methods. In 1774 there appeared the Theresan school regulations, the work of noted school reformer Abbot Johann Ignaz von FELBIGER of Sagan (Silesia). After the suppression of the Society of Jesus in 1773 and the departure of the Jesuits from the faculty of the University of Vienna, a new curriculum was organized by a disciple of FEBRONIANISM, Abbot Franz Stephan von RAUTENSTRAUCH of Braunau (Bohemia). Though viewed with suspicion because of its shortened courses in dogmatic theology, this curriculum put new stress upon Biblical and patristic study, Church history, pastoral theology and catechetics.

During the struggle to halt State encroachments upon ecclesiastical jurisdiction, Christoph Anton MIGAZZI, Archbishop of Vienna (1757–1803), papal nuncios Giuseppe GARAMPI and Giovanni Battista CAPRARA worked to preserve the relationship between Emperor Joseph II and PIUS VI, who journeyed to Vienna in the spring of 1782 in a vain attempt at conciliation. Josephinism was a more stubborn problem than Lutheranism, which disappeared from Austria almost completely during the renewed religious enthusiasm of the baroque period. After the death of Joseph II, Josephinism declined slowly during the reign of Francis I (1804–35), who declared himself hereditary emperor of Austria and abdicated (1806) the crown of the Holy Roman Empire he had assumed as Francis II in 1792. Civil functionaries attempted to keep the Church in subordination and suppressed any movement toward clerical liberty. Meanwhile there developed a type of Josephinist cleric, who was a civil officer and spiritual bureaucrat, performing his service in the office, school and church. During the Napoleonic era and the ensuing Restoration period after the Congress of Vienna (1814–15), Josephinism weakened, much of its decline due to the revival of Catholic life in Austria brought about by the Redemptorist St. Clement HOFBAUER, the ''Apostle of Vienna,'' and his disciples, Anton GÜNTHER, Johann Emmanuel Veith (1787–1876) and Cardinal Joseph Othmar von RAUSCHER, Archbishop of Vienna (1853–75).

The Modern Church: 1848–1945

The Revolution of 1848 brought liberty to the Church but also abolished the privileged position Catholicism had enjoyed as the state religion. After long negotiations, a concordat in 1855 marked the culmination of the movement for renewal. The concordat benefited the Church even though it was infected with a new type of state absolutism that did not collapse until the Austrian military defeats of Solferino and Königgrätz. Contemporary LIBERALISM opposed the concordat as a purely clerical solution of Church-State questions and even as an abdication of the State's power in the face of the Church. Count Antony Alexander of Auersperg, a liberal member of Parliament, called the concordat a printed canossa in which 19th-century Austria atoned in sackcloth and ashes for 18th-century Josephinism. Liberal opposition to the concordat assumed massive proportions after the constitution of February 1861 was promulgated. With the rise

of parliamentary government in Austria new laws doomed the concordat. The Fundamental Law of the State (1867) set forth a strongly liberal code. The May Laws (1868) placed marriages and education completely under state control. In 1870 Austria abrogated the concordat by unilateral action on the pretext that VATICAN COUNCIL I had essentially altered the nature of the papacy by its decrees on papal primacy and infallibility.

Under the leadership of Franz RUDIGIER, Bishop of Linz and Joseph Fessler, Bishop of St. Pölten and general secretary at Vatican Council I, the Austrian hierarchy vigorously opposed the May Laws and sought to mobilize Catholics. Legislation in 1874—the Law on Recognition of Churches—attempting to regulate Church-State relations almost caused a rupture with Rome and the excommunication of Emperor Francis Joseph. An open breach was averted only by the monarch's refusal to sign the legislation (see KULTURKAMPF).

During this period the Austrian Church was forced for the first time to struggle alone and fight for its rights. Aware of the growing social issues, some Catholics initiated a movement for Christian social reform and a program of social legislation in 1870. The pioneer leader in these ventures was Baron Karl von Vogelsang. Unfortunately the Church at first did not grasp all the intimations of Austria's rapid industrialization and consequent labor problems. This failure was not catastrophic because the Catholic conservative movement, supported by the nobility, successfully advocated social legislation earlier than in other countries. However, the tardiness in adapting pastoral outlooks and methods to the needs of a changing environment resulted in large-scale defections of working-class Austrians from the Church. A Christian social movement under the political leadership of Dr. Karl Lueger (d. 1910) defeated the liberal regime in Vienna. Under Franz Schindler (d. 1922) and the conservative Prince Alois of Liechtenstein, the Christian Social party ultimately became the main support of the Catholic ideal in Austria. This was effected only after painful adjustments during which the conservatives, supported by the bishops, tried to secure a papal censure of the Christian Social movement. Fortunately the zealous Joseph Scheicher (d. 1924) won over the younger clergy. In 1907 the conservatives fused with the Christian Social party; their publications were combined in 1911.

Catholics tried to influence public life by organizing unions and associations. The Catholic Union, later styled the Severin Union, originated in 1848. St. Michael's Union, whose original purpose was the defense of the papacy, concerned itself more and more with bringing Catholic interests to public notice. By 1870 popular Catholic associations of patriotic character (Casinos) and associations of journeymen developed. Christian labor unions encountered great opposition from Socialists in the 1890s. Leopold Kunschak and Anton Orel were outstanding in their efforts to aid the young workers. The Catholic Popular Union originated in 1909 as a nonpolitical central organization of Austrian Catholics, embracing all Catholic organizations and unions in the various dioceses until it ended in 1938. To some extent it exercised the functions carried out after 1945 by CATHOLIC ACTION.

The early 20th century witnessed the estrangement of a large portion of the educated classes, as well as the working classes from the Church. The LOS-VON-ROM cost the Church many members. On the other hand, there was a great increase in the number of vocations to religious congregations of women. The development of sodalities and the retreat movement strengthened Catholic life. Henry Abel, SJ, promoted an apostolate among men. Founded in 1892, the Leo-Gesellschaft, fostered Catholic scientific activities. The Catholic Associations of Academicians, especially the Austrian Cartel Unions, fought the spirit of nationalistic liberalism growing within universities and academies. The emergence of a more energetic clergy and the training of Catholic lay elite helped to reinvigorate Catholicism.

The Two World Wars. The end of the Austro-Hungarian Empire came following Austria's declaration of war on Serbia in response to the assassination of Hapsburg Archduke Franz Ferdinand. Following the acceleration of violence into World War I, the empire was dissolved and under the Treaty of St. Germain a greatly diminished Austria was reformed into a republic. While Catholics recalled the glories of the old monarchy more vividly than its shortcomings and grieved at its passing, they also focused on the catastrophic economic conditions in the postwar years. Once the monarchy was ended, hostile attention was refocused on the altar, and from 1918 to 1932 the Church became preoccupied with strong opposition from the socialist Social Democratic party. Searching for a new "secular arm" to support it, the Church discovered the Christian Social party, led by Ignaz SEIPEL. Austrian socialism was Marxist: radical, atheistic and class-conscious. Social Democrats increased their strength by profiting from the disturbed conditions after 1918; their aim was the complete separation of Church and State and the abolition of public recognition of the Church's legal character. Viewing religion as an "opiate of the people," they attacked the Church as an enemy of the proletariat and an arm of capitalism. Defections from the Church reached 30,000 between 1927 and 1928 alone. Jewish publications also joined in the attack.

In this troubled period, Cardinal PIFFL of Vienna stood out as a resolute and far-sighted leader. Ignaz Sei-pel also proved himself a Christian diplomat of European stature as planner and statesman; heading the government, he saved Austria from economic collapse, revolution and Communist rule. Among the evidences of spiritual vitality during this era were the establishment of the Canisiuswerk für Priesterberufe, a society to promote priestly vocations and the charitable association known as Caritas Socialis. New Catholic newspapers included *Wiener Kirchenblatt,* started by Monsignor Mörzinger and the *Reichspost,* published by Frederic Funder. Canon Handlos and Monsignor Rudolf opened an institute for pastoral theology.

Christian Socialist Engelbert Dollfuss became chancellor in 1932 and went to work eradicating the Socialist power base. Dollfuss ratified a concordat with the Holy See and implemented social programs influenced by Catholic thinkers Karl Sonnenschein (d. 1929) and Seipel. He also attempted to end class conflicts by putting into effect the corporative state advocated by Pius XI in the encyclical *QUADRAGESIMO ANNO.* Despite opposition within his own party, Dollfuss gave Austria a new, corporative, constitution that bucked the traditional concept of parliamentary representation and gave much autonomy to the federated states. In order to effect his lofty aims amid growing agitation by advocates of National Socialism, Dollfuss used authoritarian methods. His murder at the hands of Nazi operatives on July 25, 1934 brought an abrupt end to his reforms. In 1938, the Nazis invaded Austria, bringing about the start of World War II.

Bibliography: E. TOMEK, *Kirchengeschichte Österreichs,* 3 v. (Innsbruck 1935–59). J. WODKA, *Kirche in Österreich* (Vienna 1959). W. LORENZ, *Du bist doch in unserer Mitte. Wege der Kirche in Österreich* (Vienna 1962). E. TOMEK and K. AMON, *Geschichte der Diözese Seckau,* v.1 (Graz 1918); v. 3.1 (Graz 1960). M. HEU-WIESER, *Geschichte des Bistums Passau,* v.1 (Passau 1939). J. WODKA, *Das Bistum St. Pölten* (St. Pölten 1950). A. MAIER, *Kirchengeschichte von Kärnten,* 3 v. (Klagenfurt 1951–56). A. SPARBER, *Kirchengeschichte Tirols* (Innsbruck 1957). *Erläuterungen zum Historischen Atlas der österreichischen Alpenländer,* 2. Abteilung: *Kirchen- und Grafschaftskarte,* pt. 1–8 (Vienna 1940–58). R. NOLL, *Frühes Christentum in Österreich* (Vienna 1954). I. ZIBER-MAYR, *Noricum, Baiern und Österreich* (2d ed. Horn 1956). K. OETTINGER, *Das Werden Wiens* (Vienna 1951). H. VON SRBIK, *Die Beziehungen von Staat und Kirche in Österreich während des Mittelalters* (Innsbruck 1904). S. R. VON LAMA, *Am tiefsten Quell,* 3 v. (Vienna 1963–64); v.1 *Der Aufbau des christlichen Österreich;* v. 2 *Im Zeit alter des Kampfes um die Glaubenserneuerung;* v. 3 *Überwindung der Aufklärung.* Austrian saints, mystics since the Middle Ages. F. KLOSTERMANN et al., *Die Kirche in Österreich . . .* (Vienna 1966). W. BUCHOWIECKI, *Die gotischen Kirchen Österreichs* (Vienna 1952). K. EDER, *Studien zur Reformationsgeschichte Oberösterreichs,* 2 v. (Linz 1933–36). G. MECENSEFFY, *Geschichte des Protestantismus in Österreich* (Graz 1956). A. CORETH, *Pietas Austriaca. Ursprung und Entwicklung barocker Frömmigkeit in Österreich* (Munich 1960). F. MAASS, *Der Josephinismus,* 5 v. (Vienna 1951–61). F. ENGEL-JANOSI, *Österreich und der Vatikan,* 2 v. (Graz 1958–60). E. WEINZIERL-FISCHER, *Die österreichischen Kon-*

kordate von 1855 und 1933 (Vienna 1961). F. FUNDER, *Vom Gestern ins Heute* (Vienna 1955); *Als Österreich den Sturm bestand* (Vienna 1957). A. DIAMANT, *Austrian Catholics and the First Republic: Democracy, Capitalism, and the Social Order, 1918–1934* (Princeton 1960). A. HUDAL, *Der Katholizismus in Österreich* (Innsbruck 1931). K. RUDOLF, *Aufbau im Widerstand* (Salzburg 1947). L. LENTNER, "Custos quid de nocte?", *Festschrift Michael Pfliegler* (Vienna 1961). E. BODZENTA, *Die Katholiken in Österreich: Ein religions-soziologischer Überblick* (Vienna 1962). J. WODKA, *Lexikon für Theologie und Kirche*, eds., J. HOFER and K. RAHNER, 10 v. (2d, new ed. Freiburg 1957–65) 7:1279–84. *Bilan du Monde*, 2:109–118. K. S. LATOURETTE, *Christianity in a Revolutionary Age: A History of Christianity in the Nineteenth and Twentieth Centuries*, 5 v. (New York 1958–62) v.1, 4. F. ENGEL-JANOSI, *Die politische Korrespondenz der Päpste mit den österreichischen Kaisern, 1804–1918* (Vienna 1964). *Annuario Pontificio* has annual data on all dioceses.

[J. WODKA]

The Church after 1945

During Nazi occupation, the Church was blamed for the defects of the Dollfuss regime and oppression began without delay. Some 1,400 establishments under clerical control were closed, while Catholic societies and youth organizations were disbanded. Numerous charitable and Church institutions were seized, and over 200 convents were suppressed. The Nazi government systematically hindered pastoral work and religious instruction and curbed clerical training. About 300,000 withdrew from the Church rather than make the requested contributions to it. Of the 724 priests arrested, 110 were sent to concentration camps, where 27 of them died and 15 others were executed.

After the war ended in 1945, the Church regained its freedom, although it now confined itself to the private sector. The concordat of 1934, negotiated between the Vatican and the Dollfuss government but abrogated when the Nazis seized power in 1938, was recognized in principle by the new republic in 1957. It is this concordat that instituted a state tax to support the Church. In 1960 the government also agreed to indemnify the Church for loss of property during the Nazi era, and in turn the Church abandoned its claims to properties confiscated by the state in the eighteenth century.

Leaving the realm of politics after World War II, the Church began to focus all its energies on confronting the worldliness of the 20th century. Since all Church associations had been destroyed during Nazi occupation, Catholic Action was organized under episcopal control; it soon became an important element in public life. Arrangements were made with the Holy See about the Religious Fund, the school problem and the creation of the Dioceses of Eisenstadt and Innsbruck.

Reforms of Vatican II. The Austrian Church supported the Second Vatican Council and embraced many of its reforms. Pius PARSCH of Klosterneuburg had long promoted the liturgical movement in Austria. Austrians Karl RAHNER, Josef Andreas JUNGMANN and Ferdinand Klostermann played important roles at the Council as periti. After Vatican II the bishops organized diocesan and national synods to discuss its teachings and implement its directives. Most dioceses encouraged the ordination of permanent deacons. Dioceses and parishes formed advisory councils, which encouraged the laity to take an active role in decision-making and Church ministry. One of the most notable features of lay involvement was the dramatic increase in the number of women working as pastoral assistants in parishes.

After Vatican II dioceses organized a series of synods to implement the conciliar directives. Rome gave special permission for the laity to participate in these meetings as voting members. The Austrian Episcopal Conference, first held in 1849, worked closely with the German and Swiss episcopal conferences on reform in the liturgy. At their meeting in 1968, the Austrian Bishops's Conference issued a statement in support of Pope Paul VI's encyclical *Humanae vitae*, but indicated that individual couples had to make their own decisions in the matter of family planning. Austrian bishops would continue to issue statements on education, the Church in society, economics, the role of women and the treatment of Gastarbeiter ("guest workers") and were active in the support of refugees and worldwide mission activity. In 1997 the Austrian hierarchy hosted a major ecumenical conference in Graz.

Church Benefits from Able Leadership. From 1956 to 1985 the Church profited from the able leadership of Franz König (b. 1905), archbishop of Vienna and head of the Austrian Episcopal Conference. Named a cardinal in 1958, he played a leading role at Vatican II, where he strongly supported the schemata calling for the liturgical renewal. In one of his more memorable interventions he addressed the schema on the Church, commenting that it should expand on the Church's duties and its obligation to preach the Gospel, so that people could realize that humanity and not merely individuals had been redeemed by Christ.

König also pioneered the Church's *Ostpolitik*. In 1963 he began a series of visits to Cardinal Mindszenty, confined in the American Embassy in Budapest, that resulted in Mindszenty's departure from Hungary. In 1964 Cardinal König established Pro Oriente, a center that brought together Roman Catholics, Orthodox, non-Chalcedonian Christians and Nestorians. In 1965 when Pope Paul VI established the Secretariat for Non-Believers to find a "basis for accommodation" with communists, atheists and other non-believers, König agreed to become its first president. Interested in the dialogue between faith and science, the Austrian cardinal organized numerous conferences on nuclear energy and nuclear armaments; the strong antinuclear movement in Austria owes much to his early work in the area. König also worked to heal the rift between the Catholic Church and the Austrian Socialist party.

Austria Restabilizes. By the mid-20th century Austria had regained a sense of identity and become a prosperous nation. It was ruled by a succession of coalition governments made up of representatives of the conservative Austrian People's Party, the ultra-conservative Freedom Party of Austria, and other liberal and socialist parties. In 1986 former U. N. secretary general Kurt Waldheim was elected president, despite evidence appearing to link him to Nazi war crimes; his government would be replaced by a liberal/conservative coalition. Because of its location adjacent to many Communist-bloc countries, until the end of the Cold War in the early 1990s Austria served as a "first stop" for political and economic refugees seeking asylum in the West; the end of the decade would find it equally useful for refugees from the former Yugoslavia.

In the year 2000 there were 4,240 secular and 2,225 religious priests in Austria, an almost 50 percent decrease over 1960 levels. There were 387 seminarians, while religious men numbered about 545 and religious women 6,701. Statistics indicated a dramatic decrease in the number of ordinations to the priesthood from over 100 per year at the time of Vatican II to fewer than 40 per year by 2000. Most Austrians attended state schools, and classes in religious education were obligatory, although parents were able to request exemptions for the their children. Religion in Austria was supported by a state Church tax collected on the basis of one's religious affiliation. While individuals officially declaring "no denomination" were not taxed, they also gave up a right to a church marriage, a church burial and the baptism of their children in a church.

Among the challenges confronting the Church in Austria during the 1990s was the increasing number of Catholics opting to officially leave the Church in order to stop paying the Church tax. In 2000 alone, 43,632 Catholics left the church, signaling economic repercussions on a Church structure used to regular infusions of money whether or not members attend services. In 2000, 78 percent of Austrians identified themselves as Roman Catholics, down from 89 percent in 1961.

Cardinal König continued to head the Austrian Episcopal Conference until 1985. He was succeeded by Karl Cardinal Berg of Salzburg, who in turn was succeeded by Hans Hermann Cardinal Groer, König's successor as archbishop of Vienna. Although elected to a second six-year term in 1995, Groer stepped down in the face of accusations of sexual misconduct and was succeeded by Cardinal Christoph Schönborn. While the damage to the Church's public image in the aftermath of charges of sexual abuse among its hierarchy proved daunting, Cardinal Schönborn was quick to assure Catholics that faith allows believers to overcome such problems.

Moving into the 21st Century. As the Church celebrated the millennium, areas of concern revolved chiefly around Austria's liberalized views regarding sexual ethics, marriage and education. Despite Church opposition and a petition signed by almost a million people, in 1974 the socialist-controlled government had legalized abortion on demand during the first trimester of pregnancy. The government also instituted a law requiring a civil ceremony for all marriage, Church weddings to be performed as an optional secondary ceremony. During its years in power, the Socialist government passed laws permitting divorce upon mutual consent and eased penalties for homosexual acts and adultery. The political pendulum swung in the other direction at the start of the 21st century, as the February 2000 elections resulted in a conservative coalition. While the new government's right-of-center views were believed to be more in line with the Church's social policies, there was also cause for concern, particularly about representatives of the nationalist Freedom Party, whose leader had been accused of anti-Semitic viewpoints and statements supportive of several Nazi policies. Church leaders were quick to respond, Cardinal Schönborn commenting that any growth of anti-Semitic feeling within Austria was a cause for concern to all. The Vatican planned to closely monitor government policies to guard against actions "contrary to Christian morality," according to a representative of the Holy See.

Because of the liberal social legislation passed during the late 1900s, Pope John Paul II developed a particular concern for the Church in Austria. During a meeting in 1997, the pope told the country's new ambassador that the mission of Austria is "to give Europe a soul," and encouraged efforts at developing a culture established on "spiritual principals." The pope visited Austria twice during the 1980s and 1990s, and attended a concert in Rome that was sponsored by the Austrian government in celebration of the anniversary of the Holy Father's ordination as a priest. In 1998 he visited Salzburg for the third time, focusing his comments on Austria's role in the reunification of post-communist Europe and encouraging Catholics to return to the Church, "Come back to her, to receive the joyous message."

Church leaders in Austria openly recognized that the Church existed in an environment indifferent to religion, even when most Catholic families had their children baptized and participated in compulsory religious education. In response, they encouraged faith-based efforts on the part of both the clergy and the laity. The international group Pax Christi had an active group in Austria. Lay groups such as Catholic Action, the Austrian Laity Council, Catholic Family Action, the Catholic Women's Movement and the Catholic Federation of Families remained active with Church financial support. These groups worked to spread the model of the modern Christian family. A variety of youth organizations also performed outreach to Austria' young people. Intellectual groups such as the Vienna Catholic Academy and the Federation of Catholic Intellectuals opened dialogue between Roman Catholicism and modern science. The Catholic Bible Work produced popular works based on modern historical critical scholarship. Austria's cultural heritage, deeply rooted in Catholicism, continued as a witness to the Christian tradition and inspired hope of renewed religious vitality.

Bibliography: *Kardinal König,* ed. A. FENZL (Vienna 1985). *Die Furche. Österreichishche Wochenzeitung für Politik, Wissenschaft, Kultur und Religion* (Vienna). *Hirtenbriefe aus Deutschland, Österreich, und der Schweiz,* eds., INSTITUT FÜR KIRCHLICHE ZEITGESCHICHTE, vol. 1–3 (Vienna 1966); vol. 4 (Salzburg 1971). A. KOHL, ''Katholikentag und Papstbesuch 1983: Eine kritische Würdigung,'' in *Österreichisches Jahrbuch für Politik 1984* (Vienna 1985) 401–435. F. LEITNER, *Kirche und Parteien in Österreich nach 1945: Ihr Verhältnis unter dem Gesichtspunkt der Äquidistanzdiskussion, Politik- und kommunikationswissenschaftliche Veröffentlichungen der Görres-Gesellschaft,* v. 4 (Paderborn 1988). *Kirche in Österreich 1938–1988: Eine Dokumentation,* ed. M. LEIBMANN (Graz 1990). F. LOIDL, *Geschichte des Erzbistums Wien* (Munich 1983). T. PIFFLE-PERCEVIC, *Kirche in Österreich: Berichte, Überlegungen, Entwürfe* (Graz 1979). E. WEINZIERL, ''Kirche seit 1970,'' in *Der österreichische Weg 1970–1985* (Beiträge zum wissenschaftlichen Symposium des Dr Karl-Renner-Instituts, abgehalten vom 27 Februar bis 1 März 1985 in Wien), ed. E. FRÖSCHLE (Vienna 1986) 239–47.

[A. BUNNELL/EDS.]

AUTHORITY

A moral power that exercises an essential function as a cause of united action. Using a twofold analysis, one negative and the other positive, this article considers respectively the disrepute into which authority has fallen, the kind of case briefed by antiauthoritarian philosophies, what is meant by the essential function of authority, and various views of its source.

Disrepute of Authority. In a century devoted to excessive egalitarianism, authority is held in considerable disrepute. Some writers have gone so far as to suggest that one ought to talk about what authority ''was'' and

not what it ''is'' (e.g., H. Arendt). Long before the current disrepute, G. W. F. HEGEL suggested that the leading thought of his day was the principle of ''interiority,'' which regards both externality and authority as impertinent and lifeless.

Generally speaking, social philosophers rarely question the fact that social happiness depends on a felicitous combination of authority and freedom. No matter how well-defined they are, however, the terms authority and freedom imply, even on the level of ordinary understanding, a kind of opposition and a kind of complementary quality. The opposition arises because authority suggests coerciveness, and coerciveness at once is considered antinomical to freedom. And indeed, even ordinary analysis suggests that unless authority is balanced by freedom, tyranny is almost inevitable. But if freedom is taken as an absolute and if it be not balanced by some kind of authority, then it leads to chaos or degenerates inevitably into abusive license. An excess of the one or the other, of freedom or of authority, leads to mutual self-destruction.

A more critical analysis of the suspicion against authority has been furnished by Yves SIMON. Persons in authority enjoy positions of privilege and have access to goods and honors not available to the majority of men; thus it seems that authority is in ''conflict with justice.'' And because vitality is evidenced by immanence and spontaneity, it may appear that the core of freedom is weakened by authority, which is in ''conflict with life.'' Sometimes authority seems to be in ''conflict with truth,'' since lovers of truth see all too often that authority is a kind of tool used to keep people in a state of ignorance favoring the *status quo.* Even more, many think that law can take the place of authority, that law is stable and orderly, free from the contingencies of the exercise of authority; thus they envision authority as in ''conflict with order.'' Despite all of these suspicions that continue to undermine authority in the 20th century, however, every community manifests an undeniable form of authority. It must be cautioned that there is no necessary connection between authority and any specific form in which it is embodied. But embodied it must be, if any community is to continue in existence.

Philosophers have long claimed that it is natural for man to live in SOCIETY, to unite with others. Society in this sense implies only reasonable members, not in any superficial connotation of acting reasonably, but as human beings who belong together by nature and exist together by reason of their common end. Natural sociability is not like membership in a club or union, into which one enters at will or from which he may withdraw arbitrarily. Aristotle states this truth most powerfully: ''He who is unable to live in society, or who has no need because he is sufficient for himself, must be either a beast or a god'' (*Pol.* 1253a 28). It is because society is natural to man, whether it be the society of the family or of the state, that authority is necessary. For authority has a necessary function to perform in attaining the goal of any society.

Antiauthoritarian Philosophies. Some antiauthority theorists assert that authority is necessary only on a provisional basis because of the ''insufficiency'' of its members, as in the case of children, the illiterate, and the primitive. The implication of this position is that once (and if) the deficiency is removed, authority is no longer necessary. A subtle justification of sterilization and euthanasia has sometimes found its roots in such a theory. The basis of the deficiency theory of authority springs from the myth that there is a direct proportion between social progress and the progress of personal freedom. The next logical step in the theory is to equate social development and personal freedom with the inevitable or proportionate decay of authority.

The Comtian ideal of a society based on enlightened reason is summarized in the famous formula ''Savoir pour prévoir pour pouvoir.'' Although covert antiauthority theories of society originating in some sociological circles have not been fully developed in technical fashion, they tend to imply constructs such as Edward Shils's ''consensual collectivity,'' in which a so-called process of illumination is thought to modify individuals and finally result in collective self-transformations. The theory of enlightened reason is expressed by Shils thus: ''. . . the very difference between the states of mind induced by attachment to or repulsion from authority and the detached and dispassionate states of mind induced by the exercise of sociological analysis means that different images of man, the world, and the authoritative self will almost inevitably persist.''

The function of authority extends beyond the work of merely supplying for deficiency or waiting for the dawn of enlightened reason. The natural sociability of man demands association not for material needs alone, and not merely for defense against animal life, hunger, and disease. Man needs man for the furtherance of knowledge, for reciprocal spiritual profundity, for the enrichment of the ''otherness'' that underlies FRIENDSHIP in a profoundly existential sense. The endless quest for totality is proper to man. This totality is one and the same for the single individual and for the collection of individuals; it is the totality that is, in fact, what was meant initially by the term common good. The glory of human society goes beyond the glory of the individual it is meant to serve, a collective glory to which each individual

brings himself as a proper gift and contributor. The human community so understood is a good itself that stands to serve mankind and every individual. It is this kind of good that demands a kind of common life wherein authority is properly necessary.

It is, of course, conceivable that some communities will attain their end without authority. In such instances, it merely happens that the good of one member coincides with that of another; here it is sufficient that an arbitrary contract effect the desired end. In these cases, the collective action can be achieved by a ''consensual collectivity,'' since what is desired is not a proper common good but the interdependence of private goods. Even in these instances, however, if bad faith or some unforeseen circumstance intervenes, authority may have to be invoked to achieve the end sought through the contract. The authority of the courts would then be invoked to achieve a judgment in line with the laws governing contractual relationships. An unrealistic view of society might lead one to suggest that all of human society could be composed of such simple partnerships. Were this possible, authority would not be necessary save for accidental reasons.

It may be noted here, however, that there is an authentic substitutional function to authority in the society of the family. In this case, parental authority is necessary for survival and for education of offspring. Children go through periods of insufficiency in which the authority proper to the home is provisionally indispensable. In case of parental deficiency in this matter or in case of death, society takes over the exercise of such a parental function. Authority on this level aims at its own disappearance. In fact, the postponement of the period of self-determination is a genuine deficiency in any theory of parental control and child training.

Essential Function of Authority. A more realistic view of human societies suggests that few if any societies can survive for any length of time unless there is a firm and stable principle at work to assure, by unified action, the achievement of their common end. A multiplicity of practical judgments is inevitable in every nontheoretical situation. The weakness of every social theory of the ''consensual collectivity'' type is its inability to assure uniformity of action in such a way that it can extend to all the concrete particulars of a social situation. Unanimity cannot be such a principle since it overlooks the obvious differences existing among humans, such as those traceable to ignorance, ill will, selfishness, vested interests, and the like. All judgments made for an action are surrounded with contingencies that make it impossible to demonstrate the necessity of any given prudential judgment. It is true that certain circumstances may generate a kind of spontaneity, such as that which takes place in times of emergency—e.g., an unjust attack or a natural disaster. Even here, however, society has to fight against plunder and treachery, factors that make unanimity highly improbable. Simon states that "unanimity is a precarious principle of united action whenever the common good can be attained in more than one way."

The main thesis of this article, then, is that authority is a moral power exercising an essential function as a cause of united action. The basis of this proposition is that the rich plurality of means for achieving the common good of any society demands the election of one from among many. The power to make such a choice lies in authority, which is a moral power residing in the regulator of the society. The desired unified action that is indispensable for the attainment of the common end comes from compliance with rules that bind all the members of the society in question. Therefore, except for the cases mentioned above, authority must exercise a vital function to guarantee consistent unified action.

It must be pointed out, however, that the need for authority in society and the need for any given form of governing personnel are quite distinct; the confusion of the two leads to multiple confusions. The power to issue commands for the sake of a common action neither implies nor excludes the actual use of coercion or persuasion. It is commonly held that the actual use of coercion or persuasion implies a failure of authority. The basis of this position is that persons who hold positions of authority and those who are said to be under authority must recognize that they are not equals; but persuasion ought to exist only among equals; therefore persuasion in society implies a contradiction. But if authority lacks the power to enforce the rules it makes for common action, then it is inefficacious. Thus the right to influence opinion by persuasion belongs to authority as a fitting instrument, just as the right to use coercion belongs to it, and both for the sake of the common good. It goes without saying that both persuasion and coercion are valid instruments only insofar as they respect the intrinsic dignity of the human PERSON.

Source of Authority. The position stated above stands in direct opposition to that of J. J. ROUSSEAU, whose dialectic of authority led to the SOCIAL CONTRACT. In the latter analysis, one is led to the myth of the general will, in which the individual human will is annihilated by an initial voluntary act; this theory terminates in a general formality making authority a power that resides in a multitude, i.e., as an attribute of multitude itself. Such power, then, could emerge without authority and makes possible the usurpation of power by the STATE. The 20th century has already provided many examples of such a rise to power without authority.

It is generally held among Catholics that civil authority is of God, not by any specifically divine institution, but by the fact that God is the author of nature and nature demands authority. In this general position, submission to authority is enjoined. The designation theory holds that the power proper to authority comes from God but that human beings designate the ruling person by cultural conventions. This is a modification of the divine-right theory, which holds that power is from God and that the person in whom it is vested also is designated by God. The transmission theory holds that civil authority is proper to the civil multitude; that the multitude not only designates the ruling person but also transmits to him the authority originally given them by God. Both the designation and the transmission theories guard the integrity of the individual while enjoining obedience to authority. The position of T. HOBBES and that of Rousseau, on the other hand, ascribe the source of authority to the multitude alone, who yield all powers to the state (Leviathan), thereby destroying the freedoms of the individual.

Teaching Authority. Sometimes authority is used in reference to a pedagogical process. In such a case, authority is, once again, properly substitutional and is necessary only as long as the learner fails to observe the relations between mind and object. In SCIENCE, properly speaking, there can be no authority, since DEMONSTRATION begets the kind of authentic objectivity that alone can necessitate the mind to its assent.

Totalitarianism. A persistent tendency in the 20th century would identify authority with totalitarianism. This tendency is rooted in the confusing of authority with TYRANNY. A proper authority ultimately rests on LAW, whereas every form of tyranny springs from the subjective interests of the tyrant. Power in totalitarianism rests on sources external to the political structure itself; these are unlike the legitimate sources of power in a properly democratic government or society. In all circles, familial, political, and ecclesiastical, authority does, indeed, imply OBEDIENCE, but an obedience that is consonant with a proper freedom. If one fails to see that the source of authority transcends not only power but also those who are in power, then he has little hope of escaping a deepening suspicion of every kind of authority. Continuing aversion to authority springs from apodictic and authoritarian statements concerning its nature.

Conclusion. Reduced to its essence, then, authority is indispensable for the achievement of the common welfare of any society. It is not necessary as a contract, nor is it established by convention or force, nor is it the result of sin. It is necessary because the nature of society demands it. The moment the connection between authority and the common good is severed, the community begins to weaken and finds itself preparing the way for the kind of ANARCHISM espoused by L. N. TOLSTOI. If and when authority is abused and issues into arbitrariness, such an issue is traceable only to accidental causes and is not proper to authority as such. Justice and a proper political friendship are the cement of society and are assumed in any reasonable theory of authority. It should be noted that the common good here mentioned, referring as it does to any and all natural societies, is not the absolute end of the person. Authority on the human level, whether familial or political, is thus indirectly related to the absolutely ultimate end of man, viz, eternal life. Therefore authority in the political community ought to look with equity and justice toward the possibility of each person's achieving his ultimate destiny. In the overall view, this demands that there be an authority that is proportionate to the natural and supernatural destiny of man (*see* AUTHORITY, CIVIL; AUTHORITY, ECCLESIASTICAL).

See Also: SOCIETY.

Bibliography: Y. SIMON, *A General Theory of Authority* (Notre Dame, Ind. 1962); *The Nature and Function of Authority* (Aquinas Lecture; Milwaukee 1940); *Philosophy of Democratic Government* (Chicago 1951). J. MARITAIN, ''Democracy and Authority,'' in his *Scholasticism and Politics* (New York 1940). H. ARENDT, ''What Is Authority?,'' in her *Between Past and Future: Six Exercises in Political Thought* (New York 1961). G. J. LYNAM, *The Good Political Ruler According to St. Thomas* (Washington 1953). J. WRIGHT, ''Reflections on Conscience and Authority,'' *Critic* 22 (April–May 1964) 11–15, 18–28. M. WEBER, ''The Types of Authority,'' in *Theories of Society,* ed. T. PARSONS et al., 2 v. (New York 1961) 1:626–32. C. BERNARD, ''The Theory of Authority,'' *ibid.* 1:632–41. E. SHILS, ''The Calling of Sociology,'' *ibid.* 2:1405–48. R. MICHELS, *Encyclopedia of the Social Sciences*, ed. E. R. SELIGMAN and A. JOHNSON, 15 v. (New York 1930–35) 1:319–21.

[G. J. MCMORROW]

AUTHORITY, CIVIL

The duty of respect for lawful civil authority, even when this was exercised by non-Christian rulers, was too plainly spelled out in the NT to be reasonably questioned by anyone professing to accept the Christian revelation. Christ Himself had acknowledged a duty to Caesar (Mt 22.21; Mk 12.17; Lk 20.25). Christians were admonished to accept civil authority as coming from God (Rom 13.1–7; Ti 3.1; 1 Tm 2.2), to regard those vested with it as sent by God (Rom 13.16; 1 Pt 2.14), to be subject to them for the Lord's sake (1 Pt 2.13), to give them their due (Rom 13.7), to look upon resistance to them as resistance to the ordinance of God (Rom 13.2).

In the early Church these plain statements of Christian duty were enough to forestall any tendency to civil anarchy or disobedience that might have arisen among Christians in consequence of the severity with which they were treated in times of persecution. But if they did not deny the rights of civil authority, the recognition they accorded it was limited by the distinction, inadmissible in the Roman state, that they drew between civil and religious authority. Christianity professed no essential antagonism to the secular claims of the state, for Christianity was not a political theory and offered no political program, but was merely a doctrine and a way of salvation. My kingdom, Christ had said, is not of the world (Jn 18.36). But if the rights of the civil ruler within his own legitimate sphere of authority were not to be questioned, there could be no compromise with the religious pretensions of the Roman state. Nevertheless, apart from this, the Christian was as willing to cooperate civilly with the government as any other citizen of the Empire. His faith did not free him from his obligation to obey or set him apart from the social community or the order of justice. On the contrary, it provided him with a new motive for submission by making him see the civil ruler as the minister of God's justice. Moreover, the virtues inculcated by Christianity, such as charity, justice, piety, and temperance, tended to make him a better and more reliable citizen.

Origin. St. Paul's insistence on the coercive function of the civil ruler made it possible for most of the Fathers to think that civil government had no other purpose and that it existed simply as a remedy to disorders arising from sin. This was the view taken by St. Augustine, who held that, had men continued in a state of innocence, no man would have been master of his fellows and neither slavery nor civil subjection would have existed (*Civ.* 19.15). Gregory the Great and Isidore of Seville held the same opinion. There is some superficial resemblance between this position and the political idealism of Seneca, Rousseau, and others who dreamed of a lost Eden in which men were free. Through the schoolmen, however, the influence of Aristotle prevented this from becoming the dominant view of Catholic theologians. According to Aristotle, political organization and government are conditions necessary for civilized life and indispensable means for bringing man to the full development of his powers. This opinion was adopted by St. Thomas Aquinas (*Summa Theologiae* 1a, 96.3–4), and has been commonly accepted by theologians since the 13th century.

The NT makes it clear that civil authority is from God, but this does not mean that God establishes it apart from the agency of secondary causes. By the 13th century theologians explicitly recognized that authority was derived from the people as a whole. Civil obedience is not submission to force, however benign, but a free acceptance of government. Some theologians, such as Suárez, have held that the people themselves first possess this power collectively, and then transmit it to the individuals they choose to govern them. In this view authority comes from God through the people. Others have thought that God immediately vests the ruler with authority, the intervention of the people being confined to the designation of the person or persons upon whom God confers it.

Limitations. The first and major limitation of the authority of the civil ruler, as this has been understood in Christian thought, arises from the distinction between civil and religious authority. The Christian sees himself, in effect, as a citizen of two cities, one temporal and the other spiritual, existing side by side and institutionally distinct, each autonomous in its own sphere. The doctrine of the two authorities, recognized in practice from the beginning of the Church, was expressly formulated by Pope GELASIUS I in a letter to the Emperor Anastasius in 494 (see Denz 347), and is known as the Gelasian doctrine, or the doctrine of the two swords. It holds that human society is subject to dual organization and control, based on the difference in kind of the values that need to be secured: spiritual interests and salvation are the concern of the Church; secular interests, on the other hand, such as the maintenance of peace, order, and justice, are the concern of civil government. Thus the authority of the civil ruler is restricted to the temporal and secular order; moreover, the ruler himself, if he is a Christian, is subject to the Church in spiritual matters, as St. Ambrose declared to the Emperor Valentinian (*Ep.* 21.4).

Other limitations took longer to be distinctly recognized. The doctrine that the ruler's authority comes from God, together with the notion that God has given men rulers as a remedy for sin—which was understood to mean that God may give men evil rulers to punish them for sin—tended to make some of the Fathers hesitate to question the legitimacy of *de facto* authority or of authority used wickedly or tyrannously (e.g., see Irenaeus, *Adv. Haer.,* 5.24; Augustine, *Civ.,* 5.19; Isidore of Seville, *Sententiae,* 3.48; St. Gregory the Great, *Regulae pastoralis lib.,* 3.4). Instead of concluding that there can be a wicked authority that does not come from God, they were disposed rather to think of the ruler as the representative of God regardless of how he came by his authority or how he conducted himself in its use.

In the changed political climate of later times, Christian philosophers and theologians from John of Salisbury onward were more forthrightly critical of bad government, and came to assert other limitations. These depended on considerations of natural and positive law determining the nature and purpose of civil authority and the conditions of its rightful establishment and exercise. Great stress was laid on legitimacy—authority must be

legitimate or at least legitimized; otherwise the ruler is such in name only and possesses no real authority. In the exercise of his office the ruler may make no demands that exceed the powers vested in him, nor may he impose useless or unjust burdens on his subjects. Indeed, unjust laws or ordinances are not, from the moral point of view, binding at all, and thus the obedience owed by subjects is always conditioned by the rightful exercise of authority (see, for example, St. Thomas Aquinas, ST 1a2ae, 96.1–6; 2a2ae, 42.2 ad 3; 104.5–6; *De reg. princ.* 3.10–12).

See Also: OBEDIENCE; CHURCH AND STATE.

Bibliography: THOMAS AQUINAS, *Selected Political Writings,* ed. A. PASSERIN D'ENTRÈVES, tr. J. G. DAWSON (Oxford 1948). T. GILBY, *The Political Thought of Thomas Aquinas* (Chicago 1958). R. W. and A. J. CARLYLE, *A History of Mediaeval Political Theory in the West,* 6 v. (New York 1903–36).

[P. K. MEAGHER]

AUTHORITY, ECCLESIASTICAL

Authority in the Church, or ecclesiastical authority, will verify, though in its own way, the concept already developed in the general treatment of the term AUTHORITY. If the Church is a true SOCIETY of human beings, a group seeking a common end through concerted action, it is inevitable that there is need of control, some power to determine ways and means, to allot functions, to redress grievances—in a word, to protect against the centrifugal tendencies that jeopardize communal action. Men in the SUPERNATURAL order still display the diversity of viewpoint that makes authority necessary wherever life is to be lived within community structures.

Early Church. From the beginning the Church was conscious of this need for persons who could decide points of conflict, administer community goods, preside over community assemblies; and the Church recognized that those so empowered owed their selection and their rights not to any decision by the community, but to Christ's own determination.

As the Gospels testify to the preparation of the TWELVE as surrogates of Christ, so the Acts of the Apostles and the Pauline Epistles testify that the Twelve and PAUL (as one later raised to the same dignity and functions) directed community life. In ch. 6 of Acts St. Luke describes the first major rift in community relations, the outburst of the Hellenist group against the Hebrews on the grounds that the Hellenist widows were being slighted in the distribution of community alms. He makes it clear that the plaintiffs instinctively brought their grievances to the APOSTLES for adjudication. He makes it clear too that the Twelve without hesitation acknowledged its competence to apply a remedy by setting up a subordinate commission.

Within the Pauline communities the same picture emerges and nowhere more clearly than in 1 Corinthians, where Paul rules on the exclusion from the community of the incestuous man (5.1–5), on the handling of quarrels among the brethren (6.1–8), on the licitness of eating flesh of animals sacrificed in pagan rites (ch. 8–10, esp. 10.23–30), on the attire of women at religious services (11.2–16), on the conduct to be observed at the Lord's Supper (11.17–34), on the discipline to be observed in the exercise of charisms (ch. 12–14, esp. 14.26–40), and on the manner of gathering alms for the relief of the brethren in Jerusalem (16.1–4). The pastorals, too, whether from the hand of Paul or in the spirit of Paul, are filled with instructions that cover nearly every aspect of community life and chart for Titus and Timothy the course they are to follow in arranging ecclesiastical life in Crete and at Ephesus. This claim to direct is always based on the mandate from the Lord, who entrusted them in His place with powers of BINDING and loosing (Mt 18.18) and of teaching the baptized to observe whatever He had commanded (Mt 28.20). And as He will be with them constantly till the end of time, this claim will be reiterated by those who succeed the original Apostles, who are as such "not from men nor by man, but by Jesus Christ and God the Father" (Gal 1.1).

A description of ecclesiastical authority would be inadequate and misleading if it were confined to the area of external Church order. For the competence of the Apostles is also a doctrinal one; i.e., they are commissioned to propose the message of SALVATION, and in such a way that their presentation is not that of simple messengers. From the start it was to the "teaching of the apostles" as well as to "communion of the breaking of the bread and prayers" (Acts 2.42) that the community devoted itself. The gospel is that "which also you received, wherein also you stand, through which also you are being saved, if you hold it fast, as I preached it to you" (1 Cor 15.1–2). And Paul is always ready to explain further and authoritatively the sense in which he and the other Apostles had preached it. He did not deliver the message of salvation once for all; he constantly renewed and deepened their intelligence, so that he could claim not only that he delivered the gospel but that through the gospel he had begotten them in Christ Jesus (1 Cor 4.15). The gospel is in St. Paul not something merely to be brought externally to the attention of others, but a principle of fecundity by which he generates offspring in Christ and assumes the direction incumbent on a parent: to develop and train those whom he has procreated.

Adequate Concept. Real and pervasive as this authority is in the Catholic understanding, it need not operate to smother the activity of those who are subject to it. The Christian life is not to be thought a mechanical execution of impulses externally received; those begotten in the gospel are the human children of God and must develop internal principles too of SUPERNATURAL life by which they continually grow. The very need for authority arises in part from the need of pruning the exuberance of Christian activity and from the need of maintaining free from aberration doctrines not passively received sometime in the past but doctrines constantly pondered and daily being reduced to principles of action. Authority is not to hinder fructification, but through its divine-human action to prune every branch that does bear fruit that it may bear more fruit (Jn 15.2).

See Also: HIERARCHY; GOVERNANCE, POWER OF; KEYS, POWER OF; SOCIETY (CHURCH AS); CHURCH, ARTICLES ON.

Bibliography: E. DUBLANCHY, *Dictionnaire de théologie catholique*, ed. A. VACANT et al., 15 v. (Paris 1903–50; Tables Générales 1951–) 4.2:2175–2207. *Dictionnaire de théologie catholique*, ed. A. VACANT et al., 15 v. (Paris 1903–50; Tables Générales 1951–) tables générales 1:1125–26. K. MÖRSDORF, *Lexikon für Theologie und Kirche*, ed. J. HOFER and K. RAHNER, 10 v. (2d, new ed. Freiburg 1957–65); suppl., *Das Zweite Vatikanische Konzil: Dokumente und Kommentare*, ed. H. S. BRECHTER et al., pt. 1 (1966) 6:218–221. J. GEWIESS and O. KARRER, H. FRIES ed., *Handbuch theologischer Grundbegriffe*, 2 v. (Munich 1962–63) 1:31–49. S. GRUNDMANN, *Die Religion in Geschichte und Gegenwart*, 7 v. (3d ed. Tübingen 1957–65) 3:1434–35. L. BOUYER, *The Word, Church and Sacraments in Protestantism and Catholicism*, tr. A. V. LITTLEDALE (New York 1961). T. D. ROBERTS, *Black Popes: Authority, Its Use and Abuse* (New York 1954).

[S. E. DONLON]

AUTO-DA-FÉ

The Portuguese term (Spanish, *auto de fé* Latin, *actus fidei*) for the public ceremonies surrounding the proclamation of sentences that terminated INQUISITION TRIALS, especially in Spain. *Autos* never included burning at the stake. The first was at Seville (1481); the last, in Mexico (1850). The Spanish solemnities, derived from the medieval Inquisition's *sermo generalis,* acquired a harsh, show-trial atmosphere, to impress and instruct the populace. Increasingly elaborate and expensive, *autos* were staged in the city plaza; a concourse of people surrounded two platforms, one of prisoners and the other of inquisitors with dignitaries. These cautionary exercises usually included a lengthy procession (prisoners wore penitential *sambenito* gowns with miter), a sermon, oaths, interminable reading of sentences, abjurations, reconciliations, and "relaxation" of the obdurate to the secular authorities.

An early *auto* (Toledo 1486) lasted six hours for 750 prisoners; later *autos* could take all day. The presence of Charles V at Valencia (1528) set the precedent for the attendance of rulers at these spectacles. After 1515, *autos* could be held only where an inquisitorial court functioned. Victims were usually apostate former Jews and former Muslims, then *alumbrados* and some Protestants, and occasionally bigamists, sorcerers, etc. Barcelona had 30 *autos* between 1488 and 1498; Saragossa had 61 between 1484 and 1502. The major Protestant *autos* were in 1559 at Valladolid (14 ''relaxed'') and Seville (55). Of all the Spanish possessions, the Netherlands suffered the most, 2,000 dying within 50 years. After 1600, *autos* became ever less frequent and gradually assumed the tone of popular fetes. *Autos* often included no death penalties and never involved executions. If a death sentence was given, it was executed later, usually outside the town.

Bibliography: J. GUIRAUD, *Histoire de l'inquisition au moyen âge,* 2 v. (Paris 1935–38). B. LLORCA, *La Inquisición en España* (3d ed. Barcelona 1954). E. CANETTI, *Auto-da-fé,* C. V. WEDGWOOD, tr. (New York 1969). H. KAMEN, *Inquisition and Society in the Sixteenth Centuries* (London 1985). E. W. MONTER, *Frontiers of Heresy* (Cambridge 1990).

[R. I. BURNS]

AUTOCEPHALY

In Greek, αὐτός (self) and κεφαλή (head), literally ''self-headed,'' a term in common usage in the Christian East. It refers to a self-governing church with the power to appoint its own primate (patriarch, catholicos or metropolitan) and other exarchs (bishops), and the right to resolve its internal problems on its own. Autocephalous churches are also to be distinguished from autonomous churches. Although they share many common elements, they differ from each other on the crucial question of jurisdiction. Autocephalous churches are not dependent on another church for leadership, ecclesial life, and mission. Autonomous churches, while having the autonomy to regulate their daily affairs, are nevertheless canonically dependent on, and subordinated to, an autocephalous church. In practical terms, this means that important decisions such as the appointment of a leader (metropolitan or major archbishop) must be ratified by the holy synod of the parent autocephalous church.

Historically, autocephaly denoted an ecclesiastical independence within the framework of Church organization and, legally, meant a juridical exemption from any subordination to such established authority on a *praeter legem* basis. Some of these Churches existed entirely within the boundaries of one state (ethnarch), others within a political framework comprising various nationalities,

in accordance with former metropolitan provinces and their dioceses whose bishops met regularly in synod and elected their own primate. Their relative rank was determined by a kind of hierarchy of honor, with the Ecumenical patriarch of Constantinople at its head. Among the ancient patriarchates of Alexandria, Antioch, and Jerusalem, the order of precedence was fixed at the Council of Chalcedon, and, later, the Patriarchate of Moscow (established in 1589) assumed fifth place. Other autocephalous Churches were assigned rank in accordance with the date of their achieving ecclesiastical independence—the Church of Cyprus (431), the Church of Sinai (sixth century), the Bulgarian Church (927), the Serbian Church (1220), the Church of Georgia, under its own Catholicos, the Church of Greece (1833), the Czechoslovak Orthodox Church (1923), the Church of Finland (1923), the Polish Orthodox Church (1924), the Albanian Church (1937), and so forth. As for the Church of Georgia, its original autocephalous status dated from the fifth century. In 1817 this status was abolished, and it was annexed to the Russian Church and governed by a Russian exarch. In 1917 it recovered its autocephalous status, which was recognized by the patriarch of Moscow in 1943.

Bibliography: D. ATTWATER, *The Christian Churches of the East,* 2 v. (Milwaukee 1946–47). J. HACKETT, *A History of the Orthodox Church of Cyprus* (London 1901). J. MEYENDORFF, *The Orthodox Church,* tr. J. CHAPIN (New York 1962). S. H. SCOTT, *The Eastern Churches and the Papacy* (London 1928).

[L. NEMEC/EDS.]

AUTOS SACRAMENTALES

The literal meaning, from the Latin *actus sacramentales,* is ''sacramental plays.'' Though variant types exist, an *auto* (as it was often called in abbreviation) may be defined as a one-act play presenting, with personified abstractions as characters, an allegorical action about ideas closely or loosely related to the Holy Eucharist, and, from the 16th to the 18th century, performed in Castilian Spanish during the Octave of Corpus Christi before outdoor audiences.

The institution of the Feast of CORPUS ET SANGUINIS CHRISTI by Urban IV in 1264 gave Christendom a new holy day, rooted in dogma and conducive of joy. It was characterized early by street processions in which the Host, attended by the clergy, was borne from the sanctuary for public adoration. In Spain the procession also featured less solemn marchers—giants, dancers, and figures of fantastic animals. Floats carried statues representing biblical or allegorical scenes; in time the statues were replaced by men, who gradually relaxed their frozen postures, and performed slight choreographic movements.

Eventually, at the stations, or stopping places, of the procession, the masqueraders acted, first in dumb show and then with improvised speech, the scenes they had portrayed as *tableaux vivants.* Drama had entered the procession, and from this stage to the presentation of written sacramental plays was but a short step.

By the end of the 15th century, Spain, unlike other European countries, was still producing only simple liturgical dramas based on the *Officium pastorum.* But she progressed rapidly in the 16th century. Out of these primitive works emerged piece by piece the great secular and religious theater of the golden age. The *autos sacramentales* were but one of several lines of development. *The Officium pastorum* plays had three parts: the appearance of the shepherds, the angel's announcement of the birth of Christ, and the adoration of the shepherds. In the plays that anticipate the *autos,* the angel is replaced by a hermit or a friar, who answers the questions of the simple shepherds. The next step was to substitute for the learned informant a personification of Faith. Meanwhile, the shepherds had themselves become individuated and made to represent some idea. The plays became wholly allegorized.

By the 17th century it was customary, in the capital and other large cities, to erect trestle stages in the plazas. Huge wagons, on which elaborate scenery had been constructed, were drawn up around the stage. After each performance the wagons, bearing the props and actors, would move to the next plaza. Performances of as many as four plays might be given each day in four locations. The city commissioned poets to write *autos* and bore the cost of the entire production. Intercity rivalry led to lavish expenditures. The actors, men and women, were professionals from the secular theater, attracted to the *autos* by their devotion and the financial rewards. In addition to the fees, the municipality offered a substantial prize to the best troupe. Dignitaries sat near the stage; the citizenry was free to stand and watch. The poetry was often lost in the hubbub, and action and spectacle were thus almost as important as the words. The *autos* were the main contribution of the civic authorities to the religious feast.

Allegory was the proper form for a Eucharistic play. A Sacrament, says St. Thomas, is *signum rei sacrae,* and a sign serves *per nota ad ignota pervenire.* The *autos* played their part in helping man to grasp the unknown through analogy with the known. During the 16th century the allegorization process continued in the works of Diego Sánchez (before 1550), the 100 anonymous plays of the *Códice de autos viejos* (c. 1575), and the *autos* written or edited by Juan de Timoneda (d. 1583). The genre approached its maturity in the works of Lope de VEGA and José de Valdivielso (1560?–1638). These dramatists wrote essentially penitential *autos,* designed to move spectators to compunction, Confession, and Communion. Their *autos* were not yet great intellectual constructions illuminating with poetic intuitions the mysteries of theology.

It was left to Calderón to raise the *autos* to these heights. Interpreting the Eucharist as an all-embracing Sacrament, Calderén explored, in daring allegories, a wide range of dogmatic themes. An abundance of allegorical personifications—Judaism, Nature, Grace, Thought, Beauty, Night—carry the profound religious action. His art was best described by the poet himself: ''Sermons set in verse, problems of Sacred Theology set in representable ideas, which my words cannot explain or comprehend, inclining man to joyfulness on this Corpus Christi day.'' With Calderón's enormous production—some 80 *autos*—the sacramental play reached its perfection.

Rationalists in the 18th century found the *autos* incomprehensible and irreverent, and in 1765 Carlos III banned their performance. Since that time *autos* have survived in occasional performances only as archaic curiosities.

Bibliography: E. GONZÁLEZ PEDROSO, ed., *Autos sacramentales* (Biblioteca de Autores Españoles 58; Madrid 1865). P. CALDERÓN DE LA BARCA, *Autos sacramentales,* ed. A. VALBUENA PRAT, 2 v. (Clásicos Castellanos 69 and 74; Madrid 1926–27); ''The Great Theatre of the World,'' tr. M. H. SINGLETON in *Masterpieces of the Spanish Golden Age,* ed. A. FLORES (pa. New York 1957) 368–395. B. W. WARDROPPER, *Introducción al teatro religioso del Siglo de Oro* (*La evolución del auto sacramental: 1500–1648*) (Madrid 1953). A. A. PARKER, *The Allegorical Drama of Calderón* (New York 1943).

[B. W. WARDROPPER/EDS.]

AUTPERT, AMBROSE, ST.

Benedictine preacher and writer; b. southern Gaul, early eighth century; d. Italy, January 30, 784. He entered the monastery of St. Vincent on the Volturno near Benevento in 754 and after ordination devoted himself especially to preaching. He soon acquired a reputation for learning and holiness and in 777 was elected abbot by the Frankish monks of the monastery; a rival group of Lombard monks elected another abbot. Although in the conflict Autpert resigned, Charlemagne ordered the matter to be submitted to the pope. On the way to Rome Autpert died. The Benedictine chronicler calls him ''sanctissimus'' because of his great virtue, the Bollandists gave him the title ''saint'', and his cultus has been approved. Autpert was one of the most outstanding men of his time, far in advance of his contemporaries in learning, culture, and spiritual insight. Though a prolific writer, he remained comparatively unknown for many centuries, and his writings were ascribed to famous men of preceding ages, including SS. Augustine, Ambrose, Gregory the Great, Leo the Great, and Isidore of Seville. Recent scholarship has reestablished much of Autpert's literary heritage. Among his works are a long commentary on the Apocalypse [*Speculum parvulorum in Maxima Bibliotheca vet. Patrum* (v. 13 Lyons 1677) 403–657]; an ascetical treatise very widely read in the Middle Ages under the name of other authors, *Conflictus vitiorum atque virtutum* (*Patrologia Latina* 83:1131–44); the lives of several saints; and a number of sermons and homilies.

Feast: July 19.

Bibliography: J. WINANDY, *Ambroise Autpert: Moine et théologien* (Paris 1953); ''L'Oeuvre littéraire d' A. A.,'' *Revue Bénédictine* 60 (1950) 93–119. U. BERLIÈRE, *Dictionnaire d'histoire et de géographie ecclésiastiques*, ed. A. BAUDRILLART et al. (Paris 1912) 2:1115–16. L. BERGERON, *Dictionnaire de spiritualité ascétique et mystique. Doctrine et histoire*, ed. M. VILLER et al. (Paris 1932) 1:429.

[M. J. BARRY]

AUTUN

Autun is an ancient city and diocese containing the entire area of Saôneet–Loire in southern France, about 60 miles southwest of Dijon. Christianity came to Autun (*Augustodunum*) from Lyons at the beginning of the 3rd century. The famous 3d-century Christian epitaph (in Greek) of PECTORIUS was discovered (1830) in the cemetery of St. Peter l'Estrier, a few miles from Autun. Sacked by the warriors of Tetricus in 269, Autun became an independent city (*c.* 300); and tradition designates St. Amator as its first bishop (*c.* 250). But the first recorded bishop was St. Reticius, who assisted at a council in Rome in 313 (Eusebius, *Ecclesiastical History,* 5.5). In 542 Bishop Nectarius brought the relics of St. Nazarius from Milan for his cathedral; St. Syagrius was the first bishop of Autun to receive the pallium. SS. Léger and Ansbert restored the monuments of the city (7th century) and founded the diocesan legacy. Under the Merovingians a number of monasteries were founded, including St. Symphorian (5th century), St. Martin (*c.* 589) by Brunhilde, and St. Andochius (restored in the 8th century).

In the 11th century the monks of Cluny effected a reform that was destined to spread to the Church at large and to constitute a powerful aid to the papacy. Bishops Valterius (975–1024) and Stephen of Bâgé (1112–36) favored the reform, and Norgaud (1098–112) opposed it in favor of episcopal rights. The great Abbey of CLUNY was located in Autun. Romanesque in architectural style, it

was completed early in the 12th century and until the erection of the basilica of St. Peter in Rome was the largest ecclesiastical building in Europe. For many centuries the library of Cluny was one of the richest and most important in France and the storehouse of a vast number of valuable manuscripts. The conclave that elected Pope CALLISTUS II (1119–24 was held at Cluny. The main structure of the cathedral of Saint-Lazare dates from the 11th and 12th centuries, though the Gothic central towers and the chapels were added in the 15th century by Nicolas Rolin, chancellor of Burgundy, who was born in Autun.

The first council at Autun was held in 589. A second council took place during the episcopate of Bishop Léger (659–678); it acknowledged the Rule of St. Benedict as the normal monastic rule. Another council in 1065 reconciled Robert, Duke of Burgundy, with the bishop of Autun. In 1077 Pope Gregory VII convened a council in Autun that deposed Manasses, Archbishop of Reims, for simony and usurpation of the see. In 1094 Hugues, Archbishop of Lyons, renewed the excommunications of Henry IV of Germany and of Guibert, the antipope. Autun was sacked by the Protestant adherents of Coligny in 1570; but the Counter Reformation was inaugurated by Bp. Peter IV Saulnier (1588–1612), who installed the Capuchins (1606), Minims, and Jesuits. Bishop Claude de Ragny (1621–25) renewed the diocesan clergy and with the aid of St. Vincent de Paul reformed the local monasteries. The seminary was founded by Bp. Gabriel de Raquette and entrusted to the Sulpicians; and he introduced the Daughters of Charity at Paray-le-Monial, where St. Margaret Mary (d. 1690) had the apparitions of the Sacred Heart.

Bibliography: É. GRIFFE, *La Gaule chrétienne à l'époque romaine* (Paris 1947–) 1:48–50. A. DE CHARMASSE, ed., *Cartulaire de l'église d'Autun,* 3 pts. in 2 v. (Autun 1865–1900).

[D. KELLEHER/EDS.]

AUTUN, COUNCILS OF

A number of Church councils held at the diocesan seat of AUTUN, France, near Lyons and CLUNY.

In 589 a council under St. Syagrius, Bishop of Autun, restored order in the monastery of Sainte-Radegonde at Poitiers by excommunicating the two nuns who were in rebellion against their abbess.

A council, *c.* 670, under Bp. LEODEGAR of Autun, promulgated a number of disciplinary canons including one requiring priests to know the Apostles' and Athanasian Creeds and one demanding monastic stability and the strict observance of the BENEDICTINE Rule. Sacramental communion by all Christians was required at Christmas, Easter, and Pentecost. Priests were to be punished for celebrating Mass unworthily.

In 1065 the archbishops of Lyons and Besanmnçon and the bishops of Chalon-sur-Sâone, Mâcon, and Autun met to consider the misrule of Duke Robert I of Burgundy whom Abbot HUGH OF CLUNY is said to have then brought to repentance.

In 1077 a council promoting Pope GREGORY VII'S reforms was held by the papal legate HUGH OF DIE. It had to restore order after the violence of the late Duke Robert. It promulgated the law forbidding lay INVESTITURE, a subject raised when the council regularized the position of GERARD, Bishop of Cambrai. The council found Abp. MANASSES of Reims guilty of simony and suspended him. Manasses then became an open supporter of Emperor HENRY IV and the antipope GUIBERT of Ravenna.

On Oct. 15, 1094, another council under Hugh of Die renewed the excommunications of Henry IV and Guibert. Eudes I of Burgundy returned some Church property. In 1100 famine forced the council scheduled for Autun to be held instead at VALENCE.

Bibliography: C. J. VON HEFELE, *Histoire des conciles d'après les documents originaux,* tr. and continued by H. LECLERCQ, 10 v. in 19 (Paris 1907–38) 3:307–308; 4:1233–34; 5:387–388. V. TERRET, *Dictionnaire d'histoire et de géographie ecclésiastiques,* ed. A. BAUDRILLART (Paris 1912–) 5:922–925.

[A. CONDIT]

AUXERRE

Located on the left bank of the Yonne River, in Yonne department, Archdiocese of Sens, central France. The See of Auxerre (4th–18th century) lost its territory at various times to Sens, ORLÉANS, and Nevers (detached from Auxerre *c.* 500); Auxerre's history, reflects its position between Sens, the Loire Valley, and Burgundy.

The Roman *Autissiodorum* was constituted in the late third century near the Gallic *Autricum.* By 400 it was one of the seven cities of the civil province *Lugdunensis IV.* It was in Frankish hands when its bishop Theodosius signed the acts of the Council of Orléans in 511. From the 10th century there was a hereditary county of Auxerre, which John IV conveyed to Charles V of France (1370). The territory passed to the Duke of Burgundy (1435), but was reannexed to the French crown after the death of Charles the Bold (1477).

Local tradition records the martyrdom of Priscus (Bris) and his companions in flight from Besançon during the reign of Emperor Aurelian (270–275). Peregrinus,

who heads the episcopal list, may have been an itinerant evangelist. From Marcellian (306?–335?) can be traced a true succession, which includes AMATOR (388?–418); GERMAIN (418–448), who was active in Britain (Bede, *Ecclesiastical History* 1:17–21); AUNARIUS (561–605), under whom a diocesan synod assembled; and Wala (872–79), in whose pontificate the *Gesta pontificum Autissiodorensium* (*Patrologia Latina*, ed. J. P. Migne [Paris 1878–90] 138:219–394) was inaugurated. The episcopal domain, established by 700 and confiscated by Pepin the Short (751–768), was restored under Bps. Herbert I (971–995) and Hugh (999–1039). Later bishops were as much feudal lords as prelates, and the diocese was rent by the Hundred Years War and the Wars of Religion. Jansenism was strong, especially under Bp. Charles G. de Caylus (1704–54). The 106th prelate, J. B. M. Champion de Cicé (1760–90; d. 1805), saw the diocese suppressed in 1790 and the territory assigned to Sens. The CONCORDAT OF 1801 gave the area to TROYES, but the restoration of Sens as an archdiocese (1822) brought about Sens's jurisdiction over all Yonne, except the commune of Pontigny (since 1954). In 1823 the archbishop of Sens added Auxerre to his title.

Auxerre produced famous philosophers: HEIRIC (d. 876), REMIGIUS (d. 908), WILLIAM (d. *c.* 1237), and Lambert (*c.* 1250). The artistic worth of the city's three parishes is considerable. The former cathedral of St. Étienne, with stained glass of the 13th and 16th centuries, has a crypt (11th century) and an upper church with an elegant Gothic choir (13th century,) and nave (14th–15th century). The Church of St. Eusèbe (12th–16th century) is graced with a Romanesque nave. The Gothic St. Pierre (16th–17th century) boasts a late Renaissance façade. Significant too are the remnants of the 12th–century, episcopal palace incorporated into the Prefecture, and the abbey church of St. Germain, founded in the early 6th century, with 9th–century crypts (Carolingian frescoes) and an upper church (13th–century choir and 15th–century nave).

Bibliography: P. R. BARBIER, *Auxerre et l'Auxerrois, pays d'art et d'histoire* (Paris 1936). G. LEBRAS, *S. Germain d'Auxerre et son temps* (Auxerre 1950). R. LOUIS, *Les Églises d'Auxerre des origines au XIe siècle* (Paris 1952). *Congrès archéologique de France: 116e session: Auxerre* (Paris 1959). E. JARRY, *Catholicisme* 1:1100–03.

[H. G. J. BECK/EDS.]

AUXILIUS OF NAPLES

Frankish priest and polemicist; date and place of birth and death unknown. He was ordained in Rome by Pope FORMOSUS (891–896), and may have either established himself as a grammarian near Naples, or entered MONTE CASSINO, where a necrology mentions an ''Auxilius'' as author of a commentary on Genesis. When SERGIUS III (904–911) reenacted the decrees of the ''cadaveric synod,'' which had declared all actions of Pope Formosus invalid and threatened with excommunication those who exercised Holy Orders conferred by him unless they were reordained, Auxilius and EUGENIUS Vulgarius became spokesmen of the position. In several pamphlets they defended the legality of the election of Formosus and the validity of the Holy Orders conferred by him. According to Auxilius, the validity of Orders did not depend on the personal worthiness of the bishop and, therefore, he opposed REORDINATION. Despite the prerogatives of the Apostolic See, Auxilius believed a council was necessary to vindicate Formosus, and to judge Sergius. His pamphlets included *De ordinationibus a Formoso papa factis* (*Patrologia latina* 129:1059–74, completed in Dümmler 107–116); *Infensor et defensor* (*Patrologia latina* 129: 1073–1102); *In defensionem sacrae ordinationis papae Formosi* (Dümmler 59–95); and *In defensionem Stephani episcopi et prefatae ordinationis* (Dümmler 96–105).

Bibliography: E. DÜMMLER, ed., *Auxilius und Vulgarius* (Leipzig 1866). L. SALTET, *Les Réordinations: Étude sur le sacrament de l'ordre* (Paris 1907) 143–145, 152–163. M. MANITIUS, *Geschidte der lateinischen Literatur des Mittelaiters*, 3v. (Munich 1911–13) 1:437–439, 2:805. D. POP, *La Défense du pape Formose* (Paris 1933). J. POZZI, ''Le Manuscrit Tomus XVIIIus de la Vallicelliana et le Libelle 'De Episcoporum Transmigratione''' *Apollinaris* 31 (1958) 313–350. S. LINDEMANS, ''Auxilius et le Manuscrit Vallicellan Tome XVIII,'' *Revue d'histoire ecclésiastique* 57 (1962) 470–484.

[S. P. LINDEMANS]

AVARICE

A vice, and one of the capital SINS, consisting in excessive appetite for wealth; it is directly opposed, by defect, to the virtue of liberality, which controls desire for possessions, and is indirectly subversive of many other virtues. While earthly wealth in itself can be considered a good thing and even a blessing from God, it is also a dangerous thing, and the inordinate desire of it or excessive preoccupation with acquiring it is dangerous. Christ condemned avarice ''because a man's life does not consist in the abundance of his possessions'' (Lk 12.15). If a man lives primarily for riches, he will have no part in the kingdom of heaven (Mt 19.24) ''for you cannot serve God and Mammon'' (Mt 6.24; Lk 16.13). Avarice in its extreme form would occur in the case of an individual who attaches such value to wealth and possessions that he makes the accumulation and retention of them the

major goal of his life, to which he subordinates all else. Such a perversion of values would obviously be mortally sinful and totally disruptive of the moral life. So basically disordered a desire for wealth, however, is probably a rare thing, occurring only in the true miser, whose preoccupation with money is so manifestly foolish that it must be explained in terms of some deep distortion of the psyche. But an individual's unreasonable pursuit of riches does not not necessarily mean that he makes an ultimate goal of them. He may seek wealth for what he gets by means of it. Money can buy gratification of many kinds—pleasures, fame, power, the envy of others, etc.—and those immoderately dedicated to gathering riches may also be lavish in their expenditures, which indicates that the wealth is sought as a means rather than an end. But this can also involve a perversion of values more or less seriously sinful depending on the objectives that are sought through wealth or the good things that are sacrificed in its pursuit. Evidently, too, avarice can be seriously sinful when it is so uncontrolled as to cause one to sin gravely against other virtues, such as justice or charity. The error of attaching too great an importance to wealth is generally committed in the practical rather the theoretical order. St. Thomas Aquinas called it an error of common (*vulgares*) men, but the ''common'' is to be understood in distinction to philosophers and not as implying that the fault is more prevalent among rude and uncultured folk. Indeed, primitive peoples, and generally those whose culture is unsophisticated, tend to be more content with their relative indigence, and even to lack something of the *auri sacra fames* (the accursed love of gold) of which Vergil spoke (*Aeneid* 3.57). In a more complex society, particularly one based economically on the principle of individual competition, men feel the need of reassurance against their fears of hostility, failure, and insecurity, and too often it is sought in an intensified quest for possessions (see K. Horney, *The Neurotic Personality of Our Time* [New York 1937] ch. 10).

In earlier times avarice was considered a more reprehensible moral fault than prodigality, which is its opposite extreme (St. Thomas Aquinas, *Summa theologiae* 2a2ae, 19.3). The latter was deemed to stand nearer to, or to have more affinity with, the mean, which is liberality, than the former, as is apparent in the terms themselves: one who gives too freely has a greater likeness to the ideally liberal man than another who gives too sparingly. In later times when bourgeois thinking had dignified trade and moneymaking with ethical or near-ethical values, the virtuous mean shifted in popular thought from a position nearer the extreme of prodigality to one more closely approaching avarice. The older term ''liberality'' accordingly became less appropriate and was largely replaced in popular use by ''thrift'' and ''frugality.'' But in the more recent stage of the economic development of society the encouragement of consumption is seen as desirable for the stimulation of industry and production. Thrift and frugality have therefore lost something of the respectability they formerly enjoyed. Nevertheless this does not appear to have resulted in a new shift in the mean popularly considered desirable between avarice and prodigality, so much as in a change in the relative values assigned to different kinds of possessions an individual will desire—for example, consumer goods, such as homes, cars, appliances, which give comfort and status to the possessor, as compared with money.

St. Thomas noted that the inclination to avarice tends to grow stronger in the aged. Because their strength and prospects are diminishing, it may seem more urgent to them to compensate for this deficiency by storing up external goods and holding onto them more tenaciously.

See Also: POVERTY, RELIGIOUS.

Bibliography: THOMAS AQUINAS, *Summa theologiae* 2a2ae, 118.1–8. A. BEUGNET, *Dictionnaire de théologie catholique,* ed. A. VACANT et al., 15 v. (Paris 1903–50; Tables générales 1951–) 1.2:2623–27. R. H. TAWNEY, *Religion and the Rise of Capitalism* (Baltimore 1947; New York 1958). G. VANN, ''Money,'' *Furrow* 13 (1962) 151–159.

[P. K. MEAGHER]

AVARS

European state from *c.* A.D. 559 to 796. They closely resembled the Huns in appearance, way of life, and warfare. They came into contact with Justinian in 558, and under Khan Baian swept across southern Russia to the Frankish borders where they were checked in 561 and 566. With Lombard aid they conquered the Hungarian plain (Pannonia) from the Gepids and, after the Lombards' departure in 568, established themselves there. They gained ascendancy over the more numerous Slavs, assumed leadership of the Slavs' southward migration, probably their most significant achievement, and indirectly contributed to the separation of the West and South Slavs. The combined horde of Avars and Slavs took Singidunum and Sirmium *c.* 582 and by 597 reached Thessalonika. Driven back across the Danube by 601, they destroyed the Antes in Bessarabia in 602. In 617 they ravaged the Balkans and reached Constantinople. In 622 the West Slavs revolted from the Avars, and in 626 the South Slavs, after an Avar defeat at Constantinople, did the same with Bulgar help. The Avars thereafter remained confined in Hungary until Charlemagne's campaign of 791 to 796 ended their history, although uprisings against the Franks occurred until 803. After 805 the Avars became Christian. Many of them were absorbed by the Bulgars.

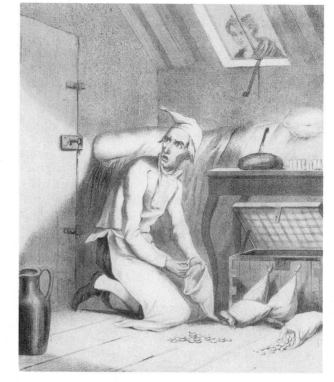

''Avarice,'' in kitchen, mid-19th-century drawing, by Louis Boilly. (©Historical Picture Archive/CORBIS)

Bibliography: F. DVORNIK, *The Slavs: Their Early History and Civilization* (Boston 1956). G. OSTROGORSKY, *History of the Byzantine State,* tr. J. HUSSEY (New Brunswick, N.J. 1957). E. KLEBEL, *Lexikon für Theologie und Kirche,* ed. J. HOFER and K. RAHNER, 10 v. (2d new ed. Freiburg 1957–65) 1:1139–40.

[R. H. SCHMANDT]

AVE MARIA (ANTIPHON)

That the text of *Ave Maria* is composed of three segments—Lk 1.28, Lk 1.42, and a prayer appended in the 15th century—is reflected in its musical settings. The Antiphonary of Hartker, for example, a 10th century source from St. Gall (*Paléographie musicale,* Ser. 2, 2), contains an antiphon that sets only the first segment followed by ''Alleluia'' (also in *Antiphonale monasticum* 228 and, in slightly different form, in *Liber usualis* 1416). Essentially the same melody is given in the 12th century Codex Worcester F. 160 (*Paléographie musicale* 12:301). The text is also used twice as an offertory antiphon—once with only the text previously mentioned and a modern melody (*Liber usualis* 1318) and once, with Lk 1.42 added and with a medieval melody (*Liber usualis* 355, found in various early MSS, among them the Codex Montpellier H. 159, PalMus 8:283, where it has two verses beginning "Quomodo in me" and "Ideo quod nascetur"). An even shorter segment of the text, ending with the words "Dominus tecum," is used as an invitatory antiphon in the Codex Worcester, and appears there with two different melodies. None of these four different medieval melodies sets the complete prayer in use today.

Renaissance polyphonists only rarely quoted any of these medieval melodies in setting the *Ave Maria*. The most celebrated early monument of music printing, *Harmonice Musices Odhecaton A* (Petrucci, 1501) begins with an *Ave Maria* by Marbriano de Orto (d. 1529) in which the melody of the first antiphon is only briefly quoted (if at all), and the text ends "Dominus tecum." Vittoria set the text twice without referring to the chant melodies. However, Josquin Desprez's setting opens with a figure very much like that beginning the antiphon, and continues with figures derived from the chant as the basis for sections in polyphonic style on the words "gratia plena," "Dominus tecum," and "benedicta tu"; but from there on his setting seems to be unrelated to the chant. His text includes Lk 1.28 and 1.42 and appends a few more lines, not part of the modern prayer, that replace the section beginning "Sancta Maria." Similarly, the text set for four voices by Palestrina is almost entirely different from the usual text after the words "Sancta Maria." Giacomo Fogliano (1473–1548), however, provided a simple four-part setting for the complete modern text. The best-known of Renaissance settings of the *Ave Maria*, that attributed to ARCADELT, is really a 19th century adaptation of the music of a secular song by Arcadelt, *Nous voyons que les hommes*, to the sacred text. Ave Maria has been set by many composers since the Renaissance— Schubert's setting is particularly well known— and contemporary composers, including Stravinsky, have continued to write music for it.

Bibliography: G. REESE, *Music in the Middle Ages* (New York 1940). R. H. LECLERCQ, *Dictionnaire d'archéologie chrétienne et de liturgie*, ed. F. CABROL, H. LECLERCQ, and H. I. MARROU (Paris 1907–53) 10.2:2043–62.

[R. STEINER]

AVE MARIS STELLA

The first verse of an unrhymed accentual hymn in honor of Our Lady. There are seven strophes of four lines each, written in trochaic dimeter brachycatalectic with three trochees to each line. It was first recorded in the Codex Sangallensis 95, found in the Abbey of Sankt Gallen, dating from the 9th century. The hymn has been attributed to various authors: St. BERNARD OF CLAIRVAUX, PAUL THE DEACON, and Venantius FORTUNATUS are the most frequently mentioned, although the MS date makes

it obvious that it could not have been the work of Bernard. It was one of the most popular hymns used for MARIAN FEASTS in the Middle Ages and was historically assigned in the Roman BREVIARY as the VESPERS hymn for the Common of feasts of the Blessed Virgin Mary as well as for the Saturday Office and the Little Office of Our Lady. The title by which Mary's intercession is sought, *maris stella*, is similar to those used in the Litany of Loreto. In the first strophe Mary is referred to as the gate of heaven, *caeli porta*, while the second stanza contrasts Mary's place in the work of redemption with Eve's responsibility for the Fall. The third stanza appeals for help and enlightenment, and in the fourth Mary is asked to use a mother's influence with her Son on our behalf. The fifth strophe recognizes the virtues we should follow if we are to reach the salvation described in the sixth stanza, *ut videntes Iesum*. The last stanza is a brief doxology. The poem, with great beauty and moving simplicity, has been translated many times, most notably by E. Caswall. The complete text with notes has been edited by C. Blume [*Analecta Hymnica* 51 (1908) 140–142].

Bibliography: F. J. MONE, ed., *Lateinische Hymnen des Mittelalters,* 3 v. (Freiburg 1853–55) 2:216–229. F. B. PLAINE, "Hymni Marialis *Ave Maris Stella* Expositio," *Studien und Mitteilungen aus dem Benedictiner-und Cistercienser Orden* 14 (1893) 244–255. G. M. DREVES, "Der Hymnus vom Meerestern," *Stimmen aus Maria Laach* 50 (1896) 558–569. P. WAGNER, "Le due melodie dell'inno *Ave Maris Stella,*" *Rassegna Gregoriana* 1 (1902) 73–75. G. BAS, *Rhythme Grégorien* (Rome 1906) 15–19. E. COSTANZI, "Quando invaluerit disciplina genuflectendi ad 1 stroph. Hymni *Ave Maris Stella,*" *Ephemerides liturgicae* 42 (1928) 322–326. M. BRITT, ed., *The Hymns of the Breviary and Missal* (new ed. New York 1948) 347–349. A. DAL ZOTTO, "Ricerche sull'autore dell' *Ave Maris Stella,*" *Aevum* 25 (1951) 494–503. J. CARCIA and E. R. PANYAGUA, "Estudios de *Ave Maris Stella,*" *Helmantica* 8 (1959) 421–475. A. MOLIEN, *Catholicisme* 1:1111–12. H. LAUSBERG, *Lexikon für Theologie und Kirche*, ed. J. HOFER and K. RAHNER (Freiburg 1957–65) 1:1141–42. J. SZÖVÉRFFY, *Die Annalen der lateinischen Hymnendichtung* (Berlin 1964–65) 1:219–220.

[B. J. COMASKEY]

AVE REGINA CAELORUM

One of the four Marian antiphons, *Ave Regina caelorum* was traditionally sung at the end of Compline from the Feast of the Lord's Presentation (Feb. 2) until Wednesday in Holy Week. Its original role in the liturgy, however, seems to have been to precede and follow the chanting of a psalm. Peter Wagner found it assigned to None on the Feast of the Assumption in a 12th century source. The more elaborate of the two melodies for this antiphon is apparently the older. The structure of the text, consisting of two pairs of similar phrases followed by an unmatched pair, is reflected in the musical form, which may be outlined as: *a a', b c, b' c, d' e.*

Bibliography: G. REESE, *Music in the Renaissance* (New York 1959). W. APEL, *Gregorian Chant* (Bloomington IN 1958). P. WAGNER, *Einführung in die gregorianische Melodien* (Hildesheim 1962). B. STÄBLEIN, ''Antiphon,'' *Die Musik in Geschichte und Gegenwart* 1:523–545.

[R. STEINER]

AVE VERUM CORPUS

Short Eucharistic hymn, no longer in liturgical use. Although regarded as a SEQUENCE, it was actually sung during the EUCHARISTIC ELEVATION, a part of the Mass introduced only in the 12th century. The hymn has been ascribed to Pope Innocent VI (1352–62), but this is improbable since the text is found in MSS from the late 13th or early 14th centuries. This hymn excels the many similar texts written during the 14th and 15th centuries (e.g., the MS of the *Orationale Augiense* contains some 26 pieces of similar character). At one time it was more popular than the *ADORO TE DEVOTE*. It originated probably in northern Italy, and it is written in trochaic tetrameter, rhyming at the caesura and at the end of lines. The last two lines reverse the roles Christ and Mary play in the famous *SALVE REGINA (Mater) Misericordiae*. Of the many musical compositions composed for this text, Mozart's motet is particularly appropriate to its spirit.

Bibliography: G. MARSOT, *Catholicisme* 1.1112–13. J. SZÖVÉRFFY, *Die Annalen der lateinischen Hymnendichtung* (Berlin 1964–65) 2:298–299. J. CONNELLY, *Hymns of the Roman Liturgy* (Westminster MD 1957) 130. *Analecta hymnica* 54:257.

[J. SZÖVÉRFFY]

AVELLANA COLLECTIO

A canonical collection of the letters of emperors and popes, beginning with a rescript of Valentinian I, dated 368, and ending with a letter of Pope VIGILIUS to Justinian, dated May 14, 553. Evidence available indicates that the collection was prepared shortly after A.D. 553. The collection reproduces in succession: letters of the emperors (from Valentinian to Honorius) interspersed with a few letters addressed to the emperors, letters of the popes from Innocent I to Vigilius, and letters and acts from the pontificate of Pope St. HORMISDAS. (The best edition is the work of O. Günther in *Corpus scriptorum ecclesiasticorum* 35.) The interest of the collection lies above all in the compiler's intention of providing texts not included in collections then in existence, and of seeking them directly in the archival deposits, e.g., a reference to the use of the *gesta* after Hormisdas' letter. But the author also collected apocryphal writings, e.g., the correspondence of Peter of Antioch relating to monophysitism. The col-

lection was not widely disseminated because the Gelasian Collections had summarized ancient law, and the legislative activity of the papacy suffered as a result of political crises. However, through the *Avellana Collectio,* we know a good portion of the letters of Vigilius and certain imperial letters.

Bibliography: P. FOURNIER and G. LEBRASM, *Histoire des collections canoniques en occident depuis les fausses décrétales jusqu'au Déret de Gratien* 1:35–41. F. MAASSEN, *Geschichte der Quellen und der Literatur des canonischen Rechts im Abendlande bis dem Ausgang des Mittelalters* 787–792. O. GÜNTHER, ''Avellana-Studien,'' *Sitzungsberichte der Akademie der Wissenschaften in Wien* 134.5 (1896). R. NAZ, ed., *Dictionnaire de droit canonique* 1:1491.

[J. GAUDEMET]

AVELLINO, ANDREW, ST.

Preacher and reformer; b. Castronuovo, Naples, 1521; d. Naples, Nov. 10, 1608. His parents, who were of the nobility, named him Lancelot at Baptism. He pursued his studies in various cities and in 1537 became a cleric. After ordination in 1545, he undertook the study of canon and civil law at Naples in 1547. In 1548 he made the spiritual exercises under the Jesuit James Laynez. This experience, as well as his remorse at the recollection of a lie he had told in pleading a legal case led to his determination to devote himself completely to the care of souls. He was badly beaten by men who resented his effort to reform a convent in Baiano, and was taken to the Theatine house of St. Paul in Naples where he recovered.

In 1556 he joined the Theatines and took the name Andrew. He evidenced qualities suitable for a spiritual director and promoter of ecclesiastical discipline, and in 1567 became superior of his community in Naples. At the request of Charles Borromeo he founded a Theatine house in Milan in 1570, and the next year went to Piacenza where he directed the diocesan seminary and a house of penitent women. Three times he acted as visitor of the Theatine houses in Lombardy. In 1582 he returned to Naples. In 1590 he officially visited the Theatine houses of the Roman and Neapolitan provinces, and successfully pleaded that he be excused from elevation to the hierarchy. An articulate and cultivated man, he left about 3,000 letters of spiritual direction, a little more than 1,000 of which were published in Naples (1731–32). Other works, including conferences, were published in Naples (1733–34). He was canonized in 1712. Naples and Sicily honor him as a patron.

Feast: Nov. 10.

Bibliography: *Acta Sanctorum* Nov. 4:609–622. G. M. MAGENIS, *Vita di S. Andrea Avellino* (Venice 1714). A. PALMIERI, *Dic-*

tionnaire d'histoire et de géographie ecclésiastiques, ed. A. BAUDRILLART et al. (Paris 1912) 1635–37, bibliog.

[W. BANGERT]

AVEMPACE (IBN BĀJJAH, ABŪ BAKR MUHAMMAD IBN YAHYĀ)

Arab philosopher who flourished in Spain; b. Saragossa (date unknown) and went to Seville in 1118; d. at the Almoravid court at Fez, 1138. He wrote works on medicine and mathematics, and commented on Aristotle's *Physica, Meteorologica, De generatione et corruptione, De generatione animalium,* and *De partibus animalium.* His main philosophical writings include treatises on logic, the *Regime* or *Guide of the Solitary, On the Contact of the Intellect with Man,* a treatise on the soul, and a letter of farewell. The last three were cited by AVERROËS in his *Commentarium magnum* on Aristotle's *De anima.*

In the *Regime of the Solitary,* according to a synopsis given by a 14th-century Jewish writer, Moses of Narbonne, Avempace tries to show how man can achieve union with the Agent Intellect. By seeking not merely forms of material things but also universal spiritual forms or ideas, the human intellect can gradually work up to a level where it grasps ideas of ideas. Thus, by its own power, it can come to know separated substances. In other works, too, Avempace holds that through a progressive abstraction of quiddities man's intellect can reach a QUIDDITY that has no further quiddities, i.e., the quiddity of a separated substance. Averroës reports these views and notes their author's abiding concern with the question of how man's intellect can achieve its end: union with the separated Agent Intellect. That question, says Averroës, never left the thought of Avempace, "not even for the space of time it takes to blink an eye" (*Comm. de anim.* 3.36, 487 Med. Acad. ed.). Aquinas restates Avempace's views and criticizes them as "frivolous" (*C. gent.* 3.41).

Avempace's commentary on the *Physica* seems to have been influential in the formulation of Galileo's law of falling bodies.

See Also: ARABIAN PHILOSOPHY; INTELLECT, UNITY OF; SCIENCE (IN THE MIDDLE AGES).

Bibliography: AVEMPACE, "Ibn Bājjah's Tadbīru'l-Mutawahhīd (Rule of the Solitary)," ed. and tr. D. M. DUNLOP, *Journal of the Royal Asiatic Society* (1945) 61–81, partial text in Arabic and Eng. S. MUNK, *Mélanges de philosophie juive et arabe* (new ed. Paris 1955). M. CLAGGET, *The Science of Mechanics in the Middle Ages* (Madison, Wis. 1959). E. A. MOODY, "Galileo and Avempace: The Dynamics of the Leaning Tower Experiment," *Journal of the History of Ideas* 12 (1951) 163–193, 375–422.

[B. H. ZEDLER]

AVENDAÑO, DIEGO DE

Jesuit specialist in law for the Indies; b. Segovia, Spain, Sept. 29, 1596; d. Lima, Peru, Aug. 30, 1688. After studying philosophy at Seville, he went to Lima in 1610, and while a student at its Colegio de San Martín, he entered the Society of Jesus on April 21, 1612. He completed his studies at the Jesuit college in Lima and taught philosophy in Cuzco, where he became rector in 1628. He made his profession on May 24, 1629. He was professor of theology in the Jesuit University of Chuquisaca (today Sucre, Bolivia), rector of the major seminary of Lima during two periods (1651, 1667), and provincial from 1663 to 1666. In his great work *Thesaurus indicus* he formulated, discussed, and resolved a varied range of legal topics, no doubt submitted to him for study, as an expert in canon, civil, and moral law, by the episcopal tribunals and the Spanish-American courts. In it he showed his fine speculative talent, his rigidly scholastic education, his eclecticism, and his extensive and up-to-date reading. He was an illustrious example of 17th-century education in Lima. He neither tried to be nor was original, but he was useful for the correct administration of justice. His intrinsic value lay in having adapted the traditional doctrine of both bodies of law to the native Peruvian environment and to its particular problems.

Bibliography: M. DE MENDIBURU, *Diccionario histórico-biográfico del Perú,* 11 v. (2d ed. Lima 1931–34) 2:291–294. J. E. DE URIARTE and M. LECINA, *Biblioteca de escritores de la Compañía de Jesús . . . ,* 2 v. (Madrid 1925–30).

[A. DE EGAÑA]

AVERROËS (IBN RUSHD)

Muslim philosopher whose writings influenced medieval Christian thinkers; b. Córdoba, Spain, 1126; d. Morocco, 1198. Averroës came from a distinguished family of judges. He studied law, medicine, theology, and philosophy and served in high positions under two Almohad rulers: Ya'qūb Yusūf and his successor, Yusūf Ya'qūb al-Mansūr. When the latter persecuted the philosophers (1196–97), Averroës was banished from Córdoba, but he was later restored to favor.

Averroës wrote a general work on medicine, *Kullīyāt*—known to the Latins as *Colliget* and used as a textbook in medieval universities. His main philosophical works include *Sermo de substantia orbis; Fasl al-maqāl (On the Harmony of Religion and Philosophy); Tahāfut al-Tahāfut* (or, in the Latin version, *Destructio destructionis philosophiae Algazelis*); commentaries on many works of Aristotle including the *Metaphysics, Physics, De generatione et corruptione, Nicomachean Ethics, De anima, De caelo et mundo, Posterior Analytics;* and a paraphrase of Plato's *Republic.*

Teaching. The Aristotelian commentaries, written at the request of Ya'qūb Yusūf, were of three types. The great commentary reproduced in the order of the original text each paragraph of Aristotle's work and explained it in a detailed way. The middle commentary cited only the first words of each of Aristotle's paragraphs before proceeding to some exposition. The paraphrase was a summary that followed the order that seemed most suitable to Averroës; this was not necessarily the order of the book he was explaining. The commentaries reflected Averroës's great admiration for ARISTOTLE. Although he was influenced also by PLATO, Aristotle, for him, was the master, the "exemplar that Nature found to show forth the highest human perfection" [*Comm. mag. in Arist. de anim. lib.* 3.14 (Mediaeval Academy ed. 433)].

Notion of Intellect. In his commentary on the *De anima* Averroës discussed a problem that had arisen from a text in book 3: Does each man have his own intellect or is there one intellect for all men? Some of the Arabs, among them Avicenna (980–1037), had thought that although each man has his own possible intellect, the active, or agent, intellect is a separated substance and one for all men. Averroës held that the possible, or "material," intellect, as well as the agent intellect, was a separated substance and one for all men. In his view the individual man has no spiritual intellect; but because man's imagination, memory, and cogitative power supply and prepare sensory data for the use of the separated intellect, he thought man shared in the latter's knowledge. For Averroës, the separated agent intellect actuates the intelligible species potentially present in man's phantasms and thus enables the separated possible intellect to become the subject in which knowledge exists (*Comm. mag.* 3.4, 383–385; 3.5, 388–389, 412; 3.18, 439–440; 3.19, 441; 3.33, 476). St. THOMAS AQUINAS was to point out that to say man provides the objects of knowledge for a separated intellect is not to explain how the individual man knows; and to deny to the individual man a spiritual power of knowing is to destroy the philosophical basis for the personal immortality of the soul (*De unit. intell.* proem.; 3). Averroës himself was not content with his own explanation, but tried to keep the intellect separate from matter to ensure its function of knowing UNIVERSALS (*Comm. mag.* 3.4, 383–384; 3.5, 388–389; 3.19, 441; 3.36, 502). He had no awareness of a spiritual intellective soul that could be the form of the body without being immersed in matter.

Concept of Being. In metaphysics Averroës found the clue to the meaning of being in the book of his Master. Aristotle had seemed to identify being with substance and substance with "what" a thing is (*Meta.* 1028a 13–14). Averroës taught that being is eminently substance and that substance is eminently form [*In 7 meta.*

"Allegory of the Catholic Religion," detail of a fresco by Taddeo Gaddi, showing Averroës, located in the Cappella degli Spagnoli of the Church of Santa Maria Novella, Florence, 14th century.

1 (Venice 1574)]. He criticized Avicenna for teaching that existence is an accident of essence. "Avicenna sinned much," he said, "in this that he thought that 'one' and 'being' signify dispositions added to the essence of a thing" (*In 4 meta.* 2, fol. 67r–v). For Averroës "to be" is in no way an addition to essence: "This name *ens* that is imposed from the 'to be' of a thing, signifies the same reality as the name that is imposed from its essence" (*In 4 meta.* 2, fol. 67r). Being means nothing else than "that which is." To him it seemed that Avicenna had mixed up theological teachings with metaphysics.

Averroës also rejected Avicenna's version of emanation, which provided a cosmological framework for showing that existence is something that "happens" to a possible essence [*Tahāfut al-Tahāfut* 3 (tr. S. van den Bergh 118–119)]. It is wrong, Averroës thought, to insist that from the one, only one can proceed. In Averroës's cosmology this principle applies more evidently to the lower world—made up of beings composed of matter and form—than it does to the realm of Intelligences. Rather, the first effect possesses plurality, a plurality that depends on unity (*ibid.* 3.107–109, 148–149, 154).

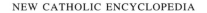

God and the World. Averroës agreed with Avicenna that there are many Intelligences and that their number and their rank are determined by the number and physical rank (i.e., the size and speed) of the celestial bodies they move, but this hierarchy of rank is not a sequence of production. Although some are subordinate to others in rank, the whole hierarchy of Intelligences is related to God as its formal and final cause. God is the First Principle, "the principle of all these principles" (*ibid.* 3.111–115; 138).

In Averroës's context the heavens, motion, time, and primary matter are all eternal. The world must be eternal, he thought; to deny its eternity would be to imply that something could prevent God's act from being eternally connected with His existence. But such a constraint upon His activity would point to an inadmissible lack of power and perfection in God (*ibid.* 1.56). The assumption that an eternal effect must necessarily result from God's eternal action was later opposed by St. Thomas Aquinas (*C. gent.* 2.35; *Summa theologiae* 1a, 46.1 ad 10).

Averroës's God was the productive cause of the things of the sublunary world. As such, He made sensible things to be by bringing into actual existence forms that existed potentially in eternal matter. Although this God might seem to a Christian to be only a First Mover and not a Creator, Averroës called Him a cause of existence, since to his way of thinking, "the bestower of the conjunction of matter and form is the bestower of existence" (*Tahāfut* 3.108).

Religion. This and other conclusions of Averroës seemed incompatible with traditional teachings of the religion of Islam, which he also accepted. Did he then teach a doctrine of double truth, as some later interpreters claimed? The answer is negative. In his *Faṣl al-maqāl* (*On the Harmony of Religion and Philosophy*) he tried to show that religion points through symbolic representations to the same truths that philosophical knowledge attains. For most people, he held, the religious approach is best (*Faṣl al-maqāl*, ch. 2, 3; *Tahāfut* [About the Natural Sciences] 1, 4). But by implying that only the philosopher, and not the believer, sees truth as it is, Averroës seemed to accept the speculative primacy of reason.

Influence. The thought of Averroës did not have much influence in his own Muslim world, but many of his works were preserved in Hebrew and Latin translations. As "The Commentator," he was used by Christians as an aid in reading Aristotle and became the source of a new movement of thought that opposed, on some points, the teachings of faith. This Latin Averroism of 13th-century Paris was succeeded by a second Averroism in 14th-, 15th-, and 16th-century Italy, especially at Padua. Petrarch declared that for some thinkers, Aristotle held the place of Christ, and Averroës that of St. Peter

[quoted by J. R. Charbonnel, *La Pensée italienne au XIVᵉ siècle* (Paris 1919) 178].

See Also: AVERROISM, LATIN; DOUBLE TRUTH, THEORY OF; INTELLEC, UNITY OF; ARABIAN PHILOSOPHY; SCHOLASTICISM.

Bibliography: Works. *Commentarium magnum in Aristotelis De anima libros,* ed. F. S. CRAWFORD (Cambridge, Mass. 1953), and other Mediaeval Academy eds. of his commentaries; *Commentarium in Aristotelis Metaphysicorum libros,* in ARISTOTLE, *Opera cum Averrois commentariis,* 9 v. in 11 and 3 suppl. (Venice 1562–74; repr. Frankfurt A. M. 1962); *Commentary on Plato's Republic,* ed. and tr. E. I. J. ROSENTHAL (Cambridge, Eng. 1956); *On the Harmony of Religion and Philosophy,* tr. G. F. HOURANI (London 1961); *Tahāfut al-Tahāfut (The Incoherence of the Incoherence),* tr. S. VAN DEN BERGH, 2 v. (London 1954); *Destructio destructionum philosophiae Algazelis in the Latin Version of Calo Calonymos,* ed. B. H. ZEDLER (Milwaukee 1961). Literature. M. ALLARD, *Le Rationalisme d'Averroës d'après une étude sur la création* (Paris 1955). L. GAUTHIER, *Ibn Rochd (Averroës)* (Paris 1948). É. H. GILSON, *Being and Some Philosophers* (2d ed. Toronto 1952); *History of Christian Philosophy in the Middle Ages* (New York 1955). E. RENAN, *Oeuvres philosophiques: Averroës et l'averroïsme . . . ,* v. 3 of *Oeuvres complètes* (Paris 1949). H. A. WOLFSON, "Revised Plan for the Publication of a *Corpus commentariorum Averrois in Aristotelem,*" *Speculum* 38 (1963) 88–98.

[B. H. ZEDLER]

AVERROISM, LATIN

A philosophical movement originating in the 13th century among masters of the faculty of arts in the University of Paris; also called integral, radical, and heterodox ARISTOTELIANISM. Its main source was the philosophy of ARISTOTLE as interpreted by AVERROËS.

Origins. In the early Middle Ages Aristotle's philosophy was known in western Europe chiefly through Latin translations of his minor logical works. In the second half of the 12th and the first half of the 13th century, the rest of his works were translated, decisively influencing the development of philosophy and theology. Along with the *corpus aristotelicum* a rich and varied Arabic philosophical and scientific literature, including some of the works of AVICENNA and Averroës, was also translated into Latin. Averroës's commentaries on Aristotle were so highly regarded that he was called the Commentator.

The portion of Avicenna's works known in the Christian West was translated in the 12th century, and its influence was felt in the first decades of the 13th century. The impact of Averroës's works came shortly afterward. They were translated between 1220 and 1235 and were first quoted in the 1230s and 1240s by theologians such as WILLIAM OF AUVERGNE, PHILIP THE CHANCELLOR, and St. ALBERT THE GREAT. At this time the scholastics used Averroës's works without suspecting how dangerous they could be to Christian thought. There is no indication of a Christian following of Averroës at this early date.

On March 16, 1255, a statute of the faculty of arts at Paris prescribed the teaching of the works of Aristotle (*Chartularium universitatis Parisiensis* 1:277). This date marks the official reception of Aristotelianism into the university. Since Aristotle's works were usually read along with Averroës's commentaries on them, it was to be expected that Averroës's influence would grow with Aristotle's.

The first criticisms of the errors of Averroës appeared shortly afterward. In 1256 St. Albert wrote his *De unitate intellectus contra Averroem* at the request of Pope Alexander IV. A few years later St. THOMAS AQUINAS refuted Averroës's doctrine of the oneness of the intellect in his *Summa contra Gentiles* (2.73–76). These works were directed against Averroës's own teachings. They give no hint that he was acquiring a following among the philosophers at Paris. In 1270, however, St. Thomas directed his *De unitate intellectus contra Averroistas* against Parisian Averroists, especially Siger of Brabant. In the first chapter he says that "for some time now the error concerning the intellect has been implanted in many minds, originating in the statements of Averroës." The criticism by St. BONAVENTURE of the heterodox Parisian masters of arts in 1267 and the official condemnation of the Averroists in 1270 by the bishop of Paris are conclusive evidence of the existence at this time of a Latin Averroist movement.

Principal Proponents. Not all the medieval philosophers and theologians who used and admired Averroës's commentaries can be called Averroists. Masters of arts such as ADAM OF BUCKFIELD, ROGER BACON, and John Sackville used them when lecturing on Aristotle; and theologians such as St. Albert and St. Thomas found the works of Averroës helpful, though they did not subscribe to his heterodox positions. The true Averroists were those who, like Averroës, tended to identify Aristotle's philosophy with philosophy itself, and generally accepted the Averroist interpretation of Aristotle. Like Averroës, they also advocated the freedom of philosophy from the influence of religion. The doctrine of Averroës that most clearly identified a scholastic as an Averroist was the oneness of the possible intellect in all men.

The leading Averroist in the 13th century was SIGER OF BRABANT, a master of arts at Paris from about 1260 to 1273. Writing in 1492, A. NIFO, himself an Averroist in his youth, called Siger the originator of the Averroist school. Siger taught an Aristotelianism strongly influenced by Averroës and to a lesser extent by the NEOPLATONISM of Avicenna. Another leading figure in the movement was BOETHIUS OF SWEDEN (Dacia). From his

few works that have survived and have been edited, he is known to have been an important logician and exponent of an Aristotelianism on some points contrary to the faith. One of the oldest manuscripts containing the heterodox propositions condemned by the bishop of Paris in 1277 names him as their principal exponent. While striving to find a *modus vivendi* for philosophy and theology, he advocated their strict separation. He also stressed the freedom of the philosopher to teach, even if his conclusions run counter to the faith. Other names associated with the condemnation of Averroism in the 13th century are Bernier of Nivelles and Goswin of La Chapelle. Nothing is known of their doctrine.

Unedited manuscripts, some anonymous, attest to the widespread influence of heterodox Aristotelianism in the late 13th and the early 14th century. A group of commentaries on Aristotle's *Nicomachean Ethics* reveals a naturalism in ethics opposed to Christian morality. James of Douai probably wrote one of these commentaries about 1275; another was written by Giles of Orléans in the beginning of the 14th century. Both were influenced by the ethical writings of Siger of Brabant and Boethius of Sweden. James of Douai was a man of moderate views, and in his Questions on the *De anima* he argued against the Averroistic doctrine of the oneness of the intellect.

Main Teachings. In the late Middle Ages and in the Renaissance the Averroists were conscious of forming a distinct school of philosophy. Averroism in the 13th century had not reached this stage of self-awareness but its characteristic spirit and general positions were already apparent.

The Averroists taught that the world and all species are eternal, and consequently that there was no first man. They adopted the Greek cyclical view of history, according to which all events, ideas, and religions eternally recur. For Siger and Boethius, this was a necessary conclusion of the philosophy of nature. God acts only indirectly on the world; hence miracles are unintelligible. God, the primary efficient cause, produced the world through intermediary separate substances, according to Siger of Brabant, reflecting the views of Avicenna; or God is only the final cause of the world, according to John of Jandun, following Averroës. God and all other celestial causes act on the world with necessity; contingency and indetermination are found only in the sublunar world, owing to the presence of matter. God's knowledge does not directly extend to contingent events.

Perhaps the most distinctive Averroistic tenet was the oneness of the possible intellect for the whole human race. This distinguishes Averroism from Avicennism, according to which the agent intellect is one for all men but each man possesses his own possible intellect. For the Averroists, the possible intellect is a separate substance that uses the sense faculties of individual men, and they can be said to understand insofar as their powers cooperate in the act of knowing. Since the individual does not possess his own intellective soul, human reason cannot demonstrate personal immortality. The ultimate end of man, or happiness, is in the present life. The highest felicity of man consists in philosophical contemplation.

The Latin Averroists did not deny their Christian faith, even though they taught doctrines contrary to it in their philosophy. In their view, the faith is true because it rests on the supernatural light of revelation. The conclusions of reason are less certain, being known by the inferior light of the human intellect. Hence a conclusion can be probable, or even necessary, in philosophy, while contradicting a revealed truth. To the theologians this was tantamount to a double truth, one for philosophy and another contradictory one for faith. The Latin Averroists themselves carefully avoided proposing a double truth. In cases of conflict between reason and faith, they invariably placed truth on the side of faith. It is difficult, if not impossible, to know whether this was done sincerely or as a cloak for unbelief (*see* DOUBLE TRUTH, THEORY OF).

Theological Reaction. Latin Averroism was immediately opposed by the theologians. The Franciscan school, headed by St. Bonaventure, took the lead in attacking the Aristotelians who, mainly under the influence of Averroës, taught doctrines contrary to the faith. In his commentary on the *Sentences* (*c.* 1250), St. Bonaventure had argued against Aristotelian doctrines such as the eternity of the world. Later, in his *Collationes de decem praeceptis* (1267), he criticized Parisian masters who erroneously taught that the world is eternal, that there is only one intellect in all men, and that a mortal being cannot attain immortality. The following year, in his *De donis Spiritus Sancti,* he opposed an even longer list of errors taught by the philosophers at Paris. His most vigorous polemic against Aristotle and his medieval followers is in the *Collationes in Hexaemeron* (1273). The threat of Greek and Arabian philosophy to the faith was clearly growing stronger at this time.

In 1270 St. Thomas wrote the *De unitate intellectus contra Averroistas* in opposition to the masters in the Parisian faculty of arts who taught the Averroistic doctrine of the unity of the intellect. This treatise seems to have been the first to use the term Averroists. In the next few centuries the term was widely used. St. Thomas wrote his own commentaries on Aristotle, using the new and more accurate translations of his works by WILLIAM OF MOERBEKE, to make available an Aristotelianism unadulterated by Arabian interpretations.

In 1270 GILES OF ROME exposed the errors of Aristotle, Avicenna, Averroës, and other non-Christian philosophers in his *De erroribus philosophorum,* and in his *De plurificatione intellectus possibilis* (*c.* 1272–75) he launched a direct attack on Averroism, based mainly on St. Thomas. About the same time GILES OF LESSINES sent St. Albert in Cologne a list of 15 propositions "taught by the most eminent masters in the schools of Paris." St. Albert replied in a treatise entitled *De quindecim problematibus,* criticizing the teaching of the Aristotelian masters at Paris as contrary not only to theology but also to sound philosophy.

Ecclesiastical Condemnations. The ecclesiastical authorities also tried to stem the rising tide of Aristotelian naturalism and Averroism. In 1270 the Bishop of Paris, Étienne TEMPIER, condemned 13 propositions traceable to Aristotle as interpreted by Averroës and his followers at Paris, and he excommunicated those who knowingly taught them. The condemned errors included the oneness of the intellect, the eternity of the world and the human species, the mortality of the human soul, the denial of providence and free will, and the necessitating influence of the heavenly bodies on the sublunar world.

On Jan. 18, 1277, Pope John XXI asked Tempier to inform him of the errors taught at Paris and of the names of the masters who taught them. No report of the bishop to the pope is extant. On March 7, 1277, the bishop, seemingly on his own authority, condemned 219 propositions, all of which were linked with philosophical naturalism and Aristotelianism. Among the condemned propositions were some upheld by St. Thomas. No written source has been discovered for some of the proscribed theses, e.g., that the Christian religion hinders education, that this religion like others contains errors, and that theology rests on myths. Other theses exalt philosophy at the expense of faith, e.g., that there is no state superior to that of the philosopher. This was taught by Boethius of Sweden. Some propositions denied the Christian moral life and ultimate end of man. In the prologue to the condemnation the bishop censured those "who say that these things are true according to philosophy but not according to the Catholic faith, as though there were two contrary truths . . ." (*Chartularium universitatis Parisiensis* 1:543). On March 18, 1277, ROBERT KILWARDBY, Archbishop of Canterbury, condemned a similar list of 30 propositions.

Later Averroism. After the condemnations, Averroism continued to be attacked by theologians, such as Raymond LULL, who wrote several treatises against Averroës and his followers. Despite these criticisms, Averroism remained alive at Paris and spread to England and Italy.

The outstanding Averroist in Paris in the early 14th century was JOHN OF JANDUN, the self-styled "ape of

Averroës.'' Jandun praised Averroës as the ''most perfect and glorious friend and defender of philosophical truth.'' Associated with him at Paris was MARSILIUS OF PADUA. Both Marsilius and John of Jandun were adversaries of the pope and, with WILLIAM OF OCKHAM, took refuge with the Emperor Louis of Bavaria. Marsilius's *Defensor pacis* is an example of political Averroism, advocating the separation of Church and State and the subordination of the former to the latter.

The Englishman JOHN BACONTHORP was called ''the prince of the Averroists'' during the Renaissance, though in fact he accepted none of the heterodox teachings of Averroës. He wrote outstanding and somewhat benign commentaries on Aristotle and Averroës that won him the acclaim of Renaissance Averroists. Another 14th-century Englishman, THOMAS OF WILTON, was more favorable to Averroism. A master of arts and theology at Paris and chancellor of St. Paul's in London, Thomas believed that human reason left to itself cannot refute the doctrine of Averroës.

Through PETRARCH, a violent anti-Averroist, it is known that Averroism reached Italy in the early 14th century, accompanied by skepticism in religion. Among the radical Italian Averroists was Anthony of Parma, a master of arts and famous doctor and philosopher of nature. Averroistic Aristotelianism was represented at Bologna by Thaddaeus of Parma and Angelo of Arezzo. Angelo's Averroism is evident even in his logical treatises. A. Maier has recently added two more names to the list of Bolognese Averroists, Matthew of Gubbio and Anselm of Como.

From Bologna Averroism made its way to Padua and Venice, where its main representatives were Paolo VENETO, Gaetano da Thiene (*see* CAJETAN, ST.), Alexander Achillini (1463–1512), and Nicoletto Vernia (1420–99). Pietro POMPONAZZI was a product of Paduan Averroism. Though he sharply criticized the Averroist doctrine of the soul in his *De immortalitate animae,* the spirit of Averroism is reflected in his naturalism and in his separation of faith and reason.

Appreciation. Latin Averroism was a serious danger to the Church because it set reason in conflict with faith. According to Christian tradition, as expressed by the Fathers of the Church and the great scholastic theologians, natural knowledge cannot be contrary to divine revelation because God is the source of both (see St. Thomas, *C. gent.* 1.7). Although the Latin Averroists wished to exalt reason and philosophy, in fact they degraded them by opposing them to the truth of faith. They misunderstood the nature of philosophy, making it an inquiry into the thought of the great philosophers of the past, especially Aristotle, rather than an investigation of reality. Centered as it was on the texts of Aristotle and his commentators, Latin Averroism was one of the most pedantic and unprogressive philosophical movements in the Middle Ages. It disappeared with the eclipse of Aristotelianism in the 16th and 17th centuries.

See Also: ARABIAN PHILOSOPHY

Bibliography: E. RENAN, *Averroès et l'averroïsme* (2d ed. Paris 1860). P. F. MANDONNET, *Siger de Brabant et l'averroïsme latin au XIIIe siècle*, 2 v. (Les Philosophes belges 6–7; 2d ed. Louvain 1908–11). F. VAN STEENBERGHEN, *Siger de Brabant d'après ses oeuvres inédites*, 2 v. (*ibid.* 12–13; Louvain 1931–42); *Aristotle in the West*, tr. L. JOHNSTON (Louvain 1955). M. GRABMANN, *Der lateinische Averroismus des 13. Jahrhunderts und seine Stellung zur christlichen Weltanschauung* (Munich 1931); *Mittelalterliches Geistesleben*, v.2 (Munich 1936). R. DE VAUX, ''La première entrée d'Averroès chez les Latins,'' *Revue des sciences philsophiques et théologiques* 22 (1933) 193–245. R. A. GAUTHIER, ''Trois commentaires averroistes sur l'Ethique à Nicomaque,'' *Archives d'histoire doctrinale et littéraire du moyen-âge* 22–23 (1947–48) 187–336. A. MAIER, *An der Grenze von Scholastik und Naturwissenschaft* (Essen 1943; 2d ed. Rome 1952); *Die Vorläufer Galileis im 14. Jahrhundert* (Rome 1949). B. NARDI, *Sigieri di Brabante nel pensiero del Rinascimento italiano* (Rome 1945); *Saggi sull' Aristotelismo Padovano dal secolo XIV al XVI* (Florence 1958). É. H. GILSON, *History of Christian Philosophy in the Middle Ages* (New York 1955). H. LEY, *Studie zur Geschichte des Materialismus im Mittelalter* (Berlin 1957).

[A. MAURER]

AVERSA, RAPHAEL

Theatine theologian; b. Sanseverino, Italy, 1588; d. Rome, June 10, 1657. He served five times as superior general of the Clerks Regular Minor and was greatly respected for his learning and his ability as a theologian. He twice refused the episcopacy offered him by Innocent X and Alexander VII. His most notable work was a complete treatment of scholastic theology, *Theologia scholastica universa ad mentem s. Thomae,* divided into six parts and published in nine volumes appearing at various times and under various titles at Rome, Venice, Genoa, and Bologna between 1631 and 1642. He also wrote *Logica* (Rome 1623) and *Philosophia* (2 v. Rome 1625–27).

Bibliography: H. HURTER *Nomenclator literarius theologiae catholicae,* 5 v. (3d ed. Innsbruck 1903–13) 3:934–935. G. FUSSENEGGER, *Lexikon für Theologie und Kirch,* ed. J. HOFER and K. RAHNER, 10 v. (2d ed. Freiburg 1957–65) 1:1146–47.

[J. C. WILLKE]

AVESTA

The sacred book of the Parsees, the modern Persian followers of the ancient religion of ZOROASTER. Its oldest part, the GĀTHĀS, dates back probably to Zoroaster himself. Its most recent parts may be as late as the Sassanian period (3d cent.–7th cent. A.D.). The Avesta is composed in two different dialects of a very archaic language, probably of equal antiquity with Vedic Sanskrit. This language was already obsolete in Sassanian times, when it became necessary to furnish the text with a paraphrase and commentary in the vernacular Pahlavi, or language of the Sassanians. Because such commentaries were called *zand,* the Avesta has been mistakenly designated as the *Zand-Avesta* or *Zend-Avesta.* A summary of the contents of the Avesta surviving in Pahlavi shows that the Sassanian Avesta was about four times longer than the extant form. It contained 21 books, but only one has been preserved intact, the *Videvdat* or ''Code against the Demons.'' The rest of the extant Avesta is made up of fragments of the other 20 books, arranged for liturgical purposes.

The first part of the Avesta is the *Yasna* or ''Sacrifice,'' a text recited during the performance of the chief ceremony of the Zoroastrian ritual, a sacrifice—faintly suggestive of the Catholic Mass—of sacred liquor and water before an ever-burning fire. In the *Yasna* are embedded the *Gāthās,* metrical discourses and revelations of Zoroaster. The *Visprat,* or ''All the patrons,'' is a collection of additions to the *Yasna,* recited in more solemn circumstances.

The second part of the Avesta is a series of 21 *Yashts* or ''Hymns'' to as many divinities, including ancient gods whom Zoroaster had ignored or combated, but whose cult had crept again into Zoroastrianism. The chief divinities are Mithra, the goddess Anahita, the star-god Tishtrya, and others. There are also hymns to the spirits of the deceased, to the FRAVASHIS, to the Xvarnah or Royal Fortune, etc. The third part is the *Videvdat,* cited above. In addition there are several minor sections.

Although the Avesta is valuable to the historian of religion, only the *Gāthās* and parts of the *Yashts* have any literary value.

Bibliography: R. C. ZAEHNER, *The Dawn and Twilight of Zoroastrianism* (New York 1961). J. DUCHESNE-GUILLEMIN, *La Religion de l'Iran ancien* (Paris 1962).

[J. DUCHESNE-GUILLEMIN]

AVIAT, FRANCESCA SALESIA, BL.

Baptized Leonie (Leonia), educator and co-founder of the Sister Oblates of Saint Francis de Sales; b. Sézanne, France, Sept. 16, 1844; d. Perugia, Umbria, Italy, Jan. 10, 1914. Leonie wanted to join the Visitation Nuns, but her family opposed her vocation. Her spiritual director,

Father Louis Alexander Alphonse Brisson, suggested that she found a women's religious congregation. Thus, in Troyes, France (1866), animated by the spirit of Saint Francis de Sales, the Oblates began providing Christian education to young women working in the mills that sprang up during the Industrial Revolution. The first sisters took their vows in 1871 with Aviat as their superior general. Because of anti-Church legislation adopted in France at the turn of the 20th century, Mother Aviat moved (1903) to Perugia, Italy, where she began the order anew, wrote the order's constitution, and received the approval of Pope Saint PIUS X (1911). She died at age 69, having seen her work extended throughout Europe and to South Africa and Ecuador. She was declared venerable in 1978 and beatified Sept. 27, 1992 by John Paul II, following the inexplicable healing of a 12-year-old South African boy in 1991. A second miracle attributed to her intercession, the spontaneous healing of a 14-year-old girl with a tethered spine in the Archdiocese of Philadelphia in 1992, was approved Dec. 18, 2000. Mother Francesca Salesia was canonized Nov. 25, 2001.

Feast: Jan. 10.

Bibliography: M.-A. D'ESMAUGES, *Leonie Aviat, Mutter Franziska Salesia, die Gründerin der Oblatinnen des hl. Franz von Sales* (Eichstatt 1993), tr. from Italian *Leonie Aviat Madre Francesca di Sales* (Padua 1992).

[K. I. RABENSTEIN]

AVICEBRON (IBN GABIROL, SOLOMON BEN JUDAH)

Jewish philosopher and poet; b. Malaga, Spain, *c.* 1021; d. Valencia, Spain, *c.* 1058. Avicebron has two distinct careers in history. As Ibn Gabirol (Shĕlōmōh ben Yĕhūdāh) he stood in the first rank of medieval Hebrew poets; as Avicebron (Avicembron, Avicenbrol, Avencebrol) he was an Arabian philosopher whose work was translated into Latin *c.* 1150 by DOMINIC GUNDISALVI and JOHN OF SPAIN under the title of *Fons Vitae* (Fountain of Life) and became a subject of scholastic controversy. Not until 1846 was the identification of the philosopher with the poet effected. Avicebron's philosophical work evoked little interest in medieval Spain; severely criticized by one of the earliest of the Spanish Aristotelians, Abraham ibn Daoud (Avendauth, *c.* 1110–80), it was ignored by Moses MAIMONIDES and thus dismissed from the tradition. The true philosophical home of Avicebron is in the ZOHAR and in the speculative sections of the CABALA.

Avicebron's universe displays the usual Neoplatonic ''chain of being.'' At the summit is God, a being in pure act. Through His agent, Will—a being that is identified with God and that plays a role analogous to that of the Logos of PHILO JUDAEUS—God confers His gift of being through the descending ranks of His creation: spiritual essences, the celestial bodies, the corporeal sublunary world. Although this is similar to Plotinus's EMANATION-ISM, the crucial and, for the theologians of the University of Paris, disturbing point was that Avicebron taught that the *entire* created universe was composed of matter and form—everything but the Will itself. Since, for him, all forms are modified and not limitless, the limiting principle (matter) extends into the realm of simple substances. When there is substance there must be composition, he argued, because form demands the support of matter.

The scholastic opposition to, and defense of, Avicebron took place in a context larger than that of the controversy over the *Fons Vitae.* The Spanish Jew's position actually echoed one held by the Franciscan adherents of St. AUGUSTINE at Paris, such as ALEXANDER OF HALES and St. BONAVENTURE. The attack against it by St. THOMAS AQUINAS, answered by DUNS SCOTUS and others, thus involved issues at question among contemporary theologians: the nature of spiritual substances, the existence of ''spiritual matter,'' and, indeed, the nature of matter itself.

The other works of Ibn Gabirol circulated solely in Jewish circles in Spain. The *Improvement of Moral Qualities,* an ethical treatise written in Arabic and later translated into Hebrew, ultimately derives from the peripatetic ethical tradition, but bears a distinctly Jewish character. Similarly, the *Choice of Pearls,* which is probably Ibn Gabirol's, addresses to the common reader a selection of moral aphorisms. Ibn Gabirol continues to be read and studied as the author of the *Kingly Crown,* a collection of religious poems in Hebrew that has gone through frequent editions and translations and still forms part of the Sephardic ritual for Yom Kippūr.

See Also: NEOPLATONISM; SCHOLASTICISM; FORMS, UNICITY AND PLURALITY OF.

Bibliography: Works. *Fons Vitae,* Latin tr. C. BAEUMKER, *Beiträge zur Geschichte der Philosophie und Theologie des Mittelalters* (Münster 1891–) 1.2–4 (1892–95); Heb. paraphrase, ed. and tr. S. MUNK, *Mélanges de philosophie juive et arabe,* (new ed. Paris 1955), Heb. text in appendix; Eng. *Fountain of Life,* tr. A. B. JACOB (Philadelphia 1954); tr. H. E. WEDICK (New York 1962), from Baeumker's Latin text; *The Improvement of Moral Qualities,* tr. S. S. WISE (Columbia U. Oriental Studies 1; New York 1902); *Solomon Ibn Gabirol's Choice of Pearls,* tr. A. COHEN (New York 1925); *Selected Religious Poems of Ibn Gabirol,* tr. I. ZANGWILL (Philadelphia 1923), Eng. and Heb.; *Kether Malkuth,* ed. J. SEIDMAN (Jerusalem 1950); Eng. *Solomon Ibn Gabirol: The Kingly Crown,* tr. B. LEWIS (London 1961). Studies. Bibliog. in J. SCHIRMANN and J. KLAUSNER, *Encyclopaedia Judaica: Das Judentum in Geschichte und Gegenwart* (Berlin 1928–34) 7:10–11, 23–24. Also

Sketch of Bl. Francesca Salesia Aviat behind Alexander Palmieri, chancellor of the archdiocese of Philadelphia and the Vatican's vice postulator. (AP/Wide World Photos)

in G. VAJDA, *Jüdische Philosophie* (Bern 1950) 14–16; *Introduction à la pensée juive du moyen âge* (Paris 1947) 75–83. S. MUNK, *op. cit.* 151–306. I. HUSIK, *A History of Medieval Jewish Philosophy* (2d ed. New York 1959) 59–79. É. H. GILSON, *History of Christian Philosophy in the Middle Ages* (New York 1955). M. WITTMANN, ''Die Stellung des Hl. Thomas von Aquin zu Avencebrol,'' *Beiträge zur Geschichte der Philosophie und Theologie des Mittelalters* (Münster 1891–) 3.3 (1900). J. GOHEEN, *The Problem of Matter and Form in the 'De Ente et Essentia' of Thomas Aquinas* (Cambridge, Mass. 1940).

[F. E. PETERS]

AVICENNA (IBN SĪNĀ, ABŪ 'ALĪAL-ḤUSAYN)

Arab physician, scholar, and philosopher, one of the greatest names in Arabian-Iranian Muslim culture; b. Afshana, near Bukhārā, in 370 of the HIJRA (A.D. 980); d. Hamadhān, 428 Hijra (A.D. 1037).

Life. Avicenna wrote an autobiography, completed by his pupil and secretary Jūzajāni after his death. He writes that he had an astonishing precociousness. Having surpassed all his teachers in the study of the Islamic religious sciences, logic, geometry, and astronomy, he pursued his work alone, notably in medicine and philosophy. Among the Arabian translations of Greek science, he encountered the works of Aristotle. After reading the *Metaphysics* 40 times without understanding it, he found help in the Arabian commentary of his predecessor ALFARABI. For this help he gave thanks at the mosque and distributed generous alms among the poor.

He was not yet 20 years old when he healed the Sultan of Bukhārā, who, through gratitude, invited him to use his rich library. Within a few years, Avicenna acquired as complete a culture as possible for that time. He started to write on his own when he was about 21. An orphan and master of his fortune at 22, he led an agitated and dangerous life. The favorite and vizier (prime minister) of the Emir of Hamadhān, then of the Emir of Ispahān, he spent some time in prison. While he was engaged in military expeditions under the latter emir, his books were pillaged, and some of his MSS disappeared. In the course of such an expedition, an illness, long before contracted as a result of "excesses of every sort," became worse. He died after freeing his slaves, distributing his goods among the poor, and reciting the entire Qur'ān.

Works. Avicenna's bibliography, thoroughly examined by G. C. Anawati (in Arabic) and Yahra Mahdavi (in Persian), is immense. His great medical treatise is *Qānūn fi l-Ṭibb*. His best known philosophical writings are the Summa of the *Shifā'* (Healing) and the compendium of the *Najāt* (Salvation). He left several small "treatises" (*rasā';'il*) exhibiting occasional gnostic characteristics. One of the treatises, *al-Risāla al-aḍhawiyya*, teaches that the bodily resurrection professed in the Muslim faith has only symbolic value. His last great work, *al-Ishārāt wa l-tanbīhāt* (Directives and Remarks), goes beyond the Aristotelian structures of the *Shifā'*. The works of the last part of his life refer to an Oriental Philosophy (or Wisdom), *al-Ḥikma almashriqiyya,* left incomplete (or lost). What remains of this work are his logic and certain chapters included in the *Ishārāt,* as well as preliminary small treatises from other sources. Another work, the *Insāf*, refuted the Baghdad commentators on Aristotle; only a rough draft of this work survived a pillage. Then there are three commentaries extant only in rough drafts, namely, on Book V of the *Metaphysics,* the *De anima,* and especially the spurious *Theology of Aristotle;* the latter, comprising extracts from the *Enneads* of Plotinus, for many centuries was falsely attributed to the Stagirite.

Teaching. Avicenna is representative of the so-called school of the *falāsifa* (philosophers), namely, Muslim Hellenistic philosophers who were nourished with the thought of Plato and Aristotle (the latter called "the Prime Teacher") and wrote in Arabic and Persian. Others of this school are al-KINDĪ, Alfarabi, AVEMPACE, AVERROËS, and Abū-Bakr Ibn-Tufail. Official ISLAM took a stand against the *falāsifa* in the East during the second half of the 11th century and the beginning of the 12th. AL-GAZEL, an orthodox thinker—deemed an Aristotelian because of a misinterpretation of the Latin Middle Ages—tried to refute Alfarabi and Avicenna in his famous *Tahāfut al-falāsifa* (The Collapse of the Philosophers). A century later, Averroës gave his answer in his *Tahāfut al-Tahāfut* (The Collapse of the Collapse), where he took his great predecessor to task and made certain "errors" of Avicenna responsible for Algazel's criticisms. Despite such explanations, however, the *falāsifa* never fully recovered from the attacks of the Muslims, and the teaching of the great mosques manifests a solid distrust toward them to this day.

Religion and Philosophy. Avicenna presents himself as a believing Muslim, but he places his philosophy and the "revealed law" (*shar'*) expressed in the Qur'ān on the same level. He thought that he succeeded in reconciling the two because of his theory about prophetism, which was in turn dependent upon his theory of knowledge. All the *falāsifa* held that the human spirit rises to intellectual knowledge only by illumination received from a single, separated Agent Intellect. For Avicenna, philosophy, like prophecy, receives illumination from the universal Intellect, the summation of separated Intellects. Yet prophecy alone receives, in its imaginative power, added lights from the Souls of the Heavenly Bodies, and these lights enable it to adapt purely intelligible truths to the masses, under a veil of symbols and allegories. This explains how religious beliefs are formed. Moreover, this influx of the heavenly Souls enables prophecy to know and teach religious practices that most aptly guarantee the fidelity of hearts. On the basis of these postulates, the "philosopher" does not hesitate to "interpret" the scriptural texts in accord with his own view of the world.

Because his era was completely imbued with influences of Shī'ite Islam and esoteric and gnostic tendencies and there was no living teaching authority, one can conclude that Avicenna was sincere in claiming his "accord" between religion and philosophy. Yet one can also understand why Algazel later stated that such notorious theses as those about the temporal eternity of the created world, God's ignorance about the singular as such, and the allegorical interpretation anent bodily resurrection are "tarnished with impiety."

Being and Emanation. Avicenna's highly constructed view of the world is hardly consonant with the creationism and divine voluntarism of the Qur'ān. His cosmogony is related with the conceptions of time—the arranged tiers of eight or ten heavenly spheres, in successive triads of separated Intellects, Souls, and Heavenly Bodies, terminating in the Active Intellect of the sublunary world, in the multiplicity of individuated human souls, each having a passive intellect, and in the "world of generation and corruption." In this system, creation seems to be a necessary and voluntary emanation from the First Being, a necessary and voluntary participation of being and light, traversed by a returning movement of natural, necessitated love of the part for the Whole. Thus a universal determinism corresponds to the necessary participation; in Avicenna's universe, there is no place for existential contingency. Yet the notion of contingency is found on the level of essence, since Avicenna's "transunivocity" of being does not destroy a certain inferior analogy between the First Being and "possible" beings, in which not only is the essence really distinct from the existence, but the existence is, in some way, an accident of the essence. Finally, according to him, the human soul is the "form" of its body, but the body remains a mere instrument of the soul; a "form of corporeity" is joined with the soul, the subsistent form. Freed from the body through death, the soul "returns" to the world of the intelligibles to which it naturally belongs.

These ideas are based on notions contained in the works of Aristotle, Plato, and Plotinus, reexamined and coordinated according to Avicenna's own dialectic. In general, Avicenna's thought is more Plotinian than Aristotelian. Abetted by influences and myths from ancient Iran, his thought is decisively Plotinian in his aforementioned Oriental Philosophy (or Wisdom).

Influence. The most illustrious aspect of Avicenna's great and immediate renown is probably a result of his studies in chemistry, astronomy, and medicine. But his philosophical work was the most durable and had a profound influence even on Muslim thought, especially in Shiïte Islam. His adversaries in Sunnite Islam attacked it, but they became imbued with it, and many Islam "theologians" followed them. Later SUFISM (Muslim mysticism) derived its great theses on the MONISM of being from him. During the 12th and 13th centuries, Latin translations were made of the *Shifā'* (Lat. *Sufficientia*), the *Qānūn fi l-Ṭibb* (Lat. *Canon*), and various commentaries or treatises, in Spain and Italy. Avicenna's thought made a deep impression on certain currents in medieval Christian SCHOLASTICISM. THOMAS AQUINAS made use of Avicenna's philosophical structures, even though he criticized them. But possibly the most profound influence of Avicenna in the West was on John DUNS SCOTUS.

See Also: ARABIAN PHILOSOPHY; EMANATIONISM; FORMS, UNICITY AND PLURALITY OF.

Bibliography: Eng. selections in R. LERNER and M. MAHDI, *Medieval Political Philosophy: A Sourcebook* (Glencoe, Ill. 1963). *Avicenna's Psychology,* tr. and ed. F. RAHMAN (New York 1952). É. H. GILSON, *History of Christian Philosophy in the Middle Ages* (New York 1955). A. M. GOICHON, *Enciclopedia filosofica* (Venice-Rome 1957) 1:525–535; *La Philosophie d'Avicenne et son influence en Europe médiévale* (2d ed. Paris 1951). M. M. ANAWATI, *Mu' allafāt Ibn Sīnā* (Cairo 1950); "La Tradition manuscrite orientale de l'oeuvre d'Avicenne," *Revue thomiste,* 51 (Paris 1951) 407–440. Y. MAHDAVI, *Bibliographie d'Ibn Sina* (Tehran 1954). L. GARDET, *La Pensée religieuse d'Avicenne (Ibn Sīnā)* (Paris 1951). M. CRUZ HERNÁNDEZ, *La metafisica de Avicenna* (Granada 1949). B. H. ZEDLER, "Saint Thomas and Avicenna in the 'De potentia Dei,' *Traditio* 6 (1948) 105–159.

[L. GARDET]

AVIGNON

Capital of Vaucluse department, on the left bank of the Rhone River in southeast France. The Archdiocese of Avignon (*Avenionensis*) was raised to the status of a metropolitan see in 1475.

Originally under nearby MARSEILLES and in the first century a Roman colony, with its first known bishop (Nectarius) in 439, Avignon became a commune in the 12th century under the suzerainty of the Counts of TOULOUSE and PROVENCE; in 1251 it went to France and the House of ANJOU. In 1309 Clement V (1305–14) installed the Holy See in Avignon, with his successors remaining there until 1376: John XXII (1316–34), Benedict XII (1334–42), Clement VI (1342–52), Innocent VI (1352–62), Urban V (1362–70) and Gregory XI (1370–78). Clement VII (1378–94) and Benedict XIII (1394–1411) resided there during the Western Schism.

Benedict XII's purchase of Avignon from the countess of Provence (1348) extended the STATES OF THE CHURCH to France, where the popes had held the adjoining county of Venaissin since the end of the Albigensian war. The first stay of the popes in Avignon, part of the Holy Roman Empire, was justified by the impossibility of their staying in their Italian states, which were in constant revolt. But the nearness of the kings of France to the popes, who were French, gave the impression that the kings ran the affairs of the Church, thus leading the Italians to call this period the Babylonian Captivity. The development of papal taxation and centralization dates from this stay in Avignon, when the popes required money to live, build their palace and maintain a court (*see* AVIGNON PAPACY).

After the departure of the popes, Avignon was governed as papal territory by a cardinal legate until 1693 and thereafter by a congregation in Rome through a vice-legate. Both legate and vice-legate had the spiritual powers of a LEGATE in the provinces of Vienne, Arles, Aix, Embrun and Narbonne. The Avignon papal states, having

Ruins of Bridge of St. Benezet, 12th century, Avignon, France. (©Charles and Josette Lenars/CORBIS)

been seized several times by French kings in dispute with the Holy See (1663, 1668, 1768–74), were occupied by Revolutionaries (1790) and annexed to France (1791). This annexation influenced the general policy of the popes toward the French Revolution. As the capital of Vaucluse, Avignon soon lost importance in Church history.

The Cathedral of Notre-Dames-des-Doms (12th century) was existent before the popes, built the walls and a Gothic palace (161,400 square feet in area) that is also a fortress. The Old Palace (1334–42) adjoins the New Palace (1342–52) and there are rooms for the supreme pontiff and his servants, spacious halls for business (tribunal, consistory, conclave, treasury), chapels, kitchens, etc. The Abbot of Saint-Ruf (1039–1793) became head of an Augustinian order, presiding over 20 men's and 20 women's communities (350 women *c.* 1750).

Avignon had many penitent confraternities: grays (1226), blacks (1448), whites (1527), blues (16th century), violets (1622), reds (1700), each with its chapel; some still survive. The university established by Boniface VIII (1303) flourished with seven colleges to 1791. The colleges of the Jesuits (1564) and of the Brothers of Christian Schools (1703) were noteworthy. Charitable es-

tablishments included hospitals, hospices, two orphanages and two houses of repentant girls (14th and 18th centuries).

Many councils (and diocesan synods) were held in Avignon: 1060, 1080, 1209 (excommunication of the count of Toulouse, who favored ALBIGENSES), 1260, 1279, 1282, 1326, 1327 (John XXII condemned antipope NICHOLAS V), 1337, 1457 (canons of the Council of Basel confirmed), 1594 (canons of the Council of Trent applied) and 1725. Of 57 known synodal statutes, 14 date from the 70-year period of the Avignon papacy.

Sixtus IV made Avignon a metropolitan see (1475) so that his nephew (the future Julius II), recently created bishop, would not be under the archbishop of Arles; the suffragans (Carpentras, Cavaillon and Vaison) were all in papal territory. The CONCORDAT OF 1801 made Avignon a vast bishopric (Vaucluse and Gard departments) under Aix. In 1822, when Names (Gard) was restored, Avignon became a metropolitan again with its present suffragans.

Bishop Geoffrey (1143–68) developed the domain of the Church; Zoen Tencarari (1240–61) fought heresy, installed mendicant orders and was several times papal legate; Cardinal Georges d'ARMAGNAC was bishop (1577–85). César de BUS (1544–1607), a missionary in the Protestant areas of Cévennes, founded the Fathers of Christian Doctrine and, with Jean-Baptiste Romillon (1553–1622), introduced the Ursulines in France.

Several former cathedrals are in the diocese: Apt (11th–12th century), Carpentras in flamboyant Gothic (15th century), Cavaillon in Romanesque (enlarged 14th–18th century), Orange with a Provençal Romanesque interior and Vaison with its cloister (6th, 11th–13th century). The Cistercian Abbey of Sénanque (1148) was restored in 1854.

Bibliography: J. GIRARD, *Dictionnaire d'histoire et de géographie ecclésiastiques,* ed. A. BAUDRILLART et al., (Paris 1912–) 5:1121–53. J. SAUTEL et al., *Vaucluse. Essai d'histoire locale* (Avignon 1944). G. MOLLAT, *Les Papes d'Avignon* (9th ed. rev.; Paris 1949), Eng. tr. J. LOVE (New York 1963); *Catholicisme* (Paris 1947–) 1:1 129–30. Y. RENOUARD, *La Papauté à Avignon* (Paris 1954). *Annuario Pontificio* (1964) 45. B. GUILLEMAIN, *La Cour pontificale d'Avignon (1309–76): Étude d'une société* (Paris 1962).

[E. JARRY]

AVIGNON PAPACY

The name given to the papacy (1308–78) because of its residence for some 70 years at AVIGNON instead of at Rome.

Reasons for Residence at Avignon. The popes took up residence at Avignon for reasons that were partly historical, partly personal, and partly political. The papacy was still suffering from the shattering effects of the pontificate of BONIFACE VIII, which had created external enemies and internally split the College of Cardinals (*see* CARDINAL). The brief pontificate of BENEDICT XI did not help matters. The cardinals were anxious to elect a pontiff who had been connected in no way with any previous papal measures and who could be seen as a "neutral" both in external and internal affairs. The long vacancy after Benedict's death testifies to the serious efforts made by the cardinals to find a man who fulfilled the requirements. After several abortive ballots in conclave—one of the candidates was the English Dominican provincial, Walter Winterbourne—the choice fell on Abp. Bertrand de Got of Bordeaux (CLEMENT V).

Clement had not been a member of the Curia, was politically a subject of the English King but culturally thoroughly French, and seemed to be exactly the man to steer the papacy through difficult times. Although he intended to go to Rome after his election, Clement was prevented by a number of circumstances, chiefly by the posthumous trial of Boniface VIII. Clement considered it more prudent to be near the French King to dissuade him from resuming the trial against the dead pope, to convene the General Council at Vienne, and to direct affairs arising from PHILIP IV's sudden arrest of the TEMPLARS. Moreover, the absence of the Curia from Rome since the death of Benedict had made Rome and Italy more insecure than ever, especially as the peninsula was seething with the strife between GUELFS AND GHIBELLINES, and as the new Luxembourg emperor, HENRY VII, pursued a policy in Italy diametrically opposed to that of the papacy.

In 1308 the papal court came to reside at Avignon, which provided easy communication with both France and Italy. Avignon belonged to vassals of the Roman Church and was not then on French soil. It was intended merely as a temporary abode until the questions between the French King and the papacy were solved and the Council of Vienne had finished its work. The council ended May 6, 1312, but the state of Clement's health did not permit the arduous move back to Rome; he seems to have suffered from cancer and died two years later. Although the situation in Italy had meanwhile deteriorated, JOHN XXII nevertheless planned to return to Italy and to reside at BOLOGNA; but that city was as unruly and insecure as any other place in Italy, and soon the plan was dropped.

Each succeeding pope entertained the idea of moving back to Italy. URBAN V did in fact return to Rome, but he found himself confronted by the hostility of the Roman populace, even though the papal emissary, Cardinal ALBORNOZ, had shortly before established some sort of order in the STATES OF THE CHURCH. Realizing also that if he were nearer the French king he might hope to mediate the struggle between England and France, Urban V resumed residence at Avignon. Under his successor, GREGORY XI, the papacy finally effected a return to Rome. A further motive for the prolonged residence at Avignon was the perhaps illusory plan of a crusade, continuously entertained by virtually all the Avignon popes. A crusading appeal, it was thought, would find a readier response if the war between England and France were brought to a speedy end.

Assessment. The Abignonese papacy has prompted many adverse judgments. One of the most frequently voiced criticisms is that it came entirely under French influence and was in fact an appendix of French policy. This is a highly colored view, rising, on the one hand, from the hostility of contemporary English sources, which understandably linked the papacy with French political designs, and on the other hand from contemporary German sources, which also were colored by the antagonism between Emperor LOUIS IV and the papacy. The one-sided judgments of PETRARCH, St. CATHERINE OF SIENA, and St. BRIDGET OF SWEDEN also added to the pe-

Ruins of the papal palace, built when the papal court moved to Avignon in 1305, Provence, France. (©Charles and Josette Lenars/ CORBIS)

jorative bias that has ever since distorted the view of the Avignon papacy.

On balance, however, the constant peace efforts of the Avignon popes showed that they stood above the turmoil of regal rivalries. Moreover, so far from being in the tow of France, they frequently pursued policies, particularly in regard to Italy, that would be quite inexplicable had the popes been mere tools of the French kings. A proper assessment of the Avignon papacy must never lose sight of the somewhat artificial situation in which the popes found themselves. This situation, which the popes had done nothing to bring about and of which they had become the victims, bred in them a sense of insecurity that may explain the restlessness and impetuosity of papal measures initiated at Avignon. Torn though they were from their natural abode, the popes of Avignon accelerated the process of bringing principles of government to their logical conclusion and theoretical perfection.

It is perhaps a paradox that the full élan and vigor of papal principles of government were to be witnessed on ''foreign'' soil and in a period not unjustifiably called the waning of the Middle Ages. One thing is clear, however—the papacy itself introduced no new principles while at Avignon. What it did was to create a highly advanced system out of what had so far grown in an unsystematic manner. The administrative and organizational measures of the Avignon papacy were designed to create the machinery that was to serve the perfected system of government. And some of these measures continued to be practiced long after the return to Rome.

Measures Adopted at Avignon. The administration was thoroughly overhauled, mainly during John XXII's pontificate. There were four main departments that constituted the hub of the papal government at work.

Apostolic Camera. This was the supreme financial office, exercising supervision and control over all papal tax collectors operating in distant lands and over all financial transactions within and without the Curia itself. The papal exchequer also controlled the papal mint. Attached to it was the secretariat that conducted the secret correspondence of the pope through specially appointed *secretarii,* as well as all diplomatic correspondence not of a routine nature. The chamberlain, the head of the apostolic chamber, was the pope's most trusted adviser.

At Avignon ecclesiastical finance was perfected. It was precisely because of demands made by a stringent financial system that numerous categories of taxes, fees, and profits were rigorously collected. By contemporary standards, the expenditures of the Roman Church at Avignon reached astronomical figures. Rigorous tax collection caused understandable opposition, especially in the ranks of the lower clergy. Large expenditure was caused also by many undertakings financed by the papacy, such as the wars in Italy, the missions to distant lands, the support of universities, and the financing of inquisitorial machinery for the suppression of heresy. However, it is also true that the Curia at Avignon had become the most splendidly equipped in Europe. Cardinals and other members of the Curia displayed an amount of luxury and pomp that was both unnecessary and inadvisable in view of the current demand that the Church return to apostolic poverty.

The Chancery. Also highly developed at Avignon, the chancery was the nerve center of the pope's government in practice. It was concerned with the drafting, registration, and dispatch of papal administrative acts, letters, and decrees, and was headed by the vice-chancellor. All routine business went through the chancery.

Judicial Department. This department dealt with all litigations and contentious matters not primarily of a financial nature. It was subdivided into several branches, of which the most important was the consistory, headed by the pope himself, assisted by the cardinals. The consistory dealt with major issues and was also the supreme court of appeal. Subsidiaries of the consistory were the *audientia sacri palatii* and the *audientia litterarum contradictarum,* both consisting of trained lawyers. The former, also called the Rota, was concerned primarily with purely ecclesiastical matters, such as collation of Benefices, provisions, reservations, and immunities; the latter dealt with proper litigations.

Apostolic Penitentiary. This department handled matters concerning interdict, excommunication, and other ecclesiastical censures, as well as the removal of canonical matrimonial impediments. The head was a cardinal who functioned as grand penitentiary.

Organization and Reform. The proliferation of offices and departments at Avignon should not lead to the view that the papacy was nothing but a gigantic administrative machine. It was a highly complicated organization which, if it were to function properly, had to be effectively controlled. For this purpose central offices and departments were a necessity. It was precisely through its first-class organization that the Avignon papacy was enabled to continue old policies and to initiate new ones. Most no-

table among the former were the reform measures concerning the state of the clergy and above all the religious orders, especially the friars. Among the latter must be mentioned the initiation of missionary enterprises on a scale much larger than hitherto envisaged.

The missions to Asia, as far as China and Persia, India and Turkestan, testify to the earnestness of the Avignon papacy to spread Christianity in regions that offered nothing but risks and unimaginable hazards. What needs special emphasis is the promotion by the Avignon papacy of educational work, notably in the universities, and the establishment of new fields of study, such as Arabic.

On the other hand, the variegated nature of the Avignon papacy at work brought about noteworthy constitutional practices, virtually dictated by governmental exigencies. The cardinals began *de facto* to assume powers which amounted, in practice, to an oligarchic form of government; the pope was virtually bound to take counsel from the cardinals in charge of special departments. It was a symptom of the increased power of the cardinals that they hit upon the device of the so-called papal electoral pacts (*see* CAPITULATIONS) first recorded in 1352, according to which the pope was to be severely restricted in the exercise of his monarchic powers. The outbreak of the WESTERN SCHISM, soon after the pope's return to Rome, was to no small extent the result of the assumption of cardinalitial power. The peculiarities and achievements of the Avignon papacy can be understood only when viewed against the historical background.

Bibliography: Sources. É. BALUZE, *Vitae paparum Avenionensium,* ed. G. MOLLAT, 4 v. (Paris 1914–27), Bibliothèque des Écoles françaises d'Athènes et de Rome, *Lettres des papes d'Avignon se rapportant à la France* (Paris 1899–). F. BOCK, *Einführung in das Registerwesen des avignonesischen Papsttums,* 2 v. (Rome 1941). O. BERTHOLD, ed. and tr., *Kaiser, Volk, und Avignon: Ausgewählte Quellen zur antikurialen Bewegung in Deutschland in der ersten Hälfte des 14. Jahrhunderts* (Berlin 1960). Literature. G. MOLLAT, *The Popes at Avignon, 1305–1378,* tr. J. LOVE (London 1963). E. KRAACK, *Rom oder Avignon? Die römische Frage unter den Päpsten Clemens V. und Johann XXII* (Marburg 1929). E. DUPRÉ THESEIDER, *Problemi del papato avignonese* (Bologna 1961). B. GUILLEMAIN, *La Cour pontificale d'Avignon (1309–76): Étude d'une société* (Paris 1962). N. HOUSLEY, *The Avignon Papacy and the Crusades, 1305–1378* (Oxford 1986). Y. RENOUARD, *The Avignon Papacy, 1305–1403,* trans. D. BETHELL (London 1970). D. WILLMAN, *The Right of Spoil of the Popes of Avignon, 1316–1415* (Philadelphia 1988).

[W. ULLMANN]

ÁVILA, FRANCISCO DE

Quechua scholar and crusader against Amerindian idolatry; b. Cuzco, Peru, 1573; d. Lima, Sept. 17, 1647. He was a foundling and took his name from Beatriz de

Ávila, wife of Cristóbal Rodríguez, who cared for him as a child. He began his studies in Cuzco and was ordained in 1591. He studied civil and Canon Law in the University of San Marcos in Lima and received a doctorate in 1606. In 1597 he became pastor of San Damián (Huarochirí) and began his campaign to wipe out native idolatry and superstition. He was accused of exceeding his authority in this matter, but Abp. Toribio de MOGROVEJO exonerated him during his visitation, and this was ratified by the visitor general of the archdiocese in 1600–01. Using his knowledge of Quechua, Ávila continued his work against idolatry. In 1608, in his zeal he held an *auto-da-fé* in which a number of idols were burned and the Amerindian Hernando Paucar was scourged for idolatry and for being a friend of the devil. Ávila subsequently spent some time in prison, but he was absolved in 1609. The chronicler Huamán Poma de Ayala criticized Ávila for depriving the native Peruvians of their idols and other objects of worship. Archbishop Lobo de Guerrero appointed Ávila the first Visitador de Idolatrías, but in the course of his duties he became ill and had to return to Lima. His writings are extensive. In 1608 he wrote *Tratado y relación de los errores, falsos dioses y otras supersticiones y ritos diabólicos en que vivían antiguamente los indios de las provincias de Huarochirí, Mama y Chaclla y hoy también viven engañados con gran perdición de sus almas* (published in 1942). His *Oratio habita in ecclesia cathedrali limensi* was printed in 1610. The next year he wrote a *Memoria* on a visit to the towns in the Province of Huarochirí, later published by Medina as *Cura de Huánacu*. In 1646 he wrote his most literary book, *Tratado de los evangelios*. The second volume of this was published posthumously as was a collection of sermons in Quechua and Spanish titled *De los misterios de nuestra Santa Fe*. The work of Ávila, along with that of Hernando de Avendaño, is considered to represent the transition from the Quechua of evangelism to the Quechua of literature.

Bibliography: F. DE ÁVILA, *Dämonen und Zauber im Inkareich,* ed. and tr. H. TRIMBORN (Leipzig 1939). H. TRIMBORN, ''Francisco de Ávila,'' *Ciencias* 3 (1936) 163–174. J. T. POLO, ''Un Quechuista,'' *Revista histórica del Instituto histórico del Perú* 1 (1906) 24–38.

[C. D. VALCÁRCEL]

AVITUS (AVY), ST.

Abbot of Micy; b. Auvergne, France, mid-fifth century; d. Châteaudun, France, June 17 c. 530. He entered religious life between 485 and 490 at the abbey of Ménat near Clermont. Desiring to embrace the life of a hermit, he left Ménat and journeyed with CARILEFFUS through the Loire Valley, finally settling at the abbey of Micy. Max-

iminus, who had been abbot there since c. 508, permitted him to lead a solitary existence nearby, but when Maximinus died in 520 the monks of the community sought out Avitus and made him their abbot. GREGORY OF TOURS relates (*Monumenta Germaniae Historica: Scriptores rerum Merovingicarum* 1:113, 810) that the abbot pleaded unsuccessfully with King Clodimir, the son of CLOVIS I, to spare the lives of SIGISMUND of Burgundy and his family who had been captured in war. Avitus was buried in the church of Saint-Georges at Orléans. His oldest biography dates from the ninth century and some modern scholars conjecture that the vita confuses two monks named Avitus, one who was abbot of Micy and the other, a monk at Ménat.

Feast: June 17.

Bibliography: *Monumenta Germaniae Historica: Scriptores rerum Merovingicarum* 3:380–385. *Acta Sanctorum* June 4:282–291. *Bibliotheca hagiograpica latina antiquae et mediae aetatis* (Brussels 1898–1901) 879–883. A. PONCELET, *Analecta Bollandiana* 24 (1905) 5–97. C. BELMON, *Dictionnaire d'histoire et de géographie ecclésiastiques,* ed. A. BAUDRILLART et al. (Paris 1912) 5:1204–05. A. BUTLER, *The Lives of the Saints,* ed. H. THURSTON and D. ATTWATER (New York 1956) 2:564–565.

[B. J. COMASKEY]

AVITUS OF VIENNE, ST.

Fifth-century bishop; b. probably Vienne, France, c. 450; d. Vienne, c. 519. Alcimus Ecdicius Avitus succeeded his father, St. Hesychius (Isicius) in the See of Vienne (c. 490) and became a leader of the Gallo-Roman episcopate. Prominent at several synods, especially Epaon (517), he persuaded the Burgundian King Gundobad, though an Arian, to extend protection to the Catholic faith. Gundobad's son and successor, Sigismund, was converted by Avitus and made him his adviser in ecclesiastical matters. Avitus contended against heresy in his diocese, especially ARIANISM, and was an ardent defender of the primacy of Rome. Magnus Felix Ennodius of Pavia, Gregory of Tours, Isidore of Seville, and Fortunatus praised his charity, learning, and literary achievement. Some 80 historically valuable letters have been preserved together with three complete sermons and fragments of possibly 30 others, the *De spiritualis historiae gestis* (a series of five poems inspired by Genesis), and a poem in praise of virginity.

Feast: Feb. 5.

Bibliography: *Opera,* ed. R. PEIPER (*Monumenta Germaniae Historica: Auctores antiquissimi* 6.2; 1883); *Oeuvres complètes,* ed. U. CHEVALIER (Lyon 1890). M. BURCKHARDT, *Die briefsammlung des bischofs Avitus von Vienne* (Berlin 1938). *Acta Sanctorum* Feb. 1:666–675. O. BARDENHEWER, *Geschichte der altkirchlichen*

Literatur (Freiburg 1913–32) 5:337–345. S. COSTANZA, *Avitiana . . .* (Messina 1968). H. J. E. GOELZER, *Le latin de saint Avit, évêque de Vienne* (Paris 1909). G. BARDY, *Catholicisme* 1:1134–35. H. LECLERCQ, *Dictionnaire d'archéologie chrétienne et de liturgie,* ed. F. CABROL, H. LECLERCQ, and H. I. MARROU (Paris 1907–53) 15.2:3061–63. J. H. FISCHER, *Lexicon für Theologie und Kirche,* ed. J. HOFER and K. RAHNER (Freiburg 1957–65) 1:1154–55.

[G. M. COOK]

AVIZ, ORDER OF

Portuguese military religious order, known originally as the Order of Evora. In 1166 the fortress of Evora, in the province of Alemtejo, was taken from the Moors. Ten years later the king ceded various properties to the master and knights of Evora, *promovendis ordinem sancti Benedicti.* This is the first authentic document concerning the order. Whether it began as an independent community or as a branch of the Castilian Order of CALATRAVA is debatable. Considering that properties given to the Order of Evora are listed among Calatrava's possessions in 1187, an affiliation of the two orders before that date seems certain. This is implied in INNOCENT III's bull of 1201 granting the privileges of Calatrava to the knights of Evora, *professis ordinem de Calatrava.* As a result of Afonso II's donation of Aviz in 1211, the knights transferred their headquarters to that fortress. Henceforth the order was known as Aviz. The visitation of Aviz in 1238 by the master of Calatrava reveals that Aviz was affiliated to Calatrava just as Calatrava was affiliated to the Cistercian abbey of MORIMOND. In 1385 the master of Aviz was elected King João I of Portugal; his dynasty came to be known as Aviz. He attempted to free the order from any dependency on Calatrava; in the 15th century the administration of the order was entrusted to royal princes. In 1551 Pope JULIUS III annexed the mastership to the crown in perpetuity.

Bibliography: A. L. JAVIERRE MUR, ''La Orden de Calatrava en Portugal,'' *Boletín de la Real Academia de la Historia* 130 (1952) 323–376. M. DE OLIVEIRA, ''A milicia de Évora e a Ordem de Calatrava,'' *Lusitania Sacra* 1 (1956) 51–67.

[J. F. O'CALLAGHAN]

AVRANCHES, COUNCIL OF

Famous Church council held at the former diocesan seat of Avranches, Normandy, to confirm the peace between the Church and King HENRY II OF ENGLAND after the murder of Thomas BECKET. An initial meeting of Henry, papal legates, and bishops bore fruit; and on May 21, 1172, at St. Andrew's Cathedral in Avranches, Henry, in the presence of Pope ALEXANDER III's legates and the bishops, was solemnly reconciled with the Church, swearing innocence of the murder. He vowed to obey the pope, to permit appeals to Rome, to make restitution, and to support the CRUSADE. It was at Avranches, September 27–28, that same year, that Henry convoked a council of his bishops. This council, which was attended by the papal legates, promulgated 12 disciplinary canons. It forbade granting children rights to benefices that had the care of souls; it forbade also the giving to priests' children their fathers' churches. It urged priests of large churches to take assistants; it prohibited the ordaining of a priest without a definite title or source of income; it barred married persons ordinarily from entering religion during the spouse's lifetime. The Council also commended fasting during Advent and forbade priests to participate in civil tribunals.

Bibliography: C. J. VON HEFELE, *Histoire des conciles d'après les documents originaux,* tr. and continued by H. LECLERCQ, 10 v. in 19 (Paris 1907–38) 5.2:1054–57. J. C. ROBERTSON, ed., *Materials for the History of Thomas Becket,* 7 v. (*Rerum Brittanicarum medii aevi scriptores* 67; 1875–85) 7:513–523. J. D. MANSI, *Sacrorum Conciliorum nova et amplissima collectio,* 31 v. (Florence-Venice 1757–98); reprinted and continued by L. PETIT and J. B. MARTIN, 53 v. in 60 (Paris 1889–1927; repr. Graz 1960–) 22:135–140. L. DUCHESNE, *Fastes épiscopaux de l'ancienne Gaule,* 3 v. (2d. ed. Paris 1907–15); 2:222–225.

[A. CONDIT]

AVRIL, PHILIPPE

Jesuit missionary; b. Angoulême, France, July 21, 1654; d. 1698. While teaching mathematics and philosophy in Paris (1684), he was assigned to find an overland route to China independent of the Portuguese. Avril went by Aleppo to Kurdistan and Armenia. Detained at Astrakhan, he turned north by the Volga to Moscow, but was expelled from Russia. After a long stay in Warsaw he returned to France by Constantinople in 1690. His *Voyages* (1692), an account of his travels, was translated into many languages, including English in 1693. A promised history of Muscovy did not appear. On his second attempt to reach the Far East he was lost at sea.

Bibliography: E. LAMALLE, *Dictionnaire d'histoire et de géographie ecclésiastiques,* ed. A. BAUDRILLART et al. (Paris 1912—) 5:1251. J. BALTEAU, *Dictionnaire de biographie française,* (Paris 1929—) 4:905. J. SEBES, *The Jesuits and the Sino-Russian Treaty of Nerchinsk, 1689* (Rome 1961).

[B. LAHIFF]

AVVAKUM

Russian archpriest and author; b. Grigorovo, Province of Nijni Novgorod, 1620; d. Pustozersk, April 24

(N.S.; April 14, O.S.), 1682. The son of a village priest, he received a wide ecclesiastical and secular education. He was involved early in a movement for church reform, and, first as pastor in a small town and later as archpriest of Iourevets on the Volga, he ruled his flocks with a vigorous hand. After exile because of his reforming zeal, he went to Moscow to serve as archpriest at Notre Dame of Kazan; he was a member of the Friends of God, a group protected by Czar Alexis and his confessor Stephen. When Nikon was elected patriarch (1652) and reoriented the reform toward adopting the customs of the Greek Church, the group refused to follow him (*see* NIKON, PATRIARCH OF MOSCOW).

The conflict grew worse under the violence of Nikon. Avvakum was exiled to Siberia in 1653 as assistant to the Pashkov expedition, organized to gain control of regions along the Sakhalin River. For protesting this shameless adventure, he suffered the knout and several times narrowly escaped death. Nikon was deposed in 1662 and Avvakum was recalled to Moscow, only to be exiled again (to Mezen) for denouncing the growing abuses of the official church. He was repatriated and again exiled by the Synod of Moscow (1666) to Pustozersk on the Arctic Ocean. Though confined (1670) in an underground prison, he stayed in contact with the Old Believers throughout Russia: he was their spiritual director from afar, their consoler, and their prophet. In 1672 he wrote his *Life,* which, particularly because of its deep and pure religious inspiration, is a masterpiece of 17th-century Russian literature. Under the harsh decrees against the Old Believers passed by the council of 1682, Avvakum was burned to death in Pustozersk Square. His memory has remained sacred to the Old Believers and his works were collected and handcopied until the end of the 19th century.

Bibliography: Collected Works. *Russkaĭa istoricheskaĭa biblioteka,* 39 v. (Leningrad 1927); *Zhitie protopopa Avvakuma, im samim napisannoe i drugie ego sochineniĭa,* ed. N. K. GUDZIĬA (Moscow 1960). Autobiography. *The Life of the Archpriest Avvakum by Himself,* tr. J. HARRISON and H. MIRRLEES (London 1924); *La Vie de l'archiprêtre Avvakum,* tr. P. PASCAL (Paris 1961); *Vita dell'arciprete Avvakum,* tr. L. RADOYCE (Turin 1962). Literature. P. PASCAL, *Avvakum et les débuts du Raskol* (new ed. The Hague-Paris 1964).

[P. PASCAL]

AXIOLOGY

Term in modern philosophy generally used to designate theory of value. It is taken from the Greek ἄξιος, value or worth, and λόγος, study of or science of. As a general synonym for value theory, axiology was first used extensively by Paul Lapie (*Logique de la volonté,* 1902)

and Eduard von HARTMANN (*Grundriss der Axiologie,* 1908). Among English speaking philosophers the term received popularization through the numerous books and articles written by Wilbur Marshall Urban, the most notable of which is *Valuation* (1909).

There is no universal agreement among philosophers that the term axiology is completely satisfactory. Those who defend its usage, such as Urban and Nicolai HARTMANN, point out that the term properly emphasizes the necessity of a metaphysical investigation into the nature and status of values as a prelude to further ethical, epistemological, and psychological studies. The term value theory is of sufficient significance in sociology, anthropology, and economics that confusions might easily be avoided if philosophy had its own term to designate its approach to problems of value. Others, such as Louis LAVELLE (*Traité des Valeurs,* 1951), judge that value theory is a more suitable term since it is not so pedantic and thus conveys immediately to all the fact that there are many ramifications of value study and value problems. The current tendency is generally to favor the usage of value theory over axiology.

In those areas where value is especially relevant, especially metaphysics and ethics, scholastic philosophers have preferred to speak in terms of GOOD in its various senses. Complete understanding between scholastics and other axiologists is hampered by the lack of adequate translation of their vocabularies.

See Also: VALUE, PHILOSOPHY OF; VALUE JUDGMENT

Bibliography: *Enciclopedia filosofica,* 4 v. (Venice-Rome 1957) 1:536. W. M. URBAN, ''Value, Theory of,'' *Encyclopedia Brittanica* 22 (New York 1965) 961–963.

[R. R. KLINE]

AXIOMATIC SYSTEM

A type of deductive theory, such as those used in mathematics, of which Euclid's *Elements* is one of the early forms. Long a model for scientific theorizing, the axiomatic system has been studied intensively only since the end of the 19th century, and this in conjunction with the development of mathematical, or symbolic, logic in research on the foundations of logic and of mathematics (*see* LOGIC, SYMBOLIC). In its earlier sense the axiomatic system was considered as having a meaning content, whereas more recently it has been understood in a purely formal sense—as practically synonymous, in fact, with the formal system (*see* FORMALISM). According to H. B. Curry, the notion of formal system is more restricted than that of axiomatic system, whereas for other authors the formal system is more general since it lacks the conditions of effectiveness that should characterize the axiomatic system.

General Characterization. A scientific theory is made up of propositions that are in turn composed of terms. One can establish the validity of a PROPOSITION by deducing it from other propositions, but it is impossible to proceed in this way to infinity. In the same manner, one can explain the sense of a TERM by defining it through the use of other terms, but again it is impossible to proceed to infinity. To build a theory it is therefore necessary to start from terms that are accepted without DEFINITION and from propositions that are considered as valid without DEMONSTRATION. To these primitive elements are then added rules of definition, with whose help it is possible to define new terms from the undefined primitive terms or from terms already defined, and rules of deduction, with whose help it is possible to obtain new propositions from the primitive propositions or from propositions already deduced. The primitive propositions are called the axioms of the theory. The propositions that can be deduced by means of the rules of deduction are said to be proved or demonstrated. The axioms and the proved propositions are the theorems of the theory.

According to the earlier view, an axiomatic system expresses a certain order of TRUTH. A deductive SCIENCE is based on postulates or FIRST PRINCIPLES that express self-evident truths or on propositions demonstrated by a superior science. The whole order of demonstrative knowledge is thus founded on self-evident propositions. The primitive terms are taken with their natural meaning, while the rules of deduction are those of ordinary logic and are not considered to be part of the theory.

According to the modern view, however, an axiomatic system is considered simply as expressing an order of possible deductions. The axioms are not considered to be true, but only as propositions provisionally accepted as valid. An axiomatic system is thus nothing but a hypotheticodeductive system. The undefined terms are not understood with regard to their intuitive meaning, but are understood in terms of what is asserted about them in the axioms. On the other hand, the logic that is used is explicitly incorporated into the system. This complete formalization of the deductive process is what is referred to as formal axiomatic method.

Interpretation. A formal axiomatic system must be considered as a pure system of deduction. Such a system, however, has interest only to the extent that it can be used to investigate the properties of theories having a factual content, i.e., to the extent that there are relationships between this system and "contensive statements," to use Curry's terminology. A contensive statement is a statement that pertains to some factual domain and is such that its truth or falsity can be established by appropriate methods that take account of the facts such statements concern; these may be mathematical or empirical in nature. An interpretation of an axiomatic system is a many-to-one correspondence between some propositions of the system and some contensive statements belonging to a given field. An interpretation is valid if every contensive statement corresponding to a theorem is true.

The advantage of the formal axiomatic method is that it offers the possibility of studying in a synthetic manner the properties of all theories having the same form, such as those of the different empirical domains of the physical sciences. The construction of such theories raises the problem of the choice of the appropriate axioms, which itself is related to the problem of INDUCTION. Such theories must also be located with reference to empirical facts by way of interpretation, and this is connected with the problem of VERIFICATION.

Abstract Characterization. Curry refers to axiomatic systems as deductive theories, themselves a particular type of theory. A THEORY is defined as a class of statements belonging to a certain definite class of statements that are previously postulated. (A statement must be distinguished from a sentence, which is a linguistic expression designating a statement.) A class is said to be definite if some effective process exists that makes it possible to determine whether a given object is a member of the class or not. The statements that belong to a theory are called its theorems. A theory is said to be deductive when it constitutes an inductive class of statements. An inductive class is a class whose elements are generated from certain initial elements (forming a definite class) by means of certain specified modes of combination that have an "effective character"—in the sense that some effective method exists that makes it possible to determine whether a given element has been actually produced from given elements of the class. (It should be noted that an inductive class is not necessarily definite.) The initial statements of a deductive theory form a definite class of statements; they are called the axioms of the theory. The modes of combination of a deductive theory are its rules of deduction; when applied to an appropriate number of theorems, such a rule produces a new theorem. Every construction of a theorem from given theorems by means of the rules of deduction is called a demonstration. The theorems of the deductive theory are then the statements for which demonstrations exist.

Formal System. When it is specified that the statements assert that certain formal objects have particular properties or stand in particular relation to each other, a theory is called a *system* or, more explicitly, a formal system. To describe such a system, one identifies a particular class of objects, called formal objects, and a particular class of predicates, called basic predicates. The statements of the system are formed by applying a basic predicate to an appropriate number of formal objects.

Types. There are two types of systems: syntactical systems and ob systems. In a syntactical system, the formal objects are taken as the expressions of a particular language. In an ob system, the formal objects form a monotectonic inductive class—monotectonic in the sense that, for every element, there exists only one construction that produces it. The elements of this class are called obs; its initial elements, atoms; and the modes of combination, operations.

Epitheory. When a system is constituted, it can be studied as a given object; such a study is then referred to as an epitheory. The main epitheoretical questions pertaining to an axiomatic system concern its consistency (the impossibility of deducing within the system both a proposition and its negation), its independence (the impossibility of deducing any axiom from the others), and its completeness (every proposition formulable in the terms of the system is provable or refutable, in which case its negation is provable, within the system). Also of interest is the decision problem, which is concerned with formulating an effective method that makes it possible to determine, for every proposition formulable in the terms of the system, whether the proposition is provable in the system. One of the most famous epitheoretical theorems is the incompleteness theorem of K. Gödel: in every consistent system that is sufficient to formalize ordinary arithmetic there are undecidable propositions, i.e., propositions that are neither provable nor refutable.

Bibliography: A. TARSKI, *Introduction to Logic and to the Methodology of Deductive Sciences* (New York 1941), first pub. in Polish 1936. H. B. CURRY, *Foundations of Mathematical Logic* (New York 1963). J. A. LADRIÈRE, *Les Limitations internes des formalismes* (Louvain 1957).

[J. A. LADRIÈRE]

AYMARD, BL.

Third abbot of Cluny; d. Cluny, Oct. 5, 965. He was elected between April 21 and June 13, 942 to succeed St. ODO OF CLUNY, whose work in the CLUNIAC REFORM he continued. During his short administration the possessions of CLUNY increased considerably. In 948 Pope Agapetus II confirmed the direct dependence of Cluny and its dependencies on the Apostolic See. Because he had become blind, Aymard resigned his office in 948, having provided for the election of MAJOLUS OF CLUNY as fourth abbot. In 1063 PETER DAMIAN collected the oral

testimony of Aymard's patience, simplicity, and humility.

Feast: Oct. 5 (Benedictines).

Bibliography: J. MABILLON, *Acta sanctorum ordinis S. Benedicti,* 9 v. (Paris 1668–1701; 2d ed. Venice 1733–40) 7:316–323. M. MARRIER and A. DUCHESNE, *Bibliotheca cluniacensis* (Paris 1614; repr. Mâcon 1915). PETER DAMIAN, *Op. 33, Patrologia Latina,* ed. J. P. MIGNE, 217 v. (Paris 1878–90) 145:570–572. A. BRUEL, *Recueil des chartes de l'abbaye de Cluny,* 6 v. (Paris 1876–1903) v.1–2. E. SACKUR, *Die Cluniacenser,* 2 v. (Halle 1892–94) *passim.* P. SCHMITZ, *Histoire de l'Ordre de Saint-Benoî,* 7 v. (Maredsous, Belgium 1942–56) 1:132–133.

[R. GRÉGOIRE]

AYMER DE LA CHEVALERIE, HENRIETTE

Cofoundress of the Sisters of the SACRED HEARTS; b. at the de la Chevalerie chateau in Poitou, France, Aug. 11, 1767; d. Paris, Nov. 23, 1834. She was of noble birth and was imprisoned, along with her mother, during the French Revolution for giving asylum to two priests (1794). When released she joined a pious association of laywomen in Poitiers devoted to charitable works and perpetual adoration of the Blessed Sacrament. Abbé COUDRIN, their spiritual director, persuaded her to act as cofoundress of the Sisters of the Sacred Hearts and Perpetual Adoration. The congregation had its beginnings in Poitiers when a residence was purchased in 1797. Henriette acted as superior of a few former members of the association. The small group received local ecclesiastical approval and pronounced religious vows (1800). Papal approval came in 1817. In 1804 headquarters were moved to Rue Picpus in Paris. Henriette remained as superior general during life and saw the institute grow to 18 houses in France and its apostolate extend to the religious education of children, along with perpetual adoration.

Bibliography: *Mère Henriette and Her Work,* tr. from Fr. (St. Louis 1926). F. TROCHU, *La Servante de Dieu, Henriette Aymer de la Chevalerie* (Lyons 1950). H. CHOMON, *Dictionnaire de biographie française* (Paris 1929–) 4:947–948.

[P. HERAN]

AYMER DE LUSIGNAN

Bishop of Winchester, one of King Henry III's Poitevin favorites; d. Paris, Dec. 4, 1260. He was the younger son of Isabella, widow of King John, by Hugh X, Count of La Marche, and thus a half-brother of Henry III. Aymer went to England in 1247 and studied at Oxford.

In 1250 HENRY III secured his election to the bishopric of WINCHESTER, whose revenues he is said to have spent extravagantly. He was consecrated in Rome by Alexander IV, in May of 1260. On a few occasions he spoke in favor of ecclesiastical reform, as in 1253, when, ironically, he pressed the king to allow free episcopal elections. But Aymer, unlike Bishop WALTER of Cantelupe, opposed the political reform outlined in the Provisions of Oxford in 1258, and he and his brothers were forced by the barons to leave the country. The barons' document, which justified this action to the pope was notable: it maintained that the Lusignan brothers by their irresponsibility had harmed the crown and that the *communitas* would never tolerate their return.

Bibliography: W. HUNT, *The Dictionary of National Biography from the Earliest Times to 1900,* 63 v. (London 1885–1900) 1:758–760. A. B. EMDEN, *A Biographical Register of the University of Oxford to A. D. 1500,* 3 v. (Oxford 1957–59) 2:1179–80. F. M. POWICKE, *King Henry III and the Lord Edward,* 2 v. (Oxford 1947). H. S. SNELLGROVE, *The Lusignans in England, 1247–1258* (Albuquerque 1950).

[H. MAYR–HARTING]

Henriette Aymer de la Chevalerie.

AZEVEDO, IGNACIO DE, BL.

Missionary, martyr; b. Oporto, Portugal, 1526; martyred off the Canary Islands, July 15, 1570. Ignacio became a Jesuit in 1548 and was named rector of the College of St. Anthony in Lisbon in 1553. Eight years later he became rector of the new college established at Braga by the saintly Dominican, Archbishop Bartholomew of the Martyrs. As a superior, Ignacio was distinguished by his thoughtful concern for his subjects and his heroic service to the poor and sick of the area. His desire to serve God on the foreign missions was fulfilled in 1566 when the general, Francis Borgia, appointed him visitor of the Jesuit Missions in Brazil. Azevedo, finding the missions flourishing but severely short of manpower, received permission to return to Europe to recruit volunteers. His infectious zeal inspired 69 young Europeans to volunteer for the Brazilian mission. They sailed in two groups on June 5, 1570. The *Santiago* on which Ignatius and 39 companions embarked was captured by five Huguenot privateers commanded by Jacques Sourie, on Saturday, July 15, 1570. Though the others aboard were spared, Ignacio and his 39 companions were brutally slaughtered and thrown into the sea. Pius IX beatified these martyrs on May 11, 1854.

Azevedo's companions in martyrdom include one priest, James de Andrade (b. Pedrógão Grande, Portugal, c. 1531); seven professed brothers; 14 Jesuit scholastics; 16 novices; and one candidate for admittance to the order,

John, the nephew of the ship's captain. Among the brothers are Alphonsus de Baena (b. Villatobas near Toledo, Spain, c. 1539), Francis Álvares (b. Covilhã, Portugal, c. 1539), Gaspar Álvares (b. Oporto, Portugal), Gregory Escribano (b. Logroño, Spain), Manuel Álvares (b. Estremoz, Portugal, c. 1536), Peter Fontoura (b. Braga, Portugal), and Stephen Zuraire (b. Zudaire, Portugal). The scholastics include Álvaro Borralho Mendes (b. Alvas, Portugal), Andrew Gonçalves (b. Viana de Alvito near Alentejo, Portugal), Antony Soares (b. Vila de Trancoso, Portugal), Bento de Castro (b. Vila de Chacim, Portugal, c. 1543), Ferdinand Sánchez (b. Old Castile, Spain), Gonçalo Henriques (deacon, b. Oporto, Portugal), James Mimoso Pires (b. Nisa near Portalegre, Portugal), John Fernandes (b. Lisbon, Portugal, c. 1551), Louis Correia (b. Évora, Portugal), Manuel Fernandes (b. Celorico da Beira, Portugal), Manuel Pacheco (b. Ceuta, North Africa, of Portuguese parents), Manuel Rodrigues (b. Alcochete, Portugal), Peter Nunes (b. Vila da Fronteira near Alentejo, Portugal), and Simon Lopes (b. Ourém, Portugal). Alexis Delgado (b. Elvas, Portugal), Amaro Vaz (b. Bemfazer near Oporto, Portugal, c. 1554), Antony Correia (b. Oporto, Portugal, c. 1553), Antony Fernandes (b. Montemór-o-Novo, Portugal, c. 1552), Bras Ribeiro (b. Braga, Portugal, c. 1546), Dominic Fernandes (b. Vila de Borba, Portugal, c. 1551), Francis de Magalhães (b. Vila de Alcácer do Sal, Portugal, *c.* 1549), Francis Pérez Godoy (b. Torrijos near Toledo, Spain, *c.* 1540), John Fernandes (b. Braga, Portugal, *c.* 1547), John de Mayorga (b. Saint Jean Pied de Port, Gascony, *c.* 1533), John de San Martín (b. Yuncos near Toledo, Spain, *c.* 1550), John de Zafra (b. Jerez de Badajoz, Spain), Louis Rodrigues (b. Évora, Portugal, *c.* 1554), Mark Caldeira (b. Vila de Feira, Portugal, *c.* 1547), Nicholas Dinis (b. Braganza, Portugal, *c.* 1553), and Simon da Costa (b. Oporto, Portugal, 1570) were the martyred novices.

Feast: Jan. 19 (Jesuits).

Bibliography: G. F. DE BEAUVAIS, *La vie du venerable pere Ignace Azevedo* (Paris 1744). F. J. CORLEY and R. J. WILLMES, *Wings of Eagles: The Jesuit Saints and Blessed* (Milwaukee 1941). M. G. DA COSTA, *Ignácio de Azevedo* (Braga, Port. 1946). J. N. TYLENDA, *Jesuit saints & martyrs* (2d ed. Chicago 1998) 202–7.

[F. A. SMALL]

AZEVEDO, LUIZ DE

Missionary in India and Ethiopia; b. Carrazzedo, Montenegro, Portugal, 1573; d. Dambea, Ethiopia, Feb. 22, 1634. After entering the Society of Jesus (1588), he spent the first years of his priesthood in India (1592–1604), where he was successively master of novices at Goa and rector of the college at Thana. In 1605 he began his fruitful labors of 28 years as a missionary in Ethiopia, particularly among the Agaus, many of whom left the schismatic Church of Ethiopia for the Catholic church. Later, however, his converts were forced to return to schism, and his fellow missionaries were expelled from the country. Too infirm to accompany them, he remained and died in Ethiopia. To assist his fellow missionaries and to aid his converts, Azevedo prepared an Ethiopic grammar and translated into Ethiopic the New Testament, a catechism, and instructions on the Apostles' Creed. His letters were published in Lisbon (1609) and Lyons (1625).

Bibliography: C. SOMMERVOGEL et al., *Bibliothèque de la Compagnie de Jésus,* 11 v. (Brussels-Paris 1890–1932) 1: 735–737. *Dictionnaire d'histoire et de géographie ecclésiastiques,* ed. A. BAUDRILLART et al. (Paris 1912–) 5:1352. H. HURTER, *Nomenclator literarius theologiae catholicae,* 5 v. (3d ed. Innsbruck 1903–13) 3:800.

[L. F. HARTMAN]

AZOR, JUAN

Jesuit moral theologian; b. Lorca, Spain, 1535, or more probably 1536; d. Rome, Feb. 19, 1603. Besides teaching extensively in Spain and Rome, Azor served from 1584 on the committee that drafted the RATIO STUDIORUM, the program of studies for Jesuit institutions. Since the Ratio required, in addition to a course explaining the *Summa,* another course on "cases of conscience," Azor wrote his *Institutiones morales* (3 v., Rome 1600–11), a new type of moral treatise in which the basic division followed that of the commandments, not the virtues. This was intended to supplant the smaller *Summae confessorum* and is rightly considered the forerunner of the modern manuals of moral theology.

Bibliography: J. E. DE URIARTE and M. LECINA, *Biblioteca de escritores de la Compañía de Jesús* (Madrid 1925–30) 1:394–399. E. MOORE, *La moral en el siglo XVI y primera mitad del XVII* (Granada 1956) 78–79. B. HÄRING, *The Law of Christ,* tr. E. G. KAISER, 3 v. (Westminster, Md. 1961–) 1:18–20.

[R. A. COUTURE]

AZTEC RELIGION

The Aztec Empire constituted one of the important civilizations of the New World at the time of Spanish conquest. Although the heart of the Empire was concentrated in the Valley of Mexico, its influence and control spread over a large part of Mexico. Aztec religion was a result of a mixture of its own tribal concepts of the supernatural world and that of the other cultures with which it came into contact. As a result, its mythology, worldview, and religious organization were unusually complex. Of extreme importance for the continuance of daily life was the propitiation of the many gods.

One of the most important of these was Huitzilopochtli, war god and symbol of the sun. In order for life to continue, Huitzilopochtli had to be well nourished, vigorous, and healthy. Since his major source of sustenance was human blood, human sacrifice was a necessary part of religious rites and the securing of victims through warfare an important function of the Empire.

According to the Aztecs, the creation of the world was achieved in four ages ruled over by four different gods and called: (1) Four Ocelot, ruled by Tezcatlipoca; (2) Four Wind, ruled by Quetzalcoatl; (3) Four Rain, ruled by Tlaloc; and (4) Four Sun, ruled by Chalchihuitlicue. The present age, the fifth, is to be extinguished by earthquakes. The basic cosmic principle uniting the multiplicity of gods was that of duality or the opposition of male and female, darkness and light, life and death, which were personified by the struggle of Quetzalcoatl and Tezcatlipoca or by Quetzalcoatl and the Death God. The world was divided in two ways, vertically and horizontally, into areas of religious significance. The horizontal universe recognized five directions—four cardinal points and the center. The vertical world was divided into heavens and hells that had little moral significance. Each of the deities was thought to consist of four forms, each corresponding to one of the four horizontal directions and associated with a particular color.

The priestly order consisted of: (1) two high priests of equal rank—one was the high priest of the cult of Huitzilopochtli, the second was the high priest of the cult of Tlaloc; (2) a priest in charge of the tribal religious school for the sons of the nobility; (3) priests, junior priests, and initiates concerned with the cult of each important god. According to some, the priests had great control over the actions of ordinary people. Religious ceremonies were intimately connected with the calendar and recurred every month (20 days). These required feasts, dances and songs, individual confessions and penances, prayers, torture, and sacrifice.

Bibliography: C. C. VAILLANT, *The Aztecs of Mexico* (Baltimore 1956) 168–181. A. CASO, *The Aztecs: People of the Sun* (Norman, Okla. 1958). G. LANCZKOWSKI, ''Quetzalcoatl—Mythos und Geschichte,'' *Numen* 9 (1962) 17–36. K. A. READ, ''The Fleeting Moment: Cosmogony, Eschatology, and Ethics in Aztec Religion and Society,'' *Journal of Religious Ethics* 14 (1986) 113–138. M. GRAULICH, ''Miccailhuitl: the Aztec Festivals of the Deceased,'' *Numen. International Review for the History of Religions*, 36 (Leiden 1989) 43–71. D. CARRASCO, ed. *To Change Place: Aztec Ceremonial Landscapes* (Niwot 1991). M. LEÓN-PORTILLA, ''Those Made Worthy by Divine Sacrifice: The Faith of Ancient Mexico,'' in *South and Meso-American Native Spirituality* (New York 1993) 41–64.

[J. RUBIN/EDS.]

ISBN 0-7876-4005-0

90000

9 780787 640057